2002 Standard Catalog of®

FIREARMS

THE COLLECTOR'S PRICE & REFERENCE GUIDE

12TH EDITION

NED SCHWING

© 2001 by
Krause Publications, Inc.

Published by

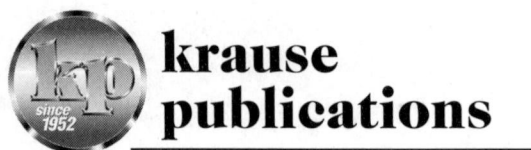

krause
publications

700 E. State Street • Iola, WI 54990-0001
Telephone: 715/445-2214

Please call or write for our free catalog of publications.
Our toll-free number to place an order or obtain a free catalog is 800-258-0929
or please use our regular business telephone 715-445-2214.

Library of Congress Catalog Number: 90-62405

ISBN: 0-87349-331-1

Printed in the United States of America

CONTENTS

——— FIREARMS DIRECTORY ———

4 •

FIREARMS DIRECTORY

FIREARMS DIRECTORY

── FIREARMS DIRECTORY ──

—— FIREARMS DIRECTORY ——

FIREARMS DIRECTORY

—— FIREARMS DIRECTORY ——

ACKNOWLEDGMENTS

Orvel Reichert is a collector of World War II-era semi-automatic pistols, especially the P38, and has been an invaluable help in sorting out a sometimes confusing array of pistol variations. He can be reached at P. O. Box 67, Vader, WA 98593, 360-245-3492, email address: mr.p38@localaccess.com

Joe Gaddini, of SWR, has provided invaluable technical assistance on Class III firearms and suppressors. He can be reached at 119 Davis Road, Suite G-1, in Martinez, GA 30907, 706-481-9403.

David Moore of William Larkin Moore & Co. provided expert information on B. Rizzine, Garbi, F. Rizzine, Piotti, and Lebeau Courally. He can be reached at 8340 E. Raintree Dr. Suite B-7, Scottsdale, AZ, 85260. Phone 480-951-8913.

John Dougan, Ruger expert, who supplied us with information on the Great Western Arms Co.

Burt O'Neill is an experienced collector of Browning "P" Grades and helped with that pricing. He can be reached at 610-793-3256

Thanks to Smith & Wesson expert Roy Jinks, of Smith & Wesson, who wrote the introduction to that section in this book.

C.W. Slagle, of Scottsdale, Arizona, for his expertise in antique firearms.

Thanks to Eric M. Larson for his knowledgeable information on federal gun laws.

A special thanks to Simeon Stoddard, curator of the Cody Firearms Museum, for his research and contribution on the M-1 Garand rifle.

A special thanks to all the manufacturers and importers who supplied us with information and photographs on their products.

Thanks to the Lew Horton Distributing Company for its invaluable information on Colt Custom Shop products and Smith & Wesson Performance Center products.

Thanks to Jerry Cummings of Manawa, Wisconsin, and William "Pete" Harvey of Falmouth, Massachusetts, who contributed photos and research information.

Many thanks to Harold Hamilton of Hershey, Pennsylvania, for his invaluable assistance with Hamilton rifles.

Michael McIntosh gave generously of his expert knowledge of A.H. Fox Company and its guns.

Ed Buehlman, a longtime firearms dealer, shared his knowledge of Colt New Frontier models. He can be reached at 847-381-2276.

Special appreciation to Joe McBride of McBride's Guns in Austin, Texas, for his expert assistance.

Walter C. Snyder is the "Chronicler of the Ithaca Gun Company" and has devoted a great deal of time and effort to making the Ithaca section the most comprehensive of any price guide on the market.

Tom Turpin is a big help with his invaluable knowledge of F.W. Heym Company and its product line.

Horst Held of Midlothian, Texas, provided us with information on interesting and seldom seen antique semi-automatic pistols.

Ted Willems and Bruce Wolberg of *Gun List* have been most helpful with information and locating hard-to-find firearms.

I also want to thank the members of the Ruger Collectors' Association for their invaluable input.

Thanks to all the readers who have taken the time to contact the editor with corrections, omissions and additional information.

PHOTO CREDITS

John Gallo, president of Butterfield and Butterfield auction house in San Francisco, made available a wealth of fine photographs and other auction information that has improved the quality of this publication. Through the efforts of Butterfield and Butterfield, firearms collecting has reached a level of interest on par with the fine art world.

Thanks to the Milwaukee Public Museum, 800 W. Wells St., Milwaukee, WI 53233; and the Buffalo Bill Historical Center, Cody Firearms Museum, P.O. Box 1000, Cody, WY 82414, for supplying us with photographs. We also wish to thank the Remington Arms Company for its kind assistance in providing us with photos of out-of-production Remington firearms.

Many thanks to the following who loaned us their firearms to photograph for this book:

Thomas W. Radcliffe

Brook Davis

Thomas F. Swearengen
Chip Johnson of Direct Firearms, St. Joseph, Missouri
C. Roy Jones of C. Roy's Gunsmithing, Kaiser, Missouri
Mike and Wanda Moutray of Mike's Gun Sales, Grant City, Missouri
Will Parsons of Parsons Gun Shop
Joe Lech of Ironwork Armco, Raytown, Missouri
Guns of the World, Kansas City, Missouri
J.M. Stanley of Stan's Gun Shop, Joplin, Missouri
H.L. Hoeflicker of HLH Enterprises, Shawnee Mission, Kansas
S.T. Sinclair
Pat Morgan
Steve Comus
William H. Lehman of B & B Guns, Brighton, Colorado
James D. McKenzie and Samuel Baum of Kentucky Rifle, Union City, Pennsylvania

Dean Parr of Dean's Gun Shop, St. Joseph, Missouri
E.K. Tryon of Philadelphia, Pennsylvania
Bob's Gun Rack of Lee's Summit, Missouri
Pat McWilliams
J.M. Stanley
Ken Waughtal of Merriam, Kansas
Armond Beetch of Quapaw, Oklahoma
Jim Rankin
Eric M. Larson
Jim Taylor of Mt. Vernon, Missouri
C. Hadley Smith
Walter C. Snyder
Ithaca Gun Company
Tom Turpin
Horst Held
Gary Gelson Photography of Boise, Idaho
Paul Goodwin Creative Services
Karl Karash

INTRODUCTION

This 12th edition of the *Standard Catalog of® Firearms* marks the first for a new feature we call "Snap Shots," a short, quick personal review of selected firearms, both old and new, that will hopefully give the reader a sense of what the gun is really like to shoot and look at. It puts a more personal face on firearms that we think the reader will appreciate and enjoy. Our contributors are acknowledged experts in their field and survey a wide variety of firearms to suit just about every taste and interest.

This new edition of the catalog features an all new color section of outstanding auction firearms for the year. Prices continue to be reviewed and updated. New models are added for the year 2001 so that the reader will be current will the newest developments in firearms. And our articles on the state of the industry, firearms legislation, and collecting continue to keep the reader informed on the latest trends in the firearms field. An interesting short article on the advantages of having a Curio and Relic firearms license will be of benefit to some collectors whose collections encompass these guns.

This year also serves as the beginning of an exciting new era with the introduction, in the fall of 2001, of a new companion volume entitled the *Standard Catalog of® Military Firearms, 1870 to the Present*. This new book will cover, in great detail, all of the collectable military firearms of the last 130 years from all over the world. It features more models, more variations, more photos, more prices, and more coverage of military firearms than has ever been attempted before. This is an outstanding new project, well worth the wait.

Good luck with your collecting and be safe in your shooting.

Ned Schwing
Editor

GRADING SYSTEM

In the opinion of the editor, all grading systems are subjective. It is our task to offer the collector and dealer a measurement that most closely reflects a general consensus on condition. The system we present seems to come closest to describing a firearm in universal terms. We strongly recommend that the reader acquaint himself with this grading system before attempting to determine the correct price for a particular firearm's condition. Remember, in most cases condition determines price.

NIB-New in Box
This category can sometimes be misleading. It means that the firearm is in its original factory carton with all of the appropriate papers. It also means the firearm is new; that it has not been fired and has no wear. This classification brings a substantial premium for both the collector and shooter.

Excellent
Collector quality firearms in this condition are highly desirable. The firearm must be in at least 98 percent condition with respect to blue wear, stock or grip finish, and bore. The firearm must also be in 100 percent original factory condition without refinishing, repair, alterations or additions of any kind. Sights must be factory original as well. This grading classification includes both modern and antique (manufactured prior to 1898) firearms.

Very Good
Firearms in this category are also sought after both by the collector and shooter. Modern firearms must be in working order and retain approximately 92 percent original metal and wood finish. It must be 100 percent factory original, but may have some small repairs, alterations, or non-factory additions. No refinishing is permitted in this category. Antique firearms must have 80% original finish with no repairs.

Good
Modern firearms in this category may not be considered to be as collectable as the previous grades, but antique firearms are considered desirable. Modern firearms must retain at least 80 percent metal and wood finish, but may display evidence of old refinishing. Small repairs, alterations, or non-factory additions are sometimes encountered in this class. Factory replacement parts are permitted. The overall working condition of the firearm must be good as well as safe. The bore may exhibit wear or some corrosion, especially in antique arms. Antique firearms may be included in this category if their metal and wood finish is at least 50 percent original factory finish.

Fair
Firearms in this category should be in satisfactory working order and safe to shoot. The overall metal and wood finish on the modern firearm must be at least 30 percent and antique firearms must have at least some original finish or old re-finish remaining. Repairs, alterations, nonfactory additions, and recent refinishing would all place a firearm in this classification. However, the modern firearm must be in working condition, while the antique firearm may not function. In either case the firearm must be considered safe to fire if in a working state.

Poor
Neither collectors nor shooters are likely to exhibit much interest in firearms in this condition. Modern firearms are likely to retain little metal or wood finish. Pitting and rust will be seen in firearms in this category. Modern firearms may not be in working order and may not be safe to shoot. Repairs and refinishing would be necessary to restore the firearm to safe working order. Antique firearms will have no finish and will not function. In the case of modern firearms their principal value lies in spare parts. On the other hand, antique firearms in this condition may be used as "wall hangers" or as an example of an extremely rare variation or have some kind of historical significance.

Pricing Sample Format

NIB	Exc.	V.G.	Good	Fair	Poor
550	450	400	350	300	200

PRICING

The prices given in this book are <u>RETAIL</u> prices.

Unfortunately for shooters and collectors, there is no central clearinghouse for firearms prices. The prices given in this book are designed as a guide, not as a quote. This is an important distinction because prices for firearms vary with the time of the year and geographical location. For example, interest in firearms is at its lowest point in the summer. People are not as interested in shooting and collecting at this time of the year as they are in playing golf or taking a vacation. Therefore, prices are depressed slightly and guns that may sell quickly during the hunting season or the winter months may not sell well at all during this time of year. Geographical location also plays an important part in pricing. Political pundits are often heard to say that all politics is local. Well, the same can be said, in many ways, for the price of firearms. For instance, a Winchester Model 70 in a .264 caliber will bring a higher price in the Western states than along the Eastern seaboard. Smaller gauges and calibers seem to be more popular along both coasts and mid-sections of the United States than in the more open western sections of the country.

It is not practical to list prices in this book with regard to time of year or location. What is given is a reasonable price based on sales at gun shows, auction houses, *Gun List* prices, and information obtained from knowledgeable collectors and dealers. The firearms prices listed in this book are **RETAIL PRICES** and may bring more or less depending on the variables discussed previously. If you choose to sell your gun to a dealer you will not receive the retail price but a wholesale price based on the markup that particular dealer needs to operate. Also, in certain cases there will be no price indicated under a particular condition but rather the notation "**N/A**" or the symbol "—." This indicates that there is no known price available for that gun in that condition or the sales for that particular model are so few

that a reliable price cannot be given. This will usually be encountered only with very rare guns, with newly introduced firearms, or more likely with antique firearms in those conditions most likely to be encountered. Most antique firearms will be seen in the good, fair and poor categories.

One final note. The prices listed here come from a variety of sources: retail stores, gun shows, individual collectors, and auction houses. Due to the nature of business, one will usually pay higher prices at a retail store than at a gun show. In some cases, auctions will produce excellent buys or extravagant prices, depending on any given situation. Collectors will sometimes pay higher prices for a firearm that they need to fill out their collection when in other circumstances they will not be willing to pay market price if they don't have to have the gun. The point here is that prices paid for firearms is an ever-changing affair based on a large number of variables. The prices in this book are a **GENERAL GUIDE** as to what a willing buyer and willing seller might agree on. You may find the item for less, and then you may have to pay more depending on the variables of your particular situation.

Sometimes we lose sight of our collecting or shooting goals and focus only on price. Two thoughts come to mind. First, one long time collector told me once that, "you can never pay too much for a good gun." Second, Benjamin Franklin once said, "the bitterness of poor quality lingers long after the sweetness of a low price."

In the final analysis, the prices listed here are given to assist the shooter and collector in pursuing their hobby with a better understanding of what is going on in the marketplace. If this book can expand one's knowledge, then it will have fulfilled its purpose.

ADDITIONAL CONSIDERATIONS

As stated in the pricing section, this publication offers a general guide to prices. There are many factors that may affect the value of a firearm. We have attempted to be as comprehensive as possible, but we cannot cover all possible factors that may influence the worth of any given firearm. Some of these circumstances will be discussed so that the shooter and collector will have a better idea of how certain factors may affect prices.

Firearms have been admired and coveted, not only for their usefulness, but also for their grace and beauty. Since the beginning of the 19th century, firearms makers have adorned their guns with engraving, fine woods, or special order features that set their products apart from the rest. There is no feasible way to give the collector every possible variation of the firearms presented in this book. However, in a general way, certain special factors will significantly influence the price of a firearm.

Perhaps the most recognizable special feature collectors agree affects the price of a firearm is engraving. The artistry, beauty, and intricate nature of engraving draw all collectors toward it. But, firearms engraving is a field unto itself requiring years of experience to determine proper chronological methods and the ability to identify the engraver in question. Factory

engraving generally brings more of a premium than after-market engraving. To be able to determine factory work is a difficult task, full of pitfalls. In some cases, factories like Colt and Winchester may have records to verify original factory engraving work. Whereas other manufacturers such as Parker, Remington, or Savage may not have these records. Whenever a firearm purchase is to be made with respect to an engraved gun, it is in the collector's best interest to secure an expert opinion and/or a factory letter prior to the purchase. Engraved firearms are expensive. A mistake could cost the collector thousands of dollars; proceed with caution.

The 18th century was also a time when pistols and rifles were purchased by or given to historically important individuals. Firearms have also been an important part of significant historical events such as the Battle of the Little Bighorn or the Battle of Bull Run or some other meaningful event in our nation's history. Many of these firearms are in museums where the public can enjoy, see and appreciate them. Others are in private collections that seldom, if ever, are offered for sale. If the collector should ever encounter one of these historically important firearms, it cannot be stressed strongly enough to secure an expert determination as to authenticity. Museum curators are perhaps the best source of information for these types of firearms. As with engraved guns, historical firearms are usually expensive, and without documentation their value is questionable.

Special features and variations are also a desirable part of firearms collecting. As with engraving, special order guns can bring a considerable premium. The Colt factory has excellent records regarding its firearms and will provide the collector with a letter of authenticity. Winchester records are not as comprehensive, but rifles made prior to 1908 may have documentation. Other firearm manufacturers either do not have records or do not provide the collector with documentation. This leaves the collector in a difficult position. Special order sights, stocks, barrel lengths, calibers, and so forth must be judged on their own merits. As with other factors, an expert should be consulted prior to purchase. Sometimes this can be difficult.

Experienced collectors, researchers, and museums will generally provide the kind of information a collector needs before purchasing a special order or unique firearm.

Perhaps the best advice is for the collector to take his time. Do not be in a hurry, and do not allow yourself to be rushed into making a decision. Learn as much as possible about the firearms you are interested in collecting or shooting. Try to keep current with prices through *Gun List* and this publication. Go to gun shows, not just to buy or sell, but to observe and learn. It is also helpful to join a firearms club or association. These groups have older, experienced collectors who are glad to help the beginner or veteran. Firearms collecting is a rewarding hobby. Firearms are part of our nation's history and represent an opportunity to learn more about their role in that American experience. If done skillfully, firearms collecting can be a profitable hobby as well.

AUCTION HOUSE CREDITS

The following auction houses were kind enough to allow the catalog to report unusual firearms from their sales. The directors of these auction concerns are acknowledged for their assistance and support.

Amoskeag Auction Company, Inc.
250 Commercial Street, Unit #3011
Manchester, NH 03101
Attention: Jason or Melissa Devine
603-627-7383
603-627-7384 FAX

Butterfield & Butterfield
220 San Bruno Avenue
San Francisco, CA 94103
Attention: James Ferrell
415-861-7500 ext. 327
415-861-8951 FAX

James D. Julia, Inc.
Rte. 201 Skowhegan Rd.
Fairfield, ME 04937
Attention: Wendie Carbone
207-453-7125
207-453-2502 FAX

Old Town Station Ltd.
P.O. Box 15351
Lenexa, KS 66285
Attention: Jim Supica
913-492-3000
913-492-3022 FAX

Rock Island Auction Company
1050 36th Avenue
Moline, IL 61265
Attention: Patrick Hogan
800-238-8022
309-797-1655 FAX

Little John's Auction Service, Inc.
1740 W. La Veta
Orange, CA 92868
Attention: Carol Watson
714-939-1170
714-939-7955 FAX

THE EDITOR

Ned Schwing is the author of:

The Winchester Model 42, Winchester's Finest: The Model 21, Winchester Slide Action Rifles, Volume I: The Model 1890 and Model 1906, Winchester Slide Action Rifles, Volume II: The Model 61 and Model 62, The Browning Superposed: John M. Browning's Last Legacy, and the *Standard Catalog of Military Firearms, 1870 to the Present*. He is also the firearms contributor to the *Standard Catalog of Winchester*. His articles have appeared in the *American Rifleman, Guns Illustrated, Shooting Sportsman, Waffen Digest, Double Gun Journal*, and other firearm publications.

CONTRIBUTING EDITORS

J.B. Barnes
Stevens single shot rifles and pistols
29 Ridgeview Dr.
Dry Ridge, KY 41035
859-824-5086

David Bichrest
Winchester lever action rifles
P.O. Box 8179
Lumberton, TX 77657
409-751-6256
FAX 409-755-0947
Email: lethabichrst@email.msm.com
Web Site:
www.davidsfirearmsltd.com

John Callahan
Savage Historian
53 Old Quarry Road
Westfield, MA 01085

Douglas Carlson
Colt percussion & Colt conversion
revolvers
Antique Remington handguns
P.O. Box 71035
Des Moines, IA 50325
515-224-6552

Jim Cate
J.P. Sauer pistols
406 Pine Bluff Dr.
Chattanooga, TN 37412
423-892-6320

Kevin Cherry
Winchester and Colt
Commemoratives
3402 West Wendover Avenue
Greensboro, NC 27407
336-854-4182

Joseph Cornell, Ph.D., A.M.A.
Ferlach Guild
Accredited Master Appraiser
2655 West 39th Avenue
CO 80211
303-455-1717
Email: joe80211@aol.com

Don Criswell
Winchester Model 21 shotguns
Parker shotguns
P.O. Box 277
Yorba Linda, CA 92686
714-970-5934

Bert O'Neill
Belgian Browning shotguns and rifles
1573 Camp Linden Rd.
West Chester, PA 19382
610-793-3256

John Dougan
Ruger & Great Western
2000 Saul Kleinfeld Dr. #110
El Paso, TX 79936
915-857-1992

Richard Freer
Belgium Browning shotguns
Winchester pre-64 shotguns
8928 Spring Branch Drive
Houston, TX 77080
713-467-3016

William Hammond
L.C. Smith shotguns
128 Pearson Lane
Rochester, NY 14612
716-227-5360

David Hunter
Marlin lever action rifles
6618 Parker Road
Wadesville, IN 47638
812-985-7448

Karl Karash
Colt Model 1911 & 1911A1
288 Randall Road
Berlin, MA 01503
978-838-9401
FAX 987-589-2060

Chuck Karwan
Colt New Service, Browning
High-Power, Lee-Enfield,
Webley revolvers
958 Cougar Creek Road
Oakland, OR 97462
541-459-4134

Rick Kennerknecht
Official Randal Firearms/Pistol Assoc.
P.O. Box 1180
Mills, WY 82644-1180
Web: www.Randal45.com
Email: Historian@Randal45.com
Phone: 877-464-0180 Ext. 319
U.S.: Fax 419-464-1080
Euro Fax: 44(0870) 131-2598

Richard M. Kumor Sr.
c/o Ricky's Gun Room
WWII era military firearms
P.O. Box 286
Chicopee, MA 01021
413-592-5000

Eric Larson
H&R Handy Guns
Smoothbore Pistols
P.O. Box 5497
Takoma Park, MD 20913
301-270-3450
e-mail:
Eric_Larson@alumni.utexas.net

Roger Lenzmeier
Ithaca Shotguns
2322 Viking Cr. N.W.
Rochester, MN 55901

Karl Lippard
First National Gun Banque
Perazzi, Fabbri, Famars
P.O. Box 60719
Colorado Springs, CO 80960
719-444-0786
www.fngbcorp.com
karl@fngbcorp.com

Joe McBride
McBride's Guns
Modern Colts, Winchester,
Remington, Browning
30th at North Lamar
Austin, TX
512-472-3532
512-478-9958 FAX

Duke McCaa
   Kimber, Current Brownings,
   Colt SAA,
   & Winchester
   5243 Gulf Breeze Parkway
   Gulf Breeze, FL 32561
   850-932-4867

Rich Machniak
   Ruger
   237 Groveland Dr.
   Howell, MI 48843
   517-546-7446
   Email: dejay@ismi.net

Gale Morgan
   Luger and Mauser pistols
   Pre-World War I pistols
   P.O. Box 72
   Lincoln, CA 95648
   916-645-1720

J.R. Moody
   Contemporary Military small arms
   c/o Ned Schwing
   Krause Publications
   700. E State St.
   Iola, WI 54990

Jeff Munnel
   Seville & El Dorado revolvers
   633 Long Run Road
   McKeesport, PA 15132

Doug Murray
   Savage Model 99 and early Savage
   rifles
   20 Polo Lane
   Westbury, NY 11590
   516-333-6874

Nick Niles
   Stevens, Savage Fox B, and
   Davis doubles
   528 Central Ave.
   Naples, FL 34106
   941-261-9592

Jim Rankin
   Walther pistols
   3615 Anderson Road
   Coral Gables, FL 33134
   305-446-1792

Orvel Reichert
   World War II-era semiautomatic
   pistols
   P.O. Box 67
   Vader, WA 98593
   360-245-3492
   email: mr.p38@localaccess.com

Dean "Winchester Man" Rinehart
   Pre-1964 Winchesters & Colt
   Woodsman
   101 Orchard Hill Road
   Gallibolis, OH 45631
   740-446-9430

Joe Schroeder
   Steyer/Mannlicher pistols
   P.O. Box 406
   Glenview, IL 60025
   847-724-8816
   827-657-6500
   847-724-8831 FAX

Dan Sheil
   Merkel shotguns and rifles
   9240 Southwest 140 Street
   Miami, FL 33176
   305-253-5984

Don Stika
   CZ pistols
   BRNO and Mauser sporting rifles
   Mannlicher rifles
   P.O. Box 882
   Bensenville, IL 60106
   630-766-4617

John Stimson, Jr.
   High Standard pistols
   540 W 92nd Street
   Indianapolis, IN 46260
   317-844-5889
   FAX-317-844-0034
   e-mail J.Stimson@home.com

Jim Supica
   Smith & Wesson
   P.O. Box 15351
   Lenexa, KS 66285
   913-492-3000

Walt Snyder
   Ithaca shotguns
   225 South Valley Rd.
   Southern Pines, NC 28387
   910-692-7324

Allan Wilson
   Winchester Model 70 & Model 52
   109 Backhill
   Plainfield, NH 03781
   603-298-8085

SNAP SHOTS

This is a new feature for the catalog that intends to give the reader a firsthand look at selected firearms, both antique and modern, from the writer's individual perspective. Due to space limitations, these reviews are kept to a 300-word maximum. Despite this restrictions, we think these commentaries are valuable to the reader. We hope that this will personalize and bring to life what otherwise might be a dispassionate rendition of technical facts and descriptions. We all have our likes and dislikes when it comes to firearms. I hope our readers enjoy our contributors' personal opinions and insights.

CONTRIBUTORS

Tom Turpin

Tom Turpin has been writing on the subject of guns, hunting, and shooting for more than 25 years. His first byline appeared in *Guns & Ammo* in 1973 and the subject of that first story was engraving. He is currently the special projects editor for *Guns Magazine* and a contributing editor for *Petersen's Rifleshooter Magazine,* as well as contributing to *Digest Books* and numerous other magazines. He has written more than 200 articles for various major publications and has contributed to several books both here and in Europe. He is the author of *Modern Custom Guns* and *Modern Firearms Engraving*, both published by Krause Publications. He usually has several articles and two or three book manuscripts in the works at any given time. He is one of the few writers today to write extensively on the subject of custom guns and engraving. He, his wife Pauline, his nine Labrador retrievers and 20 Japanese Koi fish live in southeastern Arizona. See his reviews under:

> Sako bolt action rifles, Marlin Model 39, Pre-64 Winchester Model 70, Blaser R93, Heym Big Bore Double rifle, Mannlicher Schoenauer rifle, Remington Model 700 rifle, Heym SR-20.

Walter Rauch

Upon receiving his bachelor of science degree from Carnegie Tech and completing service as a special agent in U.S. Army Intelligence, Walt Rauch was a special agent with the U.S. Secret Service and an investigator with the Warrant Unit, First Judicial District, Penn. where he made over 2,000 felony arrests. He now operates his own consulting company, Rauch & Company, Ltd., for defense-weapon and tactical training. Rauch & Company services expert witness testimony on firearms use and tactics. He is also a writer and lecturer in the firearms filed. He is published regularly in national and international publications including *Combat Handguns, Guns & Weapons for Law Enforcement*, and other Harris Publications specialty magazines. He is also the author of a book on self-defense, titled *REAL-WORLD SURVIVAL! What Has Worked For Me*. See his reviews under:

> Luger pistol, Glock pistol, Kimber 1911 pistol, Remington Model 870 shotgun, Smith & Wesson K-frame revolvers, Smith & Wesson J-frame revolvers, Colt Detective Special, Colt Model 1911

John Taffin

John Taffin has been a staff writer for the *American Handgunner* and *Guns* magazines for the past 15 years, assigned to do feature articles, as well as two regular columns, "Taffin Test" and "The Sixgunner." He also contributes regular columns and features to *Shoot!Magazine*, *Freedom Arms Collectors Journal*, and *Handguns Hunter International,* as well as the *Digest* annuals from Krause Publications. His main interests are big-bore sixguns, lever-action rifles, and single-shot rifles and pistols, and he has hunted extensively with handguns in America and Africa. Taffin is the author of two books from Krause Publications, *Big Bore Sixguns* and *Action Shooting Cowboy Style* and more than 750 articles. See his reviews under:

> Colt Single Action Army, Colt Model 1860 Army, Colt Model 1877, Model 1860 Henry rifle, Winchester Model 1892, Winchester Model 1897, Smith & Wesson Model 3 Russian, Sharps rifles, Freedom Arms Model 83 .454 Casull, Smith & Wesson Model 29, Ruger Super Blackhawk, Ruger .480 Super Redhawk, Dan Wesson, Smith & Wesson Schofield, Marlin Cowboy, Taurus .454 Raging Bull.

J.R. Moody

J. R. Moody, a degreed historian, has been collecting and shooting Class III firearms for 20 years because he enjoys the historical and technological aspects of these firearms. He competes successfully at sub-machine matches across the country. On several occasions, he has defeated the national champion. In addition, he works as a consultant to Knight's Armament Company, one of the country's leading small arms contractors to U.S. military forces and law enforcement agencies. See his reviews under:

> Accuracy International AW Sniper rifle, Remington 700 PSS rifle, Colt AR15A2 HB rifle, SIG SSG 3000 rifle, Sako TRG 21 Sniper rifle, Heckler and Koch P9S pistol, Steyr SSG 69/P II.

Ned Schwing

Your editor of the catalog does more than just sit behind a computer. He actually gets out from time to time to do what he likes best: shoot. For more years than he chooses to think about, he has hunted and fooled around with guns of all kinds. He's not an expert shot, he's more like an every-man shot, but he loves to shoot and appreciates accurate firearms of all kinds. His opinions offer the reader down-to-earth impressions, as well as historical looks at those guns he has reviewed. See his reviews under:

> Browning Superposed, H&K USP Tactical, Parker Shotguns, Winchester Model 61, Winchester Model 1890 Winchester Model 42, Winchester 21

2001 HAD MORE UPS THAN DOWNS FOR FIREARMS INDUSTRY

By Robert Hausman

The final outcome of the 2000 presidential election spelled the beginning of a year of defeats for the proponents of gun control. The ascendancy of George W. Bush to the presidency virtually took gun control off the radar screens of Congress.

Advocacy for gun control was one of the issues that cost presidential candidate Al Gore, and many other Democrats, the 2000 election. While Al Gore may have edged George W. Bush in the popular vote, he carried only a small number of populous states. Largely due to his anti-gun position on firearms civil rights, Gore lost in many traditionally Democratic states, including his home state of Tennessee and Clinton's home state of Arkansas.

New Label, Same Package

In an attempt to make the organization more palatable to the public, Handgun Control, Inc., the leading gun control lobbying organization in Washington, D.C., changed its name to the Brady Campaign to Prevent Gun Violence. The name change, which was obviously done to make the organization appear more moderate (i.e. being against violence, rather than firearms) did not seem to work as several months later 20 percent of its staff was laid off.

The financially-strapped "Million" Mom March merged with the Brady Campaign after letting go 30 of its 35 paid staff members. Turnout was barely noticeable at the organization's Mother's Day rally held in Washington, D.C., in the spring, and turnout at similar events held around the country was a fraction of what it had been in 2000.

New Anti-Gun Strategy

In a revealing article appearing in the *Washington Post* on July 31, former Clinton advisor and press secretary Joe Lockhart acknowledged gun control is a losing issue for Democrats, but he also revealed its new strategy to separate Americans from their guns.

"So what should Democrats do now on gun safety issues?" Lockhart began in a reference to the new strategy of imposing additional controls on firearms, such as the mandatory use of trigger locking devices in the guise of "common sense gun safety."

"Serious and thoughtful party leaders are privately warning candidates to stay away from the gun debate completely," Lockhart said . But while these important Democrats have diagnosed the disease correctly, they're prescribing the wrong medicine: a full retreat from the issue.

"No one doubts Democrats will have a hard time winning elections if they ignore or insult the values of gun-owning Americans," Lockhart continued. "Democrats should em-

brace a 'third way' on guns that treats gun ownership as neither an absolute right nor an absolute wrong, but as a balance between rights and responsibilities." Lockhart added that more than 90 percent of the nation's gun owners are not NRA members and that while most people believe gun ownership is a right, poll results suggest they believe that right "allows for sensible gun laws."

As further affirmation that the results of the 2000 elections have decidedly trounced the dark forces of gun control, the U.S. Justice Department drafted a formal legal opinion that the Second Amendment to the U.S. Constitution does in fact ensure the rights of individuals to own firearms. That view was earlier espoused by Attorney General John Ashcroft during his Senate confirmation hearings, and again in a letter from Ashcroft to the National Rifle Association last May.

Although in his letter Ashcroft commented that the Constitution does not prohibit Congress from enacting some firearm restrictions, he stressed that "... the Second Amendment clearly protects the rights of individuals to keep and bear arms. Like the First and Fourth amendments, the Second Amendment protects the rights of 'the people,' which the Supreme Court has noted is a term of art that should be interpreted consistently throughout the Bill of Rights."

The new government position is a complete reversal from the Clinton Administration's policy that aggressively promoted the view that the Second Amendment conferred only a collective right to own guns through the establishment of state militias and was not an individual right.

The Bush Administration's Department of Housing and Urban Development (HUD) announced on July 23 that it was terminating the controversial funding of gun buy-ups (at $50 per gun from public housing tenants) that cost the government $15 million since they were begun by the Clinton White House in November 1999. An attempt by Sen. Charles Schumer (D-NY) to keep the program alive was resoundingly defeated by the Senate on August 2 in a 65-33 vote.

HUD spokeswoman Nancy Segerdahl said the agency's focus was shifting back to affordable housing, and that HUD is no longer participating in the Communities for Safer Guns Coalition begun by former HUD Secretary Andrew Cuomo.

The Bush Administration has also backed away from the government's landmark deal (forged during the Clinton Administration) in which gunmaker Smith & Wesson agreed to step up greater oversight of its retailers and other measures in exchange from relief from the costly lawsuits filed against it by municipalities and anti-gun groups. The Clinton Administration saw the pact as a backdoor way to establish gun control proposals it couldn't get through Congress. While the agreement was not being enforced, Smith & Wesson remained a defendant in many cases.

U.S. Sen. John McCain (R-AZ) stepped up his stumping for gun control efforts during the year. Forging an alliance with a group called "Americans for Gun Safety," a sham organization bankrolled by a former Handgun Control, Inc. board member, McCain appeared in advertisements screened in movie theaters where he touted his support for the use of trigger-locks. McCain also became a co-sponsor [along with Sen. Joseph Lieberman (D-CT)] of a bill that would ban gun shows.

Sen. James Jeffords of Vermont bolted the Republican party in late May declaring himself an Independent who will organize with the Democrats. His move gave control of the U.S. Senate to the Democrats for the first time since 1994, with anti-gun Sen. Tom Daschle (D-SD) as the new majority leader. The results of Jeffords' action, as far as gun owners are concerned, could be ominous on important gun issue votes, although none had come up as this publication goes to press.

In contrast, U.S. Rep. Carolyn McCarthy (D-NY), who was originally elected as a strident gun control advocate while playing upon the fact that her husband was killed and son wounded in the 1993 Long Island Railroad massacre, angered her fellow control colleagues in September by stepping back from support for imposing a three-day waiting period on sales of firearms at gun shows. Saying she would settle for a maximum 24-hour delay, McCarthy made the astounding declaration (for her) to the *New York Daily News* that, "It's the right of every law-abiding American to own guns."

Attendance at the 2000 NRA annual meetings was the second best ever, with some 47,500 persons present. Charlton Heston was unanimously re-elected to an unprecedented fourth term as NRA president. Though traditionally NRA membership drops when there are no major threats to gun rights, the organization reported its membership is holding steady at some 4.3 million.

Legal Victories

The summer of 2000 marked a string of legal victories for gun owners. These included dismissal in early August of a suit filed by New York State Attorney General Eliot Spitzer attempting to hold firearms manufacturers responsible for criminal violence. There was also a decision in the San Francisco law firm massacre case by the California Supreme Court in early August affirming that under state law, firearms manufacturers cannot be held responsible for the criminal misuse of a legally sold and non-defective product.

And the Louisiana Supreme Court dismissed a suit against firearms manufactures filed by the city of New Orleans and its mayor, Marc Morial. Morial's suit was the first of some 30 such city and county lawsuits against the firearms industry instigated by anti-gun interests.

On Aug. 30, a very major victory was sustained with a ruling of the Second Circuit U.S. Court of Appeals reversing the 1999 federal jury trial decision in *Hamilton v. Accu-Tek, et al*, and dismissing the case. The suit was originally filed against 49 gun manufacturers in January 1995 by relatives of victims of violent crimes, supported by anti-gun activist lawyers and organizations. It received national attention as the first case in which a handful of private individuals were allowed to proceed to trial on a claim for damages against virtually the entire firearms industry.

After a jury trial, three manufacturers were ordered to pay damages. They appealed to the Second Circuit Court of Appeals then asked the New York State Court of Appeals to de-

cide two key questions of state law. After consideration, the state appeals court ruled that long-standing court decisions and simple fairness dictate that a manufacturer of a lawfully manufactured and distributed product cannot be held liable because a criminal decides to misuse that product. The resultant August ruling by the federal appeals court affirmed the decision of New York's highest court and directed that the "Hamilton case" against firearms manufacturers be dismissed.

These wins were capped off in early October by the Connecticut Supreme Court's unanimous decision upholding the dismissal of the city of Bridgeport's lawsuit against the industry. The 5-0 ruling spelled an end to Bridgeport's and its mayor, Joseph P. Ganim's attempt the hold the firearms industry legally and financially responsible for the city's crime and social problems. Bridgeport joined Camden County, N.J.; Chicago, Cincinnati, Gary, Ind.; Miami, New York and Philadelphia in having their politically-motivated suits dismissed.

In early May, Florida Gov. Jeb Bush signed a bill into law to prevent local municipalities from filing such unjustified lawsuits against the firearms industry. In doing so, Florida became the 26th state to have adopted similar provisions, meaning legislatures in more than half of the country have determined such suits will not be sanctioned.

International Victory

Much concern was expressed by American gun owners over a July meeting of the United Nations in New York on the worldwide trade in small arms. The conference, which was billed as having its focus on the global trafficking in illegal arms, instead entertained a variety of proposals that would have amounted to banning civilian firearms ownership in much of the world. A refusal by the American representatives present, to go along with such measures, was credited with leading to their withdrawal.

U.S. Undersecretary of State John Bolton told the world that the U.S. would not sign onto any international protocol that undercut the U.S. Constitution's Second Amendment. Instead, firearms marking proposals, similar to those required for firearms manufactured in or imported into the U.S., were adopted as a way to better track the origin and movement of firearms around the world.

A report presented during the U.N. conference revealed that more than half (56 percent) of the world's estimated 551 million firearms are legally owned by private citizens. Just some 910,000 (0.2 percent) are in the hands of rebels or anti-government insurgents. Government military forces account for about 226 million arms (41 percent), and police forces hold some 18 million (3 percent). It was estimated that some 250 million firearms are legally owned in the U.S. alone. America, according to the report, has more than half of the approximately 600 firearms makers and leads all nations in the manufacture and export of small arms and ammunition.

Gun owners in the Irish Free State won a significant legal battle when the country's high court ruled against the Garda Siochana (Irish Police) in a suit challenging a police directive requiring all gun owners to install gun cabinets in their homes and allow police inspection of same. The court found that since the government had enacted no such law, the police lacked authority to issue the regulations. The court added that the demand to inspect homes without legal authority, violated the Irish Constitution's guarantees that the family home shall be inviolable.

Terrorist Attacks

One unintended consequence of the terrorist attacks has been a renewed interest in acquiring firearms on the part of the public. From the afternoon of Sept. 11 and for several weeks afterward, many retailers (particularly on the East Coast) reported crowds of customers flocking into their stores to buy firearms (particularly handguns, tactical rifles and shotguns) along with large quantities of ammunition. Survival gear, such as gas masks, freeze-dried food, candles, wood-burning stoves and other basics sold quickly in a repeat of the "Y2K" scenario of two years before. Two chain stores, Dick's Sporting Goods and Kmart, discontinued sales of firearms and ammunition temporarily, but were back in operation a day later.

Roll Call, the Capitol Hill newspaper, reported some members of Congress, "including some advocates of strict controls on handguns" were now "seeking firearms training in hopes of protecting themselves if the need should arise."

The rush of average citizens buying guns caused the Brady Campaign to send out a press release telling people they were at greater risk with a gun in the house. Some of Osama bin Laden's henchmen, who were alleged to still be in the country, must have gotten a great laugh out of that one.

Airline pilots began calling for greater ability to carry side-arms in the cockpit. Although federal regulations allowed pilots to carry arms onboard at the time of the attacks, pilots had to meet rigid training and other criteria which effectively prevented the practice. Meanwhile, the Federal Aviation Administration, to the contrary, was preparing to issue an outright ban on guns in the cockpit at presstime. Sen. Bob Smith (R-NH) offered an amendment to the Aviation Security Act that would preempt the FAA's gun ban regulation and allow pilots to use firearms to defend their passengers and planes. It would also provide for reinforcing the doors on commercial aircraft.

While there had not been much of a push for gun control after the attacks (as the incidents did not involve firearms) there was a great rush to enact many curtailments of other civil liberties, many of which had originally been proposed during the Clinton Administration.

A coalition of public interest groups from across the political spectrum formed into a new organization to try to stop Congress from rushing to enact counter-terrorism legislation before considering its effect on Americans' privacy and other civil rights. Tentatively named, In Defense of Freedom, the group expressed concerns about expanded electronic surveillance measures sought by the U.S. Justice Department, a proposal to allow federal agencies to jail people for up to a year without filing charges, fingerprinting and photographing persons desiring to travel by air, and requiring all persons to be issued and to carry a national identification card on their persons at all times.

"What is disturbing to people is just how swiftly Congress began grasping for anything to appear responsive to the outrage of the attacks," said a spokesman. Concerns were also voiced about the excesses of past crises, such as the internment of Japanese Americans after the bombing of Pearl Harbor in 1941.

State Level

Taking a look at happenings at the state level, opponents of Michigan's new shall-issue concealed carry law gave up on plans for a ballot proposal to overturn it in 2002. Representatives of the group "People Who Care About Kids," said they wouldn't mount a petition drive to place the issue before voters as they didn't have the money to run a campaign.

New Jersey State Troopers must now call a supervisor before they can ask a motorist's permission to search his or her car under new guidelines. Some motorists either did not realize they had a right to refuse a search request, or they had been intimidated into allowing the search to be conducted. There have been cases where motorists were pulled over and their cars searched for firearms simply because they had an NRA decal in the window.

Handgun licensing bills had passed muster by the state legislature in California, but it was uncertain, at presstime, if the state's governor, Gray Davis, would sign the new measures into law.

Handgun sales in Alaska were reported as being particularly brisk throughout the year. So much so, that Kmart, the nation's number two retailer, which earlier in the year announced it would discontinue the sale of most handgun ammunition, continues to offer not only handgun ammunition but recently began stocking handguns as well in its Fairbanks store. Kmart discontinued offering handguns in the lower 48 states in the 1970s.

The Federal Bureau of Investigation (FBI) sent a letter on June 15 to the Pennsylvania State Police directing the state to discontinue their practice of keeping a database of handgun purchasers approved under the state Point of Contact background check system. The FBI said the database of law-abiding gun owners is illegal under both state and federal laws which prevent establishment of such gun owner registries.

Yes, reporting on gun news during 2001 has been pleasant –much more enjoyable than it had been during the Clinton-Gore years.

***

A veteran journalist on the firearms scene, Robert M. Hausman is also publisher of **The Firearms Trade,** *a bimonthly newsletter written for a professional audience and covering the marketing, legal and regulatory aspects of the firearms industry. For a sample copy and subscription information, send an e-mail to: FirearmsTrade@aol.com.*

Is a COLLECTOR'S FEDERAL FIREARMS LICENSE for you?

By Jim Supica, Old Town Station, Ltd., Armchairgunshow.com

Many readers of *Standard Catalog of® Firearms* are familiar with the Dealer's Federal Firearms License ("FFL"). This is a license issued by the Bureau of Alcohol, Tobacco, and Firearms that allows the licensee to engage in the business of buying and selling guns for profit. An FFL Dealer must comply with many requirements, including zoning and sales tax compliance and maintaining a fixed place of business. The FFL holder must keep a record of all sales and purchases, filing of a 4473 "Yellow Form" for each sale with NICS instant background check or state equivalent. The licensee may buy guns for resale and have them mailed or shipped directly from distributors and other sources. This dealer FFL is not available to private individuals who want to purchase guns for their personal use or collections.

However, there is another, less well known, type of FFL that is designed specifically for individuals who want to buy certain types of gun for their personal collection. It's called a Collector's Federal Firearms License, sometimes called a Curios and Relics (C&R) FFL. It is designed specifically to enable collectors to buy certain types of older and other collectible guns without having to go through a Licensed Dealer.

What can you do with a Collector FFL?

The licensed collector can buy "Curio & Relic" (C&R) firearms directly from a distributor, dealer, or other persons without having to go through a licensed dealer. Many licensed collectors order guns directly from sources on the Internet or listings in publications like Gun List.

What is a C&R firearm?

Federal regulations define C&R guns as those "which are of special interest to collectors by reason of some quality other than those associated with firearms intended for sporting use or ... as weapons." To be considered a C&R, such a gun must fall into one of three categories:

- Any gun which is at least 50 years old;
  A gun which has been certified by the curator of a government museum as of museum interest; or
  A gun whose value is substantially derived from its novelty, rarity, oddity, or historical attribution.

Of these, the "50 years old" is the broadest and most definite group. If you can prove that the gun in question (not the model, but the specific gun) is at least 50 years old, it is a C&R gun, eligible for licensed collector purchase.

The other two classes are a bit more subjective. Presumably, you could rely on the "curator's certification" of C&R status if you kept a copy of the certification with the gun. The "value derived" class is quite subjective. The BATF will make a determination as to whether such a gun is a C&R on written application from a licensed collector. C&R status based on this class has often been given to commemorative firearms. The BATF publishes a list of previously approved C&R firearms, upon which a licensed collector may rely.

What are the obligations of a licensed collector?

A licensed collector must keep a record of all the C&R purchases made with his license in a "bound book", recording make, model, serial number, caliber, type of gun, and the name and address (or FFL number) of the seller, with date. When he sells, trades, or disposes of the gun, he must enter the name, address and other information for the buyer, with the date in the book. The BATF has the right to inspect these records on an annual basis. The licensed collector can decide whether this inspection will be at the location of the collection or at the BATF office. Realistically, licensed collector records are rarely inspected unless there has been a specific problem that has come to the attention of the BATF. Unlike a Licensed Dealer, the Licensed Collector is not required to send his records to the BATF upon expiration of his license.

What are the restrictions on a Licensed Collector?

Most importantly, a Collector FFL does NOT permit the holder to engage in the business of buying and selling guns for profit. The guns purchased on a C&R license must be for the collector's personal collection, and not for resale. This does not prevent a collector from selling or trading guns in his collection to improve the collection. When doing so, he is generally subject to the same laws as any other private citizen selling personal guns, with the addition of needing to list the sale in his bound book. In addition, a Licensed Collector does not have any special privileges when buying a modern non-C&R gun.

To apply, or for more information:

This article is a general summary, and is not legal advice. Probably the best source for definitive information is the BATF website - http://www.atf.treas.gov where you can find the full text of the laws, plus a form to apply for a Collector FFL. You can also request information from the U.S. Government Printing Office, PO Box 5650, Springfield VA 22150-5950. Publication ATF P 5300.4 is the Federal Firearms Regulations Reference Guide; ATF P 5300.11 is the Firearms Curio and Relics List; and ATF F 5310.16 is the application form for a C&R Collector License. The fee is $30 for a three-year license.

GUN COLLECTING — 2001

By Joseph Schroeder

During the first two-thirds of 2001 the marketplace for collectible firearms maintained itself at a steady, if not spectacular, pace. Gun shows were well attended, auctions lively, every issue of "Gun List" and "Shotgun News" was filled with attractive offerings, and an ever-increasing number of savvy collectors were discovering that surfing the Internet uncovered a burgeoning number of Web sites offering guns, collectible or otherwise, for sale or at auction.

The inauguration of George W. Bush and the establishment of a more gun-friendly administration was certainly an encouraging boost for the gun collecting fraternity. The previous administration's open hostility to guns and gun ownership had led a number of collectors to question the wisdom of even maintaining, much less adding to, their collections. Now that's changed, at least for the present, and as 2001 began it was back to serious collecting again. Let's take a look at what's happened during the year.

The focus of interest for most U.S. collectors has long been and continues to be on certain U.S. and foreign makers and military arms of various eras. Among U.S. makers Colt always seems to remain the leader, though there's been some drop-off in interest in some Colt offerings. Prices of Single Actions of recent as well as early vintage remain strong; their "Romance of the West" aura, classic looks, and - for some collectors - shooting fun seem destined to make the "Hogleg" a top collectible forever! Colt percussion revolvers continue to provide an on-going favorite collecting field, though the limited availability and high (and apparently increasing) prices of really nice examples does limit the number of active players in this area.

Among the cartridge Colts the big-bore revolvers such as the New Service have pretty much held their own, but there seems to have been some weakening in interest for the Police Positive and other small-frame Colts. Among the automatics the early locked-breech models - 1900-1905 - have flattened out somewhat after seeing a significant run-up in value over the past few years. However, the faithful 1911 and its derivatives including the Super 38 and Aces have continued to attract a strong following and the prices of nice examples continue to rise. Colt long guns, on the other hand, comprise a relatively narrow field of interest, and a market where prices have remained fairly stable.

Smith & Wesson, after suffering a pretty bad black eye among collectors as well as shooters for its knuckling under to the Clinton administration's "gun control" efforts, seems to be coming back into favor thanks to new company ownership and policies. Of course the serious S&W collectors never left, but there for a time it did seem as if almost everyone else was giving Smiths the cold shoulder. S&W products of all vintages are coming back in favor, hopefully to stay, with early post-WWII models attracting an increasing amount of attention.

Winchester is another American maker whose products attract wide collector interest. Winchester lever actions, like Colt single actions, still are and - as they've always seemed to be - popular, though prices for nice '73s, '86s and '95s (not to mention '66s) are getting to the point where they're beyond reach for many collectors. As a result the 1892s and 1894s have been attracting more collector interest. Pre-'64 Model 70s continue strong, and among Winchester rimfires the target model prices seem to be rising though the pumps have settled down after increasing in the past decade. Among the smaller U.S. makers Hi Standard and Ruger are still in vogue, though with possibly a bit less enthusiasm than they received a few years ago.

Though Civil War and earlier U.S. military ordnance is still popular, the 20th Century small arms are where the action is for current serious military collectors. Military shotguns have become particularly strong, with a growing collector base and prices escalating accordingly. On the rifle side, Springfield 1903 and M-1 Garand models, along with the ever popular M-1 Carbine, have seen no slackening in interest either, with prices of all of them on the increase.

Military small arms of all nations also remain strong with collectors. Among pistol collectors, Lugers and Walthers - particularly P-38s - remain very popular. Recent imports of large numbers of both of them from eastern Europe have fueled rather than filled the demand, and prices for nice examples of scarcer variations continue to rise. Mauser's pistols, both the 1896 "Broomhandle" and the various pocket models, have seemed to flatten a bit in the past year or so, although Mauser rarities like C96 six-shots still bring very good prices indeed. Mauser rifles, sporting as well as military, also remain popular.

Webleys, particularly Webley revolvers, have lost a lot of their luster for collectors in the past few years, and prices of many have dropped noticeably. European revolvers of all types are also slow movers, and their prices have softened considerably. Japanese revolvers are a significant exception to this downward trend, and Japanese automatics are doing quite well. Nice Nambus, especially the later common models, have been going up steadily in price as have the notoriously crude Model 94s. Japanese rifles are enjoying the same renaissance, with nice examples with crests that have not been ground bringing a lot more than they did just a few years ago.

That's pretty much the way gun collecting was in the U.S. before September 11, 2001: shows were well attended, and dealers catering primarily to collectors were recording a comfortable level of business. Where the gun business had been hurting was in sales of new guns, with those dealers reporting gun sales going very slowly and manufacturers and importers alike singing the blues.

However, all that changed dramatically on September 11. Following the dastardly terrorist attacks on the World Trade Center and Pentagon, Americans everywhere were robbed of a lot of that sense of security that we'd always enjoyed thanks to those two big oceans that had effectively insulated us from much of the world's problems. There was new sense of our vulnerability, individual as well as collective, and with it came a need to do something about it.

For many people that need translated to protection. With it also came the realization that they might sometime even need to provide their own protection... and the best means to do that might very well be with a gun. Gun dealers across the country reported a surge in gun and ammunition sales to many first-time buyers, and those dealers offering gun training found their classes booked for weeks in advance.

As we move toward the end of 2001 dealers report that gun sales are continuing well ahead of the pace just a few weeks ago and show little immediate sign of slackening. Gun shows since September 11 have also been crowded, with sales of the still serviceable but less expensive collectibles particularly active.

So what does this new and apparently more positive attitude toward gun ownership mean to the immediate and long-term future of gun collecting? First, it's likely a lot of the new gun-owning Americans will find their newly acquired "tools" to hold more than simply "new tool" interest. This could translate into a shooting interest, casual or even serious. In some cases it could even manifest itself into a new collecting hobby!

These new gun owners do provide a marvelous opportunity for all of us who share a serious passion for the gun-related hobbies. First of all, what better chance will we ever have to bring new blood into our ranks? For example, the counter people at gun shops can stoke this new-found interest by paying special attention to obviously inexperienced new customers, answering the novice's inevitable "dumb" questions with patience and, when indicated, directing them to appropriate books or magazines. Above all, they should sign them up for NRA membership - even offer to pay a part of it!

Those of us who attend gun shows or hang out at shooting ranges should also become mentors to these newcomers. Let's welcome and help out these potential recruits. We all love guns and love talking about them, so why not share that love (and our knowledge) with someone other than our fellow advanced collectors or serious shooters? A few minutes invested in sharing your passion for collecting or shooting with a neophyte might very well plant a seed that will grow into a serious collector or competition shooter!

It's no secret that the various gun interests, from collecting and shooting and even to hunting, have been suffering from declining popularity for quite some time. Take a look around next time you're at a gun show, gun shop, or shooting range. There's more gray hair every year! We're not attracting new blood like we used to. Of course, this slump is not peculiar to the shooting sports; it's also being experienced in many, if not most, hobby areas.

In the gun-related areas, though, we have a particular problem. The on-going barrage of political and media anti-gun sentiment has taken its toll, with the word "gun" becoming a "four-letter word" in many people's vocabulary. That's why this opportunity is so important to we gun people; it's probably the best opportunity we'll ever have to swing a substantial number of on-the-fence or even mildly hostile people to our side of the gun issue.

Politically, there's yet another positive factor for us in this crisis-induced surge in gun ownership. It's now in the best interest of all of these newly minted gun owners to view with a much more jaundiced eye, the future efforts of the "gun grabbers." With hard earned dollars invested in that new bureau drawer pistol or closet shotgun, they're far less likely to ignore, much less support, future anti-gun legislation.

Though it's impossible to predict just what the long-term fallout from the events of September 11 will be, it certainly seems likely that our legislators at every level will have far more weighty matters to wrestle with than fiddling with new gun control matters. In addition, the effects of the slowing economy on gun collecting are also certainly matters of concern. The job layoffs and stock market slump that followed September 11 have certainly hit some collectors very hard. How soon they and the economy return to some degree of normalcy is an open question.

Under the present circumstances, the one collecting field that will almost certainly remain strong is military small arms, foreign as well as U.S. With military action, albeit probably limited, likely for some extended period, this is the one area where interest and activity should remain high. Similarly, for patriotic reasons U.S. makers, particularly Colt, should retain a strong following.

Now, let's take a different tack for a moment. The experiences of over half a century immersed in the gun collecting field, dealing with fellow collectors both at home and abroad, has led me to recognize a number of "truths" as they apply to our passion. Here are some of them, in no particular order of importance, for your consideration:

10 Commandments for Gun Collectors

1. When you find a rare goodie that belongs in your collection and the price seems appropriate, buy it whether you can afford it or not! You can always somehow find some way to pay for it, but you can never count on finding it again when you can afford it! Remember, the pleasure remains when the price is forgotten.

2. Always deal within the law. That means never buying or selling "off paper" or "under the table," and avoiding such temptations as unregistered machine guns like the plague. It also means, if you're dealing for profit, getting a dealer's FFL plus a state tax stamp and a local business license, where they're required. Pushing the gun laws can cost you not only your collection but your freedom - NO deal is worth that!

3. Never butt in on someone else's deal. Gun show etiquette requires that you shut up while a buyer and seller are negotiating, even if you're willing to pay twice the price under discussion. Until he lays it back on the table, it's the prospective buyer's gun!

4. Whenever you buy a gun, buy a gun book. Knowledge is power, and the more you learn about your collecting interest, the better equipped you'll be to make wise collecting decisions. Without knowledge you are not a collector, but merely a gatherer.

5. Always describe a gun you're selling at a distance accurately and completely, as you'd like it described to you. "It's even better than you said!" is a lot more pleasant to hear, when the buyer receives it, than "I want my money back, you crook!" And always stand behind your sale and take an item back when the buyer isn't satisfied.

6. Always treat all guns, yours and other people's, with respect. First and foremost from the safety standpoint, always check them for empty and always point them away from others. Second, preserve them by proper maintenance and safe, secure, storage.

7. Always be a "straight arrow" in all your gun-related activities. Your good reputation within the collecting fraternity will bring you buying

opportunities as well as respect, and will build respect for our hobby from the public, news media, and authorities as well.

8. Maintain an accurate and up-to-date inventory - with current values - and share it with your wife. After all, your gun collection should be an asset of ever-increasing value, and that up-to-date inventory is the best way there is to keep her from being robbed by vultures if something should happen to you.

9. Share your knowledge but always be ready to admit ignorance. You may be the very top expert on your collecting specialty, but no one knows everything about anything and even the rankest beginner has seen guns you haven't and knows things you don't!

And finally...

10. Invest in the preservation of the future of gun collecting by:

   • Doing your homework, so you can adequately and intelligently defend collecting to friends and acquaintances;

   • Carefully monitoring the political scene, always being ready to contribute time and money when needed to defend your collecting hobby; and

   • Being a mentor, introducing interested friends and relatives to the pleasures of collecting and assisting the newcomers you meet at shows or gun shops in their collecting efforts.

Great Collecting!

2001: The Year in Review

By Dave Tinker

The September 11 terrorist attacks on New York and Washington shocked and saddened all Americans but they also awakened a new sense of patriotism in the United States and reversed almost every trend in the firearms industry for most of 2001.

Sudden demand for just about every product this industry sells caught most manufacturers and wholesalers by surprise. The attacks came as most companies were eliminating inventory and scaling back manufacturing rates while they set up production lines for 2002. The instant demand rapidly ate up inventories of such items as web gear, gas masks, mace, body armor and just about every firearm that might have a military, law enforcement or home defense application.

The U.S. government was the largest and best customer in the weeks following the attacks. Federal law enforcement agencies and some military branches that normally place orders through the General Services Administration began buying directly from wholesalers in an effort to speed deliveries. State and local law enforcement departments were similarly active.

Ammunition demand continued to surprise two weeks after the attacks. Spot shortages of certain calibers, mainly .223, 7.62 and .45 ACP have been reported around the country but so far, manufacturers have held the line on prices. They are not, however, giving the same discounts they were offering earlier in the month.

Major brands weren't the only ones being snapped up, distributors said. The market surge has worked its way down the list of brand names.

"We sold out of just about everything," one marketer noted. "We moved more Blazer than I ever thought we would and lesser known brands like Fiocchi and Dynamit Nobel also sold out. The problem is that most of the companies had cut back on their manufacturing rates and inventory before all this happened. Now it is almost impossible to get anything in a timely manner."

The market for inexpensive imported brands like **Russian-made Wolf**--the star of the low price products--tightened quickly and replacement costs were much higher. Although retailers are still selling the stuff for around $99 a case, they are being quoted prices as high as $149 for future deliveries.

On the firearm side, the market grew predictably tighter for AR-style rifles. **Bushmaster** has been a strong seller for many distributors all summer and continues to be during the crisis. Demand was also high for **Colt AR** rifles but they were almost impossible to get.

"Colt's will make rifles for us but they are asking for payment up front, with no guaranteed delivery date," a market source said. "The company did say that anyone who bought into the program would get priority on deliveries. Maybe somebody will buy, but we don't plan to right now."

As welcome as the extra business might be, it is business the industry would have preferred to find under different circumstances.

Before the tragic events of September 11, the industry was enduring yet another season of lackluster sales. The trend began developing early in the year.

The SHOT Show made an inauspicious return to New Orleans in January, setting a record for square feet of exhibit space but falling well short of what the industry had hoped for in terms of dealer buying activity.

National Shooting Sports Foundation officials sold more than 486,000 square feet of booth space at the New Orleans show, establishing a new record. But that was tempered by a drop in the number of buyers. Those who did go to New Orleans didn't exactly burn up the old checkbook. Most manufacturers and distributors described the purchasing as "conservative" and suggested that fears of an economic slowdown may have hurt business.

Firearms sales in the first three months of 2001 were off anywhere from 10 to 20 percent, a decline almost wholly the result of terrible February sales. March was comparatively better although market observers detected some quiet discounting as manufacturers tried to get inventory moving through the pipeline.

Sturm, Ruger & Company was a shining example of the market in the first half of 2001. Firearm shipments dropped by almost 40 percent. Ruger's first quarter sales of $43.9 million were $16 million lower than in the same period a year earlier when sales came to $59.9 million. Firearm sales accounted for $35.8 million, compared to $51 million last year. Net income for the quarter was $4.1 million, less than half the $9 million Ruger made in the same quarter in 2000.

Through the first six months of 2001, Ruger sales came to $81.5 million, down from $108.8 million in 2000. Net income for the six-month period was $5.9 million. Firearm sales were down sharply for the quarter and for the six months. Second quarter volumes came to $29.5 million, about $8 million lower than in the corresponding period last year. For the six months, gun sales totaled $65.4 million, compared to $88.7 million last year.

The same conditions were evident in the ammunition and accessories markets.

Blount Inc., owner of **Federal Cartridge**, **CCI**, **Simmons**, **Weaver** and a host of other brands, had a disappointing first quarter. The group reported first quarter sales of $55.5 million, a 24.4 percent drop from the $73.4 million posted in 2000. The group ended the quarter with a manufacturing backlog of $24.1 million, down from $36.3 million in 2000.

The company said ammunition markets outside law enforcement were hurt by slow retail sales, high distributor inventories and competitive discounting. Those developments hurt sales and margins as well, although Blount implemented cost reduction measures and production cuts partially offset the weak market.

Olin's Winchester unit was not a strong first-quarter performer. The ammunition division lost $700,000 on $55.6 million in sales. In the same period a year earlier, Winchester rang up $61.6 million in sales, good for an operating income of $4.7 million.

Winchester's second quarter sales came to $62.4 million, a 7 percent reduction from last year's $67.4 million. The ammunition producer made $2.3 million in the quarter, exactly half what it earned last year at the same time.

Through the first six months of the year, Winchester booked $118 million in sales, down $11 million from last year's $129 million. Operating income for the year came to $1.6 million, compared to $9.3 million last year.

Remington Arms Company got hit on both sides of the market. For the six months, sales came to $177.3 million, down from $198.1 million in 2000. Remington's net income came to $5.1 million. In 2000, the firm made $6 million.

In the first six months of the year, firearms sales came to $96.8 million, down slightly from the $100.3 million Remington showed last year. The downturn was blamed on weak shotgun markets, although higher rifle prices helped offset the trend.

Ammunition was down 24 percent in the second quarter, slipping to $29.2 million from $38.4 million at the same time in 2000. Through the first six months of the year, Remington's ammo sales came to $56.7 million. Last year, ammo sales hit $72.4 million.

"The decrease in ammunition is largely attributable to a decline in demand," the company said. "Management believes the slowdown was caused by a number of factors relating to the current economic slowdown, including reduction of customer inventories. In addition, we have faced competitive price reductions in many categories. This softness in demand and pricing may continue through 2001."

A good part of the ammunition manufacturers' market problems could be traced to ultra-cheap foreign-made product. Russian-made Wolf ammunition made a major if unexpected impact on the market early in the year when it landed here at less than $70 a case and prices got even lower as 2001 progressed. By fall, distributors were paying a little under $60 per 1,000 rounds.

At least one major producer decided to fight fire with fire. **Winchester** had .223 ball ammunition made in Israel, a move that freed its loaders for lines that had better margins.

As firearm markets continued to languish into the summer, manufacturers brought out the big guns--or at least some guns that had sold well in the past.

Colt's Manufacturing Company reprised some of its old favorites after being practically out of the handgun market for several months. The company started its marketing effort with a custom shop offering that was be an exact replication of the original **1911A1**, including packaging.

Part of a limited run of just 4,000 guns, the 1911 pistols featured a pre-Series 70 firing system, original World War II roll marks, parkerized finish, and wide spur hammers, safeties and slide stops with original serrations. It came with two magazines.

Colt's also re-introduced its **Python .357 Magnum** and the **Anaconda .44 Magnum** revolvers. Both are made of stainless steel. The Python comes with a 6-inch barrel while the Anaconda will be available with 6-inch or 8-inch barrels.

Bringing the Anaconda and Python back was a good move for Colt's, not just because revolvers were one of the few bright spots in the handgun market. A scheduled late summer delivery date had dealers hoping the gun would sell well. There is no doubt that it interests the customers because the price shot up to about $1,500 when Colt discontinued the Anaconda.

"It's all about timing with the Anaconda because it's a hunting gun and people want to buy their hunting guns in the fall," a wholesaler observed. "Colt's always had the gun out in January or February, when nobody wanted it."

Other manufacturers took a more direct route to draw consumers into the stores by offering attractive cash rebates to retail buyers of some of their slower-moving lines. It was the first time consumers got cash-back deals in almost 10 years.

Remington gave $25 cash back to consumers who buy a **Model 870 Express** shotgun in any of the 30 versions the company produces. Ruger's program gave back $40 to consumers who bought from its **P-Series** line of pistols. **Mark II** and **22/45** pistol buyers got back $20. It was, by all accounts, an early success.

"This plan is going to work; It is already having an effect on sales," one Ruger distributor commented. "This is the first 'pull through' program they've done in a long time so it should help."

No other companies matched the Remington and Ruger rebates. Many didn't have the wherewithal to do it. Others claimed it wasn't necessary.

"Our new products have inspired a lot of interest and business is brisk, so we don't feel the need to give money away," said one executive. "When you have what the market is looking for, your sales will rise."

Ironically, the rebates came as handgun sales were beginning to improve. At retail, sales improvements had as much to do with circumstance as brilliant marketing. For example, Michigan's new concealed carry law has been a major factor in strong sales of smaller pistols and revolvers. The new lightweight wheel guns are particularly popular, dealers said.

Taurus International Manufacturing said its new **CIA revolver** has been a smashing success everywhere. Marketing executives said demand for the gun was heavy from its introduction, noting that "Brazil can't make them fast enough."

Smith & Wesson didn't fare well in the market but it did find a new owner in May. The company hopes the change will stimulate a return to the market status it enjoyed before making settlement deals that required major changes to its manufacturing and marketing practices.

The new owner is **Saf-T-Hammer Corporation,** a small lock and safety device manufacturer run by former S&W executive Robert Scott. Although Saf-T-Hammer reported almost no sales, it purchased Smith & Wesson from Tomkins PLC for $15 million in cash. The firm paid $5 million upon closing and the balance due in May 2002.

Saf-T-Hammer incurred significant debt to buy Smith & Wesson from British conglomerate Tomkins PLC for $15 million, much of it due within a year, according to documents the firm filed with the U.S. Securities and Exchange Commission.

The $5 million down payment Saf-T-Hammer paid Tomkins was borrowed from Colton Melby, the former owner of a Washington aerospace company. That note is due in May 2002, as is the remaining $10 million owed Tomkins. On top of those obligations, the firm also assumed a $30 million note Smith & Wesson owed Tomkins.

"Smith & Wesson, a brand name for 147 years, would be at the top of any list of immediately identifiable corporate logos recognized worldwide," said Scott, who was named president of his former company. "We are proud to return this storied company to American ownership. We intend to maximize the value of the name and to fully utilize the manufacturing, marketing and worldwide distribution assets of the company to create appreciation and value for our shareholders.

"We also plan to increase the company's revenues through expanded branding activities and strategic acquisitions that will complement the company's current product lines," Scott added. "As part of the synergy between our two companies, we plan to incorporate Saf-T-Hammer products into the firearms manufactured by Smith & Wesson."

The company has a long way to go before it can return to profitability. In the year following its agreement with the U.S. Department of Housing and Urban Development and its settlement of the Boston lawsuit, **Smith & Wesson** lost more than $57 million

Sales for the fiscal year ended April 28, 2001 came to $70.7 million, down $41.3 million from the prior year. S&W reported an operating loss of $48.4 million for the period, which included a $29 million write-off of goodwill related to the 1987 purchase of the company by British conglomerate Tomkins PLC. The bleeding continued through the end of July, with the manufacturer losing another $6 million on a little more than $11 million in sales.

One of the shooting sports industry's best-known accessories brands changed ownership when **Michael's of Oregon** purchased **Hoppe's** from **Brunswick Corporation.**

Michael's was already among the largest accessories manufacturers with its holster lines. The Hoppe's acquisition gave the company a well-known brand with which to strengthen its position in the gun cleaning and maintenance market. Michael's also manufactures **BoreSnake** bore cleaners.

"We're excited to welcome Hoppe's into Michael's growing family of shooting products and accessories," said **Michael's President Dennis Pixton**. "The Hoppe's name is synonymous with quality gun care and we're ecstatic to be able to expand the breadth of our line with these products."

Gun manufacturers fared better in court than in the marketplace.

The industry posted an impressive string of legal successes through the summer, highlighted by the Second Circuit U.S. Court of Appeals' unanimous reversal of a jury verdict in *the Hamilton v. Accu-Tek* negligent marketing lawsuit and dismissal of the case. The panel's decision affirmed an earlier ruling by the **New York Court of Appeals** that said there was no basis in law to hold manufacturers liable for the criminal misuse of their products.

"We trust this puts the final nail in the coffin of this distasteful experiment to harass legal and responsible manufacturers through unproven and convoluted legal theory," said **National Shooting Sports Foundation President Bob Delfay**.

Just two weeks before the federal appeals court ruled on the Hamilton case, **New York Judge Louis B. York** granted a motion to dismiss a public nuisance claim brought against the industry by **Attorney General Eliot Spitzer**.

"The parties most directly responsible for the unlawful use of handguns are the individuals who unlawfully use them," Judge York said. "But for their conduct, the nuisance alleged would not exist. The relief sought would have the potential effect of preventing defendants from engaging in activities they are permitted to engage in by law, in an area strongly controlled by various federal and state statutes."

Continuing the trend, the **Louisiana Supreme Court** threw out **New Orleans'** lawsuit seeking to hold the industry responsible for the costs of the city's crime and gun violence problems.

The 5-2 decision reversed last year's lower court ruling that allowed the suit to proceed despite a state law preempting such actions. The law, passed in 1999, may be retroactively applied to New Orleans' 1998 lawsuit, justices said. The U.S. and Louisiana constitutions protect private citizens, not local governments, against retroactive enforcement of laws.

The ruling called the New Orleans suit "an indirect attempt to regulate the lawful design, manufacture, marketing and sale of firearms," a power which the state gave itself with the 1999 law. State regulation of firearms is of vital interest to the citizens of Louisiana. Allowing municipalities to regulate the industry by lawsuit "could conceivably threaten the public safety and welfare by resulting in haphazard and inconsistent rules."

The **California Supreme Court** said gun manufacturers cannot be held liable for the criminal misuse of their products, a decision that could have a national impact on similar litigation. **101 California**, as the case is known throughout the industry, was dismissed and reinstated at least three times since it was filed in 1994 with the help of **Handgun Control, Inc**.

The 5-1 decision reversed a ruling by the California **First District Court of Appeals** that said victims of the 1993 incident should be allowed to sue the manufacturer of the gun. The killer, **Gian Luigi Ferri**, purchased the gun in Nevada and brought it to San Francisco.

A key element in the case was whether **Navegar, Inc.,** maker of the TEC-DC9 pistol used in a shooting rampage at a San Francisco law firm, should be responsible for damages because it allegedly marketed its gun to "criminal elements" and "directed its sales toward people with violent tendencies."

Justice Ming W. Chin, writing for the majority, said a 1983 California law prohibits lawsuits against makers of nondefective products on the grounds that the benefits of the products are outweighed by the dangers they pose.

"We are not insensitive to the terrible tragedy that occurred on July 1, 1993, or the devastating effect of Ferri's rampage on his victims and their loved ones," Ming wrote. "But to rule for the victims would open the doors for virtually every person injured by a gun to sue."

In yet another devastating loss for those who want to change the industry via litigation, the **Connecticut Supreme Court** said the **City of Bridgeport** had no legal basis to sue gun manufacturers. The October 1 decision affirmed a lower court's dismissal of the lawsuit. It was the ninth dismissal of a municipal suit in the last two years.

"In light of the events of September 11, we must all unite as never before," said Ruger Senior Executive Vice President and General Counsel Stephen L. Sanetti. "We respectfully submit that our cities should not spend one more minute or one more dime wrongly attacking those companies which have proudly armed our police, military and law-abiding citizens in times of peril. We again stand ready to assist our nation as the great arsenal of democracy."

PRICING CLASS III FIREARMS

Text by J. R. Moody

The market price for NFA weapons as been steadily increasing, although in the past year or so the increase has been quite dramatic. Twenty years ago a new M16 rifle cost approximately $350; today it's about $4,500. During the same period a German light machine gun, the MG42, cost about $900. Today, if one can be found, its cost is approximately $10,000 or more. The most important aspects of the pricing formula are rarity, desirability, and historical significance. Keep in mind that these guns are not bought on the world market at prices much lower than private sales to individuals. These guns bring a premium because the buyer is in essence purchasing the grandfathered registration paperwork of the weapon plus the weapon itself.

In order to better understand the pricing structure of NFA weapons it is necessary to understand the different chronological sequences that NFA weapons went through. There were periods of time which gradually decreased the incoming supply of NFA weapons entering the NFA registry. The Gun Control Act of 1968 was one of the most crucial. Pursuant to NFA weapons the 1968 Act stipulated that no more imported machine guns could be brought into the system. As a result pre-1968 imported guns command a premium because of their original manufacture. During 1968 the NFA branch of the ATF allowed a one-year amnesty period so that returning servicemen from Vietnam could register their war trophies. It was during this period that many AK47s, PPSH41s, and MP40 machine guns were put into the system. Many more U.S. and foreign manufactured guns were also registered at this time as well. All of these guns command a premium because of their originality and registration.

Domestic production of NFA weapons continued until 1986 when the 1986 Gun Control Act prohibited the registration of domestic machine guns. Thus the door was closed to any further production of machine guns available to individuals. NFA weapons already registered could remain in the system and be transferred to qualified individuals. This situation drove prices higher and continues to do so. This group of weapons consist of many desirable semi-automatic that were legally converted into fully automatic weapons. These include the HK94s converted to the MP5, the HK91s converted to the G3, and the HK93 converted to the HK33. There were many Browning .30 and .50 caliber machine guns manufactured during this time frame as well. But remember pedigree determines price. An original pre-1968 Israeli-manufactured Uzi will fetch over $9,000 where as a U.S. manufactured Uzi built during the same time period will only bring $2,700.

Those individuals who wish to be Class III dealers in machine guns have many more NFA weapons to choose from especially the newer, more contemporary designs. Pre-1986 dealer samples, imported before 1986, can be transferred between dealers only and retained personally by them after they surrender their Class III licenses. Only people who wish to engage in active business of buying and selling machine guns should do this as it entails much more paperwork and responsibility. These dealers samples can only be transferred to other dealers. Some of these contemporary guns are very rare and desirable. For example, a pre-1986 dealer sample FN MAG machine gun in excellent condition will bring upwards of $50,000 because only about six of these guns were imported into the country before 1986. Supply and demand rule here.

Post-1986 dealer samples are even more restrictive. Only dealers who can produce a law enforcement letter wishing to demonstrate these weapons can obtain them. Unlike the pre-1986 samples these post-1986 samples cannot be retained after their license is surrendered. It is for this reason that post-1986 dealer sample prices are not given.

It is always important to keep in mind that these NFA firearms are heavily regulated and strict federal rules must be adhered to. Always follow NFA rules. When in doubt call or write the ATF for clarification.

J. R. Moody, a degreed historian, has been collecting and shooting Class III firearms for twenty years because he enjoys the historical and technological aspects of these firearms. He competes successfully at sub-machine matches across the country. On several occasions he has defeated the National Champion. In addition he works as a consultant to Knight's Armament Company, one of the country's leading small arms contractors to U.S. military forces and law enforcement agencies.

ADVISORY: For those readers who are interested in advancing their knowledge and understanding of Class III firearms it is recommended that they subscribe to *Small Arms Review*, a first rate publication that has many informative and useful features. There are sections on the law, new products, and illuminating articles on all aspects of NFA weapons and their history. *Small Arms Review* may be contacted at Moose Lake Publishing, 223 Sugar Hill Rd., Harmony, ME 04942. Telephone 207-683-2959 or FAX 203-683-2172. E-mail SARreview@aol/com. Website-http://www. smallarmsreview.com.

NOTE: *The prices listed in this section reflect the most current information as of publication date. Class III firearms are very volatile with rapid and sudden price changes. It is highly recommended that the latest market prices be verified in a particular market prior to a sale.*

SUB-MACHINE GUNS

NOTE: Prices listed below reflect the gun only with one magazine and no accessories.

Beretta Model 1938A

Pre-1968

Exc.	V.G.	Fair
5500	5200	4700

Pre-1986 conversions

Exc.	V.G.	Fair
4500	4200	3750

Pre-1986 Dealer samples

Exc.	V.G.	Fair
3500	3000	2500

Beretta Model 38/42

Pre-1968

Exc.	V.G.	Fair
4750	4200	3750

Pre-1986 conversions

Exc.	V.G.	Fair
N/A	N/A	N/A

Pre-1986 Dealer samples

Exc.	V.G.	Fair
2500	2200	2000

Beretta Model 12

Pre-1968 (Rare)

Exc.	V.G.	Fair
8000	7500	6500

Pre-1986 conversions

Exc.	V.G.	Fair
N/A	N/A	N/A

Pre-1986 Dealer samples

Exc.	V.G.	Fair
3500	3000	2500

Beretta Model 12S

Pre-1968

Exc.	V.G.	Fair
N/A	N/A	N/A

Pre-1986 conversions

Exc.	V.G.	Fair
N/A	N/A	N/A

Pre-1986 Dealer samples

Exc.	V.G.	Fair
5000	4500	4000

MP18/1 (WWI)

Pre-1968

Exc.	V.G.	Fair
5250	4500	4000

Pre-1986 conversions

Exc.	V.G.	Fair
N/A	N/A	N/A

Pre-1986 Dealer samples

Exc.	V.G.	Fair
2500	2250	2000

MP18/1 (Post-war)

Pre-1968

Exc.	V.G.	Fair
4750	4000	3500

Pre-1986 conversions

Exc.	V.G.	Fair
N/A	N/A	N/A

Pre-1986 Dealer samples

Exc.	V.G.	Fair
N/A	N/A	N/A

Bergman MP28

Pre-1968

Exc.	V.G.	Fair
4500	4000	3500

Pre-1986 conversions

Exc.	V.G.	Fair
N/A	N/A	N/A

Pre-1986 Dealer samples

Exc.	V.G.	Fair
2750	2500	2000

Carl Gustav 45

Pre-1968

Exc.	V.G.	Fair
7500	7000	6500

Pre-1986 conversions

Exc.	V.G.	Fair
4250	3750	3250

Pre-1986 Dealer samples

Exc.	V.G.	Fair
3000	2500	2000

NOTE: Add 33% for M45/B model which features a different non-removable magazine well, green finish, and improved bolt retention.

Colt 9mm

Pre-1968

Exc.	V.G.	Fair
N/A	N/A	N/A

Pre-1986 conversions, for OEM add 20%

Exc.	V.G.	Fair
6500	6000	5500

Pre-1986 Dealer samples

Exc.	V.G.	Fair
N/A	N/A	N/A

Danish Hovea Model 49

Pre-1968

Exc.	V.G.	Fair
9000	8000	7500

Pre-1986 conversions

Exc.	V.G.	Fair
N/A	N/A	N/A

Pre-1986 Dealer samples

Exc.	V.G.	Fair
N/A	N/A	N/A

Erma EMP

Pre-1968

Exc.	V.G.	Fair
5000	4000	3500

Pre-1986 conversions

Exc.	V.G.	Fair
N/A	N/A	N/A

Pre-1986 Dealer samples

Exc.	V.G.	Fair
3000	2500	2000

Franchi LF-57

Pre-1968

Exc.	V.G.	Fair
5500	4750	4500

Pre-1986 conversions

Exc.	V.G.	Fair
N/A	N/A	N/A

Pre-1986 Dealer samples

Exc.	V.G.	Fair
2500	2000	1750

H&K MP5

Pre-1968 (Rare)

Exc.	V.G.	Fair
12000	11000	10500

Pre-1986 conversions

Exc.	V.G.	Fair
9750	9250	9000

NOTE: Add 15% for registered receiver using OEM parts.

Pre-1986 Dealer samples

Exc.	V.G.	Fair
5000	4500	4000

HK MP5 K

Pre-1968 (Rare)

Exc.	V.G.	Fair
N/A	N/A	N/A

Pre-1986 conversions

Exc.	V.G.	Fair
8500	8000	7000

NOTE: Add 15% for registered receiver using OEM parts.

Pre-1986 Dealer samples

Exc.	V.G.	Fair
5500	5000	4750

HK MP5 SD

Pre-1968

Exc.	V.G.	Fair
N/A	N/A	N/A

Pre-1986 conversions

Exc.	V.G.	Fair
10500	9500	9000

NOTE: Add 15% for registered receiver using OEM parts.

Pre-1986 Dealer samples

Exc.	V.G.	Fair
5500	5250	5000

HK53

Pre-1968

Exc.	V.G.	Fair
N/A	N/A	N/A

Pre-1986 conversions

Exc.	V.G.	Fair
8750	8000	7500

Pre-1986 Dealer samples

Exc.	V.G.	Fair
6000	5000	4500

Ingram Model 10

Pre-1968

Exc.	V.G.	Fair
1500	1200	1000

Pre-1986 conversions

Exc.	V.G.	Fair
N/A	N/A	N/A

Pre-1986 Dealer samples

Exc.	V.G.	Fair
N/A	N/A	N/A

Japan 100/44

Pre-1968

Exc.	V.G.	Fair
4750	4500	4000

Pre-1986 conversions

Exc.	V.G.	Fair
N/A	N/A	N/A

Pre-1986 Dealer samples

Exc.	V.G.	Fair
N/A	N/A	N/A

Lanchester

Pre-1968

Exc.	V.G.	Fair
6000	5500	5000

Pre-1986 conversions

Exc.	V.G.	Fair
N/A	N/A	N/A

Pre-1986 Dealer samples

Exc.	V.G.	Fair
3500	3000	2500

Madsen M50

Pre-1968

Exc.	V.G.	Fair
4000	3500	3000

Pre-1986 conversions

Exc.	V.G.	Fair
2900	2500	2000

Pre-1986 Dealer samples

Exc.	V.G.	Fair
2500	2000	1500

MAS 38

Pre-1968

Exc.	V.G.	Fair
3000	2500	2000

Pre-1986 conversions

Exc.	V.G.	Fair
N/A	N/A	N/A

Pre-1986 Dealer samples

Exc.	V.G.	Fair
N/A	N/A	N/A

MAT 49

Pre-1968

Exc.	V.G.	Fair
8000	7500	7000

Pre-1986 conversions

Exc.	V.G.	Fair
N/A	N/A	N/A

Pre-1986 Dealer samples

Exc.	V.G.	Fair
N/A	N/A	N/A

Mauser Schnellfeuer (Model 712)

Pre-1968

Exc.	V.G.	Fair
7500	7000	6500

Pre-1986 conversions

Exc.	V.G.	Fair
N/A	N/A	N/A

Pre-1986 Dealer samples

Exc.	V.G.	Fair
5000	4500	4000

MP35

Pre-1968

Exc.	V.G.	Fair
5000	4500	4000

Pre-1986 conversions

Exc.	V.G.	Fair
N/A	N/A	N/A

Pre-1986 Dealer samples

Exc.	V.G.	Fair
N/A	N/A	N/A

MP38

Pre-1968 (Rare)

Exc.	V.G.	Fair
11000	10500	9500

Pre-1986 conversions (or U.S. manufactured parts)

Exc.	V.G.	Fair
5750	5500	5000

Pre-1986 Dealer samples

Exc.	V.G.	Fair
N/A	N/A	N/A

MP40

Pre-1968

Exc.	V.G.	Fair
7500	7000	6000

Pre-1986 conversions (or U.S. manufactured receivers)

Exc.	V.G.	Fair
5000	4500	4000

Pre-1986 Dealer samples

Exc.	V.G.	Fair
3000	2500	2500

MP41

Pre-1968 (Rare)

Exc.	V.G.	Fair
11000	10500	9000

Pre-1986 conversions

Exc.	V.G.	Fair
N/A	N/A	N/A

Pre-1986 Dealer samples

Exc.	V.G.	Fair
N/A	N/A	N/A

Owen

Pre-1968

Exc.	V.G.	Fair
5000	4500	4000

Pre-1986 conversions

Exc.	V.G.	Fair
N/A	N/A	N/A

Pre-1986 Dealer samples

Exc.	V.G.	Fair
2500	2250	2000

PPD-1940

Pre-1968

Exc.	V.G.	Fair
7500	6500	5500

Pre-1986 conversions

Exc.	V.G.	Fair
N/A	N/A	N/A

Pre-1986 Dealer samples

Exc.	V.G.	Fair
N/A	N/A	N/A

PPS-43

Pre-1968

Exc.	V.G.	Fair
7500	6500	5500

Pre-1986 conversions

Exc.	V.G.	Fair
N/A	N/A	N/A

Pre-1986 Dealer samples

Exc.	V.G.	Fair
N/A	N/A	N/A

PPsh-41

Pre-1968

Exc.	V.G.	Fair
7000	6000	5000

Pre-1986 conversions

Exc.	V.G.	Fair
N/A	N/A	N/A

Pre-1986 Dealer samples

Exc.	V.G.	Fair
N/A	N/A	N/A

Reising 50

Pre-1968

Exc.	V.G.	Fair
2500	2000	1500

Pre-1986 conversions

Exc.	V.G.	Fair
N/A	N/A	N/A

Pre-1986 Dealer samples

Exc.	V.G.	Fair
1500	1000	750

Star Z-70

Pre-1968

Exc.	V.G.	Fair
6000	5500	5000

Pre-1986 conversions

Exc.	V.G.	Fair
N/A	N/A	N/A

Pre-1986 Dealer samples

Exc.	V.G.	Fair
3500	2500	2000

Sten Mark II

Pre-1968

Exc.	V.G.	Fair
4000	3500	3500

Pre-1986 conversions (or U.S. manu-factured receivers)

Exc.	V.G.	Fair
2500	2000	2000

Pre-1986 Dealer samples

Exc.	V.G.	Fair
2000	1500	1000

Sten Mark V

Pre-1968

Exc.	V.G.	Fair
4750	4250	4000

Pre-1986 conversions

Exc.	V.G.	Fair
3500	3000	2750

Pre-1986 Dealer samples

Exc.	V.G.	Fair
2000	1500	1000

Sterling

Pre-1968 (Rare)

Exc.	V.G.	Fair
9000	8500	8000

Pre-1986 conversions

Exc.	V.G.	Fair
5000	4500	4500

Pre-1986 Dealer samples

Exc.	V.G.	Fair
5000	4500	3250

Steyr Mpi69

Pre-1968 (Rare)

Exc.	V.G.	Fair
9000	8500	8000

Pre-1986 conversions

Exc.	V.G.	Fair
N/A	N/A	N/A

Pre-1986 Dealer samples

Exc.	V.G.	Fair
2500	2250	2000

Suomi Model 1931

Pre-1968

Exc.	V.G.	Fair
8000	7500	7000

Pre-1986 conversions

Exc.	V.G.	Fair
N/A	N/A	N/A

Pre-1986 Dealer samples

Exc.	V.G.	Fair
3500	3000	2500

Suomi Model 1944

Pre-1968

Exc.	V.G.	Fair
8000	7500	7000

Pre-1986 conversions

Exc.	V.G.	Fair
N/A	N/A	N/A

Pre-1986 Dealer samples

Exc.	V.G.	Fair
3500	3000	2500

Thompson Model 1921/21AC/21A

Pre-1968

Exc.	V.G.	Fair
25000	17500	12000

Pre-1986 conversions

Exc.	V.G.	Fair
N/A	N/A	N/A

Pre-1986 Dealer samples

Exc.	V.G.	Fair
N/A	N/A	N/A

Thompson Model 1928 Commercial

Pre-1968

Exc.	V.G.	Fair
18000	15000	10000

Pre-1986 conversions

Exc.	V.G.	Fair
N/A	N/A	N/A

Pre-1986 Dealer samples

Exc.	V.G.	Fair
9000	7500	5000

NOTE: For Model 1928A1 .45ACP guns built by Auto Ordnance in West Hurley, NY deduct 60%, for .22 caliber version deduct 70%.

Thompson Model 1928A1 U.S. Military

Pre-1968

Exc.	V.G.	Fair
12000	10000	8000

Pre-1986 conversions

Exc.	V.G.	Fair
N/A	N/A	N/A

Pre-1986 Dealer samples

Exc.	V.G.	Fair
6000	5000	4000

Thompson M1/M1A1

Pre-1968

Exc.	V.G.	Fair
10500	8500	7000

Pre-1986 conversions

Exc.	V.G.	Fair
N/A	N/A	N/A

Pre-1986 Dealer samples

Exc.	V.G.	Fair
5000	4000	3500

NOTE: For Model 1928A1 guns built by Auto Ordnance in West Hurley, NY deduct 30%.

UD (United Defense) M42

Pre-1968

Exc.	V.G.	Fair
6000	5500	5000

Pre-1986 conversions

Exc.	V.G.	Fair
N/A	N/A	N/A

Pre-1986 Dealer samples

Exc.	V.G.	Fair
N/A	N/A	N/A

US M3

Pre-1968

Exc.	V.G.	Fair
6500	6000	5500

Pre-1986 conversions (or current U.S. manufacture)

Exc.	V.G.	Fair
5000	4500	4200

Pre-1986 Dealer samples

Exc.	V.G.	Fair
3500	3000	2000

US M3A1

Pre-1968

Exc.	V.G.	Fair
9000	8000	7000

Pre-1986 conversions (or current U.S. manufacture)

Exc.	V.G.	Fair
6000	5500	5000

Pre-1986 Dealer samples

Exc.	V.G.	Fair
4000	3500	3000

UZI

Pre-1968 (Very Rare)

Exc.	V.G.	Fair
10000	9000	8000

Pre-1986 conversions

Exc.	V.G.	Fair
3000	2500	2300

Vector Uzi pre-1986 conversion

Pre-1986 conversions

NIB/Exc.	V.G.	Fair
3000	2500	2300

Mini-UZI

Pre-1968

Exc.	V.G.	Fair
N/A	N/A	N/A

Pre-1986 conversions

Exc.	V.G.	Fair
5000	4500	4000

Pre-1986 Dealer samples

Exc.	V.G.	Fair
3500	2750	2500

Vietcong K-50M

Pre-1968

Exc.	V.G.	Fair
7000	6500	6000

Pre-1986 conversions

Exc.	V.G.	Fair
N/A	N/A	N/A

Pre-1986 Dealer samples

Exc.	V.G.	Fair
N/A	N/A	N/A

Walter MPK and MPL

Pre-1968 (Rare)

Exc.	V.G.	Fair
12000	10000	9000

Pre-1986 conversions

Exc.	V.G.	Fair
N/A	N/A	N/A

Pre-1986 Dealer samples

Exc.	V.G.	Fair
2500	2000	1900

Smith & Wesson Model 76

Pre-1968

Exc.	V.G.	Fair
3500	3000	2750

Pre-1986 conversions (or Model 760)

Exc.	V.G.	Fair
2250	1750	1500

Pre-1986 Dealer samples

Exc.	V.G.	Fair
N/A	N/A	N/A

Yugoslav Model 49

Pre-1968

Exc.	V.G.	Fair
6500	6000	5000

Pre-1986 conversions

Exc.	V.G.	Fair
N/A	N/A	N/A

Pre-1986 Dealer samples

Exc.	V.G.	Fair
4000	3500	2750

Yugoslav Model 56

Pre-1968

Exc.	V.G.	Fair
7500	5500	4000

Pre-1986 conversions

Exc.	V.G.	Fair
5500	4500	4000

Pre-1986 Dealer samples

Exc.	V.G.	Fair
3500	3200	3000

AUTOMATIC RIFLES

NOTE: Prices listed below reflect the gun only with one magazine and no accessories.

Armalite AR-18

Pre-1968

Exc.	V.G.	Fair
4500	4200	4000

Pre-1986 conversions

Exc.	V.G.	Fair
3000	3000	3000

Pre-1986 Dealer samples

Exc.	V.G.	Fair
N/A	N/A	N/A

Beretta Model BM59

Pre-1968

Exc.	V.G.	Fair
5500	5000	4500

Pre-1986 conversions

Exc.	V.G.	Fair
4500	4000	3500

Pre-1986 Dealer samples

Exc.	V.G.	Fair
N/A	N/A	N/A

Beretta AR70/.223

Pre-1968 (Rare)

Exc.	V.G.	Fair
12000	8000	8000

Pre-1986 conversions

Exc.	V.G.	Fair
10000	7500	5000

Pre-1986 Dealer samples

Exc.	V.G.	Fair
6500	5000	5000

Beretta SC70

Pre-1968

Exc.	V.G.	Fair
12000	9500	8500

Pre-1986 conversions

Exc.	V.G.	Fair
10000	8000	6500

Pre-1986 Dealer samples

Exc.	V.G.	Fair
8000	6500	5500

Chinese Type 56 Rifle

Pre-1968

Exc.	V.G.	Fair
14000	12000	10000

Pre-1986 conversions

Exc.	V.G.	Fair
7500	6500	6000

Pre-1986 Dealer samples

Exc.	V.G.	Fair
5000	4000	3850

FG 42

Pre-1968 (Extremely Rare)

Exc.	V.G.	Fair
35000	30000	25000

Pre-1986 conversions

Exc.	V.G.	Fair
N/A	N/A	N/A

Pre-1986 Dealer samples

Exc.	V.G.	Fair
N/A	N/A	N/A

FN FAL

Pre-1968 (Rare)

Exc.	V.G.	Fair
9000	8500	8000

Pre-1986 conversions

Exc.	V.G.	Fair
5500	5000	4500

Pre-1986 Dealer samples

Exc.	V.G.	Fair
4000	3500	3000

FN CAL

Pre-1968 (Rare)

Exc.	V.G.	Fair
10000	9000	8500

Pre-1986 conversions

Exc.	V.G.	Fair
8500	8000	7500

Pre-1986 Dealer samples

Exc.	V.G.	Fair
5000	5000	6800

FN FNC

Pre-1968

Exc.	V.G.	Fair
N/A	N/A	N/A

Pre-1986 conversions

Exc.	V.G.	Fair
5500	4500	4000

Galil ARM

Pre-1968

Exc.	V.G.	Fair
N/A	N/A	N/A

Pre-1986 conversions

Exc.	V.G.	Fair
10000	7500	7000

Pre-1986 Dealer samples (Rare)

Exc.	V.G.	Fair
10000	9000	8500

Galil SAR

Pre-1968

Exc.	V.G.	Fair
N/A	N/A	N/A

Pre-1986 conversions

Exc.	V.G.	Fair
10000	9000	8500

Pre-1986 Dealer samples

Exc.	V.G.	Fair
10000	9000	8500

HK G3

Pre-1968

Exc.	V.G.	Fair
9000	8750	8500

Pre-1986 conversions

Exc.	V.G.	Fair
7000	6500	6000

Pre-1986 Dealer samples

Exc.	V.G.	Fair
4500	3800	3500

HK33

Pre-1968 (Very Rare)

Exc.	V.G.	Fair
10000	9500	9000

Pre-1986 conversions

Exc.	V.G.	Fair
8000	7500	7000

Pre-1986 Dealer samples

Exc.	V.G.	Fair
3500	3200	3000

Pre-1986 Dealer samples

Exc.	V.G.	Fair
4000	3800	3500

NOTE: The HK33K is the same as the HK33 with the exception of a 13" barrel. Prices may differ slightly for the 33 K version.

HK41
Pre-1968

Exc.	V.G.	Fair
N/A	N/A	N/A

Pre-1986 conversions

Exc.	V.G.	Fair
N/A	N/A	N/A

Pre-1986 Dealer samples (Very Rare)

Exc.	V.G.	Fair
9000	8000	7500

Kalashnikov AK-47
Pre-1968

Exc.	V.G.	Fair
21000	12000	9500

Pre-1986 conversions

Exc.	V.G.	Fair
6500	6000	5750

Pre-1986 Dealer samples

Exc.	V.G.	Fair
5000	4000	3750

AKM
Pre-1968

Exc.	V.G.	Fair
15000	11500	11000

Pre-1986 conversions

Exc.	V.G.	Fair
7000	6500	5500

Pre-1986 Dealer samples (Rare)

Exc.	V.G.	Fair
9000	9000	8500

MP 44
Pre-1968

Exc.	V.G.	Fair
7000	6500	5500

Pre-1986 conversions

Exc.	V.G.	Fair
N/A	N/A	N/A

Pre-1986 Dealer samples

Exc.	V.G.	Fair
N/A	N/A	N/A

Ruger AC-556
Pre-1968

Exc.	V.G.	Fair
3500	3300	3000

Pre-1986 conversions

Exc.	V.G.	Fair
3000	2800	2500

Pre-1986 Dealer samples

Exc.	V.G.	Fair
N/A	N/A	N/A

Santa Barbara CETME Model L
Pre-1968

Exc.	V.G.	Fair
N/A	N/A	N/A

Pre-1986 conversions

Exc.	V.G.	Fair
N/A	N/A	N/A

Pre-1986 Dealer samples

Exc.	V.G.	Fair
5000	5000	5000

SIG SG510-4
Pre-1968 (Rare)

Exc.	V.G.	Fair
9000	8500	8000

Pre-1986 conversions

Exc.	V.G.	Fair
6000	5500	5000

Pre-1986 Dealer samples

Exc.	V.G.	Fair
5000	4500	4000

SIG SG540
Pre-1968

Exc.	V.G.	Fair
N/A	N/A	N/A

Pre-1986 conversions

Exc.	V.G.	Fair
N/A	N/A	N/A

Pre-1986 Dealer samples (Rare)

Exc.	V.G.	Fair
7500	7500	7000

Simonov AVS-36
Pre-1968

Exc.	V.G.	Fair
4500	4250	4000

Pre-1986 conversions

Exc.	V.G.	Fair
N/A	N/A	N/A

Pre-1986 Dealer samples

Exc.	V.G.	Fair
N/A	N/A	N/A

Steyr AUG
Pre-1968

Exc.	V.G.	Fair
N/A	N/A	N/A

Pre-1986 conversions

Exc.	V.G.	Fair
8500	8000	7500

Pre-1986 Dealer samples

Exc.	V.G.	Fair
N/A	N/A	N/A

Exc.	V.G.	Fair
7500	7300	7000

U.S. M2 Carbine
Pre-1968

Exc.	V.G.	Fair
4000	3500	3000

Pre-1986 conversions

Exc.	V.G.	Fair
3000	2750	2500

Pre-1986 Dealer samples

Exc.	V.G.	Fair
2500	2750	2500

U.S. M4 Carbine
Pre-1968

Exc.	V.G.	Fair
N/A	N/A	N/A

Pre-1986 conversions or OEM/Colt (Rare)

Exc.	V.G.	Fair
9000	7000	6500

Pre-1986 Dealer samples

Exc.	V.G.	Fair
N/A	N/A	N/A

U.S. M14
Pre-1968

Exc.	V.G.	Fair
6500	6300	6000

Pre-1986 conversions (or U.S. manufacture/M1A Springfield Armory)

Exc.	V.G.	Fair
3500	3250	3000

Pre-1986 Dealer samples

Exc.	V.G.	Fair
N/A	N/A	N/A

U.S. M16 Standard Rifle
Pre-1968

Exc.	V.G.	Fair
7000	6500	6000

Pre-1986 conversions, for OEM A1 add 40%

Exc.	V.G.	Fair
5500	5500	5500

Pre-1986 Dealer samples

Exc.	V.G.	Fair
2500	2500	2250

U.S. M16 A2
Pre-1968

Exc.	V.G.	Fair
N/A	N/A	N/A

Pre-1986 OEM/Colt

Exc.	V.G.	Fair
10000	9000	8500

Pre-1986 Dealer samples (Rare)

Exc.	V.G.	Fair
N/A	N/A	N/A

Valmet M76

Pre-1968

Exc.	V.G.	Fair
N/A	N/A	N/A

Pre-1986 conversions

Exc.	V.G.	Fair
5000	4750	4500

Pre-1986 Dealer samples

Exc.	V.G.	Fair
4000	4000	3850

NOTE: For rifles in 7.62x39mm caliber add a 20% premium.

Zastava M70B1

Pre-1968

Exc.	V.G.	Fair
N/A	N/A	N/A

Pre-1986 conversions

Exc.	V.G.	Fair
N/A	N/A	N/A

Pre-1986 Dealer samples

Exc.	V.G.	Fair
5000	4500	4500

MACHINE GUNS

NOTE: Prices listed below reflect the gun only with one magazine and no accessories. The prices for medium and heavy machine guns do not include bipods or tripods. These necessary items are extra. Buyer and seller should note that machine gun mounts come in various configurations. Mounts may range in price from several hundred dollars to several thousand dollars depending on type.

Armalite AR-10

Pre-1968 (Very Rare)

Exc.	V.G.	Fair
15000	15000	14000

Pre-1986 conversions

Exc.	V.G.	Fair
7500	6500	5000

Pre-1986 Dealer samples

Exc.	V.G.	Fair
2500	2500	2000

Beretta M70/78

Pre-1968

Exc.	V.G.	Fair
N/A	N/A	N/A

Pre-1986 conversions

Exc.	V.G.	Fair
N/A	N/A	N/A

Pre-1986 Dealer samples (Rare)

Exc.	V.G.	Fair
9000	9000	8500

Breda Model 30

Pre-1968

Exc.	V.G.	Fair
6000	5000	4500

Pre-1986 conversions

Exc.	V.G.	Fair
N/A	N/A	N/A

Pre-1986 Dealer samples

Exc.	V.G.	Fair
N/A	N/A	N/A

Breda Model 37

Pre-1968

Exc.	V.G.	Fair
6000	5500	5000

Pre-1986 conversions

Exc.	V.G.	Fair
N/A	N/A	N/A

Pre-1986 Dealer samples

Exc.	V.G.	Fair
N/A	N/A	N/A

Bren

Pre-1968 (Very Rare)

Exc.	V.G.	Fair
22000	17500	15000

Pre-1986 conversions

Exc.	V.G.	Fair
N/A	N/A	N/A

Pre-1986 Dealer samples

Exc.	V.G.	Fair
14000	10000	6000

Browning M1917A1

Pre-1968

Exc.	V.G.	Fair
13000	11000	9000

Pre-1986 conversions (Non-Martial current U.S. manufacture)

Exc.	V.G.	Fair
9000	8500	8000

Pre-1986 Dealer samples

Exc.	V.G.	Fair
N/A	N/A	N/A

Browning M1919 A4

Pre-1968

Exc.	V.G.	Fair
12000	11000	10000

Pre-1986 conversions (Non-Martial current U.S. manufacture)

Exc.	V.G.	Fair
8000	7000	6500

Pre-1986 Dealer samples

Exc.	V.G.	Fair
4500	4500	4000

Browning M1919 A6

Pre-1968

Exc.	V.G.	Fair
12000	11000	10000

Pre-1986 conversions (Non-Martial current U.S. manufacture)

Exc.	V.G.	Fair
8000	7000	6500

Pre-1986 Dealer samples

Exc.	V.G.	Fair
4500	4500	4000

Browning M2HB .50

Pre-1968

Exc.	V.G.	Fair
15000	14000	13000

Pre-1986 conversions (Non-Martial current U.S. manufacture)

Exc.	V.G.	Fair
11000	10000	9000

Pre-1986 Dealer samples

Exc.	V.G.	Fair
N/A	N/A	N/A

Browning Automatic Rifle (BAR)

Pre-1968 (Rare)

Exc.	V.G.	Fair
15000	14000	12000

Pre-1986 conversions

Exc.	V.G.	Fair
10000	9000	8500

Pre-1986 Dealer samples

Exc.	V.G.	Fair
5500	5500	5500

Degtyarev DP28

Pre-1968

Exc.	V.G.	Fair
12000	11000	10000

Pre-1986 conversions

Exc.	V.G.	Fair
9000	8000	8000

Pre-1986 Dealer samples

Exc.	V.G.	Fair
N/A	N/A	N/A

Degtyarev RPD

Pre-1968 (Very Rare)

Exc.	V.G.	Fair
25000	23000	20000

Pre-1986 conversions

Exc.	V.G.	Fair
N/A	N/A	N/A

Pre-1986 Dealer samples

Exc.	V.G.	Fair
N/A	N/A	N/A

Pre-1986 conversions (Non-Martial current U.S. manufacture)

Exc.	V.G.	Fair
8000	7000	6500

Pre-1986 conversions (Non-Martial current U.S. manufacture)

Exc.	V.G.	Fair
N/A	N/A	N/A

Pre-1986 Dealer samples

Exc.	V.G.	Fair
N/A	N/A	N/A

FN BAR Type D

Pre-1968 (Very Rare)

Exc.	V.G.	Fair
14000	13000	12000

Pre-1986 conversions

Exc.	V.G.	Fair
N/A	N/A	N/A

Pre-1986 Dealer samples

Exc.	V.G.	Fair
5500	5250	5000

FN MAG

Pre-1968 (Extremely Rare, only 1 known)

Exc.	V.G.	Fair
85000	—	—

Pre-1986 conversions

Exc.	V.G.	Fair
N/A	N/A	N/A

Pre-1986 Dealer samples

Exc.	V.G.	Fair
60000	58000	55000

NOTE: This is an extremely rare machine gun with prices based on scarcity and high demand.

FN Minimi

Pre-1968

Exc.	V.G.	Fair
N/A	N/A	N/A

Pre-1986 conversions

Exc.	V.G.	Fair
N/A	N/A	N/A

Pre-1986 Dealer samples (Extremely Rare, only 6 known)

Exc.	V.G.	Fair
50000	45000	43000

Goryunov SG43

Pre-1968 (Very Rare)

Exc.	V.G.	Fair
20000	17000	15000

Pre-1986 conversions

Exc.	V.G.	Fair
N/A	N/A	N/A

Pre-1986 Dealer samples

Exc.	V.G.	Fair
N/A	N/A	N/A

H&K 21 (HK21E-HK23E)

Pre-1968-Model 21 only

Exc.	V.G.	Fair
10000	9000	8000

Pre-1986 conversions

Exc.	V.G.	Fair
7500	7500	7500

Pre-1986 Dealer samples

Exc.	V.G.	Fair
5500	5500	5500

NOTE: The HK21E and HK23E will bring a premium of 75% over the older HK21.

Japanese Type 3

Pre-1968

Exc.	V.G.	Fair
8000	7000	6500

Pre-1986 conversions

Exc.	V.G.	Fair
N/A	N/A	N/A

Pre-1986 Dealer samples

Exc.	V.G.	Fair
N/A	N/A	N/A

Japanese Type 11

Pre-1968

Exc.	V.G.	Fair
6000	5000	4500

Pre-1986 conversions

Exc.	V.G.	Fair
N/A	N/A	N/A

Pre-1986 Dealer samples

Exc.	V.G.	Fair
N/A	N/A	N/A

Japanese Type 89

Pre-1968

Exc.	V.G.	Fair
11000	10000	9500

Pre-1986 conversions

Exc.	V.G.	Fair
N/A	N/A	N/A

Pre-1986 Dealer samples

Exc.	V.G.	Fair
N/A	N/A	N/A

Japanese Type 92

Pre-1968

Exc.	V.G.	Fair
9000	8000	7500

Pre-1986 conversions

Exc.	V.G.	Fair
N/A	N/A	N/A

Pre-1986 Dealer samples

Exc.	V.G.	Fair
N/A	N/A	N/A

Japanese Type 96

Pre-1968

Exc.	V.G.	Fair
6000	5000	4500

Pre-1986 conversions

Exc.	V.G.	Fair
N/A	N/A	N/A

Pre-1986 Dealer samples

Exc.	V.G.	Fair
N/A	N/A	N/A

Japanese Type 97

Pre-1968

Exc.	V.G.	Fair
7000	6000	5500

Pre-1986 conversions

Exc.	V.G.	Fair
N/A	N/A	N/A

Pre-1986 Dealer samples

Exc.	V.G.	Fair
N/A	N/A	N/A

Japanese Type 98

Pre-1968

Exc.	V.G.	Fair
8500	7500	7000

Pre-1986 conversions

Exc.	V.G.	Fair
N/A	N/A	N/A

Pre-1986 Dealer samples

Exc.	V.G.	Fair
N/A	N/A	N/A

Japanese Type 99

Pre-1968

Exc.	V.G.	Fair
10000	9000	8500

Pre-1986 conversions

Exc.	V.G.	Fair
N/A	N/A	N/A

Pre-1986 Dealer samples

Exc.	V.G.	Fair
N/A	N/A	N/A

Johnson M1941 & 1944

Pre-1968

Exc.	V.G.	Fair
10000	9000	9000

Pre-1986 conversions

Exc.	V.G.	Fair
N/A	N/A	N/A

Pre-1986 Dealer samples

Exc.	V.G.	Fair
N/A	N/A	N/A

Lewis Mark 1
Pre-1968

Exc.	V.G.	Fair
15000	13000	11000

Pre-1986 conversions

Exc.	V.G.	Fair
N/A	N/A	N/A

Pre-1986 Dealer samples

Exc.	V.G.	Fair
N/A	N/A	N/A

Madsen
Pre-1968

Exc.	V.G.	Fair
10000	9000	8000

Pre-1986 conversions

Exc.	V.G.	Fair
N/A	N/A	N/A

Pre-1986 Dealer samples

Exc.	V.G.	Fair
5500	5250	5000

Madsen-Satter
Pre-1968 (Very Rare)

Exc.	V.G.	Fair
25000	23000	22000

Pre-1986 conversions

Exc.	V.G.	Fair
N/A	N/A	N/A

Pre-1986 Dealer samples (Rare)

Exc.	V.G.	Fair
20000	18000	17000

Maxim '08/15
Pre-1968

Exc.	V.G.	Fair
8500	7500	7000

Pre-1986 conversions

Exc.	V.G.	Fair
N/A	N/A	N/A

Pre-1986 Dealer samples

Exc.	V.G.	Fair
N/A	N/A	N/A

MG15 Aircraft Gun
Pre-1968

Exc.	V.G.	Fair
13000	12000	11500

Pre-1986 conversions

Exc.	V.G.	Fair
N/A	N/A	N/A

Pre-1986 Dealer samples

Exc.	V.G.	Fair
N/A	N/A	N/A

MG15 Water Cooled Ground Gun
Pre-1968

Exc.	V.G.	Fair
12000	11000	10500

Pre-1986 conversions

Exc.	V.G.	Fair
N/A	N/A	N/A

Pre-1986 Dealer samples

Exc.	V.G.	Fair
N/A	N/A	N/A

MG34
Pre-1968

Exc.	V.G.	Fair
27000	25000	22000

Pre-1986 conversions

Exc.	V.G.	Fair
N/A	N/A	N/A

Pre-1986 Dealer samples

Exc.	V.G.	Fair
15000	12000	11000

MG42-MG42/59-MG1-MG3
Pre-1968

Exc.	V.G.	Fair
25000	22000	20000

Pre-1986 conversions

Exc.	V.G.	Fair
N/A	N/A	N/A

Pre-1986 Dealer samples

Exc.	V.G.	Fair
13000	11000	10000

NOTE: For post-war guns add 50% premium.

Stoner Model 63A
Pre-1968 (Very Rare, less than 6 known)

Exc.	V.G.	Fair
35000	32000	30000

Pre-1986 conversions (Non-martial current U.S. manufacture)

Exc.	V.G.	Fair
30000	28000	27000

Pre-1986 Dealer samples

Exc.	V.G.	Fair
20000	19000	18000

U.S. M60
Pre-1986 OEM/Maremont manufacture

Exc.	V.G.	Fair
20000	19000	17000

Pre-1986 conversions

Exc.	V.G.	Fair
15000	14000	13000

Pre-1986 Dealer samples

Exc.	V.G.	Fair
N/A	N/A	N/A

U.S. M60E3
Pre-1986 OEM/Maremont manufacture

Exc.	V.G.	Fair
25000	24000	23000

Pre-1986 conversions

Exc.	V.G.	Fair
15000	14000	13500

Pre-1986 Dealer samples

Exc.	V.G.	Fair
N/A	N/A	N/A

Valmet M78
Pre-1968

Exc.	V.G.	Fair
N/A	N/A	N/A

Pre-1986 conversions

Exc.	V.G.	Fair
8500	7000	7000

NOTE: For guns chambered for 7.62x39 add 20%.

Pre-1986 Dealer samples

Exc.	V.G.	Fair
6000	5500	5000

Vickers Mark 1
Pre-1968

Exc.	V.G.	Fair
12000	11000	10000

Pre-1986 conversions (Non-Martial current U.S. manufacture)

Exc.	V.G.	Fair
8000	7000	6000

Pre-1986 Dealer samples

Exc.	V.G.	Fair
N/A	N/A	N/A

A.A.
Azanza & Arrizabalaga
Eibar, Spain

A.A.

A 6.35mm and 7.65mm caliber semiautomatic pistol with a 6- and 9-shot magazine. Many of these pistols are identifiable by the trademark "AA" on their frames.

Photo courtesy James Rankin

Exc.	V.G.	Good	Fair	Poor
225	175	150	100	50

Reims

A 6.35mm or 7.65mm caliber semiautomatic pistol with 6- or 8-round magazine capacity. Most of the pistols have their slides marked "1914 Model Automatic Pistol Reims Patent".

Photo courtesy James Rankin

Exc.	V.G.	Good	Fair	Poor
225	175	150	100	50

A.A.A.
Aldazabal
Eibar, Spain

Modelo 1919

A 7.65mm semiautomatic pistol with 9-round magazine capacity. The trademark of a knight's head over three As is on the side of the slide and the grips.

Photo courtesy James Rankin

Exc.	V.G.	Good	Fair	Poor
225	175	150	100	50

A & R SALES SOUTH
El Monte, California

45 Auto

An alloy-frame version of the Colt Model 1911 semiautomatic pistol.

NIB	Exc.	V.G.	Good	Fair	Poor
450	300	200	150	125	100

Mark IV Sporter

A semiautomatic copy of the M-14 military rifle. Manufactured in .308 cal. (7.65mm Nato) only.

NIB	Exc.	V.G.	Good	Fair	Poor
750	450	300	200	150	100

AFC
Auguste Francotte
Liege, Belgium

This was one of the most prolific makers of revolvers in Liege during the last half of the 19th century. It is estimated that over 150 different revolvers were made and marketed by them before they were forced out of business by the German occupation of 1914. Francotte produced many variations from Tranter copies to pinfires, early Smith & Wesson designs to the 11mm M1871 Swedish troopers revolver. They made break-open revolvers and produced only one semiauto, a 6.35mm blowback design. A good portion of their pistols were produced for the wholesale market and were sold under other names. These particular revolvers will bear the letters "AF" stamped somewhere on the frame. Because of the vast number and variety of pistols produced by this company, cataloging and pricing is beyond the scope of this or any general reference book. It is suggested that any examples encountered be researched on an individual basis. The lone semiauto, produced in 1912, can be priced rather easily since it is the only one the company ever manufactured.

For more information on Francotte see the information under that listing.

Model 1895

On of the earliest Francotte pistols. Chambered for the 8mm cartridge and is a self loader. Marked "A. Francotte & Co. Makers" on the top of the slide.

Photo courtesy James Rankin

Exc.	V.G.	Good	Fair	Poor
3500	3000	2500	2000	1500

Trainer

A single shot training pistol made for Switzerland in .22 caliber short. AFC trademark on the left side of the frame.

Photo courtesy James Rankin

Exc.	V.G.	Good	Fair	Poor
3000	2750	2500	2000	1500

Semiauto

A 6.35mm, 6-shot detachable magazine pocket pistol with blue finish. This model was marked "Francotte Liege" or "AFC".

Photo courtesy James Rankin

Exc.	V.G.	Good	Fair	Poor
350	275	200	125	90

A. J. ORDNANCE

This is a delayed blowback action that is unique in that every shot was double action. This pistol was chambered for the .45 ACP cartridge and had a 3.5" stainless steel barrel with fixed sights and plastic grips. The detachable magazine held 6 shots, and the standard finish was matte blue. Chrome plating was available and would add approximately 15 percent to the values given.

NIB	Exc.	V.G.	Good	Fair	Poor
550	450	400	350	275	150

AMAC
American Military Arms Corporation
formerly Iver Johnson
Jacksonville, Arkansas

The Iver Johnson Arms Co. was founded in 1871 in Fitchsburg, Massachusetts. It was one of the oldest and most successful of the old-line arms companies on which our modern era has taken its toll. In 1984 the company moved to Jacksonville, Arkansas; in 1987 it was purchased by the American Military Arms Corporation. This company has released some of the older designs as well as some new models. In 1993 the company went out of business. The original Iver Johnson line will be listed under its own heading later in this text.

U.S. Carbine .22

This is a semiautomatic, military-style carbine that is patterned after the M1 of WWII fame. It is chambered for the .22 l.r. cartridge, has an 18.5" barrel and features military-style peep sights and a 15-shot detachable magazine.

NIB	Exc.	V.G.	Good	Fair	Poor
250	150	125	100	75	50

Wagonmaster Lever Action Rifle

This model is chambered for the .22 rimfire cartridge, has an 18.5" barrel and is styled after the Win. 94. The stock has a straight grip; and the forend, a barrel band. There are adjustable sights and a tube magazine that holds 15 l.r. cartridges.

NIB	Exc.	V.G.	Good	Fair	Poor
200	150	120	100	75	50

Wagonmaster .22 Magnum

This model is the same as the Wagonmaster except that it is chambered for the .22 rimfire magnum.

NIB	Exc.	V.G.	Good	Fair	Poor
250	175	120	100	75	50

Targetmaster Pump Action Rifle

This model is a slide or pump action that is chambered for the .22 rimfire cartridges. It has an 18.5" barrel with adjustable sights and a straight grip stock. It holds 12 l.r. cartridges.

NIB	Exc.	V.G.	Good	Fair	Poor
225	150	120	100	75	50

Li'L Champ Bolt Action Rifle

This model is a scaled-down single shot that is chambered for the .22 rimfire cartridges. It has a 16.25" barrel, adjustable sights, a molded stock, and nickel-plated bolt. This model is 33" overall and is designed to be the ideal first rifle for a young shooter.

NIB	Exc.	V.G.	Good	Fair	Poor
125	75	60	45	35	20

M .30 Cal. Carbine

A military-style carbine styled after the M1 of WWII fame. It is chambered for the .30 Carbine cartridge and has an 18" barrel with military-style sights and hardwood stock. There are detachable 5-, 15-, and 30-round magazines available.

NIB	Exc.	V.G.	Good	Fair	Poor
275	225	200	175	125	90

Paratrooper .30 Carbine

This model is similar to the M1 model with a folding stock.

NIB	Exc.	V.G.	Good	Fair	Poor
325	250	225	200	150	100

Enforcer .30 Carbine

This is a 9.5" pistol version of the M1 Carbine. It has no buttstock.

NIB	Exc.	V.G.	Good	Fair	Poor
400	300	250	200	150	100

Long Range Rifle System

This is a specialized long-range, bolt action rifle chambered for the .50 Cal. Browning Machine gun cartridge. It has a 33" barrel and a special muzzle brake system. A custom order version in the .338 or .416 caliber is also available.

NIB	Exc.	V.G.	Good	Fair	Poor
8500	7000	5000	3500	2000	1000

TP-22 and TP-25

This model is a compact, double action, pocket automatic that was styled after the Walther TP series. Chambered for either the .22 rimfire or the .25 centerfire cartridges, it has a 2.75" barrel, fixed sights and black plastic grips. The detachable magazine holds 7 shots and the finish is either blue or nickel-plated. The nickel-plated version is worth 10 percent more than the blue.

NIB	Exc.	V.G.	Good	Fair	Poor
225	175	150	100	75	50

AMAC 22 Compact or 25 Compact

This is a compact, single action, semiautomatic pocket pistol that is chambered for the .22 rimfire or the .25 ACP cartridge. It has a 2" barrel, 5-shot magazine, plastic grips and blue or nickel finish. The nickel finish is 10 percent higher in cost than the blue.

NIB	Exc.	V.G.	Good	Fair	Poor
175	125	100	80	55	35

AMT
formerly Arcadia Machine and Tool
Irwindale, California
See also-Galena Industries Inc.

In May of 1998 Galena Industries Inc. purchased rights to produce most (not all) of AMT developed firearms. Galena Industries also purchased the logo and rights to use the trade name "AMT". Galena Industries did not purchase Arcadia Machine and Tool Inc.

NOTE: The firearms listed below are for AMT-built guns only. As of the present edition these guns are no longer in production. For currently manufactured firearms see *Galena Industries.*

Lightning

A single action, semiautomatic .22 caliber pistol. Available with barrel lengths of 5" (Bull only), 6.5", 8.5", 10.5" and 12.5" (either Bull or tapered), and adjustable sights, as well as the trigger. The grips are checkered black rubber. Manufactured between 1984 and 1987 this model resembled the Ruger.

Courtesy John J. Stimson, Jr.

Exc.	V.G.	Good	Fair	Poor
250	200	175	125	85

Bull's Eye Regulation Target

As above, with a 6.5" vent rib bull barrel, wooden target grips, and an extended rear sight. Manufactured in 1986 only.

Exc.	V.G.	Good	Fair	Poor
350	300	250	200	100

Baby Automag

Similar to the above with an 8.5" ventilated rib barrel, and Millett adjustable sights. Approximately 1,000 were manufactured. No longer in production.

Exc.	V.G.	Good	Fair	Poor
450	350	275	225	150

Automag II

A stainless steel, semiautomatic .22 Magnum Pistol. Available with 3-3/8", 4.5", and 6" barrel lengths and Millett adjustable sights, grips of black, grooved, plastic. Was first manufactured in 1987. Still in production.

NIB	Exc.	V.G.	Good	Fair	Poor
375	300	225	150	100	80

Automag III

This semiautomatic pistol is chambered for the .30 Carbine cartridge and the 9mm Winchester Magnum cartridge. Barrel length is 6.37" and overall length is 10.5". The magazine capacity is 8 rounds. Fitted with Millett adjustable rear sight and carbon fiber grips. Stainless steel finish. Pistol weighs 43 oz.

NIB	Exc.	V.G.	Good	Fair	Poor
450	350	250	225	100	80

Automag IV
Similar in appearance to the Automag III this pistol is chambered for the .45 Winchester Magnum. Magazine capacity is 7 rounds and weight is 46 oz.

NIB	Exc.	V.G.	Good	Fair	Poor
575	475	400	300	200	100

Automag V
Introduced in 1993 this model is similar in appearance to the Automag models but is chambered for the .50 caliber cartridge. A limited production run of 3000 pistols with special serial number from "1 of 3000 to 3000 of 3000". Barrel length is 6.5" and magazine capacity is 5 rounds. Weighs 46 oz. Production stopped in 1995.

NIB	Exc.	V.G.	Good	Fair	Poor
750	600	500	400	300	150

Back Up Pistol
This is a small semiautomatic pocket pistol chambered for the .22 l.r. and the .380 ACP cartridges. This is fitted with a 2.5" barrel and is offered with either black plastic or walnut grips. The pistol weighs 18 oz. Magazine capacity is 5 rounds. Originally manufactured by TDE, then Irwindale Arms Inc., it is now currently produced by AMT.

NIB	Exc.	V.G.	Good	Fair	Poor
300	225	175	125	100	85

Back Up-.45 ACP, .40 S&W, 9mm

NIB	Exc.	V.G.	Good	Fair	Poor
300	250	200	150	100	85

Back Up-.38 Super, .357 Sig, .400 CorBon

NIB	Exc.	V.G.	Good	Fair	Poor
350	300	250	200	150	100

.380 Back Up II

Introduced in 1993 this pistol is similar to the Back Up model but with the addition of a double safety, extended finger grip on the magazine, and single action only. This is a special order pistol only.

NIB	Exc.	V.G.	Good	Fair	Poor
350	300	250	200	150	100

Hardballer/Government Model
This model is similar to the Colt Gold Cup .45 ACP. It is offered in two versions. The first has fixed sights and rounded slide top while the second has adjustable Millett sights and Matte rib. Magazine capacity is 7 rounds. Wraparound rubber grips are standard. Long grip safety, beveled magazine well, and adjustable trigger are common to both variations. Weight is 38 oz.

Hardballer-Adjustable sights

NIB	Exc.	V.G.	Good	Fair	Poor
450	400	350	275	200	125

Government Model-Fixed sights

NIB	Exc.	V.G.	Good	Fair	Poor
400	350	300	250	150	100

Hardballer Longslide
Similar to the Hardballer Model but fitted with a 7" barrel. Magazine capacity is 7 rounds. Pistol weighs 46 oz.

NIB	Exc.	V.G.	Good	Fair	Poor
450	400	325	275	200	125

.400 Accelerator
Similar to the models above but chambered for .400 CorBon cartridge and fitted with a 7" barrel. Fully adjustable sights. Introduced in 1997.

NIB	Exc.	V.G.	Good	Fair	Poor
500	450	375	—	—	—

Commando

Built on a Government model type action and chambered for .40 S&W cartridge. Fitted with a 5" barrel and fully adjustable sights. Introduced in 1997.

NIB	Exc.	V.G.	Good	Fair	Poor
400	350	300	—	—	—

On Duty

This semiautomatic pistol features a double action-only trigger action or double action with decocker and is chambered for the 9mm, .40 S&W, or .45 ACP calibers. Barrel length is 4.5" and overall length is 7.75". The finish is a black anodized matte finish. Carbon fiber grips are standard. Furnished with 3-dot sights. Weighs 32 oz. No longer in production.

NIB	Exc.	V.G.	Good	Fair	Poor
450	350	250	200	150	100

Skipper

Identical to the Hardballer with a 1" shorter barrel and slide, discontinued in 1984.

Exc.	V.G.	Good	Fair	Poor
400	325	275	200	125

Combat Skipper

Similar to the Colt Commander. Discontinued in 1984.

Exc.	V.G.	Good	Fair	Poor
350	300	250	200	125

Lightning Rifle

Patterned after the Ruger 10/22, this rifle has a 22" barrel and a 25-round, detachable magazine with a folding stock. Introduced in 1986. No longer in production.

NIB	Exc.	V.G.	Good	Fair	Poor
300	225	175	150	125	100

Small Game Hunter

As above with a full stock and 10-round magazine. Introduced in 1986. No longer in production.

NIB	Exc.	V.G.	Good	Fair	Poor
300	225	175	150	125	100

Small Game Hunter II

This semiautomatic rifle is chambered for the .22 Long Rifle cartridge. Stock is a checkered black matte nylon and is fitted with a removable recoil pad for ammo, cleaning rod, and knife. Rotary magazine holds 10 rounds. Stainless steel action and barrel. Barrel is a heavy weight target type 22" long. Weight is 6 lbs. No longer in production.

NIB	Exc.	V.G.	Good	Fair	Poor
300	225	175	150	125	100

Hunter Rifle

This semiautomatic rifle is chambered for the .22 Rimfire Magnum cartridge. Stock is checkered black matte nylon. Other features are similar to the Small Game Hunter II including weight. No longer in production.

NIB	Exc.	V.G.	Good	Fair	Poor
350	250	200	150	125	100

Magnum Hunter

Introduced in early 1993 this new addition to the AMT line is chambered for the .22 Magnum cartridge and is fitted with a 22" accurized barrel. Barrel and action are stainless steel. It comes standard with a 5-round magazine and composite stock but a laminated stock is available at an extra cost as is a 10-round magazine.

NIB	Exc.	V.G.	Good	Fair	Poor
450	400	350	250	200	150

Target Model

A semiautomatic rifle chambered for .22 L.R. cartridge and fitted with a 20" target barrel. Weight is about 7.5 lbs. Choice of Fajen or Hogue stock. For Hogue stock deduct $50.00.

NIB	Exc.	V.G.	Good	Fair	Poor
575	500	450	300	200	—

Challenge Edition

This is a custom ordered .22 caliber semiautomatic rifle built on a Ruger 10/22-like receiver. Offered in either 18" or 22" barrel lengths with all stainless steel construction, McMillan fiberglass stock, and Weaver-style scope mounts.

NIB	Exc.	V.G.	Good	Fair	Poor
990	800	550	400	300	—

Single Shot Standard Rifle

Custom-built rifle with choice of barrel length, composite stock adjustable trigger, post '64 Winchester action all in stainless and chrome moly steel. Chambered for all standard calibers. First offered in 1996.

NIB	Exc.	V.G.	Good	Fair	Poor
840	675	500	350	200	—

Single Shot Deluxe Rifle

Custom built rifle on a Mauser-type action with choice of match grade barrel lengths and custom Kevlar stock. Built from stainless and chrome moly steel. Chambered for all standard calibers. First offered in 1996.

NIB	Exc.	V.G.	Good	Fair	Poor
1800	1400	950	650	400	—

Bolt Action Repeating Rifle-Standard

Similar in construction and features to the Standard Single shot rifle.

NIB	Exc.	V.G.	Good	Fair	Poor
840	675	500	350	200	—

Bolt Action Repeating Rifle-Deluxe

Similar in construction and features to the Deluxe Single shot rifle.

NIB	Exc.	V.G.	Good	Fair	Poor
1800	1400	950	650	400	—

A-SQUARE
Bedford, Kentucky

Hannibal Grade

Utilizing the P-17 Enfield action, with a 22" to 26" barrel, this rifle is chambered for 32 calibers from 7mm Rem. Mag. up to and including the 500 A-Square Mag. and .577 Tyrannosaur. Blued with a checkered walnut pistol grip stock. Introduced in 1986. Weights range from 9 lbs. to 13.25 lbs. depending on caliber.

NIB	Exc.	V.G.	Good	Fair	Poor
2900	2400	1500	950	500	300

NOTE: Add $350 for synthetic stock.

Caesar Grade

Utilizing a Remington Model 700 action and chambered for the same cartridges as the above with the exception that A-Square proprietary cartridges are not available. Also made in the left hand version. Introduced in 1986. Weights are in the 8.5 to 11 lbs. range.

NIB	Exc.	V.G.	Good	Fair	Poor
2900	2400	1500	950	500	300

NOTE: Add $350 for synthetic stock.

Hamilcar Grade

This model is a smaller and lighter version of the Hannibal Grade. It was introduced in 1994. It is designed to be chambered in cartridges in the 30-.06 size. Weights are around 8 to 8.5 lbs. Introduced in 1994.

NIB	Exc.	V.G.	Good	Fair	Poor
2900	2400	1500	950	500	300

NOTE: Add $350 for synthetic stock.

Genghis Khan Model

This model is designed for varmint shooting and is fitted with a heavyweight barrel. Offered in .22-250, .243 Win., 6mm Rem., .25-06, 257 Wby., and .264 Win. Barrel length is to customer's specifications as is length of pull. No iron sights are fitted to this model. Weight is approximately 11 lbs.

NIB	Exc.	V.G.	Good	Fair	Poor
2900	2400	1500	950	500	300

NOTE: These rifles are offered with a number of options that can affect price.

ATCSA
Armas De Tiro Y Casa
Eibar, Spain

Colt Police Positive Copy

A .38 caliber 6-shot revolver resembling a Colt Police Positive.

Exc.	V.G.	Good	Fair	Poor
200	125	100	60	40

Target Pistol

A .22 caliber single shot target pistol utilizing a revolver frame.

Exc.	V.G.	Good	Fair	Poor
250	175	125	100	55

AGUIRREY ARANZABAL (AYA)
Eibar, Spain
Side-x-Side Shotguns
Current Importers-Armes de Chasse, John Rowe, Fieldsport, New England Custom Gun Service, Ltd., British Game Gun.

SIDE-BY-SIDE

Matador Side-x-Side

A 12, 16, 20, 28 or .410 bore boxlock double barrel shotgun with 26", 28" or 30" barrels, single selective trigger and automatic ejectors. Blued with a walnut stock. Manufactured from 1955 to 1963.

28 gauge and .410-Add 20%.

Exc.	V.G.	Good	Fair	Poor
500	400	350	300	200

Matador II Side-x-Side

As above, in 12 or 20 gauge with a ventilated rib.

Exc.	V.G.	Good	Fair	Poor
600	425	375	300	200

Matador III Side-x-Side

As above, with 3" chambers.

NIB	Exc.	V.G.	Good	Fair	Poor
950	750	600	450	350	250

Bolero Side-x-Side

As above, with a non-selective single trigger and extractors. Manufactured until 1984.

Exc.	V.G.	Good	Fair	Poor
500	400	300	250	200

Iberia Side-x-Side

A 12 or 20 gauge Magnum boxlock double barrel shotgun with 26", 28" or 30" barrels, double triggers and extractors. Blued with a walnut stock.

NIB	Exc.	V.G.	Good	Fair	Poor
600	500	425	325	250	200

Iberia II Side-x-Side

Similar to the above, in 12 or 16 gauge with 28" barrels and 2-3/4" chambers. Still in production.

NIB	Exc.	V.G.	Good	Fair	Poor
600	500	425	325	250	200

Model 106 Side-x-Side

A 12, 16, or 20 gauge boxlock double barrel shotgun with 28" barrels, double triggers and extractors. Blued with a walnut stock. Manufactured until 1985.

NIB	Exc.	V.G.	Good	Fair	Poor
600	500	400	300	250	200

Model 107-LI Side-x-Side

As above, with the receiver lightly engraved and an English-style stock. In 12 or 16 gauge only.

NIB	Exc.	V.G.	Good	Fair	Poor
700	600	525	450	300	250

Model 116 Side-x-Side

A 12, 16 or 20 gauge sidelock double barrel shotgun with 27" to 30" barrels, double triggers and ejectors. Engraved, blued with a walnut stock. Manufactured until 1985.

NIB	Exc.	V.G.	Good	Fair	Poor
950	800	600	475	350	275

Model 117 Side-x-Side

As above, with 3" chambers.

NIB	Exc.	V.G.	Good	Fair	Poor
850	700	500	425	300	250

Model 117 "Quail Unlimited" Side-x-Side

As above in 12 gauge only with 26" barrels and the receiver engraved "Quail Unlimited of North America". Forty-two were manufactured.

NIB	Exc.	V.G.	Good	Fair	Poor
1500	1200	875	650	425	300

Model 210 Side-x-Side

An exposed hammer, 12 or 16 gauge, boxlock shotgun with 26" to 28" barrels and double triggers. Blued with a walnut stock. Manufactured until 1985.

NIB	Exc.	V.G.	Good	Fair	Poor
800	675	550	400	325	225

Model 711 Boxlock Side-x-Side

A 12 gauge boxlock double barrel shotgun with 28" or 30" barrels having ventilated ribs, single selective trigger and automatic ejectors. Manufactured until 1984.

NIB	Exc.	V.G.	Good	Fair	Poor
900	800	700	500	350	250

Model 711 Sidelock Side-x-Side

As above, with sidelocks. Manufactured in 1985 only.

NIB	Exc.	V.G.	Good	Fair	Poor
1000	900	750	500	400	300

Senior Side-x-Side

A custom order 12 gauge double barrel sidelock shotgun, gold inlaid and engraved. Made strictly to individual customer's specifications.

NIB	Exc.	V.G.	Good	Fair	Poor
15000	12500	9000	7000	4500	2250

OVER/UNDERS

Model 79 "A" Over/Under

A 12 gauge boxlock Over/Under double barrel shotgun with 26", 28" or 30" barrels, single selective trigger and automatic ejectors. Blued with a walnut stock. Manufactured until 1985.

NIB	Exc.	V.G.	Good	Fair	Poor
1250	1050	925	750	500	300

Model 79 "B" Over/Under

As above, with a moderate amount of engraving.

NIB	Exc.	V.G.	Good	Fair	Poor
1350	1150	950	800	575	350

Model 79 "C" Over/Under

As above, with extensive engraving.

NIB	Exc.	V.G.	Good	Fair	Poor
2000	1800	1500	1150	675	400

Model 77 Over/Under

As above, patterned after the Merkel shotgun.

NIB	Exc.	V.G.	Good	Fair	Poor
3000	2700	2000	1500	1000	500

Coral "A" Over/Under

A 12 or 16 gauge Over/Under boxlock double barrel shotgun with 26" or 28" barrels having ventilated ribs, double triggers and automatic ejectors. Fitted with a Kersten cross bolt. Manufactured until 1985.

NIB	Exc.	V.G.	Good	Fair	Poor
1250	900	700	500	300	200

Coral "B" Over/Under

As above, with an engraved French case hardened receiver.

NIB	Exc.	V.G.	Good	Fair	Poor
1400	1100	750	600	350	250

CURRENTLY IMPORTED SHOTGUNS
Current Importers-Armes de Chasse, John Rowe, Fieldsport, New England Custom Gun Service, Ltd., British Game Gun.

SIDELOCK/SIDE-BY-SIDE

AYA sidelock shotguns use the Holland and Holland system. They feature double triggers, articulated front trigger, cocking indicators, bushed firing pins, replaceable firing pins, replaceable hinge pins, and chopper lump barrels. Frame and sidelocks are case-colored. These shotguns weigh between 5 and 7 pounds depending on gauge and barrel length. Barrel lengths are offered in 26", 27", 28", and 29" depending on gauge. All stocks are figured walnut with hand checkering and oil finish. These guns are available with several extra cost options that may affect price. Also influencing price of new guns is the fluctuating dollar in relation to Spanish currency.

Model No. 1

This model is offered in 12 gauge and 20 gauge with special English scroll engraving. Fitted with automatic ejectors and straight grip stock with exhibition quality wood.

NIB	Exc.	V.G.	Good	Fair	Poor
5500	3000	1500	1000	750	500

Model No. 2

The Model 2 is offered in 12, 16, 20, and 28 gauge as well as .410 bore. It has automatic ejectors and straight grip select walnut stock.

NIB	Exc.	V.G.	Good	Fair	Poor
2500	1500	1000	750	600	450

Model No. 53

Chambered for 12, 16, and 20 gauge, this model features three locking lugs and side clips. It also has automatic ejectors and straight grip stock.

NIB	Exc.	V.G.	Good	Fair	Poor
3750	2250	1500	950	650	400

Model No. 56

This model is available in 12 gauge only and features three locking lugs, side clips, special wide action body, and raised matted rib. Select walnut straight grip stock.

NIB	Exc.	V.G.	Good	Fair	Poor
6500	4000	2500	1200	800	400

Model XXV-sidelock

Offered in 12 gauge and 20 gauge only this model is fitted with a Churchill-type rib. Automatic ejectors and select straight grip walnut stock are standard.

NIB	Exc.	V.G.	Good	Fair	Poor
3250	1750	1200	750	500	300

BOXLOCK SIDE-BY-SIDE

These AYA guns utilize an Anson & Deeley system with double locking lugs with detachable cross pin and separate trigger plate that gives access to the firing mechanism. Frame is case-colored. The barrels are chopper lump, firing pins are bushed, automatic safety and automatic ejectors are standard. Barrel lengths are offered in 26", 27", and 28" depending on gauge. Weights are between 5 and 7 pounds depending on gauge.

Model XXV-Boxlock

This model is available in 12 and 20 gauge only. The select walnut stock is hand checkered with straight grip stock.

NIB	Exc.	V.G.	Good	Fair	Poor
2500	1250	800	600	350	250

Model No. 4

This model is available in 12, 16, 20, and 28 gauge as well as .410 bore. It is fitted with select hand checkered walnut stock with straight grip. Light scroll engraving on this model.

NIB	Exc.	V.G.	Good	Fair	Poor
1500	800	650	450	350	200

Model No. 4 Deluxe

Same as above but with select walnut stock and slightly more engraving coverage.

NIB	Exc.	V.G.	Good	Fair	Poor
2500	2000	1500	1000	550	350

OVER/UNDER

These AYA shotguns are similar in design and appearance to the Gebruder Merkel over and under sidelocks with three part forend, Kersten cross bolt, and double under locking lugs.

Model No. 37 Super

MODELO 37 SUPER A

This model is available in 12 gauge only with ventilated rib, automatic ejectors, internally gold-plated sidelocks. Offered with three different types of engraving patterns: ducks, scroll, or deep cut engraving. Very few of this model were imported into the U.S.

NIB	Exc	V.G.	Good	Fair	Poor
11000	8500	5000	3500	2000	1000

Model Augusta

This is the top-of-the-line AYA model offered in 12 gauge only. It features presentation wood and deep cut scroll engraving. Very few of this model were imported into the U.S.

NIB	Exc.	V.G.	Good	Fair	Poor
20000	15000	8000	4500	3500	1500

NOTE: For extra cost options add approximately:
Pistol grip-$90
Rubber recoil pad-$190
Left-hand gun-$775
Length of pull longer than 15"-$125
Select wood-$235
Deluxe wood-$550
Single non-selective trigger-$400
Single selective trigger-$600
Chrome lined barrels-$140
Churchill rib-$375
Raised rib-$180
Extra set of barrels-$1500

ABADIE
Liege, Belgium

System Abadie Model 1878
A 9mm double action revolver with a 6-shot cylinder, octagonal barrel and integral ejector rod.

Exc.	V.G.	Good	Fair	Poor
400	225	175	125	90

System Abadie Model 1886
A heavier version of the above.

Exc.	V.G.	Good	Fair	Poor
400	200	150	110	75

ABBEY, F.J. & CO.
Chicago, Illinois

The Abbey Brothers produced a variety of percussion rifles and shotguns which are all of individual design. The prices listed below represent what a plain F.J. Abbey & Company firearm might realize.

Rifle

Exc.	V.G.	Good	Fair	Poor
—	950	500	250	125

Shotgun

Exc.	V.G.	Good	Fair	Poor
—	1250	600	300	150

ABBEY, GEORGE T.
Utica, New York, and Chicago, Illinois

George T. Abbey originally worked in Utica, New York, from 1845 to 1852. He moved to Chicago in 1852 and was in business until 1874. He manufactured a wide variety of percussion and cartridge firearms. The values listed represent those of his most common products.

Single Barrel .44 Cal.

Exc.	V.G.	Good	Fair	Poor
—	1500	750	400	200

Side-x-Side Double Barrel-.44 Cal.

Exc.	V.G.	Good	Fair	Poor
—	2250	1000	525	250

Over/Under Double Barrel-.44 Cal.

Exc.	V.G.	Good	Fair	Poor
—	2500	1000	525	250

ABESSER & MERKEL
Suhl, Germany

Empire Grade
This shotgun is a side-by-side with an Anson-Deeley action. The receiver is fully engraved with game birds and fine scroll. The stock is carved behind the action. Checkering is a fine skip line-style. Auto ejectors. Pistol or straight grip stock. With or without Monte Carlo and cheekpiece. Prices below are for pre-war guns with fluid steel barrels.

Courtesy Dan Sheil

Exc.	V.G.	Good	Fair	Poor
12000	10000	8000	—	—

NOTE: Add 50% for 20 gauge guns and 100% for 28 gauge or .410 bore guns.

Diamond Grade
This model is a side-by-side gun offered in 12, 16, 20, and 28 gauge as well as .410 bore. Auto ejectors. Double triggers. Full coverage engraving with artistic stock carving behind the frame. Skip line checkering. Many extras offered on this grade will affect price. Barrel lengths from 25" to 32". Weights are from 6.5 lbs. to 7 lbs. Prices are for standard gun with no extras.

Courtesy Dan Sheil

Exc.	V.G.	Good	Fair	Poor
10000	8000	7000	—	—

NOTE: Add 50% for 20 gauge guns and 100% for 28 gauge or .410 bore guns.

Excelsior Grade
This side-by-side gun is fitted with engraved side plates. Anson-Deeley action with double triggers. Fine line checkering. Figured walnut stock. All gauges offered from 12 to .410. Barrel lengths from 25" to 32". Many extra cost options available.

Courtesy Dan Sheil

Exc.	V.G.	Good	Fair	Poor
7500	6500	5000	—	—

NOTE: Add 50% for 20 gauge guns and 100% for 28 gauge or .410 bore guns.

Diana Grade

This is an over and under combination gun with Greener cross bolt action. Safety is located on the side of the pistol grip. Iron sights. Set trigger for rifle barrel. A wide variety of centerfire calibers offered with barrel lengths from 26" to 30".

Courtesy Dan Sheil

Exc.	V.G.	Good	Fair	Poor
8000	7000	5000	—	—

Vandalia Grade

This is an over and under gun chambered for 4.75" 12 gauge shells. Barrel lengths from 28" to 32". Walnut stock with pistol or straight grip with skip line checkering. Double triggers with extractors. This model may be fitted with factory multi-barrel combinations. An appraisal is recommended for this option.

Courtesy Dan Sheil

Exc.	V.G.	Good	Fair	Poor
6000	5000	3500	—	—

Nimrod

This is a drilling with a Greener cross bolt action and double under bolt. Safety is located on side of grip. Top two barrels may be 12, 16, or 20 gauge. The bottom barrel is offered in a variety of centerfire calibers. Iron sights. Pistol or straight grip stock. Receiver engraved with game scenes.

Courtesy Dan Sheil

Exc.	V.G.	Good	Fair	Poor
8500	7000	5000	—	—

NOTE: Add 50% for 20 gauge guns.

Crown Grade

This model is a single barrel Trap gun with Greener cross bolt action with two underbolt locks. Offered in 12 gauge with barrel lengths from 28" to 34". Ventilated rib standard. Ship line checkering. Pistol or straight grip stock. Gun weight is between 7 and 7.5 lbs. Engraved receiver with game scenes.

Courtesy Dan Sheil

Exc.	V.G.	Good	Fair	Poor
5500	4500	3500	—	—

Magazine Rifle

A bolt action rifle offered in a wide variety of calibers. Barrel lengths from 24" to 30". Calibers from 6.5mm to .404 Rimless. This model may have a Zeiss scope or other special order features that will affect price. Seek an expert appraisal prior to a sale.

Courtesy Dan Sheil

Exc.	V.G.	Good	Fair	Poor
4000	3000	2500	—	—

NOTE: Add $2000 for magnum actions.

ACCU-MATCH
Mesa, Arizona

Accu-Match Custom Pistol

This is a competition pistol built on the Colt 1911 design. Chambered for the .45 ACP it is fitted with a 5-1/2" match grade stainless steel barrel, stainless steel slide and frame with extended slide release and safety. Fitted with a beavertail grip safety and wraparound finger groove rubber grips, this pistol has a threaded three port compensator and dual action recoil spring system with three dot sight system.

NIB	Exc.	V.G.	Good	Fair	Poor
900	700	550	—	—	—

ACCU-TEK
Chino, CA

BL-9

This is a semiautomatic double action-only pistol chambered for 9mm cartridge and furnished with a 5-round magazine. Barrel length is 3". Grips are black composition. Finish is black. Weight is approximately 22 oz. Introduced in 1997.

NIB	Exc.	V.G.	Good	Fair	Poor
200	160	130	—	—	—

BL-380

Similar to the Model BL-9 but chambered for the .380 ACP cartridge. Also introduced in 1997.

NIB	Exc.	V.G.	Good	Fair	Poor
200	160	130	—	—	—

CP-9SS

This semiautomatic double action-only stainless steel pistol is chambered for the 9mm cartridge and is fitted with a 3.2" barrel with adjustable for windage rear sight. Magazine capacity is 8 rounds. Grips are black checkered nylon. Weight is about 28 oz. Introduced in 1992.

NIB	Exc.	V.G.	Good	Fair	Poor
250	200	160	120	90	—

CP-45SS

Similar to the Model CP-9SS but chambered for the .45 ACP cartridge. Furnished with a 6-round magazine. Introduced in 1996.

NIB	Exc.	V.G.	Good	Fair	Poor
250	200	160	120	—	—

CP-40SS

Introduced in 1992 and similar to the CP-9SS but chambered for .40 S&W cartridge. Furnished with a 7-round magazine.

NIB	Exc.	V.G.	Good	Fair	Poor
250	200	160	120	—	—

AT-380SS

Introduced in 1991 this semiautomatic pistol is chambered for the .380 ACP cartridge. Fitted with a 2.75" barrel with adjustable for windage rear sight. Black composition grips. Stainless steel construction. Furnished with a 5-round magazine. Weight is about 20 oz.

NIB	Exc.	V.G.	Good	Fair	Poor
180	150	125	100	—	—

HC-380SS

This .380 ACP semiautomatic pistol has a 2.75" barrel. Stainless steel finish. Weight is about 28 oz. Furnished with a 10-round magazine. Introduced in 1993.

NIB	Exc.	V.G.	Good	Fair	Poor
230	180	150	120	—	—

AT-32SS

Similar to the Model AT-380SS but chambered for the .32 ACP cartridge. Introduced in 1991.

NIB	Exc.	V.G.	Good	Fair	Poor
175	150	125	100	—	—

ACCURACY INTERNATIONAL
England

This English company provides its rifles to military forces in over 40 countries, and these models have been used in Northern Ireland, Sri Lanka, Somalia, Bosnia, Rwanda, and in Desert Storm. Most of these rifles are currently NATO codified.

Model AW

Chambered for the 5.56 NATO cartridge and the 7.62x51 NATO cartridge, this bolt action rifle is fitted with a 26" heavy match grade barrel with muzzle brake. Magazine capacity is 8 rounds for the 5.56 and 10 rounds for the 7.62x51. Olive green stock with adjustable butt stock. Bipod, scope, and other accessories are included in the complete kit. Prices below are for rifle only. Weight is about 14.25 lbs.

Exc.	V.G.	Good	Fair	Poor
5200	—	—	—	—

WHAT'S IT LIKE-THE ACCURACY INTERNATIONAL AW

England is a country that is synonymous with fine rifle manufacturing. The Accuracy International group is a British company that is relatively new to the production of small arms. AI was the winning design in the shoot-off in the British Sniper Trials in 1986, beating out great names like Parker Hale and others. Since then the British Army and other military forces have used, to good effect, the L96A1 or PM model bolt action sniper rifle manufactured by Accuracy International. The Accuracy people further evolved this very accurate sniper rifle system into an even better one; the Model AW or Arctic Warfare Model. Both the Model PM and Model AW utilize a revolutionary new chassis receiver system which produces a much more rigid and accurate rifle. This new system also allows a rapid barrel change, much more so than previous sniper rifle systems. The AW rifle is a bolt action, three lug bolt locking design incorporating a detachable magazine. The surgical precision accuracy of this rifle is nothing short of amazing. One quarter inch, 5-shot groups at 100 yards are the norm, but I know of groups printed under 2-1/5" at 600 yards; truly phenomenal. So astounding is the accuracy and durability of this rifle that the German Armed Forces adopted it as its own sniper rifle. Other countries followed suit. Sweden, Belgium, Canada, Australia, and many others are fielding the British Accuracy International Model AW sniper rifle system. As terrorism continues, government counterterrorist military and police units will continue to adopt the best equipment available. I have no doubt the Accuracy International Company will be a name at the top of the list.

J.R. Moody

Model AWP

Similar to the Model AW but with black stock and metal and 24" barrel. Offered in .243 and .308 calibers. Weight is about 14 lbs.

Exc.	V.G.	Good	Fair	Poor
4300	—	—	—	—

Model AWS

A suppressed version of the AW model. Weight is about 13 lbs.

Exc.	V.G.	Good	Fair	Poor
N/A	—	—	—	—

Model AWM

Similar to the Model AW but chambered for the .300 Winchester Magnum or .338 Lapua Magnum cartridge. Fitted with a 26" barrel with muzzle brake. Magazine capacity is 5 rounds. Weight is about 15.5 lbs.

Exc.	V.G.	Good	Fair	Poor
5625	—	—	—	—

Model AW 50

Chambered for the .50 caliber Browning cartridge. Barrel length is 27" with muzzle brake. Magazine capacity is 5 rounds. Weight is about 33 lbs. Supplied with metal case, spare magazine, carry handle, cling, and tool kit.

Exc.	V.G.	Good	Fair	Poor
10950	—	—	—	—

ACHA
Domingo Acha
Vizcaya, Spain

Atlas

A 6.35mm caliber semiautomatic pistol manufactured during the 1920s in the style of the Model 1906 Browning. Grips are plain checkered hard rubber. Some grips had the ACHA trademark of the Count's head. The name Atlas appears on the slide. Later models incorporated a grip safety.

Photo courtesy James Rankin

Exc.	V.G.	Good	Fair	Poor
200	150	100	75	50

Looking Glass (Ruby Style)

This is a 7.65mm semiautomatic pistol in the Ruby style. These pistols were furnished with a 7-, 9-, or 12-round magazine.

Photo courtesy James Rankin

Exc.	V.G.	Good	Fair	Poor
200	150	100	75	50

Looking Glass

A 6.35mm or 7.65mm caliber semiautomatic pistol. Various markings are seen on these pistols and their grips as they were sold in both France and Spain by different distributors. The pistols pictured has two trademarks; Domingo Acha on the grips and on the slide is Fabrique D'Arms de Guerre De Grande Presision.

Photo courtesy James Rankin

Exc.	V.G.	Good	Fair	Poor
200	150	100	75	50

ACME
SEE—Davenport Arms Co., Maltby Henley & Co., and Merwin & Hulbert & Co.

ACME ARMS
New York, New York

A trade name found on .22, .32 caliber revolvers and 12 gauge shotguns marketed by the Cornwall Hardware Company.

.22 Revolver
A 7-shot single action revolver.

Exc.	V.G.	Good	Fair	Poor
350	275	175	125	75

.32 Revolver
A 5-shot single action revolver.

Exc.	V.G.	Good	Fair	Poor
375	300	200	150	100

Shotgun
A 12 gauge double barrel shotgun with external hammers.

Exc.	V.G.	Good	Fair	Poor
350	275	175	125	75

ACME HAMMERLESS
Made by Hopkins & Allen
Norwich, Connecticut

Acme Hammerless
A .32 or .38 caliber 5-shot revolver with either exposed hammer or enclosed hammer. Sometimes known as the "Forehand 1891."

Exc.	V.G.	Good	Fair	Poor
—	350	200	75	50

ACTION
Eibar, Spain
Maker—Modesto Santos

Action
A 6.35mm or 7.65mm semiautomatic pistol marked on the slide "Pistolet Automatique Modele 1920." Often found bearing the trade name "Corrientes" as well as the maker's trademark "MS".

Exc.	V.G.	Good	Fair	Poor
200	150	100	80	60

ACTION ARMS LTD.
Philadelphia, Pennsylvania

AT-84, AT-88
A 9mm or .41 Action Express caliber semiautomatic pistol with a 4.75" barrel and either 15-shot (9mm) or 10-shot (.41) magazine. Blued or chrome plated with walnut grips.

NIB	Exc.	V.G.	Good	Fair	Poor
600	500	425	350	300	150

AT-84P, AT-88P
As above, with a 3.7" barrel and smaller frame.

NIB	Exc.	V.G.	Good	Fair	Poor
700	600	525	450	400	200

AT-88H
As above with a 3.4" barrel and smaller frame.

NIB	Exc.	V.G.	Good	Fair	Poor
600	500	425	350	300	150

Timber Wolf Carbine

Introduced in 1989, this slide action carbine features an 18.5" barrel with adjustable rear sight and blade front sight. Chambered for the .357 Magnum or .38 Special cartridges, it is offered in either blue or hard chrome finish. Weight is approximately 5.5 lbs. Built in Israel by Israel Military Industries.

NIB	Exc.	V.G.	Good	Fair	Poor
450	400	300	200	150	100

ADAMS
Deane, Adams & Deane
London, England
London Armoury Co. (After 1856)

Revolvers based upon Robert Adams' patents were manufactured by the firm of Deane, Adams & Deane. Although more technically advanced than the pistols produced by Samuel Colt, Adams' revolvers were popular primarily in England and the British Empire.

Adams Model 1851 Self-Cocking Revolver
A .44 caliber double action percussion revolver with a 7.5" octagonal barrel and 5-shot cylinder. The barrel and frame are blued, the cylinder case hardened and the grips are walnut. The top strap is marked "Deane, Adams and Deane 30 King William St. London Bridge." This revolver does not have a hammer spur and functions only as a double action.

Exc.	V.G.	Good	Fair	Poor
—	1500	1000	700	400

Adams Pocket Revolver
As above, in .31 caliber with a 4.5" barrel.

Exc.	V.G.	Good	Fair	Poor
—	1750	1200	850	400

Beaumont-Adams Revolver
As above, fitted with a Tranter Patent loading lever and the hammer made with a spur.

Exc.	V.G.	Good	Fair	Poor
—	1450	850	625	300

A Confederate inscribed Beaumont Adams revolver sold at auction for $6,900. Condition was fair to good. This revolver belonged to Colonel Tandy Walker. Butterfield & Butterfield, May 1999

ADAMY GEBRUDER
Suhl, Germany

Over/Under Shotgun
A 12 or 16 gauge double barrel Over/Under shotgun with 26" to 30" barrels, double triggers and a walnut stock.

Exc.	V.G.	Good	Fair	Poor
1850	1500	1100	750	400

ADIRONDACK ARMS CO. or
A.S. BABBITT CO.
Plattsburgh, New York

Orvil M. Robinson Patent Rifle
The Robinson tube-fed repeating rifle was made in New York between 1870 and 1874. The early models, 1870-1872, are marked "A.S. Babbitt"; the later models, 1872-1874, "Adirondack Arms Co." The Company was sold to Winchester in 1874, but they never produced the Robinson after that date. The rifle has been found in two styles: The first with small fingers on the hammer to cock and operate the mechanism; the second with buttons on the receiver to retract the bolt and cock the hammer. The rifle was made in .44 cal. with an octagonal barrel usually found in 26" or 28" length. The frames were predominantly brass; but some iron frames have been noted, and they will bring a premium of approximately 25 percent. The barrel and magazine tube have a blued finish.

First Model

Exc.	V.G.	Good	Fair	Poor
—	4000	1750	750	300

Courtesy Buffalo Bill Historical Center, Cody, Wyoming

Second Model

Exc.	V.G.	Good	Fair	Poor
—	4000	1750	750	300

ADLER
Engelbrecht & Wolff
Blasii, Germany

An extremely rare and unusually designed semiautomatic pistol adapted for the 7.25mm Adler cartridge. Produced in very limited numbers. Prospective purchasers are advised to secure a qualified appraisal prior to acquisition.

Courtesy James Rankin

Courtesy James Rankin

Exc.	V.G.	Good	Fair	Poor
—	5000	2500	1000	500

ADVANCED SMALL ARMS INDUSTRIES
Solothurn, Switzerland
Imported by Magnum Research
Minneapolis, Minnesota

one Pro .45

Introduced in 1997 and built in Switzerland by ASAI this pistol features a 3" barrel chambered for the .45 ACP cartridge. It is based on a short recoil operation and is available in double ac-

tion or double action only. Also available is a kit (purchased separately) to convert the pistol to .400 Cor-Bon caliber. The pistol weighs about 24 oz. empty. The conversion kit has a retail price of $209.00.

NIB	Exc.	V.G.	Good	Fair	Poor
650	525	—	—	—	—

ADVANTAGE ARMS U.S.A., INC.
Distributed by Wildfire Sports
St. Paul, Minnesota

Model 422

A .22 or .22 Magnum caliber 4 barrel derringer with 2.5" barrels. Entirely made of an aluminum alloy. Finished in either blue or nickel-plate. Manufactured in 1986 and 1987.

NIB	Exc.	V.G.	Good	Fair	Poor
175	125	100	85	65	45

AERO
Manufactura De Armas De Fuego
Guernica, Spain

Model 1914

A 7.65mm caliber semiautomatic pistol with a 3.25" barrel in the Ruby design. The Aero name is on the slide along with an airplane. Magazine capacity is 7 rounds, weight is about 23 oz.

Exc.	V.G.	Good	Fair	Poor
300	250	200	125	95

AETNA ARMS CO.
New York

A .22 caliber spur trigger revolver with an octagonal barrel and 7-shot cylinder. The barrel marked "Aetna Arms Co. New York". Manufactured from approximately 1870 to 1880.

Exc.	V.G.	Good	Fair	Poor
—	—	600	300	150

AFFERBACH, W. A.
Philadelphia, Pennsylvania

This maker is known to have produced copies of Henry Derringer's percussion pocket pistols. Though uncommon, their values would be approximately as listed below.

Exc.	V.G.	Good	Fair	Poor
—	—	1500	750	300

AGNER (SAXHOJ PRODUCTS INC.)
Copenhagen, Denmark
Importer: Beeman Arms
Santa Rosa, California

Model M 80

A .22 caliber single shot stainless steel target pistol with a 5.9" barrel, adjustable sights and walnut grips. This pistol is fitted with a dry fire mechanism. Also available in a left-hand version. Imported from 1981 to 1986.

Exc.	V.G.	Good	Fair	Poor
1000	700	500	300	150

AGUIRRE
Eibar, Spain

Basculant

A 6.35mm semiautomatic pistol marked on the slide "Cal. 6.35 Automatic Pistol Basculant".

Exc.	V.G.	Good	Fair	Poor
200	125	100	75	50

LeDragon

As above, with the slide marked "Cal. 6.35 Automatic Pistol LeDragon" and a stylized dragon molded into the grips.

Exc.	V.G.	Good	Fair	Poor
200	125	100	75	50

AIR MATCH
Importer: Kendall International
Paris, Kentucky
Air Match 500

A .22 caliber single shot target pistol with a 10.5" barrel, adjustable sights and adjustable front-mounted counterweights. Blued with walnut grips. Imported from 1984 to 1986.

NIB	Exc.	V.G.	Good	Fair	Poor
700	550	400	300	250	125

AJAX ARMY

Single Action Unknown

A spur-trigger, single action, solid-frame revolver that was chambered for the .44 rimfire cartridge. It had a 7" barrel and was blued with walnut grips. It was manufactured in the 1880s.

Exc.	V.G.	Good	Fair	Poor
—	—	1000	500	200

ALAMO RANGER
Alamo Ranger Spain

A typical low-quality, early Spanish copy of the Colt Police Positive, chambered for the .38 caliber centerfire, and the cylinder held 6 shots. The finish was blued; grips were checkered hard rubber. The maker of this pistol is unknown.

Exc.	V.G.	Good	Fair	Poor
150	125	100	75	45

ALASKA
SEE—Hood Firearms Co.
Norwich, Connecticut

ALDZABAL
Eibar, Spain
Aldazabal, Leturiondo & CIA

Aldazabal

Another typical low-quality, "Eibar"-type semiautomatic. It was a Browning blowback copy, chambered for the 7.65mm cartridge. It had a 7-shot detachable magazine and blued finish with checkered wood grips. This company ceased production before the Spanish Civil War.

Exc.	V.G.	Good	Fair	Poor
175	125	95	65	40

ALERT
SEE—Hood Firearms Co.
Norwich, Connecticut

ALEXIA
SEE—Hopkins & Allen
Norwich, Connecticut

ALFA
SEE—Armero Especialistas Reunides
Eibar, Spain

ALKARTASUNA FABRICA DE ARMAS
Guernica, Spain

This company began production during World War I to help Gabilondo y Urresti supply sidearms to the French. After the hostilities ceased, they continued to produce firearms under their own name. They produced a number of variations in both 6.35mm and 7.65mm marked "Alkar." Collector interest is very thin. The factory burned down in 1920, and by 1922 business had totally ceased.

Alkar

A 6.35mm semiauitomatic pistol with a cartridge counter in the grip plates was one variation on many built in either 6.35mm or 7.65mm.

Courtesy James Rankin

Exc.	V.G.	Good	Fair	Poor
300	250	200	150	100

Alkar (Ruby Style)

A 7.65mm semiautomatic pistol built in the Ruby style. This pistol was supplied to the French government during World War I.

Courtesy James Rankin

Exc.	V.G.	Good	Fair	Poor
275	225	175	125	90

ALLEN, ETHAN
Grafton, Massachusetts

The company was founded by Ethan Allen in the early 1800s. It became a prolific gun making firm that evolved from Ethan Allen to Allen & Thurber, as well as the Allen & Wheelock Company. It was located in Norwich, Connecticut, and Worcester, Massachusetts, as well as Grafton. It eventually became the Forehand & Wadsworth Company in 1871 after the death of Ethan Allen. There were many and varied firearms produced under all of the headings described above. If one desires to collect Ethan Allen firearms, it would be advisable to educate oneself, as there are a number of fine publications available on the subject. The basic models and their values are as follows:

First Model Pocket Rifle

Manufactured by Ethan Allen in Grafton, Massachusetts. It was a bootleg-type, under-hammer, single shot pistol chambered for .31 percussion. Larger-caliber versions have also been noted. It had barrel lengths from 5" to 9" that were part-octagon in configuration. It had iron mountings and was blued with walnut grips. The barrel was marked, "E. Allen/Grafton/Mass." as well as "Pocket Rifle/Cast Steel/ Warranted." There were approximately 2,000 manufactured from 1831 to 1842.

Exc.	V.G.	Good	Fair	Poor
—	—	1100	500	200

Second Model Pocket Rifle

A rounded-frame, round-grip version of the First Model.

Exc.	V.G.	Good	Fair	Poor
—	—	1000	400	200

Bar Hammer Pistol

A double action pistol with a top-mounted bar hammer. It was chambered for .28 to .36 caliber percussion. The half-octagon barrels were from 2" to 10" in length. They screwed out of the frame so it was possible to breech load them. The finish was blued with rounded walnut grips. They were marked, "Allen & Thurber/Grafton Mass." There were approximately 2,000 manufactured between the early 1830s and 1860.

Exc.	V.G.	Good	Fair	Poor
—	—	1000	400	200

Tube Hammer Pistol

This version was similar to the Bar Hammer with a curved hammer without a spur. There were only a few hundred manufactured between the early 1830s and the early 1840s.

Exc.	V.G.	Good	Fair	Poor
—	—	2250	950	400

Side Hammer Pistol

A single-shot, target-type pistol that was chambered for .34, .41, and .45 caliber percussion. It had a part-octagon barrel that was from 6" to 10" in length. There was a wooden ramrod mounted under the barrel. This model had a good quality rear sight that was adjustable. The ornate triggerguard had a graceful spur at its rear. The finish was blued with a rounded walnut grip. The barrel was marked, "Allen & Thurber, Worchester." There were approximately 300 manufactured in the late 1840s and early 1850s.

Exc.	V.G.	Good	Fair	Poor
—	—	850	400	200

Center Hammer Pistol

A single action chambered for .34, .36, or .44 percussion. It had a half-octagon barrel from 4" to 12" in length. It had a centrally mounted hammer that was offset to the right side to allow for sighting the pistol. The finish was blued with walnut grips. It was marked, "Allen & Thurber, Allen Thurber & Company." Some specimens are marked, "Allen & Wheelock." There were several thousand manufactured between the late 1840s and 1860.

Exc.	V.G.	Good	Fair	Poor
—	—	600	300	100

Double Barrel Pistol

A SxS, double barrel pistol with a single trigger. It was chambered for .36 caliber percussion with 3" to 6" round barrels. The finish was blued with walnut grips. Examples with a ramrod mounted under the barrel have been noted. The flute between the barrels was marked, "Allen & Thurber," "Allen Thurber & Company," or "Allen & Wheelock." There were approximately 1,000 manufactured in the 1850s.

Exc.	V.G.	Good	Fair	Poor
—	—	700	300	100

Allen & Wheelock Center Hammer Pistol

A single action pocket pistol chambered for .31 to .38 caliber percussion. It had octagon barrels from 3" to 6" in length. The finish was blued with square butt walnut grips. The barrel was marked, "Allen & Wheelock." There were approximately 500 manufactured between 1858 and 1865.

Exc.	V.G.	Good	Fair	Poor
—	—	600	250	100

Allen Thurber & Company Target Pistol

A deluxe, single action target pistol that was chambered for .31 or .36 caliber percussion. It had a heavy, octagon barrel that was from 11" to 16" in length. There was a wooden ramrod mounted underneath the barrel. The mountings were of German silver, and there was a detachable walnut stock with a deluxe, engraved patchbox. This weapon was engraved, and the barrel was marked, "Allen Thurber & Co./Worchester/Cast Steel." This firearm was furnished in a fitted case with the stock, false muzzle, and various accessories. It was considered to be a very high grade target pistol in its era. The values shown are for a complete-cased outfit. There were very few manufactured in the 1850s.

Exc.	V.G.	Good	Fair	Poor
—	—	7500	3000	1000

NOTE: For pistols without attachable stock deduct 75%.

Ethan Allen Pepperboxes

During the period from the early 1830s to the 1860s, this company manufactured over 50 different variations of the revolving, pepperbox-type pistol. They were commercially quite successful and actually competed successfully with the Colt revolving handguns for more than a decade. They were widely used throughout the United States, as well as in Mexico, and during our Civil War. They are widely collectible because of the number of variations that exist. The potential collector should avail himself of the information available on the subject. These pepperboxes can be divided into three categories.

No. 1—Manufactured from the 1830s until 1842, at Grafton, Massachusetts.

No. 2—Manufactured from 1842 to 1847, at Norwich, Connecticut.

No. 3—Manufactured from 1847 to 1865, at Worchester, Massachusetts.

There are a number of subdivisions among these three basic groups that would pertain to trigger type, size, barrel length etc. It would be impossible to cover all 50 of these variations in a text of this type. We strongly suggest that qualified, individual appraisal be secured if contemplating a transaction. The values of these pepperbox pistols in excellent condition would be between $1,500 and $5,000. Most examples will be seen in the fair to good condition and will bring $1,000 to 2,000 depending on variation.

Large Frame Pocket Revolver

A double action pocket revolver that was chambered for .34 caliber percussion. It had an octagon barrel from 3" to 5" in length. There were no sights. The 5-shot, unfluted cylinder was game scene engraved. The finish was blued with rounded walnut grips. It had a bar-type hammer. This was the first conventional revolver manufactured by this company, and it was directly influenced by the pepperbox pistol for which Ethan Allen had become famous. It was marked, "Allen & Wheelock" as well as "Patented April 16, 1845." There were approximately 1,500 manufactured between 1857 and 1860.

Courtesy Milwaukee Public Museum, Milwaukee, Wisconsin

Exc.	V.G.	Good	Fair	Poor
—	—	750	300	125

Small Frame Pocket Revolver

This version was similar to the Large Frame Pocket Revolver except chambered for .31 caliber percussion, with a 2" to 3.5" octagon barrel. It was slightly smaller in size, finished and marked the same. There were approximately 1,000 made between 1858 and 1860.

Exc.	V.G.	Good	Fair	Poor
—	—	750	300	125

Side Hammer Belt Revolver

A single action revolver chambered for .34 caliber percussion. It had an octagon barrel from 3" to 7.5" in length. It featured a hammer that was mounted on the right side of the frame and a 5-shot, engraved, unfluted cylinder. The cylinder access pin is inserted from the rear of the weapon. The finish is blued with a case-colored hammer and triggerguard and flared-butt walnut grips. It is marked, "Allen & Wheelock." There were two basic types. Values for the early model, of which 100 were manufactured between 1858 and 1861, are as follows:

Exc.	V.G.	Good	Fair	Poor
—	—	950	400	200

Standard Model

The second type was the Standard Model, with a spring-loaded catch on the triggerguard as opposed to a friction catch on the early model. There were approximately 1,000 manufactured between 1858 and 1861.

Courtesy Milwaukee Public Museum, Milwaukee, Wisconsin

Exc.	V.G.	Good	Fair	Poor
—	—	750	325	150

Side Hammer Pocket Revolver

This version was chambered for .28 caliber percussion and had a 2" to 5" octagon barrel. The frame was slightly smaller than the belt model.

Courtesy Milwaukee Public Museum, Milwaukee, Wisconsin

Early Production, 100 Manufactured

Exc.	V.G.	Good	Fair	Poor
—	—	800	325	150

Standard Production, 1,000 Manufactured

Exc.	V.G.	Good	Fair	Poor
—	1500	600	200	100

Side Hammer Navy Revolver

This was a large-frame, military-type revolver that was similar to the Side Hammer Belt Model, chambered for .36 caliber percussion. It features an octagon, 5.5" to 8" barrel with a 6-shot, engraved cylinder. There was an early-production type with a friction catch on the triggerguard. There were approximately 100 manufactured between 1858 and 1861.

Exc.	V.G.	Good	Fair	Poor
—	—	3250	1500	500

Standard Model, 1,000 Manufactured

Exc.	V.G.	Good	Fair	Poor
—	—	2500	1150	500

Center Hammer Army Revolver

A large, military-type, single action revolver that was chambered for .44 caliber percussion. It had a 7.5", half-octagon barrel and a 6-shot, unfluted cylinder. The hammer was mounted in the center of the frame. The finish was blued with a case-colored hammer and triggerguard and walnut grips. The barrel was marked, "Allen & Wheelock. Worchester, Mass. U.S./Allen's Pt's. Jan. 13, 1857. Dec. 15, 1857, Sept. 7, 1858." There were approximately 700 manufactured between 1861 and 1862.

Courtesy Milwaukee Public Museum, Milwaukee, Wisconsin

Courtesy Milwaukee Public Museum, Milwaukee, Wisconsin

Exc.	V.G.	Good	Fair	Poor
—	—	3250	1250	500

Center Hammer Navy Revolver

Similar to the Army Revolver except chambered for .36 caliber percussion with a 7.5", full-octagon barrel. Examples have been noted with 5", 6", or 8" barrels. Otherwise, it was similar to the Army model.

Exc.	V.G.	Good	Fair	Poor
—	—	2750	950	400

Center Hammer Percussion Revolver

A single action revolver chambered for .36 caliber percussion. It had an octagonal, 3" or 4" barrel with a 6-shot, unfluted cylinder. The finish was blued with walnut grips. This model supposedly was made for the Providence, Rhode Island, Police Department and has become commonly referred to as the "Providence Police Model." There were approximately 700 manufactured between 1858 and 1862.

Exc.	V.G.	Good	Fair	Poor
—	—	1000	450	150

Lipfire Army Revolver

A large, military-type, single action revolver that was chambered for the .44 lipfire cartridge. It had a 7.5", half-octagon barrel with a 6-shot, unfluted cylinder that had notches at its rear for the cartridge lips. The finish was blued with a case-colored hammer and triggerguard and square butt walnut grips. The barrel was marked, "Allen & Wheelock, Worchester, Mass." It resembled the Center Hammer Percussion Army Revolver. There were two basic variations, with a total of 250 Lipfire Army Revolver manufactured in the early 1860s.

Early Model—Top Hinged Loading Gate

Exc.	V.G.	Good	Fair	Poor
—	—	2500	1000	500

Late Model—Bottom Hinged Loading Gate

Exc.	V.G.	Good	Fair	Poor
—	—	2000	850	400

Lipfire Navy Revolver

Similar to the Army model, except chambered for the .36 lipfire cartridge, with an octagonal, 4", 5", 6", 7.5", or 8" barrel. There were approximately 500 manufactured in the 1860s.

Exc.	V.G.	Good	Fair	Poor
—	—	1750	750	300

Lipfire Pocket Revolver

A smaller version chambered for the .32 lipfire cartridge, with an octagonal, 4", 5", or 6" barrel. There were approximately 200 manufactured in the early 1860s.

Exc.	V.G.	Good	Fair	Poor
—	—	1250	550	200

.32 Side Hammer Rimfire Revolver

A single action, spur-trigger, pocket revolver chambered for the .32 caliber rimfire cartridge. It had octagonal barrels from 3" to 5" in length. The finish was blued with flared-butt, walnut grips. It was marked "Allen & Wheelock Worchester, Mass." There were three variations with a total of approximately 1,000 manufactured between 1859 and 1862.

First Model—Rounded Top Strap

Exc.	V.G.	Good	Fair	Poor
—	—	750	350	125

Second Model—July 3, 1860 Marked on Frame

Exc.	V.G.	Good	Fair	Poor
—	—	650	300	100

Third Model—1858 and 1861 Patent Dates

Exc.	V.G.	Good	Fair	Poor
—	—	500	200	100

.22 Side Hammer Rimfire Revolver

A smaller version of the .32 revolver, chambered for the .22 rimfire cartridge. It has octagonal barrels from 2.25" to 4" in length. It has a 7-shot, unfluted cylinder. There were approximately 1,500 manufactured between 1858 and 1862. There were many variations.

Early Model First Issue—Access Pin Enters from Rear

Exc.	V.G.	Good	Fair	Poor
—	—	700	300	100

Second Issue—Access Pin Enters from Front

Exc.	V.G.	Good	Fair	Poor
—	—	700	300	100

Third Issue—Separate Rear Sight

Exc.	V.G.	Good	Fair	Poor
—	—	850	400	150

Fourth to Eighth Issue—Very Similar, Values the Same

Exc.	V.G.	Good	Fair	Poor
—	—	350	150	75

Single Shot Center Hammer

A single-shot derringer-type pistol that was chambered for the .22 caliber rimfire cartridge. It had part-octagon barrels from 2" to 5.5" in length that swung to the right side for loading. Some had automatic ejectors; others did not. The frame was either brass or iron with birdshead or squared butt walnut grips. It was marked "Allen & Wheelock" or "E. Allen & Co." There were very few manufactured in the early 1860s.

Early Issue

Full-length, octagon barrel and a round, iron frame. It is rarely encountered.

Exc.	V.G.	Good	Fair	Poor
—	—	700	300	100

Standard Issue—Squared-Butt or Birdshead

Exc.	V.G.	Good	Fair	Poor
—	—	350	150	100

.32 Single Shot Center Hammer

A larger-frame pocket pistol chambered for the .32 rimfire cartridge. It has a part-octagon or full-octagon barrel of 4" or 5" in length. It swung to the right side for loading. Otherwise, this model was similar to the .22-caliber version.

Exc.	V.G.	Good	Fair	Poor
—	—	600	300	100

Vest Pocket Derringer

A small pocket pistol chambered for the .22 rimfire cartridge. It had a 2", part-octagon barrel that swung to the right-hand side for loading. The cartridges were manually extracted. It featured a brass frame with a blued or plated barrel and walnut, birdshead grips. The barrel was marked "Allen & Co. Makers." This was an extremely small firearm, and there were approximately 200 manufactured between 1869 and 1871.

Exc.	V.G.	Good	Fair	Poor
—	—	600	300	100

.32 Derringer

Similar to the Vest Pocket version, larger in size, and chambered for the .32 rimfire cartridge. It had a part-octagon barrel from 2" to 4" in length that swung to the right for loading. This

version featured an automatic extractor. The barrel was marked "E. Allen & Co. Worchester, Mass." This was a very rare firearm, made between 1865 and 1871.

Exc.	V.G.	Good	Fair	Poor
—	—	500	250	100

.41 Derringer

The same size and configuration as the .32 caliber model except it was chambered for the .41 rimfire cartridge with barrel lengths of 2.5" to 2.75" in length. The markings were the same. There were approximately 100 manufactured between 1865 and 1871.

Exc.	V.G.	Good	Fair	Poor
—	—	1750	800	350

Center Hammer Muzzleloading Rifle

A single-shot rifle chambered for .44 caliber percussion. It had a 36" round barrel with an octagonal breech. It had a center-mounted hammer that was offset to the right for sighting. It had iron mountings. The finish was browned with a case-colored lock. There was a ramrod mounted under the barrel. It had a walnut buttstock with a crescent buttplate and no forearm. There were approximately 100 manufactured in the 1850s.

Exc.	V.G.	Good	Fair	Poor
—	—	1250	500	250

Side Hammer Muzzleloading Rifle

Similar to the Center Hammer model, with the hammer mounted on the right side of the lock. It was chambered for .38 caliber percussion, with an octagon barrel from 28" to 32" in length. It is occasionally found with a patchbox. The barrel is browned with a case-colored lock and a walnut stock with crescent buttplate. There were several hundred manufactured from the early 1840s to the 1860s.

Exc.	V.G.	Good	Fair	Poor
—	—	2500	800	350

Combination Gun

Either an Over/Under or SxS rifle chambered for 12 gauge and .38 caliber percussion. The barrels were from 28" to 34" in length. It had two hammers and double triggers with a ramrod mounted either beneath or on the right side of the barrels. The finish was browned with a walnut stock. Examples with a patchbox have been noted. Production was very limited, with the Over/Under versions worth approximately 20 percent more than the SxS values given. They were manufactured between the 1840s and the 1860s.

Exc.	V.G.	Good	Fair	Poor
—	—	3000	1000	450

Side Hammer Breech-loading Rifle

A unique rifle chambered for .36 to .50 caliber percussion. It was offered with various-length, part-octagon barrels. It had an unusual breech mechanism that was activated by a rotating lever which resembled a water faucet. The barrel was browned with a case-colored lock and a walnut stock. It was marked "Allen & Wheelock/ Allen's Patent July 3, 1855." There were approximately 500 manufactured between 1855 and 1860.

Courtesy Buffalo Bill Historical Center, Cody, Wyoming

Exc.	V.G.	Good	Fair	Poor
—	—	2750	1250	500

Drop Breech Rifle

This single-shot rifle was chambered for the .22 through the .44 rimfire cartridges. It had a part-octagon barrel from 23" to 28" in length. The breech was activated by the combination triggerguard action lever. Opening the breech automatically ejected the empty cartridge. The external hammer was manually cocked, and it featured an adjustable sight. The barrel was blued with a case-colored frame and a walnut stock. It was marked "Allen & Wheelock/ Allen's Pat. Sept. 18, 1860." There were approximately 2,000 manufactured between 1860 and 1871.

Courtesy Milwaukee Public Museum, Milwaukee, Wisconsin

Exc.	V.G.	Good	Fair	Poor
—	—	750	300	125

Lipfire Revolving Rifle

A six-shot, cylinder-type rifle chambered for the .44 caliber lipfire cartridge. It had an unfluted cylinder with slots at its rear to allow for the cartridge lips. The round barrels were 26" to 28" in length with an octagon breech. The finish was blued with a case-colored frame and a walnut buttstock. This model was not marked with the maker's name. There were approximately 100 manufactured between 1861 and 1863.

Courtesy Buffalo Bill Historical Center, Cody, Wyoming

Exc.	V.G.	Good	Fair	Poor
—	—	15000	6000	2000

Double Barrel Shotgun

A SxS gun chambered for 10 or 12 gauge. The barrel length was 28". It was loaded by means of a trapdoor-type breech that had a lever handle. The finish was blued with checkered walnut stock. There were a few hundred manufactured between 1865 and 1871.

Exc.	V.G.	Good	Fair	Poor
—	—	1250	600	250

ALLEN & THURBER
SEE—Ethan Allen

ALLEN & WHEELOCK
SEE—Ethan Allen

ALLEN FIREARMS
Santa Fe, New Mexico
SEE—Aldo Uberti

ALL RIGHT F. A. CO.
Lawrence, Massachusetts

Little All Right Palm Pistol

Squeezer-type pocket pistol invented by E. Boardman and A. Peavy in 1876, was made in .22 cal. and had a 5-shot cylinder with a 1-5/8" or 2-3/8" barrel. The barrel is octagonal with a tube on top of it which houses the sliding trigger. The finish is nickel. The black hard rubber grips have "Little All Right" & "All Right Firearms Co., Manufacturers Lawrence, Mass. U.S.A." molded into them. There were several hundred produced in the late 1870s.

Courtesy Milwaukee Public Museum, Milwaukee, Wisconsin

Exc.	V.G.	Good	Fair	Poor
—	2250	1000	500	250

ALPHA ARMS CO.
Flower Mound, Texas

Alpha Arms Co. produced high-grade bolt action rifles on a semi-custom basis. It manufactured a number of standard models but offered many options at additional cost. Some of these options were custom sights and finishes and an octagonal barrel. These extra features would add to the value of the models listed. This company operated from 1983 until 1987.

Alpha Jaguar Grade I

Built on a Mauser-type action with barrel lengths from 20" to 24". It was chambered for most calibers between .222 Rem. and .338 Win. Mag. The stock was made from a synthetic laminated material that the company called Alphawood. This model was introduced in 1987 and only produced that year.

NIB	Exc.	V.G.	Good	Fair	Poor
900	750	500	400	300	200

Jaguar Grade II

Similar to the Grade I with a Douglas Premium barrel.

NIB	Exc.	V.G.	Good	Fair	Poor
1000	850	650	500	400	250

Jaguar Grade III

Has the Douglas barrel plus a hand-honed trigger and action and a three-position safety like the Winchester Model 70.

NIB	Exc.	V.G.	Good	Fair	Poor
1200	1000	850	700	400	200

Jaguar Grade IV

Has all the features of the Grade III with a specially lightened action and sling-swivel studs.

NIB	Exc.	V.G.	Good	Fair	Poor
1300	1100	950	800	500	250

Alpha Grand Slam

Features the same high quality as the Jaguar models and is available in a left-hand model. It has a fluted bolt, laminated stock, and a matte blue finish.

NIB	Exc.	V.G.	Good	Fair	Poor
1200	1000	850	700	450	250

Alpha Custom

Similar to the Grand Slam with a select grade stock.

NIB	Exc.	V.G.	Good	Fair	Poor
1500	1275	1000	750	500	250

Alpha Alaskan

Similar to the Grand Slam but chambered for the .308 Win., .350 Rem. Mag., .358 Win. and the .458 Win. Mag. It features all stainless steel construction.

NIB	Exc.	V.G.	Good	Fair	Poor
1500	1275	1000	750	500	250

Alpha Big - Five

Similar to the Jaguar Grade IV chambered for the .300 Win. Mag., .375 H&H Mag. and the .458 Win. Mag. It had a reinforced through-bolt stock to accommodate the recoil of the larger caliber cartridges for which it was chambered. It also had a decelerator recoil pad. This model was manufactured in 1987 only.

NIB	Exc.	V.G.	Good	Fair	Poor
1600	1375	1100	850	600	300

ALSOP, C.R.
Middletown, Connecticut

This firearms manufacturer made revolvers during 1862 and 1863. They made two basic models, the Navy and the Pocket model. Some collectors consider the Alsop to be a secondary U.S. martial handgun, but no verifying government contracts are known to exist.

First Model Navy Revolver

A .36 cal. revolver with a 3.5", 4.5", 5.5", or 6.5" barrel length and a 5-shot cylinder. It has a blued finish, wood grips, and a peculiar hump in its backstrap. The first model has a safety device which blocks the spur trigger. This device is found on serial numbers 1-100. Markings are as follows: "C.R. Alsop Middletown, Conn. 1860 & 1861" on the barrel. The cylinder is marked "C.R. Alsop" & "Nov. 26th, 1861"; the side plate, "Patented Jan. 21st, 1862."

Exc.	V.G.	Good	Fair	Poor
—	—	3500	1250	500

Standard Model Navy Revolver

Exactly the same as the First Model without the safety device. They are serial numbered 101 to 300.

Exc.	V.G.	Good	Fair	Poor
—	—	3000	850	300

Pocket Model Revolver

A .31 cal. 5-shot revolver with spur trigger, 4" round barrel, blued finish, and wood grips. It is very similar in appearance to the Navy model but smaller in size. It is marked "C.R. Alsop Middletown, Conn. 1860 & 1861" on the barrel. The cylinder is marked "C.R. Alsop Nov. 26th, 1861." They are serial numbered 1-300.

Courtesy Milwaukee Public Museum, Milwaukee, Wisconsin

Exc.	V.G.	Good	Fair	Poor
—	—	1250	500	200

AMERICAN ARMS
Garden Grove, California

Eagle .380

This pistol was a stainless steel copy of the Walther PPKS. It was a semiauto blowback that was chambered for the .380 ACP. It was double action and had a 3.25" barrel and a 6-shot detachable magazine. An optional feature was a black teflon finish that would increase the value by 10 percent. This company ceased production in 1985.

Exc.	V.G.	Good	Fair	Poor
300	225	175	150	100

AMERICAN ARMS CO.
Boston, Massachusetts

The history of American Arms is rather sketchy, but it appears the company was formed in 1853 as the G. H. Fox Co. and then became the American Tool & Machine Co. in 1865. In 1870 they formed a new corporation called American Arms Company with George Fox as the principle stockholder. This corporation was dissolved in 1873; a second American Arms Co. was incorporated in 1877 and a third in 1890. It is unclear if these corporations had essentially the same owners, but George H. Fox appears as a principal owner in two of the three. One could assume that financial problems forced them to bankrupt one corporation and reorganize under another. American Arms manufactured firearms in Boston, Massachusetts, from 1866 until 1893. In 1893 they moved to Bluffton, Alabama and manufactured guns until 1901.

Fox Model "Swing Out" Hammer Double

Manufactured from 1870 to 1884, designed by George H. Fox, not to be confused with A.H. Fox. This model is unusual in that the barrel swings to the right for loading and the barrel release is located on the tang. It comes in 10 and 12 gauge, 26", 28", 30" and 32", with twist, Damascus or laminated barrels. Early production models have conventional soldered together barrels. Later variations after 1878 feature a unique design in that the barrels are dovetailed together. These guns could be ordered with several options and choices of finish; this would add premium value to a particular gun.

Exc.	V.G.	Good	Fair	Poor
1500	900	600	300	150

Semi-Hammerless Double

Manufactured from 1892 to 1901. This model features a cocking lever that cocks an internal firing pin. It comes in 12 gauge with 30" twist barrels.

Exc.	V.G.	Good	Fair	Poor
1200	800	400	250	150

Whitmore Model Hammerless Double

Manufactured from 1890 to 1901. It comes in 10, 12, and 16 gauge with 28", 30" or 32" twist, laminated or Damascus barrels. It is marked Whitmore's patent.

Courtesy Nick Niles, Photo Paul Goodwin

Exc.	V.G.	Good	Fair	Poor
1000	700	500	250	150

Semi-Hammerless Single Barrel

Manufactured from 1882 to 1901. It comes in 10, 12, and 16 gauge with 28", 30" or 32" twist or Damascus barrel.

Exc.	V.G.	Good	Fair	Poor
1000	600	400	200	100

TOP BREAK REVOLVERS

Courtesy Milwaukee Public Museum, Milwaukee, Wisconsin

Spur Trigger - Single Action Five-Shot Revolver

These revolvers were made between 1883 and 1887 in .38 S&W only. They feature an unusual manual ring extractor and double-fluted cylinder. They are nickel plated with hard rubber grips and are marked "American Arms Company Boston Mass."

Exc.	V.G.	Good	Fair	Poor
—	350	250	100	75

Standard Trigger Double Action Model 1886 Revolver

This model has a standard trigger and triggerguard, comes in .32 short and .38 S&W with a 3.5-inch barrel, in blue or nickel finish. The early models are equipped with the ring extractor and double fluted cylinder. Later variations have a standard star extractor and single fluted cylinder.

Exc.	V.G.	Good	Fair	Poor
—	600	250	100	75

Hammerless Model 1890 Double Action

These guns were manufactured from 1890 to 1901. It has an adjustable single- or double-stage trigger pull and several unusual safety devices. It comes in .32 and .38 S&W with a 3.25" ribbed barrel, fluted cylinder, nickel finish, hard rubber grips with logo and ivory or mother of pearl grips. It is marked "American Arms Co. Boston/Pat. May 25, 1886." The top strap is marked "Pat. Pending" on early models and "Pat's May 25'86/Mar 11'89/June 17'90" on later models.

Exc.	V.G.	Good	Fair	Poor
—	600	250	100	75

DOUBLE BARREL DERRINGERS

American Arms Co. manufactured a two-barrel derringer-style pocket pistol. The barrels were manually rotated to load and fire the weapon. The pistol had a nickel-plated brass frame, blued barrels, and walnut grips. The markings were as follows: "American Arms Co. Boston, Mass." on one barrel and "Pat. Oct. 31, 1865" on the other barrel. There were approximately 2,000-3,000 produced between 1866 and 1878.

Combination .22 caliber R.F. and .32 caliber R.F.

A two-caliber combination with 3" barrel, square butt only. The most common variation.

Exc.	V.G.	Good	Fair	Poor
—	—	600	250	100

.32 cal. R.F., Both Barrels

3" barrel with square butt.

Courtesy Milwaukee Public Museum, Milwaukee, Wisconsin

Exc.	V.G.	Good	Fair	Poor
—	—	750	300	100

.32 caliber R.F., Both Barrels

2-5/8" barrel with birdshead grips.

Exc.	V.G.	Good	Fair	Poor
—	—	850	400	100

.38 caliber R.F. Both Barrels

2-5/8" barrel with birdshead grips. A rare variation.

Exc.	V.G.	Good	Fair	Poor
—	—	1750	800	200

.41 caliber R.F. Both Barrels

2-5/8" barrel with square butt only.

Exc.	V.G.	Good	Fair	Poor
—	—	1250	600	150

AMERICAN ARMS, INC.
North Kansas City, Missouri

Basically an importer of firearms: shotguns from Spain, rifles from Yugoslavia, and handguns from Germany and Yugoslavia. They also manufacture in the U.S.A. There are certain rifles that they are no longer allowed to import because of the Bush administration's ban on foreign semiautomatic rifles. These weapons are listed for reference but are not priced due to the extreme fluctuations in values as this is written.

NOTE: American Arms has been sold to Tristar Ltd. Sporting Arms.

SHOTGUNS SIDE-BY-SIDE

Gentry - York

These two designations cover the same model. Prior to 1988 this model was called the York. In 1988 the receiver was case-colored and the designation was changed to the Gentry. This model was chambered for 12, 20, 28 gauge and .410. It had chrome-lined barrels from 26" to 30" in length, double triggers, 3" chambers, and automatic ejectors. The boxlock action featured scroll engraving, and the walnut stock was hand checkered. It was introduced in 1986.

NIB	Exc.	V.G.	Good	Fair	Poor
750	625	450	300	200	150

10 Gauge Magnum Shotgun

A 10 gauge with 3.5" chambers and 32" barrels. It featured a scroll-engraved, chromed boxlock action and double triggers. It was imported from Spain in 1986 only.

NIB	Exc.	V.G.	Good	Fair	Poor
850	750	550	350	250	150

12 Gauge Magnum Shotgun

As above but chambered for 12 gauge 3-1/2" magnum shell.

NIB	Exc.	V.G.	Good	Fair	Poor
800	700	500	300	200	150

Brittany

Chambered for 12 and 20 gauge with 27" or 25" barrels with screw-in choke tubes. It had a solid matted rib and a case-colored, engraved boxlock action. Automatic ejectors and a single selective trigger were standard on this model, as was a hand checkered, walnut, straight grip stock with semi-beavertail forend. This model was introduced in 1989.

NIB	Exc.	V.G.	Good	Fair	Poor
850	750	600	450	375	200

Turkey Special

A utilitarian model designed to be an effective turkey hunting tool. It is chambered for the Magnum 10 and 12 gauges and has 26" barrels. The finish is parkerized, and the stock is also finished in a non-glare matte. Sling-swivel studs and a recoil pad are standard. This model was introduced in 1987.

NIB	Exc.	V.G.	Good	Fair	Poor
800	700	450	350	250	150

Waterfowl Special

This model is similar to the Turkey Special but chambered for the 10 gauge only. It is furnished with a camouflaged sling. It was introduced in 1987.

NIB	Exc.	V.G.	Good	Fair	Poor
950	850	550	350	250	150

Specialty Model

Similar to the Turkey Special and offered in 12 gauge 3-1/2" magnum.

NIB	Exc.	V.G.	Good	Fair	Poor
875	750	500	300	200	150

Derby

Chambered for the 12 and 20 gauge. It has 26" or 28" barrels with 3" chambers and automatic ejectors. Either double or single selective triggers are offered, and the sidelock action is scroll engraved and chromed. The checkered straight grip stock and forearm are oil-finished. This model was introduced in 1986. No longer imported.

NIB	Exc.	V.G.	Good	Fair	Poor
825	700	600	500	350	200

Grulla #2

Top-of-the-line model chambered for 12, 20 and 28 gauge and .410. The barrels are 26" or 28" with a concave rib. The hand-fitted full sidelock action is extensively engraved and case-colored. There are various chokes, double triggers, and automatic ejectors. The select walnut, straight grip stock and splinter forend is hand checkered and has a hand-rubbed oil finish. This model was introduced in 1989. No longer imported.

NIB	Exc.	V.G.	Good	Fair	Poor
2500	1750	1250	900	500	250

SHOTGUNS O/U

F.S. 200

A trap or skeet model that was chambered for 12 gauge only. It had 26" Skeet & Skeet barrels or 32" full choke barrels on the trap model. The barrels were separated and had a vent rib. The boxlock action had a Greener crossbolt and was either black or matte chrome-plated. It featured a single selective trigger, automatic ejectors, and a checkered walnut pistol grip stock. The F.S. 200 was imported in 1986 and 1987 only.

Exc.	V.G.	Good	Fair	Poor
675	575	465	350	150

F.S. 300

Similar to the F. S. 200 with lightly engraved side plates and a 30" barrel offered in the trap grade. It was imported in 1986 only.

Exc.	V.G.	Good	Fair	Poor
800	675	565	450	250

F.S. 400

Similar to the F.S. 300 with an engraved, matte chrome-plated receiver. It was imported in 1986 only.

Exc.	V.G.	Good	Fair	Poor
1100	950	800	650	350

F.S. 500

Similar to the F.S. 400 with the same general specifications. It was not imported after 1985.

Exc.	V.G.	Good	Fair	Poor
1150	1000	850	700	350

Waterfowl Special

Chambered for the 12 gauge Magnum with 3.5" chambers. It has 28" barrels with screw-in choke tubes. There are automatic ejectors and a single selective trigger. The finish is parkerized with a matte finished stock, sling swivels, and camouflaged sling and a recoil pad. It was introduced in 1987.

NIB	Exc.	V.G.	Good	Fair	Poor
875	700	500	350	300	150

Waterfowl 10 Gauge

The same as the Waterfowl Special but is chambered for the 10 gauge Magnum with double triggers.

NIB	Exc.	V.G.	Good	Fair	Poor
975	850	600	400	300	200

Turkey Special

Similar to the Waterfowl Special 10 gauge with a 26" barrel with screw-in choke tubes.

NIB	Exc.	V.G.	Good	Fair	Poor
975	850	600	350	300	200

Lince

Chambered for the 12 and 20 gauge and had 26" or 28" barrels with 3" chambers and various chokes. The boxlock action had a Greener crossbolt and was either blued or polished and chrome-plated. The barrels were blued with a ventilated rib. It had a single selective trigger and automatic ejectors. The Lince was imported in 1986 only.

Exc.	V.G.	Good	Fair	Poor
500	425	350	300	200

Silver Model

Similar to the Lince with a plain, unengraved, brushed-chrome-finished receiver. It was imported in 1986 and 1987.

Exc.	V.G.	Good	Fair	Poor
500	425	350	300	200

Silver I

Similar to the Silver but is available in 28 gauge and .410, as well as 12 and 20 gauge. It also has a single selective trigger, fixed chokes, extractors, and a recoil pad. It was introduced in 1987.

NIB	Exc.	V.G.	Good	Fair	Poor
650	550	325	275	200	175

NOTE: Add $25 for 28 gauge and .410 bore guns.

Silver II

Similar to the Silver I with screw-in choke tubes, automatic ejectors, and select walnut. It was introduced in 1987.

NIB	Exc.	V.G.	Good	Fair	Poor
750	650	450	350	300	150

NOTE: Add $25 for 28 gauge and .410 bore guns.

Silver II Lite

Introduced in 1994 this model is designed as an upland game gun. Offered in 12, 20, and 28 gauge with 26" barrels. Chambered for both 2-3/4" and 3" shells. Frame is made from a lightweight steel alloy. No longer imported.

NIB	Exc.	V.G.	Good	Fair	Poor
875	775	550	400	300	150

Silver Competition/Sporting

Offered in 12 gauge with a choice of 28" or 30" barrels which are made from chrome moly. Barrels have elongated forcing cones, chromed bores and are ported to help reduce recoil. Comes with interchangeable choke tubes. The single selective trigger is mechanical. Weighs about 7-1/2 pounds. In 1996 a 20 gauge model was added with 28" barrel and 3" chambers.

NIB	Exc.	V.G.	Good	Fair	Poor
950	800	600	400	300	150

Silver Hunter

Introduced in 1999 this model is offered in 12 and 20 gauges with 26" and 28" barrels. Single selective trigger with extractors. Choke tubes standard. Weight is about 7 lbs.

NIB	Exc.	V.G.	Good	Fair	Poor
625	500	400	—	—	—

Bristol (Sterling)

Chambered for 12 and 20 gauge. It has various barrel lengths with a vent rib and screw-in choke tubes. The chambers are 3", and the chrome-finished action is a boxlock with Greener crossbolt and game scene engraved side plates. There are automatic ejectors and a single selective trigger. It was introduced in 1986, and in 1989 the designation was changed to the Sterling. No longer imported.

NIB	Exc.	V.G.	Good	Fair	Poor
825	750	675	500	400	200

Sir

Chambered for the 12 and 20 gauge with 3" chambers, various barrel lengths and chokings and a ventilated rib. The chrome-finished sidelock action has a Greener crossbolt and is engraved with a game scene. There are automatic ejectors and a single selective trigger. This model was imported in 1986. No longer imported.

Exc.	V.G.	Good	Fair	Poor
875	750	625	500	250

Royal

Chambered for the 12 and 20 gauge. It is manufactured in various barrel lengths and chokes with a vent rib and 3" chambers. The chrome-finished sidelock action has a Greener crossbolt and is profusely scroll-engraved. It has automatic ejectors and a single selective trigger. The select pistol grip walnut stock is hand checkered and oil-finished. This model was imported in 1986 and 1987. No longer imported.

Exc.	V.G.	Good	Fair	Poor
1500	1275	1000	800	400

Excelsior

Similar to the Royal with extensive deep relief engraving and gold inlays. This model was imported in 1986 and 1987. No longer imported.

Exc.	V.G.	Good	Fair	Poor
1750	1500	1200	875	450

SINGLE BARREL SHOTGUNS

AASB

The standard single-barrel, break-open, hammerless shotgun. It is chambered for 12 and 20 gauge and .410. It has a 26" barrel with various chokes and 3" chambers. It has a pistol grip stock and a matte finish. It was introduced in 1988. No longer imported.

AASB

NIB	Exc.	V.G.	Good	Fair	Poor
100	85	75	60	45	25

Campers Special

Similar to the standard model with a 21" barrel and a folding stock. It was introduced in 1988. No longer imported.

NIB	Exc.	V.G.	Good	Fair	Poor
107	95	85	70	50	35

Single Barrel Shotguns Youth Model

Chambered for the 20 gauge and .410 and has a 12.5" stock with a recoil pad. It was introduced in 1989. No longer imported.

NIB	Exc.	V.G.	Good	Fair	Poor
115	100	80	65	50	35

Slugger

This version has a 24" barrel with rifle sights. It is chambered for the 12 and 20 gauge and has a recoil pad. No longer imported.

AASB SLUGGER

NIB	Exc.	V.G.	Good	Fair	Poor
115	100	80	65	50	35

10 Gauge Model

Chambered for the 10 gauge 3.5" Magnum. It has a 32" full choke barrel and a recoil pad. This model was introduced in 1988. No longer imported.

NIB	Exc.	V.G.	Good	Fair	Poor
150	135	100	85	60	45

Combo Model

Similar in appearance to the other single-barrel models but is offered in an interchangeable-barreled rifle/shotgun combination—the 28" barreled .22 Hornet and the 12 gauge, or the 26" barreled .22 l.r. and 20 gauge. This model was furnished with a fitted hard case to hold the interchangeable barrels. It was introduced in 1989. No longer imported.

AASB COMBO

NIB	Exc.	V.G.	Good	Fair	Poor
250	200	175	145	110	75

SEMIAUTO SHOTGUNS

Phantom Field

Chambered for 12 gauge and fitted with choice of 24", 26", or 28" barrels. Fitted with 3" chamber. Gas operated action. Choke tubes standard. Five-round magazine. Checkered walnut stock. Weight is about 7 lbs. Introduced in 1999.

NIB	Exc.	V.G.	Good	Fair	Poor
425	350	300	—	—	—

Phantom Synthetic

Same as model above but furnished with checkered synthetic stock. Weight is about 6.75 lbs. Introduced in 1999.

NIB	Exc.	V.G.	Good	Fair	Poor
425	350	300	—	—	—

Phantom HP

This model features a 19" threaded barrel for external choke tubes. Five-round magazine. Weight is about 6.75 lbs. Introduced in 1999.

NIB	Exc.	V.G.	Good	Fair	Poor
450	375	325	—	—	—

RIFLES

Model ZCY.223

A gas-operated, semiautomatic rifle that is chambered for the .223. It is the civilian version of the Yugoslavian Military rifle and was never actually imported — only advertised. This is another model that would have wildly fluctuating values; and if one were to be located for sale, it would be a market-will-bear situation.

NOTE: These rifles are listed for reference purposes only. An independent appraisal should be secured if a transaction is contemplated.

Model ZCY.308

Essentially the same rifle as the ZCY.223 — only it is chambered for the .308 cartridge. This model was imported in 1988 only.

AKY39

The semiautomatic version of the Soviet AK-47 as it is manufactured by Yugoslavia. It is offered with folding tritium night sights and a wooden fixed stock. It was imported in 1988 and is now banned from further importation.

AKF39

The same rifle as the AKY39 with a metal folding stock.

AKC47

Basically the same rifle as the AKY39 without the tritium night sights. Importation is no longer allowed.

AKF47

The same rifle as the AKC47 with a metal folding stock.

EXP-64 Survival Rifle

A .22 caliber, semiautomatic takedown rifle. It is self-storing in a floating, oversized plastic stock. The rifle has a 21" barrel with open sights and a crossbolt safety. There is a 10-shot detachable magazine. Importation by American Arms began in 1989.

NIB	Exc.	V.G.	Good	Fair	Poor
165	150	125	95	75	50

SM-64 TD Sporter

A .22 l.r. semiautomatic with a takedown 21" barrel. It has adjustable sights and a checkered hardwood stock and forend. Importation commenced in 1989.

NIB	Exc.	V.G.	Good	Fair	Poor
150	135	110	85	65	45

1860 Henry

Replica of lever action Henry rifle. Brass frame. Steel half-octagon barrel with tube magazine. Chambered for .44-40 or .45 Long Colt. Offered in 24" or 18.5" barrels. Weight with 24" barrel is about 9.25 lbs. Built by Uberti.

NIB	Exc.	V.G.	Good	Fair	Poor
950	800	650	—	—	—

1866 Winchester

Replica of Winchester 1866. Offered in .44-40 or .45 Long Colt. Barrel lengths in 24" or 19". Brass frame. Weight is about 8.25 lbs. for 24" barrel model. Built by Uberti.

NIB	Exc.	V.G.	Good	Fair	Poor
725	625	475	—	—	—

1873 Winchester

Replica of Winchester Model 1873. Offered with choice of 24" or 30" barrels. Chambered for .44-40 or .45 Long Colt. Case hardened steel frame. Weight is about 8.25 lbs. for 24" model. Built by Uberti.

NIB	Exc.	V.G.	Good	Fair	Poor
850	700	550	—	—	—

NOTE: Add $80 for 30" barrel.

1885 Single Shot High Wall

Chambered for .45-70 cartridge this Winchester replica is fitted with a 28" round barrel. Weight is about 8.75 lbs. Built by Uberti.

NIB	Exc.	V.G.	Good	Fair	Poor
800	650	500	—	—	—

Sharps Cavalry Carbine

This Sharps replica is fitted with a 22" round barrel and chambered for the .45-70 cartridge. Adjustable rear sight. Weight is about 8 lbs.

NIB	Exc.	V.G.	Good	Fair	Poor
650	500	350	—	—	—

Sharps Frontier Carbine

Similar to the Cavalry carbine but with a 22" octagonal barrel and double set triggers. Weight is about 7.75 lbs.

NIB	Exc.	V.G.	Good	Fair	Poor
675	525	375	—	—	—

Sharps Sporting Rifle

This model features a 28" octagonal barrel chambered for either the .45-70 or .45-120 cartridge. Double set triggers. Adjustable rear sight. Checkered walnut stock. Weight is about 9 lbs.

NIB	Exc.	V.G.	Good	Fair	Poor
675	525	375	—	—	—

Sharps 1874 Deluxe Sporting Rifle

Similar to the above model but with browned barrels.

NIB	Exc.	V.G.	Good	Fair	Poor
700	550	400	—	—	—

HANDGUNS

Model TT Tokarev

The Yugoslavian version of the Soviet Tokarev chambered for 9mm Parabellum and with a safety added to make importation legal. It has a 4.5" barrel, 9-shot magazine and a blued finish with checkered plastic grips. Importation began in 1988.

NIB	Exc.	V.G.	Good	Fair	Poor
275	225	175	150	125	100

Model ZC-.380

A scaled-down version of the Tokarev that is chambered for the .380 ACP. It has a 3.5" barrel and holds 8 shots. The finish and grips are the same as on the full-sized version. Importation from Yugoslavia began in 1988.

NIB	Exc.	V.G.	Good	Fair	Poor
275	225	175	150	125	100

Model EP-.380

A high-quality, stainless steel pocket pistol that is chambered for the .380 ACP cartridge. It is a double action semiautomatic that holds 7 shots and has a 3.5" barrel. The grips are checkered walnut. This pistol has been imported from West Germany since 1988.

NIB	Exc.	V.G.	Good	Fair	Poor
450	400	350	275	225	100

Model PK-22

A domestic semiautomatic that is chambered for the .22 l.r. It is a double action with a 3.5" barrel and an 8-shot finger extension magazine. It is made of stainless steel and has black plastic grips. This model is manufactured in the U.S.A. by American Arms.

NIB	Exc.	V.G.	Good	Fair	Poor
200	175	150	125	100	75

Model CX-22

A compact version of the PK-22 with a 2.75" barrel and a 7-shot magazine. Manufacture began in 1989.

NIB	Exc.	V.G.	Good	Fair	Poor
200	175	150	125	100	75

Aussie Model

Introduced in 1996 this is an Australian designed semiautomatic pistol made in Spain. Chambered for the 9mm or .40 S&W cartridge it has a polymer frame with nickeled steel slide. Sold with 10-shot magazine. Barrel length is 4-3/4" and weight is 23 oz.

NIB	Exc.	V.G.	Good	Fair	Poor
400	350	300	250	200	100

Mateba Auto-Revolver

This is a combination semiauto pistol and revolver. It has a blued steel frame and walnut grips. It is chambered for the .357 Magnum/.38 Special. Barrel length is 4", 6", or 8". This handgun can be fired single or double action. The cylinder rotates when the gun is fired. Weight is about 44 oz. Six-round capacity.

NIB	Exc.	V.G.	Good	Fair	Poor
850	650	500	400	—	—

Regulator

Built by Uberti this single action revolver has a case hardened frame, polished brass triggerguard and backstrap. Barrel and cylinder are blued. One piece walnut grips. Choice of chambers in .44-40, .45 LC, or .357 Magnum. Barrel lengths from 4.75", 5.5", to 7.5". Weight is about 34 oz. with 5.75" barrel.

NIB	Exc.	V.G.	Good	Fair	Poor
320	250	200	—	—	—

Regulator Deluxe

Same as above but with steel triggerguard and backstrap. Chambered in .45 Long Colt only.

NIB	Exc.	V.G.	Good	Fair	Poor
350	300	175	—	—	—

AMERICAN BARLOCK WONDER
SEE—Crescent Arms Co.

AMERICAN DERRINGER CORP.
Waco, Texas

Model 1 Derringer

Fashioned after the Remington O/U derringer this is a high quality, rugged pistol. It is built from high tensile strength stainless steel. There are over 60 different rifle and pistol calibers to choose from on special order. The upper barrel can be chambered different from the lower barrel on request. Available in a high polish finish or a satin finish. Offered with rosewood, bacote, walnut, or blackwood grips. Ivory, bonded ivory, stag, or pearl are available at extra cost. Overall length is 4.8", barrel length is 3", width across the frame is .9", width across the grip is 1.2". Typical weight is 15 oz. in .45 caliber. All guns are furnished with French fitted leatherette case. Prices are determined by caliber.

Caliber: .22 Long Rifle through .357 Mag. and .45 ACP

NIB	Exc.	V.G.	Good	Fair	Poor
300	225	150	125	100	75

Calibers: .41 Mag., .44-40, .44 Special, .44 Mag., .45 Long Colt, .410 Bore, .22 Hornet, .223 Rem., 30-30, and .47-70 Gov't.

NIB	Exc.	V.G.	Good	Fair	Poor
375	300	250	200	150	100

NOTE: Add $25 for optional extra high polish finish.

Model 1 Texas Commemorative

Built with a solid brass frame and stainless steel barrel. Dimensions are same as Model 1. Grips are stag or rosewood and offered in .45 Colt, .44-40, or .38 Special. Barrels marked "Made in the 150th Year of Texas Freedom". Limited to 500 pistols in each caliber.

Caliber: .38 Special

NIB	Exc.	V.G.	Good	Fair	Poor
325	250	200	150	100	75

Calibers: .45 Colt and .44-40

NIB	Exc.	V.G.	Good	Fair	Poor
400	325	250	200	125	100

Deluxe Engraved

Special serial number engraved on back strap.

NIB	Exc.	V.G.	Good	Fair	Poor
900	750	550	350	250	150

Model 1 Lady Derringer

Similar to the Model 1 but chambered for the .38 Special, .32 Magnum, .45 Colt, or .357 Magnum. Offered in two grades.

Deluxe Grade

High polished stainless steel with scrimshawed ivory grips with cameo or rose design.

NIB	Exc.	V.G.	Good	Fair	Poor
325	250	200	150	100	75

Deluxe Engraved Grade

Same as above but hand engraved in 1880s style.

NIB	Exc.	V.G.	Good	Fair	Poor
650	550	500	450	250	150

NOTE: For .45 Colt and .45/.410 add $75. For .357 magnum add $50.

Model 1 125th Anniversary Commemorative

Built to commemorate the 125th anniversary of the derringer, 1866 to 1991. Similar to the Model 1 but marked with the patent date December 12, 1865. Brass frame and stainless steel barrel. Chambered for .440-40, .45 Colt, or .38 Special.

NIB	Exc.	V.G.	Good	Fair	Poor
300	250	225	175	125	100

Deluxe Engraved

NIB	Exc.	V.G.	Good	Fair	Poor
650	550	500	450	250	150

Model 1 NRA 500 Series

Limited edition of 500. Also available in gold and blue finishes over stainless steel.

NIB	Exc.	V.G.	Good	Fair	Poor
350	300	250	200	150	100

Model 2-Pen Pistol

Introduced in 1993 this is a legal pistol that cannot be fired from its pen position but requires that it be pulled apart and bent 80 degrees to fire. Made from stainless steel it is offered in .22 LR, .25 ACP, and .32 ACP. The length in pen form is 5.6" and in pistol form is 4.2". Barrel length is 2". Diameter varies from 1/2" to 5/8". Weight is 5 oz. No longer in production.

NIB	Exc.	V.G.	Good	Fair	Poor
300	175	135	115	100	85

Model 3

This model is a single barrel derringer. Barrel length is 2.5" and swing down to load. Frame and barrel are stainless steel. Offered in .38 Special or .32 Magnum. Weighs about 8 oz. Production of this model has been temporary halted.

NIB	Exc.	V.G.	Good	Fair	Poor
150	100	85	75	65	50

Model 4

Similar in appearance to the Model 3 but fitted with a 41" barrel. Overall length is 6" and weight is about 16.5 oz. Chambered for 3" .410 bore, .45 Long Colt, .44 Magnum, or .357 Magnum.

NIB	Exc.	V.G.	Good	Fair	Poor
375	300	275	250	200	125

NOTE: For .45-70 add $150. For .44 magnum add $100.

Model 4-Engraved

NIB	Exc.	V.G.	Good	Fair	Poor
1500	1200	—	—	—	—

Model 4-Alaskan Survival Model

Similar to the Model 4 but with upper barrel chambered for .45-70 and lower barrel for .45 LC or .410. Both barrels can also be chambered for .44 Magnum or .45-70. Comes with oversized rosewood grips.

NIB	Exc.	V.G.	Good	Fair	Poor
425	350	275	200	150	100

NOTE: For extra high polish add $25.00.

Model 6

This double barrel derringer is fitted with a 6" barrel chambered for the .45 LC or .410 bore. Weighs about 21 oz. Rosewood grips are standard. Optional calibers are .357 Magnum or .45 ACP. Oversize grips are optional and add about $35 to value.

NIB	Exc.	V.G.	Good	Fair	Poor
400	350	250	200	150	100

Model 6-Engraved

NIB	Exc.	V.G.	Good	Fair	Poor
1700	1400	—	—	—	—

High Standard Double Action Derringer

This double barrel derringer is chambered for the .22 Long Rifle or .22 Magnum cartridge. Its barrel length is 3.5" and overall length is 5.125". Weighs approximately 11 oz. The finish is blue with black grips. Production temporarily halted.

NIB	Exc.	V.G.	Good	Fair	Poor
170	150	125	100	85	75

DA 38 Double Action Derringer

This is a two-barrel model featuring a double action trigger. Overall length is 4.9" and barrel length is 3". Weight is about 15 oz. Chambered for .38 Special, .357 magnum, 9mm Luger, and .40 S&W. Finish is satin stainless. Grip is made from aluminum. Grips are rosewood or walnut.

NIB	Exc.	V.G.	Good	Fair	Poor
400	325	250	200	150	100

NOTE: For .40 S&W add $40.

MINI COP-4 SHOT

This is a four-barrel derringer chambered for the .22 Magnum Rimfire cartridge. Production is temporarily halted.

NIB	Exc.	V.G.	Good	Fair	Poor
310	285	250	225	175	125

COP-4 SHOT

Same as above but chambered for the .357 Magnum cartridge. Production is temporarily halted.

NIB	Exc.	V.G.	Good	Fair	Poor
375	350	325	300	225	150

Model 7 Derringer-Lightweight

Manufactured as a backup gun for police officers. The frame and barrels are made of aircraft aluminum alloy; the other parts are stainless steel. This gun weighs 7.5 oz. Its appearance and function are similar to the Model 1. The finish is a gray matte with thin, matte-finished grips of rosewood or bacote. This model is chambered for and priced as follows:

.32 S&W Long/.32 Magnum

NIB	Exc.	V.G.	Good	Fair	Poor
275	225	150	100	80	50

.38 S&W and .380 ACP

NIB	Exc.	V.G.	Good	Fair	Poor
275	225	150	100	80	50

.22 L.R. and .38 Special

NIB	Exc.	V.G.	Good	Fair	Poor
275	225	150	100	80	50

.44 Special

NIB	Exc.	V.G.	Good	Fair	Poor
525	450	375	300	250	150

Model 8

This is a single action two-shot target pistol with a manually operated hammer block safety. Safety automatically disengages when the hammer is cocked. Barrel length is 8". Chambered for the .45 Colt and .410 shotshell. Weight is 24 oz.

NIB	Exc.	V.G.	Good	Fair	Poor
475	400	325	250	175	100

Model 8-Engraved

NIB	Exc.	V.G.	Good	Fair	Poor
1850	1500	—	—	—	—

Model 10 Derringer

Similar to the Model 1 with a frame of aluminum alloy and all other parts, including the barrels, stainless steel. It has a grey matte finish and thin grips of rosewood or bacote. It weighs 10 oz. and is chambered for the .38 Special, .45 ACP or the .45 Colt.

NIB	Exc.	V.G.	Good	Fair	Poor
250	200	175	140	110	80

NOTE: For .45 Colt add $75.

Model 11 Derringer

A stainless steel barrel and all other parts aluminum. It weighs 11 oz. and is chambered for the .38 Special, .380 Auto, .32 Mag., .22 LR, and .22 Magnum. The grips and finish are the same as on the Model 10.

NIB	Exc.	V.G.	Good	Fair	Poor
275	225	150	125	100	75

Semmerling LM-4

This gun has been in production for approximately 10 years, built by various companies. This latest offering by American Derringer may, with the right marketing and manufacturing approach, be the one that makes a commercial success of this fine firearm concept. The LM-4 was designed as the ultimate police backup/defense weapon. It is a manually operated, 5-shot repeater only 5.2" long, 3.7" high, and 1" wide. It is chambered for the .45 ACP and is undoubtedly the smallest 5-shot .45 ever produced. The LM-4 is made of a special tool steel and is either blued or, at extra cost, hard chrome-plated. A stainless steel version is also available. The LM-4 is not a semiautomatic, although it physically resembles one. The slide is flicked forward and back after each double action squeeze of the trigger. This weapon is virtually hand-built and features high visibility sights and a smooth trigger. It is an extremely limited production item, and the company produces only two per week. The price and availability may fluctuate, so the company should be contacted for accurate figures. The values for the guns produced before American Derringer's involvement will be found in the section dealing with the Semmerling. These values are for the latest production by American Derringer. Prices listed below may change due to supply and demand.

Hard Chrome-Add $200.00.

Stainless steel-Add 35%.

NIB	Exc.	V.G.	Good	Fair	Poor
2500	2000	1500	—	—	—

LM-5

Built of stainless steel this semiauto is chambered for the .32 Mag. or .25 Auto. The barrel length is 2.25" and the overall length is 4", height is 3". Wooden grips are standard. Offered in limited quantities. Weight is approximately 15 oz.

NIB	Exc.	V.G.	Good	Fair	Poor
300	250	200	150	100	75

Millennium Series 2000

This model chambered for .38 Special, .45 Colt, or .44-40. Single action. Fitted with scrimshaw grips with a yellow rose of Texas on the left side and the Lone Star flag on the right side. Weight is about 15 oz. Supplied with red velvet box with silver inlay. Introduced in 1999.

NIB	Exc.	V.G.	Good	Fair	Poor
400	325	—	—	—	—

Gambler Millennium 2000

Similar to the Millennium Series above but fitted with rosewood grips with etched Lone Star of Texas. Supplied with brown leatherette box with copper logo inlay.

NIB	Exc.	V.G.	Good	Fair	Poor
400	325	—	—	—	—

Women of Texas Series

This model has the same features as the Millennium Series 2000. Stamped "Women of Texas Series 2000".

NIB	Exc.	V.G.	Good	Fair	Poor
400	325	—	—	—	—

Cowboy Series 2000

This model has the same features as the Gambler Millennium 200 but with "Cowboy Series 2000" stamped on the barrel.

NIB	Exc.	V.G.	Good	Fair	Poor
400	325	—	—	—	—

AMERICAN F.A. MFG. CO., INC.
San Antonio, Texas

This company operated between 1972 and 1974, producing a .25 ACP pocket pistol and a stainless steel .38 Special derringer. A .380 auto was produced on an extremely limited basis.

American .25 Automatic

A small, blowback, semiautomatic pocket pistol that was chambered for the .25 ACP cartridge. It had a 2" barrel and was made of either stainless steel or blued carbon steel. The grips were of plain uncheckered walnut, and the detachable magazine held 7 shots. It was manufactured until 1974.

Stainless Steel-Add 20%.

Exc.	V.G.	Good	Fair	Poor
200	150	125	100	75

American .380 Automatic

Similar to the .25 except larger. The barrel was 3.5", and the gun was made in stainless steel only. The grips were of smooth walnut, and it held 8 shots. There were only 10 of these .380's manufactured between 1972 and 1974. They are extremely rare, but there is little collector base for this company's products, and the value is difficult to estimate.

Exc.	V.G.	Good	Fair	Poor
600	550	475	375	200

American .38 Special Derringer

A well-made, stainless steel O/U derringer that was similar in appearance and function to the old Remington O/U. It had 3" barrels that pivoted upward for loading. This gun was a single action that had an automatic selector and a spur trigger. The smooth grips were of walnut. There were approximately 3,500 manufactured between 1972 and 1974.

Exc.	V.G.	Good	Fair	Poor
200	180	150	125	90

AMERICAN FRONTIER FIREARMS
Aguanga, California

This firm began importing Italian-made parts for its single action revolver line in 1996. These parts are then fitted and finished in its California facility. The first of these metallic cartridge revolvers was ready for delivery in late 1996. In addition to its standard guns the company also offers special finishes and is ready to fill special orders. For this reason only standard prices are given.

1871-72 Open Top Standard Model

Offered in .38 or .44 caliber with non-rebated cylinder. Barrel lengths are 7.5" or 8" in round. Blued finish except silver backstrap and triggerguard. Walnut grips.

NIB	Exc.	V.G.	Good	Fair	Poor
795	625	500	400	—	—

Richards & Mason Conversion 1851 Navy Standard Model

Offered in .38 and .44 calibers with Mason ejector assembly and non-rebated cylinder with a choice of octagon barrels in 4.75", 5.5", or 7.5". Blued finish with blued backstrap and triggerguard. Walnut grips.

NIB	Exc.	V.G.	Good	Fair	Poor
795	325	500	400	—	—

1860 Richards Army Model

Chambered for .44 Colt and .38 caliber. Rebated cylinder with or without ejector assembly. Barrel length is 7.5". High polish blue finish with silver triggerguard and case hardened frame.

NIB	Exc.	V.G.	Good	Fair	Poor
795	325	500	400	—	—

NOTE: Guns shipped without ejector assembly will be supplied with a ramrod and plunger typical of the period.

AMERICAN GUN CO., NEW YORK
Norwich, Connecticut
Crescent Firearms Co.—Maker
H. & D. Folsom Co.—Distributor

Side-x-Side Shotgun

A typical trade gun made around the turn of the century by the Crescent Firearms Co. to be distributed by H. & D. Folsom. These are sometimes known as "Hardware Store Guns," as that is where many were sold. This particular gun was chambered for 12, 16, and 20 gauges and was produced with or without external hammers. The length of the barrels varied, as did the chokes. Some were produced with Damascus barrels; some, with fluid steel. The latter are worth approximately 25% more.

Knickerbocker Pistol
(See Knickerbocker)

NOTE: For a full listing of most of the variations of the Crescent Arms Co., and shotguns marked with American Gun Co. see "Crescent F.A. Co.".

AMERICAN HISTORICAL FOUNDATION
Richmond, Virginia

The American Historical Foundation is a private organization that commissions historical commemoratives. Secondary market sales are infrequent and are difficult to confirm. The American Historical Foundation sells only direct and not through dealers or distributors. For information on past and current issues contact the American Historical Foundation at 1142 West Grace Street, Richmond, VA 23220.

AMERICAN INDUSTRIES
Cleveland, Ohio
Renamed CALICO
Bakersfield, California

Calico M-100

A semiautomatic carbine that has a 16.1" barrel with a flash suppressor. It is chambered for the .22 l.r. and features a folding stock, full shrouding hand guards, a 100-round capacity, helical feed, and detachable magazine. It features an ambidextrous safety, pistol grip storage compartment, and a black finished alloy frame and adjustable sights. This model was introduced in 1986.

NIB	Exc.	V.G.	Good	Fair	Poor
400	300	250	175	125	100

Calico M-100P/M-110

Similar to the M-100 .22 rimfire with a 6" barrel with muzzle brake and no shoulder stock.

NIB	Exc.	V.G.	Good	Fair	Poor
325	275	225	175	100	75

Calico M-100S Sporter/M-105

Similar to the Model 100 with a futuristically styled walnut buttstock and forearm.

NIB	Exc.	V.G.	Good	Fair	Poor
350	275	250	200	100	75

Calico M-101 Solid Stock Carbine

Introduced in 1994 this rifle features a 100-round magazine and a composite buttstock that is removable.

NIB	Exc.	V.G.	Good	Fair	Poor
375	300	275	200	100	75

Calico M-900

A black polymer-stocked rifle that is similar to the M-100S, chambered for the 9mm Parabellum. It has a delayed blow-back action and features a stainless steel bolt and alloy receiver. The cocking handle is non-reciprocating, and the rear sight is fixed with an adjustable front. There is a 50-round magazine standard and a 100-round capacity model optional. This model was introduced in 1989.

NIB	Exc.	V.G.	Good	Fair	Poor
500	425	375	300	225	100

Calico M-950 Pistol

Similar to the Model 900 rifle with a 6" barrel and no shoulder stock.

NIB	Exc.	V.G.	Good	Fair	Poor
475	400	350	275	200	100

Calico M-951

The M-951 is a tactical carbine with a sliding buttstock. The barrel is 16" in length. It weighs about 7 pounds.

NIB	Exc.	V.G.	Good	Fair	Poor
500	425	375	300	225	100

Calico M-951S

Same as above but furnished with more conventional buttstock. Referred to as a light tactical carbine. Weighs about 7-1/4 pounds.

NIB	Exc.	V.G.	Good	Fair	Poor
500	425	375	300	225	100

AMERICAN INTERNATIONAL
Salt Lake City, Utah
A/K/A American Research & Development

American 180 Carbine

This firearm, imported from Austria, is a semiautomatic, 16.5" barreled carbine chambered for the .22 l.r. The sights are adjustable, and the stock is made of high-impact plastic. The unique drum magazine holds 177 rounds and is affixed to the top of the receiver. There is a select-fire version available for law enforcement agencies only and an optional laser lock sight system. This firearm was discontinued and recently has become available again from Feather Industries in Boulder, Colorado. It is now known as the SAR-180.

NIB	Exc.	V.G.	Good	Fair	Poor
650	500	400	300	200	100

N.P. AMES PISTOLS
Springfield, Massachusetts

Overall length-11-5/8"; barrel length-6"; caliber-.54. Markings: on lockplate, forward of hammer "N.P. AMES/SPRING-FIELD/MASS", on tail, either "USN" or "USR" over date; on barrel, standard U.S. Navy inspection marks. N. P. Ames of Springfield, Massachusetts received a contract from the U.S. Navy in September 1842 for the delivery of 2,000 single shot muzzleloading percussion pistols. All are distinguished by having a lock mechanism that lies flush with the right side of the stock. On the first 300 Ames pistols, this lock terminates in a point; the balance produced were made with locks with a rounded tail. This "box lock" had been devised by Henry Nock in England, and was adapted to the U.S. Navy for the percussion pistols they ordered from Ames and Derringer. In addition to the 2,000 pistols for the Navy, the U.S. Revenue Cutter Service purchased 144 (distinguished by the "U S R" marks) for the forerunner of the U.S. Coast Guard. The latter commands triple the price over the "U S N" marked pistols, while the Navy pistols with pointed tails quadruple the value.

Courtesy Milwaukee Public Museum, Milwaukee, Wisconsin

Courtesy Milwaukee Public Museum, Milwaukee, Wisconsin

Exc.	V.G.	Good	Fair	Poor
—	—	2500	1000	400

AMES SWORD CO.
Chicopee Falls, Massachusetts

Turbiaux Le Protector

Ames Sword Co. became one of three U.S. companies that produced this unique, French palm-squeezer pistol. The design consists of a round disk with a protruding barrel on one side and a lever on the other. The disk contains the cylinder that holds either seven 8mm rimfire or ten 6mm rimfire cartridges. The barrel protrudes between the fingers, and the lever trigger is squeezed to fire the weapon. The design was patented in 1883 and sold successfully in France into the 1890s. In 1892 Peter Finnegan bought the patents and brought them to Ames Sword. He contracted with them to produce 25,000 pistols for the Minneapolis Firearms Company. After approximately 1,500 were delivered, Finnegan declared insolvency, and after litigation, Ames secured the full patent rights. The Ames Company produced Protector Revolvers until at least 1917.

(See Chicago Firearms Co. and Minneapolis Firearms Co.)

Exc.	V.G.	Good	Fair	Poor
—	—	1500	600	300

ANCION & CIE
(of Liege, Belgium
See—French Military Firearms)

ANCION MARX
Liege, Belgium

This company began production in the 1860s with a variety of cheaply-made pinfire revolvers. They later switched to solid-frame, centerfire, "Velo-Dog"-type revolvers chambered for 5.5mm or 6.35mm. They were marketed in various countries under many different trade names. Some of the names that they will be found under are Cobalt, Extracteur, LeNovo, Lincoln, and Milady. The quality of these revolvers is quite poor; and collector interest, almost non-existent. Values do not usually vary because of trade names.

Exc.	V.G.	Good	Fair	Poor
—	175	125	75	45

ANDERSON
Anderson, Texas

Anderson Under Hammer Pistol
An unmarked, under hammer percussion pistol that was chambered for .45 caliber. It had a 5" half-round/half-octagonal barrel with an all steel, saw handle-shaped frame. There was a flared butt with walnut grips. The finish was blued. There is little information on this pistol, and its origin is strongly suspected but not confirmed.

Exc.	V.G.	Good	Fair	Poor
—	—	750	350	100

ANDRUS & OSBORN
Canton, Connecticut

Andrus & Osborn Under Hammer Pistol
This pistol is of the percussion type and chambered for .25 caliber. The part-round/part-octagonal barrel is 6" long and features small silver star inlays along its length. The barrel is marked "Andrus & Osborn/Canton Conn." with an eagle stamped beside it. It is marked "Cast Steel" near the breech. The grips are of walnut, and the finish is browned. Active 1863 to 1867.

Exc.	V.G.	Good	Fair	Poor
—	—	1000	450	150

ANSCHUTZ
Ulm, Germany

Mark 10 Target Rifle
A single-shot, bolt action rifle that is chambered for the .22 l.r. cartridge. It has a 26" heavy barrel with adjustable target-type sights. The finish was blued, and the walnut target stock had an adjustable palm rest. It was manufactured between 1963 and 1981.

NIB	Exc.	V.G.	Good	Fair	Poor
350	300	250	210	150	100

Model 1407
Similar to the Mark 10 but is furnished without sights. It was known as the "I.S.U." model. It was discontinued in 1981.

NIB	Exc.	V.G.	Good	Fair	Poor
375	325	275	235	175	100

Model 1408
A heavier-barreled version of the Model 1407.

NIB	Exc.	V.G	Good	Fair	Poor
375	325	275	235	175	100

Model 1411
Designed specifically to be fired from the prone position.

NIB	Exc.	V.G.	Good	Fair	Poor
350	300	250	210	150	100

Model 1413 Match
A high-grade, competition version with a heavy target barrel that is furnished without sights. The walnut stock has an adjustable cheekpiece.

NIB	Exc.	V.G.	Good	Fair	Poor
550	500	450	400	275	150

Model 1416D Classic
This sporting rifle is chambered for the .22 Long Rifle cartridge and is fitted with an American-style stock of European walnut or hardwood. Built on Anschutz Match 64 action. Left handed model also offered.

NIB	Exc.	V.G.	Good	Fair	Poor
650	500	400	300	200	100

Model 1516D Classic

Same as above but chambered for .22 Magnum cartridge.

NIB	Exc.	V.G.	Good	Fair	Poor
700	500	400	300	200	100

Model 1416D Custom

Chambered for the .22 Long Rifle cartridge, this model features a European-style stock with Monte Carlo cheekpiece, and schnabel forend.

NIB	Exc.	V.G.	Good	Fair	Poor
750	550	450	300	200	100

Model 1516D Custom

Same as above but chambered for .22 Magnum cartridge.

NIB	Exc.	V.G.	Good	Fair	Poor
750	550	450	300	200	100

Model 1733D Mannlicher

Introduced in 1993 this model features a Mannlicher stock built on a Match 54 action. The stock has a rosewood schnabel tip and checkering is done in a skip-line pattern. Chambered for .22 Hornet. Weighs about 6-1/4 pounds.

NIB	Exc.	V.G.	Good	Fair	Poor
1250	950	700	500	300	200

Model 1418D Mannlicher

A hunting rifle with a full-length, Mannlicher-type stock made with hand checkered walnut. Chambered for .22 Long Rifle.

NIB	Exc.	V.G.	Good	Fair	Poor
1100	850	600	350	200	150

Model 1518D Mannlicher

Same as above but chambered for the .22 Magnum.

NIB	Exc.	V.G.	Good	Fair	Poor
1100	850	600	350	200	150

Model 1418/19

A lower-priced sporter model that was formerly imported by Savage Arms.

NIB	Exc.	V.G.	Good	Fair	Poor
300	250	200	150	125	85

Model 184

A high-grade, bolt action sporting rifle chambered for the .22 l.r. cartridge. It has a 21.5" barrel with a folding-leaf sight. The finish is blued with a checkered walnut, Monte Carlo stock with a schnabel forend. It was manufactured between 1963 and 1981.

NIB	Exc.	V.G.	Good	Fair	Poor
375	335	280	220	150	100

Model 54 Sporter

A high-grade, bolt action sporting rifle chambered for the .22 l.r. cartridge. It has a 24" tapered round barrel and a 5-shot detachable magazine. It features a folding leaf-type rear sight. The finish is blued with a checkered walnut, Monte Carlo stock. It was manufactured between 1963 and 1981.

NIB	Exc.	V.G.	Good	Fair	Poor
650	575	500	350	250	125

Model 54M

This version is chambered for the .22 rimfire Magnum cartridge.

NIB	Exc.	V.G.	Good	Fair	Poor
700	600	525	375	275	125

Model 141

A bolt action sporter chambered for the .22 l.r. cartridge. It has a 23" round barrel with a blued finish and walnut Monte Carlo stock. It was manufactured between 1963 and 1981.

NIB	Exc.	V.G.	Good	Fair	Poor
350	300	250	200	150	100

Model 141M

Chambered for the .22 rimfire Magnum cartridge.

NIB	Exc.	V.G.	Good	Fair	Poor
375	325	275	225	175	100

Model 164

This bolt action rifle is fitted with a 23" round barrel chambered for the .22 Long Rifle cartridge. It has a Monte Carlo stock with open sights. Magazine holds 5 rounds.

NIB	Exc.	V.G.	Good	Fair	Poor
400	325	275	225	175	100

Model 164M

Same as model above but chambered for the .22 Win. Magnum cartridge.

NIB	Exc.	V.G.	Good	Fair	Poor
450	350	275	225	175	100

Model 153

A bolt action sporting rifle chambered for the .222 Remington cartridge. It has a 24" barrel with folding-leaf rear sight. The finish is blued with a checkered French walnut stock featuring a rosewood forend tip and pistol grip cap. It was manufactured between 1963 and 1981.

NIB	Exc.	V.G.	Good	Fair	Poor
575	500	385	300	225	150

Model 153-S

This version was offered with double-set triggers.

NIB	Exc.	V.G.	Good	Fair	Poor
625	550	435	350	275	150

Model 64

A single shot, bolt action rifle that is chambered for the .22 l.r. cartridge. It has a 26" round barrel and is furnished without sights. The finish is blued, and the walnut target-type stock featured a beaver-tail forearm and adjustable buttplate. It was manufactured between 1963 and 1981.

NIB	Exc.	V.G.	Good	Fair	Poor
375	300	250	200	150	100

Model 64MS

This version was designed for silhouette shooting and has a 21.25" barrel, blued finish, and a target-type walnut stock with a stippled pistol grip.

NIB	Exc.	V.G.	Good	Fair	Poor
750	600	525	400	300	200

Model 64P

Bolt action pistol with adjustable trigger. The action is grooved for scope mounts, and the stock is synthetic. Barrel length is 10" and is chambered for .22 long rifle cartridge. Weight is approximately 3 lb. 8 oz. Introduced in 1998.

NIB	Exc.	V.G.	Good	Fair	Poor
450	350	—	—	—	—

Model 64P Mag

Same as model above but chambered for .22 WMR cartridge.

NIB	Exc.	V.G.	Good	Fair	Poor
450	350	—	—	—	—

Model 54.18MS

A high-grade silhouette rifle chambered for the .22 l.r. cartridge. It has a 22" barrel and a match-grade action with fully adjustable trigger. It is furnished without sights. The finish is blued with a target-type walnut stock.

NIB	Exc.	V.G.	Good	Fair	Poor
1250	950	750	500	300	200

Model 54.MS REP

A repeating rifle with a 5-shot, detachable magazine with a thumbhole stock with vented forearm.

NIB	Exc.	V.G.	Good	Fair	Poor
1650	1350	900	500	300	200

Model 2000 MK

This single shot rifle was chambered for the .22 l.r. cartridge. It has a 26" round barrel with target-type sights. The finish was blued and has a checkered walnut stock. It was not imported after 1988.

NIB	Exc.	V.G.	Good	Fair	Poor
350	300	250	200	150	100

Model 2007 Supermatch

Introduced in 1993 this target rifle is chambered for the .22 long rifle cartridge. It has a 19-3/4" barrel fitted to a Match 54 action. Trigger is a two-stage. The stock is standard ISU configuration with adjustable cheekpiece. Weighs about 10.8 pounds. Offered in left-hand model.

NIB	Exc.	V.G.	Good	Fair	Poor
2250	1750	1250	750	350	200

Model 2013 Supermatch

Similar to the above model but fitted with an International stock with palm rest and buttstock hook. Weighs about 12.5 pounds.

NIB	Exc.	V.G.	Good	Fair	Poor
3100	2500	1750	1250	600	300

Model 1403D

A single-shot target rifle chambered for the .22 l.r. cartridge. It has a 26" barrel and is furnished without sights. It has a fully adjustable trigger and a blued finish with a walnut target-type stock.

NIB	Exc.	V.G.	Good	Fair	Poor
700	650	575	500	375	250

Model 1803D

A high-grade target rifle chambered for the .22 l.r. cartridge. It has a 25.5" heavy barrel with adjustable target sights. It features an adjustable trigger. The finish is blued with a light-colored wood stock with dark stippling on the pistol grip and forearm. The stock features an adjustable cheekpiece and buttplate. It was introduced in 1987.

NIB	Exc.	V.G.	Good	Fair	Poor
810	750	675	600	450	200

Model 1808DRT Super

A single shot, running-boar type rifle that is chambered for the .22 Long Rifle cartridge. It has a 32.5" barrel furnished without sights. The finish is blued with a heavy target-type walnut stock with thumbhole. It is furnished with barrel weights. Rifle weighs about 9.4 pounds. Also available in a left-hand version.

NIB	Exc.	V.G.	Good	Fair	Poor
1400	1200	1050	750	450	250

Model 1903D

Designed for the advanced junior shooter this target rifle has a 25-1/2" barrel on a Match 64 action with a single stage trigger. The walnut stock is fully adjustable. Weighs about 9.5 pounds and is offered in a left-hand model.

NIB	Exc.	V.G.	Good	Fair	Poor
850	700	600	400	300	200

Model 1907ISU Standard Match

Chambered for the .22 Long Rifle cartridge this rifle is designed for both prone and position shooting with a weight of

11.2 pounds. Built on a Match 54 action and fitted with a 26" barrel this rifle has a two-stage trigger with a removable cheekpiece and adjustable buttstock.

NIB	Exc.	V.G.	Good	Fair	Poor
1500	1250	900	450	300	200

Model 1910 Super Match II

A high-grade, single shot target rifle chambered for the .22 Long Rifle cartridge. It has a 27.25" barrel and is furnished with diopter-type target sights. The finish is blued with a walnut thumbhole stock with adjustable cheekpiece and buttplate. Hand rest and palm rest are not included.

NIB	Exc.	V.G.	Good	Fair	Poor
2200	1750	1300	900	500	250

Model 1911 Prone Match

This version has a stock designed specifically for firing from the prone position.

NIB	Exc.	V.G.	Good	Fair	Poor
1750	1450	950	650	400	250

Model 1913 Super Match

A virtually hand-built, match target rifle. It is chambered for the .22 l.r. cartridge and features a single-shot action. It has adjustable, diopter-type sights on a 27.25" heavy barrel. This is a custom-made gun that features every target option conceivable. The finish is blued with a fully adjustable walnut stock.

NIB	Exc.	V.G.	Good	Fair	Poor
2600	2000	1500	1000	500	250

Model 1827B Biathlon

A repeating, bolt action target rifle chambered for the .22 l.r. cartridge. It is specially designed for the biathlon competition. Production is quite limited and on a custom basis.

NIB	Exc.	V.G.	Good	Fair	Poor
1750	1400	1050	800	400	250

Model 1827BT Biathlon

Similar to the above model but features a straight pull Fortner bolt system. Available in left-hand model.

NIB	Exc.	V.G.	Good	Fair	Poor
2800	2250	1650	1000	500	250

Model 1433D

This is a centerfire version of the Model 54 target rifle chambered for the .22 Hornet. It is a special-order item and features a set trigger and a 4-round, detachable magazine. The finish was blued with a full length Mannlicher stock. It was discontinued in 1986.

NIB	Exc.	V.G.	Good	Fair	Poor
1000	850	600	400	200	100

Model 1451R

This is a bolt action target rifle chambered for the .22 long rifle cartridge and fitted with a target-style stock and 22" heavy barrel. Furnished with no open sights. Two stage target trigger is standard. Weight is approximately 6.5 lbs.

NIB	Exc.	V.G.	Good	Fair	Poor
525	400	300	200	150	100

Model 1451D Custom

Similar to the above model but fitted with a checkered walnut sporting stock with Monte Carlo comb and cheekpiece. Barrel length is 22.75" with open sights. Weight is about 5 lbs.

NIB	Exc.	V.G.	Good	Fair	Poor
450	375	300	200	150	100

Model 1451D Classic

Similar to the Model 1451 Custom with the exception of a straight walnut stock. Weight is about 5 lbs.

NIB	Exc.	V.G.	Good	Fair	Poor
350	300	250	200	150	100

Achiever

Introduced in 1993 this target rifle is chambered for the .22 Long Rifle cartridge. Designed for the beginning shooter it is furnished with a 5-shot clip but can be converted to a single shot with an adaptor. Barrel length is 19-1/2". Action is Mark 2000 with two-stage trigger. Stock pull is adjustable from 12" to 13". Weighs about 5 pounds.

NIB	Exc.	V.G.	Good	Fair	Poor
325	250	200	150	125	100

Achiever Super Target

Designed for the advanced junior shooter this model has a 22" barrel. Weighs about 6-1/2 pounds.

NIB	Exc.	V.G.	Good	Fair	Poor
400	325	250	175	125	100

Bavarian 1700

A classic-style sporting rifle chambered for the .22 l.r., .22 rimfire Magnum, .22 Hornet, and the .222 Remington cartridges. It features a 24" barrel with adjustable sights. It has a detachable magazine and a blued finish with a checkered walnut, European-style Monte Carlo stock with cheekpiece. It was introduced in 1988.

NIB	Exc.	V.G.	Good	Fair	Poor
800	650	500	400	300	200

Classic 1700

Similar in appearance to the Bavarian but furnished with an American-style stock with fluted comb. Furnished in same calibers as Bavarian but weighs 6-3/4 pounds.

NIB	Exc.	V.G.	Good	Fair	Poor
1200	900	700	400	300	200

NOTE: For fancy wood stocks "Meister Grade" add $175.

Custom 1700

Similar to the Bavarian and Classic in caliber offerings but offered with a fancy European walnut stock with roll-over cheekpiece with Monte Carlo. The pistol grip has a palm swell and is fitted with a white lined rosewood grip cap with a white diamond insert. Forend is schabel type and stock is checkered in ship line pattern.

NIB	Exc.	V.G.	Good	Fair	Poor
1250	950	750	400	300	200

NOTE: For fancy wood stocks "Meister Grade" add $175.

Model 1700 Mannlicher

Similar to the 1700 Classic but fitted with a full-length stock.

NIB	Exc.	V.G.	Good	Fair	Poor
1550	1200	850	550	350	200

NOTE: For fancy wood stocks "Meister Grade" add $175.

Model 1700 FWT

This model has same specifications as the 1700 Custom but is fitted with a McMillan laminated fiberglass stock. Weighs about 6-1/4 pounds.

NIB	Exc.	V.G.	Good	Fair	Poor
950	800	700	500	300	200

Model 1700 FWT Deluxe

Same as above but fitted with a laminated wood grain stock.

NIB	Exc.	V.G.	Good	Fair	Poor
1125	900	800	550	300	200

Model 520/61

A blowback-operated, semiautomatic rifle that is chambered for the .22 l.r. cartridge. It has a 24" barrel and a 10-round, detachable magazine. The finish is blued with a checkered walnut stock. This rifle was discontinued in 1983.

NIB	Exc.	V.G.	Good	Fair	Poor
275	200	150	125	100	85

Model 525 Sporter

This semiautomatic rifle is chambered for the .22 long rifle cartridge. It has a 24" barrel with adjustable sights and a 10-round, detachable magazine. The finish is blued with a check-

ered Monte Carlo-type stock. It was introduced in 1984. A carbine version with a 20" barrel was originally offered but was discontinued in 1986.

NIB	Exc.	V.G.	Good	Fair	Poor
435	375	300	225	175	100

Exemplar

A bolt action pistol that is built on the Model 64 Match Action. It is chambered for the .22 l.r. cartridge and has a 10" barrel with adjustable sights and a 5-shot, detachable magazine. It features an adjustable two-stage trigger with the receiver grooved for attaching a scope. The walnut stock and forend are stippled. It was introduced in 1987.

NIB	Exc.	V.G.	Good	Fair	Poor
400	325	275	210	150	100

Exemplar XIV

Similar to the standard Exemplar with a 14" barrel. It was introduced in 1988.

NIB	Exc.	V.G.	Good	Fair	Poor
420	370	275	200	150	100

Exemplar Hornet

Chambered for the .22 Hornet cartridge. It was introduced in 1988.

NIB	Exc.	V.G.	Good	Fair	Poor
750	600	400	300	200	100

ANTI GARROTTER
English

Percussion belt pistol, marked Balls Pat. Steel oval is 7 inches long and the barrel protrudes 1-1/2 inches, approximately 45 caliber. A cord runs from the lock up and through the sleeve and is fired by pulling the cord.

Exc.	V.G.	Good	Fair	Poor
—	6000	2500	800	400

APACHE
Eibar, Spain
SEE—Ojanguren Y Vidosa

APALOZO HERMANOS
Zumorraga, Spain

Spanish manufacturer from approximately 1920 to 1935. Their trademark, a dove-like bird, is normally found impressed into the grips.

Apaloza
Copy of a Colt Police Positive Revolver.

Exc.	V.G.	Good	Fair	Poor
175	125	100	65	45

Paramount
Copy of the Model 1906 Browning chambered for the 6.35mm. Standard marking "Paramount Cal. .25" normally found on the slide.

Exc.	V.G.	Good	Fair	Poor
175	125	100	65	45

Triomphe
The slide is inscribed "Pistolet Automatique Triomphe Acier Comprime."

Exc.	V.G.	Good	Fair	Poor
175	125	100	65	45

ARCUS
Bulgaria
Importer-Miltex, Inc., Waldorf, MD

Arcus-94
Introduced in 1998 this is a semiautomatic pistol chambered for the 9mm cartridge. Fitted with an ambidextrous safety and 10-round magazine. Imported from Bulgaria.

NIB	Exc.	V.G.	Good	Fair	Poor
400	300	250	200	150	100

ARIZAGA, G.
Eibar, Spain

Spanish manufacturer during the first half of the twentieth century.

Arizaga
7.65mm semiautomatic pistol.

Exc.	V.G.	Good	Fair	Poor
175	125	100	65	45

Mondial
Resembling a Savage semiautomatic pistol externally, this model is based on John M. Browning's design. Examples are known with and without a grip safety. The grips are stamped with an owl in a circle trademark and "Mondial".

Exc.	V.G.	Good	Fair	Poor
175	125	100	75	50

Pinkerton
Arizaga's standard model known to exist with a cartridge counter. Slide is marked "Pinkerton Automatic 6.35".

Exc.	V.G.	Good	Fair	Poor
150	100	75	50	35

Warwinck
As above but chambered for 7.65mm cartridges, the slide is marked "Automatic Pistol 7.65 Warwinck".

Exc.	V.G.	Good	Fair	Poor
175	125	100	75	50

ARIZMENDI, FRANCISCO
Eibar, Spain

Originally founded in the 1890s, the company was reformed in 1914 and manufactured semiautomatic pistols.

Singer
The Singer was manufactured in a number of different variations and in calibers 6.35mm and one 7.65mm. It was earlier called the Victor. The 6.35mm models resembled the Browning 1906. The 7.65mm model resembled the Browning Model 1910.

6.35mm

Courtesy James Rankin

Exc.	V.G.	Good	Fair	Poor
150	100	75	50	35

7.65mm

Courtesy James Rankin

Exc.	V.G.	Good	Fair	Poor
150	100	75	50	35

Teuf Teuf
The Teuf Teuf was chambered in calibers 6.35mm and 7.65mm. The 7.65mm was only slightly larger than the 6.35mm model. The pistol copied its name from the Browning Model 1906 and from the Belgium Teuf Teuf. The pistol shown is a cartridge indicator model.

Courtesy James Rankin

6.35mm

Exc.	V.G.	Good	Fair	Poor
150	100	75	50	35

7.65mm

Exc.	V.G.	Good	Fair	Poor
150	100	75	50	35

Walman

The Walman was manufactured in a number of variations, and in calibers 6.35mm, 7.65mm, and .380. Earliest semiautomatic production was in 1908 through 1926. Certain variations were called the American Model. The model in .380 caliber had a squeeze grip safety.

6.35mm

Courtesy James Rankin

Exc.	V.G.	Good	Fair	Poor
150	100	75	50	35

7.65mm

Courtesy James Rankin

Exc.	V.G.	Good	Fair	Poor
175	125	90	60	35

.380

Courtesy James Rankin

Exc.	V.G.	Good	Fair	Poor
175	125	90	60	35

Arizmendi

Solid-frame, folding-trigger revolver chambered for 7.65mm or .32 caliber revolver. Normal markings are the trademark "FA" and a circled five-pointed star.

Exc.	V.G.	Good	Fair	Poor
175	125	80	50	25

Boltun - 1st Variation

The Bolton semiautomatic pistol was made in both calibers 6.35mm and 7.65mm. It was almost an exact copy of the Belgian Pieper. The 7.65mm model was only slightly larger than the 6.35mm model.

6.35mm

Exc.	V.G.	Good	Fair	Poor
175	125	90	60	35

7.65mm

Exc.	V.G.	Good	Fair	Poor
175	125	90	60	35

Boltun - 2nd Variation

The Boltun 2nd variation is chambered for the 7.65mm cartridge and is almost an exact copy of the Browning Model 1910. It was made into the 1930s.

Exc.	V.G.	Good	Fair	Poor
175	125	90	60	35

Puppy

A variation of the "Velo-Dog" revolver with the barrel stamped "Puppy" and the frame bearing the "FA" trademark.

Exc.	V.G.	Good	Fair	Poor
175	125	80	50	25

Pistolet Automatique

Normal markings include the "FA" trademark.

Exc.	V.G.	Good	Fair	Poor
175	125	80	50	25

Kaba Spezial

A 6.35mm semiautomatic pistol patterned after the Browning Model 1906. The Kaba Spezial was originally made by August Menz of Suhl, Germany and sold by Karl Bauer of Berlin, Germany. The name "Kaba" was derived from the first two initials of Karl Bauer. These two pistols do not look alike.

Courtesy James Rankin

Exc.	V.G.	Good	Fair	Poor
150	100	75	50	35

Roland

Chambered for 6.35 and 7.65mm cartridges, this model was manufactured during the 1920s. The 7.65mm was only slightly larger than the 6.35mm model.

Courtesy James Rankin

6.35mm

Exc.	V.G.	Good	Fair	Poor
175	125	90	60	35

7.65mm

Exc.	V.G.	Good	Fair	Poor
175	125	90	60	35

Ydeal

The Ydeal was manufactured in four variations and in calibers 6.35mm, 7.65mm, and .380. All four variations resemble the Browning Model 1906 with the 7.65mm and .380 caliber being slightly larger.

Courtesy James Rankin

6.35mm

Exc.	V.G.	Good	Fair	Poor
175	125	90	60	35

7.65mm

Exc.	V.G.	Good	Fair	Poor
175	125	90	60	35

.380

Exc.	V.G.	Good	Fair	Poor
175	125	90	60	35

ARIZMENDI ZULAICA
Eibar, Spain

Cebra

A semiautomatic 7.65mm pistol patterned after the Ruby style of Spanish automatics. The slide is marked "Pistolet Automatique Cebra Zulaica Eibar," together with the letters "AZ" in an oval. Generally found with checkered wood grips.

Courtesy James Rankin

Exc.	V.G.	Good	Fair	Poor
150	100	75	50	35

Cebra Revolver

Copy of a Colt Police Positive revolver marked "Made in Spain" with the word "Cebra" cast in the grips.

Exc.	V.G.	Good	Fair	Poor
175	125	125	75	50

ARMALITE, INC.
Costa Mesa, California
Geneseo, Illionis (current production)

In 1995 Eagle Arms purchased the Armalite trademark and certain other assets. The new companies are organized under the Armalite name. The original company, formed in the mid 1950s, developed the AR-10, which in turn led to the development of the M-16 series of service rifles still in use today. All current models are produced at the Geneseo, Illinois facility.

AR-17 Shotgun

A gas-operated semiautomatic 12 gauge shotgun, with a 24" barrel and interchangeable choke tubes. The receiver and the barrel are made of an aluminum alloy, with an anodized black or gold finish. The stock and forearm are of plastic. Approximately 2,000 were manufactured during 1964 and 1965.

NIB	Exc.	V.G.	Good	Fair	Poor
550	450	400	300	225	100

AR-7 Explorer Rifle

A .22 l.r. semiauto carbine with a 16-inch barrel. The receiver and barrel are partially made of an alloy. The most noteworthy feature of this model is that it can be disassembled and the component parts stored in the plastic stock. Manufactured between 1959 and 1973. Reintroduced in 1999.

NIB	Exc.	V.G.	Good	Fair	Poor
170	125	100	75	50	—

AR-7 Custom

As above with a walnut cheekpiece stock, manufactured between 1964 and 1970.

NIB	Exc.	V.G.	Good	Fair	Poor
150	125	100	80	50	35

AR-180

A gas-operated semiautomatic rifle chambered for the .223 or 5.56mm cartridge. The AR-180 is the civilian version of the AR18 that is fully automatic. It is a simple and efficient rifle that was tested by various governments and found to have potential. This rifle was also manufactured by Howa Machinery Ltd. and Sterling Armament Co. of England. The most common version is manufactured by Sterling. Those built by Armalite and Howa bring a small premium.

NIB	Exc.	V.G.	Good	Fair	Poor
750	700	650	550	450	200

AR-10A4 Rifle

Introduced in 1995 this model features a 20" stainless steel heavy barrel chambered for the .308 Win. or .243 Win. cartridge. Has a flattop receiver, optional two-stage trigger, detachable carry handle, scope mount. Equipped with two 10-round magazines. Weight is about 9.6 lbs.

NIB	Exc.	V.G.	Good	Fair	Poor
1500	1250	900	700	500	—

NOTE: For stainless steel barrel add $100.

AR-10A4 Carbine

Similar to above model but chambered for .308 Win. cartridge and fitted with a 16" barrel. Flattop receiver. Sold with two 10-round magazines. Weight is approximately 9 lbs.

NIB	Exc.	V.G.	Good	Fair	Poor
1500	1250	900	700	500	—

NOTE: For stainless steel barrel add $100.

AR-10A2 Rifle

This model has a 20" heavy barrel chambered for the .308 cartridge but without the removable carry handle. Weight is about 9.8 lbs.

NIB	Exc.	V.G.	Good	Fair	Poor
1500	1250	900	700	500	—

NOTE: For stainless steel barrel add $100.

AR-10A2 Carbine

Similar to model above but fitted with a 16" barrel. Weight is approximately 9 lbs.

NIB	Exc.	V.G.	Good	Fair	Poor
1500	1250	900	700	500	—

NOTE: For stainless steel barrel add $100.

AR-10B

Chambered for the .308 cartridge and fitted with a 20" barrel. The trigger is a single-stage or optional 2-stage match type. This model has several of the early M16 features such as a tapered handguard, pistol grips, and short buttstock in original brown color. Fitted with early charging handle. Limited production. Weight is about 9.5 lbs. Introduced in 1999.

NIB	Exc.	V.G.	Good	Fair	Poor
1600	1250	900	—	—	—

AR-10(T) Rifle

This model features a 24" heavy barrel with a two-stage trigger. The front sight and carry handle are removable. The handguard is fiberglass. Weight is approximately 10.4 lbs.

NIB	Exc.	V.G.	Good	Fair	Poor
2400	1950	1500	1100	800	—

AR-10(T) Carbine

Similar to the AR-10T but fitted with a 16.25" target weight barrel. Weight is approximately 8.5 lbs.

NIB	Exc.	V.G.	Good	Fair	Poor
2400	1950	1500	1100	800	—

M15A2 HBAR

This model was introduced in 1995 and features a 20" heavy barrel chambered for .223 cartridge. A2 style forward assist, recoil check brake. Sold with a 10-round magazine. Weight is approximately 8.2 lbs.

NIB	Exc.	V.G.	Good	Fair	Poor
1000	850	600	500	—	—

M15A2 National Match

Chambered for the .223 cartridge this variation features a 20" stainless steel match barrel with two-stage trigger, A2 style forward assist and hard coated anodized receiver. Equipped with a 10-round magazine. Weight is about 9 lbs.

NIB	Exc.	V.G.	Good	Fair	Poor
1500	1200	850	600	—	—

M15A2- M4A1C Carbine

Similar to the M15A2 heavy barrel but with a 16" heavy barrel. Flattop receiver with detachable carry handle. Introduced in 1995.

NIB	Exc.	V.G.	Good	Fair	Poor
1250	900	700	500	—	—

M15A2-M4C Carbine

Similar to the M4A1C Carbine but with the flattop receiver and detachable carry handle.

NIB	Exc.	V.G.	Good	Fair	Poor
1000	850	600	500	—	—

M15A4(T)-Eagle Eye

Chambered for the .223 cartridge and fitted with a 24" stainless steel heavy weight barrel this rifle has a National Match two-stage trigger, Picatinny rail, NM fiberglass handguard tube. Sold with a 7-round magazine and 4-section cleaning rod with brass tip, sling, owner's manual, and lifetime warranty.

NIB	Exc.	V.G.	Good	Fair	Poor
1500	1100	800	600	—	—

M15A4 Special Purpose

This model is fitted with a 20" heavy barrel with detachable front sight, detachable carry handle with NM sights, Picatinny rail. Weight is about 7.8 lbs.

NIB	Exc.	V.G.	Good	Fair	Poor
1200	900	750	600	—	—

M15A4-Action Master

This variation features a 20" stainless steel heavy barrel with two-stage trigger, Picatinny rail, and fiberglass handguard tube. Weight is approximately 9 lbs.

NIB	Exc.	V.G.	Good	Fair	Poor
1450	1000	850	600	—	—

M15A4-Eagle Spirit

This version is similar to the Action Master above but fitted with a 16" stainless steel barrel. Weight is about 7.6 lbs.

NIB	Exc.	V.G.	Good	Fair	Poor
1450	1000	850	600	—	—

AR-30M

Chambered for the .338 Lapua or the .300 Winchester Magnum cartridges. This model is a reduced version of the AR-50.

NIB	Exc.	V.G.	Good	Fair	Poor
—	—	—	—	—	—

AR-50

Introduced in 2000 this rifle is chambered for the .50BMG cartridge. Fitted with a 31" tapered barrel threaded for recoil check (muzzle brake). Trigger is single-stage. Stock is a 3 section type with extruded forend. Packmayer buttplate. Picatinny rail. Buttplate is adjustable. Finish is magnesium phosphated steel and hard anodized aluminum. Weight is about 33 lbs.

NIB	Exc.	V.G.	Good	Fair	Poor
2600	2000	—	—	—	—

PRE-BAN MODELS

Golden Eagle

Fitted with a 20" stainless extra heavy barrel with NM two-stage trigger and NM sights. Sold with a 30-round magazine. Weight is about 9.4 lbs.

NIB	Exc.	V.G.	Good	Fair	Poor
1500	1200	950	800	—	—

HBAR

This pre-ban rifle has a 20" heavy barrel, a 30-round magazine, and sling. Weight is approximately 8 lbs.

NIB	Exc.	V.G.	Good	Fair	Poor
1300	1000	850	700	—	—

M4C Carbine

This pre-ban variation is fitted with a 16" heavy barrel, collapsible stock, and fixed flash suppressor. Weight is about 6.2 lbs.

NIB	Exc.	V.G.	Good	Fair	Poor
1300	1000	850	700	—	—

ARMAS DE FUEGO
Guernica, Spain
See Alkar

ARMERO ESPECIALISTAS
Eibar, Spain

Alfa

"Alfa" was a trademark given a number of revolvers based upon both Colt and Smith & Wesson designs in calibers ranging from .22 to.44.

Exc.	V.G.	Good	Fair	Poor
200	150	100	75	50

Omega

A semiautomatic 6.35 or 7.65mm pistol marked "Omega" on the slide and grips.

Exc.	V.G.	Good	Fair	Poor
200	150	100	75	50

ARMES DE CHASSE
Chadds Ford, Pennsylvania

Importer of firearms manufactured by P. Beretta, and other arms manufactured in Germany.

Model EJ

An O/U Anson & Deeley action 12 gauge shotgun with double triggers as well as automatic ejectors. Blued barrels, silver finished receiver and checkered walnut stock. Manufactured in Germany and introduced in 1989.

NIB	Exc.	V.G.	Good	Fair	Poor
1000	950	800	650	500	250

Model EU

As above with a ventilated rib barrel and a nonselective single trigger. Introduced in 1989.

NIB	Exc.	V.G.	Good	Fair	Poor
1200	1000	850	650	500	250

Highlander

A side-by-side double barrel 20 gauge shotgun with a boxlock action. Available in various barrel lengths and choke combinations, with double triggers and manual extractors. Blued with a checkered walnut stock. Manufactured in Italy and introduced in 1989.

NIB	Exc.	V.G.	Good	Fair	Poor
700	600	500	350	250	125

Chesapeake

As above but chambered for the 3.5" 12 gauge shell. The bores are chrome-lined and suitable for steel shot. Fitted with automatic ejectors and double triggers. Manufactured in Italy, it was introduced in 1989.

NIB	Exc.	V.G.	Good	Fair	Poor
800	700	600	475	400	200

Balmoral

English-style straight grip 12, 16, or 20 gauge boxlock shotgun, fitted with false side plates. Receiver and side plates case hardened, the barrels blued. Fitted with a single trigger and automatic ejectors. Manufactured in Italy and introduced in 1989.

NIB	Exc.	V.G.	Good	Fair	Poor
800	725	625	500	400	200

Model 70E

A 12, 16, or 20 gauge side-by-side shotgun fitted with 27" or 28" barrels. The action based upon the Anson & Deeley design with a Greener crossbolt. The receiver is case hardened, barrels are blued and the walnut stock checkered. Manufactured in Germany and introduced in 1989.

NIB	Exc.	V.G.	Good	Fair	Poor
800	725	625	500	400	200

Model 74E

As above with game scene engraving and more fully figured walnut stock. Introduced in 1989.

NIB	Exc.	V.G.	Good	Fair	Poor
1000	925	775	625	500	250

Model 76E

As above with engraved false side plates and fully figured walnut stock. Introduced in 1989.

NIB	Exc.	V.G.	Good	Fair	Poor
1500	1150	900	750	600	300

ARMINEX LTD.
Scottsdale, Arizona

Tri-Fire

A semiautomatic pistol chambered for 9mm, .38 Super or .45 ACP cartridges. Available with conversion units that add approximately $130 if in excellent condition. Fitted with 5", 6", or 7" stainless steel barrels. Presentation cases were available at an extra cost of $48. Approximately 250 were manufactured from 1981 to 1985.

NIB	Exc.	V.G.	Good	Fair	Poor
500	400	250	175	125	90

Target Model

As above with a 6" or 7" barrel.

NIB	Exc.	V.G.	Good	Fair	Poor
550	450	300	175	125	100

ARMINUS
SEE—Freidrich Pickert
Zelia-Mehlis, Germany
Hermann Weirauch
Melrichstadt, Germany
F. 1. E.
Hialeah, Florida

ARMITAGE INTERNATIONAL, LTD.
Seneca, South Carolina

Scarab Skorpion
A blowback-operated, semiautomatic pistol, patterned after the Czechoslovakian Scorpion submachine gun. Chambered for the 9mm cartridge with a 4.6" barrel having military-type sights. Fitted with a 32-round, detachable box magazine. The standard finish is matte black and the grips are of plastic.

NIB	Exc.	V.G.	Good	Fair	Poor
450	300	200	150	125	90

ARMS CORPORATION OF THE PHILIPPINES
Armscor Precision
Foster City, California

Armscor Precision is an importer of a variety of firearms made in the Philippines.

KBI, Inc. also distributes some .22 caliber Armscor rifles.

SHOTGUNS
Model 30D
A slide action 12 gauge shotgun fitted with either 28" or 30" barrels with various chokes. The magazine holds 6 cartridges. Weight is about 7.6 lbs.

NIB	Exc.	V.G.	Good	Fair	Poor
200	175	150	125	100	75

Model 30DG
As above with a 20" barrel, fitted with rifle sights and a 7-shot magazine. Weight is about 7.2 lbs.

NIB	Exc.	V.G.	Good	Fair	Poor
175	150	125	100	80	70

Model 30R
As above with shotgun bead sights, 20" or 18.5" barrel. Weight is between 7 and 7.2 lbs. depending on barrel length.

NIB	Exc.	V.G.	Good	Fair	Poor
175	150	125	100	80	70

Model 30RP
As above with an auxiliary black composition pistol grip and an 18.5" barrel.

NIB	Exc.	V.G.	Good	Fair	Poor
175	150	125	100	80	70

RIFLES
Model M14P
A .22 caliber bolt action rifle fitted with a 23" barrel, open sights, and a 5-shot detachable magazine. Stock of mahogany.

NIB	Exc.	V.G.	Good	Fair	Poor
100	90	75	50	35	25

Model M14D
As above with an adjustable rear sight and checkered stock. Manufactured in 1987 only.

NIB	Exc.	V.G.	Good	Fair	Poor
125	100	85	60	40	25

Model 14Y
This bolt action rifle is chambered for .22 long rifle cartridge. It is fitted with an 18" barrel and 10-round magazine. Weight is approximately 5.2 lbs.

NIB	Exc.	V.G.	Good	Fair	Poor
150	125	100	—	—	—

Model 12Y
This bolt action rifle is a single-shot and chambered for the .22 long rifle. It is fitted with an 18" barrel. Weight is about 5 lbs.

NIB	Exc.	V.G.	Good	Fair	Poor
125	100	75	—	—	—

Model 1400
This is a bolt action rifle chambered for the .22 long rifle cartridge. Fitted with a 22.5" barrel and a 10-round magazine. Weight is about 6.5 lbs.

NIB	Exc.	V.G.	Good	Fair	Poor
200	175	150	125	100	75

Model M1500
A .22 Magnum bolt action rifle fitted with a 22.5" barrel, open sights, 5-shot magazine and checkered mahogany stock. Weight is approximately 6.5 lbs.

NIB	Exc.	V.G.	Good	Fair	Poor
200	175	150	125	100	75

Model M1600
A .22 caliber copy of the U.S. M16 rifle having an 18" barrel and detachable 15-round magazine. Weight is about 6.2 lbs.

NIB	Exc.	V.G.	Good	Fair	Poor
200	150	125	100	75	50

Model M1600R

As above with a stainless steel collapsible stock and shrouded barrel. No longer in production.

NIB	Exc.	V.G.	Good	Fair	Poor
250	200	150	125	100	75

Model M1600C

As above with a 20" barrel and fiberglass stock. No longer in production.

NIB	Exc.	V.G.	Good	Fair	Poor
135	110	90	70	50	35

Model M1600W

As above with a mahogany stock. No longer in production.

NIB	Exc.	V.G.	Good	Fair	Poor
150	125	100	75	50	35

Model M1800

A .22 Hornet bolt action rifle fitted with a 22.5" barrel, 5-shot magazine and a mahogany Monte Carlo-style stock. Weight is approximately 6.6 lbs.

NIB	Exc.	V.G.	Good	Fair	Poor
150	125	100	75	50	35

Model 20C

Chambered for .22 long rifle with a 15-round magazine and fitted with an 18.25" barrel. Weight is about 6.2 lbs.

NIB	Exc.	V.G.	Good	Fair	Poor
150	120	90	70	50	40

Model M20P

A .22 caliber 15-shot semiautomatic rifle fitted with a 20.75" barrel, open sights and plain mahogany stock. Weight is about 6.3 lbs.

NIB	Exc.	V.G.	Good	Fair	Poor
100	80	65	50	35	25

Model M2000

As above with adjustable sights and a checkered stock. Weight is approximately 6.4 lbs.

NIB	Exc.	V.G.	Good	Fair	Poor
120	90	70	50	35	25

Model AK22S

A .22 caliber semiautomatic rifle resembling the Russian AKA47. Barrel length of 18.5", 15-round magazine and mahogany stock. Weight is about 7.5 lbs.

NIB	Exc.	V.G.	Good	Fair	Poor
160	140	125	100	75	50

Model AK22F

As above with a folding stock. No longer in production.

NIB	Exc.	V.G.	Good	Fair	Poor
200	175	150	100	75	50

HANDGUNS

Model M100

A double action, swing-out cylinder revolver chambered for .22, .22 Magnum, and the .38 Special cartridges. Having a 4" ventilated rib barrel. Six-shot cylinder and adjustable sights. Blued with checkered mahogany grips. No longer in production.

NIB	Exc.	V.G.	Good	Fair	Poor
200	175	150	110	80	50

Model 200P

Introduced in 1990 this 6-shot revolver is chambered for the .38 Special cartridge. It is fitted with a 4" barrel, fixed sights and wood or rubber grips. Weighs about 26 ozs.

NIB	Exc.	V.G.	Good	Fair	Poor
180	150	125	100	85	60

Model 200TC

Introduced in 1990 this model is similar to above but is fitted with adjustable sights and checkered wood grips. Weight is about 28 oz.

NIB	Exc.	V.G.	Good	Fair	Poor
200	175	150	125	100	75

Model 200DC

Similar to the Model 200P but fitted with a 2.5" barrel. Weight is about 22 oz.

NIB	Exc.	V.G.	Good	Fair	Poor
175	150	125	100	85	60

Model 201S

Similar to the Model 200P but in stainless steel.

NIB	Exc.	V.G.	Good	Fair	Poor
200	175	150	125	100	75

Model 1911-A1

A semiautomatic pistol similar in design to the Colt Model 1911 pistol. Chambered for the .45 ACP cartridge and fitted with a 5" barrel. Blued finish. Magazine capacity is 8 rounds. Weight is about 39 oz.

NIB	Exc.	V.G.	Good	Fair	Poor
500	400	—	—	—	—

Model 1911-A2

Same as above but fitted with a double column magazine with a 13-round capacity. Weight is approximately 43 oz.

NIB	Exc.	V.G.	Good	Fair	Poor
600	500	—	—	—	—

ARMSCORP OF AMERICA
Baltimore, Maryland

RIFLES

M-14R

A civilian version of the U.S. M14 rifle manufactured from new and surplus parts. Introduced in 1986.

NIB	Exc.	V.G.	Good	Fair	Poor
600	500	400	300	200	100

M-14 National Match

As above but built to A.M.T.U. MIL specifications. Introduced in 1987.

NIB	Exc.	V.G.	Good	Fair	Poor
1500	1150	800	500	400	200

FAL

A civilian version of the FN FAL rifle assembled from new and Argentine surplus parts. Introduced in 1987.

NIB	Exc.	V.G.	Good	Fair	Poor
800	650	500	400	300	150

M36 Israeli Sniper Rifle

A specialized weapon built upon the Armscor M-14 receiver in the Bullpup style. Barrel length 22" and of free floating design for accuracy, chambered for the .308 cartridge. There is an integral flash suppressor and a bipod. It is furnished with a 20-shot detachable magazine. This civilian version was first offered for sale in 1989.

NIB	Exc.	V.G.	Good	Fair	Poor
3000	2500	2000	1500	850	400

Expert Model

A .22 caliber semiautomatic rifle with a 21" barrel, open sights, and 10-shot magazine. Introduced in 1989.

NIB	Exc.	V.G.	Good	Fair	Poor
225	200	175	145	100	80

HANDGUNS

Hi-Power

An Argentine-made version of the Browning semiautomatic pistol chambered for 9mm with a 4.75" barrel. Matte finished with checkered synthetic grips. Introduced in 1989.

NIB	Exc.	V.G.	Good	Fair	Poor
400	350	300	250	200	100

Detective HP - Compact

As above with a 3.5" barrel.

NIB	Exc.	V.G.	Good	Fair	Poor
450	400	350	275	200	100

SD9

An Israeli-made 9mm double action semiautomatic pistol with a 3" barrel. Assembled extensively from sheet metal stampings. Loaded chamber indicator and 6-round magazine. This model is also known as the Sirkus SD9 manufactured by Sirkus Industries in Israel. Introduced in 1989.

NIB	Exc.	V.G.	Good	Fair	Poor
300	250	200	150	100	75

P22

A copy of the Colt Woodsman .22 caliber semiautomatic pistol available with either 4" or 6" barrels and a 10-shot magazine. Finish blued, grips of checkered hardwood. Introduced in 1989.

NIB	Exc.	V.G.	Good	Fair	Poor
200	150	125	100	75	50

ARMY & NAVY CO-OPERATIVE SOCIETY
London, England
SEE—British Double Guns

ARNOLD ARMS
Arlington, Washington

This company offers a wide range of rifles and calibers including its own proprietary cartridges, from the 6mm Arnold to the .458 Arnold. Rifles are built on a choice of actions including the Apollo, Remington, Sako, and Winchester. These action choices affect the base price of the rifle. In addition to action choice the buyer has a choice of metal finish such as matte blue, standard polish blue, hi-luster blue and matte stainless steel. There is also a choice of black Teflon finish. Thus, the choice of finish and action affects the price. Arnold Arms offers a number of extra-cost options such as muzzle brakes, sights, barrel length, engraving, checkered bolts, and extra-cost fancy wood. It is strongly suggested that the buyer or seller seek an expert appraisal before a sale if any extra cost items are involved in the sale.

NOTE: The prices listed below are for a base rifle with Remington actions and matte blue finish unless otherwise noted.

Varminter I

This model features a heavy match grade barrel with straight taper. Lengths are from 24" to 26". Calibers are from .222 Rem. to .257 Arnold magnum. Choice of McMillian Varmint stock in various finishes and Pacific Research Varmint stock in flat black. Rifles weigh from 9 to 11 lbs. depending on caliber and configuration.

NIB	Exc.	V.G.	Good	Fair	Poor
2600	2000	—	—	—	—

NOTE: For Apollo action add approximately $1,100.

Varminter II

This variation features a 24" to 26" medium weight match barrel with choice of McMillan or Pacific Research sporter stocks. Choice of triggers. Weight is 7.5 to 9 lbs. depending on configuration. Calibers from .223 Rem. to .257 Arnold Magnum.

NIB	Exc.	V.G.	Good	Fair	Poor
2600	2000	—	—	—	—

NOTE: For Apollo action add approximately $1,100.

Alaskan Rifle

This is a bolt action rifle chambered for calibers from .223 to .338 Win. Mag. Barrel lengths are from 22" to 26" depending on caliber. Stocks are synthetic in black woodland or arctic camo. Sights are optional. Rifle is drilled and tapped for scope mounts. Trigger is fully adjustable. Choice of chrome moly steel or stainless steel. Introduced in 1996.

NIB	Exc.	V.G.	Good	Fair	Poor
2600	2000	—	—	—	—

NOTE: Add $1,100 for Apollo action.

Alaskan Trophy Rifle

Similar to the Bush Rifle except chambered for .300 Magnums to .458 Win. Mag. Barrel lengths are 24" to 26" depending on caliber. Choice of walnut, synthetic, or fibergrain stock. Fitted with iron sights. Choice of stainless or chrome moly steel. Introduced in 1996.

NIB	Exc.	V.G.	Good	Fair	Poor
3100	2500	—	—	—	—

NOTE: Add $1,100 for Apollo action.

Alaskan Guide Rifle

This model is offered in choice of calibers from .257 to .338 Magnum. Barrel lengths are 22" to 26" depending on caliber. Buyer has a choice of "A" English walnut stock or deluxe synthetic stock. No open sights.

Synthetic stock

NIB	Exc.	V.G.	Good	Fair	Poor
3700	2900	—	—	—	—

Walnut Stock

NIB	Exc.	V.G.	Good	Fair	Poor
4300	3400	—	—	—	—

NOTE: For Apollo action add approximately $1,100.

Grand Alaskan Rifle

This version is fitted with AAA fancy select or exhibition wood. Built in calibers from 300 Mag. to .458 Win. Mag.

"AAA" English walnut

NIB	Exc.	V.G.	Good	Fair	Poor
6300	5000	—	—	—	—

"Exhibition" Grade walnut

NIB	Exc.	V.G.	Good	Fair	Poor
7400	6000	—	—	—	—

NOTE: for Apollo action add $1,100.

Safari Rifle

Introduced in 1996 this model features calibers from .223 to .458 Win. Mag. Barrel lengths are from 22" to 26" depending on caliber. The Apollo is a controlled or push feed type with one piece cone head bolt. Fully adjustable trigger with chrome moly or stainless steel construction. Sights are optional but the rifle is drilled and tapped for scope mounts. Choice of A fancy English or AA fancy English walnut.

"A" Fancy English Walnut

NIB	Exc.	V.G.	Good	Fair	Poor
4300	3500	—	—	—	—

"AA" Fancy English Walnut

NIB	Exc.	V.G.	Good	Fair	Poor
4400	3500	—	—	—	—

NOTE: For Apollo action add $1,100.

African Trophy Rifle

Similar to the Safari Rifle except stocked in AAA fancy walnut with wraparound checkering.

NIB	Exc.	V.G.	Good	Fair	Poor
6300	5000	—	—	—	—

NOTE: For Apollo action add $1,100.

Grand African Rifle

Similar to the Safari rifle with the addition of Exhibition Grade wood. Calibers are from .338 to .458.

NIB	Exc.	V.G.	Good	Fair	Poor
7600	6100	—	—	—	—

NOTE: For Apollo action add $1,100.

Serengeti Synthetic Rifle

Similar to the Safari rifle with a fibergrain stock in classic or Monte Carlo-style. Checkering or stipple finish. Calibers are .243 to 300 Magnum. Introduced in 1996.

NIB	Exc.	V.G.	Good	Fair	Poor
2600	2100	—	—	—	—

NOTE: For Apollo action add $1,100.

African Synthetic Rifle

Similar to the Safari rifle with fibergrain stock, checkering or stipple finish. Calibers are .338 Mag. to .458 Mag.

NIB	Exc.	V.G.	Good	Fair	Poor
3300	2600	—	—	—	—

NOTE: For Apollo action add $1,100.

Neutralizer Rifle Mark I

Built on a Remington 700 or Winchester action this bolt action rifle is chambered in a choice of calibers from .223 to .300 Win. Mag. Barrel lengths are from 24" to 26" depending on caliber with Magnum barrels up to 28". A fiberglass tactical stock with adjustable cheekpiece and buttplate is standard in various finishes. Winchester action is $400 less.

NIB	Exc.	V.G.	Good	Fair	Poor
2900	2300	—	—	—	—

Neutralizer Rifle Mark II

Same as above but with Apollo action.

NIB	Exc.	V.G.	Good	Fair	Poor
4000	3200	—	—	—	—

Benchrest Rifles

Custom built. Unable to price individual rifles.

Prone rifles

Custom built. Unable to price individual rifles.

X-Course Rifles

Custom built. Unable to price individual rifles.

1,000 Yard Match Rifles

Custom built. Unable to price individual rifles.

Fully Accurized Production Rifles

These rifles are offered in standard blue or stainless steel with walnut or synthetic stock. Chambered from .223 to .338 Win. mag. and built on Remington, Ruger, or Winchester actions.

NIB	Exc.	V.G.	Good	Fair	Poor
1250	—	—	—	—	—

AROSTEGUI, EULOGIO
Eibar, Spain

Azul, Royal (Model 31)

A semiautomatic or full automatic pistol in calibers 7.63 Mauser, 9mm Bergmann, or 38 ACP. Manufactured between 1935 and 1940. Fitted with a 10-round integral magazine.

Courtesy James Rankin

Exc.	V.G.	Good	Fair	Poor
2200	1500	1000	500	300

NOTE: Add 200% for fully automatic machine pistol version.

Super Azul (M-34)

A semiautomatic or full automatic pistol in 7.63mm Mauser, 9mm Bergmann, and .38 ACP. Manufactured between 1935 and 1940. It has a removable box magazine with capacity of 10, 20, or 30 rounds. Also known as the War Model or the Standard Model.

Courtesy James Rankin

Exc.	V.G.	Good	Fair	Poor
2200	1500	1000	500	300

NOTE: Add 300% for fully automatic machine pistol version.

Azul 6.35mm.

A 6.35mm semiautomatic pistol copied after the Model 1906 Browning. The frame is marked with the letters "EA" in a circle and a retriever is molded in the grips. Magazine capacity is 6 or 9 rounds.

Exc.	V.G.	Good	Fair	Poor
250	200	150	100	75

Azul 7.65mm

A 7.65mm semiautomatic pistol copied after the Model 1910 FN. Magazine capacity is 7 or 9 rounds.

Exc.	V.G.	Good	Fair	Poor
250	200	150	100	75

Velo-Dog

A folding trigger 5.5mm or 6.35mm revolver bearing the trademark "EA" on the grips.

Exc.	V.G.	Good	Fair	Poor
125	100	75	50	30

ARRIETA S.L. ELQOLBAR
Spain
Importers
Jack J. Jansma, Orvis, New England Arms, Quality Arms

This company produces a wide variety of double-barrel shotguns in a price range from $450 to above $14,000. It is recommended that highly engraved examples as well as small bore arms be individually appraised.

490 Eder

A double barrel boxlock shotgun with double triggers and extractors. Discontinued in 1986.

Exc.	V.G.	Good	Fair	Poor
475	425	325	250	100

500 Titan

A Holland & Holland-style sidelock double barrel shotgun with French case hardened and engraved locks. Double triggers on extractors. No longer imported after 1986.

Exc.	V.G.	Good	Fair	Poor
575	500	400	300	150

501 Palomara
As above, but more finely finished. Discontinued in 1986.

Exc.	V.G.	Good	Fair	Poor
700	600	500	400	200

505 Alaska
As above, but more intricately engraved. Discontinued in 1986.

Exc.	V.G.	Good	Fair	Poor
800	700	600	500	250

510 Montana
A Holland & Holland-style sidelock double barrel shotgun with the internal parts gold-plated.

NIB	Exc.	V.G.	Good	Fair	Poor
2200	1750	1250	850	500	250

550 Field
As above, without the internal parts being gold-plated.

NIB	Exc.	V.G.	Good	Fair	Poor
2200	1750	1250	850	500	250

557 Standard
As above, but more finely finished.

NIB	Exc.	V.G.	Good	Fair	Poor
2750	2000	1750	1250	800	400

558 Patria
As above, but more finely finished.

NIB	Exc.	V.G.	Good	Fair	Poor
2650	2150	1750	1250	800	400

560 Cumbre
As above, but featuring intricate engraving.

NIB	Exc.	V.G.	Good	Fair	Poor
2800	2200	1800	1200	800	400

570 Lieja

NIB	Exc.	V.G.	Good	Fair	Poor
3400	2500	2000	1500	750	500

575 Sport

NIB	Exc.	V.G.	Good	Fair	Poor
3750	2750	2250	1700	1200	750

578 Victoria
This model is engraved in the English manner with floral bouquets.

NIB	Exc.	V.G.	Good	Fair	Poor
3500	2750	2000	1250	750	350

585 Liria
As above, but more finely finished.

NIB	Exc.	V.G.	Good	Fair	Poor
3800	3000	2250	1500	900	400

588 Cima

NIB	Exc.	V.G.	Good	Fair	Poor
3800	3000	2250	1500	900	400

590 Regina

NIB	Exc.	V.G.	Good	Fair	Poor
4250	3500	2700	1750	1000	500

595 Principe
As above, but engraved with relief-cut hunting scenes.

NIB	Exc.	V.G.	Good	Fair	Poor
6500	5000	4000	3000	2000	1000

600 Imperial
This double barrel shotgun has a self-opening action.

NIB	Exc.	V.G.	Good	Fair	Poor
5000	4250	3250	2000	1000	500

601 Imperial Tiro
As above, but nickel-plated. Fitted with a self-opening action.

NIB	Exc.	V.G.	Good	Fair	Poor
5750	5000	4000	3000	2000	1000

801
A detachable sidelock, self-opening action, double barrel shotgun engraved in the manner of Churchill.

NIB	Exc.	V.G.	Good	Fair	Poor
7950	7000	6500	4000	3000	1500

802

As above, with Holland & Holland-style engraving.

NIB	Exc.	V.G.	Good	Fair	Poor
7950	7000	6500	4000	3000	1500

803

As above, with Purdey-style engraving.

NIB	Exc.	V.G.	Good	Fair	Poor
5850	5000	4000	3000	2000	1000

871

This model features hand detachable sidelocks with Holland ejectors. Scroll engraving.

NIB	Exc.	V.G.	Good	Fair	Poor
4300	3600	2500	1500	1000	750

872

This model has same features as the Model 871 with the addition of more engraving coverage using a tighter scroll.

NIB	Exc.	V.G.	Good	Fair	Poor
9800	8250	7000	4000	3000	1000

873

This model features hand detachable sidelocks and game scene engraving.

NIB	Exc.	V.G.	Good	Fair	Poor
6850	5800	4500	3000	1500	750

874

Same features as above model but with the addition of a blued frame with gold line outlines.

NIB	Exc.	V.G.	Good	Fair	Poor
8000	6750	5500	4500	3000	1000

875

A custom manufactured sidelock, double barrel shotgun built solely to the customer's specifications.

NIB	Exc.	V.G.	Good	Fair	Poor
13000	10500	8500	6000	3000	1000

R-1 Double Rifle

NIB	Exc.	V.G.	Good	Fair	Poor
8950	7500	6000	4000	2000	1000

R-2 Double Rifle

NIB	Exc.	V.G.	Good	Fair	Poor
13000	10500	8500	6000	3000	1000

NOTE: Add 5% for gauges smaller than 16 gauge. Add 10% for matched pairs. There are a number of extra cost options that will affect the price of individual guns. Seek expert advice before a sale.

ARRIZABALAGA, HIJOS de C.
Eibar, Spain

Arrizabalaga

A 7.65mm semiautomatic pistol with a 9-shot magazine and a lanyard ring fitted to the butt. Checkered wood grips. ARRIZABALAGA on the slide.

Courtesy James Rankin

Exc.	V.G.	Good	Fair	Poor
225	175	125	75	50

Campeon

A the Model 1919 6.35mm, 7.65mm, or 9mm Kurtz semiautomatic pistol with the slide marked "Campeon Patent 1919" and the plastic grips "Campeon". Supplied with 6- or 8-round magazines. CAMPEON appears on the slide.

Courtesy James Rankin

Exc.	V.G.	Good	Fair	Poor
225	175	125	75	50

NOTE: Add 25% for 9mm Kurtz.

Sharpshooter

A 6.35mm, 7.65mm or 9mm Corto (short) semiautomatic pistol fitted with a cocking lever. The barrel tips up for cleaning or when using the pistol as a single shot. SHARPSHOOTER appears on the slide.

Courtesy James Rankin

Exc.	V.G.	Good	Fair	Poor
300	250	200	125	75

Jo Lo Ar

The Model 1924 semi automatic pistol with a tip-up barrel, cocking lever, and no triggerguard. The Jo La Ar was built in five calibers: 6.35mm, 7.65mm, 9mm, kurtz, and .45 ACP. Jo La Ar appears on the slide and the grips.

Courtesy James Rankin

Exc.	V.G.	Good	Fair	Poor
350	300	275	200	100

NOTE: The .45 caliber version is worth approximately 700% more than the values listed above.

ASCASO
Cataluna, Spain
Spanish Rebublican Government

A copy of the Astra Model 400 chambered for the 9mm Largo cartridge. The barrel marked "F. Ascaso Tarrassa" in an oval. Built by the Spanish government during the Spanish Civil War. Very few were made during the Spanish Civil War.

Courtesy James Rankin

Exc.	V.G.	Good	Fair	Poor
850	750	550	300	200

ASHEVILLE ARMORY
Asheville, North Carolina

Enfield Type Rifle

A .58 caliber percussion rifle with a 32.5" barrel and full stock secured by two iron barrel bands. Finished in the white brass triggerguard and buttplate with a walnut stock. The lockplate is marked "Asheville, N.C." Approximately 300 were made in 1862 and 1863. Prospective purchasers are advised to secure a qualified appraisal prior to acquisition.

Courtesy Milwaukee Public Museum, Milwaukee, Wisconsin

Exc.	V.G.	Good	Fair	Poor
—	—	30000	12500	2500

ASHTON, PETER & WILLIAM
Middletown, Connecticut

Ashton Under Hammer Pistol

A .28 to .38 caliber single shot percussion revolver with 4" or 5" half-octagonal barrels marked "P.H. Ashton" or "W. Ashton." Blued or browned with walnut grips. Active 1850s.

Exc.	V.G.	Good	Fair	Poor
—	—	750	300	100

H. ASTON/H. ASTON & CO. PISTOLS
Middleton, Connecticut

Overall length 14"; barrel length 8-1/2"; caliber .54. Markings: on lockplate, forward of hammer "U S/H. ASTON" or "U S/H. ASTON & CO.," on tail "MIDDTN/CONN/(date)"; on barrel, standard government inspection marks. Henry Aston of Middleton, Connecticut received a contract from the U.S. War Department in February 1845 for 30,000 single shot percussion pistols. These were delivered between 1846 and 1852, after which Ira N. Johnston continued production under a separate contract. Three thousand of these pistols were purchased for Navy usage and many of these were subsequently marked with a small anchor on the barrel near the breech. These Navy purchases will command a slight premium.

Courtesy Milwaukee Public Museum, Milwaukee, Wisconsin

Exc.	V.G.	Good	Fair	Poor
—	—	4000	1750	500

ASTRA-UNCETA SA
Guernica, Spain

Astra is a brand name placed on guns built by Esperanza y Unceta and then Unceta y Cia. This Spanish company has now incorporated its trade name into its corporate name and is now know as Astra-Unceta SA. The firm under the direction of Don Pedron Unceta and Don Juan Esperanza began business in Eibar on July 17, 1908 and moved to Guernica in 1913. The Astra trademark was adopted on November 25, 1914. Esperanza began production of the Spanish Army's Campo Giro pistol in 1913. The Model 1921 was marketed commercially as the Astra 400. After the Spanish Civil War Uncerta was one of only four handgun companies permitted to resume manufacturing operations. An interesting and informative side note is that pistols with 1000 to 5000 model numbers were made after 1945.

Victoria

A 6.36mm semiautomatic pistol with a 2.5" barrel. Blued with black plastic grips. Manufactured prior to 1913.

Exc.	V.G.	Good	Fair	Poor
350	250	200	150	100

Astra 1911

As above, renamed in November of 1914 and chambered additionally for the 7.65mm cartridge.

Exc.	V.G.	Good	Fair	Poor
350	250	175	100	75

Astra 1924

A 6.35mm semiautomatic pistol with a 2.5" barrel. The slide marked "Esperanza y Unceta Guernica Spain Astra Cal 6.35 .25." Blued with black plastic grips.

Exc.	V.G.	Good	Fair	Poor
300	200	125	100	75

Astra 100

A different tradename for the Model 1911 in 7.65mm caliber.

Exc.	V.G.	Good	Fair	Poor
350	225	200	150	100

Astra 200

A 6.35mm semiautomatic pistol with a 2.5" barrel and 6-shot magazine fitted with a grip safety. Also known as the "Firecat" in the United States. Manufactured from 1920 to 1966.

Exc.	V.G.	Good	Fair	Poor
300	200	125	100	75

Astra 400 or Model 1921

A 9x23 Bergman caliber semiautomatic pistol with a 6" barrel. Blued with black plastic grips. This model was adopted for use by the Spanish Army. Approximately 106,000 were made prior to 1946. Recent importation has depressed the price of these guns. Any with Nazi proofs marks are worth a 100% premium, but caution is advised.

Exc.	V.G.	Good	Fair	Poor
325	275	150	75	40

Astra 300

As above, in 7.65mm or 9mm short. Those used during World War II by German forces bear Waffenamt marks. Approximately 171,000 were manufactured prior to 1947.

Nazi-Proofed-Add 25%.

Courtesy Orvel Reichert

Exc.	V.G.	Good	Fair	Poor
400	350	250	150	100

Astra 600

Similar to the Model 400, but in 9mm Parabellum. In 1943 and 1944 approximately 10,500 were manufactured. Some of these World War II guns will have Nazi proof stamp and bring a premium. A further 49,000 were made in 1946 and commercially sold.

Exc.	V.G.	Good	Fair	Poor
350	250	200	150	100

Astra 700

The Model 400 in 7.65mm caliber. Approximately 4,000 were made in 1926.

Exc.	V.G.	Good	Fair	Poor
600	450	400	300	150

Astra 800

Similar to the Model 600 with an external hammer and loaded chamber indicator. Blued with plastic grips having the trade-name "Condor" cast in them. Approximately 11,400 were made from 1958 to 1969.

Exc.	V.G.	Good	Fair	Poor
1250	850	750	500	250

Astra 900

A copy of the Mauser Model C96 semiautomatic pistol. Blued with walnut grips.

Exc.	V.G.	Good	Fair	Poor
2250	1750	1250	750	500

Astra 1000

A postwar version of the Model 200 with a 4" barrel and 12-shot magazine.

Exc.	V.G.	Good	Fair	Poor
550	450	400	300	150

Astra 2000

As above, in .22 or 6.35mm caliber without a grip safety and with an external hammer. Blued with plastic grips.

Exc.	V.G.	Good	Fair	Poor
350	250	200	150	90

Astra 3000

The Model 300 in 7.65mm or 9mm short with a 6- or 7-shot magazine and loaded chamber indicator. Manufactured from 1948 to 1956.

Paul Goodwin Photo

Exc.	V.G.	Good	Fair	Poor
400	300	250	200	100

Astra 4000

As above, with an external hammer and also chambered in .22 caliber. Blued with plastic grips.

Exc.	V.G.	Good	Fair	Poor
300	225	200	150	75

Astra 5000

A .22, 7.65mm or 9mm short semiautomatic pistol (resembling a Walther PP Pistol) with a 3.5" barrel. Blued, chrome-plated or stainless steel with plastic grips. Also available with a 6" barrel as a sport model. Introduced in 1965.

Exc.	V.G.	Good	Fair	Poor
350	250	200	150	75

Astra 7000

An enlarged version of the Model 2000 in .22 caliber.

Exc.	V.G.	Good	Fair	Poor
300	250	200	150	75

Constable A-60

A .380 caliber double action semiautomatic pistol with a 3.5" barrel, adjustable sights and 13-shot magazine. Blued with plastic grips. Introduced in 1986.

NIB	Exc.	V.G.	Good	Fair	Poor
400	300	200	150	100	75

Astra A-80

A .38 Super, 9mm or .45 caliber double action semiautomatic pistol with a 3.75" barrel and either a 9- or 15-shot magazine depending upon the caliber. Blued or chrome-plated with plastic grips. Introduced in 1982.

NIB	Exc.	V.G.	Good	Fair	Poor
450	350	300	250	200	100

Astra A-90

As above, in 9mm or .45 caliber only. Introduced in 1986.

NIB	Exc.	V.G.	Good	Fair	Poor
400	350	300	250	200	100

Astra Cadix

A .22 or .38 Special double action swing-out cylinder revolver with a 4" or 6" barrel and either 9- or 5-shot cylinder. Blued with plastic grips. Manufactured from 1960 to 1968.

Exc.	V.G.	Good	Fair	Poor
200	150	125	90	70

.357 Double Action Revolver

As above, in .357 Magnum caliber with a 3", 4", 6", or 8.5" barrel, adjustable sights and 6-shot cylinder. Blued or stainless steel with walnut grips. Manufactured from 1972 to 1988.

Stainless steel-Add 10%.

NIB	Exc.	V.G.	Good	Fair	Poor
250	200	150	125	100	75

.44/.45 Double Action Revolver

As above, in .41 Magnum, .44 Magnum or .45 ACP caliber with 6" or 8.5" barrels and a 6-shot cylinder. Blued or stainless steel with walnut grips. Manufactured from 1980 to 1987.

Stainless steel-Add 25%.

Exc.	V.G.	Good	Fair	Poor
350	300	250	200	100

Terminator

As above, in .44 Special or .44 Magnum with a 2.75" barrel, adjustable sights and 6-shot cylinder. Blued or stainless steel with rubber grips.

Stainless steel version-Add 10%.

Exc.	V.G.	Good	Fair	Poor
350	300	250	200	100

Convertible Revolver

Similar to the .357 D/A revolver but accompanied by a cylinder chambered for 9mm cartridges. Barrel length 3". Blued with walnut grips. Introduced in 1986.

Exc.	V.G.	Good	Fair	Poor
300	250	200	150	100

CURRENTLY IMPORTED PISTOLS
IMPORTER-EUROPEAN AMERICAN ARMORY
Hialeah, FL

Model A-100

This semiautomatic service pistol is chambered for the 9mm Parabellum, .40 S&W, or .45 ACP cartridges. The trigger action is double action for the first shot, single action for follow-up shots. Equipped with a decocking lever. The barrel is 3.8" long and the overall length is 7.5". Magazine capacity for the 9mm is 17 rounds, .40 S&W is 13 rounds, while the .45 holds 9 rounds. A blue or nickel finish is standard. Weight is approximately 34 oz. Also available in a featherweight model 9mm only at 26.5 oz.

NIB	Exc.	V.G.	Good	Fair	Poor
400	350	300	250	200	100

NOTE: Add $35 for nickel finish.

Model A-100 Carry Comp

Similar to the Model A-100 but fitted with a 4.25" barrel and 1" compensator. Blue finish only. Weight is approximately 38 oz. Magazine capacity for 9mm is 17 rounds and for the .40 S&W and .45 ACP 10 rounds.

NIB	Exc.	V.G.	Good	Fair	Poor
475	375	—	—	—	—

Model A-70

This is a lightweight semiautomatic pistol chambered for the 9mm cartridge or .40 S&W cartridge. It is fitted with 3-dot combat sights. The barrel is 3.5" long and the magazine capacity is 8 rounds for 9mm and 7 rounds for the .40 S&W. Black plastic grips and blue finish are standard. Weight is 29 oz.

NIB	Exc.	V.G.	Good	Fair	Poor
325	275	225	175	150	100

NOTE: Add $35 for nickel finish.

Model A-75

Introduced in 1993 this model features all of the standard features of the Model 70 plus selective double or single trigger action and decocking lever. Chambered for 9mm, .40 S&W, or .45 ACP. Offered in blue or nickel finish and steel or alloy frame in 9mm only. Weight for steel frame in 9mm and .40 S&W is 31 oz., for .45 ACP weight is 34.4 oz. Featherweight 9mm weight is 23.5 oz.

NIB	Exc.	V.G.	Good	Fair	Poor
375	325	250	200	150	100

NOTE: Add $35 for nickel finish.

ATKIN, HENRY
London, England
SEE—British Double Guns

AUBREY, A.J.
Meriden, Connecticut

Double Barrel Shotguns

Good quality doubles made for Sears. Value depends on condition, grade, and model. Price range between $100 and $1,500. Seek an expert appraisal prior to sale.

AUER, B.
Louisville, Kentucky

Auer Pocket Pistol

A .60 caliber percussion pocket pistol with a 4" octagonal barrel and a long tang extending well back along the grip. Browned, silver furniture and a checkered walnut stock. The lock is marked "B. Auer". Produced during the 1850s.

Exc.	V.G.	Good	Fair	Poor
—	—	1500	600	250

AUGUSTA MACHINE WORKS
Augusta, Georgia

1851 Colt Navy Copy

A .36 caliber percussion revolver with an 8" barrel and 6-shot cylinder. Unmarked except for serial numbers with either 6 or 12 stop cylinder slots. Blued with walnut grips. This is a very rare revolver. Prospective purchasers are advised to secure a qualified appraisal prior to acquisition.

Exc.	V.G.	Good	Fair	Poor
—	—	30000	12500	2500

AUSTIN & HALLECK, INC.
Weston, MO

Model 320 LR BLU

An in-line percussion, bolt action rifle fitted with a 26" half octagon-half round barrel in .50 caliber. Receiver and barrel are blue. Adjustable trigger and receiver drilled and tapped for scope mount. Stock is black synthetic with checkering. Weight is about 7.87 lbs.

NIB	Exc.	V.G.	Good	Fair	Poor
450	375	—	—	—	—

Model 320 S/S

Similar to the above model but fitted with stainless steel barrel and action.

NIB	Exc.	V.G.	Good	Fair	Poor
500	400	—	—	—	—

Model 420 LR Classic

Similar to the Model 320 series but fitted with a standard lightly figured Maple stock in classic configuration. Available in blue or stainless steel.

NIB	Exc.	V.G.	Good	Fair	Poor
500	425	—	—	—	—

NOTE: Add $100 for fancy wood, add $200 for hand select wood, add $800 for Exhibition wood.

Model 420 LR Monte Carlo

Same as classic series but with Monte Carlo stock and cheekpiece.

Hand Select wood

NIB	Exc.	V.G.	Good	Fair	Poor
500	425	—	—	—	—

NOTE: Add $100 for fancy wood, add $200 for hand select wood, add $800 for Exhibition wood.

Mountain Rifle

This is a .50 caliber percussion or flintlock rifle with double set triggers, 32" octagonal barrel, buckhorn sights, curly Maple stock and crescent steel buttplate. Weight is approximately 7.5 lbs.

NIB	Exc.	V.G.	Good	Fair	Poor
500	400	—	—	—	—

NOTE: Add $100 for hand select wood.

AUSTRALIAN AUTOMATIC ARMS LTD.
Tasmania, Australia
Importer-North American Sales International, Inc.
Midland, Texas

SAR

A 5.56mm semiautomatic rifle with a 16.25" or 20" barrel, 5-shot or 20-shot magazine, black plastic stock and forend. Imported from 1986 to 1989.

NIB	Exc.	V.G.	Good	Fair	Poor
1000	800	500	350	250	125

SAP

A 10.5" barreled pistol version of the above. Imported from 1986 to 1989.

NIB	Exc.	V.G.	Good	Fair	Poor
1000	800	500	350	250	125

SP

A sporting rifle version of the SAR, fitted with a wood stock and 5-shot magazine. Introduced in 1989.

NIB	Exc.	V.G.	Good	Fair	Poor
800	650	500	350	250	125

AUSTRIAN MILITARY FIREARMS

The end of the Napoleonic Wars found the army of the Austria Hungarian Empire armed with a variety of flintlock firearms. The foot troops carried either the M1798 or the M1807 musket or the M1807 yager rifle. The mounted forces were armed with either the M1798 dragoon carbine, the M1798 Hussarcarbine, the M1798 rifled cavalry carbine, the M1781 Cuirassier musketoon, and the M1798 pistol. In 1828 a new flintlock musket superseded the M1798 pattern, only to be modified again in 1835. In the latter years, however, the Austrian military also began experimenting with a variation of the percussion system invented by Giuseppe Console, utilizing a small elongated copper cylinder filled with fulminate. In 1840, the flintlock muskets adopted in 1835 were adapted to a variation of this percussion system as modified by Baron von Augustin. This system was made army-wide in 1842 with the adoption of a new musket and yager rifle with locks specifically manufactured for the Augustin tubelocks. In 1849, a new rifle replaced the M1842 pattern; both of these rifles were based on the Devilgne chambered breech. In 1850, a cavalry carbine and a horse pistol were added to the tubelock series. All of these arms were either .69 or .71 caliber. The tubelock, however, was short-lived; in 1854, Austria abandoned the tubelock system in favor of standard percussion cap then widely used by the armies of Europe. At the same time it adopted a new smaller caliber (.54) which it applied to the new M1854 rifle-musket and the M1855 yager rifle. A horse pistol based on the same system (Lorenz's compressed, elongated ball) was adopted in 1859.

Large numbers of the Austrian longarms were imported to the United States in the first two years of the American Civil War. Beginning in 1863, the Confederate States also imported large numbers of the M1854 series rifle-muskets. Most of the tubelocks first being modified to standard percussion in Belgium before importation, arms of prime interest to American collectors, accordingly demand higher prices.

In 1867, the Austria-Hungarian Empire adopted two different breechloading mechanisms and the self-contained metallic cartridge. Those muzzleloading arms deemed acceptable for alteration (the M1854 series of rifle-muskets and rifles) were adapted to the Wanzel system. Newly made arms (the M1867 rifle) were made in conformity with Werndl's breechloading design.

During the period within the scope of this catalog, Austrian arms were generally made on contract with the major gun makers in and near Vienna ("Wien" in Austrian). These makers usually marked their products with their name upon the barrel of the arm, near the breech. The major makers included BENTZ, FERD. FRUWIRTH (who also simply marked his arms "F. F."), CARL HEISER, JOSEF JESCHER, ANNA OSTERLIEN, PIRKO, TH. ROTTME, G. SCHLAGER, TH. SEDERE, F. UMFAURER, WANZEL, and ZEILINGER (with the "Z" usually backwards). Lockplates were marked with the government ownership mark (a small double-headed eagle) and the date of manufacture (deleting the number "1" from the year, such as "847" for "1847".) Since the arms were not interchangeable, mating numbers are usually found on all the metal parts.

Austrian Musket, M1828

Overall length 57-3/4"; barrel length 42-1/2"; caliber .69. Basically following the pattern of the French M1822 musket, this arm still accepted the quadrangular M1799 bayonet, distinguished by having a solid socket with a hook ring at its rear, like the Prussian bayonet for the M1808 musket.

Exc.	V.G.	Good	Fair	Poor
—	—	1000	550	400

Austrian Musket, M1835

Overall length 57-3/4"; barrel length 42-1/2"; caliber .69. The M1835 musket follows the pattern of the Austrian M1807 musket, but is adapted for the Consule tubelock percussion system, which essentially replaced the frizzen and pan with a hinged tube retainer. This arm still uses the M1799 quadrangular bayonet.

Exc.	V.G.	Good	Fair	Poor
—	—	1500	600	350

Austrian Musket, M1840

Overall length 57-3/4"; barrel length 42-1/2"; caliber .69. The M1840 musket was manufactured in flint. Its primary differences from the M1828 musket lie in its furniture (mainly the front band) and the bayonet attachment, which consists of a lug beneath the barrel and an elongated hook projecting from the forend of the stock to accept the new M1840 quadrangular bayonet. The bayonet is distinguished by having a straight slot in its socket, closed by a bridge.

Exc.	V.G.	Good	Fair	Poor
—	—	1500	600	350

Austrian Musket, M1842

Overall length 57-3/4"; barrel length 42-1/2"; caliber .69 (.71). The M1842 musket was manufactured in Augustin tubelock. Its main distinction from the M1840 flintlock musket is the lock, which in addition to having the integral hinged tubelock mechanism in lieu of the frizzen, has a distinctly rounded rear tail. Although 25,000 of these muskets were imported into the United States for use by Fremont's forces in Missouri in 1861, many were subsequently altered to percussion. The Cincinnati contractors, Hall, Carroll & Co. or Greenwood & Co. accounted for 10,000 of these arms, all of which were altered to percussion by means of the cone-in-barrel system. These were also rifled and a portion of them sighted with a long range rear sight similar to the Enfield P1853 rifle-musket. Many of the balance were subsequently sent to the Frankfort Arsenal in Philadelphia, where they were subcontracted to Henry Leman of Lancaster for alteration to standard percussion. Those altered by Leman are distinguished by having a new breechpiece with integral bolster, the latter with a cleanout screw through its face. In addition to the 25,000 imported for Fremont, the firm of H. Boker & Co. of New York imported approximately 8,000 Austrian M1842 muskets which it had altered to percussion in Belgium. The French method of adding a reinforced bolster to the top right-hand side of the barrel was used. Many of those were also rifled and sighted in the manner of the French adaptations fashionable in Europe. George Heydecker of New York City imported another 4,000 in 1863 that were seized in transit to Canada, reputedly for delivery to Mexican republican forces.

Courtesy Milwaukee Public Museum, Milwaukee, Wisconsin

In original tubelock!

Exc.	V.G.	Good	Fair	Poor
—	—	1750	850	500

Altered to percussion (Cincinnati contractors)

Exc.	V.G.	Good	Fair	Poor
—	—	950	450	250

Altered to percussion (Leman)

Courtesy Milwaukee Public Museum, Milwaukee, Wisconsin

Exc.	V.G.	Good	Fair	Poor
—	—	750	350	200

Altered to percussion and rifled (Boker)

Exc.	V.G.	Good	Fair	Poor
—	—	750	350	200

Austrian M1844 "Extra Corps" Musketoon

Overall length 48-3/8"; barrel length 33-1/2"; caliber .69 (.71). Is essentially a shortened version of the Austrian M1842 musket. In original Augustin tubelock, it is virtually unknown. Most of the production is thought to have been purchased by arms speculators at the beginning of the American Civil War and altered to standard percussion in Liege, Belgium. The Belgian alteration followed the second pattern adopted by that government to alter arms to percussion and consisted of brazing a "lump" of metal to the upper right-hand side of the barrel, into which a cone was threaded. The arms so altered were also rifled and sighted. The sights either copied the Austrian M1854 rifle-musket folding sight or the French "ladder" rear sight using the pattern utilized on the M1829 rifled cavalry musketoon. Over 10,000 of these arms were imported into the United States in 1861-1862 by Herman Boker & Co. of New York City.

Courtesy Milwaukee Public Museum, Milwaukee, Wisconsin

Altered to percussion and rifled (Boker)

Exc.	V.G.	Good	Fair	Poor
—	—	950	400	200

Austrian M1842 yager rifle

Overall length 48-1/4"; barrel length 33-1/4"; caliber .69/.71. The Austrian M1842 yager rifle ("Kammer Busche") was originally manufactured in tubelock for the rifle battalions of the Austrian Army. Its bore terminated in a Delvigne breech, i.e. a chamber of lesser diameter than the caliber whose lip served as a base for disfiguring the projectile to fill the rifling. Made obsolete by the Thouvenin and Minie systems, many M1842 yager rifles were altered in 1860 in Belgium to standard percussion and sold to the Italian revolutionaries led by Giuseppe Garibaldi, giving the gun that nickname. Two methods of alteration were applied. One, the "Belgian" system, brazed a "lump" of iron to the upper right surface of the breech, which was tapped for a standard percussion cone. The other, the "Prussian," involved fitting the breech with a new barrel section incorporating a new bolster. At least 500 of these altered arms were imported into the United States during the American Civil War, where they (and the M1849 yager rifles similarly altered) were called "Garibaldi Rifles."

Courtesy Milwaukee Public Museum, Milwaukee, Wisconsin

Exc.	V.G.	Good	Fair	Poor
—	—	1000	450	150

Austrian M1849 yager rifle

Overall length 48"; barrel length 33-1/4"; caliber .71. The successor to the M1842 Austrian "Kammer Busche," the M1849 model is distinguished by having its barrel wedge fastened rather than retained by bands. Both the M1842 and the M1849 yager rifles were adapted to socket bayonets having long straight knife blades; both socket types were slotted. That of

the M1842 was secured to the barrel by the same method as the M1842 Austrian musket; that of the M1849, however, locked onto a lug on the right side of the barrel and was secured by a rotating ring on the back of the socket. Adapted to standard percussion in the same manner as the M1842 yager rifles, more than 25,000 were sold to the U.S. War Department in 1862 and 1863.

Courtesy Milwaukee Public Museum, Milwaukee, Wisconsin

Austrian M1850 horse pistol

Overall length 16"; barrel length 8-7/8"; caliber .69. A bulky brass mounted pistol with lanyard ring, this arm was made originally in tubelock. However, a small quantity appear to have been altered to standard percussion locks in Liege, Belgium. In the process the double-strapped front bands of the original were removed and the forestock cut away to adapt the stock to an iron ramrod. (In Austrian service the ramrod was hung from the crossbelt of the mounted trooper.) Quantities imported into the United States are uncertain but may have been included among the 346 foreign horse pistols purchased by the U.S. War Department from P.S. Justice in 1861.

Exc.	V.G.	Good	Fair	Poor
—	—	750	350	150

Austrian M1850 carbine

Overall length 30"; barrel length 14-1/2"; caliber .71. Originally manufactured in tubelock for Austrian cavalry service, this large caliber, short-barreled rifled carbine (12-groove rifling) saw service in the United States when 10,000 were purchased by U.S. purchasing agent George Schuyler in 1861. Those purchased for U.S. service, however, had been altered in Liege, Belgium for standard percussion locks in the same manner that the Austrian M1842 and M1849 yager rifles had been altered.

Courtesy Milwaukee Public Museum, Milwaukee, Wisconsin

M1854 rifle-musket (The "Lorenz")

Overall length 52"; barrel length 37-1/4"; caliber .54 (and .58). Adopted in 1854 as a replacement for its smoothbore muskets, the Austrian M1854 rifle-musket was made in three variants. The standard infantry arm had a simple block sight for mass volley fire. The rifles for the "rear rank" men were similar but with a folding leaf sight with windows graduated to 900 paces. A similar sight was also applied to the rifles for sharpshooter battalions, which also had a cheekpiece built into the buttstock. The quadrangular socket bayonet locked onto the front sight, whose sides were angled to accept the diagonal slot in the bayonet's socket. The Austrian M1854 rifle-musket was the second most prolifically imported arm during the American Civil War, with some 89,000 being imported into the Confederacy and more than 175,000 into the Union. Thousands of the latter were bored up to .58 caliber before being imported.

Courtesy Milwaukee Public Museum, Milwaukee, Wisconsin

Exc.	V.G.	Good	Fair	Poor
—	—	950	400	200

M1854 yager rifle

Overall length 43"; barrel length 28"; caliber .54. Designed for the rifle battalions of the Austrian army to replace the M1842 and M1849 rifles, the M1854 yager rifles are distinguished by having an octagonal, wedge-fastened barrel turned round near the muzzle to accept a socket bayonet with a long straight knife blade. An angled lug on the turned section engaged the diagonal slot in the bayonet's socket. The rear sight for these rifles is unusual, consisting of a curved slide that traverses two upright walls and can be locked with a turn key on its right side for various ranges up to 900 paces. These rifles were made for Austrian service without provision for a ramrod (that device being affixed to a crossbelt of the individual soldier). But the approximately 2,500 that were imported for U.S. service during the American Civil War were adapted for a ramrod by inletting a channel under the forestock.

Courtesy Milwaukee Public Museum, Milwaukee, Wisconsin

Exc.	V.G.	Good	Fair	Poor
—	—	1250	600	200

Austrian M1859 horse pistol

Overall length 16" (less stock); barrel length 10-3/8"; caliber .54. The M1850 tubelock pistol was replaced in the Austrian service in 1859 with a new standard percussion rifled horse pistol firing the Lorenz "compression" elongated ball. Like the U.S. M1855 horse pistol, this new pistol had a detachable shoulder stock so that it could be used as a carbine. Like its predecessors, no provision was made for a ramrod, which continued to be attached to a belt crossing the trooper's torso.

Exc.	V.G.	Good	Fair	Poor
—	—	750	350	200

Austrian M1854/67 "Wanzel" alteration to breechloader

Overall length 52-1/4"; barrel (bore) length; 34-1/2"; caliber .54. The "Wanzel" breechloading mechanism applied to the Austrian M1854 rifle-muskets is much like the Allin "trapdoor" applied in the U.S. to long arms during the period 1865-1873. A breech block that hinges forward upon the barrel is released by a lever on the right side of the block, permitting insertion of a brass cartridge. In the process of altering these arms to breechloaders the sling swivels were moved from the middle band and triggerguard bow to the middle of the forestock and the buttstock.

Courtesy Milwaukee Public Museum, Milwaukee, Wisconsin

Exc.	V.G.	Good	Fair	Poor
—	—	750	350	200

Austrian M1867 "Werndl" breechloading rifle

Overall length 48-1/4"; barrel (bore) length 31-1/4"; caliber 11mm. In 1867 the Austrian military adopted the breechloading system that had been invented by Joseph Werndl, director of the Austrian armory at Steyr. The breech of Werndl's design is rotated by means of a lever on its left side to expose the chamber for loading and extraction of cartridges. WERNDL appears on the top of the barrel in recognition of the designer's invention. In 1888 the Werndl rifles were superseded by the Mannlicher smokeless powder arms.

Courtesy Milwaukee Public Museum, Milwaukee, Wisconsin

Exc.	V.G.	Good	Fair	Poor
—	—	1000	450	200

AUTAUGA ARMS INC.
Prattville, AL

Autauga MK II

This is .32 ACP semiautomatic blow back pistol with a double action trigger. Barrel length is 2.25". Fixed sights. Overall length 4.25". Weight is about 13.5 oz. Magazine capacity is 6 rounds. Introduced in 1999.

NIB	Exc.	V.G.	Good	Fair	Poor
400	325	—	—	—	—

AUTO MAG
Various Manufacturers

This popular stainless steel semiautomatic pistol was developed by the Sanford Arms Company of Pasadena, California, in the 1960s and was chambered for a special cartridge known as the .44 AMP which had a 240 grain .44 caliber bullet. Production of this arm has been carried out by a number of companies over the past 30 years. It is believed that less than 10,000 have been produced by the eight manufacturers involved.

AUTO MAG CORP.
Pasadena, California
Serial number range A0000 through A3300, made with a 6.5" vent rib barrel, chambered in .44 AMP only.

NIB	Exc.	V.G.	Good	Fair	Poor
2250	1700	1200	850	600	300

TDE CORP.
North Hollywood, California
Serial number range A3400 through A05015, made with a 6.5" vent rib barrel, chambered in .44 AMP and .357 AMP.

.44 AMP

NIB	Exc.	V.G.	Good	Fair	Poor
1950	1500	1100	850	600	300

.357 AMP

NIB	Exc.	V.G.	Good	Fair	Poor
2150	1650	1200	900	600	300

TDE CORP.
El Monte, California
Serial number range A05016 through A08300, 6.5" vent rib barrel standard. Also available in 8" and 10" barrel lengths chambered for .44 AMP and .357 AMP.

.44 AMP

NIB	Exc.	V.G.	Good	Fair	Poor
1800	1450	1000	800	600	300

.357 AMP

NIB	Exc.	V.G.	Good	Fair	Poor
1600	1200	900	700	500	300

HIGH STANDARD
New Haven, Connecticut
High Standard made 113 guns, all with "H" prefix serial numbers between numbers H 198 and H 17219 through H 17222. High Standard also added less than 1000 guns between serial numbers A 05278 through A 07637. These pistols were chambered for .357 and .44 caliber.

NIB	Exc.	V.G.	Good	Fair	Poor
2000	1750	1250	900	600	300

TDE-OMC
This is known as the solid-bolt or "B" series. The serial number range is B00001 through B00370. Either 6.5" vent rib or 10" tapered barrels are available.

NIB	Exc.	V.G.	Good	Fair	Poor
2400	2000	1500	1000	600	300

AMT "C" SERIES
There were 100 guns produced in this series. The first 50 were serial numbered with a "C" prefix. The second 50 were serial numbered "LAST 1" through "LAST 50." They were available with a 6.5" vent rib or 10" tapered barrel.

NIB	Exc.	V.G.	Good	Fair	Poor
2400	2000	1500	1250	700	350

L. E. JURRAS CUSTOM
This custom maker produced a limited number of Auto Mag pistols in 1977. These arms are worth approximately 35-50% more than standard production models.

KENT LOMONT
As pistols made by this maker are essentially prototypes, it is advised that potential purchasers secure a qualified appraisal.

AUTO MAG, INC.
Irwindale, California
In 1998 this company was formed to produce 1,000 Harry Sanford Commemorative pistols. Chambered for .44 AMP cartridge. Each pistol comes in a walnut display case with special serial number with Harry Sanford's signature and the name Auto Mag on the receiver.

The current retail price for the Auto Mag is $2,750.

AUTO ORDNANCE CORP.
West Hurley, New York
In 1999 Kahr Arms purchased Auto Ordnance Corp.

An Auto Ordnance 1911A1 cut-away pistol was sold at auction for $1,035. Condition was excellent. Amoskeag Auction Co., Inc., November 1999

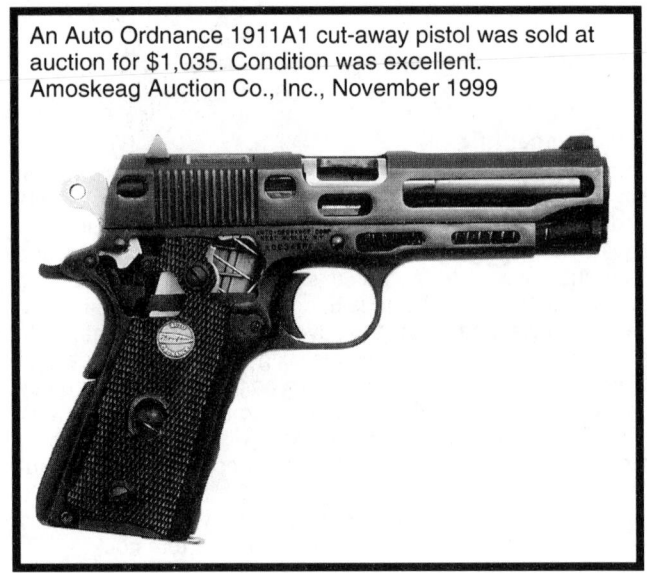

Thompson 1911 A1-Standard
A 9mm, .38 Super or .45 caliber copy of the Colt Model 1911 A1. Pistol weighs 39 oz.

NIB	Exc.	V.G.	Good	Fair	Poor
375	300	250	200	150	100

NOTE: For 9mm and .38 Super add $20 to above prices. The 9mm and .38 Super models were discontinued in 1997.

Thompson 1911 A1-Deluxe

Same as above but Hi-profile 3 white dot sight system. Grips are black textured, rubber wraparound grips.

NIB	Exc.	V.G.	Good	Fair	Poor
400	325	275	225	150	100

Thompson 1911 A1 Custom High Polish

Introduced in 1997 this model features a special high polish blued finish with numerous special options. Stocks are rosewood with medallion. Fitted with 5" barrel and chambered for .45 ACP. Weight is about 39 oz.

NIB	Exc.	V.G.	Good	Fair	Poor
575	475	—	—	—	—

Thompson 1911 A1-10mm

Same as above but chambered for the 10mm cartridge. Magazine capacity is 8 rounds. Discontinued in 1997.

NIB	Exc.	V.G.	Good	Fair	Poor
425	350	300	250	175	100

Thompson 1911 A1-Duo Tone

Chambered for the .45 ACP, the slide is blued and the frame is satin nickel. Discontinued in 1997.

NIB	Exc.	V.G.	Good	Fair	Poor
400	325	275	225	150	100

Thompson 1911 A1-Satin Nickel

Chambered for .45 ACP or .38 Super the finish is a satin nickel on both frame and slide. Blade front sight and black checkered plastic grips. Discontinued in 1997.

NIB	Exc.	V.G.	Good	Fair	Poor
400	325	275	225	150	100

Thompson 1911 A1-Competition

Chambered for .45 ACP or .38 Super the pistol is fitted with a 5" barrel with compensator and other competition features such as custom Commander hammer, flat mainspring housing, beavertail grip safety, full length recoil guide rod, extended ejector, slide stop and thumb safety. Pistol weight 42 oz. and is 10" overall. Discontinued in 1997.

NIB	Exc.	V.G.	Good	Fair	Poor
600	525	400	350	300	150

NOTE: For .38 Super add $10 to above prices.

Thompson 1911 A1-Parkerized

NIB	Exc.	V.G.	Good	Fair	Poor
375	295	250	225	200	150

Thompson 1911 A1-Pit Bull

Chambered for .45 ACP and fitted with a 3-1/2" barrel this model has high profile sights and black textured rubber wraparound grips. Magazine capacity is 7 rounds and weight is 36 oz.

NIB	Exc.	V.G.	Good	Fair	Poor
400	350	300	250	200	150

Thompson 1911 A1-General

This is a Commander-size pistol with 4-1/2" barrel, high profile sights. Chambered for .45 ACP or .38 Super. Weighs 37 oz. Discontinued in 1997.

NIB	Exc.	V.G.	Good	Fair	Poor
400	325	275	225	150	100

ZG-51 "Pit Bull"

Same as above, with a 3.5" barrel in .45 caliber. Introduced in 1988 and renamed "PIT BULL" in 1994. Discontinued.

NIB	Exc.	V.G.	Good	Fair	Poor
375	325	275	225	200	150

Thompson 1927 A1 Standard

A semiautomatic version of the Thompson submachine gun, chambered for the .45 ACP cartridge with a 16-1/2" barrel that is 18" with compensator. Blued with walnut stock. Weight is 13 lbs.

NIB	Exc.	V.G.	Good	Fair	Poor
550	450	300	250	200	150

1927 A1 Deluxe

As above, with a finned barrel, adjustable sights, pistol grip forearm, and a 50-round drum magazine costing an additional $140. The violin-shaped carrying case adds approximately $115 to the values listed below.

NIB	Exc.	V.G.	Good	Fair	Poor
750	650	575	500	350	150

1927 A1C

As above, with an aluminum alloy receiver. Introduced in 1984.

NIB	Exc.	V.G.	Good	Fair	Poor
725	625	550	500	350	150

1927 A1 Commando

Introduced in 1998 this version features a 16.5" finned barrel with compensator. The finish is parkerized with black wood finish. Furnished with 30-round magazine and black nylon sling. Weight is about 13 lbs.

NIB	Exc.	V.G.	Good	Fair	Poor
800	700	—	—	—	—

1927 A5

A reduced-size version of the Model 1927 A1 with a 13" finned barrel, aluminum alloy receiver and no shoulder stock.

NIB	Exc.	V.G.	Good	Fair	Poor
725	625	550	500	350	150

1927 A3

A .22 caliber variation of the Model 1927 A1 with a 16" barrel and aluminum alloy receiver. No longer in production.

NIB	Exc.	V.G.	Good	Fair	Poor
450	400	350	275	200	100

Thompson Submachine Gun NFA

Auto Ordnance manufactured fully automatic reproductions of the Thompson Submachine Gun from approximately 1975 until the Firearm Owners Protection Act (Public Law 99-308, effective May 19, 1986) prohibited the transfer to private citizens of any machine guns that were not lawfully registered on the effective date of the 1986 Act. Some fully automatic .22 caliber Thompsons were manufactured, but their serial numbers are different from the .45 caliber guns described here, and are unavailable at this time.

With the exception of the .22 caliber guns earlier noted, all West Hurley Thompsons were caliber .45 automatic, manufactured in Model 1928 and M1 versions; however, the M1 designation "is actually incorrect, as the guns are in the M1A1 Thompson configuration" (see "The West Hurley M1 Thompson SMG," by Frank Iannamico, *Machine Gun News*, June 1995, pages 40-42). All of the so-called "West Hurley" Thompsons have the letter "A" suffix in the serial number and the West Hurley, New York, address stamped on the right side of the receiver. The Model 1928 has a 10.5" finned barrel with Cutts compensator (which adds about 2" to the barrel length); the M1 has a 10.5" plain barrel and no compensator.

The quality of the West Hurley Thompsons has been and continues to be actively debated. Some early guns were not well manufactured and required considerable work, while guns of later manufacture were of superior manufacture and expertly fitted, with some of varying quality in between. Auto Ordnance assembled many early guns with GI parts, and many collectors and shooters have replaced key parts with GI parts, in some cases to improve shooting performance. Each gun must be evaluated individually by a qualified professional gunsmith and test fired to assess its quality of manufacture and/or mechanical/shooting proficiency, and the advisability of switching out factory parts for GI parts.

The original wholesale price of each model was $525 ($750 retail), and these values have risen dramatically along with the prices of many other machine guns, as demand has begun to catch up with the limited supply of "transferables" that was "frozen" by the 1986 Act. The M1 was manufactured only during 1985-86, and relatively few were made compared with the Model 1928, although the Model 1928 has so far been consistently valued higher. West Hurley Thompsons were originally considered "shooters" rather than collector's items, but the M1 (the so-called "Private Ryan" gun, after the movie), was recently ruled to be a "curio or relic" by ATF, and it seems reasonable to assume that the Model 1928 will eventually follow. The prices listed here are approximate, and reflect the premium that many people are willing to pay to own even a reproduction Thompson.

Total Model 1928 production was 3,306 guns, including Commemorative engraved Thompsons with various serial numbers, whose current retail prices may range from about $7,500 to $10,000 or more. (In 1992 there was a special run of 141 guns made for export or law enforcement only). The number of Commemorative guns manufactured are: World War II, 85 guns; Korean War, 145 guns; and Vietnam War, 17 guns. Total M1 production was 609 guns. There were also various special serial numbers included in the M1 production that are not listed; the factory would honor any request for a "special serial number," and these were not in the normal serial number ranges.

Model 1928 (serial numbered from 100A to 3159A(?)

Exc.	V.G.	Good	Fair	Poor
6500	5750	5500	5000	4750

M1 serial numbered from M11A to M717A

Exc.	V.G.	Good	Fair	Poor
6000	5500	4750	4500	4250

The Violent Crime Control and Law Enforcement Act of 1994 (Public Law 103-322, effective September 13, 1994) has banned the production of certain so-called "assault weapons" and high-capacity ammunition feeding devices until 2004. Although those manufactured before September 13, 1994, can be and are imported regularly, some members of Congress have repeatedly introduced legislation that would prohibit their importation. As magazines wear out and replacements are sought, the prices and availability of high-capacity magazines continue to rise and vary dramatically. Standard GI Thompson 20- or 30-round stick magazines that once were plentiful and sold for $5 to $6, have increased to $20 or more. Original Thompson drums have always been relatively costly, and prices of even West Hurley drums of modern manufacture suggest a high demand. New-in-box 50-round West Hurley L drums that last year were priced from $350 to $700 have risen to minimum asking prices of $650, but not much higher; and 100-round C drums that last year were offered from $750 to $1,000, have risen to $1,000 and higher. The quality of the West Hurley drums, particularly the 100-round C drums have been vastly criticized, and buyers would be well advised to request a demonstration before closing a purchase. As is the case with West Hurley Thompsons, some drums run flawlessly, others need work, and still others apparently are virtually unusable. The prices for vintage Thompson L drums range from $650 and up, while the much-sought-after C drum commands $3,000 or more. The uneven demand for these drum magazines precludes establishing firm retail prices at this time.

AUTO POINTER
Yamamoto Co.
Tokyo, Japan

Auto - Pointer Shotgun

A 12 or 20 gauge semiautomatic shotgun with 26", 28" or 30" barrels and an aluminum alloy frame. Blued with a checkered walnut stock. Originally imported by Sloan's but no longer available.

Exc.	V.G.	Good	Fair	Poor
350	250	200	150	100

AXTELL RIFLE CO.
(Riflesmith Inc.)
Sheridan, MT

#1 Long Range Creedmore

This single shot rifle is chambered for the 40-50BN, 40-70SS, 40-70BN, 40-90, 45-70, 45-90, 45-100. Weight is about 10 lbs. Numerous options will affect price.

NIB	Exc.	V.G.	Good	Fair	Poor
4700	3750	—	—	—	—

New Model Sharps 1877

Chambered for the 45-90, 45-100, and the 45-70 cartridges and fitted with a choice of 30" to 34" 1/2 round-1/2 octagon barrel with double set triggers.

NIB	Exc.	V.G.	Good	Fair	Poor
5200	4000	—	—	—	—

#2 Long Range

The Long Range #2 rifle is chambered for all the same calibers as the #1 Long Range Creedmore. Weight is about 10 lbs.

NIB	Exc.	V.G.	Good	Fair	Poor
3900	3000	—	—	—	—

Lower Sporting Rifle

Chambered for same calibers as above. Weight is between 9 and 12 lbs. depending on barrel options.

NIB	Exc.	V.G.	Good	Fair	Poor
2600	2000	—	—	—	—

Business Rifle

Same calibers as above. Weight is about 8.5 lbs.

NIB	Exc.	V.G.	Good	Fair	Poor
2400	1800	—	—	—	—

Overbaugh Schuetzen

Chambered for the 40-50BN and the 40-50 straight. Weight is 11 to 14 lbs. depending on barrel options.

NIB	Exc.	V.G.	Good	Fair	Poor
4400	3500	—	—	—	—

AZPIRI
Eibar, Spain

Avion

A 6.35mm semiautomatic pistol copied after the model 1906 Browning. Marked "Pistolet Automatique Avion Brevete." Manufactured from 1914 to 1918.

Exc.	V.G.	Good	Fair	Poor
250	150	125	95	65

Colon

As above, in 6.35mm caliber and marked "Automatic Pistol Colon".

Exc.	V.G.	Good	Fair	Poor
200	125	100	75	50

B

B.R.F.
South Africa

B.R.F.

This is a .25 caliber semiautomatic pistol similar to the P.A.F. with a 2" barrel and 6-shot magazine. U-SA means Union of South Africa. Little is known about the manufacturer of this pistol, its origin, or dates of manufacture.

Exc.	V.G.	Good	Fair	Poor
200	175	125	100	70

BSA GUNS LTD.
Birmingham, England
Birmingham Small Arms

Established in 1861, this firm has produced a wide variety of firearms over the years. The more common of these arms that are currently available in the United States are as follows:

SINGLE SHOT

No. 12 Cadet Martini

A .310 caliber single shot Martini action rifle with a 29" barrel, adjustable sights and straight-gripped walnut stock. Approximately 80,000 were manufactured from 1911 to 1913. Many of those imported into the United States were altered to .22 caliber.

Exc.	V.G.	Good	Fair	Poor
400	300	200	150	100

Centurian Match Rifle

As above, in .22 caliber with a 24" barrel, adjustable sights and a pistol-grip walnut stock.

Exc.	V.G.	Good	Fair	Poor
500	350	300	200	100

Model 13 Sporter

As above, in .22 Hornet with hunting sights.

Exc.	V.G.	Good	Fair	Poor
450	325	300	225	100

Martini International Match

As above, with a heavy match barrel, ISU style sights and a match stock. Manufactured from 1950 to 1953.

Exc.	V.G.	Good	Fair	Poor
500	375	325	250	125

Martini International Light

As above, with a 26" barrel of lighter weight.

Exc.	V.G.	Good	Fair	Poor
500	375	325	250	125

Martini International ISU

As above, meeting ISU specifications with a 28" barrel. Manufactured from 1968 to 1976.

Exc.	V.G.	Good	Fair	Poor
600	450	400	325	200

BOLT ACTIONS

Royal

A bolt-action sporting rifle manufactured in a variety of calibers and a 24" barrel, with a checkered French walnut stock.

Exc.	V.G.	Good	Fair	Poor
400	300	250	200	100

Majestic Deluxe

A .22 Hornet, .222, .243, 7x57mm, .308 or .30-06 bolt action sporting rifle with a 22" barrel, having a folding rear sight and a checkered walnut stock with a schnabel forend tip. Imported from 1959 to 1965.

Exc.	V.G.	Good	Fair	Poor
400	300	250	200	100

Majestic Deluxe Featherweight

As above, in .270 or .458 Magnum with a thinner barrel.

Exc.	V.G.	Good	Fair	Poor
400	300	250	200	100

Monarch Deluxe

As above, drilled and tapped for telescopic sight and also available in a heavy barreled varmint version in .222 or .243 caliber. Imported from 1966 to 1974.

Exc.	V.G.	Good	Fair	Poor
450	325	275	225	100

Herters U9
The firm of Herters, Inc. of Waseca, Minnesota, imported BSA rifle actions beginning in 1965 which were used for custom made rifles. Commencing in 1986, BSA began production of a new line of bolt action sporting rifles on the Model CF-2 action. The standard production models are as follows:

Sporter/Classic
A hunting rifle available in a variety of calibers with a checkered walnut stock. Introduced in 1986.

Exc.	V.G.	Good	Fair	Poor
400	325	275	200	100

Varminter
As above, with a matte-finished heavy barrel in .222, .22-250 or .243 caliber. Introduced in 1986.

Exc.	V.G.	Good	Fair	Poor
350	275	225	175	100

Stutzen Rifle
As above, with a 20.5" barrel and a Mannlicher style stock.

Exc.	V.G.	Good	Fair	Poor
450	350	275	225	100

Regal Custom
As above, with an engraved receiver, checkered walnut stock and an ebony forend. Imported only in 1986.

Exc.	V.G.	Good	Fair	Poor
925	750	600	500	250

CFT Target Rifle
A .308 caliber single shot version of the above with a 26.5" barrel and adjustable sights. Imported only in 1987.

Exc.	V.G.	Good	Fair	Poor
750	600	550	400	200

BABCOCK, MOSES
Charlestown, Massachusetts
Babcock Under Hammer Cane Gun
A .52 caliber percussion cane gun having a 27" barrel and overall length of approximately 33". Folding trigger, under hammer with a wood handle. The hammer is marked "Moses Babcock/Charlestown." Active 1850s and 1860s.

Exc.	V.G.	Good	Fair	Poor
—	—	2000	800	250

BABBIT, A. S.
Plattsburgh, New York
SEE—Adirondack Arms

BACON ARMS CO.
Norwich, Connecticut
Bacon Arms operated from 1862 until 1891. They have become known primarily for the production of cheaply made, solid-frame, rim-fire revolvers known as "Suicide Specials." Bacon manufactured and sold under a number of different trademarks. They were: Bacon, Bonanza, Conqueror, Express, Gem, Governor, Guardian, and Little Giant. Collector interest is low, and values for all trademarks are quite similar.

Courtesy Milwaukee Public Museum, Milwaukee, Wisconsin

Exc.	V.G.	Good	Fair	Poor
—	300	150	100	75

BAER CUSTOM, LES
Hillsdale, Ilinois
This long standing 1911 pistolsmith is now producing custom quality 1911 pistols on a semi-production basis. Each pistol features a large number of custom characteristics such as forged steel frame and full slide recoil rod, double serrated slide, beveled magazine well, checkered front strap, beavertail safety, extended magazine release button, Bo-Mar sights, and many others depending on the specific model.

COMPETITION PISTOLS

Baer 1911 Ultimate Master Combat Pistol-Compensated
Chambered for the .45 ACP and fitted with a triple port, tapered cone compensator.

NIB	Exc.	V.G.	Good	Fair	Poor
2300	1750	1000	750	600	300

Baer 1911 Ultimate Master Steel Special
Designed for steel targets and Bianchi style competition this model is similar to above but designed for light loads. Chambered for .38 Super. Hard Chrome finish.

NIB	Exc.	V.G.	Good	Fair	Poor
2900	2250	1500	950	750	350

Baer 1911 Ultimate Master Combat Pistol
Similar to the other Baer Master series pistols this model is offered in .45 ACP, .400 COR-BON, and .38 Super. It is fitted with a large number of special features.Offered in a 5" or 6" version. The 5" version is also offered in 9x23 caliber.

6" Model

NIB	Exc.	V.G.	Good	Fair	Poor
2400	1900	1300	850	650	350

5" Model

NIB	Exc.	V.G.	Good	Fair	Poor
2500	1800	1200	800	600	350

Baer 1911 Ultimate Master Para

Designed for IPSC competition and offered either in Unlimited version with compensator and scope or Limited version with iron sights and no compensator.

Unlimited Model-.45ACP, .38 Super, 9x23

NIB	Exc.	V.G.	Good	Fair	Poor
3200	2500	1750	1200	850	400

Limited Model-.45ACP, .38 Super, 9x23

NIB	Exc.	V.G.	Good	Fair	Poor
2700	2000	1500	900	650	300

Baer 1911 IPSC Action Pistol

Chambered for .45ACP with blued slide and frame.

NIB	Exc.	V.G.	Good	Fair	Poor
1500	1150	850	600	450	300

Baer 1911 Nationale Match Hardball Pistol

Designed for DCM matches. Chambered for .45 ACP.

NIB	Exc.	V.G.	Good	Fair	Poor
1225	900	700	500	400	200

Baer 1911 Bullseye Wadcutter Pistol

Designed for use with wadcutter loads only. Chambered for .45 ACP.

NIB	Exc.	V.G.	Good	Fair	Poor
1500	1100	800	600	500	250

NOTE: This version is also offered with a Baer Optical mount. Add $125 for this option. For a 6" slide with LoMount BoMars sight add $200.

Baer 1911 Target Master

Designed for NRA centerfire matches. Chambered for .45ACP.

NIB	Exc.	V.G.	Good	Fair	Poor
1250	1000	750	550	450	250

Baer 1911 P.P.C. Distinguished Match

Introduced in 1999 this pistol features a 5" barrel with an adjustable Aristrocrat rear sight. Many, many special features such as double serrated slide lowered and flared ejection port extended ambi safety, checkered front strap, etc. Offered in .45ACP, and 9mm with supported chamber. Blued finish and one magazine.

NIB	Exc.	V.G.	Good	Fair	Poor
1600	1300	—	—	—	—

NOTE: Add approximately $300 for 9mm model.

Baer 1911 P.P.C. Open Class
Similar to the model above but fitted with a 6" barrel and slide. Chambered for .45ACP, and 9mm with supported chamber. Blued finish. Introduced in 1999.

NIB	Exc.	V.G.	Good	Fair	Poor
1700	1350	—	—	—	—

NOTE: Add approximately $300 for 9mm model.

DUTY & DEFENSE PISTOLS

Baer 1911 Premier II
Designed as a duty or defense pistol this model is chambered for the .45 ACP, .400 COR-BON, and 9x23 cartridges. Fitted with a 5" slide.

NIB	Exc.	V.G.	Good	Fair	Poor
1425	1150	900	600	450	250

NOTE: For stainless steel version add $150 to above prices. Add $100 for .400 COR-BON and $250 for 9x23.

Baer 1911 Premier II-6" barrel
Same as above but fitted with a 6" match grade barrel.

NIB	Exc.	V.G.	Good	Fair	Poor
1700	1400	1100	900	700	350

NOTE: Add $100 for .400 COR-BON and $300 for .38 Super. 9x23 not offered with 6" slide.

Baer 1911 Premier II-Light Weight (LW1)
Has the same features as the standard Premier II but with reduced weight aluminum frame. Furnished with low mount LCB adjustable rear sight. Offered in .45ACP only.

NIB	Exc.	V.G.	Good	Fair	Poor
1700	1400	1100	900	700	350

Baer 1911 Premier II-Light Weight (LW2)
Same as above but with fixed combat style rear sight.

NIB	Exc.	V.G.	Good	Fair	Poor
1700	1400	1100	900	700	350

Baer 1911 Premier II Super-Tac
Similar to the standard Premier II models but with low mount adjustable rear night sight and front sight. Special BEAR COAT finish. Offered in .45ACP, .40S&W, .400 Cor-Bon.

NIB	Exc.	V.G.	Good	Fair	Poor
1900	1500	1200	900	700	350

NOTE: Dual caliber .45ACP/.400 Cor-Bon combo add $200.

Baer 1911 Custom Carry-Commanche Length

Chambered for .45ACP this model has several options including 4-1/2" barrel, stainless steel slide and frame, lightweight aluminum frame with blued steel slide. As of 2000 this model is furnished with night sights.

NIB	Exc.	V.G.	Good	Fair	Poor
1640	1200	950	600	450	250

NOTE: For stainless steel add $40. For lightweight frame add $130.

Baer Custom Carry-5"

Same as above but offered with 5" slide. Not offered in aluminum frame.

NIB	Exc.	V.G.	Good	Fair	Poor
1600	1200	950	600	450	250

NOTE: Add $40 for stainless steel.

Baer 1911 Thunder Ranch Special

This model features a steel frame and slide with front and rear serrations. Deluxe fixed rear sight with tritium insert. Checkered front strap. Numerous special features. Slim line grips with Thunder Ranch logo. Seven round magazine standard. Special serial numbers with "TR" prefix. Offered in .45ACP.

NIB	Exc.	V.G.	Good	Fair	Poor
1600	1200	950	600	450	250

Baer 1911 Thunder Ranch Special Engraved Model

As above but with engraved frame and slide.

NIB	Exc.	V.G.	Good	Fair	Poor
6000	4750	—	—	—	—

Baer 1911 Prowler III

Similar to the Premier II but with a tapered cone stub weight, a full length guide rod, and a reverse plug. Special order only.

NIB	Exc.	V.G.	Good	Fair	Poor
1800	1500	1200	950	700	350

Baer 1911 Prowler IV

Chambered for .45 ACP or .38 Super this model is built on a Para-Ordnance oversize frame. Fitted with a 5" slide. Special order only.

NIB	Exc.	V.G.	Good	Fair	Poor
2300	1750	1250	900	650	300

NOTE: For optional 6" barrel and slide add $300.

Baer S.R.P. (Swift Response Pistol)

Chambered for .45ACP and built on a Para-Ordnance frame this unit is similar to the one supplied to the FBI. Supplied with wooden presentation box.

NIB	Exc.	V.G.	Good	Fair	Poor
2800	2350	1750	1200	850	400

NOTE: For S.R.P. models built on a Baer frame or shorter 4-1/2" frame subtract $300 from NIB through Fair prices.

Baer 1911 Monolith

Introduced in 1999 this model features a 5" barrel and slide with extra long dust cover. Chambered in .45ACP, .400 COR-BON, .40S&W, 9x23, 9mm, or .38 Super all with supported chamber. Many special features such as BoMar sights, Commander style hammer, speed trigger, etc. Blued finish with 1 magazine. Weight is approximately 37 oz.

NIB	Exc.	V.G.	Good	Fair	Poor
1650	1300	—	—	—	—

NOTE: For all other supported calibers add $250.

Baer 1911 Monolith Heavyweight

Introduced in 1999 this model is similar to the Monolith but with the addition of a heavier frame that adds 3.5 oz. Same calibers as available on the Monolith. Weight is approximately 40 oz.

NIB	Exc.	V.G.	Good	Fair	Poor
1650	1300	—	—	—	—

NOTE: For all other supported calibers add $200.

Baer 1911 Monolith Tactical Illuminator

This model, introduced in 1999, has the same features as the Monolith Heavyweight above but with the addition of light mounted under the dust cover. Offered in .45ACP and .40S&W with supported chamber. Weight with light is approximately 44 oz.

NIB	Exc.	V.G.	Good	Fair	Poor
1850	1500	—	—	—	—

NOTE: For all other supported calibers add $275.

Baer 1911 Monolith Commanche

Fitted with a 4.25" slide and a dust cover that covers the length of the slide. Has all the features of the standard Monolith. Comes with night sights and a deluxe fixed rear sight. Edges rounded for tactical carry. Chambered in .45ACP only. Introduced in 2001.

NIB	Exc.	V.G.	Good	Fair	Poor
1600	1250	—	—	—	—

Baer 1911 Monolith Heavyweight

Exactly as above but with thicker dust cover to add an additional 2 oz. of weight. Introduced in 2001.

NIB	Exc.	V.G.	Good	Fair	Poor
1650	1275	—	—	—	—

Baer 1911 Stinger

This model features a shorter Officer's grip frame and Commanche slide and barrel. Many special features. Offered in .45ACP. Choice of aluminum frame with blued slide, aluminum frame with stainless steel slide and stainless steel frame and slide. Weight in aluminum is about 28 oz., with stainless steel about 34 oz. Introduced in 1999.

NIB	Exc.	V.G.	Good	Fair	Poor
1500	1200	—	—	—	—

NOTE: For aluminum frame and blued slide with supported calibers add $300. For aluminum frame with stainless slide and supported chamber add $340. For stainless frame and slide with supported chamber add $140.

Baer 1911 Stinger Stainless

Same as above but with stainless steel frame and slide. Introduced in 2001.

NIB	Exc.	V.G.	Good	Fair	Poor
1500	1200	—	—	—	—

NEW CONCEPTS PISTOLS

This line of 1911 pistols offers custom features at a slightly lower cost. Each succeeding grade offers a few more features.

Baer 1911 Concept I

Chambered for .45 ACP and fitted with BoMar sights.

NIB	Exc.	V.G.	Good	Fair	Poor
1400	1150	900	750	550	300

Baer 1911 Concept II

Same as above but fitted with Baer adjustable sights.

NIB	Exc.	V.G.	Good	Fair	Poor
1400	1150	900	750	550	300

Baer 1911 Concept III

Same as above but with stainless steel frame with blued steel slide with BoMar sights.

NIB	Exc.	V.G.	Good	Fair	Poor
1520	1250	950	800	550	300

Baer 1911 Concept IV

Same as above but with Baer adjustable sights.

NIB	Exc.	V.G.	Good	Fair	Poor
1500	1250	950	800	550	300

Baer 1911 Concept V

This model has both stainless steel slide and frame with BoMar sights.

NIB	Exc.	V.G.	Good	Fair	Poor
1550	1350	1000	850	600	300

Baer 1911 Concept V 6"

This model is identical to the Concept V with the addition of a 6" barrel and slide. Introduced in 1999.

NIB	Exc.	V.G.	Good	Fair	Poor
1700	1350	—	—	—	—

Baer 1911 Concept VI

Same as above but fitted with Baer adjustable sights.

NIB	Exc.	V.G.	Good	Fair	Poor
1550	1350	975	850	600	300

Baer 1911 Concept VI L.W.

Same as above but built on aluminum frame with supported chamber and Nation match barrel.

NIB	Exc.	V.G.	Good	Fair	Poor
1750	1400	1000	—	—	—

Baer 1911 Concept VII

Features all blued 4-1/2" steel frame and slide with Baer adjustable fixed night sights.

NIB	Exc.	V.G.	Good	Fair	Poor
1500	1250	950	800	550	300

Baer 1911 Concept VIII

Same as above but with stainless steel slide and frame. Fixed combat night sights standard.

NIB	Exc.	V.G.	Good	Fair	Poor
1550	1350	1000	850	600	300

Baer 1911 Concept IX

This version has a lightweight aluminum frame with 4-1/2" steel slide.

NIB	Exc.	V.G.	Good	Fair	Poor
1600	1350	1000	850	600	300

Baer 1911 Concept X

This model features a 4-1/2" stainless steel slide with a lightweight aluminum frame.

NIB	Exc.	V.G.	Good	Fair	Poor
1600	1350	1000	850	600	300

Baer Lightweight .22 caliber 1911 Models

4-1/2" Model with fixed sights

NIB	Exc.	V.G.	Good	Fair	Poor
1425	1200	950	800	550	300

5" Model with fixed sights

NIB	Exc.	V.G.	Good	Fair	Poor
1425	1200	950	800	550	300

5" Model with Bo-Mar sights

NIB	Exc.	V.G.	Good	Fair	Poor
1500	1275	1000	850	600	300

Baer Limited Edition Presentation Grade 1911.

A fully hand engraved Baer 1911 with special bluing in presentation wooden box.

NIB	Exc.	V.G.	Good	Fair	Poor
6000	—	—	—	—	—

RIFLES

AR .223 Super Varmint

Fitted with a choice of 18", 20", or 24" heavy barrels with 1-in-12 twist. Flat top rail. Choice of single or two-stage trigger. Aluminum free floating handguard. Bear Coat finish. Introduced in 2000.

NIB	Exc.	V.G.	Good	Fair	Poor
1975	1600	—	—	—	—

AR .223 M4-A2 Flat

This model features a flat top rail and match bolt and carrier. The 16" barrel has a integral compensator. Single stage trigger. Knights Armament Systems rail adapter. Bear Coat finish. Introduced in 2000.

NIB	Exc.	V.G.	Good	Fair	Poor
2175	1700	—	—	—	—

AR .223 IPSC Action Model

Similar to the model above but with 18" Super Match heavy barrel with integral compensator. Introduced in 2000.

NIB	Exc.	V.G.	Good	Fair	Poor
2175	1700	—	—	—	—

Bullpup Muzzleloader

This .50 caliber muzzleloader is fitted with a 28" stainless steel barrel with a Williams front sight and M16 National Match rear sight. Maple or synthetic stock. Internal ignition system.

NIB	Exc.	V.G.	Good	Fair	Poor
320	250	—	—	—	—

NOTE: Add $30 for maple stock and stainless steel.

BAFORD, ARMS, INC.
Bristol, Tennessee
C.L. Reedy & Assoc.-Distributors
Melbourne, Florida

Thunder Derringer

A .410 bore or .44 Special single shot pistol with 3" interchangeable barrels and a spur trigger. Additional interchangeable barrels are chambered in calibers from .22 to 9mm. Also available with a scope. Blued with a walnut grip. Introduced in 1988.

NIB	Exc.	V.G.	Good	Fair	Poor
150	100	85	70	55	35

NOTE: Add $100 for interchangeable barrel.

Fire Power Model 35

A 9mm semiautomatic pistol with a 4.75" barrel, Millett adjustable sights and 14-shot magazine. Fitted with a combat safety and hammer, and Pachmayr grips. Stainless steel. Introduced in 1988.

NIB	Exc.	V.G.	Good	Fair	Poor
475	425	350	300	250	125

BAIKAL
Russia

Baikal IJ-27E1C

A 12 or 20 gauge Magnum O/U shotgun with 26" skeet-skeet or 28" modified-full ventilated rib barrels, single selective trigger and extractors. Blued with a walnut stock.

Mfg. List Price
$449.95

NIB	Exc.	V.G.	Good	Fair	Poor
350	275	200	150	100	75

Baikal TOZ - 34

A 12 or 28 gauge double-barrel shotgun with 26" or 28" barrels, double triggers, cocking indicators and extractors. Blued with a checkered walnut stock. This model was also available with a silver-plated receiver.

Mfg. List Price
$465.95

NIB	Exc.	V.G.	Good	Fair	Poor
375	300	250	200	100	75

Model MC-8-0

A 12 gauge double barrel shotgun with 26" skeet-skeet or 28" full-modified barrels, hand fitted action and engraved receiver.

Mfg. List Price
$2,295.00

NIB	Exc.	V.G.	Good	Fair	Poor
1800	1250	950	700	500	250

Model MC-5-105

The Model TOZ-34 with an engraved receiver.

Mfg. List Price
$1,325.00

NIB	Exc.	V.G.	Good	Fair	Poor
1050	850	700	500	300	150

Model MC-7

As above, with a relief engraved receiver.

Mfg. List Price
$2,695.00

NIB	Exc.	V.G.	Good	Fair	Poor
2100	1750	1200	800	550	250

Model MC-109

A custom made O/U shotgun with detachable sidelocks. Produced in limited quantities and most often to the purchaser's specifications.

Mfg. List Price
$3,695.00

NIB	Exc.	V.G.	Good	Fair	Poor
2850	2000	1500	950	600	300

CURRENTLY IMPORTED
BAIKAL SHOTGUNS
Importer-European American Armory

IZH-43K

Introduced in 1999 this is a 12 gauge 3" side by side hammer gun with choice of barrel lengths of 18.5", 20", 24", 26", and 28". Single selective trigger or double trigger. Engraved side plates. Walnut stock with pistol grip. Weight is about 7.3 lbs.

NIB	Exc.	V.G.	Good	Fair	Poor
375	300	250	—	—	—

NOTE: Deduct $40 for double triggers.

MP-213 Coach Gun

Similar to the above model but with internal hammers. Single or double triggers. Weight is about 7 lbs.

NIB	Exc.	V.G.	Good	Fair	Poor
275	255	175	—	—	—

NOTE: Deduct $40 for double triggers. Add $80 for 20 gauge.

IZH-43

This side by side gun is available in 12, 16, 20, 28, and .410 bore. In barrel lengths for 20" to 28" depending on gauge. Internal hammers. Single selective trigger, ejectors. Walnut stock.

NIB	Exc.	V.G.	Good	Fair	Poor
350	275	200	—	—	—

NOTE: Add $80 for 28 gauge and .410 bore guns.

IZH-43K

Same as the model above but with external hammers. In 12 gauge only.

NIB	Exc.	V.G.	Good	Fair	Poor
425	350	275	—	—	—

IZH-18

This is a single barrel shotgun chambered for 12, 20, or .410 bore. Choice of 26.5" or 29.5" barrels. Hardwood stock. Ejectors. Introduced in 1999.

NIB	Exc.	V.G.	Good	Fair	Poor
95	75	50	—	—	—

IZK-18MAX

Similar to the above model but with polished nickel receiver, vent rib, walnut stock, screw-in chokes, and ejectors. Offered in 12 and 20 gauge as well as .410 bore.

NIB	Exc.	V.G.	Good	Fair	Poor
170	125	100	—	—	—

IZH-27

This is an over/under gun chambered for 12, 20, 28, and .410 bore. Choice of 26.5" or 28.5" barrels. Walnut stock. Single trigger with ejectors. Fixed chokes.

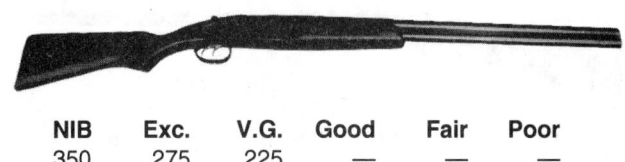

NIB	Exc.	V.G.	Good	Fair	Poor
350	275	225	—	—	—

NOTE: Add $35 for screw-in chokes. Add $85 for 28 gauge and .410 bore guns.

MP-233

This over/under gun is chambered for the 12 gauge 3" shell with a choice of 26", 28", or 30" barrels. Walnut checkered stock. Single or double triggers. Screw-in chokes. Removable trigger assembly. Weight is about 7.3 lbs. Introduced in 1999.

NIB	Exc.	V.G.	Good	Fair	Poor
700	550	—	—	—	—

IZH-94

This is an over/under combination gun with a 12 gauge upper barrel and centerfire rifle barrel on the under barrel. Barrel length is 24" or 26". This model is offered as an over/under rifle in calibers from .222 to .30-06. Walnut stock single or double trigger. Weight is about 7.3 lbs. Open sights.

NIB	Exc.	V.G.	Good	Fair	Poor
600	475	—	—	—	—

IZH-81

This is a pump action shotgun chambered for 12 gauge 3" shells. Barrel lengths are a choice of 20", 26", or 28". Five round detachable magazine. Walnut stock.

NIB	Exc.	V.G.	Good	Fair	Poor
250	200	—	—	—	—

NOTE: Add $60 for vent rib.

MP-131K

This is a pump action shotgun with a choice of two different feeding sources: a tubular magazine or a detachable 3-round or 5-round box magazine.

NIB	Exc.	V.G.	Good	Fair	Poor
350	275	225	—	—	—

MP-133

This is a slide action shotgun chambered for the 12 gauge 3.5" shell. Available with barrel lengths of 20", 24", 26", or 28". Vent rib or all barrel lengths except 20". Walnut stock. Choke tubes for all barrel lengths except 20" (cylinder choke). Introduced in 2001.

NIB	Exc.	V.G.	Good	Fair	Poor
275	225	—	—	—	—

MP-153

This is a semiautomatic shotgun chambered for 12 gauge 3" shell. Choice of 26" or 28" barrels. Choice of walnut or black synthetic stock. Weight is about 7.8 lbs. Screw-in chokes. Introduced in 1999.

NIB	Exc.	V.G.	Good	Fair	Poor
300	250	—	—	—	—

IZH 35

This is a semiautomatic pistol chambered for the .22 Long Rifle cartridge. Fully adjustable target grip, adjustable trigger assembly, cocking indicator, detachable scope. Fitted with a 6" barrel. Introduced in 2000.

NIB	Exc.	V.G.	Good	Fair	Poor
500	400	350	—	—	—

BAILONS GUNMAKERS, LTD.
Birmingham, England

Most of the products of this company are produced strictly on custom order.

Hunting Rifle

A bolt-action sporting rifle produced in a variety of calibers with a 24" barrel having open sights, double-set triggers and a 3- or 4-shot magazine. Blued with a well figured walnut stock. The values listed below are for a standard grade rifle.

NIB	Exc.	V.G.	Good	Fair	Poor
2250	1700	1250	900	600	300

BAKER GAS SEAL
London, England

A .577 caliber percussion revolver with a 6.5" octagonal barrel and 6-shot cylinder. When the hammer is cocked, the cylinder is forced forward tightly against the barrel breech, thus creating a gas seal. Blued, case hardened with walnut grips.

Exc.	V.G.	Good	Fair	Poor
1200	700	600	475	250

BAKER GUN & FORGING CO.
Batavia, New York

The Baker Gun & Forging Company was founded in early 1890, by Elias Baker, brother of William Baker (see below). Made from drop forged parts, Baker single and double barrel shotguns quickly gained a reputation for strength and reliability among shooters of the period. Offered in a wide variety of grades, from plain utilitarian to heavily embellished models, Baker shotguns have in recent years become highly collectable. The company was sold on December 24, 1919, to H. & D. Folsom Arms Company of Norwich, Connecticut. The Folsom company had for almost 20 years been the Baker company's sole New York City agent and had marketed at least one Baker model that was only made for them. From 1919 to approximately 1923, Folsom continued to assemble and make Baker shotguns. Late model Bakers were made by the Crescent Firearms Company and have serial numbers with an "F" suffix.

The Baker Gun & Forging Company was the first American arms manufacturer to:

1. Make a single barrel trap shotgun.

2. Make a single barrel trap shotgun with a ventilated rib.

3. Make arms with an intercepting firing pin block safety.

4. Make a double barrel shotgun with hammers directly behind the firing pins.

5. Use a long swinging sear that once adjusted gave consistent trigger pull throughout the working life of an arm.

Those Baker shotguns manufactured between 1913 and 1923 that were engraved by Rudolph J. Kornbrath command substantial price premiums over the values listed below. Prospective purchasers of Kornbrath decorated Bakers are advised to secure a qualified appraisal prior to acquisition.

Baker Trap Gun

A 12, gauge single barrel boxlock shotgun with either a 30" or 32" barrel. Blued, case hardened with a walnut stock.

Exc.	V.G.	Good	Fair	Poor
1500	1250	900	500	250

Elite Grade (standard scrollwork and simple game scenes engraved on receiver)

"ELITE" GRADE

Exc.	V.G.	Good	Fair	Poor
2000	1500	1000	500	250

Superba (heavily engraved on receiver and sides of barrel breech)

Exc.	V.G.	Good	Fair	Poor
4000	3000	1500	750	500

Black Beauty Double Shotgun

Made solely for H. & D. Folsom Arms Company. A 12 or 16 gauge double barrel shotgun with sidelocks and 26", 28", 30", or 32" barrels in 12 gauge and 26", 28", or 30" barrels in 16 gauge. the barrels blued, the receiver case hardened and the sideplates finished with black oxide and the stock of walnut. Automatic ejectors and single trigger extra cost options.

Exc.	V.G.	Good	Fair	Poor
850	750	650	500	250

Grade S Double Shotgun

As above, with simple engraving.

Exc.	V.G.	Good	Fair	Poor
1200	1000	750	400	250

Grade R Double Shotgun

As above, with case hardened sideplates and engraved with simple scrollwork as well as game scenes.

Exc.	V.G.	Good	Fair	Poor
1500	1250	900	500	300

Paragon Grade Shotgun

As above, with finely cut scrollwork and detailed game scenes engraved on the sideplates. The stock of finely figured walnut.

Exc.	V.G.	Good	Fair	Poor
2000	1750	1200	900	500

Paragon Grade - Model NN

As above, but more finely engraved. Built on special order only. Automatic ejectors.

Exc.	V.G.	Good	Fair	Poor
3000	2250	1400	900	500

Expert Grade Double Shotgun

The highest grade shotgun manufactured by the Baker Gun & Forging Company. General specifications as above. The stock of imported English or French walnut. The engraving of full coverage type and partially chiselled. Automatic ejectors and single trigger if requested. Built on special order only.

Exc.	V.G.	Good	Fair	Poor
5000	4000	2000	1500	750

Deluxe Grade Double Shotgun

The designation given those Expert Grade shotguns produced by H. & D. Folsom from 1919 to 1923. Characteristics and values identical to those listed for the Baker Expert grade Double Shotgun.

Batavia Special

A 12 or 16 gauge double barrel shotgun with sidelocks and 28", 30", or 32" barrels in 12 gauge and 28" or 30" barrels in 16 gauge. Blue, case hardened with a walnut stock and double triggers.

Exc.	V.G.	Good	Fair	Poor
500	325	275	225	175

Batavia Brush Gun

A 12 or 16 gauge double barrel shotgun with sidelocks and 26" barrels. Blue, case hardened with walnut stock. Sling rings and swivels optional.

Exc.	V.G.	Good	Fair	Poor
400	325	275	225	175

Batavia Leader

A 12 or 16 gauge double barrel shotgun with sidelocks and 26", 28", 30", or 32" barrels in 12 gauge and 26", 28", or 30" barrels in 16 gauge. Blue, case hardened with a walnut stock and double triggers.

Exc.	V.G.	Good	Fair	Poor
500	425	375	325	275

Batavia Damascus

As above with Damascus barrels.

Exc.	V.G.	Good	Fair	Poor
400	325	275	225	175

Baker Hammer Gun

A 10, 12, or 16 gauge double barrel shotgun with sidehammers and 30" and 32" barrels in 10 gauge, 26" to 32" barrels in 12 gauge and 26" to 30" barrels in 16 gauge. Browned, case hardened with walnut stock and double triggers.

Exc.	V.G.	Good	Fair	Poor
300	250	175	125	100

Batavia Automatic Rifle

A .22 caliber semiautomatic rifle with a 24" round barrel and a detachable 7-shot magazine. Blue with a walnut stock.

Exc.	V.G.	Good	Fair	Poor
400	300	200	100	50

BAKER, WILLIAM
Marathon, Syracuse and Ithaca, New York

William Baker designed and built double barrel shotguns from approximately 1869 until his death in 1889. His hammerless designs were used by the Baker Gun & Forging Company of Batavia, New York, which was established by his brother Elias in early 1890.

BAKER, M.A.
Fayetteville, North Carolina

In business from 1857 through 1862, Baker produced sporting arms prior to the Civil War. During the Civil War Baker altered muskets and "common rifles." In addition, it is thought that Baker made rifles for the State of North Carolina with lockplates stamped M.A. BAKER/FAYETTEVILLE/N.C. These rifles resembled the U.S. Model 1841 Rifle and had the following characteristics: Overall length 51-1/2"; Barrel length 35-1/8"; Caliber .50. Number made in excess of 65. Prospective purchasers are strongly advised to secure a qualified appraisal prior to acquisition.

Exc.	V.G.	Good	Fair	Poor
—	—	25000	12500	2500

BAKER, THOMAS

Baker shotguns and rifles were extensively imported into the United States during the nineteenth and early twentieth centuries. As these arms are often marked with his address, the following list of the London premises he occupied should prove useful.

1 Stonecutter Street	1838-1844
Bury Street, St. James's	1844-1850
34 St. James's Street	1850
88 Fleet Street	1851-1881
88 Fleet Street & 21 Cockspur Street	1882-1898
88 Fleet Street & 29 Glasshouse Street	1899-1905
29 Glasshouse Street	1905-1915
64 Haymarket	1915

BALL REPEATING CARBINE
Lamson & Co.
Windsor, Vermont

Ball Repeating Carbine

A .50 caliber lever-action repeating carbine with a 20.5" round barrel and 7-shot magazine. The receiver is marked "E.G. Lamson & Co./Windsor, Vt./U.S./Ball's Patent/June 23, 1863/Mar. 15, 1864." Blued, case hardened with a walnut stock. Late production examples of this carbine have been noted with browned or bright barrels. In excess of 1,500 were made between 1864 and 1867.

Courtesy Milwaukee Public Museum, Milwaukee, Wisconsin

Exc.	V.G.	Good	Fair	Poor
—	5000	2500	900	400

BALLARD PATENT ARMS
(until 1873; after 1875, see MARLIN)

On Nov. 5, 1861, C.H. Ballard of Worcester, Massachusetts, received a patent for a breechloading mechanism that would remain in production for nearly thirty years. Ballard patented a breechblock that tilted down at its front to expose the breech by activating the lever/triggerguard. During the twelve years that followed, Ballard rifles, carbines, and shotguns were produced by five interrelated companies. Four of these were successive: Ball & Williams, R. Ball & Co. (both of Worcester, Massachusetts), Merrimack Arms & Manufacturing Co. and Brown Manufacturing Company (both of Newburyport, Massachusetts). These four companies produced Ballard arms in a successive serial range (1 through approximately 22,000), all marked upon the top of the frame and the top of the barrel where it joins the frame. In 1863, another company, Dwight, Chapin & Company of Bridgeport, Connecticut also produced Ballard rifles and carbines in a larger frame size, but in a different serial range (1 through about 1,900), usually marked on the left side of the frame below the agents' mark. The large frame carbines and rifles were produced to fulfill a U.S. War Department contract initially for 10,000 of each, subsequently reduced to 1,000 of each, issued to Merwin & Bray, the sole agents for the Ballard patent arms between 1862 and 1866. Most of the production during this period concentrated on military contracts, either for the U.S. War Department or the state of Kentucky, although the state of New York also purchased 500 for its state militia.

Ballard (Ball & Williams) sporting rifles, first type.
(Serial numbers 1-100)

Barrel length 24"; caliber .38 rimfire. Markings: BALL & WILLIAMS/Worcester, Mass., and BALLARD'S PATENT/Nov. 5, 1861 on octagonal barrel. The distinctive feature of the earliest production of the Ballard rifles is the presence of an internal extractor conforming to the patent specifications. After approximately 100 rifles, this feature was dropped in favor of a manual extractor located under the barrel.

Courtesy Milwaukee Public Museum, Milwaukee, Wisconsin

Exc.	V.G.	Good	Fair	Poor
—	—	2000	1100	450

Ballard (Ball & Williams) sporting rifles, second type.
(Serial numbers 200-1600, and 1600 through 14,000, interspersed with martial production)

Barrel length 24", 28", or 30", usually octagonal, but part round/part-octagonal as well; calibers .32, .38, and .44 rimfire. Markings: BALL & WILLIAMS/Worcester, Mass., BALLARD'S PATENT/Nov. 5, 1861, and MERWIN & BRAY, AGT'S/ NEW YORK, on facets of barrel until about serial no. 9000, thereafter the patent name and date on the right side of the frame and the manufacturer and agents on the left side of the frame. On early production (200 to 1500), the extractor knob is smaller and crescent shaped. Early production (prior to about serial no. 10,000) have solid breechblocks; after that number breechblocks are made in two halves. A few of these arms were made with bronze frames to facilitate engraving and plating. These should command a higher premium.

Exc.	V.G.	Good	Fair	Poor
—	—	1000	500	200

Ballard (Ball & Williams) sporting rifles, third type.
(Serial numbers 14,000 to 15,000)

These arms are essentially the same as the second type in characteristics but have Merwin & Bray's alternate percussion mechanism built into the breechblock. The hammer is accordingly marked on the left side "PATENTED JAN. 5, 1864."

Exc.	V.G.	Good	Fair	Poor
—	—	1000	500	200

Ballard (Ball & Williams) military carbines. (Serial numbers 1500 through 7500, and 8500 through 10,500)

Overall length 37-1/4"; barrel (bore) length 22"; caliber .44 rimfire. Markings: same as Ballard/Ball & Williams sporting rifles, second type. Additional marks on U.S. War Department purchases include inspector's initials "MM" or "GH" on left side of frame, and "MM" on barrel, breechblock, buttplate, and on left side of buttstock in script within an oval cartouche. Three thousand of the earlier production (serial numbers 1700 through about 5000) of these carbines were sold to the state of Kentucky under an August 1862 contract, extended in April 1863. In November 1863, Kentucky contracted for an additional 1,000 carbines. In the interim, the state of New York purchased 500 for distribution to its militia. The U.S. War Department ordered 5,000 under a contract signed in January of 1864, but Ball & Williams delivered only 1,500 (serial numbers noted in range of 9800 through 10,600) while concentrating production on their more lucrative Kentucky contract. Another 600 of the federal contract were partially inspected (serial numbers about 6500 to 7100-MM in cartouche in stock only) but were rejected because the barrels had been rifled prior to proofing; these were sold to Kentucky in September 1864 on an open market purchase. The carbines marked with federal inspection marks usually bring a premium.

Courtesy Milwaukee Public Museum, Milwaukee, Wisconsin

Exc.	V.G.	Good	Fair	Poor
—	—	3500	1000	400

Ballard (Ball & Williams) "Kentucky" half-stock rifles

Overall length 45-3/8"; barrel (bore) length 30"; caliber .44 rimfire. These half-stock rifles bear the standard Ball & Williams markings upon their barrels and in addition have the state ownership mark ("KENTUCKY") on the barrel forward of the rear sights. A total of 1,000 (serial numbers about 7100 through 8550) were contracted for by Kentucky in November 1863 and delivered between January and April 1864.

Courtesy Milwaukee Public Museum, Milwaukee, Wisconsin

Exc.	V.G.	Good	Fair	Poor
—	—	1250	700	300

Ballard (Ball & Williams) "Kentucky" full stock rifles

Overall length 45-1/4"; barrel (bore) length 30"; caliber .46 rimfire. Marked on the frame with standard Ball & Williams manufacturer (left), agent (left), and patent (right) markings, these rifles are additionally distinguished by the state ownership mark "KENTUCKY" stamped into the top of the frame near the breech. Kentucky contracted for 3,000 of these arms in November 1863, initially in .56 caliber. However, by mutual consent of the state and the contractors, in February 1864 the caliber of the arms was changed to .46. All deliveries were made in this caliber, beginning in July 1864 and continuing until March 1865 (serial numbers 10,400 to 14,500).

Courtesy Milwaukee Public Museum, Milwaukee, Wisconsin

Exc.	V.G.	Good	Fair	Poor
—	—	1100	500	250

Ballard (Dwight, Chapin & Co.) carbines

Overall length 37-3/4"; barrel (bore) length 22"; caliber .56 rimfire. Markings: On left side of round-topped frame "BALLARD'S PATENT/NOV. 5 1861"; on right side of frame "DWIGHT, CHAPIN & CO./BRIDGEPORT CONN." (through serial no. about 125, deleted after that number) over "MERWIN & BRAY/AGT'S N.Y." over serial no. Inspection letters "D" frequently appear on carbines with the Dwight, Chapin, & Co. markings, indicative of preliminary inspection by E. M. Dustin, of the U.S. Ordnance Department.

Often mistaken as early Ballard production from a fictitious Fall River, Massachusetts factory, these carbines and their complementing rifles were in fact not placed into production until 1863, as evident by the split, two-piece breechblocks. Both carbines and rifles originated from a contract entered into between the U.S. War Department and Merwin & Bray in October 1862 for 10,000 of each arm, subsequently reduced to 1,000 of each by the Commission on Ordnance and Ordnance Stores. Because Ball & Williams facilities were tied up with Kentucky contracts, Merwin & Bray turned to the small parts maker of Dwight, Chapin & Co. in Bridgeport, Connecticut. Although they tooled for production, they fell short of scheduled delivery dates, and although about 100 carbines had been inspected, no deliveries were accepted (due to caliber problems) by the U.S. government, effectively bankrupting Dwight, Chapin & Co. The completed carbines and unfinished parts were sent to Worcester and assembled by Ball & Williams, and Merwin & Bray sold all 1,000 carbines in Kentucky in April 1864 on an open market purchase.

Courtesy Milwaukee Public Museum, Milwaukee, Wisconsin

Exc.	V.G.	Good	Fair	Poor
—	—	1500	650	275

Ballard (Dwight, Chapin & Co.) full-stock rifle

Overall length 53"; barrel (bore) length 30"; caliber .56 rimfire. Markings: same as Dwight, Chapin & Co. carbines, but none found with "DWIGHT, CHAPIN & CO./BRIDGEPORT, CONN." stamping above agents marks. The history of these rifles is the same as the .56 caliber carbines, with serial numbers interspersed in the production of the carbines (1 through 1850). Evidently only about 650 of the rifles were completed of the 1,000 set up. Of these, 35 were sold to a U.S. agent in Flor-

ida in February 1864 and 600 to Kentucky in April 1864 with the 1,000 carbines.

Exc.	V.G.	Good	Fair	Poor
—	—	1250	500	250

Ballard (R. Ball) & Co. sporting rifles

Overall length varies according to barrel length; barrel (bore) length usually 24", 28", and 30"; calibers .32, .38, .44, and .46 rimfire. Markings: The frame markings of R. Ball & Co. rifles are similar to Ball & Williams production, only eliminating the Ball & Williams marking on the left side. Cartridge size, e.g. "No. 44", usually also stamped upon the top of the barrel or frame. Merwin & Bray's patented alternate ignition device usually present with left side of hammer usually marked "PATENTED JAN. 5, 1864." Serial numbers (which follow in sequence with Ball & Williams production. i.e. after no. about 15,800) appear on top of barrel and top of frame. After William Williams withdrew from the Ball & Williams partnership in mid-1865, the business continued under the name of R. Ball & Co., with Richard Ball's son-in-law, E.J. Halstead, in charge after the former's paralytic stroke in the fall of 1865.

Ballard (R. Ball) & Co. carbines

Overall length 37-1/4"; barrel (bore) length 22" caliber .44 rimfire. Markings: same as R. Ball & Co. sporting rifles; "No. 44" on top of frame near breech. Although firm evidence is elusive, approximately 1,000 of these carbines were manufactured in anticipation of a Canadian contract, which never came to fruition. Serial numbers are interspersed with sporting rifles, in the 16,400 through 17,700 range. All are equipped with the Merwin & Bray dual ignition block.

Exc.	V.G.	Good	Fair	Poor
—	—	1000	500	200

Ballard (Merrimack Arms & Manufacturing Co.) sporting rifles

Overall length varies with barrel length; usual barrel lengths 24", 28", 30"; calibers .22, .32, .44, .46, .50 rimfire. Markings: left side of frame marked with both manufacturing and patent marks, "MERRIMACK ARMS & MFG. CO./NEWBURYPORT, MASS." over "BALLARD'S PATENT/ NOV. 5, 1861". Caliber usually marked on top of barrel or frame, e.g. "No. 38" together with serial no. Left side of hammer marked "PATENTED JAN. 5, 1864" if breech fitted with Merwin & Bray's alternate ignition device. In the spring of 1866, Edward Bray of Brooklyn, New York, and former partner of Joseph Merwin purchased the Ballard machinery from R. Ball & Co. and set up a new plant in Newburyport, Massachusetts, primarily for the production of sporting rifles. The glut of surplus arms on the market following the American Civil War, however, forced him into bankruptcy in early 1869, after producing only about 2,000 Ballard rifles, carbines and a limited number of 20 gauge shotguns. Serial numbers continue in the sequence of the Ball & Williams/R. Ball & Co. production (serial numbers about 18,000 through 20,300). Prices of these rifles will vary considerably depending on the degree of finish or engraving.

Exc.	V.G.	Good	Fair	Poor
—	—	950	400	275

Ballard (Merrimack Arms & Manufacturing Co.) carbines

Overall length 37-1/4"; barrel (bore) length 22"; caliber .44 rimfire. Markings: same as Merrimack Arms & Mfg. Co. sporting rifles. In March 1866, the state of New York purchased 100 Ballard carbines (serial numbers about 18,500 to 18,600) for use by its prison guards. In January 1870, an additional 70 (serial numbers 19,400 to 19,500) were purchased from New York City arms merchants Merwin, Hulbert & Co. to arm guards at Sing Sing Prison. Between these two purchases Merrimack Arms & Mfg. Co. had shortened its new "tangless" frames by 1/8", the prime distinction between the two purchases. Despite the rarity of both types of carbines, they do not command high prices.

Exc.	V.G.	Good	Fair	Poor
—	—	1000	500	300

Ballard (Brown Manufacturing Co.) sporting rifles
Dimensions: same as Merrimack Arms & Mfg. Co. sporting rifles. Markings: left side of frame marked with manufacturer, "BROWN MFG. CO. NEWBURYPORT, MASS." over patent, "BALLARD'S PATENT/ NOV. 5, 1861." Serial no. on top of barrel and frame. Upon the failure of Merrimack Arms & Manufacturing Company in early 1869, the plant was purchased by John Hamilton Brown, who continued producing Ballard patent rifles until 1873 in a serial range consecutive with that of its three predecessors (Ball & Williams, R. Ball & Co., and Merrimack Arms & Mfg. Co.). Approximately 2,000 Ballard arms were produced during the period of Brown's manufacture of the Ballard (serial numbers about 20,325 through 22,100). Brown made Ballards tend to exhibit finer finishing than earlier produced rifles, accounting for their average higher value. Special features, such as breakdown facility and side extractors (on .22 cal. rifles) will also positively affect the prices.

Exc.	V.G.	Good	Fair	Poor
—	—	2500	950	400

Ballard (Brown Mfg. Co.) full-stock military rifles
Overall length 52-1/2" barrel (bore) length 30"; caliber .46 rimfire. Markings: The same as Brown Mfg. Co. sporting rifles, with the addition of the caliber marking, "No. 46", on the top of the barrel forward of the rear sight. The cause for the production of the Ballard/Brown military rifle has yet to be determined, but it has been speculated that they were possibly manufactured in anticipation of a sale to France during the Franco-Prussian War. In any event, the sale was not culminated, and many, if not most, of the estimated 1,000 produced were "sporterized" by shortening the forestock and sold by commercial dealers in the United States. Serial numbers concentrate in the 20,500 through 21,600 range, with sporting rifles interspersed in the sequence. Rifles that have not been sporterized command a premium.

Exc.	V.G.	Good	Fair	Poor
—	—	1500	700	300

BALLARD, C. H.
Worcester, Massachusetts
Single Shot Derringer
A .41 caliber rimfire spur trigger single shot pistol with a 2.75" barrel marked "Ballard's". Blued with silver-plated frame and walnut grips. Manufactured during the 1870s.

Iron Frame Model-Add 20%.

Exc.	V.G.	Good	Fair	Poor
—	—	1000	500	200

BALLARD RIFLE AND CARTRIDGE CO.
Cody, Wyoming
All models feature American black walnut stocks, case hardening, and rust blued barrels. There are a number of special order features that are available with these rifles. These extra costs items should be appraised prior to a sale.

No. 1-3/4 Far West Rifle
Offered with 30" round barrel in standard or heavy weight. Single or double set triggers, S lever, ring style lever, blade front sight, and Rocky Mountain rear sight. Offered in calibers from .32-40 to .50-90. Weight with standard 30" barrel is approximately 10.5 lbs. With heavy weight barrel 11.75 lbs.

NIB	Exc.	V.G.	Good	Fair	Poor
1850	1500	—	—	—	—

No. 4-1/2 Mid Range Model
This model features checkered fancy walnut stock, standard or heavy weight half octagon barrel 30" or 32" with single or double set triggers, pistol grip, hard rubber or steel shotgun butt, horn forend cap, full loop lever, and globe front sight. Offered in calibers from .32-40 to .40-70. Weight with standard barrel 10.75 lbs. and with heavy barrel 11.5 lbs.

NIB	Exc.	V.G.	Good	Fair	Poor
2650	2000	—	—	—	—

No. 5 Pacific Model
This model features a 30" or 32" octagon barrel in either standard or heavy weight, stocks in rifle or shotgun configuration, double set triggers, ring lever, blade front sight, and Rock Mountain rear sight. Calibers from .38-55 to .50-90. Weight with standard 30" barrel is 10.75 lbs. with heavy weight barrel 12 lbs.

NIB	Exc.	V.G.	Good	Fair	Poor
2375	1850	—	—	—	—

No. 7 Long Range Model
This model features a fancy walnut checkered stock with 32" or 34" standard or heavy weight half octagon barrel. Pistol grip stock with rubber or steel shotgun butt, single or double set triggers, full loop lever, horn forend cap, and globe front sight. Calibers from .32-40 to .45-110. Weight with standard 32" barrel 11.75 lbs. with heavy weight barrel 12.25 lbs.

NIB	Exc.	V.G.	Good	Fair	Poor
2650	2000	—	—	—	—

No. 1-1/2 Hunter's Rifle
This model features a 30" round barrel, single trigger, S lever, plain forend, and rifle butt stock. Blade front sight and Rocky Mountain rear sight are standard. Calibers from .32-40 to .50-70. Weight is about 10.5 lbs.

NIB	Exc.	V.G.	Good	Fair	Poor
1650	1250	—	—	—	—

No. 2 Sporting Model

Stocked in plain walnut with crescent butt and offered in 24", 26", 28", or 30" octagon barrel with blade front and Rocky Mountain rear sights. A straight grip action with S lever in calibers from 38-40, 44-40, and .45 Colt.

NIB	Exc.	V.G.	Good	Fair	Poor
1650	1250	—	—	—	—

No. 3 Gallery Rifle

Chambered for the .22 caliber rimfire cartridge this model features a choice of 24", 26", or 30" lightweight octagon barrel with rifle style butt stock with steel crescent butt plate, S lever, blade and Rocky Mountain sights. Weight with standard 26" barrel is about 7.5 lbs.

NIB	Exc.	V.G.	Good	Fair	Poor
1650	1250	—	—	—	—

No. 3F Fine Gallery Rifle

Same as above model but with fancy checkered walnut stock, pistol grip, single or double set triggers, full loop lever, light Schuetzen buttstock, Globe front sight and gallery tang sight. Weight with standard 26" barrel is approximately 7.75 lbs.

NIB	Exc.	V.G.	Good	Fair	Poor
2650	2000	—	—	—	—

No. 4 Perfection Model

This model features a plain walnut stock with rifle or shotgun butt. Offered in 30" or 32" octagon barrel with blade front sight and Rocky Mountain rear sight. Straight grip action with single or double set triggers with S lever or ring lever in calibers from .32-40 to .50-90.

NIB	Exc.	V.G.	Good	Fair	Poor
1850	1500	—	—	—	—

No. 5-1/2 Montana Model

This model has a fancy walnut stock, double set triggers, and ring lever. Shotgun steel butt. Barrels are either 30" or 32" extra heavy octagon in calibers .45-70, .45-110, and .50-90. Under barrel wiping rod. Weight is approximately 14.5 lbs.

NIB	Exc.	V.G.	Good	Fair	Poor
2525	2000	—	—	—	—

No. 6 Off-Hand Rifle Model

This rifle features a fancy walnut checkered stock with hand rubbed finish, heavy Schuetzen buttplate, and horn insert on forend. Choice of 30", 32", or 34" half octagon barrel with Globe front sight. Straight grip action with double set triggers, Schuetzen ball and spur lever and deluxe rust blueing. Offered in .22 Long Rifle, .32-40, .38-55, 40-65, and .40-70 calibers.

NIB	Exc.	V.G.	Good	Fair	Poor
2950	2350	—	—	—	—

No. 8 Union Hill Model

This model features a 30" or 32" half octagon standard or heavy barrel, single or double set triggers, pistol grip stock with cheekpiece full loop lever, hook Schuetzen buttplate and fancy walnut checkered stock. Offered in calibers from .22 Long Rifle to 40-70. Weight with standard barrel in .32 caliber 10.5 lbs, with heavy weight barrel in .40 caliber 11 .5 lbs. This model is not furnished with sights.

NIB	Exc.	V.G.	Good	Fair	Poor
2650	2000	—	—	—	—

Model 1885 High Wall

This single shot rifle is chambered for a wide variety of calibers from .18 Bee to .577 Express. Barrel lengths to 34". American walnut stock. Many options to choose from that will effect price. Introduced in 2000.

NIB	Exc.	V.G.	Good	Fair	Poor
1850	1500	—	—	—	—

BALLESTER—MOLINA
SEE—Hafdasa

BARNETT
SEE—English Military Firearms

BARRETT F.A. MFG. CO.
Murfreesboro, Tennessee

Model 82 Rifle

A .50 caliber Browning semiautomatic rifle with a 37" barrel and 11-shot magazine. The barrel fitted with a muzzle brake, and the receiver with a telescope. Approximate weight 35 lbs. Parkerized. Manufactured from 1985 to 1987.

NIB	Exc.	V.G.	Good	Fair	Poor
4200	3500	2750	2250	—	—

Model 82AI

As above, with a 29" barrel without sights, and a 10 round magazine. A 10X telescope and iron sights are optional. Comes with hard carrying case. Weight is 28.5 lbs.

NIB	Exc.	V.G.	Good	Fair	Poor
6750	5200	4000	2750	—	—

Model 95

Introduced in 1995 this .50 caliber BMG bolt action model features a 29" barrel and 5 round magazine. Scope optional. Weight is 22 lbs.

NIB	Exc.	V.G.	Good	Fair	Poor
4500	4000	3000	2000	—	—

Model 99

This model is a single shot bolt action rifle chambered for the .50 BMG cartridge. Barrel length is 33". Rifle weight is about 25 lbs.

NIB	Exc.	V.G.	Good	Fair	Poor
2800	2250	—	—	—	—

NOTE: Add $200 for fluted barrel.

BARRETT, J. B. and A.B. & CO.
Wytheville, Virginia

Barrett Muskets and Rifled Muskets

Overall length 57-3/4"; barrel length 41-1/2" - 42"; caliber .69. Markings: Although the Barretts placed no marks of their own on their alterations, most were effected on Virginia Manufactory muskets, whose lockplates are marked "VIRGINIA/Manufactory" forward of the hammer and "RICHMOND/(date)" on the tail.

For many years collectors considered the adaptations of Hall rifles and carbines from breechloaders to muzzleloaders to be the product of J.B. Barrett & Co. of Wytheville. Recent evidence, however, confirms that those adaptations were actually effected in Danville, Virginia, by another firm (see READ & WATSON). Nevertheless, the Barretts of Wytheville did adapt arms during the early years of the American Civil War. The adaptation, effected almost exclusively upon Virginia Manufactory flintlock muskets consisted of percussioning by means of the cone-in-barrel and rifling of the barrels with seven narrow grooves. In 1861 and 1862, the Barretts percussioned a total of 1250 muskets, of which 744 were rifled.

Courtesy Milwaukee Public Museum, Milwaukee, Wisconsin

Exc.	V.G.	Good	Fair	Poor
—	—	12500	6000	2000

BAR-STO PRECISION MACHINE
Burbank, California

Bar-Sto 25

A .25 caliber semiautomatic pistol with a brushed stainless steel receiver and slide. Walnut grips. Produced in 1974.

Exc.	V.G.	Good	Fair	Poor
200	175	150	125	100

BASCARAN, MARTIN A.
Eibar, Spain

Martian

A 6.35mm or 7.65mm caliber semiautomatic pistol. The slide is marked "Automatic Pistol Martian". Blued with black plastic grips having the monogram "MAB" cast in them.

Exc.	V.G.	Good	Fair	Poor
250	175	135	100	75

Thunder

As above, in 6.35mm caliber. The slide is not marked, but the tradename "Thunder" is cast in the grips.

Exc.	V.G.	Good	Fair	Poor
275	200	165	125	90

BAUER F. A. CORP.
Fraser, Michigan

Bauer 25 Automatic

A .25 caliber semiautomatic pistol made of stainless steel with a 2.5" barrel and 6-shot magazine. Walnut or imitation pearl grips. Manufactured from 1972 to 1984. After 1984 this pistol was produced under the name of Fraser for a few years.

Courtesy James Rankin

Exc.	V.G.	Good	Fair	Poor
200	175	150	110	80

The Rabbit

A .22 caliber by .410 bore combination rifle/shotgun, with a tubular metal stock. Manufactured between 1982 and 1984.

Exc.	V.G.	Good	Fair	Poor
150	110	90	75	50

BAYARD
SEE—Pieper, H. & N. and Bergmann
Herstal, Belgium

BAYONNE, MANUFACTURE D'ARMES
Bayonne, France
A/K/A MAB

MAB Model A

Manufactured in 1921 and chambered for the 6.35mm cartridge. Patterned after the Browning Model 1906. Squeeze grip safety with a 6-round magazine.

Courtesy James Rankin

Exc.	V.G.	Good	Fair	Poor
175	150	90	75	50

MAB Model B

Manufactured in 1932 and chambered for the 6.35mm cartridge. The pistol has an exposed hammer, no grip safety, and a 6-round magazine.

Courtesy James Rankin

Exc.	V.G.	Good	Fair	Poor
175	150	90	75	50

MAB Model C

Manufactured in 1933 and chambered for the 7.65mm and .380 cartridge. Patterned after the Browning Model 1910. Seven-round magazine.

Courtesy James Rankin

Exc.	V.G.	Good	Fair	Poor
275	225	200	125	90

MAB Model D

Manufactured in 1933 and chambered for the 7.65mm and .380 cartridge. Basically a Model C with a longer barrel and a 9-round magazine.

NOTE: Add 100% for Nazi marked pistols.

Courtesy Richard M. Kumor, Sr.

Courtesy James Rankin

Exc.	V.G.	Good	Fair	Poor
225	200	150	125	100

MAB Model E

Manufactured in 1949 and chambered for the 6.35mm cartridge. Patterned after the Model D with streamlined grips and a 10-round magazine.

Exc.	V.G.	Good	Fair	Poor
250	225	200	150	125

MAB Model F

Manufactured in 1950 and chambered for the .22 Long Rifle cartridge. Interchangeable barrel lengths, target grips, and a 10-round magazine.

Courtesy James Rankin

Exc.	V.G.	Good	Fair	Poor
250	225	200	150	125

MAB Model G

Manufactured in 1951, chambered for the .22 Long Rifle cartridge and 7.65mm cartridge. Some with Dural frames. Magazine capacity is 10 rounds for .22 LR and 8 rounds for the 7.65mm.

Courtesy James Rankin

Exc.	V.G.	Good	Fair	Poor
275	245	225	150	125

MAB Model GZ

Manufactured in calibers .22 Long Rifle, 6.35mm, 7.65mm, and .380. Almost identical to the Model G. Dural frames and two tone finishes on some variations.

Exc.	V.G.	Good	Fair	Poor
275	2455	225	150	125

MAB Model R

Manufactured in caliber 7.65mm Long in 1951 the Model R was similar to the Model D. Model Rs were later produced in several calibers. The .22 Long Rifle was furnished with a 10-round magazine and two different barrel lengths. The 7.65mm had a 9-round magazine while the .380 and 9mm Parabellum were fitted with 8-round magazines.

.22 Long Rifle

Exc.	V.G.	Good	Fair	Poor
275	245	225	150	125

7.65mm & 7.65mm Long & .380

Exc.	V.G.	Good	Fair	Poor
275	245	225	150	125

9mm Parabellum

Exc.	V.G.	Good	Fair	Poor
350	290	250	150	125

MAB Model R PARA Experimential

In the late 1950s MAB began experimenting with the Model R in caliber 9mm Parabellum. There was a large number of these experimental-type pistols and the 8-round, rotating barrel Model R shown led directly to the Model P-15 series.

Courtesy James Rankin

Exc.	V.G.	Good	Fair	Poor
1500	1250	1000	500	250

MAB Model P-8 & P-15

In 1966 MAB manufactured the Model P-8 and Model P-15 in 9mm Parabellum with 8- and 15-round magazine capacity. Basically the same gun with different magazine capacities. The Model P-15 went to the French military as well as some commercial sales.

Courtesy James Rankin

Exc.	V.G.	Good	Fair	Poor
400	350	300	250	175

Model P-15 M1 Target

The MAB Model P-15 was manufactured for target shooting using the 9mm Parabellum cartridge. Most M1 Target MABs were purchased by the French military for their target teams.

Courtesy James Rankin

Exc.	V.G.	Good	Fair	Poor
450	400	350	275	175

Model "Le Chasseur"

Manufactured in 1953 the Le Chasseur was a target model in .22 Long Rifle and had a 9-round magazine. It had an external hammer, target sights, and target grips.

Exc.	V.G.	Good	Fair	Poor
250	200	150	125	90

NOTE: MAB pistols that were sold in the U.S.A. were retailed by the Winfield Arms Company of Los Angeles, California, and are marked "Made in France for WAC." This does not affect values to any appreciable degree.

BEATTIE, J.
London, England

Beattie produced a variety of revolvers during the percussion period, some of which were imported into the United States. During the period this firm was in business, it was located at the following London addresses:

43 Upper Marylebone Street	1835-1838
52 Upper Marylebone Street	1838-1842
52 Upper Marylebone Street & 223 Regent Street	1842-1846
205 Regent Street	1851-1882
104 Queen Victoria Street	1882-1894

Beattie Gas Seal Revolver

A .42 caliber single action percussion revolver with a 6.25" octagonal barrel. When the hammer is cocked, the cylinder is forced forward against the barrel breech, thus effecting a gas seal. Blued, case hardened with walnut grips.

Exc.	V.G.	Good	Fair	Poor
—	4500	3000	2000	1000

BEAUMONT
Maastrict, Netherlands
1873 Dutch Service Revolver, Old Model

A 9.4mm double-action 6-shot revolver weighing 2 lbs. 12 oz.

Exc.	V.G.	Good	Fair	Poor
—	300	200	150	100

1873 Dutch Service Revolver, New Model

As above, with a 6-shot cylinder.

Exc.	V.G.	Good	Fair	Poor
—	300	200	150	100

1873 KIM, Small Model

As above, with an octagonal barrel and 5-shot cylinder.

Exc.	V.G.	Good	Fair	Poor
—	350	250	175	100

BEAUMONT, ADAMS
SEE—Adams

BEAUMONT-VITALI
Holland

Beaumont-Vitali

An 11mm caliber bolt-action rifle with a 30" barrel and full stock secured by two barrel bands. Essentially this rifle is a modification of the Dutch Model 1871 single shot rifle fitted with a Vitali box magazine.

Courtesy Milwaukee Public Museum, Milwaukee, Wisconsin

Exc.	V.G.	Good	Fair	Poor
—	250	125	90	65

BECKER AND HOLLANDER
Suhl, Germany

Beholla

A 7.65mm caliber semiautomatic pistol produced under contract for the German War Department. The right side of the slide is marked "Becker U Hollander Waffenbau Suhl" and the left side "Selbstlade Pistol Beholla Cal. 7.65."

Exc.	V.G.	Good	Fair	Poor
500	300	225	175	100

BEEMAN PRECISION ARMS, INC.
Santa Rosa, California

Although primarily known as an importer and retailer of airguns, Beeman Precision Arms, Inc. has marketed several firearms.

MP-08

A .380 caliber semiautomatic pistol with a 3.5" barrel and 6-shot magazine, resembling the German Luger. Blued. Introduced in 1968.

NIB	Exc.	V.G	Good	Fair	Poor
400	350	250	200	175	100

P-08

As above, in .22 caliber with an 8-shot magazine and walnut grips. Introduced in 1969.

NIB	Exc.	V.G.	Good	Fair	Poor
400	350	250	200	175	100

SP Standard

A .22 caliber single shot target pistol with 8" to 15" barrels. Fitted with adjustable sights and walnut grips. Imported in 1985 and 1986.

NIB	Exc.	V.G.	Good	Fair	Poor
225	200	175	150	125	75

SP Deluxe

As above, with a walnut forend.

NIB	Exc.	V.G.	Good	Fair	Poor
250	225	200	175	125	75

BEERSTECHER, FREDERICK
Philadelphia, Pennsylvania (1846-1856)
Lewisburg, Pennsylvania (1857-1868)

Superposed Load Pocket Pistol

A .41 caliber superposed load percussion pistol with an average barrel length of 3", German silver mounts and walnut stock. The hammer is fitted with a moveable twin striker head so that the first charge in the barrel can be fired and then the second fired. The lock is normally marked "F. Beerstecher's/Patent 1855". Prospective purchasers are advised to secure a qualified appraisal prior to acquisition.

Exc.	V.G.	Good	Fair	Poor
5000	4500	4000	3000	1500

BEESLEY, FREDERICK
London, England
SEE—British Double Guns

BEHOLLA
SEE—Becher and Hollander

BEISTEGUI, HERMANOS
Eibar, Spain

Beistegui "RUBY"

A 7.65mm caliber semiautomatic pistol copied after the Ruby. The slide marked "1914 Model Automatic Pistol Beistegui Hermanos Eiber (Espana)."

Exc.	V.G.	Good	Fair	Poor
200	150	125	80	50

Bulwark #1

The Bulwark is a fixed-barrel, external-hammer, blowback semiautomatic chambered for the 7.65mm cartridge. It bears no external markings except the monogram "B&H" molded into the grips.

Exc.	V.G.	Good	Fair	Poor
175	125	100	75	50

Bulwark #2

A copy of the Browning .25 caliber semiautomatic pistol. The slide marked "Fabrique de Armes de Guerre de Grand Precision Bulwark patent Depose No. 67259."

Exc.	V.G.	Good	Fair	Poor
175	125	100	75	50

Libia

As above, with the mark "Libia".

Exc.	V.G.	Good	Fair	Poor
175	125	100	75	50

Benelli USA

BENELLI
Italy
Importer-Benelli USA
Accokeek, Maryland

NOTE: Benelli, USA is now owned by Beretta Holding Co..

SHOTGUNS

Model SL-121 V

This is a semiautomatic 12 gauge with 3" chambers and various barrel lengths and chokes. It has a black anodized alloy receiver and was discontinued in 1985.

NIB	Exc.	V.G.	Good	Fair	Poor
500	450	400	350	300	150

Model SL 121 Slug

This model is similar to the SL-121 V with a 21" cylinder-bore barrel and rifle sights. It, too, was discontinued in 1985.

NIB	Exc.	V.G.	Good	Fair	Poor
500	450	400	350	300	150

Model SL-123 V

This model has the improved, fast, third-generation action. Otherwise it resembles the earlier SL-121.

NIB	Exc.	V.G.	Good	Fair	Poor
550	475	425	350	300	150

Model SL 201

This is a 20 gauge with a 26", improved cylinder barrel. It is similar in appearance to the SL-123.

NIB	Exc.	V.G.	Good	Fair	Poor
500	475	425	350	300	150

M3 Super 90

This is an improved version of the Benelli pump action and semiautomatic inertia recoil system. The shotgun can be converted from pump to semiautomatic by turning a spring loaded ring located at the end of the forearm. It has a rotating bolt system and is chambered for 12 gauge, with a 3" chamber. This model has a 19.75" barrel with cylinder bore and rifle sights with a 7-round tubular magazine. It has a matte black finish and a black fiberglass pistol grip stock and forearm. This model was introduced in 1986.

NIB	Exc.	V.G.	Good	Fair	Poor
1000	750	700	600	450	300

M3 Super 90 Folding Stock

Same as above but furnished with a folding tubular steel stock.

NIB	Exc.	V.G.	Good	Fair	Poor
2000	1500	1150	850	600	300

M4 Super 90

Adopted by the U.S. Marine Corps this 12 gauge shotgun features a choice of three modular buttstock and two barrel configurations. Top mounted Picatinny rail. Barrel length is 18.5". Magazine capacity is 6 rounds. Ghost-ring sights. Weight is about 8.4 lbs. Matte black finish. Deliveries in 2000.

NIB	Exc.	V.G.	Good	Fair	Poor
N/A	—	—	—	—	—

M1 Super 90 Tactical

This is a semiautomatic 12 gauge shotgun with an inertia recoil system. It features a 18.5" plain barrel with 3 screw in choke tubes. Available in either standard polymer stock or pistol grip stock. Ghost ring sights are standard. Gun weighs 6.5 lbs. First introduced in 1993.

NIB	Exc.	V.G.	Good	Fair	Poor
900	700	600	500	450	250

M1 Practical

This model was designed for IPSC events and features an oversized safety, speed loader, larger bolt handle, muzzle brake, and adjustable ghost ring sight and optics rail. Offered with 26" barrel with extended magazine tube. Weighs about 7.6 lbs.

NIB	Exc.	V.G.	Good	Fair	Poor
1150	900	750	500	—	—

M1 Super 90 Defense Gun

Comes standard with polymer pistol grip stock, 19.75" barrel, plain sights, or ghost ring sights. Offered in 12 gauge only. Weighs 7.1 lbs.

NIB	Exc.	V.G.	Good	Fair	Poor
900	700	600	500	450	250

M1 Super 90 Slug Gun

Equipped with a standard black polymer stock with 19.75" plain barrel. Fitted with a 7-shot magazine. Ghost ring sights are an option. Weighs 6.7 lbs. Camo model introduced in 2000.

NIB	Exc.	V.G.	Good	Fair	Poor
1000	750	550	450	350	250

NOTE: Add $100 for Camo model.

M1 Super 90 Entry Gun

This model is fitted with a black polymer pistol grip stock with 14" plain barrel. Magazine holds 5 shells. Plain or ghost ring sights available. **CAUTION: NFA Weapon, Restricted sale, Class III Transfer required.** Manufacturer's retail price is $900.

M1 Super 90 Field

This model is similar to other Super 90 series guns with a 21", 24", 26", or 28" vent rib barrel with screw-in choke tubes. In 1998 this model was available with 24" rifled bore with matte rib. Add $80 for this barrel. Left hand model added in 2000. In 2001 this model was offered in 20 gauge as well.

NIB	Exc.	V.G.	Good	Fair	Poor
900	650	600	550	450	200

M1 Super 90 Camo Field

Same as above but with camouflage receiver, barrel, butt stock and forearm. Offered in 24", 26", and 28" vent rib barrels. Introduced in 1997. In 1998 this model was also offered with a 21" vent rib barrel. Left hand model added in 2000. In 2001 this model was offered in 20 gauge as well.

M1 20 gauge

NIB	Exc.	V.G.	Good	Fair	Poor
950	750	700	600	500	400

M1 Super 90 Sporting Special

Introduced in 1993 this 12 gauge shotgun is similar to the Super 90 with the addition of non-reflective surfaces, 18.5" plain barrel with 3 choke tubes (IC, Mod, Full). The gun is fitted with ghost ring sights.

NIB	Exc.	V.G.	Good	Fair	Poor
725	600	500	400	350	200

Montefeltro Super 90

Introduced in 1987, this model is similar to the Super 90 Field with a checkered walnut stock and forearm with gloss finish. Offered with 21", 24", 26", or 28" vent rib barrel. Available in 12 gauge only with 3" chambers. This shotgun offered in left-hand model also.

NIB	Exc.	V.G.	Good	Fair	Poor
900	700	600	500	450	350

Montefeltro 20 Gauge

Introduced in 1993, this model features a walnut checkered stock with 26" vent rib barrel. In 1995 a 24" vent rib barrel was offered as well. Gun weighs 5.75 lbs.

NIB	Exc.	V.G.	Good	Fair	Poor
900	700	600	500	450	350

NOTE: Add $75 for short stock model

Montefeltro 20 Gauge Camo

Same as above with Realtree Camo finish and offered with 26" vent rib barrel. Introduced in 1998.

NIB	Exc.	V.G.	Good	Fair	Poor
950	750	—	—	—	—

Montefeltro 20 Gauge Limited

Introduced in 1995 this version features a finely etched nickel plate receiver with scroll and game scenes highlighted in gold. The stock is a select grade walnut and is fitted with a 26" vent rib barrel.

NIB	Exc.	V.G.	Good	Fair	Poor
1750	1250	800	500	400	350

Super Black Eagle

This model is similar to the Montefeltro Super 90 Hunter with a polymer or walnut stock and forearm. It is offered with a 24", 26", or 28" vent rib-barrel with 5 screw-in choke tubes. Chambered for 12 gauge from 2-3/4" to 3-1/2". It was introduced in 1989. The 24" barrel was introduced in 1993.

NIB	Exc.	V.G.	Good	Fair	Poor
1200	800	750	600	500	400

Super Black Eagle Left Hand

Introduced in 1999 this model is the same as the Black Eagle but in a left hand version. A Camo version is available.

NIB	Exc.	V.G.	Good	Fair	Poor
1200	950	750	—	—	—

NOTE: Add $75 for Camo version.

Super Black Eagle Custom Slug Gun

This 12 gauge model has a 24" rifled barrel with 3" chamber. It comes standard with matte metal finish. Gun weighs 7.6 lbs.

NIB	Exc.	V.G.	Good	Fair	Poor
1100	800	750	600	500	350

Super Black Eagle Camo Gun

Introduced in 1997 this model features 24", 26", or 28' vent rib barrels chambered for 12 gauge shells. Has a Realtree Xtra Brown Camo finish. Stock is camo polymer as is forearm.

NIB	Exc.	V.G.	Good	Fair	Poor
1300	1000	750	600	500	400

Super Black Eagle Limited Edition

Introduced in 1997 this shotgun features a 26" vent rib barrel, matte metal finish, and satin select grade wood stock. The nickel plated receiver is finely etched with scroll and game scenes. Limited to 1,000 guns.

NIB	Exc.	V.G.	Good	Fair	Poor
2000	1500	—	—	—	—

Black Eagle Competition Gun

Offered in 12 gauge only this model is fitted with an etched receiver, mid rib bead, competition stock, and 5 screw-in choke tubes. Available in either 26" or 28" vent rib barrel. The upper receiver is steel while the lower receiver is lightweight alloy. Weighs 7.3 lbs.

NIB	Exc.	V.G.	Good	Fair	Poor
1300	800	750	700	600	450

Black Eagle

Similar to the Black Eagle Competition Model but with standard grade wood and matte black finish on the receiver. Introduced in 1997.

NIB	Exc.	V.G.	Good	Fair	Poor
900	600	—	—	—	—

Black Eagle Executive Series

Offered in 12 gauge only this is a special order only shotgun. It is offered with a choice of 21", 24", 26", 28" vent rib barrels. Each grade or level of gun is engraved with increasing levels of coverage. The stock is fancy walnut.

Grade I

NIB	Exc.	V.G.	Good	Fair	Poor
5000	4000	2500	—	—	—

Grade II

NIB	Exc.	V.G.	Good	Fair	Poor
5700	4500	3000	—	—	—

Grade III

NIB	Exc.	V.G.	Good	Fair	Poor
6600	5000	—	—	—	—

Legacy

This model features a coin finished alloy receiver and is chambered for the 12 gauge 2-3/4" or 3" shell. It is fitted with a choice of 26" or 28" vent rib barrel with mid and front sights. Weight is about 7.5 lbs. Butt stock and forearm are select walnut.

NIB	Exc.	V.G.	Good	Fair	Poor
1300	1000	750	—	—	—

Legacy-20 Gauge

Offered for the first time in 1999 this model is chambered for 20 gauge shells and is fitted with either 24" or 26" vent rib barrels. Weight is about 6 lbs.

NIB	Exc.	V.G.	Good	Fair	Poor
1300	1000	—	—	—	—

Legacy Limited Edition

Offered in both 12 and 20 gauge this model features select walnut stock and etched game scenes with gold filled accents. The 12 gauge features waterfowl scenes while the 20 gauge has upland game scenes. The 12 gauge is fitted with a 28" barrel while the 20 gauge has a 26" barrel. This model was introduced in 2000 and is limited to 250 guns in each gauge.

Limited Edition right side-12 gauge

NIB	Exc.	V.G.	Good	Fair	Poor
1600	1200	—	—	—	—

Sport Model

This model was introduced in 1997 and is the first shotgun with removable, interchangeable carbon fiber vent ribs. This model is offered in 12 gauge only with choice of 26" or 28" barrels. Butt pad is adjustable. Weight is 7 lbs. for 26" models and 7.3 lbs. for 28" models.

NIB	Exc.	V.G.	Good	Fair	Poor
1300	1000	650	—	—	—

Nova

Introduced in 1999 this model features polymer molded frame with steel cage chambered for 3-1/2" shells. Choice of 24", 26", or 28" vent rib barrels. A 18.5" slug barrel is also offered. Two- or four-shot magazine extensions are offered as well. Weight with 28" barrel is 8 lbs. Choice of camo or black synthetic pistol grip stock. In 2001 this model was offered in 20 gauge as well.

Nova Pump with vent rib barrel

Nova Camo Model

Nova 20 Gauge

NIB	Exc.	V.G.	Good	Fair	Poor
375	275	—	—	—	—

NOTE: Add $75 for Camo version.

Nova Slug

This 12 gauge shotgun has a 18.5" cylinder bore barrel with open rifle or ghost-ring sights. Black synthetic stock. Chambered for 2.75", 3", or 3.5" shells. Magazine capacity is 4 rounds. Weight is about 7.2 lbs. Introduced in 2000.

NIB	Exc.	V.G.	Good	Fair	Poor
300	250	200	—	—	—

NOTE: Add $40 for ghost ring-sights.

Nova Rifled Slug

Introduced in 2000 this 12 gauge model features a 24" rifled barrel with open rifle sights. Black synthetic stock. Chambered

for 2.75" or 3" shells. Magazine capacity is 4 rounds. Weight is about 8 lbs.

NIB	Exc.	V.G.	Good	Fair	Poor
525	425	350	—	—	—

HANDGUNS

Model B-76

This is an all-steel, double-action semiautomatic chambered for the 9mm Parabellum. It has a 4.25" barrel, fixed sights, and an 8-round detachable magazine.

NIB	Exc.	V.G.	Good	Fair	Poor
450	400	350	300	200	100

Model B-76S

This is the target version of the B-76. It has a 5.5" barrel, adjustable sights, and target grips.

NIB	Exc.	V.G.	Good	Fair	Poor
550	500	400	300	200	100

Model B-77

This model is similar to the B-76 except that it is chambered for the .32 ACP.

NIB	Exc.	V.G.	Good	Fair	Poor
350	300	250	200	150	100

Model B-80

This is another model similar to the B-76 except that it is chambered for the .30 Luger cartridge.

NIB	Exc.	V.G.	Good	Fair	Poor
400	350	300	200	150	100

Model B-80S

This is the target version of the B-80 with a 5.5" barrel and adjustable sights. It also features target grips.

NIB	Exc.	V.G.	Good	Fair	Poor
500	450	400	300	200	100

Model MP90S Match (World Cup)

This is a semiautomatic single action pistol chambered for the .22 Short, .22 Long Rifle, or .32 S&W wadcutter. It is fitted with a 4-3/8" barrel with walnut match style fully adjustable grips, blade front sight and fully adjustable rear sight. Barrel has adjustable weights below. Magazine capacity is 5 rounds.

Weight is about 39 oz. Previously imported by European American Armory, now imported by Benelli USA.

NIB	Exc.	V.G.	Good	Fair	Poor
1200	950	700	500	—	—

Model MP95E Match (Atlanta)

Similar to the above model but with anatomically shaped grips. Choice of blue or chrome finish. Previously imported by European American Armory, now imported by Benelli USA.

NIB	Exc.	V.G.	Good	Fair	Poor
750	600	450	350	—	—

NOTE: Add $60 for chrome finish.

BENSON FIREARMS
Seattle, Washington
SEE—Aldo Uberti

Formerly the importer of the fine Italian Uberti firearms. Their arrangement ended in 1989, and these guns are now imported by Uberti U.S.A., Inc.

BENTLEY, DAVID
Birmingham

Bentley was a prolific maker of both percussion and cartridge arms between 1845 and 1883. Those arms in cases can be dated by the addresses listed.

New Church Street	1845-1849
55 Hockley Street	1849-1854
5 Lower Loveday Street	1855-1860
61 & 62 Lower Loveday Street	1860-1863
44 Shadwell Street	1863-1871
Tower Works, Aston	1871-1883

BENTLEY, JOSEPH
Birmingham and Liverpool

Best known for his transitional and later patented percussion revolvers, Bentley worked at the following addresses:

Birmingham	11 Steelhouse Lane	1829-1837
	14 St. Mary's Row	1840-1864
Liverpool	143 Dale Street	1840-1842
	12 South Castle Street	1842-1851
	40 Lime Street & 65 Castle	1852-1857
	65 Castle & 37 Russell Street	1857-1862

Bentley Revolver

A .44 caliber double action percussion revolver with a 7" barrel and 5-shot cylinder. Blued, case hardened with walnut grips.

Exc.	V.G.	Good	Fair	Poor
—	4000	2500	1500	500

BENTZ
SEE—Austrian Military Firearms

BERETTA, DR. FRANCO
Brescia, Italy

Black Diamond Field Grade

A boxlock O/U shotgun produced in a variety of gauges and barrel lengths with single triggers and automatic ejectors. Blued, French case hardened with a walnut stock.

NIB	Exc.	V.G.	Good	Fair	Poor
975	850	700	575	450	200

The above model is produced in four embellished grades as follows:

Grade One

NIB	Exc.	V.G.	Good	Fair	Poor
1150	900	700	550	400	200

Grade Two

NIB	Exc.	V.G.	Good	Fair	Poor
1700	1250	900	700	500	300

Grade Three

NIB	Exc.	V.G.	Good	Fair	Poor
2500	1750	1200	850	600	300

Grade Four

NIB	Exc.	V.G.	Good	Fair	Poor
3250	2750	2200	1250	700	350

Gamma Standard

A 12, 16, or 20 gauge boxlock O/U shotgun with 26" or 28" barrels, single trigger and automatic ejectors. Blued, French case hardened with a walnut stock. Imported from 1984 to 1988.

NIB	Exc.	V.G.	Good	Fair	Poor
450	375	300	225	150	100

Gamma Deluxe

As above, but more finely finished.

NIB	Exc.	V.G.	Good	Fair	Poor
650	575	500	400	250	125

Gamma Target

As above, in a trap or skeet version. Imported from 1986 to 1988.

NIB	Exc.	V.G.	Good	Fair	Poor
600	500	450	375	300	150

America Standard

A .410 bore boxlock O/U shotgun with 26" or 28" barrels. Blued, French case hardened with a walnut stock. Imported from 1984 to 1988.

NIB	Exc.	V.G.	Good	Fair	Poor
325	275	225	175	150	100

America Deluxe

As above, but more finely finished.

NIB	Exc.	V.G.	Good	Fair	Poor
400	325	275	220	175	100

Europa

As above, with a 26" barrel and engraved action. Imported from 1984 to 1988.

NIB	Exc.	V.G.	Good	Fair	Poor
400	325	275	225	175	100

Europa Deluxe

As above, but more finely finished.

NIB	Exc.	V.G.	Good	Fair	Poor
475	375	300	250	200	125

Francia Standard

A .410 bore boxlock double-barrel shotgun with varying barrel lengths, double triggers and manual extractors. Blued with a walnut stock. Imported from 1986 to 1988.

NIB	Exc.	V.G.	Good	Fair	Poor
250	200	175	150	125	100

Alpha Three

A 12, 16, or 20 gauge boxlock double-barrel shotgun with 26" or 28" barrels, single triggers and automatic ejectors. Blued, French case hardened with a walnut stock. Imported from 1984 to 1988.

NIB	Exc.	V.G.	Good	Fair	Poor
400	350	300	225	150	100

Beta Three

A single-barrel, break-open, field-grade gun chambered for all gauges and offered with a ventilated rib barrel from 24" to 32" in length. The receiver chrome-plated, and the stock of walnut. Imported from 1985 to 1988.

NIB	Exc.	V.G.	Good	Fair	Poor
150	125	100	75	60	40

BERETTA, PIETRO
Brescia, Italy
IMPORTER - Beretta U.S.A. Corp.
Accokeek, Maryland

Fabbrica d'Armi Pierto Beretta, of Gardone Val Trompia, near Milan, Italy is one of the world's oldest industrial concerns. A leading maker of sporting, military, and civilian firearms, this firm has been in existence for almost 500 years. Founded by Bartolomeo Beretta, a master gunbarrel maker, in 1526. His son Giovannino followed his father's footsteps and subsequent generations have developed this firm into a worldwide success. Beretta manufactured its first pistol, the Model 1915, in 1915 as a wartime project.

Spread over 500,000 square feet and employing 2,200 employees this old world firm captured the United States military contract in 1985 for its standard issue sidearm, the Model 92F. These pistols are currently manufactured at Beretta U.S.A.'s plant in Maryland. Besides the affiliate in the United States, Beretta has three others located in France, Greece, and Rome.

The American affiliate was formed in 1977 to handle U.S. demand. A year later it began to manufacture some firearms, namely the Model 92F. At the present time Beretta has delivered over 250,000 Model 92F pistols to the U.S. military. Beretta continues to produce sidearms for the U.S. military and law enforcement agencies throughout the U.S.

NOTE: In 1994 Beretta changed its model designations with a new nomenclature system that brings back some of the old product names and the addition of new names instead of numbered models. Beretta will continue to use the numbered model designation along with the new product names so that both will complement the other.

PISTOLS

Model 1915

A 7.65mm and 9mm Glisenti caliber semiautomatic pistol with 3.5" barrel, fixed sights and 8-shot magazine. Blued with walnut grips. The slide is marked "Pietro Beretta Brescia Casa Fondata nel 1680 Cal. 7.65mm Brevetto 1915." Manufactured between 1915 and 1922. Replaced by the Model 1915/19.

Exc.	V.G.	Good	Fair	Poor
850	700	500	350	250

Model 1915/1919

This model is an improved version of the above pistol but chambered for the 7.65mm cartridge. It also incorporates a new barrel-mounting method and a longer cutout in the top of the slide.

Courtesy Orvel Reichert

Courtesy Orvel Reichert

Exc.	V.G.	Good	Fair	Poor
350	300	225	150	100

Model 1919

Similar to Model 1915, in 6.35mm caliber. Manufactured with minor variations and different names between 1919 and the 1940s.

Courtesy James Rankin

Exc.	V.G.	Good	Fair	Poor
500	400	300	250	100

Model 1923

A 9mm caliber semiautomatic pistol with 4" barrel and 8-shot magazine. Blued with steel grips. The slide is marked, "Brev 1915-1919 Mlo 1923." Manufactured from 1923 to 1935.

Exc.	V.G.	Good	Fair	Poor
525	425	350	225	150

Model 1931

A 7.65mm caliber semiautomatic pistol with 3.5" barrel and open-top slide. Blued with walnut grips and marked, "RM" separated by an anchor.

Exc.	V.G.	Good	Fair	Poor
450	375	275	200	150

Model 1934

As above, with 9mm short caliber. The slide is marked, "P. Beretta Cal. 9 Corto-Mo 1934 Brevet Gardone VT." This inscription is followed by the date of manufacture that was given numerically, followed by a Roman numeral that denoted the year of manufacture on the Fascist calendar which began in 1922. Examples are marked, "RM" (Navy), "RE" (Army), "RA" (Air Force), and "PS" (Police). Manufactured between 1934 and 1959.

Courtesy Orvel Reichert

Courtesy Orvel Reichert

Exc.	V.G.	Good	Fair	Poor
375	325	225	150	100

Air Force "RA" marked

Exc.	V.G.	Good	Fair	Poor
550	475	325	225	150

Navy "RM" marked

Exc.	V.G.	Good	Fair	Poor
625	550	375	250	175

Model 1934 Rumanian Contract

This model is identical to the Model 1934 except the slide is marked "9mm Scurt" instead of 9mm Corto.

Exc.	V.G.	Good	Fair	Poor
475	425	325	225	125

Model 1935

As above, in 7.65mm caliber. Postwar versions are known. Manufactured from 1935 to 1959.

Courtesy Orvel Reichert

Exc.	V.G.	Good	Fair	Poor
375	325	225	150	100

Model 318

An improved version of the old Model 1919 with the butt reshaped to afford a better grip. Chambered for the .25 ACP cartridge and has a 2.5" barrel. Variety of finishes with plastic grips. In the United States it is known as the "Panther." Manufactured between 1935 and 1946.

Exc.	V.G.	Good	Fair	Poor
300	250	200	150	100

Model 418

As above, with a rounded grip and a cocking indicator. It is known as the "Bantam" in the U.S. Introduced in 1947.

Exc.	V.G.	Good	Fair	Poor
250	200	150	125	90

Model 420

An engraved and chrome-plated Model 418.

Exc.	V.G.	Good	Fair	Poor
350	300	275	200	150

Model 421

An engraved, gold-plated Model 418 with tortoise-shell grips.

Exc.	V.G.	Good	Fair	Poor
475	425	325	250	150

Model 948

A .22 l.r. version of the Model 1934. It has either a 3.5" or 6" barrel.

Exc.	V.G.	Good	Fair	Poor
350	300	200	125	90

Model 949 Olympic Target

A .22 caliber semiautomatic pistol with 8.75" barrel, adjustable sights and muzzle break. Blued with checkered, walnut grips. Manufactured from 1959 to 1964.

Exc.	V.G.	Good	Fair	Poor
750	600	500	400	200

Beretta 70 Series

These pistols began production in 1958 replacing Models 1934, 1935, 948, and 949. During the late 1960s several of these models briefly utilized a 100 series designation for the U.S. market. During the latter part of the 1970s a magazine safety was added to the 70 series and the pistols became known as the Model 70S. The 70S designation replaced model designations 70 through 75 making these older model numbers obsolete. Only the Model 76 designation continued.

The 70 Series design included a cross bolt safety, sear block safety, a slide hold open device, and a push button magazine release. Shorty after its introduction the cross bolt safety pushbutton was replaced with a lever-type sear block safety located in the same place.

NOTE: The above information was supplied by contributing editor John Stimson, Jr.

Model 70 (Model 100)

The Model 948 with cross bolt safety, hold-open device, and a push button magazine release. Fixed sights. There are a number of subvariations available chambered for the .22 l.r., .32 ACP, and the .380 ACP cartridges. Available with a 3.5" or 5.9" barrel and has a detachable magazine. Also known as the "Puma" when marketed in the U.S. by J.L. Galef & Sons. It was introduced in 1958 and discontinued in 1985.

NIB	Exc.	V.G.	Good	Fair	Poor
325	275	200	175	125	85

Model 70S

This is an improved Model 70. Chambered for the 7.65 (.32ACP), 9mm Corto (.380ACP), and the 22 Long rifle cartridge. Magazine capacity is 7, 8, and 8 rounds respectively.

NIB	Exc.	V.G.	Good	Fair	Poor
325	275	200	175	125	85

Model 71/Jaguar (Model 101)

Similar to above model and chambered for .22 l.r. cartridge. Magazine capacity is 10 rounds. Frame is alloy and is fitted with a 5.9" barrel. Models imported into the US prior to 1968 were fitted with 3.5" barrels.

NIB	Exc.	V.G.	Good	Fair	Poor
350	275	225	175	125	100

Model 72

This is essentially a Model 71 but sold with 2 sets of barrels; a 3.5" and 5.9". Fixed sights.

NIB	Exc.	V.G.	Good	Fair	Poor
350	300	275	225	150	125

Model 73

The Model 73 was a Model 72 with a 5.9" barrel. Fixed sights mounted on the barrel.

NIB	Exc.	V.G.	Good	Fair	Poor
N/A	—	—	—	—	—

Model 74

This model was a Model 73 with an adjustable rear sight mounted on the barrel. Magazine capacity is 10 rounds.

NIB	Exc.	V.G.	Good	Fair	Poor
N/A	—	—	—	—	—

Model 75

This model is a Model 72 with a 5.9" barrel only.

NIB	Exc.	V.G.	Good	Fair	Poor
N/A	—	—	—	—	—

Model 76 (102)

This is a .22 Long rifle target pistol. The barrel is shrouded with an aluminum sleeve with the rear part of the sleeve extended above the slide to hold an adjustable rear sight. Marketed in the U.S. as the Sable. Magazine capacity is 10 rounds. Briefly after 1968 imported into the U.S. as the Model 102, the New Sable.

Courtesy John J. Stimson, Jr.

NIB	Exc.	V.G.	Good	Fair	Poor
N/A	—	—	—	—	—

Model 950/Jetfire

A .22 caliber semiautomatic pistol with 2.25" barrel hinged at the front that could be pivoted forward for cleaning or loading, making this either a semiauto or single-shot pistol. Blued with plastic grips. Introduced in 1955. A 4" barrel version also available. This model was known as the "Minx" in the U.S.

NIB	Exc.	V.G.	Good	Fair	Poor
200	150	135	110	85	50

Model 950B/Jetfire

As above, in .25 caliber, known as the "Jetfire" in the United States.

NIB	Exc.	V.G.	Good	Fair	Poor
200	150	135	110	85	50

Model 950 Jetfire Inox
Same as the Model 950 Jetfire but with stainless steel finish. Introduced in 2000.

NIB	Exc.	V.G.	Good	Fair	Poor
250	200	—	—	—	—

Model 3032 Tomcat
This is a double action semiautomatic pistol similar in appearance to the Model 950 but chambered for the .32 ACP cartridge. Barrel length is 2.45" and overall length is 5". Fixed blade front sight and drift adjustable rear sight. Plastic grips. Seven round magazine. Blued or matte black finish. Weight is 14.5 oz.

NIB	Exc.	V.G.	Good	Fair	Poor
325	225	150	125	100	75

NOTE: For blued finish add $30.

Model 3032 Tomcat Inox
Same as above but with stainless steel finish. Introduced in 2000.

NIB	Exc.	V.G.	Good	Fair	Poor
400	325	—	—	—	—

Model 3032 Tomcat Titanium
Same as above but with titanium finish and plastic grips. Weight is about 16 oz. Introduced in 2001.

NIB	Exc.	V.G.	Good	Fair	Poor
550	450	—	—	—	—

Alley Cat
Introduced in 2001 as a special limited run promotion pistol. Chambered for the .32 ACP cartridge this model is a Tomcat with special features such as AO Big Dot night sights. Supplied with an Alcantara inside-the-pants holster.

Alley Cat AO Big Dot night sights

NIB	Exc.	V.G.	Good	Fair	Poor
350	275	—	—	—	—

Model 951

A 9mm caliber semiautomatic pistol with 4.5" barrel and fixed sights. Blued with plastic grips. It was also known as the "Brigadier" at one time. Manufactured from 1952 to present day.

Exc.	V.G.	Good	Fair	Poor
350	300	200	150	100

Model 20

A .25 ACP double-action pistol with 2.5" barrel and 9-shot magazine. Blued with either walnut or plastic grips. Discontinued in 1985.

NIB	Exc.	V.G.	Good	Fair	Poor
200	175	150	125	90	75

Model 21/21 Bobcat

This small frame semiautomatic pistol, chambered for the .22 Long Rifle or .25 ACP cartridge, features a 2.4" tip-up barrel with fixed sights and a magazine capacity of 8 rounds (.25 ACP) or 7 rounds (.22 L.R.). Comes with either plastic or walnut grips and a deluxe version with gold line engraving. Pistol weighs about 11 to 11.8 oz. depending on caliber.

Standard model

NIB	Exc.	V.G.	Good	Fair	Poor
200	175	150	125	100	75

Model 21EL-Gold Engraved Model

NIB	Exc.	V.G.	Good	Fair	Poor
350	250	200	—	—	—

Model 21 Inox-Stainless steel

NIB	Exc.	V.G.	Good	Fair	Poor
300	225	175	—	—	—

Model 90

A double-action, semiautomatic pocket pistol with a 3.5" barrel and 8-round magazine. Manufactured from 1969 to 1983.

Exc.	V.G.	Good	Fair	Poor
275	250	200	150	125

Model 92

A 9mm caliber double action, semiautomatic pistol with a 5" barrel, fixed sights and a 16-round, double-stack magazine. Blued with plastic grips. Introduced in 1976 and is now discontinued.

NIB	Exc.	V.G.	Good	Fair	Poor
500	400	375	300	250	200

Model 92SB-P

As above, but with a polished finish. Manufactured from 1980 to 1985.

NIB	Exc.	V.G.	Good	Fair	Poor
550	425	375	325	250	200

Model 92SB Compact

As above, with a 4.3" barrel and a shortened grip frame that holds a 14-shot magazine. Either blued or nickel-plated with wood or plastic grips. The nickel version would be worth an additional 15 percent. The wood grips would add $20 to the value. Introduced in 1980 and discontinued in 1985.

NIB	Exc.	V.G.	Good	Fair	Poor
500	425	375	325	250	200

Model 92FS

The current production Model 92 chambered for the 9mm Parabellum cartridge. Barrel length is 4.9" and rear sight is a 3-dot combat drift adjustable. The magazine capacity is 15 rounds. This semiautomatic pistol features a double or single action operation. The safety is manual type. The frame is a light alloy sandblasted and anodized black. The barrel slide is steel. Grips are plastic checkered with black matte finish. Equipped with spare magazine cleaning rod, and hard carrying case. Pistol weighs 34.4 oz. empty.

NIB	Exc.	V.G.	Good	Fair	Poor
550	450	350	300	200	150

Model 92FS Inox

Introduced in 2001 this pistol is chambered for the 9mm cartridge and fitted with a 4.9" barrel. The slide is black stainless steel with lightweight frame and combat-style triggerguard, reversible magazine release, and ambidextrous safety. Grey wrap-around grips. Weight is about 34 oz.

NIB	Exc.	V.G.	Good	Fair	Poor
725	575	—	—	—	—

Model 96

Identical to Model 92FS but fitted with a 10-round magazine and chambered for the .40 S&W. Introduced in 1992.

NIB	Exc.	V.G.	Good	Fair	Poor
550	450	350	300	200	150

Model 96 Combat

Introduced in 1997 this model is single action only with a competition tuned trigger. Developed for practical shooting competition. The barrel length is 5.9" and is supplied with a weight as standard. Rear sight is adjustable target type. Tool kit included as standard. Weight is 40 oz.

NIB	Exc.	V.G.	Good	Fair	Poor
1700	1300	—	—	—	—

Model 96 Stock

Similar to the Model 96 but in double/single action with a halfcock notch for cocked and locked carry. Fitted with a 4.9" barrel with fixed sights. Three interchangeable front sights are supplied as standard. Weight is 35 oz. Introduced in 1997. No longer in the U.S. product line.

NIB	Exc.	V.G.	Good	Fair	Poor
1350	950	—	—	—	—

Model 92/96FS Inox

Same as above except the barrel, slide, trigger, extractor, and other components are made of stainless steel. The frame is made of lightweight anodized aluminum alloy. **NOTE:** The Model 96FS was discontinued in 1993.

NIB	Exc.	V.G.	Good	Fair	Poor
650	550	450	350	300	200

Model 92/96FS Centurion

Chambered for either the 9mm or .40 S&W this model features a 4.3" barrel but yet retains a full grip to accommodate a 15-round magazine (9mm) or 10 rounds (.40 S&W). Pistol weighs approximately 33.2 oz. Introduced in 1993. Black sandblasted finish.

NIB	Exc.	V.G.	Good	Fair	Poor
550	450	400	300	200	150

Model 92FS/96 Brigadier

Same as the 92FS and 96 but with a heavier slide to reduce felt recoil. Removable front sight. Weight is about 35 oz.

NIB	Exc.	V.G.	Good	Fair	Poor
700	550	400	—	—	—

Model 92FS/96 Brigadier Inox

Same as above but with stainless steel finish. Introduced in 2000.

NIB	Exc.	V.G.	Good	Fair	Poor
750	600	—	—	—	—

Model 92F

A 9mm Parabellum caliber double action semiautomatic pistol with a 4.9" barrel, fixed sights and a 15-shot double-stack magazine with an extended base. Matte-blued finish with walnut or plastic grips. Introduced in 1984. No longer in production.

NIB	Exc.	V.G.	Good	Fair	Poor
500	400	350	300	200	150

Model 92F Compact

As above, with a 4.3" barrel and a 13-shot magazine. No longer in production.

NIB	Exc.	V.G.	Good	Fair	Poor
500	400	350	300	200	150

Model 92/96 Compact "Type M"
Essentially the same as the Model 92FS Compact but with the exception of a single column magazine that holds 8 rounds and reduces the grip thickness of the pistol. Pistol weighs 30.9 oz. Discontinued in 1993 and reintroduced in 1998. The Model 96 version (.40S&W) was introduced in 2000.

NIB	Exc.	V.G.	Good	Fair	Poor
700	550	350	300	200	150

NOTE: Add $90 for Tritium night sights.

Model 92/96 Compact Inox
Same as above but with stainless steel slide and frame. Introduced in 2000.

NIB	Exc.	V.G.	Good	Fair	Poor
700	550	—	—	—	—

Model 92D Compact Type M
Same as above but with double action only trigger function.

NIB	Exc.	V.G.	Good	Fair	Poor
550	450	350	300	200	150

NOTE: Add $90 for Tritium night sights.

Model 92FS Deluxe
Identical dimensions to the full size Model 92FS with the addition of gold plated engraved frame with gold plated extra magazine in fitted leather presentation hard case. Grips are walnut briar with gold initial plate. Introduced in 1993.

NIB	Exc.	V.G.	Good	Fair	Poor
3750	3000	2000	1000	750	500

Model 92FS "470th Anniversary" Limited Edition
This model is limited to only 470 pistols worldwide. Features high polish finish with stainless steel, gold filled engravings, walnut grips, Anniversary logo on top of slide and on the back of the chrome plated magazine. Supplied with walnut case.

NIB	Exc.	V.G.	Good	Fair	Poor
2075	—	—	—	—	—

Model 92/96D
Same specifications as the standard Model 92 and Model 96 except that this variation has no visible hammer and is double action only. This model has no manual safety. Pistol weighs 33.8 oz.

NIB	Exc.	V.G.	Good	Fair	Poor
425	375	325	275	200	150

Model 92/96DS
Same as above but with the same manual safety as found on the 92FS pistol. Introduced in 1994.

NIB	Exc.	V.G.	Good	Fair	Poor
425	375	325	275	200	150

Model 92G/96G
Designed for the French Gendarmerie, this model has now been adopted for the French Air Force as well as other government agencies. This model features a hammer drop lever that does not function as a safety when the lever is released

but lowers the hammer and returns to the ready to fire position automatically. Offered to law enforcement agencies only.

Model 92 Competition Conversion Kit

The kit includes a 7.3" barrel with counterweight and elevated front sight, semiautomatic, walnut grips, and fully adjustable rear sight. Comes in special carrying case with the basic pistol.

Kit Price Only:

NIB	Exc.	V.G.	Good	Fair	Poor
500	350	300	200	150	100

Model 92/96 Combo

This model features a specially designed Model 96 pistol with an extra 92FS slide and barrel assembly. Barrel lengths are 4.66". Sold with one 10-round magazine in both 9mm and .40 S&W.

NIB	Exc.	V.G.	Good	Fair	Poor
900	725	—	—	—	—

Model M9 Limited Edition

Introduced in 1995 to commemorate the 10th anniversary of the U.S. military's official sidearm this 9mm pistol is limited to 10,000 units. Special engraving on the slide with special serial numbers. Slide stamped "U.S. 9MM M9-BERETTA U.S.A.-65490".

Standard Model

NIB	Exc.	V.G.	Good	Fair	Poor
750	600	400	300	200	100

Deluxe Model-Walnut grips with gold plated hammer and grip screws.

NIB	Exc.	V.G.	Good	Fair	Poor
850	700	450	350	200	100

Model 92 Billennium

Introduced in 2001 this is a limited production pistol of 2,000 units world wide. Chambered for the 9mm cartridge. Steel frame with checkered front and back strap. Nickel alloy finish with unique engraving. Carbon fiber grips. Interchangeable sights with adjustable rear sight. Carry case standard.

NIB	Exc.	V.G.	Good	Fair	Poor
1275	—	—	—	—	—

ELITE TEAM SERIES

In 1999 Beretta introduced a new series of pistols based on the company's M92/96 pistol. Each of these pistols has specific features for specific shooting requirements.

Model 92G/96G Elite

Chambered for 9mm or .40S&W calibers this pistol is fitted with a 4.7" stainless steel barrel and heavy-duty Brigadier-style slide. The action is decock only. Slide has both front and rear serrations. Hammer is skeletonized. Beveled magazine well. Special "ELITE" engraving on the slide.

NIB	Exc.	V.G.	Good	Fair	Poor
750	600	450	—	—	—

Model 92/96 Border Marshall

This is the commercial version of the pistol built for the Immigration and Naturalization Service. It is fitted with a heavy-duty steel slide and short 4.7" I.N.S. style barrel. Rubber grips and night sights are standard. "BORDER MARSHALL" engraved on the slide. Offered in either 9mm or .40S&W calibers.

NIB	Exc.	V.G.	Good	Fair	Poor
750	600	—	—	—	—

Model 92/96 Custom Carry

This model is fitted with a 4.3" barrel, shortened grip, and low profile control levers. Safety lever is left side only. Magazine capacity is 10 rounds. "CUSTOM CARRY" engraved on the slide. Chambered for either 9mm or .40S&W calibers.

NIB	Exc.	V.G.	Good	Fair	Poor
625	500	—	—	—	—

Model 92FS INOX Tactical

This model has a satin matte finish on its stainless steel slide. The frame is anodized aluminum. Black rubber grips and night sights are standard. Offered in 9mm only.

NIB	Exc.	V.G.	Good	Fair	Poor
775	625	—	—	—	—

COUGAR SERIES

Model 8000/8040/8045 Cougar

This is a compact size pistol using a short recoil rotating barrel. It features a firing pin lock, chrome lined barrel, anodized aluminum alloy frame with Bruniton finish. Overall length is 7", barrel length is 3.6", overall height 5.5", and unloaded weight is 33.5 oz. Offered in double/single action as well as double action only. Magazine holds 10 rounds. Available in 9mm or 40 S&W. In 1998 Beretta added the .45ACP caliber to this model.

NIB	Exc.	V.G.	Good	Fair	Poor
625	525	400	350	250	150

NOTE: Add $50 for .45ACP models

Model 8000/8040/8045 Mini Cougar

This pistol was introduced in 1997 and is similar in design to the full size model. Offered in 9mm or 40 S&W or .45 ACP. The pistol is fitted with a 3.6" barrel (3.7" on .45 ACP). Empty weight is 27 oz. Offered in double/single action or double action only. Magazine capacity is 10 rounds for 9mm and 8 rounds for .40 S&W model. Weight is between 27 oz. and 30 oz. depending on caliber.

NIB	Exc.	V.G.	Good	Fair	Poor
650	550	—	—	—	—

NOTE: Add $50 for .45 ACP models

Model 9000F

Introduced in 2000 this pistol is chambered for the 9mm or .40S&W cartridge. It is fitted with a 3.4" barrel and has a polymer frame. The "F" type has a single action/double action trigger. Fixed sights. Magazine capacity is 10 rounds. Weight is about 27 oz. Overall length is 6.6" and overall height is 4.8". External hammer and black finish.

NIB	Exc.	V.G.	Good	Fair	Poor
550	450	—	—	—	—

NIB	Exc.	V.G.	Good	Fair	Poor
550	450	—	—	—	—

Model 9000D

Same as above but with double action only trigger.

NIB	Exc.	V.G.	Good	Fair	Poor
550	450	—	—	—	—

Model 9000S

This model is chambered for the 9mm or .40 S&W cartridges. Magazine capacity is 10 rounds. With optional spacer Model 92/96 magazines can also be used. Three dot sight system. An accessory magazine bottom that extends when griped but retracts when holstered is standard. Steel alloy frame and slide. Weight is about 27 oz. Introduced in 2001.

CHEETAH SERIES

Model 84/Cheetah

This is a small semiautomatic pistol chambered for the .380 cartridge. It has a double column magazine that holds 13 rounds. Offered in blue or nickel finish. Grips are checkered black plastic or checkered wood.

NIB	Exc.	V.G.	Good	Fair	Poor
450	375	325	275	200	150

Model 84BB

Similar to the Model 84 but incorporates different features such as a firing pin blocking device and loaded chamber indicator. Single column magazine holds 8 rounds of .380 shells. Discontinued in 1993.

NIB	Exc.	V.G.	Good	Fair	Poor
425	375	325	275	200	150

Model 85/Cheetah

Similar in appearance to the Model 84 but features a single column magazine with a capacity of 8 rounds. Available in blue or nickel finish. Grips are checkered black plastic. Pistol weighs 22 oz.

NIB	Exc.	V.G.	Good	Fair	Poor
550	425	300	250	200	150

Model 87 Target

This is a .22 caliber single action target pistol. It features an adjustable rear sight, integral scope base, and external hammer. Anodized aluminum frame. Weight is about 41 oz. Introduced in 2000.

NIB	Exc.	V.G.	Good	Fair	Poor
405	375	325	275	200	150

Model 86/Cheetah

This .380 ACP semiautomatic pistol has a 4.4" tip-up barrel. Magazine capacity is 8 rounds. Furnished with checkered wood grips. Pistol weighs 23 oz.

NIB	Exc.	V.G.	Good	Fair	Poor
650	500	—	—	—	—

Model 89/Gold Standard

A .22 caliber, semiautomatic target pistol with adjustable sights, and 10-shot, detachable magazine. Matte finish with hand-fitting walnut grips. Introduced in 1988.

NIB	Exc.	V.G.	Good	Fair	Poor
425	350	300	250	200	150

Model 87/Cheetah

A .22 caliber double-action, semiautomatic target pistol with a 3.8" or 6" barrel, adjustable sights with a 7-shot magazine. Blued with checkered walnut grips. Introduced in 1986.

NIB	Exc.	V.G.	Good	Fair	Poor
800	625	475	400	300	150

RIFLES

AR-70

A .223 caliber, semiautomatic rifle with a 17.7" barrel, adjustable diopter sights, and an 8, or 30-shot magazine. Black epoxy finish with a synthetic stock. Weight is approximately 8.3 lbs. No longer imported into the U.S.

NIB	Exc.	V.G.	Good	Fair	Poor
2500	2200	1900	1500	1000	—

BM-59 Standard Grade

A gas operated semiautomatic rifle with detachable box magazine. Chambered for .308 cartridge. Walnut stock. Barrel length is 19.3" with muzzle brake. Magazine capacity is 5,10, or 20 rounds. Weight is about 9.5 lbs.

NIB	Exc.	V.G.	Good	Fair	Poor
1600	1400	1100	700	400	—

Model 500 Custom

A bolt-action sporting rifle chambered for a variety of calibers with a 24" barrel, open sights, three action lengths and a 3- or 4-shot magazine. Blued with a checkered walnut stock.

Exc.	V.G.	Good	Fair	Poor
600	525	400	325	275

This model was offered in five grades:

Model 500S

Exc.	V.G.	Good	Fair	Poor
625	550	425	350	300

Model 500DL

Exc.	V.G.	Good	Fair	Poor
1400	1250	1000	775	650

Model 500DEELL

Exc.	V.G.	Good	Fair	Poor
1600	1450	1200	975	800

Model 500DEELLS

Exc.	V.G.	Good	Fair	Poor
1625	1475	1225	1000	825

Model 501

A .243 or .308 caliber bolt-action rifle with a 23" barrel, furnished without sights and a 6-shot magazine. Blued with a checkered walnut stock. It was discontinued in 1986. It was offered in the same variations as the Model 500 series-501S, 501DL, 501DLS, 501EELL, and 501EELLS. The values for this series are the same as for the 500 series rifles.

Model 502

A .270, 7mm Remington Magnum, and the .30-06 caliber bolt action rifle with a 24" barrel, without sights and a 5-shot magazine. Blued with a checkered walnut stock. Discontinued in 1986. It is also available in the same variations as the Model 500 and the Model 501 but is valued at approximately 10 percent higher in each variation.

Mato Deluxe

This bolt action rifle was introduced into the Beretta product line in 1997. It is based on the Mauser 98 action and is fitted with a drop-out box magazine. The stock is XXX Claro walnut with a hand rubbed oil finish and black forend tip. Chambered

for .270 Win., .280, .30-06, 7mm magnum, .300 magnum, .338 magnum, and .375 H&H. Weight is about 8 lbs.

NIB	Exc.	V.G.	Good	Fair	Poor
2000	1500	1000	750	—	—

Mato Standard

Same as above but fitted with a matte gray Kevlar and graphite composite stock. Weight is approximately 7.9 lbs.

NIB	Exc.	V.G.	Good	Fair	Poor
1550	1200	800	600	—	—

PREMIUM RIFLES

Model S689 Sable

A 9.3x74R or the .30-06 caliber O/U rifle with a boxlock action, 23" ribbed barrels and express-type sights. Blued, case hardened or nickel-plated with checkered walnut stock. Double triggers and automatic ejectors. Offered in three grades.

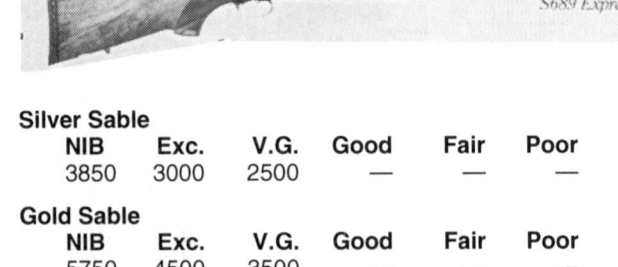

Silver Sable

NIB	Exc.	V.G.	Good	Fair	Poor
3850	3000	2500	—	—	—

Gold Sable

NIB	Exc.	V.G.	Good	Fair	Poor
5750	4500	3500	—	—	—

Diamond Sable

NIB	Exc.	V.G.	Good	Fair	Poor
12750	10000	7500	—	—	—

NOTE: Extra 20 gauge barrel with forearm add $1,200. Scope with claw mounts add $2,000.

SSO Express

A .375 Holland & Holland and .458 Winchester Magnum caliber O/U, double-barrel rifle with 23" barrels, folding express sights, double triggers, and automatic ejectors. Furnished with a fitted case. This firearm is available on a custom-order basis and should be individually appraised.

NIB	Exc.	V.G.	Good	Fair	Poor
18000	13000	9500	—	—	—

SS05 Express

A more finely finished version of the above.

NIB	Exc.	V.G.	Good	Fair	Poor
20000	15000	11000	—	—	—

SS06

This is a premium grade sidelock over and under express rifle. Equipped with double triggers. It is offered in 9.3x74R, .375 H&H Magnum, and .458 Win. Magnum. It is fitted with a 24" barrel with express sights. Claw mounts and Ziess are available from the factory. The receiver is case-colored with light scroll engraving. Special select walnut is used in the stock and forearm with fine line checkering. Stock comes with cheek-piece and rubber recoil pad. Furnished with leather case. Rifle weighs about 11 lbs.

NIB	Exc.	V.G.	Good	Fair	Poor
39500	32000	24000	—	—	—

SS06 EELL

Offered in the same calibers as above but furnished with hand engraved game scenes with gold inlays. Walnut stock is special select briar with fine diamond line checkering.

NIB	Exc.	V.G.	Good	Fair	Poor
42500	32500	27000	—	—	—

Model 455

This is a premium grade side by side express rifle with slide locks. Available in the following calibers: .375 H&H Magnum, .458 Win. Magnum, .470 Nitro Express, .500 Nitro Express, and .416 Rigby. The receiver is case-colored without engraving and the walnut stock is highly figured with fine line checkering. Comes supplied with express sights. Claw mounts and Zeiss scope offered at customers request only on .375, .458, and .416. Weighs about 11 lbs.

NIB	Exc.	V.G.	Good	Fair	Poor
53000	40000	30000	—	—	—

Model 455 EELL

Same as above model but furnished with case-colored game scene engraving with gold inlays. Walnut briar stock with fine diamond line checkering. Supplied with leather case and accessories.

NIB	Exc.	V.G.	Good	Fair	Poor
72500	50000	—	—	—	—

SHOTGUNS

Beretta shotguns are marked with a symbol or 0 stamping to indicate the type of fixed choke in the barrel or barrels. Usually this stamping is on the side of the barrel in the rear near the receiver on semiautomatics and near the ejectors on double barrel shotguns. Beretta shotguns with screw-in Mobilchoke tubes will have notches cut in them to indicate the amount of choke placed in the tube.

Fixed Chokes & Beretta Mobilchoke Designations		Mobilchoke Rim Notches
O(*)	F(Full)	I
OO(**)	IM(Improved Modified)	II
OOO(***)	M(Modified)	III
OOOO(****)	IC(Improved Cyl.)	IIII
COOOO(C****)	CL(Cylinder)	IIIII
SK	SK(Skeet)	No Notches

The BL series of O/U shotguns were manufactured between 1968 and 1973. They are chambered for 12 or 20 gauge and were offered with 26", 28", or 30" vent ribbed barrels with various choke combinations. They feature boxlock actions and were offered with either single or double triggers, and manual extractors or automatic ejectors. The finishes are blued with checkered walnut stocks. The configurations differ basically in the quality of materials and workmanship and the degree of ornamentation.

BL-1

Exc.	V.G.	Good	Fair	Poor
500	450	350	225	150

BL-2

Exc.	V.G.	Good	Fair	Poor
425	375	300	250	200

BL-2/S (Speed Trigger)

Exc.	V.G.	Good	Fair	Poor
450	400	325	275	225

BL-2 Stakeout (18" Barrel)

Exc.	V.G.	Good	Fair	Poor
400	350	275	225	175

BL-3

Exc.	V.G.	Good	Fair	Poor
600	550	475	425	350

BL-3 Competition

Exc.	V.G.	Good	Fair	Poor
650	600	525	475	400

BL-4

Exc.	V.G.	Good	Fair	Poor
800	750	650	525	425

BL-4 Competition

Exc.	V.G.	Good	Fair	Poor
850	800	700	575	450

BL-5

Exc.	V.G.	Good	Fair	Poor
900	850	725	575	450

BL-5 Competition

Exc.	V.G.	Good	Fair	Poor
950	900	775	600	475

BL-6 (Sidelock)

Exc.	V.G.	Good	Fair	Poor
1250	1150	1000	850	675

BL-6 Competition

Exc.	V.G.	Good	Fair	Poor
1300	1200	1050	900	725

Model S55B

A 12 or 20 gauge O/U shotgun with 26", 28", or 30" ventilated rib barrels, various choke combinations and boxlock action with a single selective trigger and extractors. Blued with a checkered walnut stock.

Exc.	V.G.	Good	Fair	Poor
550	500	400	325	275

Model S56 E

As above, but more finely finished.

Exc.	V.G.	Good	Fair	Poor
600	550	450	375	325

Model S58 Competition

As above, with either 26" or 30" barrels, wide vent ribs and competition-type stocks.

Exc.	V.G.	Good	Fair	Poor
700	650	550	475	400

Silver Snipe

A 12 or 20 gauge O/U shotgun with 26", 28", or 30" barrels, boxlock action with a double trigger and extractors. Blued with a checkered walnut stock. Manufactured from 1955 through 1967. A single selective trigger version with ventilated rib and automatic ejectors would be worth approximately 50 percent additional.

Exc.	V.G.	Good	Fair	Poor
475	375	325	275	200

Golden Snipe

As above with a ventilated rib and automatic ejectors. If it has a single selective trigger, add 10%.

Exc.	V.G.	Good	Fair	Poor
675	600	500	350	200

Model 57 E

As above, but more finely finished. Manufactured between 1955 and 1967.

Exc.	V.G.	Good	Fair	Poor
825	775	600	475	250

ASEL Model

A 12 or 20 gauge O/U shotgun with 26", 28", or 30" ventilated rib barrel with various choke combinations. Single selective trigger and automatic ejectors. Blued with a checkered pistol grip stock. Manufactured between 1947 and 1964. Prices below are for 20 gauge guns.

Exc.	V.G.	Good	Fair	Poor
4250	2500	1200	750	400

NOTE: For 12 gauge guns deduct $1000 from Exc. condition price. For EELL grade add 30%.

Model 409 PB

A 12, 16, 20, and 28 gauge boxlock, double-barrel shotgun with 27", 28", or 30" barrels with double triggers and extractors and various choke combinations. Blued with a checkered walnut stock. Manufactured between 1934 and 1964.

Exc.	V.G.	Good	Fair	Poor
775	700	625	500	250

Model 410 E

As above, but more finely finished.

Exc.	V.G.	Good	Fair	Poor
900	825	650	500	275

Model 410

As above, with a 32" full-choke barrel. Blued with a checkered walnut stock. Introduced in 1934.

Exc.	V.G.	Good	Fair	Poor
1000	925	750	600	300

Model 411 E

The Model 410 with false sideplates and more heavily engraved. Manufactured between 1934 and 1964.

Exc.	V.G.	Good	Fair	Poor
1200	1125	950	800	425

Model 424

A 12 and 20 gauge boxlock shotgun with 26" or 28" barrels, double triggers, various choke combinations, and extractors. Blued with a checkered walnut stock. In 20 gauge it is designated the Model 426 and would be worth an additional $100.

Exc.	V.G.	Good	Fair	Poor
950	875	675	500	225

Model 426 E

As above, with silver inlays and heavier engraving, single selective trigger and automatic ejectors. Not imported after 1983.

Exc.	V.G.	Good	Fair	Poor
1150	1075	875	700	350

Model 625

A 12 or 20 gauge boxlock, double-barrel shotgun with 26", 28", or 30" barrels, various choke combinations, double triggers and extractors. Moderately engraved and blued with a checkered walnut grip. Imported between 1984 and 1986.

Exc.	V.G.	Good	Fair	Poor
800	750	600	500	250

Silver Hawk

A 10 or 12 gauge boxlock, double-barrel shotgun with 30" barrels, double triggers and extractors. Blued with a silver-finished receiver and a checkered walnut stock. The 10 gauge version would be worth an additional 20 percent. Discontinued in 1967.

Exc.	V.G.	Good	Fair	Poor
500	450	375	250	150

Model 470 Silver Hawk

Introduced in 1997 to commemorate Beretta's 470 years in the gun making business, this shotgun is offered in either 12 or 20 gauge configurations. The receiver is silver chrome with engraving. The top lever is checkered with a gold inlaid hawk's head. The gun is fitted with a straight grip stock with splinter forearm of select walnut with oil finish. Choice of 26" or 28" barrels with auto ejection or manual extraction. Weight of 12 gauge about 6.5 lbs. The 20 gauge weighs approximately 6 lbs.

NIB	Exc.	V.G.	Good	Fair	Poor
3600	2800	1500	—	—	—

BERETTA "SO" SERIES & OTHER PREMIUM SHOTGUNS

These over and under shotguns were fitted with side locks, automatic ejectors, single or double triggers. Barrel ranges in length from 26" to 30" with a wide variety of choke combinations. These guns were introduced in 1948 in 12 gauge only and no longer imported as a production gun in 1986. Many of these SO guns were sold through the firm of Garcia, a sporting goods firm and distributor. The various grades are priced according to quality of wood, finish engraving coverage, and the like. Do not confuse these earlier Beretta shotguns with the present line of premium grade Berettas now being imported into the U.S.

Model SO-1

Exc.	V.G.	Good	Fair	Poor
2000	1600	1200	800	400

Model SO-2

Exc.	V.G.	Good	Fair	Poor
3000	1900	1500	900	500

Model SO-3

Exc.	V.G.	Good	Fair	Poor
4500	4000	2500	1500	1000

Model SO-4 (Garcia SO3EL)

Exc.	V.G.	Good	Fair	Poor
7500	6500	3500	2000	1500

NOTE: For fully engraved Garcia Model SO3EL add 80%.

Model SO-5 (Garcia SO3EELL)

Exc.	V.G.	Good	Fair	Poor
8000	7500	5000	3500	2500

Model SO-6 (450 or 451EL) Side-x-Side

This model is fitted with Holland and Holland-style side locks and third fastener.

Exc.	V.G.	Good	Fair	Poor
7000	6000	5000	3500	2500

Model SO-7 (451EELL) Side-x-Side

Exc.	V.G.	Good	Fair	Poor
8000	7000	5500	4000	3000

SO-5 Trap

A premium grade Beretta over and under shotgun built for competition trap shooting. Available in 12 gauge with 30" vent rib barrels standard. Barrels in 28" and 32" may be special ordered. Receiver is silver with light scroll engraving. The stock is select highly figured walnut with pistol grip and offered in International or Monte Carlo dimensions. Special trap rubber recoil pad is furnished. Weighs 8 lbs. 2 oz. Furnished with leather case and tools.

NIB	Exc.	V.G.	Good	Fair	Poor
19500	15000	—	—	—	—

SO-5 Trap 2 BBL Set

NIB	Exc.	V.G.	Good	Fair	Poor
22500	17500	—	—	—	—

SO-5 Skeet

Same general specifications as above but furnished to skeet dimensions. Offered in 12 gauge only with 26" or 28" vent rib barrels choked sheet. Weighs 7 lbs. 8 oz.

NIB	Exc.	V.G.	Good	Fair	Poor
19500	15000	—	—	—	—

SO-5 Sporting Clays

Offered in 12 gauge only with choice of 28", 30", or 32" barrels; 26" on special order. Sporting clay dimension walnut stock with pistol grip and rubber recoil pad. Weighs 7 lbs. 8 oz.

SO5 sidelocks

NIB	Exc.	V.G.	Good	Fair	Poor
19500	9000	—	—	—	—

SO-6EL

This is a premium grade Beretta that is available in several different configurations similar to the SO-5. Available in 12 gauge only. It features a true side lock action, single selective or non-selective trigger, fixed or screw-in choke tubes. The receiver is offered either in silver finish or case hardened without engraving. The walnut is highly select walnut with fine line checkering. A choice of pistol grip or straight grip is offered. Supplied with a leather fitted hard case. Weighs about 7 lbs. 4 oz. depending on barrel length.

SO6 receiver

SO-6 Trap

NIB	Exc.	V.G.	Good	Fair	Poor
25500	12000	—	—	—	—

SO-6 Skeet

NIB	Exc.	V.G.	Good	Fair	Poor
25500	12000	—	—	—	—

SO-6 Sporting Clays

NIB	Exc.	V.G.	Good	Fair	Poor
25500	12000	—	—	—	—

SO-6 EELL

A higher grade in the SO-6 series that features a silver receiver with custom engraving with scroll or game scenes. Gold inlays are available on request. Choice of barrel lengths from 26" to 30". Choice of pistol grip or straight grip. All of the same features of the SO 6, but with higher fit and finish. Offered in 12 gauge only.

NIB	Exc.	V.G.	Good	Fair	Poor
42750	32500	—	—	—	—

SO-6EESS

Same specifications as the SO-6 EELL grade but with ruby, sapphire, or emerald side plates with diamond brilliants.

NIB	Exc.	V.G.	Good	Fair	Poor
86850	—	—	—	—	—

SO-7

One of Beretta's best-grade, sidelock, double-barrel shotgun. It is elaborately engraved and has the highest grade walnut in the stock. No longer in production.

Exc.	V.G.	Good	Fair	Poor
9500	7850	6750	5500	4500

SO-9

This model O/U is Beretta's highest grade. Offered in 12, 20, and 28 gauge, and .410 bore. The true side lock (removable) receiver is highly engraved with scroll or game scenes by Italy's finest craftsmen. Barrel lengths are offered from 26" to 30"

with solid hand filed rib. The walnut stock is the finest available with either pistol grip or straight grip. Stock dimensions to customers request. A custom fitted leather case with accessories is supplied with gun. A custom order gun. An independent appraisal is strongly suggested prior to a sale.

Suggester Retail Price: from $44,500 to $90,000

Jubilee Field Grade

This model was introduced in 1998 and is Beretta's finest boxlock over/under shotgun. The model is fitted with sideplates without screws. Offered in 12, 20, 28, and .410 bore with 26" to 30" barrel depending on gauge. Each gun is richly engraved with fine scroll and signed by master engravers. Highly figured walnut with pistol or straight grip. Weights range from about 7 lbs. in 12 gauge to 5.5 lbs. in .410 bore.

Single Gun

NIB	Exc.	V.G.	Good	Fair	Poor
13750	11000	—	—	—	—

Matched Pair

NIB	Exc.	V.G.	Good	Fair	Poor
31650	—	—	—	—	—

Jubilee Sporting Grade

Similar to the above model in terms of finish but offered in 12 gauge only with choice of 30" or 32" barrels. Pistol grip standard.

NIB	Exc.	V.G.	Good	Fair	Poor
13750	11000	—	—	—	—

NOTE: For 2 barrel combination with 20 gauge barrel with extended chokes add $1,500.

Jubilee II

This is a side-by-side model offered in 12 or 20 gauge only with straight grip stocks. Choice of 26" or 28" barrels. Full coverage scroll engraving and highly figured walnut. Double triggers are by special order only. The 12 gauge weighs about 6.5 lbs. while the 20 gauge weighs about 6 lbs.

Single Gun

NIB	Exc.	V.G.	Good	Fair	Poor
13750	11000	—	—	—	—

Matched Pair

NIB	Exc.	V.G.	Good	Fair	Poor
31650	—	—	—	—	—

ASE Deluxe Sporting

This boxlock over/under gun is offered in 12 gauge only with choice of 28" or 30" barrels. Classic European scroll engraving. Offered in both field and competition configuration. Weights are about 7.5 lbs. for the 12 gauge.

NIB	Exc.	V.G.	Good	Fair	Poor
24000	17500	—	—	—	—

Model 687 EELL Gallery Special

A special version of this model. These are especially engraved guns with upgraded wood that are only made for the Beretta Galleries. Offered in 12, 20, 28, and .410 bore.

Single Gun

NIB	Exc.	V.G.	Good	Fair	Poor
7500	—	—	—	—	—

Special Combo-20/28Gauge

NIB	Exc.	V.G.	Good	Fair	Poor
8500	—	—	—	—	—

Matched Pair

NIB	Exc.	V.G.	Good	Fair	Poor
16100	—	—	—	—	—

Model 451 Series

A custom order sidelock shotgun. The lowest priced version would be worth approximately $8,000 in excellent condition; and the top-of-the-line model, approximately $25,000. Prospective purchasers are advised to secure a qualified appraisal prior to acquisition.

Model 450 Series

This model is the same as the 451 series with the exception of being a Holland & Holland sidelock design. Prospective purchasers are advised to secure a qualified appraisal prior to acquisition.

Model 452

This is a premium grade side-by-side shotgun fitted with slide locks (removable). Offered in 12 gauge only with 26", 28", or 30" solid rib barrels. The receiver is a highly polished silver finish without engraving. Triggers may be double, single selective, or single non-selective. The stock and forearm are special select walnut with fine line checkering with a choice of pistol or straight grip. Comes with leather hard case. Weighs about 6 lbs. 13 oz.

NIB	Exc.	V.G.	Good	Fair	Poor
22000	17000	12500	8500	4500	2500

Model 452 EELL

Same as above but furnished with fine scroll or game scene engraving. The highest grade of walnut is furnished for the stock and forearm. Leather case with accessories furnished.

NIB	Exc.	V.G.	Good	Fair	Poor
31000	27500	19500	12000	7500	3500

BERETTA 682 SERIES

Model 682/682 Gold

This is a high grade, quality built O/U shotgun. Offered in 12 and 20 gauge, it is also available in some configurations in 28 gauge and .410 bore with barrel lengths from 26" to 34" depending on the type of shooting required. It is fitted with single selective trigger and automatic ejectors. Barrels are fitted with ventilated rib and various fixed or screw-in choke combinations are available. The stock is a high grade walnut with fine checkering in stock dimensions to fit the function of the gun. The frame is silver with light scroll borders on most models. This model covers a wide variety of applications and these are listed below by grade and/or function:

NOTE: The Beretta Competition series shotguns have been renamed as of 1994. These shotguns are also referred to as the 682 Gold Competition Series guns, such as Model 682 Gold Trap or Model 682 Gold X Trap Combo and so forth.

682 Super Skeet

This model is offered in 12 gauge only with 28" vent rib barrels choked skeet and skeet. Single selective trigger and auto ejectors are standard. This Super Skeet features ported barrels and adjustable length of pull and drop. A fitted hard case is standard. Gun weighs 7 lbs. 8 oz.

NIB	Exc.	V.G.	Good	Fair	Poor
2600	1850	1500	1250	950	750

682 Skeet

This is the standard 12 gauge skeet model that features a choice of 26" or 28" vent rib barrels choked skeet and skeet. Walnut stock is of International dimensions with special skeet rubber recoil pad. Gun is supplied with hard case. Weighs 7 lbs. 8 oz.

NIB	Exc.	V.G.	Good	Fair	Poor
2300	1850	1500	1250	950	700

682 4 BBL Set

This skeet gun is fitted with 4 barrels in 12, 20, 28 gauge, and .410 bore. Each barrel is 28", choked skeet and skeet, and fitted with a vent rib.

NIB	Exc.	V.G.	Good	Fair	Poor
5000	4000	3500	3000	2000	950

682 Super Sporting/682 Gold Sporting Ported

Built for sporting clays this 12 gauge or 20 gauge model features ported barrel and adjustable length of pull and drop. Fitted with 28" or 30" vent barrel with screw-in chokes; fixed chokes on special order. Checkered walnut stock with pistol grip and recoil pad. Supplied with case. Introduced in 1993. Weight of 12 gauge is 7 lbs. 8 oz. and 20 gauge weighs 6 lbs. 3 oz.

NIB	Exc.	V.G.	Good	Fair	Poor
2600	1000	750	—	—	—

682 Sporting/682 Gold Sporting

The standard version of the 12 gauge or 20 gauge Super Sporting model with a choice of 28" or 30" vent rib barrel with screw-in chokes. Checkered walnut stock with recoil pad. Introduced in 1993.

NIB	Exc.	V.G.	Good	Fair	Poor
2600	1750	1500	1250	950	350

682 Sporting Combo

Similar to the 682 Sporting with the addition of two 12 gauge 28" and 30" barrel fitted with screw-in chokes. Supplied with hard case.

NIB	Exc.	V.G.	Good	Fair	Poor
3200	2500	2250	1750	1250	650

Models 682 Skeet (top), 682 Super Trap (middle) and 682 Trap (bottom)

682 Super Trap

This 12 gauge trap model (a 20 gauge set of barrels is available on special order) features ported 30" or 32" ventilated rib barrels with either fixed or screw-in chokes. Automatic ejectors are standard as is a single non-selective trigger. The checkered walnut stock can be adjusted for length of pull and drop of comb and is offered in either Monte Carlo or International dimensions. Weight is approximately 8 lbs. 6 oz.

NIB	Exc.	V.G.	Good	Fair	Poor
2600	1850	1500	1250	950	500

682 Top Single Super Trap

Same as the Super Trap but available in a single barrel configuration of either 32" or 34".

NIB	Exc.	V.G.	Good	Fair	Poor
2400	1950	1600	1350	950	500

682 Top Combo Super Trap

This configuration features a single barrel and a O/U barrel both interchangeable. The combinations are: 30", 32", and 30", 34".

NIB	Exc.	V.G.	Good	Fair	Poor
3000	2750	2250	1750	1250	650

682 Trap

This model is the standard variation Beretta Trap gun. This 12 gauge comes standard with 30" vent rib barrels. However, 28" and 32" barrel can be special ordered. Fixed or screw-in chokes are available. The three-position sliding trigger allows for adjustable length of pull. A checkered walnut stock with recoil pad is standard. Stock is available in either Monte Carlo or International dimensions. Customer has choice of either silver or black receiver. Comes cased.

NIB	Exc.	V.G.	Good	Fair	Poor
2600	1750	1500	1250	900	450

682 Top Single Trap

This 12 gauge single barrel trap gun is available in 32" or 34" vent rib barrel.

NIB	Exc.	V.G.	Good	Fair	Poor
2100	1750	1500	1250	900	450

682 Mono Combo Trap

A special configuration that features a single barrel with vent rib set to place single barrel in bottom position of what would normally be an O/U setup. A second barrel that is an O/U is also provided as part of the set. Single barrel is 34" and the O/U set is 32" in length.

NIB	Exc.	V.G.	Good	Fair	Poor
2700	2350	1850	1350	950	500

682 Top Combo

This trap combination features a standard placement single barrel with an interchangeable O/U barrel. Barrel available in 30", 32"; 30", 34"; and 32", 34". Barrels are fitted with ventilated rib.

NIB	Exc.	V.G.	Good	Fair	Poor
2700	2350	1850	1350	950	500

682 Gold Trap with Adjustable Stock

Introduced in 1998 this over and under features a choice of 30" or 32" barrels with Monte Carlo stock and adjustable drop, cast, and comb. Trigger is adjustable for length of pull. Selected walnut stock with oil finish. Black rubber recoil pad standard. Weight is approximately 8.8 lbs.

NIB	Exc.	V.G.	Good	Fair	Poor
3700	2800	—	—	—	—

NOTE: Add $800 for Top Combo set.

682 Gold Skeet with Adjustable Stock

Introduced in 1999 this 12 gauge model features skeet stock with adjustable comb. Stock drop and cast may also be adjusted. Greystone receiver. Comes with case. Offered in choice of 28" or 30" barrels. Single selective trigger adjustable for length of pull. Black rubber recoil pad standard. Weight is about 7.5 lbs.

NIB	Exc.	V.G.	Good	Fair	Poor
3400	2700	—	—	—	—

682 Gold "Live Bird"

Introduced in 1995 this model has a gray receiver with select walnut stock. Single selective is adjustable for length of pull. Offered in 12 gauge only with 30" barrels. Average weight is 8.8 lbs.

NIB	Exc.	V.G.	Good	Fair	Poor
2250	1750	1450	1150	850	400

S682 Gold E Trap

Chambered for 12 gauge 3" chambers with choice of 30" or 32" barrels with overbore and choke tubes. Highly select walnut stock with black rubber pad. Single selective trigger with adjustable length of pull. Beavertail forend. Adjustable Monte Carlo stock. Front white bead with mid bead sight. Carry case standard. Weight is about 8.8 lbs. Introduced in 2001.

NIB	Exc.	V.G.	Good	Fair	Poor
4300	3500	—	—	—	—

S682 Gold E Trap Combo
Offers the same features as the Trap model but with interchangeable over and under barrels and top single barrel with under rib. Introduced in 2001.

NIB	Exc.	V.G.	Good	Fair	Poor
5300	4200	—	—	—	—

S682 Gold E Skeet
This 12 gauge skeet gun features a special skeet-style stock with beavertail forend. Adjustable stock. Barrel lengths are 28" or 30". Single selective trigger. Weight is about 7.5 lbs. Introduced in 2001.

NIB	Exc.	V.G.	Good	Fair	Poor
4300	3400	—	—	—	—

S682 Gold E Sporting
This 12 gauge model has a choice of 28", 30", or 32" barrels with extended choke tubes and tapered top rib with white front sight and mid bead. Sporting clay-style stock of select walnut. Weight is about 7.6 lbs. Introduced in 2001.

NIB	Exc.	V.G.	Good	Fair	Poor
3850	3000	—	—	—	—

Model 685
A lower-priced O/U chambered for 12 or 20 gauge with 3" chambers, a satin-chromed boxlock action with a single trigger and extractors. Not imported after 1986.

Exc.	V.G.	Good	Fair	Poor
650	600	500	375	200

BERETTA 686 SERIES
Model 686/686 Silver Perdiz Sporting
This Beretta O/U shotgun is available in a number of different configurations. This basic model features ventilated rib barrels from 24" to 30"; 30" being a special order. Screw-in chokes or fixed chokes are available. All configurations are offered in 12 gauge and 20 gauge with 28 gauge and .410 bore available in special order only. The gun is fitted with checkered American walnut stock with black rubber recoil pad and special grip cap.

Some models have silver receiver with scroll engraving and others have black receivers with gold filled contours.

NOTE: This 686 series also renamed in 1994.

Model 686 Essential/Silver Essential
Introduced in 1994 this 686 model is designed to be an entry level 686. It offers all of the mechanical features of the 686 series without any of the frills. Offered in 12 gauge only with 26" or 28" barrels with open-side rib. Plain walnut stock with checkering and plain blue receiver. Weighs about 6.7 lbs. Renamed the Silver Essential in 1997.

Beretta 686 Silver Essential close-up

NIB	Exc.	V.G.	Good	Fair	Poor
900	750	600	450	350	200

686 Ultra Light Onyx
This model features a black anodized light alloy receiver accented with an engraved gold-filled "P. Beretta" signature. Available in 12 gauge only with 26" or 28" vent rib barrels. Chokes are either fixed or screw-in type. Weighs 5 lbs. 1 oz.

NIB	Exc.	V.G.	Good	Fair	Poor
1050	850	750	600	500	400

686 Onyx
Similar in appearance to the Ultra Light Onyx, but available in either 12 gauge or 20 gauge with vent rib barrel lengths from 26" to 28". Chambers are either 3" or 3.5". Checkered walnut stock offered in pistol grip or straight grip. Choice of choke types. Weight of 12 gauge 6 lbs. 13 oz.; 20 gauge 6 lbs. 3 oz. A 12 gauge version with 3-1/2" chambers and 28" barrel is offered (new in 1999) with matte wood finish, matte black receiver, beavertail forend with fingerwells, and silver finish trigger.

NIB	Exc.	V.G.	Good	Fair	Poor
1100	850	750	650	500	400

686 Onyx 2 BBL Set
Same as above but supplied with a 20 gauge 28" vent rib barrel and a 28 gauge 26" vent rib barrel.

NIB	Exc.	V.G.	Good	Fair	Poor
1600	1250	1000	800	650	500

686 Silver Receiver
This model is the basic 686. It features a plain semi-matte silver receiver and is available in either 12 or 20 gauge; 28 gauge available on special order. Vent rib barrels are offered in lengths from 24" to 30" with fixed chokes or choke tubes.

NIB	Exc.	V.G.	Good	Fair	Poor
1100	850	750	650	500	400

686 L/686 Silver Perdiz
Same as above but furnished with a scroll engraved silver receiver. Offered in 28 gauge with 26" or 28" vent rib barrels. Gun weighs 5 lbs. 5 oz.

NIB	Exc.	V.G.	Good	Fair	Poor
1100	850	750	650	500	400

686 Silver Pigeon
Introduced in 1996 this model replaces the Silver Perdiz. It has an electroless nickel finish on a scroll engraved receiver. Offered in 12, 20, and 28 gauge with 26" or 28" barrels. Average weight is 6.8 lbs. A new variation, introduced in 1999, features a 20 gauge gun with 28" barrels, straight grip stock, and matte nickel receiver.

NIB	Exc.	V.G.	Good	Fair	Poor
1700	1350	950	600	—	—

686 Silver Pigeon Sporting
NIB	Exc.	V.G.	Good	Fair	Poor
1400	950	750	600	500	300

686 Silver Pigeon Trap (30")
NIB	Exc.	V.G.	Good	Fair	Poor
1700	1300	—	—	—	—

686 Silver Pigeon Trap Top Mono (32" or 34")

NIB	Exc.	V.G.	Good	Fair	Poor
1700	1300	—	—	—	—

686E Sporting
Offered in 12 or 20 gauge with choice of 28" or 30" barrels. Five Beretta screw-in chokes. Modern ellipsis receiver engraving. Special carrying case. Introduced with new styling in 2001.

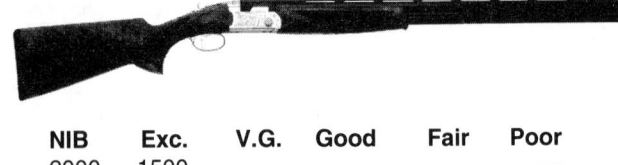

NIB	Exc.	V.G.	Good	Fair	Poor
2000	1500	—	—	—	—

686 EL/Gold Perdiz
This model is available in 12 gauge or 20 gauge with 26" or 28" vent rib barrels. The receiver is silver with scroll engraving and fitted with side plates. A fitted hard case comes with the gun.

NIB	Exc.	V.G.	Good	Fair	Poor
1800	1250	1000	800	700	350

686 Hunter Sport
A sporting clays 12 gauge or 20 gauge shotgun that features a silver receiver with scroll engraving. Wide 12.5mm target rib. Radiused recoil pad. Offered in 26" or 28" vent rib barrels with screw-in chokes. Offered for the first time in 1993.

NIB	Exc.	V.G.	Good	Fair	Poor
1100	850	750	600	500	250

686 Onyx Hunter Sport
Same as above but offered in 12 gauge only with matte black finish on receiver and barrels. Weighs 6 lbs.13 oz. Introduced in 1993.

NIB	Exc.	V.G.	Good	Fair	Poor
1000	850	750	600	500	250

686 Whitewing
Introduced in the fall of 1998, this over and under shotgun is chambered for the 12 gauge shell and fitted with 26" or 28" barrels with Beretta's choke system. The receiver is polished nickel with engraved game scenes, and gold-plated trigger. Walnut pistol grip stock with gloss finish.

NIB	Exc.	V.G.	Good	Fair	Poor
1250	975	—	—	—	—

686 Sporting Combo
Same specifications as the Hunter Sport with the addition of an interchangeable 30" 12 gauge barrel.

NIB	Exc.	V.G.	Good	Fair	Poor
1800	1500	1250	1000	800	550

686 Collection Trap

Introduced in 1996 this model features a special multi-colored stock and forend. Offered in 12 gauge only with 30" barrels. Factory recoil pad standard. Average weight is 7.7 lbs.

NIB	Exc.	V.G.	Good	Fair	Poor
1400	900	750	500	400	300

686 Collection Sport

Similar to above but offered with 28" barrels.

NIB	Exc.	V.G.	Good	Fair	Poor
1400	900	750	500	400	300

Ultralight

This over and under model is chambered for 12 gauge 4-3/4" shells and fitted with a choice of 26" or 28" barrels. The receiver is light aluminum alloy with nickel finish with game scene engraving. Black rubber recoil pad is standard. Single selective trigger, pistol grip, and schnabel forearm. Weight is approximately 5.75 lbs.

Ultralight Receiver

NIB	Exc.	V.G.	Good	Fair	Poor
1700	1300	850	600	—	—

Ultralight Deluxe

Similar to the above model but offered only with 28" barrels. Nickel receiver is gold game scene engraved. First offered in 1998.

NIB	Exc.	V.G.	Good	Fair	Poor
1900	1500	—	—	—	—

BERETTA 687 SERIES

Model 687/687 Silver Pigeon Sporting

This model is similar to the Model 686 but in a slightly more ornate version.

NOTE: This series renamed in 1994.

687 L/Silver Pigeon

This model is offered in 12 gauge or 20 gauge with 26" or 28" vent rib barrels. The boxlock receiver is scroll engraved with game scenes. Auto ejectors and double or single triggers are offered.

NIB	Exc.	V.G.	Good	Fair	Poor
1800	1100	950	800	650	300

687 Silver Pigeon II

Introduced in 1999, this model features a deep relief game scene engraving on a silver receiver. Select walnut stock with oil finish. Available in 12 gauge only with choice of 26" or 28" vent rib barrels. Single selective trigger. Weight is about 6.8 lbs.

NIB	Exc.	V.G.	Good	Fair	Poor
2000	1600	—	—	—	—

687 Silver Pigeon Sporting

A sporting clays version available in 12 or 20 gauge with 28" or 30" barrels.

NIB	Exc.	V.G.	Good	Fair	Poor
1900	1400	1000	700	550	350

687 Silver Pigeon II Sporting

Introduced in 1999, this model features a deep relief engraving with oil finished select walnut stock with schnabel forend. Single selective trigger. Offered in 12 gauge only with choice of 28" or 30" barrels. Black rubber recoil pad. Weight is about 7.7 lbs.

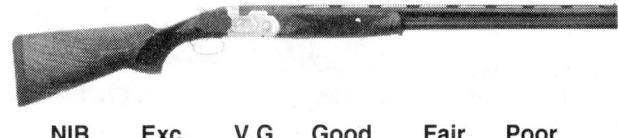

NIB	Exc.	V.G.	Good	Fair	Poor
2100	1500	1100	—	—	—

687 Sporting Combo

Offered in 12 gauge only with two sets of 12 gauge interchangeable vent rib barrels in 28" and 30".

NIB	Exc.	V.G.	Good	Fair	Poor
2400	2100	1850	1500	1150	600

687 EL/687 Gold Pigeon

This model is offered with scroll engraved gold inlaid game animals. Fitted with side plates. The stock is highly figured walnut with fine line checkering. Available in 12, 20, 28 gauge or .410 bore in 26" or 28" vent rib barrels with screw-in chokes. Comes with fitted hard case. Weights for 12 gauge: 6 lbs. 13 oz.; 20 gauge: 6 lbs. 3 oz.; 28/.410: 5 lbs. 5 oz.

NOTE: Series renamed in 1994.

In 2001 Beretta enhanced the engraving on the Model 687EL Gold Pigeon

687 EL 12 gauge and 20 gauge

NIB	Exc.	V.G.	Good	Fair	Poor
3200	2450	1800	1200	750	350

687 EL 28/.410

NIB	Exc.	V.G.	Good	Fair	Poor
3200	2500	1850	1250	800	400

687 EL Gold Pigeon Sporting

A sporting clays model chambered for 12 gauge and fitted with 28" or 30" vent rib barrels. Offered new in 1993. Comes with fitted hard case.

NIB	Exc.	V.G.	Good	Fair	Poor
3200	2250	1750	1250	900	450

687 EELL/Diamond Pigeon

Same as above, including gauge and barrel offerings, but furnished with more fully figured walnut and finer checkering. Fitted with side plates that are scroll engraved with fine cut game scenes. This grade is also available in a straight grip English stock version in 20 gauge as well as a combo set of 20 gauge and 28 gauge interchangeable 26" barrels. All 687 EELL Models are fitted with hard case.

NOTE: Series renamed in 1994.

687 EELL 12 and 20 gauge

NIB	Exc.	V.G.	Good	Fair	Poor
5000	2500	2000	1500	1000	500

687 EELL 28 gauge and .410 bore

NIB	Exc.	V.G.	Good	Fair	Poor
5000	3000	2200	1700	1100	550

687 EELL Combo

NIB	Exc.	V.G.	Good	Fair	Poor
5500	3750	2750	2000	1500	1000

687 EELL Diamond Pigeon Skeet

Same as above with the addition of a skeet configuration. A 12 gauge version is offered with 28" vent rib barrels choked skeet and skeet. Weighs about 7 lbs. 8 oz. A 4 barrel set is also offered with interchangeable 12, 20, 28 gauge, and .410 bore barrels choked skeet and skeet.

687 EELL 12 gauge

NIB	Exc.	V.G.	Good	Fair	Poor
4700	3700	2500	—	—	—

687 EELL 4 BBL Set

NIB	Exc.	V.G.	Good	Fair	Poor
6200	5000	4500	3750	2500	1500

687 EELL Diamond Pigeon Skeet with Adjustable Stock

Same as the Skeet version above but with adjustable comb, drop and cast. Introduced in 1999.

NIB	Exc.	V.G.	Good	Fair	Poor
6200	4500	—	—	—	—

687 EELL Diamond Pigeon Sporting

A sporting clays version of the 687 EELL in 12 gauge only with 28" vent rib barrels fitted with screw-in chokes.

NIB	Exc.	V.G.	Good	Fair	Poor
4800	3250	2500	1700	1100	600

687 EELL Trap

This model is fitted with either International or Monte Carlo trap stock dimensions. Offered in 12 gauge with 30" vent rib barrels fixed or screw-in choke tubes. Weighs about 8 lbs. 6 oz.

NIB	Exc.	V.G.	Good	Fair	Poor
3800	3000	2500	2000	1500	1000

687 EELL Top Combo

A single barrel trap gun with choice of one single barrel set and one Over/Under steel rod barrel in either 30" and 32" or 32" and 34".

NIB	Exc.	V.G.	Good	Fair	Poor
4500	3500	3000	2250	2000	1000

Model 626 Field Grade

A 12 or 20 gauge boxlock double barrel shotgun with a 26" or 28" barrel, various choke combinations, single trigger and automatic ejectors. Engraved, blued with a checkered walnut stock. Imported between 1984 and 1988.

Exc.	V.G.	Good	Fair	Poor
900	825	700	575	475

626 Onyx

This model is a boxlock side-by-side shotgun offered in 12 gauge and 20 gauge. With choice of 26" or 28" solid rib barrels with screw-in chokes. Double triggers are standard but single trigger is available on request. Receiver is anti-glare black matte finish. Stock is walnut with hand checkering and pistol grip. The 12 gauge weighs 6 lbs. 13 oz. and the 20 gauge weighs 6 lbs. 13 oz.

NIB	Exc.	V.G.	Good	Fair	Poor
1250	950	850	750	500	400

627 EL

This model is offered in 12 gauge only with choice of 26" or 28" solid rib barrels. The walnut is highly figured and fine cut checkered. The receiver is silver with side plates engraved with scroll. Comes with hard case.

627EL Sport

NIB	Exc.	V.G.	Good	Fair	Poor
2500	2000	1750	1500	1250	650

627 EELL

Same as above but fitted with scroll engraved side plates with game scenes. Walnut is highly figured with fine line checkering. A straight grip stock is also offered in this model. Comes with hard case.

NIB	Exc.	V.G.	Good	Fair	Poor
3750	3500	3000	2500	1500	1000

Model FS-1

A single barrel boxlock shotgun in all gauges and a 26" or 28", full choke barrel. Blued with a checkered walnut stock. This model was also known as the "Companion."

Exc.	V.G.	Good	Fair	Poor
250	225	175	125	90

TR-1 Trap

A 12 gauge, single barrel boxlock trap gun, 32" ventilated rib, full choke barrel. Blued with a checkered, Monte Carlo stock. Manufactured between 1968 and 1971.

Exc.	V.G.	Good	Fair	Poor
275	250	200	150	100

TR-2 Trap

As above, with a high, competition-type vent rib. It was manufactured between 1969 and 1973.

Exc.	V.G.	Good	Fair	Poor
300	275	225	175	125

Mark II Trap

A 12 gauge, boxlock single barrel trap shotgun with a 32" or 34", full choke barrel, competition-type rib and automatic ejector. Blued with a checkered, Monte Carlo type, walnut stock. Manufactured between 1972 and 1976.

Exc.	V.G.	Good	Fair	Poor
700	625	525	450	275

Model ASE 90/Gold Series

This is a competition trap model Over/Under shotgun. It features a trigger lock assembly that is removable in the field so a spare can be used in the event of failure. The single non-selective trigger has a three way adjustment. The ventilated rib is wide and the side ribs are also ventilated. Walnut stock and forearms are interchangeable. Special trap recoil pad is standard. Receiver is silver with gold inlays or blued on special order. The ASE 90 weighs about 8 lbs. 6 oz.

ASE 90 Pigeon

Equipped with 28" barrels choked Improved Modified and Full.

NIB	Exc.	V.G.	Good	Fair	Poor
6500	5250	3750	2750	1500	1000

ASE 90 Trap

Comes standard with 30" vent rib barrels.

NIB	Exc.	V.G	Good	Fair	Poor
5750	5250	3750	2750	1500	1000

ASE 90 Gold X Trap Combo

Introduced in 1993 this set features a single barrel and interchangeable Over/Under barrels in 30", 32"and 30", 34" combinations.

NIB	Exc.	V.G.	Good	Fair	Poor
6750	2500	—	—	—	1000

ASE 90 Skeet

This model is a skeet version of the ASE 90 series. Features the same basic specifications as the trap model but configured for competition skeet. Offered in 12 gauge only with 28" skeet and skeet chokes. Weighs about 7 lbs. 11 oz.

NIB	Exc.	V.G.	Good	Fair	Poor
5750	2500	—	—	—	1000

ASE 90 Sporting Clay

Configured for sporting clay competition. Offered in 12 gauge only with 28" or 30" vent rib barrels.

NIB	Exc.	V.G.	Good	Fair	Poor
6750	5000	4000	3000	1500	1000

Model SL-2

A 12 gauge slide action shotgun, 26", 28", or 30", ventilated rib barrels with various chokes. Blued with a checkered walnut stock. Manufactured between 1968 and 1971.

Exc.	V.G.	Good	Fair	Poor
350	300	250	200	150

Pigeon Series

As above, in three grades.

Silver Pigeon

Exc.	V.G.	Good	Fair	Poor
300	250	200	150	110

Gold Pigeon

Exc.	V.G.	Good	Fair	Poor
450	400	300	250	200

Ruby Pigeon

Exc.	V.G.	Good	Fair	Poor
600	550	450	375	275

DT 10 TRIDENT SERIES

These shotguns feature removable trigger mechanism, overbored barrels, and special choke tubes.

DT 10 Trident Trap

This is a 12 gauge over/under gun with a number of options. The barrel is 30" or 32" and the highly select walnut stock is fitted with a Monte Carlo comb. Stock is also adjustable. Rib type is 3/8" with progressive step. Full black rubber recoil pad. Weight is about 8.8 lbs. A top single model is also offered with 34" barrel. Introduced in 2000.

NIB	Exc.	V.G.	Good	Fair	Poor
9450	7000	—	—	—	—

DT 10 Trident Trap Combo Top

Same as above with both over/under barrels and single barrel combo.

NIB	Exc.	V.G.	Good	Fair	Poor
11995	9500	—	—	—	—

DT 10 Trident Trap Bottom Single

Introduced in 2001 this model features a choice of 30"/34" barrel combo o r 32"/34" barrel combo. Select walnut stock. Fitted with an adjustable point-of-impact rib. Weight is about 8.8 lbs.

NIB	Exc.	V.G.	Good	Fair	Poor
12250	9500	—	—	—	—

DT 10 Trident Skeet

This 12 gauge skeet model is fitted with either 28" or 30" barrel. Walnut stock is adjustable. Weight is about 8 lbs. Introduced in 2000.

NIB	Exc.	V.G.	Good	Fair	Poor
9450	7000	—	—	—	—

DT 10 Trident Sporting

This 12 gauge over/under gun is fitted with a choice of 28", 30", or 32" barrels. Highly figured walnut stock with Schnabel forearm. Weight is about 8 lbs. Introduced in 2000.

NIB	Exc.	V.G.	Good	Fair	Poor
9200	7000	—	—	—	—

SEMIAUTOMATIC SHOTGUNS

AL Series

A 12 or 20 gauge semiautomatic shotgun with 26", 28", or 30" barrels and various choke combinations. Blued with a checkered walnut stock. Manufactured between 1969 and 1976.

AL-1

Exc.	V.G.	Good	Fair	Poor
400	375	300	225	150

AL-2

Exc.	V.G.	Good	Fair	Poor
350	300	250	175	125

AL-2 Competition

Exc.	V.G.	Good	Fair	Poor
400	350	300	225	175

AL-2 Magnum

Exc.	V.G.	Good	Fair	Poor
425	375	325	250	200

AL-3

Exc.	V.G.	Good	Fair	Poor
400	350	300	225	175

AL-3 Deluxe Trap

Exc.	V.G.	Good	Fair	Poor
775	700	600	500	425

Model 301

Improved version of the AL Series manufactured between 1977 and 1982. It is also available as a slug gun with a 22" barrel with rifle sights.

Exc.	V.G.	Good	Fair	Poor
400	350	300	225	175

Model 1200 Field Grade

A 12 gauge semiautomatic shotgun, 28" ventilated rib barrel, screw-in choke tubes and a 4-round, tubular magazine. Matte blued with either a checkered walnut or black synthetic stock. Introduced in 1984.

NIB	Exc.	V.G.	Good	Fair	Poor
585	525	425	325	250	200

Model 1200 Magnum (3" Chamber)

NIB	Exc.	V.G.	Good	Fair	Poor
585	525	425	325	250	200

Model 1200 Riot (20" Cyl. Bore Barrel)

NIB	Exc.	V.G.	Good	Fair	Poor
585	525	425	325	250	200

Model 1201

This 12 gauge semiautomatic shotgun has a short recoil system and features a synthetic stock with matte black finish and lightweight alloy receiver. Available in two basic configurations: the Field Grade with choice of 24", 26", and 28" vent rib barrel with screw-in chokes and Riot Models with 18" plain cylinder choked barrel with either full stock or pistol grip only stock (introduced in 1993). Field Grade weighs about 6 lbs. 12 oz. and the Riot Model about 6 lbs. 5 oz.

Field Grade

NIB	Exc.	V.G.	Good	Fair	Poor
450	400	350	300	200	150

Riot Model

NIB	Exc.	V.G.	Good	Fair	Poor
650	500	400	350	250	175

NOTE: For Riot Models with pistol grip add $40. For Riot Models with Tritium sights add $75. For Ghost Ring sights add $100.

Model 302

A 12 or 20 gauge semiautomatic shotgun using 2.75" or 3" shells interchangeably, various barrel lengths and screw-in choke tubes. Blued with a checkered walnut stock. Manufactured between 1982 and 1987.

Exc.	V.G.	Good	Fair	Poor
400	350	275	200	150

Model 302 Super Lusso

As above, with a heavily engraved receiver and gold plated, contrasting parts. Presentation-grade walnut was used for the hand checkered stock. Discontinued in 1986.

Exc.	V.G.	Good	Fair	Poor
2150	2000	1600	1050	850

Model Vittoria/Pintail

This semiautomatic 12 gauge shotgun was introduced to the Beretta product line in 1993. It has a short recoil operation and is offered with a 24" or 26" vent rib barrel with screw-in chokes. A 24" rifled choke tube version for slugs is also available. A nonreflective matte finish is put on all wood and metal surfaces. Equipped with sling swivels and walnut stock. Weighs about 7 lbs.

NOTE: Renamed in 1994.

NIB	Exc.	V.G.	Good	Fair	Poor
600	550	500	400	350	250

ES100 Pintail Synthetic

Introduced in 1999, this model is essentially the same as the Pintail model above with the addition of a black synthetic stock. Offered with a choice of 24", 26", or 28" vent rib barrels with screw-in chokes. Weight is about 7 lbs.

NIB	Exc.	V.G.	Good	Fair	Poor
800	650	—	—	—	—

ES100 Pintail Rifled Slug

Introduced in 1997 this model features a 24" fully rifled barrel with adjustable rear sight and removable blade front sight. The receiver is drilled and tapped for scope mount. Hardwood stock with matte finish. Anodized aluminum alloy receiver. Weight is approximately 7 lbs. Fitted with 3" chambers.

NIB	Exc.	V.G.	Good	Fair	Poor
1000	800	600	—	—	—

ES100 Rifled Slug

This variation is the same as the Pintail Rifled Slug model above with the addition of a black synthetic stock. Introduced in 1999.

NIB	Exc.	V.G.	Good	Fair	Poor
900	725	—	—	—	—

ES100 Rifles Slug Combo

Same as above but with the addition of a 28" smooth bored barrel.

NIB	Exc.	V.G.	Good	Fair	Poor
1000	800	—	—	—	—

ES100 NWTF Special Camo

This 12 gauge model is fitted with a 24" barrel with 3" chambers. Stock is Mossy Oak camo. Metal is black matte finish. Weight is about 7.3 lbs. Introduced in 1999.

NIB	Exc.	V.G.	Good	Fair	Poor
925	750	—	—	—	—

A-303 Series

A 12 or 20 gauge semiautomatic shotgun, 26", 28", 30", or 32" ventilated rib barrels with screw-in choke tubes. Blued with a checkered walnut stock. Introduced in 1987. The various models offered differ slightly in configuration and/or quality of materials.

Model A-303

NIB	Exc.	V.G.	Good	Fair	Poor
650	600	475	375	300	250

Model A-303 Upland (24" Barrel)

NIB	Exc.	V.G.	Good	Fair	Poor
680	650	525	425	350	300

Model A-303 Sporting Clays

NIB	Exc.	V.G.	Good	Fair	Poor
735	700	575	475	400	350

Model A-303 Competition (Trap or Skeet)

NIB	Exc.	V.G.	Good	Fair	Poor
675	650	530	425	350	300

Model A-303 Slug Gun (22" Barrel with Sights)

NIB	Exc.	V.G.	Good	Fair	Poor
680	650	525	425	350	300

Model 303 Youth Gun

This version of the Model 303 is available in 20 gauge with a shorter length of pull, 13.5", than standard. It is fitted with a rubber recoil pad, screw-in choke tubes, and checkered walnut stock.

NIB	Exc.	V.G.	Good	Fair	Poor
500	450	400	300	250	200

Model A-303 Ducks Unlimited

A commemorative version of the Model 303. It is chambered for 12 or 20 gauge. There were 5,500 manufactured in 12 gauge in 1986 and 1987. There were 3,500 manufactured in 20 gauge in 1987 and 1988. These are commemorative firearms and are collectible when NIB with all furnished materials.

12 Gauge

NIB	Exc.	V.G.	Good	Fair	Poor
575	500	425	325	275	225

20 Gauge

NIB	Exc.	V.G.	Good	Fair	Poor
675	600	525	425	375	325

Model AL390/Mallard Series

This series of 12 gauge semiautomatic shotguns features a self compensating gas operating recoil system. All loads from target to 3" magnums can be used in the same gun. The Field Model features an anodized light alloy receiver with scroll engraving and matte black receiver top. Magazine capacity is 3 rounds. Checkered walnut stock with recoil pad. Available in vent rib barrel lengths from 24" to 30" with 32" on special request. A 22" or 24" slug plain barrel is also available. Chokes are fixed or screw-in at customer's option. Shotgun weighs about 7 lbs. Beginning in 1996 Beretta will offer the Silver mallard shotguns chambered for the 20 gauge shell and available with 24", 26, or 28" barrels. Average weight for these 20 gauge guns is 6.4 lbs.

Field Grade/AL390 Silver Mallard

NIB	Exc.	V.G.	Good	Fair	Poor
800	600	450	350	300	200

Slug Gun/AL390 Silver Mallard

NIB	Exc.	V.G.	Good	Fair	Poor
800	600	450	350	300	200

AL390 Silver Mallard-Synthetic Stock

NIB	Exc.	V.G.	Good	Fair	Poor
800	600	450	350	300	200

AL390 Silver Mallard-Camouflage

NIB	Exc.	V.G.	Good	Fair	Poor
800	600	450	—	—	—

Deluxe Grade/Gold Mallard

Gold filled game animals and select walnut stock.

NIB	Exc.	V.G.	Good	Fair	Poor
700	650	500	350	300	200

AL390 Trap

NIB	Exc.	V.G.	Good	Fair	Poor
675	600	500	400	300	200

AL390 Super Trap

Features ported barrels in 30" or 32", adjustable length of pull, adjustable comb.

NIB	Exc.	V.G.	Good	Fair	Poor
1000	800	600	500	300	200

AL390 Skeet

NIB	Exc.	V.G.	Good	Fair	Poor
625	550	450	350	250	200

AL390 Super Skeet

Features ported barrel, adjustable cast and length of pull, and adjustable drop. 12 gauge only.

NIB	Exc.	V.G.	Good	Fair	Poor
1000	800	600	500	300	200

AL390 Sporting

NIB	Exc.	V.G.	Good	Fair	Poor
700	550	450	350	250	200

AL390 Sporting-20 gauge

Same as above but in 20 gauge. Introduced in 1997. Weight about 6.8 lbs.

NIB	Exc.	V.G.	Good	Fair	Poor
800	600	—	—	—	—

AL390 Sporting Ported

NIB	Exc.	V.G.	Good	Fair	Poor
725	650	550	400	300	200

AL390 Sport Gold Sporting

Introduced in 1997 this model is similar to above models but with silver sided receiver with gold engraving. Select walnut stock. 12 gauge only with choice of 28" or 30" vent rib barrels. Weight about 7.6 lbs.

NIB	Exc.	V.G.	Good	Fair	Poor
1100	900	—	—	—	—

AL390 Sport Sporting Youth

This semiautomatic shotgun is offered in 20 gauge only with 26" vent rib barrel. Length of pull is 13.5" with adjustable drop and cast on the butt stock. Introduced in 1997. Weight is approximately 6.7 lbs.

NIB	Exc.	V.G.	Good	Fair	Poor
825	675	—	—	—	—

AL390 NWTF Special Youth

Introduced in 1999, this model features a shortened walnut stock with 24" 20 gauge vent rib barrel. Black matte finish. Weight is about 6.4 lbs.

NIB	Exc.	V.G.	Good	Fair	Poor
900	700	—	—	—	—

AL390 Sport Sporting Youth Collection

Same as above but with multi-colored stock and forearm. Introduced in 1997.

NIB	Exc.	V.G.	Good	Fair	Poor
900	750	—	—	—	—

AL390 Sport Diamond Sporting

Introduced in 1998 this model features a silver sided receiver with gold engraving. Select walnut stock with oil finish and adjustable for drop and cast. Available in 12 gauge with 28" or 30" barrels. Sold with spare trigger group and orange front sight beads. Weight is approximately 7.6 lbs.

NIB	Exc.	V.G.	Good	Fair	Poor
3850	3000	—	—	—	—

AL390 Camo

This 12 gauge shotgun is offered with either a 24" or 28" vent rib barrel. Barrel, receiver, stock and forearm have woodland camo finish. Weight is about 7.5 lbs. Offered for first time in 1997.

NIB	Exc.	V.G.	Good	Fair	Poor
995	775	—	—	—	—

Waterfowl/Turkey Model-Matte Finish

NIB	Exc.	V.G.	Good	Fair	Poor
550	500	450	350	300	250

NWTF Special Camo

NIB	Exc.	V.G.	Good	Fair	Poor
1100	875	—	—	—	—

NWTF Special Synthetic

NIB	Exc.	V.G.	Good	Fair	Poor
925	750	—	—	—	—

Super Trap-Ported barrels, adjustable comb and L.O.P.

NIB	Exc.	V.G.	Good	Fair	Poor
975	800	650	500	—	—

Super Skeet-Ported barrels, adjustable comb and L.O.P.

NIB	Exc.	V.G.	Good	Fair	Poor
950	800	650	500	—	—

AL 391 URIKA SERIES

Urika

Introduced in 2000 this semi-automatic shotgun is offered in both 12 and 20 gauge. Choice of barrels from 24" to 30" depending on gauge. Stock is walnut with checkered grip and forend. Rubber recoil pad. Gold trigger. Choke tubes. Weight for 12 gauge is about 7.3 lbs. while the 20 gauge is about 6 lbs.

NIB	Exc.	V.G.	Good	Fair	Poor
850	750	600	—	—	—

Urika Synthetic

Same as above but fitted with a black synthetic stock with gripping inserts. Offered in 12 gauge only. Introduced in 2000.

NIB	Exc.	V.G.	Good	Fair	Poor
950	750	—	—	—	—

Urika Camo

This 12 gauge model is offered with either Realtree Hardwoods camo or Advantage Wetlands camo. In 24" or 26" barrels. Weight is about 7.3 lbs. First introduced in 2000.

NIB	Exc.	V.G.	Good	Fair	Poor
1050	800	—	—	—	—

Urika Gold

This model features a 26" or 28" barrels with choke tubes. The black receiver model is offered in both 12 and 20 gauge with a weight of about 7.3 lbs. The silver receiver model (lightweight) is available in 12 gauge only and weighs about 6.6 lbs. Both configurations are fitted with highly figured walnut stock. Gold trigger. Introduced in 2000.

AL391 Gold receiver

NIB	Exc.	V.G.	Good	Fair	Poor
1150	900	—	—	—	—

Urika Youth

This 20 gauge model features a walnut with a shorter length of pull than standard and a 24" barrel. Weight is about 6 lbs. Introduced in 2000.

NIB	Exc.	V.G.	Good	Fair	Poor
950	750	—	—	—	—

Urika Sporting

This model is offered in both 12 and 20 gauge. Fitted 28" or 30" barrels. Select walnut checkered stock. Gold trigger. Chambered for 3" shells. Weight of 12 gauge is about 7.3 lbs. and the 20 gauge is about 6 lbs. Introduced in 2000.

NIB	Exc.	V.G.	Good	Fair	Poor
1000	750	—	—	—	—

Urika Gold Sporting

This model is offered in 12 gauge with a choice of black or silver receiver. The 20 gauge models are offered with black receiver only. Fitted with 28" or 30" barrels. Highly select checkered walnut stock. Chambered for 3" shells. Introduced in 2000.

NIB	Exc.	V.G.	Good	Fair	Poor
1195	950	—	—	—	—

NOTE: Add $30 for 12 gauge silver receiver.

Urika Trap

This 12 gauge model is fitted with a choice of 30" or 32" barrels. Select checkered walnut stock with Monte Carlo comb. Chambered for 3" shells. Weight is about 7.2 lbs. Introduced in 2000.

NIB	Exc.	V.G.	Good	Fair	Poor
1000	750	—	—	—	—

Urika Gold Trap

This model is similar to the standard Urika Trap but with highly selected checkered walnut stock and black receiver.

NIB	Exc.	V.G.	Good	Fair	Poor
1195	950	—	—	—	—

Urika Parallel Target RL/SL

This 12 gauge competition model is fitted with 28" or 30" barrels and select walnut Monter Carlo stock. The "RL" has standard stock configurations while the "SL" has a shorter length of pull.

NIB	Exc.	V.G.	Good	Fair	Poor
1000	750	—	—	—	—

BERGER, JEAN MARIUS
St. Etienne, France

Berger

The Berger was a magazine fed repeating pistol in 7.65mm. It was a self loader and self cocker. It had all the characteristics of a semiautomatic except for the recoil operating system.

Courtesy James Rankin

Exc.	V.G.	Good	Fair	Poor
5000	4500	3750	3000	2000

BERGMANN, THEODOR
Gaggenau, Germany

Theodor Bergmann was a successful industrialist, designer and sometimes inventor with a deep interest in firearms based in Gaggenau, Germany. His first automatic pistol patent dates from 1892, and by 1894 he had prototype pistols, refined with the help of Louis Schmeisser, being evaluated by various governments. When his designs went into commercial production in 1896, however, they were actually manufactured by the firm of V. Charles Schilling in Suhl, the heart of German arms manufacture. Later he licensed manufacture of his "Mars" pistol to Anciens Establishment Pieper ("Bayard"), and after WWI affiliated with the Lignose firm, producing a line of .25 caliber pocket pistols, first under the Bergmann name but later marketed as Lignose. Still later several pistol designs from the August Menz firm were marketed under the "Bergmann Erben" trademark, though it's doubtful if the Bergmann firm actually had much part in their production or sale.

Model 1894 Bergmann Schmeisser

The Model 1894 was made in prototype form only, with only a few examples surviving and known serial numbers no higher than the mid teens. Most are large framed and chambered for the 8mm Bergmann-Schmeisser cartridge, though at least one was made in 7.5mm Swiss revolver for Swiss army testing and a few very compact versions, with a unique folding trigger, for 5mm Bergmann. Early Bergmann pistols had no extractor, counting on gas pressure to blow the fired (rimless-grooveless) cartridge from the chamber. Too rare to price.

Model 1896, Number 2

The 1896 Number 2 pistols were quite compact and chambered for the 5mm Bergmann cartridge. Early Number 2s also featured a folding trigger and no extractor, but after serial 500 or so reverted to a more conventional in-the-frame trigger and an extractor was added. About 2000 of the later model were produced. Cased sets are known, and add about 50% to the value.

Folding Trigger Number 2

Exc.	V.G.	Good	Fair	Poor
3500	2750	2200	1200	800

Conventional Number 2

Exc.	V.G.	Good	Fair	Poor
2500	2000	1500	900	600

Model 1896 Number 3

The Number 3 was a larger version of the Number 2, chambered for the 6.5mm Bergmann cartridge. Early examples had a slim gripframe and, up to about serial 800, were made without extractor like the early Number 2s. These bring about a 20% premium over the later examples. Number 3 serials range to a little over 4000. Add about 20% for dealer markings (usually English), and 50% for cased sets. A few target models, with long barrel, adjustable sights and set triggers are known and will bring about three times the price of a standard Number 3.

Exc.	V.G.	Good	Fair	Poor
2500	2000	1600	1000	700

Model 1886 Number 4

The Number 4 is a Number 3, chambered for a unique 8mm Bergmann cartridge and serialed in the same series with the Number 3. Both the Number 4 and its cartridge are rare; probably fewer than 200 were ever made.

Exc.	V.G.	Good	Fair	Poor
4500	3750	2500	1750	1250

Model 1897 Number 5

The was Bergmann's first attempt at a more powerful arm for the military market, with a unique side-moving locking system and a 10-shot removable box magazine. The 7.8mm cartridge resembled the 7.63mm Mauser, but with a longer neck. Add 60% for original metal framed leather holster-stock.

Exc.	V.G.	Good	Fair	Poor
7500	6000	4500	2750	1750

Model 1897 Number 5a Carbine

A limited number of the approximately 1000 Bergmann Model 5s were made with a 12-inch barrel and solid wood detachable buttstock and marked "Karabiner Bergmann" on the action cover. A very few were made with a full-length Mannlicher-type stock and sold as the Bergmann Model 1897/07 Sporting Carbine; these are worth about 50% more than the long barreled pistol with detachable stock.

Exc.	V.G.	Good	Fair	Poor
15000	12000	9000	6000	4000

Bergmann Simplex

The Simplex combined some features of the 1896 pistols with improvements developed from the "Mars," resulting in a reasonable compact pocket pistol that came on the market in the early 1900s. It was chambered for the unique Bergmann-Simplex 8mm cartridge, however, and that and competition from better Browning and other designs doomed it to a short production life. Very early examples had checkered wood grips and bring a premium, as do very late examples (above serial 3000) that have the magazine release behind the magazine instead of on the front of the frame.

Exc.	V.G.	Good	Fair	Poor
3250	2800	2000	900	600

Bergmann "Mars"

The Mars was Bergmann's first really successful pistol aimed at the military market. Early examples, about 100 of the total 1000 or so Mars pistols made, were chambered for the 7.63mm Mauser cartridge but later Mars pistols, identified by a large "9mm" on the chamber, were chambered for the special 9mm cartridge that later became known as the 9mm Bergmann-Bayard. The Mars was adopted by the Spanish government in 1905 as their first military automatic pistol, but none were ever delivered by Bergmann. At least two Mars pistols were also made in .45 caliber for U.S. Army trials in 1906, but did not perform well and were dropped from the trials; these are too rare to price. Add 25% for a low serial number gun chambered for 7.63mm Mauser; add 50% for original Bergmann Mars holster stock.

Exc.	V.G.	Good	Fair	Poor
5000	4250	3500	2200	1350

Bergmann Bayard Model 1908

Shortly after receiving the Spanish contract for the Mars pistol, Bergmann's arrangement with Schilling to produce Bergmann pistols ended. However, he negotiated an arrangement with Anciens Establishment Pieper (Bayard) to produce the Mars and, after some minor modifications, AEP filled the Spanish contract. They also marketed the gun commercially, and later secured a production contract from the Danish army as the Model 1910. Spanish contract (proofed with a small circle divided into three segments) and very early commercial pistols have hard rubber grips that proved very fragile in service; these bring a premium as do original unmodified Danish contract guns (with a contract number and Danish letter D proof). A few Model 1908 Bergmann Bayards were equipped with leather and wood holster stocks; a complete rig is worth at least twice the price of an unslotted pistol.

Exc.	V.G.	Good	Fair	Poor
1350	1200	850	700	500

Bergmann Model 1910-21

At the end of WWI the Danish army needed more Bergmann Bayard pistols, but AEP could or would not supply them. The Danes then undertook manufacture in their national arsenals (Haerens Tojus and Haerens Rustkammer), adding an enlarged grip and improved takedown, as their Model 1910-21; most original AEP Bergmann Bayards were also modified in the 1920s into the 1910-21 configuration and were so marked on the frame rail.

Exc.	V.G.	Good	Fair	Poor
1250	1000	750	650	450

Bergmann Post War Pistols

Shortly after WWI ended Bergmann came on the market with a line of .25 caliber pocket pistols; the 2 and 3 were conventional vest pocket designs with a short and long gripframe respectively; the 2a and 3a were identical except for an "Einhand" (one-hand) feature that enabled the user to cycle the slide by pulling the front of the triggerguard with his trigger finger. Soon into production (at about serial 8000) Bergmann affiliated with the Lignose firm and later Model 2 and 3 pistols were marketed under the Lignose name.

Courtesy James Rankin

Model 2 and 3

Exc.	V.G.	Good	Fair	Poor
275	225	175	125	100

Model 2a and 3a

Exc.	V.G.	Good	Fair	Poor
350	275	225	175	125

Bergmann Erben Pistols

The Bergmann Erben pistols appear to be an attempt by the Bergmann family to keep the Bergmann name associated with firearms without actually investing any design or production effort. The Bergmann Erben pistols were all August Menz designs, and were undoubtedly made by Menz as well. Most noteworthy was the "Spezial" model, a very sophisticated double action .32 pocket pistol that could be cocked for single action fire by pulling and then releasing the trigger. Also noteworthy were several compact vest pocket .25s that also bore the Bergmann Erben name.

Bergmann Erben Spezial

Exc.	V.G.	Good	Fair	Poor
1250	950	750	500	300

Bergmann Erben .25 Pistols

Exc.	V.G.	Good	Fair	Poor
350	275	225	150	100

Bergmann Einhand

See Lignose.

BERN, WAFFENFABRIK
Bern, Switzerland

NOTE: For history, technical data, descriptions, photos, and prices see the *Standard Catalog of Military Firearms, 1870 to the Present* under Switzerland.

BERNARDELLI, VINCENZO
Brescia, Italy
Importer
Armsport-Miami, Florida

Established in the 1721, this company originally manufactured military arms and only entered the commercial sporting arms market in 1928.

HANDGUNS

Vest Pocket Model

Similar to the Walther Model 9, in a 6.35mm caliber semiautomatic pistol with a 2.25" barrel, and 5-shot magazine. An extended 8-shot version was also available. Blued with plastic grips. Manufactured between 1945 and 1948.

Exc.	V.G.	Good	Fair	Poor
300	225	155	100	75

Pocket Model

As above, in 7.65mm caliber. This model was also offered with extended barrels that protruded beyond the end of the slide. Introduced in 1947.

Exc.	V.G.	Good	Fair	Poor
275	200	150	100	75

Baby Model

As above, in .22 short or long rifle. Manufactured between 1949 and 1968.

Exc.	V.G.	Good	Fair	Poor
275	200	150	100	75

Sporter Model

A .22 caliber semiautomatic pistol with 6", 8", or 10" barrels and adjustable sights. Blued with walnut grips. Manufactured between 1949 and 1968.

Exc.	V.G.	Good	Fair	Poor
300	225	175	125	100

Revolvers

A .22 rimfire and .32 caliber double-action revolver with 1.5", 2", or 5" barrels. A .22 caliber, 7" barrel version with adjustable sights also available. Manufactured between 1950 and 1962.

Exc.	V.G.	Good	Fair	Poor
225	150	125	100	75

Model 60

A .22, .32 ACP or .380 ACP caliber semiautomatic pistol with 3.5" barrel and fixed sights. Blued with plastic grips. Manufactured since 1959.

Exc.	V.G.	Good	Fair	Poor
250	175	150	125	90

Model 68

A .22 rimfire caliber or .25 ACP semiautomatic pistol with a 2" barrel and 5-shot magazine. Blued with plastic grips. No longer imported into the U.S.

Exc.	V.G.	Good	Fair	Poor
175	125	100	75	50

Model 80

A .22 or .380 ACP caliber semiautomatic pistol with a 3.5" barrel and adjustable sights. Blued with plastic grips. Imported between 1968 and 1988.

Exc.	V.G.	Good	Fair	Poor
225	175	125	100	80

Model USA

A .22, .32 ACP or .380 ACP caliber semiautomatic pistol with a 3.5" barrel, adjustable sights, steel frame and a loaded chamber indicator. Blued with plastic grips.

NIB	Exc.	V.G.	Good	Fair	Poor
450	350	200	150	100	90

Model AMR

As above, with a 6" barrel.

NIB	Exc.	V.G.	Good	Fair	Poor
450	350	200	150	100	90

Model 69

A .22 caliber semiautomatic target pistol with a 6" heavy barrel, and a 10-shot magazine. Blued with checkered walnut grips.

NIB	Exc.	V.G.	Good	Fair	Poor
450	375	300	225	150	100

Model P010

A .22 caliber, single action, semiautomatic target pistol with a 6" barrel, adjustable target sights, barrel weights, and an adjustable trigger. Matte-black finish with stippled walnut grips. Introduced in 1989. Weight 40 oz. sold with special hard case.

NIB	Exc.	V.G.	Good	Fair	Poor
800	700	500	300	200	100

Model PO 18

A 7.65mm or 9mm Parabellum caliber, double action, semiautomatic pistol with a 4.75" barrel and a 16-shot, double stack, detachable magazine. All-steel construction. Blued with plastic grips. Walnut grips are available for an additional $40. Introduced in 1985.

NIB	Exc.	V.G.	Good	Fair	Poor
650	550	400	275	200	100

Model PO 18 Compact

As above, with a 4" barrel and a shorter grip frame with a 14-shot, double-column magazine. Introduced in 1989.

NIB	Exc.	V.G.	Good	Fair	Poor
650	550	400	275	200	100

Model P One

A full size semiautomatic pistol chambered for the 9mm or 40S&W calibers. Fitted with a 4.8" barrel. Can be fired double action or single. 10 shot magazine. Weight is 2.14 lbs. Available in black or chrome finish. Add $50 for chrome finish.

NIB	Exc.	V.G.	Good	Fair	Poor
625	525	400	275	200	100

Model P One-Compact

Same as above but with 4" barrel and offered in .380 caliber as well as 9mm and 40S&W. Weight is 1.96 lbs.

NIB	Exc.	V.G.	Good	Fair	Poor
650	550	400	275	200	100

Practical VB Target

Designed for Practical shooting this 9mm pistol has a 6" barrel with choice of 2 or 4 port compensator. It is fitted with numerous extra features. Weights is 2.2 lbs.

NIB	Exc.	V.G.	Good	Fair	Poor
1500	1200	850	600	400	200

Practical VB Custom

As above but designed for IPSC rules.

NIB	Exc.	V.G.	Good	Fair	Poor
2250	1900	1400	900	600	300

SHOTGUNS

Model 115 Series

A 12 gauge Over/Under, boxlock, double-barrel shotgun with various barrel lengths and choke combinations, single triggers and automatic ejectors.

Model 115

NIB	Exc.	V.G.	Good	Fair	Poor
1525	1250	900	700	550	300

Model 115S

NIB	Exc.	V.G.	Good	Fair	Poor
2000	1750	1200	800	600	300

Model 115L

NIB	Exc.	V.G.	Good	Fair	Poor
2500	2000	1500	900	650	300

Model 115E

NIB	Exc.	V.G.	Good	Fair	Poor
5200	4800	4200	3500	2500	1850

Model 115 Trap

NIB	Exc.	V.G.	Good	Fair	Poor
2200	1950	1400	950	750	600

Model 115S Trap

NIB	Exc.	V.G.	Good	Fair	Poor
2700	2450	1900	1450	1150	900

Model 115E Trap

NIB	Exc.	V.G.	Good	Fair	Poor
5250	4800	4200	3500	2500	1850

Model 190 Series

A 12 gauge, Over/Under shotgun with various barrel lengths and choke combinations, a single selective trigger and automatic ejectors. Engraved and silver-finished with a checkered walnut stock. Introduced in 1986. The various versions differ in the degree of ornamentation and quality of materials utilized in construction.

Model 190

NIB	Exc.	V.G.	Good	Fair	Poor
1050	950	750	600	475	400

Model 190MC

NIB	Exc.	V.G.	Good	Fair	Poor
1150	1050	850	700	575	500

Model 190 Special

NIB	Exc.	V.G.	Good	Fair	Poor
1350	1150	950	800	675	600

Model 190 Combo Gun

A .243, .308 or .30-06 caliber and 12, 16, or 20 gauge combination Over/Under rifle shotgun with a boxlock action, double triggers and automatic ejectors. Blued with a checkered walnut stock. Introduced in 1989.

NIB	Exc.	V.G.	Good	Fair	Poor
1325	1125	925	775	650	575

Orione Series

A 12 gauge boxlock Over/Under shotgun with various barrel lengths and choke combinations. Finishes and triggers were optional, as were extractors or automatic ejectors.

Orione

NIB	Exc.	V.G.	Good	Fair	Poor
1150	900	700	500	400	200

Orione S

NIB	Exc.	V.G.	Good	Fair	Poor
1150	900	700	500	400	200

Orione L

NIB	Exc.	V.G.	Good	Fair	Poor
1250	1000	800	600	500	250

Orione E

NIB	Exc.	V.G.	Good	Fair	Poor
1350	1150	850	600	500	250

S. Uberto I Gamecock

A 12, 16, 20, or 28 gauge boxlock side by side shotgun with either 25.75" or 27.5" barrels, various chokes, double triggers and extractors. Automatic ejectors were available and would be worth a 20 percent premium. Blued with a checkered stock.

Exc.	V.G.	Good	Fair	Poor
950	700	500	350	250

Brescia

A 12, 16, or 20 gauge sidelock double-barrel shotgun with exposed hammers, various barrel lengths, choke combinations, a sidelock action, double triggers, and manual extractors. Blued with an English-style, checkered walnut stock.

NIB	Exc.	V.G.	Good	Fair	Poor
1850	900	700	450	350	225

Italia
This is a higher-grade version of the Brescia.

NIB	Exc.	V.G.	Good	Fair	Poor
2250	1250	750	600	400	250

Italia Extra
This is the highest grade hammer gun that Bernardelli produces.

NIB	Exc.	V.G.	Good	Fair	Poor
5900	2750	1500	1000	750	300

Uberto Series
A 12, 16, 20 or 28 gauge, Anson & Deeley boxlock double-barrel shotgun with various barrel lengths and choke combinations. The increased value of the various models depends on the degree of engraving, options, and quality of materials and workmanship utilized in their construction.

S. Uberto I

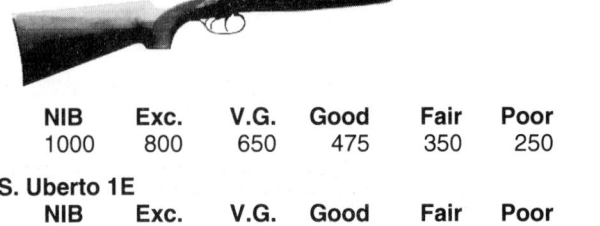

NIB	Exc.	V.G.	Good	Fair	Poor
1000	800	650	475	350	250

S. Uberto 1E
NIB	Exc.	V.G.	Good	Fair	Poor
1100	900	700	500	350	250

S. Uberto 2

NIB	Exc.	V.G.	Good	Fair	Poor
1500	1100	800	500	350	250

S. Uberto 2E
NIB	Exc.	V.G.	Good	Fair	Poor
1750	1350	950	600	400	250

S. Uberto F.S.

NIB	Exc.	V.G.	Good	Fair	Poor
2000	1500	1100	800	400	250

S. Uberto F.S.E.
NIB	Exc.	V.G.	Good	Fair	Poor
2250	1750	1200	800	400	250

Roma Series
Similar to the S. Uberto Series with false sideplates. The value of the respective variations result from the degree of ornamentation and quality of materials and workmanship utilized in the construction.

Roma 3

NIB	Exc.	V.G.	Good	Fair	Poor
1550	1200	800	600	300	200

Roma 3E
NIB	Exc.	V.G.	Good	Fair	Poor
1750	1300	900	650	300	200

Roma 4

NIB	Exc.	V.G.	Good	Fair	Poor
1950	1400	1100	750	400	250

Roma 4E
NIB	Exc.	V.G.	Good	Fair	Poor
2000	1500	1200	750	400	250

Roma 6

NIB	Exc.	V.G.	Good	Fair	Poor
2100	1750	1400	850	500	250

Roma 6E
NIB	Exc.	V.G.	Good	Fair	Poor
2200	1800	1400	850	500	250

Roma 7
NIB	Exc.	V.G.	Good	Fair	Poor
2900	2500	1800	1200	700	350

Roma 8
NIB	Exc.	V.G.	Good	Fair	Poor
3500	3000	2250	1550	850	400

Roma 9
NIB	Exc.	V.G.	Good	Fair	Poor
4000	3500	2750	1700	950	450

Elio
A 12 gauge, boxlock double-barrel shotgun with various barrel lengths and choke combinations, lightweight frame, double triggers and extractors. Scroll-engraved, silver finished receiver, blued barrels and a select, checkered walnut stock.

NIB	Exc.	V.G.	Good	Fair	Poor
1000	800	600	500	350	250

Elio E

As above, with automatic ejectors.

NIB	Exc.	V.G.	Good	Fair	Poor
1100	900	700	550	350	250

Hemingway

As above, with coin-finished receiver, engraved with hunting scenes, 23.5" barrels, double triggers or single trigger and a select, checkered walnut stock. Available in 12, 20 and 28 gauge.

NIB	Exc.	V.G.	Good	Fair	Poor
1750	1350	900	700	400	250

Hemingway Deluxe

Same as above but fitted with full side plates.

NIB	Exc.	V.G.	Good	Fair	Poor
2250	1750	1200	800	400	250

Las Palomas Pigeon Model

A live Pigeon gun in 12 gauge with single trigger.

NIB	Exc.	V.G.	Good	Fair	Poor
3800	3250	2500	2000	1500	750

Holland V.B. Series

A 12 or 20 gauge sidelock shotgun with various barrel lengths, detachable Holland & Holland-type locks, single triggers, and automatic ejectors. The various models listed below vary in the amount of engraving and the quality of their wood. Prospective purchasers are advised to secure a qualified appraisal prior to acquisition.

Holland V.B. Liscio

NIB	Exc.	V.G.	Good	Fair	Poor
8000	5500	4000	3000	2000	1000

Holland V.B. Inciso

NIB	Exc.	V.G.	Good	Fair	Poor
10250	7500	5250	4000	2500	1250

Holland V.B. Lusso

NIB	Exc.	V.G.	Good	Fair	Poor
11000	8000	6000	4500	2500	1250

Holland V.B. Extra

NIB	Exc.	V.G.	Good	Fair	Poor
13000	10000	7500	5500	3000	1500

Holland V.B. Gold

NIB	Exc.	V.G.	Good	Fair	Poor
45000	30000	22500	15000	7500	3000

Luck

An over and under shotgun with single selective trigger or double triggers, automatic ejectors with choice of fixed chokes or choke tubes. Available in 12 gauge. Blued or coin finish receiver.

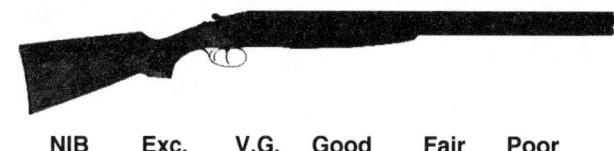

NIB	Exc.	V.G.	Good	Fair	Poor
1400	1100	850	600	400	200

Giardino

This is a semiautomatic shotgun chambered for the 9mm shot cartridge. Fitted with a 4-round magazine. Weight is 5 lbs.

NIB	Exc.	V.G.	Good	Fair	Poor
400	350	300	250	200	100

RIFLES

Carbina VB Target

A semiautomatic carbine chambered for the .22LR cartridge. Barrel is 20.8" and magazine capacity is 10 rounds.

NIB	Exc.	V.G.	Good	Fair	Poor
650	550	400	300	200	100

Comb 2000

A rifle shotgun combination in 12 or 16 gauge with a variety of centerfire calibers to choose from. Barrels are 23.5" long. Set trigger special rib for scope mount and cheekpiece stock with pistol grip. Weight is 6-3/4 lbs.

NIB	Exc.	V.G.	Good	Fair	Poor
2200	1700	1200	800	400	250

Express 2000

An over and under double rifle chambered for a variety of European calibers Express with automatic ejectors, double set triggers or single trigger, muzzle adjustment device. Barrel length is 23.5".

NIB	Exc.	V.G.	Good	Fair	Poor
2750	2350	1700	1200	600	300

Express VB

A side by side double rifle chambered for a variety of European calibers up to .375 H&H. Double or single trigger auto ejectors, and finely engraved receiver with beavertail forearm and cheekpiece stock with pistol grip.

NIB	Exc.	V.G.	Good	Fair	Poor
5500	4700	3750	2000	1000	750

Express VB Deluxe

Same as above but with side plates and select walnut stock finely checkered.

NIB	Exc.	V.G.	Good	Fair	Poor
5600	4800	3750	2000	1000	750

Minerva

A side by side double rifle with exposed hammers chambered for the 9.3x74R cartridge. Fitted with fancy walnut stock, double triggers, hand cut rib, and other high quality features.

NIB	Exc.	V.G.	Good	Fair	Poor
6000	5600	4250	2500	1200	750

BERNARDON MARTIN
St. Etienne, France

1907/8 Model

A 7.65mm caliber semiautomatic pistol. The left side of the slide is marked "Cal. 7.65mm St. Etienne." The trademark "BM" is molded into the grips. Sometimes found with a 32-round horseshoe magazine.

Courtesy James Rankin

Exc.	V.G.	Good	Fair	Poor
400	300	225	175	100

NOTE: Add $400 for horseshoe magazine.

Occasionally the Bernardon Martin pistol will be noted with the word "Hermetic" stamped on the slide in letters that do not match the other markings on the weapon.

BERNEDO, VINCENZO
Eibar, Spain

B C

The B C is in caliber 6.35mm and most of the barrel is exposed. The recoil spring is housed in the rear of the receiver. The B C closely resembles the Tanque pistol.

Courtesy James Rankin

Exc.	V.G.	Good	Fair	Poor
175	125	90	60	35

Bernado

This model 7.65mm is in the Spanish style of the Ruby automatic pistols.

Courtesy James Rankin

Exc.	V.G.	Good	Fair	Poor
175	125	90	60	35

BERSA
Ramos Mejia, Argentina
Importer-Eagle Imports

The firm Fabrica de Armas Bersa SA has been selling pistols in this country since about the mid-1970s.

Model 644

This model is a blowback pocket pistol chambered for the .22 Long Rifle. The trigger system is single action. Barrel length is 3.5", overall length is 6.57", and empty weight is approximately 28 oz. This is the basic Bersa model from which its other models derive their design and function.

NIB	Exc.	V.G.	Good	Fair	Poor
225	175	150	125	100	75

Model 622

Similar to the Model 644 but with a slightly longer barrel.

NIB	Exc.	V.G.	Good	Fair	Poor
225	175	150	125	100	75

Model 23

A .22 rimfire caliber, double-action, semiautomatic pistol with a 3.5" barrel and 10-shot detachable magazine. Either blued or satin nickel-plated with checkered walnut grips.

NIB	Exc.	V.G.	Good	Fair	Poor
225	200	150	125	100	75

Model 223

As above, with a squared triggerguard and nylon grips. Imported after 1988.

Exc.	V.G.	Good	Fair	Poor
225	175	125	100	75

Model 224

As above, with a 4" barrel. Imported after 1988.

Exc.	V.G.	Good	Fair	Poor
225	175	125	100	75

Model 225

As above, with a 5" barrel. Discontinued in 1986.

Exc.	V.G.	Good	Fair	Poor
225	175	125	100	75

Model 226

As above, with a 6" barrel. Discontinued in 1988.

Courtesy John J. Stimson, Jr.

Exc.	V.G.	Good	Fair	Poor
225	175	125	100	75

Model 323

A .32 ACP caliber single-action semiautomatic pistol, with a 3.5" barrel, fixed sights and a 7-shot detachable magazine. Blued with molded plastic grips. Not imported after 1986.

Exc.	V.G.	Good	Fair	Poor
150	125	100	75	50

Model 383

As above, in .380 caliber. Discontinued in 1988.

Exc.	V.G.	Good	Fair	Poor
175	150	125	90	75

Model 383A

A .380 ACP caliber double-action semiautomatic pistol with a 3.5" barrel with fixed sights and 7-shot magazine. Blued with checkered walnut grips. Overall length is 6.6" and weight is about 24 oz. Available in blue or nickel finish.

NIB	Exc.	V.G.	Good	Fair	Poor
225	200	150	125	100	75

Model 83

Similar to the above model but with double action operating system. Weighs about 26 oz. Introduced in 1988.

NIB	Exc.	V.G.	Good	Fair	Poor
225	200	150	125	100	75

Model 85

As above, with a double-column magazine. Introduced in 1988.

NIB	Exc.	V.G.	Good	Fair	Poor
275	250	200	150	100	75

Model 97

This model is a slightly larger version of the Model 644 chambered for the 9mm Short.

NIB	Exc.	V.G.	Good	Fair	Poor
200	175	150	125	100	75

Model 86

Similar to the Model 85 .380 caliber, but features a matte blue or satin nickel finish, wrap around rubber grips, and three-dot sight. Magazine capacity is 13 rounds.

NIB	Exc.	V.G.	Good	Fair	Poor
295	250	225	200	150	100

Thunder 9

Introduced in 1993 this model is a double action 9mm pistol that features ambidextrous safety, reversible extended magazine release, ambidextrous slide release, adjustable trigger stop, combat style hammer, three-dot sights, and matte blue finish. Magazine capacity is 15 rounds.

NIB	Exc.	V.G.	Good	Fair	Poor
300	275	250	200	150	100

Series 95

This is a semi-automatic double action pistol chambered for the .380 cartridge. Choice of matte blue or nickel finish. Barrel length is 3.5". Fixed sights. Magazine capacity is 7 rounds. Weight is about 23 oz.

NIB	Exc.	V.G.	Good	Fair	Poor
250	200	150	100	—	—

Thunder Deluxe

This semi-automatic double action pistol is chambered for the .380 cartridge. Blued finish. Fixed sights. Barrel length is 3.5". Weight is about 23 oz. Magazine capacity is 9 rounds.

NIB	Exc.	V.G.	Good	Fair	Poor
275	225	175	100	—	—

BERTHIER
French State

The Berthier bolt-action rifle was adopted as the French service rifle in 1890 and was made in two styles: a Carbine with a 17.5" barrel, and a rifle with a 31.5" barrel. Both were chambered for the 8mm Lebel cartridge and originally had three-shot magazines. After World War I, many of these arms were modified so that a 5-shot magazine could be used.

Berthier Carbine

Exc.	V.G.	Good	Fair	Poor
—	350	175	125	75

Berthier Rifle

Exc.	V.G.	Good	Fair	Poor
—	300	150	100	50

BERTRAND, JULES
Liege, Belgium
Le Novo

A 6.35mm caliber double-action revolver. Manufactured in the 1890s. The only identifying markings are the "JB" trademark on the grips.

Exc.	V.G.	Good	Fair	Poor
—	150	75	35	20

Lincoln

As above, in 7.65mm caliber.

Exc.	V.G.	Good	Fair	Poor
—	150	75	35	20

Le Rapide

A 6.35mm caliber, semiautomatic pistol marked "Man Gr/d'Armes et Munitions Cal. Browning 6.35 Le Rapide." The grips are marked "Le Rapide" and "JB."

Exc.	V.G.	Good	Fair	Poor
—	175	90	50	25

BERTUZZI
Brescia, Italy
Importer-New England Arms
Kittery Point, Maine

SHOTGUNS OVER/UNDER

Zeus

A 12 gauge sidelock shotgun with automatic ejectors, single selective trigger, and deluxe checkered walnut stock. Custom order in various barrel lengths and chokes. Engraved. Rarely seen on the used gun market.

NIB	Exc.	V.G.	Good	Fair	Poor
10000	8500	6500	4500	3500	2500

Zeus Extra Lusso

As above, but available on special order only.

NIB	Exc.	V.G.	Good	Fair	Poor
15000	12000	8500	6000	4500	3500

SHOTGUNS SIDE-SIDE

Orione

A 12-gauge boxlock shotgun with Anson & Deeley through bolt, in various barrel lengths and chokes, single selective trigger and automatic ejectors. Hand checkered, walnut stock with a semi-beavertail forearm.

NIB	Exc.	V.G.	Good	Fair	Poor
3500	3000	2500	1850	1500	1000

Best Quality Sidelock

A custom order sidelock shotgun in various gauges with barrel lengths and chokes to suit the customer. Extensively engraved with a walnut stock.

NIB	Exc.	V.G.	Good	Fair	Poor
7500	7000	6000	4500	3500	2500

BIGHORN ARMS CO.
Watertown, South Dakota

Target Pistol

A .22 caliber single shot pistol resembling a semiautomatic. Ventilated rib barrel 6" in length. Stock of molded plastic.

Exc.	V.G.	Good	Fair	Poor
175	125	100	85	65

Shotgun

A single shot 12 gauge shotgun with a 26" barrel. Blued with a plastic stock.

Exc.	V.G.	Good	Fair	Poor
125	85	65	50	30

BIGHORN RIFLE CO.
Orem, Utah

Bighorn Rifle

Custom order in any caliber, double-barrel, bolt-action rifle with optional barrel lengths and finishes. Double trigger and walnut stock.

NIB	Exc.	V.G.	Good	Fair	Poor
2000	1750	1500	1000	750	400

BILHARZ, HALL, & CO.
CONFEDERATE CARBINES

During the American Civil War, the Southern Confederacy made valiant but often futile efforts to produce small arms for its forces. The small firm of Bilharz, Hall, & Co. of Pittsylvania Court House (currently Chatham), Virginia, exemplifies one such effort to furnish the Confederate cavalry with arms. Unfortunately, because their arms were never marked with the name of the manufacturer, they have been mistaken for the products of other small arms makers of the Confederacy.

Bilharz, Hall & Co. breechloading ("Rising Breech") carbine

Overall length 40"; barrel length 21"; caliber 54. Markings: either "P" or "P/CS" on upper left side of barrel and top of rising breech. The peculiar feature of this carbine is the manner in which the breechblock exposes the chamber. A box-like chamber at the rear of the barrel rises vertically to expose the chamber for a paper cartridge by activating the lever/triggerguard mechanism. Only 100 of this type were delivered to the Confederacy in September 1862. Two types of front sight blades are known, but neither affects the value.

Courtesy Milwaukee Public Museum, Milwaukee, Wisconsin

Exc.	V.G.	Good	Fair	Poor
—	—	40000	15000	3500

Bilharz, Hall & Co. muzzleloading carbine

Overall length 37-1/2"; barrel length 22"; caliber .58. Markings: "P/CS" on upper left of barrel near breech; "CSA" on top near breech. Modeled after the Springfield U.S. M1855 rifle carbine, the Bilharz, Hall & Co. muzzleloading carbine has often been mistakenly identified as a product of D.C. Hodgkins & Sons of Macon, Georgia. Serial numbers (found internally) belie that identification. Instead these arms are part of deliveries made to Richmond from the middle of 1863 until March 1864. Serial numbers, noted in excess of 700, suggest that about 1,000 were produced. Two basic types, the earlier (through serial number 300) were made with brass nosecaps; the later type (about serial number 310 through at least 710) have pewter nosecaps on the short forestock; neither type affects value.

Exc.	V.G.	Good	Fair	Poor
—	—	20000	10000	3000

BILLINGHURST, WILLIAM
Rochester, New York

Billinghurst originally worked for James and John Miller of Rochester. After James Miller's death in 1837, Billinghurst established his own shop where he produced revolving rifles based upon Miller's 1829 patent. While these arms were originally made with percussion ignition systems (either pill or percussion cap), later examples using self-contained metallic cartridges are sometimes encountered. Billinghurst also established a well-deserved reputation for making extremely accurate percussion target pistols and rifles.

Revolving Rifle

Calibers vary from .40 to .50 with barrels from 24" to 29"; walnut stocks. The barrels marked: "W. Billinghurst, Rochester, N.Y.," or "W. Billinghurst."

Exc.	V.G.	Good	Fair	Poor
—	—	7500	3000	950

A Billinghurst full stocked revolving sporting rifle sold at auction for $8,050. Chambered for .45 caliber with 35.5" octagon barrel. Condition of metal is brown patina with 50% faded case colors. All original.
Amoskeag Auction Company, November 2000

W. Billinghurst Under Hammer Pistol

This pistol is somewhat different than most of the under hammers encountered. The barrels are 12" to 18" in length and of a heavy octagonal construction. They are chambered from .30 to .38 caliber and utilize the percussion ignition system. Higher grade versions feature a part-round barrel, and it is important to note that no two pistols are alike. These pistols were furnished with detachable shoulder stocks, and a good many were cased with telescopic sights and false muzzles. This is a high quality weapon; and if encountered with the optional accessories, it would definitely warrant an individual appraisal. This firearm was manufactured in the 1850s and 1860s.

Shoulder Stock-Add 50%.

Exc.	V.G.	Good	Fair	Poor
—	—	3500	1500	800

BILLINGS
Location Unknown

Billings Pocket Pistol

A .32 rimfire caliber single shot spur trigger pistol with a 2.5" round barrel and an unusually large grip. The barrel is stamped "Billings Vest Pocket Pistol Pat. April 24, 1866." Blued with walnut grips. Manufactured between 1865 and 1868.

Exc.	V.G.	Good	Fair	Poor
—	—	3000	1250	500

BINGHAM LTD.
Norcross, Georgia

PPS 50

A .22 rimfire caliber semiautomatic rifle patterned after the Soviet PPSH submachine gun with 16" barrel and a 50-round drum magazine. Blued, walnut or beech stock with a vented handguard. Manufactured between 1976 and 1985.

Exc.	V.G.	Good	Fair	Poor
350	250	175	125	100

AK-22

A .22 rimfire caliber semiautomatic rifle patterned after the Soviet AK-47 with either a 15- or 29-shot magazine. Walnut or beech stock. Manufactured between 1976 and 1985.

Exc.	V.G.	Good	Fair	Poor
250	200	150	100	75

Bantam

A .22 rimfire or .22 rimfire Magnum caliber bolt-action rifle with an 18.5" barrel. Manufactured between 1976 and 1985.

Exc.	V.G.	Good	Fair	Poor
100	85	70	50	35

BISMARCK
Location Unknown

Bismarck Pocket Revolver

A .22 caliber spur trigger revolver with a 3" round-ribbed barrel and a 7-shot, unfluted cylinder. Brass frame and the remainder was plated with rosewood grips. The barrel is marked "Bismarck." Manufactured in the 1870s.

Exc.	V.G.	Good	Fair	Poor
—	—	400	150	90

BITTERLICH, FRANK J.
Nashville, Tennessee

A .41 caliber single shot percussion pistol in a variety of octagonal barrel lengths, German silver mounts, walnut stock. The barrel and locks are marked "Fr.J. Bitterlich/Nashville, Tenn." Produced between 1861 and 1867.

Exc.	V.G.	Good	Fair	Poor
—	—	4000	1750	750

BITTNER, GUSTAV
Wieport, Bohemia

Bittner

A 7.7mm Bittner caliber self-loading pistol with a 4.5" barrel. The bolt containing the firing pin is fully mounted within the frame and is operated by the finger lever trigger. Manufactured in 1893. Less than 500 were made.

Exc.	V.G.	Good	Fair	Poor
6000	5000	3500	2000	1000

A cased Bittner was sold at auction for $19,800. Condition was excellent to mint. All accessories in case. Faintich Auction Services, Inc., September 1998

BLAKE, J. H.
New York, New York

Blake Bolt Action Rifle

A .30-40 Krag caliber bolt action rifle with a 30" barrel, and a 7-shot magazine. The stock is secured by three barrel bands. Blued with a walnut stock. Manufactured between 1892 and 1910.

Courtesy Milwaukee Public Museum, Milwaukee, Wisconsin

Exc.	V.G.	Good	Fair	Poor
—	750	500	375	200

BLANCH, JOHN
London, England

Blanch Percussion Pistol

A .69 caliber single shot, percussion pistol with a 5" Damascus barrel. Engraved frame and hammer with a walnut grip. Manufactured in the 1830s.

Exc.	V.G.	Good	Fair	Poor
—	5000	2500	1300	800

Double Barrel Shotguns
SEE—British Double Guns

BLAND, THOMAS & SONS
London, England

Established in 1840, this firm has produced or marketed a wide variety of percussion and cartridge arms. Over the years, the firm has occupied a variety of premises in London, some of them concurrently.

41 Whittall Street	1840-1867
41, 42, 43 Whittall Street	1867-1886
106 Strand	1872-1900
430 Strand	1886-1900
2 William IV Street	1900-1919
4-5 William IV Street	1919-1973
New Row, St. Martin's Lane	1973-

T. Bland & Sons is perhaps best known for their double barrel rifles and shotguns, which were made in a variety of grades.

Double Barrel Shotguns
SEE—British Double Guns

BLASER JAGDWAFFEN
Germany
Importer-SIG Arms, Inc. Exeter, NH

Model K77

A single shot rifle chambered in a variety of calibers with a 24" barrel and silver-plated as well as engraved receiver. Walnut stock. Introduced in 1988.

Extra Barrels-Add $750 Per Barrel.

NIB	Exc.	V.G.	Good	Fair	Poor
2300	1850	1500	1200	900	450

Model R-84

A bolt action sporting rifle chambered in a variety of calibers with either a 23" or 24" barrel. Interchangeable barrels are available for this model. Walnut stock. Imported beginning in 1988.

NIB	Exc.	V.G.	Good	Fair	Poor
2300	1850	1500	1200	900	450

Model R-93 LX

This is a straight pull back bolt action rifle with interchangeable barrels in calibers from .22-250 to .416 Rem. Mag. Barrel length for standard calibers is 22" and for Magnum calibers 26". Magazine capacity is 3 rounds. Receiver is drilled and tapped for Blaser scope mounts. Weight is approximately 7 lbs. Two piece walnut stock. Introduced by SIG Arms into the U.S. in 1998.

NIB	Exc.	V.G.	Good	Fair	Poor
1800	1400	—	—	—	—

NOTE: Add $200 for left-hand rifles, add $800 for .416 Remington Magnum.

Model R-93 Classic

Similar to the model above in choice of calibers and barrel lengths but with the addition of highly figured walnut stock and game scene engraved receiver.

NIB	Exc.	V.G.	Good	Fair	Poor
3500	2750	—	—	—	—

NOTE: Add $200 for left-hand rifles, add $800 for .416 Remington Magnum.

Model R-93 Synthetic

Also available in the same wide range of interchangeable barrels and calibers. This model features a 1 piece black synthetic stock.

NIB	Exc.	V.G.	Good	Fair	Poor
1500	1200	—	—	—	—

NOTE: Add $200 for left hand rifles, add $800 for .416 Remington Magnum.

Model R-93 Attache

This model features a custom made stock of highly figured walnut with cheekpiece, leather covered butt plate, silver pistol grip cap, ebony forend tip, and custom checkering. Sold with a leather carrying case.

NIB	Exc.	V.G.	Good	Fair	Poor
5100	4000	—	—	—	—

NOTE: Add $200 for left hand rifles.

Model R-93 Safari Synthetic

This model is chambered for the .416 Remington Magnum cartridge and fitted with a 24" heavy barrel with open sights. Weight is 9.5 lbs. Black synthetic stock. Other Blaser barrels will interchange on this model.

NIB	Exc.	V.G.	Good	Fair	Poor
2100	1700	—	—	—	—

Model R-93 Safari LX

Same as the R-93 Safari Synthetic with the exception of a 2 piece walnut stock.

NIB	Exc.	V.G.	Good	Fair	Poor
2500	2000	—	—	—	—

Model R-93 Safari Classic

This model features an engraved receiver and fancy walnut stock.

NIB	Exc.	V.G.	Good	Fair	Poor
2500	2000	—	—	—	—

Model R-93 Safari Attache

This is a top-of-the-line version of the R-93 series. It features engraved receiver, fancy walnut stock and other custom options found on the R-93 Attache model.

NIB	Exc.	V.G.	Good	Fair	Poor
5800	4500	—	—	—	—

Model R-93 Long Range Sporter

Introduced in 1998, this bolt action rifle is chambered for the .308 Win. cartridge. The barrel length is 24" without muzzle brake. Removable box magazine holds 10 rounds. The stock is aluminum and fully adjustable. Weight is approximately 10.4 lbs. No longer in production.

NIB	Exc.	V.G.	Good	Fair	Poor
2130	1700	—	—	—	—

Model R-93 (LRS2)

This model, introduced in 2000, is a 2nd generation version of the Long Range Sporter model above. It is chambered for the .300 Win. Mag and the .308 both of which are interchangeable. It is also chambered for the .338 Lapua cartridge which does not interchange with the other calibers. The cheekpiece is improved and a new front rail has been added to this model. Barrel length is 24" without muzzle brake. Weight is about 10.4 lbs.

NIB	Exc.	V.G.	Good	Fair	Poor
3475	2700	—	—	—	—

NOTE: For .338 Lapua add $350.

WHAT'S IT LIKE-THE BLASER R93

As a German design, one might expect an engineering sensation and the R93 certainly fits that description. When shouldering one for the first time, the shooter finds several differences between it and a "normal" Mauser design. Most obvious, at least at first, is its looks. The buttstock and forend are pretty much traditional looking but between the two pieces of European walnut there is a frame of steel (or is it aircraft grade aluminum) not covered by the stock. The next most obvious difference grabs you when operating the bolt. It doesn't turn, like a Mauser. Rather, it pulls straight to the rear. In addition, it is manually cocked by pushing forward on a knob at the rear of the bolt. It features modular construction so switching calibers is simply a matter of switching components. If one wanted to do so and could afford it, 15 different standard and magnum calibers could be mated to one rifle. It is built like a bank vault and functions flawlessly. Not lifting the bolt takes a little getting used to, as does manually cocking the rifle, but a couple range sessions fix that potential problem. Otherwise, it is pretty much straightforward like any other fine magazine rifle.

Like most European goods these days the Blaser R93 is a bit pricey and it is certainly unconventional. It is a highly functional rifle though and for one wanting something a bit different, the Blaser would be an excellent candidate.

Tom Turpin

Model R-93 Grand Luxe

Offered in the same wide range of calibers as other Blaser models with the addition of a high grade walnut stock, fully hand engraved receiver, and matching scroll sideplates. Introduced in 1999.

NIB	Exc.	V.G.	Good	Fair	Poor
4675	3700	—	—	—	—

NOTE: Add $200 for left hand rifles.

Model K-95 Standard

This is a single shot model with break-open action. The receiver is aluminum with engraving on the side plates. Barrel length is 23.6" for standard calibers and 25.6" for magnum calibers. Oil finish Turkish walnut stock. Interchangeable barrels in calibers from .243 to .300 Wby. Magnum. Weight is about 5.5 lbs. Introduced in 2001.

NIB	Exc.	V.G.	Good	Fair	Poor
2250	1750	—	—	—	—

Model K-95 Luxus

Same as above but with fancy Turkish walnut stock and hand-graving on receiver and side plates.

NIB	Exc.	V.G.	Good	Fair	Poor
2600	2000	—	—	—	—

Ultimate Bolt Action

As above, with a silver-plated and engraved receiver as well as a set trigger.

NIB	Exc.	V.G.	Good	Fair	Poor
1500	1300	1050	825	700	375

Special Order Ultimate

The above model is available in a variety of finishes and degrees of decoration as follows:

Ultimate Deluxe

NIB	Exc.	V.G.	Good	Fair	Poor
1600	1400	1150	925	800	400

Ultimate Super Deluxe

NIB	Exc.	V.G.	Good	Fair	Poor
4250	3750	3250	2500	2000	1000

Ultimate Exclusive

NIB	Exc.	V.G.	Good	Fair	Poor
5700	5000	4500	3500	2600	1300

Ultimate Super Exclusive

NIB	Exc.	V.G.	Good	Fair	Poor
8900	7900	6800	5000	4000	2000

Ultimate Royal

NIB	Exc.	V.G.	Good	Fair	Poor
11500	9500	7500	6000	4000	2000

NOTE: Extra interchangeable caliber barrels for the above rifles are available at $700 to $1,200 per barrel depending on the grade.

BLISS, F. D.
New Haven, Connecticut

Bliss Pocket Revolver

A .25 caliber spur trigger revolver with a 3.25" octagon barrel, 6-shot magazine, and a square butt. Blued with either hard rubber or walnut grips. The barrel is stamped "F.D. Bliss New Haven, Ct." There was an all-brass framed version made early in the production, and this model would be worth approximately 50 percent more than the values listed here for the standard model. Approximately 3,000 manufactured circa 1860 to 1863.

Exc.	V.G.	Good	Fair	Poor
—	—	700	300	100

BLISS & GOODYEAR
New Haven, Connecticut

Pocket Model Revolver

A .28 caliber percussion revolver with a 3" octagonal barrel, 6-shot magazine, unfluted cylinder and a solid frame with a removable sideplate. Blued with a brass frame and walnut grips. Approximately 3,000 manufactured in 1860.

Exc.	V.G.	Good	Fair	Poor
—	—	950	450	200

BLISSETT
SEE—English Military Firearms

BLUNT & SYMS
New York, New York

Under Hammer Pepperbox

Pepperboxes produced by Blunt & Syms are noteworthy for the fact that they incorporate a ring trigger cocking/revolving mechanism and a concealed under hammer. They were produced in a variety of calibers and the standard finish was blued. Normally these pistols are found marked simply "A-C" on the face of the barrel group. Some examples though are marked "Blunt & Syms New York".

This firm was in business from approximately 1837 to 1855.

Small Frame Round Handle .25-.28 Caliber

Exc.	V.G.	Good	Fair	Poor
—	—	1000	600	200

Medium Frame Round Handle .31 Caliber

Exc.	V.G.	Good	Fair	Poor
—	—	750	350	150

Round Handle Dragoon .36 Caliber

Exc.	V.G.	Good	Fair	Poor
—	—	1500	700	300

Medium Frame Saw Handle .31 Caliber

Exc.	V.G.	Good	Fair	Poor
—	—	950	500	250

Saw Handle Dragoon .36 Caliber

Exc.	V.G.	Good	Fair	Poor
—	—	1750	800	350

Dueling Pistol

A .52 caliber percussion single shot pistol with an octagonal barrel normally of 9" length. Steel furniture with a walnut stock. Barrel marked "B&S New York/Cast Steel".

Exc.	V.G.	Good	Fair	Poor
—	—	1500	650	300

A .36 caliber single-shot percussion pistol with a 6" half octagonal barrel and a bar hammer. Blued or browned with walnut grips. Marked as above.

Exc.	V.G.	Good	Fair	Poor
—	—	900	400	200

Side Hammer Pocket Pistol

A .31 or .35 caliber single shot percussion pistol with a 2.5" to 6" octagonal barrel. Blued with walnut grips.

Exc.	V.G.	Good	Fair	Poor
—	—	650	300	175

Side Hammer Belt Pistol

As above, in calibers ranging from .36 to .44 with barrel lengths of 4" or 6".

Exc.	V.G.	Good	Fair	Poor
—	—	750	350	250

Ring Trigger Pistol

A .36 caliber percussion single shot pistol with a 3" to 5" half octagonal barrel and a ring trigger. Blued with walnut grips.

Exc.	V.G.	Good	Fair	Poor
—	—	600	300	150

Double Barrel Pistol

A .36 to .44 caliber percussion double barrel pistol with 7.5" barrels and walnut grips. A ring trigger variation of this model is known.

Exc.	V.G.	Good	Fair	Poor
—	—	700	300	150

Double Barrel Under Hammer Pistol

As above, with two under hammers and in .34 caliber with 4" barrels.

Exc.	V.G.	Good	Fair	Poor
—	—	900	400	200

Derringer Style Pistol

A .50 caliber single shot percussion pistol with a 3" barrel, German silver mounts and a walnut stock. The lock is marked "Blunt & Syms/New York".

Exc.	V.G.	Good	Fair	Poor
—	—	1000	475	250

BODEO
Italian Service Revolver

System Bodeo Modello 1889 (Enlisted Model)

Exc.	V.G.	Good	Fair	Poor
—	250	150	100	75

Modello 1889 (Officers Model)

Exc.	V.G.	Good	Fair	Poor
—	250	150	100	75

BOLUMBURO, G.
Eibar, Spain

A 6.35 and 7.65mm caliber semiautomatic pistol under the trade name Bristol, Giraida, Gloria, Marina, Regent, and Rex. The values on these would be quite similar, and they may be regarded the same.

Exc.	V.G.	Good	Fair	Poor
200	125	85	65	45

BOND
SEE—English Military Firearms

BOND ARMS INC.
Grandbury, Texas

Texas Defender

This is a stainless steel over and under derringer chambered for a variety of calibers such as .45 Colt/.410, .357 Magnum, 9mm, .45 ACP, and .44 Magnum. Barrels are interchangeable. Grips are laminated black ash or rosewood. Barrel length is 3" with blade front sight and fixed rear sight. Weight is approximately 21 oz. Introduced in 1997.

BOOM

SEE—Shaftuck, C.S.
Hatfield, Massachusetts

BORCHARDT

Berlin, Germany
Waffenfabrik Lowe

Borchardt

A forerunner of the German Luger. The Borchardt was a semi-automatic pistol chambered for the 7.65mm Borchardt cartridge. It was fitted with a 6.5" barrel and the magazine held 8 rounds. The pistol was designed by Hugo Borchardt and manufactured by Ludwig Lowe of Berlin. Later models were manufactured by DWM, Deutsch Waffen Und Munitionsfabriken, Berlin. Most Borchardts come with a case which holds shoulder stock, holster, extra magazines, and numerous other accessories. Prospective purchasers should secure a qualified appraisal prior to acquisition.

Exc.	V.G.	Good	Fair	Poor
320	275	—	—	—

A cased Borchardt with accessories sold at auction for $17,250. Built by Loewe. Condition was excellent. Butterfield & Butterfield, May 1999

Courtesy James Rankin

Pistol Only

Exc.	V.G.	Good	Fair	Poor
14000	10000	7500	5000	2500

Pistol with Case and Accessories

Exc.	V.G.	Good	Fair	Poor
19000	15000	10000	8000	4500

A Borchardt Model 1893 pistol was sold at auction for $14,950. Produced by DWM. Original stock. No case, pistol only. Condition was very good to excellent.
Amoskeag Auction Co. Inc., May 2000

BORSIG
East Germany

The Borsig is the East German version of the Soviet Makarov pistol. It is a double action, chambered for the Soviet 9X18mm cartridge. Its appearance is nearly identical to the Makarov.

Exc.	V.G.	Good	Fair	Poor
250	175	150	100	75

BOSIS, LUCIANO
Brescia, Italy

Bosis is a maker of high grade sidelock over and under and side by side guns in gauges 12, 20, 28, and .410. These guns are made on a custom order basis.

Over and Under

Values for used guns in excellent condition begin at $30,000. Secure an expert appraisal prior to sale.

Side-by-Side

Values for used guns in excellent condition begin at $20,000. Secure an expert appraisal prior to sale.

NOTE: Small gauge guns will bring a premium of 20%.

BOSS & CO.
London, England
SEE—British Double Guns

A cased pair of Boss & Co. sidelock shotguns was sold at auction for $51,750. Chambered for 12 gauge with 28" self-opening barrels. Scroll engraved receiver and sidelocks. Straight grip stocks. Double triggers. Condition was excellent. Built in 1961.
Butterfield & Butterfield, August 2000

BOSWELL, CHARLES
London, England

One of England's more established makers of best-quality rifles and shotguns. In 1988 the company was purchased by an American consortium and the Cape Horn Outfitters of Charlotte, North Carolina, was appointed their sole agent.

Double Rifle, Boxlock

A .300 Holland & Holland, .375 Holland & Holland or .458 Winchester Magnum double-barrel boxlock rifle with double triggers and a walnut stock. Other features were made to the customer's specifications. A .600 Nitro Express version was also available.

.600 Nitro Express-Add 25%.

Exc.	V.G.	Good	Fair	Poor
40000	32500	25000	17500	12500

Double Rifle, Sidelock

As above, with Holland & Holland-style sidelocks.
.600 Nitro Express-Add 25%.

Exc.	V.G.	Good	Fair	Poor
55000	40000	30000	20000	17500

Double Barrel Shotguns
SEE—British Double Guns

BOSWORTH, B. M.
Warren, Pennsylvania

Bosworth Under Hammer Pistol

A .38 caliber single-shot percussion pistol with an under hammer and a 6" half octagonal barrel. The frame is marked "BM Bosworth". Browned with brass grips forming part of the frame. Made circa 1850 to 1860.

Exc.	V.G.	Good	Fair	Poor
—	—	1000	450	200

BRAENDLIN ARMOURY
London, England

A .450 caliber 8-barrel pistol with hinged barrels, rotating firing pin and double-action lock. Manufactured during the 1880s.

Exc.	V.G.	Good	Fair	Poor
—	7500	4500	2750	1500

BRAND
E. Robinson, Maker
New York

Brand Breech Loading Carbine

A .50 rimfire caliber carbine with a 22" barrel secured by one barrel band. The frame is marked "Brand's Patent July 29,1862/E. Robinson Manfr/New York." This carbine was produced in limited numbers, primarily for trial purposes.

Exc.	V.G.	Good	Fair	Poor
—	—	4750	2000	900

BREDA, ERNESTO
Milan, Italy

Andromeda Special

A 12 gauge boxlock shotgun with various barrel lengths and chokes, single selective triggers and automatic ejectors. Engraved, satin-finished with checkered walnut stock.

Exc.	V.G.	Good	Fair	Poor
700	650	550	425	300

Vega Special

A 12 gauge boxlock Over/Under shotgun with 26" or 28" barrels, various choke combinations, single selective trigger and automatic ejectors. Engraved and blued with a checkered walnut stock.

Exc.	V.G.	Good	Fair	Poor
650	600	500	375	275

Vega Special Trap

As above with a competition-styled stock and 30" or 32" barrels with full chokes.

Exc.	V.G.	Good	Fair	Poor
1150	900	750	500	350

Sirio Standard

Similar to the Vega with extensive engraving and a higher degree of finishing. There is a 28" barreled skeet version available in this model.

Exc.	V.G.	Good	Fair	Poor
2250	2000	1750	1250	650

Standard Semiautomatic

A 12 gauge semiautomatic shotgun with 25" or 27" ventilated rib barrels, screw-in choke tubes, an engraved receiver, and checkered walnut stock.

Exc.	V.G.	Good	Fair	Poor
325	275	225	175	125

Grade I

As above, with more engraving and finer wood.

Exc.	V.G.	Good	Fair	Poor
550	475	325	225	175

Grade II

A more elaborately engraved version of the Grade I.

Exc.	V.G.	Good	Fair	Poor
675	600	450	375	250

Grade III

The most deluxe version in this line with select walnut and extensive engraving.

Exc.	V.G.	Good	Fair	Poor
875	800	650	575	250

Magnum Model

Same as the standard, 12 gauge Magnum.

Exc.	V.G.	Good	Fair	Poor
475	400	350	275	200

Gold Series Antares Standard

A 12 gauge semiautomatic shotgun with a 25" or 27" ventilated rib barrel and screw-in choke tubes. Blued with a checkered walnut stock.

Exc.	V.G.	Good	Fair	Poor
500	400	350	275	225

Gold Series Argus

As above, with alloy frame.

Exc.	V.G.	Good	Fair	Poor
525	425	375	300	250

Gold Series Aries

As above, except in 12 gauge Magnum.

Exc.	V.G.	Good	Fair	Poor
550	450	400	325	275

BREN 10
Dornaus & Dixon Inc.
Huntington Beach, California

Manufactured from 1983 until 1986.

Standard Bren 10

A 10mm caliber double action semiautomatic pistol with a 5" barrel and 11-shot magazine. Stainless frame and satin-blued slide. Manufactured between 1983 and 1986.

NIB	Exc.	V.G.	Good	Fair	Poor
1500	1100	800	500	300	200

M & P Model

As above, with a matte black finish.

NIB	Exc.	V.G.	Good	Fair	Poor
1500	1100	800	500	300	200

Special Forces Model

Chambered for 10mm cartridge and is similar to the M&P model. Offered in two models: Model D has a dark finish while Model L has a light finish. Prices below are for Model D, add 25% for Model L.

NIB	Exc.	V.G.	Good	Fair	Poor
1500	1200	900	700	500	250

Pocket Model

This model is fitted with a 4" barrel and 9-shot magazine.

NIB	Exc.	V.G.	Good	Fair	Poor
1150	1100	800	500	300	200

Dual-Master Presentation Model

As above, with a .45 caliber, extra barrel and slide and a fitted walnut case.

NIB	Exc.	V.G.	Good	Fair	Poor
3500	2500	1250	700	500	300

Marksman Model

Similar to the Standard Model but in .45 caliber. There were 250 manufactured for the "Marksman Shop" in Chicago, Illinois.

NIB	Exc.	V.G.	Good	Fair	Poor
1400	1000	750	500	300	200

Initial Commemorative

There were supposed to be 2,000 of these manufactured in 1986, but no one knows how many were actually produced. They are chambered for the 10mm and have a high-gloss blue finish with 22 kt. gold-plated details. The grips are laser engraved, and the whole affair is furnished in a walnut display case.

NIB	Exc.	V.G.	Good	Fair	Poor
3500	2500	—	—	—	—

BRETTON
Ste. Etienne, France
Baby Standard

A 12 or 20 gauge Over/Under shotgun with various barrel lengths and choke combinations and double triggers. Blued, checkered walnut stock.

NIB	Exc.	V.G.	Good	Fair	Poor
800	725	625	500	400	325

Deluxe Grade

A 12, 16, and 20 gauge Over/Under shotgun. Engraved, coin-finished receiver with walnut stock.

NIB	Exc.	V.G.	Good	Fair	Poor
1000	800	650	500	400	325

BRIGGS, H. A.
Norwich, Connecticut

Briggs Single Shot Pistol

A .22 caliber single shot spur trigger pistol with a 4" part-round/part-octagonal barrel with a downward rotating breech-block. Blued with walnut grips. Frame is marked "H.A. Briggs/Norwich, Ct." Manufactured in the 1850s and 1860s.

Exc.	V.G.	Good	Fair	Poor
—	—	2500	1100	400

BRILEY MANUFACTURING INC.
Houston, Texas

El Presidente Model-Unlimited

This 1911 style pistol can be built on a Caspian Arms, STI, or SVI frame. Includes scope mount, compensator, match barrel, cocking sight, lowered and flared ejection port, front and rear serrations, aluminum guide rod, and numerous other custom features. Offered in most calibers. Blued finish.

NIB	Exc.	V.G.	Good	Fair	Poor
2400	2000	—	—	—	—

Versatility Plus Model-Limited

Built on a 1911 frame with BoMar sight, checkered mainspring housing and checkered front strap. Many other custom features. Available in .45 ACP, .40 S&W, and 9mm.

NIB	Exc.	V.G.	Good	Fair	Poor
1750	1500	—	—	—	—

Versatility Model-Limited

Similar to the above model but without several features such as the checkered front strap. Available in .45 ACP, .40 S&W, 9mm.

NIB	Exc.	V.G.	Good	Fair	Poor
1250	1000	—	—	—	—

Lightning Model-Action Pistol

Built on a 1911 frame this pistol features many custom components including a titanium compensator. Weight no more than 40 oz. Available in 9mm and .38 Super only.

NIB	Exc.	V.G.	Good	Fair	Poor
2200	1800	—	—	—	—

Carry Comp Model-Defense

Built on a 1911 frame this model features a dual port cone compensator with many custom features. Barrel length is about 5". Offered in .45 ACP only.

NIB	Exc.	V.G.	Good	Fair	Poor
2150	1800	—	—	—	—

BRITISH DOUBLES

By Douglas Tate

British double barrel shotguns have never been more popular. Tougher laws in Britain have encouraged gun owners there to sell at just the same time as shotgunners here have attained enough sophistication to recognize that even a mid-grade gun such as a Webley is a better weapon than a machine-made American classic.

The result has been unprecedented opportunities for shooters/collectors but also a bit of confusion. Several lessons have emerged but the most important is that traditional methods of evaluating American shotguns will not work for British guns and that each one must be individually evaluated on its own merits.

For instance "Exc., V.G., Good, Fair, & Poor" are almost meaningless with English shotguns because you will frequently find guns which are cosmetically in the first category but which paper thin barrels and out of proof bores have consigned to the last category.

In just the same way that there are only three important elements to game management; habitat, habitat, habitat, there are only three significant elements to appraising British guns; barrels, barrels and barrels. This is because most problems with second-hand British guns when fixed will add value to the gun but replacement barrels are prohibitively expensive. A $4000 gun with sound barrels is a bargain but an identical gun bought for $400 with duff barrels is a dud because it will cost $10,000 for new ones. Barrel condition is then the essential component of value.

If a 12 bore gun was originally proofed at .729 and still measures .729, (this figure represents the interior bore diameter 9 inches from the breech) and if the wall thicknesses—9 inches from the muzzle—are well above the gun trade recommended minimum of 20 thou, then the gun is excellent regardless of its appearance, because cosmetic problems are easily rectified.

If, on the other hand, it was proofed at .729 and now measures .750 and has wall thicknesses in the low teens, it is virtually worthless regardless of how lovely it may look. If you have neither the gauges nor the skills to check these measurements out yourself, send the gun to one of the English gun makers working in North America listed at the end of this essay.

This type of thing is more common than one might think. I learned about such a gun recently which was externally new in the box condition but must have been put away dirty because the barrels were pitted beyond redemption. An unscrupulous seller could easily have the pits lapped out and offered it as a new gun with mirror bores. Only careful gauging would reveal that the gun was out of proof and potentially dangerous.

Also, it is a mistake to think that original condition has the same significance for British as it does for American guns. The most desirable 23,000 / 24,000 serial number Purdeys were built with hard use in mind and consequently left the factory with the wood slightly proud. The idea was that at the end of every season the gun would be returned to the maker for routine maintenance, and also to have the barrels and furniture reblacked, the color case revarnished and the wood refinished as need be.

A philistine seeing two guns, one with proud wood and one with the wood refinished to the metal, might assume the former was a restock and the latter an original gun. Such are the pitfalls for the uninitiated. But the point is that broadly speaking, a properly maintained gun will command a high resale value and completely unfired guns from the golden era are so rare as to be virtual non-existent. The exception: a pair of Boss's from the 1930's sold at Sotheby's in London on Tuesday, May 17th, 1994 for £58,700, over $90,000.

The major distinction between a reconditioned and re-case colored Parker and a sympathetically restored Purdey is that the latter is perfectly acceptable while the former is a corporal offense.

Another significant difference is that model designations mean very little in the U.K. Although most makers offered a variety of models in their catalogues, the actual guns rarely resemble the catalogue pictures and model names almost never appear on the guns themselves. The exception here is W. W. Greener, who offered an unbelievable one hundred and fifty one (151) grades of guns many of which seem to have the model name or number on the gun. Moreover certain models such as the Churchill "Hercules" were of quite different qualities before and after WWII while the model known as the "Utility" in the thirties became the "Regal" in the fifties with out any noticeable change of quality.

To avoid confusion the British—to all intents and purposes—ignore model designation. Instead they have adopted a system which divides any given makers output into boxlock non-ejector, boxlock ejector, sidelock nonejector, sidelock ejector, over unders and hammer guns. It's a system that works well for the Brits and one that worked well for Don Gustine in his essay in Birmingham Gunmakers (see pages 162-164.) I hope it is one which will work well here but ultimately, of course, because of their bespoke nature, the only way to evaluate British guns is one at a time.

ENGLISH GUNMAKERS IN NORTH AMERICA

Dale Tate
P.O. Box 3016
Gonzales, CA 93926
408 675 2473

David Trevallion
9 Old Mountain Road
Cape Neddick, ME 03902
207 361 1130

John F. Rowe
P.O. Box 86
2501 Rockwood Road
Enid, OK 73702
405 233 5942

Kirk Merrington
207 Sierra Road
Kerrville, TX 78028
830 367 2937

Les Paul
R.R. 1, Roseneath, Ontario
Canada K0K 2X0
905 721 1876

Paul Hodgins
P.O. Box 3546
Logan, UT 84323
435 753 2796

Alfred W. Gallifent
P.O. Box 34
Warrington, PA 18976
215 343 3974

Following is an alphabetic listing of British makers whose guns are most frequently encountered with dealers and at auctions.

Army & Navy Co-operative Society Limited, London

Started in 1871 as an organization by which military men could buy wine wholesale, the membership soon increased to include diplomats and foreign service bureaucrats, while the catalogue expanded to include every manner of household and sporting goods. Most guns were acquired in the Birmingham trade and many were Webley & Scott products.

Estimates listed below range from guns barely in proof with marginal wall thicknesses to those with barrel specifications as proofed.

Boxlock non-ejectors $1,000 to $3,000
Boxlock ejectors $1,500 to $5,000
Sidelock non-ejectors $2,000 to $7,000
Sidelock ejectors $3,000 to $15,000
Hammer Guns $1,000 to $3,000

Henry Atkin

The first Henry Atkin was one of James Purdey's original workman, his son started the family business in 1878. J. P. Morgan and Gough Thomas were both Atkin customers because they felt the Atkin's offered the same quality as Purdey's without as high a cost.

Estimates listed below range from guns barely in proof with marginal wall thicknesses to those with barrel specifications as proofed.

Boxlock non-ejectors $1,500 to $4,000
Boxlock ejectors $2,000 to $8,500
Sidelock non-ejectors $2,000 to $10,000
Sidelock ejectors $4,000 to $30,000
Hammer Guns $2,000 to $10,000

Frederick Beesley

Frederick Beesley served his apprenticeship with Moore and Grey and worked for several London gun makers including James Purdey and Son before establishing his own business in 1879. His claim to fame is the self opening system he patented (No. 31 of 1880) and licensed to James Purdey for "five shillings for every gun made." To this day every side-by-side gun by Purdey is built on this system.

Estimates listed below range from guns barely in proof with marginal wall thicknesses to those with barrel specifications as proofed.

Boxlock non-ejectors $1,500 to $4,000
Boxlock ejectors $2,000 to $8,500
Sidelock non-ejectors $2,000 to $10,000
Sidelock ejectors $4,000 to $30,000
Hammer Guns $2,000 to $10,000
Over & Unders $5,000 to $30,000

John Blanch

John Blanch apprenticed with Jackson Mortimer and married his master's daughter. Later he working with John Manton. Today the Blanch name is perhaps best remembered for *"A Century of Guns"* first published in 1909 and written by H. J. Blanch grandson of the founder.

Estimates listed below range from guns barely in proof with marginal wall thicknesses to those with barrel specifications as proofed.

Boxlock non-ejectors $1,500 to $4,000
Boxlock ejectors $2,000 to $8,500
Sidelock non-ejectors $2,000 to $10,000
Sidelock ejectors $4,000 to $30,000
Hammer Guns $2,000 to $10,000

Thomas Bland

Thomas Bland started in business in 1840 in Birmingham. Bland moved to London in 1875 and occupied a variety of premises close to Charing Cross Station until at least the 1960s. They well known for their wildfowling guns, particularly the "Brent" model which enjoyed a wide following. The Bland firm is still in business in Benton, Pennsylvania.

Estimates listed below range from guns barely in proof with marginal wall thicknesses to those with barrel specifications as proofed.

Boxlock non-ejectors $1,000 to $3,000
Boxlock ejectors $1,500 to $5,000
Sidelock non-ejectors $2,000 to $7,000
Sidelock ejectors $3,000 to $15,000
Hammer Guns $1,000 to $3,000

Boss & Co.

Thomas Boss worked for the great Joseph Manton before becoming an outworker to the London trade. In 1891 John Robertson, a Scotsman, was taken in as a partner. Under Robertson's control the firm established itself as London's best gun maker rivaled only by Purdey's. Beyond intrinsic quality Boss is famous for their single trigger and over and under designs which are both widely copied. A scarce 20 bore assisted opening over and under by Boss sold as Sotheby's, Glen-eagles sale in August 1998 for $76,500.

Estimates listed below range from guns barely in proof with marginal wall thicknesses to those with barrel specifications as proofed.

Boxlock non-ejectors $1,500 to $4,000
Boxlock ejectors $2,000 to $8,500
Sidelock non-ejectors $2,000 to $10,000
Sidelock ejectors $4,000 to $30,000
Hammer Guns $2,000 to $10,000
Over & Unders $20,000 to $100,000

Charles Boswell

Charles Boswell worked for Thomas Gooch and the Enfield factory before establishing himself in 1872. He was a skillful pigeon shot and the firm's reputation rested for many years on their ability to build live bird guns. The records are currently in the hands of G. R. Beckstead in Florida.

Estimates listed below range from guns barely in proof with marginal wall thicknesses to those with barrel specifications as proofed.

Boxlock non-ejectors $1,000 to $3,000
Boxlock ejectors $1,500 to $5,000

Sidelock non-ejectors $2,000 to $7,000
Sidelock ejectors $3,000 to $15,000
Hammer Guns $1,000 to $3,000

A.A. Brown

Albert Arthur Brown established his business in Whittal St., Birmingham in 1930. The firm has maintained a reputation as one of the finest makers to the trade having built guns for Churchill, H & H and Westley Richards. They still make guns today in Alverchurch, not far from Birmingham.

Estimates listed below range from guns barely in proof with marginal wall thicknesses to those with barrel specifications as proofed.

Boxlock non-ejectors $1,000 to $3,000
Boxlock ejectors $1,500 to $5,000
Sidelock non-ejectors $2,000 to $7,000
Sidelock ejectors $3,000 to $15,000

David McKay Brown

David McKay Brown started his apprenticeship with Alex Martin in Glasgow and completed it with John Dickson in Edinburgh. His renown rest on his ability with traditional Scottish round action guns and his own patent over/under based on a trigger plate action. He works in Bothwell just outside Glasgow. A fine pair of 20 bore assisted opening round action guns by David McKay Brown sold at Sotheby's, Gleneagles sale in August 1998 for $52,200.

Estimates listed below range from guns barely in proof with marginal wall thicknesses to those with barrel specifications as proofed.

Round Action & O/U Guns $20,000 to $100,000

E.J. Churchill

Edwin John Churchill served his time with William Jeffery & Son and was famous as a pigeon shot. Today the firm is best remembered for its 25" barreled guns introduced by Robert Churchill in the 1920s. The firm is still in business in West Wycombe, England.

Estimates listed below range from guns barely in proof with marginal wall thicknesses to those with barrel specifications as proofed.

Boxlock non-ejectors $1,500 to $4,000
Boxlock ejectors $2,000 to $8,500
Sidelock non-ejectors $2,000 to $10,000
Sidelock ejectors $4,000 to $30,000
Hammer Guns $2,000 to $10,000
Over & Unders $10,000 to $50,000

Cogswell & Harrison

Benjamin Cogswell claimed to be in business from 1770. The firm's reputation rests on its self-opening game guns. Today this tradition continues with ex-Purdey craftsman Allen Crewe. building fine Beesley action self-openers and Woodward-style O/U's. They are in Royal Berkshire just west of London.

Estimates listed below range from guns barely in proof with marginal wall thicknesses to those with barrel specifications as proofed.

Boxlock non-ejectors $1,000 to $3,000
Boxlock ejectors $1,500 to $5,000
Sidelock non-ejectors $2,000 to $7,000
Sidelock ejectors $3,000 to $30,000
Hammer Guns $1,000 to $3,000
Over & Unders $10,000 to $50,000

John Dickson

John Dickson served his time with J. Wallace in Edinburgh. In 1882 he registered the first of a series of patents which would culminate in the famous Scottish round action gun. Dickson's continue to build these guns to this day at their Frederick Street premises.

Estimates listed below range from guns barely in proof with marginal wall thicknesses to those with barrel specifications as proofed.

Boxlock non-ejectors $1,000 to $3,000
Boxlock ejectors $1,500 to $5,000
Sidelock non-ejectors $2,000 to $7,000
Sidelock ejectors $3,000 to $15,000
Hammer Guns $2,000 to $10,000
Round Action Guns $5,000 to $50,000

William Evans

William Evans worked for both Purdey and H & H before setting up on his own in 1883. Many of the Evans guns appear to have been made by Webley & Scott and other Birmingham gun makers. Today the firm builds its own guns and is located in St. James, central London.

Estimates listed blow range from guns barely in proof with marginal wall thicknesses to those with barrel specifications as proofed.

Boxlock non-ejectors $1,000 to $3,000
Boxlock ejectors $1,500 to $5,000
Sidelock non-ejectors $2,000 to $7,000
Sidelock ejectors $3,000 to $50,000
Hammer Guns $1,000 to $3,000

Daniel Fraser

Daniel Fraser apprenticed with Alexander Henry in Edinburgh before opening his own business on Leith St. He is perhaps best remembered for his rifles and distinctive, fancy back boxlocks. The firm he founded is once again in business in Scotland.

Estimates listed below range from guns barely in proof with marginal wall thicknesses to those with barrel specifications as proofed.

Boxlock non-ejectors $1,000 to $3,000
Boxlock ejectors $1,500 to $5,000
Sidelock non-ejectors $2,000 to $7,000
Sidelock ejectors $3,000 to $50,000
Hammer Guns $1,000 to $3,000

Stephen Grant

Stephen Grant was apprenticed to Kavanagh of Dublin before working with Charles Lancaster and Thomas Boss in London. The firm is perhaps best remembered for its distinctive sidelever guns with fluted fences. The guns are made today in Essendon, Herts, England.

Estimates listed below range from guns barely in proof with marginal wall thicknesses to those with barrel specifications as proofed.

Boxlock non-ejectors $1,500 to $4,000
Boxlock ejectors $2,000 to $8,500
Sidelock non-ejectors $2,000 to $10,000
Sidelock ejectors $4,000 to $50,000
Hammer Guns $2,000 to $10,000

George Gibbs

The Gibbs Company has been in Bristol, England since the 1830s. Though they have built many fine shotguns the name is also strongly associated with rifles. The firm is now owned by Ian Crudgington famous for his book *"The British Shotgun, Vol. I & II."*

Estimates listed below range from guns barely in proof with marginal wall thicknesses to those with barrel specifications as proofed.

Boxlock non-ejectors $1,000 to $3,000
Boxlock ejectors $1,500 to $5,000
Sidelock non-ejectors $2,000 to $7,000
Sidelock ejectors $3,000 to $15,000
Hammer Guns $1,000 to $3,000

W.W. Greener

William Greener apprenticed with Burnand of Newcastle before working with John Manton in London. His son, W.W. Greener, took over in 1869 and built his reputation with "a medium-priced weapon of sound workmanship. The name will forever be associated with the "Greener crossbolt." In recent years the company, still based in Birmingham, has built a small quantity of high grade guns.

Estimates listed below range from guns barely in proof with marginal wall thicknesses to those with barrel specifications as proofed.

Boxlock non-ejectors $1,000 to $3,000
Boxlock ejectors $1,500 to $50,000
Sidelock non-ejectors $2,000 to $7,000
Sidelock ejectors $3,000 to $100,000
Hammer Guns $1,000 to $3,000

Charles Hellis

Charles Hellis was established in 1884 in Westbourne Park, London. The most frequently encountered Hellis guns here in the U.S. are probably the 2" 12 bore and "featherweight" models. Charles Hellis is once again doing business from the west end of London.

Estimates listed below range from guns barely in proof with marginal wall thicknesses to those with barrel specifications as proofed.

Boxlock non-ejectors $1,000 to $3,000
Boxlock ejectors $1,500 to $5,000
Sidelock non-ejectors $2,000 to $7,000
Sidelock ejectors $3,000 to $15,000

Alexander Henry

Alexander Henry has been Edinburg's rifle maker since 1853. Between 1860 and 1882 Henry registered over a dozen patents, mostly for falling black and double rifles. Henry built rifles for Queen Victoria, her husband Prince Albert and their son The Duke of Edinburg. The name and records were eventually acquired by Alex Martin of Glasgow and now reside with Dickson's in Edinburg.

Estimates listed below range from guns barely in proof with marginal wall thicknesses to those with barrel specifications as proofed.

Boxlock non-ejectors $1,500 to $3,000
Boxlock ejectors $2,000 to $6,000
Sidelock non-ejectors $2,000 to $9,000
Sidelock ejectors $4,000 to $15,000

Holland & Holland

Pair of H&H Royal Deluxe Self-Opening Ejector Guns

Harris Holland started as a tobacconist but moved into guns around 1848. Famous for presentation quality guns built for figures as diverse as President Theodore Roosevelt and The Nizam of Hydrabad, they continue to trade under the auspices of Channel, the well-known French luxury goods company.

Estimates listed below range from guns barely in proof with marginal wall thicknesses to those with barrel specifications as proofed.

Boxlock non-ejectors $1,5000 to $4,000
Boxlock ejectors $2,000 to $9,000

Sidelock non-ejectors $2,000 to $10,000
Sidelock ejectors $4,000 to $100,000
Hammer Guns $2,000 to $10,000
Over & Unders $8,000 to $100,000

Thomas Horsley

The firm was founded by Thomas Horsley in about 1832 in York, Yorkshire. Famous for their sliding thumb piece toplever hammer guns they are considered by many to be the best of the provincial gun makers. No longer in business.

Estimates listed below range from guns barely in proof with marginal wall thicknesses to those with barrel specifications as proofed.

Boxlock non-ejectors $1,000 to $3,000
Boxlock ejectors $1,500 to $5,000
Sidelock non-ejectors $2,000 to $7,000
Sidelock ejectors $3,000 to $15,000
Hammer Guns $1,000 to $3,000

William Horton

William Horton was a Burmingham gunmaker who moved to Whitehaven in north-west England before settling in Glasgow in 1863. He died in 1896 but his son Oliver continued registering a series of patents that culminated in the firm's distinctive boxlock gun. Horton was acquired by another Glasgow gunmaker, Arthur Allen, in 1924.

Estimates listed below range from guns barely in proof with marginal wall thicknesses to those with barrel specifications as proofed.

Boxlock non-ejectors $1,500 to $3,000
Boxlock ejectors $2,000 to $6,000
Sidelock non-ejectors $2,000 to $9,000
Sidelock ejectors $4,000 to $15,000

W.J. Jeffrey

William Jackman Jeffery managed Philip Webley's London showroom from 1887 to 1894. The business he established retailed more of the massive .600 double rifles than any other London maker. but these were likely made by Leonard of Birmingham. John Saunders, also of Birmingham, made many of his sidelock ejectors. The company records are with Holland & Holland in London.

Courtesy Butterfield & Butterfield

Estimates listed below range from guns barely in proof with marginal wall thicknesses to those with barrel specifications as proofed.

Boxlock non-ejectors $1,000 to $3,000
Boxlock ejectors $1,500 to $5,000
Sidelock non-ejectors $2,000 to $7,000
Sidelock ejectors $3,000 to $15,000
Hammer Guns $1,000 to $3,000

Charles Lancaster

The original Charles Lancaster was a barrel maker for both Joseph Manton and the first James Purdey. In 1878 the business was acquired by A.A. Thorn who established the firm's name with "The Art of Shooting," which ran to at least 14 editions and which he wrote under the pseudonym of "Charles Lancaster." The firm was famous for its four barrel pistols/rifles/shotguns and continues today from Bishopswood, Somerset.

Estimates listed below range from guns barely in proof with marginal wall thicknesses to those with barrel specifications as proofed.

Boxlock non-ejectors $1,000 to $3,000
Boxlock ejectors $1,500 to $5,000
Sidelock non-ejectors $2,000 to $7,000
Sidelock ejectors $3,000 to $15,000
Hammer Guns $1,000 to $3,000
Over & Unders $5,000 to $20,000

Joseph Lang

Joseph Lang worked for Alexander Wilson before starting out on his own in 1821. The firm is best remembered for its "Vena Contracta" gun which had a 12 bore breech that tapered to 16 bore at the muzzle. The company was until recently owned by a Texan but has since returned to England.

Estimates listed below range from guns barely in proof with marginal wall thicknesses to those with barrel specifications as proofed.

Boxlock non-ejectors $1,000 to $3,000
Boxlock ejectors $1,500 to $5,000
Sidelock non-ejectors $2,000 to $7,000
Sidelock ejectors $3,000 to $35,000
Hammer Guns $1,000 to $3,000

G.E. Lewis

George Edward Lewis was born in 1829 and apprenticed in "all branches" of the Birmingham gun trade. His fame rests on his magnum "gun of the period" which was popular with generations of wildfowlers. The firm continues today from Halesowen, West Midlands.

Estimates listed below range from guns barely in proof with marginal wall thicknesses to those with barrel specifications as proofed.

Boxlock non-ejectors $1,500 to $4,000
Boxlock ejectors $2,000 to $8,500
Sidelock non-ejectors $2,000 to $10,000
Sidelock ejectors $4,000 to $30,000
Hammer Guns $2,000 to $10,000

MacNaughton & Son

James MacNaughton started in business in 1864 in Edinburgh. His fame rests on his patent Edinburgh round action gun of 1879. The firm is back in business in Edinburgh.

Estimates listed below range from guns barely in proof with marginal wall thicknesses to those with barrel specifications as proofed.

Boxlock non-ejectors $1,000 to $3,000
Boxlock ejectors $1,500 to $5,000
Sidelock non-ejectors $2,000 to $7,000
Sidelock ejectors $3,000 to $15,000
Hammer Guns $2,000 to $10,000
Round Action Guns $3,000 to $20,000

W.R. Pape

William Rochester Pape started his business in 1858 enlarging a game dealership owned by his family. He is credited with the earliest patent for choke boring (1866) and rivals Horsley as the best of the provincial gun makers. A 16 bore Pape, once owned by the Grandson of the firm's founder, sold at Sotheby's, London for $14,904 in March 1999.

Estimates listed below range from guns barely in proof with marginal wall thicknesses to those with barrel specifications as proofed.

Boxlock non-ejectors $1,000 to $3,000
Boxlock ejectors $1,500 to $15,000
Sidelock non-ejectors $2,000 to $7,000
Sidelock ejectors $3,000 to $15,000
Hammer Guns $1,000 to $3,000

William Powell

William Powell started out in Birmingham in 1802. Their top "lift uplever" are considered highly desirable. They continue in Birmingham today.

Estimates listed below range from guns barely in proof with marginal wall thicknesses to those with barrel specifications as proofed.

Boxlock non-ejectors $1,000 to $3,000
Boxlock ejectors $1,500 to $5,000
Sidelock non-ejectors $2,000 to $7,000
Sidelock ejectors $3,000 to $35,000
Hammer Guns $1,000 to $3,000

Courtesy Butterfield & Butterfield

James Purdey & Son

James Purdey, one of Joseph Manton's earliest gun makers, starting in about 1803. The famous Purdey underbolt, developed in 1863 is perhaps the most widely disseminated of all shotgun patents. Today the company is still considered the world's greatest gun makers. A pair of Purdey 16 bore guns, once were owned by Edward VIII when he was Prince of Wales, sold at Sotheby's, Geneva, in 1991 for $196,428.

Estimates listed below range from guns barely in proof with marginal wall thicknesses to those with barrel specifications as proofed.

Boxlock non-ejectors $1,5000 to $4,000
Boxlock ejectors $2,000 to $9,000
Sidelock non-ejectors $2,000 to $10,000
Sidelock ejectors $4,000 to $100,000
Hammer Guns $2,000 to $10,000
Over & Unders $8,000 to $100,000

John Rigby

John Rigby started for himself in Dublin in 1775. The company enjoys a 200-year reputation as fine rifle makers and are famous for their .416 propriety cartridge. They were recently sold and moved to California.

Estimates listed below range from guns barely in proof with marginal wall thicknesses to those with barrel specifications as proofed.

Boxlock non-ejectors $1,500 to $4,000
Boxlock ejectors $2,000 to $8,500
Sidelock non-ejectors $2,000 to $10,000
Sidelock ejectors $4,000 to $35,000
Hammer Guns $2,000 to $10,000

Pair of Sidelock Ejector guns by J. Purdey was sold at auction for $101,500. They were the property of Edward, Prince of Wales, later Edward VIII, King of England. The pair is 16 gauge with 28.5" barrels. Cased. Condition was excellent. Butterfield & Butterfield, August, 1999.

C. S. Rosson & Co.

C. S. Rosson was a provincial maker active from the turn of the century in Norwich. They produced a slide opener, self openers built on the Edwin V. Smith patent and a 2" chambered gun they called the "Twentieth Century." They failed in 1957.

Estimates listed below range from guns barely in proof with marginal wall thicknesses to those with barrel specifications as proofed.

Boxlock non-ejectors $1,000 to $3,000
Boxlock ejectors $1,500 to $5,000
Sidelock non-ejectors $2,000 to $7,000
Sidelock ejectors $3,000 to $15,000
Hammer Guns $1,000 to $3,000

W & C Scott

William Scott served an apprenticeship with a Bury St. Edmund's gun maker, possibly Ben or Charles Parker. In 1865 the firm contributed to the perfection of the English gun by developing the standard spindle, which connects the Purdey bolt to the top lever. They no longer trade.

Estimates listed below range from guns barely in proof with marginal wall thicknesses to those with barrels specifications as proofed.

Boxlock non-ejectors $1,000 to $3,000
Boxlock ejectors $1,500 to $5,000
Sidelock non-ejectors $2,000 to $7,000
Sidelock ejectors $3,000 to $15,000
Hammer Guns $1,000 to $3,000

A Watson Brothers boxlock .410 bore with ejectors was sold at auction for $8,625. Fitted with 27" barrels choked full and full. Built in 1929. Action has full coverage scroll engraving. Highly figured walnut stock. Condition is 97% blue and 95% case colors. Cased.
Faintich Auction Services, Inc., November 2000

Watson Brothers

Watson Brothers date from 1875 and are famous for their small bore guns. In recent years the company has been resuscitated by Mike Louca, who is establishing himself as a builder of round bodied over and unders.

Estimates listed below range from guns barely in proof with marginal wall thicknesses to those with barrel specifications as proofed.

Boxlock non-ejectors $1,000 to $3,000
Boxlock ejectors $1,500 to $5,000
Sidelock non-ejectors $2,000 to $7,000
Sidelock ejectors $3,000 to $15,000
Hammer Guns $1,000 to $3,000
Over & Unders $30,000 to $100,000

Webley & Scott

Philip Webley began his apprenticeship as a lockmaker in 1827, probably with Ryan & Watson. In 1897 he merged with W. & C. Scott and built semi machine-made shotguns using techniques previously employed on revolvers. The firm ceased operations in 1991.

Estimates listed below range from guns barely in proof with marginal wall thicknesses to those with barrel specifications as proofed.

Boxlock non-ejectors $1,000 to $3,000
Boxlock ejectors $1,500 to $5,000
Sidelock non-ejectors $2,000 to $7,000
Sidelock ejectors $3,000 to $15,000
Hammer Guns $1,000 to $3,000

Westley Richards

William Westley Richards founded his own company in 1812 at 82 High St., Birmingham. In 1975 two of the firms workforce developed the famous Anson & Deeley boxlock action which was made hand detachable in 1897. The firm continues in Bournebrook to this day.

Estimates listed below range from guns barely in proof with marginal wall thicknesses to those with barrel specifications as proofed.

Boxlock non-ejectors $1,500 to $4,000
Boxlock ejectors $2,000 to $8,500
Sidelock non-ejectors $2,000 to $10,000
Sidelock ejectors $4,000 to $30,000
Hammer Guns $2,000 to $10,000
Over & Unders $10,000 to $100,000

John Wilkes

Current Importer/Distributor FNGB, Colorado Springs, CO

The first John Wilkes was established in Birmingham in 1830. The firm's reputation rests on the intrinsic high quality of their work. They continue on Beak St., Soho.

New guns built today have interchangeable parts and locks. Special Series over and under sidelock guns in 20 gauge only with custom features retail for $28500. Only 25 are to be built.

Estimates listed below range from guns barely in proof with marginal wall thicknesses to those with barrel specifications as proofed.

Boxlock non-ejectors $2,000 to $3,000
Boxlock ejectors $2,000 to $4,500
Sidelock non-ejectors $20,000 to $25,000
Sidelock ejectors $20,000 to $250,000
Hammer Guns $4,000 to $15,000

James Woodward

James Woodward worked for Charles Moore, becoming a partner before establishing his own company. The firm's reputation rests in large part on its "Automatic" double rifles and to an even greater extent on its over and under shotguns, which are the only ones that have ever rivaled Boss's. A .410 Woodward over and under sold at auction by J. C. Devine in April 1999 for $200,500.

Estimates listed below range from guns barely in proof with marginal wall thicknesses to those with barrel specifications as proofed.

Boxlock non-ejectors $1,500 to $4,000
Boxlock ejectors $2,000 to $8,500
Sidelock non-ejectors $2,000 to $10,000
Sidelock ejectors $4,000 to $30,000
Hammer Guns $2,000 to $10,000
Over & Unders $20,000 to $200,000

BRIXIA
Brescia, Italy

Model 12

A commercial version of the Model 1910 Glisenti in 9mm Glisenti caliber. The Brixia was a simplified Glisenti and was made to replace the Glisenti for the military market. The Italian military did not accept them and only a few were made for the commercial market. The only markings are the monogram Eagle holding a shield cast in the grips.

Courtesy James Rankin

Exc.	V.G.	Good	Fair	Poor
900	650	500	300	200

BRNO ARMS
Uhersky Brod, Czech Republic
Importer-Euro Imports

NOTE: Some but not all of the BRNO models listed in this section are currently imported into the U.S.

ZG-47

A bolt action rifle based on the Mauser system. Chambered for .270, 7x57, 7x64, .30-06, 8x57, 8x60, 8x64S, 9.3x62, and on special order 10.75x68. Barrel length is 23.6". Adjustable trigger. Hinged floorplate. Weight is about 7.7 lbs.

Standard

Exc.	V.G.	Good	Fair	Poor
950	850	750	600	350

Deluxe

Exc.	V.G.	Good	Fair	Poor
1000	850	750	550	350

ZH-Series

A double barrel Over/Under boxlock series of shotguns with interchangeable barrels in shotgun and rifle configurations, of various lengths, double triggers and automatic ejectors. The models listed below represent the different gauges and/or calibers offered.

ZH-300

NIB	Exc.	V.G.	Good	Fair	Poor
800	675	575	400	325	250

ZH-301-12ga/12ga

Exc.	V.G.	Good	Fair	Poor
600	500	400	350	200

ZH-302-12ga/12ga Skeet

Exc.	V.G.	Good	Fair	Poor
600	550	450	400	250

ZH-30312ga/12ga Trap

Exc.	V.G.	Good	Fair	Poor
600	550	450	400	250

ZH-304-12ga/7x57R

Exc.	V.G.	Good	Fair	Poor
700	600	500	400	250

ZH-305-12ga/6x52R

Exc.	V.G.	Good	Fair	Poor
700	600	500	400	225

ZH-306-12ga/6x50R Mag.

Exc.	V.G.	Good	Fair	Poor
700	550	450	350	200

ZH-308-12ga/7x65R

Exc.	V.G.	Good	Fair	Poor
700	600	500	400	225

ZH-309-12ga/8x57 JRS

Exc.	V.G.	Good	Fair	Poor
700	600	500	400	225

ZH-321-16ga/16ga

Exc.	V.G.	Good	Fair	Poor
650	550	450	400	225

ZH-324-16ga/7x57R

Exc.	V.G.	Good	Fair	Poor
700	600	500	400	225

ZH-328-16ga/7x65R

Exc.	V.G.	Good	Fair	Poor
700	600	500	400	225

NOTE: For ZH models with set triggers and cheekpiece add $75. For interchangeable barrels add between $300 and $400 depending on gauge and caliber.

Model 300 Combo

The model ZH-300 with 8 interchangeable barrels in a fitted case. Introduced in 1986.

NIB	Exc.	V.G.	Good	Fair	Poor
5800	5000	4000	2750	2000	1500

Model 500

The model ZH-300 with acid etched decoration, automatic ejectors and in 12 gauge.

NIB	Exc.	V.G.	Good	Fair	Poor
1000	800	600	425	350	275

ZP-49

A 12 gauge sidelock double-barrel shotgun with double triggers and automatic ejectors. Blued with a walnut stock. Imported in 1986 only.

Exc.	V.G.	Good	Fair	Poor
950	800	650	450	325

ZP-149

As above, without engraving.

NIB	Exc.	V.G.	Good	Fair	Poor
700	600	500	400	300	200

ZP-349

As above, with the buttstock having a cheekpiece and a beavertail forearm.

Exc.	V.G.	Good	Fair	Poor
700	600	500	350	250

ZBK-100

A single barrel shotgun in 12 or 20 gauge with 27" barrel and walnut stock. Weight is approximately 5.5 lbs.

NIB	Exc.	V.G.	Good	Fair	Poor
200	150	100	—	—	—

RIFLES

ZKW-465 (Hornet Sporter)

A .22 Hornet caliber bolt-action rifle with a 23" barrel, express sights and double set triggers. Blued with a walnut stock.

Exc.	V.G.	Good	Fair	Poor
1300	1100	950	800	550

Model 21H

A 6.5x57mm, 7x57mm or 8x57mm caliber bolt-action sporting rifle with a 23-5/8" barrel, express sights and double set triggers. Blued with a walnut stock.

Exc.	V.G.	Good	Fair	Poor
1100	1000	900	700	550

Model 22F

As above, with a Mannlicher-style stock. Barrel length is 20-1/2".

Exc.	V.G.	Good	Fair	Poor
1250	1100	900	650	500

Model I

A .22 caliber bolt-action rifle with a 22.75" barrel having folding leaf rear sights. Blued with a walnut stock.

Exc.	V.G.	Good	Fair	Poor
500	400	300	250	200

Model II

As above, with a more finely figured walnut stock.

Exc.	V.G.	Good	Fair	Poor
550	450	350	300	225

ZKM 611

This is a semiautomatic rifle chambered for the .22 WRM cartridge. It is fitted with a 20" barrel and has a magazine capacity of 6 rounds. Weight is approximately 6.2 lbs.

NIB	Exc	V.G.	Good	Fair	Poor
450	400	300	200	175	125

ZKM 451

This is a semiautomatic rifle chambered for the .22 Long rifle cartridge and fitted with a 22" barrel. Magazine capacity is 7 rounds. Weight is about 5.25 lbs.

NIB	Exc.	V.G.	Good	Fair	Poor
250	200	150	—	—	—

ZKM 451 LUX

Same as above but with select walnut stock.

NIB	Exc.	V.G.	Good	Fair	Poor
300	250	200	—	—	—

ZBK 680

A .22 Hornet or .222 caliber bolt-action rifle with a 23.5" barrel, double set triggers and 5-shot magazine. Blued with a walnut stock.

NIB	Exc.	V.G.	Good	Fair	Poor
800	700	550	400	325	225

Super Express Rifle

An Over/Under sidelock double barrel rifle, with 23.5" barrels, double triggers and automatic ejectors. Engraved, blued with a walnut stock. Available in 6 grades as below:

Standard Model

NIB	Exc.	V.G.	Good	Fair	Poor
4500	3750	3000	2500	1750	1250

Grade I

NIB	Exc.	V.G.	Good	Fair	Poor
6500	5500	4750	4500	3600	3250

Grade II

NIB	Exc.	V.G.	Good	Fair	Poor
5500	4750	4000	3500	2750	2250

Grade III

NIB	Exc.	V.G.	Good	Fair	Poor
5250	4500	3950	3250	2750	2250

Grade IV

NIB	Exc.	V.G.	Good	Fair	Poor
5000	4000	3500	3000	2500	2250

Grade V

NIB	Exc.	V.G.	Good	Fair	Poor
4750	3850	3250	2750	2250	1750

Grade VI

NIB	Exc.	V.G.	Good	Fair	Poor
4600	3950	3100	2600	1950	1500

ZH-344/348/349

An over and under rifle chambered for 7x57R, 7x65R, or 8x57JRS.

NIB	Exc	V.G.	Good	Fair	Poor
1100	850	600	—	—	—

Model 98 Standard

This bolt action rifle is chambered for a variety of calibers from the 7x64 to the 9.3x62. It is fitted with a 23" barrel and figured walnut stock with butt plate and open sights. Weight is approximately 7.25 lbs.

NIB	Exc.	V.G.	Good	Fair	Poor
600	550	400	300	200	150

NOTE: For set trigger add $100.

Model 98 Full Stock

Same as above but with full one-piece stock and set trigger.

NIB	Exc.	V.G.	Good	Fair	Poor
700	600	500	400	350	200

ZK 99

This is a tip-up centerfire rifle chambered for a wide variety of calibers from 6.5x57R to .30-06. Barrel length is 23" and weight is about 5.75 lbs.

NIB	Exc.	V.G.	Good	Fair	Poor
900	700	550	—	—	—

ZBK 110

This is a single shot tip-open rifle chambered for the .22 Hornet, .222 Rem., the 5.6x50R Mag., and the 5.6x52R. Barrel length is 23.5". Open sights. Walnut stock without checkering. Weight is about 6 lbs.

NIB	Exc.	V.G.	Good	Fair	Poor
250	200	150	—	—	—

ZBK 110 LUX

Same as above but with select walnut stock with checkering. Open sights.

NIB	Exc.	V.G.	Good	Fair	Poor
340	275	—	—	—	—

ZBK 110 Super Lux

Same as above but with fancy walnut stock with checkering. Open sights.

NIB	Exc.	V.G.	Good	Fair	Poor
450	350	—	—	—	—

HANDGUNS

ZKR 551

This is a double action or single action revolver with 6 round cylinder. Adjustable rear sight. Walnut grips. Fitted with 6" barrel. Chambered for .38, .32 S&W Long, and .22 Long Rifle. Weight is about 35 oz.

NIB	Exc.	V.G.	Good	Fair	Poor
1500	1200	—	—	—	—

BROLIN ARMS
Le Verne, California

This California company began business in 1995 with the manufacturing of 1911 type pistols. These pistols are manufactured and assembled in the U.S. Because these pistols were first introduced in 1996 only limited prices will be given. Very little price history has been established. Since 1997 the company has expanded its product line to include shotguns, single action revolvers, Mauser rifles, semiautomatic .22 caliber pistols, and a custom shop.

NOTE: This company ceased operations in 1999.

LEGEND SERIES-1911 AUTO PISTOL

Model L45-Standard Auto Pistol

This is the standard model with 5" barrel chambered for the .45 ACP. Fitted with throated match barrel, polished feed ramp, lowered ejection port, beveled magazine well and fixed sights. Other custom features as well. Finish is matte blue with 7-round magazine. Weight is about 36 oz.

NIB	Exc.	V.G.	Good	Fair	Poor
450	350	—	—	—	—

Model L45C-Compact Auto Pistol

Similar to the above standard model with the same features but with a 4.5" barrel. Weight is about 32 oz.

NIB	Exc.	V.G.	Good	Fair	Poor
460	350	—	—	—	—

Model L45T

This version of the L45 series was introduced in 1997 and is fitted with a compact slide on a full size frame. Weight is 36 oz.

NIB	Exc.	V.G.	Good	Fair	Poor
460	350	—	—	—	—

NOTE: For Novak sights add $50.

PATRIOT SERIES-DPC CARRY-COMP PISTOLS

Model P45 Comp-Standard Carry Comp

This model features a 4" barrel with integral compensator cut into the slide. Other features are a custom beavertail grip safety, adjustable aluminum trigger, flat top slide, and checkered wood grips. Weight is about 37 oz. For two-tone finish add $20.

NIB	Exc.	V.G.	Good	Fair	Poor
650	500	—	—	—	—

Model P45C Comp-Compact Carry Comp

Similar to the above model but fitted with a 3.25" barrel. Weight is about 33 oz. For two-tone finish add $20.

NIB	Exc.	V.G.	Good	Fair	Poor
680	500	—	—	—	—

Model P45T

This addition to the Patriot Series was introduced in 1997 and has all of the features of the Patriot pistols but is fitted with a compact slide and full size frame. Weight is about 35 oz. Also available in two-tone finish for an additional $20.

NIB	Exc.	V.G.	Good	Fair	Poor
690	500	—	—	—	—

NOTE: For Novak sights add $50.

TAC SERIES-TACTICAL 1911 PISTOLS

Model TAC-11

This series and model were introduced in 1997 and have all of the features of the L45 series with the additions of a special 5" conical match barrel, Novak Low Profile sights, black rubber contour grips, "iron claw" extractor, and optional night sights. Chambered for the .45 ACP the pistol is supplied with an 8-round magazine. Weight is approximately 37 oz.

NIB	Exc.	V.G.	Good	Fair	Poor
650	525	—	—	—	—

NOTE: For Tritium night sights add $90.

TAC SERIES-DOUBLE ACTION PISTOLS

MS45

This is a full size double action pistol chambered for the .45 ACP cartridge. It is fitted with an 8 round magazine and low profile 3-dot sights. Standard finish is matte blue. Add $20 for royal blue finish.

NIB	Exc.	V.G.	Good	Fair	Poor
400	300	—	—	—	—

M45

Similar to the model above but with a longer barrel. Chambered for .45 ACP and 8 round magazine. Add $20 for royal blue finish.

NIB	Exc.	V.G.	Good	Fair	Poor
400	300	—	—	—	—

M40

Same as M45 but chambered for .40 S&W cartridge. Magazine capacity is 10 rounds. Add $20 for royal blue finish.

NIB	Exc.	V.G.	Good	Fair	Poor
400	300	—	—	—	—

M90

Same as M45 model but chambered for 9mm cartridge. Magazine capacity is 10 rounds. Add $20 for royal blue finish.

NIB	Exc.	V.G.	Good	Fair	Poor
400	300	—	—	—	—

MC40

This is compact version of the full size double action models. It is fitted with a full size frame but shorter slide. Chambered for .40 S&W cartridge. Magazine capacity is 10 rounds. Add $20 for royal blue finish.

NIB	Exc.	V.G.	Good	Fair	Poor
400	300	—	—	—	—

MC90

Same as above but chambered for 9mm cartridge.

NIB	Exc.	V.G.	Good	Fair	Poor
400	300	—	—	—	—

MB40

This is super compact version double action pistol. Features a concealed hammer. Chambered for .40 S&W cartridge. Magazine capacity is 6 rounds. Add $20 for royal blue finish.

NIB	Exc.	V.G.	Good	Fair	Poor
430	350	—	—	—	—

MB90

Same as above but chambered for 9mm cartridge.

NIB	Exc.	V.G.	Good	Fair	Poor
430	350	—	—	—	—

PRO SERIES-COMPETITION PISTOL

Model Pro-Stock-Competition Pistol

Chambered for the .45 ACP, this pistol is designed for the competition shooter. Many special features are standard such as full length recoil guide, front strap high relief cut, serrated flat mainspring housing, ambidextrous thumb safety and fully adjustable rear sight. Barrel length is 5" and weight is about 37 oz. For two-tone finish add $20.

NIB	Exc.	V.G.	Good	Fair	Poor
780	600	—	—	—	—

Model Pro-Comp-Competition Pistol
Similar to the competition model above but fitted with an integral compensator and 4" barrel. Weight is about 37 oz. For two-tone finish add $20.

NIB	Exc.	V.G.	Good	Fair	Poor
900	700	—	—	—	—

SHOTGUNS

LAWMAN SERIES—PERSONAL SECURITY SHOTGUN

Model HL18SB
This is a pump action 12 gauge shotgun with an 18.5" barrel with black synthetic stock with bead sights. Weight is about 7 lbs. Introduced in 1997.

NIB	Exc.	V.G.	Good	Fair	Poor
250	200	—	—	—	—

Model HL18SR
Same as above but fitted with rifle sights.

NIB	Exc.	V.G.	Good	Fair	Poor
260	200	—	—	—	—

Model HL18SBN
Same as above but with nickel finish and bead sights.

NIB	Exc.	V.G.	Good	Fair	Poor
270	200	—	—	—	—

Model HL18WB
This version has a wood stock and bead sights.

NIB	Exc.	V.G.	Good	Fair	Poor
250	200	—	—	—	—

Model HL18WR
Same as above but fitted with rifle sights.

NIB	Exc.	V.G.	Good	Fair	Poor
260	200	—	—	—	—

FIELD SERIES-PUMP ACTION FIELD GUN

Model HF24SB
This is a 12 gauge pump action shotgun with a 24" barrel, matte finish, and black synthetic stock with bead sights. Weight is about 7.3 lbs. Introduced in 1997.

NIB	Exc.	V.G.	Good	Fair	Poor
270	200	—	—	—	—

Model HF28SB
Same as above but fitted with a 28" barrel. Weight is 7.4 lbs.

NIB	Exc.	V.G.	Good	Fair	Poor
270	200	—	—	—	—

Model HF24WB
This model features a 24" barrel with wood stock.

NIB	Exc.	V.G.	Good	Fair	Poor
270	200	—	—	—	—

Model HF28WB
Same as above but with 24" barrel.

NIB	Exc.	V.G.	Good	Fair	Poor
270	200	—	—	—	—

Slug Special
This slide action shotgun is chambered for 3" 12 gauge shells and is available with choice of 18.5" or 22" barrels with rifle or

ghost ring sights. Available with fixed improved cylinder choke, 4" extended rifled choke, or fully rifled barrel. Choice of wood or synthetic stocks.

NIB	Exc.	V.G.	Good	Fair	Poor
270	200	—	—	—	—

Turkey Special
This 12 gauge 3" model is fitted with a 22" extra full choke vent rib barrel with a choice of wood or synthetic stock.

NIB	Exc.	V.G.	Good	Fair	Poor
270	200	—	—	—	—

SEMIAUTOMATIC SHOTGUNS

BL-12 Security
This 12 gauge shotgun has a 3" chamber and 5 round magazine. It is fitted with a 18.5" vent rib barrel. Synthetic stock is standard.

NIB	Exc.	V.G.	Good	Fair	Poor
430	350	—	—	—	—

BL-12 Field
Similar to the above model but with a 28" vent rib barrel and choice of wood or synthetic stock.

NIB	Exc.	V.G.	Good	Fair	Poor
470	375	—	—	—	—

SAS-12 Security
This 12 gauge shotgun is chambered for 2.75" 12 gauge shells and fitted with 24" vent rib barrel or rifle sight barrel. Detachable box magazine; 3 round standard, 5 round optional. Synthetic stock.

NIB	Exc.	V.G.	Good	Fair	Poor
500	400	—	—	—	—

FIELD COMBO-TWO BARREL COMBO SET

Model HC28SB
This set consists of an 18.5" barrel and 28" barrel with synthetic stock pistol grip, and bead sights.

NIB	Exc.	V.G.	Good	Fair	Poor
300	250	—	—	—	—

Model HC28SR
Same as above but with rifle and bead sights.

NIB	Exc.	V.G.	Good	Fair	Poor
320	250	—	—	—	—

Model HC28WB
This model features a wood stock, pistol grip, and bead sights.

NIB	Exc.	V.G.	Good	Fair	Poor
300	250	—	—	—	—

Model HC28WR
Same as above but with wood stock with rifle and bead sights.

NIB	Exc.	V.G.	Good	Fair	Poor
320	250	—	—	—	—

RIFLES

Legacy
This is a .50 caliber muzzle loader with in-line ignition system. It has a walnut stain hardwood stock with recoil pad. Finish is blue or chrome. Add $20 for Chrome finish.

NIB	Exc.	V.G.	Good	Fair	Poor
180	150	—	—	—	—

Mitchell PPS-50
This is a semiautomatic rifle chambered for the .22 LR cartridge. It has a detachable 10-round magazine. It is a copy of the Russian PPSh machine gun used in WWII.

NIB	Exc.	V.G.	Good	Fair	Poor
400	325	—	—	—	—

MAUSER RIFLES
All of these Mauser rifles were introduced in 1998 to the Brolin product line.

Lightning Model
This model features a sliding bolt that locks directly into the barrel. Chambered for 7.62x39mm cartridge as well as the .308 Win. Blue finish with choice of colored synthetic stocks. Open sights are standard.

NIB	Exc.	V.G.	Good	Fair	Poor
550	450	—	—	—	—

Lightning Hunter Model
This model features a detachable magazine, recoil pad, blued finish, checkered wood stock, and choice of open sights or no sights with scope mounts included. Calibers from .243 to .300 Win. Mag. Add $50 for open sights, $50 for stainless steel.

NIB	Exc.	V.G.	Good	Fair	Poor
750	600	—	—	—	—

Lightning Hunter All Weather Model
Same as above but with black synthetic stock.

NIB	Exc.	V.G.	Good	Fair	Poor
700	550	—	—	—	—

Lightning Varmint Model
The features of this model are the same as the Lightning Hunter Model with the addition of a heavy fluted barrel with special varmint wood or synthetic stock. Chambered for .22-250 and .243 cartridges.

NIB	Exc.	V.G.	Good	Fair	Poor
1000	800	—	—	—	—

Lightning Sniper
This model features a heavy fluted barrel with detachable magazine and a choice of special wood or synthetic stock with built-in bi-pod rail. Offered in .308 or 300 Win. Mag. calibers.

NIB	Exc.	V.G.	Good	Fair	Poor
1000	800	—	—	—	—

Lightning Professional
This model has a heavy fluted barrel, no sights, and recoil compensator. A tuned trigger system is standard. All weather

adjustable stock with pistol grip. Available in .308 or .300 Win. Mag. calibers.

NIB	Exc.	V.G.	Good	Fair	Poor
1000	800	—	—	—	—

Model 2000 Classic

The 2000 Classic features an interchangeable caliber system for cartridges in the same action length. Detachable magazine. High grade walnut stock with cut checkering and rosewood forend. Single set trigger is standard. Offered in .270, .308, .30-06, 7mm Rem. Mag., and .300 Win. Mag.

NIB	Exc.	V.G.	Good	Fair	Poor
1800	1400	—	—	—	—

Model 2000 Varmint

This model features a heavy fluted barrel with special varmint wood stock with accessory rail. Offered in .22-250, and .243 calibers. Standard without sights.

NIB	Exc.	V.G.	Good	Fair	Poor
2200	1700	—	—	—	—

Model 2000 Sniper

This model features an interchangeable caliber system, heavy fluted barrel, no sights, single set trigger, all weather stock with built-in bi-pod rail. Offered in .308 and .300 Win. Mag. calibers.

NIB	Exc.	V.G.	Good	Fair	Poor
2200	1750	—	—	—	—

Model 2000 Professional

This model has all of the features of the Sniper rifle with the addition of a recoil compensator and special all weather pistol grip stock. Each rifle is custom built.

NIB	Exc.	V.G.	Good	Fair	Poor
3500	2750	—	—	—	—

Model 20/22

This is a high quality .22 bolt action rifle chambered for the .22 l.r. of .22 magnum cartridge. Available in both a standard and deluxe configuration. Add $100 for Deluxe version.

NIB	Exc.	V.G.	Good	Fair	Poor
700	550	—	—	—	—

Model 1898 Commemorative

This model celebrates the 100 year anniversary of the '98 Mauser. Chambered for the 8mm Mauser cartridge. This is a limited edition rifle.

NIB	Exc.	V.G.	Good	Fair	Poor
2300	—	—	—	—	—

Model 98

This is the original Mauser action built to Safari calibers. Chambered for .375 H&H or .416 Rigby.

NIB	Exc.	V.G.	Good	Fair	Poor
10000	8000	—	—	—	—

CUSTOM SHOP

Formula One RZ

This is a high performance competition race gun with many special features such as supported barrel chamber, 6 port compensator, tuned trigger, extended magazine release, and many other options as standard. Chambered for .38 Super, .40 S&W cartridges. Blue finish. Add $400 for double action.

NIB	Exc.	V.G.	Good	Fair	Poor
2500	2000	—	—	—	—

Formula One RS

Designed as a Limited Class competition gun with 5" barrel and chambered for .38 Super, .40 S&W, or .45 ACP calibers. Features adjustable rear sight, tuned trigger, checkered front

strap and mainspring housing and other special features. Add $300 for double action.

NIB	Exc.	V.G.	Good	Fair	Poor
2000	1600	—	—	—	—

Formula Z

This model is a custom built combat pistol chambered for .40 S&W, .400 Cor-Bon, or .45 ACP calibers. Fitted with a 5" or 4" barrel. Features many extra cost features as standard.

NIB	Exc.	V.G.	Good	Fair	Poor
1300	1000	—	—	—	—

MITCHELL SINGLE ACTION REVOLVERS

Single Action Army Model

Offered in 4.75", 5.5", or 7.5" barrel lengths and chambered for the .45 Long Colt, .357 Magnum, or .44-40 calibers. Offered in blue finish with case hardened frame or nickel finish. Also available with dual cylinders, i.e. .45LC/.45ACP. Add $50 for nickel finish, and $150 for dual cylinders models.

NIB	Exc.	V.G.	Good	Fair	Poor
450	350	—	—	—	—

BRONCO
SEE—Arizmendi
Eibar, Spain

BROOKLYN F. A. CO.
Brooklyn, New York

Slocum Pocket Revolver

A .32 caliber spur trigger revolver with a 3" round barrel. The frame is silver-plated brass and scroll engraved; the remainder is either blued or plated with walnut grips. The barrel is marked "B.A. Co. Patented April 14, 1863." Approximately 10,000 were manufactured in 1863 and 1864. The cylinder has five individual tubes that slide forward to open for loading and then for ejecting the spent cartridges.

Exc.	V.G.	Good	Fair	Poor
—	—	750	300	100

Slocum Unfluted Cylinder Pocket Revolver

As above, but in .22 or .32 caliber with 5- or 7-shot cylinder. Approximately 250 were manufactured in .32 rimfire and 100 in .22 rimfire.

.22 Caliber-Add 25%.

Exc.	V.G.	Good	Fair	Poor
—	—	900	400	200

BROWN, A.A.
Birmingham, England
SEE—British Double Guns

BROWN, DAVID MCKAY
Glasgow, Scotland
SEE—British Double Guns

BROWN, E.A. MANUFACTURING CO.
Akron, Ohio

Brown Classic Single Shot Pistol

This is a falling block single shot pistol with 15" match grade barrel. Chambered for calibers from .17 Ackley to .45-70 Gov't. Walnut thumbrest grips. Handfitted. Introduced in 1998.

NIB	Exc.	V.G.	Good	Fair	Poor
500	400	—	—	—	—

Brown Model 97D Single Shot Rifle

This is a single shot falling block rifle chambered for calibers from .17 Ackley to .45-70 Gov't. Barrels lengths up to 26". Sporter style stock with pistol grip, cheekpiece, and schnabel forend. Blue/black finish. Weight is about 6 lbs. No sights.

NIB	Exc.	V.G.	Good	Fair	Poor
600	475	—	—	—	—

BROWN, ED CUSTOM
Perry, Missouri

RIFLES

NOTE: There are a number of extra cost options that are offered by this company on its rifles that may affect value. Consult the company or an expert prior to a sale.

Model 702, Savanna

Fitted with a long action and chambered for calibers from .257 Ackley to .338 Win. Mag. Barrel is a lightweight 24" for standard calibers and a 24" medium weight for magnum calibers. Talley scope mounts included. Fiberglass stock, recoil pad, steel triggerguard and floorplate are standard.

NIB	Exc.	V.G.	Good	Fair	Poor
2800	2250	—	—	—	—

Model 702, Ozark

This rifle is built on a short action with a blind magazine. A 21" lightweight barrel is fitted for standard calibers and a medium weight 21" barrel for magnum calibers. Chambered for calibers from .22-250 to .308. Talley scope mounts are included as is a fiberglass stock, recoil pad, steel triggerguard and floorplate.

NIB	Exc.	V.G.	Good	Fair	Poor
2500	2000	—	—	—	—

Model 76, Bushveld

This model is based on a Dakota controlled feed action. Fitted with a 24" medium or heavy weight barrel. Calibers from .330 Dakota to .458 Win. Mag. Detachable box magazine. Monte Carlo fiberglass stock, recoil pad, steel trigger and floorplate

are standard as is Talley scope mounts. Weight is approximately 8.5 lbs.

NIB	Exc.	V.G.	Good	Fair	Poor
3400	2750	—	—	—	—

Model 702, Light Tactical

This is short action rifle with light weight floorplate and triggerguard. Fitted with a 21" medium weight barrel. Black fiberglass stock with aluminum bedding block. Available in calibers from .22-250 to .308.

NIB	Exc.	V.G.	Good	Fair	Poor
2800	2250	—	—	—	—

Model 702, Tactical

This is similar to the above model but built on a long action with heavy weight 26" blued barrel. McMillian A-3 black tactical stock. Available in .308 and .300 Win. Mag.

NIB	Exc.	V.G.	Good	Fair	Poor
3200	2500	—	—	—	—

Model 702, Varmint

This is a custom made rifle with a short single shot action. 26" medium weight barrel or 24" heavy weight barrel. H-S Precision stock. Available in calibers from .222 to 6.5/.284.

NIB	Exc.	V.G.	Good	Fair	Poor
2500	2000	—	—	—	—

Model 702, Peacekeeper

This is single shot long action rifle chambered for .30/378 Wby., .338/378 Wby., or the .338 Lapua caliber. Fitted with a heavy 26" barrel with muzzle brake. Fiberglass tactical stock with recoil pad. Leupold Mark 4 scope mounts standard. Weight is approximately 13 lbs.

NIB	Exc.	V.G.	Good	Fair	Poor
3500	2750	—	—	—	—

BROWN, ED PRODUCTS, INC.
Perry, MO

PISTOLS

NOTE: There are a number of extra options offered on these pistols that may affect value. Consult the company or an expert prior to a sale.

Commander Bobtail

This model features a 4.25" barrel chambered for the .45 ACP, .400 Cor-Bon, .40 S&W, .38 Super, 9x23, or 9mm Luger cartridge. Modified Hogue grips from exotic wood are standard. This pistol is completely handmade and is built to the customer's specifications. Many available options. Retail prices begin at $2,400.

Classic Custom

Chambered for the .45 ACP cartridge. This is a custom built pistol with many extra features such as Videki trigger, Ed Brown wide thumb safety, stainless steel thumb safety, and extended safety, adjustable rear sight, etc. All hand fitted parts.

NIB	Exc.	V.G.	Good	Fair	Poor
2750	2000	—	—	—	—

Class A Limited

This is a custom built pistol offered in a number of different calibers from .45 ACP to 9mm Luger. Fitted with a 4.25" Commander length slide. Many special features. Price listed below is for the basic pistol.

NIB	Exc.	V.G.	Good	Fair	Poor
2250	1750	—	—	—	—

BROWN MANUFACTURING CO.
Newburyport, Massachusetts
ALSO SEE—Ballard

Courtesy W. P. Hallstein III and son Chip

Southerner Derringer

A .41 caliber spur trigger single shot pocket pistol with a pivoted 2.5" or 4" octagonal barrel marked "Southerner". Silver-plated or blued with walnut grips. This pistol was manufactured by the Merrimack Arms Co. from 1867 to 1869 and by the Brown Manufacturing Co. from 1869 to 1873.

Brass Framed 2.5" Barrel

Exc.	V.G.	Good	Fair	Poor
—	—	700	300	125

Iron Frame 2.5" Barrel (Brown Mfg. Only)

Exc.	V.G.	Good	Fair	Poor
—	—	800	400	200

Brass Frame 4" Barrel

Exc.	V.G.	Good	Fair	Poor
—	—	2500	950	400

Brown Mfg. Co./Merrill Patent breechloading rifles

Overall length 54-3/4"; barrel (bore) length 35"; caliber .577. Markings: On breechblock-bolt mechanism, "BROWN MFG. CO. NEWBURYPORT, MASS./PATANTED OCT. 17, 1871." The patent issued to George Merrill in 1871, permitted the Brown Manufacturing Co. to alter probably up to 1,000 English P1853 rifle-muskets to a single shot breechloading system. The large bolt handle projecting upward at the end of the breech readily distinguishes these arms.

Courtesy Milwaukee Public Museum, Milwaukee, Wisconsin

Exc.	V.G.	Good	Fair	Poor
—	—	1000	500	275

BROWN PRECISION, INC.
Los Molinos, California

Although known as a manufacturer of stocks, this company also produces custom order rifles.

High Country Standard

A .243 to .30-06 bolt action rifle with a 22" barrel and Kevlar stock. Gray camo stock, stainless barrel and Leupold 2.5 x 10 Scope-Add $650.

NIB	Exc.	V.G.	Good	Fair	Poor
985	775	600	500	400	200

Open Country Varmint Rifle

Similar to the above, with a heavy barrel. Introduced in 1989.

NIB	Exc.	V.G.	Good	Fair	Poor
1100	800	650	550	400	200

Law Enforcement Model
A .308 caliber Remington Varmint action rifle with a 20" barrel, Zeiss telescope and Kevlar stock.

NIB	Exc.	V.G.	Good	Fair	Poor
1050	800	650	550	400	200

Pro-Hunter
A .375 Holland & Holland or .458 Winchester Magnum bolt action rifle. Blued, electroless nickel-plated or Teflon coated.

NIB	Exc.	V.G.	Good	Fair	Poor
1800	1400	950	700	500	250

A .270 or .30-06 bolt-action rifle with a 22" featherweight barrel and Kevlar stock.

NIB	Exc.	V.G.	Good	Fair	Poor
600	475	350	250	150	100

Blaser Rifle
Built on the Camex-Blaser action with a Brown Precision stock.

NIB	Exc.	V.G.	Good	Fair	Poor
1400	1100	750	550	400	200

BROWNING ARMS CO.
Morgan, Utah

Contrary to popular belief, the firm of Browning Arms has really manufactured only one gun in its long and colorful history. This was the Model 1878 single shot rifle, which was actually the first gun that the prolific inventor John M. Browning patented. This firm was founded in 1880 as J. M. Browning & Bro. in Ogden, Utah. John Browning is considered by many to be the greatest firearms genius of all time. He created 80 firearms designs and held 128 individual patents. He sold designs to Winchester, Stevens, Remington, and Colt, as well as to the Belgian firm of Fabrique Nationale (FN). He was directly responsible for designing many of the firearms with which we have come to be familiar, including the 1911 Colt Government Model, the 1885 Winchester Single Shot (evolved from the Model 1878 that was actually Browning-manufactured), the Models 1886, 1892, 1894, and 1895 Lever Action Rifles, as well as the Model 1897 Shotgun. He was also directly responsible for producing the Model 1935 Hi-Power that achieved worldwide service pistol acceptance. In the 1890s Browning had difficulty dealing with the American arms corporations, so he went to Europe and established a lasting relationship with the firm of Fabrique Nationale in Herstal, Belgium. This agreement has lasted until 1977 when FN purchased the Browning Company. In the early 1970s, the Browning corporation contracted with the firm of B. C. Miroku in Japan and has since marketed guns produced by them. In 1991 GIAT, a French state-owned firm, purchased FN and Browning. One should be cognizant of the fact that in the opinion of many experts Miroku-produced Browning firearms are as high in quality as any others produced; collector interest dictates greater values on the Belgian-manufactured versions.

> **CAUTION**
> Certain Browning long guns and pistols used wood that was salt-cured, causing a rusting problem to the underside of barrels and actions. This problem occurred from about 1966 to 1972. This should be carefully checked before purchase.

Early Semiautomatic Pistols
In the period between 1900 and the development of the Model 1935 Hi-Power Pistol, Browning had a number of semiautomatic pistols manufactured by Fabrique Nationale of Herstal, Belgium. They were the Models 1900, 1903, 1905, 1910, 1922, the Baby, and the 1935 Model Hi-Power. These firearms will be listed in more detail with their respective values in the Fabrique Nationale section of this text.

Hi-Power Modern Production
This version of the FN Model 1935 is quite similar in appearance to the original described in the FN section. It is chambered for the 9mm Parabellum cartridge and has a 4.75" barrel. Models built before the passage of the crime bill have a double column, 13-round, detachable box magazine and is blued with checkered walnut grips. It has fixed sights and has been produced in its present configuration since 1954. Add a 10 percent premium for adjustable sights. A matte-nickel version, offered between 1980 and 1984, was also available and would be worth approximately 15% additional.

Spur Hammer Version

NIB	Exc.	V.G.	Good	Fair	Poor
525	450	350	300	275	200

Round Hammer Version

NIB	Exc.	V.G.	Good	Fair	Poor
650	550	400	350	300	200

Hi-Power-.30 Luger

This version is similar to the standard Hi-Power except that it is chambered for the .30 Luger cartridge. There were approximately 1,500 imported between 1986 and 1989. The slide is marked "FN." The Browning-marked versions are quite rare and worth approximately 30 percent additional.

Exc.	V.G.	Good	Fair	Poor
500	400	300	250	150

Tangent Sight Model

This version is similar to the standard Hi-Power with the addition of an adjustable rear sight calibrated to 500 meters. There were approximately 7,000 imported between 1965 and 1978. If the grip frame is slotted to accept a detachable shoulder stock, add approximately 20 percent to the value; but be wary of fakes. Add an additional 10% for "T" series serial numbers.

Exc.	V.G.	Good	Fair	Poor
850	725	550	400	300

Renaissance Hi-Power

This is a heavily engraved version with a matte-silver finish. It features synthetic-pearl grips and a gold-plated trigger. Import on this model ended in 1979.

Spur Hammer Model

NIB	Exc.	V.G.	Good	Fair	Poor
1500	1200	1050	800	250	100

Ring Hammer Model

NIB	Exc.	V.G.	Good	Fair	Poor
1600	1400	1000	800	500	250

Adjustable Sight Spur Hammer Model

NIB	Exc.	V.G.	Good	Fair	Poor
1675	1150	850	600	500	250

Renaissance .25 Caliber

NIB	Exc.	V.G.	Good	Fair	Poor
900	750	600	400	300	150

Renaissance .380 Caliber

With pearl grips

NIB	Exc.	V.G.	Good	Fair	Poor
1400	1150	850	600	400	200

Renaissance .380 Caliber (Model 1971)

With wood grips and adjustable sights.

NIB	Exc.	V.G.	Good	Fair	Poor
1000	800	600	400	325	175

Cased Renaissance Set

This features one example of a fully engraved and silver-finished .25 ACP "Baby," one .380 ACP pistol, and one Hi-Power. The set is furnished in a fitted walnut case or black leatherette and was imported between 1955 and 1969.

NIB	Exc.	V.G.	Good	Fair	Poor
4500	3500	2500	1800	1100	900

NOTE: For early coin finish sets add 30%.

Louis XVI Model

This is a heavily engraved Hi-Power pistol that features a leaf-and-scroll pattern. It is satin-finished and features checkered walnut grips. It is furnished in a fitted walnut case. To realize its true potential, this pistol must be NIB. It was imported between 1980 and 1984.

Diamond Grip Model

NIB	Exc.	V.G.	Good	Fair	Poor
1200	775	650	550	300	200

Medallion Grip Model

NIB	Exc.	V.G.	Good	Fair	Poor
950	700	600	350	225	150

Hi-Power Centennial Model

This version is similar to the standard fixed-sight Hi-Power but is chrome-plated with the inscription, "Browning Centennial/1878-1978" engraved on the slide. It is furnished with a fitted case. There were 3,500 manufactured in 1978. As with all commemorative pistols, in order to realize its collector potential, this model should be NIB with all supplied material. Prices are for pistols built in Belgium

NIB	Exc.	V.G.	Good	Fair	Poor
875	550	450	300	200	150

Hi-Power Capitan

This is a new version of the Hi-Power model fitted with tangent sights. Introduced in 1993. Furnished with walnut grips. Weighs about 32 oz. Assembled in Portugal.

NIB	Exc.	V.G.	Good	Fair	Poor
650	475	350	300	250	200

Hi-Power Practical

First introduced in 1993 this version is furnished with a blued slide and chrome frame. Has Pachmayr wraparound rubber grips, round style serrated hammer, and removable front sight. As available with adjustable sights. Weighs 36 oz. Assembled in Portugal.

NIB	Exc.	V.G.	Good	Fair	Poor
650	475	350	300	250	200

Hi-Power Silver Chrome Model

Furnished in hard chrome and fitted with wraparound Pachmayr rubber grips. Weighs 36 oz. Assembled in Portugal. Add 10% for models with all Belgian markings. This pistol was introduced in 1981 and dropped from the Browning product line in 1984. It was reintroduced in 1991.

NIB	Exc.	V.G.	Good	Fair	Poor
650	425	325	275	225	200

Hi-Power Mark III

The pistol, introduced in 1991, has a matte blued finish with low profile fixed sights, and two-piece molded grips with thumb rest. Weighs 32 oz.

NIB	Exc.	V.G.	Good	Fair	Poor
550	400	300	225	200	175

Hi-Power 40 S&W

Introduced in 1994, this new version of the Hi-Power is furnished with adjustable sights, molded grips, 5" barrel and a 10-round magazine. Weighs about 35 oz.

NIB	Exc.	V.G.	Good	Fair	Poor
600	450	350	300	250	200

BDA-380

This is a double action, semiautomatic pistol chambered for the .380 ACP cartridge. It features a 3.75" barrel with a 14-round, double-stack, detachable magazine. The finish is either blued or nickel-plated with smooth walnut grips. This pistol was manufactured in Italy by Beretta and introduced in 1977. Add 10% for nickel finish.

NIB	Exc.	V.G.	Good	Fair	Poor
500	375	325	275	200	150

Model BDA

This is a double action, semiautomatic pistol manufactured between 1977 and 1980 for Browning by Sig-Sauer of Germany. It is identical to the Sig-Sauer Model 220. It is chambered for

9mm Parabellum, .38 Super, and the .45 ACP cartridges. The .38 Super would be worth approximately 30 percent additional.

Exc.	V.G.	Good	Fair	Poor
500	425	375	300	235

BDM Pistol

This is a double action, semiautomatic pistol chambered for the 9mm cartridge. The pistol is fitted with a selector switch that allows the shooter to choose between single action model or double action model. It features a 4.75" barrel with adjustable rear sight. The magazine capacity is 15 rounds. Weighs 31 oz. First introduced in 1991.

NIB	Exc.	V.G.	Good	Fair	Poor
560	500	450	400	300	200

Model BDM Silver Chrome

This variation of the BDM was introduced in 1997 and features a silver chrome finish on the slide and frame. The balance of the pistol is in a contrasting matte blue finish.

NIB	Exc.	V.G.	Good	Fair	Poor
560	500	450	400	300	200

Model BDM Practical

This model, also introduced in 1997, is the same as above but with the silver chrome on the frame only.

NIB	Exc.	V.G.	Good	Fair	Poor
560	500	450	400	300	200

Model BPM-D

Introduced in 1997 this new version of the BDM (Browning Pistol Model Decocker) features a double action pistol with the first shot fired double action and subsequent shots fired single action. There is no manual safety. A decock lever also releases the slide.

NIB	Exc.	V.G.	Good	Fair	Poor
525	475	425	375	275	200

Model BRM-DOA

This 9mm pistol is a redesigned version of the Model BDM but the initials stand for "Browning Revolver Model-Double Action Only". This pistol also has a finger support triggerguard for two-handed control. All other features are the same as the BPM-D pistol. Weight is approximately 31 oz.

NIB	Exc.	V.G.	Good	Fair	Poor
525	475	425	375	275	200

Nomad

This is a blowback-operated, semiautomatic pistol chambered for the .22 l.r. cartridge. It was offered with a 4.5" or 6.75" barrel. It has a 10-round, detachable magazine with adjustable sights and all-steel construction. The finish is blued with black plastic grips. It was manufactured between 1962 and 1974 by FN.

NIB	Exc.	V.G.	Good	Fair	Poor
300	250	200	150	75	50

Challenger

This is a more deluxe target pistol chambered for the .22 l.r. cartridge. It was offered with a 4.5" or 6.75" barrel and has a 10-round magazine. It is constructed entirely of steel and has adjustable sights. The finish is blued with a gold-plated trigger and checkered, wraparound, walnut grips. It was manufactured between 1962 and 1974 by FN.

Courtesy John J. Stimson, Jr.

NIB	Exc.	V.G.	Good	Fair	Poor
500	375	300	250	200	140

Renaissance Challenger

This version is fully engraved with a satin-nickel finish and furnished with a fleece lined pouch.

NIB	Exc.	V.G.	Good	Fair	Poor
1600	1300	1000	750	500	350

Gold Line Challenger

This version is blued and has a gold-inlaid line around the outer edges of the pistol. It was cased in a fleece lined pouch. Built in Belgium.

NIB	Exc.	V.G.	Good	Fair	Poor
1600	1300	1000	750	500	350

Challenger II

This is a blowback-operated, semiautomatic pistol chambered for the .22 l.r. cartridge. It has a 6.75" barrel with an alloy frame. The finish is blued with phenolic impregnated hardwood grips. This pistol was manufactured between 1976 and 1982 in Salt Lake City, Utah.

Exc.	V.G.	Good	Fair	Poor
250	225	175	140	100

Challenger III

This version features a 5.5" bull barrel with adjustable sights. It was manufactured between 1982 and 1984 in Salt Lake City, Utah. A 6.75", tapered-barrel version was also available and known as the Sporter.

Exc.	V.G.	Good	Fair	Poor
250	200	150	125	90

Medalist

This is a high-grade, semiautomatic target pistol chambered for the .22 l.r. cartridge. It has a 6.75", vent rib barrel with adjustable target sights. It was supplied with three barrel weights and a dry-fire-practice mechanism. The finish is blued with target type, thumbrest, walnut grips. It was manufactured between 1962 and 1974 by FN. There were four additional high-grade versions of this pistol that differed in the degree of ornamentation.

NIB	Exc.	V.G.	Good	Fair	Poor
900	750	575	475	375	250

International Medalist

About 700 were sold in the U.S. from 1977 to 1980. Barrels were 5-7/8" long. Built in Belgium.

Courtesy John J. Stimson, Jr.

NIB	Exc.	V.G.	Good	Fair	Poor
950	800	600	450	300	150

Second Model International Medalist.

Same as above but with flat-sided barrel, dull finish, and adjustable palm rest. Built in Belgium.

Courtesy John J. Stimson, Jr.

NIB	Exc.	V.G.	Good	Fair	Poor
825	725	450	300	200	150

Gold Line Medalist

Introduced in 1962 and discontinued in 1974 with only an estimated 400 guns produced.

NIB	Exc.	V.G.	Good	Fair	Poor
1750	1600	1250	1000	750	500

Renaissance Medalist

This model was built entirely in Belgium from 1970 to 1974. Built with a one-piece grip.

NIB	Exc.	V.G.	Good	Fair	Poor
2250	1900	1500	1200	900	700

Browning Collector's Association Edition-Fully Engraved, 100 Manufactured

This model was fitted with a two piece grip.

NIB	Exc.	V.G.	Good	Fair	Poor
2500	2000	—	—	—	—

Buck Mark

This is a blowback-operated, semiautomatic pistol chambered for the .22 l.r. cartridge. It has a 5.5" bull barrel with adjustable sights. It has an 11-round, detachable magazine and is matte blued with skip-line checkered synthetic grips. It was introduced in 1985. Produced in the U.S.

NIB	Exc.	V.G.	Good	Fair	Poor
240	175	150	135	110	85

Buck Mark Plus

This version is similar to the standard with plain wood grips. It was introduced in 1987. Produced in the U.S.

NIB	Exc.	V.G.	Good	Fair	Poor
275	210	185	150	120	100

Buck Mark Plus Nickel

Introduced in 1991. Add $30 to above prices.

Buck Mark Varmint

This version has a 9.75" bull barrel with a full length ramp to allow scope mounting. It has no sights. It was introduced in 1987 and produced in the U.S.

NIB	Exc.	V.G.	Good	Fair	Poor
320	285	250	200	175	125

Buck Mark Silhouette

This version features a 9.75" bull barrel with adjustable sights. Introduced in 1987.

NIB	Exc.	V.G.	Good	Fair	Poor
350	325	285	220	185	140

Buck Mark 22 Micro

This version of the Buck Mark 22 is fitted with a 4" bull barrel. Available in blue, matte blue, or nickel finish. Also available in Micro Plus variation with walnut grips. Weighs 32 oz. Introduced in 1992.

NIB	Exc.	V.G.	Good	Fair	Poor
250	200	150	125	100	70

Micro Plus

NIB	Exc.	V.G.	Good	Fair	Poor
275	225	175	150	125	90

Micro Plus Nickel

Introduced in 1996. Add $30 to above price.

Buck Mark 5.5

This .22 caliber pistol has a 5.5" heavy bull barrel fitted with target sights. It is offered in three separate models:

5.5 Blued Target

This version has a blued finish, contoured walnut grips, target sights. Weighs 35.5 oz. Introduced in 1990.

NIB	Exc.	V.G.	Good	Fair	Poor
300	275	250	200	150	100

5.5 Gold Target

Same as above but has a gold anodized frame and top rib. Slide is blue. Walnut grips. Introduced in 1991.

NIB	Exc.	V.G.	Good	Fair	Poor
325	300	275	225	175	125

5.5 Field

Same action and barrel as the Target Model but with adjustable field sights. Sights are hoodless. Slide and barrel is blued while the rib and frame are anodized blue. Grips are walnut. Introduced in 1991.

NIB	Exc.	V.G.	Good	Fair	Poor
300	275	250	200	150	100

Buck Mark Bullseye

Introduced in 1996 this pistol is designed for metallic silhouette competition. The fluted barrel is 7-1/4" long. Adjustable trigger pull, adjustable rear sight removable barrel are some of the features. Weight is about 36 oz. Choice of laminated wood grips or rubber grips.

NIB	Exc.	V.G.	Good	Fair	Poor
325	275	225	175	125	75

NOTE: For Rosewood target grips add $90.

Buck Mark Unlimited Match

This pistol is fitted with a 14" barrel with top rib. The front sight hood is slightly rearward of the muzzle for a maximum sight radius of 15". All other features are the same as the Silhouette model. Weighs 64 oz.

NIB	Exc.	V.G.	Good	Fair	Poor
375	325	275	225	175	125

Buck Mark Challenge

Introduced in 1999 this model features a lightweight 5.5" barrel with adjustable rear sight. Smaller grip diameter. Matte blue finish and 10 round magazine capacity. Weight is about 25 oz.

NIB	Exc.	V.G.	Good	Fair	Poor
300	250	—	—	—	—

Buck Mark Micro

This model is essentially the same as the Buck Mark Challenge but with a 4" barrel. Weight is approximately 23 oz. Introduced in 1999.

NIB	Exc.	V.G.	Good	Fair	Poor
300	250	—	—	—	—

Buck Mark Camper

This model is fitted with a heavy 5.5" barrel and has a matte blue finish. Ten round magazine capacity. Weight is about 34 oz. Introduced in 1999.

NIB	Exc.	V.G.	Good	Fair	Poor
250	200	150	125	—	—

Buck Mark Limited Edition 25th Anniversary

This model is limited to 1,000 pistols and features a 6.75" barrel with matte blued finish and scrimshaw etched ivory grips. Pistol rug standard.

NIB	Exc.	V.G.	Good	Fair	Poor
435	350	—	—	—	—

CAUTION

Certain Browning long guns used wood that was salt-cured, causing a rusting problem to the underside of barrels and actions. This should be carefully checked before purchase. This problem is most prevalent during the years 1966 to 1972.

SHOTGUNS

SUPERPOSED SHOTGUNS

This series of Over/Under, double-barrel shotguns is chambered for 12, 20, and 28 gauges, as well as the .410 bore and is offered with vent rib barrels from 26.5" to 32" in length. It features various choke combinations. This shotgun is built on a boxlock action and features either double or single selective triggers and automatic ejectors. There were a number of versions offered that differ in the amount of ornamentation and the quality of the materials and workmanship utilized in manufacture. Values for small-bore models are generally higher. This series was introduced in 1930 and is manufactured by Fabrique Nationale in Belgium. For factory restored guns or very fine non-factory restorations Superposed guns will bring close to factory original prices.

For extra factory installed barrels add $1000 to $2500 depending on the grade of the gun.

PREWAR SUPERPOSED, 1930-1940

Browning Superposed shotgun prices are divided into three different categories. The first category is for prewar guns built from 1930 to 1940. *These prewar Superposed guns were manufactured in 12 gauge only* from serial number 1 to around 17,000. These shotguns were offered in four different grades: Grade I, Pigeon, Diana, and Midas.

Grade I

Exc.	V.G.	Good	Fair	Poor
2000	1500	1000	450	300

Pigeon

Exc.	V.G.	Good	Fair	Poor
3200	2200	1400	500	400

Diana

Exc.	V.G.	Good	Fair	Poor
5500	5000	3000	900	500

Midas

Exc.	V.G.	Good	Fair	Poor
8000	6800	3500	1200	750

NOTE: For Twin-Single triggers add 15%.
For Vent Rib add 10%.
For recoil pads or shorter than standard stocks deduct 25%.

SUPERPOSED FROM 1947-1959

The second category of Superposed was produced and sold from 1947 to 1959. These were built in 12 and 20 gauge as well as the 28 gauge and .410 bore which were introduced in 1959. These shotguns were graded using a Roman numeral system instead of names. They are: Grade I, Grade II, Grade III, Grade IV, Grade V, and Grade VI. The values listed below are for 12 gauge. Add the premium or deductions as listed below.

20 Gauge-Add 30%.
28 Gauge- Add 70% (1959 only).
.410-Add 35% (1959 only).

Trap-Deduct 35%

Standard Weight 12 gauge Grade I-Deduct 10%.

Grade I (marked Lightning on frame)

NIB	Exc.	V.G.	Good	Fair	Poor
2700	2000	1100	900	300	200

Grade II

NIB	Exc.	V.G.	Good	Fair	Poor
4000	3200	2000	1200	600	300

Grade III

NIB	Exc.	V.G.	Good	Fair	Poor
4500	3600	2600	1800	750	300

Grade IV

NIB	Exc.	V.G.	Good	Fair	Poor
7000	5500	3800	2400	1200	500

Grade V

NIB	Exc.	V.G.	Good	Fair	Poor
7000	5500	3800	2400	1200	600

Grade VI (Built in 1957 through 1959 only)

NIB	Exc.	V.G.	Good	Fair	Poor
12000	9000	6000	4000	2200	700

NOTE: The number of Grade VIs sold in North America is unknown, but it was most likely very small. This is a very rare grade. Proceed with caution.
The number of 28 gauge and .410 bore guns sold in late 1959 number less than 100.

SUPERPOSED FROM 1960-1976

Browning Superposed shotguns built from 1960 to 1976 revert back to the older grade names. They are Grade I, Pigeon, Pointer, Diana, and Midas. These shotguns were available in 12, 20, and 28 gauge as well as .410 bore. This last production period is a little more complicated due to manufacturing changes that some collectors consider important such as round knobs, long tangs.

Prices below reflect Superposed field guns produced from 1960 to 1965 in round pistol grip knob with long triggerguard tang in 12 gauge. For all other variations during this period one should consider the following:

For salt wood damage deduct a minimum of 50%.
For round knob short tang (circa 1966-1969) deduct 40%.
For flat knob short tang (circa 1969-1971) deduct 40%.
For flat knob long tang (circa 1971-1976) deduct 15%.
For New Style Skeet and Lightning Trap (recoil pad, flat knob, full beavertail forearm) with long triggerguard tang (1971-1976) deduct 35%; with short triggerguard tang deduct 40%; if Broadway rib deduct an additional 10%.
For skeet chokes on field guns deduct 5%.
For recoil pads on 2-3/4" chambered field guns deduct 20%.
For Master engraver signed guns (Funken, Watrin, Vrancken) add 10%.
For Standard Weight Grade I guns deduct 10%.
For shorter than standard stock length deduct 25%.
For 20 gauge add 30%.
For 28 gauge add 70%.
For .410 bore add 25%.

Grade I (Lightning marked on frame)

NIB	Exc.	V.G.	Good	Fair	Poor
2750	2250	1200	700	500	250

Pigeon Grade

NIB	Exc.	V.G.	Good	Fair	Poor
4500	3700	2500	1600	900	450

Pointer Grade-Rare

NIB	Exc.	V.G.	Good	Fair	Poor
6500	5500	4000	2500	1600	800

Diana Grade

NIB	Exc.	V.G.	Good	Fair	Poor
7500	6000	4000	2600	1800	800

Midas Grade

NIB	Exc.	V.G.	Good	Fair	Poor
9500	7750	5750	3500	2000	1000

Comment: FN also built Exhibition Grades that were sold in this country under the Browning name. Collectors consider a true Exhibition Grade as one not having a "C" prefix in the serial number. These particular guns are considered quite desirable and should be appraised on an individual basis. Superposed in this catageory can range in price from $10,000 to $20,000 depending on gauge, engraving coverage, and options.

The second type of Exhibition Grade is know as the "C" type that was first sold in the United States from about 1973 to 1977 and is so called because of the "C" prefix in the serial number. There were about 225 of these guns sold in the United States They came in quite a few grades and some were specially ordered. Although the lower grades are not considered by some to be true exhibitions (pre-C series) the highest "C" series grades are a match to the best of the older exhibitions. In 2000, an all option Superlight 2 barrel set with sideplates engraved by Vranken sold for $22,000. Generally, depending on the gun, prices will range between $6,000 and $25,000. These "C" grade guns should also be appraised individually.

WHAT'S IT LIKE-THE BROWNING SUPERPOSED

The Superposed shotgun was John M. Browning's' last legacy before he died in 1926. This over and under gun, with its single sighting plain, and single selective trigger is Browning's genius at its most obvious. The consequence is a fast pointing gun with well distributed weight between the hands. The gun's hinge pin, placed well forward, requires a fair amount of space to open far enough to actuate the ejectors. The positive side of this equation is strength and long lasting fit between barrel and action. The barrel selector switch, part of the safety located on the upper tang, can be awkward at times but with practice satisfactory. During the decade before World War II the Superposed was built only in 12 gauge. These early examples are a tribute to the Belgian craftsmen who built the guns. After Fabrique Nationale reopened its factory in Herstal, Belgium following the war the company produced a 20 gauge in addition to the 12 gauge. Not nearly as heavy, the 20 gauge Superposed proved to be the most popular over and under gun in North America over the next three decades. During the late 1950s Browning began to offer the Superposed in 28 gauge, as well as the .410 bore. These additions proved to be very popular with skeet shooters and hunters alike. The Grade I with its tasteful scroll is understated elegance and the higher grade Superposed, engraved by some of Europe's best, are truly breathtaking. My favorite is the Pointer Grade, but all are works of art. All of these features were accomplished while keeping the gun in a price range more accessible than other foreign over and under guns. Today the Superposed offers beauty, value, superb handling, and reliability at a cost well below many other European doubles.

Ned Schwing

SUPERPOSED SUPERLIGHT

This model was first introduced in 1967 in 12 gauge and 1969, in 20 gauge. Special order 28 gauge as well as .410 bore are also seen. It was offered in 26.5" barrel lengths with 27.5" barrls in 12 gauge and 28" barrels in smaller bores available on special order. It features a rounded frame and straight grip stock with tapered solid or vent rib barrels. Regular production on the Superlight ended in 1976 for the grades listed below. Production did continue for the Superlight in the P series begun in 1977.

NOTE: For 20 gauge guns add a 30% premium.
For 28 gauge guns add a 70% premium.
For .410 bore guns add 25% premium for high grades guns and 30% for Grade I.

Grade I

NIB	Exc.	V.G.	Good	Fair	Poor
3000	2500	1500	600	400	200

Pigeon Grade

NIB	Exc.	V.G.	Good	Fair	Poor
4250	3350	2300	1200	750	500

Pointer Grade-Rare

NIB	Exc.	V.G.	Good	Fair	Poor
6500	5200	3900	2000	1200	800

Diana Grade

NIB	Exc.	V.G.	Good	Fair	Poor
7500	6000	4100	2200	1200	800

Midas Grade

NIB	Exc.	V.G.	Good	Fair	Poor
9500	7500	5500	3500	2000	900

SUPERPOSED PRESENTATION GRADE SERIES

The following superposed shotguns were manufactured between 1977 and 1984 by FN in Belgium. The following models differ in the amount of ornamentation and the quality of materials and workmanship utilized in construction. This series was also available in a superlight configuration.

NOTE: Due to the tremendous variation of P-Series guns, prices here reflect the Superlight configuration. An all option superlight with a checkered butt, oil finish, and three piece forend will bring 25% to 30% more. For all other variations one should consider the following:
For trap guns deduct 25%.
For new style skeet deduct 25%.
For skeet choked field guns deduct 5%.
For recoil pads on field guns deduct 20%.
For flat knob long tang hunting guns with no options deduct 25%.
For flat knob long tang hunting guns with all options add 25%.
For guns signed by J. Baerten add 5%.
For P-4V guns with no gold deduct 20%.
For hand filed vent rib add 5%.
For Presentation Grade guns with extra sets of barrels add approximately $1,250 to $1,500 depending on gauge and combination.

For P1, P2, and P3 grades add the following premium:

For 20 gauge guns-30%.
For .28 gauge guns-60%.
For .410 bore-25%.

For the P4 grade add the following premium:

For 20 gauge guns-35%.
For 28 gauge guns-70%.
For .410 bore-30%.

Presentation I (without gold inlays)

NIB	Exc.	V.G.	Good	Fair	Poor
3200	2700	1200	1000	600	500

Presentation 1 Gold-inlaid

NIB	Exc.	V.G.	Good	Fair	Poor
4200	3400	2400	1300	700	500

Presentation 2 (without gold inlays)

NIB	Exc.	V.G.	Good	Fair	Poor
4700	3900	2700	1700	800	600

Presentation 2 Gold-inlaid

NIB	Exc.	V.G.	Good	Fair	Poor
6400	5650	3750	2250	1000	700

NOTE: For early hand-engraved P3 models (approximately 25 produced) add 40%. These early guns are rare, proceed with caution.

Presentation 3 Gold-inlaid

NIB	Exc.	V.G.	Good	Fair	Poor
7750	6500	4600	3000	1300	800

Presentation 4 Gold-inlaid

NIB	Exc.	V.G.	Good	Fair	Poor
10500	9500	7500	5500	3000	2500

NOTE: For P4 Grade guns with no gold deduct approximately 20%.

SUPERPOSED WATERFOWL LIMITED EDITION SERIES

This model was issued in three different versions; Mallard, Pintail, and Black Duck. Each edition was limited to 500 guns, all in 12 gauge. It has been observed that some of these guns were stocked with salt cured wood. Salt wood stocks will drastically affect price. Caution should be exercised when a sale is contemplated. Prices reflect the absence of salt wood damage.

1981 Mallard Issue

NIB	Exc.	V.G.	Good	Fair	Poor
6000	4500	3500	2500	1300	900

1982 Pintail Issue

NIB	Exc.	V.G.	Good	Fair	Poor
6000	4500	3500	2500	1300	900

1983 Black Duck Issue

NIB	Exc.	V.G.	Good	Fair	Poor
6000	4500	3500	2500	1300	900

Bicentennial Model

Produced in 1976 to commemorate the 200 year anniversary of America. A total of 53 guns were built in this special edition. All of these Superposed were 12 gauge with 28" barrels and each was numbered for one of the fifty states plus the District of Columbia. Two additional guns were built for the Smithsonian Institution and the Liege Firearms Museum. All were fitted with side plates with gold inlays. To reflect true value guns must be in unfired condition in their original case with all the papers.

NIB	Exc.	V.G.	Good	Fair	Poor
10000	7500	5000	2750	1500	1000

NOTE: Price often depends on the state.

FN/Browning Superposed

A number of FN Browning Superposed B-25 shotguns were imported into this country by Browning in various grades. These Superposed were intended originally for FN's European market. There are a large number of variations and grades. It is strongly suggested that an expert appraisal be sought prior to the sale. As a general rule these prices for NIB guns are: A grade-$1,200-1,600; B grade $1,600-2,500; C grade $2,500-3,500; D grade $3,500-5,000. These guns are marked with both the Browning and FN barrel address.

Classic

Produced in 1986 this model was offered in 20 gauge with 26" barrels. About 2,500 guns were produced. Silver gray receiver with engraving.

NIB	Exc.	V.G.	Good	Fair	Poor
1900	1400	—	—	—	—

Gold Classic

This shotgun was similar to the above model but more finely finished and engraved with gold inlays. About 350 of these guns were built in 1986.

NIB	Exc.	V.G.	Good	Fair	Poor
8000	5500	—	—	—	—

Custom Shop B25 & B125 Superposed

These special order Superposed are currently available with a delivery time of 6 to 8 months. A number of options are offered that effect price. B125 guns are assembled in Belgium with components made in other countries to hold down costs. The B25 is made entirely in Belgium and is the more expensive version of the Superposed. Prices listed are retail only. Buyer and seller are urged to seek an expert appraisal before a sale.

B-125

Trap   Retail Price-$8,125

12 Gauge Sporting

A Style   Retail Price-$4,475

B Style   Retail Price-$4,800

C Style   Retail Price-$5,275

12 & 20 Gauge Hunting and Superlight

A Style   Retail price-$4,475

B Style   Retail price-$4,800

C Style   Retail price-$5,275

B-25

Grade I   Retail price-$6,850

Pigeon Grade   Retail price-$8,625

Pointer Grade   Retail price-$9,950

Diana Grade   Retail price-$10,350

Midas Grade   Retail price-$14,500

Custom Shop BSL

This is a side by side shotgun is equiped with Browning side lock barrel, Holland & Holland type lockswith double trigger and auto ejectors. the gun is assembled and finished by Labeau-Courally. It is offered in both 12 and 20 gauge. Engraved grayed receiver or case colored receiver. Introduced into the Browning product line in 2001.

Case Colored Receiver

NIB	Exc.	V.G.	Good	Fair	Poor
10200	—	—	—	—	—

BROWNING CUSTOM SHOP

Engraved Gray Receiver

NIB	Exc.	V.G.	Good	Fair	Poor
12275	—	—	—	—	—

Liege

This is an Over/Under shotgun chambered for 12 gauge. It was offered with 26.5", 28", or 30" vent rib barrels with various choke combinations. It features a boxlock action with a nonselective single trigger and automatic ejectors. The finish is blued with a checkered walnut stock. There were approximately 10,000 manufactured between 1973 and 1975. U.S. versions were marked Browning Arms Company on the barrel.

NIB	Exc.	V.G.	Good	Fair	Poor
825	650	550	450	300	200

B27

This improved version of the Liege was imported into the U.S., some without the Browning Arms Company markings and only the FN barrel address. Others may have both barrel addresses. It was offered in a number of variations that differed in the amount of ornamentation and quality of materials and workmanship utilized. It features the same action as the Liege Over/Under gun.

Standard

NIB	Exc.	V.G.	Good	Fair	Poor
700	550	450	350	250	200

Deluxe

NIB	Exc.	V.G.	Good	Fair	Poor
1000	900	650	500	350	250

Deluxe Trap

NIB	Exc.	V.G.	Good	Fair	Poor
950	825	550	450	300	250

Deluxe Skeet

NIB	Exc.	V.G.	Good	Fair	Poor
950	825	550	450	300	250

Grand Deluxe

NIB	Exc.	V.G.	Good	Fair	Poor
1350	1100	775	650	500	400

City of Liege Commemorative-250 Manufactured

NIB	Exc.	V.G.	Good	Fair	Poor
1300	1050	725	600	450	300

ST-100

This is an Over/Under trap gun that features separated barrels with an adjustable point of impact. It is chambered for 12 gauge and has a 30" or 32" barrel with full choke and a floating ventilated rib. It features a single trigger and automatic ejectors. The finish is blued with a checkered walnut stock. It was manufactured by FN between 1979 and 1981.

NIB	Exc.	V.G.	Good	Fair	Poor
2000	1700	1400	1000	700	400

CITORI SERIES

This is an Over/Under, double-barrel shotgun chambered for all gauges and offered with vent rib barrels of 26" through 30" in length. It has a boxlock action with a single selective trigger and automatic ejectors. The various grades differ in the amount of ornamentation and the quality of materials and workmanship utilized in construction. This series is manufactured in Japan by B.C. Miroku and was introduced in 1973.

Grade I

NIB	Exc.	V.G.	Good	Fair	Poor
900	800	725	550	425	300

NOTE: Add premium of 30% for 16 gauge guns.

Upland Special-Grade I

Offered with straight grip stock and 24" rib barrels. Available in 12 gauge or 20 gauge. Weighs 6 lbs. 11 oz. in 12 gauge and 6 lbs. in 20 gauge. Introduced in 1984.

NIB	Exc.	V.G.	Good	Fair	Poor
1050	850	700	600	400	300

Grade II-1978 to 1983

Exc.	V.G.	Good	Fair	Poor
1500	1200	1000	650	400

Grade II-Choke Tubes

NIB	Exc.	V.G.	Good	Fair	Poor
1600	1400	1000	775	650	400

Grade V-1978 to 1984

NIB	Exc.	V.G.	Good	Fair	Poor
2600	2100	1600	950	750	400

Grade V-with side plates-1981 to 1984

NIB	Exc.	V.G.	Good	Fair	Poor
2900	2500	2100	1500	800	400

NOTE: Add 10% for small gauges.

Grade VI-Choke Tubes-Introduced 1983

NIB	Exc.	V.G.	Good	Fair	Poor
1750	1500	1200	1000	750	500

Citori Hunter

This model features a full pistol grip stock with beavertail forearm with high gloss walnut. Chambered for 12 with 2.75", 3", or 3.5" chambers and choice of 26", 28" or 30" barrels in 12 gauge. The 20 gauge models have a choice of 26" or 28" barrels. Twelve gauge guns weigh from 7 lbs. 13 ozs. to 8 lbs. 9 ozs. depending on barrel length. Twenty gauge guns weigh about 6.75 lbs. Add $75 for 3.5" models.

NIB	Exc.	V.G.	Good	Fair	Poor
1300	1000	850	650	550	450

Citori Sporting Hunter

This model has the same features as the Hunting model with the exception of the stock configuration. The Sporting Hunter has a Sporting model butt stock and a Superposed style forearm. Fitted with a contoured sporting recoil pad. Introduced in 1998. Add $75 for 3.5" models.

NIB	Exc.	V.G.	Good	Fair	Poor
1400	1300	1050	750	550	450

Citori Satin Hunter

This model is chambered for 12 gauge shells, has a hunting style stock, choice of 26" or 28" barrels, and a special satin wood finish with matte black receiver and barrels. Offered in Grade I only. Weight is about 8 lbs. Introduced in 1999.

NIB	Exc.	V.G.	Good	Fair	Poor
1250	1000	—	—	—	—

NOTE: Add $100 for 3.5" chamber.

Citori Lightning

This is a lightweight version that features a slimmer profile and has a checkered, round-knob, pistol-grip stock. It is offered in all gauges and in the same barrel lengths as the standard Citori. It features screw-in choke tubes known as invectors. It was introduced in 1988. The models differ in the amount of ornamentation and quality of materials and workmanship utilized.

Grade I

NIB	Exc.	V.G.	Good	Fair	Poor
1100	950	775	600	450	375

Grade III

NIB	Exc.	V.G.	Good	Fair	Poor
1600	1450	1050	825	650	500

Grade VI

NIB	Exc.	V.G.	Good	Fair	Poor
1900	1650	1350	1100	750	500

Citori Lightning Feather

Introduced in 1999 this model features a lightweight alloy receiver. Offered in 12 gauge Grade I only with choice of 26" or 28" barrels. Weight with 28" barrels is about 7 lbs. 11 ozs. In 2000 this model was offered in 20 gauge as well with 26" or 28" barrels with 3" chambers. Weight of 20 gauge is about 6.5 lbs.

NIB	Exc.	V.G.	Good	Fair	Poor
1575	1200	—	—	—	—

Citori Lightning Feather Combo

This model features a 20 gauge and 28 gauge barrel, both 27" long. The 20 gauge with 3" chambers the 28 gauge with 2.75" chambers. Pistol grip stock. Weight is about 6.25 lbs. Supplied with Browning luggage case. Introduced in 2000.

NIB	Exc.	V.G.	Good	Fair	Poor
2300	1995	1700	1500	—	—

Citori Feather XS

This model is offered in 12, 20, 28, and .410 bore. It has a lightweight alloy receiver. Fittted with a walnut stock with pistol grip and black recoil pad and Schnabel forearm. Triple trigger system and Hi-Viz Comp sight system standard. Weight is about 7 lbs. for 12 gauge; 6.5 lbs. for 20 gauge; 6 lbs. for 28 gauge; and 6 lbs. for .410 bore. Introduced in 2000.

NIB	Exc.	V.G.	Good	Fair	Poor
2000	1500	—	—	—	—

Citori Sporting Clays

Specifically design for sporting clays shooting. Offered in 12 gauge only, each model is back-bored, ported and fitted with Invector-Plus choke tubes. Barrels are chrome-plated. Receiver is blued with gold inscription. Pigeon Grade has gold detailing and high grade gloss walnut stock. Signature Grade features a red and black print on the stock with gold decals. Trigger is adjustable to three length of pull positions. Comes with three interchangeable trigger shoes. Each model is fitted with rubber recoil pad.

Lightning Sporting Model

This model features a rounded pistol grip and Lightning forearm with choice of high or low vent rib. Chambered for 3" shells. Offered in 28" or 30" barrels. Weighs about 8.5 lbs. Introduced in 1989.

NIB	Exc.	V.G.	Good	Fair	Poor
1200	1000	8000	600	450	300

Pigeon Grade

NIB	Exc.	V.G.	Good	Fair	Poor
1350	1100	900	650	450	300

Golden Clays

First introduced in 1994.

NIB	Exc.	V.G.	Good	Fair	Poor
2600	2250	1650	900	450	300

Citori Privilege

This high grade model features game scene engraved sideplates, unique checkering pattern, oil finish high-grade walnut stock with pistol grip. Offered in 12 gauge only with choice of 26" or 28" barrels. Weight is about 8 lbs. Introduced in 2000. In 2001 a 20 gauge version with 26" or 28" barrels was introduced.

Citori Privilege

Citori Privilege Left Side

NIB	Exc.	V.G.	Good	Fair	Poor
5375	4250	—	—	—	—

Citori XS Sporting Clays

Introduced in 1999, this model features silver nitride receiver with gold accents and European-style stock with schnabel forend. Available in 12, 20, and 28 gauge as well as .410 bore. Choice of 28" or 30" barrels. Weight varies from 8 lbs. in 12 gauge to 6 lbs. 7 ozs. in .410 bore. Offered in Grade I only.

NIB	Exc.	V.G.	Good	Fair	Poor
2000	1600	—	—	—	—

Citori Ultra XS Skeet

This model is offered in 12 gauge only with choice of 28" or 30" ported barrels chambered for 2.75" shells. Semi-beavertail forearm. Triple trigger system standard. Adjustable comb optional. Walnut stock with pistol grip and black recoil pad. Weight is about 7.75 lbs. Introduced in 2000. In 2001 a 20 gauge version was introduced with a choice of 28" or 30" barrels.

NIB	Exc.	V.G.	Good	Fair	Poor
2375	1800	—	—	—	—

Citori Plus

This model features an adjustable point of impact from 3" to 12" above point of aim. Receiver on Grade I is blued with scroll engraving. Walnut stock is adjustable and forearm is a modified beavertail style. Available in 30" or 32" barrels that are backbored and ported. Non-ported barrels are optional. Weighs about 9 lbs. 6 oz. Introduced in 1989.

Grade I

NIB	Exc.	V.G.	Good	Fair	Poor
1200	1000	750	500	400	300

Pigeon Grade

NIB	Exc.	V.G.	Good	Fair	Poor
1750	1500	950	700	500	300

Signature Grade

NIB	Exc.	V.G.	Good	Fair	Poor
1650	1450	950	700	500	300

Golden Clays

First introduced in 1994.

NIB	Exc.	V.G.	Good	Fair	Poor
2750	2250	1500	900	450	300

Trap Combination Set

This version is offered in Grade I only and features a 34" single barrel and a 32" set of Over/Under barrels. It is furnished in a fitted case and has been discontinued.

Exc.	V.G.	Good	Fair	Poor
1200	1050	950	800	700

GTI Model

This model features a 13mm wide rib, ventilated side ribs, pistol grip stock, semi-beavertail forearm. Offered in 28" or 30" barrel. Weighs about 8 lbs. This model not offered in Pigeon Grade. Introduced in 1989.

Grade I

NIB	Exc.	V.G.	Good	Fair	Poor
1100	900	750	600	450	300

Signature Grade

NIB	Exc.	V.G.	Good	Fair	Poor
1100	900	750	600	450	300

Golden Clays

First introduced in 1994.

NIB	Exc.	V.G.	Good	Fair	Poor
2350	1900	1250	900	450	300

Ultra Sporter-Sporting Clays

This model was introduced in 1995 and replaces the GTI model. It features a 10mm to 13mm tapered rib and is offered with either a blued or grey receiver with walnut stock with pistol grip and semi-beavertail forearm. Fitted with adjustable comb. Adjustable length of pull. Offered in 12 gauge only with 28" or 30" barrels. Average weight is 8 lbs.

NIB	Exc.	V.G.	Good	Fair	Poor
1450	1100	800	550	400	300

Ultra Sporter Sporting Clays-Golden Clays

NIB	Exc.	V.G.	Good	Fair	Poor
2750	2200	1600	1100	750	400

NOTE: For Ultra Sporters with adjustable comb add $200 to NIB price.

Citori Superlight

This is a lighter-weight version of the Citori chambered for all gauges and offered with the same features as the Lightning Series. The grades differ in the amount of ornamentation and quality of materials and workmanship utilized. This series was introduced in 1983.

Citori Superlight Feather

Introduced in 1999 this model features a straight grip stock with schnabel forend. Lightweight alloy receiver. Offered in 12 gauge Grade I only with choice of 26" or 28" barrels. Weight with 28" barrels is about 6 lbs. 6 ozs.

NIB	Exc.	V.G.	Good	Fair	Poor
1600	1250	—	—	—	—

Micro Lightning

Offered in 20 gauge only and has reduced dimensions for smaller shooters. Available with 24" vent rib barrels. Weighs 6 lbs. 3 oz. Introduced in 1991.

NIB	Exc.	V.G.	Good	Fair	Poor
950	850	700	600	400	300

Gran Lightning

This is essentially a Grade I Lightning with a high grade select walnut stock with satin finish. Receiver and barrels are blued. Offered in 12 gauge and 20 gauge with choice of 26" or 28" vent rib barrels. Choke tubes standard. Weighs about 8 lbs. in 12 gauge and 6 lbs. 11 oz. in 20 gauge. Introduced in 1990.

NIB	Exc.	V.G.	Good	Fair	Poor
1400	1100	850	650	450	300

Grade I

NIB	Exc.	V.G.	Good	Fair	Poor
1100	950	750	500	425	350

Grade III

NIB	Exc.	V.G.	Good	Fair	Poor
1500	1350	1050	750	550	450

Grade V-Discontinued 1984

Exc.	V.G.	Good	Fair	Poor
1600	1250	950	750	500

Grade VI

NIB	Exc.	V.G.	Good	Fair	Poor
1800	1600	1300	1000	800	500

Citori White Lightning

Introduced in 1998 this model features a silver nitride scroll engraved receiver. Offered in 3" 12 and 3" 20 gauge with choice of 26" or 28" barrels. Weight is approximately 8 lbs. for 12 gauge models and 6.8 lbs. for 20 gauge models. Invector-Plus chokes standard. Lightning-style stock.

NIB	Exc.	V.G.	Good	Fair	Poor
1400	1100	—	—	—	—

Citori White Upland Special

Introduced in 2000 this model features a shortened straight grip stock, Schnabel forearm, and 24" barrel. Fitted with 2.75" chambered for 12 gauge and 20 gauge only. Weight is about 6.75 lbs.

NIB	Exc.	V.G.	Good	Fair	Poor
—	—	—	—		

Citori Skeet

This series of guns was chambered for all gauges and was designed for competition skeet shooting. It is similar to the standard Citori with a high-post target rib and 26" or 28" barrels. The versions differ in the amount of engraving and the quality of materials and workmanship utilized.

Grade I

NIB	Exc.	V.G.	Good	Fair	Poor
1000	925	750	550	425	350

Grade II-Discontinued 1983

Exc.	V.G.	Good	Fair	Poor
1000	900	750	450	300

Grade III

NIB	Exc.	V.G.	Good	Fair	Poor
1500	1200	900	750	450	300

Grade V-Discontinued 1984

NIB	Exc.	V.G.	Good	Fair	Poor
1600	1200	900	750	450	300

Grade VI

NIB	Exc.	V.G.	Good	Fair	Poor
2000	1750	1200	900	450	300

Golden Clays

First introduced in 1994.

NIB	Exc.	V.G.	Good	Fair	Poor
2400	2000	1500	900	450	300

3 Gauge Set

Consists of 20 gauge, 28 gauge, and .410 bore interchangeable 28" vent rib barrels. Introduced in 1987.

Grade I

NIB	Exc.	V.G.	Good	Fair	Poor
2100	1950	1700	1250	900	700

Grade III

NIB	Exc.	V.G.	Good	Fair	Poor
2500	2250	1900	1400	1100	800

Grade VI

NIB	Exc.	V.G.	Good	Fair	Poor
2950	2500	2000	1500	1200	900

4 Gauge Set

This set has a 12 gauge, 20 gauge, 28 gauge, and .410 bore interchangeable vent rib barrels in either 26" or 28" lengths. Introduced in 1981.

Grade I

NIB	Exc.	V.G.	Good	Fair	Poor
3300	2750	2250	1700	1250	900

Grade III

NIB	Exc.	V.G.	Good	Fair	Poor
3400	2900	2500	1900	1350	900

Grade VI

NIB	Exc.	V.G.	Good	Fair	Poor
3800	3300	2900	2250	1400	950

Citori Trap

This version is similar to the standard Citori, offered in 12 gauge only with 30" or 32" barrels. It features a high rib and a Monte Carlo-type stock with recoil pad. The versions differ as to the amount of ornamentation and the quality of materials and workmanship utilized.

Grade I

NIB	Exc.	V.G.	Good	Fair	Poor
1000	900	750	550	425	350

Plus Trap-Adjustable Rib and Stock-Introduced 1989

NIB	Exc.	V.G.	Good	Fair	Poor
1500	1350	1000	750	600	500

Grade II-Discontinued 1983

Exc.	V.G.	Good	Fair	Poor
1000	850	675	450	350

Grade III

NIB	Exc.	V.G.	Good	Fair	Poor
1500	1350	1000	750	600	500

Grade V-Discontinued 1984

Exc.	V.G.	Good	Fair	Poor
1400	1250	900	650	450

Grade VI

NIB	Exc.	V.G.	Good	Fair	Poor
2100	1800	1550	1250	1000	800

Citori XT

Introduced in 1999, this Trap model is fitted with contoured beavertail with Monte Carlo stock with or without adjustable comb. The grayed receiver is highlighted in gold with light scroll work. Choice of 32" or 30" barrels. Weight is approximately 8 lbs. 11 ozs.

NIB	Exc.	V.G.	Good	Fair	Poor
2000	1600	—	—	—	—

Golden Clays

First introduced in 1994.

NIB	Exc.	V.G.	Good	Fair	Poor
2750	2250	1500	900	450	300

Signature Grade

NIB	Exc.	V.G.	Good	Fair	Poor
1150	950	800	600	450	300

Model 325 Sporting Clays

Introduced in 1993 this model has a European design that features a grayed receiver scroll engraved, schnabel forearm, 10mm wide vent rib, three interchangeable and adjustable trigger shoes, back-bore barrels that are ported and fitted with choke tubes. Available in 12 gauge and 20 gauge. The 12 gauge is offered with 28", 30", or 32" barrels while the 20 gauge is offered with 28" or 30" barrel fitted with conventional chokes. The 12 gauge weighs about 7 lbs. 14 oz., while the 20 gauge weighs about 6 lbs. 12 oz.

325 Sporting Clays

NIB	Exc.	V.G.	Good	Fair	Poor
1350	1200	900	700	450	300

Special Sporting

Similar to the Sporting model but fitted with a 2-3/4" chamber and choice of 28", 30", or 32" barrels. Barrels are ported. Barrels are also fitted with a high post rib. Stock has a full pistol grip and optional adjustable comb. Depending on barrel length weighs about 8.3 lbs.

Grade I

NIB	Exc.	V.G.	Good	Fair	Poor
1150	900	750	600	450	300

Signature Grade

NIB	Exc.	V.G.	Good	Fair	Poor
1150	900	750	600	450	300

Pigeon Grade

NIB	Exc.	V.G.	Good	Fair	Poor
1300	1100	850	600	450	300

Golden Clays

NIB	Exc.	V.G.	Good	Fair	Poor
2400	1900	1250	900	450	300

Model 425 Sporting Clays

This Citori over and under gun is offered in both 12 and 20 gauge with a choice of 28" and 30" barrel with 32" barrels available on the 12 gauge as well. The 425 is adjustable for length of pull and has an adjustable comb. Barrel are fitted with a 10mm wide rib. Invector chokes are standard. Average weight is 7 lbs. 14 oz. Introduced in 1995.

NIB	Exc.	V.G.	Good	Fair	Poor
1550	1200	850	600	450	300

Model 425 Golden Clays

Same as above but with high grade wood and engraved receiver.

NIB	Exc.	V.G.	Good	Fair	Poor
2950	2350	1650	1100	600	300

NOTE: For Model 425 with adjustable comb add $200 to NIB price.

Light Sporting 802ES (Extended Swing)

Introduced in 1996 this model features a 28" vent rib barrel with 2" stainless steel extension tubes for an extended swing of 30". An additional 4" extension is also included. Thus the barrel can be 28", 30" or 32" according to needs. Chambered for 12 gauge with adjustable length of pull. Walnut stock with pistol grip and schnabel forearm. Weight is about 7.5 lbs.

NIB	Exc.	V.G.	Good	Fair	Poor
1700	1400	900	700	500	250

BT-99

This is a break-open, single-barrel trap gun chambered for 12 gauge only. It is offered with a 32" or 34", vent rib barrel with screw-in choke tubes. It features a boxlock action with automatic ejectors. The finish is blued with a checkered walnut stock and beavertail forearm. It was introduced in 1968 by B.C. Miroku.

NIB	Exc.	V.G.	Good	Fair	Poor
800	700	600	500	400	350

Citori Plus Combo

This model features a single barrel trap and an interchangeable Over/Under set of barrels. Other features are similar to Citori Plus Grade 1. Barrel combinations are 32" Over/Under with 34" single barrel or 30" Over/Under barrel with 32" or 34" single barrel. Introduced in 1989.

NIB	Exc.	V.G.	Good	Fair	Poor
2500	2100	1750	1 100	700	450

BT-99 Stainless

First introduced in 1993.

NIB	Exc.	V.G.	Good	Fair	Poor
1275	1150	900	700	550	350

BT-99 Signature Grade I

First introduced in 1993.

NIB	Exc.	V.G.	Good	Fair	Poor
975	850	700	600	500	300

BT-99 Pigeon Grade

First introduced in 1993.

NIB	Exc.	V.G.	Good	Fair	Poor
1200	950	800	650	500	300

BT-99 Golden Clays

First introduced in 1994.

NIB	Exc.	V.G.	Good	Fair	Poor
2250	1750	1250	900	450	300

BT-99 Plus

This version features an adjustable vent rib and a recoil reduction system. It has an adjustable stock and recoil pad, as well as a back-bored barrel. It was introduced in 1989.

NIB	Exc.	V.G.	Good	Fair	Poor
1350	1200	900	700	500	300

BT-99 Plus Stainless-Grade I

Same as standard version but offered in stainless steel. First introduced in 1993. Available in 32" and 34" barrels. Weighs about 8 lbs. 11 oz.

NIB	Exc.	V.G.	Good	Fair	Poor
1600	1350	900	700	500	350

BT-99 Plus-Pigeon Grade

NIB	Exc.	V.G.	Good	Fair	Poor
1500	1200	900	800	550	350

BT-99 Plus-Signature Grade

NIB	Exc.	V.G.	Good	Fair	Poor
1400	1100	850	700	500	300

BT-99 Plus-Golden Clays

First introduced in 1994.

NIB	Exc.	V.G.	Good	Fair	Poor
2600	2250	1750	900	450	300

BT-99 Plus Micro

Slightly reduced dimensions and offered in barrel lengths from 28" to 34". Weighs about 8 lbs. 6 oz. Introduced in 1991.

NIB	Exc.	V.G.	Good	Fair	Poor
1350	1100	900	700	500	300

BT-99 Plus-Pigeon Grade

NIB	Exc.	V.G.	Good	Fair	Poor
1500	1200	900	800	550	350

BT-99 Plus-Signature Grade

NIB	Exc.	V.G.	Good	Fair	Poor
1400	1150	900	750	500	300

Model BT-100

First introduced in 1995 this single barrel trap features an adjustable trigger pull and length of pull. The stock has either a Monte Carlo version or an adjustable comb version. Barrel is either 32" or 34". Choice of blue or stainless finish. Weight is about 8.9 lbs.

NIB	Exc.	V.G.	Good	Fair	Poor
1850	1200	900	700	500	300

Model BT-100 Satin

Introduced in 1999, this model features a matte black receiver and barrels without ejector selector. Available in 32" or 34" barrels. Available in Grade I only.

NIB	Exc.	V.G.	Good	Fair	Poor
1650	1300	—	—	—	—

Model BT-100 Thumbhole

This model is the same as the standard BT-100 but with the additional feature of a thumbhole stock. Offered in both blue and stainless.

NIB	Exc.	V.G.	Good	Fair	Poor
2375	1900	—	—	—	—

Recoilless Trap

First introduced in 1993 this model features an advanced design that eliminates recoil up to 72 percent. The receiver is a special bolt action single shot. Receiver is black anodized. It is fitted with an adjustable ventilated rib so the point of impact can be moved. Adjustable length of pull. The Standard Model is a 12 gauge with 30" barrel while the Micro Model is fitted with 27" barrels. Choke tubes are supplied. Standard Model weighs 9 lbs. 1 oz., while the Micro Model weighs 8 lbs. 10 oz.

NIB	Exc.	V.G.	Good	Fair	Poor
1500	1300	900	700	500	350

BSS

This is a SxS, double-barrel shotgun chambered for 12 or 20 gauge. It was offered with a 26", 28", or 30" barrel with various choke combinations. It features a boxlock action and automatic ejectors. Early guns had a nonselective single trigger; late production, a selective trigger. The finish is blued with a checkered walnut stock and beavertail forearm. It was manufactured between 1978 and 1987 by B.C. Miroku.

Single-Selective Trigger-Add 20%.
20 Gauge add 20%.

Exc.	V.G.	Good	Fair	Poor
1200	950	775	650	400

BSS Sporter

This version features an English-style, straight-grip stock and a splinter forearm. The stock was oil-finished. It was offered with a 26" or 28" barrel.

For 20 gauge add 20%.

Exc.	V.G.	Good	Fair	Poor
1200	950	775	650	400

BSS Grade II

This version features game scene engraving and a satin, coin finished receiver. It was discontinued in 1984.

Exc.	V.G.	Good	Fair	Poor
1750	1350	1100	850	500

BSS Sidelock

This version features an engraved sidelock action and was offered in 12 or 20 gauge. It was offered with a 26" or 28" barrel and has a straight-grip stock and splintered forearm. It was manufactured in Korea between 1983 and 1987.

NIB	Exc.	V.G.	Good	Fair	Poor
2400	2100	1600	1250	800	500

NOTE: Add 10% to above prices for 20 gauge guns.

AUTO-5 SHOTGUN

Early Production Auto-5

This series of recoil-operated, semiautomatic shotguns was designed by John M. Browning and was offered in 12 or 16 gauge. The barrel lengths were 26", 28", 30", or 32" with various chokes and ribs. It has a unique, square-back action that has become instantly recognizable. The finish is blued with a checkered, walnut, round-knob stock. The various versions differ in the amount of ornamentation, type of rib, and quality of materials and workmanship utilized in construction. This series was manufactured in Belgium by FN between 1903 and 1939. The first example appeared in the United States in 1923. Pre-WWI 16 gauge guns, introduced in 1936, had 2-9/16" chambers; early models should be inspected by a qualified gunsmith before firing.

NOTE: For 16 gauge not converted to 2-3/4" chamber deduct 30 percent. Grade III or Grade IV prices are not nearly as affected by chamber length because of their rarity. Original prewar barrels were serial numbered to the gun. For extra barrels serial numbered to the gun add $100 for plain barrels, $200 for matte rib barrels, $275 for vent rib barrels. For extra barrels on Grade IV guns add an additional 30% to these barrel prices. Prices given below are for guns with original barrels serial numbered to the gun. Remember the safety is located in front of the triggerguard.

Grade I-Plain Barrel

Exc.	V.G.	Good	Fair	Poor
500	400	300	250	150

Grade I-Matte Rib

Exc.	V.G.	Good	Fair	Poor
650	550	375	300	175

Grade I-Vent Rib

Exc.	V.G.	Good	Fair	Poor
825	650	475	375	200

Grade II-Plain Barrel

Exc.	V.G.	Good	Fair	Poor
550	450	300	250	150

Grade II-Matte Rib

Exc.	V.G.	Good	Fair	Poor
825	650	450	350	175

Grade II-Vent Rib

Exc.	V.G.	Good	Fair	Poor
1400	850	600	400	200

Grade III-Plain Barrel

Exc.	V.G.	Good	Fair	Poor
1900	1500	850	500	250

Grade III-Matte Rib

Exc.	V.G.	Good	Fair	Poor
3000	2500	1350	600	250

Grade III-Vent Rib

Exc.	V.G.	Good	Fair	Poor
3000	2500	1350	600	300

Grade IV-Plain Barrel

Exc.	V.G.	Good	Fair	Poor
4000	3250	2250	850	350

Grade IV-Matte Rib

Exc.	V.G.	Good	Fair	Poor
4850	4150	3000	1000	400

Grade IV-Vent Rib

Exc.	V.G.	Good	Fair	Poor
5500	4750	3500	1500	500

American Browning Auto-5

This recoil-operated, semiautomatic shotgun was another variation of the early-production Auto-5. It was chambered for 12, 16, or 20 gauge and was manufactured by the Remington Company for Browning. It is quite similar to Remington's Model 11 shotgun but features the Browning logo and a different type of engraving. There were approximately 45,000 manufactured between 1940 and 1942.

Vent Rib add 20%.
20 Gauge add 10%.

Exc.	V.G.	Good	Fair	Poor
600	475	350	250	175

MID-PRODUCTION AUTO-5-FN MANUFACTURE STANDARD WEIGHT

This version of the recoil-operated, semiautomatic Auto-5 shotgun was manufactured by FN in Belgium between 1952 and 1976. It was offered in 12 or 16 gauge with 26" through 32" barrels with various chokes. The finish is blued with a checkered walnut stock and a black buttplate that was marked "Browning Automatic" with "FN" in center oval. Guns made prior to 1967 will be found with round knob pistol grips. The flat-bottom variation was introduced in 1967.

NOTE: Add 25% for guns with round knob pistol grip and 35% for straight grip stock. Add 20% for 20 gauge guns. Add 40% for 16 and 20 gauge guns NIB.

Plain Barrel

NIB	Exc.	V.G.	Good	Fair	Poor
750	600	475	400	250	175

Matte Rib

NIB	Exc.	V.G.	Good	Fair	Poor
825	725	500	400	275	200

Vent Rib

NIB	Exc.	V.G.	Good	Fair	Poor
950	800	600	450	300	250

Auto-5 Lightweight

This version was chambered for 12 or 20 gauge and featured a lighter-weight, scroll-engraved receiver. It was manufactured between 1952 and 1976 by FN. The 20 gauge was not introduced until 1958.

Vent Rib-Add 20%.
For 20 Gauge-Add 20%.

NIB	Exc.	V.G.	Good	Fair	Poor
895	750	600	450	275	200

Auto-5 Magnum

This version featured 3" chambers and was offered with 26" through 32", full-choke barrels. It was manufactured between 1958 and 1976 by FN. The 12 gauge was introduced in 1958 and the 20 gauge brought out in 1967.

Vent Rib-Add 20%.

Exc.	V.G.	Good	Fair	Poor
700	600	475	375	250

Auto-5 Skeet

This version is similar to the Lightweight Model, chambered for 12 or 20 gauge with a 26" or 28", vent rib, skeet-choked barrel.

Exc.	V.G.	Good	Fair	Poor
795	575	525	425	250

Auto-5 Trap Model

This version is similar to the standard-weight model except chambered for 12 gauge only, with a 30", vent rib, full-choke barrel. It was manufactured by FN until 1971.

Exc.	V.G.	Good	Fair	Poor
525	475	400	300	225

Sweet Sixteen

This version is similar to the standard-weight and is chambered for 16 gauge only. It has a gold plated trigger and was manufactured by FN between 1936 and 1976.

Matte Rib-Add 25%.
Vent Rib-Add 50%.

NIB	Exc.	V.G.	Good	Fair	Poor
1000	750	600	400	300	200

Buck Special

This version features a 24", cylinder-bore barrel with adjustable rifle sights. It was produced in 12 and 20 gauge 2-3/4" and 3" magnum, and in 16 gauge with 2-3/4" chambers. It was manufactured by FN between 1963 and 1976. Prices are for 12 gauge guns.

Exc.	V.G.	Good	Fair	Poor
650	600	475	350	250

Two Millionth Commemorative

This version commemorated the two millionth Auto-5 shotgun produced by FN. It was engraved with a special high-polish blue finish and high-grade, checkered walnut in the stock. It was furnished in a black fitted case along with a book on the Browning Company. There were 2,500 manufactured between 1971 and 1974. As with all commemoratives, it must be NIB to realize its top potential.

NIB	Exc.	V.G.	Good	Fair	Poor
2250	1500	850	500	—	—

LATE PRODUCTION AUTO-5-B.C. MIROKU MANUFACTURE

In 1976 production of the Auto-5 shotgun was begun by B.C. Miroku in Japan. This move was accomplished after approximately 2,750,000 Auto-5 shotguns were manufactured by FN in Belgium between 1903 and 1976. The Japanese manufactured guns in the opinion of many knowledgeable people show no less quality or functionality but are simply not as desirable from a collector's standpoint.

NOTE: In 1998 Browning announced its intent to discontinue production of the Auto-5 shotgun.

Auto-5 Light 12

This version is chambered for 12 gauge 2-3/4" chamber only and is offered with a lightweight receiver. The barrel has a vent rib and choke tubes. It was introduced in 1975.

NIB	Exc.	V.G.	Good	Fair	Poor
650	550	400	300	250	150

Auto-5 Light 20

This version is similar to the Light 12 except chambered for 20 gauge only.

NIB	Exc.	V.G.	Good	Fair	Poor
700	550	450	325	250	150

Auto-5 Magnum

This version features 3" chambers and is offered with 26", 28", 30", or 32" barrels. It was introduced in 1976 by Miroku and discontinued in 1996.

NIB	Exc.	V.G.	Good	Fair	Poor
600	475	400	300	250	150

Auto-5 Buck Special

This version has a 24" barrel cylinder-bored with adjustable sights. It was introduced by Miroku in 1976.

NIB	Exc.	V.G.	Good	Fair	Poor
600	500	400	300	250	150

Auto-5 Skeet

This is a competition model that features 26" or 28", skeet-bored barrels with a vent rib. It was manufactured between 1976 and 1983 by Miroku.

NIB	Exc.	V.G.	Good	Fair	Poor
750	475	375	275	225	150

Sweet Sixteen

This version is similar to the Belgian-produced Sweet Sixteen, but is offered standard with a vent rib and screw-in invector choke tubes. It was introduced in 1988 by Miroku and discontinued in 1992.

NIB	Exc.	V.G.	Good	Fair	Poor
1150	900	600	300	250	150

A-5 DU 50th Anniversary

This was a high-grade version of the Auto-5 produced to commemorate the 50th anniversary of Ducks Unlimited. It is highly engraved and features high-gloss bluing and a fancy checkered walnut stock. There were approximately 5,500 manufactured by Miroku in 1987. They were auctioned by the Ducks Unlimited chapters to raise money for the organization, and because of this fact, it is difficult to furnish an accurate value. This is a commemorative firearm and, as such, must be NIB with all furnished materials to command premium collector value. We furnish what we feel is a general value.

NIB	Exc.	V.G.	Good	Fair	Poor
1450	975	750	500	350	250

A-5 DU Sweet Sixteen

This was a special version of the Miroku-manufactured Sweet Sixteen that was auctioned by the Ducks Unlimited chapters in 1988. There were 5,500 produced. All specifications and cautions that were furnished for the 50th Anniversary gun also apply here.

NIB	Exc.	V.G.	Good	Fair	Poor
1250	950	750	500	350	250

Auto-5 Classic

This is a special limited edition series of A-5 shotguns built in 12 gauge only. The Classic is photo-etched with game scenes on a silver gray receiver. 5,000 of these guns were manufactured in 1984. The Gold Classic is similar in appearance but features gold inlays and is limited to 500 guns.

Classic

NIB	Exc.	V.G.	Good	Fair	Poor
1550	1200	900	650	500	300

Gold Classic-Produced by FN

NIB	Exc.	V.G.	Good	Fair	Poor
4500	3250	2500	2000	1000	500

Auto-5 Light Buck Special

This model is a lightweight version of the Buck Special. Chambered for the 2-3/4" shell and fitted with a 24" vent rib barrel. Conventional choked for slug or buckshot. Barrel has adjustable rear sight and ramp front sight. Weighs 8 lbs.

NIB	Exc.	V.G.	Good	Fair	Poor
600	500	400	300	225	150

Auto-5 Stalker

New for 1992 this model is available in either a lightweight version or a Magnum version. The Light Stalker is available in 12 gauge with either 26" or 28" barrel with choke tubes. The Magnum Stalker is offered in 12 gauge (3" chamber) with 28" or 30" barrel and choke tubes. The Light Stalker weighs 8 lbs. 4 oz. and the Magnum Stalker weighs 8 lbs. 11 oz.

Light Stalker

NIB	Exc.	V.G.	Good	Fair	Poor
575	500	425	325	250	150

Magnum Stalker

NIB	Exc.	V.G.	Good	Fair	Poor
575	500	425	325	250	150

Auto-5 Final Tribute Limited Edition

Introduced in 1999, this commemorative A-5 is limited to 1,000 shotguns. It represents the final production of this model. Chambered for the 12 gauge shell and fitted with a 28" vent rib barrel this shotgun has a special engraved receiver.

NIB	Exc.	V.G.	Good	Fair	Poor
1600	1300	—	—	—	—

Double Automatic Shotgun

This is a short recoil-operated, semiautomatic shotgun chambered for 12 gauge only. It was offered with a 26", 28", or 30" barrel that was either plain or vent ribbed. It has various chokes. The receiver is steel, and the finish is blued or silver with a checkered walnut stock. The tubular magazine holds only two shots—hence its name. It was manufactured between 1954 and 1972.

Vent Rib add 25%.

Exc.	V.G.	Good	Fair	Poor
450	400	325	250	200

Twelvette Double Auto

This version is similar to the Double Automatic except that it has an aircraft aluminum alloy frame color-anodized in either blue, silver, green, brown, or black. Red-, gold-, or royal blue-colored receivers were the rarest colors and would command approximately a 50 percent premium. It was offered with either a plain or vent rib barrel. There were approximately 65,000 produced between 1954 and 1972.

Vent Rib add 25%.

Exc.	V.G.	Good	Fair	Poor
675	525	350	275	225

Twentyweight Double Auto

This version is similar in all respects to the Twelvette except that it is three-quarters of a pound lighter and was offered with a 26.5" barrel. It was manufactured between 1952 and 1971.

Vent Rib add 25%.

Exc.	V.G.	Good	Fair	Poor
750	575	375	300	250

2000 SERIES

B-2000

This is a gas-operated, semiautomatic shotgun chambered for 12 or 20 gauge and offered with a 26", 28", or 30", vent rib barrel with various chokes. The finish is blued with a checkered walnut stock. This shotgun was assembled in Portugal from parts that were manufactured by FN in Belgium. There were approximately 115,000 imported between 1974 and 1981.

NIB	Exc.	V.G.	Good	Fair	Poor
550	450	400	250	200	150

B-2000 Magnum

This version features a barrel with 3" chambers and was offered standard with a recoil pad.

NIB	Exc.	V.G.	Good	Fair	Poor
550	450	400	250	200	150

B-2000 Buck Special

This version has a 24", cylinder-bored barrel with rifle sights.

NIB	Exc.	V.G.	Good	Fair	Poor
550	450	400	250	200	150

B-2000 Trap

This version has a 30", full-choke barrel with a floating rib and a Monte Carlo-type trap stock.

NIB	Exc.	V.G.	Good	Fair	Poor
550	450	400	250	200	150

B-2000 Skeet

This version features a 26", skeet-bored barrel with a floating vent rib and a skeet-type stock.

Exc.	V.G.	Good	Fair	Poor
450	375	325	275	200

NOTE: Add 20% for 20 gauge guns.

Model B-80

This is a gas-operated, semiautomatic shotgun chambered for 12 or 20 gauge. It features 3" magnum potential by simply exchanging the barrel. It features various-length barrels and was offered with screw-in invector chokes as of 1985. The receiver is either steel or lightweight aluminum alloy. The finish is blued with a checkered walnut stock. This gun was assembled in Portugal from parts manufactured by Beretta in Italy. It was manufactured between 1981 and 1988.

Exc.	V.G.	Good	Fair	Poor
500	450	375	325	225

NOTE: Add 20% for 20 gauge guns.

Model B-80 Buck Special

This version features a 24", cylinder-bored barrel with rifle sights. It was discontinued in 1984.

Exc.	V.G.	Good	Fair	Poor
450	400	350	300	200

Model B-80 DU Commemorative

This version was produced to be auctioned by American Ducks Unlimited chapters. In order to realize the collector potential, it must be NIB with all supplied materials. Values supplied are general.

NIB	Exc.	V.G.	Good	Fair	Poor
900	700	500	375	300	250

GOLD SERIES

Model Gold 10

Introduced for the first time in 1993 this is a gas operated 5-shot semiautomatic shotgun chambered for the 10 gauge shell. Offered with 26", 28", or 30" vent rib barrel. The standard model has a walnut stock, blued receiver and barrel while the Stalker Model is fitted with a graphite composite stock with nonglare finish on receiver and barrel. Both models are fitted with choke tubes. Weighs about 10 lbs. 10 oz.

NIB	Exc.	V.G.	Good	Fair	Poor
950	700	550	450	300	150

Gold 10 Gauge Light Camo

This 10 gauge model is offered with 26" or 28" barrels with Mossy Oak or Shadow Grass camo. Lightweight alloy receiver reduces weight to 9 lb. 10 oz. Introduced in 2001.

NIB	Exc.	V.G.	Good	Fair	Poor
1225	975	—	—	—	—

Gold 10 Gauge Combo

This 10 gauge model has a choice of two vent rib barrels in lengths of 24" and 26", or 24" and 28". Walnut stock with black ventilated recoil pad. Weight with 28" barrels is about 10 lbs. 10 ozs.

NIB	Exc.	V.G.	Good	Fair	Poor
1050	800	—	—	—	—

Gold Stalker Model

NIB	Exc.	V.G.	Good	Fair	Poor
925	700	550	450	300	150

Gold Classic Staker

Introduced in 1999 this model features a classic Browning squared receiver and fully adjustable stock. This model is chambered for 12 gauge shells with choice 26" or 28" vent rib barrels. Gun has 3" chambers. Black synthetic stock. Weight is about 7 lbs. 3 ozs.

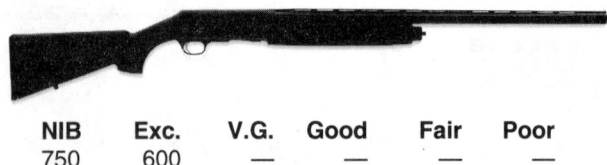

NIB	Exc.	V.G.	Good	Fair	Poor
750	600	—	—	—	—

Gold 3-1/2" 12 Gauge

Introduced in 1997 this model features a 3-1/2" chamber. It can operate 2-3/4", or 3" shells as well. Choice of barrel lengths from 26" to 30". Invector Plus chokes. Magazine capacity is four 2.75" shells or three 3" shells or three 3.5" shells. The weight is approximately 7 lbs. 10 oz.

NIB	Exc.	V.G.	Good	Fair	Poor
900	700	550	450	—	—

Gold 12 Gauge Hunter

Introduced in 1994 this semiautomatic shotgun is built on the same gas operating system as the Gold 10. Offered with 26", 28", or 30" barrel it has a magazine capacity of four 3" shells. Walnut stock has full checkered pistol grip with black rubber recoil pad. Invector plus choke tubes supplied. Weighs about 7.5 lbs. Also available (1998) in Stalker version with non-glare matte metal parts and stocks.

NIB	Exc.	V.G.	Good	Fair	Poor
650	525	400	300	200	150

Gold Classic Hunter

Introduced in 1999, this model features a squared receiver, fully adjustable stock, selected walnut stock, and deep blued barrels. Choice of 26", 28", or 30" vent rib barrel. Offered with 3" chamber 12 gauge only.

NIB	Exc.	V.G.	Good	Fair	Poor
750	600	—	—	—	—

Gold Classic 20 Gauge

Offered with choice of 26" or 28" vent rib barrels with select walnut stock. Adjustable comb. Squared receiver. Weight is about 6 lbs. 12 ozs. Introduced in 1999.

NIB	Exc.	V.G.	Good	Fair	Poor
750	600	—	—	—	—

Gold Classic High Grade

Introduced in 1999, this model features a traditional square receiver with engraved silver grey finish. Offered in 12 gauge only with 3" chambers and 28" vent rib barrel. Select walnut stock. Weight is about 7 lbs. 6 ozs.

NIB	Exc.	V.G.	Good	Fair	Poor
1400	1100	—	—	—	—

Gold Deer Hunter

Introduced in 1997, this model features a choice of a fully rifled barrel or a smooth bore barrel with invector choke system. Both versions come with a cantilever scope mount. Stock and forearm are of select walnut. Receiver has non-glare black finish. Barrel is satin finish. Barrel length is 22" on both barrels. Weight is about 7 lbs. 12 oz. Price below is for smooth bore barrel.

NIB	Exc.	V.G.	Good	Fair	Poor
775	600	500	400	200	150

NOTE: For fully rifled version add $40.

Gold Deer Hunter-20 gauge

Same as above but chambered for 20 gauge 3" shell. Furnished with fully rifled 22" barrel. Cantilever scope mount. Introduced in 2001.

NIB	Exc.	V.G.	Good	Fair	Poor
975	800	—	—	—	—

Gold Deer Stalker

This model, introduced in 1999, is the same as the model above but fitted with a black synthetic stock.

NIB	Exc.	V.G.	Good	Fair	Poor
800	650	—	—	—	—

Gold Deer-Mossy Oak

Introduced in 1999 with camo finish.

NIB	Exc.	V.G.	Good	Fair	Poor
825	675				

Gold Waterfowl-Mossy Oak Shadow Grass

Introduced in 1999 with camo finish.

NIB	Exc.	V.G.	Good	Fair	Poor
850	700	—	—	—	—

Gold Waterfowl-Mossy Oak Breakup

Introduced in 2000 with camo finish.

NIB	Exc.	V.G.	Good	Fair	Poor
850	700	—	—	—	—

Gold Turkey/Waterfowl-Mossy Oak

Introduced in 1999 with camo finish.

NIB	Exc.	V.G.	Good	Fair	Poor
850	700	—	—	—	—

Gold Turkey/Waterfawl Stalker

Introduced in 1999, this model features a black synthetic stock, 24" barrel, Hi-Viz sight, and 3" or 3.5" chambers. Weight is approximately 7 lbs. 4 ozs.

NIB	Exc.	V.G.	Good	Fair	Poor
800	650	—	—	—	—

Gold Turkey/Waterfowl Hunter

This 12 gauge 3" or 3.5" chambered gun is offered with 24" vent rib barrel. Select walnut stock with black ventilated recoil pad. Weight is about 7 lbs. Introduced in 1999.

NIB	Exc.	V.G.	Good	Fair	Poor
775	625	—	—	—	—

Gold NWTF Series

This model is finished in a Mossy Oak Breakup pattern and bears the NWTF logo on the buttstock. Fitted wtih a 24" barrel, Hi-Viz front sight, X-full extended Turkey choke. Offered in the following configurations:

Gold Light 10 Gauge

NIB	Exc.	V.G.	Good	Fair	Poor
1250	950	—	—	—	—

Gold 12 Gauge-3.5" Chamber

NIB	Exc.	V.G.	Good	Fair	Poor
1175	900	—	—	—	—

Gold 12 Gauge-3" Chamber

NIB	Exc.	V.G.	Good	Fair	Poor
1000	775	—	—	—	—

Gold 20 Gauge Hunter

Same as above but chambered for 20 gauge and offered in 26" or 28" barrel lengths. Weighs about 6.8 lbs.

NIB	Exc.	V.G.	Good	Fair	Poor
650	525	400	300	200	150

Gold Sporting Clays

Introduced in 1996, this model features a ported barrel in 28" or 30" lengths. Recoil pad is standard. Weight is about 7.5 lbs.

NIB	Exc.	V.G.	Good	Fair	Poor
700	575	475	375	200	150

Gold Ladies/Youth Sporting Clays

Offered in 12 gauge only with 2.75" chambers this model features a 28" vent rib barrel. Overall dimensions have been adjusted to fit women. Black solid recoil pad. Weight is about 7 lbs. 6 ozs. Introduced in 1999.

NIB	Exc.	V.G.	Good	Fair	Poor
800	650	—	—	—	—

Gold Micro

Introduced in 2001 this model features a 20 gauge gun with 26" barrel, smaller pistol grip, shorter length of pull, and backbored barrel with choke tubes. Weight is about 6 lb. 10 oz.

NIB	Exc.	V.G.	Good	Fair	Poor
890	650	—	—	—	—

Gold Upland

Offered in 12 or 20 gauge. The 12 gauge offered with 24" barrel and the 20 gauge with 26" barrel. Straight grip stock with 3" chamber. Weight is 7 lbs. for 12 gauge and 6.75 lbs. for 20 gauge. Introduced in 2001.

NIB	Exc.	V.G.	Good	Fair	Poor
900	700	—	—	—	—

Gold Fusion

This model features a new style vent rib, adjustable comb pro-comp sight, and five choke tubes. Offered in 12 gauge with 3" chambers with 26" or 28" barrels. Introduced in 2001.

NIB	Exc.	V.G.	Good	Fair	Poor
975	800	—	—	—	—

Golden Clays

Introduced in 1999, this model features chambered for the 12 gauge shell with 2.74" chambers. Choice of 28" or 30" vent rib ported barrels. Engraved silver grey receiver. Select walnut stock. Weight is about 7 lbs. 3 ozs.

NIB	Exc.	V.G.	Good	Fair	Poor
1250	1000	—	—	—	—

500 SERIES

A-500

This is a self-adjusting, gas-operated, semiautomatic shotgun chambered for 12 gauge only. It is offered with 26", 28", or 30" barrels with a vent rib and screw-in invector choke tubes. It has 3" chambers and can fire any load interchangeably. The finish is blued with a checkered walnut stock and recoil pad. It features light engraving. It was introduced in 1987.

NIB	Exc.	V.G.	Good	Fair	Poor
560	490	425	350	275	225

A-500G Sporting Clays

This gas operated version is designed for sporting clays and features a choice of 28" or 30" vent rib barrel with semi-gloss finish with gold lettering "Sporting Clays". Ventilated recoil pad standard. Weighs about 8 lbs.

NIB	Exc.	V.G.	Good	Fair	Poor
520	425	350	300	200	150

A-500R Hunting Model

Similar in appearance to the A-500G with the exception that this model operates on a short recoil design. The butt stock features a full pistol grip. Available with 26", 28", or 30" vent rib barrels. Choke tubes standard. Weighs about 7 lbs. 13 oz.

NIB	Exc.	V.G.	Good	Fair	Poor
475	385	300	250	200	150

A-500R Buck Special

Same as Hunting Model with the addition of adjustable rear sight and contoured front ramp sight with gold bead. Choke tubes standard as is 24" barrel. Weighs 7 lbs. 11 oz.

NIB	Exc.	V.G.	Good	Fair	Poor
500	425	350	300	225	150

BPS SERIES

This is a slide action shotgun chambered for 10, 12, or 20 gauge. It is offered with various length vent rib barrels with screw-in invector chokes. It features 3" magnum chambers and a bottom-ejection system that effectively makes it ambidextrous. It has double slide bars and a 5-shot tubular magazine. It is constructed of all steel. It was introduced by B.C. Miroku in 1977.

BPS Field Grade

NIB	Exc.	V.G.	Good	Fair	Poor
435	390	325	275	200	150

BPS Field Grade-28 Gauge

Introduced in 1994. Weight approximately 7 lbs.

NIB	Exc.	V.G.	Good	Fair	Poor
425	325	250	150	100	—

BPS Magnum Model-10 or 12 Gauge, 3.5" Chambers

NIB	Exc.	V.G.	Good	Fair	Poor
510	400	350	300	250	150

BPS 12 Gauge Waterfowl Camo (1999)

NIB	Exc.	V.G.	Good	Fair	Poor
525	425	—	—	—	—

BPS 12 Gauge Waterfowl Mossy Oak Break-Up

NIB	Exc.	V.G.	Good	Fair	Poor
—	—	—	—	—	—

BPS 10 Gauge-Mossy Oak Shadow Grass Camo (1999)

NIB	Exc.	V.G.	Good	Fair	Poor
600	475	—	—	—	—

BPS NWTF Series

This model is finished in a Mossy Oak Breakup pattern and bears the NWTF logo on the buttstock. Fitted with a 24" barrel, Hi-Viz front sight, X-full extended Turkey choke. Introduced in 2001. Offered in the following configurations:

BPS 10 Gauge

NIB	Exc.	V.G.	Good	Fair	Poor
625	475	—	—	—	—

BPS 12 Gauge-3.5" Chamber

NIB	Exc.	V.G.	Good	Fair	Poor
625	475	—	—	—	—

BPS 12 Gauge-3" Chamber

NIB	Exc.	V.G.	Good	Fair	Poor
550	450	—	—	—	—

BPS Upland Special-22" Barrel, Straight Stock

NIB	Exc.	V.G.	Good	Fair	Poor
435	390	325	275	200	150

BPS Stalker Model-Matte Finish, Black Stock

NIB	Exc.	V.G.	Good	Fair	Poor
435	390	325	275	200	150

BPS Stalker Model-Combo

A combination of a 28" vent rib barrel and a choice of 22" fully rifles barrel or 20.5" Invector barrel with extra full Turkey choke. Introduced in 2000.

NIB	Exc.	V.G.	Good	Fair	Poor
650	525	—	—	—	—

BPS 10 Gauge Turkey

Fitted with a 24" vent rib barrel and black synthetic stock with black solid recoil pad, this model was introduced in 1999. Weight is about 9 lbs. 2 ozs.

NIB	Exc.	V.G.	Good	Fair	Poor
525	425	—	—	—	—

BPS Game Gun

These models are designed for turkey and deer with 20.5" barrels with Invector chokes or rifled barrels. Deer model has 5" rifled choke tube while the turkey model has Extra Full choke tube. The Cantilever model has a fully rifled barrel. Weight is approximately 7.7 lbs. Introduced in 1998. Add $30 for deer model and $60 for Cantilever model.

NIB	Exc.	V.G.	Good	Fair	Poor
450	350	300	250	—	—

BPS Micro 20 Gauge

This model features a 22" vent rib barrel with shorter pistol grip stock and lighter weight. Weight is about 6.75 lbs. Introduced in 2001.

NIB	Exc.	V.G.	Good	Fair	Poor
450	350	—	—	—	—

BPS Upland Special

This model is chambered for the 20 gauge shell and fitted with a 22" vent rib barrel. The walnut stock is a straight grip. Weight is about 6.5 lbs.

NIB	Exc.	V.G.	Good	Fair	Poor
450	350	—	—	—	—

BPS Small Gauge

Introduced in 2000 this model is chambered for the 28 gauge and the .410 bore. The 28 gauge is offered with a choice of 26" or 28" vent rib barrel with Invector chokes. The .410 is available with 26" vent rib barrel with Invector chokes. Both the 28 gauge and .410 bore weigh about 6.75 lbs.

NIB	Exc.	V.G.	Good	Fair	Poor
450	350	—	—	—	—

BPS Pigeon Grade

Furnished in 12 gauge only with high grade walnut stock and gold trimmed receiver.

NIB	Exc.	V.G.	Good	Fair	Poor
500	400	300	225	175	125

Game Gun

Offered in 12 gauge only this model is available in either a Turkey Special or a Deer Special. Both have 20.5" plain barrel and drilled and tapped receivers. The stock is walnut. The turkey gun is fitted with an extra full choke. The deer gun has a special rifled choke tube for slugs. Both weigh about 7 lbs. 7 oz.

NIB	Exc.	V.G.	Good	Fair	Poor
250	200	175	125	100	50

Buck Special-24" Barrel With Sights

NIB	Exc.	V.G.	Good	Fair	Poor
450	400	350	300	225	175

Trap Model-Discontinued 1984

Exc.	V.G.	Good	Fair	Poor
375	325	275	200	150

Youth Model-Short Stock, 22" Barrel

NIB	Exc.	V.G.	Good	Fair	Poor
435	390	325	275	200	150

Waterfowl Deluxe

This version is chambered for 12 gauge with a 3" chamber and features an etched receiver with a gold-plated trigger. Otherwise, it is similar to the standard BPS.

Exc.	V.G.	Good	Fair	Poor
600	525	425	325	250

Ducks Unlimited Versions

These were limited-edition guns produced to be auctioned by Ducks Unlimited. They were furnished with a case and must be NIB with furnished materials to realize their collector potential.

NIB	Exc.	V.G.	Good	Fair	Poor
650	525	425	325	250	175

BROWNING CHOKE TUBE SELECTION

Rim Notches	Pattern w/Lead Shot	Pattern w/Steel Shot
12 Gauge Invector-Plus for Back-Bored Guns		
Knurled	X-Full Turkey	Do not use
I	Full	Do not use
II	Imp. Modified	Full
III	Modified	Full
IIII	Imp. Cylinder	Modified
IIIII	Skeet	Imp. Cylinder
No Notches	Cylinder	Cylinder
10 Gauge Invector		
Knurled	X-Full Turkey	Do not use
I	Full	Do not use
II	Modified	Full
III	Imp. Modified	Modified
16 Gauge Invector		
I	Full	Do not use
II	Modified	Full
III	Imp. Cylinder	Modified
IIII	Skeet	Imp. Cylinder
No Notches	Cylinder	Imp. Cylinder
20 Gauge Invector		
I	Full	Full
II	Modified	Imp. Modified
III	Imp. Cylinder	Modified
IIII	Skeet	Modified
No Notches	Cylinder	Imp. Cylinder

CAUTION: Do not interchange invector choke tubes with Invector-Plus choke tubes. May cause personal injury.

Model 12-Grade I

This is a slide-action shotgun chambered for 20 gauge with a 26", modified choke, vent rib barrel. It is a reproduction of the Winchester Model 12 shotgun. It has a 5-round, tubular magazine with a floating, high-post rib. It has a takedown feature and is blued with a walnut stock. Introduced in 1988, total production will be limited to 8,500 guns.

NIB	Exc.	V.G.	Good	Fair	Poor
725	625	425	300	250	200

Model 12-Grade V

This is an extensively engraved version of the Grade I Model 12. It features a select walnut stock with deluxe checkering and a high-gloss finish. There are gold inlays. It was introduced in 1988, and production will be limited to 4,000 guns.

NIB	Exc.	V.G.	Good	Fair	Poor
1300	950	700	450	300	200

Limited Edition Model 42

A new version of the .410 bore pump shotgun that was last produced by Winchester in 1963. Available in two grades both fitted with 26" vent rib barrels. The Grade I features a plain blued receiver with walnut stock. The Grade V features a blued receiver with scroll engraving and gold inlays. Both models are choked full and weigh 6 lbs. 4 oz.

Grade I

NIB	Exc.	V.G.	Good	Fair	Poor
700	600	500	400	300	200

Grade V

NIB	Exc.	V.G.	Good	Fair	Poor
1150	900	700	500	350	200

A-Bolt Shotgun

Introduced in 1995 this bolt action shotgun is offered in 12 gauge with 3" chamber. Rifled barrel version is 22" long while the invector barrel version is 23" long with a 5" rifle tube installed. Has a 2-shot detachable magazine. Average weight is about 7 lbs.

Hunter Version

NIB	Exc.	V.G.	Good	Fair	Poor
625	550	450	300	200	100

Stalker Version

NIB	Exc.	V.G.	Good	Fair	Poor
500	400	300	250	200	100

NOTE: For invector rifled choke tube model deduct $50.

RIFLES

High-Power Bolt Action Rifle

This was a high-grade, bolt-action sporting rifle manufactured by FN in Belgium (from 1959 to 1975) or Sako of Finland (from 1961 to 1975). It was built on either a Mauser or a Sako action and chambered for a number of popular calibers from the .222 Remington up to the .458 Winchester Magnum. There were three basic grades that differed in the amount of ornamentation and the quality of materials and workmanship utilized. Certain calibers are considered to be rare and will bring a premium from collectors of this firearm. We recommend securing a qualified appraisal on these rifles if a transaction is contemplated. We furnish general values only.

NOTE: From 1959 through 1966 FN Mauser actions with long extractors were featured. These Mauser actions will bring a premium depending on caliber. From 1967 on, FN Supreme actions with short extractors were used. *Only* .30-06 and .270 calibers continued with long extractor Mauser actions.

CAUTION: For buyer and seller alike some rare calibers may be worth as much as 100 percent or more over prices listed below for rare calibers such as .284 Win., .257 Roberts, 300 H&H, and .308 Norma Magnum. The High-Power bolt action rifles seemed to be particularly hard hit by salt wood. No factory replacement stocks are known to still be available. Proceed with caution.

Safari Grade-Standard Model, Standard Calibers

Exc.	V.G.	Good	Fair	Poor
900	750	575	450	300

Medallion Grade-Scroll Engraved

Exc.	V.G.	Good	Fair	Poor
1500	1250	1000	750	500

Olympian Grade-Extensive Game Scene Engraving

Exc.	V.G.	Good	Fair	Poor
2750	2000	1750	1450	1000

Model BBR

This is a bolt-action sporting rifle chambered for various popular calibers. It has a 24" barrel with an adjustable trigger and fluted bolt. It features a detachable magazine under the floorplate and was furnished without sights. The finish is blued with a checkered, walnut, Monte Carlo stock. It was manufactured between 1978 and 1984 by Miroku.

Exc.	V.G.	Good	Fair	Poor
475	400	350	275	200

BOSS™ SYSTEM

Introduced by Browning in 1994 this new accuracy system allows the shooter to fine-tune his Browning rifle to the particular load he is using. Consists of a tube on the end of the rifle muzzle that allows the shooter to select the best setting for the ammunition type. The system also reduces recoil. BOSS stands for Ballistic Optimizing Shooting System. This option will add approximately $80 to the value of the particular Browning rifle on which it is fitted.

A-BOLT SERIES

A-Bolt Hunter

This is the current bolt-action rifle manufactured by B.C. Miroku. It is chambered for various popular calibers and offered with a 22", 24", or 26" barrel. It has either a short or long action, an adjustable trigger, and a detachable box magazine that is mounted under the floorplate. It is furnished without sights and is blued with a checkered walnut stock. It was introduced in 1985.

NIB	Exc.	V.G.	Good	Fair	Poor
450	400	350	300	250	200

A-Bolt II Hunter

Introduced in 1994 this new model features a newly designed anti-bind bolt and improved trigger system. In 2001 the .300 Winchester Short Magnum cartridge was offered for this model.

NIB	Exc.	V.G.	Good	Fair	Poor
450	400	350	300	250	200

A-Bolt II Micro Hunter

Introduced in 1999, this model features a shorter length of pull and a shorter barrel length than the Hunter model. Offered in .22 Hornet, .22-250, 7mm-08, .308, .243, and .260 calibers. Weight is about 6 lbs.

NIB	Exc.	V.G.	Good	Fair	Poor
550	450	—	—	—	—

A-Bolt II Classic

This model features a Monte Carlo stock, low luster bluing, select walnut, and double bordered checkering. Offered in 30-06, .270, 7mm Rem. Mag., and .300 Win. Mag. No sights. Weight is about 7 lbs. Introduced in 1999.

NIB	Exc.	V.G.	Good	Fair	Poor
625	500	—	—	—	—

Composite Stalker

Supplied with composite stock and matte finish bluing. Offered in .338 Win. Mag., .300 Win. Mag., 7mm Rem. Mag., .25-06, .270, .280, .30-06. Introduced in 1988. In 2001 the .300 Winchester Short Magnum cartridge was offered for this model.

NIB	Exc.	V.G.	Good	Fair	Poor
400	350	300	250	200	150

A-Bolt II Composite Stalker

Same as above but with 1994 improvements.

NIB	Exc.	V.G.	Good	Fair	Poor
450	400	350	300	250	200

Stainless Stalker

This version is chambered for the .270, .30-06, and the 7mm Remington Magnum cartridges. IN 2001 this model was available in .300 Remington Ultra Mag and .338 Rem. Ultra Mag. It is constructed of stainless steel and has a black, painted wood stock. It was introduced in 1987. In 2001 the .300 Winchester Short Magnum cartridge was offered for this model.

NIB	Exc.	V.G.	Good	Fair	Poor
580	525	450	350	300	250

NOTE: For .300 and .338 calibers add $200.

A-Bolt II Composite Stainless Stalker

Same as above but with 1994 improvements.

NIB	Exc.	V.G.	Good	Fair	Poor
580	525	450	350	300	250

A-Bolt Carbon Fiber Stainless Stalker

This model features a Christensen Arms patent carbon barrel. Chambered for .22-250 or .300 Win. Mag. Weight is about 6.25 lbs. for short action and 7 lbs. for long action. Introduced in 2000. In 2001 the .300 Winchester Short Magnum cartridge was offered for this model.

NIB	Exc.	V.G.	Good	Fair	Poor
1400	1200	1000	900	700	—

A-Bolt II Heavy Barrel Varmint

Introduced in 1994 this model features all of the A-Bolt II improvements in a heavy barrel varmint rifle. Offered in .22-250 and .223 Rem. calibers with 22" barrel. Equipped with black laminated wood stock.

NIB	Exc.	V.G.	Good	Fair	Poor
685	600	525	425	325	250

A-Bolt Eclipse M-1000

This version of the Eclipse was introduced in 1997 and is offered in .300 Win. Mag. The rifle is fitted with a 26" barrel with BOSS system. The stock is a laminated hardwood with gray/black finish. The forearm is a benchrest style. Weight is approximately 9 lbs. 13 oz.

NIB	Exc.	V.G.	Good	Fair	Poor
900	700	600	450	350	250

A-Bolt Eclipse Varmint

Introduced in 1996 this model features a thumbhole stock made from gray/black laminated hardwood. Offered in two version: a short action heavy barrel version and a long and short action with standard weight barrel. Eclipse varmint weighs about 9 lbs. and the standard barrel version weighs about 7.5 lbs. depending on caliber.

NIB	Exc.	V.G.	Good	Fair	Poor
950	800	600	500	400	250

Euro-Bolt

First introduced in 1993 this A-Bolt variation features a rounded bolt shroud, Mannlicher-style bolt handle, continental style stock with cheekpiece, schnabel style forearm. The finish is a low luster blue. Offered in .270, .30-06, and 7mm Rem. Mag. calibers. Weighs about 7 lbs.

EURO-BOLT
Bolt Action Rifle

NIB	Exc.	V.G.	Good	Fair	Poor
550	500	450	350	250	150

A-Bolt II Euro Bolt

Same as above but with 1994 improvements.

NIB	Exc.	V.G.	Good	Fair	Poor
550	500	450	350	250	150

A-Bolt Medallion Model

This is a deluxe version of the A-Bolt Hunter with a high polish blue finish and a select walnut stock with rosewood pistol grip cap and forend tip. Introduced in 1985. In 2001 this model was available in .300 and .338 Rem. Ultra Mag calibers. In 2001 the .300 Winchester Short Magnum cartridge was offered for this model.

NIB	Exc.	V.G.	Good	Fair	Poor
525	475	400	350	300	250

NOTE: Add $200 for .300 and .338 calibers.

A-Bolt II Medallion

Same as above but with 1994 improvements.

NIB	Exc.	V.G.	Good	Fair	Poor
525	475	400	350	300	250

Gold Medallion

This version has a fancy grade walnut stock with a cheekpiece. It is lightly engraved and has gold-inlaid letters. It was introduced in 1988.

NIB	Exc.	V.G.	Good	Fair	Poor
690	625	550	450	400	325

A-Bolt II Gold Medallion

Same as above but with 1994 improvements.

NIB	Exc.	V.G.	Good	Fair	Poor
690	625	550	450	400	325

A-Bolt II White Gold Medallion

This model features a gold engraved stainless receiver and barrel, select walnut stock with brass spacers and rosewood caps. European-style cheekpiece. No sights. Introduced in 1999. Offered in 30-06, .270, 7mm Rem. Mag., and .300 Win. Mag. Weight is about 7 lbs. 8 ozs.

NIB	Exc.	V.G.	Good	Fair	Poor
600	500	350	300	250	200

A-Bolt Custom Trophy

Introduced in 1998 this model features gold highlights on the barrel and receiver, select walnut stock, with shadowline cheekpiece and skeleton pistol grip. The barrel is octagonal. Chambered for .270 and .30-06 with 24" barrel and 7mm Rem. Mag. and .300 Win. Mag. with 26" barrel. Weight varies from 7 lbs. 11 oz. to 7 lbs. 3 oz. depending on caliber.

NIB	Exc.	V.G.	Good	Fair	Poor
1300	1000	—	—	—	—

Big Horn Sheep Issue

This is a high grade version of the A-Bolt chambered for the .270 cartridge. It features a deluxe skipline checkered walnut stock with a heavily engraved receiver and floorplate. It has two gold sheep inlays. There were 600 manufactured in 1986 and 1987.

NIB	Exc.	V.G.	Good	Fair	Poor
1050	800	600	450	400	325

Pronghorn Issue

This is a deluxe version of the A-Bolt chambered for the .243 cartridge. It is heavily engraved and gold inlaid and features a presentation-grade walnut stock with skipline checkering and pearl-inlaid borders. There were 500 manufactured in 1987.

NIB	Exc.	V.G.	Good	Fair	Poor
1300	1000	750	500	400	325

Micro-Medallion Model

This is a smaller version of the A-Bolt Hunter chambered for popular cartridges that fit a short action. It has a 20" barrel without sights and a 3-round magazine. It was introduced in 1988.

NIB	Exc.	V.G.	Good	Fair	Poor
525	475	400	350	300	250

A-Bolt II Micro-Medallion

Same as above but with 1994 improvements.

NIB	Exc.	V.G.	Good	Fair	Poor
525	475	400	350	300	250

Acera Straight Pull Rifle

Introduced in 1999, this model features a straight action bolt system. It is chambered for the 30-06 with a 22" barrel and the .300 Win. Mag. with 24" barrel. Open sights are optional as is the BOSS system. Detachable box magazine. Checkered walnut stock. Prices below are for .30-06 with no sights and no BOSS.

NIB	Exc.	V.G.	Good	Fair	Poor
845	675	—	—	—	—

NOTE: Add $85 for .300 Win. Mag with no sights and no BOSS.

Grade I A-Bolt .22

This is a bolt-action sporting rifle chambered for the .22 l.r. or .22 Magnum cartridges. It features a 60-degree bolt and a 22" barrel available either with or without open sights. It has a 5-round, detachable magazine and an adjustable trigger. The finish is blued with a checkered walnut stock. It was introduced in 1986.

.22 Magnum-Add 15%.

NIB	Exc.	V.G.	Good	Fair	Poor
340	275	210	150	125	100

Gold Medallion A-Bolt.22

This deluxe, high-grade version features a select stock with rosewood pistol-grip cap and forend tip. It is lightly engraved and has gold-filled letters. It was introduced in 1988.

NIB	Exc.	V.G.	Good	Fair	Poor
450	400	350	300	225	175

T-Bolt Model T-1

This is a unique, straight-pull, bolt-action sporting rifle chambered for .22 caliber cartridges. It has a 22" barrel with open sights and a 5-round magazine. The finish is blued with a plain walnut stock. It was manufactured between 1965 and 1974 by FN. Many T-Bolt rifles were affected by salt wood. Proceed with caution.

Exc.	V.G.	Good	Fair	Poor
350	300	250	150	100

T-Bolt Model T-2

This version is similar to the T-1 with a select, checkered walnut stock and a 24" barrel.

Exc.	V.G.	Good	Fair	Poor
450	380	300	250	200

Model 52 Limited Edition

This model is based on the design of the original Winchester Model 52 .22 caliber bolt action rifle. Fitted with a 24" barrel and walnut stock with oil finish. Metal pistol grip cap and rosewood forend tip. Drilled and tapped for scope. Five round detachable magazine. Blued finish. Weight is about 7 lbs. From 1991 to 1992 5,000 Model 52s were built.

NIB	Exc.	V.G.	Good	Fair	Poor
500	400	325	225	—	—

Trombone Model

This is a slide-action rifle chambered for the .22 l.r. cartridge. It has a 24" barrel with open sights and a takedown design. It has a tubular magazine and a hammerless action. There were approximately 150,000 manufactured by FN between 1922 and 1974. Approximately 3,200 were imported by Browning in the 1960s. They are marked with either the FN barrel address or the Browning Arms address. The Browning marked guns are worth approximately 20 percent additional. The values given are for FN-marked guns.

NIB	Exc.	V.G.	Good	Fair	Poor
900	750	600	450	375	275

BPR-22

This is a short-stroke, slide action rifle chambered for the .22 Magnum cartridge. It has a 20.25" barrel with open sights and an 11-round, tubular magazine. The finish is blued with a checkered walnut stock. It was manufactured between 1977 and 1982.

Exc.	V.G.	Good	Fair	Poor
275	200	150	125	95

NOTE: Add $100 for models chambered for .22 Magnum.

BPR-22 Grade II
This version is engraved and has a select walnut stock.

Exc.	V.G.	Good	Fair	Poor
500	375	275	225	150

NOTE: Add 20% for models chambered for .22 Magnum.

.22 CALIBER SEMIAUTO
This is a blowback-operated, semiautomatic rifle chambered for the .22 Long Rifle or Short cartridge. It features a takedown barrel design with a 19.25" barrel and an 11-round, tubular magazine inside the buttstock. It is loaded through a hole in the middle of the buttstock. The finish is blued with a checkered walnut stock and beavertail forearm. This lightweight, compact firearm was manufactured by FN between 1956 and 1974 for U.S. marked guns. There are a number of versions that differ in the amount of ornamentation and the quality of materials and workmanship utilized.

Early Wheel Sight manufactured 1956-1960-Add 10%.

Grade I

NIB	Exc.	V.G.	Good	Fair	Poor
650	475	400	325	220	125

NOTE: For Grade I short add 20%.

Grade II-French Greyed Receiver

NIB	Exc.	V.G.	Good	Fair	Poor
1500	1200	900	700	300	200

NOTE: For Grade II short add 300%.

Grade III-French Greyed Receiver

NIB	Exc.	V.G.	Good	Fair	Poor
3000	2400	1900	1200	700	400

NOTE: For premium engravers add 40 percent to Grade III. For Grade III short add 800%. For unsigned Grade III, 1956-1960, deduct 20%.

.22 Semiauto (Miroku Mfg.)
This model is similar to the Belgian FN except that it was produced as of 1976 by B.C. Miroku in Japan. Collector interest is not as high as in the FN version.

Grade I

NIB	Exc.	V.G.	Good		
325	275	200	175	125	100

Grade II-Discontinued 1984

NIB	Exc.	V.G.	Good	Fair	Poor
475	400	325	275	225	150

Grade III-Discontinued 1983

NIB	Exc.	V.G.	Good	Fair	Poor
750	675	500	400	300	200

Grade VI-Gold Plated Animals

NIB	Exc.	V.G.	Good	Fair	Poor
725	650	500	425	325	275

BAR-22
This is a blowback-operated, semiautomatic rifle chambered for the .22 l.r. cartridge. It has a 20.25" barrel with open sights and

a 15-round, tubular magazine. It features a polished, lightweight alloy receiver. It was finished in blue with a checkered walnut stock. It is manufactured between 1977 and 1985 by Miroku.

Exc.	V.G.	Good	Fair	Poor
275	225	190	160	125

BAR-22 Grade II

This is a deluxe version with an engraved, silver-finished receiver. It has a select walnut stock. It was discontinued in 1985.

Exc.	V.G.	Good	Fair	Poor
475	300	200	150	120

Buck Mark Rifle

This model uses the same design as the Buck Mark pistol. It is fitted with an 18" barrel (heavy on the target model) and thumbhole pistol grip. Magazine capacity is 10 rounds. Integral rail scope mount. Introduced in 2001.

Sporter Model

NIB	Exc.	V.G.	Good	Fair	Poor
500	400	—	—	—	—

Target Model

NIB	Exc.	V.G.	Good	Fair	Poor
500	400	—	—	—	—

Patent 1900 High Power

This is a semiautomatic sporting rifle chambered for the .35 Remington cartridge. It is similar in configuration to the Remington Model 8 rifle. It has a 22" barrel with open sights and a 5-round, integral magazine. The finish is blued with a plain walnut stock. There were approximately 5,000 manufactured between 1910 and 1931. A deluxe model with a ribbed barrel and checkered walnut stock was also available and would be worth approximately 15 percent additional.

Exc.	V.G.	Good	Fair	Poor
675	600	500	375	300

BAR HIGH POWER RIFLE

This is a gas-operated, semiautomatic sporting rifle chambered for various popular calibers from the .243 up to the .338 Magnum cartridges. It was offered with either a 22" or 24" barrel with folding leaf sight until 1980. The finish is blued with a checkered walnut stock. The various grades offered differed in the amount of ornamentation and the quality of materials and workmanship utilized. Earlier models were manufactured in Belgium by FN; these guns would be worth approximately 15 percent additional over guns assembled in Portugal from parts manufactured by FN. The early .338 Magnum model is rarely encountered and would be worth approximately 25 percent additional. The Grade I values furnished are for Portuguese-assembled guns from 1977 until the introduction of the BAR Mark II in 1993. This model was introduced in 1967 and discontinued in 1977.

Grade I

NIB	Exc.	V.G.	Good	Fair	Poor
600	425	350	275	225	100

Grade I Magnum

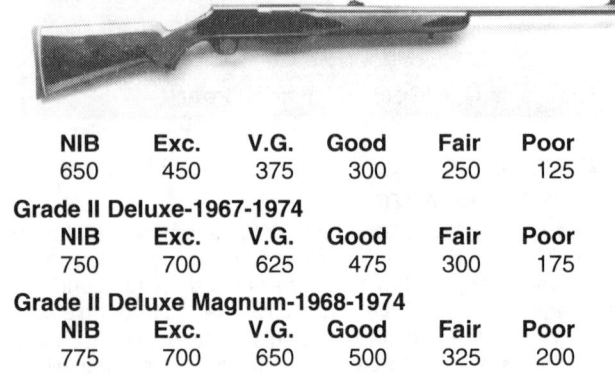

NIB	Exc.	V.G.	Good	Fair	Poor
650	450	375	300	250	125

Grade II Deluxe-1967-1974

NIB	Exc.	V.G.	Good	Fair	Poor
750	700	625	475	300	175

Grade II Deluxe Magnum-1968-1974

NIB	Exc.	V.G.	Good	Fair	Poor
775	700	650	500	325	200

Grade III-Discontinued 1984

NOTE: The Grade III was offered in two variations. The first was hand engraved and produced in Belgium. The second was photo etched and built in Belgium and assembled in Portugal. This second variation will not be as valuable as the first.

NIB	Exc.	V.G.	Good	Fair	Poor
1250	1000	700	550	375	250

Grade III Magnum-Discontinued 1984

NIB	Exc.	V.G.	Good	Fair	Poor
1400	1200	850	600	400	275

NOTE: Prices indicated above are for 1970 through 1974 production. For guns assembled in Portugal deduct 30%. .338 Win. Mag caliber is rare in Grade III. Add 75% premium.

Grade IV-Gamescene Engraved

This grade was hand engraved from 1970 through 1976 then was etched thereafter. Grade IV rifles were discontinued in 1984.

Pre-1977 rifles add 40%.
Premium engravers add 10%.

NIB	Exc.	V.G.	Good	Fair	Poor
1700	1300	950	800	650	400

Grade IV Magnum

NIB	Exc.	V.G.	Good	Fair	Poor
1800	1300	975	850	650	425

Grade V-Gold Inlaid-1971-1974

NIB	Exc.	V.G.	Good	Fair	Poor
3000	2700	2300	1800	1200	600

Grade V Magnum-1971-1974

NIB	Exc.	V.G.	Good	Fair	Poor
3500	3200	2500	1850	1250	600

NOTE: For special order variations on Grade V rifles add up to 100%.

North American Deer Rifle Issue

This is a deluxe version of the BAR chambered for .30-06 only. It features a photo etched, silver-finished receiver and a deluxe, checkered walnut stock. There were 600 produced and furnished with a walnut case and accessories. This model was discontinued in 1983. As with all commemoratives, it must be NIB to command premium values.

NIB	Exc.	V.G.	Good	Fair	Poor
2700	1800	1400	1000	450	250

BAR Mark II Safari Rifle

This is an improved version of the BAR first introduced by Browning in 1967. Announced in 1993 this Mark II design uses a new gas system with a newly designed buffering system to improve reliability. This model also has a new bolt release lever, a new easily removable trigger assembly. Available with or without sights. Walnut stock with full pistol grip and recoil pad on Magnum gun are standard. The receiver is blued with scroll engraving. Rifles with Magnum calibers have a 24" barrel while standard calibers are fitted with a 22" barrel. Available in .243, .308, .270, .30-06, 7mm Rem. Mag., .300 Win. Mag., .338 Win. Mag. Standard calibers weigh about 7 lbs. 9 oz. and Magnum calibers weigh about 8 lbs. 6 oz.

BAR Mark II Rifle

NIB	Exc.	V.G.	Good	Fair	Poor
525	450	400	350	250	150

NOTE: Add 30% for .270 Wby. Mag. which was made for one year only.

BAR Mark II Lightweight

This version of the Mark II was introduced in 1997 and features a lightweight alloy receiver and shortened 20" barrel. It is offered in .30-06, .270 Win., .308 Win., and .243 Win. calibers. It is not offered with the BOSS system. Weight is approximately 7 lbs. 2 oz.

NIB	Exc.	V.G.	Good	Fair	Poor
700	550	400	300	—	—

BAR Composite Stalker

Introduced in 2001 this model features a composite butt stock and forend with removable magazine. It is offered in short action (.243 and .308) with sights, and in standard action (.270 and .30-06) with no sights. In magnum calibers (7mm, .330 Win., and .338) it is offered with no sights and with the BOSS system as well.

NIB	Exc.	V.G.	Good	Fair	Poor
800	625	—	—	—	—

NOTE: For magnum calibers add $75, and for BOSS add $140.

BAR High Grade Models

These models will feature high grade walnut stock with highly polished blued barrel. Receivers will be grayed with game animals: mule deer and whitetail on the standard calibers (.270 and .30-06) and elk and moose on magnum calibers (7mm magnum and .300 Win. Mag).

NIB	Exc.	V.G.	Good	Fair	Poor
1825	1450	—	—	—	—

Model BPR

The initials "BPR" stand for Browning Pump Rifle. It was introduced in 1997 and is similar in appearance to the BAR. Offered in both long action and short action calibers with barrel lengths from 22" to 24". Short action calibers are: .243 Win., and .308 Win. Long Action calibers are: .270 Win., .30-06, 7mm Rem. Mag., and .300 Win. Mag. Weight is about 7 lbs. 3 oz.

NIB	Exc.	V.G.	Good	Fair	Poor
650	475	—	—	—	—

BL-22 Grade I

This is a lever action rifle chambered for the .22 rimfire cartridge. It has an 18" barrel with a tubular magazine and a folding leaf rear sight. It is a Western-style firearm that features an exposed hammer. The finish is blued with a walnut stock. It was introduced in 1970 by Miroku.

NIB	Exc.	V.G.	Good	Fair	Poor
350	250	200	150	125	100

BL-22 Grade II

This version is similar with a scroll-engraved receiver and a checkered, select walnut stock.

NIB	Exc.	V.G.	Good	Fair	Poor
325	250	225	175	150	125

BL-22 Classic

This model was introduced in 1999 and has the same features as the BL-22 Grade I.

NIB	Exc.	V.G.	Good	Fair	Poor
350	250	—	—	—	—

Model 81 BLR

This is a contemporarily designed, lever action sporting rifle chambered for various popular calibers from .22-250 up to .358 Winchester. It has a 20" barrel with adjustable sights. It features a 4-round, detachable magazine and a rotary locking bolt. The finish is blued with a checkered walnut stock and recoil pad. It was introduced in 1971 and manufactured that year in Belgium. In 1972 manufacture moved to Miroku in Japan.

Belgian manufactured version add 20%.

NIB	Exc.	V.G.	Good	Fair	Poor
525	450	325	275	200	150

Model BLR Lightning

Introduced in 1996 this model features a lightweight aluminum receiver with walnut stock with checkered pistol grip. Offered in both long and short action calibers from .223 Rem. to 7mm Rem. Mag. Barrel length is 20" for short action calibers and 22" to 24" for long action calibers. Open sights are standard. Weight is about 7 lbs. depending on caliber.

NIB	Exc.	V.G.	Good	Fair	Poor
600	500	350	275	200	150

Model 65 Grade I

This was a limited-edition, lever action rifle chambered for the .218 Bee cartridge. It has a tapered, round, 24" barrel with open sights. It was patterned after the Winchester Model 65 rifle. It has a 7-round, tubular magazine. The finish is blued with a plain walnut stock and metal buttplate. There were 3,500 manufactured in 1989.

NIB	Exc.	V.G.	Good	Fair	Poor
600	525	450	350	275	200

Model 65 High Grade

This is a deluxe version that features a silver-finished, scroll engraved receiver with gold animal inlays and a gold-plated trigger. It features a select, checkered walnut stock. There were 1,500 manufactured in 1989.

NIB	Exc.	V.G.	Good	Fair	Poor
900	825	650	550	450	300

Model 53

Offered in 1990 this model is a reproduction of the Winchester Model 53 and like the original is chambered for the .32-20 cartridge. This is a limited edition offering confined to 5,000 rifles. It features hand cut checkering, high grade walnut stock with full pistol grip and semi-beavertail forend. Pistol grip is fitted with a metal grip cap. Barrel length is 22" and the finish is blue.

NIB	Exc.	V.G.	Good	Fair	Poor
725	625	550	450	325	200

Model 71 Grade I

This was a reproduction of the Winchester Model 71, chambered for the .348 cartridge. It has either a 20" or 24" barrel with open sights and a 4-round, tubular magazine. The finish is blued with a plain walnut stock. There were 4,000 twenty-inch carbines and 3,000 24" rifles manufactured in 1986 and 1987.

Exc.	V.G.	Good	Fair	Poor
650	550	450	325	225

Model 71 High Grade

This version was similar to the Grade I except that it had a scroll engraved, grayed receiver with a gold-plated trigger and gold inlays. There were 3,000 rifles and 3,000 carbines manufactured in 1986 and 1987.

Exc.	V.G.	Good	Fair	Poor
1000	825	650	550	400

Jonathan Browning Centennial Mountain Rifle

This is a limited edition black powder rifle chambered for the .50 ball. It is fitted with a 30" octagon barrel with single set trigger. Figured walnut stock and engraved lock plate. Cased with powder horn. Limited to 1,000 rifles in 1978.

NIB	Exc.	V.G.	Good	Fair	Poor
950	750	—	—	—	—

Jonathan Browning Mountain Rifle

Same as above but without fancy wood, case, or engraving. Also chambered for .45 or .54 caliber.

NIB	Exc.	V.G.	Good	Fair	Poor
650	500	400	300	—	—

Model 1878

Based on John M. Browning's first patent this single shot rifle was the only firearm manufactured by the Browning brothers. Offered in several calibers only a few hundred probably exist with the Ogden, Utah, barrel address. This design was later sold to Winchester and sold under that company's name as the Model 1885 High Wall.

Exc.	V.G.	Good	Fair	Poor
4500	3500	2500	1500	500

Model B-78

Introduced in 1973 this single shot, lever action falling block was offered in several calibers from .22-250 to .45-70. Barrel lengths from 24" to 26" in either round or octagonal shape with no sights except .45-70. Checkered walnut stock. First built in 1973 and discontinued in 1983.

NOTE: Add 15% for .45-70 caliber.

NIB	Exc.	V.G.	Good	Fair	Poor
800	650	550	300	200	100

Model 1885 High Wall

This is a single shot rifle with falling block action and octagonal free floating barrel similar to the Model 78. Introduced in 1985. The stock is a high grade walnut with straight grip and recoil pad. Furnished with 28" barrel it is offered in the following calibers: .223, .22-250, .270, .30-06, 7mm Rem. Mag., .45-70 Gov't. Weighs about 8 lbs. 12 oz.

NIB	Exc.	V.G.	Good	Fair	Poor
800	650	550	300	200	100

Model 1885 Low Wall

Introduced in 1995 this rifle is similar to the above but in a more accurate version of the original Low Wall. The thin octagon barrel is 24" in length. Trigger pull is adjustable. The walnut stock is fitted with a pistol grip and schnabel forearm. Offered in .22 Hornet, .223 Rem. and the .243 Win. calibers. Weight is about 6.4 lbs.

NIB	Exc.	V.G.	Good	Fair	Poor
750	600	500	400	300	150

Model 1885 Low Wall Traditional Hunter

Introduced in 1998 this model is similar to the Low Wall but with a half octagon half round 24" barrel chambered for the .357 Magnum, .44 Magnum, and .45 Colt cartridges. Case colored receiver and crescent butt with tang sight are also features. Weight is approximately 6.5 lbs.

NIB	Exc.	V.G.	Good	Fair	Poor
900	750	—	—	—	—

Model 1885 BPCR (Black Powder Cartridge Rifle)

This model was introduced in 1996 for BPCR metallic silhouette shoots. Chambered for the .45-70 or .40-60 caliber the receiver is case colored and the 28" round barrel is fitted with vernier sight with level. The walnut stock has a checkered pistol grip and is fitted with a tang sight. Weight is approximately 11 lbs.

NIB	Exc.	V.G.	Good	Fair	Poor
1500	1300	800	400	300	150

Model 1885 BPCR Creedmore Type

Introduced in 1998 this model is chambered for the 45/90 cartridge and features a 34" heavy half round barrel with long range tang sight and wind gauge front sight. Weight is approximately 11 lbs. 13 oz.

NIB	Exc.	V.G.	Good	Fair	Poor
1250	1000	—	—	—	—

Model 1885 High Wall Traditional Hunter

This variation of the Model 1885 series was introduced in 1997. It is fitted with an oil finish walnut stock with crescent buttplate. The barrel is octagonal and 28" in length. The rear sight is buckhorn and the rifle is fitted with a tang mounted peep sight. The front sight is gold bead classic style. The rifle is chambered for the 30-30, .38-55, and .45-70 cartridges. Weight is approximately 9 lbs. In 1998 the .454 Casull caliber was added to this rifle.

NIB	Exc.	V.G.	Good	Fair	Poor
1100	900	700	—	—	—

Model 1886 Grade I

This was a lever-action sporting rifle patterned after the Model 1886 Winchester rifle. It was chambered for the .45-70 cartridge and has a 26", octagonal barrel with a full-length, tubular magazine. The finish is blued with a walnut stock and crescent buttplate. There were 7,000 manufactured in 1986.

NIB	Exc.	V.G.	Good	Fair	Poor
1350	950	725	600	450	300

Model 1886 Grade I Carbine

NIB	Exc.	V.G.	Good	Fair	Poor
850	650	550	400	325	250

Model 1886 High Grade

This deluxe version of the Model 1886 features game scene engraving with gold accents and a checkered, select walnut stock. "1 of 3,000" is engraved on the top of the barrel. There were 3,000 manufactured in 1986.

NIB	Exc.	V.G.	Good	Fair	Poor
1600	1150	900	700	550	425

Model 1886 High Grade Carbine

NIB	Exc.	V.G.	Good	Fair	Poor
1200	950	750	600	450	300

Model 1886 Montana Centennial

This version is similar to the High Grade with a different engraving pattern designed to commemorate the centennial of the State of Montana. There were 2,000 manufactured in 1986. As with all commemoratives, it must be NIB with all supplied materials to command collector interest.

NIB	Exc.	V.G.	Good	Fair	Poor
1300	950	750	600	450	375

B-92 Carbine

This is a lever-action sporting rifle patterned after the Winchester Model 92. It was chambered for the .357 Mag. and the .44 Mag. cartridges. It has a 20" barrel with an 11-round, tubular magazine. The finish is blued with a walnut stock. It was discontinued in 1986.

NOTE: Add 10% for Centennial Model.

Exc.	V.G.	Good	Fair	Poor
400	325	195	150	120

NOTE: For .357 Magnum add 30 percent.

Model 1895 Grade I

This is a lever-action sporting rifle chambered in .30-.40 Krag and the .30-06 cartridge. It was patterned after the Model 1895 Winchester rifle. It has a 24" barrel and a 4-round, integral box magazine. It has a buckhorn rear sight and a blade front. The finish is blued with a walnut stock. There were 6,000 manufac-

tured in .30-06 and 2,000 chambered for the .30-40 Krag. It was manufactured in 1984.

Exc.	V.G.	Good	Fair	Poor
600	525	450	375	275

NOTE: For .30-06 caliber add 15 percent.

Model 1895 High Grade

This is the deluxe engraved version of the Model 1895. It has gold-inlaid game scenes and a gold-plated trigger and features a checkered select walnut stock. There were 2,000 produced in 1984—1,000 in each caliber.

Exc.	V.G.	Good	Fair	Poor
1000	900	700	575	400

NOTE: For .30-40 caliber deduct 20 percent.

Express Rifle

This is an Over/Under, superposed rifle chambered for the .270 Winchester or the .30-06 cartridges. It has 24" barrels with folding express sights and automatic ejectors. It features a single trigger. The receiver is engraved and is finished in blue with a deluxe checkered walnut stock. Introduced in 1980 and discontinued in 1986.

Exc.	V.G.	Good	Fair	Poor
2200	1800	1500	1100	800

Continental Set

This consists of an Express Rifle chambered for the .30-06 cartridge and furnished with an extra set of 20 gauge, Over/Under barrels. The shotgun barrels are 26.5" in length. There is a single trigger, automatic ejectors, and a heavily engraved receiver. The select walnut stock is hand checkered and oil-finished. It was furnished with a fitted case. There were 500 manufactured between 1978 and 1986.

Exc.	V.G.	Good	Fair	Poor
3500	2750	2200	1750	1000

BROWNING.
Automatic-5 Shotguns
(Photo G-3)

3 inch Magnum 12 gauge

12 gauge

16 gauge

20 gauge

Challenger

Medalist

Nomad

BROWNING.
.22 Automatic Pistols
Photo G-5

BROWNING
Automatic Pistols
(Photo G-8)

Top 9mm

Center .380 caliber

Bottom .25 caliber

Safari Grade with Browning 4X Scope.

Magnum Safari Grade

Medallion Grade

Olympian Grade

BROWNING
High-Power Rifles
(Photo G-13)

Grade I .22 Long Rifle

Grade I .22 Long Rifle with Browning 4X scope

Grade III .22 Long Rifle

BROWNING
.22 Automatic Rifles
(Photo G-7)

Grade I .22 Short

BROWNING

AUTOMATIC RIFLE

Grade II

BROWNING
High-Power Rifles
(Photo G-33)

Safari Grade Rifle and Browning 4X Scope. Calibers available: .270W, 30 06, 308W, .264W.

Safari Grade Rifle and Browning 3X - 9X Variable Scope. Calibers Available: 7mm Rem. Magnum, 300W Magnum, 300H&H Magnum, .308 Norma Magnum, .338W Magnum, 375H&H, .458W Magnum.

Safari Grade Rifle with Lightweight Sporter Barrel and 2X - 7X Variable Scope. Heavy target barrel optional. Calibers Available: .243W or .22 250 (Wildcat)

Safari Grade Rifle with Heavy Target Barrel and Browning 6X Scope. Lightweight Sporter barrel optional. Calibers Available: .222 Remington or .222 Remington Magnum.

BROWNING
SUPERPOSED SHOTGUN
New Super-Light Field Model
20 GAUGE

T-2

T-1 with Browning 4X .22 Riflescope

BROWNING

T-BOLT .22 CALIBER BOLT ACTION RIFLE

An entirely new concept in bolt action design.

(Photo G-37)

BRUCE & DAVIS
Webster, Massachusetts

Double Barreled Pistol

A .36 caliber double-barrel percussion pistol with 3" to 6" round barrels. The barrel rib marked "Bruce & Davis". Blued with walnut grips. Manufactured during the 1840s.

Exc.	V.G.	Good	Fair	Poor
—	—	750	350	150

BRUCHET
Ste. Etienne, France

Model A Shotgun

A 12 or .410 bore side by side shotgun with double triggers, and automatic ejectors. The barrel lengths and chokes are to customer specifications. Produced on a limited basis (50 per year) since 1982. Base Price as Follows.

NIB	Exc.	V.G.	Good	Fair	Poor
2000	1750	1500	1250	1000	500

Model B

As above, with a finer finish and a spring assisted action opener. Imported since 1982.

NIB	Exc.	V.G.	Good	Fair	Poor
6250	5250	4000	3000	2250	1250

BRUFF, R.P.
New York, New York

Bruff Pocket Pistol

A .41 caliber single shot percussion pistol with 2.5" to 3" barrels The pistol is marked "R.P. Bruff NY" in an arch and "Cast Steel." German silver with a checkered walnut stock. Manufactured between 1861 and 1870.

Exc.	V.G.	Good	Fair	Poor
—	—	1250	500	200

BUCO
Germany

Buco Gas Pistol

This odd firearm looks more like a telescope than a pistol. It is chambered for a 10.55mm gas cartridge and is a single shot. Overall it is approximately 5.5" long in its open or cocked position. The barrel is smooth bore and 3.75" in length. This pistol has no sights and no safety—one simply pulls the inner tube back much like extending a telescope, unscrews the end cap, inserts the round, and screws the cap back into place. When it is needed, a thumbnail is used to depress the sear and fire the pistol. They are marked on the end cap "Buco DRGM." No more information is available as to quantity or year of manufacture.

Exc.	V.G.	Good	Fair	Poor
—	350	200	150	100

BUDISCHOWSKY
Mt. Clemens, Michigan

TP-70

A .22 or .25 ACP caliber semiautomatic pistol with a 2.5" barrel, fixed sights and 6-shot magazine. Stainless steel with plastic grips. Manufactured between 1973 and 1977.

.22 Rimfire Caliber

NIB	Exc.	V.G.	Good	Fair	Poor
475	425	350	300	225	150

.25 ACP Caliber

NIB	Exc.	V.G.	Good	Fair	Poor
400	325	250	200	175	125

NOTE: After 1977, Norton Arms produced this pistol; values are approximately 40 percent less than those made by Budischowsky.

BUL TRANSMARK LTD.
Tel-Aviv, Israel
Importer-All American Sales, Memphis, Tennessee

Model M5

Introduced for the first time in the U.S. in 1996 this semiautomatic pistol bears a resemblance to the Model 1911. The frame is polymer and the slide is stainless steel. Available in 9mm, .38 Super, .40 S&W, and .45 ACP. Magazine limited to 10 rounds.

NIB	Exc.	V.G.	Good	Fair	Poor
750	600	450	350	—	—

BULLARD REPEATING ARMS CO.
Springfield, Massachusetts

Designed by James H. Bullard, the following rifles were manufactured in competition with those produced by the Whitney Arms Company and the Winchester Repeating Arms Company. Approximately 12,000 were made between 1886 and 1890.

Courtesy Milwaukee Public Museum, Milwaukee, Wisconsin

Small Frame

A .32-40 and .38-45 caliber lever action rifle with a 26" octagonal barrel and either a half or full length magazine tube. Blued or case hardened with a walnut stock. The receiver is stamped "Bullard Repeating Arms Company/Springfield, Mass., U.S.A. Pat. Aug. 16, 1881." The caliber is marked on top of the frame.

Exc.	V.G.	Good	Fair	Poor
—	2500	1000	600	300

A Bullard large frame rifle was sold at auction for $6,037.50. Chambered for .40 caliber and fitted with a 30" tapered octagon barrel with full magazine. No provision for rear sight. Fitted with an adjustable tang sight. Unique adjustable trigger pull. Figured walnut stock. Condition was excellent.
Amoskeag Auction Co. Inc., May 2000

Large Frame

A .40-75 through .45-85 caliber lever-action rifle with 28" octagonal barrel. Other features and markings as above. Can be custom ordered in .50-95 and .50-115.

Exc.	V.G.	Good	Fair	Poor
—	3500	1500	800	400

Carbine

A .45-70 caliber lever-action rifle with a 22" round barrel and a sliding dust cover on the receiver. Marking and finish as above.

Exc.	V.G.	Good	Fair	Poor
—	5500	2750	1250	500

Musket

A .45-70 caliber lever-action rifle with a 30" round barrel with a full-length stock secured by two barrel bands. There is a rod under the barrel, military sights, and the same sliding cover on the receiver as found on the Carbine. There have been examples noted without the manufacturer's markings.

Exc.	V.G.	Good	Fair	Poor
—	5000	2500	1250	500

BULLDOG SINGLE SHOT PISTOL
Connecticut Arms & Manufacturing Co.
Naubuc, Connecticut

Bulldog

A .44 or .50 caliber single shot spur trigger pistol with 4" or 6" barrels, and a pivoting breechblock that moves to the left for loading. Blued, case hardened and stamped "Connecticut Arms & Manf. Co. Naubuc Conn. Patented Oct. 25, 1864." There were only a few hundred manufactured, and the .50 caliber, 6" barreled versions would be worth an additional 40 percent. Produced between 1866 and 1868.

Exc.	V.G.	Good	Fair	Poor
—	1000	600	250	150

BURGESS GUN CO.
Buffalo, New York
ALSO SEE—Colt and Whitney

One of the most prolific 19th century designers was Andrew Burgess who established his own company in 1892. The Burgess Gun Company manufactured slide action shotguns and rifles operated by a unique pistol grip prior to their being purchased by the Winchester Repeating Arms Company in 1899. Arms based on Burgess' patents were manufactured by a variety of American gun makers. Serial numbers for all Burgess shotguns begin at 1000.

12 Gauge Slide Action Shotgun

A 12 gauge slide action shotgun with a 28" or 30" barrel. Blued with a walnut stock. This model was available with 6 grades of engraving. The values listed below are for the standard, plain model.

Burgess engraving grades (1-4)

Exc.	V.G.	Good	Fair	Poor
—	1250	600	250	125

Folding Shotgun

As above, with a 19.5" barrel that is hinged so that it may be folded back against the buttstock.

Exc.	V.G.	Good	Fair	Poor
—	3500	1500	650	300

Slide Action Rifle

An extremely rare rifle based upon the shotgun design described above. Manufactured in at least three calibers with varying barrel lengths. Blued with a walnut stock.

Exc.	V.G.	Good	Fair	Poor
—	3000	1250	500	250

BURGSMULLER, K.
Krelensen, Germany

Burgo

The Rohm RG10 under another name. It is a poor quality, inexpensive .38 caliber revolver. The examples marketed by Burgsmuller are so marked.

Exc.	V.G.	Good	Fair	Poor
150	100	75	50	25

Regent

The Regent is a .22 caliber revolver that resembles the Colt Police Positive in appearance. It is of a higher quality than the Burgo. The manufacturer is not known.

Exc.	V.G.	Good	Fair	Poor
175	125	100	75	50

BURNSIDE RIFLE CO.
Providence, Rhode Island
Bristol Firearms Co.

Bristol, Rhode Island

This is an historically desirable firearm for Civil War collectors as the designer, Ambrose E. Burnside, was to become a well known Union general. The rifle, of which there were four distinct models, was used quite extensively in the Civil War.

This carbine was manufactured first by the Bristol Firearms Co., which made the entire production of the first model and also some of the second model. In 1862 the Burnside Firearms Co. was formed, and they produced the remainder of the second models and all of the third and fourth models. Production ceased entirely in 1865.

Burnside Carbine 1st Model

This model was produced by Bristol and was chambered for the .54 caliber. It is a breechloader that uses the percussion ignition system but features a cartridge of sorts made of copper, and a tape priming device that was located inside the frame. It has a 22" round barrel with no forend and a walnut stock with inspector's cartouche. The finish is blued and case-colored, and the frame is stamped "Burnside's /Patent/March 25th/1856." There were approximately 250 1st Models manufactured.

Exc.	V.G.	Good	Fair	Poor
—	—	12000	5000	1500

2nd Model

The 2nd Model features an improved breechblock opening mechanism located inside the triggerguard. The barrel is 21" long, and the other features are similar to the 1st Model. They are marked either "Bristol Firearm Co." or "Burnside Rifle Co./Providence-R.I." The barrel is marked "Cast Steel 1861," and some of the breechblock devices are marked "G.P. Foster Pat./April 10th 1860." There were approximately 1,500 2nd Models manufactured in 1861 and 1862.

Courtesy Milwaukee Public Museum, Milwaukee, Wisconsin

Exc.	V.G.	Good	Fair	Poor
—	—	5000	2000	750

3rd Model

This model differs from the 2nd Model in that it has a forend with a barrel band and a slightly modified hammer. The markings are the same as the Burnside-manufactured 2nd Models. There were approximately 2,000 produced in 1862.

Exc.	V.G.	Good	Fair	Poor
—	—	3500	1250	500

4th Model

This model differs from the others in that it features a hinged breech that permits simpler loading of the odd-shaped Burnside percussion cartridge. The frame is marked "Burnside's Patent/Model of 1864." The other features are similar to the 3rd Model. There were approximately 50,000 manufactured between 1862 and 1865.

Courtesy Milwaukee Public Museum, Milwaukee, Wisconsin

Exc.	V.G.	Good	Fair	Poor
—	3500	2000	800	400

BUSHMASTER FIREARMS INC.
Windham, Maine

As of 1996 the company had a limited supply of pre-ban rifles similar to those listed below but fitted with flash suppressor, bayonet lug, and telescoping stocks. These pre-ban guns have a retail price of $1,000. This price may be higher or lower depending on your area and the current mood surrounding "assault weapons".

Bushmaster XM15-E2S Shorty Carbine

This is a "post-ban" model of the M16 gas operated semiautomatic rifle chambered for the .223 Remington cartridge. It is fitted with a heavy 16" barrel and a 30-round magazine (while supplies last). Overall length is 35" and empty weight is 6.72 lbs.

NIB	Exc.	V.G.	Good	Fair	Poor
900	750	600	500	350	250

NOTE: Add $50 for fluted barrel. Add $75 for A3 Type carry handle.

Bushmaster XM15-E2S Dissipator

Similar to the above model with a 16" barrel but fitted with a longer plastic handguard to give a longer sight radius. Weight is 7.2 lbs.

NIB	Exc.	V.G.	Good	Fair	Poor
900	750	600	450	350	250

NOTE: Add $75 for A3 carry handle.

Bushmaster XM15-E2S Target Model

Furnished with a 20" heavy barrel and A-2 stock. Weight is 8.35 lbs.

NIB	Exc.	V.G.	Good	Fair	Poor
900	750	600	450	350	250

NOTE: Add $10 for 24" barrel and $20 for 26" barrel. Add $75 for A3 carry handle.

Bushmaster XM15-E2S V-Match Competion Rifle

This model is a specially designed competition rifle with 20", 24", or 26" barrel lengths. Fitted with a black anodized aluminum handguard. Weight is about 8.1 lbs.

NIB	Exc.	V.G.	Good	Fair	Poor
950	800	650	500	400	275

NOTE: Add $75 for A3 carry handle.

Bushmaster XM15-E2S V-Match Carbine

As above but with 16" barrel. Weight is about 6.9 lbs.

NIB	Exc.	V.G.	Good	Fair	Poor
1015	800	—	—	—	—

NOTE: Add $75 for A3 carry handle.

Bushmaster M4 Post-Ban Carbine

Introduced in 2001 this rifle features a 14.5" barrel with permanently attached Mini Y Comp muzzle brake (total length 16") and pinned and fixed length Tele-style stock. Chambered for .223 caliber. M16A2 rear sight. Supplied with 10-round magazine. Weight is about 6.6 lbs.

NIB	Exc.	V.G.	Good	Fair	Poor
1020	800	—	—	—	—

Bushmaster M4A3 Post-Ban Carbine

Same as above but with removable carry handle. Introduced in 2001.

NIB	Exc.	V.G.	Good	Fair	Poor
1095	875	—	—	—	—

Bushmaster DCM Competition Rifle

This model features a 20" extra heavy barrel with free floating forend. Competition sights and trigger. Supplied with buttstock weight and hard carrying case. 10-round magazine.

NIB	Exc.	V.G.	Good	Fair	Poor
1525	1200	—	—	—	—

Bushmaster M17S Bullpup

This model is a gas operated semiautomatic rifle in the bullpup design. Chambered for the .223 cartridge and fitted with a 21.5" barrel. Weight is 8.2 lbs.

NIB	Exc.	V.G.	Good	Fair	Poor
725	575	475	375	250	150

BUTLER, WM. S.
Rocky Hill, Connecticut

Butler Single Shot Pistol

A .36 caliber single shot percussion pocket pistol with a 2.5" barrel and the frame and grip made in one piece. The frame marked "Wm. S. Butler's Patent/Patented Feb.3, 1857."

Exc.	V.G.	Good	Fair	Poor
—	—	750	300	150

BUTTERFIELD, JESSE
Philadelphia, Pennsylvania

Butterfield Army Revolver

A .41 caliber revolver with a 7" octagonal barrel, an unfluted 5-shot cylinder and features a special priming device, a disk that was loaded in front of the triggerguard. A brass frame, blued with walnut grips. The frame is stamped "Butterfield's Patent Dec. 11, 1855/Phila." Approximately 650 manufactured in 1861 and 1862.

Courtesy Milwaukee Public Museum, Milwaukee, Wisconsin

Exc.	V.G.	Good	Fair	Poor
—	—	5250	2000	800

Butterfield Pocket Pistol

A .41 caliber single-shot percussion pistol with a 2" to 3.5" barrel. German silver with walnut stocks. The lock is marked "Butterfield's/Patent Dec 11, 1855." Extremely rare. Manufactured in the 1850s.

Exc.	V.G.	Good	Fair	Poor
—	—	8500	3750	1500

CZ
(Ceska Zbrojovka)
Uhersky Brod, Czech Republic

Established by Karel Bubla and Alois Tomiska in 1919. This company later merged with Hubertus Engineering Company. In 1949 the company was nationalized. CZ regularly exports 90% of its production to over 80 countries.

Fox

A 6.35mm caliber semiautomatic pistol with a 2.5" barrel, tubular slide, a folding trigger and no triggerguard. Blued with plastic grips. Manufactured between 1919 and 1926.

Exc.	V.G.	Good	Fair	Poor
375	275	225	150	125

CZ 1922

As above with a conventional trigger and guard. Blued with checkered plastic grips. Manufactured between 1921 and 1923.

Exc.	V.G.	Good	Fair	Poor
650	500	350	200	150

CZ 1924

The first military pistol produced by CZ.

Exc.	V.G.	Good	Fair	Poor
475	375	300	200	100

CZ 1927

A semiautomatic pistol chambered for the 7.65mm cartridge, marked the same as the CZ 1924, but the cocking grooves on the slide are cut vertically instead of sloped as on the earlier model. This model was blued with checkered, wrap-around, plastic grips. These early guns were beautifully made and marked, "Ceska Zbrojovka AS v Praze." After the war, these pistols continued in production until 1951. There were over 500,000 manufactured.

Nazi-Proofed add 50%.

Commercial markings

Courtesy Orvel Reichert

Exc.	V.G.	Good	Fair	Poor
450	375	300	200	165

NOTE: Some of these pistols were made with an extended barrel for the use of a silencer. This variation brings a large premium. Less than 10 CZ27s were made in .22 caliber. An expert opinion is suggested if a sale is contemplated.

CZ 1936

A 6.35mm caliber semiautomatic pistol with 2.5" barrel, and double-action-only lockwork. Discontinued in 1940 because of wartime production.

Exc.	V.G.	Good	Fair	Poor
350	250	200	125	100

CZ 1938

Exc.	V.G.	Good	Fair	Poor
450	400	350	250	175

CZ 45

This model is a small .25 caliber (6.35mm) pocket pistol that is double action only. It was produced and sold after World War II. It is a modified version of the CZ 1936. Approximately 60,000 were built between 1945 and 1949.

Exc.	V.G.	Good	Fair	Poor
350	300	250	175	125

CZ 1950

This is a blowback-operated, semiautomatic, double action pistol chambered for the 7.65mm cartridge. It is patterned after the Walther Model PP with a few differences. The safety catch is located on the frame instead of the slide; and the triggerguard is not hinged, as on the Walther. It is dismantled by means of a catch on the side of the frame. Although intended to be a military pistol designed by the Kratochvil brothers, it proved to be underpowered and was adopted by the police. There were few released on the commercial market.

Exc.	V.G.	Good	Fair	Poor
250	200	150	100	75

Model 1970

This model was an attempt to correct dependability problems with the Model 50. There is little difference to see externally between the two except for markings and the grip pattern. Production began during the 1960s and ended in 1983.

Courtesy Rock Island Auction Company

Exc.	V.G.	Good	Fair	Poor
250	200	150	100	75

CZ 1952

Exc.	V.G.	Good	Fair	Poor
175	150	100	75	65

RIFLES

Model 52

Exc.	V.G.	Good	Fair	Poor
300	275	250	—	—

Model 52/57

Exc.	V.G.	Good	Fair	Poor
350	300	250	—	—

CURRENTLY IMPORTED CZ RIFLES
CZ-USA
Kansas City, Kansas

CZ first entered the U.S. market in 1990 through various distributors. In January 1998 CZ-USA opened its office in Kansas City, Kansas. This office includes full sales and warranty service as well as an on-site gunsmith.

LONG GUNS

CZ 452-2E LUX

This bolt action rifle is chambered for the .22 l.r. or .22 Win. Mag. cartridge. It is fitted with a 24.8" barrel with hooded front and adjustable rear sight. Trigger is adjustable for pull. The pistol grip stock is a European-style Turkish walnut. Supplied with a 5-round magazine. Blued finish. Weight is approximately 6.6 lbs.

NIB	Exc.	V.G.	Good	Fair	Poor
335	275	225	150	125	—

NOTE: Add $40 for .22 WMR.

CZ ZKM-452D

As above, with a walnut, Monte Carlo-style stock.

Exc.	V.G.	Good	Fair	Poor
275	225	150	100	—

CZ 452-2E ZKM Style

Similar to the above model but chambered for .22 l.r. only and fitted with a black synthetic stock and matte nickel finish. Fitted with a 22.5" barrel. Weight is about 6 lbs.

NIB	Exc.	V.G.	Good	Fair	Poor
345	275	225	175	125	—

CZ 452 American Classic

This model is chambered for the .22 l.r. and .22 Win. Mag. cartridge and features an American-style Circassian walnut stock with 18 lpi checkering. Fitted with a 21" barrel with recessed target crown. Supplied with a 5-round magazine. Blued finish. Weight is about 6.5 lbs. Introduced in 1999.

NIB	Exc.	V.G.	Good	Fair	Poor
375	300	—	—	—	—

NOTE: Add $40 for .22 WMR.

CZ 452 Varmint

This bolt action rifle is chambered for the .22 l.r. cartridge and is fitted with a 20" barrel. American-style Turkish walnut stock. Blued finish. Weight is about 7.5 lbs.

NIB	Exc.	V.G.	Good	Fair	Poor
370	300	250	200	150	—

CZ 452 Scout

This model is designed for the younger shooter and features a shortened buttstock, 16.2" barrel, and reduced weight receiver. Chambered for the .22 Long Rifle cartridge. Open adjustable sights. Weight is 3.9 lbs. Introduced in 2000.

NIB	Exc.	V.G.	Good	Fair	Poor
250	200	—	—	—	—

CZ 511

This is a semiautomatic rifle chambered for the .22 l.r. cartridge. Fitted with a 22" barrel. Two position rear sight. Supplied with an 8-round magazine. Cross bolt safety. Turkish walnut stock. Blued finish. Weight is approximately 5.4 lbs.

NIB	Exc.	V.G.	Good	Fair	Poor
350	275	225	175	125	—

CZ 527 LUX

This is a bolt action center fire rifle chambered for the .22 Hornet, .222 Rem., or the .223 Rem. cartridge. Fitted with a 23.6" barrel with a hooded front sight and fixed rear sight. The trigger is an adjustable single set type. The Turkish walnut stock is in the Bavarian style. Blued finish. Supplied with a 5-round magazine. Weight is approximately 6.6 lbs.

NIB	Exc.	V.G.	Good	Fair	Poor
540	425	350	250	—	—

CZ 527 Premium (Lux)

Introduced in 2000 this model features hand fitted actions, fancy walnut stock, 18 LPI checkering, and satin finish. Offered in .22 Hornet and .223 Rem. Barrel length is 22". Magazine capacity is 5 rounds. Weight is about 6.2 lbs.

NIB	Exc.	V.G.	Good	Fair	Poor
650	525	—	—	—	—

CZ Model 527

This bolt action model is chambered for the .22 Hornet, .222 Rem., and the .223 Rem. The rear sight is adjustable and the checkered stock is walnut. Barrel length is 23.6" and magazine capacity is 5 rounds. Weight is approximately 6.2 lbs.

NIB	Exc.	V.G.	Good	Fair	Poor
600	500	400	300	225	—

CZ 527 FS

Similar to the above model but fitted with a 20.5" barrel with Mannlicher-style stock. Blued finish. Weight is about 6 lbs.

NIB	Exc.	V.G.	Good	Fair	Poor
600	475	375	250	—	—

CZ 527 American Classic

Introduced in 1999, this model features a 20.5" barrel with American-style Turkish walnut stock. Weight is approximately 7.6 lbs. Blued finish.

NIB	Exc.	V.G.	Good	Fair	Poor
540	425	—	—	—	

CZ 527 Prestige

An upgraded CZ 527 American with jeweled bolt and semi-fancy Turkish walnut with hand rubbed finish. Chambered for the .22 Hornet or .223 Remington cartridges. Barrel length is 21.9". Weight is about 6.2 lbs. Introduced in 2001.

NIB	Exc.	V.G.	Good	Fair	Poor
620	500	—	—	—	—

CZ 527 Carbine

This model, introduced in 2000, is chambered for the 7.62x39 cartridge and fitted with a 18.5" barrel. Detachable magazine capacity is 5 rounds. Open sights. Weight is about 6 lbs.

NIB	Exc.	V.G.	Good	Fair	Poor
525	425	—	—	—	—

Model 537

This bolt action rifle is chambered for the .270, .308, and .30-06 cartridges. The rear sight is adjustable and the stock is checkered walnut. Barrel length is 23.6". Magazine capacity is 5 rounds. Weight is approximately 7.9 lbs.

NIB	Exc.	V.G.	Good	Fair	Poor
600	475	375	250	200	—

CZ 550

This center fire bolt action rifle is chambered for a number of cartridges from .22-250 to .30-06. Fitted with a 20.5" barrel and Bavarian-style Turkish walnut stock. Blued finish. Weight is about 7.6 lbs.

NIB	Exc.	V.G.	Good	Fair	Poor
600	475	375	250	200	—

CZ 550 American Classic

Similar to the Model CZ 550 this rifle is chambered for the .243, .308, .270, and .30-06 cartridges. It is fitted with a 20.5" barrel and American-style Turkish walnut stock. No sights. Supplied with 5-round internal magazine. Blued finish. Weight is about 7.6 lbs. Introduced in 1999.

NIB	Exc.	V.G.	Good	Fair	Poor
600	475	—	—	—	—

CZ Model 550

Chambered for the .243, .270, .308, and .30-06 cartridges, this bolt action rifle features a 24" barrel and high comb walnut stock. No open sights. Weight is about 7.25 lbs.

NIB	Exc	V.G.	Good	Fair	Poor
600	475	375	250	200	—

CZ Model 550 Battue Lux

Chambered for the .30-06 cartridge. Ramp rear sight. Barrel length is 20.25". Weight is approximately 7.25 lbs. Checkered walnut stock.

ZKM452

CZ527

CZ550

ZKK602

NIB	Exc.	V.G.	Good	Fair	Poor
675	550	450	325	—	—

CZ Model 550 FS Battue

Same as above but with full length stock.

NIB	Exc.	V.G.	Good	Fair	Poor
750	600	500	375	—	—

CZ Model 550 Minnesota

This model is chambered for the .270 Win. and .30-06 calibers. Barrel length is 23.5". Weight is approximately 7.25 lbs. No sights. Supplied with recoil pad.

NIB	Exc.	V.G.	Good	Fair	Poor
650	550	450	325	—	—

CZ Model 550 Minnesota DM

Same as above but with detachable magazine. Calibers are .270 Win. and .308.

NIB	Exc.	V.G.	Good	Fair	Poor
725	575	475	350	—	—

CZ 550 Prestige

This model is similar to the CZ 550 American with the added features of jeweled bolt, semi-fancy walnut and hand rubbed finish. Chambered for the .270 or .30-06 cartridges with 23.6" barrel. Weight is approximately 7.3 lbs. Introduced in 2001.

NIB	Exc.	V.G.	Good	Fair	Poor
620	500	—	—	—	—

CZ 550 Medium Magnum

This model is designed around a mid-sized magnum action. Fitted with a 23.6" barrel and has a fixed magazine capacity of 5 rounds. Chambered for the .300 Win. Mag or the 7mm Rem. Mag. Single set trigger and adjustable rear sight. Weight is about 7.3 lbs. Introduced in 2001.

NIB	Exc.	V.G.	Good	Fair	Poor
620	500	—	—	—	—

CZ 550 Magnum

Chambered for the .300 Win. Mag., .375 H&H, .458 Win. Mag., and the .416 Rigby cartridges, this bolt action rifle is fitted with a 25" barrel and 5-round internal magazine. Sights are 1 standing and 2 folding express rear with a hooded front sight. Blued finish. Bavarian-style Turkish walnut stock. Weight is about 9.2 lbs.

NIB	Exc.	V.G.	Good	Fair	Poor
700	550	—	—	—	—

CZ 550 Premium

Introduced in 2000 this model features a hand fitted action with fancy walnut stock and 18 LPI checkering. Chambered for .30-06 and .270 Win. cartridges. Barrel length is 23.6". Weight is about 7.3 lbs.

NIB	Exc.	V.G.	Good	Fair	Poor
700	550	—	—	—	—

CZ 550 Special Order

Custom built rifles with special engraving, fancy wood, custom checkering and other extra cost options. These rifles are built to order.

NIB	Exc.	V.G.	Good	Fair	Poor
N/A	—	—	—	—	—

CZ-581

A 12 gauge O/U double barrel boxlock shotgun with 28" ventilated rib barrels, single trigger, and automatic ejectors. Blued with a walnut stock.

NIB	Exc.	V.G.	Good	Fair	Poor
800	700	600	450	400	—

CZ-584

A combination 12 gauge/7x57Rmm, .222 or .308 caliber Over/Under combination rifle/shotgun with 24.5" ventilated rib barrels, single triggers and automatic ejectors. Blued with a walnut stock.

NIB	Exc.	V.G.	Good	Fair	Poor
850	700	600	500	—	—

CZ 589 Stopper

This is an over/iunder rifle with a Kersten-style action. Fitted with 21.7" barrels and chambered for the .458 Winchester Magnum cartridge. Weight is about 9.3 lbs. Introduced in 2001.

NIB	Exc.	V.G.	Good	Fair	Poor
3000	2500	—	—	—	—

NOTE: Add $1,000 for special engraved model with side plates.

CZ ZKK 600

Offered in 7x57mm, 7x64mm, .270, or .30-06. Features a Mauser-type bolt action with controlled feed, non-rotating extractor, and dovetailed receiver in three action lengths.

NIB	Exc.	V.G.	Good	Fair	Poor
700	600	500	425	325	—

NOTE: Add $100 to prices for pop-up receiver sight that was discontinued in 1977.

CZ ZKK 601

As above, in .243 or .308 caliber.

NIB	Exc.	V.G.	Good	Fair	Poor
700	600	500	425	325	—

CZ ZKK 602

As above, in .300 Holland & Holland, .375 Holland & Holland or .458 Winchester Magnum.

NIB	Exc.	V.G.	Good	Fair	Poor
800	700	600	500	400	—

CZ 700 Sniper M1

Introduced in 2001 this rifle is chambered for the .308 Winchester cartridge and fitted with a 25.6" heavy barrel. Receiver has permanently attached Weaver rail. Laminated stock has adjustable cheekpiece and buttplate with adjustable trigger. Magazine capacity is 10 rounds. Weigh is approximately 12 lbs.

NIB	Exc.	V.G.	Good	Fair	Poor
2100	1700	—	—	—	—

PISTOLS

All currently imported CZ pistols can be ordered with tritium night sights with the exception of models CZ 97B and CZ 100. Add $80 for this option.

CZ 75

Designed by the Koucky brothers in 1975, this model bears little resemblance to previous CZ pistols. Considered by many to be the best pistol ever to come from the Czech Republic. Chambered for the 9mm Parabellum cartridge it is copied in many countries. This pistol has a breech lock system utilizing a Browning-style cam. The slide rides on the inside of the slide rails. Magazine capacity is 15 rounds, barrel length is 4.72", overall length is 8", and the empty pistol weighs 34.5 oz. Offered in black paint, matte or polished blue finish.

NIB	Exc.	V.G.	Good	Fair	Poor
600	500	425	400	325	250

CZ 75 B

Introduced in 1994 this CZ model is an updated version of the original CZ 75. It features a pinned front sight, a commander hammer, non-glare ribbed barrel, and a squared triggerguard. Also offered in 40 S&W chamber.

NIB	Exc.	V.G.	Good	Fair	Poor
450	350	300	250	175	125

NOTE: For .40 S&W add $30. For glossy blue add $20, for dual tone finish $25, and for nickel add $25. For tritium night sights add $80.

CZ 75 BD

Has all the same features as the Model 75B but with the addition of a decocking double action.

NIB	Exc.	V.G.	Good	Fair	Poor
450	350	300	—	—	—

CZ BD Compact

Introduced in 2001 this model features a 3.9" barrel with decocking lever. Chambered for the .40 S&W cartridge. Blued finish. Magazine capacity is 10 rounds. Weight is about 32 oz. All other features same as CZ 75 B Compact.

NIB	Exc.	V.G.	Good	Fair	Poor
450	350	—	—	—	—

CZ BD Compact Carry

Same as the model above but with rounded edges including triggerguard.

NIB	Exc.	V.G.	Good	Fair	Poor
—	—	—	—		

CZ 75B SA

This model was introduced in 2000 and features a single action trigger designed for competitive shooting that can be carried in condition one. Fitted with a straight trigger, manual safety, and chambered for the 9mm cartridge. Weight is about 35 oz.

NIB	Exc.	V.G.	Good	Fair	Poor
450	350	—	—	—	—

CZ 75 DAO

This model is similar to the CZ 75 but with a double action only trigger, no safety lever and a spurless hammer. Offered in 9mm and .40S&W. Barrel length is 4.7". Weight is about 35 oz. Introduced in 2000.

NIB	Exc.	V.G.	Good	Fair	Poor
450	350	—	—	—	—

CZ 75 Compact

Introduced in 1992, this is a compact version of the CZ 75. The barrel length is 3.9", the overall length is 7.3", and the weight is about 32 oz. Offered in black paint, matte or polished blue finish. Traditional single action double action.

NIB	Exc.	V.G.	Good	Fair	Poor
450	350	300	250	175	125

NOTE: For .40 S&W add $30. For glossy blue add $20, for dual tone finish $25, and for nickel add $25. For tritium night sights add $80.

CZ 75 Compact D

Essentially the same as the CZ 75 Compact but with a decocking double action system and lightweight alloy frame. Weight approximately 25 oz.

NIB	Exc.	V.G.	Good	Fair	Poor
525	—	—	—	—	—

NOTE: Only 20 of these pistols were imported into the U.S. No longer in production. Expert appraisal suggested prior to sale. Only the NIB retail price is listed above.

CZ 75 D PCR Compact

Introduced in 2000 this pistol is chambered for the 9mm cartridge and features a light alloy frame and 3.9" barrel. Trigger is both single and double action with decocking lever. Low profile sights. Serrated front and rear back strap. Designed for the Czech national police force. Magazine capacity is 10 rounds. Weight is about 27 oz.

NIB	Exc.	V.G.	Good	Fair	Poor
525	425	—	—	—	—

CZ 75 Semi-Compact

This model was introduced in 1994 and has the same barrel length as the Compact (3.9") but has the same full size grip as the CZ 75. Magazine capacity is 15 rounds of 9mm. Overall length is 7.3".

NIB	Exc.	V.G.	Good	Fair	Poor
450	350	300	250	175	—

CZ 75 Champion

This model is chambered for the .40 S&W, 9mm, and 9x21 cartridges. Single action only trigger with straight trigger. Fitted with a 4.5" barrel with low profile adjustable sights and three port compensator. Furnished with blue slide and nickel frame. Hand fitted. Weight is about 36 oz.

NIB	Exc.	V.G.	Good	Fair	Poor
1475	1150	—	—	—	—

CZ 75 Standard IPSC (ST)

Designed and built for IPSC competition. Chambered for .40 S&W and fitted with a 5.4" barrel. Single action only trigger. Special high profile sights. Weight is about 45 oz.

NIB	Exc.	V.G.	Good	Fair	Poor
1025	825	—	—	—	—

CZ 75 M IPSC

Similar to the CZ 75 Standard IPSC with the addition of a 2 port compensator with blast shield to protect frame mounted optics. Slide racker standard. Red Dot optics. Barrel length is 3.9". Weight is about 45 oz. Introduced in 2001.

NIB	Exc.	V.G.	Good	Fair	Poor
1500	1200	—	—	—	—

CZ 75 Silver Anniversary Model

This model commemorates the 25th anniversary of the CZ Model 75 pistol. It features a high polish nickel finish with walnut grips. The number "25" is inlaid in the grips. A total of 1000 pistols will be produced with about 500 allocated for the U.S. market.

NIB	Exc.	V.G.	Good	Fair	Poor
700	—	—	—	—	—

CZ 85 B

This model is similar in appearance to the CZ 75 but offers some new features such as ambidextrous safety and slide stop levers, squared triggerguard, adjustable sight, and ribbed slide. Caliber, magazine capacity, and weight are same as CZ 75.

NIB	Exc.	V.G.	Good	Fair	Poor
450	350	300	250	175	125

NOTE: For .40 S&W add $30. For glossy blue add $20, for dual tone finish $25, and for nickel add $25.

CZ 85-Combat

Similar to the CZ 85 but with the addition of adjustable sights, walnut grips, round hammer, and free dropping magazine.

NIB	Exc.	V.G.	Good	Fair	Poor
450	350	300	250	175	125

NOTE: For .40 S&W add $30. For glossy blue add $20, for dual tone finish $25, and for nickel add $25.

CZ Kadet

Chambered for the .22 l.r. cartridge and fitted with a 4.7" barrel. This model is a fixed barrel blowback semiautomatic pistol. Adjustable sights and blue finish. Weight is about 36 oz.

NIB	Exc.	V.G.	Good	Fair	Poor
485	375	300	225	—	—

CZ 75 Kadet Conversion

This is a separate conversion kit for the CZ 75/85 series. It converts these pistols to .22 Long Rifle. Adjustable rear sight. supplied with 10-round magazine.

NIB	Exc.	V.G.	Good	Fair	Poor
275	225	200	—	—	—

CZ 83

This is a fixed barrel .380 caliber pistol. It features an ambidextrous safety and magazine catch behind the triggerguard. The pistol is stripped by means of a hinged triggerguard. Barrel length is 3.8", overall length is 6.8", and weight is about 23 oz.

NIB	Exc.	V.G.	Good	Fair	Poor
315	250	200	175	150	125

NOTE: For nickel finish add $5.

NOTE: In 1993 Special Editions of the above pistols were introduced. These Special Editions consist of special finishes for the then currently imported CZ pistols. They are high polish blue, nickel, chrome, gold, and a combination of the above finishes. These Special Edition finishes may affect price and the buyer and seller should be aware of the initial extra cost that added between $100 and $250 to the cost of the pistol when new.

CZ Engraved Model 75 and Model 83 Pistols

CZ USA imports into this country factory engraved CZ 75 and CZ 83 pistols. These engraved pistols are special order and prices are quoted at the time of the order. It is strongly advised that a qualified appraisal be given before a sale.

Model CZ 75 Grade I

Model CZ 75 Grade II

Model CZ 75 Grade III

Model CZ 83 Grade I

Model CZ 83 Grade II

CZ 97B

This pistol was planned for production in the summer of 1997. It is chambered for the .45 ACP cartridge. It is fitted with a 4.8" barrel and has a single action double action mode. Magazine capacity is 10 rounds. Wood grips with blue finish. Weight is approximately 40 oz.

NIB	Exc.	V.G.	Good	Fair	Poor
600	475	375	250	—	—

CZ 100

This is a semiautomatic pistol, introduced in 1996, chambered for the 9mm or .40 S&W cartridge. It has a plastic frame and steel slide. Barrel length is 3.75". Weight is approximately 24 oz. U.S. magazine capacity is 10 rounds.

NIB	Exc.	V.G.	Good	Fair	Poor
425	300	200	—	—	—

CABANAS, INDUSTRIAS S.A.
Aguilas, Mexico

This company manufactures a variety of bolt-action single shot rifles that utilize .22 caliber blanks to propel a .177 caliber pellet.

Mini-82 Youth

NIB	Exc.	V.G.	Good	Fair	Poor
75	65	50	40	30	20

R-83 Larger Youth

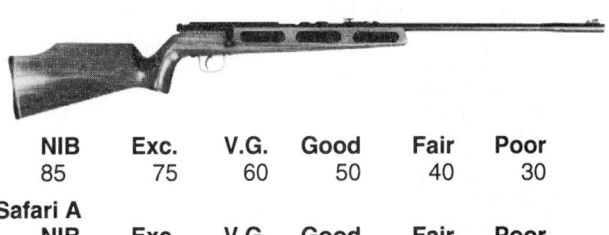

NIB	Exc.	V.G.	Good	Fair	Poor
85	75	60	50	40	30

Safari A

NIB	Exc.	V.G.	Good	Fair	Poor
100	90	75	50	40	30

Varmint

NIB	Exc.	V.G.	Good	Fair	Poor
125	110	90	75	50	35

Espronceda IV

NIB	Exc.	V.G.	Good	Fair	Poor
125	110	90	75	50	35

Leyre

NIB	Exc.	V.G.	Good	Fair	Poor
140	125	100	85	65	50

Master

NIB	Exc.	V.G.	Good	Fair	Poor
150	130	110	100	75	60

CABELAS, INC.
Sidney, Nebraska

AYA Grade II Custom

A 12, 16, and 20 gauge boxlock shotgun in various barrel lengths and chokes, a single selective trigger, and automatic ejectors. Engraved with a hand checkered walnut stock. This model is no longer available.

Exc.	V.G.	Good	Fair	Poor
1250	1175	950	700	575

Hemingway Model

A 12 or 20 gauge boxlock shotgun with 28" barrels, various chokes, a single selective trigger and automatic ejectors. Engraved with a hand checkered walnut stock.

NIB	Exc.	V.G.	Good	Fair	Poor
975	900	750	600	525	450

CALICO
See—American Industries, Inc.
Cleveland, Ohio

CAMEX-BLASER USA, INC.
See—Blaser Jagwaffen
Ft. Worth, Texas

CAMPO GIRO
Eibar, Spain

Esperanza y Unceta Model 1904

Designed by Lt. Col. Venancio Aguirre. This pistol was produced in limited numbers. Prospective purchasers are advised to secure a qualified appraisal prior to acquisition.

Exc.	V.G.	Good	Fair	Poor
1500	1000	800	600	450

Model 1910

Similar to the above, in 9mm Largo. Tested, but not adopted, by the Spanish army.

Exc.	V.G.	Good	Fair	Poor
1200	800	650	500	450

Model 1913

An improved version of the above.

Courtesy James Rankin

Courtesy James Rankin

Exc.	V.G.	Good	Fair	Poor
950	750	650	500	450

Model 1913/16

An improved version of the above.

Courtesy James Rankin

Courtesy James Rankin

Exc.	V.G.	Good	Fair	Poor
550	450	375	300	200

CARCANO
Turin, Italy

Fucile Modello 91

Exc.	V.G.	Good	Fair	Poor
165	135	85	40	20

Model 91/24 T.S. Carbine

Exc.	V.G.	Good	Fair	Poor
165	135	85	40	20

Model 91/28 Carbine

NOTE: Model 91/28 Carbine is rare and will command a substantial premium. Models in excellent condition can sell as high as $4,300. This model is encountered so seldom that prices are not given. Consult an expert prior to a sale.

Cavalry Carbine

Exc.	V.G.	Good	Fair	Poor
165	135	85	40	20

Fucile Modello 38 T.S. Carbine

Exc.	V.G.	Good	Fair	Poor
165	135	85	40	20

Cavalry Carbine

Exc.	V.G.	Good	Fair	Poor
165	135	100	65	40

Italian Carcano Model 1941 Rifle

Exc.	V.G.	Good	Fair	Poor
195	160	110	—	—

Italian Youth Rifle

Exc.	V.G.	Good	Fair	Poor
500	400	275	150	75

Italian Model 1889 Military Revolver-10.4mm caliber

Exc.	V.G.	Good	Fair	Poor
225	175	150	—	—

CARD, S. W.
Unknown

Under Hammer Pistol

A .34 caliber single shot percussion pocket pistol with a 7.75" half octagonal barrel marked "S.W. Card" and "Cast Steel". Blued with walnut grips.

Exc.	V.G.	Good	Fair	Poor
—	—	750	300	125

CARLTON, M.
Haverhill, New Hampshire

Under Hammer Pistol

A .34 caliber percussion under hammer single shot pistol with a 3.5" to 7.75" half-octagonal barrel marked "M. Carleton & Co." Browned with walnut grips. Active 1830s and 1840s.

Exc.	V.G.	Good	Fair	Poor
—	—	900	400	175

CASARTELLI, CARLO
Brescia, Italy
Importer-New England Arms Co.
Kittery Point, Maine

Sidelock Shotgun

Custom order sidelock shotgun that is available in any gauge, barrel length, choke, automatic ejectors and single selective trigger and choice of engraving style.

NIB	Exc.	V.G.	Good	Fair	Poor
15000	13500	10000	8250	6000	4000

Kenya Double Rifle

Custom order, full sidelock rifle that is available in all standard and magnum calibers. The customer may literally design this firearm if one desires and if one can afford it.

NIB	Exc.	V.G.	Good	Fair	Poor
30000	27000	22500	18000	13000	9000

Africa Model

A bolt-action rifle built on a square-bridge magnum Mauser action. It is chambered for the heavy magnum calibers and can be taken down for transport. The other features are on a custom order basis.

NIB	Exc.	V.G.	Good	Fair	Poor
8750	8000	7000	5750	4750	3750

Safari Model

Built on a standard Mauser bolt-action and is chambered for the non-magnum calibers.

NIB	Exc.	V.G.	Good	Fair	Poor
7000	6500	5500	4500	3250	2500

CASE WILLARD & CO.
New Hartford, Connecticut

Under Hammer Pistol

A .31 caliber single shot percussion pistol with a 3" half-octagonal barrel marked "Case Willard & Co./New Hartford Conn." Blued, brass frame with walnut grips.

Exc.	V.G.	Good	Fair	Poor
—	—	750	350	150

CASPIAN ARMS, LTD.
Hardwick, Vermont

Government Model

Similar to the Colt 1911, a .45 ACP caliber semiautomatic pistol with interchangeable slides for 9mm and .38 Super available. This model features high profile sights, an adjustable trigger, carbon steel or stainless steel and walnut grips. Manufactured since 1986.

NIB	Exc.	V.G	Good	Fair	Poor
550	475	425	375	300	225

Model 110

A fully customized version of the Colt 1911, .45 ACP or .38 Super caliber semiautomatic pistol with all the custom features one could cram on the Government Model. Manufactured since 1988.

NIB	Exc.	V.G.	Good	Fair	Poor
900	825	700	600	475	300

Viet Nam Commemorative

Government Model engraved by J.J. Adams and nickel-plated. The walnut grips have a branch service medallion inlaid, and gold plating was available for an additional $350. There were 1,000 manufactured in 1986.

NIB	Exc.	V.G.	Good	Fair	Poor
1200	1000	800	600	475	300

CASULL ARMS, INC.
Afton, WY

CA 2000

Chambered for the .22 caliber Long Rifle cartridge this stainless steel revolver has a 5-round cylinder with fold-up trigger. Double action only. Palm sized.

NIB	Exc.	V.G.	Good	Fair	Poor
400	325	250	—	—	—

CA 3800

Chambered for the .38 Casull cartridge (124 gr. 1800+fps) this pistol is fitted with a 6" match barrel and has a magazine capacity of 8 rounds. Full-length two-piece guide rod. Checkering on front strap and mainspring housing is 20 lpi. Match trigger and numerouis other special features. Weight is about 40 oz. Introduced in 2000.

NIB	Exc.	V.G.	Good	Fair	Poor
2495	2000	1500	—	—	—

NOTE: Add $300 for extra .45 ACP barrel.

CENTURY GUN CO.
Greenfield, Indiana

This was formerly a handmade revolver produced in Evansville, Indiana, and chambered for the .45-70 cartridge. This model was discontinued after only 524 were manufactured. They are now back in production as of 1986. The original guns are valued separately from the new production version.

Model 100 Revolver

A .30-30, .375 Winchester, .444 Marlin, .45-70, and .50-70 caliber revolver with barrel lengths from 6.5" to 15", 6-shot steel cylinder and a manganese bronze alloyed frame, a crossbolt safety, adjustable sights, and walnut grips. A limited-production item, with only 600 produced since 1976. The .45-70 is considered the standard caliber, and all other calibers are custom-order only.

.45-70 Caliber

NIB	Exc.	V.G.	Good	Fair	Poor
750	700	600	500	400	325

All Other Calibers

NIB	Exc.	V.G.	Good	Fair	Poor
1600	1400	1200	1000	800	600

Original Evansville Model 100

NIB	Exc.	V.G.	Good	Fair	Poor
2500	2250	2000	1600	1250	950

CENTURY INTERNATIONAL ARMS CO.
St. Albans, Vermont

Century International Arms is a leading importer of military firearms primarily of foreign manufacture. These low-cost firearms are excellent shooters and many have been restocked to make satisfactory hunting rifles. The listing below offers a representative sample of imports from Century. The company is always providing new surplus firearms that may not appear in this edition.

Centurion Shotgun

This is a new Over/Under shotgun in 12 gauge with 2-3/4" chambers. The walnut stock is checkered. The receiver is blue. Offered in 26" or 28" vent rib barrels in full and modified chokes. Weight is about 7 lbs.

Exc.	V.G.	Good	Fair	Poor
280	225	200	175	125

Centurion 98 Sporter

This is a refinished and rebuilt on a surplus German Mauser 98 action with new commercial 22" barrel. No sights. A synthetic stock with recoil pad is standard. Chambered for .270 or .30-06. Weighs about 7 lbs. 13 oz.

Exc.	V.G.	Good	Fair	Poor
230	200	175	150	100

Century Centurion 14

This bolt action rifle uses an Enfield Pattern 14 action drilled and tapped for scope mount. Barrel is 24" and chambered for 7mm Rem. Mag. Walnut stock is checkered with pistol grip and Monte Carlo comb. No sights.

NIB	Exc.	V.G.	Good	Fair	Poor
275	225	175	—	—	—

Enfield Sporter No. I Mark III

This refinished rifle has a cut down Sporter-style stock. Action and sights are original. Caliber is .303.

Exc.	V.G.	Good	Fair	Poor
120	80	60	50	40

Enfield Sporter No. 4 Mark I

Similar to above with cut down stock. Caliber .303.

Exc.	V.G.	Good	Fair	Poor
120	80	60	50	40

With new walnut stock.

LEE ENFIELD
No 4 Mark I Sporter
RI682 / 10LE41S
Nov 11, 1992
New Walnut Stock

Exc.	V.G.	Good	Fair	Poor
160	125	100	75	50

TOZ-17

An original Russian rifle chambered for the .22 l.r. Has a 21" barrel and 5-round magazine. Checkered stock and iron sights. Weighs about 5.4 lbs.

Exc.	V.G.	Good	Fair	Poor
120	80	60	50	40

TOZ-17-1

Same as above with hooded front sight and tangent rear sight. Receiver is grooved for scope mount.

Exc.	V.G.	Good	Fair	Poor
80	65	50	40	35

Mexican Mauser Model 1910 Sporter

This rifle has been converted from a military rifle to a sporter by cutting down the stock. The metal is refinished and the barrel has been rebored and rechambered for the .30-06 cartridge. The box magazine holds 5 rounds. Barrel is 23" and rifle weighs about 8 lbs.

Exc.	V.G.	Good	Fair	Poor
175	140	125	100	75

FAL Sporter

This is a refinished FAL receiver and barrel installed in a synthetic thumbhole stock. The flash suppressor and bayonet lug have been removed. Barrel is 20.75" and weight is approximately 10 lbs.

NIB	Exc.	V.G.	Good	Fair	Poor
625	500	350	300	250	150

M-14 Rifle

Imported from China by Century International this rifle features a 22" barrel chambered for the .308 Win. cartridge. Stock is walnut with rubber pad. Parkerized finish. Weight is approximately 8.25 lbs.

NIB	Exc.	V.G.	Good	Fair	Poor
450	350	250	200	150	100

Tiger Dragunov Rifle

This is a shortened version of the Russian SVD sniper rifle. Fitted with a 20.8" barrel and chambered for the 7.62x54R cartridge the rifle is sold with a 5-round magazine and a 4x range finding scope. Imported from Russia. Weight is about 8.5 lbs.

NIB	Exc.	V.G.	Good	Fair	Poor
1350	1100	800	—	—	—

CETME
Madrid, Spain

Cetme Autoloading Rifle

A .308 caliber semiautomatic rifle with a fluted chamber, a 17.74" barrel, an aperture rear sight and a 20-round detachable magazine. Black with a military-style wood stock. It is identical in appearance to the H&K 91 assault rifle.

NIB	Exc.	V.G.	Good	Fair	Poor
2500	2000	1500	900	—	—

CHAMELOT-DELVIGNE
Liege, Belgium

NOTE: For full details, prices, and photos by country of issue see the *Standard Catalog of Military Firearms*.

CHAMPLIN FIREARMS
Enid, Oklahoma

Champlin Firearms Company manufactures custom order rifles built to the customer's specifications. Prospective purchasers are advised to secure a qualified appraisal prior to acquisition.

Bolt Action Rifle

These arms featured round or octagonal barrels, set triggers, a variety of sights and well figured walnut stocks.

NIB	Exc.	V.G.	Good	Fair	Poor
5500	4500	3500	2900	2200	1500

CHAPMAN C.
Unknown

Chapman Rifle

This rare Confederate weapon was patterned after the U.S. Model 1841. It is chambered for .58 caliber and utilizes the percussion ignition system. The round barrel is 33" long, with a full-length stock and two barrel bands. The mountings are brass, and the stock is walnut. "C.Chapman" was stamped on the lock. This weapon was manufactured somewhere in the Confederate States of America during the Civil War, but little else is known.

CHAPMAN CHARLES
Chattanooga, Tennessee

Chapman produced a limited number of percussion carbines and rifles during the Civil War. Carbines had an overall length of 39-1/2" and .54 caliber barrels 24" in length. Their furniture was of brass. Chapman rifles resembled the U.S. Model 1841

Rifle, but did not have patchboxes. Overall length 48-1/2", barrel length 33", caliber .58. Chapman rifles and carbines are marked "C. CHAPMAN" on the lockplates.

Prospective purchasers are strongly advised to secure an expert appraisal prior to acquisition.

Courtesy Milwaukee Public Museum, Milwaukee, Wisconsin

Exc.	V.G.	Good	Fair	Poor
—	—	30000	12500	2500

CHAPMAN, G. & J.
Philadelphia, Pennsylvania

Chapman Pocket Revolver

A .32 caliber revolver with a 4" round barrel and 7-shot cylinder. The frame is made of brass while the barrel and cylinder are of steel. The barrel is marked "G.& J. Chapman/Philada/Patent Applied For/1861." Manufactured during the 1860s.

Exc.	V.G.	Good	Fair	Poor
—	—	1800	750	250

CHAPIUS
France

RG Progress

A 12, 16, or 20 gauge boxlock shotgun. Most options are available on order.

NIB	Exc.	V.G.	Good	Fair	Poor
2500	2250	2000	1800	1250	900

RG Express Model 89

A 7 x 65R, 8 x 57 JRS, 9.3 x 74R, and .375 Holland & Holland caliber sidelock, double barreled rifle. The other features are at the customer's order.

NIB	Exc.	V.G.	Good	Fair	Poor
6500	5750	4800	4000	3000	1500

Utility Grade Express Model

A side-by-side boxlock action double rifle with case colored or coin finish receiver. Offered in a variety of calibers: 9.3x74R, 8x57JRS, 7x65R, 8x75RS, and .30-06. Checkered walnut stock with pistol grip.

NIB	Exc.	V.G.	Good	Fair	Poor
6000	4800	4000	3000	1500	750

St. Bonnet Model

This model is a side-by-side shotgun with sideplates on a boxlock action. Scroll engraved case colored receiver. Straight grip stock and double triggers. Offered in 12, 16, or 20 gauge.

NIB	Exc.	V.G.	Good	Fair	Poor
4000	3250	2000	1250	800	500

African PH Model Grade I

A boxlock action double rifle offered in a wide variety of calibers. Caliber determines retail price. Hand engraved case colored receiver. Pistol grip stock with European-style cheekpiece.

.470 Nitro & .416 Rigby

NIB	Exc.	V.G.	Good	Fair	Poor
12500	9500	—	—	—	—

375 H&H

NIB	Exc.	V.G.	Good	Fair	Poor
9500	7500	—	—	—	—

.300 Win. Mag.

NIB	Exc.	V.G.	Good	Fair	Poor
8500	6500	—	—	—	—

.30-06, 9.3x74 R

NIB	Exc.	V.G.	Good	Fair	Poor
8000	6000	—	—	—	—

African PH Model Grade II

Same as above but with master engraving with game scenes. Add 20% to 25% to above NIB prices.

CHARLEVILLE
("Manufre Royle de Charleville"
See—French Military Firearms)

CHARTER 2000, INC.
Shelton, CT

Bulldog

Chambered for the .44 Special cartridge and fitted with a 2.5" barrel. Stainless steel frame with 5-round cylinder. Round butt and fixed sights. Weight is 21 oz.

NIB	Exc.	V.G.	Good	Fair	Poor
275	225	175	125	—	—

Undercover

Chambered for the .38 Special cartridge and fitted with a 2" barrel. Stainless steel frame with 5-round cylinder. Round butt. Weight is about 20 oz.

NIB	Exc.	V.G.	Good	Fair	Poor
250	200	175	150	100	75

Mag Pug

Chambered for the .357 Magnum cartridge and fitted with a 2.2" ported barrel. Stainless steel frame. Weight is about 24 oz.

NIB	Exc.	V.G.	Good	Fair	Poor
275	225	175	125	—	—

Field King Rifle

Available with blue or stainless steel finish and chambered for .25-06, .270, .30-06, or .308 with 22" barrel. Magazine capacity is 4 rounds. Checkered fiberglass stock with cheekpiece. Weight is about 8 lbs.

NIB	Exc.	V.G.	Good	Fair	Poor
300	225	175	125	—	—

Field King Carbine

Same as above but with 18" barrel with compensator (20" total) and chambered for .308.

NIB	Exc.	V.G.	Good	Fair	Poor
350	250	200	150	—	—

CHARTER ARMS CORP.
Ansonia, Connecticut

Police Undercovers

This model is chambered for the .38 Special or the .32 Magnum. It is fitted with a 2" barrel in blue or stainless steel finish. Offered with walnut or rubber grips. The overall length is 6.25" and weight is between 16 oz. and 19 oz. depending on grips and finish. This model is currently in production.

NIB	Exc.	V.G.	Good	Fair	Poor
250	200	175	150	100	75

Undercover Stainless Steel

As above, in stainless steel.

NIB	Exc.	V.G.	Good	Fair	Poor
300	250	225	175	125	100

Undercoverette

As above, with a thinner grip and in .32 S&W.

Exc.	V.G.	Good	Fair	Poor
200	150	125	100	75

Pathfinder

Similar to the above, but in .22 or .22 Magnum caliber with a 2", 3", or 6" barrel with adjustable sights.

NIB	Exc.	V.G.	Good	Fair	Poor
250	200	175	150	100	75

Pathfinder Stainless Steel

As above, in stainless steel.

NIB	Exc.	V.G.	Good	Fair	Poor
300	250	200	175	125	100

Bulldog

Similar to the Undercover model, but in .44 Special caliber with a 2.5" or 3" barrel and 5-shot cylinder.

NIB	Exc.	V.G.	Good	Fair	Poor
250	200	175	150	125	100

Stainless Steel Bulldog

As above, in stainless steel.

NIB	Exc.	V.G.	Good	Fair	Poor
300	250	225	175	150	110

Target Bulldog

As above, in .357 Magnum or .44 Special with a 4" barrel fitted with adjustable rear sights. Blued with walnut grips. Manufactured from 1986 to 1988.

NIB	Exc.	V.G.	Good	Fair	Poor
225	185	160	145	110	80

Bulldog Pug

Chambered for the .44 Special cartridge it is fitted with a 2.5" barrel. Available with walnut or neoprene grips in blue or stainless steel finish with choice of spur or pocket hammer. The cylinder holds 5 rounds. Overall length is 7" and weight is between 20 oz. and 25 oz. depending on grip and finish. This model is currently in production.

NIB	Exc.	V.G.	Good	Fair	Poor
250	200	175	150	100	75

Stainless Steel Bulldog

As above, in stainless steel.

NIB	Exc.	V.G.	Good	Fair	Poor
300	250	225	175	150	125

Bulldog Tracker

As above, with a 2.5", 4", or 6" barrel in .357 Magnum only.

NIB	Exc.	V.G.	Good	Fair	Poor
275	225	200	165	140	110

Police Bulldog

As above, in .32 H&R Magnum, .38 Special or .44 Special with 3.5" or 4" barrel.

NIB	Exc.	V.G.	Good	Fair	Poor
250	200	175	150	125	100

Stainless Steel Police Bulldog

As above, in stainless steel and available also in .357 Magnum.

NIB	Exc.	V.G.	Good	Fair	Poor
300	250	210	175	145	110

Off Duty

Chambered for the .38 Special or .22 Long Rifle this revolver is fitted with a 2" barrel. Offered with either walnut or rubber grips in blue or stainless steel finish with choice of spur or pocket hammer. Weight of the .38 special version is between 17 oz. and 23 oz., depending on grip and finish. The .22 l.r. version weighs between 19 oz. and 22 oz. The overall length is 4.75". This model is currently in production. A nickel finish with rubber grips is also offered.

NIB	Exc.	V.G.	Good	Fair	Poor
200	150	125	100	75	60

Pit Bull

A 9mm Federal, .38 Special or .357 Magnum caliber double action revolver with a 2.5", 3.5", or 4" barrel. Blued with rubber grips.

NIB	Exc.	V.G.	Good	Fair	Poor
300	250	200	175	125	90

Explorer 11 Pistol

A .22 caliber semiautomatic pistol with 6", 8", or 10" barrels. Available with a camo, black, silver, or gold finish and plastic grips. Discontinued in 1986.

NIB	Exc.	V.G.	Good	Fair	Poor
125	100	75	65	45	25

Model 40

A .22 caliber double action semiautomatic pistol with a 3.5" barrel and 8-shot magazine. Stainless steel with plastic grips. Manufactured from 1984 to 1986.

Exc.	V.G.	Good	Fair	Poor
275	225	200	150	100

Model 79K

A .32 or .380 caliber double action semiautomatic pistol with a 3.5" barrel and 7-shot magazine. Stainless steel with plastic grips. Manufactured from 1986 to 1988.

Exc.	V.G.	Good	Fair	Poor
350	300	250	180	125

Model 42T

A .22 caliber semiautomatic pistol with a 6" barrel and adjustable sights. Blued with walnut grips. Manufactured in 1984 and 1985.

NIB	Exc.	V.G.	Good	Fair	Poor
500	450	400	325	—	200

AR - 7 Explorer Rifle

A .22 caliber semiautomatic rifle with a 16" barrel, 8-shot magazine and hollow plastic stock which can house the barrel when detached.

NIB	Exc.	V.G.	Good	Fair	Poor
175	125	100	80	60	40

CHASSEPOT
French Military

MLE 1866

An 11mm caliber bolt-action rifle with a 32" barrel, a full-length walnut stock held on by two barrel bands, a cleaning rod mounted under the barrel and a bayonet lug that allows the attaching of a brass-handled, saber-type bayonet. White with a walnut stock.

Courtesy Milwaukee Public Museum, Milwaukee, Wisconsin

Exc.	V.G.	Good	Fair	Poor
1500	850	500	150	100

CHICAGO F. A. CO.
Chicago, Illinois

Protector Palm Pistol
A .32 caliber radial cylinder revolver designed to fit in the palm of the hand and to be operated by a hinged lever mounted to the rear of the circular frame. The sideplates are marked "Chicago Firearms Co., Chicago, Ill." and "The Protector". Blued with hard rubber grip panels or nickel-plated with pearl grip panels. Manufactured by the Ames Manufacturing Company.

Standard Model Nickel-Plated/Black Grips

Exc.	V.G.	Good	Fair	Poor
—	2500	1000	500	250

Blued Finish add 50%.
Pearl Grips add 20%.

A Chicago Palm Pistol was sold at auction for $1,725. Nickel plated with pearl grips. Condition was excellent. Rock Island Auction Company, August 1999

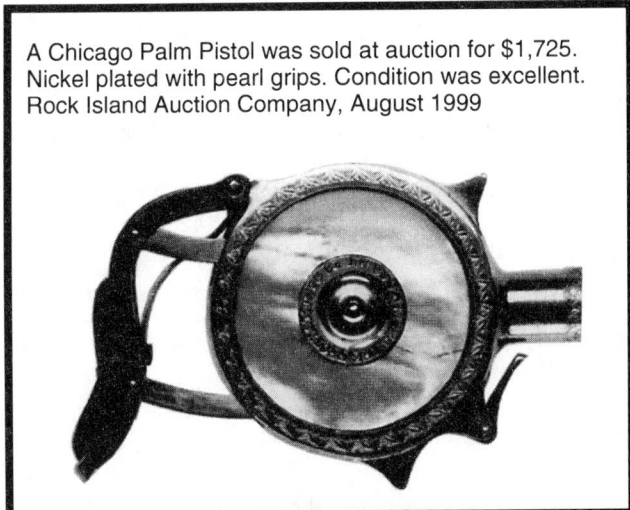

CHIPMUNK RIFLES
Prospect, Oregon

Chipmunk Single Shot Standard Rifle
A .22 or the .22 rimfire Magnum caliber bolt-action rifle with 16.25" barrel, and open sights. Weight is approximately 3.5 lbs.

NIB	Exc.	V.G.	Good	Fair	Poor
185	150	125	100	80	60

Deluxe Chipmunk
As above, with a hand-checkered walnut stock.

NIB	Exc.	V.G.	Good	Fair	Poor
230	180	135	100	80	60

Special Edition
This model features a fancy hand checkered stock, hand engraved receiver, barrel, and bolt.

NIB	Exc.	V.G.	Good	Fair	Poor
NA	—	—	—	—	—

Silhouette Pistol
A .22 caliber bolt-action pistol with a 14.5" barrel, open sights and rear pistol-grip walnut stock.

NIB	Exc.	V.G.	Good	Fair	Poor
150	125	100	80	60	40

CHRISTENSEN ARMS
St. George, Utah

Carbon One
This is a bolt action rifle with Remington 700 action chambered for .17 through .243 caliber. It is fitted with a custom trigger, Match grade stainless steel barrel and black synthetic stock. Weight is about 6 lbs.

NIB	Exc.	V.G.	Good	Fair	Poor
2750	2250	—	—	—	—

Carbon Lite
This model is similar to above but weighs about 5 lbs.

NIB	Exc.	V.G.	Good	Fair	Poor
2750	2250	—	—	—	—

Carbon King
This model utilizes a Remington 700 BDL long action and is chambered for .25 caliber through .30-06. Stainless steel barrel, custom trigger, and black synthetic stock are standard. Weight is approximately 6.5 lbs.

NIB	Exc.	V.G.	Good	Fair	Poor
2750	2250	—	—	—	—

Carbon Cannon
Similar to above model and chambered for belted magnum calibers. Weight is about 7 lbs.

NIB	Exc.	V.G.	Good	Fair	Poor
2750	2250	—	—	—	—

Carbon Challenge I
This rifle is built on a Ruger 10/22 action. It is fitted with a Volquartsen trigger, bull barrel of stainless steel and black synthetic stock. Weight is approximately 3.5 lbs.

NIB	Exc.	V.G.	Good	Fair	Poor
995	800	—	—	—	—

Carbon Challenge II

Similar to above model but fitted with an AMT action and trigger. Weight is about 4.5 lbs.

NIB	Exc.	V.G.	Good	Fair	Poor
1095	900	—	—	—	—

Carbon Tactical

This bolt action model uses a Remington 700 BDL action and is available in most any caliber. It is fitted with a custom trigger, Match grade stainless steel barrel, and black synthetic stock. Weight is about 7 lbs.

NIB	Exc.	V.G.	Good	Fair	Poor
2750	2250	—	—	—	—

CHURCHILL
Importer-Ellet Bros.
Chapin, South Carolina

Windsor I

A 10, 12, 16, 20, 28, and .410 bore Anson & Deeley double barrel boxlock shotgun with barrel lengths from 23" through 32", various choke combinations, double triggers and extractors. Scroll-engraved, silver-finished, with checkered walnut pistol grip and forend.

NIB	Exc.	V.G.	Good	Fair	Poor
750	600	500	400	300	200

Windsor II

As above, in 10, 12, and 20 gauge only with automatic ejectors. Not imported after 1987.

NIB	Exc.	V.G.	Good	Fair	Poor
750	600	550	450	350	250

Windsor VI

As above with sidelocks. Chambered for 12 and 20 gauge only with automatic ejectors. Not imported after 1987.

NIB	Exc.	V.G.	Good	Fair	Poor
1000	800	750	650	500	350

Royal

A 12, 20, 28 and .410 bore boxlock double-barrel shotgun with various barrel lengths and chokes, double triggers and extractors. Case hardened with checkered walnut stock. Introduced in 1988.

NIB	Exc.	V.G.	Good	Fair	Poor
650	500	425	350	275	125

OVER/UNDERS

Monarch

A 12, 20, 28, or .410 bore Over/Under shotgun with a boxlock action, 25", 26", or 28" ventilated-rib barrels, either double or a single selective trigger, extractors, and a checkered walnut stock.

NIB	Exc.	V.G.	Good	Fair	Poor
600	475	425	375	300	150

Windsor III

A 12 and 20 and .410 bore boxlock double-barrel shotgun with 27" or 30" ventilated-rib barrels, extractors, a single selective trigger, scroll-engraved, silver finished and a checkered walnut stock.

NIB	Exc.	V.G.	Good	Fair	Poor
700	575	525	475	400	200

Windsor IV

As above, with screw-in choke tubes standard. Introduced in 1989.

NIB	Exc.	V.G.	Good	Fair	Poor
975	775	650	500	425	200

Regent

As above, in 12 and 20 gauge with 27" ventilated-rib barrels, screw-in choke tubes, scroll-engraved false sideplates, automatic ejectors, a single selective trigger, and a checkered walnut stock. Not imported after 1986.

NIB	Exc.	V.G.	Good	Fair	Poor
950	750	650	550	450	250

Regent II

As above with finer overall finishing.

NIB	Exc.	V.G.	Good	Fair	Poor
1250	1000	850	750	500	250

Regent Shotgun Rifle Combination

A .222, .223, .243, .270, .308, or .30-06 caliber/12 gauge Over/Under rifle/shotgun with a 25" ventilated rib, automatic ejectors and single selective trigger. Silver finished, scroll engraved with a checkered walnut stock.

NIB	Exc.	V.G.	Good	Fair	Poor
1050	825	725	600	450	250

Windsor Grade Semiautomatic

A 12 gauge semiautomatic shotgun with 26", 28", or 30" ventilated-rib barrels and screw-in choke tubes. An etched and anodized alloy receiver with a checkered walnut stock.

NIB	Exc.	V.G.	Good	Fair	Poor
475	375	325	275	225	175

Regent Grade Semiautomatic

Chambered for 12 gauge with choice of 26", 28", or 30" barrels. Standard chokes or choke tubes. walnut stock with pistol grip. Introduced in 1984 and discontinued in 1986. Weight is about 7-1/2 lbs.

NIB	Exc.	V.G.	Good	Fair	Poor
475	375	325	275	225	175

Windsor Grade Slide Action

A 12 gauge slide action shotgun with a 26" through 30" ventilated-rib barrel, various chokes, double slide rails, and an anodized alloy receiver. Checkered walnut stock. Discontinued in 1986.

Exc.	V.G.	Good	Fair	Poor
475	375	300	250	175

RIFLES

Highlander

A .25-06 through .300 Winchester Magnum caliber bolt-action rifle with a 22" barrel, with or without sights, a 3-shot magazine, and a checkered walnut stock.

NIB	Exc.	V.G.	Good	Fair	Poor
525	425	375	300	250	200

Regent

As above, with a Monte Carlo-style comb and cheekpiece. Discontinued in 1988.

Exc.	V.G.	Good	Fair	Poor
625	500	425	350	275

CHURCHILL, E. J. LTD.
London, England

One of One Thousand Rifle

A .270 to .458 Magnum caliber bolt-action rifle with 24" barrel and a select French walnut stock with a trap pistol-grip cap and recoil pad. Only 100 produced for the 20th anniversary of Interarms in 1973.

Exc.	V.G.	Good	Fair	Poor
15000	12500	10000	7000	5500

Double Barrel Shotgun
See—British Double Guns

CHYLEWSKI, WITOLD
Switzerland

A 6.35mm caliber semiautomatic pistol with a 6-round magazine, marked "Brevete Chylewski" and bears the name Neuhausen on the left side of the pistol. Approximately 1,000 were made between 1910 and 1918. This pistol was designed to be cocked with one hand.

Exc.	V.G.	Good	Fair	Poor
—	1000	650	400	200

CIMARRON F. A. MFG. CO.
Fredericksburg, Texas

In business since 1984 this company imports quality single action revolvers and rifles from Uberti, Armi San Marco, and Pedersoli.

Model No. 3 Schofield

This version of the Schofield is manufactured for Cimarron by Armi San Marco in Italy. Its parts are interchangeable with the original. It is offered in several variations and calibers.

Schofield Civilian Model

Fitted with 7" barrel and offered in .44 Russian & .44 Special, .44 WCF, .45 Schofield, .45 Long Colt.

NIB	Exc.	V.G.	Good	Fair	Poor
849	650	—	—	—	—

Schofield Military Model

Essentially the same as the Civilian Model except for its markings.

NIB	Exc.	V.G.	Good	Fair	Poor
849	650	—	—	—	—

Schofield Wells Fargo

Similar to the Military and Civilian Model but fitted with a 5" barrel. Calibers are the same.

NIB	Exc.	V.G.	Good	Fair	Poor
849	650	—	—	—	—

NOTE: For standard nickel finish add $100.00 and for custom nickel finish add $150.00.

Cimarron Arms reproduction of the 1873 Colt Single Action Army revolver comes in two basic configurations. First is the "Old Model" with the black powder frame screw-in cylinder pin retainer and circular bull's eye ejector head. Second is the "prewar Model" style frame with spring loaded cross-pin cylinder retainer and half moon ejector head. Old Model revolvers are available in authentic old style charcoal blue finish at an extra charge. Unless otherwise stated all of these Colt reproductions are produced by Uberti of Italy. Plain walnut grips are standard unless noted.

Model 1872 Open Top

Offered with 5.5" barrel or 7.5" barrel and chambered for the .38 Colt & S&W Special, .44 Colt & Russian, .45 S&W Schfield. Walnut grips. Choice of early Navy-style brass or later Army steel style grip frame. Finish is blue, charcoal blue, nickel, or original finish.

NIB	Exc.	V.G.	Good	Fair	Poor
469	350	—	—	—	—

General Custer 7th Cavairy Model

Has US military markings and is fitted with 7-1/2" barrel on an Old Model frame. Offered in .45 Long Colt only.

NIB	Exc.	V.G.	Good	Fair	Poor
499	375	—	—	—	—

Rough Rider U.S. Artillery Model

This version of the Old Model is fitted with a 5-1/2" barrel and chambered for .45 Long Colt.

NIB	Exc.	V.G.	Good	Fair	Poor
499	675	—	—	—	—

Frontier Six Shooter

This revolver is offered with a choice of 4-3/4", 5-1/2", or 7-1/2" barrel. It is chambered for .38 WCF, .357 Magnum, .44 WCF, .45 Long Colt, or .45LC with extra .45 ACP cylinder. For charcoal blue finish add $40.00 to NIB price. For extra .45 ACP cylinder add $30.00.

NIB	Exc.	V.G.	Good	Fair	Poor
469	350	—	—	—	—

Sheriff's Model w/No ejector

Fitted with a 3" barrel and chambered in .44 WCF or .45 Long Colt. Built on an Old Model frame.

NIB	Exc.	V.G.	Good	Fair	Poor
469	350	—	—	—	—

New Sheriff's Model w/ejector

This variation is fitted with a 3-1/2" barrel with ejector and is available in .357 Magnum, .44 WCF, .44 Special, and .45 Long Colt. For checkered walnut grips add $35.00.

NIB	Exc.	V.G.	Good	Fair	Poor
469	350	—	—	—	—

New Thunderer

The frame is based on the Old Model fitted with a bird's head grip with a choice of plain or checkered walnut grips. Offered in 3-1/2" or 4-3/4" barrel lengths. First offered for 1997 are barrel lengths in 5-1/2". Chambered for .357 Magnum, .44 WCF, .44 Special, or .45 Long Colt/.45 ACP. Add $35.00 for checkered grips.

NIB	Exc.	V.G.	Good	Fair	Poor
470	350	—	—	—	—

Thunderer Long Tom

Same as the New Thunderer except for a barrel length of 7.5".

NIB	Exc.	V.G.	Good	Fair	Poor
470	350	—	—	—	—

Lightning

Similar to the Thunderer but with a smaller grip frame. Chambered for the .38 Special cartridge and fitted with 3.5", 4.75", or 5.5" barrel. Finish is blue with case hardened frame.

NIB	Exc.	V.G.	Good	Fair	Poor
389	300	—	—	—	—

New Model P

Offered in either Old Model or prewar styles in a choice of 4-3/4", 5-1/2", or 7-1/2" barrel. Chambered for .32 WCF, .38 WCF, .44 WCF, .44 Special, or .45 Long Colt.

NIB	Exc.	V.G.	Good	Fair	Poor
469	350	—	—	—	—

A.P. Casey Model P U.S. Cavalry

Fitted with a 7-1/2" barrel and chambered for .45 Long Colt this revolver has US markings (APC) on an Old Model frame.

NIB	Exc.	V.G.	Good	Fair	Poor
499	375	—	—	—	—

Rinaldo A. Carr Model P U.S. Artillery

This is a Model P built on an Old Model frame and chambered for .45 Long Colt and fitted with a 5-1/2" barrel. US markings (RAC).

NIB	Exc.	V.G.	Good	Fair	Poor
499	375	—	—	—	—

Model P Jr.

Similar to the Model P but sized 20% smaller. Chambered for the .38 Special cartridge and fitted with 3.5" or 4.75" barrels. Blue with case hardened frame.

NIB	Exc.	V.G.	Good	Fair	Poor
389	300	—	—	—	—

Cimarron 1880 Frontier Flat Top

Introduced in 1998 this model is a target version of the Colt single action army. Rear sight is adjustable for windage and front adjustable for elevation. Offered with choice of 4.75", 5.5", or 7.5" barrels and chambered for .45 Colt, .45 Schofield, .44 WCF, and .357 Magnum. Choice of model P frame or prewar frame.

NIB	Exc.	V.G.	Good	Fair	Poor
480	350	—	—	—	—

Cimarron Bisley

Exact copy of the Colt Bisley with case hardened frame. Choice of 4.75", 5.5", or 7.5" barrels and calibers from .45 Colt, .45 Schofield, .44WCF, to .357 Magnum. Introduced in 1998.

NIB	Exc.	V.G.	Good	Fair	Poor
500	375	—	—	—	—

Cimarron Bisley Flat Top

Offered in the same barrel lengths and caliber as the standard Bisley with the addition of a windage adjustable rear sight and elevation adjustable front sight. Introduced in 1998.

NIB	Exc.	V.G.	Good	Fair	Poor
500	375	—	—	—	—

El Pistolero

This budget priced revolver was introduced in 1997 and features a brass backstrap and triggerguard with plain walnut grips. Offered in 4-3/4", 5-1/2", and 7-1/2" barrel lengths. Chambered for .45 Long Colt or .357 Magnum.

NIB	Exc.	V.G.	Good	Fair	Poor
340	250	—	—	—	—

NOTE: Cimarron also sells Uberti manufactured black powder Colt reproductions from the Patterson to the Model 1862 Pocket. For prices and specifications on these models see the Uberti section.

RICHARDS CONVERSIONS

Model 1851

Chambered for .38 Special, .38 Colt, and .44 Colt. Fitted with 5" or 7" barrels.

NIB	Exc.	V.G.	Good	Fair	Poor
550	450	—	—	—	—

Model 1861

Chambered for .38 Special, .38 Colt, and .44 Colt. Fitted with 5" or 7" barrels.

NIB	Exc.	V.G.	Good	Fair	Poor
550	450	—	—	—	—

Model 1860

Chambered for .38 Special, .38 Colt, and .44 Colt. Fitted with 5" or 7.5" barrels.

NIB	Exc.	V.G.	Good	Fair	Poor
550	450	—	—	—	—

Relic Finish

Offered by Cimarron as an extra cost item on its revolvers. This finish duplicates the old worn antique finish seen on many used historical Colts. Add $40 to the NIB price for any Cimarron revolver with this finish.

Relic finish

RIFLES

Henry Civil War Model

Offered in .44 WCF or .45 Long Colt with 24-1/4" barrel. For charcoal blue or white finish add $80.00.

NIB	Exc.	V.G.	Good	Fair	Poor
1050	850	—	—	—	—

Henry Civilian Model

Same as above but without military markings.

NIB	Exc.	V.G.	Good	Fair	Poor
1025	825	—	—	—	—

Model 1866 Yellowboy Carbine

Reproduction of the Winchester model 1866. Fitted with a 19" barrel and chambered for .38 Special, .44 WCF, or .45 Long Colt. For charcoal blue add $40.00.

NIB	Exc.	V.G.	Good	Fair	Poor
825	625	—	—	—	—

Model 1866 Yellowboy Rifle

Same as above but fitted with a 24-1/4" barrel. For charcoal blue add $40.00.

NIB	Exc.	V.G.	Good	Fair	Poor
835	625	—	—	—	—

Model 1873 Winchester Rifle

This lever action rifle is offered in .357 Magnum, .44 WCF, or .45 Long Colt. Fitted with a 24-1/4" barrel. For charcoal blue add $40.00. For pistol grip option add $140.00.

NIB	Exc.	V.G.	Good	Fair	Poor
950	775	—	—	—	—

Model 1873 Long Range Rifle

Similar to the Model 1873 but fitted with a 30" barrel. For pistol grip option add $140.00. For 1 of 1000 engraving option add $1,250.00.

NIB	Exc.	V.G.	Good	Fair	Poor
1000	800	—	—	—	—

Model 1873 Carbine

Same as the standard Model 1873 but fitted with a 19" barrel. Add $40.00 for charcoal blue.

NIB	Exc.	V.G.	Good	Fair	Poor
950	775	—	—	—	—

Model 1873 Short Rifle

This model is fitted with a 20" barrel. Add $40.00 for charcoal blue. Production ceased in 1998.

NIB	Exc.	V.G.	Good	Fair	Poor
950	775	—	—	—	—

Billy Dixon Model 1874 Sharps

A reproduction of the Model 1874 Sharps rifle chambered for the .45-70 cartridge. Fitted with a 32" tapered octagon barrel. Stock is hand checkered with oil finish walnut. Double set triggers standard. First introduced to the Cimarron product line in 1997.

NIB	Exc.	V.G.	Good	Fair	Poor
1500	1200	—	—	—	—

Remington Rolling Block

This Remington reproduction was introduced to Cimarron in 1997 and represents the Rolling Block Sporting rifle with 30" tapered octagon barrel and chambered for .45-70 cartridge. Hand checkered stock with satin finished walnut stock.

NIB	Exc.	V.G.	Good	Fair	Poor
1300	1000	—	—	—	—

Model 1885 High Wall

Reproduction of the Winchester Model 1885 chambered for .45-70, .40-65, or .38-65 cartridges. Fitted with a 30" barrel. Walnut stock and case colored receiver.

NIB	Exc.	V.G.	Good	Fair	Poor
995	800	—	—	—	—

Sharps Silhoutte

Offered in .45-70 or .40-65 calibers with 32" octagon barrel. Introduced in 1998.

NIB	Exc.	V.G.	Good	Fair	Poor
1095	850	—	—	—	—

Quigley Sharps Sporting Rifle

This rifle is chambered for the .45-70 or .45-120 caliber and fitted with a heavy 34" octagon barrel. Introduced in 1998.

NIB	Exc.	V.G.	Good	Fair	Poor
1495	1200	—	—	—	—

Springfield Trapdoor Carbine

Based on the famous Springfield design. Chambered for the .45-70.

NIB	Exc.	V.G.	Good	Fair	Poor
995	800	—	—	—	—

Springfield Trapdoor Officers Model

This is the Officers version of the Springfield Trapdoor model. Chambered for .45-70.

NIB	Exc.	V.G.	Good	Fair	Poor
1150	900	—	—	—	—

CLAPP, HOFFMAN & CO.
CLAPP, GATES & CO. RIFLES
Alamance, North Carolina

Clapp, Hoffman & Co. and its successor, Clapp, Gates & Co., both of Alamance (Guilford County), North Carolina, entered into several contracts with the state of North Carolina for the delivery of rifles. These contracts included an escalator clause that allowed the contractors to charge costs plus a percentage. Under their contracts, Clapp, Gates & Co. delivered 1,078 rifles in four varieties, before the state bought out the balance of the contract in 1864 due to the exorbitant prices caused by inflation.

Overall length: Types I, II, & III 51-1/4" to 52", Type IV varies between 46-1/2" and 51"; barrel length: Types I, II, & III 35-1/4" to 36", Type IV varies between 31-1/4" and 35-7/8"; caliber: Types I, II, & III .50, Type IV .577; markings: none. Despite the absence of makers marks, the Clapp, Gates & Co. products are readily distinguished by their part-round, part-octagonal (octagonal section on Types I to III, about 4" long, 4-3/4" to 5-1/2" on Type IV rifles) barrels having only a slightly raised bolster projecting from the upper right quarter. This small bolster accommodates the boxlock that distinguished the first 100 rifles produced. This gave way to a standard percussion lock on subsequent production, which required that the hammer bend sharply to the left to strike the cone. Type I and Type II rifles were adapted to a "footprint" saber bayonet lug on the right side of the barrel; Types III and IV also had a saber bayonet lug on the right side of the barrel but of the standard pattern. Types III and IV are distinguished by their caliber, the former being .50, the latter .577. Prices reflect Type II through IV production; Type I (while extant) has never been offered for sale and would presumably bring a significantly higher premium.

Exc.	V.G.	Good	Fair	Poor
—	—	25000	10000	2500

CLARK, F. H.
Memphis, Tennessee

Pocket Pistol

A .41 caliber single shot percussion pistol with a 3.5" to 5" barrel, German silver mounts and end cap, and the barrel is stamped "F.H. Clark & Co./Memphis." Manufactured in the 1850s and 1860s.

Exc.	V.G.	Good	Fair	Poor
—	—	3500	1500	500

CLASSIC DOUBLES
Tochigi City, Japan
Importer-Classic Doubles International
St. Louis, Missouri

Importer of the Japanese shotgun formerly imported by Winchester as the Model 101 and Model 23. These models were discontinued by Winchester in 1987.

Model 201 Classic

A 12 or 20 gauge boxlock double-barrel shotgun with 26" ventilated-rib barrels, screw-in choke tubes single selective trigger and automatic ejectors. Blued with checkered walnut stock and beavertail forearm.

NIB	Exc.	V.G.	Good	Fair	Poor
2400	1950	1700	1500	1250	900

Model 201 Small Bore Set

As above, with a smaller receiver and two sets of barrels chambered for 28 gauge and .410. The barrels are 28" in length.

NIB	Exc.	V.G.	Good	Fair	Poor
3850	3200	2750	2250	1750	1250

Model 101 Classic Field Grade I

A 12 or 20 gauge Over/Under shotgun with 25.5" or 28" ventilated-rib barrels, screw-in choke tubes, automatic ejectors and a single-selective trigger. Engraved, blued with checkered walnut stock.

NIB	Exc.	V.G.	Good	Fair	Poor
2150	1750	1500	1250	1000	700

Classic Field Grade II

As above, in 28 gauge and .410, highly engraved with a coin-finished receiver and a deluxe walnut stock with a round knob pistol grip and fleur-de-lis checkering.

NIB	Exc.	V.G.	Good	Fair	Poor
2500	2000	1750	1500	1250	900

Classic Sporter

As above, in 12 gauge only with 28" or 30" barrels, ventilated rib and screw-in choke tubes. The frame is coin-finished with light engraving and a matted upper surface to reduce glare. The stock is select walnut. This model was designed for "Sporting Clays."

NIB	Exc.	V.G.	Good	Fair	Poor
2250	1800	1500	1250	1000	700

Waterfowl Model

As above with 30" barrels having 3" chambers, vent rib, and screw-in choke tubes. The overall finish is a subdued matte with light engraving.

NIB	Exc.	V.G.	Good	Fair	Poor
1650	1350	1000	850	650	500

Classic Trap Over/Under

Designed for competition trap shooting with 30" or 32" barrels having a ventilated center and top rib, automatic ejectors, screw-in choke tubes, and a single trigger. Blued with light engraving and a walnut stock in straight or Monte Carlo style.

NIB	Exc.	V.G.	Good	Fair	Poor
2250	1750	1500	1250	1000	700

Classic Trap Single

As above, with a single 32" or 34" barrel.

NIB	Exc.	V.G.	Good	Fair	Poor
2250	1800	1500	1250	1000	700

Classic Trap Combo

As above, with a single barrel and a set of Over/ Under barrels.

NIB	Exc.	V.G.	Good	Fair	Poor
3000	2500	2000	1750	1250	1000

Classic Skeet

As above, with 27.5" barrels.

NIB	Exc.	V.G.	Good	Fair	Poor
2250	1750	1500	1250	1000	700

Classic Skeet 4 Gauge Set

As above, furnished with four sets of barrels chambered for 12, 20, 28 gauge, and .410.

NIB	Exc.	V.G.	Good	Fair	Poor
3700	3000	2500	2250	1850	1500

CLEMENT, CHAS.
Liege, Belgium

Model 1903

A 5.5mm Clement semiautomatic pistol.

Exc.	V.G.	Good	Fair	Poor
700	500	450	375	250

Model 1907

As above, but in 6.35mm and 7.65mm caliber.

Courtesy Orvel Reichert

Courtesy Orvel Reichert

Exc.	V.G.	Good	Fair	Poor
375	300	250	200	150

Model 1908
As above with grip frame and a repositioned magazine release.

Exc.	V.G.	Good	Fair	Poor
475	400	350	300	200

Model 1910
Redesigned version of the above with the barrel and housing all one piece. This unit is held in position by the triggerguard.

Courtesy Orvel Reichert

Exc.	V.G.	Good	Fair	Poor
475	400	350	300	250

Model 1912
A 6.35mm caliber semiautomatic rifle marked "Clement's Patent"; others, "Model 1912 Brevet 243839."

Exc.	V.G.	Good	Fair	Poor
750	650	550	400	325

American Model
Revolver copy of the Colt Police Positive. It was chambered for .38 caliber.

Exc.	V.G.	Good	Fair	Poor
300	250	200	125	90

CLERKE PRODUCTS
Santa Monica, California

Hi-Wall
A copy of the Winchester Model 1885 High Wall rifle with the action activated by a lever, and the receiver is case colored. This rifle is chambered for almost all of the modern calibers and features a 26" barrel and a walnut stock with a pistol grip and a schnabel forend. It was manufactured between 1972 and 1974.

NIB	Exc.	V.G.	Good	Fair	Poor
500	400	200	150	100	80

Deluxe Hi-Wall
As above, with a half-round/half-octagonal barrel, select walnut stock, and a recoil pad. It was manufactured between 1972 and 1974.

NIB	Exc.	V.G.	Good	Fair	Poor
600	450	250	200	150	100

CLIFTON ARMS
Grand Prairie, Texas
Although this company primarily is a manufacturer of composite laminated stocks, they will on special order build custom rifles. Due to the unique nature of each rifle, a qualified appraisal is necessary.

COBRAY INDUSTRIES
Atlanta, Georgia
S.W.D., Inc.

M-11 Pistol
A 9mm caliber semiautomatic pistol. It fires from the closed bolt and is made of steel stampings with a parkerized finish. It is patterned after, though a good deal smaller than, the Ingram Mac 10. It is currently out of production and difficult to accurately price. If purchase or sale is contemplated, please check local values.

Exc.	V.G.	Good	Fair	Poor
250	200	150	100	75

NOTE: Add $70 for stainless steel. Add $150 for pre-ban models.

M-12
Same as above but chambered for the .380 ACP cartridge.

Exc.	V.G.	Good	Fair	Poor
250	200	150	100	75

NOTE: Add $150 for pre-ban models.

TM-11 Carbine
As above in 9mm caliber, with a 16.25" shrouded barrel and a telescoping metal shoulder stock.

Exc.	V.G.	Good	Fair	Poor
350	250	200	150	100

TM-12 Carbine
As above but chambered for the .380 ACP cartridge.

Exc.	V.G.	Good	Fair	Poor
350	250	200	150	100

Terminator Shotgun
A single shot 12 or 20 gauge shotgun that fires from an open bolt position. The cocked bolt is released to slam home on the shell when the trigger is pulled. The 18" barrel is cylinder bored. There is a telescoping wire stock and the finish is parkerized.

Exc.	V.G.	Good	Fair	Poor
125	100	80	60	40

COCHRAN TURRET
C. B. Allen
Springfield, Massachusetts

Under Hammer Turret Rifle
A .36 or .40 caliber percussion radial cylinder rifle with 31" or 32" octagonal barrels and walnut stocks. The barrel marked "Cochrans/Many/Chambered/&/Non Recoil/Rifle" and the top strap "C.B. Allen / Springfield." These rifles were produced in the variations listed below. Manufactured during the late 1830s and 1840s.

1st Type
Fitted with a circular top strap secured by two screws. Serial numbered from 1 to approximately 30.

Exc.	V.G.	Good	Fair	Poor
—	—	10500	4000	1250

2nd Type
Fitted with a rectangular hinged top strap, the locking catch of which serves as the rear sight. Serial numbered from approximately 31 to 155.

Exc.	V.G.	Good	Fair	Poor
—	—	9000	3500	1500

3rd Type
As above, with a smaller hammer and a plain triggerguard.

Exc.	V.G.	Good	Fair	Poor
—	—	9000	3500	1500

Pistol
Action similar to above with 4" to 7" barrels.

Exc.	V.G.	Good	Fair	Poor
—	—	14000	6000	2000

CODY, MICHAEL & SONS
Nashville, Tennessee

Received a contract with the State of Tennessee for "Mississippi" rifles with brass patchboxes in late 1861. Barrel length 36"; caliber .54. Cody often used reworked Model 1817 Rifle barrels and sporting pattern single screw lockplates. Rifles are unmarked except for large engraved serial number on top of breech plug tang.

Prospective purchasers are strongly advised to secure a qualified appraisal prior to acquisition.

Exc.	V.G.	Good	Fair	Poor
—	—	22500	9000	1500

COFER, T. W.
Portsmouth, Virginia

Cofer Navy Revolver
A .36 caliber spur trigger percussion revolver with a 7.5" octagonal barrel and 6-shot cylinder. The top strap is marked "T.W. Cofer's/Patent." and the barrel "Portsmouth, Va." This revolver was manufactured in limited quantities during the Civil War. Prospective purchasers are advised to secure a qualified appraisal prior to acquisition.

Exc.	V.G.	Good	Fair	Poor
—	—	100000	35000	5000

COGSWELL
London, England

Cogswell Pepperbox Pistol
A .47 caliber 6-shot percussion pepperbox with case hardened barrels, German silver frame and walnut grips. Normally marked "B. Cogswell, 224 Strand, London" and "Improved Revolving Pistol."

Exc.	V.G.	Good	Fair	Poor
—	—	3000	1250	750

COGSWELL & HARRISON, LTD.
London, England
See—British Double Guns

COLTS PATENTS ARMS MANUFACTURING COMPANY
Hartford, Connecticut

Of all the American firearms manufacturers, perhaps the best known is the Colt Company. Indeed, this recognition is so widespread that some popular writers have used the name Colt to indicate a revolver or semiautomatic pistol.

Originally founded in 1836 as the Patent Arms Manufacturing Company (Paterson, New Jersey) to produce percussion revolvers designed by Samuel Colt, the concern was initially a failure. However, the company formed in 1847 to manufacture revolvers of an improved form was a success. Even after Samuel Colt's death in 1862, his company thrived. With the introduction of the Model 1873 Single Action Army Revolver, the myth of the Colt became part of the American legend for that revolver was to be used by adventurers, cowboys, farmers, soldiers and a host of others for better than 70 years.

In 1897 the Colt's Patent Fire Arms Manufacturing Company entered into an agreement with John M. Browning to produce self-loading pistols of his design. One result of this association was to be the .45 caliber Model 1911 Semiautomatic Pistol, which was the standard issue sidearm of the U.S. Armed Forces from 1911 to the late 1980s.

Because of their romance, form and variation, Colt revolvers, pistols and longarms are most sought after by collectors. Due to this, however, caution should be exercised and the opinion of experts should be sought when the purchase of rare or pristine examples is contemplated.

COLT PATERSON MODELS
Paterson, New Jersey

Pocket or Baby Paterson Model No. 1

The Paterson was the first production revolver manufactured by Colt. It was first made in 1837. The Model 1 or Pocket Model is the most diminutive of the Paterson line. The revolver is serial numbered in its own range, #1 through #500. The numbers are not visible without dismantling the revolver. The barrel lengths run from 1.75" to 4.75". The standard model had no attached loading lever. The chambering is .28 caliber percussion and it holds five shots. The finish is all blued, and the grips are varnished walnut. It has a roll-engraved cylinder scene, and the barrel is stamped "Patent Arms Mfg. Co. Paterson N.J.Colt's Pt."

Exc.	V.G.	Good	Fair	Poor
—	—	30000	12500	—

Belt Model Paterson No. 2

The Belt Model Paterson is a larger revolver with a straight-grip and an octagonal barrel that is 2.5" to 5.5" in length. It is chambered for .31 caliber percussion and holds five shots.

The finish is all blued, with varnished walnut grips and no attached loading lever. It has a roll-engraved cylinder scene, and the barrel is stamped "Patent Arms Mfg. Co. Paterson N.J. Colt's Pt." The serial number range is #1-#850 and is shared with the #3 Belt Model. It was made from 1837-1840.

Courtesy Buffalo Bill Historical Center, Cody, Wyoming

Exc.	V.G.	Good	Fair	Poor
—	—	30000	12500	—

Belt Model Paterson No. 3

This revolver is quite similar to the Model #2 except that the grips are curved outward at the bottom to form a more hand-filling configuration. They are serial numbered in the same #1-#850 range. Some attached loading levers have been noted on this model, but they are extremely rare and would add approximately 35 percent to the value.

Exc.	V.G.	Good	Fair	Poor
—	—	35000	12500	—

Ehlers Model Pocket Paterson

John Ehlers was a major stockholder and treasurer of the Patent Arms Mfg. Co. when it went bankrupt. He seized the assets and inventory. These revolvers were Pocket Model Patersons that were not finished at the time. Ehlers had them finished and marketed them. They had an attached loading lever, and the abbreviation "Mfg Co." was deleted from the barrel stamping. There were 500 revolvers involved in the Ehlers variation totally, and they were produced from 1840-1843.

Exc.	V.G.	Good	Fair	Poor
—	—	30000	12000	—

Ehlers Belt Model Paterson
The same specifications apply to this larger revolver as they do to the Ehlers Pocket Model. It falls within the same 500 revolver involvement and is rare.

Exc.	V.G.	Good	Fair	Poor
—	—	30000	12000	—

Texas Paterson Model No. 5
This is the largest and most sought after of the Paterson models. It is also known as the Holster Model. It has been verified as actually seeing use by both the military and civilians on the American frontier. It is chambered for .36 caliber percussion, holds five shots, and has an octagonal barrel that ranges from 4" to 12" in length. It has been observed with and without the attached loading lever, but those with it are rare. The finish is blued, with a case-colored hammer. The grips are varnished walnut. The cylinder is roll-engraved; and the barrel is stamped "Patent Arms Mfg. Co. Paterson, N.J. Colts Pt." Most Texas Patersons are well used and have a worn appearance. One in excellent or V.G. condition would be highly prized. A verified military model would be worth a great deal more than standard, so qualified appraisal would be essential. The serial number range is #1-#1000, and they were manufactured from 1838-1840. The attached loading lever brings approximately a 25 percent premium.

Exc.	V.G.	Good	Fair	Poor
—	—	85000	35000	—

COLT REVOLVING LONG GUNS 1837-1847

First Model Ring Lever Rifle
This was actually the first firearm manufactured by Colt; the first revolver appeared a short time later. There were 200 of the First Models made in 1837 and 1838. The octagonal barrel of the First Model is 32" long and browned, while the rest of the finish is blued. The stock is varnished walnut with a cheekpiece inlaid with Colt's trademark. The ring lever located in front of the frame is pulled to rotate the 8-shot cylinder and cock the hammer. The rifle is chambered for .34, .36, .38, .40, and .44 caliber percussion. The cylinder is roll-engraved, and the barrel is stamped "Colt's Patent/Patent Arms Mfg. Co., Paterson, N. Jersey." This model has a top strap over the cylinder. They were made both with and without an attached loading lever. The latter is worth approximately 10 percent more.

Courtesy Butterfield & Butterfield, San Francisco, California

Exc.	V.G.	Good	Fair	Poor
—	—	30000	12500	—

Second Model Ring Lever Rifle
This model is quite similar in appearance to the First Model. Its function is identical. The major difference is the absence of the top strap over the cylinder. It had no trademark stamped on the cheekpiece. The Second Model is offered with a 28" and a 32" octagonal barrel and is chambered for .44 caliber percussion, holding 8 shots. There were approximately 500 produced from 1838-1841. The presence of an attached cheekpiece would add approximately 10 percent to the value.

Courtesy Butterfield & Butterfield, San Francisco, California

Exc.	V.G.	Good	Fair	Poor
—	—	25000	9500	—

Model 1839 Carbine
This model has no ring but features an exposed hammer for cocking and rotating the 6-shot cylinder. It is chambered for .525 smoothbore and comes standard with a 24" round barrel. Other barrel lengths have been noted. The finish is blued, with a browned barrel and a varnished walnut stock. The cylinder is roll-engraved, and the barrel is stamped "Patent Arms Mfg. Co. Paterson, N.J.-Colt's Pt." There were 950 manufactured from 1838-1841. Later variations of this model are found with the attached loading lever standard, and earlier models without one would bring approximately 25 percent additional. There were 360 purchased by the military and stamped "WAT" on the stock. These would be worth twice what a standard model would bring. Anyone considering the purchase of one would be well advised to proceed with extreme caution.

Courtesy Butterfield & Butterfield, San Francisco, California

Exc.	V.G.	Good	Fair	Poor
—	—	25000	9500	—

Model 1839 Shotgun
This model is quite similar in appearance to the 1839 Carbine. It is chambered for 16 gauge and holds six shots. It has a Damascus pattern barrel, and the most notable difference is a 3.5" (instead of a 2.5") long cylinder. There were only 225 of these made from 1839-1841. The markings are the same as on the Carbine.

Courtesy Butterfield & Butterfield, San Francisco, California

Exc.	V.G.	Good	Fair	Poor
—	—	17500	7500	—

Model 1839/1850 Carbine

In 1848 Colt acquired a number of Model 1839 Carbines (approximately 40) from the state of Rhode Island. In an effort to make them marketable they were refinished and the majority fitted with plain cylinders (brightly polished) having integral ratchets around the arbor hole.

Barrel length 24"; caliber .525; barrel browned; cylinder polished; frame blued; furniture case hardened; walnut stock varnished.

Exc.	V.G.	Good	Fair	Poor
—	—	17500	7500	—

Model 1854 Russian Contract Musket

In 1854 Colt purchased a large number of U.S. Model 1822 flintlock muskets that the company altered to percussion cap ignition and rifled. The reworked muskets are dated 1854 on the barrel tang and at the rear of the lockplate. In most instances the original manufactory marks, such as Springfield or Harpers Ferry at the rear of the lockplate, have been removed, while the U.S. and eagle between the hammer and bolster remain. The percussion nipple bolster is marked COLT'S PATENT. Some examples have been noted with the date 1858.

Barrel length 42"; caliber .69; lock and furniture burnished bright; walnut stock oil finished.

Exc.	V.G.	Good	Fair	Poor
4000	3000	2000	1500	750

Breech loading examples made in two styles are also known. Production of this variation is believed to have only taken place on an experimental basis.

Exc.	V.G.	Good	Fair	Poor
6500	6000	5000	2500	1000

COLT WALKER-DRAGOON MODELS
Hartford, Connecticut

Walker Model Revolver

The Walker is a massive revolver. It weighs 4 lbs., 9 oz. and has a 9" part-round/part-octagonal barrel. The cylinder holds six shots and is chambered for .44 caliber percussion. There were 1,000 Walker Colts manufactured in 1847, and nearly all of them saw extremely hard use. Originally this model had a roll-engraved cylinder, military inspection marks, and barrel stamping that read "Address Saml. Colt-New York City." Practically all examples noted have had these markings worn or rusted beyond recognition. Because the Walker is perhaps the most desirable and sought-after Colt from a collector's standpoint and because of the extremely high value of a Walker in any condition, qualified appraisal is definitely recommended. These revolvers were serial numbered A, B, C, and D Company 1-220, and E Company 1-120.

Courtesy Buffalo Bill Historical Center, Cody, Wyoming

Exc.	V.G.	Good	Fair	Poor
—	—	300000	150000	50000

Civilian Walker Revolver

This model is identical to the military model but has no martial markings. They are found serial numbered 1001 through 1100.

Exc.	V.G.	Good	Fair	Poor
—	—	300000	150000	50000

Whitneyville Hartford Dragoon

This is a large, 6-shot, .44 caliber percussion revolver. It has a 7.5" part-round/part-octagonal barrel. The frame, hammer, and loading lever are case colored. The remainder is blued, with a brass triggerguard and varnished walnut grips. There were only 240 made in late 1847. The serial numbers run from 1100-1340. This model is often referred to as a Transitional Walker. Some of the parts used in its manufacture were left over from the Walker production run. This model has a roll-engraved cylinder scene, and the barrel is stamped "Address Saml. Colt New York-City." This is an extremely rare model, and much care should be taken to authenticate any contemplated acquisitions.

Exc.	V.G.	Good	Fair	Poor
—	—	45000	35000	18500

Walker Replacement Dragoon

This extremely rare Colt (300 produced) is sometimes referred to as the "Fluck" in memory of the gentleman who first identified it as a distinct and separate model. They were produced by Colt as replacements to the military for Walkers that were no longer fit for service due to mechanical failures. They were large, 6-shot, .44 caliber percussion revolvers with 7.5" part-round/part-octagonal barrels. Serial numbers ran from 2216 to 2515. The frame, hammer, and loading lever are case-colored; the remainder, blued, The grips, which are longer than other Dragoons and similar to the Walkers, are of varnished walnut and bear the inspectors mark "WAT" inside an oval cartouche on one side and the letters "JH" on the other. The frame is stamped "Colt's/ Patent/U.S." The letter "P" appears on various parts of the gun. This is another model that should definitely be authenticated before any acquisition is made.

Exc.	V.G.	Good	Fair	Poor
—	—	35000	25000	6000

First Model Dragoon

Another large, 6-shot, .44 caliber percussion revolver. It has a 7.5" part-round/part-octagonal barrel. The frame, hammer, and loading lever are case colored; the remainder, blued with a brass grip frame and square backed triggerguard. The triggerguard is silver-plated on the Civilian Model only. Another distinguishing feature on the First Model is the oval cylinder stop notches. The serial number range is 1341-8000. There were approximately 5,000 made. The cylinder is roll-engraved; and the barrel stampings read "Address Saml. Colt, New York City." "Colt's Patent" appears on the frame. On Military Models the letters "U.S." also appear on the frame.

Military Model

Exc.	V.G.	Good	Fair	Poor
—	65000	35000	20000	3500

Civilian Model

Exc.	V.G.	Good	Fair	Poor
—	45000	25000	18000	3000

Second Model Dragoon

Most of the improvements that distinguish this model from the First Model are internal and not readily apparent. The most obvious external change is the rectangular cylinder-stop notches. This model is serial numbered from 8000-10700, for a total production of approximately 2,700 revolvers manufactured in 1850 and 1851. There is a Civilian Model, a Military Model, and an extremely rare variation that was issued to the militias of New Hampshire and Massachusetts (marked "MS."). Once again, caution is advised in acquisition.

Civilian Model

Exc.	V.G.	Good	Fair	Poor
—	55000	35000	25000	3500

Military Model

Exc.	V.G.	Good	Fair	Poor
—	60000	45000	30000	3000

Militia Model

Exc.	V.G.	Good	Fair	Poor
—	55000	45000	30000	3000

Third Model Dragoon

This is the most common of all the large Colt percussion revolvers. Approximately 10,500 were manufactured from 1851 through 1861. It is quite similar in appearance to the Second Model, and the most obvious external difference is the round triggerguard. The Third Model Dragoon was the first Colt revolver available with a detachable shoulder stock. There are three basic types of stocks, and all are quite rare as only 1,250 were produced. There are two other major variations we will note—the "C.L." Dragoon, which was a militia-issued model and is rare, and the late-issue model with an 8" barrel. These are found over serial number 18000, and only 50 were produced. Qualified appraisal should be secured before acquisition as many fakes abound.

Courtesy Buffalo Bill Historical Center, Cody, Wyoming

Civilian Model

Exc.	V.G.	Good	Fair	Poor
55000	45000	25000	15000	2500

Military Model

Exc.	V.G.	Good	Fair	Poor
—	45000	27500	17500	3000

Shoulder Stock Cut Revolvers

Exc.	V.G.	Good	Fair	Poor
50000	40000	27500	17500	2500

Shoulder Stocks

Exc.	V.G.	Good	Fair	Poor
15000	12000	8000	4000	2000

C.L. Dragoon (Hand Engraved, Not Stamped)

Exc.	V.G.	Good	Fair	Poor
—	55000	35000	15000	2500

8" Barrel Late Issue

Exc.	V.G.	Good	Fair	Poor
55000	45000	35000	25000	4000

Hartford English Dragoon

This is a variation of the Third Model Dragoon. The only notable differences are the British proofmarks and the distinct #1-#700 serial number range. Other than these two features, the description given for the Third Model would apply. These revolvers were manufactured in Hartford but were finished at Colt's London factory from 1853-1857. Some bear the hand-engraved barrel marking "Col. Colt London." Many of the English Dragoons were elaborately engraved, and individual appraisal would be a must.

Two hundred revolvers came back to America in 1861 to be used in the Civil War. As with all the early Colts, caution is advised in acquisition.

Exc.	V.G.	Good	Fair	Poor
45000	35000	20000	12000	3500

Model 1848 Baby Dragoon

This is a small, 5-shot, .31 caliber percussion revolver. It has an octagonal barrel in lengths of 3", 4", 5", and 6". Most were made without an attached loading lever, although some with loading levers have been noted. The frame, hammer, and loading lever (when present) are case colored; the barrel and cylinder, blued. The grip frame and triggerguard are silver-plated brass. There were approximately 15,500 manufactured between 1847 and 1850. The serial range is between #1-#5500. The barrels are stamped "Address Saml. Colt/New York City." Some have been noted with the barrel address inside brackets. The frame is marked "Colt's/Patent." The first 10,000 revolvers have the Texas Ranger/Indian roll-engraved cylinder scene; the later guns the stagecoach holdup scene. This is a popular model, and many fakes have been noted.

Attached Loading Lever add 15%.

Courtesy Butterfield & Butterfield, San Francisco, California

Texas Ranger/Indian Scene

Exc.	V.G.	Good	Fair	Poor
35000	20000	12000	6500	2000

Stagecoach Holdup Scene

Exc.	V.G.	Good	Fair	Poor
35000	20000	12000	6500	2000

Model 1849 Pocket Revolver

This is a small, either 5- or 6-shot, .31 caliber percussion revolver. It has an octagonal barrel 3", 4", 5", or 6" in length. Most had loading gates, but some did not. The frame, hammer, and loading lever are case colored; the cylinder and barrel are blued. The grip frame and round triggerguard are made of brass and are silver plated. There are both large and small triggerguard variations noted. This is the most plentiful of all the Colt percussion revolvers, with approximately 325,000 manufactured over a 23-year period, 1850-1873. There are over 200 variations of this model, and one should consult an expert for individual appraisals. There are many fine publications specializing in the field of Colt percussion revolvers that would be helpful in the identification of the variations. The values represented here are for the standard model.

Courtesy Butterfield & Butterfield, San Francisco, California

Exc.	V.G.	Good	Fair	Poor
5500	4000	1800	1200	300

London Model 1849 Pocket Revolver

Identical in configuration to the standard 1849 Pocket Revolver, the London-made models have a higher quality finish and their own serial number range, #1-#11000. They were manufactured from 1853 through 1857. They feature a roll-engraved cylinder scene, and the barrels are stamped "Address Col. Colt/London." The first 265 revolvers, known as early models, have brass grip frames and small round triggerguards. They are quite rare and worth approximately 50 per-

cent more than the standard model that has a steel grip frame and large oval triggerguard.

Exc.	V.G.	Good	Fair	Poor
5000	3500	1600	1000	300

Model 1851 Navy Revolver

This is undoubtedly the most popular revolver Colt produced in the medium size and power range. It is a 6-shot, .36-caliber percussion revolver with a 7.5" octagonal barrel. It has an attached loading lever. The basic model has a case colored frame hammer, and loading lever, with silver-plated brass grip frame and triggerguard. The grips are varnished walnut. Colt manufactured approximately 215,000 of these fine revolvers between 1850 and 1873. The basic Navy features a roll-engraved cylinder scene of a battle between the navies of Texas and Mexico. There are three distinct barrel stampings—serial number 1-74000, "Address Saml. Colt New York City"; serial number 74001-101000 "Address Saml. Colt. Hartford, Ct."; and serial number 101001-215000 "Address Saml. Colt New York U.S. America." The left side of the frame is stamped "Colt's/Patent" on all variations. This model is also available with a detached shoulder stock, and values for the stocks today are nearly as high as for the revolver itself. Careful appraisal should be secured before purchase. The number of variations within the 1851 Navy model designation makes it necessary to read specialized text available on the subject. We furnish values for the major variations but again caution potential purchasers to acquire appraisals.

Courtesy Milwaukee Public Museum, Milwaukee, Wisconsin

Square Back Triggerguard 1st Model Serial #1-1000

Exc.	V.G.	Good	Fair	Poor
—	—	35000	25000	5500

Square Back Triggerguard 2nd Model Serial #1001-4200

Exc.	V.G.	Good	Fair	Poor
—	35000	25000	10000	2500

Small Round Triggerguard Serial #4201-85000

Exc.	V.G.	Good	Fair	Poor
18000	14000	5000	2500	500

Large Round Triggerguard Serial #85001-215000

Exc.	V.G.	Good	Fair	Poor
15000	8000	4000	2200	500

Martial Model

"U.S." stamped on the left side of frame; inspector's marks and cartouche on the grips.

Exc.	V.G.	Good	Fair	Poor
40000	25000	12000	4000	1000

Shoulder Stock Variations

1st and 2nd Model Revolver cut for stock only. An expert appraisal is recommended prior to a sale of these very rare variations.

Stock Only

Exc.	V.G.	Good	Fair	Poor
3500	2500	2000	1750	1250

3rd Model Cut For Stock
Revolver Only

Exc.	V.G.	Good	Fair	Poor
25000	15000	8000	2500	800

Stock

Exc.	V.G.	Good	Fair	Poor
2500	2000	1750	1250	850

London Model 1851 Navy Revolver
These revolvers are physically similar to the U.S.-made model with the exception of the barrel address, which reads "Address Col. Colt. London." There are also British proofmarks stamped on the barrel and cylinder. There were 42,000 made between 1853 and 1857. They have their own serial-number range, #1-#42,000. There are two major variations of the London Navy, and again a serious purchaser would be well advised to seek qualified appraisal as fakes have been noted.

1st Model
Serial #1-#2,000 with a small round brass triggerguard and grip frame. Squareback guard worth a 40 percent premium.

Exc.	V.G.	Good	Fair	Poor
10000	7000	4000	2500	700

2nd Model
Serial #2,001-#42,000, steel grip frame, and large round triggerguard.

Exc.	V.G.	Good	Fair	Poor
8000	6000	3000	1800	600

A Colt Model 1851 London Navy 2nd Model was sold at auction for $10,637. All matching. Condition is 30% original blue with 90% case colors and 95% original varnish. Cased with accessories.
Amoskeag Auction Co. Inc., August 2001

Hartford Manufactured Variation
Serial numbers in the 42,000 range.

Exc.	V.G.	Good	Fair	Poor
25000	16000	4500	3000	600

COLT SIDE HAMMER MODELS

Model 1855 Side Hammer "Root" Pocket Revolver
The "Root", as it is popularly known, was the only solid-frame revolver Colt ever made. It has a spur trigger and walnut grips, and the hammer is mounted on the right side of the frame. The standard finish is a case colored frame, hammer, and loading lever, with the barrel and cylinder blued. It is chambered for both .28 caliber and .31 caliber percussion. Each caliber has its own serial number range-#1-#30000 for the .28 caliber and #1-#14000 for the .31 caliber. The model consists of seven basic variations, and the serious student should avail himself of the fine publications dealing with this model in depth. Colt produced the Side Hammer Root from 1855-1870.

Models 1 and 1A Serial #1-#384
3.5" octagonal barrel, .28 caliber, roll-engraved cylinder, Hartford barrel address without pointing hand.

Exc.	V.G.	Good	Fair	Poor
8500	6000	5000	3500	1200

Courtesy Milwaukee Public Museum, Milwaukee, Wisconsin

Model 2 Serial #476-#25000
Same as Model 1 with pointing hand barrel address.

Exc.	V.G.	Good	Fair	Poor
4000	3000	1800	1200	500

Model 3 Serial #25001-#30000
Same as the Model 2 with a full fluted cylinder.

Exc.	V.G.	Good	Fair	Poor
4000	3000	1800	1200	500

Model 3A and 4 Serial #1-#2400
.31 caliber, 3.5" barrel, Hartford address, full fluted cylinder.

Exc.	V.G.	Good	Fair	Poor
5000	4000	2500	1500	600

Model 5 Serial #2401-#8000
.31 caliber, 3.5" round barrel, address "Col. Colt New York."

Exc.	V.G.	Good	Fair	Poor
5000	4000	2500	1500	600

Model 5A Serial #2401-#8000
Same as Model 5 with a 4.5" barrel.

Courtesy Milwaukee Public Museum, Milwaukee, Wisconsin

Exc.	V.G.	Good	Fair	Poor
6500	5200	3200	1600	600

Models 6 and 6A Serial #8001-#11074

Same as Model 5 and 5A with roll-engraved cylinder scene.

Exc.	V.G.	Good	Fair	Poor
6000	5000	3000	1500	600

Models 7 and 7A Serial #11075-#14000

Same as Models 6 and 6A with a screw holding in the cylinder pin.

Exc.	V.G.	Good	Fair	Poor
6500	5000	3500	2200	800

COLT SIDE HAMMER LONG GUNS

1855 Sporting Rifle, 1st Model

This is a 6-shot revolving rifle chambered for .36 caliber percussion. It comes with a 21", 24", 27", or 30" round barrel that is part octagonal where it joins the frame. The stock is walnut with either an oil or a varnish finish. The frame, hammer, and loading lever are case colored; the rest of the metal, blued. The hammer is on the right side of the frame. The 1st Model has no forend, and an oiling device is attached to the barrel underlug. The triggerguard has two spur-like projections in front and in back of the bow. The roll-engraved cylinder scene depicts a hunter shooting at five deer and is found only on this model. The standard stampings are " Colt's Pt./1856" and "Address S. Colt Hartford, Ct. U.S.A."

Early Model

Low serial numbers with a hand-engraved barrel marking "Address S. Colt Hartford, U.S.A."

Exc.	V.G.	Good	Fair	Poor
—	—	12500	3500	1000

Production Model

Exc.	V.G.	Good	Fair	Poor
—	—	9500	3000	1000

1855 1st Model Carbine

Identical to the 1st Model Rifle but offered with a 15" and 18" barrel.

Courtesy Milwaukee Public Museum, Milwaukee, Wisconsin

Exc.	V.G.	Good	Fair	Poor
—	—	9500	3000	1000

1855 Half Stock Sporting Rifle

Although this rifle is quite similar in appearance and finish to the 1st Model, there are some notable differences. It features a walnut forend that protrudes halfway down the barrel. There are two types of triggerguards—a short projectionless one or a long model with a graceful scroll. There is a 6-shot model chambered for .36 or .44 caliber or a 5-shot model chambered for .56 caliber. The cylinder is fully fluted. The markings are "Colt's Pt/1856" and "Address Col. Colt/Hartford Ct. U.S.A." There were approximately 1,500 manufactured between 1857 and 1864.

Courtesy Milwaukee Public Museum, Milwaukee, Wisconsin

Exc.	V.G.	Good	Fair	Poor
—	—	8500	3000	1000

1855 Full Stock Military Rifle

This model holds 6 shots in its .44 caliber chambering and 5 shots when chambered for .56 caliber. It is another side hammer revolving rifle that resembles the Half Stock model. The barrels are round and part-octagonal where they join the frame. They come in lengths of 21", 24", 27", 31", and 37". The hammer and loading lever are case colored; the rest of the metal parts, blued. The walnut buttstock and full length forend are oil finished. The cylinder is fully fluted. Military models have provisions for affixing a bayonet and military-style sights and bear the "U.S." martial mark on examples that were actually issued to the military. The standard stampings found on this model are "Colt's Pt/1856" and "Address Col. Colt Hartford, Ct. U.S.A." There were an estimated 9,300 manufactured between 1856 and 1864.

Courtesy Milwaukee Public Museum, Milwaukee, Wisconsin

Courtesy Milwaukee Public Museum, Milwaukee, Wisconsin

Martially Marked Models

Exc.	V.G.	Good	Fair	Poor
—	—	20000	7500	2000

Without Martial Markings

Exc.	V.G.	Good	Fair	Poor
—	—	7500	3500	1000

1855 Full Stock Sporting Rifle

This model is similar in appearance to the Military model, with these notable exceptions. There is no provision for attaching a bayonet, there are no sling swivels, and it has sporting-style sights. The buttplate is crescent shaped. This model has been noted chambered for .56 caliber in a 5-shot version and chambered for .36, .40, .44, and .50 caliber in the 6-shot variation. They are quite scarce in .40 and .50 caliber and will bring a 10 percent premium. The standard markings are "Colt's Pt/1856" and "Address Col. Colt/Hartford Ct. U.S.A." Production on this model was quite limited (several hundred at most) between the years 1856 and 1864.

Exc.	V.G.	Good	Fair	Poor
—	—	9500	4000	1000

Model 1855 Revolving Carbine

This model is similar in appearance to the 1855 Military Rifle. The barrel lengths of 15", 18", and 21" plus the absence of a forend make the standard Carbine Model readily identifiable. The markings are the same. Approximately 4,400 were manufactured between 1856 and 1864.

Exc.	V.G.	Good	Fair	Poor
—	—	8500	3500	1000

Model 1855 Artillery Carbine
Identical to the standard carbine but chambered for .56 caliber only, it has a 24" barrel, full-length walnut forend, and a bayonet lug.

Exc.	V.G.	Good	Fair	Poor
—	—	14000	4000	1200

Model 1855 British Carbine
This is a British-proofed version with barrel lengths of up to 30". It has a brass triggerguard and buttplate and is chambered for .56 caliber only. This variation is usually found in the 10000-12000 serial number range.

Exc.	V.G.	Good	Fair	Poor
—	—	8000	3250	1000

Model 1855 Revolving Shotgun
This model very much resembles the Half Stock Sporting Rifle but was made with a 27", 30", 33", and 36" smoothbore barrel. It has a 5-shot cylinder chambered for .60 or .75 caliber (20 or 10 gauge). This model has a case colored hammer and loading lever; the rest of the metal is blued, with an occasional browned barrel noted. The buttstock and forend are of walnut, either oil or varnish-finished. This model has no rear sight and a small triggerguard with the caliber stamped on it. Some have been noted with the large scroll triggerguard; these would add 10 percent to the value. The rarest shotgun variation would be a full stocked version in either gauge, and qualified appraisal would be highly recommended. This model is serial numbered in its own range, #1-#1100. They were manufactured from 1860-1863.

Courtesy Amoskeag Auction Company

.60 Caliber (20 gauge)

Exc.	V.G.	Good	Fair	Poor
—	—	6500	3000	1000

.75 Caliber (10 gauge)

Exc.	V.G.	Good	Fair	Poor
—	—	6500	3000	1000

Model 1861 Single Shot Rifled Musket
With the advent of the Civil War, the army of the Union seriously needed military arms. Colt was given a contract to supply 112,500 1861-pattern percussion single shot muskets. Between 1861 and 1865, 75,000 were delivered. They have 40" rifled barrels chambered for .58 caliber. The musket is equipped with military sights, sling swivels, and a bayonet lug. The metal finish is bright steel, and the stock is oil-finished walnut. Military inspector's marks are found on all major parts. "VP" over an eagle is stamped on the breech along with a date. The Colt address and a date are stamped on the lockplate. A large number of these rifles were altered to the Snyder breech loading system for the Bey of Egypt.

Courtesy Milwaukee Public Museum, Milwaukee, Wisconsin

Production Model

Exc.	V.G.	Good	Fair	Poor
—	4000	1800	750	450

PERCUSSION REVOLVERS
Model 1860 Army Revolver
This model was the third most produced of the Colt percussion handguns. It was the primary revolver used by the Union Army during the Civil War. Colt delivered 127,156 of these revolvers

to be used during those hostilities. This is a 6-shot .44 caliber percussion revolver. It has either a 7.5" or 8" round barrel with an attached loading lever. The frame, hammer, and loading lever are case colored; the barrel and cylinder are blued. The triggerguard and front strap are brass, and the backstrap is blued steel. The grips are one-piece walnut. The early models have the barrels stamped "Address Saml. Colt Hartford Ct." Later models are stamped "Address Col. Saml. Colt New-York U.S. America." "Colt's/Patent" is stamped on the left side of the frame; ".44 Cal.," on the triggerguard. The cylinder is roll engraved with the naval battle scene. There were a total of 200,500 1860 Army Revolvers manufactured between 1860 and 1873.

Martial Marked Model

Exc.	V.G.	Good	Fair	Poor
35000	20000	6500	3500	900

Civilian Model

This model is found in either 3-or-4 screw variations and it may or may not be cut for a shoulder stock. Civilian models are usually better finished.

Courtesy Milwaukee Public Museum, Milwaukee, Wisconsin

Exc.	V.G.	Good	Fair	Poor
20000	10000	5000	3000	800

Full Fluted Cylinder Model

Approximately 4,000 Army's were made with full fluted cylinders. They appear in the first 8,000 serial numbers.

Courtesy Milwaukee Public Museum, Milwaukee, Wisconsin

Exc.	V.G.	Good	Fair	Poor
40000	30000	15000	7000	2000

Courtesy Milwaukee Public Museum, Milwaukee, Wisconsin

A shoulder stock for a Colt Model 1860 Army revolver was sold at auction for $4,600. Condition was excellent. 95% silver plated finish.
Butterfield & Butterfield, August 1999

Courtesy Milwaukee Public Museum, Milwaukee, Wisconsin

Shoulder Stock 2nd Type (Fluted Cylinder Model)
NOTE: Expert appraisals should be acquired before a sale. These are rare accouterments.

Shoulder Stock 3rd Type (Standard Model)
NOTE: Expert appraisals should be acquired before a sale. These are rare accouterments.

Model 1861 Navy Revolver

This model is a 6-shot, 7.5" round-barreled, .36 caliber percussion revolver. The frame, hammer, and attached loading lever are case colored. The barrel and cylinder are blued. The grip frame and triggerguard are silver-plated brass. The grips are of one-piece walnut. The cylinder has the roll-engraved naval battle scene, and the barrel stamping is "Address Col. Saml. Colt New-York U.S. America." The frame is stamped "Colts/Patent" with "36 Cal." on the triggerguard. There are not many variations within the 1861 Navy model designation, as less than 39,000 were made between 1861 and 1873.

Courtesy Butterfield & Butterfield, San Francisco, California

Civilian Model

Exc.	V.G.	Good	Fair	Poor
35000	20000	6000	3500	900

Military Model

Marked "U.S." on frame, inspector's cartouche on grip. 650 were marked "U.S.N." on the butt.

Exc.	V.G.	Good	Fair	Poor
50000	35000	12000	5500	1800

Shoulder Stock Model

Only 100 3rd-type stocks were made. They appear between serial #11000-#14000. These are very rare revolvers. Cautions should be exercised.

Revolver

NOTE: Expert appraisals should be acquired before a sale.

Stock

NOTE: Expert appraisals should be acquired before a sale. These are rare accouterments.

Fluted Cylinder Model

Approximately the first 100 were made with full fluted cylinders.

NOTE: Expert appraisals should be acquired before a sale. These are very rare.

Model 1862 Pocket Navy Revolver

This is a smaller, 5-shot, .36 caliber percussion revolver that resembles the configuration of the 1851 Navy. It has a 4.5", 5.5", or 6.5" octagonal barrel with an attached loading lever. The frame, hammer, and loading lever are case colored; the barrel and cylinder, blued. The grip frame and triggerguard are silver-plated brass; and the one-piece grips, of varnished walnut. The stagecoach holdup scene is roll-engraved on the cylinder. The frame is stamped "Colt's/Patent"; and the barrel, "Address Col. Saml. Colt New-York U.S. America." There were approximately 19,000 manufactured between 1861 and 1873. They are serial numbered in the same range as the Model 1862 Police. Because a great many were used for metallic cartridge conversions, they are quite scarce today.

The London <u>Address</u> Model with blued steel grip frame would be worth more than the standard model.

Standard Production Model

Exc.	V.G.	Good	Fair	Poor
20000	12000	4000	3000	1000

NOTE: Longer barrels will bring a premium over the 4.5" length.

Model 1862 Police Revolver

This is a slim, attractively designed revolver that some consider to be the most aesthetically pleasing of all the Colt percussion designs. It has a 5-shot, half-fluted cylinder chambered for .36 caliber. It is offered with a 3.5", 4.5", 5.5", or 6.5" round barrel. The frame, hammer, and loading lever are case colored; the barrel and cylinder, blued. The grip frame is silver-plated brass; and the one-piece grips, varnished walnut. The barrel is stamped "Address Col. Saml Colt New-York U.S. America"; the frame has "Colt's/Patent" on the left side. One of the cylinder flutes is marked "Pat Sept. 10th 1850." There were approximately 28,000 of these manufactured between 1861 and 1873. Many were converted to metallic cartridge use, so they are quite scarce on today's market.

The London <u>Address</u> Model would be worth approximately twice the value of the standard model.

Courtesy Milwaukee Public Museum, Milwaukee, Wisconsin

Standard Production Model

Exc.	V.G.	Good	Fair	Poor
12000	6000	3500	2000	800

NOTE: Longer barrels will bring a premium over the 3.5" or 4.5" length.

METALLIC CARTRIDGE CONVERSIONS

Thuer Conversion Revolver

Although quite simplistic and not commercially successful, the Thuer Conversion was the first attempt by Colt to convert the percussion revolvers to the new metallic cartridge system. This conversion was designed around the tapered Thuer cartridge and consists of a ring that replaced the back part of the cylinder, which had been milled off. This ring is stamped "Pat. Sep. / 15. 1868." The ejection position is marked with the letter "E." These conversions have rebounding firing pins and are milled to allow loading from the front of the revolver. This conversion was undertaken on the six different models listed below; and all other specifications, finishes, markings, etc., not directly affected by the conversion would be the same as previously described. From a collectible and investment standpoint, the Thuer Conversion is very desirable. Competent appraisal should be secured if acquisition is contemplated.

Model 1849 Pocket Conversion

Exc.	V.G.	Good	Fair	Poor
35000	20000	10000	4000	2000

Model 1851 Navy Conversion

Exc.	V.G.	Good	Fair	Poor
25000	20000	10000	3500	1800

Courtesy Milwaukee Public Museum, Milwaukee, Wisconsin

Model 1860 Army Conversion

Exc.	V.G.	Good	Fair	Poor
20000	14000	8000	5000	2000

Model 1861 Navy Conversion

Exc.	V.G.	Good	Fair	Poor
25000	16000	10000	6000	3000

A Model 1851 Navy Thuer Conversion was sold at auction for $19,550. The revolver was cased with British proofs and a New York address. Condition was very good. Butterfield & Butterfield, August 1999

Models 1862 Police Conversion

Exc.	V.G.	Good	Fair	Poor
20000	12000	8000	5000	3000

Model 1862 Pocket Navy Conversion

Exc.	V.G.	Good	Fair	Poor
20000	12000	8000	5000	3000

NOTE: Blued models will bring higher prices than nickel models in the same condition.

Richards Conversion, 1860 Army Revolver

This was Colt's second attempt at metallic cartridge conversion, and it met with quite a bit more success than the first. The Richards Conversion was designed for the .44 Colt cartridge and has a 6-shot cylinder and an integral ejector rod to replace the loading lever that had been removed. The other specifications pertaining to the 1860 Army Revolver remain as previously described if they are not directly altered by the conversion. The Richards Conversion adds a breechplate with a firing pin and its own rear sight. There were approximately 9,000 of these Conversions manufactured between 1873 and 1878.

Civilian Model

Exc.	V.G.	Good	Fair	Poor
18000	10000	5000	3000	1200

Martially Marked Variation

This variation is found with mixed serial numbers and a second set of conversion serial numbers. The "U.S." is stamped on the left side of the barrel lug, and inspector's cartouche appears on the grip. This is a very rare Colt revolver.

Exc.	V.G.	Good	Fair	Poor
—	35000	20000	8000	3000

NOTE: Blued models will bring higher prices than nickel models in the same condition.

Transition Richards Model

This variation is marked by the presence of a firing pin hammer.

Courtesy Butterfield & Butterfield, San Francisco, California

Exc.	V.G.	Good	Fair	Poor
16000	10000	4000	3000	1200

NOTE: Blued models will bring higher prices than nickel models in the same condition.

Richards-Mason Conversion, 1860 Army Revolver

This conversion is different from the Richards Conversion in a number of readily apparent aspects. The barrel was manufactured with a small lug much different in appearance than seen on the standard 1860 Army. The breechplate does not have its own rear sight, and there is a milled area to allow the hammer to contact the base of the cartridge. These Conversions were also chambered for the .44 Colt cartridge, and the cylinder holds 6 shots. There is an integral ejector rod in place of the loading lever. The barrels on some are stamped either "Address Col. Saml. Colt New-York U.S. America" or "Colt's Pt.

F.A. Mfg. Co. Hartford, Ct." The patent dates 1871 and 1872 are stamped on the left side of the frame. The finish of these revolvers, as well as the grips, were for the most part the same as on the unconverted Armies; but for the first time, nickel-plated guns are found. There were approximately 2,100 of these Conversions produced in 1877 and 1878.

Exc.	V.G.	Good	Fair	Poor
25000	16000	6000	4000	2000

NOTE: Blued models will bring higher prices than nickel models in the same condition.

Richards-Mason Conversions 1851 Navy Revolver

These revolvers were converted in the same way as the 1860 Army previously described, the major difference being the caliber .38, either rimfire or centerfire. Finishes are mostly the same as on unconverted revolvers, but nickel-plated guns are not rare.

Courtesy Butterfield & Butterfield, San Francisco, California

Production Model Serial #1-3800

Exc.	V.G.	Good	Fair	Poor
12000	8000	4000	2500	1200

U.S. Navy Model Serial #41000-91000 Range

"USN" stamped on butt; steel grip frame.

Exc.	V.G.	Good	Fair	Poor
24000	16000	7000	3500	1800

NOTE: Blued models will bring higher prices than nickel models in the same condition.

Richards-Mason Conversion 1861 Navy Revolver

The specifications for this model are the same as for the 1851 Navy Conversion described above, with the base revolver being different. There were 2,200 manufactured in the 1870s.

Courtesy Wallis & Wallis, Lewes, Sussex, England

Standard Production Model Serial #100-#3300 Range

Exc.	V.G.	Good	Fair	Poor
12000	6500	3500	2500	1200

U.S. Navy Model #1000-#9999 Serial Range

Exc.	V.G.	Good	Fair	Poor
24000	13000	6500	3500	1800

NOTE: Blued models will bring higher prices than nickel models in the same condition.

Model 1862 Police and Pocket Navy Conversions

The conversion of these two revolver models is the most difficult to catalogue of all the Colt variations. There were approximately 24,000 of these produced between 1873 and 1880. There are five basic variations with a number of sub-variations. The confusion is usually caused by the different ways in which these were marked. Depending upon what parts were utilized, caliber markings could be particularly confusing. One must also consider the fact that many of these conversion revolvers found their way into secondary markets, such as Mexico and Central and South America, where they were either destroyed or received sufficient abuse to obliterate most identifying markings. The five basic variations are all chambered for either the .38 rimfire or the .38 centerfire cartridge. All held 5 shots, and most were found with the round roll-engraved stagecoach holdup scene. The half-fluted cylinder from the 1862 Police is quite rare on the conversion revolver and not found at all on some of the variations. The finishes on these guns were pretty much the same as they were before conversion, but it is not unusual to find nickel-plated specimens. Blued models will bring a premium over nickel in the same condition. The basic variations are as follows.

Courtesy Butterfield & Butterfield, San Francisco, California

Round Barrel Pocket Navy with Ejector

Exc.	V.G.	Good	Fair	Poor
4500	3800	2200	1600	800

3.5" Round Barrel Without Ejector

Exc.	V.G.	Good	Fair	Poor
2500	2000	1000	650	300

4.5" Octagonal Barrel Without Ejector

Exc.	V.G.	Good	Fair	Poor
4000	3200	1600	1200	700

Courtesy Butterfield & Butterfield, San Francisco, California

NOTE: Blued models will bring higher prices than nickel models in the same condition.

Model 1862 Pocket Navy Octagon Barrel with Ejector

Half-fluted cylinder add 20%.

Exc.	V.G.	Good	Fair	Poor
5000	4500	2000	1500	600

Model 1862 Police Round Barrel with Ejector

Exc.	V.G.	Good	Fair	Poor
5000	4500	2000	1500	600

NOTE: Blued models will bring higher prices than nickel models in the same condition.

Model 1871-1872 Open Top Revolver

This model was the first revolver Colt manufactured especially for a metallic cartridge. It was not a conversion. The frame, 7.5" or 8" round barrel, and the 6-shot cylinder were produced for the .44 rimfire metallic cartridge. The grip frame and some internal parts were taken from the 1860 Army and the 1851 Navy. Although this model was not commercially successful and was not accepted by the U.S. Ordnance Department, it did pave the way for the Single Action Army that came out shortly thereafter and was an immediate success. This model is all blued, with a case colored hammer. There are some with silver-plated brass grip frames, but most are blued steel. The one-piece grips are of varnished walnut. The cylinder is roll-engraved with the naval battle scene. The barrel is stamped "Address Col. Saml. Colt New-York U.S. America." The later production revolvers are barrel stamped "Colt's Pt. F.A. Mfg. Co. Hartford, Ct. U.S.A." The first 1,000 revolvers were stamped "Colt's/Patent." After that, 1871 and 1872 patent dates appeared on the frame. There were 7,000 of these revolvers manufactured in 1872 and 1873.

1860 Army Grip Frame

Exc.	V.G.	Good	Fair	Poor
35000	20000	12000	8000	3500

A Colt Open Top revolver sold at auction for $57,500. The condition was 95% blue and 98% case color. Very rare in this condition.
Butterfield & Butterfield, May 1999

1851 Navy Grip Frame

Exc.	V.G.	Good	Fair	Poor
40000	25000	15000	10000	4000

NOTE: Blued models will bring higher prices than nickel models in the same condition.

COLT DERRINGERS AND POCKET REVOLVERS

First Model Derringer

This is a small all-metal single shot. It is chambered for the .44 rimfire cartridge. The 2.5" barrel pivots to the left and downward for loading. This model is engraved with a scroll pattern and has been noted blued, silver, or nickel-plated. The barrel is stamped "Colt's Pt. F.A. Mfg. Co./Hartford Ct. U.S.A/ No.1." ".41 Cal." is stamped on the frame under the release catch. There were approximately 6,500 of this model manufactured from 1870-1890. It was the first single shot pistol Colt produced.

Courtesy Butterfield & Butterfield, San Francisco, California

Exc.	V.G.	Good	Fair	Poor
4000	3000	1800	1200	400

Second Model Derringer

Although this model has the same odd shape as the First Model, it is readily identifiable by the checkered varnished walnut grips and the "No 2" on the barrel after the address. It is also .41 rimfire and has a 2.5" barrel that pivots in the same manner as the First Model. There were approximately 9,000 of these manufactured between 1870 and 1890.

Courtesy Wallis & Wallis, Lewes, Sussex, England

Exc.	V.G.	Good	Fair	Poor
3500	2200	1400	900	400

Third Model Derringer

This model was designed by Alexander Thuer who was also responsible for Colt's first metallic cartridge conversion. It is often referred to as the "Thuer Model" for this reason. It is also chambered for the .41 rimfire cartridge and has a 2.5" barrel that pivots to the right (but not down) for loading. The Third Model has a more balanced appearance than its predecessors, and its commercial success (45,000 produced between 1875 and 1910) reflects this. The barrel on this model is stamped "Colt" in small block letters on the first 2,000 guns. The remainder of the production features the "COLT" in large italicized print. The ".41 Cal." is stamped on the left side of the frame. This model will be found with the barrel blued or plated in either silver or nickel and the bronze frame plated. The grips are varnished walnut.

First Variation, Early Production

This has a raised area on the underside of the frame through which the barrel screw passes, and the spur is not angled. Small block "Colt" lettering on barrel.

Exc.	V.G.	Good	Fair	Poor
6000	5000	3000	1800	1000

First Variation, Late Production

This is similar to early production but has large italicized "COLT" on barrel.

Exc.	V.G.	Good	Fair	Poor
3600	2600	2000	1500	600

Courtesy Butterfield & Butterfield, San Francisco, California

Production Model

Exc.	V.G.	Good	Fair	Poor
1500	1000	600	400	200

NOTE: Blued models will bring a premium over nickel in the same condition.

A cased pair of Third Model Colt derringers was sold at auction for $4,830. Nickel finish on both pistols. Condition was good. Condition of grips was excellent.
Rock Island Auction Company, August 1999

House Model Revolver

There are two basic versions of this model. They are both chambered for the .41 rimfire cartridge. The 4-shot version is known as the "Cloverleaf" due to the shape of the cylinder when viewed from the front. Approximately 7,500 of the nearly 10,000 House revolvers were of this 4-shot configuration. They are offered with a 1.5" or 3" barrel. The 1.5" length is quite rare, and some octagonal barrels in this length have been noted. The 5-shot round-cylinder version accounts for the rest of the production. It is found with serial numbers over

6100 and is offered with a 2-7/8" length barrel only. This model is stamped on the top strap "Pat. Sept. 19, 1871." This model has brass frames that were sometimes nickel-plated. The barrels are found either blued or plated. The grips are varnished walnut or rosewood. There were slightly fewer than 10,000 of both variations manufactured from 1871-1876.

NOTE: Blued models will bring a premium over nickel in the same condition.

Cloverleaf with 1.5" Round Barrel

Exc.	V.G.	Good	Fair	Poor
4500	3400	2200	1800	800

Courtesy Buffalo Bill Historical Center, Cody, Wyoming

Cloverleaf with 3" Barrel

Exc.	V.G.	Good	Fair	Poor
3000	2000	1400	800	400

House Pistol with 5-Shot Round Cylinder

Exc.	V.G.	Good	Fair	Poor
3600	2200	1600	1200	600

Open Top Pocket Revolver

This is a .22-caliber rimfire, 7-shot revolver that was offered with either a 2-3/8" or a 2-7/8" barrel. The model was a commercial success, with over 114,000 manufactured between 1871 and 1877. There would undoubtedly have been a great deal more sold had not the cheap copies begun to flood the market at that time, forcing Colt to drop this model from the line. This revolver has a silver or nickel-plated brass frame and a nickel-plated or blued barrel and cylinder. The grips are varnished walnut. The cylinder bolt slots are found toward the front on this model. "Colt's Pt. F.A. Mfg. Co./Hartford, Ct. U.S.A." is stamped on the barrel and ".22 Cal." on the left side of the frame.

NOTE: Blued models will bring a premium over nickel in the same condition.

Early Model With Ejector Rod

Exc.	V.G.	Good	Fair	Poor
3000	2000	1400	800	400

Production Model Without Ejector Rod

Exc.	V.G.	Good	Fair	Poor
1200	800	500	300	150

New Line Revolver .22

This was the smallest framed version of the five distinct New Line Revolvers. It has a 7-shot cylinder and a 2.25" octagonal barrel. The frame is nickel-plated, and the balance of the revolver is either nickel-plated or blued. The grips are of rosewood. There were approximately 55,000 of these made from 1873-1877. Colt also stopped production of the New Lines rather than try to compete with the "Suicide Specials." "Colt New .22" is found on the barrel; and ".22 Cal.," on the frame. The barrel is also stamped "Colt's Pt. F.A. Mfg.Co./Hartford, Ct. U.S.A."

Courtesy Butterfield & Butterfield, San Francisco, California

1st Model
Short cylinder flutes.

Exc.	V.G.	Good	Fair	Poor
1600	1000	500	400	200

2nd Model
Long cylinder flutes.

Exc.	V.G.	Good	Fair	Poor
1600	1000	500	400	200

NOTE: Blued models will bring higher prices than nickel models in the same condition.

New Line Revolver .30

This is a larger version of the .22 New Line. The basic difference is the size, caliber, caliber markings, and the offering of a blued version with case colored frame. There were approximately 11,000 manufactured from 1874-1876.

Courtesy Wallis & Wallis, Lewes, Sussex, England

Exc.	V.G.	Good	Fair	Poor
1800	1000	600	400	200

NOTE: Prices above are for nickel finish. Blued models will bring a premium of 100%.

New Line Revolver .32

This is the same basic revolver as the .30 caliber except that it is chambered for the .32-caliber rimfire and .32-caliber centerfire and is so marked. There were 22,000 of this model manufactured from 1873-1884. This model was offered with the rare 4" barrel, and this variation would be worth nearly twice the value of a standard model.

Courtesy Butterfield & Butterfield, San Francisco, California

Exc.	V.G.	Good	Fair	Poor
1600	800	600	400	200

NOTE: Prices above are for nickel finish. Blued models will bring a premium of 100%.

New Line Revolver .38

There were approximately 5,500 of this model manufactured between 1874 and 1880. It is chambered for either the .38 rimfire or .38 centerfire caliber and is so marked. This model in a 4" barrel would also bring twice the value.

Exc.	V.G.	Good	Fair	Poor
1800	1200	800	600	300

NOTE: Blued models will bring a premium over nickel in the same condition.

New Line Revolver .41

This is the "Big Colt," as it was sometimes known in advertising of its era. It is chambered for the .41 rimfire and the .41 centerfire and is so marked. The large caliber of this variation makes this the most desirable of the New Lines to collectors. There were approximately 7,000 of this model manufactured from 1874-1879. A 4"-barreled version would again be worth a 100 percent premium.

Exc.	V.G.	Good	Fair	Poor
2000	1200	800	600	300

NOTE: Prices above are for nickel finish. Blued models will bring a premium of 100%.

New House Model Revolver

This revolver is similar to the other New Lines except that it features a square butt instead of the bird's head configuration, a 2.25" round barrel without ejector rod, and a thin loading gate. It is chambered for the .32 (rare), .38, and the .41 centerfire cartridges. The finish was either full nickel-plated or blued, with a case colored frame. The grips are walnut, rosewood or (for the first time on a Colt revolver) checkered hard rubber, with an oval around the word "Colt." The barrel address is the same as on the other New Lines. The frame is marked "New House," with the caliber. There were approximately 4,000 manufactured between 1880-1886. .32 caliber model would bring a 10 percent premium.

Courtesy Milwaukee Public Museum, Milwaukee, Wisconsin

Exc.	V.G.	Good	Fair	Poor
2200	1600	1000	600	300

NOTE: Prices above are for nickel finish. Blued models will bring a premium of 100%.

New Police Revolver

This was the final revolver in the New Line series. It is chambered for .32, .38, and .41 centerfire caliber. The .32 and .41 are quite rare. It is offered in barrel lengths of 2.25", 4.5", 5.5", and 6.5". An ejector rod is found on all but the 2.5" barrel. The finish is either nickel or blued and case colored. The grips are hard rubber with a scene of a policeman arresting a criminal embossed on them; thusly the model became known to collectors as the "Cop and Thug" model. The barrel stamping is as the other New Lines, and the frame is stamped "New Police .38." There were approximately 4,000 of these manufactured between 1882-1886.

NOTE: The .32 and .41 caliber versions of this model will bring a 40-50 percent premium. Blued models and models with 5.5" or 6.5" barrels will bring a premium. Short barrel model will bring about 50% of the listed prices.

Courtesy Milwaukee Public Museum, Milwaukee, Wisconsin

Long Barrel model with ejector

Exc.	V.G.	Good	Fair	Poor
4200	3200	2200	1400	700

COLT'S SINGLE ACTION ARMY REVOLVER

The Colt Single Action Army, or Peacemaker as it is sometimes referred to, is one of the most widely collected and recognized firearms in the world. With few interruptions or changes in design, it has been manufactured from 1873 until the present. It is still available on a limited production basis from the Colt Custom Shop. The variations in this model are myriad. It has been produced in 30 different calibers and barrel lengths from 2.5" to 16", with 4.75", 5.5", and 7.5" standard. The standard finish is blued, with a case colored frame. Many are nickel-plated. Examples have been found silver- and gold-plated, with combinations thereof. The finest engravers in the world have used the SAA as a canvas to display their artistry. The standard grips from 1873-1883 were walnut, either oil-stained or varnished. From 1883 to approximately 1897, the standard grips were hard rubber with eagle and shield. After this date, at serial number 165000, the hard rubber grips featured the Rampant Colt. Many special-order grips were available, notably pearl and ivory, which were often checkered or carved in ornate fashion. The variables involved in establishing values on this model are extreme. Added to this, one must also consider historical significance, since the SAA played a big part in the formative years of the American West. Fortunately for those among us interested in the SAA, there are a number of fine publications available dealing exclusively with this model. It is my strongest recommendation that they be acquired and studied thoroughly to prevent extremely expensive mistakes. The Colt factory records are nearly complete for this model, and research should be done before acquisition of rare or valuable specimens.

For our purposes we will break down the Single Action Army production as follows:

Antique or Black Powder, **1873-1898, serial #1-#175000**

The cylinder axis pin is retained by a screw in the front of the frame.

Prewar, **1899-1940, serial #175001-#357859**

The cylinder axis pin is retained by a spring-loaded button through the side of the frame. This method is utilized on the following models, as well.

Postwar 2nd Generation, **1956-1978, serial #0001SA-99999SA**

3rd Generation, **1978-Present, serial #SA1001.** A breakdown of production by caliber will follow the chapter. It is important to note that the rarer calibers and the larger calibers bring higher values in this variation.

COLT *ANTIQUE* SINGLE ACTION ARMY REVOLVER

WHAT'S IT LIKE-THE COLT SINGLE ACTION ARMY

Pick up a Colt Single Action Army, run your fingers lovingly over the graceful contours. Let your eyes feast on the most beautiful sixgun silhouette ever discovered by man. I say discovered as the legendary Single Action Army is so grand it has to be a supernatural design! As you hold it, carefully cock the hammer slowly and you'll hear the mechanism spell out C-O-L-T. As you let the hammer down, your imagination takes over and you smell bacon and beans sizzling over an open campfire; your nostrils fill with the dust of 1000 longhorns trailing north; your ears pick up the tinkling of the ivories from a piano at the Long Branch. As you close your eyes you see a century of history of the Old West and men like Jesse James, Wyatt Earp, John Wesley Hardin, and Theodore Roosevelt. You visualize Lt. George Patton beginning his illustrious career packing a fully engraved ivory stocked Colt as he accompanied Black Jack Pershing in 1917 after Pancho Villa. The Colt Single Action Army has been in near continuous production since 1873 except for the years from 1941 to 1956. It was made obsolete with the coming of the Smith & Wesson M & P in 1899. It survived. The arrival of the 1911 would surely put an end to the obsolete frontier design. It survived. Only the arrival of World War II and worn out machinery could stop it. But not for long. It survived the coming of the Magnums, the Wonder Nines, and black plastic guns. For the past 125 years plus it has been offered in over three dozen chamberings; from .44 Henry Rimfire to .357 Magnum with the most popular chambering being the .45 Colt. It is hopelessly out-dated, terribly overpriced, requires a tune-up from a master gunsmith, and yet it survives. The Old West is pretty much a thing of the past. The Colt and the coyote remain. May it ever be so.

John Taffin

1st Year Production "Pinched Frame" 1873 Only
It is necessary to categorize this variation on its own. This is one of the rarest and most interesting of all the SAAs-not to mention that it is the first. On this model the top strap is pinched or constricted approximately one-half inch up from the hammer to form the rear sight. The highest surviving serial number having this feature is #156, the lowest #1. From these numbers, it is safe to assume that the first run of SAAs were all pinched-frame models; but there is no way to tell how many

there were, since Colt did not serial number the frames in the order that they were manufactured. An educated guess would be that there were between 50 and 150 pinched frame guns in all and that they were all made before mid-July 1873. The reason for the change came about on the recommendation of Capt. J.R. Edie, a government inspector who thought that the full fluted top strap would be a big improvement in the sighting capabilities of the weapon. The barrel length of the first model is 7.5"; the standard caliber, .45 Colt; and the proper grips were of walnut. The front sight blade is German silver. Needless to say, this model will rarely be encountered; and if it is, it should never be purchased without competent appraisal.

Exc.	V.G.	Good	Fair	Poor
N/A	N/A	75000	45000	15000

Early Military Model 1873-1877

The serial number range on this first run of military contract revolvers extends to #24000. The barrel address is in the early script style with the # symbol preceding and following. The frame bears the martial marking "US," and the walnut grips have the inspector's cartouche stamped on them. The front sight is steel as on all military models; the barrel length, 7.5". The caliber is .45 Colt, and the ejector rod head is the bull's-eye or donut style with a hole in the center of it. The finish features the military polish and case colored frame, with the remainder blued. Authenticate any potential purchase; many spurious examples have been noted.

Exc.	V.G.	Good	Fair	Poor
N/A	35000	18000	12000	6000

NOTE: Certain 3-digit and 4-digit serial numbers will command a substantial premium. Seek an expert appraisal prior to sale.

Early Civilian Model 1873-1877

This model is identical to the Early Military Model but has no military acceptance markings or cartouches. Some could have the German silver front sight blade. The early bull's-eye ejector rod head is used on this model. The Civilian Model has a higher degree of polish than is found on the military models, and the finish on these early models could be plated or blued with a case colored frame. This model also has a script barrel address. The grips are standard one-piece walnut. Ivory-grip models are worth a premium.

Exc.	V.G.	Good	Fair	Poor
35000	18000	12000	6000	3000

NOTE: Certain 3-digit and 4-digit serial numbers will command a substantial premium. Blued models will command a premium. Seek an expert appraisal prior to sale.

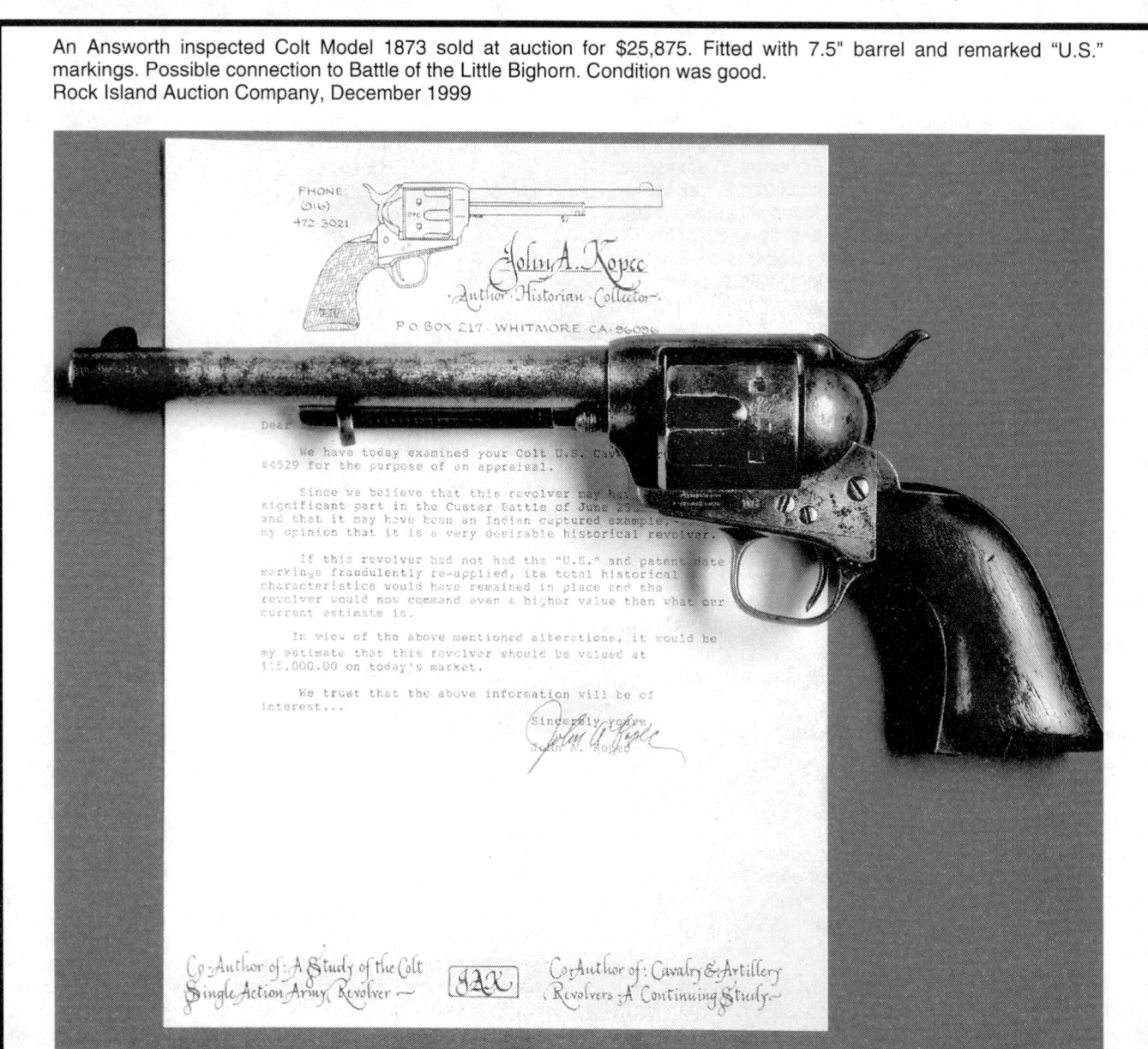

An Answorth inspected Colt Model 1873 sold at auction for $25,875. Fitted with 7.5" barrel and remarked "U.S." markings. Possible connection to Battle of the Little Bighorn. Condition was good.
Rock Island Auction Company, December 1999

.44 Rimfire Model 1875-1880

This model was made to fire the .44 Henry Rimfire cartridge. It was to be used as a compatible companion sidearm to the Henry and Winchester 1866 rifles that were used extensively during this era. However, this was not the case; and the .44 Rimfire was doomed to economic failure as soon as it appeared on the market. By that time, it had already been established that large-caliber centerfire cartridges were a good deal more efficient than their rimfire counterparts. The large-caliber rimfires were deemed obsolete before this Colt ever hit the market. The result of this was that Colt's sales representatives sold most of the production to obscure banana republics in South and Central America, where this model received much abuse. Most had the original 7.5" barrels cut down; and nearly all were denied even the most basic maintenance, making the survival rate of this model quite low. All this adds to its desirability as a collector's item and makes the risk of acquiring a fake that much greater. This model is unique in that it was the only SAA variation to have its own serial number range, starting with #1 and continuing to #1892, the latest known surviving specimen. The block style barrel markings were introduced during this production run. At least 90 of these revolvers were converted by the factory to .22 rimfire, and one was shipped chambered for .32 rimfire.

Exc.	V.G.	Good	Fair	Poor
N/A	35000	20000	8000	3000

NOTE: Blued models will command a significant premium.

Late Military Model 1878-1891

The later Military Models are serial numbered to approximately #136000. They bear the block-style barrel address without the # prefix and suffix. The frames are marked "US," and the grips have the inspector's cartouche. The finish is the military-style polish, case colored frame; and the remainder, blued. Grips are oil-stained walnut. On the military marked Colts, it is imperative that potential purchases be authenticated as many fakes have been noted.

Exc.	V.G.	Good	Fair	Poor
35000	20000	12000	7000	3000

NOTE: Revolvers produced from 1878 to 1885 will command a premium. Seek an expert appraisal prior to sale.

Artillery Model 1895-1903

A number of "US" marked SAAs were returned either to the Colt factory or to the Springfield Armory, where they were altered and refinished. These revolvers have 5.5" barrels and any combination of mixed serial numbers. They were re-marked by the inspectors of the era and have a case colored frame and a blued cylinder and barrel. Some have been noted all blued within this variation. This model, as with the other military marked Colts, should definitely be authenticated before purchase. Some of these revolvers fall outside the 1898 antique cutoff date that has been established by the government and, in our experience, are not quite as desirable to investors. They are generally worth approximately 20 percent less.

Exc.	V.G.	Good	Fair	Poor
8000	6000	4000	3000	1500

London Model

These SAAs were manufactured to be sold through Colt's London Agency. The barrel is stamped "Colt's Pt. F.A. Mfg. Co. Hartford, Ct. U.S.A. Depot 14 Pall Mall London." This model is available in various barrel lengths. They are generally chambered for .45 Colt, .450 Boxer, .450 Eley, .455 Eley, and rarely .476 Eley, the largest of the SAA chamberings. A good many of these London Models were cased and embellished, and they should be individually appraised. This model should be authenticated as many spurious examples have been noted.

Exc.	V.G.	Good	Fair	Poor
15000	12000	7000	4000	1500

NOTE: Revolvers chambered for .476 Eley will command a 100% premium. Blued models will command a premium.

A factory engraved Colt Single Action Army with London barrel address was sold at auction for $31,625. Cased with mother of pearl grips. Caliber is .450. Condition was excellent.
Butterfield & Butterfield, November 1999

Frontier Six-Shooter 1878-1882

Several thousand SAAs were made with the legend "Colt's Frontier Six Shooter" acid-etched into the left side of the barrel instead of being stamped. This etching is not deep, and today collectors will become ecstatic if they discover a specimen with mere vestiges of the etched panel remaining. These acid-etched SAAs are serial numbered #45000-#65000. They have various barrel lengths and finishes, but all are chambered for the .44-40 caliber.

Exc.	V.G.	Good	Fair	Poor
28000	18000	8000	4000	2000

NOTE: Blued models will command a premium.

Sheriff's or Storekeeper's Model 1882-1898

This model was manufactured with a short barrel (2.5"-4.75"). Most have 4" barrels. It features no ejector rod or housing, and the frame is made without the hole in the right forward section to accommodate the ejector assembly. The Sheriff's or Storekeeper's Model is numbered above serial #73000. It was manufactured with various finishes and chambered for numerous calibers. This model continued after 1898 into the smokeless or modern era. Examples manufactured in the prewar years are worth approximately 20 percent less. Although faking this model is quite difficult, it has been successfully attempted.

Courtesy Butterfield & Butterfield, San Francisco, California

Exc.	V.G.	Good	Fair	Poor
40000	30000	20000	8000	4000

NOTE: Blued models will command a premium.

Flattop Target Model 1888-1896

This model is highly regarded and sought after by collectors. It is not only rare (only 925 manufactured) but is an extremely attractive and well-finished variation. It is chambered for 22 different calibers from .22 rimfire to .476 Eley. The .22 rimfire, .38 Colt, .41, and .45 Colt are the most predominant chamberings. The 7.5" barrel length is the most commonly encountered.

A cased Colt London Flat-Top Target was sold at auction for $10,350. Condition was good to very good. Butterfield & Butterfield, February 1999

The serial number range is between #127000-#162000. Some have been noted in higher ranges. The finish is all blued, with a case colored hammer. The checkered grips are either hard rubber or walnut. The most readily identifying feature of the flattop is the lack of a groove in the top strap and the sight blade dovetailed into the flattop. The front sight has a removable blade insert. The values given are for a standard production model chambered for the calibers previously mentioned as being the most common. It is important to have other calibers individually appraised as variance in values can be quite extreme.

Exc.	V.G.	Good	Fair	Poor
20000	16000	8000	5500	3500

NOTE: Nickel models will command a premium.

Bisley Model 1894-1915

This model was named for the target range in Great Britain, where their National Target Matches were held since the nineteenth century. The model was designed as a target revolver with an odd humped-back grip that was supposed to better fill the hand while target shooting. It is also easily identified by the wide low profile hammer spur, wide trigger, and the name "Bisley" stamped on the barrel. The Bisley production fell within the serial number range #165000-#331916. There were 44,350 made.

It was offered in 16 different chamberings from .32 Colt to .455 Eley. The most common calibers were .32-20, .38-40, .41, .44-40, and .45 Colt. The barrel lengths are 4.75", 5.5", and 7.5". The frame and hammer are case-colored; the remainder, blued. Smokeless powder models produced after 1899 utilized the push-button cylinder pin retainer. The grips are checkered hard rubber. This model was actually designed with English sales in mind; and though it did sell well over there, American sales accounted for most of the Bisley production. The values we provide here cover the standard calibers and barrel lengths. Rare calibers and/or other notable variations can bring greatly fluctuating values, and qualified appraisals should be secured in such cases.

NOTE: Bisleys manufactured before 1898 are worth approximately 50 percent more.

Exc.	V.G.	Good	Fair	Poor
6500	5500	3500	1250	750

Bisley Model Flattop Target 1894-1913

This model is quite similar to the Standard Bisley Model, with the flattop frame and dovetailed rear sight feature. It also has the removable front sight insert. It has an all-blued finish with case-colored hammer only and is available with a 7.5" barrel. Smokeless powder models produced after 1899 utilized the push-button cylinder pin retainer. The calibers are the same as the standard Bisley. Colt manufactured 976 of these revolvers. The advice regarding appraisal would also apply.

Exc.	V.G.	Good	Fair	Poor
16000	10000	7000	3500	1500

NOTE: Nickel models will command a premium.

Standard Civilian Production Models 1876-1898

This final designated category for the black powder or antique SAAs includes all the revolvers not previously categorized. They have barrel lengths from 4.75", 5.5", and 7.5" and are chambered for any one of 30 different calibers. The finishes could be blued, blued and case colored, or plated in nickel, silver, gold, or combinations thereof. Grips could be walnut, hard rubber, ivory, pearl, stag, or bone. The possibilities are endless. The values given here are for the basic model, and we again strongly advise securing qualified appraisal when not completely sure of any model variation.

NOTE: For Standard Civilian Production Models with screw-in frame, serial number to 163,000 add a 25% to 100% premium depending on year built. Seek an expert appraisal prior to sale.

Exc.	V.G.	Good	Fair	Poor
15000	10000	6000	3500	1600

NOTE: At this time it is important to note that the Colt's Single Action Army Revolvers we have discussed to this point are in the antique category as established by our federal government. The arbitrary cutoff date of 1898 has been established, and any weapon made prior to this date is considered an antique and, as such, not subject to the restraints placed on collectors and dealers by the Gun Control Act of 1968. This is important because firearms falling into this category will usually bring higher values due to the demand by pure investors who do not relish paperwork on collectible investments. There will be those who disagree with me on this line of reasoning, but my experience tells me that it is correct.

COLT PREWAR SINGLE ACTION ARMY REVOLVER 1899-1940

Standard Production Prewar Models

The 1899 cutoff has been thoroughly discussed, but it is interesting to note that the actual beginning production date for smokeless models was 1900. The Prewar Colts are, all in all, quite similar to the antiques—the finishes, barrel lengths, grips, etc. Calibers are also similar, with the exception of the obsolete ones being dropped and new discoveries added. The most apparent physical difference between the smokeless powder and black powder models is the previously discussed method of retaining the cylinder axis pin. The prewar Colts utilized the spring-loaded button through the side of the frame. The black powder models utilized a screw in the front of the frame. The values we furnish for this model designation are for these standard models only. The serial number range on the prewar SAAs is 175001-357859. Note that any variation can have marked effects on value fluctuations, and qualified appraisal should be secured.

Exc.	V.G.	Good	Fair	Poor
9500	6750	4000	2500	1500

A Colt Single Action Army revolver was sold at auction for $46,000. Fitted with a 5.5" barrel. Chambered for the .45 ACP cartridge. Display case. Shipped in 1934. Condition is 98%.
Rock Island Auction Company, October 2000

Long Fluted Cylinder Model 1913-1915

Strange as it may seem, the Colt Company has an apparent credo they followed to never throw anything away. That credo was never more evident than with this model. These Long Flute Cylinders were actually left over from the model 1878 Double Action Army Revolvers. Someone in the hierarchy at Colt had an inspiration that drove the gunsmiths on the payroll slightly mad: to make these cylinders fit the SAA frames. There were 1,478 of these Long Flutes manufactured. They are chambered for the .45 Colt, .38-40, .32-20, .41 Colt, and the .44 Smith & Wesson Special. They were offered in the three standard barrel lengths and were especially well-polished, having what has been described as Colt's "Fire Blue" on the barrel and cylinder. The frame and hammer are case colored. They are fitted with checkered hard rubber grips and are particularly fine examples of Colt's craft.

Exc.	V.G.	Good	Fair	Poor
12000	8500	6000	3250	1700

COLT POSTWAR SINGLE ACTION ARMY REVOLVER

Standard Postwar Model 1956-1975

In 1956 the shooting and gun-collecting fraternity succeeded in convincing Colt that there was a market for a re-introduced SAA. The revolver was brought back in the same external configuration. The only changes were internal. The basic specifications as to barrel length and finish availability were the same. The calibers available were .38 Special, .357 Magnum, .44 Special, and .45 Colt. The serial number range of the re-introduced 2nd Generation, as it is sometimes known, Colt is #000ISA-73000SA. Values for the standard postwar Colts are established by four basic factors: caliber (popularity and scarcity), barrel length, finish, and condition. Shorter barrel lengths are generally more desirable than the 7.5". The .38 Special is the rarest caliber, but the .45 Colt and .44 Special are more sought after than the .357 Magnum. Special feature revolvers, such as the 350 factory-engraved guns produced during this period, must be individually appraised. The ivory situation in the world today has become quite a factor, as ivory grips are found on many SAAs. We will attempt to take these factors into consideration and evaluate this variation as accurately and clearly as possible. Remember as always, when in doubt secure a qualified appraisal.

4.75" Barrel add 25%.
5.5" Barrel add 15%.
Nickel Finish add 20%.
Ivory Grips add $250.

A Colt Single Action 2nd generation revolver was sold at auction for $2,970. Fitted with 4-3/4" barrel and nickel finish. Condition was mint with original box.
Amoskeag Auction Company, May 1999

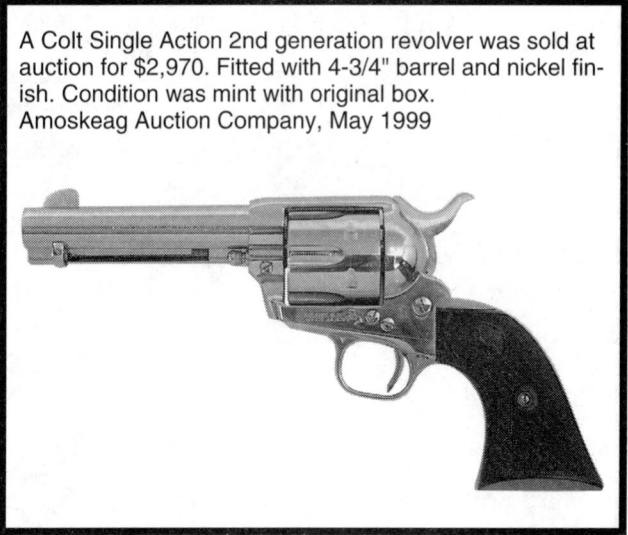

Values for 7.5" Barrel Model

.38 Special

NIB	Exc.	V.G.	Good	Fair	Poor
2450	1850	1200	900	700	600

.357 Magnum

NIB	Exc.	V.G.	Good	Fair	Poor
1850	1350	900	750	700	650

.44 Special

NIB	Exc.	V.G.	Good	Fair	Poor
2950	2250	1750	1100	1000	750

.45 Colt

NIB	Exc.	V.G.	Good	Fair	Poor
2000	1650	1400	1000	900	750

A consecutively numbered pair of 2nd generation Single Action Armys sold at auction for $4,180 for the pair. Condition was mint with original boxes.
Amoskeag Auction Company, May 1999

Paul Goodwin Photo

Sheriff's Model 1960-1975

Between 1960 and 1975, there were approximately 500 Sheriff's Models manufactured. They have 3" barrels and no ejec-

A pair of 2nd generation Colt Single Action revolvers with Buscadero rig were sold at auction for $27,500. They were presented to the Lone Ranger's business manager and were worn by Clayton Moore during the TV series. Condition was near mint.
Faintich Auction Service, October 1999

A Colt Single Action Army was sold at auction for $39,387.50. It was built in 1908 and factory engraved. Chambered for .45 Colt cartridge. Ivory grips with full coverage engraving. Condition is 75% case colors and 35% blue. Grips are excellent.
Amoskeag Auction Company, March 1999

tor rod assemblies. The frames were made without the hole for the ejector rod to pass through. They were blued, with case colored frames; 25 revolvers were nickel-plated and would bring a sizable premium if authenticated. The barrels are marked "Colt Sheriff's Model." The serial number has an "SM" suffix. They are chambered for the .45 Colt cartridge.

Nickel Finish add 20%.

NIB	Exc.	V.G.	Good	Fair	Poor
3000	2200	1800	1200	850	600

Buntline Special 1957-1975

The "Buntline Special" was named after a dime novelist named Ned Buntline, who supposedly gave this special long barrel revolver to Wyatt Earp. The story is suspected to be purely legend as no Colt records exist to lend it credence. Be that as it may, the Colt factory decided to take advantage of the market and produced the 12" barreled SAA from 1957-1974. There were approximately 3,900 manufactured. They are chambered for the .45 Colt cartridge and are offered in the blued and case colored finish. Only 65 Buntlines are nickel-plated, making this an extremely rare variation that definitely should be authenticated before purchase. Walnut grips are the most commonly noted, but they are also offered with the checkered hard rubber grips. The barrels are marked on the left side "Colt Buntline Special .45." Nickel finish add 60%.

NIB	Exc.	V.G.	Good	Fair	Poor
1950	1400	1100	750	600	500

New Frontier 1961-1975

The New Frontier is readily identified by its flattop frame and adjustable sight. It also has a high front sight. Colt manufactured approximately 4,200 of them. They are chambered for the .357 Magnum, .45 Colt, .44 Special (255 produced), and rarely (only 49 produced) in .38 Special. A few were chambered for the .44-40 cartridge. The 7.5" barrel length is by far the most common, but the 4.75" and 5.5" barrels are also offered. The standard finish is case colored and blued. Nickel-plating and full blue are offered but are rarely encountered. Standard grips are walnut. The barrel is stamped on the left side "Colt New Frontier S.A.A." The serial has the "NF" suffix.

4.75" Barrel add 25%.
5.5" Barrel add 20%.
Full Blue add 50%.
.38 Special add 50%.
.44 Special add 30%.
44-40 add 30%

NIB	Exc.	V.G.	Good	Fair	Poor
1850	1400	1000	800	600	500

New Frontier Buntline Special 1962-1967

This model is rare, as Colt only manufactured 70 during this five-year period. They are similar to the standard Buntline, with a 12" barrel. They are chambered for .45 Colt only.

NIB	Exc.	V.G.	Good	Fair	Poor
5000	4000	3000	2000	1400	700

COLT THIRD GENERATION SINGLE ACTION ARMY 1976-1981

In 1976 Colt made some internal changes in the SAA. The external configuration was not altered. The serial number range began in 1976 with #80000SA, and in 1978 #99999SA was reached. At this time the suffix became a prefix, and the new serial range began with #SA01001. This model's value is determined in much the same manner as was described in the section on the 2nd Generation SAAs. Caliber, barrel length, finish, and condition are once again the four main determining factors. The prevalence of special-order guns was greater during this period, and many more factory-engraved SAAs were produced. Colt's Custom Shop was quite active during this period. We feel that it is not advisable to undertake evaluation of specially embellished guns and strongly advise that competent appraisal be secured on any firearms that deviate from the standard. There are, quite frankly, too many fraudulent Colt SAAs out there; and the financial risks are great.

4.75" Barrel add 25%.
5.5" Barrel add 10%.
Nickel Plated add 10%.
Ivory Grips add $250.

Values with 7.5" Barrel

.357 Magnum

NIB	Exc.	V.G.	Good	Fair	Poor
1400	1150	895	750	600	500

.44-40

NIB	Exc.	V.G.	Good	Fair	Poor
1500	1250	900	750	600	500

.44-40 Black Powder Frame (Screw Retaining Cylinder Pin)

NIB	Exc.	V.G.	Good	Fair	Poor
1700	1400	1150	1000	800	600

.44 Special

NIB	Exc.	V.G.	Good	Fair	Poor
1400	1200	900	700	550	500

.45 Colt

NIB	Exc.	V.G.	Good	Fair	Poor
1500	1300	900	750	600	500

Sheriff's Model 3rd Generation

This model is similar to the 2nd Generation Sheriff's Model. The serial number and the fact that this model is also chambered for the .44-40 are the only external differences. Colt offered this model with interchangeable cylinders—.45 Colt/.45 ACP or .44-40/.44 Special-available in 3" barrel, blued and case colored finish standard.

Interchangeable Cylinders add 30%.
Nickel Finish add 10%.
Ivory Grips add $250.

NIB	Exc.	V.G.	Good	Fair	Poor
1050	875	750	600	450	400

Buntline Special 3rd Generation

This is the same basic configuration as the 2nd Generation with the 12" barrel. Standard finish blued and case-colored, it is chambered for .45 Colt and has checkered hard rubber grips.

Nickel Finish add 10%.

NIB	Exc.	V.G.	Good	Fair	Poor
1050	875	750	600	450	400

New Frontier 3rd Generation

This model is similar in appearance to the 2nd Generation guns. The 3rd Generation New Frontiers have five-digit serial numbers; the 2nd Generation guns, four-digit numbers. That and the calibers offered are basically the only differences. The 3rd Generations are chambered for the .44 Special and .45 Colt and are rarely found in .44-40. Barrel lengths are 7.5" standard, with the 4.75" and 5.5" rarely encountered.

.44-40 add 20%.
4.75" Barrel add 35%.
5.5" Barrel add 25%.

NIB	Exc.	V.G.	Good	Fair	Poor
950	725	650	550	500	400

Colt Single Action Army Production Breakdown by Caliber Antique and Prewar

CALIBER	SAA	FLATTOP SAA	BISLEY	FLATTOP BISLEY
.22 R.F.	107	93	0	0
.32 R.F.	1	0	0	0
.32 Colt	192	24	160	44
.32 S&W	32	30	18	17
.32-44	2	9	14	17
.32-20	29,812	30	13,291	131
.38 Colt (1914)	1,011	122	412	96
.38 Colt (1922)	1,365	0	0	0
.38 S&W	9	39	10	5
.38 Colt Sp.	82	7	0	0
.38 S&W Sp.	25	0	2	0
.38-44	2	11	6	47
.357 Mag.	525	0	0	0
.380 Eley	1	3	0	0
.38-40	38,240	19	12,163	98
.41	16,402	91	3,159	24
.44 SmBr.	15	0	1	0
.44 R. F.	1,863	0	0	0
.44 Germ.	59	0	0	0
.44 Russ.	154	51	90	62
.44 S&W	24	51	29	64
.44 S&W Sp.	506	1	0	0
.44-40	64,489	21	6,803	78
.45 Colt	150,683	100	8,005	97
.45 SmBr.	4	0	2	0
.45 ACP	44	0	0	0
.450 Boxer	729	89	0	0
.450 Eley	2,697	84	5	0
.455 Eley	1,150	37	180	196
.476 Eley	161	2	0	0
Total	**310,386**	**914**	**44,350**	**976**

The above chart covers the production by caliber of the Single Action Army Revolvers manufactured between 1873 and 1940. These are the antique and the prewar firearms. This chart readily informs us as to which are the rare calibers.

COLT CURRENT PRODUCTION SINGLE ACTION ARMY 1982-PRESENT

Standard Single Action Army

The SAA, it is sad to note, has all but faded from the firearms picture. They are currently available as a special-order custom shop proposition. The cost is great; and the availability, low. The heyday of one of the most venerable firearms of them all is pretty much at an end. The SAAs have been available in .357 Magnum, .38-40, .44-40, .44 Special, and .45 Colt. Barrels were available in 3" through 10" lengths. The finishes are nickel-plated and blued, with case-colored frames. A number of optional finishes are available on request. Grips are available on a custom order basis. This model is available on special-order only.

NOTE: As of 2000 the Custom Shop is offering this revolver in the following configurations:

P1840-Blued .45 Colt with 4.75" barrel
P1841-Nickel .45 Colt with 4.75" barrel
P1850-Blued .45 Colt with 5.5" barrel
P1856-Nickel .45 Colt with 5.5" barrel
P1940-Blued .44-40 with 4.75" barrel
P1941-Nickel .44-40 with 4.75" barrel
P1950-Blued .44-40 with 5.5" barrel
P1956-Nickel .44-40 with 5.5" barrel

Optional Features:

Nickel Finish add $125.
Royal Blue Finish add $200.
Mirror Brite Finish add $225.
Gold Plate add $365.
Silver Plate add $365.
Class A Engraving add $875.
Class B Engraving add $1,200.
Class C Engraving add $1,500.
Class D Engraving add $1,750.
Buntline Engraving add 15%.

NIB	Exc.	V.G.	Good	Fair	Poor
1750	1350	1150	—	—	—

Colt Cowboy (CB1850)

Introduced in 1998 this model is a replica of the Single Action Army that features a modern transfer bar safety system. Offered with 5.5" barrel and chambered for .45 Colt. Sights are fixed with walnut grips. Blued barrel with case colored frame. Weight is about 42 oz.

NIB	Exc.	V.G.	Good	Fair	Poor
650	500	—	—	—	—

Colt Single Action Army "The Legend"

A limited edition revolver built to commemorate Colt's official PRCA sponsorship. Limited to 1,000. Chambered for .45 Long Colt fitted with a 5-1/2" barrel. Nickel finish Buffalo horn grips with gold medallions. Machine engraved and washed in gold.

NIB	Exc.	V.G.	Good	Fair	Poor
2750	2250	—	—	—	—

COLT SCOUT MODEL SINGLE ACTION ARMY

Frontier Scout 1957-1971

This is a scaled-down version of the SAA that is chambered for the .22 l.r. with an interchangeable .22 Magnum cylinder. It is offered with a 4.25", 4.75", or a 9.5" barrel. The frame is alloy. First year production frame were duotone with frame left in the white and the balance of the revolver blued. All blue models and wood grips became available in 1958. In 1961 the duotone model was dropped from production. A .22 Magnum model was first offered in 1959. In 1964 dual cylinders were introduced. These revolvers have "Q" or "F" serial number suffixes. In 1960 the "K" series Scout was introduced and featured a heavier frame, nickel plating, and wood grips. The majority of commemorative revolvers are of this type. This series was discontinued in 1970. Prices are about 15% higher than for the "Q" and "F" series guns.

9.5" Buntline add 50%.
Extra Cylinder add 10%.

NIB	Exc.	V.G.	Good	Fair	Poor
450	325	200	175	125	90

Peacemaker Scout & New Frontier

This model is similar to the Frontier Scout, with a steel case-colored or blued frame. Fitted with old style black plastic eagle grips. The barrel lengths offered are 4.75", 6", or 7.5" (Buntline model). It also has an interchangeable .22 Magnum cylinder. Most of these revolvers had a "G" suffix although some built in 1974 had a "L" suffix. In 1982 through 1986 a New Frontier model with cross-bolt safety was offered. This model is often referred to as the "GS" series. This revolver was offered with adjustable sights only. No Peacemakers were offered in this series.

NIB	Exc.	V.G.	Good	Fair	Poor
550	475	300	200	150	100

Scout Model SAA 1962-1971

This is basically a scaled-down version of the SAA chambered for the .22 l.r. cartridge. This model is offered with a 4.75", 6", or 7" barrel. The earlier production has case-colored frames with the remainder blued; later production is all blued. Grips are checkered hard rubber. This model was discontinued in 1986.

NIB	Exc.	V.G.	Good	Fair	Poor
400	275	200	150	100	75

NOTE: Anyone wishing to procure a factory letter authenticating a Single Action Army should do so by writing to: COLT HISTORIAN, P.O. BOX 1868, HARTFORD, CT 06101. There is a charge of $35 per serial number for this service. If Colt cannot provide the desired information, $10 will be refunded. Enclose the Colt model name, serial number, and your name and address, along with the check.

COLT ANTIQUE LONG ARMS

Berdan Single Shot Rifle

This is a scarce rifle on today's market. There were approximately 30,200 manufactured, but nearly 30,000 of them were sent to Russia. This rifle was produced from 1866-1870. It is a trapdoor-type action chambered for .42 centerfire. The standard model has a 32.5" barrel; the carbine, 18.25". The finish is blued, with a walnut stock. This rifle was designed and the patent held by Hiram Berdan, Commander of the Civil War "Sharpshooters" Regiment. This was actually Colt's first cartridge arm. The 30,000 rifles and 25 half-stocked carbines that were sent to Russia were in Russian Cyrillic letters. The few examples made for American sales have Colt's name and Hartford address on the barrel.

Courtesy Milwaukee Public Museum, Milwaukee, Wisconsin

Rifle Russian Order, 30,000 Manufactured

Exc.	V.G.	Good	Fair	Poor
—	2000	750	450	—

Carbine Russian Order, 25 Manufactured

Exc.	V.G.	Good	Fair	Poor
—	5500	3000	1250	—

Rifle U.S. Sales, 100 Manufactured

Exc.	V.G.	Good	Fair	Poor
—	5000	2250	1250	—

Carbine U.S. Sales, 25 Manufactured

Exc.	V.G.	Good	Fair	Poor
—	9500	4500	2000	—

Colt-Franklin Military Rifle

This is a rifle that was not a successful venture for Colt. The patents were held by William B. Franklin, a vice-president of the company. This was a bolt action rifle with a primitive, gravity-fed box magazine. It is chambered for the .45-70 government cartridge, has a 32.5" barrel, and is blued, with a walnut stock. The rifle has the Colt Hartford barrel address and is stamped with an eagle's head and U.S. inspectors marks. There were only 50 of these rifles produced, and it is believed that they were prototypes intended for government sales. This was not to be, and production ceased after approximately 50 were manufactured in 1887 and 1888.

Exc.	V.G.	Good	Fair	Poor
—	8000	4500	2000	—

Colt-Burgess Lever Action Rifle

This represented Colt's only attempt to compete with Winchester for the lever action rifle market. It is said that when Winchester started to produce revolving handguns for prospective marketing, Colt dropped the Burgess from its line. This rifle is chambered for .44-40. It has a 25.5" barrel and a 15-shot tubular magazine. The Carbine version has a 20.5" barrel and 12-shot magazine. The finish is blued, with a case-colored hammer and lever. The stock is walnut with an oil finish. The Colt Hartford address is on the barrel, and "Burgess Patents" is stamped on the bottom of the lever. There were 3,775 rifles manufactured—1,219 with round barrels and 2,556 with octagonal barrels. There were also 2,593 Carbines. The Burgess was produced from 1883-1885.

Courtesy Buffalo Bill Historical Center, Cody, Wyoming

Rifle, Octagonal Barrel

Exc.	V.G.	Good	Fair	Poor
—	—	3500	1500	550

Rifle, Round Barrel

Exc.	V.G.	Good	Fair	Poor
—	—	3500	1500	550

Carbine

Exc.	V.G.	Good	Fair	Poor
—	—	5000	2000	950

Baby Carbine, Lighter Frame and Barrel (RARE)

Exc.	V.G.	Good	Fair	Poor
—	—	6000	2500	1150

Lightning Slide Action, Medium Frame

This was the first slide action rifle Colt produced. It is chambered for .32-20, .38-40, and .44-40 and was intended to be a companion piece to the SAAs in the same calibers. The rifle has a 26" barrel with 15-shot tube magazine; the carbine, a 20" barrel with 12-shot magazine. The finish is blued, with case-colored hammer; the walnut stock is oil-finished; and the forend, usually checkered. The Colt name and Hartford address are stamped on the barrel along with the patent dates. There were approximately 89,777 manufactured between 1884 and 1902.

Courtesy Butterfield & Butterfield, San Francisco, California

Rifle

Exc.	V.G.	Good	Fair	Poor
—	2500	1250	750	400

Carbine

Exc.	V.G.	Good	Fair	Poor
—	3500	1750	800	500

Military Rifle or Carbine

.44-40 caliber, short magazine tube, bayonet lug, and sling swivels.

Exc.	V.G.	Good	Fair	Poor
—	4250	2000	1000	600

Baby Carbine, 1 lb., Lighter Version of Standard Carbine

Courtesy Richard M. Kumor Sr.

Exc.	V.G.	Good	Fair	Poor
—	5000	2500	1250	750

San Francisco Police Rifle

.44-40 caliber, #SFP 1-SFP401 on bottom tang.

Exc.	V.G.	Good	Fair	Poor
—	3250	1250	800	500

Lightning Slide Action Small Frame

This is a well-made rifle and the first of its type that Colt manufactured. It is chambered for the .22 Short and Long. The standard barrel length is 24"; the finish, blued with a case-colored hammer. The stock is walnut; some were checkered; some, not. The barrel is stamped with the Colt name and Hartford address and the patent dates. There were 89,912 manufactured between 1887 and 1904.

Courtesy Butterfield & Butterfield, San Francisco, California

Exc.	V.G.	Good	Fair	Poor
2750	1250	700	500	300

Lightning Slide Action, Large Frame

This rifle is similar in appearance to the Medium Frame Lightning, though larger in size. It is chambered in larger rifle calibers of the era, from .38-56 up to .50-95 Express. The larger calibers are more desirable from a collector's standpoint. The rifle has a 28" barrel; the carbine, a 22" barrel. The finish is blued, with a case-colored hammer. The stock is oiled walnut; the forend, checkered. The Colt name and Hartford address

are stamped on the barrel along with the patent dates. This rifle is quite large and has come to be known as the "Express model." Colt manufactured 6,496 between 1887 and 1894.

Rifle, 28" Octagonal Barrel

Exc.	V.G.	Good	Fair	Poor
—	4500	2000	750	500

Rifle, 28" Round Barrel

Exc.	V.G.	Good	Fair	Poor
—	4000	1750	750	500

Carbine, 22" Barrel

Exc.	V.G.	Good	Fair	Poor
—	7500	3500	1500	750

Baby Carbine, 22" Barrel 1 lb. Lighter

Exc.	V.G.	Good	Fair	Poor
—	10000	5000	2250	950

A Colt Lightning Semi-Deluxe rifle in .22 caliber was sold at auction for $2,645. Fitted with a 24" tapered barrel. Shipped in 1888. Condition was very good. Lyman No. 15 tang sight.
Amoskeag Auction Co. Inc., May 2000

Model 1878 Double Barrel Shotgun

This model is chambered in 10 or 12 gauge and has 28", 30", or 32" barrels. It is a sidelock double-trigger hammer gun with case-colored locks and breech. The barrels are browned Damacus-patterned. The checkered walnut stock is varnished or oil-finished. The Colt's Hartford address is stamped on the barrel rib; and Colt's name, on the lock. This has been regarded as one of the finest shotguns made in America, although Colt had difficulty competing with the less expensive European imports of the day. They ceased production after only 22,690 were manufactured between 1878 and 1889.

Fully Engraved Model add 300%.

Exc.	V.G.	Good	Fair	Poor
—	1250	600	400	250

Model 1883 Double Barrel Shotgun

This model is a hammerless boxlock, chambered for 10 or 12 gauge. The barrels are 28", 30", or 32"; and it features double triggers. The frame and furniture are case-colored; the barrels, browned with Damascus pattern. The checkered walnut stock is varnished or oil-finished. Colt's Hartford address is stamped on the barrel rib. "Colt" is stamped on each side of the frame. Again, as in the Model 1878, this is rated as one of the finest of all American-made shotguns. There were many special orders, and they require individual appraisal. Colt manufactured 7,366 of these guns between 1883 and 1895.

Fully Engraved Model add 300%.

Exc.	V.G.	Good	Fair	Poor
—	1750	800	500	250

Double Barrel Rifle

This is one of the rarest of all Colt firearms and is a prize for the Colt collector. There were only 35 of these guns manufactured. They were said to be the special interest of Caldwell Hart Colt, Samuel Colt's son, who was an avid arms collector. It is said that most of the 35 guns produced wound up in his collection or those of his friends. This gun is chambered for .45-70 or one of the larger variations thereof. It is an exposed hammer sidelock with double triggers. The locks, breech, and furniture are case-colored; the barrels, browned or blued. The barrels are 28" in length, and the checkered stock was oil-finished or varnished walnut. The barrel rib is stamped with the Colt name and Hartford address. The locks are also stamped "Colt." One must exercise extreme caution in dealing with this model as there have been model 1878 Shotguns converted into double rifles. Colt manufactured the 35 guns over the period 1879-1885.

Courtesy Butterfield & Butterfield, San Francisco, California

Exc.	V.G.	Good	Fair	Poor
—	25000	10000	5000	1500

COLT DOUBLE ACTION REVOLVERS

Model 1877 "Lightning" and "Thunderer"

The Model 1877 was Colt's first attempt at manufacturing a double-action revolver. It shows a striking resemblance to the Single Action Army. Sales on this model were brisk, with over 166,000 produced between 1877 and 1909. Chambered for two different cartridges, the .38 Colt, known as the "Lightning", and .41 Colt, as the "Thunderer." The standard finishes are blued, with case-colored frame and nickel plate. The bird's-head grips are of checkered rosewood on the early guns and hard rubber on the majority of the production run. The barrel lengths most often encountered are 2.5" and 3.5" without an ejector rod, and 4.5" and 6" with the rod. Other barrel lengths from 1.5" through 10" were offered. The Model 1877 holds 6 shots in either caliber. There were quite a few different variations found within this model designation. Values furnished are for the standard variations. Antiques made before 1898 would be more desirable from an investment standpoint.

.41 Caliber "Thunderer" add 10%.
Over 6" Barrel add 50%.
London Barrel Address add 20%.
.32 Caliber add 50%.
Rosewood Grips add 10%.

Without Ejector, 2.5" and 3.5" Barrel

Exc.	V.G.	Good	Fair	Poor
3000	2000	1000	500	350

With Ejector, 4.5" and 6" Barrel

Exc.	V.G.	Good	Fair	Poor
3000	1800	1000	750	450

NOTE: Premium for blued guns-25%.
NOTE: Premium for shorter than 2-1/2"-50%.

WHAT'S IT LIKE-COLT'S DOUBLE ACTION MODEL OF 1877

All of Colt's big bore sixguns from the 1847 Walker through the 1873 Single Action Army had one thing in common. They could be fired accurately or they could be fired quickly but it was a rare individual that could operate them so they did both. Colt took care of this problem in 1877 with the introduction of the first practical double action revolver, the New Double Action Self-Cocking Central-Fire Six-Shot Revolver, which fortunately is better known by its much shorter name, the Lightning Model. Actually there were two versions of the 1877 Model: the Lightning in .38 Long Colt and the .41 Long Colt Thunderer. Both of these double action sixguns were a radical departure from the single actions not only in the shape of the grip frame, but also the fact that the hammer no longer had to be cocked as this little gun could be fired by simply pulling the trigger. They still loaded and unloaded the same as the Single Action Army. That is they had a loading gate and a sliding ejector rod. Hold a Lightning or Thunderer in your hand and you realize what a great idea this was. The grip frame is very comfortable and both trigger and hammer are easy to reach. Such gunfighters as Billy the Kid, Doc Holliday, and John Wesley Hardin saw the great advantage of having a sixgun that was self-cocking. The Model of 1877 had a well-deserved reputation for being very prone to breakage. However, such fire-eaters as the three men mentioned must have thought that its assets far outweighed its liabilities. If you come upon a Model 1877 that looks like it should be a good shooter don't pass it by. There are men today who specialize in making these little guns sing a new song.

John Taffin

Model 1878 "Frontier"

This model is a large and somewhat ungainly looking revolver. It has a solid frame with a removable triggerguard. The cylinder does not swing out, and there is a thin loading gate. It has bird'shead grips made of checkered hard rubber; walnut would be found on the early models. The finish is either blued and case-colored or nickel-plated. The Model 1878 holds 6 shots, and the standard barrel lengths are 4.75", 5.5", and 7.5" with an ejector assembly and 3", 3.5", and 4" without. The standard chamberings for the Model 1878 are .32-20, 38-40, .41 Colt, .44-40, and .45 Colt. This model was fairly well received because it is chambered for the large calibers that were popular in that era. Colt manufactured 51,210 between 1878 and 1905. Antique models made before 1898 would be more desirable from an investment standpoint.

NOTE: Add a 15% premium for blued revolvers. Add 10% to 50% premium for calibers other than .44-40 or .45.

Courtesy Butterfield & Butterfield, San Francisco, California

Model 1878 "Frontier" Standard

Exc.	V.G.	Good	Fair	Poor
4200	3000	1200	800	400

Model 1878 "Frontier" Omnipotent

This is a special order version of the model above with the name "Omnipotent" stamped on the barrel.

Exc.	V.G.	Good	Fair	Poor
16000	10000	6000	3000	1000

Sheriffs Model

Chambered for .44-40 or .45 Colt with barrels lengths of 3.5" or 4".

Exc.	V.G.	Good	Fair	Poor
6000	4000	2000	1000	800

Model 1902 (Philippine or Alaskan Model)

This is a U.S. Ordnance contract Model 1878. It has a 6" barrel and is chambered for .45 Colt. The finish is blued, and there is a lanyard swivel on the butt. This model bears the U.S. inspector's marks. It is sometimes referred to as the Philippine or the Alaskan model. The triggerguard is quite a bit larger than standard.

Courtesy Butterfield & Butterfield

Exc.	V.G.	Good	Fair	Poor
5500	3500	1800	1000	600

Model 1889 Navy-civilian model

The 1889 Navy is an important model from a historical standpoint as it was the first double action revolver Colt manufactured with a swing-out cylinder. They produced 31,000 of them between 1889 and 1894. The Model 1889 is chambered for the .38 Colt and the .41 Colt cartridges. The cylinder holds 6 shots. It is offered with a 3", 4.5", or 6" barrel; and the finish was either blued or nickel-plated. The grips are checkered hard rubber with the "Rampant Colt" in an oval molded into them. The patent dates 1884 and 1888 appear in the barrel marking, and the serial numbers are stamped on the butt.

NOTE: For 3" Barrel add 20%.

Exc.	V.G.	Good	Fair	Poor
3000	1500	1000	600	300

NOTE: Add premium for blued models.

Model 1889 U.S. Navy-martial model

This variation has a 6" barrel, is chambered for .38 Colt, and is offered in blued finish only. "U.S.N." is stamped on the butt. Most of the Navy models were altered at the Colt factory to add the Model 1895 improvements. An original unaltered specimen would be worth as much as 50 percent premium over the altered values shown.

Courtesy Butterfield & Butterfield, San Francisco, California

Exc.	V.G.	Good	Fair	Poor
9000	5000	2500	1000	500

Model 1892 "New Army and Navy"-civilian model

This model is similar in appearance to the 1889 Navy. The main differences are improvements to the lockwork function. It has double bolt stop notches, a double cylinder locking bolt, and shorter flutes on the cylinder. The .38 Smith & Wesson and the .32-20 were added to the .38 Colt and .41 Colt chamberings. The checkered hard rubber grips are standard, with plain walnut grips found on some contract series guns. Barrel lengths and finishes are the same as described for the Model 1889. The patent dates 1895 and 1901 appear stamped on later models. Colt manufactured 291,000 of these revolvers between 1892 and 1907. Antiques before 1898 are more desirable from an investment standpoint.

NOTE: For 3" Barrel add 20%.

Exc.	V.G.	Good	Fair	Poor
2000	800	500	200	100

Model 1892 U.S. Navy-martial model

Exc.	V.G.	Good	Fair	Poor
3500	2000	800	600	400

Courtesy Butterfield & Butterfield, San Francisco, California

Courtesy Butterfield & Butterfield, San Francisco, California

Model 1892 U.S. Army-martial model

Exc.	V.G.	Good	Fair	Poor
3500	2000	800	600	400

Model 1896/1896 Army

Exc.	V.G.	Good	Fair	Poor
3500	2000	800	600	400

Model 1905 Marine Corps

This model is a variation of the New Army and Navy Model. It was derived from the late production with its own serial range #10001-10926. With only 926 produced between 1905 and 1909, it is quite rare on today's market and is eagerly sought after by Colt Double Action collectors. This model is chambered for the .38 Colt and the .38 Smith & Wesson Special cartridges. It holds 6 shots, has a 6" barrel, and is offered in a blued finish only. The grips are checkered walnut and are quite different than those found on previous models. "U.S.M.C." is stamped on the butt; patent dates of 1884, 1888, and 1895 are stamped on the barrel. One hundred twenty-five of these revolvers were earmarked for civilian sales and do not have the Marine Corps markings; these will generally be found in better condition. Values are similar.

Courtesy Faintich Auction Services, Inc. Photo Paul Goodwin

Exc.	V.G.	Good	Fair	Poor
4500	3500	2000	1500	750

New Service Model

This model was in continual production from 1898 through 1944. It is chambered for 11 different calibers: .38 Special, .357 Magnum, .38-40, .44 Russian, .44 Special, .44-40, .45 ACP, .45 Colt, .450 Eley, .455 Eley, and .476 Eley. It is offered in barrel lengths from 2" to 7.5", either blued or nickel-plated. Checkered hard rubber grips were standard until 1928, and then checkered walnut grips were used with an inletted Colt medallion. This was the largest swing-out cylinder double action revolver that Colt ever produced, and approximately 356,000 were manufactured over the 46 years they were made. There are many different variations of this revolver, and one should consult a book dealing strictly with Colt for a thorough breakdown and description.

Courtesy Wallis & Wallis, Lewes, Sussex, England

Early Model, #1-21000

Exc.	V.G.	Good	Fair	Poor
1000	650	350	200	125

Early Model Target, #6000-15000

Checkered walnut grips, flattop frame, 7.5" barrel.

Courtesy Faintich Auction Services, Inc. Photo Paul Goodwin

Exc.	V.G.	Good	Fair	Poor
3000	1500	550	300	200

Improved Model, #21000-325000

Has internal locking improvements.

Courtesy Faintich Auction Services, Inc. Photo Paul Goodwin

Exc.	V.G.	Good	Fair	Poor
850	550	300	175	150

Improved Target model, #21000-325000

Courtesy Faintich Auction Services, Inc. Photo Paul Goodwin

Exc.	V.G.	Good	Fair	Poor
2250	1500	550	300	200

U.S. Army Model 1909, #30000-50000
5.5" barrel, .45 Colt, walnut grips, "U.S. Army model 1909" on butt.

Courtesy Faintich Auction Services, Inc. Photo Paul Goodwin

Exc.	V.G.	Good	Fair	Poor
1850	1200	650	300	200

U.S. Navy Model 1909, #50000-52000
Same as above with "U.S.N." on butt.

Exc.	V.G.	Good	Fair	Poor
2600	1800	1000	350	250

U.S. Marine Corps Model 1909, #21000-23000
Checkered walnut grips, "U.S.M.C." on butt.

Exc.	V.G.	Good	Fair	Poor
3000	2000	1200	650	450

U.S. Army Model 1917, #150000-301000
Smooth walnut grips, 5.5" barrel, .45 ACP. Model designation stamped on butt.

Courtesy Faintich Auction Services, Inc. Photo Paul Goodwin

Exc.	V.G.	Good	Fair	Poor
850	600	400	300	225

Model 1917 Civilian, #335000-336000
Approximately 1,000 made in .45 ACP only from Army parts overrun. No military markings.

Exc.	V.G.	Good	Fair	Poor
750	550	400	250	200

Late Model New Service, #325000-356000
Checkered walnut grips and internal improvements.

Exc.	V.G.	Good	Fair	Poor
850	650	400	200	125

Shooting Master, #333000-350000
Round butt, checkered walnut grips with Colt medallion, 6" barrel, "Colt Shooting Master" on barrel, flattop frame with target sights. Chambered for the .38 Special cartridge.

Courtesy Faintich Auction Services, Inc. Photo Paul Goodwin

Exc.	V.G.	Good	Fair	Poor
1500	1200	850	400	300

NOTE: Add 100% premium for .357 Magnum, .44 Special, .45 ACP, and .45 Colt.

Magnum Model New Service, Over #340000
Chambered for .357 Magnum, .38 Special.

Exc.	V.G.	Good	Fair	Poor
800	600	350	250	200

NOTE: Deduct $100 for .38 Special

New Pocket Model
This was the first swing-out cylinder, double action pocket revolver made by Colt. It is chambered for .32 Colt and .32 Smith & Wesson. It holds 6 shots and is offered with barrel lengths of 2.5", 3.5", 5", and 6". The finish is blued or nickel-plated, and the grips are checkered hard rubber with the oval Colt molded into them. "Colt's New Pocket" is stamped on the frame. 1884 and 1888 patent dates are stamped on the barrel of later-production guns. There were approximately 30,000 of these manufactured between 1893 and 1905. Antiques made before 1898 are more desirable.

Early Production Without Patent Dates add 25%.
5" Barrel add 10%.

Exc.	V.G.	Good	Fair	Poor
600	450	300	250	150

Pocket Positive
Externally this is the same revolver as the New Pocket, but it has the positive lock feature. It was manufactured between 1905 and 1940.

Exc.	V.G.	Good	Fair	Poor
500	375	275	225	125

New Police Model

This model appears similar to the New Pocket Model. The frame is stamped "New Police." It is chambered for the .32 Colt, .32 Colt New Police, and .32 Smith & Wesson cartridges. The barrel lengths are 2.5", 4", and 6". The finishes are blued or nickel-plated. Colt manufactured 49,500 of this model from 1896-1907. The New York City Police Department purchased 4,500 of these revolvers, and the backstraps are so marked. There was also a target model of this revolver, which features a 6" barrel with a flattop frame and target sights, of which 5,000 were produced.

New York Police Marked add 10%.
Target model add 20%.

Exc.	V.G.	Good	Fair	Poor
400	250	200	150	100

Police Positive

This is externally the same as the New Police with the addition of the positive lock feature and two new chamberings—the .38 New Police and the .38 Smith & Wesson. They were manufactured from 1905-1947.

Exc.	V.G.	Good	Fair	Poor
400	300	250	200	150

Police Positive Target

This is basically the same as the New Police Target with the positive lock feature. It is chambered in .22 l.r., the .22 WRF, as well as the other cartridges offered in the earlier model.

Exc.	V.G.	Good	Fair	Poor
650	550	400	300	200

NOTE: A .22 caliber Police Positive chambered for the .22 short and long cartridge may be seen with British proofs. Several such revolvers were sold to London Armory in this configuration during the late 1920s. A NIB example recently sold for $1,200.

Police Positive Special

This model is similar to the Police Positive but has a slightly larger frame to accept the longer cylinder needed to chamber more powerful cartridges such as the .38 Special, in addition to the original chamberings. They were manufactured from 1907-1973.

Exc.	V.G.	Good	Fair	Poor
350	275	225	150	100

Police Positive Special Mark V

Introduced in 1994 this is an updated version of the Police Positive Special. This model features an underlug 4" barrel with rubber grips and fixed sights. The butt is rounded. The revolver is rated to fire .38 caliber +P rounds. Overall length is 9" and weighs approximately 30 oz.

NIB	Exc.	V.G.	Good	Fair	Poor
350	250	200	150	100	85

Army Special Model

This is a heavier-framed improved version of the New Army and Navy revolver. It is chambered for the .32-20, .38 Colt, .38 Smith & Wesson, and .41 Colt. It is offered with a 4", 4.5", 5", and 6" barrel. The finish is blued or nickel-plated, and the grips are checkered hard rubber. The serial number range is #291000-#540000, and they were manufactured between 1908-1927.

Exc.	V.G.	Good	Fair	Poor
550	400	250	200	150

Officer's Model Target 1st Issue

This revolver is chambered for the .38 Special cartridge. It has a 6" barrel and is blued. It has a flattop frame with adjustable target sights. Colt manufactured this model from 1904-1908.

Exc.	V.G.	Good	Fair	Poor
1000	750	350	300	200

Officer's Model Target 2nd Issue

Courtesy Faintich Auction Services, Inc. Photo Paul Goodwin

This model is similar to the 1st Issue but is offered in .22 l.r. and .32 Police Positive caliber, as well as in .38 Special. It also is furnished with a 4", 4.5", 5", 6", and 7.5" barrel in .38 Special only. It has checkered walnut grips. Colt manufactured this model between 1908 and 1940.

Exc.	V.G.	Good	Fair	Poor
700	550	300	250	150

Camp Perry Single Shot

This model was created by modifying an Officer's Model frame to accept a special flat single shot "cylinder." This flat chamber pivots to the left side and downward for loading. The pistol is chambered for .22 l.r. and is offered with an 8" (early production) or 10" (late production) barrel. The finish is blued, with checkered walnut grips. The name "Camp Perry Model" is stamped on the left side of the chamber; the caliber is on the barrel. Colt named this model after the site of the U.S. Target Competition held annually at Camp Perry, Ohio. They manufactured 2,525 of these between 1920 and 1941.

Exc.	V.G.	Good	Fair	Poor
1750	1250	750	500	350

Officers Model Match

Introduced in 1953 this model is similar to the Officers Model Target and chambered for either the .22 caliber cartridge or the .38 Special with 6" barrel. The revolver is fitted with a heavy tapered barrel and wide hammer spur with adjustable rear sight and ramp front sight. It was sold with checkered walnut target grips. Blued finish is standard. Discontinued in 1970. The standard of long action could be fired both double or single action. The .22 caliber version prices are listed below. Officers Model Match in .38 caliber will bring approximately 20% less.

Exc.	V.G.	Good	Fair	Poor
750	600	450	350	250

.22 Caliber in Short Action-Single Action Only

Exc.	V.G.	Good	Fair	Poor
1000	750	600	500	350

Official Police

This was a popular revolver in the Colt line for many years. It was manufactured from 1927 to 1969. It is chambered for .32-20 and .41 Colt. These calibers were discontinued in 1942 and 1930, respectively. The .38 Special was chambered throughout the entire production run, and .22 l.r. was added in 1930. This model holds 6 shots, has a square butt, and is offered with 2", 4", 5", and 6" barrel lengths. The grips are checkered walnut. The finish is either blued or nickel-plated.

Nickel-Plated add 10%.
.22 l.r. add 20%.

Exc.	V.G.	Good	Fair	Poor
400	300	250	200	150

Commando Model

This model, for all intents and purposes, is an Official Police chambered for .38 Special, with a 2", 4", or 6" barrel. This model is parkerized and stamped "Colt Commando" on the barrel. There were approximately 50,000 manufactured between 1942-1945 for use in World War II.

NOTE: Add 30% for 2" barrel.

Courtesy Richard M. Kumor, Sr.

Exc.	V.G.	Good	Fair	Poor
550	450	275	150	100

Marshall Model

This is an Official Police that is marked "Colt Marshall" on the barrel and has an "M" suffix in the serial number. It has a 2" or 4" barrel and a round butt. The finish is blued. There were approximately 2,500 manufactured between 1954 and 1956.

Exc.	V.G.	Good	Fair	Poor
500	400	300	250	150

Bankers Special

The Bankers Special is a 2" barreled, easily concealed revolver. It was designed with bank employees in mind. It is chambered for .38 Special and was offered in blued finish. The grips are rounded but full-sized, and Colt utilized this feature in advertising this model. The U.S. Postal Service equipped its railway mail clerks with this model. There were approximately 35,000 manufactured between 1926 and 1943.

Exc.	V.G.	Good	Fair	Poor
1200	800	300	250	150

NOTE: Nickel models will command a premium.

Detective Special 1st Issue

This model is actually a duplication, as it is nothing more than a Police Positive Special with a 2" barrel standard. It was originally chambered for .32 New Police, .38 New Police, (which were discontinued) and .38 Special, which continued until the end of the production run. The finish is blued, and it is offered with wood or plastic grips. There were over 400,000 manufactured between 1926 and 1972.

Exc.	V.G.	Good	Fair	Poor
900	650	250	175	100

Detective Special 2nd Issue

This is basically a modernized, streamlined version of the 1st issue. It is similar except that it has a 2" or 3" barrel with a shrouded ejector rod and wraparound checkered walnut grips and is chambered for .38 Special. It was finished in blue or nickel plate. Reintroduced in 1993.

Left View

Right View

NEW Colt Detective Special®
Blue finish, 2" barrel, black composition grips.
Model number D1425.

NIB	Exc.	V.G.	Good	Fair	Poor
375	275	225	175	125	75

Add $25 for nickel finish.

COLT REVOLVERS

If there is one quintessential Colt revolver, other than the Colt Single-Action (at least to the generation that grew up with TV in the 1950s), it is the Colt Detective Special. For the '50s crowd, we learned that no self-respecting detective, be he federal, local or private, would ever be seen carrying or using anything other than the Colt medium-frame, six-shot, 2"-barrel, blued revolver (carried in a cross-draw rig, of course). I, naturally, had to have one, but was disappointed. The Colt double-action gets heavier just before it releases the hammer and I was already accustomed to my S&W revolvers with a different release.

I also joined in, vicariously, with the ongoing debate of the time which was choosing between the five-shot S&W and the six-shot Colt 2"- barreled guns for concealment and self-defense. The debate went along the lines of, "is it better to have six rounds with the increased cylinder width or go with five and have better concealment?" The debate was never resolved for me.

The early version Colt didn't fit my hand well, because the "Disk Special" as it came to be called, had rounded and, to me, ill-shaped grips. The later versions had a more hand-filling grip design and I was able to de credible double-action work with them. (As far as how I finally stood on the debate, I went with the S&W five-shooters, but hedged my bet and carried two of them so I had ten rounds!)

Walt Rauch

Colt .38 SF-VI

Introduced in 1995 this model is essentially a Detective Special in stainless steel with a new internal mechanism. Has a transfer bar safety mechanism. Fitted with a 2" barrel and cylinder holds 6 rounds of .38 Special. A 4" barrel in bright stainless steel is also available. Weight is 21 oz. and overall length is 7".

NIB	Exc.	V.G	Good	Fair	Poor
400	325	275	225	150	100

Colt .38 SF-VI Special Lady

Introduced in 1996 this 2" barrel version is similar to the above model with the addition of a bright finish and bobbed hammer. Weight is 21 oz.

NIB	Exc.	V.G.	Good	Fair	Poor
400	325	275	225	150	100

Detective Special II (DS-II)

Introduced in 1997 this version of the Detective special features new internal lock work and a transfer bar safety mechanism. It is fitted with a 2" barrel, has a capacity of six rounds, and is chambered for the .38 Special. In 1998 this model was offered chambered for .357 Magnum cartridge as well. Rubber combat style grips are standard. Weight is approximately 21 oz. Stainless steel finish.

NIB	Exc.	V.G.	Good	Fair	Poor
450	350	275	225	—	—

Colt Magnum Carry

Introduced in 1998 this model is essentially a renamed Detective Special II. Stainless steel finish. Weight is 21 oz.

NIB	Exc.	V.G.	Good	Fair	Poor
450	350	275	—	—	—

Cobra 1st Issue

The Cobra is simply an alloy-framed lightweight version of the Detective Special. It weighs only 15 oz. The Cobra is chambered for .32, .38 Special, and .22 l.r. This model is available in either a round butt or square butt version with a 4" barrel only. They were manufactured between 1950 and 1973.

Exc.	V.G.	Good	Fair	Poor
500	300	225	150	100

Cobra 2nd Issue

The same as the 1st Issue in .38 Special only, this is streamlined with wraparound walnut grips and shrouded ejector rod.

Exc.	V.G.	Good	Fair	Poor
400	300	225	150	100

NOTE: For nickel add 30%.

Agent 1st Issue

This revolver is basically the same as the 1st Issue Cobra with a shortened grip frame. This was done to make the Agent more concealable. Colt manufactured the Agent 1st Issue from 1955-1973.

Exc.	V.G.	Good	Fair	Poor
400	300	200	125	100

Agent L.W. 2nd Issue

This is a streamlined version with the shrouded ejector rod. In the last four years of its production, it was matte finished. Colt manufactured this model between 1973 and 1986.

Exc.	V.G.	Good	Fair	Poor
350	250	200	175	150

Border Patrol

This model is quite rare, as Colt manufactured only 400 of them in 1952. It is basically a Police Special with a heavy 4" barrel. It is chambered for the .38 Special and was built to be strong. The finish is blued and serial numbered in the 610000 range.

Exc.	V.G.	Good	Fair	Poor
5000	3000	2000	1000	500

Air Crewman Special

This model was especially fabricated for the Air Force to be carried by their pilots for protection. It is extremely lightweight at 11 oz. The frame and the cylinder are made of aluminum alloy. It has a 2" barrel and is chambered for the .38 Special. The finish was blued, with checkered walnut grips. There were approximately 1,200 manufactured in 1951, and they are marked "U.S." or "A.F."

Exc.	V.G.	Good	Fair	Poor
4500	2500	1500	800	250

Courier

This is another version of the Cobra. It features a shorter grip frame and a 3" barrel. This model is chambered for .32 and .22 rimfire. There were approximately 3,000 manufactured in 1955 and 1956.

.22 Rimfire add 20%.

Exc.	V.G.	Good	Fair	Poor
850	750	600	500	350

Trooper

This model was designed specifically by Colt to fill the need for a large, heavy-duty, powerful revolver that was accurate. The Trooper filled that need. It was offered with a 4" or 6" barrel and blued or nickel finishes with checkered walnut grips. The Trooper is chambered for the .38 Special/.357 Magnum, and there is a .22 rimfire version for the target shooters. This model was manufactured between 1953 and 1969.

Exc.	V.G.	Good	Fair	Poor
400	250	200	150	100

Colt .357 Magnum

This is a deluxe version of the Trooper. It is offered with a special target wide hammer and large target-type grips. The sights are the same as Accro target model. It features a 4" or 6" barrel and a blued finish and was manufactured between 1953 and 1961. There were less than 15,000 produced.

Exc.	V.G.	Good	Fair	Poor
500	350	300	200	150

Diamondback

This model is a medium-frame, duty-type weapon suitable for target work. It has the short frame of the Detective Special with the ventilated rib 2.5", 4", or 6" barrel. It is chambered for .38 Special and .22 rimfire for the target shooters. The finish is blued or nickel-plated, with checkered walnut grips. The Diamondback features adjustable target sights, wide target hammer, and a steel frame. It was manufactured between 1966 and 1986.

Nickel Finish add 15%.

NIB	Exc.	V.G.	Good	Fair	Poor
600	450	350	300	250	150

NOTE: For .22 caliber 2.5" barrel add 30%. If finish is nickel add $500.

Viper

This is an alloy-framed revolver chambered for the .38 Special. It has a 4" barrel and was manufactured between 1977 and 1984. The Viper is essentially a lightweight version of the Police Positive.

NIB	Exc.	V.G.	Good	Fair	Poor
450	375	200	175	125	100

Python

The Python is the Cadillac of the Colt double-action line. It has been manufactured since 1955 and is still the flagship of the Colt line. It is chambered for the .357 Magnum cartridge, holds 6 shots, and has been offered in barrel lengths of 2.5", 3", 4", 6", and 8". This revolver is offered finished in high polished Colt Royal Blue, nickel-plate, matte-finish stainless steel, or what is known as "The Ultimate"—a high polished stainless steel. The 3" barrel, as well as the nickel plating, has been discontinued. The grips are checkered walnut. It is possible that the nickel-plated specimens may bring a 10 percent premium. In my experience this is not always the case as many potential purchasers have a definite preference for the blued finish. No longer in production.

NIB	Exc.	V.G.	Good	Fair	Poor
850	700	600	500	400	225

Matte Stainless Steel

NIB	Exc.	V.G.	Good	Fair	Poor
900	800	700	600	500	275

"The Ultimate" Bright Stainless

NIB	Exc.	V.G.	Good	Fair	Poor
900	800	700	600	500	300

Python .38 Special

This is an 8" barreled Python chambered for the .38 Special only. It was a limited-production venture that was not a success. It was offered in blue only.

Exc.	V.G.	Good	Fair	Poor
600	500	400	300	225

Python Hunter

The Hunter was a special 8" .357 Magnum Python with an extended eye relief Leupold 2X scope. The grips are neoprene with gold Colt medallions. The revolver, with mounted scope and accessories, was fitted into a Haliburton extruded aluminum case. The Hunter was manufactured in 1981 only.

NIB	Exc.	V.G.	Good	Fair	Poor
1000	800	650	500	400	300

Metropolitan MK III

This revolver is basically a heavier-duty version of the Official Police. It is chambered for .38 Special and fitted with a 4" heavy barrel. It is finished in blue only and was manufactured from 1969-1972.

NIB	Exc.	V.G.	Good	Fair	Poor
400	300	150	125	100	75

Lawman MK III

This model is offered chambered for the .357 Magnum with a 2" or 4" barrel. It has checkered walnut grips and is either blued or nickel-plated. Colt manufactured the Lawman between 1969 and 1983.

Exc.	V.G.	Good	Fair	Poor
350	300	200	150	100

Lawman MK V

This is an improved version of the MK III. It entailed a redesigned grip, a shorter lock time, and an improved double action. It was manufactured 1982-1985.

NIB	Exc.	V.G.	Good	Fair	Poor
400	350	300	200	150	100

Trooper MK III

This revolver was intended to be the target-grade version of the MK III series. It is offered with a 4", 6", or 8" vent-rib barrel with a shrouded ejector rod similar in appearance to the Python. It is chambered for the .22 l.r. and the .22 Magnum, as well as .357 Magnum. It features adjustable target sights, checkered walnut target grips, and is either blued or nickel-plated. This model was manufactured between 1969 and 1983.

NIB	Exc.	V.G.	Good	Fair	Poor
375	275	250	200	150	100

Trooper MK V

This improved version of the MK III was manufactured between 1982 and 1985.

NIB	Exc.	V.G.	Good	Fair	Poor
375	275	250	200	150	100

Boa

This is basically a deluxe version of the Trooper MK V. It has all the same features plus the high polished blue found on the Python. Colt manufactured 1,200 of these revolvers in 1985, and the entire production was purchased and marketed by Lew Horton Distributing Company in Southboro, Massachusetts.

NIB	Exc.	V.G.	Good	Fair	Poor
450	400	350	300	250	150

Peacekeeper

This model was designed as a duty-type weapon with target capabilities. It is offered with a 4" or 6" barrel chambered for .357 Magnum. It features adjustable sights and neoprene combat-style grips and has a matte blued finish. This model was manufactured between 1985 and 1987.

NIB	Exc.	V.G.	Good	Fair	Poor
375	275	225	200	150	100

King Cobra

This model has become the workhorse of the Colt revolver line. The King Cobra has a forged steel frame and barrel and a full length ejector rod housing. The barrel is fitted with a solid rib. This model is equipped with an adjustable, white outline rear sight and a red insert front sight. Colt black neoprene combat style grips are standard. The blued model is no longer offered.

Blued

NIB	Exc.	V.G.	Good	Fair	Poor
450	350	300	250	200	100

Stainless Steel

Offered in 4" or 6" barrel lengths. In 1997 this model was introduced with optional barrel porting. No longer in production.

NOTE: For 1998 all King Cobras are drilled and tapped for scope mounts.

NIB	Exc.	V.G.	Good	Fair	Poor
475	350	300	250	200	125

High Polish Stainless Steel

NIB	Exc.	V.G.	Good	Fair	Poor
500	450	400	300	250	125

Anaconda

This double-action .44 Magnum revolver was introduced in 1990. It is offered with 4", 6", or 8" barrel lengths. The 4" model weighs 47 oz., the 6" model weighs 63 oz., and the 8" model weighs 59 oz. The Anaconda holds 6 rounds and is available with a matte stainless steel finish. For 1993 a new chambering in .45 Colt was offered for the Anaconda. This model was offered with a 6" or 8" barrel in a matte stainless steel finish revolver chambered for the .44 Remington Magnum cartridge. It is currently offered with a 6" or 8" barrel and adjustable red-insert front and white-outline rear sights. It is constructed of matte-finished stainless steel and has black neoprene finger-groove grips with gold Colt medallions. In 1996 the Realtree model was offered with 8" barrel. Chambered for the .44 Magnum cartridge. Furnished with either adjustable rear sight and ramp front sights or special scope mount. No longer in production.

NOTE: In 1998 the Anaconda was drilled and tapped for scope mounts and buyers had the option of barrel porting.

NIB	Exc.	V.G.	Good	Fair	Poor
550	450	—	—	—	—

COLT SEMIAUTOMATIC PISTOLS

The Colt Firearms Co. was the first of the American gun manufacturers to take the advent of the semiautomatic pistol seriously. This pistol design was becoming popular among European gun makers in the late 1880s and early 1900s. In the United States, however, the revolver was firmly ensconced as the accepted design. Colt realized that if the semiauto could be made to function reliably, it would soon catch on. The powers that be at Colt were able to negotiate with some of the noted inventors of the day, including Browning, and to secure or lease the rights to manufacture their designs. Colt also encouraged the creativity of their employees with bonuses and incentives and, through this innovative thinking, soon became the leader in semiauto pistol sales—a position that they have never really relinquished to any other American gun maker. The Colt semiautomatic pistols represent an interesting field for the collector of Colt handguns. There were many variations with high enough production to make it worthwhile to seek them out. There are a number of fine books on the Colt semiautomatics, and anyone wishing to do so will be able to learn a great deal about them. Collector interest is high in this field, and values are definitely on the rise.

Model 1900

This was the first of the Colt automatic pistols. It was actually a developmental model with only 3,500 being produced. The Model 1900 was not really a successful design. It was quite clumsy and out of balance in the hand and was not as reliable in function as it should have been. This model is chambered for the .38 Rimless smokeless cartridge. It has a detachable magazine that holds seven cartridges. The barrel is 6" in length. The finish is blued, with a case-colored hammer and safety/sight combination. The grips are either plain walnut, checkered walnut, or hard rubber. This pistol is a Browning design, and the left side of the slide is stamped "Browning's Patent" with the 1897 patent date. Colt sold 200 pistols to the Navy and 200 to the Army for field trials and evaluation. The remaining 3,300 were sold on the civilian market. This model was manufactured from 1900-1903.

Civilian Model with Sight/Safety Combination add 40%.

Standard Civilian Production

Colt Anaconda with optional ported barrel with optional Colt optics

.44 Magnum

NIB	Exc.	V.G.	Good	Fair	Poor
600	500	400	300	250	200

.45 Colt

NIB	Exc.	V.G.	Good	Fair	Poor
600	500	400	300	250	200

Realtree Camo Model-Adjustable sights

NIB	Exc.	V.G.	Good	Fair	Poor
675	625	500	400	300	200

Realtree Camo Model-Scope mounts

NIB	Exc.	V.G.	Good	Fair	Poor
900	800	650	500	400	250

Colt Multi Caliber

Introduced into the Colt product line in 1999, this model is based on the Phillips & Rodgers multi caliber design. This revolver has the capability of using 11 different cartridges in the same cylinder. They are: 9x18, 9x19, 9x23, 9mm, 9 Ruger, 9mm Largo, .380, .38 Super, .38 Special, .38 Special + P, and .357 Magnum. Barrel length is 3" and capacity is 5 rounds. Rubber combat style grips. Fixed rear sight. Stainless steel finish. Weight is about 22 oz. No longer in production.

Exc.	V.G.	Good	Fair	Poor
7500	4000	2250	1250	750

U.S. Navy Military Model

Exc.	V.G.	Good	Fair	Poor
7500	6000	5000	2500	1000

U.S. Army Military Model-1st contract

Exc.	V.G.	Good	Fair	Poor
20000	15000	10000	4000	2000

U.S. Army Military Model-2nd contract

Exc.	V.G.	Good	Fair	Poor
10000	7500	5500	2000	1500

Model 1902 Sporting Pistol

This model is chambered for the .38 Rimless smokeless cartridge. It has a 7-round detachable magazine and a 6" barrel and is blued, with checkered hard rubber grips featuring the "Rampant Colt" molded into them. The most notable features of the 1902 Sporting Model are the rounded butt, rounded hammer spur, dovetailed rear sight, and the 1897-1902 patent dates. Colt manufactured approximately 7,500 of these pistols between 1903 and 1908.

Paul Goodwin Photo

Exc.	V.G.	Good	Fair	Poor
3500	2000	1250	750	450

Model 1902 Military Pistol

Early Model with Front of Slide Serrated

Exc.	V.G.	Good	Fair	Poor
3500	2000	1250	750	450

Standard Model with Rear of Slide Serrated

Exc.	V.G.	Good	Fair	Poor
2500	1750	1000	500	400

U.S. Army Marked, #15001-15200 with Front Serrations

Exc.	V.G.	Good	Fair	Poor
6000	5000	2500	1250	600

Model 1903 Pocket Pistol

This was the first automatic pocket pistol Colt produced. It is essentially identical to the 1902 Sporting Model with a shorter slide. The barrel length is 4.5", and it is chambered for the .38 Rimless smokeless cartridge. It is blued, with a case-colored hammer, with checkered hard rubber grips that have the "Rampant Colt" molded into them. The detachable magazine holds 7 rounds. There were approximately 26,000 manufactured between 1903 and 1929.

Paul Goodwin Photo

Exc.	V.G.	Good	Fair	Poor
1100	850	650	350	200

Model 1903 Hammerless, .32 Pocket Pistol

Courtesy Orvel Reichert

Model 1903 Hammerless with 4" barrel

Courtesy Richard M. Kumor, Sr.

This was the second pocket automatic Colt manufactured. It was another of John Browning's designs, and it developed into one of Colt's most successful pistols. This pistol is chambered for the .32 ACP cartridge. Initially the barrel length was 4"; this was shortened to 3.75". The detachable magazine holds 8 rounds. The standard finish is blue, with quite a few nickel plated. The early model grips are checkered hard rubber with the "Rampant Colt" molded into them. Many of the nickel plated pistols had pearl grips. In 1924 the grips were changed to checkered walnut with the Colt medallions. The name of this model can be misleading as it is not a true hammerless but a concealed hammer design. It features a slide stop and a grip safety. Colt manufactured 572,215 civilian versions of this pistol and approximately 200,000 more for military contracts. This model was manufactured between 1903 and 1945.

Early Model 1897 Patent Date add 40%.
Nickel Plated With Pearl Grips add $100.
4" Barrel to #72,000 add 20%.

Exc.	V.G.	Good	Fair	Poor
550	500	450	300	200

U.S. Military Model
Serial prefix M, marked "U.S. Property" on frame, parkerized finish.

NOTE: Pistols issued to General Officers will command a premium.

Exc.	V.G.	Good	Fair	Poor
1200	850	400	300	250

Model 1908 Hammerless .380 Pocket Pistol
This model is essentially the same as the .32 Pocket Pistol, chambered for the more potent .380 ACP, also known as the 9mm Browning short. Other specifications are the same. Colt manufactured approximately 138,000 in this caliber for civilian sales. An unknown number were sold to the military.

Standard Civilian Model
Nickel with pearl grips add $100.

Exc.	V.G.	Good	Fair	Poor
800	650	475	350	250

Military Model
Serial prefix M, marked "U.S. Property" on frame, parkerized finish.

Exc.	V.G.	Good	Fair	Poor
1500	1000	750	500	300

Model 1908 Hammerless .25 Pocket Pistol
This was the smallest automatic Colt made. It is chambered for the .25 ACP cartridge, has a 2" barrel, and is 4.5" long overall. It weighs a mere 13 oz. This is a true pocket pistol. The detachable magazine holds 6 shots. This model was offered in blue or nickel-plate, with grips of checkered hard rubber and

checkered walnut on later versions. This model has a grip safety, slide lock, and a magazine disconnector safety. This was another Browning design, and Fabrique Nationale manufactured this pistol in Belgium before Colt picked up the rights to make it in the U.S. This was a commercial success by Colt's standards, with approximately 409,000 manufactured between 1908 and 1941.

Courtesy Orvel Reichert

Civilian Model
Exc.	V.G.	Good	Fair	Poor
500	350	300	200	100

Military Model
"U.S. Property" marked on right frame. Very rare.

Exc.	V.G.	Good	Fair	Poor
2500	1500	600	450	300

A Colt Model 1908 Hammerless Pocker pistol in 25 ACP sold at auction for $2,875. Serial number 25. Condition is 95% blue with 70% case colors. All original. Amoskeag Auction Company, January 2001

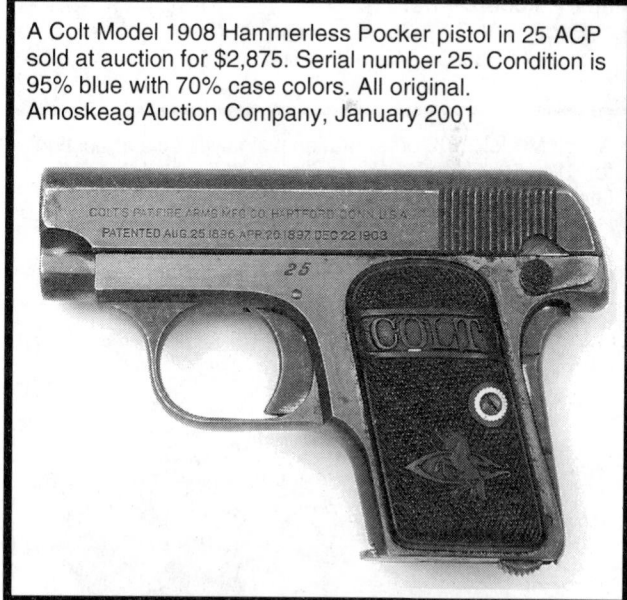

Model 1905 .45 Automatic Pistol
The Spanish American War and the experiences with the Moros in the Philippine campaign taught a lesson about stopping power or the lack of it. The United States Army was convinced that they needed a more powerful handgun cartridge. This led Colt to the development of a .45-caliber cartridge suitable for the semiautomatic pistol. The Model 1905 and the .45 Rimless round were the result. In actuality, this cartridge was not nearly powerful enough to satisfy the need, but it led to the development of the .45 ACP. Colt believed that this pistol/cartridge combination would be a success and was geared up for mass production. The Army actually bought only 200 of them, and

the total production was approximately 6,300 from 1905 to 1911. The pistol has a 5" barrel and detachable 7-shot magazine and is blued, with a case-colored hammer. The grips are checkered walnut. The hammer was rounded on the first 3,600 pistols and was changed to a spur hammer on the later models. The right side of the slide is stamped "Automatic Colt / Calibre 45 Rimless Smokeless." This model was not a commercial success for Colt—possibly because it has no safety whatsoever except for the floating inertia firing pin. The 200 military models have grip safeties only. A small number (believed to be less than 500) of these pistols were grooved to accept a shoulder stock. The stocks were made of leather and steel and made to double as a holster. These pistols have been classified "Curios and Relics" under the provisions of the Gun Control Act of 1968.

Civilian Model
Exc.	V.G.	Good	Fair	Poor
4000	3500	1750	950	400

Military Model, Serial #1-201
Exc.	V.G.	Good	Fair	Poor
8500	6500	4500	1500	500

A Colt Model 1905 presentation pistol was sold at auction for $14,950. Chambered for the .45 ACP cartridge and fitted with a 4.875" barrel. Shipped 1910. Inscribed to Howard Russell Hickock on top of slide. Condition is 99% original blue with 98% case colors. Grips are excellent. Rock Island Auction Company, September 2001

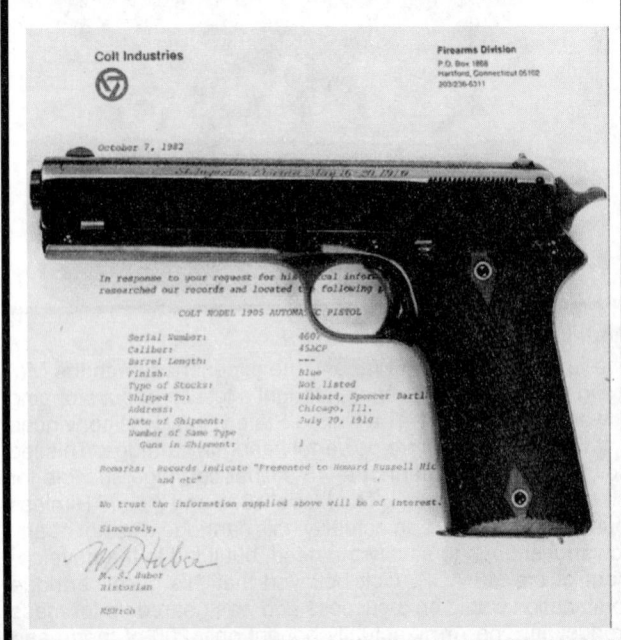

COLT 1911
Model designations and prices by Karl Karash

The Colt Government Model is one of the most recognizable handguns in the world. Its popularity is second only to the Colt Single Action Army among firearm collectors in the world today. It was this pistol that re-established Colt as the leader among handgun manufacturers. The advent of this semiautomatic pistol was timely from a historic point of view. It appeared in time for the beginning of WWI and was able to prove its worth on the battlefields of Europe and the Pacific in WWI, WWII, the Korean War and Vietnam War. The Colt .45 Auto may have been John Browning's crowning achievement, and shall always be the most respected of the Colt Auto line. There are over 200 factory variations and the unsurpassed production run from 1911 continues today.

Yet only recently has collector interest become widespread, but along with widespread collector interest has come widespread counterfeiting and fakery. Only by education in depth can the collector "hold his own" with these scoundrels and avoid costly mistakes. There are four reference books on the Colt .45 Service pistols so indispensable to collecting that they will be mentioned by name: *Colt .45 Service Pistols, Model of 1911 and 1911A1, Colt .45 Government Models (Commerical Series), and Collectors Guide to Colt .45 Service Pistols, Model 1911 and 1911A1*, all by Charles Clawson. *U.S Military Automatic Pistols 1894-1920* by Edward S. Meadows.

Model 1911 Automatic Pistol Commercial Series

The commercial or civilian version of the 1911 .45 is distinguishable by the "C" prefix in the serial number. This model commenced production in 1911 with serial number C1 and was superceded in 1924/1925 by the Model of 1911A1. The improvements built into the Model of 1911A1 were gradually phased into the pistols in the range C131000 to C138000. However the four major changes (shortening the trigger, arching the mainspring housing, lengthening the grip safety, and adding the frame finger cutouts) did not occur until about C136000. The 1911 is a large-frame semiautomatic with a 5" barrel. The finish of the early pistols (under serial C4500 to C5500) is a brilliant mirror-like high polish blue. Pistols under about C4500 had most of the visible small parts finished in a spectacular brilliant blue that can best be compared to the blue in a peacock's tail feathers. Pistols after about C5500 generally had less of a degree of polishing than the earlier pistols. The checkered walnut grips feature a raised uncheckered diamond relief around the screw holes. The 1911 has a thin front sight blade, long trigger, short spur on the hammer, and short tang on the grip safety. (The hammer spur was later lengthened at about SN C100,000.) The mainspring housing is flat, and there is no finger cut on the frame behind the trigger. The pistol is chambered for the .45 ACP and has a 7-round detachable magazine. Pistols under about C5000 had fully blued barrels and were marked "Government Model" on the right front of the frame. After about C5000, the barrels were polished and the "Government Model" marking was moved to above the trigger on the right side. All Government Model 1911s generally had a "Verified Proof" mark on the upper left triggerguard bow. There are a large number of variations of this model if all of the part, finish, and marking changes are included. The major variations are listed, but even now new information is surfacing and there may be as yet unknown variations. Be cautious of absolute statements, because these pistols were made in a real factory with real shipping schedules where "exceptions to the rule" sometimes occur.

MPORTANT PRICING INFORMATION: Generally a collectable pistol MUST have ALL original parts and original finish. Without BOTH of these, the pistols values quickly to the utility range ($250-$350). All prices are for COMPLETELY original pistols, and since most 1911/1911A1 parts generally interchange, many pistols have had parts changed. A single replaced part will reduce the value of a collectable 1911 considerably. Prices are shown based on a pistol with all screws intact and NO pits, rust, or defects, only normal wear, and no modifications. Extra deductions should be made for any defect. For common collectable pistols, (99%-100% add 20%-30%). For rare pistols the premium can be +100%. Reblued pistols will equal fair to poor condition. Be extra cautious with near new pistols, as restored pistols usually appear near new.

Early Government Models
Serial numbers through C4500, with high polish and fire blue, 3 digit serial number add 20%. 2 digit serial number add 40%. For 99%-100% add 30%-50%.

Courtesy Karl Karash collection

Exc.	V.G.	Good	Fair	Poor
5500	2900	1600	900	500

Standard Commercial 1911 Pistol
Above serial # C4500, no fire blue. Polished finished but not mirror finish. (99%-100% add 20%-30%.)

Exc.	V.G.	Good	Fair	Poor
2500	1500	900	500	300

Model 1911 With Un-numbered Slide
This variation will be found to about serial #C127300. (99% to 100% add 20% to 30% premium.)

Exc.	V.G.	Good	Fair	Poor
2500	1500	900	500	300

Model 1911 With Numbered Slide
This variation will be found from about serial #C127300 to C136000. (99% to 100% add 20% to 30% premium.)

Exc.	V.G.	Good	Fair	Poor
3000	1700	1000	500	300

FOREIGN CONTRACTS
Argentine Contract
Multiple contracts were awarded Colt by Argentina between 1914 and 1948 to supply .45 caliber pistols to their armed forces, police, and government agencies. These pistols are usually marked with an Argentine crest as well as the normal Colt commercial markings including the C prefix serial number. Colt also supplied Argentina the "MODELO 1927" that had its own serial number range of #1 to #10000 with no C prefix. Most of these pistols were well used, reblued, had mixed parts, and have import markings. Prices shown are for completely original pistols. Reblue=Fair/Poor. (99%-100% add 20%-30%.)

Exc.	V.G.	Good	Fair	Poor
950	650	400	300	200

1911 Russian Order
This variation is chambered for .45 ACP and has the Russian version of "Anglo Zakazivat" stamped on the frame. There were about 51,000 of these blued pistols manufactured in 1915-1916. They are found between serial numbers C21000 and C89000.

This variation is rarely encountered today, but a few have recently been imported and advertised. One should be extremely cautious and secure qualified appraisal if contemplating a purchase, as fakes have been noted. (99%-100% add 20%-30%.) Despite market uncertainies demand for original pistols is high.

Exc.	V.G.	Good	Fair	Poor
4000	2650	1750	1100	625

WWI British Contract
This series is chambered for the British .455 cartridge and is so marked on the right side of the slide. The British "Broad Arrow" proofmark will usually be found. These pistols were made in 1915-1919 and follow the same numeric serial number sequence as the normal Government models, except that the "C" was replaced with a "W". They are commercial series pistols. All pistols in the W19001 to W19200 range as well as some in the W29000 range are believed to be JJ marked above the left triggerguard bow. Add 25% for JJ marked. (99%-100% add 20%-30%.)

Exc.	V.G.	Good	Fair	Poor
2500	1700	950	650	450

MODEL 1911 AUTOMATIC PISTOL, MILITARY SERIES
Colt Manufacture
U.S. Army marked throughout serial range.

NOTE: Below Serial #25000 add 15%. (99%-100% add 20%-30%.)

Army below Serial #10000 add 50%
Navy below Serial #10000 add 100%
Army below Serial #1000 add 250%
Navy below Serial #1000 add 400%
Above Serial #137400 deduct 25%.

Exc.	V.G.	Good	Fair	Poor
4000	2800	2200	1550	750

A consecutively numbered pair of Model 1911 U.S. Navy pistols sold at auction for $11,500. These pistols were one of the last to bear the U.S. Navy slide markings. Shipped to the Brooklyn Navy Yard in 1915. Condition is 98% original blue. Grips are excellent. Amoskeag Auction Company, March 2001

U.S.M.C. Serial Number ranges
All USMC shipped pistols were "ARMY" marked. (99%-100% add 20%-30%.)

Exc.	V.G.	Good	Fair	Poor
7000	4300	2700	1800	1000

Springfield Armory Manufacture
(99%-100% add 20%-30%.)

Exc.	V.G.	Good	Fair	Poor
6000	3900	2500	1500	900

Springfield Armory N.R.A. marked
(99%-100% add 20%-30%.)

Exc.	V.G.	Good	Fair	Poor
6500	4200	2700	1700	1000

Remington-UMC Manufacture
(99%-100% add 20%-30%.)

Exc.	V.G.	Good	Fair	Poor
5000	3200	2000	1300	750

North American Arms Co. Manufacture
(99%-100% add 20%-30%.)

Exc.	V.G.	Good	Fair	Poor
20000	15000	10000	7000	4500

British RAF Rework
(Add 80% for original pistol.)

Exc.	V.G.	Good	Fair	Poor
1000	850	700	500	400

Arsenal Reworked 1911 Military Models

Exc.	V.G.	Good	Fair	Poor
700	625	500	400	300

Norwegian Kongsberg Vapenfabrikk Pistol Model 1912
Serial Number 1-96. (99%-100% add 20%-30%.)

Exc.	V.G.	Good	Fair	Poor
3500	2200	1150	850	600

Norwegian Kongsberg Vapenfabrikk Pistol Model 1914
Serial number 97-32854. (99%-100% add 20%-30%.)

Exc.	V.G.	Good	Fair	Poor
900	675	600	400	200

Kongsberg Vapenfabrikk Model 1914 (Norwegian) copy
Serial Number 29615 to 30535. Waffenamt marked on slide and barrel. (99%-100% add 20%-30%.) CAUTION: Fakes have been reported.

Exc.	V.G.	Good	Fair	Poor
3000	1900	1150	850	600

4 Digit X Numbered Rework
These pistols were renumbered when their original serial numbers were either defaced, obliterated, or became too light to read during rebuilding or refinishing. The four digit X prefix numbers (X1000 through X4385) were assigned after WWI (1924) and were used by Springfield through 1953. All are considered "Arsenal Refinished."

Exc.	V.G.	Good	Fair	Poor
1000	800	650	475	350

MODEL 1911A1 SEMIAUTOMATIC PISTOL, COMMERCIAL SERIES

It is said that the period between the two wars saw the finest of the Colt Automatics produced. The civilian configurations of the 1911 and 1911A1 were known as the "Government Model"(s). With the exception of the fit, finish, and markings, they were identical to the military models. However commercial production of 1911A1 pistols was stopped when WWII started and production changes to the 1911A1 were not carried over to contemporary commercial pistols because there were no contemporary commercial production. The "C" prefix designated the commercial series until 1950, when it was changed to a "C" suffix. The "Government Model"(s) were polished and blued until about SN C230,000 when the top, bottom, and rear were matte finished. The words "Government Model" as well as the usual "Verified Proof" mark were stamped on all but about the first 500 pistols when postwar production commenced at C220,000. Prewar pistols all had checkered walnut grips. Postwar pistols generally had plastic grips until the "Midrange" series when the wood grips returned. There were a number of different commercial models manufactured. We individually list them.

PRE-WWII COMMERCIAL PISTOLS

These pistols were manufactured by Colt from 1925-1942. They fall within the #C136000-C215000 serial range. A few pistols from Serial #C202000 to C215000 will most likely not be seen as most were shipped to Brazil or renumbered into Military models. *See Model 1911A1 commercial to Military conversions.*

Standard Model 1911A1 Pre-WWII "Government Model"
These pistols have numbered slides, no foreign markings, and no additions whatsoever. (99%-100% add 30%.)

Exc.	V.G.	Good	Fair	Poor
2200	1400	1000	600	325

Standard (C)1911A1 Pre-WWII "GOVERNMENT MODEL"
This pistol has a numbered slide. Foreign crest or foreign inscription from country such as Argentina or Brazil. Many of these variations with the foreign markings are more rare than the standard domestic pistol, but with the possible exception of the Mexican pistols, which seem to have a local following on the West Coast. They do not have the collector interest that the "Standard" domestic pistol has. There are four additional factors that reduce collector interest in the foreign pistols compared to their domestic counterparts:

A Colt Model 1911A1 transitional model was sold at auction for $4,715. Serial #702xxx. Full checkered walnut grips. Condition was excellent.
Amoskeag Auction Co. Inc., March 2000

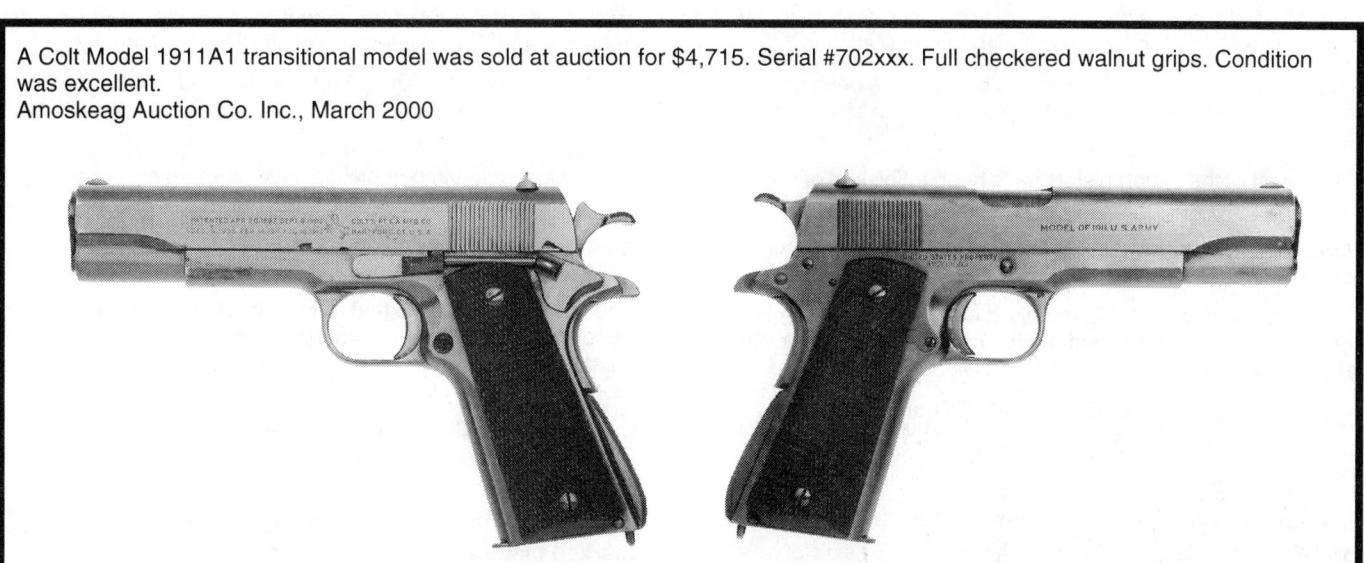

SERIAL NUMBERS ASSIGNED TO M1911 AND 1911A1 CONTRACTORS

Year	Serial No.	Manufacturer	Year	Serial No.	Manufacturer
1912	1-500	Colt	1917	186201-209586	Colt
	501-1000	Colt USN		209587-210386	Colt USMC
	1001-1500	Colt		210387-215386	Colt Frames
	1501-2000	Colt USN		215387-216186	Colt USMC
	2001-2500	Colt		216187-216586	Colt
	2501-3500	Colt USN		216587-216986	Colt USMC
	3501-3800	Colt USMC	1918	216987-217386	Colt USMC
	3801-4500	Colt		217387-232000	Colt
	4501-5500	Colt USN		232001-233600	Colt USN
	5501-6500	Colt		233601-594000	Colt
	6501-7500	Colt USN	1918	1-13152	Rem-UMC
	7501-8500	Colt	1919	13153-21676	Rem-UMC
	8501-9500	Colt USN		594001-629500	Colt
	9501-10500	Colt		629501-700000	Winchester (Assigned)
	10501-11500	Colt USN			
	11501-12500	Colt	1924	700001-710000	Colt
	12501-13500	Colt USN	1937	710001-712349	Colt
	13501-17250	Colt	1938	712350-713645	Colt
1913	17251-36400	Colt	1939	713646-717281	Colt USN
	36401-37650	Colt USMC	1940	717282-721977	Colt
	37651-38000	Colt	1941	721978-756733	Colt
	38001-44000	Colt USN	1942	756734-800000	Colt
	44001-60400	Colt		S800001-S800500	Singer
1914	60401-72570	Colt USN		800501-801000	H&R (Assigned)
	72571-83855	Springfield	1943	801001-958100	Colt
	83856-83900	Colt		1041405-1088725*	U.S. S.& S.
	83901-84400	Colt USMC		1088726-1208673	Colt
	84401-96000	Colt		1208674-1279673	Ithaca
	96001-97537	Colt		1279674-1279698	Augusta Arsenal (Renumber)
	97538-102596	Colt			
	102597-107596	Springfield		1279699-1441430	Remington-Rand
1915	107597-109500	Colt		1441431-1471430	Ithaca
	109501-110000	Colt USN		1471431-1609528	Remington-Rand
	110001-113496	Colt	1944	1609529-1743846	Colt
	113497-120566	Springfield		1743847-1890503	Ithaca
	120567-125566	Colt		1890504-2075103	Remington-Rand
	125567-133186	Springfield	1945	2075104-2134403	Ithaca
1916	133187-137400	Colt		2134404-2244803	Remington-Rand
1917	137401-151186	Colt		2244804-2380013	Colt
	151187-151986	Colt USMC		2380014-2619013	Remington-Rand
	151987-185800	Colt		2619014-2693613	Ithaca
	185801-186200	Colt USMC			

*859405-916404 Ithaca and 916405-1041404 Remington Rand

First: Most of the foreign marked pistols have been recently imported and have the legally required Import Markings.

Second: Many of the foreign marked pistols have been advertised and sold in the wholesale trade publications at utility prices.

Third: Most of the import pistols have been refinished or are in "Well Used" condition.

Fourth: Most of the foreign marked pistols have had some parts changed or mixed up.

The few of these pistols that remain in original and excellent or better condition do not command the same prices as their domestic counterparts. (99%-100% add 20-30%.)

Exc.	V.G.	Good	Fair	Poor
1100	800	600	400	250

Colt National Match Caliber, Pre-WWII, .45

(SN C162,000 - C215,000 about 3,000 pistols). This pistol was introduced at the 1930 National Matches at Camp Perry. Production began in 1932. The right side of the slide was marked "NATIONAL MATCH" and the mainspring housing had no lanyard loop. The only actual improvements to the pistol amounted to honing the firing pin stop plate, hammer link, and possibly the sear/hammer combination. (However inspection of the hammer/sear usually shows little evidence of hand honing.) It also has a selected "Match Grade" barrel and wider Patridge-type sights. Nothing was done to improve the lockup or accuracy, and it is unlikely that they shot any better than the standard "GOVERNMENT MODEL". However scores probably improved due to the wider sights and smoother trigger. The very first pistols had fixed sights, but by about SN C177,000 the "Stevens Adjustable Rear Target Sight" was available. Both fixed and adjustable sights were available thereafter throughout production. (99%-100% add 20-30%) With Adjustable Sights:

Exc.	V.G.	Good	Fair	Poor
3800	2300	1350	850	550

Fixed Sights

Exc.	V.G.	Good	Fair	Poor
2975	2150	1125	700	450

SWARTZ SAFETIES, PRE-WWII, FIRING PIN AND SEAR:

The total of pistols shipped with Swartz Safeties is probably much less than 3000.

(C)1911A1 Pre-WWII, "GOVERNMENT MODEL" marked pistol and numbered slide.

With "Swartz Safeties" No foreign markings, no additions whatsoever. (99%-100% add 20-30%.)

Exc.	V.G.	Good	Fair	Poor
3000	2000	1575	950	600

(C)1911A1 Pre-WWII, "GOVERNMENT MODEL" marked pistol and numbered slide.

With "Swartz Safeties" and foreign crest or foreign inscription from countries such as Argentina or Brazil. Many of these variations with the foreign markings are more rare than the standard domestic pistol, but with the possible exception of the Mexican pistols which seem to have a local following on the West Coast, they do not have the collector interest that the plain domestic pistol has. There are four additional factors that reduce collector interest in the foreign pistols compared to their domestic counterparts:

First: Most of the foreign marked pistols have been recently imported and have the legally required Import Markings.

Second: Many of the foreign marked pistols have been advertised and sold in the wholesale trade publications at utility prices.

Third: Most of the import pistols have been refinished or are in "Well Used" condition.

Fourth: Most of the foreign marked pistols have had some parts changed or mixed up.

The few of these pistols that remain in original and excellent or better condition do not command the same prices as their domestic counterparts. Many are reblued (100% reblue = Fair/Poor). 99%-100% add 20%.

Exc.	V.G.	Good	Fair	Poor
1400	1000	750	600	450

Standard (C)1911A1 Pre-WWII, "GOVERNMENT MODEL" marked pistol and numbered slide.

With NO "Swartz Safeties" but with Mexican crest (99%-100% add 20-30%). West Coast USA.

Exc.	V.G.	Good	Fair	Poor
2500	1800	1300	950	650

East Coast USA and Elsewhere

Exc.	V.G.	Good	Fair	Poor
1200	900	700	575	400

Argentine Contract (COLT Made) Pistols "Modelo Argentino 1927, Calibre .45"

These pistols were delivered to Argentina in 1927. The right side of the slide is marked with the two-line inscription "Ejercito Argentino Colt Cal .45 Mod. 1927." There is also the Argentine National Seal and the "Rampant Colt." SN 1-10,000. Verified proof, Assembler's mark, and Final inspectors mark under left stock by upper bushing. Most of these pistols were reblued. Reblued = Fair/Poor. (99%-100% add 20-30%.)

Exc.	V.G.	Good	Fair	Poor
1050	750	500	300	200

Colt National Match Caliber Pre-WWII, .45 With "Swartz Safeties"

(SN C186,000 - C215,000 probably less than 1500 pistols). (99%-100% add 20-30%.)

Exc.	V.G.	Good	Fair	Poor
4200	2650	1475	900	525

Fixed Sights

Exc.	V.G.	Good	Fair	Poor
3400	2400	1450	850	500

"Military to Commercial Conversions"

Some 1911 Military pistols that were brought home by GIs were subsequently returned to the Colt factory by their owners, for repair or refinishing. If the repair included a new barrel, the pistol would have been proof fired and a normal Verified proof mark affixed to the triggerguard bow in the normal commercial practice. If the pistol was refinished between about 1920 and 1942, the slide would probably be numbered to the frame again in the normal commercial practice. These pistols are really remanufactured Colt pistols of limited production and should be valued at least that of a contemporary 1911A1 commercial pistol. Very seldom seen. 99%-100% add 30%.

Exc.	V.G.	Good	Fair	Poor
2000	1200	900	500	275

"C" prefix until 1950, when it was changed to a suffix. Approximately 196,000 manufactured.

POST WWII COMMERCIAL PRODUCED 1946-1969

SN C220,000 to about C220,500

No verified proof or "GOVERNMENT MODEL" marking. Most parts are leftover military. (99% to 100% finish + 33%.)

Exc.	V.G.	Good	Fair	Poor
1500	1000	750	600	400

SN C220,500 to about C249,000 verified proof and "GOVERNMENT MODEL" marking

Many parts are leftover military. No foreign markings. (Less 30% for foreign markings.) (99% to 100% finish Add 33%.)

Exc.	V.G.	Good	Fair	Poor
1000	750	600	475	350

SN 255,000-C to about 258,000-C Slide Factory Roll Marked " PROPERTY OF THE STATE OF NEW YORK", "verified proof, and "GOVERNMENT MODEL" marking.

A few leftover military parts are still used. (99% to 100% finish +33%.) A few pairs of pistols remain as consecutive pairs. (Add 15%.)

Courtesy Karl Karash collection

Exc.	V.G.	Good	Fair	Poor
1100	800	600	500	350

SN 249,500-C to about 335,000-C verified proof and "GOVERNMENT MODEL" marking

No foreign markings. (Less 30% for foreign markings.) (99% to 100% finish add 33%.)

Exc.	V.G.	Good	Fair	Poor
850	675	550	450	300

SN 334,500-C to about 336,169-C, BB (Barrel Bushing) Marked under Serial.

About 1000 pistols. Verified proof and "GOVERNMENT MODEL" marking. (99% to 100% finish add 33%)

Exc.	V.G.	Good	Fair	Poor
1100	800	625	500	350

Super .38 1929 Model, Pre-WWII

This pistol is identical in outward physical configuration to the .45 ACP Colt Commercial. It is chambered for the .38 Super cartridge and has a magazine that holds 9 rounds. The right side of the slide is marked "Colt Super .38 Automatic" in two lines, followed by the "Rampant Colt." (99% to 100% finish add 33%.)

Paul Goodwin Photo

Exc.	V.G.	Good	Fair	Poor
3000	2000	1200	1000	600

Super Match .38 1935 Model, Pre-WWII

Only 5,000 of these specially fit and finished target-grade pistols were manufactured. They have Stevens adjustable sights, and the top surfaces are matte-finished to reduce glare. Twelve hundred of these pistols were purchased and sent to Britain in 1939, at the then costly rate of $50 per unit. Adjustable Sights. (99% to 100% finish add 33%.)

Exc.	V.G.	Good	Fair	Poor
5700	3600	2600	1300	800

Fixed Sights

Exc.	V.G.	Good	Fair	Poor
5000	3250	2400	1250	850

ACE and SERVICE MODEL ACE

Ace Model .22 Pistol

In 1930 Colt purchased advertising that, in effect, requested the shooting public to let the company know if they would be interested in a .22 rimfire pistol built similar to the Government Model. The response must have been positive because in 1931 the Colt Ace appeared on the market. The Ace uses the same frame as the Government Model with a highly modified slide and a heavy barrel. It is chambered for .22 l.r. The size is the same as the larger-caliber version, and the weight is 36 oz. The operation is straight blowback. The Ace has a 10-round detachable magazine and features the "Improved Ace Adjustable Target Sight." The markings on the left side of the slide are the same as on the Government Model; the right side reads "Colt Ace 22 Long Rifle." At first the Army purchased a few pistols (totaling 206) through 1936. It was found, however, that the function of the Ace was less than perfect, as the .22 rimfire lacked the power to consistently and reliably operate the slide. Approximately 11,000 Ace pistols were manufactured, and in 1941 they were discontinued. (99% to 100% finish add 33%.)

Paul Goodwin Photo

Exc.	V.G.	Good	Fair	Poor
2500	1750	1000	700	500

Courtesy Karl Karash collection

Exc.	V.G.	Good	Fair	Poor
850	600	450	350	225

Service Model Ace .22 R. F. Pistol

In 1937 Colt introduced this improved version of the Ace Pistol. It utilizes a floating chamber invented by David "Carbine" Williams, the firearm's designer who invented the MI carbine while serving time on a Southern chain gang. This loading chamber gave the Service Model Ace the reliability and "feel" that the public wanted. The serial number is prefixed by the letters "SM." The external configuration is the same as the Ace, and the slide is marked "Colt Service Model Ace .22 Long Rifle." Colt sold some to the Army and some on a commercial basis. There were a total of 13,803 manufactured before production ceased in 1945. (99% to 100% finish add 33%.) Parkerized pistols. (After about SN SM 3840.)

Exc.	V.G.	Good	Fair	Poor
2600	1700	1050	600	450

Blued pistols (Before about SN SM 3840)
Exc.	V.G.	Good	Fair	Poor
3500	2000	1250	800	600

Ace Service Model-Post-War

Introduced in 1978 this model is similar to the pre-war model. Production ceased in 1982.

NIB	Exc.	V.G.	Good	Fair	Poor
800	650	400	300	200	100

Conversion Units .22/.45, .45/.22

In 1938 Colt released a .22-caliber conversion unit. With this kit, one who already owned a Government Model could simply switch the top half and fire inexpensive .22 rimfire ammunition. The unit consists of a slide marked "Service Model Ace", barrel with floating chamber, ejector, slide lock, bushing, recoil spring, 10-shot magazine, and box. The Conversion Units feature the Stevens adjustable rear sight. Later that same year, a kit to convert the Service Model Ace to .45 ACP was offered. In 1942 production of these units ceased. The .22 kit was reintroduced in 1947; the .45 kit was not brought back. (99% to 100% finish add 33%.) Prewar Service Model Ace Conversion Unit (Convert .45 Cal. to .22 Cal.) SN 1-2670.

Prewar Service Model Ace

(Re-)Conversion Unit. (Convert SMA to .45 Cal. SN 1-SN 112.) (99% to 100% finish add 33%.)

Exc.	V.G.	Good	Fair	Poor
3500	2500	1500	450	350

Prewar .45/.22 Conversion Unit Unnumbered
(99% to 100% finish Add 25%.)

Exc.	V.G.	Good	Fair	Poor
450	375	325	250	150

Postwar .22 Conversion Unit Unnumbered
(99% to 100% finish add 25%.)

Exc.	V.G.	Good	Fair	Poor
350	300	250	200	130

Drake National Match Pistols

In 1964, Springfield Armory used some of these specially machined and hardened slides to build the Military National Match pistols that year. This year's pistol is perhaps the most identifiable NM pistol due to the unique slide marking. However er Drake was only the supplier of the slides that year. Colt supplied the slides in the following year (1965).

Exc.	V.G.	Good	Fair	Poor
1500	1100	750	600	400

Military National Match .45 pistols

Rebuilt from service pistols at Springfield Armory between 1955 and about 1967. These pistols were built and rebuilt each year with a portion being sold to competitors by the NRA. Each year improvements were added to the rebuild program. Four articles in the "National Rifleman" document these pistols well: August 1959, April 1963, June 1966, and July 1966. Many parts for these pistols have been available and many "Look Alike" pistols have been built by basement armorers. Pistols generally came with a numbered box and shipping papers. Prices shown are for pistols with numbered box or papers. Less box or papers -40%. When well worn, these pistols will offer little over a standard pistol.

Exc.	V.G.	Good	Fair	Poor
950	800	550	450	350

A Colt Gold Cup National Match was sold at auction for $1,265. NIB with papers.
Amoskeag Auction Co. Inc., May 2000

Gold Cup MKIII National Match

This pistol is identical to the Gold Cup .45 except that it is chambered for the .38 Mid-Range Wad Cutter round. It was manufactured from 1961 until 1974.

Paul Goodwin Photo

Exc.	V.G.	Good	Fair	Poor
1400	1000	700	550	350

Courtesy John J. Stimpson

Exc.	V.G.	Good	Fair	Poor
1050	875	600	450	350

Colt 1911A1 AMU (Army Marksmanship Unit)

Exc.	V.G.	Good	Fair	Poor
2700	2250	1450	900	400

NOTE: For Army modified pistols deduct 70%.

Gold Cup National Match (pre-series 70)

This model is chambered for the .45 ACP, features the flat mainspring housing of the 1911, and has a match-grade barrel and bushing. The parts were hand fitted, and the slide has an enlarged ejection port. The trigger is the long version with an adjustable trigger stop, and the sights are adjustable target type. The finish is blued, with checkered walnut grips and gold medallions. The slide is marked "Gold Cup National Match," and the serial number is prefixed by the letters "NM." This pistol was manufactured from 1957 until 1970.

COLT LICENSED AND UNLICENSED FOREIGN-MADE 1911A1 AND VARIATIONS

Argentine D.G.F.M.

(Direccion General de Fabricaciones Militares) made at the F.M.A.P. (Fabrica Militar de Arms Portatiles (Military Factory of Small Arms)). Licensed copies SN 24,000 to 112,494. Parts are generally interchangable with Colt. Most pistols were marked D.G.F.M. - (F.M.A.P.). Late pistols were marked FM within a cartouche on the right side of the slide. These Pistols are found both with and without import markings, often in excellent condition, currently more often in refinished condition, and with a seemingly endless variety of slide markings. None of these variations have yet achieved any particular collector status or distinction, unless "New In Box". A "New In The Box" DGFM recently sold at auction for $1200. In fact many of these fine pistols have and continue to be used as the platforms for the highly customized competition and target pistols that are currently popular.

Courtesy Karl Karash collection

Exc.	V.G.	Good	Fair	Poor
450	325	250	185	135

Brazilian Models 1911A1

Made by "Fabrica de Itajuba" in Itajuba, Brazil and the Imbel Model 973, made by "Industriade Material Belico do Brazil" in Sao Paulo, Brazil. The Itajuba is a true copy of the Colt 1911A1, and the Imbel is also believed to be a true copy, however an Imbel has yet to be examined by the author. Too Rarely seen in the U.S.A. to establish a meaningful price.

Courtesy Karl Karash collection

Exc.	V.G.	Good	Fair	Poor
575	475	375	275	225

Argentine Made Ballester Molina

UN-Licensed, Argentine Re-designed versions. (Parts are NOT interchangable with Colt except for the Barrel and Magazine.) These Pistols are found both with and without import markings. Pistols without import markings usually have a B prefix number stamped on the Left rear part of the mainspring housing and are often in excellent to New original condition. The vast majority of currently available pistols are found in excellent but refinished condition. Only the pistols with no import markings that are in excellent to New original condition have achieved any particular collector status. Most of these pistols that are being sold today are being carried and shot, rather than being collected. 99%-100% = (Exc +40%). Refinished = Fair/Poor.

MODEL 1911A1 AUTOMATIC PISTOL MILITARY MODEL

Colt Manufacture

Early models with polished and blued Finish add 100% to 1000%. (99%-100& add 30%-100.) These premiums depend on model and rarity.

Exc.	V.G.	Good	Fair	Poor
1150	850	575	450	350

Remington-Rand Manufacture

Approximate production 948,905; 1943-1945. Add 100% for first type slide, add 20% for second type slide. (99%-100% condition add 20%-30%.)

Exc.	V.G.	Good	Fair	Poor
850	750	325	500	350

thaca Manufacture

Approximate production 441,557; 1943-1945. (99%-100% condition add 20%-30%.)

Exc.	V.G.	Good	Fair	Poor
1050	950	825	600	425

Union Switch & Signal Manufacture

55,000 produced in 1943 only, between serial number 1041405 and 1096404. (99%-100% condition add 20%-30%.

Exc.	V.G.	Good	Fair	Poor
2000	1450	1050	825	600

Singer Manufacture

Five hundred produced in 1942 only. Exercise caution if contemplating purchase, as the extreme rarity of this model has encouraged fakery. Reblued, restored deduct 90% to 95%. (99%-100% condition add 30%-100%.)

Exc.	V.G.	Good	Fair	Poor
25000	18000	12000	7000	3500

7 Digit X Numbered Rework

These pistols were renumbered when their original serial numbers were either defaced, obliterated, or became too light to read during rebuilding or refinishing. The seven digit X prefix numbers (X2693614 through X2695212) were assigned to various arsenals from 1949 to 1957. Some of the reworks are done in small batches and are more distinctive and collectable than the 4 digit X numbers. All are considered "Arsenal Refinished."

Exc.	V.G.	Good	Fair	Poor
1100	850	700	500	350

MODEL 1911A1 SEMIAUTOMATIC PISTOL

The Model 1911A1 was manufactured by Colt until 1971 when the Series 70 Government Model superceded it. The modifications in the new model were a slightly heavier slide and a slotted collet barrel bushing. In 1983 Colt introduced the Series 80 models which had an additional passive firing pin safety lock. The half-cock notch was also redesigned. At the beginning of 1992 another change was made to the Model 1911A1 model in the form of an enhanced pistol. Included were the Government models, the Commander, the Officer's model, the Gold Cup, and the Combat Elite. These modifications are the result of Colt's desire to meet the shooters demand for a more "customized" pistol. Colt chose some of the most popular modifications to perform on their new enhanced models. They include beavertail safety grip, a slotted Commander-style hammer, a relief cut under the triggerguard, a beveled magazine well, a slightly longer trigger, a flat top rib, and angled slide serrations. The Model 1911A1 may be the most modified handgun in the world.

MKIV Series 70 Government Model

This model is essentially a newer version of the 1911A1. It has the prefix "70G" from 1970-1976, "G70" from 1976-1980, and "70B" from 1980-1983, when production ceased. This model is offered in blue or nickel plate and has checkered walnut grips with the Colt medallion. It is chambered for .45 ACP, .38 Super, 9mm, and 9mm Steyr (foreign export only).

NIB	Exc.	V.G.	Good	Fair	Poor
600	500	400	300	250	200

MKIV Series 70 Gold Cup National Match

This is the newer version of the 1957 National Match. It features a slightly heavier slide and Colt Elliason sights. The chambering is .45 ACP only. The Accurizer barrel and bushing was introduced on this model. It was manufactured from 1970-1983.

NIB	Exc.	V.G.	Good	Fair	Poor
800	700	600	550	500	400

A factory engraved pre-war Colt 1911A1 built in 1930 was sold at auction for $15,525. Carved ivory grips. Full coverage engraving. Only 32 .38 Super pistols were factory engraved before WWII. Condition was mint.
Rock Island Auction, March 1999

COLT 1911

The 1911 is a professional's gun and is well-suited to the most demanding of pro-active and reactive defensive use. I'm biased, though, for I've carried a 1911 my entire adult life, using it for self-defense, law enforcement and competition, which included formal bullseye as well as self-defense-based contests. The good part of the 1911 is it lends itself to all these with or without modification. For me, ising it is simply reflexive. I "know" when the gun is ready to fire. I grip the gun to automatically depress the grip safety and my thumb moves the manual safety to "off" as the gun muzzle comes to bear on the target. The grip angle is, technically, less than ideal for me and I must flex my wrist upward slightly to point it effectively. But, based on years of use, it has become second nature.

For me, the 1911 is well-suited for concealed carry, for it is flat enough where it matters and rounded where otherwise an edge would be at least an irritant and at worst an impediment. The 1911 delivers the bullet where I want it – on demand – and this directly attributable to the short-moving single-action trigger.

I'm totally comfortable with the 1911, but I also recognize that this isn't an "every man's gun, despite its use for over seventy years by the U.S. and foreign militaries. Like the Luger, it was the right gun at the right place at the right time.

Walt Rauch

COLT ENHANCED GOVERNMENT MODELS

In 1992 Colt introduced a new set of features for its Model 1911A1 series pistols. These new features include: a flattop slide, angled rear slide serrations, scalloped ejection port, combat style hammer, beavertail grip safety, relief cut under triggerguard, and long trigger. The models that are affected by this new upgrade are the: Delta Elite, Combat Elite, Government Model, Combat Commander, Lightweight Commander, Officer's ACP, Officer's ACP Lightweight.

Commander

This is a shortened version of the Government model. It has a 4.25" barrel, a lightweight alloy frame, and a rounded spur hammer. The total weight of the Commander is 27.5 oz. The serial number has the suffix "LW." The Commander is chambered for the .45 ACP, 9mm, and .38 Super. The latter two have been discontinued. Some were chambered for 7.65 Parabellum for export only. The Commander was introduced in 1949 and is still being manufactured. No longer in production.

NIB	Exc.	V.G.	Good	Fair	Poor
700	550	450	350	300	200

Combat Commander

The Combat Commander was produced in response to complaints from some quarters about the excessive recoil and rapid wear of the alloy-framed Commander. This model is simply a Commander with a steel frame. The Combat Commander weighs 32 oz. and is offered in blue or satin nickel with walnut grips. No longer in production.

Left View

Right View

NIB	Exc.	V.G.	Good	Fair	Poor
700	550	475	375	300	200

MK IV Series 80 Government Model

This model was introduced in 1983. It is, for all purposes, the same externally as the Series 70. The basic difference is the addition of the new firing pin safety on this model. No longer in production.

NOTE: In 1997 Colt offered this model with fixed white dot sights.

Blued

NIB	Exc.	V.G.	Good	Fair	Poor
650	500	400	350	300	250

Nickel Plated

NIB	Exc.	V.G.	Good	Fair	Poor
750	600	500	375	300	250

Stainless Steel

NIB	Exc.	V.G.	Good	Fair	Poor
675	625	500	400	325	275

NIB	Exc.	V.G.	Good	Fair	Poor
550	450	350	300	150	125

NOTE: This pistol was offered in stainless steel in 1996. Add $50 to the above prices.

Polished Stainless Steel

NIB	Exc.	V.G.	Good	Fair	Poor
750	650	550	450	350	300

Colt 1991A1

Introduced in 1992 this Colt Government Model is designed to resemble the original GI service issue Government Model. Offered in .45 ACP, a 5" barrel, 7-round magazine, black composition grips, and a special parkerized finish. In 1996 this model was also chambered for the 9x23 cartridge. No longer in production.

M1991A1 Commander

Chambered for the .45 ACP this model has all of the same features as the standard M1991A1 with a slightly shorter 4.25" barrel. No longer in production.

NOTE: In 1997 Colt offered this model in stainless steel with fixed white dot sights. Add $50 to NIB price.

Left View

Right View

NIB	Exc.	V.G.	Good	Fair	Poor
550	400	250	200	150	125

M1991A1 Compact

Chambered for the .45 ACP this model has a 3.25" barrel. It is 1.5" shorter than the standard M1991A1 model and .375" shorter in height. Its magazine holds 6 rounds. No longer in production.

NOTE: In 1997 Colt offered this model in stainless steel with fixed white dot sights. Add $50 to NIB price.

Left View

Right View

NIB	Exc.	V.G.	Good	Fair	Poor
550	400	250	200	150	125

MK IV Series 80 Gold Cup National Match

Externally the same as the Series 70 Gold Cup with the new firing pin safety. No longer in production.

Blued

NIB	Exc.	V.G.	Good	Fair	Poor
850	725	600	500	350	250

Stainless Steel

NIB	Exc.	V.G.	Good	Fair	Poor
925	775	650	500	400	300

Polished Stainless Steel

NIB	Exc.	V.G.	Good	Fair	Poor
975	850	725	600	450	350

Officers ACP

This is a shortened version of the Government Model. It has a 3.5" barrel and weighs 37 oz. It is chambered for the .45 ACP only and has checkered walnut grips. The Officers ACP was introduced in 1985. No longer in production.

Blued

NIB	Exc.	V.G.	Good	Fair	Poor
625	500	400	325	250	200

Matte Blued

NIB	Exc.	V.G.	Good	Fair	Poor
600	475	375	300	225	200

Satin Nickel (Discontinued 1985)

Exc.	V.G.	Good	Fair	Poor
450	350	275	200	150

Stainless Steel

NIB	Exc.	V.G.	Good	Fair	Poor
750	625	450	350	300	250

Lightweight Officers ACP

This is an alloy-framed version that weighs 24 oz. It was introduced in 1986. No longer in production.

NIB	Exc.	V.G.	Good	Fair	Poor
675	550	450	375	300	200

Concealed Carry Officer Model

This model features a lightweight aluminum frame with stainless steel Commander slide. Barrel length is 4.25" and it is chambered for .45 ACP cartridge. Fitted with lightweight trigger, combat style hammer, and Hogue grips. Weight is approximately 34 oz. Introduced in 1998. No longer in production.

NIB	Exc.	V.G.	Good	Fair	Poor
800	650	—	—	—	—

Delta Gold Cup

Introduced in 1992 the Delta Gold Cup is chambered for the 10mm, features a 5" barrel, stainless steel finish, adjustable Accro sights, special trigger, and black rubber wraparound stocks. Features all of the new "Enhanced" model features. No longer in production.

NIB	Exc.	V.G.	Good	Fair	Poor
1000	825	700	600	400	200

Delta Elite

This model is chambered for the 10mm Norma cartridge. It is offered in blue or stainless steel. The grips are black neoprene with the Delta medallion. It features a high-profile three-dot combat sight system. The Delta Elite was introduced in 1987. No longer in production.

Blued

NIB	Exc.	V.G.	Good	Fair	Poor
700	525	425	350	300	250

Stainless Steel

NIB	Exc.	V.G.	Good	Fair	Poor
750	575	450	375	300	250

Polished Stainless Steel

NIB	Exc.	V.G.	Good	Fair	Poor
850	675	550	425	350	250

Combat Elite

This is a specialized Government model that has a 5" barrel and adjustable Accro sights. It is chambered either in .45 ACP or .38 Super. It weighs 38 oz. and has an 8-round magazine for the .45 ACP and a 9-round magazine for the .38 Super. Finish can be either blue or matte stainless steel. No longer in production.

NIB	Exc.	V.G.	Good	Fair	Poor
775	625	500	400	300	200

Combat Target Model

Introduced in 1996 this 5" barrel 1911 model features a fitted barrel, Gold Cup style trigger, tuned action, flat top slide, relieved ejection port, skeletonized hammer, wide grip safety, high cut triggerguard, beveled magazine well, and adjustable sights. Weight is 39 oz. Offered in both blue and stainless steel. In 1996 this model was also chambered for the new 9x23 cartridge as well as the .45 ACP and the .38 Super. No longer in production.

NOTE: In 1997 Colt expanded this Target Model to include a number of different variations. They are listed below.

NIB	Exc.	V.G.	Good	Fair	Poor
800	650	550	500	400	200

NOTE: Add $50 for stainless steel version.

Combat Target Combat Commander

Barrel length is 4-1/4". Chambered for .45 ACP. Stainless steel finish. Weight is 36 oz. Has all other Combat Target features. No longer in production.

NIB	Exc.	V.G.	Good	Fair	Poor
800	675	575	500	400	200

Combat Target Officer's ACP

Fitted with a 3-1/2" barrel and chambered for .45 ACP. Stainless steel finish. Weight is about 34 oz. Has all other Combat Target features. No longer in production.

NIB	Exc.	V.G.	Good	Fair	Poor
800	675	575	500	400	200

XS SERIES MODEL O PISTOLS

Introduced in 1999, these models are an enhanced version of the Colt 1911 and features front slide serrations, checkered, double diamond rosewood grips, adjustable McCormick trigger, 3 dot dovetail rear sights, ambidextrous safety, enhanced tolerances, aluminum frame, and stainless steel slide. Chambered for .45 ACP cartridge.

Colt O-Model Government (01070XS)

Fitted with a 5" barrel and 8-round magazine.

NIB	Exc.	V.G.	Good	Fair	Poor
950	750	—	—	—	—

Colt O-Model Concealed Carry Officers (09850XS)

Fitted with a 4.25" barrel and 7-round magazine.

NIB	Exc.	V.G.	Good	Fair	Poor
950	750	—	—	—	—

Colt O-Model Commander (04012XS)

Fitted with a 4.25" barrel and 8-round magazine.

NIB	Exc.	V.G.	Good	Fair	Poor
950	750	—	—	—	—

Colt O-Model Lightweight Commander (04860XS)

Fitted with a 4.25" barrel and 8-round magazine. Weight is about 26 oz.

NIB	Exc.	V.G.	Good	Fair	Poor
950	750	—	—	—	—

1991 SERIES MODEL O PISTOLS

This series of pistol was introduced in 1999 and is to replace the standard Colt 1911 series pistols. These pistols feature checkered rubber composite grips, smooth trigger, fixed sights, beveled magazine well and standard thumb safety and service style grip safety. Chambered for .45 ACP cartridge and 7-round magazines.

Colt O-Model Government Matte (01991)

Fitted with a 5" barrel, black matte finish, carbon steel frame and slide.

NIB	Exc.	V.G.	Good	Fair	Poor
645	500	—	—	—	—

Colt O-Model Government Stainless (01091)

Fitted with a 5" barrel, mattel stainless finish on stainless steel frame and slide.

NIB	Exc.	V.G.	Good	Fair	Poor
800	625	—	—	—	—

Colt O-Model Commander Stainless (04091U)

Fitted with a 4.25" barrel and matte stainless finish with stainless steel frame and slide.

NIB	Exc.	V.G.	Good	Fair	Poor
800	625	—	—	—	—

Colt O-Model Commander (04691)

Fitted with a 4.25" barrel and black matte finish with carbon steel frame and slide.

NIB	Exc.	V.G.	Good	Fair	Poor
645	500	—	—	—	—

Colt O-Model Gold Cup

This model has the same features as the O-Model Commander with the addition of a 5" barrel with a stainless steel frame and slide. Slide top is rounded. Magazine capacity is 8 rounds. Weight is about 39 oz. Introduced in 1999.

NIB	Exc.	V.G.	Good	Fair	Poor
1100	850	—	—	—	—

Colt Defender

This single action pistol was introduced in 1998. This model features a lightweight aluminum alloy frame and stainless steel slide. It is chambered for the .45 ACP or .40S&W cartridge and is fitted with a 3" barrel. Magazine capacity is 7 rounds. Rubber wraparound grips. Weight is approximately 23 oz. and overall length is 6.75". No longer in production.

NIB	Exc.	V.G.	Good	Fair	Poor
750	600	475	—	—	—

Colt Defender Model O (07000D)

This model takes the place of Defender and was introduced in 2000. It has a brushed stainless finish with a 3" barrel. Skeletonized composite trigger, beveled magazine well, extended thumb safety and upswept beavertail with palm swell. Chambered for .45 ACP only.

NIB	Exc.	V.G.	Good	Fair	Poor
750	600	—	—	—	—

Pocket Nine

This double action semiautomatic pistol is chambered for the 9mm cartridge. The frame is aluminum alloy and the slide is stainless steel. Barrel length is 2.75". Magazine capacity is 6 rounds. Wraparound rubber grips standard. Overall length is 5.5". Weight is approximately 17 oz. No longer in production.

NIB	Exc.	V.G.	Good	Fair	Poor
550	450	325	—	—	—

Tac Nine

Introduced in 1999, this double-action-only semiautomatic pistol is chambered for the 9mm cartridge. It has a 2.75" barrel with an aluminum alloy frame and stainless steel slide. Sight is Tritium night sights. Wraparound rubber grips are standard. The finish is black oxide. Enhanced tolerances. Weight is about 17 oz. No longer in production.

NIB	Exc.	V.G.	Good	Fair	Poor
725	575	—	—	—	—

Double Eagle

This is a double-action semiautomatic pistol chambered for the 10mm Auto and the .45 ACP cartridges. It has a 5" barrel and an 8-round detachable box magazine. It is constructed of stainless steel and has checkered black synthetic grips. The sights are fixed and utilize the three-dot system. No longer in production.

Left View

NIB	Exc.	V.G.	Good	Fair	Poor
500	425	350	300	250	200

Double Eagle Officer's Model

This is a compact version of the double-action Double Eagle pistol chambered for .45 ACP only. No longer in production.

NIB	Exc.	V.G.	Good	Fair	Poor
480	425	375	300	250	6200

Double Eagle Combat Commander

Based on the standard Double Eagle design but with a slightly shorter 4.25" barrel, the Double Eagle Combat Commander fits between the standard model and the smaller Officer's Model. Available in .45 ACP and .40 S&W (1993) this model weighs about 36 oz., holds 8 rounds, has white dot sights, and checkered Xenoy grips. The finish is matte stainless steel. No longer in production.

NIB	Exc.	V.G.	Good	Fair	Poor
625	550	500	400	300	200

Double Eagle First Edition

This version of the double-action Double Eagle pistol is chambered for the 10mm Auto and is furnished with a Cordura holster, double-magazine pouch, and three magazines, as well as a zippered black Cordura case.

NIB	Exc.	V.G.	Good	Fair	Poor
700	650	550	475	375	300

.380 Series 80 Government Model

This is a single-action, blowback-operated semiautomatic pistol chambered for the .380 ACP cartridge. It has a 3.25" barrel and a 7-round magazine. The sights are fixed. It is available either blued, nickel plated, or stainless steel. It has synthetic grips and was introduced in 1985. No longer in production.

Nickel Finish add 10%.
Stainless Steel add 10%.

NIB	Exc.	V.G.	Good	Fair	Poor
350	300	250	200	175	125

Mustang

This is a more compact version of the .380 Government Model. It has a 2.75" barrel and a 5-round detachable magazine. No longer in production.

Nickel Finish add 10%.
Stainless Steel add 10%.

NIB	Exc.	V.G.	Good	Fair	Poor
350	300	250	200	175	125

Mustang Plus II

This version of the Mustang pistol features the 2.75" barrel with the longer grip frame that accommodates a 7-round magazine. It was introduced in 1988 and is offered in blue, as well as stainless steel. No longer in production.

Stainless Steel add 10%.

Left View

Right View

NIB	Exc.	V.G.	Good	Fair	Poor
385	300	250	200	175	125

Mustang PocketLite

A lightweight version of the Mustang that features an aluminum alloy receiver. The finish is blued only, and it has synthetic grips. It was introduced in 1987. No longer in production.

NIB	Exc.	V.G.	Good	Fair	Poor
450	300	250	200	175	125

Government Pocketlite LW

Similar to the Mustang but fitted with a 3.25" barrel and a 7" round magazine. This model has an aluminum frame and stainless steel slide. Fixed sights. Black composition grips. Weight is approximately 15 oz. No longer in production.

NIB	Exc.	V.G.	Good	Fair	Poor
450	300	250	200	175	125

Colt Pony

Introduced in 1997 this semiautomatic pistol is chambered for the .380 ACP. It is fitted with a 2-3/4" barrel and a bobbed hammer. It is double action only. The grips are black composition. Sights are a ramp front with fixed rear. Finish is Teflon and stainless steel. Magazine capacity is 6 rounds. Overall length is 5-1/2". Weight is 19 oz. No longer in production.

NIB	Exc.	V.G.	Good	Fair	Poor
475	400	300	—	—	—

Colt Pony PocketLite

Same as above but with aluminum and stainless steel frame. Weight is approximately 13 oz. No longer in production.

NIB	Exc.	V.G.	Good	Fair	Poor
550	475	350	275	—	—

Colt Model 2000

Introduced in 1992, the Model 2000 is a new departure for Colt from its traditional service style semiautomatic pistols. Chambered for the 9mm, the Model 2000 is a double action only pistol with a 4.5" barrel and a choice between a polymer frame or an aluminum alloy frame. The polymer frame model weighs 29 oz. while the aluminum alloy frame weighs 33 oz. Grips are black composition and sights are white dot. Pistol was dropped from the Colt line in 1994.

NIB	Exc.	V.G.	Good	Fair	Poor
450	400	350	300	250	200

Colt CZ40

Introduced in 1998 this double action .40 S&W pistol is built for Colt by CZ in the Czech Republic. It is fitted with a 4" barrel and has black polymer grips. The frame is alloy with a carbon steel slide with blue finish. Magazine capacity is 10 rounds. Weight is approximately 34 oz. No longer in production.

NIB	Exc.	V.G.	Good	Fair	Poor
750	600	—	—	—	—

COLT .22 RIMFIRE SEMIAUTOMATIC PISTOLS

Pre-Woodsman Model

This pistol was designed by John Browning. The name Woodsman was not used until 1927, but some collectors use it to describe this pistol as it is of the same pattern. This pistol was designed for general purpose use, hunting, and informal target practice. The pistol has a 6.5" or 6.625" thin barrel and weighs 28 oz. There is a 10-round detachable magazine, and the chambering is .22 Long Rifle standard velocity only. It has a concealed hammer and a sliding thumb safety. The finish is blue, with checkered plastic grips. On early models checkered walnut grips and a brass follower in magazine are seen. It was manufactured between 1915 and 1927, and there were approximately 54,000 produced.

Courtesy Orvel Reichert

Exc.	V.G.	Good	Fair	Poor
1200	950	550	350	200

1st Series Woodsman

This series was manufactured from 1927 until 1947. It was chambered for .22 l.r. standard velocity up to 1932. After that date it was redesigned to fire high-velocity ammunition. The mainspring housing on these high-velocity models is serrated instead of checkered. This change took place at serial number 83790. All Woodsmans after this fired high-velocity ammunition. This model is blued, with checkered wood grips; and the side of the frame is marked "The Woodsman." The 10-shot detachable magazine is released at the bottom. There were approximately 112,000 manufactured.

Sport Model, 4.5" Barrel

Exc.	V.G.	Good	Fair	Poor
1000	850	500	300	200

Target Model, 6.5" Barrel

Courtesy Rock Island Auction Company

Exc.	V.G.	Good	Fair	Poor
950	675	450	275	200

1st Series Woodsman Match Target

This model has a special 6.5" heavy barrel, target sights, and longer checkered walnut target grips. The side of the receiver has a "Bull's-eye" and the "Match Target" designation stamped on it. There were only 16,000 of these pistols manufactured between 1938 and 1944. They are quite scarce today.

Caution: Be sure to check wood "Elephant Ear" grips for cracks prior to sale. Magazine should be marked "MATCH TARGET MOD"

NOTE: A few of these pistols were made for the military. For those that are so marked add 50%.

Exc.	V.G.	Good	Fair	Poor
2300	1700	1250	850	400

2nd Series Woodsman

This is a totally redesigned pistol and is different from the preceding models. It has a slide stop, a hold-open device, and a push-button magazine release behind the triggerguard. It is blued, with brown plastic grips. There were approximately 146,000 manufactured between 1948 and 1955.

Sport Model, 4.5" Barrel

Exc.	V.G.	Good	Fair	Poor
850	625	475	300	250

Target Model, 6" Barrel

Exc.	V.G.	Good	Fair	Poor
800	625	500	350	250

Match Target Model, 4.5" Barrel

Exc.	V.G.	Good	Fair	Poor
1075	950	750	450	300

Match Target Model, 6" Barrel

Exc.	V.G.	Good	Fair	Poor
900	750	650	350	250

NOTE: Some black plastic grips are replacement grips. Deduct 30% for these replacement grips. Add 25% for original box, papers and targets.

3rd Series Woodsman

This model is similar to the 2nd Series except that the magazine catch is located at the bottom of the grip. It was manufactured from 1955-1960 with black plastic grips and from 1960-1977 with checkered walnut.

Sport Model, 4.5" Barrel

Exc.	V.G.	Good	Fair	Poor
750	600	450	275	225

Target Model, 6" Barrel

Exc.	V.G.	Good	Fair	Poor
750	625	450	300	200

Match Target Model, 4.5" Barrel

Exc.	V.G.	Good	Fair	Poor
850	750	600	350	225

Match Target, 6" Barrel

Exc.	V.G.	Good	Fair	Poor
775	625	450	300	200

NOTE: Add 20% for Colt-Elliason rear sights on Match Target.

Challenger Model

This pistol is simply a Woodsman with less expensive grips and sights. It has either a 4.5" or a 6" barrel, fixed sights, no hold-open device, and a bottom magazine release. It is chambered for .22 l.r. The production ran to 77,000. It was manufactured between 1950 and 1955.

Exc.	V.G.	Good	Fair	Poor
550	400	275	200	150

Huntsman Model

The only difference between the Huntsman and the Challenger is that the Huntsman utilizes a 3rd Series frame. The Huntsman had black plastic grips until 1960 and checkered walnut after that. There were approximately 100,000 manufactured between 1955 and 1977.

Exc.	V.G.	Good	Fair	Poor
475	375	275	150	100

Colt Junior Pocket Model

This diminutive unit is only 4.5" long overall and weighs 12 oz. Colt did not manufacture this pistol but rather had it made for them by Astra in Spain. The pistol was introduced in 1958 chambered for .25 ACP. One year later a .22 Short version appeared. Both had external hammers and detachable 6-round magazines. The passage of the 1968 Gun Control Act made import of a weapon of this size illegal, so Colt discontinued its relationship with Astra. The pistol was re-introduced in 1970 as an American-made product and was produced for two more years. Production ceased in 1972. Astra also made this pistol and called it the Cub.

.22 Short add 25%.

NIB	Exc.	V.G.	Good	Fair	Poor
300	250	200	175	125	75

Targetsman Model

This is essentially the Huntsman with adjustable target sights and a thumbrest grip. It is offered with a 6" barrel only. There were approximately 65,000 manufactured between 1959 and 1977.

Exc.	V.G.	Good	Fair	Poor
450	350	250	200	150

Cadet / Colt .22

Introduced in 1994 this .22 caliber semiautomatic pistol is offered with a 4-1/2" barrel and stainless steel finish. The model was renamed Colt .22 in 1995. The sights are fixed and magazine capacity is 11 rounds. Overall length is 8-5/8" and weight is approximately 33 oz.

NIB	Exc.	V.G.	Good	Fair	Poor
250	200	165	125	75	50

Colt .22 Target

Introduced in 1995 this model features a 6" bull barrel with removable front sight and adjustable rear sight. Black composite monogrip stock. Stainless steel finish. Weight is 40.5 oz.

NIB	Exc.	V.G.	Good	Fair	Poor
325	275	225	150	100	75

COLT MODERN LONG ARMS

Colteer I-22

This is a single shot bolt-action rifle chambered for .22 l.r. or .22 Magnum. It has a plain uncheckered walnut stock, 20" barrel, and adjustable sights. There were approximately 50,000 manufactured between 1957 and 1966.

Exc.	V.G.	Good	Fair	Poor
400	300	175	125	90

Stagecoach

This is a semiautomatic, saddle ring carbine. It is chambered for .22 l.r. and has a 16.5" barrel and a 13-shot tubular magazine. The stock is fancy walnut, and the receiver has the stagecoach holdup scene roll-engraved on it. There were approximately 25,000 manufactured between 1965 and 1975.

Exc.	V.G.	Good	Fair	Poor
450	350	200	150	100

Courier

This model is similar to the Stagecoach, with a pistol grip stock and beavertail forearm. It was manufactured between 1970 and 1975.

Exc.	V.G.	Good	Fair	Poor
450	350	200	125	90

Colteer

This is a less expensive version of the Stagecoach. It features a 19.5" barrel, has a 15-shot tubular magazine, and is stocked in a plainer grade walnut. There is no roll engraving. Approximately 25,000 were manufactured between 1965 and 1975.

Exc.	V.G.	Good	Fair	Poor
450	350	200	125	90

Colt "57" Bolt Action Rifle

This rifle was manufactured for Colt by the Jefferson Mfg. Co of New Haven, Connecticut. It utilizes a Fabrique Nationale Mauser action and has a checkered American walnut stock with a Monte Carlo comb. The rifle is offered with adjustable sights. It is chambered for .243 or .30-06. There is also a deluxe version that features higher-grade wood. There were approximately 5,000 manufactured in 1957.

Deluxe Version add 20%.

Exc.	V.G.	Good	Fair	Poor
550	450	350	300	225

Coltsman Bolt Action Rifle

The Coltsman was manufactured for Colt by Kodiak Arms. It utilizes either a Mauser or Sako action. The rifle is offered in .243, .308, .30-06, and .300 Winchester Magnum. It has a barrel length of 22", 24" in the Magnum chambering. The stock is checkered American walnut. There were approximately 10,000 manufactured between 1958 and 1966. There is a deluxe version that features a higher-grade, skipline-checkered walnut stock and rosewood forend tip; this is called "The Coltsman Custom."

Coltsman Custom add 50%.

Exc.	V.G.	Good	Fair	Poor
650	550	450	350	250

Coltsman Pump Shotgun

This model was manufactured by Jefferson Arms, utilizing an aluminum alloy frame made by Franchi. It is chambered for 12, 16, and 20 gauge and has a 26" or 28" plain barrel. There were approximately 2,000 manufactured between 1961 and 1965.

Exc.	V.G.	Good	Fair	Poor
350	300	275	200	150

Semiauto Shotgun

The Semiauto Shotgun was manufactured for Colt by the firm of Luigi Franchi in Italy. It features an aluminum alloy receiver and is chambered for 12 or 20 gauge. The barrel length is 26", 28", 30", or 32"—either vent rib or plain. A deluxe version, "The Custom Auto," features a fancy walnut stock and a hand engraved receiver. There were approximately 5,300 manufactured between 1962 and 1966.

Custom Auto add 25%.

Exc.	V.G.	Good	Fair	Poor
375	325	300	225	175

Double Barrel Shotgun

During 1961 and 1962, Colt had approximately 50 side-by-side shotguns made for them by a French gun manufacturer. They have the Colt name on the breech area of the barrels and are in the 467000-469000 serial range. There is little information available on this gun, and Colt never went past the test-market stage.

Exc.	V.G.	Good	Fair	Poor
1000	750	650	500	400

Colt Light Rifle

Introduced in 1999, this bolt action rifle is offered in both long and short action calibers from .243 to .300 Win. Mag. Fitted with a 24" barrel and adjustable trigger. Stock is black synthetic. Action and barrel are matte black. Long action calibers. Weight about 6 lbs. with short action rifle about 5.4 lbs. Adjustable trigger. No sights.

NIB	Exc.	V.G.	Good	Fair	Poor
600	475	—	—	—	—

Colt Sauer Bolt Action Rifle

This is a high quality and unique rifle manufactured for Colt by the firm of J.P. Sauer & Son of Germany. The rifle features a non-rotating bolt that makes the Colt Sauer action smoother functioning than most. It has a 24" barrel, skipline-checkered walnut stock with rosewood forend tip, pistol grip cap, and recoil pad. There are five basic configurations: the Standard Action, chambered for .25-06, .270 Winchester, and .30-06; the Short Action, chambered for .22-250, .243 Winchester, and .308 Winchester; the Magnum Action, chambered for .7mm Remington Magnum, .300 Winchester Magnum, and .300 Weatherby Magnum; also the "Grand Alaskan" and the "Grand African," heavier versions chambered for .375 Holland & Holland Magnum and .458 Winchester Magnum, respectively. These rifles were all discontinued by Colt in 1985.

Colt Sauer Short Action

Exc.	V.G.	Good	Fair	Poor
995	850	700	600	500

Standard Action add $50.
Magnum Action add $200.
"Grand Alaskan" add $400.
"Grand African" add $450.

Colt Sauer Drilling

This is a rather unique firearm and one with which many American enthusiasts are not familiar—a 3-barreled gun. It features a side-by-side shotgun in 12 gauge over a .30-06 or .243 rifle barrel. The name was based on the German word for three, as this is where the concept was developed. They are quite popular in Europe where the game preserve style of hunting is prevalent but have little use in America where our hunting seasons don't often overlap. This drilling has 25" barrels and pop-up sights for the rifle barrel and is nicely engraved. It was discontinued by Colt in 1985.

Exc.	V.G.	Good	Fair	Poor
3500	2750	2000	1500	1100

Colt-Sharps Rifle

Introduced in 1970 as the last word in sporting rifles, the Colt-Sharps is a falling-block action that was advertised as a modern Sharps-Borchardt. This undertaking was first-class all the way. The finish is high polish blue with a deluxe-grade hand-checkered walnut stock and forend. This rifle is chambered for .17 Remington, .22-250, .243, .25-06, 7mm Remington Magnum, .30-06, and .375 Holland & Holland Magnum; and it was offered cased with accessories. This model was manufactured between 1970 and 1977.

NIB	Exc.	V.G.	Good	Fair	Poor
2500	2000	1200	850	500	300

AR-15 Sporter (Model #6000)

A semiautomatic rifle firing from a closed bolt was introduced into the Colt product line in 1964. Similar in appearance and function to the military version, the M-16. Chambered for the .223 cartridge. It is fitted with a standard 20" barrel with no forward assist, no case deflector, but with a bayonet lug. Weighs about 7.5 lbs. Dropped from production in 1985.

Colt AR-15 and Colt Sporter Terminology

There are three different and distinct manufacturing cycles that not only affect the value of these rifles but also the legal consequences of their modifications.

Pre-Ban Colt AR-15 rifles (Pre-1989): Fitted with bayonet lug, flash hider, and stamped AR-15 on lower receiver. Rifles that are NIB have a green label. It is legal to modify this rifle with any AR-15 upper receiver. These are the most desirable models because of their pre-ban features.

Colt Sporters (Post-1989-pre-September, 1994): This transition model has no bayonet lug, but it does have a flash hider. There is no AR-15 designation stamped on the lower receiver. Rifles that are NIB have a blue label. It is legal to modify this rifle with upper receivers made after 1989, i.e. no bayonet lug. These rifles are less desirable than pre-ban AR-15s.

Colt Sporters (Post-September, 1994): This rifle has no bayonet lug, no flash hider, and does not have the AR-15 designation stamped on the lower receiver. Rifles that are NIB have a blue label. It is legal to modify this rifle only with upper receivers manufactured after September, 1994. These rifles are the least desirable of the three manufacturing periods because of their lack of pre-ban military features and current manufacture status.

NIB	Exc.	V.G.	Good	Fair	Poor
1450	1100	850	700	600	400

AR-15 Sporter w/Collapsible Stock (Model #6001)

Same as above but fitted with a 16" barrel and folding stock. Weighs approximately 5.8 lbs. Introduced in 1978 and discontinued in 1985.

NIB	Exc.	V.G.	Good	Fair	Poor
2000	1800	1100	800	600	400

AR-15 Carbine (Model #6420)

Introduced in 1985 this model has a 16" standard weight barrel. All other features are the same as the previous discontinued AR-15 models. This version was dropped from the Colt product line in 1987.

NIB	Exc.	V.G.	Good	Fair	Poor
1600	1350	1000	800	600	400

AR-15 9mm Carbine (Model #6450)

Same as above but chambered for 9mm cartridge. Weighs 6.3 lbs.

NIB	Exc.	V.G.	Good	Fair	Poor
2500	2000	1200	900	700	400

AR-15A2 Sporter II (Model #6500)

Introduced in 1984 this was an updated version with a heavier barrel and forward assist. The AR sight was still utilized. Weighs approximately 7.8 lbs.

NIB	Exc.	V.G.	Good	Fair	Poor
1800	1500	1100	750	550	400

AR-15A2 Govt. Model Carbine (Model #6520)

Added to the Colt line in 1988 this 16" standard barrel carbine featured for the first time a case deflector and the improved A2 rear sight. This model is fitted with a 4-position telescoping buttstock. Weighs about 5.8 lbs.

NIB	Exc.	V.G.	Good	Fair	Poor
2500	2000	1250	950	700	500

AR-15A2 Gov't. Model (Model #6550)

This model was introduced in 1988 is the rifle equivalent to the Carbine. It features a 20" A2 barrel, forward assist, case deflector, but still retains the bayonet lug. Weighs about 7.5 lbs. Discontinued in 1990. USMC model.

NIB	Exc.	V.G.	Good	Fair	Poor
2300	2000	1250	950	700	500

AR-15A2 H-Bar (Model #6600)

Introduced in 1986 this version features a special 20" heavy barrel. All other features are the same as the A2 series of AR15s. Discontinued in 1991. Weighs about 8 lbs.

NIB	Exc.	V.G.	Good	Fair	Poor
2500	2000	1500	950	700	500

AR- 15A2 Delta H-Bar (Model #6600DH)
Same as above but fitted with a 3x9 scope and detachable cheekpiece. Dropped from the Colt line in 1990. Weighs about 10 lbs.

NIB	Exc.	V.G.	Good	Fair	Poor
2800	2000	1500	1200	850	600

WHAT'S IT LIKE-THE AR-15 HB 16"
I have fired almost every variation of the Colt AR-15 and I have come to one conclusion. It is one of the versatile and accurate rifles manufactured in this country, contrary to what the liberal media might say. My favorite is the Colt Flat Top AR-15 A2 heavy barrel 16" with a 1 in 9 barrel twist. The 1 in 9 twist rate will stabilize both the 55 grain and 62 grain military FMJ bullets with incredible accuracy. The Flat Top does not have a carry handle on it but is furnished with a Weaver compatible rail instead. The allows the operator to install the optics of his choice. I chose a small Trijicon ACOG 4 power to keep the package compact. My 16" HBAR will deliver 1/4", one hole groups on demand with match grade ammunition. The is nothing short of astounding, considering that it is semiautomatic military; not a bolt action target rifle. Once this was witnessed at the local upscale range by two die-hard bolt action shooters. I overheard one of them say that he didn't think those assault rifles would shoot that well. I answered by saying that they don't unless you fire them properly with good ammunition and are a reasonable competent marksman, which most of the time is not me. They walked away saying how the media had lied to them-No KIDDING. The AR-15 system is a particular good one for accurate fire because of the tight lock-up of the bolt in relation to the barrel. This is due to the fact that the bolt locks directly into the barrel instead of the receiver. This gives the system its very tight bolt to chamber interface which enables accurate fire. The other part of the equation is the shot, very rigid 16" barrel which exhibits excellent barrel harmonics.

J.R. Moody

Sporter Lightweight Rifle
This lightweight model has a 16" barrel and is finished in a matte black. It is available in either a .223 Rem. caliber (Model #6530) that weighs 6.7 lbs., a (Model #6430) 9mm caliber weighing 7.1 lbs., or a (Model #6830) 7.65x39mm that weighs

---

7.3 lbs. The .223 is furnished with two five-round box magazines as is the 9mm and 7.65x39mm. A cleaning kit and sling are also supplied with each new rifle. The buttstock and pistol grip are made of durable nylon and the handguard is reinforced fiberglass and aluminum lined. The rear sight is adjustable for windage and elevation. These newer models are referred to simply as Sporters and are <u>not</u> fitted with a bayonet lug and receiver block has different size pins.

NIB	Exc.	V.G.	Good	Fair	Poor
1350	1100	900	650	400	300

NOTE: The Model 6830 will bring about $25 less than the above prices. For post-9/94 guns deduct 30%.

Sporter Target Model Rifle (Model #6551)
This 1991 model is a full size version of the Lightweight Rifle. The Target Rifle weighs 7.5 lbs. and has a 20" barrel. Offered in .223 Rem. caliber only with target sights adjustable to 800 meters. New rifles are furnished with two 5-round box magazines, sling, and cleaning kit.

NIB	Exc.	V.G.	Good	Fair	Poor
1350	1100	900	650	400	300

NOTE: For post-9/94 guns deduct 30%.

Sporter Match H-Bar (Model #6601)
This 1991 variation of the AR-15 is similar to the Target Model but has a 20" heavy barrel chambered for the .223 caliber. This model weighs 8 lbs. and has target type sights adjustable out to 800 meters. Supplied with two 5-round box magazines, sling, and cleaning kit.

NIB	Exc.	V.G.	Good	Fair	Poor
1500	1200	900	650	400	300

NOTE: For post-9/94 guns deduct 35%.

Colt AR-15 (XM16E1)
This rifle was made upon request for foreign contracts. Very rare. Proceed with caution. This variation will command a premium price over the standard AR-15 rifle. Secure an appraisal before a sale.

Courtesy Richard M. Kumor, Sr.

Courtesy Richard M. Kumor, Sr.

Sporter Match Delta H-Bar (Model #6601 DH)
Same as above but supplied with a 3x9 scope. Weighs about 10 lbs. Discontinued in 1992.

NIB	Exc.	V.G.	Good	Fair	Poor
1800	1500	1100	850	600	400

Match Target H-BAR Compensated (Model #6601C)
Same as the regular Sporter H-BAR with the addition of a compensator.

NIB	Exc.	V.G.	Good	Fair	Poor
1250	900	750	—	—	—

Sporter Competition H-Bar (Model #6700)
Introduced in 1992, the Competition H-Bar is available in .223 caliber with a 20" heavy barrel counterbored for accuracy. The carry handle is detachable with target sights. With the carry handle removed the upper receiver is dovetailed and grooved for Weaver-style scope rings. This model weighs approximately 8.5 lbs. New rifles are furnished with two 5-round box magazines, sling, and cleaning kit.

NIB	Exc.	V.G.	Good	Fair	Poor
1500	1300	950	700	500	350

NOTE: For post-9/94 guns deduct 35%.

Sporter Competition H-Bar Select w/scope (Model #6700CH)
This variation, also new for 1992, is identical to the Sporter Competition with the addition of a factory mounted scope. The rifle has also been selected for accuracy and comes complete with a 3-9X rubber armored variable scope, scope mount, carry handle with iron sights, and nylon carrying case.

NIB	Exc.	V.G.	Good	Fair	Poor
1900	1500	1150	850	600	400

Match Target Competition H-BAR Compensated (Model #6700C)
Same as the Match Target with a compensator.

NIB	Exc.	V.G.	Good	Fair	Poor
1250	900	—	—	—	—

AR-15 Carbine Flat-top Heavyweight/Match Target Competition (Model #6731)
This variation in the Sporter series features a heavyweight 16" barrel with flat-top receiver chambered for the .223 cartridge. It is equipped with a fixed buttstock. Weight is about 7.1 lbs.

NIB	Exc.	V.G.	Good	Fair	Poor
1250	1000	800	600	400	300

NOTE: For post-9/94 guns deduct 30%.

AR-15 Tactical Carbine (Model #6721)
This version is similar to the above model with the exception of the buttstock which is telescoping and adjusts to 4 positions. Chambered for the .223 cartridge with a weight of about 7 lbs. A majority of these guns were for law enforcement only.

NIB	Exc.	V.G.	Good	Fair	Poor
1900	1500	1200	—	—	—

Sporter H-Bar Elite/Accurized Rifle (Model #6724)
This variation was introduced in 1996 and features a free floating 24" stainless steel match barrel with an 11 degree target crown and special Teflon coated trigger group. The handguard is all-aluminum with twin swivel studs. Weight is approximately 9.26 lbs.

NIB	Exc.	V.G.	Good	Fair	Poor
1200	1000	800	550	—	—

COLT CUSTOM SHOP

The Colt Custom Shop has developed several models over the years that are available to the public. The basis of these offerings are standard Colt Models upgraded to perform special functions.

Special Combat Government Model (Competition)
This is a competition ready model. Chambered for the .45 ACP it comes fitted with a skeletonized trigger, upswept grip safety, custom tuned action, polished feed ramp, throated barrel, flared ejection port, cutout commander hammer, two 8-round magazines, hard chromed slide and receiver, extended thumb safety, Bomar rear sight, Clark dovetail front sight, and flared magazine funnel. The pistol has been accurized and is shipped with a certified target.

NIB	Exc.	V.G.	Good	Fair	Poor
1450	1100	800	500	300	200

Special Combat Government Model (Carry)
This model has all of the same features as the competition model except that it has a royal blue finish, special bar-dot night sights, ambidextrous safety. It has also been accurized and shipped with a certified target.

NIB	Exc.	V.G.	Good	Fair	Poor
1250	900	700	400	300	200

Gold Cup Commander
Chambered for the .45 ACP and has the following features: heavy-duty adjustable target sights, beveled magazine well, serrated front strap, checkered mainspring housing, wide grip safety, Palo Alto wood grips, and stainless steel or royal blue finish.

NIB	Exc.	V.G.	Good	Fair	Poor
875	775	650	600	500	375

Gold Cup Trophy

Introduced in 1997 this model features .45 ACP 5" barrel 1911 with a choice of stainless steel or blue finish. Several custom features such as skeletonized hammer and trigger. Adjustable rear sight and wraparound rubber grips are standard. The pistol has been accurized and is shipped with a target. Magazine capacity is 7 or 8 rounds. Weight is approximately 39 oz. Add $60.00 for stainless steel finish.

NIB	Exc.	V.G.	Good	Fair	Poor
1000	800	—	—	—	—

McCormick Commander

This is a limited edition pistol made for Lew Horton in 1995 and limited to 100 pistols. It has many special features. The slide is engraved and there is a gold rampant colt on the slide.

Suggested Retail Price: $1125

McCormick Officer

This Lew Horton exclusive pistol has factory installed McCormick parts and a hard chrome finish. A total of 500 guns were built in 1995.

Suggested Retail Price: $950

McCormick Factory Racer

This is a limited edition pistol from Lew Horton. It is a full size government model with hard chrome finish, special barrel, trigger safety, and other custom features. Each gun is rollmarked "McCormick Factory Racer" on the slide. Special serial numbers from MFR001 to MFR500.

Suggested Retail Price: $1100

U.S. Shooting Team Gold Cup

This is a limited edition Gold Cup .45 ACP with special blue, sights, grips. The U.S. Shooting Team logo is rolled on the slide. Limited to 500 pistols and built for Lew Horton.

Suggested Retail Price: $1025

Colt Classic .45 Special Edition

This Lew Horton model is limied to 400 pistols and features a royal blue polish with special "Classic .45" gold etched on the slide. Pearlite grips.

Suggested Retail Price: $960

125th Anniversary Edition Peacemaker

Introduced in 1998 this model features a V-shaped rear sight with 2 line patent date. Barrel is 4.75" and is chambered for .45 Colt cartridge. The cylinder is the second generation type and the hammer is knurled. Frame and hammer are case colored with blue barrel. Grips are two piece walnut with oil finish. Special serial number range SA74000 to SA75999.

Suggested Retail Price: $1,615

Ultimate Python

Custom tuned action with both Elliason and Accro sighting systems. Both rubber and walnut grips are included. Bright stainless steel or royal blue finish. Available only with 6" barrel.

NIB	Exc.	V.G.	Good	Fair	Poor
1150	950	800	650	450	275

Python Elite

This model has a hand tuned .357 magnum action with a choice of 4" or 6" barrel with adjustable rear sight and red ramp front sight. On the 4" barrel models grips are rubber service while on the 6" models they are rubber target style. Finish is stainless steel or royal blue. Weight is about 38 oz. with 4" barrel and 43 oz. with 6" barrel.

Suggested Retail Price: $925

Custom Anaconda

Custom tuned action, Magnaported barrel, with Elliason rear sight. The contoured trigger is polished smooth. Comes with Pachmayr grips and brushed stainless steel finish.

NIB	Exc.	V.G.	Good	Fair	Poor
650	575	500	400	300	200

Anaconda Hunter

Comes with a Leupold 2X scope, heavy-duty mounts, cleaning accessories, both walnut and rubber grips, in a hard case. Furnished only with an 8" barrel.

NIB	Exc.	V.G.	Good	Fair	Poor
975	900	800	600	400	250

Bobbed Detective Special

First offered in 1994 this model features a bobbed hammer, a front sight with night sight, and honed action. Available in either chrome or blue finish.

NIB	Exc.	V.G.	Good	Fair	Poor
475	400	300	200	150	100

Limited Class .45 ACP

Designed for tactical competition. Supplied with a parkerized matte finish, lightweight composite trigger, extended ambidextrous safety, upswept grip safety, beveled magazine well, accurized, and shipped with a signed target. Introduced in 1993.

NIB	Exc.	V.G.	Good	Fair	Poor
750	675	600	450	300	200

Compensated Model .45 ACP

This competition pistol has a hard chrome receiver, bumper on magazine, extended ambidextrous safety, blue slide with full profile BAT compensator, Bomar rear sight, and flared funnel magazine well. Introduced in 1993.

NIB	Exc.	V.G.	Good	Fair	Poor
1850	1350	900	650	400	250

Compensated .45 ACP Commander

Introduced in 1998 and limited to 500 pistols. This model is fitted with a full length guide rod, extended beavertail safety, skeletonized hammer, Novak-style sights, and checkered walnut double diamond grips.

Suggested Retail Price: $890

Nite Lite .380

Supplied with a bar-dot night sight, special foil mark on barrel slide, Teflon-coated alloy receiver, stainless slide, high capacity grip extension magazine, and a standard magazine. Shipped with a soft carrying case. Introduced in 1993.

NIB	Exc.	V.G.	Good	Fair	Poor
450	400	325	275	225	150

Standard Tactical Model

Built for 20th Anniversary of IPSC competition shooting in 1996. Built on the Colt Government model with round top slide and chamber for .45 ACP. Many special features Special serial numbers. Limited to 1,500 pistols.

Suggested Retail Price: $1400

Superior Tactical Model

Same as above but built on an enhanced frame with many custom features

Special serial numbers limited to 500 pistols.
Suggested Retail Price: $1800

Deluxe Tactical Model

Same as above but with added features. Limited to 250 Pistols.

Suggested Retail Price: $2660

The following is a list of special edition Colt pistols and revolvers produced by the Colt Custom Shop exclusively for distributor Lew Horton. These handguns are listed to provide the reader with an idea of the number of limited edition Colts sold by Lew Horton and the year they were produced with the retail price.

COLT COMMEMORATIVES

The field of commemoratives can be fascinating and frustrating, depending on one's point of view. For someone who collects things from purely an aesthetic sense, commemoratives are quite desirable. Most are embellished and have had great care put into their fit and finish. They are attractively cased, and the proliferation of them makes acquisition relatively simple except from a financial standpoint. On the other hand, the collector who has an eye for the investment potential of his collections has found that the commemorative market has been soft and as investments they historically have not done well. The reason for this is twofold. The limited production appeal is not always what it seems. Many times the amounts produced are greater than one would consider limited. It is also a fact that if one fires a commemorative, its collectibility is gone. Even excessive handling can cause this problem. This means that since the majority of these firearms are kept new in the original boxes, the supply will usually outstrip the demand. Because of the limited numbers built it is difficult to furnish accurate prices for the secondary market.

Few commemoratives are ever lost or worn out. Collectors who seek firearms for their historic significance are usually not interested in the commemoratives, as even though they may have been issued to commemorate a specific historic person or event, they are not a part of the era and are regarded as "instant" collectibles. In some areas one will find that the Colt Commemoratives are not as desirable, saleable, or expensive as the plain out-of-the-box versions. This is especially true in the Single Action Army Models. We list the commemoratives made by Colt in chronological order. Remember that the prices reflect new-in-the-box as it came from the factory—all papers, books, etc., intact and included. We also include the issue price for comparison. If the model with which you are concerned has been fired or is not in its original casing or box, deduct as much as 50 percent from these prices. It is interesting to note that in some areas shooters are taking advantage of the soft commemorative market and are buying SAAs at lower prices than the plain 3rd Generation guns—then shooting them. This can perhaps have a positive effect on appreciation.

One final note. There are a number of Colt Commemoratives that were produced by Colt but offered for sale by private companies to commemorate an event of their choosing. This publication does not cover most of these private commemoratives because it is difficult, if not impossible, to determine a secondary market value. It is also difficult to construct any meaningful comprehensive list of these private offerings. While the market for Colt factory remains soft the market for private commemoratives is usually very soft. the few that come on the market sometimes sell for less than half of their initial offering price. For those who enjoy collecting these firearms without investment goals these private commemoratives offer an additional outlet.

Model	Qty. Built	Year Made	Retail Price
Horse Pistol, SAA	100	1983	$1100.00
Ultimate Officer's .45 ACP	500	1989	777.00
Lt. Commander .45 ACP	800	1985	590.00
Combat Cobra 2-1/2"	1000	1987	500.00
Lady Colt (MKIV .380 ACP)	1000	1989	547.00
Night Commander .45 ACP	250	1989	725.00
El Presidente .38 Super	350	1990	995.00
El Comandante .38 Super	500	1991	995.00
El General .38 Super	500	1991	995.00
El Capitan	500	1991	995.00
Colt Boa-4" & 6"	600	1985	525.00
El Dorado	750	1992	1195.00
El Coronel	750	1993	995.00
El Teniente	400	1992	1195.00
Classic Gold Cup	300	1993	1849.95
Night Officer	350	1993	679.95
El Presidente Premier Edition	10	1993	3000.00

COLT COMMEMORATIVES

1961	Issue	NIB	Amount Mfg.
Geneseo, IL. 125th Anniv. Derringer	$ 28	$ 650	104
Sheriff's Model (Blue & Case)	130	1995	478
Sheriff's Model (Nickel)	140	5000	25
Kansas Statehood Scout	75	425	6,197
125th Anniv. Model SAA .45	150	1395	7,390
Pony Express Cent. Scout	80	450	1,007
Civil War Cent. Pistol	75	175	24,114
1962			
Rock Island Arsenal Cent. Scout	$ 39	$ 250	550
Columbus, OH. Sesquicent. Scout	100	550	200
Ft. Findlay, OH. Sesquicent. Scout	90	650	110
Ft. Findlay Cased Pair	185	2500	20
New Mex. Golden Anniv. Scout	80	425	1,000
Ft. McPherson, Nebraska Cent. Derringer	29	395	300
West Virginia Statehood Cent. Scout	75	425	3,452
1963			
West Virginia Statehood Cent. SAA .45	$ 150	$1395	600
Ariz. Terr. Cent. Scout	75	425	5,355
Ariz. Terr. Cent. SAA .45	150	1395	1,280
Carolina Charter Tercent Scout	75	425	300
Carolina Charter Tercent .22/.45 Comb.	240	1595	251
H. Cook 1 To 100 .22/.45 Comb.	275	1795	100
Ft. Stephenson, Oh. Sesquicent. Scout	75	550	200
Battle of Gettysburg Cent. Scout	90	425	1,019
Idaho Terr. Cent. Scout	75	425	902
Gen. J.H. Morgan Indiana Raid Scout	75	650	100
1964			
Cherry's 35th Anniv. .22/.45 Comb.	$ 275	$ 1695	100
Nevada Statehood Cent. Scout	75	425	3,984
Nevada Statehood Cent. SAA .45	150	1395	1,688
Nevada Statehood Cent. .22/.45 Comb.	240	1595	189
Nevada Statehood Cent. .22/.45 W/extra Cyls.	350	1695	577
Nevada Battle Born Scout	85	425	981
Nevada Battle Born SAA .45	175	1495	80
Nevada Battle Born .22/.45 Comb.	265	2595	20
Montana Terr. Cent. Scout	75	425	2,300
Montana Terr. Cent. SAA .45	150	1395	851
Wyoming Diamond Jubilee Scout	75	425	2,357
General Hood Cent. Scout	75	425	1,503
New Jersey Tercent Scout	75	425	1,001
New Jersey Tercent SAA .45	150	1395	250

1964	Issue	NIB	Amount Mfg.
St. Louis Bicent. Scout	$ 75	$ 425	802
St. Louis Bicent. SAA .45	150	1395	200
St. Louis Bicent. .22/.45 Comb.	240	1595	250
California Gold Rush Scout	80	450	500
Pony Express Pres. SAA .45	250	1495	1,004
Chamizal Treaty Scout	85	450	450
Chamizal Treaty SAA .45	170	1495	50
Chamizal Treaty .22/.45 Comb	280	1995	50
Col. Sam Colt Sesquicent. SAA .45	225	1395	4,750
Col. Sam Colt Deluxe SAA .45	500	2500	200
Col. Sam Colt Special Deluxe SAA .45	1000	4500	50
Wyatt Earp Buntline SAA .45	250	2500	150
1965			
Oregon Trail Scout	$ 75	$ 425	1,995
Joaquin Murietta .22/.45 Comb.	350	1695	100
Forty-Niner Miner Scout	85	425	500
Old Ft. Des Moines Reconst. Scout	90	450	700
Old Ft. Des Moines Reconst. SAA .45	170	1395	100
Old Ft. Des Moines Reconst. .22/.45 Comb.	290	1695	100
Appomattox Cent. Scout	75	425	1,001
Appomattox Cent. SAA .45	150	1395	250
Appomattox Cent. .22/.45 Comb.	240	1595	250
General Meade Campaign Scout	75	425	1,197
St. Augustine Quadracent. Scout	85	450	500
Kansas Cowtown Series Wichita Scout	85	425	500
1966			
Kansas Cowtown Series Dodge City Scout	$ 85	$ 425	500
Colorado Gold Rush Scout	85	450	1,350
Oklahoma Territory Scout	85	425	1,343
Dakota Territory Scout	85	425	1,000
General Meade SAA .45	165	1395	200
Abercrombie & Fitch Trailblazer N.Y.	275	1095	200
Abercrombie & Fitch Trailblazer Chic.	275	1095	100
Abercrombie & Fitch Trailblazer S.F.	275	1095	100
Kansas Cowtown Series Abilene Scout	95	425	500
Indiana Sesquicent. Scout	85	425	1,500
Pony Express 4-Square Set .45 4 Guns	1,400	5995	N/A
California Gold Rush SAA .45	175	1395	130
1967			
Lawman Series Bat Masterson Scout	$ 90	$ 450	3,000
Lawman Series Bat Masterson SAA .45	180	1500	500
Alamo Scout	85	425	4,250
Alamo SAA .45	165	1395	750
Alamo .22/.45 Comb.	265	1595	250
Kansas Cowtown Series Coffeyville Scout	95	425	500
Kansas Trail Series Chisolm Trail Scout	100	425	500
WWI Series Chateau Thierry .45 Auto	200	695	7,400
WWI Series Chateau Thierry Deluxe	500	1350	75
WWI Series Chateau Thierry Sp. Deluxe	1000	2750	25
1968			
Nebraska Cent. Scout	$ 100	$ 425	7,001
Kansas Trail Series Chisolm Trail Scout	100	425	500
WWI Series Belleau Wood .45 Auto	200	795	7,400
WWI Series Belleau Wood Deluxe	500	1350	75
WWI Series Belleau Wood Sp. Deluxe	1000	2750	25
Lawman Series Pat Garrett Scout	110	450	3,000
Lawman Series Pat Garrett SAA .45	220	1395	500
1969			
Nathan B. Forrest Scout	$ 110	$ 425	3,000
Kansas Trail Series Santa Fe Trail Sct.	120	425	501
WWI Ser. 2nd Battle of Marne .45 Auto	220	795	7,400
WWI Ser. 2nd Battle of Marne Deluxe	500	1350	75
WWI Ser. 2nd Battle of Marne Sp. Del.	1000	2750	25
Alabama Sesquicent. Scout	110	425	3,001
Alabama Sesquicent. SAA .45	N/A	15000	1
Golden Spike Scout	135	450	11,000

1969	Issue	NIB	Amount Mfg.
Kansas Trail Ser. Shawnee Tr. Scout	$ 120	$ 425	501
WWI Ser. Meuse-Argonne .45 Auto	220	795	7,400
WWI Ser. Meuse-Argonne Deluxe	500	1350	75
WWI Ser. Meuse-Argonne Sp. Deluxe	1000	2750	25
Arkansas Terr. Sesquicent. Scout	110	425	3,500
Lawman Ser. Wild Bill Hickok Scout	117	450	3,000
Lawman Ser. Wild Bill Hickok SAA .45	220	1395	500
California Bicent. Scout	135	425	5,000

1970	Issue	NIB	Amount Mfg.
Kansas Ft. Ser. Ft. Larned Scout	$ 120	$ 425	500
WWII Ser. European Theatre	250	795	11,500
WWII Ser. Pacific Theatre	250	695	11,500
Texas Ranger SAA .45	650	2250	1,000
Kansas Ft. Ser. Ft. Hays Scout	130	425	500
Marine Sesquicent. Scout	120	425	3,000
Missouri Sesquicent. Scout	125	425	3,000
Missouri Sesquicent. SAA .45	220	1295	900
Kansas Ft. Ser. Ft. Riley Scout	130	425	500
Lawman Ser. Wyatt Earp Scout	125	495	3,000
Lawman Ser. Wyatt Earp SAA .45	395	2500	500

1971	Issue	NIB	Amount Mfg.
NRA Centennial SAA .45	$ 250	$ 1495	5,000
NRA Centennial SAA .357 Mag.	250	1295	5,000
NRA Centennial Gold Cup .45 Auto	250	1295	2,500
U.S. Grant 1851 Navy	250	595	4,750
Robt. E. Lee 1851 Navy	250	595	4,750
Lee - Grant Set 1851 Navies	500	1350	250
Kansas Ft. Ser. Ft. Scott Scout	130	425	500

1972	Issue	NIB	Amount Mfg.
Centennial Cased Set Florida Terr. Sesquicent. Scout	$ 125	$ 425	2,001
Arizona Ranger Scout	135	425	3,001

1975	Issue	NIB	Amount Mfg.
Peacemaker Centennial SAA .45	$ 300	$ 1495	1,500
Peacemaker Centennial SAA .44-40	300	1495	1,500
Peacemaker	625	2995	500

1976	Issue	NIB	Amount Mfg.
U.S. Bicentennial Set	$ 1695	$ 2995	1,776

1977	Issue	NIB	Amount Mfg.
2nd Amendment .22	$ 195	$ 425	3,020
U.S. Cavalry 200th Anniversary Set	995	1250	3,000

1978	Issue	NIB	Amount Mfg.
Statehood 3rd Model Dragoon	$ 12500	$ 6995	52

1979	Issue	NIB	Amount Mfg.
Ned Buntline SAA N.F. .45	$ 895	$ 895	3,000
Ohio President's Spec. Edit. .45 Auto	N/A	995	250
Tombstone Cent. .45 SAA	550	1395	300

1980	Issue	NIB	Amount Mfg.
Drug Enforcement Agency .45 Auto	$ 550	$ 1100	910
Olympics Ace Spec. Edition .22	1000	1295	200
Heritage Walker .44 Percussion	1495	950	1,847

1981	Issue	NIB	Amount Mfg.
John M. Browning .45 Auto	$ 1100	$ 995	3,000

1982	Issue	NIB	Amount Mfg.
John Wayne SAA	$ 2995	$ 1995	3,100
John Wayne SAA Deluxe	10000	7500	500
John Wayne SAA Presentation	20000	12000	100

1983	Issue	NIB	Amount Mfg.
Buffalo Bill Wild West Show Cent. SAA	$ 1350	$ 1595	500
1984			
1st Edition Govt. Model .380 ACP	$ 425	$ 475	1,000
Duke Frontier .22	475	495	1,000
Winchester/Colt SAA .44-40	N/A	2250	4,000
USA Edition SAA .44-40	4995	3500	100
Kit Carson New Frontier .22	550	450	1,000
2nd Edition Govt. Model .380 ACP	525	475	1,000
Officer's ACP Commencement Issue	700	795	1,000
Theodore Roosevelt SAA .44-40	1695	1895	500
No Amer. Oilmen Buntline SAA .45	3900	3500	200
1985			
Mustang 1st Edition .380 ACP	$ 475	$ 450	1,000
Officer's ACP Heirloom Edition	1575	1550	N/A
Klay-Colt 1851 Navy	1850	1850	150
Klay-Colt 1851 Navy Engraved Edit.	3150	3150	50
Double Diamond Set .357 & .45 Auto	1575	1795	1,000
1986			
150th Anniversary SAA .45	$ 1595	$ 1795	1,000
150th Anniv. Engraving Sampler	1613	2750	N/A
150th Anniv. Engraving Sampler .45 Auto	1155	1295	N/A
Texas 150th Sesquicent. Sheriff's .45	836	1495	N/A
1987			
Combat Elite Custom Edition .45 Auto	$ 900	$ 995	500
12th Man Spirit of Aggieland .45 Auto	950	995	999
1989			
Snake Eyes Ltd. Edit. 2-2.5" Pythons	$ 2950	$ 1995	500

Bat Masterson

Abilene Commemorative

Arizona Territorial Centennial

Belleau Wood Commemorative

Buffalo Bill Wild West Show

California Gold Rush

Chateau Thierry Commemorative

Dodge City Commemorative

Florida Territorial Sesquicentennial

John Wayne Commemorative

John Wayne Deluxe

Alabama Sesquicentennial

John Wayne Presentation

REPRODUCTION COLT PERCUSSION REVOLVERS

Walker
Made from 1979 to 1981; serial numbers 1200-4120 and 32256 to 32500.

NIB	Exc.	V.G.
895	750	500

Walker Heritage Model
NIB
950

First Model Dragoon
Made from 1980 to 1982; serial numbers 24100-34500.

NIB	Exc.	V.G.
395	300	100

Second Model Dragoon
Made from 1980 to 1982; serial numbers as above.

NIB	Exc.	V.G.
395	300	100

Third Model Dragoon
Made from 1980 to 1982; serial numbers as above.

NIB	Exc.	V.G.
395	300	100

Model 1848 Pocket Pistol
Made in 1981; serial numbers 16000-17851.

NIB	Exc.	V.G.
425	300	100

Model 1851 Navy Revolver
Made from 1971 to 1978; serial numbers 4201-25100 and 24900-29150.

NIB	Exc.	V.G.
395	400	325

Model 1860 Army Revolver
Made from 1978 to 1982; serial numbers 201000-212835.

NIB	Exc.	V.G.
550	500	475

Model 1861 Navy Revolver
Made during 1980 and 1981; serial numbers 40000-43165.

NIB	Exc.	V.G.
500	450	400

Model 1862 Pocket Pistol
Made from 1979 to 1984; serial numbers 8000-58850.

NIB	Exc.	V.G.
425	350	300

Model 1862 Police Revolver
Made from 1979 to 1984; serial numbers in above range.

NIB	Exc.	V.G.
425	400	300

NOTE: The above revolvers were manufactured in a variety of styles (cylinder form, stainless steel, etc.) that affect prices. Factory engraved examples command a considerable premium over the prices listed above.

COLT BLACKPOWDER ARMS
Brooklyn, New York
These blackpowder revolvers and rifles are made under license from Colt.

1842 Paterson Colt No. 5 Holster Model
This model is a copy of the No. 5 Holster model and is chambered for the .36 caliber ball. Fitted with a 7.5" octagon barrel. Hand engraved. This is a special order revolver.

NIB	Exc.	V.G.	Good	Fair	Poor
3000	—	—	—	—	—

Special order Paterson Colt No. 5 Holster Model

Walker

This .44 caliber large frame revolver is fitted with a 9" barrel.

NIB	Exc.	V.G.	Good	Fair	Poor
475	400	350	300	200	150

Walker 150th Anniversary Model

Marked "A Company No. 1" in gold. Introduced 1997.

NIB	Exc.	V.G.	Good	Fair	Poor
600	500	—	—	—	—

Whitneyville Hartford Dragoon

Similar in appearance to the Walker colt this revolver is fitted with a 7-1/2" barrel and a silver plated iron backstrap and triggerguard. This is a limited edition with a total of 2,400 guns built with serial numbers between 1100 through 1340.

NIB	Exc.	V.G.	Good	Fair	Poor
475	400	350	300	200	150

Marine Dragoon

Special limited edition presentation grade in honor of U.S. Marine Corps.

NIB	Exc.	V.G.	Good	Fair	Poor
895	—	—	—	—	—

3rd Model Dragoon

Another large frame revolver with 7-1/2" barrel with a brass backstrap, 3-screw frame, and unfluted cylinder.

NIB	Exc.	V.G.	Good	Fair	Poor
475	400	350	300	200	150

3rd Model Dragoon-Steel Backstrap

NIB	Exc.	V.G.	Good	Fair	Poor
500	425	375	325	200	150

3rd Model Dragoon-Fluted Cylinder

NIB	Exc.	V.G.	Good	Fair	Poor
510	435	375	325	200	150

Cochise Dragoon

This is a commemorative issue Third Model with gold inlay frame and barrel with special grips.

NIB	Exc.	V.G.	Good	Fair	Poor
895	—	—	—	—	—

Colt 1849 Model Pocket

A small frame revolver chambered in .31 caliber with a 4" barrel. Fitted with one-piece walnut grips.

NIB	Exc.	V.G.	Good	Fair	Poor
435	375	325	275	200	150

Colt 1851 Model Navy

This is medium frame revolver chambered in .36 caliber with 7-1/2" barrel. Walnut grips and case color frame.

NIB	Exc.	V.G.	Good	Fair	Poor
435	375	325	275	200	150

Colt 1851 Model Navy with Dual Cylinder

NIB	Exc.	V.G.	Good	Fair	Poor
475	400	350	300	200	150

Colt Model 1860 Army

This model is chamber in .44 caliber with roll engraved cylinder and one piece walnut grips. Barrel length is 8".

NIB	Exc.	V.G.	Good	Fair	Poor
435	375	325	275	200	150

Colt Model 1860 Army with Dual Cylinder

NIB	Exc.	V.G.	Good	Fair	Poor
475	400	350	300	200	150

Colt Model 1860 Army-Fluted Cylinder

NIB	Exc.	V.G.	Good	Fair	Poor
450	400	350	300	200	150

Colt 1860 Officers Model

This is a deluxe version of the standard 1860 with a special blued finish and gold crossed sabres. This is a 4-screw frame with 8" barrel and 6-shot rebated cylinder.

NIB	Exc.	V.G.	Good	Fair	Poor
675	575	450	375	250	150

Colt Model 1860 Army Gold U.S. Cavalry

Features a gold engraved cylinder and gold barrel bands.

NIB	Exc.	V.G.	Good	Fair	Poor
650	575	450	375	250	150

Colt Model 1860 Army-Stainless Steel

NIB	Exc.	V.G.	Good	Fair	Poor
475	400	350	300	200	150

Colt 1860 Heirloom Edition

This is an elaborately engraved revolver done in the Tiffany-style and fitted with Tiffany-style grips.

NIB	Exc.	V.G.	Good	Fair	Poor
5000	—	—	—	—	—

Colt Model 1861 Navy

This .36 caliber revolver features a 7-1/2" barrel with engraved cylinder, case colored frame and one piece walnut grips.

NIB	Exc.	V.G.	Good	Fair	Poor
450	400	350	300	200	150

Colt Model 1861 Navy General Custer

Same as above but with engraved frame and cylinder.

NIB	Exc.	V.G.	Good	Fair	Poor
975	850	700	500	300	200

Colt Model 1862 Trapper-Pocket Police

This small frame revolver is fitted with a 3-1/2" barrel, silver backstrap, and triggerguard. The cylinder is semi-fluted and chambered in .36 caliber.

NIB	Exc.	V.G.	Good	Fair	Poor
435	375	325	275	200	150

Colt Model 1862 Pocket Navy

This small frame revolver is fitted with a round engraved cylinder with a 5" octagon barrel with hinged loading lever. Chambered for .36 caliber.

NIB	Exc.	V.G.	Good	Fair	Poor
435	375	325	275	200	150

Colt 1861 Musket

This Civil War musket is chambered in the .58 caliber. Lockplate, hammer, buttplate, and 3 barrel bands, and 40" barrel are finished bright. The stock is a one-piece oil-finish affair. Bayonet and accessories are extra.

NIB	Exc.	V.G.	Good	Fair	Poor
650	550	400	325	275	150

Colt 1861 Musket-Artillery Model
Same as above but fitted with a 31-1/2" barrel.

NIB	Exc.	V.G.	Good	Fair	Poor
650	550	400	325	275	150

Colt 1861 Musket Presentation 1 of 1000
Limited to 1,000 guns these are special finished with a high polish and Colt's signature in gold on the triggerguard. Sold with special custom wooden case.

NIB	Exc.	V.G.	Good	Fair	Poor
2100	1500	750	600	450	300

Colt 1861 Musket Presentation 1 of 1000-Artillery Model
Same as above but 31-1/2" barrel.

NIB	Exc.	V.G.	Good	Fair	Poor
2100	1500	750	600	450	300

Colt Gamemaster .50
Introduced in 1997 this rifle is chambered for the .50 caliber. It is fitted with a 31.5" barrel and weighs about 13 lbs.

NIB	Exc.	V.G.	Good	Fair	Poor
800	650	—	—	—	—

COLTON MANUFACTURING CO.
Toledo, Ohio

The Colton Manufacturing Co. provided Sears with its first American-made hammerless house brand double. Sears advertised their sidelock hammerless gun as "the equal of any gun made, regardless of price" in their 1900 Fall catalog No. 110. There were four models: three sideplated boxlock-types and a unique unitized coil spring driven striker assembly version. All these, especially the latter, were designed to be mass produced. Many of the distinctive sidelock-within-a-sideplated model were produced but they are seldom seen today either because they were used-up or did not hold up well and were scrapped. Sears replaced Colton with the more traditional design Fryberg gun in 1902. Values depend on grade. There appear to be a least two levels of quality and condition ranging from $300 to $1,500. Colton marked guns are scarce.

Courtesy Nick Niles. Photo Paul Goodwin

COLUMBIA ARMORY
Columbia, Tennessee

A trade name applied to a variety of solid frame cartridge revolvers made by John T. Smith Company of Rock Falls, Connecticut. They were marked "SAFETY HAMMERLESS REVOLVER". This model was made under several trade names.

Exc.	V.G.	Good	Fair	Poor
—	200	100	75	50

COLUMBUS F. A. MFG. CO.
Columbus, Georgia

Columbus Revolver

A .36-caliber double action percussion revolver with a 6-shot, unfluted cylinder and a 7.5" octagonal barrel. Similar in appearance to the 1851 Colt Navy. The pistol is browned steel, with brass gripstraps and walnut grips. The barrel is marked "Columbus Fire Arms Manuf. Co/Columbus Ga." 100 revolvers were manufactured in 1863 and 1864.

Exc.	V.G.	Good	Fair	Poor
—	—	50000	25000	5000

COMBLAIN
Belgium and Brazil

Single Shot Rifle

A 11x53Rmm caliber rifle with a falling block action. Manufactured both in a hammerless and hammer version. Full stock secured by two barrel bands.

Courtesy Milwaukee Public Museum, Milwaukee, Wisconsin

Exc.	V.G.	Good	Fair	Poor
750	650	500	350	250

COMMANDO ARMS
Knoxville, Tennessee

Formerly known as Volunteer Enterprises. The name change took place in 1978.

Mark III Carbine

A .45 ACP caliber semiautomatic rifle with a 16.5" barrel, a peep rear sight and a vertical foregrip. Manufactured between 1969 and 1976.

NIB	Exc.	V.G.	Good	Fair	Poor
400	300	250	200	150	100

Mark 9 Carbine

As above, in 9mm caliber.

NIB	Exc.	V.G.	Good	Fair	Poor
400	300	250	200	150	100

Mark.45

The new designation for the Mark III after the company changed its name.

NIB	Exc.	V.G.	Good	Fair	Poor
400	300	250	200	150	100

COMPETITOR CORP.
New Ipswich, New Hampshire

Competitor Single Shot

This single shot pistol is chambered for calibers from .22 Long Rifle to .50 Action Express. Choice of barrels lengths from 10.5", 14", and 16". Ramp front sight. Adjustable single stage trigger. Interchangeable barrels. Matte blue finish. Weight is approximately 59 oz. depending on barrel length. Introduced in 1988.

NIB	Exc.	V.G.	Good	Fair	Poor
400	325	275	225	175	125

CONNECTICUT ARMS CO.
Norfolk, Connecticut

Pocket Revolver

A .28 caliber spur trigger revolver with 3" octagonal barrel, 6-shot unfluted cylinder, using a cup-primed cartridge and loads from the front of the cylinder. There is a hinged hook on the side of the frame under the cylinder that acts as the extractor. Silver-plated brass, blued with walnut grips. The barrel is marked "Conn. Arms Co. Norfolk, Conn." Approximately 2,700 manufactured in the 1860s.

Exc.	V.G.	Good	Fair	Poor
—	—	750	300	100

CONNECTICUT VALLEY ARMS CO.
Norcross, Georgia

RIFLES

Express Rifle

A .50 caliber double barrel percussion rifle with 28" barrels. Blued with a walnut stock.

Deluxe Version add 100%.

NIB	Exc.	V.G.	Good	Fair	Poor
550	450	400	350	300	200

Over/Under Rifle

A .50 caliber double-barrel Over/Under rifle with 26" barrels. Blued with a walnut stock.

NIB	Exc.	V.G.	Good	Fair	Poor
575	450	400	350	300	200

Hawken Rifle

A .50 caliber with a 28" octagonal barrel, double set triggers and a walnut stock.

NIB	Exc.	V.G.	Good	Fair	Poor
400	325	275	225	150	100

Presentation Grade Hawken

As above, with an engraved lock, patchbox, and finely figured stock.

NIB	Exc.	V.G.	Good	Fair	Poor
500	425	375	325	275	200

Pennsylvania Long Rifle

A .50 caliber flintlock rifle with a 40" octagonal barrel, double set triggers and a walnut stock.

NIB	Exc.	V.G.	Good	Fair	Poor
475	400	350	300	250	175

Kentucky Rifle

A .45 caliber percussion rifle with a 33.5" octagonal barrel and walnut stock.

NIB	Exc.	V.G.	Good	Fair	Poor
275	225	175	150	100	75

Mountain Rifle

A .50 or .54 caliber percussion half-stock rifle.

NIB	Exc.	V.G.	Good	Fair	Poor
300	225	175	125	100	75

Blazer Rifle

A .50 caliber percussion rifle with a 28" octagonal barrel and walnut stock.

NIB	Exc.	V.G.	Good	Fair	Poor
150	125	100	85	65	45

Apollo Shadow SS

Introduced in 1993 this rifle features an in-line stainless steel bolt spring action, a 24" blued round barrel with octagonal one piece receiver, drilled and tapped. Stock is black hardwood-textured with Dura Grip with pistol grip and recoil pad. Offered in either .50 or .54 caliber. Weighs about 9 lbs.

NIB	Exc.	V.G.	Good	Fair	Poor
175	150	125	100	75	50

Apollo Classic

Similar to the above Apollo Model but with dark brown stained laminated hardwood stock with pistol grip, raised comb, and recoil pad. Weighs about 8-1/2 lbs.

NIB	Exc.	V.G.	Good	Fair	Poor
215	175	150	125	100	75

Apollo Carbelite

Offered in .50 caliber with percussion bolt and 27" blued round taper barrel with octagonal receiver, drilled and tapped. Fitted with Carbelite composite stock with Monte Carlo and cheekpiece with pistol grip. Weighs approximately 7-1/2 lbs.

NIB	Exc.	V.G.	Good	Fair	Poor
280	225	175	150	100	75

Apollo Starfire

Chambered for the .50 caliber bullet this rifle is an in-line type with 24" stainless steel barrel with synthetic stock with checkered pistol grip, raised comb, and cheekpiece. Weight is about 6.5 lbs.

NIB	Exc.	V.G.	Good	Fair	Poor
225	175	150	125	100	75

Apollo Eclipse Rifle

Offered in either .50 or .54 caliber with 24" round barrel with blued steel receiver. Synthetic stock with checkered pistol, raised comb, and cheekpiece. Approximate weight is 6.5 lbs.

NIB	Exc.	V.G.	Good	Fair	Poor
175	150	1250	100	85	65

Apollo Dominator

Fitted with a synthetic thumbhole stock and a 24" round barrel this rifle is chambered for the .50 caliber bullet. Introduced in 1996. Weight is approximately 8.5 lbs.

NIB	Exc.	V.G.	Good	Fair	Poor
300	225	175	150	100	75

Apollo Brown Bear

This .50 caliber rifle is fitted with a hardwood stock with pistol grip with raised comb and cheekpiece. The barrel is round and 24". Introduced in 1996. Weight is about 6.5 lbs.

NIB	Exc.	V.G.	Good	Fair	Poor
200	175	150	125	100	75

Frontier Carbine

Fitted with a 24" blued barrel this rifle is offered in .50 caliber percussion or flintlock. Case hardened lock with hardwood stock. Weighs about 6-3/4 lbs.

NIB	Exc.	V.G.	Good	Fair	Poor
150	125	100	85	75	50

Plainsman rifle

This .50 caliber percussion rifle has a 26" octagonal barrel with case hardened lock and hardwood stock. Weight is about 6-1/2 lbs.

NIB	Exc.	V.G.	Good	Fair	Poor
130	115	100	85	75	50

Panther Carbine

This percussion rifle is available in either .50 or .54 caliber. It is fitted with a 24" blued octagonal barrel with Hawken-style case hardened lock. Stock is textured black Dura Grip over hardwood with Monte Carlo comb, cheekpiece, and pistol grip. Weight approximately 7-1/2 lbs.

NIB	Exc.	V.G.	Good	Fair	Poor
150	125	100	85	75	50

Bushwacker Rifle

This .50 caliber percussion rifle is fitted with a 26" octagonal barrel with case hardened engraved lock and brown stained hardwood stock with rounded nose. Weight is about 7-1/2 lbs.

NIB	Exc.	V.G.	Good	Fair	Poor
135	115	100	85	75	50

Trophy Carbine

This carbine is fitted with a 24" half-round half-octagon barrel with Hawken-style lock. The stock is walnut with Monte Carlo comb, cheekpiece, and pistol grip. Offered in .50 or .54 caliber percussion and weighs about 6-3/4 lbs.

NIB	Exc.	V.G.	Good	Fair	Poor
215	175	150	125	100	75

Varmint Rifle

This is a lightweight percussion rifle in .32 caliber with 24" octagon barrel and case-colored lock. The stock is hardwood. Weighs about 6-3/4 lbs.

NIB	Exc.	V.G.	Good	Fair	Poor
175	150	125	100	85	75

Woodsman Rifle LS

Introduced in 1994 this rifle features a 26" blued octagon barrel with dark brown stained laminated hardwood stock. Offered in .50 or .54 caliber percussion. Weighs about 6-1/2 lbs.

NIB	Exc.	V.G.	Good	Fair	Poor
135	115	100	85	75	50

Frontier Hunter Carbine

Offered in either .50 or .54 caliber this percussion rifle is fitted with a 24" blued octagon barrel and case hardened 45° offset hammer. The stock is dark stained laminated hardwood. Weighs about 7-1/2 lbs.

NIB	Exc.	V.G.	Good	Fair	Poor
170	150	125	100	75	50

Grey Wolf Rifle

Offered in either .50 or .54 caliber percussion this rifle is fitted with a 26" matte blue octagon barrel with a case hardened engraved lock. The stock is matte gray composite with raised comb, checkered pistol grip, and buttplate. Weighs about 6-1/2 lbs.

NIB	Exc.	V.G.	Good	Fair	Poor
160	125	100	85	75	50

Lone Grey Wolf Rifle
Introduced in 1994 this .50 caliber percussion rifle features a 26" matte blued octagon barrel. The triggerguard is oversized. The composite stock is black and has a raised comb, checkered pistol grip, and recoil pad. Weighs about 6-1/2 lbs.

NIB	Exc.	V.G.	Good	Fair	Poor
185	150	125	100	75	50

Timber Wolf Rifle
Introduced in 1994 this model is similar to the above model but is furnished with Realtree composite stock with raised comb, checkered pistol grip, and buttplate. Weighs about 6-1/2 lbs.

NIB	Exc.	V.G.	Good	Fair	Poor
185	165	140	100	75	50

Tracker Carbine LS
Introduced in 1994 this carbine is fitted with a 21" blued, half-round, half-octagon barrel with a Hawken-style lock. The stock is laminated dark brown with matte finish, and straight grip. Chambered for .50 caliber percussion. Weighs about 6-1/2 lbs.

NIB	Exc.	V.G.	Good	Fair	Poor
185	165	140	100	75	50

Stag Horn
Introduced in 1996 this in-line rifle is chambered for the .50 or .54 caliber bullet. The round barrel is 24" with blued finish. The stock is synthetic with checkered pistol grip, raised comb, and cheekpiece. Weight is about 6.5 lbs.

NIB	Exc.	V.G.	Good	Fair	Poor
175	150	1250	100	85	65

SHOTGUNS
Brittany 11 Shotgun
A .410 bore double-barrel percussion shotgun with 24" barrels, double triggers and a walnut stock.

NIB	Exc.	V.G.	Good	Fair	Poor
170	150	125	100	75	50

Trapper Shotgun
A 12 gauge percussion single barrel shotgun with a 28" barrel threaded for choke tubes and a walnut stock.

NIB	Exc.	V.G.	Good	Fair	Poor
225	200	175	150	100	75

Classic Turkey Double-Barrel Shotgun
This is a 12 gauge percussion breech loading shotgun with 28" barrel. The stock is European walnut with straight grip checkered stock. Weighs about 9 lbs.

NIB	Exc.	V.G.	Good	Fair	Poor
325	275	225	150	125	100

Trapper Shotgun
This is a single barrel 12 gauge shotgun with a 28" barrel. The stock is a straight grip hardwood with checkering. Supplied with three interchangeable chokes. Weighs about 6 lbs.

NIB	Exc.	V.G.	Good	Fair	Poor
185	165	140	100	75	50

PISTOLS
Siber
A .45 caliber percussion pistol patterned after the Swiss Siber.

NIB	Exc.	V.G.	Good	Fair	Poor
400	325	275	225	150	100

Kentucky
A .45 caliber single shot percussion pistol with a 10" barrel and walnut stock.

NIB	Exc.	V.G.	Good	Fair	Poor
140	125	100	80	60	40

Philadelphia Derringer
A .45 caliber single shot percussion pistol with a 3.25" barrel and walnut stock.

NIB	Exc.	V.G.	Good	Fair	Poor
75	65	50	40	30	20

Sheriff's Model
A .36 caliber percussion revolver, nickel-plated with walnut grips.

NIB	Exc.	V.G.	Good	Fair	Poor
225	200	175	150	125	100

3rd Model Dragoon
NIB	Exc.	V.G.	Good	Fair	Poor
225	200	175	150	125	100

Colt Walker Replica
NIB	Exc.	V.G.	Good	Fair	Poor
275	250	225	200	175	150

Remington Bison
NIB	Exc.	V.G.	Good	Fair	Poor
250	225	200	175	150	125

Pocket Police
NIB	Exc.	V.G.	Good	Fair	Poor
135	110	100	85	65	45

Pocker Revolver

Chambered for .31 caliber. Fitted with 4" octagon barrel. Cylinder holds five bullets. Solid brass frame. Weighs about 15 oz.

NIB	Exc.	V.G.	Good	Fair	Poor
125	100	85	75	60	50

Wells Fargo

NIB	Exc.	V.G.	Good	Fair	Poor
165	145	125	100	75	50

1851 Navy

NIB	Exc.	V.G.	Good	Fair	Poor
135	110	100	85	65	45

1861 Navy

NIB	Exc.	V.G.	Good	Fair	Poor
150	135	110	90	75	50

1860 Army

NIB	Exc.	V.G.	Good	Fair	Poor
220	200	175	150	125	100

1858 Remington

NIB	Exc.	V.G.	Good	Fair	Poor
175	150	125	100	75	50

1858 Remington Target

As above, but fitted with adjustable sights.

NIB	Exc.	V.G.	Good	Fair	Poor
235	200	175	125	100	75

Bison

A 6-shot .44 caliber revolver with 10-1/4" octagonal barrel. Solid brass frame. Weighs about 48 oz.

NIB	Exc.	V.G.	Good	Fair	Poor
160	130	100	85	75	50

Hawken Pistol

This is a .50 caliber percussion pistol with 9-3/4" octagon barrel. The stock is hardwood. Weighs about 50 oz.

NIB	Exc.	V.G.	Good	Fair	Poor
135	110	85	75	65	50

CONSTABLE, R.
Philadelphia, Pennsylvania

Pocket Pistol

A single shot percussion pistol with a 3" round or octagonal barrel. German-silver mounts and walnut stock. These pistols are marked "R. Constable Philadelphia" and were manufactured during the late 1840s and 1850s.

Exc.	V.G.	Good	Fair	Poor
—	1750	900	500	200

CONTENTO/VENTUR
Importer-Ventura
Seal Beach, California

This high-grade, double-barrel shotgun is no longer imported.

SIDE-BY-SIDE

Model 51

A 12, 16, 20, 28, and .410 bore boxlock double-barrel shotgun with 26", 28", 30", and 32" barrels, various chokes, extractors and double triggers. Checkered walnut stock. Introduced in 1980 and discontinued in 1985.

Exc.	V.G.	Good	Fair	Poor
500	350	300	225	150

Model 52

As above in 10 gauge.

Exc.	V.G.	Good	Fair	Poor
500	350	300	225	150

Model 53

As above, with scalloped receiver, automatic ejectors and available with a single selective trigger. Discontinued in 1985. Single-Selective Trigger add 25%.

Exc.	V.G.	Good	Fair	Poor
550	400	350	250	200

Model 62

A 12, 20, or 28 gauge Holland & Holland sidelock shotgun with various barrel lengths and chokes, automatic ejectors, cocking indicators, a floral engraved receiver, a checkered, walnut stock. Discontinued in 1982.

Exc.	V.G.	Good	Fair	Poor
950	800	750	600	450

Model 64

As above, but more finely finished. No longer in production.

Exc.	V.G.	Good	Fair	Poor
1150	900	850	700	550

OVER/UNDER

A 12 gauge Over/Under shotgun with 32" barrels, screw-in choke tubes, a high ventilated rib, automatic ejectors, and a standard single selective trigger. Checkered, with Monte Carlo walnut stock.

Exc.	V.G.	Good	Fair	Poor
1050	900	750	600	500

Mark 2

As above, with an extra single barrel and fitted in a leather case.

Exc.	V.G.	Good	Fair	Poor
1350	1200	1050	900	800

Mark 3

As above, but engraved with a finely figured walnut stock.

Exc.	V.G.	Good	Fair	Poor
1600	1500	1250	1100	950

Mark 3 Combo

As above, with an extra single barrel and fitted in a leather case.

Exc.	V.G.	Good	Fair	Poor
2800	2600	2250	1750	1300

CONTINENTAL
RWM
Cologne, Germany

Continental Pocket Pistol

A 6.35mm caliber semiautomatic pistol with a 2" barrel, internal hammer, and a 7-shot detachable magazine. Blued with plastic grips, and the slide is marked "Continental Kal. 6.35."

Exc.	V.G.	Good	Fair	Poor
250	150	125	100	75

CONTINENTAL ARMS CO.
Liege, Belgium

Double Rifle

A .270, .303, .30-40, .30-06, .348, 375 H&H, .400 Jeffreys, .465, .475, .500, and .600 Nitro Express caliber Anson & Deeley boxlock double-barreled rifle with 24" or 26" barrels, and double triggers. Checkered walnut stock.

Exc.	V.G.	Good	Fair	Poor
6500	4500	3750	3000	2250

CONTINENTAL ARMS CO.
Norwich, Connecticut

Pepperbox

A .22 caliber 5-barrel pepperbox with a spur trigger and 2.5" barrels marked "Continental Arms Co. Norwich Ct. Patented Aug. 28, 1866." Some examples of this pistol are to be found marked "Ladies Companion."

Courtesy Milwaukee Public Museum, Milwaukee, Wisconsin

Exc.	V.G.	Good	Fair	Poor
—	1850	850	350	250

COOK & BROTHER RIFLES AND CARBINES
New Orleans

In early 1861, Ferdinand W.C. Cook and his brother, Francis L. Cook, both English emigres, joined to form Cook & Brother in New Orleans to manufacture rifles and carbines following the English P1853 series for the newly seceded state of Louisiana and its neighbors. Between June 1861 and the federal occupation of New Orleans in April 1862, this firm produced about 200 cavalry and artillery carbines and about 1000 rifles. Having successfully moved the armory's machinery before federal occupation, the firm continued manufacture of rifles in Selma, Alabama, during 1862, probably completing another 1,000 rifles with the New Orleans lock markings from the parts brought with them. Re-established in Athens, Georgia, in early 1863, the firm continued to build both carbines and rifles, manufacturing more than 5,500 above the New Orleans production through 1864. The firm's products were clearly among the best small arms made within the Confederacy

Cook & Brother Rifles (New Orleans & Selma production)

Overall length 48-3/4"; barrel length 33"; caliber .58. Markings: representation of a Confederate flag ("Stars & Bars") and "COOK & BROTHER/N.O./1861 (or) 1862" on lock; same usually on barrel, together with serial number and "PROVED" near breech. Rifles in the early production have long range rear sights and unusual two piece block and blade front sights as well as an integral bayonet lug with guide on right side of barrel. Later production utilizes a brass clamping ring for the bayonet, a block open rear sight and a simple block and blade front sight. Earlier production will claim a premium if in good condition.

Courtesy Milwaukee Public Museum, Milwaukee, Wisconsin

Exc.	V.G.	Good	Fair	Poor
—	—	15000	7500	3000

Cook & Brother Carbines (New Orleans production)

Overall length 40" (artillery), 37" (cavalry); barrel length 24" (artillery), 21"-21-1/2"; caliber .58. Markings: As on Cook & Brother rifles (New Orleans production) artillery and cavalry carbines were produced in New Orleans in a separate serial range from the rifles. Total production is thought not to have exceeded 225, divided evenly between 1861 and 1862 dates. In addition to the overall and barrel lengths, the main difference between the artillery and cavalry carbines is the manner in which they were carried. The former bears standard sling rings on the upper band and the triggerguard strap, the latter has a bar with a ring on the left side of the stock. Both are exceedingly rare.

Exc.	V.G.	Good	Fair	Poor
—	—	15000	6500	5000

Cook & Brother Rifles (Athens production)

Overall length 49"; barrel length 33"; caliber .58. Markings: representation of a Confederate flag ("Stars & Bars") and "COOK & BROTHER/ATHENS GA./date (1863 or 1864), and serial number on lock; "PROVED" on barrel near breech; serial number on various metal parts. After re-establishing their plant at Athens, Georgia, in the spring of 1863, Cook & Brother continued to manufacture rifles in a consecutive serial range after their New Orleans/Selma production (beginning about serial number 2000) and continued to make arms well into 1864 (through at least serial number 7650) until Sherman's army threatened the plant and necessitated the employment of its workforce in a military capacity as the 23rd Battalion Georgia State Guard.

Courtesy Milwaukee Public Museum, Milwaukee, Wisconsin

Exc.	V.G.	Good	Fair	Poor
—	—	15000	7500	3000

Cook & Brother Carbines (Athens production)

Overall length 40" (artillery) or 37" (cavalry); barrel lengths 24" (artillery) or 21"-21-1/2" (cavalry); caliber .58. Markings: same as on Athens production rifles. Artillery and cavalry carbines were manufactured in the same serial range as the Athens production rifles (about 2000 through 7650). As in New Orleans production, the artillery and cavalry carbines are distinguished from one another by their respective lengths. Unlike New Orleans/Selma production, however, some of the cavalry carbines are mounted with sling swivels of the artillery style, while others bear the sling ring on the left side and additionally have a swivel ring to secure the ramrod.

Courtesy Milwaukee Public Museum, Milwaukee, Wisconsin

Courtesy Milwaukee Public Museum, Milwaukee, Wisconsin

Exc.	V.G.	Good	Fair	Poor
—	—	15000	6500	5000

COONAN ARMS CO.
Maplewood, Minnesota

Model A

A .357 Magnum semiautomatic pistol with a 5" barrel, a 7-shot, detachable magazine, and fixed sights. Stainless steel with walnut grips. Introduced in 1981 and discontinued in 1984.

NIB	Exc.	V.G.	Good	Fair	Poor
700	550	425	—	—	—

Model B

An improved version of the above with a linkless barrel system, extended grip safety, enclosed trigger bar, and a more contoured grip. A 6" barrel is available, as are adjustable sights, as extra cost options. A .38 Special conversion is also available. Introduced in 1985. A number of other options are also available which will effect value.

NOTE: For 6" Barrel add $40, Bomar Adjustable Sights add $130, .38 Special Conversion add $40, Checkered walnut grips add $40, with Teflon slide add $100, with Teflon frame add $100.

NIB	Exc.	V.G.	Good	Fair	Poor
735	600	475	—	—	—

Comp I

As above, with 6" barrel and attached compensator and a stippled front grip strap. Introduced in 1989.

NIB	Exc.	V.G.	Good	Fair	Poor
1000	800	650	—	—	—

NOTE: For 6" Barrel add $40, Bomar Adjustable Sights add $130, .38 Special Conversion add $40, Checkered walnut grips add $40, with Teflon slide add $100, with Teflon frame add $100.

Comp I Deluxe

As above, with a blued stainless steel slide, checkered grip straps, and a finer finishing.

NIB	Exc.	V.G.	Good	Fair	Poor
1650	1350	1150	950	800	600

Classic

This model features an integrated compensator with 5" barrel. Pistol is supplied with checkered walnut grips, Millett adjustable rear sight, and two-tone Teflon finish. Magazine capacity is 7 rounds, weight is 42 oz., and overall length is 8.3".

NIB	Exc.	V.G.	Good	Fair	Poor
1400	1100	850	—	—	—

.41 Magnum Model

Introduced in 1997 this model is chambered for the .41 Magnum cartridge and fitted with a 5" barrel with smooth walnut grips and fixed sights.

NIB	Exc.	V.G.	Good	Fair	Poor
825	650	—	—	—	—

NOTE: For 6" Barrel add $40, Bomar Adjustable Sights add $130, .38 Special Conversion add $40, Checkered walnut grips add $40, with Teflon slide add $100, with Teflon frame add $100.

Cadet

Chambered for the .357 magnum cartridge this model has a 3.9" barrel with smooth walnut grips, and fixed rear sight. Magazine capacity is 6 rounds; weight is about 39 oz., and overall length is 7.8". Height of the pistol is 5.3". Coonan Arms refers to this model as the "Short Grip".

NIB	Exc.	V.G.	Good	Fair	Poor
855	675	—	—	—	—

NOTE: For 6" Barrel add $40, Bomar Adjustable Sights add $130, .38 Special Conversion add $40, Checkered walnut grips add $40, with Teflon slide add $100, with Teflon frame add $100.

Cadet II
Same as above but with a standard grip. Magazine capacity of this model is 7 rounds.

NIB	Exc.	V.G.	Good	Fair	Poor
855	675	—	—	—	—

NOTE: For 6" Barrel add $40, Bomar Adjustable Sights add $130, .38 Special Conversion add $40, Checkered walnut grips add $40, with Teflon slide add $100, with Teflon frame add $100.

COOPER ARMS
Stevensville, Montana

Model 36 Marksman
This is a premium bolt action rifle chambered for the .22 Long Rifle cartridge and in centerfire calibers of .17 CCM and .22 Hornet. The 23" Shilen barrel is mated to a solid bar stock receiver. High grade walnut is used in stocks that are fine-lined checkered.

Standard

NIB	Exc.	V.G.	Good	Fair	Poor
1400	800	700	500	300	—

Classic

NIB	Exc.	V.G.	Good	Fair	Poor
1600	1100	800	600	400	—

Custom Classic

NIB	Exc.	V.G.	Good	Fair	Poor
1900	1550	1150	850	600	—

Western Classic-octagon barrel & case color metal

INIB	Exc.	V.G.	Good	Fair	Poor
2200	1800	—	—	—	—

BR-50 w/Jewell Trigger

NIB	Exc.	V.G.	Good	Fair	Poor
1800	1450	1100	800	600	—

IR-50-50 w/Jewell Trigger

NIB	Exc.	V.G.	Good	Fair	Poor
1800	1450	1100	800	600	—

Featherweight w/Jewell Trigger

NIB	Exc.	V.G.	Good	Fair	Poor
1800	1450	1100	800	600	—

Model 38/40
This bolt action rifle is chambered for the .17 AK Hornet, .22 K Hornet, or the .22 Hornet.

Classic

NIB	Exc.	V.G.	Good	Fair	Poor
1800	1500	1100	800	600	—

Custom Classic

NIB	Exc.	V.G.	Good	Fair	Poor
2000	1750	1250	850	600	—

Western Classic-octagon barrel & case color metal

INIB	Exc.	V.G.	Good	Fair	Poor
2200	1800	—	—	—	—

Model 21
This bolt action rifle is chambered for the following cartridges: .221 Fireball, .222, .223, .6x45, 6x47, .17 Mach IV, and the .17 Rem. A 24" stainless steel Shilen match grade barrel is fitted. AAA claro walnut is used with oval forearm, ambidextrous palm swell, 22 line to the inch checkering, oil finish, and Pachmayr butt pad are all standard features. Weighs approximately 8 lbs.

Varmint Extreme

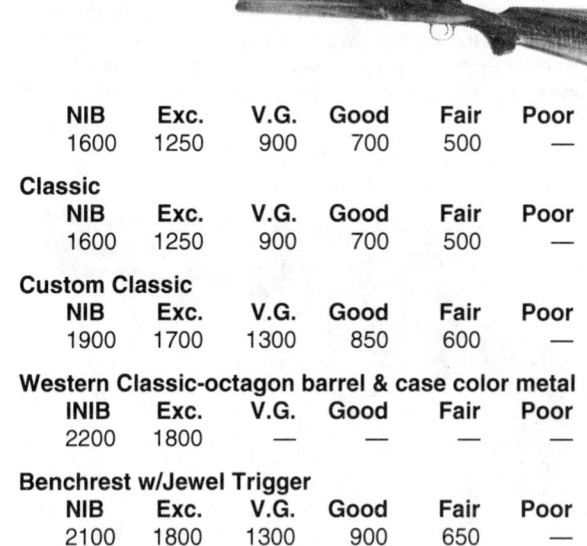

NIB	Exc.	V.G.	Good	Fair	Poor
1600	1250	900	700	500	—

Classic

NIB	Exc.	V.G.	Good	Fair	Poor
1600	1250	900	700	500	—

Custom Classic

NIB	Exc.	V.G.	Good	Fair	Poor
1900	1700	1300	850	600	—

Western Classic-octagon barrel & case color metal

INIB	Exc.	V.G.	Good	Fair	Poor
2200	1800	—	—	—	—

Benchrest w/Jewel Trigger

NIB	Exc.	V.G.	Good	Fair	Poor
2100	1800	1300	900	650	—

Model 22
This is a bolt action single rifle chambered for a variety of calibers: 6.PPC, 22-250, .220 Swift, .243, .25-06, .308, .22 BR, 7.62X39, 6.5X55. A Pachmayr decelerator pad is standard. Weight is approximately 8.5 lbs.

Pro Varmint Extreme

NIB	Exc.	V.G.	Good	Fair	Poor
1750	1500	1200	800	600	—

Benchrest w/Jewel Trigger

NIB	Exc.	V.G.	Good	Fair	Poor
2100	1800	1300	900	650	—

Model 22 Repeater
Same as above but with magazine and chambered for .22-25, .308, 7mm-08, and .243.

Classic

NIB	Exc.	V.G.	Good	Fair	Poor
2400	2000	1750	1250	800	—

Custom Classic

NIB	Exc.	V.G.	Good	Fair	Poor
2650	2200	1850	1400	900	—

Western Classic-octagon barrel & case color metal

INIB	Exc.	V.G.	Good	Fair	Poor
2200	1800	—	—	—	—

Model 72/Montana Plainsman
Introduced in 1997 this High Wall single shot rifle is available in a wide variety of calibers. It is offered with single or double set triggers.

NIB	Exc.	V.G.	Good	Fair	Poor
2200	1800				

NOTE: There are a number of extra cost options that can effect the price of each of these models. Options such as Skelton butt plate, quarter ribs ribbon checkering etc. can add hundreds of dollars to the price of the gun. Check these options carefully before a sale.

COOPER, J. M. & CO.
Philadelphia, Pennsylvania

Pocket Revolver

A .31 caliber percussion double action revolver with 4", 5", or 6" octagonal barrel, and a 6-shot unfluted cylinder. Blued with walnut grips. During the first two years of production they were made in Pittsburgh, Pennsylvania, and were so marked. Approximately 15,000 were manufactured between 1864 and 1869.

Pittsburgh-Marked Models add 20%.

Courtesy Milwaukee Public Museum, Milwaukee, Wisconsin

Courtesy Milwaukee Public Museum, Milwaukee, Wisconsin

Exc.	V.G.	Good	Fair	Poor
—	—	700	350	150

COOPERATIVA OBRERA
Eibar, Spain

Longines

A 7.65mm caliber semiautomatic pistol. The slide is marked "Cal. 7.65 Automatic Pistol Longines."

Exc.	V.G.	Good	Fair	Poor
250	175	150	110	85

COPELAND, FRANK
Worcester, Massachusetts

Copeland Pocket Revolver .22

A .22 cartridge spur trigger revolver with a 2.5" barrel, 7-shot magazine, an unfluted cylinder and lock notches on the front. Frame is brass, blued walnut, or rosewood grips. The barrel marked "F. Copeland, Worcester, Mass." Manufactured in the 1860s.

Exc.	V.G.	Good	Fair	Poor
—	650	300	125	100

Copeland .32 Revolver

A .32 caliber spur trigger revolver with a 5-shot fluted cylinder and an iron frame. Nickel-plated. The barrel marked "F. Copeland, Sterling, Mass." Manufactured in the 1860s.

Exc.	V.G.	Good	Fair	Poor
—	650	300	150	75

COSMI, A. & F.
Torrette, Italy
Importer-New England Arms
Kittery Pt., Maine

Semiautomatic

A 12 and 20 gauge semiautomatic shotgun with various barrel lengths and chokes, an 8-shot magazine, and a ventilated rib. This is basically a custom-built, made-to-order gun. There is a standard and a deluxe model, with the differences being in the degree of embellishment.

Standard Model

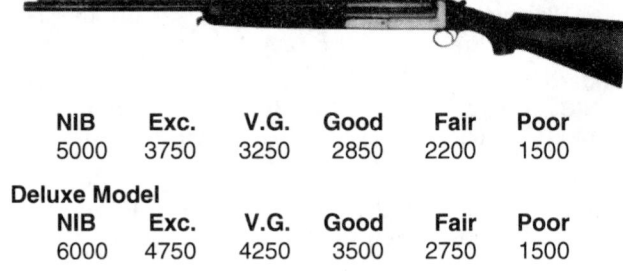

NIB	Exc.	V.G.	Good	Fair	Poor
5000	3750	3250	2850	2200	1500

Deluxe Model

NIB	Exc.	V.G.	Good	Fair	Poor
6000	4750	4250	3500	2750	1500

COSMOPOLITAN ARMS CO.
Hamilton, Ohio

Breech Loading Rifle

A .52 single shot percussion rifle with a 31" round barrel. The frame marked "Cosmopolitan Arms Co. Hamilton 0. U.S./Gross Patent." Blued with a walnut buttstock. Approximately 100 were made between 1859 and 1862.

Exc.	V.G.	Good	Fair	Poor
—	—	4500	1750	500

COWLES & SON
Chicopee, Massachusetts

Single Shot

A .22 or .30 caliber single shot spur trigger pistol with a 3.25" round barrel. Silver-plated brass frame, blued with walnut grip. Approximately 200 manufactured in 1865.

Courtesy Richard M. Kumor Sr.

Exc.	V.G.	Good	Fair	Poor
—	950	400	250	100

CARL PHILLIP CRAUSE
MUSKETS AND RIFLES
Herzberg, Germany

Carl Phillip Crause (who signed his products only with his last name) operated a gun manufactory in Herzberg on the Harz in the northwestern German kingdom of Hannover from the close of the Napoleonic Wars until 1857. The main production of his factory was devoted to military arms for Hannover and the surrounding principalities. Weapons of his manufacture included the Brunswick M1835 and M1848 rifles, the Hannovarian M1850 and M1854 rifle-muskets and yager rifles, and the M1840 and M1849 rifle-muskets of the Hanseatic League (a coalition of the north German states of Oldenberg, Hamburg, Bremen, and Lubeck). The latter two arms were subsequently altered to accept the elongated projectiles popular during the 1850s, and a few thousand evidently were imported into the United States and saw service during the American Civil War.

Hanseatic League M1840 Rifled Musket

Overall length 55-1/2"; barrel length 40-1/4"; caliber .70. Markings: on lockplate forward of hammer, "Crause in Herzberg" in script, the "s" in the archaic form, appearing as an "f." Of the 6,000 muskets of this type made, approximately half were sent to the United States in 1861 during the arms crisis that accompanied the outbreak of the American Civil War. A total of 2,680 of these were issued to Ohio and at least one regiment (the 56th Ohio) was armed with these rifled muskets. These arms were mistakenly identified during the period as being Saxon due to the similarity of the large squared off foresection of the lockplate.

Courtesy Milwaukee Public Museum, Milwaukee, Wisconsin

Exc.	V.G.	Good	Fair	Poor
—	850	475	375	250

Oldenberg M1849 Rifled Musket

Overall lengths 55-1/2"-56-5/8" (long version), 49-1/2" (short version); barrel lengths 39"-39-1/8" (long version), 33" (short version); caliber .69-.72 (rifled). Markings: "Crause in Herzberg" inscribed in script on the backstrap of the hammer housing, the "s" in archaic form, appearing as an "f." Nicknamed the "Cyclops" because its large, center-hung hammer is pierced with a large window that served as its rear sight, a few hundred of these clumsy rifled muskets may have been intermixed with the shipments of "Saxon" muskets imported in 1861 or 1862 into the United States during the American Civil War.

Courtesy Milwaukee Public Museum, Milwaukee, Wisconsin

Exc.	V.G.	Good	Fair	Poor
—	900	500	350	225

CRESCENT F. A. CO.
Norwich, Connecticut

Text and prices by Nick Niles

The company made good quality inexpensive single and double barrel shotguns at its Norwich works, beginning about 1892. It was bought by H&D Folsom of New York City, large importers and distributors of firearms and sporting goods, so they could add an American-made sidelock hammer, side by side to their extensive range of imported guns. The Crescent guns were offered in 12, 16, 20, and 28 gauges and later, 44XL shot caliber with Damascus twist laminated or Armory steel barrels depending on the shooter's wants. In 1898 VL&D said these were the best American hammer guns in the market for the money.

Huge quantities of these "Hardware Guns" were produced in a profusion of private brands as well as in Folsom's house brand "American Gun Co. of NY". In 1922 the Crescent brand replaced the "American Gun Co. of NY" and can be found on many thousands of doubles. In 1905 Crescent's first hammerless sidelock was introduced as the American Gun Co. "Knickerbocker" Model No. 6. This very popular model became the Crescent "Peerless" No. 6 in 1922. In 1928 it became the Crescent "Empire" No. 60 and in 1931 the Crescent-Davis "New Empire" No. 88, "New Empire" No. 9, and "Empire" No. 9.

Crescent was bought by J. Stevens Arms Co., Division of Savage Arms Corp. about 1930. It was merged with Davis-Warner Arms Corp. successors to N.R. Davis & Sons Co. and became Crescent-Davis Arms Corp. In 1932 the operation was moved to the Stevens plant at Springfield, Mass. where some sidelock doubles were assembled, Crescent-Davis brand guns remained in Steven's full line catalog until 1941 but from 1937 to 1941 the doubles sold in the C-D brand were on either Stevens or Davis boxlock frames.

DOUBLES

Triumph-Hammerless Boxlock

Exc.	V.G.	Good	Fair	Poor
700	600	400	300	200

Model 2655-Laminated Barrels Hammer Sidelock

Exc.	V.G.	Good	Fair	Poor
500	400	300	200	150

Model 2665-Damascus Barrels Hammer Sidelock

Exc.	V.G.	Good	Fair	Poor
500	400	300	200	150

Crescent American Hammer Gun No. 0-Hammer Sidelock

Exc.	V.G.	Good	Fair	Poor
350	300	250	200	100

Knickerbocker No. 6 Armory-Hammerless Sidelock

Courtesy Nick Niles. Photo Paul Goodwin

Exc.	V.G.	Good	Fair	Poor
400	300	250	200	100

Knickerbocker No. 7 Hammerless Sidelock

Exc.	V.G.	Good	Fair	Poor
400	300	250	200	100

Knickerbocker No. 8-Damascus Barrels Hammerless Sidelock

Exc.	V.G.	Good	Fair	Poor
500	400	300	250	200

American Gun Co. NY No. 1 Armory-Hammerless Sidelock

Exc.	V.G.	Good	Fair	Poor
400	300	250	200	100

American Gun Co. NY No. 2-Hammerless Sidelock

Exc.	V.G.	Good	Fair	Poor
500	400	300	250	200

American Gun Co. No. 3-Damascus Barrels Hammer Sidelock

Exc.	V.G.	Good	Fair	Poor
600	500	400	300	250

American Gun Co. No. 4-Hammer Sidelock

Exc.	V.G.	Good	Fair	Poor
700	600	500	400	300

American Gun Co. No. 5-Damascus Barrels Hammer Sidelock

Exc.	V.G.	Good	Fair	Poor
800	700	600	450	350

American Machine Made 2641-Hammer Sidelock

Exc.	V.G.	Good	Fair	Poor
400	350	300	250	200

American Machine Made 2650-Hammer Sidelock

Exc.	V.G.	Good	Fair	Poor
500	400	350	300	250

American Machine Made 2660-Damascus Barrels Hammer Sidelock

Exc.	V.G.	Good	Fair	Poor
600	500	450	350	300

Folsom Arms Co. No. 0 Armory-Hammer Sidelock

Exc.	V.G.	Good	Fair	Poor
400	300	250	200	100

Folsom Arms Co. No. 2-Hammer Sidelock

Exc.	V.G.	Good	Fair	Poor
500	400	300	200	150

Folsom Arms Co. No. 3 Damascus Barrel

Exc.	V.G.	Good	Fair	Poor
600	450	350	300	200

New Knickerbocker Armory-Hammerless Sidelock

Exc.	V.G.	Good	Fair	Poor
400	300	250	200	100

New Knickerbocker WT-Hammerless Sidelock

Courtesy Nick Niles. Photo Paul Goodwin

Exc.	V.G.	Good	Fair	Poor
450	350	250	200	150

New Knickerbocker Damascus Barrels-Hammerless Sidelock

Exc.	V.G.	Good	Fair	Poor
500	400	300	250	200

American Gun Co. Small Bore No. 28 Straight Stock-Hammer Sidelock

Exc.	V.G.	Good	Fair	Poor
800	700	600	400	300

American Gun Co. Small Bore No. 44 Straight Stock-Hammer Sidelock

Exc.	V.G.	Good	Fair	Poor
900	750	650	450	350

American Gun Co. No. 0 Armory Straight Stock-Hammer Sidelock

Courtesy Nick Niles. Photo Paul Goodwin

Exc.	V.G.	Good	Fair	Poor
350	300	250	200	100

American Gun Co. No. 28 Nitro Straight Stock-Hammer Sidelock

Exc.	V.G.	Good	Fair	Poor
800	650	550	400	300

American Gun Co. No. 44 Nitro Straight Stock-Hammer Sidelock

Exc.	V.G.	Good	Fair	Poor
900	750	600	450	350

American Gun Co. Midget Field No. 28-Hammer Sidelock

Exc.	V.G.	Good	Fair	Poor
800	650	400	400	300

American Gun Co. Midget Field No. 44-Hammer Sidelock

Courtesy Nick Niles. Photo Paul Goodwin

Exc.	V.G.	Good	Fair	Poor
900	750	650	500	350

Crescent 1922 Model No. 66 Quali-Hammerless Sidelock

Exc.	V.G.	Good	Fair	Poor
600	500	450	350	250

Crescent Firearms Co. No. 0-Hammer Sidelock

Exc.	V.G.	Good	Fair	Poor
400	350	250	200	150

Crescent Firearms Co. No. 0 Nickel-Hammer Sidelock

Exc.	V.G.	Good	Fair	Poor
500	400	350	250	200

Crescent Firearms Co. No. 6 Peerless-Hammerless Sidelock

Exc.	V.G.	Good	Fair	Poor
400	350	250	200	150

Crescent Firearms Co. No. 6E Peerless Engraved-Hammerless Sidelock

Exc.	V.G.	Good	Fair	Poor
600	450	350	250	200

Crescent Firearms Co. No. 66 Quali-Hammerless Sidelock

Exc.	V.G.	Good	Fair	Poor
650	500	400	300	200

Crescent Firearms Co. No. 60 Empire-Hammerless Sidelock

Courtesy Nick Niles. Photo Paul Goodwin

Exc.	V.G.	Good	Fair	Poor
450	400	350	300	200

Crescent Firearms Co. No. 6 Peerless-Hammerless Sidelock

Courtesy Nick Niles. Photo Paul Goodwin

Exc.	V.G.	Good	Fair	Poor
400	350	300	200	150

Crescent Firearms Co. No. 44 Improved-Hammer Sidelock

Exc.	V.G.	Good	Fair	Poor
700	600	500	400	300

New Crescent Empire Red Butt-Hammerless Sidelock

Exc.	V.G.	Good	Fair	Poor
400	350	250	200	150

Crescent New Empire No. 88-Hammerless Sidelock

Exc.	V.G.	Good	Fair	Poor
400	350	250	200	150

Crescent New Empire No. 9-Hammerless Sidelock

Courtesy Nick Niles. Photo Paul Goodwin

Exc.	V.G.	Good	Fair	Poor
350	300	250	200	100

Crescent Empire No. 60-Hammerless Sidelock

Exc.	V.G.	Good	Fair	Poor
350	300	250	200	100

Crescent Certified Empire No. 60-Hammerless Sidelock

Exc.	V.G.	Good	Fair	Poor
400	300	250	200	150

Crescent Certified Empire No. 9-Hammerless Sidelock

Exc.	V.G.	Good	Fair	Poor
450	350	300	250	200

Crescent Certified Empire No. 88-Hammerless Sidelock

Courtesy Nick Niles. Photo Paul Goodwin

Exc.	V.G.	Good	Fair	Poor
500	450	400	350	300

Crescent Davis No. 600-Hammerless Boxlock

Courtesy Nick Niles. Photo Paul Goodwin

Exc.	V.G.	Good	Fair	Poor
400	350	300	250	200

Crescent Davis No. 900-Hammerless Boxlock

Exc.	V.G.	Good	Fair	Poor
500	450	400	350	300

Single Shot

Made in 12, 16, 20, and 28 gauge and .410. Barrel lengths were 26", 28", 30", and 32", with various chokes. It had an exposed hammer, fluid steel barrel, and walnut pistol grip stock.

Exc.	V.G.	Good	Fair	Poor
175	125	100	75	50

Revolver

A typical S&W copy made by Crescent in Norwich, Connecticut. It was a top-break, double action, that was found either blued or nickel-plated with checkered, black hard rubber grips. The cylinder held 5 shots and was chambered for the .32 S&W cartridge.

Exc.	V.G.	Good	Fair	Poor
200	150	125	85	40

Crescent Certified Shotgun NFA, CURIO OR RELIC

The Crescent Certified Shotgun is a .410 smooth bore pistol with a 12.25" barrel manufactured from approximately 1930 to 1932 by the Crescent-Davis Arms Corp., Norwich, Connecticut, and possibly thereafter until 1934 by the J. Stevens Arms Co., which purchased the company. In various distributor catalogs it is termed the "Ever-Ready" Model 200, and advertised with a blued frame. Specimens have been observed with "tiger-stripe" (like an H&R Handy-Gun) or Colt SAA or Winchester-type case hardening. Total production is unknown but serial numbers ranging from 1305 to 3262 have been observed, suggesting it may have been fewer than 4,000. The Treasury Department ruled the .410 Crescent to be a "firearm" in the "any other weapon" category under the NFA in 1934, when its retail price was about $11.

Exc.	V.G.	Good	Fair	Poor
850	650	500	350	250

NOTE: Add $100 to $300 for original cardboard box.

The barrel is marked *PROOF TESTED 410 GAUGE* on top and **2-1/2IN SHELLS** on the middle left side. The receiver's left side is stamped **CRESCENT CERTIFIED SHOTGUN/CRESCENT-DAVIS ARMS CORPORATION/NORWICH, CONN., U.S.A.** The earliest guns also have **.410** stamped at the top of the left side of the receiver near the breech, but this marking does not appear on later guns. It is a rather heavy (57 oz. unloaded) handgun.

Crescent Auto & Burglar Gun CURIO OR RELIC, NFA

The Crescent Auto & Burglar Gun is a hammerless .410 bore or 20 gauge smooth bore pistol with 12.25" double barrels. The triggerguard and double trigger designs are identical to those of the .410 Crescent Certified Shotgun. An extremely rare firearm whose total production and years of manufacture are unknown at this time, its only known documentation is an advertisement by "Saul Ruben, The Gun Store, 68 E. Long St., Columbus, Ohio," on page 44 of the October 1932 issue of *Hunter-Trader-Trapper*, which lists a $14.75 retail price. At this time, four specimens are known, all in .410 bore, bearing serial numbers S-1, S-13, S-18, and S-19. The serial number appears under the forestock on the metal. The left side of its receiver is marked **Crescent Fire Arms Co./Norwich, Conn. U.S.A.**, and the right side is stamped **NEW EMPIRE**. Establishing a reliable value may be difficult, but could be logically expected to approximate those for a nonstandard or special-order Ithaca Auto & Burglar Gun. The Crescent Auto & Burglar Gun may have been distributed by the H.&D. Folsom Arms Co. of New York City through its manufacturing division, the Crescent Firearms Co., Norwich, Connecticut. Crescent's sellers included the Belknap Hardware Co., Louisville, Kentucky, and Hibbard-Spencer-Bartlett Co., Chicago, Illinois.

Victor Ejector Pistol NFA

The Victor Ejector Pistol is a .410 smooth bore pistol with a 12" barrel manufactured sometime before 1930 by the Crecent Fire Arms Co. of Norwich, Connecticut, but is not listed in any Crescent or other trade catalog. It may be a predecessor or factory prototype of the Crescent Certified Shotgun .410 pistol, because both were manufactured by Crescent, and most design features are identical. The single known example of the Victor Ejector Pistol bears serial number 755004. Because of its extreme rarity, a reliable value cannot be determined at this time.

The left side of the receiver is stamped **Victor Ejector/Crescent Fire Arms Co./Norwich, Conn. U.S.A.**; and **.410** is stamped at the top left side of the receiver near the breech (as in the earliest variations of the Crescent Certified Shotgun). The barrel is stamped **GENUINE ARMORY STEEL** on the top near the breech, chambered only for 2.5" shells, with serial number 755004 stamped on the left side of the barrel lug. The configuration of the receiver, triggerguard, barrel latch lever, and wooden forend (the number 5004 is stamped on the forend metal) are identical to those of the Crescent Certified Shotgun.

The major differences between the Victor Ejector and Crescent Certified Shotgun is the latter's (1) pistol grip style, and (2) weight. The Victor pistol grip represents the average that would result from combining the Colt Single Action Army and Colt Bisley grips. The Victor is unusually heavy, exactly 74 oz. (about 4.6 lbs) unloaded, versus 57 oz. (about 3.5 lbs) for the Crescent. Whether the pistol grip part of the Victor Ejector receiver was brazed on or cast with the rest of the receiver is unclear, and additional specimens of this firearm may shed some light on this question. The Victor Ejector was probably redesigned to eliminate some of the weight.

BRAND NAMES USED BY CRESCENT ARMS

American Bar Lock Wonder made for Sears, Roebuck & Co.

American Boy made for Townley Metal & Hardware Co.

American Gun Co. (H & D Folsom house brand)

American Gun Company of New York

American Nitro

Armory Gun Co.

Baker Gun Co. (if no foreign proof marks)

T. Barker New York-if a sidelock hammerless double without proofs.

Bellmore Gun Co.

Berkshire No. 3000 made for Shapleigh Hardware Co. of St. Louis, MO

Black Beauty-hammerless doubles

Bluefield Clipper

Bluegrass Arms Co. made for Belknap Hardware Co. of Louisville, KY

Blue Whistler

Bridge Black Prince

Bridge Gun Co.

Bridge Gun Works

Bridgeport Arms Co. (if no foreign proof marks)

Bright Arms Co.

Canadian Belle

Carolina Arms Co. made for Smith Wadsworth Hardware Co. of Charlotte, NC

Caroline Arms

Central Arm Co. made for Shapleigh Hardware Co. of St. Louis, MO

Chatham Arms Co.

Cherokee Arms Co. made for C. M. McClung Co. of Knoxville, TN

Chesapeake Gun Co.

Chicago Long Range Wonder 1908-1918 made for Sears, Roebuck & Co. of Chicago, IL

Colonial

Columbian New York Arms Co.

Compeer made for Van Camp Hardware & Iron Co. of Indianapolis, IN

Connecticut Arms Co.

Cumberland Arms Co.

Crescent Fire Arms Co.

Creve Cour (if no foreign proof marks) made for Isaac Walker Hardware Co. of Peoria, IL

Cruso

Daniel Boone Gun Co. made for Belknap Hardware Co. of Louisville, KY

Delphian Arms Co. (some models without foreign proof marks) made for Supplee-Biddle Hardware Co. of Philadelphia, PA

Delphian Manufacturing Co. (some models)

Diamond Arms Co. (some models) made for Shapleigh Hardware Co. of St. Louis, MO

Dunlap Special made for Dunlap Hardware Co. of Macon, GA

E.C. Mac made for E.C. Meacham Arms Co. of St. Louis, MO

Elgin Arms Co. made for Strauss & Schram and Fred Biffar & Co. both of Chicago, IL

Elmira Arms Co.

Empire Arms Co. made for Sears, Roebuck & Co. of Chicago, IL

Empire State Arms Co.

Enders Oakleaf made for Shapleigh Hardware Co. of St. Louis, MO

Enders Special Service made for Shapleigh Hardware Co.

Enders Royal Service made for Shapleigh Hardware Co.

Essex made for Belknap Hardware Co. of Louisville, KY

Excel made for Montgomery Ward & Co. of Chicago, IL

Farwell Arms Co. made for Farwell, Ozmun & Kirk of St. Paul, MN

Faultless made for John M. Smythe Co. of Chicago, IL

Faultless Goose Gun made for John M. Smyth Co. of Chicago, IL

The Field after 1894

Folsom Arms Co. (also used by H & D Folsom on Belgian imports)

F.F. Forbes (H & D Folsom house brand)

Fort Pitt Arms Co.

Fremont Arms Co. (also used on Belgian imports)

Gold Medal Wonder

Greenfield (some models) made for Hibbard, Spencer, Bartlett & Co. of Chicago, IL

H.B.C. (some models) made for Hudson's Bay Co. of Canada.

H.S.B. & Co. (some models) made for Hibbard, Spencer, Bartlett & Co. of Chicago, IL

Hanover Arms Co. (if no foreign proof marks)

S.H. Harrington (if no foreign proof marks)

Hartford Arms Co. made for both Simmons Hardware and Shapleigh Hardware Co. of St. Louis, MO

Harvard (H & D Folsom house brand)

Hermitage (some models) made for Grey-Dusley Hardware Co. of Nashville, TN

Hip Spe Bar (some models) made for Hibbard, Spencer, Bartlett & Co. of Chicago, IL

Hibbard (some models) made for Hibbard, Spencer, Bartlett & Co. of Chicago, IL

Howard Arms Co. made for Fred Biffar & Co. of Chicago, IL

Hudson (some models) made for Hibbard, Spencer, Bartlett & Co. of Chicago, IL

Hunter made for Belknap Hardware Co. Louisville, KY

Interstate Arms Co. made for Townley Metal & Hardware Co. of Kansas City, MO

Jackson Arms Co. made for C.M. McClung & Co. of Knoxville, TN

Joseph Arms Co. Norwich, Conn.

K K and Keen Kufter (some models) made for Shapleigh Hardware Co. of St. Louis, MO

Kingsland Special and Kingsland 10 Star made for Geller, Ward & Hasner of St. Louis, MO

Kirk Gun Co. made for Farwell, Ozmun & Kirk of St. Paul, MN

Knickerbocker (up to 1915, H & D Folsom house brand)

Knockabout (before 1925) made for Montgomery Ward & Co. of Chicago, IL

Knoxall (only hammerless doubles)

Laclede Gun Co.

Lakeside made for Montgomery Ward & Co. of Chicago, IL

Leader Gun Co. made for Charles Williams Stores of New York, NY

Lee's Special and Lee's Munner Special made for Lee Hardware Co. of Salina, KS

Long Range Marvel, Long Range Winner, and Long Range Wonder made between 1893 to 1909 for Sears, Roebuck & Co. of Chicago, IL F.A. Loomis

Marshwood

Massachusetts Arms Co. made before 1920 for Blish, Mizet and Silliman Hardware Co. of Atchison, KS

Mears (if no foreign proof marks)

Metropolitan made for Siegal-Cooper Co. of New York, NY

Minnesota Arms Co. made for Farwell, Ozmun, Kirk & Co. of St. Paul, MN

Mississippi Arms Co. St. Louis (some models) made for Shepleigh Hardware Co. of St. Louis, MO

Mississippi Valley Arms Co. (some models) made for Shapleigh Hardware Co. of St. Louis, MO

Mohawk made for Glish, Mizet and Lilliman Hardware Co. of Atchinson, KS

Monitor

R. Murdock, National Firearms Co. (some models)

National Arms Co. hammer doubles (without foreign proof marks) and hammerless doubles made for May Hardware Co. of Washington, D.C. and Moskowitz and Herbach Co. of Philadelphia, PA

New Britain Arms Co.'s Monarch

New Elgin Arms Co.

New Empire

New England (some models after 1914) made for Sears, Roebuck & Co.

New England Arms Co. (some models)

Newport Model CN made for Hibbard, Spencer, Bartlett and Co. of Chicago

Newport Model WN (some models) made for Hibbard, Spencer, Bartlett and Co. of Chicago

New Rival made for Van Camp Hardware and Iron Co. of Indianapolis, IN

New York Arms Co. made for Garnet Carter Co. of Chattanooga, TN

New York Machine Made (some models)

New York Match Gun (some models)

New York Nitro Hammerless

Nitro Bird made for Conover Hardware Co. of Kansas City, MO

Nitro Hunter made for Belknap Hardware Co. of Louisville, KY

Nitro King 1908 to 1917 made for Sears, Roebuck & Co. of Chicago, IL

Norwich Arms Co.

Not-Noc Manufacturing Co. made for Belknap Hardware Co. of Louisville, KY and Canton Hardware Co. of Canton, OH

Osprey made for Lou J. Eppinger, Detroit, MI

Oxford made for Belknap Hardware Co. of Louisville, KY

Peerless (H & D Folsom house brand)

Perfection made for H. G. Lipscomb & Co. of Nashville, TN
Piedmont made for Piedmont Hardware Co. of Danville, PA

Piedmont Arms Co.

Pioneer Arms (if no foreign proof marks) made for Kruse and Baklmann Hardware Co. of Cincinnati, OH

No. 66—410 GAUGE QUAIL MODEL

Quail (H & D Folsom house brand)

Queen City made for Elmira Arms Co. of Elmira, NY

Red Chieftan (model 60) made for Supplee Biddle Hardware Co. of Philadelphia, PA

Rev-O-Noc (some models) made for Hibbard, Spencer, Bartlett & Go. of Chicago, IL

Rich-Con made for Richardson & Conover Hardware Co.

Charles Richter (some models) made for New York Sporting Goods Co. of New York, NY

Rickard Arms Co. made for J. A. Rickard Co. of Schenectady, NY

Rival (some models) made for Van Camp Hardware and Iron Co.of Indianapolis, IN

Rocket Special

Royal Service made for Shapleigh Hardware Co. of St. Louis, MO

Rummel Arms Co. made for A. J. Rummel Arms Co. of Toledo, OH

Ruso (if no foreign proof marks)

St. Louis Arms Co. (sidelock hammerless doubles) made for Shapleigh Hardware Co. of St. Louis, MO

Seminole (hammerless) unknown

Shue's Special made for Ira M. Shue of Hanover, PA

Smithsonian (some models)

John M. Smythe & Co. made for John M. Smythe Hardware Co. of Chicago, IL

Southern Arms Co. (some models)

Special Service made for Shapleigh Hardware Co. of St. Louis, MO

Spencer Gun Co. made for Hibbard, Spencer, Bartlett & Co. of Chicago, IL

Sportsman (some models) made for W. Bingham & Co. of Cleveland, OH

Springfield Arms Co. used until 1930. (H & D Folsom house brand). This brand was also used by Stevens and James Warner guns.

Square Deal made for Stratton, Warren Hardware Co. of Memphis, TN

Star Leader (some models)

State Arms Co. made for J.H. Lau & Co. of New York, NY

Sterling Arms Co.

Sullivan Arms Co. made for Sullivan Hardware Co. of Anderson, SC

Superior (some models) made for Paxton & Gallagher Co. of Omaha, NE

Syco (some models) made for Wyeth Hardware Co. of St. Joseph, MO

Ten Star & Ten Star Heavy Duty (if no foreign proof marks) made for Geller, Ward & Hasner Co. of St. Louis, MO

Tiger (if no foreign proof marks) made for J.H. Hall & Co. of Nashville, TN

Townley's Pal and Townley's American Boy made for Townley Metal & Hardware Co. of Kansas City, MO

Trap's Best made for Watkins, Cottrell Co. of Richmond, VA

Triumph (some models) made for Sears, Roebuck & Co. of Chicago, IL

Tryon Special (some models) made for Edward K. Tryon Co. of Philadelphia, PA

U.S. Arms Co. (if no foreign proof marks) made for Supplee-Biddle Hardware Co. of Philadelphia, PA

U.S. Field

Utica Firearms Co. (some models) made for Simmons Hardware Co. of St. Louis, MO

Victor & Victor Special made for Hibbard, Spencer, Bartlett & Co. of Chicago, IL

Virginia Arms Co. made for Virginia-Carolina Co. of Richmond, VA

Volunteer (some models) made for Belknap Hardware Co. of Louisville, KY

Vulcan Arms Co. made for Edward K. Tryon Co. of Philadelphia, PA

Warren Arms Co. (if no foreign proof marks)

Washington Arms Co. (some models)

Wauregan (some models)

Wautauga (some models) made for Wallace Hardware Co. Morristown, TN

Wildwood made for Sears, Roebuck & Co. of Chicago, IL

Wilkinson Arms Co. (if no foreign proof marks) made for

Richmond Hardware Co. of Richmond, VA

Wilshire Arms Co. made for Stauffer, Eshleman & Co. of New Orleans, LA

Winfield Arms Co. (H & D Folsom house brand)

Winoca Arms Co. made for Jacobi Hardware Co. of Philadelphia, PA

Witte Hardware Co. (some models) made for Witte Hardware Co. of St. Louis, MO

Wolverine Arms Co. made for Fletcher Hardware Co. of Wilmington, NC

Worthington Arms Co. made for George Worthington Co. of Cleveland, OH

CRISPIN, SILAS
New York, New York

Crispin Revolver

A .32 Crispin caliber 5- or 6-shot revolver produced in limited quantities. Some are marked "Smith Arms Co., New York City. Crispin's Pat. Oct. 3, 1865." The most noteworthy feature of these revolvers is that the cylinder is constructed in two pieces so that the belted Crispin cartridge can be used. It is believed that these revolvers were only made on an experimental basis, between 1865 and 1867.

Exc.	V.G.	Good	Fair	Poor
—	—	10000	5000	2500

CROSSFIRE
Lagrange, Georgia

This combination rifle/shotgun is manufactured by Saco Defense, Inc. for Crossfire. It is the first production firearm to combine the shotgun and rifle into a pump action, multi-shot weapon.

MK-1

This model is designed to fire both a .223 Rem. cartridge and a 12 gauge 3" shotgun shell from two different barrels. It is a dual action long gun operated with a pump action. Overall length of the gun is 38". The shotgun has a 4-round detachable magazine while the rifle has an AR-15 type 5-round magazine. Shotgun barrel is furnished with choke tubes. Offered in black oxide finish or camo finish. Weight is approximately 8.6 lbs. Introduced in 1999.

NIB	Exc.	V.G.	Good	Fair	Poor
1895	—	—	—	—	—

NOTE: Add $100 for camo finish.

CRUCELEGUI, HERMANOS
Eibar, Spain

A 5mm, 6.35mm, 7.65mm, and 8mm caliber double-action revolver. The trade names used were; Puppy, Velo-Mith, LeBrong, Bron-Sport, C.H., and Brong-Petit.

Exc.	V.G.	Good	Fair	Poor
150	100	80	60	35

CUMMINGS, O. S.
Lowell, Massachusetts

Cummings Pocket Revolver

A .22 caliber spur trigger revolver with a 3.5" ribbed round barrel, and a 7-shot fluted cylinder. Nickel-plated with rosewood grip. The barrel is stamped "O.S. Cummings Lowell, Mass." Approximately 1,000 manufactured in the 1870s.

Exc.	V.G.	Good	Fair	Poor
—	650	300	150	100

CUMMINGS & WHEELER
Lowell, Massachusetts

Pocket Revolver

Similar to the Cummings Pocket Revolver with subtle differences such as the length of the flutes on the cylinder and the size and shape of the grip. The barrel is slightly longer and is marked "Cummings & Wheeler, Lowell, Mass."

Exc.	V.G.	Good	Fair	Poor
—	700	350	150	100

CUSTOM GUN GUILD
Doraville, Georgia

Wood Model IV

A falling block single shot rifle produced in a number of popular calibers with barrel lengths from 22" to 28". The stock of select checkered walnut. This is a lightweight rifle, at approximately 5.5 lbs. It was manufactured for one year only, 1984, and is not often encountered on today's market.

Exc.	V.G.	Good	Fair	Poor
3250	2750	2500	1750	1000

D

D (anchor) C
**(probably either "Dejardine & Cie," "L. Demousse & Cie,"
or "DeFooze & Cie," all of Liege, Belgium
SEE—English Military Firearms**

DPMS
Becker, MN

Panther Bull A-15

This A-15 type rifle is chambered for the .223 cartridge and fitted with a 20" stainless steel bull barrel. A2 style buttstock. No sights. Barrel has 1:9 twist. Flat top receiver. Handguard is aluminum free float tube.Upper and lower receivers are hard coated black. Weight is about 9.5 lbs. Each rifle comes standard with two 7-round magazines, sling, and cleaning kit.

NIB	Exc.	V.G.	Good	Fair	Poor
900	700	550	—	—	—

Panther Bull 24

Similar to the model above but fitted with a 24" bull barrel. Flat top receiver. Weight is about 10 lbs.

NIB	Exc.	V.G.	Good	Fair	Poor
950	750	600	—	—	—

Panther Deluxe Bull 24 Special

This model is fitted with a 24" stainless steel fluted bull barrel. Adjustable A2 style buttstock. Flat top receiver. Adjustable sniper pistol grip. Weight is about 10 lbs.

NIB	Exc.	V.G.	Good	Fair	Poor
1150	900	750	—	—	—

Panther Extreme Super Bull 24

This model is fitted with a 24" stainless steel extra heavy bull barrel (1.150" dia.). Skeletonized stock. Flat top receiver. Weight is about 11.75 lbs.

NIB	Exc.	V.G.	Good	Fair	Poor
1200	800	650	—	—	—

Panther Bulldog

Fitted with a 20" stainless steel fluted bull barrel with black synthetic A2 style buttstock. Flat top receiver. Adjustable trigger. Weight is about 10 lbs.

NIB	Exc.	V.G.	Good	Fair	Poor
1200	975	800	—	—	—

Panther Bull Sweet 16

This model is fitted with a 16" stainless steel bull barrel with flat top receiver. Weight is about 7.75 lbs.

NIB	Exc.	V.G.	Good	Fair	Poor
875	700	550	—	—	—

Panther Bull SST 16

Similar to the model above but with stainless steel lower receiver. Weight is about 9 lbs.

NIB	Exc.	V.G.	Good	Fair	Poor
875	700	550	—	—	—

Panther Bull Classic

This model is fitted with a 20" 4150 steel bull barrel. Square front post sight, adjustable A2 rear sight. Weight is about 9.75 lbs.

NIB	Exc.	V.G.	Good	Fair	Poor
900	650	500	—	—	—

Panther Arctic

This model is similar to the model above but with 20" fluted bull barrel and flat top receiver. Black A2 style buttstock with white coat finish on receiver and handguard. Black teflon finish on barrel. Weight is about 8.25 lbs.

NIB	Exc.	V.G.	Good	Fair	Poor
1075	850	700	—	—	—

Panther Classic

Fitted with a 20" 4150 steel heavy barrel with square front post sight and A2 rear sight. A2-round handguard. Weight is about 9.5 lbs.

NIB	Exc.	V.G.	Good	Fair	Poor
775	600	500	—	—	—

Panther DCM

This model is similar to the model above but with 20" stainless steel heavy barrel and NM rear sight. DCM free float handguard. Adjustable trigger. Weight is about 9.5 lbs.

NIB	Exc.	V.G.	Good	Fair	Poor
1075	750	600	—	—	—

Panther Classic 16 Post Ban

This model is fitted with a 1" 4150 steel heavy barrel. A2 style sights. Round handguard. Weight is about 7.25 lbs.

NIB	Exc.	V.G.	Good	Fair	Poor
775	600	500	—	—	—

Panther Free Float 16 Post Ban

Similar to the model above with 16" barrel but fitted with a vented free floated barrel and vented free float tube handguard. Weight is approximately 7.25 lbs.

NIB	Exc.	V.G.	Good	Fair	Poor
825	650	550	—	—	—

Panther Southpaw Post Ban

This model is fitted with a 20" 4150 steel heavy barrel with A2 style sights. Upper receiver has been modified for left hand ejection. Weight is about 9.5 lbs.

NIB	Exc.	V.G.	Good	Fair	Poor
875	700	600	—	—	—

Panther A-15 Pump Rifle

This model has a 20" 4150 steel heavy barrel with A2 style sights. Fitted with an A2 compensator and modified to slide action. Weight is about 8.5 lbs.

NIB	Exc.	V.G.	Good	Fair	Poor
1700	1400	1000	—	—	—

Panther A-15 Pump Pistol

Same as above but fitted with a 10.5" barrel. Weight is about 5 lbs.

NIB	Exc.	V.G.	Good	Fair	Poor
1600	1250	850	—	—	—

D. W. M.
Berlin, Germany
ALSO SEE—Luger & Borchardt

Model 22

A 7.65mm caliber semiautomatic pistol with 3.5" barrel. Blued with walnut grips; later changed to plastic grips. Approximately 40,000 manufactured between 1921 and 1931.

Exc.	V.G.	Good	Fair	Poor
750	675	500	400	250

DAEWOO
Pusan, Korea

DH-40

This semiautomatic pistol is chambered for the .40 S&W cartridge. It has a 4.13" barrel and a magazine capacity of 11 rounds. Weight is approximately 32 oz.

NIB	Exc.	V.G.	Good	Fair	Poor
450	350	300	250	175	100

DP-51B

This semiautomatic pistol is chambered for the 9mm cartridge and is fitted with a 4.13" barrel. Magazine capacity is 13 rounds. Overall length is 7.5" and weight is approximately 28 oz.

NIB	Exc.	V.G.	Good	Fair	Poor
375	325	275	225	175	100

DP-51SB

This is a more compact design with 3.6" barrel and 10-round magazine. Weight is 27 oz. Stainless steel finish.

NIB	Exc.	V.G.	Good	Fair	Poor
400	350	275	225	175	100

DP-51CB

Same as above but fitted with a 3.6" barrel. Magazine capacity is 10 rounds. Weight is about 26 oz.

NIB	Exc.	V.G.	Good	Fair	Poor
425	375	300	250	175	100

DP-52

This semiautomatic pistol is chambered for the .22 Long Rifle cartridge. It has a 3.82" barrel length and a magazine capacity of 10 rounds. It operates in double action and single action modes. Overall length is 6.7" and weight is approximately 23 oz.

NIB	Exc.	V.G.	Good	Fair	Poor
350	300	250	200	150	100

DH380

Introduced in 1996 this semiautomatic pistol is chambered for the .380 ACP cartridge. It is fitted with a 3.8" barrel and has a magazine capacity of 8 rounds. The firing model is double or single action. Weight is approximately 24 oz.

NIB	Exc.	V.G.	Good	Fair	Poor
375	325	275	225	150	100

DR200

Introduced in 1996 this semiautomatic rifle is chambered for the .223 Rem. cartridge. It features a black matte finish with a synthetic thumbhole stock. Barrel length is 18.3". Uses AR15 magazines not included with the rifle. Weight is about 9 lbs.

NIB	Exc.	V.G.	Good	Fair	Poor
675	625	500	400	300	150

Max I

A 5.56mm caliber semiautomatic rifle with an 18" barrel, gas operated rotary bolt action, magazines interchangeable with those from the M-16. Black. Introduced in 1985, but is no longer imported.

Max II

This rifle is quite similar to the Max I with a folding composite stock.

DAISY
Rogers, Arkansas

WL Rifle

A .22 combustible cartridge single shot rifle with an 18" barrel and plastic stock. Cartridge is ignited by compressed air. Manufactured during 1968 and 1969. It is believed that less than 20,000 were made.

NIB	Exc.	V.G.	Good	Fair	Poor
150	100	85	75	50	25

VL Presentation Model

As above, with a walnut stock. Approximately 4,000 were made in 1968 and 1969.

NIB	Exc.	V.G.	Good	Fair	Poor
225	150	125	100	75	50

WL Cased Presentation Model

As above, with a gold plaque inlaid in the stock and with a fitted case containing 300 VL cartridges.

NIB	Exc.	V.G.	Good	Fair	Poor
275	200	175	125	100	75

Model 2201/2211

A bolt action single shot rifle chambered for .22 long rifle cartridge. Fitted with a 19" barrel with octagon shroud. Ramp blade front sight with adjustable notch rear sight. Synthetic stock on Model 2211 and walnut stock on Model 2201. Trigger is adjustable. Weight is about 6.5 lbs.

The American Legend

NIB	Exc.	V.G.	Good	Fair	Poor
150	100	75	60	50	25

NOTE: Add $10 for synthetic stock.

Model 2202/2212
Similar to the above model in appearance but fitted with a 10-round rotary magazine. The synthetic stock is Model 2212 and the walnut stock is Model 2202. Weight is about 6.5 lbs.

NIB	Exc.	V.G.	Good	Fair	Poor
150	100	75	60	50	25

NOTE: Add $10 for synthetic stock.

Model 2203/2213
This is a semiautomatic rifle chambered for .22 long rifle cartridge. Has a 7-round magazine and a 19" barrel. The synthetic stock is Model 2213 and the walnut stock is Model 2203. Weight is approximately 6.5 lbs.

NIB	Exc.	V.G.	Good	Fair	Poor
150	100	75	60	50	25

NOTE: Add $10 for synthetic stock.

DAKIN GUN CO.
San Francisco, California

Model 100
A 12 and 20 gauge boxlock double barrel shotgun with 26" or 28" barrels, various chokes, extractors and double triggers. Engraved, blued, with a checkered walnut stock. Manufactured in the 1960s.

Exc.	V.G.	Good	Fair	Poor
400	325	275	200	100

Model 147
As above, with ventilated rib barrels.

Exc.	V.G.	Good	Fair	Poor
450	375	250	200	100

Model 160
As above with a single selective trigger.

Exc.	V.G.	Good	Fair	Poor
475	400	350	250	150

Model 215
As above, but more finely finished.

Exc.	V.G.	Good	Fair	Poor
950	850	700	500	250

Model 170
A 12, 16, and 20 gauge Over/Under shotgun with 26" or 28" ventilated rib barrels, various chokes, and double triggers. Blued and lightly engraved. Discontinued in the 1960s.

Exc.	V.G.	Good	Fair	Poor
500	425	350	275	150

DAKOTA ARMS, INC.
Sturgis, South Dakota
This company was formed by Don Allen. He is a fine craftsmen in the field of custom rifles. The company offers four basic

models with a number of options to fit the customers' needs or wants. The workmanship and materials are of the highest quality. They have been in business since 1987.

NOTE: All prices are base prices. Dakota offers a number of extra cost options that can greatly effect the value of its rifles and shotguns.

Dakota 76 Classic

A .257 Roberts, .270 Winchester, .280 Remington, .3006, 7mm Remington Magnum, .338, .300 Winchester Magnum, and the .458 Winchester Magnum bolt action rifle with a 23" barrel, and Mauser-type extractor. Checkered walnut stock. Manufactured in 1987.

NIB	Exc.	V.G.	Good	Fair	Poor
3495	2750	1500	950	800	400

Dakota 76 Varmint

Introduced in 1996 this rifle is chambered for a variety of cartridges from the .22 Hornet to the 6mm PPC. This is a single shot bolt action design available in right or left hand versions. Barrel length is 24". The Varmint style stock is semi-fancy walnut with oil finish and no checkering. Many extra cost options are offered for this model. This model is no longer in production as of 1998.

NIB	Exc.	V.G.	Good	Fair	Poor
2500	2200	1650	1100	850	400

Varmint Grade

Offered in a wide variety of calibers from the .222 Rem. to the .22-250 Rem. Furnished with X grade English walnut. This model discontinued in 1998.

NIB	Exc.	V.G.	Good	Fair	Poor
2000	1850	1500	1200	900	400

Varmint Hunter

This model is built on a Model 97 action. Standard features are fiberglass stock, round action single shot, adjustable trigger, and black recoil pad. Barrel length is 24". Offered in calibers from .220 Swift to .308 Winchester. Weight is about 8 lbs. Introduced in 1999.

NIB	Exc.	V.G.	Good	Fair	Poor
1795	1400	1000	—	—	—

Safari Grade

As above, in .375 Holland & Holland, .458 Winchester Magnum, and other short Magnum calibers with an ebony forend tip, one-piece magazine assembly and features open sights. Weighs approximately 8-1/2 lbs.

NIB	Exc.	V.G.	Good	Fair	Poor
4495	3250	2000	—	—	—

Alpine Grade

As above, but lighter in weight and chambered for .22-250, .243, 6mm, 250-3000, 7mm/08, .308, and .358. Introduced in 1989. This model is no longer in production.

NIB	Exc.	V.G.	Good	Fair	Poor
1850	1750	1400	1250	800	400

African Grade

As above in .416 Rigby, .416 Dakota, .404 Jeffery, and .450 Dakota with walnut especially selected for strength, with crossbolts through the stock. Weighs between 9 and 10 lbs.

NIB	Exc.	V.G.	Good	Fair	Poor
4995	3750	2500	—	—	—

Model 10 Single Shot

Built on a single shot falling action this rifle features a 23" barrel and choice of XX grade wood with oil finish. Fine line checkering, steel gripcap, and 1/2" recoil pad are also standard. Weighs about 5.5 lbs.

NIB	Exc.	V.G.	Good	Fair	Poor
3495	2500	1750	—	—	—

Model 10 Single Shot Magnum

Same as above but in calibers .338 Win. Mag to .416 Dakota. Weight about 6.5 lbs.

NIB	Exc.	V.G.	Good	Fair	Poor
3595	2600	1850	—	—	—

Dakota .22 Long Rifle Sporter

Fitted with a 22" barrel and X grade oil finish walnut with fine line checkering and steel gripcap. A 1/2" black recoil pad is standard. Weighs about 6-1/2 lbs. This model no longer in production.

NIB	Exc.	V.G.	Good	Fair	Poor
1250	1000	800	650	500	300

Model 97 Long Range Hunter

Introduced in 1997 this bolt action rifle is offered in 13 calibers: .250-6, .257 Roberts, .270 Win., .280 Rem., 7mm Rem. Mag., 7mm Dakota Mag., .30-06, .300 Win. Mag., .300 Dakota Mag., .338 Win. mag., .330 Dakota Mag., .375 H&H, .375 Dakota Mag. Barrel lengths depend on caliber but are either 24" or 26". The trigger is fully adjustable. Many other special features. Stock is black synthetic with one-piece bedding. Black recoil pad is standard. Weight is approximately 7.7 lbs.

NIB	Exc.	V.G.	Good	Fair	Poor
1795	1250	—	—	—	—

Model 97 Lightweight Hunter

Introduced in 1998 this rifle features barrel lengths from 22" to 24" in both short and long actions. A special lightweight composite stock is used. Calibers offered range from .22-250 to .330 Dakota Magnum. Weights are between 6.15 to 6.5 lbs. depending on caliber and barrel length.

NIB	Exc.	V.G.	Good	Fair	Poor
1795	1250	—	—	—	—

Model T-76 Longbow Tactical Rifle

This long range tactical bolt action rifle is available in 3 calibers: .338 Lapua, .300 Dakota Mag., and .330 Dakota Mag. The fiberglass stock is an A-2 McMillan in black or olive green. Adjustable length of pull with bipod spike in forearm. The 28" stainless steel is .950 diameter at the muzzle with muzzle brake. The rifle is sold with a number of accessories such as a case with bipod, tool kit and tool box. Weight is about 13.7 lbs.

NIB	Exc.	V.G.	Good	Fair	Poor
4250	3000	—	—	—	—

NOTE: Dakota offers a wide variety of options to all of its grades. Some of these options are quite expensive and will add a considerable sum to the value of the gun. It is advisable to secure a knowledgeable appraisal before the sale.

Model 76 Traveler

This model was introduced in 1999 and is built on a modified Model 76 design and stocked in wood. Disassembly is threadless. It is offered in standard length action, short magnum action, and long actions in both left and right hand. Offered in three grades.

Traveler Classic

NIB	Exc.	V.G.	Good	Fair	Poor
4495	3200	—	—	—	—

Traveler Safari

NIB	Exc.	V.G.	Good	Fair	Poor
5495	3900	—	—	—	—

Traveler African

NIB	Exc.	V.G.	Good	Fair	Poor
5995	4500	—	—	—	—

Double Rifle

Available in most common calibers. Fitted with exhibition walnut with pistol grip. Barrel is 25". Round action with selective ejectors, recoil, pad and hard case. Prices listed below are for guns without engraving.

NIB	Exc.	V.G.	Good	Fair	Poor
25000	—	—	—	—	—

SHOTGUNS

Dakota American Legend

Introduced in 1996, this side-by-side shotgun is offered in 12, 20, 28 gauge and .410 bore with 27" barrels, concave rib, splinter forearm, double triggers, straight grips stock, and full scroll engraving on the frame. Many additional extra cost options are offered which can greatly affect the price. The base price is listed below.

NIB	Exc.	V.G.	Good	Fair	Poor
18000	14000	—	—	—	—

Dakota Shotgun

Similar to the American Legend but offered in two grades of finish. These new grades were first offered in 1997.

Classic Grade

This grade features a case colored round action with straight grip and fancy walnut oil finish stock. Forearm is splinter type. Double trigger standard with choice of chokes. This model no longer in production.

NIB	Exc.	V.G.	Good	Fair	Poor
7950	12500	—	—	—	—

Premier Grade

This grade features a case colored round action with 50% engraving coverage. Exhibition grade English walnut stock with straight grip and splinter forearm. Oil rubbed finish. Double triggers are standard with choice of chokes.

NIB	Exc.	V.G.	Good	Fair	Poor
13950	9500	—	—	—	—

NOTE: Add 10% for 28 gauge and .410 bore.

DAKOTA ARMS INC.- FERLIB SHOTGUNS

In 2000 Dakota Arms Inc. became the exclusive importer of Ferlib shotgun in the U.S. The following is a list of those models imported and sold by Dakota Arms Inc.

Model 7

NIB	Exc.	V.G.	Good	Fair	Poor
10950	8000	—	—	—	—

Prince Model

NIB	Exc.	V.G.	Good	Fair	Poor
11950	9000	—	—	—	—

Prince Model Side Lever

NIB	Exc.	V.G.	Good	Fair	Poor
14500	10500	—	—	—	—

Rex

NIB	Exc.	V.G.	Good	Fair	Poor
14950	11000	—	—	—	—

Premier
NIB	Exc.	V.G.	Good	Fair	Poor
16950	12500	—	—	—	—

Sideplate Model
NIB	Exc.	V.G.	Good	Fair	Poor
14400	10500	—	—	—	—

Sideplate Model with Gold
NIB	Exc.	V.G.	Good	Fair	Poor
15100	11250	—	—	—	—

Sideplate with Scroll
NIB	Exc.	V.G.	Good	Fair	Poor
14000	10500	—	—	—	—

Hammer Gun
NIB	Exc.	V.G.	Good	Fair	Poor
19000	14000	—	—	—	—

H.H. Model-no engraving
NIB	Exc.	V.G.	Good	Fair	Poor
20000	15000	—	—	—	—

Esposizione
NIB	Exc.	V.G.	Good	Fair	Poor
25500	18000	—	—	—	—

L'Inglesina
NIB	Exc.	V.G.	Good	Fair	Poor
25500	18000	—	—	—	—

Model E "Fantasy"

NIB	Exc.	V.G.	Good	Fair	Poor
39500	27500	—	—	—	—

Boss-no engraving
NIB	Exc.	V.G.	Good	Fair	Poor
29500	20000	—	—	—	—

DALY, CHARLES
Importer-KBI, Inc.
Harrisburg, Pennsylvania

An importer of German, Japanese, and Italian shotguns and combination guns.

CHARLES DALY, EARLY PRUSSIAN GUNS

Commanidor Over/Under Model 100

A boxlock Over/Under Anson & Deeley action shotgun chambered all gauges, choice of barrel length and chokes, double triggers (standard) or single selective trigger. Blued with a checkered walnut stock. Manufactured in Belgium in the late 1930s.

Exc.	V.G.	Good	Fair	Poor
800	600	475	275	200

Commanidor Over/Under Model 200

As above, with a better-grade walnut stock.

Exc.	V.G.	Good	Fair	Poor
900	700	500	300	200

Superior Side-x-Side

As above, with an Anson & Deeley boxlock action and double triggers. Blued with a walnut stock. Not manufactured after 1933.

Exc.	V. G.	Good	Fair	Poor
1200	850	650	450	250

Empire Side-x-Side

As above, but engraved with a better grade of walnut.

Exc.	V.G.	Good	Fair	Poor
2500	2000	1750	1250	600

Diamond Grade Side-x-Side

A deluxe version of the above.

Exc.	V.G.	Good	Fair	Poor
5000	4500	3750	3000	1200

A Charles Daly Diamond Grade side-by-side gun sold at auction for $6,440. Chambered for the 20 gauge shell and fitted with 26" barrels choked improved cylinder and modified. Engraved with scroll and game scenes. Condition is 95% blue and about 50% case colors. Solid rubber pad. Leg-of-mutton case.
Amoskeag Auction Company, January 2001

Regent Diamond Grade Side-x-Side
A custom order version of the above.

Exc.	V.G.	Good	Fair	Poor
10000	8500	7000	5500	2500

Empire Over/Under
A 12, 16, and 20 gauge Anson & Deeley boxlock shotgun with choice of barrel length and choke, double triggers and automatic ejectors. Engraved with fine quality scrollwork and walnut stock. Discontinued in 1933.

Exc.	V.G.	Good	Fair	Poor
2250	2000	1500	1150	500

Diamond Grade Over/Under
As above, but more finely finished.

Exc.	V.G.	Good	Fair	Poor
5000	4500	3750	3000	1250

SEXTUPLE SINGLE BARREL TRAP
Empire Grade
A 12 gauge boxlock single barrel shotgun with 30"-34" full choke barrels, a ventilated rib and automatic ejectors. The action features six locking lugs and is strong. Engraved with a walnut stock. Manufactured after 1933.

Exc.	V.G.	Good	Fair	Poor
2500	2250	1850	1500	750

Regent Diamond Grade
As above, with more engraving and a better grade walnut stock.

Exc.	V.G.	Good	Fair	Poor
7000	6300	5500	4500	2000

DRILLINGS
Superior Grade Drilling
A 12, 16, and 20 gauge Over/Under rifle/shotgun with a rifle barrel in .25-20, .25-35, or .30-30 running beneath them. Engraved with a walnut stock. Not manufactured after 1933.

Exc.	V.G.	Good	Fair	Poor
2500	2250	1800	1450	800

Diamond Grade Drilling
As above, with more engraving and a better grade of walnut in the stock.

Exc.	V.G.	Good	Fair	Poor
4500	4000	3750	3000	1500

Regent Diamond Grade Drilling
As above, with elaborate engraving and the highest quality walnut stock.

Exc.	V.G.	Good	Fair	Poor
10000	8500	7200	5800	3000

CHARLES DALY, B.C. MIROKU GUNS
Empire Grade Side-By-Side
A 12, 16, and 20 gauge Anson and Deeley boxlock shotgun with 26", 28", and 30" barrels, various chokes, extractors, and a single trigger. Blued with a checkered walnut stock. Manufactured between 1968 and 1971.

Add 10% for ventilated rib barrels and/or 20 gauge.

Exc.	V.G.	Good	Fair	Poor
600	450	300	200	100

Superior Grade Single Barrel Trap
A 12 gauge boxlock shotgun with 32" or 34" ventilated rib barrels, full choke, and automatic ejector. Blued with Monte Carlo walnut stock. Manufactured between 1968 and 1976.

Exc.	V.G.	Good	Fair	Poor
550	500	450	350	200

Over/Unders
A 12, 20, and 28 gauge and .410 bore boxlock shotgun with 26", 28", and 30" barrels with ventilated ribs. Various choke combinations were offered with single selective triggers and automatic ejectors. Blued with checkered walnut stocks. The differences between the grades are the degree and quality of the engraving and the grade of walnut used for the stock. The smaller-bore guns bring a premium as follows. Manufactured between 1963 and 1976 by B.C. Miroku.

20 Gauge add 10%.
28 Gauge add 20%.
.410 add 30%.

Venture Grade

Exc.	V.G.	Good	Fair	Poor
550	500	450	375	200

Venture Grade Skeet or Trap
Offered with either 26" Skeet & Skeet or 30" full choke.

Exc.	V.G.	Good	Fair	Poor
575	525	475	375	200

Field Grade
Chambered for 12 and 20 gauge only.

Exc.	V.G.	Good	Fair	Poor
650	575	500	425	200

Superior Grade
Exc.	V.G.	Good	Fair	Poor
750	675	600	525	200

Superior Grade Trap

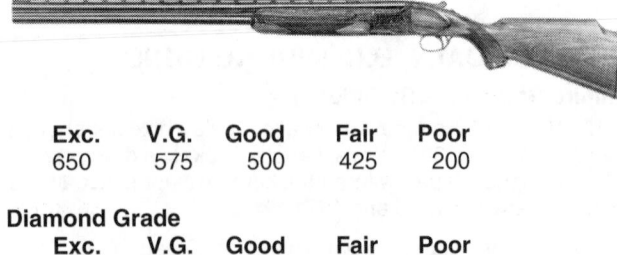

Exc.	V.G.	Good	Fair	Poor
650	575	500	425	200

Diamond Grade
Exc.	V.G.	Good	Fair	Poor
1000	900	750	600	300

Diamond Grade Trap or Skeet
With either 26" Skeet & Skeet or 30" full choke barrels and Monte Carlo stocks.

Wide Rib add 5%.

Exc.	V.G.	Good	Fair	Poor
1050	950	800	650	350

CHARLES DALY, ITALIAN MANUFACTURE
Manufactured by the firm of Breda in Milan, Italy. The semiautomatic "Novamatic" was produced in 1968. All other models began Italian production in 1976. Imported by KBI, Inc.

SEMIAUTOMATIC SHOTGUNS

Novamatic Lightweight
A 12 gauge semiautomatic shotgun with a 26" or 28" ventilated-rib barrel and screw-in choke tubes. The receiver is alloy, with checkered walnut stock. Imported under the Daly name in 1968 only.

Exc.	V.G.	Good	Fair	Poor
300	275	225	175	125

Novamatic Trap
As above, with a Monte Carlo stock and a 30" full choke barrel.

Exc.	V.G.	Good	Fair	Poor
350	300	250	200	150

Charles Daly Automatic
A 12 gauge Magnum semiautomatic shotgun with 26" or 28" ventilated rib barrels, screw-in choke tubes and a 5-shot magazine. There is a slug gun available with rifle sights. Checkered walnut grip in two versions—a pistol grip and an English-style straight grip. The choke-tube model would be worth a 10% premium.

Exc.	V.G.	Good	Fair	Poor
375	325	275	225	150

Field Grade
Introduced in 1999, this model has several variations all in 12 gauge. The standard gun has a choice of 24", 26", 28", or 30" barrels with screw-in chokes and synthetic stocks. A slug gun is offered with 22" barrel in blue or nickel finish. A full coverage camo model is offered in the same configurations as the field grade.

NIB	Exc.	V.G.	Good	Fair	Poor
400	350	—	—	—	—

NOTE: Add $30 for nickel slug gun, add $100 for camo gun.

Superior Grade Hunter
Offered in 12 gauge with choice of 26", 28", or 30" vent rib barrels. Walnut stock with hand checkering. Gold trigger and gold highlights. Introduced in 1999.

NIB	Exc.	V.G.	Good	Fair	Poor
500	400	—	—	—	—

Superior Grade Sporting
Same as above but with a 28" or 30" ported barrel.

NIB	Exc.	V.G.	Good	Fair	Poor
525	425	—	—	—	—

Superior Grade Trap
This 12 gauge model is offered with a choice of 30" or 32" vent rib barrel. Walnut stock with hand checkering. Introduced in 1999.

NIB	Exc.	V.G.	Good	Fair	Poor
550	450	—	—	—	—

PUMP SHOTGUNS

Field Grade
This 12 gauge pump gun is offered with 24", 26", 28", or 30" barrels. With fixed chokes. A slug gun is offered with 18.5" barrels with blue or nickel finish. A camo version is also offered. First introduced in 1999.

NIB	Exc.	V.G.	Good	Fair	Poor
250	200	—	—	—	—

NOTE: Add $10 for nickel gun, add $80 for full camo gun.

OVER/UNDER GUNS

Charles Daly Field Grade Over/Under
A 12, 20, 28, and .410 gauge Over/Under shotgun with 26" or 28" chrome-lined ventilated rib barrels with a crossbolt boxlock action, single selective trigger, and extractors. Blued with a stamped checkered walnut stock. Introduced in 1989. Weight for 12 gauge guns about 7 lbs. Weight for 28 and .410 guns about 6.75 lbs. Add $150 for ejectors.

NIB	Exc.	V.G.	Good	Fair	Poor
700	550	400	300	250	200

Charles Daly Field Ultra Light

Introduced in 1999, this model is offered in either 12 or 20 gauge with 26" barrel choke-improved cylinder/modified. The receiver is aluminum alloy. Walnut stock with pistol grip and slim forend. Weight is approximately 5.5 lbs.

NIB	Exc.	V.G.	Good	Fair	Poor
850	675	—	—	—	—

Charles Daly Empire Over/Under

As above with automatic ejectors, screw-in choke tubes, and a silver-finished receiver. The walnut stock is hand-checkered. Introduced in 1989.

NIB	Exc.	V.G.	Good	Fair	Poor
1250	1000	750	500	400	200

Empire Sporting

This model is offered in 12 gauge with a choice of 28" or 30" barrels. Fitted with a Monte Carlo stock and automatic ejectors.

NIB	Exc.	V.G.	Good	Fair	Poor
1450	1150	800	600	—	—

Empire Grade Combination

This is an over and under with a 12 gauge top barrel and a rifle lower barrel. Rifle calibers are .22 Hornet, .223 Rem., .22-250, .243, .270, .308 and .30-06. Barrel length is 23.5". Weight is about 7.25 lbs.

NIB	Exc.	V.G.	Good	Fair	Poor
1700	1350	900	650	—	—

Empire Trap

This 12 gauge model features a Monte Carlo stock with 30" barrels.

NIB	Exc.	V.G.	Good	Fair	Poor
1450	1150	800	600	—	—

Empire Trap Mono

This is a single barrel trap gun with choice of 30" or 32" barrels. Automatic ejectors and Monte Carlo fully adjustable stock.

NIB	Exc.	V.G.	Good	Fair	Poor
2150	1700	1250	900	—	—

NOTE: Deduct $600 for non-adjustable stock.

Empire Grade Trap Combo

This model features a 30" over/under barrel with an additional 32" single barrel. Buttstock has fully adjustable comb. Introduced in 1999.

NIB	Exc.	V.G.	Good	Fair	Poor
2950	2400	1700	—	—	—

NOTE: Deduct $600 for non-adjustable stock.

Diamond Grade Over/Under

As above in 12 and 20 gauge Magnum with various barrel lengths and screw-in choke tubes, single trigger, automatic ejectors, and select walnut stock. Extra fancy walnut stock and hand engraved frame.

NIB	Exc.	V.G.	Good	Fair	Poor
5400	4250	2500	1250	900	450

Diamomd Grade Sporting

This 12 gauge model features a choice of 28" or 30" barrels with automatic ejectors and Monte Carlo stock.

NIB	Exc.	V.G.	Good	Fair	Poor
5600	4500	2750	1250	—	—

Diamond Grade Trap or Skeet

As above, with 26" or 30" barrels. Available in 1989.

NIB	Exc.	V.G.	Good	Fair	Poor
5200	4000	1750	950	500	250

Diamond Grade Mono

This model has a fully adjustable stock. Barrel choice is 30". Automatic ejectors are standard.

NIB	Exc.	V.G.	Good	Fair	Poor
6300	5000	3500	2000	—	—

Diamond Grade Trap Combo

This model has a fully adjustable stock. Choice of 30" over/under barrels and 32" single barrel.

NIB	Exc.	V.G.	Good	Fair	Poor
7100	5500	4000	2500	—	—

Presentation Grade Over/Under

As above, with a Purdy-type boxlock action and engraved false sideplates. The stock is of deluxe French walnut. Discontinued in 1986.

Exc.	V.G.	Good	Fair	Poor
5000	3500	1500	900	450

Superior Over/Under

A 12, 20, 28, and .410 gauge Over/Under shotgun with 26" or 28" ventilated rib barrels, various chokes, single trigger, and automatic ejectors. Engraved, blued with a walnut stock. Weight for 12 and 20 gauge guns about 7 lbs. For 28 and .410 guns weight is about 6.75 lbs.

NIB	Exc.	V.G.	Good	Fair	Poor
1100	875	600	450	350	200

Superior Grade Sporting

This 12 gauge model is fitted with a choice of 28" or 30" barrels. Monte Carlo stock and automatic ejectors.

NIB	Exc.	V.G.	Good	Fair	Poor
1200	950	700	500	—	—

Superior Grade Trap

This 12 gauge gun is fitted with 30" barrels, Monte Carlo stock and automatic ejectors.

NIB	Exc.	V.G.	Good	Fair	Poor
1250	1000	750	500	—	—

Superior Grade Combination

This is an over and under with a 12 gauge top barrel and a rifle lower barrel. Rifle calibers are .22 Hornet, .223 Rem., and .30-06. Barrel length is 23.5". Weight is about 7.25 lbs.

NIB	Exc.	V.G.	Good	Fair	Poor
1200	950	650	450	—	—

SIDE-BY-SIDE GUNS

Field Grade Side-x-Side

A side-by-side box lock gun chambered for 10, 12, 20, 28 and .410. Barrel length from 26" to 32" depending on gauge. Extractors are standard. Add $100 for ejectors. Weight from 8.75 lbs. to 6.75 lbs. depending on gauge. Nickel receiver with game scene engraving.

NIB	Exc.	V.G.	Good	Fair	Poor
750	600	500	350	250	125

NOTE: Add $40 for 28 and .410 guns, add $100 for automatic ejectors.

Superior Grade Side-x-Side

A 12, 20, and 28 gauge boxlock double barrel shotgun with 26" or 28" barrels, various chokes, a boxlock action and single trigger. Blued with a walnut stock.

NIB	Exc.	V.G.	Good	Fair	Poor
950	800	600	400	—	—

NOTE: Add $50 for 28 gauge guns.

Empire Side-x-Side

Offered in 12 and 20 gauge with 26" or 28" barrels. Chokes are fixed. Weight is about 7 lbs. Silver receiver with game scene engraving, straight stock, splinter forearm, automatic ejectors.

NIB	Exc.	V.G.	Good	Fair	Poor
1250	1000	750	500	—	—

Diamond Side-x-Side

Offered in 12, 20, 28, and .410 with 26" or 28" barrels and fixed chokes. Fancy walnut straight grip stock, hand detachable sidelocks, 100% hand engraving coverage. Hand fit and finished. Weight for 12 and 20 gauge guns is about 6.75 lbs. while the 28 and .410 guns weigh about 5.75 lbs.

NIB	Exc.	V.G.	Good	Fair	Poor
6700	5000	3500	1500	—	—

NOTE: Add $450 for 28 and .410 bores.

Country Squire Side-by-Side Folding

This model features a folding stock with 25.5" barrels, gold double triggers and walnut stock. Chokes are full and full.

NIB	Exc.	V.G.	Good	Fair	Poor
475	375	275	—	—	—

Country Squire Over/Under Folding

Same as the model above but with over and under vent rib barrels 25.5" in length.

NIB	Exc.	V.G.	Good	Fair	Poor
550	450	325	—	—	—

RIFLES

Field Grade Mauser 98

This bolt action rifle is offered in a wide variety of calibers from .243 Win. to .458 Win. Mag. Barrel length is 23" for all calibers. Stock is black synthetic. Open sights. Add $175 for .375 H&H and .458 Win. Mag.

NIB	Exc.	V.G.	Good	Fair	Poor
360	300	—	—	—	—

Field Grade Mini-Mauser 98

This version is chambered for short cartridges such as the .22 Hornet, .223, .22-250, and 7.62x39mm. Barrel length is 19.25". Magazine capacity is 5 rounds.

NIB	Exc.	V.G.	Good	Fair	Poor
400	325	—	—	—	—

Superior Grade Mauser 98

This model is similar to the Field Grade Mauser with the addition of a hand checkered walnut stock.

NIB	Exc.	V.G.	Good	Fair	Poor
420	350	—	—	—	—

Superior Grade Mini-Mauser 98

Same as the Field Grade Mini-Mauser with the addition of a hand checkered walnut stock.

NIB	Exc.	V.G.	Good	Fair	Poor
450	350	—	—	—	—

Field Grade Rimfires

Chambered for .22 Long Rifle cartridge and fitted with a 22" barrel in the bolt action version, 20" barrel in semiauto version or 17.5" barrel in bolt action. Youth model or 16.25" barrel in bolt action single shot True Youth model. Add $25 for True Youth model.

NIB	Exc.	V.G.	Good	Fair	Poor
120	100	—	—	—	—

Superior Grade Rimfire

Chambered for .22 Long Rifle or .22 Mag, or .22 Hornet in bolt action or .22 LR semiauto. Walnut stock with checkering. Open sights.

NIB	Exc.	V.G.	Good	Fair	Poor
170	130	—	—	—	—

NOTE: Add $20 for .22 Mag. model and $170 for .22 Hornet model.

Empire Grade Rimfire

Empire Grade has select walnut stock with 24 lpi hand cut checkering. Grip and forearm caps highly polished and blued metal finish. Same configurations as Superior Grade rifles.

NIB	Exc.	V.G.	Good	Fair	Poor
335	275	—	—	—	—

NOTE: Add $20 For .22 Mag. model and $100 for .22 Hornet model.

PISTOLS

Field 1911-A1

Chambered for .45 ACP with a choice of 5", 4", or 3.5" barrel and various special features such as front and rear slide serrations, extended beavertail safety, and lightweight trigger. Magazine capacity is 8 rounds. Overall length is 8.75".

NIB	Exc.	V.G.	Good	Fair	Poor
430	350	300	—	—	—

Superior 1911-A1
Same as the Field Grade described above but a blued frame and stainless steel slide. Introduced in 1999.

NIB	Exc.	V.G.	Good	Fair	Poor
475	375	—	—	—	—

Empire 1911-A1
Same as the Field Grade but in full stainless with both stainless steel slide and frame. Introduced in 1999.

NIB	Exc.	V.G.	Good	Fair	Poor
500	400	—	—	—	—

Field 1911-A2P
Same as above but with 10-round magazine.

NIB	Exc.	V.G.	Good	Fair	Poor
570	450	—	—	—	—

.22 Caliber Conversion Kit
Offered with adjustable sights for models with 5" barrel only. First offered in 1999.

NIB	Exc.	V.G.	Good	Fair	Poor
200	150	—	—	—	—

Field 1911-A1 PC
This model is fitted with a 4" barrel and slide. It also has a polymer frame. Produced under license from STI. Introduced in 1999.

NIB	Exc.	V.G.	Good	Fair	Poor
500	400	—	—	—	—

Superior 1911-A1 PC
Same as the model above but with stainless steel slide and black polymer frame. Introduced in 1999.

NIB	Exc.	V.G.	Good	Fair	Poor
525	425	—	—	—	—

DAN ARMS OF AMERICA
Allentown, Pennsylvania
These are Italian-made shotguns manufactured by Silmer and imported by Dan Arms of America. They are no longer produced as of 1988.

SIDE-X-SIDES
Field Grade
A boxlock shotgun chambered for all gauges with 26" or 28" barrels, various choke combinations, double triggers and extractors. Blued with a walnut stock.

Exc.	V.G.	Good	Fair	Poor
300	265	225	150	125

Deluxe Field Grade
As above, with a single trigger and automatic ejectors.

Exc.	V.G.	Good	Fair	Poor
450	400	325	250	200

OVER/UNDERS
Lux Grade I
A 12 and 20 gauge Over/Under shotgun with a 26", 28" or 30" ventilated rib barrels, double triggers and extractors. Blued finish with a walnut stock.

Exc.	V.G.	Good	Fair	Poor
275	250	200	150	100

Lux Grade II
As above, in 12 gauge only with a single trigger.

Exc.	V.G.	Good	Fair	Poor
325	300	250	200	150

Lux Grade III
As above, in 20 gauge only with automatic ejectors.

Exc.	V.G.	Good	Fair	Poor
400	325	275	225	175

As above in 12 gauge only with screw-in choke tubes.

Exc.	V.G.	Good	Fair	Poor
450	375	325	275	200

Silver Snipe

A 12 or 20 gauge shotgun manufactured to custom order with engraved false sideplates and a select walnut stock.

Exc.	V.G.	Good	Fair	Poor
1250	1000	800	600	350

DANCE & BROTHERS
CONFEDERATE REVOLVERS
Columbia, Texas

J.H., G.P., and D.E. Dance began production of percussion revolvers for the Confederate States of America in Columbia, Texas, in mid-1862, moving to Anderson, Texas, in early 1864. Based on surviving serial numbers, the combined output at both places did not exceed 350 pistols. Most of these were in the "Army" (.44 caliber) size but a limited number of "Navy" (.36 caliber) were also manufactured. Nearly all are distinguished by the absence of a "recoil shield" on the frame behind the cylinders. As Colt M1851 "Navy" revolvers closely resemble the Dance Navy revolvers, great care must be exercised in examining revolvers purported to be Dance Navies.

.44 Caliber

Exc.	V.G.	Good	Fair	Poor
—	—	25000	8000	2000

.36 Caliber

Courtesy Milwaukee Public Museum, Milwaukee, Wisconsin

Exc.	V.G.	Good	Fair	Poor
—	—	27500	8500	3000

C DANDOY/A LIEGE
SEE—French Military Firearms

DANSK REKYLRIFFEL SYNDIKAT
Copenhagen, Denmark

Schouboe 1902/1903

A 7.65mm caliber semiautomatic pistol with a conventional blowback design. Production ended in 1910, with less than 1,000 manufactured.

Exc.	V.G.	Good	Fair	Poor
—	4000	3000	2500	1200

Model 1907

An 11.35mm caliber semiautomatic pistol designed to fire a 55-grain, copper-aluminum-and-wood projectile at a velocity of 1625 ft./sec. Five hundred were manufactured before production stopped in 1917.

Exc.	V.G.	Good	Fair	Poor
—	5000	4000	3000	2000

Combination holster/shoulder stocks were made for this model, but are extremely rare. If present with a pistol, they would add approximately 50% to the value.

DARDICK CORP.
Hamden, Connecticut

Perhaps one of the most unusual firearms to have been designed and marketed in the United States during the 20th century. It utilizes "tround," which is a triangular plastic case enclosing a cartridge. The action of these arms consists of a revolving carrier that brings the trounds from the magazine into line with the barrel. Discontinued in 1962.

Series 1100 (3" barrel)
Chambered in .38 Dardick only.

Exc.	V.G.	Good	Fair	Poor
800	650	550	400	200

Series 1500 (6" barrel)
Chambered for the .22, .30, and the .38 Dardick.

Exc.	V.G.	Good	Fair	Poor
950	850	750	600	300

A carbine conversion kit consisting of a long barrel and shoulder stock was available and would bring a premium of $250 to $400 depending on the condition.

DARLING, B. & B. M.
Belingham, Massachusetts

Darling Pepperbox Pistol

A .30 caliber percussion 6-shot pepperbox with 3.25" length barrels. Blued with walnut grips. This is one of the rarest American pepperboxes and copies are known to have been made.

Consequently, prospective purchasers are advised to secure a qualified appraisal prior to acquisition. Manufactured during the late 1830s.

Exc.	V.G.	Good	Fair	Poor
—	—	3500	1000	550

DARNE, S. A.
St. Etienne, France

Darne Side-x-Side Shotguns

A 12, 16, 20, or 28 gauge sliding breech double barrel shotgun manufactured in a variety of barrel lengths and with numerous optional features. Manufactured from 1881 to 1979.

Model R11

Exc.	V.G.	Good	Fair	Poor
1000	900	750	600	350

Model R15

Exc.	V.G.	Good	Fair	Poor
2500	2000	1750	1500	750

Model V19

Exc.	V.G.	Good	Fair	Poor
3250	3000	2750	2250	1250

Model V22

Exc.	V.G.	Good	Fair	Poor
3750	3500	3000	2500	1200

Model V Hors Series No. I

Exc.	V.G.	Good	Fair	Poor
4500	4000	3750	3250	1500

DAUDETEAU
St. Denis, France

Model 1896

A 6.5mm caliber bolt action rifle with a 26" barrel, full length stock secured by two barrel bands and a fixed magazine. Blued with a walnut stock.

Exc.	V.G.	Good	Fair	Poor
—	250	175	100	75

DAVENPORT FIREARMS CO.
Providence, Rhode Island
Norwich, Connecticut

Double Barrel Shotguns

Text and prices by Nick Niles

William Hastings Davenport's company also made and marked double barrel, visible hammer guns in Providence, R.I. on Orange St., 1880-1882 and in Norwich, Conn. ca. 1890-1909. All are monbloc designs of which there were four models. The 1st model made at Providence, ca. 1881, had hammers rising out of the boxlock frame. The 2nd model, made in Norwich, Conn. about 1898, is a typical boxlock. The 3rd model made in Norwich, Conn., ca. 1909, has small sidelocks set in larger boxlock frames. Its barrels have unnotched extensions and notched underlugs. The 4th model, also from Norwich, possibly made after the 1901 takeover by Hopkins & Allen, also has sidelocks set in boxlock frames but the barrels have half moon lugs and notched barrel extensions. Few Davenport doubles are seen although single barrel guns are often found.

1st Model

Exc.	V.G.	Good	Fair	Poor
1000	800	500	400	300

2nd Model

Courtesy Nick Niles

Exc.	V.G.	Good	Fair	Poor
600	400	300	200	150

3rd Model

Exc.	V.G.	Good	Fair	Poor
1000	800	500	400	300

4th Model

Exc.	V.G.	Good	Fair	Poor
800	400	300	250	200

Single Barrel Shotgun

A 10, 12, 16, or 20 gauge side hammer single barrel shotgun with 26" to 36" barrels and extractors. Blued, case hardened with a walnut stock. Manufactured from approximately 1880 to 1915.

Exc.	V.G.	Good	Fair	Poor
—	400	300	150	75

8 Gauge Goose Gun

As above, in 8 gauge.

Exc.	V.G.	Good	Fair	Poor
—	500	250	175	100

Falling Block Single Shot Rifle

A .22, .25, or .32 rimfire single shot rifle with a 24" round barrel and exposed hammer. Blued with a walnut stock. The barrel marked "The W.H. Davenport Fire Arms Co. Norwich, Conn. U.S.A. Patented Dec. 15, 1891." Manufactured between 1891 and 1910.

Exc.	V.G.	Good	Fair	Poor
—	600	425	325	200

DAVIDSON F. A.
Eibar, Spain

Arms bearing this name were manufactured in Spain by Fabrica De Armas.

Model 63B

A 12, 16, 20, 28, or .410 bore double barrel boxlock shotgun with 25" to 30" barrels. Engraved, nickel-plated with a walnut stock. Made from 1963 to 1976.

Exc.	V.G.	Good	Fair	Poor
275	225	200	150	100

Model 69 SL

A 12 or 20 gauge sidelock double barrel shotgun with 26" or 28" barrels and finished as above.

Exc.	V.G.	Good	Fair	Poor
400	350	300	225	125

Stagecoach Model 73

A 12 or 20 gauge Magnum sidelock double barrel shotgun with 20" barrels and exposed hammers.

Exc.	V.G.	Good	Fair	Poor
275	225	175	150	100

DAVIS, A. JR.
Stafford, Connecticut

Under Hammer Pistol

A .31 caliber single shot under hammer percussion pistol with a 7.5" half octagonal barrel and brass frame. The grips are of maple and formed with a bottom tip. The top strap marked "A. Davis Jr./Stafford Conn."

Exc.	V.G.	Good	Fair	Poor
—	950	600	300	100

DAVIS, N.R. & CO.
DAVIS, N.R. & SONS

Manufacturer of percussion, and later, cartridge shotguns from 1853 to 1919. The cartridge shotguns embodied Nathan R. Davis' patented improvements of 1879, 1884, and 1886. Though only made in plain, serviceable grades, Davis shotguns were extremely well made and lived up to the company's motto "As Good as the Best."

Grade A and B Hammerless Shotguns

Made in 12 or 16 gauge with 28", 30", or 32" barrels.

Exc.	V.G.	Good	Fair	Poor
750	600	400	200	100

Grade C Hammerless Shotgun

Made in 10 gauge with 30" or 32" barrels.

Exc.	V.G.	Good	Fair	Poor
750	600	400	200	100

Grade D and DS Hammer Shotguns

Made in 12 or 16 gauge with 28", 30", or 32" barrels.

Exc.	V.G.	Good	Fair	Poor
750	600	400	200	100

Grade E and F Single Barrel Shotguns

Made in 12 or 16 gauge with 30" or 32" barrels.

Exc.	V.G.	Good	Fair	Poor
250	200	100	75	50

N.R. DAVIS BRANDS

1st Button Opener-Hammer Boxlock

Exc.	V.G.	Good	Fair	Poor
400	300	250	150	100

1st Sidelever-Hammer Boxlock

Exc.	V.G.	Good	Fair	Poor
400	300	250	150	100

2nd Sidelever-Hammer Boxlock

Courtesy Nick Niles. Photo Paul Goodwin

Exc.	V.G.	Good	Fair	Poor
400	300	250	150	100

1st Toplever-Hammer Boxlock

Courtesy Nick Niles. Photo Paul Goodwin

Exc.	V.G.	Good	Fair	Poor
400	300	250	150	100

2nd Toplever-Hammer Boxlock

Exc.	V.G.	Good	Fair	Poor
400	300	250	150	100

3rd Toplever-Hammer Boxlock

Exc.	V.G.	Good	Fair	Poor
400	300	250	150	100

1879 1st Model-Hammer Boxlock

Exc.	V.G.	Good	Fair	Poor
400	300	250	150	100

1879 2nd Model Damascus Barrels-Hammer Boxlock

Exc.	V.G.	Good	Fair	Poor
400	300	250	150	100

1885 "Hammerless"-Hammerless Boxlock

Exc.	V.G.	Good	Fair	Poor
400	300	250	150	100

1886 Rival-Hammerless Boxlock

Exc.	V.G.	Good	Fair	Poor
300	250	200	150	100

1886 Rival Improved-Hammerless Boxlock

Exc.	V.G.	Good	Fair	Poor
300	250	200	150	100

1897 "G"-Hammer Sidelock

Exc.	V.G.	Good	Fair	Poor
300	250	200	150	100

N.R. DAVIS & SONS BRAND

Hammerless 1900-Hammerless Boxlock

Exc.	V.G.	Good	Fair	Poor
300	250	200	150	100

Hammerless A Damascus Barrels-Hammerless Boxlock

Exc.	V.G.	Good	Fair	Poor
300	250	200	150	100

Hammerless B-Hammerless Boxlock

Exc.	V.G.	Good	Fair	Poor
300	250	200	150	100

Hammerless C Engraved Damascus Barrel-Hammerless Boxlock

Exc.	V.G.	Good	Fair	Poor
350	300	250	150	100

Hammerless D Engraved-Hammerless Boxlock

Exc.	V.G.	Good	Fair	Poor
400	350	300	250	200

New Model-Hammerless Boxlock

Exc.	V.G.	Good	Fair	Poor
300	250	200	150	100

"D.S." Straight Stock-Engraved-Hammerless Boxlock

Exc.	V.G.	Good	Fair	Poor
300	250	200	150	100

Davis Special-Hammerless Boxlock

Exc.	V.G.	Good	Fair	Poor
800	600	500	400	250

Davis "B" Manga Steel-Hammerless Boxlock

Exc.	V.G.	Good	Fair	Poor
800	600	500	400	250

DAVIS-WARNER BRANDS

See Davis-Warner
CRESCENT-DAVIS BRANDS
Model No. 600-Hammerless Boxlock

Exc.	V.G.	Good	Fair	Poor
600	500	300	200	100

Model No. 900-Hammerless Boxlock

Exc.	V.G.	Good	Fair	Poor
600	500	300	200	100

DAVIS & BOZEMAN
Central, Alabama

Pattern 1841 Rifle

A .58 caliber single shot percussion rifle with a 33" round barrel, full walnut stock, 2 barrel bands, brass furniture and an iron ramrod. The lock marked "D. & B. Ala." as well as the serial number and date of manufacture. Prospective purchasers are advised to secure a qualified appraisal prior to acquisition.

Exc.	V.G.	Good	Fair	Poor
—	—	14000	5000	2000

DAVIS INDUSTRIES
Mira Loma, California

This company was founded in 1982 by Jim Davis in Chino, California. At the present time the company produces all of its handguns in a 50,000 square foot plant in Mira Loma, California. All Davis guns have a lifetime warranty. Any malfunction will be repaired or replaced free of charge.

D-Series Deringer

A .22 Long Rifle, .22 WMR, .25 ACP and .32 ACP caliber double barrel Over/Under derringer with 2.4" barrels. Black Teflon or chrome plated finish with laminated wood grips. Weighs approximately 9.5 oz.

NIB	Exc.	V.G.	Good	Fair	Poor
60	50	40	30	25	20

Big Bore D-Series

Similar to the above model but chambered for the .38 Special and .32 H&R Magnum. Barrel length is 2.75". Weighs about 11.5 oz.

NIB	Exc.	V.G.	Good	Fair	Poor
80	60	45	30	25	20

Long Bore D-Series

Introduced in 1994 this two-shot pistol is chambered for the .22 Long Rifle, .22 WMR, .32 ACP, .32 H&R Mag., .380 ACP, 9mm, and .38 Special cartridges. Barrel length is 3.75", overall length is 5.65" and weight is approximately 13 oz.

NIB	Exc.	V.G.	Good	Fair	Poor
80	60	45	30	25	20

P-32

A .32 caliber semiautomatic pistol with a 2.8" barrel and 6-shot magazine. Black Teflon or chrome-plated finish with laminated wood grips. Overall length is 5.4". Weighs approximately 22 oz.

NIB	Exc.	V.G.	Good	Fair	Poor
85	75	60	45	35	25

P-380

As above, in .380 caliber.

NIB	Exc.	V.G.	Good	Fair	Poor
100	80	65	50	40	30

DAVIS-WARNER ARMS CORPORATION
Norwich, Connecticut

Established in 1917, when N.R. Davis & Sons purchased the Warner Arms Company. Manufactured shotguns, as well as revolvers and semiautomatic pistols. Ceased operations in 1930. The Crescent Arms Company purchased the proprietary rights to the name and briefly assembled shotguns under the name (probably from parts acquired in the purchase) until Crescent was in turn purchased by J.C. Stevens.

Initially, the Davis-Warner shotguns were identical to those made by Davis, (page 360), but they subsequently made a Davis Grade B.S. Hammerless, Davis-Warner Expert and Davis Grade D.S. The pistols made by the company included .32 caliber revolvers and two Browning Patent semiautomatics made in Belgium for the company.

Davis Grade B.S. Hammerless Shotgun
Made in 12, 16, or 20 gauge with 28", 30", or 32" barrels.

Courtesy William Hammond

Exc.	V.G.	Good	Fair	Poor
750	600	400	200	100

Davis-Warner Expert Hammerless
Made in 12, 16, or 20 gauge with 26", 28", 30", or 32" barrels.

Courtesy Nick Niles. Photo Paul Goodwin

Exc.	V.G.	Good	Fair	Poor
750	600	400	200	100

"BS"-Hammerless Boxlock
Exc.	V.G.	Good	Fair	Poor
300	250	200	150	100

"Maximin"-Hammerless Boxlock

Courtesy Nick Niles. Photo Paul Goodwin

Exc.	V.G.	Good	Fair	Poor
400	300	250	200	150

"DS"-Hammerless Boxlock
Exc.	V.G.	Good	Fair	Poor
300	250	200	150	100

Deluxe-Hammerless Boxlock
Exc.	V.G.	Good	Fair	Poor
300	250	200	150	100

Premier-Hammerless Boxlock
Exc.	V.G.	Good	Fair	Poor
300	250	200	150	100

Peerless Ejector-Hammerless Boxlock

Courtesy Nick Niles. Photo Paul Goodwin

Exc.	V.G.	Good	Fair	Poor
400	300	250	200	150

Hypower-Hammerless Boxlock
Exc.	V.G.	Good	Fair	Poor
400	300	250	200	150

Ajax-Hammerless Boxlock

Courtesy Nick Niles. Photo Paul Goodwin

Exc.	V.G.	Good	Fair	Poor
300	250	200	150	100

Certified (Savage)

Courtesy Nick Niles. Photo Paul Goodwin

Exc.	V.G.	Good	Fair	Poor
400	300	250	150	100

Deluxe Special (Model 805)-Automatic Ejectors
Exc.	V.G.	Good	Fair	Poor
500	400	300	200	150

Premier Special (Model 802)
Exc.	V.G.	Good	Fair	Poor
500	400	300	200	150

Premier (Model 801)
Exc.	V.G.	Good	Fair	Poor
400	300	250	150	100

Ajax (Model 800)

Courtesy Nick Niles. Photo Paul Goodwin

Exc.	V.G.	Good	Fair	Poor
400	300	250	150	100

Davis-Warner Swing Out Revolver

Double action .32 caliber revolver with a 5" or 6" barrel.

Exc.	V.G.	Good	Fair	Poor
150	125	100	75	50

Davis-Warner Semiautomatic Pistols

Browning Patent .25 ACP, .32 ACP or .380 caliber pistols.

Exc.	V.G.	Good	Fair	Poor
300	250	175	125	75

Warner Infallible Semiautomatic Pistol

Freyberg Patent .32 ACP.

Exc.	V.G.	Good	Fair	Poor
300	250	175	125	75

DAW, G. H.
London, England

Daw Revolver

A .38 caliber double action percussion revolver with a 5.5" barrel marked "George H. Daw, 57 Threadneedle St. London, Patent No. 112." Blued, with walnut grips. Manufactured in the 1860s.

Exc.	V.G.	Good	Fair	Poor
—	5000	3000	1750	1000

A cased factory engraved Daw's revolver was sold at auction for $4,600. Condition was good. Butterfield & Butterfield, August 1999

DEANE, ADAMS & DEANE
London, England
SEE—Adams

DEANE-HARDING
London, England

Deane-Harding Revolver

A .44 caliber percussion revolver with a 5.25" barrel and 5-shot cylinder. Blued, case hardened with walnut grips. Manufactured during the late 1850s.

Courtesy Butterfield & Butterfield, San Francisco, California

Exc.	V.G.	Good	Fair	Poor
—	3000	1750	1250	800

DECKER, WILHELM
Zella St. Blasii, Germany

A 6.35mm double action revolver with a 6-shot cylinder and concealed hammer. Blued with plastic grips. Manufactured prior to 1914.

Exc.	V.G.	Good	Fair	Poor
—	750	450	300	100

DEFIANCE ANTI-BANDIT GUN
Distributed by California Arms Co.
San Francisco, California

Defiance Anti-Bandit Gun CURIO OR RELIC, NFA

The Defiance Anti-Bandit Gun is a double barreled smooth bore pistol designed for 2.5" 20 gauge shotgun or tear gas shells. It was manufactured in 1926-27 by The American Machine Company for the California Arms Co., San Francisco, California, a law enforcement supply manufacturer and distributor, and distributed by them from about 1926-30. Because few specimens exist establishing reliable values may be difficult, but could logically be expected to approximate those for a nonstandard or special-order Ithaca Auto & Burglar Gun.

DEMIRETT, J.
Montpelier, Vermont

Under Hammer Pistol

A .27 caliber single shot percussion pistol with 3" to 8" barrels and an under hammer. The barrel marked "J. Demerrit / Montpelier / Vermont." Blued with maple, walnut or stag horn grips. Active from 1866 to the mid-1880s.

Exc.	V.G.	Good	Fair	Poor
—	—	1500	600	300

DEMRO
Manchester, Connecticut

XF-7 Wasp Carbine

A 9mm or .45 caliber semiautomatic carbine with a 16.5" barrel and folding stock.

Exc.	V.G.	Good	Fair	Poor
500	350	250	200	150

T.A.C. Model 1

As above, with a fixed stock.

Exc.	V.G.	Good	Fair	Poor
500	350	250	200	150

DERINGER REVOLVER AND PISTOL CO.
Philadelphia, Pennsylvania

After Henry Deringer's death, his name was used by I.J. Clark who manufactured rimfire revolvers on Charles Foehl's patents between 1870 and 1879.

Deringer Model I

A .22 caliber spur trigger revolver with a hinged octagonal barrel and 7-shot cylinder. Manufactured circa 1873.

Exc.	V.G.	Good	Fair	Poor
—	—	450	200	150

Deringer Model II

As above, with a round barrel and also available in .32 caliber.

Exc.	V.G.	Good	Fair	Poor
—	—	350	175	100

Centennial 1876

A .22, .32, or .38 caliber solid frame revolver.

Exc.	V.G.	Good	Fair	Poor
—	—	800	450	200

HENRY DERINGER RIFLES AND PISTOLS
Philadelphia, Pennsylvania

Henry Deringer Sr. and his son, Henry Jr., were well established in Philadelphia by the close of the War of 1812, having made both sporting and military rifles at that place since the turn of the century. Henry Jr. continued in the gun trade until the outbreak of the American Civil War, primarily producing flintlock and percussion military rifles, at least 2,500 "Northwest guns" and 1,200 rifles for the Indian trade, a few percussion martial pistols, but most importantly the percussion pocket pistols that became so popular that they took on his misspelled name as a generic term, the "derringers."

Deringer U.S. M1814 Military Rifle

Overall length 48-1/2"; barrel length 32-3/4"; caliber .54. Markings: on lockplate, "US/H. DERINGER/PHILADA", on top flat of barrel, "H. DERINGER/PHILADA" and standard U.S. proofmarks. The U.S. M1814 rifle is distinguished by its part octagonal barrel, whose bands were secured by wedge-shaped spring bands, and the distinctive finger ridges on the triggerguard strap. Henry Deringer Sr. received a contract for 2,000 of these rifles in 1814, but delivered only 50 that year, devoting his resources instead to a more lucrative Pennsylvania state contract for rifles.

Exc.	V.G.	Good	Fair	Poor
—	4000	1600	1200	850

Deringer U.S. M1817 Military Rifle (Types I & II)

Overall length 51-1/4"; barrel length 36"; caliber .54. Markings: on lockplate, "US/H. DERINGER/PHILADA" forward of cock, date on tail; standard U.S. proofmarks on barrel. The U.S. M1817 "common" rifle followed much of the same design elements as its predecessor, the U.S. M1814 rifle; however, the barrel is fully round with its bands secured by full band springs, and on the earlier production, the finger ridges on the triggerguard strap were eliminated in favor of a plain strap formed into a handgrip. On the 6,000 rifles manufactured under his 1840 contract, Deringer eliminated the "pistol grip" in favor of a plain strap, distinguishing Type 11 production from Type 1. As one of the four major contractors for the U.S. M1817 rifle, Deringer produced a total of 111,000 rifles for the U.S. War Department. Many of the rifles from first two contracts (2,000 in 1821, 3,000 in 1823) were distributed to Southern states under the 1808 Militia Act. Accordingly, Deringer M1817 rifles altered to percussion by traditional Southern methods may generate a premium.

(in flintlock)

Exc.	V.G.	Good	Fair	Poor
—	4000	1500	1200	800

(altered to percussion)

Exc.	V.G.	Good	Fair	Poor
—	2000	700	550	400

Deringer Original Percussion Martial Rifles (Types I & II)

Overall length 51-1/4"; barrel length 36"; caliber .54. Markings: Type I-on lockplate forward of hammer "DERINGER/PHILA"; also known to exist with standard U.S. M1817 lock markings and barrel marks; Type II-on lockplate forward of hammer "US/DERINGER/PHILADELA" or "DERINGER/PHILADELA" and same on top of barrel.

Although the Type I rifle of this series appears at first glance to be a late contract rifle altered to percussion by means of the cone-in barrel method, in fact it is an original percussion rifle made by Deringer from modified spare parts that remained after the completion of his 1840 contract. The Type 11 rifle also evidences having been made from modified parts; however, its cone is set in an elongated bolster brazed to the right side of the barrel. Speculation concerning these rifles is rampant; however, the available evidence indicates that Deringer produced about 600 of these most likely produced at the beginning of the American Civil War.

Courtesy Milwaukee Public Museum, Milwaukee, Wisconsin

Exc.	V.G.	Good	Fair	Poor
—	2500	900	650	450

Deringer Original Percussion Rifle-Muskets

Overall length 57-3/4"; barrel length 42"; caliber .69. Markings: on lock forward of hammer, "US/DERINGER/PHILADELA". Just as the original percussion rifle appears to be an altered arm, the rare Deringer rifle muskets at first appear to have been flintlocks. However, these arms are original percussion, having been made from spare or rejected parts from the U.S. M1816 muskets. The brazed bolsters are identical in style to that of the Type 11 original percussion rifles made by Deringer. Barrels are rifled with seven grooves, and the barrels accordingly bear a rear sight. Deringer probably assembled a hundred of these rifles in 1861 to arm some company of Pennsylvania's early war regiments.

Courtesy Milwaukee Public Museum, Milwaukee, Wisconsin

Exc.	V.G.	Good	Fair	Poor
—	2500	900	650	450

Deringer U.S. Navy Contract "Boxlock" Pistols

Overall length 11-5/8"; barrel length 6"; caliber .54. Markings: on lockplate, "US/DERINGER/ PHILADELIA" or merely "DE-RINGER/PHILADEL'A" in center, the tail either plain or marked "U.S.N./(date)"; barrels sometimes marked with U.S. Navy inspection marks.

Deringer was granted a contract with the U.S. Navy in 1845 for 1,200 of the new "boxlock" percussion pistols also made by Ames. All of these appear to have been delivered. From the extra parts, Deringer is thought to have assembled several hundred extra pistols, some of which he rifled. The latter bring a premium, even though quantities remain enigmatic.

Exc.	V.G.	Good	Fair	Poor
—	3500	1400	1100	750

Deringer Percussion Pocket Pistols

Overall length varies with barrel length; barrel length 1-1/2" to 6" in regular 1/8" gradiants; caliber .41 (usually, other calibers known). Markings: "DERINGER/PHILADELA" on back action lock and rear section of top barrel flat; "P" impressed in circle with serrated edges on left side of breech; agent marks occasionally on top of barrel.

Courtesy Milwaukee Public Museum, Milwaukee, Wisconsin

The most famous of Henry Deringer's products, an estimated 15,000 were produced between the Mexican War through the Civil War, usually in pairs. The popularity of the pistol is attested in the large number of imitations and the nickname "Derringer" applied to them, even when clearly not Deringer's products. Prices can fluctuate widely based on agent marks occasionally found on barrel. Care is advised in purchasing purported "true" derringers.

Exc.	V.G.	Good	Fair	Poor
—	4500	1600	1200	800

Principal Makers of Deringer-Style Pocket Pistols

William AFFLERBACH, Philadelphia, PA

Balthaser AUER, Louisville, KY

Frederick BEERSTECHER, Philadelphia and Lewisburg, PA

Franz J. BITTERLICH, Nashville, TN

BLUNT & SYMS, New York, NY

Richard P. BRUFF, New York, NY

Jesse S. BUTTERFIELD, Philadelphia, PA

Daniel CLARK, Philadelphia, PA

Richard CONSTABLE, Philadelphia, PA

DELONG & SON, Chattanooga, TN

MOSES DICKSON, Louisville, KY

Horace E. DIMICK, St. Louis, MO

Gustau ERICHSON, Houston, TX

B.J. EUSTACE & Company, St. Louis, MO

James E. EVANS, Philadelphia, PA

W.S. EVANS, Philadelphia, PA

FIELD, LANGSTROTH & Company, Philadelphia, PA

Daniel FISH, New York, NY

FOLSOM BROTHERS & Company, New Orleans, LA

August G. GENEZ, New York, NY

George D. H. GILLESPIE, New York, NY

Frederick G. GLASSICK, Memphis, TN

James GOLCHER, Philadelphia, PA

Joseph GRUBB & Company, Philadelphia, PA

John H. HAPPOLDT, Charlestown, SC

John M. HAPPOLDT, Columbus, George, and Charlestown, SC

HAWS & WAGGONER, Columbia, SC

HODGKINS & SONS, Macon, GA

Louis HOFFMAN, Vicksburg, MS

HYDE & GOODRICH, New Orleans, LA

Joseph JACOB, Philadelphia, PA

William W. KAYE, Philadelphia, PA

Benjamin KITTERIDGE, Cincinnati, OH

Peter W. KRAFT, Columbia, SC

John KRIDER, Philadelphia, PA

Jacob KUNTZ, Philadelphia, PA

Martille La FITTE, Natchitoches, LA

A. Frederichk LINS, Philadelphia, PA

C. LOHNER, Philadelphia, PA

John P. LOWER, Denver, CO

A.R. MENDENHALL, Des Arc, AK

John MEUNIER, Milwaukee, WI

William D. MILLER, New York, NY

MURPHY & O'CONNELL, New York, NY

—— NEWCOMB, Natchez, MS

Charles A. OBERTEUFFER, Philadelphia, PA

Stephen O'DELL, Natchez, MS

Henry C. PALMER, St. Louis, MO

R. PATRICK, New York, NY

REID & TRACY, New York, NY

William ROBERTSON, Philadelphia, PA

ROBINSON & KRIDER, Philadelphia, PA

Ernst SCHMIDT & Company, Houston, TX

SCHNEIDER & GLASSICK, Memphis, TN

W.A. SEAVER, New York, NY

Paul J. SIMPSON, New York, NY

SLOTTER & Company, Philadelphia, PA

Patrick SMITH, Buffalo, NY

SPRANG & WALLACE, Philadelphia, PA

Adam W. SPIES, New York, NY

Casper SUTER, Selma, AL

Jacob F. TRUMPLER, Little Rock, AK

Edward TRYON, Jr., Philadelphia, PA

George K. TRYON, Philadelphia, PA

TUFTS & COLLEY, New York, NY

WOLF, DASH & FISHER, New York, NY

Alfred WOODHAM, New York, NY

Andrew WURFFLEIN, Philadelphia, PA

John WURFFLEIN, Philadelphia, PA

Agent Names Found On Deringer Pocket Pistols

W.C. ALLEN, San Francisco, CA

W.H. CALHOUN, Nashville, TN

CANFIELD & BROTHERS, Baltimore, MD

F. H. CLARK & CO., Memphis, TN

COLEMAN & DUKE, Cahaba, AL

M.W. GALT & BROTHER, Washington, DC

J.B. GILMORE, Shreveport, LA

A.B. GRISWOLD & CO., New Orleans, LA

HYDE & GOODRICH, New Orleans, LA

LULLMAN & VIENNA, Memphis, TN

A.J. MILLSPAUGH, Shreveport, LA

H.G. NEWCOMB, Natchez, MS

A.J. PLATE, San Francisco, CA

J.A. SCHAFER, Vicksburg, MS

S.L. SWETT, Vicksburg, MS

A.J. TAYLOR, San Francisco, CA

WOLF & DURRINGER, Louisville, KY

DESENZANI, LABORATORIES ARMI
Brescia, Italy

This firm builds high grade over and under and side-by-side sidelock shotguns. Production is only about 25 guns per year. These guns will be seen in gauges of 12, 20, 28 and .410. It is strongly suggested that an expert appraisal is obtained prior to sale.

Over and Under

These custom made guns are all unique. Used guns in excellent condition will bring $30,000. Values increase depending on the small gauges and amount and coverage of engraving.

Side-by-Side

These custom made guns are all unique. Used guns in excellent condition will bring $20,000. Values increase depending on the small gauges and amount and coverage of engraving.

DESERT EAGLE
Imported by Magnum Research
Minneapolis, Minnesota

The Desert Eagle is a semiautomatic gas operated pistol chambered for the .357 Magnum, .41 Magnum, .44 Magnum, and .50 Action Express. It is produced by Israel Military Industries. The pistols are furnished with a standard 6" barrel but 10" and 14" interchangeable barrels are offered as options. Also available are these interchangeable barrels that are Mag-Na-Ported. The standard material used for frame is steel, but stainless and aluminum are also available. The standard finish for these pistols are black oxide but custom finishes are available on special order. These special finishes are: gold, stainless steel, satin nickel, bright nickel, polished blue, camo, matte chrome, polished chrome, brushed chrome, and matte chrome with gold. All of these special order finishes as well as the optional barrels will affect the prices of the pistols. Prices listed here will reflect standard pistols only.

Desert Eagle .357 Magnum

Standard with 6" barrel and black oxide finish. Magazine capacity is 9 rounds. Standard weight is 58 oz.

NIB	Exc.	V.G.	Good	Fair	Poor
650	600	550	500	400	250

Desert Eagle .41 Magnum/.44 Magnum

Standard barrel length is 6" with black oxide finish. Magazine capacity is 8 rounds. Weight for standard pistol is 63 oz.

NIB	Exc.	V.G.	Good	Fair	Poor
750	700	600	550	450	275

Desert Eagle .50 Action Express

Standard barrel length is 10" with black oxide finish. Magazine capacity is 7 rounds. Standard weight is 72 oz.

NIB	Exc.	V.G.	Good	Fair	Poor
1200	950	800	700	600	375

Desert Eagle Mark XIX

Introduced in 1996 this new design is manufactured in the U.S. and allows the interchangeability of barrels to switch calibers between the same receiver. A single receiver can be turned into 6 different pistols in 3 Magnum calibers. Available are the .50 A.E., .44 Mag., and .357 Mag. in barrel lengths of 6" or 10". Separate magazines are also required. Eight different finishes are offered as well. A separate bolt assembly is necessary to convert the .44/.50 calibers to the .357. There are so many different possibilities with this design that only the basic pistol prices are given. Extra barrel assemblies are an additional cost. Prices range from $280 to $160 depending on caliber and length.

.50A.E. w/6" Barrel

NIB	Exc.	V.G.	Good	Fair	Poor
1000	800	650	450	—	—

.50A.E. w/10" Barrel

NIB	Exc.	V.G.	Good	Fair	Poor
1100	900	700	450	—	—

.44 Mag. w/6" Barrel

NIB	Exc.	V.G.	Good	Fair	Poor
1000	800	650	450	—	—

.44 Mag. w/10" Barrel

NIB	Exc.	V.G.	Good	Fair	Poor
1100	900	700	450	—	—

.357 Mag. w/6" Barrel

NIB	Exc.	V.G.	Good	Fair	Poor
1000	800	650	450	—	—

.357 Mag. w/10" Barrel

NIB	Exc.	V.G.	Good	Fair	Poor
1100	900	700	450	—	—

.440 Cor-Bon w/6" Barrel (1999)

NIB	Exc.	V.G.	Good	Fair	Poor
1200	950	—	—	—	—

.440 Cor-Bon w/10" Barrel (1999)

NIB	Exc.	V.G.	Good	Fair	Poor
1300	1000	—	—	—	—

Bolt Assembly-.44/.50 or .357

NIB	Exc.	V.G.	Good	Fair	Poor
125	100	—	—	—	—

Mark XIX Component System

Introduced in 2000 this system features a Mark XIX frame with a .44 magnum 6" and 10" barrels; .50AE with 6" and 10" barrel; and .357 magnum with 6" and 10" barrel. Supplied with ICC aluminum case. Also offered with 6" only barrel components or 10" only barrel components.

6" & 10" Component System

NIB	Exc.	V.G.	Good	Fair	Poor
3690	—	—	—	—	

6" Component System

NIB	Exc.	V.G.	Good	Fair	Poor
2395	—	—	—	—	

10" Component System

NIB	Exc.	V.G.	Good	Fair	Poor
2655	—	—	—	—	

Baby Eagle

The Baby Eagle is a smaller version of the Desert Eagle. It is an all steel construction, extra long slide rail, nylon grips, combat style triggerguard, ambidextrous thumb safety, decocking safety. It is a double action design and available in 9mm, .40 S&W, .41 Action Express. Standard finish is black oxide but matte chrome and brushed are offered as optional finishes. Fixed sights are standard. Fixed night sights and adjustable night sights are options.

Baby Eagle 9mm

Fitted with a 4.7" barrel and black oxide finish this model has a magazine capacity of 16 rounds. Empty weight is 35 oz.

NIB	Exc.	V.G.	Good	Fair	Poor
450	400	350	300	250	200

Baby Eagle .40 S&W

Supplied with 4.7" barrel and black oxide finish it has a magazine capacity of 10 rounds. Empty weight is 35 oz.

NIB	Exc.	V.G.	Good	Fair	Poor
450	400	350	300	250	200

Baby Eagle .41 Action Express

This model also has a 4.7" barrel and black oxide finish. Magazine capacity is 11 rounds. Empty weight is 35 oz.

NIB	Exc.	V.G.	Good	Fair	Poor
450	400	350	300	250	200

Baby Eagle Short Barrel

This 9mm model features a 3.6" barrel with frame mounted safety. Magazine holds 10 rounds.

NIB	Exc.	V.G.	Good	Fair	Poor
450	400	350	300	250	200

Baby Eagle Short Barrel/Short Grip

This 9mm version has a 3.6" barrel and shorter grip than standard. Magazine capacity is still 10 rounds. Frame mounted safety.

NIB	Exc.	V.G.	Good	Fair	Poor
450	400	350	300	250	200

NOTE: Custom shop finishes for Desert Eagle pistols are available as follows: Satin Nickel, Bright Nickel, Polished and deep blued, Matte hard chrome, Polished hard chrome, Brushed hard chrome, 24K Gold. All finishes *except* gold add $195 to price of pistol. For Gold finish add $500. For gold appointments add $195.

Mountain Eagle

This semiautomatic pistol is chambered for the .22 Long Rifle cartridge. It features a 6.5" barrel with adjustable rear sight. The grip is a one-piece molded plastic, checkered with raised side panels. The magazine capacity is 15 rounds with 20-round magazine available as an option. A black oxide finish is standard. The pistol weighs 21 oz.

NIB	Exc.	V.G.	Good	Fair	Poor
200	175	150	125	100	75

Mountain Eagle-Target Edition

Similar to the standard Mountain Eagle but fitted with an 8" accurized barrel, two-stage target trigger, jeweled bolt, adjustable sights with three interchangeable blades, and range case.

NIB	Exc.	V.G.	Good	Fair	Poor
250	200	175	150	125	85

Mountain Eagle Compact Edition

Similar to above but fitted with a 4.5" barrel and short grip.

NIB	Exc	V.G.	Good	Fair	Poor
200	150	125	100	85	70

Lone Eagle

This is a single shot rotating breech pistol designed to fire centerfire cartridges. The standard finish is a black oxide blue luster. The barrel is drilled and tapped for scope mounts. Standard barrel length is 14". Fixed, adjustable, or silhouette sights are offered as options. Stock assembly is made from Lexan. The handgun is offered in the following calibers: .22-250, .223, .22 Hornet, .243, .30-30, .30-06, .308, .357 Mag., .358 Win., .35 Rem., .44 Mag., .444 Marlin, 7mm-08, 7mm

Bench Rest. Weighs between 4 lbs. 3 oz. to 4 lbs. 7 oz. depending on caliber.

NIB	Exc.	V.G.	Good	Fair	Poor
325	300	275	250	200	125

Lone Eagle (New Model)

Introduced in 1996 this new Lone Eagle model features 15 interchangeable barreled actions from .22 Hornet to .444 Marlin. Available in both black and chrome actions with or without muzzle brake. The 7.62X39 action was introduced in 1996 also. Sights can be fixed, adjustable or silhouette type. Weight is from 4 lbs. 3 oz. to 4 lbs. 7 oz. depending on caliber. Prices below reflect black action and fixed sights.

NIB	Exc.	Good	Good	Fair	Poor
280	225	175	150	125	100

NOTE: Add $100 for muzzle brake; $30 for chrome action; $35 for adjustable sights; $130 for silhouette sights.

Mountain Eagle Rifle

A limited edition rifle (1,000) with a Sako action and composite stock. Chambered for the .270, .280, .30-06, .300 Win., .338 Win, 7mm Mag. Introduced in 1994. Additional calibers are .300 Weatherby, .375 H&H, .416 Rem., and 7mm STW. Barrel length is 24". Average weight is about 7.74 lbs.

NIB	Exc.	V.G.	Good	Fair	Poor
1500	1200	850	700	500	—

NOTE: For muzzle brake add $150. For .375 H&H and .416 Rem. add $300. For left hand actions add $100.

Mountain Eagle Varmint Edition

Chambered for the .222 Rem. and the .223 Rem. cartridges and fitted with a 26" stainless Krieger barrel. Kevlar-graphite stock. Weight is approximately 9 lbs. 13 oz.

NIB	Exc	V.G.	Good	Fair	Poor
1600	1250	900	800	500	—

Magnum Lite Rimfire Rifles

These rifles are built with Ruger 10/22 actions and graphite barrels. There are several variations depending on stock configuration.

Hogue and Fajen Scope-Hi stock

NIB	Exc.	V.G.	Good	Fair	Poor
600	475	400	—	—	—

Fajen Thumbhole Sporter

NIB	Exc.	V.G.	Good	Fair	Poor
700	550	450	—	—	—

Fajen Thumbhole Silhouette

NIB	Exc.	V.G.	Good	Fair	Poor
800	650	500	—	—	—

Turner Barracuda

NIB	Exc.	V.G.	Good	Fair	Poor
800	650	500	—	—	—

NOTE: For Clark Custom Upgrades add $130 to price of each Magnum Lite rifle.

Magnum Lite Centerfire Rifles

These rifles are built on Sako actions and are fitted with graphite barrels. Introduced in 1999. Offered in two configurations, both with synthetic stock.

Heavy Barrel

Fitted with a 26", 1.2" diameter barrel with a 1 in 14 twist. Chambered for .223 cartridge. Weight is approximately 7.8 lbs.

NIB	Exc.	V.G.	Good	Fair	Poor
2295	1750	—	—	—	—

Sport Taper Barrel

Fitted with a 24" tapered barrel and chambered for the .280 Rem., 7mm Mag, .30-06, .300 Win. Mag. Weight is about 6.4 lbs.

NIB	Exc.	V.G.	Good	Fair	Poor
2295	1750	—	—	—	—

Tactical Rifle

Introduced in 2000 this rifle features a 26" match grade barrel chambered for the .223, .22-250, .308, or .300 Win. MAg. cartridges. The barrel is made from carbon fiber. the action is a Remington Model 700. The stock is an H-S Precesion tactical stock with adjustable comb. Adjustable trigger. Weight is approximately 8.3 lbs.

NIB	Exc.	V.G.	Good	Fair	Poor
2400	1900	—	—	—	—

DESTROYER CARBINE
Spain

Destroyer Carbine

A 9mm Bayard caliber bolt action rifle with a 20" barrel and 7-shot magazine. Full length stock with two barrel bands.

Exc.	V.G.	Good	Fair	Poor
200	125	90	65	35

DETONICS MANUFACTURING CORP.
Bellevue, Washington

This company manufactured semiautomatic pistols based upon the Colt Model 1911. This company is no longer in business.

Mark I

A .45 caliber semiautomatic pistol with a 3.25" barrel and 6-shot magazine. Matte blued with walnut grips. Discontinued in 1981.

Exc.	V.G.	Good	Fair	Poor
550	450	400	300	200

Mark II
As above, with satin nickel-plated finish. Discontinued in 1979.

Exc.	V.G.	Good	Fair	Poor
550	450	400	300	200

Mark III
As above, with hard chrome plating. Discontinued in 1979.

Exc.	V.G.	Good	Fair	Poor
600	500	450	350	250

Mark IV
As above, with polished blue finish. Discontinued in 1981.

Exc.	V.G.	Good	Fair	Poor
550	450	400	300	200

Combat Master
The Mark I in 9mm, .38 Super, or .45 caliber.

NIB	Exc.	V.G.	Good	Fair	Poor
975	800	600	500	400	250

Combat Master Mark V
As above, in stainless steel with a matte finish. Discontinued in 1985.

NIB	Exc.	V.G.	Good	Fair	Poor
975	800	600	500	400	250

Combat Master Mark VI
As above, with adjustable sights and the sides of the slide polished. 1,000 were made in .451 Detonics Magnum caliber.

.451 Detonics Magnum add 40%.

NIB	Exc.	V.G.	Good	Fair	Poor
900	750	600	500	400	250

Combat Master Mark VII
As above, without sights.

.451 Detonics Magnum add 40%.

NIB	Exc.	V.G.	Good	Fair	Poor
900	750	600	500	400	250

Military Combat MC2
As above, in 9mm, .38 Super or .45 caliber with fixed sights, dull finish and Pachmayr grips. Discontinued in 1984.

NIB	Exc.	V.G.	Good	Fair	Poor
675	600	500	425	300	200

Scoremaster
As above, in .45 or .451 Detonics Magnum with a 5" or 6" barrel, Millet sights and a grip safety.

NIB	Exc.	V.G.	Good	Fair	Poor
1250	1000	800	600	400	250

Janus Competition Scoremaster
As above, in .45 caliber with a compensated barrel. Introduced in 1988.

NIB	Exc.	V.G.	Good	Fair	Poor
1750	1450	1250	850	650	300

Servicemaster
As above, with a 4.25" barrel, interchangeable sights and matte finish. Discontinued in 1986.

Exc.	V.G.	Good	Fair	Poor
1000	800	600	400	200

Pocket 9
A 9mm double action semiautomatic pistol with a 3" barrel and 6-shot magazine. Matte finish stainless steel. Discontinued in 1986.

Exc.	V.G.	Good	Fair	Poor
400	350	275	225	175

DEUTSCHE WERKE
Erfurt, Germany

Ortgies
A 7.65mm or 9mm short semiautomatic pistol marked on the slide "Deutsche Werke Erfurt". The walnut grips inlaid with a brass medallion cast with an ornate "D".

6.35mm
Exc.	V.G.	Good	Fair	Poor
375	225	175	125	90

DEVISME, F. P.
Paris, France

One of the more popular French gunsmiths of the mid-19th century, F.P. Devisme manufactured a wide variety of firearms including single shot percussion pistols, double barrel percussion rifles and shotguns, percussion revolvers and cane guns. After 1858 this maker manufactured cartridge weapons of the same style as his percussion arms. The quality of all of his products is uniformly high and it is impossible to provide generalized price guide. Prospective purchasers are advised to secure a qualified appraisal prior to acquisition.

DICKINSON
SEE—Dickinson, E.L.

DICKINSON, E. L. & J.
Springfield, Massachusetts

Ranger
A .32 caliber spur trigger revolver with a 6-shot cylinder.

Exc.	V.G.	Good	Fair	Poor
—	—	400	200	100

Single Shot
A .32 caliber single shot pistol with a 3.75" hinged barrel, silver plated brass frame, blued barrel and walnut grips.

Exc.	V.G.	Good	Fair	Poor
—	—	500	250	100

DICKSON, JOHN
Edinburg, Scotland
SEE—British Double Guns

DICKSON, NELSON & CO.
Dawson, Georgia

Dickson, Nelson Rifle
A .58 caliber single shot percussion rifle with a 34" barrel, full stock secured by two barrel bands, brass furniture and iron loading rod. The lock marked "Dickson/Nelson & Co./C.S." as well as "Ala." and the date of manufacture. Prospective purchasers are advised to secure a qualified appraisal prior to acquisition. A carbine version of this arm is known and has a 24" barrel.

Exc.	V.G.	Good	Fair	Poor
—	—	17500	7500	3000

DIMICK, H.E.
St. Louis, Missouri

While this maker is primarily known for half stock Plains Rifles, he also manufactured a limited number of percussion pistols. These vary in length, caliber, stock form and type of furniture. The values listed below should only be used as a rough guide. Prospective purchasers should secure a qualified appraisal prior to acquisition. Active 1849 to 1873.

Exc.	V.G.	Good	Fair	Poor
—	—	5000	2000	900

DOMINGO ACHA
See Acha

DOMINO
Brescia, Italy
Importer - Mandall Shooting Supplies
Scottsdale, Arizona

Model OP 601 Match Pistol
A .22 caliber short semiautomatic pistol with a 5.6" vented barrel, target sights, adjustable and removable trigger. Blued with adjustable walnut grips.

NIB	Exc.	V.G.	Good	Fair	Poor
1300	1000	800	550	—	—

Model SP 602 Match Pistol
As above, in .22 l.r. caliber.

Courtesy John J. Stimsom, Jr.

NIB	Exc.	V.G.	Good	Fair	Poor
1300	1000	800	550	—	—

DORMUS
Austria

8MM Special

Made in Austrai in 1894 by M. Dormus from a design by Carlos Salvador. Fired an 8mm Special cartridge.

Courtesy James Rankin

Exc.	V.G.	Good	Fair	Poor
5500	5000	4500	2500	1500

DORNHAUS & DIXON
Huntington Beach, California
SEE—Bren 10

DORNHEIM, G.C.
Suhl, Germany

Gecado

A 6.35mm or 7.65mm semiautomatic pistol bearing the name "Gecado" on the slide. Marketed by G.C. Dornheim.

Exc.	V.G.	Good	Fair	Poor
225	150	125	75	50

DOUG TURNBULL RESTORATION, INC.
Bloomfield, NY

This company began operation in 1983 as a one man shop. Today the company numbers 14 people and does finish work for most major firarms manufactures. The company also installes Miller single triggers. The models listed below are a series of special run firearms produced by Turnbull.

DT Colt

This model is a current Colt SAA reworked to look like the pre-1920 SAA. Assigned serisl numbers beginning with 001DT these revoluersd are offered in .45 Colt, .44-40, and .38-40 calibers. Barrel lengths are 4.75", 5.5", and 7.5:. The standard Dt has color case hardened frame and the rest of the gun charchol blue. Cylinder flutes are enlarged and the fron of the of the cylinder is beveled. Many special optios offered which will effect cost. Prices listed below are for standard revolvers.

Year Offered-1998

NIB	Exc.	V.G.	Good	Fair	Poor
1495	—	—	—	—	—

Year Offered-1999

NIB	Exc.	V.G.	Good	Fair	Poor
1995	—	—	—	—	—

Year Offered-2000

NIB	Exc.	V.G.	Good	Fair	Poor
2200	—	—	—	—	—

EHBM Colt

This is a Colt SAA current production revolver limited to 50 guns chambered of the .45 Colt and fitted with a 5.5" barrel. Special features. Serial numbers EHBM01 to EHBM50. First offered in 2000.

NIB	Exc.	V.G.	Good	Fair	Poor
2150	—	—	—	—	—

DOWNSIZER CORPORATION
Santee, California

Model WSP

Introduced in 1998, this is billed as the world's smallest pistol by the manufacturer. It is a single shot, double action-only pistol with tip-up barrel. It is chambered for .22 Mag., .32 Mag, .357 Mag., 9mm, .40 S&W, and .45 ACP cartridges. Barrel length is 2.1". Overall length is 3.25". Height is 2.25", thickness is .9". Weight is approximately 11 oz. Built from stainless steel.

NIB	Exc.	V.G.	Good	Fair	Poor
330	250	—	—	—	—

DREYSE
SEE—Rheinmetall

DRISCOLL, J.B.
Springfield, Massachusetts

Single Shot Pocket Pistol

A small pistol chambered for .22 rimfire. It has a 3.5" octagonal barrel that pivots downward for loading after a trigger-like hook under the breech is pulled. It has a spur trigger, silver-plated brass frame, and a blued barrel. The square butt is flared at the bottom, and the grips are walnut. There were approximately 200 manufactured in the late 1860s.

Exc.	V.G.	Good	Fair	Poor
—	—	600	200	100

DSA, INC.
Round Lake, Illinois

DSA, Inc. began selling its rifles to the public in 1996. Based on actual blueprints of the famous FN/FAL rifle DSA rifles are made in the US. All SA58 rifles are fitted with fully adjustable gas system, Type I forged receiver, hand-lapped barrel, muzzle brake, elevation adjustable post front sight, windage adjustable rear peep sight with 5 settings from 200 to 600 meters, detachable metric magazine, adjustable sling and hard case.

SA58 24" Bull
Fitted with a 24" stainless steel barrel with .308 match chamber. Overall length is 44.5". Weight is approximately 11.5 lbs.

NIB	Exc.	V.G.	Good	Fair	Poor
1800	1400	1050	800	—	—

SA58 21" Bull
Same as the above but fitted with a 21" stainless steel barrel. Weight is about 11.1 lbs.

NIB	Exc.	V.G.	Good	Fair	Poor
1800	1400	1050	800	—	—

SA58 Medium Contour
This model is offered with a 21" barrel in either stainless steel or blued steel. Weight is about 10.5 lbs.

Medium contour stainless steel

Medium contour blued

NIB	Exc.	V.G.	Good	Fair	Poor
1600	1300	950	750	—	—

NOTE: Add $75 for stainless steel.

SA58 Carbine
This model is fitted with a 16.5" barrel. Barrel is cut for factory light bipod. Blued finish. Overall length is 38.25". Weight is about 9.2 lbs.

NIB	Exc.	V.G.	Good	Fair	Poor
1500	1200	900	700	—	—

SA58 Standard
This model has a 21" barrel cut for factory light bipod. Weight is about 9.5 lbs. Blued finish.

NIB	Exc.	V.G.	Good	Fair	Poor
1500	1200	900	700	—	—

DUBIEL ARMS CO.
Sherman, Texas

Established in 1975 by Joseph Dubiel and Dr. John Tyson. They are engaged in the manufacture of high quality, custom built, bolt action rifles. The rifles are constructed from patented Dubiel actions that feature a 5-lug bolt locking mechanism and a 36-degree bolt rotation. They are chambered for all calibers from .22-250 through .458 Winchester Magnum. Barrel lengths, weights, and stock styles are made to the customer's order. Douglas Premium barrels and Canjar triggers are used, and there are six basic stock designs available. The rifles are guaranteed to group in 1.5" at 100 yards with factory ammunition. The values listed are basic retail prices, and appraisal should be secured as options will drastically affect prices.

NIB	Exc.	V.G.	Good	Fair	Poor
2500	2000	1500	950	700	—

DUMOULIN
Herstal, Belgium
Importer - Midwest Gunsport
Zebulon, North Carolina

The guns produced by Ernest Dumoulin are essentially handmade to the customer's order. They are of the highest quality, both in materials and workmanship. There are many options available that have a tremendous impact on value fluctuations. The models and values listed here are base prices. If a sale or purchase is contemplated, individual competent appraisal should be secured.

SHOTGUNS
Europa Model
A side-x-side double barrel chambered for 12, 20, and 28 gauge and .410 bore. It is available in any length barrel and choke combination, with an Anson & Deeley boxlock action and automatic ejectors. One has the option of double or single selective triggers and a choice of six different moderate engraving patterns. The select walnut stock is oil-finished. This model was introduced in 1989.

Basic Values:

NIB	Exc.	V.G.	Good	Fair	Poor
3350	2750	1950	1250	800	—

Leige Model

A side-x-side double chambered for 12, 16, 20, and 28 gauge. It is similar to the Europa, with a greater degree of finish and more engraving. The walnut is of a higher grade. This model was introduced in 1986.

NIB	Exc.	V.G.	Good	Fair	Poor
5300	4200	2750	1500	950	—

Continental Model

A side-x-side chambered for 12, 20, and 28 gauge and .410. Barrel lengths and chokes are on a custom-order basis. This is a true sidelock action with automatic ejectors and choice of triggers. There are six different engraving patterns, and the stock is made of high grade, hand-checkered, oil-finished walnut. This model was introduced in 1989.

NIB	Exc.	V.G.	Good	Fair	Poor
7500	6000	4500	3000	1500	—

Etendart Model

A side-x-side chambered for 12, 20, and 28 gauge. This best grade side-x-side is built on a purely made-to-order basis. It is profusely engraved and uses exhibition grade walnut in its stock. There are 12 different engraving patterns from which to choose, and the cost is according to embellishments chosen. Values given here are for the basic model.

NIB	Exc.	V.G.	Good	Fair	Poor
14500	11000	8500	4000	3000	—

Superposed Express International

An Over/Under chambered for 20 gauge and is furnished with a set of rifle barrels in the customer's choice of seven calibers. The walnut is of a deluxe grade, and engraving is available at extra cost. This is a made-to-order gun, and the value here is for the most basic model. This gun was discontinued in 1985.

Exc.	V.G.	Good	Fair	Poor
2500	2000	1250	750	—

Boss Royal Model

The best grade Over/Under, chambered for 12, 20, and 28 gauge. It is a full sidelock gun that is made to the customer's specification using the finest materials and workmanship available. This model was introduced in 1987.

NIB	Exc.	V.G.	Good	Fair	Poor
18500	15000	12000	8000	4500	—

Eagle Model Combination Gun

This model has a rifle barrel or the shotgun barrel that is chambered for 12 or 20 gauge. The rifle calibers available are .22 Hornet, .222 Remington, .222 Remington Magnum, 6mm, .243, .25-06, .30-06, 6.5 x 57R, 7 x 57R, 8 x 57JRS, and 9.3 x 74R. The action is a boxlock with automatic ejectors, and the other specifications are on a custom-order basis. This model was introduced in 1989.

NIB	Exc.	V.G.	Good	Fair	Poor
2750	2250	1500	950	750	—

DOUBLE RIFLES

Europa I

A made-to-order, Over/Under, double barreled rifle available in the same calibers as the Eagle Combination gun. It has an Anson & Deeley boxlock and all other options to the customer's specifications.

NIB	Exc.	V.G.	Good	Fair	Poor
5000	4000	3000	2000	1000	—

Continental I Model

A more deluxe Over/Under rifle with a true sidelock action. The calibers are the same as the Europa. The specifications are to the customer's order with 12 engraving patterns to choose from at extra cost. This model was introduced in 1989.

NIB	Exc.	V.G.	Good	Fair	Poor
8500	6750	5500	4000	2000	—

Pionier Express Rifle

A side-x-side double rifle chambered for the .22 Hornet through the .600 Nitro Express. It has the Anson & Deeley boxlock action and is quite deluxe throughout. The specifications are to the customer's order, and there are basically 12 models available (P-1 through P-XII). The differences among these models are in the degree of ornamentation and quality of the walnut used for the stock. The prices of these models would have to be ascertained through appraisal, as a book of this nature could not possibly consider the variables that one could encounter with a gun of this type. Values range from approximately $8,000 to $12,000 for the basic models.

Aristocrat Model

A low-profile single shot chambered for all calibers up to .375 Holland & Holland. This is a deluxe, made-to-order rifle with exhibition-grade walnut and 12 engraving patterns available.

Exc.	V.G.	Good	Fair	Poor
9000	7000	5500	3000	—

BOLT ACTION RIFLES

Centurion Model

A custom-order rifle built on a Mauser or Sako action and chambered for all calibers from .270 to .458 Winchester Magnum. The barrel lengths available were 21.5", 24", and 25.5"; and there were many engraving options from which to choose. The stock is of deluxe French walnut, with rosewood forend tip and pistol gripcap. This rifle was discontinued in 1986.

NIB	Exc.	V.G.	Good	Fair	Poor
800	650	500	400	300	200

Centurion Classic

Similar to the Mauser-actioned Centurion chambered for the non-Magnum calibers only. The walnut used for the stock is a better grade.

NIB	Exc.	V.G.	Good	Fair	Poor
950	750	600	500	400	200

Diane

A more deluxe version of the Centurion Classic.

NIB	Exc.	V.G.	Good	Fair	Poor
1550	1250	900	650	500	300

Amazone

A 20" barreled, full-length stocked, upgraded version of the Diane.

NIB	Exc.	V.G.	Good	Fair	Poor
1750	1400	950	700	500	300

Bavaria Deluxe

Similar to the Centurion, with the same barrel lengths and calibers available. The engraving styles available are more deluxe. This model was discontinued in 1985.

NIB	Exc.	V.G.	Good	Fair	Poor
1900	1500	1000	800	500	300

Safari Model

Similar to the Bavaria Deluxe, but it is chambered for the heavy Magnum calibers only.

NIB	Exc.	V.G.	Good	Fair	Poor
2400	1900	1450	900	500	300

Safari Sportsman

Built on a Magnum Mauser action and is chambered for the .375 Holland & Holland, .404 Jeffreys, .416 Rigby, and the .505 Gibbs. This is a true big game rifle that was made available in 1986.

NIB	Exc.	V.G.	Good	Fair	Poor
4000	3250	2000	1250	900	—

African Pro

A more deluxe version of the Safari Sportsman, with a folding leaf rear sight, hooded front sight, and an ebony or buffalo horn forend tip.

NIB	Exc.	V.G.	Good	Fair	Poor
4800	3750	2500	1500	1000	—

NOTE: Again we feel it is important to note that all values furnished in this section are estimates based on the most basic model in each designation. There are many options that will radically affect values, and a competent appraisal should be secured if a sale or purchase is contemplated.

DURLOV
Czech Republic

This company was part of the national co-operative under communist rule when the Czech Republic was part of Czechoslovakia. The company was formed in 1948. The company specialized in low-cost but well made rimfire target pistols.

Durlov Model 70 Standard

This model is a bolt action single shot pistol chambered for the .22 long rifle. A knob at the rear of the frame opened the bolt. When the bolt is closed the firing pin is cocked. The barrel is 9.75" long with an adjustable front sight for windage. The rear sight is adjustable for elevation. Wooden wraparound grips with thumb rest are standard. Weighs about 44 oz.

Exc.	V.G.	Good	Fair	Poor
250	200	175	100	75

Durlov Model 70 Special

Same as above but with the addition of a set trigger.

Exc.	V.G.	Good	Fair	Poor
300	250	200	150	100

Durlov Model 75

This model features a set trigger, better sights, and grip. The rear sight is fully adjustable.

Exc.	V.G.	Good	Fair	Poor
350	300	250	200	150

Pav

This target pistol was introduced between World War I and World War II. It is an inexpensive pistol with a fixed front sight and a notch for the rear sight. Like the other models above it is also a single shot chambered for the .22 long rifle cartridge. The barrel is 10.25" and weighs about 35 oz.

Courtesy Orvel Reichert

Exc.	V.G.	Good	Fair	Poor
175	150	100	75	50

DUSEK, F.
Opocno, Czech Republic

Dusek commenced business in the mid-1920s and continued to make firearms through WWII. They manufactured pistols for Nazi Germany under the contract code "aek." After the war the communists took over, and Dusek's designs were relegated to the CZ factory.

Duo

Introduced in 1926, this 6.35mm pistol is based on the 1906 Browning design. It has a 2.25" barrel and 6-shot detachable magazine. The Duo was successful from a commercial standpoint and was exported throughout the world. During WWII the slide markings were in German; and the name "Eblen", Dusek's German sales agent, may sometimes be found on the slide. The Duo may also be found marked Ideal, Jaga, and Singer.

Nazi-marked examples will bring a 25% premium.

Exc.	V.G.	Good	Fair	Poor
250	200	150	100	80

Perla

This 6.35mm pistol has a fixed barrel and open-topped slide. It resembles a Walther design and is striker-fired. The slide is marked "Automat Pistole Perla 6.35mm"; the grips, "Perla 6.35." Dusek made this model from the early 1930s until WWII.

Exc.	V.G.	Good	Fair	Poor
250	200	150	100	80

E

E.M.F. CO., INC.
Santa Ana, California
SEE—Uberti, Aldo

An importer and a distributor of quality Italian-made reproduction firearms. Its offerings are listed in the section dealing with Aldo Uberti firearms. Included below are new products for this company as of 1997.

Hartford Bisley

This single action revolver is fitted with a Colt Bisley grip. Chambered for .45 Long Colt as well as .32-20, .357 Magnum, .38-40, and .44-40 calibers. Barrel lengths are 4-3/4", 5-1/2", and 7-1/2". Plain walnut grips.

NIB	Exc.	V.G.	Good	Fair	Poor
450	350	—	—	—	—

Hartford Express

A single Colt SAA frame and barrel with a Colt Lightning style grip. Chambered for .45 Long Colt in 4-3/4", 5-1/2", or 7-1/2" barrel lengths.

NIB	Exc.	V.G.	Good	Fair	Poor
450	350	—	—	—	—

Hartford Pinkerton

This model features a 4" barrel with ejector and a bird's head grip. Chambered for 45 Long Colt, .32-20, .357 Magnum, .38-40, .44-40, and .44 Special.

NIB	Exc.	V.G.	Good	Fair	Poor
450	350	—	—	—	—

EAGLE ARMS CO.
New Haven, Connecticut
SEE—Plant Manufacturing Co.

EAGLE ARMS
Division of Armalite
Geneseo, Illinois

PRE-BAN MODELS

Golden Eagle

This model is identical in design to the AR-15. Fitted with a 20" stainless steel extra heavy barrel with National Match sights and two stage trigger. Weight is about 9.4 lbs.

NIB	Exc.	V.G.	Good	Fair	Poor
1500	1200	850	—	—	—

HBAR

Similar to the above model but with a heavy 20" barrel. Weight is approximately 8 lbs.

NIB	Exc.	V.G.	Good	Fair	Poor
1100	800	600	—	—	—

SPR

This is similar to the above model with the exception of a detachable carry handle. Weight is about 7.6 lbs.

NIB	Exc.	V.G.	Good	Fair	Poor
1150	850	650	—	—	—

M4C Carbine

This model features a 16" barrel with a 4.33" flash suppressor. Retractable stock. Weight is approximately 6.2 lbs.

NIB	Exc.	V.G.	Good	Fair	Poor
1100	800	600	—	—	—

M4A1C Carbine
Similar to the above model but with detachable carry handle. Weight is about 6 lbs.

NIB	Exc.	V.G.	Good	Fair	Poor
1150	800	600	—	—	—

POST-BAN MODEL
Golden Eagle
This model features a 20" stainless steel extra heavy barrel with two stage trigger. Weight is about 9.2 lbs.

NIB	Exc.	V.G.	Good	Fair	Poor
1200	900	700	—	—	—

ECHAVE & ARIZMENDI
Eibar, Spain

Founded in 1911, this company produced the usual poor quality, early Spanish semiautomatic pistols. They did improve their quality later on and were permitted to return to gun manufacturing after the Spanish civil war. They were one of the few pistol makers to survive this period. They imported many models, and their products are not particularly of interest to collectors.

Basque, Echasa or Dickson Special Agent
These two pistols are the same under different names. They are chambered for 7.65mm and are double action, blowback operated, semiautomatic copies of the Walther PP. The disassembly methods and the quality are the two differences. The finish is blued, and the grips are checkered wood. The slides are marked either "Basque" or "Echasa" and "Made in Spain Cal. .3 2".

Exc.	V.G.	Good	Fair	Poor
200	150	125	100	75

Bronco
A copy of the Browning 1906 chambered for 7.65mm and 6.35mm. It has a grip safety and is marked "1918 Model Automatic Pistol Bronco Patent No. 66130". This model was manufactured at the end of WWI.

Exc.	V.G.	Good	Fair	Poor
175	125	100	75	50

Echasa
Similar to the 6.35mm Bronco, without a grip safety. It is marked "Model 1916".

Exc.	V.G.	Good	Fair	Poor
175	125	100	75	50

Fast
Similar to the Echasa except that it is chambered for the .22 l.r. and the 9mm short, as well as the 7.65mm and the 6.35mm. There is one version that is chrome-plated with white plastic grips.

Exc.	V.G.	Good	Fair	Poor
200	150	125	100	75

Lightning
A renamed version of the Bronco in 6.35mm.

Exc.	V.G.	Good	Fair	Poor
175	125	100	75	50

Lur Panzer
A copy of the Luger toggle-lock action, chambered for .22 rimfire. This is an almost exact copy except for a different trigger assembly and a less robust mainspring. It is marked "Lur Cal.22 LR Made in Spain." The plastic grips have "Panzer" molded into them.

Exc.	V.G.	Good	Fair	Poor
250	200	150	125	100

Pathfinder
The 6.35mm Bronco with another name for export purposes.

Exc.	V.G.	Good	Fair	Poor
175	125	100	75	50

Protector
Similar to the Echasa, chambered for 6.35mm. There is a slight difference in the triggerguard and the magazine catch. The grips have molded flowers and the caliber in a circle.

Exc.	V.G.	Good	Fair	Poor
175	125	100	75	50

Selecta
Similar to the Protector, chambered for 7.65mm.

Exc.	V.G.	Good	Fair	Poor
175	125	100	75	50

ECHEVERRIA, STAR-BONIFACIO SA
Eibar, Spain

An old-line Spanish company that survived the Spanish civil war. It was founded in 1908 by Jean Echeverria, but the early records of the company were lost during the civil war. The early pistols the company produced were patterned after the Mannlicher designs, and the trade name Star was the closest thing to Steyr that could be used. After the close of WWI, the company began production of the open-topped slide Star for which they have become known. They also produced a large 1911-type pistol that was successful. During the civil war, the plant was damaged and the company records destroyed; but after the cessation of hostilities, they were one of only three gun companies that were allowed to remain in business. They survive to this day and are known for the manufacture of quality firearms.

Star Model 1908
The first pistol produced under the Star banner. It is a Mannlicher copy that is chambered for 6.35mm. It has a 3" fixed barrel and an open-topped slide. The detachable magazine holds 8 shots. The finish is blued, and the grips are checkered plastic. The slide is marked "Automatic Pistol Star Patent."

Exc.	V.G.	Good	Fair	Poor
300	250	200	150	100

Star Model 1914
Similar to the Model 1908, with a 5" barrel and larger grips that have the Star name molded into them. This model was the first to have the six-pointed star surrounded by rays of light (that became the Star trademark) stamped on its slide.

Exc.	V.G.	Good	Fair	Poor
300	250	200	150	100

Star Model 1919
Also a copy of a Mannlicher design and differs from its predecessors chiefly in the way the pistol is disassembled. This model has a spring catch at the top of the triggerguard. This model also has a small spur on the hammer, and the magazine release was relocated to a button behind the triggerguard instead of a catch at the bottom of the butt. This model was chambered for 6.35mm, 7.65mm and 9mm short, with various barrel lengths offered. The maker's name, as well as the Star trademark, is stamped into the slide. This model was produced until 1929.

Exc.	V.G.	Good	Fair	Poor
300	250	200	150	100

Modelo Militar
Represents the first pistol Star produced that was not a Mannlicher design copy. This model was copied from the Colt 1911. It was chambered initially for the 9mm Largo in hopes of securing a military contract. When this contract was awarded to Astra, Star chambered the Model 1919 for the .38 Super and the .45 ACP and put it on the commercial market. This model is like the Colt 1911—it has a Browning-type swinging

link and the same type of lock up. However there is no grip safety, and the thumb safety functions differently. This model was produced until 1924.

Exc.	V.G.	Good	Fair	Poor
300	250	200	175	125

Star Model A

A modification of the Model 1919, chambered for the 7.63 Mauser, 9mm Largo, and the .45 ACP cartridge. The slide is similar in appearance to the 1911 Colt, and the spur hammer has a small hole in it. Early models had no grip safety, but later production added this feature. Some models are slotted for addition of a shoulder stock.

Exc.	V.G.	Good	Fair	Poor
375	275	175	150	100

Star Model B

Similar to the Model A except that it is almost an exact copy of the Colt 1911. It is chambered for 9mm Parabellum and has a spur hammer with no hole. This model was introduced in 1928.

Courtesy Orvel Reichert

Exc.	V.G.	Good	Fair	Poor
350	250	200	175	125

Star Model C

The Model B chambered for the 9mm Browning long cartridge. It was manufactured in the 1920s.

Exc.	V.G.	Good	Fair	Poor
250	175	150	125	90

Star Model CO

A pocket pistol similar to the early open-topped Star pistols. It is chambered for the 6.35mm cartridge, and the finish is blued with checkered plastic grips that bear the Star name and logo. This model was manufactured between 1930 and 1957.

Exc.	V.G.	Good	Fair	Poor
250	150	125	100	75

Star Model D

A medium-sized pistol that is similar in appearance to a smaller Model A. It is chambered for the 9mm short cartridge and was called the "Police and Pocket Model" after it was adopted by the Spanish police. It was manufactured between 1930 and 1941.

Exc.	V.G.	Good	Fair	Poor
275	175	150	110	80

Star Model E

A pocket pistol chambered for the 6.35mm cartridge. It has a 2.5" barrel and an external hammer. The detachable magazine holds 5 rounds, and the finish is blued with checkered plastic grips. This model was manufactured between 1932 and 1941.

Exc.	V.G.	Good	Fair	Poor
225	175	150	110	80

Star Model F

The first of the .22 caliber Star pistols. It has a 4" barrel, a 10-shot magazine, and fixed sights. The finish is blued, and the plastic grips are checkered. This model was manufactured between 1942 and 1967.

Exc.	V.G.	Good	Fair	Poor
225	175	125	100	75

Star Model F Target

Similar to the Model F, with a 6" barrel.

Exc.	V.G.	Good	Fair	Poor
250	200	150	125	100

Star Model F Sport

Has a 5" barrel and was also manufactured between 1962 and 1967.

Exc.	V.G.	Good	Fair	Poor
225	175	150	125	100

Star Model F Olympic

Has a 6" barrel and adjustable sights. It is furnished with a muzzle brake and barrel weights. It was manufactured between 1942 and 1967.

Exc.	V.G.	Good	Fair	Poor
325	225	175	150	125

Star Model F Olympic Rapid Fire

Similar to the Olympic but is chambered for .22 short only.

Exc.	V.G.	Good	Fair	Poor
325	225	175	150	125

Star Model FR

Has an adjustable sight and a slide stop. The 4" barrel is heavier, with flattened sides. It was manufactured between 1967 and 1972.

Exc.	V.G.	Good	Fair	Poor
225	175	145	125	100

Star Model FRS

Similar to the Model FR, with a 6" barrel. It is also available chrome-plated with white checkered plastic grips. It was introduced in 1967 and is still in production.

Exc.	V.G.	Good	Fair	Poor
225	175	145	125	100

Star Model FM

A heavier-framed version of the Model FRS. It has a 4.5" barrel and is available in blue or chrome-plated. It was introduced in 1972 and is still made.

Exc.	V.G.	Good	Fair	Poor
225	175	145	125	100

Star Model H

Similar to the old Model CO—only larger in size. It is chambered for the 7.65mm cartridge and was manufactured between 1932 and 1941.

Exc.	V.G.	Good	Fair	Poor
225	175	150	125	100

Star Model HK

A pocket-sized version of the Model F chambered for .22 short. It has a 2.5" barrel and is quite scarce on today's market.

Exc.	V.G.	Good	Fair	Poor
250	200	150	125	100

Star Model HN

Simply the Model H chambered for the 9mm short cartridge. It was manufactured and discontinued at the same time as the Model H was.

Exc.	V.G.	Good	Fair	Poor
250	200	150	125	100

Star Model I

An improved version of the Model H with a 4" barrel and a re-contoured grip. It was chambered for 7.65mm and was produced until 1941. After the war it was resumed and survived until the mid-1950s, when it was replaced by the modernized Model IR that would be valued approximately the same.

Exc.	V.G.	Good	Fair	Poor
200	150	125	100	75

Star Model M

Similar to the Model B, chambered for the .38 Auto cartridge.

Exc.	V.G.	Good	Fair	Poor
275	225	175	125	100

Star Model P

The postwar version of the Model B, fitted with a 5" barrel and chambered for the .45 ACP cartridge. Checkered walnut grips and blued finish.

Exc.	V.G.	Good	Fair	Poor
350	300	225	175	125

Star Model CU "Starlet"

Similar to the Model CO, with an alloy frame that was anodized in black, blue, gray, green, or gold. It has a steel slide that is blued or chrome-plated. It has checkered, white plastic grips and is chambered for the .25 ACP cartridge. It has a 2.5" barrel, fixed sights, and a 5-shot magazine. This model was introduced in 1975 and was not imported after 1986.

Exc.	V.G.	Good	Fair	Poor
200	150	125	100	75

Star Model 1941 S

Add 100% to prices listed below for pistols issued to Spanish Air Force with box, cleaning rod, instruction sheet, and 2 numbered magazines.

Courtesy Richard M. Kumor Sr.

Exc.	V.G.	Good	Fair	Poor
200	175	150	100	75

Star Model BKS "Starlight"

The smallest locked-breech automatic chambered for the 9mm cartridge at the time. It has an alloy frame and a 4.25" barrel. It is similar in appearance to a scaled-down Colt 1911 without a grip safety. It has an 8-shot magazine and is either blued or chrome-plated, with checkered plastic grips. This model was manufactured between 1970 and 1981.

Exc.	V.G.	Good	Fair	Poor
275	225	200	150	125

Star Model PD

Chambered for the .45 ACP cartridge and has a 4" barrel. It has an alloy frame and a 6-shot magazine and adjustable sights and is blued with checkered walnut grips. It was introduced in 1975.

NIB	Exc.	V.G.	Good	Fair	Poor
400	325	275	225	175	125

Star Model BM

A steel-framed 9mm that is styled after the Colt 1911. It has an 8-shot magazine and a 4" barrel. It is available either blued or chrome-plated.

NIB	Exc.	V.G.	Good	Fair	Poor
350	300	250	200	150	125

Star Model BKM

Similar to the BM, with an alloy frame.

NIB	Exc.	V.G.	Good	Fair	Poor
375	325	275	225	175	125

Star Model 28

The first of Star's Super 9s. It is a double action semiautomatic chambered for the 9mm Parabellum cartridge. It has a 4.25" barrel and a steel frame. The magazine holds 15 shots. The construction of this pistol was totally modular, and it has no screws at all in its design. It is blued with checkered synthetic grips and was manufactured in 1983 and 1984.

NIB	Exc.	V.G.	Good	Fair	Poor
400	300	250	200	150	100

Star Model 30M

An improved version of the Model 28, that is quite similar in appearance. It was introduced in 1985.

NIB	Exc.	V.G.	Good	Fair	Poor
450	350	300	250	200	125

Star Model 30/PK

Similar to the Models 28 and 30M, with a lightweight alloy frame.

NIB	Exc.	V.G.	Good	Fair	Poor
450	350	300	250	200	125

ECHEVERRIA
(Star)

Megastar

This is a double action semiautomatic pistol chambered for the 10mm or .45 ACP cartridge. It features a three position ambidextrous selective decocking lever, rubber grips, combat style triggerguard, slotted hammer, and checkered mainspring housing. Barrel length is 4.6" and the magazine capacity is 12 rounds. Available in either blue or starvel (brushed chrome). The pistol weighs 47.6 oz.

NIB	Exc.	V.G.	Good	Fair	Poor
400	300	250	200	150	100

Firestar Plus

This is a lightweight version of the Firestar Series with the addition of a double column magazine. Offered in the 9mm caliber in either blue or Starvel finish this pistol has a magazine capacity of 10 rounds and weighs 24 oz. Introduced in 1992.

NIB	Exc.	Good	Good	Fair	Poor
450	350	300	250	175	125

Starfire Model 31P

This model evolved from the Models 28 and 30. It is chambered for either the 9mm Parabellum or .40 S&W. The trigger action is double action/single action. Barrel length is 3.9". It is fitted with a two position safety/decocking lever. The magazine capacity for the 9mm is 15 rounds while the .40 S&W holds 11 rounds. The pistol weighs 39 oz.

NIB	Exc.	V.G.	Good	Fair	Poor
425	350	300	250	200	100

NIB	Exc.	V.G.	Good	Fair	Poor
500	450	350	250	200	100

Firestar-M/43, M/40, and M45

This is a compact large caliber semiautomatic pistol offered in 9mm, the M43, .40 S&W, the M40, and the .45 ACP, the M45. It features an ambidextrous safety, steel frame and slide, checkered rubber grips. The barrel is 3.4" on the M43 and M40 and 3.6" on the M45. Choice of finish is blue or starvel (brushed chrome). A finger rest magazine is optional. Weight for the M43 and M40 is 30 oz. while the M56 weighs 35 oz. Introduced in 1990.

Starfire Model 31PK

Similar to the Model 31P but built on an alloy frame. Chambered for 9mm only with a 15-round magazine capacity. Weight is 30 oz.

NIB	Exc.	V.G.	Good	Fair	Poor
400	325	275	225	200	100

Ultrastar

Introduced in 1994 this compact 9mm or .40 S&W semiautomatic pistol with a polymer frame features a 3.57" barrel, a 9-round magazine, a blued finish and an overall length of 7". It weighs about 26 oz. It has a double action operating system, a windage adjustable rear sight, and an ambidextrous two-position safety.

NIB	Exc.	V.G.	Good	Fair	Poor
475	375	325	275	200	100

ECLIPSE
Pittsburgh, Pennsylvania
Enterprise Gun Works

Single Shot Derringer

This pocket pistol was made by the firm of James Bown & Son, doing business as the Enterprise Gun Works. It is chambered for .22 or .32-caliber rimfire cartridges. A few in .25 rimfire have been noted and would add approximately 25% to the values listed. The barrel is 2.5" in length and is part-round/part-octagonal. It pivots sideways for loading. It has a spur trigger and a bird's head grip. The barrel is stamped "Eclipse." It is made of nickel-plated iron, with walnut grips. There were approximately 10,000 manufactured between 1870 and 1890.

Exc.	V.G.	Good	Fair	Poor
—	600	250	100	75

84 GUN CO.
Eighty Four, Pennsylvania

In business for a brief time in the early 1970s. They produced three basic bolt action rifles—each in four grades that differ in amounts of embellishment and grades of wood. There is little known about this company and its products. An accurate appraisal with hands-on would be the only proper way to place a value on these rifles as there are not enough traded in to establish correct values in a book of this nature. The basic models are as follows:

Classic Rifle
Grade 1-Grade 4 available
450—1600

Lobo Rifle
Grade 1-Grade 4 available
425—2500

Pennsylvania Rifle
Grade 1-Grade 4 available
425—2500

EL DORADO ARMS
SEE United Sporting Arms, Inc.

ELGIN CUTLASS
Springfield, Massachusetts

Manufactured by two companies—C.B. Allen of Springfield, Massachusetts, and Morill, Mosman and Blair of Amherst, Massachusetts. It is a unique pistol that has an integral knife attachment affixed to the gun barrel. It was designed and patented by George Elgin and simultaneously produced by the two companies. The inspiration for this weapon was supposedly Jim Bowie, who at that time had made a name as a knife fighter with his large "Bowie" knife. The blades for these pistols were supplied by N.P. Ames of the famed Ames Sword Co. These pistols are much sought after, and one must exercise caution as fraudulent examples have been noted.

C. B. Allen-Made Pistols
U.S. Navy Elgin Cutlass Pistol

Chambered for .54 caliber percussion and has a 5" octagonal smooth-bore barrel. The Bowie-style blade is 11" long by 2" wide and is forged together with the triggerguard and the knuckle guard that protects the grip. The handle is walnut. This pistol was issued to the U.S. Navy's Wilkes-South Sea Exploration Expedition, and the markings are "C.B. Allen / Springfield / Mass." "Elgin's Patent" and the letters "CB", "CBA" along with the date 1837. If the sheath that was issued with this knife pistol is included and in sound condition, it would add approximately $700 to the value. There were 150 manufactured for the U.S. Navy in 1838.

Exc.	V.G.	Good	Fair	Poor
—	10000	8000	6500	4750

Civilian Model

Chambered for .35 or .41 caliber percussion and has a 4" octagonal barrel with a 7.5"-10" knife blade. It has a round triggerguard but does not have the knuckle bow across the grip, as found on the military model. They are marked "C.B. Allen Springfield, Mass." Blades marked "N.P. Ames" have been noted. There were approximately 100 manufactured in 1837.

Exc.	V.G.	Good	Fair	Poor
—	9000	6000	3250	2750

Morill, Mosman and Blair-Made Pistols
Small Model

The main difference in the pistols of the two makers is that this model has a round barrel and a square-back triggerguard that comes to a point at the rear. This version is chambered for .32 caliber percussion and has a 2.75" barrel. The knife blade is 7.5" in length and is screwed to the frame. This model is unmarked except for a serial number. The number produced is unknown, and they were manufactured in 1837.

Exc.	V.G.	Good	Fair	Poor
—	9000	6000	3250	2750

Large Model

Chambered for .36 caliber percussion and has a 4" round barrel and a 9" knife blade. The pistol is usually marked "Cast Steel" and serial numbered. The blade is etched with an American eagle, stars, and an urn with flowers. "Elgin Patent" is etched in the center. This model was also manufactured in 1837.

Courtesy Milwaukee Public Museum, Milwaukee, Wisconsin

Exc.	V.G.	Good	Fair	Poor
—	10000	7000	3500	3000

ELLS, JOSIAH
Pittsburgh, Pennsylvania

Pocket Revolver

Three distinct variations of this percussion revolver. They are chambered for .28 and .31 caliber and have 6-shot unfluted cylinders. They have been noted with 2.5", 3", and 3.75" octagonal barrels.

Model 1

The first model has an open-topped frame and is chambered for .28 caliber. The cylinder holds 5 or 6 shots, and the hammer is of the bar type. It was offered with a 2.5" or 3" barrel. The markings are "J. Ells; Patent; 1854." There were approximately 625 manufactured between 1857 and 1859.

Courtesy Milwaukee Public Museum, Milwaukee, Wisconsin

Exc.	V.G.	Good	Fair	Poor
—	1200	500	275	200

Model 2

The second model is similar to the first, with a solid-topped frame. They have 5-shot cylinders and 3.75" long barrels. There were approximately 550 manufactured.

Courtesy Milwaukee Public Museum, Milwaukee, Wisconsin

Exc.	V.G.	Good	Fair	Poor
—	1500	800	350	200

Model 3

The third model is radically different from its forerunners. It has a closed-top frame and a conventional spur-type hammer that strikes from the right side. It functions either as a double- or single action. It is chambered for .28 caliber and has a 5-shot cylinder and a 3.75" barrel. There were only about 200 manufactured between 1857 and 1859.

Exc.	V.G.	Good	Fair	Poor
—	1500	800	350	200

ENDERS, CARL
Suhl, Germany

Side-by-Side Shotgun

Precussion damascus double barrel side-by-side in 12 gauge. Ornate checkering with cheekpiece and engraved metal work. Made circa 1850-1860.

Courtesy Jim Cate

Exc.	V.G.	Good	Fair	Poor
—	750	500	—	—

ENFIELD ROYAL SMALL ARMS FACTORY
Middlesex, England

NOTE: For technical details, descriptions, photos, and prices see the *Standard Catalog of Military Firearms* under Great Britian, Handguns and Rifles.

ENFIELD AMERICAN, INC.
Atlanta, Georgia

MP-45

A blowback-operated, semiautomatic assault pistol chambered for the .45 ACP cartridge. It was offered with a barrel length of 4.5" through 18.5". The long barrel features a shroud. The finish is parkerized, and there were four different magazines available in 10, 20, 30, and 50-round capacities. This firearm was manufactured in 1985 only.

Exc.	V.G.	Good	Fair	Poor
300	275	225	175	125

ENGLISH MILITARY FIREARMS
Enfield, England

Until the establishment of the Royal Armory at Enfield in 1816, the government of England relied solely upon the contract system to obtain small arms for its naval and military forces. Even after the Enfield Armory began is first major production in 1823, the contractors continued to dominate the production of arms for the military. These contractors were concentrated in two major cities, Birmingham and London. Although a number of makers from Birmingham were capable of manufacturing arms, "lock, stock, and barrel," and of assembling them, most of the makers of that city specialized in the making of specific parts, which could be assembled into complete arms on the "factory system" then prevalent in Liege. When the English War Department was the purchaser, the parts were usually delivered to the Tower of London for assembly. Most military arms made in Birmingham accordingly are seldom marked with a single maker's name. Rather they bear the English crown and the name "TOWER" on the lock. Those barrels that passed proof at Birmingham after 1813 were marked with the view and proofmarks derived from Ketland's only proofmarks; these consisted of a pair of crowned, crossed scepters, one pair of which had the letter "V" in the lower quarter and the other of which had the letters "B," "C," and "P" respectively in the left, right, and lower quarters. In contrast, the arms manufactured at London were almost always completed by their manufacturers, and bear their names usually upon the lockplates and barrels. The London gunmakers also marked their barrels with a pair of proofmarks, consisting of a crown over a "V" and a crown over an intertwined "G" and "P." Prominent martial arms makers in the London trade through the 1860s included, "BOND," "BARNETT," "BLISSETT," "GREENER," "HOLLIS & SONS," "LONDON ARMORY CO," "KERR," "PARKER, FIELD & SONS," "PRITCHETT," "POTTS & HUNT," "ROBERT WHEELER," "WILSON & CO.," and "YEOMANS." (It should be noted that most of these London makers also manufactured sporting and other trade arms, which will bear similar marks.) During the period of transition from the contract system to the reliance upon the works at Enfield (roughly 1816 through 1867), the arms themselves underwent major transitions, first from flintlock to percussion ignition systems and then from smoothbore to rifled bore, first in large and then in small bore sizes. The major infantry types include:

New Land Pattern Musket
Overall length 58-1/2"; barrel length 42"; caliber .75. The mainstay of the British Army during the Napoleonic Wars, this flintlock arm continued, primarily, in service until 1838, with major quantities (5,000 from each) being ordered from Enfield and from the contractors as late as 1823.

Exc.	V.G.	Good	Fair	Poor
—	2500	1500	850	600

Pattern of 1839 (P1839) Musket
Overall length 55"; barrel length 39"; caliber .76. In 1838 the British War Department contracted for the parts for 30,000 new flintlock arms. However, before these arms could be assembled, the War Department adopted the percussion system of ignition and ordered that these arms be made as percussion. Obsolete by 1861, large numbers were purchased by the Southern Confederacy and imported for use in the American Civil War. Arms with firm evidence of Confederate military usage increases the value of the arm considerably.

Exc.	V.G.	Good	Fair	Poor
—	1000	500	450	350

Pattern of 1842 (P1842) Musket (and Rifled Musket)
Overall length 55"; barrel length 39-1/4"; caliber .75. The first English-made as percussion musket to be issued to the Line Regiments of the British Army, continued in production through the Crimean War. The final production (1851-1855) of 26,400 were made with rifled barrel and a long range rear sight soldered to the barrel, similar in configuration to that of the P1851 rifle-musket. These rifled versions of the P1842 musket will command a premium.

Courtesy Milwaukee Public Museum, Milwaukee, Wisconsin

Exc.	V.G.	Good	Fair	Poor
—	1000	650	450	350

"Brunswick" Rifles (first model or P1837) and (second model or P1845)
Overall length 46-1/2" (Pl837), 45-3/4" (Pl845); barrel length 33" (Pl837), 30" (Pl845); caliber .704. The "Brunswick" rifle differed from its predecessors (the "Baker rifle") adopted for the English "Rifle Brigade" in having a large bore cut with only two spiraling grooves. These grooves engaged a specially cast ball having a raised belt circumventing it. The first model of the "Brunswick rifle" adopted in 1837 is primarily distinguished by having a "backaction" percussion lock, which continued in production until 1844 despite having been officially changed to the standard "barlock" in 1841. Those made after 1844 bear the standard percussion lock. The value of these rifles is enhanced by virtue of the importation of at least 2,000 (probably first model variants) into the Southern Confederacy during the American Civil War. (It should be noted that Russia also adopted a variant of the "Brunswick" style rifle, having them made in Liege, Belgium and so marked with Liege proofmarks. These rifles are distinguished by having a distinctive rear sight with an adjustable arcing ladder.)

Courtesy Milwaukee Public Museum, Milwaukee, Wisconsin

Exc.	V.G.	Good	Fair	Poor
—	1500	900	700	450

Pattern of 1851 (P1851) Rifle-Musket
Overall length 55"; barrel length 39"; caliber .702. With the success of the "Minie ball" projectile in France, England in 1851 adopted its first production rifle musket. Externally resembling the P1842 musket, the P1851 is distinguished by the long range rear sight soldered to the barrel and its smaller caliber (.70) rifled bore. Approximately 35,000 were manufactured until 1855, with a substantial number being imported to the United States during the early years of the American Civil War.

Courtesy Milwaukee Public Museum, Milwaukee, Wisconsin

Exc.	V.G.	Good	Fair	Poor
—	1750	1000	700	450

Pattern of 1853 (P1853) Rifle Musket (first through fourth types)
Overall length 55" (54" on fourth type); barrel length 39"; caliber .577. The P1853 rifle musket underwent several changes during the span of its production. The earliest type (first model) was made with clamping bands. Due to problems with the bands slipping, the bands were modified in late 1855 to solid, spring fastened (second model), the upper wider than the other two. However, in 1858 the government reverted to clamping bands continuing production in this style through 1863. Those made at Enfield after 1859 were one inch shorter in the butt stock, but the contractors continued to deliver them in 55-inch length well into the 1860s. The fourth model is distinguished by the "Baddeley patent" clamping barrel bands, wherein the screwheads are recessed into the bands. The third model saw the greatest production, with more than 600,000 being imported into the north and about 300,000 into the south during the American Civil War. P1853 rifle muskets with early Confederate importation marks on the stock and butt plate will command a premium if authentic.

Courtesy Milwaukee Public Museum, Milwaukee, Wisconsin

Exc.	V.G.	Good	Fair	Poor
—	1500	650	450	350

American Made Copies of the English P1853 Rifle Musket

Three firms during the period from 1855 through 1862 produced copies of the P1853 rifle musket, Robbins & Lawrence of Windsor, Vermont; Orison Blunt of New York City; and John Moore of New York City. All three types command a premium over the standard imported muskets and may be distinguished as follows:

Robbins & Lawrence P1853 Rifle Muskets

During the Crimean War, Robbins & Lawrence received a contract for 25,000 P1853 rifle muskets of the second model. Due to production delays, the company had delivered only 10,400 when the war ended. Due to the penalties for non-deliveries, Robbins & Lawrence declared bankruptcy. An additional 5,600 arms were made on the firms machinery while in receivership by the "Vermont Arms Co." before the machinery was sold to Sharps and Eli Whitney, Jr. The Robbins & Lawrence-made P1853 rifle muskets are distinguished by the lock marking "WINDSOR" beneath the date (such as "1856") on the forward part of the lock and by non-English proofmarks on the barrel. Many of these arms saw service in the American Civil War, with Alabama obtaining several hundred in 1861. Arms with confirmed southern usage will bring substantial premiums.

Exc.	V.G.	Good	Fair	Poor
—	2500	1300	850	600

Orison Blunt P1853 Rifle Muskets

At the beginning of the Civil War, Orison Blunt of New York City attempted to produce a copy of the P1853 rifle musket but with a 40-inch barrel and in .58 caliber. After making several hundred, his proposed contract with the U.S. War Department was declined. Nevertheless, in mid-1862, it is thought that about 1,000 of his rifle muskets were purchased by the U.S. government and sent to Illinois to arm volunteers. Blunt "Enfields" are distinguished by two distinct markings. While most lockplates are totally unmarked, a few are known with the mark "UNION" on the forward part of the lockplate and an eagle impressed into the rounded tail. More importantly, Blunt barrels bear an oval with the letters "DP/B" near the breech. (Note: Not all P1853 rifle muskets with 40-inch barrels were made by Blunt; Birmingham and Liege contractors supplied the Spanish government with a 40-inch barrel copy of the P1853 English rifle musket as well, and some of these were diverted to the American market during the Civil War. These are usually distinguished by the letter "C" in a diamond near the breech of the barrel surrounded by proofmarks.)

Courtesy Milwaukee Public Museum, Milwaukee, Wisconsin

Exc.	V.G.	Good	Fair	Poor
—	1750	1000	750	475

John P. Moore P1853 Rifle Muskets

During the American Civil War arms merchant John P. Moore of New York City received a contract for the delivery of 20,000 P1853 rifle muskets, supposedly to be made in the United States. In fact, most of his contract was made in Birmingham, England, with only 1,080 completely made in the United States. These are distinguished by having an unusual script proofmark on the barrel near the breech instead of the standard Birmingham crossed scepters. These script letters have been interpreted as either "V LB" or "EP I" depending on how they are read. All of Moore's P1853 deliveries bear a distinctive lock marking, consisting of the date forward of the hammer ("1861", "1862," or "1863") and an eagle perched on a shield on the tail. The shield bears the letter "M" in its chief. Moore also delivered 999 short rifles (33" barrels) with the same lock markings. Likewise, all of the barrels on the Moore P1853 rifle musket contract are serially numbered, either on the forward side near the muzzle or on the side of the bayonet lug/front sight. Because the Moore rifles have been misidentified as a product of a North Carolina arms merchant, they tend to command higher prices than are warranted by their numbers.

Exc.	V.G.	Good	Fair	Poor
—	1500	850	600	450

"Brazilian Naval Rifle"

Overall length 48"; barrel length 32"; caliber .58. Markings: on lockplate forward of hammer "D (anchor) C"; the same mark stamped in the wood and metal in various places on the rifle; on barrel, same mark and Liege proofmarks (an oval encompassing the letters E/LG/(star). Although neither made for the English government nor in England, this rifle copies so many features of the English P1856 series rifles (see next page) as to be easily mistaken for it. The major differences consist of a longer (3-3/8") sight base than the English rifles and a front band/nosecap that also serves as the ramrod funnel. These Liege-made rifles were supposedly made for the Brazilian government, but at the beginning of the American Civil War they were diverted to the United States, about 10,000 being imported. To show their new ownership, a brass shield bearing the U.S. coat of arms was screwed into the wrist of the stock.

Courtesy Milwaukee Public Museum, Milwaukee, Wisconsin

Exc.	V.G.	Good	Fair	Poor
—	1250	650	450	275

Patterns of 1856, 1858, 1860, and 1861 (P1856, P1858, P1860, P1861) Sergeant's Rifles

Overall length 49"; barrel length 33"; caliber .577. The four variations of the short rifle adopted for sergeants in the British Army in 1856 are relatively minor. The P1856 is mainly distinguished by having a short (1/2") key forward of the saber bayonet lug on the right side of the barrel. The P1858 rifle moved this lug to the forward band, permitting the extension of the length of the forestock. (A brass furnished rifle also without the key but with the lug on the barrel was also adopted in 1858 for the Navy; it is distinguished by having its rear sling swivel attached to the triggerguard bow instead of the tail of the triggerguard strap.) The P1860 rifle differed from its predecessors by having five groove rifling instead of three groove. The introduction of a new gunpowder in 1861 permitted the resighting of the ladder on the P1861 rifle to 1,250 yards instead of the 1,100 yards that had been previously used. Significant quantities of these rifles were purchased by both billigerents during the American Civil War; those with proven southern history will command a premium.

Courtesy Milwaukee Public Museum, Milwaukee, Wisconsin

Courtesy Milwaukee Public Museum, Milwaukee, Wisconsin

Exc.	V.G.	Good	Fair	Poor
—	1500	800	650	450

Pattern of 1853 (P1853) Artillery Carbine (First, Second, and Third Models)

Overall length 40"; barrel length 24"; caliber .577. Designed for the gunners of the Royal Artillery, this carbine was meant to be slung over the shoulder and accordingly has a sling swivel on the upper band and upon a lug inset into the buttstock. The first model (adopted in 1853), like the sergeant's rifle has a 112" key forward of the saber bayonet lug on the right side of the barrel; in addition to other minor improvements, this key was eliminated in the second model, adopted in 1858. In 1861, a third model was adopted, having five groove rifling and improved rear sight. Approximately 1,000 of the latter type saw service in the American Civil War. Carbines with Confederate stock and buttplate markings will command a premium.

Courtesy Milwaukee Public Museum, Milwaukee, Wisconsin

Exc.	V.G.	Good	Fair	Poor
—	1500	700	550	400

Patterns of 1856 (P1856) and Pattern of 1861 (P1861) Cavalry Carbines

Overall length 37" (P1856), 36-1/2" (P1861) barrel length 21"; caliber .577. Due to inadequacies in the various breechloading carbines tried by the British mounted service, in 1856 the War Department adopted a muzzleloading carbine incorporating the features of the P1853 series small arms. The earlier version had three groove rifling and a small rear sight with two leaves. In 1861 this was replaced by a larger ladder sight and five groove rifling adopted. More than 6,000 P1856 carbines were imported by the Southern Confederacy during the Civil War to make up for the inadequate supply of carbines. Carbines with verifiable Southern history will command a premium.

Courtesy Milwaukee Public Museum, Milwaukee, Wisconsin

Exc.	V.G.	Good	Fair	Poor
—	1500	725	600	375

ENTREPRISE ARMS, INC.
Irwindale, California

Elite Series

This is the basic model with stainless steel barrels, fixed sights, squared triggerguard, adjustable match trigger, checkered slide release, high ride grip safety, flat mainspring housing, and a number of other special features. Magazine capacity is 10 rounds.

Elite P500

Chambered for .45 ACP and fitted with a 5" barrel. Weight is about 40 oz.

NIB	Exc.	V.G.	Good	Fair	Poor
740	600	—	—	—	—

Elite P425

This model has a 4.25" barrel. Weight is approximately 38 oz.

NIB	Exc.	V.G.	Good	Fair	Poor
740	600	—	—	—	—

Elite 325

This model has a 3.25" barrel with a weight of 36 oz.

NIB	Exc.	V.G.	Good	Fair	Poor
740	600	—	—	—	—

Tactical Series

This model has an ambidextrous thumb lock with lightweight match hammer with matching sear. National match barrel with match extractor, full length one-piece guide rod, Novak sights, dovetail front sight, matte black finish, and a host of other features. Magazine capacity is 10 rounds.

Tactical P500

This model is chambered for the .45 ACP cartridge and has a 5" barrel and a weight of approximately 40 oz.

NIB	Exc.	V.G.	Good	Fair	Poor
980	780	—	—	—	—

Tactical P425

This model is fitted with a 4.25" barrel and weighs about 38 oz.

NIB	Exc.	V.G.	Good	Fair	Poor
980	780	—	—	—	—

Tactical P325

This model is fitted with a 3.25" barrel and has a weight of 36 oz.

NIB	Exc.	V.G.	Good	Fair	Poor
980	780	—	—	—	—

Tactical P325 Plus

This model features a 3.25" barrel and is fitted to a full size Government model frame. Weight is about 37 oz.

NIB	Exc.	V.G.	Good	Fair	Poor
1050	800	—	—	—	—

Titleist National Match Series

This model is chambered for either the .45 ACP or .40 S&W cartridge. It has all the features of the Elite Series with an adjustable rear sight and dovetail Patridge front sight. Many other special features.

Titleist P500

This model is fitted with a 5" barrel. Add $20 for .40 S&W chambering. Weight is about 40 oz.

NIB	Exc.	V.G.	Good	Fair	Poor
980	780	—	—	—	—

Boxer Model

Chambered for the .45 ACP cartridge and fitted with a 5" barrel this model features a ramped bull barrel, wide ambi safety and high mass chiseled slide. Weight is approximately 44 oz.

NIB	Exc.	V.G.	Good	Fair	Poor
1100	875	—	—	—	—

Tournament Series

These are the top of the line models that feature all of the Elite Series features plus oversized magazine release button, checkered front strap, and flared extended magazine well.

TSM I

This is a limited class competition pistol. All these model are hand crafted. Fitted with a 5" barrel and choice of calibers. Weight is about 40 oz.

NIB	Exc.	V.G.	Good	Fair	Poor
2300	1750	—	—	—	—

TSM II

This is a long slide model with cocking serrations on front and rear of slide. Barrel is 6". Weight is about 44 oz.

NIB	Exc.	V.G.	Good	Fair	Poor
2000	1500	—	—	—	—

TSM III

This is an open class pistol designed for scope mount. Barrel is 5.5" long. Fitted with 7 port compensator. Many other custom features. Weight is about 44 oz.

NIB	Exc.	V.G.	Good	Fair	Poor
2700	2000	—	—	—	—

ERA
Brazil

Era Double Barrel Shotgun

An inexpensive shotgun chambered for 12 and 20 gauge, as well as .410. It was offered with 26", 28", or 30" barrels with various choke combinations. It has double triggers and extractors, with a checkered hardwood pistol-grip stock. This gun is also available as a Quail model with a 20" barrel and as a Riot model with an 18" barrel. These two models are not offered in .410 bore.

Exc.	V.G.	Good	Fair	Poor
200	150	125	100	75

Era Over/Under Shotgun

Chambered for 12 or 20 gauge, with 28" ventilated rib barrels that were choked full and modified. It is a boxlock with double triggers, extractors, and a hardwood stock. It was also offered in a trap model and a skeet model chambered for 12 gauge only and appropriately choked. These latter two models would be worth a 10% premium over the values shown.

Exc.	V.G.	Good	Fair	Poor
325	275	250	200	150

ERICHSON, G.
Houston, Texas

Erichson Pocket Pistol

A close copy of the Philadelphia-style Henry Deringer. It is chambered for .45-caliber percussion and has a 3.25" barrel. The mountings are German silver and not engraved; the stock is walnut. The hammer is deeply fluted; and the forend, carved. The barrel is marked "G. Erichson / Houston, Texas." The number produced is unknown, but examples are scarce. They were manufactured in the 1850s and 1860s.

Exc.	V.G.	Good	Fair	Poor
—	—	6000	3000	1000

ERMA WERKE WAFFENFABRIK
Erfurt, Germany
Postwar
Dachau, Germany

Known primarily as a manufacturer of submachine guns, but they are also in the handgun and rifle business. In 1933 they answered the German army's need for an inexpensive practice weapon by producing a .22 rimfire conversion unit for the

Luger pistol. This was marketed commercially and was available for many years. The success of this unit led the company to produce other inexpensive target and plinking pistols. After the war they were reorganized in the western sector and resumed submachine gun production. In 1964 they returned to the sporting firearms business with the introduction of their .22 rimfire Luger-lookalike pistol. Since then, they have produced many like-quality firearms. They were imported by Excam of Hialeah, Florida. This association is now terminated, and they are currently imported by Beeman Precision in Santa Rosa, California, and Mandell Shooting Supplies in Scottsdale, Arizona.

Erma .22 Luger Conversion Unit

Produced for the German army in 1933 and then became a successful commercial item. It would turn a standard 9mm or 7.65mm Luger into an inexpensive-to-shoot .22 rimfire. The unit consists of a barrel insert, a breech block, and toggle unit with its own lightened recoil spring, and a .22 magazine. This unit was furnished with a wooden box. There were many different sized units to fit various caliber and barrel-length Lugers, but all used the same parts and concept. These units have become desirable to Luger collectors.

Exc.	V.G.	Good	Fair	Poor
500	425	350	275	200

.22 Target Pistol (Old Model)

An inexpensive, blowback-operated, semiautomatic pistol chambered for the .22 rimfire cartridge. This model has a 4" barrel and an open-topped slide. The frame is made from a cast zinc alloy, and there is an external hammer. There are adjustable sights, and balance weights were available. This pistol was manufactured in 1936.

Exc.	V.G.	Good	Fair	Poor
250	225	175	125	100

.22 Target Pistol (New Model)

An improved version of the old model, that features a new grip angle and a magazine and takedown device that is like that of the Luger. There were interchangeable barrels and three basic models—the "Sport," "Hunter," and the "Master." The difference was the length of the barrels—4", 5", and 6", respectively. These pistols were manufactured between 1937 and 1940, when they were discontinued due to Erma's involvement in the war effort.

Exc.	V.G.	Good	Fair	Poor
275	250	200	150	125

KGP-Series

Made to resemble the Luger quite closely. They utilized the mechanical features of the .22 conversion unit and developed a pistol around it. There are many different versions of this pistol chambered for .22 rimfire, .32 ACP, and .380 ACP. The original designation was the KGP-68; but the Gun Control Act of 1968 required that a magazine safety be added, and the model was redesignated the KGP-68A. The last designations for the three calibers are KGP-22, KGP-32, and KGP-38. These pistols were manufactured between 1964 and 1986, and their values are as follows:

KGP-68

A 4" barrel and is chambered for the .32 ACP and the .380 ACP cartridges. It has a 6-shot magazine and an anodized alloy receiver. This model is also known as the Beeman MP-08.

Exc.	V.G.	Good	Fair	Poor
500	400	300	200	100

KGP-69

A .22 rimfire version of this series, with an 8-shot magazine capacity. It is also known as the Beeman P-08.

Exc.	V.G.	Good	Fair	Poor
300	200	150	100	75

ET-22 Luger Carbine

A rare firearm. According to some estimates only 375 were produced. It features a 11.75" barrel and is chambered for the .22 rimfire cartridge. It has an artillery Luger-type rear sight and checkered walnut grips, with a smooth walnut forend. The pistol was furnished with a red-felt-lined, black leatherette case.

Exc.	V.G.	Good	Fair	Poor
400	350	300	200	150

KGP-22

The later version of the KGP-69 chambered for .22 rimfire.

Exc.	V.G.	Good	Fair	Poor
350	300	250	200	125

KGP-32 & KGP-38

These two designations are the later versions of the KGP-68 and 68A.

Exc.	V.G.	Good	Fair	Poor
350	300	250	200	125

ESP 85A

A high quality target pistol imported by Mandall Shooting Supply. It features an interchangeable barrel system that converts the chambering from .22 rimfire to .32 S&W long wad cutter. The barrels are both 6" in length, and there are adjustable and interchangeable sights and a 5- or 8-shot detachable magazine. The finish is blued, and the grips are stippled target types. The gun is furnished in a padded hard case with two extra magazines and takedown tools. This unit was introduced in 1989.

NIB	Exc.	V.G.	Good	Fair	Poor
1100	1000	850	700	550	450

RX-22

A .22 rimfire copy of the Walther PPK. It has a 3.25" barrel, an 8-shot detachable magazine, and a blued finish with checkered black plastic grips. It was assembled in the U.S.A. from parts made in West Germany. It was discontinued in 1986.

Exc.	V.G.	Good	Fair	Poor
200	175	150	125	100

REVOLVERS

ER-772 Match

A target revolver chambered for the .22 rimfire and has a 6" shrouded barrel with a solid rib. The swing-out cylinder holds 6 shots, and the sights are adjustable. The finish is blued, with stippled target grips. This model was introduced in 1989.

NIB	Exc.	V.G.	Good	Fair	Poor
500	450	400	350	250	200

ER-773 Match

Similar to the ER-772 except that it is chambered for the .32 S&W long cartridge.

NIB	Exc.	V.G.	Good	Fair	Poor
500	450	400	350	250	200

ER-777

Basically a similar revolver to the ER-773 except that it has a 4.5" or 5" barrel and is chambered for the .357 Magnum cartridge. The revolver is larger and has standard sport grips. This model was also introduced in 1989.

NIB	Exc.	V.G.	Good	Fair	Poor
500	450	400	350	250	200

RIFLES

EMI.22

A semiautomatic .22 rimfire version of the MI Carbine. It has an 18" barrel and a 15-round magazine. It was manufactured between 1966 and 1976.

Exc.	V.G.	Good	Fair	Poor
200	175	150	125	100

EG-72, EG-722

A 15-shot slide action carbine chambered for .22 rimfire, with a 18.5" barrel and open sights. The finish is blued, and it was manufactured between 1970 and 1985.

Exc.	V.G.	Good	Fair	Poor
150	110	100	75	50

EG-712, EG-73

A lever copy of the Winchester 94 Carbine chambered for the .22 rimfire or the .22 rimfire Magnum (EG-73). It has an 18.5" barrel and holds 15 shots in a tubular magazine. It was manufactured between 1973 and 1985.

Exc.	V.G.	Good	Fair	Poor
200	175	150	125	100

SR-100

This is long range precision bolt action rifle chambered for .308 Win., .300 Win. Mag., or .338 Lapua calibers. Barrel length on the .308 Win. caliber is 25.25", other calibers are 29.25". All barrels are fitted with a muzzle brake. Trigger is adjustable. Stock is laminated with thumbhole and adjustable recoil pad and cheekpiece. Weight is approximately 15 lbs.

NIB	Exc.	V.G.	Good	Fair	Poor
8800	7000	—	—	—	—

ERQUIAGA
Eibar, Spain

Another Spanish company that commenced business during WWI as a subcontractor on the French "Ruby" contract. They manufactured the usual poor quality, 7.65mm Eibar-type pistol.

Fiel

The trade name found on the Ruby subcontract pistol described above. It is marked "Erquiaga y Cia Eibar Cal. 7.65 Fiel".

Exc.	V.G.	Good	Fair	Poor
200	150	125	100	75

Fiel 6.35

After the end of WWI, a 1906 Browning copy was made. It is chambered for the 6.35mm cartridge. The markings are "Automatic Pistol 6.35 Fiel No. 1". Later models had "EMC" molded into the grip.

Exc.	V.G.	Good	Fair	Poor
175	125	100	75	50

Marte

Another poor-quality "Eibar"-type pistol that is chambered for the 6.35mm and that was made in the early 1920s.

Exc.	V.G.	Good	Fair	Poor
175	125	100	75	50

ERRASTI, A.
Eibar, Spain

Errasti manufactured a variety of inexpensive yet serviceable pistols from the early 1900s until the Spanish civil war.

Velo-Dog

Usual cheap solid frame folding trigger revolvers one associates with the model designation. They were chambered in 5.5mm and 6.35mm and were made in the early 1900s.

Exc.	V.G.	Good	Fair	Poor
175	125	100	75	50

M1889

In 1915-1916 Errasti produced the 10.4mm Italian army service revolver. The quality was reasonably good. They were marked "Errasti Eiber" on the right side of the frame.

Exc.	V.G.	Good	Fair	Poor
225	175	150	100	75

Errasti

Two "Eibar" type Browning copies were made under this trade name. One was chambered for the 6.35mm, the other the 7.65mm. They were both marked "Automatic Pistol Errasti."

Exc.	V.G.	Good	Fair	Poor
175	125	100	75	50

Errasti Oscillante

Manufactured in the 1920s, these revolvers were copied from the Smith & Wesson Military & Police design. They were chambered for the .32, .38, and .44 calibers with the .38 being the most frequently encountered.

Exc.	V.G.	Good	Fair	Poor
175	125	100	75	50

Dreadnaught, Goliath and Smith Americano

These three trade names were found on a group of poor quality nickel-plated revolvers. They were made from 1905 through 1920 and were obvious copies of the Iver Johnson design. They had break-open actions, ribbed barrel, and were chambered for .32, .38, and .44 calibers. They are scarce today, as most have long since fallen apart.

Exc.	V.G.	Good	Fair	Poor
175	125	100	75	50

ESCODIN, M.
Eibar, Spain

This company made a Smith & Wesson revolver copy from 1924 through 1931. It is chambered for the .32 and the .38 Special. The only marking is a coat of arms stamped on the left side of the frame.

Exc.	V.G.	Good	Fair	Poor
175	125	100	75	50

ESPIRIN, HERMANOS
Eibar, Spain

Euskaro

This poor-quality, often unsafe revolver was manufactured from 1906 until WWI. They are copies of the Iver Johnson design break-open actions, chambered for .32. .38, and .44. This product epitomizes the worst Eibar had to offer during the pre-Civil War era.

Exc.	V.G.	Good	Fair	Poor
—	125	75	50	25

EUROARMS OF AMERICA
Winchester, Virginia

An importer of black powder muzzle-loading firearms, primarily replicas of early American weapons.

REVOLVERS

1851 Navy

A replica of the Colt revolver chambered for .36 or .44 caliber percussion. It has a squareback, silver-plated triggerguard and a 7.5" barrel.

NIB	Exc.	V.G.	Good	Fair	Poor
175	125	110	80	65	45

1851 Navy Police Model

Chambered for .36 caliber with a 5-shot, fluted cylinder and a 5.5" barrel.

NIB	Exc.	V.G.	Good	Fair	Poor
175	125	110	80	65	45

1851 Navy Sheriff's Model

A 5" barrelled version of the Navy Model.

NIB	Exc.	V.G.	Good	Fair	Poor
150	100	80	60	50	35

1851 "Schneider & Glassick" Navy

A replica of the Confederate revolver chambered for .36 or .44 caliber percussion.

NIB	Exc.	V.G.	Good	Fair	Poor
150	100	80	60	50	35

1851 "Griswold & Gunnison" Navy

A replica of this Confederate revolver chambered for .36 or .44 caliber percussion.

NIB	Exc.	V.G.	Good	Fair	Poor
150	90	75	60	40	25

1862 Police

A replica of the Colt Model 1862 chambered for .36 caliber percussion, with a 7.5" barrel and a steel frame.

NIB	Exc.	V.G.	Good	Fair	Poor
175	125	110	90	65	45

1860 Army

A replica of the Colt revolver chambered for .44 caliber percussion. It was offered with a 5" or 8" barrel.

NIB	Exc.	V.G.	Good	Fair	Poor
175	125	100	75	50	30

1861 Navy

A replica of the Colt revolver chambered for .36 caliber percussion.

NIB	Exc.	V.G.	Good	Fair	Poor
175	135	110	80	60	40

1858 Remington Army or Navy

Replicas of the Remington percussion revolvers chambered for .26 or .44 caliber.

NIB	Exc.	V.G.	Good	Fair	Poor
200	150	125	100	75	50

RIFLES

The following rifles are modern replicas of early American and British firearms. They are of good quality and are quite serviceable. There is little collector interest, and we list them along with their values.

Cook & Brother Carbine

NIB	Exc.	V.G.	Good	Fair	Poor
375	325	250	100	150	100

1863 J.P. Murray

NIB	Exc.	V.G.	Good	Fair	Poor
350	300	225	175	125	100

1853 Enfield Rifled Musket

NIB	Exc.	V.G.	Good	Fair	Poor
400	350	300	250	175	125

1858 Enfield Rifled Musket

NIB	Exc.	V.G.	Good	Fair	Poor
375	325	250	200	150	100

1861 Enfield Musketoon

NIB	Exc.	V.G.	Good	Fair	Poor
350	300	225	175	125	90

1803 Harper's Ferry

NIB	Exc.	V.G.	Good	Fair	Poor
500	425	350	300	225	150

1841 Mississippi Rifle

NIB	Exc.	V.G.	Good	Fair	Poor
475	400	325	275	200	125

Pennsylvania Rifle

NIB	Exc.	V.G.	Good	Fair	Poor
300	250	225	200	150	100

Hawken Rifle

NIB	Exc.	V.G.	Good	Fair	Poor
300	250	200	150	100	80

Cape Gun

NIB	Exc.	V.G.	Good	Fair	Poor
400	350	275	225	175	125

Buffalo Carbine

NIB	Exc.	V.G.	Good	Fair	Poor
400	350	300	250	175	100

1862 Remington Rifle

NIB	Exc.	V.G.	Good	Fair	Poor
300	250	225	200	125	60

Zouave Rifle

NIB	Exc.	V.G.	Good	Fair	Poor
325	275	225	175	125	90

Duck Gun

A single-barreled percussion fowling piece chambered for 8, 10, or 12 gauge. It has a 33" smooth-bore barrel and a case-colored hammer and lock. The stock is walnut with brass mountings. This model was introduced in 1989.

NIB	Exc.	V.G.	Good	Fair	Poor
400	350	300	250	175	100

A side-by-side, chambered for 12 gauge percussion. It has 28" barrels with engraved locks and a walnut stock.

NIB	Exc.	V.G.	Good	Fair	Poor
425	375	325	275	200	125

EUROPEAN AMERICAN ARMORY CORP.
Importers
Sharpes, Florida

Witness Pistols

These quality pistols are produced by Tanfoglio, an Italian firm, and imported into the U.S. by European American Armory. These handguns are based on the CZ design and offer many features that are sought after by the shooter such as: competition sights, double action/single action trigger system, and internal firing pin lock. The firm was founded by Giuseppe Tanfoglio after WWII. He formed a partnership with Antonio Sabbati and began to manufacture small caliber pistols. During the 1960s the firm also produced derringers and Colt SAA copies. In 1980 the Tanfoglio company decided to enter the service pistol market and copied the respected Czech CZ design. The Tanfoglio company currently produces the P9 series for Springfield Armory and the Desert Eagle line for IMI. In 1993 EAA converted from two frame sizes to one and redesigned the triggerguard and beavertail. This redesigned frame enables all of the different caliber slide assemblies to be interchangeable with one frame. This new configuration began to appear in mid-1993. The buyer should be aware that the EAA Custom Shop offers a wide variety of accessories for its pistols, such as compensators, hammers, ported barrels, grips, etc., that will affect price.

EAA Witness P-Series Full Size

Introduced in 1998 this is a full size polymer frame pistol chambered for 9mm, .40 S&W, .45 ACP, .38 Super, and 10mm cartridges. Barrel length is 4.55". Overall length is 8.5" with an empty weight of 31oz. Rear sight is adjustable for windage. Magazine capacity for 9mm and .40 S&W is 10 rounds while the .45 ACP model holds 8 rounds.

NIB	Exc.	V.G.	Good	Fair	Poor
425	325	250	—	—	—

NOTE: Add $30 for ported barrel

EAA Witness P-Series Carry-Comp

This model is fitted with a 4.25" ported barrel. Chambered for .45 ACP.

NIB	Exc.	V.G.	Good	Fair	Poor
425	350	300	—	—	—

EAA Witness P-Series Compact

Similar to the above model but with a barrel length of 3.55". Weight is about 26 oz.

NIB	Exc.	V.G.	Good	Fair	Poor
385	300	250	—	—	—

NOTE: Add $30 for ported barrel

EAA Witness P-S Series
Built on a different frame size from the P-Series pistols. This model is chambered for the .22 Long Rifle, 9mm, or .40S&W cartridges. Barrel length is 4.55". Weight is about 31 oz.

NIB	Exc.	V.G.	Good	Fair	Poor
400	325	275	—	—	—

EAA Witness Standard
Available in 9mm, .41 AE, 40 S&W, and .45 ACP with 4.5" barrel. Magazine capacity: 9mm-16 rounds, .41 AE-11 rounds, .40 S&W-12 rounds, .45 ACP-10 rounds. Offered in blue, chrome, two-tone, and stainless steel. Weighs approximately 33 oz.

Old Configuration

NIB	Exc.	V.G.	Good	Fair	Poor
385	325	275	225	175	125

New Configuration

NIB	Exc.	V.G.	Good	Fair	Poor
400	325	275	225	175	125

NOTE: For chrome, two-tone, and stainless steel add 5% to above prices.

EAA Witness Subcompact
Offered in the same calibers as the standard model but fitted with a 3.66" barrel and shorter grip. Magazine capacity: 9mm-13 rounds, .41 AE-9 rounds, .40 S&W 9 rounds, .45 ACP-8 rounds. Weighs about 30 oz. Offered in blue, chrome, two-tone, and stainless steel.

Old Configuration

NIB	Exc.	V.G.	Good	Fair	Poor
385	325	275	225	175	125

New Configuration

NIB	Exc.	V.G.	Good	Fair	Poor
400	325	275	225	175	125

NOTE: For chrome, two-tone, and stainless steel add 5% to above prices.

EAA Witness Carry Comp
This model is offered in 9mm, .41 AE, .40 S&W, and .45 ACP. It features a 1" steel compensator. The barrel is 41" long. Overall length is the same as the standard model as is magazine capacity. Offered in blue or blue chrome finish. Weighs 34 oz.

Old Configuration

NIB	Exc.	V.G.	Good	Fair	Poor
500	450	375	325	250	175

New Configuration

NIB	Exc.	V.G.	Good	Fair	Poor
425	350	300	250	200	175

NOTE: For .45 ACP add 15% to above prices.

EAA Witness Combo 9/40

This model offers a 9mm conversion kit, and a .40 S&W conversion kit. These kits consist of a slide, barrel, recoil spring and guide, and magazine. Available in standard or subcompact size in blue, chrome, or two-tone finish.

NIB	Exc.	V.G.	Good	Fair	Poor
550	475	400	350	275	175

NOTE: For chrome or two-tone finish add 5% to above prices.

EAA Witness Sport L/S

This model features a longer slide for its 4.75" barrel. Offered in 9mm, .41 AE, .40 S&W, and .45 ACP. Magazine capacity: 9mm-19 rounds, .41 AE-13 rounds, .40 S&W 14 rounds, and .45 ACP-11 rounds. This model is also fitted with adjustable rear sight and extended safety. Available in two-tone finish. Weighs about 34.5 oz. A ported barrel is offered as an option.

Old Configuration

NIB	Exc.	V.G.	Good	Fair	Poor
625	550	500	400	300	200

New Configuration

NIB	Exc.	V.G.	Good	Fair	Poor
625	550	500	400	300	200

NOTE: For .45 ACP add 10% to prices.

EAA Witness Sport

This model is built on the standard Witness frame with the addition of an adjustable rear sight and extended safety. Offered in 9mm, .41 AE, .40 S&W, .45 ACP in standard model magazine capacity. Weighs 33 oz. Available in two-tone finish.

Old Configuration

NIB	Exc.	V.G.	Good	Fair	Poor
550	475	400	300	200	150

New Configuration

NIB	Exc.	V.G.	Good	Fair	Poor
550	475	400	300	200	150

NOTE: For .45 ACP add 10% to above prices.

EAA Witness Silver Team Match

This is designed as a competition pistol. It is fitted with a 5.25" barrel. It has the following features: dual chamber compensator, single action trigger, extended safety, competition hammer, paddle magazine release, checkered walnut grips, and adjustable rear sight or drilled and tapped for scope mount. Offered in 9mm-19 rounds, .40 S&W 14 rounds, .41 AE-13 rounds, .45 ACP-11 rounds, and 9 x 21. Finish is blue and weight is approximately 34 oz.

NIB	Exc.	V.G.	Good	Fair	Poor
900	800	700	600	450	300

EAA Witness Gold Team Match

This is a full race competition pistol with triple chamber compensator, beaver tail grip safety, beveled magazine well, adjustable rear sight or drilled and tapped for scope mount, extended safety and magazine release, competition hammer, square triggerguard, checkered front and back strap, competition grips, and hard chrome finish. Same barrel length, magazine capacity, and calibers as the Silver Team Match. Weighs 38 oz.

NIB	Exc.	V.G.	Good	Fair	Poor
1600	1250	900	750	600	400

NIB	Exc.	V.G.	Good	Fair	Poor
1500	1200	850	600	300	200

NOTE: Any of the above EAA Witness pistol can be supplied with double action only triggers at no additional charge.

OTHER EAA IMPORTED FIREARMS

EAA Big Bore Bounty Hunter

This model is a single action revolver made in Germany. It features three-position hammer, forged barrel, and walnut grips. Offered in .357 Mag., .45 Long Colt, and .44 Mag. in 4.5", 5.5", or 7.5" barrel lengths. Choice of finish includes blue or case-colored frame, chrome, gold, or blue and gold.

EAA Witness Limited Class Pistol

This model is built on the Witness Match frame with competition grips, high capacity magazine, extended safety and magazine release, single action trigger, long slide with adjustable rear sight, and match grade barrel. Offered in 9mm, .40 S&W, .38 Super, and .45 ACP with blue finish.

NIB	Exc.	V.G.	Good	Fair	Poor
300	225	175	150	125	100

NOTE: For chrome, gold, or blue and gold finish add 20%.

EAA Small Bore Bounty Hunter

This is a single action .22 caliber revolver. It has wood grips and is available in blue or blue and brass finish. Barrel lengths are 4.75", 6", and 9". It is chambered for .22 Long Rifle or .22 Winchester Rimfire Magnum.

NIB	Exc.	V.G.	Good	Fair	Poor
225	175	125	100	75	60

EAA Bounty Hunter Shotgun-External Hammers

This is a side-by-side shotgun with external hammers chambered for 10, 12, 16, 20, 28, and .410 bores. It is offered in barrel lengths of 20", 24", and 26".

NIB	Exc.	V.G.	Good	Fair	Poor
900	775	650	550	400	300

EAA Witness Multi Class Pistol Package

This package consists of one Witness Limited Class pistol with a complete unlimited class top half. The top half is made up of a standard length slide with super sight, recoil guide and spring, match grade competition barrel (threaded for compensator), and a dual chamber compensator. Available in 9mm, .40 S&W, 9 x 21, .45 ACP, 9 x 23, and .38 Super. Finish is blue.

NIB	Exc.	V.G.	Good	Fair	Poor
375	300	250	—	—	—

EAA Bounty Hunter Shotgun-Traditional

Same as above but with internal hammers. Offered in 12 or 20 gauge.

NIB	Exc.	V.G.	Good	Fair	Poor
300	250	200	—	—	—

EAA F.A.B. 92 Pistol

This model is a semiautomatic pistol similar to the Witness, but fitted with a hammer drop safety and slide mounted safety, that is both a double action or single action. It is available in either a full size (33 oz.) or compact size (30 oz.). The full size version has a 4.5" barrel while the compact is fitted with a 3.66" barrel. Offered in 9mm or .40 S&W in blue, two-tone, or chrome finish.

NIB	Exc.	V.G.	Good	Fair	Poor
350	275	225	175	125	100

EAA European Standard Pistol

This is a single action semiautomatic pistol with external hammer, slide grip serrations, wood grips, and single column magazine. The barrels length is 3.2" and overall length is 6.5". Chambered for .22 Long Rifle, 380 ACP, .32 ACP. The magazine capacity is 10 rounds for the .22 LR, 7 rounds for .380, and 7 rounds for .32. Offered in blue, blue/chrome, chrome, blue/gold. Weighs 26 oz.

NIB	Exc.	V.G.	Good	Fair	Poor
165	135	110	95	75	50

EAA European Target Pistol

This model features adjustable rear sight, external hammer, single action trigger, walnut target grips, and adjustable weight system. Chambered for .22 Long Rifle. Offered in blue finish and weighs 40 oz.

NIB	Exc.	V.G.	Good	Fair	Poor
325	275	225	175	150	100

EAA Windicator Standard Grade

This German built model is a double action revolver chambered for the .22 Long Rifle, .22 Winchester Rimfire Magnum, .32 H&R, and .38 Special. It is offered in 2", 4", and 6" barrel lengths. The cylinder capacity for the .22 LR/.22WRM is 8 rounds, .32 H&R is 7 rounds, and the .38 Special is 6 rounds. The cylinder is unfluted. Finish is blue.

NIB	Exc.	V.G.	Good	Fair	Poor
185	140	120	95	75	60

EAA Windicator Basic Grade

This model is chambered for the .38 Special or the .357 Magnum with 2" barrel. The fluted cylinder holds 6 rounds. Finish is blue.

NIB	Exc.	V.G.	Good	Fair	Poor
175	130	110	85	65	50

EAA Windicator Tactical Grade

This model is similar in appearance to the standard grade but is chambered for the .38 Special with 2" or 4" barrel. The 4" barrel has an integral compensator. Finish is blue.

2" Barrel

NIB	Exc.	V.G.	Good	Fair	Poor
190	150	125	100	80	60

4" Barrel

NIB	Exc.	V.G.	Good	Fair	Poor
250	200	150	125	100	75

EAA Windicator Target Grade

This model has the following special features: adjustable trigger pull, walnut grips, adjustable rear sight, drilled and tapped for scope mount, target hammer, adjustable trigger stop. Fitted with 6" target barrel. Chambered for .22 Long Rifle, .38 Special, .357 Mag. Blue finish.

NIB	Exc.	V.G.	Good	Fair	Poor
350	275	225	200	150	100

EAA PM2 Shotgun

This is a pump action 12 gauge shotgun with 6-round box magazine. Barrel length is 20" and finish is either blue or chrome. Stock is black composite. Weight is 6.8 lbs. This model was discontinued in 1993.

NIB	Exc.	V.G.	Good	Fair	Poor
450	350	300	250	200	150

NOTE: Add $100 for optional night sights.

EAA HW 60 Rifle

This German made target rifle is chambered for the .22 Long Rifle. It features an adjustable trigger and other target and match grade components. The barrel length is 26.8", the stock is stippled walnut, and the finish is blue. Weighs approximately 10.8 lbs.

Target Grade

NIB	Exc.	V.G.	Good	Fair	Poor
670	575	500	400	300	200

Match Grade

NIB	Exc.	V.G.	Good	Fair	Poor
760	650	550	450	350	250

EAA Sabatti

These firearms are made by the Sabatti firm in Gardone, Italy. It is a old line company, having been in the firearms business since 1674. The company also produces and supplies component parts to many of Italy's premier gun makers. These shotguns and rifles are manufactured for the cost-conscious buyer.

EAA Sabatti Falcon

This is a field grade Over/Under shotgun with checkered walnut stock with pistol grip, boxlock action, double triggers, and extractors. Offered in 12 or 20 gauge with 3" chambers. Also available in 28 gauge and .410 bore with 26" or 28" barrels. Barrel lengths are available in 26", 28", or 30". Chokes are fixed.

NIB	Exc.	V.G.	Good	Fair	Poor
575	425	400	350	300	250

28/.410

NIB	Exc.	V.G.	Good	Fair	Poor
625	480	425	375	325	275

EAA Sporting Clay Basic

This model features a single selective trigger, extractors, checkered walnut stock with pistol grip, extra wide rib, and blued receiver with scroll engraving. Offered in 12 gauge only with 28" fixed choke barrel.

NIB	Exc.	V.G.	Good	Fair	Poor
350	275	250	200	150	100

EAA Sporting Clay Pro

This model is similar to the basic sporting clay model with the addition of a select walnut stock, screw in choke tubes, automatic ejectors, recoil pad. Comes with hard shell case.

NIB	Exc.	V.G.	Good	Fair	Poor
950	720	650	550	450	300

EAA Sporting Clay Pro Gold

Same as above but with gold inlay receiver.

NIB	Exc.	V.G.	Good	Fair	Poor
1000	750	650	550	450	300

EAA Saba

This model is a side-x-side shotgun that features an engraved silver boxlock receiver, double or single triggers, selective ejectors, solid raised matted rib, and select European walnut checkered stock. Offered in 12, 20, and 28 gauge as well as .410 bore. Barrel length are 26" or 28" with fixed chokes.

NIB	Exc.	V.G.	Good	Fair	Poor
775	600	500	400	300	250

EAA/BAIKAL SHOTGUNS

See Baikal

EAA/Saiga Shotgun

A semiautomatic shotgun based on the AK-47 design. Chambered for the 12, 20 and .410 bore. Barrel length are 20", 24", 26", or 28". Blued finish with optional camo finish. Detachable 5-round box magazine. Introduced in 1999.

NIB	Exc.	V.G.	Good	Fair	Poor
450	350	—	—	—	—

NOTE: Deduct $175 for .410 variation.

EAA/Saiga Rifle

Same as above but chambered for 7.62x39 or .308 cartridge. Fitted with a 20" barrel. Introduced in 1999.

NIB	Exc.	V.G.	Good	Fair	Poor
275	225	—	—	—	—

NOTE: Add $100 for .308 caliber.

EAA Rover 870

This is a high quality bolt action rifle. The walnut stock is checkered with rubber recoil pad. Adjustable rear sight and receiver is drilled and tapped for scope mount. Barrel length is 22". Chambered for the following cartridges: .22-250, .243, .25-06, .270, .308, .30-06, 7mm Rem. Mag., .300 and .338 Win. Mag.

NIB	Exc.	V.G.	Good	Fair	Poor
560	425	375	300	200	125

EAA SP 1822

This Sabatti rifle is chambered for the .22 Long Rifle. It is a semiautomatic carbine with a two-piece stock and adjustable stock.

NIB	Exc.	V.G.	Good	Fair	Poor
200	150	125	100	85	60

EAA SP 1822H

This a heavy barrel version of the above model without sights. The receiver is fitted with scope mount base.

NIB	Exc.	V.G.	Good	Fair	Poor
200	150	125	100	85	60

EAA SP 1822TH

This variation also has a heavy barrel without sights but with base mounts. A one-piece Bell and Carlson thumb hole stock is the feature of this model.

NIB	Exc.	V.G.	Good	Fair	Poor
350	260	225	175	125	90

EAA Benelli Silhouette Pistol

This is a specialized competition pistol with a semiautomatic action. The stocks are match type walnut with stippling. The palm shelf is adjustable. The barrel is 4.3" long. Fully adjustable sights. It is chambered for the .22 Long Rifle, .22 Short, and the .32 WC. Supplied with loading tool and cleaning rod. The .22 Caliber version weighs 38.5 oz. Overall length is 11.7".

NIB	Exc.	V.G.	Good	Fair	Poor
1850	1250	950	750	600	400

EAA Astra Pistol
See—Astra

EVANS REPEATING RIFLE CO.
Mechanic Falls, Maine

Incorporated in 1873, this firm produced repeating rifles based upon patents issued to Warren R. Evans (1868-1871) and later George F. Evans (1877, 1878 and 1879). The most distinctive feature of these arms is that they used a butt magazine operating on the principle of an Archimedean screw. Distributed by Merwin, Hulbert & Company, as well as Schuyler, Hartley & Graham, Evans rifles met with some success. One of their earliest advocates was William F. Cody (Buffalo Bill). The company ceased operations in 1879, after approximately 15,000 arms had been made.

Lever Action Rifle

This rifle is totally unique for a number of reasons. It holds the most rounds of any repeating rifle that did not have a detachable magazine, with capacities up to 38 rounds on some models. This rifle was chambered for its own cartridge—the .44 Evans of which there were two versions: a 1" cartridge in the "Old Model" and the "Transition Model" and a 1.5" cartridge in the "New Model". The finish on these rifles is blued, with nickel-plated levers and buttplates noted on some examples. The stocks are walnut. There were approximately 12,250 of all models manufactured between 1873 and 1879.

Old Model

This variation is chambered for the 1" .44 Evans cartridge and has a butt stock that covers only the top half of the revolving 34-shot magazine located in the butt of the rifle. The buttplate appears as if it is reversed, and the markings on the "Old Model" are "Evans Repeating Rifle/Pat. Dec. 8, 1868 & Sept. 16, 1871." There are three versions of the Old Model as follows. They were manufactured between 1874 and 1876 and serial numbered 1-500.

Military Musket

This version has a 30" barrel, with two barrel bands and provisions for a bayonet. There were only 50 estimated manufactured.

Exc.	V.G.	Good	Fair	Poor
—	—	2500	1500	500

Sporting Rifle

Approximately 300 of this model produced with a 26", 28", or 30" octagonal barrel.

Courtesy Milwaukee Public Museum, Milwaukee, Wisconsin

Exc.	V.G.	Good	Fair	Poor
—	—	1500	800	400

Carbine

This variation has a 22" barrel, with one barrel band and a sling swivel. There were 150 produced.

Courtesy Milwaukee Public Museum, Milwaukee, Wisconsin

Exc.	V.G.	Good	Fair	Poor
—	—	1750	900	550

Transitional Model

Has a butt stock that covers both the top and bottom of the rotary magazine, with an exposed portion in the middle of the butt. The buttplate does not have the backward appearance, and the barrel is marked "Evans Repeating Rifle Mechanic Falls Me./Pat Dec. 8, 1868 & Sept. 16, 1871". This version was manufactured in 1876 and 1877 and was serial numbered between 500-2185, for a total of approximately 1,650 manufactured.

Military Musket

Has a 30" barrel and two barrel bands. 150 were produced.

Exc.	V.G.	Good	Fair	Poor
—	—	1800	1200	450

Carbine

Four hundred-fifty of these produced, with a 22" barrel and one barrel band.

Exc.	V.G.	Good	Fair	Poor
—	—	1300	700	375

Sporting Rifle

Has a 26", 28", or 30" barrel. There were 1,050 produced.

Exc.	V.G.	Good	Fair	Poor
—	—	1000	500	300

"Montreal Carbine"

A special issue marked "Montreal," sold by R.H. Kilby, Evans' Canadian sales agent. There were between 50 and 100 produced.

Exc.	V.G.	Good	Fair	Poor
—	—	1800	1000	450

New Model

Approximately 10,000 of the New Model produced, chambered for the 1.5" .44 Evans cartridge with a magazine capacity reduced to 28. The frame was redesigned and rounded at the top, and the forend fit flush to the receiver. The lever and hammer are streamlined, and there is a dust cover over the loading gate. The markings are the same as on the Transitional Model with "U.S.A." added to the last line. This version was not serial numbered, and any numbers found are assembly numbers only.

Military Musket

3,000 produced, with a 30" barrel and two barrel bands.

Courtesy Butterfield & Butterfield, San Francisco, California

Exc.	V.G.	Good	Fair	Poor
—	—	1650	1000	450

Carbine

4,000 produced with a 22" barrel, one barrel band, and a sling swivel.

Courtesy Buffalo Bill Historical Center, Cody, Wyoming

Exc.	V.G.	Good	Fair	Poor
—	—	1000	550	400

Sporting Rifle

3,000 produced with 26", 28", or 30" octagonal barrels.

Exc.	V.G.	Good	Fair	Poor
—	1500	750	500	275

EVANS, J. E.
Philadelphia, Pennsylvania

Evans Pocket Pistol

A copy of the Philadelphia-made Henry Deringer pistol and is chambered for .41 caliber. It utilizes the percussion ignition system and has barrels from 2.5" to 3" in length. The stock is of walnut with a checkered grip, and the mountings are scroll engraved German silver. The barrel is marked "J.E. Evans Philada." These pistols were manufactured in the 1850s.

Exc.	V.G.	Good	Fair	Poor
—	—	1500	550	350

EVANS, WILLIAM
London, England
SEE—British Double Guns

EXCAM
Hialeah, Florida

An importer of firearms is not a manufacturer. The Erma and Uberti products they import are under their own heading in this book. The other products that they import are listed here. They are no longer in business.

TA 76

Patterned after the Colt Single Action Army and is chambered for the .22 rimfire cartridge. It has a 4.75", 6", or 9" barrel and blue finish with wood grips. It is offered with brass triggerguard and backstrap and also offered chrome-plated. A combo model with an extra .22 Magnum cylinder is available and would add 10% to the listed values.

Exc.	V.G.	Good	Fair	Poor
100	75	65	40	25

TA 38 Over/Under Derringer

A two-shot derringer patterned after the Remington derringer. It is chambered for the .38 Special cartridge, has 3" barrels that pivot upward for loading, and is blued with checkered nylon grips. This model was discontinued in 1985.

Exc.	V.G.	Good	Fair	Poor
100	75	65	40	25

TA 90

A double action, semiautomatic copy of the CZ-75 that some experts rate as the finest combat handgun in the world. It is chambered for the 9mm Parabellum and has a 4.75" barrel. It is constructed of steel and is finished with a matte blue or chrome with checkered wood or rubber grips. The detachable magazine holds 15 rounds.

NIB	Exc.	V.G.	Good	Fair	Poor
425	375	325	275	200	150

BTA-90B

A compact version of the TA 90, that has a 3.5" barrel and a 12-round detachable magazine. It is similar in all other respects to the standard model, with rubber grips only.

NIB	Exc.	V.G.	Good	Fair	Poor
425	375	325	275	200	150

TA 90 SS

A competition version of the TA 90, that is similar to the standard model except that it is compensated and features adjustable sights. It is offered either blued or chrome-plated and was introduced in 1989.

NIB	Exc.	V.G.	Good	Fair	Poor
650	575	500	400	325	225

TA 41, 41C, and 41 SS

This series of pistols is identical to the TA 90 series except that they are chambered for the .41 Action Express cartridge. Their values are about 10 percent higher than the 9mm versions. They were introduced in 1989.

Warrior Model W 722

A double action revolver chambered for the .22 rimfire and the .22 rimfire magnum with an interchangeable cylinder. It has a 6" barrel, adjustable sights, and an 8-shot cylinder capacity. It is blued, with checkered plastic grips. This model was not imported after 1986.

Exc.	V. G.	Good	Fair	Poor
100	75	50	35	20

Model W384

A double action revolver chambered for the .38 Special cartridge, with a 4" or 6" vent rib barrel, blued finish, and plastic grips. It was discontinued in 1986.

Exc.	V.G.	Good	Fair	Poor
175	125	100	75	50

Model W357

Similar to the W384 except that it is chambered for the .357 Magnum cartridge. It was discontinued in 1986.

Exc.	V.G.	Good	Fair	Poor
200	150	125	100	75

Targa GT 26

A blowback-operated, semiautomatic pistol chambered for the .25 ACP cartridge. It has a 2.5" barrel and a 6-shot detachable magazine. It is finished in blue or matte chrome, with a choice of alloy or steel frame. The grips are wood.

Steel Frame Version

NIB	Exc.	V.G.	Good	Fair	Poor
125	90	75	50	40	30

Alloy Frame Version

NIB	Exc.	V.G.	Good	Fair	Poor
100	75	50	35	30	25

GT 22

A semiautomatic pistol chambered for the .22 l.r. cartridge. It has a 4" barrel, fixed sights, and a 10-round magazine. It is available either blued or matte chrome-plated and has wooden grips.

NIB	Exc.	V.G.	Good	Fair	Poor
200	175	150	125	90	70

GT 22T

Similar to the GT 22, with a 6" barrel and adjustable target-type sights.

NIB	Exc.	V.G.	Good	Fair	Poor
225	200	175	150	100	75

GT 32

A blowback-operated semiautomatic pistol chambered for the .32 ACP cartridge. It has a 7-round magazine and is either blued or matte chrome-plated with wood grips.

NIB	Exc.	V.G.	Good	Fair	Poor
200	175	150	125	90	75

GT 380

Similar to the GT 32 except that it is chambered for the .380 ACP cartridge.

NIB	Exc.	V.G.	Good	Fair	Poor
225	175	150	125	100	75

GT 380XE

Similar to the GT 380, with an 11-shot, high-capacity, detachable magazine.

NIB	Exc.	V.G.	Good	Fair	Poor
225	200	175	150	125	100

EXEL ARMS OF AMERICA
Gardner, Massachusetts
SEE—Lanber
Laurona & Ugartechia

This firm was engaged in the import of Spanish shotguns. They ceased importing them in 1967, and the specific models will be found listed under the manufacturers' names.

F

F.A.S.
Italy
Importer - Beeman Prec. Arms
Santa Rosa, California
Osbourne's
Cheboygan, Michigan

Model 601
A high-grade, competition target pistol chambered for the .22 short cartridge. It is a semiautomatic, with a 5.5" barrel and adjustable target sights. The detachable magazine holds 5 rounds, and the finish is blued with wraparound target grips. This model was discontinued in 1988.

Exc.	V.G.	Good	Fair	Poor
1250	1000	750	550	300

Model 602
Similar to the Model 601 except that it is chambered for the .22 l.r. It was discontinued in 1987.

Exc.	V.G.	Good	Fair	Poor
1100	900	700	500	250

Model 603
Chambered for the .32 S&W wad cutter cartridge and features adjustable grips. It was discontinued in 1987.

Exc.	V.G.	Good	Fair	Poor
1100	900	700	500	250

FEG
(FEGYVERGYAR)
Budapest, Hungary
Importer—Century International Arms Co. & KBI, Inc.
St. Albans, Vermont & Harrisburg, Pennsylvania

Rudolf Frommer was a first-class engineer who became associated with Fegyvergyar in 1896. In 1900 he became the manager and held that position until his retirement in 1935. He died one year later in 1936. His designs were successful and prolific. They were used militarily and sold on the commercial market as well.

Model 1901
An odd pistol that was not successful at all. It was chambered for an 8mm cartridge that was the forerunner of the 8mm Roth Steyr. It has a long, slender barrel, which was actually a collar with the barrel within. It has a rotary bolt and external hammer and is recoil-operated. There is a 10-round integral magazine, and it is loaded from the top via a stripper clip. This pistol was manufactured from 1903 to 1905.

Exc.	V.G.	Good	Fair	Poor
2000	1600	950	700	350

Model 1906
An improved version of the 1901, chambered for the 7.65mm Roth-Sauer cartridge. It is, for all intents and purposes, the same action; but on later models a detachable 10-round magazine was adopted. It was manufactured between 1906 and 1910 in small quantity.

Exc.	V.G.	Good	Fair	Poor
2000	1600	950	700	350

Model 1910
The final version in this series of pistols and is similar with the addition of a grip safety. Chambered for 7.65mm Browning.

Courtesy James Rankin

Exc.	V.G.	Good	Fair	Poor
1250	1000	750	550	300

Model Stop
Exc.	V.G.	Good	Fair	Poor
300	225	200	150	100

Baby Model
A smaller version of the Stop that was designed as a pocket pistol with a 2" barrel and chambered for the same calibers. It was manufactured at the same time as the Stop Model.

Courtesy James Rankin

Exc.	V.G.	Good	Fair	Poor
300	225	175	125	75

Lilliput

This pocket pistol is chambered for 6.35mm and outwardly resembles the Baby. It is actually a simple, blowback-operated, semiautomatic pistol and was a good deal less complex to produce. This model was introduced in 1921.

Courtesy James Rankin

Exc.	V.G.	Good	Fair	Poor
250	200	150	125	75

Model 1929
Exc.	V.G.	Good	Fair	Poor
400	300	200	175	125

Model 1937

Nazi Proofed 7.65mm Version
Exc.	V.G.	Good	Fair	Poor
275	250	200	150	100

9mm Short Hungarian Military Version
Exc.	V.G.	Good	Fair	Poor
250	225	175	125	75

Model R-9

A copy of the Browning Hi-Power semiautomatic pistol. It is chambered for 9mm Parabellum and has a 4.75" barrel. The frame is steel, and the finish is blued with checkered wood

grips. The detachable magazine holds 13 shots, and the sights are fixed. This model was imported in 1986 and 1987 only.

Exc.	V.G.	Good	Fair	Poor
275	225	200	150	100

Model PPH

A copy of the Walther PP, chambered for the .380 ACP cartridge. It is a double action semiautomatic with a 3" barrel, alloy frame, and a blued finish, with thumb rest checkered plastic grips. It was imported in 1986 and 1987 only.

Exc.	V.G.	Good	Fair	Poor
225	175	150	100	75

Model B9R

This semiautomatic pistol is chambered for the .380 ACP cartridge and fitted with a 4" barrel, it features double or single action trigger operation. The frame is alloy and weighs about 25 oz. Magazine capacity is 15 rounds.

NIB	Exc.	V.G.	Good	Fair	Poor
250	200	175	150	125	75

Model AP9

Chambered for the .380 ACP this pistol is a copy of the Walther PP. It has a aluminum alloy frame and a magazine capacity of 7 rounds. The barrel is 3.94" in length and the pistol is 6.89" overall. The trigger is double action.

Exc.	V.G.	Good	Fair	Poor
150	100	85	70	50

Model PA63

Same as above but chambered for the 9mm Makarov (9x18mm) cartridge.

Exc.	V.G.	Good	Fair	Poor
125	90	75	60	50

Model FP9

This model is a copy of the Browning Hi-Power pistol. Chambered for the 9mm Luger cartridge. It features a walnut checkered grip with blue finish. Barrel is 5" and overall length is 8". The top of the slide features a full length ventilated rib with fixed sights. Weighs 35 oz. Magazine capacity is 14 rounds.

NIB	Exc.	V.G.	Good	Fair	Poor
225	175	150	125	90	70

Model P9R

This is similar to the model above and follows the Browning Hi-Power lines with the exception of the ventilated rib. Barrel length is 4.66" and the pistol is offered in blue or chrome finish. Magazine capacity is 15 rounds.

Blue

NIB	Exc.	V.G.	Good	Fair	Poor
225	200	150	125	90	70

Chrome

NIB	Exc.	V.G.	Good	Fair	Poor
250	225	175	150	120	80

Model P9RK

Similar to model above but fitted with 4.12" barrel and 7.5" overall length. Finger grooves on front strap and back strap is serrated. Weighs about 34 oz.

NIB	Exc.	V.G.	Good	Fair	Poor
230	200	150	25	90	70

RIFLES

SA-2000-M

Introduced in 1999, this model is a semiautomatic rifle chambered for the 7.62x39mm cartridge or the .223 cartridge. Fitted with a detachable 10 round magazine, synthetic stock and muzzle brake.

NIB	Exc.	V.G.	Good	Fair	Poor
435	350	—	—	—	—

F.I.E.
Hialeah, Florida

Firearms Import and Export was engaged in the business of importing the Franchi shotgun (which is listed under its own heading) and the Arminius revolver (which is made in Germany). They were also distributors for the Titan semiautomatic pistols, which are manufactured in the U.S.A. They were also importing a series of 9mm pistols from Italy that are produced by Tanfoglio and known as the TZ series. F.I.E. was no longer in business as of 1990.

TZ 75

A copy of the CZ 75 Czechoslovakian combat pistol produced by Tanfoglio in Italy. It is a 9mm, double action semiautomatic with a 4.75" barrel, all-steel construction, fixed sights, and a 15-shot magazine. It is offered either blued or matte chrome plated, with wood or rubber grips.

NIB	Exc.	V.G.	Good	Fair	Poor
400	350	300	250	200	150

TZ 75 Series 88

An improved version that is also chambered for the .41 Action Express cartridge. It has a firing pin safety and can be carried cocked and locked. There are a few other minor changes. It was introduced in 1988.

NIB	Exc.	V.G.	Good	Fair	Poor
425	375	325	250	200	150

KG-99

A blowback-operated, semiautomatic assault pistol chambered for the 9mm Parabellum cartridge. It has a 36-round magazine. It was discontinued in 1984.

NIB	Exc.	V.G.	Good	Fair	Poor
500	450	350	250	200	150

Spectre Assault Pistol

An assault-type semiautomatic pistol chambered for the 9mm Parabellum. It has a 30- or 50-round magazine available. It was introduced in 1989.

NIB	Exc.	V.G.	Good	Fair	Poor
650	575	475	400	300	200

NOTE: Recent firearms legislation creates an uncertain market for this type of pistol.

Titan II .22

A semiautomatic pistol chambered for the .22 l.r. It has a 10-shot magazine and a blued finish with walnut grips. It is made in the U.S.A.

NIB	Exc.	V.G.	Good	Fair	Poor
200	150	100	75	50	25

Titan E32

A single action, blowback-operated, semiautomatic pistol that was chambered for the .32 ACP and is now chambered for the .380 ACP cartridge. The finish is blue or chrome-plated, and the grips are walnut.

NIB	Exc.	V.G.	Good	Fair	Poor
225	175	150	125	100	75

Super Titan 11

Similar to the Titan except that it has a 12-round, high-capacity magazine.

NIB	Exc.	V.G.	Good	Fair	Poor
250	200	175	150	100	75

Titan 25

A smaller version of the Titan Series chambered for the .25 ACP cartridge. It is blued or chrome-plated.

NIB	Exc.	V.G.	Good	Fair	Poor
100	75	50	40	30	20

Titan Tigress

Similar to the Titan 25 except that it is gold-plated and cased.

NIB	Exc.	V.G.	Good	Fair	Poor
150	115	90	75	50	30

D38 Derringer

A two-shot, Over/Under, Remington-style derringer chambered for the .38 Special cartridge. It is chrome-plated and was dropped from the line in 1985.

NIB	Exc.	V.G.	Good	Fair	Poor
85	60	45	35	25	20

D86 Derringer

A single-shot derringer with a 3" barrel. It is chambered for the .38 Special cartridge and is chrome-plated. There is an ammunition storage compartment in the butt and a transfer bar safety that makes it safer to carry. This model was introduced in 1986.

NIB	Exc.	V.G.	Good	Fair	Poor
100	80	65	50	35	20

There is a series of single action, .22 caliber revolvers that were patterned after the Colt Single Action Army. They were manufactured in the U.S.A. or Brescia, Italy. They are inexpensive and of fair quality. The differences between these models are basically barrel lengths, type of sights, and finish. They all are chambered for the .22 l.r. and have interchangeable .22 Magnum cylinders. We list them for reference purposes.

Cowboy

NIB	Exc.	V.G.	Good	Fair	Poor
100	75	50	40	35	20

Gold Rush

NIB	Exc.	V.G.	Good	Fair	Poor
150	125	100	80	75	50

Texas Ranger

NIB	Exc.	V.G.	Good	Fair	Poor
100	85	75	50	35	20

Buffalo Scout

NIB	Exc.	V.G.	Good	Fair	Poor
95	80	70	50	35	20

Legend S.A.A.

NIB	Exc.	V.G.	Good	Fair	Poor
125	110	85	65	50	30

Hombre

A single action made in Germany by Arminius. It is patterned after the Colt Single Action Army revolver. The Hombre is chambered for the .357 Magnum, .44 Magnum, and .45 Colt cartridges. It is offered with a 5.5", 6", or 7.5" barrel, case-colored frame, and blued barrel and cylinder, with smooth walnut grips. The backstrap and triggerguard are offered in brass and will bring a 10% premium.

NIB	Exc.	V.G.	Good	Fair	Poor
225	200	175	125	100	75

ARMINIUS REVOLVERS

Model 522TB

A swing-out cylinder, double action revolver chambered for the .22 rimfire cartridge. It has a 4" barrel and is blued with wood grips.

NIB	Exc.	V.G.	Good	Fair	Poor
150	125	100	75	50	30

722

Similar to the 522, with an 8-shot cylinder and a 6" barrel. It is available with a chrome finish.

NIB	Exc.	V.G.	Good	Fair	Poor
150	125	100	75	50	30

532TB

A 7-shot, double action revolver chambered for the .32 S&W cartridge. It has a 4" barrel and adjustable sights and is finished in either blue or chrome.

NIB	Exc.	V.G.	Good	Fair	Poor
160	130	110	80	60	40

732B

Similar to the 532TB, with a 6" barrel and fixed sights. It was discontinued in 1988.

NIB	Exc.	V.G.	Good	Fair	Poor
120	100	80	65	50	35

Standard Revolver

A double action, swing-out cylinder revolver chambered for .32 Magnum or .38 Special. It has a 4" or 6" barrel and fixed sights and is blued with wood grips. This model is made in the U.S.A. and was introduced in 1989.

NIB	Exc.	V.G.	Good	Fair	Poor
125	100	75	50	35	20

Models 384TB and 386TB

These two models are double action chambered for the .38 Special cartridge. The 384 has a 4" barrel; and the 386, a 6" barrel. They are available in blue or chrome plate and were discontinued in 1985.

NIB	Exc.	V.G.	Good	Fair	Poor
165	125	100	85	65	50

Model 357TB

Similar to the 384TB except that it is chambered for the .357 Magnum cartridge and is offered with a 3", 4", or 6" barrel.

NIB	Exc.	V.G.	Good	Fair	Poor
200	175	150	125	90	75

222, 232, and 382TB

These models are double action swing-out cylinder revolvers chambered for .22 rimfire, .32 S&W, and .38 Special. They are 2"-barreled snub-nosed revolvers, with either blued or chrome-plated finishes. They were discontinued in 1985.

NIB	Exc.	V.G.	Good	Fair	Poor
125	100	75	50	40	25

Model 3572

A similar revolver to the 382TB except that it is chambered for the .357 Magnum cartridge. It was discontinued in 1984.

NIB	Exc.	V.G.	Good	Fair	Poor
225	200	175	125	100	75

SHOTGUNS AND RIFLES

Model 122

A bolt action rifle chambered for .22 rimfire, with a 21" barrel and adjustable sights. It has a 10-shot magazine and a walnut Monte Carlo stock. It was introduced in 1986.

NIB	Exc.	V.G.	Good	Fair	Poor
125	95	75	50	35	25

Single Shot

Brazilian made and chambered for 12 or 20 gauge and .410. It is a single-barreled break open, with 25" through 30" barrel and various chokes. It is blued with a wood stock and was introduced in 1985.

NIB	Exc.	V.G.	Good	Fair	Poor
100	80	60	45	35	25

S.O.B.
Similar to the single shot, with an 18.5" barrel and a pistol grip instead of a standard stock. This model was discontinued in 1984.

NIB	Exc.	V.G.	Good	Fair	Poor
100	80	60	45	35	25

Sturdy Over/Under
Chambered for 12 and 20 gauge and has 3" chambers and 28" vent rib barrels with various chokes. This is an Over/Under with double triggers and extractors. The frame is engraved and silver finished. It was manufactured in Italy by Maroccini and imported between 1985 and 1988.

NIB	Exc.	V.G.	Good	Fair	Poor
300	275	225	175	150	100

Brute
A side-x-side chambered for 12 and 20 gauge and .410. It has 19" barrels, double triggers, and extractors. It has a wood stock and was dropped from the line in 1984.

NIB	Exc.	V.G.	Good	Fair	Poor
200	175	125	100	75	50

SPAS-12
A unique shotgun in that it can function as a pump or an automatic with the touch of a button. It is a paramilitary-type shotgun chambered for 12 gauge, with a 21.5" barrel and a 9-shot tube magazine. It has an alloy receiver and a folding stock. The finish is all black. This model is manufactured by Franchi in Italy.

NIB	Exc.	V.G.	Good	Fair	Poor
2000	1500	900	650	400	300

Law-12
A paramilitary-type, 12-gauge, semiautomatic shotgun that is gas-operated and has a 9-shot tube magazine. The barrel is 21.5" in length and choked cylinder bore. It has a military special black finish and a black synthetic stock.

NIB	Exc.	V.G.	Good	Fair	Poor
650	550	400	300	200	100

SAS-12
A paramilitary-type, slide action shotgun chambered for 12 gauge. It has a 21.5" barrel, choked cylinder bore. The finish is similar to the LAW-12, and it is manufactured by Franchi in Italy.

NIB	Exc.	V.G.	Good	Fair	Poor
750	650	500	400	300	200

F.L. SELBSTLADER
This is not a manufacturer but the German designation for the self-loader used on pistols made by Friedrich Langenhan. SEE—LANGENHAN

F&T
(Falise & Trappman of Liege, Belgium)
SEE—French Military Firearms

FABARM
Brescia, Italy
Importer - Heckler & Koch, Inc.
Sterling, Virginia
In 1998 H&K took over the importation of the Fabarm shotgun line in the U.S.

SEMIAUTOMATIC SHOTGUNS
Ellegi Standard
A gas-operated, semiautomatic shotgun chambered for 12 gauge. It has a 28" vent rib barrel with choice of choke. The receiver is blue anodized alloy with a photo-etched game scene, and the stock and forearm are checkered walnut. This model was introduced in 1989.

NIB	Exc.	V.G.	Good	Fair	Poor
700	625	525	450	350	250

The Ellegi Model is available in six other configurations. The differences are in the barrel length and choke, type of choke tubes, and finish. Basically the guns are quite similar to the standard model. These variations are as follows:

Ellegi Multichoke
NIB	Exc.	V.G.	Good	Fair	Poor
700	625	525	450	350	250

Ellegi Innerchoke
NIB	Exc.	V.G.	Good	Fair	Poor
725	650	550	475	375	275

Ellegi Magnum
NIB	Exc.	V.G.	Good	Fair	Poor
725	650	550	475	375	275

Ellegi Super Goose
NIB	Exc.	V.G.	Good	Fair	Poor
800	725	625	550	450	350

Ellegi Slug
NIB	Exc.	V. G.	Good	Fair	Poor
775	700	600	525	425	325

Ellegi Police
NIB	Exc.	V. G.	Good	Fair	Poor
575	500	450	400	300	225

SLIDE ACTION SHOTGUNS
Model S.D.A.S.S.
Chambered for 12 gauge with a 3" chamber. It is offered with a 20" or 24.5" barrel threaded for external choke tubes. This model has an 8-shot tube magazine, twin action bars, an alloy receiver, and a matte black finish. It is a defensive-type shotgun and has been imported since 1989.

NIB	Exc.	V.G.	Good	Fair	Poor
500	450	400	350	250	175

The Special Police and the Martial Model are variations of the basic slide action and differ in barrel length and choke. The Police Model has a shrouded barrel.

Special Police

NIB	Exc.	V.G.	Good	Fair	Poor
525	475	425	350	275	200

Martial Model

NIB	Exc.	V.G.	Good	Fair	Poor
475	425	375	300	225	175

SINGLE SHOT SHOTGUNS

Omega Standard

Has an alloy receiver and is chambered for 12 and 20 gauge, as well as .410. It has 26" or 28" barrels with various chokes. The finish is black with a beech stock. It was introduced in 1989.

NIB	Exc.	V.G.	Good	Fair	Poor
150	125	100	75	50	40

Omega Goose Gun

Chambered for 12 gauge only, with a 35.5" full-choke barrel.

NIB	Exc.	V.G.	Good	Fair	Poor
160	140	125	100	75	50

SIDE-X-SIDE SHOTGUNS

Beta Model

This double-barrel is chambered for 12 gauge only, with choice of barrel length and choke. It has a boxlock action with false side plates. It has a single trigger and automatic ejectors, and the finish is blued with a checkered, select walnut stock. This model was introduced in 1989.

NIB	Exc.	V.G.	Good	Fair	Poor
925	850	750	600	450	300

Beta Europe

A deluxe version that features single selective triggers and a game scene engraved, coin-finished receiver. The stock is the straight English style with a splinter forend. This model was introduced in 1989.

NIB	Exc.	V.G.	Good	Fair	Poor
1750	1500	1250	1000	750	500

OVER/UNDER SHOTGUNS

Field Model

Chambered for 12 gauge and has 29" vent rib barrels with various chokes. The receiver is coin-finished, and the stock is checkered walnut. This Model was discontinued in 1985.

NIB	Exc.	V.G.	Good	Fair	Poor
900	700	600	500	400	300

Gamma Field

Chambered for 12 or 20 gauge and is offered with 26", 28", or 29" vent rib barrels and various choke combinations. Screw-in choke tubes are available and would be worth a 10% premium. This model has a boxlock, coin-finished receiver that is moderately engraved and a checkered walnut stock.

NIB	Exc.	V.G.	Good	Fair	Poor
925	850	775	650	500	350

Gamma Paradox Gun

Chambered for 12 gauge only, and the top barrel is rifled for accurate placement of slugs. The barrels are 25" long with vent rib, and the bottom barrel has three screw-in choke tubes. This model has a single selective trigger and automatic ejectors. The finish is similar to the Field Model. It was introduced in 1989.

NIB	Exc.	V.G.	Good	Fair	Poor
1000	900	825	750	600	450

Gamma Trap or Skeet

Competition-grade guns with either a 27.5" barrel with five screw-in choke tubes on the skeet model or a 29" barrel with screw-in trap chokes. Both models feature single selective triggers and automatic ejectors; and the trap model has a Monte Carlo stock. They have moderately engraved, coin-finished boxlock actions and were introduced in 1989.

NIB	Exc.	V.G.	Good	Fair	Poor
1000	900	825	750	600	450

Gamma Sporting Competition Model

Designed for Sporting Clays and is chambered for 12 gauge only. The 29" barrel has a wide rib and is furnished with five screw-in choke tubes. It has a single selective trigger, automatic ejectors, and a checkered walnut stock with a competition recoil pad. It is finished like the skeet and trap models and was introduced in 1989.

NIB	Exc.	V.G.	Good	Fair	Poor
1000	900	825	750	600	450

CURRENTLY IMPORTED SHOTGUNS
(H&K- POST 1997)

SEMIAUTOMATIC & PUMP SHOTGUNS

Red Lion

This is a 12 gauge semiauto with 3" chambers, three shot magazine, matte finish, walnut stock, rubber vented recoil pad with leather cover, and set of five choke tubes. Available with 24", 26", or 28" vent rib barrel. Weight is about 7 lbs.

NIB	Exc.	V.G.	Good	Fair	Poor
800	650	500	—	—	—

Red Lion Ducks Unlimited 2001

This model is offered only through the Ducks Unlimited banquet program only. This is a 12 gauge 28" barrel with select walnut stock. Oil finish. Unique serial numbers from 0001DU2001 to 3600DU2001. Receiver is engraved with waterfowl scene and DU logo. Comes with lockable case. Limited to 3,600 shotguns.

NIB	Exc.	V.G.	Good	Fair	Poor
N/A	—	—	—	—	—

Gold Lion

Has many of the features of the Red Lion model with the addition of a high-grade oil-finished walnut stock with Olive wood pistol grip cap. Trigger is gold plated.

NIB	Exc.	V.G.	Good	Fair	Poor
900	700	—	—	—	—

Camo Lion

Introduced in 1999, this 12 gauge model features a ported barrel system in 24", 26", or 28" lengths. Wetlands camo finish. Five chokes tubes and hard plastic case included. Weight is about 7 lbs.

NIB	Exc.	V.G.	Good	Fair	Poor
975	775	—	—	—	—

Sporting Clays Lion

This model, introduced in 1999, features a ported barrel and special "TriBore" system. Offered in 12 gauge with 28" barrel. Walnut stock with rubber recoil pad, gold-plated trigger, matte blue finish, red front sight bar, 10mm channeled rib, two extra front sights (green and white), and a set of five choke tubes. Weight is about 7.2 lbs.

NIB	Exc.	V.G.	Good	Fair	Poor
950	750	—	—	—	—

Sporting Clays Extra

Introduced in 2000 this model features a 28" or 30" vent rib barrel with carbon fiber finish on both barrel and receiver. This model also supplied with 8 competition choke tubes. Stock is adjustable. Supplied with fitted luggage case. Weight is about 7.3 lbs.

NIB	Exc.	V.G.	Good	Fair	Poor
1250	950	—	—	—	—

Tactical Semi-Auto

This is a 12 gauge semiautomatic shotgun fitted with a 20" barrel threaded for chokes. Receiver mounted Picatinny rail. Flip-up front sight. Optional magazine extension has 7-round capacity. Weight is about 6.6 lbs. Introduced in 2001.

NIB	Exc.	V.G.	Good	Fair	Poor
—	—	—	—	—	—

FP6 Field Pump

Introduced in 2001 this model features a black alloy receiver with screw-in chokes. Chambered for 12 gauge with 28" barrel. Black synthetic stock Optional 24" rifles barrel. Weight is about 7 lbs.

NIB	Exc.	V.G.	Good	Fair	Poor
400	325	—	—	—	—

FP6 Field Pump Camo

Same as above but with Mossy Oak Break-up camo pattern.

NIB	Exc.	V.G.	Good	Fair	Poor
460	350	—	—	—	—

FP6

This model is a 12 gauge slide action shotgun with 3" chamber, 20" barrel with heat shield, black polymer stock, threaded barrel for exterior chokes. Weight is about 6.6 lbs. This model is also available with a carbon fiber finish.

NIB	Exc.	V.G.	Good	Fair	Poor
475	375	—	—	—	—

FP6 with Rail

Introduced in 1999, this model is similar to the standard FP6 with the addition of a Picatinny rail mounted on the top of the receiver. Also fitted with a flip-up front sight.

NIB	Exc.	V.G.	Good	Fair	Poor
500	400	—	—	—	—

NOTE: This model is also available with 14" barrel. This requires a BATF tax and all NFA rules apply to purchase and sale of this restricted shotgun. An accessory wire stock are available and pistol grip are for an additional $150.

OVER/UNDER GUNS

Max Lion

This over/under gun is chambered for the 12 or 20 gauge, 3" shell and fitted with single selective trigger, auto ejectors, high grade walnut stock, leather covered recoil pad, set of 5 choke tubes and a fitted luggage-style case. Choice of 26", 28", or 30" barrels on 12 gauge guns and 26" or 28" on 20 gauge guns. Weight is about 7.5 lbs. for 12 gauge and 7 lbs. for 20 gauge.

Max Lion 12 gauge

Max Lion 20 gauge

NIB	Exc.	V.G.	Good	Fair	Poor
1800	1400	1050	—	—	—

NOTE: In 1999 the Max Lion was offered with the TriBore barrel system. For models with this system add $70 to above NIB prices.

Max Lion Light

Introduced in 2000 this model features 24" barrels in both 12 and 20 gauge. Receiver has gold game bird enlay. Single trigger automatic ejectors and select walnut stock. Weight is about 7 lbs.

NIB	Exc.	V.G.	Good	Fair	Poor
1925	1450	—	—	—	—

Sporting Clays Competition Lion

This model is available in 12 or 20 gauge with 28" 10mm channeled rib barrels. Single selective trigger and automatic ejectors. Recoil reducer installed in buttstock. Ported barrels. Set of 5 choke tubes standard. Leather covered recoil pad. High grade walnut stock. Introduced in 1999.

NIB	Exc.	V.G.	Good	Fair	Poor
1350	1050	—	—	—	—

Sporting Clays Competition Extra

This 12 gauge model features a a choice of 28" or 30" barrels. Walnut stock is adjustable. Finish is carbon fiber. Gun is supplied with set of 8 choke tubes. Introduced in 2000. Weight is about 7.8 lbs.

NIB	Exc.	V.G.	Good	Fair	Poor
1750	1300	—	—	—	—

Black Lion Competition

Similar to the Max Lion in choice of gauges and barrel lengths and features but with less figured walnut stock and black receiver finish.

Black Lion 12 gauge

Black Lion 20 gauge

NIB	Exc.	V.G.	Good	Fair	Poor
1525	1200	—	—	—	—

Monotrap

This is a single barrel trap gun with 30" vent rib barrel. Forearm has built-in recoil reduction system. Single selective trigger and automatic ejectors. Adjustable comb. This shotgun is a 12 gauge built on a 20 gauge receiver. Weight is about 6 lbs. Introduced in 2000.

NIB	Exc.	V.G.	Good	Fair	Poor
1825	1350	—	—	—	—

Silver Lion

This model is available in both 12 and 20 gauge and with 26", 28" barrel and 30" barrels in 12 gauge. The silver finish receiver is etched and stock is high quality walnut with leather covered pad. Scalable forearm is standard and is single selective trigger and auto ejectors. 5 chokes tubes are included. Weight is about 7.5 lbs. for 12 gauge guns and 7 lbs. for 20 gauge.

Silver Lion 12 gauge

Silver Lion 20 gauge

NIB	Exc.	V.G.	Good	Fair	Poor
1325	1050	—	—	—	—

Silver Lion Youth

This 20 gauge over and under features a shortened buttstock and 24" ported barrels. Single selective trigger and automatic ejectors standard. Walnut stock. Rubber recoil pad. Silver steel receiver. Weight is approximately 6 lbs. Introduced in 1999.

NIB	Exc.	V.G.	Good	Fair	Poor
1325	1050	—	—	—	—

Super Light Lion Youth

Similar to the Silver Lion Youth model but chambered for 12 gauge shells. Aluminum receiver and 24" ported barrels. Introduced in 1999. Weight is about 6.5 lbs.

NIB	Exc.	V.G.	Good	Fair	Poor
1050	800	—	—	—	—

Ultra Mag Lion

This model is a 12 gauge gun with 3.5" chambers, black receiver, single selective trigger, auto ejectors, blackened walnut stock, leather covered recoil pad, and set of 5 choke tubes. Barrel length is 28". Weight is 7.9 lbs.

NIB	Exc.	V.G.	Good	Fair	Poor
1100	875	—	—	—	—

Super Light Lion

This model features a lightweight alloy receiver with 12 gauge 24" barrels, single selective trigger, non-auto ejectors, walnut stock, 5 choke tubes, and leather covered recoil pad. Weight is about 6.5 lbs.

NIB	Exc.	V.G.	Good	Fair	Poor
1050	850	—	—	—	—

NOTE: For TriBore system add $125 to NIB price.

Camo Turkey Mag.

Introduced in 1999, this model features an unported TriBore 20" barrel. Receiver has Picatinny rail on top. Full extra brown camo finish. Chambered for 12 gauge with 3.5" chambers. Weight is about 7.5 lbs.

NIB	Exc.	V.G.	Good	Fair	Poor
1275	1025,	—	—	—	—

Ultra Camo Mag. Lion

This 12 gauge 3.5" model is fitted with 28" barrels. Wetlands camo pattern finish. Non-automatic ejectors. Weight is about 8 lbs. Introduced in 1999. Standard with steel screw-in chokes and regular screw-in chokes.

NIB	Exc.	V.G.	Good	Fair	Poor
1100	875	—	—	—	—

SIDE-BY-SIDE GUNS

Classic Lion Grade I

Offered in 12 gauge with 3" chambers, single selective trigger, auto-ejectors, walnut stock, butt plate, and fitted with 26" barrels. Weight is about 7 lbs.

NIB	Exc.	V.G.	Good	Fair	Poor
1475	1175	—	—	—	—

Classic Lion Grade II

Similar to the Grade I but with the addition of oil finished stock and removable sideplates with game scene engraving. Weight is 7.2 lbs.

NIB	Exc.	V.G.	Good	Fair	Poor
2100	1650	—	—	—	—

FABBRI, ARMI
Gardone V.T., Italy

Fabbri Armi currently manufactures one of the best shotguns in the world. They are available as a custom made-to-order item, and they are not often seen in the used gun market. The values for guns of this nature and quality are impossible to accurately establish in a book of this nature as there are so many options and conditions that make the prices fluctuate greatly. We give an estimate figure as a base starting point but strongly urge individual appraisal should a transaction involving one of these fine firearms be contemplated. See Karl Lippard's book *Fabbri Shotguns*, Colorado Springs, Colorado, VM Publications, 1998, for more value details

Side-x-Side Shotgun

Chambered for 12 or 20 gauge with all other features on a custom-order basis. This model is no longer in production.

NIB	Exc.	V.G.	Good	Fair	Poor
38500	25000	17500	15000	10000	8000

Over/Under Shotgun

Chambered for 12 or 20 gauge with all other features on a custom-order basis. Prices listed below are for Boehler barrels.

NIB	Exc.	V.G.	Good	Fair	Poor
76000	50000	30000	20000	15000	10000

NOTE: Add 50% for Vaecum Arc Romelt barrels.

FABRIQUE NATIONALE
Herstal, Belgium

In 1889 Fabrique Nationale (or FN) was founded by a group of Belgian investors for the purpose of manufacturing Mauser rifles for the Belgian army. This was to be accomplished under license from Mauser, with the technical assistance of Kudwig Loewe of Berlin. A few years later, in the late 1890s, John Browning arrived in Europe seeking a manufacturer for his semiautomatic shotgun. He had severed his ties with Winchester after a disagreement. This led to a long association that worked out extremely well for both parties. Later Browning became associated with Colt, and the world market was divided—with the Eastern Hemisphere going to FN and the Western Hemisphere to Colt.

In this section, we list arms that bear the FN banner. The FN-manufactured firearms produced under the Browning banner are listed in the Browning section of this book.

Model 1900

A blowback-operated semiautomatic pistol chambered for the 7.65mm cartridge. It has a 4" barrel and fixed sights and is blued with molded plastic grips. This model is notorious as the pistol that was used to assassinate Archduke Ferdinand, an event that touched off WWI. It was manufactured between 1899 and 1910. This model is referred to as the "Old Model."

Exc.	V.G.	Good	Fair	Poor
400	325	275	200	150

Model 1903

A considerable improvement over the Model 1900. It is also a blowback-operated semiautomatic; but the recoil spring is located under the barrel, and the firing pin travels through the slide after being struck by a hidden hammer. The barrel is held in place by five locking lugs that fit into five grooves in the frame. This pistol is chambered for the 9mm Browning long cartridge and has a 5" barrel. The finish is blued with molded plastic grips, and the detachable magazine holds 7 rounds. There is a detachable shoulder stock/holster along with a 10-round magazine that was available for this model. These accessories are extremely rare and if present would make the package worth approximately five times that of the pistol alone. There were approximately 58,000 manufactured between 1903 and 1939. This model was one of the Browning patents that the Eibar Spanish gunmakers did so love to copy because of the simplicity of the design.

Exc.	V.G.	Good	Fair	Poor
500	425	375	275	175

Model 1906

A smaller version of the Model 1903, designed to be a pocket pistol and chambered for the 6.35mm cartridge. It became known as the "Vest Pocket" model and was also the basis for many Eibar copies. It has a 2.5" barrel and was produced in two distinct variations. The first variation had no safety lever or slide lock and relied on the grip safety. The second variation, that occurred at approximately serial number 100000, added this safety lever and slide lock, which helped simplify dismantling of the pistol. This model was available either blued or nickel-plated. The plated models would bring a 10% premium. There were approximately 1,086,100 manufactured between 1906 and 1959.

1st Variation Under Serial Number 100000

Exc.	V.G.	Good	Fair	Poor
350	300	250	200	125

2nd Variation Over Serial Number 100000

Exc.	V.G.	Good	Fair	Poor
325	275	200	175	100

Model 1910 "New Model"

Chambered for 7.65mm and 9mm short. It has a 3.5" barrel, is blued, and has molded plastic grips. The principal difference between this model and its predecessors is that the recoil spring on the Model 1910 is wrapped around the barrel. This gives the slide a more graceful tubular appearance instead of the old slab-sided look. This model has the triple safety features of the 1906 Model 2nd variation and is blued with molded plastic grips. This model was adopted by police forces around the world. It was manufactured between 1912 and 1954.

Courtesy Orvel Reichert

Exc.	V.G.	Good	Fair	Poor
350	300	250	175	125

Model 1922

Exc.	V.G.	Good	Fair	Poor
275	225	175	125	100

"Baby" Model

A smaller and lighter version of the Model 1906. It is chambered for the 6.35mm cartridge and has a 2" barrel. There is no grip safety or slide lock on this model, and it appears to be more square in shape than the Model 1906. This model was offered in blue, with molded plastic grips. Early models have the word "Baby" molded into the grips; post-1945 versions do not. There is also a nickel-plated version with pearl grips. There were over 500,000 of these manufactured between 1931 and 1983.

Courtesy Orvel Reichert

Courtesy Orville Reichert

Exc.	V.G.	Good	Fair	Poor
400	325	300	225	150

Model 1935

The last design from John Browning and was developed between 1925 and 1935. This pistol is known as the Model 1935, the P-35, High-Power or HP, and also as the GP (which stood for "Grand Puissance") and was referred to by all those names at one time or another. The HP is essentially an improved version of the Colt 1911 design. The swinging link was replaced with a fixed cam, which was less prone to wear. It is chambered for the 9mm Parabellum and has a 13-round detachable magazine. The only drawback to the design is that the trigger pull is not as fine as that of the 1911, as there is a transfer bar

instead of a stirrup arrangement. This is necessary due to the increased magazine capacity resulting in a thicker grip. The barrel is 4.75" in length. It has an external hammer with a manual and a magazine safety and was available with various finishes and sight options and was furnished with a shoulder stock. The Model 1935 was used by many countries as their service pistol as such there are many variations. We list these versions and their approximate values. There are books available specializing in this model, and it would be beneficial to gain as much knowledge as possible if one contemplates acquisition of this fine and highly collectible pistol.

Prewar Commercial Model

Found with either a fixed sight or a sliding tangent rear sight and is slotted for a detachable shoulder stock. It was manufactured from 1935 until 1940.

Wood Holster Stock-Add 50%.

Fixed Sight Version

Exc.	V.G.	Good	Fair	Poor
600	525	475	375	275

Tangent Sight Version

Exc.	V.G.	Good	Fair	Poor
1000	850	675	550	400

Prewar Military Contract

The Model 1935 was adopted by many countries as a service pistol, and they are as follows:

Belgium

Exc.	V.G.	Good	Fair	Poor
1200	1050	900	600	375

Canada and China (*See John Inglis & Company*)

Denmark

Exc.	V.G.	Good	Fair	Poor
1250	1100	950	650	400

Great Britain

Exc.	V.G.	Good	Fair	Poor
1150	1000	850	550	325

Estonia

Exc.	V.G.	Good	Fair	Poor
1200	1050	900	600	375

Holland

Exc.	V.G.	Good	Fair	Poor
1250	1100	950	650	400

Latvia

Exc.	V.G.	Good	Fair	Poor
1500	1350	1050	775	500

Lithuania

Exc.	V.G.	Good	Fair	Poor
1250	1100	950	650	400

Romania

Exc.	V.G.	Good	Fair	Poor
1500	1350	1050	775	500

German Military Pistole Modell 640(b)

In 1940 Germany occupied Belgium and took over the FN plant. The production of the Model 1935 continued, with Germany taking the output. The FN plant was assigned the production code "ch," and many thousands were produced. The finish on these Nazi guns runs from as fine as the Prewar Commercial series to downright crude, and it is possible to see how the war was progressing for Germany by the finish on their weapons. One must be cautious with some of these guns as there have been fakes noted with their backstraps cut for shoulder stocks, producing what would appear to be a more expensive variation. Individual appraisal should be secured if any doubt exists.

Fixed Sight Model

Exc.	V.G.	Good	Fair	Poor
500	450	400	300	250

Tangent Sight Model - 50,000 Manufactured

Courtesy Orvel Reichert

Courtesy Orvel Reichert

Exc.	V.G.	Good	Fair	Poor
800	750	700	550	400

Captured Prewar Commercial Model

These pistols were taken over when the plant was occupied. They are slotted for stocks and have tangent sights. There were few produced between serial number 48,000 and 52,000. All noted have the WA613 Nazi proof mark. Beware of fakes!

Exc.	V.G.	Good	Fair	Poor
1500	1400	1150	750	500

Postwar Military Contract

Manufactured from 1946, and they embody some design changes—such as improved heat treating and barrel locking. Pistols produced after 1950 do not have barrels that can interchange with the earlier model pistols. The earliest models have an "A" prefix on the serial number and do not have the magazine safety. These pistols were produced for many countries, and there were many thousands manufactured.

Fixed Sight

Exc.	V.G.	Good	Fair	Poor
475	425	375	300	250

Tangent Sight

Exc.	V.G.	Good	Fair	Poor
750	675	575	400	300

Slotted and Tangent Sight

Exc.	V.G.	Good	Fair	Poor
1150	1050	750	500	400

Postwar Commercial Model

Introduced in 1950 and in 1954. Those imported into the U.S.A. are marked Browning Arms Co. These pistols have the commercial polished finish.

Fixed Sight

Exc.	V.G.	Good	Fair	Poor
500	425	350	300	250

Tangent Sight

Exc.	V.G.	Good	Fair	Poor
750	650	500	400	350

Slotted and Tangent Sight

Exc.	V.G.	Good	Fair	Poor
1200	1100	800	550	450

Model Forty-Nine

This pistol is built by FN Manufacturing, Inc. in Columbia, SC. It has a polymer frame and stainless steel slide. Chambered for 9mm or .40S&W cartridge. Barrel length is 4.25". Magazine capacity is 16 rounds for law enforcement and 10 rounds for commercial sales. It features a repeatable secure striker trigger system. Offered in stainless steel slide or black coated slide. Weight is about 26 oz. Offered primarily for sale to law enforcement agencies. Introduced in 2000.

NIB	Exc.	V.G.	Good	Fair	Poor
465	375	—	—	—	—

Model HP-DA/HP-DAO

This model is offered in two different configurations. The first is with double action/single action trigger while the second is double action only. Chambered for the 9mm cartridge the pistol is fitted with fixed sights. Magazine capacity is 15 rounds for law enforcement and 10 rounds for commerical sales. Weight is about 31 oz. Intended primarily for law enforcement sales. Introduced in 2000.

NIB	Exc.	V.G.	Good	Fair	Poor
640	475	—	—	—	—

> **WARNING:** A large number of counterfeit FN Hi-Powers have been shipped to the United States, possibly from the Balkans. The slides are marked just like the FN originals but the fit and finish is of poor quality. These pistols are missing numerous small proof stamps and markings normally found on FN pistols. These counterfeits have a serial number on the front of the grip strap with a single letter prefix. All are fitted with the late style extractor. Metal finish is either a military matte blue or a commercial high gloss blue.

RIFLES

Model 1889

Exc.	V.G.	Good	Fair	Poor
275	250	200	125	100

Model 1949 or SAFN 49

NOTE: The Egyptian model has recently been imported in large numbers and is worth approximately 20% less. For .30-06 caliber-Add 20%.

Exc.	V.G.	Good	Fair	Poor
500	400	300	225	150

Model 30-11 Sniper Rifle

Exc.	V.G.	Good	Fair	Poor
5000	4500	3500	2750	2000

FN-FAL

50.00-21" Rifle Model

NIB	Exc.	V.G.	Good	Fair	Poor
3500	3000	2300	1900	1200	1000

50.63-18" Paratrooper Model

NIB	Exc.	V.G.	Good	Fair	Poor
4000	3600	3000	2000	1300	1100

50.64-21" Paratrooper Model

NIB	Exc.	V.G.	Good	Fair	Poor
2800	2400	2000	1800	1200	1000

50.41-Synthetic Butt H-Bar

NIB	Exc.	V.G.	Good	Fair	Poor
2800	2400	2000	1800	1200	1000

50.42-Wood Butt H-Bar

NIB	Exc.	V.G.	Good	Fair	Poor
2800	2400	2000	1800	1200	1000

FN FAL "G" Series (Type I Receiver)

Standard

NIB	Exc.	V.G.	Good	Fair	Poor
5000	4500	4000	3000	2000	1000

Lightweight

NIB	Exc.	V.G.	Good	Fair	Poor
5000	4500	4000	3000	2000	1000

FN CAL

NIB	Exc.	V.G.	Good	Fair	Poor
7000	6500	5000	3000	1500	1000

FNC

Standard-Fixed stock, 16" or 18" barrel

NIB	Exc.	V.G.	Good	Fair	Poor
3000	2800	2500	2000	1500	1000

Paratrooper Model-Folding stock, 16" or 18" barrel

NIB	Exc.	V.G.	Good	Fair	Poor
3000	2800	2500	2000	1500	1000

NOTE: The above prices are for Belgian made guns only.

Musketeer Sporting Rifles

A bolt action rifle built on the Mauser action chambered for various popular cartridges. It has a 24" barrel and is blued, with a checkered walnut stock. It was manufactured between 1947 and 1963.

Exc.	V.G.	Good	Fair	Poor
450	350	300	250	200

Deluxe Sporter

A higher-grade version of the Musketeer with the same general specifications. It was also manufactured between 1947 and 1963.

Exc.	V.G.	Good	Fair	Poor
550	450	400	275	200

FN Supreme

Chambered for the popular standard calibers and has a 24" barrel with an aperture sight and a checkered walnut stock. It was manufactured between 1957 and 1975.

Exc.	V.G.	Good	Fair	Poor
800	650	500	400	400

Supreme Magnum Model

Similar to the standard Supreme except that it is chambered for .264 Win. Mag., 7mm Rem. Mag., and .300 Win. Mag. It is furnished with a recoil pad and was manufactured between the same years as the standard model.

Exc.	V.G.	Good	Fair	Poor
800	650	500	400	400

FN-Mini-Hecate

Chambered for the .308 cartridge this bolt action rifle features a free-loading match grade barrel, etc. Introduced in 2001.

NIB	Exc.	V.G.	Good	Fair	Poor
N/A	—	—	—	—	—

FAIRBANKS, A. B.
Boston, Massachusetts

Fairbanks All Metal Pistol

This odd pistol was produced of all metal, with a one-piece cast brass frame and handle and an iron barrel and lock system. It is chambered for .33 caliber and utilizes the percussion ignition system. The barrel lengths noted are of 3" to 10". The barrels are marked "Fairbanks Boston. Cast Steel." They were manufactured between 1838 and 1841.

Exc.	V.G.	Good	Fair	Poor
—	—	600	300	150

FALCON FIREARMS
Northridge, California

Portsider

A copy of the Colt 1911 built for a left-handed individual. It is constructed of stainless steel and is similar in all other respects to the Colt. It was introduced in 1986.

NIB	Exc.	V.G.	Good	Fair	Poor
575	500	425	375	300	225

Portsider Set

A matching serial numbered pair consisting of a left-handed and a right-handed version of this model. It was cased, and there were only 100 manufactured in 1986 and 1987.

NIB	Exc.	V.G.	Good	Fair	Poor
1400	1250	1000	750	600	475

Gold Falcon

The frame was machined from solid 17-karat gold. The slide is stainless steel, and the sights have diamond inlays. It was engraved to the customer's order, and there were only 50 manufactured.

NIB	Exc.	V.G.	Good	Fair	Poor
30000	25000	20000	15000	—	—

FAMARS, A. & S.
Brescia, Italy

The Famars shotgun is one of the world's finest and is available on a custom-order basis. This makes it quite difficult to accurately establish values in a book of this nature. Each individual gun must be appraised if a transaction is contemplated as the array of options available makes the values fluctuate greatly. We list them and give an estimated value in their basic form only.

NOTE: In 2001 Famars guns are sold directly through the manufacturer. Prices have been increased by as much as 42%. Also a new grade system has been put in place of the old one listed below. No details are yet avaivable on these new grades.

Engraving Pattern Descriptions
(Older Discontinued Patterns)

S2-Traditional fully engraved fine English scroll with coverage highlighting selected areas of the receiver and forend metal. Wood grade is AA.

S3-Traditional hand-engraved scroll with some open areas around the scroll coverage on the receiver and forend metal. Wood grade is AAA.

S4-Traditional full coverage, intricate and high in detail. Patterns may be English, German, or game scene. Wood grade is AAAA.

S5-Grade S4 patterns with animals inlaid in 24k gold. Wood grade is AAAAA.

S4E-Extremely high detail scenes and elaborate ornamental work where the subject matter is selected by the customer. Wood grade is AAAAA.

S5E-Similar to the S4E level but with raised or flush gold inlay work. Wood grade is AAAAA.

SXO-The best work by the world's best engravers. Museum quality. Wood grade is AAAAAA.

Zeus

An engraved side-by-side boxlock in 12, 20, 28, and .410 bore.

In the white

NIB	Exc.	V.G.	Good	Fair	Poor
19000	12000	—	—	—	—

D2 pattern

NIB	Exc.	V.G.	Good	Fair	Poor
20000	12000	—	—	—	—

S3 pattern

NIB	Exc.	V.G.	Good	Fair	Poor
22000	20000	—	—	—	—

NOTE: Add 10% for smaller gauges.

Tribute

An engraved side-by-side droplock offered in 12 or 20 gauge.

In the white

NIB	Exc.	V.G.	Good	Fair	Poor
21400	20800	—	—	—	—

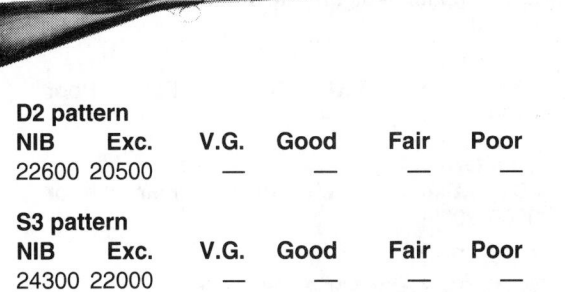

D2 pattern

NIB	Exc.	V.G.	Good	Fair	Poor
22600	20500	—	—	—	—

S3 pattern

NIB	Exc.	V.G.	Good	Fair	Poor
24300	22000	—	—	—	—

Venus

A side-by-side sidelock shotgun with choice of engraving patterns and coverage. Offered in 12, 20, 28, or .410 bore.

In the white

NIB	Exc.	V.G.	Good	Fair	Poor
32700	30500	—	—	—	—

D2 pattern

NIB	Exc.	V.G.	Good	Fair	Poor
33900	31500	—	—	—	—

D3 pattern

NIB	Exc.	V.G.	Good	Fair	Poor
37000	10500	—	—	—	—

D4 pattern

NIB	Exc.	V.G.	Good	Fair	Poor
42800	39000	—	—	—	—

D5 pattern

NIB	Exc.	V.G.	Good	Fair	Poor
48200	42000	—	—	—	—

D4E pattern

NIB	Exc.	V.G.	Good	Fair	Poor
53500	47500	—	—	—	—

D5E pattern

NIB	Exc.	V.G.	Good	Fair	Poor
58500	51500	—	—	—	—

DXO pattern

NIB	Exc.	V.G.	Good	Fair	Poor
85000	55000	—	—	—	—

Veneri

A side-by-side sidelock shotgun.

NIB	Exc.	V.G.	Good	Fair	Poor
32000	30000	—	—	—	—

D2 pattern

NIB	Exc.	V.G.	Good	Fair	Poor
32700	30500	—	—	—	—

Jorema Royal

An over and under shotgun with sidelocks. Offered in 12, 20, 28, and .410 bore

In the white

NIB	Exc.	V.G.	Good	Fair	Poor
32700	26000	—	—	—	—

S2 pattern

NIB	Exc.	V.G.	Good	Fair	Poor
33900	20000	—	—	—	—

S3 pattern

NIB	Exc.	V.G.	Good	Fair	Poor
37300	29500	—	—	—	—

S4 pattern

NIB	Exc.	V.G.	Good	Fair	Poor
42900	33500	—	—	—	—

S5 pattern

NIB	Exc.	V.G.	Good	Fair	Poor
48200	29500	—	—	—	—

S4E pattern

NIB	Exc.	V.G.	Good	Fair	Poor
53500	42500	—	—	—	—

S5E pattern

NIB	Exc.	V.G.	Good	Fair	Poor
53500	42500	—	—	—	—

SXO pattern

NIB	Exc.	V.G.	Good	Fair	Poor
85000	66500	—	—	—	—

NOTE: Add 15% for smaller gauges.

Excaliber BL

An over and under shotgun with removable trigger group. Offered in 12, 20, 28, and .410 bore with single trigger.

NIB	Exc.	V.G.	Good	Fair	Poor
11800	6500	—	—	—	—

Excalibur BL Extra

Finer engraving than standard.

NIB	Exc.	V.G.	Good	Fair	Poor
15455	8900	—	—	—	—

Excalibur BL Prestige

Finer engraving than BL Extra.

NIB	Exc.	V.G.	Good	Fair	Poor
17820	10750	—	—	—	—

Excalibur BLX

Over and under shotgun with sideplates.

NIB	Exc.	V.G.	Good	Fair	Poor
11150	9000	—	—	—	—

Excalibur BLX Extra

Same as above but with finer engraving.

NIB	Exc.	V.G.	Good	Fair	Poor
16759	14000	—	—	—	—

Excalibur BLX Prestige

Finer engraving than the BLX Extra.

NIB	Exc.	V.G.	Good	Fair	Poor
16900	13750	—	—	—	—

Excalibur SL

Over and under shotgun with sidelocks.

NIB	Exc.	V.G.	Good	Fair	Poor
26125	14800	—	—	—	—

Excalibur SL Extra

Same as above with finer engraving.

NIB	Exc.	V.G.	Good	Fair	Poor
30000	16000	—	—	—	—

Excalibur SL Prestige

Finer engraving than the SL Extra.

NIB	Exc.	V.G.	Good	Fair	Poor
33000	18000	—	—	—	—

Excalibur Express

An over and under double rifle in calibers from 7x65R to .375 H&H.

NIB	Exc.	V.G.	Good	Fair	Poor
20196	11500	—	—	—	—

Excalibur Express Extra
Same as above but with finer engraving.

NIB	Exc.	V.G.	Good	Fair	Poor
27060	12000	—	—	—	—

Excalibur Express Prestige
Finer engraving than the Express Extra.

NIB	Exc.	V.G.	Good	Fair	Poor
32065	15250	—	—	—	—

African Express
A side-by-side boxlock double rifle. Calibers from .22 Long Rifle to .600 NE.

NIB	Exc.	V.G.	Good	Fair	Poor
34000	17500	—	—	—	—

Venus Express Professional
A side-by-side double rifle with sidelocks.

NIB	Exc.	V.G.	Good	Fair	Poor
45000	34500	—	—	—	—

Venus Express Extra
A side-by-side double rifle with sidelocks. Calibers from .375 H&H to .500 NE.

NIB	Exc.	V.G.	Good	Fair	Poor
95750	50000	—	—	—	—

FARQUHARSON, JOHN
London, England
Not a gunmaker but the designer of what is perhaps the finest single shot action ever developed. It was patented on May 25, 1872, and has been used as the basis for some of the world's best single shot rifles manufactured by top English gunmakers throughout the years. There will be references to this action under sections dealing with these makers.

FARROW ARMS CO.
Holyoke, Massachusetts
Mason, Tennessee
Farrow Falling Block Rifle
Designed by W.M. Farrow, a target shooter who had worked on the Ballard rifles for the Marlin company. The Farrow rifles are chambered for various calibers and have barrel lengths from 28"-36" of octagonal configuration. They feature tang sights and are either all blued or have a nickel-plated receiver.

The stocks are walnut. There were two grades offered that varied according to the grade of wood used. These rifles are quite scarce on today's market, and the number manufactured between 1885 and 1900 is unknown.

No. 1 Model
Fancy walnut with checkering and a Schutzen buttplate.

Exc.	V.G.	Good	Fair	Poor
—	—	6500	3000	1750

No. 2 Model
Plainer wood and no checkering.

Exc.	V.G.	Good	Fair	Poor
—	—	5500	2500	1400

FAYETTEVILLE ARMORY PISTOLS AND RIFLES
Fayetteville, North Carolina
In 1861, the U.S. Arsenal at Fayetteville, North Carolina, was seized by the officials of that state and later turned over to the government of the Confederate States of America. While still controlled by the state of North Carolina, a number of inferior flintlock arms were altered at the arsenal from flint to percussion, including a number of U.S. M1836 pistols and U.S. M1819 Hall rifles (the latter also shortened and remodeled into cavalry carbines). In accordance with an agreement between the governors of Virginia and North Carolina, the rifle machinery seized at the former U.S. Armory at Harpers Ferry, Virginia, was also sent to Fayetteville, where in 1862 the Confederacy began the construction of rifles modeled after the U.S. M1855 rifle. Production continued until 1865 when the advance of Sherman's armies necessitated the evacuation of the armory.

Fayetteville Armory Percussion Pistols
(U.S. M1836 Pistols, Altered)
Overall length 13-1/4"; barrel length 8-1/2"; caliber .54. Markings: same as U.S. M1836 contact pistols, i.e. the locks either marked with eagle head over "A. WATERS/MILBURY MS./(date)" or "US/R. JOHNSON/MIDDN CONN./(date)" and various barrel proofmarks; also occasionally marked "N. CAROLINA".

The Fayetteville Armory altered approximately 900 U.S. M1836 pistols from flintlock to percussion. These arms were altered by enlarging the flint touchhole and screwing in a cylindrical drum in place of the pan and frizzen. The distinguishing feature of the Fayetteville alteration is the clean-out screw at the face of the cylinder and the "S" shaped hammer, not unlike that used on post-1862 dated rifles.

Courtesy Milwaukee Public Museum, Milwaukee, Wisconsin

Exc.	V. G.	Good	Fair	Poor
—	—	2500	1200	900

Fayetteville Armory Rifles (Types I through IV)
Overall length 49-1/8"; barrel length 33"; caliber .58. Markings: on barrel, an eagle over "C.S.A./FAYETTEVILLE" forward of the hammer and the date on the rounded tail. "CSA"

also found on buttplates; date on top of barrel; proofmarks (eagle head, "V" and "P") on left quarter of barrel near breech.

From 1862 to early 1865, the Fayetteville Armory produced four variants of the old U.S. M1855 rifle on the machinery that had been lent to North Carolina by Virginia after its capture in April 1861. The earliest 1862 production (Type I) utilized unmilled lockplates captured at Harpers Ferry and are distinguished by having a "hump" (where the Maynard primer would have been milled) that extends to the arc of the hammer. Type II production utilized the newly made locks received from Richmond during the balance of 1862; they had a relatively low "hump" whose upper surface matched the contour of the stock. By the end of 1862, Fayetteville was producing its own lock, the plate of which resembled the U.S. M1861 rifle musket, but with a distinctive "S" shaped hammer. This lock distinguishes both type III and type IV production. All rifles made through 1863 continued to bear a saber bayonet lug on the right side of the barrel. In 1864, however, this was eliminated in favor of a triangular socket bayonet. The absence of the saber bayonet lug and remodeled front sight distinguishes type IV production. Because the barrel machinery went to Richmond, production at Fayetteville was continually hindered, seldom reaching more than 300 per month in the three years that the Fayetteville rifle was manufactured. (Note: The rarity of Type I production will usually generate a premium for that variant.)

Courtesy Milwaukee Public Museum, Milwaukee, Wisconsin

Courtesy Milwaukee Public Museum, Milwaukee, Wisconsin

Exc.	V.G.	Good	Fair	Poor
—	—	11500	4500	3750

FEATHER INDUSTRIES, INC.
Trinidad, Colorado

AT-22
A blowback-operated semiautomatic chambered for the .22 l.r. cartridge. It has a removable, shrouded 17" barrel and a folding metal stock. There are adjustable sights, and the finish is black. There is a detachable 20-round magazine. This model was introduced in 1986.

NIB	Exc.	V.G.	Good	Fair	Poor
250	200	175	150	110	75

AT-9
Similar to the AR-22 except that it is chambered for the 9mm Parabellum cartridge and has a 16" barrel and 32-round magazine. It was introduced in 1988.

NIB	Exc.	V.G.	Good	Fair	Poor
325	275	250	225	175	125

KG-9
A 9mm, semiautomatic assault rifle that was introduced in 1989.

NIB	Exc.	V.G.	Good	Fair	Poor
575	500	425	375	300	250

KG-22
Similar in appearance to the KG-9 except that it is chambered for .22 l.r. and has a 20-round detachable magazine. It was introduced in 1989.

NIB	Exc.	V.G.	Good	Fair	Poor
300	275	225	175	125	100

A Fayetteville Armory Type III Rifle was sold at auction for $46,000. Condition was near mint. Possibly never issued. Butterfield & Butterfield, November 1999

SAR-180

The current incarnation of the old American 180, which was manufactured in Austria a number of years ago. It is chambered for .22 l.r. and has a 17.5" barrel. It is a blowback-operated semiautomatic that has a 165-round drum magazine that sits on top of the action on the flat side. The rear sight is adjustable, and the finish is blued with a walnut stock, pistol grip, and forend. This model was revived by Feather Industries in 1989.

NIB	Exc.	V.G.	Good	Fair	Poor
500	450	400	350	275	200

Mini-AT

A blowback-operated semiautomatic pistol chambered for the .22 l.r. cartridge. It is a 5.5"-barreled version of the AT-22 rifle and has a 20-round magazine. This model was manufactured between 1986 and 1989.

NIB	Exc.	V.G.	Good	Fair	Poor
350	200	175	150	125	100

Guardian Angel

A two-shot, Over/Under, derringer-styled pistol. It is chambered for the 9mm Parabellum and can be converted to fire the .38 Super cartridge. It is constructed of stainless steel and has an internal hammer and fully enclosed trigger. It was introduced in 1988.

NIB	Exc.	V.G.	Good	Fair	Poor
150	125	100	75	50	40

FEDERAL ENGINEERING CORP.
Chicago, Illinois

XC-220

A blowback-operated, semiautomatic rifle chambered for the .22 l.r. cartridge. It has a 16.5" barrel and a steel receiver that is blued. The stock is black synthetic. This model was introduced in 1984.

NIB	Exc.	V.G.	Good	Fair	Poor
450	300	275	225	175	125

XC-450

Similar in appearance to the XC-220 except that it is chambered for the .45 ACP cartridge. It has a 30-round detachable magazine.

NIB	Exc.	V.G.	Good	Fair	Poor
650	525	450	400	300	250

XC-900

A 9mm Parabellum version of the same basic firearm. It has a 32-round magazine and was introduced in 1984.

NIB	Exc.	V.G.	Good	Fair	Poor
600	500	425	350	275	200

FEDERAL ORDNANCE, INC.
South El Monte, California

An importer as well as a manufacturer that basically fabricates new and custom firearms out of existing older military parts. The firearms they import are military surplus weapons that will be covered in their own sections of this book. The firearms covered here are of Federal Ordnance manufacture.

M-14 Semiautomatic

A semiautomatic version of the M-14 service rifle. It is constructed of a newly manufactured receiver that has no selector and select surplus G.I. parts. The rifle is refinished to original specifications and furnished with a 20-round magazine and either a wood or fiberglass stock. This model was introduced in 1986. Although this model is a battle rifle and falls into the category affected by the wild price fluctuations we have been experiencing, prices for this gun have stayed fairly stable due to a fairly constant supply. This model has been manufactured since 1986.

Exc.	V.G.	Good	Fair	Poor
650	600	550	450	375

Model 714 Broomhandle Mauser

A remanufactured C96-type pistol chambered for 7.63mm or 9mm Parabellum. It utilizes a new manufactured frame and surplus parts. It features a 10-round detachable magazine, adjustable sights, and walnut grips. A Bolo Model with a smaller grip was produced in 1988 only.

NIB	Exc.	V.G.	Good	Fair	Poor
650	500	400	300	250	100

Model 713 Mauser Carbine

A 16"-barreled version of the Mauser with a fixed walnut stock. It has a standard magazine and is chambered for 7.63mm or 9mm Parabellum. It is refinished and was introduced in 1987.

Exc.	V.G.	Good	Fair	Poor
1250	1000	900	700	575

Model 713 Deluxe

Chambered for 7.63mm and has a 16" barrel with a detachable shoulder stock made of deluxe walnut. It has been modified to accept detachable magazines and is furnished with two 20-shot units. It has a 1000-meter adjustable sight and is furnished in a fitted leather case. There were only 1,500 manufactured in 1986.

NIB	Exc.	V.G.	Good	Fair	Poor
2000	1750	1500	1250	1000	800

Standard Broomhandle

A refurbished surplus C-96 Mauser pistol with a new 7.63mm or 9mm barrel. All springs are replaced, and the entire gun is refinished. It is furnished with a shoulder stock/holster of Chinese manufacture.

NIB	Exc.	V.G.	Good	Fair	Poor
725	650	525	450	350	275

Ranger 1911A1

Federal Ordnance's version of the 1911A1 Colt service pistol. It is made of all steel, is chambered for .45 ACP, and has checkered walnut grips. It was introduced in 1988.

NIB	Exc.	V.G.	Good	Fair	Poor
450	375	325	275	225	150

FEINWERKBAU
Oberndorf, Germany
Importer - Beeman Precision Arms
Santa Rosa, California

Known predominately for the production of high quality, extremely accurate air rifles and pistols. They also produce some of the most accurate target .22 caliber firearms in the world today. These firearms are listed:

Model 2000 Universal

A single-shot, bolt action target rifle chambered for the .22 rimfire cartridge. It has a 26.5" barrel with adjustable aperture sights and a fully adjustable trigger. There were four different stock configurations offered with stippled pistol grips and forearms. An electronic trigger was available as a $450 option. This model was discontinued in 1988.

Exc.	V.G.	Good	Fair	Poor
1350	1050	850	650	550

Mini 2000

Has a 22" barrel, and the electronic trigger was available at the additional cost.

Exc.	V.G.	Good	Fair	Poor
1100	850	750	550	450

Running Boar Rifle

Has a thumbhole stock with an adjustable cheekpiece and is furnished without sights. It was specially designed for the off-hand Running Boar Competitions.

Exc.	V.G.	Good	Fair	Poor
1350	1050	850	650	550

Match Rifle

Has a 26.75" barrel and an adjustable cheekpiece stock.

Exc.	V.G.	Good	Fair	Poor
1200	950	750	550	450

Model 2600 Ultra Match Free Rifle

Similar to the Model 2000, with a laminated thumbhole stock and a heavy 26" barrel, fully adjustable sights, and trigger. It is offered with an electronic trigger for an additional $400. This model was introduced in 1986.

NIB	Exc	V.G.	Good	Fair	Poor
1500	1200	1000	850	650	550

FEMARU
Budapest, Hungary

Hungary became a communist satellite in the mid-1950s. At this time the Femaru company was designated to replace the firm of Fegyvergyar as the official Hungarian arms manufacturer. The products are of good quality.

Model 37

This semiautomatic pistol was built in both 7.65mm and 9mm Short calibers. It is well designed pistol of quality construction. It is fitted with a grip safety and exposed hammer. The Hungarian military adopted the pistol in 1937. It was produced until the late 1940s. Early guns were marked "Femaru Fegyver es Gepgyar RT Budapest" but during the war the Nazi code for these guns was "jhv". The 9mm models have a 7-round magazine while the 7.65 models have an 8-round magazine. During World War II the Germans designed this pistol the "Pistol Mod 37 Kal 7.65 (Ung)". Add 75% for Nazi proofed examples.

Courtesy Richard M. Kumor, Sr.

Exc.	V.G.	Good	Fair	Poor
350	275	225	150	100

Hege

A complete copy of the Walther PP. It is chambered for the 7.65mm and manufactured to be sold by Hegewaffen of Germany. The slide is so marked, along with a Pegasus in a circle. The designation "AP 66 Cal.7.65" also appears. The pistol was intended for export sales in the U.S. and other western countries.

Exc.	V.G.	Good	Fair	Poor
250	225	175	125	100

Tokagypt

15,000 of these pistols were built in 1958, under contract for the Egyptian army. It is a modified version of the Soviet TT-33 Tokarev chambered for the 9mm Parabellum with a safety added. This is a well-made, serviceable pistol; and it is difficult to understand why Egypt reneged on the contract. The balance were sold commercially-some under the trademark "Firebird."

Exc.	V.G.	Good	Fair	Poor
400	350	275	200	125

Walam

Another Walther PP copy of excellent quality chambered for the 9mm short or .380 ACP. Egypt was also to be the recipient of this contract, but again they mysteriously cancelled. The pistols were sold on the commercial market—some designated Model 48.

Exc.	V.G.	Good	Fair	Poor
250	225	175	125	100

FERLACH
Ferlach, Austria
Text by Joseph M. Cornell Ph.D., A.M.A.

The history of gun making in Ferlach began in the early 1500s and continues to the present. Today, there are 13 companies making guns in this beautiful city of about 5,000 inhabitants, which is located in a remote corner of southern Austria. These companies make guns that are among the world's most beautiful and finest. Their price range, at the low end, for a bolt action rifle is from $5,000 to the high end, for one of their high art guns, at $500,000, or perhaps even more.

These companies are family groupings. Many of these families have been making guns for centuries. For them, gun making is an all-consuming tradition. Some of the best known of these families, and most often encountered in the United States, have names such as Just, Hauptmann, Winkler, Michelitsch, Hambrusch, Scheiring, and Borovnik, etc. Other less well-known makers include Juch, Fanzoj, Glanzig, Koschat, Hofer and Zauner. Some of the companies from the past, such as Franz Sodia are no longer in business and guns from these now extinct companies will be occasionally encountered. But whether or not the families are still in business, Ferlach guns are some of the most beautiful and remarkable examples of the gunmaker's art that are to be found anywhere in the world. A Ferlach gun can be recognized, although not always easily, by the following:

1. Many times the city name "Ferlach" will be found on the gun.

2. Many times a recognizable Ferlach maker's name will be found on the guns, such as ones listed above, but not all Ferlach-made guns will have a maker's name on the gun.

3. Ferlach guns are usually made in the typical "German" style.

4. Ferlach guns usually have a unique type of serial number, which contains a two-digit number followed by a period, ".", e.g. XX.XXX. This serial number can sometimes by used to identify the maker.

Along with the companies in Ferlach, which make guns, there is also a Gunmaker's Consortium, which is owned by 12 of these companies. This Consortium provides a variety of services and products for gun makers both in Ferlach and in other locations as well. The Consortium acts as an engineering and mechanical "Center" that is an essential resource for many of the Ferlach gun makers. The Consortium uses three basic types of the steel to make the barrels: Boehler Antinit, Blitz and Super Blitz. The latter allows the thickness of the barrels to be reduced to a minimum, thus reducing the gun's final weight. Antinit is the most often encountered steel and the least expensive of the steel used in Ferlach guns.

While it is not generally known, many of the makers outside Ferlach, who make some of the world's most expensive guns, do not make their own barreled actions. They buy the actions and put their names on them. This is not true of the Ferlach maker. The actions used in their guns, with the exception of bolt action rifles, are made right there in Ferlach by the Consortium and then finished by the individual maker. This allows for maximum efficiency and the technical control of the guns being made.

Ferlach gun makers produce almost all types of hunting weapons; these include bolt action rifles, double rifles, three barreled rifles, drillings, shotguns, guns combining both rifles and shotguns called "combination guns", four barreled guns and even five barreled guns. Ferlach makers are very talented gunsmiths and as a result not only can they make the finest possible guns but they are also able to make guns that would be difficult or impossible for other makers to construct. Furthermore, Ferlach is one of the few centers of gun making in the world where it is still possible to order guns in almost any configuration and in almost any caliber from the small 22LR to the .600 nitro express or even larger.

In addition to the companies that manufacture guns, Ferlach is the home of many of the world's best engravers. Many of the Ferlach makers have in-house engravers but many do not and almost all the companies send out work for special situations. A list of some of the engravers whose work will be found on Ferlach guns would include names such as Krondorfer, Mack, Orou, Schaschl, Singer, Maurer, Widmann, Stogner, de Florian, Plucher and Obiltschnig.

Almost all Ferlach guns are "custom" made guns. This makes each gun somewhat unique, which makes their valuation difficult. There is, however, as with other gunmakers, almost always a relationship between quality, complexity of construction, functionality, beauty, rarity and value/pricing.

It is suggested for proper pricing and evaluation of Ferlach-made guns that an expert be consulted.

FERLIB
Gardone V.T., Italy
Importers-Dakota Arms Inc.
SEE ALSO Dakota Arms Inc.

Model F.VI
A high-grade, side-x-side shotgun chambered for all gauges and is essentially custom-ordered. It is available in various barrel lengths and chokes and has an Anson and Deeley boxlock action, double triggers, and automatic ejectors. The action is case-colored, and the stock is hand-checkered select walnut. Single selective triggers are available for an additional $375.

28 Gauge and .410-Add 10%.

NIB	Exc.	V.G.	Good	Fair	Poor
4500	3500	—	—	—	—

Model F.VII
Has a scroll-engraved, coin-finished frame but otherwise is similar to the Model F.VI. Single trigger option and small gauge premium are the same.

NIB	Exc.	V.G.	Good	Fair	Poor
11000	8000	—	—	—	—

Model F.VII/SC
A more deluxe version with gold inlays and a game scene-engraved receiver. Options and premium are the same.

NIB	Exc.	V.G.	Good	Fair	Poor
12000	9000	—	—	—	—

Model F. VII Sideplate
Features false sideplates that are completely covered with game scene engraving. This model is standard with a single-selective trigger, but the small gauge premium is applicable.

NIB	Exc.	V.G.	Good	Fair	Poor
14000	10000	—	—	—	—

Model F.VII/SC Sideplate
The false sideplate model with gold inlays accenting the full coverage engraving.

28 Gauge and .410-Add 10%.

NIB	Exc.	V.G.	Good	Fair	Poor
15000	11000	—	—	—	—

Hammer Gun
Features a boxlock action with external hammers. Its other features are custom ordered to the purchaser's specifications.

NIB	Exc.	V.G.	Good	Fair	Poor
19000	14000	—	—	—	—

FERRY, ANDREWS & CO.
Stafford, Connecticut

Under Hammer Pistol
This boot pistol is chambered for .36 caliber percussion and has a 3" part-round, part-octagonal barrel. They are similar to the other under hammer pistols that were produced in Connecticut and Massachusetts. The top strap was marked "Andrews Ferry & Co." The number manufactured is unknown. They were produced in the 1850s.

Exc.	V.G.	Good	Fair	Poor
—	1250	600	350	125

FIALA ARMS COMPANY
New Haven, Connecticut

Fiala Repeating Target Pistol

A different type of pistol than what is commonly encountered. Outwardly it resembles a semiautomatic Colt Woodsman; in actuality it is a manually operated firearm that must be cycled by hand after every shot. It was chambered for the .22 rimfire and was offered with interchangeable barrels in lengths of 3", 7.5", and 20". The finish is blued, and the grips are ribbed walnut. The rear sight is a square notched blade which tips up into an elevation adjustable peep sight. They are marked "Fiala Arms and Equipment Co. Inc. / New Haven Conn. / Patents Pending" on the right side of the frame behind the grip and Model 1920/Made in U.S.A. on the right side of the frame above the triggerguard. The left side of the frame was marked "FIALA ARMS" above the image of the polar bear with the "TRADE MARK" below the polar bear in the area above the triggerguard. This pistol was furnished with a detachable shoulder stock in a leather trunk case that held the gun, three barrels, stock, and cleaning tools. A 7.5" smoothbore barrel was catalogued as a silencer. Some 20.0" smoothbore barrels were produced. Some pistols bear the names "Columbia Arms Company, and Botwinik Brothers. The government has classified this pistol with its stock as a "Curio and Relic"; and in its complete state it is a very desirable collectible.

NOTE: *See also Schall & Co.*

Courtesy Butterfield & Butterfield, San Francisco, California

Complete, Three Barrels, Stock, Tools, and Case

Exc.	V.G.	Good	Fair	Poor
2500	2100	1250	675	550

Gun Only

Courtesy Dr. Jon Miller

Courtesy Dr. Jon Miller

Exc.	V.G.	Good	Fair	Poor
600	400	325	250	175

FINNISH LION
Valmet, Sweden

ISU Target Rifle

A single shot, bolt action rifle chambered for the .22 rimfire cartridge. It has a 27" heavy barrel and a target stock with accessories. It features target adjustable sights and was manufactured between 1966 and 1977.

Exc.	V.G.	Good	Fair	Poor
350	300	250	200	125

Champion Free Rifle

Has a 29" heavy barrel and double-set triggers. Otherwise it is similar to the ISU model. It was manufactured between 1965 and 1972.

Exc.	V.G.	Good	Fair	Poor
700	525	450	375	275

Match Rifle

Similar to the Champion rifle, with a thumbhole stock and an adjustable butt plate. It was manufactured between 1937 and 1972.

Exc.	V.G.	Good	Fair	Poor
600	425	350	275	200

FIOCCHI OF AMERICA, INC.
Ozark, Missouri
SEE—Pardini and A. Zoli

Imports the above firearms, and they are listed in their own respective sections.

FIREARMS INTERNATIONAL
Washington, D.C.
SEE—Star

Was once the importer of the Star Model D as it was sold in the U.S.A. They also imported various other .25 caliber Colt copies that are not considered collectible and would be valued in the $150-and-under range.

FIRESTORM
Argentina
Importer-SGS, Wanamassa, NJ

Firestorm .22 L.R.

A semiautomatic pistol chambered for the .22 long rifle cartridge. Ten-round magazine capacity. Matte blue finish or duotone.

NIB	Exc.	V.G.	Good	Fair	Poor
240	185	—	—	—	—

Firestorm .380

This semiauto double action pistol is chambered for the .380 ACP cartridge and fitted with a 3.5" barrel. Fixed 3 dot combat sights. Matte blue or duotone finish. Magazine capacity is 7 rounds. Weight is about 23 oz.

NIB	Exc.	V.G.	Good	Fair	Poor
240	185	—	—	—	—

Mini Firestorm 9mm

This 9mm semiauto double action pistol is fitted with a 3.5" barrel. White outline drift adjustable target sights. Matte blue finish. Polymer grips. Magazine capacity is 10 rounds. Weight is about 25 oz.

NIB	Exc.	V.G.	Good	Fair	Poor
350	275	—	—	—	—

Mini Firestorm .40 S&W

As above but chambered for the .40 S&W cartridge.

NIB	Exc.	V.G.	Good	Fair	Poor
350	275	—	—	—	—

Firestorm .25 Gov't

This is a single action semiautomatic pistol chambered for the .45 ACP cartridge. Fitted with a 5.125" barrel and 3 dot fixed combat sights. Magazine capacity is 7 rounds. Black rubber grips. Matte blue or duotone finish. Weight is about 36 oz.

NIB	Exc.	V.G.	Good	Fair	Poor
300	250	—	—	—	—

Compact Firestorm .45 Gov't

As above but with 4.25" barrel. Weight is about 34 oz.

NIB	Exc.	V.G.	Good	Fair	Poor
300	250	—	—	—	—

Mini Firestorm .45 Gov't

As above but with 3.14" barrel. Black polymer grips and magazine capacity of 10 rounds. Weight is about 31 oz.

NIB	Exc.	V.G.	Good	Fair	Poor
325	275	—	—	—	—

FLETCHER BIDWELL, LLC
Viroqua, WI

Spencer 1860 Military Carbine

Introduced in 2001 this is a faithful reproduction of the original Spencer Carbine. It is chambered for the 56-50 black powder cartridge but in centerfire. Fitted with a blued 22" round barrel. Magazine capacity is 7 rounds in butt tube. Bone charcoal case hardened receiver. Walnut stock. Blade front sight with ladder rear sight adjustable to 800 yards. Weight is about 9 lbs. Built in U.S.

NIB	Exc.	V.G.	Good	Fair	Poor
2395	—	—	—	—	—

FLORENCE ARMORY
Florence, Guilford County, North Carolina

Founded in 1862 as a repair facility to alter sporting arms for military use. Majority of work done by H.C. Lamb & Company. In 1862, Captain Z. Coffin ordered stocks, barrels and locks to assemble newly made rifles. Furniture of these arms varied, either being supplied by Glaze & Company or being the remainders from Searcy & Moore's production. Number made estimated to be in excess of 300 rifles in both .50 and .54 calibers. These arms (particularly the barrels) exhibit characteristics of North Carolina contract pieces.

Prospective purchasers are strongly advised to secure an expert appraisal prior to acquisition.

Exc.	V.G.	Good	Fair	Poor
—	—	7500	6000	4000

FOEHL, C.
Philadelphia, Pennsylvania

Foehl Derringer

A .41 caliber percussion single shot pistol with a 2" barrel, German silver mounts and a walnut stock. The lock marked "C. Foehl".

Exc.	V.G.	Good	Fair	Poor
—	—	1750	750	300

FOEHL & WEEKS
Philadelphia, Pennsylvania

Columbian

A .32 or .38 caliber revolver marked with the patent date "20 January 1891".

Exc.	V.G.	Good	Fair	Poor
—	250	100	75	50

Columbian Automatic

A .38 caliber revolver with a hinged barrel and cylinder assembly.

Exc.	V.G.	Good	Fair	Poor
—	275	125	100	75

Perfect

As above, with a concealed hammer and also in .32 caliber.

Exc.	V.G.	Good	Fair	Poor
—	275	125	100	75

FOGARTY
American Repeating Rifle Co.
Boston, Massachusetts

Fogarty Repeating Rifle and Carbine

A limited number of repeating rifles and carbines based upon Valentine Fogarty's patents were produced between 1866 and 1867. The calibers of these arms varies and the normal barrel lengths are 20" and 28". Blued, casehardened with walnut stocks. The American Repeating Rifle Company was pur-

chased by the Winchester Repeating Arms Company in 1869. Prospective purchasers are advised to secure a qualified appraisal prior to acquisition.

Rifle

Courtesy Buffalo Bill Historical Center, Cody, Wyoming

Exc.	V.G.	Good	Fair	Poor
—	—	5000	3000	1250

Carbine

Courtesy Buffalo Bill Historical Center, Cody, Wyoming

Exc.	V.G.	Good	Fair	Poor
—	—	5000	3000	1250

FOLSOM, H.
St. Louis, Missouri

Derringer

A .41 caliber single shot percussion pocket pistol with a 2.5" barrel, German silver mounts and a walnut stock. The barrel marked "H. Folsom".

Exc.	V.G.	Good	Fair	Poor
—	—	800	350	275

FOLSOM, H&D ARMS CO.

Double Barrel Shotguns

Large distributor of double and single barrel shotguns produced by Crescent Firearms Co., Norwich, CT. Folsom owned and later sold to Savage Arms Co. the Crescent Firearms Co., Davis Warner Co., and Baker Gun Co. around 1930. For more information see also Crescent Firearms Co.

FOREHAND & WADSWORTH
Worcester, Massachusetts

Established in 1871 and operated under the above name until 1890 when it became the Forehand Arms Company. Hopkins & Allen purchased the company in 1902.

Single Shot Derringer

A .22 caliber single shot pocket pistol with a 2" half-octagonal pivoted barrel, spur trigger and nickel- or silver-plated frame. Walnut grips. The barrel marked "Forehand & Wadsworth Worcester".

Exc.	V.G.	Good	Fair	Poor
—	1250	500	250	100

Single Shot .41 Derringer

As above in .41 caliber with a 2.5" round barrel.

Courtesy Milwaukee Public Museum, Milwaukee, Wisconsin

Exc.	V.G.	Good	Fair	Poor
—	—	750	450	200

Side Hammer .22

A .22 caliber spur trigger revolver with a 2.25" to 4" octagonal barrel and 7-shot cylinder. Blued or nickel-plated with walnut grips.

Exc.	V.G.	Good	Fair	Poor
—	300	200	150	100

Center Hammer

A .32 caliber spur trigger revolver with a 3.5" octagonal barrel and 6-shot cylinder. Blued or nickel-plated with rosewood or walnut grips. The top strap commonly found marked "Terror".

Courtesy Milwaukee Public Museum, Milwaukee, Wisconsin

Exc.	V.G.	Good	Fair	Poor
—	350	150	175	125

Old Model Army Single Action Revolver

A .44 Russian caliber revolver with a 7.5" round barrel and 6-shot cylinder. The barrel marked "Forehand & Wadsworth, Worchester, Mass. U.S. Patd. Oct. 22, '61, June 27, '71 Oct. 28, '73." Blued with walnut grips. Approximately 250 were manufactured between 1872 and 1878.

Exc.	V.G.	Good	Fair	Poor
—	—	1500	850	500

New Model Army Single Action Revolver

Similar to the above, with a 6.5" barrel and half-cock notch on the hammer. Approximately 250 were made between 1878 and 1882.

Exc.	V.G.	Good	Fair	Poor
—	—	1750	1000	500

Double Action Revolver

A .32 or .38 caliber double action revolver with a 3.5" barrel and 6-shot cylinder. The .32 caliber version marked "Forehand & Wadsworth Double Action", and the .38 caliber "American Bulldog". Manufactured from 1871 to 1890.

Exc.	V.G.	Good	Fair	Poor
—	—	200	125	75

British Bulldog

A solid frame double action revolver similar to the above.

Exc.	V.G.	Good	Fair	Poor
—	—	200	125	75

British Bulldog .44

As above in .44 S&W caliber with a 5" barrel and 5-shot cylinder.

Exc.	V.G.	Good	Fair	Poor
—	—	200	125	75

Swamp Angel

A .41 caliber single action revolver with a 3" barrel and 5-shot cylinder. The top strap marked "Swamp Angel".

Exc.	V.G.	Good	Fair	Poor
—	—	200	100	50

Forehand Arms Co. 1898-1902
Perfection Automatic

A .32 or .38 caliber double action revolver with a hinged barrel and cylinder assembly. Varying barrel lengths. Blued or nickel-plated with hard rubber grips.

Exc.	V.G.	Good	Fair	Poor
—	250	100	75	50

Double Barrel Shotguns

Good quality hammer and hammerless doubles but few produced until taken over by Hopkins and Allen Firearms Co. Values from $100 to $1,000 depending on grade and condition.

FOWLER, B. JR.
Hartford, Connecticut

Percussion Pistol

A .38 caliber single shot percussion pistol with a 4" half octagonal barrel, iron frame and maple grips. The barrel marked "B. Fowler, Jr." Manufactured between 1835 and 1838.

Exc.	V.G.	Good	Fair	Poor
—	950	500	300	150

FOX, A. H.
Philadelphia, Pennsylvania

Ansley H. Fox established the Fox Gun Company in Baltimore, Maryland, in 1896. Subsequently, he made arms under the name Philadelphia Gun Company. As of 1905, he operated under the name A.H. Fox. In 1930, this company was purchased by the Savage Arms Company who continued manufacturing all grades of Fox shotguns. As of 1942, the Savage Company only made the plainer grades.

NOTE: Fox Model B double shotguns see Savage Arms Co.

Sterlingworth

A 12, 16, or 20 gauge boxlock double-barrel shotgun with 26", 28", or 30" barrels, double triggers and extractors. Automatic ejectors were also available and would add approximately 30% to the values listed below. Blued, casehardened with a walnut stock. Manufactured from 1911 to 1946.

20 Gauge-Add 50%.

Courtesy Nick Niles. Photo Paul Goodwin

Exc.	V.G.	Good	Fair	Poor
1250	1000	800	500	275

Sterlingworth Deluxe

As above, with an ivory bead, recoil pad and optional 32" barrel.

20 Gauge-Add 50%.

Exc.	V.G.	Good	Fair	Poor
1450	1250	1000	700	400

SP Grade

A 12, 16, or 20 gauge boxlock double-barrel shotgun with varying length barrels, double triggers and extractors.

20 Gauge-Add 35%.

Automatic Ejectors-Add 15%.

Exc.	V.G.	Good	Fair	Poor
1000	850	750	450	225

HE Grade

Similar to the early A Grade and offered in 12 and 20 gauge. Chambers were 2-1/4" standard with 3" chambers available on request. This model is marked on the barrel "Not Warranted". this referred to pattern density, not barrel quality. Only 60 20 gauge HE Grades appear in factory records. Manufactured from 1923 to 1942.

Single Selective Trigger-Add 20%.

Exc.	V.G.	Good	Fair	Poor
2500	2150	1750	1000	650

High Grade Guns A-FE

The Fox Company as well as the Savage Arms Company produced a variety of shotguns decorated in varying grades. They were available in 12, 16, and 20 gauge. As the value for these arms depends on the particular features of these arms, prospective purchasers are advised to secure a qualified appraisal prior to acquisition.

A Grade-built from 1905 to 1942

Exc.	V.G.	Good	Fair	Poor
1450	1150	850	600	400

AE Grade (Automatic Ejectors)-built from 1905 to 1946

Exc.	V.G.	Good	Fair	Poor
1750	1450	1150	900	700

B Grade-built from 1905 to 1918

Exc.	V.G.	Good	Fair	Poor
2400	2100	1600	1100	500

BE Grade-built from 1905 to 1918

Exc.	V.G.	Good	Fair	Poor
2800	2500	2000	1500	900

C Grade-built from 1905 to 1913

Exc.	V.G.	Good	Fair	Poor
2600	2200	1700	1100	550

CE Grade-built from 1905 to 1946

Exc.	V.G.	Good	Fair	Poor
3000	2600	2100	1550	950

XE Grade-built from 1914 to 1945

Courtesy William Hammond

Exc.	V.G.	Good	Fair	Poor
5500	5000	3500	1850	1100

D Grade-built from 1906 to 1913

Exc.	V.G.	Good	Fair	Poor
8000	7000	4500	2500	1000

DE Grade-built from 1906 to 1945

Exc.	V.G.	Good	Fair	Poor
8500	7500	5000	3000	1500

F Grade-built from 1906 to 1913

Exc.	V.G.	Good	Fair	Poor
22500	15000	8000	5000	3000

FE Grade-built from 1906 to 1940

Exc.	V.G.	Good	Fair	Poor
25000	18500	10000	7000	5000

Single Barrel Trap Guns

A 12 gauge single barrel boxlock shotgun with 30" or 32" ventilated rib barrels and automatic ejector. There were approximately 571 single barrel trap guns manufactured. Produced in four grades as listed below:

J Grade-built from 1919 to 1936

Exc.	V.G.	Good	Fair	Poor
2350	1950	1250	950	600

K Grade-built from 1919 to 1931
Approximately 75 built

Exc.	V.G.	Good	Fair	Poor
3500	2750	2000	1500	950

L Grade-built from 1919 to 1931
Approximately 25 built

Exc.	V.G.	Good	Fair	Poor
4750	3300	2700	1950	1200

M Grade-built from 1919 to 1932
A total of 9 guns built

Exc.	V.G.	Good	Fair	Poor
11500	8750	5500	4000	2500

CURRENTLY MANUFACTURED A.H. FOX SHOTGUNS

In 1993 the Connecticut Manufacturing Company of New Britain, Connecticut, announced the production of the A.H. Fox shotgun in 20 gauge exclusively. The gun is hand-built and constructed to the same dimensions and standards as the original Fox. The gun is offered in five grades with many standard features and several optional ones as well. Each shotgun is built to order. Because these guns are newly built and have no pricing history, only manufacturer's retail price for the base gun will be given. Extra sets of barrels, single triggers, and other extra costs options will greatly affect price.

CE Grade

Receiver engraved with fine scroll and game scene engraving with Turkish Circassian walnut stock, fine line hand checkering. Choice of full, half, or straight grip with splinter forend. Double triggers, automatic ejectors, automatic safety, choice of chokes, and barrel lengths in 26, 28, and 30 inches.

Retail price: $5,650

XE Grade

Same features as above with the addition of chiseled scroll work with engraved game scenes and higher quality Circassian walnut.

Retail price: $8,500

DE Grade

Same features as above with more intricate and extensive engraving. Even higher quality wood with diamond pattern checkering.

Retail price: $12,500

FE Grade

This grade features gold inlays and distinctive scroll work. Best quality wood with very fine line diamond pattern checkering.

Retail price: $17,500

Exhibition Grade

This is the company's highest grade and features any optional detail the customer desires including custom engraving and exhibition quality wood. Each Exhibition Grade Fox will be unique and should be appraised on an individual basis.

Retail price: $25,000

FRANCHI, L.
Brescia, Italy
Importer - Benelli USA

SIDE-X-SIDE-SHOTGUNS

Astore

A 12 gauge boxlock shotgun manufactured in a variety of barrel lengths with double triggers and automatic ejectors. Blued with a straight walnut stock. Manufactured from 1937 to 1960.

NIB	Exc.	V.G.	Good	Fair	Poor
1100	900	750	500	350	200

Astore II

As above, but more finely finished.

NIB	Exc.	V.G.	Good	Fair	Poor
1350	1100	900	700	450	250

Astore 5

As above, but more finely finished.

NIB	Exc.	V.G.	Good	Fair	Poor
2250	1750	1250	950	600	300

Airone
Similar to the Astore. Manufactured during the 1940s.

NIB	Exc.	V.G.	Good	Fair	Poor
1300	1050	950	750	500	250

Sidelock Double Barrel Shotguns
A 12, 16, or 20 gauge sidelock double-barrel shotgun manufactured in a variety of barrel lengths with a single selective trigger and automatic ejectors. Produced in the following grades they differ as to engraving coverage and quality of wood:

Condor

NIB	Exc.	V.G.	Good	Fair	Poor
7500	6500	4500	3500	2500	1250

Imperial

NIB	Exc.	V.G.	Good	Fair	Poor
10000	8500	6000	4500	3250	1500

Imperiales

NIB	Exc.	V.G.	Good	Fair	Poor
10500	9000	6500	5000	3500	1500

No. 5 Imperial Monte Carlo

NIB	Exc.	V.G.	Good	Fair	Poor
15000	12500	9000	7500	5000	2000

No. 11 Imperial Monte Carlo

NIB	Exc	V.G.	Good	Fair	Poor
16000	13500	10000	8000	5500	2000

Imperial Monte Carlo Extra

NIB	Exc.	V.G.	Good	Fair	Poor
20000	17500	12500	9500	7500	3500

OVER/UNDER SHOTGUNS

Priti Deluxe Model
A 12 or 20 gauge Over/Under boxlock double-barrel shotgun with 26" or 28" ventilated rib barrels, single trigger and automatic ejectors. Introduced in 1988.

NIB	Exc.	V.G.	Good	Fair	Poor
400	350	300	250	200	150

Falconet
A 12, 16, 20, and 28 gauge as well as .410 bore boxlock double-barrel shotgun with single selective trigger and automatic ejectors. The receiver was anodized in tan, ebony, or silver finishes. Manufactured from 1968 to 1975.

Silver Receiver-Add 10%.
28 Gauge and .410-Add 25%.

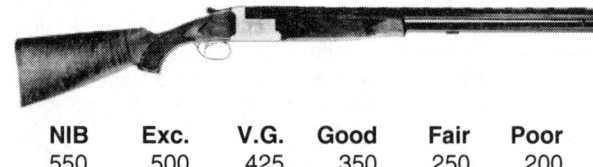

NIB	Exc.	V.G.	Good	Fair	Poor
550	500	425	350	250	200

Falconet Skeet
As above, with a 26" skeet barrel with a wide rib and the receiver casehardened. Manufactured from 1970 to 1974.

NIB	Exc.	V.G.	Good	Fair	Poor
950	850	700	550	450	250

Falconet International Skeet
As above, but more finely finished.

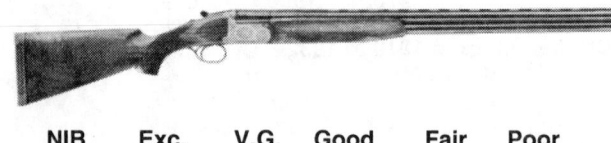

NIB	Exc.	V.G.	Good	Fair	Poor
1000	900	750	600	475	250

Falconet Trap
As above, with a 30" modified and full choke barrel, and trap stock. Manufactured from 1970 to 1974.

NIB	Exc.	V.G.	Good	Fair	Poor
950	850	700	550	450	250

Falconet International Trap
As above, but more finely finished.

NIB	Exc.	V.G.	Good	Fair	Poor
1000	900	750	600	475	250

Peregrine Model 451
A 12 gauge boxlock double-barrel shotgun with 26" or 28" ventilated rib barrels, alloy receiver, single selective trigger and automatic ejectors. Manufactured in 1975.

NIB	Exc.	V.G.	Good	Fair	Poor
600	525	450	375	275	200

Peregrine Model 400
As above, with a steel frame.

NIB	Exc.	V.G.	Good	Fair	Poor
650	575	500	400	300	200

Aristocrat
Similar to the above, with 26", 28", or 30" ventilated rib barrels. Manufactured from 1960 to 1969.

NIB	Exc.	V.G.	Good	Fair	Poor
650	575	500	400	300	200

Aristocrat Magnum
As above, with 3" chambers and 32" full choke barrels.

NIB	Exc.	V.G.	Good	Fair	Poor
650	575	500	400	300	200

Aristocrat Silver King

As above, with a French casehardened receiver, and available in four grades of decoration.

NIB	Exc.	V.G.	Good	Fair	Poor
750	675	575	475	350	200

Aristocrat Deluxe

NIB	Exc.	V.G.	Good	Fair	Poor
1000	800	675	575	400	200

Aristocrat Supreme

NIB	Exc.	V.G.	Good	Fair	Poor
1450	1200	850	700	575	250

Aristocrat Imperial
NIB	Exc.	V.G.	Good	Fair	Poor
2750	2250	1750	1250	950	450

Aristocrat Monte Carlo
NIB	Exc.	V.G.	Good	Fair	Poor
3500	3000	2750	2000	1500	750

Model 2003 Trap

A 12 gauge boxlock double-barrel shotgun with 30" or 32" ventilated rib barrels, single selective trigger and automatic ejectors. Manufactured in 1976.

NIB	Exc.	V.G.	Good	Fair	Poor
1250	1100	800	650	500	250

Model 2004 Trap

A single-barreled version of the Model 2003.

NIB	Exc.	V.G.	Good	Fair	Poor
1250	1100	800	650	500	250

Model 2005 Combination Trap

The Model 2003 with both a single and set of Over/Under barrels.

NIB	Exc.	V.G.	Good	Fair	Poor
2500	2200	1750	1200	950	450

Model 3000 "Undergun"

As above, with a single barrel fitted with a high ventilated rib so that it fires from the lower barrel position.

NIB	Exc.	V.G.	Good	Fair	Poor
2750	2450	2000	1500	1200	600

Alcione Field Model

A 12 gauge boxlock double-barrel shotgun with 26" or 28" ventilated rib barrels, single selective trigger and automatic ejectors. Engraved silver receiver. Weight is about 7.5 lbs.

NIB	Exc.	V.G.	Good	Fair	Poor
975	750	550	400	250	150

Alcione Sporting

This over/under gun is designed for sporting clays competition. Fitted with mechanical triggers and ported barrels. Offered in 12 gauge only with 30" barrels. Select walnut stock. Removable sideplates. Weight about 7.5 lbs.

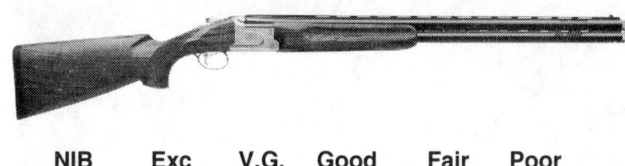

NIB	Exc	V.G.	Good	Fair	Poor
1300	950	700	—	—	—

Alcione LF

This 12 or 20 gauge model features barrels of 26" and 28" in 12 gauge and 26" in 20 gauge. Both gauges are chambered for 3" shells. Walnut stock. Receiver is aluminum alloy with etched games scenes with gold fill. Weight is about 6.8 lbs.

Alcione LF receiver-Right side view

NIB	Exc	V.G.	Good	Fair	Poor
1100	800	600	—	—	—

Alcione SL

As above, but more finely finished and with a French casehardened receiver.

NIB	Exc	V.G.	Good	Fair	Poor
1250	900	700	—	—	—

Alcione Field SX

This model is fitted with a high grade walnut stock, fine checkering, and engraved receivers with gold filled etched side plates. Offered with 28" or 26" barrels. Weight is about 7.3 lbs.

NIB	Exc	V.G.	Good	Fair	Poor
1635	1250	—	—	—	—

Veloce

Introduced in 2001 this model is chambered for the 20 or 28 gauge only with 26" or 28" barrels for 20 gauge guns and 26" barrels for 28 gauge guns. Aluminum alloy receiver. Engraved side plates with gold filled game scenes. Mechanical trigger. Select walnut stock. Weight of 20 gauge guns is about 5.8 lbs. and 28 gauge guns about 5.5 lbs.

NIB	Exc	V.G.	Good	Fair	Poor
1380	1100	—	—	—	—

SEMIAUTOMATIC SHOTGUNS

Standard Model
A 12 or 20 gauge semiautomatic shotgun with 24" to 30" ventilated rib barrels (those made after 1989, threaded for choke tubes) and an alloy receiver. Walnut stock. Manufactured since 1950.

Magnum Model-Add 10%.

NIB	Exc.	V.G.	Good	Fair	Poor
500	450	350	300	250	150

Hunter Model
As above with an etched receiver and more finely figured wood.

Magnum Model-Add 10%.

NIB	Exc.	V.G.	Good	Fair	Poor
400	350	300	250	200	150

Eldorado
As above, but more finely finished. Manufactured from 1954 to 1975.

NIB	Exc.	V.G.	Good	Fair	Poor
475	425	325	250	200	150

Crown Grade, Diamond Grade, Imperial Grade
As above, with hand-done engraving and finely figured walnut stocks.

Crown Grade

NIB	Exc.	V.G.	Good	Fair	Poor
1500	1250	1000	700	475	250

Diamond Grade

NIB	Exc.	V.G.	Good	Fair	Poor
2000	1750	1250	900	675	300

Imperial Grade

NIB	Exc.	V.G.	Good	Fair	Poor
2500	2250	1750	1250	950	450

Model 500
A 12 gauge semiautomatic shotgun with a 28" ventilated rib barrel and walnut stock. Introduced in 1976.
Deluxe Version-Add 10%.

NIB	Exc.	V.G.	Good	Fair	Poor
350	325	275	200	150	100

Model 520 "Eldorado Gold"
An engraved and gold inlaid version of the above.

NIB	Exc.	V.G.	Good	Fair	Poor
1000	850	650	450	300	150

Model 530 Trap
The Model 500 with a 30" or 32" ventilated rib barrel and trap stock.

NIB	Exc.	V.G.	Good	Fair	Poor
675	600	500	400	300	150

Prestige Model
A 12 gauge semiautomatic shotgun manufactured in a variety of barrel lengths. After 1989 the barrels threaded for choke tubes. Alloy receiver and walnut stock.

NIB	Exc.	V.G.	Good	Fair	Poor
575	500	425	350	250	150

Elite Model
As above, with an etched receiver and more finely figured stock.

NIB	Exc.	V.G.	Good	Fair	Poor
600	500	425	350	250	150

SPAS12
A 12 gauge slide action or semiautomatic shotgun with a 21.5" barrel and 9-shot magazine. Anodized, black finish with a composition folding or fixed stock.

NIB	Exc.	V.G.	Good	Fair	Poor
950	800	600	500	400	300

Black Magic Game Model

A 12 gauge Magnum semiautomatic shotgun with 24" to 28" ventilated rib barrels threaded for choke tubes, gold anodized alloy receiver, blackened barrel and walnut stock. Also available in trap or skeet configuration.

Skeet Model-Add 10%.
Trap Model-Add 15%.

NIB	Exc.	V.G.	Good	Fair	Poor
400	350	275	200	150	100

Black Magic Hunter

A 12 gauge Magnum double-barrel shotgun with 28" ventilated rib barrels threaded for choke tubes, single selective triggers and automatic ejectors. Blued with a walnut stock. Introduced in 1989.

NIB	Exc.	V.G.	Good	Fair	Poor
975	850	650	400	300	150

Black Magic Lightweight Hunter

As above, with 26" barrels and 2.75" chambers.

NIB	Exc.	V.G.	Good	Fair	Poor
975	850	650	400	300	150

Variomax 912

Introduced in 2001 this model is chambered for the 12 gauge 3.5" shell. It is offered with a choice of 24", 26", 28", or 30" barrels with vent rib. Black synthetic stock. Weight is about 7.6 lbs. Choke tubes.

NIB	Exc.	V.G.	Good	Fair	Poor
940	750	—	—	—	—

Variomax 912 Camo

Same as above but with Advantage Timber camo finish.

NIB	Exc.	V.G.	Good	Fair	Poor
1035	825	—	—	—	—

Variopress 612 Sporting

This is a 12 gauge semiautomatic gas operated shotgun with 30" ported barrel. Extended choke tubes. Select walnut stock with stock drop kit. Magazine capacity is 5 rounds. Weight is about 7 lbs. First imported in 2000.

NIB	Exc	V.G.	Good	Fair	Poor
900	650	—	—	—	—

Variopress 612 Field

This 12 gauge model is offered with barrel lengths from 24" to 28". Stock configurations are walnut, synthetic, or camo. Magazine capacity is 5 rounds. Weight is about 7 lbs. depending on barrel length.

NIB	Exc	V.G.	Good	Fair	Poor
600	475	375	—	—	—

Variopress 612 Defense

This 12 gauge gun is fitted with an 18.5" barrel and black synthetic stock. Matte black finish. Choke is cylinder. Weight is about 6.5 lbs. Magazine capacity is 5 rounds. First imported in 2000.

NIB	Exc	V.G.	Good	Fair	Poor
500	400	—	—	—	—

Variopress 620 Field

This model is offered in 20 gauge with a choice of walnut or camo stock. Barrel lengths from 24" to 28". Magazine capacity is 5 rounds. Weight is about 6 lbs.

NIB	Exc	V.G.	Good	Fair	Poor
600	475	375	—	—	—

NOTE: Add $50 for camo stock.

Variopress 620 Short Stock

Same as above but with 12.5" length of pull and walnut stock. First imported in 2000.

NIB	Exc	V.G.	Good	Fair	Poor
600	475	—	—	—	—

AL 48

This is a long recoil operated semiautomatic shotgun offered in 12, 20, and 28 gauge. Walnut stock. Barrel length are 24" to 28" in 12 and 20 gauge and 26" in 28 gauge. Magazine capacity is 5 rounds. Blued finish. The 12 gauge weight is about 6.7 lbs.; 20 gauge about 5.6 lbs.; and the 28 gauge about 5.4 lbs.

NIB	Exc	V.G.	Good	Fair	Poor
600	475	375	—	—	—

NOTE: Add $75 for 28 gauge model.

AL 48 Short Stock

Same as above but in 20 gauge with shorter length of pull. First imported in 2000.

NIB	Exc	V.G.	Good	Fair	Poor
600	475	—	—	—	—

AL 48 Deluxe

This is a deluxe version of the AL 48 that features upgraded walnut stock and a high polish blue finish. Offered in 20 and 28 gauge with 26" barrel. Weight is about 5.5 lbs. First imported in 2000.

NIB	Exc	V.G.	Good	Fair	Poor
700	550	—	—	—	—

NOTE: For 28 gauge model add $100.

RIFLES

Centennial Semiautomatic

A .22 caliber semiautomatic rifle with a 21" barrel, adjustable sights, Alloy receiver and walnut stock. Manufactured in 1968 only.

Deluxe Engraved Model-Add 20%.

NIB	Exc.	V.G.	Good	Fair	Poor
500	350	300	250	175	125

FRANCOTTE, A.
Liege, Belgium

For pistols and revolvers see-AFC

Jubilee

A 12, 16, 20, and 28 gauge Anson & Deeley boxlock double-barrel shotgun with various barrel lengths and chokes, automatic ejectors, double triggers and walnut stock.

Exc.	V.G.	Good	Fair	Poor
1650	1350	1100	850	450

No. 14

Photo courtesy William Hammond

Exc.	V.G.	Good	Fair	Poor
2250	1850	1600	1300	650

No. 18

Exc.	V.G.	Good	Fair	Poor
2750	2250	2000	1500	750

No. 20

Exc.	V.G.	Good	Fair	Poor
3250	2500	2250	1750	900

No. 25

Exc.	V.G.	Good	Fair	Poor
3750	3000	2750	2000	1000

No. 30

Photo Courtesy William Hammond

Exc.	V.G.	Good	Fair	Poor
4800	4000	3500	3000	1500

Eagle Grade No. 45

Exc.	V.G.	Good	Fair	Poor
3750	3000	2500	2000	1000

Knockabout

A plain version of the Jubilee Model in 12, 16, 20, 28 and .410 bore.

20 Gauge-Add 20%.
28 Gauge-Add 30%.
.410-Add 40%.

Exc.	V.G.	Good	Fair	Poor
1250	1100	850	650	500

Sidelock Side-x-Side

A 12, 16, 20, and 28 and .410 bore sidelock shotgun ordered per customer's specifications. Extensive scroll engraving, deluxe walnut stock and finely checkered. The .410 will bring a premium of from $1,200-$1,500.

NIB	Exc.	V.G.	Good	Fair	Poor
12650	10000	8000	6500	5000	3500

Deluxe Sidelock Side-x-Side

As above, with gold-inlaid hunting scenes.

NIB	Exc.	V.G.	Good	Fair	Poor
15000	12500	10000	8000	5750	4800

FRANCOTTE, A.
Liege, Belgium
CURRENTLY IMPORTED SHOTGUNS AND RIFLES
Importer - Armes De Chasse
Chadds Ford, Pennsylvania

Francotte currently imports side-by-side boxlock or sidelock shotguns, double rifles, and single shot rifles as well as bolt action rifles into the United States through Armes De Chasse. These shotguns and rifles are all custom built to the customers specifications. Gauge (including 24 and 32 gauge), caliber, barrel length, engraving, wood type and style are all individually produced. No two all alike. These shotguns and rifles should be individually appraised before the sale. Prices listed below reflect a range that the original buyer paid and also reflect the value of the changing dollar.

Custom Side-x-Side Shotguns

Available in 12, 16, 20, 28 gauge and .410 bore in either boxlock or sidelock actions. Barrel length, engraving, wood type and style are at the customer's discretion. Retail prices range from:

Basic Boxlock with 27.5" barrels and walnut stock with double triggers in 12, 16, and 20 gauge without engraving-$15,000

Basic Boxlock in 28 gauge or .410 bore without engraving-$11,000

Basic Boxlock with 26.5" or 28" barrels and deluxe walnut stock with scroll engraving, and double triggers in 12, 16, and 20 gauge-$20,000

Basic Boxlock in 28 gauge or .410 bore-$25,000

Prices for 24 and 32 gauge are extra. These prices do not include engraving.

Custom Double Rifles

These custom built double rifles are offered in calibers from 9.3x74R to .470 Nitro Express in boxlock or sidelock actions. Barrel length, engraving, wood type and style are at the customer's discretion. Retail prices range from:

Prices for 24 and 32 gauge are extra. These prices do not include engraving.

Boxlock in 9.3x74R, 8x57JRS and other European calibers-$11,800

Boxlock in.375 H&H and.470 NE-$15,700

Sidelock in 9.3x74R, etc.-$23,700 Sidelock in large calibers-$28,500

Custom Single Shot Mountain Rifles

These single shot rifles are offered in rimmed cartridges but rimless cartridge rifles can be built on special request. Barrel length, engraving, wood type and style are at the customer's discretion. Retail prices range from:

Boxlock in rimmed calibers-Prices start at $10,000

Sidelock in 7x65R and 7mm Rem. Mag.-Prices start at $21,000

Custom Bolt Action Rifles

These bolt action rifles utilize a Mauser 98 type action with adjustable trigger. They are offered in calibers from .17 Bee to .505 Gibbs. Barrel lengths are 21" to 24.5", engraving wood type and style are at the customers' discretion. Retail prices range from:

Standard bolt action calibers: .270, .30-06, 7x64, 8x60S and 9.3x62-Prices start at $5,650

Short action calibers: .222, .223-Prices start at $7,100

Magnum action calibers: 7mm Rem. Mag., .300 Win. Mag., .338 Win. Mag., .375 H&H, and .458 Win. Mag.-Prices start at $6,400

African calibers: .416 Rigby, .460 Wby., .505 Gibbs-Prices start at $10,250. **NOTE:** Please note that the above prices are for the basic models. They do not reflect the extensive list of options available on these custom firearms.

Francotte engraving patterns

FRANKLIN, C. W.
Liege, Belgium

Manufacturer of utilitarian shotguns with either exposed or enclosed hammers. Circa 1900.

Single Barrel
Exc.	V.G.	Good	Fair	Poor
150	75	50	35	20

Damascus Barrel Double
Exc.	V.G.	Good	Fair	Poor
250	150	125	100	65

Steel Barrel Double
Exc.	V.G.	Good	Fair	Poor
300	175	150	125	90

FRANKONIAJAGD
Favorit, Germany

Chambered for various European calibers, this bolt action rifle has a 24" barrel and set triggers. Blued, with a checkered walnut stock.

Exc.	V.G.	Good	Fair	Poor
400	275	250	175	125

Favorit Deluxe
As above, with a more finely figured stock.

Exc.	V.G.	Good	Fair	Poor
450	300	275	200	150

Safari Model
As above, in Magnum calibers.

Exc.	V.G.	Good	Fair	Poor
650	450	375	275	200

Heeren Rifle
A best quality single shot rifle with a 26" octagonal barrel, double-set triggers, and adjustable sights. Engraved with hand checkered, high-grade walnut. Blued. Produced in a variety of calibers.

Exc.	V.G.	Good	Fair	Poor
4500	2650	2200	1700	1250

FRASER, DANIEL & SON
Edinburgh, Scotland

This renowned rifle maker was an apprentice of Alexander Henry. Fraser had retail stores at the following addresses:

22 Greenside Place	1873-1874
18 Leith Walk	1874-?
4 Leith Street Terrace	?-1916

A cased .475 Nitro Express double rifle by Daniel Fraser sold at auction for $21,850. 60% scroll engraving on case-hardened action. Condition was excellent. Butterfield & Butterfield, November 1999

FRASER F. A. CORP.
Fraser, Michigan

Fraser 25 cal.

A .25 ACP caliber semiautomatic pistol with a 2.25" barrel and 6-round magazine. Stainless steel with black nylon grips. There is a 24 kt. gold-plated model that is worth approximately $100 additional.

NIB	Exc.	V.G.	Good	Fair	Poor
175	125	100	75	50	35

FREEDOM ARMS
Freedom, Wyoming

Bostonian

As above, with a 3" barrel.

NIB	Exc.	V.G.	Good	Fair	Poor
175	150	125	100	80	60

"Percussion" Mini-Revolver

A .22 caliber spur trigger revolver with 1", 1.75", or 3" barrel lengths, 5-shot cylinder and a bird's-head grip. Stainless steel. A belt buckle is available that houses the pistol for an additional $40.

NIB	Exc.	V.G.	Good	Fair	Poor
200	175	150	125	100	75

Patriot

As above, in .22 l.r. caliber.

NIB	Exc.	V.G.	Good	Fair	Poor
150	125	100	85	65	45

Minuteman

As above, with a 3" barrel. Discontinued in 1988.

NIB	Exc.	V.G.	Good	Fair	Poor
150	125	100	85	65	45

Ironsides

As above, in .22 Magnum with a 1" or a 1.75" barrel.

NIB	Exc.	V.G.	Good	Fair	Poor
175	150	125	100	80	60

Celebrity

As above, with the belt buckle mount for either .22 or .22 Magnum revolvers.

.22 Magnum Model-Add $25.

NIB	Exc.	V.G.	Good	Fair	Poor
325	300	250	200	150	100

PREMIER AND FIELD GRADES

Both grades use the same materials and machining tolerances. The difference is in the finish, standard components, and warranty.

The **Premier Grade** has a bright brushed finish, screw adjustable rear sight, laminated hardwood grips, and a limited lifetime warranty.

The **Field Grade** has a matte finish, adjustable rear sight for elevation only, Pachmayr rubber grips, and a one year warranty.

WHAT'S IT LIKE-FREEDOM ARMS MODEL 83 .454 CASULL

Constructed of 17-4PH stainless steel, the Freedom Arms .454 Casull speaks quality from its near perfect cylinder/barrel alignment, to the precise fitting of the specially designed grip frame that helps tame felt recoil as few others, to the 1:24 twist barrel that has proven to be the best for the pressures and velocities that the .454 attains. The Freedom Arms is a traditionally styled, but completely modern single action revolver. Its roots go all the way back to the original Colt Single Action Army maintaining the look and feel of the old black powder frontier sixguns while at the same time having the portable power to handle anything that walks. Everything about the Freedom Arms Model 83 speaks of tremendous strength and yet it is only slightly larger than other single action revolvers. Most large caliber single action sixguns have very little steel between chambers. Freedom Arms builds a "five-gun", that is, the cylinder is a five-shot affair that allows a lot of beef between the chambers. One also notices that the cylinder does not have the "play" that is common to most factory produced revolvers. My original .454 has had thousands upon thousands of heavy, very heavy, loads through it and yet the cylinder remains as tight as it was in 1986 with virtually no side movement or front to back movement. The reason is simple. Although Freedom Arms revolvers are produced in a factory they are in reality custom built. No long assembly lines here. All .454's are carefully, meticulously put together by employees who care about turning out what is the best built revolver of all times. The Model 83 .454 has been produced by Freedom Arms in the beautiful Star Valley of Wyoming since 1983. It has now been joined by chamberings in .44 Magnum, .357 Magnum, .41 Magnum, .50 Action Express, and most recently, the .475 Linebaugh.

John Taffin

Casull Field Grade Model 83

A .454 Casull Magnum revolver with a 4.75", 6", 7.5", and a 10" barrel and standard fixed sights. Fires a 225-grain bullet. Also offered in .50 AE, 475 Linebaugh, .44 Rem. Mag, 41 Magnum, and .357 Magnum. Adjustable sights available as a $75 option. Matte stainless steel with black rubber "Pachmayr" grips. Introduced in 1988.

NIB	Exc.	V.G.	Good	Fair	Poor
1500	1000	750	550	400	300

Casull Premier Grade Model 83

A .454 Mag., .44 Rem. Mag., .45 Win. Mag., .475 Limbaugh, and .50 AE, with replaceable forcing and walnut grips. The finish is a brush stainless steel. The adjustable sights are an extra cost option on this model as well. Offered in barrel lengths of 4.75", 6", 7.5", and 10" except for .475 Casull.

NIB	Exc.	V.G.	Good	Fair	Poor
1950	1400	950	700	500	300

NOTE: Extra cylinders are available for these models in .45 Colt, .45 Win. Mag., and .45 ACP. Add $250 to the price of the gun for each cylinder.

Casull Premier Grade Model 97

This model is similar to the Model 83 except that it offered in .45 Colt, .41 Rem. Mag., and .357 Mag. (6 shot). Barrel lengths are 4.25", 5.5", and 7.5".

NIB	Exc	V.G.	Good	Fair	Poor
1550	1100	800	600	—	—

Model 353

Chambered for .357 magnum cartridge with choice of 4.75", 6", 7.5", or 9" barrel length. Adjustable sights.

Field Grade

NIB	Exc.	V.G.	Good	Fair	Poor
1100	900	750	550	400	300

Premier Grade

NIB	Exc.	V.G.	Good	Fair	Poor
1500	1200	900	700	500	300

Signature Edition

As above, with a highly polished finish, rosewood grips, 7.5" barrel only and a fitted case. The serial numbers are DC1-DC2000. (The DC represents Dick Casull, the designer of the firearm.) A total of 2,000 were made.

NIB	Exc.	V.G.	Good	Fair	Poor
2000	1750	1500	1250	900	600

Model 252

This is a stainless steel version of the large frame revolver chambered for the .22 Long Rifle cartridge. Available in 5.12", 7.5", or 10" barrel lengths. Matte finish. Optional .22 magnum cylinder available for $250.

Silhouette Class-10" barrel

NIB	Exc.	V.G.	Good	Fair	Poor
1700	1150	850	600	450	250

Varmint Class-5.12" or 7.5" barrel

NIB	Exc.	V.G.	Good	Fair	Poor
1700	1150	850	600	450	250

Mid Frame Revolver

Introduced in 1997 this 6-round single action is chambered for the .357 magnum cartridge and is fitted with either a 5.5" or 7.5" barrel. It is offered with adjustable sights or fixed sights. The frame is slightly smaller than the company's large frame revolvers.

NIB	Exc.	V.G.	Good	Fair	Poor
1360	1100	—	—	—	—

Model 757

Introduced in 1999, this five shot revolver is chambered for the .475 Linebaugh cartridge. Fitted with adjustable sights and offered in both Field and Premier Grades. Choice of 4.75", 6", or 7.5" barrel.

Field Grade

NIB	Exc.	V.G.	Good	Fair	Poor
1400	1100	—	—	—	—

Premier Grade

NIB	Exc.	V.G.	Good	Fair	Poor
1800	1450	—	—	—	—

Model 654

This five shot revolver is chambered for the .41 Magnum cartridge. Adjustable sights. Introduced in 1999.

Field Grade

NIB	Exc.	V.G.	Good	Fair	Poor
1325	1050	—	—	—	—

Premier Grade

NIB	Exc.	V.G.	Good	Fair	Poor
1750	1400	—	—	—	—

Model 1997

This revolver is chambered for either the .357 Magnum or .45 Long Colt cartridge. Available in Field or Premier Grades. Available with a choice of 5.5" or 7.5" barrel. Optional .45 ACP cylinder of .45 Colt and optional .38 special cylinder for .357 Magnum model.

NIB	Exc.	V.G.	Good	Fair	Poor
1500	1200	—	—	—	—

NOTE: There are a number of extra cost options that will affect the price. Some of these options are extra costs sights, grips, Mag-Na-Port barrels, slings and trigger overtravel screws.

FREEMAN, AUSTIN T.
Hoard's Armory
Watertown, New York

Freeman Army Model Revolver

A .44 caliber percussion revolver with a 7.5" round barrel and a 6-shot unfluted cylinder with recessed nipples. Blued, case-hardened rammer and hammer, and walnut grips. The frame is marked "Freeman's Pat. Dec. 9, 1862/Hoard's Armory, Watertown, N.Y." Several thousand were manufactured in 1863 and 1864.

Exc.	V.G.	Good	Fair	Poor
—	—	3000	1250	500

FRENCH MILITARY FIREARMS
(including copies made in Liege, Belgium)
Charleville, St. Etienne, Chatellrault,
Mutzig and Tulle Armories

Most of these firearms were the products of five major armories, the old Charleville Armory and St. Etienne works, and the newer armories at Chatellrault, Mutzig, and Tulle. The armory of manufacture was invariably inscribed in script upon the lock, usually preceeded by an abbreviation "Manufactire Roy le de" or M re R le de" until 1848, "M re N le de" from 1848 until 1852, and "M re Imp ale de" after 1852, respectively representing, "The Royal Manufactory at ..." "The National Manufactory at ...," and, "The Imperial Manufactory at ..." In addition to these lock markings, the specific model year was usually marked upon the barrel tang, preceded by an "M". If the model had been altered, a "T" (for "transformed") was added after the date, and if subsequently remodeled, the script ("bis" was added after that (for "again"). Date of manufacture usually appears upon the barrel, and also within the pressed circle surrounding the "touch mark" on the right side of the buttstock. Numerous inspection marks also appear on the metal parts of the gun.

The arms manufactured for the French military were widely copied in Europe's major firearms center, Liege, Belgium. The Liege gun trade, however, was based on the "factory" system. Each specialist, working out of his own cottage, manufactured one type of part on subcontract and delivered it to an assembler. Many of the final assemblers in Liege did not mark their products or did so only with crowned initials. Those that did usually marked their "products" upon the lockplates. Among the better known Liege assemblers' marks during the middle of the 19th century were ANCION & CIE/A LIEGE, A F (A. Francofte), B F (Beuret Freres), C D (probably for Charles Dandoy), D (anchor) C (probably Dejerdine & Co., Demousse & Co., or DeFooz & Co.), D L (DeLoneux) C. DANDOY/A LIEGE, A. & CH DE LONEUX DRISKET & WAROUX, G M (Gulikers Marquinay), V. GULIKERS/A LIEGE, J L (Joseph LeMille), L (anchor) C or L. LAMBIN & CIE/LIEGE, LE MILLE/A LIEGE, P.J. MALHEREBE & CIE/LIEGE, E. MUNSEUR/LIEGE, J.A. PETRY/A LIEGE, G. SCHOPEN/A LEIGE, TANNER & CIE., T. TILKEN/A/LIEGE, AND V P (Vivario-Plombeur). It should be noted, however, that these makers produced not only copies of French arms, but also accepted contracts for arms from other European powers, notably Russia, Spain, the Piedmont, Saxony, and England. Whether marked on the lock or not, all Liege barrels were required to pass a proof of strength, and having done so were marked near their breech with a small tower and the Liege black powder proof, an oval encompassing the letters "E/LG/"(star). The main French firearms produced or copied during the muzzle-loading era were:

French M 1816 Flintlock Musket
(for Infantry/Light Infantry)

Overall length 58-1/8"/ 56"; barrel length 42-7/8"/ 40-1/2"; caliber .69 This musket is basically the French M1777 musket with minor improvements. Although the French did not subsequently alter this model to percussion, the Kingdom of Wurtemberg obtained several thousand from the Charleville Armory, which were altered to percussion and then rifled and sighted after their own models of 1842 and 1855, the barrel receiving a long range French style rear sight after rifling. As many as 2,000 of these may have been imported into the United States in 1862 by Marcellus Hartley.

(in flintlock)

Exc.	V.G.	Good	Fair	Poor
—	2500	1700	1350	700

Courtesy Milwaukee Public Museum, Milwaukee, Wisconsin

(altered to percussion, rifled and sighted)

Exc.	V.G.	Good	Fair	Poor
—	950	500	400	275

French M 1822 Flintlock Musket
(for Infantry/Light Infantry)

Overall length 58"/55-7/8"; barrel length 42-5/8"/ 40-5/8" (40-5/8" for both types if "T bis"); caliber .69 (.71 for rifled versions). The French M1822 musket in either full infantry length or the shorter version for light infantry (voltiguers), set the pattern for most of the muskets subsequently adopted by the European powers during the second quarter of the 19th century.

In the 1840s many were "transformed," i.e. altered to percussion by adding a convex bolster to the upper right side of the barrel near the breech for a cone and replacing the flintlock battery with a percussion hammer. With the adoption of the Minie ball projectile, it was determined to further upgrade these arms; however, because a new caliber had been adopted, the old barrels were deemed too thin to both enlarge and rifle. Accordingly new barrels were made in .71 caliber. The percussioned version was copied in Liege (by Ancion, Francotte, and Falise & Trapmann) for the Kingdom of Piedmont as its M1844 musket and M1860 rifle musket. These are distinguished by the enlarged tip of the hammer spur, a peculiar rear sight added to the breech and tang, and Liege markings.

(in flintlock)

Exc.	V. G.	Good	Fair	Poor
—	2500	1700	1350	700

(altered to percussion, and rifled)

Exc.	V. G.	Good	Fair	Poor
—	950	500	400	275

French M 1822 Cavalry Flintlock Pistol (and "T bis")

Overall length 13-1/4"; barrel length 7-7/8"; caliber .69 (.71 in "T bis"). The M1822 cavalry or horse pistol served as the secondary arm of the French mounted forces, with a pair assigned to each horseman to be kept in saddle holsters astride the pommel of the saddle. Like the M1822 muskets, these were altered ("transformed") to percussion after 1842 in the same manner as the muskets. In 1860, the ordnance department decided to rifle them as well ("transformed again"—hence "Tbis") but this required a new barrel since the adoption of the new caliber (.71) precluded rifling the thin old barrels.

(in flintlock)

Exc.	V.G.	Good	Fair	Poor
—	1250	600	450	375

(in percussion and rifled)

Exc.	V.G.	Good	Fair	Poor
—	750	500	375	250

French M1822 Cavalry and Lancer Flintlock Musketoons (and "T")

Overall length 34-5/8"; barrel length 19-5/8"; caliber .69. The main difference between the carbines carried by the cavalry and that of the lancers was the manner of slinging, with the latter having sling rings attached to the upper band and to a projection set into the buttstock. The ramrod was carried separately, consequently there was no inletting of the forestock. After 1842, both types were altered to percussion in the same manner as the M1822 muskets and pistols.

(in flintlock)

Exc.	V.G.	Good	Fair	Poor
—	1250	650	450	375

(in percussion and rifled)

Exc.	V.G.	Good	Fair	Poor
—	750	450	350	250

French M1829 Artillery Flintlock Carbine (and "T bis")

Overall length 37-1/4"/38-1/4" (for "T bis"); barrel length 23-5/8"; caliber .69/.71 (for "T bis"). The carbine for artillerists was similar in configuration to that for the cavalry and lancers, differing primarily in having a ramrod in a channel below the barrel. After 1841, these arms were altered to percussion and after 1846 a bayonet lug with long guide was added to the right side of the barrel to accommodate the French M1847 yatagan saber bayonet. At the same time, a number of these arms were sighted, rifled, and a "tige" (a metal column or pillar) was inserted into the breech of the bore that permitted the arm to fire the Thouvenin projectile. After 1857 new barrels were manufactured that permitted the introduction of the standard Minie projectile of .71 caliber.

Courtesy Milwaukee Public Museum, Milwaukee, Wisconsin

Exc.	V.G.	Good	Fair	Poor
—	1250	650	450	375

(in percussion and rifled)

Exc.	V.G.	Good	Fair	Poor
—	750	450	350	250

French M1837 Rifle 4" Carbine a la Poncharra")

Overall length 51-5/8"; barrel length 34-1/4"; caliber .69. The first of the French percussion arms for the general services, the M1837 rifle was designed on the Poncharra system. In this system, a chamber of lesser diameter than the bore was affixed to the barrel. A projectile of the diameter across the lands and its "sabot" was rammed into the barrel, and upon striking the lip of the chamber theoretically expanded into the rifling.

Courtesy Milwaukee Public Museum, Milwaukee, Wisconsin

Exc.	V.G.	Good	Fair	Poor
—	1850	1250	850	450

French M1840 Rifle ("Carbine de Munition")

Overall length 48-1/8"; barrel 32-5/8"; caliber .71. After the success of the M1837 carbine, the rifle went into production at the armories at Mutzig and Chatellrault as the M1840 "carbine Tierry" or "carbine de munition." It was modified in 1842. The design was modified by adding a projection to the lower end of the buttplate. Herman Boker of New York City imported 25,000 of the M1840 rifles in 1862, but the slow twist of the rifling caused them to be classified as "4th class" weapons and none were issued.

Courtesy Milwaukee Public Museum, Milwaukee, Wisconsin

Exc.	V.G.	Good	Fair	Poor
—	1250	600	450	300

French M1840 and M1842 Percussion Muskets (Infantry/Light Infantry)

Overall length 58-1/4" / 55-1/4"; barrel length 42-5/8"/ 40-1/2"; caliber .71. The M1840 and M1842 muskets were the first percussion arms adopted for general infantry service in the French army, both being distinguished by employing back action percussion locks. The M1840 was distinguished from the M1842 by having a screwed in "patent" breech integrating the bolster, while the bolster of the M1842 musket was forged integral to the barrel, both flush with the right side of the barrel. The M1842 musket was later "transformed" to the M1842T by rifling the barrel with four broad grooves. The Belgian gun trade copied the M1842T both with and without the block rear sight that stood on the breechplug tang.

Courtesy Milwaukee Public Museum, Milwaukee, Wisconsin

Courtesy Milwaukee Public Museum, Milwaukee, Wisconsin

Exc.	V.G.	Good	Fair	Poor
—	950	475	400	275

French M1853 Musket, M1853 "T" and M1857 Rifle-Muskets

Overall length 58-1/8" (M1853 infantry musket only)/ 55-1/4"; barrels 42-5/8" (MI853 only) /40-1/2"; caliber .71. In 1853, the

M1842 series of arms was modified slightly, the most visible difference being the right face of the bolster, which stands away from the right side of the barrel. After the adoption of the "Minie ball" as the main projectile of the French army, the new M1857 rifle musket was introduced. It was essentially the same as the M1853 "T" light infantry musket but its bore was rifled with four broad grooves. Subsequent to the adoption of the M1857 rifle musket the M1853 muskets were "transformed," the light infantry muskets simply by rifling them, and the infantry muskets by shortening them to 55-1/4" with 40-1/2" barrels and rifling them. Both types were widely copied by the Belgian gun trade, who exported thousands to the United States in 1861, many with French style long range sights affixed to the barrels.

Courtesy Milwaukee Public Museum, Milwaukee, Wisconsin

Exc.	V.G.	Good	Fair	Poor
—	950	475	425	300

French M1846 and M1853 Rifles ("Carbine a tige")

Overall length 49-1/4"; barrel length 34-1/4"; caliber .71. In 1846 the French abandoned the Delvigne chamber rifles in favor of a different method of compressing the projectile into the rifling, that of M. Thouvenin. In Thouvenin's system, the chamber with a lip was replaced with a metal column or pillar "a tige" extending from the breechplug into the bore. After the powder settled around the "tige" the bullet was rammed into the bore and compressed against the tige to expand it into the rifling. The rifle adopted in 1853 differed from the original model adopted in 1846 only in the bolster configuration, the latter extending away from the right side of the barrel. At least a thousand Belgian made "carbines a tige" were imported into the Confederacy in 1861. Accordingly, Belgian "tige" rifles with proven Southern usage should command a premium over those without such history.

Exc.	V.G.	Good	Fair	Poor
—	1250	650	475	350

French M1853 "T" and M1859 Rifles ("Carbine de Vincennes")

Overall length 49-1/4"; barrel length 34-1/4"; caliber .71. With the adoption of the self expanding "Minie ball" in 1857, the French ordnance soon adopted a rifle which was suitable for it, the M1859 "carbine de Vincennes." Beginning in 1860, the M1853 "tige" rifles were "transformed" by the removal of the pillars from the breechplugs and fitting them with the rear sight leaves of the M1859 rifle. The M1853 "T" and M1859 French rifle was widely copied in Liege, and thousands were exported to the United States during the American Civil War, while most of the French made M1859 rifles reposed in French arsenals. Like the M1840 and M1846 and M1853 rifles, the M1859 rifle took a long yatagan blade saber bayonet that was affixed to a lug with a guide on the right side of the barrel.

Courtesy Milwaukee Public Museum, Milwaukee, Wisconsin

Exc.	V.G.	Good	Fair	Poor
—	1250	700	525	425

FRENCH STATE
Manufactured by MAS
Etienne, France
SACM
Cholet, France
MAC
Chatellerault, France
MAT
Tulle, France

NOTE: For history, technical data, descriptions, and prices see the *Standard Catalog of Military Firearms, 1870 to the Present* under France.

FRIGON
Clay Center, Kansas

An importer of guns manufactured by Marocchi of Italy.

FT I
A 12 gauge boxlock single-barrel shotgun with a 32" or 34" ventilated rib barrel, full choke, automatic ejector and interchanged stock. Blued. Introduced in 1986.

NIB	Exc.	V.G.	Good	Fair	Poor
950	750	650	550	450	300

FTC
As above, with two sets of barrels (a single ventilated rib trap barrel and a set of Over/Under ventilated rib barrels). In a fitted case. Introduced in 1986.

NIB	Exc.	V.G.	Good	Fair	Poor
1750	1400	1150	800	650	500

FS-4
A four gauge set (12, 20, and 28 gauge and .410 bore). Introduced in 1986.

NIB	Exc.	V.G.	Good	Fair	Poor
2500	2100	1750	1500	1100	750

FROMMER
SEE—Fegyvergyar

FRUHWIRTH
Austria

M1872 Fruhwirth System Rifle
An 11mm bolt action rifle with a 25" barrel and 6-shot magazine. Blued with a full length walnut stock.

Exc.	V.G.	Good	Fair	Poor
500	300	250	175	100

FUNK, CHRISTOPH
Suhl, Germany

Christoph Funk began his gun business before 1900. The vast majority of long guns were best quality. Some collectors believe that J.P. Sauer built receivers for Funk but this is not known for certain. Funk produced shotguns, shotgun-rifle combinations, and double rifles. Some were exported to England and the U.S. Most of the U.S. imports are in the more common North American calibers such as .300 Savage, 30-30, 32-20 Winchester, and 12 or 16 gauge. Most are found with only a right hand extension arm which locks into the receiver, but some higher grades have both extension arms. The quality of these guns is extremely high. Guns were probably not made after 1940. Quality of engraving and caliber determines value. American calibers will command a higher price. Prices listed below are for American calibers.

Courtesy Jim Cate

Exc.	V.G.	Good	Fair	Poor
2800	2000	1250	600	400

FURR ARMS
Prescott, Arizona
J. & G. Sale, Inc.
Prescott, Arizona

In addition to producing reproductions of various cannon, this company also manufactured one-tenth to three-quarter scale reproductions of Gatling guns. Prospective purchasers are advised to secure a qualified appraisal prior to acquisition.

FYRBERG, ANDREW
Worcester and Hopkinton, Massachusetts

Double Barrel Shotguns
Fyrberg did work for Iver Johnson and C.S. Shattuck Co. of Hatfield, Mass. He began producing a hammerless double about 1902, a well designed boxlock with coil mainsprings. An estimated 2,000 were produced at Hopkinton and Worcester, Mass. Some have been made at Meriden, Conn. Sears cataloged the Fyrberg guns in 1902 to about 1908.

Exc.	V.G.	Good	Fair	Poor
500	400	300	200	150

Revolvers
A 3"-barreled .32 caliber and a 3.5" .38 caliber revolver with round ribbed barrels and round butts. The grips bear the trademark, "AFCo." This model was most likely made by Iver Johnson for Andrew Fyrburg.

Exc.	V.G.	Good	Fair	Poor
200	125	100	75	50

G

G M
(Gulikers Marquinay of Liege, Belgium)
SEE—French Military Firearms

GABBET - FAIRFAX, H.
Leamington Spa, England

Mars

Designed by Hugh Gabbet-Fairfax, this semiautomatic pistol was produced on an experimental basis by Webley Scot Revolvers in the 1890s. After Webley gave up on the idea an extremely limited number were built by the Mars Automatic Pistol Syndicate, Ltd., 1897 to 1901. The pistol was produced in four calibers; the 8.5mm Mars, 9mm Mars, .45 Mars Short Case, and .45 Mars Long Case. This was the most powerful handgun cartridge of its time and remained so until well after World War II. It is estimated that only about 80 of these pistols were ever produced. This is a rare and desirable collectible, and prospective purchasers are advised to acquire a qualified appraisal prior to the sale.

Courtesy James Rankin

Exc.	V.G.	Good	Fair	Poor
25000	15000	9000	5000	3000

GABILONDO Y CIA
SEE—Llama

GABILONDO Y URRESTI
Guernica, Spain
Elgoibar, Spain
SEE—Llama

This Spanish firm was founded in 1904 to produce inexpensive revolvers of the Velo-Dog type. Sometime around 1909 the firm began to manufacture the Radium revolver. In 1914 the company produced a semiautomatic pistol distributed as the Ruby. This pistol soon became the mainstay of the company with orders of 30,000 pistols a month for the French army. With the end of WWI Gabilondo Y Urresti moved to Elgoeibar, Spain. The company produced a Browning 1910 replica pistol until the early 1930s. It was at this point that Gabilondo began to manufacture a Colt Model 1911 copy that became known as the Llama. For information of specific Llama models see the Llama section. The pistols listed below reflect the pre-Llama period and are so marked with the trade name of that particular model. The monogram "GC" frequently appears on the grips but not on the slide.

Velo-Dog Revolver

A 6.35mm double action revolver with a 1.5" barrel, folding trigger and concealed hammer. Blued with walnut grips. Manufactured from 1904 to 1914.

Exc.	V.G.	Good	Fair	Poor
175	125	100	75	50

Radium

A 6.35mm caliber semiautomatic pistol with a 2.5" barrel and 6-shot magazine. The slide is marked "Firearms Manufacturing Automatic Pistol Radium Cal. 6.35." Produced between 1909 and 1914.

Exc.	V.G.	Good	Fair	Poor
200	150	125	100	75

Ruby

A 7.65mm caliber semiautomatic pistol. Discontinued in 1930.

Exc.	V.G.	Good	Fair	Poor
225	175	150	100	75

Bufalo

A 6.35mm, 7.65mm, and 9mm short caliber semiautomatic pistol. Blued with black plastic grips. Marked "Automatica Piastola Espana Bufalo." The caliber is also stamped on the slide. Manufactured between 1919 and 1925 under this name and for a number of years more under different names.

Exc.	V.G.	Good	Fair	Poor
200	150	125	100	75

Danton

As above, without the grip safety. "Danton" stamped on the side. Manufactured between 1925 and 1933.

Exc.	V.G.	Good	Fair	Poor
200	150	125	100	75

Perfect

This semiautomatic pistol was chambered for the 6.35mm and 7.65mm cartridges. It was a cheap, low priced pistol marketed by Mugica. These pistols usually have the word "Perfect" on the grips. The slide may be stamped with the name MUGICA but many are not.

Exc.	V.G.	Good	Fair	Poor
225	175	150	100	75

Plus Ultra

This pistol was chambered for the 7.65mm cartridge and was built from 1925 to 1933. It had a 20-round magazine that gave the pistol an unusual appearance.

Exc.	V.G.	Good	Fair	Poor
250	200	175	125	100

GALAND, C.F.
Liege, Belgium

Galand, Galand & Sommerville, Galand Perrin

A 7mm, 9mm, and 12mm caliber double action revolver with a 6-shot cylinder, open frame, a unique ejection system that, by means of rotating a lever downward from the triggerguard, causes the barrel and cylinder to slide forward, leaving the ejector and the spent cases behind. Circa 1870.

Exc.	V.G.	Good	Fair	Poor
—	500	275	200	150

Velo-Dog

A 5.5mm Velo-Dog caliber fixed trigger and guard double action revolver with open-top design. Later models (.22 and 6.35mm caliber) feature folding triggers and no triggerguards.

Exc.	V.G.	Good	Fair	Poor
200	125	100	75	50

Le Novo

As above, with a concealed hammer and in 6.35mm caliber.

Exc.	V.G.	Good	Fair	Poor
225	175	125	100	75

Tue-Tue

A .22 short, 5.5mm Velo-Dog, and 6.35mm caliber double action revolver with a concealed hammer, folding trigger, and a swing-out cylinder with central extractor. Introduced in 1894.

Exc.	V.G.	Good	Fair	Poor
225	175	150	100	75

GALAND & SOMMERVILLE
Liege, Belgium
SEE—Galand

GALEF
Zabala Hermanos & Antonio Zoli
Spain

Zabala Double

A 10, 12, 16, and 20 caliber boxlock shotgun with a 22" to 30" barrel and various chokes. Hardwood stock.

Exc.	V.G.	Good	Fair	Poor
300	200	150	100	75

Companion

A folding 12 to .410 bore single shot underlever shotgun with a 28" or 30" barrel.

Exc.	V.G.	Good	Fair	Poor
175	100	75	50	25

Monte Carlo Trap

A 12 gauge underlever single shot shotgun with a 32" ventilated rib barrel.

Exc.	V.G.	Good	Fair	Poor
225	175	150	100	75

Silver Snipe, Golden Snipe, and Silver Hawk
SEE—Antonio Zoli

GALENA INDUSTRIES INC.
Sturgis, South Dakota

In 1998 Galena Industries purchased the rights to use the AMT trademark and manufacturing rights to many, but not all, AMT designs. For AMT models made by AMT see that section.

AMT Backups

This model features a double action only trigger system and is offered in both stainless steel and matte black finish. The small frame .380 Backup weighs 18 oz. with its 2.5" barrel. The large frame Backups are fitted with a 3" barrel and are offered in 9mm, .38 Super, .357 Sig., .40S&W, .400 CorBon, and .45ACP. Weights are approximately 23 oz. and magazine capacity is 5 to 6 rounds, depending on caliber.

Galena .380 DAO Backup

Galena 45ACP DAO Backup

NIB	Exc	V.G.	Good	Fair	Poor
320	225	175	—	—	—

NOTE: Add $50 for .38 Super, .357 Sig, and .400 CorBon.

Automag II

This semiautomatic pistol is chambered for the .22 WMR cartridge. Offered in 3.38", 4.5", or 6" barrel lengths. Magazine capacity is 9 rounds except for the 3.38" model where capacity is 7 rounds. Weight is about 32 oz.

Automag II with 4" barrel

NIB	Exc	V.G.	Good	Fair	Poor
425	300	250	—	—	—

Automag III

This pistol is chambered for the .30 Carbine cartridge. Barrel length is 6.38" and weight is about 43 oz. Stainless steel finish.

NIB	Exc	V.G.	Good	Fair	Poor
525	400	325	—	—	—

Automag IV

This model is chambered for the .45 Winchester Magnum cartridge. It is fitted with a 6.5" barrel and has a magazine capacity of 7 rounds. Weight is approximately 46 oz.

NIB	Exc	V.G.	Good	Fair	Poor
600	450	350	—	—	—

Automag .440 CorBon

This semiautomatic pistol is chambered for the .440 CorBon cartridge and fitted with a 7.5" barrel. Magazine capacity is 5

rounds. Finish is matte black. Weight is about 46 oz. Checkered walnut grips. Introduced in 2000. Special order only.

NIB	Exc	V.G.	Good	Fair	Poor
900	750	—	—	—	—

Galena Hardballer

This pistol is based on the Colt Model 1911 design and is chambered for the .45ACP cartridge. It is fitted with a 5" barrel and has a magazine capacity of 7 rounds. Finish is stainless steel. Adjustable trigger and beveled magazine well. Also offered chambered for the .40S&W and .400 CorBon cartridges. Weight is about 38 oz.

NIB	Exc	V.G.	Good	Fair	Poor
445	325	275	—	—	—

Galena Longslide

This model is chambered for the .45 ACP cartridge and fitted with a 7" barrel. Magazine capacity is 7 rounds with weight about 46 oz. Finish is stainless steel.

NIB	Exc	V.G.	Good	Fair	Poor
525	400	325	—	—	—

Galena Accelerator

This model has a 7" barrel built on a 1911 frame and is chambered for the .400 CorBon. Magazine capacity is 7 rounds. Weight is about 46 oz. Finish is stainless steel.

NIB	Exc	V.G.	Good	Fair	Poor
550	425	350	—	—	—

Galena Commando

The Cammando is chambered for the .40S&W cartridge and fitted with a 4" barrel. Magazine capacity is 8 rounds. Weight is about 38 oz. Finish is stainless steel.

NIB	Exc	V.G.	Good	Fair	Poor
425	300	250	—	—	—

GALESI, INDUSTRIA ARMI
Brescia, Italy

Rino Galesi Armi, Collebeato, Italy manufactured shotguns, revolvers, and automatic pistols. The firm's name changed from Rino Galesi Armi to Industria Armi Galesi, to Rigarmi di Rino Galesi. Their semiautomatic pistols were designated by model year, model number, and a 500 Series. Most models named in the 500 Series came after the firm changed its name to Industria Armi Galesi.

Model 1923

A 6.35mm and 7.65mm caliber semiautomatic pistol.

Courtesy James Rankin

Exc.	V.G.	Good	Fair	Poor
250	175	100	75	50

Model 1930

A 6.35mm and 7.65mm caliber semiautomatic pistol. A very few were made in 1946 in 9mm parabellum. Based on the 1910 Browning design. Blued with plastic grips. The slide marked "Brevetto Mod. 1930."

Exc.	V.G.	Good	Fair	Poor
250	175	100	75	50

Courtesy James Rankin

9mm Parabellum

Exc.	V.G.	Good	Fair	Poor
600	500	400	300	100

Model 6

Updated Model 1930. Manufactured approximately 1938 to 1948 in calibers; 22 short, .22 long, .22 long rifle, 6.35mm, 7.65mm, and 9mm short.

Courtesy James Rankin

Exc.	V.G.	Good	Fair	Poor
350	175	100	75	50

Model 9

Manufactured from approximately 1947 to 1956 in calibers .22 short, .22 long, .22 long rifle, 6.35mm, 7.65mm, and 9mm short. Also, listed under the 500 Series.

Courtesy James Rankin

Exc.	V.G.	Good	Fair	Poor
350	175	100	75	50

GALIL
Israel Military Industries
Israel

Model AR

NIB	Exc.	V.G.	Good	Fair	Poor
2800	2400	2000	1500	900	700

Model ARM

NIB	Exc.	V.G.	Good	Fair	Poor
3000	2700	2000	1500	900	700

Sniper Rifle

NIB	Exc.	V.G.	Good	Fair	Poor
8500	7500	6000	4000	3000	2000

Hadar II

NIB	Exc.	V.G.	Good	Fair	Poor
1300	1100	800	650	500	400

GALLAGER
Richardson & Overman
Philadelphia, Pennsylvania

Courtesy Milwaukee Public Museum, Milwaukee, Wisconsin

Gallager Carbine

A .50 caliber single shot percussion carbine with a 22.25" barrel, saddle ring and walnut stock. Blued and case hardened. Approximately 23,000 were made during the Civil War.

Percussion Model

Exc.	V.G.	Good	Fair	Poor
—	3250	2000	1250	500

As above, in .56-62 rimfire caliber. Approximately 5,000 of this model were made.

Spencer Cartridge Model

Exc.	V.G.	Good	Fair	Poor
—	2750	1500	950	400

GAMBA, RENATO
Gardone V. T., Italy
Importer-Gamba, USA
Colorado Springs, Colorado

SIDE-X-SIDE SHOTGUNS

Hunter Super

A 12 gauge Anson & Deeley boxlock double barrel shotgun with a variety of barrel lengths and chokes, double triggers and extractors. Engraved and silver-plated.

NIB	Exc.	V.G.	Good	Fair	Poor
1250	900	700	550	450	250

Principessa

A 12 or 20 gauge boxlock shotgun. Engraved, checkered stock.

NIB	Exc.	V.G.	Good	Fair	Poor
1850	1250	900	700	500	250

Oxford 90

A 12 or 20 gauge sidelock shotgun with various barrel lengths and chokes, the Purdey locking system, double triggers, and automatic ejectors. Walnut stock.

NIB	Exc.	V.G.	Good	Fair	Poor
4250	3250	1700	900	600	300

Oxford Extra

Same as above but with fine engraving.

NIB	Exc.	V.G.	Good	Fair	Poor
5200	4000	2250	1500	900	450

Gamba 624 Prince

Fitted with a Wesly Richards type frame, select walnut stock, and fine hand engraving. Offered in 12 gauge with 28" barrels.

NIB	Exc.	V.G.	Good	Fair	Poor
4800	3900	2500	1500	850	400

Gamba 624 Extra

Same as above but with deep floral engraving.

NIB	Exc.	V.G.	Good	Fair	Poor
8000	6500	4500	2500	1250	600

London

A 12 or 20 gauge Holland & Holland sidelock shotgun with various barrel lengths and chokes, double or single selective trigger, automatic ejectors. Walnut stock.

NIB	Exc.	V.G.	Good	Fair	Poor
9000	7000	4500	2500	1250	700

London Royal
As above with engraved hunting scenes.

NIB	Exc.	V.G.	Good	Fair	Poor
11000	9000	6500	3750	2000	950

Ambassador Gold and Black
A 12 and 20 gauge Holland & Holland sidelock shotgun with various barrel lengths and choke combinations, single selective trigger, automatic ejectors, and a single gold line engraved on the barrels and the frame. Walnut stocks.

NIB	Exc.	V.G.	Good	Fair	Poor
25000	19000	13500	9500	5000	2500

Ambassador Executive
Gamba's best quality shotgun produced in 12 or 20 gauge to the customer's specifications.

NIB	Exc.	V.G.	Good	Fair	Poor
34000	27000	18500	10000	5000	2500

OVER AND UNDER SHOTGUNS

Country Model
A 12 and 20 gauge Over/Under shotgun with 28" or 30" barrels with ventilated rib, double triggers, extractors, and walnut stock.

NIB	Exc.	V.G.	Good	Fair	Poor
650	550	400	300	275	200

Grifone Model
A 12 and 20 gauge Over/Under shotgun with 26", 28", or 30" ventilated rib barrels, a single selective trigger, and automatic ejectors. The boxlock action is silver-plated, with walnut stock. Available with screw-in chokes, and this would add 10% to the values.

NIB	Exc.	V.G.	Good	Fair	Poor
800	650	550	350	250	200

Europa 2000
A 12 gauge Over/Under shotgun in various barrel lengths and choke combinations, single selective trigger, and automatic ejectors. Engraved, silver-plated, boxlock action with false sideplates with walnut stock.

NIB	Exc.	V.G.	Good	Fair	Poor
1250	900	700	550	350	250

Grinta Trap and Skeet
A 12 gauge Over/Under shotgun with 26" skeet or 30" full choke barrels, a single selective trigger, automatic ejectors, and some engraving. Walnut stock.

NIB	Exc.	V.G.	Good	Fair	Poor
1350	900	700	550	350	250

Victory Trap and Skeet
As above, but more finely finished.

NIB	Exc.	V.G.	Good	Fair	Poor
1650	1150	850	600	400	250

Edinburg Match
As above, with slightly different engraving patterns.

NIB	Exc.	V.G.	Good	Fair	Poor
1650	1150	850	600	400	250

Boyern 88 Combination Gun
A 12 gauge combination Over/Under rifle/shotgun with double triggers, and extractors. Engraved game scenes and coin-finished with walnut stock.

NIB	Exc.	V.G.	Good	Fair	Poor
1250	900	700	500	400	250

Daytona Series
This is a competition shotgun, first introduced into the US in 1986 as the Type I. The Type I was available in different configurations with the base model selling for about $4,000 until 1991. In 1994 Gamba introduced the Daytona in a wide variety of configurations and grades under a new designation called the Type II. The primary difference was in the location of the stock bolt. Only about 80 Daytona Type II shotguns are allocated to the US per year. They are a high quality shotgun with an excellent reputation. Prices are listed for 12 gauge guns. 20 gauge guns are available on special request.

Daytona Trap
Offered in 12 gauge with 30" or 32" barrels. Select walnut stock with hand checkering. Removable trigger group, improved Boss lock-up, and boxlock receiver.

NIB	Exc.	V.G.	Good	Fair	Poor
5900	4750	3000	2250	1200	600

Daytona Sporting
Available in 12 gauge with 30" barrel with screw-in chokes and single selective trigger.

NIB	Exc.	V.G.	Good	Fair	Poor
6600	5250	3750	2800	1400	700

Daytona Skeet
Offered in 12 gauge with 29" barrels and single selective trigger.

NIB	Exc.	V.G.	Good	Fair	Poor
5900	4750	3000	2250	1200	600

Daytona America Trap
Offered in 12 gauge with 30" or 32" barrels, high adjustable rib, adjustable stock, and single trigger.

NIB	Exc.	V.G.	Good	Fair	Poor
7450	6000	4000	3000	1500	750

Daytona Game
Offered in 12 gauge with 28" barrels and single trigger.

NIB	Exc.	V.G.	Good	Fair	Poor
5900	4750	3000	2250	1200	600

NOTE: Add $300 for black frame with gold inlaid names and logo.

Daytona Grade 6 Engraving
Fine English scroll hand engraving edged with gold line work.

Daytona Trap and Skeet Models

NIB	Exc.	V.G.	Good	Fair	Poor
13000	10500	7500	5000	2500	1200

Daytona Sporting Model

NIB	Exc.	V.G.	Good	Fair	Poor
13500	11000	8000	5000	2500	1200

Daytona Grade 5 Engraving
Deep relief floral engraving with gold inlaid griffons.

Daytona Trap and Skeet Models
NIB	Exc.	V.G.	Good	Fair	Poor
14000	11250	8000	5000	2500	1200

Daytona Sporting Model
NIB	Exc.	V.G.	Good	Fair	Poor
14500	11500	8500	5000	2500	1200

Daytona Grade 4 Engraving
A flying eagle in a landscape and very fine English scroll by master engravers.

Daytona Trap and Skeet Models
NIB	Exc.	V.G.	Good	Fair	Poor
16250	13000	9000	6000	3000	1500

Daytona Sporting Model
NIB	Exc.	V.G.	Good	Fair	Poor
16750	13250	9500	6000	3000	1500

Daytona SL Grade 3 Engraving
Fitted with sideplates with engraved game scenes and fine English scroll by master engravers.

Daytona Trap and Skeet Models
NIB	Exc.	V.G.	Good	Fair	Poor
18750	15000	11000	7500	3500	1750

Daytona Sporting Model
NIB	Exc.	V.G.	Good	Fair	Poor
19250	15500	11250	7500	3500	1750

Daytona Game
NIB	Exc.	V.G.	Good	Fair	Poor
18750	15000	11000	7500	3500	1750

Daytona SLHH Grade 2 Engraving
Fitted with sideplates and Boss lock-up system, automatic ejectors, figured walnut stock, and fine game scene engraving signed by a master. Offered in 12 gauge with 28" barrels.

NIB	Exc.	V.G.	Good	Fair	Poor
36250	29000	20000	12500	6000	3000

Daytona SLHH Grade 1 Gold Engraving
Same as above but with gold inlaid game scenes and floral style engraving signed by master engraver. Offered in 12 gauge with 28" barrels.

NIB	Exc.	V.G.	Good	Fair	Poor
43500	35000	25000	15000	7500	3500

Daytona SLHH "One of Thousand"
Same as above but game scene is executed at customers direction and is a totally custom ordered gun. Available in all configurations.

NIB	Exc.	V.G.	Good	Fair	Poor
106000	85000	40000	20000	10000	5000

Concorde Game Shotguns
This over and under model is offered as a slightly less expensive alternative to the Daytona Series guns. The base gun is available with a blued or chromed action. Extra barrel are interchangeable in both 12 and 20 gauges with 28" barrels and single triggers.

NIB	Exc.	V.G.	Good	Fair	Poor
5600	4500	3200	1700	950	450

Concorde Trap
Available in 12 gauge with 30" or 32" barrels with single trigger.

NIB	Exc.	V.G.	Good	Fair	Poor
5600	4500	3200	1700	950	450

Concorde Skeet
Available in 12 gauge with 29" barrels and single trigger.

NIB	Exc.	V.G.	Good	Fair	Poor
5600	4500	3200	1700	950	450

Concorde Sporting
Offered in 12 gauge with 30" barrels, screw in chokes, and single selective trigger.

NIB	Exc.	V.G.	Good	Fair	Poor
6100	5000	3500	2000	1000	500

Concorde Game Grade 7 Engraving
Game scene engraving with fine English scroll.

NIB	Exc.	V.G.	Good	Fair	Poor
8700	7000	4000	2500	1200	600

Concorde Game Grade 8 Engraving
English scroll engraving.

NIB	Exc.	V.G.	Good	Fair	Poor
6250	5000	3500	2000	1000	500

RIFLES

Safari Express
A 7x65R, 9.3x74R, or .375 H&H caliber boxlock double barrel rifle with 25" barrels, open sights double triggers, automatic ejectors, and a coin-finished scroll engraved receiver. Walnut stock.

NIB	Exc.	V.G.	Good	Fair	Poor
5500	4000	2500	1500	750	350

Mustang
A 5.6x50, 6.5x57R, 7x65R, .222 Rem., .270 Win., or.30-06 caliber sidelock single barrel rifle with double-set triggers, engraved sidelock action and walnut stock.

NIB	Exc.	V.G.	Good	Fair	Poor
10500	8000	6000	3500	1750	800

RGZ 1000
7x64, .270 Win., 7mm Rem. Mag., and .300 Win. Mag. caliber Mauser 98 bolt action with a 20.5" barrel. Walnut pistol grip stock with a cheekpiece.

NIB	Exc.	V.G.	Good	Fair	Poor
1100	900	750	550	400	200

RGX 1000 Express
As above, with double-set triggers and a 23.75" barrel.

NIB	Exc.	V.G.	Good	Fair	Poor
1250	950	750	550	400	200

PISTOLS

SAB G90
A 7.65 Parabellum or 9mm caliber double action semiautomatic pistol with a 4.75" barrel, and 15-shot magazine. Blued or chrome-plated with walnut grips.

NIB	Exc.	V.G.	Good	Fair	Poor
575	450	350	300	250	175

SAB G91 Compact
As above, with a 3.5" barrel and a 12-shot magazine.

NIB	Exc.	V.G.	Good	Fair	Poor
550	400	325	275	225	150

Trident Fast Action
A .32 S&W or the .38 Special caliber double action revolver with a 2.5" or 3" barrel, 6-shot cylinder and is double actioned. Blued, with walnut grips.

NIB	Exc.	V.G.	Good	Fair	Poor
500	400	300	250	200	150

Trident Super
As above, with a 4" ventilated rib barrel.

NIB	Exc.	V.G.	Good	Fair	Poor
550	400	325	275	225	150

Trident Match 900
As above, with 6" heavy barrel, adjustable sights and target type, walnut grips.

NIB	Exc.	V.G.	Good	Fair	Poor
850	700	550	400	350	200

GARAND
(U.S. M1 Rifle)
U.S. Rifle, CAL. M1 (Garand)
NOTE: For history, technical data, descriptions, and prices see the *Standard Catalog of Military Firearms, 1870 to the Present* under United States, Rifles.

GARATE, ANITUA
Eibar, Spain

Charola
A 5.5mm Clement semiautomatic pistol with the magazine located in front of the trigger and having an exposed hammer. Normally encountered with a nickel-plated finish and composition grips.

Exc.	V.G.	Good	Fair	Poor
325	225	175	125	90

Cosmopolite

A .38 caliber copy of the Colt Police Positive. Manufactured from 1920 to 1930.

Exc.	V.G.	Good	Fair	Poor
250	150	125	100	75

El Lunar

Resembling the Colt Police Positive in 88mm Lebel caliber, this revolver was made for the French government in 1915 and 1916.

Exc.	V.G.	Good	Fair	Poor
300	175	150	125	100

G.A.C.

A copy of the Smith & Wesson Military & Police revolver, manufactured between 1930 and 1936, in .32-20 caliber. Marked "G.A.C. Firearms Mfg. Co."

Exc.	V.G.	Good	Fair	Poor
250	150	125	100	75

Garate, Anitua

A 7.65mm caliber "Eibar" semiautomatic pistol with 8-shot magazine.

Exc.	V.G.	Good	Fair	Poor
225	125	100	75	50

Garate, Anitua

A .455 caliber double action break-open revolver with a 5" barrel, adopted by the Royal Army in November of 1915 and known as "Pistol OP No. 1 Mark 1".

Exc.	V.G.	Good	Fair	Poor
450	250	200	150	100

La Lira

A copy of the Mannlicher Model 1901 in .32ACP caliber with removable magazine marked "System La Lira" on the breech; "Para Cartoucho Browning 7.65mm," on the barrel; and "G.A.C.," on the grips. Produced prior to WWI.

Exc.	V.G.	Good	Fair	Poor
275	175	150	125	100

L'Eclair

A 5.5mm Velo-Dog caliber folding trigger double action revolver with 6-shot cylinder. Manufactured from 1900-1914.

Exc.	V.G.	Good	Fair	Poor
225	125	100	75	50

Sprinter

A 6.35mm caliber semiautomatic pistol marked "The Best Automatique Pistol Sprinter Patent 6.35mm Cartridge." Manufactured before WWI.

Exc.	V.G.	Good	Fair	Poor
225	125	100	75	50

Triumph

Identical to the La Lira model but marked "Triumph Automatic Pistol."

Exc.	V.G.	Good	Fair	Poor
300	175	150	125	100

GARATE, HERMANOS
Ermua, Spain

Cantabria

A 6.35mm caliber folding trigger double action revolver with a concealed hammer, cocking spur and a short barrel resembling the slide on a semiautomatic. The name "Cantabria" is stamped on the left side.

Exc.	V.G.	Good	Fair	Poor
300	175	125	100	75

Velo-Stark

A double action folding trigger revolver with concealed hammer.

Exc.	V.G.	Good	Fair	Poor
250	150	100	75	50

GARBI
Eibar, Spain
Importer-W. L. Moore and Co.
Scottsdale, Arizona

Model 51-B

As above, in 16 and 20 gauge, as well as 12 gauge, with automatic ejectors, case hardened or coin-finished receiver.

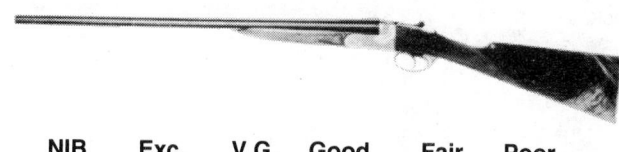

NIB	Exc.	V.G.	Good	Fair	Poor
1600	1200	850	600	—	—

Model 62-B

Similar to the above, but chambered for 16 and 20 gauge as well as 12 gauge. Engraved, case hardened or coin-finished receiver and walnut stock.

NIB	Exc.	V.G.	Good	Fair	Poor
1250	1050	850	650	—	—

Model 71

A 12, 16, or 20 gauge Holland & Holland sidelock shotgun with various barrel lengths and choke combinations, automatic ejectors and a single selective trigger. Engraved with fine English style scrollwork and walnut stock. Discontinued in 1988.

NIB	Exc.	V.G.	Good	Fair	Poor
2500	2000	1800	1500	—	—

Model 100

A 12, 16, or 20 gauge Holland & Holland sidelock shotgun with chopper-lump barrels, automatic ejectors, and a single trigger. Engraved in the Purdy style, with walnut stock.

NIB	Exc.	V.G.	Good	Fair	Poor
3500	3000	2500	2000	—	—

Model 101

As above, with floral engraving. Discontinued in 1988 in this form then furnished with hand engraved Contentinal scroll with round body action.

NIB	Exc.	V.G.	Good	Fair	Poor
6100	4500	2250	—	—	—

Model 102

As above, with Holland & Holland style, engraving and also in 28 gauge. Discontinued in 1988.

NIB	Exc.	V.G.	Good	Fair	Poor
4500	3750	3200	—	—	—

Model 103A

This model has Purdey-style engraving with high grade wood and checkering.

NIB	Exc.	V.G.	Good	Fair	Poor
7500	5500	4250	—	—	—

Model 103A Royal

Same as above but with special high quality engraving, very fancy wood, hand matted rib.

NIB	Exc.	V.G.	Good	Fair	Poor
11000	7750	6000	—	—	—

Model 103B

In 12, 16, 20, or 28 gauge Holland & Holland sidelock shotgun with various barrel lengths and choke combinations, chopper-lump barrels, Holland & Holland easy-opening mechanism, automatic ejectors, single selective trigger, and Purdy-type scroll engraving.

NIB	Exc.	V.G.	Good	Fair	Poor
10500	7750	6000	—	—	—

Model 103B Royal

Same as above but with high quality engraving, very fancy wood, hand matted rib.

NIB	Exc.	V.G.	Good	Fair	Poor
14750	11000	8000	—	—	—

Model 120

As above, with engraved hunting scenes. Discontinued in 1988.

NIB	Exc.	V.G.	Good	Fair	Poor
7500	6000	4000	—	—	—

Model 200

As above, Magnum proofed, double locking screws and 100% floral scroll engraving.

NIB	Exc.	V.G.	Good	Fair	Poor
10000	7500	6000	—	—	—

Model Special

A special order gun. Seek an expert appraisal prior to a sale.

NIB	Exc.	V.G.	Good	Fair	Poor
N/A	—	—	—	—	—

Express Rifle

This is best quality sidelock side by side double rifle. Stock has pistol grip and cheekpiece. Choice of English scroll or floral engraving. Calibers are 7x65R, 9.3x74R, or .375H&H.

NIB	Exc.	V.G.	Good	Fair	Poor
21000	15000	12000			

GARCIA

Garcia Bronco

A single shot .410 shotgun with swing out action. Barrel length is 18.5". Stock is a one piece metal skeletonized affair. Weight is approximately 3.5 lbs. Introduced in 1968 and discontinued in 1978. Built in Italy.

NIB	Exc.	V.G.	Good	Fair	Poor
125	100	85	75	50	30

Garcia Bronco 22/.410

This is an over and under shotgun rifle combination. The over barrel is .22 long rifle and the under barrel is chambered for .410 bore. Barrel length is 18.5". One piece metal skeletonized stock. Introduced in 1976 and discontinued in 1978. Weight is about 4 lbs.

NIB	Exc.	V.G.	Good	Fair	Poor
150	125	100	80	60	40

Garcia Musketeer

This model is a bolt action rifle chambered for the .243, .264, .270, .30-06, .307 Win. Mag., .308 Norma, 7mm Rem. Mag., and .300 Win. Mag. Fitted with a checkered walnut stock, open sights, pistol grip, hinged floorplate, and adjustable trigger. Introduced in 1970 and discontinued in 1972.

NIB	Exc.	V.G.	Good	Fair	Poor
600	500	350	250	200	150

GARRET, J. & F. CO.
Greensboro, North Carolina

Garrett Single Shot Pistol

A .54 caliber single shot percussion pistol with an 8.5" round barrel, swivel ramrod, walnut stock and brass mounts. Marked on the barrel breech "G.W." or "S.R." Approximately 500 were made in 1862 and 1863.

Courtesy Butterfield & Butterfield

Exc.	V.G.	Good	Fair	Poor
—	—	2500	1500	1000

GASSER, LEOPOLD
Ottakring, Austria

M1870

An 11mm caliber double action revolver with a 14.75" or 9.3" barrel, and 6-shot cylinder. Marked "Gasser Patent, Guss Stahl." It also bears an Austrian eagle and an apple pierced by an arrow, with the words "Schutz Mark."

Exc.	V.G.	Good	Fair	Poor
450	325	250	175	125

M1870/74

As above, with a steel frame.

Exc.	V.G.	Good	Fair	Poor
450	325	250	175	125

Gasser-Kropatschek M1876

An M1870/74 weighing 1 lb., 11 oz. and 9mm caliber.

Exc.	V.G.	Good	Fair	Poor
350	225	175	125	100

Montenegrin Gasser

A 10.7mm caliber double action revolver with 5" or 6" barrels, and 5-shot cylinder. Engraved, silver and gold inlay, and ivory or bone grips. Values given are for the plain, unadorned model. Embellished models will need individual appraisal.

Exc.	V.G.	Good	Fair	Poor
450	325	250	200	150

Rast & Gasser M1898

A 8mm caliber double action revolver with 4.75" barrel, 8-shot cylinder, solid-frame revolver with loading gate and an integral ejector rod.

Exc.	V.G.	Good	Fair	Poor
350	225	175	125	100

GATLING ARMS CO.
Birmingham, England

Established in 1888, this company remained in operation until approximately 1890. Although primarily involved with the marketing of Gatling Guns, it did market the one revolver listed below.

Kynoch-Dimancea

A .38 or .45 caliber double action hammerless revolver with a 6-shot cylinder. The loading system is rather unusual—a spur that resembles a hammer is pulled down, allowing the barrel and cylinder to pivot and to be pulled forward. During this motion the empty cases are ejected and new ones could be inserted. Marked "The Gatling Arms and Ammunition Co. Birmingham"; some are also marked "Dimancea Patent."

Exc.	V.G.	Good	Fair	Poor
—	1750	700	500	325

GAUCHER
France
Importer-Mandel Shooting Supplies

GN 1

This is a single-shot, bolt action pistol chambered for the .22 Long Rifle. It is fitted with a 10" barrel with blade front sight and adjustable rear sight. Adjustable trigger. Hardwood target grips. Weight is approximately 38 oz. Introduced in 1990.

NIB	Exc.	V.G.	Good	Fair	Poor
525	425	350	—	—	—

GAULOIS
St. Etienne, France
SEE—Le Francaise

GAVAGE, A.
Liege, Belgium

A 7.65mm caliber semiautomatic pistol with a fixed barrel and a concealed hammer. Similar in appearance to the Clement. Markings with "AG" molded into the grips. Some have been found bearing German Waffenamts. Manufactured from 1930s to 1940s.

Exc.	V.G.	Good	Fair	Poor
400	300	225	150	100

GAZANAGA, ISIDRO
Eibar, Spain

Destroyer M1913

A 6.35mm caliber semiautomatic pistol copied after the 1906 Browning. Produced through WWI.

Exc.	V.G.	Good	Fair	Poor
200	125	100	75	50

Destroyer M1916

A 7.65mm caliber "Eibar" design semiautomatic pistol with a 7- or 9-shot magazine. Marked "Pistolet Automatique Destroyer l Gaztanaga Eibar."

Exc.	V.G.	Good	Fair	Poor
200	125	100	75	50

Destroyer Revolver
A good quality .38 caliber copy of the Colt Police Positive.

Exc.	V.G.	Good	Fair	Poor
225	150	125	100	75

Super Destroyer
A 7.65mm caliber copy of the Walther PP. The slide is stamped "Pistola Automatica 7.65 Super Destroyer."

Exc.	V.G.	Good	Fair	Poor
225	150	125	100	75

Surete
As above in 7.65mm caliber. Marked "Cal. 7.65 Pistolet Automatique Surete" with "IG" stamped on the frame.

Exc.	V.G.	Good	Fair	Poor
225	150	125	100	75

GECO
SEE—Genschow, Gustave
Hamburg, Germany

GEHA
Germany
An altered Mauser 98 rifle rebarreled for use with 12 gauge shotgun shells. Barrel length 26.5", military stock shortened to half length and the butt inlaid with a brass medallion marked "Geha". Manufactured from approximately 1919 to 1929.

Exc.	V.G.	Good	Fair	Poor
250	200	150	100	75

GEM
Bacon Arms Company
Norwich, Connecticut
SEE—Bacon Arms Company under their separate listing

Gem Pocket Revolver
A .22 caliber spur trigger revolver with a 1.25" octagonal barrel. The frame is iron, engraved, nickel-plated, with walnut or ivory grips. The barrel marked "Gem." Manufactured between 1878 and 1883.

Exc.	V.G.	Good	Fair	Poor
—	1750	1000	600	300

GENEZ, A. G.
New York, New York
Located at 9 Chambers Street, Genez made a wide variety of firearms during his working life (ca. 1850 to 1875). The most commonly encountered of his arms today are single shot percussion pistols and percussion double barrel shotguns. More rarely seen are single shot percussion target rifles. A number of the arms he made were decorated by Louis D. Nimschke. Genez products signed by Nimschke command considerable premiums over the values for the standard firearms listed below and prospective purchasers of Nimschke engraved pieces are strongly advised to secure a qualified appraisal prior to acquisition.

Double Barrel Shotgun
Most often encountered in 12 gauge with varying barrel lengths; blued steel furniture, and walnut stock.

Exc.	V.G.	Good	Fair	Poor
—	—	2000	1500	500

Pocket Pistol
A .41 caliber single shot percussion pistol with a 3" barrel, German silver mountings and a walnut stock. Manufactured in the 1850s and 1860s.

Exc.	V.G.	Good	Fair	Poor
—	—	2750	1000	500

GENSCHOW, G.
Hamburg, Germany

Geco
A 6.35mm, 7.65mm, .32 long, and 8mm Lebel caliber folding trigger double action revolver.

Exc.	V.G.	Good	Fair	Poor
225	150	100	75	50

German Bulldog
A .32, .38, and .45 caliber folding trigger double action revolver with solid frames, integral ejector rods, and loading gates. The proofmarks indicate Belgian manufacture.

Exc.	V.G.	Good	Fair	Poor
225	150	100	75	50

GEORGIA ARMORY
Milledgeville, George
Established in 1862, this concern produced a rifle based upon the U.S. Model 1855 Harper's Ferry Rifle. Nearly identical in all respects to the Harpers Ferry, the Georgia Armory rifle had a lockplate patterned after the U.S. Model 1841 Rifle. Lock marked "G.A. ARMORY" over the date (1862 or 1863). Buttplate tangs marked with serial numbers. The highest known serial number is 309. These rifles were fitted with saber bayonets.

Prospective purchasers are strongly advised to secure an expert appraisal prior to acquisition.

Exc.	V.G.	Good	Fair	Poor
—	—	15000	10000	5000

GERING, H. M. & CO.
Arnstadt, Germany

Leonhardt
Identical to the "Beholla" made by Becker.

Exc.	V.G.	Good	Fair	Poor
300	250	200	150	100

GERMAN WWII MILITARY RIFLES
NOTE: For history, technical data, descriptions, and prices see the *Standard Catalog of Military Firearms, 1870 to the Present* under Germany, Rifles.

GERSTENBERGER & EBERWEIN
Gussenstadt, Germany

Em-Ge, G.& E., Omega & Pic
A series of poor-quality revolvers sold in the U.S.A. before 1968. .22 and .32 calibers with 2.25" barrels, and 6-shot cylinder.

Exc.	V.G.	Good	Fair	Poor
—	100	70	50	25

GEVARM
St. Etienne, France

Model A-6
This .22 caliber semiautomatic rifle fires from an open bolt. It is fitted with a one piece stock. Furnished with a 10-round magazine. The E-1 20 magazine will not fit the A-6 without hand fitting.

Exc.	V.G.	Good	Fair	Poor
250	200	175	125	75

E-1 Autoloading Rifle
A .22 caliber semiautomatic rifle with a 19" barrel, 10-shot magazine, blued with walnut grips. Two piece stock. A 20-round magazine is an option.

Exc.	V.G.	Good	Fair	Poor
350	250	200	150	100

GIB
Eibar, Spain

10 Gauge Shotgun

A 10 gauge Magnum boxlock double barrel shotgun with 32" matte-ribbed barrels. Case hardened, blued with walnut grips.

Exc.	V.G.	Good	Fair	Poor
300	250	225	150	100

GIBBS
New York, New York

Gibbs Carbine

A .52 caliber single shot percussion carbine with a sliding 22" round barrel. Blued, case hardened with a walnut stock. The lock marked with an American eagle and "Wm. F. Brooks/Manf New York/I863." The breech marked "L.H. Gibbs/Patd/Jany 8, 1856." There were only 1,050 produced.

Courtesy Milwaukee Public Museum, Milwaukee, Wisconsin

Courtesy Milwaukee Public Museum, Milwaukee, Wisconsin

Exc.	V.G.	Good	Fair	Poor
—	—	4000	1750	500

Gibbs Pistol

A caliber percussion pistol made by Hull & Thomas of Ilion, New York in 1855 or 1856.

Courtesy Milwaukee Public Museum, Milwaukee, Wisconsin

Exc.	V.G.	Good	Fair	Poor
—	—	2750	1250	400

GIBBS, J. & G.
LATER GIBBS, GEORGE
Bristol, England
SEE—British Double Guns

Established in 1835, this concern continues in business to this day.

J. & G. Gibbs	4 Redcliffe Street	1835-1842
George Gibbs	142 Thomas Street	
	Clare Street	
	39 Corn Street	

While initially known for exceptionally accurate single shot rifles, the firm subsequently established a reputation for first quality bolt action magazine rifles in a variety of large bore calibers.

GIBBS GUNS, INC.
Greenback, Tennessee

Mark 45 Carbine

A .45 ACP caliber semiautomatic rifle with a 16.5" barrel, a 5-, 15-, 30-, or 90-shot magazine. Blued, with a walnut buttstock and forend. A nickel-plated model was available as an option and would bring approximately $25 additional. Discontinued in 1988.

NIB	Exc.	V.G.	Good	Fair	Poor
300	225	175	150	125	100

GIBBS RIFLE COMPANY
Martinsburg, West Virginia
See also Parker Hale

This company imports Parker Hale black powder replicas and WW II surplus military firearms such as the Mauser Model 1888, Model 71/84, and the Israeli K98. The company also produced historical remakes and specialty rifles.

Enfield No. 5 Jungle Carbine

This is a remake of the original British rifle. Chambered for the .303 cartridge and fitted with a 20" barrel with flash hider. Magazine capacity is 10 rounds. Weight about 7.75 lbs. New stock.

NIB	Exc.	V.G.	Good	Fair	Poor
190	140	100	—	—	—

Enfield No.7 Jungle Carbine

This model is chambered for the .308 Winchester cartridge. Fitted with a 20" barrel with flash hider. Magazine capacity is 12 rounds. Adjustable rear sight. Original wood. Weight is about 8 lbs.

NIB	Exc.	V.G.	Good	Fair	Poor
200	150	125	—	—	—

Quest Extreme Carbine

An updated design of the No. 5 Jungle Carbine. Chambered for .303 cartridge with 20" barrel. Nickel finish and new hardwood stock. Brass butt trap. Weight is about 7.75 lbs.

NIB	Exc.	V.G.	Good	Fair	Poor
250	200	150	—	—	—

Quest II Extreme Carbine

Updated version of the No. 7 Jungle Carbine with nickel finish, see through scope mount and hardwood stock. Chambered for the .308 cartridge. Magazine capacity is 12 rounds. Barrel length is 20" and weight is about 8 lbs.

NIB	Exc.	V.G.	Good	Fair	Poor
280	225	150	—	—	—

Summit 45-70 Carbine

This bolt action is built on the Enfield No. 4 action and rebarreled to .45-70 caliber. Fitted to a 21" barrel. MIL SPEC peep sight and checkered walnut stock. Weight is about 8.5 lbs.

NIB	Exc.	V.G.	Good	Fair	Poor
375	275	225	—	—	—

Mauser M71/84

Chambered for the 11mm Mauser cartridge and fitted with a 31.5" barrel. This model has been arsenal reconditioned but is otherwise original. Weight is about 10 lbs.

NIB	Exc.	V.G.	Good	Fair	Poor
300	250	175	—	—	—

Mauser M88 Commission Rifle

Fitted with a 30" barrel and chambered for the 8mm cartridge. This model has been arsenal reconditioned but is otherwise original. Weight is about 10 lbs.

NIB	Exc.	V.G.	Good	Fair	Poor
100	75	60	—	—	—

GIBBS TIFFANY & CO.
Sturbridge, Massachusetts

Under Hammer Pistol

A .28 caliber single shot percussion pistol with 3" to 8" barrels. A browned iron frame, walnut or maple pointed handle trimmed with brass. The top strap is marked "Gibbs Tiffany & Co." Active 1820 to 1838.

Exc.	V.G.	Good	Fair	Poor
—	—	750	400	250

GILLAM & MILLER
High Point, North Carolina

Established in 1862, this firm produced two types of rifles, one for the State of North Carolina and one for the Confederate Government. Six hundred and seventy six (676) were accepted by North Carolina in 1863. These arms had an overall length of 48-3/4"; barrel length 33" in .577 caliber. These rifles marked in comb of stock "GILLAM &/MILLER". Confederate contract rifles of the U.S. Model 1841 Pattern were made in .577 caliber in the same style as the state contract rifles. However, their lockplates have a pointed tail. Serial numbered inside of the lockplate. Number made in excess of 125.

Prospective purchases are strongly advised to secure an expert appraisal prior to acquisition.

GILLESPIE
New York, New York

Derringer Type Pocket Pistol

A .41 caliber single shot percussion pistol with a 2.5" barrel and a walnut stock. Manufactured from 1848 to 1870.

Exc.	V.G.	Good	Fair	Poor
—	—	2500	1200	500

GLAZE, W. & CO.
Columbia, South Carolina
SEE—B. & B. M. Darling

GLISENTI
Turin, Italy

Glisenti Model 1906-1910

A semiautomatic pistol in calibers 7.65mm and 9mm Gilesenti. Developed for the Italian Army who accepted it in 7.65mm in 1906 and 9mm in 1910.

WARNING: *Standard 9x19 ammo must not be shot in this gun.*

Courtesy James Rankin

Exc.	V.G.	Good	Fair	Poor
900	650	500	300	200

GLOCK
Austria
Importer - Glock Inc.
Smyrna, Georgia

Glock Inc. is an Austrian company founded by Gaston Glock in 1963. What originally began as a commercial appliance manufacturing company developed into a line of products that involved military and police products. In 1982 Glock bid on and won the right to manufacture a new state-of-the-art semiautomatic 9mm pistol for the Austrian Army. This new pistol used polymer as a basic component material along with steel. The slide is steel, while the grip and slide base are polymer. The result is a lightweight, strong, and highly reliable military and police pistol. In 1984 the Norwegian Army chose the Glock 17 as its service pistol. With its growing success in Europe, Glock established an American subsidiary in Smyrna, Georgia in 1985 to sell its Glock 17 to American police forces and civilian shooters. By 1990 over 2,700 law enforcement agencies were using the Glock pistol as a duty weapon. One of its unusual design features is a trigger-activated safety. From its introduction as the 9mm Glock 17, the company has expanded its caliber offerings to include the 10mm, .357 Sig, .40 S&W and the .45 ACP.

Since September of 1994 all Glock pistols sold to the civilian market have a maximum magazine capacity of 10 rounds. Magazine capacities listed over 10 apply to pistols sold to law enforcement or pistols sold prior to September, 1994.

NOTE: In August 1995, with the introduction of the Glock sub-compact models, Glock produced these pistols with finger grooves. During the following years, the rest of the Glock pistol line began to receive these finger grooves on their grips. In January of 1998 Glock introduced the light rail on the front of its pistol frames on all Glock pistols. By early 1999 all Glock pistols had both finger grooves and rails. Older models will have the original pebble finish grips without finger grooves.

GLOCK

As the Luger and the 1911 pistols set the standard for handguns at the beginning of the 20th Century, so too has the Glock pistol raised the bar for the 21st Century. The Glock design has captivated legions of satisfied users. Other handgun makers had previously used polymer for their frames but none had moved forward enough to eliminate external levers and none had developed a workable alternative to the long double action trigger, thought to be mandatory in any modern semi-automatic pistol. I had been a dyed-in-the-wool 1911 user, along with my S&W revolvers, until the Glock came along. I now find that I spend as much if not more time shooting the "black" gun. (Gaston Glock, like Henry Ford, will make a gun in any color you want as long as the color is black.)

I find Glocks in most of the calibers and sizes (standard, compact and sub-compact) to be good carry guns and now I've moved them over to my action shooting competition, for they are equally effective in this field as well. I own more Glocks (and 1911s) than I should and, right now, it's a toss up between my first love, the 1911, and a Glock. The Glock Safe-Action Trigger has been deemed a double action trigger system for import purposes by the U.S. Treasury Department's Bureau of Alcohol, Tobacco and Firearms, but the Safe-Action is neither double action nor single action. Working the trigger, I operate it with the thought that it is more akin to a very smooth, short, revolver double action. The grip angle is more severe compared to the 1911 and for me takes an adjustment period when I transition from one to the other, since I have learned to cant my wrist upward to compensate for the 1911's natural tendency to point low. Regardless, the Glock gun is very close to being - if it's not already - the "every man's" pistol.

Walt Rauch

Glock 17

This model is chambered for the 9mm Parabellum cartridge. It is a double action only semiautomatic that has a 4.49" barrel and a 17-shot detachable magazine. The empty weight of this pistol is 21.91 oz. This pistol is offered with either fixed or adjustable sights at the same retail price. The finish is black with black plastic grips. It is furnished in a plastic case with an extra magazine. This pistol was introduced in 1985 and is still currently produced.

NOTE: Add $70.00 if equipped with Meprolight night sights. Add $90 if equipped with Trijicon night sights. Add $30 if equipped with adjustable sights.

NIB	Exc.	V.G.	Good	Fair	Poor
600	450	325	300	275	175

NOTE: Add $70.00 if equipped with Meprolight night sights. Add $90 if equipped with Trijicon night sights. Add $30 if equipped with adjustable sights.

Glock 17C

Similar to the Model 17 but with the additional feature of an integral ported barrel. Specifications are the same except for weight: 17C weighs 21.9 oz.

NIB	Exc.	V.G.	Good	Fair	Poor
650	475	350	300	275	175

NOTE: Add $70.00 if equipped with Meprolight night sights. Add $90 if equipped with Trijicon night sights. Add $30 if equipped with adjustable sights.

Glock 17CC

Introduced in 1998 this is a compensated competition version of the C variation. It is fitted with an extended slide stop lever, extended magazine release, adjustable sights and a target trigger pull. This is special order item only.

NIB	Exc.	V.G.	Good	Fair	Poor
760	600	500	—	—	—

Glock 17L Competition Model

This version features a 6" compensated barrel and adjustable sights. The trigger is fine-tuned to provide between a 5 to 8 lbs. trigger pull. This model was introduced in 1988 and is still being manufactured. In 1990 this pistol won the I.P.S.C. World Stock Gun Championship. This pistol has limited availablity in the U.S.

NIB	Exc.	V.G.	Good	Fair	Poor
700	550	450	350	300	225

Glock 22

Almost identical in appearance to the Model 17, the Model 22 is chambered for the .40 S&W cartridge. It comes standard with a 15-round clip. It has a slightly larger and heavier slide. Weight is 22.36 oz.

NIB	Exc.	V.G.	Good	Fair	Poor
600	450	325	300	275	175

NOTE: Add $70.00 if equipped with Meprolight night sights. Add $90 if equipped with Trijicon night sights. Add $30 if equipped with adjustable sights.

Glock 22C

Same as the Glock 22 model but with the addition of an integral ported barrel. Weight is 22.5 oz.

NIB	Exc.	V.G.	Good	Fair	Poor
650	475	350	300	275	175

NOTE: Add $70.00 if equipped with Meprolight night sights. Add $90 if equipped with Trijicon night sights. Add $30 if equipped with adjustable sights.

Glock 22CC

Introduced in 1998 this is a compensated competition version of the C variation. It is fitted with an extended slide stop lever, extended magazine release, adjustable sights and a target trigger pull. This is special order item only.

NIB	Exc.	V.G.	Good	Fair	Poor
760	600	500	—	—	—

Glock 19

This is similar in appearance to the Model 17 but is a compact version with a 4" barrel and a smaller grip that will accept either a 15-round or the standard 17-round magazine that protrudes a bit. Weight for this model is 20.99 oz. empty. The grip straps on this model are serrated as they are on the other Glock models. It was introduced in 1988 and is currently in production.

NIB	Exc.	V.G.	Good	Fair	Poor
650	450	325	300	275	175

NOTE: Add $70.00 if equipped with Meprolight night sights. Add $90 if equipped with Trijicon night sights. Add $30 if equipped with adjustable sights.

Glock 19C

Same as above but with integral ported barrel. Weight is 20.7 oz.

NIB	Exc.	V.G.	Good	Fair	Poor
700	550	350	300	275	175

NOTE: Add $70.00 if equipped with Meprolight night sights. Add $90 if equipped with Trijicon night sights. Add $30 if equipped with adjustable sights.

Glock 19CC

Introduced in 1998 this is a compensated competition version of the C variation. It is fitted with an extended slide stop lever, extended magazine release, adjustable sights and a target trigger pull. This is special order item only.

NIB	Exc.	V.G.	Good	Fair	Poor
760	600	500	—	—	—

Model 23

Model 23 is chambered for the .40 S&W cartridge. Its slide is slightly heavier and larger than the Model 19. Weight is 21.67 oz. The Glock 23 magazine holds 13 rounds.

NIB	Exc.	V.G.	Good	Fair	Poor
600	450	350	300	275	175

NOTE: Add $70.00 if equipped with Meprolight night sights. Add $90 if equipped with Trijicon night sights. Add $30 if equipped with adjustable sights.

Glock 23C

Same as above but with integral ported barrel. Weight is 20.9 oz.

NIB	Exc.	V.G.	Good	Fair	Poor
650	475	350	300	275	175

NOTE: Add $70.00 if equipped with Meprolight night sights. Add $90 if equipped with Trijicon night sights. Add $30 if equipped with adjustable sights.

Glock 23CC

Introduced in 1998 this is a compensated competition version of the C variation. It is fitted with an extended slide stop lever, extended magazine release, adjustable sights and a target trigger pull. This is special order item only.

NIB	Exc.	V.G.	Good	Fair	Poor
760	600	500	—	—	—

Glock 24

Chambered for the .40 S&W cartridge, it is fitted with a 6" barrel. It had a magazine capacity of 15 rounds before the Assault Weapons ban. Weight is 26.5 oz.

NIB	Exc.	V.G.	Good	Fair	Poor
600	450	400	350	300	175.

NOTE: Add $70.00 if equipped with Meprolight night sights. Add $90 if equipped with Trijicon night sights. Add $30 if equipped with adjustable sights.

Glock 24C

Same as above but with a ported barrel.

NIB	Exc.	V.G.	Good	Fair	Poor
650	475	400	300	250	200

NOTE: Add $70.00 if equipped with Meprolight night sights. Add $90 if equipped with Trijicon night sights. Add $30 if equipped with adjustable sights.

Glock 24CC

Introduced in 1998 this is a compensated competition version of the C variation. It is fitted with an extended slide stop lever, extended magazine release, adjustable sights and a target trigger pull. This is special order item only.

NIB	Exc.	V.G.	Good	Fair	Poor
760	600	500	—	—	—

Glock 20 and Glock 21

Both of these models are identical in physical appearance except for the caliber: the Model 20 is chambered for the 10mm cartridge while the Model 21 is chambered for the .45 ACP. Both have a barrel length of 4.60". The Model 20 has a 15-round clip and weighs 26.35 oz. while the Model 21 has a 13-round magazine and weighs 25.22 oz.

NIB	Exc.	V.G.	Good	Fair	Poor
700	525	375	300	250	200

NOTE: Add $70.00 if equipped with Meprolight night sights. Add $90 if equipped with Trijicon night sights. Add $30 if equipped with adjustable sights.

Glock 20C and 21C

Same as above but with integral ported barrel.

NIB	Exc.	V.G.	Good	Fair	Poor
700	525	400	325	250	200

NOTE: Add $70.00 if equipped with Meprolight night sights. Add $90 if equipped with Trijicon night sights. Add $30 if equipped with adjustable sights.

Glock 20CC/21CC

Introduced in 1998 this is a compensated competition version of the C variation. It is fitted with an extended slide stop lever, extended magazine release, adjustable sights and a target trigger pull. This is special order item only.

NIB	Exc.	V.G.	Good	Fair	Poor
760	600	500	—	—	—

Glock 26 and Model 27

Both of these models are identical except for caliber. Introduced in 1995 these are subcompact versions of the full size Glock's. The Model 26 is chambered for the 9mm cartridge, while the Model 27 is chambered for the .40 S&W cartridge. The 9mm version magazine capacity is 10 rounds and the 40 caliber version holds 9 rounds. The overall length is 6-1/4" with a barrel length of 3-1/2". The height is 4-3/16" and the width is 1-1/4". Weight for both models is about 20 oz. Standard are a dot front sight with white outline rear adjustable sight.

NIB	Exc.	V.G.	Good	Fair	Poor
600	450	300	250	200	150

NOTE: Add $70.00 if equipped with Meprolight night sights. Add $90 if equipped with Trijicon night sights. Add $30 if equipped with adjustable sights.

Comparison - Other Pistols

Model 30 with 10-round magazine

NIB	Exc.	V.G.	Good	Fair	Poor
700	525	400	325	—	—

NOTE: Add $70.00 if equipped with Meprolight night sights. Add $90 if equipped with Trijicon night sights. Add $30 if equipped with adjustable sights.

Glock 36

Introduced in 1999, this model is similar to the Model 30 but fitted with a single column magazine with a capacity of 6 rounds. The width of the pistol is .14" less than the Model 30. Barrel length is 3.78". Weight is 20 oz.

NIB	Exc.	V.G.	Good	Fair	Poor
700	525	400	325	—	—

NOTE: Add $70.00 if equipped with Meprolight night sights. Add $90 if equipped with Trijicon night sights. Add $30 if equipped with adjustable sights.

Glock 29 and Glock 30

These two pistols were introduced in 1997. The Model 29 is chambered for the 10mm cartridge while the Model 30 is chambered for the .45 ACP cartridge. Barrel length is 3.78". Weight is about 24 oz. Overall length is 6.77". The Model 29 has a magazine capacity of 10 rounds while the Model 30 has a standard capacity of 10 rounds with an optional capacity of 9 rounds. With the 10-round magazine in place the Model 30 magazine protrudes slightly below the grip. With the 9-round magazine in place the magazine fits flush with the bottom of the grip.

Model 29

Glock 31

Chambered for the .357 SIG cartridge this pistol is fitted with a 4.5" barrel and a a magazine capacity of 10 rounds (15 rounds law enforcement). Overall length is 7.3" and the height is 5.4". Weight is about 23.3 oz. Introduced in 1998.

NIB	Exc.	V.G.	Good	Fair	Poor
600	450	375	—	—	—

NOTE: Add $70.00 if equipped with Meprolight night sights. Add $90 if equipped with Trijicon night sights. Add $30 if equipped with adjustable sights.

Glock 31C

Same as the Model 31 but with an integral compensator.

NIB	Exc.	V.G.	Good	Fair	Poor
650	525	450	—	—	—

NOTE: Add $70.00 if equipped with Meprolight night sights. Add $90 if equipped with Trijicon night sights. Add $30 if equipped with adjustable sights.

Glock 31CC

Introduced in 1998 this is a compensated competition version of the C variation. It is fitted with an extended slide stop lever, extended magazine release, adjustable sights and a target trigger pull. This is special order item only.

NIB	Exc.	V.G.	Good	Fair	Poor
760	600	500	—	—	—

Glock 32

Similar to the Glock 31 except fitted with a 4" barrel. Overall length is 6.85" and height is 5". Magazine capacity is 10 rounds (13 rounds law enforcement). Weight is approximately 21.5 oz. Introduced in 1998.

NIB	Exc.	V.G.	Good	Fair	Poor
600	475	375	—	—	—

NOTE: Add $70.00 if equipped with Meprolight night sights. Add $90 if equipped with Trijicon night sights. Add $30 if equipped with adjustable sights.

Glock 32C

Same as above but fitted with integral ported barrel and slide.

NIB	Exc.	V.G.	Good	Fair	Poor
700	550	400	325	—	—

Glock 32CC

Introduced in 1998 this is a compensated competition version of the C variation. It is fitted with an extended slide stop lever, extended magazine release, adjustable sights and a target trigger pull. This is special order item only.

NIB	Exc.	V.G.	Good	Fair	Poor
760	600	500	—	—	—

Glock 33

This .357 SIG model has a 3.5" barrel and an overall length of 6.3". Height is 4.2" and weight is about 17.7 oz. Introduced in 1998.

NIB	Exc.	V.G.	Good	Fair	Poor
600	500	425	—	—	—

NOTE: Add $70.00 if equipped with Meprolight night sights. Add $90 if equipped with Trijicon night sights. Add $30 if equipped with adjustable sights.

Glock 34

This model is chambered for the 9x19 cartridge and has a 5.3" barrel, overall length of 8.2", and a magazine capacity of 10 rounds. Empty weight is approximately 23 oz.

NIB	Exc.	V.G.	Good	Fair	Poor
750	600	475	—	—	—

NOTE: Add $70.00 if equipped with Meprolight night sights. Add $90 if equipped with Trijicon night sights. Add $30 if equipped with adjustable sights.

Glock 35

The Glock 35 is chambered for the .40 S&W cartridge. It has the same dimensions as the Glock 34 except for weight, which is 24.5 oz.

NIB	Exc.	V.G.	Good	Fair	Poor
750	600	475	—	—	—

NOTE: Add $70.00 if equipped with Meprolight night sights. Add $90 if equipped with Trijicon night sights. Add $30 if equipped with adjustable sights.

GODDARD
SEE—B. & B. M. Darling

GOLDEN EAGLE
Tochigi, Japan
Nikko Limited

SHOTGUNS

Golden Eagle Model 5000 Grade I

A 12 or 20 gauge Over/Under shotgun with of 26", 28", and 30" barrels with ventilated ribs and various choke combinations, a single selective trigger and automatic ejectors. Blued, with a walnut stock that has an eagle's head inlaid into the pistol grip cap. Manufactured between 1976 and the early 1980s.

Exc.	V.G.	Good	Fair	Poor
900	750	600	475	250

Grade I Skeet

As above, with a 26" or 28" barrel having a wide competition rib.

Exc.	V.G.	Good	Fair	Poor
950	800	700	550	275

Grade I Trap

Similar to the skeet model, with a 30" or 32" barrel.

Exc.	V.G.	Good	Fair	Poor
950	800	700	550	375

Model 5000 Grade II

As above, but more finely finished with an eagle head inlaid in the receiver in gold.

Exc.	V.G.	Good	Fair	Poor
1000	850	750	600	325

Grandee Grade III

As above, but more elaborately engraved.

Exc.	V.G.	Good	Fair	Poor
2500	2000	1750	1400	850

RIFLES

Model 7000 Grade I

A Mauser bolt action rifle chambered for all popular American calibers with a 24" or 26" barrel, walnut stock and a rosewood pistol-grip cap and forend tip.

NIB	Exc.	V.G.	Good	Fair	Poor
700	600	500	400	325	250

Model 7000 African

As above in .375 H&H and .458 Win. Mag. caliber with open sights.

NIB	Exc.	V.G.	Good	Fair	Poor
700	600	500	400	325	250

Model 7000 Grade II

As above, but engraved.

Exc.	V.G.	Good	Fair	Poor
650	550	475	375	300

GONCZ CO.
Hollywood, California

GC Carbine

A 7.63mm Mauser, 9mm Parabellum, .38 Super, and the .45 ACP caliber semiautomatic rifle with a 16.1" barrel. Black with a walnut stock. All current production models are now stainless steel.

NIB	Exc.	V.G.	Good	Fair	Poor
500	400	325	275	200	125

GC Stainless

As above, in stainless steel. Introduced in 1987.

NIB	Exc.	V.G.	Good	Fair	Poor
550	450	375	325	250	175

GC Collector's Edition

A limited edition with hand-polished finish.

NIB	Exc.	V.G.	Good	Fair	Poor
800	600	500	425	350	225

Halogen Carbine

The GC Carbine with a powerful light source mounted under the barrel. Chambered for 9mm and .45 ACP only.

NIB	Exc.	V.G.	Good	Fair	Poor
550	450	375	325	250	175

Laser Carbine

As above, with a laser sighting system effective to 400 yards.

NIB	Exc.	V.G.	Good	Fair	Poor
1500	1250	1000	750	650	500

GA Pistol

The GC Carbine with a 9.5" shrouded barrel and a 16- or 18-shot magazine. Black with a one-piece grip. Manufactured between 1985 and 1987.

NIB	Exc.	V.G.	Good	Fair	Poor
425	350	275	200	150	100

GAT-9 Pistol
As above, in a 9mm caliber with an adjustable trigger and hand-honed action.

NIB	Exc.	V.G.	Good	Fair	Poor
600	475	375	300	225	150

GA Collectors Edition
A hand-polished stainless steel limited production of the above.

NIB	Exc.	V.G.	Good	Fair	Poor
825	675	600	500	400	300

GS Pistol
The Model GA with a plain 5" barrel. In 1987 pistols were made in stainless steel.

NIB	Exc.	V.G.	Good	Fair	Poor
350	275	225	175	125	75

GS Collectors Edition
A hand-polished, limited-production, stainless steel version of the GS.

NIB	Exc.	V.G.	Good	Fair	Poor
775	625	550	475	350	250

GOUDRY, J.F.
Paris, France
Double action 10-shot turret pistol. Marked on barrel rib J.F. Goudry Paris and Systeme A. Norl. By raising the gate on the left side the turret can be removed and reloaded or another preloaded turret inserted.

Exc.	V.G.	Good	Fair	Poor
—	5500	3500	2000	1000

GOVERNOR
Norwich, Connecticut
Governor Pocket Revolver
A .22 caliber spur trigger revolver with a 3" barrel and 7-shot cylinder. These revolvers were made from modified Bacon pepperboxes. The top strap marked "Governor". Manufactured from approximately 1868 to 1874.

Exc.	V.G.	Good	Fair	Poor
—	—	450	200	100

GRABNER G.
Kolibri Rehberg, Austria
Kolibri
A 2.7mm or 3mm caliber semiautomatic pistol with a 3-grain bullet. Muzzle velocity is approximately 500 feet per second. Fitted with a 5-round magazine. Manufactured from 1914 to about the mid 1920s.

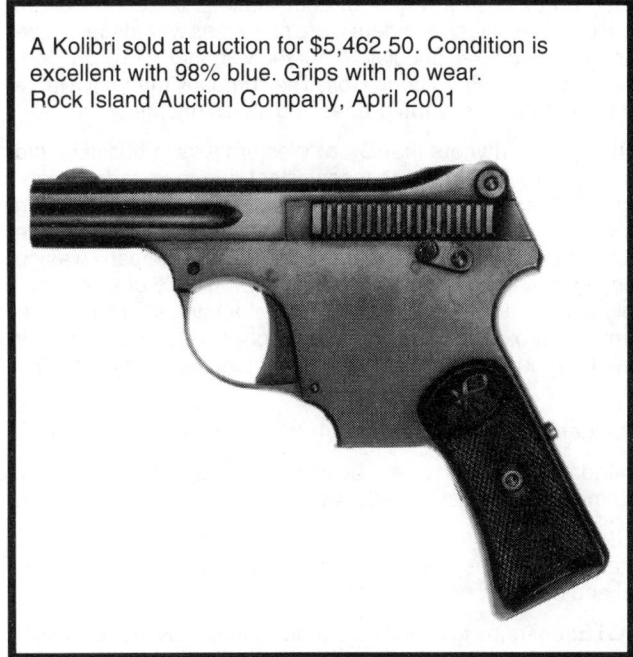

A Kolibri sold at auction for $5,462.50. Condition is excellent with 98% blue. Grips with no wear. Rock Island Auction Company, April 2001

Exc.	V.G.	Good	Fair	Poor
—	750	500	400	200

GRAND PRECISION
Eibar, Spain
A retailer of Spanish-made firearms

GRANGER, G.
St. Etienne, France
Importer-Wes Gilpin
Dallas, Texas
Side-x-Side Shotgun
A custom-order 12, 16, and 20 gauge boxlock double barrel shotgun. Manufactured since 1902. This is a custom order shotgun and an independent appraisal is strongly recommended. Because the gun is imported the value of the dollar frequently determines price movement.

Exc.	V.G	Good	Fair	Poor
15000	12000	8000	4000	1500

GRANT, STEPHEN
London, England
SEE—British Double Guns

GRAS
France
Model 1874
An 11mm caliber bolt action rifle with a 32" barrel with a walnut stock, a barrel band and a metal tip. The bayonet is a spike blade with a wood handle and a brass butt cap.

Exc.	V.G.	Good	Fair	Poor
325	275	200	150	75

GREAT WESTERN ARMS COMPANY

A certain amount of confusion surrounds Great Western Arms Company firearms. Collectors believe that this company's Colt single action and Remington derringer look-alikes were produced in Italy or Spain and imported into the U.S. under the West Coast distributor H.Y. Hunter. In fact all major components were built of the finest alloys using investment castings and assembled in Los Angeles, California. Great Western offered an extensive variety of combinations of caliber, finish, and grips. Auxiliary cylinders were offered as well in the following chambers: .44 Special/44-40/.44 Magnum, .357/.38 Special and .45 ACP/.45 Long Colt. The company made available to its customers several grades and styles of engraving.

During the ten years that Great Western was in business the quality of its firearms was inconsistent due to uncertain management and finances. This left the company's reputation damaged and allowed Colt and Ruger to dominate the single action market. By 1961 Great Western Arms Company was no longer able to compete. Despite the company's unstable history there is a small but growing collector interest in these firearms. Approximately 22,000 single action revolvers were built and less than 3,500 derringers were manufactured from 1953 to 1961.

Standard barrel lengths were: 4-3/4, 5-1/2, and 7-1/2 inches.

Standard calibers were: .38 Special, .357 Magnum, .357 Atomic, .44 Special, 44-40, .44 Magnum, .45 Long Colt, and .22 Long Rifle.

Standard finishes were: Case hardened frame and blued barrel and cylinder, or all blue finish.

NOTE: For guns to be in NIB condition they must have original boxes and paper work. Factory engraved guns must be supported by some type of invoice, letter, or other provenance to realize full value.

Centerfire Single Action

Courtesy John C. Dougan

Courtesy John C. Dougan

Exc.	V.G.	Good	Fair	Poor
500	425	350	250	200

.22 Long Rifle Single Action

Exc.	V.G.	Good	Fair	Poor
335	295	250	200	150

Target Model-Flattop with Micro Sights

Exc.	V.G.	Good	Fair	Poor
550	475	400	300	225

Fast Draw Model-Brass Back Strap and Triggerguard

Exc.	V.G.	Good	Fair	Poor
550	475	400	300	225

Deputy Model-4 inch Barrel with Full Length Sight Rib

Exc.	V.G.	Good	Fair	Poor
1000	850	750	650	550

NOTE: For calibers other than standard such as .22 Hornet, 3220, .45 ACP, .22 Magnum, .30 Carbine add 10% premium.

For factory plated pistols-Add 10%.
For factory cased pistols-Add 20%.
For Sheriff's Model or Buntline Special-Add 15%.

Courtesy John C. Dougan

For factory ivory grips add $175; for stag grips add $95, and for pearl grips add $150.

Factory engraved guns will add $750 to $3,500 to above prices depending on coverage.

Unassembled Kit Gun-in the White

N.I.B.	Exc.	V.G.	Good	Fair
350	300	—	—	—

NOTE: Assembled Kit Gun will bring between $100 and $200 depending on condition.

Derringer Model .38 Special & .38 S&W

Courtesy John C. Dougan

Exc.	V.G.	Good	Fair	Poor
300	250	200	150	100

Derringer Model-.22 Magnum RF

Exc.	V.G.	Good	Fair	Poor
400	350	250	200	150

NOTE: Factory Engraved Derringers add $350 to $500.

Courtesy John C. Dougan

Courtesy John C. Dougan

Courtesy John C. Dougan

Courtesy John C. Dougan

GREEN, E.
Cheltenham, England

Green

A .450 and .455 caliber double action revolver, popular with its military users in the late 1800s.

Exc.	V.G.	Good	Fair	Poor
—	500	350	275	150

GREENE
Milbury, Massachusetts

Greene Breechloading Rifle

A .53 caliber single shot bolt action percussion rifle with a 35" barrel, under hammer and full length walnut stock secured by three barrel bands. Marked "Greene's Patent/Nov. 17, 1857". Approximately 4,000 were made by the A.H. Waters Armory between 1859 and 1862.

Courtesy Milwaukee Public Museum, Milwaukee, Wisconsin

Exc.	V.G.	Good	Fair	Poor
—	—	2000	950	400

GREENER, W. W. LTD.
Birmingham, England
SEE—British Double Guns

Perhaps the best known manufacturer of double barrel shotguns in England during the nineteenth century, Greener was also a prolific author.

GREIFELT & CO.
Suhl, Germany

OVER/UNDER SHOTGUNS

Grade No. 1

A 12, 16, 20, 28 and .410 bore Anson & Deeley boxlock Over/Under shotgun with 26" to 32" ventilated rib barrels, various choke combinations, automatic ejectors, and double triggers. A single selective trigger was available and would increase the value approximately 15 percent. Walnut stock in a straight or pistol grip stock. The values are for the standard 12 gauge version.

28 Gauge and .410-Add 25%.

Exc.	V.G.	Good	Fair	Poor
3500	3000	2750	1750	1000

Grade No. 3

Similar to the No. 1, with less engraving. Manufactured prior to WWII.

28 Gauge and .410-Add 25%.

Exc.	V.G.	Good	Fair	Poor
3000	2500	1750	1250	750

Model 143E

The postwar version of the No. 1. Not made in 28 gauge or .410 bore.

Exc.	V.G.	Good	Fair	Poor
2500	2150	1500	1200	750

Combination Gun

A combination Over/Under rifle shotgun manufactured in all bores and a variety of rifle calibers with 24" or 26" barrels. Made prior to 1939.

Deduct 40% if rifle caliber is obsolete.
28 Gauge and .410-Add 25%.
Automatic Ejectors-Add 10%.

Exc.	V.G.	Good	Fair	Poor
5500	4500	3750	2500	1250

SIDE-X-SIDE SHOTGUNS

Model 22

A 12 or 20 gauge boxlock double barrel shotgun with 28" or 30" barrels, sideplates, double triggers and extractors. Blued, case hardened with a walnut stock. Manufactured after 1945.

Exc.	V.G.	Good	Fair	Poor
2250	1800	1500	1200	750

Model 22E

As above, with automatic ejectors.

Exc.	V.G.	Good	Fair	Poor
2500	2000	1500	1200	750

Model 103

A 12 and 16 gauge boxlock shotgun with a 28" or a 30" barrel, double triggers and extractors. Walnut stock with a pistol or straight English-style grip. Postwar model.

Exc.	V.G.	Good	Fair	Poor
2250	1800	1500	1200	750

Model 103E

As above, with automatic ejectors.

Exc.	V.G.	Good	Fair	Poor
2500	2000	1500	1200	750

Drilling

A 12, 16, or 20 gauge double barrel shotgun fitted with a rifle barrel, chambered for a variety of cartridges. Barrel length 26", boxlock action, double triggers, extractors and folding rear sight. Manufactured prior to 1939.

Deduct 40% if rifle caliber is obsolete.
20 Gauge-Add 10%.

Exc.	V.G.	Good	Fair	Poor
3500	3000	2750	1750	1000

GRENDEL, INC.
Rockledge, Florida

P-10 Pistol

A .380 caliber semiautomatic pistol with a 3" barrel, 11-shot magazine, matte black finish with black plastic grips. The pistol has a plastic frame with plastic magazine. It is offered in electroless nickel-plate, as well as a green Teflon finish for a slightly higher price.

Green Finish-Add $5.
Electroless Nickel-Add $15.

NIB	Exc.	V.G.	Good	Fair	Poor
175	125	100	75	65	40

P-12

This semiautomatic double action pistol is chambered for the .380 ACP cartridge. Fitted with a 3" barrel, checkered polymer grips, and blued finish. Magazine capacity is 10 rounds. Weight is about 13 oz. Introduced in 1992.

NIB	Exc.	V.G.	Good	Fair	Poor
175	125	100	85	70	50

P-30

Introduced in 1990 this is a double action semiautomatic pistol chambered for the .22 WMR cartridge. Fitted with a 5" barrel or 8" barrel. Fixed sights. Magazine capacity is 30 rounds. Weight is about 21 oz. Discontinued in 1994.

NIB	Exc.	V.G.	Good	Fair	Poor
200	150	125	100	85	75

P-30L

Same as above model but in 8" barrel only. Also discontinued in 1994.

NIB	Exc.	V.G.	Good	Fair	Poor
225	175	150	100	85	75

P-30M

Similar to the P-30 but fitted with a removable muzzle brake.

NIB	Exc.	V.G.	Good	Fair	Poor
225	175	150	100	85	75

P-31

This is a semiautomatic pistol chambered for .22 WMR cartridge. Fitted with an 11" barrel, muzzle brake. Black matte finish. Weight is approximately 48 oz. Introduced in 1991 but no longer in production.

NIB	Exc.	V.G.	Good	Fair	Poor
300	250	200	150	125	100

RIFLES

SRT-20F Compact Rifle

A .308 caliber bolt action rifle with 20" finned matchgrade barrel, 9-shot magazine, a folding synthetic stock, integral bipod and no sights.

Courtesy Jim Supice, Old Town Station

NIB	Exc.	V.G.	Good	Fair	Poor
525	475	400	325	250	100

SRT-24

As above, with a 24" barrel. Discontinued in 1988.

NIB	Exc.	V.G.	Good	Fair	Poor
550	450	375	300	250	100

R-31 Carbine

This semiautomatic carbine was introduced in 1991 and is chambered for the .22 WMR cartridge. Fitted with a 16" barrel with muzzle brake and a telescoping tubular stock. Magazine capacity is 30 rounds. Weight is about 4 lbs. Discontinued in 1994.

NIB	Exc.	V.G.	Good	Fair	Poor
300	250	200	150	125	100

GRIFFIN & HOWE
New York, New York

Established in 1923, this firm manufactured on custom order a variety of bolt action sporting rifles. As these arms essentially were all built to specific customer's specifications, prospective purchasers should secure a qualified appraisal prior to purchase.

GRIFFON
South Africa
Importer-Griffon USA, Forth Worth, Texas

Griffon 1911 A1 Combat

This semiautomatic single action pistol is chambered for the .45ACP cartridge and fitted with a 4" ported barrel. Aluminum trigger and high profile sights are standard. Frame is chrome and slide is blued. Magazine capacity is 7 rounds.

NIB	Exc.	V.G.	Good	Fair	Poor
500	400	—	—	—	—

GRISWOLD & GIER
SEE-Griswold & Gunnison

GRISWOLD & GUNNISON
Griswoldville, Georgia

1851 Navy Type

A .36 caliber percussion revolver with a 7.5" barrel and 6-shot cylinder. The frame and grip straps made of brass and the barrel as well as cylinder made of iron. Approximately 3,700 were made between 1862 and 1864, for the Confederate government.

NOTE: This revolver is sometimes referred to as the Griswold and Grier.

Courtesy Milwaukee Public Museum, Milwaukee, Wisconsin

Exc.	V.G.	Good	Fair	Poor
—	—	8500	4500	2500

GROSS ARMS CO.
Tiffin, Ohio

Pocket Revolver

A .25 and .30 caliber spur trigger revolver with a 6" octagonal barrel, a 7-shot cylinder and marked "Gross Arms Co., Tiffin, Ohio." Blued, with walnut grips. Only a few hundred were manufactured between 1864 and 1866.

Exc.	V.G.	Good	Fair	Poor
—	—	1000	550	300

GRUBB, J. C. & CO.
Philadelphia, Pennsylvania

Pocket Pistol

A .41 caliber single shot percussion pistol with various barrel lengths. German silver, walnut stock and engraved lock and triggerguard. The lock is marked "J.C. Grubb." Several hundred were manufactured between 1860 and 1870.

Exc.	V.G.	Good	Fair	Poor
—	—	1000	650	300

GUEDES-CASTRO
Steyr, Austria

Model 1885

An 8x60mm Guedes single shot dropping block rifle with a 28" barrel, full length walnut stock and iron mounts. Made in Austria under contract for the Portuguese army in 1885.

Exc.	V.G.	Good	Fair	Poor
650	400	350	250	125

GUIDE LAMP
Detroit, Michigan
Division General Motors

Liberator

NIB	Exc.	V.G.	Good	Fair	Poor
2000	1200	750	400	300	175

GUION, T. F.
New Orleans, Louisiana

Pocket Pistol

A .41 caliber single shot percussion pistol with a 2.5" barrel, German silver mountings, and a walnut stock. Manufactured in the 1850s.

Exc.	V.G.	Good	Fair	Poor
—	—	1750	500	275

V. GULIKERS/A LIEGE
SEE—French Military Firearms

GUNWORKS LTD.
Buffalo, New York

Model 9 Derringer

An Over/Under derringer chambered in 9mm, .38 Special, .38 Super, and .357 Magnum caliber with 2.5" barrels, with a spur trigger and Millet sights. Nickel-plate, with walnut grips. Manufacturing ceased in 1986.

Exc.	V.G.	Good	Fair	Poor
125	100	90	75	50

GUSTAF, CARL
Eskilstuna, Sweden

Bolt Action Rifle

A 6.5x55, 7x64, .270, 7mm Magnum, .308, .30-06, and 9.3x62 caliber bolt action rifle with a 24" barrel. Blued with a walnut stock in either the classic style or with a Monte Carlo cheekpiece. Manufactured between 1970 and 1977.

Exc.	V.G.	Good	Fair	Poor
550	425	350	275	150

Grade II

As above, with better walnut and a rosewood pistol grip cap and forend tip.

Exc.	V.G.	Good	Fair	Poor
650	525	450	375	175

Grade III

As above, with a high-gloss finish and a finely figured walnut stock.

Exc.	V.G.	Good	Fair	Poor
775	625	550	475	275

Deluxe Bolt Action

As above, with an engraved floorplate and triggerguard, a Damascened bolt, and a high-grade French walnut stock. Manufactured between 1970 and 1977.

Exc.	V.G.	Good	Fair	Poor
800	725	650	575	300

Varmint Model

A .222, .22-250, .243, and 6.5x55 caliber bolt action rifle with 27" barrel and a large bolt knob made of Bakelite. Furnished without open sights and has a heavy target-type stock. Manufactured in 1970 only.

Exc.	V.G.	Good	Fair	Poor
525	425	350	275	150

Grand Prix Target

A .22 caliber single-shot, bolt action rifle with a 27" barrel and adjustable weights. Furnished without sights and with an adjustable butt target stock. Only manufactured in 1970.

Exc.	V.G.	Good	Fair	Poor
600	475	400	325	175

Model 2000

A 6.5x55, .243, .270, .308, and .30-06 caliber bolt action rifle with a 60 percent bolt lift and a cold swagged barrel and action. Furnished with open sights. Blued, walnut stock with a Monte Carlo cheekpiece. Manufactured until 1985.

Exc.	V.G.	Good	Fair	Poor
625	500	400	300	150

Courtesy Milwaukee Public Museum, Milwaukee, Wisconsin

GWYN & CAMPBELL
Hamilton, Ohio

Union Carbine

A .52 caliber single shot breech loading percussion carbine with a round/octagonal 20" barrel marked "Gwyn & Campbell/ Patent/1862/ Hamilton,O." Blued, case hardened with a walnut stock. Approximately 8,500 were made between 1862 and 1865.

Courtesy Milwaukee Public Museum, Milwaukee, Wisconsin

Exc.	V.G.	Good	Fair	Poor
—	—	1750	750	350

H

HDH, SA.
Henrion, Dassy & Heuschen
Liege, Belgium

Cobold

A 9.4mm Dutch, 10.6mm German, .38, and .45 caliber double action five shot revolver with solid frame, octagonal barrel, and an odd safety catch that locks the cylinder.

Exc.	V.G.	Good	Fair	Poor
250	175	125	100	75

Puppy

A 5.5mm to 7.65mm caliber folding trigger, double action revolver. Most are "Velo-Dogs".

Exc.	V.G.	Good	Fair	Poor
175	125	100	75	50

Lincoln

A .22 caliber folding trigger, double action revolver with a solid frame, imitation pearl or ivory grips, and engraving.

Exc.	V.G.	Good	Fair	Poor
175	125	100	75	50

Lincoln-Bossu

A 5.5mm or 6.35mm caliber folding trigger double action revolver ("Velo-Dog" type) with solid-frame and hammerless.

Exc.	V.G.	Good	Fair	Poor
175	125	100	75	50

Left Wheeler

A Colt Police Positive copy in .32 or .38 caliber. The last revolver HDH manufactured.

Exc.	V.G.	Good	Fair	Poor
200	150	125	100	75

H.J.S. INDUSTRIES, INC.
Brownsville, Texas

Frontier Four Derringer

A .22 caliber four barreled pocket pistol with 2.5" sliding barrels, stainless steel frame and barrel grip and walnut grips.

Exc.	V.G.	Good	Fair	Poor
150	100	75	50	25

Lone Star Derringer

A .38 Special caliber single shot spur trigger pistol with a 2.5" barrel. Stainless steel with wood grips.

Exc.	V.G.	Good	Fair	Poor
175	125	100	75	50

H&R 1871, LLC
Gardner, MA
SEE-Harrington & Richardson

H-S PRECISION, INC.
Rapid City, SD

SPR Sporter Rifle

This bolt action rifle is offered in both long and short actions with any standard SAAMI caliber. Match grade stainless steel barrel lengths are 22", 24", or 26" with optional muzzle brake available. Synthetic stock is offered in various colors. Weight is between 7.5 and 7.75 lbs. depending on barrel length. Magazine capacity is 4 rounds for standard calibers and 3 rounds for magnum calibers.

NIB	Exc.	V.G.	Good	Fair	Poor
1850	1500	—	—	—	—

PHR Professional Hunter Rifle

This bolt action rifle is chambered for magnum calibers only and is fitted with 24" or 26" stainless steel match grade fluted barrel (except .416 Rigby). Built in recoil reduced in synthetic stock with choice of colors. Matte black finish. Weight is between 7.75 lbs. and 8.25 depending on barrel length and caliber. Offered in any standard SAAMI caliber. Magazine capacity is 3 rounds.

NIB	Exc.	V.G.	Good	Fair	Poor
2000	1650	—	—	—	—

VAR Varmint Rifle

Offered in long or short action with .17 Rem., 6mm PPC, and .223 Rem. in single shot. Fitted with match grade stainless steel fluted barrel in 24" or 26" lengths. Also available is a light-weight 20" barrel. Synthetic stock in choice of colors with 20" barrel guns offered with thumbhole stocks. Blach matte finish. Weight is between 8 and 8.25 lbs. for standard rifles and 7.5 and 7.75 lbs. for 20" barrel guns. Available in any standard SAAMI caliber.

NIB	Exc.	V.G.	Good	Fair	Poor
1850	1500	—	—	—	—

Varmint Take-Down Rifle

This take-down bolt action rifle is offered in a stainless steel long or short action with 24" stainless steel match grade fluted barrel. Matte black finish. Weight is between 8.5 and 9 lbs.

NIB	Exc.	V.G.	Good	Fair	Poor
2100	1750	—	—	—	—

NOTE: Add $1,000 for extra barrel with same head size caliber and $1,200 for extra barrel with different head size caliber.

Professional Hunter Take-Down Rifle

This take-down rifle is offered in magnum and super magnum calibers with 24" fluted stainless steel barrel. Built in recoil reducer. Matte black finish. Weight is between 8.25 and 8.75 lbs.

NIB	Exc.	V.G.	Good	Fair	Poor
2200	1750	—	—	—	—

Varmint Pistol

Bolt action single shot pistol chambered for a wide variety of calibers from .17 Rem. to 7mm BR. Fitted with a heavy contour fluted stainless steel match barrel. Synthetic stock with center grip. Matte black finish. Weight is about 5.25 to 5.5 lbs.

NIB	Exc.	V.G.	Good	Fair	Poor
1250	1000	—	—	—	—

Silhouette Pistol

Same as above but with sporter contoured barrel. Weight is about 4.5 lbs.

NIB	Exc.	V.G.	Good	Fair	Poor
1250	1000	—	—	—	—

HTR Heavy Tactical Rifle

This bolt action model features a stainless steel long or short action with fluted stainless steel 24" heavy barrel. Stock is synthetic with adjustable cheekpiece and length of pull. Any standard SAAMI caliber is available. Weight is about 10.75 to 11.25 lbs. Matte black finish.

NIB	Exc.	V.G.	Good	Fair	Poor
2000	1600	—	—	—	—

RDR Rapid Deployment Rifle

This is similar ot the model above but with 20" stainlees steel fluted barrel and smaller stock. Thumbhole stock on request. Magazine is 4 rounds. Matte black finish. Offered in any short action SAAMI calibers. Weight is between 7.5 and 7.75 lbs.

NIB	Exc.	V.G.	Good	Fair	Poor
1850	1500	—	—	—	—

TTD Tactical Take-Down System

This take-down rifle is chambered for any standard SAAMI caliber and fitted with a 24" fluted heavy stainless steel barrel. Magazine capacity is 4 rounds for standard calibers and 3 rounds for magnum calibers. Synthetic stock that is adjustable for length of pull and cheekpiece. Matte black finish. Weight is between 11.25 and 11.75 lbs.

NIB	Exc.	V.G.	Good	Fair	Poor
2400	1850	—	—	—	—

HWP INDUSTRIES
Milwaukee, Wisconsin

Sledgehammer

A .500 HWP caliber double action revolver with a shrouded 4" barrel, 5-shot, swing-out cylinder. Stainless steel with Pachmayr grips. Introduced in 1989.

Exc.	V.G.	Good	Fair	Poor
1300	1000	900	650	350

HAENEL, C. G.
Suhl, Germany

Established in 1840, this company began to manufacture semiautomatic pistols after Hugo Schmeisser joined the firm in 1921 as its chief engineer.

Model 1

A 6.35mm caliber semiautomatic pistol with a 2.48" barrel, striker fired, a 6-shot magazine and the left side of the slide is stamped "C.G. Haenel Suhl-Schmeisser Patent." Each grip panel is marked "HS" in an oval.

Exc.	V.G.	Good	Fair	Poor
400	300	225	175	100

Model 2

As above, but shorter and lighter in weight. "Schmeisser" is molded into the grips.

Courtesy Orvel Reichert

Exc.	V.G.	Good	Fair	Poor
450	325	250	200	125

HAFDASA
Buenos Aires, Argentina

Ballester-Molina
A copy of the Colt Model 1911 semiautomatic pistol differing only in the absence of a grip safety, smaller grip and the finger grooves on the slide. The slide stamped "Pistola Automatica Cal. .45 Fabricado por HAFDASA Patentes Internacional Ballester Molina Industria Argentina" on the slide. Introduced in 1930s.

Exc.	V.G.	Good	Fair	Poor
475	400	300	225	100

Criolla
A .22 caliber automatic pistol, similar to the Ballester-Molina. Some were sold commercially under the trademark "La Criolla."

Exc.	V.G.	Good	Fair	Poor
1000	800	650	500	250

Hafdasa
A .22 caliber semiautomatic pistol with a tubular receiver. A true hammerless, striker-fired, with an angled grip. Markings are "HA" on the butt.

Exc.	V.G.	Good	Fair	Poor
400	325	275	200	100

Zonda
As above, but marked "Zonda".

Exc.	V.G.	Good	Fair	Poor
400	325	275	200	100

HAKIM
Egypt
A 7.92x57mm caliber semiautomatic rifle copied from the Swedish Model 42 Ljungman. Manufactured by Maadi Military and Civil Industries Co.

Exc.	V.G.	Good	Fair	Poor
275	225	200	150	100

HAHN, WILLIAM
New York, New York

Pocket Pistol
A .41 caliber single shot percussion pistol with a 2.5" round barrel, German silver mountings, and a walnut stock. Manufactured in the 1860s and 1870s.

Exc.	V.G.	Good	Fair	Poor
—	—	1500	900	400

HALE, H. J.
Bristol, Connecticut

Under Hammer Pistol
A .31 caliber single shot, under hammer percussion pistol with a 5" or 6" part-round, part-octagonal barrel and an iron frame with either a pointed or a round walnut butt. Markings read "H.J.Hale/Warranted/Cast Steel." Manufactured during the 1850s.

Exc.	V.G.	Good	Fair	Poor
—	—	650	300	200

HALE & TULLER
Hartford, Connecticut

Under Hammer Pistol
A .44 caliber single shot under hammer percussion pistol with a 6" tapered round barrel and a pointed walnut grip. Manufactured at the Connecticut State Prison between 1837 and 1840.

Exc.	V.G.	Good	Fair	Poor
—	—	600	300	200

HALL, ALEXANDER
New York, New York

Revolving Rifle
A .58 caliber percussion revolving rifle with a 15-shot open centered cylinder. The frame was made of brass, the barrel and cylinder of iron and the stock of walnut. Manufactured during the 1850s in limited quantities. Prospective purchasers should secure a qualified appraisal prior to acquisition. This is a very rare firearm.

Exc.	V.G.	Good	Fair	Poor
—	—	15000	7500	3000

HALL-NORTH
Middletown, Connecticut

Model 1840 Carbine
This carbine was manufactured by Simeon North and was chambered for .52 caliber percussion. It is a single shot, breech-loading, smoothbore with a 21" round barrel. It has a full-length stock held on by two barrel bands. There is a ramrod mounted under the barrel, and the mountings are of iron. The lock is case hardened, and the barrel is brown. The stock is walnut. The markings are "US/S. North/Midltn/ Conn." There are two distinct variations, both produced under military contract.

Type 1 Carbine
This model has a squared, right-angled breech lever mounted on the trigger plate. There were 500 of these manufactured in 1840.

Exc.	V.G.	Good	Fair	Poor
—	—	3500	2500	1200

Type 2 Carbine
This variation features a curved, breech-operating lever that is known as a fishtail. There were approximately 6,000 of these manufactured from 1840 to 1843. Some have an 8" bar and ring.

Exc.	V.G.	Good	Fair	Poor
—	—	2500	1750	750

HAMBUSH, JOSEPH
Ferlach, Austria

Boxlock Side-x-Side Shotgun
A custom-order boxlock double barrel shotgun chambered for all gauges, single selective or double trigger and automatic ejectors. It features workmanship of a high order, and all specification could vary with the customer's wishes. Engraved with hunting scenes. This is a rare gun and is not often encountered on today's market.

NOTE: Pricing is only estimated as not enough are traded to provide accurate values.

Exc.	V.G.	Good	Fair	Poor
1250	1000	800	550	350

Sidelock Side-x-Side Shotgun
Similar to the above, but features a full sidelock action.

Exc.	V.G.	Good	Fair	Poor
2500	2000	1800	1500	1250

HAMILTON RIFLE COMPANY
Plymouth, Michigan
Manufacturer of inexpensive .22 caliber rifles established by Clarence J. Hamilton and his son Coello. The company was established in 1898 in Plymouth, Michigan. The company ceased production in 1945. Over 1 million rifles were produced between 1900 and 1911.

NOTE: Despite the fact that there were many Hamilton rifles sold, most of these little guns were used hard and many did not survive. Hamilton rifles in excellent condition are hardly ever encountered. No prices are quoted for rifles in this condition as few exist. Further information about these rifles is gratefully accepted by the editor.

Hamilton Model 7

Courtesy William F. Krause

Model 7

The first rifle produced by the company, it was made entirely of castings and stampings. It was nickel plated. Chambered for the .22 Short cartridge with am 8" brass lined barrel that pivots for loading. The stock was a metal skeleton. Production ceased in 1901 with a total of 44,000 rifles produced.

Exc.	V.G.	Good	Fair	Poor
—	350	250	200	150

Model 11

Similar to the Model 7 but fitted with a board-like walnut stock. There are markings stamped into the buttstock: HAMILTON RIFLES CO., PLYMOUTH, MICH., PAT. PENDING NO.11. The Model 11 was produced from 1900 to 1902 and approximately 22,000 were sold.

Exc.	V.G.	Good	Fair	Poor
—	400	300	200	150

Model 15

Produced from 1901 to 1910 the Model 15 was chambered for the .22 Short with an 8" brass lined barrel. Walnut stock. The design was an under lever single shot with the loading port under the barrel. The cocking knob is located at the rear of the frame. Blued finish. Approximately 234,000 of these rifles were sold.

Exc.	V.G.	Good	Fair	Poor
—	300	200	150	100

Model 19

This is similar to the Model 15 with a modified loading port and a 12" barrel. A few Model 19s have been seen with 13" barrels. these will bring a premium. Produced from 1903 to 1910 there were about 59,000 of these models sold.

Exc.	V.G.	Good	Fair	Poor
—	400	300	200	150

Model 23

This was the first bolt action rifle made by the company. The receiver is a steel tube with a loading port in the top where the barrel joins the receiver. The bolt handle is located at the extreme rear of the bolt. The cocking knob must be operated manually. Walnut stock either rounded or flat. Chamber for the .22 Short and .22 Long cartridges. 15" brass lined barrel. Blued finish. Weighs about 3 lbs. Produced from 1905 to 1909. About 25,000 guns were sold.

Exc.	V.G.	Good	Fair	Poor
—	400	300	200	150

Model 27

Single shot tip-up .22 caliber rifle with stamped steel receiver. Barrel length 16" brass lined or 14-7/8"; overall length 30". First produced in 1906.

Exc.	V.G.	Good	Fair	Poor
—	250	200	150	100

Model 27

As above with a walnut stock. First produced in 1908.

Exc.	V.G.	Good	Fair	Poor
—	250	200	150	100

Model 31

Introduced in 1910 this single shot rifle is chambered for the .22 Short and Long cartridge. Fitted with a 15-3/4" barrel with brass liner. It is a tip-up design. Blued finish. Weighs about 2.25 lbs.

Exc.	V.G.	Good	Fair	Poor
—	500	350	250	200

Model 35 or Boys' Military Rifle

Single shot .22 caliber rifle with a full length oval walnut straight grip stock and 15-3/4" brass lined barrel. Produced from 1915 to 1918. Sold with a stamped steel bayonet. Few bayonets survive.

Exc.	V.G.	Good	Fair	Poor
—	350	250	150	100

NOTE: Add $100 for bayonet to above prices.

Model 39

This was the only repeating rifle built by the company. It is a hammerless slide action design with a tubular magazine. Magazine capacity is 15 rounds of .22 Short. Barrel length is 16" with brass liner. Walnut stock with blade front sight. Produced from 1922 to 1930. Weighs about 4 lbs.

Exc.	V.G.	Good	Fair	Poor
—	250	200	150	100

Model 43

This is a bolt action design with the loading port on the top of the barrel. There is no external cocking knob but the bolt is pulled to the rear when in the locked position. Chambered for the .22 Short and .22 Long cartridges. 15.75" brass lined barrel. Fitted with an oval walnut stock with blade front sight and open non-adjustable rear sight. Weighs about 3 lbs. Built from 1924 to 1932.

Exc.	V.G.	Good	Fair	Poor
—	250	200	150	100

Model 47

This is a bolt action single shot rifle with the loading port located on top of the barrel. It was chambered for the .22 Short and Long cartridges. The cocking knob is located at the rear of the bolt handle. Early Model 47 were built with 16" brass lined barrels. Later examples were fitted with 18.25" steel lined barrels. Early guns had an oval buttstock while later guns had a pistol grip stock. Very late guns had an all steel barrel. Produced form 1927 to 1932.

Exc.	V.G.	Good	Fair	Poor
—	400	300	200	150

Model 51

This was a conventional type bolt action rifle with the cocking knob located at the rear of the bolt. Two styles of buttstocks were used: a flat style or later an oval shape. This was the first Hamilton rifle chambered for the .22 Long Rifle cartridge. Barrel was 20" steel. Finish was blue. Weight was approximately 3.5 lbs. Produced from 1935 to 1941.

Exc.	V.G.	Good	Fair	Poor
—	350	250	200	150

Model 55

This bolt action rifle was chambered for the .22 Short, Long, and Long Rifle cartridges. Fitted with a 20" steel barrel with bead front sight and open adjustable rear sight. Walnut stock. This is the rarest Hamilton rifle. Only one example is known. Produced from late 1941 to early 1942. No price has yet been established.

HAMMERLI, SA
Lenzburg, Switzerland

RIFLES

Model 45 Smallbore Rifle

A .22 caliber bolt action single shot, with a 27.5" heavy barrel, an aperture rear and globe target front sight and a match rifle-type thumbhole stock. Manufactured between 1945 and 1957.

Exc.	V.G.	Good	Fair	Poor
725	600	525	425	225

Model 54 Smallbore Rifle

As above, with an adjustable buttplate. Manufactured between 1954 and 1957.

Exc.	V.G.	Good	Fair	Poor
750	625	550	450	250

Model 503 Smallbore Free Rifle

Similar to the Model 54, with a free rifle style stock.

Exc.	V.G.	Good	Fair	Poor
700	575	500	400	200

Model 506 Smallbore Match Rifle.

The later version of the Smallbore target series. Manufactured between 1963 and 1966.

Exc.	V.G.	Good	Fair	Poor
750	625	650	550	350

Olympic 300 Meter

A 7x57, .30-06, or .300 H&H Magnum caliber bolt action, single shot, rifle with a 20.5" heavy barrel, an aperture rear, globe target front sight, double-set triggers and a free rifle-type, adjustable thumbhole stock with a wide beaver tail forearm and Schutzen-style buttplate. Manufactured between 1945 and 1959.

Exc.	V.G.	Good	Fair	Poor
950	800	650	500	300

Sporting Rifle

A bolt action, single shot rifle chambered for many popular calibers (American and European), double-set triggers and a classic-style stock.

Exc.	V.G.	Good	Fair	Poor
700	575	500	400	325

PISTOLS

Model 100 Free Pistol

A .22 caliber single shot Martini action target pistol with an 11.5" octagonal barrel, adjustable sights, single set trigger and walnut stocks. Manufactured from 1933 to 1949.

Exc.	V.G.	Good	Fair	Poor
900	725	650	500	300

Model 101

As above, with a heavy round barrel and more sophisticated target sights. A matte-blued finish and was manufactured between 1956 and 1960.

Exc.	V.G.	Good	Fair	Poor
900	725	650	500	300

Model 102

As above, with highly polished blue finish. Manufactured between 1956 and 1960.

Exc.	V.G.	Good	Fair	Poor
900	725	650	500	300

Model 103

Similar to the Model 101, with a lighter-weight octagonal barrel, high polished blued finish. Manufactured between 1956 and 1960.

Exc.	V.G.	Good	Fair	Poor
1000	825	750	600	400

Model 104

As above, with a lightweight round barrel. Manufactured between 1961 and 1965.

Exc.	V.G.	Good	Fair	Poor
750	625	550	450	300

Model 105

As above, with a redesigned stock and an improved action. Manufactured between 1962 and 1965.

Exc.	V.G.	Good	Fair	Poor
1000	825	750	600	400

Model 106

As above, with an improved trigger.

Exc.	V.G.	Good	Fair	Poor
1100	900	750	600	400

Model 107

This variation is fitted with a five-level set trigger. Introduced in 1965 and discontinued in 1971.

Exc.	V.G.	Good	Fair	Poor
750	600	500	300	—

Model 107 Deluxe

As above, but engraved and with a carved stock.

Exc.	V.G.	Good	Fair	Poor
1500	1250	900	800	500

Model 120-1 Free Pistol

A bolt action, single shot pistol in .22 l.r. caliber with a a 9.9" barrel, adjustable target sights, activated for loading and cocking by an alloy lever on the side of the bolt. Blued, with checkered walnut grips.

Exc.	V.G.	Good	Fair	Poor
450	375	300	225	150

Model 120-2

As above with contoured grips.

Exc.	V.G.	Good	Fair	Poor
475	400	325	250	175

Model 120 Heavy Barrel

As above, with a 5.7" heavy barrel.

Exc.	V.G.	Good	Fair	Poor
450	375	300	225	150

Model 150

A single shot, Martini action .22 caliber pistol with an 11.25" barrel, adjustable sights, contoured grips and a single-set trigger. Blued with walnut stocks.

Exc.	V.G.	Good	Fair	Poor
2150	1800	1500	1250	800

Model 152

As above, with an 11.25" barrel, and an electronic release trigger.

Exc.	V.G.	Good	Fair	Poor
2300	1950	1750	1500	900

International Model 206

A .22 caliber semiautomatic pistol with a 7.5" barrel, an integral muzzle brake, adjustable sights, and walnut grips. Manufactured between 1962 and 1969.

Exc.	V.G.	Good	Fair	Poor
725	600	475	375	275

International Model 207

As above, with adjustable grips.

Exc.	V.G.	Good	Fair	Poor
750	625	500	400	200

International Model 208

A .22 caliber semiautomatic pistol with a 6" barrel, adjustable sights and an 8-shot magazine, adjustable trigger, and target grips. The barrel is drilled and tapped for the addition of barrel weights. Manufactured between 1966 and 1988.

Exc.	V.G.	Good	Fair	Poor
1850	1550	1250	1000	750

International Model 208 Deluxe

As above, with an engraved receiver, and carved grips. Discontinued in 1988.

Exc.	V.G.	Good	Fair	Poor
3250	2750	2500	2000	1500

International Model 209

A .22 short caliber semiautomatic pistol with a 4.75" barrel, a muzzle brake, adjustable target sights, and 5-shot magazine. Blued, with walnut grips. Manufactured between 1966 and 1970.

Exc.	V. G.	Good	Fair	Poor
850	700	600	450	350

International Model 210

As above, with adjustable grips.

Exc.	V.G.	Good	Fair	Poor
850	700	600	450	350

International Model 211

As above, with non-adjustable thumb rest grips.

Exc.	V.G.	Good	Fair	Poor
1850	1550	1250	1000	750

Model 212

A .22 caliber semiautomatic pistol with a 5" barrel, and adjustable sights. Blued with walnut grips.

Exc.	V.G.	Good	Fair	Poor
1500	1275	1000	750	650

Model 230

A .22 Short caliber semiautomatic pistol with a 6.3" barrel, a 5-shot magazine, adjustable sights and walnut grip. Manufactured between 1970 and 1983.

Exc.	V.G.	Good	Fair	Poor
725	600	500	400	200

Model 232

A .22 short caliber semiautomatic pistol with a 5" barrel, adjustable sights, and a 6-shot magazine. Contoured walnut grips. Introduced in 1984.

Exc.	V.G.	Good	Fair	Poor
1500	1300	1150	850	550

Model 280

This is the new state-of-the-art target pistol from Hammerli. It features a modular design and has a frame of carbon fiber material. It has a 4.6" barrel with adjustable sights, trigger, and grips. It is chambered for .22 l.r. or .32 wad cutter. The magazine holds 5 rounds, and the pistol was introduced in 1988.

Exc.	V.G.	Good	Fair	Poor
1800	1500	1350	1000	600

Model SP 20

Introduced in 1998, this pistol has a very low sight line and features a wide variety of special items such as adjustable buffer system, anatomically shaped trigger in various sizes, various receiver colors, change over caliber system from .22 Long Rifle to .32 S&W.

NIB	Exc.	V.G.	Good	Fair	Poor
N/A	—	—	—	—	—

Dakota

A single action revolver based on the Colt SAA design. It has a solid frame and is loaded through a gate. It is chambered for .22 l.r., .357 Magnum .44-40, and .45 Colt and was offered with barrel lengths of 5", 6", and 7.5". It has a 6-shot cylinder and is blued, with a brass triggerguard and walnut grips.

Exc.	V.G.	Good	Fair	Poor
150	125	100	75	50

Large Calibers

Exc.	V.G.	Good	Fair	Poor
225	175	150	125	100

Super Dakota

Similar to the Dakota but is chambered for .41 and .44 Magnum, with adjustable sights.

Exc.	V.G.	Good	Fair	Poor
275	225	175	150	100

Virginian

Basically a more deluxe version of the Dakota. It is chambered for the .357 and .45 Colt cartridge. The triggerguard and back strap are chrome plated, with the frame case colored and the remainder blued. This model features the "Swissafe" safety system that allows the cylinder axis pin to be locked back to prevent the hammer from falling.

Exc.	V.G.	Good	Fair	Poor
300	250	200	175	125

HAMMERLI-WALTHER
Lenzburg, Switzerland

These target pistols were produced by Hammerli under license from Walther after WWII. This project continued until approximately 1963, when production was ceased.

Olympia Model 200 Type 1952

A .22 caliber semiautomatic pistol with a 7.5" barrel, a 10-shot magazine, adjustable target sights, and a blued with walnut grips. Manufactured between 1952 and 1958.

Exc.	V.G.	Good	Fair	Poor
700	575	475	375	300

Model 200 Type 1958

As above with an integral muzzle brake. Manufactured between 1958 and 1963.

Exc.	V.G.	Good	Fair	Poor
750	625	525	425	325

Model 201

A Model 200 Type 1952 with a 9.5" barrel. Manufactured between 1955 and 1957.

Exc.	V.G.	Good	Fair	Poor
700	575	475	375	300

Model 202

Similar to the Model 201, with adjustable walnut grips. Manufactured between 1955 and 1957.

Exc.	V.G.	Good	Fair	Poor
750	625	525	425	325

Model 203

Similar to the Model 200, with the adjustable grips, available with or without a muzzle brake.

Exc.	V.G.	Good	Fair	Poor
750	625	525	425	325

Model 204

A .22 caliber semiautomatic pistol with a 7.5" barrel, a muzzle brake, and barrel weights. Manufactured between 1956 and 1963.

Exc.	V.G.	Good	Fair	Poor
800	675	575	475	375

Model 205

As above, with adjustable target grips. Manufactured between 1956 and 1963.

Exc.	V.G.	Good	Fair	Poor
925	775	675	575	450

HAMMOND BULLDOG
Connecticut Arms & Mfg. Co.
Naubuc, Connecticut

Hammond Bulldog

A .44 rimfire single shot spur trigger pistol with a 4" octagonal barrel that pivots to open. Blued with checkered walnut grips. Manufactured from 1864 to approximately 1867.

Exc.	V.G.	Good	Fair	Poor
—	900	500	375	250

HAMMOND, GRANT MFG. CO.
New Haven, Connecticut

Military Automatic Pistol

A .45 ACP caliber semiautomatic pistol with a 6.75" barrel and an 8-shot magazine. Blued, with checkered walnut grips. Marked on the right of the slide "Grant Hammond Mfg. Corp. New Haven, Conn." The left side shows the patent dates. Manufactured in 1917. As all the known specimens of this pistol exhibit differences, it is believed that they were only made as prototypes. The highest serial number known is under 20. It is strongly suggested that an expert appraisal be obtained before the sale.

Courtesy Horst Held

Exc.	V.G.	Good	Fair	Poor
7000	5500	4000	3000	1000

HANKINS, WILLIAM
Philadelphia, Pennsylvania

Pocket Revolver

A .26 caliber spur trigger percussion revolver with a 3" octagonal barrel, and a 5-shot unfluted cylinder. Blued with walnut grips. Approximately 650 were manufactured in 1860 and 1861.

Courtesy Milwaukee Public Museum, Milwaukee, Wisconsin

Exc.	V.G.	Good	Fair	Poor
—	—	1750	1000	475

HANUS, BILL
Newport, Oregon

Bill Hanus Classic

Built in Spain by Ignacio Ugartechea these side-by-side shotgun are offered in 16, 20, 28 gauge, as well as .410 bore. They are fitted with 27" barrel with concave ribs and are choked IC/M. Stock is straight grip with splinter forearm. Double triggers are standard as are automatic ejectors.

NIB	Exc.	V.G.	Good	Fair	Poor
1600	1250	—	—	—	—

HARPERS FERRY ARMORY MUSKETS AND CARBINES
Harpers Ferry, Virginia

Established at Harpers Ferry, Virginia, in 1798 as the new nation's "Southern Armory," production finally began in 1800 and continued at the "musket works" until the facilities were seized by Virginia state militia in April 1861. With the signing of a contract in 1819 between the government and J.H. Hall, the latter was permitted to construct a separate facility for the production of his patent breechloading rifles, which continued to be known as the "rifle works" after the discontinuation of Hall production until it, too, was seized by Virginia militia in 1861. The machinery of the former was sent to Richmond to be used in the manufacture of the "Richmond rifle musket" while the rifle machinery was sent to Fayetteville, North Carolina, where it was employed in making "Fayetteville rifles."

Harpers Ferry U.S. M1816 Muskets (Types I to III)

Overall length 57-3/4"; barrel length 42"; caliber .69. Markings: on lockplate eagle over "US" forward of cock, "HARPERS/FERRY/(date)" on tail. Barrel tang also bears the date, and barrel should show proofmarks on upper left side near breech. The 45605 (type 1) muskets produced at Harpers Ferry from 1817 through 1821 were made with a lower sling swivel that was attached to a separate lug extending from the forward strap of the triggerguard. In 1822, this piece was eliminated and the balance of the production (216,116) officially known as the M1822 musket, incorporated the lower sling swivel directly to the triggerguard bow. Until 1832, these muskets were manufactured with a "browned" barrel to inhibit rusting. The brown barrels of these 107,684 muskets distinguish them as Type II production. The balance of production until 1844 (98,432) were made with bright barrel, distinguishing Type III muskets. Despite the large numbers produced, most were altered to percussion during the 1850s. Most by the "cone-in-barrel" (so called arsenal) method. Many of these were altered again during the American Civil War, usually with a "Patent Breech," and were then rifled and sighted.

Courtesy Milwaukee Public Museum, Milwaukee, Wisconsin

Courtesy Milwaukee Public Museum, Milwaukee, Wisconsin

(in flintlock)

Exc.	V.G.	Good	Fair	Poor
—	—	3500	1500	500

(altered to percussion)

Exc.	V.G.	Good	Fair	Poor
—	—	1000	600	300

NOTE: Add 100% for Type III flintlock muskets (rare).

Harpers Ferry U.S. M1842 Musket

Overall length 57-3/4"; barrel length 42"; caliber .69. Markings: on lockplate, eagle over "US" forward of hammer, "HARPERS/FERRY/(date)" on tail; barrel tang also shows date; upper left quarter of barrel near breech includes proofmarks (an eagle head, a "V", and a "P") and inspector's initials. Between 1844 and 1855, Harpers Ferry manufactured 106,629 of these smoothbore muskets, many of which were subsequently rifled and sighted; the latter will bring a slight premium.

Exc.	V.G.	Good	Fair	Poor
—	—	2500	950	400

Harpers Ferry U.S. M1819 Hall Rifle (Types I and II)

Overall length 52-3/4"; barrel (bore) length 32-5/8"; caliber .52. Markings: on top of receiver, either "J.H. HALL/H.FERRY/(date)/U.S." or "J.H. HALL.S./(date)." The 2,000 rifles manufactured between 1824 and 1826 (Type I) are distinguished by having their barrel bands retained by band springs on the right side of the stock. The balance of production (17,680), made between 1828 and 1840, have pins driven through the bands and the stock, distinguishing Type II production. Many of these rifles were altered to percussion just before and in the early months of the American Civil War. Those with evidence of having been altered in the South will command a premium.

(in flintlock)

Exc.	V.G.	Good	Fair	Poor
—	—	3000	1750	750

Courtesy Milwaukee Public Museum, Milwaukee, Wisconsin

Courtesy Milwaukee Public Museum, Milwaukee, Wisconsin

(altered to percussion)

Exc.	V.G.	Good	Fair	Poor
—	—	1750	800	400

NOTE: For Type I flintlocks add 250%.

Harpers Ferry U.S. M1841 Hall Rifle

Overall length 52-3/4"; barrel (bore) length 32-5/8"; caliber .52. Markings: on top of receiver, either "J.H. HALL/H.FERRY/US/(date)." With the general adoption of the percussion system of ignition, the manufacture of Hall's rifles was changed to conform to the new system, a cone tapped directly into the breechblock substituting for the frizzen and pan, and a hammer replacing the flint cock. The newly made percussion arms also incorporated the newly adopted "fishtail" latch for levering the breechblock. Two-thirds of the 4,213 rifles made were still in storage at the arsenal when it was burned in 1861, enhancing the rarity of the arm.

Exc.	V.G.	Good	Fair	Poor
—	—	4000	1750	650

Harpers Ferry U.S. M1836 Hall Carbine (Types I & II)

Overall length 43"; barrel (bore) length 23"; caliber .64. Markings: on top of receiver, "J.H. HALL/U.S./(date)." To furnish the newly raised 2nd Regiment U.S. Dragoons raised in 1836, Harpers Ferry Armory was directed to construct 1,003 Hall carbines, differing in length and caliber over the M1833 model produced by the North for the 1st Regiment, but were not ready when the unit was sent to Florida. Another 1,017 were made during 1839-1840 with the addition of a tool compartment in the buttstock, distinguishing type II production.

Courtesy Milwaukee Public Museum, Milwaukee, Wisconsin

Exc.	V.G.	Good	Fair	Poor
—	—	4000	1500	650

Harpers Ferry U.S. M1842 Hall Carbine

Overall length 40"; barrel (bore) length 21"; caliber .52. Markings: on top of receiver, "H. FERRY/U S/1842." To meet the needs of the U.S. Dragoons for replacement carbines, Harpers Ferry manufactured 1,001 carbines in 1842, differing only from the North M1840 (Type II—"fishtail lever") carbine by being brass instead of iron mounted.

Courtesy Milwaukee Public Museum, Milwaukee, Wisconsin

Exc.	V.G.	Good	Fair	Poor
—	—	8000	3000	1500

Harpers Ferry U.S. M 1841 Muzzleloading Rifle-The "Mississippi Rifle"

Overall length 49"; barrel length 33"; caliber .54 (altered to .58 after 1857). Markings: on lockplate, eagle over "US" forward of hammer; "HARPERS/FERRY/(date)" on tail; date also on tang of breechplug; inspector's initials "AW/P" or "WW/P" and proofmarks (eagle head, "V" and "P" on upper left side of barrel). With the discontinuance of production of the Hall patent arms, Hall's Rifle Works was transformed into the production of the new U.S. rifle adopted in 1841. From 1846 until 1855 a total of 25,296 were manufactured at Harpers Ferry. Approximately 10,000 of these rifles were subsequently adapted for long range firing and to saber bayonets at Harpers Ferry between 1855 and 1861. The adaptations in chronological order included the adoption of the Snell bayonet and Benton long range "screw" sight, the adoption of a saber bayonet lug with guide and the Benton sight, the adoption of the saber bayonet lug with guide and the Burton "ladder" long range sights, the adoption of the U.S. M1855 (Type 1) rifle sights and bayonet lug (first in .54 and then in .58 caliber), and finally the adoption of the U.S. M1855 (Type II) rifle sights and bayonet lug (in .58 caliber). A few thousand were also adapted to the Colt revolving rifle sights and split ring bayonet adaptor in 1861-1862, but that adaptation was not restricted to Harpers Ferry-made rifles.

Courtesy Milwaukee Public Museum, Milwaukee, Wisconsin

Courtesy Milwaukee Public Museum, Milwaukee, Wisconsin

Exc.	V.G.	Good	Fair	Poor
—	—	4500	1750	750

Harpers Ferry U.S. M1842 Musket

Overall length 57-3/4"; barrel length 42"; caliber .69. Markings: on lockplate, eagle over "US" forward of hammer; "HARPERS/FERRY/(date)" on tail; date also on tang of breechplug; inspector's initials and proofmarks on barrel near breech. Harpers Ferry manufactured a total of 106,629 of these smoothbore muskets between 1844 and 1855. Many of these muskets were subsequently rifled and sighted from 1855 to 1858 or simply rifled during the early years of the American Civil War.

Exc.	V.G.	Good	Fair	Poor
—	—	3000	1500	750

Harpers Ferry U.S. M1855 Rifle-Musket (Type I & II)

Overall length 56"; barrel length 40"; caliber .58. Markings: on lockplate, eagle on Maynard primer door; "US/HARPERS FERRY" forward of hammer; date on tail; date also on top of barrel near breech plus proofmarks (eagle head, "V", and "P"). Between 1857 and 1858 Harpers Ferry produced 15,071 of these rifles, but many were still unsighted at the end of the fiscal year. This early production (Type I) is distinguished from the later production (1859-1860) by the absence of the iron "patchbox" on the right side of the buttstock, a long range rear sight, and a brass nosecap. The "patchbox" was added in 1859 together with a short base rear sight with leaves graduated to only 300 and 500 yards. The brass nosecaps were gradually phased out during 1859.

Exc.	V.G.	Good	Fair	Poor
—	—	4750	2000	800

Harpers Ferry U.S. M1855 Rifles (Type I & II)

Overall length 49"; barrel length 33"; caliber .58. Markings: on lockplate, eagle on Maynard primer door; "U S/HARPERS FERRY" forward of hammer; date on tail; date also on top of barrel near breech plus proofmarks (eagle head, "V", and "P"). Designed as the replacement of the U.S. M1841 rifle, production of the U.S. M1855 rifle began at John Hall's old "Harpers Ferry Rifle Works" in 1857. The production of 1857 and 1858 (Type I), numbering only 3,645 rifles, were all brass mounted, bore a long range rear sight on the browned barrel, and bore a "patchbox" inletted for a special crosshair figure "8" detachable front sight, though many were still without their rear sights at the end of the fiscal year due to the intervention of the Secretary of War. Most of these were never issued and were subsequently destroyed when the arsenal was set afire in April 1861 to prevent the capture of its arms by Virginia forces. The 3,771 rifles produced between 1858 and April 1861 (Type II) were all iron mounted (though a transitional period continued to utilize the brass nosecaps), eliminated the special front sight (permitting the cavity to be enlarged for greased patches), and employed a short base long range rear sight similar to that of the Type II M 1855 rifle musket.

Courtesy Milwaukee Public Museum, Milwaukee, Wisconsin

Courtesy Milwaukee Public Museum, Milwaukee, Wisconsin

(Type I)

Exc.	V.G.	Good	Fair	Poor
—	—	10000	5500	1750

(Type II)

Exc.	V.G.	Good	Fair	Poor
—	—	6500	3500	1250

HARRINGTON & RICHARDSON, INC.
Worcester, Massachusetts

Established in 1877 by G.H. Harrington and W.A. Richardson. The arms originally produced by this company were marketed under the trade name Aetna. The firm is now located in Gardner, Massachusetts.

NOTE: In November of 2000 the Marlin Firearms Company purchased the assets of Harrington & Richardson. This new company is now known as H&R 1871, LLC.

Model No. I

A .32 or .38 caliber spur-trigger single action revolver with a 3" octagonal barrel, solid frame, a 7-shot or a 5-shot cylinder, depending on the caliber. Nickel-plated with checkered rubber bird's-head grips. Barrel marked "Harrington & Richardson Worcester, Mass." Approximately 3,000 were manufactured in 1877 and 1878.

Exc.	V.G.	Good	Fair	Poor
300	250	200	125	75

Model 1-1/2

A .32 caliber spur-trigger, single action revolver with a 2.5" octagonal barrel and a 5-shot cylinder. Nickel-plated, round-butt rubber grips with an "H&R" emblem molded in. Approximately 10,000 were manufactured between 1878 and 1883.

Exc.	V.G.	Good	Fair	Poor
175	150	125	75	50

Model 2-1/2

As above, with a 3.25" barrel and a 7-shot cylinder. Approximately 5,000 were manufactured between 1878 and 1883.

Exc.	V.G.	Good	Fair	Poor
175	150	125	75	50

Model 3-1/2

Similar to the Model 2-1/2 except in .38 rimfire caliber with a 3.5" barrel and a 5-shot cylinder. Approximately 2,500 were manufactured.

Exc.	V.G.	Good	Fair	Poor
200	175	150	100	75

Model 4-1/2

A .41 rimfire caliber spur trigger revolver with a 2.5" barrel and 5-shot cylinder. Approximately 1,000 were manufactured.

Exc.	V.G.	Good	Fair	Poor
250	200	175	125	90

Model 1880

A .32 or .38 S&W centerfire caliber double action revolver with a 3" round barrel, a solid frame, and a 5- or 6-shot cylinder, depending on the caliber. Nickel-plated with hard rubber grips. Marked "Harrington & Richardson Worchester, Mass." Approximately 4,000 were manufactured between 1880 and 1883.

Exc.	V.G.	Good	Fair	Poor
250	200	175	125	90

The American Double Action

A .32, .28, or .44 centerfire caliber double action revolver with a 2.5", 4.5", or 6" round or octagonal barrel, a 5- or 6-shot fluted cylinder, depending on the caliber, and solid frame, nickel-plated, with some blue models noted. The grips are of hard rubber. Marked "The American Double Action." Some noted are marked "H&R Bulldog." Approximately 850,000 were manufactured between 1883 and 1940.

Exc.	V.G.	Good	Fair	Poor
125	100	85	65	40

The Young America Double Action

A .22 rimfire or .32 S&W centerfire caliber, double action revolver, with 2", 4.5", or 6" round or octagonal barrels, solid frame, and a 5- or 7-shot cylinder, depending on the caliber. Blued or nickel-plated, with hard rubber grips. Marked "Young

America Double Action" or "Young America Bulldog." Approximately 1,500,000 were manufactured between 1884 and 1941.

Exc.	V.G.	Good	Fair	Poor
125	100	85	65	40

First Model Hand Ejector

A .32 or .38 centerfire caliber double action revolver with a 3.25" ribbed round barrel. This version does not feature the automatic ejection found on later models. Nickel-plated, with hard rubber grips. The company name is marked on the barrel. Approximately 6,000 were manufactured between 1886 and 1888.

Exc.	V.G.	Good	Fair	Poor
200	150	125	90	65

Model 1 Double Action Revolver

A .32, .32 long, and the .38 S&W caliber double action revolver with a 3.25" ribbed round barrel, and a 5- or 6-shot cylinder, depending on the caliber. Nickel-plated, with hard rubber grips. Approximately 5,000 were manufactured between 1887 and 1889.

Exc.	V.G.	Good	Fair	Poor
175	145	110	80	50

Model 2

Similar to the Model 1, with 2.5", 3.25", 4", 5", or 6" barrels. The grips feature the H&R target logo. There were approximately 1,300,000 manufactured between 1889 and 1940.

Exc.	V.G.	Good	Fair	Poor
125	100	80	65	40

Knife Model

The Model 2 with a 4" ribbed round barrel having a folding 2.25" double-edged knife mounted under the barrel. Blued or nickel-plated. Approximately 2,000 were manufactured between 1901 and 1917.

Exc.	V.G.	Good	Fair	Poor
450	400	350	250	150

Self-Loader

A 6.35mm or the 7.65mm semiautomatic pistol with a 2" or 3.5" barrel, a 6- or 8-shot magazine. The larger 7.65 model has a grip safety. Blued or nickel-plated with checkered, hard rubber grips that bear the H&R monogram. The slide is marked, "H&R Self-Loading" with 1907 or 1909 patent dates. Approximately 16,500 were manufactured in 6.35mm between 1912 and 1916 and 34,500 in 7.65mm manufactured between 1916 and 1924.

Courtesy Orvel Reichert

Courtesy Orvel Reichert

Courtesy Orvel Reichert

Courtesy Orvel Reichert

Exc.	V.G.	Good	Fair	Poor
300	250	200	150	100

Hunter

A .22 caliber double action revolver with a 10" octagonal barrel and a 9-shot fluted cylinder. Blued, with checkered walnut grips.

Courtesy Mike Stukslager

Exc.	V.G.	Good	Fair	Poor
200	150	125	100	75

Trapper
As above, with a 6" octagonal barrel and a 7-shot cylinder. Otherwise it is similar to the Hunter.

Courtesy Mike Stuckslager

Exc.	V.G.	Good	Fair	Poor
200	150	125	100	75

Model 922 First Issue
A .22 caliber double action revolver with a 2.5", 4", or 6" barrel. Blued, with checkered walnut grips.

Exc.	V.G.	Good	Fair	Poor
150	125	100	75	50

Target Model
A .22 l.r. or .22 rimfire Magnum caliber double action revolver with 7-shot cylinder, a break-open frame and a 6" barrel with fixed sights. Blued, with checkered walnut grips.

Exc.	V.G.	Good	Fair	Poor
150	125	100	75	50

.22 Special
A .22 l.r. or the .22 rimfire Magnum double action, break-open revolver with a 6" barrel and a 7-shot cylinder. Blued, with checkered walnut grips.

Exc.	V.G.	Good	Fair	Poor
175	150	125	90	65

Expert
As above, with a 10" barrel.

Exc.	V.G.	Good	Fair	Poor
150	125	100	75	50

No. 199 Sportsman
A .22 caliber single action, break-open revolver with a 6" barrel, adjustable target sights and a 9-shot cylinder. Blued, with checkered walnut grips.

Exc.	V.G.	Good	Fair	Poor
200	175	150	100	75

Ultra Sportsman
As above, but more finely finished and with a special, wide target hammer and an improved action.

Exc.	V.G.	Good	Fair	Poor
225	200	175	125	90

Defender
A .38 S&W caliber double action, break-open revolver with a 4" or 6" barrel and fixed sights. Blued, with plastic grips.

Exc.	V.G.	Good	Fair	Poor
150	125	100	75	50

New Defender
A .22 caliber double action, break-open revolver with a 2" barrel and a 9-shot cylinder. Blued with checkered, walnut round-butt grips.

Exc.	V.G.	Good	Fair	Poor
225	200	175	125	90

.22 U.S.R.A./Model 195 Single Shot Match Target Pistol
Also called the Model 195, this pistol underwent nearly constant modifications from its inception in 1928 until production ceased in 1941. Its development was greatly influenced by the United States Revolver Association (USRA), which established certain rules for target pistol shooting. The lack of any H&R-published model chronology for the estimated 3,500 guns manufactured makes model determination by examination complicated; a further difficulty is that H&R supplied newly designed parts to owners of older variations, who would then retrofit their pistols with newer triggers, hammers, sights, and triggerguards. Extracted from the available literature, the parts represent approximately: 14 different stocks and virtually endless custom variations by Walter F. Roper; 5 different triggerguards; 3 different triggers; 2 different hammers; 2 different extractors; 3 barrel lengths (7", 8", 10"); and 3 barrel rib styles. From this array of potential characteristics, at least four distinct variations can be identified.

.22 U.S.R.A./Model 195 pistol, Variations 1 to 3

Exc.	V.G.	Good	Fair	Poor
450	350	325	275	200

.22 U.S.R.A./Model 195 pistol, Variation 4

Exc.	V.G.	Good	Fair	Poor
500	400	350	325	250

Variation 1, pre-U.S.R.A., 1928-30: Not marked **U.S.R.A.**, and known as the "H&R Single Shot Pistol." There is no finger rest between the triggerguard and front grip strap; it was advertised with "sawhandle" shape grip copied from the Model 1 or 2 smooth bore H&R Handy-Gun, manufactured with a 10" "hourglass" barrel with a deeply undercut rib. These are the first 500 pistols.

Variation 2, U.S.R.A. Keyhole Barrel, 1930-31: This is the standard "early" model marked **U.S.R.A.**, has a finger rest, and non-sawhandle grips; however, several grip shapes were offered as options. The grip screw goes from rear of grip into threaded hold in back grip strap.

Variation 3, Modified Keyhole Barrel, 1931: Modification of Variation 2 to improve rear sight, barrel catch changed, reduced spent cartridge force by replacing cylindrical extractor with less powerful hinged type, and the hammer cocking spur and finger rest were made wider. The 8" barrel was offered as an option to standard 10" length, and the number of different grip shapes was increased. This is a transition model between "early" Variation 2 and "final" Variation 4 designs.

Variation 4, Tapered Slabside Barrel, 1931-41: New "truncated teardrop" barrel cross section shape; new standard barrel length of 7", with 10" optional; adjustable trigger; new sear; grip screw location was changed to front of grip; and front sight was adjustable for elevation. The trigger design was changed from curved to straight beveled type with relocated cocking surfaces, and the number of grip shapes increased further to 13 types. A front sight protector was supplied as standard equipment, and luggage style case offered as an option. It appears that Variation 4 was introduced around 1931; the 1932 advertisements describe the fully redesigned gun, but picture Variation 2, indicating H&R probably did not re-photograph the new design. The final variation has a special, tight bore .217" in diameter, with bullet seating .03125" (1/32") into rifling, and is among the most accurate of single-shot .22 caliber pistols. The Model 195/U.S.R.A. was relatively expensive, costing approximately $30 in 1932, and increased to slightly more than $36 by the time production ended in 1941, yet was the least expensive of all single-shot .22 target pistols of quality.

Information about specific U.S.R.A. pistols (serial number and other descriptive information) is being sought by L. Richard Littlefield, P.O. Box 9, Jaffrey, New Hampshire 03452, telephone (603) 532-8004, FAX (603) 532-4501.

Model 504

A .32 H&R Magnum caliber double action, swing-out cylinder revolver with a 4" or 6" heavy barrel, adjustable sights, and 5-shot cylinder. Blued, with either black plastic or walnut grips. Smaller version manufactured with a 3" or 4" barrel and a round butt.

Exc.	V.G.	Good	Fair	Poor
175	150	125	90	65

Model 532

As above, but with a cylinder that has to be removed for loading. Manufactured in 1984 and 1985.

Exc.	V.G.	Good	Fair	Poor
100	75	50	40	25

Model 586

A .32 H&R Magnum caliber double action revolver with a 4.5", 5.5", 7.5", or 10" barrel, adjustable sights and a 5-shot cylinder. Blued, with either black plastic or walnut grips.

Exc.	V.G.	Good	Fair	Poor
175	150	125	100	75

Model 603

A .22 rimfire Magnum caliber double action revolver with a 6" flat-sided barrel and swing-out 6-shot cylinder. Blued, with smooth walnut grips.

Exc.	V.G.	Good	Fair	Poor
165	140	110	85	60

Model 604

As above, with a 6", ribbed, heavy barrel.

Exc.	V.G.	Good	Fair	Poor
175	150	125	90	65

Model 622

A .22 caliber solid-frame double action revolver with a 2.5" or 4" barrel. Blued, with round-butt plastic grips.

Exc.	V.G.	Good	Fair	Poor
100	80	65	50	25

Model 623

As above, but nickel-plated.

Exc.	V.G.	Good	Fair	Poor
125	100	80	60	40

Model 632

As above in .32 centerfire.

Exc.	V.G.	Good	Fair	Poor
110	90	75	60	30

Model 642

As above, in .22 rimfire Magnum.

Exc.	V.G.	Good	Fair	Poor
100	80	65	50	25

Model 649

The Model 622, with a 5.5" or 7.5" barrel.

Exc.	V.G.	Good	Fair	Poor
150	125	100	75	50

Model 650

As above, but nickel-plated.

Exc.	V.G.	Good	Fair	Poor
150	125	100	75	50

Model 660

A .22 caliber solid-frame, Western-style revolver with a 5.5" barrel and is a double action. Blued, with walnut grips. It is also known as the "Gunfighter."

Exc.	V.G.	Good	Fair	Poor
100	80	65	45	25

Model 666

A .22 or .22 rimfire Magnum caliber double action revolver with a 6" barrel and a 6-shot cylinder. Blued, with plastic grips. Manufactured between 1976 and 1982.

Exc.	V.G.	Good	Fair	Poor
100	80	65	45	25

Model 676

Similar to the Model 660. Blued, with a case colored frame. It has walnut grips. Manufactured between 1976 and 1982.

Exc.	V.G.	Good	Fair	Poor
150	125	100	75	50

Model 686

Similar to the Model 660 "Gunfighter" with a 4.5", 5.5", 7.5", 10", or 12" barrel.

Exc.	V.G.	Good	Fair	Poor
175	150	125	100	75

Model 732

A .32 caliber double action, solid-frame revolver with a swing-out cylinder, a 2.5" or 4" barrel and a 6-shot cylinder. Blued, with black plastic grips. Also known as the "Guardsman."

Exc.	V.G.	Good	Fair	Poor
125	100	80	65	45

Model 733

As above, but nickel-plated and a 2.5" barrel.

Exc.	V.G.	Good	Fair	Poor
150	125	100	75	50

Model 900

A .22 caliber solid-frame revolver with a removable cylinder, a 2.5" or 4" barrel and a 9-shot cylinder. Blued, with black plastic grips. Manufactured between 1962 and 1973.

Exc.	V.G.	Good	Fair	Poor
100	90	80	60	40

Model 901

As above, but chrome-plated with white plastic grips. Manufactured in 1962 and 1963 only.

Exc.	V.G.	Good	Fair	Poor
100	90	80	60	40

Model 903

As above, with a swing-out cylinder, a flat-sided, 6" barrel, and a 9-shot cylinder. Blued, with walnut grips.

Exc.	V.G.	Good	Fair	Poor
125	100	90	75	50

Model 904

As above, with a ribbed heavy barrel.

Exc.	V.G.	Good	Fair	Poor
150	125	100	75	50

Model 905

As above, but nickel-plated.

Exc.	V.G.	Good	Fair	Poor
165	140	110	80	65

Exc.	V.G.	Good	Fair	Poor
125	100	85	65	45

Model 922 Second Issue

A .22 rimfire caliber solid-frame revolver with a 2.5", 4", or 6" barrel. Blued, with black plastic grips. Manufactured between 1950 and 1982.

Exc.	V.G.	Good	Fair	Poor
100	90	80	60	40

Model 923

As above, but nickel-plated.

Exc.	V.G.	Good	Fair	Poor
110	90	80	60	40

Model 925

A .38 S&W caliber double action, break-open, hand ejector revolver with a 2.5" barrel, adjustable sights and a 5-shot cylinder. Blued, with a one-piece wraparound grip. Manufactured between 1964 and 1984.

Exc.	V.G.	Good	Fair	Poor
150	125	100	75	50

Model 935

As above, but nickel-plated.

Exc.	V.G.	Good	Fair	Poor
150	125	100	75	50

Model 929

A .22 rimfire solid-frame, swing-out revolver with a 2.5", 4", or 6" barrel and a 9-shot cylinder. Blued, with plastic grips. It is also known as the "Sidekick". Manufactured between 1956 and 1985.

Model 929 Sidekick-New Model

Reintroduced in 1996 this single and double action revolver chambered for the .22 Short, Long, or Long Rifle cartridges. Cylinder holds 9 rounds. Sold with a lockable storage case, nylon holster, and gun oil and gun grease samples. Weighs about 30 oz.

NIB	Exc.	V.G.	Good	Fair	Poor
150	125	—	—	—	—

Model 929 Sidekick Trapper Edition

Same as above but with grey laminate grips and special "NTA" Trapper Edition roll stamp on barrel.

NIB	Exc.	V.G.	Good	Fair	Poor
175	150	—	—	—	—

Model 930

As above, but nickel-plated and not available with a 6" barrel.

Exc.	V.G.	Good	Fair	Poor
125	100	85	65	45

Model 939 Ultra Sidekick

As above, with a ventilated rib, flat sided 6" barrel, adjustable sights, thumb rest grips and features a safety device whereby the pistol could not be fired unless it was unlocked by a furnished key. Manufactured between 1958 and 1982.

Exc.	V.G.	Good	Fair	Poor
125	100	85	65	45

Model 939 Premier

Similar to the above models but fitted with a 6" barrel with sighting rib, adjustable rear sight, hard wood grips, high polished blued finish. Weighs about 36 oz.

NIB	Exc.	V.G.	Good	Fair	Poor
150	125	100	85	65	45

Model 940

A round-barreled version of the above.

Exc.	V.G	Good	Fair	Poor
100	90	80	65	45

Model 949

A .22 caliber double action, Western-type revolver with a 5.5" barrel with an ejector rod, 9-shot, gate-loaded cylinder and adjustable sights. Blued, with walnut grips. Manufactured between 1960 and 1985.

Exc.	V.G.	Good	Fair	Poor
125	100	80	65	40

Model 949 Western

Similar to the above model this revolver is offered with a choice of 5.5" or 7.5" barrel. Adjustable rear sight, walnut grips, and case colored frame and backstrap with blued cylinder and barrel. Weight is about 36 oz.

NIB	Exc.	V.G.	Good	Fair	Poor
150	125	100	80	65	40

Model 950

As above, but nickel-plated.

Exc.	V.G.	Good	Fair	Poor
125	100	80	65	40

Model 976

As above, with a case hardened frame.

Exc.	V.G.	Good	Fair	Poor
100	80	65	45	30

Model 999 Sportsman

A .22 rimfire caliber double action, break-open, self ejecting revolver with a 6"or 4" barrel ventilated rib barrel and windage adjustable sights. Blued, with walnut grips. Weighs about 30 oz. with 4" barrel and 34 oz. with 6" barrel.

Exc.	V.G.	Good	Fair	Poor
200	150	125	90	65

Engraved Model 999

As above, but engraved.

Exc.	V.G.	Good	Fair	Poor
425	350	300	200	125

Amtec 2000

This is a German designed and American built double action revolver introduced in 1996. Offered in 2" or 3" barrel and chambered for .38 Special cartridge. Pachmayr composition grips. Cylinder holds 5 rounds. Weight is approximately 25 oz.

NIB	Exc.	V.G.	Good	Fair	Poor
250	200	—	—	—	—

SHOTGUNS

Hammerless Double

A 10 or 12 gauge Anson & Deeley hammerless boxlock double barrel shotgun with a 28", 30", or 32" Damascus barrels in various choke combinations, double triggers and extractors. Engraved, case hardened and walnut stock. Four grades were available. They differ in the amount of engraving and the quality of materials and workmanship utilized. Approximately 3,500 were manufactured between 1882 and 1885.

D Grade

Exc.	V.G.	Good	Fair	Poor
650	550	425	300	175

C Grade

Exc.	V.G.	Good	Fair	Poor
750	650	500	400	275

B Grade

Exc.	V.G.	Good	Fair	Poor
900	750	600	500	350

A Grade

Exc.	V.G.	Good	Fair	Poor
2000	1750	1500	1000	550

Harrich No. I

A 12 gauge boxlock single barrel shotgun with a 32" or 34", ventilated rib, full-choke barrel and automatic ejector. Engraved, blued with a checkered, walnut stock. Imported between 1971 and 1975.

Exc.	V.G.	Good	Fair	Poor
1750	1500	1150	850	650

Harrington & Richardson manufactured a series of single barrel, break-open shotguns between 1908 and 1942. They were chambered for various gauges and had various barrel lengths and chokes. The finishes were blued with walnut stocks. There is little collector interest in these guns and, if in sound condition, are desirable as shooters only. They are the Models 3, 5, 6, 7, 8, and 9, as well as a hinged-frame, folding design. Values are as follows:

Exc.	V. G.	Good	Fair	Poor
125	100	85	65	40

Turkey Mag

A single shot break-open side release gun chambered for the 12 gauge 3-1/2" shell with screw-in full choke. The hardwood stock has a Mossy Oak finish. Barrel length is 24" with a bead front sight. Weight is about 6 lbs.

NIB	Exc.	V.G.	Good	Fair	Poor
175	150	125	100	75	50

Youth Turkey Gun

Similar in appearance to the Turkey Mag. but on a smaller scale. Chambered for the 20 gauge 3" shell with 22" barrel. Weighs about 5.5 lbs.

NIB	Exc.	V.G.	Good	Fair	Poor
165	140	115	90	60	40

Topper (New production)

This is a break-open side release single shot available in 12 and 20 gauge as well as .410 bore. The 12 gauge is offered with 28" barrel while the others are fitted with 26" barrels. Blued finish with hardwood stock in black finish with semi-pistol grip. Weight is approximately 6 lbs.

NIB	Exc.	V.G.	Good	Fair	Poor
125	100	80	60	45	30

Topper Deluxe

NIB	Exc.	V.G.	Good	Fair	Poor
140	115	90	70	50	40

Topper Jr. in 20 Gauge and .410 Bore Only

NIB	Exc.	V.G.	Good	Fair	Poor
125	100	80	60	45	30

Topper Jr. Classic

Similar to the Topper Jr. Features a black walnut stock with butt checkering. White line spacer and black recoil pad. Weighs about 7.5 lbs.

NIB	Exc.	V.G.	Good	Fair	Poor
125	100	80	60	45	30

Topper Deluxe Slug

This 12 gauge single shot has a 24" full rifles barrel with built in compensator.

NIB	Exc.	V.G.	Good	Fair	Poor
150	115	90	70	50	40

Tamer

This single shot gun is chambered for the .410 shell with 3" chamber. It is fitted with a 19-1/2" barrel and had a matte nickel finish. The stock is matte black polymer. Weighs about 6 lbs.

NIB	Exc.	V.G.	Good	Fair	Poor
130	100	80	60	45	30

Ultra Slug Hunter

Introduced in 1995 this model uses a heavy 10 gauge action fitted with a 24" 12 gauge barrel. Weight is about 8 lbs.

NIB	Exc.	V.G.	Good	Fair	Poor
150	115	90	70	50	40

Ultra Slug Hunter Deluxe-20 Gauge

Introduced in 1997 this model is chambered for 20 gauge shells and features a hand checkered camo laminated wood stock. Fitted with a fully rifled heavy slug barrel 24" long.

NIB	Exc.	V.G.	Good	Fair	Poor
225	175	—	—	—	—

Ultra Slug Hunter Deluxe-12 Gauge

Same as above but in 12 gauge with 3" chamber.

NIB	Exc.	V.G.	Good	Fair	Poor
225	175	—	—	—	—

Ultra Slug Youth Model

As above but chambered for 20 gauge shell. Weight is approximately 7 lbs.

NIB	Exc.	V.G.	Good	Fair	Poor
130	100	80	60	45	30

Ultra Slug Hunter-Bull Barrel

Same as above but chambered for 20 gauge.

NIB	Exc.	V.G.	Good	Fair	Poor
130	100	80	60	45	30

Ultra Slug Youth Bull Barrel

Same as above but with 22" barrel.

NIB	Exc.	V.G.	Good	Fair	Poor
130	100	80	60	45	30

Camo Laminate Turkey NWTF Edition

Introduced in 1999 this single barrel model features a 12 gauge 3.5" 22" barrel choked Turkey full. Polished receiver has laser engraved NWTF logo. Stock is hand checkered and is hardwood laminate with a green, brown, and black pattern. Ventilated recoil pad and sling swivels and camo sling are standard.

NIB	Exc.	V.G.	Good	Fair	Poor
170	130	—	—	—	—

Camo Laminate Turkey Youth NWTF Edition

Similar to the Camo Turkey above but chambered for 20 gauge with 3" chambers. Stock is laminated hardwood but with special shorter dimensions.

NIB	Exc.	V.G.	Good	Fair	Poor
170	130	—	—	—	—

H&R Handy-Gun (rifled barrel) CURIO OR RELIC

Rifled-barrel H&R Handy-Guns were manufactured about 1930-34, but details of their production are not well documented. In H&R catalogue #19 (copyright 1931) and #20, the .22 and .32-20 are listed as available with blued frame only, 12.25" barrel, with an optional ($1.50) detachable shoulder stock. Whether the .22 W.R.F. version listed on page 83 of the 1932 *Stoeger's Bible* was manufactured is unknown. Guns that were originally factory fitted for the shoulder stock (all are extremely rare) have **H.&R. ARMS COMPANY/WORCESTER, MASS.U.S.A./PAT.PENDING** stamped on the bottom of the grip in .125" letters. Production of the rifled-barrel H&R Handy-Gun was halted in 1934 when the Treasury Department classified it as a "firearm" under the NFA, because it was available with a shoulder stock. Any rifled-barrel H&R Handy-Gun is (and always was) exempt from the NFA, if not accompanied by a shoulder stock.

H&R catalog descriptions imply the .32-20 is like the .22 (i.e., blued, and with a flat grip); however, H&R flyers illustrate it with a case hardened frame and spur grip, and all known specimens are in the latter configuration. It is unclear if the .32-20, whose production likely predates the .22 rimfire, was serial numbered in the same run as the smooth bore H&R Handy-Gun. Observed serial number ranges for each caliber justify estimates of relatively low production totals of fewer than 225 in .22 and fewer than 100 in .32-20. Allows any qualified person to "make" such a firearm (which includes "putting

together" parts not controlled under the NFA) by filing ATF Form 1 (Firearms), paying a $200 tax, and obtaining ATF approval before possessing both the stock and the pistol, but ATF has cautioned that filing a Form 1 under these circumstances would be a prosecutable felony offense (for perjury, that is, "making a false statement to the Government") because it would constitute reassembling a prohibited firearm. Collectors who wish to mate a pistol to a stock in this instance are advised to seek legal counsel.

The .32-20 H&R Handy-Gun has a case hardened (hot cyanide dip) receiver and grip identical to the Model 2, Type II or III smooth bore H&R Handy-Gun, with a 12.25" rifled barrel marked **32-20 W.C.F.** The barrel has a front target sight identical to that on the .22 rimfire variation, and a rear Patridge-type nonadjustable sight fitted into a slot cut behind the barrel markings. Its serial number range and dates of manufacture are uncertain, but could have begun as early as 1929. Whether the .32-20s were serial numbered separately is unknown (the size of the serial numbers is the same as those on the smooth bore H&R Handy-Gun.

The number of .32-20 H&R Handy-Guns manufactured is not well understood, and may range from approximately 25 to 86 or more. According to a letter from H&R to ATF dated November 27, 1953, only about 25 were manufactured as sales samples. But the serial numbers of 9 known guns range from 43851 to 43937, suggesting that as many as 86 could have been made. A 10th gun, bearing serial number 46854, suggests that this range may be larger or may represent a special-order gun. Without definitive factory records, it may be impossible to conclusively document the total production of this firearm.

32-20 W.C.F. serial range mostly from 43851 (?) to 43937 (?)

Exc.	V.G.	Good	Fair	Poor
1,400	900	800	700	600

Much hand fitting is evident on the .22 rimfire H&R Handy-Gun, which was made using the same high-quality machinery that produced the unusually accurate rifling perfected for H&R's .22 caliber Model 195/U.S.R.A. match target pistol. Consequently, there is significant collector and shooter demand for the .22 rimfire H&R Handy-Gun. The .15" serial numbers are smaller than the .20" serial numbers used on smooth bore H&R Handy-Guns, which probably indicates the .22 rimfire variation has its own serial number range. Based on the serial numbers of 23 guns, a serial range from approximately 1 to 223 can be established, with 223 being considered an upper limit. The reason is that known guns from number 215 forward are "parts" guns; that is, the serial number(s) of the barrel, forend iron, and receiver do not match, indicating they probably were assembled from leftover parts. All known commercial .22 rimfire models have blued frames with markings and grips otherwise identical to the Model 3 smooth bore H&R Handy-Gun, a 12.25" tapered barrel marked **.22 RIMFIRE**, and a fixed peep or flip aperture/peep (adjustable for elevation and windage) sight built into the barrel. Some nonstandard or experimental .22 caliber H&R Handy-Guns exist, but expert opinion must be sought to authenticate their originality. Some .410 bore H&R Handy-Guns have been expertly altered to .22 rimfire, and their values approximate those for a standard 12.25" barrel .410, and the alterations are obvious.

.22 rimfire serial range from 1 (?) to 223 (?)

Exc.	V.G.	Good	Fair	Poor
1200	900	750	650	500

Rifled-barrel H&R Handy-Guns in calibers other than .22 rimfire and .32-20 Winchester have been reported, but are controversial because (1) none have been made available for inspection, and (2) their production has apparently never been confirmed by the H&R factory. One collector has reported (but has not himself observed) that H&R Handy-Guns were manufactured in .25-20 (25 W.C.F.), 22 Hornet, and .30-30 Winchester (30 W.C.F.). The owner of a .30 caliber carbine H&R Handy-Gun, who lives in Canada, advised this writer that the gun was expertly altered by a mechanical engineer.

H&R Handy-Gun (smooth bore) NFA, CURIO OR RELIC

The .410 bore or 28 gauge H&R Handy-Gun is a single-shot pistol with an 8" or 12.25" smooth bore barrel, made from 1921 to 1934 by the Harrington & Richardson Arms Co., Worcester, Massachusetts. It shares internal parts with H&R's Model 1915 (No. 5) shotgun, but the Handy-Gun's shorter receiver is designed for a pistol grip, its barrels won't fit the No. 5, and these firearms are serial numbered separately. About 54,000 H&R Handy-Guns were manufactured, nearly all for 2.5" shells. Production was halted after the government ruled the H&R Handy-Gun to be a "firearm" in the "any other weapon" category under the NFA, when its retail price was about $16. An H&R Handy-Gun with an 18" smooth bore barrel is subject to the NFA, but exempt if accompanied by an original (detachable) wire shoulder stock.

More than 50 H&R Handy-Gun variations exist, and their serial number ranges demonstrate that production of some was extremely limited. The rarest is probably the Model 3, Type III, 18" barrel .410, which apparently was manufactured in an unsuccessful attempt to continue a version of the Handy-Gun that was exempt from the NFA. The H&R Handy-Gun has not achieved its full potential as a collectible because ATF continues to require its registration under the NFA, although it could be administratively removed from the NFA as a collector's item. ATF's position is illogical, because (1) at least 500,000 modern rifled-barred .410 handguns have been manufactured since 1968, all these firearms are exempt from the NFA, and none have been identified as being used in crimes; (2) Congress determined in 1960 that firearms like the Handy-Gun are unlikely to be used as weapons by criminals; and (3) the supply of available Handy-Guns is relatively small (probably fewer than 6,000 have survived), is concentrated among collectors, who highly prize them and thus tightly control their ownership. Removing the Handy-Gun from the NFA would probably significantly raise its value and demand among collectors; at present, they are not bought and sold frequently enough to establish reliable values. Prices below are for a typical 12.25" choked-barrel .410 and unchoked 28 gauge (serial number on receiver and barrel lug should match), though there may be significant local variation in these prices depending upon the geographic area and collector demand.

.410 bore, Model 2, Types II and III

Exc.	V.G.	Good	Fair	Poor
500	375	300	250	175

28 gauge, Model 2, Type I

Exc.	V.G.	Good	Fair	Poor
1200	900	700	650	500

NOTE: Rare variations command premiums: 8" barrel, 25 to 50 percent; 18" barrel (rarest), 200 to 300 percent; unchoked .410, 20 to 30 percent; 28 gauge or Model 3 (only) with factory-equipped original detachable shoulder stock, 150 percent or more; holster, $75 to $200; serial matching box, $100 to $200 or more (i.e., a box for an 8" barrel 28 gauge could be quite expensive).

Nine major variations of the smooth bore H&R Handy-Gun have been identified. These are derived from three Models which can each be further categorized according to three types, based on differences in receiver finish and markings, barrel latch levers, barrel types and markings, and triggerguards and grips. H&R termed some late-model .410 and 28 gauge Handy-Guns Models 141 and 128, respectively, but earlier variations were not assigned model numbers. During 1947-57, H&R sold the .410 Handy-Gun through its factory in Drummondville, Quebec, Canada, as the Model 625, but all these guns actually were manufactured in Worcester in or before 1934. This writer has defined the "Models" and "Types" described here arbitrarily. The number of possible combinations of characteristics noted below exceeds 50.

Model 1 has a blued receiver made of malleable (ductile) iron and a spur pistol grip, also termed the "saw-handle" grip, plain triggerguard, and a heavy cylinder bore (unchoked) barrel marked **410-12m/m** or **28 GAUGE**. Model 1, Type I has a 1.71" barrel latch lever secured by a screw, with apparently hand-cut knurling, here termed Type A. The left side of the receiver is stamped **Harrington & Richardson Arms Co/Worcester, Mass. U.S.A.** Model 1, Type II is the same as Model 1, Type I except for a smaller 1.5" barrel latch lever that is not secured by a screw, with cast knurling, here termed Type B. Model 1, Type III is the same as Model 1, Type II except that the H&R manufacturer's identification was moved to the right side of the receiver, and the left side is stamped **H.&R. "HANDY-GUN."**

Model 2 has a receiver whose so-called "tiger stripe" finish was produced by hot cyanide dip, which resembles but is not true case hardening. Model 2, Type I is identical to Model 1, Type III, except for the receiver's "tiger stripe" finish. Model 2, Type II is identical to Model 2, Type I except that in .410 bore, the barrel is choked and its markings are **410-12m/mCHOKE**. In .410 bore, Model 2, Type III is identical to Model 2, Type II except for barrel markings **MADE IN U.S.A. 410 GA.CHOKE**, and a new 1.81" barrel latch lever with indented dish checkered knurling, covering the serial number, here termed Type C. In 28 gauge, the Model 2, Type I barrel marking is **28 GAUGE** (2.5" shell), with a Type B barrel latch lever. The 28 gauge Model 2, Type III is designed for 2.75" shells (the measured chamber length is 3.125"), has barrel markings **MADE IN U.S.A. 28 GA.CHOKE**, and a Type C barrel latch lever. Whether Model 2, Type II exists is currently unknown; if so, it would probably have barrel markings **MADE IN U.S.A. 28 GA.CHOKE**, be designed for 2.75" shells, and have a Type B barrel latch lever. Some Model 2 guns have overlapping characteristics by Type; the exact number involved is unknown, but appears relatively small. I have classified serial number 38335 as Model 2, Type II, because it has a Type B barrel latch lever, although it has Type III barrel markings (**MADE IN U.S.A. 410 GA.CHOKE**).

Model 3 has a flat grip mounted at a 70° angle to the barrel, in contrast with the 80° bore-to-grip angle on Models 1 and 2, and the receiver was shortened about .312", probably by grinding, to accommodate it. Model 3, Type I is identical to Model 2, Type III except for the new flat grip. Model 3, Type II is identical to Model 3, Type I except that a hook was added to the triggerguard for the middle finger to assist in stabilizing recoil. Model 3, Type III is identical to Model 3, Type II except that the number **3** is stamped in the lower right-hand corner of the left side of the barrel lug, designating the barrel was H&R factory chambered for the 3" .410 shotshell of 1933. Only one 28 gauge Model 3 H&R Handy-Gun (an 8" barrel Type I with barrel markings **MADE IN U.S.A. 28 GA.CHOKE** and a 3.125" chamber) has been observed.

H&R manufactured "private-branded" or "trade-branded" H&R Handy-Guns for other distributors. One variation has **ESSEX GUN WORKS** on the left side of the receiver. Another has **HIBBARD** stamped on the left side, and **MODEL W.H.** stamped on the right; a holster with identical stampings was also available. Most have nickel-plated receivers and are serial numbered within the same ranges as, and have other characteristics identical to, regular-production H&R Handy-Guns, by variation. None of those inspected during this research had any markings identifying H&R as the original manufacturer. Anecdotal evidence suggests H&R manufactured a Handy-Gun for an independent telephone company in Colorado; none were located during this research.

Because few factory records have been located, serial number ranges and years of manufacture for the nine variations are not well understood, although there is strong evidence that Handy-Guns were serial numbered from 1 to approximately 54,000, and that .410 and 28 gauge variations were included within this range and not numbered separately. These data are estimated, based on serial numbers of 331 H&R Handy-Guns and very limited original records, including sales records, early NFA paperwork, H&R advertisements, and other records, as shown below. Although these data are in one sense limited because of the small number of observations, they nevertheless (1) reveal a great deal about the number of each variation that was originally manufactured, and (2) establish fairly reliable minimum and maximum production ranges for many (but not all) variations.

Variation	Estimated year(s) of manufacture	Observed serial number ranges .410 bore	28 gauge
Model 1			
Type I	1921-22	167 to 4981	5 to 4527
Type II	1922-23	5052 to 6588	5554 to 6274
Type III	1923-24	unknown to 6817	6973 to 7067
Model 2			
Type I	1924-25	8276 to 14660	10539 to 29731
Type II	1925-27	15159 to 38761	none observed
Type III	1927-30	39060 to 47528	44228 to 44247
Model 3			
Type I	1931	47642 to 48218	unknown to 48566
Type II	1932-33	48819 to 51655	none observed
Type III	1933-34	51920 to 53691	none observed

These materials are copyright © 1998 by Eric M. Larson.

Topper

A single shot, break-open shotgun chambered for various gauges with various barrel lengths, chokes. Blued, with a hardwood stock. Introduced in 1946.

Exc.	V.G.	Good	Fair	Poor
110	95	75	60	40

Model 088

An external hammer single shot, break-open shotgun chambered for all gauges with various barrel lengths, chokes and an automatic ejector. Blued, with a case colored frame and hardwood stock.

Exc.	V.G.	Good	Fair	Poor
80	65	50	40	30

Model 099

As above, but matte, electroless, nickel-plated.

Exc.	V.G.	Good	Fair	Poor
110	95	75	60	40

Model 162

A 12 or 20 gauge boxlock single shotgun with a 24" barrel with rifle sights.

Exc.	V.G.	Good	Fair	Poor
125	100	80	65	45

Model 176

A 10-gauge, 3.5" Magnum caliber boxlock single barrel shotgun with a heavyweight 36" barrel and a full choke. Manufactured between 1977 and 1985.

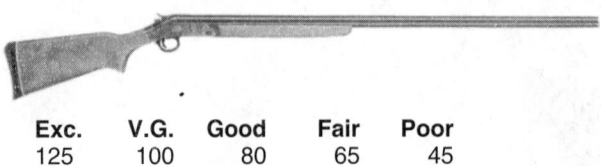

Exc.	V.G.	Good	Fair	Poor
125	100	80	65	45

Model 400

A 12, 16, or 20 gauge slide action shotgun with a 28" full-choke barrel. Blued, with a hardwood stock. Manufactured between 1955 and 1967.

Exc.	V.G.	Good	Fair	Poor
150	125	100	75	50

Model 401

As above, with a variable choke device. Manufactured between 1956 and 1963.

Exc.	V.G.	Good	Fair	Poor
175	150	125	90	65

Model 402

As above, in a .410 bore. Manufactured between 1959 and 1967.

Exc.	V.G.	Good	Fair	Poor
175	150	125	90	65

Model 440

A 12, 16, or 20 gauge slide action shotgun with a 26", 28", or 30" barrel in various chokes. Blued, with a hardwood stock. Manufactured between 1968 and 1973.

Exc.	V.G.	Good	Fair	Poor
150	125	100	75	50

Model 442

As above with a ventilated rib barrel and a checkered stock. Manufactured between 1969 and 1973.

Exc.	V.G.	Good	Fair	Poor
175	150	125	90	65

Model 403

A .410 bore semiautomatic shotgun with a 26", full choke barrel. Blued, with a hardwood stock. Manufactured in 1964.

Exc.	V.G.	Good	Fair	Poor
200	175	150	100	75

Model 404

A 12, 20, or .410 bore boxlock double barrel shotgun with 26" or 28" barrels, double triggers and extractors. Blued with a walnut stock. Manufactured by Rossi in Brazil and imported between 1969 and 1972.

Exc.	V.G.	Good	Fair	Poor
175	150	125	90	65

Model 1212

A 12 gauge Over/Under boxlock shotgun with 28" ventilated rib barrels. Blued with a walnut stock. Also available with 30" barrels having 3" chambers. Manufactured by Landbar Arms of Spain and imported after 1976.

Exc.	V.G.	Good	Fair	Poor
300	250	200	150	100

Long Tom Classic

Introduced in 1996 this limited edition single barrel shotgun features a case hardened frame with 32" full choked barrel. Stock is hand checkered black walnut with crescent buttplate. Chambered for 12 gauge. Weight is about 7.5 lbs. About 1,000 of these shotguns will be built each year.

NIB	Exc.	V.G.	Good	Fair	Poor
300	250	—	—	—	—

RIFLES

Model 058

A 20 gauge, .22 Hornet, .30-30, .357 Magnum, or .44 Magnum caliber combination Over/Under rifle/shotgun. Blued, with a hardwood stock.

Exc.	V.G.	Good	Fair	Poor
125	100	80	65	40

Model 258

As above, but with a matte, electroless nickel-plate finish.

Exc.	V.G.	Good	Fair	Poor
175	150	125	90	65

Reising Model 60

A .45 ACP caliber semiautomatic rifle with an 18.25" barrel and a 12- or 20-round detachable magazine. Blued, with a walnut stock. It operates on a retarded blowback system and was developed to be used as a police weapon. Manufactured between 1944 and 1946.

Courtesy Richard M. Kumor, Sr.

Exc.	V.G.	Good	Fair	Poor
1400	1200	500	250	100

Model 65 Military

A .22 l.r. caliber semiautomatic rifle with a 23" barrel and Redfield peep sights. Blued, with a walnut stock. Manufactured between 1944 and 1956.

NOTE: Add 100% if USMC marked.

Courtesy Richard M. Kumor, Sr.

Exc.	V.G.	Good	Fair	Poor
350	300	200	125	90

Model 150

A .22 l.r. caliber semiautomatic rifle with a 20" barrel and a 5-shot magazine. Blued, with a walnut stock. Manufactured between 1949 and 1953.

Exc.	V.G.	Good	Fair	Poor
100	80	60	45	30

Model 155

This is a single shot, break-open rifle chambered for the .44 Magnum or the .45-70 cartridge. It has a 20" barrel with fixed sights. The finish is blued, with a walnut stock. It was introduced in 1972.

Exc.	V.G.	Good	Fair	Poor
125	100	80	60	40

Model 157

As above in .22 Magnum, .22 Hornet, and the .30-30 caliber.

Exc.	V.G.	Good	Fair	Poor
125	100	80	60	40

Model 158

A .357 or .44 Magnum single shot side lever rifle with a 22" barrel. Blued, case hardened with a walnut stock. Available with an interchangeable 26" 20 gauge barrel. Manufactured prior to 1986.

Exc.	V.G.	Good	Fair	Poor
100	80	60	45	30

Model 171

A reproduction of the Model 1873 Trapdoor Springfield Carbine with a 22" barrel. Blued, with a case colored receiver and a walnut stock.

Exc.	V.G.	Good	Fair	Poor
300	250	200	150	100

Model 171-DL

As above, but more finely finished.

Exc.	V.G.	Good	Fair	Poor
350	300	250	200	125

Model 300 Ultra

A .22-250 up to the .300 Winchester Magnum caliber, bolt action rifle with a 22" or 24" barrel and without sights. High polished blue, and checkered walnut stock. Manufactured between 1965 and 1978.

Exc.	V.G.	Good	Fair	Poor
450	400	350	275	175

Model 301 Carbine

As above with an 18" barrel and a full-length, Mannlicher-style stock.

Exc.	V.G.	Good	Fair	Poor
450	400	350	275	175

Model 317 Ultra Wildcat

A .17 Rem., .17-223, .222 Rem., and the .223 Rem. caliber short Sako bolt action rifle with a 20" barrel furnished without sights. Blued, with a checkered walnut stock. Manufactured between 1968 and 1976.

Exc.	V.G.	Good	Fair	Poor
450	400	350	275	175

Ultra Varmint Rifle

This single shot rifle is chambered for the .223 Rem. or the .22-250 cartridge. It is fitted with a 22" heavy barrel. The stock is hand checkered curly maple with Monte Carlo cheekpiece. Comes with no sights but scopes mounts are included. Weighs about 7.5 lbs.

NIB	Exc.	V.G.	Good	Fair	Poor
175	150	100	80	60	40

Model 317P

As above, but more finely finished. Manufactured between 1968 and 1976.

Exc.	V.G.	Good	Fair	Poor
550	500	450	375	250

Ultra Rifle-Hunting

Single shot rifle chambered for .25-06, .308 Win., and .357 Rem. Max. The .25-06 has a 26" barrel, the other two are fitted with 22" barrels. A Cinnamon laminated stock is standard. Weight is about 7 lbs. In 2001 the .450 Marlin cartridge was added.

NIB	Exc.	V.G.	Good	Fair	Poor
225	175	125	100	75	50

Ultra Rifle-Varmint

Same as above but chambered for .223 Rem. with 22" barrel. Laminated stock with checkered pistol grip.

NIB	Exc.	V.G.	Good	Fair	Poor
225	175	125	100	75	50

Ultra .22 Magnum Rifle

Same as above but chambered for the .22 Winchester Magnum. Introduced in 2001.

NIB	Exc.	V.G.	Good	Fair	Poor
225	175	—	—	—	—

Ultra Rifle-Comp

Introduced in 1997 this single shot rifle features an integral muzzle brake on the end of the barrel. Available in .270 Win. and .30-06 calibers with 24" barrels. Camo laminated stock.

NIB	Exc.	V.G.	Good	Fair	Poor
275	225	—	—	—	—

Ultra Rifle Rocky Mountain Elk Foundation Commemorative

A limited edition single rifle chambered for the .35 Whelen cartridge. Selected laminated stock with Monte Carlo. Barrel length is 26".

NIB	Exc.	V.G.	Good	Fair	Poor
450	400	—	—	—	—

Ultra Rifle Whitetails Unlimited 1997 Commemorative Edition

Introduced in 1997 and chambered for the .45-70 Gov't cartridge this model features a hand checkered black walnut stock. Special laser engraving on the action and pewter finished medallion inletted into stock. Barrel length is 22".

NIB	Exc.	V.G.	Good	Fair	Poor
275	225	—	—	—	—

Wesson & Harrington Brand 125th Anniversary Rifle

Introduced in 1996 this rifle commemorates the 125th anniversary of the partnership. This special rifle is chambered for the .45-70 Government cartridge. The receiver is hand engraved. The barrel length is 32". The stock is American black walnut with crescent steel butt.

NIB	Exc.	V.G.	Good	Fair	Poor
500	400	—	—	—	—

Buffalo Classic

This rifle was first produced in 1995. It is chambered for the .45-70 cartridge. Barrel length is 32" with no sights but dovetail front and drilled and tapped rear. Hand checkered walnut stock with case colored crescent steel buttplate. Weight is approximately 8 lbs. Since its introduction in 1995 there have been about 2,000 guns produced. The factory anticipates about 1,000 of these rifles being built each year.

NIB	Exc.	V.G.	Good	Fair	Poor
300	250	—	—	—	—

Model 333

The Model 300 in 7mm Mag. caliber. Manufactured in 1974.

Exc.	V.G.	Good	Fair	Poor
250	200	175	125	100

Model 340

A .243 to .308 Winchester caliber bolt action rifle with a 22" barrel and a 5-shot magazine. Blued, with a checkered walnut stock.

Exc.	V.G.	Good	Fair	Poor
400	350	300	225	150

Model 360 Ultra Automatic

A .243 Win. and the .308 Win. caliber semiautomatic rifle with a 22" barrel, adjustable sights and a 3-shot detachable magazine. Blued, with a checkered walnut stock. Manufactured between 1965 and 1978.

Exc.	V.G.	Good	Fair	Poor
350	300	250	175	100

Model 451 Medalist

A .22 l.r. caliber bolt action rifle with a 26" barrel, open sights and a 5-shot detachable magazine. Blued, with a walnut stock. Manufactured between 1948 and 1961.

Exc.	V.G.	Good	Fair	Poor
175	150	125	100	75

Model 700

A .22 rimfire Magnum caliber, semiautomatic rifle with a 22" barrel, adjustable sights and a 5-round, detachable magazine. Blued, with a checkered walnut stock. Manufactured between 1977 and 1985.

Exc.	V.G.	Good	Fair	Poor
225	200	150	125	85

Model 700 DL

As above, with a checkered walnut stock and with a 4X scope. Manufactured until 1985.

Exc.	V.G.	Good	Fair	Poor
300	250	200	150	100

Model 750

A .22 l.r. bolt action single shot rifle with a 22" barrel with sights and a short stock. Blued, and the stock is hardwood.

Exc.	V.G.	Good	Fair	Poor
100	80	60	45	25

Model 865

A .22 l.r. caliber bolt action rifle with a 22" barrel, open sights and a 5-shot magazine. Blued, with a hardwood stock.

Exc.	V.G.	Good	Fair	Poor
100	80	60	45	25

Model 5200

A .22 l.r. caliber bolt action, single shot rifle with a 28" heavy barrel without sights, and an adjustable trigger. Blued, with a target-type walnut stock.

Exc.	V.G.	Good	Fair	Poor
400	350	300	225	125

Model 5200 Sporter

A .22 l.r. caliber bolt action rifle with a 24" barrel, adjustable sights and a 5-shot magazine. Blued with a walnut stock. Not manufactured after 1983.

Exc.	V.G.	Good	Fair	Poor
400	350	300	225	125

100th Anniversary Officer's Model

A commemorative replica of the Officer's Model 1873 Trapdoor Springfield Rifle, with a 26" barrel. Engraved, and an anniversary plaque mounted on the stock. Blued, with a case colored receiver and a pewter forend tip. There were 10,000 manufactured in 1971. As with all commemoratives, this model is desirable only when NIB with all supplied material.

NIB	Exc.	V.G.	Good	Fair	Poor
450	350	300	275	200	125

Custer Memorial Issue

A limited production issue commemorating George Armstrong Custer's Battle of the Little Bighorn. Heavily engraved and gold inlaid with a high-grade checkered walnut stock. Furnished in a mahogany display case that included two books dealing with the subject. There were two versions produced—an Officer's Model, of which 25 were issued commemorating the 25 officers that fell with Custer, and another version commemorating the 243 enlisted men who lost their lives at the Little Bighorn. As with all commemoratives, to be collectible they must be NIB with all furnished material.

Officer's Model-25 Manufactured

NIB	Exc.	V.G.	Good	Fair	Poor
2700	2000	1500	1000	600	400

Enlisted Men's Model-243 Manufactured

NIB	Exc.	V.G.	Good	Fair	Poor
1500	1000	750	500	350	250

Model 174

A plain copy of the Springfield Model 1873 Carbine in .45-70 caliber with a 22" barrel. Manufactured in 1972.

Exc.	V.G.	Good	Fair	Poor
400	350	300	250	175

Model 178

A copy of the Springfield Model 1873 rifle with a 32" barrel. Manufactured from 1973 to 1984.

Exc.	V.G.	Good	Fair	Poor
325	300	250	200	125

HARRIS GUNWORKS
Phoenix, Arizona

National Match Rifle

Introduced in 1989 this model features a bolt action rifle chambered for the 7mm-08 or .308 with 5-round magazine. It is fitted with a 24" stainless steel match grade barrel with Canjar trigger. The stock is fiberglass with adjustable buttplate. Weight is about 11 lbs.

NIB	Exc.	V.G.	Good	Fair	Poor
3500	2750	1750	950	—	—

Model 86 Sniper Rifle

Chambered for .308, .30-06, .300 Win. Mag. with 24" heavy match grade barrel. The stock is a special design McHale fiberglass with textured grip and forearm. Fitted with a recoil pad. Supplied with a bipod. Weight is about 11.25 lbs.

NIB	Exc.	V.G.	Good	Fair	Poor
2700	2100	1600	—	—	—

NOTE: Add $100 for take-down model.

Model 87 Series

These are single shot rifles chambered for 50 BMG. Fitted with a 29" barrel with muzzlebrake. Fiberglass stock. Introduced in 1987. Weight is approximately 21.5 lbs.

NIB	Exc.	V.G.	Good	Fair	Poor
3700	2900	2000	—	—	—

NOTE: For Model 87R 5 shot repeater add $400. For Model 87 5 shot repeater add $300. For Model 92 Bullpup add $300.

Model 88

These bolt action .50 BMG rifles are offered in two different configurations. One is fitted with a 20" carbon graphite barrel with add-on recoil arrestor with black teflon finish. The second variation is fitted with a 16.5" stainless steel barrel with integral recoil arrestor. Both rifles weigh about 14 lbs. Titanium action is available for further weight reduction.

NIB	Exc.	V.G.	Good	Fair	Poor
3600	2850	—	—	—	—

Model 89 Sniper Rifle

This bolt action rifle is chambered for .308 cartridge. Fitted with a 28" barrel. Supplied with a bipod. Stock is fiberglass with adjustable length of pull and fitted with a recoil pad. Weight is about 15.25 lbs.

NIB	Exc.	V.G.	Good	Fair	Poor
2700	2100	1600	—	—	—

Model 93

Bolt action .50 BMG rifle with folding hinge stock assembly. Furnished with a 10-round or 20-round magazine. Barrel length is 29". Weight is approximately 21 lbs.

Model 93 folding model

NIB	Exc.	V.G.	Good	Fair	Poor
4450	3500	—	—	—	—

Model 95

This is a lightweight variation of the .50 BMG models featuring Titanium and graphite. Supplied with bipod. Barrel length is 29". Weight is approximately 18 lbs.

NIB	Exc.	V.G.	Good	Fair	Poor
5200	4000	—	—	—	—

Model 96

This is a gas operated semiautomatic .50 BMG sniper rifle. Barrel length is 29". Detachable 5-round magazine. Weight is approximately 25 lbs.

NIB	Exc.	V.G.	Good	Fair	Poor
6800	5500	—	—	—	—

Long Range Rifle

Chambered for a variety of cartridges such as the .300 Win. Mag., 7mm Rem. Mag., .300 Phoenix, .338 Lapua. This is a single shot rifle fitted with a 26" match grade stainless steel barrel. Fiberglass stock with adjustable buttplate and cheekpiece. Weight is about 14 lbs.

NIB	Exc.	V.G.	Good	Fair	Poor
3600	2850	1500	—	—	—

Target/Benchrest Rifle on top and Long Range Rifle on bottom

Target/Benchrest Rifle

Offered in .243, .308, 6mm BR, 6mm PPC, and 6mm Rem. This model is custom built for the customer. Available in both left and right hand. Weight is about 11 lbs.

NIB	Exc.	V.G.	Good	Fair	Poor
3000	2500	—	—	—	—

Antietam Sharps Rifle

This is a replica of the Sharps Model 1874 sidehammer introduced in 1994. Chambered for the .40-65 or the .45-70. Choice of 30" or 32" octagon or round barrel. Stock is fancy walnut with either straight, pistol grip, or Creedmoor with schnabel forearm. Many optional sights offered. Weight is about 11.25 lbs.

NIB	Exc.	V.G.	Good	Fair	Poor
2400	1850	1200	—	—	—

Signature Classic Sporter

This is a left or right handed bolt action model introduced in 1987 with a choice of calibers from .22-250 to .375 H&H. Barrel lengths are 22", 24", or 26" depending on caliber. Choice of fiberglass stocks in green, beige, brown, or black. A wood stock is optional. Weight is about 7 lbs. for short action calibers.

NIB	Exc.	V.G.	Good	Fair	Poor
2900	2250	1500	—	—	—

Signature Classic Stainless Sporter

Same as above but with barrel and action made from stainless steel. A .416 Rem. Mag is available in this variation also. This model is also available with interchangeable barrels. Add $600 for this option.

NIB	Exc.	V.G.	Good	Fair	Poor
2700	2000	1500	—	—	—

Signature Super Varminter

Similar to the Classic Sporter except fitted with a heavy contoured barrel, adjustable trigger, and special hand-bedded fiberglass stock. Chambered for .223, .22-250, .220 Swift, .243, 6mm Rem., .25-06, 7mm-08, 7mm BR, .308, .350 Rem. Introduced in 1989.

NIB	Exc.	V.G.	Good	Fair	Poor
2700	2000	1500	—	—	—

Signature Alaskan

Similar to the Classic Sporter except fitted with a match grade barrel with single leaf rear sight. Nickel finish. Walnut Monte Carlo stock with cheekpiece and palm swell grip. Chambered for .270 to .375 H&H. Introduced in 1989.

NIB	Exc.	V.G.	Good	Fair	Poor
3800	3000	2000	—	—	—

Signature Titanium Mountain Rifle

Similar to the Classic Sporter except action is made of titanium alloy and barrel of chrome molly-steel. Stock is graphite reinforced fiberglass. Chambered for .270 to .300 Win. Mag. Weight is about 5.5 lbs. Introduced in 1989. Add $400 for graphite steel barrel.

NIB	Exc.	V.G.	Good	Fair	Poor
3300	2600	1750	—	—	—

Talon Safari Rifle

This bolt action rifle is chambered for 16 different calibers from .300 Win. Mag. to .460 Whthy. Mag. The finish is a matte black with fiberglass Safari stock. Weight is between 9 and 10 lbs. depending on caliber.

NIB	Exc.	V.G.	Good	Fair	Poor
3900	3150	2000	—	—	—

Talon Sporter Rifle

This bolt action rifle, introduced in 1991, uses a pre-64 Model 70 type action with cone breech. Barrel and action are stainless steel. Chambered for a wide variety of calibers from .22-250 to .416 Rem. Mag. Choice of walnut or fiberglass stock. Most barrel lengths are 24". Weight is about 7.5 lbs. depending on caliber.

NIB	Exc.	V.G.	Good	Fair	Poor
2900	2500	1750	—	—	—

Sportsman 97

This bolt action rifle is chambered for a variety of calibers from .270 Win. to .338 Win. The stock is fancy grade walnut, Bastogne, or English. A Talon action is fitted.

NIB	Exc.	V.G.	Good	Fair	Poor
2800	2250	—	—	—	—

Double Rifle/Shotgun

This side-by-side gun is offered in .470 NE or .500 NE as well as 12 and 20 gauge guns. Engraved receiver, AAA fancy walnut stocks and 3-leaf express sights are standard. Offered in box lock and side lock models.

Box Lock

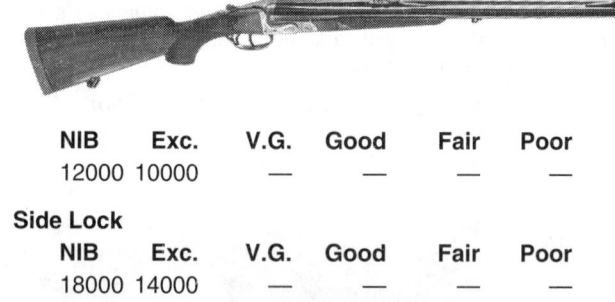

NIB	Exc.	V.G.	Good	Fair	Poor
12000	10000	—	—	—	—

Side Lock

NIB	Exc.	V.G.	Good	Fair	Poor
18000	14000	—	—	—	—

NOTE: There are a wide range of extra costs options for all Harris Gunworks models that in many cases will dramatically effect price. Caution is advised before a sale.

HARTFORD ARMS & EQUIPMENT CO.
Hartford, Connecticut

Established in 1925, this firm was purchased by the High Standard Company in 1932.

Single Shot Target

A .22 caliber single shot pistol with a 6.75" round barrel, fixed sights and either walnut or composition grips. The frame marked "Manfd. by the/ Hartford Arms and Equip. Co./ Hartford, Conn./ Patented .22 cal./ Long Rifle" on the left side in front of ther breach. Although this pistol resembles a semiautomatic, it is in fact a single shot manually operated pistol.

Add $150 premium for guns in original Hartford Arms box numbered to the gun. Add $250 premium for guns in original High Standard box numbered to the gun.

Courtesy John J. Stimson, Jr.

Exc.	V.G.	Good	Fair	Poor
600	425	350	280	250

Repeating Pistol

Although listed in this and other price guides, the existence of this pistol is in doubt. If encountered please have the gun checked by an expert for authenticity and advise the editor. The interrelationship of Fiala, Schall, and Hartford through a common gun designer suggest that if the Hartford repeating pistol exists, then it is probably a Hartford marked repeater like the Fiala and Schall. Numerous examples exist of unmarked Schall pistols and some have confused the Schall as a Hartford repeater.

Exc.	V.G.	Good	Fair	Poor
N/A	—	—	—	—

Model 1925

Semiautomatic pistol chambered for .22 caliber with 6.75" round barrel, checkered hard black rubber grips or ribbed walnut grips. Magazine capacity is 10 rounds. The frame is marked, "MANFD. BY/ THE HARTFORD ARMS AND EQUIP. CO./ HARTFORD, CONN./ PATENTED/ .22 CAL/LONG RIFLE" on the left side in front of the breach Approximately 5,000 were produced from 1925 to 1932.

Courtesy John J. Stimson, Jr.

Exc.	V.G.	Good	Fair	Poor
600	425	350	280	250

HATFIELD RIFLE COMPANY
St. Joseph, Missouri

Squirrel Rifle

A flintlock or percussion rifle in .32 to .50 caliber with a 39" barrel, double set triggers, adjustable sights, brass mounts and maple stocks. Available in a wide variety of forms, which affect the values. The values listed below are for plain, standard models.

NIB	Exc.	V.G.	Good	Fair	Poor
475	400	350	300	225	150

SHOTGUNS

Uplander Grade I

A 20 gauge boxlock double barrel shotgun with a 26" improved cylinder and modified barrel with a matte raised rib, single selective trigger and automatic ejectors. Case hardened, blued with a deluxe-grade, hand-checkered walnut stock. Introduced in 1987.

NIB	Exc.	V.G.	Good	Fair	Poor
1150	1050	750	600	475	400

Uplander Pigeon Grade II

As above, with scroll engraving with a fitted leather case.

NIB	Exc.	V.G.	Good	Fair	Poor
2000	1750	1275	900	650	500

Uplander Super Pigeon Grade III

As above, with deep-relief cut engraving and a leather case.

NIB	Exc.	V.G.	Good	Fair	Poor
2500	2200	1700	1400	1000	700

Uplander Golden Quail Grade IV

A gold inlaid version of the above.

NIB	Exc.	V.G.	Good	Fair	Poor
4000	3500	2750	2000	1700	1300

Uplander Woodcock Grade V

As above, with seven 24 kt. gold inlays and best quality engraving. Furnished with a leather case.

NIB	Exc.	V.G.	Good	Fair	Poor
5600	5000	4250	3500	2750	2000

HAVILAND & GUNN
Ilion, New York

Gallery Pistol

A .17 caliber rimfire single shot pistol with a 5" barrel. The barrel and frame made of one piece of iron and nickel plated. There are no markings on these pistols whatsoever. Believed to have been made during the 1870s.

Exc.	V.G.	Good	Fair	Poor
—	—	750	300	175

HAWES
Los Angeles, California
An importer of handguns primarily made in Europe

Courier

A .25 caliber, blowback, semiautomatic pocket pistol manufactured by Galesi.

Exc.	V.G.	Good	Fair	Poor
125	100	75	50	25

Diplomat

A .380 ACP pistol with an external hammer.

Exc.	V.G.	Good	Fair	Poor
150	125	100	75	50

Trophy

A J.P. Sauer & Sohn, manufactured revolver with a swing-out cylinder and a 6" barrel. Chambered for the .22 l.r. and the .38 Special. Has adjustable sights.

Exc.	V.G.	Good	Fair	Poor
250	200	175	125	90

Medalion

As above, with a 3", 4", or 6" barrel and fixed sights.

Exc.	V.G.	Good	Fair	Poor
200	175	125	100	75

J. P. Sauer also made a Western-styled series for Hawes based in appearance on the Colt Single Action Army.

Silver City Marshal

A .22 l.r. or .22 rimfire Magnum caliber single action revolver with a 5.5" barrel, 6-shot cylinder, and fixed sights.

Exc.	V.G.	Good	Fair	Poor
125	100	75	50	25

Western Marshal

A .357 Magnum, .44 Magnum, .45 Colt, .45 ACP, .44-40, 9mm, .22 l.r., and .22 rimfire Magnum single action revolver with fixed sights. Blued.

Exc.	V.G.	Good	Fair	Poor
175	150	125	100	75

Chief Marshal

A .357 Magnum, .44 Magnum, and the .45 Colt caliber revolver with a 6.5" barrel, and 6-shot cylinder and adjustable sights. Blued.

Exc.	V.G.	Good	Fair	Poor
175	150	125	100	75

Texas Marshal

As above, but nickel plated.

Exc.	V.G.	Good	Fair	Poor
185	160	135	100	75

Montana Marshal

The Western Marshal with a brass backstrap and triggerguard.

Exc.	V.G.	Good	Fair	Poor
175	150	125	100	75

Deputy Marshal

A .22 l.r. and .22 rimfire Magnum single action revolver with a 5.5" barrel, and 6-shot cylinder.

Exc.	V.G.	Good	Fair	Poor
125	100	75	50	25

Federal Marshal

A 6-shot single action revolver in .357 Magnum, .44 Magnum, and the .45 Colt caliber.

Exc.	V.G.	Good	Fair	Poor
175	150	125	100	75

HAWES & WAGGONER
Philadelphia, Pennsylvania

Pocket Pistol

A .41 caliber single shot percussion pistol with a 3" barrel, German silver mountings, and a walnut stock. Manufactured in the 1850s.

Exc.	V.G.	Good	Fair	Poor
—	1250	500	350	250

HAWKEN
St. Louis, Missouri

During the early part of the 19th century, Jacob and Samuel Hawken manufactured a variety of flintlock, percussion and cartridge rifles, shotguns and pistols. They are best known, however, for half stock Plains Rifles. Though of a plain nature, these arms were recognized for their accuracy and dependability. Prospective purchasers are advised to secure a qualified appraisal prior to acquisition. Early Hawken rifles will be worth a substantial premium over later examples. Some examples in very good condition may be worth as much as $25,000. Proceed with caution.

HEAVY EXPRESS INC.
Colorado Springs, Colorado

This company builds custom-built rifles using its proprietary nonbelted cartridges from .260 Heavy Express Magnum to the .416 Heavy Express Magnum. The company's rifles are built on Ruger Model 77 Mark II and Winchester Model 70 Classic actions. Barrels are 4140 Chrome-moly blue and 416R stainless steel. Stocks include factory walnut, laminated, or composite designs. The prices listed below are for the basic guns. Options are not included and will affect price.

Heavy Express Premier-Ruger M77 Mk II

This rifle is chambered for the .260HE Mag., .284 HE mag., or .300 HE Mag. Choice of walnut, laminated, or composite stocks.

NIB	Exc.	V.G.	Good	Fair	Poor
1200	—	—	—	—	—

NOTE: Add $200 for stainless steel.

Heavy Express Premier-Winchester M 70 Classic

This rifle is built on a Ruger M77 Mk II action in .260 HE Mag., .284 HE Mag., or .300 HE Mag. Choice of stocks.

NIB	Exc.	V.G.	Good	Fair	Poor
1300	—	—	—	—	—

NOTE: Add $200 for stainless steel.

Heavy Express Monarch-Ruger 77 MK II

This rifle is built on a Ruger M 77 action and is chambered for the .338, .350, .375, .416, and .460 HE Magnum cartridges. Choice of stocks.

NIB	Exc.	V.G.	Good	Fair	Poor
1475	—	—	—	—	—

NOTE: Add $200 for stainless steel.

Heavy Express Monarch-Winchester M 70 Classic

Same as above but built on a Winchester M 70 Classic action. Choice of stocks.

Close-up of Model 70 Classic stainless steel action

NIB	Exc.	V.G.	Good	Fair	Poor
1575	—	—	—	—	—

NOTE: Add $200 for stainless steel.

Heavy Express Single Shot-Ruger #1

This rifle is chambered in .300, .338, .350, and .416 HE Magnum cartridges. Choice of stocks.

NIB	Exc.	V.G.	Good	Fair	Poor
1500	—	—	—	—	—

NOTE: Add $200 for stainless steel.

HECKLER & KOCH
Oberndorf/Neckar, Germany

At the end of WWII, the French dismantled the Mauser factory as part of their reparations; and the buildings remained idle until 1949, when firearms production was again allowed in Germany. Heckler & Koch was formed as a machine tool enterprise and occupied the vacant Mauser plant. In the early 1950s Edmund Heckler and Theodor Koch began to produce the G3 automatic rifle based on the Spanish CETME design and progressed to machine guns and submachine guns and eventually to the production of commercial civilian rifles and pistols. In 1990 the company got into financial difficulties because of a failed contract bid. In December of 1990 the French state consortium GIAT announced the purchase of Heckler and Koch, but a little more than a year later the contract was cancelled. Later in 1991 the company was purchased by Royal Ordnance of Britain.

Model 91

This rifle is recoil-operated, with a delayed-roller lock bolt. It is chambered for the .308 Winchester cartridge and has a 17.7" barrel with military style aperture sights. It is furnished with a 20-round detachable magazine and is finished in matte black with a black plastic stock. Some areas of the country have made its ownership illegal.

NIB	Exc.	V.G.	Good	Fair	Poor
3500	2750	2300	1550	1200	800

Model 91 A3

This model is simply the Model 91 with a retractable metal stock.

NIB	Exc.	V.G.	Good	Fair	Poor
3700	3000	2500	1600	1300	900

Model 93

This model is similar to the Model 91 except that it is chambered for the .223 cartridge and has a 16.4" barrel. The magazine holds 25 rounds, and the specification are the same as for the Model 91.

NIB	Exc.	V.G.	Good	Fair	Poor
3500	2750	2300	1500	1200	800

Model 93 A3

This is the Model 93 with the retractable metal stock.

NIB	Exc.	V.G.	Good	Fair	Poor
3700	3000	2500	1650	1300	900

Model 94

This is a carbine version chambered for the 9mm Parabellum cartridge, with a 16.5" barrel. It is a smaller-scaled weapon that has a 15-shot magazine.

NIB	Exc.	V.G.	Good	Fair	Poor
4200	3850	3300	2750	2200	1500

Model 94 A3

This model is a variation of the Model 94 with the addition of a retractable metal stock.

NIB	Exc.	V.G.	Good	Fair	Poor
4500	3900	3400	2900	2300	1500

Model 270

This model is chambered for the .22 l.r. cartridge. It is a sporting-styled rifle with a 16.5" barrel. It is furnished with either a 5- or a 20-round magazine and is blued, with a checkered walnut stock. This rifle was discontinued in 1985.

NIB	Exc.	V.G.	Good	Fair	Poor
600	500	450	350	250	150

Model 300

This model is similar to the Model 270 except that it is chambered for the .22 rimfire Magnum cartridge. It was not imported after 1988.

NIB	Exc.	V.G.	Good	Fair	Poor
800	675	500	350	250	150

Model 630

This model is chambered for the .223 and features the same roller-delayed semiautomatic action as found on the paramilitary-type weapons. This is a sporting style rifle that has a polished blue finish and a checkered walnut stock. The barrel is 17.7" long, and the magazines offered hold either 4 or 10 rounds. Importation was discontinued in 1986.

NIB	Exc.	V.G.	Good	Fair	Poor
1100	850	600	450	350	300

Model 770

This model is similar to the Model 630 except that it is chambered for the .308 Winchester cartridge and has 19.7" barrel. It was not imported after 1986.

NIB	Exc.	V.G.	Good	Fair	Poor
1100	950	600	450	350	300

Model 820

This rifle is a falling design and chambered for the .30-06 cartridge. Two of these rifle are known in the U.S., one of which is in the H&K museum.

NIB	Exc.	V.G.	Good	Fair	Poor
3500	3000	—	—	—	—

Model 877

This rifle is a breech loading rifle chambered for .30-06 or .22-250 cartridge. Two of these rifles are known in the U.S., one of which is the H&K museum.

NIB	Exc.	V.G.	Good	Fair	Poor
3500	3000	—	—	—	—

Model 940

This model is essentially the same as the Model 770 except that it is chambered for the .30-06 cartridge. It has a 21" barrel and was not imported after 1986.

NIB	Exc.	V.G.	Good	Fair	Poor
1450	1100	800	600	400	300

Model SL6

This is Heckler & Koch's current sporting rifle chambered for the .223 cartridge. It has a 17.7" barrel and features the same basic action as the military versions. It has a matte black finish and a walnut stock with a vented walnut hand guard. The magazine holds 4 rounds.

NIB	Exc.	V.G.	Good	Fair	Poor
1100	850	600	450	350	300

Model SL7

This model is similar to the SL6 except that it is chambered for the .308 Winchester cartridge and has a 3-round magazine.

NIB	Exc.	V.G.	Good	Fair	Poor
1100	850	600	450	350	300

Model SR9

This model was introduced into the U.S. market after the federal government prohibited the importation of H&K's other semiautomatic rifles. The SR9 is similar to the HK91 but has been certified by the BATF as a sporting rifle. This model features a special thumb hole stock made of Kevlar reinforced fiberglass. The action is a delayed-roller locked bolt semiautomatic design chambered for the .308 Winchester cartridge. The barrel is 19.7" in length and features adjustable rear sight with hooded front sight. The rifle weighs 10.9 lbs.

NIB	Exc.	V.G.	Good	Fair	Poor
2000	1700	1400	1000	700	500

Model SR9 (T) Target

Similar to the standard model SR9 but with the addition of a special MSG90 adjustable buttstock, PSG 1 trigger group, and a PSG 1 contoured hand grip. Rifle weighs 10.6 lbs.

NIB	Exc.	V.G.	Good	Fair	Poor
3000	2800	2200	1650	1050	800

Model SR9 (TC) Target Competition

Similar to the Model SR9 (T) but with the addition of the PSG 1 adjustable buttstock. Rifle weighs 10.9 lbs.

NIB	Exc.	V.G.	Good	Fair	Poor
3300	3000	2300	1950	1100	900

PSG-1

This rifle is a high precision sniping rifle that features the delayed-roller semiautomatic action. It is chambered for the .308 Winchester cartridge and has a 5-shot magazine. Barrel length is 25.6". It is furnished with a complete array of accessories including a 6x42-power illuminated Hensoldt scope. Rifle weighs 17.8 lbs.

NIB	Exc.	V.G.	Good	Fair	Poor
14500	12500	9000	7500	6000	4000

BASR Model

This is a bolt action rifle chambered for various popular calibers. It has a stainless steel barrel and was essentially custom built to the customer's specifications. The stock is of Kevlar. This model is quite rare since only 100 were manufactured in 1968.

Exc.	V.G.	Good	Fair	Poor
1750	1200	900	650	400

Model SL8-1

This is a new generation .223 rifle modeled after the military Model G36 and introduced in 2000. It is built of carbon fiber polymer and is gas operated. Thumbhole stock with cheekpiece. Barrel length is 20.8". Magazine capacity is 10 rounds. Adjustable sights. Weight is approximately 8.6 lbs.

NIB	Exc.	V.G.	Good	Fair	Poor
1600	1200	—	—	—	—

SLB 2000

Introduced in 2001 this gas operated semiautomatic rifle is chamberd for the .30-06 cartridge. The receiver is built of lightweight alloy. The barrel is 16.7" in length and will accept interchangeable barrels at some future date. Oil finished walnut stock. Open sights with both barrel and receiver drilled and tapped for scope mounts. Magazine capacity is 2, 5, or 10 rounds. Weight is about 7.25 lbs.

NIB	Exc.	V.G.	Good	Fair	Poor
N/A	—	—	—	—	—

Model USC

Introduced in 2000 this semiautomatic blowback carbine is derived from H&K's UMP submachine gun. Chambered for the .45ACP cartridge and fitted with a 16" barrel. Skeltonized stock. Accessory rail on top of receiver. Adjustable sights. Magazine capacity is 10 rounds. Weight is approximately 6 lbs.

NIB	Exc.	V.G.	Good	Fair	Poor
1200	900	—	—	—	—

PISTOLS

HK4

This is a blowback-operated semiautomatic pistol based on the Mauser HSc design. It is chambered for .22 l.r., .25 ACP, .32 ACP, and .380. These calibers were easily converted by switching the barrels, recoil springs and magazines. The rimfire model could be changed by rotating the breechface. The conversion kits were available for all calibers. The barrel is 3" long; and the finish is blued, with molded plastic thumb rest grips. This pistol was sold from 1968-1973 as the Harrington & Richardson HK4 and is so marked. It was completely discontinued in 1984.

.22 Caliber or .380 Caliber

Exc.	V.G.	Good	Fair	Poor
475	350	250	200	100

.25 Caliber or .32 Caliber

Exc.	V.G.	Good	Fair	Poor
350	300	250	200	100

Conversion Units

Exc.	V.G.	Good	Fair	Poor
150	125	90	60	30

P9

This is a single action, delayed-blowback semiautomatic pistol chambered for 9mm or 7.65mm Parabellum. The action is based on the G-3 rifle mechanism. The barrel is 4" in length, and the pistol has an internal hammer and a thumb-operated hammer drop and decocking lever. There is also a manual safety and a loaded-chamber indicator. The finish is parkerized, and the grips are molded plastic and well contoured. It has fixed sights. This model was manufactured between 1977 and 1984. This model is rarer than the P9S model.

NIB	Exc.	V.G.	Good	Fair	Poor
800	650	500	400	300	200

P9S

This model is similar to the Model P9 except that the action features a double action capability and it is chambered for the .45 ACP and the 9mm Parabellum with a 5.5" barrel. This model was also manufactured between 1977 and 1984.

NIB	Exc.	V.G.	Good	Fair	Poor
800	650	500	400	300	200

NIB	Exc.	V.G.	Good	Fair	Poor
1100	850	700	600	500	300

P9S COMPETITION

Similar to the P9S target but with the addition of barrel weights and special competition grips.

NIB	Exc.	V.G.	Good	Fair	Poor
2000	1500	1200	—	—	—

VP 70Z

This is a blowback-operated semiautomatic chambered for the 9mm Parabellum cartridge. It is striker-fired and double action only. The barrel is 4.5" long, and the double-column magazine holds 18 rounds. The finish is blued, and the receiver and grip are molded from plastic. This model was discontinued in 1984.

NIB	Exc.	V.G.	Good	Fair	Poor
550	450	350	300	250	200

P7 PSP

This was the first of the squeeze-cocked H&K pistols. It is a single action semiautomatic that is placed in the firing position by pressure on the front of the grip strap. This moves the striker into battery; and firing is then accomplished by a single action pressure on the trigger, releasing the grip strap cocking device and decocking the mechanism. This particular model does not have the extended finger guard on the trigger and

---

WHAT'S IT LIKE-THE H&K P9S

The Heckler and Koch Company of Germany got its start in the world of military small arms during the post WWII years. The H&K P9S was a very successful pistol design for the company. It was adopted by many armies around the world. This pistol, imported into the U.S. from the early 1870s to the late 1980s, was one of the first pistols to utilize plastic in its receiver. The Navy Seals used the pistol for many years, not only because of its great accuracy and reliability but also for its capacity to utilize a suppressor. This feature was due to the fact that the pistol's barrel was fixed. It did not move as the gun cycled. The fixed barrel resulted in excellent accuracy. It does not matter how loose the slide to barrel interface is, the gun still shoots very well because the barrel is locked into the receiver. The P9S was made in 6 configurations: the P9s Combat, P9S Target, and the P9S Competition. All of which were available in either 9mm or .45 ACP caliber. The P9S Combat has fixed sights with a double action trigger and decocker. The P9S Target is the same size but with high visibility adjustable sights. More importantly, the Target model utilizes an adjustable trigger that would put to shame most match .22 caliber pistols. The P9S Competition incorporates a 1 1/2" longer barrel with barrel weight and front sight located at the barrels' end that increases sights radius and helps to balance the weapon. The Competition model is also fitted with ergonomically designed target grips.

J.R. Moody

P9S Target Model

This version is similar to the Model P9S chambered for the 9mm or .45 ACP cartridges, with adjustable sights, and an adjustable trigger. It was discontinued in 1984.

also does not have an ambidextrous safety. It was discontinued in 1984.

NIB	Exc.	V.G.	Good	Fair	Poor
800	700	600	500	400	200

P7 M8

This is the 8-shot newer version of the "squeeze cocker." It has the heat-shield finger guard and the ambidextrous safety. It has a 4" barrel and a 3-dot sight system. The finish is matte blue or nickel with stippled black plastic grips.

NIB	Exc.	V.G.	Good	Fair	Poor
1000	800	700	600	500	300

NOTE: For night sights, introduced in 1993, add $100.

P7 M10

A new addition to the P7 series in 1993, this variation is chambered for the .40 S&W cartridge. Magazine holds 10 rounds and the finish is available in either blue or nickel. Pistol weighs 2.69 lbs.

NIB	Exc.	V.G.	Good	Fair	Poor
1200	1000	800	650	500	300

NOTE: For night sights add $100.

P7 M13

This version is similar to the P7 M8 except that it has a double column 13-shot magazine.

NIB	Exc.	V.G.	Good	Fair	Poor
1300	1000	800	650	500	300

NOTE: For night sights add $100.

P7 K3

This is the "Squeeze Cocker" chambered for either the .380 or .22 L.R. caliber. It has a recoil buffer that is oil-filled and a 3.8" barrel. The magazine holds 8 rounds. This model was introduced in 1988.

NIB	Exc.	V.G.	Good	Fair	Poor
1000	900	750	650	500	300

.22 Caliber Conversion Kit

This unit will convert the P7 K3 to fire the .22 Long Rifle cartridge.

NIB	Exc.	V.G.	Good	Fair	Poor
575	400	350	300	150	75

.32 ACP Caliber Conversion Kit

NIB	Exc.	V.G.	Good	Fair	Poor
200	175	150	100	75	50

SP89

Introduced in the early 1990s, this is a large frame semiautomatic pistol chambered for the 9mm cartridge. It features a 15-round magazine and a square notch rear sight with a hooded front sight. The pistol has a 4.5" barrel and is 13" overall. It weighs 4.4 lbs. In August 1993 this model was no longer imported due to a ban on assault pistols.

NIB	Exc.	V.G.	Good	Fair	Poor
4000	3600	3200	2500	1800	1000

USP SERIES

NOTE: Late in 1999 H&K began shipping its USPs and Mark 23s with an internal locking system. This lock-out is installed in the grip and blocks the movement of the hammer, trigger, and slide. It is operated with a two pronged key, supplied with the pistol. This system is in addition to the traditional trigger lock that is sold with each H&K firearm.

NOTE: In 2001 the stainless steel version of these pistols was discontinued.

USP40

Introduced in 1993 this new semiautomatic H&H pistol features a new design that incorporates a short recoil modified Browning action. Chambered for the .40 S&W cartridge this model has a 4.13" barrel and a magazine capacity of 13 rounds. Stainless steel model introduced in 1996. It weighs 1.74 lbs. Available in seven different variations from traditional double action to double action only and various safety locations and styles. These variants are numbered by H&K as follows:

1. DA/SA with safe position and control lever on left side of frame.
2. DA/SA with safe position and control lever on right side of frame.
3. DA/SA without safe position and decocking lever on left side of frame.
4. DA/SA without safe position and decocking lever on left side of frame.
5. DA only with safe position and safety lever on left side of frame.
6. DA only with safe position and safety lever on right side of frame.
7. DA only without control lever.
9. DA/SA with safe position and safety lever on left side of frame.
10. DA/SA with safety lever on the right side of frame.

NIB	Exc.	V.G.	Good	Fair	Poor
600	500	400	300	250	—

NOTE: For stainless steel model add $45.

USP9

Same as the USP40 but chambered for the 9mm cartridge. Magazine holds 16 rounds and pistol weighs 1.66 lbs. This model also has the choice of seven variations as listed above for the USP40. New for 1993.

NIB	Exc.	V.G.	Good	Fair	Poor
600	500	400	300	250	—

NOTE: For stainless steel model add $45.

USP45

Introduced in 1995 this version is slightly larger than the 9mm and .40 S&W models. Barrel length is 4.41" and overall length is 7.87". Weight is 1.9 lb. The USP45 is available in the same variants as the other USP models.

NIB	Exc.	V.G.	Good	Fair	Poor
675	575	450	350	250	—

NOTE: For stainless steel model add $45.

NIB	Exc.	V.G.	Good	Fair	Poor
625	500	425	—	—	—

H&K Stainless Steel Model

USP 9 Compact

Introduced in 1997 this 9mm model is a smaller version of the full size USP9. There are some internal differences due to size. Barrel length is 3.58". Overall length is 6.81". Magazine capacity is 10 rounds. Weight is approximately 26 oz. Also available with stainless steel slide. Add $45 to NIB price.

NIB	Exc.	V.G.	Good	Fair	Poor
625	500	425	—	—	—

USP 40 Compact

Same as 9mm Compact model but chambered for 40 S&W cartridge. Weight is about 27 oz. All other dimensions are the same.

From top to bottom is the USP45, the USP40, and the USP40 Compact

USP45 Match

Introduced in 1997 this model is a match grade variation of the USP. It is chambered for the .45 ACP cartridge. Fitted with a 6.02" barrel with barrel weight assembly. Adjustable rear sight and target front sight. Adjustable trigger stop. Blued finish. Weight is approximately 38 oz. Also available in a stainless steel version. Add $60.00 for stainless steel.

NIB	Exc.	V.G.	Good	Fair	Poor
1370	1100	—	—	—	—

USP 45 Compact

Introduced in 1997 this pistol is chambered for the .45 ACP cartridge. It has a 3.8" barrel and an overall length of 7.1". It weighs approximately 28 oz. Magazine capacity is 8 rounds.

NIB	Exc.	V.G.	Good	Fair	Poor
650	500	400	—	—	—

USP .357 Compact

Introduced in mid-1998 this pistol is built on the same frame as the .40 S&W Compact but chambered for the .357 Sig cartridge. Magazine capacity is 10 rounds. Weight is about 28 oz.

NIB	Exc.	V.G.	Good	Fair	Poor
700	550	—	—	—	—

USP 45 Tactical

This pistol was introduced in 1998. It is an enhanced version of the USP 45. It is fitted with a 4.9" threaded barrel with adjustable high profile target sights. Overall length is 8.6" and weight is approximately 36 oz. Magazine capacity is 10 rounds. Availability limited to between 1,000 and 2,500 pistols.

NIB	Exc.	V.G.	Good	Fair	Poor
950	750	—	—	—	—

USP .45 Expert

Introduced in the fall of 1998, this .45 ACP pistol is fitted with a 5.2" barrel and slide and 10-round magazine. Overall length is 8.7" and height is 1.87". Weight is approximately 30 oz. Adjustable low-profile sights. Limited availability of between 1,000 and 2,500 pistols.

NIB	Exc.	V.G.	Good	Fair	Poor
1370	1100	—	—	—	—

USP .45 50th Anniversary Commemorative

Limited to 1,000 pistols this pistol features a high polish blue with 50th anniversary logo engraved in gold and silver. Supplied with custom-made wooden box with commemorative coin. Introduced in 2000.

NIB	Exc.	V.G.	Good	Fair	Poor
1000	—	—	—	—	—

WHAT'S IT LIKE- THE HK USP TACTICAL

I am not a competitive pistol shooter nor am I a first-rate pistol shot, perhaps better than average but certainly not by much. So what? Because when I pick up a .45 ACP USP Tactical I become a much better pistol shot than usual. It's because the Tactical has a superior double action and single action trigger pull and feel than standard USPs. With a handy adjustable trigger over-travel stop the operator can set it just to his liking. The manual safety also serves as a decocking lever on variant 1 pistols. Different variants mean that the pistol can be set up in numerous configurations to suit the shooter. Mounting grooves on the frame under the barrel provide a method of installing lights or lasers. The grip is comfortable in my average size hand, and the sights look good even to my aging eyes. They are adjustable as well, the sights I mean. The barrel is 4.9" in length threaded for a suppressor. More importantly the barrel has a neat little rubber O ring behind the threads that aid barrel fit and increases accuracy. Because of its secondary captive recoil spring, barrel jump and felt recoil are noticeably reduced giving faster follow-up shots and less time away from point of aim. I find the pistol very comfortable to shoot even for extended periods of time. I have fired over a thousand round through my Tactical and have never had a problem. So is it perfect? No. It weighs 36 ounces and is over 8 1/2 inches long overall; a bit large and heavy to carry. But it shoots great, is very reliable, and for me that's what a pistol needs to be to earn its keep around the house.

Ned Schwing

USP ACCESSORIES

The items listed below are factory options for the USP pistol and may be encountered when a sale is contemplated. We have listed the retail price of the factory item.

Tritium Sights
MSRP-$95.00

Mark II UTL (Universal Tactical Light)
MSRP-$267.00

Quik-Comp
MSRP-$184.00 (Discontinued 1997)

Optical Sight/Scope Mount

Optical sight/scope mount and Quik-Comp

MSRP-$221.00

Mark 23

Very similar to the H&K's US government contract pistol developed for special Operation Units. Chambered for the .45 ACP and fitted with a 5.87" barrel, this pistol has a polymer frame with steel slide. Magazine capacity is 10 rounds on civilian models and 12 rounds on law enforcement models. Barrel is threaded for noise suppressor. Weight is about 42 oz. Limited availability in fall 1996 to about 2,000 pistols.

NIB	Exc.	V.G.	Good	Fair	Poor
1900	1550	1250	—	—	—

Mk 23 Suppressor

This unit can be fitted to the threaded barrel of the MK 23 and be compensated for point of aim. With water the dB sound reduction is 33-35dB. Produced by Knight Armament Corp. of Vero Beach, FL. This suppressor, with a different piston assembly, can be fitted to the USP Tactical.

NIB	Exc.	V.G.	Good	Fair	Poor
1250	—	—	—	—	—

NOTE: Suppressors require a Class III transfer tax. All NFA rules apply to the sale or purchase of these suppressors.

HEINZELMANN, C.E.
Plochipnam Neckar, Germany

Heim

A 6.35mm semiautomatic pistol with a 2" barrel. Detachable magazine holds 6 rounds. Manufactured during the 1930s and marked on the frame "C.E. Heinzelmann Plochingen A.N. Patent Heim-6.35."

Exc.	V.G.	Good	Fair	Poor
800	675	550	400	200

HEISER, CARL
SEE—Austrian Military Firearms

HELFRICHT
Zella-Mehlis, Germany

Model 3 Pocket Pistol

A 6.35mm semiautomatic pistol with a 2" barrel and 6-shot magazine. Blued with black plastic grips having the monogram "KH" cast in them.

Exc.	V.G.	Good	Fair	Poor
475	400	350	275	150

Model 4 Pocket Pistol

As above, without the barrel extension.

Exc.	V.G.	Good	Fair	Poor
425	350	300	225	100

HELLIS, CHARLES
London, England
SEE—British Double Guns

HENRION & DASSY
Liege, Belgium

Semiautomatic

A 6.35mm semiautomatic pistol with a 2.5" barrel and 5-shot magazine. Blued with black plastic grips. Marked "H&D".

Exc.	V.G.	Good	Fair	Poor
600	500	450	375	275

HENRY
SEE—Winchester

HENRY, ALEXANDER
Edinburgh, Scotland

Noted for both the rifling system he developed and the falling block single shot rifles he made, Alexander Henry conducted business at the following locations:

12 South Street, Andrew Street	1853-1858
8 South Street, Andrew Street	1858-1862
12 South Street, Andrew Street	1862-1871
12 and 14 South Street, Andrew Street	1871-1875
12 South Street, Andrew Street	1875-1895
18 Frederick Street	1895-1911
22 Frederick Street	1911

Rifles made by this maker are highly sought after and prospective purchasers are strongly advised to secure a qualified appraisal prior to acquisition.

Single Shot Rifle

A high-grade single shot that features a true falling-block action that is activated by a side lever on the action. It was available in the popular European cartridges of the era, and the barrel length varies from 22" to 28" in length. This rifle exhibits fine quality materials and workmanship. The select-grade walnut stock and schnabel forend are hand checkered. The finish of the rifle is scroll-engraved and blued. This company manufactured firearms from 1869 until 1895.

Exc.	V.G.	Good	Fair	Poor
—	3500	1750	800	400

Double Rifle

A side-x-side, double barreled Express Rifle chambered for the .500/450 Black Powder Express cartridge. It has Damascus barrels and double triggers. This gun is hammerless and features ornate scroll engraving as well as a high-grade hand checkered walnut stock and forend. It was furnished with a fitted leather case and accessories. This rifle was manufactured in the 1890s.

Exc.	V.G.	Good	Fair	Poor
—	6000	3500	1250	600

HENRY REPEATING ARMS COMPANY
Brooklyn, New York

Henry Lever Action

Chambered for the .22 Long Rifle, Long, and Short cartridges It is fitted with a 18.25" barrel and weighs 5.5 lbs. Magazine capacity is 15 for the .22 Long Rifle cartridge. Rear sight is adjustable and the front sight is hooded.

NIB	Exc.	V.G.	Good	Fair	Poor
225	175	125	—	—	—

Henry Carbine

Similar to the above model but with an overall length of 34". It features a large loop lever.

NIB	Exc.	V.G.	Good	Fair	Poor
225	175	125	—	—	—

Henry Youth Model

Similar to the carbine model above but with an overall length of 33".

NIB	Exc.	V.G.	Good	Fair	Poor
225	175	125	—	—	—

Henry Pump Action Rifle

Introduced in 1999 this .22 caliber is fitted with a 18.25" barrel and chambered for the .22 long rifle cartridge. Walnut stock and adjustable rear sight. Weight is approximately 5.5 lbs.

NIB	Exc.	V.G.	Good	Fair	Poor
250	200	—	—	—	—

Henry U.S. Survival Rifle

This model is an improved version of the AR-7 .22 caliber survival rifle issued to the Air Force. It is a breakdown design and features a waterproof stock, a steel-lined barrel and adjustable sights. Furnished with two 8-round magazines. Overall length when broken down is 16.5".

NIB	Exc.	V.G.	Good	Fair	Poor
165	130	100	—	—	—

HERITAGE MANUFACTURING, INC.
Opa Locka, Florida

Stealth

This is a 9mm semiautomatic pistol. It has a black polymer frame with stainless steel slide. Barrel length is 3.9" with overall length at 6.3". Magazine capacity is 10 rounds. Weight is approximately 20 oz. A .40 S&W version is scheduled to be introduced in the summer of 1996. Offered with a black finish, two-tone black chrome with stainless steel side panels, or black chrome.

NIB	Exc.	V.G.	Good	Fair	Poor
300	225	175	150	125	100

Model H25S

A semiautomatic pistol chambered for the .25 ACP cartridge. Barrel length is 2.25" and overall length is 4.58". Weight is about 13.5 oz. Frame mounted safety. Single action only. Available in blue or nickel.

NIB	Exc.	V.G.	Good	Fair	Poor
150	125	100	85	65	50

Sentry

This is a double action revolver chambered for the .38 Special. Cylinder holds 6 rounds. Barrel length is 2". Weight is about 23 oz. Blue or nickel finish.

NIB	Exc.	V.G.	Good	Fair	Poor
130	100	85	65	50	30

Rough Rider

Single action revolver chambered for the .22 caliber cartridges. Barrel lengths are 4.75", 6.5", and 9". Cylinder holds 6 rounds. Weight is about 34 oz. Available in blue or nickel finish.

NIB	Exc.	V.G.	Good	Fair	Poor
130	100	75	50	40	30

With Combination Cylinder-.22 Mag.

NIB	Exc.	V.G.	Good	Fair	Poor
150	125	85	65	50	35

With Birds Head Grip & Combo Cylinder

NIB	Exc.	V.G.	Good	Fair	Poor
150	125	85	65	50	35

HEROLD
Franz Jaeger
Suhl, Germany

Bolt Action Rifle

A .22 Hornet bolt action sporting rifle with a 24" ribbed barrel, adjustable sights, double set triggers and walnut stock. Imported by Charles Daly and Stoeger Arms prior to WWII.

Exc.	V.G.	Good	Fair	Poor
1500	850	600	400	250

HERTERS
Waseca, Minnesota

An importer and retailer of European made firearms. Active until approximately 1980.

REVOLVERS

Guide

A .22 caliber double action swing-out cylinder revolver with a 6" barrel and 6-shot cylinder. Blued with walnut grips.

Exc.	V.G.	Good	Fair	Poor
100	80	50	35	25

Power-Mag Revolver

A .357 Magnum, .401 Herters Power Magnum, and .44 Magnum caliber single action revolver with a 4" or 6" barrel and 6-shot cylinder. Blued, with walnut grips.

Exc.	V.G.	Good	Fair	Poor
150	125	80	60	50

Western

As above, in .22 caliber.

Exc.	V.G.	Good	Fair	Poor
85	75	60	45	25

RIFLES

J-9 or U-9 Hunter
Mauser action sporting rifles manufactured in England (J-9) and Yugoslavia (U-9), with 24" barrels and Monte Carlo-style walnut stocks.

Exc.	V.G.	Good	Fair	Poor
225	185	135	100	75

J-9 or U-9 Presentation or Supreme
As above, with checkering and sling swivels.

Exc.	V.G.	Good	Fair	Poor
250	225	200	150	100

HESSE ARMS
Inver Grove Heights, Minn.
This company has been in business since 1986. It offers a one-year warranty on all of its rifles and a lifetime warranty on its receivers.

FAL-H RIFLES
All FAL-H rifles include the following features: military spec internal parts, new or as new barrel, military finish, post ban legal muzzle break, one magazine, new metric pattern Type 3 receiver, adjustable gas system, refinished or new pistol grip, hard case, carry handle, sling, and manual. All rifles chambered for .308 Winchester cartridge. Additional calibers in .22-250 and .243 are also available. Weights are from 8.5 to 14 lbs. depending on model.

FALO Tactical Rifle
This model features a free floating handguard assembly.

NIB	Exc.	V.G.	Good	Fair	Poor
1150	900	700	—	—	—

FALO Heavy Barrel
This model features a heavy barrel and is based on the Israeli FALO rifle.

NIB	Exc.	V.G.	Good	Fair	Poor
950	750	600	—	—	—

FAL-H High Grade
This model is available in any configuration and features a new walnut stock, pistol grip, and handguard. Trigger is gold plated.

NIB	Exc.	V.G.	Good	Fair	Poor
1350	1050	850	—	—	—

FAL-H Standard Grade
This is standard model that is similar in appearance to the original FAL.

NIB	Exc.	V.G.	Good	Fair	Poor
950	750	600	—	—	—

FAL-H Congo Rifle
This model features a 16" barrel.

NIB	Exc.	V.G.	Good	Fair	Poor
1000	800	650	—	—	—

FALO Congo Rifle
Similar to the model above but fitted with a 16" heavy barrel.

NIB	Exc.	V.G.	Good	Fair	Poor
1000	800	650	—	—	—

HAR-15 RIFLES
All of the HAR-15 rifles have the following features: military spec internal parts, heavy match grade barrels, post ban legal muzzle break, A2 upper receiver, A2 round handguards with heat shields, A2 stock, A2 lower receiver. Each rifle comes with hard case, manual, and sling. Rifles are chambered for .223 Remington but can be chambered in other calibers as well. These are: .17 Rem. add $145, 9mm NATO add $85, 6mm PPC add $145, 6mmx45 add $95, .300 Fireball add $195, 7.62x39 add $45.

Omega Match
Fitted with a 1" diameter stainless steel barrel, adjustable match trigger, E2 stock, flat top receiver, free floating handguard.

NIB	Exc.	V.G.	Good	Fair	Poor
1000	800	650	—	—	—

HAR-15A2 Standard Rifle
This model has all of the standard features offered for HAR-15 rifles.

NIB	Exc.	V.G.	Good	Fair	Poor
725	575	475	—	—	—

HAR-15A2 National Match

This model is fitted with special bolt carrier, adjustable match trigger. Designed as Match grade rifle.

NIB	Exc.	V.G.	Good	Fair	Poor
1000	800	650	—	—	—

HAR-15A2 Bull Gun

This model is fitted with a 1" stainless steel barrel with special front sight base.

NIB	Exc.	V.G.	Good	Fair	Poor
775	600	475	—	—	—

HAR-15A2 Dispatcher

Fitted with a 16" barrel with full length handguard.

NIB	Exc.	V.G.	Good	Fair	Poor
725	575	450	—	—	—

HAR-15A2 Carbine

Fitted with a 16" heavy barrel and a non-collapsing stock with short handguard.

NIB	Exc.	V.G.	Good	Fair	Poor
725	575	475	—	—	—

H-22 RIFLES

All H-22 rifles include the following features: new internal parts interchangeable with Ruger 10/22 rifle, heavy stainless steel barrel with match chamber, stainless steel receiver, laminated stock, hard case, magazine, and manual. All rifle are chambered for .22 Long Rifle. For an additional $250 charge any H-22 rifle can be converted to .22 Magnum. Weight of these rifles is approximately 7 lbs.

H-22 Tigershark

Special forearm and skeleton stock with heavy fluted barrel. Special trigger pack with over travel screw and glass bedded stock.

NIB	Exc.	V.G.	Good	Fair	Poor
800	650	525	—	—	—

H-22 Competition Rifle

This model features a gloss finished laminated competition thumbhole stock.

NIB	Exc.	V.G.	Good	Fair	Poor
550	450	350	—	—	—

H-22 Wildcat

This model has a screwed in heavy barrel and a special laminated stock.

NIB	Exc.	V.G.	Good	Fair	Poor
550	450	350	—	—	—

H-22 Standard Rifle

Has all the standard features of the H-22 rifle with a buttstock with cheekpiece.

NIB	Exc.	V.G.	Good	Fair	Poor
475	375	300	—	—	—

M14-H Standard Rifle

This is a semiautomatic version of the M14 rifle chambered for the .308 cartridge. It is fitted with a new receiver, walnut stock or synthetic stock. Each rifle is sold with a sling, annual, and 10-round magazine and an extra original M145 stock.

NIB	Exc.	V.G.	Good	Fair	Poor
1000	800	650	—	—	—

M14-H Brush Rifle

This model has the same features as the standard rifle but with an 18" barrel.

NIB	Exc.	V.G.	Good	Fair	Poor
1050	800	650	—	—	—

Hesse Model 47 Rifle

This is a copy of the AK-47 and it is chambered for the 7.63x39 cartridge. It is also available in .223 caliber.

NIB	Exc.	V.G.	Good	Fair	Poor
600	475	375	—	—	—

HEYM, F. W.
Suhl, Germany

Established in 1865 in Suhl, Germany, this company was re-established after WWII in Munnerstadt. The company remained there until 1996 when it moved back to a suburb of Suhl. Postwar arms were originally imported by Paul Jaeger of Grand Junction, Tennessee. At the present time there is no American importer of Heym and guns are not entering this country as of 2000.

SINGLE SHOT RIFLES

Model HR-30

Built on the Ruger No. 1 falling-block action and chambered for most calibers with a 24" round barrel or a 26" barrel in the magnum calibers. There is a quarter rib with express sights, and the single-set trigger is made by Canjar. The rifle is engraved with a game scene motif, and the stock is deluxe, hand checkered French walnut with a classic European-style cheekpiece. French case hardened and blued.

Exc.	V.G.	Good	Fair	Poor
3000	2750	2250	1750	1250

Model HR-38

As above, with an octagonal barrel.

Exc.	V.G.	Good	Fair	Poor
3500	3250	2500	2000	1500

DOUBLE RIFLE

Model 77B/55B Over/Under Rifle

An Over/Under rifle manufactured in a variety of calibers with 25" barrels having open sights: and a boxlock action with Kersten double cross bolts. The action is heavily engraved with a game scene motif and is silver plated. This model has double triggers, cocking indicators, automatic ejectors, and select walnut stock. The barrels machined to accept a Zeiss scope with claw mounts.

Exc.	V.G.	Good	Fair	Poor
5000	4500	4000	3250	2500

Model 55BSS

As above with sidelocks.

Exc.	V.G.	Good	Fair	Poor
9500	8500	7500	5000	3500

WHAT'S IT LIKE-A BIG BORE DOUBLE

The big bore double rifle has always been mostly associated with Africa and dangerous game hunting. There is ample good reason for this association. Properly crafted, no rifle is more dependable to face a life or death situation. There are several reasons for this reliability. First of all is the double's ease of pointing. Built like a fine bird gun, it points almost naturally and is extremely fast to trigger a shot. More importantly, with two triggers, it is basically two single shot rifles joined together. If one firing pin breaks, there is another. If a hammer spring fails, there is another. The chances of two of anything failing at the same time is almost non-existent. For a period of years, the double rifle was essentially dead. Kynoch stopped making ammunition for the big nitro express calibers and collectors rapidly snapped them up. As the supply dried up, the double rifles became big, expensive paper weights.

In the last few years though, thanks in large measure to Jim Bell, ammo again became available and that fact brought many doubles out of forced retirement. It also motivated a small number of manufacturers to add a large caliber double rifle to their line. Heym, Krieghoff, several Italian double manufacturers, and, of course, the old British firms, all started producing big bore double rifles. The legendary firm of Holland & Holland even one-upped everyone by introducing a .700 Nitro Express double! Supposedly an American customer stopped by the H&H showroom and inquired about Holland building him a .600 NE rifle. When asked why he wanted such a behemoth, he supposedly answered "because you don't make a .700!" Thus a seed was sown. Double rifles have a charisma that no other type seems to inspire. When holding one, even in the confines of one's den, the smell of the African veldt permeates the room. No other type rifle does that.

Tom Turpin

Model 55BF/77BF

Similar to the Model 55B, except one barrel is rifled and the other smooth in 12, 16, or 20 gauge.

Exc.	V.G.	Good	Fair	Poor
5000	4500	4000	3250	2500

Model 55BFSS

As above, with sidelocks.

Exc.	V.G	Good	Fair	Poor
9500	8500	7500	5000	3500

Model 88 B

A large bore double barrel boxlock rifle with 24" barrels, automatic ejectors, double triggers, and select walnut stock.

Exc.	V.G.	Good	Fair	Poor
9500	8750	7750	5500	4000

Model 88 BSS
As above with sidelocks.

Exc.	V.G.	Good	Fair	Poor
14000	12500	9500	6500	5250

Model 88 Safari
As above, but chambered for .375 Holland & Holland, .458 Winchester Magnum, .470, or .500 Nitro Express calibers with 25" barrels.

Exc.	V.G.	Good	Fair	Poor
13500	12000	9000	6000	4750

Model 22 Safety
An Over/Under combination rifle/shotgun chambered for 16 or 20 gauge over .22 Hornet, .22 WMR, .222 Remington, .222 Remington Magnum, .223, 5.6x50Rmm, 6.5x57Rmm, and 7x57Rmm with 24" barrels. Boxlock action with a single trigger, automatic ejectors, and automatic decocking mechanism. French case hardening, blued with a walnut stock.

Exc.	V.G.	Good	Fair	Poor
2500	2000	1750	1200	900

DRILLINGS
Model 33
A boxlock drilling manufactured in a variety of American and European calibers and gauges with 25" barrels, double triggers and extractors. Case hardened, blued with a walnut stock.

Exc.	V.G.	Good	Fair	Poor
6000	5000	4250	2750	2000

Model 33 Deluxe
Same as above but with game scene engraving.

Exc.	V.G.	Good	Fair	Poor
7500	6000	4750	3500	2500

Model 37
Similar to the Model 33 Standard but with full sidelocks.

Exc.	V.G.	Good	Fair	Poor
12500	10000	7500	5000	2500

Model 37 Deluxe
Similar to the above Model 37 but with hand engraved scroll work and fancy walnut stock.

Exc.	V.G.	Good	Fair	Poor
15000	12000	8500	6000	3000

BOLT ACTION RIFLES
Model SR-20
A Mauser action sporting rifle manufactured in a variety of calibers with 21", 24", or 26" barrels, open sights, adjustable trigger or set trigger. Blued with a walnut stock.

NIB	Exc.	V.G.	Good	Fair	Poor
1450	1250	950	750	600	450

Model SR-20 Alpine
As above with a 20" barrel and Mannlicher stock. Introduced in 1989.

NIB	Exc.	V.G.	Good	Fair	Poor
2650	2250	1750	1250	850	600

SR-20 Classic Safari

As above, but chambered for .404 Jeffries, .425 Express, and the .458 Winchester Magnum with a 24" barrel having express sights. Introduced in 1989.

NIB	Exc	V.G.	Good	Fair	Poor
3500	3000	2750	2000	1250	750

SR-20 Classic Sportsman

This model features a round barrel without sights. Chambered for many calibers from .243 to .375 H&H. Introduced in 1988. Add $100 for Magnum calibers.

NIB	Exc.	V.G.	Good	Fair	Poor
1650	1250	900	700	500	300

SR-20 Trophy

Similar to the above Classic Sportsman model but with German bead ramp sight and open quarter rib rear sight. Select walnut stock with oil finish. Octagonal barrel and rosewood grip cap.

NIB	Exc.	V.G.	Good	Fair	Poor
2500	2000	1250	800	500	300

Heym Magnum Express

This bolt action rifle is chambered for .338 lapua, .375 H&H, .416 Rigby, .500 Nitro Express.500 A-Square, and a few were built in .600 Nitro Express. Fitted with a 24" barrel. Adjustable front sight, three leaf rear express sight. Select hand checkered European walnut stock, and many other special features. Introduced in 1989.

NOTE: Add $4,000 for 600 N.E.

NIB	Exc.	V.G.	Good	Fair	Poor
5800	4500	3000	1500	750	500

HI-POINT FIREARMS
MKS Supply
Dayton, Ohio

Model C

This is a 9mm single action compact semiautomatic pistol with a 3.5" barrel. Magazine capacity is 8 rounds. Black or chrome finish. Weight is 32 oz.

NIB	Exc	V.G.	Good	Fair	Poor
125	100	85	75	65	50

Model C-Polymer

Same as above but with polymer frame. Weight is 28 oz.

NIB	Exc	V.G.	Good	Fair	Poor
125	100	85	75	65	50

Model C Comp

Introduced in 1998 this 9mm model features a 4" barrel with compensator, adjustable sights and 10-round magazine.

NIB	Exc.	V.G.	Good	Fair	Poor
150	120	—	—	—	—

Model JH

All steel construction chambered for .45ACP with 4.5" barrel. Magazine capacity is 7 rounds. Weight is 39 oz.

NIB	Exc	V.G.	Good	Fair	Poor
150	125	100	85	75	50

Model 40S&W

Same as above but chambered for .40S&W cartridge. 8-round magazine capacity. Weight is 39 oz.

NIB	Exc	V.G.	Good	Fair	Poor
150	125	100	85	75	50

Model CF

This pistol is chambered for the .380 ACP cartridge and is fitted with a polymer frame. Magazine capacity is 8 rounds. Barrel length is 3.5". Weight is 29 oz.

NIB	Exc	V.G.	Good	Fair	Poor
80	70	50	40	30	25

Carbine

This semiautomatic carbine is chambered for the 9mm cartridge and fitted with a 16.5" barrel and a 10-round magazine. In 1999 this model was offered chambered for 40 S&W cartridge. It has a polymer stock and a rear peep sight. Available in parkerized or chrome finish.

NIB	Exc	V.G.	Good	Fair	Poor
170	150	125	100	85	65

HIGGINS, J. C.

Chicago, Illinois

The Sears, Roebuck & Company of Chicago used the trade name J.C. Higgins on the firearms and other sporting goods it sold between 1946 and 1962. Arms bearing this tradename were manufactured by a variety of American gunmakers.

HIGH STANDARD MANUFACTURING CORPORATION

New Haven, Hamden, and East Hartford Connecticut

The High Standard Manufacturing Company was established in 1926, by Carl Swebilius and Gustave Beck to produce drills and machine tools. In 1932, the firm purchased the Hartford Arms & Equipment Company (q.v.) and began the manufacture of the latter's Model 1925 Semiautomatic Pistol as the Hi-Standard Model "B".

Throughout the High Standard Manufacturing Corporation's business life, its products were highly regarded for both their design and quality. While the company was originally located in New Haven, in early 1950 it moved to Hamden, Connecticut. In 1976 it moved to East Hartford, Connecticut. Operations ceased in 1984. In the spring of 1993 the High Standard Manufacturing Co, Inc. of Houston, Texas acquired the company assets and trademarks as well as the .22 Target Pistols. These original assets were transfered from Connecticut to Houston, Texas in July 1993. The first shipments of Houston manufactured pistols began in March of 1994. Prices listed here are separated for both the Connecticut and Houston models. Collectors will pay a premium for the Connecticut pistols.

Model descriptions, photos, and prices by John J. Stimson, Jr.

Letter Models

These are the first models made using letters to designate the various models. A few guns from this series were sold after WWII. Catalog numbers for this series were assigned after the war in order to utilize the record keeping system of that time. This design series utilized three different take-downs. Types I-A and I-B take-downs have the take-down lever on the left side of the frame. Type I-A take-down has a round retracting rod protuding through the rear of the slide off center to the left side. Type I-B take-down is an improved, more durable design with a rectangular retracting rod. Type II take-down has a take-down lever in the right side of the frame with a round pick-up button on the top of the slide. Type I-A take-down was utilized from 1932 to February 1938 and the Type I-B take-down was utilized from that time until August 1939. Models B and C are the only models with the Type I-A take-down. The other Letter Models utilized Type I-B and II take-downs. Guns with original boxes and original papers can add significant premium but like the guns the condition is very important as is the requirement that the box be numbered to the gun.

Model B

A .22 LR caliber semiautomatic pistol with either a 4.5" or a 6.75" round barrel and a 10-shot magazine. Blues came with checkered hard rubber grips (later production versions have checkered grips impressed with the High Standard monogram). Introduced 1932, with serial numbers beginning at 5000. Early production utilized Hartford parts. Approximately 65,000 made. Add $75 premium for Type-I-B take-down. Add a $75 premium for early models with Hartford Arms front sight, safety, and take-down levers. Box with papers add premium of 15%.

Catalog number 9000 for 4.5" barrel, 9001 for 6.75" barrel.

Exc.	V.G.	Good	Fair	Poor
525	300	225	150	125

Model B-US

A version of the Model B with slight modifications to the frame. 14,000 made for the US government 1942-1943. Monogrammed hard rubber grips. Available with a 4.5" round barrel. Type II take-down only. Box with papers add premium of 20%.

Exc.	V.G.	Good	Fair	Poor
750	500	275	180	150

Model C

Like the Model B except in .22 short. Introduced 1936; approximately 4,700 made. Both plain and monogrammed hard rubber grips. Available with either a 4.5" or a 6.75" round barrel. Early production in separate serial number series beginning with 500 and continuing through 3116. Joined regular serial number series at 42806. There are numerous Model Cs in the regular serial number series earlier than 42806 around 25600 which shipped a date later than the Model Bs in the same serial number range.

Add $75 premium for I-A take-down. Add $175 premuim for I-B take-down. Box with papers add premium of 15%.

Catalog number 9061 for 4.5" barrel, 9062 for 6.75" barrel.

Exc.	V.G.	Good	Fair	Poor
825	525	375	225	150

Model A

Similar to the Model B but with checkered walnut grips over an extended grip and an adjustable sight. Introduced 1938; approximately 7,300 made. Available with either a 4.5" or a 6.75" round barrel. The same light barrel as the model B.

Add $175 premium for I-B take-down. Box with papers add premium of 15%.

Catalog number 9005 for 4.5" barrel, 9006 for 6.75" barrel.

Exc.	V.G.	Good	Fair	Poor
700	500	300	180	150

Model D

Similar to a Model A but with a heavier weight barrel. (The middle weight barrel.) Available with either a 4.5" or a 6.75" barrel and optional checkered walnut grips. Introduced 1938; approximately 2,500 made.

Add $175 premium for I-B take-down. Box with papers add premium of 15%.

Catalog number 9063 for 4.5" barrel, 9064 for 6.75" barrel.

Exc.	V.G.	Good	Fair	Poor
850	550	400	280	180

Model E

Like the Model D but with a still heavier weight barrel. (The heavy weight barrel.) Available with either a 4.5" or a 6.75" barrel. Checkered walnut grips with thumb rest. Introduced 1938; approximately 2,600 made. Add $175 for I-B take-down. Box with papers add premium of 18%.

Catalog number 9067 for 4.5" barrel, 9068 for 6.75" barrel.

Exc.	V.G.	Good	Fair	Poor
1050	650	450	350	200

Model S

Not a production model. Like the model B but with a smooth bore. Nine registered as Model S. Additional five with Model C slides are registered, Model C/S. Note Ivory bead front sight. Others may exist but only 14 are registered with BATF. Values for both variations are equal. 6.75" barrels.

Exc.	V. G.	Good	Fair	Poor
4750	3500	3000	—	—

Hammer Letter Models

Second models made. Like the letter models with external hammers. They still use letters to designate the various models. Mostly produced before the war but a few exist with postwar serial numbers. Catalog numbers for this series were assigned after the war in order to utilize the record keeping system of that time. Type II take-down only. Guns with original boxes and original papers can add significant premium but like the guns the condition is very important as is the requirement that the box be numbered to the gun.

Model H-B, Type 1 Prewar

Like the Model B but with exposed hammer. Introduced 1940; approximately 2,100 made. Box with papers add premium of 15%.

Exc.	V. G.	Good	Fair	Poor
725	475	250	200	175

Model H-B, Type 2 Postwar

Postwar variation has an external safety. Approximately 25,000 made. Box with papers add premium of 15%.

Catalog number 9003 for 4.5" barrel, 9004 for 6.75" barrel.

Exc.	V. G.	Good	Fair	Poor
575	400	240	200	175

Model H-A

Like the Model A but with exposed hammer. Introduced 1940; approximately 1,040 made. Box with papers add premium of 15%.

Catalog number 9007 for 4.5" barrel, 9008 for 6.75" barrel.

Exc.	V. G.	Good	Fair	Poor
1100	575	400	250	200

Model H-D

Like the Model D but with exposed hammer. Introduced 1940; approximately 6,900 made. Box with papers add premium of 15%.

Catalog number 9065 for 4.5" barrel, 9066 for 6.75" barrel.

Exc.	V. G.	Good	Fair	Poor
1100	500	400	250	200

Model H-E

Like the Model E but with exposed hammer. Introduced 1940; approximately 2,100 made. Box with papers add premium of 15%.

Catalog number 9026 for 4.5" barrel, 9027 for 6.75" barrel.

Exc.	V. G.	Good	Fair	Poor
1600	900	700	425	225

Model USA-Model HD

Similar to the Model HD but 4.5" barrel only. Had fixed sights, checkered black hard rubber grips and an external safety. Early models blued; later model parkerized. Introduced 1943; approximately 44,000 produced for the US government. Box with papers add premium of 20%.

Exc.	V.G.	Good	Fair	Poor
750	550	400	250	175

Model USA-Model HD-MS

A silenced variation of the USA Model HD. Approximately 2000 produced for the OSS during 1944 and 1945. 6.75" shrouded barrel. Early models blued; later model parkerized. Only a few registered with BATF for civilian ownership.

Exc.	V.G.	Good	Fair	Poor
6000	5000	—	—	—

Model H-D Military

Similar to the HD but with external safety. Early production had checkered plastic grips; later production changed to checkered walnut. Introduced 1946; approximately 150,000 produced. Box with papers add premium of 15%.

Catalog number 9050 for 4.5" barrel, 9051 for 6.75" barrel.

Exc.	V.G.	Good	Fair	Poor
500	350	240	180	150

Lever Letter Models

Third design models which incorporate interchangeable barrels with a lever take-down. The .22 caliber guns evolved from the model G .380, High Standard's first production removable barrel gun. Like the letter models with external hammers, these .22 caliber models still used letters to designate the various models. New to this series was the adjustable Davis sight. Also introduced in this series was a breach face shrouded by the slide. Significant premiums for guns with the combination of both barrels if verified by factory records that the gun shipped as a combination. Many "combinations" have been created after leaving the factory. Non-factory combinations should have the additional value of the extra barrel. Guns with original boxes and original papers can add significant premium but like the guns, the condition is very important, as is the requirement that the box be numbered to the gun.

G-.380

A .380 caliber semiautomatic pistol with a 5" barrel and 6-shot magazine. Blues with checkered plastic grips. Fixed sights. Introduced 1947, discontinued 1950; approximately 7,400 made. Box with papers add premium of 10%.

High Standard's only production centerfire pistol.

Catalog number 9060.

Exc.	V.G.	Good	Fair	Poor
525	400	225	175	150

G-B

Similar characteristics with the Model B but with interchangeable 4.5" or 6.75" barrels. Sold with either barrel or as a combination with both barrels. Fixed sights. Blued with monogrammed plastic grips. Last short frame model produced. Introduced 1949, discontinued 1950; approximately 4,900 produced. Box with papers add premium of 15%.

Add $225 premium for factory combination.

Catalog number 9010 for 4.5" barrel, 9011 for 6.75" barrel, 9012 for combination.

Exc.	V.G.	Good	Fair	Poor
575	390	225	175	150

G-D

Similar characteristics with the Model D but with interchangeable 4.5" or 6.75" barrels. Sold with either barrel or as a combination with both barrels. Adjustable sights. Blued with checkered walnut grips. Optional checkered thumb rest walnut grips. Introduced 1949, discontinued 1950; approximately 3,300 produced.

Add $325 premium for factory combination, $50 premium for factory target grips. Box with papers add premium of 15%.

Catalog number 9020 for 4.5" barrel, 9021 for 6.75" barrel, 9022 for combination for std grips.
Catalog number 9023 for 4.5" barrel, 9024 for 6.75" barrel, 9025 for combination for tgt grips.

Exc.	V.G.	Good	Fair	Poor
857	450	325	225	175

G-E

Similar characteristics with the Model E but with interchangeable 4.5" or 6.75" barrels. Sold with either barrel or as a combination with both barrels. Adjustable sights. Blued with checkered thumb rest walnut grips. Introduced 1949, discontinued 1950; approximately 2,900 produced.

Add $375 premium for factory combination. Box with papers add premium of 15%.

Catalog number 9030 for 4.5" barrel, 9031 for 6.75" barrel, 9032 for combination.

Exc.	V. G.	Good	Fair	Poor
1275	825	450	300	225

OLYMPIC (commonly called "G-O")

New gun design for competitive shooting in .22 short caliber. 4.5" or 6.75" barrels. Sold with either barrel or as a combination with both barrels. Grooved front and back straps on frame. Adjustable sights. Blued with checkered thumb rest walnut grips. Introduced 1949, discontinued 1950; approximately 2,900 produced. This model uses a special curved magazine. A few guns will utilize a straight magazine only or a specially modified curved magazine.

Add $375 premium for factory combination. Box with papers add premium of 15%. Add $300 for the straight magazine variation.

Catalog number 9040 for 4.5" barrel, 9041 for 6.75" barrel, 9042 for combination.

Exc.	V. G.	Good	Fair	Poor
1500	850	475	325	250

Lever Name Models

Fourth design models evolving from the lever letter series designs with slight changes. This series followed the precedent of naming the models instead of utilizing letters set by the Olympic (G-O). The upscale models, Supermatic and Olympic, incorporated a rib dovetailed to the top of the barrel and a dovetail slot on the bottom of the barrel for mounting balance weights. This series continued the breach face shrouded by the slide. Significant premiums for guns with the combinations of both barrels if verified by factory records that the gun shipped as a combination. Many "combinations" have been created after leaving the factory. Non-factory combinations should have the additional value equal to the value of the extra barrel. Adjustable sight models continued to use the Davis

sight. This series produced 1951 to 1953. Guns with original boxes and original papers can add significant premium but like the guns the condition is very important as is the requirement that the box be numbered to the gun.

Supermatic

.22 LR caliber pistol with 10-shot magazine. Heavy weight round barrel, blued finish; adjustable sights and brown plastic thumb rest grips. Grooved front and back straps on frame. Available with 4.5" or 6.75" barrels or combination with both barrels. Ribbed barrels and provisions for weights. A 2 oz. and a 3 oz. weight were provided with this model, as was a filler strip for when the weights were not used.

Add $250 for factory combination. Box with papers add premium of 15%.

Catalog number 9070 for 4.5" barrel, 9071 for 6.75" barrel, 9072 for combination.

Exc.	V. G.	Good	Fair	Poor
675	425	280	200	150

Olympic

.22 short caliber pistol with 10-shot magazine. Heavy weight round barrel, blued finish, adjustable sights and brown plastic thumb rest grips. Grooved front and back straps on frame. Available with 4.5" or 6.75" barrels or combination with both barrels. Ribbed barrels and provisions for weights. A 2 oz. and a 3 oz. weight were provided with this model, as was a filler strip for when the weights were not used.

Add $250 for factory combination. Box with papers add premium of 15%.

Catalog number 9043 for 4.5" barrel, 9044 for 6.75" barrel, 9045 for combination.

Exc.	V. G.	Good	Fair	Poor
900	575	375	260	200

Field King

.22 LR caliber pistol with 10-shot magazine. Heavy weight round barrel, blued finish, adjustable sights and brown plastic thumb rest grips. Available with 4.5" or 6.75" barrels or combination with both barrels. No rib on barrels or provisions for weights.

Add $225 premium for factory combination. Box with papers add premium of 15%.

Catalog number 9090 for 4.5" barrel, 9091 for 6.75" barrel, 9092 for combination.

Exc.	V. G.	Good	Fair	Poor
575	350	235	160	125

Sport King

.22 caliber pistol with 10-shot magazine. Light weight round barrel, blued finish, fixed sights and brown plastic thumb rest grips. Available with 4.5" or 6.75" barrels or combination with both barrels. Early models did not have a slide hold back when magazine empty. Early variation without hold back were produced in about twice the quantity as the later models incorporating this feature. Add a $25 premium for guns with holdback feature.

Add $200 premium for factory combination. Box with papers add premium of 15%.

Catalog number 9080 for 4.5" barrel, 9081 for 6.75" barrel, 9082 for combination.

Exc.	V. G.	Good	Fair	Poor
425	300	225	160	125

100 Series Models

Fifth design models evolving from the lever name series designs. This series introduced the small pushbutton barrel release take-down and deletes the shrouded breach. The upscale models continued the ribbed barrel and a dovetail slot on the bottom of the barrel for mounting balance weights. Adjustable sight models continued to use the Davis sight. New to this series is the introduction of an aluminum frame on the Flite King and the Sport King lightweight. Also included in this series is a new striker-fired design called the Dura-Matic as a low cost Plinker. Significant premiums for guns with the combinations of both barrels if verified by factory records that the gun shipped as a combination. Many "combinations" have been created after leaving the factory. Non-factory combinations should have the additional value equal to the value of the extra barrel. Guns with original boxes and original papers can add significant premium but like the guns, the condition is very important, as is the requirement that the box be numbered to the gun.

Supermatic S-100

Like the lever take-down Supermatic but with new take-down. Available with 4.5", 6.75", or a combination with both barrel lengths. Grooved front and back straps on frame. This model produced briefly in 1954. A 2 oz. and a 3 oz. weight were provided with this model, as was a filler strip for when the weights were not used.

Add $250 for factory combination. Box with papers add premium of 15%.

Catalog number 9109 for 4.5" barrel, 9110 for 6.75" barrel, 9111 for combination.

Exc.	V. G.	Good	Fair	Poor
775	450	280	200	150

Olympic O-100

Like the lever take-down Olympic but with new take-down. Available with 4.5", 6.75", or a combination with both barrel lengths. Grooved front and back straps on frame. This model produced briefly in 1954. A 2 oz. and a 3 oz. weight were provided with this model, as was a filler strip for when the weights were not used.

Add $250 for factory combination. Box with papers add premium of 15%.

Catalog number 9112 for 4.5" barrel, 9113 for 6.75" barrel, 9114 for combination.

Exc.	V. G.	Good	Fair	Poor
1100	700	375	260	190

Field King FK-100

Like the lever take-down Field King but with new take-down. Available with 4.5", 6.75", or a combination with both barrel lengths. This model produced briefly in 1954.

Add $225 premium for factory combination. Box with papers add premium of 15%.

Catalog number 9106 for 4.5" barrel, 9107 for 6.75" barrel, 9108 for combination.

Exc.	V. G.	Good	Fair	Poor
675	425	240	160	125

Sport King SK-100

Like the lever take-down Sport King but with new take-down. Available with 4.5", 6.75", or a combination with both barrel lengths. This model produced 1954 to 1957.

Add $200 premium for factory combination. Box with papers add premium of 10%.

Catalog number 9100 for 4.5" barrel, 9101 for 6.75" barrel, 9102 for combination.

Exc.	V.G.	Good	Fair	Poor
400	280	225	160	125

Sport King Lightweight SK-100

Aluminum frame like Flite King LW-100 but in .22 LR caliber. Produced 1956 to 1964. Also available nickel plated 1957 to 1960.

Add $150 premium for nickel finish, $200 premium for factory combination. Box with papers add premium of 12%.

Blued: Catalog number 9156 for 4.5" barrel, 9157 for 6.75" barrel, 9158 for combination.
Nickel: Catalog number 9166 for 4.5" barrel, 9167 for 6.75" barrel, 9168 for combination.

Exc.	V.G.	Good	Fair	Poor
475	350	225	160	125

Flite King LW-100

.22 short caliber semiautomatic pistol with 10-shot magazine. Blued finish with black anodized aluminum frame and slide. Brown plastic checkered thumb rest grips. Fixed sights. Available with 4.5", 6.75", or a combination with both barrel lengths. This model produced 1954 to 1957.

Add $200 for factory combination. Box with papers add premium of 12%.

Catalog number 9103 for 4.5" barrel, 9104 for 6.75" barrel, 9105 for combination.

Exc.	V.G.	Good	Fair	Poor
525	325	210	160	125

Dura-Matic M-100

.22 LR caliber semiautomatic pistol with 10-shot magazine. Striker fired, fixed sights, blued finish, brown checkered plastic

one-piece grip. Take-down by thumb nut. Available with 4.5", 6.50", or a combination with both barrel lengths. This model produced briefly in 1954.

Add $150 premium for factory combination. Box with papers add premium of 12%.

Catalog number 9124 for 4.5" barrel, 9125 for 6.5" barrel, 9126 for combination.

Exc.	V.G.	Good	Fair	Poor
325	240	190	160	125

101 Series Models

Sixth design models evolving from the 100 series. This series continued the small pushbutton barrel release take-down. The ribbed barrel was dropped from the upscale models but the dovetail slot on the bottom of the barrel for mounting balance weights continued. Adjustable sight models continued to use the Davis sight. Note the Flight King, Sport King and Sport King lightweight did not upgrade to this series. Significant premiums for guns with the combinations of both barrels if verified by factory records that the gun shipped as a combination. Many "combinations" have been created after leaving the factory. Non-factory combinations should have the additional value equal to the value of the extra barrel. Add $250 for factory combination. This series produced 1954 through 1957. Guns with original boxes and original papers can add significant premium but like the guns, the condition is very important, as is the requirement that the box be numbered to the gun.

Supermatic SK-101

A .22 LR caliber semiautomatic pistol with a 10-shot magazine. Heavy weight round barrel, blued finish, adjustable sights and brown plastic thumb rest grips. Grooved front and back straps on frame. Available with 4.5", 6.75", or a combination with both barrel lengths. The 6.75" barrel incorporates a muzzle brake with one slot on either side of the front sight. Also produced with U.S. marking for the military.

Add $250 premium for factory combination. Box with papers add premium of 13%.

Catalog number 9118 for 4.5" barrel, 9119 for 6.75" barrel, 9120 for combination.

Exc.	V.G.	Good	Fair	Poor
700	400	275	195	150

Olympic O-101

A .22 Short caliber semiautomatic pistol with a 10-shot magazine. Heavy weight round barrel, blued finish, adjustable sights and brown plastic thumb rest grips. Grooved front and back straps on frame. Available with 4.5" , 6.75", or a combination with both barrel lengths. The 6.75" barrel incorporates a muzzle brake with one slot on either side of the front sight.

Add $250 premium for factory combination. Box with papers add premium of 13%.

Catalog number 9121 for 4.5" barrel, 9122 for 6.75" barrel, 9123 for combination.

Exc.	V.G.	Good	Fair	Poor
950	650	360	240	175

Field King FK-101

A .22 LR caliber semiautomatic pistol with a 10-shot magazine. Heavy weight round barrel, blued finish, adjustable sights and brown plastic thumb rest grips. Available with 4.5", 6.75", or a combination with both barrel lengths.

Add $225 premium for factory combination. Box with papers add premium of 13%.

Catalog number 9115 for 4.5" barrel, 9116 for 6.75" barrel, 9117 for combination.

Exc.	V.G.	Good	Fair	Poor
575	400	240	160	125

Dura-Matic M-101

Like the Dura-matic M-100 with slightly different locking method for thumb nut take-down. Produced 1954 to 1970.

Add $150 premium for factory combination. Box with papers add premium of 10%.

Later appeared renamed "Plinker" M-101 in 1971 to 1973. Plinker not available with both barrel combinations. A slightly modified version was sold by Sears Roebuck & Co. as the J. C. Higgins M-80.

Catalog number 9124 for 4.5" barrel, 9125 for 6.5" barrel, 9126 for combination Duramatic.
Catalog number 9133 for 4.5" barrel, 9134 for 6.5" barrel, 9135 for combination for Sears M-80 guns.
Catalog number 9214 for 4.5" barrel, 9215 for 6.5" barrel Plinker.

Exc.	V.G.	Good	Fair	Poor
300	220	190	150	125

Conversion Kits

These kits convert .22 LR to .22 short and include a barrel, an aluminum slide, and magazine for .22 short to .22 LR in which case the slide is steel. Prices are for the kit in original factory boxes.

For 101 Series: Catalog numbers 9150 through 9155

Exc.	V.G.
500	400

NOTE: First advertised for 101 series guns. Later, versions were produced for lever take-down guns. Catalog numbers unknown for conversion kits for lever take-down guns.

102 & 103 Series Models

The 102 Series was a major design change incorporating a new frame with a large pushbutton take-down release. Also new was a superb adjustable sight. There is little difference between the two series. These series are marked Model 102 or Model 103 on right side of the slide. Three variations of ejectors utilized during 102 Series. No premium for these variations. Significant premiums for guns with the combinations of both barrels if verified by factory records that the gun shipped as a combination. Many "combinations" have been created after leaving the factory. Non-factory combinations should have the additional value equal to the value of the extra barrel. The 102 Series was produced 1957 to 1960. The 103 Series was produced 1960 to 1963 except the Sport King, see below. Guns with original boxes and original papers can add significant premium but like the guns, the condition is very important, as is the requirement that the box be numbered to the gun.

A High Standard 102 Supermatic Trophy pistol was sold at auction for $1,380. Fitted with an 8" barrel with weights and brake. Cased with papers. Condition was mint. Amoskeag Auction Company, August 1999

Supermatic Trophy

A .22 LR caliber semiautomatic pistol with a 10-shot magazine. A tapered barrel with an enlarged register at the muzzle end to hold a removable muzzle brake. Super polished blue finish; adjustable sights; 2 and 3 oz. adjustable weights and checkered walnut thumb rest grips. Grooved front and back straps on frame. Available with 6.75", 8" or 10" barrels. Occasionally sold as a combination including two barrels. Premiums for 10" barrels and combinations in original boxes. 5.5" bull barrel available in 103s after April 1962, 7.25" fluted barrels available in 103s after April 1963.

Add $125 premium for 8" barrel and $225 premium for 10.0" barrel. Box with papers add premium of 12%. Occasionally found with the optional light oak case, which will command a premium of about 14%.

Catalog number 9250 for 6.75" barrel, 9251 for 8" barrel, 9252 for 10" barrel.
Catalog number 9254 for 5.5" barrel, 9255 for 7.25" barrel.

Exc.	V.G.	Good	Fair	Poor
1000	675	400	240	200

Supermatic Citation

Like the Supermatic Trophy with checkered plastic grips. Blued finish without the trophy's super polished finish. Grooved front and back straps on frame. 5.5" bull barrel available in 103s after April 1962. Also produced with U.S. marking for the military.

Add $100 premium for 8" barrel and $200 premium for 10.0" barrel. Box with papers add premium of 12%. Occasionally found with optional light oak case, which will command a premium of about 14%.

Catalog number 9260 for 6.75" barrel, 9261 for 8" barrel, 9262 for 10" barrel.
Catalog number 9263 for 5.5" barrel.

Exc.	V.G.	Good	Fair	Poor
700	400	340	215	180

Supermatic Tournament

A .22 LR caliber semiautomatic pistol with a 10-shot magazine. Barrels are round and tapered. Blued finish, adjustable sights and checkered plastic grips. Available with 4.5", 6.75", or a combination with both barrels. Combinations available in 102 Series only. 5.5" bull barrel replaced the 4.5" barrel in early 1962. Also produced with **U.S.** marking for the military.

Add $200 premium for factory combination. Box with papers add premium of 12%.

Catalog number 9270 for 4.5" barrel, 9271 for 6.75" barrel, 9272 for combination.
Catalog number 9275 for 5.5" barrel.

Exc.	V.G.	Good	Fair	Poor
600	400	290	200	175

Olympic

A .22 short caliber version of the Supermatic Citation. Early models marked Olympic Citation. Grooved front and back straps on frame. 6.75", 8" and 10" barrels produced. 5.5" bull barrel available on later 103 production.

Add $125 premium for 8" barrel and $225 premium for 10.0" barrel and $250 premium for "Olympic Citation" marked guns. Box with papers add premium of 12%.

Catalog number 9280 for 6.75" barrel, 9281 for 8" barrel, 9282 for 10" barrel.

Exc.	V.G.	Good	Fair	Poor
1100	600	315	240	200

A High Standard 103 Olympic pistol sold at auction for $1,840. Produced in 1961 and fitted with a 10" barrel with weights and brake. Condition was mint.
Amoskeag Auction Company, August 1999

Olympic ISU

Like an Olympic but only available with a 6.75" barrel with integral muzzle brake. Grooved front and back straps on frame.

Catalog number 9299 for 6.75" barrel. Box with papers add premium of 12%.

Exc.	V.G.	Good	Fair	Poor
1050	600	325	240	200

Olympic Trophy ISU

An Olympic ISU with a Supermatic Trophy finish. Grooved front and back straps on frame. Produced in the 103 Series only. Fewer than 500 produced. Box with papers add premium of 10%.

Catalog number 9289 for 6.75" barrel.

Exc.	V.G.	Good	Fair	Poor
2100	700	330	240	200

Sport King

A .22 LR caliber semiautomatic pistol with a 10-shot magazine. Barrels are lightweight, round, and tapered. Blued finish; fixed sights and checkered plastic grips. Available with 4.5", 6.75", or a combination with both barrel lengths. Produced 1957 to 1970 and 1974 to 1977. Also available 1974 to 1977 with nickel finish. $100 premium for nickel finish and $200 premium for factory combination. Note later production not marked 103. Box with papers add premium of 10%.

Catalog number 9200 for 4.5" barrel, 9201 for 6.75" barrel, 9202 for combination blued.
Catalog number 9208 for 4.5" barrel, 9209 for 6.75" barrel nickel.

Exc.	V.G.	Good	Fair	Poor
350	265	200	175	150

Flite King

A .22 short caliber version of the Sport King Models 102 and 103. Note these models have steel frames.

Add $200 premium for factory combination. Box with papers add premium of 12%.
Catalog number 9220 for 4.5" barrel, 9221 for 6.75" barrel, 9222 for combination.

Exc.	V.G.	Good	Fair	Poor
450	350	225	185	150

Conversion Kits-102-104 Series

These kits convert .22 LR to .22 short and include a barrel, an aluminum slide, and magazine. Prices are for kits in original boxes.

Catalog # 9286 Trophy to 6.75" barrel Olympic

Exc.	V. G.
500	400

Catalog # 9287 Trophy to 8.0" barrel Olympic

Exc.	V. G.
625	515

Catalog # 9288 Trophy to 10.0" barrel Olympic

Exc.	V. G.
725	600

Catalog # 9283 Citation to 6.75" barrel Olympic

Exc.	V. G.
600	500

Catalog # 9284 Citation to 8.0" barrel Olympic

Exc.	V. G.
725	600

Catalog # 9285 Citation to 10.0" barrel Olympic

Exc.	V. G.
825	700

NOTE: Kits below convert .22 short to .22 LR and include a barrel, a steel slide, and magazine.

Catalog # 9263 Olympic to 6.75" Citation

Exc.	V. G.
500	400

Catalog # 9264 Olympic to 8.0" barrel Citation

Exc.	V. G.
625	515

Catalog # 9265 Olympic to 10.0" barrel Citation

Exc.	V. G.
725	600

104 Series Models

The last of the slant grip gun designs. The early production marked model 104. Later production is unmarked. The trigger stop screw moved from the right side of the frame to the trigger on the upscale model with that feature. During the production of this series the accessories were deleted in lieu of a price increase. The serial numbers of later guns produced after mid 1975 utilized a new serial numbering system with the slant grip models utilizing a "G" prefix on the serial number. This series produced 1964 to 1977. Guns with original boxes and original papers can add significant premium but like the guns, the condition is very important, as is the requirement that the box be numbered to the gun.

Supermatic Trophy

A .22 LR caliber semiautomatic pistol with a 10-shot magazine. Super polished blue finish; adjustable sights; 2 and 3 oz. adjustable weights, checkered walnut thumb rest grips. Grooved front and back straps on frame. Available with 5.5" bull or 7.25" fluted barrels. Both barrels accept the removable muzzle brake. Discontinued 1965.

Add $100 premium for high polish blue finish. Box with papers add premium of 12%.

Catalog number 9254 for 5.5" barrel, 9255 for 7.25" barrel.

Exc.	V.G.	Good	Fair	Poor
1000	650	425	310	200

Supermatic Citation

A .22 LR caliber semiautomatic pistol with a 10-shot magazine. Blue finish; adjustable sights; 2 and 3 oz. adjustable weights, checkered walnut thumb rest grips. Grooved front and back straps on frame. Available with 5.5" bull, 6.75", 8" or 10" barrels. All but 5.5" barrel discontinued before 1966. Box with papers add premium of 12%.

Catalog number 9260 for 6.75" barrel, 9261 for 8." barrel, 9262 for 10" barrel.
Catalog number 9263 for 5.5" barrel.

Exc.	V.G.	Good	Fair	Poor
700	425	310	215	200

Supermatic Tournament

Like the late 103 models with 5.5" bull barrel or 6.75" tapered barrel. Discontinued 1965. Box with papers add premium of 12%.

Catalog number 9275 for 5.5" barrel, 9271 for 6.75" barrel.

Exc.	V.G.	Good	Fair	Poor
625	400	290	200	175

Olympic

Like the 103 series 5.5" and 8" barrel models. Box with papers add premium of 12%.

Catalog number 9281 for 8" barrel.
Catalog number 9295 for 5.5" barrel with accessories, 9294 for 5.5" barrel without accessories.

Exc.	V. G.	Good	Fair	Poor
1100	600	315	240	200

Olympic ISU

Like the 102/103 models. 6.75" barrel with integral brake. Box with papers add premium of 12%.

Catalog number 9237 without accessories, 9299 with accessories.

Exc.	V. G.	Good	Fair	Poor
1050	600	315	240	200

Victor

A .22 LR caliber semiautomatic pistol with a 10-shot magazine. 4.5" and 5.5" slab-sided barrels with either ventilated or solid ribs. The adjustable sights are integral with the rib. Blue finish, barrel tapped for weight, checkered walnut thumb rest grips. Grooved front and back straps on frame.

Add $75 premium for steel rib, $200 premium for solid rib, and $200 premium for 4.5" barrel. Box with papers add premium of 15%.

Produced in 1973 and 1974.
Catalog number 9218 for 4.5" barrel, 9219 for 6.75" barrel steel or aluminum vent rib.
Steel rib available 1973 only.
Catalog number 9226 for 4.5" barrel, 9229 for 6.75" barrel aluminum solid rib.

Exc.	V. G.	Good	Fair	Poor
2750	1500	900	400	250

Sharpshooter

A .22 LR caliber semiautomatic pistol with a 10-shot magazine. 5.5" bull barrel, blued finish, adjustable sights, checkered plastic grips. Some produced with Model 103 marked slides. Although the 103 marked guns have 1969 and later serial numbers they were shipped after the introduction of the Sharpshooter in 1971 and were probably converted from unsold Sport Kings. No premium for 103 marked. Variation without series marked on slide is the most plentiful. Produced 1971 to 1977. Box with papers add premium of 12%.

Catalog number 9205.

Exc.	V. G.	Good	Fair	Poor
380	300	230	200	175

106 Series Models

Referred to as military models, this series was designed to provide the same grip angles and feel of the Colt military model 1911. This design was introduced in 1965 and continued through most of 1968. The design utilized the tooling of the 104 Series guns which resulted in the occasional appearance of a bullet shaped brass design in the rear grip strap when the spring hole was not properly plugged. This design appears as both a full bullet shape or only the outline. There is no premium for this feature. The magazines in this series have a red plastic bottom. The right side of the frame is marked MILITARY. During the production of this series the accessories were deleted in lieu of a price increase. This resulted in two catalog numbers for each model. Guns with original boxes and original papers can add significant premium but like the guns, the condition is very important, as is the requirement that the box be numbered to the gun.

Supermatic Trophy

Like the 104 series Supermatic Trophy with the new military frame. Stippled front and back straps on frame.

Add $1000 premium for high polish blue finish, $200 premium for guns with boxes and accessories if factory records verify model numbers. Box with papers add premium of 12%.

Catalog number 9245 for 5.5" barrel, 9246 for 7.25" barrel with accessories.
Catalog number 9247 for 5.5" barrel, 9248 for 7.25" barrel without accessories.

Exc.	V. G.	Good	Fair	Poor
900	500	325	210	175

Supermatic Citation

Like the 104 Series Supermatic Citation with the new military frame. Stippled front and back straps on frame.

Add $150 premium for guns with boxes and accessories if factory records verify model numbers. Box with papers add premium of 12%.

Catalog number 9240 for 5.5" barrel, 9241 for 7.25" barrel with accessories.
Catalog number 9242 for 5.5" barrel, 9243 for 7.25" barrel without accessories.

Exc.	V. G.	Good	Fair	Poor
650	425	315	210	175

Supermatic Tournament

Like the 104 Series Supermatic Tournament with the new military frame. Stippled front and back straps on frame.

Add $125 premium for guns with boxes and accessories if factory records verify model numbers. Box with papers add premium of 12%.

Catalog number 9230 for 4.5" barrel, 9231 for 6.75" barrel with accessories.
Catalog number 9232 for 4.5" barrel, 9233 for 6.75" barrel without accessories.

Exc.	V.G.	Good	Fair	Poor
575	375	290	200	165

Olympic

Listed in catalog but not in shipping records. Catalog number 9235 for 5.5" barrel.

WARNING: There is no evidence that this model was actually produced.

Exc.	V.G.	Good	Fair	Poor
N/A	N/A	N/A	N/A	N/A

Olympic ISU

Like the 104 Series Olympic ISU with the new military frame. Stippled front and back straps on frame.

Add $200 premium for guns with boxes and accessories if factory records verify model numbers. Box with papers add premium of 12%.

Catalog number 9238 for 6.75" barrel with accessories.
Catalog number 9236 for 6.75" barrel without accessories.

Exc.	V.G.	Good	Fair	Poor
1050	600	325	235	200

107 Series Models

The evolutionary successor to the 106 Series. This series had the frame redesigned to eliminate the plugging of the spring hole produced with the old tooling. During the time of this series production, the MILITARY marking on the frame was removed and then later reappeared near the end of the end of the traditional serial number series. The MILITARY marking is absent from the guns with the ML prefixed serial numbers. There is no premium associated with these variations. The Model 107 marking was also deleted about 1972. This was not a change in design series only a change in markings. The serial numbers of later guns produced after mid-1975 utilized a new serial numbering system. The military models utilized a "ML" prefix on the serial number. Early production utilized the red-bottomed magazines. Later guns had a blued steel bottom. The 107 Series was produced from 1968 until 1982. Production at Hamden, CT 1968 to 1976. At East Hartford 1976 to 1982. Collectors prefer Hamden guns. Prices are for Hamden guns. Discount about 5% For East Hartford guns. Guns with original boxes and original papers can add significant premium but like the guns, the condition is very important, as is the requirement that the box be numbered to the gun.

Supermatic Trophy

Like the 106 Series Supermatic Trophy. Box with papers add premium of 12%.

Catalog number 9247 for 5.5" barrel, 9248 for 7.25" barrel.

Exc.	V.G.	Good	Fair	Poor
900	500	325	210	175

Supermatic Trophy 1972 Commemorative

A limited edition of the 107 Supermatic Trophy with 1000 being planned. "T" prefix on serial numbers from 0001 to 1000. Engraved, right side of slide has the five gold ring Olympic logo. Offered with lined presentation case. 107 guns listed in the shipping records, plus one frame. A couple of prototypes believed to exist in the regular serial number series. Prices are for guns in original presentation cases.

Catalog number 9207.

NIB	Exc.	V.G.	Good	Fair	Poor
5000	4000	—	—	—	—

Supermatic Citation

Like the 106 Series Supermatic Citation. Box with papers add premium of 12%.

Catalog number 9242 for 5.5" barrel, 9243 for 7.25" barrel.

Exc.	V.G.	Good	Fair	Poor
600	400	315	210	175

Supermatic Tournament

Like the 106 Series Supermatic Tournament. Smooth front and back straps on frame. Box with papers add premium of 12%.

Catalog number 9232 for 5.5" barrel, 9233 for 6.75" barrel.

Exc.	V.G.	Good	Fair	Poor
550	375	290	200	175

Olympic ISU

Like the 106 Series Olympic ISU. Box with papers add premium of 12%.

Catalog number 9238 for 6.75" barrel.

Exc.	V.G.	Good	Fair	Poor
1050	600	375	225	200

Olympic ISU 1980 Commemorative

A limited edition of the 107 Olympic ISU with 1000 being produced. "USA" prefix on serial numbers from 0001 to 1000. Engraved, right side of slide has the five gold ring Olympic logo. Offered with lined presentation case.

Prices are for guns with box, papers, and presentation case, otherwise deduct $250 For guns in excellent condition.

Catalog number 9239.

Exc.	V.G.	Good	Fair	Poor
1200	750	475	300	215

Victor

A .22 LR caliber semiautomatic pistol with a 10-shot magazine. 4.5" and 5.5" slab-sided barrels with either ventilated or solid ribs. The adjustable sights are integral with the rib. Blue finish, barrel tapped for weight, checkered walnut thumb rest grips. Stippled front and back straps on frame. Early ventilated ribs were steel; aluminum replaced the steel on later ventilated ribs. Still later a clearance groove was added for spent shell ejection behind the barrel. Early models marked THE VICTOR, later guns marked simply VICTOR.

Add $125 premium for steel ribs, $150 premium for solid rib guns, premium for 4.5" barreled guns, $140 premium for Hamden guns (7 digit serial numbers and ML prefix serial numbers below ML 25,000). Box with papers add premium of 12%.

Catalog number 9216 for 4.5" barrel, 9217 for 6.75" barrel steel vent rib 1972/1973.
Catalog number 9206 for 4.5" barrel, 9211 for 6.75" barrel aluminum solid rib 1974/1977.
Catalog number 9216 for 4.5" barrel, 9217 for 6.75" barrel aluminum vent rib 1973/1982.

Exc.	V.G.	Good	Fair	Poor
635	450	325	200	175

Sport King

Like the 103 Series Sport King with the military frame. Box with papers add premium of 12%.

Catalog number 9258 for 4.5" barrel, 9259 for 6.75" barrel blued.

Exc.	V.G.	Good	Fair	Poor
325	250	200	175	150

Sharpshooter

Like the 103 Series Sharpshooter with the military frame. Box with papers add premium of 12%.

Catalog number 9210 for 5.5" barrel.

Exc.	V.G.	Good	Fair	Poor
380	300	230	200	150

Survival Kit

An electroless nickel Sharpshooter with 5.5" barrel in a canvas carrying case with an extra electroless nickel magazine. Deduct $75 for guns without the case and $50 for guns without the extra magazine for guns in excellent condition.

Catalog number 9424 gun.

Exc.	V.G.	Good	Fair	Poor
625	425	325	250	200

10-X

A .22 LR caliber semiautomatic pistol with a 10-shot magazine. Matte blue finish, adjustable sights, checkered walnut thumb rest grips painted black. Stippled front and back straps on frame. Available with 5.5" bull barrel. Assembled by a master gunsmith. Gunsmith's initials stamped in frame under left grip panel. Produced in 1981.

Prices are for guns with box and papers including test target. Otherwise deduct $150.

Catalog number 9372 for 5.5" barrel.

Exc.	V.G.	Good	Fair	Poor
2400	1400	800	400	200

SH Series Models

The final design produced by High Standard. A change in take-down from the large pushbutton introduced with the 102 Series and continuing through the 107 Series, to a hex socket head cap screw take-down. This was a cost reduction design change. The ML prefix of the 107 Series was replaced with "SH." Near the end of production a "V" suffix was added to some visually impaired guns which were sold at discount. These guns were guaranteed to function properly but the company would not allow them to be returned for appearance reasons. This series sells at discount to more desirable series. Both series were produced in 1982 through 1984. Guns with original boxes and original papers can add significant premium but like the guns, the condition is very important, as is the requirement that the box be numbered to the gun.

Supermatic Trophy

Like the 107 Supermatic Trophy with a new take-down. Box with papers add premium of 10%.

Catalog number 9247 for 5.5" barrel, 9248 for 7.25" barrel.

Exc.	V.G.	Good	Fair	Poor
600	375	225	190	160

Supermatic Citation

Like the 107 Supermatic Citation with a new take-down. Box with papers add premium of 10%.

Catalog number 9242 for 5.5" barrel, 9243 for 7.25" barrel.

Exc.	V.G.	Good	Fair	Poor
500	325	215	190	160

Citation II

A new gun like the Supermatic Citation but with the barrel slabbed on the sides like the Victor and smooth front and back straps on frame. 5.5" and 7.25" barrels available. Blued finish, adjustable sights. Electroless nickel version utilized in some survival kits. Box with papers add premium of 10%.

Catalog number 9348 for 5.5" barrel, 9349 for 7.25" barrel.

Exc.	V.G.	Good	Fair	Poor
475	325	215	190	160

Sport King

Like the 107 Sport King with a new take-down. Electroless nickel finish also available. Box with papers add premium of 10%.

Catalog number 9258 for 4.5" barrel, 9259 for 6.75" barrel blued.
Catalog number 9450 for 4.5" barrel, 9451 for 6.75" barrel electroless nickel.

Exc.	V.G.	Good	Fair	Poor
325	250	200	175	140

Victor

Like the 107 Victor with a new take-down. Only available with 5.5" barrel. Box with papers add premium of 10%.

Catalog number 9217 for 5.5" barrel.

Exc.	V.G.	Good	Fair	Poor
550	325	215	175	150

Sharpshooter

Like the 107 Supermatic Sharpshooter with a new take-down. Electroless nickel version utilized in some survival kits. Box with papers add premium of 10%.

Catalog number 9210 for 5.5" barrel.

Exc.	V.G.	Good	Fair	Poor
380	275	200	175	150

10-X

Like the 107 10X with a new take-down. Also available with 7.25" fluted barrel and a 5.5" ribbed barrel like a Victor.

Prices are for guns with box and papers including test target. Otherwise deduct $150. Add $500 premium for 7.25" barrel, $1,000 for ribbed barrel like Victor.

Catalog number 9372 for 5.5" barrel, 9249 for 7.25" barrel, 9234 for 5.5" ribbed.

Exc.	V.G.	Good	Fair	Poor
2100	1400	600	300	250

Survival kit

Either an electroless nickel Sharpshooter or Citation II with 5.5" barrel in a canvas carrying case with an extra electroless nickel magazine. Two different fabrics utilized during production. Deduct $75 for guns without the case and $50 for guns without the extra magazine for guns in excellent condition.

Catalog number 9424 either gun.

Exc.	V.G.	Good	Fair	Poor
625	425	325	250	200

Conversion Kits for Military Frame Guns

These kits convert .22 LR to .22 short and include a barrel, an aluminum slide, and 2 magazines. Prices are for kits in original boxes.

Catalog # 9371 with 5.5" bull barrel & Catalog # 9370 with 5.0" Victor type barrel

Exc.	V.G.
550	350

CURRENTLY MANUFACTURED HOUSTON MODELS

Sport King-currently manufactured model

Chambered for .22 Long Rifle and fitted with a 4.5" or 6.75" barrel. Adjustable rear sight. Weight is about 44 oz.

NIB	Exc	V.G.	Good	Fair	Poor
350	300	225	150	100	80

Supermatic Tournament-currently manufactured model

Chambered for .22 Long Rifle and fitted with a 5.5" barrel. Matte blue finish. Weight is approximately 44 oz.

NIB	Exc	V.G.	Good	Fair	Poor
400	325	250	200	175	100

Supermatic Citation-currently manufactured model

Chambered for the .22 Long Rifle and fitted with a 5.5" barrel. Matte blue or parkerized finish. Weight is about 44 oz.

NIB	Exc	V.G.	Good	Fair	Poor
425	325	275	225	175	100

Supermatic Citation MS-currently manufactured model

Designed for metallic silhouette shooting and introduced in 1996. Fitted with a 10" barrel. Weight is approximately 49 oz.

NIB	Exc	V.G.	Good	Fair	Poor
675	575	425	350	250	125

Supermatic Trophy-currently manufactured model

Offered with 5.5" or 7.25" barrels and chambered for .22 Long Rifle. Adjustable trigger, barrel weights, gold-plated trigger, safety, slide stop and magazine catch. Matte blue or parkerized finish. Weight is about 45 oz.

NIB	Exc	V.G.	Good	Fair	Poor
500	425	350	250	150	100

Olympic Model-currently manufactured model

Chambered for .22 Short and fitted with a 5.5" bull barrel. Blued finish. Weight is approximately 44 oz.

NIB	Exc	V.G.	Good	Fair	Poor
525	425	300	250	200	100

Olympic ISU-currently manufactured model

Similar to the previous model but fitted with a 6.75" barrel with internal stabilizer. Magazine capacity is 5 rounds. Checkered walnut grips. Weight is approximately 45 oz. This model was discontinued in 1995.

NIB	Exc	V.G.	Good	Fair	Poor
500	400	350	300	200	150

Olympic Rapid Fire-currently manufactured model

Introduced in 1996. Chambered for the .22 short cartridge with a 4" barrel, integral muzzle brake and forward mounted compensator. Special grips. Weight is about 46 oz.

NIB	Exc	V.G.	Good	Fair	Poor
1995	1550	1200	900	600	—

Victor-currently manufactured model

With 4.5" barrel and blue or parkerized finish.

NIB	Exc	V.G.	Good	Fair	Poor
525	425	350	300	200	125

10-X-currently manufactured model

Fitted with 5.5" barrel. Weight is about 44 oz.

NIB	Exc	V.G.	Good	Fair	Poor
850	700	550	450	350	200

10-X-Shea model

Fitted with a 4.5" or 5.5" barrel. Limited to 150 pistols a year.

NIB	Exc	V.G.	Good	Fair	Poor
1100	850	700	500	350	200

DERRINGERS

A .22 caliber or .22 Magnum caliber Over/Under double action derringer with 3.5" barrels. Early models marked "HI-STANDARD" / "DERRINGER" and had the eagle logo on the left side of the barrel. These models were marked D-100 for the .22 caliber and DM-101 for the .22 Magnum on the left side of the frame. Date range 1962 to about 1967.

Later models were marked "HI-STANDARD" / "Derringer" and had the trigger logo. These models were also marked D-100 for the .22 caliber and DM-101 for the .22 Magnum on the left side of the frame. Date range 1967 to about 1968.

Still later models were marked "HIGH-STANDARD" / "DER-RINGER" and had the trigger logo. These models were also marked D-100 for the .22 caliber and DM-101 for the .22 Magnum on the left side of the frame. Date range about 1969.

The latest models were marked simply "DERRINGER" without HI STANDARD, HIGH-STANDARD or either logo. These models were also marked D-101 for the .22 caliber and DM-101 for the .22 Magnum on the left side of the frame. Date range about 1969 to 1983.

Serial numbers: included with the other High Standard handgun serial numbers from about 1,263,4XX until changing to a "D" prefix beginning with serial number D 01001 in July 1975. E. Hartford derringer D 13000 in April 1977 through D 92099 in July 1983.

Catalog number 9193 for blued with white grips .22 cal.
Catalog number 9194 for blued with white grips .22 Magnum cal.

Exc.	V.G.	Good	Fair	Poor
225	165	125	90	75

Catalog number 9193 for nickel with black grips .22 cal.
Catalog number 9194 for nickel with black grips .22 Magnum cal.

Exc.	V.G.	Good	Fair	Poor
250	185	125	90	75

Catalog number 9193 for electroless nickel with Walnut grips .22 cal. (1982).
Catalog number 9194 for electroless nickel with Walnut grips .22 Magnum cal. (1982).

Exc.	V.G.	Good	Fair	Poor
275	200	135	90	75

Silver-Plated Derringer

A .22 Magnum derringer with a presentation case. Gray grips. 501 made. Serial numbers SP 0 through SP 500. Produced in 1981. Catalog number 9341.

Exc.	V.G.	Good	Fair	Poor
375	250	150	125	100

Gold-Plated Derringer

A .22 caliber or .22 Magnum caliber derringer with a presentation case. Consecutive numbered pair in a presentation case were also available.

Serial numbers: The earliest were in a separate series beginning with 1 through 123 less than 100 guns, although few were included with the other High Standard handgun serial numbers. These guns were in the 1960s time frame.

A DM prefix was used in 1974/1975 time frame. DM 0000 through DM 416.
A GP prefix was used in 1980 time frame. GP 0000 through GP 1000 less than 1000 guns.
A few special prefix serial numbers exist on about 10 guns, probably by special order.
Catalog number 9195 for Gold with black grips .22 cal.
Catalog number 9196 for Gold with black grips .22 Magnum cal.
Catalog number 9196 for Gold with Walnut grips .22 Magnum cal. GP prefix guns.
Catalog number 9197 for Gold with black grips .22 cal. consecutive numbered pair.
Catalog number 9198 for Gold with black grips .22 Magnum cal. consecutive numbered pair.

Exc.	V.G.	Good	Fair	Poor
350	225	175	150	100

Prices are for GP serial number guns.
$150 premium for DM prefix guns in Exc. condition.
$250 premium for 1960s gold guns in Exc. condition.
Significant premium for cased consecutively numbered pair.

High Standard Revolvers
POLICE STYLE REVOLVERS
Sentinel Aluminum frames

A nine shot single action or double action revolver with swing out cylinder for .22 short, long, or long rifle cartridges. Fixed sights. Beginning with R-102 series the ejector had a spring return. Available in configurations below.

Catalog numbers

3.0" barrel, brown square butt plastic grips.
blue   9127: 1955-1960   nickel 9136: 1956-1960

5.0" barrel, brown square butt plastic grips.
blue   9128: 1955-1955

6.0" barrel, brown square butt plastic grips.
blue   9128: 1956-1964   nickel 9137: 1956-1964

4.0" barrel, brown square butt plastic grips.
blue   9159: 1957-1964   nickel 9160: 1957-1964

2.375" barrel, Ivory colored round butt plastic grips.
blue   9144: 1957-1966   nickel 9145: 1957-1966

Exc.	V.G.	Good	Fair	Poor
135	110	95	75	50

Add $15 premium for nickel. Deduct $15 for early models without spring return ejector.

From 1957 through 1962 High Standard offered the 2.375" snub barreled sentinel in three different color anodized frames. These guns had Nickel plated cylinders, triggers, and hammers. The grips were round butt ivory colored plastic.

Gold
Catalog Number 9161

Exc.	V.G.	Good	Fair	Poor
300	225	160	100	75

Turquoise
Catalog Number 9162

Exc.	V.G.	Good	Fair	Poor
325	240	160	100	75

Pink
Catalog Number 9163

Exc.	V.G.	Good	Fair	Poor
325	240	160	100	75

The Sentinel Imperial

Has two piece walnut square butt grips, ramp front and adjustable rear sights and was produced 1962 through 1964.

4.0" barrel Catalog Number 9187

6.0" barrel Catalog Number 9188

Exc.	V.G.	Good	Fair	Poor
150	125	100	75	50

The Sentinel Deluxe

Has two piece walnut square butt grips and fixed sights.

4.0" barrel
blue   Catalog Number 9146: 1965-1969 & 1972-1973
nickel Catalog Number 9148: 1965-1973

6.0" barrel
blue   Catalog Number 9147: 1965-1969 & 1972-1973
nickel Catalog Number 9149: 1965-1973.

Exc.	V.G.	Good	Fair	Poor
150	125	100	75	50

Add $20 premium for Nickel.

The Sentinel Snub

Has a 2.375 barrel with round butt grips.

Brown round butt plastic grip.
blue   9344: 1967-1969 & 1972-1973

Ivory colored round butt plastic grip.
nickel 9345: 1967-1969 & 1972-1973

Exc.	V.G.	Good	Fair	Poor
150	125	100	75	50

Add $15 premium for nickel

Sentinel Steel Frames

This model is like the Mark I sentinels without the Mark I markings.

Catalog numbers

2.0" barrel Fixed Sights   9390: 1977–1984
4.0" barrel Adjustable Sights 9392: 1977–1984

Exc.	V.G.	Good	Fair	Poor
150	125	100	75	50

Kit Gun

A nine shot single action or double action revolver with swing out cylinder for .22 short, long, or long rifle cartridges. Blue finish, aluminum frame, 4.0" barrel, and adjustable sights. Wood round butt grips. R-109.

Catalog number 9304   Produced 1971 through 1973.

Exc.	V.G.	Good	Fair	Poor
150	125	100	75	50

Sentinel Mark I

A nine shot single action or double action revolver with swing out cylinder for .22 short, long, or long rifle cartridges. Steel frame, and fixed sights. Available with blue and nickel finishes in 2.0", 3.0", and 4.0" barrels. Adjustable sights available on 3.0" and 4.0" barreled guns only. Wood square butt grips.

Catalog numbers

2.0" barrel fixed sights
blue   9350: 1974–1976   nickel 9351: 1974–1976.

3.0" barrel fixed sights
blue   9352: 1974–1974   nickel 9354: 1974–1974

3.0" barrel adjustable sights
blue   9353: 1974–1974   nickel 9355: 1974–1974

4.0" barrel fixed sights
blue   9356: 1974–1976   nickel 9358: 1974–1976.

4.0" barrel adjustable sights
blue   9357: 1974–1984   nickel 9359: 1974–1976

Exc.	V.G.	Good	Fair	Poor
180	150	120	100	75

Add $25 premium for adjustable sights. Add $25 for nickel.

Sentinel Mark IV

Like the Mark I above except in .22 Magnum.

Catalog numbers:

2.0" barrel fixed sights
blue   9360: 1974–1984   nickel 9361: 1974–1976

3.0" barrel fixed sights
blue   9362: 1974–1976   nickel 9363: 1974–1976

3.0" barrel Adjustable sights
blue   9364: 1974–1976   nickel 9365: 1974–1976

4.0" barrel fixed sights
blue   9366: 1974–1976   nickel 9367: 1974–1976

4.0" barrel adjustable sights
blue   9368: 1974–1984   nickel 9369: 1974–1976

Exc.	V.G.	Good	Fair	Poor
200	160	120	75	50

Add $25 premium for nickel. $25 premium for adjustable sights.

Sentinel Mark II

A .357 Magnum single action or double action 6-shot revolver with swing out cylinder. Blue finish, steel frame, fixed sights. Produced by Dan Wesson for High Standard Sold 1974 through 1975.

Catalog numbers

2.5" barrel 9401; 4.0" barrel 9402; 6.0" barrel 9403

Exc.	V.G.	Good	Fair	Poor
225	175	125	100	75

Sentinel Mark III

Like the Mark II above except with adjustable sights. Sold 1974 through 1975.

Catalog numbers

2.5" barrel 9407; 4.0" barrel 9408; 6.0" barrel 9409

Exc.	V.G.	Good	Fair	Poor
250	200	150	100	75

Camp Gun

A nine-shot single action or double action revolver with swing out cylinder for .22 short, long, or long rifle cartridges or for.22 mag. Also available as a combination with both cylinders. Blue finished steel frame, adjustable sights.

Catalog numbers

.22 S / L / LR   9342: 1976–1976
.22 Magnum   9343: 1976–1976
Combination   9393: 1977–1984

Exc.	V.G.	Good	Fair	Poor
180	140	100	75	50

Power Plus

A five-shot single action or double action revolver with swing out cylinder for .38 special cartridges. Blue finished steel frame.

Catalog number 9438   Produced 1983–1984

Exc.	V.G.	Good	Fair	Poor
500	350	175	110	80

Crusader

A .44 Magnum or .45 Colt caliber double action swing out cylinder revolver with a unique geared action. Adjustable sights. 6-shot cylinder. The first fifty one guns had the long barrels, special engraving, a gold crusader figure on the side plate, and an aniversary rollmark to commemorate High Standard's fiftieth anniversary.

Catalog numbers

.357 Mag. 4.25" barrel. Cataloged 1979-1980	9458: NEVER PRODUCED	
.357 Mag. 6.50" barrel. Cataloged 1979-1980	9459: NEVER PRODUCED	
.44 Mag. 4.25" barrel. Cataloged 1979-1980	9452: NEVER PRODUCED	
.44 Mag. 6.50" barrel. Cataloged 1979-1980	9453: NEVER PRODUCED	
.44 Mag. 8.375" barrel. Cataloged 1979-1980	9454: NEVER PRODUCED	
.45 Colt 4.25" barrel. Cataloged 1979-1980	9455: NEVER PRODUCED	
.45 Colt 6.50" barrel. Cataloged 1979-1980	9456: NEVER PRODUCED	
.45 Colt 8.375" barrel. Cataloged 1979-1980	9457: NEVER PRODUCED	
.44 Mag. 8.375" barrel. First 51 of 501 commemoratives	9601: 1978-1983	
44 Mag. 6.50" barrel. Balance of 501 commemoratives	9603: 1978-1983	
.45 Colt 8.375" barrel. First 51 of 501 commemoratives	9600: 1978-1983	
.45 Colt 6.50" barrel. Balance of 501 commemoratives	9602: 1978-1983	

Prices for serial numbers 0 through 50 with the 8.375" barrels.

Exc.	V.G.	Good	Fair	Poor
1200	1000	800	600	450

Prices for serial numbers 51 through 500 with the 6.50" barrels.

Exc.	V.G.	Good	Fair	Poor
550	475	400	325	250

WESTERN STYLE REVOLVERS

Double Nine

A nine shot single action or double action revolver for .22 short, long, or long rifle cartridges for all aluminum frame guns. One model has grip straps and triggerguard with gold plating contrasting with the blue frame.

Catalog numbers

Aluminum frame Blued with ivory colored plastic grip	9169: 1958–1965
Aluminum frame Nickel with black plastic grips	9170: 1958– 1970
Aluminum frame Sears version, blued, "Ranger"	9171
Aluminum frame Sears version, nickel, "Ranger"	9174
Aluminum frame Blue/Gold colored trim, stag-style grips	9129: 1966–1966
Aluminum frame Blue, stag-style grips	9329: 1967–1970

Exc.	V.G.	Good	Fair	Poor
200	165	100	75	50

Add $20 premium for Nickel.

Double Nines With Steel Frame

guns available as .22 S / L / LR, .22 mag, or a combination with both cylinders.

Catalog numbers

Steel frame, Blue, Combination	9320: 1971 – 1979
Steel frame, Blue, .22 Mag.	9321: 1971–1973
Steel frame, Nickel, Combination	9322: 1971–1973
Steel frame, Nickel, .22 Mag.	9323: 1971–1976
Steel frame Blue, Combination, adjustable sights,	9324: 1971–1984
Steel frame, Blue, .22 Mag. adjustable sights,	9325: 1971–1973

Exc.	V.G.	Good	Fair	Poor
225	175	115	80	50

Add $25 premium for combination models $20 premium for Nickel.

Longhorn

 A nine shot single action or double action revolver for .22 short, long, or long rifle cartridges for all aluminum frame guns. Blue finish, fixed sights, and square butt grips. One model has grip straps and triggerguard with gold plating contrasting with the blue frame.

Catalog numbers

Aluminum frame 4.5" barrel, ivory colored plastic grips	9175: 1961–1961
Aluminum frame 5.5" barrel, ivory colored plastic grips	9176: 1961–1961
Aluminum frame 9.5" barrel, ivory colored plastic grips	9177: 1961–1961
Aluminum frame 4.5" barrel, pearl-style plastic grips	9178: 1961–1965
Aluminum frame 5.5" barrel, stag-style plastic grips	9179: 1961 –1965
Aluminum frame 9.5" barrel, walnut grips	9180: 1961–1965
Aluminum frame Sears version	9184
Aluminum frame 9.5" barrel, walnut grips, gold colored trim	9199: 1966–1966
Aluminum frame 9.5" barrel, walnut grips	9399: 1967–1970

Exc.	V.G.	Good	Fair	Poor
200	160	125	100	75

Longhorns With Steel Frame

Guns available as .22 S / L / LR, .22 mag., or a combination with both cylinders.

Steel frame 9.5" barrel, .22 S / L / LR	9397: 1984–1984
Steel frame 9.5" barrel .22 Mag	9327: 1971–1974
Steel frame 9.5" barrel, combination	9326: 1971–1976
Steel frame 9.5" barrel, combination, adjustable sights	9328: 1976–1984

Exc.	V.G.	Good	Fair	Poor
250	180	125	100	75

Marshall

A nine shot single action or double action revolver for .22 short, long, or long rifle cartridges. Blue finish. Aluminum frame, 5.50" long barrel, fixed sights and square butt stag style plastic grips. Offered in a special promotion package with a holster, trigger lock and spray can of G-96 gun scrubber.

Catalog number 9330 Produced 1971 through 1973

Exc.	V.G.	Good	Fair	Poor
180	150	120	100	75

Posse

A nine shot single action or double action revolver for .22 short, long, or long rifle cartridges. Blue finish with brass colored grip straps and triggerguard. Aluminum frame, 3.50" long barrel, fixed sights and square butt walnut grips.

Catalog numbers

9181 Produced 1961–1965   Sears version   9183

Exc.	V.G.	Good	Fair	Poor
150	125	100	75	50

Natchez

A nine shot single action or double action revolver for .22 short, long, or long rifle cartridges. Aluminum frame, 4.50" long barrel, fixed sights and bird's head style ivory colored plastic grips.

Catalog numbers

9182   Produced 1961–1965   Sears version   9186

Exc.	V.G.	Good	Fair	Poor
200	175	130	100	75

Hombre

A nine shot single action or double action revolver for .22 short, long, or long rifle cartridges. Blue or nickel finish. Aluminum frame, 4.0" long barrel, fixed sights and square butt walnut grips.

Catalog numbers

Blue   9300: 1970–1972
Nickel 9301: 1970–1972

Exc.	V.G.	Good	Fair	Poor
175	150	125	100	75

Durango

A nine shot single/double action revolver for .22 short, long, or long rifle cartridges. Blue or nickel finish. Aluminum or steel frame, 4.50" or 5.50" long barrel, fixed or adjustable sights and square butt walnut grips. Two models have their grip straps and triggerguard with contrasting plating to the blue frame.

Catalog numbers

Aluminum frame 4.5" barrel, blue with brass trim	9302: 1970– 1973
Aluminum frame 5.5" barrel, blue	9307: 1971–1973
Aluminum frame 5.5" barrel, nickel	9308: 1971–1973
Steel frame 5.5" barrel, blue with nickel trim	9316: 1974– 1974
Steel frame 5.5" barrel, nickel	9317: 1974–1974
Steel frame 5.5" barrel, adjustable sights, blue / nickel	9318: 1974–1974

Exc.	V.G.	Good	Fair	Poor
175	150	125	100	75

Add $20 premium for nickel.

High Sierra

A nine shot single/double action revolver for .22 short, long, or long rifle cartridges. Also available as a combination model with a second cylinder in .22 Mag. Blued finish with gold plated grip straps and triggerguard. Steel frame, 7.0" long octagonal barrel, fixed or adjustable sights and square butt walnut grips.

Catalog numbers

.22 S / L / LR, in a case	9313: 1974-1974
Combination, in a case	9314: 1974-1974
Combination, in a case, adjustable sights	9315: 1974-1974
Combination, without a case	9374: 1975-1975
Combination, without a case, adjustable sights	9375: 1975-1984
.22 S / L / LR, without a case	9379: 1984-1984

Exc.	V.G.	Good	Fair	Poor
225	175	140	100	75

Add $40 premium for presentation case. Add $25 premium for combination models.

BLACK POWDER REVOLVERS

These guns were a series of .36 caliber cap and ball revolvers which began production in 1974 and ran through 1976.

Griswold & Gunnison

Blued finish with a brass frame. Six shot single action. Commemorative gun came wtih a pine presentation case and a brass belt plate depicting the Georgia state seal.

Catalog number 9331 (Serial numbers 00501 through 02600)

Catalog number 9333 Commemorative (Serial numbers 00001 through 00500)

Price is for gun in case with accessories. Deduct $100 for gun only in Exc. condition.

Exc.	V.G.
350	175

Leech & Rigdon

Blued finish with a steel frame. Six shot single action. Commemorative gun came with a presentation case and a reproduction of a Civil War belt buckle.

Catalog number 9332 (Serial numbers 00501 through 01199)

Catalog number 9334 Commemorative (Serial numbers 00001 through 00500)

Price is for gun in case with accessories. Deduct $100 for gun only in Exc. condition.

Exc.	V.G.
350	175

Schneider & Glassick

Blued finish with a steel frame. Six shot single action. Commemorative gun came with a presentation case and a modern version of a Confederate "D" guard Bowie knife.

Catalog number 9335 (Serial numbers 0 through 1000)

Exc.	V.G.
375	200

Bicentennial 1776-1976

Blued finish with a steel frame. Six shot single action. Guns came with two versions of presentation case. One case is pine, marked High Standard and the trigger logo is on the lid with a powder flask and silver dollar-sized medallion inside. The other is a brown leatherette covered case with American Bicentennial 1776-1976 and contains a pewter Bicentennial belt buckle. The U.S.-prefixed guns are specials but the specifics are presently not known.

Catalog number 9336 (Serial numbers A 0000 through A 2028)

Catalog number 9337 Steel (Serial numbers US 001 through US 010)

Catalog number 9339 Steel (Serial numbers US 011 through US 050)

Catalog number 9338 Brass (Serial numbers US 001 through 010)

Catalog number 9340 Brass (Serial numbers US 011 through US 050)

Exc.	V.G.
350	250

High Standard Shotguns

High Standard began making shotguns for Sears Roebuck in the late 1940's. In 1960 High Standard began marketing shotguns under their own name and the approximately 200 models in the following listing is derived from the catalogs and price lists of the 1960's and 1970's. Additionally, there are over 70 catalog numbers not listed which represent models with High Standard markings, but with special roll marking or other features which High Standard produced for several large distributors. A redesign of the shotgun line occurred with new models introduced in 1966. In 1973 High Standard introduced their new "Trophy Line" of shotguns and this marked a change in catalog numbers from the number beginning with the numeral 8 to the number beginning with the numeral 6. At this time the previous catalog numbers were referred to as the "Regular Line". Some regular line guns were catalogued in 1973 but this was the last year for them except the Police models. The 12 gauge pumps in the Trophy Line were guns which had interchangeable barrels. Serial numbers began appearing on the High Standard shotguns during mid to late 1967.

The choke markings used by High Standard are: * Full, ** Modified, *** Improved Cylinder, and **** Skeet Bore. Cylinder Bore has no mark.

SEMIAUTOMATIC SHOTGUNS

Supermatic Field

Gas operated semiautomatic shotgun. Blued finish, plain pistol grip walnut stock and forearm. 4-round magazine capacity. Supermatic Field models were superceded by models in the Supermatic Deluxe group beginning in 1966.

Catalog numbers

12 ga.	28" barrel	Full choke	8200: 1960-1965
12 ga.	28" barrel	Modified choke	8201: 1960-1965
12 ga.	26" barrel	Improved cylinder	8202: 1960-1965
12 ga.	30" barrel	Full choke	8203: 1962-1965
20 ga.	28" barrel	Full choke	8270: 1963-1965
20 ga.	28" barrel	Modified choke	8271: 1963-1965
20 ga.	27" barrel	Improved cylinder	8273: 1965-1965

Slight premium for 20 gauge.

Exc.	V.G.	Good	Fair	Poor
200	175	150	100	75

Supermatic Special

Like the Supermatic Field except with 27" barrel with 6 position click stop adjustable choke. Supermatic Special models were superceded by models in the Supermatic Deluxe group beginning in 1966.

Catalog numbers

12 ga.	27" barrel	Adjustable Choke	8250: 1961-1965
20 ga.	27" barrel	Adjustable Choke	8272: 1963-1965

Exc.	V.G.	Good	Fair	Poor
200	175	150	100	75

Supermatic Deluxe

Gas operated semiautomatic shotgun. Blued finish, Checkered pistol grip walnut stock and forearm. 4 round magazine capacity. The adjustable choke had 6 click stop positions. Recoil pad beginning 1966.

Catalog numbers

12 ga.	28" barrel	Full choke	8204: 1966-1972
12 ga.	28" barrel	Modified choke	8205: 1966-1972
12 ga.	26" barrel	Improved cylinder	8206: 1966-1972
12 ga.	30" barrel	Full choke	8207: 1966-1972
12 ga.	27" barrel	Adjustable choke	8251: 1967-1971
12 ga.	28" barrel	Full choke	8210: 1960-1962
12 ga.	28" barrel	Modified choke	8211: 1960-1962
12 ga.	26" barrel	Improved cylinder	8212: 1960-1962
12 ga.	30" barrel	Full choke	8213: 1961-1962
12 ga.	30" barrel	Full choke, vent rib	8214: 1961-1965
12 ga.	28" barrel	Full choke, vent rib	8215: 1961-1965
12 ga.	28" barrel	Mod. choke, vent rib	8216: 1961-1965
12 ga.	26" barrel	Imp. cylinder, vent rib	8217: 1961-1965
12 ga.	30" barrel	Full choke, vent rib	8224: 1966-1972
12 ga.	28" barrel	Full choke, vent rib	8225: 1966-1972
12 ga.	28" barrel	Mod. choke, vent rib	8226: 1966-1972
12 ga.	26" barrel	Adj. choke, vent rib	8232: 1966-1972
12 ga.	28" barrel	Modified choke	6205: 1973-1975
12 ga.	30" barrel	Full choke	6207: 1973-1975
12 ga.	30" barrel	Full choke, vent rib	6224: 1973-1975
12 ga.	28" barrel	Full choke, vent rib	6225: 1973-1975
12 ga.	28" barrel	Mod. choke, vent rib	6226: 1973-1975
12 ga.	27" barrel	Adj. choke, vent rib	6232: 1973-1975
20 ga.	28" barrel	Full choke	8274: 1963-1965
20 ga.	28" barrel	Modified	8276: 1963-1965
20 ga.	28" barrel	Full choke	8280: 1966-1972
20 ga.	28" barrel	Modified choke	8283: 1966-1972
20 ga.	26" barrel	Improved cylinder	8279: 1966-1972
20 ga.	27" barrel	Adjustable choke	8275: 1966-1972
20 ga.	28" barrel	Full choke, vent rib	8284: 1966-1973
20 ga.	28" barrel	Mod. choke, vent rib	8285: 1966-1973

20 ga.	27" barrel	Imp. cylinder, vent rib	8282: 1966-1973
20 ga.	26" barrel	Imp. cylinder	6279: 1973-1975
20 ga.	28" barrel	Full choke	6280: 1973-1975
20 ga.	27" barrel	Click adj., vent rib	6282: 1973-1975
20 ga.	28" barrel	Modified choke	6283: 1973-1975
20 ga.	28" barrel	Full choke, vent rib	6284: 1973-1975
20 ga.	28" barrel	Mod. choke, vent rib	6285: 1973-1975

Exc.	V.G.	Good	Fair	Poor
250	200	160	110	75

Add $75 Premium for vent rib versions.

Supermatic Citation

Same as Trophy except without ventilated rib. 6 click stop adjustable choke. Catalog number 8220 has a compensator integral with the adjustable choke.

Catalog numbers

| 12 ga. | 27" barrel | Adjustable choke | 8220: 1960-1960 |
| 12 ga. | 27" barrel | Adjustable choke | 8221: 1961-1962 |

Exc.	V.G.	Good	Fair	Poor
220	180	130	95	65

Supermatic Trophy

Gas operated semiautomatic shotgun. Blued finish, checkered walnut stock and foreend. 4-round magazine capacity. 6 click stop adjustable choke. Catalog number 8230 has a compensator integral with the adjustable choke.

Catalog numbers

12 ga.	27" barrel	Adj. choke, vent rib	8230: 1960-1960
12 ga.	27" barrel	Adj. choke, vent rib	8231: 1961-1965
20 ga.	27" barrel	Adj. choke, vent rib	8281: 1963-1965

Exc.	V.G.	Good	Fair	Poor
230	190	140	100	75

Supermatic Duck

Gas operated semiautomatic shotgun chambered for 3" magnum and suitable for all 2-3/4" shells. Blued finish. Checkered pistol grip walnut stock and forearm. 4-round magazine capacity. Magazine capacity 5 - 2-3/4" shells, 4 - 3" shells. Recoil pad.

Catalog numbers

12 ga. 3"	30" barrel	Full choke, vent rib	8240: 1960-1960
12 ga. 3"	30" barrel	Full choke	8241: 1961-1962
12 ga. 3"	30" barrel	Full choke, vent rib	8242: 1961-1965
12 ga. 3"	30" barrel	Full choke	8243: 1963-1965
12 ga. 3"	30" barrel	Full choke	8244: 1966-1973
12 ga. 3"	30" barrel	Full choke, vent rib	8247: 1966-1973
12 ga. 3"	30" barrel	Full choke, vent rib	6247: 1973-1975

Exc.	V.G.	Good	Fair	Poor
270	200	150	100	75

Add $75 premium for vent rib versions.

Supermatic Deer Gun

Like Supermatic Deluxe with rifle sight. Recoil pad. Receiver tapped for peep sight on catalog number 8246.

Catalog numbers

| 12 ga. | 22" barrel | Cylinder bore | 8245: 1965-1965 |
| 12 ga. | 22" barrel | Cylinder bore | 8246: 1966-1972 |

Exc.	V.G.	Good	Fair	Poor
225	175	150	100	75

Supermatic Skeet

Same features as Supermatic Deluxe except select American walnut stock and forearm and no recoil pad.

Catalog numbers

12 ga.	26" barrel	Skeet choke, vent rib	8260: 1962-1963
12 ga.	26" barrel	Skeet choke, vent rib	8262: 1964-1965
12 ga.	26" barrel	Skeet choke, vent rib	8264: 1966-1972
12 ga.	26" barrel	Skeet choke, vent rib	6264: 1973-1975
20 ga.	26" barrel	Skeet choke, vent rib	8277: 1964-1965
20 ga.	26" barrel	Skeet choke, vent rib	8287: 1966-1972
20 ga.	26" barrel	Skeet choke, vent rib	6287: 1973-1975

Exc.	V.G.	Good	Fair	Poor
300	250	190	125	85

Supermatic Trap

Same features as Supermatic Deluxe except select American walnut stock and forearm. Recoil pad. Catalog number 8266 is the Executive Trap model with Fajen Monte Carlo stock.

Catalog numbers

12 ga.	30" barrel	Full choke, vent rib	8261: 1962-1963
12 ga.	30" barrel	Full choke, vent rib	8263: 1964-1965
12 ga.	30" barrel	Full choke, vent rib	8265: 1966-1972
12 ga.	30" barrel	Full choke, vent rib	8266: 1970-1972
12 ga.	30" barrel	Full choke, vent rib	6265: 1973-1975

Exc.	V.G.	Good	Fair	Poor
250	200	150	100	75

PUMP SHOTGUNS

Flite King Field

Slide action shotgun. Blued finish, plain pistol grip walnut stock and forearm. 5-round magazine capacity. Catalog number 8450, magazine capacity: 5 - 2 1/2" shells, 4 - 3" shells.

Catalog numbers

12 ga.	28" barrel	Full choke	8100:1960-1965
12 ga.	28" barrel	Modified choke	8101:1960-1965
12 ga.	26" barrel	Improved cylinder	8102:1960-1965
12 ga.	30" barrel	Full choke	8103: 1961-1965
16 ga.	28" barrel	Full choke	8300: 1961-1964
16 ga.	28" barrel	Modified choke	8301:1961-1964
16 ga.	26" barrel	Improved cylinder	8302: 1961-1964
20 ga.	28" barrel	Full choke	8400: 1961-1965
20 ga.	28" barrel	Modified choke	8401: 1961-1965

20 ga.	26" barrel	Improved cylinder	8402: 1961-1965
.410 bore	26" barrel	Full coke	8450: 1962-1965

Exc.	V.G.	Good	Fair	Poor
175	150	125	100	65

Flite King Brush

Like the Flite King Field except has adjustable rifle sights. Receiver is tapped for the Williams sight and provision exist for sling swivels. Deluxe models have Williams receiver sight, a leather sling with swivels, and a recoil pad.

Catalog numbers

12 ga.	20" barrel	Cylinder bore	8105: 1962-1965
12 ga.	20" barrel	Cylinder bore, deluxe	8106: 1964-1965
12 ga.	26" barrel	Cylinder bore	8107: 1962- 963
12 ga.	26" barrel	Cylinder bore, deluxe	8108: 1964-1965
12 ga.	18" barrel	Cylinder bore	8109: 1964-1965
12 ga.	20" barrel	Cylinder bore	8116: 1966-1972
12 ga.	20" barrel	Cylinder bore, deluxe	8117: 1966-1972
12 ga.	20" barrel	Cylinder bore	6116: 1973-1975

Premium for deluxe model.

Exc.	V.G.	Good	Fair	Poor
175	1560	125	100	65

Flite King Special

Like the Flite King Field except for a 27" barrel with 6 click stop adjustable choke.

Catalog numbers

12 ga.	27" barrel	Adjustable choke	8110: 1961-1965
16 ga.	27" barrel	Adjustable choke	8310: 1961-1964
20 ga.	27" barrel	Adjustable choke	8410: 1961-1965

Exc.	V.G.	Good	Fair	Poor
175	150	125	100	65

Flite King Deluxe

Slide action shotgun. Blued finish, checkered pistol grip walnut stock and forearm. 5-round magazine capacity. Available with and without a vent rib. 8411 and 6411 were the boys "Converta Pump" sold with two stocks: one youth size and one full size. The adjustable choke had 6 click stop positions Recoil pad beginning 1966 except .410 models.

Catalog numbers

12 ga.	27" barrel	Adjustable	8115: 1966-1973
12 ga.	28" barrel	Full choke	8120: 1960-1962
12 ga.	28" barrel	Modified choke	8121: 1960-1962
12 ga.	26" barrel	Improved cylinder	8122: 1960-1962

12 ga.	30" barrel	Full choke	8123: 1961-1962
12 ga.	28" barrel	Full choke	8124: 1962-1965
12 ga.	28" barrel	Modified choke	8125: 1962-1965
12 ga.	26" barrel	Improved cylinder	8126: 1962-1965
12 ga.	30" barrel	Full choke	8127: 1962-1964
12 ga.	28" barrel	Full choke	8132: 1966-1973
12 ga.	28" barrel	Modified choke	8133: 1966-1973
12 ga.	26" barrel	Improved cylinder	8134: 1966-1973
12 ga.	30" barrel	Full choke	8135: 1966-1973
12 ga.	30" barrel	Full choke, vent rib	8136: 1966-1973
12 ga.	28" barrel	Full choke, vent rib	8137: 1966-1973
12 ga.	28" barrel	Mod. choke, vent rib	8138: 1966-1973
12 ga.	27" barrel	Adjustable, vent rib	8142: 1966-1973
12 ga.	27" barrel	Click adjustable	6115: 1973-1975
12 ga.	28" barrel	Full choke	6132: 1973-1975
12 ga.	28" barrel	Modified choke	6133: 1973-1975
12 ga.	26" barrel	Improved cylinder	6134: 1973-1975
12 ga.	30" barrel	Full choke	6135: 1973-1975
12 ga.	30" barrel	Full choke, vent rib	6136: 1973-1975
12 ga.	28" barrel	Full choke, vent rib	6137: 1973-1975
12 ga.	28" barrel	Mod. choke, vent rib	6138: 1973-1975
12 ga.	27" barrel	Click adj., vent rib	6142: 1973-1975
16 ga.	28" barrel	Full choke	8320: 1961-1962
16 ga.	28" barrel	Modified choke	8321: 1961-1962
16 ga.	26" barrel	Improved cylinder	8322: 1961-1962
16 ga.	28" barrel	Full choke, vent rib	8324: 1961-1962
16 ga.	28" barrel	Mod. choke, vent rib	8326: 1962-1965
16 ga.	26" barrel	Imp. cylinder, vent rib	8327: 1962-1965
20 ga.	28" barrel	Full choke	8420: 1961-1962
20 ga.	28" barrel	Modified choke	8421: 1961-1962
20 ga.	26" barrel	Improved cylinder	8422: 1961-1962
20 ga.	28" barrel	Full choke	8425: 1961-1965
20 ga.	28" barrel	Modified choke	8426: 1961-1965
20 ga.	26" barrel	Improved cylinder	8427: 1961-1965
20 ga.	26" barrel	Full choke	8403: 1966-1971
20 ga.	26" barrel	Modified choke	8304: 1966-1971
20 ga.	26" barrel	Imp. cylinder, vent rib	8411: 1971-1973
20 ga.	26" barrel	Improved cylinder	8305: 1966-1971
20 ga.	26" barrel	Full choke	8429: 1966-1971
20 ga.	26" barrel	Full choke	8430: 1966-1971
20 ga.	26" barrel	Full choke	8442: 1966-1971
20 ga.	26" barrel	Imp. cylinder, vent rib	8443: 1972-1973
20 ga.	28" barrel	Full choke	6403: 1973-1975
20 ga.	28" barrel	Modified choke	6404: 1973-1975
20 ga.	26" barrel	Improved cylinder	6411: 1973-1975
20 ga.	28" barrel	Full choke, vent rib	6429: 1973-1975
20 ga.	28" barrel	Mod. choke, vent rib	6430: 1973-1975
20 ga.	27" barrel	Click adj., vent rib	6442: 1973-1975
20 ga.	26" barrel	Imp. cylinder, vent rib	6443: 1973-1975
28 ga.	26" barrel	Full choke	8332: 1968-1972
28 ga.	26" barrel	Modified choke	8333: 1968-1972
28 ga.	26" barrel	Full choke, vent rib	8334: 1968-1972
28 ga.	26" barrel	Mod. choke, vent rib	8335: 1968-1972
28 ga.	26" barrel	Full choke	6332: 1973-1973
28 ga.	26" barrel	Modified choke	6333: 1973-1973

28 ga.	26" barrel	Full choke, vent rib		6334: 1973-1973
28 ga.	26" barrel	Mod. choke, vent rib		6335: 1973-1973
.410 bore	26" barrel	Full choke, vent rib		8451: 1963-1965
.410 bore	26" barrel	Skeet choke, vent rib		8452: 1963-1963
.410 bore	26" barrel	Full choke		8453: 1966-1973
.410 bore	26" barrel	Full choke, vent rib		8454: 1966-1973
.410 bore	26" barrel	Full choke		6453: 1973-1975
.410 bore	26" barrel	Full choke, vent rib		6454: 1973-1975

Exc.	V.G.	Good	Fair	Poor
190	150	130	100	65

Flite King Citation

Like the Flite King Trophy without the vent rib. Catalog number 8130 has a compensator integral with the 6 position click stop adjustable choke.

Catalog numbers

12 ga.	26 1/2" barrel	Adjustable choke	8130: 1960-1960
12 ga.	27" barrel	Adjustable choke	8131: 1961-1962
16 ga.	27" barrel	Adjustable Choke	8331: 1961-1962

Exc.	V.G.	Good	Fair	Poor
185	155	125	100	75

Flite King Trophy

Slide action shotgun. Blued finish, checkered pistol grip walnut stock and forearm. 5-round magazine capacity. Ventilated rib. Catalog number 8140 has a compensator integral with the adjustable choke.

Catalog numbers

12 ga.	26.5" barrel	Adj. choke, vent rib	8140: 1960-1960
12 ga.	27" barrel	Adj. choke, vent rib	8141: 1961-1965
16 ga.	27" barrel	Adj. choke, vent rib	8341: 1961-1964
20 ga.	__" barrel	Adj. choke, vent rib	8441: 1962-1965

Exc.	V.G.	Good	Fair	Poor
200	175	130	100	75

Flite King Skeet

Same features as Flite King Deluxe except select American walnut stock and forearm and no recoil pad.

Catalog numbers

12 ga.	26" barrel	Skeet bore, vent rib	8160: 1962-1963
12 ga.	26" barrel	Skeet bore, vent rib	8162: 1964-1965
12 ga.	26" barrel	Skeet bore, vent rib	8164: 1966-1972
12 ga.	26" barrel	Skeet bore, vent rib	6164: 1973-1975
20 ga.	26" barrel	Skeet bore, vent rib	8428: 1964-1965
20 ga.	26" barrel	Skeet bore, vent rib	8431: 1966-1972
20 ga.	26" barrel	Skeet bore, vent rib	6431: 1973-1975
28 ga.	26" barrel	Skeet bore, vent rib	8336: 1968-1972
28 ga.	26" barrel	Skeet bore, vent rib	6336: 1973-1973
.410 bore	26" barrel	Skeet bore, vent rib	8452: 1964-1965

.410 bore	26" barrel	Skeet bore, vent rib	8455: 1968-1972
.410 bore	26" barrel	Skeet bore, vent rib	6455: 1973-1973

Exc.	V.G.	Good	Fair	Poor
275	225	180	110	85

Flite King Trap

Same features as Flite King Deluxe except select American walnut stock and forearm. Recoil pad. 8166 is the Executive Trap model with Fajen Monte Carlo stock. Catalog number 6165 is a model with provisions for interchangeable barrels.

Catalog numbers

12 ga.	30" barrel	Full choke, vent rib	8161: 1962-1963
12 ga.	30" barrel	Full choke, vent rib	8163: 1964-1965
12 ga.	30" barrel	Full choke, vent rib	8165: 1966-1972
12 ga.	30" barrel	Full choke, vent rib	8166: 1970-1971
12 ga.	30" barrel	Full choke, vent rib	6165: 1973-1975

Exc.	V.G.	Good	Fair	Poor
250	200	160	110	85

BOLT ACTION

Model 514

The Sears version of this shotgun was recalled for safety considerations in the late 1990's. The catalog numbers shown are from a parts book which does not provide production dates.

Catalog numbers

12 ga.	Full choke	8370
16 ga.	Full choke	8371
20 ga.	Full choke	8372
12 ga.	Adjustable choke	8370
16 ga.	Adjustable choke	8371
20 ga.	Adjustable choke	8372
12 ga.	Full choke, single shot	8370
16 ga.	Full choke, single shot	8371
20 ga.	Full choke, single shot	8372

Exc.	V.G.	Good	Fair	Poor
125	100	—	—	—

Police Shotguns

Semiautomatic

A gas operated semiautomatic 12 ga. shotgun. Plain oiled pistol grip walnut stock and forearm. Magazine capacity 4. Recoil pad.

Catalog numbers

12 ga.	20" barrel	Cylinder bore	8294: 1969-1969
12 ga.	20" barrel	Cyl. bore, rifle sights	8295: 1969-1969

Exc.	V.G.	Good	Fair	Poor
220	175	140	105	75

Model 10-A

A gas operated semiautomatic 12 ga. shotgun in bullpup configuration with pistol grip. Integral carrying handle and integral flashlight on top of gun. Magazine capacity 4.

Catalog numbers

12 ga.	18" barrel	Cylinder bore	8290: 1967-1969

Exc.	V.G.	Good	Fair	Poor
700	600	450	325	225

Model 10-B

A gas operated semiautomatic 12 ga. shotgun in bullpup configuration with pistol grip. Fitted with a integral folding carrying handle and mounting provisions for a flashlight. Magazine capacity 4. Carrying case catalog number 50284 and attachable flashlight catalog number 50285 sold optionally. Prices are for gun with flashlight otherwise deduct $75.

Catalog numbers

12 ga.   18.13" barrel   Cylinder bore   8291: 1970-1977

Exc.	V.G.	Good	Fair	Poor
650	575	450	350	250

Pump

A slide action 12 ga. shotgun. Plain pistol grip oiled walnut stock & forearm—changed from walnut to stained and lacquered birch in the mid 70's. 8111/8113 magazine capacity 6. 8104/8129 magazine capacity 5. A 1963 flyer mentions the #8105 Flite King Brush 20" and the #8107 Flite King Deluxe 20" as riot guns. The data on the #8105 and #8107 is listed under Flite King Brush.

Catalog numbers

12 ga.	20" barrel	Cylinder bore	8104: 1963-1977
12 ga.	18" barrel	Cylinder bore	8111: 1964-1978
12 ga.	18" barrel	Cyl. bore, rifle sights	8113: 1965-1978
12 ga.	20" barrel	Cyl. bore, rifle sights	8129: 1976-1977
12 ga.	20" barrel	Cylinder bore	8112: 1964-1965
12 ga.	18" barrel	Cyl. bore, rifle sights	8128: 1976-1977

Exc.	V.G.	Good	Fair	Poor
200	160	130	100	75

IMPORTED SHOTGUNS

Supermatic Shadow Automatic

A gas operated semiautomatic shotgun in 12 and 20 gauge, interchangeable barrels. Checkered walnut stock and forearm. Special "airflow" rib. Imported from Nikko in Japan.

Catalog numbers

12 ga. 2.75"	28" barrel	Imp. / Mod. choke	54200: 1974-1975
12 ga. 2.75"	28" barrel	Mod. choke	54201: 1974-1975
12 ga. 2.75"	26" barrel	Imp. choke	54202: 1974-1975
12 ga. 2.75"	26" barrel	Skeet choke	54203: 1974-1975
12 ga. 2.75"	28" barrel	Full choke	54204: 1974-1975
12 ga. 2.75"	30" barrel	Full choke	54205: 1974-1975
12 ga. 2.75"	30" barrel	Trap choke	54206: 1974-1975
12 ga. 2.75"	30" barrel	Imp. mod. choke	54207: 1974-1975
20 ga. 3.0"	28" barrel	Imp. / Mod. choke	54210: 1974-1975
20 ga. 3.0"	28" barrel	Mod. choke	54211: 1974-1975
20 ga. 3.0"	26" barrel	Imp. choke	54212: 1974-1975
20 ga. 3.0"	26" barrel	Skeet choke	54213: 1974-1975
20 ga. 3.0"	28" barrel	Full choke	54214: 1974-1975

Exc.	V.G.	Good	Fair	Poor
375	280	225	150	100

Supermatic Shadow Indy O/U

A boxlock over and under 12 gauge shotgun with selective auto ejectors and single trigger. Receiver is fully engraved. Skipline checkered walnut stock with pistol grip. Ventilated forearm. Recoil pad. Special "airflow" rib. Imported from Nikko in Japan.

Catalog numbers

12 ga. 2.75"	27.5" barrel	Skeet / Skeet choke	54230: 1974-1975
12 ga. 2.75"	29.75" barrel	Full / Full choke	54231: 1974-1975
12 ga. 2.75"	29.75" barrel	Imp.mod. / Full choke	54232: 1974-1975

Exc.	V.G.	Good	Fair	Poor
850	740	625	500	400

Supermatic Shadow Seven O/U

Like the Shadow Indy but with a standard size vent rib, conventional forearm, no recoil pad, standard checkering, and less engraving. Imported from Nikko in Japan.

Catalog numbers

12 ga. 2.75"	27.5" barrel	Skeet / Skeet choke	54220: 1974-1975
12 ga. 2.75"	27.5" barrel	Mod. / Imp. Choke	54221: 1974-1975
12 ga. 2.75"	27.5" barrel	Full / Mod. Choke	54222: 1974-1975
12 ga. 2.75"	29.75" barrel	Full / Full Choke	54223: 1974-1975
12 ga. 2.75"	29.75" barrel	Imp. Mod. / Full choke	54224: 1974-1975

Exc.	V.G.	Good	Fair	Poor
675	600	500	425	350

RIFLES

RIMFIRE PUMP

Flite King

A .22 caliber slide action rifle capable of using S / L / LR ammunition interchangeably. 24.25" barrel, open sights, and a tubular magazine. Magazine capacity 21 S, 17 L or 15 LR. Monte Carlo walnut stock with pistol grip.

Catalog number 8004. Manufactured between 1963 and 1965. Catalog number 8006. Manufactured between 1966 and 1971. Catalog number 6006. Manufactured between 1973 and 1976

Exc.	V.G.	Good	Fair	Poor
130	100	80	65	45

RIMFIRE SEMIAUTO

Sport King Field

A .22 caliber semiauto rifle capable of using S / L / LR ammunition interchangeably. 24.25" barrel, open sights, and a tubular magazine. Magazine capacity 21 S, 17 L, or 15 LR. Walnut stock.

Catalog number 8000. Manufactured between 1960 and 1965.

Exc.	V.G.	Good	Fair	Poor
100	90	75	55	40

Sport King Special

Like the Sport King Field except Monte Carlo walnut stock with pistol grip.

Catalog number 8001. Manufactured between 1960 and 1965.

Exc.	V.G.	Good	Fair	Poor
160	125	100	60	40

Sport King Deluxe

The Sport King Special with a new name. Catalog number 6005 is also the same gun but called just Sport King.

Catalog number 8005. Manufactured between 1966 and 1971.
Catalog number 6005. Manufactured between 1973 and 1976.

Exc.	V.G.	Good	Fair	Poor
185	140	110	80	50

Sport King Carbine

A .22 carbine semiautomatic rifle capable of using S / L / LR ammunition interchangeably. 18.25" barrel, open sights, and a tubular magazine. Magazine capacity 17 S, 14 L, or 12 LR. Straight grip walnut stock with barrel band and sling.

Catalog number 8002. Manufactured between 1962 and 1971.

Exc.	V.G.	Good	Fair	Poor
180	140	110	80	50

CENTERFIRE

Hi-Power Field Grade

A .270 or .30-06 caliber bolt action rifle with a 22" barrel, open sights and a 4-shot magazine. Blued with a walnut stock. Manufactured between 1962 and 1965.

Catalog numbers .30-06 8507, .270 8509.

Exc.	V.G.	Good	Fair	Poor
325	250	225	150	100

Hi-Power Deluxe

Like the Field Grade except has a Monte Carlo-style stock. Also available in .243 and .308 calibers in later part of 1965.

Catalog numbers .30-06 8506, .270 8508, .308 8511, .243 8513.

Exc.	V.G.	Good	Fair	Poor
375	300	275	200	150

HILL, W.J.
Birmingham, England

Hill's Self Extracting Revolver

A .32 caliber double action folding trigger revolver with a 3.75" barrel and 6-shot cylinder. Marked "Hill's Patent Self Extractor". Blued with walnut grips.

Exc.	V.G.	Good	Fair	Poor
—	700	350	250	150

HILLIARD, D. H.
Cornish, New Hampshire

Under Hammer Pistol

A .34 caliber under hammer percussion pistol with varying barrel lengths. Blued with walnut grips. Active 1842 to 1877.

Exc.	V.G.	Good	Fair	Poor
—	—	650	350	200

HINO-KOMURA
Tokyo, Japan

A 7.65mm or 8mm Nambu semiautomatic pistol manufactured in limited quantities between 1905 and 1912. The operation of this pistol involves pulling the muzzle forward until the slide engages a catch on the trigger assembly. Pulling the trigger at this point allows the barrel to move back and engage the cartridge nose into the chamber. Squeezing the grip safety then allows the barrel to slam back into the fixed firing pin on the breechblock. Prospective purchasers are advised to secure a qualified appraisal prior to acquisition.

Exc.	V.G.	Good	Fair	Poor
3500	3250	2750	2000	1000

HODGKINS, D. C. & SONS
Macon, Georgia
SEE—Bilharz, Hall & Co.

HOFER, P.
Feriach, Austria

A gunmaker specializing in double barrel rifles made strictly to custom order. Prospective purchasers should secure a qualified appraisal prior to acquisition.

HOFFMAN, LOUIS
Vicksburg, Mississippi

Pocket Pistol

A .41 caliber percussion pocket pistol with a 3" barrel, German silver mounts and walnut stock. Active 1857 to 1886.

Exc.	V.G.	Good	Fair	Poor
—	—	750	450	200

HOLDEN, C. B.
Worcester, Massachusetts

Open Frame Rifle

A .44 r.f. single shot rifle with a 28" barrel, open sights, silver plated bronze frame and walnut stock. The barrel marked "C.B. Holden Worcester-Mass." Produced in limited quantities during the mid-1860s.

Exc.	V.G.	Good	Fair	Poor
—	—	750	475	300

HOLECK, EMANUEL
Czechoslovakia

Holeck Rifle

Chambered for the .276 cartridge this semiautomatic rifle was submitted for testing for U.S. military trials in the 1920s. Barrel length is 21.5" with upper portion slotted for operating handle. Rotating dial at barrel band. Rarely encountered.

NOTE: Thanks to Jim Supica for his research found in his *Old Town Station Dispatch* in which one of these rifles was offered for sale.

Exc.	V.G.	Good	Fair	Poor
3900	—	—	—	—

HOLLAND & HOLLAND, LTD.
London, England
SEE—British Double Guns

Established in 1835, Holland & Holland has manufactured a wide variety of shotguns and rifles during its existence. The greater part of these arms were made to custom order and, therefore, prospective purchasers are advised to secure a qualified appraisal prior to acquisition.

DOUBLE RIFLES

No. 2 Grade Double Rifle
A sidelock double barrel rifle produced in a variety of calibers with 24" barrels, double triggers, automatic ejectors and express sights. Obsolete cartridges could be worth less.

Exc	V.G.	Good	Fair	Poor
15000	12500	8500	7000	4000

Royal Side-x-Side Rifle
Price depends on caliber.

Prices start at $90,000 and go to $115,000 for .600 Nitro Express. Each rifle is unique. An independent appraisal is a must for this gun.

H&H .700 Bore Side-x-Side Rifle
A .700 Holland & Holland double barrel rifle with a weight of approximately 18 lbs. Currently manufactured. Due to the uniqueness of the piece, buyers should seek qualified appraisal. The last known quoted retail price for this rifle was $152,000.

BOLT ACTION RIFLES

Best Quality Rifle
A bolt action rifle produced in calibers up to .375 Holland & Holland with a 24" barrel, express sights and 4-shot magazine.

Price depends on caliber and extra cost options. Retail prices for magazine rifles begin around $30,000, depending on the value of the dollar. Due to the uniqueness of each rifle an independent appraisal is a must prior to a sale.

HOLLIS & SONS
SEE—English Military Firearms

HOLLOWAY ARMS CO.
Ft. Worth, Texas

HAC Model 7
A 7.62x54mm semiautomatic rifle with a 20" barrel, adjustable sights, integral telescope mount and 20-shot magazine. Black anodized finish with folding stock. No longer in production.

NIB	Exc.	V.G.	Good	Fair	Poor
1250	1000	800	600	400	250

HAC Model 7C
As above, with a 16" barrel.

NIB	Exc.	V.G.	Good	Fair	Poor
1250	1000	800	600	400	250

HAC Model 7S
As above, with a heavy barrel.

NIB	Exc.	V.G.	Good	Fair	Poor
1250	1000	800	600	400	250

HOLMES FIREARMS
Wheeler, Arkansas

MP-22
A .22 caliber semiautomatic pistol with a 6" barrel and alloy receiver. Anodized black finish with a walnut grip. Manufactured in 1985.

NIB	Exc.	V.G.	Good	Fair	Poor
425	325	250	200	150	100

MP-83
Similar to the above, but in 9mm or .45 caliber. Manufactured in 1985.

NIB	Exc.	V.G.	Good	Fair	Poor
550	425	325	250	200	125

NOTE: Several of the Holmes pistols have been declared machine guns by the BATF because of their easy conversion to full automatic. Make sure before purchase that a Class III license is not required.

HOOD F. A. CO.
Norwich, Connecticut

A manufacturer of spur trigger .22 or .32 caliber revolvers with varying length barrels and finishes. Many of these revolvers are found stamped only with trade names. This type of handgun is often referred to as a suicide special to denote its poor quality and lack of reliability.

Exc.	V.G.	Good	Fair	Poor
—	175	100	75	50

HOPKINS & ALLEN
Norwich, Connecticut
ALSO SEE—Bacon Arms Co. & Merwin Hulbert & Co.

Established in 1868, this company produced a variety of spur trigger revolvers in .22, .32, .38, or .41 caliber often marked with trade names such as: Acme, Blue Jacket, Captain Jack, Chichester, Defender, Dictator, Hopkins & Allen, Imperial Arms Co., Monarch, Mountain Eagle, Ranger, Tower's Police Safety, Universal and XL.

Courtesy Milwaukee Public Museum, Milwaukee, Wisconsin

Exc.	V.G.	Good	Fair	Poor
—	—	300	150	75

Some of these revolvers are hinged-frame, double action break-opens with round-ribbed barrels of various lengths. Blued or nickel-plated, with checkered plastic grips.

Exc.	V.G.	Good	Fair	Poor
—	—	300	150	75

Dictator

A .36 caliber percussion or .38 r.f. single action revolver with a 4" barrel and 5-shot cylinder. Blued with walnut grips. The barrel marked "Dictator". Approximately 6,000 percussion revolvers were made and 5,000 rimfire.

Exc.	V.G.	Good	Fair	Poor
—	—	350	150	75

Falling Block Rifle

A .22 to .38-55 caliber single shot rifle with a 24", 26", or 28" octagonal barrel. Blued with a walnut stock. Manufactured between 1888 and 1892.

Exc.	V.G.	Good	Fair	Poor
—	750	400	200	100

Schuetzen Rifle

A .22 or .25-20 caliber single shot rifle with a 26" octagonal barrel, double-set trigger and a Schuetzen-type buttplate. Blued with a walnut stock.

Exc.	V.G.	Good	Fair	Poor
—	2000	950	500	200

Navy Revolver

A .38 caliber single action revolver with a 6.5" barrel marked, "Hopkins & Allen Mfg. Co., Pat. Mar. 28, 71, Apr. 27, 75" and a 6-shot cylinder. The top strap marked "XL Navy". Blued or nickel-plated with walnut grips. Several hundred were made between 1878 and 1882.

Exc.	V.G.	Good	Fair	Poor
—	—	800	400	175

Army Revolver

As above, in .44 r.f. with a 4.5", 6", or 7.5" barrel. The top strap marked "XL No. 8." Several hundred were manufactured between 1878 and 1882.

Exc.	V.G.	Good	Fair	Poor
—	—	1000	600	250

Derringer

A .22 caliber single shot pistol with a hinged 1.75" barrel that pivots downwards for loading. Blued or nickel-plated with walnut, ivory, or pearl grips. The frame marked, "Hopkins & Allen

Arms Co., Norwich, Conn. U.S.A." Several hundred were manufactured in the 1880s and 1890s.

Exc.	V.G.	Good	Fair	Poor
—	—	1500	600	250

Double Barrel Shotguns

Hopkins & Allen also made good quality single and double barrel shotguns in large numbers. Many were sold under private brand names such as Seminole and King Nitro. Both hammer and hammerless versions were offered. Values vary from $100 to $1,000 depending on model and condition.

HORSLEY, THOMAS
York, England
SEE—British Double Guns

HOTCHKISS
Winchester Arms Co.
New Haven, Connecticut

HOWA MACHINE COMPANY
Japan

This company manufactured bolt action rifles for Smith & Wesson until 1985 and then for Mossberg in 1986 and 1987. Presently, Howa firearms are imported by Interarms of Alexandria, Virginia.

Model 1500 Hunter

A .22-250, .223, .243, .270, 7mm Remington Magnum .308, .30-06, .300 Win. Mag., and .338 Winchester Magnum caliber bolt action sporting rifle with a 22" or 24" barrel and 3- or 5-shot magazine. Blued or stainless steel with a checkered walnut stock. Weight is approximately 7.6 lbs. Imported by Interarms.

NIB	Exc.	V.G.	Good	Fair	Poor
450	350	275	225	175	100

NOTE: Add $10 for stainless steel

Model 1500 Trophy

As above, but with more finely figured walnut stocks and checkering. Introduced in 1988. No longer imported.

NIB	Exc.	V.G.	Good	Fair	Poor
500	400	300	250	200	150

Model 1500 Varmint

As above, in .22-250 or .223 caliber with a 24" heavy barrel. Choice of walnut or synthetic stock, in blue or stainless. Weight is about 9.3 lbs. Introduced in 1988.

NIB	Exc.	V.G.	Good	Fair	Poor
450	350	250	225	200	150

NOTE: Add $70 for stainless steel and $20 for walnut stock.

Realtree Camo Rifle

Introduced in 1993, this bolt action model features a composite stock and a 22" barrel. Both the metal and stock finish are a brown leaf pattern. The receiver is a mono-block system. The floorplate is hinged and the magazine holds 5 rounds. The receiver is drilled and tapped for scope mounts. Fitted with a sling swivel and recoil pad. Offered in .30-06 and .270 calibers. Weighs 8 lbs.

NIB	Exc.	V.G.	Good	Fair	Poor
500	450	400	350	300	200

Model 1500 Lightning Rifle

Introduced in 1993, this model has a black composite checkered stock with schnabel forend. The buttstock is Monte Carlo. Choice of blue or stainless steel. Offered in .223, .22-250, .243, .270, .308, .30-06, 7mm Rem. Mag., .300 and .338 Win. Mag. Weighs about 7.5 lbs.

NIB	Exc.	V.G.	Good	Fair	Poor
425	350	300	250	200	150

Model 1500 PCS (Police Counter Sniper)

This bolt action is offered in .308 Winchester and fitted with a 24" heavy barrel. Magazine capacity is 5 rounds. Available in blue or stainless steel and walnut or synthetic stock. Weight is approximately 9.3 lbs.

NIB	Exc.	V.G.	Good	Fair	Poor
450	350	300	250	—	—

HOWARD-WHITNEY
New Haven, Connecticut
SEE—Whitney Arms Co.

HUNT
New Haven, Connecticut
SEE—Winchester Repeating Arms Co.

HUNTER ARMS CO.
Fulton, New York
SEE—L. C. Smith

HUSQVARNA
Husqvarna, Sweden

PISTOLS

Model 1907

This pistol is a copy of the FN Browning Model 1903 made for the Swedish Army. It is identical in every way to the FN model. Many were converted to the .380 caliber and imported into the U.S. If converted to .380 caliber reduce values by 50%.

Courtesy Orvel Reichert

Exc.	V.G.	Good	Fair	Poor
350	250	200	150	100

Lahti

A 9mm caliber semiautomatic pistol with a 5.5" barrel and 8-shot magazine. Designed by Aino Lahti and adopted as the standard Swedish sidearm in 1940.

Exc.	V.G.	Good	Fair	Poor
425	350	275	225	150

BOLT ACTION RIFLES

Hi-Power

A bolt action sporting rifle manufactured in a variety of calibers with a 24" barrel, open sights and beechwood stock. Manufactured between 1946 and 1951.

Exc.	V.G.	Good	Fair	Poor
400	300	275	200	150

Model 1100 Deluxe

As above, with a walnut stock. Manufactured between 1952 and 1956.

Exc.	V.G.	Good	Fair	Poor
475	400	325	250	200

Model 1000 Super Grade

As above, with a Monte Carlo-style stock. Manufactured between 1952 and 1956.

Exc.	V.G.	Good	Fair	Poor
475	400	325	250	200

Model 3100 Crown Grade

A bolt action sporting rifle manufactured in a variety of calibers with a 24" barrel, walnut stock with a black composition forend tip and pistol grip cap. Manufactured between 1954 and 1972.

Exc.	V.G.	Good	Fair	Poor
575	475	350	300	200

Model 4100 Lightweight

As above, with a schnabel forend tip. Manufactured between 1954 and 1972.

Exc.	V.G.	Good	Fair	Poor
575	475	350	300	200

Model 456

As above, with a full length Mannlicher-style stock. Manufactured between 1959 and 1970.

Exc.	V.G.	Good	Fair	Poor
425	350	300	250	200

Model 6000

The Model 4100 with express folding sights and a finely figured walnut stock. Manufactured between 1968 and 1970.

Exc.	V.G.	Good	Fair	Poor
600	500	400	300	200

Model 9000 Crown Grade

A bolt action sporting rifle manufactured in a variety of calibers with a 23.5" barrel, open sights, adjustable trigger and walnut stock. Manufactured in 1971 and 1972.

Exc.	V.G.	Good	Fair	Poor
500	425	350	300	250

Model 8000 Imperial Grade

As above, with an engraved magazine floor plate, machine jeweled bolt and finely figured walnut stock. Manufactured in 1971 and 1972.

Exc.	V.G.	Good	Fair	Poor
675	550	475	400	300

HY-HUNTER, INC.
Burbank, California

Chicago Cub

A .22 caliber folding trigger double action revolver with a 2" barrel and 6-shot cylinder.

Exc.	V.G.	Good	Fair	Poor
50	40	30	25	20

Detective

A .22 or .22 WMR caliber double action revolver with a 2.5" barrel and 6-shot cylinder. Blued with plastic grips.

Exc.	V.G.	Good	Fair	Poor
65	50	40	30	25

Frontier Six Shooter

A .22 or .22 WMR caliber single action revolver with a 6-shot cylinder.

Exc.	V.G.	Good	Fair	Poor
75	65	50	40	30

Frontier Six Shooter

As above, in .357 Magnum, .44 Magnum or .45 Colt.

Exc.	V.G.	Good	Fair	Poor
125	100	85	75	50

Maxim

A .25 caliber semiautomatic pistol with a 2" barrel and 5-shot magazine.

Exc.	V.G.	Good	Fair	Poor
75	65	50	40	30

Military

A .22, .32 or .380 caliber double action semiautomatic pistol with a 4" barrel and 6-shot magazine.

Exc.	V.G.	Good	Fair	Poor
100	80	60	50	40

Stingray

A .25 caliber semiautomatic pistol with a 2.5" barrel and 5-shot magazine.

Exc.	V.G.	Good	Fair	Poor
75	65	50	40	30

Panzer

A .22 caliber semiautomatic pistol with a 4" barrel and 7-shot magazine.

Exc.	V.G.	Good	Fair	Poor
75	65	50	40	30

Stuka

Similar to the above.

Exc.	V.G.	Good	Fair	Poor
75	65	50	40	30

Automatic Derringer

A .22 caliber Over/Under pocket pistol patterned after the Remington Double Derringer.

Exc.	V.G.	Good	Fair	Poor
50	40	30	25	20

Accurate Ace

A .22 caliber Flobert action pistol.

Exc.	V.G.	Good	Fair	Poor
50	40	30	25	20

Favorite

A .22 or .22 WMR caliber copy of the Steven's single shot pistol with a 6" barrel and nickel-plated frame.

Exc.	V.G.	Good	Fair	Poor
100	80	70	50	25

Gold Rush Derringer

A .22 caliber spur trigger single shot pistol with a 2.5" barrel.

Exc.	V.G.	Good	Fair	Poor
50	40	30	25	20

Target Model

A .22 or .22 WMR bolt action single shot pistol with a 10" barrel, adjustable sights and walnut grip.

Exc	V.G.	Good	Fair	Poor
50	40	30	25	20

HYDE & SHATTUCK
Hatfield, Massachusetts

Queen Derringer

A .22 caliber spur trigger single shot pistol with a 2.5" half octagonal barrel. Blued or nickel-plated with walnut grips. The barrel normally marked "Queen", but sometimes "Hyde & Shattuck". Manufactured between 1876 and 1879.

Exc.	V.G.	Good	Fair	Poor
—	—	450	300	150

HYPER
Jenks, Oklahoma

Single Shot Rifle

A custom made falling block action single shot rifle manufactured in a variety of calibers, barrel lengths, barrel types, and stock styles. As these rifles were made to custom order, prospective purchasers should secure a qualified appraisal prior to acquisition. Manufactured until 1984.

Exc.	V.G.	Good	Fair	Poor
2500	2000	1750	1450	800

IAB
Brescia, Italy
Industria Armi Bresciane

Imported by Puccinelli & Company of San Anselmo, California, and by Sporting Arms International of Indianola, Mississippi.

S-300
A 12 gauge boxlock single barrel trap gun with 30" or 32" barrels having a wide ventilated rib and walnut trap-style stock.

Exc.	V.G.	Good	Fair	Poor
1500	1250	1000	850	450

C-300 Combo
A 12 gauge Over/Under boxlock double-barrel shotgun with 30" or 32" barrels, single selective trigger, automatic ejectors, trap-style walnut stock, accompanied by two extra single barrels.

Exc.	V.G.	Good	Fair	Poor
2750	2250	1850	1500	800

C-300 Super Combo
As above, but more finely finished.

Exc.	V.G.	Good	Fair	Poor
3500	2750	2250	1750	900

IAI-AMERICAN LEGENDS
Houston, Texas

RIFLES

M-888 M1 Carbine
A recreation of the U.S. M1 Carbine in .30 caliber. Barrel length is 18". Weight is about 5.5 lbs. Uses surplus magazines of 15 to 30 rounds. Comes with 10-round magazine. Options of wooden are metal handguard and walnut or birchwood stock.

NIB	Exc.	V.G.	Good	Fair	Poor
600	450	—	—	—	—

M-333 M1 Garand
This is a remanufactured firearms to GI specifications. Fitted with 24" barrel and GI wood stock. Eight round capacity. Parkerized finish. Weight is about 9.5 lbs.

NIB	Exc.	V.G.	Good	Fair	Poor
800	600	—	—	—	—

PISTOLS

M-2000
This is a Gov't model .45ACP pistol fitted with a 5" barrel and 7-round magazine. Fixed sights. Wood grips. Parkerized finish. Weight is about 38 oz.

NIB	Exc.	V.G.	Good	Fair	Poor
475	350	—	—	—	—

M-999
Similar to the above model but with rubber style combat grips, extended slide stop, safety, and magazine release. Fixed sights. Offered with stainless steel slide and blued frame or all stainless steel. Supplied with 7-round magazine. Weight is about 38 oz.

NIB	Exc.	V.G.	Good	Fair	Poor
475	350	—	—	—	—

NOTE: Add $25 for stainless steel frame.

M-777
Same as M-999 but fitted with 4.25" barrel. Weight is about 36 oz.

NIB	Exc.	V.G.	Good	Fair	Poor
475	350	—	—	—	—

NOTE: Add $25 for stainless steel frame.

M-6000
This .45ACP pistol is fitted with a 5" barrel, plastic grips, extended slide stop, safety, and magazine release. Safety is ambidextrous. Magazine capacity is 8 rounds. Fixed sights. Weight is about 38 oz.

NIB	Exc.	V.G.	Good	Fair	Poor
400	300	—	—	—	—

M-5000
This model is similar to the M-6000 but fitted with a 4.25" barrel. Weight is about 36 oz.

NIB	Exc.	V.G.	Good	Fair	Poor
400	300	—	—	—	—

IAR
San Juan Capistrano, California

This company is an importer of Italian made reproduction pistol and rifles. For a complete listing see *Uberti*. IAR also imports military surplus firearms.

IGA
Veranopolis, Brazil
Importer-Stoeger Industries
Hackensack, New Jersey

Single Barrel Shotgun
A 12 or 20 gauge or .410 bore single barrel shotgun with an exposed hammer, 28" barrel and hardwood stock.

NIB	Exc.	V.G.	Good	Fair	Poor
125	90	75	50	40	30

Single Barrel Shotgun Youth Model
Offered in 20 gauge and .410 bore this model features a 22" barrel and shorter than standard buttstock. Weighs 5 lbs.

NIB	Exc.	V.G.	Good	Fair	Poor
125	100	80	60	50	35

Coach Gun
A 12 and 20 gauge as well as .410 bore boxlock double-barrel shotgun with 20" barrels, double triggers and extractors. Blued with a hardwood stock.

NIB	Exc.	V.G.	Good	Fair	Poor
400	325	250	150	100	75

NOTE: Add $50 for nickel finish. Add $60 for engraved butt stock.

Standard Side-x-Side Uplander Model
Offered in 12, 20, 28 gauge, and .410 bore with 26" and 28" barrels. Checkered hardwood stock with pistol grip or straight grip in 20 gauge only. Weighs 6.75 lbs.

NIB	Exc.	V.G.	Good	Fair	Poor
425	325	250	150	100	75

NOTE: Add $40 for choke tubes.

Uplander Youth Model
Same as above but offered in .410 bore with 24" barrel or 20 gauge with 24" barrels. Shorter length of pull. Recoil pad standard.

NIB	Exc.	V.G.	Good	Fair	Poor
450	325	250	150	100	75

Uplander Supreme
Introduced in 2000 this model features a high grade walnut stock with checkering, single selective trigger, choke tubes, and automatic ejectors. Offered in 12 and 20 gauge with 26" or 28" barrels. Chambered for 3" shells. Soft rubber recoil pad standard.

NIB	Exc.	V.G.	Good	Fair	Poor
600	450	—	—	—	—

Standard O/U Condor I
This model is offered in 12 or 20 gauge with 26" or 28" barrels. Fitted with extractors and single trigger. Choke tubes are standard. Checkered hardwood stock with pistol grip and recoil pad. Weighs 8 lbs.

NIB	Exc.	V.G.	Good	Fair	Poor
300	250	225	200	150	100

Condor II
Same as above but with double triggers and plastic buttplate.

NIB	Exc.	V.G.	Good	Fair	Poor
275	225	200	150	100	75

Condor Supreme Deluxe
This model is similar to the standard Condor model but has a high grade walnut stock, hand checkering, recoil pad, single selective trigger, and automatic ejectors. Offered in 12 and 20

gauge with 26" or 28" vent rib barrels. Chambered for 3" shells. Choke tubes standard. First offered in 2000.

NIB	Exc.	V.G.	Good	Fair	Poor
550	400	—	—	—	—

Deluxe O/U ERA 2000
Offered in 12 gauge only with 26" or 28" barrels. Fitted with single trigger and extractors. Choke tubes are standard. Barrels are chrome lined and stock is hand checkered.

NIB	Exc.	V.G.	Good	Fair	Poor
400	325	275	225	175	125

I.G.I.
Zingone de Tressano, Italy
Itaiguns International

Domino SP602
A .22 caliber semiautomatic target pistol with a 6" barrel and 5-shot magazine (that is inserted into the action from the top), adjustable trigger and customized grips.

Exc.	V.G.	Good	Fair	Poor
900	700	600	450	250

Domino OP601
As above, but in .22 short caliber.

Exc.	V.G.	Good	Fair	Poor
900	700	600	450	250

INDIAN ARMS CORP.
Detroit, Michigan

Indian Arms .380
A .380 caliber semiautomatic pistol with a 3.25" barrel and 6-shot magazine. Made of stainless steel and finished either in the white or blued with walnut grips. Manufactured from 1975 to 1977.

Exc.	V.G.	Good	Fair	Poor
400	325	275	175	100

INGLIS, JOHN & COMPANY
Toronto, Canada

NOTE: For history, technical data, descriptions, and prices see the *Standard Catalog of Military Firearms, 1870 to the Present* under Canada, Handguns.

INDUSTRIA ARMI GALESI
Brescia, Italy
SEE—Galesi

INGRAM
Atlanta, Georgia
Military Armament Corp.

MAC10
A 9mm or .45 caliber semiautomatic pistol with a 5.75" barrel and 32-shot magazine. Anodized with plastic grips.

Accessory Kit (Barrel Extension and Extra Magazine)-Add 20%.

NIB	Exc.	V.G.	Good	Fair	Poor
1100	800	650	500	400	200

MAC 10AI
As above, but firing from a closed bolt.

Accessory Kit-Add 20%.

NIB	Exc.	V.G.	Good	Fair	Poor
450	350	250	200	150	100

MAC 11
As above in a smaller version and chambered for the .380ACP cartridge.

Accessory Kit-Add 20%.

NIB	Exc.	V.G.	Good	Fair	Poor
1000	800	600	400	300	150

INTERARMS
Alexandria, Virginia

An importer of arms made by Howa Machine, Star and Walther. This firm is no longer in business.

RIFLES

Mark X Viscount
Bolt action sporting rifle made in a variety of calibers with a 24" barrel, open sights, adjustable trigger and magazine holding either 3 or 5 cartridges. Manufactured in Yugoslavia. Blued with a walnut stock.

NIB	Exc.	V.G.	Good	Fair	Poor
350	300	250	200	175	125

Mark X Lightweight
As above, with a 20" barrel and composition stock. Introduced in 1988.

NIB	Exc.	V.G.	Good	Fair	Poor
350	300	250	200	175	125

Mini Mark X
As above, with a short action in .223 caliber only with a 20" barrel, open sights, adjustable trigger and 5-shot magazine. Introduced in 1987.

NIB	Exc.	V.G.	Good	Fair	Poor
350	300	250	200	175	125

Mark X American Field
As above, with a finely figured walnut stock, ebony forend tip, pistol grip cap, sling swivels and recoil pad. Introduced in 1984.

NIB	Exc.	V.G.	Good	Fair	Poor
450	400	350	300	250	175

Whitworth Express Rifle
A .375 Holland & Holland or .458 Winchester Magnum bolt action sporting rifle with a 24" barrel, express sights and 3-shot magazine. Blued with a walnut stock. Introduced in 1974.

NIB	Exc.	V.G.	Good	Fair	Poor
550	500	450	350	250	200

Whitworth Mannlicher Carbine
A .243, .270, 7x57mm, .308, and the .30-06 caliber bolt action rifle with a 20" barrel, open sights, sling swivels and a full length stock. Manufactured between 1984 and 1987.

Exc.	V.G.	Good	Fair	Poor
450	400	350	250	200

Cavalier
A bolt action sporting rifle made in a variety of calibers with a modern styled stock having a rollover cheekpiece. Discontinued.

Exc.	V.G.	Good	Fair	Poor
325	275	250	200	150

Mannlicher Carbine

As above, with a 20" barrel and full length stock. Discontinued.

Exc.	V.G.	Good	Fair	Poor
325	275	250	200	150

Continental Carbine

As above, with double set triggers. Discontinued.

Exc.	V.G.	Good	Fair	Poor
350	300	250	200	150

Alaskan Model

Similar to the Mark X, in .375 Holland & Holland or .458 Winchester Magnum with a 24" barrel. Discontinued in 1985.

Exc.	V.G.	Good	Fair	Poor
450	400	350	300	200

22-ATD

A .22 caliber semiautomatic rifle with a 19.4" barrel, open sights, and 11-shot magazine. Blued with a hardwood stock. Manufactured by Norinco. Introduced in 1987.

NIB	Exc.	V.G.	Good	Fair	Poor
125	100	80	60	50	40

HANDGUNS

Helwan Brigadier

A 9mm semiautomatic pistol with a 4.5" barrel, fixed sights, and 8-shot magazine. Blued with plastic grips. Introduced in 1988.

NIB	Exc.	V.G.	Good	Fair	Poor
250	225	200	175	125	100

FEG R-9

A 9mm semiautomatic pistol patterned after the Browning 35 with a 13-shot magazine. Blued with walnut grips. Manufactured in 1986 and 1987.

Exc.	V.G.	Good	Fair	Poor
275	225	185	145	100

FEG PPH

A .380 caliber double action semiautomatic pistol with a 3.5" barrel and 6-shot magazine. Blued with plastic grips.

Exc.	V.G.	Good	Fair	Poor
200	175	150	125	100

Mark II AP

A copy of the Walther PP. Chambered for the .380 ACP or .22 LR cartridge.

NIB	Exc.	V.G.	Good	Fair	Poor
225	175	125	100	—	—

Mark II APK

A copy of the Walther PPK. Chambered for the .380 ACP cartridge only.

NIB	Exc.	V.G.	Good	Fair	Poor
225	175	125	100	—	—

Virginian Dragoon

A .44 Magnum single action revolver with a 6", 7.5", 8.75", or 12" barrel, adjustable sights and 6-shot cylinder. Originally made in Switzerland and then in the U.S.A. Discontinued in 1984.

Exc.	V.G.	Good	Fair	Poor
250	150	125	100	75

Stainless Dragoon

As above, in stainless steel.

Exc.	V.G.	Good	Fair	Poor
275	175	150	125	100

Virginian .22 Convertible

As above, in .22 caliber with a 5.5" barrel.

Exc.	V.G.	Good	Fair	Poor
250	150	125	100	75

Virginian Stainless .22 Convertible

As above, in stainless steel.

Exc.	V.G.	Good	Fair	Poor
275	175	150	100	80

Mauser Parabellum Karabiner

A 9mm caliber semiautomatic carbine with an 11.75" barrel and detachable shoulder stock. Fitted in a leather case.

NOTE: Only 100 were imported into the United States and this arm is subject to BATF registration.

NIB	Exc.	V.G.	Good	Fair	Poor
6500	5750	5000	4000	3000	2250

Mauser Parabellum Cartridge Counter

A reproduction of the cartridge counter Luger. Fitted in a leather case with only 100 units imported into the United States.

NIB	Exc.	V.G.	Good	Fair	Poor
3600	3000	2500	2000	1500	1000

INTERDYNAMICS OF AMERICA
Miami, Florida

KG-9

A 9mm caliber semiautomatic pistol with a 3" barrel and 36-shot magazine. Manufactured from 1981 and 1983.

Exc.	V.G.	Good	Fair	Poor
800	650	575	500	300

KG-99

As above, with a barrel shroud. Manufactured from 1981 and 1984.

Exc.	V.G.	Good	Fair	Poor
300	225	175	125	100

KG-99 Stainless

As above, in stainless steel. Manufactured in 1984.

Exc.	V.G.	Good	Fair	Poor
350	275	225	150	125

KG-99M

A more compact version of the above. Manufactured in 1984.

Exc.	V.G.	Good	Fair	Poor
250	200	150	125	100

INTRATEC USA, INC.
Miami, Florida

TEC-9

A 9mm caliber semiautomatic pistol with a 5" shrouded barrel and 36-shot magazine. Introduced in 1985.

NIB	Exc.	V.G.	Good	Fair	Poor
250	200	175	150	125	100

TEC-9C

As above, with a 16" barrel and a folding stock. Manufactured in 1987.

Exc.	V.G.	Good	Fair	Poor
275	225	200	150	100

TEC-9M

As above, with a 3" barrel and 20-shot magazine. Also made in stainless steel.

NIB	Exc.	V.G.	Good	Fair	Poor
300	200	175	150	100	75

TEC-22 "Scorpion"

Similar to the above, but in .22 caliber with a 4" barrel and 30-shot magazine.

NIB	Exc.	V.G.	Good	Fair	Poor
250	150	125	100	75	50

TEC-38

A .38 caliber Over/Under double action derringer with 3" barrels. Manufactured between 1986 and 1988.

Exc.	V.G.	Good	Fair	Poor
125	100	80	65	45

IRVING, W.
New York, New York

Single Shot Derringer

A .22 caliber spur trigger single shot pistol with a 2.75" half octagonal barrel. Silver plated brass frame, blued barrel and rosewood grips. The barrel marked "W. Irving". Manufactured in the 1860s. The .32 caliber variation has a 3" barrel and is worth approximately 40% more than the values listed below.

Exc.	V.G.	Good	Fair	Poor
—	900	500	300	125

POCKET REVOLVER

1st Model

A .31 caliber spur trigger percussion revolver with a 3" octagonal barrel, 6-shot cylinder and brass frame. The barrel marked "W. Irving". Approximately 50 were made between 1858 and 1862.

Exc.	V.G.	Good	Fair	Poor
—	800	500	350	250

2nd Model

A .31 caliber percussion revolver with a 4.5" round barrel, loading lever and either brass or iron frame. The barrel marked "Address W. Irving. 20 Cliff St. N.Y." Approximately 600 manufactured with a brass frame and 1,500 with a frame of iron. The brass-frame version will bring a premium of about 35%.

Exc.	V.G.	Good	Fair	Poor
—	700	400	300	200

IRWINDALE ARMS, INC.
Irwindale, California
SEE—AMT

ISRAELI MILITARY INDUSTRIES
Israel

Civilian firearms manufactured by this firm have been retailed by Action Arms Limited, Magnum Research, and Mossberg.

ITHACA GUN CO.
Ithaca, New York

The following material was supplied by Walter C. Snyder and is Copyrighted in his name. Used with the author's permission.

The Ithaca Gun Company was founded by William Henry Baker, John VanNatta, and Dwight McIntyre. Gun production started during the latter half of 1883 at an industrial site located on Fall Creek, Ithaca, New York. Leroy Smith joined the company by 1885 and George Livermore joined the firm in 1887. By 1894 the company was under the exclusive control of Leroy Smith and George Livermore. Many of the company's assets were purchased by the Ithaca Acquisition Corporation in 1987 and moved to King Ferry, New York, where it operated until May, 1996. Ithaca Acquisition's assets were purchased in 1996 by the Ithaca Gun Company, LLC and they continue operations to this day at the King Ferry site.

HAMMER MODELS

Ithaca Baker Model

The first model produced by the company was designed by W.H. Baker and was manufactured from 1883 through 1887. It was offered in six grades; Quality A ($35.00) through Quality F ($200.00) in either 10 or 12 gauge. All Ithaca produced Baker models had exposed hammers. Grades above Quality B are seldom encountered and an expert appraisal is recommended.

Quality A

Courtesy Walter C. Snyder

Exc.	V.G.	Good	Fair	Poor
700	500	300	200	100

Quality B

Exc.	V.G.	Good	Fair	Poor
1000	700	350	200	100

New Ithaca Gun

The New Ithaca Gun was introduced in 1888 and discontinued during 1915. Like its predecessor, it was introduced in the same seven grades, Quality A through Quality F. Later, the Quality F was discontinued. By 1900, a "Condensed Steel" barreled model, named Quality X, was introduced. The New Ithaca Gun was produced in gauges 10, 12, and 16, and very rarely, 20. Lower grade models carried the logo, "New Ithaca Gun", usually within a banner, on each side of the frame. Like its predecessor, grades above Quality B are seldom encountered, and an expert appraisal is recommended. Sixteen gauge guns command a 30% price premium. The extremely rare 20 gauge model requires an expert appraisal.

Quality A

Courtesy Walter C. Snyder

Exc.	V.G.	Good	Fair	Poor
1000	700	250	150	100

Quality AA

Exc.	V.G.	Good	Fair	Poor
1000	700	300	150	100

Quality B

Exc.	V.G.	Good	Fair	Poor
1200	800	400	200	100

Quality X

Exc.	V.G.	Good	Fair	Poor
1200	800	400	200	100

NOTE: Sixteen gauge guns command a 30% premium. the extremely rare 20 gauge model requires an expert appraisal.

The "New Double Bolted Hammer Gun"

During 1915, the Ithaca Gun Company replaced the New Ithaca Gun with a model it referred to as "our new model two bolt hammer gun". The new hammer gun had coil springs powering the external hammers. The "two bolt" lock up was accomplished by a bottom bolt and by the top lever engagement with the rear nub of the rib extension. Lower grade models were marked on both sides of the frame with a setter dog and the logo, "Ithaca Gun Co." The 1915 catalog is the last year hammer guns were advertised but the old records indicate a few were sold as late as 1919.

Grades offered were X, A, AA, B, C, D, and E. The 1915 catalogue advertised a price of $29.00 for an A Quality model and $150.00 for the elaborately engraved Quality E. All grades were available in 10, 12, and 16 gauges. Like the New Ithaca Gun, grades above Quality B are seldom encountered, and an expert appraisal is recommended. Sixteen gauge guns command a 30% price premium. The extremely rare 20 gauge model requires an expert appraisal.

Quality A

Exc.	V.G.	Good	Fair	Poor
1200	800	300	200	100

Quality AA

Exc.	V.G.	Good	Fair	Poor
1500	1000	400	200	100

Quality B

Exc.	V.G.	Good	Fair	Poor
1500	1000	400	200	100

Quality X

Exc.	V.G.	Good	Fair	Poor
1500	1000	450	200	100

HAMMERLESS MODELS

The first hammerless Ithaca gun was introduced in 1888. All Ithaca double guns were discontinued in 1948.

The gauge and grade can usually be found on the left front corner of the water table of the frame, the serial number is usually found on the right side of the same water table, on the barrel flats, and on the forend iron.

Crass Model

The Crass Model, named after Ithaca's Frederick Crass who designed it, was introduced in 1888. It was offered in Quality 1 through Quality 7. The Quality 1P, a model with no engraving, was introduced in 1898. The Crass Model underwent three major frame redesigns before it was discontinued during 1901. The gun was available in 10, 12, and 16 gauge. Automatic ejectors were introduced in 1893 and were available in any quality gun at extra cost.

NOTE: Sixteen gauge guns will command a 20% price premium. Guns above Quality 4 are seldom encountered, and an expert appraisal is necessary. For automatic ejectors add $250.00. The serial number range for the Crass Model is approximately 7,000 to 50,000.

Quality 1

Exc.	V.G.	Good	Fair	Poor
800	500	350	200	100

Quality 1-1/2

Exc.	V.G.	Good	Fair	Poor
800	500	350	200	100

Quality 1P

Exc.	V.G.	Good	Fair	Poor
800	500	350	200	100

Quality 2

Courtesy Walter C. Snyder

Exc.	V.G.	Good	Fair	Poor
1200	800	550	200	100

Quality 3

Exc.	V.G.	Good	Fair	Poor
1700	1200	700	300	100

Quality 4

Exc.	V.G.	Good	Fair	Poor
2000	1750	1000	300	100

Lewis Model

Chester Lewis, an Ithaca Gun employee, was credited with the design of the gun that now bears his name. The gun was bolted through the rib extension in addition to the traditional under bolt. The model was available from 1901 through 1906, and was offered in Qualities 1 through 7. It was made in 10, 12, and 16 gauge, and after 1906, 20 gauge. Automatic ejectors were offered at added cost.

Qualities offered: 1, 1 Special, 1-1/2, 2, 3, 4, 5, 6, 7. The 1 Special had Nitro Steel barrels.

NOTE: Automatic ejectors add about $250.00 to grades below Quality 4. The serial number range for the Lewis Model is approximately 55,000 to 123,600.

Quality 1

Exc.	V.G.	Good	Fair	Poor
800	500	300	150	100

Quality 1 Special

Courtesy Walter C. Snyder

Exc.	V.G.	Good	Fair	Poor
800	500	300	150	100

Quality 1-1/2

Exc.	V.G.	Good	Fair	Poor
850	550	300	150	100

Quality 2

Exc.	V.G.	Good	Fair	Poor
1000	600	400	200	100

Quality 3

Exc.	V.G.	Good	Fair	Poor
1700	1400	800	400	100

Quality 4

Exc.	V.G.	Good	Fair	Poor
2500	2200	1800	400	100

Quality 5

Exc.	V.G.	Good	Fair	Poor
3500	3000	2000	700	300

Quality 6

Exc.	V.G.	Good	Fair	Poor
6000	4500	3000	700	300

Quality 7

Exc.	V.G.	Good	Fair	Poor
6000	4500	3000	700	300

Minier Model

The Minier Model, named after Ithaca's David Minier, was introduced in 1906 and was available through 1908. It was offered in Qualities Field through 7 and any grade could be ordered with ejectors. The Minier Model was the first Ithaca gun to use coil springs to power the internal hammers. This model was triple bolted, e.g., two fastenings at the rib extension and the under bolt. Gauges 10, 12, 16, and 20 were offered.

Grades offered: Field, 1, 1 Special, 1-1/2, 2, 3, 4, 5, 6, 7.

NOTE: Automatic ejectors add $250.00 to guns below Quality 4. The serial number range for the Minier Model is approximately 130,000 to 151,000.

Field Grade

Exc.	V.G.	Good	Fair	Poor
1000	500	300	150	100

Quality 1

Exc.	V.G.	Good	Fair	Poor
1000	500	300	150	100

Quality 1 Special

Exc.	V.G.	Good	Fair	Poor
1000	500	300	150	100

Quality 1-1/2

Exc.	V.G.	Good	Fair	Poor
1000	550	300	150	100

Quality 2

Exc.	V.G.	Good	Fair	Poor
1200	600	400	200	100

Quality 3

Quality 3 Minier Model   Courtesy Walter Snyder

Exc.	V.G.	Good	Fair	Poor
2000	1000	500	400	100

Quality 4

Exc.	V.G.	Good	Fair	Poor
2500	1200	800	400	100

Quality 5

Exc.	V.G.	Good	Fair	Poor
3500	2500	1500	700	300

Quality 6

Exc.	V.G.	Good	Fair	Poor
5000	4000	1500	700	300

Quality 7

Exc.	V.G.	Good	Fair	Poor
5000	4000	1500	700	300

Flues Model

The Flues Model Ithaca gun was built on a three piece lock mechanism invented and patented by Emil Flues. Introduced in 1908, it remained in production through 1926 when it was replaced by the Ithaca New Double. It was offered in gauges 10, 12, 16, 20, and 28, and enjoyed the longest production life of any Ithaca double gun. Several grades were offered beginning with the Field grade and ending with the Sousa Special. The Flues Model had the same bolting system as used on the Minier Model. Any grade could have been ordered with automatic ejectors at extra cost. A single selective trigger made by the Infallible Trigger company was offered after 1914 and was the first single trigger offered from the company.

Qualities offered were: Field, 1, 1 Special, 1-1/2, 2, 3, 4, 5, 6, 7, and Sousa.

NOTE: Add $200.00 for factory ordered single trigger, add $200.00 for automatic ejectors on grades lower than Grade 4. Small gauges command a price premium. A 20 gauge gun may command up to a 50% price premium; a 28 gauge field grade perhaps as much as 100%. The serial number range for the Flues is approximately 175,000 to 399,000. Expert appraisals are recommended on higher grade, small gauge models as they are seldom encountered.

Field Grade

Flues Model Field Grade   Courtesy Walter Snyder

Exc.	V.G.	Good	Fair	Poor
1000	600	300	150	100

Grade 1

Exc.	V.G.	Good	Fair	Poor
1000	750	400	150	100

Grade 1 Special

Exc.	V.G.	Good	Fair	Poor
1000	750	400	150	100

Grade 1-1/2

Exc.	V.G.	Good	Fair	Poor
1100	750	400	150	100

Grade 2

Exc.	V.G.	Good	Fair	Poor
1200	800	400	200	100

Grade 3

Exc.	V.G.	Good	Fair	Poor
2000	1500	800	300	100

Grade 4

Exc.	V.G.	Good	Fair	Poor
2000	1600	1200	300	100

Grade 5

Exc.	V.G.	Good	Fair	Poor
2500	2000	1500	500	200

Grade 6

Photo courtesy of Walter C. Snyder

Exc.	V.G.	Good	Fair	Poor
9000	5000	2500	1000	300

Exc.	V.G.	Good	Fair	Poor
9000	5000	2500	1000	300

Grade 7

Exc.	V.G.	Good	Fair	Poor
8000	4500	2000	1000	300

Sousa

Exc.	V.G.	Good	Fair	Poor
15000	10000	6000	3000	N/A

The New Ithaca Double

The New Ithaca Double, commonly referred to as the NID, was manufactured from 1926 to 1948. It has the distinction of being the last double gun manufactured by the factory. The NID was bolted by a single rotary top bolt and was considered of all Ithaca double guns manufactured up to that time. External cocking indicators were standard on all NID models until about 1934 when they were eliminated from the design. Selective and non-selective single triggers and automatic ejectors were optional at additional costs. A special variation of the NID was introduced in 1932 to accommodate 10 gauge 3-1/2" magnum ammunition and was named, appropriately, the Magnum 10. All NID were available in grades Field, 1, 2, 3, 4, 5, 7, and Sousa (renamed the $1,000 grade after 1936). Gauges Magnum 10, standard 10, 12, 16, 20, 28, and .410 bore were offered.

NOTE: Like most collectable double guns, the smaller gauges command a price premium over the gauge model. A 16 gauge field grade may command a 25% price premium, a 20 gauge field grade may command up to a 50% price premium, and the 28 gauge, and .410 caliber field grade models perhaps as much as 100%. It is recommended that an expert opinion be sought for the valuation of high grade, small gauge models. Of late, the Magnum 10 gauge model also commands a price premium. Few of these guns trade, and the advise of an expert appraiser is suggested.

Non-selective Single Trigger-Add $150.
Single Selective Trigger-Add $250.
Ventilated Rib-Add $300.
Automatic Ejectors for grade below Grade 4-Add $300.
Beavertail Forearm-Add $200.

Monte Carlo buttstock-Add $300.

Field Grade

Exc.	V.G.	Good	Fair	Poor
800	600	300	150	100

Grade 1

Exc.	V.G.	Good	Fair	Poor
1000	700	400	200	100

Grade 2

Courtesy Walter C. Snyder

Exc.	V.G.	Good	Fair	Poor
1200	800	650	300	100

Grade 3

Exc.	V.G.	Good	Fair	Poor
2000	1400	1000	400	100

Grade 4

Exc.	V.G.	Good	Fair	Poor
3000	2500	1500	400	100

Grade 5

Grade 5 NID

Courtesy Walter Snyder

Exc.	V.G.	Good	Fair	Poor
4000	3200	2000	700	200

Grade 7

Exc.	V.G.	Good	Fair	Poor
10000	7000	4000	1000	300

Sousa Grade

Exc.	V.G.	Good	Fair	Poor
20000	10000	6000	3000	500

The New Ithaca Double (Modern-1999)

Reborn in 1999 under the company name Ithaca Classic Doubles of Victor, New York the reintroduction of the NID will begin with serial number 470000. The last recorded production number from the Ithaca factory for NID was 469999. Only about 50 guns will be produced per year.

Special Skeet Grade

This side-by-side double is offered in 20, 28, and .410 bore with a choice of matted rib barrel lengths of 26", 28", or 30". Ivory bead front sight. The action is case colored with light line border engraving. The stock is feather crotch black walnut with 22 l.p.i. checkering. Choice of pistol or straight grip. Double trigger is standard. Weight in 20 gauge is about 5 lbs. 14 oz. 28 gauge is about 5 lbs. 8 oz., and .410 bore weighs about 5 lbs. 5 oz.

NIB	Exc.	V.G.	Good	Fair	Poor
3150	—	—	—	—	—

Grade 4E

This model is also available in 20, 28, and .410 with 26", 28", and 30" barrels. This model has gold plated triggers jeweled barrel flats and hand tuned locks. Black walnut stock has 28 l.p.i. checkering with a fleur-de-lis pattern. Pistol or straight grip stock. Action is hand engraved with three game scenes and bank note scroll. Case colored frame.

NIB	Exc.	V.G.	Good	Fair	Poor
4200	—	—	—	—	—

Grade 7E

This model has all of the gauges and barrel lengths of the above guns. Action is hand engraved with gold two tone inlays. Exhibition grade black walnut stock with elaborate patterns. Custom built dimensions.

NIB	Exc.	V.G.	Good	Fair	Poor
8400	—	—	—	—	—

Sousa Grade

This model, available in the same gauges and barrel lengths as the above guns is stocked with presentation grade black walnut, hand carved with 32 l.p.i. checkering. The action is hand engraved with bank note scroll and gold inlays. The entire gun is hand fitted and polished. Extremely limited availability. Special order only.

Sousa Grade

The famous Sousa mermaid in raised gold inlay

NIB	Exc.	V.G.	Good	Fair	Poor
10500	—	—	—	—	—

LEFEVER ARMS COMPANY, INC.

During 1921, Ithaca Gun, under the name "The Lefever Arms Company, Inc." introduced a line of lower costs, box lock guns. See the Lefever Arms Company section of this book for prices concerning those guns.

WESTERN ARMS CORPORATION

During 1929 the Ithaca Gun Company created the Western Arms Corporation which introduced a new, low cost double gun. That new double gun was named The Long Range Double and it was produced in 12, 16, and 20 gauges, and .410 caliber. Twenty gauge guns often command a 20% premium, a .410 caliber can command up to a 50% premium. This model was last made at the start of World War II.

The Long Range Double

The Long Range Double had walnut stocks that were not checkered.

Single trigger guns will add $100 and automatic ejectors will add $200.

Exc.	V.G.	Good	Fair	Poor
450	350	200	150	N/A

The Long Range Double Deluxe

Usually made exclusively for the Montgomery Ward Company and sold by them under the name, Western Field Deluxe. This model had a line checkering pattern at the grip and on the splinter forend. Many of the Ithaca produced Western Field Deluxe guns had automatic ejectors and that fact was stamped into the right barrel.

Single triggers add $100.
Automatic ejectors add $200.

Exc.	V.G.	Good	Fair	Poor
450	350	250	150	N/A

ITHACA SINGLE BARREL TRAP GUNS

The Ithaca Gun Company introduced a single barrel trap gun in 1914. This gun was based upon the Emil Flues three piece lock design used for the double gun and has become known as the Flues Model Single Barrel Trap. The Flues Model was discontinued during 1922 and was replaced that year by a model designed by Ithaca's Frank Knickerbocker, commonly referred to as the "Knick". The Knick Model was discontinued in 1988, shortly after the Ithaca Acquisition Corp. purchased the assets of the Ithaca Gun Company. For many years, The Ithaca Single Barrel Trap Gun was the gun of choice for many champion shooters.

Flues Model Single Barrel Trap Gun (1914 to 1922)

The Flues Model trap gun was introduced in 1914 and offered in Grades 4, 5, 6, and 7. A lower cost Victory grade was introduced in 1919 and the highest cost variety, the Sousa Special was introduced in 1918. All Flues model trap guns were made within the same serial number sequence as the double guns but do have the letter "T" for Trap following the serial number. All Flues Models with the exception of the Victory Grade were produced with an automatic ejector. A rubber anti-recoil pad was an option. Guns having a pre-1916 engraving pattern will command the highest prices.

Courtesy Walter C. Snyder

Victory Grade

Exc.	V.G.	Good	Fair	Poor
1200	800	650	300	N/A

Grade 4E

Exc.	V.G.	Good	Fair	Poor
2200	1800	1250	400	N/A

Grade 5E

Grade 5E Flues Model

Courtesy Walter Snyder

Exc.	V.G.	Good	Fair	Poor
4000	3000	2500	600	N/A

Grade 6E

Exc.	V.G.	Good	Fair	Poor
6000	5000	3000	800	N/A

Grade 7E

Exc.	V.G.	Good	Fair	Poor
8000	6000	4000	1000	N/A

Sousa Grade

Exc.	V.G.	Good	Fair	Poor
15000	10000	8000	2000	N/A

Knick Model Single Barrel Trap

The Knick Model trap gun was introduced during 1922 and was based on a design credited to Frank Knickerbocker. The design was simple and very serviceable, had been in continues production until 1988 when it was discontinued. The model was available in Victory, 4, 5, 7, and Sousa Special Grades. The Sousa was replaced by the $1,000 Grade in about 1936 which was replaced by the $2,000 Grade by 1952, the $2,500 Grade by 1960, the $3,000 Grade by 1965, the $5,000 Grade by 1974, and finally, the Dollar Grade in the early 1980s as the cost of production increased. All Knick models were produced with an automatic ejector and a rubber anti-recoil pad.

Victory Grade

Courtesy William Hammond

NIB	Exc.	V.G.	Good	Fair	Poor
2000	1200	800	650	300	N/A

Grade 4E

Courtesy C. Hadley Smith

NIB	Exc.	V.G.	Good	Fair	Poor
3000	2200	1800	1000	500	N/A

Grade 5E

NIB	Exc.	V.G.	Good	Fair	Poor
5000	4000	3000	2500	800	N/A

Grade 7E

Grade 7 Knick Model

Courtesy Walter Snyder

NIB	Exc.	V.G.	Good	Fair	Poor
8000	5000	4000	3000	1000	N/A

Sousa Grade

NIB	Exc.	V.G.	Good	Fair	Poor
25000	15000	10000	8000	2000	N/A

$1,000 to $2,500 Grades

$2,000 Grade Knick Model

Courtesy Walter Snyder

NIB	Exc.	V.G.	Good	Fair	Poor
15000	12000	8000	6000	2000	N/A

$3,000 through the Dollar Grade

NIB	Exc.	V.G.	Good	Fair	Poor
12000	10000	6000	5000	2000	N/A

Century Grade Trap (SKB)

A 12 gauge boxlock single barrel shotgun with a 32" or 34" ventilated rib barrel and automatic ejector. Blued with a walnut stock. Manufactured by SKB during the 1970s.

Exc.	V.G.	Good	Fair	Poor
600	500	450	350	300

Century II (SKB)

An improved version of the above model.

Exc.	V.G.	Good	Fair	Poor
650	550	500	400	350

Model 66-1963-1978

A 12, 20 or .410 bore lever action single shot shotgun with a 24" barrel. Blued with a walnut stock. The 20 gauge and .410 bore command a 50% price premium.

Courtesy C. Hadley Smith

NIB	Exc.	V.G.	Good	Fair	Poor
175	150	125	75	50	—

Model 66 Youth Grade

A special gun offered for the youth market in 20 gauge and .410 bore.

NIB	Exc.	V.G.	Good	Fair	Poor
225	150	125	100	50	—

Model 66 Buck Buster (RS Barrel)

As above, in 20 gauge with a Deerslayer 22" barrel fitted with rifle sights.

NIB	Exc.	V.G.	Good	Fair	Poor
225	150	125	100	50	—

Model 66 Vent Rib

NIB	Exc.	V.G.	Good	Fair	Poor
225	150	125	100	50	—

ITHACA AUTO & BURGLAR GUN NFA, CURIO OR RELIC

The Ithaca Auto & Burglar Gun is a double barreled 20 gauge smooth bore pistol manufactured by Ithaca Gun Company, Ithaca, New York, from 1922 to 1934. Total production was approximately 4,500. They were made by modifying Ithaca's standard field grade double barrel shotgun by shortening the barrels and fitting the receiver with a pistol grip. Standard factory guns had blued 10" barrels, case hardened receivers with the legend **Auto & Burglar Gun/ Ithaca Gun Co./Ithaca, New York**, and the figure of a pointing dog stamped on each side. The barrel length on 21 guns inspected varied to 10.25" (typically in increments divisible by .125"), apparently from inexact factory quality control. Ithaca set a $37.50 retail price when the gun was in production, but some dealers sold it for $40 or more. Production was halted when the government ruled the Ithaca Auto & Burglar Gun to be a "firearm" in the "any other weapon" category under the National Firearms Act (NFA) of 1934.

There are two variations, termed Model A and Model B. Model A utilizes the so-called Flues frame (named after Emil Flues, who designed it in 1908), and its distinctive grip has a curving butt and a large spur. Model A is designed for 2.5" shells, and is not considered safe to fire using modern ammunition. Approximately 2,500 Model A Auto & Burglar Guns were manufactured from 1922 to 1925, when the Flues model was discontinued.

Model B utilizes the so-called N.I.D. frame (short for New Ithaca Double), introduced in 1926 and discontinued in 1948. The N.I.D. is designed for modern ammunition and 2.75" shells, has cocking indicators, and a different pistol grip that is perpendicular to the barrel and which lacks the distinctive spur. Some Model Bs have been observed with rosettes or "stars" engraved in each side of the receiver; their significance is unknown at this time, but they probably are decorations. Approximately 2,000 Model B Auto & Burglar Guns were manufactured from 1926 to 1934.

Model A, serial numbered from 343336 to 398365

Exc.	V.G.	Good	Fair	Poor
1,500	1,000	900	750	550

Model B, serial numbered from 425000 to 464699

Exc.	V.G.	Good	Fair	Poor
1,300	950	750	550	450

NOTE: Nonstandard or special order guns command premiums of 100 percent or more. Original holsters (marked Auto and Burglar Gun/MADE BY/ITHACA GUN CO./ITHACA, N.Y.) are extremely rare and worth $300 to $500 or more.

Ithaca Auto & Burglar Gun serial numbers are interspersed among those of sporting guns assembled during the same production runs, in lots of approximately 100. Their dates of manufacture generally correspond those by serial number reported by the Ithaca Gun Co., but some guns were assembled later than the reported years of manufacture (see *The World's Fighting Shotguns*, by Thomas F. Swearengen. Alexandria, Virginia: Ironside International Publishers, Inc., 1978, pages 80-85).

Swearengen reports approximately 20 special-order Auto & Burglar Guns were manufactured; so far 11 have been documented, and are listed below. Nonstandard (other than 10") barrel lengths were produced on special-order or were experimental or prototype guns. The 12" barrels on serial number 354442 are probably original to the gun, whose low serial number and hand engraved (rather than stamped) **Auto & Burglar Gun** legend indicates it could have been the first gun assembled. A hand-engraved legend is probably a useful diagnostic in determining the authenticity of the earliest specimens. The 18.5" barreled guns may have been exempt from the NFA when originally manufactured, but today are not because their overall lengths are less than 26" (a requirement established in 1960). Data on Model A guns, which may include experimental or prototype models, are from L. Franklin Moore, Jr. (354442); Cliff Schisler (360142); and Michael McIntosh (361452, in *Sporting Classics*, January/February 1986, page 73), respectively. Data on Model B guns, Flues and N.I.D. serial numbers, and dates of manufacture, are from Walter Claude Snyder's book *The Ithaca Gun Company From the Beginning* (Spencerport, New York: Cook and Uline Publishing Co., 1991, page 211), and reproduced here with Mr. Snyder's kind permission. Note that some N.I.D. serial numbers for 1935 and 1936 are nonsequential.

Model A (Flues frame)			Model B (N.I.D. frame)		
Factory serial number ranges			Factory serial number ranges		
From	To	Year	From	To	Year
343336	356513	1921	425000	425299	1925
356514	361849	1922	425300	439199	1926
361900	372099	1923	439200	451099	1927
372100	390499	1924	451100	454530	1928
390500	398352	1925	454600	457299	1929
398353	398365	1926	457300	458399	1930
			458400	459139	1931
			459140	459162	1932
			459163	459195	1933
			459196	459637	1935
			459638	459649	1936
			459650	460799	1935
			460800	462899	1936
			462900	464699	1937

ITHACA MODEL 37 REPEATER

The Ithaca Model 37 Repeater was introduced in 1937 in 12 gauge, 1938 in 16 gauge, and in 1939 in 20 gauge. It underwent very few design changes throughout its long life which ended 1987 when the Ithaca Acquisition Corp. acquired the assets of the Ithaca Gun Company during 1987 and renamed the gun the Model 87. The name has recently been changed again to the M37 after the assets of the Ithaca Acquisition Corp. were purchased in May of 1996 by the Ithaca Gun Company, LLC. All Model 37 guns were chambered only for 2-3/-5/4" ammunition until 1983, when the Magnum with 3" chamber was introduced to some configurations. Most Model 37 guns had blued metal and walnut stocks with the exception of the Model 37 Field Grade series which had matte finished metal and Birch stocks. Sixteen gauge guns were discontinued in 1973.

NOTE: Twenty gauge guns made before 1968 will generally command a price premium.

Model 37/Standard Grade-1937 to 1983
Guns made before 1968 will enjoy a 15% price premium; those made before World War II, a 30% price premium.

Courtesy C. Hadley Smith

Exc.	V.G.	Good	Fair	Poor
350	200	175	125	75

Model 37S/Skeet Grade-1937 to 1953
Guns made before World War II will enjoy a 50% price premium.

Exc.	V.G.	Good	Fair	Poor
600	400	350	250	100

Model 37T/Trap-1937 to 1953
Guns made before World War II will enjoy a 50% price premium.

Exc.	V.G.	Good	Fair	Poor
600	400	350	250	100

Model 37T/Target-1954 to 1961

Exc.	V.G.	Good	Fair	Poor
600	400	350	250	100

Model 37R/Solid Rib-1940-1967
Guns made before World War II will enjoy a 50% price premium.

Courtesy Walter Snyder

Exc.	V.G.	Good	Fair	Poor
400	275	225	200	75

Model 37 Military Marked (WWII)
This is one of the scarcest military shotguns. It was built in three different configurations; 30" barrel, 20" barrel, and 20" barrel with handguard and bayonet lug (Trench Gun). A scarce shotgun, proceed with caution.

Model 37 with 20" barrel and release papers

Courtesy Richard M. Kumor, Sr.

Exc.	V.G.	Good	Fair	Poor
2000	1800	1500	—	—

NOTE: Add $200 for government release papers and 150% for Trench Gun configuration.

Model 37RD/Deluxe Solid Rib-1954 to 1962

Courtesy C. Hadley Smith

Exc.	V.G.	Good	Fair	Poor
500	375	300	200	100

Nonstandard or Special Order Ithaca Auto & Burglar Guns

Serial number	Bore/ Model	Barrel gauge	length	Customer	Date
354442	A	28	12"	Unknown	circa 1921-22
360142	A	28	10"	Unknown	circa 1921-22, Grade No. 1
361452	A	28	10"	Unknown	circa 1922, Grade No. 4
452245	B	.410	26"	Wray-Richards	August 17, 1928
452246	B	.410	26"	Emil F. Flues	August 17, 1928
452251	B	.410	12.5"	Leslie Hawks	March 29, 1929
452252	B	.410	10"	L. M. Armstrong	March 29, 1929
459357	B	16	18.5"	Montgomery & Crawford	September 28, 1935
460388	B	20	18.5"	Montgomery & Crawford	January 9, 1936
463375	B	20	18.5"	Lawrence D. Bell	September 2, 1937
461194	B	.410	18.5"	Unknown	June 22, 1938

Model 37 Deerslayer-1959 to 1987
All Deerslayer models made before 1968 will enjoy a 10% to 20% price premium.

Courtesy C. Hadley Smith

Exc.	V.G.	Good	Fair	Poor
300	250	200	125	75

Model 37 Deluxe Deerslayer-1959 to 1971
Exc.	V.G.	Good	Fair	Poor
300	250	225	125	75

Model 37 Super Deluxe Deerslayer-1959-1987

Courtesy C. Hadley Smith

Exc.	V.G.	Good	Fair	Poor
350	325	275	200	100

Model 37 Supreme Grade-1967 to 1987
Exc.	V.G.	Good	Fair	Poor
600	450	350	200	100

Model 37 Field Grade Standard-1983 to 1985
Exc.	V.G.	Good	Fair	Poor
250	200	150	125	75

Model 37 Field Grade Vent-1983 to 1986
Exc.	V.G.	Good	Fair	Poor
275	250	200	125	75

Model 37 Basic Featherlight-1979 to 1983
Manufactured in 12 gauge only.

Courtesy Walter Snyder

Exc.	V.G.	Good	Fair	Poor
275	250	200	125	75

Model 37V/Vent Rib-1961-1983
Guns made before 1968 will enjoy a 10% to 20% price premium.

Exc.	V.G.	Good	Fair	Poor
250	200	175	150	75

Model 37RV/Deluxe Vent Rib-1961-1966

Courtesy Walter Snyder

Exc.	V.G.	Good	Fair	Poor
500	375	300	200	75

Model 37D/Deluxe-1955 to 1977
Guns made before 1968 will enjoy a 10% to 20% price premium.

Courtesy C. Hadley Smith

Exc.	V.G.	Good	Fair	Poor
275	225	175	125	75

Model 37DV/Deluxe Vent Rib-1961 to 1987
Guns made before 1968 will enjoy a 10% to 20% price premium.

Exc.	V.G.	Good	Fair	Poor
400	300	200	150	100

Model 37 Magnum-3" Chamber-1978 to 1987
Exc.	V.G.	Good	Fair	Poor
325	275	225	125	75

Model 37 Field Grade Magnum-1984-1987

Exc.	V.G.	Good	Fair	Poor
300	225	175	125	75

Model 37 UltraLight-1978 to 1987

The UltraLight had an aluminum alloy frame and trigger plate. The barrels are marked Ultra Featherlight and the serial number is prefaced with the mark, "ULT". Both the 12 and 20 gauges were offered.

Exc.	V.G.	Good	Fair	Poor
475	400	300	150	100

Model 37 English UltraLight-1982 to 1987

This gun is the same as the Model 37 UltraLight, but has an English style straight grip stock.

Exc.	V.G.	Good	Fair	Poor
500	450	350	150	100

Model 37 CAMO

Introduced in 1985, this model is available with either a green or brown camouflage finish and was offered only in 12 gauge.

Exc.	V.G.	Good	Fair	Poor
350	300	200	150	100

Model 37 Bicentennial

A special model produced during 1976 to commemorate the 200 year anniversary of the United States. The gun came with a full length trunk style hard case and a pewter belt buckle number to the gun. The serial number was prefaced with "U.S.A." Subtract 35% if the original case and belt buckle are missing.

NIB	Exc.	V.G.	Good	Fair	Poor
650	500	300	200	125	75

Model 37 Ducks Unlimited Commemorative, Auction Grade

Special edition made during 1977. Serial number sequence was 40-DU0001 to 40-DU1125.

NIB	Exc.	V.G.	Good	Fair	Poor
650	400	300	150	100	75

Model 37 Ducks Unlimited Commemorative, Trade Grade

Special edition made during 1977. Lower grade version of the Auction Grade. Serial number preceded with the mark, DU37040.

Model 37 2500 Series Centennial

A commemorative Model 37 12 gauge shotgun with silver-plated receiver and press checkered stocks. Manufactured in 1984.

NIB	Exc.	V.G.	Good	Fair	Poor
800	500	300	150	100	75

Model 37 Presentation Series Centennial

A commemorative Mode 37 12 gauge with a gold-plated receiver and high grade hand checkered stocks. It was manufactured during 1980, but is still available as of August, 1997.

NIB	Exc.	V.G.	Good	Fair	Poor
1500	800	500	150	100	—

Hi-Grade Ithaca Model 37 Guns

The Ithaca Gun company offered custom engraving services either from its in-house engraver, one of which was retained until about 1972, or through an outside contract engraver who was usually William Mains. Many customers requested some degree of custom work and guns with various patterns turn up from time to time. There were four standard engraving patterns offered to customers, Grade 1, Grade 2, Grade 3, and the very elaborate $1,000 Grade pattern. Increasing production costs forced the $1,000 Grade to become the $2,000 Grade, the $2,500, and finally the $3,000 Grades over the years.

NOTE: All factory engraved Model 37 guns are rare and require an expert appraiser to determine an accurate value.

Model 37 $1,000 Grade

The Model 37 with an engraved receiver, gold inlays, and a well-figured walnut stock. Manufactured between 1940 and 1942.

NIB	Exc.	V.G.	Good	Fair	Poor
10000	5000	3000	2000	N/A	N/A

Model 37 $2,000 Grade

Manufactured from 1946 to 1957

NIB	Exc.	V.G.	Good	Fair	Poor
10000	5000	3000	2000	N/A	N/A

Model 37 $3,000 Grade

As above. Manufactured from 1958 to 1967.

NIB	Exc.	V.G.	Good	Fair	Poor
8000	4000	2500	1500	N/A	N/A

Model 37 Law Enforcement Weapons

The Ithaca Gun Company entered the law enforcement market in 1962 when it introduced the Model 37 Military and Police (M&P) and the Model 37DS Police special (DSPS). The M&P Model was styled after the riot guns made for various military contracts. The DSPS was styled after the Ithaca Deerslayer. Both models were offered with 8-shot capacity after 1968. A chrome finish was an available option after 1976. Both models usually had ring turned slide handles. Only those models available to the general public, i.e. barrel lengths of 18" or longer, are listed.

Model 37 Military and Police (M&P) 1962-1986

Add 20% for an 8-shot model in NIB or EXC. condition, and add an additional 15% for chrome plated models in similar condition.

NIB	Exc.	V.G.	Good	Fair	Poor
350	300	250	200	125	75

Model 37 DS Police Special-1962-1986

Add 20% for an 8-shot model in NIB or EXC. condition, and add an additional 15% for chrome plated models in similar condition.

NIB	Exc.	V.G.	Good	Fair	Poor
400	350	250	200	125	75

ITHACA MODEL 87 REPEATER

During 1987 many of the assets of the bankrupt Ithaca Gun Company were purchased by the Ithaca Acquisition Corporation. Manufacture of the Model 37 was resumed that summer after the gun was renamed the Model 87. Many of the Models offered by the old company were continued. All Model 87 field guns were produced with ventilated ribs. All Deerslayer models continued the rifle sights used on the Model 37 guns.

Model 87 Basic-1989-1994

Early models had birch stocks, later production had walnut stocks. All had ring turned slide handles.

NIB	Exc.	V.G.	Good	Fair	Poor
250	200	175	150	125	75

Model 87 Magnum

A 12 or 20 gauge Magnum slide action shotgun with a 25" barrel fitted with screw-in choke tubes, ventilated rib that is similar to the Model 37. Blued with a walnut stock.

NIB	Exc.	V.G.	Good	Fair	Poor
300	250	200	175	125	100

The Model 87 was manufactured in the following styles as of 1989:

Model 87 Field Grade-1987-1990

Stocks were walnut with pressed checkering.

NIB	Exc.	V.G.	Good	Fair	Poor
300	250	200	175	125	75

Model 87 Camo-1987-1994

NIB	Exc.	V.G.	Good	Fair	Poor
300	250	200	175	125	75

Model 87 Turkey Gun-1987-1996

Photo by Walter C. Snyder

NIB	Exc.	V.G.	Good	Fair	Poor
300	250	200	175	125	75

Model 87 Deluxe-1987-1996

The buttstocks and slide handle were walnut with a machine cut checkered pattern.

Photo by Walter C. Snyder

NIB	Exc.	V.G.	Good	Fair	Poor
300	275	250	200	125	75

Model 87 Ultralite-1987-1990

All IAC manufactured Ultralite guns carry the old Model 37 serial number.

Photo by Walter C. Snyder

NIB	Exc.	V.G.	Good	Fair	Poor
500	350	250	175	125	75

Model 87 English-1993-1996

Hand checkered walnut stocks. The slide handle was styled after the pre-war Model 37 slide handle.

NIB	Exc.	V.G.	Good	Fair	Poor
400	350	250	175	125	75

Model 87 Ultralite Deluxe

NIB	Exc.	V.G.	Good	Fair	Poor
400	350	300	250	125	75

Model 87 Supreme Grade-1987-1996

High grade walnut stocks with hand checkering. Metal had extra fine polish and finish.

Photo by Walter C. Snyder

NIB	Exc.	V.G.	Good	Fair	Poor
1000	700	500	—	—	—

Model 87 Deerslayer Basic-1989-1996

Walnut, oil finish butt and slide handle stocks. Slide handle was classic ring turned style.

NIB	Exc.	V.G.	Good	Fair	Poor
300	275	250	200	125	75

Model 87 Deerslayer-1989-1996

It was sometimes advertised as the Model 87 Deerslayer Field. Buttstock and slide handle were walnut and usually had a pressed checkered pattern. The slide handle was the beavertail style.

Photo by Walter C. Snyder

NIB	Exc.	V.G.	Good	Fair	Poor
350	300	250	200	125	75

Model 87 Deluxe Deerslayer-1989-1996

Butt stock and slide handle were walnut with a machine cut checkering pattern. The slide handle was beavertail.

NIB	Exc.	V.G.	Good	Fair	Poor
400	350	250	200	125	75

Model 87 Deerslayer II-1988-1996

This model had a fixed rifle barrel and a Monte Carlo buttstock. A small number of guns were specially made with a fast twist barrel to handle Brenneke ammunition and are marked "BRENNEKE" on the receiver. Brenneke marked guns will command a 30% price premium.

Photo by Walter C. Snyder

NIB	Exc.	V.G.	Good	Fair	Poor
450	400	350	200	125	75

Model 87 Home Protection and Law Enforcement models

The Ithaca Acquisition Corporation continued production of many of the law enforcement firearms produced by the Ithaca Gun Company. Only those models available to the general public are listed.

Model 87 Military & Police-1987-1996

Generally produced with a non-checkered walnut buttstock and a ring turned slide handle, both of which were oil finished. Add 20% for an 8-shot model in NIB or excellent condition. Add an additional 15% for chrome plated models in similar condition.

NIB	Exc.	V.G.	Good	Fair	Poor
350	300	250	200	125	75

Model 87 DS Police Special-1987-1996

Produced from either a pressed checkered or a non-checkered walnut buttstocks, and a ring turned slide handle, both lacquer finished. The metal was usually finished with a commercial polished blue but a chrome plated finish was also available. Add 20% for an 8-shot model in NIB or excellent condition, and add an additional 15% for a chrome plated models in similar condition.

NIB	Exc.	V.G.	Good	Fair	Poor
400	350	250	200	125	75

NEW MODEL 37

During 1996, the assets of the bankrupt Ithaca Acquisition Corporation were purchased by a new company named the Ithaca Gun Company, LLC. One of the first public actions of the new firm was to rename the Model 87 the Model 37, before resuming production later that year, the serial number of the new Model 37 is prefaced with the letter "M". A used market for the new Model 37 has not been established at this time. Suggested retail prices for each model currently produced are listed.

In 2001 a Legacy Edition upgrade featuring a laser carved handwritten message in the stock was available for an additional $125.00.

Model 37 Deerslayer II

This model is offered in both 12 and 20 gauge. Fitted with either 20" or 25" barrels with rifled bores. These barrel are fixed to the receiver. Magazine capacity is 5 rounds. Walnut stock. Weight is approximately 7 lbs. In 2001 a 16 gauge version with fixed rifled barrel was offered.

NIB	Exc.	V.G.	Good	Fair	Poor
565	450	375	—	—	—

Smooth Bore Deluxe

Offered in 12, 16, or 20 gauge with interchangeable barrels in 20" or 25" with smooth bore for deer. Walnut stock. Magazine capacity is 5 rounds. Weight is approximately 6.75 lbs.

NIB	Exc.	V.G.	Good	Fair	Poor
515	400	350	—	—	—

Rifled Deluxe

Same as above but in 12 and 20 gauge only with rifled barrels.

NIB	Exc.	V.G.	Good	Fair	Poor
515	400	350	—	—	—

Model 37 Deluxe Field

This model is offered in 12, 16, and 20 gauge with interchangeable vent rib barrels of 26", 28", or 30" (12 gauge only). Walnut stock. Magazine capacity is 5 rounds. Weight is about 7 lbs.

NIB	Exc.	V.G.	Good	Fair	Poor
545	450	375	—	—	—

Model 37 Deluxe Field English Style

This model is offered in 20 gauge only with 24", 26", or 28" vent rib barrels. Walnut stock. Weight is about 7 lbs. Magazine capacity is 5 rounds.

NIB	Exc.	V.G.	Good	Fair	Poor
545	450	375	—	—	—

Model 37 Ultra Featherlight Grouse Special

Based on the Classic Model 37 with bottom ejection this model features an aluminum receiver and 24" vent rib barrel with choke tubes. Straight grip stock of American black walnut.

NIB	Exc.	V.G.	Good	Fair	Poor
600	475	—	—	—	—

Model 37 Ultra Featherlight Youth

Similar to the above model but with a 22" barrel and 12.75" length of pull buttstock with ventilated recoil pad.

NIB	Exc.	V.G.	Good	Fair	Poor
600	475	—	—	—	—

Model 37 Sporting Clays

This model features a choice of 24", 26", or 28" wide vent rib barrels with Briley choke tubes. Receiver has an antiqued finish with scroll engraving and high grade American black walnut.

NIB	Exc.	V.G.	Good	Fair	Poor
1350	1000	—	—	—	—

Model 37 Trap

This model has similar features as the sporting clays but with 30" wide vent rib barrel.

NIB	Exc.	V.G.	Good	Fair	Poor
1350	1000	—	—	—	—

Model 37 Women's Endowment Shotgun

Offered in 16 or 20 gauge with straight grip stock and a length of pull designed for the woman's height of 5'5". American walnut stock with cut checkering.

NIB	Exc.	V.G.	Good	Fair	Poor
635	500	—	—	—	—

Model 37 Turkeyslayer

This model is offered in 12 gauge with 22" full choke barrel. Choice of 22" ported barrel. Also, a 20 gauge youth model is offered with 22" barrel. Camo stock is standard. Weight is about 7 lbs.

NIB	Exc.	V.G.	Good	Fair	Poor
565	450	375	—	—	—

NOTE: Add $15 for ported barrel option.

Model 37 Waterfowler

Available in 12 gauge only with 28" steel shot barrel. Camo pattern stock. Weight is about 7 lbs. Magazine capacity is 5 rounds.

NIB	Exc.	V.G.	Good	Fair	Poor
595	475	375	—	—	—

Model 37 New Classic

Available in 12, 20, or 16 gauge with hand checkered walnut stock and high polish bolt and other component parts. Sunburst recoil pad. Interchangeable vent rib barrels in either 26" or 28". Weight is about 7 lbs.

NIB	Exc.	V.G.	Good	Fair	Poor
695	550	—	—	—	—

MODEL 51 SERIES

A 12 or 20 gauge semiautomatic shotgun with 26", 28", or 30" ventilated rib barrels. Blued with a walnut stock. Manufactured from 1970 to 1985 as follows:

Model 51A Standard-Plain Barrel
Vent Rib-Add $100.

Photo by C. Hadley Smith

Exc.	V.G.	Good	Fair	Poor
275	225	200	150	75

Model 51A Magnum-3" Chamber
Vent Rib-Add $100.

Exc.	V.G.	Good	Fair	Poor
300	250	225	175	75

Model 51A Waterfowler-Matte Finished

Exc.	V.G.	Good	Fair	Poor
425	375	325	250	75

Model 51A Deerslayer

Photo by C. Hadley Smith

Exc.	V.G.	Good	Fair	Poor
325	275	225	150	75

Model 51A Turkey Gun

Photo by Walter C. Snyder

Exc.	V.G.	Good	Fair	Poor
325	275	225	150	75

Model 51 Supreme Trap

Exc.	V.G.	Good	Fair	Poor
425	375	325	250	75

Model 51 Supreme Skeet

Exc.	V.G.	Good	Fair	Poor
450	400	350	275	200

Model 51 Ducks Unlimited Commemorative

NIB	Exc.	V.G.	Good	Fair	Poor
475	400	375	325	275	200

Model 51 Presentation-Engraved Receiver

NIB	Exc.	V.G.	Good	Fair	Poor
1500	1250	1000	750	500	N/A

Mag-10 Series

A 10 gauge Magnum semiautomatic shotgun manufactured in a variety of barrel lengths, styles and finishes. Manufactured from 1975 to 1986 in as follows:

Standard Grade

Exc.	V.G.	Good	Fair	Poor
750	700	650	300	250

Standard Vent Rib Grade

Exc.	V.G.	Good	Fair	Poor
850	775	700	550	250

Deluxe Vent Rib Grade

Exc.	V.G.	Good	Fair	Poor
1000	850	775	600	250

Supreme Grade

Exc.	V.G.	Good	Fair	Poor
1200	1050	850	700	250

Roadblocker-Military and Police Model

Exc.	V.G.	Good	Fair	Poor
650	575	500	400	200

Presentation Grade-Engraved, Gold-inlaid, 200 Made

NIB	Exc.	V.G.	Good	Fair	Poor
1875	1500	1100	900	750	300

National Wild Turkey Federation-1985 Manufacture

NIB	Exc.	V.G.	Good	Fair	Poor
850	700	600	550	450	350

Shotguns manufactured by Perazzi and Japanese firms that were marketed by Ithaca are listed under the respective manufacturer's name.

Model X5-C

A .22 caliber semiautomatic rifle with a 7-shot magazine. A 10-shot magazine was available as an extra cost option. Blued with a walnut stock. Manufactured between 1958 and 1964.

NIB	Exc.	V.G.	Good	Fair	Poor
400	200	150	100	75	—

Model X5T Lightning

A .22 caliber tubular feed auto loading rifle produced between 1959 and 1963. Some models were stocked with curly maple stocks. These guns will command a 25% price premium.

NIB	Exc.	V.G.	Good	Fair	Poor
450	175	150	100	75	—

Model X-15 Lightning
Similar to the above, but manufactured between 1964 and 1966.

NIB	Exc.	V.G.	Good	Fair	Poor
450	175	150	100	75	—

Model 49 Saddlegun-1961-1979
A .22 caliber lever action single shot rifle with an 18.5" barrel, fixed sights, alloy receiver and hardwood stock. It was offered chambered for the .22 Magnum in 1962.

Photo by C. Hadley Smith

NIB	Exc.	V.G.	Good	Fair	Poor
250	150	125	100	50	—

Model 49 Saddlegun Deluxe Grade
Fitted with gold plated trigger, hammer, and equipped with sling and sling swivels.

NIB	Exc.	V.G.	Good	Fair	Poor
350	250	150	100	50	—

Model 49 Saddlegun Presentation Grade
High grade wood and engraved frame.

NIB	Exc.	V.G.	Good	Fair	Poor
400	300	250	200	50	—

Model 49R-1968-1971
A lever action .22 caliber tubular feed rifle. Magazine capacity is 15 Long Rifle cartridges. No other chambers were offered.

NIB	Exc.	V.G.	Good	Fair	Poor
350	250	200	150	50	—

Model 72 Saddlegun-1973-1979
A .22 or .22 Magnum caliber lever action rifle with an 18.5" barrel, tubular magazine, open sights and walnut stock. Made by Erma in Germany.

NIB	Exc.	V.G.	Good	Fair	Poor
375	275	225	200	100	—

LSA-55 or 65 Series
A bolt action sporting rifle manufactured in a variety of calibers and barrel lengths by Tikka of Finland. Imported between 1969 and 1977 in the following models:

LSA-55 Standard
Exc.	V.G.	Good	Fair	Poor
500	350	300	250	175

LSA-55 Deluxe
Exc.	V.G.	Good	Fair	Poor
600	375	325	275	200

LSA-55 Varmint-Heavy Barrel
Exc.	V.G.	Good	Fair	Poor
600	400	350	300	225

LSA-65-Long Action
Exc.	V.G.	Good	Fair	Poor
500	350	300	250	175

LSA-65 Deluxe
Exc.	V.G.	Good	Fair	Poor
600	375	325	275	200

LSA-55 Turkey Gun
A 12 gauge by .222 Remington caliber Over/Under combination rifle/shotgun with 24.5" barrels, single trigger, exposed hammer and walnut stock. Manufactured in Finland by Tikka between 1970 and 1981.

Exc.	V.G.	Good	Fair	Poor
850	600	450	350	275

X-Caliber
A .22 to .44 Magnum caliber single shot pistol with 10" or 15" barrels featuring a dual firing pin system so that interchangeable barrels could be used. The Model 20 is blued, the Model 30 is Teflon coated. Introduced in 1988.

NIB	Exc.	V.G.	Good	Fair	Poor
275	225	200	175	145	100

IVER JOHNSON ARMS, INC.
Middlesex, New Jersey
SEE—AMAC
Established in 1883 in Fitchburg, Massachusetts, this company has produced a wide variety of firearms during its existence.

Trade Name Revolvers
A series of spur trigger revolvers were made by Iver Johnson bearing only the trade names such as those that follow: Encore, Eclipse, Favorite, Tycoon, and Eagle. In general, the value for these revolvers is as follows:

Exc.	V.G.	Good	Fair	Poor
200	170	120	95	65

Safety Automatic Double Action
A .22, .32CF, or .38CF caliber double action revolver produced in a variety of barrel lengths with or without exposed hammers. Manufactured between 1893 and 1950.

Exc.	V.G.	Good	Fair	Poor
200	170	120	95	65

Model 1900

A .22 to .38 caliber double action revolver with a 2.5", 4.5", or 6" barrel. Blued or nickel-plated with rubber grips and no cartridge ejecting system. Manufactured between 1900 and 1947.

Exc.	V.G.	Good	Fair	Poor
200	170	120	95	65

Safety Cycle Automatic

Similar to the Safety Automatic with a 2" barrel.

Exc.	V.G.	Good	Fair	Poor
200	170	120	95	65

Petite

A .22 short caliber double action folding trigger revolver with a 1" barrel and 7-shot cylinder. Nickel-plated with rubber grips. Introduced in 1909.

Exc.	V.G.	Good	Fair	Poor
350	250	200	150	100

Supershot Sealed 8

A .22 caliber double action revolver with a 6" barrel and counterbored 8-shot cylinder. Blued with rubber grips. Manufactured from 1919 to 1957.

Exc.	V.G.	Good	Fair	Poor
200	170	120	95	65

Protector Sealed 8

As above, with a 2.5" barrel.

Exc.	V.G.	Good	Fair	Poor
200	170	120	95	65

Supershot 9

Similar to the Supershot Sealed 8 with a 9-shot uncounterbored cylinder. Manufactured between 1929 and 1949.

Exc.	V.G.	Good	Fair	Poor
200	170	120	95	65

Trigger Cocker Single Action

A .22 caliber single action revolver with a 6" barrel and 8-shot counterbored cylinder. Blued with walnut grips. Manufactured between 1940 and 1947.

Exc.	V.G.	Good	Fair	Poor
150	125	100	50	25

.22 Target Single Action

As above, with adjustable sights and adjustable grips. Manufactured between 1938 and 1948.

Exc.	V.G.	Good	Fair	Poor
225	190	150	125	65

Model 844

A .22 caliber double action revolver with a 4.5" or 6" barrel, adjustable sights, and an 8-shot cylinder. Manufactured in the 1950s.

Exc.	V.G.	Good	Fair	Poor
175	140	100	80	40

Model 855

As above, but single action with a 6" barrel. Manufactured in the 1950s.

Exc.	V.G.	Good	Fair	Poor
175	140	100	80	40

Model 55A Sportsmen Target

A .22 caliber single action revolver with a 4.75" or 6" barrel, fixed sights and 8-shot cylinder. Blued with walnut grips.

Exc.	V.G.	Good	Fair	Poor
140	125	100	75	35

Model 55S-A Cadet

A .22 to .38 caliber single action revolver with a 2.5" barrel and fixed sights. Blued with plastic grips. Introduced in 1955.

Exc.	V.G.	Good	Fair	Poor
200	170	120	95	65

Model 57A Target

As above, with a 4.5" or 6" barrel and adjustable sights. Manufactured between 1955 and 1975.

Exc.	V.G.	Good	Fair	Poor
135	110	85	60	35

Model 66 Trailsman

A .22 caliber double action revolver with a 6" barrel, adjustable sights, and 8-shot cylinder. Blued with walnut grips. Manufactured between 1958 and 1975.

Exc.	V.G.	Good	Fair	Poor
100	75	65	50	25

Model 67 Viking

As above, with a safety hammer.

Exc.	V.G.	Good	Fair	Poor
100	75	65	50	25

Model 67S Viking Snub

Same as above but fitted with 2" barrel.

Exc.	V.G.	Good	Fair	Poor
100	75	65	50	25

Model 50

A .22 or .22 Magnum single action revolver with a 4.75" or 6" barrel, 8-shot cylinder and either fixed or adjustable sights. Also known as the Sidewinder. Manufactured between 1961 and 1975.

Exc.	V.G.	Good	Fair	Poor
100	75	65	50	25

American Bulldog

A .22 to .38 caliber double action revolver with a 2.5" or 4" barrel and adjustable sights. Blued or nickel-plated with plastic grips. Manufactured between 1974 and 1976.

Exc.	V.G.	Good	Fair	Poor
125	100	75	50	25

Rookie

A .38 caliber revolver with a 4" barrel and 5-shot cylinder. Blued or nickel-plated with plastic grips.

Exc.	V.G.	Good	Fair	Poor
125	100	75	50	25

Cattleman Series
Manufactured by Aldo Uberti and listed under that name in this book.

Model X300 Pony
A .380 semiautomatic pistol with a 3" barrel and 6-shot magazine. Blued with plastic grips. Introduced in 1975.

Exc.	V.G.	Good	Fair	Poor
225	195	165	135	85

Trailsman
A .22 caliber semiautomatic pistol with a 4.5" or 6" barrel and 10-shot magazine. Blued with plastic or walnut grips.

Exc.	V.G.	Good	Fair	Poor
225	195	165	135	85

TP Pistol
A .22 or .25 ACP caliber double action semiautomatic pistol with a 2.8" barrel and 7-shot magazine. Blued or nickel-plated with plastic grips.

Exc.	V.G.	Good	Fair	Poor
225	195	165	135	85

RIFLES

Model X
Bolt action .22 caliber single shot rifle fitted with 22" barrel with open sights, pistol grip. Manufactured between 1927 and 1932.

Exc.	V.G.	Good	Fair	Poor
135	110	90	70	40

Model XA
As above but with Lyman receiver sight, swivels, leather strap, and ivory bead. Manufactured between 1927 and 1932.

Exc.	V.G.	Good	Fair	Poor
275	225	175	130	80

Model 2X
Fitted with a 24" heavy barrel and adjustable sights. Manufactured between 1932 and 1955.

Exc.	V.G.	Good	Fair	Poor
350	300	250	150	100

Li'L Champ
Chambered for the .22 Long Rifle cartridge this is a bolt action single shot rifle that weighs about 3 lbs.

Exc.	V.G.	Good	Fair	Poor
100	85	70	50	30

Long Range Rifle
This is a single shot bolt action rifle chambered for the .50 caliber Browning cartridge. Fitted with a 29" fluted barrel and adjustable trigger. Bipod. Comes supplied with a 20 power Leopold scope. Limited production. Weight is about 36 lbs. Manufactured between 1988 and 1993.

Exc.	V.G.	Good	Fair	Poor
4600	4000	3000	2500	1000

JJ9MM Carbine
This is a copy of the U.S. military M1. Blued finish and hardwood stock. Magazine is 20 rounds. Chambered for the 9mm cartridge. Built between 1985 and 1986.

Exc.	V.G.	Good	Fair	Poor
260	200	150	100	80

NOTE: Add 10% for folding stock. Deduct 5% for plastic stock.

Delta-786 Carbine
Similar to the M1 carbine but in 9mm only. Matte finish. Manufactured in 1989.

Exc.	V.G.	Good	Fair	Poor
650	550	400	300	150

Carbine .30 Caliber
Similar to the M1 carbine and chambered for the .30 carbine cartridge. Offered in various stock configurations. Built from 1985 to 1986 and again in 1988 to 1993.

Exc.	V.G.	Good	Fair	Poor
350	285	215	150	100

NOTE: For paratrooper model add $50, for Johnson 5.7mm caliber deduct $75, no premium for stainless steel.

U.S. Carbine .22 Caliber
Same as above but chambered for the .22 Long Rifle or .22 Magnum cartridge. Built in 1985 and 1986 and again in 1988. Fitted with 15-round magazine.

Exc.	V.G.	Good	Fair	Poor
175	145	125	85	50

Slide Action Targetmaster
Chambered for the .22 Long Rifle or .22 Magnum cartridge this rifle has a 15-round tubular magazine. Manufactured between 1985 and 1988 and again in 1990.

Exc.	V.G.	Good	Fair	Poor
200	170	125	100	50

Wagonmaster Model EW .22 HBL Lever Action
Chambered for the .22 Long Rifle or .22 Magnum cartridge and fitted with a hardwood stock. Blued finish. Grooved scope mounts. Built in 1985 and 1986 and again between 1988 and 1990.

Exc.	V.G.	Good	Fair	Poor
200	175	130	100	500

Model IJ .22 HB Semiautomatic (Trail Blazer)
Chambered for .22 Long Rifle only with 10-round magazine. Manufactured in 1985 only.

Exc.	V.G.	Good	Fair	Poor
150	130	100	60	40

SHOTGUNS

Champion

A single barrel shotgun manufactured in a variety of gauges as well as .44 or .45 caliber with 26" to 32" barrels, external hammers, and automatic ejectors. Blued with a walnut stock. Manufactured between 1909 and 1956.

Exc.	V.G.	Good	Fair	Poor
125	100	75	50	25

Matted Rib Grade

As above, in 12, 16, or 20 gauge with a matte rib barrel. Manufactured between 1909 and 1948.

Exc.	V.G.	Good	Fair	Poor
150	125	100	75	50

Trap Grade

As above, in 12 gauge with a 32" ventilated rib barrel. Manufactured between 1909 and 1942.

Exc.	V.G.	Good	Fair	Poor
375	300	250	175	100

Hercules Grade

A boxlock double barrel shotgun manufactured in a variety of gauges with 26" to 32" barrels, double triggers and extractors. Blued with a walnut stock.

Exc.	V.G.	Good	Fair	Poor
1100	950	700	500	350

NOTE: Add premium for following features:
Single trigger-200%
Ejectors-200%
28 gauge-200%
.410 bore-150%
20 gauge-75%
16 gauge-10%
Engraving-200%
Vent rib-25%

Skeeter Model

As above, but more finely finished. Discontinued in 1946.

Exc.	V.G.	Good	Fair	Poor
2000	1500	1000	750	500

NOTE: Add premium for following features:
Single trigger-200%
Ejectors-200%
28 gauge-200%
.410 bore-150%
20 gauge-75%
16 gauge-10%
Engraving-200%
Vent rib-25%

Super Trap

A 12 gauge boxlock single barrel shotgun with a 32" barrel, and extractors. Discontinued in 1942.

Exc.	V.G.	Good	Fair	Poor
1100	950	700	500	375

Silver Shadow

A 12 gauge boxlock Over/Under shotgun with a 26" or 28" ventilated rib barrels, double triggers and extractors. Blued with a walnut stock. Also available with a single trigger, which would increase the values listed below by approximately 25%. Manufactured in Italy and imported by Iver Johnson.

Exc.	V.G.	Good	Fair	Poor
500	400	350	300	200

IXL
New York, New York

Pocket Revolver

A .31 caliber double action percussion revolver with a 4" octagonal barrel and 6-shot cylinder. Blued with walnut grips. The barrel marked "IXL N.York." Approximately 750 were made without hammer spurs and 150 with side mounted hammers during the 1850s.

Exc.	V.G.	Good	Fair	Poor
—	—	1100	600	300

Navy Revolver

As above in .36 caliber. Approximately 100 were made with both center and side mounted hammers during the 1850s.

Exc.	V.G.	Good	Fair	Poor
—	—	2750	1200	500

Courtesy Milwaukee Public Museum, Milwaukee, Wisconsin

J

JACQUEMART, JULES
Liege, Belgium

Le Monobloc

A 6.35mm semiautomatic pistol with a 2" barrel and 6-shot magazine. The slide marked "Le Monobloc/Pistolet Automatique/Brevefte." Blued with composition grips. Production ceased in 1914.

Exc.	V.G.	Good	Fair	Poor
—	450	250	200	125

JACQUITH, ELIJAH
Brattleboro, Vermont

Revolving Under Hammer Rifle

An extremely rare .40 caliber percussion revolving rifle with a 34" round-octagonal barrel and 8-shot cylinder. It is believed that approximately 25 of these rifles were made in 1838 and 1839. The barrel marked "E. Jaquith Brattleboro. Vt." Prospective purchasers should secure a qualified appraisal prior to acquisition.

Exc.	V.G.	Good	Fair	Poor
—	—	11000	5500	2000

JAGER WAFFENFABIK
Suhl, Germany

Jager Semiautomatic Pistol

A 7.65mm caliber semiautomatic pistol with a 3" barrel and 7-shot magazine. Largely made from steel stampings. Blued with plastic grips. The slide marked "Jager-Pistole DRP Angem." Approximately 5,500 were made prior to 1914.

NOTE: Add 50% for Imperial proofed examples.

Courtesy Richard M. Kumor, Sr.

Exc.	V.G.	Good	Fair	Poor
450	350	300	175	100

JAPANESE STATE MILITARY WEAPONS
Japan

NOTE: For history, technical data, descriptions, and prices see the *Standard Catalog of Military Firearms, 1870 to the Present,* under Japan.

JEFFERY, W. J. & CO. LTD.
London, England

This company produced high quality shotguns and rifles. Their products have been used by wealthy sportsmen for many years. They produced guns under their own banner and also as contractors for other distributors. They made the guns sold by the Army & Navy Department Store in London. Guns of this type were basically custom-ordered and as such are extremely hard to evaluate on a general basis. We supply an estimated value for a standard model but strongly urge that one secure an individual appraisal if a transaction is contemplated.

SHOTGUNS-See British Double Guns

RIFLES

Single Shot

Built on the Farquharson Falling Block action and was chambered for many calibers up to the .600 Nitro Express. This was also a custom-order gun, and the barrel length was optional. There are usually folding express sights, and the finish is usually blued with a select, hand-checkered walnut stock. These were high quality firearms, and the values would be determined, for the most part, by the options and embellishments on the particular specimen. Individual appraisal is definitely advised. The caliber in which a rifle is chambered will also have an effect on the value. Obsolete calibers bring less, and the larger express calibers bring more.

Exc.	V.G.	Good	Fair	Poor
4000	3250	2500	1750	900

Boxlock Double Rifle

A boxlock chambered for many different calibers. It can be found with either a top or underlever action and has folding express sights. The stock and forearm are select, hand-checkered walnut, and the finish is usually blue. This was a custom-order proposition, and values can be affected by many variables such as caliber, options, and embellishment. Damascus barreled hammerguns are worth approximately 50 percent less.

Exc.	V.G.	Good	Fair	Poor
8000	6500	4500	3500	2500

Sidelock Double Rifle

Has detachable sidelocks and otherwise is comparable to the boxlock version. Individual appraisal is recommended.

Exc.	V.G.	Good	Fair	Poor
12500	10000	7500	5000	4000

JENISON, J. & CO.
Southbridge, Connecticut

Under Hammer Pistol

A .28 caliber single shot under hammer percussion pistol with a 4" half-octagonal barrel marked "J.Jenison & Co./Southbridge, Mass." Blued with a maple or oak grip. Manufactured during the 1850s.

Exc.	V.G.	Good	Fair	Poor
—	—	950	500	200

JENKS CARBINE
Springfield, Massachusetts
N. P. Ames Manufacturer

Jenks "Mule Ear Carbine"

A .54 caliber percussion side hammer carbine with a 24.5" round barrel and full length stock secured by two barrel bands. The lock case hardened, the barrel browned and the furniture of brass. The lock marked "N.P.Ames/Springfield/Mass." The barrel stamped "Wm.Jenks/USN" followed by the inspector's initials. The buttstock carries an inspector's cartouche. Approximately 4,250 were made between 1841 and 1846. Some were marked "USR" for the "U.S. Revenue Cutter Service," and these would bring approximately an 80 percent premium over the values listed below. However, prospective purchasers should secure a qualified appraisal prior to acquisition.

Courtesy Milwaukee Public Museum, Milwaukee, Wisconsin

Exc.	V.G.	Good	Fair	Poor
—	—	3500	1500	600

Jenks Navy Rifle

As above, with a 30" round barrel and full length stock secured by three barrel bands. Approximately 1,000 were made for the U.S. Navy in 1841.

Courtesy Milwaukee Public Museum, Milwaukee, Wisconsin

Exc.	V.G.	Good	Fair	Poor
—	—	5500	2500	950

JENKS-HERKIMER
New York
Manufacturer-E. Remington & Son

Jenks Carbine

Identical to the Jenks Carbine listed in the previous entry except that the barrel length is 24.25" and the lock is fitted with a Maynard tape primer. The lock marked "Remington's/Herkimer/N.Y." The barrel is marked "W. Jenks/USN/RC/P/Cast Steel." Approximately 1,000 of these carbines manufactured circa 1846.

Exc.	V.G.	Good	Fair	Poor
—	—	3750	1500	650

JENKS-MERRILL
Baltimore, Maryland

An alteration of the Jenks Carbine listed previously to a breech loading system developed by J.H. Merrill. The conventional sidelock marked "J. H. Merrill Balto./Pat. July 1858." The breech retains the mark "Wm.Jenks/USN." Approximately 300 were altered between 1858 and 1860.

Exc.	V.G.	Good	Fair	Poor
—	—	6750	3000	950

JENNINGS
Windsor, Vermont
Manufacturer - Robbins & Lawrence
SEE—Winchester Repeating Arms

JENNINGS F. A., INC.
Carson City, Nevada

Distributors of arms manufactured by Calwestco in Chino, California, and Bryco Firearms in Carson City, Nevada.

J-22

A .22 caliber semiautomatic pistol with a 2.5" barrel and 6-shot magazine. Aluminum, finished in bright chrome, Teflon, or satin nickel with plastic or wood grips.

Exc.	V.G.	Good	Fair	Poor
75	65	50	35	25

Bryco Model 25

A .25 caliber semiautomatic pistol with a 2.5" barrel and 6-shot magazine. Constructed and finished as above.

Exc.	V.G.	Good	Fair	Poor
90	75	65	50	35

Bryco Model 38

A .22, .32, or .380 semiautomatic pistol with a 2.8" barrel and 6-shot magazine. Constructed and finished as above.

Exc.	V.G.	Good	Fair	Poor
90	75	65	50	35

Bryco Model 48

Similar to the above, with a redesigned triggerguard with a squared forward section. Introduced in 1988.

Exc.	V.G.	Good	Fair	Poor
90	75	65	50	35

JERICHO
Israeli Military Industries, Israel

Jericho

A 9mm or .41 Action Express double action semiautomatic pistol with a 4.72" barrel, polygonal rifling, ambidextrous safety and fixed sights. Blued with plastic grips. No longer imported.

Exc.	V.G.	Good	Fair	Poor
475	400	350	300	200

JIEFFCO
Robar et Cie
Liege, Belgium

Pocket Pistol

A .25 or .32 caliber semiautomatic pistol with a 3" barrel and 6-shot magazine. Blued with composition grips. Manufactured prior to WWI.

Exc.	V.G.	Good	Fair	Poor
—	350	200	150	100

New Model Melior

A .25 caliber semiautomatic pistol with a 2" barrel and 6-shot magazine. Blued with composition grips. Manufactured during the 1920s and imported by Davis-Warner.

Exc.	V.G.	Good	Fair	Poor
350	225	175	125	90

JOHNSON AUTOMATIC RIFLE
Cranston Arms Co.
Providence, Rhode Island

NOTE: For history, technical data, descriptions, and prices see the STAN JOHNSON, BYE & CO.

Worcester, Massachusetts

Established in 1871 by Martin Bye and Iver Johnson. This company primarily manufactured inexpensive pistols. In 1883 Johnson assumed full control of the company and renamed it the Iver Johnson Arms Company.

Defender, Eagle, Encore, Eureka, Favorite, Lion, Smoker, and Tycoon

A .22, .32, .38, or .44 caliber spur trigger revolver manufactured with various barrel lengths and normally nickel-plated. The barrel marked with one of the above trade names.

Exc.	V.G.	Good	Fair	Poor
—	125	75	50	25

Eclipse

A .22 caliber spur trigger single shot pistol with a 1.5" barrel. Blued with walnut grips.

Exc.	V.G.	Good	Fair	Poor
—	125	75	50	25

American Bulldog

A .22, .32, or .38 caliber double action revolver with a 3" barrel. Blued or nickel-plated with walnut or composition grips.

Exc.	V.G.	Good	Fair	Poor
—	125	75	50	25

JOSEF JESCHER
SEE—Austrian Military Firearms

JOSLYN
Milbury, Massachusetts
A.H. Waters-Manufacturer

Model 1855 Carbine

A .54 caliber breech loading single shot percussion carbine with a 22.5" barrel secured to the forend by one barrel band. Blued, case hardened with brass mounts. The lock marked "A.H.Waters & Co./Milbury, Mass.", and the patent dates stamped on the breech lever. Approximately 1,000 manufactured in 1855 and 1856.

Exc.	V.G.	Good	Fair	Poor
—	—	3500	2000	950

Model 1855 Rifle

Similar to the above, in .58 caliber with a 38" barrel secured by three barrel bands. Several hundred were made in 1856.

Exc.	V.G.	Good	Fair	Poor
—	—	6000	3000	1100

JOSLYN FIREARMS COMPANY
Stonington, Connecticut

Model 1862 Carbine

A .52 rimfire breech loading single shot carbine with a 22" round barrel secured by one barrel band. Blued, case hardened with brass mounts. The lock marked "Joslyn Firearms Co./Stonington/Conn.", and the patent date marked on the barrel. The trigger plate is 8" long, and the upper tang measures 4.5". Approximately 4,000 manufactured in 1862.

Courtesy Milwaukee Public Museum, Milwaukee, Wisconsin

Exc.	V.G.	Good	Fair	Poor
—	—	2500	950	400

Model 1864 Carbine

As above, with case hardened iron mounts, a 7" trigger plate and 2" upper tang. Approximately 12,000 were made in 1864 and 1865.

Courtesy Milwaukee Public Museum, Milwaukee, Wisconsin

Exc.	V.G.	Good	Fair	Poor
—	—	2250	900	500

Army Model Revolver

A .44 caliber side hammer percussion revolver with an 8" octagonal barrel and 5-shot cylinder. Blued, case hardened with walnut grips. The barrel marked "B. F. Joslyn/Patd. May 4, 1858." Martially marked examples are worth a premium of approximately 25 percent over the values listed below. The two models of this revolver are as follows:

First Model

With a brass triggerguard and iron butt cap. Approximately 500 made in 1861.

Exc.	V.G.	Good	Fair	Poor
—	—	4250	1750	650

Second Model

Fitted with an iron triggerguard and without a butt cap. Approximately 2,500 were made in 1861 and 1862.

Exc.	V.G.	Good	Fair	Poor
—	—	3500	1500	500

JOSLYN
Springfield, Massachusetts
Manufacturer-Springfield Armory

Joslyn Breechloading Rifle

The first mass-produced, true breechloading cartridge firearm manufactured in a national armory. The actions were supplied by the Joslyn Firearms Company, and the rifles were chambered for the .56-50 rimfire cartridge. This rifle has a 35.5" round barrel and a full-length stock that is held on by three barrel bands. The lock is marked "U.S./Springfield" with "1864" at the back. The barrel is marked "B. F. Joslyn's Patent/ Oct. 8th, 1861 / June 24th, 1862." There were approximately 3,000 of these manufactured circa 1865. They were probably issued to Union forces, but it is unknown if they saw action before the end of the Civil War.

Exc.	V.G.	Good	Fair	Poor
—	—	2250	950	500

.50-70 Alteration

Approximately 1,600 Joslyn rifles were re-chambered to fire the .50-70 centerfire cartridge. The conversion consisted of re-chambering and drilling a new firing pin hole after the rimfire pin was sealed. There was no specific serial number range in which these conversions were done. Most of these weapons were eventually converted to smoothbores and sold in Africa. The original military specimens are extremely scarce.

Exc.	V.G.	Good	Fair	Poor
—	—	2500	1500	750

JURRAS, LEE
Prescott, Arizona
SEE—Auto-Mag

While Jurras is best known for manufacturing the last model of the Auto-Mag, he also produced the following pistol sold by J. & G. Sales in Prescott, Arizona.

Howdah Pistol

A .375, .416, .460, .475, .500, and the .577 caliber single shot pistol with a 12" barrel, adjustable sights and Nitex finish, built upon a Thompson Center Contender frame.

Exc.	V.G.	Good	Fair	Poor
1200	1000	800	650	500

JUSTICE, P. S.
Philadelphia, Pennsylvania

Percussion Rifle

A .58 caliber percussion rifle with a 35" round barrel secured by two barrel bands, browned barrel, polished lock and brass furniture. The lock marked "P.S. Justice/Philada." Approximately 2,500 were manufactured in 1861.

Courtesy Milwaukee Public Museum, Milwaukee, Wisconsin

Exc.	V.G.	Good	Fair	Poor
—	—	1750	800	450

K

KBI, INC.
Harrisburg, Pennsylvania

PSP-25

A .25 caliber semiautomatic pistol with a 2" barrel manufactured in Charlottesville, Virginia, under license from Fabrique Nationale. Introduced in 1989.

NIB	Exc.	V.G.	Good	Fair
225	200	175	150	100

KDF, INC.
Seguin, Texas
Kleinguenther Distinctive Firearms

The former importer of Voere and Mauser rifles into the U.S.

Condor

A 12 gauge boxlock Over/Under shotgun with 28" barrels with ventilated ribs, single selective trigger and automatic ejectors. Blued with a walnut stock. Manufactured in Italy.

Exc.	V.G.	Good	Fair	Poor
650	600	525	375	275

Brescia

A 12 gauge boxlock double barrel shotgun with 28" barrels, double triggers and extractors. Blued with a walnut stock. Manufactured in Italy.

Exc.	V.G.	Good	Fair	Poor
350	325	300	200	125

K-14 Insta Fire Rifle

A bolt action sporting rifle manufactured in a variety of calibers with 24" or 26" barrels furnished without sights. Blued with a Monte Carlo-style walnut stock.

Exc.	V.G.	Good	Fair	Poor
600	550	450	325	250

K-15

Similar to the above, with a 60-degree bolt angle and an accurized barrel guaranteed to fire a .5" group at 100 yards. Manufactured with a variety of optional features.

Exc.	V.G.	Good	Fair	Poor
1000	850	750	550	300

K-15 Pro-Hunter

As above, matte blued or electroless nickel-plated with a fiberglass stock.

Exc.	V.G.	Good	Fair	Poor
1400	1250	1000	700	500

K-15 Swat Rifle

A 7.62x54mm caliber bolt action rifle with a 24" or 26" barrel furnished without sights, 4-shot magazine and parkerized finish. Walnut stock.

Exc.	V.G.	Good	Fair	Poor
1500	1300	1100	800	550

K-15 Dangerous Game

As above, in .411 KDF caliber.

Exc.	V.G.	Good	Fair	Poor
2000	1600	1300	1000	700

K-16

A bolt action sporting rifle manufactured in a variety of calibers with a 24" or 26" barrel furnished without sights, single stage adjustable trigger, accurized barrel and Dupont Rynite stock. Produced with a variety of optional features.

Exc.	V.G.	Good	Fair	Poor
775	675	500	400	200

Titan Menor

A .222 or .223 caliber bolt action rifle with a 24" or 26" barrel furnished without sights and Monte Carlo-style or standard schnabel tipped walnut stock. Blued.

Exc.	V.G.	Good	Fair	Poor
650	600	550	400	200

Titan II Standard

As above, with a mid-sized action.

Exc.	V.G.	Good	Fair	Poor
900	800	700	500	250

Titan II Magnum

As above, with a long action. Discontinued in 1988.

Exc.	V.G.	Good	Fair	Poor
1000	850	750	550	250

Titan .411 KDF Mag.

As above, in .411 KDF with a 26" barrel having an integral muzzle brake. Blued or electroless nickel-plated with a walnut stock. Discontinued in 1988.

Exc.	V.G.	Good	Fair	Poor
1200	1050	850	650	350

K-22

A .22 caliber bolt action rifle with a 21" free floating barrel furnished without sights, adjustable trigger, and 5-shot magazine. Also known as the Mauser 201

Exc.	V.G.	Good	Fair	Poor
300	275	250	175	100

K-22 Deluxe

Exc.	V.G.	Good	Fair	Poor
400	375	350	275	125

K-22 Deluxe Custom

Exc.	V.G.	Good	Fair	Poor
650	550	450	375	225

K-22 Deluxe Special Select

Exc.	V.G.	Good	Fair	Poor
1000	850	750	650	325

Model 2005

A .22 caliber semiautomatic rifle with a 19.5" barrel, open sights, and 5-shot magazine. Blued with a walnut stock. Also available in a deluxe model. Imported in 1986.

NIB	Exc.	V.G.	Good	Fair	Poor
125	100	80	60	40	30

Model 2107

A .22 or .22 Magnum caliber bolt action rifle with a 19.5" barrel, open sights, and 5-shot magazine. Blued with a walnut stock.

Exc.	V.G.	Good	Fair	Poor
175	150	125	100	75

Model 2112

The deluxe version of the Model 2107.

Exc.	V.G.	Good	Fair	Poor
250	200	175	125	90

K.F.C.

Japan
Importer-LaPaloma Marketing
Tucson, Arizona

E-1 Trap or Skeet Over/Under

A 12 gauge boxlock double barrel shotgun with 26" or 30" barrels, competition rib, single selective trigger and automatic ejectors. Engraved, blued with a walnut stock. Manufactured until 1986.

Exc.	V.G.	Good	Fair	Poor
950	800	700	500	300

E-2 Trap or Skeet Over/Under

As above, but more finely finished.

Exc.	V.G.	Good	Fair	Poor
1400	1250	1000	750	350

Field Grade Over/Under

As above, with a narrow rib and 26" or 28" barrels. Discontinued in 1986.

Exc.	V.G.	Good	Fair	Poor
650	575	500	400	275

Model 250

A 12 gauge semiautomatic shotgun with 26", 28", or 30" barrels fitted for choke tubes. Matte blued with a walnut stock. Manufactured from 1980 to 1986.

Exc.	V.G.	Good	Fair	Poor
350	300	275	200	100

KSN INDUSTRIES
Israel
Importer-J.O. Arms, Houston, Texas

Golan

A semiautomatic pistol, introduced in 1996, chambered for the 9mm or .40 S&W cartridge. Double action trigger with ambidextrous controls. Barrel length is 3.9" and magazine capacity is 10 rounds in US. In rest of the world 15 rounds for 9mm and 11 rounds for the .40 S&W. Weight is 29 oz.

NIB	Exc.	V.G.	Good	Fair	Poor
650	525	400	325	—	—

Kareen MK II

This single action semiautomatic pistol is chambered for the 9mm cartridge. The barrel length is 4.5". Ambidextrous safety and rubber grips. Steel slide and frame. Weight is about 34 oz.

NIB	Exc.	V.G.	Good	Fair	Poor
400	325	250	200	150	100

Kareen MK II-Compact

Same as above but fitted with a 3.9" barrel. Weight is about 32 oz.

NIB	Exc.	V.G.	Good	Fair	Poor
500	400	300	250	200	150

GAL

Same as the full size Kareen but chambered for the .45 ACP cartridge.

NIB	Exc.	V.G.	Good	Fair	Poor
400	325	250	200	150	100

KAHR ARMS
Blauvelt, New York

Kahr K9

This is a semiautomatic pistol chambered for the 9mm cartridge. It is a ultra-compact size. The barrel length is 3.5" and the overall length is 6". The width at the slide is .9". The magazine capacity is 7 rounds. Available in blue or electroless nickel finish. Weight is 25 oz.

NIB	Exc.	V.G.	Good	Fair	Poor
500	425	350	300	250	150

Kahr Lady K9

Same as above but with lightened recoil spring.

NIB	Exc.	V.G.	Good	Fair	Poor
500	425	350	300	250	150

Kahr P9 Compact Polymer

Introduced in 1999 this 9mm model features a 3.5" barrel with double action only trigger. Black polymer frame with stainless steel slide. Overall length is 6", height is 4.5". Weight is about 18 oz. Magazine capacity is 7 rounds.

NIB	Exc.	V.G.	Good	Fair	Poor
525	425	325	—	—	—

Kahr K9 Compact Polymer Covert

Same as the model above but with 1/2" shorter grip frame. Weight is about 17 oz. Magazine capacity is 6 rounds. Introduced in 1999.

NIB	Exc.	V.G.	Good	Fair	Poor
525	425	325	—	—	—

Kahr K40

This model is similar to the K9 but is chambered for the .40S&W cartridge. Magazine capacity is 6 rounds. Weight is 26 oz.

NIB	Exc.	V.G.	Good	Fair	Poor
550	450	350	300	250	150

K40 Elite

NOTE: For night sights add $90.00. For Nickel finish add $70.00. For Black Titanium finish add $100.00. For the K40 Stainless steel version add $50.00. Add $50 for Elite models.

Kahr K40 Covert

Similar to the K40 with a 1/2" shorter grip frame and flush fitting 5-round magazine. Barrel length is 3.5". Weight is about 25 oz. Finish is matte stainless steel.

NIB	Exc.	V.G.	Good	Fair	Poor
600	475	—	—	—	—

Kahr MK 40

This .40S&W model is fitted with a 3" barrel. Its overall length is 5.4" and height is 4". Finish is matte stainless steel. Magazine capacity is 5 rounds. Uses same magazines as K40 Covert. Introduced in 1999.

NIB	Exc.	V.G.	Good	Fair	Poor
600	475	375	—	—	—

Kahr P40

Similar to the P9 but chambered for the .40 S&W cartridge. Fitted with a 3.5" match grade barrel and matte stainless steel slide and black polymer frame. Supplied with 2 6-round stainless steel magazines. Weight is approximately 19 oz. Introduced in 2001.

NIB	Exc.	V.G.	Good	Fair	Poor
575	450	—	—	—	—

Kahr MK9

This is a 9mm model with double action only trigger. Barrel length is 3". Overall length is 5.5" and height is 4". Weight is approximately 22 oz. One 6-round magazine and one 7-round magazine with grip extension standard. This model is fitted with a specially designed trigger for shorter trigger stroke.

NIB	Exc.	V.G.	Good	Fair	Poor
600	475	375	—	—	—

NOTE: Add $150 for two-tone finish, add $50 for Elite stainless steel finish.

Wilson Combat Kahr Pistols

Offered in both the K9 and K40 models this is a customized pistol by Wilson's Gun Shop. It features hard chrome frame, black slide, 30 lpi checkering on front strap, beveled magazine well and several other special features. Initial production for the K40 is 50 pistols and for the K9 25 pistols.

NIB	Exc.	V.G.	Good	Fair	Poor
1300	1050	—	—	—	—

Model 1911PKZ

This model uses the Auto-Ordnance 1911 pistols re-engineered by Kahr Arms. This model includes a parkerized finish, lanyard loop and U.S. Army roll mark of the slide. Seven-round magazine standard. Introduced in 2001.

NIB	Exc.	V.G.	Good	Fair	Poor
	—	—			

Model T1911 Standard

This model features a blued finish, plastic grips with Thompson medallion and bullet logo on the slide. Seven-round magazine. Introduced in 2001.

NIB	Exc.	V.G.	Good	Fair	Poor
	—				

Model 1911WGS Deluxe

This model has a blued finish, rubber wrap-around grips with Thompson medallion, high profile white dot sights, and Thompson bullet logo on the slide. Seven-round magazine. Introduced in 2001.

NIB	Exc.	V.G.	Good	Fair	Poor
	—		—		

KASSNAR IMPORTS, INC.
Harrisburg, Pennsylvania
Currently the following firearms are imported by this company.

Standard Over/Under

A 12, 20, 28 or .410 bore boxlock double barrel shotgun with 26" or 28" barrels, ventilated ribs, single trigger and extractors. Blued with a walnut stock.

NIB	Exc.	V.G.	Good	Fair	Poor
350	275	225	200	150	100

Deluxe Over/Under
As above, with a more finely figured stock.

NIB	Exc.	V.G.	Good	Fair	Poor
400	325	250	225	175	100

Standard Side-by-Side

A 20, 28 or .410 bore boxlock folding double barrel shotgun with 26" barrels, double triggers and extractors. Blued with a walnut stock.

NIB	Exc.	V.G.	Good	Fair	Poor
250	200	175	150	100	75

Deluxe Side-by-Side
As above, in .410 bore only and with more finely figured wood.

NIB	Exc.	V.G.	Good	Fair	Poor
300	250	200	175	125	75

KEBERST INT.
Kendall International
Paris, Kentucky

Keberst Model 1A

A .338 Lapua Magnum, .338-416 Rigby, and the .338-06 caliber bolt action rifle with a 24" barrel having an integral muzzle brake, and fitted with a 3-9 power Leupold telescope. Matte blued with a camouflaged composition stock. Manufactured in 1987 and 1988.

Exc.	V.G.	Good	Fair	Poor
3750	3000	2500	1800	900

KEL-TEC CNC INDUSTRIES
Cocoa, Florida

P-11

This is a semiautomatic pistol chambered for the 9mm cartridge. It is double action only with a barrel length of 3.1". Overall length is 5.6". Weight is 14 oz. Magazine capacity is 10 rounds. Standard model has blued slide with black grip. Stainless steel and parkerized finish are offered as well.

NIB	Exc.	V.G.	Good	Fair	Poor
300	225	175	150	125	100

NOTE: Add $100 for stainless steel and $40 for parkerized finish. Add $60 for hard chrome.

P-32

This .32 caliber semiautomatic pistol is fitted with a 2.68" barrel. The action is double action only. Overall length is 5", overall height is 3.5". Magazine capacity is 7 rounds. Weight is about 6.6 oz. Blued slide and frame.

NIB	Exc.	V.G.	Good	Fair	Poor
300	225	—	—	—	—

NOTE: Add $40 for parkerized finish. Add $60 for hard chrome.

P-40

This model is similar to the P-11 but chambered for the .40S&W cartridge. Barrel length is 3.3". Magazine capacity is 9 rounds. Weight is approximately 16 oz. Blued finish.

NIB	Exc.	V.G.	Good	Fair	Poor
325	250	—	—	—	—

NOTE: Add $40 for parkerized finish. Add $60 for hard chrome.

SUB-9 Rifle

Introduced in 1996 this is a semiautomatic rifle chambered for the 9mm cartridge. The barrel length is 16.1". The rifle can be folded closed with an overall length of 16". Weight is approximately 4.6 lbs. Different grip assembly can be fitted to this rifle allowing for the use of different magazines.

NIB	Exc.	V.G.	Good	Fair	Poor
650	500	—	—	—	—

KEMPER, SHRIVER & COMPANY
Nashville, Tennessee

Delivered rifles made from sporting arm parts to the Ordnance Department at Nashville from December 1861 to March 1862. In all 150 arms were assembled. Overall length 48-1/2"; octagonal barrels shortened 33" and bored to .48 caliber; some fitted with saber bayonet lugs; stocks of military with brass furniture.

Prospective purchasers are strongly advised to secure an expert appraisal prior to acquisition.

Exc.	V.G.	Good	Fair	Poor
—	—	4500	2000	1500

KENDALL, INTERNATIONAL
Paris, Kentucky
SEE—Keberst International

KENDALL, NICANOR
Windsor, Vermont

Under Hammer Pistol

A .31 to .41 caliber under hammer percussion pistol with 4" to 10" octagonal/round barrels marked "N.Kendall/Windsor,Vt." Browned or blued with brass mounts and maple grips. Manufactured in the 1850s.

Exc.	V.G.	Good	Fair	Poor
—	—	1500	600	200

KENO
Unknown

Derringer

A .22 caliber single shot spur trigger pistol with a 2.5" barrel, brass frame, and walnut grips. The barrel blued or nickel-plated and marked "Keno".

Exc.	V.G.	Good	Fair	Poor
—	—	400	175	100

KEPPLINGER, HANNES
Kufstein, Austria

3-S Rifle System

A short action rifle chambered for all popular American and European cartridges. The major parts are constructed of a high strength alloy, and it features a de-cocking lever that allows manual cocking and de-cocking of the firing-pin spring. The barrel is 23" in length, and the detachable magazine holds 3 rounds. This is essentially a custom-built gun and is rarely encountered on the market. The engraving varies with the customer's wishes; and the walnut stock, either full-length Mannlicher style or with a schnabel forend, is made of the highest

grade wood available. This company does not have an importer at this time. We are not able to evaluate, as there are too few traded. It is listed for reference only.

KERR
London, England

Kerr Revolver

A .44 caliber double action percussion revolver with a 5.5" barrel and 6-shot cylinder. Blued with walnut grips. The frame marked "Kerr's Patent 648"; and "London Armoury Bermondsey."

Courtesy Butterfield & Butterfield, San Francisco, California

Exc.	V.G.	Good	Fair	Poor
—	2250	1250	600	300

KERR
SEE—English Military Firearms

KESSLER ARMS CORPORATION
Silver Creek, New York

Bolt Action Shotgun

A 12, 16, or 20 gauge shotgun with 26" or 28" barrels. Blued with a walnut stock. Manufactured between 1951 and 1953.

Exc.	V.G.	Good	Fair	Poor
125	75	50	30	20

Levermatic Shotgun

A 12, 16, or 20 gauge lever action shotgun with a 26" or 28" barrel. Blued with a walnut stock. Manufactured between 1951 and 1953.

Exc.	V.G.	Good	Fair	Poor
150	100	75	50	25

KETTNER, EDWARD
Suhl, Germany

Drilling

This is a high quality three barreled firearm chambered for 12x12 gauge or 16x16 gauge over various metric rifle cartridges. The barrels are 25" in length and feature ejectors, selective triggers, and pop-up rifle sights that appear when the rifle barrel is selected. This gun is deep-relief engraved in the German style and has a high-grade checkered walnut stock. It was manufactured between 1922 and 1939.

Exc.	V.G.	Good	Fair	Poor
—	3000	1750	950	500

KIMBALL ARMS COMPANY
Detroit, Michigan

Semiautomatic Pistol
A .30 carbine caliber semiautomatic pistol with a 3.5" or 5" barrel. Blued with plastic grips. Also believed to have been made in .22 Hornet and .357 Magnum, though few legitimate examples have been seen. Manufactured from 1955 to 1958. Approximately 238 were made.

Exc.	V.G.	Good	Fair	Poor
1250	750	500	300	200

KIMBER MFG., INC
Yonkers, New York

Kimber of Oregon was established in April 1979 by Greg and Jack Warne. The company produced high quality rimfire and centerfire rifles until going out of business in early 1991. Kimber produced approximately 60,000 rifles during its operation. In April 1993, Greg Warne opened Kimber of America in Clackamas, Oregon. This new company presently manufactures the same high quality rifles built on an improved Model 82 Sporter action and stock but in rimfire only. In 1995 the company expanded its product line to include centerfire rifles as well as a 1911 .45 ACP Semiautomatic pistol line. In 1997 manufacturing operations were consolidated in the New York pistol factory and the two factories in Oregon were closed.

DISCONTINUED MODELS
NOTE: For Model 82 Series rifles in .22 Magnum caliber add 10%. For rifles chambered for .22 Hornet add 15%.

Model 82 Classic
A .22, .22 Magnum, or .22 Hornet bolt action rifle with a 22" barrel furnished without sights and 4- or 5-shot magazine. Blued with a walnut stock. Discontinued in 1988.

Exc.	V.G.	Good	Fair	Poor
700	600	550	450	350

Cascade Model
As above, with a Monte Carlo-style stock.

Exc.	V.G.	Good	Fair	Poor
750	650	600	500	400

Custom Classic Model
As above, in .218 Bee or .25-20.

Exc.	V.G.	Good	Fair	Poor
800	725	650	400	300

Mini Classic
The Model 82 with an 18" barrel. Manufactured in 1988.

Exc.	V.G.	Good	Fair	Poor
600	550	475	400	300

Deluxe Grade
Similar to the Custom Classic. Introduced in 1989.

NIB	Exc.	V.G.	Good	Fair	Poor
1000	850	650	550	450	350

Model 82A Government
A .22 caliber bolt action rifle with a 25" heavy barrel fitted with telescope mounts. Matte blued with a walnut stock. Introduced in 1987.

NIB	Exc.	V.G.	Good	Fair	Poor
675	550	450	375	300	200

Continental
Similar to the Custom Classic with a 20" barrel, open sights, and full length Mannlicher-style stock. Introduced in 1987.

NIB	Exc.	V.G.	Good	Fair	Poor
850	750	650	500	400	300

Super Continental
As above, but more finely finished. Discontinued in 1988.

NIB	Exc.	V.G.	Good	Fair	Poor
1200	1100	1000	750	600	300

Super America
The Model 82 but more finely finished. Discontinued in 1988.

NIB	Exc.	V.G.	Good	Fair	Poor
1500	1200	950	850	650	500

Super Grade
As above, introduced in 1989.

NIB	Exc.	V.G.	Good	Fair	Poor
1200	1000	900	750	600	475

Centennial
A commemorative rifle moderately engraved including a special match barrel, skeleton buttplate, hand-selected walnut stock, and light engraving. Issued to commemorate the 100th anniversary of the 22 l.r. cartridge. One hundred were manufactured in 1987.

NIB	Exc.	V.G.	Good	Fair	Poor
2500	2250	2000	1750	1500	1150

Brownell
In 1986, 500 commemorative rifles were produced in honor of Leonard Brownell, featuring a high-grade, Mannlicher-style, full-length walnut stock.

NIB	Exc.	V.G.	Good	Fair	Poor
1500	1250	1000	800	600	500

Model 84 Series-Discontinued Models
A bolt action rifle manufactured in a variety of smallbore calibers with a 22" or 24" barrel and 5-shot magazine. Blued with a walnut stock. Variations are as follows:

Classic Model

NIB	Exc.	V.G.	Good	Fair	Poor
700	650	600	400	250	200

Custom Classic Model

NIB	Exc.	V.G.	Good	Fair	Poor
900	800	700	500	350	200

Deluxe Grade Sporter

NIB	Exc.	V.G.	Good	Fair	Poor
1200	1000	850	750	500	250

Continental

NIB	Exc.	V.G.	Good	Fair	Poor
975	900	800	700	500	250

Super Continental

NIB	Exc.	V.G.	Good	Fair	Poor
1300	1100	850	700	575	250

Super America

NIB	Exc.	V.G.	Good	Fair	Poor
1500	1000	925	825	600	300

Super Grade

NIB	Exc.	V.G.	Good	Fair	Poor
1250	1100	1000	850	650	300

Ultra Varmint

As above, with a 24" stainless steel barrel and laminated birch wood stock. Introduced in 1989.

NIB	Exc.	V.G.	Good	Fair	Poor
1150	1000	900	750	550	250

Super Varmint

As above with a walnut stock. Introduced in 1989.

NIB	Exc.	V.G.	Good	Fair	Poor
1250	1100	1000	850	650	300

Predator

A .221 Fireball, .223 Rem., 6mm TCU, 7mm TCU, or the 6x45mm caliber single shot bolt action pistol based upon the Model 84 action with a 14.75" barrel adopted for a telescope. Blued with a walnut stock and available in two grades as follows. Manufactured in 1987 and 1988 only.

Hunter Grade

Exc.	V.G.	Good	Fair	Poor
800	650	575	400	300

Super Grade

Exc.	V.G.	Good	Fair	Poor
1000	850	675	500	400

Model 89 Series/BRG (Big Game Rifles)

A bolt action sporting rifle produced in .270 Winchester to .375 Holland & Holland caliber with a 22" or 24" barrel. Blued with a walnut stock. The variations of this model are as follows:

Classic Model

NIB	Exc.	V.G.	Good	Fair	Poor
800	650	550	400	300	200

Custom Classic Model

NIB	Exc.	V.G.	Good	Fair	Poor
1000	850	650	450	350	250

Deluxe Grade

NIB	Exc.	V.G.	Good	Fair	Poor
1400	1150	900	650	450	250

Super America

NIB	Exc.	V.G.	Good	Fair	Poor
1800	1250	900	700	500	250

Super Grade

NIB	Exc.	V.G.	Good	Fair	Poor
1800	1250	900	700	500	250

MODEL 82C SERIES

NOTE: As of 1998 the Model 82C series rifles went out of production.

Model 82C Classic

Bolt action rifle chambered for the .22 long rifle cartridge. Receiver drilled and tapped for sights. Fitted with a 22" barrel. Detachable magazine holds 4 rounds. Stock is plain with standard grade Claro Walnut. Checkering is 18 lines to the inch with 4 point side panel pattern. Red rubber butt pad and polished steel pistol grip cap are standard. Weight is approximately 6-1/2 lbs.

NIB	Exc.	V.G.	Good	Fair	Poor
900	650	500	400	—	—

Model 82C SuperAmerica

Same as above but fitted with AAA fancy grade Claro Walnut with ebony tip and beaded cheekpiece. Hand checkering is 22 lines to the inch in a full coverage pattern. Steel buttplate and steel pistol grip cap are standard.

NIB	Exc.	V.G.	Good	Fair	Poor
1475	1100	750	450	—	—

Model 82C-Custom Match

This bolt action .22 caliber has a 22" barrel. The stock is AA French walnut with full coverage checkering. Finish is rust blued. Weight is about 6.75 lbs.

NIB	Exc.	V.G.	Good	Fair	Poor
2000	1600	950	700	—	—

Model 82C Custom Shop SuperAmerica (Basic)

Same as above but furnished with a number of special order options that greatly effect the value. Seek an independent appraisal before the sale. Prices begin at $1,650.00.

Model 82C Stainless Classic Limited Edition

Introduced in 1996 this limited edition Model 82C is chambered for the .22 long rifle cartridge The stainless steel barrel is 22" long. A 4-shot magazine is included. Production limited to about 600 rifles.

NIB	Exc.	V.G.	Good	Fair	Poor
900	750	—	—	—	—

Model 82C SVT (Short/Varmint/Target)

First introduced in 1996 this .22 caliber rifle is a single shot. It is fitted with an 18" stainless steel fluted barrel. The walnut stock is a target style with no checkering. Weight is about 7.5 lbs.

NIB	Exc.	V.G.	Good	Fair	Poor
900	700	500	400	—	—

Model 82C HS (Hunter Silhouette)

Introduced in 1997 this model features a 24" half-fluted barrel. Chambered for .22 long rifle cartridge. Stock is American walnut with high comb. Trigger is fully adjustable. Four-round magazine is standard. Weight is about 7 lbs.

NIB	Exc.	V.G.	Good	Fair	Poor
750	600	500	—	—	—

MODEL 84C SERIES

NOTE: As of 1998 the Model 84C series rifle went out of production.

Model 84C-Single Shot Varmint

Chambered for the .17 Rem. or .223 Rem. cartridge this rifle is fitted with a 25" stainless steel fluted barrel. Claro walnut stock with varmint style forearm. Weight is approximately 7.5 lbs.

NIB	Exc.	V.G.	Good	Fair	Poor
1000	750	600	500	400	200

Kimber Sporterized Model 98 Swedish Mausers

These are reconditioned and reworked Mausers which are fitted with new match grade stainless steel fluted barrels in 24" or 26" depending on caliber. The stock is new synthetic checkered. Chambered in .257 Roberts, .270 Win., .280 Rem., .30-06, 7mm Rem. Mag., .300 Win. Mag., .338 Win. Mag., and the .220 Swift with a 25" barrel.

Suggested retail price is $535 for standard calibers and $560 for Magnums.

Kimber Sporterized Model 96 Swedish Mausers

Similar to the above in terms of reworking and reconditioning. Chambered for the following calibers:

22-250 w/stainless steel heavy barrel fluted-Retail $500.
.243 Win.-$400 to $465 depending on finish.
6.5x55mm-$340 to $370 depending on finish.
7mm-08 Rem.-$415 to $465 depending on finish.
.308 Win.-$415 to 520 depending on finish and barrel configuration.

CURRENT PRODUCTION MODELS

KIMBER 22 SERIES

In 1999 Kimber introduced a new line of bolt action .22 caliber rimfire rifles. First deliveries were made early in 2000. This series is built on a totally new design from bolt, to magazine, to barrel. All rifles in this series have a 5 round magazine capacity. This line replaces the Model 82-C series of rifles.

Classic

This .22 caliber rifle is fitted with a 22" barrel with fully adjustable trigger. Stock is A grade Claro walnut with 18 lpi checkering. Fitted with a Model 70 style safety. Blued finish. Weight is about 6.5 lbs.

NIB	Exc.	V.G.	Good	Fair	Poor
950	750	—	—	—	—

SuperAmerica

This model features a 22" barrel with fully adjustable trigger. Stock is AAA grade Claro walnut with 22 lpi wrap-around checkering and ebony forend tip. Black recoil pad. Weight is about 6.5 lbs.

NIB	Exc.	V.G.	Good	Fair	Poor
1550	1200	—	—	—	—

SVT (Short Varmint/Target)

Fitted with an 18" fluted stainless steel barrel and gray laminated wood stock with high target comb. This model weighs about 7.5 lbs.

NIB	Exc.	V.G.	Good	Fair	Poor
950	750	—	—	—	—

HS (Hunter Silhouette)

This model is fitted with a 24" medium sporter match grade barrel with match chambered and half fluting. Walnut stock with 18 lpi checkering and Monte Carlo comb. Weight is about 7 lbs.

NIB	Exc.	V.G.	Good	Fair	Poor
775	575	—	—	—	—

MODEL 84M SERIES

Model 84M Classic

Introduced in 2001 this centerfire bolt action rifle is chambered for the .243 Win., .260 Rem., .7mm-08 Rem., and the .308 Win. Fitted with a 22" light sporter match grade barrel Claro walnut stock with 20 lpi checkering and satin wood finish. Matted blue finish. Fitted with a 1" Pachmayr Decelerator recoil pad. Weight is about 5.75 lbs.

NIB	Exc.	V.G.	Good	Fair	Poor
895	700	—			

Model 84M Varmint

Similar to the Classic but fitted with a stainless steel 26" match grade barrel. Chambered for the .22-250 Rem. cartridge. Fitted with a .5" solid recoil pad. Weight is approximately 7.4 lbs.

NIB	Exc.	V.G.	Good	Fair	Poor
780	625	—			

KIMBER CLASSIC .45 PISTOLS

First introduced in 1996 this is a quality built American made 1911 designed by Chip McCormick for Kimber.

NOTE: In 2001 Kimber phased in a new safety system on its pistols: the Kimber firing pin safety. Models with this new firing pin safety will bear the designation "II" as part of its model name.

Custom

Barrel length is 5" with black oxide finish fixed sights. Black synthetic grips. Magazine capacity is 8 rounds. Weight is about 38 oz.

NIB	Exc.	V.G.	Good	Fair	Poor
650	500	350	—	—	—

NOTE: For Walnut grips add $10.00. For night sights add $100.

Custom Heritage Edition

Chambered for .45 ACP cartridge and fitted with a 5" barrel. Magazine capacity is 7 rounds. Checkered front strap, ambidextrous thumb safety, aluminum trigger, hand checkered rosewood grips, a special edition markings on slide. Sights are low profile fixed. Weight is about 38 oz. Introduced in 2000.

NIB	Exc.	V.G.	Good	Fair	Poor
1065	850	—	—	—	—

Custom Stainless

As above but in stainless steel.

NIB	Exc.	V.G.	Good	Fair	Poor
750	500	425	—	—	—

NOTE: For night sights add $100.

Stainless Limited Edition

Similar to the Custom Stainless except for black thumb release, black grip safety, black magazine release button, and black barrel bushing. Limited to approximately 1,200 pistols.

NIB	Exc.	V.G.	Good	Fair	Poor
745	600	525	—	—	—

Custom Target

The Custom Target has the same features as the Custom with the addition of an adjustable rear sight.

NIB	Exc.	V.G.	Good	Fair	Poor
750	600	525	—	—	—

Stainless Target

Same as the Custom Target with the addition of a slide and frame machined from stainless steel. Weight is 38 oz.

NIB	Exc.	V.G.	Good	Fair	Poor
850	675	550	—	—	—

Stainless Target Limited Edition

Similar to the Stainless Target but with black thumb safety, black grip safety, black slide release, and black barrel bushing. This model is limited to approximately 700 pistols. Introduced in 1998.

NIB	Exc.	V.G.	Good	Fair	Poor
825	650	—	—	—	—

Custom Royal

This has all the features of the Custom plus a high polish blue finish, hand checkered walnut grips, and long guide rod.

NIB	Exc.	V.G.	Good	Fair	Poor
775	625	525	—	—	—

Gold Match

All of the features of the Custom Royal plus BoMar adjustable sights, fancy checkered diamond grips.

NIB	Exc.	V.G.	Good	Fair	Poor
975	775	600	—	—	—

Stainless Gold Match

Similar to the Gold Match except slide and frame are stainless steel. Introduced in 1998.

NIB	Exc.	V.G.	Good	Fair	Poor
1150	900	—	—	—	—

Polymer

This model features a polymer frame with a matte black oxide slide. Sights are McCormick low profile. Barrel length is 5" and overall length is 8.75". Weight is about 34 oz. Magazine is 14 rounds. One 14-round magazine is supplied with gun when new.

NIB	Exc.	V.G.	Good	Fair	Poor
850	675	550	—	—	—

Polymer Stainless

Similar to the Polymer model but with a stainless steel slide. Weight is the same as the Polymer model; 34 oz.

NIB	Exc.	V.G.	Good	Fair	Poor
925	750	600	—	—	—

Polymer Target

Introduced in 1998 this pistol has a matte black oxide slide with adjustable sights. Magazine is 14 rounds. Weight is about 34 oz.

NIB	Exc.	V.G.	Good	Fair	Poor
950	750	—	—	—	—

Polymer Stainless Target

Same as above but with stainless steel slide. Introduced in 1998.

NIB	Exc.	V.G.	Good	Fair	Poor
1025	825	650	—	—	—

Polymer Pro Carry Stainless

Chambered for the .45ACP cartridge with a 4" barrel. McCormick Low Profile sights. Stainless steel slide with black polymer frame. Weight is about 32 oz. Magazine capacity is 14 rounds. Introduced in 1999.

NIB	Exc.	V.G.	Good	Fair	Poor
875	700	—	—	—	—

Polymer Pro Carry

Same as model above but with blued steel slide.

NIB	Exc.	V.G.	Good	Fair	Poor
800	650	—	—	—	—

Polymer Ultra Ten II

Introduced in 2001 this pistol is chambreerd for the .45 ACP cartridge and fitted with a 3" barrel. Stainless steel slide and black Polymer frame. Supplied with 10-round magazine. McCormick low profile sights. Weight is about 24 oz.

NIB	Exc.	V.G.	Good	Fair	Poor
895	725	—	—	—	—

Polymer Gold Match

This .45ACP 5" barrel model has all of the standard features of the Gold Match with a black Polymer frame and blued steel slide. Magazine capacity is 14 rounds. Weight is approximately 34 oz.

NIB	Exc.	V.G.	Good	Fair	Poor
1075	850	—	—	—	—

Polymer Stainless Gold Match

This model is similar to the Polymer Gold Match with the addition of a stainless steel slide. This model is also chambered for several calibers: .45 ACP, .40 S&W, 9mm, and .38 Super. Weight is about 34 oz.

NIB	Exc.	V.G.	Good	Fair	Poor
1250	1000	—	—	—	—

Compact

These steel frame and slide pistols are fitted with a 4" bull barrel and shortened grip (.4" shorter than full size). Offered in .45 ACP. Finish is matte black oxide. Grips are black synthetic. Overall length is 7.7". Weight is about 43 oz. Introduced in 1998.

NIB	Exc.	V.G.	Good	Fair	Poor
675	550	—	—	—	—

Compact Aluminum

This model has the same appearance as the Compact but with an aluminum frame. Matte black finish. Weight is approximately 28 oz. Introduced in 1998.

NIB	Exc.	V.G.	Good	Fair	Poor
675	550	450	—	—	—

Compact Stainless

Same as the Compact model but with a stainless steel slide and frame. Offered in both .45ACP and .40S&W. Introduced in 1998.

NIB	Exc.	V.G.	Good	Fair	Poor
775	625	475	—	—	—

Compact Stainless Aluminum

Offered in both .45ACP and .40S&W this model features a 4" barrel with stainless steel slide and aluminum frame. Weight is about 28 oz.

NIB	Exc.	V.G.	Good	Fair	Poor
750	600	475	—	—	—

NOTE: Add $25 for .40S&W models.

Pro Carry

Introduced in 1998 this .45ACP or .40S&W model features a full size aluminum frame and 4" slide and bull barrel. Other features are match grade trigger, beveled magazine well, full length guide rod, low profile combat sights, and 7-round magazine. Finish is matte black oxide. Weight is approximately 28 oz.

NIB	Exc.	V.G.	Good	Fair	Poor
675	550	—	—	—	—

Pro Carry Stainless

Same as above but with stainless steel slide.

NIB	Exc.	V.G.	Good	Fair	Poor
750	600	—	—	—	—

Ultra Carry

This model is chambered for the .45ACP or .40S&W cartridge. It is fitted with a 3" barrel with McCormick low profile sights. Grips are black synthetic. Magazine capacity is 7 rounds. Weight is about 25 oz. Black oxide finish. Introduced in 1999.

NIB	Exc.	V.G.	Good	Fair	Poor
675	550	—	—	—	—

Ultra Carry Stainless

Same as above but with stainless steel slide.

NIB	Exc.	V.G.	Good	Fair	Poor
750	600	—	—	—	—

NOTE: Add $25 for .40S&W model.

```
/////////////////////////////////
```
KIMBER 1911

Going from handling and shooting a GI-type 1911 to a Kimber 1911 is similar to going from driving a VW Beetle to a Porsche. I get shots on target or a ride in both instances, but there certainly is a noticeable difference. The Kimber 1911 is a recent entry in a crowded 1911 field, but the Kimber has elbowed its way to the front of the pack in a few short years simply based on quality, price and the inclusion of previously-custom touches.

The basic Kimber comes with some necessary improvements to the original 1911A1 design. Until I learned about lowered and scalloped ejection ports, I just thought that dented cases were a cross I had to bear if I chose to shoot a 1911. The Kimber also comes with a widened and rounded grip safety. This is instant elimination of hammer bite, which is caused by the hammer catching the web of your shooting hand between it and the grip safety tang. For years, this hammer bite and the remaining scars were viewed and exhibited to others by 1911 afficionados as their equivalent of Prussian facial dueling scars - a mark of a rite of passage, as it were. Higher and more visible sights have replaced the functional but less-than-optimal sights on previous factory-produced 1911s, and an extended and wider thumb safety as well as a slightly-raised magazine catch is standard equipment, making these controls easier to use. Among my custom 1911s I now include the factory-produced Kimber. It's a good fighting machine.

Walt Rauch

Kimber .22 Long Rifle Conversion Kit

Introduced in 1998 this Kimber kit features a complete upper assembly: slide, barrel, guide rod, shock buffer, and 10-round magazine. Finish is satin silver or satin blue. Will fit all Kimber 1911 .45 ACP models.

NIB	Exc.	V.G.	Good	Fair	Poor
300	250	—	—	—	—

CUSTOM SHOP PISTOLS

Royal Carry

This is a limited edition of 600 pistols. Chambered for .45 ACP and fitted with a 4" barrel with night sights. Hand checkered rosewood grips. Steel slide and aluminum frame. High polish blue finish. Magazine capacity is 7 rounds. Weight is approximately 28 oz. Introduced in 1998.

NIB	Exc.	V.G.	Good	Fair	Poor
900	725	575	—	—	—

Elite Carry

Introduced in 1998 this custom shop pistol is limited to 1,200 pistols. Chambered for .45 ACP with a 4" barrel with night sights. Frame is aluminum with black oxide finish. Slide is steel with stainless steel finish. Ambidextrous extended thumb safety, checkered front strap, match trigger, and hand checkered rosewood grips. Magazine capacity is 7 rounds. Weight is about 28 oz.

NIB	Exc.	V.G.	Good	Fair	Poor
1000	800	650	—	—	—

Gold Guardian

This limited edition Custom shop pistol is limited to 300 pistols. Chambered for .45 ACP and fitted with a 5" barrel with fixed night sights. Stainless steel slide and frame. Ambidextrous extended thumb safety, match grade barrel, extended magazine well, match trigger, and special markings and serial number. Magazine capacity is 8 rounds and weight is about 38 oz. Introduced in 1998.

NIB	Exc.	V.G.	Good	Fair	Poor
1350	1050	850	—	—	—

Combat Carry

This 4" barrel pistol is chambered for the .45 ACP or .40 S&W cartridge. Many custom features. Special markings. Stainless steel slide and blued frame. Night sights standard. Weight is approximately 28 oz. Introduced in 1999.

NIB	Exc.	V.G.	Good	Fair	Poor
1025	800	—	—	—	—

Gold Combat

This full size pistol is chambered for the .45 ACP cartridge. Many custom features. Night sights standard. Special markings. Weight is about 38 oz. Blued slide and frame. Introduced in 1999.

NIB	Exc.	V.G.	Good	Fair	Poor
1475	1150	—	—	—	—

Gold Combat Stainless

Same as the model above but with stainless steel slide.

NIB	Exc.	V.G.	Good	Fair	Poor
1425	1100	—	—	—	—

Super Match

This is Kimber's most accurate .45ACP pistol. Fitted with a 5" barrel and many special features. Adjustable sights. Weight is about 38 oz. Stainless steel slide and frame with two tone finish. Introduced in 1999.

NIB	Exc.	V.G.	Good	Fair	Poor
1700	1300	—	—	—	—

CDP SERIES (Custom Defense Package)
Ultra CDP

This custom shop model features a 3" barrel, night sights, hand checkered rosewood grips, numerous custom features. Finish is stainless steel slide and matte black frame. Chambered for .45ACP cartridge. Magazine capacity is 6 rounds. Weight is about 25 oz. Introduced in 2000.

NIB	Exc.	V.G.	Good	Fair	Poor
1140	900	—	—	—	—

Compact CDP

This model, introduced in 2000, features a 4" bull barrel, night sights, hand checkered rosewood grips, and other custom features. Stainless steel slide and matte black frame. Chambered for .45ACP cartridge. Magazine capacity is 6 rounds. Weight is about 28 oz.

NIB	Exc.	V.G.	Good	Fair	Poor
1140	900	—	—	—	—

Pro CDP

This model is similar to the Compact CDP but with a full length grip. Magazine capacity is 7 rounds and weight is about 28 oz. Introduced in 2000.

NIB	Exc.	V.G.	Good	Fair	Poor
1140	900	—	—	—	—

Custom CDP

This .45 ACP full size pistol is fitted with a 5" match grade barrel and stainless steel slide with front and rear beveled serrations. Matte black steel frame with checkered rosewood grips. Night sights standard. Introduced in 2001.

NIB	Exc.	V.G.	Good	Fair	Poor
1140	900	—	—	—	—

KIMBER OF OREGON, INC.
Clackamas, Oregon
SEE—Kimber Mfg., Inc

NOTE: Firearms marked Kimber, Clackamas, Oregon will be found under Kimber Mfg., Inc. Usually firearms produced in the Oregon facility will be stamped in this manner.

KIMBER OF AMERICA
Yonkers, New York
SEE—Kimber Mfg., Inc.

NOTE: Firearms marked Kimber of America or Kimber, Yonkers, NY will be found under Kimber Mfg., Inc.

KING PIN
Unknown

Derringer

A .22 caliber spur trigger brass constructed single shot pistol with a 2.5" barrel and walnut grips. Believed to have been made during the 1880s.

Exc.	V.G.	Good	Fair	Poor
—	—	500	200	100

KIRRIKALE, ENDUSTRISI
Ankara, Turkey

Kirrikale Pistol

A 7.65 or 9mm short caliber semiautomatic pistol with a 3.5" barrel and 6-shot magazine. Blued with plastic grips. The slide marked "MKE"; and "Kirrikale Tufek Fb Cal.—." Imported by Firearms Center in Victoria, Texas, and also by Mandall Shooting Supplies. This was an unauthorized copy of the Walther PP which was imported into the US briefly.

NIB	Exc.	V.G.	Good	Fair	Poor
400	350	275	225	150	100

KLIPZIG & COMPANY
San Francisco, California

Pocket Pistol

A .41 caliber single shot percussion pistol with a 2.5" barrel, German silver mounts and walnut stocks. Manufactured during the 1850s and early 1860s.

Exc.	V.G.	Good	Fair	Poor
—	—	1500	900	400

KNICKERBOCKER

Made by Crescent Fire Arms Co.

Knickerbocker Pistol NFA

The Knickerbocker is a 14" double barreled 20 gauge smooth bore pistol manufactured by Crescent Fire Arms Co. of Norwich, Connecticut. On the basis of its hammerless design and the dates of production of similarly designed firearms by Crescent, the Knickerbocker was probably manufactured sometime during the early 1900s. The receiver is case hardened, and the barrels are nickel-plated. The right side of the receiver is stamped **AMERICAN GUN CO./ NEW YORK U S A**; the left side is stamped **KNICKERBOCKER**. It probably was intended for law enforcement and/or defensive purposes, and manufactured using the same techniques used to produce the Ithaca Auto & Burglar Gun. The receiver is fitted with a checkered pistol grip resembling that of the Model 1 and Model 2 smooth bore H&R Handy-Gun. The only known specimen of the Knickerbocker bears serial number 200114. The Knickerbocker was classified as an "any other weapon" under the NFA in 1934 because it was originally designed as "a so-called shotgun with a pistol grip" and because it is concealable (see Treasury Department ruling S.T. 772, dated August 6, 1934). Its rarity precludes being able to reliably estimate its value at this time.

The Knickerbocker is a so-called "Hardware Gun" of the type produced under direct contract to distributors, mail order houses, hardware stores and other retail outlets. The Knickerbocker is apparently not listed in any Crescent or other trade catalog, and its total production is unknown at this time--but there seems little doubt it was originally manufactured in its present condition.

The design of the Knickerbocker confirms that it is an "any other weapon" rather than a short barreled shotgun or a weapon made from a shotgun. Upon inspecting the barrels for choke using a simple plug-type gauge, both barrels were determined to be full choke, a physical impossibility had the barrels simply been cut down. The triggerguard is bent at approximately 80° and extends down the front of the grip--a design feature that is identical on the Model A 20 gauge Ithaca Auto & Burglar Gun. The pistol grip attachment is no different from that of a shoulder-fired sidelock shotgun; there is no through-bolt, but 2 screws that pass through the upper and lower tangs and the stock. Upon disassembly, no serial number is evident on the stock; the triggerguard is serialized 00114--the number 2 is missing--and the 4 is very indistinct. The complete serial number is also stamped on the left side of the barrel lug, left side of the water table, forend metal, and forend wood. The weight of the Knickerbocker is just under 5 lbs. Although no written documentation of this firearm has been located, the foregoing physical examination distinguishes the Knickerbocker from a sawed-off shotgun.

Double Barrel Shotgun

Knickerbocker was a popular Dutch name for a New Yorker and was used as a brand on many hammerless sidelock doubles made by Crescent Firearms Co. Valued from $100 to $700 depending on model and condition,

KNIGHT RIFLES

Centerville, Iowa

This company was started in 1985 by Tony Knight. The company produces in-line black powder muzzleloading rifles and a complete line of accessories

Disc Magnum

Available in .50 caliber with a choice of blued or stainless steel 24"" or 26" barrel. Adjustable rear sight. Checkered stock with palm swell and rubber recoil pad. Stock also offered in black or camo. Adjustable trigger. Weight is approximately 8 lbs.

NIB	Exc.	V.G.	Good	Fair	Poor
450	350	300	250	200	150

NOTE: Add $50 for camo finish, $70 for stainless steel.

Bighorn Magnum

Available in .50 caliber with choice of 22" or 26" blued or stainless steel barrel. Adjustable rear sight. Checkered stock with rubber recoil pad. Stock also offered in black or camo. Adjustable trigger. Weight is about 7.7 lbs.

NIB	Exc.	V.G.	Good	Fair	Poor
325	250	200	175	150	100

NOTE: Add $50 for camo finish, $70 for stainless steel.

T-Bolt Magnum

Available in .50 caliber with choice of blue or stainless steel 22" or 26" barrel. Adjustable rear sight. Composite stock with rubber recoil pad. Stock also available in camo. Adjustable trigger. Weight is about 8 lbs.

NIB	Exc.	V.G.	Good	Fair	Poor
400	325	275	225	150	100

NOTE: Add $50 for camo finish, $70 for stainless steel.

LK-93 Wolverine

Available in .50 or .54 caliber with a choice of 22" blued or stainless steel barrel. Adjustable rear sight. Composite skeleton or thumbhole stock. Stock also available in black or camo. Adjustable trigger. Weight is about 6.5 lbs.

NIB	Exc.	V.G.	Good	Fair	Poor
265	200	150	100	75	—

NOTE: Add $50 for camo finish, $70 for stainless steel, $40 for thumbhole stock.

LK-93 Wolverine Youth

Same as model above but with shorter length of pull. Offered in black stock only.

NIB	Exc.	V.G.	Good	Fair	Poor
275	225	175	125	100	75

American Knight

Available in .50 caliber with 22" blued barrel. Adjustable rear sight. Black composite stock. Non-adjustable trigger. Weight is approximately 6.3 lbs.

NIB	Exc.	V.G.	Good	Fair	Poor
200	150	100	75	—	—

MK-85 Hunter

This model is offered in .50 or .54 caliber with blued finish and walnut stock.

NIB	Exc.	V.G.	Good	Fair	Poor
550	450	375	325	250	200

MK-85 Predator

This is a stainless steel version of the Hunter model. Offered with composite stock or various camo finishes.

NIB	Exc.	V.G.	Good	Fair	Poor
650	525	450	300	250	200

NOTE: Add $50 for camo finish.

MK-85 Stalker

This model is offered in .50 or .54 caliber with a variety of stock options. Standard stock is composite. Blued finish.

NIB	Exc.	V.G.	Good	Fair	Poor
565	450	375	325	250	200

NOTE: Add $50 for camo finish.

MK-85 Knight Hawk

This model is offered in .50 or .54 caliber with black composite stock and stainless steel.

NIB	Exc.	V.G.	Good	Fair	Poor
750	600	500	400	300	200

MK-86 Shotgun

Available in 12 gauge with 24" extra full choked barrel. Black composite stock with blued finish.

NIB	Exc.	V.G.	Good	Fair	Poor
600	475	375	250	200	150

HK-94 Hawkeye Pistol

This is a .50 caliber pistol fitted with a 12" barrel and an overall length of 20" and a weight of 52 oz. Offered in stainless steel or blued finish. First offered in 1993 and discontinued in 1998.

NIB	Exc.	V.G.	Good	Fair	Poor
400	300	250	200	150	100

NOTE: Add $70 for stainless steel.

KNIGHT'S MANUFACTURING CO.
Vero Beach, Florida

STONER SR-15 RIFLES

SR-15 Match

Chambered for .223 Win. and fitted with a target contour 20" free floating barrel. Two stage match trigger. Flat top receiver. No sights. Weight is approximately 7.9 lbs.

NIB	Exc.	V.G.	Good	Fair	Poor
1595	1250	950	750	500	—

SR-15 M-5 Rifle

This .223 is fitted with a 20" standard weight barrel with 2 stage target trigger. Handguard employs RAS accessory system. Fitted with flip-up low profile rear sight. Weight is about 7.6 lbs.

NIB	Exc.	V.G.	Good	Fair	Poor
1295	1000	800	600	400	—

SR-15 M-4 Carbine

This model also includes the RAS system and has a flip-up rear sight. Two stage target trigger and 16" lightweight barrel. Weight is about 6.8 lbs.

NIB	Exc.	V.G.	Good	Fair	Poor
1295	1000	800	600	400	—

STONER SR-25 RIFLES

SR-25 Match

This rifle is chambered for the .308 caliber and fitted with a 24" target contour free floating barrel. Special rifling and twist rate. No sights. Weight is about 10.75 lbs.

NIB	Exc.	V.G.	Good	Fair	Poor
2995	2250	1500	900	—	—

SR-25 Lightweight Match

This .308 rifle is fitted with a 20" free floating barrel. No sights. Weight is about 9.5 lbs.

NIB	Exc.	V.G.	Good	Fair	Poor
2995	2250	1500	900	—	—

SR-25 Stoner Carbine

Fitted with a 16" free floating barrel and special short non-slip handguard. Weight is about 7.75 lbs.

NIB	Exc.	V.G.	Good	Fair	Poor
2995	2250	1500	900	—	—

SR-25 Competition Match

This rifle is chambered for either .308 or .260 cartridge and has a 26" match barrel. Fitted with a special forearm which rotates in 15 degree increments. Trigger is adjustable two-stage with extended triggerguard. Special bolt stop and charging handle. Adjustable buttstock. This model may be fitted with several extra costs options that will affect price.

NIB	Exc.	V.G.	Good	Fair	Poor
6000	4750	3000	—	—	—

SR-50 Rifle

This is a semiautomatic rifle chambered for the .50 BMG cartridge. Magazine feed. Weight is approximately 31 lbs.

NIB	Exc.	V.G.	Good	Fair	Poor
7000	5500	4000	—	—	—

KOHOUT & SPOLECNOST
Kdyne, Czechoslovakia

Mars

A 6.35 or 7.65mm caliber semiautomatic pistol, the larger caliber having a grip safety. Blued with plastic grips impressed with the word "Mars". The slide marked "Mars 7.65 (or 6.35) Kohout & Spol. Kdyne." Manufactured between 1928 and 1945.

Exc.	V.G.	Good	Fair	Poor
350	250	200	150	100

Niva, PZK

Similar to the above in 6.35mm caliber.

Exc.	V.G.	Good	Fair	Poor
350	250	200	150	100

KOLB, HENRY M.
Philadelphia, Pennsylvania

The revolvers listed below were manufactured by Henry Kolb and Charles Foehl until 1912 when R.F. Sedgely replaced Foehl. Manufacture continued until approximately 1938.

Baby Hammerless

A .22 caliber folding trigger double action revolver with an enclosed hammer and 5-shot cylinder.

Exc.	V.G.	Good	Fair	Poor
—	350	200	150	100

New Baby Hammerless

Similar to the above, with a hinged barrel to facilitate loading.

Exc.	V.G.	Good	Fair	Poor
—	350	200	150	100

KOLIBRI
Frederich Pfannl
Rehberg, Austria

2.7mm

A 2.7mm semiautomatic pistol with a 7-round magazine. F.P. trademark are on the grips as well as the Kolibri name at the bottom of the grips.

Courtesy James Rankin

Exc.	V.G.	Good	Fair	Poor
1800	1500	1200	—	—

3mm

A 3mm semiautomatic pistol with a 6-round magazine. The 3mm version is the rarer of the two Kolibri pistols. The F.P. trademark is on the grips.

Courtesy James Rankin

Exc.	V.G.	Good	Fair	Poor
300	250	200	150	90

Model 3

A 6.35mm semiautomatic pistol with a 9-round magazine. The Kommer name is on the slide and the TH.K. trademark is on the grips. Same as the Model 2 with extended grips straps for longer magazine.

Courtesy James Rankin

Courtesy James Rankin

Exc.	V.G.	Good	Fair	Poor
2500	2000	1500	—	—

KOMMER, THEODOR WAFFENFABRIK
Zella Mehlis, Germany

Model 1

A 6.35mm semiautomatic pistol with an 8-shot magazine. Blued with plastic grips. Kommer name is both on the slide and the frame with T.K. trademark on the grips. Manufactured during the 1920s.

Exc.	V.G.	Good	Fair	Poor
300	250	200	150	90

Model 4

A 7.65mm caliber semiautomatic pistol with a 7-shot magazine and without a grip safety. Similar to the FN Model 1901. The slide marked "Waffenfabrik Kommer Zella Mehlis Kal. 7.65". Manufactured between 1936 and 1940.

Courtesy James Rankin

Exc.	V.G.	Good	Fair	Poor
300	250	200	150	90

Model 2

A 6.35mm semiautomatic pistol with a 6-round magazine similar to the Model 1906 Browning. The Kommer name is on the slide. The late TH.K. trademark is on the grips. Manufactured in the 1930s.

Courtesy James Rankin

Exc.	V.G.	Good	Fair	Poor
375	325	275	175	100

KONGSBERG
Norway
Importer-Kongsberg America
Fairfield, Connecticut

Thumbhole Sporter

Introduced in 1993, this bolt action rifle is chambered of the .22-250 and .308 Win. cartridges. It is fitted with a 23" heavy barrel. The stock is American walnut with stippled thumbhole grip and wide forend. Cheekpiece is adjustable for height. Weight is about 8.5 lbs. Available in both right- and left-hand configurations.

NIB	Exc.	V.G.	Good	Fair	Poor
1575	1250	900	—	—	—

NOTE: Add 10% for left hand model.

Classic Rifle

This model was also introduced in 1993 and is chambered for a wide variety of calibers from .22-250 to .338 Win. Mag. Fitted with a 23" barrel for standard calibers and a 26" barrel for magnum calibers. European walnut stock with straight comb. Hand checkered. Open sights. Weight is about 7.5 lbs. depending on caliber. Offered in both left and right hand configurations.

NIB	Exc.	V.G.	Good	Fair	Poor
995	800	650	—	—	—

NOTE: Add 10% for left hand models and 10% for magnum calibers.

KORRIPHILIA
Germany
Importer-Intertex
Pineville, North Carolina

HSP

A 7.65mm Luger, .38 Special, 9mm Police, 9mm Luger, 9mm Steyr, 10mm ACP, and the .45 ACP caliber double action semiautomatic pistol with a 4" barrel made of stainless steel.

NIB	Exc.	V.G.	Good	Fair	Poor
7500	6000	—	—	—	—

HSP-Single Action Only
NIB	Exc.	V.G.	Good	Fair	Poor
7500	6000	—	—	—	—

Odin's Eye

Essentially the same model as above in the same calibers with choice of barrel lengths of 4" or 5". Frame and slide are made of Damascus steel.

NIB	Exc.	V.G.	Good	Fair	Poor
14000	10000	—	—	—	—

KORTH
Germany

NOTE: This company is no longer in business as of 2000.

Semiautomatic Pistol

A 9mm caliber double action semiautomatic pistol with a 4.5" barrel, adjustable sights and 13-shot magazine. Matte or polished blue with walnut grips. Introduced in 1985.

NIB	Exc.	V.G.	Good	Fair	Poor
3500	2500	2000	1500	750	400

Revolver

A .22 l.r., .22 Magnum, .357 Magnum, and 9mm caliber revolver with a 3", 4", or 6" barrel and 6-shot cylinder. The barrels and cylinders are interchangeable, matte or polished blue with walnut grips.

NIB	Exc.	V.G.	Good	Fair	Poor
2450	1950	1500	950	600	400

KRAG JORGENSEN
Springfield, Massachusetts

NOTE: For history, technical data, descriptions, and prices see the *Standard Catalog of Firearms, 1870 to the Present* under United States, Norway, Denmark, Rifles

KRAUSER, ALFRED
Zella Mehlis, Germany

Helfricht or Helkra
A 6.35mm semiautomatic pistol with a 2" barrel. Produced in four models, the 4th having an enclosed barrel. Blued with composition grips. Manufactured from 1921 to 1929.

Exc.	V.G.	Good	Fair	Poor
475	400	350	250	150

KRICO
Stuttgart, West Germany
Importer-Mandall Shooting Supplies

Sporting Rifle
A .22 Hornet or .222 caliber bolt action rifle with 22", 24", or 26" barrels, single or double set trigger, adjustable sights and a 4-shot magazine. Blued with a walnut stock. Manufactured between 1956 and 1962.

Exc.	V.G.	Good	Fair	Poor
650	550	475	375	275

Sporting Carbine
As above, with a 20" barrel and full length stock.

Exc.	V.G.	Good	Fair	Poor
675	575	500	400	300

Varmint Special Rifle
The Sporting Rifle with a heavier barrel.

Exc.	V.G.	Good	Fair	Poor
650	550	475	375	275

Model 300
A .22 caliber bolt action rifle with a 23.5" barrel, 5-shot magazine and grooved receiver. Blued with a walnut stock. Imported prior to 1989.

Exc.	V.G.	Good	Fair	Poor
700	600	550	400	300

Model 302 and 304
Variations of the above. Discontinued in 1986.

Exc.	V.G.	Good	Fair	Poor
700	600	550	400	300

Model 311 Smallbore
A .22 caliber bolt action rifle with a 22" barrel, double set triggers, adjustable sights and a 5- or 10-shot magazine. Blued with walnut stock. Not imported after 1988.

Exc.	V.G.	Good	Fair	Poor
325	275	225	150	100

Model 320
As above, with a 19.5" barrel and full length stock. Discontinued in 1988.

Exc.	V.G	Good	Fair	Poor
700	600	550	400	300

Model 340
A .22 caliber bolt action rifle with a 21" heavy barrel furnished without sights, adjustable trigger and 5-shot magazine. Blued with a walnut stock. Not imported after 1988.

Exc.	V.G.	Good	Fair	Poor
750	625	575	425	325

Model 340 Mini-Sniper
As above, but matte finished, the barrel fitted with a muzzle brake and the stock with a raised cheekpiece as well as ventilated hand guard.

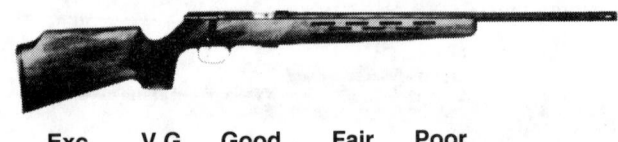

Exc.	V.G.	Good	Fair	Poor
1000	850	750	500	400

Model 340 Kricotronic
The Model 340 fitted with an electronic trigger. Not imported after 1988.

Exc.	V.G.	Good	Fair	Poor
1250	1000	850	600	500

Model 360S Biathlon Rifle
Introduced in 1991 this model features a 22 Long rifle straight pull bolt action with 5-round magazine and fitted with a 21.25" barrel. Walnut stock with high comb and adjustable buttplate. Fully adjustable match peep sight. Fitted with 17 oz. match trigger. Weight is approximately 9.25 lbs.

NIB	Exc.	V.G.	Good	Fair	Poor
1600	1350	850	—	—	—

Model 360S2 Biathlon Rifle
Same as above but fitted with a black epoxy finished walnut stock with pistol grip. Weight is 9 lbs.

NIB	Exc.	V.G.	Good	Fair	Poor
1500	1250	800	—	—	—

Model 400 Match
Chambered for the 22 Long Rifle or the .22 Hornet this bolt action rifle is fitted with a heavy match 23" barrel and a 5-round magazine. The match style stock is of European walnut. Fitted with a double set of match trigger. Weight is about 8.8 lbs.

NIB	Exc.	V.G.	Good	Fair	Poor
900	775	650	500	300	150

Model 400 Sporter

A .22 Hornet caliber bolt action rifle with a 23.5" barrel, open sights and 5-shot magazine. Blued with a walnut stock. Not imported after 1988.

Exc.	V.G.	Good	Fair	Poor
750	625	550	425	325

Model 420

As above, with a 19.5" barrel, double set triggers, and a full length stock. Discontinued in 1988.

Exc.	V.G.	Good	Fair	Poor
900	750	675	500	400

Model 440

Similar to the Model 340. Not imported after 1988.

Exc.	V.G	Good	Fair	Poor
950	800	700	500	375

Model 500 Kricotronic Match Rifle

Chambered for the .22 Long Rifle this bolt action rifle is fitted with a 23.6" barrel with tapered bore. Walnut stock with match type adjustable buttplate. Electronic ignition system gives fastest lock time. Weight is approximately 9.4 lbs.

NIB	Exc.	V.G.	Good	Fair	Poor
3900	3000	—	—	—	—

Model 600 Sporter

A .17 Remington to .308 Winchester caliber bolt action rifle with a 23.5" barrel, open sights and 3-shot magazine. Blued with a walnut stock. Not imported after 1988.

Exc.	V.G.	Good	Fair	Poor
1150	950	875	700	575

Model 600 Sniper Rifle

This bolt action rifle is chambered for the .222, .223, .22-250, .243, and 308. It is fitted with a 25.6" heavy barrel with flack hider. The stock is walnut with adjustable rubber buttplate. Magazine holds 4 rounds. Weight is about 9.2 lbs.

NIB	Exc.	V.G.	Good	Fair	Poor
2600	2000	1500	—	—	—

Model 600 Match Rifle

Chambered for the same calibers as the 600 Sniper with the addition of the 5.6x50 Mag. Fitted with a 23.6" barrel. The match stock is vented in forearm for cooling. Wood is walnut with cheekpiece. Weight is approximately 8.8 lbs.

NIB	Exc.	V.G.	Good	Fair	Poor
1200	900	750	600	—	—

Model 620

As above, with a 20.5" barrel, double set triggers, and full length stock.

Exc.	V.G.	Good	Fair	Poor
1200	1000	900	750	600

Model 640 Varmint Rifle

Similar to the above, in .22-250, .222 or .223 caliber with a 23.5" heavy barrel. Not imported after 1988.

Exc.	V.G.	Good	Fair	Poor
1250	1025	925	775	625

Model 640 Sniper Rifle

As above, but matte finished. Discontinued in 1988.

Exc.	V.G.	Good	Fair	Poor
1300	1100	950	750	600

Model 640 Deluxe Sniper Rifle

As above, in .223 or .308 caliber with a 23" barrel, stippled stock, and adjustable trigger. Not imported after 1988.

Exc.	V.G.	Good	Fair	Poor
1500	1250	1000	750	650

Model 700 Sporter

A .270 or .30-06 caliber bolt action rifle with a 23.5" barrel, open sights, single set trigger, and 3-shot magazine. Blued with a walnut stock. Discontinued in 1988.

Exc.	V. G.	Good	Fair	Poor
1050	850	750	600	500

Model 720

As above, with a 20.5" barrel, double set triggers, and full length stock. Discontinued in 1988.

Exc.	V.G.	Good	Fair	Poor
1050	850	750	600	500

Model 720 Limited Edition

As above, in .270 caliber only with gold-plated furniture and gold highlighted engraving. Not imported after 1988.

Exc.	V.G.	Good	Fair	Poor
2500	2000	1750	1400	900

KRIDER, J. H.
Philadelphia, Pennsylvania

Pocket Pistol

A .41 caliber percussion pocket pistol with a 3" barrel, German silver furniture and walnut stock. The barrel marked "Krider Phila." Manufactured during the 1850s and 1860s.

Exc.	V.G.	Good	Fair	Poor
—	—	1500	700	300

Militia Rifle

A .58 caliber percussion rifle with a 39" barrel and full length stock secured by two barrel bands. The barrel browned, the lock marked "Krider". Case hardened and furniture of brass. Several hundred were manufactured in 1861.

Courtesy Milwaukee Public Museum, Milwaukee, Wisconsin

Courtesy Milwaukee Public Museum, Milwaukee, Wisconsin

Exc.	V.G.	Good	Fair	Poor
—	—	4250	2000	750

KRIEGHOFF, HEINRICH, GUN CO.
Ulm, Germany
Importer-Krieghoff International
Ottisville, Pennsylvania

NOTE: Krieghoff manufactured Lugers are listed in the Luger section.

DRILLINGS AND COMBINATION GUNS

Plus Model
A 3 barrel combination rifle/shotgun produced in a variety of gauges and calibers with 25" barrels, double triggers, and automatic ejectors. Blued with a walnut stock. Introduced in 1988.

NIB	Exc.	V.G.	Good	Fair	Poor
6000	4750	3750	—	—	—

Trumpf Model
A combination rifle/shotgun produced in a variety of calibers and gauges with 25" barrels and double triggers. Blued with a walnut stock.

NIB	Exc.	V.G.	Good	Fair	Poor
10000	7000	4750	—	—	—

Trumpf Dural
As above, lightweight boxlock with a Duraluminum frame.

NIB	Exc.	V.G.	Good	Fair	Poor
10000	7000	4750	—	—	—

NOTE: For single trigger add $1,850. For free-floating barrel add $450.

Neptun Model
A combination Over/Under rifle/shotgun with sidelocks produced in a variety of gauges and calibers. Engraved, blued with a walnut stock.

NIB	Exc.	V.G.	Good	Fair	Poor
16500	12500	9500	—	—	—

A Krieghoff drilling was sold at auction for $10,500. It was chambered for 16x16 gauge over 7x57R with 23.62" barrels. Engraved sideplates. Two Zeiss scopes with claw mounts. Cased. Condition was excellent.
Amoskeag Auction Company, March 1999

Neptun Dural
As above, lightweight boxlock with a Duraluminum frame.

NIB	Exc.	V.G.	Good	Fair	Poor
16500	12500	9500	—	—	—

Neptun Primus Model
The Neptun with relief engraving and detachable sidelocks.

NIB	Exc.	V.G.	Good	Fair	Poor
24500	18500	12500	—	—	—

Neptun Primus Dural
As above, lightweight sidelock with a Duraluminum frame.

NIB	Exc.	V.G.	Good	Fair	Poor
24500	18500	12500	—	—	—

DOUBLE RIFLES

Teck Over/Under
A boxlock Over/Under rifle manufactured in a variety of calibers with 25" barrels, double triggers, extractors, and express sights. Blued with a walnut stock.

NIB	Exc.	V.G.	Good	Fair	Poor
10500	7500	6000	—	—	—

NOTE: For .458 Win. Mag add $1,500.

Ulm Model

As above, with sidelocks.

NIB	Exc.	V.G.	Good	Fair	Poor
17900	14000	10000	—	—	—

Ulm Primus

As above, with detachable sidelocks.

NIB	Exc.	V.G.	Good	Fair	Poor
26000	20000	15000	—	—	—

Ultra

This boxlock over and under rifle is offered with several different options such as same caliber rifle barrels or different caliber rifle barrels. Built on a 20 gauge frame with game scene engraving. Weights are depending on calibers and combinations of calibers but are between 6.5 lbs. and 8 lbs.

NIB	Exc.	V.G.	Good	Fair	Poor
6900	5500	4000	—	—	—

Classic

This is a side-by-side rifle with sideplates. Offered in 7x65R to 9.3x74R calibers with an optional interchangeable 20 gauge shotgun barrel. Single trigger. Choice of standard stock with cheekpiece or classic Bavaria style. Weight is approximately 7.25 to 8 lbs. depending on calibers.

Classic with sideplates

NIB	Exc.	V.G.	Good	Fair	Poor
7850	6250	—	—	—	—

Classic Big Five

Similar to the Classic but chambered for .375 H&H, .375 NE, .458 Win. Mag., .416 Rigby, .470 NE, and .500 NE 3". Double trigger with hinged front trigger. Weight is approximately 9.25 to 10 lbs. depending on caliber. Interchangeable barrel are optional.

NIB	Exc.	V.G.	Good	Fair	Poor
9400	7500	—	—	—	—

NOTE: There are many optional engraving patterns available for these double rifles that may effect price. Consult an expert prior to a sale.

SHOTGUNS

Model 32 Standard

A 12, 20, 28 or .410 bore boxlock Over/Under shotgun with 26.5" to 32" barrels, single selective trigger and automatic ejectors. Blued with a walnut stock. Discontinued in 1980.

28 Gauge or .410 Two Barrel Set-Add 50%.
4 barrel Skeet Set-Add 100%.as

Exc.	V.G.	Good	Fair	Poor
2000	1750	1500	1000	750

Model 32 San Remo Grade

Exc.	V.G.	Good	Fair	Poor
3250	2500	1750	1250	1000

Model 32 Monte Carlo Grade

Exc.	V.G.	Good	Fair	Poor
4750	3500	2500	1500	1250

Model 32 Crown Grade

Courtesy Butterfield & Butterfield

Exc.	V.G.	Good	Fair	Poor
7000	5000	3000	2000	1500

Model 32 Super Crown Grade

NIB	Exc.	V.G.	Good	Fair	Poor
10000	7000	5000	3500	2500	2000

Model 32 Single Barrel Trap Gun

The Model 32 with a single 32" to 34" barrel.

Exc.	V.G.	Good	Fair	Poor
1750	1400	1100	750	600

Teck

Similar to the Teck double rifle but offered in 12 and 16 gauge.

NIB	Exc.	V.G.	Good	Fair	Poor
7750	6250	—	—	—	—

Teck Dural

Same as above but with lightweight aluminum frame.

NIB	Exc.	V.G.	Good	Fair	Poor
7750	6250	—	—	—	—

Ulm

This sidelock over and under is offered in both 12 and 16 gauge.

NIB	Exc.	V.G.	Good	Fair	Poor
14500	11000	—	—	—	—

Ulm Dural

This is a lightweight version of the above model.

NIB	Exc.	V.G.	Good	Fair	Poor
14500	11000	—	—	—	—

Ulm Primus

This is a deluxe version of the Ulm series with sidelocks and extensive engraving.

NIB	Exc.	V.G.	Good	Fair	Poor
22800	17500	—	—	—	—

Ulm Primus Dural

This is a lightweight version of the above model.

NIB	Exc.	V.G.	Good	Fair	Poor
22800	17500	—	—	—	—

Ultra

This is a lightweight over and under gun offered in 12 or 20 gauge.

NIB	Exc.	V.G.	Good	Fair	Poor
5000	4000	3000	—	—	—

KS-5 Single Barrel Trap

This model is a boxlock 12 gauge only trap gun with 32" or 34" ventilated tapered rib barrel and case hardened frame with a satin gray finish. The barrel features an adjustable point of impact and is offered with screw-in choke tubes. Weight is approximately 8.6 lbs.

NIB	Exc.	V.G.	Good	Fair	Poor
2850	2250	1750	1500	1250	800

KS-5 Special

Same as above but furnished with adjustable rib and adjustable comb.

NIB	Exc.	V.G.	Good	Fair	Poor
3500	3000	2500	2000	1500	1000

KS-80 Trap

This is a boxlock 12 gauge shotgun built to trap dimensions. This model is offered in many variations. Available is Over/Under trap with choice of 30" or 32" vent tapered step rib barrels. Also a single barrel is offered in 32" or 34" tapered step rib lengths. These single barrels are adjustable for point of impact. A top single barrel is available as well in 34" length. Trap combos are offered also. All barrels are offered with or without choke tubes. The checkered walnut stock is offered in Monte Carlo or straight trap dimensions. Trap guns weigh approximately 8.75 lbs. Prices below are for Standard Grade.

Over/Under Trap

NIB	Exc.	V.G.	Good	Fair	Poor
5400	4900	4000	3500	2000	1000

Unsingle Trap

NIB	Exc.	V.G.	Good	Fair	Poor
5800	5300	4500	4000	2250	1250

Top Single Trap

NIB	Exc.	V.G.	Good	Fair	Poor
7500	6500	5000	4000	3000	1500

Trap Combos

NIB	Exc.	V.G.	Good	Fair	Poor
8200	7000	6000	4000	3000	1500

Bavaria Grade-Add 70%.
Danube Grade-Add 100%.
Gold Target Grade-Add 200%.

K-80 Sporting Clays

The frame is the same as the trap model with the addition of a lightweight alloy model and is available in 12 gauge only. Barrel lengths for standard weight model are 28", 30", or 32" with tapered flat rib. The lightweight model is offered with 28" or 30" flat rib barrels. Select European walnut stock with hand checkering and supplied with a #3 Sporting stock with schnabel forearm. The standard weight model weighs about 8.25 lbs. while the lightweight model weighs 7.75 lbs. Prices below are for the Standard Grade.

NIB	Exc.	V.G.	Good	Fair	Poor
5800	5250	4500	3000	2000	1000

Bavaria Grade-Add 70%.
Danube Grade-Add 100%.
Gold Target Grade-Add 200%.

K-80 Skeet

This model is offered in a number of variations. The standard weight skeet with 28" or 30" tapered or parallel ribs, lightweight skeet with 28" or 30" tapered or parallel ribs, International skeet with 28" parallel broadway rib, and the 4 barrel skeet set in 12, 20, and 28 gauge as well as .410 bore with 8mm rib. Stock is hand checkered select European walnut with a choice of several skeet dimensions. Prices below are for Standard Grade.

Standard Weight Skeet

NIB	Exc.	V.G.	Good	Fair	Poor
5000	4500	3500	2500	1750	1250

Lightweight Skeet

NIB	Exc.	V.G.	Good	Fair	Poor
5000	4500	3500	2500	1750	1250

International Skeet

NIB	Exc.	V.G.	Good	Fair	Poor
5500	5000	3750	2750	1950	1300

4 Barrel Set

NIB	Exc.	V.G.	Good	Fair	Poor
11250	8000	6000	4000	3000	2000

Bavaria Grade-Add 70%.
Danube Grade-Add 100%.
Gold Target Grade-Add 200%.

Optional Engravings available by special order on NIB or Exc. conditions guns add:

Parcours-Add $1500.
Parcours Special-Add $2800.
Super Scroll -Add $1100.
Gold Super Scroll-Add $2900.

Custom Bavaria $4700 over Bavaria Grade price.

Standard

Super Scroll

Parcours

Bavaria

Danube

Gold Target

KRNKA, KAREL
Vienna, Austria

Karel Krnka was a talented firearms inventor born in 1858. He began his career in firearms design as a member of the Austro-Hungarian army. He made many improvements to their service rifle design. After he left the military, he took the job of head engineer with the ill-fated and short-lived "Gatling Gun Company." This company ceased operations in 1890, and then Krnka went to work for the patent office and remained there for a few years. In 1898 he became foreman of the Roth Cartridge Company and worked with Roth on firearms designs until the death of Roth in 1909. After this he became associated with the Hertenberger Cartridge Company; and finally in 1922 he moved to Czechoslovakia, where he became a firearms designer for the firm of C.Z. He remained at this post until his death in 1926. He recorded his first firearm patent in 1888 for a mechanical repeater with a ring trigger. His best known innovations are the internal butt magazine that is loaded by means of a stripper clip and the rotating locked bolt with internal firing pin. These designs were never actually turned into a mass-marketed pistol but were major contributions in the development of a practical semiautomatic pistol design.

Model 1892

Exc.	V.G.	Good	Fair	Poor
—	7500	5000	2000	950

KROPATSCHEK
Steyr-Werke
Steyr, Austria

Model 1878

An 11mm caliber bolt action rifle with a 32" barrel, full length stock secured by three barrel bands, and 7-shot magazine. Finished in the white with a walnut stock.

Exc.	V.G.	Good	Fair	Poor
—	300	200	125	75

KUFAHL, G. L.
Sommerda, Germany

Kufahl Needle-Fire Revolver

Designed and patented in Britain in 1852 by G.L. Kufahl, who tried unsuccessfully to interest a British company in producing it. He then went to the firm of Rheinmettal Dreyse, where a needle-fire gun was produced in 1838. This company manufactured his design. This revolver was chambered for a unique, totally consumed .30 caliber "cartridge." A lead projectile had the ignition percussion cap affixed to its base, with the propellant powder in the rear. The firing pin had to be long enough to penetrate the powder charge and hit the percussion cap. This does not sound efficient, but realize that these were the days before cartridges. This revolver has a 3.2" barrel and an unfluted cylinder that holds six shots. It is not bored all the way through but is loaded from the front. The finish is blued, with a modicum of simple engraving and checkered wood grips that protrude all the way over the trigger. The markings are "Fv.V. Dreyse Sommerda."

Exc.	V.G.	Good	Fair	Poor
—	2500	1250	600	400

KYNOCH GUN FACTORY
Birmingham, England

Established by George Kynoch in approximately 1886, this company ceased operation in 1890.

Early Double Trigger Revolver

A .45 caliber double trigger revolver with a 6" barrel, 6-shot cylinder and enclosed hammer. Blued with walnut grips. Manufactured in 1885.

Exc.	V.G.	Good	Fair	Poor
—	1250	600	450	350

Late Double Trigger Revolver

Similar to the above, but in .32, .38, or .45 caliber with the cocking trigger enclosed within the triggerguard. Approximately 600 of these revolvers were made between 1896 and 1890.

Exc.	V.G.	Good	Fair	Poor
—	1500	700	550	450

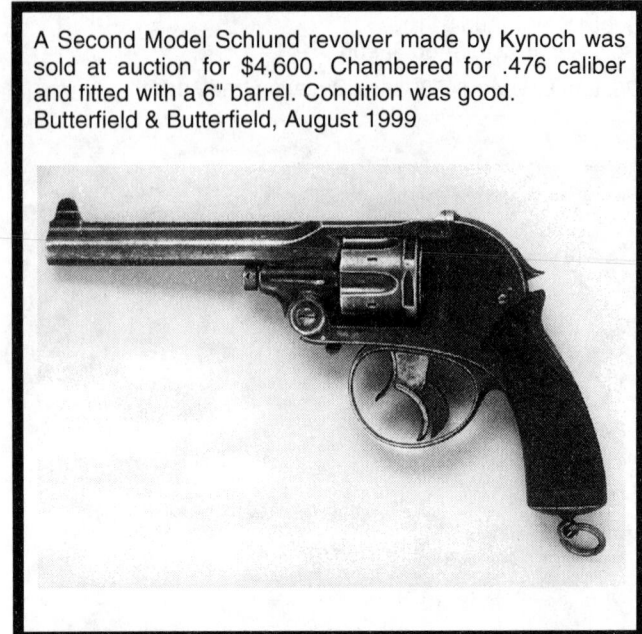

A Second Model Schlund revolver made by Kynoch was sold at auction for $4,600. Chambered for .476 caliber and fitted with a 6" barrel. Condition was good.
Butterfield & Butterfield, August 1999

LAR MFG. CO.
West Jordan, Utah

Grizzly Mark I

A .357 Magnum, .45 ACP, 10mm, or .45 Winchester Magnum semiautomatic pistol with a 5.4", 6.5", 8", or 10" barrel, Millett sights, ambidextrous safety and 7-shot magazine. Parkerized, blued, or hard-chrome plated with rubber grips. Available with cartridge conversion units, telescope mounts, or a compensator. Weight is approximately 48 oz. Introduced in 1984.

NIB	Exc.	V.G.	Good	Fair	Poor
900	775	650	500	400	200

Grizzly Mark II

As above, with fixed sights and without the ambidextrous safety. Manufactured in 1986.

Exc.	V.G.	Good	Fair	Poor
650	600	500	375	300

Grizzly Mark IV

Similar to the Mark I but chambered for the .44 Magnum cartridge. Barrel length is 5.4" or 6.5". Choice of blue or parkerized finish.

NIB	Exc.	V.G.	Good	Fair	Poor
900	775	650	500	400	200

Grizzly Mark V

Same as above model but chambered for .50 AE cartridge. Empty weight is 56 oz.

NIB	Exc.	V.G.	Good	Fair	Poor
1100	875	700	550	425	200

Grizzly State Pistol

This is a limited edition of 50 Grizzly pistols with serial numbers that match the order in which each state was admitted into the union. Each pistol features the state outline, the state seal, and the name of the state engraved in gold. Supplied with a cherry wood fitted case with glass top. Chambered for .45 Win. Mag cartridge.

NIB	Exc.	V.G.	Good	Fair	Poor
3500	—	—	—	—	—

Grizzly 50 Big Boar

A single shot breech loading rifle chambered for the .50 caliber BMG cartridge. The barrel is 36" in length and the rifle weighs approximately 30 lbs.

NIB	Exc.	V.G.	Good	Fair	Poor
2500	2150	1500	800	600	300

NOTE: Add $100 for parkerized finish. Add $250 for nickel frame, and $350 for full nickel finish.

LES, INC.
Skokie, Illinois

Rogak P-18

A 9mm caliber double action semiautomatic pistol with a 5.5" barrel and 18-shot magazine. Stainless steel. Discontinued.

Exc.	V.G.	Good	Fair	Poor
350	300	275	200	150

LAGRESE
Paris, France

Lagrese Revolver

A large ornate revolver chambered for the .43 rimfire cartridge. It has a 6.25" barrel and a 6-shot fluted cylinder. This revolver has no top strap; and the frame, as well as the grip straps, are cast in one piece with the barrel screwed into the frame. It is loaded through a gate and has double action lockwork. The outstanding feature about this well-made revolver is its extremely ornate appearance. There are more sweeps and curves than could be imagined. It is engraved and blued, with well-figured curved walnut grips. It is marked "Lagrese Bte a Paris" and was manufactured in the late 1860s.

Exc.	V.G.	Good	Fair	Poor
—	—	2500	1150	800

LAHTI
Finland
SEE—Husqvarna

Lahti

Exc.	V.G.	Good	Fair	Poor
1250	1000	800	550	300

LAKELANDER
Gulfport, Mississippi

Model 389 Premium

This bolt action rifle is chambered for .270 Win., .308 Win., and .30-06 calibers. It is fitted with a 22" lightweight barrel. The stock is oil finished walnut with diamond checkering. Rosewood forend cap, black recoil pad, and Monte Carlo buttstock. Weight is approximately 7.6 lbs. Introduced in 1997.

NIB	Exc.	V.G.	Good	Fair	Poor
1600	1250	850	—	—	—

Model 389 Classic

Similar to the Premium grade rifle above but offered with traditional stock and checkering and less fancy walnut stock. Weight is approximately 7.3 lbs. Introduced in 1997.

NIB	Exc.	V.G.	Good	Fair	Poor
1650	1300	900	—	—	—

Model 389 Match-Maker

This bolt action is chambered for the .308 cartridge and is fitted with a 21.7" barrel. The stock is target style with adjustable chin support with benchrest style butt pad. Weight is approximately 8.4 lbs. Introduced in 1997.

NIB	Exc.	V.G.	Good	Fair	Poor
2050	1650	1250	—	—	—

NOTE: Add $50 for magnum calibers.

LAMB, H. C. & CO.
Jamestown, North Carolina

Muzzle Loading Rifle

Chambered for .58 caliber and utilizes the percussion ignition system. It has a 33" barrel and a full-length oak stock held on by two barrel bands. There is a ramrod mounted under the barrel that is made of iron. All other trim is brass, and there is a bayonet lug at the muzzle. This rifle was made for the Confederacy; and the workmanship was crude, as it was on most CSA weapons. The stock is marked "H.C.Lamb & Co., N.C." There were supposedly 10,000 rifles ordered, but actually there were approximately 250 manufactured between 1861 and 1863. The rarity of the guns of the Confederacy gives them a great deal of collector appeal. One should always be aware that there have been fraudulent examples noted, and a qualified independent appraisal is definitely advisable when dealing with weapons of this nature.

Courtesy Milwaukee Public Museum, Milwaukee, Wisconsin

Exc.	V.G.	Good	Fair	Poor
—	—	30000	10000	2500

LAMES
Chiavari, Italy

Skeet or Trap Grade

An Over/Under shotgun chambered for 12 gauge with either 26" skeet-and-skeet barrels or 30" or 32" full-choked barrels. It has a competition-style wide vent rib and automatic ejectors. The trigger is single selective, and the finish is blued. The trap gun has a Monte Carlo stock of checkered walnut. Both models feature recoil pads.

Exc.	V.G.	Good	Fair	Poor
600	500	450	350	200

California Trap Grade

This Over/Under is similar to the standard trap model, with separated barrels. All other features are the same.

Exc.	V.G.	Good	Fair	Poor
700	600	550	450	225

Field Grade

Similar in design to the standard trap model, with 3" chambers and barrel lengths of 26", 28", or 30" and a field dimensioned stock. It features various choke combinations and was also available with the separated barrels of the California Trap for an additional 20 percent in cost.

Exc.	V.G.	Good	Fair	Poor
400	350	300	225	150

LANBER ARMAS S.A.
Vizcaya, Spain
Lanber Arms of America
Adrian, Michigan

Model 844 ST

A 12-gauge Over/Under shotgun with 26" or 28" vent rib barrels. The chokes vary, and the gun features a single-selective trigger, extractors, and an engraved receiver with a blued finish and a walnut stock. This gun was manufactured until 1986, when the entire line was no longer imported.

Exc.	V.G.	Good	Fair	Poor
425	350	300	250	175

Model 844 MST
Similar to the Model 844 ST except that it is chambered for 3" Magnum and has 30" full-and-modified barrels.

Exc.	V.G.	Good	Fair	Poor
425	350	300	250	175

Model 844 EST
Similar to the others, but it features automatic ejectors.

Exc.	V.G.	Good	Fair	Poor
475	400	350	300	200

Model 844 EST CHR
Has automatic ejectors and double triggers. All other features are the same as the EST.

Exc.	V.G.	Good	Fair	Poor
450	375	325	275	175

Model 2004 LCH
An Over/Under chambered for 12 gauge and features 28" vent rib barrels with screw-in choke tubes. It has a single selective trigger, automatic ejectors, and an engraved boxlock action that is matte finished, with a hand-checkered walnut stock. This model was also discontinued in 1986.

Exc.	V.G.	Good	Fair	Poor
775	650	550	475	375

Model 2008 LCH and Model 2009 LCH
The trap and skeet versions of the series. The basic differences are in the barrel lengths and the stock dimensions.

Model 2008 LCH

Model 2009 LCH

Exc.	V.G.	Good	Fair	Poor
900	750	650	575	475

LANCASTER, CHARLES
London, England
SEE—British Double Guns

4 Barreled Pistol
A unique pistol for several reasons. It is chambered for the .476 rimfire cartridge and has four 6.25" barrels. The bore has a slightly twisted oval pattern that imparts a spin to the bullet. The barrels are hinged at the bottom and break downward for loading. It is a double action type lockwork with a long, difficult trigger pull. The pistol is well made; and the caliber, suitably

heavy to insure stopping power. The primary goal was military; and it was successful, seeing action in the Sudan campaigns of 1882 and 1885. This powerful weapon was also popular with big game hunters as a backup sidearm. The finish is blued, with checkered walnut grips. It is marked "Charles Lancaster (Patent) 151 New Bond St. London." This model was introduced in 1881. There are smaller-caliber versions of this pistol with shorter barrels. They are not as well known as the large-caliber version, and the values would be similar as their rarity would be balanced by the desirability of the large bore models.

Exc.	V.G.	Good	Fair	Poor
—	—	2500	1000	750

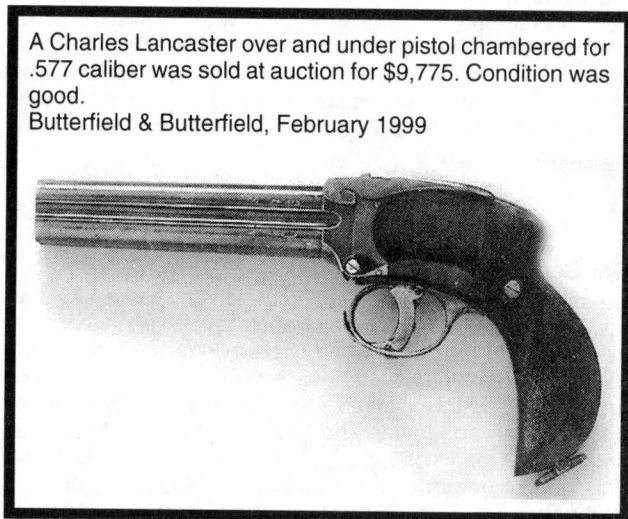

A Charles Lancaster over and under pistol chambered for .577 caliber was sold at auction for $9,775. Condition was good.
Butterfield & Butterfield, February 1999

2 Barreled Pistol
Similar to the 4 barreled version, with only two superposed barrels chambered for a variety of calibers from .320 to .577. It was also chambered for the 20 gauge and .410 bore shotshell. The advantage to the 2 barreled pistol is that it is lighter and better balanced. The two barrel is less common than the four barrel version.

Courtesy James Rankin

Exc.	V.G.	Good	Fair	Poor
—	3000	2000	900	600

4 Barreled Shotgun
This company also produced a shotgun in the 4 barrel configuration. It is chambered for 12 or 16 gauge and has 28" barrels. The gun is, as one would imagine, quite heavy and poorly balanced; and it was not a great success.

Exc.	V.G.	Good	Fair	Poor
—	2000	1300	900	600

Bolt Action Rifle
A high-grade sporting rifle chambered for various different calibers. The barrel is 24" in length; and the finish is blued with a

classic-styled, hand-checkered walnut stock. This rifle was discontinued in 1936.

Exc.	V.G.	Good	Fair	Poor
1750	1000	800	550	400

LANG, J.
London, England
SEE—British Double Guns

Percussion Pistol

Chambered for .60 caliber percussion. It is a single barreled, muzzle-loading pistol with a 3.25" barrel. This is essentially a defensive weapon that was well made, with Damascus barrels and an ornate engraved hammer and frame. The grips are finely checkered walnut, and there is a hinged ramrod under the barrel. There is a spring steel belt hook mounted to the left side of the frame. This pistol was manufactured circa 1836 and was marked "J. Lang."

Exc.	V.G.	Good	Fair	Poor
—	—	4500	2750	1000

Gas Seal Revolver

Chambered for the .42 caliber percussion and has a 4.75" barrel. The unfluted cylinder holds 6 shots and is spring-loaded to be forced into the barrel when cocked, in order to obtain the "Gas Seal" feature desired. This revolver was well made and finished. It is lightly engraved, with a case-colored cylinder and a blued barrel and frame. The grips are finely checkered walnut, and the markings are "J.Lang 22 Cockspur St. London." This type of firearm was the forerunner of later designs such as the Russian Nagant. This revolver was manufactured in the 1850s.

Exc.	V.G.	Good	Fair	Poor
—	2750	1250	900	550

LANGENHAN, FRIEDRICH
Zella Mehlis, Germany

Langenhan Army Model

A blowback-operated semiautomatic pistol chambered for the 7.65mm Auto Pistol cartridge. It has a 4" barrel and a detachable magazine that holds 8 rounds. The pistol was made with a separate breechblock that is held into the slide by a screw. This feature doomed this pistol to eventual failure as when this screw became worn, it could loosen when firing and allow the breechblock to pivot upwards—and the slide would then be propelled rearward and into the face of the shooter. This is not a comforting thought. This pistol was produced and used in WWI only and was never offered commercially. It is marked "F.L. Selbstlade DRGM." The finish is blued, and the grips are molded rubber, with "F.L." at the top.

Exc.	V.G.	Good	Fair	Poor
300	225	200	150	100

Model 2

A blowback-operated semiautomatic pistol chambered for the 6.35mm cartridge. It has a 3" barrel and an 8-round detachable magazine. The pistol fires by means of a concealed hammer, and the breechblock is separate from the rest of the slide and is held in place by a heavy crossbolt. The finish is blued, and the grips are molded checkered black plastic with the monogram "F.L." at the top. The slide is marked "Langenhan 6.35." This model was manufactured between 1921 and 1936.

Exc.	V.G.	Good	Fair	Poor
300	250	225	175	125

Model 3

Similar to the Model 2 except that it is somewhat smaller. The barrel is 2.25" in length, and the butt is only large enough to house a 5-round detachable magazine. The markings are the same with the addition of "Model 111" on the slide. This model was also manufactured until 1936.

Exc.	V.G.	Good	Fair	Poor
325	275	250	200	150

LASALLE
France

Slide Action Shotgun

Chambered for 12 or 20 gauge and is offered with a 26", 28", or 30" barrel with improved-cylinder, modified, or full chokes. The receiver is alloy, anodized blue; and the vent rib barrel is blued. The stock is checkered walnut.

Exc.	V.G.	Good	Fair	Poor
325	250	200	150	100

Semiautomatic Shotgun

A gas-operated semiautomatic shotgun chambered for 12 gauge only, with the same barrel length and choke combinations as are available on the Slide Action model. The receiver is also alloy, and the stock is checkered walnut.

Exc.	V.G.	Good	Fair	Poor
350	275	225	175	100

LASERAIM ARMS
Little Rock, Arkansas

Series I

Offered in 10mm or .45 ACP this single action semiautomatic pistol is fitted with a 6" barrel with compensator. Adjustable rear sight. Stainless steel frame and barrel with mate black Teflon finish. Introduced in 1993. Magazine capacity for 10mm is 8 rounds and 7 rounds for .45 ACP. Weight is about 46 oz

NIB	Exc.	V.G.	Good	Fair	Poor
550	475	400	—	—	—

Series II

This is similar to the Series I except this model has no compensator. It is fitted with a 5" barrel and stainless steel finish. A compact version has a 3-3/8" barrel. Introduced in 1993. Weight is 43 oz. for 5" barrel and 37 oz. for compact version.

NIB	Exc.	V.G.	Good	Fair	Poor
350	300	250	—	—	—

Series III

This model is similar to the Series II except it is offered with 5" barrel only with a dual port compensator. Introduced in 1994. Weight is about 43 oz

NIB	Exc.	V.G.	Good	Fair	Poor
500	400	300	—	—	—

LAURONA
Eibar, Spain
Importer - Galaxy Imports
Victoria, Texas

NOTE: The "G" in the model designation stands for Gemini for "twin" for the unique double selective trigger system. The "G" triggers will function either as a single or double triggers. The front trigger is non-selective firing in bottom to top sequence and the back trigger in top to bottom sequence. The "U" models are models with non-selective single triggers. The version listed first was the normal production configuration and the version listed second was the special order or optional configuration.

The list of models that appear below was compiled by Thomas E. Barker of Galaxy Imports, Ltd., Inc.

Model 67 (G&U)
The first over/under Laurona chambered for 12 gauge only with double triggers and 28" vent rib barrels with extractors. The boxlock action and barrels are blued, and the stock is checkered walnut in 20 lpi. skip line checkering.

Exc.	V.G.	Good	Fair	Poor
500	400	300	200	150

Model 71 (G&U)
Similar to the Model 67 with minor cosmetic changes and improvements to facilitate ease of manufacturing. Receiver is bright chromed with roll engraving depicting dogs on the right side and birds on the left. This model was imported and sold by Sears & Robuck in about 1973 and 1974. The earlier models had traditional solid center ribbed blued barrels, the later models having Black Chrome finished solid ribbed barrels.

Exc.	V.G.	Good	Fair	Poor
500	400	350	300	200

MODEL 82 (G&U)
Similar to the Model 71 with auto-ejectors. Chambered for 12 gauge only. All barrels separated without center rib with Black Chrome finish and hard chrome bores with long forcing cones in chambers. Firing pins changed to traditional round type. Many internal parts improved for reliability. Checkering changed from skip diamond to standard 20 lpi. In most respects the 82 Models are representative of present day Laurona over and under shotguns and will share most internal parts.

Model 82 Game (G&U)
Barrels are 28" with 2-3/4" or 3" chambers, long forcing cones, hard chrome bores, 5mm rib, and chokes ****/**(IC/IM) or ***/*(M/F). Finish on barrels is black chrome with nickel receiver with Louis XVI style engraving. Tulip forend, field style stock with plastic buttplate. Weights approximately 7 lbs.

Exc.	V.G.	Good	Fair	Poor
550	400	350	300	200

Model 82 Super Game (G&U)
Similar to the Model 82 Game except with more elaborate and very delicate engraving

Exc.	V.G.	Good	Fair	Poor
575	450	350	300	200

Model 82 Trap Combi (U&G)
Similar to the Model 82 Game except for 28" or 29" barrels. The rib is 8mm. The Trap stock is fitted with a rubber recoil pad. Weight is about 7.4 lbs.

Exc.	V.G.	Good	Fair	Poor
550	400	350	300	200

Model 82 Trap Competition (U only)
Similar to the Model 82 Trap Combi except for the 13mm aluminum rib with long white sight. Engraving consist of motifs on sides of receiver. Beavertail fluted forend and Monte Carlo Trap stock with black rubber special Trap recoil pad. Weight is approximately 8 lbs.

Exc.	V.G.	Good	Fair	Poor
600	500	400	350	300

Model 82 Super Trap (U only)
Similar to the Model 82 Trap Competition except for special trap Pachmayr recoil pad with imitation leather face. Engraving very delicate fine scroll. Weight is 7 lbs., 12 oz.

Exc.	V.G.	Good	Fair	Poor
675	575	450	400	350

Model 82 Super Skeet
Similar to the Model 82 Super Trap except fitted with 28" barrels choked sheet with field style buttstock with plastic buttplate. Weight is approximately 7 lbs.

Exc.	V.G.	Good	Fair	Poor
600	500	400	350	300

Model 82 Pigeon Competition (U only)
Similar to the Model 82 Trap Competition except fitted with 28" barrels. Recoil pad is special competition style Pachmayr with imitation leather face. Weight is about 7 lbs., 13 oz.

Exc.	V.G.	Good	Fair	Poor
650	550	450	400	350

Model 82 Super Pigeon (U only)
Similar to the Model 82 Super Trap except fitted with 28" barrels. Weight is approximately 7 lbs., 9 oz.

Exc.	V.G.	Good	Fair	Poor
675	575	450	400	350

NOTE: The following Super Models have nickel finish receivers with delicate fine scroll engraving with black chrome relief. All barrels have a very durable rust resistance black chrome finish.

Model 84S Super Game
Similar to the Model 82 Super Game except for the new Single Selective Trigger which is designated by "S" in the model number. Chambered for the 12 gauge 3" magnum with 28" barrels with 8mm rib. Weight is approximately 7 lbs.

Exc.	V.G.	Good	Fair	Poor
800	700	650	600	500

NOTE: The following Super Game models were available with an extra set of 20 gauge multi-choke barrels in 26" or 28". Add $400 to **Exc.** value for these barrels. For models with cast-on stocks for left hand shooters add $50 to **Exc.** value.

Model 83MG Super Game
Similar to the Model 82 Super Game except this model was the advent of Laurona's new multi-choke. **CAUTION!** The Laurona multi-choke is not compatible with any other brand of screw-in chokes because the black chrome plating of the met-

ric threads. Do not attempt to interchange with other guns. Barrel for this model in 12 gauge are 28" in length and for the 20 gauge 26" or 28". Both are chambered for the 3" shell. Rib is 8mm. Weight is about 7 lbs.

Exc.	V.G.	Good	Fair	Poor
1000	850	750	650	600

Model 85MS Super Game
Similar to the Model 83MG Super Game except for the Single Selective Trigger. Chambered for the 12 or 20 gauge 3" Magnum. Weight is about 7 lbs.

Exc.	V.G.	Good	Fair	Poor
1000	850	750	650	600

Model 84S Super Trap
Single selective trigger with 29" barrels. Chambered for 2-3/4" shells with long forcing cones. The aluminum rib is 13mm wide. Auto ejectors. Receiver is nickel plated with fine scroll engraving with black chrome relief. Beavertail forearm and choice of Monte Carlo or standard Trap stock. Weight is about 7 lbs., 12 oz.

Exc.	V.G.	Good	Fair	Poor
1250	1000	800	700	600

Model 85MS Super Trap
Similar to the Model 82S Super Trap except multi-choke in bottom barrel with fixed choke on top barrel. Weight is about 7 lbs., 12 oz.

Exc.	V.G.	Good	Fair	Poor
1250	1000	800	700	600

Model 85MS Super Pigeon
Similar to the Model 85MS Super Trap except with 28" barrels with fixed IM choke on top barrel and multi-choke on bottom barrel. Intended for live bird competition. Weight is about 7 lbs., 4 oz.

Exc.	V.G.	Good	Fair	Poor
1250	1000	800	700	600

Model 85MS Special Sporting
Similar to the Model 85MS Super Pigeon except for field style buttstock with plastic buttplate. Intended for upland game. Weight is approximately 7 lbs., 4 oz.

Exc.	V.G.	Good	Fair	Poor
1250	1000	800	700	600

Model 84S SuperSkeet
Similar to the Model 85MS Special Sporting except choked skeet and skeet. Weight is approximately 7 lbs.

Exc.	V.G.	Good	Fair	Poor
1000	800	700	600	500

LAURONA O/U MODELS SILHOUETTE 300
These guns are basically the same as the Super series above with the exception of the following. They are readily identified by the white and black chrome stripped receiver with the model engraved on the side of the receiver. Barrels are multi-choked on both bores and have 11mm steel ribs. **NOTE:** Two types of chokes were used. Some guns came with knurl head type as in the Super models and others were made with the flush invector style. A later option for ease of changing chokes is the knurl long choke which is a flush type with a knurl head added. Both later type chokes, the flush and the knurl long type, can be used in the early multi-choke models with some extension showing.

Silhouette 300 Trap
This model has barrels 29" with 2-3/4" chambers and long forcing cones with hard chrome bores and 11mm rib. Beavertail forearm and straight comb trap stock fitted with a ventilated black rubber recoil pad are standard. Weight is approximately 8 lbs.

Exc.	V.G.	Good	Fair	Poor
1250	1000	800	700	600

Silhouette 300 Sporting Clays
Similar to the Model 300 Trap except with 28" barrels. Some guns came with 3" chambers. The buttstock is field style with plastic buttplate or hard rubber sporting clays pad. Weight is about 8 lbs.

Exc.	V.G.	Good	Fair	Poor
1250	1000	800	700	600

Silhouette 300 Ultra Magnum
Similar to the Model 300 Sporting Clays except with 3-1/2" chamber in 12 gauge for waterfowl hunting. This unique gun with its ability to shoot any type and size 12 gauge ammunition along with its non-rusting Black Chrome finish makes it the most versatile O/U on the market for either hunting or competition. Weight is about 7 lbs., 8 oz.

Exc.	V.G.	Good	Fair	Poor
1265	1000	900	800	750

LAURONA SIDE-BY-SIDE SHOTGUNS
Models with "X" after the model number were made after 1975 and finished with non-rusting Black Chrome on barrels and action with hard chrome bores. Guns were made in 12, 16, and 20 bore. Smaller gauges were made on special order. Side-by-side shotguns were discontinued by Laurona after 1978 to concentrate on the O/U market.

Model 11
Box lock action with triple Greener type round crossbolt. Independent firing pins bushed into the face of the action. Barrels of "Bellota" steel. Made in 12, 16, and 20 bore.

Exc.	V.G.	Good	Fair	Poor
400	350	300	200	150

Model 13

Similar to the Mode 11 except with Purdey type bolting system. Extractor of double radius.

Exc.	V.G.	Good	Fair	Poor
400	350	300	200	150

Model 13X

Barrels and action finished in Black Chrome and hard chrome bores.

Exc.	V.G.	Good	Fair	Poor
500	400	300	250	200

Model 13E

Similar to the Model 13 except with automatic ejectors.

Exc.	V.G.	Good	Fair	Poor
500	400	300	250	200

Model 13XE

Similar to the Model 13E except Black Chrome finish and hard chrome bores.

Exc.	V.G.	Good	Fair	Poor
600	500	400	350	300

Model 15 Economic Pluma

Similar to the Model 13 except first model to have hard chrome bores.

Exc.	V.G.	Good	Fair	Poor
450	400	300	250	200

Model 15X

Similar to the Model 15 except Black Chrome finish and hard chrome bores.

Exc.	V.G.	Good	Fair	Poor
500	400	300	250	200

Model 15E Economic Pluma

Similar to the Model 15 except with automatic ejectors.

Exc.	V.G.	Good	Fair	Poor
550	450	350	300	250

Model 15XE

Similar to the Model 15E except Black Chrome finish and hard chrome bores.

Exc.	V.G.	Good	Fair	Poor
600	500	400	350	300

Model 52 Pluma

Box lock action with back of action scalloped and artistically engraved in fine English style scroll. Churchill rib and double radius extractor. Hard chrome bores. Weight is about 6 lbs.

Exc.	V.G.	Good	Fair	Poor
750	650	500	400	350

Model 52E Pluma

Similar to the Model 52 except with automatic ejectors. Weight is approximately 6 lbs., 2 oz.

Exc.	V.G.	Good	Fair	Poor
850	750	600	500	450

LAURONA SIDE-BY-SIDE SIDE LOCKS

Model 103

Blued side lock with some light border engraving. Triple Purdey type bolting system. Extractor of double radius. Barrels of special "Bellota" steel with hard chrome bores. Made in 12, 16, and 20 bore.

Exc.	V.G.	Good	Fair	Poor
900	800	700	500	400

Model 103E

Similar to the Model 103 except with automatic ejectors.

Exc.	V.G.	Good	Fair	Poor
1000	800	700	600	500

Model 104X

Case colored side locks with Purdey type bolting system. Extractor with double radius. Fine double safety side locks. Gas relief vents. Articulated trigger. Hard chrome bores. Demi-block barrels of special "Bellota" steel. Black Chrome barrels. Produced in 12, 16, and 20 bore with smaller bores available on special order.

Exc.	V.G.	Good	Fair	Poor
1200	1000	800	700	600

Model 104XE

Same as Model 104X but with Holland automatic selective ejectors.

Exc.	V.G.	Good	Fair	Poor
1350	1100	900	800	700

Model 105X Feather

Same as the Model 104X but with concave rib. Weight in 12 gauge is approximately 6 lbs., 2 oz.

Exc.	V.G.	Good	Fair	Poor
1250	1000	800	700	600

Model 105 XE Feather

Same as Model 105X but with Holland automatic selective ejectors.

Exc.	V.G.	Good	Fair	Poor
1400	1250	1000	800	750

Model 502 Feather

Fine side lock with Purdey type bolting system. Very fine double safety side locks, hand detachable. Gas relief vents. Holland automatic selective ejectors. Articulated trigger. Inside hard chromed demi-block barrels of special "Bellota" steel. Outside Black Chrome finish. Fine English style scroll engraving. Marble gray or Laurona Imperial finish. churchill or concave type rib. Weight is 12 bore is approximately 6.25 lbs. Offered in 12, 16, and 20 bore.

Exc.	V.G.	Good	Fair	Poor
2200	1800	1600	1500	1400

Model 801 Deluxe

Same as the Model 502 Feather but engraving is a true deluxe Renaissance style. Fully hand made with Imperial finish. First grade walnut stock and forearm.

Exc.	V.G.	Good	Fair	Poor
4400	4000	3750	2750	2250

Model 802 Eagle

Same as the Model 801 Deluxe except highly artistic base relief hand engraving of hunting scenes.

Exc.	V.G.	Good	Fair	Poor
5000	4500	4000	3500	3250

LAW ENFORCEMENT ORDNANCE CORP.
Ridgeway, Pennsylvania

Striker 12

A semiautomatic shotgun designed for self-defense. It is chambered for 12 gauge and has an 18.25" cylinder bored barrel. The unique feature about this gun is its 12-round drum magazine. The barrel is shrouded, and the stock folds. A fixed-stock model is also available. This gun was introduced primarily as a law enforcement tool, and the original models had 12" barrels and were legal for law enforcement agencies and Class 3 licensed individuals only. The 18.25" version is legal for private ownership and was introduced in 1986. This shotgun is no longer imported into the U.S. This shotgun is now classified as a Class III weapon and subject to restrictions of the B.A.T.F. Be certain that the particular shotgun is transferable before purchase. If there are any questions contact B.A.T.F. before purchase.

Striker 12 shotguns in excellent condition may sell for as much as $1500.

LAZZERONI ARMS COMPANY
Tucson, Arizona

Model 2000 ST-F

This model, as with all Lazzeroni models, is chambered for the company's own proprietary calibers. The 6.17 (.243) Spitfire, 6.53 (.257) Scramjet, 6.71 (.264) Phantom, 7.21 (.284) Tomahawk, 7.82 (.308) Patriot, and the 8.59 (.338) Galaxy. Fitted with a 27" match grade barrel with fully adjustable trigger, and removable muzzle brake. Conventional fiberglass stock.

NIB	Exc.	V.G.	Good	Fair	Poor
3700	3000	—	—	—	—

Model 2000 ST-W

As above but fitted with a conventional black wood laminate stock. No longer offered.

NIB	Exc.	V.G.	Good	Fair	Poor
4800	3900	—	—	—	—

Model 2000ST-FW

As above but fitted with a conventional fiberglass stock and an additional black wood laminate stock. No longer offered.

NIB	Exc.	V.G.	Good	Fair	Poor
5300	4250	—	—	—	—

Model 2000ST-28

This model is a 28" barrel variation of the Model 2000 ST chambered for the 7.82 Warbird cartridge. Introduced in 1999.

NIB	Exc.	V.G.	Good	Fair	Poor
5300	4250	—	—	—	—

Model 2000SLR

This model has a 28" extra heavy fluted barrel with conventional fiberglass stock. Chambered for the 6.53 Scramjet, 7.21 Firehawk, and the 7.82 Warbird.

NIB	Exc.	V.G.	Good	Fair	Poor
3900	3100	—	—	—	—

Model 2000SP-F

This model is fitted with a 23" match grade and Lazzeroni thumbhole fiberglass stock. Chambered for all Lazzeroni calibers.

NIB	Exc.	V.G.	Good	Fair	Poor
3700	2950	—	—	—	—

Model 2000SP-W

Same as above but with black wood laminate thumbhole stock. No longer offered.

NIB	Exc.	V.G.	Good	Fair	Poor
4800	3850	—	—	—	—

Model 2000SP-FW

Same as above model but is supplied with two stocks: a thumbhole fiberglass stock and a black wood laminate stock. No longer offered.

NIB	Exc.	V.G.	Good	Fair	Poor
5300	4250	—	—	—	—

Model 2000SA

Designed as a lightweight mountain rifle. Chambered for .308, .284, or .338 propriety calibers. Barrel length is 24" and fluted except for .338 caliber. Offered in both right and left hand models. Stock has Monte Carlo cheekpiece. Weight is approximately 6.8 lbs.

NIB	Exc.	V.G.	Good	Fair	Poor
4000	3250	—	—	—	—

Model 2000DG

Offered in Saturn and Meteor calibers only and fitted with a 24" barrel this rifle weight about 10 lbs. Fibergrain stock finish, removable muzzle brake, and threaded muzzle protector are standard.

NIB	Exc.	V.G.	Good	Fair	Poor
4400	3500	—	—	—	—

Model 700ST

This rifle is built around a modified Remington 700 action and fitted with a 26" barrel. Chambered for all Lazzeroni long action calibers except Saturn and Meteor. Weight is about 8 lbs. synthetic stock.

NIB	Exc.	V.G.	Good	Fair	Poor
2400	1850	—	—	—	—

Swarovski P.H. 3-12x50 Rifle

NIB	Exc.	V.G.	Good	Fair	Poor
1400	1150	—	—	—	—

Savage 16 LZ

Introduced in 2001 this model features a 24" stainless steel barrel, synthetic stock. It is chambered for the 7.82 Patriot and 7.21 Tomahawk cartridges. Weight is approximately 6.8 lbs. Base price listed below.

NIB	Exc.	V.G.	Good	Fair	Poor
700	575	—	—	—	—

Sako TRG-S

This model is fitted with a 26" stainless steel barrel and synthetic stock. It is chambered for the 7.82 Warbird and 7.21 Firebird cartridges. Weight is about 7.9 lbs. Base price listed below.

NIB	Exc.	V.G.	Good	Fair	Poor
900	750	—	—	—	—

LEBEAU COURALLY
Liege, Belgium

This company has been in business since 1865 and has more guns for royalty than any other gun company world wide. The prices listed below are for guns without engraving. There are other extra cost options that will effect price. Consult an expert prior to a sale.

Boxlock Side-by-Side

NIB	Exc.	V.G.	Good	Fair	Poor
23000	17500	—	—	—	—

NOTE: Add $3,000 to $8,400 for engraving

Sidelock Side-by-Side

NIB	Exc.	V.G.	Good	Fair	Poor
47000	35000	—	—	—	—

NOTE: Add $3,600 to $20,000 for engraving

Over and Under Boss-Verees

NIB	Exc.	V.G.	Good	Fair	Poor
81000	55000	—	—	—	—

NOTE: Add $6,000 to $20,000 for engraving

Express Rifle

NIB	Exc.	V.G.	Good	Fair	Poor
51000	37500	—	—	—	—

NOTE: Add $3,600 to $20,000 for engraving, and $2,250 for .470 NE caliber.

LEBEL
French State

NOTE: For history, technical data, descriptions, and prices see the *Standard Catalog of Military Firearms, 1870 to the Present* under France.

LEE FIREARMS CO.
Milwaukee, Wisconsin

Lee Single Shot Carbine

A rare single shot break-open carbine that pivots to the right side for loading. It is chambered for the .44 rimfire cartridge and has a 21.5" barrel with a hammer mounted in the center of the frame. The carbine has a walnut buttstock but no forearm and is marked "Lee's Firearms Co. Milwaukee, Wisc." There were approximately 450 manufactured between 1863 and 1865. There are few surviving examples, and one should be wary of fakes.

Courtesy Milwaukee Public Museum, Milwaukee, Wisconsin

Exc.	V.G.	Good	Fair	Poor
—	—	5000	2000	900

Lee Sporting Rifle

Similar to the military carbine except that it has a longer octagonal barrel. The barrel length was varied, and there were more of these manufactured. The survival rate appears to have been better than for the carbine model.

Courtesy Milwaukee Public Museum, Milwaukee, Wisconsin

Exc.	V.G.	Good	Fair	Poor
—	—	1250	600	300

LEE-ENFIELD
Middlesex, England

NOTE: For history, technical data, descriptions, and prices see the *Standard Catalog of Military Firearms, 1870 to the Present* under Great Britian.

LEE-METFORD
Great Britain

NOTE: For history, technical data, descriptions, and prices see the *Standard Catalog of Military Firearms, 1870 to the Present* under Great Britian.

LEECH & RIGDON
Greensboro, Georgia

Leech & Rigdon Revolver

This Confederate revolver was patterned after the 1851 Colt Navy. It is chambered for .36 caliber percussion and has a 6-shot unfluted cylinder. The 7.5" barrel is part-octagonal and has a loading lever beneath it. The frame is open-topped; and the finish is blued, with brass grip straps and walnut one-piece grips. The barrel is marked "Leech & Rigdon CSA." There were approximately 1,500 revolvers manufactured in 1863 and 1864. These were all contracted for by the Confederacy and are considered to be a prime acquisition for collectors. Be wary of fakes, and trust in qualified independent appraisals only.

Exc.	V.G.	Good	Fair	Poor
—	—	25000	10000	2500

LEFAUCHAUX, CASIMER & EUGENE
Paris, France

Pinfire Revolver

The pinfire ignition system was invented by Casimir Lefauchaux in 1828 but was not widely used until the 1850s. It consists of a smooth rimless case that contains the powder charge and a percussion cap. A pin protrudes from the side of this case at the rear and when struck by the hammer is driven into the cap, thereby igniting the charge and firing the weapon. The pistols for this cartridge are slotted at the end of the cylinder to allow the pins to protrude and be struck by the downward blow of the hammer. This particular revolver is chambered for .43 caliber and has a 5.25" barrel. The cylinder holds 6 shots; and the finish is blued, with checkered walnut grips. This revolver was manufactured after 1865 and was selected for service by the French military.

Exc.	V.G.	Good	Fair	Poor
—	—	575	250	125

LEFEVER ARMS CO.
Syracuse, New York

Founded by Dan Lefever, who was a pioneer in the field of breech-loading firearms. This company was founded in 1884, with Lefever as the president. He was referred to as "Uncle Dan" within the firearms industry. He was responsible for many improvements in the double barrel shotgun design. He developed the automatic hammerless system in the late 1880s. He also developed a compensating action that allowed simple adjustments to compensate for action wear. In 1901 he was forced out of the company and organized another company—the D.M. Lefever, Sons & Company—also in Syracuse. Dan Lefever died in 1906, and his new company went out of business. The original company was acquired by Ithaca in 1916. They continued to produce Lefever guns until 1948.

Sidelock Shotgun

A double barrel, side-by-side shotgun chambered for 10, 12, 16, or 20 gauge. It was offered with 26", 28", 30", or 32" barrels with various choke combinations. The barrels are either Damascus or fluid steel. Damascus guns have become collectible and in better condition—very good to excellent—can bring nearly the same price as the fluid-steel guns. It features a full sidelock action. Double triggers are standard. The finish is blued, with a checkered walnut stock. There are a number of variations that differ in the amount of ornamentation and the quality of materials and workmanship utilized in their construction. Automatic ejectors are represented by the letter "E" after the respective grade designation. This shotgun was manufactured between 1885 and 1919. We strongly recommend that a qualified appraisal be secured if a transaction is contemplated.

20 Gauge-Add 25%.
Single Selective Trigger-Add 10%.

DS Grade

Exc.	V.G.	Good	Fair	Poor
1250	800	650	450	250

DSE Grade

Exc.	V.G.	Good	Fair	Poor
1750	1450	1100	750	400

H Grade

Exc.	V.G.	Good	Fair	Poor
1250	800	650	450	250

HE Grade

Exc.	V.G.	Good	Fair	Poor
2000	1650	1300	1000	500

G Grade

Exc.	V.G.	Good	Fair	Poor
1500	1300	1000	750	400

GE Grade

Exc.	V.G.	Good	Fair	Poor
3000	1800	1500	1200	650

F Grade

Exc.	V.G.	Good	Fair	Poor
1500	1000	800	650	375

FE Grade

Exc.	V.G.	Good	Fair	Poor
4500	3000	1750	1250	650

E Grade

Exc.	V.G.	Good	Fair	Poor
2000	1800	1550	1000	800

EE Grade

Exc.	V.G.	Good	Fair	Poor
5500	3500	2000	1500	1000

D Grade

Exc.	V.G.	Good	Fair	Poor
2500	2200	1650	1050	800

DE Grade

Exc.	V.G.	Good	Fair	Poor
5500	3500	2000	1500	1000

C Grade

Exc.	V.G.	Good	Fair	Poor
6000	4000	2850	2000	1250

CE Grade

Exc.	V.G.	Good	Fair	Poor
8500	6000	4000	3000	1500

B Grade

Exc.	V.G.	Good	Fair	Poor
6000	5000	4000	3000	2250

BE Grade

Exc.	V.G.	Good	Fair	Poor
10000	8000	4500	3500	2500

A Grade

Exc.	V.G.	Good	Fair	Poor
13000	9000	5000	3500	2500

AA Grade

Exc.	V.G.	Good	Fair	Poor
18500	12000	6000	4000	3000

There was also an Optimus Grade and a Thousand Dollar Grade offered. These are extremely high-grade, heavily ornamented firearms inlaid with precious metals. They are extremely rare, and evaluating them on a general basis is impossible.

LEFEVER ARMS COMPANY, INC. (ITHACA)

During 1916, the Ithaca Gun company purchased the gunmaking assets of the Syracuse, New York based, Lefever Arms Company. Between then and World War I, they continued to manufacture the same sidelock gun that had been made in Syracuse until about 1919 when they were discontinued. Prices for those guns are listed above. During 1921, Ithaca Gun Company, under the name the Lefever Arms Company, Inc., introduced a line of lower costs, boxlock guns. Eventually, six different models were produced. Ithaca's Lefever guns were produced in 12, 16, and 20 gauges, and in .410 bore. Twenty gauge guns often command a price premium of 20%, a .410 bore gun may command up to a 100% premium.

Nitro Special

A side-by-side, double barrel shotgun chambered for 12, 16, or 20 gauge, as well as .410. The barrels were offered in lengths of 26" to 32" with various choke combinations. It features a boxlock action with double triggers and extractors standard. The finish is blued, with a case-colored receiver and a checkered walnut stock. This model was manufactured between 1921 and 1948; and incredible as it may seem, its price at introduction was $29.

Single Selective Trigger-Add $100
Automatic ejectors-Add $200

Exc.	V.G.	Good	Fair	Poor
600	400	250	200	—

Long Range Single Barrel Trap and Field (Model 2)
Manufactured from 1927 to 1947, the Model 2 was a single barrel gun with no rib. Like the Nitro Special, it had walnut stocks that were line cut checkered at the grip area of the buttstock and on the forend.

Exc.	V.G.	Good	Fair	Poor
300	250	200	100	—

Single Barrel Trap Ventilated Rib (Model 3)
Manufactured from 1927 to 1942, the Model 3 was a single barrel gun with the same ventilated rib that was used on the "Knick" trap gun. The walnut stocks had line cut checkering at the grip area of the buttstock and on the forend.

Exc.	V.G.	Good	Fair	Poor
400	300	250	100	—

Double Barrel Ventilated Rib Trap (Model 4)
Manufactured during 1929 but catalogued until 1939, the Model 4 was a double barrel gun with a ventilated rib barrel. The walnut stocks had line cut checkering at the grip area of the buttstock and on the beavertail forend. Only about 200 units were produced.

Exc.	V.G.	Good	Fair	Poor
2000	1200	1000	700	—

A Grade (Model 5)
Manufactured from 1936 to 1939, the A Grade was a double barreled gun. The walnut stocks had pointed checkering cut at the grip area of the buttstock and on the splinter forend. A line engraving outlined its nicely sculptured frame.

NOTE: Single trigger add $200, automatic ejectors add $200, beavertail forend add $300.

Photo by Walter C. Snyder

Exc.	V.G.	Good	Fair	Poor
800	600	400	300	—

Skeet Special (Model 6)
Manufactured from 1936 to 1939, the A Grade was a double barreled gun. The walnut stocks had pointed checkering cut at the grip area of the buttstock and on the beavertail forend. A beavertail forend, single trigger, automatic ejectors, a recoil pad, and ivory center and front sight were standard. The frame was sculptured and line engraved like the Model 5.

Exc.	V.G.	Good	Fair	Poor
1500	1200	1000	400	—

LEFEVER, D. M., SONS & COMPANY
Syracuse, New York
"Uncle Dan" Lefever founded the Lefever Arms Company in 1884. In 1901 he was forced out of his company and founded the D.M. Lefever, Sons & Company. He continued to produce high-grade, side-by-side, double ceased operations. There were approximately 1,200 shotguns of all variations produced during this period, making them extremely rare and difficult to evaluate on a general basis. We list the models and average values but strongly suggest securing qualified appraisal if a transaction is contemplated.

Lefever Double Barrel Shotgun

A side-by-side, double-barrel shotgun chambered for 12, 16, or 20 gauge. It was offered with various-length barrels and choke combinations that were made to order. It features double triggers and automatic ejectors. A single selective trigger was available as an option. The finish is blued, with a checkered walnut stock. The individual grades differ in the amount of ornamentation and the general quality of the materials and workmanship utilized in their construction. This model was discontinued in 1906.

Single Selective Trigger-Add 10%.
20 Gauge-Add 25%.

O Excelsior Grade-Extractors

Exc.	V.G.	Good	Fair	Poor
2500	2000	1650	950	700

Excelsior Grade-Auto Ejectors

Exc.	V.G.	Good	Fair	Poor
3000	2500	2000	1250	900

F Grade, No. 9

Exc.	V.G.	Good	Fair	Poor
3000	2750	2250	1500	1100

G Grade-10 Gauge, Damascus Barrels

Exc.	V.G.	Good	Fair	Poor
3500	3100	2600	2000	1350

E Grade, No. 8

Exc.	V.G.	Good	Fair	Poor
4000	3500	3000	2400	1700

D Grade, No. 7

Exc.	V.G.	Good	Fair	Poor
4500	3900	3400	2750	2000

C Grade, No. 6

Exc.	V.G.	Good	Fair	Poor
5000	4500	3750	3000	2500

B Grade, No. 5

Exc.	V.G.	Good	Fair	Poor
6500	5750	4800	3500	3000

AA Grade, No. 4

Exc.	V.G.	Good	Fair	Poor
9000	7800	6500	4200	2750

There is an "Uncle Dan" grade, which is the top-of-the-line version, that features extremely high quality in materials and workmanship and a great deal of ornamentation. This firearm is extremely rare and seldom found in today's market. It is impossible to evaluate it on a general basis.

LE FORGERON
Liege, Belgium
Importer - Midwest Guns
Zebulon, North Carolina

Model 6020 Double Rifle

A boxlock-actioned side-x-side rifle that is chambered for the 9.3x74R cartridge. It has 25" barrels with double triggers and automatic ejectors. The finish is blued, and the pistol grip stock is checkered walnut.

Exc.	V.G.	Good	Fair	Poor
5500	4500	4000	3000	1250

Model 6040

Simply the Model 6020 with false sideplates. All other specifications are the same.

Exc.	V.G.	Good	Fair	Poor
6250	5200	4500	3500	1500

Model 6030

A double rifle that has a true sidelock action and is engraved. It has a deluxe French walnut stock.

Exc.	V.G.	Good	Fair	Poor
10000	8000	7250	5500	2000

Boxlock Shotgun

This is a side-x-side, double-barreled shotgun chambered for 20 or 28 gauge. The barrel lengths are optional, as are the choke combinations. This gun has a single selective trigger and automatic ejectors. It is engraved and blued, with a deluxe French walnut stock.

False Sideplates-Add 20%.

Exc.	V.G.	Good	Fair	Poor
5000	4000	3250	2250	1000

Sidelock Shotgun

Has similar specifications to the boxlock except that it has a true sidelock action and is generally more deluxe in materials and workmanship.

Exc.	V. G.	Good	Fair	Poor
11500	10500	8500	6500	2500

LE FRANCAIS
St. Etienne, France
Francais D'Armes et Cycles de St. Etienne

Gaulois

An 8mm palm pistol designed by Brun-Latrige and manufactured by Le Francais. Furnished with a 5-round magazine.

Courtesy James Rankin

Exc.	V.G.	Good	Fair	Poor
950	750	550	400	300

Le Francais Model 28 (Type Armee)

A unique pistol chambered for the 9mm Browning cartridge. It is a large pistol, with a 5" barrel that was hinged with a tip-up breech. This is a blowback-operated semiautomatic pistol that has no extractor. The empty cases are blown out of the breech by gas pressure. The one feature about this pistol that is desirable is that it is possible to tip the barrel breech forward like a shotgun and load cartridges singly, while holding the contents of the magazine in reserve. This weapon has fixed sights and a blued finish, with checkered walnut grips. It was manufactured in 1928.

Courtesy James Rankin

Exc.	V.G.	Good	Fair	Poor
1250	950	750	500	200

Police Model (Type Policeman)

A blowback-operated, double action semiautomatic that is chambered for the .32 ACP cartridge. It has a 3.5" barrel and a 7-round magazine. It has the same hinged barrel feature of the Model 28 and is blued, with fixed sights and Ebonite grips. This model was manufactured 1913 to 1914.

Courtesy James Rankin

Exc.	V.G.	Good	Fair	Poor
800	650	450	300	150

Officers Model (Pocket Model)

May also be referred to a "Staff Model". Also a blowback-operated semiautomatic chambered for the .25 ACP cartridge. It has a 2.5" barrel and a concealed hammer. It has fixed sights and the finish is blued. The grips are Ebonite. This model was manufactured between 1914 and 1938 in two variations: early and second type.

Early variation Pocket

Courtesy James Rankin

Second variation Pocket

Courtesy James Rankin

Exc.	V.G.	Good	Fair	Poor
300	250	200	150	100

Target Model (Type Champion)

Chambered for 6.35mm cartridge and fitted with a 6" barrel. Extended magazine base is for grip purchase, not additional cartridges.

Courtesy James Rankin

Exc.	V.G.	Good	Fair	Poor
900	700	550	400	275

LEMAN, H. E.
Lancaster, Pennsylvania

Leman Militia Rifle

A .58 caliber percussion muzzleloader that has a 33" round barrel. The stock is full-length and is held on by two barrel bands. There is a ramrod mounted under the barrel. The trim is brass; and the barrel is browned, with a case-colored lock. The lock is marked "H.E.Leman/Lancaster, Pa." There were approximately 500 manufactured between 1860 and 1864. They are believed to have been used by the Pennsylvania State Militia in the Civil War.

Courtesy Milwaukee Public Museum, Milwaukee, Wisconsin

Courtesy Milwaukee Public Museum, Milwaukee, Wisconsin

Exc.	V.G.	Good	Fair	Poor
—	—	4250	2000	750

LE MAT
Paris, France

Le Mat

Has a somewhat unique background that makes it a bit controversial among collectors. It is a foreign-made firearm manufactured in Paris, France, as well as in Birmingham, England. It was designed and patented by an American, Jean Alexander Le Mat of New Orleans, Louisiana; and it was purchased for use by the Confederate States of America and used in the Civil War. This is a curious firearm as it is a huge weapon that has two barrels. The top 6.5" barrel is chambered for .42 caliber percussion and is supplied by a 9-shot unfluted cylinder that revolves on a 5", .63 caliber, smoothbore barrel that doubles as the cylinder axis pin. These two barrels are held together by a front and a rear ring. The rear sight is a

notch in the nose of the hammer, and there is an attached ramrod on the side of the top barrel. The weapon is marked "Lemat and Girards Patent, London". The finish is blued, with checkered walnut grips. There were fewer than 3,000 manufactured, of which approximately one-half were purchased by the Confederate States of America. They were made between 1856 and 1865.

Courtesy Milwaukee Public Museum, Milwaukee, Wisconsin

Exc.	V.G.	Good	Fair	Poor
—	25000	10000	5000	1750

A LeMat revolver was sold at auction for $28,750. It was the property of Captain Albert Hervey, CSA. Condition is very good with some light pitting.
Butterfield & Butterfield, September 2000

Baby Le Mat

Similar in appearance (though a good deal smaller in size) to the standard model pistol. It is chambered for .32 caliber percussion and has a 4.25" top barrel and a .41 caliber smoothbore lower barrel. The cylinder is unfluted and holds 9 shots. The barrel is marked "Systeme Le Mat Bte s.g.d.g. Paris". It has British proofmarks and is blued, with checkered walnut grips. This is the scarcest model Le Mat, as there were only an estimated 100 manufactured and used by the Confederate States of America in the Civil War.

Exc.	V.G.	Good	Fair	Poor
—	—	20000	9500	3000

LEONARD, G.
Charlestown, Massachusetts

Pepperbox

A .31-caliber, four barreled pepperbox with a concealed hammer. The barrels are 3.25" in length. There is a ring trigger used to cock the weapon, while a smaller trigger located outside the ring is used to fire the weapon. The barrels on this pistol do not revolve. There is a revolving striker inside the frame that turns to fire each chamber. The barrels must be removed for loading and capping purposes. The frame is iron and blued, with engraving. The rounded grips are walnut. The barrel is stamped "G. Leonard Jr. Charlestown." There were fewer than 200 manufactured in 1849 and 1850.

Exc.	V.G.	Good	Fair	Poor
—	—	1500	650	300

LE PAGE SA.
Liege, Belgium

Pinfire Revolver

Was in the business of revolver manufacture in the 1850s, producing a .40 caliber pinfire revolver that was similar to the Lefauchaux and other pinfires of the day. The barrel lengths vary, and the unfluted cylinder holds 6 shots. These pistols are double action and are sometimes found with ornate but somewhat crude engraving. The finish is blued, with wood grips. The quality of these weapons is fair. They were serviceable; but the ammunition created somewhat of a problem, as it is rather fragile and difficult to handle with the protruding primer pin to contend with.

Exc.	V.G.	Good	Fair	Poor
—	500	300	200	125

Semiautomatic Pistol

Was dormant for many years and was revived in 1925 to produce this blowback-operated semiautomatic with an open-topped slide and exposed barrel. It is chambered for the 7.65mm, 9mm Short, and the 9mm Browning Long cartridges. The barrel is 4" in length, and the grip is oversized, has finger grooves, and houses a 12-shot magazine. The pistol was not a commercial success, and there were not a great many manufactured.

Exc.	V.G.	Good	Fair	Poor
—	400	200	150	100

LEWIS, G.E.
Halesowen, England
SEE—British Double Guns

LIDDLE & KAEDING
San Francisco, California

Pocket Revolver

Manufactured by Forehand and Wadsworth and stamped with the above name. This company was a dealer in California and had nothing whatever to do with the production of this revolver. It is chambered for the .32 rimfire cartridge and has a 3.25" octagonal barrel and a 5-shot fluted cylinder. The frame is iron; and the finish is blued, with walnut grips. There were a few hundred manufactured between 1880 and 1886. The dealer's name is marked on the top strap.

Exc.	V.G.	Good	Fair	Poor
—	—	450	200	75

LIEGEOISE D ARMES
Liege, Belgium

Side-x-Side Boxlock Shotgun

This double barreled gun is chambered for 12 and 20 gauge. The barrels are 28" or 30" in length, and the choke combinations are varied. It has a single trigger and automatic ejectors. The action is moderately engraved; and the finish is blued, with a checkered walnut stock.

Exc.	V.G.	Good	Fair	Poor
900	700	500	400	200

LIGNOSE
Suhl, Germany

In 1921, Bergmann Industriewerke was incorporated under Aktiengesellschaft Lignose, Berlin with a marketing division in Suhl. Most of the firearms there after had the Bergmann nomenclature on the pistol with Lignose on the grip.

Einhand Model 2A

This unique design resembled the Chelewski. It allows the shooter to cock and fire this blowback-operated semiautomatic pistol with one hand (Einhand). It is chambered for the 6.35mm cartridge and has a 2" barrel. The magazine holds 6 shots; and the finish is blued, with molded rubber grips marked "Lignose." The triggerguard on this pistol has a reverse curve that fits the finger, and it moves backward to cock the slide. The short grip model without Einhard feature was the Model 2; the long grip model without Einhand was the Model 3. the first 9,000 to 10,000 examples (all four variations serial numbered in the same series) were marketed under the Bergmann name; only later Lignose. It was manufactured in 1917 by the Bergman Company, but the rights were then sold to Lignose where it was produced after 1921.

Courtesy James Rankin

Exc.	V.G.	Good	Fair	Poor
750	650	500	400	250

Einhand Model 3

The same as the Model 2 but with a 9-round magazine capacity.

Exc.	V.G.	Good	Fair	Poor
500	400	350	250	150

Einhand Model 3A

Similar to the Model 2A, with a longer grip that houses a 9-shot magazine. All other specifications are the same as the Model 2A.

Courtesy James Rankin

Exc.	V.G.	Good	Fair	Poor
500	400	350	250	150

Model 4/5
Same general design as the Model 2 and 3 except larger and produced in calibers 7.65mm and 9mm short.

Exc.	V.G.	Good	Fair	Poor
450	400	350	250	150

Liliput Model I
Manufactured in caliber 6.35mm during the 1920s.

Courtesy Orvel Reichert

Exc.	V.G.	Good	Fair	Poor
850	700	650	500	300

Model 2
The Taschen Model 1 Pocket Model in 6.35mm caliber. Almost identical with the pre-WWI Bergmann model.

Courtest James Rankin

Exc.	V.G.	Good	Fair	Poor
650	500	450	300	150

Spezial
See Bergmann.

LILLIPUT
SEE—Menz

LINDE A.
Memphis, Tennessee

Pocket Pistol
This company manufactured a small, concealable firearm patterned after the Henry Deringer Philadelphia-type pistol. It is chambered for .41 caliber percussion and has a 2.5" barrel, German silver mountings, and a walnut stock. It was manufactured in the 1850s.

Exc.	V.G.	Good	Fair	Poor
—	—	1750	700	300

Courtesy James Rankin

Exc.	V.G.	Good	Fair	Poor
450	400	350	250	150

Bergmann Erben Model II
Manufactured in calibers 6.35mm, 7.65mm, and 9mm Short.

LINDSAY, JOHN P.
Naugatuck, Connecticut
Union Knife Company

The Union Knife Company manufactured the Lindsay 2-shot pistols for the inventor, John P. Lindsay. There are three separate and distinct models as follows.

2 Shot Belt Pistol

An oddity. It is a single barreled, .41 caliber percussion pistol with a double chamber that contains two powder charges and projectiles that are simultaneously fired by two separate hammers. The hammers are released by a single trigger that allows them to fall in the proper sequence. The 5.5" octagonal barrel is contoured into a radical stepped-down shape, and there is a spur trigger. The frame is brass and has scroll engraving. The barrel is blued and is marked "Lindsay's Young America". There were estimated to be fewer than 100 manufactured between 1860 and 1862.

Exc.	V.G.	Good	Fair	Poor
—	—	2750	1250	700

2 Shot Pocket Pistol

A smaller version of the Belt Pistol. It is chambered for the same caliber but has a 4" barrel. There were approximately 200 manufactured between 1860 and 1862.

Courtesy W. P. Hallstein III and son Chip

Exc.	V.G.	Good	Fair	Poor
—	—	2000	750	400

2 Shot Martial Pistol

A large version of the Lindsay design. It is chambered for .45 caliber smoothbore and has an 8.5" part-round, part-octagonal barrel. In other respects it is similar to the smaller models. The inventor tried to sell this pistol to the government but was unsuccessful. It was estimated that there were 100 manufactured between 1860 and 1862.

Exc.	V.G.	Good	Fair	Poor
—	—	4500	2000	700

A two-shot Martial pistol was sold at auction for $5,175. Its price reflects its condition which was excellent. Butterfield & Butterfield, August 1998

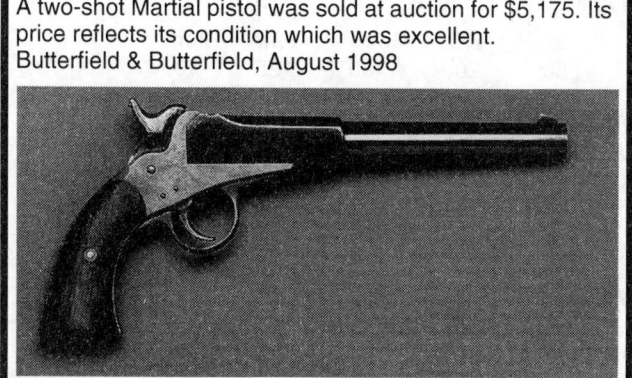

LINS, A. F.
Philadelphia, Pennsylvania

Pocket Pistol

Chambered for .41 caliber percussion and is a copy of the Henry Deringer pistol. It has a 3" barrel and a walnut stock and is marked "A. Fred. Lins. Philada." This pistol was manufactured between 1855 and 1860.

Exc.	V.G.	Good	Fair	Poor
—	—	1750	800	350

Rifled Musket

A single shot, muzzleloading, percussion rifle chambered for .58 caliber. It has a 39" barrel and a full-length walnut stock held on by three barrel bands. There is an iron ramrod mounted under the barrel. The mountings are iron, and there is a bayonet lug combined with the front sight. The lock is marked "A. Fred. Lins/Philada." This is a rare weapon that was used by Union forces in the Civil War. There were approximately 200 manufactured in 1861 and 1862.

Courtesy Milwaukee Public Museum, Milwaukee, Wisconsin

Exc.	V.G.	Good	Fair	Poor
—	—	4000	1750	750

LITTLE ALL RIGHT FIREARMS CO.
Lawrence, Massachusetts

Little All Right Palm Pistol

An unusual-appearing pocket-sized palm pistol. It is chambered for the .22 Short rimfire cartridge and has a 1.75" barrel. The cylinder holds 5 shots. The trigger is mounted on the top of the barrel at the muzzle and is hinged and connected to a rod that cocks the concealed hammer, cycles the cylinder, and fires the weapon in double action fashion. The grip was designed to be fit into the palm and not gripped as in a conventional pistol. The finish is nickel-plated, and the grips are pearl.

Exc.	V.G.	Good	Fair	Poor
—	—	2000	750	300

LJUNGMAN
Eskilstuna, Sweden
Carl Gustav

NOTE: For history, technical data, descriptions, and prices see the *Standard Catalog of Military Firearms, 1870 to the Present* under Sweden.

LJUTIC INDUSTRIES
Yakima, Washington

Bi-Matic Semiautomatic

A custom-built, gas-operated, semiautomatic shotgun that is known for its low level of felt recoil. It is chambered for 12 gauge and has 26" to 32" barrels choked for either skeet or trap. The stock specifications are to the customer's order. There are options available that affect the value, so we recommend an individual appraisal.

Exc.	V.G.	Good	Fair	Poor
2000	1500	1000	800	400

Dynatrap Single Barrel

A single shot trap gun chambered for 12 gauge. It has a 33" vent rib full-choke barrel and features a push-button opener and a manual extractor. The stock is made to trap specifications. There are many options that affect the value; independent appraisal is recommended.

Exc.	V.G.	Good	Fair	Poor
2000	1500	1000	800	400

Model X-73 Single Barrel

Similar features to the Dynatrap, with a high competition rib. Appraisal is recommended.

Exc.	V.G.	Good	Fair	Poor
2500	2000	1500	950	500

Mono Gun Single Barrel

Chambered for 12 gauge and has a 34" vent rib barrel. It is essentially a custom-order proposition that is available with a standard, as well as a release, trigger. There are many value-affecting options available. Appraisal is recommended.

NIB	Exc.	V.G.	Good	Fair	Poor
3800	3000	2250	1500	900	500

LTX Model

A deluxe version of the Mono Gun with a 33" medium-height vent rib and a high-grade walnut stock with fine hand checkering. Options raise values drastically. Appraisal is recommended.

NIB	Exc.	V.G.	Good	Fair	Poor
5000	4000	3000	1500	900	500

Space Gun

A unique single barrel gun chambered for 12 gauge, with trap choking. It has a stock and forearm that reminds one of a crutch in appearance but which allows the shooter to have in-line control with little felt recoil. The barrel, forearm, and stock are all on one line. There is a recoil pad and a high ventilated rib.

NIB	Exc.	V.G.	Good	Fair	Poor
3750	3000	2250	1500	900	500

Bi-Gun O/U

An Over/Under double chambered for 12 gauge. It has 30" or 32" vent ribbed barrels that are separated. The choking is to trap specifications, and the stock is deluxe hand-checkered walnut.

NIB	Exc.	V.G.	Good	Fair	Poor
10000	8000	6000	4000	2000	1000

Bi-Gun Combo

The Over/Under Bi-Gun supplied with a high-ribbed single barrel in addition to the separated Over/Under barrels. It is furnished in a fitted case, and the walnut is of exhibition grade.

NIB	Exc.	V.G.	Good	Fair	Poor
17000	13000	7000	4000	2000	1000

LM-6 Super Deluxe

This is a custom built over and under gun made to the customer's specifications. Available in 12 gauge with barrel lengths from 28" to 34". All other specifications are custom. Expert appraisal recommended prior to sale.

NIB	Exc.	V.G.	Good	Fair	Poor
18000	13500	8000	—	—	—

NOTE: Extra single barrel add $7,000.

LLAMA
Manufactured by
Gabilondo Y Cia
Vitoria, Spain
Importers - Import Sports, Inc.

This is the same firm that was founded in 1904 and produced several inexpensive revolvers and pistols prior to 1931. In 1931 the company began to produce a semiautomatic pistol based on the Colt Model 1911. They were of high quality and have been sold around the world. After the Spanish civil war the company moved its facilities to Vitoria, Spain, where it continued to build handguns under the Llama trade name. In the 1980s the firm introduced a new line of pistols that were more modern in design and function. The Llama pistol is still produced today. For Llama pistols built prior to 1936 the slide marking reads: "GABILONDO Y CIA ELOEIBAR (ESPANA) CAL 9MM/.380IN LLAMA." For pistols built after 1936 the slide marking reads: "LLAMA GABILONDO Y CIA ELOEIBAR (ESPANA) CAL 9MM .380." Current production Llama pistols will show a slide marking with either "LLAMA CAL..." or "GABILONDO Y CIA VITORIA (ESPANA)" and the Llama logo.

LLAMA AUTOMATICS

Model I-A

This is a 7.65mm blowback design introduced in 1933. Magazine capacity is 7 rounds. The barrel was 3.62", overall length 6.3", and weight about 19 oz.

Exc.	V.G.	Good	Fair	Poor
225	175	125	100	75

Model II

Chambered for the 9mm Short introduced in the same year. Identical to the Model I. Discontinued in 1936.

Exc.	V.G.	Good	Fair	Poor
250	200	150	125	100

Model III

An improved version of the Model II. Introduced in 1936 and discontinued in 1954.

Exc.	V.G.	Good	Fair	Poor
250	200	150	125	100

Model III-A

Similar to the Model III, chambered for the .380 ACP, but with the addition of the Colt type grip safety. Introduced in 1955. Weight is about 23 oz

Exc.	V.G.	Good	Fair	Poor
250	200	150	125	100

Model IV

Chambered for the 9mm Largo or .380 ACP. Is not fitted with a grip safety. Introduced in 1931, it is the first of the Llama designs.

Exc.	V.G.	Good	Fair	Poor
250	200	150	100	75

Model V

The same as the Model IV but was intended for export to the United States and is stamped "made in Spain" on the slide.

Exc.	V.G.	Good	Fair	Poor
250	200	150	100	75

Model VI

Chambered for the 9mm Short and without a grip safety.

Exc.	V.G.	Good	Fair	Poor
250	200	150	100	75

Model VII

This model was introduced in 1932 and manufactured until 1954. It is chambered for the .38 Super Auto cartridge. It does not have a grip safety.

Exc.	V.G.	Good	Fair	Poor
250	200	150	125	100

Model VIII

This model was introduced in 1955 and is chambered for the .45 ACP, .38 Super, or 9mm Largo. It is fitted with a grip safety. Barrel length is 5", overall length is 8.5", and weight is about 38 oz. Magazine capacity is 7 rounds

Exc.	V.G.	Good	Fair	Poor
300	250	175	125	100

Model IX

Chambered for the 7.65mm Para, 9mm Largo, or .45 ACP, this model has a locked breech with no grip safety. Built from 1936 to 1954.

Exc.	V.G.	Good	Fair	Poor
325	275	200	150	100

Model IX-A

This version of the Model IX is fitted with a grip safety. Current production models are chambered for the .45 ACP only. Weighs about 30 oz. with 5" barrel.

Exc.	V.G.	Good	Fair	Poor
275	225	150	125	100

Model IX-B

This version of the Model IX series is chambered in .45 ACP. It is fitted with an extended slide release, black plastic grips, and target type hammer. Offered in blue or satin chrome finish.

NIB	Exc.	V.G.	Good	Fair	Poor
350	300	250	175	125	100

Model IX-C

This is the current large frame version of the Model IX. It is chambered for the .45 ACP and is fitted with a 5.125" barrel. Blade front sight with adjustable rear sight. Magazine capacity is 10 rounds. Weight is approximately 41 oz.

NIB	Exc.	V.G.	Good	Fair	Poor
350	300	250	200	150	100

Model IX-D

This model is a compact frame version with a 4.25" barrel and chambered for the .45 ACP cartridge. Stocks are black rubber. Fixed front sight with adjustable rear. Introduced in 1995. Magazine capacity is 10 rounds. Weight is about 39 oz.

NIB	Exc.	V.G.	Good	Fair	Poor
350	300	—	—	—	—

Model X

First produced in 1935, this model is chambered for the 7.65mm cartridge. It has no grip safety.

Exc.	V.G.	Good	Fair	Poor
250	200	150	100	75

Model X-A

This version is similar to the Model X but with a grip safety. Produced from 1954 to the present.

Exc.	V.G.	Good	Fair	Poor
250	200	150	100	75

Model XI

Chambered for the 9mm Parabellum cartridge this model is different from previous models with a longer curved butt, ring hammer, and vertically grooved walnut grips. Magazine capacity is 9 rounds. Barrel length is 5". Discontinued in 1954.

Exc.	V.G.	Good	Fair	Poor
275	225	175	125	100

Model XI-B

(Currently imported by Century International Arms Co.)
Similar to the Model XI but with a spur hammer and shorter barrel. Currently in production.

NIB	Exc.	V.G.	Good	Fair	Poor
250	200	150	125	100	75

Model XII-B

This model is chambered for the .40 S&W cartridge. It has a compact frame. Currently in production.

NIB	Exc.	V.G.	Good	Fair	Poor
325	275	225	175	125	100

Model XV

Chambered for the .22 long rifle this model is marked "Especial". It is fitted with a grip safety and comes in several finishes and with different grip styles. The barrel length is 3.6", the overall length is 6.5", and the weight is about 17 oz.

Exc.	V.G.	Good	Fair	Poor
225	175	150	125	100

Model XVI

This is a deluxe version of the Model XV with engraving, ventilated rib, and adjustable sights.

Exc.	V.G.	Good	Fair	Poor
350	275	200	150	100

Model XVII

This model is chambered for the .22 Short. It is small version of the Model XV with a finger-shaped grip.

Exc.	V.G.	Good	Fair	Poor
300	250	175	125	100

Model Max-I

Introduced in 1995 this 1911 design single action model features a choice of 9mm or .45 ACP chambers with a 4.25" barrel or a 5.125" barrel. Black rubber grips with blade front sight and adjustable rear sight. Weight is 34 oz. for compact model and 36 oz. for Government model.

NIB	Exc.	V.G.	Good	Fair	Poor
300	250	200	150	—	—

NOTE: For compact model add $25. For Duo-tone model add $25.

Model Mini-Max

This version is chambered for the 9mm, .40 S&W, or .45 ACP. Furnished with a 6-round magazine. Barrel length is 3.5". Checkered rubber grips. Introduced in 1996. Weight is about 35 oz. choice of blue, duo-tone, satin chrome, or stainless steel.

NIB	Exc.	V.G.	Good	Fair	Poor
300	250	200	—	—	—

NOTE: Add $40 for satin chrome finish. Add $60 for stainless. Add $20 for duo-tone finish.

Mini-Max Sub Compact

This semiautomatic is chambered for the 9mm, .40S&W, or .45ACP cartridge. It is fitted with a 3.14" barrel with an overall length of 6.5" and a height of 4.5". Skeletonized combat style hammer. Grips are black polymer. Weight is about 31 oz. Introduced in 1999.

NIB	Exc.	V.G.	Good	Fair	Poor
325	250	200	—	—	—

NOTE: Add $40 for satin chrome finish. Add $60 for stainless. Add $20 for duo-tone finish.

Model Max-I with Compensator
Similar to the Max-I with the addition of a compensator. This model introduced in 1996. Weight is about 42 oz.

NIB	Exc.	V.G.	Good	Fair	Poor
450	400	—	—	—	—

Micro-Max
This pistol is chambered for the .32ACP or .380 cartridge. It operates on a straight blowback system with a single action trigger. Black polymer grips. Barrel length is 3.6". Overall length is 6.5" and height is 4.37". Weight is approximately 23 oz. Introduced in 1999.

NIB	Exc.	V.G.	Good	Fair	Poor
275	200	150	125	100	—

NOTE: Add $20 for satin chrome finish.

Model 82
This is a large frame double action semiautomatic pistol. It features plastic grips, ambidextrous safety, 3-dot sights. The barrel length is 4.25" and overall length is 8". Weight is approximately 39 oz. Choice of blue or satin chrome finish.

NIB	Exc.	V.G.	Good	Fair	Poor
750	600	450	300	200	100

Mugica
Eibar gun dealer Jose Mugica sold Llama pistols under his private trade name. They are marked "mugica-ebir-spain" on the slide. These pistols do not seem to have any additional value over and above their respective Llama models. For the sake of clarification the Mugica models will be listed with their Llama counterparts:

Mugica Model 101	Llama Model X
Mugica Model 101-G	Llama Model X-A
Mugica Model 105	Llama Model III
Mugica Model 105-G	Llama Model III-A
Mugica Model 110	Llama Model VII
Mugica Model 110-G	Llama Model VIII
Mugica Model 120	Llama Model XI

Tauler
In an arrangement similar to Mugica a gun dealer in Madrid sold Llama pistols under his own brand name. Most of these pistols were sold in the early 1930s to police and other government officials. The most common Llama models were Models I to VIII. Slide inscriptions were in English and had the name Tauler in them. No additional value is attached to this private trademark.

REVOLVERS

Ruby Extra Models
These revolvers were produced in the 1950s and were copies of Smith & Wessons. They were marked "RUBY EXTRA" on the left side of the frame. At the top of the grips was a Ruby medallion. The barrel address is stamped: gabilondo y cia el-goeibar espana. The Ruby Extra Models represent the company's attempts to produce and sell a low cost revolver.

Model XII
This model is chambered for the .38 Long cartridge and is fitted with a 5" barrel and a squared butt.

Exc.	V.G.	Good	Fair	Poor
200	150	125	100	75

Model XIII
(Currently imported by Century International Arms Co.) Chambered for the .38 Special, this revolver has a round butt with 4" or 6" ventilated rib barrel. The 6" barreled gun was fitted with adjustable sights and target grips.

Exc.	V.G.	Good	Fair	Poor
200	150	125	100	75

Model XIV
Offered in .22 Long Rifle or .32 caliber, this model was available in a wide choice of barrel lengths and sights.

Exc.	V.G.	Good	Fair	Poor
200	150	125	100	75

Model XXII Olimpico
This model was designed as a .38 Special target revolver. It features an adjustable anatomic grip, adjustable rear sight, ventilated rib barrel, and a web that joins the barrel to the ejector shroud.

Exc.	V.G.	Good	Fair	Poor
275	225	150	125	100

Model XXVI
Chambered for the .22 Long Rifle, it features traditional grips and shrouded ejector rod.

Exc.	V.G.	Good	Fair	Poor
175	150	125	100	75

NIB	Exc.	V.G.	Good	Fair	Poor
250	225	175	125	100	75

Model XXVII

Similar to the model above but fitted with a 2" barrel and chambered for the .32 Long cartridge.

Exc.	V.G.	Good	Fair	Poor
175	150	125	100	75

Model XXVIII

This model is chambered for the .22 l.r. and is fitted with a 6" barrel. It has a ramp front sight and adjustable rear sight.

Exc.	V.G.	Good	Fair	Poor
200	175	150	100	75

Model XXIX Olimpico

This is the Model XXI I chambered for the .22 Long Rifle.

Exc.	V.G.	Good	Fair	Poor
250	200	150	125	100

Model XXXII Olimpico

This model is a .32 target revolver with an unusual cylinder and frame design.

Exc.	V.G.	Good	Fair	Poor
275	225	150	125	100

Llama Omni

A .45 ACP and the 9mm caliber double action semiautomatic pistol with a 4.25" barrel and a 7-shot detachable magazine (.45 caliber) and a 13-shot magazine (9mm), a double sear bar and three distinct safeties. Steel with a blued finish. Discontinued in 1986.

Exc.	V.G.	Good	Fair	Poor
275	250	200	150	100

Llama Small Frame Semiautomatic

A .22, .32 ACP, and the .380 ACP caliber semiautomatic pistol with a 3-11/16" barrel and 7-shot detachable magazine. Either blued or satin chrome finished.

Satin Chrome Finish-Add $75.

NIB	Exc.	V.G.	Good	Fair	Poor
200	175	150	125	100	75

Llama Compact Frame Semiautomatic

A 9mm or the .45 ACP caliber semiautomatic pistol with a 4.25" barrel and either a 7- or 9-shot detachable magazine. Blued. Introduced in 1986.

Llama Large Frame Semiautomatic

A 9mm, .38 Super or .45 ACP caliber semiautomatic pistol with a 5.25" barrel and either a 7- or 9-shot detachable magazine, depending on the caliber. Blued or satin chrome.

Satin Chrome Finish-Add $125

NIB	Exc.	V.G.	Good	Fair	Poor
250	225	175	125	100	75

Llama Model 82

A 9mm Parabellum caliber double action semiautomatic pistol with a 4.25" barrel, a 3-dot sighting system, 15-shot detachable magazine, a loaded-chamber indicator, and an ambidextrous safety. Blued, with black plastic grips. Introduced in 1988.

NIB	Exc.	V.G.	Good	Fair	Poor
400	350	300	250	200	100

Llama Model 87 Competition

As above with a compensator special barrel bushing, a beveled magazine well, a squared and checkered triggerguard, with an adjustable trigger. Blued. Introduced in 1989.

NIB	Exc.	V.G.	Good	Fair	Poor
850	700	500	300	200	100

Llama Martial

A .22 or the .38 Special caliber double action revolver with a 6-round swingout cylinder, a 4" or 6" barrel and adjustable sights. Blued, with checkered hardwood grips. Manufactured between 1969 and 1976.

Exc.	V.G.	Good	Fair	Poor
225	175	150	110	85

Llama Comanche I

As above, in .22 caliber.

Exc.	V.G.	Good	Fair	Poor
250	200	175	125	100

Llama Comanche II

As above, in .38 Special caliber. Manufactured between 1977 and 1982.

Exc.	V.G.	Good	Fair	Poor
250	200	175	125	100

Llama Comanche III

As above, in .357 Magnum with a 4", 6", or 8.5" barrel and adjustable sights. Introduced in 1975.

Satin Chrome Finish-Add 20%.

NIB	Exc.	V.G.	Good	Fair	Poor
275	225	175	125	100	75

Llama Super Comanche

As above, in .44 Magnum with a 6" or 8.5" ventilated rib barrel and adjustable sights. Blued, with walnut grips.

NIB	Exc.	V.G.	Good	Fair	Poor
350	275	200	150	100	75

LOEWE, LUDWIG & CO.
Berlin, Germany
SEE—Borchardt

During the 1870s and 1880s this firm manufactured a close copy of the Smith & Wesson Russian Model for the Russian government. They are marked "Ludwig Loewe Berlin" on the top of the barrel.

Loewe Smith & Wesson Russian Revolver

Exc.	V.G.	Good	Fair	Poor
—	400	200	125	75

LOHNER, C.
Philadelphia, Pennsylvania

Pocket Pistol

A .44 caliber single shot percussion pistol with a 5" barrel, German silver mounts and walnut grip. The barrel marked "C. Lohner." Manufactured during the 1850s.

Exc.	V.G.	Good	Fair	Poor
—	—	1250	550	250

LOMBARD, H. C. & CO.
Springfield, Massachusetts

Pocket Pistol

A .22 caliber single shot spur trigger pistol with a 3.5" octagonal barrel. The frame is silver plated, barrel blued and grips are of walnut. Barrel marked "H.C. Lombard & Co. Springfield, Mass."

Exc.	V.G.	Good	Fair	Poor
—	—	450	200	100

LONDON ARMOURY COMPANY
London

This firm was established in 1856, by Robert Adams. In addition to marketing revolvers based upon Adams' designs, the London Armoury Company were major retailers of other arms, particularly Enfield Pattern 53 Percussion Rifles. During the 1870's, the London Armoury distributed Colt pistols. During its business life, the London Armoury Company was located at the following addresses:

Henry Street	1857-1863
36 King William Street	1864-1868
54 King William Street	1868-1883
118 Queen Victoria Street	1884-1886
114 Queen Victoria Street	1887-1905
1 Lawrence Pounty Hill	1905-1910
31 Bury Street, St. James's	1910-1939
10 Ryder Street, St. James's	1940-1950

Although the firm continued in business after 1950, its operations were restricted to the trade of used arms.

LONE STAR RIFLE COMPANY
Conroe, Texas

This company builds custom black powder rifles. They are built on the rolling block design and are offered in two basic configurations. There are a wide number of options that will affect the price of these rifles. Prospective purchasers are urged to seek expert assistance before a sale takes place.

Sporting Rifle

This is a basic configuration that features a straight grip stock with semi-crescent butt. Offered in a wide variety of calibers from .32-40 to .50-90. Barrel lengths, barrel configurations, wood, triggers, sights, engraving, finishes, hammers, and accessories will greatly effect the final price.

Basic retail price: $1850.

Target Rifle

This is a basic configuration that features a straight grip stock with semi-crescent butt. Offered in a wide variety of calibers from .32-40 to .50-90. Barrel lengths, barrel configurations, wood, triggers, sights, engraving, finishes, hammers, and accessories will greatly effect the final price.

Basic retail price: $1850.

LORCIN ENGINEERING CO., INC.
Mira Loma, California

NOTE: This company is no longer in business.

Model L-25

A .25 caliber semiautomatic pistol with a 2.5" barrel and 7-shot magazine. Weight is 14.5 oz. Overall length is 4.8". Introduced in 1989.

NIB	Exc.	V.G.	Good	Fair	Poor
75	60	50	40	30	20

Model LT-25

Same as above but with aluminum alloy frame. Introduced in 1989.

NIB	Exc.	V.G.	Good	Fair	Poor
100	75	60	50	40	30

Model L-22

Chambered for the .22 Long Rifle cartridge with a 2.5" barrel. Magazine capacity is 9 rounds. Introduced in 1989. Weight is 16 oz.

NIB	Exc.	V.G.	Good	Fair	Poor
90	65	55	45	35	25

Model L-380

This semiautomatic pistol is chambered for the .380ACP cartridge. Barrel length is 3.5" with a magazine capacity of 7 rounds. Introduced in 1992. Weight is about 23 oz.

NIB	Exc.	V.G.	Good	Fair	Poor
120	95	80	50	40	30

Model I-380 10th Anniversary

Same as above but frame and slide are plated in 24 karat gold. Limited edition model.

NIB	Exc.	V.G.	Good	Fair	Poor
150	—	—	—	—	—

Model L-32

Same as above but chambered for the .32 ACP cartridge. Introduced in 1992

NIB	Exc.	V.G.	Good	Fair	Poor
100	80	70	50	40	30

Model LH-380

This semiautomatic pistol is chambered for the .380 ACP cartridge. The barrel length is 4.5" and the magazine capacity is 10 rounds. Offered in black, Satin or Bright Chrome finishes.

NIB	Exc.	V.G.	Good	Fair	Poor
150	125	100	75	60	50

Model L-9mm

Same as above but chambered for 9mm cartridge. Weight is 36 oz.

NIB	Exc.	V.G.	Good	Fair	Poor
150	125	100	75	60	50

Derringer

This over and under pistol is chambered for the .38 Special, .357 Magnum, and .45 ACP. Barrel length is 3.5". Overall length is 6.5".

NIB	Exc.	V.G.	Good	Fair	Poor
140	120	95	65	50	40

LOWELL ARMS CO.
SEE—Rollin White Arms Co.

LOWER, J. P.
SEE—Slotter & Co.

LUGERS
Various Manufacturers

Just before the turn of the twentieth century, Georg Luger redesigned the Borchardt semiautomatic pistol so that its mainspring was housed in the rear of the grip. The resulting pistol was to prove extremely successful and his name has become synonymous with the pistol despite the fact his name never appeared on it.

The following companies manufactured Luger pattern pistols at various times.

1. DWM - Deutsch Waffen und Munitions - Karlsruhe, Germany

2. The Royal Arsenal of Erfurt Germany

3. Simson & Company - Suhl, Germany

4. Mauser - Oberndorf, Germany

5. Vickers Ltd. - England

6. Waffenfabrik Bern - Bern, Switzerland

7. Heinrich Krieghoff - Suhl, Germany

Those interested in these pistols are advised to read the various books written about the marque which are listed in the bibliography at the close of this book.

THE LUGER PISTOL
(Pistole Parabellum)

I must be the only person who finds the Luger pistol in its most common version, the Model 08 with 3 5/8" barrel, not to be the natural-pointing handgun everyone claims it to be. But I do believe that everyone should probably have a Luger in their collection if for no other reason than it is an excellent example of the golden age of precision metal working that will never again be done, given the cost of labor and the use of computer-run machinery.

About once a year or so, I pull my WWII-era Luger out of safekeeping and touch off 50 rounds or so. Nothing changes year to year, though. The gun is still too muzzle-light and the grip feels more like an axe handle than a pistol grip in my hand. The trigger is not bad but I can see, in my mind's eye, the various parts all trying to work together to get the gun to fire. Of course, the sights don't help much either since the rear notch is just that, a shallow V in which I'm supposed to put the equally-difficult-to-use front sight.

Once I get everything going the Luger does work reliably, contrary to the same common wisdom that says the Luger is prone to malfunctions due to its toggle-link design. Mine works because I use the correct ammunition in the gun—a 124-grain round-nose FMJ bullet, factory-loaded to the upper end of SAAMI specifications. The Luger is more than sufficiently accurate for its purpose, and its adoption and use in battle at one time or another by almost every army in the world indicates that the Luger is a proven design—and that I'm the exception to the rule.

Walt Rauch

Swiss Cross & Sunburst   Courtesy Gale Morgan

Exc.	V.G.	Good	Fair	Poor
5500	4000	2000	1500	1000

1900 Commercial
4.75" barrel, 7.65mm caliber. The area above the chamber is blank. The serial range is 01-19000, and there were approximately 5,500 manufactured for commercial sale in Germany or other countries. Some have "Germany" stamped on the frame. These pistols were imported into the U.S., and some were even stamped after blueing.

Courtesy Gale Morgan

Exc.	V.G.	Good	Fair	Poor
5000	3700	2000	1000	650

DEUTSCH WAFFEN UND MUNITIONS

1899/1900 Swiss Test Model
4.75" barrel, 7.65mm caliber. The Swiss Cross in Sunburst is stamped over the chamber. The serial range runs to three digits. With less than 100 manufactured and only one known to exist, it is one of the rarest of the Lugers and the first true Luger that was produced. This model is far too rare to estimate an accurate value.

1900 Swiss Contract
4.75" barrel, 7.65mm caliber. The Swiss Cross in Sunburst is stamped over the chamber. The military serial number range is 2001-5000; the commercial range, 01-21250. There were approximately 2,000 commercial and 3,000 military models manufactured.

Wide Trigger-Add 20%.

1900 American Eagle

4.75" barrel, 7.65mm caliber. The American Eagle crest is stamped over the chamber. The serial range is between 2000-200000, and there were approximately 11,000-12,000 commercial models marked "Germany" and 1,000 military test models without the commercial import stamp. The serial numbers of this military lot have been estimated at between 6100-7100.

Exc.	V.G.	Good	Fair	Poor
4500	3200	1500	850	600

1900 Bulgarian Contract

An old model, 1900 Type, with no stock lug. It has a 4.75" barrel and is chambered for the 7.65mm cartridge. The Bulgarian crest is stamped over the chamber, and the safety is marked in Bulgarian letters. The serial range is 20000-21000, with 1,000 manufactured. This is a military test model and is quite rare as most were rebarreled to 9mm during the time they were used. Even with the 9mm versions, approximately 10 are known to exist. It was the only variation to feature a marked safety before 1904.

Exc.	V.G.	Good	Fair	Poor
12000	8000	4000	2500	1800

1900 Carbine

11.75" barrel, 7.65mm caliber. The carbines have a gracefully contoured and finely checkered walnut forearm and detachable shoulder stock. The rear sight on this extremely rare variation is a five-position sliding model located on the rear link. The area above the chamber is blank. The serial range is three digits or under, and this may have been a prototype as less than 100 were produced. This model is far too rare to estimate an accurate value.

1902 Prototype

6" barrel, 7.65mm caliber. The serial numbers are in the 10000 range with a capital B, and the chamber is blank. The 6" barrel is of a heavy contour, and there were less than 10 manufactured. The rarity of this variation precludes estimating value.

1902 Carbine

11.75" barrel, 7.65mm caliber. The sight has four positions and is silver-soldered to the barrel. A stock and forearm were sold with this weapon. The serial range was 21000-22100 and 23500-24900. There were approximately 2,500 manufactured for commercial sale in and out of Germany. Many were imported into the United States, but none here have been noted with the "Germany" import stamp.

With stock-Add 50%.

Courtesy Gale Morgan

Exc.	V.G.	Good	Fair	Poor
13000	9500	6000	3500	2500

1902 Commercial-"Fat Barrel"

Thick 4" barrel, 9mm caliber. The area above the chamber is blank. It is chambered for the 9mm cartridge, and the serial numbers fall within the 22300-22400 and the 22900-23500 range. There were approximately 600 manufactured, and the greater part of those noted were marked "Germany" for export purposes.

Exc.	V.G.	Good	Fair	Poor
9000	7500	5000	2000	1100

1902 American Eagle

As above, with an American Eagle stamped over the chamber. It is chambered for the 9mm cartridge, and the serial numbers fall within the 22100-22300 and the 22450-22900 range. This model was solely intended for export sales in the U.S.A., and all are marked "Germany" on the frame. There were approximately 700 manufactured.

Exc.	V.G.	Good	Fair	Poor
8500	7000	5000	3000	1200

1902 American Eagle Cartridge Counter

As above, with a "Powell Indicating Device" added to the left grip. A slotted magazine with a numbered window that allows visual access to the number of cartridges remaining. There were 50 Lugers altered in this way at the request of the U.S. Board of Ordnance, for U.S. Army evaluation. The serial numbers are 22401-22450. Be especially wary of fakes!

Exc.	V.G.	Good	Fair	Poor
29000	22000	16000	6000	3500

1902 Presentation Carbine

11.75" barrel, 7.65mm caliber. These carbines have the initials of the owner gold-inlaid above the chamber. They are furnished with a checkered walnut stock and forearm. Only four have been noted in the 9000C serial number range. They have the initials "GL" for Georg Luger on the back of the rear toggle. They are too rare to estimate value.

1902/06 Carbine (Transitional)

11.75" barrel, 7.65mm caliber. Assembled from Model 1902 parts with a new toggle assembly. They have the four-position sliding sight, silver-soldered to the barrel, and a checkered walnut stock and forearm. There were approximately 100 manufactured in the 23600 serial number range.

With stock-Add 25%.

Exc.	V.G.	Good	Fair	Poor
15000	10000	8000	5000	3000

A Model 1902 Carbine presented to Dr. Gerald Webb by President Theodore Roosevelt sold at auction for $12,650. Condition was very good, stock excellent. Butterfield & Butterfield, May 1999

Paul Goodwin Photo

1903 Commercial

4" barrel, 7.65mm caliber. The chamber area is blank. There were approximately 50 manufactured for export to France, serial numbered 25000-25050. The extractor on this model is marked "CHARGE".

Exc.	V.G.	Good	Fair	Poor
12000	9000	5000	3200	2500

1904 Navy

6" thick barrel, 9mm caliber. The chamber area is blank, and the extractor is marked "Geladen". The safety is marked "Gesichert". There were approximately 1,500 manufactured in the one- to four-digit serial range, for military sales to the German Navy. The toggle has a "lock" comparable to 1900 types.

Exc.	V.G.	Good	Fair	Poor
40000	30000	16000	6000	4500

1906 Navy Commercial

This is a new model, 1906 Type, with stock lug. It has a 6" barrel and is chambered for the 9mm cartridge. The chamber is blank, and the extractor is marked "Geladen." The safety is marked "Gesichert," and some have the "Germany" export stamp. The proper magazine has a wood bottom with concentric circles on the sides. There were approximately 2,500 manufactured in the 25050-65000 serial range. They were produced for commercial sales in and outside of Germany.

Exc.	V.G.	Good	Fair	Poor
6000	4500	2700	1500	1000

1906 Commercial

4" barrel, 9mm caliber. The extractor is marked "Geleden," and the area of the frame under the safety in its lower position is polished and not blued. The chamber is blank. There were approximately 4,000 manufactured for commercial sales. Some have the "Germany" export stamp. The serial range is 26500-68000.

Courtesy Orvel Reichert

Courtesy Orvel Reichert

Exc.	V.G.	Good	Fair	Poor
3500	2500	1000	800	600

1906 Commercial (Marked Safety)

As above, with the area of the frame under the safety in its lowest position is marked "Gesichert" and the barrel is 4.75" in length and chambered for the 7.65mm cartridge. There were approximately 750 manufactured, serial numbered 25050-26800.

Exc.	V.G.	Good	Fair	Poor
4000	3000	2000	800	600

1906 American Eagle

4" barrel, 9mm caliber. The chamber area has the American Eagle stamped upon it. The extractor is marked "Loaded", and the frame under the safety at its lowest point is polished and not blued. This model has no stock lug. There were approximately 3,000 manufactured for commercial sale in the U.S.A. in the serial range 25800-69000.

Exc.	V.G.	Good	Fair	Poor
3400	2500	1200	700	500

NOTE: Add 10% premium for "CAL. 9MM" mag.

1906 American Eagle (Marked Safety)

4.75" barrel, 7.65mm caliber. The frame under the safety at its lowest point is marked "Gesichert." There were approximately 750 manufactured in the 25100-26500 serial number range.

Courtesy Gale Morgan

Exc.	V.G.	Good	Fair	Poor
4200	3200	1500	1200	800

1906 American Eagle 4.75" Barrel

As above but with polished bright safety area. Approximately 8,000 manufactured in the 26500-69000 serial range.

Exc.	V.G.	Good	Fair	Poor
3200	2200	1100	700	450

1906 U.S. Army Test Luger .45 Caliber

5" barrel, .45 ACP caliber. Sent to the United States for testing in 1907. The chamber is blank; the extractor is marked "Loaded", and the frame is polished under the safety lever. The trigger on this model has an odd hook at the bottom. Only five of these pistols were manufactured.

1906 Swiss Commercial

4.75" barrel, 7.65mm caliber. The Swiss Cross in Sunburst appears over the chamber. The extractor is marked "Geladen," and the frame under the safety is polished. There is no stock lug, and the proofmarks are commercial. There were approximately 1,000 manufactured in the 35000-55000 serial number range.

Courtesy Butterfield & Butterfield, San Francisco, California

Exc.	V.G.	Good	Fair	Poor
5000	3500	2500	1400	800

1906 Swiss Military

As the Swiss Commercial, except with military proofmarks.

Exc.	V.G.	Good	Fair	Poor
4500	3100	2000	900	700

1906 Swiss Police Cross in Shield

As above, with a shield replacing the sunburst on the chamber marking. There were 10,215 of both models combined. They are in the 5000-15215 serial number range.

Courtesy Gale Morgan

Exc.	V.G.	Good	Fair	Poor
4700	3700	2000	1000	700

1906 Dutch Contract

4" barrel, 9mm caliber. It has no stock lug, and the chamber is blank. The extractor is marked "Geleden" on both sides, and the safety is marked "RUST" with a curved upward pointing arrow. This pistol was manufactured for military sales to the Netherlands, and a date will be found on the barrel of most examples encountered. The Dutch refinished their pistols on a regular basis and marked the date on the barrels. There were approximately 4,000 manufactured, serial numbered between 1 and 4000.

Courtesy Gale Morgan

Exc.	V.G.	Good	Fair	Poor
4200	3000	1500	800	600

1906 Royal Portuguese Navy

4" barrel, 9mm caliber, and has no stock lug. The Royal Portuguese Naval crest, an anchor under a crown, is stamped above the chamber. The extractor is marked "CARREGADA" on the left side. The frame under the safety is polished. There were approximately 1,000 manufactured with one- to four-digit serial numbers.

Exc.	V.G.	Good	Fair	Poor
12000	9000	6500	4000	2500

1906 Royal Portuguese Army (M2)

4.75" barrel, 7.65mm caliber. It has no stock lug. The chamber area has the Royal Portuguese crest of Mannuel II stamped upon it. The extractor is marked "CARREGADA". There were approximately 5,000 manufactured, with one- to four-digit serial numbers.

Portugese "M2" Photo Courtesy Gale Morgan

Exc.	V.G.	Good	Fair	Poor
3200	2700	1200	600	500

1906 Republic of Portugal Navy

4" barrel, 9mm caliber. It has no stock lug, and the extractor was marked "CARREGADA". This model was made after 1910, when Portugal had become a republic. The anchor on the chamber is under the letters "R.P." There were approximately 1,000 manufactured, with one- to four-digit serial numbers.

Exc.	V.G.	Good	Fair	Poor
11000	9000	5500	3500	2500

1906 Brazilian Contract

4.75" barrel, 7.65mm caliber. It has no stock lug, and chamber area is blank. The extractor is marked "CARREGADA", and the frame under the safety is polished. There were approximately 5,000 manufactured for military sales to Brazil.

Exc.	V.G.	Good	Fair	Poor
3000	2400	1100	750	450

1906 Bulgarian Contract

4.75" barrel, 7.65mm caliber. It has no stock lug, and the extractor and safety are marked in cyrillic letters. The Bulgarian crest is stamped above the chamber. Nearly all of the examples located have the barrels replaced with 4" 9mm units. This was done after the later 1908 model was adopted. Some were refurbished during the Nazi era, and these pistols bear Waffenamts and usually mismatched parts. There were approximately 1,500 manufactured, with serial numbers of one- to four-digits.

Exc.	V.G.	Good	Fair	Poor
9500	7000	5000	3500	1500

1906 Russian Contract

4" barrel, 9mm caliber. It has no stock lug, and the extractor and safety are marked with cyrillic letters. Crossed Nagant rifles are stamped over the chamber. There were approximately 1,000 manufactured, with one- to four-digit serial numbers; but few survive. This is an extremely rare variation, and caution should be exercised if purchase is contemplated.

Courtesy Gale Morgan

Exc.	V.G.	Good	Fair	Poor
14000	12000	6500	4000	2500

1906 Navy 1st Issue

6" barrel, 9mm caliber. The safety and extractor are both marked in German, and the chamber area is blank. There is a stock lug, and the unique two-position sliding Navy sight is mounted on the rear toggle link. There were approximately 12,000 manufactured for the German Navy, with serial numbers of one- to five-digits. The wooden magazine bottom features concentric rings.

NOTE: Many of these pistols had their safety changed so that they were "safe" in the lower position. Known as "1st issue altered." Value at approximately 20% less.

Courtesy Gale Morgan

Exc.	V.G.	Good	Fair	Poor
6000	4500	2000	1300	950

1906 Navy 2nd Issue

As above, but manufactured to be safe in the lower position. Approximately 11,000 2nd Issue Navies manufactured, with one- to five-digit serial numbers—some with an "a" or "b" suffix. They were produced for sale to the German Navy.

Courtesy Gale Morgan

Exc.	V.G.	Good	Fair	Poor
4900	3500	1500	950	700

1908 Commercial

4" barrel, 9mm caliber. It has no stock lug, and the chamber area is blank. The extractor and the safety are both marked in German, and many examples are marked with the "Germany" export stamp. There were approximately 9,000 manufactured in the 39000-71500 serial number range.

Exc.	V.G.	Good	Fair	Poor
2400	1800	750	600	450

1908 Navy Commercial

6" barrel, 9mm caliber. It has a stock lug, no grip safety, and the characteristic two-position sliding sight mounted on the rear toggle link. The chamber area is blank, and the safety and extractor are both marked. The "Germany" export stamp appears on some examples. There were approximately 1,500 manufactured, in the 44000-50000 serial number range.

Exc.	V.G.	Good	Fair	Poor
5600	4700	2500	1750	1250

1908 Navy

As above, with the "Crown M" military proof. They may or may not have the concentric rings on the magazine bottom. There were approximately 40,000 manufactured, with one- to five-digit serial numbers with an "a" or "b" suffix. These Lugers are quite scarce as many were destroyed during and after WWI.

Exc.	V.G.	Good	Fair	Poor
4200	3200	2000	1100	800

1914 Navy

Similar to the above, but stamped with the dates from 1914-1918 above the chamber. Most noted are dated 1916-1918. There were approximately 30,000 manufactured, with one- to five-digit serial numbers with an "a" or "b" suffix. They are scarce as many were destroyed as a result of WWI.

Exc.	V.G.	Good	Fair	Poor
4500	3000	1500	950	700

A DWM 1914 Navy was sold at auction for $6,600. Pistol has all matching serial numbers with matching stock, three matching magazines, all marked with Naval acceptance proofs. All accessories. Condition was very good to excellent.
Faintich Auction Service, June 2000

Paul Goodwin Photo

1908 Military 1st Issue

4" barrel, 9mm caliber. It has no stock lug, and the extractor and safety are both marked in German. The chamber is blank. There were approximately 20,000 manufactured, with one- to five-digit serial numbers—some with an "a" suffix.

Exc.	V.G.	Good	Fair	Poor
1800	1200	600	500	350

1908 Military Dated Chamber (1910-1913)

As above, with the date of manufacture stamped on the chamber.

Exc.	V.G.	Good	Fair	Poor
1300	1000	600	500	350

1914 Military

As above, with a stock lug.

Exc.	V.G.	Good	Fair	Poor
1150	900	650	500	350

1913 Commercial

As above, with a grip safety. Approximately 1,000 manufactured, with serial numbers 71000-72000; but few have been noted, and it is considered to be quite rare.

Exc.	V.G.	Good	Fair	Poor
2800	1700	1300	850	600

1914 Artillery

8" barrel, 9mm caliber. It features a nine-position adjustable sight that has a base that is an integral part of the barrel. This model has a stock lug and was furnished with a military-style flat board stock and holster rig (see Accessories). The chamber is dated from 1914-1918, and the safety and extractor are both marked. This model was developed for artillery and machine gun crews; and many thousands were manufactured, with one- to five-digit serial numbers—some have letter suffixes. This model is quite desirable from a collector's standpoint and is rarer than its production figures would indicate. After the war many were destroyed as the allies deemed them more insidious than other models, for some reason.

Courtesy Gale Morgan

Exc.	V.G.	Good	Fair	Poor
2500	2000	1300	900	600

NOTE: For models stamped with 1914 date add 50%.

DWM Double Dated

4" barrel, 9mm cartridge. The date 1920 or 1921 is stamped over the original chamber date of 1910-1918, creating the double-date nomenclature. These are arsenal-reworked WWI military pistols and were then issued to the German military and/or police units within the provisions of the Treaty of Versailles. Many thousands of these Lugers were produced.

Exc.	V.G.	Good	Fair	Poor
1100	800	550	400	300

1920 Police Rework

As above, except that the original manufacture date was removed before the rework date was stamped. There were many thousands of these produced.

Exc.	V.G.	Good	Fair	Poor
800	650	500	350	300

1920 Commercial

Similar to the above, with 3.5" to 6" barrels in 7.65mm or 9mm and marked "Germany" or "Made in Germany" for export. Others are unmarked and were produced for commercial sale inside Germany. Some of these pistols are military reworks with the markings and the proofmarks removed; others were newly manufactured. The extractors and safety are both marked, and the chamber is blank. The serial number range is one to five digits, and letter suffixes often appear

NOTE: Add 15% for 9mm.

Exc.	V.G.	Good	Fair	Poor
1200	800	600	450	350

1920 Commercial Navy

6" barrel, 9mm caliber. Some have a stock lug; others have been noted without. The chamber area is generally blank, but some have been found with 1914-1918 dates stamped upon them. These were reworked by DWM from Military Navy Lugers after WWI for commercial sales. They are marked "Germany" or "Made in Germany" and were sold by Stoeger Arms, among others. The extractor and safety are both marked, and the unique Navy sight is on the rear toggle link. No one knows exactly how many were produced, but they are quite scarce.

Exc.	V.G.	Good	Fair	Poor
4000	3000	1600	1100	850

1920 Commercial Artillery

8" barrel, 9mm caliber. Erfurt-manufactured pistols, as well as DWM-manufactured pistols, were reworked in this manner. The export markings "Germany" or "Made in Germany" are found on most examples. The number produced is not known, but examples are quite scarce.

Exc.	V.G.	Good	Fair	Poor
3000	2300	1100	700	450

1920 Long Barrel Commercial

10" to 24" barrels, 7.65mm or 9mm caliber. The extractor and safety are both marked, and an artillery model rear sight is used. This model was often built to a customer's specifications. They are rare, and the number manufactured is not known.

Exc.	V.G.	Good	Fair	Poor
3000	2000	1500	1000	800

1920 Carbine

11.75" barrel, 7.65mm caliber. The chamber is blank, and the extractor is marked either "Geleden" or "Loaded". The safety is not-marked. The carbine has a checkered walnut forearm and stock, and most have the "Germany" or "Made in Germany" export stamp. There were few of these carbines manufactured for commercial sales in and outside of Germany, and they are highly prized by collectors.

With stock-Add 25%.

Exc.	V.G.	Good	Fair	Poor
9000	6000	5000	2500	1500

1920 Navy Carbine

Assembled from surplus Navy parts with the distinctive two position, sliding navy sight on the rear toggle link. Most are marked with the export stamp and have the naval military proofmarks still in evidence. The safety and extractor are marked, and rarely one is found chambered for the 9mm cartridge. Few were manufactured.

Exc.	V.G.	Good	Fair	Poor
6250	5000	3000	1800	900

1920 Swiss Commercial

3.5"-6" barrels, 7.65mm or 9mm caliber. The Swiss Cross in Sunburst is stamped over the chamber, and the extractor is marked "Geladen." The frame under the safety is polished. There were a few thousand produced, with serial numbers in the one- to five-digit range, sometimes with a letter suffix.

Exc.	V.G.	Good	Fair	Poor
4000	3000	1600	1000	800

1923 Stoeger Commercial

3.5" to 24" barrels, 7.65mm or 9mm caliber. There is a stock lug. The chamber area is either blank or has the American Eagle stamped on it. The export stamp and "A.F.Stoeger Inc. New York" is found on the right side of the receiver. The extractor and safety are marked in German or English. This was the model that Stoeger registered with the U.S. Patent office to secure the Luger name, and some examples will be so marked. There were less than 1,000 manufactured, with one- to five-digit serial numbers without a letter suffix. Individual appraisal must be secured on barrel lengths above 6". Be wary as fakes have been noted. The values given here are for the shorter barreled models.

Courtesy Gale Morgan

Exc.	V.G.	Good	Fair	Poor
5000	4000	1800	1000	700

NOTE: For barrel lengths over 8"-Add 25%.

Abercrombie & Fitch Commercial 100

Swiss Lugers were made for commercial sale in the United States by "Abercrombie & Fitch Co. New York. Made in Switzerland."—in either one or two lines—is stamped on the top of the barrel. The barrel is 4.75" in length, and there were 49 chambered for 9mm and 51 chambered for the 7.65mm cartridge. This pistol has a grip safety and no stock lug. The Swiss Cross in Sunburst is stamped over the chamber. The extractor is marked, but the safety area is polished. The serial range is four digits—some with a letter suffix. This is a rare and desirable Luger. Be careful of fakes on models of this type and rarity.

Exc.	V.G.	Good	Fair	Poor
10000	7000	5000	3000	2000

1923 Commercial

7-1/2" barrel, 7.65mm caliber. It has a stock lug, and the chamber area is blank. The extractor and safety are both marked in German. These pistols were manufactured for commercial sales in and outside of Germany. There were approximately 18,000 produced, with serial numbers in the 73500-96000 range.

Exc.	V.G.	Good	Fair	Poor
1300	1100	800	600	450

1923 Commercial Safe & Loaded

As above, except that the extractor and safety are marked in English "Safe" & "Loaded". There were approximately 7,000 manufactured in the 73500-96000 serial number range.

Courtesy Gale Morgan

Exc.	V.G.	Good	Fair	Poor
2500	1800	1000	800	500

1923 Dutch Commercial & Military

4" barrel, 9mm caliber. It has a stock lug, and the chamber area is blank. The extractor is marked in German, and the safety is marked "RUST" with a downward pointing arrow. This model was sold commercially and to the military in the Netherlands. There were approximately 1,000 manufactured in the one- to three-digit serial range, with no letter suffix.

Exc.	V.G.	Good	Fair	Poor
3500	2400	1000	850	550

Royal Dutch Air Force

4" barrel, 9mm caliber. Marked with the Mauser Oberndorf proofmark and serial numbered in the 10000 to 14000 range. The safety marked "RUST".

Exc.	V.G.	Good	Fair	Poor
3700	2500	1000	800	550

VICKERS LTD.

1906 Vickers Dutch

4" barrel, 9mm caliber. There is no stock lug, and it uses a grip safety. The chamber is blank, and the extractor is marked "Geleden." "Vickers Ltd." is stamped on the front toggle link. The safety is marked "RUST" with an upward pointing arrow. Examples have been found with an additional date as late as 1933 stamped on the barrel. These dates indicate arsenal refinishing and in no way detract from the value of this variation.

Arsenal reworks are matte-finished, and the originals are a higher-polished rust blue. There were approximately 10,000 manufactured in the 1-10100 serial-number range.

Exc.	V.G.	Good	Fair	Poor
3500	2800	1800	1200	750

ERFURT ROYAL ARSENAL

1908 Erfurt

4" barrel, 9mm caliber. It has no stock lug; and the year of manufacture, from 1910-1913, is stamped above the chamber. The extractor and safety are both marked in German, and "ERFURT" under a crown is stamped on the front toggle link. There were many thousands produced as Germany was involved in WWI. They are found in the one- to five-digit serial range, sometimes with a letter suffix.

Exc.	V.G.	Good	Fair	Poor
1200	950	600	400	350

1914 Erfurt Military

4" barrel, 9mm caliber. It has a stock lug and the date of manufacture over the chamber, 1914-1918. The extractor and safety are both marked in German, and the front link is marked "ERFURT" under a crown. The finish on this model is rough; and as the war progressed in 1917 and 1918, the finish got worse. There were many thousands produced with one- to five-digit serial numbers, some with letter suffixes.

Exc.	V.G.	Good	Fair	Poor
1000	800	600	400	350

1914 Erfurt Artillery

8" barrel, 9mm caliber. It has a stock lug and was issued with a flat board-type stock and other accessories which will be covered in the section of this book dealing with same. The sight is a nine-position adjustable model. The chamber is dated 1914-1918, and the extractor and safety are both marked in German. "ERFURT" under a crown is stamped on the front toggle link. There were a great many manufactured with one- to five-digit serial numbers, some with a letter suffix. This model is similar to the DWM Artillery except that the finish is not as fine.

Exc.	V.G.	Good	Fair	Poor
2700	1700	1100	800	600

Double Date Erfurt

4" barrel, 9mm caliber. The area above the chamber has two dates: the original 1910-1918, and the date of rework, 1920 or 1921. The extractor and safety are both marked in German, and this model can be found with or without a stock lug. "ERFURT" under a crown is stamped on the front toggle link. Police or military unit markings are found on the front of the grip straps more often than not. There were thousands of these produced by DWM as well as Erfurt.

Exc.	V.G.	Good	Fair	Poor
750	600	500	400	350

WAFFENFABRIK BERN

See separate section on Bern.

SIMSON & CO. SUHL, GERMANY

Simson & Co. Rework

4" barrels, 7.65 or 9mm caliber. The chamber is blank, but some examples are dated 1917 or 1918. The forward toggle link is stamped "SIMSON & CO. Suhl". The extractor and safety are marked in German. Most examples have stock lugs; some have been noted without them. The only difference between military models and commercial models is the proofmarks.

Exc.	V.G.	Good	Fair	Poor
2000	1300	900	600	500

Simson Grip Safety Rework

4" barrel, 9mm caliber and a grip safety was added. There is a stock lug. The chamber area is blank; the extractor is marked but the safety is not. There were only a few of these commercial reworks manufactured, and caution should be taken to avoid fakes.

Exc.	V.G.	Good	Fair	Poor
3000	2200	1500	850	550

Simson Dated Military

4" barrel, 9mm caliber. There is a stock lug, and the year of manufacture from 1925-1928 is stamped above the chamber. The extractor and the safety are both marked in German. The checkered walnut grips of Simson-made Lugers are noticeably thicker than others. This is an extremely rare variation. Approximately 2,000 were manufactured with one- to three-digit serial numbers, and few seem to have survived.

Exc.	V.G.	Good	Fair	Poor
3200	2200	1800	900	650

Simson S Code

4" barrel, 9mm caliber. The forward toggle link is stamped with a Gothic S. It has a stock lug, and the area above the chamber is blank. The extractor and the safety are both marked. The grips are also thicker. There were approximately 12,000 manufactured with one- to five-digit serial numbers—some with the letter "a" suffix. This pistol is quite rare on today's market.

Exc.	V.G.	Good	Fair	Poor
4000	3000	1500	1000	750

EARLY NAZI ERA REWORKS MAUSER

Produced between 1930 and 1933, and normally marked with Waffenamt markings.

Deaths Head Rework

4" barrel, 9mm caliber. It has a stock lug; and a skull and crossbones are stamped, in addition to the date of manufacture, on the chamber area. This date was from 1914-1918. The extractor and safety are both marked. The Waffenamt proof is present. It is thought that this variation was produced for the 1930-1933 era "SS" division of the Nazi Party. Mixed serial numbers are encountered on this model and do not lower the value. This is a rare Luger on today's market, and caution should be exercised if purchase is contemplated.

Exc.	V.G.	Good	Fair	Poor
2500	1500	950	600	450

Kadetten Institute Rework

4" barrel, 9mm caliber. It has a stock lug, and the chamber area is stamped "K.I." above the date 1933. This stood for Cadets Institute, an early "SA" and "SS" officers' training school. The extractor and safety are both marked, and the Waffenamt is present. There were only a few hundred reworked, and the variation is quite scarce. Be wary of fakes.

Exc.	V.G.	Good	Fair	Poor
3200	2500	1100	800	600

Mauser Unmarked Rework

4" barrel, 9mm caliber. The entire weapon is void of identifying markings. There is extensive refurbishing, removal of all markings, rebarreling, etc. The stock lug is present, and the extractor and safety are marked. The Waffenamt proofmark is on the right side of the receiver. The number manufactured is not known.

Exc.	V.G.	Good	Fair	Poor
1450	1000	850	600	450

MAUSER MANUFACTURED LUGERS
1930-1942 DWM

Mauser Oberndorf

4" barrel, 9mm caliber. It has a stock lug, blank chamber area and a marked extractor and safety. This is an early example of Mauser Luger, and the front toggle link is still marked DWM as leftover parts were intermixed with new Mauser parts in the production of this pistol. This is one of the first Lugers to be finished with the "Salt" blue process. There were approximately 500 manufactured with one- to four-digit serial numbers with the letter "v" suffix. This is a rare variation.

Exc.	V.G.	Good	Fair	Poor
4000	3200	2000	1500	900

1934/06 Swiss Commercial Mauser

4.75" barrel, 7.65mm caliber. There is no stock lug, but it has a grip safety. The Swiss Cross in Sunburst is stamped above the chamber. The extractor and safety are marked in German. The front toggle link is marked with the Mauser banner. There were approximately 200 manufactured for commercial sale in Switzerland. This variation is very well finished, and the serial numbers are all four digits with a "v" suffix.

Exc.	V.G.	Good	Fair	Poor
7500	5500	4000	1800	1000

1935/06 Portuguese "GNR"

4.75" barrel, 7.65mm caliber. It has no stock lug but has a grip safety. The chamber is marked "GNR," representing the Republic National Guard. The extractor is marked "Carregada"; and the safety, "Seguranca". The Mauser banner is stamped on the front toggle link. There were exactly 564 manufactured according to the original contract records that the Portuguese government made public. They all have four-digit serial numbers with a "v" suffix.

Exc.	V.G.	Good	Fair	Poor
3400	2900	1600	900	750

1934 Mauser Commercial

4" barrel, 7.65mm or 9mm caliber. It has a stock lug, and the chamber area is blank. The extractor and the safety are marked. The Mauser banner is stamped on the front toggle link. The finish on this pistol was very good, and the grips are either checkered walnut or black plastic on the later models. There were a few thousand manufactured for commercial sales in and outside of Germany.

Exc.	V.G.	Good	Fair	Poor
3500	2800	1650	1100	700

S/42 K Date

4" barrel, 9mm caliber. It has a stock lug, and the extractor and safety are marked. This was the first Luger that utilized codes to represent maker and date of manufacture. The front toggle link is marked S/42 in either Gothic or script; this was the code for Mauser. The chamber area is stamped with the letter "K," the code for 1934, the year of manufacture. Approximately 10,500 were manufactured with one- to five-digit serial numbers—some with letter suffixes.

Exc.	V.G.	Good	Fair	Poor
4600	3800	2200	1200	1000

S/42 G Date

As above, with the chamber stamped "G", the code for the year 1935. The Gothic lettering was eliminated, and there were many thousands of this model produced.

Courtesy Orvel Reichert

Exc.	V.G.	Good	Fair	Poor
2000	1500	1000	650	450

Dated Chamber S/42

4" barrel, 9mm caliber. The chamber area is dated 1936-1940, and there is a stock lug. The extractor and safety are marked. In 1937 the rust blue process was eliminated entirely, and all subsequent pistols were salt blued. There were many thousands manufactured with one- to five-digit serial numbers—some with the letter suffix.

Exc.	V.G.	Good	Fair	Poor
1600	1100	750	500	400

NOTE: Rarest variation is early 1937 with rust blued and strawed parts, add 20%.

S/42 Commercial Contract

4" barrel, 9mm caliber. It has a stock lug, and the chamber area is dated. It has a marked extractor and safety. The unusual feature is that, although this was a commercial pistol, the front toggle link is stamped S/42, which was the military code for Mauser. There were only a few hundred manufactured, so perhaps the toggles were left over from previous military production runs. The serial number range is four digits with the letter "v."

Exc.	V.G.	Good	Fair	Poor
2800	2000	1000	750	450

Code 42 Dated Chamber

4" barrel, 9mm caliber. The new German code for Mauser, the number 42, is stamped on the front toggle link. There is a stock lug. The chamber area is dated 1939 or 1940. There were at least 50,000 manufactured with one- to five-digit serial numbers; some have letter suffixes.

Exc.	V.G.	Good	Fair	Poor
1100	850	650	400	350

41/42 Code

As above, except that the date of manufacture is represented by the final two digits (e.g. 41 for 1941). There were approximately 20,000 manufactured with the one- to five-digit serial number range.

Exc.	V.G.	Good	Fair	Poor
1600	1350	900	700	500

byf Code

As above, with the "byf" code stamp on the toggle link. The year of manufacture, either 41 or 42, is stamped on the chamber. This model was also made with black plastic, as well as walnut grips. There were many thousands produced with the one- to five-digit serial numbers— some with a letter suffix.

Exc.	V.G.	Good	Fair	Poor
1200	950	750	450	350

Persian Contract 4"

4" barrel, 9mm caliber. It has a stock lug, and the Persian crest is stamped over the chamber. All identifying markings on this variation—including extractor, safety and toggle—are marked in Farsi, the Persian alphabet. There were 1,000 manufactured. The serial numbers are also in Farsi.

Exc.	V.G.	Good	Fair	Poor
6500	5000	3500	2500	2000

Persian Contract Artillery

As above, with an 8" barrel and nine-position adjustable sight on the barrel. This model is supplied with a flat board stock. There were 1,000 manufactured and sold to Persia.

Exc.	V.G.	Good	Fair	Poor
3500	2850	1800	1300	1000

1934/06 Dated Commercial

4.75" barrel, 7.65mm caliber. It has a grip safety but no stock lug. The year of manufacture, from 1937-1942, is stamped above the chamber, and the Mauser banner is stamped on the front link. The extractor is marked, but the safety is not. There were approximately 1,000 manufactured with one- to three-digit serial numbers—some with the letter suffix.

Exc.	V.G.	Good	Fair	Poor
3000	2200	1400	900	500

1934 Mauser Dutch Contract

4" barrel, 9mm caliber. The year of manufacture, 1936-1940, is stamped above the chamber. The extractor is marked "Geladen," and the safety is marked "RUST" with a downward pointing arrow. The Mauser banner is stamped on the front toggle link. This was a military contract sale, and approximately 1,000 were manufactured with four-digit serial numbers with a letter "v" suffix.

Exc.	V.G.	Good	Fair	Poor
3500	3000	2000	1100	850

1934 Mauser Swedish Contract

4.75" barrel, 9mm or 7.65mm caliber. The chamber is dated 1938 or 1939. The extractor and safety are both marked in German, and there is a stock lug. The front toggle link is stamped with the Mauser banner. There were only 275 dated 1938 and 25 dated 1939 in 9mm. There were only 30 chambered for 7.65mm dated 1939. The serial number range is four digits with the letter "v" suffix.

Exc.	V.G.	Good	Fair	Poor
4000	3000	2000	1500	700

1934 Mauser Swedish Commercial

4" barrel, 7.65mm caliber. 1940 is stamped over the chamber; "Kal. 7.65" is stamped on the left side of the barrel. The extractor and safety are both marked, and the Mauser banner is stamped on the front toggle link. There is a stock lug. This model is rare as there were only a few hundred manufactured with four digit serial numbers with the letter "w" suffix.

Exc.	V.G.	Good	Fair	Poor
3000	2000	1200	850	600

1934 Mauser German Contract

4" barrel, 9mm caliber. The chamber is dated 1939-1942, and the front toggle link is stamped with the Mauser banner. There is a stock lug, and the extractor and safety are both marked. The grips are either walnut or black plastic. There were several thousand manufactured with one- to five-digit serial num-

bers—some with letter suffixes. They were purchased for issue to police or paramilitary units.

Exc.	V.G.	Good	Fair	Poor
2800	2300	1500	800	550

Austrian Bundes Heer (Federal Army)

4" barrel, 9mm caliber. The chamber is blank, and there is a stock lug. The extractor and safety are marked in German, and the Austrian Federal Army Proof is stamped on the left side of the frame above the triggerguard. There were approximately 200 manufactured with four digit serial numbers and no letter suffix.

Exc.	V.G.	Good	Fair	Poor
2500	1850	1200	700	500

Mauser 2 Digit Date

4" barrel, 9mm caliber. The last two digits of the year of manufacture—41 or 42—are stamped over the chamber. There is a stock lug, and the Mauser banner is on the front toggle link. The extractor and safety are both marked, and the proofmarks were commercial. Grips are either walnut or black plastic. There were approximately 2,000 manufactured for sale to Nazi political groups. They have one- to five-digit serial numbers; some have the letter suffix.

Courtesy Gale Morgan

Exc.	V.G.	Good	Fair	Poor
2800	2200	1500	900	650

Ku Luger (Prefix or suffix)

A 4" barrel, 9mm Luger probably manufactured by Mauser for the German Luftwaffe in the early 1940s. The serial number (on the left side receiver area) has a Ku prefix or suffix. Total production is estimated at 5000 pieces.

Exc.	V.G.	Good	Fair	Poor
3000	1800	1200	900	550

KRIEGHOFF MANUFACTURED LUGERS

1923 DWM/Krieghoff Commercial

4" barrel, 7.65mm or 9mm caliber. The chamber is dated 1921 or left blank. There is a stock lug. The front toggle is marked DWM, as they manufactured this Luger to be sold by Krieghoff. "Krieghoff Suhl" is stamped on the back above the lanyard loop. The second "F" in Krieghoff was defective, and all specimens have this distinctive die strike. The safety and extractor are marked in German. There were only a few hundred manufactured with four-digit serial numbers with the letter "i" suffix.

Exc.	V.G.	Good	Fair	Poor
2000	1500	950	650	500

DWM/Krieghoff Commercial

As above, but marked "Heinrich Krieghoff Waffenfabrik Suhl" on the right side of the frame. Some examples have the "Germany" export stamp. There were several hundred manufactured with four-digit serial numbers with a letter suffix.

Exc.	V.G.	Good	Fair	Poor
3500	2850	2000	950	800

Krieghoff Commercial Inscribed Side Frame

4" or 6" barrel, 7.65mm or 9mm caliber. 1,000 were marked "Heinrich Krieghoff Waffenfabrik Suhl" on the right side of the frame, and 500 were devoid of this marking. All have the dagger and anchor trademark over "H.K. Krieghoff Suhl" on the front toggle link. The extractor and the safety are both marked. There is a stock lug, and the grips are of brown checkered plastic. There were approximately 1,500 manufactured with one- to four-digit serial numbers with a "P" prefix.

Exc.	V.G.	Good	Fair	Poor
6000	5000	3000	2000	1000

S Code Krieghoff

4" barrel, 9mm caliber. The Krieghoff trademark is stamped on the front toggle link, and the letter "S" is stamped over the chamber. There is a stock lug, and the extractor and safety are both marked. The grips are wood on early manufactured pistols and brown checkered plastic on later examples. There were approximately 4,500 manufactured for the Luftwaffe with one- to four-digit serial numbers.

Exc.	V.G.	Good	Fair	Poor
4000	3200	1800	950	750

Grip Safety Krieghoff

4" barrel, 9mm caliber. The chamber area is blank, and the front toggle link is stamped with the Krieghoff trademark. There is a stock lug and a grip safety. The extractor is marked "Geleden," and the safety is marked "FEUER" (fire) in the lower position. The grips are checkered brown plastic. This is a rare Luger, and the number produced is not known.

Exc.	V.G.	Good	Fair	Poor
6000	4000	2800	1400	900

36 Date Krieghoff

4" barrel, 9mm caliber. It has a stock lug and the Krieghoff trademark on the front toggle link. The safety and extractor are marked, and the grips are brown plastic. The two-digit year of manufacture, 36, is stamped over the chamber. There were approximately 700 produced in the 3800-4500 serial number range.

Exc.	V.G.	Good	Fair	Poor
4500	3850	2200	1200	950

4 Digit Dated Krieghoff

As above, with the date of production, 1936-1945, stamped above the chamber. There were approximately 9,000 manufactured within the 4500-14000 serial number range.

Courtesy Gale Morgan

Exc.	V.G.	Good	Fair	Poor
3750	3000	1850	950	750

2nd Series Krieghoff Commercial

4" barrel, 9mm caliber. There is a stock lug, and the Krieghoff trademark is stamped on the front link. The chamber area is

blank, and the extractor and safety are marked. There were approximately 500 manufactured for commercial sales inside Germany. The date of manufacture is estimated at 1939-1940, as this variation has the dark finish that results from blueing without polishing the surface, which was done during these years. The grips are coarsely checkered black plastic. The serial number range is one to three digits with a "P" prefix.

Exc.	V.G.	Good	Fair	Poor
4000	3000	2000	1300	800

Postwar Krieghoff

4" barrel, 9mm caliber. There is a stock lug, and the chamber area is blank. The extractor and safety are marked, and the serial numbers in the one- to three-digit range are unusually large—about 3/16ths of an inch. There were 300 of these postwar Lugers produced for the occupation forces. They were assembled from leftover parts, and only 150 have the Krieghoff trademark on the front toggle link—the second 150 have blank links.

Exc.	V.G.	Good	Fair	Poor
3500	1500	1000	750	650

Krieghoff Postwar Commercial

As above, in 7.65mm caliber and the extractor not marked. Approximately 200 manufactured with standard-sized two- or three-digit serial numbers. They were supposedly sold to the occupation forces in the PX stores.

Exc.	V.G.	Good	Fair	Poor
3000	2000	1000	700	550

LUGER ACCESSORIES

Detachable Carbine Stocks

Approximately 13" in length, with a sling swivel and horn buttplate.

Exc.	V.G.	Good	Fair	Poor
4000	3500	1500	700	500

Artillery Stock with Holster

The artillery stock is of a flat board style approximately 13.75" in length. There is a holster and magazine pouches with straps attached. This is a desirable addition to the Artillery Luger.

Exc.	V.G.	Good	Fair	Poor
1500	1000	500	400	300

Navy Stock without Holster

As above, but 12.75" in length with a metal disc inlaid on the left side.

Exc.	V.G.	Good	Fair	Poor
2000	1500	1000	500	400

NOTE: With holster add 100%.

Ideal Stock/Holster with Grips

A telescoping metal tube stock with an attached leather holster. It is used in conjunction with a metal-backed set of plain grips that correspond to the metal hooks on the stock and allow attachment. This Ideal Stock is U.S. patented and is so marked.

Exc.	V.G.	Good	Fair	Poor
2000	1400	1000	700	450

Drum Magazine 1st Issue

A 32-round, snail-like affair that is used with the Artillery Luger. It is also used with an adapter in the German 9mm submachine gun. The 1st Issue has a telescoping tube that is used to wind the spring. There is a dust cover that protects the interior from dirt.

Exc.	V.G.	Good	Fair	Poor
1000	800	600	350	300

Drum Magazine 2nd Issue
As above, with a folding spring winding lever.

Exc.	V.G.	Good	Fair	Poor
800	700	500	350	300

Drum Magazine Loading Tool
This tool is slipped over the magazine and allows the spring to be compressed so that cartridges could be inserted.

Exc.	V.G.	Good	Fair	Poor
600	550	500	300	200

Drum Magazine Unloading Tool
The origin of this tool is unknown and caution should be exercised prior to purchase.

Drum Carrying Case
The same caveat as above applies.

Exc.	V.G.	Good	Fair	Poor
250	200	125	100	50

Holsters
Produced in a wide variety of styles.

Exc.	V.G.	Good	Fair	Poor
350	275	150	60	50

LATE PRODUCTION MAUSER LUGERS MANUFACTURED DURING THE 1970S

P.08 Interarms
4" or 6" barrel, 7.65mm or 9mm caliber.

NIB	Exc.	V.G.	Good	Fair	Poor
1200	750	500	400	350	300

Swiss Eagle Interarms
Swiss-style straight front grip strap and the American Eagle crest over the chamber. It is chambered for 7.65mm or 9mm and is offered with a 4" or 6" barrel.

NIB	Exc.	V.G.	Good	Fair	Poor
700	550	450	350	325	300

Cartridge Counter
Chambered for 9mm cartridge and fitted with a slotted grip to show cartridge count in magazine.

NIB	Exc.	V.G.	Good	Fair	Poor
3700	3000	2200	1000	N/A	N/A

Commemorative Bulgarian
The Bulgarian crest is stamped over the chamber. There were only 100 produced.

NIB	Exc.	V.G.	Good	Fair	Poor
2500	1500	1200	950	650	450

Commemorative Russian
Crossed Nagant rifles are stamped over the chamber. There were 100 produced.

NIB	Exc.	V.G.	Good	Fair	Poor
2500	1500	1200	950	650	450

Modern Production Carbine
This splendid reproduction was produced on a limited basis. The workmanship is excellent, and the carbine and stock are furnished in a case.

NIB	Exc.	V.G.	Good	Fair	Poor
6000	4500	4000	3200	2500	2000

JOHN MARTZ CUSTOM LUGERS

Martz Luger Carbine
16" barrel. Approximately 80 were manufactured.

Mint	Exc.	V.G.	Good	Fair	Poor
8000	6000	4500	—	—	—

.45 ACP
6" barrel, .45 ACP caliber. Assembled from two Luger pistols that were split and welded together. 50 manufactured.

Mint	Exc.	V.G.	Good	Fair	Poor
5500	4000	3000	—	—	—

Baby Luger 9mm & 7.65mm
A compact Luger pistol. Approximately 200 were produced.

Courtesy Gale Morgan

Mint	Exc.	V.G.	Good	Fair	Poor
3500	2500	1500	1000	—	—

Baby Luger .380 ACP
As above, in .380 caliber. Approximately 7 were manufactured.

Courtesy Gale Morgan

Mint	Exc.	V.G.	Good	Fair	Poor
6500	5000	4000	—	—	—

LUNA
Zella-Mehlis, Germany

Model 200 Free Pistol
A .22 caliber Martini action single shot pistol with an 11" barrel, adjustable sights, and walnut grips. Manufactured prior to WWII.

Exc.	V.G.	Good	Fair	Poor
1150	850	700	500	300

Model 300 Free Pistol

This model is a single shot target pistol chambered for .22 Short cartridge. Fitted with an 11" barrel, set trigger, walnut stocks and forearm with adjustable palm rest. Built from about 1929 to 1939

Exc.	V.G.	Good	Fair	Poor
950	750	650	400	300

Target Rifle

A .22 or .22 Hornet caliber Martini action single shot rifle with a 20" barrel, adjustable sights, and walnut stock. Manufactured prior to WWII.

Exc.	V.G.	Good	Fair	Poor
1000	850	650	500	250

LYMAN
Middletown, Connecticut

Lyman In-Line

Introduced in 1998 this in-line muzzle loader is offered in either .50 or .54 caliber. Fitted with a 22" barrel. Hardwood stock. Add $80 for stainless steel version.

NIB	Exc.	V.G.	Good	Fair	Poor
300	250	200	—	—	—

Deerstalker Rifle

Available in either .50 or .54 caliber percussion or flintlock. Fitted with a 24" barrel and hardwood stock. A stainless steel version is also offered for an additional $80

NIB	Exc.	V.G.	Good	Fair	Poor
300	250	200	—	—	—

Deerstalker Carbine

Same as above but with 21" barrel. Offered in .50 caliber only.

NIB	Exc.	V.G.	Good	Fair	Poor
325	275	225	—	—	—

Great Plains Rifle

This rifle is offered in .50 or .54 caliber flint or percussion. Barrel length is 32". Hardwood stock. Add $25 for flintlock version and $10 for left hand rifles.

NIB	Exc.	V.G.	Good	Fair	Poor
425	350	300	—	—	—

Trade Rifle

This rifle is offered in either .50 or .54 caliber with 28" octagonal barrel and hardwood stock. Polished brass furniture. Add $25 for flintlock rifle.

NIB	Exc.	V.G.	Good	Fair	Poor
300	250	200	—	—	—

Plains Pistol

Available in .50 or .54 caliber percussion

NIB	Exc.	V.G.	Good	Fair	Poor
225	175	150	—	—	—

M

MAB
SEE—Bayonne

MAC
SEE—Ingram

MAS
St. Etienne, France
Manufacture d'Armes de St. Etienne

NOTE: For history, technical data, descriptions, and prices see the *Standard Catalog of Military Firearms, 1870 to the Present* under France.

MBA GYROJET
San Ramon, California

Established in 1960, by R. Maynard and Art Biehl, MBA manufactured a pistol as well as carbine that utilized a spin stabilized rocket. Initially, these arms were of 13mm caliber and later of 12mm.

NOTE: It is reported that this ammo is selling for $20 to $25. About 20% of this ammo still functions.

Mark I Pistol

Exc.	V.G.	Good	Fair	Poor
700	600	500	400	200

Mark I Carbine

This model is similar to the pistol except that it has an 18" barrel and a buttstock with a pistol grip.

Exc.	V.G.	Good	Fair	Poor
1250	1050	850	600	300

MK ARMS, INC.
Irvine, California

K 760

A 9mm caliber semiautomatic carbine with a 16" shrouded barrel, fixed sights, and 14-, 24- or 36-shot magazine. Parkerized with a folding stock. Introduced in 1983.

NIB	Exc.	V.G.	Good	Fair	Poor
500	450	375	300	250	125

MKE
Ankara, Turkey
Importer - Mandall Shooting Supplies
Scottsdale, Arizona

Kirrikale

A 7.65 or 9mm short semiautomatic pistol with a 4" barrel and 7-shot magazine. It is an unauthorized copy of the Walther PP. Blued with plastic grips.

NIB	Exc.	V.G.	Good	Fair	Poor
400	350	275	225	150	100

M.O.A. CORP.
Maximum Dayton, Ohio

A single shot pistol manufactured in a variety of calibers from .22 rimfire to .454 Casull with an 8.5", 10", or 14" barrel, adjustable sights, stainless steel receiver blued barrel and walnut grip. Introduced in 1986.

NIB	Exc.	V.G.	Good	Fair	Poor
800	600	475	325	250	—

NOTE: Add $75 for stainless steel barrel.

Carbine

As above with an 18" barrel. Manufactured during 1986 and 1987.

NIB	Exc.	V.G.	Good	Fair	Poor
900	675	525	350	275	—

MACNAUGHTON & SON
Edinburg, Scotland-Carrizo Springs, Texas
SEE—British Double Guns

MADSEN
Copenhagen, Denmark

Model 47

Exc.	V.G.	Good	Fair	Poor
500	425	300	—	—

NOTE: Add $75 for rifles with numbered matching bayonet.

MAGNUM RESEARCH, INC.
SEE ALSO—Desert Eagle

Magnum BFR Maxine
This is a single action revolver with a long cylinder chambered for .45 Long Colt or .410 with 7.5" barrel or .45-70 caliber with 7.5" or 10" barrel and .444 Marlin with 10" barrel. Fitted with adjustable sights and stainless steel finish. Introduced in 1998.

NIB	Exc.	V.G.	Good	Fair	Poor
1000	750	550	—		

Magnum BFR Little Max
This single action revolver has a standard cylinder chambered for the .454 Casul (6.5", 7.5", or 10" barrel), .45 Long Colt (6.5" or 7.5" barrel), .22 Hornet (7.5" barrel), or .50 A.E (7.5" barrel). Introduced in 1998.

NIB	Exc.	V.G.	Good	Fair	Poor
1000	750	550	—		

MAKAROV
Former Soviet Union, Warsaw Pact Nations, and China
Importer - Century International Arms Co.
St. Albans, Vermont

NOTE: For history, technical data, descriptions, and prices see the *Standard Catalog of Military Firearms, 1870 to the Present* under Russia.

MALIN, F. E.
London, England
Importer - Cape Horn Outfitters
Charlotte, North Carolina

Boxlock and sidelock shotguns made by Malin were imported into the United States for a number of years. As these arms were all essentially built to specific customer's requirements, standard values cannot be provided. Prospective purchasers are advised to secure a qualified appraisal prior to acquisition.

Boxlock
Features an Anson & Deeley action and high-grade walnut. All other specification were on a custom-order basis. This gun should definitely be individually appraised as values will fluctuate greatly with options.

Basic Model Estimated Value Only
NIB	Exc.	V.G.	Good	Fair	Poor
4000	3500	3000	2500	1850	1000

Sidelock
Features a Holland & Holland-type detachable sidelock action, and all other features (as on the boxlock) were on a custom-order basis. This model should also be appraised individually.

Basic Model Estimated Value Only
NIB	Exc.	V.G.	Good	Fair	Poor
5500	5000	4250	3000	2500	1250

MALTBY, HENLEY AND CO.
New York, New York

Spencer Safety Hammerless Revolver
A .32 caliber double action revolver with a 3" barrel and 5-shot cylinder. The frame and barrel made of brass and the cylinder of steel. The barrel marked "Spencer Safety Hammerless Pat. Jan. 24, 1888 & Oct. 29, 1889." Several thousand were manufactured during the 1890s.

Courtesy Mike Stuckslager

Exc.	V.G.	Good	Fair	Poor
—	350	225	125	75

MANHATTAN FIREARMS COMPANY
Norwich, Connecticut
Newark, New Jersey

Bar Hammer Pistol
A .31, .34, or .36 caliber single shot percussion pistol with a 2" or 4" barrel. The hammer marked "Manhattan F.A. Mfg. Co. New York." Blued with walnut grips. Approximately 1,500 were made during the 1850s.

Exc.	V.G.	Good	Fair	Poor
—	—	400	250	150

Shotgun Hammer Pistol
A .36 caliber bar hammer single shot percussion pistol with a 5.5" half octagonal barrel marked as above. Blued with walnut grips. Approximately 500 were made.

Exc.	V.G.	Good	Fair	Poor
—	600	375	225	175

Pepperbox
A .28 or .31 caliber double action percussion pepperbox with 3", 4", or 5" barrels and 5- or 6-shot barrel groups. Blued, case hardened with walnut grips. Marked as above and also "Cast Steel". The major variations of this pistol are as follows:

Courtesy Milwaukee Public Museum, Milwaukee, Wisconsin

Three-shot with 3" Barrel
Manually rotated barrels.

Exc.	V.G.	Good	Fair	Poor
—	—	750	450	350

Five-shot with 3", 4", 5" Barrel
Automatically rotated barrels.

Exc.	V.G.	Good	Fair	Poor
—	—	650	350	250

Six-shot with 3" or 4" Barrel
Automatic rotation.

Exc.	V.G.	Good	Fair	Poor
—	—	650	350	250

Six-shot with 5" Barrel
Automatic rotation.

Exc.	V.G.	Good	Fair	Poor
—	—	750	450	350

Pocket Revolver
A .31 caliber percussion revolver with a 4", 5", or 6" barrel and either 5-shot or 6-shot cylinder. Blued, case hardened with walnut grips. The barrel marked, "Manhattan Firearms/Manufg. Co. New York" on the 5-shot model, serial numbers from 1 to approximately 1,000, and "Manhattan Firearms Mfg. Co. New York" on the 6-shot model. The frame marked "December 27, 1859".

Courtesy Milwaukee Public Museum, Milwaukee, Wisconsin

First Model - 5-Shot

Exc.	V.G.	Good	Fair	Poor
—	—	600	250	150

Second Model - 6-Shot

Exc.	V.G.	Good	Fair	Poor
—	—	550	200	100

London Pistol Company
As above, but marked "London Pistol Company". Approximately 200 manufactured between 1859 and 1861.

Exc.	V.G.	Good	Fair	Poor
—	—	900	400	200

.36 Caliber Percussion Revolver
A .36 caliber percussion revolver with a 4", 5", or 6.5" octagonal barrel and 5- or 6-shot cylinder. Blued, case hardened with walnut grips. Approximately 78,000 were made between 1859 and 1868. There were five variations—see below.

Courtesy Milwaukee Public Museum, Milwaukee, Wisconsin

Model I
A 5-shot cylinder marked "Manhattan Firearms Mfg. Co. New York." The serial numbers from 1 through 4200. The 6" barreled version would be worth a 15% premium.

Exc.	V.G.	Good	Fair	Poor
—	—	850	400	250

Model II
As above with the 1859 patent date marked on the barrel. The serial range is 4200 to 14500.

Exc.	V.G.	Good	Fair	Poor
—	—	700	300	200

Model III
A 5-shot cylinder and marked, "Manhattan Firearms Co. Newark NJ," together with the 1859 patent date. The serial numbers are from 14500 to 45200.

Exc.	V.G.	Good	Fair	Poor
—	—	700	300	150

Model IV
As above, with a modified recoil shield and the patent date March 8, 1864, added to the barrel inscription. Serial numbers from 45200 to 69200.

Exc.	V.G.	Good	Fair	Poor
—	—	700	300	150

Model V
As above, with a 6-shot cylinder and numbered 1 to approximately 9000.

Exc.	V.G.	Good	Fair	Poor
—	—	750	350	200

.22 Caliber Pocket Revolver
A .22 caliber spur trigger revolver with a 3" barrel and 7-shot cylinder. Blued, silver plated with walnut or rosewood grips. Approximately 17,000 were made during the 1860s.

Courtesy Milwaukee Public Museum, Milwaukee, Wisconsin

Exc.	V.G.	Good	Fair	Poor
—	—	400	200	100

Manhattan-American Standard Hero
A .34 caliber single shot percussion pistol with a 2" or 3" round barrel that unscrews for loading. Blued, brass frame with walnut grips. Marked "A.S.T. Co./HERO". Made by the American Standard Tool Company, Manhattan's successor. Approximately 30,000 manufactured between 1868 and 1873.

Manhattan Manufactured
Marked, "HERO/M.F.A.Co." Approximately 5,000 were produced.

Exc.	V.G.	Good	Fair	Poor
—	—	250	150	100

American Standard Manufactured
Approximately 25,000 were produced.

Exc.	V.G.	Good	Fair	Poor
—	—	200	100	75

MANN, FRITZ
Suhl, Germany

6.35mm Pocket Pistol
A 6.35mm caliber semiautomatic pistol with a 1.65" barrel and 5-shot magazine. Blued with plastic grips having the name "Mann" cast in them. This pistol, which weighs only 9 oz., is

one of the smallest semiautomatic pistols ever manufactured. Made between 1920 and 1922.

Exc.	V.G.	Good	Fair	Poor
325	250	200	150	100

7.65mm Pocket Pistol
A 7.65mm or 9mm short semiautomatic pistol with a 2.35" barrel and 5-shot magazine. Blued with plastic grips having the name "Mann" cast in them. Manufactured between 1924 and 1929.

Exc.	V.G.	Good	Fair	Poor
375	300	250	200	125

MANNLICHER PISTOL
Steyr, Austria
SEE—Steyr

MANNLICHER SCHOENAUER
Steyr, Austria

NOTE: For military models and their history, technical data, descriptions, and prices see the *Standard Catalog of Military Firearms, 1870 to the Present* under Austria-Hungry.

High Velocity Rifle
As above, but in 7x64mm Brenneke, .30-06, 8x60Smm Magnum, 9.3x62mm, and the 10.75x68mm caliber with a 23.5" barrel and folding-leafsight. Half-length walnut stock.

Takedown Model-Add 75%.

Exc.	V.G.	Good	Fair	Poor
2750	2250	1750	1000	500

All of the above models were discontinued prior to WWII.

Model 1950
A .257 Roberts, .270 Winchester, and the .30-06 caliber bolt action rifle with a 24" barrel and 5-shot rotary magazine. Blued with a half length walnut stock. Manufactured between 1950 and 1952.

Exc.	V.G.	Good	Fair	Poor
1250	1000	800	650	450

Model 1950 Carbine
As above, with a 20" barrel and a full-length stock.

Exc.	V.G.	Good	Fair	Poor
1300	1050	900	700	350

Model 1950 6.5 Carbine
As above, in 6.5x54mm Mannlicher Schoenauer caliber with a 18.5" barrel and full-length stock.

Exc.	V.G.	Good	Fair	Poor
1500	1100	850	650	300

Model 1952
Similar to the above, with a turned back bold handle. Manufactured between 1952 and 1956.

Exc.	V.G.	Good	Fair	Poor
1500	1200	1000	750	600

Model 1952 Carbine
Similar to the Model 1950 carbine, but additionally in 7x57mm caliber. Manufactured between 1952 and 1956.

Exc.	V.G.	Good	Fair	Poor
1500	1200	1000	750	600

Model 1952 6.5mm Carbine
As above, in 6.5x54mm Mannlicher Schoenauer caliber with an 18.5" barrel. Manufactured between 1952 and 1956.

Exc.	V.G.	Good	Fair	Poor
1500	1100	850	650	300

Model 1956 Rifle
A .243 or .30-06 caliber bolt action rifle with a 22" barrel and Monte Carlo-style stock. Manufactured between 1956 and 1960.

Exc.	V.G.	Good	Fair	Poor
1250	1100	900	700	600

Model 1956 Carbine
As above, with a 20" barrel and full-length stock. Manufactured between 1956 and 1960.

Exc.	V.G.	Good	Fair	Poor
1450	1100	900	700	600

Model 1961 MCA Rifle
As above, but modified for easier use with a telescopic sight.

Exc.	V.G.	Good	Fair	Poor
1450	1250	1100	700	600

Model 1961 MCA Carbine
As above, with a 20" barrel and half-length stock.

Exc.	V.G.	Good	Fair	Poor
1300	1200	1000	650	550

Model M72 LM Rifle
Fitted with a 23" fluted barrel, double set or single trigger and full-length stock. Manufactured between 1972 and 1980.

Exc.	V.G.	Good	Fair	Poor
1100	850	650	500	400

WHAT'S IT LIKE—THE MANNLICHER-SCHOENAUER

As a kid, I occasionally would come across a Stoeger catalog. In it, I would marvel over the many strange (to me at least) and wonderful imported firearms. One model that was of particular interest to me was a beautiful carbine type rifle made in Austria. It was called the Mannlicher-Schoenauer. Even though I had never seen an actual example of such a rifle, the photos of the various models in the catalog kept me enthralled. It wasn't until years later that I actually had a chance to play with one.

The company was started by Ferdinand Ritter Von Mannlicher and Otto Schoenauer in 1903. Although there have been numerous changes over the years, they are still in production (as the Steyr-Mannlicher) even today. The pre-WWII and early post-WWII models are the ones that I am most familiar with. Even though the rifle earned its enviable reputation in the carbine version, a few full length rifles were also produced. All featured the split bridge action that was both a bane and a blessing. The good news is that, paired with the M/S rotary magazine, it was silky smooth to operate. The down side was that it was a bear to mount a scope on without resorting to very special and expensive mounts. The rifle predated lightweight mountain rifles so popular today by several decades—actually, almost a century. It was such a rifle though and the jaegers (hunters) hunting in the Alps demanded them for that reason. The little 18 inch barreled rifle chambered for the metric 6.5mm cartridge was particularly popular among Alpine hunters. It was and is a wonderful rifle, one of the best—and a joy to shoot and even more so, to carry.

Tom Turpin

For Currently Imported Mannlicher Rifles-see Steyr

MANUFRANCE
St. Etienne, France
SEE—Le Francais

Auto Stand
A .22 caliber semiautomatic pistol manufactured by Pyrenees and sold by Manufrance under the trade name Auto Stand.

Exc.	V.G.	Good	Fair	Poor
250	225	200	150	100

Buffalo Stand
A .22 caliber bolt action pistol with a 12" barrel and adjustable sights. Blued with a walnut stock. Manufactured prior to 1914.

Exc.	V.G.	Good	Fair	Poor
250	225	200	150	100

Le Agent
An 8mm caliber double action revolver with a 5" barrel. Blued with walnut grips.

Exc.	V.G.	Good	Fair	Poor
200	100	175	150	75

Le Colonial
As above, with an enclosed hammer.

Exc.	V.G.	Good	Fair	Poor
200	175	150	100	75

MANURHIN
Mulhouse, France

This company manufactured the Walther PP and PPK models under license and these are marked "Manufacture de Machines du Haut-Rhin" on the left front of the slide and "Lic Excl. Walther" on the left rear. These arms were imported into the U.S.A. in the early 1950s by Thalson Import Company of San Francisco, California, and later by Interarms. The latter are marked "Mark 11" and "Made in France."

New Production
Currently, the Matra Manurhin Defense Corp. is manufacturing handguns, and they are imported by Atlantic Business Organizations of New York.

Model 73 Defense Revolver
A .38 Special or .357 Magnum caliber double action swing-out cylinder revolver with a 2.5", 3", or 4" barrel having fixed sights. Blued with walnut grips.

NIB	Exc.	V.G.	Good	Fair	Poor
1150	1000	850	750	500	350

Model 73 Gendarmerie
As above, with a 5.5", 6", or 8" long barrel and adjustable sights.

NIB	Exc.	V.G.	Good	Fair	Poor
1250	1100	900	800	550	400

Model 73 Sport
Similar to the above, with a shortened lock time and target style adjustable sights.

NIB	Exc.	V.G.	Good	Fair	Poor
1250	1100	900	800	550	400

Model 73 Convertible
As above, with interchangeable .22, .32, or .38 caliber barrels and cylinders.

NIB	Exc.	V.G.	Good	Fair	Poor
2250	1850	1600	1400	950	750

Model 73 Silhouette
Similar to the Model 73 Sport, but in .22 to .357 Magnum caliber with a 10" or 10.75" shrouded barrel and formfitting walnut grips,

NIB	Exc.	V.G.	Good	Fair	Poor
1200	1050	850	750	500	350

Model PP
Similar to the Walther Model PP, with a revised safety.

Exc.	V.G.	Good	Fair	Poor
400	350	300	225	150

Model PPK/S

Similar to the Walther Model PPK/S, with a revised safety.

Exc.	V.G.	Good	Fair	Poor
400	350	300	225	150

Model PP Sports

This is a target version of the PP chambered for the .22 caliber shell. Available in various barrel lengths.

Exc.	V.G.	Good	Fair	Poor
400	350	300	225	150

MARATHON PRODUCTS, INC.
Santa Barbara, California

.22 First Shot

A .22 caliber single shot bolt action rifle with a 16.5" barrel and overall length of 31". Blued with a walnut stock. Manufactured between 1985 and 1987.

Exc.	V.G.	Good	Fair	Poor
75	55	45	30	25

.22 Super Shot

As above, with a 24" barrel. Manufactured between 1985 and 1987.

Exc.	V.G.	Good	Fair	Poor
75	55	45	30	25

.22 Hot Shot Pistol

A .22 caliber bolt action pistol with a 14.5" barrel. Blued with a walnut stock. Manufactured in 1986 and 1987.

Exc.	V.G.	Good	Fair	Poor
75	55	45	30	25

Centerfire Rifle

A bolt action sporting rifle manufactured in a variety of calibers with a 24" barrel, open sights, adjustable trigger and 5-shot magazine. Blued with a walnut stock. Manufactured in 1985 and 1986.

Exc.	V.G.	Good	Fair	Poor
325	250	200	150	125

MARBLE'S ARMS & MFG. CO.
Gladstone, Michigan

Marble's Game Getter Gun NFA, CURIO OR RELIC

The Game Getter has 12", 15", or 18" separated over/under rifled/smooth bore barrels in .22/.44 or .22/.410, a manually pivoted hammer striker to select the upper or lower barrel, an attached folding steel skeleton stock, and is intended to be fired from the shoulder. The tip-up barrels are opened by pulling back the triggerguard. Two versions, Model 1908 and Model 1921, indicating their first years of production, were made. Both apparently were designed by Webster L. Marble (1854-1930), and manufactured by Marble Safety Axe Co. of Gladstone, Michigan, which became Marble's Arms & Mfg. Co. in 1911.

A Marble's Game Getter Model 1908 sold at auction for $3,162.50. Chambered for .22 rimfire over .44 smooth-bore. Barrels are 18". Tang sight. Original folding stock and original leather holster. Condition was excellent. Amoskeag Auction Co. Inc., March 2000

Marble's suspended sales of the Game Getter in the United States after the Treasury Department ruled it was a "firearm" under the NFA, but continued sales abroad. Its retail price in 1934 was about $24 (12" or 15" barrels) to $26 (18" barrels). The Bureau of Internal Revenue removed the 18" barrel variation from the NFA in a Letter Ruling dated March 1, 1939. Today, the 12" and 15" barrel variations are controlled under the NFA in the "any other weapon" category. If the shoulder stock is removed from a 12", 15", or 18" barreled Game Getter, however, ATF has ruled it to be an NFA "firearm" subject to a $200 transfer tax.

Model 1908, serial numbered from A to M; then 001 to 10000

Exc.	V.G.	Good	Fair	Poor
1,500	900	750	550	425

Model 1921, serial numbered from 10001 to 20076

Exc	V.G.	Good	Fair	Poor
900	750	550	450	375

NOTE: Boxed guns (wooden box, Model 1908; cardboard box, Model 1921) with accessories, or 18" barrel variations, nonstandard calibers (.25-20, .32-20, .38-40, etc.) command premiums of 50 to 200 percent or more; an original holster is $75 to $150. Two new-in-box Model 1908 with 15" and 18" barrels sold for $2,700 and $3,600, respectively, in 1994. An original wooden Model 1908 box alone may sell for $500 to $900. All 18" barrel variations are rare.

The Model 1908 was available in two variations. Model 1908A has a flexible rear tang sight, and the Model 1908B has a filler block. Some confusion about the serial numbering exists because some Marbles factory representatives gave out incorrect information during the 1960s and 1970s. According to some letters from this period on Marble's factory letterhead, serial numbers began with number 700 and ended with 9999. Original factory records, however, disclose that the Model 1908 was first shipped from the factory in 1909, and serial numbered with letters from A through M, before beginning numerically with serial number 001 through 10000, when production ended in May, 1914. Serial number 001 was shipped from the factory on March 3, 1909, and the last Model 1908 was shipped on May 22, 1918.

The markings on the Model 1908 are:

	Type I (serial 1 to about 4000)	Type II (about serial 4000 to 9999)
LEFT SIDE:	**MANUFACTURED BY THE** MARBLE SAFETY AXE CO. GLADSTONE, MICH. U.S.A. **MARBLE ARMS & MFG. CO.**	**MANUFACTURED BY THE** MARBLE SAFETY AXE CO. GLADSTONE, MICH. U.S.A. SUCCESSOR
RIGHT SIDE:	*Calibers 22 & 44* *Patent Allowed*	*Calibers 22 & 44* *Patent Allowed*

Each of the markings on the right side is enclosed within an elongated circle.

OTHER CHARACTERISTICS: Separate flat buttplate attached with two screws up to approximately serial number 1200; afterwards, a flattened buttplate was integrally formed from the same round steel used to form the skeleton stock. Early stocks have drop adjustment with a knurled collar 3/8" diameter by 13/16" long; at approximately serial number 2500, the collar was changed to 1/2" by 5/8" long. The hammer spur is curved down up to approximately serial number 2,000, then the curve at hammer is up.

The Model 1908 was originally designed for .22 Short, Long or Long Rifle and .44 shot and ball ammunition, but the most satisfactory load was the long-cased .44-40 that held the shot in place with a disk and mouth crimp. The 1915 Marble's catalog stated the Model 1908 was available for use with the 2" .410 shotgun shell; chambering is slightly different from that of the .44-40, but is seldom encountered.

Production of the Model 1908 was not resumed because of World War I. To meet the continuing demand for this extremely popular firearm, Marble's produced an entirely new gun in 1921. The grip, folding stock (made from cold-rolled sheet metal and nickel-plated), and other features were redesigned. The serial number range for the Model 1921 is 10001 (shipped in October 1921) to 20076. Most production of the Model 1921 apparently ended around the time of World War II; however, factory records disclose that Marble's was exporting 15" barrel Model 1921s into Canada in 1955, where their registration was not required at that time. Marble's also assembled approximately 200 Model 1921s from parts circa 1960-61, and sold them (without the holster) for $200 each.

The Model 1921 was originally designed from the 2" .410 shotgun shell, but Marble's changed the extractor marking on some guns to 2-1/2" or 2 1/2" to indicate factory rechambering for the 2.5" shell, which has been reported to have started in 1924. However, the change to a 2-1/2" chamber may not have been uniform, because both 2" and 2-1/2" marked guns have been observed in low (14000) and high (19000) serial number ranges. The lowest serial number with 2" marking observed so far is 14601. The range from approximately 14500 to 17000 have plastic rather than walnut grips, a single-bladed rear sight rather than multiple-blade, and blued rather than case-hardened hammer. Outside this range, only 19288 has the 2" marking; and number 19692 is marked 2-1/2". No Model 1921 Game Getters are known to have been factory chambered for the 3" .410 shell.

The markings on the Model 1921 are:

The markings on the Model 1921 are:

LEFT SIDE: **MARBLE'S**

 Game Getter Gun

Marble Arms & Mfg.Co.

 Gladstone, Mich.U.S.A.

RIGHT SIDE: ***UPPER BARREL 22 S.L. LR.&N.R.A***

LOWER BARREL .44GG & .410 2"

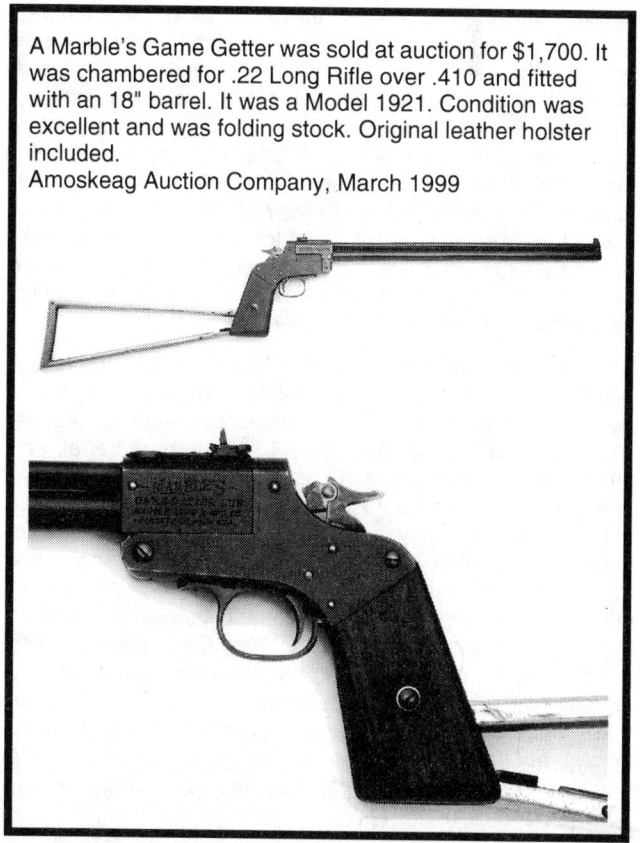

A Marble's Game Getter was sold at auction for $1,700. It was chambered for .22 Long Rifle over .410 and fitted with an 18" barrel. It was a Model 1921. Condition was excellent and was folding stock. Original leather holster included.
Amoskeag Auction Company, March 1999

OTHER CHARACTERISTICS: Other barrel markings for the Model 1921 in .410 are *.410 2-1/2"* and *.410 2-1/2"*; the latter appears in the serial number range from approximately 15000 to 16600, and in the low 19000 range. Plastic grips were used in the serial range from approximately 14600 to 17000.

The Model 1921 was originally designed for the 2" .410 shotgun shell, but Marble's changed the extractor marking on some guns to **2-1/2"** or **2-1/2"** to indicate factory rechambering for the 2.5" shell, apparently on a random or special-order basis (both 2" and 2-1/2" marked guns have been observed in low (14000) and high (19000) serial number ranges). The lowest serial number with 2?" marking observed so far is 14601. The range from approximately 14500 to 17000 have plastic rather than walnut grips, single-bladed rear sight rather than multiple-blades, and blued rather than case hardened hammer. Outside this range, only 19288 has the 2?" marking; number 19692 is marked **2-1/2"**. No Model 1921 Game Getters are known to have been factory chambered for the 3" .410 shell.

Marble's Game Getter Pistol and other special-order or experimental Game Getters NFA, CURIO OR RELIC

Contemporary articles and advertisements in *Hunter-Trader-Trapper*, and some early Marble's catalogs, state that a small number of Model 1908 Game Getters were originally manufactured (with rifled barrels) for .25-20, .32-20, and .38-40 cartridges. An illustrated advertisement in a 1910 issue of *Hunter-Trapper-Trader* states that 12", 15" and 18" barrel Game Getters were available for delivery in .25-20, .32-20 and .38-40, and that these firearms were designed as over-and-under rifles with rifled barrels. An article in the October 1913 issue of *Outdoor Life* states that Marble's was manufacturing a Game Getter pistol, with 10" barrels, and that any barrel length could be ordered.

Original factory records have confirmed the manufacture of the foregoing Game Getters, and clarified their designs. All original guns are thus correctly classified as experimental or special-order guns, and all are extremely rare. Factory records disclose that about 20 each of the Model 1908 were manufactured with .22/25-20 and .22/.32-20 over-and-under rifled barrels, but the barrel lengths are not specified. No .22/.38-40 Model 1908 Game Getters are listed in the factory records, but that may not have precluded a later factory alteration to that configuration. It is important to note that any Model 1908 Game Getter with over-and-under rifled barrels less than 18" in length is currently subject to registration under the NFA as a short barreled rifle, with a $200 transfer tax. Under current law, if these firearms are not registered they are contraband and cannot be legally owned unless ATF administratively removes them from the NFA as collector's items.

Factory records disclose that eight Model 1908 Game Getter pistols were manufactured, and all were shipped to a Minneapolis hardware store. Two specimens have been located: serial number 3810, with a 8" .22/.44 smooth bore barrel, and serial number 3837, with a 10" .22/.44 smooth bore barrel. Inspection of serial numbers 3810 and 3837 (including removal of the grips) reveal they were never fitted with shoulder stocks, because the portion of the frame which would have accommodated the stock was never machined out to receive one. Under current law, an original Marble's Game Getter pistol is subject to registration under the NFA as an "Any Other Weapon" with a $5 transfer tax. According to very incomplete factory records, a relatively small number—about a dozen—Model 1921 Game Getters were manufactured with .22/.38-40 rifled barrels, but the barrel lengths are not specified. It is possible that other factory-original configurations exist, such as .22/.25-20 and others.

MARGOLIN
Tula, Soviet State Arsenal

Model MT Sports

This is a semiautomatic .22 caliber pistol with no barrel weights and is not threaded for a compensator. Barrel length is 7.5". Furnished with a black plastic case with spare magazine and repair parts.

Courtesy Orvel Reichert

Exc.	V.G.	Good	Fair	Poor
600	500	400	300	200

Model MTS- I

A .22 short semiautomatic pistol with a 5.9" barrel having an integral muzzle brake (7.4" overall), adjustable walnut grips and a 6-shot magazine. Normally, accompanied by a wooden case with cleaning accessories.

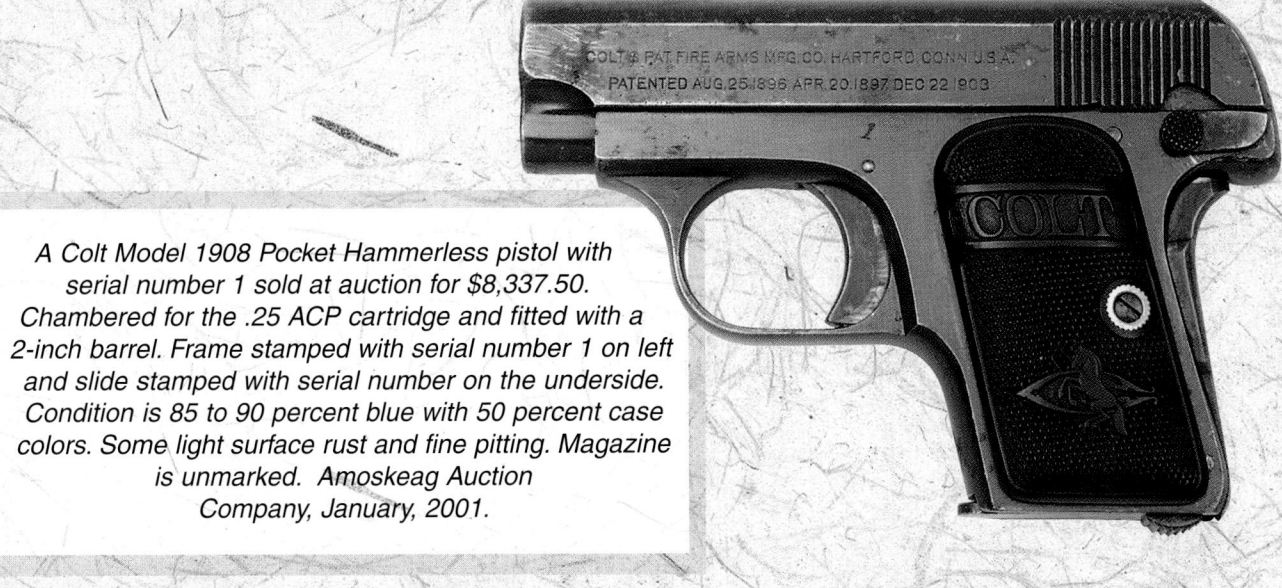

A Colt Model 1908 Pocket Hammerless pistol with serial number 1 sold at auction for $8,337.50. Chambered for the .25 ACP cartridge and fitted with a 2-inch barrel. Frame stamped with serial number 1 on left and slide stamped with serial number on the underside. Condition is 85 to 90 percent blue with 50 percent case colors. Some light surface rust and fine pitting. Magazine is unmarked. *Amoskeag Auction Company, January, 2001.*

Three examples of the engraving and gold inlay of Wilbur A. Glahn. At top, Police, engraved (grade C), N. R. Webster inscription gold inlaid, checkered f Hoegee Company, Los Angeles, California, February 16, 1931.

At center, Officers Model Target revolver number 515559; inscribed on the b gold and silver plated, ivory grips with steerhead motif relief carved on each *Hunter, Trader, and Trapper* magazine.

Bottom, Police Positive Special number 363377; engraved in grade 2½; shipp 1928. The gun is cased, and on the lid is a large silver plaque indicating prese Clarence M. Dunbar from his friends. *(David S. Woloch Collection/Photograph, Ti*

290

A cased factory engraved gold inlaid Colt Official Police revolver was sold at auction for $25,300. Chambered for the .38 Long Colt cartridge and fitted with a 6-inch barrel. Ivory grips. Full coverage engraving with gold inlays and the inscription, "N.R. WEBSTER/COMM. OF POLICE/LOS ANGELES". Condition is mint blue. Appears unfired. Cased. *Rock Island Auction Company, September, 2001.*

A Colt Model 1877 Lightning revolver sold at auction for $12,650. London agency cased. Chambered for .38 caliber and fitted with a 4.4-inch barrel. Nickel finish. Two-piece hard rubber grips. Condition is as new and unfired as is the case. Butterfield & Butterfield, December, 2000.

A factory engraved and gold inlaid Winchester Model 1886 rifle was sold at auction for $57,750. Chambered for the 45-70 cartridge with half octagon barrel, checkered stock, pistol grip, Lyman hunting front sight, flat top sporting rear sight, 2/3 magazine, shotgun butt with rubber plate, and inscription engraved. Engraving is scroll and game scenes with gold inlaid line work surrounding the inscription with the name, "George W. La Rue, 1895". Signed by Ulrich. Condition is 95 percent blue and about 85 percent case colors. Stock is very good to excellent. Little John's Auction Service, Inc., May, 2001.

A factory engraved deluxe Maynard carbine sold at auction for $17,250. Fitted with a 20 inch half round barrel chambered for .50 caliber. Scroll engraved frame with game scenes. Vernier tang sight. Deluxe burl walnut stock with engraved patchbox. Condition is excellent with about 95 percent finish. Butterfield & Butterfield, December, 2000.

A factory engraved Colt Model 1855 Root Sidehammer with Charter Oak grips sold at auction for $23,000. Fitted with a 28 caliber 3.5-inch barrel. Frame, topstrap, loading lever, hammer, and backstrap full scroll engraved. Grips mounted with silver medallion inscribed: "Sylvester Bliss presented by Col. Colt Aug. 1857-Stock of The Charter Oak". Cased with accessories. Condition is very good with some light pitting. Butterfield & Butterfield, December, 2000.

A cased pair of Smith & Wesson Model No. 2 Army revolvers sold at auction for $12,925. Fitted with 6-inch barrel and chambered for .32 caliber. Nickel plated finish. Rosewood grips. Cased with oiler and UMC cartridge box. Condition is excellent with 98 percent finish. Butterfield & Butterfield, February, 2001.

A Nimschke-engraved Smith & Wesson No. 2 Army revolver with mother-of-pearl grips sold at auction for $40,625. Fitted with 6-inch barrel chambered for .32 caliber. Frame with full scroll engraving and scroll down barrel flats. Carved mother-of-pearl grips. Case is burl wood with ivory mountings. Condition is 97 percent finish with excellent grips. Butterfield & Butterfield, February, 2001.

A cased pair of Smith & Wesson Model No. 2 Army revolvers were sold at auction for $26,250. Fitted with 6-inch barrels and chambered for .32 caliber. Blued finish. Rosewood grips. English oak case with cleaning rod, screwdriver, UMC cartridge box. Also extra un-numbered cylinder. Condition is 75 percent blue on barrels and frame with 95 percent blue on cylinders. Excellent grips. Case very good. Butterfield & Butterfield, February, 2001.

Winchester Model 1890 Deluxe Grade sold at auction for $14,950. Second Model case colored frame, and 24-inch barrel. Checkered butt stock and slide handle with deluxe walnut. About 255 Deluxe Model 1890 rifles were built with pistol grip. Condition is very good with 95 percent blue and 90 percent case colors. Butterfield & Butterfield, December, 2000.

A Colt single action Buntline revolver sold at auction for $165,000. It is chambered for the .44 caliber cartridge and is fitted with a 10-inch barrel. It also has an original nickel plated shoulder stock. Revolver is furnished with factory original peep and globe sights. Shipped in 1878 from Colt. Condition is 85 percent original blue with about 65 percent case colors. Grips have about 85 percent original varnish. Little John's Auction Service Inc., May, 2001.

A 1st Model Manhattan .22 caliber revolver was sold at auction for $209,000. Inscribed on the backstrap "B.G. George A. Custer from U.S.V. 1863". Condition is 45 percent thinning blue. Pearl grips are very good. A Civil War period writing desk included along with velvet lined gutta percha case. Little John's Auction Service, Inc., May, 2001.

O.F Winchester
New Haven, Ct
U.S.A.

F WINCHESTER.
Magazine Fire-Arm.

Patented

Oliver Fisher Winchester

An 1860 Henry rifle was sold at auction for $143,000. This rifle is inscribed, "O.F. Winchester, New Haven, CT, U.S.A.". The rifle is also fitted with a prototype magazine cut-off feature. Condition is about 55 percent blue with very good wood. Bore is excellent. Little John's Auction Service, Inc., May, 2001.

An Ithaca 4E Grade single barrel trap gun owned by Annie Oakley was sold at auction for $43,125. Gun was fitted with 32-inch barrel chambered for 12 gauge. Double ivory sights. Scroll engraved frame. Monte Carlo stock with pistol grip. Built in 1916. Condition is very good with 90 percent blue with some light pitting. Butterfield & Butterfield, December, 2000.

A Winchester Model 21 Grand American was sold at auction for $40,250. Engraved by Winchester factory engraver Nick Kusmit and fitted with three barrels: two 20-gauge and one .410 bore. All barrels are 28 inches with vent ribs. Cased. Condition is near mint. Rock Island Auction Company, October, 2000.

A Colt single action pinch-frame revolver was sold at auction for $264,000. Serial number 14. Unaltered original .44 S&S caliber. Condition is 15 percent blue on barrels with 75 percent case colors on frame. Grips are 85 percent original varnish. Little John's Auction Service, Inc., May, 2001.

TEN BEST ARMS
AWARD

NRA   2000   NRA

A deluxe engraved 1860 Henry sold at auction for
$115,500. Chambered for the .44 rimfire cartridge and fur-
nished with original silver plated frame and deluxe walnut
stock. Condition is 90 percent original silver plate with
near 98 percent original varnish. Blue is about 90 percent.
Little John's Auction Service, Inc., May, 2001.

A Smith & Wesson 1st Model American revolver sold at auction for $143,000. It was the property of western lawman and gunfighter Dallas Stoudenmire. Condition is 95 percent nickel with some lifting. Original ivory grips have some minor cracking. Little John's Auction Service, Inc., May, 2001.

A Winchester Model 1894 saddle ring carbine sold at auction for $16,675. Serial number 46. Chambered for the 38-55 cartridge and fitted with a 20-inch barrel with excellent bore. Factory records show that this was the first Model 1894 carbine built at the factory. Condition is 95 percent blue with some faint rust. Stock has 95 percent finish. All original. Amoskeag Auction Company, March, 2001

A Colt Bisley flat-top revolver with long flutes sold at auction for $28,750. Fitted with a 7.5-inch barrel and chambered for the 45 Colt cartridge. Condition is excellent with 97 percent blue and vivid case colors on hammer. Rock Island Auction Company, April, 2001.

An engraved Model 1861 Colt Navy revolver sold at auction for $172,500. Engraved extra-deluxe by Gustave Young with almost full coverage. There are a total of eleven animals engraved inside the scroll; each is crying. Cased with accessories. Condition is excellent with 97 percent blue and 90 percent case colors. Checkered ivory grips are excellent. Rosewood case is excellent. Rock Island Auction Company, September, 2001.

A factory inscribed Colt Single Action Army revolver was sold at auction for $50,000. Chambered for .45 Colt Cartridge and fitted with a 4.75-inch barrel. Ivory grips. Inscribed to, "PAUL SPOFFORD PEARSALL/ROUGH RIDER U.S.A.". Shipped 1911. No front sight. Condition is excellent with 99 percent blue, 99 percent case colors and excellent ivory grips. Rock Island Auction Company, September, 2001.

A Colt Single Action Army sold at auction for $14,950. Shipped in 1915 and fitted with a 4.75-inch barrel and chambered for the .38-40 cartridge. Cylinder has long flutes. Furnished with original box. Condition is 97 percent blue on barrel and 90 percent on cylinder. Case colors are about 95 percent. Rock Island Auction Company, April, 2001.

Courtesy Orvel Reichert

Exc.	V.G.	Good	Fair	Poor
800	700	600	450	350

Model MTS-2

As above, in .22 l.r. with a 5.9" barrel.

Exc.	V.G.	Good	Fair	Poor
800	700	600	450	350

Courtesy Orvel Reichert

The above photos are of an unusual Margolin .22 caliber Olympic Model with wrap around square barrel weights and wooden case.

MARIETTE BREVETTE
Liege, Belgium

A number of European manufacturers produced percussion pepperbox pistols based upon a patent issued to Mariette during the 1840s and 1850s. These pistols have detachable barrels that are loaded at the breech, double action ring triggers, and internally mounted hammers. They are normally blued and foliate engraved.

6 Barrel Pepperbox

Exc.	V.G.	Good	Fair	Poor
—	—	2000	900	400

4 Barreled Pepperbox

Exc.	V.G.	Good	Fair	Poor
—	—	2000	900	400

MARLIN FIREARMS CO.
New Haven, Connecticut

Ballard Rifles

Established by John Mahlon Marlin in 1863. Marlin manufactured pistols until 1875 when he began production of Ballard rifles. In 1881 he made his first lever action repeating rifle for which his company became famous.

The Marlin Firearms Company has the distinction of being the oldest family owned firearms company in the United States.

The Ballard single shot rifle was invented by C.H. Ballard of Worcester, Massachusetts. It was patented in 1861. The first of the Ballard rifles was manufactured by the Ball and Williams Co. of Worchester, Massachusetts. In 1866 Merwin and Bray purchased the firm, calling it Merrimack Arms Company, and operated until 1869, when they sold it to the Brown Manufacturing Company of New York City. This venture took a decidedly negative turn, and in 1873 mortgage foreclosure forced the sale to Schoverling and Daly of New York City. These gentlemen were arms dealers, not manufacturers, so they entered into an agreement with John M. Marlin to produce the Ballard rifle. The rifles produced during this period are regarded as some of the finest single shots ever made, and the venture finally became successful. In 1881 the business became incorporated as the Marlin Firearms Company, and the Ballard was produced under this banner until it was discontinued around the year 1891. The popularity of the repeating rifle simply eroded the demand for the fine single shot until it was no longer a profitable venture.

BALL & WILLIAMS BALLARDS
First Model

This model was the first Ballard produced. It was introduced in 1861 and was offered with a 24" or 28" octagonal barrel. The frame is case colored, and the barrel is blued. The walnut stock is varnished. The major identifying feature of this model is the inside extractor. This was the only Ballard that had this feature before Marlin began to manufacture the rifle in 1875. The barrel is stamped "Ball & Williams/Worchester, Mass."

and "Ballards Patent/Nov. 5, 1861." There were approximately 100 manufactured and serial numbered from 1-100.

Exc.	V.G.	Good	Fair	Poor
—	—	1500	800	400

Military Rifle

There is not enough known about these rifles and probably never will be. They were chambered most frequently for the .44 and .54 rimfire cartridges and feature the outside tangs and extractors. They were offered with a 30" round barrel and full-length forearm. There are three barrel bands and sling swivels. The government ordered only 35 of these for use in the Civil War; and if one was to be definitely authenticated as a genuine martial specimen, it would be quite valuable. Many of these rifles were marked "Kentucky" on top of the receiver because the militia of that state armed its men with the Ballard rifles and carbines. This marking was a sales aid used by the company and does not indicate militia ownership. The amount manufactured is not known. Barrel markings are as on the First Model.

Exc.	V.G.	Good	Fair	Poor
—	—	1000	500	250

Civil War Military Carbine

This model has a 22" part-round, part-octagonal barrel and is chambered for the .44 rimfire cartridge. It has the outside tang and extractor. The stock and forearm are walnut with a barrel band sling swivel. The buttstock bears an oval cartouche surrounding the inspector's marks, "MM." These letters also appear stamped on major metal parts. There were 1,509 ordered by the government for use in the Civil War. The barrel was marked the same as the rifle.

Exc.	V.G.	Good	Fair	Poor
—	—	1000	500	250

Sporting Rifle

This model is chambered for the .32, .38, and .44 rimfire cartridges. The octagonal barrel is 24", 26", or 28" in length and is blued. The frame is case colored. The stock and forearm are varnished walnut, and there is a knob that protrudes in front of the frame to operate the outside manual extractor. There is a crescent buttplate standard. There were approximately 6,500 manufactured, and barrel markings are the same as on the First Model.

Exc.	V.G.	Good	Fair	Poor
—	—	750	400	200

Sporting Carbine

This model is similar in appearance to the Sporting Rifle with a 22" part-round, part-octagonal barrel. It is chambered for the .44 and .54 caliber cartridge, and the sling swivel is found on a barrel band in the front. The knob on the bottom activates the outside extractor. There have been some encountered with "Kentucky" stamped on the top, but this does not affect the value. The markings are the same as on the previous models. There are no production figures available, but some estimate approximately 2,000 were manufactured.

Exc.	V.G.	Good	Fair	Poor
—	—	1000	500	250

Dual Ignition System

This system allows the use of the rimfire cartridge or percussion method by simply turning the striker on the hammer from one position to the other. This model features a percussion nipple mounted on the breechblock, and the hammer is marked "Patented Jan. 5, 1864." The patent was held by Merwin and Bray. This swivel system is usually found on the sporting models and would increase the value of the weapon by 20 percent.

Merrimack Arms Co. and Brown Manufacturing Co.

The values for the Ballard rifles manufactured by these two firms are the same, and the specifications are similar. The

identifying difference is in the markings, "Merrimack Arms & Mfg. Co./Newburyport Mass." or "Brown Mfg. Co. Newburyport, Mass." Merrimack produced approximately 3,000 of these rifles between 1867 and 1869 serial numbered in the 18000-20000 range. Brown produced approximately 1,800 between 1869 and 1873 in the 20000-22000 serial number range.

Sporting Rifle

This model was produced in .22 (rare), .32, .38, .44, .46, and .52 caliber rimfire or percussion, as most encountered featured the dual ignition system and had the nipple in the breechblock. They have either a round or octagonal barrel in 24", 26", or 28" lengths. The appearance and finish is similar to the Ball & Williams rifles; and the major difference is the inside tang. The extractor was still outside mounted and manually activated. Exact production breakdown is unknown. There is no premium for the dual ignition system on these later guns.

Exc.	V.G.	Good	Fair	Poor
—	—	750	350	200

Sporting Carbine

This model is quite similar in appearance to the Sporting Rifle, with a 22" part-round, part-octagonal barrel.

Exc.	V.G.	Good	Fair	Poor
—	—	950	550	300

Military Rifle

The Military Rifle is similar to the sporting version except that it has a 30" round barrel and full-length forearm with three barrel bands. It is chambered for the .44 and .52 caliber rimfire or percussion with the dual ignition system.

Exc.	V.G.	Good	Fair	Poor
—	—	1100	550	300

Shotgun

This model is similar to the Sporting Rifle in appearance but is chambered for 24 gauge, with a 30" round barrel. There is a groove milled in the top of the frame to use as a sight. The buttplate is shotgun-style instead of the usual crescent shape.

Exc.	V.G.	Good	Fair	Poor
—	—	550	300	200

Marlin-Ballard Rifles

Commencing in 1875 the Ballard single-shot rifle was made by John Marlin for Schoverling and Daly. In 1881 the business was incorporated and became the Marlin Firearms Co. All the Ballards made from then until 1891, when they were discontinued, were produced under this banner. The only real difference in the rifles manufactured during these periods was in the markings. The earlier rifles are stamped "J.M. Marlin New Haven. Conn. U.S.A./Ballards Patent. Nov. 5, 1861"; and the post-1881 models are stamped "Marlin Firearms Co. New Haven Ct. U.S.A./Patented Feb. 9, 1875/Ballards Patent Nov. 5, 1861." The major difference between Marlin-made Ballards and the earlier models is the inside tang and the internal extractor on the Marlin-made rifles. All of the Marlin-made Ballards have an octagonal frame top, and the Marlin Firearms Co. models have grooved receiver sides. The standard finish on all these later rifles is case colored frames and blued octagonal or part-round, part-octagonal barrels. There are many variations in these rifles as to types of sights, stock, engraving, and other special order features-such as barrel lengths, weights, and contours. These rifles must be considered individually and competently appraised. There is also the fact that many of these Ballards have been rebarreled and rechambered over the years, as they were known for their shooting ability and were used quite extensively. This can seriously affect the value in a negative manner unless it can be authenticated that the work was done by the likes of Harry Pope or

George Schoyen and other noted and respected gunsmiths of that era. This can add considerably to the value of the rifle. One must approach this model with caution and learn all that can be learned before purchasing.

Ballard Hunters Rifle

This model resembles the earlier Brown Manufacturing Company rifles, and it utilizes many leftover parts acquired by Marlin. It is chambered for the .32, .38, and .44 rimfire and centerfire and features John Marlin's unique reversible firing pin that allows the same gun to use both rimfire and centerfire ammunition simply by rotating the firing pin in the breechblock. This model still had the external ejector and bears the J.M. Marlin markings. There were approximately 500 manufactured in the 1 to 500 serial range. They were produced in 1875 and 1876.

Exc.	V.G.	Good	Fair	Poor
—	—	1750	800	400

Ballard No. I Hunters Rifle

This model bears the early J.M. Marlin marking only, as it was manufactured from 1876 until 1880 and was discontinued before the incorporation. It has a 26", 28", and 30" barrel and is chambered for the .44 rimfire or centerfire cartridge. It has the reversible firing pin and also the new internal extractor. Production figures are not available, but the serial number range is between 500 and 4000.

Exc.	V.G.	Good	Fair	Poor
—	1750	650	300	100

Ballard No. 1-1/2 Hunters Rifle

This model is similar to the No. 1 except that it is chambered for the .45-70, .40-63, and the .40-65 cartridges and does not have the reversible firing pin. The barrel length is 30" and 32". It was manufactured between 1879 and 1883. This model is found with both early and later markings.

Exc.	V.G.	Good	Fair	Poor
—	2500	1200	700	300

Ballard No. 1-3/4 "Far West" Hunters Rifle

This model was made by J. M. Marlin only and is similar to the 1-1/2, the difference being the addition of double-set triggers and a ring on the opening lever. It was manufactured in 1880 and 1881.

Exc.	V.G.	Good	Fair	Poor
—	2500	1200	700	300

Ballard No. 2 Sporting Rifle

This model is chambered for the .32, .38 rimfire or centerfire cartridges, and the .44 centerfire. It has the reversible firing pin and was offered in 26", 28", and 30" barrel lengths. This model features "Rocky Mountain" sights and was manufactured between 1876 and 1891. It is found with both early and late markings.

Courtesy Milwaukee Public Museum, Milwaukee, Wisconsin

Exc.	V.G.	Good	Fair	Poor
—	1250	600	300	100

Ballard No. 3 Gallery Rifle

This model is similar to the No. 2 rifle but is chambered for the .22 rimfire cartridge and has a manually operated external extractor. The sights are the same; and a 24" barrel was offered in addition to the 26", 28", and 30". This rifle was manufactured between 1876 and 1891.

Exc.	V.G.	Good	Fair	Poor
1700	1250	600	300	100

Ballard No. 3F Gallery Rifle

This is a deluxe version of the No. 3. It has a pistol grip stock, a nickel-plated Schutzen-style buttplate, and an opening lever like a repeating rifle. It features a 26" octagonal barrel and an oil-finished stock. It was manufactured in the late 1880s and is quite scarce in today's market.

Exc.	V.G.	Good	Fair	Poor
3200	2500	1000	550	250

Ballard No. 4 Perfection Rifle

This model is chambered for a number of centerfire calibers from .32-40 to .50-70. The barrel lengths are from 26" to 30", and the sights are of the "Rocky Mountain" type. This model was manufactured between 1876 and 1891.

Exc.	V.G.	Good	Fair	Poor
—	2500	1000	550	250

Ballard No. 3-1/2 Target Rifle

This model is similar to the No. 4 Perfection Rifle except that it has a checkered stock with a shotgun-style buttplate, a 30" barrel, and a tang peep sight with globe front sight. It was chambered for the .40-65 cartridge and was manufactured from 1880-1882.

Exc.	V.G.	Good	Fair	Poor
—	2500	1000	550	250

Ballard No. 4-1/2 Mid Range Rifle

This model is also a variation of the No. 4 Perfection model. It has a higher-grade checkered stock with a shotgun buttplate. It has a 30" part-round, part-octagonal barrel and is chambered for the .38-40, .40-65, and the .45-70 cartridges. It features a Vernier tang peep sight and a globe front sight. It was manufactured between 1878 and 1882.

Exc.	V.G.	Good	Fair	Poor
—	2800	1500	800	400

Ballard No. 4-1/2 A-1 Mid Range Target Rifle

This is a deluxe version of the No. 4-1/2 rifle. It features scroll engraving on the frame with "Ballard A-1" on the left and "Mid-Range" on the right. It is chambered for the .38-50 and the .40-65 cartridge and has a high-grade checkered stock with a horn forend tip. The sights are the highest-grade Vernier tang sight and a spirit lever front sight. The shotgun or rifle-style butt was optional. This model was manufactured between 1878 and 1880.

Courtesy Milwaukee Public Museum, Milwaukee, Wisconsin

Exc.	V.G.	Good	Fair	Poor
—	5000	2250	1150	500

Ballard No. 5 Pacific Rifle

This model has a 30" or 32" medium to heavyweight barrel, with a ramrod mounted underneath. It is chambered for many different calibers from .38-50 to .50-70. This model features "Rocky Mountain" sights, a crescent butt, double-set triggers, and a ring-style opening lever. It was manufactured between 1876 and 1891.

Courtesy Milwaukee Public Museum, Milwaukee, Wisconsin

Exc.	V.G.	Good	Fair	Poor
—	2800	1500	800	400

Ballard No. 5-1/2 Montana Rifle

This model is similar to the Pacific Rifle, with an extra heavy-weight barrel, and is chambered for the .45 Sharps cartridge only. It features a checkered steel shotgun-style buttplate. It was manufactured from 1882-1884 and has the late markings only.

Courtesy Milwaukee Public Museum, Milwaukee, Wisconsin

Exc.	V.G.	Good	Fair	Poor
—	6500	2850	1300	650

Ballard No. 6 Schuetzen Off Hand Rifle

This model has a 30" or 32" octagonal barrel and is chambered for the .40-65, .44-75, and the .38-50 cartridges. The stock is of select walnut in the high-combed Schuetzen style. The buttplate is nickel-plated, and the receiver is not engraved. The sights are Vernier tang type on the rear and a spirit lever front. The triggers are double set, and the opening lever has a ring and a spur. This model is marked J.M. Marlin only and was manufactured between 1876 and 1880.

Exc.	V.G.	Good	Fair	Poor
—	5000	2250	1150	500

Ballard No. 6 Schuetzen Rifle

This model is similar to the Off Hand model but was produced by the later Marlin Firearms Company and was so marked. It is a more deluxe version with checkered stock, horn forend tip, and a fully engraved receiver. This model was chambered for the .32-40 and the .38-55 cartridges and was manufactured between 1881 and 1891.

Courtesy Milwaukee Public Museum, Milwaukee, Wisconsin

Courtesy Milwaukee Public Museum, Milwaukee, Wisconsin

Exc.	V.G.	Good	Fair	Poor
—	6250	2850	1300	650

Ballard No. 6-1/2 Off Hand Mid Range Rifle

This model is chambered for the .40-54 Everlasting cartridge only. It has a 28" or 30" part-round, part-octagonal barrel, a Schuetzen-style stock, and a plain non-engraved receiver. It was manufactured between 1880 and 1882.

Exc.	V.G.	Good	Fair	Poor
—	3600	1500	800	500

Ballard No. 6-1/2 Rigby Off Hand Mid Range Rifle

This model is chambered for the .38-50 and the .40-65 cartridges. It features the Rigby ribbed-style barrel in 26" and 28" lengths, with Vernier rear and globe front sights and a high grade, checkered walnut, Schuetzen-style stock with horn forend tip, and pistol grip cap. The buttplate is nickel-plated, and the opening lever is of the ring type with a single trigger and extensively engraved receiver. This model was manufactured from 1880 to 1882.

Exc.	V.G.	Good	Fair	Poor
—	5750	2500	1300	650

Ballard No. 6-1/2 Off Hand Rifle

This model is chambered for the .32-40 and .38-55 cartridges and features barrel lengths of 28" and 30". It has a checkered, high-grade walnut, Schuetzen-style stock with nickel-plated buttplate. The forend tip and pistol grip cap are of horn, and the receiver is engraved. This model has a single trigger, full-ring opening lever, Vernier tang rear sight, and spirit lever front sight. The 6-1/2 Off Hand was made by the Marlin Firearms Company between 1883 and 1891 and is found with the later markings only.

Exc.	V.G.	Good	Fair	Poor
—	5750	2750	1300	650

Ballard No. 7 "Creedmore A-1" Long Range Rifle

This model is commonly chambered for the .44-100 or the .45100 cartridges. It has a 34" part-round, part-octagonal barrel and a high grade checkered pistol grip stock, with a horn forend tip and shotgun-style butt. The sights are a special 1,300-yard Vernier tang rear and a spirit level front. There is another sight base on the heel of the stock for mounting the rear sight for ultra long-range shooting. The opening lever is similar to a repeating rifle, and a single trigger is featured. The receiver is engraved and marked "Ballard A-1" on the left and "Long Range" on the right. This model was manufactured between 1876 and 1886 and is found with both early and late markings.

Courtesy Milwaukee Public Museum, Milwaukee, Wisconsin

Exc.	V.G.	Good	Fair	Poor
—	6250	2850	1500	700

Ballard No. 7 Long Range Rifle

This model is similar to the "Creedmore A-1" but is slightly less deluxe. The engraving is less elaborate, and the lettering on the receiver is absent. This model was manufactured between 1883 and 1890 and is found with the later markings only.

Exc.	V.G.	Good	Fair	Poor
—	6250	2850	1500	700

Ballard No. 7A-1 Long Range Rifle

This model is a higher grade version of the "Creedmore A-I," with fancier walnut and a checkered straight stock. Better sights and deluxe engraving are also featured. This model was manufactured between 1879 and 1883 and is found with both markings.

Exc.	V.G.	Good	Fair	Poor
—	6250	2850	1500	700

Ballard No. 7A-1 Extra Long Range Rifle
This is the highest grade version of the No. 7 rifles. It features a 34" "Rigby"-type ribbed, round barrel. This was usually a special-order rifle with most features to customer specifications. The model was manufactured in limited numbers between 1879 and 1883. It is found with both markings.

Exc.	V.G.	Good	Fair	Poor
—	7250	3500	2000	700

Ballard No. 8 Union Hill Rifle
This model has a 28" and 30" part-round, part-octagonal barrel and is chambered for the .32-40 and the .38-55 cartridges. It has a checkered pistol grip stock with nickel-plated buttplate; and the opening lever is fully enclosed ring, as on the repeaters. There is a double-set trigger and a tang peep with globe front sight. The receiver is not engraved. This model was manufactured between 1884 and 1890 and is found only with the late markings. This was one of the most popular rifles in the Ballard line.

Courtesy Milwaukee Public Museum, Milwaukee, Wisconsin

Exc.	V.G.	Good	Fair	Poor
—	3250	1500	750	300

Ballard No. 9 Union Hill Rifle
This model is similar to the No. 8 except that it features a single trigger and better sights. It was manufactured between 1884 and 1891 and has the later markings only.

Courtesy Butterfield & Butterfield, San Francisco, California

Exc.	V.G.	Good	Fair	Poor
—	2950	1250	650	300

Ballard No. 10 Schuetzen Junior Rifle
This model is simply a heavier barreled version of the No. 9. The barrel is 32" long, and the checkered pistol grip stock is of the off-hand style. The rear sight is a Vernier Mid Range model, and the front sight is a spirit-level type. This was a popular model that was manufactured between 1885 and 1891. It is found with the later markings only.

Exc.	V.G.	Good	Fair	Poor
—	3500	1500	850	400

MARLIN HANDGUNS
The first firearm that was manufactured by John M. Marlin was actually a derringer-type single shot that was small enough to be hidden in the palm of the hand. From this beginning evolved the company that became known for its highly accurate and dependable rifles. The Marlin Company manufactured handguns up to the turn of the century, discontinuing their last and only double action model in 1899.

1st Model Derringer

Courtesy Milwaukee Public Museum, Milwaukee, Wisconsin

This was the first handgun produced by Marlin. The barrel is 2-1/16" long and pivots to the side for loading. There is a plunger under the frame that is depressed to free the barrel. This device is a Ballard patent. This pistol is chambered for the .22 rimfire cartridge, and there is no extractor. The frame is brass and usually nickel-plated. It has two grooves milled beneath the blued barrel. The grips are of rosewood. The barrel is stamped "J.M. Marlin, New Haven, Ct." There were approximately 2,000 manufactured between 1863 and 1867. They are quite scarce on today's market.

Exc.	V.G.	Good	Fair	Poor
—	—	550	250	100

O.K. Model Derringer
The O.K. Model is chambered for .22, .30, and .32 rimfire cartridges. The barrel is 2-1/8" or 3-1/8" on the .32. There is no extractor, and it functions as the 1st Model. The frame is plated brass with flat sides, and the barrel is found either blued or nickel-plated. The grips are rosewood. The markings are the same as on the 1st Model but are located on the right side of the barrel. The top of the barrel is marked "O.K." There were approximately 5,000 manufactured between 1863 and 1870.

Exc.	V.G.	Good	Fair	Poor
—	—	450	225	100

Victor Model Derringer
This model is similar in appearance to the "O.K." Model but is larger in size and is chambered for the .38-caliber rimfire cartridge. The barrel is 2 11/16" long; and there was, for the first time, an extractor. The finish and function were unchanged. The right side of the barrel is stamped "J.M. Marlin/New Haven, Ct./Pat. April 5.1870." "Victor" is stamped on the top of the barrel. There were approximately 4,000 manufactured between 1870 and 1881.

Exc.	V.G.	Good	Fair	Poor
—	—	750	300	150

Nevermiss Model Derringer
This model was made in three different sizes chambered for the .22, .32, and .41 rimfire cartridges. The barrel is 2.5" long and swings sideways for loading. The frame is plated brass, and the barrels are either blued or nickel-plated. The grips are rosewood. The frame is grooved under the barrels as on the 1st model. There is an extractor on this model. The barrel markings are the same as on the "Victor," with the top of the barrel marked "Nevermiss." There were approximately 5,000 manufactured between 1870 and 1881.

.22 Caliber Model

Exc.	V.G.	Good	Fair	Poor
—	—	500	300	100

.32 Caliber Model

Exc.	V.G.	Good	Fair	Poor
—	—	400	250	100

.41 Caliber Model

Exc.	V.G.	Good	Fair	Poor
—	—	1500	800	400

Stonewall Model Derringer

This model is identical to the .41-caliber "Nevermiss," but the top of the barrel is marked "Stonewall." It is rarely encountered.

Exc.	V.G.	Good	Fair	Poor
—	—	2500	1500	650

O.K. Pocket Revolver

This is a solid-frame, spur-trigger, single action revolver chambered for the .22 rimfire short. The round barrel is 2.25", and the 7-shot cylinder is unfluted. The frame is nickel-plated brass with a blue or nickel-plated barrel, and the bird's-head grips are rosewood. The cylinder pin is removable and is used to knock the empty cases out of the cylinder. The top of the barrel is marked "O.K." and "J.M. Marlin. New Haven, Conn. U.S.A." There were approximately 1,500 manufactured between 1870 and 1875.

Exc.	V.G.	Good	Fair	Poor
—	500	250	125	75

Little Joker Revolver

This model is similar in appearance to the "O.K." Model except that it features engraving and ivory or pearl grips. There were approximately 500 manufactured between 1871 and 1873.

Exc.	V.G.	Good	Fair	Poor
—	600	300	150	100

J. M. MARLIN STANDARD POCKET REVOLVERS

In 1872 Marlin began production of its Smith & Wesson look-alike. The Manhattan Firearms Company had developed a copy of the Model 1 S&W .22 cartridge revolver. In 1868 the company ceased business, and the revolvers were produced by the American Standard Tool Company until their dissolution in 1873. In 1872 Marlin had entered into an agreement with this company to manufacture these revolvers, which were no longer protected by the Rollin White patent after 1869. The Marlin revolvers are similar to those made by American Standard, the only real difference being that Marlin grips are of the bird's-head round configuration. A contoured grip frame and a patented pawl spring mechanism is utilized on the Marlin revolvers.

Marlin XXX Standard 1872 Pocket Revolver

This is the first in the series of four Standard model revolvers. It is chambered for the .30 caliber rimfire. The earlier model has an octagonal 3-1/8" barrel; and the later, a round 3" barrel. There are round and octagonal barrel variations (with unfluted cylinder) and round barrel variations (with short and long fluted cylinders). All of the barrels are ribbed and tip up for loading. They have plated brass frames, and the barrels are nickel-plated. The bird's-head grips are of rosewood or hard rubber, bearing the monogram "M.F.A. Co." inside a star. There is a spur trigger. The markings "J.M. Marlin-New Haven Ct." appear on the earlier octagonal barreled models. "U.S.A. Pat. July 1. 1873" was added to the later round barreled models. All barrels are marked "XXX Standard 1872." There were approximately 5,000 of all types manufactured between 1872 and 1887.

Octagon Barrel-Early Variation

Exc.	V.G.	Good	Fair	Poor
—	500	300	150	75

Round Barrel-Non-Fluted Cylinder

Exc.	V.G.	Good	Fair	Poor
—	550	325	175	100

Round Barrel-Short Fluted Cylinder

Exc.	V.G.	Good	Fair	Poor
—	300	150	100	75

Round Barrel-Long Fluted Cylinder

Exc.	V.G.	Good	Fair	Poor
—	300	150	100	75

Marlin XX Standard 1873 Pocket Revolver

This model is similar in appearance to the XXX 1872 model except that it is chambered for the .22 long rimfire and is marked "XX Standard 1873." There are three basic variations: the early octagonal barrel model with non-fluted cylinder, the round barrel model with non-fluted cylinder, and the round barrel with fluted cylinder. Function and features are the same as described for the "XXX Standard 1872" model. There were approximately 5,000 manufactured between 1873 and 1887.

Early Octagon Barrel Model

Exc.	V.G.	Good	Fair	Poor
—	500	250	125	75

Round Barrel-Non-Fluted Cylinder

Exc.	V.G.	Good	Fair	Poor
—	550	275	150	100

Round Barrel-Fluted Cylinder

Exc.	V.G.	Good	Fair	Poor
—	300	150	100	75

Marlin No. 32 Standard 1875 Pocket Revolver

This model is also similar in appearance to the "XXX Standard 1872" model except that it is chambered for the .32 rimfire cartridge. The 3" barrel is round with a rib, and the 5-shot cylinder is fluted and is in two different lengths to accommodate either the .32 Short or Long cartridge. The finish, function, and most markings are the same as on previous models with the exception of the barrel top marking "No. 32 Standard 1875." There were approximately 8,000 manufactured between 1875 and 1887.

Exc.	V.G.	Good	Fair	Poor
—	300	175	125	80

Marlin 38 Standard 1878 Pocket Revolver

This model is different than its predecessors in that it features a steel frame and flat bottom butt, with hard rubber monogram grips. There was still a spur trigger, and the 3.25" ribbed round barrel still tipped up for loading. This model is chambered for the .38 centerfire cartridge. The finish is full nickel plate, and the top of the barrel is marked "38 Standard 1878." There were approximately 9,000 manufactured between 1878 and 1887.

Exc.	V.G.	Good	Fair	Poor
—	400	200	150	75

Marlin 1887 Double Action Revolver

This is the last handgun that Marlin produced and the only double action. It is chambered for the .32 or the .38 caliber centerfire cartridges and is of the break-open auto-ejector type. The fluted cylinder holds 6 shots in .32 and 5 shots in .38 caliber. The round ribbed barrel is 3.25" in length, and the frame is made of steel. The standard finish is nickel-plated with a blued triggerguard. Many full-blued examples have been noted. The round butt grips are hard rubber, and the top of the barrel is marked "Marlin Firearms Co. New Haven Conn. U.S.A./Patented Aug. 9 1887." There were approximately 15,000 manufactured between 1887 and 1899.

Exc.	V.G.	Good	Fair	Poor
—	325	175	100	75

EARLY PRODUCTION MARLIN RIFLES

Model 1881 Lever Action Rifle

This was the first of the Marlin lever action rifles and has always been regarded as a high quality rifle. It is capable of handling the large calibers and was well received by the shooting public. The rifle is chambered for the .32-40, .38-55, .40-60, .45-70, and the .45-85. The 24", 28", or 30" octagonal barrel is standard. Round barrels were offered and are scarce today. There is a tubular magazine beneath the barrel, and the rear sight is the buckhorn type with a blade on the front. This model ejects its empty cartridges from the top. The finish is blued, with a case colored hammer, lever, and buttplate. The walnut stock is varnished. There were approximately 20,000 manufactured between 1881 and 1892 but this is not easy to ascertain, as the factory records on Marlin rifles are quite incomplete.

Courtesy Butterfield & Butterfield, San Francisco, California

Courtesy Butterfield & Butterfield, San Francisco, California

Exc.	V.G.	Good	Fair	Poor
—	1750	1100	600	300

Lightweight Model-Thinner Frame, Lever, and Barrel .32-40 and .38-55 Caliber Only-24" and 28" Barrel

Exc.	V.G.	Good	Fair	Poor
—	1750	750	550	300

NOTE: Add 200-300% premium for 1st Models prior to serial number 600. Add 15% premium for .45-70 caliber.

Model 1888 Lever Action Rifle

This model is chambered for the .32-20, .38-40, and the .44-40 cartridges. This is a shorter action that was designed (chiefly by Lewis Hepburn) to handle the pistol cartridges for which it was chambered. The standard barrel was octagonal, but round barrels were available as special-order items. This is a top ejecting action. It has a buckhorn rear and a blade front sight. The finish is blued with a case colored hammer, lever, and buttplate. The walnut stock is varnished. There were approximately 4,800 manufactured in 1888 and 1889. As with most of these fine old rifles, many special-order options were available that affect today's market value. Individual appraisal would be necessary for these special models, to ascertain both value and authenticity.

Exc.	V.G.	Good	Fair	Poor
—	2500	1100	600	350

NOTE: Add 40% premium for half octagon barrel. Add 20% premium for round barrel.

Model 1889 Lever Action Rifle

This was Marlin's first side-eject, solid-top rifle. It is chambered for .25-20, .32-20, .38-40, and the .44-40 cartridges. It features either octagonal or round barrels in lengths from 24" to 32" with buckhorn rear and blade front sights. The finish is blued with a case colored hammer, lever, and buttplate. The plain walnut stock is varnished. The barrel is stamped "Marlin Fire-Arms Co. New Haven Ct. U.S.A./Patented Oct.11 1887 April 2.1889." This model features a lever latch, and many options were offered. Again one must urge individual appraisal on such variations. Values fluctuate greatly due to some seemingly insignificant variation. There were approximately 55,000 manufactured between 1889 and 1899.

A factory engraved Marlin Model 1889 rifle was sold at auction for $167,500. It was the property of Annie Oakley. Chambered for .32 caliber and fitted with a 22" part round, part octagon barrel. The receiver was scroll engraved and nickel plated. Deluxe walnut stock with fine checkering. Condition was excellent as refinished. Butterfield & Butterfield, February 2000

Production Model 24" Barrel

Exc.	V.G.	Good	Fair	Poor
—	1200	700	350	150

Carbine 20" Barrel and Saddle Ring on Left Side of Receiver

Exc.	V.G.	Good	Fair	Poor
—	1500	800	500	250

Musket 30" Barrel with Full-length Stock-68 Made in .44-40

Exc.	V.G.	Good	Fair	Poor
—	5000	2750	1250	650

Model 1891 Lever Action Rifle

This was Marlin's first rifle designed to fire the .22 rimfire and the first repeating rifle to accept the .22 Short, Long, and Long Rifle cartridges interchangeably. It was also chambered for the .32 rimfire and centerfire. The 24" octagonal barrel is standard, with a buckhorn rear and blade front sight. The finish is blued with a case colored hammer, lever, and buttplate. The stock is plain walnut. The first variation is marked "Marlin Fire-Arms Co. New Haven, Ct. U.S.A./Pat'd Nov.19.1878.April 2.1889. Aug.12 1890" on the barrel, with the solid-topped frame marked "Marlin Safety." The second variation was marked the same with "March 1,1892" added. There were approximately 18,650 manufactured between 1891 and 1897.

1st Variation .22 Rimfire Only-Side Loading-Appr. 5,000

Exc.	V.G.	Good	Fair	Poor
2500	1500	1000	550	300

2nd Variation-.22 and .32 Rimfire, .32 Centerfire, Tube Loading, Model 1891 on Later Model Tangs (3rd variation)

Exc.	V.G.	Good	Fair	Poor
1500	800	500	300	150

NOTE: Add 20% for .22 rifle with "1891" stamped on tang. Deduct 50% for .32 caliber.

Model 1892 Lever Action Rifle

This is basically an improved version of the Model 1891 and is similar to the second variation of the 1891. The only notable exceptions were the tang marking "Model 1892" and "Model 92" on later models. The .22 rimfire was scarce in the Model 1892. There were approximately 45,000 manufactured between 1895 and 1916. There were many options, and these special-order guns must be individually appraised to ascertain value and authenticity.

Antique (Pre-1898)-Add 20%.

Exc.	V.G.	Good	Fair	Poor
1200	700	400	250	150

.32 Rimfire and Centerfire

Exc.	V.G.	Good	Fair	Poor
700	400	200	150	100

Model 1893 Lever Action Rifle

This model was the first rifle Marlin designed for the then new smokeless powder cartridges. It is chambered for the .25-36, .30-30, .32 Special, .32-40, and the .38-55. It was offered standard with either a round or octagonal barrel, in lengths of 24" to 32". Buckhorn rear and blade front sights were also standard. The receiver, lever, hammer, and buttplate are case colored, and the rest is blued. The stock is varnished walnut.

As with all of these early Marlins, many options were offered and, when encountered, will drastically alter the value of the particular rifle. For this reason we supply the values for the basic model and urge securing competent appraisal on non-standard specimens. The barrel on earlier guns is marked "Marlin FireArms Co. New Haven, Ct.U.S.A./ Patented Oct.11. 1887.April 2.1889.Aug.1.1893." In 1919 the markings were changed to "The Marlin Firearms Corporation/ New Haven, Conn.U.S.A.Patented." The rifles manufactured after 1904 are marked "Special Smokeless Steel" on the left side of the barrel. The upper tang is marked "Model 1893" on early guns; and "Model 93," on later specimens. There were approximately 900,000 manufactured between 1893 and 1935. Factory records are incomplete on the Model 1893.

Antique Production Pre-1898

Courtesy Butterfield & Butterfield, San Francisco, California

Exc.	V.G.	Good	Fair	Poor
1600	1000	650	450	275

Modern Production 1899-1935

Exc.	V.G.	Good	Fair	Poor
1400	850	550	350	225

NOTE: Add 100% premium for musket. Deduct 50% for B model with blued receiver.

Model 1894 Lever Action Rifle

This model is similar to the Model 1893, with a shorter action. It is chambered for the .25-20, .32-20, .38-40, and the .44-40. 24" to 32" round or octagonal barrels with full-length magazine tubes are standard, as are buckhorn rear and blade front sights. The finish is case colored receiver, lever, hammer, and buttplate, with the rest blued. The walnut stock is varnished. The first versions were marked "Marlin Fire-Arms Co., New Haven, Ct.U.S.A./Patented Oct.11, 1887. April 2,1889." The top of the frame is marked "Marlin Safety," and the model designation is not stamped on the tang. These early rifles were chambered for .38-40 and .44-40 only. The later rifles added the patent date "Aug. 1, 1893"; and "Model 1894" was stamped on the tang. On the latest versions this was shortened to "Model 94." There were approximately 250,000 manufactured between 1894 and 1935. This model was also produced with a great many options. Individual appraisal should be secured when confronted with these features.

Antique Production (Pre-1898)

Exc.	V.G.	Good	Fair	Poor
1700	1000	650	450	275

Modern Production (1899-1935)
Exc.	V.G.	Good	Fair	Poor
1600	850	550	350	225

NOTE: Add 100% premium for musket. Add 25% premium for saddle ring carbine. Add 30% premium for "Baby" carbine.

Model 1895 Lever Action Rifle

This is a large rifle designed to fire the larger hunting cartridges. It is chambered for the .33 W.C.F., .38-56, .40-65, .40-70, .40-83, .45-70, and the .45-90. It came standard with round or octagonal barrels from 26" to 32" in length. A bull-length magazine tube was also standard, as were buckhorn rear and blade front sights. The finish is case colored receiver, lever, and hammer; the rest is blued with a varnished walnut stock. The barrel markings are the same as the Model 1894, and the top tang is marked "Model 1895." After 1896 "Special Smokeless Steel" was stamped on the barrel. There were also many options available for this model, and they have a big effect on the value. There were approximately 18,000 manufactured between 1895 and 1917.

Antique Production (Pre-1898)
Exc.	V.G.	Good	Fair	Poor
3500	2750	2000	1250	600

Modern Production (1899-1917)

Exc.	V.G.	Good	Fair	Poor
2400	1500	875	650	500

Model 1895M Guide Gun

This lever action model is chambered for the .450 Marlin cartridge and is fittted with a 18.5" barrel. Adjustable rear sight. Blued finish is sandblasted receiver top. Checkered walnut stock is Mar-Shield finish. Weight is about 7 lbs.

NIB	Exc.	V.G.	Good	Fair	Poor
—	—	—	—	—	—

Model 1895 Century Limited

Introduced in 1995 to commemorate the 100th anniversary of the Marlin Model 1895, as well as the 125th anniversary of the Marlin Company. The rifle is chambered for the 45-70 Gov't cartridge. It features a 24" half round/half octagon barrel, a crescent buttplate, semi-fancy American black walnut stock. and French greyed engraved receiver. Production limited to 2,500 guns.

NIB	Exc.	V.G.	Good	Fair	Poor
800	650	500	350	275	200

Model 1897 Lever Action Rifle

This model is an improved version of the Model 1892. It was chambered for the .22 rimfire only and came standard with a 24", 26", or 28" round, octagonal, or part-round, part-octagonal barrel. The standard sights are buckhorn rear and blade front, and all were manufactured as takedown rifles. They have case colored receiver, lever, and hammer. The rest is blued, and the walnut stock is varnished. There were approximately 125,000 manufactured between 1897 and 1917. In 1922 production was begun with the designation changed to Model 39 which is produced to this day. There were also options offered with this rifle that have great effect on the value; take this into consideration and seek qualified appraisal.

NOTE: For First Year Production Antique-Add 40%.

Standard Production Rifle

Exc.	V.G.	Good	Fair	Poor
1500	1000	650	350	200

Deluxe Rifle with checkering and fancy pistol grip stock
Exc.	V.G.	Good	Fair	Poor
2500	1500	850	500	300

MODERN PRODUCTION MARLIN RIFLES

Model 18 Slide Action Rifle

This model is chambered for the .22 rimfire cartridges. It was offered standard with a 20" round or octagonal barrel, open sights, and a straight walnut stock. It has an exposed hammer and blued finish with blued steel buttplate. There is a half-length tubular magazine, and the stock features a quick takedown screw on the top tang which was marked "Model 18." This rifle was manufactured between 1906 and 1909.

Exc.	V.G.	Good	Fair	Poor
350	300	250	150	100

Model 20 Slide Action Rifle

The Model 20 was chambered for the .22 rimfire cartridges and was offered standard with a 24" octagonal barrel and open sight, with an exposed hammer. This rifle was only made as a "Takedown" receiver model and is blued, with a straight walnut stock. It was manufactured between 1907 and 1909.

Exc.	V.G.	Good	Fair	Poor
350	300	250	150	100

Model 25 Slide Action Rifle

This model was chambered for the .22 Short only and was not a commercial success. The 23" round or octagonal barrel is standard, as are open sights. It is called a takedown model, but only the stock is removable—the receiver does not separate. It has an exposed hammer, tubular magazine, and straight walnut stock. The finish is blued. This rifle was manufactured in 1910.

Exc.	V.G.	Good	Fair	Poor
375	325	275	175	125

Model 27 Slide Action Rifle

This is a centerfire rifle chambered for the .25-20 and .32-20 cartridges. It features a 24" octagonal barrel with two-thirds-length magazine tube that holds 7 shots. It has open sights, a blued finish, and straight walnut stock with crescent buttplate. It was manufactured in 1909 only.

Exc.	V.G.	Good	Fair	Poor
350	300	250	150	100

Model 27S Slide Action Rifle

The Model 27S is similar to the Model 27 but with a sliding button on the right side of the receiver that permitted the gun to be opened while a cartridge was in the chamber. It was offered with a round (1913) or octagonal 24" barrel. The .25 rimfire cartridge was added in 1913 to those already available. This model was introduced in 1910 and was manufactured until 1932.

Exc.	V.G.	Good	Fair	Poor
350	300	250	150	100

Model 29 Slide Action Rifle

This model is identical to the Model 20 with a 23" round barrel and smooth walnut forend instead of a grooved one as found on the Model 20. It was manufactured between 1913 and 1916.

Exc.	V.G.	Good	Fair	Poor
350	300	250	150	100

Model 32 Slide Action Rifle

This model was the first of the hammerless slide action rifles. It is chambered for the .22 rimfire and has a 24" octagonal barrel and half-length magazine tube. The Model 32 is a takedown rifle with adjustable sights and features "Ballard" rifling. It is blued, with a pistol grip walnut stock. The advent of WWI and the need for Marlin to produce military arms cut short the production of this model. It was manufactured in 1914 and 1915 only.

Exc.	V.G.	Good	Fair	Poor
450	350	250	150	100

Model 37 Slide Action Rifle

This model is the same as the Model 29 with a 24" round barrel and full-length magazine tube. It was manufactured between 1913 and 1916.

Exc.	V.G.	Good	Fair	Poor
350	300	250	150	100

Model 38 Slide Action Rifle

This was the hammerless model introduced after the end of WWI to replace the Model 32. It is similar in appearance but features a Rocky Mountain adjustable rear and an ivory bead front sight instead of the distinctive round Swebilius sight on the Model 32. The Model 38 was manufactured between 1920 and 1930.

Exc.	V.G.	Good	Fair	Poor
450	350	250	150	100

Model 40 Slide Action Rifle

This model is identical to the Model 27S centerfire rifle except that the barrel is marked "Marlin-Rockwell." The top tang is stamped "Marlin/Mod. 40." This is a rare model, and not many marked in this manner have been noted.

Exc.	V.G.	Good	Fair	Poor
400	300	250	150	100

Model 47 Slide Action Rifle

This model is similar to the Model 20, with a 23" round barrel and an improved magazine tube. The Model 47 has a case colored receiver and a checkered buttstock. This model was not offered for sale nor was it listed in Marlin's catalog but was offered free of charge to anyone purchasing four shares of Marlin stock for $100. One other fact about this model is that it was the first Marlin to be case colored with the new cyanide method; this created a tiger-striped pattern that is peculiar to the Model 47 Rifle.

Exc.	V.G.	Good	Fair	Poor
450	300	250	150	100

Model 1936 Lever Action Rifle or Carbine

This model is a direct descendant of the Model 1893. It is chambered for the .30-30 and the .32 Special cartridge. The stock is streamlined with a pistol grip added and a 20" round barrel. A barrel band and improved sights are utilized. It has a 7-shot tube magazine and a semi-beavertail forearm. The receiver, lever, and hammer are case colored; and the rest is blued. This model was manufactured between 1936 and 1948. It was designated the Model 36 in 1937.

1st Variation (early 1936)

This variation has a slight "fish-belly" forearm, long tang, case colored receiver, lever, and hammer, with no serial number prefix. These are rare.

Exc.	V.G.	Good	Fair	Poor
1000	700	300	175	125

2nd Variation (late 1936-1947)

This variation has thicker forearm, short tang, and "B" serial number prefix.

Exc.	V.G.	Good	Fair	Poor
550	400	250	150	100

Model 36 Lever Action Rifle or Carbine (1937-1948)

First and Second variations both have case colored receiver and "C" serial number prefix. Second variation tapped for receiver sight.

Exc.	V.G.	Good	Fair	Poor
600	450	325	195	125

Third Variation-Blued Receiver

Exc.	V.G.	Good	Fair	Poor
450	325	275	175	100

Model 36 Sporting Carbine

This model is similar to the 1936 Carbine, with a 20" barrel. It features a two-thirds-length magazine tube and holds 6 shots instead of 7. The front sight is a ramp sight with hood.

Exc.	V.G.	Good	Fair	Poor
325	275	225	175	125

Model 36A-DL Lever Action Rifle

This model is similar to the Model 36A, with a deluxe checkered stock. It features sight swivels and is furnished with a leather sling.

Exc.	V.G.	Good	Fair	Poor
675	550	300	225	150

Model 336

Information and prices on the Model 336 were provided by Doug Murray, author and publisher of *The 336* (1983).

Model 336 Carbine (R.C. Regular Carbine)

This model was introduced in 1948 and was an improved version of the Model 36. It features a new-type round bolt, chrome-plated with improved extractor and redesigned cartridge carrier that improved feeding. It is chambered for the .30-30 and the .32 Special cartridges and has a 20" tapered round barrel with Ballard-type rifling. The finish is blued, with the receiver top matted to reduce reflections. The pistol grip stock and semi-beavertail forend are of American walnut. It features Rocky Mountain-style rear and bead front sights, and the hammer is lowered to facilitate scope mounting.

Exc.	V.G.	Good	Fair	Poor
285	200	175	125	100

Model 336C

The same as the Model 336 Carbine. In 1951 the catalog model designation was changed. In 1952 the .35 Remington cartridge was added to the line.

Exc.	V.G.	Good	Fair	Poor
285	200	175	125	100

Model 336A

This model is similar to the 336C, with a 24" barrel and steel forend tip instead of a barrel band. The magazine tube is two-thirds-length and holds 6 shots. This model was introduced in 1948 and built until 1962. It was reintroduced in 1973 and discontinued in 1980.

Exc.	V.G.	Good	Fair	Poor
350	275	200	150	125

Model 336 ADL

This model differs from the Model 336A by having a checkered stock and forend, swivels, better grade walnut stock, and a sling.

Exc.	V.G.	Good	Fair	Poor
475	375	225	150	125

Model 336 SC (Sporting Carbine)

This is basically a 336A with forend tip and two-thirds magazine but has a 20" barrel instead of the 24" found on the 336A.

Exc.	V.G.	Good	Fair	Poor
285	200	175	150	100

Model 336 SD (Sporting Deluxe Carbine)

This is the 336 SC in a deluxe checkered stock version, with swivels and supplied with a sling.

NOTE: This is a scarce model as only 4,392 were built.

Exc.	V.G.	Good	Fair	Poor
750	500	275	175	125

Model 336 Micro Groove Zipper

This model was advertised as a fast-handling, lever action carbine chambered for the .219 Zipper cartridges flat trajectory, varmint-type round. It has a 20" heavy barrel, which was the feature that doomed it to failure as this was too short to coax the maximum performance and accuracy from the cartridge. The "MicroGroove" rifling that was used did not yield long barrel life; and the model survived from 1955 through 1959, when it was discontinued. It is externally similar to the 336 SC.

Exc.	V.G.	Good	Fair	Poor
650	450	300	200	150

NOTE: First few thousand zippers made in standard weight barrels, not heavy weight. These are scarce add 100%.

Model 336T (Texan)

This is a straight-stock version of the 336C, chambered for the .30-30 cartridge, with an 18.5" barrel. It was manufactured from 1954-1983.

Exc.	V.G.	Good	Fair	Poor
250	200	175	125	100

Model 336 DT

A deluxe-stock version of the "Texan," with the map of Texas and a longhorn carved on the butt. It was manufactured between 1962 and 1964.

Exc.	V.G.	Good	Fair	Poor
300	250	225	175	125

Model 336 "Marauder"

This is simply a 336 T with a 16.25" barrel and a slimmer forend. It is chambered for either the .30-30 or .35 Remington cartridges, has a gold trigger, and is drilled and tapped for both scope mounts and receiver sights. It was manufactured in 1963 and 1964.

Exc.	V.G.	Good	Fair	Poor
400	300	200	150	100

Model 336 .44 Magnum

This is the 336 "Marauder" with a 20" Micro-Groove barrel chambered for the .44 Magnum cartridge. It holds 10 shots and was introduced in 1963.

Exc.	V.G.	Good	Fair	Poor
275	250	200	150	100

Model 336 T "Centennial"

In 1970 a 100th year medallion was embedded into the buttstock of every rifle manufactured.

Exc.	V.G.	Good	Fair	Poor
325	250	200	150	100

1970 100th Year Commemorative Matched Pair

This is a deluxe octagonal barreled .30-30 with an engraved receiver and deluxe wood with an inlaid medallion, accompanied by a matching Model 339 .22 rimfire rifle. They are numbered the same and are furnished in a deluxe luggage case. There were 1,000 sets manufactured in 1970. These are commemoratives, and as such it should be noted that collectors usually will only show interest if they are new and uncocked in the original packaging. All accessories and brochures should be included for them to be worth top dollar. Once a commemorative has been used, it has no more value than as a shooter.

NIB	Exc.	V.G.	Good	Fair	Poor
1000	850	650	500	400	300

Model 336 "Zane Grey Century"

This model was introduced in 1972, the 100th anniversary of the birth of Zane Grey, the famous Western author. This model has a 22" octagonal barrel chambered for the .30-30. The stock is high grade walnut and features a brass buttplate and pistol grip cap. A Zane Grey medallion is inlaid into the receiver. There were 10,000 manufactured in 1972. This is a commemorative rifle and must be new in the box to generate the top collector appeal.

NIB	Exc.	V.G.	Good	Fair	Poor
350	300	250	200	150	100

Model 336 Octagon

This model was introduced to utilize the octagonal barrel making equipment that was on hand from the manufacture of the commemoratives. It is essentially a 336T with a 22" tapered octagonal barrel chambered for .30-30 only. It features a full-length magazine tube, slim forend with steel cap, and a classic-style hard rubber buttplate. The walnut stock is straight, and the lever is square. The finish, including the trigger, is blued. This model was made in 1973 only.

NIB	Exc.	V.G.	Good	Fair	Poor
600	500	325	175	150	100

Model 336 ER (Extra Range)

This model was introduced in 1983 and was advertised as being chambered for the .307 Winchester and the .356 Winchester cartridges. The .307 was never produced. The .356 Winchester was supposed to add new capabilities to this classic rifle, but it never caught on with the shooting public and was discontinued in 1986 after only 2,441 Model ERs were manufactured. It has a 20" barrel and 5-shot tube magazine.

Exc.	V.G.	Good	Fair	Poor
500	400	300	250	150

Model 336 CS

This is the current carbine model of this line. It has a hammer-block safety and is chambered for the .30-30, .35 Remington, and until 1988 the .375 Winchester. The barrel is 20", and the magazine tube holds 6 shots. The pistol grip stock and semi-beavertail forearm are American walnut. This model has been manufactured since 1984. The 1983 model was known as the 336C and had no hammer-block safety. Weight is approximately 7 lbs.

NIB	Exc.	V.G.	Good	Fair	Poor
275	225	200	175	150	100

Model 336 LTS

This is the latest version of the old "Marauder" carbine. It was dubbed the LTS or "Lightweight" model instead of the Marauder as it was feared that the latter designation would be inappropriate in today's society. The model features a 16.5" barrel with full-length tube magazine that holds 5 shots. The walnut stock has a straight grip, and there is a barrel band on the forearm. The butt has a rubber rifle pad. This model was introduced in 1988.

NIB	Exc.	V.G.	Good	Fair	Poor
350	300	250	200	150	100

Model 336 Cowboy

This model is similar to the Model 336 CS. It is available in both .30-30 and .38-55 calibers. It is fitted with 24" tapered octagon barrel. Rear sight is Marble buckhorn. Tubular magazine holds 6 rounds. Straight grip walnut stock has a hard rubber buttplate. Weight is about 7.5 lbs. First introduced in 1999.

NIB	Exc.	V.G.	Good	Fair	Poor
650	525	—	—	—	—

WHAT'S IT LIKE: THE MARLIN COWBOY

Several years ago, three of us, Bob Baer, Brian Pearce, and myself, all met with the powers to be at Marlin to discuss what we felt Marlin should consider offering shooters as far as leverguns. The three of us have several things in common not the least of which is our love and appreciation for Marlin lever action rifles. My love affair for Marlins goes way back to my grade school days and Marlin advertisements in Outdoor Life. The Marlin Texan looked to my young eyes like the perfect rifle for wood's use and nothing has happened in these intervening years to change my mind. As the three of us conversed with the men from Marlin we emphasized, among other things, straight grip stocks and the old calibers. I am not going to tell you that we were responsible for the Marlin Cowboy as I am sure they were already thinking in that direction and we just reinforced their thoughts. Whatever the case I am more than happy that the Marlin Cowboy is a reality. The Marlin Cowboy lever action rifles are available in the sixgun chamberings of .357 Magnum, .44 Magnum, .44-40, and .45 Colt as well as the .30-30, .38-55, and .45-70. Without a doubt these are extremely popular leverguns with Cowboy Action Shooters many of whom also uses their leverguns for hunting. Versatility is the watchword as there are four ways to use the Marlin Cowboy and that should be considered a bargain in anyone's book. They can be used with the original sights for Cowboy Action Shooting or tang sights can be added for competition. For hunting use, they are drilled and tapped for either receiver sights or scope mounting using the Marlin base and Weaver rings. Even the old time cowboys did not have this many choices. Now if Marlin would just add the .38-40 to their list of chamberings I would call it perfect!

John Taffin

Model 336M
Introduced in 2000 this model is chambered for the .30-30 cartridge. It features a stainless steel receiver and barrel all other parts are nickel plated. Barrel length is 20". Magazine capacity is 6 rounds. Checkered walnut stock has a Mar-Shield finish. Rubber butt pad. Weight is about 7 lbs.

NIB	Exc.	V.G.	Good	Fair	Poor
—	—	—	—		

Model 336 CC
Chambered for the .30-30 cartridge and fitted with a 20" barrel this model features a Mossy Oak Break-Up camo finish. Adjustable rear sight. Weight is about 7 lbs. Introduced in 2001.

NIB	Exc.	V.G.	Good	Fair	Poor
—	—	—	—		

Model 30 AS
This model is similar to the 336 CS, but the stock is made of walnut-finished hardwood instead of genuine American walnut. It is chambered for .30-30 only.

Marlin 30AS with scope

NIB	Exc.	V.G.	Good	Fair	Poor
285	250	200	175	125	100

Model 375 Lever Action
This model was introduced in 1980. It has a 20" Micro-Groove barrel and is chambered for the .375 Winchester cartridge. This should have been a popular rifle; but perhaps because of difficulty in obtaining ammunition, it was not a commercial success. Its appearance is much the same as the Model 336, with walnut pistol stock and steel forend tip. This model was discontinued in 1983 after 16,315 were manufactured.

Exc.	V.G.	Good	Fair	Poor
350	225	175	125	100

Model 444 Lever Action
This model was introduced in 1965. It is chambered for the .444 Marlin, a large and powerful cartridge that has the capability of dropping any game in North America, theoretically speaking. The rifle is essentially a Model 336 action modified to accept the larger cartridge. It has a 24" round barrel that was cut back to 22" in 1971. It holds 5 shots total and, when introduced, featured a straight-gripped Monte Carlo stock and semi-beavertail forend with barrel band. Another band holds the two-thirds-length magazine tube in place. In 1971 the stock was changed to a pistol grip without the Monte Carlo comb.

Exc.	V.G.	Good	Fair	Poor
325	250	175	125	100

Model 444 S
This model was introduced in 1972 and is essentially the later 444 with a steel forend tip instead of the barrel bands.

Exc.	V.G.	Good	Fair	Poor
250	200	175	150	125

Model 444 SS
In 1984 the company added a crossbolt hammer-block safety to the 444 S and redesignated it the 444 SS. This Model is currently in production.

NIB	Exc.	V.G.	Good	Fair	Poor
395	300	225	175	150	125

Model 444P Outfitter

Introduced in 1999 this model is chambered for the .444 Marlin cartridge. It is fitted with a 18.5" ported barrel. Tubular magazine capacity is 5 rounds. Walnut stock with straight grip and ventilated recoil pad standard. Weight is approximately 6.75 lbs.

NIB	Exc.	V.G.	Good	Fair	Poor
575	450	—	—	—	—

Model 1894 Lever Action

The production of the Model 336 in .44 Magnum was a frustrating experience as the action was simply too long for a short pistol case. In 1969 Marlin reintroduced the Model 1894 chambered for the .44 Magnum cartridge. The barrel is 20", and the full-length magazine tube holds 10 rounds. It features an adjustable rear and a ramp-type front sight. The finish is blued, with a matted receiver top. The walnut stock has a straight grip; and the forend, a barrel band. From 1969 to 1971 there was a brass saddle ring.

NIB	Exc.	V.G.	Good	Fair	Poor
300	275	225	175	125	100

Model 1894 Octagon Barrel

This is basically the same as the Model 1894, with a 20" octagonal barrel and a steel forend tip instead of the barrel band. There were 2,957 manufactured in 1973 only.

Exc.	V.G.	Good	Fair	Poor
375	275	175	125	100

Model 1894 Sporter

This variation has a 20" round barrel, half-length magazine tube that holds 6 shots, and a hard rubber classic-style buttplate. Only 1,398 were manufactured in 1973.

NIB	Exc.	V.G.	Good	Fair	Poor
475	325	250	175	125	100

Model 1894P

This model was introduced in 2000 and is chambered for the .44 Magnum or .44 Special cartridges. Barrel length is 16.25". Magazine capacity is 8 rounds. Adjustable rear sight. Blued finish with bead blasted receiver top. Drilled and tapped for scope mount. Weight is about 5.75 lbs.

NIB	Exc.	V.G.	Good	Fair	Poor
—	—	—	—	—	—

Model 1894 CS Lever Action

This model is chambered for the .38 Special and .357 Magnum cartridges. It features an 18.5" round barrel, with full-length magazine tube and two barrel bands. It holds 9 shots and has a walnut straight-grip stock. This model was manufactured between 1969 and 1984. In 1984 a hammer-block cross-bolt safety was added, and the model number was changed to 1894 CS. All other specifications remained the same.

Exc.	V.G.	Good	Fair	Poor
325	250	175	125	100

Model 1894 M Lever Action Rifle

This model is similar to the other 1894 rifles except that it is chambered for the .22 Magnum cartridge and features an outside loading tube magazine that holds 11 shots. The barrel is 20" long, and there is a steel forend tip instead of a barrel band.

It is important to note that this model will not function properly with any cartridge except the .22 Magnum and that injury could result from attempting to chamber and fire the shorter .22 l.r. This model was manufactured between 1983 and 1988 and was only produced with the crossbolt safety.

Exc.	V.G.	Good	Fair	Poor
275	225	175	150	100

Model 1894 S Lever Action Rifle

This model was introduced in 1984. It is chambered for the .41 Magnum and the .44 Special/.44 Magnum cartridges. In 1988 the .45 Colt chambering was offered. This model has a 20" barrel and a straight-grip stock. The forend has a steel cap. This model is currently produced and features the hammer-block safety.

NIB	Exc.	V.G.	Good	Fair	Poor
350	325	250	200	175	125

Model 1894 CL (Classic) Lever Action Rifle

This model was introduced in 1988 and is the same basic rifle chambered for the old .25-20 and .32-20 cartridges. The rifle is also chambered for the .218 Bee cartridge. The barrel is 22", and the half-length magazine tube holds 6 shots. The walnut stock has no white spacers and has a black buttplate. Discontinued in 1993.

NIB	Exc.	V.G.	Good	Fair	Poor
425	350	250	150	125	100

NOTE: Collector interest has been growing in this model since it was discontinued in 1993.

Model 1894 Century Limited

An anniversary edition of the Marlin Model 1894 is limited to 2,500 rifles chambered in 44/40 caliber. Frame engraved and case colored. It is fitted with a 24" octagon barrel with 10-round magazine tube. The stock is semi-fancy walnut with straight grip and cut checkering with brass crescent buttplate.

NIB	Exc.	V.G.	Good	Fair	Poor
950	700	425	—	—	—

Model 1894 Century Limited Employee Edition

Same as above but limited to 100 rifles. The gun has a finer grade wood and the Marlin Man on the Horse logo is inlaid in gold on the right side of the receiver.

NIB	Exc.	V.G.	Good	Fair	Poor
1500	825	—	—	—	—

Model 1894 Cowboy

Introduced in 1996 this lever action rifle features a 24" tapered octagon barrel with a 10-round tubular magazine. It is chambered for the .45 Long Colt, a popular cartridge for "Cowboy Action Shooting". Straight grip checkered stock with blued steel forearm cap. Weight is approximately 7.5 lbs.

NIB	Exc.	V.G.	Good	Fair	Poor
600	450	300	—	—	—

Model 1894 Cowboy II

Introduced in 1997 and is the same as the Model 1894 Cowboy but is chambered for several cartridges. Available in .44-40, .357 Mag., .38 Special, and .44 Mag/.44 Special.

NIB	Exc.	V.G.	Good	Fair	Poor
600	450	300	—	—	—

Model 1894 CP

This mdoel is chambered for the .375 Magnum cartridge and fitted with a 16.25" ported barrel. Tubular magazine holds 8 rounds. Checkered American black walnut stock. Adjustable semi-buckhorn rear sight. Receiver drilled and tapped for scope mount. Weight is about 5.75 lbs. Introduced in 2001.

NIB	Exc.	V.G.	Good	Fair	Poor
—	—	—	—	—	—

Model 1895 Lever Action SS

The model 1895 was reintroduced on the Model 336 action that had been modified to handle the .45-70 cartridge. This was done to capitalize on the nostalgia wave that descended on the country in the early 1970s. This model features a 22" round barrel with a two-thirds-length magazine tube that holds 4 shots. The walnut stock had a straight grip until the Model 1895 S was released in 1980, when a pistol grip stock was used. In 1983 the Model 1895 SS with the crossbolt hammer-block safety was added; and it is currently produced in this configuration.

Exc.	V.G.	Good	Fair	Poor
350	275	225	150	100

NOTE: For early "B" prefix guns below serial number 12,000 add 25%.

Model 1895 Century Limited

Chambered for the .45-70 cartridge this model features a 4-shot tubular magazine, 24" half round/half octagon barrel, semi-fancy walnut stock with pistol grip. The receiver is French greyed and engraved with the Marlin Man on one side and two bears on the other. Weight is about 7.5 lbs.

NIB	Exc.	V.G.	Good	Fair	Poor
995	750	—	—	—	—

Model 1895 Century Limited Employee Edition

Similar to the above model but limited to 100 rifles. The company logo is inlaid in gold on the right side and the left side has two cow elk and a bull elk.

NIB	Exc.	V.G.	Good	Fair	Poor
1450	—	—	—	—	—

Model 1895G

This model is chambered for the .45-70 Gov't cartridge. It has a 18.5" ported barrel. Straight grip walnut stock with cut checkering and ventilated recoil pad. Adjustable rear sight. Weight is about 6.75 lbs. Introduced in 1998.

NIB	Exc.	V.G.	Good	Fair	Poor
425	350	—	—	—	—

Model 1895 GS

Introduced in 2001 this .45-70 rifle is fitted with a 18.5" ported barrel with 4-round magazine. Stainless steel receiver and barrel. American black walnut stock with cut checkering and ventilated recoil pad. Adjustable rear semi-buckhorn sight. Weight is about 7 lbs.

NIB	Exc.	V.G.	Good	Fair	Poor
—	—	—	—	—

Model 1895 Cowboy

This rifle is chambered for the .45-70 cartridge and fitted with a 26" tapered octagon barrel. Tubular magazine has a 9-round capacity. Adjustable semi-buckhorn rear sight. American black stock with cut checkering. Hard rubber butt. Weight is about 8 lbs. Introduced in 2001.

NIB	Exc.	V.G.	Good	Fair	Poor

Model 1897 Century Limited

Introduced in 1997 this model is chambered for the .22 caliber cartridge and commemorates the 100th anniversary of the Model 1897. It is fitted with a 24" half round/half octagon barrel with adjustable Marble rear sight and Marble front sight with brass bead. Blued receiver is engraved and gold inlayed with semi-fancy walnut stock and hard rubber buttplate. Weight is about 6.5 lbs.

NIB	Exc.	V.G.	Good	Fair	Poor
750	600	—	—	—	—

Model 1897 Century Limited Employee Edition

Similar to the model above but with additional gold engraving on the lever. Limited to 100 rifles.

NIB	Exc.	V.G.	Good	Fair	Poor
1300	—	—	—	—	—

Model 1897 Annie Oakley

Introduced in 1998 this .22 caliber model features an 18.5" tapered octagon barrel, adjustable Marble rear sight and Marble front sight. The Blued receiver is roll engraved with gold signature. Stock is straight grip with blued end cap and hard rubber buttplate. Weight is approximately 5.5 lbs.

NIB	Exc.	V.G.	Good	Fair	Poor
800	650	500	—	—	—

Model 1897 Cowboy

This .22 caliber lever action rifle is fitted with a 24" tapered octagon barrel with adjustable Marble buckhorn sight and Marble front sight with brass bead. Full length tubular magazine holds 26 Shorts, 21 Longs, and 19 Long Rifle cartridges. Walnut straight grip stock with hard rubber buttplate. Weight is 7.5 lbs. Introduced in 1999.

NIB	Exc.	V.G.	Good	Fair	Poor
650	525				

Marlin Glenfield Lever Action Rifles

The Glenfield line of rifles was designed to be sold in large outlet chain stores and were simply cheaper versions that were to be sold for less money. The rifles functioned fine, but birch was used instead of walnut and pressed checkering instead of handcut. These rifles were manufactured under the Glenfield name between 1964 and 1983. There are five models of Lever Action Glenfields: the 36G, 30, 30A, 30 GT, and the 30 AS. They are chambered for the .30-30 cartridge, and the basic differences are slight and, in most cases, merely cosmetic. They are good, serviceable rifles but have little or no collector interest or investment potential.

NIB	Exc.	V.G.	Good	Fair	Poor
150	125	100	90	75	50

Model 30AW

This lever action rifle is chambered for the .30-30 cartridge. It has a 20" barrel and 6-round magazine tube. The stock is walnut finished birch with pistol grip cap and hard rubber buttplate. Introduced in 1998.

NIB	Exc.	V.G.	Good	Fair	Poor
300	250	—	—	—	—

Model 39 Lever Action Rifle

This model originally evolved from the Model 1891 invented by L.L. Hepburn. The 1891 rifle became the 1892 and eventually developed into the takedown Model 1897. The latter two were produced until 1915, when they were discontinued in favor of machine gun production for WWI. In 1922, when the company was sold to John Moran and became the Marlin Firearms Corp., the .22 rimfire lever action was reintroduced as the Model 39. It has been in production in one form or another ever since.

Model 39

As it was introduced in 1922, the Model 39 was chambered for the .22 rimfire and had a 24" octagonal barrel and a takedown receiver. It has a full-length magazine tube which holds 25 shorts, 20 longs, or 18 Long Rifle cartridges. Most Model 39s had a spring-loaded button outer magazine tube release. Very early variations had the Model '97 type knurled latch release. As the Model 39As were being phased in around 1939 many have the more modern removable inner magazine tube. It has a solid top frame and side ejection, a Rocky Mountain rear, and ivory bead front sight. The receiver, lever, and hammer are case colored; the barrel is blued. The pistol grip stock and steel-capped forearm are varnished walnut. This model was manufactured in this form between 1922 and 1938 with a number of options that could affect value and would warrant individual appraisal. Model 39s with a "star" stamped on the tang were considered high grade guns by the factory inspector and will command a premium in better condition examples.

Standard Rifle

Exc.	V.G.	Good	Fair	Poor
1500	850	475	300	200

Deluxe Rifle-Factory checkering, fancy wood & "star" stamp on tang

Exc.	V.G.	Good	Fair	Poor
2500	1500	850	500	300

NOTE: Model 39s made prior to 1932 that have either no prefix or the prefix S to the serial number should not be used with high-speed ammunition. The prefix HS indicates the improved bolt that is safe for this ammunition.

WHAT'S IT LIKE - THE MARLIN MODEL 39

As a kid growing up in eastern Kentucky, my dad could get rid of me all Saturday afternoon for 25 cents. The Saturday afternoon matinee for kids under 12 cost 15 cents, a coke added a nickel and so did a bag of popcorn. Gene Autry, Roy Rogers, William Boyd (a.k.a. Hopalong Cassidy), Lash LaRue, Randolph Scott and many others became my heros. All the movie cowboys were armed with Colt Peacemakers and Winchester Model 92 saddle carbines. How I longed for one of each for myself. Unfortunately, at the time, neither was in production even if I have been fortunate enough to have the purchase price. The closest thing to the saddle carbine was either the Winchester Model 94 - chambered for the .30-30, or the, for me at least much more useful, Marlin Model 39 in .22 rimfire. It would take several years, but I finally got one.

I have always had a fondness for Marlin rifles. The second rifle that I ever owned was a Model 81-DL bolt repeater which dad bought for me when I was somewhere around 8 years old. I still have it. The Model 39 was a much nicer rifle though and filled a nostalgia gap. The action was smooth as glass and the rifle would really shoot. It was my favorite squirrel rifle for a time and I always felt a bit John Wayneish when armed with it. Made of walnut and steel, not plastic and aluminum, it was a fine rifle. When I outgrew the Saturday oaters, my interest in the Marlin waned and I swapped it to something else. I wish I still owned it. Living in Arizona as I now do and in an area where many of the old westerns were filmed, it would come in mighty handy.

Tom Turpin

Model 39A Lever Action Rifle

This is an improved version of the Model 39. It has a heavier, tapered round barrel and semi-beavertail forearm and a redesigned pistol grip stock. The rubber buttplate was replaced by

one of a synthetic fiber; otherwise, specifications were similar to the Model 39. This model was manufactured from 1939 to 1960. Several variations are listed below:

Prewar (1939-1941)-Case colored receiver, no serial number prefix (1939) or "B" prefix (1940-1941)

Exc.	V.G.	Good	Fair	Poor
1200	800	450	250	150

Postwar Variations (1945-1953)-Serial number prefixes up to letter "K"
NOTE: Add 20% premium of C prefix 1st post-war variation with figured wood.

Ballard Type Deep Rifling.

Exc.	V.G.	Good	Fair	Poor
500	375	275	150	100

Postwar Variations (1954-1956)-Serial number prefixes L, M, N, with Micro-Groove barrel

Exc.	V.G.	Good	Fair	Poor
395	275	175	125	100

"Golden 39A's" (1954-1963)-Gold trigger, micro groove rifling Serial number prefixes L through W

Exc.	V.G.	Good	Fair	Poor
395	275	175	125	100

Model 39A Mountie

This is basically a carbine version of the Model 39A. It features a 20" tapered round barrel, straight grip walnut stock, and slimmed-down forearm. It was manufactured between 1953 and 1960.

1st Variation w/K prefix and 24" barrel-fat forearm

Exc.	V.G.	Good	Fair	Poor
600	450	300	—	—

NOTE: Add 20% for slim forearm.

Standard

Exc.	V.G.	Good	Fair	Poor
275	225	175	125	100

Model 39A 1960 Presentation Model

Released in 1960, this was Marlin's 90th Anniversary model. It is similar to the 39A but has a chrome-plated barrel and receiver with a high grade, checkered walnut stock and forend. There is a squirrel carved on the right side of the buttstock. There were 500 produced in 1960. This is a commemorative and as such will be desirable to collectors only if NIB with all boxes and papers with which it was originally sold. Once used, it becomes a shooter and is not easily sold.

NIB	Exc.	V.G.	Good	Fair	Poor
1200	900	500	300	175	125

Model 39M Mountie 1960 Presentation Model

This is the carbine version of the 90th Anniversary model. This is the same as the 39A with a 20" barrel and straight-grip stock. There were 500 of this model manufactured in 1960.

NIB	Exc.	V.G.	Good	Fair	Poor
1200	900	500	300	175	125

Model 39ADL Lever Action Rifle

This model is the same as the 90th Anniversary issue except that it is blued instead of chrome-plated. There were 3,306 manufactured between 1960 and 1963.

NIB	Exc.	V.G.	Good	Fair	Poor
1000	850	500	300	175	125

Golden 39A Lever Action Rifle

This model is similar to the 39A, with a gold-plated trigger and sling swivels. It was manufactured between 1960 and 1983.

Exc.	V.G.	Good	Fair	Poor
200	175	150	100	75

Model 39 Carbine

This is a slimmer, lighter version of the Model 39A. It features a slimmer forend and thinner barrel. There were 12,140 manufactured between 1963 and 1967.

Exc.	V.G.	Good	Fair	Poor
175	150	125	90	60

Model 39 Century Limited

The introduction of this model marked the 100th Anniversary of the Marlin Company. This model features a 20" octagonal barrel with semi-buckhorn rear and brass blade front sight. The stock is fancy walnut, with a straight grip and a brass forend tip and buttplate. There is a medallion inlaid into the right side of the receiver and a brass plate on the stock. There were 34,197 manufactured in 1970. As a commemorative this model needs to be as it came from the factory to command collector interest.

NIB	Exc.	V.G.	Good	Fair	Poor
350	250	200	150	125	100

Model 39A Article II

This model commemorated the National Rifle Association's 100th Anniversary in 1971. It has a 24" octagonal barrel, high grade walnut pistol grip stock, and brass forend tip and buttplate. The right side of the receiver has the NRA's Second Amendment "Right to Keep and Bear Arms" medallion inlaid. There were 6,244 of these .22 rifles manufactured in 1971.

NIB	Exc.	V.G.	Good	Fair	Poor
450	350	200	150	125	100

Model 39M Article II

This model is the same as the Model 39A Article II except that it is a carbine version with a 20" octagonal barrel and a straight grip stock. There were 3,824 manufactured in 1971. As commemoratives NIB condition is essential to collector interest.

NIB	Exc.	V.G.	Good	Fair	Poor
450	350	200	150	125	100

Model 39A Octagon

This model was produced because the company had the machinery and some leftover barrels from the two commemorative models produced in 1970 and 1971. This was a regular production run that was meant to be used and was not a special issue. It has a 24", tapered octagonal barrel and is chambered for the .22 rimfire cartridges. It has a pistol grip walnut stock, with steel forend tip. There were 2,551 manufactured in 1972 and 1973. This was not a commercially successful model, and it was discontinued for that reason.

NIB	Exc.	V.G.	Good	Fair	Poor
750	600	400	250	200	175

Model 39M Octagon

This is the 20", octagonal barreled carbine version with a straight-grip stock. There were 2,140 manufactured in 1973.

NIB	Exc.	V.G.	Good	Fair	Poor
750	600	400	250	200	175

Model 39D Lever Action Rifle

This is essentially the Model 39M carbine, 20" barrel version with a pistol grip stock. It was manufactured in 1971 and reintroduced in 1973.The 1971 version has white line spacers and pistol grip caps. The 1973 version has neither of these features.

Exc.	V.G.	Good	Fair	Poor
275	200	125	75	50

Model 39AS Lever Action Rifle

This is the current production model of this extremely popular .22 rifle. It features the hammer-block crossbolt safety and sling swivel studs. It is similar in appearance to its predecessors and still boasts a genuine walnut pistol grip stock and the same quality fit and finish we have come to expect from Marlin.

NIB	Exc.	V.G.	Good	Fair	Poor
340	275	225	200	150	100

Model 39TDS Lever Action Rifle

This is another current production model. It is similar to the Model 39AS, with a 20" carbine barrel and straight-grip stock. It replaced the Model 39M and was introduced in 1988.

NIB	Exc.	V.G.	Good	Fair	Poor
375	325	250	225	150	100

Model 39 AWL

This is a limited edition of 2,000 rifles distributed solely through Wal-Mart. Fitted with a 24.5" octagon barrel, select checkered walnut stock, gold filled engraving, and stamped "Wildlife For Tomorrow".

NIB	Exc.	V.G.	Good	Fair	Poor
700	500	—	—	—	—

Model 56 Levermatic Rifle

This is a streamlined version of the lever action. It features a short lever throw and a one-piece walnut stock. The 22" barrel is round and is chambered for the .22 rimfire cartridges. There is a 7-shot detachable magazine, open sights, and a gold-plated trigger. The receiver on this model was made of aluminum after 1956. There were 31,523 manufactured between 1955 and 1964.

Exc.	V.G.	Good	Fair	Poor
180	125	100	75	50

Model 56 "Clipper King" Levermatic

This is the same as the Model 56 except that it is specially packaged and comes with a 4X .22 scope. The name "Clipper King" is stamped on the barrel, and the buttplate is red hard rubber. There were only 152 of these manufactured in 1959.

Exc.	V.G.	Good	Fair	Poor
250	175	125	100	75

Model 57 Levermatic Rifle

This model is similar to the Model 56, with a tube magazine and Monte Carlo stock. In 1960 Marlin went back to a steel receiver on this model. There were 34,628 manufactured from 1959 to 1965.

Exc.	V.G.	Good	Fair	Poor
200	155	100	75	50

Model 57M Levermatic Rifle

This is the Model 57 chambered for the .22 Magnum cartridge. There were 66,889 manufactured between 1959 and 1969.

Exc.	V.G.	Good	Fair	Poor
200	155	125	100	75

Model 62 Levermatic Rifle

This model is similar in appearance to the Model 57 except that it is chambered for the centerfire .256 Magnum cartridge and has a 4-shot magazine. In 1966 the .30 carbine cartridge was added. This model has a 23" "Micro-Groove" barrel with open sights and a walnut one-piece stock. The first 4,000 Model 62s were shipped without serial numbers in violation of federal law. The company recalled the rifles for numbering; and, to this day, the owner of a centerfire Model 62 can return the rifle for numbering. There were 15,714 manufactured between 1963 and 1969.

Exc.	V.G.	Good	Fair	Poor
325	250	125	100	75

NOTE: From 1969 to 1972, the first digit of the serial number indicates the year of manufacture. In 1973, the system was changed by having the first two digits subtracted from 100 to find the year of production. For example: 2717793=100-27=1973.

It is important to note that the year of manufacture of Marlin modern production rifles made between 1946 and 1968 can be ascertained by the letter prefix on the serial number. The prefixes are as follows:

1946 - C	1951 - H	1956 - N	1961 - U	1966 - AB
1947 - D	1952 - J	1957 - P	1962 - V	1967 - AC
1948 - E	1953 - K	1958 - R	1963 - W	1968 - AD
1949 - F	1954 - L	1959 - S	1964 - Y, Z	
1950 - G	1955 - M	1960 - T	1965 - AA	

The Marlin Firearms Company produced a great many bolt action rifles, both single shot and repeaters, starting in 1930 and continuing today. These rifles were low-priced and designed primarily as utility rifles. They also manufactured many autoloaders of the same type during these years. The Glenfield name will also be found on these models, as many were produced to be marketed by the large chain outlets. These rifles have no collectible value of which I am aware, and they sell for under $100 in today's market. This list is for reference purposes.

BOLT ACTIONS	AUTOLOADERS
Model 65 - SS- 1935-37	Model 50 - 1931-34
Model 65E - SS- 1935-37	Model 50E - 1931-34
Model 100 - SS- 1935-59	Model A-1 - 1935-46
Model 80 - Rep- 1935-59	Model A-1 E - 1935-46
Model 80E - Rep- 1935-39	Model A-1C - 1940-46
Model 100S - SS- 1937-38	Model A-1 DL - 1940-46
Model 81 - Rep- 1939	Model 88-C - 1947-56
Model 81E - Rep- 1939	Model 88-DL - 1953-56
Model 80B - Rep- 1940	Model 89-C - 1950-61
Model 80BE - Rep-1940	Model 89-DL - 1950-61
Model 81B - Rep-1940	Model 98 - 1950-61
Model 81BE - Rep-1940	Model 99 - 1959-61
Model 101 - SS- 1941-77	Model 99C - 1962-78
Model 101 DL - SS- 1941-45	Model 99G - 1960-65
Model 80C - Rep-1941-71	Model DL - 1960-65
Model 80DL - Rep-1941-64	Model 60 - 1960-Pres.
Model 80 CSB - Rep-1941	Model 49 - 1968-71
Model 100 SB - SS- 1941	Model 49DL - 1971-78
Model 101 - SS- 1959	Model 990 - 1979-87
Model 122 - SS- 1962-65	Model 995 - 1979-Pres.
Model 980 - Rep- 1966-71	
Model 780 - Rep- 1971-88	
Model 781- Rep- 1971-88	
Model 782 - Rep- 1971-88	
Model 783 - Rep- 1971-88	
Model 880 - Rep- 1988—	
Model 881 - Rep- 1988—	
Model 882 - Rep- 1988—	
Model 883 - Rep- 1988—	

MARLIN Model 99C

NIB	Exc.	V.G.	Good	Fair	Poor
310	275	225	175	125	100

Model 70P "Papoose"

This model is quite unique in that it is a total package concept. It is a semiautomatic takedown carbine chambered for the .22 rimfire family of cartridges. It has a 16.25" barrel and a 7-shot detachable magazine. It is supplied with 4X scope and bright red case that will float if dropped overboard. The stock is walnut-finished birch, with a pistol grip and rubber buttplate. It was introduced in 1986.

Model 45 Carbine

This is the same as the 9mm version but is chambered for the .45 ACP cartridge and has a 7-shot detachable magazine.

NIB	Exc.	V.G.	Good	Fair	Poor
160	140	110	85	75	50

Model 70HC

This is the Model 70 .22 rimfire that has been produced since 1983 with a high-capacity, 25-round "Banana" magazine.

NIB	Exc.	V.G.	Good	Fair	Poor
160	140	110	85	75	50

Model 70PSS

Same as above but furnished with a 10-round magazine and finished in stainless steel.

NIB	Exc.	V.G.	Good	Fair	Poor
310	275	225	175	125	100

Model 922M

First offered in 1993 this model is a semiautomatic .22 Win. Magnum Rimfire rifle. It features a 7-shot clip, 20.5" Micro-Grove barrel. The receiver is sandblasted and drilled and tapped for scope mounting. Monte Carlo black walnut stock with rubber rifle buff pad. Adjustable rear sight and ramp front sight with hood. Rifle weighs 6.5 lbs.

NIB	Exc.	V.G.	Good	Fair	Poor
180	150	125	100	85	60

NIB	Exc.	V.G.	Good	Fair	Poor
275	250	200	150	125	110

Model 9 Camp Carbine

This model has a 16.5" barrel and is chambered for the 9mm Parabellum pistol cartridge. It has a 12- or 20-shot detachable magazine, walnut-finished hardwood pistol grip stock, and a sandblasted matte-blued finish. There are open sights, and the receiver is drilled and tapped for scope mounting. This model was introduced in 1985.

Model 995

Semiautomatic .22 Long Rifle only rifle features a 7-shot clip, 18" Micro-Grove barrel. Receiver is grooved for scope mount and receiver has a serrated non-glare top. Adjustable sights.

Monte Carlo American black walnut stock with checkered pistol grip and forearm. White buttplate spacer is standard. Rifle weighs 5 lbs. Introduced in 1979 and still in production.

NIB	Exc.	V.G.	Good	Fair	Poor
125	100	80	70	60	40

Model 995SS

Same as above but with stainless steel finish and black fiberglass stock. Introduced in 1995.

NIB	Exc.	V.G.	Good	Fair	Poor
150	125	100	85	60	50

Model 990L

This semiautomatic .22 Long Rifle Marlin features a tubular 14-round magazine with 22" Micro-Grove barrel. The trigger is gold plated. The receiver is grooved for a scope mount while the stock is a two-tone brown birch Monte Carlo. Rubber rifle butt pad is standard. Rifle weighs 5.75 lbs.

NIB	Exc.	V.G.	Good	Fair	Poor
140	120	100	80	65	50

Model 7000

This model was first offered in 1997 and is a semiautomatic .22 caliber rifle with 18" heavy barrel. Magazine holds 10 rounds. Black synthetic stock with Monte Carlo comb and molded checkering. Receiver grooved for scope mount. No sights included. Weight about 6 lbs.

NIB	Exc.	V.G.	Good	Fair	Poor
200	150	125	100	—	—

Model 7000 T

This target rifle is fitted with an 18" barrel with recessed muzzle. No sights. The stock is red, white, and blue laminated stock with pistol grip. Serrated rubber buttplate is adjustable for length of pull, height, and angle. Weight is about 7.5 lbs. Introduced in 1999.

NIB	Exc.	V.G.	Good	Fair	Poor
425	375	—	—	—	—

Model 795

Similar to the model above but with an 18" standard weight barrel. Weight is about 5 lbs. Also available with 4X scope. Add $5.00 for scope.

NIB	Exc.	V.G.	Good	Fair	Poor
150	115	—	—	—	—

Model 60

A Marlin promotional model. This semiautomatic 14-shot .22 caliber Long Rifle features a 22" MicroGroove barrel with adjustable rear sight. Receiver is grooved for scope mount and stock is birch with Monte Carlo comb. Rifle weighs 5.5 lbs. Introduced in 1960 and still in current production.

NIB	Exc.	V.G.	Good	Fair	Poor
100	85	70	60	50	40

Model 60SS

Introduced in 1993 this model is similar to the Model 60 except that it features a stainless barrel, bolt, and magazine tube. All other metal parts are nickel plated. The stock is a two-tone black and gray laminated birch Monte Carlo.

NIB	Exc.	V.G.	Good	Fair	Poor
160	135	100	80	60	50

Model 60SB

Introduced in 1998 this model features a stainless steel 22" barrel, bolt and magazine tube. The stock is birch with Monte Carlo and hard rubber buttplate.

NIB	Exc.	V.G.	Good	Fair	Poor
160	125	—	—	—	—

Model 60SSK

Similar to the Model 60SB with the addition of a black synthetic Monte Carlo stock with checkering.

NIB	Exc.	V.G.	Good	Fair	Poor
175	125	—	—	—	—

Model 60C

Similar to the Model 60 but with Mossy Oak Break-Up camo finish. Introduced in 2000.

NIB	Exc.	V.G.	Good	Fair	Poor
—	—	—	—		

Model 9N

Similar to the Model 9mm Carbine but furnished with nickel-plated metal parts.

NIB	Exc.	V.G.	Good	Fair	Poor
270	245	210	175	125	100

Model 322 Bolt Action Rifle

This model is chambered for the .222 cartridge and has a 24" medium-weight barrel with MicroGroove rifling. It has a checkered walnut pistol grip stock. The magazine holds 4 shots, and the adjustable trigger and sights are Sako products. The Sako receiver is fitted for Sako scope mounting bases. The MicroGroove rifling in the barrel was not successful for this caliber, and accuracy fell off after as few as 500 shots—so this model was dropped and replaced. The serial numbers were Sako, and there were 5,859 manufactured between 1954 and 1959.

Exc.	V.G.	Good	Fair	Poor
375	325	250	175	125

Model 422 Bolt Action Rifle

This model is the successor to the Model 322. It is simply the same rifle fitted with a 24", featherweight, stainless steel barrel and named the "Varmint King." The stock features a Monte Carlo stock with a cheekpiece. There were only 354 manufactured between 1956 and 1958.

Exc.	V.G.	Good	Fair	Poor
375	325	275	175	125

Model 455 Bolt Action Rifle

This model is built on the Fabrique Nationale Belgian Mauser action. It is chambered for the .308 and the .30-06 cartridges. It has a stainless steel barrel made by Marlin and has a 5-shot magazine. It has a Bishop checkered walnut stock with detachable sling swivels and a leather sling. The rear sight is a Lyman 48, and the front is a ramp type with a detachable hood. The receiver is drilled and tapped for scope mounts. The trigger is an adjustable Sako unit. There were 1,079 manufactured in .3006 and only 59 in .308 between 1955 and 1959.

Exc.	V.G.	Good	Fair	Poor
375	325	275	175	125

Model 2000

This is a bolt action single shot target rifle chambered for the .22 Long Rifle. The barrel is a 22" long MicroGroove design with match chamber and recessed muzzle. The rear sight is a fully adjustable target peep sight with a hooded front sight supplied with 10 aperture inserts. The stock is a Marlin blue fiberglass/Kevlar material with adjustable buttplate. There is an aluminum forearm rail with forearm stop and quick detachable swivel. Rifle weighs 8 lbs.

NIB	Exc.	V.G.	Good	Fair	Poor
350	300	250	200	150	125

Model 2000A

This is an ungraded 1996 version of the Model 2000 introduced in 1994 that features an adjustable comb and an ambidextrous pistol grip. A Marlin logo is molded into the side of the buttstock. Weighs approximately 8-1/2 lbs.

NIB	Exc.	V.G.	Good	Fair	Poor
350	300	250	200	—	—

Model 2000L

Introduced in 1996 this version of the Model 2000 features a black/grey laminated stock. It is fitted with a heavy 22" barrel with a match chamber. Fitted with a two-stage target trigger and a rubber buttplate that is adjustable for length of pull, height and angle. Weight is about 8 lbs.

NIB	Exc.	V.G.	Good	Fair	Poor
625	500	450	—	—	—

Model 880

This is a bolt action clip-fed rifle chambered for the .22 Long Rifle caliber. The clip is a 7-shot magazine. The MicroGroove barrel is 22" and has adjustable folding rear sight and ramp front sight with hood. Rifle weighs 5.5 lbs. and was introduced in 1988 and is still in production.

NIB	Exc.	V.G.	Good	Fair	Poor
160	135	110	90	75	50

Model 880SS

Introduced in 1994 this .22 caliber rifle features a synthetic stock and a stainless steel receiver and barrel. The barrel is 22" long and a 7-shot magazine is standard.

NIB	Exc.	V.G.	Good	Fair	Poor
225	175	150	125	75	60

Model 880SQ

Similar to the Model 880 but fitted with a 22" heavy barrel and no sights. Introduced in 1996. Weight is approximately 7 lbs.

NIB	Exc.	V.G.	Good	Fair	Poor
285	225	200	—	—	—

Model 881

Bolt action .22 caliber rifle has a tubular magazine that holds 25 Shorts, 19 Longs, and 17 Long rifles. A 22" MicroGroove barrel has adjustable folding rear sight and ramp front sight with hood. Stock is black walnut with Monte Carlo and a rubber rifle butt pad with sling swivels. Rifle weighs 6 lbs. First offered in 1988 and still in production.

NIB	Exc.	V.G.	Good	Fair	Poor
175	150	125	100	80	60

Model 882SS

This bolt action magazine rifle is chambered for the .22 Magnum cartridge. It has a stainless steel barrel and action with black synthetic stock. It has Marlin "Fire Sights" installed. Introduced in 1998.

NIB	Exc.	V.G.	Good	Fair	Poor
225	175	—	—	—	—

Model 25N

A Marlin promotional model. Bolt action rifle chambered for the .22 Long Rifle only. Seven-shot clip magazine with a 22" MicroGroove barrel. Receiver grooved for scope mount. Walnut finished birch stock. Gun weighs 5.5 lbs.

NIB	Exc.	V.G.	Good	Fair	Poor
100	90	80	70	50	40

Model 25NC

Similar to the model above but with Mossy Oak Break-Up camo finish. Introduced in 2000.

NIB	Exc.	V.G.	Good	Fair	Poor
125	100	—	—	—	—

Model 25MN

Same as above but chambered for the .22 Win. Magnum Rimfire cartridge. Gun weighs 6 lbs.

NIB	Exc.	V.G.	Good	Fair	Poor
120	100	85	75	65	50

Model 25 MNC

Similar to the above model but with Mossy Oak Break-Up camo finish. Weight is about 6 lbs. Introduced in 2001.

NIB	Exc.	V.G.	Good	Fair	Poor
—	—	—	—	—	—

Model 15YN

A Marlin promotional model referred to as the "Little Buckaroo". A bolt action .22 caliber single shot rifle for the beginner. Features a MicroGroove 16.25" barrel adjustable rear sight and receiver grooved for scope mount. Birch stock. Rifle weighs 4.25 lbs.

NIB	Exc.	V.G.	Good	Fair	Poor
125	100	75	60	50	40

Model 15N

This bolt action rifle is chambered for all three .22 caliber rim-cartridges. It is fitted with an adjustable rear sight. It has a full size birch interchangeable with the Model 15YN. Weight is about 4.25 lbs. Introduced in 1998.

NIB	Exc.	V.G.	Good	Fair	Poor
150	125	—	—	—	—

Model 81TS

This is a bolt action rifle chambered for the .22 Long, Short, and Long Rifle cartridges. It is fitted with a 22" barrel and has a tubular magazine. It comes with a black Monte Carlo synthetic stock and adjustable rear sight. Weight is about 6 lbs. Introduced in 1998.

NIB	Exc.	V.G.	Good	Fair	Poor
140	100	—	—	—	—

Model 882

Bolt action rifle chambered for .22 Win. Magnum Rimfire cartridge. A 7-shot clip is standard. A MicroGroove 22" barrel with adjustable rear sight and ramp front sight with hood. Receiver grooved for scope mount. Black walnut stock with Monte Carlo and rubber rifle butt. Rifle weighs 6 lbs. Introduced in 1988 and still in production.

NIB	Exc.	V.G.	Good	Fair	Poor
150	125	100	80	65	50

Model 882L

Same as above but furnished with a two-tone brown hardwood Monte Carlo stock. Rifle weighs 6.25 lbs.

NIB	Exc.	V.G.	Good	Fair	Poor
180	155	130	100	80	60

Model 882SS

Same as above but furnished in stainless steel. With black fiberglass stock. Introduced in 1995.

NIB	Exc.	V.G.	Good	Fair	Poor
180	155	130	100	80	60

Model 882SSV

This variation of the Model 882, introduced in 1997, is all in stainless steel and chambered for the .22 WMR cartridge. It is fitted with a nickel plated 7-round magazine and 22" barrel. The stock is black synthetic with molded checkering. Receiver is grooved for scope mount. 1" brushed aluminum scope ring mounts included. Weighs about 7 lbs.

NIB	Exc.	V.G.	Good	Fair	Poor
275	200	—	—	—	—

Model 83 TS

Chambered for the .22 Win. Mag cartridge and fitted with a 22" barrel with 12-round tubular magazine. Adjustable rear sight. Bolt action with synthetic stock. Weight is about 6 lbs. Introduced in 2001.

NIB	Exc.	V.G.	Good	Fair	Poor
—	—	—	—		

Model 883

Bolt action rifle chambered for .22 Win. Magnum cartridge with 12-shot tubular magazine. Furnished with a 22" MicroGroove barrel and adjustable rear sight, ramp front sight with hood. Checkered American black walnut stock with Monte Carlo. Rifle weighs 6 lbs. Introduced in 1988 and still in production.

NIB	Exc.	V.G.	Good	Fair	Poor
160	125	100	80	65	50

Model 883N

Same as above but furnished with stainless steel barrel, receiver, front breech bolt, and striker. All other metal parts, except for sights, are nickel plated.

NIB	Exc.	V.G.	Good	Fair	Poor
180	155	130	100	80	60

Model 883SS

Introduced in 1993 this model is similar to the Model 883 but with all metal parts in stainless steel or nickel and the stock is a two-tone brown birch Monte Carlo that is not checkered.

NIB	Exc.	V.G.	Good	Fair	Poor
170	150	125	100	80	60

MR-7

Introduced in 1996, this is an American made bolt action centerfire rifle of a totally new design. Chambered for the .25-06 (first offered in 1997), .243, .270 Win. .280, .308, or .30-06 cartridges it is fitted with a 22" barrel. It has an American black walnut stock and a 4-shot detachable box magazine. Offered with or without sights. Weight is approximately 7.5 lbs.

NIB	Exc.	V.G.	Good	Fair	Poor
450	350	300	250	—	—

Model MR-7B

Similar to the MR-7 but fitted with a 4-round blind magazine and birch stock. Offered in .30-06 or .270 with or without sights. Introduced in 1998.

NIB	Exc.	V.G.	Good	Fair	Poor
375	300	—	—	—	—

MARLIN SHOTGUNS

Model 1898 Slide Action Shotgun

This model was made in 12 gauge, with an exposed hammer. It has a takedown receiver and walnut pistol grip stock and forend.

There is a 5-shot tube magazine, and the barrel lengths are from 26" and 32". They were manufactured between 1898 and 1905.

Grade A

This variation has a 38", 30", or 32" barrel, is full choke, and is the plainest grade.

Exc.	V.G.	Good	Fair	Poor
350	275	200	100	75

Grade A Brush or Riot

This is the same shotgun with a 26" cylinder-bore barrel.

Exc.	V.G.	Good	Fair	Poor
350	275	200	100	75

Grade B

This is the same as the Grade A with a special smokeless steel barrel and a checkered stock.

Exc.	V.G.	Good	Fair	Poor
500	400	300	200	100

Model 1898 Grade C

This is a more deluxe version with engraving and fancier wood.

Exc.	V.G.	Good	Fair	Poor
700	550	450	275	125

Grade D

This variation has a Damascus barrel and the greatest amount of engraving.

Exc.	V.G.	Good	Fair	Poor
1400	1100	825	600	400

Model 16 Slide Action Shotgun

This model is exactly the same as the Model 1898 except that it is chambered for 16 gauge only. The four grades are the same also. They were manufactured between 1903 and 1910.

Grade A

Exc.	V.G.	Good	Fair	Poor
400	350	300	250	150

Grade B

Exc.	V.G.	Good	Fair	Poor
500	450	400	350	225

Grade C

Exc.	V.G.	Good	Fair	Poor
650	575	500	425	300

Grade D

Exc.	V.G.	Good	Fair	Poor
1400	1200	1000	700	550

Model 17 Slide Action Shotgun

This model is an exposed-hammer gun with a solid frame and a straight-grip stock. It is chambered for 12 gauge, with a 30" or 32" barrel. The Model 17 was manufactured between 1906 and 1908.

Exc.	V.G.	Good	Fair	Poor
350	235	195	150	75

Model 17 Brush Gun

This variation is similar to the standard Model 17, with a 26" cylinder-bore barrel.

Exc.	V.G.	Good	Fair	Poor
375	325	275	200	100

Model 17 Riot Gun

This variation has a 20" cylinder-bore barrel.

Exc.	V.G.	Good	Fair	Poor
350	235	195	150	75

Model 19 Slide Action Shotgun

This is a takedown gun, chambered for 12 gauge. It is basically an improved and lightened version of the Model 1898. It is available in the same four grades. It was manufactured in 1906 and 1907.

Grade A
Exc.	V.G.	Good	Fair	Poor
400	350	300	250	150

Grade B
Exc.	V.G.	Good	Fair	Poor
500	450	400	350	225

Grade C
Exc.	V.G.	Good	Fair	Poor
650	575	500	425	300

Grade D
Exc.	V.G.	Good	Fair	Poor
1400	1200	1000	700	550

Model 21 "Trap" Slide Action Shotgun

This model is basically the same as the Model 19 with a straight-grip stock. The 1907 catalog listed it as a Trap model. This model was manufactured in 1907 and 1908. The four grades are similar to the previous models.

Grade A
Exc.	V.G.	Good	Fair	Poor
400	350	300	250	150

Grade B
Exc.	V.G.	Good	Fair	Poor
500	450	400	350	225

Grade C
Exc.	V.G.	Good	Fair	Poor
650	575	500	425	300

Grade D
Exc.	V.G.	Good	Fair	Poor
1400	1200	1000	700	550

Model 24 Slide Action Shotgun

This model is actually an improved version of the Model 21. It has a pistol grip stock and exposed hammer. It features an automatic recoil lock on the slide and a matte rib barrel. Otherwise, it is quite similar to its predecessor. It was manufactured between 1908 and 1917.

Grade A
Exc.	V.G.	Good	Fair	Poor
350	300	250	200	100

Grade B
Exc.	V.G.	Good	Fair	Poor
500	450	400	350	225

Grade C
Exc.	V.G.	Good	Fair	Poor
650	575	500	425	300

Grade D
Exc.	V.G.	Good	Fair	Poor
1400	1200	1000	700	550

Marlin "Trap Gun"

This model is unique in that it has no numerical designation and is simply known as the "Trap Gun." It is a takedown gun with interchangeable barrels from 16" to 32". It has a straight-grip buttstock and is quite similar in appearance to the Model 24. It was manufactured between 1909 and 1912.

Exc.	V.G.	Good	Fair	Poor
450	400	350	250	175

Model 26 Slide Action Shotgun

This model is similar to the Model 24 Grade A, with a solid frame. It has 30" or 32" barrels.

Exc.	V.G.	Good	Fair	Poor
275	225	175	125	100

Model 26 Brush Gun

This model has a 26" cylinder-bored barrel.

Exc.	V.G.	Good	Fair	Poor
300	250	200	150	125

Model 26 Riot Gun

This variation has a 20" cylinder-bored barrel.

Exc.	V.G.	Good	Fair	Poor
250	200	150	100	75

Model 28 Hammerless Slide Action Shotgun

This model was the first of the Marlin hammerless shotguns. It is a takedown 12 gauge, with barrels from 26" to 32" in length.

The stock has a pistol grip, and it comes in four grades like its predecessors. The Model 28 was manufactured between 1913 and 1922.

Grade A
Exc.	V.G.	Good	Fair	Poor
300	235	165	125	75

Grade B
Exc.	V.G.	Good	Fair	Poor
500	450	400	350	225

Grade C
Exc.	V.G.	Good	Fair	Poor
650	575	500	425	300

Grade D
Exc.	V.G.	Good	Fair	Poor
1400	1200	1000	700	550

Model 28 TS Trap Gun

This variation is the same as the Model 28 with a 30" full-choke barrel with matted rib and a high-comb straight grip stock. It was manufactured in 1915.

Exc.	V.G.	Good	Fair	Poor
425	375	300	225	175

Model 28T Trap Gun

This variation is the deluxe model, similar to the Model 28TS, with engraving, high-grade walnut, and hand checkering. It was manufactured in 1915.

Exc.	V.G.	Good	Fair	Poor
600	525	450	375	250

Model 30 Slide Action Shotgun

This model is an improved version of the Model 16, 16 gauge shotgun. Its features are similar, with the addition of the improved takedown system and the automatic recoil lock on the slide. This model was manufactured between 1910 and 1914.

Grade A
Exc.	V.G.	Good	Fair	Poor
400	350	300	250	150

Grade B
Exc.	V.G.	Good	Fair	Poor
500	450	400	350	225

Grade C

Exc.	V.G.	Good	Fair	Poor
650	575	500	425	300

Grade D

Exc.	V.G.	Good	Fair	Poor
1400	1200	1000	700	550

Model 30 Field Grade

This model is similar to the Model 30 Grade B, with a 25" modified-choke barrel and a straight-grip stock. It was manufactured in 1913 and 1914.

Exc.	V.G.	Good	Fair	Poor
400	350	300	225	150

Model 31 Slide Action Shotgun

This model is a smaller version of the Model 28 hammerless takedown shotgun, chambered for 16 and 20 gauge. It was produced with barrel lengths of 26" and 28" and was available in the usual four grades, with various different chokes. This model was manufactured between 1915 and 1922.

Grade A

Exc.	V.G.	Good	Fair	Poor
400	350	300	250	150

Grade B

Exc.	V.G.	Good	Fair	Poor
500	450	400	350	225

Grade C

Exc.	V.G.	Good	Fair	Poor
650	575	500	425	300

Grade D

Exc.	V.G.	Good	Fair	Poor
1400	1200	1000	700	550

Model 42/42A Slide Action Shotgun

This model was originally listed as the Model 42; but in the second year of production, the designation was changed to 42/A for no more apparent reason than standardization of models. This model is similar to the Model 24 except that the barrel markings are different. It is still an exposed hammer takedown gun chambered for 12 gauge. It was manufactured between 1922 and 1933.

Exc.	V.G.	Good	Fair	Poor
275	250	200	150	100

Model 43A Slide Action Shotgun

This hammerless model was quite similar to the Model 28, with different markings and less attention to finishing detail. It was manufactured between 1923 and 1930.

Exc.	V.G.	Good	Fair	Poor
350	300	250	200	150

Model 43T Slide Action Shotgun

This model is the same as the Model 43A takedown hammerless with a 30" or 32" matte-rib barrel. The straight-grip stock is of high grade walnut, with a non-gloss oil finish and fitted recoil paid. This model was manufactured between 1922 and 1930.

Exc.	V.G.	Good	Fair	Poor
400	350	300	250	200

Model 43TS Slide Action Shotgun

This is a custom-order version of the Model 43T, the same in all respects except that the stock could be ordered to any specifications the shooter desired. It was manufactured between 1922 and 1930.

Exc.	V.G.	Good	Fair	Poor
600	550	500	350	275

Model 44A Slide Action Shotgun

This model is similar to the Model 31 and was advertised as its successor. It is a hammerless takedown chambered for the 20 gauge. It features an improved bolt opening device located in the triggerguard area instead of at the top of the receiver and has a shorter 4-shot magazine tube. The model was manufactured from 1922 until 1933.

Exc.	V.G.	Good	Fair	Poor
375	325	275	225	175

Model 44S Slide Action Shotgun

This model is similar to the Model 44A, with a higher grade walnut stock that featured hand-cut checkering.

Exc.	V.G.	Good	Fair	Poor
450	400	350	300	225

Model 49 Slide Action Shotgun

This model is a 12-gauge, exposed-hammer takedown that combines features of the Model 42 and the Model 24. It is basically a lower-priced model that was never listed in the Marlin catalog. This model was part of Frank Kenna's money-raising program—anyone who purchased four shares of stock for $25 per share was given one, free of charge. This model was manufactured between 1925 and 1928.

Exc.	V.G.	Good	Fair	Poor
450	400	350	275	200

Model 53 Slide Action Shotgun

This model is a hammerless, takedown, 12 gauge that was not in production for long. It is theorized that the Model 53 was produced to use up old parts on hand when the Model 43 was introduced. It was manufactured in 1929 and 1980.

Exc.	V.G.	Good	Fair	Poor
350	300	250	175	125

Model 63 Slide Action Shotgun

This was the last of the slide action shotguns produced by Marlin until the Model 120 in 1971. It is a hammerless, takedown 12 gauge and replaced the Model 43A in the Marlin catalog. This model had improvements over the earlier guns, but its introduction during the Depression did little to bolster sales. This model was also offered free of charge to anyone purchasing four shares of Marlin stock at $25 per share. It was manufactured between 1931 and 1933.

Exc.	V.G.	Good	Fair	Poor
350	300	250	175	125

Model 63T Slide Action Shotgun

This is the trap-grade version of the Model 63. It has a better grade hand-checkered stock, with a fitted recoil pad and oil finish. It was manufactured between 1931 and 1933.

Exc.	V.G.	Good	Fair	Poor
375	325	275	200	150

Model 63TS Slide Action Shotgun

This variation is the same as the Model 63T except that the stock dimensions were custom-made to the customer's specifications. It was manufactured between 1931 and 1933.

Exc.	V.G.	Good	Fair	Poor
400	350	300	225	175

Model 60 Single Barrel Shotgun

This is a break-open, exposed-hammer, top lever-opening 12 gauge with either 30" or 32" full-choke barrel. It has a pistol grip stock. There were approximately 60 manufactured in 1923.

Exc.	V.G.	Good	Fair	Poor
200	175	150	125	100

Model .410 Lever Action Shotgun

This was a unique venture for the Marlin Company—a lever action shotgun based on the Model 1893 action with a longer loading port, modified tube magazine that held 5 shots, and a smoothbore barrel chambered for the .410 shot shell. The finish of this gun is blued, with a walnut pistol grip stock and grooved beavertail forend. It has a hard rubber rifle-type buttplate. The model was available with either a 22" or 26" full-choke barrel. This gun was also part of the stock purchase plan and was given free of charge to anyone purchasing four shares at $25 per share. It was also cataloged for sale and was manufactured between 1929 and 1932.

Courtesy Mike Stuckslager

Exc.	V.G.	Good	Fair	Poor
1200	900	550	400	250

Model .410 Deluxe

This variation was never cataloged and is essentially the same as the standard version with a hand-checkered stock. The forend does not have the grooves found on the standard model. Be wary of fakes!

Exc.	V.G.	Good	Fair	Poor
1600	1000	700	500	300

Model 90 Over/Under Shotgun

This gun was produced in response to a request from Sears Roebuck that Marlin should manufacture an Over/Under shotgun for Sears to market in their stores. The guns produced for Sears have the prefix 103 in their serial numbers and were marked "Ranger" before WWII and "J.C. Higgins" after the war. Prior to 1945 they were not marked Marlin; after that date Sears requested that the company stamp their name on the guns. They were also produced as the Marlin Model 90 during the same period and were chambered for 12, 16, and 20 gauge, as well as .410 bore. The 16 and 20 gauge guns were first offered in 1937 with 26" or 28" barrels. In 1939 the .410 bore was first offered with 26" barrel and 3" chambers. The barrels are either 26", 28", or 30", with various chokes. The action is a boxlock with extractors. Guns made prior to 1950 were solid between the barrels; after that date there was a space between the barrels. They can be found with double or single triggers and a checkered walnut stock. A ventilated rib was also offered as an option beginning in 1949. Be aware that this model was also available as a combination gun in .22 LR/.410, .22 Hornet/.410, and .218 Bee/.410. There were approximately 34,000 Model 90s manufactured between 1937 and 1963.

EDITOR'S NOTE: Collectors should be aware that this model has a receiver of malleable iron. It will not blue by the usual bluing methods. The barrels and ribs are soft soldered and cannot take hot bluing. Use caution.

Exc.	V.G.	Good	Fair	Poor
500	425	350	275	200

NOTE: Single Trigger-Add 35%. Add 25% for 20 gauge guns and 25% for .410 bores. Add a 50% premium for combination guns. There are other rare gauge and barrel combinations that may affect value. If in doubt seek an expert appraisal.

Premier Mark I Slide Action Shotgun

This model was made by Manufrance and called the LaSalle. Marlin was able to purchase them without the barrels at a good enough price for them to barrel and market them under their own name. This model is 12 gauge only, with an alloy receiver and seven interchangeable barrels in 26"-30" lengths and various chokes. The plain stock is French walnut. The biggest problem with this gun is that the light weight (six pounds) produced bad recoil, and it was less than enjoyable to shoot. This model was in production from 1959 through 1963, with approximately 13,700 sold.

Exc.	V.G.	Good	Fair	Poor
225	175	150	100	75

Premier Mark II

This model is similar to the Mark I, with light engraving and a checkered stock.

Exc.	V.G.	Good	Fair	Poor
250	200	175	125	100

Premier Mark IV

This model is similar to the Mark II, with more engraving on the receiver.

Exc.	V.G.	Good	Fair	Poor
300	250	200	150	125

NOTE: Add 10% for vent rib.

Model 120 Slide Action Shotgun

This model was styled to resemble the Winchester Model 12 and was advertised as an all steel and walnut shotgun. It was offered with interchangeable barrels from 26" to 40", and various chokes were available. The checkered stock is of walnut, with a fitted recoil pad. The tube magazine holds 5 shots, 4 in 3". There was a Trap Model available (1973-1975), as well as a slug gun (1974-1984). This model was manufactured between 1971 and 1985.

Exc.	V.G.	Good	Fair	Poor
300	250	200	150	125

Model 778 Slide Action Shotgun (Glenfield)

This model is similar to the Model 120, with a walnut finished hardwood stock instead of walnut, and the Glenfield name stamped on it. It was manufactured between 1979 and 1984.

Exc.	V.G.	Good	Fair	Poor
225	175	150	125	100

Model 50 DL

This bolt action 12 gauge shotgun is available with a 28" modified barrel, black synthetic stock. Ventilated recoil pad is standard. Brass bead front sight. Weight is approximately 7.5 lbs.

NIB	Exc.	V.G.	Good	Fair	Poor
300	275	225	150	125	100

Model 55 Bolt Action Shotgun

This model is chambered for 12, 16, and 20 gauge, with full or adjustable choke and barrels of 26" or 28". It is a bolt action with 2-shot box magazine. The pistol grip stock is plain. This model was manufactured between 1950 and 1965.

Exc.	V.G.	Good	Fair	Poor
100	75	50	35	25

Model 55 Swamp Gun

This is simply the Model 55 with a 3" Magnum, 20" barrel and an adjustable choke. It was manufactured between 1963 and 1965.

Exc.	V.G.	Good	Fair	Poor
110	80	65	45	25

Model 55 Goose Gun

This is the Model 55 with a 3" chambered, 36" full choke barrel and a recoil pad and sling. It was introduced in 1962 and is still manufactured.

NIB	Exc.	V.G.	Good	Fair	Poor
230	175	140	125	100	75

Model 55S Slug Gun

This is the Model 55 with a 24" cylinder-bore barrel and rifle sights. It was manufactured between 1974 and 1983.

Exc.	V.G.	Good	Fair	Poor
150	125	100	75	50

Model 55 10 Bolt Action Shotgun

This model is chambered for the 3.5" 10 gauge. It has a 34" full-choke barrel and a recoil pad and sling. It was manufactured between 1976 and 1985.

Exc.	V.G.	Good	Fair	Poor
200	150	125	100	75

Model 55 GDL

This bolt action shotgun is fitted with a 36" full choke barrel and reinforced black synthetic stock. Magazine holds two rounds. Ventilated recoil pad is standard. First introduced in 1997. Weight is about 8 lbs.

NIB	Exc.	V.G.	Good	Fair	Poor
350	275	—	—	—	—

Model 512 Slugmaster

Introduced in 1994 this bolt action shotgun features a rifled 21" barrel. It is equipped with a two-shot detachable magazine and a ventilated recoil pad. A special scope is also provided. Weight is approximately 8 lbs.

NIB	Exc.	V.G.	Good	Fair	Poor
285	250	225	200	150	100

Model 512 DL Slugmaster

Introduced in 1997 this bolt action model features a black synthetic stock with a fully rifled 21" barrel chambered for the 12 gauge shell. A two-round magazine is standard. Adjustable rear sight with ramp front sight. Receiver drilled and tapped for scope mount. Weight is about 8 lbs.

NIB	Exc.	V.G.	Good	Fair	Poor
300	250	—	—	—	—

Model 512DL with Fire Sights

NOTE: In 1998 this model was furnished with "Fire Sights"

Model 512P

Introduced in 1999 this model is similar to the Model 512 DL with the addition of a 21" fully rifled and ported barrel. Fire sights are standard. Weight is about 8 lbs.

NIB	Exc.	V.G.	Good	Fair	Poor
350	300	—	—	—	—

Model 25 MG

This bolt action .22 Win. Mag Shot Shell only gun is fitted with a 22" smoothbore barrel. It has a 7-round magazine. Hardwood stock. Weight is about 6 lbs. First introduced in 1999.

NIB	Exc.	V.G.	Good	Fair	Poor
225	175	—	—	—	—

MODERN MUZZLELOADERS

Model MLS-50/54

These Marlin in-line muzzleloaders were introduced in 1997. They are stainless steel and available in either .50 or .54 caliber. The barrel is 22" long. Adjustable Marble rear sight, ramp front sight with brass bead. Drilled and tapped for scope mount. Black synthetic stock with molded in checkering. Weight is about 7 lbs.

NIB	Exc.	V.G.	Good	Fair	Poor
400	300	250	200	—	—

MAROCCHI, ARMI
Brescia, Italy
Importer-Precision Sales International
Westfield, Massachusetts

Model 2000

A 12 gauge Magnum single shot shotgun with a 28" barrel, exposed hammer and automatic ejector. Blued with a walnut stock.

Exc.	V.G.	Good	Fair	Poor
100	80	65	50	35

Field Master I

A 12 gauge Over/Under shotgun with 26" or 28" ventilated rib barrels fitted for choke tubes, single trigger and automatic ejectors. Blued, French case hardened with a walnut stock.

Exc.	V.G.	Good	Fair	Poor
400	350	300	200	150

Field Master II

As above, with a single selective trigger.

Exc.	V.G.	Good	Fair	Poor
425	375	325	225	175

CONQUISTA SERIES

Offered in 3 grades:

Grade I is the standard grade with a special polished steel finish and machined engraved. The stock and forearm are select walnut and hand checkered 20 lines to the inch.

Grade II has roll engraved game scenes. The stock is select figured walnut.

Grade III is hand engraved by a master engraver featuring game scenes. Finely figured walnut stock.

Sporting Clays Model

Offered in 12 gauge with 28", 30", or 32" ventilated rib barrels. Screw in chokes are standard. Adjustable trigger. Weight is approximately 8 lbs.

Grade I

NIB	Exc.	V.G.	Good	Fair	Poor
1800	1600	1100	850	600	300

Grade II

NIB	Exc.	V.G.	Good	Fair	Poor
2200	1800	1400	950	700	350

Grade III

NIB	Exc.	V.G.	Good	Fair	Poor
3200	2750	1750	1150	800	400

Sporting Light

Same as above but slightly smaller dimensions. Available in 28" or 30" barrel length. Weight is about 7.5 lbs.

Grade I

NIB	Exc.	V.G.	Good	Fair	Poor
1900	1600	1100	850	600	300

Sporting Clays Left Model

Same as Sporting Clays Model but designed for the left hand-ed shooter.

Grade I

NIB	Exc.	V.G.	Good	Fair	Poor
1900	1600	1100	850	600	300

Lady Sport Model

Offered in 12 gauge only with choice of 28" or 30" vent rib bar-rels. Slightly smaller dimensions for women. Weight 7.75 lbs.

Grade I

NIB	Exc.	V.G.	Good	Fair	Poor
1900	1600	1100	850	600	300

Spectrum Grade-Colored Frame

NIB	Exc.	V.G.	Good	Fair	Poor
1975	1650	1150	850	600	300

Lady Sport-Left Handed

Same as above but for left handed shooters.

Grade I

NIB	Exc.	V.G.	Good	Fair	Poor
1975	1650	1150	850	600	300

Spectrum-Left Handed

NIB	Exc.	V.G.	Good	Fair	Poor
2025	1700	1175	850	600	300

Trap Model

Built for the competition shooter this model features a choice of 30" or 32" vent rib barrels. Trap dimension stock. Weight approximately 8.25 lbs.

Grade I

NIB	Exc.	V.G.	Good	Fair	Poor
1875	1650	1150	850	600	300

Grade II

NIB	Exc.	V.G.	Good	Fair	Poor
2275	1850	1450	1000	750	350

Grade III

NIB	Exc.	V.G.	Good	Fair	Poor
3250	2600	1850	1500	800	400

Skeet Model

This model is designed for the competition shooter. Only a 28" vent rib barrel is offered as standard. Skeet dimension stock. Skeet chokes. Weight is approximately 7.75 lbs.

Grade I

NIB	Exc.	V.G.	Good	Fair	Poor
1875	1650	1150	850	600	300

Grade II

NIB	Exc.	V.G.	Good	Fair	Poor
2275	1850	1450	1000	750	350

Grade III

NIB	Exc.	V.G.	Good	Fair	Poor
3250	2600	1850	1500	800	400

Classic Doubles Model 92

Offered in 12 gauge only with 30" vent rib barrels. Adjustable trigger. Walnut stock with 18 lines to the inch checkering. Weight is approximately 8.12 lbs.

NIB	Exc.	V.G.	Good	Fair	Poor
1500	1250	800	600	500	250

MARS
SEE—Gabbet-Fairfax or Bergmann

MARSTON, S.W.
New York, New York

Double Action Pepperbox

A .31 caliber double action percussion pepperbox with a 5" barrel group and ring trigger. Blued with walnut grips. Manu-factured between 1850 and 1855.

Exc.	V.G.	Good	Fair	Poor
—	—	850	350	150

Two Barrel Pistol

A .31 or .36 revolving barrel 2-shot pistol with a ring trigger. The barrel marked "J.Cohn & S.W.Marston-New York." Blued, brass frame with walnut grips. Manufactured during the 1850s.

Exc.	V.G.	Good	Fair	Poor
—	—	1900	850	300

MARSTON, W. W. & CO.
New York, New York

W.W. Marston & Company manufactured a variety of firearms some of which are marked only with the trade names: Union Arms Company, Phoenix Armory, Western Arms Company, Washington Arms Company, Sprague and Marston, and Mar-ston and Knox.

Pocket Revolver

A .31 caliber percussion revolver with a 3.25" to 7.5" barrel and 6-shot cylinder. Blued with walnut grips. Approximately 13,000 were manufactured between 1857 and 1862.

Exc.	V.G.	Good	Fair	Poor
—	—	800	350	200

Navy Revolver

A .36 caliber percussion revolver with a 7.5" or 8.5" octagonal barrel and 6-shot cylinder. Blued with walnut grips. Manufac-tured between 1857 and 1862.

Exc.	V.G.	Good	Fair	Poor
—	—	2250	950	400

Double Action Single Shot Pistol

A .31 or .36 caliber bar hammer percussion pistol with a 2.5" or 5" half octagonal barrel. Blued with walnut grips. Manufac-tured during the 1850s.

Exc.	V.G.	Good	Fair	Poor
—	—	400	200	100

Single Action Pistol

A .31 or .36 caliber percussion pistol with a 4" or 6" barrel. Blued with walnut grips. Manufactured during the 1860s.

Exc.	V.G.	Good	Fair	Poor
—	—	400	200	100

Breech Loading Pistol

A .36 caliber breech loading percussion pistol with a 4" to 8.5" half octagonal barrel and either a brass or iron frame. Blued, case hardened with walnut grips. Approximately 1,000 were manufactured in the 1850s.

Courtesy Milwaukee Public Museum, Milwaukee, Wisconsin

Brass Frame

Exc.	V.G.	Good	Fair	Poor
—	—	2750	1000	300

Iron Frame

Exc.	V.G.	Good	Fair	Poor
—	—	2250	750	300

Double Action Pepperbox

A .31 caliber double action 6-shot percussion pepperbox with 4" or 5" barrel groups and a bar hammer. Blued, case hardened with walnut grips. Manufactured during the 1850s.

Courtesy Milwaukee Public Museum, Milwaukee, Wisconsin

Courtesy Milwaukee Public Museum, Milwaukee, Wisconsin

Exc.	V.G.	Good	Fair	Poor
—	—	1750	750	250

3 Barreled Derringer

A .22 caliber 3 barreled spur trigger pocket pistol with a sliding knife blade mounted on the left side of the 3" barrel group. Blued, silver-plated with walnut grips. The barrel marked "Wm. W. Marston/New York City." Approximately 1,500 were manufactured between 1858 and 1864.

Knife Bladed Model

Courtesy Milwaukee Public Museum, Milwaukee, Wisconsin

Exc.	V.G.	Good	Fair	Poor
—	—	3250	1400	400

Model Without Knife

Courtesy Milwaukee Public Museum, Milwaukee, Wisconsin

Exc.	V.G.	Good	Fair	Poor
—	—	1600	700	200

.32 Caliber 3 Barrel Derringer

Similar to the above, but in .32 caliber with either 3" or 4" barrels and not fitted with a knife blade. Approximately 3,000 were manufactured between 1864 and 1872.

Courtesy Milwaukee Public Museum, Milwaukee, Wisconsin

Exc.	V.G.	Good	Fair	Poor
—	—	1250	500	200

MASQUELIER S. A.
Liege, Belgium

Carpathe

A .243, .270, .7x57mm, 7x65Rmm, or .30-06 caliber single shot rifle with a 24" barrel, adjustable trigger and adjustable sights. Blued, with an engraved receiver and walnut stock. Imported until 1986.

Exc.	V.G.	Good	Fair	Poor
3500	2750	1950	1250	750

Express

A .270, .30-06, 8x57JRSmm, or 9.3x74Rmm caliber Over/Under double barrel rifle with 24" barrels, single selective trigger and automatic ejectors. Blued, engraved with a walnut stock. Not imported after 1986.

Exc.	V.G.	Good	Fair	Poor
3500	2750	1950	1250	750

Ardennes

As above, but made on custom order only. Discontinued in 1986.

Exc.	V.G.	Good	Fair	Poor
6500	5250	3750	2500	1000

Boxlock Side-by-Side Shotgun

A 12 gauge boxlock double barrel shotgun manufactured in a variety of barrel lengths with a single selective trigger and automatic ejectors. Blued with a walnut stock. Imported prior to 1987.

Exc.	V.G.	Good	Fair	Poor
4500	3250	2500	1500	850

Sidelock Side-by-Side Shotgun

Similar to the above, but with detachable sidelocks and finely engraved. Imported prior to 1987.

Exc.	V.G.	Good	Fair	Poor
13000	10500	7000	5000	1750

MASSACHUSETTS ARMS CO.
Chicopee Falls, Massachusetts

Wesson & Leavitt Dragoon

A .40 caliber percussion revolver with a 7" round barrel, 6-shot cylinder and side mounted hammer. Blued, case hardened with walnut grips. Approximately 800 were manufactured in 1850 and 1851.

Early Model with 6" Barrel-Approximately 30 Made

Exc.	V.G.	Good	Fair	Poor
—	—	5000	2000	750

Fully Marked 7" Barrel Standard Model

Exc.	V.G.	Good	Fair	Poor
—	—	4500	1500	650

Wesson & Leavitt Belt Revolver

A .31 caliber percussion revolver with a 3" to 7" round barrel and 6-shot cylinder. Similar in appearance to the above. Approximately 1,000 were manufactured in 1850 and 1851.

Exc.	V.G.	Good	Fair	Poor
—	—	1500	500	200

Maynard Primed Belt Revolver

Similar to the above, with a Maynard tape primer. Approximately 1,000 were manufactured between 1851 and 1857.

Exc.	V.G.	Good	Fair	Poor
—	—	2000	700	250

Maynard Primed Pocket Revolver

Similar to the above, but in .28 or .30 caliber with 2.5" to 3.5" octagonal or round barrels. Approximately 3,000 were made between 1851 and 1860.

Courtesy Milwaukee Public Museum, Milwaukee, Wisconsin

Exc.	V.G.	Good	Fair	Poor
—	—	1000	450	150

Adams Patent Navy Revolver

As above, in .36 caliber with a 6" octagonal barrel. Approximately 600 of the 1,000 made were purchased by the U.S. government. Those bearing inspection marks will bring approximately a 20% premium over the values listed below.

Exc.	V.G.	Good	Fair	Poor
—	—	1150	500	200

Single Shot Pocket Pistol

A .31 caliber single shot percussion pistol with a 2.5" to 3.5" half octagonal barrel and a Maynard tape primer. The barrel marked "Mass. Arms Co/Chicopee Falls" and the primer door "Maynard's Patent Sept. 22, 1845." Blued, case hardened with walnut grips. Manufactured in the 1850s.

Exc.	V.G.	Good	Fair	Poor
—	—	2500	850	300

Maynard Carbine

This is a single-shot breechloader chambered for .35 or .50 caliber percussion. The barrel is round and 20" in length. The triggerguard is the lever that pivots the barrel in break-open fashion when it is lowered. The finish is blued, with a case colored frame. The buttstock is walnut, and there is no forend. This carbine was designed by the same Maynard who invented the tape primer system. There are two models—a 1st and a 2nd. They were made for both sporting use and as a U.S. Martial carbine. The 2nd Model was used considerably during the Civil War.

1st Model

This model is marked "Maynard Patentee/May 27, 1851/June 17, 1856." It has an iron patchbox and a curved buttplate. It has a Maynard tape primer system and a tang sight. Later production was fitted with a sling swivel. There are approximately 400 of these carbines that are U.S. marked, but the total manufactured in the late 1850s is unknown.

Courtesy Milwaukee Public Museum, Milwaukee, Wisconsin

U.S. Martially Marked and AUTHENTICATED

Exc.	V.G.	Good	Fair	Poor
—	—	5000	2000	500

Commercial Model

Exc.	V.G.	Good	Fair	Poor
—	—	3500	1000	350

2nd Model

This model is chambered for .50 caliber only and does not have the tape primer system or the tang sight. There is no patchbox, and the buttplate is not as curved as on the 1st Model. It is marked "Manufactured By/Mass. Arms Co./Chicopee Falls." There were approximately 20,000 manufactured between 1860 and 1865. This model was used by Union forces during the Civil War.

Courtesy Milwaukee Public Museum, Milwaukee, Wisconsin

Exc.	V.G.	Good	Fair	Poor
—	—	1500	650	350

Maynard Patent Sporting Rifles

Courtesy Milwaukee Public Museum, Milwaukee, Wisconsin

Courtesy Milwaukee Public Museum, Milwaukee, Wisconsin

Sporting rifles bearing the designations Model 1865, 1873 and 1882 were manufactured in a wide variety of calibers, gauges, stock styles, finishes, and options. As these features affect the values of individual arms considerably, it is recommended that prospective purchasers are advised to secure a qualified appraisal prior to acquisition.

Exc.	V.G.	Good	Fair	Poor
—	—	1000	600	200

MATERA ARMS
Italy
Importer-Kiesler's Wholesale

AutoRevolver

Introduced in 2000 this revolver is chambered for the .357 magnum or .44 Magnum with 4", 6", or 8" barrel. The gun features a single action trigger that has a reciprocating cylinder that fires from the bottom chamber rather than the top. The firing of the gun cocks the hammer and cycles the action for the next round. Available with or without compensator. Offered in blue or nickel finish. Extra barrels available.

NIB	Exc.	V.G.	Good	Fair	Poor
1149	—	—	—	—	—

NOTE: Guns without compensator deduct $80. For nickel finish add $50. For extra barrel add $140.

MATRA MANURHIN DEFENSE
Mulhouse, France
SEE—Manurhin

MAUSER WERKE
Oberndorf-am-Neckar, Germany

Established in 1869 by Peter and Wilhelm Mauser, this company came under the effective control of Ludwig Loewe and Company of Berlin in 1887. In 1896 the latter company was re-organized under the name *Deutsches Waffen und Munition* or as it is better known, DWM.

NOTE: For historical information, technical details, and photos and prices see the *Standard Catalog of Military Firearms, 1870 to the Present* under Germany.

Early Sporting Rifles

A wide variety of commercial Model 98 Sporting Rifles were made, most of which had 23.5" ribbed barrels, open sights, 5-shot magazines, single or double set triggers, and either full or semi-pistol grip stocks.

NOTE: While the following values are representative, it is suggested that prospective purchasers secure a qualified appraisal prior to acquisition. Mauser rifles almost always have extra cost features that can greatly affect price.

Type A-Short Action

Exc.	V.G.	Good	Fair	Poor
4000	3500	3000	1750	1100

Type A-Medium Action

Exc.	V.G.	Good	Fair	Poor
3000	2500	2000	1500	1000

Type A-Long Action

Exc.	V.G.	Good	Fair	Poor
4250	3750	3250	2500	2000

Type B

Exc.	V.G.	Good	Fair	Poor
3000	2500	1750	1250	1000

Type K-21.65" Barrel

Exc.	V.G.	Good	Fair	Poor
4250	3750	3200	2250	1000

Type M-Full-length Stock, Spoon Bolt Handle

Exc.	V.G.	Good	Fair	Poor
4250	3750	3000	1750	1100

Type S-Full-length Stock, No Forend Cap

Exc.	V.G.	Good	Fair	Poor
4250	3750	3000	1750	1100

MODEL 1896
"BROOMHANDLE MAUSER PISTOL"

Manufactured from 1896 to 1939, the Model 1896 Pistol was produced in a wide variety of styles as listed below. It is recommended that those considering the purchase of any of the following models should consult Breathed & Schroeder's System Mauser (Chicago 1967) as it provides detailed descriptions and photographs of the various models. A correct, matching stock/holster will add approximately 40 percent to value of each category.

Large Ring Cutaway   Courtesy Gale Morgan

"BUYER BEWARE" ALERT by Gale Morgan: As noted in previous editions of the *Standard Catalog of Firearms* over the past several years large quanities of "Broomhandle" Mausers and Astra "copies" have been imported into the United States. Generally these are in poor or fair condition and have been offered for sale in the $125 to $300 price range, primarily as shooters or parts guns. Over the past year or so, a cottage industry has sprung up where these very common pistols have been "converted" to "rare, exotic, near mint, original" specimens selling well into the four figure price range. I have personallly seen English Crest, the U.S. Great Seal, unheard-of European dealers, aristocratic Coats-of-Arms, and Middle East Medallions beautifully photo-etched into the magazine wells and rear panels of some really common wartime commercials with price tags that have been elevated to $2,500 plus. They are quite eye-catching and if they are sold as customized/modified Mausers, the seller can price the piece at whatever the market will bear. However, if sold as a factory original-BUYER BEWARE.

Courtesy Wallis & Wallis, Lewes, Sussex, England

Six-Shot Step-Barrel Cone Hammer

A 7.63mm semiautomatic pistol with a 5.5" barrel, fixed rear sight and checkered walnut grips. Marked "Ruecklauf Pistole System Mauser, Oberndorf am/Neckar 1896." Fewer than 200 were manufactured. Too rare to price.

Courtesy Joe Schroeder

Twenty-Shot Step-Barrel Cone Hammer

As above, with a 20-shot extended magazine and tangent rear sight. Engraved "SYSTEM MAUSER" on top of chamber. Too rare to price.

Courtesy Joe Schroeder

System Mauser Cone Hammer

As above, with either fixed or tangent rear sight. Magazine capacity 10 rounds.

Courtesy Rock Island Auction Company

Exc.	V.G.	Good	Fair	Poor
17000	15000	10000	8000	7000

Six-Shot Standard Cone Hammer

Similar to the above but with no step in the barrel, 6-shot magazine and marked "Waffenfabrik Mauser, Oberndorf A/N" over the chamber. May have fixed or rarely tangent rear sight.

Exc.	V.G.	Good	Fair	Poor
11000	10000	6000	5000	3000

Twenty-Shot Cone Hammer

As above, with an extended magazine holding 20 cartridges.

Exc.	V.G.	Good	Fair	Poor
30000	25000	15000	10000	7000

Standard Cone Hammer

As above, with a 10-shot magazine and 23 groove grips.

Exc.	V.G.	Good	Fair	Poor
4000	3000	2400	1400	800

Fixed Sight Cone Hammer

Similar to the standard Cone Hammer except that a fixed, integral sight is machined into the barrel extension.

Courtesy Joe Schroeder

Exc.	V.G.	Good	Fair	Poor
4700	4000	2000	1500	1000

Turkish Contract Cone Hammer

As above, but marked in Turkish script and bearing the crest of Sultan Abdul-Hamid II on the frame. Approximately 1,000 were made.

Courtesy Joe Schroeder

Courtesy Gale Morgan

Exc.	V.G.	Good	Fair	Poor
12000	8000	6500	3000	2000

Early Transitional Large Ring Hammer

This variation has the same characteristics of the "Standard Cone Hammer" except the hammer has a larger, open ring.

Courtesy Joe Schroeder

Exc.	V.G.	Good	Fair	Poor
3500	2800	2500	1150	800

Model 1899 Flat Side-Italian Contract

Similar to the above, with a 5.5" barrel, adjustable rear sight and the frame sides milled flat. Left flat of chamber marked with "DV" proof. Approximately 5,000 were manufactured in 1899.

Courtesy Joe Schroeder

Exc.	V.G.	Good	Fair	Poor
4000	3000	1500	1200	900

Early Flat Side

Similar to the above, except with "pinned" rear sight and without the Italian markings.

Exc.	V.G.	Good	Fair	Poor
3000	2700	1500	1000	750

Late Flat Side

Similar to the above, with an integral pin mounted adjustable rear sight and often marked with dealer's names such as "Von Lengerke & Detmold, New York".

Exc.	V.G.	Good	Fair	Poor
2700	2200	1500	1000	750

Flat Side Bolo

Similar to the above, but with a 3.9" barrel, fixed sights, and checkered walnut grips. Very rare.

Exc.	V.G.	Good	Fair	Poor
7500	6000	4000	3000	2000

Early Large Ring Hammer Bolo

As above, with a milled frame, adjustable rear sight, and grooved wood or hard rubber grips cast with a floral pattern. 10-shot magazine.

Exc.	V.G.	Good	Fair	Poor
4500	3700	2000	1500	1000

Shallow-Milled Panel Model

Similar to the above, with a 5.5" barrel and either 23 groove walnut or checkered hard rubber grips.

Exc.	V.G.	Good	Fair	Poor
3300	2400	1000	750	500

Deep-Milled Panel Model

As above, with deeper milled panels on the sides of the receiver.

Exc.	V.G.	Good	Fair	Poor
3300	2000	1500	1000	750

Late Large Ring Hammer Bolo

Similar to the Early Large Ring Hammer Bolo, but with the late style adjustable rear sight.

Exc.	V.G.	Good	Fair	Poor
3000	2500	1500	1000	750

Six-Shot Large Ring Bolo

Similar to the above Large Ring Bolo but with six-shot magazine. This model is usually equipped with fixed sights.

Courtesy James Rankin

Exc.	V.G.	Good	Fair	Poor
8000	7000	5000	3000	1800

Early Small Ring Hammer Model, Transitional

The Model 96 with an early long extractor and a hammer having a small diameter hole and a 5.5" barrel. The grips with 34 grooves.

Courtesy Joe Schroeder

Exc.	V.G.	Good	Fair	Poor
3200	2500	1500	1000	500

Early Small Ring Hammer Bolo Model

As above, with a 3.9" barrel and hard rubber grips cast with a floral pattern. Serial numbers in the 40,000 range.

Exc.	V.G.	Good	Fair	Poor
3500	3000	2000	1500	600

Six-Shot Small Ring Hammer Model

As above, with 27 groove walnut grips.

Exc.	V.G.	Good	Fair	Poor
8000	6500	4000	2250	1600

Standard Prewar Commercial

A Model 96 with a 5.5" barrel, late-style adjustable rear sight and either 34 groove walnut grips or checkered hard rubber grips. Often found with dealers markings such as "Von Lengerke & Detmold."

Courtesy Joe Schroeder

Exc.	V.G.	Good	Fair	Poor
2200	1800	1200	650	300

9mm Export Model

As above, in 9mm Mauser with 34 groove walnut grips.

Exc.	V.G.	Good	Fair	Poor
2500	2250	1500	1000	700

Mauser Banner Model

Standard pre-war features except chamber stamped with the Mauser Banner trademark and 32 groove walnut grips. Approximately 10,000 were manufactured.

Courtesy Joe Schroeder

Exc.	V.G.	Good	Fair	Poor
3700	3200	2300	1100	600

Persian Contract

Persian rampant lion on left rear panel. Prospective purchasers should secure a qualified appraisal prior to acquisition. Serial numbers in the 154000 range.

Exc.	V.G.	Good	Fair	Poor
4200	3500	2250	1400	1000

Standard Wartime Commercial

Identical to the prewar Commercial Model 96, except that it has 30 groove walnut grips and the rear of the hammer is stamped "NS" for new safety. Many also bear German or Austrian military acceptance proofs.

Courtesy Gale Morgan

Exc.	V.G.	Good	Fair	Poor
1800	1300	1000	500	350

9mm Parabellum Military Contract

As above, in 9mm Parabellum caliber with 24 groove grips, stamped with a large "9" filled with red paint.

Mauser 9mm Military Contract "Red 9" rig

Courtesy Gale Morgan

Exc.	V.G.	Good	Fair	Poor
2400	1700	1200	700	450

1920 Rework

A Model 96 modified to a barrel length of 3.9" and in 7.63mm Mauser or 9mm Parabellum caliber. Often encountered with police markings.

Courtesy Joe Schroeder

Courtesy Butterfield & Butterfield, San Francisco, California

Exc.	V.G.	Good	Fair	Poor
1500	1000	500	400	350

Luger Barreled 1920 Rework

Similar to the above, but fitted with a Luger barrel of 4" in length. 23 groove walnut grips and of 9mm caliber.

Courtesy Gale Morgan

Exc.	V.G.	Good	Fair	Poor
2100	1500	750	500	450

French Gendarme Model

A standard Model 96 fitted with a 3.9" barrel and checkered hard rubber grips. Although reputed to have been made under a French contract, no record of that has been found to date.

Courtesy James Rankin

Exc.	V.G.	Good	Fair	Poor
3000	2500	1500	800	400

Early Postwar Bolo Model

A Model 96 in 7.63mm caliber with a 3.9" barrel, adjustable rear sight and 22-groove walnut grips.

Exc.	V.G.	Good	Fair	Poor
1800	1200	700	400	200

Late Postwar Bolo Model

As above, with the Mauser Banner trademark stamped on the left rear panel.

Courtesy Gale Morgan

Courtesy James Rankin

Exc.	V.G.	Good	Fair	Poor
1800	1200	700	400	200

Early Model 1930

A 7.63mm caliber Model 96 with a 5.2" stepped barrel, 12-groove walnut grips and late style safety.

Courtesy Gale Morgan

Exc.	V.G.	Good	Fair	Poor
2700	2200	1200	800	500

Late Model 1930

Identical to the above, except for solid receiver rails.

Exc.	V.G.	Good	Fair	Poor
2500	2000	1000	700	400

Model 1930 Removable Magazine

Similar to the above, but with a detachable magazine. Prospective purchasers should secure a qualified appraisal prior to acquisition. Too rare to price.

CARBINE MODELS

Cone Hammer Flat Side Carbine

A 7.63mm caliber carbine with an 11.75" barrel, early adjustable sight, flat frame and detachable buttstock. Prospective purchasers should secure a qualified appraisal prior to acquisition. Too rare to price.

Large Ring Hammer Transitional Carbine

Similar to the above, with milled frame panels. Prospective purchasers should secure a qualified appraisal prior to acquisition.

Exc.	V.G.	Good	Fair	Poor
23000	18000	11000	5000	3000

Large Ring Hammer Carbine

Similar to the above, with a 14.5" barrel. Prospective purchasers should secure a qualified appraisal prior to acquisition.

A large ring transitional carbine was sold at auction for $23,000. Low two digit serial number. Engraved "WESTLEY RICHARDS & CO./LONDON" on left milled panel. Condition was excellent.
Amoskeag Auction Co. Inc., November 1999

Exc.	V.G.	Good	Fair	Poor
22000	18000	10000	4000	3000

Small Ring Hammer Carbine with serial numbers 1035 and 1045, the highest known manufactured by Mauser.

Courtesy Gale Morgan

Small Ring Hammer Carbine

Similar to the above, with the hammer having a smaller diameter hole at its tip. Prospective purchasers should secure a qualified appraisal prior to acquisition.

Exc.	V.G	Good	Fair	Poor
26000	20000	12000	5000	3000

CHINESE COPIES

Chinese Marked, Handmade Copies

Crude copies of the Model 96 and unsafe to fire.

Exc.	V.G.	Good	Fair	Poor
500	400	350	250	175

Taku-Naval Dockyard Model

Approximately 6,000 copies of the Model 96 were made at the Taku-Naval Dockyard. Values listed below include a correct shoulder stock/holder.

Exc.	V.G.	Good	Fair	Poor
2500	1500	1000	500	400

Shansei Arsenal Model

Approximately 8,000 Model 96 pistols were manufactured in .45 ACP caliber.

Shansei Panel Marking

Courtesy Gale Morgan

Exc.	V.G.	Good	Fair	Poor
5000	3500	2250	1500	1300

NOTE: Within the past several years, a large quantity of Model 96 pistols exported to or made in China have been imported into the United States. It has been reported that some *newly* made copies of the Shansei .45 were recently exported from China. **Proceed with caution**.

Copies of the Model 96 were made by Unceta (Astra) and Zulaica y Cia (Royal) and marketed by the firm of Beistegui Hermanos. These copies are covered in their own sections of this text.

MAUSER POCKET PISTOLS

Model 1910

A 6.35mm (.25 ACP) caliber pistol with a 3" barrel, 9-shot magazine and either a checkered walnut or (scarce) hard rubber wraparound grip. Early examples (below serial 60,000 or so) have a pivoting takedown latch above the triggerguard and are identified as "Sidelatch" models by collectors. Later production Models 1910s are often identified as the Model 1910/14. Manufactured from 1910 to 1934.

Sidelatch Model

Exc.	V.G.	Good	Fair	Poor
600	450	300	200	150

Later Production (Model 1910/14)

Exc.	V.G.	Good	Fair	Poor
375	275	200	150	100

Model 1914

A larger version of the Model 1910, chambered for 7.65mm Browning (.32 ACP) with a 3.5" or (rarely) 4.5" barrel. Very early examples up to serial 2500 or so had an odd hump on the slide and are called "Humpbacks" by collectors; these bring a considerable premium. Model 1914s with police or military markings bring a small premium. Manufactured between 1914 and 1934.

Model 1914 "Humpback"

Exc.	V.G.	Good	Fair	Poor
2500	2000	1500	800	400

Model 1914 (later)

Exc.	V.G.	Good	Fair	Poor
400	300	200	150	100

Model 1912/14

While Mauser's pocket pistols were very successful on the commercial market, Mauser was also trying to develop a larger caliber pistol for military use. The most successful of these was the Model 1912/14, though only about 200 were ever made. A few of these did reach the commercial market, and it's likely the pistol would have continued in production had WWI not broken out. Higher serial numbered guns were slotted for a Model 1896-style holster stock, and a few of these also had tangent sights. Add 25% for shoulder stock.

Exc.	V.G.	Good	Fair	Poor
20000	15000	11000	8000	4000

Model WTP 1

This was Mauser's first post-WWI new design and first vest pocket pistol, with a 2.5" barrel and 6-shot magazine capacity. Grips were plastic wraparound, with one, two or three grip screws depending on production period! Production ended in the late '30s, when the WTP II was introduced.

Exc.	V.G.	Good	Fair	Poor
400	300	250	175	125

Model WTP II

The WTP II was a much more compact design that its predecessor, with a 2" barrel and separate grip panels instead of Mauser's usual wraparound grip. Production was limited by the outbreak of WWII, so the WTP II is much scarcer than the WTP I. Under French occupation at least several hundred WTP IIs were assembled and sold; these can be identified by their very low electric penciled serial numbers and lack of German proofing, and bring a slight premium over the prewar German manufactured pistols.

Courtesy Gale Morgan

Exc.	V.G.	Good	Fair	Poor
600	450	325	250	175

Model 1934

In response to competition from Walther and others, in 1934 Mauser spruced up its aging 1910/14 and 1914 pistols with a new high polish finish and form-fitting swept back grips. Nickel finish was also offered, but is very rare (50% premium, but beware of renickeled blued guns!). The 7.65mm pistols became popular with both the military and police, but those so marked can bring a considerable premium (see prices at right).

Courtesy Orvel Reichert

Courtesy Orvel Reichert

Courtesy Gale Morgan

Model 1934 6.35mm

Exc.	V.G.	Good	Fair	Poor
450	325	250	200	125

Model 1934 7.65mm Commercial

Exc.	V.G.	Good	Fair	Poor
400	325	250	200	125

Model 1934 7.65mm Eagle L proofed

Exc.	V.G.	Good	Fair	Poor
550	450	300	250	150

Model 1934 7.56mm Large Eagle over M (Navy)

Exc.	V.G.	Good	Fair	Poor
800	650	450	300	200

Model HSc

The HSc was a totally new design, chambered for 7.65mm Browning and featuring double action lockwork and a partially concealed external hammer. Introduced just as WWII broke out, the HSc was produced through the war for both commercial sale and military use. Serials started at 700,000, and the first 1500 or so had the grip screws located near the bottom of the grip and bring a large premium. Finish deteriorated as the war progressed, and some HSc pistols were even produced after the war ended under French occupation.

Add 20% for Waffenamt markings, and 50% for Navy marked front straps.

Courtesy Orvel Reichert

Bottom Grip Screw pistols

Exc.	V.G.	Good	Fair	Poor
3000	2500	2000	1500	800

Later, but still high polish finish

Exc.	V.G.	Good	Fair	Poor
450	375	300	250	150

Late Wartime Production with dull finish

Exc.	V.G.	Good	Fair	Poor
350	275	225	175	150

Model HSc Postwar Production

In the late 1960s Maser resumed production of the HSc in both 7.65mm and 9mm Browning short (.380). Five thousand postwar HSc pistols were specially marked with an American eagle, and bring a slight premium over standard marked pistols. In the '80s Mauser licensed HSc production to Gamba in Italy, who produced an enlarged frame version of the HSc with a double column magazine. In both German and Italian production, 380s bring about a 20% premium over .32s.

Mauser Production (.32)

Exc.	V.G.	Good	Fair	Poor
325	250	200	175	125

Gamba Production

Exc.	V.G.	Good	Fair	Poor
250	200	175	150	100

NOTE: In recent years Mauser has licensed several firms other than Gamba to produce pistols bearing the Mauser trademark, such as a Browning Hi Power knockoff made in Hungary. In 1999 Mauser was bought by SIG Sauer, and a new large caliber Mauser pistol was announced.

Low Grip Screw Model

As above, with screws that attach the grip located near the bottom of the grip. Highly-polished blue, checkered walnut grips and the early address without the lines and has the Eagle N proof. Some have been observed with Nazi Kreigsmarine markings. Approximately 2,000 were manufactured.

Exc.	V.G.	Good	Fair	Poor
3500	3000	1800	750	650

Early Commercial Model

A highly-polished blued finish, checkered walnut grips, the standard Mauser address on the slide, and the Eagle N proofmark. The floorplate of the magazine stamped with the Mauser Banner.

Exc.	V.G.	Good	Fair	Poor
650	500	350	175	125

Transition Model

As above, but not as highly finished.

Exc.	V.G.	Good	Fair	Poor
525	400	300	150	100

Early Nazi Army Model

Courtesy Orvel Reichert

Exc.	V.G.	Good	Fair	Poor
650	550	400	200	125

Late Nazi Army Model

Exc.	V.G.	Good	Fair	Poor
450	375	250	150	100

Early Nazi Navy Model

Exc.	V.G.	Good	Fair	Poor
1000	800	550	400	300

Wartime Nazi Navy Model

Exc.	V.G.	Good	Fair	Poor
700	600	500	400	200

Early Nazi Police Model

Exc.	V.G.	Good	Fair	Poor
600	500	425	250	175

Wartime Nazi Police Model

Exc.	V.G.	Good	Fair	Poor
500	400	350	250	175

Wartime Commercial Model

As above, without acceptance markings on the triggerguard.

Exc.	V.G.	Good	Fair	Poor
425	350	300	200	125

French Manufactured Model

Blued or parkerized with walnut or plastic grips and the trigger-guard marked on the left side with the monogram "MR".

Exc.	V.G.	Good	Fair	Poor
325	275	225	150	100

American Eagle HSc

Only 5,000 of this pistols were produced in both .380 and .32 caliber.

NOTE: Deduct 20% for .32 caliber model.

NIB	Exc.	V.G.	Good	Fair	Poor
375	325	275	225	150	100

Late Mauser Production Model

Manufactured from 1968 to 1981, this model was almost identical to the early Commercial Model. Built in .380 and .32 caliber.

NOTE: Deduct 20% for .32 caliber model.

Exc.	V.G.	Good	Fair	Poor
325	275	225	150	100

Interarms Import Models

As above, but made by Gamba in Italy and sold by Interarms of Alexandria, Virginia, from 1983 to 1985.

Exc.	V.G.	Good	Fair	Poor
275	250	200	150	100

MAUSER RIFLES & PISTOLS-RECENT PRODUCTION

NOTE: In February of 1999 SIG Arms announced the acquisition of the Mauser line of small arms. With the acquisition, SIG assumes the rights to the Mauser name and will integrate the Mauser product line into SIG Arms' line of small arms.

Model 2000

A .270, .308, or the .30-06 caliber bolt action rifle with a 24" barrel, open sights and a 5-shot magazine. Blued, with a checkered walnut stock. Manufactured between 1969 and 1971.

Exc.	V.G.	Good	Fair	Poor
350	300	250	200	150

Model 3000

As above, with a 22" barrel, no sights and Monte Carlo-style stock. Manufactured from 1971 to 1974.

Exc.	V.G.	Good	Fair	Poor
450	400	350	300	250

Model 3000 Magnum

As above, in 7mm Rem. Mag., .300 Win. Mag. and the .375 H&H Mag. caliber with a 26" barrel and a 3-shot integral magazine. Blued, with a checkered walnut stock.

Exc.	V.G.	Good	Fair	Poor
500	450	400	350	300

Model 4000

Similar to the Model 3000, but in .222 or .223 caliber with folding open sights.

Exc.	V.G.	Good	Fair	Poor
400	350	300	250	200

Model 225

A .243 to. 300 Weatherby Magnum caliber bolt action rifle with a 24" or 26" barrel, no sights, adjustable trigger or 3- or 5-shot magazine. Blued with a walnut stock.

NIB	Exc.	V.G.	Good	Fair	Poor
1400	1250	1000	750	600	500

Model ES340

A .22 caliber single shot bolt action rifle with a 25.5" barrel, open sights, and walnut stock. Manufactured before WWII.

Exc.	V.G.	Good	Fair	Poor
300	250	225	175	125

Model DSM34
Similar to the above, with a 25" barrel and full-length walnut stock. Manufactured prior to WWII.

Exc.	V.G.	Good	Fair	Poor
325	275	250	200	150

Model MS420B
Similar to the above, with a 25" barrel and 5-shot magazine. Manufactured before WWII.

Exc.	V.G.	Good	Fair	Poor
375	325	300	275	200

Model ES350
A .22 caliber single shot bolt action rifle with a 27.5" barrel and checkered pistol grip walnut stock. Manufactured before WWII.

Exc.	V.G.	Good	Fair	Poor
450	400	375	350	275

Model M410
Similar to the above, with a 23.5" barrel and 5-shot magazine. Manufactured before WWII.

Exc.	V.G.	Good	Fair	Poor
375	325	300	275	200

Model M420
As above, with a 25.5" barrel.

Exc.	V.G.	Good	Fair	Poor
375	325	300	275	200

Model EN310
A .22 caliber single shot bolt action rifle with a 19.75" barrel, open sights, and plain walnut stock. Manufactured before WWII.

Exc.	V.G.	Good	Fair	Poor
250	225	200	150	100

Model EL320
As above, with a 23.5" barrel and checkered walnut stock.

Exc.	V.G.	Good	Fair	Poor
275	250	225	175	125

Model KKW
A .22 caliber single shot bolt action rifle with a 26" barrel, ladder rear sight and full-length walnut stock. Manufactured prior to WWII.

Exc.	V.G.	Good	Fair	Poor
400	350	300	225	150

Model MS350B
A .22 caliber bolt action rifle with a 26.75" barrel, adjustable rear sight and 5-shot magazine. Blued with a walnut stock.

Exc.	V.G.	Good	Fair	Poor
475	400	350	275	200

Model ES340B
Similar to the above, but in single shot form.

Exc.	V.G.	Good	Fair	Poor
375	300	250	175	100

Model MM41OBN
A .22 caliber bolt action rifle with a 23.5" barrel, adjustable sights, and 5-shot magazine. Blued with a walnut stock.

Exc.	V.G.	Good	Fair	Poor
400	350	300	200	125

Model MS420B
As above, with a 26.75" barrel and target style stock.

Exc.	V.G.	Good	Fair	Poor
400	350	300	200	125

Model 107
This is a bolt action rifle chambered for the .22 Long Rifle. Barrel length is 21.6" and box magazine has a 5-shot capacity. The beechwood checkered Monte Carlo stock is full size with pistol grip, plastic buttplate. The rear sight is adjustable. Metal finish is blue. Weighs about 5 lbs.

NIB	Exc.	V.G.	Good	Fair	Poor
265	225	180	150	125	100

Model 201 Standard
This model features a 21" medium heavy free-floating barrel. The receiver accepts all rail mounts and is also drilled and tapped for scope mount. Magazine capacity is 5-shot. Chambered for .22 Long Rifle or .22 WMR cartridge. The beechwood stock is hand checkered with plastic buttplate. The Monte Carlo stock is fitted with cheekpiece. Weighs about 6.5 lbs.

NIB	Exc.	V.G.	Good	Fair	Poor
400	325	250	200	150	100

Model 201 Luxus
Same as above but features a European walnut stock with rosewood forend, hand checkering, rubber butt pad, and 1" quick disconnect sling swivels. Available with or without sights.

NIB	Exc.	V.G.	Good	Fair	Poor
550	475	400	350	300	200

Model 66 Standard
This is a centerfire bolt action rifle fitted with a European Walnut hand-checkered oil finish stock. Stock is half stock design. Rosewood forends and pistol grip caps are standard. Fitted with rubber recoil pad and 1" quick disconnect sling swivels.

Barrels are interchangeable on this model. Barrels with standard calibers is 24" and approximate weight is 7.5 lbs. Standard calibers are: .243 Win., .270, .308, .30-06, 5.6x57, 6.5x57, 7.64, and 9.3x62.

NIB	Exc.	V.G.	Good	Fair	Poor
1400	1150	850	700	550	350

Model 66 Magnum

Same as above but chambered for 7mm Rem. Mag., .300 and .338 Win. Mag., 6.5x68, 8x86S, 9.3x64. Fitted with a 26" barrel and weighs about 7.9 lbs.

NIB	Exc.	V.G.	Good	Fair	Poor
1500	1250	950	800	600	400

Model 66 Safari

Same as above but chambered for .375 H&H and .458 Win. Mag. Fitted with a 26" barrel and weighs about 9.3 lbs.

NIB	Exc.	V.G.	Good	Fair	Poor
1650	1400	1100	850	650	400

Model 66 Stuzen

Same as the Standard Model 66 but fitted with a full stock. Barrel length is 21" and calibers are same as Standard. Weighs about 7.5 lbs.

NIB	Exc.	V.G.	Good	Fair	Poor
1500	1250	950	800	600	400

IDF Mauser Rifle Model 66SP

This is a bolt action rifle chambered for the .308 Win. cartridge. Adjustable trigger for pull and travel. Barrel length is 27". Specially designed stock has broad forend and a thumb hole pistol grip. Cheekpiece is adjustable as is the recoil pad. Supplied with case. This rifle is military issue. Less than 100 imported into the U.S by Springfield Armory.

NIB	Exc.	V.G.	Good	Fair	Poor
2200	1750	—	—	—	—

Model 86 SR

Introduced in 1993 this bolt action .308 is sometimes referred to as the Specialty Rifle. Fitted with a laminated wood and special match thumbhole stock or fiberglass stock with adjustable cheekpiece. Stock has rail in forearm and an adjustable recoil pad. Magazine capacity is 9 rounds. Finish is a non-glare blue. The barrel length with muzzle brake is 28.8". Many special features are found on this rifle from adjustable trigger weight to silent safety. Mauser offers many options on this rifle as well that will affect the price. Weight is approximately 11 lbs.

NIB	Exc.	V.G.	Good	Fair	Poor
3300	2950	2500	1750	1250	750

Model 93 SR

Introduced in 1996 this is a tactical semiautomatic rifle chambered for the .300 Win. Mag. or the .338 Lapua cartridge. Barrel length is 25.5" with an overall length of 48.4". Barrel is fitted with a muzzle brake. Magazine capacity is 6 rounds for .300 and 5 rounds for .338 caliber. Weight is approximately 13 lbs.

NIB	Exc.	V.G.	Good	Fair	Poor
N/A	—	—	—	—	—

Model 99 Standard

This model is a bolt action centerfire sporting rifle. It is offered with two stock designs: a classic with straight oil finish stock or high luster with cheekpiece and schnabel forend and Monte Carlo with rosewood forend tip and pistol grip cap. Chambered for standard calibers: .243, .25-06, .270, .308, .30-06, 5.6x57, 6.5x57, 7x57, 7x64. Barrel length is 24". Weight about 8 lbs.

NIB	Exc.	V.G.	Good	Fair	Poor
900	700	600	500	400	300

Model 99 Magnum

Same as above but chambered for magnum calibers: 7mm Rem. Mag., .257 Wby., .270 Wby., .300 Wby., .300 and .338 Win. Mag., 8x68S, and 9.3x64. Fitted with 26" barrel. Weighs about 8 lbs.

NIB	Exc.	V.G.	Good	Fair	Poor
950	750	650	550	400	300

Model 96

This bolt action rifle is chambered for the .25-06, .270 Win., 7x64, .308, or .30-06 cartridge. It is fitted with a 22" barrel (24" Magnum calibers) and has a 5-round top loading magazine. Receiver is drilled and tapped. Checkered walnut stock. No sights. Approximately weight is 6.25 lbs.

NIB	Exc.	V.G.	Good	Fair	Poor
675	525	400	300	250	200

Model 98 (SIG Arms)

Built in Germany this bolt action rifle features a select walnut stock with oil finish. Express rear sight and single stage trigger. Chambered for the .416 Rigby, .450 Dakota, .458 Lott, and .500 Jeffry. Weight is approximately 8.8 lbs.

NIB	Exc.	V.G.	Good	Fair	Poor
9500	—	—	—	—	—

NOTE: Add $1,000 for .500 Jeffry.

Model 80 SA

This single action semiautomatic pistol is based on the Browning Hi-Power design. Chambered for the 9mm Parabellum cartridge it has a barrel length of 4.66" and a magazine capacity of 14 rounds. Weighs approximately 35 oz.

NIB	Exc.	V.G.	Good	Fair	Poor
300	275	225	175	125	100

Model Compact DA

Same as above but double action trigger and shorter barrel: 4.13". Weighs approximately 33 oz.

NIB	Exc.	V.G.	Good	Fair	Poor
340	320	250	175	125	100

Model 90 DA

Similar to the Model 80 but with a double action trigger.

NIB	Exc.	V.G.	Good	Fair	Poor
310	285	235	175	125	100

Model M2 (Imported by SIG Arms)

Introduced in 2000 this pistol is chambered for the .45ACP, .40S&W, or .357 SIG cartridges. It has an aluminum alloy frame and steel slide. The action is an enclosed hammerless striker-fired design. Barrel length is 3.5". Fixed sights. Weight is about 29 oz. Magazine capacity for .45ACP is 8 rounds, for .40S&W and .357 SIG capacity is 10 rounds.

NIB	Exc.	V.G.	Good	Fair	Poor
475	400	—	—	—	—

MAVERICK ARMS, INC.
Eagle Pass, Texas

Model 88

A 12 gauge Magnum slide action shotgun with 28" or 30" barrels, anodized receiver and composition stock. Introduced in 1989.

NIB	Exc.	V.G.	Good	Fair	Poor
250	150	125	100	75	50

MAYNARD/PERRY
Keen, Walker & Co.
Danville, Virginia

Brass Framed Carbine

Overall length 40"; barrel length 22.5"; caliber .54. Browned, blued barrel, brass frame and walnut stock. Manufactured in 1861 and 1862. Less than 300 produced. Prospective purchasers are advised to secure a qualified appraisal prior to acquisition.

Exc.	V.G.	Good	Fair	Poor
—	—	25000	10000	—

McMILLAN, G. & CO. INC.
Phoenix, Arizona

Competition Model

A custom order bolt action rifle in .308, 7mm/08, and the .300 Winchester Magnum caliber with the barrel length, stock type, and dimensions to the customer's specifications. Introduced in 1988.

NIB	Exc.	V.G.	Good	Fair	Poor
1700	1500	1150	800	600	300

Model 86 Sniper's Rifle

A custom order rifle in .308 Winchester or the .300 Winchester Magnum calibers with a synthetic stock and a choice of scope systems. Introduced in 1988.

NIB	Exc.	V.G.	Good	Fair	Poor
1350	1100	900	600	400	200

Model 86 System

As above, with the Ultra scope, mounting system, bipod, and fitted case. Introduced in 1988.

NIB	Exc.	V.G.	Good	Fair	Poor
2150	1850	1500	1100	550	250

Model 87 Long Range Snipers Rifle

A large stainless steel, single shot bolt action rifle in .50 BMG caliber with a 29" barrel having an integral muzzle brake. Camouflaged synthetic stock. Weight 21 lbs. Accurate to 1,500 meters. Introduced in 1988.

NIB	Exc.	V.G.	Good	Fair	Poor
2700	2200	1800	1200	600	250

Model 87 System

As above, with a bipod and a 20X Ultra scope, mounting system, and a fitted case. Introduced in 1988.

NIB	Exc.	V.G.	Good	Fair	Poor
3350	2700	2100	1500	900	400

Signature Model

A bolt action sporting rifle manufactured in a variety of calibers up to .375 Holland & Holland with a 22" or 24" stainless barrel, composition stock and either 3- or 4-shot magazine. Introduced in 1988.

NIB	Exc.	V.G.	Good	Fair	Poor
2200	1750	1250	800	600	300

Signature Stainless

Same as model above but barrel and action made of stainless steel. Fiberglass stock. Left or right hand model. The .416 Rigby is also offered in this configuration. Introduced in 1990.

NIB	Exc.	V.G.	Good	Fair	Poor
2200	1750	1250	800	600	300

Signature Alaskan

This model, introduced in 1989, is offered in .270 .280 Rem., .30-06, 7mm Rem. Mag., .300 Win. Mag., .300 Wethby Mag., .358 Win. Mag., .340 Wethby Mag., .375 H&H. Match grade barrel from 22" to 26" in length. Single leaf rear sight and barrel band front sight.

NIB	Exc.	V.G.	Good	Fair	Poor
3000	2700	2000	1500	950	500

Signature Titanium Mountain

Offered in calibers from .270 Win. to 7mm Rem. Mag. Match grade barrel is produced from titanium. Stock is graphite. Weight is about 6.5 lbs.

NIB	Exc.	V.G.	Good	Fair	Poor
3000	2500	2000	1500	950	500

Signature Varminter

Available in calibers such as .223, .22-250, .220 Swift, .243, 6mm Rem., .25-06, 7mm-08, .308. Barrel lengths from 22" to 26". Heavy barrel configuration with hand bedded fiberglass stock. Field bipod is standard. Introduced in 1989.

NIB	Exc.	V.G.	Good	Fair	Poor
2500	2000	1500	900	600	400

Talon Safari

Bolt action rifle offered in various calibers from .300 Win. Mag. to .458 Win. Mag. Stainless steel barrel is 24". Four-round magazine. Fiberglass stock. Introduced in 1989. Weight is approximately 10 lbs.

NIB	Exc.	V.G.	Good	Fair	Poor
3500	3000	2000	1500	950	500

Talon Sporter

Offered in calibers from .25-06 to .416 Rem. Mag. 24" barrel with no sights. Built on a pre-1964 Winchester Model 70 action. Choice of walnut or fiberglass stock. Weight is about 7.5 lbs.

NIB	Exc.	V.G.	Good	Fair	Poor
2500	2000	1750	1250	600	250

Model 300 Phoenix Long Range Rifle

Introduced in 1992 and chambered for the .300 Phoenix cartridge. Fitted with a 28" barrel with no sights. Fiberglass stock. Weight is approximately 12.5 lbs.

NIB	Exc.	V.G.	Good	Fair	Poor
2500	2000	1750	1250	600	250

Model 40 Sniper

This bolt action rifle chambered for the .308 cartridge was introduced in 1990. Fitted with a 24" match grade heavy weight barrel. No sights. Weight is about 9 lbs.

NIB	Exc.	V.G.	Good	Fair	Poor
2000	1500	1000	750	500	300

Model 92 Bullpup

This is a single shot rifle chambered for the .50 caliber BMG. Fitted with a 26" barrel and no sights. Fiberglass bullpup stock. First introduced in 1995.

NIB	Exc.	V.G.	Good	Fair	Poor
4000	3250	2500	2000	1000	500

Model 93 SN

This is a bolt action rifle chambered for the .50 BMG and fitted with a 29" barrel with muzzle brake. Magazine holds 10 rounds. No sights. Weight is approximately 21.5 lbs. Folding fiberglass stock. Introduced in 1995.

NIB	Exc.	V.G.	Good	Fair	Poor
4250	3750	3000	2250	1250	750

MEAD & ADRIANCE
St. Louis, Missouri

This company retailed a variety of single shot percussion pistols most of which were manufactured by Ethan Allen of Grafton, Massachusetts. In general, the value for pistols marked "Mead & Adriance" are as follows:

Exc.	V.G.	Good	Fair	Poor
—	—	1150	500	250

MEIJA
SEE—Japan State

MENDENHALL, JONES & GARDNER
Greensboro, North Carolina

Muzzle Loading Rifle

A .58 caliber percussion rifle with a 33" barrel and full-length walnut stock secured by two barrel bands. Finished in the white with the lock marked "M.J.&G.,N.C." Prospective purchasers should secure a qualified appraisal prior to acquisition.

Exc.	V.G.	Good	Fair	Poor
—	—	25000	11000	—

MENZ, AUGUST
Suhl, Germany

Established prior to WWI to manufacture Beholla pistols, this company was purchased by Lignose in 1937.

Menta

Identical to the Beholla, which is listed separately.

Exc.	V.G.	Good	Fair	Poor
350	250	200	150	100

Liliput

A 4.25mm caliber semiautomatic pistol with a 2" barrel and 6-shot magazine. Overall length 3.5", weight 10 oz. The slide marked "Liliput Kal. 4.25". Also manufactured in 6.35mm caliber. These pistols have an overall length of 4". Blued with composition grips.

Exc.	V.G.	Good	Fair	Poor
400	300	250	200	125

Menz Model II

As above in 7.65mm caliber.

Exc.	V.G.	Good	Fair	Poor
400	300	250	200	125

Menz VP Model

Similar to the Model 2, but in 6.35mm caliber with a 2.35" barrel, 6-shot magazine and fitted with a cocking indicator.

Exc.	V.G.	Good	Fair	Poor
400	300	250	200	125

Model III

A total redesign. It has a closed-top slide, and the quality is much better than the previous Menz pistols. It has a fixed barrel and is similar to the Model 1910 Browning with an exposed hammer. This model was produced until 1937.

Exc.	V.G.	Good	Fair	Poor
450	350	300	250	150

MERCURY
Liege, Belgium

Model 622 VP

A .22 caliber semiautomatic rifle with a 20" barrel, open sights and 7-shot magazine. Blued with a walnut stock. Manufactured by Robar & Son.

Exc.	V.G.	Good	Fair	Poor
325	275	250	200	125

MERCURY
Eibar, Spain

Double Barreled Shotgun

A 10, 12, or 20 gauge Magnum boxlock double barrel shotgun with 28" or 32" barrels, double triggers and extractors. Blued with a walnut stock.
10 Gauge-Add 25%.

Exc.	V.G.	Good	Fair	Poor
325	250	225	175	125

MERIDEN FIREARMS CO.
Meriden, Connecticut

Pocket Pistol

A .32 or .38 caliber double action revolver manufactured in a variety of barrel lengths and with either an exposed or enclosed hammer. Nickel-plated with rubber grips. The barrel marked "Meriden Firearms Co. Meriden, Conn. USA." Manufactured between 1895 and 1915.

Exc.	V.G.	Good	Fair	Poor
—	250	100	75	50

Double Barrel Shotguns

From 1905-1918 Meriden Fire Arms Co. successor to A.J. Aubrey, made 12, 16, and 20 gauge sidelock double barrel shotguns. These were better quality hammer and hammerless side-by-sides fitted with twist, laminated, Damascus, and steel barrels in grades A to G. Some of these guns were beautifully engraved by the same artisans who worked for Parker Bros. and other Connecticut gunmakers. Prices in 1910 ranged from $40 to $250 but they represented great value for the money as they were superior to the popular Crescent guns which they closely resembled. Current values depend on model, grade, gauge, and condition. It is difficult to find examples in excellent condition as these were sold by Sears to customers who put them to hard use. In good condition their current values range from $250 for plain Janes to $3,500 or more for the top grades of which few specimens are known.

Single Barrel Shotguns and Rifles

Meriden Fire Arms Co. also made many single barrel shotguns and rifles whose current values are determined by growing collector interest and condition.

MERKEL, GEBRUDER
Suhl, Germany
Importer-GSI, Inc.

An Introduction to Merkel Brother's Guns
by Dan Sheil

Merkel Brothers shotgun and rifle makers began production around the turn of the century in Suhl, Germany. Merkel made a number of different models but the company was most well known for its Over/Under shotgun. It also made bolt action rifles, side-by-side double express rifles, falling block single shot rifles, side-by-side shotguns, drillings, and just about anything in the way of firearms its customers desired.

Perhaps the company's greatest productive era fell between the end of World War I and the 1950s. During the 1930s most of the live pigeon shoots were won with Merkel shotguns. However, there seems to be a difference of opinion about when Merkel built its best quality guns. This is not an easy question to answer. Most shooters and collectors feel that pre-World War II guns are the best examples of Merkel craftsmanship. But, in my opinion, some of the finest Merkels I have seen were produced immediately after World War II. Outstanding examples of Merkel's quality continue to appear up to the construction of the Berlin Wall in 1961.

Another area of controversy is the high grade Merkel 300 series shotgun. Many have compared this gun to the Italian and British makers and believe it is a mass produced gun. This is not the case because all Merkel shotguns are handcrafted and as far as I know barrels will not interchange unless they are supplied with the gun from the factory. While the 100 and 200 series guns may be mass produced the 300 series is not, and that is easy to determine by looking at the serial number together with the date stamped on the barrel. Very few 300 series guns were produced in a given period.

In terms of durability, strength, and reliability, there is not an over and under shotgun that is built as strong as the Merkel. It has two Kersten style locking lugs on the upper barrel that fit into the face of the receiver while the bottom has two under lugs that give the gun a rugged four position locking system. I don't think I have ever heard of a Merkel being sent back to the gunmaker or a gunsmith to have the frame tightened. It just is not necessary; the guns will not shoot loose.

With respect to value, the Merkel over and under guns have been sleepers in the gun industry for a number of years. Until recently they have not brought the price that they deserve. I am specifically talking about the 300 series; the 303 Luxus and the 304. Generally speaking all of the special order Merkel over and under shotguns have done well. I think the shooting public will begin to recognize the quality and craftsmanship built into every one of these fine guns.

One last comment regarding special order Merkels and the company's reputation for building just about anything the customer wanted. It is impossible to cover all of the variations that the company produced in its long history, but the buyer should be aware that he may encounter some different and uncataloged Merkels along the way.

As of August 1993 Merkel Brothers declared bankruptcy. The assets of the company were reportedly purchased by Steyr. GSI, Inc. Trussville, Alabama currently imports Merkel guns.

Editor's Comment: The following Merkel gun prices are based on either one or two factors. First, they are no longer in production or second that the guns were built prior to the Berlin Wall, which generally bring a premium. An additional factor has been introduced as of 1994 when the factory began to use an alpha numeric serial number system. This new system dates the guns from 1994. The prices listed below for new Merkels are influenced by the value of the dollar to the German Mark.

MERKEL SIDE-X-SIDE SHOTGUNS
Model 117/117E

Offered in 12 and 16 gauge with various barrel lengths, this model featured a boxlock action with double triggers and extractors. Ejectors were available under the "E" designation. The boxlock action body was scrupled at the rear with fine line scroll engraving.

Exc.	V.G.	Good	Fair	Poor
3000	2500	1500	1000	500

Model 118/118E

Also offered in 12 and 16 gauge this model is similar to above model with slightly more engraving and better wood. This model also has some engraving coverage on the breech end of the barrels.

Exc.	V.G.	Good	Fair	Poor
3500	2750	1700	1200	650

Model 124/125

Similar to the above models but supplied with extractors for the Model 124 and ejectors for the Model 125. Both models have more engraving coverage with game scenes. Finer checkering and fancy wood is seen on this model.

Model 124

Exc.	V.G.	Good	Fair	Poor
3900	3500	2000	1500	700

Model 125

Exc.	V.G.	Good	Fair	Poor
4500	3750	3000	2000	1000

Model 170

This model was offered in 12 gauge only with automatic ejectors. The boxlock action was engraved with fine full coverage scroll.

Exc.	V.G.	Good	Fair	Poor
5000	4000	3200	2500	1200

Model 130

This was one of Merkel's highest side-by-side shotguns. It featured a sidelock action, extra fancy wood, fine line checkering, and full coverage game scene engraving.

Exc.	V.G.	Good	Fair	Poor
15000	12000	7500	4500	2500

Model 126

Similar to the Model 130 but fitted with removable sidelocks.

Exc.	V.G.	Good	Fair	Poor
15000	12000	7500	4500	2500

Model 127

This model was Merkel's highest and finest side-by-side shotgun. The sidelock action featured full coverage fine line scroll engraving of the best quality.

Exc.	V.G.	Good	Fair	Poor
21000	16000	12000	6000	4000

Model 8

This model has a self-cocking Deeley boxlock action side-by-side with cocking indicators. The locking mechanism is a Greener cross-bolt with double barrel locking lug. Triggers are single selective or double. The safety is automatic and tang mounted. This model has an extractor. Offered in 12 and 16 gauge with 28" solid rib barrels or 20 gauge with 26.75" barrels. Available with straight or pistol grip oil-finished walnut stock. Receiver is case colored with light scroll engraving. The 12 and 16 gauge guns weigh about 6.8 lbs. while the 20 gauge weighs approximately 6 lbs.

NIB	Exc.	V.G.	Good	Fair	Poor
1000	800	700	600	500	300

Model 47E

Same as above but fitted with ejectors. Offered in 12, 16, or 20 gauge. Supplied with fitted luggage case.

NIB	Exc.	V.G.	Good	Fair	Poor
2750	2100	1500	950	—	—

Model 147

Same as Model 8 but with silver grayed receiver with fine engraved hunting scenes, engraved border, and screws. This model has been discontinued.

NIB	Exc.	V.G.	Good	Fair	Poor
2900	2500	1750	1100	600	300

Model 147E

Same as above but fitted with ejectors. Offered in 12, 16, 20, or 28 gauge. Supplied with fitted luggage case.

NIB	Exc.	V.G.	Good	Fair	Poor
3375	2500	1750	1100	—	—

Model 147EL

Similar to the Model 147E but with fancy walnut stock. Supplied with fitted luggage case.

NIB	Exc.	V.G.	Good	Fair	Poor
4375	3250	2400	1600	—	—

Model 122

This model features the same specifications as the above models but has false sideplates. This model is fitted with ejectors and the receiver is silver grayed with fine engraved hunting scenes on false sideplates, engraved border, and screws.

NIB	Exc.	V.G.	Good	Fair	Poor
4900	3850	2750	1750	950	500

Model 47SL

Same as above but with scroll engraving in place of hunting scenes.

NIB	Exc.	V.G.	Good	Fair	Poor
5350	4000	2500	1750	1100	600

Model 147SL

This model features true Holland and Holland style side locks with cocking indicators. Gauge and barrel lengths are as above. Stock is fancy walnut. However, 20 gauge gun weighs 6.4 lbs., 28 gauge gun weighs about 6.1 lbs.

NIB	Exc.	V.G.	Good	Fair	Poor
6950	5250	3750	2500	1500	750

Model 147SSL

Similar to the Model 147SL but fitted with removable side plates. Fancy walnut stock. Supplied with fitted luggage case.

NIB	Exc.	V.G.	Good	Fair	Poor
7950	5900	4750	3000	—	—

Models 247S/347S

These models are the same as the Model 147S with the exception of the types of engraving.

Model 247S-Large scroll engraving

NIB	Exc.	V.G.	Good	Fair	Poor
7000	5250	4000	2500	—	—

Model 347S-Medium scroll engraving

NIB	Exc.	V.G.	Good	Fair	Poor
6500	5500	4500	3500	2250	1500

Model 447SL-Small scroll engraving

NIB	Exc.	V.G.	Good	Fair	Poor
9000	6750	5250	4000	—	—

NOTE: For wood upgrade add $1,200. For custom stock dimensions add $ 1,400. For left hand stocks add $900.

Model 280EL

This model features an Anson & Deely boxlock saction with engraved hunting scenes on a silver-grayed action. Double triggers. Fancy walnut with straight grip stock. Offered in 28 gauge with 28" barrels. Fitted luggage case standard. Weight is about 5.2 lbs. First imported in 2000.

NIB	Exc.	V.G.	Good	Fair	Poor
4975	3750	—	—	—	

Model 280SL

Similar to the Model 280EL but with English style scroll engraving on H&H style sidelocks with choice of pistol grip or straight grip fancy walnut stock. Fitted luggage case standard. First imported in 2000.

NIB	Exc.	V.G.	Good	Fair	Poor
7450	5500	—	—		

Model 360EL

This model is the same as the Model 280EL but chambered for the .410 shell and fitted with 28" barrels. Fancy walnut and fitted case. Weight is about 5.5 lbs. First imported in 2000.

NIB	Exc.	V.G.	Good	Fair	Poor
4975	3750	—	—	—	

Model 360SL

Same as the Model 360EL but with English style scroll engraving on H&H style sidelocks and choice of pistol grip or straight grip stock. First imported in 2000.

NIB	Exc.	V.G.	Good	Fair	Poor
7450	5500	—	—		

Model 280/360EL Two Barrel Set

This set consist of a 28 gauge 28" barrel and a .410 bore 28" barrel with engraved hunting scenes and fancy walnut stock. Double triggers and straight grip stock. First imported in 2000.

Model 280EL two barrel set

NIB	Exc.	V.G.	Good	Fair	Poor
7450	5500	—	—		

Model 280/360SL Two Barrel Set

Same as above but with English style scroll engraving and choice of pistol gip or straight grip stock. First imported in 2000.

NIB	Exc.	V.G.	Good	Fair	Poor
10975	8250	—	—		

MERKEL OVER AND UNDER SHOTGUNS

Model 102E

This was Merkel's standard over and under boxlock model. Offered in 12 gauge with 28" barrels or 16 gauge with 26" barrels. Both are fitted with double triggers, semi-pistol grip, and ejectors.

Exc.	V.G.	Good	Fair	Poor
1600	1200	1000	650	400

Model 103E

Similar to the standard but with more English scroll engraving coverage and better wood. This model was offered in 12, 16, and 20 gauge.

Exc.	V.G.	Good	Fair	Poor
2200	1500	1200	950	600

Model 204E

This model is essentially a Model 203E with finer engraving. This model was discontinued prior to 1939.

Exc.	V.G.	Good	Fair	Poor
6000	4500	3000	2200	1750

Model 301 E

This is a boxlock model with scrupled action chambered for the 12, 16, 20, 24, 28, and 32 gauge. The engraving is an English scroll and the triggerguard is horn. Double triggers and pistol grip are standard. This model was produced prior to 1939.

Exc.	V.G.	Good	Fair	Poor
4500	4000	2500	2000	1850

Model 302E

Similar to the Model 301E but fitted with side plates. The full coverage engraving features game scenes. This model produced prior to WWII.

Exc.	V.G.	Good	Fair	Poor
12000	10000	7500	4000	2000

Model 303 Luxus

This over and under Merkel is custom built to the customer's specifications. Each gun is unique and should be appraised by a knowledgeable individual who is familiar with quality European shotguns. Prices for this model start at $20,000.

Model 304E

This prewar model was the highest grade in Merkel's over and under shotgun line. A side lock gun with full coverage scroll engraving of the highest quality. Fine line checkering and extra fancy wood make this gun difficult to appraise due to its rarity. A qualified appraisal before a sale is highly recommended.

Modell 304

Model 400E

A higher grade Over/Under fitted with Kersten crossbolt, finer engraving, and fancy wood. Merkel offered this grade in 12, 16, 20, 24, 28, and 32 gauge with choice of barrel lengths. This model was produced prior to 1939.

Exc.	V.G.	Good	Fair	Poor
1800	1300	1000	600	400

Model 401E

Similar to the model above but with full coverage game scene engraving.

Exc.	V.G.	Good	Fair	Poor
2500	1850	1200	800	600

Model 200E

The action on this model is a self cocking Blitz where the hammers are attached to the trigger plates. The locking mechanism is a Kersten double cross bolt lock with release. Trigger may be either single selective or double. The manual safety is mounted on the tang. Fitted with coil spring ejectors. Offered in 12 and 16 gauge with 28" solid rib barrels or 20 gauge with 26.75" barrels. The oil-finished stock is offered with straight or pistol grip. The receiver is case colored with engraved border and screws. The 12 gauge weighs 7 lbs., the 16 gauge 6.8 lbs., and the 20 gauge 6.4 lbs.

NIB	Exc.	V.G.	Good	Fair	Poor
2700	2000	1500	1000	800	500

Model 201E

Same as above but with silver grayed receiver with fine engraved hunting scenes, engraved border, and screws.

NIB	Exc.	V.G.	Good	Fair	Poor
3350	2850	2250	1500	1000	750

Model 202E

This model has the same basic specifications as the Model 201E but is fitted with false side plates with cocking indicators.

NIB	Exc.	V.G.	Good	Fair	Poor
6500	5000	3500	2500	1500	1000

Model 203E

This model has true Holland & Holland style side locks with cocking indicators. These sideplates are removable with cranked screw. The gauge selection and barrel are the same as those listed above. The silver grayed receiver as English style large scroll engraving. This model has been discontinued.

NIB	Exc.	V.G.	Good	Fair	Poor
12000	9500	7500	5000	2500	1000

Model 303E

Same as above but with detachable side lock plates with integral retracting hook. The Model 303E also has medium scroll work engraving and Holland & Holland type ejectors.

NIB	Exc.	V.G.	Good	Fair	Poor
17000	15000	12000	7500	5000	2500

Model 303EL

This model features H&H style sidelocks that are quick detachable without tools. Receiver is engraved with hunting scenes. Offered in 12, 20 and 28 gauge. Double triggers and fancy wanut stock with pistol or straight grip. Weight for 12 gauge is about 7 lbs, for the 20 gauge about 6.4 lbs, and for the 28 gauge about 6.4 lbs. Fitted luggage case standard.

NIB	Exc.	V.G.	Good	Fair	Poor
20000	14500	11500	—	—	—

Model 200ES

This model features a Blitz action with cocking indicators and Kersten double cross bolt lock with release. The trigger is single selective with tang mounted manual safety. Coil spring ejectors are standard. Offered in 12 gauge only with 26.75" or 28" ventilated rib barrel. The walnut stock has skeet dimensions with pistol grip. Receiver is silver grayed with 112 coverage scroll engraving, engraved borders, and screws. Weighs approximately 7.3 lbs.

NIB	Exc.	V.G.	Good	Fair	Poor
4000	3250	2500	2000	1500	1000

Model 200SC (Sporting Clays)

Introduced in 1995 this model is offered in 12 gauge only with 3" chambers and 30" barrels with ventilated rib. It is fitted with a single selective trigger adjustable for length of pull. It has a special walnut oil finished stock with 26 lines to the inch checkering. Pistol grip and Pachmayr Sporting Clays recoil pad is standard. Weight is approximately 7.6 lbs.

NIB	Exc.	V.G.	Good	Fair	Poor
6500	5500	3000	1500	900	450

NOTE: With Briley choke tubes add $500.

Model 201ES

Same as model above but with full coverage scroll engraving.

NIB	Exc.	V.G.	Good	Fair	Poor
4500	3750	3000	2500	2000	1000

Model 200ET

Same as Model 200ES, but in a trap configuration. The ventilated rib barrel length offered is 30".

NIB	Exc.	V.G.	Good	Fair	Poor
4250	3500	2750	2250	1750	1000

Model 201ET

Same as Model 210ES but fitted with a 30" barrel and trap stock dimensions.

NIB	Exc.	V.G.	Good	Fair	Poor
4500	3750	3000	2500	2000	1000

Model 2000EL

This model features a Kersten cross bolt lock, scroll engraving on a silver greyed receiver and a modified Anson & Deely box lock action. This gun is offered in 12, 20, or 28 gauge with ejectors, single selective or double triggers, fancy wood, and choice of pistol or straight grip stock. Weight is about 7 lbs. for 12 gauge, 6.4 lbs. for 20 gauge, and 6.4 lbs. for 28 gauge.

NIB	Exc.	V.G.	Good	Fair	Poor
5000	4000	2750	1750	1250	750

Model 2000EL Sporter

Similar to the above model but fitted with 30" barrels on the 12 gauge, and 28" barrels on the 20 and 28 gauge.

NIB	Exc.	V.G.	Good	Fair	Poor
5000	4000	2750	1750	1250	750

Model 2001EL

Similar to the Model 2000 but with finely engraved hunting scenes. This model is offered in 28 gauge as well as 12 and 20 gauge.

NIB	Exc.	V.G.	Good	Fair	Poor
6500	4850	3250	2250	1500	1000

Model 2001EL Sporter

Same as above but with 30" barrels for 12 gauge, 28" barrels for 20 and 28 gauge.

NIB	Exc.	V.G.	Good	Fair	Poor
6500	4850	3250	2250	1500	1000

Model 2002EL

This model features finely engraved hunting scenes with arabesque style. Offered in 12, 20 and 28 gauges.

NIB	Exc.	V.G.	Good	Fair	Poor
10000	8000	6000	4000	—	—

MERKEL SHOTGUN CHOKE DESIGNATIONS		
Choke ID	**Description**	**Percentage**
1/1	Full Choke	70 to 75
3/4	Imp. Modified	65 to 70
1/2	Modified	60 to 65
1/4	Quarter Choke	55 to 60
VZ	Imp. Cylinder	45 to 50
S	Skeet Choke	70 to 75 (at 25 yds)

MERKEL RIFLE/SHOTGUN COMBINATIONS

Model 410E

Merkel's base boxlock model with ejectors. Produced prior to WWII.

Exc.	V.G.	Good	Fair	Poor
2250	1800	1200	750	500

Model 411 E

Similar to the above but with the addition of a small coverage of scroll engraving.

Exc.	V.G.	Good	Fair	Poor
2500	2000	1500	1000	600

Model 300

A box lock hammerless four barrel shotgun/rifle combination. The shotgun barrels were 12, 16, or 20 gauge, while the top rifle barrel was .22 rimfire with the bottom rifle barrel .30-30 or .25-35. Probably any combination of rifle and shotgun could be used as this was a special order gun. Very rare. An independent appraisal is strongly recommended.

Model 311E

This combination gun has additional English scroll engraving.

Exc.	V.G.	Good	Fair	Poor
7900	6500	5000	2250	1250

Model 312E

This model is fitted with sideplates and game scene engraving.

Exc.	V.G.	Good	Fair	Poor
9500	8150	6600	4000	2000

Model 313E

This model has sidelocks with fine, full coverage scroll engraving. An expert appraisal is recommended due to this model's rarity and unique features.

Exc.	V.G.	Good	Fair	Poor
11500	10500	8000	4000	2000

Model 314E

This sidelock model is also rare and unique. An expert appraisal is recommended prior to a sale. Extra barrels will frequently be seen with this model.

SINGLE SHOT AND BOLT ACTION RIFLES

Merkel built special single shot rifles and bolt action rifles. These guns were produced prior to WWII and are seldom seen in the United States. The buyer should exercise caution and seek expert assistance prior to a sale.

Model 180

This is a top lever single rifle with double under lugs built on a boxlock action. The stock is 3/4 with pistol grip. Commonly referred to as a stalking rifle. Offered in a variety of European calibers. A rare Merkel.

Exc.	V.G.	Good	Fair	Poor
3000	2100	1500	1000	500

Model 183

This top lever model features a Holland & Holland type sidelock action with the side lock on the left side and the removable side plate on the right side. Fitted with a straight grip stock and full length forearm with sling swivels, fine line checkering, and fancy wood. A rare rifle.

Exc.	V.G.	Good	Fair	Poor
7500	5000	3500	2000	1200

Model 190

This is Merkel's version of a Sporting rifle built on a Mauser action. Offered in a variety of European calibers. These were special order rifles and will be seen in a variety of configurations.

Exc.	V.G.	Good	Fair	Poor
3000	2200	1500	1000	650

DOUBLE RIFLES-COMBINATION GUNS-DRILLINGS

Merkel Side-x-Side Double Rifles Model 128E

This side-by-side rifle is a droplock design with scroll and game scene engraving. The wood is Circassion walnut with fine line checkering. Offered in a variety of European calibers. Because of the rarity and uniqueness of each rifle a qualified appraisal should be sought prior to a sale.

Model 132E

Similar to the Model 128E but with full coverage scroll engraving and fancy wood. This model also should have an expert appraisal done prior to a sale.

Model 220E O/U Double Rifle

This is a boxlock design with a Kersten double cross bolt, scroll engraved case hardened receiver, Blitz action, double triggers, and pistol grip stock with cheekpiece.

NIB	Exc.	V.G.	Good	Fair	Poor
8500	6000	4500	3800	—	—

Model 221 E Over/Under Double Rifle

Similar to the model above but with game scene engraving on a silver grayed receiver.

NIB	Exc.	V.G.	Good	Fair	Poor
10900	8500	5750	—	—	—

Model 223E Over/Under Double Rifle

This model is fitted with sidelocks and features English style arabesque engraving in large scrolls on silver grayed receiver.

NIB	Exc.	V.G.	Good	Fair	Poor
14500	12500	10000	—	—	—

Model 323E O/U Double Rifle

Similar to the above model but with finer engraving.

NIB	Exc.	V.G.	Good	Fair	Poor
22500	17500	12500	—	—	—

Model 140-1

This model features a Greener cross bolt, scroll engraving with case hardened receiver. Extractors and double triggers with pistol grip stock are standard. Offered in a wide variety of European and American calibers.

NIB	Exc.	V.G.	Good	Fair	Poor
5900	4750	3750	—	—	—

Model 140-1.1

Same as above model but with finely engraved hunting scenes.

NIB	Exc.	V.G.	Good	Fair	Poor
6800	5500	4000	—	—	—

Model 140-2

This double rifle has a Anson & Deely boxlock action. Double triggers. Barrel length is 23.6". Chambered for .375H&H, .416 Rigby, and the .470 NE. Pistol grip stock with cheekpiece on oil finish walnut. Weight is about 10.7 lbs. depending on caliber.

NIB	Exc.	V.G.	Good	Fair	Poor
8500	6750	4750	—	—	—

Model 140-2.1

This model is similar to the one above but is engraved with African game scenes.

NIB	Exc.	V.G.	Good	Fair	Poor
10000	8000	6000	—	—	—

Model 150-1

This model features an arabesque engraving on a silver greyed receiver. Extractors, double triggers, and pistol grip are standard.

NIB	Exc.	V.G.	Good	Fair	Poor
7500	6000	4750	—	—	—

Model 150-1.1

Same as above model but with finely engraved hunting scenes.

NIB	Exc.	V.G.	Good	Fair	Poor
8700	7000	5500	—	—	—

Model 160S Luxus Double Rifle

This double rifle is part of the Luxus series and features on the highest quality sidelock action, wood, and fittings. It is offered in .222 Rem., 5.6x5OR Mag., .243, 6.5x57R, 7x57, 7x65, .3006, .30R Blazer, 8x57IRS, 8x57RS, .308 Win., and 9.3x74R. Weighs approximately 8 lbs. An expert appraisal should be sought prior to a sale due to the unique nature of this model.

NIB	Exc.	V.G.	Good	Fair	Poor
13300	10500	—	—	—	—

Model 160S-1.1

Same as above but with finely engraved hunting scenes.

NIB	Exc.	V.G.	Good	Fair	Poor
14800	11500	—	—	—	—

Model 211E Rifle/Shotgun Combination

This over and under model features a gray metal boxlock action with hunting scenes. The top barrel is available in 12, 16, or 20 gauge and the bottom barrel is offered in .22 Hornet, 5.6R Mag., 5.6R, .222 Rem., .243 Win., 6.5x55, 6.5x57R, 7x57R, 7x65R, .30-06, 8x57IRS, 9.3x74R, and .375 H&H Mag. The barrel has a solid rib and the trigger is single selective. The select walnut stock is hand checkered. Weight is about 7 lbs.

NIB	Exc.	V.G.	Good	Fair	Poor
6000	4500	3500	2250	1500	—

Model 210E Rifle/Shotgun Combination

Same as above model but features a scroll engraved case hardened receiver. This model has been discontinued.

NIB	Exc.	V.G.	Good	Fair	Poor
6200	5000	4000	2750	1200	700

Model 211E Rifle/Shotgun Combination

Similar to the above model but with finely engraved hunting scenes.

NIB	Exc.	V.G.	Good	Fair	Poor
7500	6000	4500	3000	1500	—

Model 213E Rifle/Shotgun Combination

This combination gun features sidelocks with English style large scroll engraving on a silver grayed receiver. Also is fitted with double triggers and pistol grip with cheekpiece.

NIB	Exc.	V.G.	Good	Fair	Poor
11500	9500	7500	5500	—	—

Model 313E Rifle/Shotgun Combination

Same as above model but with finer scroll engraving and fancy wood.

NIB	Exc.	V.G.	Good	Fair	Poor
17500	12500	7500	6500	—	—

Model 95K Drilling

This model is a three barrel shotgun/rifle combination. The top two barrels are chambered for 12, 16, or 20 gauge and the bottom barrel is available in rifle calibers from .22 Hornet to .375 H&H Mag. The action is a boxlock design with scroll engraving on borders and screws. The stock is select grade walnut with raised comb, pistol grip with cap, cheekpiece, and plastic buttplate. Weighs about 7.7 lbs. This model has been discontinued.

NIB	Exc.	V.G.	Good	Fair	Poor
8500	6750	4250	—	—	—

Model 96K

Similar to the above model but with scroll engraving on a case hardened frame.

NIB	Exc.	V.G.	Good	Fair	Poor
6500	4750	3750	—	—	—

Model 96K-Engraved

Same as above but with finely engraved hunting scenes with arabesque engraving on a silver greyed receiver.

NIB	Exc.	V.G.	Good	Fair	Poor
8000	6000	4500	—	—	—

MERRILL
Fullerton, California

Sportsman

A single shot pistol manufactured in a variety of calibers with either a 9" or 12" octagonal barrel having a wide ventilated rib, adjustable sights, and integral telescope mounts. Blued with walnut grips.

Interchangeable Barrels-Add $75.
Wrist Support-Add $25.

Exc.	V.G.	Good	Fair	Poor
300	275	225	175	125

MERRILL, JAMES H.
Baltimore, Maryland

Merrill Rifle

A single-shot breechloading rifle that is chambered for .54 caliber and utilizes the percussion ignition system. The breech opens for loading by lifting and pulling back on a lever. The barrel is 33" in length, and there is a full-length walnut stock held on by two barrel bands. The mountings and patch box are brass; and the lock is case colored, with a browned barrel. The lock is marked "J.H. Merrill Balto./Pat. July 1858." There are military acceptance marks on the stock. There were approximately 775 of these rifles manufactured and purchased by the government for use during the Civil War. They were made in 1864 and 1865.

Courtesy Milwaukee Public Museum, Milwaukee, Wisconsin

Exc.	V.G.	Good	Fair	Poor
—	—	4750	2000	500

Merrill Carbine

Similar in appearance to the rifle except that the barrel length is 22" and the stock is only half-length with one barrel band. There are some variations that are quite subtle in appearance but which have a considerable effect on values. We recommend that an independent appraisal be secured. The values given are for the standard 1st and 2nd Types. There were approximately 15,000 total manufactured, and most were used in the Civil War.

1st Type

No eagle stamped on the lock, and the breech lever is flat.

Courtesy Milwaukee Public Museum, Milwaukee, Wisconsin

Exc.	V.G.	Good	Fair	Poor
—	—	3500	1000	500

A Merrill Civil War carbine sold at auction for $5,175. Condition was very good. This was an early example with a staple-type front sight and flat brass barrel band. Amoskeag Auction Co. Inc., November 1999

2nd Type

An eagle stamped on the lock, and the stock has no patch box. The breech lever has a round tip.

Courtesy Milwaukee Public Museum, Milwaukee, Wisconsin

Exc.	V.G.	Good	Fair	Poor
—	—	3500	1200	500

MERRILL, LATROBE & THOMAS
S. Remington-Maker
Ilion, New York

Carbine

A .58 caliber breech loading percussion carbine with an overall length of 38" and barrel length of 21". The lock marked "S. Remington/ Ilion, N.Y." and the barrel "Merrill, Latrobe & Thomas/Baltimore, Md./Patent Applied For." Approximately 170 were made in 1855. Prospective purchasers are advised to secure a qualified appraisal prior to acquisition.

Exc.	V.G.	Good	Fair	Poor
—	—	30000	10000	—

MERRIMACK ARMS
SEE—Brown Manufacturing Co.

MERWIN & BRAY
Worcester, Massachusetts

This company marketed a number of firearms produced by various manufacturers under their own name.

Merwin & Bray Pocket Pistol

A .32 caliber spur trigger single shot pistol with a 3.5" barrel. Blued, silver-plated with walnut grips. The barrel marked "Merwin & Bray New York".

Exc.	V.G.	Good	Fair	Poor
—	—	300	150	75

MERWIN HULBERT & CO.
New York, New York

By Jim Supica, Pres., Old Town Station, Ltd.

Merwin Hulbert & Co., New York City. Founder Joseph Merwin had previously been involved in Merwin & Bray. Merwin Hulbert & Co. or its principals were also involved in Phoenix Rifle, Evans Rifle Company, American Cartridge Company, and Hopkins & Allen of Norwich, CT. Most Merwin Hulbert revolvers will be marked with the Hopkins & Allen name, in addition to Merwin Hulbert. They were made for a fairly brief period, with most production apparently taking place during the 1870's & early 1880's.

There has been some confusion over a classification system for MH revolvers. The system adopted here is based on the distinctions listed in Art Phelps' book, *The Story of Merwin Hulbert & Co. Firearms*. We believe this is the first time the Phelps system has been adapted to a list format.

LARGE FRAME MERWIN HULBERT SIXGUNS

There has been a marked increase in interest in Merwin Hulbert & Co. over the past decade, with many coming to recognize them as one of the pre-eminent makers of large frame revolvers used in the American West. Total production of large frame revolvers has been estimated at a few thousand by some sources. However, the frequency with which they are encountered suggests possibly greater production.

MH used a unique system of opening, loading & unloading their revolvers which was supposed to allow selective ejection of spent shells, leaving remaining cartridges in place. A latch on the bottom of the frame is pushed toward the rear of the gun, and the barrel and cylinder are rotated to the right (clockwise, as viewed from the rear of the revolver) 90 degrees. The barrel & cylinder are then pulled forward, far enough to allow empty brass to fall free. This system required exceptional quality machining, and some modern authorities are on record as considering the Merwin Hulbert to have the finest workmanship of all revolvers of the era.

All are .44 caliber six-shot large frame revolvers. Beyond that, to fully identify a large frame Merwin Hulbert, you must specify the following:

1. MODEL DESIGNATION - First Model has an open top & scoop flutes, round barrel, and two small screws above the triggerguard. Second Model is similar to the first, except with only one screw above the triggerguard. Third Model has a topstrap with standard flutes & a round barrel. Fourth Model is similar to the third, except that it has a ribbed barrel. The open-top 1st & 2nd Models seem to be more sought after. The 4th Model is rare, and will bring a premium from a serious Merwin collector.

2. FRONTIER ARMY or POCKET ARMY - Frontier Army models have a square butt, and were made in 1st through 4th models. Pocket Army models have a birdshead butt with a pointed extension with lanyard hole, and are found in 2nd or 3rd Model configuration. Generally, the Frontier Army will bring more than the Pocket Army.

3. SINGLE ACTION or DOUBLE ACTION - The topstrap models, 3rd & 4th, were manufactured in both single action and double action. The single action models tend to bring more.

4. BARREL LENGTH - Standard barrel length on the Frontier Army 1st, 2nd, & 3rd Models is 7", with a 5-1/2" barrel common on the 4th Model. Standard barrel length on the Pocket Army was a more "pocket-sized" 3-1/2". However, somewhat ironically, birdshead butt models marked "Pocket Army" were also produced with full length 7" barrels. Generally, these longer barrels will bring a bit more than the shorter ones.

5. CALIBER - Most common is .44-40 (designated "Winchester Calibre 1873"). Merwins were also chambered for .44 Merwin Hulbert (somewhat similar to the S&W .44 American cartridge), and .44 Russian. The less common calibers may bring a small premium from serious Merwin collectors.

6. FOREIGN COPIES - The Merwin Hulbert design was relatively widely copied during the period of use, particularly in Spain. It seems that much of this production may have gone to Mexico, and some found their way to the U.S. Although these Spanish copies may bear markings such as "System Merwin Hulbert" or other usage of the words "Merwin Hulbert", they generally will not be found with the Hopkins & Allen marking. Spanish firms making Merwin copies included Orbea Hermanos and Anitua y Charola. These Spanish copies may bring half or less of what an original Merwin will bring, and it can sometimes take a fairly experienced eye to tell the difference.

7. ENGRAVING - Special order engraving was available, and it was usually executed in a distinctive and colorful "punch dot" style, which has come to be associated with Merwins (although it is occasionally encountered on other makes of firearms). For a long time, this style was somewhat dismissed as a bit crude and lacking in artistry. However, a new appreciation of Merwin engraving has emerged, and factory engraved pieces will bring a significant premium. Often, a panel scene depicts an animal, object, or landmark. These panel scenes have an almost "folk art" quality to them, and will enhance the value further. Engraved Merwins are sometimes encountered with the engraving filled with colored enamel, quite rare, and, if original, this will bring a further premium.

8. FINISH - The vast majority were nickel plated. Original blued guns will bring a premium.

Top: Open Top Pocket Army
Bottom: Top Strap Double Action Pocket Army

Courtesy Supica's Old Town Station

First Model Frontier Army, .44 open top
Two screws, square butt, 7" barrel

Exc.	V.G.	Good	Fair	Poor
—	5500	3000	1500	500

Second Model Frontier Army, .44 open top
One screw, square butt, 7" barrel

Exc.	V.G.	Good	Fair	Poor
—	4500	2750	1000	500

Second Model Pocket Army, .44 open top
Birdshead butt. 3-1/2" barrel standard, 7" will bring a premium.

Exc.	V.G.	Good	Fair	Poor
—	3500	2000	700	400

Third Model Frontier Army, Single Action, .44, topstrap
Square butt, 7" barrel.

Exc.	V.G.	Good	Fair	Poor
—	3750	2250	800	450

Third Model Frontier Army, Double Action, .44, topstrap
Square butt, 7" barrel.

Exc.	V.G.	Good	Fair	Poor
—	3250	1750	700	400

Third Model Pocket Army, Single Action, .44 topstrap
Birdshead butt. 3-1/2" barrel standard, 7" will bring a premium.

Exc.	V.G.	Good	Fair	Poor
—	3250	1750	700	400

Third Model Pocket Army, Double Action, .44, topstrap
Birdshead butt. 3-1/2" barrel standard, 7" will bring a premium.

Exc.	V.G.	Good	Fair	Poor
—	3000	1600	650	400

Fourth Model Frontier Army, Single Action.44, topstrap
Ribbed barrel, scarce. 5-1/2" barrel seems to be most common, also offered in 7" & 3-1/2".

Exc.	V.G.	Good	Fair	Poor
—	5000	2750	800	550

Fourth Model Frontier Army, Double Action, .44, topstrap
Ribbed barrel. Barrel lengths as above.

Exc.	V.G.	Good	Fair	Poor
—	4750	2500	750	550

SMALL FRAME MERWIN HULBERT POCKET REVOLVERS

Top: Single Action Pocket Revolver
Bottom: Double Action Pocket Revolver

Courtesy Supica's Old Town Station

The .32 & .38 centerfire revolvers were manufactured with the unique Merwin Hulbert twist-open system, like the large frame revolvers. They were often advertised as chambered for the .32 MH & Co. or .38 MH & Co. cartridges, but it appears as if these cartridges may have been essentially the same as the .32 S&W and .38 S&W rounds. Of course, the Merwin Hulbert revolvers were manufactured for the original lower pressure black-powder loadings of these cartridges. Saw-handled grip frames were standard, although some were manufactured with the distinctive Pocket Army type pointed "skullcrusher" birdshead grip frames, and these will generally bring a premium. Most common barrel length for most models is 3-1/2", with

5-1/2" barrels somewhat scarcer in most models, and 2-3/4" barrels quite scarce and worth a premium. A number of police departments purchased small frame Merwin Hulbert revolvers in the late 19th century. Department marked guns will bring a premium. Terminology alert -- note that the .44 caliber "Pocket Army" model is a large frame, and is listed in the section above. The .22 Merwin Hulbert revolver is the only one not to use the MH twist-open system. It is, instead, a tip-up revolver closely resembling the S&W Model One.

First Pocket Model Single Action

Spur-trigger, cylinder pin exposed at front of frame, round loading aperture in recoil shield (no loading gate), 5 shot .38, scarce

Exc.	V.G.	Good	Fair	Poor
—	1250	800	300	175

Second Pocket Model Single Action

Spur-trigger, cylinder pin exposed, sliding loading gate, 5 shot .38.

Exc.	V.G.	Good	Fair	Poor
—	1000	650	285	150

Third Pocket Model Single Action Spur-trigger

Enclosed cylinder pin, sliding loading gate, 5 shot .38

Exc.	V.G.	Good	Fair	Poor
—	950	600	225	125

Third Pocket Model Single Action w/ Triggerguard

5 shot .38.

Exc.	V.G.	Good	Fair	Poor
—	1000	675	285	150

Double Action Pocket Model, medium frame

Usually .38 five shot. Scarce .32 seven shot will bring a 25% to 50% premium. Patent marked folding hammer spur will bring a small premium.

Exc.	V.G.	Good	Fair	Poor
—	900	900	225	150

Double Action Pocket Model, small frame

.32 cal. five shot. Patent marked folding hammer spur will bring a small premium.

Exc.	V.G.	Good	Fair	Poor
—	800	550	185	125

Tip-up .22 spur-trigger

.22 rf., a S&W patent infringement, looks similar to S&W Mod. One Third Issue. Scarce. "Made by Merwin Hulbert & Co. for Smith & Wesson" marking will bring a small premium.

Exc.	V.G.	Good	Fair	Poor
—	1000	650	275	175

Merwin Hulbert Rifles

Very similar in design to Hopkins & Allen single shot breech loaders. Advertised in .22 & .32 rimfire, as well as .32 WCF, .38 WCF, and .44 WCF. May have been offered in .32-40 and .38-55 chamberings. A 20 ga. shotgun barrel was offered separately for these rifles. Features included set trigger, rebounding hammer, pistol grip stock, & takedown. Seldom encountered, the Merwin Hulbert name on these should bring a premium over standard Hopkins & Allen single shot rifles. A small frame "Merwin Hulbert & Co's. Junior" rifle was also offered, chambered for .22 rf.

METROPOLITAN ARMS CO.
New York, New York

Established in February 1864, this company manufactured copies of the Colt Model 1851 and 1861 Navy Revolvers, as well as copies of the Colt Model 1862 Police Revolver. Two of the firm's principle officers were Samuel and William Syms (formerly of Blunt & Syms) and it is believed that they were responsible for production. Curiously, although most Metropolitan pistols were produced during the 1864 to 1866 period, the company itself was not dissolved until 1920.

1851 Navy Revolver

A .36 caliber percussion revolver with a 7.5" octagonal barrel and 6-shot cylinder. Blued, case hardened with walnut grips. The barrel marked "Metropolitan Arms Co. New York." Approximately 6,000 of these revolvers were made during the 1860s. Those bearing H.E. Dimick markings are worth considerably more than the standard marked examples.

H.E. Dimick Navy Model

Exc.	V.G.	Good	Fair	Poor
—	—	6000	2750	850

Standard Navy Model

Exc.	V.G.	Good	Fair	Poor
—	—	3500	1000	500

1861 Navy Revolver

A .36 caliber percussion revolver with a 7.5" round barrel and 6-shot cylinder. The loading lever of the rack and pinion type. Blued, case hardened with walnut grips. The barrel marked "Metropolitan Arms Co. New York." Approximately 50 were made in 1864 and 1865.

Exc.	V.G.	Good	Fair	Poor
—	—	6500	3000	950

Police Revolver

A .36 caliber percussion revolver with either 4.5", 5.5" or 6.5" round barrels and a fluted 5-shot cylinder. Blued, case hardened with walnut grips. The barrel normally marked "Metropolitan Arms Co. New York," although examples have been noted without any markings. Approximately 2,750 were made between 1864 and 1866.

Exc.	V.G.	Good	Fair	Poor
—	—	1250	500	200

MILDA
Japan
Marubena America Corp.

Model 612

A 12 gauge boxlock Over/Under shotgun with 26" or 28" ventilated rib barrels, single selective trigger and automatic ejectors. Blued with a walnut stock. Imported between 1972 and 1974.

Exc.	V.G.	Good	Fair	Poor
900	750	600	400	250

Model 612 Skeet

As above, with 27" skeet choked barrels and some engraving. Imported between 1972 and 1974.

Exc.	V.G.	Good	Fair	Poor
900	750	600	400	250

Model 2100 Skeet

Similar to the Model 612 but with more engraving coverage.

Exc.	V.G.	Good	Fair	Poor
950	800	650	450	300

Model 2200 Trap or Skeet

As above, with either 30" trap or 27" skeet bored barrels and more finely engraved. Imported between 1972 and 1974.

Exc.	V.G.	Good	Fair	Poor
1100	850	700	450	300

Model 2300 Trap or Skeet

A more finely finished Model 2200. Imported from 1972 until 1974.

Exc.	V.G.	Good	Fair	Poor
1200	900	750	500	300

Model GRT Trap or GRS Skeet

A 12 gauge boxlock shotgun fitted with false sideplates, 27" skeet or 29" full choked barrels, single selective trigger and automatic ejector. Imported between 1972 and 1974.

Exc.	V.G.	Good	Fair	Poor
2250	1850	1250	800	500

MILTECH
Los Altos, CA

This company has been in business for 19 years and rebuilds and refinishes selected military firearms. All firearms are thoroughly inspected for safety and are considered safe to shoot. All firearms have their original receivers and markings. These rifles are not stamped with the Miltech name but do have a unique Miltech pine crate serial numbered to the gun as standard. The company will verify that it did the rebuild if asked. All guns come with manual, sling, and other selected accessories depending on model.

German Mauser Model 98k

NIB	Exc.	V.G.	Good	Fair	Poor
1025	—	—	—	—	—

M1 Garand

NIB	Exc.	V.G.	Good	Fair	Poor
1475	—	—	—	—	—

NOTE: For International Harvester and Winchester add $125.

M1D Garand

NIB	Exc.	V.G.	Good	Fair	Poor
2495	—	—	—	—	—

M1 Carbine

NIB	Exc.	V.G.	Good	Fair	Poor
10255	—	—	—	—	—

NOTE: For Rockola and Winchester add $100.

Model 1941 Johnson

NIB	Exc.	V.G.	Good	Fair	Poor
3000+	—	—	—	—	—

Model 1903 Springfield

NIB	Exc.	V.G.	Good	Fair	Poor
1095	—	—	—	—	—

Model 1903A3 Springfield

NIB	Exc.	V.G.	Good	Fair	Poor
1025	—	—	—	—	—

Model 1903 Mark I Springfield

NIB	Exc.	V.G.	Good	Fair	Poor
1195	—	—	—	—	—

Model 1917 U.S. Enfield

NIB	Exc.	V.G.	Good	Fair	Poor
1025	—	—	—	—	—

MINNEAPOLIS F. A. CO.
Minneapolis, Minnesota

Palm Pistol

A .32 caliber radial cylinder pistol with a 1.75" barrel manufactured by the Ames Manufacturing Company (see the Ames entry). Nickel-plated with hard rubber grips. The sideplates marked "Minneapolis Firearms Co." and "The Protector." Several thousand were sold during the 1890s.

Exc.	V.G.	Good	Fair	Poor
—	1750	850	350	100

MIROKU B. C.
Miroku, Japan

Firearms produced by this manufacturer have been imported and marketed by a variety of companies such as Charles Daly, Browning, Winchester, and SKB.

MITCHELL ARMS, INC.
Santa Ana, California

An importer and distributor of foreign-made firearms, this company is no longer in business. However, some Mitchell models are available under Brolin Arms as of 1998. Brolin Arms is no longer in business as of 1999.

M-16

A .22 rimfire copy of the Colt AR-15. Introduced in 1987.

NIB	Exc.	V.G.	Good	Fair	Poor
225	200	150	125	100	75

MAS

A .22 or .22 Magnum caliber copy of the French MAS Bullpup Service Rifle. Introduced in 1987.

NIB	Exc.	V.G.	Good	Fair	Poor
275	225	200	150	125	100

Galil

A .22 or .22 Magnum caliber copy of the Galil rifle. Introduced in 1987.

NIB	Exc.	V.G.	Good	Fair	Poor
275	225	200	150	125	100

AK-22

A .22 or.22 Magnum caliber copy of the AK47 rifle. Introduced in 1985.

NIB	Exc.	V.G.	Good	Fair	Poor
225	200	150	125	100	75

PPSH-30/50

A .22 or .22 Magnum caliber copy of the PPSH Submachine gun.

NIB	Exc.	V.G.	Good	Fair	Poor
175	150	125	100	75	60

This company also imported Yugoslavian-manufactured semi-automatic AK-47 rifles in 7.62x39mm, as well as 7.62x54mm.

NOTE: The rifles listed above are banned from further manufacture and importation under the "Assault Weapons" provisions in the 1994 Crime Law effective 9/13/94.

HANDGUNS

Trophy II

A semiautomatic pistol chambered for the .22 Long Rifle cartridge. Offered in either 7-1/4" fluted or 5-1/2" bull barrel. Barrels are interchangeable. Trigger is adjustable for weight and pull. Walnut grips with thumb rest are standard.

NIB	Exc.	V.G.	Good	Fair	Poor
400	325	275	200	150	100

Victor II

This .22 caliber pistol is built from stainless steel and has interchangeable barrels in 4-1/2" or 5-1/2" lengths. Barrels have full length ventilated ribs, checkered walnut grips with thumb rest. Gold plated trigger is adjustable.

NIB	Exc.	V.G.	Good	Fair	Poor
450	375	325	250	175	125

Victor II W/Weaver Rib

NIB	Exc.	V.G.	Good	Fair	Poor
525	450	375	275	175	125

Citation II

Similar to the Trophy II but with a matte satin finish.

NIB	Exc.	V.G.	Good	Fair	Poor
375	300	250	200	150	100

Sharpshooter II

This is a stainless steel target pistol with 5-1/2" bull barrel to which barrel weights can be added. Fully adjustable rear sight and checkered walnut grips are standard.

NIB	Exc.	V.G.	Good	Fair	Poor
325	275	225	200	150	100

Olympic I.S.U.

This competition pistol features a 6-3/4" barrel with integral stabilizer. Rear sight is adjustable as is the trigger. Barrel weights are adjustable as well as removable.

NIB	Exc.	V.G.	Good	Fair	Poor
525	475	400	300	200	100

High Standard Collectors' Association Special Editions

Limited run of Mitchell's version of the High Standard pistol with special roll marking on the slide "High Standard / Collectors Association / Special Edition" and a special serial number series with a HSCA prefix. Manufactured by Pastucek Industries, Fort Worth, Texas.

Trophy II

5.50" barrel. See standard Mitchell guns for rest of description.

NIB	Exc.
420	325

Victor II

4.50" barrel. See standard Mitchell guns for rest of description.

NIB	Exc.
450	325

Citation II

7.25" barrel. See standard Mitchell guns for rest of description.

NIB	Exc.
400	300

Three gun set

Includes Trophy II, Olympic ISU, and Victor II. Eleven sets manufactured.

NIB	Exc.
1400	1100

Six gun set

Includes 5.5" Trophy II, 6.75" Olympic II, and 4.5" Victor II, Sharpshooter II, Citation II, and 4.5" Sport King II. Nineteen sets manufactured.

NIB	Exc.
2450	1975

Skorpion

A .32 caliber semiautomatic pistol with a 4.75" barrel and either 20- or 30-shot magazine. Blued with plastic grips. Imported from Yugoslavia in 1987 and 1988 only.

Exc.	V.G.	Good	Fair	Poor
600	500	425	350	175

Spectre

A 9mm caliber semiautomatic pistol with an 8" shrouded barrel and either 30- or 50-shot magazine. Blued with plastic grips. Also produced with an 18" barrel and folding buttstock. Imported from Yugoslavia in 1987 and 1988.

Exc.	V.G.	Good	Fair	Poor
600	500	425	350	175

MODESTO SANTOS CIA.
Eibar, Spain

Action, Corrientes, and M.S.

A 6.35mm or 7.65mm caliber semiautomatic pistol of low quality marked on the slide "Pistolet Automatique Model 1920." Blued with composition grips having the monogram "M.S." cast in them. Manufactured between 1920 and 1935.

Exc.	V.G.	Good	Fair	Poor
200	125	100	75	50

MONDRAGON
Mexico City, Mexico

Firearms designed by Manuel Mondragon were produced on an experimental basis first at St. Chamond Arsenal in France and later at SIG in Neuhausen, Switzerland. The latter company was responsible for the manufacture of the two known production models; the Model 1890 and 1908.

The Model 1890 Mondragon semiautomatic rifle holds the distinction of being the first self-loading rifle to be issued to any armed forces.

Courtesy Rock Island Auction Company

Exc.	V.G.	Good	Fair	Poor
6000	4000	2000	1000	750

MONTENEGRAN-GASSER
SEE—Gasser, Leopold

MOORE-ENFIELD
SEE—English Military Firearms

MOORES PATENT FIREARMS CO.
Brooklyn, New York

In 1866 this company became known as the National Arms Company.

No. 1 Derringer

A .41 caliber spur trigger all metal pistol with a 2.5" barrel. Blued or silver-plated. Approximately 10,000 were manufactured between 1860 and 1865. This model was also marketed as the No. 1 Derringer by the Colt Company after they purchased the National Arms Company in 1870.

Courtesy Milwaukee Public Museum, Milwaukee, Wisconsin

1st Variation Marked "Patent Applied For"

Exc.	V.G.	Good	Fair	Poor
—	—	2500	1100	400

2nd Variation Marked "D. Moore Patented Feb. 19 1861"

Exc.	V.G.	Good	Fair	Poor
—	—	1500	700	250

Standard Model Marked "Moore's Pat F.A. Co."

Exc.	V.G.	Good	Fair	Poor
—	—	850	350	150

National Arms Co. Production

Courtesy Milwaukee Public Museum, Milwaukee, Wisconsin

Exc.	V.G.	Good	Fair	Poor
—	—	800	350	150

Iron Model

Exc.	V.G.	Good	Fair	Poor
—	—	1000	500	250

Pocket Revolver

A .32 teat fire caliber spur trigger revolver with a round 3.25" barrel and 6-shot cylinder. Blued or silver plated with walnut grips. Approximately 30,000 were manufactured between 1864 and 1870.

Courtesy Milwaukee Public Museum, Milwaukee, Wisconsin

Exc.	V.G.	Good	Fair	Poor
—	—	500	250	100

Belt Revolver

A .32 rimfire caliber revolver with a 4", 5", or 6" octagonal barrel and 7-shot cylinder. The barrel and cylinder blued, the brass frame sometimes silver-plated with walnut grips. The barrel marked "D. Moore Patent Sept. 18, 1860." Several thousand were manufactured between 1861 and 1863.

Exc.	V.G.	Good	Fair	Poor
—	—	950	350	150

MORGAN & CLAPP
New Haven, Connecticut

Single Shot Pocket Pistol

A .22 or .23 caliber spur trigger single shot pistol with a 3.5" octagonal barrel. Blued, silver-plated frame with walnut grips. The barrel marked "Morgan & Clapp New Haven." Active 1864 to 1867.

Exc.	V.G.	Good	Fair	Poor
—	—	450	200	100

MORINI
Italy
Importer-Nygord Precision Products
Prescott, AZ

C-80 Standard

A .22 caliber single shot pistol with a free floating 10" barrel, match sights, adjustable frame, and adjustable grips. Discontinued in 1989.

Exc.	V.G.	Good	Fair	Poor
900	800	675	550	250

CM-80 Super Competition

As above, with a trigger adjustable from 5 to 120 grams pressure, Plexiglass front sight and a polished finish. Discontinued in 1989.

Exc.	V.G.	Good	Fair	Poor
1000	900	750	650	300

Model 84E Free Pistol

Introduced in 1995 this competition pistol features an 11.4" barrel chambered for the .22 Long Rifle. It is a single shot. Adjustable sights with adjustable electronic trigger. Weight is about 44 oz.

NIB	Exc.	V.G.	Good	Fair	Poor
1450	1150	900	700	500	—

MORRONE
Hope Valley, Rhode Island
SEE—Rhode Island Arms Company

MORSE
Greenville, South Carolina
State Armory

Morse Carbine

Overall length 40"; barrel length 2"; caliber .50 (other calibers are known to have been made on an experimental basis). The round barrel is blued, the frame is of brass and the stock is of either walnut or beechwood. Approximately 1,000 were manufactured during the Civil War. Prospective purchasers are advised to secure a qualified appraisal prior to acquisition.

Courtesy Milwaukee Public Museum, Milwaukee, Wisconsin

Courtesy Milwaukee Public Museum, Milwaukee, Wisconsin

Exc.	V.G.	Good	Fair	Poor
—	—	20000	7500	1500

MOSIN-NAGANT
Russia

NOTE: For history, technical data, descriptions, and prices see the *Standard Catalog of Military Firearms, 1870 to the Present* under Russia.

MOSSBERG, O. F. & SONS, INC.
North Haven, Connecticut

Founded by Oscar F. Mossberg in 1892 at Fitchburg, Massachusetts, this company for a time was located at Chicopee Falls, Massachusetts, and since 1919 has been in North Haven, Connecticut. It is the oldest family-owned firearms manufacturer in America.

Brownie

A .22 caliber 4 barreled pocket pistol with a revolving firing pin. This pistol resembles a semiautomatic. Manufactured from 1906 to approximately 1940.

Exc.	V.G.	Good	Fair	Poor
400	325	300	225	150

RIFLES

Model K Rifle

A .22 caliber slide action rifle with a 22" barrel, tubular magazine, internal hammer and takedown system. Blued with a walnut stock. Discontinued in 1931.

Exc.	V.G.	Good	Fair	Poor
175	150	125	75	50

Model M Rifle

As above, with a 24" octagonal barrel. Manufactured from 1928 and 1931.

Exc.	V.G.	Good	Fair	Poor
175	150	125	75	50

Model L Rifle

A .22 caliber single shot takedown rifle with a 24" barrel. Manufactured from 1927 to 1932.

Exc.	V.G.	Good	Fair	Poor
300	250	200	150	100

Beginning in 1930, the Mossberg company manufactured a variety of utilitarian single shot and repeating bolt action rifles. Later they introduced a similar line of semiautomatic rifles. As these arms were intended for extensive use and were low-priced, the values for them may be categorized as follows:

Bolt Action Rifles

Model 10	Model 25	Model 340M
Model 14	Model 25A	Model 341
Model 140B	Model 26B	Model 342K
Model 140K	Model 26C	Model 346B
Model 142A	Model 30	Model 346K
Model 142K	Model 320B	Model 352K
Model 144	Model 320K	Model 450
Model 144LS	Model 321K	Model 432
Model 146B	Model 340B	Model 50
Model 20	Model 340K	Model 51
		Model 51M

Model 140 B

Exc.	V.G.	Good	Fair	Poor
100	80	65	45	20

Semiautomatic Rifles

Model 151K	Model 350K
Model 151M	Model 351C
Model 152	Model 351K
Model 152K	

Exc.	V.G.	Good	Fair	Poor
125	100	80	60	40

Model 400 Palomino

A .22 caliber lever action rifle with a 22" barrel, open sights and tubular magazine. Also made with an 18.5" barrel. Blued with a walnut stock. Manufactured from 1959 to 1964.

Exc.	V.G.	Good	Fair	Poor
150	125	100	75	50

Model 800

A bolt action rifle manufactured in a variety of calibers with a 22" barrel and folding leaf rear sight. Blued with a walnut stock. Introduced in 1967.

Exc.	V.G.	Good	Fair	Poor
225	200	150	100	75

Model 800D

As above, with a comb stock, rosewood forend tip and pistol grip cap. Manufactured from 1970 to 1973.

Exc.	V.G.	Good	Fair	Poor
300	250	200	150	100

Model 800V

As above, with a 24" heavy barrel not fitted with sights. Introduced in 1968.

Exc.	V.G.	Good	Fair	Poor
225	200	150	100	75

Model 800M

As above, with a Mannlicher-style stock.

Exc.	V.G.	Good	Fair	Poor
275	250	200	150	100

Model 800SM

As above, with a 4X scope.

Exc.	V.G.	Good	Fair	Poor
300	275	225	150	100

Model 810

A .270 to .338 Winchester Magnum caliber bolt action rifle with a 22" or 24" barrel fitted with a folding rear sight. Blued with a Monte Carlo-style stock. Introduced in 1970.

Exc.	V.G.	Good	Fair	Poor
275	250	200	150	100

Model 472C

A .30-30 or. 35 Remington Caliber lever action rifle with a 20" barrel, open sights, and tubular magazine. Blued with a walnut stock. Introduced in 1972.

Exc.	V.G.	Good	Fair	Poor
200	175	150	100	75

Model 472P

As above, with a pistol grip stock and not fitted with a saddle ring.

Exc.	V.G.	Good	Fair	Poor
200	175	150	100	75

Model 472 One In Five Thousand

As above, with an etched receiver, brass buttplate, saddle ring and barrel band. A total of 5,000 were made in 1974.

Exc.	V.G.	Good	Fair	Poor
400	350	300	200	150

Model 479 PCA

Similar to the Model 472C in .30-30 caliber with a 20" barrel. Blued with a walnut stock.

Exc.	V.G.	Good	Fair	Poor
200	175	150	100	75

Model 479 RR

As above, with a gold-plated trigger and barrel band as well as "Roy Rogers" signature. A total of 5,000 were made in 1983.

Exc.	V.G.	Good	Fair	Poor
300	250	200	150	100

SSi-One Sporter

Introduced in 2000 this is a single shot rifle chambered for the .223, .243, 270 Win., .308, and .30-06 cartridges. Fitted with a 24" barrel without sights. Matte blue finish. Checkered walnut stock. Weight is about 8 lbs. Interchangeable barrels including 12 gauge.

NIB	Exc.	V.G.	Good	Fair	Poor
475	375	—	—	—	—

SSi-One Varmint

Similar to the above model but fitted with a 24" bull barrel chambered for the .22-250 cartridge. Walnut stock. Weight is about 10 lbs. Introduced in 2000. Inchangeable barrels.

NIB	Exc.	V.G.	Good	Fair	Poor
475	375	—	—	—	—

SSi-One Slug

This model is similar to the other SSi-One guns but is fitted with a 24" fully rifled 12 gauge barrel. Walnut stock. Weight is about 8 lbs. Interchangeable barrels. Introduced in 2000.

NIB	Exc.	V.G.	Good	Fair	Poor
475	375	—	—	—	—

SSi-One Turkey

Same as above but with 24" smooth bore barrel. Will handle 3.5" magnum 12 gauge shells. Weight is about 7.5 lbs. Introduced in 2001.

NIB	Exc.	V.G.	Good	Fair	Poor
475	375	—	—	—	—

Model 1500 Series

A .223 to .338 Winchester Magnum bolt action rifle with a 22" or 24" barrel, 5- or 6-shot magazine and various sights. Blued with a hardwood or walnut stock. Manufactured by Howa in Japan and also known as the Smith & Wesson Model 1500. Offered in 1986 and 1987.

Model 1500 Mountaineer Grade I

Exc.	V.G.	Good	Fair	Poor
3050	250	225	150	125

Model 1500 Mountaineer Grade II

Exc.	V.G.	Good	Fair	Poor
325	275	250	175	125

Model 1500 Varmint-24" Heavy Barrel

Exc.	V.G.	Good	Fair	Poor
350	300	275	200	150

Model 1550

As above, but in .243, .270 or .30-06 caliber. Offered in 1986 and 1987.

Exc.	V.G.	Good	Fair	Poor
325	275	250	175	125

Model 1700 LS

Similar to the above, and in the same calibers with a 22" barrel not fitted for sights, machine jeweled bolt and knurled bolt handle. Blued with a walnut stock having a schnabel forend. Offered in 1986 and 1987.

Exc.	V.G.	Good	Fair	Poor
400	350	275	200	150

SHOTGUNS

Mossberg manufactured a variety of shotguns that were sold at low to moderate prices. The values for these arms are approximately all the same.

Bolt Action Shotguns

Model 173	Model 190D	Model 390K
Model 173Y	Model 190K	Model 390T
Model 183D	Model 195D	Model 395K
Model 183K	Model 195K	Model 395S
Model 183T	Model 385K	Model 395T
Model 185D	Model 385T	Model 73
Model 185K		

Model 190D

Exc.	V.G.	Good	Fair	Poor
90	65	50	40	25

Model 695

Introduced in 1969 this bolt action shotgun is chambered for the 12 gauge shell. Barrel length is 22" with either a rifled bore or plain bore. Finish is matte blue. In 1997 this model was offered with a 22" plain ported barrel with rifled bore. Magazine capacity is 3 rounds. Weight is about 7.5 lbs.

NIB	Exc.	V.G.	Good	Fair	Poor
275	225	175	150	125	100

Model 695 Camo

Introduced in 2000 this model is the same as the standard Model 695 with the addition of Woodlands camo finish.

NIB	Exc.	V.G.	Good	Fair	Poor
N/A	—	—	—	—	—

Model 200K

A 12 gauge slide action shotgun with a 28" barrel and Mossberg select choke. Blued with a composition slide handle and walnut stock. Manufactured from 1955 to 1959.

Exc.	V.G.	Good	Fair	Poor
150	125	100	75	50

MODEL 500 SERIES

A 12, 20 or .410 bore slide action shotgun manufactured in a variety of barrel lengths and styles, as follows:

Model 500 Regal

Exc.	V.G.	Good	Fair	Poor
250	200	150	100	75

Model 500 Field Grade

NIB	Exc.	V.G.	Good	Fair	Poor
285	250	200	150	100	75

Model 500 Steel Shot-Chrome Bore

Exc.	V.G.	Good	Fair	Poor
300	250	200	125	100

Model 500 Slugster-Crown Grade-Iron Sights

Exc.	V.G.	Good	Fair	Poor
275	250	200	150	100

Model 500 Camper-18.5" Barrel, Camo Case

Exc.	V.G.	Good	Fair	Poor
295	275	225	175	125

Model 500 Hi-Rib Trap

Exc.	V.G.	Good	Fair	Poor
275	250	200	150	100

Model 500 Super Grade

Exc.	V.G.	Good	Fair	Poor
200	175	150	100	75

Model 500 Pigeon Grade

Exc.	V.G.	Good	Fair	Poor
375	300	250	250	125

Model 500 Pigeon Grade Trap

Exc.	V.G.	Good	Fair	Poor
450	375	300	250	175

Model 500 Persuader-Riot Gun-18.5" Barrel

NIB	Exc.	V.G.	Good	Fair	Poor
250	200	175	150	125	100

Model 500 Mariner-Marinecote Finish

NIB	Exc.	V.G.	Good	Fair	Poor
350	300	225	200	150	125

Model 500 Cruiser-Pistol Grip Only

NIB	Exc.	V.G.	Good	Fair	Poor
250	200	175	150	125	100

Model 500 Muzzleloader Combo

NIB	Exc.	V.G.	Good	Fair	Poor
350	325	275	225	200	150

Model 500 Bullpup

A 12 gauge slide action Bullpup shotgun with an 18.5" or 20" shrouded barrel. Matte black finish with a composition stock. Introduced in 1986.

NIB	Exc.	V.G.	Good	Fair	Poor
400	325	250	200	150	100

Model 500 Bantam

Introduced in 1996 this model is slightly smaller overall than the full size guns. Chambered for the 20 gauge shell it is fitted with a 22" shotgun barrel or 24" rifled vent rib barrel. Walnut stock. Weight is about 6.9 lbs.

NIB	Exc.	V.G.	Good	Fair	Poor
275	225	200	150	125	100

Model 500 Slug Gun-Viking Grade

Introduced in 1996 this model is a 12 gauge gun with 24" rifled barrel with iron sights and green synthetic stock.

NIB	Exc.	V.G.	Good	Fair	Poor
250	200	175	150	125	100

NOTE: In 1997 Mossberg introduced ported barrels on some of its slug models. These ported barrels will be seen on rifled barrels only.

Model 500 Combo

The 500 series has a total of nine combination sets available to choose from. They are a combination of shotgun barrels and rifled barrels for different hunting applications they are offered in both 12 and 20 gauge sets of the same gauge only.

NIB	Exc.	V.G.	Good	Fair	Poor
400	325	275	225	175	125

Model 500 USA

Introduced in 1997 this model is similar to the military model. It has a parkerized finish with heavy duty sling swivels. Fitted with a plain 20" barrel choked cylinder. Stock is black synthetic. Magazine capacity is 6 rounds. Weight is about 7.2 lbs.

NIB	Exc.	V.G.	Good	Fair	Poor
250	200	175	150	125	100

Model 500 HS (Home Security)

This shotgun is chambered for the .410 shell and fitted with an 18.5" barrel. Five round magazine capacity. Synthetic stock and blue finish.

NIB	Exc.	V.G.	Good	Fair	Poor
250	200	175	150	125	100

NOTE: In 1999 Mossberg offered a .50 muzzleloader 24" fully rifles barrel that will fit directly onto any 6 shot Model 500.

Porting on most 500 series and 835 series vent rib and slug barrels.

MODEL 590 SERIES

Model 590 Special Purpose
Fitted with a 20" shrouded barrel, bayonet lug, parkerized or blued finish. Speed feed stock and ghost ring sights. Introduced in 1987. Weight is about 7.25 lbs.

NIB	Exc.	V.G.	Good	Fair	Poor
325	275	200	175	125	100

Model 590 Mariner-Marinecote Finish

NIB	Exc.	V.G.	Good	Fair	Poor
425	350	275	225	150	100

Model 590 Bullpup
The Model 500 with a 20" barrel and 9-shot magazine. Introduced in 1989.

NIB	Exc.	V.G.	Good	Fair	Poor
475	400	325	250	200	125

Model 590DA
This 12 gauge model, introduced in 2000, features a 6-round tubular magazine and an 18.5" barrel. Choice of plain bead sight or ghost ring sights. Choke is fixed modified. Weight is about 7 lbs. A 14" barreled model is also offered but NFA rules apply.

NIB	Exc.	V.G.	Good	Fair	Poor
500	400	—	—	—	—

NOTE: Add $50 for Ghost ring sights.

MODEL 835 SERIES

Model 835 Ulti-Mag
A 12 gauge Magnum slide action shotgun with a choice of 24" or 28" ventilated rib barrel fitted for choke tubes, 6-shot magazine and either composition camo or walnut stock. Barrel is ported. Introduced in 1988. In 1998 this model was offered with Shadow Grass camo pattern on both stock and barrel. In 1999 this model was offered with Woodland camo. Weight is 7.3 to 7.7 lbs. In 2000 this model was offered with Realtree Hardwoods camo finish.

Shadow Grass Camo pattern

Woodland Camo

NIB	Exc.	V.G.	Good	Fair	Poor
425	350	275	25	150	100

Model 835 Ulti-Mag Crown Grade
The Crown Grade features checkered walnut stock with fluted comb. It is chambered for the 12 gauge with 3.5" chamber. Offered in 24" or 28" vent rib barrels with blued or camo finish. Weight is about 7.3 to 7.7 lbs.

NIB	Exc.	V.G.	Good	Fair	Poor
350	275	225	200	150	100

Crown Grade Ulti-Mag Combo Model
Same as above but offered with both a 28" vent rib barrel and a 24" rifled barrel with iron sights.

NIB	Exc.	V.G.	Good	Fair	Poor
400	350	300	250	200	100

Model 835 Ulti-Mag Viking Grade
Introduced in 1996 this model features a 12 gauge 3.5" magnum chambered with green synthetic stock and modified choke tube. Furnished with 28" vent rib barrel.

NIB	Exc.	V.G.	Good	Fair	Poor
300	250	200	175	125	100

Model 835 Wild Turkey Federation
As above, with a Wild Turkey Federation medallion inlaid in the stock. Introduced in 1989.

NIB	Exc.	V.G.	Good	Fair	Poor
475	400	325	250	200	125

Model 835 American Field
This 12 gauge model has a checkered walnut stock, 28" ventilated rib barrel with modified choke tube. Weight is about 7.7 lbs.

NIB	Exc.	V.G.	Good	Fair	Poor
300	275	225	200	150	100

Model 3000
A 12 or 20 gauge slide action shotgun manufactured in a variety of barrel lengths and styles. Blued with a walnut stock. Also known as the Smith & Wesson Model 3000.

Exc.	V.G.	Good	Fair	Poor
325	250	175	125	75

Model 3000 Waterfowler
As above, but matte finished, fitted with sling swivels and accompanied by a camouflage sling. Produced in 1986.

Exc.	V.G.	Good	Fair	Poor
350	275	200	150	100

Model 3000 Law Enforcement
As above, with an 18.5" or 20" cylinder-bore barrel. Manufactured in 1986 and 1987.

Exc.	V.G.	Good	Fair	Poor
325	250	175	125	75

Model 1000
A 12 or 20 gauge semiautomatic shotgun manufactured in a variety of barrel lengths and styles, the receiver of an aluminum alloy and blued. Also known as the Smith & Wesson Model 1000. Offered in 1986 and 1987.

Exc.	V.G.	Good	Fair	Poor
400	325	250	200	125

Model 1000 Slug
As above, with a 22" barrel having rifle sights. Offered in 1986 and 1987.

Exc.	V.G.	Good	Fair	Poor
400	325	250	200	125

Model 1000 Super Series
As above, with a steel receiver and a self-regulating gas system that allows the use of either standard or Magnum shells.

Exc.	V.G.	Good	Fair	Poor
500	450	400	300	200

Model 1000 Super Waterfowler-Matte Finish

Exc.	V.G.	Good	Fair	Poor
500	450	400	300	200

Model 1000 Super Slug-Rifle Sights

Exc.	V.G.	Good	Fair
500	450	400	300

Model 1000 Super Trap-30" High Rib Barrel

Exc.	V.G.	Good	Fair	Poor
475	425	350	250	175

Model 1000 Super Skeet-25" Barrel

Exc.	V.G.	Good	Fair	Poor
575	525	450	350	225

Model 5500 MKI I
A 12 gauge semiautomatic shotgun supplied with either a 26" barrel for 2.75" shells or a 28" barrel for 3" shells. Blued with a walnut stock. Introduced in 1989.

NIB	Exc.	V.G.	Good	Fair	Poor
435	375	275	225	175	125

MODEL 9200 SERIES

This model has a variety of configurations. It is a 12 gauge semiautomatic with a choice of walnut stock or camo synthetic stock. Barrel lengths are from 22" to 28". Weights range from 7 to 7.7 lbs.

Model 9200 Viking Grade

NIB	Exc.	V.G.	Good	Fair	Poor
400	350	300	275	200	100

Mossy Oak Shadow Branch Camo

Model 9200 USST Crown Grade

NIB	Exc.	V.G.	Good	Fair	Poor
475	400	350	300	200	100

Model 9200 Combos

NIB	Exc.	V.G.	Good	Fair	Poor
550	475	425	350	250	150

Model 9200 Special Hunter-28" vent rib barrel with synthetic stock

NIB	Exc.	V.G.	Good	Fair	Poor
550	475	425	350	250	150

Model 9200 Deer Combo

NIB	Exc.	V.G.	Good	Fair	Poor
550	475	425	350	250	150

Model 9200 Turkey Camos

NIB	Exc.	V.G.	Good	Fair	Poor
550	475	425	350	250	150

Model 9200 Crown Grade Bantam

NIB	Exc.	V.G.	Good	Fair	Poor
475	400	350	300	250	125

Model 9200 Jungle Gun

This is a 12 gauge auto loader fitted with a plain 18.5" barrel with bead sight. Barrel choked cylinder. Chambers are 2-3/4". Magazine capacity is 5 rounds. Parkerized finish. Synthetic stock.

NIB	Exc.	V.G.	Good	Fair	Poor
475	400	—	—	—	—

MOUNTAIN RIFLES, INC.
Palmer, Alaska

Mountaineer

This bolt action rifle, introduced in 1997, is built on a Remington action with Model 70 style bolt release. A factory muzzle brake is installed with open sights. A Timney trigger is standard. Stock is fiberglass. Finish is parkerized. This model is chambered for many different calibers, from .223 Rem. to .416 Rem. Including Dakota and Weatherby cartridges. Weight starts at about 6 lbs. and is dependent on caliber. There are several options that will affect price. A left hand model is offered as an option.

NIB	Exc.	V.G.	Good	Fair	Poor
2195	1750	—	—	—	—

Super Mountaineer

Similar to the Mountaineer model but the bolt is fluted and hollow. Barrel is match grade stainless steel with muzzle brake. Kevlar/Graphite stock. Wide variety of calibers. Weight starts at about 4.25 lbs. depending on caliber.

NIB	Exc.	V.G.	Good	Fair	Poor
2895	2350	—	—	—	—

Pro Mountaineer

This model is built on a Winchester Model 70 action. Premium match grade barrel with muzzle brake. Model 70 trigger. Stainless steel matte finish. Kevlar/Graphite stock. Wide variety of calibers. Weight starts at about 6 lbs.

NIB	Exc.	V.G.	Good	Fair	Poor
2895	2350	—	—	—	—

Pro Safari

This model is built on an MRI action with controlled feed. Premium match grade barrel. Timney trigger. Matte blue finish. Exhibition grade walnut stock with custom bottom metal. Weight starts at about 7 lbs. depending on caliber. Caliber from .223 to .458 Lott.

NIB	Exc.	V.G.	Good	Fair	Poor
4495	3500	—	—	—	—

Ultra Mountaineer

Built on an MRI action with premium match grade barrel and muzzle brake. Timney trigger. Parkerized finish. Kevlar/Graphite stock. Calibers form .223 to .505 Gibbs. Weight begins at 5 lbs. depending on caliber. Add $500 for Rigby length calibers.

NIB	Exc.	V.G.	Good	Fair	Poor
2995	2500	—	—	—	—

MUGICA, JOSE
Eibar, Spain
SEE—Llama

A trade name found on Llama pistols that were manufactured by Gabilondo.

MURATA
SEE—Japan State

MURFEESBORO ARMORY
Murfeesboro, Tennessee

Established in 1861 by William Ledbetter. Made copies of U.S. Model 1841 Rifle complete with patchbox and double strapped nose cap. Barrel bands pinned to stock. Between 270 and 390 made from October of 1861 through March of 1862. Overall length 48-3/4"; barrel length 33"; .54 caliber. Unmarked except for serial number on various parts including the barrel.

Prospective purchasers are strongly advised to secure an expert appraisal prior to acquisition.

Exc.	V.G.	Good	Fair	Poor
—	—	13500	6000	2000

MURRAY, J. P.
Columbus, Georgia

Percussion Rifle

A .58 caliber percussion rifle with a 33" barrel, full stock and brass mounts. Also made with a 23.5" to 24" barrel as a carbine. The lock marked "J.P. Murray/Columbus Ga." Several hundred were manufactured between 1862 and 1864. Prospective purchasers are advised to secure a qualified appraisal prior to acquisition.

Courtesy Milwaukee Public Museum, Milwaukee, Wisconsin

Exc.	V.G.	Good	Fair	Poor
—	—	25000	8000	1500

A J.P. Murray percussion rifle was sold at auction for $13,800. Condition was fair to good. Butterfield & Butterfield, August 1999

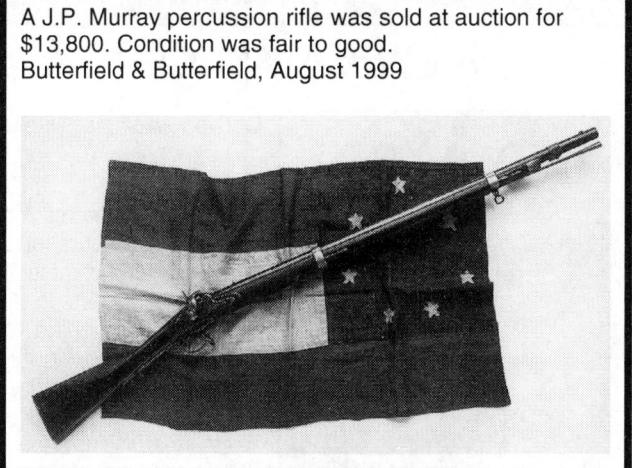

MURPHY & O'CONNEL
New York, New York

Pocket Pistol

A .41 caliber single shot percussion pocket pistol with a 3" barrel, German silver mounts and a walnut stock. Manufactured during the 1850s.

Exc.	V.G.	Good	Fair	Poor
—	—	2500	1000	450

MUSGRAVE
Republic of South Africa

RSA NR I Single Shot Target Rifle

A .308 caliber single shot bolt action rifle with a 26" barrel, match sights, adjustable trigger and target-style stock. Made of walnut. Manufactured between 1971 and 1976.

Exc.	V.G.	Good	Fair	Poor
450	325	225	175	100

Valiant NR6

A .243, .270, .308, .30-06, and 7mm Remington Magnum caliber bolt action sporting rifle with a 24" barrel, open sights and English style stock. Imported from 1971 to 1976.

Exc.	V.G.	Good	Fair	Poor
350	250	200	150	100

Premier NR5

As above, with a 26" barrel and pistol grip Monte Carlo-style stock. Discontinued in 1976.

Exc.	V.G.	Good	Fair	Poor
400	300	250	200	100

MUSKETEER RIFLES
Washington, D.C.
Importer-Firearms International

Sporter

A .243 to .300 Winchester Magnum caliber bolt action rifle with a 24" barrel without sights, and Monte Carlo-style stock. Imported between 1963 and 1972.

Exc.	V.G.	Good	Fair	Poor
350	250	200	175	100

Deluxe Sporter

As above, with an adjustable trigger and more finely figured walnut stock.

Exc.	V.G.	Good	Fair	Poor
400	300	250	200	100

Carbine

The Sporter with a 20" barrel.

Exc.	V.G.	Good	Fair	Poor
375	275	225	175	100

e-GunParts.com

Numrich Gun Parts Corporation has expanded its website to include full e-commerce purchasing. Our new virtual storefront allows shopping for all your firearms parts and accessories by manufacturer and model. 180,000 items are available to purchase from our secure site, 24 hours a day, from anywhere in the world. You can now browse and buy within four clicks. The updated e-commerce site will also offer specials, new products, and inventory closeouts.

NUMRICH GUN PARTS CORPORATION
226 Williams Lane, West Hurley, NY 12491
Orders: 845-679-2417 • Customer Svc: 845-679-4867
Toll Free Fax: 877-Gun Parts • E-mail: info@gunpartscorp.com

PRECISION RIFLE REST

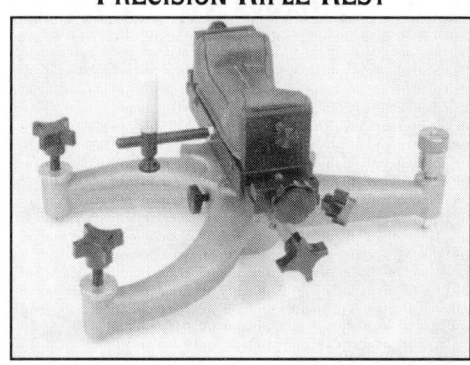

Bald Eagle Precision Machine Co. offers a rifle rest perfect for the serious benchrester or dedicated varminter.

"The Slingshot" or Next Generation has 60° front legs. The rest is constructed of aircraft-quality aluminum or fine grain cast iron and weighs 12 to 20 lbs. The finish is 3 coats of Imron clear. Primary height adjustments are made with a rack and pinion gear. Secondary adjustment uses a mariner wheel with thrust bearings for smooth operation. A hidden fourth leg allows for lateral movement on the bench.

Bald Eagle offers approximately 150 rest combinations to choose from, including windage adjustable, right or left hand, cast aluminum or cast iron.

Prices: $165.00 to $335.00

BALD EAGLE PRECISION MACHINE CO.
101-K Allison Street, Lock Haven, PA 17745
Phone: 570-748-6772 — Fax: 570-748-4443
Web: www.baldeaglemachine.com

HIGH QUALITY OPTICS

One of the best indicators of quality is a scope's resolution number. The smaller the number, the better. Our scope has a resolution number of 2.8 seconds of angle. This number is about 20% smaller (better) than other well-known scopes costing much more. It means that two .22 caliber bullets can be a hair's breath apart and edges of each still be clearly seen. With a Shepherd at 800 yards, you will be able to tell a four inch antler from a four inch ear and a burrowing owl from a prairie dog. Bird watchers will be able to distinguish a Tufted Titmouse from a Ticked-Off Field Mouse. Send for free catalog.

SHEPHERD ENTERPRISES, INC.
Box 189, Waterloo, NE 68069
Phone: 402-779-2424 • Fax: 402-779-4010
Email: shepherd@shepherdscopes.com • Web: www.shepherdscopes.com

6x18x40 VARMINT/TARGET SCOPE

Send for
Free Catalog

The Shepherd 6x18x40 Varmint/Target Scope makes long-range varmint and target shooting child's play. Just pick the ranging circle that best fits your target (be it prairie dogs, coyotes or paper varmints) and Shepherd's exclusive, patented Dual Reticle Down Range System does the rest. You won't believe how far you can accurately shoot, even with rimfire rifles.

Shepherd's superior lens coating mean superior light transmission and tack-sharp resolution.

This new shockproof, waterproof scope features 1/4 minute-of-angle clicks on the ranging circles and friction adjustments on the crosshairs that allows fine-tuning to 0.001 MOA. A 40mm adjustable objective provides a 5.5-foot field of view at 100 yards (16x setting). 16.5 FOV @ 6X.

SHEPHERD ENTERPRISES, INC.
Box 189, Waterloo, NE 68069
Phone: 402-779-2424 • Fax: 402-779-4010
Email: shepherd@shepherdscopes.com • Web: www.shepherdscopes.com

SHOOTER'S MARKETPLACE

N

NAGANT, EMILE & LEON
Liege, Belgium
NOTE: For history, technical data, descriptions, photos, and prices see the *Standard Catalog of Military Firearms, 1870 to the Present.*

NAMBU
SEE—Japan State

NATIONAL ARMS CO.
Brooklyn, New York
SEE—Moore's Patent Firearms Co.
The successor to the Moore's Patent Firearms Company in 1865. Purchased by the Colt Company in 1870.

Large Frame Teat-Fire Revolver
A .45 teat fire caliber revolver with a 7.5" barrel and 6-shot cylinder. Blued or silver-plated with walnut grips. The barrel marked "National Arms Co. Brooklyn". The exact number of these revolvers made is unknown, but it is estimated to be less than 30. Prospective purchasers are advised to secure a qualified appraisal prior to acquisition.

Exc.	V.G.	Good	Fair	Poor
—	—	10000	4000	850

No. 2 Derringer
A .41 caliber spur trigger pocket pistol with a 2.5" barrel. Blued or silver-plated with walnut grips. Later manufactured by the Colt Company as their No. 2 Derringer.

Exc.	V.G.	Good	Fair	Poor
—	—	850	400	150

NAVY ARMS COMPANY
Ridgefield, New Jersey
Founded in 1957 by Val Forgett to enhance the shooting of black powder firearms without destroying the originals. The first replica was the Colt 1851 Navy. Thus, the name of the new company, "Navy Arms". In the early 1980s Navy Arms began importing surplus firearms from European countries. Navy Arms continues to offer both black powder replicas and foreign imports. For a short period of time the company imported double barrel shotguns. This was discontinued in 1990.

SHOTGUNS
The shotguns listed below were no longer imported by Navy Arms in 1990.

Model 83
A 12 or 20 gauge Magnum Over/Under shotgun manufactured in a variety of barrel lengths and styles with double triggers and extractors. Blued, engraved, with a walnut stock. Introduced in 1985.

NIB	Exc.	V.G.	Good	Fair	Poor
385	300	275	200	175	100

Model 93
As above, with automatic ejectors.

NIB	Exc.	V.G.	Good	Fair	Poor
450	400	300	250	200	100

Model 95
As above, with a single trigger and screw-in choke tubes.

NIB	Exc.	V.G.	Good	Fair	Poor
475	375	300	250	200	100

Model 96 Sportsman
As above, in 12 gauge only with a gold-plated receiver.

NIB	Exc.	V.G.	Good	Fair	Poor
575	450	350	300	225	150

Model 100
A 12, 20, 28 or .410 bore Over/Under boxlock shotgun with 26" ventilated rib barrels, single trigger and extractors. Blued, chrome-plated, with a walnut stock. Introduced in 1989.

NIB	Exc.	V.G.	Good	Fair	Poor
300	250	200	150	100	75

Model 100 Side-by-Side
A 12 or 20 gauge Magnum boxlock double barrel shotgun with 27.5" barrels, double triggers and extractors. Blued with a walnut stock. Imported between 1985 and 1987.

Exc.	V.G.	Good	Fair	Poor
375	300	250	200	100

Model 150
As above, with automatic ejectors.

Exc.	V.G.	Good	Fair	Poor
450	350	300	225	125

Model 105
A 12, 20 or .410 bore folding single barrel shotgun with a 26" or 28" barrel, chrome-plated engraved receiver, blued barrel and hardwood stock. Introduced in 1985.

NIB	Exc.	V.G.	Good	Fair	Poor
100	80	75	65	50	35

Model 105 Deluxe
As above, with vent rib barrel and a checkered walnut stock.

NIB	Exc.	V.G.	Good	Fair	Poor
120	100	85	75	60	45

REPLICA LONG GUNS

Harpers Ferry Flint Rifle

This model is a copy of the 1803 rifle in the original .54 caliber. It features a rust blued 35" barrel. Weight is 8.5 lbs.

NIB	Exc.	V.G.	Good	Fair	Poor
600	475	350	300	200	100

Brown Bess Musket

This replica is a copy of the second model used between 1760 and 1776. Bright finish on metal and one piece walnut stock with polished brass locks. Barrel is 42" and weight is 9.5 lbs.

NIB	Exc.	V.G.	Good	Fair	Poor
800	625	500	300	200	100

Brown Bess Carbine

Same as above but fitted with a 30" barrel. Weighs 7.75 lbs.

NIB	Exc.	V.G.	Good	Fair	Poor
800	625	500	300	200	100

1777 Charleville Musket

Copy of French flintlock in .69 caliber. Fittings are steel with brass front sight and brass flashpan. Barrel length is 44.625" and weight is about 8.75 lbs.

NIB	Exc.	V.G.	Good	Fair	Poor
900	700	550	400	300	150

1777 Standard Charleville Musket

Same as above with polished steel barrel and select walnut stock.

NIB	Exc.	V.G.	Good	Fair	Poor
900	700	550	400	300	150

1816 M.T. Wickham Musket

Furnished in .69 caliber with steel ramrod with button head. Brass flashpan and walnut stock are standard.

NIB	Exc.	V.G.	Good	Fair	Poor
600	550	450	350	250	200

1808 Springfield Musket

This model is a U.S. copy of the 1763 Charleville musket with 1808 Springfield markings. Barrel length is 44" and weight is 8.75 lbs.

NIB	Exc.	V.G.	Good	Fair	Poor
950	800	600	400	200	100

Pennsylvania Long Rifle

This model is offered in either percussion or flintlock ignition and is offered in a choice of .32 caliber or .45 caliber. It has an octagonal 40.5" rust blued barrel, polished lock, double set triggers, and brass furniture on a walnut stock. Weighs 7.5 lbs.

Percussion

NIB	Exc.	V.G.	Good	Fair	Poor
450	375	250	200	150	100

Flintlock

NIB	Exc.	V.G.	Good	Fair	Poor
475	400	275	225	150	100

Kentucky Rifle

Offered in either percussion or flintlock ignition it has a blue steel barrel, case colored lockplate, and a polished brass patch box inletted into a walnut stock. The barrel length is 35" and the rifle is available in .45 oz. 50 caliber. Weight is 6 lbs. 14 oz.

Percussion

NIB	Exc.	V.G.	Good	Fair	Poor
400	325	200	150	100	75

Flintlock

NIB	Exc.	V.G.	Good	Fair	Poor
420	335	225	150	100	75

Mortimer Flintlock Rifle

Offered in .54 caliber with rust blued barrel, walnut stock with cheekpiece and checkered straight grip. It also has a external safety and sling swivels. Barrel length is 36" and weight is 9 lbs. Optional shotgun barrel.

NIB	Exc.	V.G.	Good	Fair	Poor
650	550	500	450	350	150

Optional shotgun barrel-Add $240.

Tryon Creedmoor Rifle

This .45 caliber model features a heavy blued 33" octagonal barrel, hooded front sight, adjustable tang sight, double set triggers, sling swivels, and a walnut stock. Weighs about 9.5 lbs.

NIB	Exc.	V.G.	Good	Fair	Poor
600	525	450	400	300	150

Standard Tryon Rifle

Same as above but without target sights.

NIB	Exc.	V.G.	Good	Fair	Poor
400	350	300	250	200	100

Deluxe Tryon Rifle

Same as above but with polished and engraved lock and patch box.

NIB	Exc.	V.G.	Good	Fair	Poor
425	375	325	250	200	100

Parker-Hale Whitworth Rifle

This is a replica of a British sniper rifle, .451 caliber, used by the Confederates during the Civil War. Round barrel is 36" and features a globe front sight and ladder rear sight. The walnut stock is hand checkered. Weighs 9 lbs. 10 oz.

NIB	Exc.	V.G.	Good	Fair	Poor
850	675	600	450	300	150

Limited edition telescope-Add $150.

Parker-Hale Volunteer Rifle

A .451 caliber rifle with hand checkered walnut stock. Fitted with 32" barrel with globe front sight and ladder rear sight. Weighs 9.5 lbs.

NIB	Exc.	V.G.	Good	Fair	Poor
825	650	550	400	300	150

Parker-Hale 3 Band Volunteer Rifle

Same basic specifications as Whitworth rifle but furnished with Alexander Henry rifling.

NIB	Exc.	V.G.	Good	Fair	Poor
750	650	600	400	250	50

Rigby Target Rifle

The 1880s replica is chambered for the .451 caliber. It is fitted with adjustable front sight and vernier tang sight. The lock, breech plug, triggerguard, buttplate, and escutcheons are case colored. Barrel length is 32" and weight is 7 lbs. 12 oz.

NIB	Exc.	V.G.	Good	Fair	Poor
600	500	450	300	200	100

1861 Springfield Rifle

This .58 caliber replica is fitted with an 1855-style hammer. Barrel length is 40" and weight is 10 lbs. 4 oz.

NIB	Exc.	V.G.	Good	Fair	Poor
550	425	350	300	200	100

1862 C.S. Richmond Rifle

This Confederate rifle is .58 caliber and is a faithful reproduction of those produced at the Richmond Armory. Barrel length is 40". Weighs 10 lbs. 4 oz.

NIB	Exc.	V.G.	Good	Fair	Poor
550	425	350	300	200	100

J.P. Murray Carbine

This Confederate cavalry .58 caliber carbine has a case colored lock and brass furniture on a walnut stock. Barrel length is 23.5" and weight is 8 lbs. 5 oz.

NIB	Exc.	V.G.	Good	Fair	Poor
400	325	250	200	150	100

1863 Springfield Rifle

An exact replica of the famous Springfield Musket. Barrel is 40" with 3 barrel bands. All metal parts are finished bright. Weighs 9.5 lbs.

NIB	Exc.	V.G.	Good	Fair	Poor
550	425	350	300	200	100

1841 Mississippi Rifle

Also know as the "Yager" rifle it is offered in either .54 or .58 caliber. Barrel length is 33" and weighs 9.5 lbs.

NIB	Exc.	V.G.	Good	Fair	Poor
450	325	250	200	150	100

Zouave Rifle

This Civil War replica is a .58 caliber with polished brass hardware and blued 33" barrel. Weighs 9 lbs.

NIB	Exc.	V.G.	Good	Fair	Poor
450	325	250	200	150	100

Parker-Hale 1861 Musketoon

Made by Gibbs Rifle Company using 130-year-old gauges for reference. This .577 caliber replica features a 24" barrel with folding ladder military sight. The stock is walnut and the lock is case colored. All furniture is polished brass. Weighs 7.5 lbs.

NIB	Exc.	V.G.	Good	Fair	Poor
400	325	250	200	150	100

Navy Arms Musketoon

Same as above but manufactured in Italy.

NIB	Exc.	V.G.	Good	Fair	Poor
400	325	250	200	150	100

Parker-Hale 1858 Two Band Musket

This .577 caliber model is based on the 1858 Enfield naval pattern. Fitted with a military sight graduated to 1,100 yards. Case colored lock and walnut stock with brass fittings. Barrel length is 33" and weighs 8.5 lbs.

NIB	Exc.	V.G.	Good	Fair	Poor
550	425	350	300	200	100

Navy Arms 1858 Two Band Musket

Same as above but built in Italy.

NIB	Exc.	V.G.	Good	Fair	Poor
450	325	250	200	150	100

Parker-Hale Three Band Musket

This replica is based on the design produced between 1853 and 1863. The rear sight is based on an 1853 model graduated to 900 yards. Is fitted with a case colored lock and walnut stock with brass furniture. Barrel is 39" and weighs 9 lbs.

NIB	Exc.	V.G.	Good	Fair	Poor
600	475	400	300	200	100

Navy Arms Three Band Musket

Same as above but produced in Italy.

NIB	Exc.	V.G.	Good	Fair	Poor
475	350	300	250	200	100

Navy Arms Revolving Carbine

Fitted with a 20" barrel and chambered for the .357 Magnum, .44-40, or .45 Colt cartridge. This model has a revolving 6 shot cylinder. Straight grip stock with brass buttplate and triggerguard. The action is based on the Remington Model 1874 revolver. Introduced in 1968 and discontinued in 1984.

NIB	Exc.	V.G.	Good	Fair	Poor
600	500	400	300	200	100

1859 Sharps Infantry Rifle

This is a .54 caliber copy of the three band Sharps. Barrel length is 30". Case hardened receiver and patch box. Blued barrel and walnut stock. Weight is about 8.5 lbs.

NIB	Exc.	V.G.	Good	Fair	Poor
1000	800	600	400	300	150

1859 Berdan Sharps Rifle

Similar to the 1859 Sharps above but with double set triggers.

NIB	Exc.	V.G.	Good	Fair	Poor
1075	850	650	450	325	150

1874 Sharps Infantry Rifle

This model is fitted with a 30" round barrel and chambered for the .45-70 cartridge. Blued barrel with case hardened receiver. Walnut stock with 3 barrel bands. Weight is about 8.5 lbs.

NIB	Exc.	V.G.	Good	Fair	Poor
1050	750	550	—	—	—

1874 Sharps Sniper Rifle

Same as 1874 Infantry rifle but with double set triggers.

NIB	Exc.	V.G.	Good	Fair	Poor
1100	800	600	—	—	—

Sharps Cavalry Carbine

A breech loading .54 caliber carbine with 22" blued barrel. Military style sights, walnut stocks, and saddle bar with ring are standard. Weighs 7 lbs. 12 oz.

NIB	Exc.	V.G.	Good	Fair	Poor
925	550	500	400	300	150

Sharps Cavalry Carbine Cartridge Model

Same as above but chambered for the .45-70 Government cartridge.

NIB	Exc.	V.G.	Good	Fair	Poor
925	550	500	400	300	150

1874 Sharps Plains Rifle

This model features a case colored receiver, blued barrel, and checkered walnut stock. Offered in .44-70 or .54 caliber percussion. Barrel length is 28.5". Weight is 8 lbs. 10 oz.

NIB	Exc.	V.G.	Good	Fair	Poor
1050	800	600	400	300	150

1874 Sharps Sporting Rifle

Similar to the above model but features a full pistol grip, 32" medium weight octagonal barrel, double set triggers, and case colored frame. Weight is about 10.75 lbs.

NIB	Exc.	V.G.	Good	Fair	Poor
1090	850	650	450	350	200

1874 Sharps Buffalo Rifle

Chambered for the .45-70 or .45-90 and fitted with a 28" heavy octagon barrel. Buttstock is checkered. Weight is approximately 12 lbs.

NIB	Exc.	V.G.	Good	Fair	Poor
1090	850	650	450	350	200

1874 Sharps No. 3 Long Range Rifle

Built by Pedersoli this rifle is fitted with a 34" medium weight octagon barrel, globe target front sight and match grade rear tang sight. Double set trigger. Case hardened frame. Walnut stock. Weight is about 11 lbs.

NIB	Exc.	V.G.	Good	Fair	Poor
1725	1250	900	—	—	—

1873 Winchester Rifle

This replica features a case colored receiver, blued octagon 24" barrel, and walnut stocks. Offered in either .440-40 or .45 Long Colt. Weighs about 8 lbs. 4 oz.

NIB	Exc.	V.G.	Good	Fair	Poor
900	725	600	500	400	200

1873 Winchester Carbine
Same specifications as rifle above but fitted with a 19" round barrel, blued receiver, and saddle ring. Weighs 7 lbs. 4 oz.

NIB	Exc.	V.G.	Good	Fair	Poor
800	650	575	500	400	200

1873 Winchester Sporting Rifle
This model features a 30" octagonal barrel, case colored receiver, and checkered pistol grip. Offered in .44-40 or. 45 Long Colt. Weighs about 8 lbs. 14 oz. A 24" model is also offered.

NIB	Exc.	V.G.	Good	Fair	Poor
950	750	650	525	400	200

1873 Border Model
Introduced in 2000 this model features a 20" blued octagon barrel with buckhorn rear sight. Magazine capacity is 10 rounds. Checkered pistol grip stock is walnut with oil finish. Chambered for the .357 Mag., .44-40, or .45 Colt cartridge.

NIB	Exc.	V.G.	Good	Fair	Poor
975	800	700	—	—	—

1866 "Yellowboy" Rifle
This model features a brass receiver, 24" octagon barrel, and walnut stocks. Weighs 8.5 lbs.

NIB	Exc.	V.G.	Good	Fair	Poor
675	525	450	400	300	150

1866 "Yellowboy" Carbine
Same as above but fitted with a 19" round barrel and saddle ring. Weighs 7 lbs. 4 oz.

NIB	Exc.	V.G.	Good	Fair	Poor
675	525	450	400	300	150

1866 "Yellowboy" Short Rifle
Introduced in 2000 this model features a 20" barrel with buckhorn rear sight. Walnut stock with oil finish. Receiver is yellow brass. Chambered for the .38 Special, .44-40, or .45 Colt cartridge. Magazine capacity is 10 rounds.

NIB	Exc.	V.G.	Good	Fair	Poor
700	550	450	—	—	—

Iron Frame Henry
This is a replica of the famous and rare .44-40 Iron Frame Henry that features a case colored frame. Barrel length is 24" and rifle weighs 9 lbs.

NIB	Exc.	V.G.	Good	Fair	Poor
925	750	650	500	400	200

Blued Iron Frame Henry
Same as above but furnished with a highly polished blued receiver.

NIB	Exc.	V.G.	Good	Fair	Poor
925	750	650	500	400	200

Military Henry
Based on the brass frame military version of the Henry rifle this model is furnished with sling swivels mounted on the left side. The buttplate is fitted with a trap door. Caliber is .44-40 and barrel length is 24". Weighs 9 lbs. 4 oz.

NIB	Exc.	V.G.	Good	Fair	Poor
900	725	625	500	400	200

Henry Carbine
This is the brass frame carbine version and features a 22" barrel. Chambered for the .44-40 cartridge. Weighs 8 lbs. 12 oz.

NIB	Exc.	V.G.	Good	Fair	Poor
875	700	600	500	400	200

Henry Trapper
This replica is not based on an actual Henry. Fitted with a unique 16.5" barrel, this brass frame model weighs 7 lbs. 7 oz. Chambered for the .44-40 cartridge.

NIB	Exc.	V.G.	Good	Fair	Poor
875	700	600	500	400	200

1892 Rifle
This lever action rifle is chambered for the .357 Mag., .44-40, or .45 Colt cartridge. Octagon barrel is 24.25". Walnut stock, crescent butt and blued or case colored receiver. Weight is about 6.25 lbs.

NIB	Exc.	V.G.	Good	Fair	Poor
525	425	350	300	250	200

1892 Short Rifle

Same as above but with 20" octagon barrel. Weight is about 6.25 lbs.

NIB	Exc.	V.G.	Good	Fair	Poor
525	425	350	300	250	200

1892 Carbine

Similar to the short rifle but fitted with a 20" round barrel and saddle ring on left side of receiver. Weight is about 5.75 lbs.

NIB	Exc.	V.G.	Good	Fair	Poor
450	350	300	250	200	150

1892 Brass Frame Carbine

Same as above but with polished brass receiver.

NIB	Exc.	V.G.	Good	Fair	Poor
450	350	300	250	200	150

1892 Brass Frame Rifle

This model is the same as the rifle but with polished brass receiver.

NIB	Exc.	V.G.	Good	Fair	Poor
525	425	350	300	250	200

No. 2 Creedmoor Target Rifle

This is a reproduction of the Remington No. 2 Creedmore. It features a case colored receiver, tapered 30" octagonal barrel, hooded front sight, Creedmore tang sight, and walnut stock with checkered pistol grip. Furnished in .45-70 Government. Weighs 9 lbs.

NIB	Exc.	V.G.	Good	Fair	Poor
900	725	625	500	400	200

Rolling Block Buffalo Rifle

This rifle is a replica of the Remington Buffalo rifle. It is fitted with a 26" or 30" octagonal or half octagonal barrel, case colored receiver, blade front sight, notch rear sight, brass triggerguard, with walnut stocks. Tang is drilled and tapped for tang sight.

NIB	Exc.	V.G.	Good	Fair	Poor
750	600	475	300	200	100

Half Octagon Barrel Model

NIB	Exc.	V.G.	Good	Fair	Poor
750	600	475	300	200	100

1885 High Wall

Chambered for the .45-70 cartridge this rifle is fitted with a 30" medium heavy octagon barrel. Case colored receiver, target sights and walnut stocks. Also available with 28" round barrel.

NIB	Exc.	V.G.	Good	Fair	Poor
900	725	600	500	400	200

NOTE: Reduce price by $100 for Buckhorn sights and $60 for 28" barrel.

1873 Springfield Infantry Rifle

A copy of the Trapdoor Springfield. Chambered for .45-70 and fitted with a 32.5" barrel. Walnut stock and case hardened breechlock. Weight is approximately 8.25 lbs.

NIB	Exc.	V.G.	Good	Fair	Poor
975	800	600	500	400	200

1873 Springfield Cavalry Carbine

Same as above but with 22" barrel. Weight is about 7 lbs.

NIB	Exc.	V.G.	Good	Fair	Poor
875	700	600	500	400	200

Ithaca/Navy Hawken Rifle

Offered in either .50 or. 54 caliber percussion. Features a 31.5" rust blued octagon barrel. The percussion lockplate is case colored, while the rest of the hardware is blued with the exception of the nose cap and escutcheons. Weighs about 9 lbs. 13 oz.

NIB	Exc.	V.G.	Good	Fair	Poor
350	300	250	200	150	100

Hawken Rifle

This model features a case colored lock, 28" blued octagon barrel, adjustable sights, double set triggers, and hooked breech. The polished brass furniture and patch box are mounted on a walnut stock. Weighs about 8.5 lbs.

NIB	Exc.	V.G.	Good	Fair	Poor
220	150	125	100	75	60

Hawken Hunter Rifle

Offered in .50, .54, or .58 caliber, this model features blued hardware, adjustable sights, case colored lock, and hooked breech. The walnut stock is hand checkered with a cheekpiece. Rubber recoil pad is standard. Barrel length is 28".

NIB	Exc.	V.G.	Good	Fair	Poor
240	190	150	100	75	60

Hawken Hunter Carbine

Same as above but fitted with a 22.5" barrel. Weighs about 6 lbs. 12 oz.

NIB	Exc.	V.G.	Good	Fair	Poor
240	190	150	100	75	60

Kodiak MKIV Double Rifle

Built in Europe, this model is chambered for the .45-70 cartridge and features a walnut stock with cheekpiece and hand checkering. Barrel length is 24" with adjustable sights. Engraved sideplates are polished bright. Sling swivels standard. Weighs 10.2 lbs.

NIB	Exc.	V.G.	Good	Fair	Poor
3000	2250	—	—	—	—

Mortimer Flintlock Shotgun

Replica of 12 gauge English Mortimer this model features a waterproof pan, roller frizzen, external safety. All parts are case colored. Barrel is 36" long. Weighs 7 lbs.

NIB	Exc.	V.G.	Good	Fair	Poor
650	500	450	300	200	100

Fowler Shotgun

This 12 gauge model is a side-by-side with straight gripstock. The gun features a hooked breech and 28" blued barrels. The sideplates are engraved and case colored. Double triggers and checkered walnut stock are standard. Weighs 7.25 lbs.

NIB	Exc.	V.G.	Good	Fair	Poor
325	225	150	125	100	75

Navy Arms Steel Shot Magnum

Same as above but chambered for 10 gauge shells. Weighs 7 lbs. 9 oz.

NIB	Exc.	V.G.	Good	Fair	Poor
325	225	150	125	100	75

T&T Shotgun

This turkey and trap model has a straight grip stock and 28" barrel choked full and full. Locks are case colored and engraved. Walnut stock is checkered. Weighs 7.5 lbs.

NIB	Exc.	V.G.	Good	Fair	Poor
550	425	300	250	200	100

Japanese Matchlock

This model is a .50 caliber with 41" barrels. Weighs 8.5 lbs.

NIB	Exc.	V.G.	Good	Fair	Poor
450	350	300	200	100	75

HANDGUNS

Le Page Pistol

This .44 caliber percussion pistol has a 10.25" tapered octagon barrel, adjustable single set trigger. The lock, triggerguard, and buff cap are engraved. The walnut stocks are hand checkered. Weighs 36 oz.

NIB	Exc.	V.G.	Good	Fair	Poor
400	350	300	250	200	100

Single Cased Set

NIB	Exc.	V.G.	Good	Fair	Poor
580	530	475	400	300	150

Double Cased Set

NIB	Exc.	V.G.	Good	Fair	Poor
995	875	750	600	400	200

Le Page Flintlock

Same as above but with flintlock ignition. Weighs 41 oz.

NIB	Exc.	V.G.	Good	Fair	Poor
470	425	350	250	150	100

Le Page Smoothbore Flintlock Pistol

Same as above but with a smooth bore.

NIB	Exc.	V.G.	Good	Fair	Poor
470	425	350	250	150	100

Single Cased Set

NIB	Exc.	V.G.	Good	Fair	Poor
650	600	500	400	300	150

Double Cased Set

NIB	Exc.	V.G.	Good	Fair	Poor
995	875	750	600	400	200

Kentucky Pistol

A percussion replica of a pistol developed in the 1840s. It has a 10.125" blued barrel, case colored lock, brass furniture and triggerguard with walnut stock. Weighs 32 oz.

NIB	Exc.	V.G.	Good	Fair	Poor
225	175	150	100	85	60

Single Cased Set

NIB	Exc.	V.G.	Good	Fair	Poor
350	275	225	175	125	75

Double Cased Set

NIB	Exc.	V.G.	Good	Fair	Poor
550	450	350	250	150	100

Kentucky Flintlock Pistol

Same as above but with flintlock ignition.

NIB	Exc.	V.G.	Good	Fair	Poor
225	175	150	100	75	60

Single Cased Set

NIB	Exc.	V.G.	Good	Fair	Poor
350	275	225	175	125	75

Double Cased Set

NIB	Exc.	V.G.	Good	Fair	Poor
550	450	350	275	175	100

Harpers Ferry Pistol

This pistol has a .58 caliber rifled 10" barrel. Case hardened lock and walnut stock. Weight is approximately 39 oz.

NIB	Exc.	V.G.	Good	Fair	Poor
300	250	200	150	100	75

Single Cased Set

NIB	Exc.	V.G.	Good	Fair	Poor
350	275	225	175	125	100

18th Georgia Le Mat Pistol

This 9-shot .44 caliber percussion revolver has a 7.625" blued barrel and engraved cylinder. An engraved banner on the left side of the frame reads "DEO VINDICE". Hammer and trigger are case colored. Stocks are checkered walnut. Comes with Le Mat mould and velvet draped French fitted case. Weighs 55 oz.

NIB	Exc.	V.G.	Good	Fair	Poor
795	625	500	400	300	150

Beauregard Le Mat Pistol

This is a replica of the Cavalry model. Comes cased.

NIB	Exc.	V.G.	Good	Fair	Poor
1000	800	650	550	350	200

Navy Le Mat

This model features a knurled pin barrel release and spur barrel selector.

NIB	Exc.	V.G.	Good	Fair	Poor
595	450	400	350	300	150

Army Le Mat

This model features a knurled pin barrel release and cross pin barrel selector.

NIB	Exc.	V.G.	Good	Fair	Poor
595	450	400	350	300	150

Cavalry Le Mat

This model features a lanyard ring, spur trigger, lever type barrel release, and cross pin barrel selector.

NIB	Exc.	V.G.	Good	Fair	Poor
595	450	400	350	300	150

Starr Double Action Model 1858 Army

This model is a double action revolver chambered for .44 caliber. Fitted with a 6" barrel. Blued finish. Weight is about 48 oz.

NIB	Exc.	V.G.	Good	Fair	Poor
350	250	200	—	—	—

Starr Single Action Model 1863 Army

This model is fitted with an 8" barrel and is chambered for .44 caliber. Blued finish and walnut stock. Weight is about 48 oz.

NIB	Exc.	V.G.	Good	Fair	Poor
350	250	200	—	—	—

1862 New Model Police

This replica is based on the Colt .36 caliber pocket pistol of the same name. It features a half fluted and re-dated cylinder, case colored frame and loading gate, and a polished brass triggerguard and back strap. Barrel length is 5.5" and pistol weigh 26 oz.

NIB	Exc.	V.G.	Good	Fair	Poor
290	225	175	150	100	75

1862 New Model Book-Style Cased Set

NIB	Exc.	V.G.	Good	Fair	Poor
350	250	200	150	100	75

Paterson Revolver

This replica is the five-shot. 36 caliber. The cylinder is scroll engraved with a stagecoach scene. The hidden trigger drops down when the hammer is cocked. Barrel is 9" and the pistol weighs 43 oz.

NIB	Exc.	V.G.	Good	Fair	Poor
300	225	200	150	125	100

1851 Navy

This Colt replica is offered in either .36 or .44 caliber. A naval battle scene is engraved in the cylinder. The octagon barrel length is 7.5". The triggerguard, and back strap are polished brass. The walnut grips are hand rubbed. Weighs 32 oz.

NIB	Exc.	V.G.	Good	Fair	Poor
150	125	100	75	50	40

Single Cased Set

NIB	Exc.	V.G.	Good	Fair	Poor
275	225	175	125	100	60

Double Cased Set

NIB	Exc.	V.G.	Good	Fair	Poor
450	350	300	250	200	100

NOTE: Optional shoulder stock-Add $100.

1851 Navy Conversion

This is a replica of the Colt 1851 Navy cartridge conversion. Offered in 38 Special or .38 Long Colt with choice of 5.5" or 7.5" barrels. Weight is about 40 oz.

NIB	Exc.	V.G.	Good	Fair	Poor
350	275	225	—	—	—

Augusta 1851 Navy Pistol

Available with either 5" or 7.5" barrel. Engraved with "A" coverage.

NIB	Exc.	V.G.	Good	Fair	Poor
300	250	200	150	100	75

Reb Model 1860 Pistol

This is a replica of the Confederate Griswold and Gunnison revolver. It features a blued round 7.5" barrel, brass frame, triggerguard and backstrap. Offered in .36 or .44 caliber. Weighs 44 oz.

NIB	Exc.	V.G.	Good	Fair	Poor
100	80	70	60	50	35

Reb 1860 Sheriff's Model

Same as above but fitted with a 5" barrel. Weighs 40 oz.

NIB	Exc.	V.G.	Good	Fair	Poor
100	80	70	60	50	35

Engraved Paterson Revolver

This model features hand engraving with silver inlays.

NIB	Exc.	V.G.	Good	Fair	Poor
475	375	300	250	200	50

1847 Walker Dragoon

This is a replica of the rare Colt .44 caliber revolver. The barrel and cylinder are blued while the frame and loading lever are case colored. Barrel length is 9" and pistol weighs 75 oz.

NIB	Exc.	V.G.	Good	Fair	Poor
275	225	175	150	125	100

Single Cased Set

NIB	Exc.	V.G.	Good	Fair	Poor
400	325	275	250	200	100

Single Deluxe Cased Set

NIB	Exc.	V.G.	Good	Fair	Poor
525	425	350	300	200	100

1860 Army Pistol

This .44 caliber model features a case colored frame and loading lever with blued barrel, cylinder, and back strap. The triggerguard is brass. The cylinder is engraved with a battle scene. Barrel is 8" and pistol weighs 41 oz.

NIB	Exc.	V.G.	Good	Fair	Poor
175	150	125	100	75	45

Single Cased Set

NIB	Exc.	V.G.	Good	Fair	Poor
300	250	200	150	100	75

Double Cased Set

NIB	Exc.	V.G.	Good	Fair	Poor
490	400	325	250	200	100

1860 Army Conversion

Chambered for the .38 Special or .38 Long Colt this model is fitted with either a 5.5" or 7.5" barrel. Blued finish. Walnut grips. Weight is about 40 oz.

NIB	Exc.	V.G.	Good	Fair	Poor
350	275	225	—	—	—

1858 New Model Remington-Style Pistol

This replica has a solid frame as did the original. The frame and 8" barrel are blued while the triggerguard is brass. Walnut grips are standard. Weighs 40 oz.

NIB	Exc.	V.G.	Good	Fair	Poor
170	125	100	75	60	45

Single Cased Set

NIB	Exc.	V.G.	Good	Fair	Poor
290	225	175	125	100	75

Double Cased Set

NIB	Exc.	V.G.	Good	Fair	Poor
475	375	300	250	200	100

Stainless Steel 1858 New Model Army

Same as above but in stainless steel. Weighs 40 oz.

NIB	Exc.	V.G.	Good	Fair	Poor
220	180	150	125	100	80

Single Cased Set

NIB	Exc.	V.G.	Good	Fair	Poor
300	250	200	150	125	100

Double Cased Set

NIB	Exc.	V.G.	Good	Fair	Poor
525	475	400	300	200	150

Brass Framed 1858 New Model Army

This version features a highly polished brass frame. Barrel length is 7.75".

NIB	Exc.	V.G.	Good	Fair	Poor
125	100	80	60	50	35

Single Cased Set

NIB	Exc.	V.G.	Good	Fair	Poor
250	200	150	100	75	60

Double Cased Set

NIB	Exc.	V.G.	Good	Fair	Poor
395	325	300	250	200	100

1858 Target Model

Same as above but features a patridge front sight and an adjustable rear sight. Barrel length is 8".

NIB	Exc.	V.G.	Good	Fair	Poor
175	150	125	100	75	50

Deluxe 1858 New Model Army

This replica is built to the exact dimensions as the original. The barrel is 8" with adjustable front sight. The triggerguard is silver plated. The action is tuned for competition. Weighs 46 oz.

NIB	Exc.	V.G.	Good	Fair	Poor
400	325	250	200	150	100

Spiller and Burr Pistol

This is a .36 caliber pistol with 7" blued octagon barrel. The frame is brass with walnut grips. Weighs 40 oz.

NIB	Exc.	V.G.	Good	Fair	Poor
140	100	80	65	50	40

Single Cased Set

NIB	Exc.	V.G.	Good	Fair	Poor
250	200	150	100	75	60

Double Cased Set

NIB	Exc.	V.G.	Good	Fair	Poor
425	350	300	250	200	100

Rogers and Spencer

This model features a 7.5" barrel with blued frame and barrel. Offered in .44 caliber. Walnut grips. Weighs 48 oz.

NIB	Exc.	V.G.	Good	Fair	Poor
240	200	150	100	75	50

"London Gray" Rogers and Spencer Pistol

Same as above but with a burnished satin chrome finish.

NIB	Exc.	V.G.	Good	Fair	Poor
240	200	150	125	100	80

Rogers and Spencer Target Model

Same as standard model but fitted with adjustable target sights.

NIB	Exc.	V.G.	Good	Fair	Poor
275	225	175	125	100	80

1861 Navy Conversion

Replica of the cartridge conversion of the 1861 Navy. Chambered for .38 Special or .38 Long Colt. Fitted with either a 5.5" or 7.5" barrel. Weight is about 40 oz.

NIB	Exc.	V.G.	Good	Fair	Poor
350	275	225	—	—	—

1872 Colt Open Top

This model features a 5.5" or 7.5" barrel with case hardened frame, blued barrel and cylinder, and silver plated brass trigger guard and backstrap. Walnut grips. Chambered for .38 caliber cartridge. Weight is about 40 oz.

NIB	Exc.	V.G.	Good	Fair	Poor
390	275	225	—	—	—

1873 Colt-Style Single Action Army

This replica features a case colored frame and hammer with blued round barrel in 3", 4.75", 5.5", or 7.5" lengths. Triggerguard, and cylinder are blued. Offered in .44-40 or .45 Long Colt.

NIB	Exc.	V.G.	Good	Fair	Poor
390	325	275	200	150	100

Economy Model 1873 S.A.A.

Same as above but with brass triggerguard and back strap.

NIB	Exc.	V.G.	Good	Fair	Poor
275	250	200	150	125	100

Nickel 1873 S.A.A.

NIB	Exc.	V.G.	Good	Fair	Poor
500	400	300	225	150	100

1873 U.S. Cavalry Model

This .45 Long Colt model features U.S. arsenal stampings, case colored frame, and walnut grips. Barrel length is 7.5" and pistol weighs 45 oz.

NIB	Exc.	V.G.	Good	Fair	Poor
390	325	275	200	150	100

1873 Pinched Frame Model

This is a replica of the "pinched" frame 1873 with "U" shape rear sight notch. Chambered for .45 Colt with 7.5" barrel.

NIB	Exc.	V.G.	Good	Fair	Poor
400	325	275	225	—	—

1873 Flat Top Target

This model features a windage adjustable rear sight on a flat top frame and a spring loaded front sight. Barrel length is 7.5". Offered in .45 Colt. Weight is about 40 oz. Introduced in 1998.

NIB	Exc.	V.G.	Good	Fair	Poor
425	350	—	—	—	—

Deputy Single Action Army

Similar to the Model 1873 but with a bird's head grip. Barrel lengths are 3", 3.5", 4", and 4.75". Chambered for .44-40 and .45 Colt.

NIB	Exc.	V.G.	Good	Fair	Poor
400	300	250	200	—	—

Shootist Model S.A.A.

This model is a reproduction of the Colt 1873. Parts are interchangeable with the originals. Blued barrel, cylinder, trigger guard, and backstrap. Case hardened frame and hammer. Walnut grips. Offered in 4.75", 5.5", and 7.5" barrel lengths. Chambered for .357 Magnum, .44-40, or .45 Colt.

NIB	Exc.	V.G.	Good	Fair	Poor
375	275	225	—	—	—

Bisley Model

This model features the famous Bisley grip. Barrel length is 4.75", 5.5", and 7.5". Chambered for .44-40 or .45 Colt.

NIB	Exc.	V.G.	Good	Fair	Poor
425	300	250	200	—	—

Bisley Flat Top Target

Similar to the Bisley but with 7.5" barrel with flat top frame with adjustable front sight and windage adjustable rear sight. Chambered for .440-40 or .45 Colt. Weight is about 40 oz.

NIB	Exc.	V.G.	Good	Fair	Poor
425	300	250	200	—	—

1895 U.S. Artillery Model

Same as Cavalry Model but fitted with a 5.5" barrel. Weighs 42 oz.

NIB	Exc.	V.G.	Good	Fair	Poor
475	375	300	250	200	100

1875 Remington-Style Revolver

The frame is case colored while all other parts are blued except for brass triggerguard. Available in .44-40 or .45 Long Colt. Furnished with walnut grips. Barrel length is 7.5". Weighs 41 oz.

NIB	Exc.	V.G.	Good	Fair	Poor
425	350	300	250	200	100

1890 Remington-Style Revolver

This is a modified version of the 1875 model that is also offered in .44-40 or .45 Long Colt. The web under the barrel has been eliminated. It has blued 5.5" steel barrel and frame. Lanyard loop is on bottom of walnut grips. Weighs 39 oz.

NIB	Exc.	V.G.	Good	Fair	Poor
445	350	300	250	200	100

TOP BREAK REVOLVERS

Model 1875 Schofield-Cavalry 7" barrel

A reproduction of the S&W Model 3 top break revolver in either .44/40 or .45 Long Colt. The Cavalry model has a 7" barrel while the Wells Fargo model has a 5" barrel. Weight is about 39 oz.

NIB	Exc.	V.G.	Good	Fair	Poor
750	600	450	350	200	100

Model 1875 Schofield-Wells Fargo 5" barrel

NIB	Exc.	V.G.	Good	Fair	Poor
750	600	450	350	200	100

Model 1875 Schofield-Hideout

This is a short barrel variation of the Schofield. It is fitted with a 3.5" barrel and chambered for the .44-40 or .45 Colt cartridge. Weight is about 38 oz.

NIB	Exc.	V.G.	Good	Fair	Poor
700	550	—	—	—	—

Model 1875 Schofield-Deluxe

This model has a charcoal blue finish with gold inlays and "A" style hand engraving. Available in either the Cavalry or Wells Fargo model. Special order only.

NIB	Exc.	V.G.	Good	Fair	Poor
1875	1500	—	—	—	—

Model 1875 Schofield-B Engraved

Available In Cavalry or Wells Fargo Model. This grade is "B" style engraved with 35% coverage. Special order only.

NIB	Exc.	V.G.	Good	Fair	Poor
1550	1250	—	—	—	—

Model 1875 Schofield-C Engraved

This model is available in Cavalry or Wells Fargo with "C" style engraving with 50% coverage. Special order only.

NIB	Exc.	V.G.	Good	Fair	Poor
1875	1500	—	—	—	—

New Model Russian

Built around the single action Smith & Wesson Model 3, this revolver is chambered for the .44 Russian cartridge. It is fitted with a 6.5" barrel. Case colored spur triggerguard, latch and hammer. Blued frame, barrel and cylinder. Walnut grips. Weight is about 40 oz. Introduced in 1999.

NIB	Exc.	V.G.	Good	Fair	Poor
750	600	500	—	—	—

MILITARY SURPLUS ARMS

SKS Type 56 W/Scope Rail

This semiautomatic gas operated rifle is chambered for the 7.62x39 cartridge. It has a 10-round clip. This model is fitted with a scope rail on the left side of the receiver. Barrel length is 20.5". Weight is 8 lbs.

NIB	Exc.	V.G.	Good	Fair	Poor
120	100	75	60	50	35

Standard SKS Type 56

Same as above without the scope rail.

NIB	Exc.	V.G.	Good	Fair	Poor
115	95	75	60	50	35

This model is fitted with a 2.75 power Type 89 scope an RPK style folding bipod.

NIB	Exc.	V.G.	Good	Fair	Poor
280	250	200	150	125	100

SKS "Cowboys Companion" Carbine

Barrel length on this version is 16.5". Weighs 7 lbs. 8 oz.

NIB	Exc.	V.G.	Good	Fair	Poor
135	110	85	70	60	40

This is the military version of the "Cowboys Companion" fitted with a short cruciform folding bayonet.

NIB	Exc.	V.G.	Good	Fair	Poor
145	120	90	75	60	40

SKS "Hunter" Carbine

This model has a checkered composite Monte Carlo stock with full length pull. Comes with 5-round magazine.

NIB	Exc.	V.G.	Good	Fair	Poor
195	175	150	125	100	75

TT-Olympia Pistol

This is a reproduction of the Walther target pistol. Chambered for .22 l.r. Barrel length is 4.625" and pistol weighs 27 oz.

NIB	Exc.	V.G.	Good	Fair	Poor
260	225	200	150	125	100

TU-90 Pistol

This model is based on the Tokagypt pistol. It features a wrap-around grip with thumb rest. Barrel length is 4.5" and pistol weighs 30 oz.

NIB	Exc.	V.G.	Good	Fair	Poor
125	90	80	70	50	40

TU-KKW Training Rifle

Based on the 98 Mauser and chambered for the .22 Long Rifle cartridge it is fitted with military sights, bayonet lug, cleaning rod and take down disc. Comes with detachable 5-round box magazine. Barrel length is 26" and weighs 8 lbs.

NIB	Exc.	V.G.	Good	Fair	Poor
180	150	125	100	80	60

TU-KKW Sniper Trainer

Same as above but fitted with a 2.75 power Type 89 scope and quick detachable mounting system.

NIB	Exc.	V.G.	Good	Fair	Poor
240	200	175	150	125	90

TU-33/40 Carbine

This model is based on the WWII Mauser G 33/40 mountain carbine. Chambered for the .22 Long Rifle or 7.62x39 cartridge. Barrel length is 20.75" and weighs 7.5 lbs.

NIB	Exc.	V.G.	Good	Fair	Poor
180	150	125	100	80	60

JW-15 Rifle

This model is a bolt action design based on the BRNO Model 5 action. Chambered for the .22 Long Rifle it features adjustable sights, sling swivels, an detachable 5-round magazine. The top of the receiver is dovetailed for easy scope mounting. Barrel is 24" long and rifle weighs 5 lbs. 12 oz.

NIB	Exc.	V.G.	Good	Fair	Poor
100	80	70	60	50	35

Martini Target Rifle

A .444 or .45-70 caliber single shot Martini action rifle with a 26" or 30" octagonal barrel, tang sight, and walnut stock. Offered between 1972 and 1984.

Exc.	V.G.	Good	Fair	Poor
475	425	350	275	175

Parker-Hale Sniper Rifle

See Parker-Hale section of this text.

RPKS-74

A 5.56mm or 7.62x39mm caliber semiautomatic rifle with a 19" barrel patterned after the Russian AK series rifles.

No. 5 Enfield Jungle Carbine

This replica is chambered for .303 British cartridge and fitted with cupped buttplate and flashider. Barrel length is 20.5". Magazine capacity is 10 rounds. Weight is approximately 7 lbs.

NIB	Exc.	V.G.	Good	Fair	Poor
200	150	125	100	80	60

No. 6 Enfield Jungle Carbine

This reproduction is chambered for .303 British with 20.5" barrel with flashider. Weight is about 7 lbs. Ten-round magazine.

NIB	Exc.	V.G.	Good	Fair	Poor
175	150	125	100	80	60

Ishapore 2A No. 1 MK III Rifle

This is a refinished rifle with 25" barrel and chambered for .308 Win. cartridge. Magazine capacity is 12 rounds. Weight is about 9.3 lbs.

NIB	Exc.	V.G.	Good	Fair	Poor
180	150	125	100	80	60

2A Tanker Carbine

This is a replica with a short 20" barrel. Chambered for .308 Win. Magazine capacity is 12 rounds. Weight is approximately 8.7 lbs.

NIB	Exc.	V.G.	Good	Fair	Poor
180	150	125	100	80	60

MK III Tanker Carbine

Similar to the above model but chambered for the .303 British cartridge. Magazine capacity is 10 rounds.

NIB	Exc.	V.G.	Good	Fair	Poor
180	150	125	100	80	60

Lithgow No. 1 MK III Rifle

This rifles are in unissued condition. Barrel length is 25". Chambered for .303 British cartridge. Magazine capacity is 10 rounds. Weight is about 9 lbs.

NIB	Exc.	V.G.	Good	Fair	Poor
250	200	150	125	100	75

No. 1 MK III Enfield Rifle

These rifles are standard MK III S.M.L.E. rifles that have been refinished. Barrel length is 25.25". Magazine capacity is 10 rounds of .303 British. Weight is about 9 lbs.

NIB	Exc.	V.G.	Good	Fair	Poor
180	150	125	100	80	60

No. 4 Tanker Carbine

This is a cut-down version of the No.4 MK I Enfield. Barrel length is 20.5". Chambered for .303 with magazine capacity of 10 rounds. Weight is approximately 8.2 lbs.

NIB	Exc.	V.G.	Good	Fair	Poor
180	150	125	100	80	60

No. 4 MK I Enfield Rifle

This is a reconditioned rifle. Barrel length is 25". Magazine capacity is 10 rounds of .303 British. Weight is about 8.6 lbs.

NIB	Exc.	V.G.	Good	Fair	Poor
150	125	100	80	60	—

Savage No. 4 MK I Rifle

Chambered for .303 British cartridge with 25" barrel. Stocks are unissued. Magazine capacity is 10 rounds. Weight is approximately 8.7 lbs.

NIB	Exc.	V.G.	Good	Fair	Poor
180	150	125	100	80	60

Luger

A .22 caliber semiautomatic pistol with a 4", 6", or 8" barrel, fixed sights, and 10-shot magazine. Blued with walnut grips. Manufactured in the U.S.A. in 1986 and 1987.

Exc.	V.G.	Good	Fair	Poor
175	150	125	100	75

Grand Prix Silhouette Pistol

A .30-30, .44 Magnum, 7mm Special, and .45-70 caliber single shot pistol with a 13.75" barrel, adjustable sights, and an aluminum, heat-disbursing rib. Matte-blued, walnut grips and forearm. Manufactured in 1985.

Exc.	V.G.	Good	Fair	Poor
325	275	225	175	125

NEAL, W.
Bangor, Maine

Under Hammer Pistol

A .31 caliber under hammer percussion pistol with 5" to 8" barrels, iron frame and walnut grip. The barrel marked "Wm. Neal/Bangor, Me."

Exc.	V.G.	Good	Fair	Poor
—	—	950	400	150

NEPPERHAN FIREARMS CO.
Yonkers, New York

Pocket Revolver

A .31 caliber percussion revolver with 3.5" to 6" barrels and a 5-shot cylinder. Blued, case hardened with walnut grips. The barrel marked "Nepperhan/Fire Arms Co" and on some additionally "Yonkers New York". The latter are worth a slight premium over the values listed below. Approximately 5,000 were made during the 1860s.

Exc.	V.G.	Good	Fair	Poor
—	—	900	350	200

NEWBURY ARMS CO.
Catskill, New York
Albany, New York

Pocket Pistol

A .25 caliber spur trigger pocket pistol with a 4" octagonal barrel. Blued, silver-plated with walnut grips.

Exc.	V.G.	Good	Fair	Poor
—	—	950	400	200

Pocket Revolver

A .26 caliber double action percussion revolver with a 5" barrel and C-shaped exposed trigger. Blued with an iron or brass frame and walnut grips. The barrel marked "Newbury Arms Co. Albany." Produced in limited numbers between 1855 and 1860. Prospective purchasers are advised to secure a qualified appraisal prior to acquisition.

Exc.	V.G.	Good	Fair	Poor
—	—	5500	2750	750

NEW ENGLAND FIREARMS CO.
Gardner, Massachusetts

Model R22

Magnum or .32 H&R Magnum double action revolver with a 2.5", 4", or 6" barrel and either a 6- or 9-shot cylinder. Blued or nickel-plated with walnut grips. Introduced in 1988.

NIB	Exc.	V.G.	Good	Fair	Poor
110	95	80	70	60	40

Pardner

A 12, 16, 20 or .410 bore single shot shotgun with a 24", 26", or 28" barrel. Blued with a walnut stock. Introduced in 1987.

NIB	Exc.	V.G.	Good	Fair	Poor
100	85	75	65	50	35

Pardner Youth

Similar to the above model but offered only in 20 and 28 gauge as well as .410 bore. Fitted with a 26" barrel. Weight is between 5 and 6 lbs.

NIB	Exc.	V.G.	Good	Fair	Poor
100	85	75	65	50	35

Special Purpose

This is a similar model but it is offered only in 10 gauge. It is available in several different configurations. A 10 gauge model with hardwood stock with 28" barrel, a camo model with 28"

barrel, a camo model with 32" barrel choked modified, and a black matte finish model with 24" barrel with screw in Turkey full choke. Weight is about 9.5 lbs.

NIB	Exc.	V.G.	Good	Fair	Poor
250	175	125	100	75	50

Special Purpose Waterfowl Model

Special Purpose Turkey Gun

Handi-Gun

.22 Hornet, .223, .243, .270, .280, .30-30, .44 Magnum, or .45-70 caliber version of the above with a 22" barrel fitted with open sights. Blued, with a walnut stock. Introduced in 1989.

NIB	Exc.	V.G.	Good	Fair	Poor
200	175	150	125	100	75

Survivor

Based on a single shot break action design this rifle or shotgun is fitted with a synthetic stock with integral storage compartments. Offered in .410/.45 Colt, 12 and 20 gauge, .223 Rem., and .357 Mag. Barrel length is 22". Weight is about 6 lbs.

NIB	Exc.	V.G.	Good	Fair	Poor
200	175	150	125	100	75

Tracker

This single shot break open shotgun is offered in both 12 and 20 gauge with rifled barrel or cylinder bore barrel. Both are 24" in length. Equipped with adjustable rifle sights. Weight is about 6 lbs.

NIB	Exc.	V.G.	Good	Fair	Poor
150	125	100	75	60	50

Super Light Rifles

This single shot rifle is chambered for the .22 Hornet or .223 Rem. It is fitted with a 20" light weight barrel. Choice of scope mount and no sights or adjustable rear sight and ramp front sight. Black polymer stock with semi-beavertail forend. Weight is about 5.5 lbs.

NIB	Exc.	V.G.	Good	Fair	Poor
175	125	100	75	60	50

NEWCOMB, H. G.
Natchez, Mississippi

Pocket Pistol

A .41 caliber percussion pocket pistol with a 2.5" barrel, German silver mounts and a walnut stock. Manufactured in the 1850s.

Exc.	V.G.	Good	Fair	Poor
—	—	1600	700	250

NEWTON ARMS CO.
Buffalo, New York

Also known as the Buffalo Newton Rifle Company and the Charles Newton Rifle Company. In operation from 1913 to 1932.

Newton-Mauser Rifle

A .256 Newton caliber bolt action rifle with a 24" barrel and double set triggers. Blued with a walnut stock. Manufactured circa 1914.

Exc.	V.G.	Good	Fair	Poor
900	700	550	400	275

Standard Rifle First Type

A .22, .256, .280, .30, .33, and .35 Newton as well as .30-06 caliber bolt action rifle with a 24" barrel, open or aperture sights and double set triggers. Blued with a walnut stock. Manufactured between 1916 and 1918.

Exc.	V.G.	Good	Fair	Poor
1250	1000	750	550	400

Standard Rifle Second Model

A .256, .30, or .35 Newton as well as .30-06 caliber bolt action rifle as above, but with an Enfield-style bolt handle. Manufactured after 1918.

Exc.	V.G.	Good	Fair	Poor
1100	800	650	400	350

Buffalo Newton Rifle

As above, but marked "Buffalo Newton Rifle Company".

Exc.	V.G.	Good	Fair	Poor
1100	800	650	400	350

NICHOLS & CHILDS
Conway, Massachusetts

Percussion Belt Revolver

A .34 caliber percussion revolver with a 6" round barrel and 6-shot cylinder. Blued or browned with walnut grips. It is estimated that less than 25 were made in 1838. Prospective purchasers are advised to secure a qualified appraisal prior to acquisition.

Exc.	V.G.	Good	Fair	Poor
—	—	9250	4250	1250

Revolving Percussion Rifle

A .36 or .40 caliber percussion rifle with a 22", 26", or 30" barrel and a 5-, 6-, 7- or 9-shot cylinder. Blued or browned with a walnut stock having a patch box. It is believed that approxi-

mately 150 were made between 1838 and 1840. Prospective purchasers are advised to secure a qualified appraisal prior to acquisition.

Exc.	V.G.	Good	Fair	Poor
—	—	11000	6000	2000

NOBLE
Haydenville, Massachusetts

In business between 1946 and 1971, this company manufactured a variety of plain, utilitarian firearms. In general, these arms are all worth approximately the same, that is, less than $200 in excellent condition.

RIFLES

Model 10

A .22 caliber bolt action single rifle with a 24" barrel. Pistol grip stock with no checkering. Open sights. Produced in the late 1950s.

Exc.	V.G.	Good	Fair	Poor
75	60	50	40	30

Model 20

A .22 caliber bolt action rifle fitted with a 22" barrel. Open sights. Produced from the late 1950s to the early 1960s.

Exc.	V.G.	Good	Fair	Poor
75	60	50	40	30

Model 33

This is a .22 caliber slide action rifle fitted with a 24" barrel and tubular magazine and Tenite stock. Produced from the late 1940s to the early 1950s.

Exc.	V.G.	Good	Fair	Poor
80	70	60	50	40

Model 33A

Same as above but fitted with a wood stock.

Exc.	V.G.	Good	Fair	Poor
75	60	50	40	30

Model 222

This is a single shot bolt action rifle chambered for the .22 caliber cartridge. Plain pistol grip stock.

Exc.	V.G.	Good	Fair	Poor
85	75	60	50	40

Model 236

A .22 caliber slide action rifle with a 24" barrel and tubular magazine. Plain pistol grip stock and groved slide handle.

Exc.	V.G.	Good	Fair	Poor
100	85	75	60	50

Model 275

A .22 caliber lever action rifle with tubular magazine. Fitted with a 24" barrel. The plain stock has a semi-pistol grip.

Exc.	V.G.	Good	Fair	Poor
125	100	80	60	50

SHOTGUNS

Model 40

This is a hammerless slide action shotgun chambered for the 12 gauge shell. It is fitted with a tubular magazine and 28" barrel with multi choke. Plain pistol stock with grooved slide handle.

Exc.	V.G.	Good	Fair	Poor
125	100	85	70	50

Model 50

Same as above but without the multi choke.

Exc.	V.G.	Good	Fair	Poor
115	90	80	65	50

Model 60

A hammerless slide action shotgun in 12 or 16 gauge with tubular magazine and fitted with a 28" barrel with adjustable choke. Plain pistol grip stock with grooved slide handle.

Exc.	V.G.	Good	Fair	Poor
175	150	125	100	75

Model 65

Same as above but without adjustable choke.

Exc.	V.G.	Good	Fair	Poor
150	125	100	75	60

Model 66CLP

Offered in 12 or 16 gauge this slide action shotgun is fitted with a 28" plain barrel and a keyed lock fire control system.

Exc.	V.G.	Good	Fair	Poor
160	140	110	85	70

Model 66RCLP

Similar to above but fitted with a 28" vent rib barrel and checkered pistol grip stock. Adjustable choke is standard.

Exc.	V.G.	Good	Fair	Poor
200	175	150	125	100

Model 66 RLP

Same as above but without adjustable choke.

Exc.	V.G.	Good	Fair	Poor
175	150	125	100	75

Model 66XL

Similar to the above models but with plain barrel, and checkering only on the slide handle.

Exc.	V.G.	Good	Fair	Poor
150	125	100	75	60

Model 70CLP

Similar to the Model 66 series but offered in .410 bore with 26" barrel and adjustable choke. Both the buttstock and slide handle are checkered.

Exc.	V.G.	Good	Fair	Poor
175	150	125	100	75

Model 70RCLP

This variation is fitted with a 26" ventilated rib barrel.

Exc.	V.G.	Good	Fair	Poor
200	175	150	125	100

Model 70RLP

This model has a vent rib barrel and no adjustable choke.

Exc.	V.G.	Good	Fair	Poor
175	150	125	100	75

Model 70XL

This version has no adjustable choke but is fitted with a 26" vent rib barrel. Stock is checked.

Exc.	V.G.	Good	Fair	Poor
125	100	80	70	60

Model 602RCLP

This is a hammerless slide action shotgun chambered for the 20 gauge shell. It is fitted with a 28" vent barrel and adjustable choke. Checkered pistol grip stock with slide handle.

Exc.	V.G.	Good	Fair	Poor
225	200	175	125	100

Model 602CLP

Same as above but with plain barrel.

Exc.	V.G.	Good	Fair	Poor
175	150	125	100	75

Model 602RLP

Same as Model RCLP except without the addition of an adjustable choke device.

Exc.	V.G.	Good	Fair	Poor
200	175	150	125	100

Model 602XL

Same as above but with only the slide handle checkered.

Exc.	V.G.	Good	Fair	Poor
150	125	100	75	60

Model 662

This 20 gauge slide action shotgun has a plain aluminum barrel with checkered pistol grip and slide handle. The receiver is made from aluminum. Produced in the late 1960s.

Exc.	V.G.	Good	Fair	Poor
200	175	150	125	100

Model 80

This model is a semiautomatic inertia operated shotgun chambered for the .410 shell. It is fitted with a 26" barrel, plain pistol stock with slotted forearm. Produced in the early to mid 1960s.

Exc.	V.G.	Good	Fair	Poor
250	200	150	125	100

Model 166L

This is a 12 gauge slide action shotgun with a key lock system. It is fitted with a 24" barrel bored for rifled slug. Lyman peep rear sight with post front sight. Checkered pistol and slide handle.

Exc.	V.G.	Good	Fair	Poor
250	200	150	125	100

Model 420

This shotgun is a box lock design side-by-side with double triggers and offered in 12, 16, 20 gauge, as well as .410 bore. Barrel lengths are 28" for all gauges except .410 where it is 26". Lightly engraved frame. Checkered walnut stock and splinter forearm.

Exc.	V.G.	Good	Fair	Poor
300	250	200	150	100

Model 450E

This model is similar to the Model 420 with the addition of automatic ejectors and not offered in .410 bore. Checkered pistol grip stock with beavertail forearm. Produced in the late 1960s.

Exc.	V.G.	Good	Fair	Poor
350	275	225	175	125

NORINCO
Peoples Republic of China
China North Industries Corp.

Imported by China Sports, as well as Interarms of Alexandria, Virginia.

ATD .22

A .22 caliber semiautomatic rifle with a 19.4" barrel and 11-shot magazine located in the butt. Blued with a hardwood stock. Importation began in 1987.

NIB	Exc.	V.G.	Good	Fair	Poor
200	150	125	100	75	50

EM-321

A .22 caliber slide action rifle with a 19.5" barrel and 10-shot tubular magazine. Blued with a hardwood stock. Introduced in 1989.

NIB	Exc.	V.G.	Good	Fair	Poor
150	100	85	75	65	50

Model HL-12-203 Shotgun

A 12 gauge boxlock Over/Under shotgun with 30" ventilated rib barrels fitted for choke tubes, single trigger and automatic ejectors. Blued with a hardwood stock. Introduced in 1989.

NIB	Exc.	V.G.	Good	Fair	Poor
400	325	275	225	175	125

Model HL-12-102 Shotgun

A 12 gauge slide action shotgun with a 28" barrel and 3-shot magazine. Blued with a hardwood stock. Introduced in 1989.

NIB	Exc.	V.G.	Good	Fair	Poor
275	225	200	75	125	100

Model 213 Pistol

A copy of the Browning P-35 semiautomatic pistol. Sold in 1988 only.

Exc.	V.G.	Good	Fair	Poor
250	200	150	100	75

Type 54-1 Tokarev

A 7.62x25mm caliber semiautomatic pistol with a 4.6" barrel, fixed sights, and 8-shot magazine. Blued with plastic grips. Imported in 1989.

Exc.	V.G.	Good	Fair	Poor
200	150	125	100	80

Type 59 Makarov

A .380 or 9mm Makarov caliber double action semiautomatic pistol with a 3.5" barrel and 8-shot magazine. Blued with plastic grips.

Exc.	V.G.	Good	Fair	Poor
275	250	225	175	125

SKS Rifle

A 7.62x39mm caliber semiautomatic rifle with a 20.5" barrel, folding bayonet and either a 10-shot fixed magazine or 30-shot detachable magazine. Blued with a hardwood stock. Importation began in 1988.

Exc.	V.G.	Good	Fair	Poor
125	100	75	65	50

Type 84S AK

Similar to the AKS service rifle, in 5.56mm caliber with a 16" barrel and 30-shot magazine.

Type 84S-1

As above, with an underfolding metal stock.

Type 84S-3

As above, with a composition stock.

Type 84S-5

As above, with a stock that folds to the side and without a bayonet.

Type 81S

A semiautomatic copy of the AK47.

Type 81S-1

As above, with a folding stock.

NORTH AMERICAN ARMS CORP.
Toronto, Canada

Brigadier

A .45 ACP caliber semiautomatic pistol with a 5" barrel, 8-shot magazine and alloy frame. Weight 4.5 lbs. Produced in limited quantity between 1948 and 1951. Prospective purchasers are advised to secure a qualified appraisal prior to acquisition.

Exc.	V.G.	Good	Fair	Poor
1250	1000	800	600	500

NORTH AMERICAN ARMS
Provo, Utah

Mini-Revolver

A .22 or .22 Magnum caliber spur trigger revolver with a 1" or 2.5" barrel and 5-shot cylinder. Stainless steel with plastic or laminated rosewood grips. Introduced in 1975 and made in the following styles:

Standard Rimfire Version

NIB	Exc.	V.G.	Fair	Poor
175	125	110	85	60

Magnum Version

NIB	Exc.	V.G.	Fair	Poor
190	150	125	100	75

2 Cylinder Magnum Convertible Version

NIB	Exc.	V.G.	Fair	Poor
225	175	150	125	100

Viper Belt Buckle Version

NIB	Exc.	V.G.	Fair	Poor
175	140	120	100	75

Standard 3 Gun Set

NIB	Exc.	V.G.	Fair	Poor
725	575	400	300	225

Deluxe 3 Gun Set

NIB	Exc.	V.G.	Fair	Poor
800	650	475	375	275

Cased .22 Magnum

NIB	Exc.	V.G.	Fair	Poor
350	250	200	150	125

Single Action Revolver

A polished stainless steel single action revolver chambered for the .45 Winchester Magnum and the .450 Magnum Express cartridge. It has a 7.5" barrel and a 5-shot cylinder. There is a transfer bar safety, and the grips are walnut. This model was discontinued in 1988.

Exc.	V.G.	Good	Fair	Poor
850	775	650	500	400

Companion Long Rifle

This is a .22 caliber cap and ball mini revolver. It has a 1.125" barrel. Overall length is 4.6" and weight is about 5 oz.

NIB	Exc.	V.G.	Good	Fair	Poor
140	125	100	75	50	35

Companion Magnum

Same as above but for .22 Magnum. It has a 1.62" barrel and weighs about 7 oz.

NIB	Exc.	V.G.	Good	Fair	Poor
160	140	100	75	50	35

Black Widow

This is a five shot fixed sight revolver with oversize black rubber grips with a 2" or 4" barrel. Chambered for .22 Long Rifle or .22 Win. Mag. Stainless steel. Weight is approximately 8.8 oz.

NIB	Exc.	V.G.	Good	Fair	Poor
250	200	150	100	75	50

NOTE: Add $20 for adjustable sights.

Mini-Master

This model is similar to the Black Widow with a 2" or 4" barrel. This model also gives a choice of either .22 Long Rifle or .22 Win. Mag. Stainless steel. Weight is approximately 10.7 oz.

NIB	Exc.	V.G.	Good	Fair	Poor
280	225	175	125	100	75

NOTE: Add $20 for adjustable sights.

Guardian

This is a semiautomatic double action only pocket pistol chambered for the .32 ACP cartridge. Magazine capacity is 6 rounds and the barrel length is 2.2". Overall length of the pistol is 4.4" and weight empty is 13.5 oz. Introduced in 1998.

NIB	Exc.	V.G.	Good	Fair	Poor
350	275	225	175	—	—

NORTH AMERICAN SAFARI EXPRESS
Liege, Belgium
SEE—Francotte

A trade name used by Francotte on their double rifles imported and distributed by Armes De Chasse of Chads Ford, Pennsylvania.

NORTH & COUCH
New York, New York

Animal Trap Gun

A .28 or. 30 caliber percussion pepperbox with either a 1.75" or 2.12" barrel group and a hammer made with or without a spur. Marked "North & Couch, Middletown, Conn." or "North & Couch New York." Manufactured during the 1860s.

Disk Hammer Model

Exc.	V.G.	Good	Fair	Poor
—	—	1500	700	300

Spur Hammer Model

Exc.	V.G.	Good	Fair	Poor
—	—	2250	900	350

NORTON ARMS CO.
Mt. Clemens, Michigan
SEE—Budischowsky

This firm manufactured Budischowsky Model TP-70 semiautomatic pistols prior to 1979. After that date, these arms were made by the American Arms and Amunition Company. The values for both manufacturers' products are as follows:

Exc.	V.G.	Good	Fair	Poor
350	275	200	125	100

NORWICH PISTOL CO.
Norwich, Connecticut

Established in 1875 by the New York retailer Maltby, Curtis & Company, this firm manufactured a wide variety of inexpensive spur trigger revolvers that were sold under the following trade names: America, Bulldozer, Challenge, Chieftain, Crescent, Defiance, Hartford Arms, Maltby Henley, Metropolitan Police, Nonpariel, Norwich Arms, Parole, Patriot, Pinafore, Prairie King, Protector, Spy, True Blue, U.M.C. Winfield Arms.

The company ceased operations in 1881. The value for any of its arms is approximately as follows:

Exc.	V.G.	Good	Fair	Poor
—	400	150	75	50

NOWLIN MANUFACTURING COMPANY
Claremore, Oklahoma

Match Classic

This 1911 pistol has a wide range of features. It can be chambered in 9mm, .38 Super, 9x23, .40 S&W, and .45 ACP. It has a 5" barrel, adjustable trigger, checkered main spring housing, hardwood grips, front and rear cocking serrations. The price listed below is for the basic pistols. Options will greatly effect price.

NIB	Exc.	V.G.	Good	Fair	Poor
1295	1050	800	—	—	—

Compact Carry

This pistol is similar to the Match Classic with the exception of a 4" barrel on a full-size frame. Again options will greatly effect price.

NIB	Exc.	V.G.	Good	Fair	Poor
1395	1100	875	—	—	—

Match Master

These hand built pistols offered a choice of S.T.I., Caspian Hi-Cap, or Nowlin STD Gov't frames. Available in 9mm, 9x23, .38 Super, .40 S&W, and .45 ACP. Many special features are included in standard pistol and many extra cost options are available.

NIB	Exc.	V.G.	Good	Fair	Poor
2195	1750	1200	—	—	—

NOTE: Add $140 for hard chrome finish.

O.D.I.
Midland Park, New Jersey

Viking

A .45 caliber double action semiautomatic pistol with a 5" barrel and 7-shot magazine. Stainless steel with teak grips. Manufactured in 1981 and 1982.

NIB	Exc.	V.G.	Good	Fair	Poor
600	500	400	300	200	100

Viking Combat

As above, with a 4.24" barrel.

NIB	Exc.	V.G.	Good	Fair	Poor
600	500	400	300	200	100

O.K.
Unknown
SEE—Marlin

OBREGON
Mexico City, Mexico

This is a .45 caliber semiautomatic pistol with a 5" barrel. Similar to the Colt M1911A1 but with a combination side and safety latch on the left side of the frame. The breech is locked by rotating the barrel, instead of the Browning swinging link. This unusual locking system results in a tubular front end appearance to the pistol. Originally designed for the Mexican military it was not adopted as such and only about 1,000 pistols were produced and sold commercially. The pistol is 8.5" overall and weighs about 40 ozs. The magazine holds seven cartridges. This is a rare pistol an independent appraisal is suggested prior to sale.

Exc.	V.G.	Good	Fair	Poor
4500	2500	1250	750	400

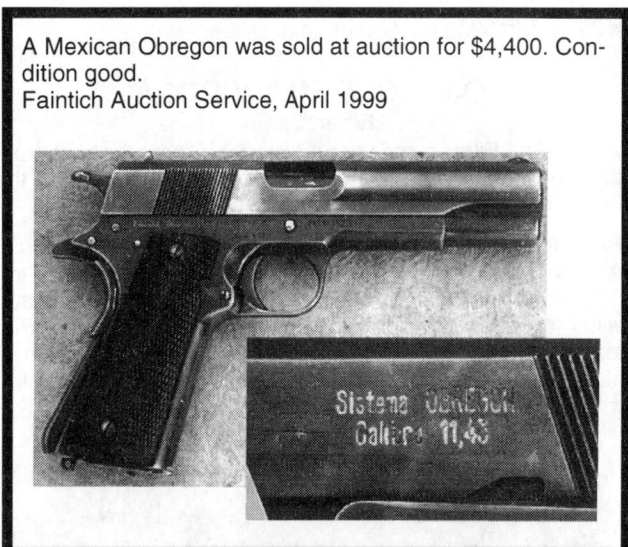

A Mexican Obregon was sold at auction for $4,400. Condition good.
Faintich Auction Service, April 1999

O'CONNELL, DAVID
New York, New York

Pocket Pistol

A .41 caliber percussion pocket pistol with a 2.5" barrel, German silver mounts, and walnut stock. Manufactured during the 1850s.

Exc.	V.G.	Good	Fair	Poor
—	—	1750	750	250

O'DELL, STEPHEN
Natchez, Mississippi

Pocket Pistol

A .34 to .44 caliber percussion pocket pistol with a 2" to 4" barrel, German silver mounts and walnut stock. Manufactured during the 1850s. Prospective purchasers are advised to secure a qualified appraisal prior to acquisition.

Exc.	V.G.	Good	Fair	Poor
—	—	4750	2000	950

OHIO ORDNANCE INC.
Chardon, Ohio

The Model 1918A3 Self-Loading Rifle

This rifle is a semiautomatic version of the famed Browning Automatic Rifle. It is chambered for the .30-06 cartridge and has a 20-round magazine. It was introduced in this configuration in 1996.

NIB	Exc.	V.G.	Good	Fair	Poor
2650	2000	1500	—	—	—

Colt Browning Water Cooled Gun

Introduced in 2001 this is a semiautomatic version of the famous Browning Model 1917 belt fed machine gun. This model features a .30-06 or 7.65 Argentine caliber belt-fed gun with tripod, wooden ammo box, water hose, water can, and one 250 cloth belt.

NIB	Exc.	V.G.	Good	Fair	Poor
5950	4750	—	—	—	—

NOTE: Add $200 for .308 or 8mm caliber guns.

OJANGUREN Y VIDOSA
Eibar, Spain

This typical Eibar company produced mediocre firearms from the early 1920s and was forced out of business during the Spanish Civil War.

Apache (Model 1920)

A typical Eibar Browning copy that is chambered for the 6.35mm cartridge. It is of the typical low quality associated with most Spanish arms of this era. The slide is marked "Pistole Browning Automatica Cal. 6.35 Apache." The finish is blued, and the plastic grips have a head with a beret and the word "Apache" molded into them.

Courtesy James Rankin

Exc.	V.G.	Good	Fair	Poor
200	150	100	75	50

Apache (Model 1920)

As above but chambered for the 7.65mm cartridge

Courtesy James Rankin

Exc.	V.G.	Good	Fair	Poor
275	225	190	100	75

Ojanguren

The trade name this company used to cover the line of revolvers they produced in the 1930s. They produced two in .32 caliber and two chambered for the. 38 Special cartridge. They are similar in appearance and have barrel lengths of either 3" or 6". The finishes are blued, and they have plastic grips. One of the .38 caliber models—the "Legitimo Tanque"—is a reasonably well-made gun that was popular with the Spanish target shooters. These guns have little collector value and little practical value and are all valued alike.

Exc.	V.G.	Good	Fair	Poor
175	125	100	75	50

Tanque

A blowback-operated semiautomatic chambered for the 6.35mm cartridge. It has a 1.5" barrel and is actually an original design, which was rarely found on Eibar guns of this period. It has an oddly shaped slide, and the barrel is retained by means of a screw in the front of the frame. It has a 6-shot magazine, and the slide is marked "6.35 Tanque Patent." The plastic grips have a tank molded into them and the word "Tanque," as well as the letters "O&V."

Exc.	V.G.	Good	Fair	Poor
175	125	100	75	50

OLD WEST GUN CO.
Houston, Texas
SEE—Cimarron Arms

An importer of reproduction firearms primarily manufactured by Aldo Uberti of Italy. In 1987 this company purchased the inventory of Allen Firearms and subsequently changed their name to Cimarron Arms.

OLYMPIC ARMS, INC.
Olympia, Washington

PISTOLS

NOTE: In 1997 Safari Arms began to offer its pistols with small serrations in the rear of the slide. As of 1999 Safari Arms still had slides in inventory with large (older style) serrations.

Black Widow

A .45 caliber semiautomatic pistol with a 3.9" barrel and 6-shot magazine. Nickel-plated with ivory Micarta grips having a spider engraved on them.

NIB	Exc.	V.G.	Good	Fair	Poor
700	575	450	350	300	200

Enforcer

A .45 caliber semiautomatic pistol with a 3.8" barrel and 6-shot magazine. Parkerized, anodized or nickel-plated with rubber grips. Weight is approximately 36 oz.

NIB	Exc.	V.G.	Good	Fair	Poor
650	500	400	350	300	200

Match Master

As above, with a 5" barrel and 7-shot magazine. Weight is about 40 oz.

NIB	Exc.	V.G.	Good	Fair	Poor
650	500	400	350	300	200

Match Master 6"

Same as above but with 6" barrel and slide. Weight is approximately 44 oz.

NIB	Exc.	V.G.	Good	Fair	Poor
675	550	400	350	300	200

Cohort
Fitted with a 4" bull barrel with a full size frame. Magazine capacity is 7 rounds. Weight is about 38 oz.

NIB	Exc.	V.G.	Good	Fair	Poor
675	550	400	350	300	200

Safari G.I.
This model is built on a Match Master frame with 5" barrel with fixed sights. Finish is flat black parkerized. Checkered walnut grips.

NIB	Exc.	V.G.	Good	Fair	Poor
550	450	400	—	—	—

Schuetzen Pistol Works Big Deuce
This model is made in Olympic Arms specialty shop called Schuetzen Pistol Works. Marked "Schuetzen Pistol Works" on the slide and "Safari Arms" on the frame. Introduced in 1995. This semiautomatic pistol is chambered for the .45 ACP cartridge and fitted with a 6" barrel, smooth walnut grips, and a number of other custom features. Magazine capacity is 7 rounds. Weight is approximately 40 oz. Black slide with stainless steel frame.

NIB	Exc.	V.G.	Good	Fair	Poor
950	800	700	500	—	—

Schuetzen Pistol Works Crest
Similar to the above model with the same markings. This version features a .45 ACP pistol with 4.5", 5", or 5.5" barrel Checkered walnut grips. Offered in both right and left hand configurations. Stainless steel finish. Introduced in 1993. Weight is about 39 oz. depending on barrel length.

NOTE: Left hand model will bring a small premium.

NIB	Exc.	V.G.	Good	Fair	Poor
700	600	500	—	—	—

Schuetzen Pistol Works Griffon
Similar to the above specialty models. This version is fitted with a 5" barrel and smooth walnut grips. Magazine capacity is 10 rounds. Stainless steel finish. Numerous custom features. Introduced in 1995.

NIB	Exc.	V.G.	Good	Fair	Poor
N/A	—	—	—	—	—

Schuetzen Pistol Works Carrier
Special built model along the lines of the Detonics Score Master with adjustable sights.

NIB	Exc.	V.G.	Good	Fair	Poor
750	600	—	—	—	—

RIFLES

SGW Ultra Match (PCR-1)
A match grade copy of the AR-15 with a 20" or 24" barrel and not fitted with a carrying handle. Weight is about 10 lbs.

NIB	Exc.	V.G.	Good	Fair	Poor
1050	850	750	500	400	200

Model PCR-2
Similar to the above model but fitted with a 16" match grade barrel, post front and E2 rear sight. Weight is approximately 8.2 lbs.

NIB	Exc.	V.G.	Good	Fair	Poor
950	800	600	500	400	200

Model PCR-3
Same as above model but with forged T-12 upper receiver.

NIB	Exc.	V.G.	Good	Fair	Poor
950	800	600	500	400	200

Model PCR-4
This version is fitted with a 20" steel barrel with post front sight and A-1 style rear sight. Weight is approximately 8.5 lbs.

NIB	Exc.	V.G.	Good	Fair	Poor
725	575	450	350	250	150

Model PCR-5
Similar to the above but fitted with a 16" barrel. Weight is about 7 lbs.

NIB	Exc.	V.G.	Good	Fair	Poor
700	550	400	300	200	100

Model PCR-6
This AR-15 style rifle is chambered for the 7.62x39 Russian short caliber. It is fitted with a 16" barrel with a post front sight and a A-1 style rear sight. Weight is about 7 lbs.

NIB	Exc.	V.G.	Good	Fair	Poor
700	550	400	300	200	100

Model PCR-7 "Eliminator"
This model is a shortened version of the PCR-4. It is fitted with a 16" barrel, A2 handguard, A2 stock, and an A2 pistol grip. Weight is about 7.6 lbs.

NIB	Exc.	V.G.	Good	Fair	Poor
825	650	500	—	—	—

Model PCR-Service Match
This .223 caliber rifle has a 20" stainless steel match barrel. It is fitted with a post front sight and a E-2 style rear sight. Weight is about 8.7 lbs.

NIB	Exc.	V.G.	Good	Fair	Poor
900	750	650	500	350	175

Ultra CSR Tactical Rifle

This is a bolt action rifle chambered for the .308 Winchester cartridge. Barrel length is 26". Magazine capacity is 5 rounds. Tactical style stock is black synthetic with aluminum bedding block. Comes complete with scope rings and Harris bipod in a hardcase. Weight is approximately 9.4 lbs.

NIB	Exc.	V.G.	Good	Fair	Poor
1200	900	—	—	—	—

Model CAR-97

Chambered for the .223 cartridge or optional 9mm, .40 S&W, or .45 ACP pistol cartridges. Fitted with a 16" barrel and non-collapsible CAR style stock. Overall length is 34". Weight is about 7 lbs.

NIB	Exc.	V.G.	Good	Fair	Poor
800	650	550	—	—	—

NOTE: Add $50 for pistol cartridge conversion.

Model OA-96

This model has a 6" barrel with pistol grip only, no buttstock. The 30-round magazine is pinned and cannot be detached. Break open action allows loading with stripper clips. Overall length is 15.75". Weight is about 4.2 lbs. BATF approved.

NIB	Exc.	V.G.	Good	Fair	Poor
900	700	600	—	—	—

Model OA-93 TG

Similar to the OA-96 but with a vertical grip. Barrel length is 7.5". Pistol grip only, no buttstock. Chambered for .223 cartridge. Weight is about 5 lbs. Overall length is 18.5". Classified by the BATF as any other weapon and subject to all NFA regulations. This weapon can only be purchased through a Class III dealer.

NIB	Exc.	V.G.	Good	Fair	Poor
1000	800	700	—	—	—

Model OA-98

Similar to the OA-93 but with lightning hoes on the grip, mount, magazine. Fitted with a 6" barrel with no vertical grip. Weight is about 3 lbs. No butt stock.

NIB	Exc.	V.G.	Good	Fair	Poor
900	700	600	—	—	—

OMEGA
Harrisburg, Pennsylvania
Importer-Kassnar

Over/Under Shotgun

A 12, 20, 28 or .410 bore boxlock Over/Under shotgun with 26" or 28" ventilated rib barrels, single trigger and extractors. Blued with a walnut stock.

Exc.	V.G.	Good	Fair	Poor
450	300	200	150	125

Side-x-Side Double Barreled Shotgun

A 20, 28 or .410 bore boxlock double-barrel shotgun with 26" barrels, double triggers and extractors. Blued with a hardwood stock.

Exc.	V.G.	Good	Fair	Poor
350	250	150	100	75

Single Barreled Shotgun

A 12, 20 or .410 bore single barrel shotgun manufactured in a variety of barrel lengths and fitted with an extractor. Blued with a hardwood stock.

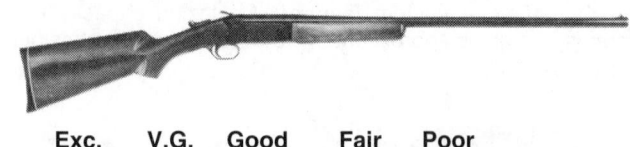

Exc.	V.G.	Good	Fair	Poor
125	85	65	50	35

OMEGA
Elbar, Spain
SEE—Armero Especialistas

OMEGA
Geneseo, Illinois
Springfield Armory

Omega Pistol

A high-grade target-type pistol that is patterned after the Colt Model 1911 type pistol, with marked improvements. It is chambered for the .38 Super, 10mm, and the .45 ACP cartridges. The barrel is either 5" or 6" in length and has polygonal rifling. The barrels are furnished either ported or plain and feature a lockup system that eliminates the barrel link and bushing associated with the normal Browning design. This pistol has a dual extractor system, adjustable sights, and Pachmayr grips. It was introduced in 1987.

NIB	Exc.	V.G.	Good	Fair	Poor
850	700	600	500	400	200

OMEGA FIREARMS CO.
Flower Mound, Texas

Bolt Action Rifle

A .25-06 to .358 Norma Magnum bolt action rifle with a 22" or 24" barrel, octagonal bolt, adjustable trigger and rotary magazine. Blued with a two-piece walnut or laminated stock. Discontinued circa 1975.

Exc.	V.G.	Good	Fair	Poor
750	600	500	400	200

OPUS SPORTING ARMS, INC.
Long Beach, California

Opus One

A .243, .270, or .30-06 caliber bolt action rifle with a 24" barrel, well figured walnut stock and an ebony pistol grip cap as well as forend tip. Built on a Model 70 Winchester action. Manufactured in 1987 and 1988.

Exc.	V.G.	Good	Fair	Poor
2000	1600	1150	700	350

Opus Two

As above, in 7mm Remington Magnum and .300 Winchester Magnum.

Exc.	V.G.	Good	Fair	Poor
2250	1750	1250	750	350

Opus Three

As above, in .375 Holland & Holland and .458 Winchester Magnum.

Exc.	V.G.	Good	Fair	Poor
2750	2000	1500	900	500

ORBEA & CIA
Eibar, Spain

Pocket Pistol

A 6.35mm semiautomatic pistol with a 2.5" barrel. Blued with plastic grips. The slide marked "Orbea y Cia Eibar Espana Pistola Automatica Cal. 6.35." Manufactured from approximately 1918 to 1936.

Exc.	V.G.	Good	Fair	Poor
175	150	125	75	50

ORTGIES, HEINRICH & CO.
Erfurt, Germany

Ortgies Pistol

A 6.35mm or 7.65mm semiautomatic pistol with a 2.75" or 3.25" barrel. Blued with walnut grips. The slide marked "Ortgies & Co. Erfurt." After 1921, these pistols were manufactured by Deutsche Werke.

An engraved Ortgies pistol was sold at auction for $2,070. Chambered for .25 ACP cartridge. Mother-of-pearl grips. Condition was excellent.
Amoskeag Auction Co. Inc., January 2000

Exc.	V.G.	Good	Fair	Poor
400	275	175	125	85

ORVIS
Dallas, Texas

An importer and retailer of sporting goods including foreign manufactured firearms.

OSBORN, S.
Canton, Connecticut

Under Hammer Pistol

A .34 caliber under hammer percussion pistol with a 7" half octagonal barrel, brass mounts and a walnut grip. The barrel marked "S. Osborn/Canton, Conn."

Exc.	V.G.	Good	Fair	Poor
—	—	550	250	125

OSGOOD GUN WORKS
Norwich, Connecticut

Duplex Revolver

A .22 caliber spur trigger revolver with two super-imposed barrels, the upper most of .22 caliber and the lower a .32 caliber. The cylinder with eight .22 chambers. The hammer fitted with a moveable firing pin so that the pistol can be used either as a revolver or as a single shot with a .32 caliber barrel. Blued or nickel-plated with hard rubber grips. The barrel marked "Osgood Gun Works-Norwich Conn." and "Duplex." An unknown quantity were manufactured during the 1880s.

Courtesy Milwaukee Public Museum, Milwaukee, Wisconsin

Exc.	V.G.	Good	Fair	Poor
—	650	300	150	100

OVERTON, JOHN
Nashville, Tennessee

Formerly armorer at Harpers Ferry Armory. He delivered 81 rifles copying the U.S. Model 1841 but with a saber bayonet lug on the right side of the barrel. Unmarked externally but are serial numbered internally. Overall length ca. 48-3/4"; barrel length 33"; .54 caliber.

Prospective purchasers are strongly advised to secure an expert appraisal prior to acquisition.

Exc.	V.G.	Good	Fair	Poor
—	—	10000	5000	2000

OWA
Vienna, Austria
Osterreiche Werke Anstalt

OWA Pocket Pistol

A 6.35mm semiautomatic pistol with a 2" barrel. Unmarked except for "OWA" logo cast in the grips. Blued with plastic grips. Manufactured between 1920 and 1925.

Courtesy Orvel Reichert

Courtesy Orvel Reichert

Exc.	V.G.	Good	Fair	Poor
300	200	175	100	75

Courtesy Orvel Reichert

P

P-38

THE GERMAN WWII SERVICE PISTOL

NOTE: For history, technical data, descriptions, photos, and prices, see the *Standard Catalog of Military Firearms, 1870 to the Present* under Germany.

WALTHER COMMERCIAL

The Commercial version of the P.38 is identified by commercial proofmarks of a crown over N or an eagle over N. Production started at around serial number 1000 and went through serial number 26659. This was the first of the commercial pistols and was a high-quality, well made gun with a complete inscription on the left slide. A few of these early pistols were equipped with checkered wooden grips. The quality decreased as the war progressed. There are many variations of these commercial models and values can vary from $1,000 to $16,000. It is suggested that these pistols be appraised and evaluated by an expert. For postwar Walther P.38 pistols see the Walther section.

A few of the Walther Commercial Model variations are listed below:

MOD HP-H Prefix w/rectangular firing pin

Exc.	V.G.	Good	Fair	Poor
2500	1750	950	750	450

MOD HP-Early w/High Gloss Blue

Exc.	V.G.	Good	Fair	Poor
1800	1200	750	600	400

MOD HP-.30 caliber, extremely rare

Exc.	V.G.	Good	Fair	Poor
16000	—	—	—	—

MOD HP-Early w/High Gloss Blue & Alloy Frame

Exc.	V.G.	Good	Fair	Poor
7500	5000	3500	2000	1000

MOD HP-Croatian contract, 100 built, 6 known

Exc.	V.G.	Good	Fair	Poor
7500	—	—	—	—

MOD HP-Late w/Military Blue Finish

Exc.	V.G.	Good	Fair	Poor
1250	1000	750	550	350

NOTE: Add $200 for "Eagle/359" on right side.

MOD P38-Late with Military Blue (1800 produced)

Exc.	V.G.	Good	Fair	Poor
1750	1200	750	600	400

P.A.F.
Pretoria, South Africa
Pretoria Small Arms Factory

P.A.F. Junior

A .22 or .25 caliber semiautomatic pistol with a 2" barrel and 6-shot magazine. Blued with plastic grips. Slide marked "Junior Verwaardig in Suid Afrika Made in South Africa". Manufactured during the 1950s.

Exc.	V.G.	Good	Fair	Poor
225	175	125	100	70

PGM PRECISION
France

Model PGM

This is a highly sophisticated semiautomatic rifle designed and built on a modular component system. Barrel change is fast and available calibers are .308 Win., .300 Savage, 7mm-08, .243, and .22-250. Match grade barrel length is 23.4". Fully adjustable trigger and buttstock with adjustable bipod. 5-round magazine is standard. Weight is approximately 13 lbs.

NIB	Exc.	V.G.	Good	Fair	Poor
8900	7000	5000	—	—	—

P.S.M.G. GUN CO.
Arlington, Massachusetts

Six In One Supreme

A .22 l.r., .30 Luger, .38 Super, .38 Special, 9mm, and the .45ACP caliber semiautomatic pistol with interchangeable 3.5", 5", or 7.5" barrels, and adjustable sights. Blued or satin nickel-plated. Introduced in 1988. Conversion kits are valued at $450 per unit.

NIB	Exc.	V.G.	Good	Fair	Poor
900	700	550	450	300	150

PTK INTERNATIONAL, INC.
Atlanta, Georgia
SEE —Poly-Technologies

PAGE-LEWIS ARMS CO.
Chicopee Falls, Massachusetts

Model A Target

A .22 caliber single-shot lever action rifle with a 20" barrel and open sights. Blued with a walnut stock. Manufactured from 1920 to 1926.

Exc.	V.G.	Good	Fair	Poor
300	225	175	125	100

Model B Sharpshooter

As above, with a 24" barrel and longer forend.

Exc.	V.G.	Good	Fair	Poor
300	225	175	125	100

Model C Olympic

As above, with a 24" barrel and improved sights.

Exc.	V.G.	Good	Fair	Poor
375	275	200	150	100

PALMER
Windsor, Vermont
E. G. Lamson & Co.

Palmer Bolt Action Carbine

A .50 caliber single-shot bolt action carbine with a 20" round barrel, walnut half stock and full sidelock. Blued and case hardened. The receiver marked "Wm. Palmer / Patent / Dec.22, 1863" and the lock "G.Lamson & Co./ Windsor, Vt." Approximately 1,000 were made in 1865.

Exc.	V.G.	Good	Fair	Poor
—	3250	1500	700	250

PANTHER ARMS
see-DPMS

PAPE, W.R.
Newcastle-Upon-Tyne, England
SEE—British Double Guns

PARA-ORDNANCE MFG. INC.
Scarborough, Ontario, Canada

Model P14.45

Similar in appearance to the Colt Government model this .45 ACP semiautomatic pistol features a 5" barrel, flared ejection port, combat style hammer beveled magazine well and a 13-round magazine capacity. Overall length is 8.5" and weight is 40 oz. for steel and stainless steel version and 31 oz. for alloy frame model. Finish is black except for stainless steel model.

NIB	Exc.	V.G.	Good	Fair	Poor
750	600	500	400	300	200

NOTE: Add $50 for steel frame, $45 for stainless steel, and $30 for duo-tone.

Model P14.45 Limited

Similar to the above model but with extra features such as full length recoil guide, beavertail grip safety, adjustable rear sight, competition hammer, lowered ejection port, front and rear slide serrations, and trigger overtravel stop. Match grade barrel. Choice of black carbon steel or stainless steel finish. Weight is about 40 oz.

NIB	Exc.	V.G.	Good	Fair	Poor
895	725	550	—	—	—

Model P14.45 LDA

This model is essentially the same as the P14.45 but with a double action trigger. Offered in black carbon steel only. Weight is about 40 oz. First introduced in 1999.

NIB	Exc.	V.G.	Good	Fair	Poor
775	625	—	—	—	—

Model P16.40

This is essentially the same as the Model 14.45 except that it is chambered for the .40 S&W cartridge. The magazine capacity is 15 rounds.

NIB	Exc.	V.G.	Good	Fair	Poor
750	600	500	400	300	200

NOTE: Add $50 for steel frame, $45 for stainless steel, and $30 for duo-tone.

Model P16.40 Limited

Similar to the above model but with extra features such as full length recoil guide, beavertail grip safety, adjustable rear sight, competition hammer, lowered ejection port, front and rear slide serrations, and trigger overtravel stop. Match grade barrel. Black carbon steel finish.

NIB	Exc.	V.G.	Good	Fair	Poor
895	725	550	425	300	200

Model P16.40 LDA

This model is a double action version of the P16-40 in black carbon steel only. First offered in 1999.

NIB	Exc.	V.G.	Good	Fair	Poor
775	625	—	—	—	—

Model P13.45

Introduced in 1994 this .45 ACP model features a 4-1/4" barrel with a 13-round magazine. The grip is 1/4" longer than the 12.45 model. Offered in light alloy, carbon, or stainless steel. Overall length is 7-3/4" and the height is 5-1/4". Weight is about 36 oz. in steel version and 28 oz. in alloy version.

NIB	Exc.	V.G.	Good	Fair	Poor
750	600	500	400	300	200

NOTE: Add $50 for steel frame, $45 for stainless steel, and $30 for duo-tone.

Model 13.45/P12.45 Limited

Similar to the above model but with extra features such as full length recoil guide, beavertail grip safety, adjustable rear sight, competition hammer, lowered ejection port, front and rear slide serrations, and trigger overtravel stop. Match grade barrel. Black carbon steel finish.

P13.45

P12.45

NIB	Exc.	V.G.	Good	Fair	Poor
895	725	550	425	300	200

Model P12.45 LDA

This model is fitted with a 3.5" barrel and has a magazine capacity of 12 rounds. It features a double action trigger. Finish is black. Weight is about 34 oz. Introduced in 2000.

NIB	Exc.	V.G.	Good	Fair	Poor
775	575	475	—	—	—

Model P12.45/P12.40

Similar to the Model P14 but in a smaller package. Introduced in 1993. Has all the same features as the Model P14 but has a magazine capacity of 11 rounds. Also available in alloy, steel, or stainless steel this model weighs 24 oz. in alloy model and 33 oz. in steel models. The P12.40 is the same model but chambered for .40 S&W cartridge.

NIB	Exc.	V.G.	Good	Fair	Poor
750	600	500	400	300	200

NOTE: Add $50 for steel frame, $45 for stainless steel, and $30 for duo-tone.

Model P10.45/P10.40/P10.9

Introduced in 1996 this model is the smallest semi-auto .45 ACP in production. Overall length is 6.5" with height of 4.5". Magazine capacity is 10 rounds. Barrel length is 3.5". Offered in stainless steel, Duotone, or black alloy finish. Also offered chambered for .40 S&W cartridge and the 9mm cartridge. Weight is about 31 oz. for stainless and 24 oz. for alloy model.

NIB	Exc.	V.G.	Good	Fair	Poor
750	600	500	400	300	200

NOTE: Add $50 for steel frame, $45 for stainless steel, and $30 for duo-tone.

Model P10.45 Limited

Similar to the above model but with extra features such as full length recoil guide, beavertail grip safety, adjustable rear sight, competition hammer, lowered ejection port, front and rear slide serrations, and trigger overtravel stop. Match grade barrel. Black carbon steel finish.

NIB	Exc.	V.G.	Good	Fair	Poor
895	725	550	425	300	200

Model P18.9

This pistol is chambered for the 9mm cartridge and is fitted with a 5" barrel. Finish is stainless steel. Rear sight is adjustable

and dovetail front sight. Magazine capacity is 18 rounds (10 rounds for US and Canada). Weight is approximately 40 oz.

NIB	Exc.	V.G.	Good	Fair	Poor
850	675	550	450	300	200

Model P18.9 LDA

This is a double action version of the P18-9. Offered in black carbon steel only. Introduced in 1999.

NIB	Exc.	V.G.	Good	Fair	Poor
775	625	—	—	—	—

PARDINI
Italy
Importer-Nygord Presision Products
Prescott, Arizona

Standard Target Pistol

A .22 caliber semiautomatic pistol with a 4.7" barrel, adjustable rear sight and adjustable trigger. Blued with two sizes of walnut grips, one suitable for use by ladies. Introduced in 1986.

NIB	Exc.	V.G.	Good	Fair	Poor
950	800	700	600	500	250

Rapidfire Pistol

Similar to the above, in .22 short with an alloy bolt, 4.6" barrel and enclosed grip. Weight is about 43 oz. Introduced in 1995.

NIB	Exc.	V.G.	Good	Fair	Poor
950	800	700	600	500	250

Centerfire Pistol

Similar to the standard model, but in .32 Smith & Wesson caliber. Introduced in 1986.

NIB	Exc.	V.G.	Good	Fair	Poor
950	800	700	600	500	250

Free Pistol

A .22 caliber single-shot pistol with a 9.8" barrel, adjustable sights and adjustable grip. Furnished with barrel weights. Weight is about 35 oz. Introduced in 1995.

NIB	Exc.	V.G.	Good	Fair	Poor
950	800	700	600	500	250

PARKER
Springfield, Massachusetts

4-Shot Pistol

A .33 caliber percussion pistol with a 4" half-octagonal barrel and a 4-shot sliding chamber. Marked "Albert Parker/Patent Secured/Springfield, Mass." Original finish unknown with walnut grips. Prospective purchasers are advised to secure a qualified appraisal prior to acquisition.

Exc.	V.G.	Good	Fair	Poor
—	—	13500	6000	2000

PARKER BROS.
Meriden, Connecticut

Perhaps the best known of all American shotgun manufacturers. Established by Charles Parker shortly after the Civil War, this company has produced a wide variety of shotguns in a number of different styles over the years. In the early 1930s the company was purchased by Remington Arms Company.

WARNING NOTE: Parker shotguns are one of the most collectible of American-made shotguns. Both the beginning and the veteran collector should be aware that originality and condition are absolutely critical in establishing such high values for these shotguns. There are numerous upgraded and refinished guns that are represented as original. Beware that such misrepresentations exist because refinished and upgraded Parker guns should sell for as much as 50 to 75 percent below the price of an original gun. Extreme caution should be exercised and we would recommend that an expert be consulted. Even the most advanced collectors may benefit from such consultations. Also, the prices indicated for guns in excellent condition may fluctuate drastically, especially in high grade or small bore guns, due to their extreme rarity.

WHAT'S IT LIKE-THE PARKER SHOTGUN

Two thoughts that come to mind when I pick up a Parker shotgun are grace and balance. The gun fits to hand, comes to shoulder, and points like no other in my experience. Parker Brothers made three styles of grip; full pistol, half pistol, and straight. All work equally well depending on the task. In gauges from 12 to .410 bore the gun is built to its own specific frame size so that each is well proportioned. A small Parker can easily be carried in the field without tiring the shooter. Butt stocks and forends are done in a tasteful walnut depending on grade, although Parker wood has never been the most extravagant around. Perhaps elegant is a better description. My favorites are the 20, 28 gauge and .410 bore with straight grip stocks, and either beavertail or splinter forend. With a straight grip stock and double triggers a Parker has one of the fastest barrel selections in the world; your trigger finger. Parker made a single trigger for its guns beginning in about 1922, and some have complained that it is not very reliable. However, for its time the trigger was a sound choice for those who wanted the handiness of a single trigger. Some Parkers are found with Miller triggers, and these are probably a little better. Despite its case hardened frame the Parker is a strong, reliable gun. With its semi-rounded frame, and depending on grade, tastefully engraved game scenes, the Parker gun brings back those days of master workmanship with attention to detail that is seldom seen today. The gun is a joy to own and shoot. This combination of utility and pride of ownership is a rare occurrence today.

Ned Schwing

In addition, uncommon extras such as single triggers, ventilated ribs, beavertail forearms, straight grip stocks, and skeleton steel buttplates may add substantial value to an individual gun. Extra sets of factory barrels that were installed at the time of delivery will add an average of a 30% premium. This premium will increase with grade and gauge; the higher the grade and smaller the gauge the higher the premium.

NOTE: Letters of authenticity are available. These letters are a must in order for any Parker gun to attain maximum value. Contact: Ronald Kirby, Exec. Secetary Parker Gun Collectors Association, 8825 Bud Smith Road, Wake Forest, SC 27587. FAX: 919-554-8120. The letter is $25 for members of the PCGA and $40 for non-members.

Editor's Comment: We now have reliable information on the production totals of Parker gauges and grades. This information comes from the book; *The Parker Story* by Gunther, Mullins, Parker, Price, and Cote (1998). **These totals reflect guns built with modern steel barrels *only* and are based on factory records.** It is the editor's opinion that while production statistics are interesting it is the relative number of guns produced in each grade and bore that are the most significant.

Trojan

A 12, 16, or 20 gauge boxlock double barrel shotgun manufactured in a variety of barrel lengths with double triggers and extractors. Only 27 Trojans were built with single triggers. Blued, case hardened receiver with a walnut stock.

*Approximately 33,000 were made: 12 gauge-21,977, 16 gauge-6,573, 20 gauge-5450, 28 gauge-only 2.
20 Gauge-Add 40%.

Exc.	V.G.	Good	Fair	Poor
2400	1500	1000	800	600

VH

A 12, 16, 20, 28 or .410 bore boxlock double barrel shotgun manufactured in a variety of barrel lengths with double triggers and extractors. Blued, case hardened receiver with a walnut stock. Only 2,297 guns had single triggers. Only 3,983 guns had straight grip stocks.

*Approximately 78,659 were made; 10 gauge-20, 12 gauge-51,901, 16 gauge-14,446, 20 gauge-10,406, 28 gauge-1,1417, .410 bore-469.

NOTE: Also made with automatic ejectors and known as the Model VHE. The E suffix was used on all models to denote automatic ejectors.
VHE-Add 40%.
20 Gauge-Add 45%.
28 Gauge-Add 120%.
.410-Add 300%.

Exc.	V.G.	Good	Fair	Poor
3250	1800	1500	1000	700

PH

Similar to the above, but with a small amount of scroll engraving. slightly better grade of walnut.

*Approximately 1,339 were made; 10 gauge-798, 12 gauge-839, 16 gauge-208, 20 gauge-204, 28 gauge-only 5, .410 bore-only 4.

PHE-Add 40%.
20 Gauge-Add 45%.
28 Gauge-Add 120%.

Exc.	V.G.	Good	Fair	Poor
3500	2200	1700	1200	900

GH

Similar to the above, with a modest amount of scroll and game scene engraving and the barrels marked "Parker Special Steel". Only about 430 G grades were built with straight grip stocks.

*Approximately 4,291 were made; 8 gauge-11, 10 gauge-63, 12 gauge-2,501, 16 gauge-607, 20 gauge-990, 28 gauge-91, .410 bore-28.

GHE-Add 35%.
16 Gauge-Add 15%.
20 Gauge-Add 40%.
28 Gauge-Add 150%.
.410-Add 400%.

Exc.	V.G.	Good	Fair	Poor
3900	2700	2200	1400	1000

DH

As above, but more finely finished. engraving coverage more profuse. Most modern D grade guns were fitted with Titanic barrels. Only about 280 were built with Parker single triggers, and only about 280 were built with ventilated ribs.

*Approximately 9,346 were made; 8 gauge-10, 10 gauge-45, 12 gauge-6,330, 16 gauge-1,178, 20 gauge-1,536, 28 gauge-187, .410 bore-60.

DHE-Add 35%.
16 Gauge-Add 10%.
20 Gauge-Add 40%.
28 Gauge-Add 150%.
.410-Add 500%.

Exc.	V.G.	Good	Fair	Poor
6500	5000	4000	2000	1500

CH

As above, with more scroll and game scene engraving coverage. Marked with Acme steel barrels. Only about 93 C grades had straight grip stocks.

*Approximately 697 were made; 8 gauge-only 2, 10 gauge only 9, 12 gauge-410, 16 gauge-105, 20 gauge-149, 28 gauge-only 16, .410 bore-only 6.

CHE-Add 35%.
16 Gauge-Add 10%.
20 Gauge-Add 40%.
28 Gauge-Add 200%.
.410-Add 700%.

Exc.	V.G.	Good	Fair	Poor
7750	5600	4300	2500	2000

A .410 bore CHE Parker was sold at auction for $46,000. Built in 1930s. Condition was 15% case colors and 95% blue. Barrels were 28".
Butterfield & Butterfield, May 1999

BH

As above, but offered in a variety of different styles of engraved decoration. Only about 66 guns had straight grip stocks, 29 had beavertail forends, 20 were built with vent ribs, and 57 had single triggers.

*Approximately 512 were made; 10 gauge-only 2, 12 gauge-317, 16 gauge-71, 20 gauge-109, 28 gauge-13.

NOTE: Prospective purchasers are advised to secure a qualified appraisal prior to acquisition.

BHE-Add 35%.
16 Gauge-Add 15%.
20 Gauge-Add 50%.
28 Gauge-Add 250%.

Exc.	V.G.	Good	Fair	Poor
10000	7500	5000	3300	2500

A Parker BHE .410 bore was sold at auction for $101,500. It was fitted with 28" barrels and straight grip stock with a skeleton butt. Condition was 35% case colors and 99% blue.
Butterfield & Butterfield, May 1999

AH

As above, but highly engraved with finely figured walnut stocks. Most had Acme steel barrels. About 42 A grade guns were built with straight grip stocks.

*Approximately 167 were made; 10 gauge-only 1, 12 gauge-92, 16 gauge-23, 20 gauge-44, 28 gauge-only 6, .410 bore-only 1.

NOTE: Due to the rarity of this grade prospective purchasers are advised to secure a qualified appraisal prior to acquisition.

AHE-Add 30%.
16 Gauge-Add 25%.
20 Gauge-Add 75%.
28 Gauge-Add 300%.
.410-Add 500%.

Exc.	V.G.	Good	Fair	Poor
18500	13000	10000	8000	5000

AAH

As above, with either Whitworth or Peerless barrels and not made in .410 bore. The engraving is more extensive and of the first quality. Only one AA grade has a ventilated rib, ten were built with single trigger and 95 had straight grip stocks.

*Approximately 238 were made; 10 gauge-only 2, 12 gauge-185, 16 gauge-19, 20 gauge-27, 28 gauge-only 5.

NOTE: Due to the rarity of this grade prospective purchasers are advised to secure a qualified appraisal prior to acquisition.

AAHE-Add 30%.
16 Gauge-Add 35%.
20 Gauge-Add 75%.
28 Gauge-Add 400%.

Exc.	V.G.	Good	Fair	Poor
35000	25000	18000	10000	7000

A Parker AAHE in 12 gauge was sold at auction for $31,625. Fitted with 28" barrels, matted rib, and pistol grip. Condition was 10% case colors and 95% blue.
Butterfield & Butterfield, May 1999

A-1 Special

As above, but made strictly on special order and not manufactured in .410 bore. Two A-1 special were built with ventilated rib, 7 had single triggers, 3 had beavertail forends, and 24 were built with straight grip stocks.

*Approximately 79 were made; 12 gauge-55, 16 gauge-only 6, 20 gauge-11, and 28 gauge-only 7.

NOTE: Due to the extreme rarity of this grade prospective purchasers are advised to secure a qualified appraisal prior to acquisition.

16 Gauge-Add 35%.
20 Gauge-Add 75%.
28 Gauge-Add 500%.

Exc.	V.G.	Good	Fair	Poor
65000	55000	42000	30000	20000

A Parker A-1 Special in 28 gauge sold at auction for $112,500. It was fitted with 26" barrel and pistol grip stock. Cased. Condition was 60% case colors and 99% blue.
Butterfield & Butterfield, May 1999

Single Barrel Trap

A 12 gauge single-shot shotgun with a 30", 32", or 34" barrel, automatic ejector and walnut stock. Produced in a variety of grades as follows. Prospective purchasers are advised to secure a qualified appraisal prior to acquisition.

S.C. Grade

Exc.	V.G.	Good	Fair	Poor
3900	2500	2000	1500	1000

S.B. Grade

Exc.	V.G.	Good	Fair	Poor
4500	3700	3000	2400	1600

S.A. Grade

Exc.	V.G.	Good	Fair	Poor
7000	5500	4000	3000	2000

S.A.A. Grade

Exc.	V.G.	Good	Fair	Poor
12000	7000	5500	3800	2400

S.A-1 Special Grade

Exc.	V.G.	Good	Fair	Poor
20000	12000	8000	6000	4000

Under Lifter Hammer Gun

A side hammer double barrel shotgun manufactured in a variety of gauges with the barrel release located in front of the triggerguards. Damascus barrels, case hardened locks, blued furniture with walnut stocks. Manufactured during the 1870s and later.

Exc.	V.G.	Good	Fair	Poor
6000	3200	1500	800	600

PARKER FIELD & SONS
SEE—English Military Firearms

PARKER FIELD & SONS
London, England

Gas Seal Revolver

A .42 caliber percussion revolver with a 6" barrel and 6-shot cylinder. Blued, case hardened with walnut grips. Manufactured during the 1860s.

Exc.	V.G.	Good	Fair	Poor
—	—	1750	850	450

PARKER HALE LTD.
Birmingham, England

S&W Victory Conversion

A .22 caliber double action revolver with a 4" barrel and 6-shot cylinder. Blued with walnut grips. An alteration of the Smith & Wesson Victor model.

Exc.	V.G.	Good	Fair	Poor
250	200	150	100	75

Model 1200

A .22-250 to .300 Winchester Magnum bolt action rifle with a 24" barrel and open sights. Blued, with walnut stock.

NIB	Exc.	V.G.	Good	Fair	Poor
700	550	450	400	350	250

Model 1100 Lightweight

As above, with a 22" barrel and 4-shot magazine. Introduced in 1985.

NIB	Exc.	V.G.	Good	Fair	Poor
600	475	400	300	250	200

Model 81 Classic

A .22-250 to 7mm Remington Magnum bolt action rifle with a 24" barrel and open sights. Blued with a walnut stock. Introduced in 1985.

NIB	Exc.	V.G.	Good	Fair	Poor
875	750	600	500	400	350

Model 81 African

As above, but in .375 Holland & Holland caliber. Introduced in 1986.

NIB	Exc.	V.G.	Good	Fair	Poor
2000	1500	1100	700	500	350

Model 84 Target

Similar to the Model 81, but in .308 caliber with adjustable rear sights and an adjustable cheekpiece.

NIB	Exc.	V.G.	Good	Fair	Poor
1500	1000	800	600	450	250

Model 85 Sniper

As above, with a telescope and bipod.

NIB	Exc.	V.G.	Good	Fair	Poor
3750	3000	2500	—	—	—

Model 640E Shotgun

A 12, 16, or 20 gauge boxlock double barrel shotgun manufactured in a variety of barrel lengths with double triggers and extractors. Blued, French case hardened with a walnut stock. Introduced in 1986.

NIB	Exc.	V.G.	Good	Fair	Poor
575	450	400	300	250	200

Model 640A

As above, with a pistol grip, beavertail forend, and single trigger. Introduced in 1986.

NIB	Exc.	V.G.	Good	Fair	Poor
675	550	500	400	300	200

Model 645E

As above, but more finely finished and engraved.

NIB	Exc.	V.G.	Good	Fair	Poor
700	550	500	400	300	200

Model 670E

A sidelock double barrel shotgun made on special order. Introduced in 1986.

NIB	Exc.	V.G.	Good	Fair	Poor
3000	2500	1850	1200	750	400

Model 680E-XXV

As above, with case hardened lockplates and 25" barrels.

NIB	Exc.	V.G.	Good	Fair	Poor
3000	2500	1850	1200	750	400

BLACK POWDER REPRODUCTIONS

Imported by Gibbs Rifle Company

1853 Enfield Rifle Musket

This is a tree band version in .577 caliber. Barrel length is 39". Rear sight graduated to 900 yards. Weight about 9 lbs.

NIB	Exc.	V.G.	Good	Fair	Poor
600	475	375	—	—	—

1858 Enfield Naval Pattern Rifle

This is the Naval version with two bands in .577 caliber. Barrel length is 33". Walnut stock with brass furniture. Rear sight adjustable to 1100 yards. Weight is approximately 8.5 lbs.

NIB	Exc.	V.G.	Good	Fair	Poor
550	425	325	—	—	—

1861 Enfield Artillery Carbine Musketoon

This is the Artillery version in .577 caliber with 24" barrel. Walnut stock with brass furniture. Rear sight adjustable to 600 yards. Weight is about 7.5 lbs.

NIB	Exc.	V.G.	Good	Fair	Poor
475	375	300	—	—	—

Whitworth Military Target Rifle

This model is in .451 caliber. Barrel length is 36". Weight is about 9.9 lbs.

NIB	Exc.	V.G.	Good	Fair	Poor
875	700	550	—	—	—

Whitworth Sniping Rifle

Same as above but with brass scope and mounts.

NIB	Exc.	V.G.	Good	Fair	Poor
1700	1350	950	—	—	—

Volunteer Percussion Target Rifle

This rifle is in .451 caliber and fitted with a 33" barrel. It is the two banned design with walnut stock and brass furniture. Adjustable rear sight. Weight is approximately 9.5 lbs.

NIB	Exc.	V.G.	Good	Fair	Poor
850	650	550	—	—	—

PARKER REPRODUCTIONS

Japan
Importer - Regent Chemical & Research
Middlesex, New Jersey

This company had exact reproductions of Parker D, DHE, B and A-1 Special shotguns made in Japan. They are of the finest quality and workmanship. The styles of engraving and features of these shotguns correspond exactly to the original Parker Arms.

D-Grade

This side-by-side shotgun is offered in 12 gauge, 20 gauge, and 28 gauge. Barrel lengths are 26" or 28" with sold matte rib. Stocks are select walnut with choice of pistol or straight grip. Choice splinter or beavertail forearms are offered. Single or double triggers are available as well. The receiver is case colored and scroll engraved with game scenes to match the original Parker DHE grade. Weight of 12 gauge is 6.75 lbs., 20 gauge is 6.5 lbs., and 28 gauge weighs 5.3 lbs.

12 or 20 Gauge

NIB	Exc.	V.G.	Good	Fair	Poor
2250	1750	1250	850	600	400

16/20 Combination

Introduced in 1993 and limited to 500 sets. Offered with 28" barrels only this set features a 16 gauge barrel on a 20 gauge frame. Weighs 6.25 lbs.

NIB	Exc.	V.G.	Good	Fair	Poor
4500	4200	3500	2500	1250	650

28 Gauge

NIB	Exc.	V.G.	Good	Fair	Poor
2250	1750	1250	850	600	400

28 Gauge/.410 Bore Combination

NIB	Exc.	V.G.	Good	Fair	Poor
4750	4250	3250	1950	1000	550

NOTE: Add $990 for an additional barrel and $170 for beavertail forearm. For the D Grade three barrels sets are offered in 16/20/20 combinations for an additional $2300.

DHE Grade Steel-Shot Special

Offered in 12 gauge only with 28" barrels. Fitted with 3" chambers and special chrome lined barrels. Weighs 7 lbs.

NIB	Exc.	V.G	Good	Fair	Poor
3500	2750	2000	1200	700	400

B-Grade Limited Edition

This model features engraving similar to the original Parker BHE Grade. Fancy walnut stocks with fine line checkering was standard. It was offered in 12 gauge, 20 gauge, and 28 gauge. A 28 gauge/.410 bore combination was also offered. Only 100 shotguns in this grade were produced in 1989.

NIB	Exc.	V.G.	Good	Fair	Poor
4000	3650	2900	1750	900	450

28 Gauge/.410 Bore Combination

NIB	Exc.	V.G.	Good	Fair	Poor
5000	4500	3500	2500	1500	750

A-1 Special

Introduced in 1988 this grade fine scroll engraving and presentation French walnut with custom checkering pattern. The stock is hand carved with fleur-de-lis and features 32 lines to the inch checkering. The grip cap is rosewood and gold or gold initial plate on straight grip guns. Gold wire is used on the breech end on the barrels. Serial numbers are in gold relief as is the word "SAFE" and "L" and "R" on models with selective single trigger. Barrels flats and frame water table is jeweled. This grade is offered in 12, 20, and 28 gauge with a few early guns sold with 28 gauge/.410 bore combinations. Furnished with English style oak and leather case with canvas and leather cover, engraved snap caps, and engraved oil bottle.

12 or 20 Gauge

NIB	Exc.	V.G.	Good	Fair	Poor
9500	8000	5000	4000	2500	1000

28 Gauge

NIB	Exc.	V.G.	Good	Fair	Poor
10500	8500	6000	5000	3000	1000

A-1 Special Custom Engraved

This model is a custom hand engraved A-1 Special to each individual customer's specifications. Only a limited number of these shotguns will be built. Initial price in 1989 was $10,500. It is strongly recommended that the prospective purchaser acquire an appraisal prior to the sale due to the unique features of each gun.

PEABODY
Providence, Rhode Island
Providence Tool Company

Peabody Rifle and Carbine

A .43 Spanish, .443, .45 Peabody, .45-70, .50 or .50-70 caliber single-shot rifle with a 33" or 20" (carbine) barrel and either a full length or half stock. The receiver marked "Peabody's Patent July 22, 1862 / Mannf'd by Providence Tool Co. Prov. R.I." Blued, with a walnut stock. Produced in large quantities during the 1860s and 1870s.

Courtesy Milwaukee Public Museum, Milwaukee, Wisconsin

Exc.	V.G.	Good	Fair	Poor
—	1700	750	300	100

Sporting Rifle

As above, in a sporting configuration with either 26" or 28" barrels. The frame marked, "Peabody's Patent, July 22, 1862 / Manf'd by Providence Tool Co., Prov. R.I." Blued, case hardened with a walnut stock. Manufactured from approximately 1866 to 1875.

Exc.	V.G.	Good	Fair	Poor
—	1200	500	300	150

PEABODY-MARTINI SPORTING RIFLES

Creedmoor

A .40-90 or .44-100 caliber Martini-action single-shot rifle with a 32" round/octagonal barrel, butt-mounted vernier rear sight, combination wind gauge and spirit level front sight. The receiver marked, "Peabody & Martini Patents" and the barrel "Manufactured by the Providence Tool Co. Providence R.I. U.S.A." Blued, case hardened with a walnut stock.

Courtesy Milwaukee Public Museum, Milwaukee, Wisconsin

Exc.	V.G.	Good	Fair	Poor
—	7500	3500	1500	550

A Peabody Martini Long Range Creedmore rifle chambered for the .44-100 caliber was sold at auction for $5,750. Engraved with light scroll. Fitted with a 32" 1/2-round barrel. Condition is 95% blue with 90% case colors. Barrel has no rear sight seat. Front sight is missing. Amoskeag Auction Company, May 2001

Creedmoor Mid-Range
Similar to the above, but in .40-70 or .40-90 caliber with a 28" round/octagonal barrel, vernier tang sight and wind gauge front sight. Blued, case hardened with a walnut stock.

Exc.	V.G.	Good	Fair	Poor
—	6000	3250	1250	400

What Cheer
The Creedmoor without a pistol grip.

Exc.	V.G.	Good	Fair	Poor
—	6000	3250	1250	400

What Cheer Mid-Range
The Mid-Range Creedmoor without a pistol grip.

Exc.	V.G.	Good	Fair	Poor
—	5000	2750	1000	300

Kill Deer
A .45-70 caliber single-shot Martini-action rifle with 28" or 30" round/octagonal barrels, adjustable tang rear sight and globe front sights. Blued, case hardened with a walnut stock.

Exc.	V.G.	Good	Fair	Poor
—	7500	4250	1500	500

PEAVY, A. J.
South Montville, Maine

Knife-Pistol
A .22 caliber single-shot knife pistol constructed of steel and brass with a folding trigger. The sideplates marked "A.J. Peavy Pat. Sept. 5, '65 & Mar. 27, '66." Produced between 1866 and 1870.

Exc.	V.G.	Good	Fair	Poor
—	—	3250	1750	500

PECARE & SMITH
New York, New York

Pepperbox
A .28 caliber 4-shot or 1-shot percussion pepperbox with a folding trigger and 4" barrel group. The barrel group enclosed within an iron casing. Blued, silver-plated frame with walnut grips. The barrel casing marked "Pecare & Smith." Manufactured during the 1840s early 1850s.

Exc.	V.G.	Good	Fair	Poor
—	—	2500	1150	350

Ten-Shot Pepperbox (rare)
Exc.	V.G.	Good	Fair	Poor
—	—	5500	2250	600

PEDERSEN, JOHN D.
Denver, CO & Jackson, WY

Pedersen Rifle
Exc.	V.G.	Good	Fair	Poor
12500	7500	—	—	—

Pedersen Carbine
Exc.	V.G.	Good	Fair	Poor
15000	8500	—	—	—

PEDERSEN CUSTOM GUNS
North Haven, Connecticut
A division of the O.F. Mossberg Company operated between 1973 and 1975.

Model 4000 Shotgun
The Mossberg Model 500 slide action shotgun in 12, 20 or .410 bore with 26", 28", or 30" ventilated rib barrels. Blued, engraved with a walnut stock. Manufactured in 1975.

Exc.	V.G.	Good	Fair	Poor
500	350	250	200	100

Model 4000 Trap
Chambered for 12 gauge only with 30" full choke barrel. Monte Carlo stock with factory recoil pad.

Exc.	V.G.	Good	Fair	Poor
550	400	300	200	100

Model 4500
As above, but with a reduced amount of engraving.

Exc.	V.G.	Good	Fair	Poor
475	325	225	175	100

Model 4500 Trap
Same as the Model 4000 Trap but with less engraving.

Exc.	V.G.	Good	Fair	Poor
500	350	250	200	100

Model 1500
A 12 gauge Magnum Over/Under shotgun with 26", 28", or 30" ventilated rib barrels, single selective trigger and automatic ejectors. Blued with a walnut stock. Weight is about 7.5 lbs. depending on barrel length. Manufactured between 1973 and 1975.

Exc.	V.G.	Good	Fair	Poor
750	600	500	400	200

Model 1500 Skeet
Similar to the above model but fitted with a skeet-style stock, 27" barrels and skeet chokes.

Exc.	V.G.	Good	Fair	Poor
825	650	550	450	200

Model 1500 Trap
This model is fitted with a Monte Carlo-style stock a choice of 30" or 32" barrels.

Exc.	V.G.	Good	Fair	Poor
825	650	550	450	200

Model 1000

As above, but manufactured in two grades of decoration. Manufactured between 1973 and 1975.

Grade I

Exc.	V.G.	Good	Fair	Poor
2250	1750	1250	800	500

Grade II

Exc.	V.G.	Good	Fair	Poor
1850	1500	1000	750	400

Model 1000 Magnum

This model is chambered for the 12 gauge 3" shell and fitted with 30" barrels.

Grade I

Exc.	V.G.	Good	Fair	Poor
2000	1600	1200	800	500

Grade II

Exc.	V.G.	Good	Fair	Poor
1750	1400	1100	750	400

Mcdel 1000 Skeet

Offered in 12 gauge only with 26" or 28" barrels. Skeet-style stock and skeet chokes.

Grade I

Exc.	V.G.	Good	Fair	Poor
2250	1750	1250	800	400

Grade II

Exc.	V.G.	Good	Fair	Poor
1850	1500	1000	750	400

Model 1000 Trap

This model is chambered for 12 gauge and fitted with 30" or 32" barrels. Trap-style Monte Carlo stock.

Grade I

Exc.	V.G.	Good	Fair	Poor
2000	1600	1200	800	500

Grade II

Exc.	V.G.	Good	Fair	Poor
1750	1400	1100	750	400

Model 2000

A 12 or 20 gauge boxlock double barrel shotgun with 26", 28", or 30" barrels, single selective trigger and automatic ejectors. Produced in two grades of decoration. Manufactured in 1973 and 1974.

Grade I

Exc.	V.G.	Good	Fair	Poor
2500	2000	1500	1000	600

Grade II

Exc.	V.G.	Good	Fair	Poor
2250	1750	1250	800	400

Model 2500

A 12 or 20 gauge boxlock double barrel shotgun with 26" or 28" barrels, double triggers and automatic ejectors. Blued with a walnut stock.

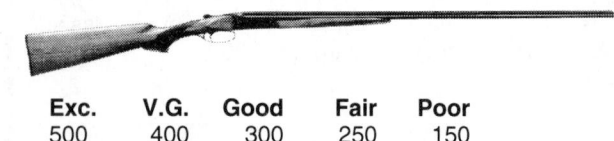

Exc.	V.G.	Good	Fair	Poor
500	400	300	250	150

Model 3000

A Mossberg Model 810 bolt action rifle manufactured in .270 to .338 Winchester Magnum caliber with a 22" or 24" barrel with open sights. Produced in three grades as follows:

Grade III -Plain

Exc.	V.G.	Good	Fair	Poor
550	450	400	350	150

Grade II

Exc.	V.G.	Good	Fair	Poor
650	525	425	350	150

Grade I

Exc.	V.G.	Good	Fair	Poor
1000	800	650	500	200

Model 4700

The Mossberg Model 472 in .30-30 or .35 Remington caliber with a 24" barrel and 5-shot tubular magazine. Blued with a walnut stock.

Exc.	V.G.	Good	Fair	Poor
250	200	150	125	100

PERAZZI
Brescia, Italy
Importer - Perazzi USA, Inc.
Monrovia, California

This company was founded in 1965. During the 1970s Ithaca and Winchester imported and sold Perazzi shotguns. Perazzi has now taken over its own importation and distribution in the United States with the creation of Perazzi USA, Inc. Many shooters consider the Perazzi to be the finest currently produced shotgun in the world.

Perazzi has an extensive variety of models to choose from. In addition, each model may be available in different grades. These grades are based on the type of finish, engraving, and wood quality. The vast majority of Perazzi shotguns that are sold in this country are Standard Grade guns. According to Perazzi USA, these Standard Grade guns account for approximately 98 percent of North American sales. Therefore, it is unlikely that the shooter or collector will encounter high grade Perazzi guns. It should be pointed out that in some models no Extra Grade or Extra Gold Grade shotguns have ever been sold in the United States.

For the benefit of the reader an approximate description of each grade follows. It is a general description because the Perazzi customer may order practically any combination of finishes or engraving patterns he or she desires. Use this list as a general guide.

PERAZZI GRADES

1. **Standard Grade:** Furnished with blued receiver and barrels with hand-checkered select walnut stock and forend.

2. **SC3 Grade:** The receiver has a silver finish with scroll engraving and choice of game scenes. Barrel is blued and stocks are a higher grade of walnut.

3. **SCO Grade:** Silver receiver with choice of Continental or English scroll with choice of game scenes. Barrels are blued and fancy walnut stocks with fine line checkering are used.

4. **Gold Grade:** Customer has a choice of several different game scenes with gold inlays. Blued barrels with fancy walnut stock. Custom checkering.

5. **SCO Grade W/Sideplates:** Similar to the SCO Grade but with more coverage available due to addition of sideplates.

6. **Gold Grade W/Sideplates:** Similar to Gold Grade but with more coverage on sideplates.

7. **Extra Grade:** This is Perazzi's finest grade. The customer has a choice of almost any pattern he desires done in a fine bank note engraving style. Only the finest walnut is used on this grade with very fine line checkering. This is a rare and seldom seen Perazzi grade.

8. **Extra Gold Grade:** Similar to all of the refinement on the Extra Grade with the addition of the birds and animals are gold inlaid. Again, this is a seldom seen grade.

SCO GRADE Engraving Patterns

SC3 GRADE Engraving Patterns

SCO GOLD GRADE Engraving Patterns

SCO GRADE With SIDEPLATES

SCO GOLD GRADE With SIDEPLATES

EXTRA GRADE

EXTRA GOLD GRADE

PRICING NOTICE: Due to a sudden oversupply of Perazzi shotguns in the U.S. prices across the board for all grades should be reduced by 40%.

NOTE: If this situation continues to exist prices will be reduced permanently in subsequent editions.

OUT OF PRODUCTION SHOTGUNS

NOTE: Very high premiums on early SCO and higher grades.

COMP1-SB TRAP

This model is a single barrel trap gun in 12 gauge only with 32" or 34" vent rib barrel.

Standard Grade

NIB	Exc.	V.G.	Good	Fair	Poor
2750	2250	1500	1000	750	500

COMP1-TRAP

This is an O/U version of the above model.

Standard Grade

NIB	Exc	V.G.	Good	Fair	Poor
3500	2750	2000	1500	900	500

Light Game Model

Offered in 12 gauge with a 27.5" vent rib barrel. Trigger group is not detachable. Produced between 1972 and 1974.

Standard Grade

NIB	Exc.	V.G.	Good	Fair	Poor
4500	3750	2750	1750	900	500

NOTE: Deduct 25% for skeet chokes.

MT-6 Model

This model was offered in 12 gauge with a tapered vent rib. The trigger group was not removable. Discontinued in 1983.

Standard Grade

NIB	Exc.	V.G.	Good	Fair	Poor
3250	2750	2000	1500	800	500

NOTE: Deduct 20% for 27.375" barrels.

MX3

This model was discontinued in 1988 and was available in 12 gauge only for single barrel Trap, O/U trap, combination trap, skeet, and sporting configurations.

Standard Grade

NIB	Exc.	V.G.	Good	Fair	Poor
4000	3500	3000	2500	2000	1000

SC3 Grade

NIB	Exc.	V.G.	Good	Fair	Poor
6500	5500	4750	3500	2200	1000

SCO Grade

NIB	Exc.	V.G.	Good	Fair	Poor
8000	6500	5500	4000	2500	1000

Gold Grade

NIB	Exc.	V.G.	Good	Fair	Poor
10000	8500	7000	5000	2700	1200

NOTE: Add 50% to above prices for Combination Trap Guns.

Grand American Special

This model was introduced in 1988 and features a high ramped rib similar to the MX3 model. The forend was grooved. Discontinued in 1991. It was offered in single barrel trap, combination trap, and O/U trap configurations.

Standard Grade

NIB	Exc.	V.G.	Good	Fair	Poor
5250	4250	3500	3000	1500	700

SC3 Grade

NIB	Exc.	V.G.	Good	Fair	Poor
6500	5250	4500	4000	1700	900

SCO Grade

NIB	Exc.	V.G.	Good	Fair	Poor
8000	6500	5500	5000	2000	1000

Gold Grade

NIB	Exc.	V.G.	Good	Fair	Poor
20000	10000	7000	—	—	—

SCO Grade W/Sideplates

NIB	Exc.	V.G.	Good	Fair	Poor
25000	21500	12500	—	—	—

Gold Grade W/Sideplates

NIB	Exc.	V.G.	Good	Fair	Poor
25000	21500	12500	—	—	—

Extra Grade

NIB	Exc.	V.G.	Good	Fair	Poor
30000	—	—	—	—	—

Extra Gold Grade

NIB	Exc.	V.G.	Good	Fair	Poor
35000	—	—	—	—	—

NOTE: The Extra Grade and Extra Gold Grade have not been imported into the US.

SHO Model

NOTE: This O/U sidelock model is available in 12 gauge only in both Type 1 and Type 2 configurations. Type 1 does not have rebounding firing pins and is worth approximately 50% less than Type 2 models that are fitted with rebounding firing pins. There are no parts available in this country or at the factory for Type 1 guns.

The SHO model features a silver finish with fine scroll engraving with game scenes to customer's specifications. Select walnut stock built to customer's dimensions with fine line checkering. A custom built shotgun. Special order only. An expert appraisal is recommended for this model due to its unique features.

DHO Model

This is a side-by-side shotgun offered in 12 gauge only. It has full sidelocks and a silver receiver finish with scroll and game scene engraving of the same quality as the SHO Model. Fancy walnut stock with fine line checkering. An expert appraisal is recommended for this model due to its unique features.

NOTE: There are no replacement parts available for the model.

DHO Extra Gold

Available in any gauge and barrel length combination. Only the finest presentation walnut and checkering. A totally custom built shotgun. Special order only. An expert appraisal is recommended for this model due to its unique features.

NOTE: There are no replacement parts available for this model.

CURRENT PRODUCTION SHOTGUNS
American Trap-Single Barrel Models

MX9

Introduced in 1993 this model features removable inserts on rib to adjust point of impact and a walnut stock with adjustable comb. Offered in 12 gauge with 32" or 34" barrel with screw in chokes. The trigger group is removable. Available in several different grades of ormentation.

Standard Grade

NIB	Exc.	V.G.	Good	Fair	Poor
4100	2800	2100	1800	1250	—

SC3 Grade

NIB	Exc.	V.G.	Good	Fair	Poor
11500	6000	5000	3000	2000	—

SCO Grade

NIB	Exc.	V.G.	Good	Fair	Poor
18000	8000	7000	3500	2000	—

Gold Grade

NIB	Exc.	V.G.	Good	Fair	Poor
20000	10000	9500	5000	2000	—

SCO Grade W/Sideplates

NIB	Exc.	V.G.	Good	Fair	Poor
28500	20000	11000	6000	2500	—

Gold Grade W/Sideplates

NIB	Exc.	V.G.	Good	Fair	Poor
31500	22500	15000	7500	3000	—

MX10

This model was introduced in 1993. It features a different method of rib height and pattern adjustment. This model also has an adjustable stock. Available in 12 gauge with 32" or 34" barrels. Chokes are fixed. Trigger is removable.

Standard Grade

NIB	Exc.	V.G.	Good	Fair	Poor
8700	3600	3000	2400	1750	—

SC3 Grade

NIB	Exc.	V.G.	Good	Fair	Poor
20800	6500	5500	5000	3000	—

SCO Grade

NIB	Exc.	V.G.	Good	Fair	Poor
31210	8000	7000	6000	3500	—

Gold Grade

NIB	Exc.	V.G.	Good	Fair	Poor
34310	9500	8000	6000	4000	—

SCO Grade W/Sideplates

NIB	Exc.	V.G.	Good	Fair	Poor
43450	20000	12500	—	—	—

Gold Grade W/Sideplates

NIB	Exc.	V.G.	Good	Fair	Poor
49300	21500	15000	—	—	—

TM I Special

This basic single barrel Perazzi Trap model is offered in 12 gauge with 32" or 34" barrel. Trigger is adjustable.

Standard Grade

NIB	Exc.	V.G.	Good	Fair	Poor
2800	1200	1000	850	700	—

SC3 Grade

(Not Offered)

SCO Grade

NIB	Exc.	V.G.	Good	Fair	Poor
13500	7000	6000	5000	2500	2000

Gold Grade

NIB	Exc.	V.G.	Good	Fair	Poor
15000	8000	7000	5500	2500	1200

TMX Special

Similar to TM I Special with select walnut.

Standard Grade

NIB	Exc.	V.G.	Good	Fair	Poor
3000	1500	1200	900	750	—

SC3 Grade
(Not Offered)

SCO Grade

NIB	Exc.	V.G.	Good	Fair	Poor
13500	7000	6000	5000	2500	2000

Gold Grade

NIB	Exc.	V.G.	Good	Fair	Poor
15000	8000	7000	5500	2500	1200

MX8 Special

This model features a low contour vent rib, adjustable trigger, and grooved forend.

NOTE: Some SCO engraving patterns on early models have sold in the $30,000 to $45,000 price range. Get an expert appraisal. Beware of counterfeits.

Standard Grade

NIB	Exc.	V.G.	Good	Fair	Poor
5800	4500	3750	3000	2000	1000

SC3 Grade

NIB	Exc.	V.G.	Good	Fair	Poor
10000	6000	5000	4000	3000	1200

SCO Grade

NIB	Exc.	V.G.	Good	Fair	Poor
16500	6000	7000	6000	3000	1500

Gold Grade

NIB	Exc.	V.G.	Good	Fair	Poor
18500	6000	7500	6000	3000	1500

SCO Grade W/Sideplates

NIB	Exc.	V.G.	Good	Fair	Poor
16000	11000	—	—	—	1500

Gold Grade W/Sideplates

NIB	Exc.	V.G.	Good	Fair	Poor
16000	11000	—	—	—	1500

MDB81 Special

This model features a high ventilated rib.

Standard Grade

NIB	Exc.	V.G.	Good	Fair	Poor
6000	3700	—	—	—	1200

SC3 Grade

NIB	Exc.	V.G.	Good	Fair	Poor
10000	4700	—	—	—	1200

SCO Grade

NIB	Exc.	V.G.	Good	Fair	Poor
17000	6500	—	—	—	1200

Gold Grade

NIB	Exc.	V.G.	Good	Fair	Poor
18750	6500	—	—	—	1500

SCO Grade W/Sideplates

NIB	Exc.	V.G.	Good	Fair	Poor
26200	11000	—	—	—	2000

Gold Grade W/Sideplates

NIB	Exc.	V.G.	Good	Fair	Poor
30200	11000	—	—	—	2000

AMERICAN TRAP-COMBO MODELS

MX7

Introduced in 1993. This an over and under trap model that is offered in 12 gauge with 29.5" or 31.5" O/U barrels with either 32" or 34" single barrel. This model has a nonrenewable trigger group feathering fixed coil spring trigger mechanism. The trigger is selective and works in conjunction with the safety catch. The vent rib is ramped on the Combo Trap model. The walnut is custom made to the customer's dimensions

Standard Grade

NIB	Exc.	V.G.	Good	Fair	Poor
5400	2700	—	—	—	1000

MX9

Offered in 12 gauge with 29.5" or 31.5" O/U barrels with 32" or 34" single barrel. All barrels are fitted with MX9 removable inserts to adjust point of impact. Walnut stock has adjustable comb. Comes with screw-in chokes. Trigger group is removable.

Standard Grade

NIB	Exc.	V.G.	Good	Fair	Poor
10000	4500	—	—	—	—

SC3 Grade

NIB	Exc.	V.G.	Good	Fair	Poor
15000	5000	—	—	—	—

SCO Grade

NIB	Exc.	V.G.	Good	Fair	Poor
22500	7000	—	—	—	—

Gold Grade

NIB	Exc.	V.G.	Good	Fair	Poor
25000	7000	—	—	—	—

SCO Grade W/Sideplates

NIB	Exc.	V.G.	Good	Fair	Poor
31750	11000	—	—	—	—

Gold Grade W/Sideplates

NIB	Exc.	V.G.	Good	Fair	Poor
35000	11000	—	—	—	—

MX10

Introduced in 1993 this model features a higher rib and different method of point of impact adjustment. Stock is adjustable for comb height. Offered in 12 gauge with 29.5" or 31.5" O/U barrels with 32" or 34" single barrel.

Standard Grade

NIB	Exc.	V.G.	Good	Fair	Poor
10000	4200	—	—	—	—

SC3 Grade

NIB	Exc.	V.G.	Good	Fair	Poor
15000	5200	—	—	—	—

SCO Grade

NIB	Exc.	V.G.	Good	Fair	Poor
23000	6000	—	—	—	—

Gold Grade

NIB	Exc.	V.G.	Good	Fair	Poor
25250	6500	—	—	—	—

SCO Grade W/Sideplates

NIB	Exc.	V.G.	Good	Fair	Poor
32000	11000	—	—	—	—

Gold Grade W/Sideplates

NIB	Exc.	V.G.	Good	Fair	Poor
36000	11000	—	—	—	—

MX8 Special

This model features a grooved forend, low contour ventilated rib, and adjustable trigger with internal selector. Same barrel combinations as above.

Standard Grade

NIB	Exc.	V.G.	Good	Fair	Poor
8200	3500	—	—	—	1000

SC3 Grade

NIB	Exc.	V.G.	Good	Fair	Poor
13000	4500	—	—	—	1500

SCO Grade

NIB	Exc.	V.G.	Good	Fair	Poor
20500	6000	—	—	—	—

Gold Grade

NIB	Exc.	V.G.	Good	Fair	Poor
23000	6500	—	—	—	—

SCO Grade W/Sideplates

NIB	Exc.	V.G.	Good	Fair	Poor
16000	11000	—	—	—	—

Gold Grade W/Sideplates

NIB	Exc	V.G	Good	Fair	Poor
33500	11000	—	—	—	—

DB81 Special

This model is similar to the above model but features a high ramped ventilated rib. Trigger is adjustable with internal selector.

Standard Grade

NIB	Exc.	V.G.	Good	Fair	Poor
8700	3700	—	—	—	1000

SC3 Grade

NIB	Exc.	V.G.	Good	Fair	Poor
13400	4900	—	—	—	—

SCO Grade

NIB	Exc.	V.G.	Good	Fair	Poor
21000	5700	—	—	—	—

Gold Grade

NIB	Exc.	V.G.	Good	Fair	Poor
23500	6200	—	—	—	—

SCO Grade W/Sideplates

NIB	Exc.	V.G.	Good	Fair	Poor
30000	11000	—	—	—	—

Gold Grade W/Sideplates

NIB	Exc.	V.G.	Good	Fair	Poor
34000	11000	—	—	—	—

COMPETITION MODELS

Competition versions are over and under shotguns in trap, skeet, pigeon, and sporting models. Stock dimensions are based on the particular model chosen. Trap models feature trap stock dimensions and forearm designed for that purpose. The other models also have their own particular specifications. However, prices are based on a common style referred to by

Perazzi as Competition. Thus, all models within this group are priced the same regardless of specific type.

MX7C

Introduced in 1993 this model is offered in 12 gauge with a nonrefillable trigger group. It has a coil spring mechanism, fully selective in conjunction with the safety. Offered in 27.5", 29.5", or 31.5" flat vent rib barrels. Screw in chokes are standard. Walnut stock is custom made to customer's dimensions. The forend is beavertail.

Standard Grade

NIB	Exc.	V.G.	Good	Fair	Poor
4900	2500	—	—	—	750

MX9

This model was introduced in 1993 and features an adjustable comb on the stock with unique vent rib inserts to correct for point of impact. Offered in 12 gauge with 29.5" or 31.5" barrels. Trigger group is removable. Comes standard with screw-in chokes.

Standard Grade

NIB	Exc.	V.G.	Good	Fair	Poor
7600	3500	—	—	—	1000

SC3 Grade

NIB	Exc.	V.G.	Good	Fair	Poor
11500	4500	—	—	—	—

SCO Grade

NIB	Exc.	V.G.	Good	Fair	Poor
18000	6000	—	—	—	—

Gold Grade

NIB	Exc.	V.G.	Good	Fair	Poor
20000	6000	—	—	—	—

SCO Grade W/Sideplates

NIB	Exc.	V.G.	Good	Fair	Poor
28000	11000	—	—	—	—

Gold Grade W/Sideplates

NIB	Exc.	V.G.	Good	Fair	Poor
32000	11000	—	—	—	—

MX10

This model was introduced in 1993 and is offered in 12 gauge and 20 gauge with choice of 29.5" or 31.5" barrel for 12 gauge and 29.5" barrel for 20 gauge. The ventilated rib height is adjustable as is the comb position on the stock. Chokes are fixed. Trigger group is removable with external selection.

Standard Grade

NIB	Exc.	V.G.	Good	Fair	Poor
6000	3500	—	—	—	1000

SC3 Grade

NIB	Exc.	V.G.	Good	Fair	Poor
6600	4500	—	—	—	—

SCO Grade

NIB	Exc.	V.G.	Good	Fair	Poor
20000	5000	—	—	—	—

Gold Grade

NIB	Exc.	V.G.	Good	Fair	Poor
23500	6000	—	—	—	—

SCO Grade W/Sideplates

NIB	Exc.	V.G.	Good	Fair	Poor
30000	11000	—	—	—	—

Gold Grade W/Sideplates

NIB	Exc.	V.G.	Good	Fair	Poor
34000	11000	—	—	—	—

MX8/20

This model was first introduced in 1993. It features a removable trigger group. Available in 20 gauge only with choice of 27.5", 28.375", 29.5" flat ventilated rib barrels. Choice of fixed or screw-in chokes on sporting model. Stock is custom made to customer's dimensions with beavertail forend.

Standard Grade

NIB	Exc.	V.G.	Good	Fair	Poor
6000	3700	—	—	—	1000

SC3 Grade

NIB	Exc.	V.G.	Good	Fair	Poor
10000	4200	—	—	—	—

SCO Grade

NIB	Exc.	V.G.	Good	Fair	Poor
17000	5500	—	—	—	—

Gold Grade

NIB	Exc.	V.G.	Good	Fair	Poor
19000	6000	—	—	—	—

SCO Grade W/Sideplates

NIB	Exc.	V.G.	Good	Fair	Poor
26000	10000	—	—	—	—

Gold Grade W/Sideplates

NIB	Exc.	V.G.	Good	Fair	Poor
30000	10000	—	—	—	—

Extra Grade

NIB	Exc.	V.G.	Good	Fair	Poor
N/A	22000	—	—	—	—

Extra Gold Grade

NIB	Exc.	V.G.	Good	Fair	Poor
N/A	—	—	—	—	—

Extra Model

Same as MX 8/20 but available in 20 gauge only with choice of barrel lengths to 31.5".

Extra Grade

NIB	Exc.	V.G.	Good	Fair	Poor
48500	40000	30000	20000	10000	5000

Extra Gold Grade

NIB	Exc.	V.G.	Good	Fair	Poor
52000	25000	—	—	—	6000

Mirage Special

This model features an adjustable trigger and is available in 12 gauge with choice of 27.5", 28.375", 29.5", or 31.5" ventilated rib barrels.

Standard Grade

NIB	Exc.	V.G.	Good	Fair	Poor
6100	2900	—	—	—	1000

Mirage Special Sporting

Similar to the Mirage Special listed above, but with external trigger selection and screw-in chokes. Offered in 12 gauge only with choice of 27.5", 28.375", or 29.5" vent rib barrels.

Standard Grade

NIB	Exc.	V.G.	Good	Fair	Poor
6400	3750	—	—	—	1250

Mirage Special Sporting Classic

This model features the same basic specifications as the Mirage Special Sporting with the addition of a scroll border on the receiver and triggerguard. The wood is of slightly higher quality. Offered in 12 gauge only with 27.5", 28.375", or 29.5" vent rib barrels.

Standard Grade

NIB	Exc.	V.G.	Good	Fair	Poor
7500	4000	—	—	—	1000

Mirage MX8
Standard Grade

NIB	Exc.	V.G.	Good	Fair	Poor
5800	3000	—	—	—	1000

MX8 Special

This model features a four position adjustable trigger. It also has a low contour rib and a grooved forearm. Offered in 12 only with choice of 29.5" or 31.5" vent rib barrels.

Standard Grade

NIB	Exc.	V.G.	Good	Fair	Poor
6100	3000	—	—	—	1000

SCO Model

This model is similar to the MX8 but offered only in 12 gauge with barrel length from 27.5" to 31.5". The trigger is adjustable instead of removable.

SCO Grade

NIB	Exc.	V.G.	Good	Fair	Poor
17000	6000	—	—	—	1500

Gold Grade

NIB	Exc.	V.G.	Good	Fair	Poor
19000	6000	—	—	—	1500

SCO Grade W/Sideplates

NIB	Exc.	V.G.	Good	Fair	Poor
16000	11000	—	—	—	3000

Gold Grade W/Sideplates

NIB	Exc.	V.G.	Good	Fair	Poor
30000	11000	—	—	—	3000

DB81 Special

This model, available in 12 gauge only, features a high ramped ventilated rib. Barrel length are 29.51, or 31.5". Adjustable trigger standard.

Standard Grade

NIB	Exc.	V.G.	Good	Fair	Poor
7000	3000	—	—	—	—

SC3 Grade

NIB	Exc.	V.G.	Good	Fair	Poor
10500	4000	—	—	—	—

SCO Grade

NIB	Exc.	V.G.	Good	Fair	Poor
17500	6000	—	—	—	—

Gold Grade

NIB	Exc.	V.G.	Good	Fair	Poor
19500	6000	—	—	—	—

SCO Grade W/Sideplates

NIB	Exc.	V.G.	Good	Fair	Poor
26500	10000	—	—	—	—

Gold Grade W/Sideplates

NIB	Exc.	V.G.	Good	Fair	Poor
30500	10000	—	—	—	—

Mirage Special 4-Gauge Set

Similar to the Mirage Special in appearance and specifications but fitted with four barrel sets with 27.62" barrels in 12, 20, 28 gauge, and .410 bore. For 28.37" barrels add $2,000 and for 29.5" barrels add $3,000.

Standard Grade

NIB	Exc.	V.G.	Good	Fair	Poor
14000	6500	5000	4000	3000	1500

SC3 Grade

NIB	Exc.	V.G.	Good	Fair	Poor
21000	6500	5000	4000	3000	—

SCO Grade

NIB	Exc.	V.G.	Good	Fair	Poor
28000	8500	6500	4500	3500	—

Gold Grade

NIB	Exc.	V.G.	Good	Fair	Poor
30000	9500	7500	5500	4500	—

SCO Grade W/Sideplates

NIB	Exc.	V.G.	Good	Fair	Poor
40000	15000	—	—	—	—

Gold Grade W/Sideplates

NIB	Exc.	V.G.	Good	Fair	Poor
44000	15000	—	—	—	—

GAME GUN MODELS

A special set of game shotguns was especially created by Perazzi. It consists of 12, 20, 28 gauge and .410 bore guns with straight grips stocks with extra fancy walnut and special engraving. The retail price of these shotguns is $285,000.

MXI2/12C

Offered in 12 gauge only with 26.75" or 27.5" vent rib barrels. The single selective trigger is nonrefillable. The walnut stock is fitted with a schnabel forend and the receiver gas a light scroll engraved border. The MX12 is supplied with fixed chokes while the MX12C is fitted with 5 screw-in choke tubes. Add $400 to MX12 prices to get MX12C values.

Standard Grade

NIB	Exc.	V.G.	Good	Fair	Poor
6250	3500	—	—	—	1000

SC3 Grade

NIB	Exc.	V.G.	Good	Fair	Poor
9900	4500	—	—	—	—

SCO Grade

NIB	Exc.	V.G.	Good	Fair	Poor
17000	5500	—	—	—	—

Gold Grade

NIB	Exc.	V.G.	Good	Fair	Poor
19000	5500	—	—	—	—

SCO Grade W/Sideplates

NIB	Exc.	V.G.	Good	Fair	Poor
26000	11000	—	—	—	—

Gold Grade W/Sideplates

NIB	Exc	V.G.	Good	Fair	Poor
30000	11000	—	—	—	—

MX20/20C

This model is offered in 20 gauge. It features a nonremovable trigger group. The frame is smaller than 12 gauge. Offered with 26" or 27.5" vent rib barrels. The MX20 has fixed chokes while the MX20C is supplied with 5 screw-in choke tubes. Add $400 to MX20 prices to get MX20C values.

Standard Grade

NIB	Exc.	V.G.	Good	Fair	Poor
8000	3250	—	—	—	1000

SC3 Grade

NIB	Exc.	V.G.	Good	Fair	Poor
10500	4250	—	—	—	1000

SCO Grade

NIB	Exc.	V.G.	Good	Fair	Poor
17000	6250	—	—	—	—

Gold Grade

NIB	Exc.	V.G.	Good	Fair	Poor
20000	6500	—	—	—	—

SCO Grade W/Sideplates

NIB	Exc.	V.G.	Good	Fair	Poor
28000	11000	—	—	—	—

Gold Grade W/Sideplates

NIB	Exc.	V.G.	Good	Fair	Poor
34000	11000	—	—	—	—

MX8/20-8/20C

Introduced in 1993 and offered in 20 gauge with 26" or 27.625" vent rib barrels. The trigger group on this model is removable. The stock is a high grade walnut custom made to customer's own specifications. The forend is round. The MX8/20 is supplied with fixed chokes while the MX8/20C has 5 screw-in choke tubes. Add $400 for MX8/20C values.

Standard Grade

NIB	Exc.	V.G.	Good	Fair	Poor
5800	3250	—	—	—	1000

SC3 Grade

NIB	Exc.	V.G.	Good	Fair	Poor
9900	4250	—	—	—	—

SCO Grade

NIB	Exc.	V.G.	Good	Fair	Poor
17000	6500	—	—	—	—

Gold Grade

NIB	Exc.	V.G.	Good	Fair	Poor
19000	6500	—	—	—	—

SCO Grade W/Sideplates

NIB	Exc.	V.G.	Good	Fair	Poor
26000	11000	—	—	—	—

Gold Grade W/Sideplates

NIB	Exc.	V.G.	Good	Fair	Poor
30000	11000	—	—	—	—

MX28 and MX410

Introduced in 1993 these two models feature a nonremovable trigger group and a special small frame for each. The MX28, .28 gauge, weighs about 5.5 lbs. while the MX410, .410 bore, weighs slightly less. Both are supplied with fixed chokes, flat ribs, custom made stocks, and round forends. Each model is offered with a choice of 26" or 27.5" barrels. Both the MX28 and MX410 are priced the same.

Standard Grade

NIB	Exc.	V.G.	Good	Fair	Poor
11500	7000	6000	4000	3000	1500

SC3 Grade

(Not Available)

SCO Grade

NIB	Exc.	V.G.	Good	Fair	Poor
22500	9000	—	—	—	2000

Gold Grade

NIB	Exc.	V.G.	Good	Fair	Poor
25000	9000	—	—	—	2500

SCO Grade W/Sideplates

NIB	Exc.	V.G.	Good	Fair	Poor
31500	16000	—	—	—	3000

Gold Grade W/Sideplates

NIB	Exc.	V.G.	Good	Fair	Poor
36000	25000	19000	12000	7500	3000

Extra Grade Models

There are three different configurations offered for this model. In Extra Grade they are chambered for 12 gauge and 20 gauge with nonremovable trigger group or 20 gauge with removable trigger group. In Extra Gold Grade they are offered in 12 gauge and 20 gauge with nonremovable trigger group and in 20 gauge with removable group. Twelve gauge guns are offered with 26.75" or 27.5" vent rib barrels while 20 gauge guns can be had with 26" or 27.5" vent rib barrels. The 20 gauge guns with removable trigger groups were first introduced in 1993.

Extra Grade

NIB	Exc.	V.G.	Good	Fair	Poor
48500	20000	—	—	—	5000

Extra Gold Grade

NIB	Exc.	V.G.	Good	Fair	Poor
52000	20000	—	—	—	5000

PERRY PATENT FIREARMS CO.

Newark, New Jersey

Perry Single-Shot Pistol

A .52 caliber breech loading percussion pistol with a 6" round barrel. Blued with walnut grips. The barrel marked "Perry Patent Firearms Co./Newark, N.J." Approximately 200 were made between 1854 and 1856 in two styles.

1st Type-Long, Contoured Triggerguard, Opening Lever

Exc.	V.G.	Good	Fair	Poor
—	—	4000	1750	500

2nd Type S Curved Shorter Triggerguard And An Automatic Primer Feed that Protrudes From The Butt

Exc.	V.G.	Good	Fair	Poor
—	—	3750	1500	500

Perry Carbine

A .54 caliber breech loading percussion carbine with a 20.75" barrel and half length walnut stock secured by one barrel band. Blued with a case hardened lock. Approximately 200 were made. Prospective purchasers are advised to secure a qualified appraisal prior to acquisition.

Courtesy Milwaukee Public Museum, Milwaukee, Wisconsin

Exc.	V.G.	Good	Fair	Poor
—	—	7500	3250	1000

PERRY & GODDARD

RENWICK ARMS CO.

New York, New York

Derringer

A .44 caliber single-shot spur trigger pistol with a 2" octagonal barrel. Blued or silver-plated with walnut or gutta-percha grips. The barrel may be swiveled so that either end can serve as the chamber and is marked "Double Header/ E.S. Renwick." Produced in limited quantities during the 1860s. Prospective purchasers are advised to secure a qualified appraisal prior to acquisition.

Exc.	V.G.	Good	Fair	Poor
—	—	16500	7000	1000

PERUGINI & VISINI
Brescia, Italy

Arms by this maker were imported by W.L. Moore of Westlake Village, California.

Liberty Model

A side-by-side 12, 20, 28 and .410 gauge shotgun having 28" barrels. Anson & Deeley action with a double Purdy lock. Blued overall with checkered walnut stock.

NIB	Exc.	V.G.	Good	Fair	Poor
5000	4000	3500	2500	1250	750

Classic Model

A 12 or 20 gauge double barrel shotgun having a Holland & Holland style sidelock with a double Purdy lock. The barrels 28" in length. Single trigger and automatic ejectors. The side-locks and mounts engraved and blued. Well figured and checkered walnut stock.

NIB	Exc.	V.G.	Good	Fair	Poor
11000	8500	6500	4000	2000	1000

Bolt Action Rifle

A Mauser type bolt action rifle available in a variety of chamberings, with 24" or 26" barrels. Sights not furnished. Well figured checkered walnut stock.

NIB	Exc.	V.G.	Good	Fair	Poor
4000	3250	2500	1500	900	500

Deluxe Bolt Action Rifle

As above with first quality walnut stocks and a case.

NIB	Exc.	V.G.	Good	Fair	Poor
4500	3750	3000	1500	1000	600

Eagle Single-Shot

An Anson & Deeley single-shot rifle fitted with either 24" or 26" barrels, open sights, automatic ejector and adjustable trigger. Stock of checkered walnut.

NIB	Exc.	V.G.	Good	Fair	Poor
5000	4000	3000	1500	1000	600

Boxlock Express Rifle

An Anson & Deeley action double barrel rifle chambered for .444 Marlin or 9.3x74R cartridges. The barrel length is 24" and is fitted with express sights. Double triggers and automatic ejectors. Receiver case hardened and the barrels as well as mounts blued. Checkered walnut stock.

NIB	Exc.	V.G.	Good	Fair	Poor
3250	2500	1750	1200	900	500

Magnum O/U

An Anson & Deeley action Over/Under rifle available .375 Holland & Holland and .458 Winchester Magnum. The barrels 24" in length and fitted with express sights. Double triggers and automatic ejectors. Receiver and barrels blued, the stock of checkered walnut.

NIB	Exc.	V.G.	Good	Fair	Poor
5500	4250	3000	2000	1500	750

Super Express Rifle

A Holland & Holland-style sidelock double barrel rifle. Having 24" barrels fitted with express sights. Available in a variety of chamberings. The receiver and sidelocks either case hardened or finished in the bright and fully engraved. Checkered walnut stock.

NIB	Exc.	V.G.	Good	Fair	Poor
9500	8000	6500	4000	2000	950

Victoria Side-x-Side Rifle

Similar to the Boxlock Express Rifle but chambered for .30-06, 7x65R, or 9.3x74R cartridges. Either 24" or 26" barrels were available. Double triggers and automatic ejectors. Blued with minimal engraving. Stock of checkered walnut.

NIB	Exc.	V.G.	Good	Fair	Poor
6500	5250	4000	3000	1500	750

Selous Side-x-Side Rifle

First quality double barrel express rifle with 24" or 26" barrels. Fully detachable Holland & Holland-style sidelocks, double triggers and automatic ejectors. Fully engraved with well figured checkered walnut stocks.

NIB	Exc.	V.G.	Good	Fair	Poor
22500	17500	12500	6000	3000	1500

PETTINGILL C. S.
New Haven, Connecticut
Rogers, Spencer & Co.
Willowvale, New York

Pocket Revolver

A hammerless, double action .31 caliber percussion revolver having a 4" octagonal barrel. The frame of brass or iron. Blued barrel, the grips of oil finished walnut. The First and Second Models are marked "Pettingill's Patent 1856" as well as "T.K. Austin." The Third Model is marked "Pettengill Patent 1856", and "Raymond and Robitaille Patented 1858." Approximately 400 were manufactured in the late 1850s and early 1860s.

1st Model with Brass Frame

Exc.	V.G.	Good	Fair	Poor
—	—	2500	1000	400

2nd Model with Iron Frame

Exc.	V.G.	Good	Fair	Poor
—	—	1500	600	200

3rd Model, Iron Frame and Improved Action

Exc.	V.G.	Good	Fair	Poor
—	—	1250	400	200

Navy Revolver

As above but in .34 caliber with a 4.5" barrel and a 6-shot cylinder. The frame of iron, blued overall, and the grips of walnut. This model is marked "Pettengill's Patent 1856" and "Raymond & Robitaille Patented 1858." Approximately 900 were manufactured in the late 1850s and early 1860s.

Courtesy Milwaukee Public Museum, Milwaukee, Wisconsin

Exc.	V.G.	Good	Fair	Poor
—	—	1750	700	250

Army Model Revolver

As above but of .44 caliber and fitted with a 7.5" barrel. The frame of iron that is case hardened, the octagonal barrel blued, the grips of oil finished walnut. Early production models are marked as the Navy models, while later production examples are marked "Petingill's Patent 1856, pat'd July 22, 1856 and July 27, 1858." Some examples will be found with government inspector's marks and are worth approximately 25% more. It is believed that 3,400 were made in the 1860s.

Courtesy Milwaukee Public Museum, Milwaukee, Wisconsin

Exc.	V.G.	Good	Fair	Poor
—	—	4500	1500	500

PFANNL, FRANCOIS
Krems, Austria

Erika

A 4.25mm semiautomatic pistol with a hinged barrel assembly. The barrel either 1.5" or 2.25" in length. The grips are marked "Erika". Approximately 3,500 made between 1912 and 1926.

Courtesy Rock Island Auction Company

Exc.	V.G.	Good	Fair	Poor
—	400	300	200	100

PHILLIPS & RODGERS INC.
Conroe, Texas

Medusa Model 47

Introduced in 1996 this unique multi-caliber revolver is designed to chamber, fire, and extract almost any cartridge using 9mm, .357, or .38 cartridges; a total of about 25 different calibers. The barrel lengths are 2.5", 3", 4", 5", or 6". Rubber grips and interchangeable front sights. Finish is matte blue.

NIB	Exc.	V.G.	Good	Fair	Poor
900	700	550	450	—	—

Ruger 50 Conversion

This conversion, executed on a new revolver, converts a .44 Magnum Ruger into a .50 Action Express. Stainless steel or blue with 5-shot cylinder. Barrel length is 6.5".

NIB	Exc.	V.G.	Good	Fair	Poor
1000	800	550	450	—	—

Wilderness Explorer

This bolt action rifle was introduced in 1997 and features an 18" match grade barrel. The boltface and barrel are quick change so four caliber can be used in the same rifle. Synthetic stock. Chambered for .22 Hornet, .218 Bee, .44 Magnum, and .50 AE calibers. Weight is approximately 5.5 lbs.

NIB	Exc.	V.G.	Good	Fair	Poor
N/A	—	—	—	—	—

PHOENIX
Lowell, Massachusetts

Pocket Pistol

A rare .25 ACP semiautomatic pistol with a 2.25" barrel and 6-round magazine. Receiver and slide blued, the grips of hard rubber. Manufactured during the 1920s.

Exc.	V.G.	Good	Fair	Poor
550	400	300	200	100

PHOENIX ARMS
Ontario, California

HP22

A pocket size semiautomatic pistol chambered for the .22 Long Rifle cartridge. Barrel length is 3". Magazine capacity is 11 rounds. Offered in bright chrome or polished blue finish with black checkered grips. Top of gun is fitted with vent rib. Overall length is 4.1" and weight is about 20 oz.

NIB	Exc.	V.G.	Good	Fair	Poor
80	60	50	40	30	20

HP25

This model is the same as above but chambered for the .25 ACP cartridge. Magazine capacity is 10 rounds.

NIB	Exc.	V.G.	Good	Fair	Poor
80	60	50	40	30	20

HP22/HP25 Target

A conversion kit to convert the HP22/HP25 into a target pistol. Kit includes extended vent rib barrel and a convertible 10-round magazine. Finish is either blue or nickel.

NIB	Exc.	V.G.	Good	Fair	Poor
125	100	75	60	—	—

Raven

A small pocket size semiautomatic pistol chambered for the .25 ACP cartridge. Magazine capacity is 6 rounds. Barrel length is 2.4" with fixed sights. Offered in 3 finishes: bright chrome, satin nickel, or polished blue. Grips are either ivory, pink pearl, or black. Overall length is 4.8" and weight is approximately 15 oz.

NIB	Exc.	V.G.	Good	Fair	Poor
65	50	40	30	25	20

PHOENIX ARMS CO.
Liege, Belgium
SEE—Robar et DeKerkhove

PICKERT, FRIEDRICH
Zella-Mehlis, Germany
Arminius Waffenfabrik

This firm produced revolvers bearing the trade name "Arminius". The revolvers manufactured by Pickert of the double action type, with or without exposed hammers. Some models are fitted with ejectors, while others have removable cylinders. Calibers and barrel lengths vary. After WWII, the trade name was acquired by Hermann Wiehauch.

Arminus 7.65mm

A five-shot concealed hammer revolver in 7.65mm caliber. The Arminus head is on the grips.

Photo courtesy James Rankin

Exc.	V.G.	Good	Fair	Poor
275	225	175	125	90

Arminus Single Shot Target Pistol

A single shot target pistol chambered for the 22 caliber cartridge. Some of these were built under the name PICKERT. The Arminus name is seen on the frame.

Photo courtesy James Rankin

Exc.	V.G.	Good	Fair	Poor
900	700	600	400	300

PIEPER, HENRI & NICOLAS
Liege, Belgium

Originally founded by Henri Pieper in 1859, the company was reorganized in 1898 when his son, Nicolas, assumed control. The firm is best known for a series of semiautomatic pistols as described below.

Pieper Model 1907

A 6.35 or 7.65mm semiautomatic pistol featuring a hinged barrel assembly 2.5" in length. Receiver and barrel blued, the grips of hard rubber with the firm's trademark cast in them. The Model 1907 variation does not have a hinged barrel assembly. The Model 1908 is also known as the "Basculant", and the Model 1918 as the "Demontant".

Courtesy Orvel Reichert

Courtesy Orvel Reichert

Exc.	V.G.	Good	Fair	Poor
200	150	125	100	75

Model 1908/Basculant

This is a tipping barrel pistol chambered for the 6.35mm Auto cartridge. Similar in appearance to the Model 1907 this model had several improvements. The front end of the barrel was retained by a pivot bolt and the recoil spring rod had a hook that engaged the lug on the slide.

Exc.	V.G.	Good	Fair	Poor
225	175	150	125	100

Courtesy Orvel Reichert

Pieper Bayard Revolver

In competition with the Nagant gas seal revolver, Henri Pieper developed a superior design. Revolvers of this type have 5" barrels and are chambered for 8mm cartridges. The first model of this revolver had an automatic ejection system, while the second version utilized a swing-out cylinder. Standard finish is blued, with checkered hard rubber grips.

Exc.	V.G.	Good	Fair	Poor
300	250	200	150	100

Legia

This model was patterned after that of the Browning, and is chambered for the 6.35mm cartridge. The standard magazine holds 6 cartridges but a 10-round magazine was also available.

Exc.	V.G.	Good	Fair	Poor
200	150	125	100	75

Bayard

A 6.35, 7.65 or 9mm short semiautomatic pistol with a 2.5" barrel. Standard magazine capacity 6 rounds. The slide stamped "Anciens Etablissement Pieper Liege, Belgium".

Exc.	V.G.	Good	Fair	Poor
200	150	125	100	75

PILSEN, ZBROVKA
Pilsen, Czechoslovakia

Pocket Pistol

Essentially a Model 1910 Browning semiautomatic pistol without a grip safety, this pistol was of 7.65mm caliber and had a 3.5" barrel with a 6-round magazine. The slide is marked "Akciova Spolecnost drive Skodovny zavody Zbrovka Plzen." Standard finish is blued, the grips of hard rubber. Manufactured during the 1920s.

Exc.	V.G.	Good	Fair	Poor
250	200	150	125	100

PIOTTI
Brescia, Italy
Importer-W. L. Moore
Scottsdale, Arizona

This Italian gunmaking firm is located in Gardone Val Trompia in the province of Brescia. Its shotguns are hand crafted and limited to a few each year. Each gun is made to individual specifications. Many consider them one of the best double shotguns made in the world today. Actions are either Anson & Deeley boxlock or Holland & Holland sidelock. Several features are offered on these shotguns at no additional cost: type of stock and forearm, barrel length and chokes, rib, action shape and finish.

Other features are considered extra cost options and will affect the value of the gun. There are: single triggers, detachable sidelocks, automatic safety, recoil pads, upgraded wood, engraving, and multi-gauge sets. With the exception of a few grades Piotti guns are available in 10, 12, 16, 20, and 28 gauge, as well as .410 bore. Depending on gauge barrel lengths are from 25" to 32".

Model Piuma (BSEE)

This model is the firm's standard boxlock offering. Available in 12 gauge to .410 bore it features ejectors and a scalloped frame. Fine scroll and rosette engraving is standard.

NOTE: Around serial number 9000, or 1989, Piotti began building the Model BSEE to the same standards as the King Model. Therefore, guns below serial number 9000 deduct about 40% from prices listed below.

NIB	Exc.	V.G.	Good	Fair	Poor
14250	10500	7500	—	—	—

Westlake Model

This was Rizzine's second quality model. It features a case colored receiver with gold line work. Offered in 12, 16, and 20 gauge. Discontinued in 1989.

NIB	Exc.	V.G.	Good	Fair	Poor
8500	6250	4750	—	—	—

Monte Carlo Model

This model was a less expensive version of the King Model. It had H&H or Purdey-style engraving. It was discontinued in 1989 and was upgraded and became part of the King Model. This occured around serial number 9000.

NIB	Exc.	V.G.	Good	Fair	Poor
14000	10000	7000	—	—	—

Model King No. I

This model features a sidelock with fine line scroll engraving with full coverage. A gold crown is inlaid on the top lever prior to 1989. H&H or Purdey-style engraving. Select walnut with hand checkering is standard. Chambered from 10 gauge to .410 bore.

NIB	Exc.	V.G.	Good	Fair	Poor
26750	20000	15000	—	—	—

Model Lunik

This model is fitted with Holland & Holland sidelocks. Engraving is Renaissance style relief cut scroll engraving. A gold crown is inlaid on the top lever. Offered in gauges from 10 to .410 bore.

NIB	Exc.	V.G.	Good	Fair	Poor
28600	21000	16000	—	—	—

Model Monaco

This sidelock model features all of the best that Piotti has to offer and extra attention is paid to hand work and fitting. Only the finest European hardwoods are used. Available in 10 gauge to 410 bore. Offered with three different types of engraving designated No. 1, No. 2, and No. 4.

Monaco No. 1 or No. 2

NIB	Exc.	V.G.	Good	Fair	Poor
35500	26500	20000	—	—	—

Monaco No. 3

38500	28500	22500	—	—	—

Monaco No. 4

NIB	Exc.	V.G.	Good	Fair	Poor
46750	35000	27500	—	—	—

Over and Under Gun

This model features King 2 engraving which has a light border scroll with 10% coverage. Custom engraving patterns available at extra charge.

NIB	Exc.	V.G.	Good	Fair	Poor
44750	33500	—	—	—	—

Model King Extra

This model is similar to the King No. 1 but with the addition of a number of engraving styles from English to game scenes with gold inlays. Because of the wide variety of engraving patterns offered on this model it is advisable to secure a qualified appraisal before purchase.

PIRKO
SEE—Austrian Military Firearms

PLAINFIELD MACHINE CO.
Dunelien, New Jersey

Super Enforcer
A cut-down version of the U.S. M1 Carbine with a 12" barrel and pistol grip. The finish is blued and stocks are walnut.

Exc.	V.G.	Good	Fair	Poor
250	200	175	125	100

NOTE: This is classified as a short barrel rifle by the ATF and must be registered as such. Proceed with caution. All NFA rules apply.

M1 Carbine
A commercial reproduction of the U.S. M1 Carbine. The finish is blued. Walnut stock.

Exc.	V.G.	Good	Fair	Poor
300	225	150	100	75

MI Paratrooper Carbine.
As above with a folding wire buttstock and walnut forend.

Exc.	V.G.	Good	Fair	Poor
350	275	200	125	100

PLAINFIELD ORDNANCE CO.
Middlesex, New Jersey

Model 71
A stainless steel .22 caliber semiautomatic pistol with a 10-shot magazine and 1" barrel. Also available in .25 ACP and conversion kits were available.

Conversion Kit
Exc.	V.G.	Good	Fair	Poor
50	40	30	25	20

.22 or .25 Caliber Pistol
Exc.	V.G.	Good	Fair	Poor
150	125	100	75	50

Model 72
As above except with an alloy frame.
Exc.	V.G.	Good	Fair	Poor
150	125	100	75	50

PLANT'S MANUFACTURING CO.
New Haven, Connecticut

Army Model Revolver
A large single action revolver chambered for a .42 caliber cup primed cartridge that loads from the front of the cylinder. Barrel length 6" and of octagonal form with a rib. And the frame is made of either brass or iron. Finish is blued, with walnut or rosewood grips. Interchangeable percussion cylinders also were made for these revolvers. If present, the values would be increased approximately 30%. This revolver was marketed by Merwin & Bray, and there were approximately 1,500 of the 1st and 2nd Models manufactured and 10,000 of the 3rd Model in the 1860s.

1st Model Brass Frame
Marked "Plant's Mfg. Co. New Haven, Ct." on the barrel, "M & B" on the side of the frame, and "Patented July 12, 1859" on the cylinder. Approximately 100 manufactured.

Exc.	V.G.	Good	Fair	Poor
—	—	1750	800	300

1st Model Iron Frame
As above with an iron frame. Approximately 500 made.

Exc.	V.G.	Good	Fair	Poor
—	—	1750	800	300

2nd Model Rounded Brass Frame
This model is distinguished by the markings "Merwin & Bray, New York" on the frame and the patent date "July 21, 1863". Approximately 300 made.

Exc.	V.G.	Good	Fair	Poor
—	—	2250	1100	400

2nd Model Iron Frame
As above with an iron frame.

Exc.	V.G.	Good	Fair	Poor
—	—	1700	750	300

3rd Model
As above with a flat brass frame.

Courtesy Milwaukee Public Museum, Milwaukee, Wisconsin

Exc.	V.G.	Good	Fair	Poor
—	—	900	350	150

Pocket Revolver
Similar to the Army model described above except chambered for .30 caliber cartridges. Barrel length 3.5", five-shot cylinder. The frame normally silver plated, barrel and cylinder blued and the grips of rosewood or walnut. This model is encountered with a variety of retailer's markings: Eagle Arms Co., New York, "Reynolds, Plant & Hotchkiss, New Haven, Ct.," and Merwin & Bray Firearms Co., N.Y." Approximately 20,000 were made.

Courtesy Milwaukee Public Museum, Milwaukee, Wisconsin

Exc.	V.G.	Good	Fair	Poor
—	—	450	200	100

POLY-TECHNOLOGIES, INC.
China
Importer-Keng's
Riverdale, Georgia
Distributor-PTK Int.
Atlanta, Georgia

SKS

A semiautomatic rifle chambered for the 7.62x39mm cartridge with a 20.5" barrel and 10-shot fixed magazine, based on the Soviet Siminov carbine. Finish is blued, and the stock and hand guard are made of a Chinese hardwood.

NIB	Exc.	V.G.	Good	Fair	Poor
150	100	80	70	50	35

AKS-762

A semiautomatic version of the Chinese-type 56 Assault rifle chambered for the 7.62x39mm cartridge with a 16.5" barrel. Furnished with a 20-round magazine and a Chinese bayonet. The finish is blued, and the stock is hardwood.

NIB	Exc.	V.G.	Good	Fair	Poor
150	100	85	70	60	50

AK-47/S

Chambered for the 7.62x39 cartridge.

NIB	Exc.	V.G.	Good	Fair	Poor
500	400	325	250	200	150

NOTE: With a Soviet style bayonet-Add $15.

M-14/S

A reproduction of the U.S. M14 rifle chambered for the 7.62mm cartridge with a 22" barrel and 20-round magazine. Finish is blued and the stock is of hardwood.

NIB	Exc.	V.G.	Good	Fair	Poor
400	300	250	200	150	100

POINTER
Hopkins & Allen
Norwich, Connecticut

Single-Shot Derringer

An unmarked Hopkins & Allen single-shot pistol stamped "Pointer" on the barrel. Barrel length 2.75", caliber .22, frame of nickel-plated brass. The barrel swings sideways for loading. Bird's-head walnut grips. It is believed that about 2,500 were made between 1870 and 1890.

Exc.	V.G.	Good	Fair	Poor
—	—	450	200	100

POND, LUCIUS, W.
Worchester, Massachusetts

Pocket Revolver

A single action, spur trigger .32 caliber revolver with octagonal barrels of 4", 5", or 6" length. The barrel top strap and cylinder pivot upwards for loading. Made with either brass or iron frames. A screwdriver is fitted in the butt. As these revolvers were an infringement of Rollin White's patent, they were discontinued. Some revolvers are to be found with the inscription "Manuf'd. for Smith & Wesson Pat'd. April 5, 1855." These examples are worth approximately 20% more than the values listed below.

Courtesy Milwaukee Public Museum, Milwaukee, Wisconsin

Courtesy Milwaukee Public Museum, Milwaukee, Wisconsin

Brass Framed Revolver

Exc.	V.G.	Good	Fair	Poor
—	—	650	300	100

Iron Framed Revolver

Exc.	V.G.	Good	Fair	Poor
—	—	550	250	75

Separate Chamber Revolver

To avoid the Rollin White patent, this revolver is chambered for .22 or .32 caliber rimfire cartridges that fit into separate steel chamber inserts that can be removed from the front of the cylinder for loading. The .22 caliber version has a 3.5" octagonal barrel with a 7-round unfluted cylinder; the .32 caliber version has a 4", 5", or 6" octagonal barrel and 6-shot unfluted cylinder. Frames are of silver-plated brass; and the barrels and cylinders are blued. Grips of walnut. Standard markings include "L.W. Pond, Worcester, Mass." and patent dates. Approximately 2,000 manufactured in .22 caliber and 5,000 in .32 caliber between 1863 and 1870.

.22 Caliber Version

Exc.	V.G.	Good	Fair	Poor
—	—	900	400	150

.32 Caliber Version

Exc.	V.G.	Good	Fair	Poor
—	—	900	400	150

PORTER, P. W.
New York, New York

Turret Revolver

An extremely rare 9-shot vertical cylinder .41 caliber percussion revolver with a 5.25" round barrel. The triggerguard is also a lever that turns the cylinder and cocks the hammer. An automatic primer system is also fitted to this revolver. Manufactured during the 1850s in an unknown quantity.

Exc.	V.G.	Good	Fair	Poor
—	—	16500	8000	1000

Turret Rifle

A 9-shot vertical cylinder .44 caliber rifle with either a 26" or 28" octagonal barrel. The only markings are "Address P.W. Porter/New York." Four variations of this rifle are known and the 22" barreled carbine would command a 25% premium. Approximately 1,250 were manufactured during the 1850s.

1st Model with Canister Magazine

Fitted with a 30-shot round canister magazine over the turret, this model was made in Tennessee and is extremely rare. Most often the canisters are not encountered and values reflect this. Approximately 25 were made.

Exc.	V.G.	Good	Fair	Poor
—	—	22500	8500	2000

2nd Model (New York)

Exc.	V.G.	Good	Fair	Poor
—	—	9000	4250	1000

3rd Model (New York)

This model has a screw-off cover over the magazine.

Exc.	V.G.	Good	Fair	Poor
—	—	9500	4750	1000

4th Model (New York)

As above but without an automatic primer magazine and the nipples are exposed.

Exc.	V.G.	Good	Fair	Poor
—	—	8000	3750	750

POWELL, W. & SON LTD.
Birmingham, England
SEE—British Double Guns

PRAGA, ZBROVKA
Prague, Czechoslovakia

Established in 1918 by A. Novotny, this company ceased operations in 1926.

VZ2L

A 7.65mm semiautomatic pistol patterned after the Model 1910 Browning, but without a grip safety. Barrel length 3.5", magazine capacity 6 rounds, grips of wood. The slide is marked "Zbrojowka Praga Praha."

Exc.	V.G.	Good	Fair	Poor
350	250	200	150	100

Praga 1921

A 6.35mm semiautomatic pistol with a slide of stamped steel cut with a finger groove at the front. Folding trigger. The barrel 2" in length. The slide is marked "Zbrojowka Praga Praha Patent Cal 6.35." The grips of molded plastic, with the name "Praga" cast in them. A dangerous feature of this pistol is that it is striker-fired with no hammer and is intended to be carried fully loaded and cocked in the pocket with absolutely no safety of any kind. The folding trigger does not spring out until the slide is drawn back slightly by using the finger groove in the front of it.

Exc.	V.G.	Good	Fair	Poor
325	225	200	150	100

PRAIRIE GUN WORKS
Winnipeg, Manitoba

M-15

This is a lightweight mountain rifle chambered for .22-250, 6mm-284, .25-284, 6.5-284, 7mm-08, .308 Win., and most short calibers.Built on a Remington 700 action with 20" lightweight barrel. Stock is Kevlar and comes in either green, black or grey. Barrel length is usually 20". Weight is approximately 4.75 lbs.

NIB	Exc.	V.G.	Good	Fair	Poor
1750	1350	—	—	—	—

M-18

Similar to the above model but chambered for long action calibers and fitted with barrel lengths from 22" to 24". Weight is approximately 5.25 lbs.

NIB	Exc.	V.G.	Good	Fair	Poor
1750	1350	—	—	—	—

PRANDELLI & GASPARINI
Brescia, Italy
Importer-Richland Arms Co.
Blissfield, Michigan

Boxlock Side-by-side Shotgun

A good quality double barrel 12 or 20 gauge shotgun with 26" or 28" barrels. Single selective trigger, automatic ejectors and an Anson & Deeley action. Blued, stock of select walnut.

Exc.	V.G.	Good	Fair	Poor
1500	1150	900	700	450

Sidelock Side-x-side Shotgun

Similar to the above, but with full sidelocks.

Exc.	V.G.	Good	Fair	Poor
2500	2150	1500	900	500

Boxlock Over/Under Shotgun

An Over/Under double barrel 12 or 20 gauge shotgun with 26" or 28" barrels, single triggers and automatic ejectors. Blued, with select walnut stock.

Exc.	V.G.	Good	Fair	Poor
1750	1250	950	700	350

Sidelock Over/Under Shotgun

As above with full sidelocks.

Exc.	V.G.	Good	Fair	Poor
3000	2500	1800	950	450

PRATT, GEORGE
Middletown, Connecticut

Trap Gun

A doubled barreled, stationary burglar alarm or animal trap gun that is chambered for .38 caliber centerfire. The barrel is 4" in length, and all of the components are made of cast iron with a galvanized finish. Barrels and action are mounted on a round base, which can turn 360 degrees. The patent date "Dec. 18, 1883" is marked on the gun. There were many manufactured between 1880 and the early 1890s.

Exc.	V.G.	Good	Fair	Poor
—	—	750	400	150

PRATT, H.
Roxbury, Massachusetts

Under Hammer Pistol

A .31 caliber percussion single-shot pistol with an 8.5" octagonal barrel. The frame marked "H. Pratt's/ Patent." Manufactured during the 1850s.

Exc.	V.G.	Good	Fair	Poor
—	—	1200	600	200

PRECISION SMALL ARMS
Beverly Hills, California

PSA-25

This is a semiautomatic pistol chambered for the .25 ACP. The barrel length is 2.13". Magazine capacity is 6 rounds. The frame and slide is steel alloy. Weight is 9.5 oz. Overall length is 4.11". Grips are black polymer. Standard finish is black oxide.

NIB	Exc.	V.G.	Good	Fair	Poor
225	175	150	125	100	75

NOTE: For brushed chrome finish add $50 and for stainless steel add $75.

Featherweight Model

Same as above but with aluminum frame and chrome slide with gold plated trigger.

NIB	Exc.	V.G.	Good	Fair	Poor
400	300	250	200	150	100

Diplomat Model

Black oxide with gold highlights and ivory grips.

NIB	Exc.	V.G.	Good	Fair	Poor
625	500	400	—	—	—

Montreaux Model

Gold plated with ivory grips.

NIB	Exc.	V.G.	Good	Fair	Poor
690	550	400	—	—	—

Renaissance Model

Same as above but with hand engraved steel frame and slide. Antique stain chrome finish.

NIB	Exc.	V.G.	Good	Fair	Poor
1100	900	600	450	—	—

Imperiale

Inlaid gold filigree over blue with scrimshawed ivory grips.

NIB	Exc.	V.G.	Good	Fair	Poor
3600	2750	—	—	—	—

PREMIER
Italy and Spain

A trade name used by various retailers on shotguns manufactured in Italy and Spain that were imported during the late 1950s and early 1960s.

Regent Side-x-Side Shotgun

A double barrel shotgun with 26" to 30" barrels available in all standard gauges. Receiver blued, stock of walnut. Normally found with a pistol grip and beavertail forend.

Exc.	V.G.	Good	Fair	Poor
350	250	200	150	100

Regent Magnum

As above but chambered for the 3.5" 10 gauge Magnum cartridge. Barrels 32" in length and choked full and full.

Exc.	V.G.	Good	Fair	Poor
400	300	250	200	150

Brush King

Identical to the Regent Model except that it is fitted with 22" modified and improved cylinder barrels and a straight grip English style stock.

Exc.	V.G.	Good	Fair	Poor
400	300	250	200	150

Ambassador Model

A more ornate version of the Regent Model.

Exc.	V.G.	Good	Fair	Poor
450	350	300	250	175

Presentation Custom Grade

A custom-order shotgun with game scenes as well as gold and silver inlays.

Exc.	V.G.	Good	Fair	Poor
1500	950	600	500	400

PRESCOTT, E. A.
Worcester, Massachusetts

Percussion Pocket Revolver

A .31 caliber percussion spur trigger revolver with either 4" or 4.25" octagonal barrel and a 6-shot cylinder. The frame of brass, and the grips of walnut. It is believed that approximately 100 were manufactured during 1860 and 1861.

Exc.	V.G.	Good	Fair	Poor
—	—	1750	700	200

Pocket Revolver

A .22 or .32 spur trigger revolver with a barrel of either 3" or 4" length. The .22 caliber version has a 7-shot cylinder and the .32 caliber version a 6-shot cylinder. The standard markings are "E.A. Prescott Worchester Mass. Pat. Oct. 2, 1860." Approximately 1,000 were manufactured between 1862 and 1867.

Exc.	V.G.	Good	Fair	Poor
—	—	750	300	100

Belt Revolver

Although similar in appearance to early Smith & Wesson revolvers, the Prescott has a solid frame. Available in either .22 or .32 caliber, the .22 caliber model has a 3" barrel and the .32 caliber a 5.75" barrel. Markings are identical found on the Pocket Revolver. Approximately 300 were manufactured between 1861 and 1863.

Exc.	V.G.	Good	Fair	Poor
—	—	750	300	100

Navy Revolver

A single action revolver fitted with a conventional trigger, chambered for .38 rimfire cartridges with a 7.25" octagonal barrel. The unfluted cylinder holds 6-shots. The frame is of either silver-plated brass or blued iron; and the barrel and cylinder are blued, with walnut grips. The barrel marked "E.A. Prescott, Worcester, Mass. Pat. Oct. 2, 1860." It is believed that several hundred were manufactured between 1861 and 1863. The Iron frame model will bring a small premium.

Courtesy Milwaukee Public Museum, Milwaukee, Wisconsin

Exc.	V.G.	Good	Fair	Poor
—	—	1250	500	200

Army Revoilver

Similar in appearance to the Navy model but with a larger frame. Chambered for .44 caliber rimfire cartridge. Fitted with a 9" octagon barrel with extractor rod and loading gate on right side of frame. Very rare.

Exc.	V.G.	Good	Fair	Poor
—	—	16500	7000	—

PRETORIA
Pretoria, South Africa
SEE—PAF

PRINZ
Germany
Importer-Helmut Hofmann
Placitas, New Mexico

Grade I Bolt Action Rifle

A high quality bolt action rifle chambered for the .243, .30-06, .308, 7mm Remington Magnum or the .300 Winchester Magnum cartridges. Barrel length 24", double-set triggers available. Finish is blued, stock of oil-finished select walnut. Introduced in 1989.

NIB	Exc.	V.G.	Good	Fair	Poor
500	400	325	275	225	150

Grade 2 Bolt Action Rifle

As above with a rosewood forend tip and pistol grip cap.

NIB	Exc.	V.G.	Good	Fair	Poor
550	450	350	300	250	150

Tip Up Rifle

A high quality single-shot rifle available in a variety of American cartridges. Barrel length 24" and not furnished with sights. Finish blued, stock of select walnut.

NIB	Exc.	V.G.	Good	Fair	Poor
2200	1700	1300	800	550	300

Model 85 "Princess"

A combination 12 gauge shotgun and rifle with 24" or 26" barrels, double triggers, and automatic ejectors. Finish blued, stock of select walnut.

NIB	Exc.	V.G.	Good	Fair	Poor
1500	1250	900	650	500	300

PRITCHETT, POTTS & HUNT
SEE—English Military Firearms

PROFESSIONAL ORDNANCE, INC.
Ontario, California

Carbon-15 Pistol-Type 97

Introduced in 1996 this semiautomatic pistol is built on a carbon fiber upper and lower receiver. Chambered for the 5.56

cartridge it has a 7.25" fluted stainless steel barrel. Ghost ring sights are standard. Magazine is AR-15 compatible. Quick detach compensator. Furnished with a 10-round magazine. Weight is approximately 46 oz.

NOTE: This pistol has several options which will affect value.

NIB	Exc.	V.G.	Good	Fair	Poor
960	750	600	500	—	—

Carbon-15 Rifle-Type 97

Similar to the above model but fitted with a 16" barrel, quick detachable buttstock, quick detach compensator, Weaver type mounting base. Overall length is 35". Weight is about 3.9 lbs.

NIB	Exc.	V.G.	Good	Fair	Poor
1120	900	700	550	—	—

Carbon -15 Rifle-Type 97S

Introduced in 2000 this rifle incorporated several new features. Its foregrip is double walled and insulated with a sheet of ultra-lightweight amumina silica ceramic fiber. The recoil buffer has been increased in size by 30% for less recoil. A new ambidextrous safety has been added, and a new multi carry silent sling with Hogue grip is standard. Weight is approximately 4.3 lbs.

NIB	Exc.	V.G.	Good	Fair	Poor
1285	1025	—	—	—	—

Carbon-15 Pistol-Type 21

Introduced in 1999 this model features a light profile stainless steel 7.25" barrel. Ghost ring sights are standard. Optional recoil compensator. A 30-round magazine is standard until supplies are exhausted. Weight is about 40 oz.

NIB	Exc.	V.G.	Good	Fair	Poor
900	725	600	500	—	—

Carbon-15 Rifle-Type 21

This model is fitted with a 16" light profile stainless steel barrel. Quick detachable stock, weaver mounting base. Introduced in 1999. Weight is approximately 3.9 lbs.

NIB	Exc.	V.G.	Good	Fair	Poor
988	800	650	550	—	—

PROTECTION
Unknown

Protection Pocket Revolver

A .28 caliber percussion spur trigger revolver with a 3.25" octagonal barrel and 6-shot cylinder roll engraved with a police arrest scene. The frame of brass and grips of walnut. The cylinder is marked "Protection". Approximately 1,000 were manufactured during the late 1850s and early 1860s.

1st Model Roll Engraved Cylinder

Exc.	V.G.	Good	Fair	Poor
—	—	700	300	100

2nd Model Plain Cylinder Above Serial No. 650

Exc.	V.G.	Good	Fair	Poor
—	—	600	250	100

PULASKI ARMORY
Pulaski, Tennessee

Founded in 1861, this firm produced rifles for the State of Tennessee. Overall length 48-1/2" - 49-1/2"; round barrels 32-1/2" - 33-1/4"; caliber .54. Resemble U.S. Model 1841 Rifles except without patchbox; had single screw sporting locks with diamond- shaped ferrules; usually marked on barrel "PULASKI T. C.S.A. 61." Production estimated to be about 300.

Prospective purchasers are strongly advised to secure an expert appraisal prior to acquisition.

Exc.	V.G.	Good	Fair	Poor
—	—	10000	5000	1500

PURDEY, J. & SONS LTD.
London, England
SEE ALSO—British Double Guns

Perhaps the finest manufacturer of shotguns, double barrel and bolt action rifles in the world. Virtually all their products are made on special order and it is impossible to establish general values for their products. Prospective purchasers are advised to seek qualified guidance prior to the acquisition of any arms made by this maker. The prices listed below are for standard guns as of 1999 with no extras. Always seek expert assistance before a sale of this size.

Hammerless Ejector Side-By-Side Game Gun

Available in 12, 16, 20, 28, and .410 bore. Engraved sidelocks.

NIB	Exc.	V.G.	Good	Fair	Poor
48000	—	—	—	—	—

NOTE: For 28 and .410 bore guns add an additional $3,000.

Hammerless Ejector Over/Under Gun

This gun is offered in 12, 16, 20, 28, and .410 bore with sidelocks.

NIB	Exc.	V.G.	Good	Fair	Poor
61000	—	—	—	—	—

NOTE: For 28 and .410 bore guns add an additional $3,500.

Double Barreled Rifle

A side-by-side double rifle with sidelocks. It can be built in any caliber. Prices listed below are for new gun in various bore sizes:

.300 bore-$77,000	.375 bore-$77,500
.470 bore-$80,500	.577 bore-$90,000
.600 bore-$92,000	

Courtesy Butterfield & Butterfield

PYRENEES
Hendaye, France

Founded in 1923 and still in operation today, this company has produced a variety of models. The most popular of which was the "Unique" series. Prior to 1939, a variety of trade names were marked on their products such as the following: Superior, Capitan, Cesar, Chantecler, Chimere Renoir, Colonial, Prima, Rapid Maxima, Reina, Demon, Demon-marine, Ebac, Elite, Gallia, Ixor, Le Majestic, St. Hubert, Selecta, Sympathique, Touriste, Le Sanspariel, Le Tout Acier, Mars, Perfect, Triomphe Francais, Unis & Vindex. Following 1939 this company's products are simply stamped "Unique".

Model 10 Unique
A 6.35mm semiautomatic pistol similar to the Model 1906 Browning. The slide is marked "Le Veritable Pistolet Francais Unique." Introduced in 1923.

Exc.	V.G.	Good	Fair	Poor
250	175	150	100	75

Model 11
As above with a grip safety and loaded chamber indicator.

Exc.	V.G.	Good	Fair	Poor
275	200	175	125	100

Model 12
As above but without the loaded chamber indicator.

Exc.	V.G.	Good	Fair	Poor
250	175	150	100	75

Model 13
As above with a 7-shot magazine.

Exc.	V.G.	Good	Fair	Poor
250	175	150	100	75

Model 14
As above with a 9-shot magazine.

Exc.	V.G.	Good	Fair	Poor
250	175	150	100	75

Model 15
As above but in 7.65mm caliber. Introduced in 1923.

Exc.	V.G.	Good	Fair	Poor
250	175	150	100	75

Model 16
As above with a 7-shot magazine.

Exc.	V.G.	Good	Fair	Poor
250	175	150	100	75

Model 17
As above with a 9-shot magazine.

Exc.	V.G.	Good	Fair	Poor
300	250	200	150	100

Model 18
A 7.65mm caliber semiautomatic pistol patterned after the Model 1920 Browning but without a grip safety.

Exc.	V.G.	Good	Fair	Poor
250	175	150	100	75

Model 19
As above with a 7-shot magazine.

Exc.	V.G.	Good	Fair	Poor
250	175	150	100	75

Model 20
As above but with a 9-shot magazine.

Exc.	V.G.	Good	Fair	Poor
275	200	175	125	100

Model 21
As above except chambered for the 9mm short cartridge.

Exc.	V.G.	Good	Fair	Poor
275	200	175	125	100

NOTE: During World War II production at this company was taken over by the Nazis. Consequently, the various models listed above will be found with German inspection marks. These arms are worth approximately 25% more than the values listed.

POSTWAR UNIQUE

Model BCF66

A 9mm short semiautomatic pistol with a 3.5" barrel, open top slide and external hammer. The slide marked "Armes Unique Hendaye BP France." Finish blued, grips of plastic.

Exc.	V.G.	Good	Fair	Poor
250	175	150	125	100

Model C

Virtually identical to the Model 17 listed above. The slide marked "7.65 Court 9 coups Unique." Finish blued, plastic grips with the trademark "PF" in a circle cast into them.

Exc.	V.G.	Good	Fair	Poor
225	150	125	100	75

Model D

A .22 caliber semiautomatic pistol with barrels ranging from 4" to 7.5" in length. The 7.5" barreled version fitted with a muzzle brake. Magazine capacity 10 rounds. Finish blued, plastic grips.

Exc.	V.G.	Good	Fair	Poor
250	175	150	125	100

Model Des 69

As above with better quality sights, special trigger and improved grips.

Exc.	V.G.	Good	Fair	Poor
300	250	200	175	125

Model DES/VO

Identical to the Model D but chambered for .22 caliber short cartridges.

Exc.	V.G.	Good	Fair	Poor
250	175	150	125	100

Model F

Identical to the Model C except chambered for 9mm short cartridges. Magazine capacity 8 rounds.

Exc.	V.G.	Good	Fair	Poor
250	175	150	125	100

Model L

Similar to the Model D except chambered for .22, .32 ACP, and 9mm short cartridges. Available with either a steel or alloy frame.

Exc.	V.G.	Good	Fair	Poor
275	225	200	150	125

Model 2000

Courtesy John J. Stimson, Jr.

NIB	Exc.	V.G.	Good	Fair	Poor
1250	950	—	—	—	—

QUACKENBUSH
Herkimer, New York

Quackenbush Safety Cartridge Rifle

A single shot, takedown boy's rifle chambered for .22 rimfire cartridges in either .22 short or .22 long. Barrel length 18". Weight was about 4.5 lbs. All metal parts nickel-plated. The breech swings to the side for loading. Stock of walnut. Manufactured between 1886 and about 1920. Approximately 50,000 were produced.

Courtesy Mike Stuckslager

Exc.	V.G.	Good	Fair	Poor
750	500	250	150	100

Junior Safety Rifle

Same as above but with skeleton stock. Built between 1893 and 1920. About 7,000 guns were manufactured. Weight was about 4 lbs.

Exc.	V.G.	Good	Fair	Poor
750	500	250	150	100

Bicycle Rifle

Chambered for the .22 cartridge this rifle was fitted with a 12" barrel. Skeleton wire pistol grip. This rifle may be classified as an "Any Other Weapon" and be subject to all NFA rules. Proceed with caution.

Exc.	V.G.	Good	Fair	Poor
850	550	350	200	150

QUINABAUG MFG. CO.
Southridge, Massachusetts

Under Hammer Pistol

A .31 caliber percussion under hammer pistol with barrels from 3" to 8" in length. Frame of blued iron, the grips of walnut or maple. The top of the frame is marked "Quinabaug Rifle M'g Co. Southbridge, Mass." The barrels are normally marked "E. Hutchings & Co. Agents". Manufactured during the 1850s.

Exc.	V.G.	Good	Fair	Poor
—	—	1100	500	200

R

R.E.
Valencia, Spain

The initials "R.E." stand for "Republica Espana". This copy of the Spanish Army Model 1921, also known as the Astra 400, was produced between 1936 and 1939 during the Spanish Civil War by the Republican forces. This variation can be identified by the "RE" monogram on the butt and the absence of any manufacturer's stampings.

Exc.	V.G.	Good	Fair	Poor
350	250	200	150	100

R. G. INDUSTRIES
Miami, Florida
Rohm Gmbh
Sontheim/Brenz, Germany

An importer of inexpensive handguns, which ceased operations in 1986.

RG-25

A .25 caliber semiautomatic pistol available with either a blued or chrome-plated finish.

Exc.	V.G.	Good	Fair	Poor
75	65	50	35	25

RG-16

A double barrel .22 caliber chrome-plated derringer.

Exc.	V.G.	Good	Fair	Poor
75	65	50	35	25

RG-17

As above except chambered for. 38 special cartridge.

Exc.	V.G.	Good	Fair	Poor
90	80	70	50	25

RG-14

A .22 caliber double action revolver with a 4" barrel and 6-shot cylinder. Blued finish, plastic grips.

Exc.	V.G.	Good	Fair	Poor
90	80	70	50	25

RG-30

A .22 l.r. or Magnum double action revolver. Blued finish, plastic grips.

Exc.	V.G.	Good	Fair	Poor
75	65	50	35	25

RG-40

A .38 special double action revolver with swing-out cylinder. Blued finish, plastic grips.

Exc.	V.G.	Good	Fair	Poor
90	80	70	50	25

RG-57

A .357 or .44 Magnum double action revolver with 6-shot cylinder. Blued finish, checkered wood grips.

Exc.	V.G.	Good	Fair	Poor
125	100	80	65	50

RG-63

A .22 caliber double action revolver resembling a Colt Model 1873.

Exc.	V.G.	Good	Fair	Poor
60	50	40	35	25

RG-66

A .22 or .22 Magnum single action revolver patterned after the Colt Model 1873.

Exc.	V.G.	Good	Fair	Poor
60	50	40	35	25

RG-66T

As above with adjustable sights.

Exc.	V.G.	Good	Fair	Poor
65	55	45	35	25

RG-74

A .22 caliber double action revolver with swing-out cylinder.

Exc.	V.G.	Good	Fair	Poor
75	65	55	45	35

RG-88

A .357 Magnum double action revolver with swing-out cylinder.

Exc.	V.G.	Good	Fair	Poor
90	80	70	60	40

RWS
Nurenberg, Germany
Dynamit Nobel

Model 820 S

A .22 caliber target rifle with 24" heavy barrel and adjustable aperture sights. The trigger fully adjustable, three position adjustable match stock with stippled pistol grip and forend. Discontinued in 1986.

NIB	Exc.	V.G.	Good	Fair	Poor
1250	800	700	550	450	250

Model 820 SF

As above with a heavier barrel. Discontinued in 1986.

NIB	Exc.	V.G.	Good	Fair	Poor
1000	800	600	500	400	250

Model 820 K

Offhand "Running Boar" model of the above with a lighter barrel. Furnished without sights. Discontinued in 1986.

NIB	Exc.	V.G.	Good	Fair	Poor
950	750	600	500	400	250

RADOM
Radom, Poland

NOTE: For history, technical data, descriptions, photos, and prices see the *Standard Catalog of Military Firearms, 1870 to the Present* under Poland.

VIS-35 Reissue

This is an exact copy of the original VIS-35 pistol. Limited to 100 pistols with less than that number imported into the U.S. The importer, "Dalvar of USA" is stamped on the barrel.

NIB	Exc.	V.G.	Good	Fair	Poor
2300	—	—	—	—	—

RANDALL FIREARMS CO.
Sun Valley, California

Randall matched set, serial-number RFOO010C. Made for the TV series "Magnum PI." (Photo by Steve Comus)

HOW TO IDENTIFY THE VARIOUS MODELS

Randall models are designated by a single letter prefix, followed by a three-digit number. Prefixes are A, B, or C. Prefix A designates a right-handed pistol. Prefix B denotes a left-handed configuration, and prefix C represented a right-handed, featherweight model.

In a logical sequence, the first numerical digit reflects the frame type, the second digit is for the slide configuration and the third number denotes caliber.

The first numerical digit is 1, 2 or 3. If the first number is 1, it means Service Model. A number 2 refers to Service Model-C or Raider, and a 3 denotes the LeMay Model.

The second digit is 1, 2, or 3. A 1 refers to round-top, fixed sight slide. A 2 stands for flat-top, fixed-sight slide, and 3 is for flat-top, adjustable-sight slide.

The third digit is 1, 2, or 3. A 1 refers to .45 ACP, a 2 is for 9mm Parabellum and a 3 is for. 38 Super.

A marketing upgrade affected most Randall pistols made from late November 1983 through the end of production. All Randalls sold had slide stops and grip safeties upgraded to "extended" and "beavertail" types, respectively. Long triggers were installed. This was not retroactive to pistols already sold. All Randalls were shipped with extended safety locks.

Having pioneered stainless steel construction and left-handed configurations, Randall carved for itself a unique place in the history of semiautomatic handguns. In two years of production, Randall cranked out an astounding 24 models in 12 variations and three different calibers.

The Randall Firearms Company officially stopped production on Dec. 15, 1984, and closed its doors on May 15, 1985. There were many reasons why Randall did not survive. To a number of industry observers, it appeared as though the fledgling firm may have attempted to accomplish too much, too quickly. The company's agenda was packed with so many innovative approaches and ideas that the production output could not keep up with the voracious R&D appetite.

NOTE: Randall prototypes can be identified by a "T" prefix. Add 50% to the price for this variety. For serial numbers under 2000 add $100 to $150.

Randall Documentation & Collectors Club: Research letters on original Randall Letterhead are available at a cost of $30 each postpaid (Randal Pistols Only). Readers and collectors interested in joining the Randall Firearms/Pistol Collectors Association contact the Randall Historian, Rick Kennerknecht at:

P.O. Box 1180, Mills, Wyoming 82644-1180
Web: www.Randall45.com
Email: Historian@Randal45.com
Phone: 877-464-0180
U.S. Fax: 419-464-0180
Euro-Fax:44-(0870) 131-2598

Model A111

Caliber is .45 Auto, barrel length 5", round-slide top, right-hand with fixed sights. Total production: 3,431.

NIB	Exc.	V.G.	Good	Fair	Poor
995	785	600	500	400	350

NOTE: For original box add a premium of $100 for Exc. through Good prices.

Model A121

Caliber is .45 Auto, barrel length 5", flat-slide top, right-hand with fixed sights. Total production: 1,067.

NIB	Exc.	V.G.	Good	Fair	Poor
1025	800	685	700	425	375

NOTE: For original box add a premium of $100 for Exc. through Good prices.

Model A131

Caliber is .45 Auto, barrel length 5", flat-slide top, right-hand with Millet sights. Total production: 2,083.

Randall A131/SO in. 451 Detonics Magnum with Randall memorabilia. (Photo by Larry Gray)

NIB	Exc.	V.G.	Good	Fair	Poor
1050	830	700	600	450	400

NOTE: For original box add a premium of $100 for Exc. through Good prices.

Model A112

Caliber is 9mm, barrel length 5", round-slide top, right-hand with fixed sights. Total production: 301.

NIB	Exc.	V.G.	Good	Fair	Poor
1250	1000	850	750	575	500

NOTE: For original box add a premium of $100 for Exc. through Good prices.

Model A122

Caliber 9mm. barrel length 5", flat-slide top, right-hand with fixed sights. Total production: 18.

NIB	Exc.	V.G.	Good	Fair	Poor
1775	1465	1245	1100	840	735

NOTE: For original box add a premium of $100 for Exc. through Good prices.

Model A211

Caliber .45 Auto, barrel length 4-1/4", round-slide top, right-hand with fixed sights. Total production: 922.

NIB	Exc.	V.G.	Good	Fair	Poor
1075	850	715	600	450	400

NOTE: For original box add a premium of $100 for Exc. through Good prices.

Model A231

Caliber .45 Auto, barrel length 4-1/4", flat-slide top, right-hand with Millet sights. Total production: 574.

NIB	Exc.	V.G.	Good	Fair	Poor
1200	975	825	700	525	450

NOTE: For original box add a premium of $100 for Exc. through Good prices.

Model A212

Caliber 9mm, barrel length 4-1/4", round-slide top, right-hand with fixed sights. Total production: 76.

NIB	Exc.	V.G.	Good	Fair	Poor
1325	1075	915	800	605	525

NOTE: For original box add a premium of $100 for Exc. through Good prices.

Model A232

Caliber 9mm. barrel length 4-1/4", flat-slide top, right-hand with Millet sights. Total production: 5.

NIB	Exc.	V.G.
2075	1750	1400

NOTE: For original box add a premium of $100 for Exc. through Good prices.

Model A311

Caliber .45 Auto, barrel length 4-1/4", round-slide top, right-hand with fixed sights. Total production: 361.

A311B black oxide LeMay special order by Soldier of Fortune magazine for field testing in El Salvador. (Photo by Steve Comus)

NIB	Exc.	V.G.	Good	Fair	Poor
1550	1260	1075	950	710	605

NOTE: For original box add a premium of $100 for Exc. through Good prices.

Model A331

Caliber .45 Auto, barrel length 4-1/4", flat-slide top, right-hand with Millet sights. Total production: 293.

NIB	Exc.	V.G.	Good	Fair	Poor
1675	1380	1175	1000	840	735

Model A312

Caliber 9mm. barrel length 4-1/4", round-slide top, right-hand with fixed sights. Total production: 2.

NIB	Exc.	V.G.	Good	Fair	Poor
3525	2995	—	—	—	—

NOTE: For original box add a premium of $100 for Exc. through Good prices.

Model A332

Caliber 9mm. barrel length 4-1/4", flat-slide top, right-hand with Millet sights. Total production: 9.

NIB	Exc.	V.G.	Good	Fair	Poor
2000	1625	1375	1200	785	735

NOTE: For original box add a premium of $100 for Exc. through Good prices.

Model B111

Caliber .45 Auto, barrel length 5", round-slide top, left-hand with fixed sights. Total production: 297.

NIB	Exc.	V.G.	Good	Fair	Poor
1775	1425	1200	1100	840	735

NOTE: For original box add a premium of $100 for Exc. through Good prices.

Model B121

Caliber .45 Auto, barrel length 5", flat-slide top, left-hand with fixed sights. Total production: 110.

NIB	Exc.	V.G.	Good	Fair	Poor
2075	1725	1450	1300	920	815

NOTE: For original box add a premium of $100 for Exc. through Good prices.

Model B122

Caliber 9mm. barrel length 5", flat-slide top, left-hand with fixed sights. Total production: 2.

NIB	Exc.	V.G.	Good	Fair	Poor
3950	3450	—	—	—	—

Model B123

Caliber .38 Super, barrel length 5", flat-slide top, left-hand with fixed sights. Total production: 2.

NIB	Exc.	V.G.	Good	Fair	Poor
3950	3450	—	—	—	—

B131/SO left-hand service model with custom Chuck Stapel knife. (Photo by Steve Comus)

Model B131

Caliber .45 Auto, barrel length 5", flat-slide top, left-hand with Millet sights. Total production: 225.

NIB	Exc.	V.G.	Good	Fair	Poor
1950	1600	1350	1200	920	815

NOTE: For original box add a premium of $100 for Exc. through Good prices.

Model B311

Caliber .45 Auto, barrel length 4-1/4", round-slide top, left-hand with fixed sights. Total production: 52.

Randall left-hand B311 with original box. Few left-hand Randalls were shipped in boxes. Most were shipped in Randall pistol rugs. (Photo by Steve Comus)

NIB	Exc.	V.G.	Good	Fair	Poor
2075	1725	1450	1300	1000	850

NOTE: For original box add a premium of $100 for Exc. through Good prices.

Model B312

Caliber 9mm. barrel length 4-1/4", round-slide top, left-hand with fixed sights. Total production: 9.

Randall B312 left-hand 9mm LeMay, one of the most sought-after of the B-series guns. Only nine were manufactured. (Photo by Steve Comus)

Randall B312 with factory 45ACP conversion unit. Only one of these factory units were made. (Photo by Steve Comus)

NIB	Exc.	V.G.	Good	Fair	Poor
3525	2995	2550	2300	1340	1100

NOTE: For pistol with .45 ACP conversion in NIB 3500. Total production of this conversion is 1 pistol. For original box add a premium of $100 for Exc. through Good prices.

Model B331

Caliber .45 Auto, barrel length 4-1/4", flat-slide top, left-hand with Millet sights. Total production: 45.

NIB	Exc.	V.G.	Good	Fair	Poor
2325	1950	1650	1500	965	850

NOTE: For original box add a premium of $100 for Exc. through Good prices.

Model C311

Caliber .45 Auto, barrel length 4-1/4", round-slide top, right-hand with fixed sights. Total production: 1.

NIB
3950

Model C332

Caliber 9mm. barrel length 4-1/4", flat-slide top, right-hand with Millet sights. Total production: 4.

NIB	Exc.	V.G.	Good
1800	1575	1350	1200

Model B321 SET

Serial Number REK I.

B321 set with gold-plated LeMay roll mark die. (Photo by Steve Comus)

Randall B321 of the B321 set, serial-number REK1. (Photo by Steve Comus)

NIB
23000

Model A111/111 Matched Set

Serial Numbers RF00000C, RF00001C, RF00010-C, RF00024C.

NIB
8600

Austrian Randall

Total production: 5.

Close-up view of Austrian proof marks. (Photo by Christopher Todd)

NOTE: Prototypes with "T" serial numbers add 50%. For serial numbers under 2000 add $200 to $300. With factory box add $100 for A111, A121, and A131. Add $200 for all other right hand models and $300 for all left hand models.

Four of the five Austrian Randalls. Each of these A111s bear cartouches from an Austrian proof house. These Randalls were proofed for the Austrian government for law enforcement evaluation. (Photo by Christopher Todd)

NIB
3000

RANDALL MAGAZINES

.45 LeMay-Right Hand

NIB	Exc.	V.G.	Good	Fair	Poor
100	90	80	80	—	—

.45 LeMay-Dogleg Right Hand

NIB	Exc.	V.G.	Good	Fair	Poor
80	70	70	70	—	—

.45 LeMay-Left Hand

NIB	Exc.	V.G.	Good	Fair	Poor
150	130	125	125	—	—

.45 LeMay-Gogleg Left Hand

NIB	Exc.	V.G.	Good	Fair	Poor
140	130	120	120	—	—

.45 Service-Right Hand

NIB	Exc.	V.G.	Good	Fair	Poor
60	45	40	40	—	—

.45 Service-Left Hand

NIB	Exc.	V.G.	Good	Fair	Poor
125	115	100	100	—	—

9mm Service-Right Hand

NIB	Exc.	V.G.	Good	Fair	Poor
125	115	100	100	—	—

9mm Service-Left Hand

NIB	Exc.	V.G.	Good	Fair	Poor
200	175	150	150	—	—

RANGER ARMS, INC.
Gainesville, Texas

Statesman

A bolt action rifle produced in various calibers with a 22" barrel, no sights, and a checkered walnut stock. Standard finish blued. Manufactured in the early 1970s.

Exc.	V.G.	Good	Fair	Poor
350	250	200	150	100

Statesman Magnum

As above, but chambered for magnum calibers and with a 24" barrel.

Exc.	V.G.	Good	Fair	Poor
400	300	250	200	100

Senator

As above with a better finish.

Exc.	V.G.	Good	Fair	Poor
450	350	300	250	125

Senator Magnum

As above chambered for magnum cartridges.

Exc.	V.G.	Good	Fair	Poor
450	350	300	250	125

Governor

As above with better walnut and finer lined checkering.

Exc.	V.G.	Good	Fair	Poor
500	400	350	250	125

Governor Magnum

As above chambered for magnum cartridges.

Exc.	V.G.	Good	Fair	Poor
500	400	350	250	125

RAPTOR ARMS CO.
Alexandria, Virginia

Raptor Bolt Action Rifle

Introduced in 1997 and chambered for the .270, .30-06, .243, .25-06, and .308 calibers. Fitted with a 22" barrel and black synthetic checkered stock with recoil pad. Adjustable trigger. Weight is about 7.5 lbs.

NIB	Exc.	V.G.	Good	Fair	Poor
300	200	150	—	—	—

RASHID
Egypt

Rashid Carbine

A gas operated 7.62x39mm caliber semiautomatic carbine with a 20.5" barrel and 10-round integral magazine. Fitted with a folded bayonet similar to that found on the Russian SKS. Blued finish and hardwood stock. This rifle is based upon the Swedish Ljungman.

Courtesy Richard M. Kumor, Sr.

Exc.	V.G.	Good	Fair	Poor
450	375	300	150	100

RAST & GASSER
SEE—Gasser

RAVELL
Barcelona, Spain

Maxim Double Rifle

A Holland & Holland-styled sidelock double-barrel rifle available in either .375 Holland & Holland or 9.3x74R with 23" barrels having express sights. Double triggers and automatic ejectors. The sidelocks and mounts engraved, stock of well figured walnut normally fitted with a recoil pad.

NIB	Exc.	V.G.	Good	Fair	Poor
4500	3500	2750	1850	1250	850

RAVEN ARMS
Industry, California

P-25

A .25 caliber semiautomatic pistol with a 2.75" barrel and 6-round magazine. Available with a blued, chrome or nickel-plated finish and walnut grips. Manufacture ceased in 1984.

Exc.	V.G.	Good	Fair	Poor
75	65	50	35	25

MP-25

As above with a die-cast frame and imitation ivory grips.

NIB	Exc.	V.G.	Good	Fair	Poor
75	65	55	45	35	25

READ & WATSON
Danville, Virginia

During 1862 and 1863, Read & Watson produced approximately 900 altered Hall rifles for the State of Virginia. These arms were made from Hall rifles issued to the state prior to the Civil War. The original breech loading mechanisms were removed and a brass breech piece or receiver was secured in their place. New buttstocks were fitted and the original Hall furniture was reused. Carbines have an overall length of 42-1/8"; barrel length of 26" and are of .52 caliber. Position and style of serial numbers varies.

Prospective purchasers are strongly advised to secure a qualified appraisal prior to acquisition.

Exc.	V.G.	Good	Fair	Poor
—	—	11500	5500	1000

RECORD-MATCH ANSCHUTZ
Zelia-Mehlis, Germany

Model 210 Free Pistol
A single shot .22 caliber target pistol using a Martini falling block action. Barrel length 11", set trigger, and adjustable sights. Blued finish with checkered walnut grips and forend. Manufactured during the 1930s.

Exc.	V.G.	Good	Fair	Poor
1250	1000	850	750	400

Model 210A
As above with a lightweight alloy frame.

Exc.	V.G.	Good	Fair	Poor
1200	950	800	700	350

Model 200 Free Pistol
As above without a set trigger.

Exc.	V.G.	Good	Fair	Poor
950	850	750	550	300

REEDER, GARY CUSTOM GUNS
Flagstaff, AZ

This company offers complete guns as listed below. It also offers custom options built on customer guns as well. An extensive number of custom options is available on any of these models. Prices listed below reflect the standard for that particular model. Retail prices only are listed below due to lack of active secondary market for these limited edition guns. Information indicates that these Gary Reeder guns hold their value well.

Black Widow
Chambered for the .44 magnum cartridge and fitted with a 4.625" barrel with black Chromix finish. Round butt with Black Cape Buffalo grips. Engraved with Black Widow on each side of the cylinder. Built on a Ruger Super Blackhawk.

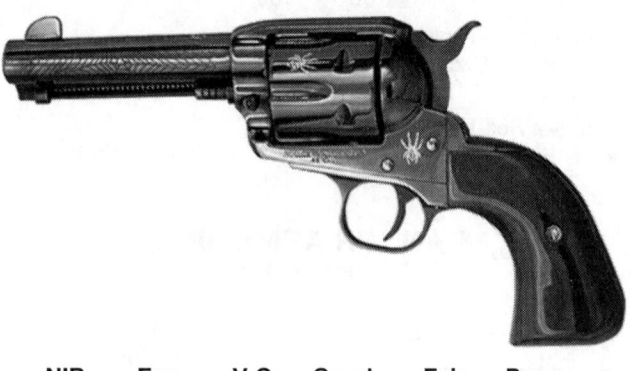

NIB	Exc.	V.G.	Good	Fair	Poor
995	—	—	—	—	—

Black Widow II
Similar to the Black Widow but chambered for the .45 Long Colt cartridge. Barrel length is 4.5".

NIB	Exc.	V.G.	Good	Fair	Poor
995	—	—	—	—	—

Arizona Ranger Classic
Built on a Ruger Vaquero this model is chambered for the .45 Long Colt cartridge and fitted with a choice of a 4.5", 5.5", or 7.5" barrel. Blue or stainlress steel finish. Special engraving with Stag grips.

NIB	Exc.	V.G.	Good	Fair	Poor
995	—	—	—	—	—

Badlands Classic
Built on a Ruger Vaquero and chambered for the .45 Long Colt cartridge with an extra .45 ACP cylinder. Fitted with a 4.5" barrel. Special engraving. Pearl grips.

NIB	Exc.	V.G.	Good	Fair	Poor
1095	—	—	—	—	—

Cowboy Classic
Built on a Ruger Vaquero and chambered for the .45 Long Colt with a 67.5" barrel. Stainless steel or Black Chromix finish. Ivory polymer or pearlite grips. Special engraving.

NIB	Exc.	V.G.	Good	Fair	Poor
995	—	—	—	—	—

Cowtown Classic
Built on a Ruger Vaquero and chambered for the .45 Long Colt with 7.5" barrel. Special engraving. Walnut grips.

NIB	Exc.	V.G.	Good	Fair	Poor
995	—	—	—	—	—

Glambers Classic
Built on a Ruger Vaquero and chambered for the .45 Long Colt with a 2.5" barrel. Stainless steel or black Chromix finish. Choice of black or white pearl grips. No ejector rod. Special engraving.

NIB	Exc.	V.G.	Good	Fair	Poor
995	—	—	—	—	—

Lone Star Classic

Built on a Ruger Vaquero and chambered for the .45 Long Colt cartridge with 7.5" barrel. Stainless steel finish. Special engraving and walnut grips with 5 notches.

NIB	Exc.	V.G.	Good	Fair	Poor
995	—	—	—	—	—

Long Rider Classic

Built on a Ruger Vaquero and chambered for the .45 Long Colt cartridge with 4.5", 5.5", or 7.5" barrel. Special engraving with black Chromix finish. Gunfighter grip with simulated pearl or ivory.

NIB	Exc.	V.G.	Good	Fair	Poor
995	—	—	—	—	—

Texas Ranger Classic

Built on a Ruger Vaquero frame and chambered for the .45 Long Colt cartridge with 4.5", 5.5", or 7.5" barrel. Stainless steel finish. Special engraving. Simulated pearl gunfighter grips.

NIB	Exc.	V.G.	Good	Fair	Poor
995	—	—	—	—	—

Trail Rider Classic

Built on a Ruger Vaquero frame and chambered for the .45 Long Colt cartridge with 7.5" barrel. Black Chromix finish. Special engraving. Simulated pearl grips.

NIB	Exc.	V.G.	Good	Fair	Poor
995	—	—	—	—	—

Tombstone Classic

Built on a Ruger Vaquero frame and chambered for the .45 Long Colt cartridge with 3.5" barrel. Black Chromix finish. Special engraving. Simulated pearl or ivory birdshead grips.

NIB	Exc.	V.G.	Good	Fair	Poor
995	—	—	—	—	—

Doc Holliday Classic

Built on a Ruger Vaquero frame and chambered for the .45 Long Colt cartridge with 3.5" barrel. Stainless steel or black Chromix finish. Special engraving. Simulated pearl gambler grips.

NIB	Exc.	V.G.	Good	Fair	Poor
995	—	—	—	—	—

Night Rider

Built on a Ruger Vaquero frame and chambered for the .44-40 cartridge with 7.5" barrel. Black Chromix finish. Special engraving. Stag grips.

NIB	Exc.	V.G.	Good	Fair	Poor
995	—	—	—	—	—

Ultimate Vaquero

Built on a Ruger Vaquero frame and chambered for the .45 Long Colt cartridge with 4" barrel. Stainless steel or black Chromix finish. Special engraving. Simulated pearl gambler grips.

NIB	Exc.	V.G.	Good	Fair	Poor
995	—	—	—	—	—

Ultimate Bisley

Built on a Ruger Vaquero frame and chambered for the .45 Long Colt or .44 magnum cartridge with 4.5", 5.5", 6.5", or 7.5" barrel. Black Chromix finish. Special engraving. Simulated pearl or ivory Bisley grips.

NIB	Exc.	V.G.	Good	Fair	Poor
1095	—	—	—	—	—

Long Colt Hunter

Built on a Ruger Blackhawk frame and chambered for the .45 Long Colt cartridge with 5.5" or 7.5" barrel. Stainless steel finish. Adjustable rear sight with gold bead front sight. Special engraving. Ebony grips.

NIB	Exc.	V.G.	Good	Fair	Poor
995	—	—	—	—	—

Long Colt Hunter II

Built on a Ruger Redhawk frame and chambered for the .45 Long Colt or .44 magnum cartridge with 5" barrel. Stainless steel finish. Special engraving. Wooden gunfighter grips.

NIB	Exc.	V.G.	Good	Fair	Poor
995	—	—	—	—	—

African Hunter

Built on a Ruger Bisley or Super Blackhawk frame and chambered for the .475 or .500 Linebaugh cartridge with 6" barrel. Available with or without muzzle break. Adjustable rear sight and interchangeable front sights. Stainless steel or black Chromix finish. Special engraving. Ebony grips.

NIB	Exc.	V.G.	Good	Fair	Poor
1195	—	—	—	—	—

Ultimate 41

Built on a Ruger Blackhawk frame and chambered for the .41 magnum or .41 GNR cartridge with 4.5", 5.5", or 7.5" barrel. Unfluted cylinder. Stainless steel finish. Adjustable rear sights. Special engraving. Ebony grips.

NIB	Exc.	V.G.	Good	Fair	Poor
950	—	—	—	—	—

Coyote Classic

Built on a Ruger frame and chambered for the .22 Hornet, .22 K Hornet, .218 Bee, .218 Mashburn Bee, .17 Ackley Bee, .17 Ackley Hornet, .256 Winchester, and .25-20 with 8" barrel. Adjustable rear sight and drilled and tapped for scope mount. Black Chromix or stainless steel finish. Special engraving. Laminated cherry grips.

NIB	Exc.	V.G.	Good	Fair	Poor
995	—	—	—	—	—

Classic Hunter

Built on a Ruger Vaquero frame and chambered for the .475 Linebaugh cartridge with heavy 6" barrel. Black Chromix finish. Special engraving. Laminated ironwood, cherry, or walnut gunfighter grips.

NIB	Exc.	V.G.	Good	Fair	Poor
1295	—	—	—	—	—

Alaskan Grizzly

Built on a Ruger Vaquero frame and chambered for the .475 or .500 Linebaugh cartridge with customer's choice of barrel. Black Chromix or stainless steel finish. Special engraving. Horn or black laminated gunfighter grips.

NIB	Exc.	V.G.	Good	Fair	Poor
1195	—	—	—	—	—

Ultimate Back Up 2

Built on a Ruger Blackhawk or Super Blackhawk frame and chambered for the .475 or .500 Linebaugh cartridge with 3.5" ported barrel. Stainless steel finish. Special engraving. Laminated wood or Buffalo horn grips.

NIB	Exc.	V.G.	Good	Fair	Poor
1295	—	—	—	—	—

Montana Hunter

Built on a Ruger Blackhawk or Super Blackhawk frame and chambered for the .45 Long Colt or .44 magnum cartridge with customer's choice of barrel. Stainless steel finish. Special engraving. Laminated gunfighter grips.

NIB	Exc.	V.G.	Good	Fair	Poor
995	—	—	—	—	—

Alaskan Survivalist

Built on a Ruger Redhawk frame and chambered for the .45 Long Colt or .44 magnum cartridge with 3" barrel. Adjustable rear sight. Stainless steel finish. Special engraving. Ebony round butt grips.

NIB	Exc.	V.G.	Good	Fair	Poor
995	—	—	—	—	—

American Hunter

Built on a Winchester Model 94 big bore frame and chambered for the .444 Marlin cartridge. Black Chromix finish. Ghost ring rear sight. Special engraving. Checkering walnut stock.

NIB	Exc.	V.G.	Good	Fair	Poor
995	—	—	—	—	—

Alaskan Classic

Built on a Marlin Model 1895 frame and chambered for the .45-70 cartridge. Barrel length is 16.5". Black Chromix finish. Ghost ring rear sight. Special engraving. Checkering walnut stock.

NIB	Exc.	V.G.	Good	Fair	Poor
1195	—	—	—	—	—

Buffalo Hunter

Built on a Marlin Model 1895 frame and chambered for the .475 GNR cartridge. Barrel length is 18". Full length magazine tube. Black Chromix finish. Peep rear sight. Special engraving. Checkering walnut stock.

NIB	Exc.	V.G.	Good	Fair	Poor
1250	—	—	—	—	—

Kodiak Hunter

Built on a Contender frame and chambered for the .50 Action Express or .454 Casull cartridge. Barrel length is 10". Black Chromix finish. Adjustable rear sight with barrel band front sight. Special engraving. Walnut grips.

NIB	Exc.	V.G.	Good	Fair	Poor
995	—	—	—	—	—

Ultimate Encore

Built on a Thompson Center frame and chambered for a variety of big bore cartridges. Fitted with a 15" barrel with muzzle brake. Black Chromix finish. Ghost ring rear sight. Special engraving.

NIB	Exc.	V.G.	Good	Fair	Poor
995	—	—	—	—	—

REFORM
Suhl, Germany
August Schuler

Reform Pistol
A 6.35 or .25ACP four barreled double action pistol constructed so that the barrel unit rises upward when the trigger is pulled. It superficially resembles a semiautomatic pistol. Blued with hard rubber grips. Manufactured between 1906 and about 1913.

Exc.	V.G.	Good	Fair	Poor
600	475	350	275	175

REICHS REVOLVER
Germany

Model 1879
Exc.	V.G.	Good	Fair	Poor
600	500	375	250	175

Model 1883
Exc.	V.G.	Good	Fair	Poor
500	400	325	225	150

REID, JAMES
New York, New York

Model 1 Revolver
A spur trigger .22 caliber revolver with a 3.5" octagonal barrel and 7-shot unfluted cylinder. Blued with walnut grips. The barrel marked "J. Reid, New York." Approximately 500 were manufactured between 1862 and 1865.

Exc.	V.G.	Good	Fair	Poor
—	—	750	300	100

Model 2 Revolver
As above but in .32 caliber, the barrel marked "Address W.P. Irving, 20 Cliff Street. N.Y." or "James P. Fitch. N.Y." Approximately 1,300 were manufactured between 1862 and 1865.

Exc.	V.G.	Good	Fair	Poor
—	—	750	300	100

Model 3 Revolver
Similar to the above, but with the grip angle sharpened. Chambered for the .32 rimfire cartridge with a 4.75" barrel. The cylinder chambers are threaded so that percussion nipples can be inserted. The barrel is marked "J. Reid N.Y. City". Approximately 300 were made between 1862 and 1865.

Exc.	V.G.	Good	Fair	Poor
—	—	1100	500	200

Model 4 Revolver
As above with barrel lengths varying from 3.75" to 8". Approximately 1,600 were manufactured between 1862 and 1865.

Exc.	V.G.	Good	Fair	Poor
—	—	950	450	150

"My Friend" Knuckle Duster
A 7-shot .22 caliber revolver constructed entirely of metal and without a barrel. The frame of silver-plated brass or blued iron and marked "My Friend Patd. Dec. 26, 1865." The grip is formed with a finger hole so that the pistol can be used as a set of brass knuckles.

Courtesy W.P. Hallstein III and son Chip

A .41 caliber Knuckle Duster was sold at auction for $10,925. Condition as defined was good to very good. Rock Island Auction Company, August 1999

Model No. 1 Knuckle Duster

As above with a 3" barrel. Approximately 350 were made between 1875 and 1880.

Courtesy W.P. Hallstein III and son Chip

Courtesy W.P. Hallstein III and son Chip

Exc.	V.G.	Good	Fair	Poor
—	—	1900	850	250

Model No. 2 Knuckle Duster

As above with a 1.75" barrel. Approximately 150 were made between 1875 and 1880.

Exc.	V.G.	Good	Fair	Poor
—	—	2250	950	350

Model No. 3 Derringer

A .41 caliber revolver with a 3" octagonal barrel and 5-shot fluted cylinder. The frame silver-plated and the barrel as well as cylinder blued. Approximately 75 were made between 1880 and 1884.

Exc.	V.G.	Good	Fair	Poor
—	—	1950	950	350

Model No. 4 Derringer

As above but with a brass frame and walnut grips and marked "Reid's Extra." Approximately 200 were made during 1883 and 1884.

Exc.	V.G.	Good	Fair	Poor
—	—	1400	700	250

New Model Knuckle Duster

Similar to the Model 2 with a 2" barrel and 5-shot cylinder. The barrel marked "Reid's New Model .32 My Friend." Approximately 150 were made in 1884.

Exc.	V.G.	Good	Fair	Poor
—	—	1750	800	250

Brass Frame

Exc.	V.G.	Good	Fair	Poor
—	—	950	500	200

Iron Frame

Exc.	V.G.	Good	Fair	Poor
—	—	1750	800	250

.32 Caliber Knuckle Duster

As above but .32 caliber. Approximately 3,400 were manufactured between 1869 and 1884.

Brass Frame

Exc.	V.G.	Good	Fair	Poor
—	—	1200	600	200

Iron Frame

Exc.	V.G.	Good	Fair	Poor
—	—	1750	800	250

.41 Caliber Knuckle Duster

As above but .41 caliber and marked "J. Reid's Derringer." Approximately 300 were manufactured between 1875 and 1878.

Exc.	V.G.	Good	Fair	Poor
—	—	10500	5500	950

REISING ARMS CO.
Hartford, Connecticut

Standard Model

A .22 caliber semiautomatic pistol with a hinged 6.5" barrel and 10-round magazine. Standard finish is blued, however, nickel-plated versions are known. The slide marked with the company's name and patent dates. The grips of bakelite impressed with a bear's head and the motto "Reising, It's A Bear". Manufactured in both New York City and Hartford, during the 1920s. **CAUTION: High velocity ammunition should not be used in these pistols**.

Courtesy John J. Stimson, Jr.

New York Manufacture

Exc.	V.G.	Good	Fair	Poor
800	500	300	200	100

Hartford Manufacture

Exc.	V.G.	Good	Fair	Poor
700	450	275	175	100

Remington.
C O U N T R Y

REMINGTON ARMS COMPANY, INC.
Madison, North Carolina

Founded in 1816 by Eliphalet Remington, this company has the distinction of being the oldest firearms manufacturing firm in the United States. Since 1856 it has been known by four different names: between 1856 and 1888, E. Remington & Sons; 1888-1910, Remington Arms Company; 1910-1925, Remington Arms U.M.C. Company (Union Metallic Cartridge Company); and 1925 to the present, Remington Arms Company.

1st Model Remington-Beals Revolver

A .31 caliber 5-shot percussion revolver with a 3" octagonal barrel. The cylinder turning mechanism is mounted on the left outside frame. Blued, case hardened, silver-plated, brass triggerguard and gutta-percha grips. The barrel marked, "F. Beal's Patent, June 24, '56 & May 26, '57" and the frame, "Remington's Ilion, N.Y." Approximately 5,000 were manufactured in 1857 and 1858.

Courtesy Milwaukee Public Museum, Milwaukee, Wisconsin

Exc.	V.G.	Good	Fair	Poor
2000	1600	1000	600	300

2nd Model Remington-Beals Revolver

A spur trigger .31 caliber 5-shot percussion revolver with a 3" octagonal barrel. Blued, case hardened with a squared gutta-percha grip. The barrel marked, "Beals Patent 1856 & 57, Manufactured by Remingtons Ilion, N.Y." Approximately 1,000 were manufactured between 1858 and 1860.

Exc.	V.G.	Good	Fair	Poor
4500	3750	2500	2000	1500

3rd Model Remington-Beals Revolver

A .31 caliber 5-shot percussion revolver with a 4" octagonal barrel. A loading lever mounted beneath the barrel. Blued, case hardened with gutta-percha grips. The barrel marked, "Beals Pat. 1856, 57, 58 and also "Manufactured by Remingtons, Ilion, N.Y." Approximately 1,500 were manufactured in 1859 and 1860.

Courtesy Milwaukee Public Museum, Milwaukee, Wisconsin

Exc.	V.G.	Good	Fair	Poor
2500	2000	1200	800	500

Remington-Rider Revolver

A double-action .31 caliber percussion revolver with a 3" barrel and 5-shot cylinder. Most of these revolvers were blued but a few were nickel-plated, case hardened with gutta-percha grips. This model is also encountered altered to .32 rimfire. The barrel marked, "Manufactured by Remingtons, Ilion, N.Y., Riders Pt. Aug. 17, 1858, May 3, 1859." Approximately 20,000 were manufactured between 1860 and 1873. The cartridge variation is worth approximately 20% less than the original percussion version.

Exc.	V.G.	Good	Fair	Poor
1800	1600	1000	500	200

Remington-Beals Army Revolver

A .44 caliber percussion revolver with an 8" barrel and 6-shot cylinder. Blued, case hardened with walnut grips. The barrel marked "Beals Patent Sept. 14, 1858 Manufactured by Remington's Ilion, New York." Approximately 2,500 were manufactured between 1860 and 1862. A martially marked example is extremely rare and would be worth approximately 35% additional.

Exc.	V.G.	Good	Fair	Poor
6000	5000	3000	2000	800

Remington-Beals Navy Revolver

Similar in appearance to Remington-Beals Army Revolver, but in .36 caliber with a 7.5" octagonal barrel. The first examples of this model were fitted with a loading lever that would not allow the cylinder pin to be completely removed. These examples are worth approximately 80% more than the standard model. Approximately 1,000 of these revolvers were purchased by the United States government and martially marked examples are worth approximately 40% more than the values listed below. Manufactured from 1860 to 1862 with a total production of approximately 15,000.

Courtesy Wallis & Wallis, Lewes, Sussex, England

Exc.	V.G.	Good	Fair	Poor
4000	3500	2500	1500	600

1861 Army Revolver

A .44 caliber percussion revolver with an 8" octagonal barrel and 6-shot cylinder. The loading lever is cut with a slot so that the cylinder pin can be drawn forward without the lever being lowered. Blued, case hardened with walnut grips. The barrel marked "Patented Dec. 17, 1861 Manufactured by Remington's, Ilion, N.Y." Some examples were converted to .46 caliber rimfire cartridge, and would be worth approximately 25% more than the original, martially marked, standard percussion model. Approximately 12,000 were manufactured in 1862. This model is also known as the "Old Army Model."

Paul Goodwin Photo

Exc.	V.G.	Good	Fair	Poor
4500	3500	1800	1000	500

1861 Navy Revolver

As above, but .36 caliber with a 7.25" octagonal barrel. Blued, case hardened with walnut grips. This model is also found altered to .38 metallic cartridge. Cartridge examples are worth approximately 35% less than the percussion versions. Approximately 8,000 were manufactured in 1862. 25% more for martial.

Paul Goodwin Photo

Exc.	V.G.	Good	Fair	Poor
4500	3500	1800	1200	500

New Model Army Revolver

A .44 caliber 6-shot percussion revolver with an 8" octagonal barrel. Blued, case hardened with walnut grips. The barrel marked "Patented Sept. 14, 1858 E. Remington & Sons, Ilion, New York, U.S.A. New Model." Approximately 132,000 were made between 1863 and 1873.

Standard Model-Military Version

Exc.	V.G.	Good	Fair	Poor
4500	3500	1800	1000	400

Civilian Model-No Government Inspector's Markings

Exc.	V.G.	Good	Fair	Poor
3800	2800	1600	800	400

.44 or .46 Cartridge Conversion

Courtesy Milwaukee Public Museum, Milwaukee, Wisconsin

Exc.	V.G.	Good	Fair	Poor
3800	3200	1800	800	400

New Model Navy Revolver

As above, but .36 caliber with a 7.23" octagonal barrel. Approximately 22,000 were made between 1863 and 1875.

Courtesy Milwaukee Public Museum, Milwaukee, Wisconsin

Military Version

Exc.	V.G.	Good	Fair	Poor
4400	3600	2200	1200	600

Civilian Version

Exc.	V.G.	Good	Fair	Poor
3800	3200	1800	1000	400

.38 Cartridge Conversion-1873 to 1888

Exc.	V.G.	Good	Fair	Poor
3200	2600	1600	800	400

New Model Single Action Belt Revolver

As above, but with a 6.5" barrel. Blued or nickel-plated, case hardened with walnut grips. This model is sometimes encountered altered to .38 cartridge. Cartridge examples are worth approximately 25% less than the values listed below. Approximately 3,000 were made between 1863 and 1873.

Paul Goodwin Photo

Exc.	V.G.	Good	Fair	Poor
3800	3200	1800	1000	400

NOTE: Blued models will command a premium.

Remington-Rider Double Action Belt Revolver

A double action .36 caliber percussion revolver with a 6.5" octagonal barrel marked, "Manufactured by Remington's, Ilion, N.Y. Rider's Pt. Aug. 17, 1858, May 3, 1859." Blued or nickel-plated, case hardened with walnut grips. This model is also found altered to cartridge and such examples would be worth approximately 20% less than the values listed below. Several hundred of this model were made with fluted cylinders and are worth a premium of about 25%. Approximately 5,000 were made between 1863 and 1873.

Courtesy Milwaukee Public Museum, Milwaukee, Wisconsin

Exc.	V.G.	Good	Fair	Poor
3600	3200	1800	1000	400

New Model Police Revolver

A .36 caliber percussion revolver with octagonal barrels ranging from 3.5" to 6.5" and with a 5-shot cylinder. Blued or nickel-plated, case hardened with walnut grips. This model is also found altered to cartridge and such examples would be worth approximately 20% less than the values listed below. Approximately 18,000 were manufactured between 1863 and 1873.

Paul Goodwin Photo

Exc.	V.G.	Good	Fair	Poor
2400	2000	1400	800	300

NOTE: Blued models will command a premium.

New Model Pocket Revolver

A .31 caliber spur trigger percussion revolver with octagonal barrels ranging from 3" to 4.5" in length and a 5-shot cylinder. Blued or nickel-plated, case hardened with walnut grips. The barrel marked, "Patented Sept. 14, 1858, March 17, 1863 E. Remington & Sons, Ilion, New York U.S.A. New Model." Approximately 25,000 were manufactured between 1863 and 1873.

1st Version-Brass Frame and Trigger

Exc.	V.G.	Good	Fair	Poor
4000	3400	1600	1200	800

2nd Version-Iron Frame, Brass Trigger

Exc.	V.G.	Good	Fair	Poor
2000	1600	1200	800	500

3rd Version-Iron Frame, Iron Trigger

Exc.	V.G.	Good	Fair	Poor
1600	1400	1000	800	400

.32 Cartridge Conversion

Exc.	V.G.	Good	Fair	Poor
1400	1200	800	500	300

NOTE: Add 15% for blued models.

Remington-Rider Derringer

A small, silver-plated brass single shot .17 caliber percussion pistol with a 3" round barrel. The barrel marked, "Rider's Pt. Sept. 13, 1859." Approximately 1,000 were manufactured between 1860 and 1863. Prospective purchasers are advised to secure a qualified appraisal prior to acquisition.

Exc.	V.G.	Good	Fair	Poor
—	—	5750	3000	900

Zig-Zag Derringer

A 6-shot .22 caliber revolving barrel pocket pistol with barrels 3.25" in length. The barrels are cut with zigzag grooves, which are part of the revolving mechanism. The trigger is formed as a ring that when moved forward and rearward turns the barrels and cocks the internal hammer. The barrel group marked "Elliot's Patent Aug. 17, 1858 May 29, 1860" as well as "Manufactured by Remington's Ilion, N.Y." Approximately 1,000 were manufactured in 1861 and 1862.

Paul Goodwin Photo

Exc.	V.G.	Good	Fair	Poor
—	—	2750	1100	450

Remington-Elliot Derringer

A 5-shot .22 or 4-shot .32 caliber pepperbox pistol with a revolving firing pin. Blued or nickel-plated with hard rubber grips. The barrel group marked "Manufactured by E. Remington & Sons, Ilion, N.Y. Elliot's Patents May 19, 1860 - Oct.1, 1861." Approximately 25,000 were manufactured between 1863 and 1888.

5-shot .22 caliber

Exc.	V.G.	Good	Fair	Poor
—	—	950	400	150

4-shot .32 caliber

4-shot .32 caliber

Courtesy W.P. Hallstein III and son Chip

Exc.	V.G.	Good	Fair	Poor
—	—	850	375	150

Vest Pocket Pistol

A .22 caliber single shot pistol with a 3.25" barrel. Blued or nickel-plated with walnut grips. The barrel marked "Remington's Ilion, N.Y. Patent Oct. 1, 1861." Early examples have been noted without any barrel markings. Approximately 25,000 were manufactured from 1865 to 1888.

NOTE: Add a 35% premium for blued models.

Paul Goodwin Photo

Exc.	V.G.	Good	Fair	Poor
—	—	750	400	200

Large-Bore Vest Pocket Pistol

As above, but in .30, .32, or .41 caliber with barrel lengths of either 3.5" or 4". Blued or nickel-plated with walnut or rosewood grips. The barrel markings as above except for the addition of the patent date, November 15, 1864. The smaller caliber versions are worth approximately 20% more than the .41 caliber. Approximately 10,000 were made from 1865 to 1888.

NOTE: Add a 35% premium for blued models.

Exc.	V.G.	Good	Fair	Poor
1600	1400	800	600	300

Remington-Elliot Derringer

A .41 caliber single shot pistol with a 2.5" round barrel. Blued or nickel-plated with walnut, ivory, or pearl grips. The barrel marked "Remingtons, Ilion, N.Y. Elliot Pat. Aug. 27, 1867." Approximately 10,000 were manufactured between 1867 and 1888.

NOTE: Add a 35% premium for blued models.

Exc.	V.G.	Good	Fair	Poor
2000	1800	1200	800	500

Remington Over/Under Derringer

A double barrel .41 caliber pocket pistol with 3" round barrels that pivot upward for loading. There is a lock bar to release the barrels on the right side of the frame. The firing pin raises and lowers automatically to fire each respective barrel. It has a spur trigger and bird's-head grip. The finish is either blued or nickel-plated; and it is featured with walnut, rosewood, or checkered hard rubber grips. Examples with factory pearl or ivory grips would be worth a small premium. Approximately 150,000 were manufactured between 1866 and 1935.

NOTE: Add a 25% premium for blued models.

Early Type I

Manufactured without an extractor, this type is marked "E". Remington & Sons, Ilion, N.Y." on one side and "Elliot's Patent Dec. 12, 1865" on the other side of the barrel rib. Only a few hundred were manufactured in 1866.

Exc.	V.G.	Good	Fair	Poor
4000	3500	1200	800	400

Type I Mid-Production

As above, but fitted with an extractor. Manufactured in the late 1860s.

Exc.	V.G.	Good	Fair	Poor
5000	4000	2500	1500	800

Type I Late Production

Fitted with an automatic extractor and marked on the top of the barrel rib. Manufactured from the late 1860s to 1888.

Exc.	V.G.	Good	Fair	Poor
2000	1600	800	500	300

Type II

Marked "Remington Arms Co., Ilion, N.Y." on the barrel rib. Manufactured between 1888 and 1911.

Exc.	V.G.	Good	Fair	Poor
1600	1200	600	400	200

Type III

Marked "Remington Arms - U.M.C. Co., Ilion, N.Y." on the barrel rib. Manufactured between 1912 and 1935.

Exc.	V.G.	Good	Fair	Poor
1400	1200	600	400	300

NOTE: For Type III models blue or nickel prices are the same.

Model 1865 Navy Rolling Block Pistol

A spur trigger single shot rolling block .50 caliber rimfire cartridge pistol with an 8.5" round barrel. Blued, case hardened with walnut grips and forend. The barrel marked "Remingtons, Ilion N.Y. U.S.A. Pat. May 3d Nov. 15th, 1864 April 17th, 1866." Examples bearing military inspection marks are worth approximately 25% more than the values listed below. Examples are also to be found altered to centerfire cartridge and these are worth approximately 10% less than the values listed below. Approximately 6,500 were manufactured between 1866 and 1870.

Exc.	V.G.	Good	Fair	Poor
5000	4000	3000	1500	800

Model 1867 Navy Rolling Block Pistol

A .50 caliber single shot rolling block pistol with a 7" round barrel. Blued, case hardened with walnut grips and forend. The majority of these pistols were purchased by the United States government and civilian examples without inspection marks are worth approximately 30% more than the values listed below.

Exc.	V.G.	Good	Fair	Poor
4000	3000	2000	1400	600

A cased pair of Model 1867 pistols sold at auction for $57,500. Gold inlaid. Caliber was .45 with 8.5" half round, half octagon barrels. Presented to Charles XV of Sweden and Norway. Condition was excellent. Butterfield & Butterfield, November 1999

Remington Rolling Block Single Shot Smooth Bore Pistol
NFA

Also called the Remington Combination Pistol-Shotgun, this firearm is a single-shot 20 gauge smooth bore pistol with a detachable shoulder stock, and is extremely rare. ATF advised this writer that it cannot be classified as a "curio or relic," because it is an antique firearm (manufactured in or before 1898) that fires fixed shotgun ammunition that is currently available in ordinary commercial channels. ATF classifies this firearm as a short-barreled shotgun under the NFA, which requires payment of a $200 tax on each ownership transfer; it is unclear whether it qualifies as an "any other weapon" (and $5 transfer tax) if unaccompanied by a shoulder stock.

John B. McClernan's article, "The Remington Combination Pistol-Shotgun" (in *The Canadian Journal of Arms Collecting*, Vol. 5, No. 1, 1967, pages 1-12), contains the most published information about this firearm at this time. He reports the barrel length is 11.75", with "no rear sight nor any sign of milling or drilling for a rear sight [and] has [an] original brass pin front sight." The outside diameter at the joint with the receiver is .843" and .406" at the opposite end. The pistol's overall length is 18.25" and 27.5" with the shoulder stock attached. The receiver's left side bears the markings: **Remington's Ilion, N.Y.U.S.A./Pat. May 3d Nov. 15th 1864 April 17th, 1866**, which he contends "dates its production period as 1867-1875." Based on documented and exhaustive original research, McClernan states: "there is no way to escape the conclusion that this gun, if not experimental, is at least a rare, special-order Remington variation."

Remington-Rider Magazine Pistol

A 5-shot .32 caliber magazine pistol with a spur trigger and 3" octagonal barrel. The magazine is located beneath the barrel and can be loaded from the front. Blued, nickel-plated or case hardened with walnut, pearl, or ivory grips. The barrel marked "E. Remington & Sons, Ilion, N.Y. Riders Pat. Aug. 15, 1871." Approximately 10,000 were manufactured between 1871 and 1888.

NOTE: For blued finish add a 50% premium.

Exc.	V.G.	Good	Fair	Poor
3000	2400	1500	800	500

Remington-Smoot No. 1 Revolver

A .30 caliber spur trigger revolver with a 2.75" octagonal barrel and 5-shot fluted cylinder. Blued or nickel-plated with walnut or hard rubber grips. The barrel rib is marked, "E. Remington & Sons, Ilion, N.Y. Pat. W. S. Smoot Oct. 21, 1873." Examples dating from the beginning of production are found with a revolving recoil shield. Such examples would command approximately a 300% premium over the values listed below.

NOTE: For blued finish add a 50% premium.

Exc.	V.G.	Good	Fair	Poor
800	600	400	200	100

Remington-Smoot No. 2 Revolver

As above, except in .32 caliber approximately 20,000 were made between 1878 and 1888.

NOTE: For blued finish add a 50% premium.

Courtesy William F. Krause

Exc.	V.G.	Good	Fair	Poor
1800	1600	800	500	300

Model 1871 Army Rolling Block Pistol

A .50 caliber rolling block single shot pistol with an 8" round barrel. Blued, case hardened with walnut grips and forend. The distinguishing feature of this model is that it has a rearward extension at the top of the grip and a squared butt. Approximately 6,000 were made between 1872 and 1888. Engraved ivory-stocked versions, as pictured below, will bring considerable premiums.

Exc.	V.G.	Good	Fair	Poor
700	600	300	200	100

Remington-Smoot No. 3 Revolver

Two variations of this spur trigger .38 caliber revolver exist. One with a rounded grip and no barrel rib, the other with a squared back, squared butt grip with a barrel rib. Centerfire versions are also known and they are worth approximately 10% more than the values listed below. Blued or nickel-plated with hard rubber grips. Approximately 25,000 were made between 1878 and 1888.

NOTE: For blued finish add a 50% premium.

Paul Goodwin Photo

Exc.	V.G.	Good	Fair	Poor
700	600	300	200	100

No. 4 Revolver

A .38 or .41 caliber spur trigger revolver with a 2.5" barrel and no ejector rod. Blued or nickel-plated with hard rubber grips. The barrel marked "E. Remington & Sons, Ilion, N.Y." Approximately 10,000 were manufactured between 1877 and 1888.

NOTE: For blued finish add a 50% premium.

Paul Goodwin Photo

Paul Goodwin Photo

Exc.	V.G.	Good	Fair	Poor
600	500	300	200	100

Remington Iroquois Revolver

A .22 caliber spur trigger revolver with a 2.25" barrel and 7-shot cylinder. Blued or nickel-plated with hard rubber grips.

The barrel marked "Remington, Ilion, N.Y." and "Iroquois." Some examples of this model will be found without the Remington markings. Approximately 10,000 were manufactured between 1878 and 1888.

NOTE: For blued finish add a 50% premium.

Exc.	V.G.	Good	Fair	Poor
800	600	400	300	200

Model 1875 Single Action Army

A .44 Remington or .44-40 or .45 caliber single action revolver with a 7.5" barrel. Blued or nickel-plated, case hardened with walnut grips. Some examples are to be found fitted with a lanyard ring at the butt. The barrel marked "E. Remington & Sons Ilion, N.Y. U.S.A." Approximately 25,000 were manufactured between 1875 and 1889.

NOTE: Blued Version-Add 40%.

Courtesy Milwaukee Public Museum, Milwaukee, Wisconsin

Exc.	V.G.	Good	Fair	Poor
5500	4500	2200	1400	800

Model 1890 Single Action Army

A .44-40 caliber single action revolver with a 5.5" or 7.5" barrel and 6-shot cylinder. Blued or nickel-plated with hard rubber grips bearing the monogram "RA" at the top. The barrel marked "Remington Arms Co., Ilion, N.Y." Approximately 2,000 were made between 1891 and 1894. Prospective purchasers are advised to secure a qualified appraisal prior to acquisition.
Blued Version-Add 40%.

Paul Goodwin Photo

Exc.	V.G.	Good	Fair	Poor
12000	8500	5000	3000	1800

Model 1891 Target Rolling Block Pistol

A .22, .25 Stevens, or .32 S&W caliber single-shot rolling block pistol with a 10" half octagonal barrel fitted with target sights. Blued, case hardened with walnut grips and forend. The barrel marked "Remington Arms Co. Ilion, N.Y.," and the frame "Remingtons Ilion N.Y. U.S.A. Pat. May 3 Nov. 15, 1864 April 17, 1866 P S." This is an extremely rare pistol, with slightly over 100 manufactured between 1892 and 1898. Prospective purchasers are advised to secure a qualified appraisal prior to acquisition.

Paul Goodwin Photo

Exc.	V.G.	Good	Fair	Poor
3000	2500	1500	800	600

Model 1901 Target Rolling Block

As above, with the exception that the bridge block thumb piece has been moved out of the line of sight and the rear sight is mounted on the frame instead of the barrel. Approximately 735 were made between 1901 and 1909. Prospective purchasers are advised to secure a qualified appraisal prior to acquisition.

Paul Goodwin Photo

Exc.	V.G.	Good	Fair	Poor
3000	2500	1500	1000	600

Mark III Signal Pistol

A 10 gauge spur trigger flare pistol with a 9" round barrel. The frame of brass and the barrel of iron finished matte black with walnut grips. The barrel marked "The Remington Arms - Union Metallic Cartridge Co., Inc. Mark III, Remington Bridgeport Works Bridgeport, Connecticut U.S.A." Approximately 25,000 were manufactured between 1915 and 1918.

Paul Goodwin Photo

Exc.	V.G.	Good	Fair	Poor
—	275	125	75	55

Remington 1911 and 1911A1

See the Colt section of this book for pistols of this type.

Model 51

A .32 or .380 caliber semiautomatic pistol with a 3.5" barrel and magazines capable of holding either 7 or 8 cartridges depending on the caliber. Blued with hard rubber grips having the legend "Remington UMC" in a circle at the top. The slide marked "The Remington Arms - Union Metallic Cartridge Co., Inc. Remington Ilion Wks. Ilion, N.Y. U.S.A. Pedersen's Pat-

ents Pending." Later versions carried a 1920 and a 1921 patent date. The early examples have nine grooves on the slide; later models have 15 grooves with the frame marked "Remington Trademark." Early variations are worth approximately 10% more than the values listed below and .32 caliber examples are worth approximately 25% additional. Approximately 65,000 were manufactured between 1918 and 1934.

Courtesy Orvel Reichert

Exc.	V.G.	Good	Fair	Poor
—	500	275	125	75

Model 53

Manufactured in 1917 in .45ACP. Similar to the Model 51 except for size and an external hammer. Tested by the US Army and Navy. Overall length is 8.25", weight is about 35 oz., and magazine capacity is 7 rounds.

Courtesy James Rankin

Exc.	V.G.	Good	Fair	Poor
7000	5500	4000	2500	2000

Model 1841 "Mississippi Rifle"

A .54 caliber percussion rifle with a 33" barrel and full stock secured by two barrel bands. The lock (marked Remington's Herkimer N.Y.) is case hardened, the barrel browned and the furniture of brass. The stock is fitted with a brass patch box on the right side. Approximately 20,000 were made between 1846 and 1855.

Paul Goodwin Photo

Exc.	V.G.	Good	Fair	Poor
—	—	4500	1750	750

Model 1861 U.S. Rifle Musket

A .58 caliber percussion rifle with a 40" barrel and full length stock secured by three barrel bands. The lock marked "Remington's Ilion, N.Y." Finished in the white with a walnut stock. Approximately 40,000 were made between 1864 and 1866.

Paul Goodwin Photo

Exc.	V.G.	Good	Fair	Poor
—	—	2500	950	400

Model 1863 Zouave Rifle

Paul Goodwin Photo

A .58 caliber percussion rifle with a 33" barrel and full length stock secured by two barrel bands. The lock case hardened and marked "Remington's Ilion N.Y.", the barrel blued and the furniture of brass. Approximately 12,500 were manufactured between 1862 and 1865.

Exc.	V.G.	Good	Fair	Poor
—	4500	2500	950	350

Breech-Loading Carbine

A .46 or .50 rimfire single shot rolling block carbine with a 20" barrel. Blued, case hardened with a walnut stock. The tang marked "Remington's Ilion, N.Y. Pat. Dec. 23, 1863 May 3 & Nov. 16, 1864." The .50 caliber version is worth approximately 15% more than the .46 caliber. Approximately 15,000 .50-caliber variations were made, most of which were sold to France. Approximately 5,000 carbines were made in .46 caliber. Manufactured from 1864 to 1866.

Paul Goodwin Photo

Exc.	V.G.	Good	Fair	Poor
—	—	3000	1250	500

Revolving Rifle

A .36 or. 44 caliber revolving rifle with either 24" or 28" octagonal barrels with a 6-shot cylinder. The triggerguard formed with a scrolled finger extension at the rear. Blued, case hardened with a walnut stock. These rifles are also encountered altered to cartridge and would be worth approximately 20% less than the percussion values listed below. The barrel marked "Patented Sept. 14, 1858 E. Remington & Sons, Ilion, New York, U.S.A. New Model." The .44 caliber model will bring a premium of about 15% and is rare. Approximately 1,000 were manufactured between 1866 and 1879.

Courtesy Milwaukee Public Museum, Milwaukee, Wisconsin

Courtesy Buffalo Bill Historical Center, Cody, Wyoming

Exc.	V.G.	Good	Fair	Poor
—	—	4250	1500	500

Remington-Beals Rifle

A .32 or. 38 caliber sliding barrel single shot rifle with octagonal barrels of 24", 26", or 28" length. The barrel can be moved forward by lowering the triggerguard/lever. This model is to be found with either frames made of brass or iron, the latter being worth approximately 20% more than the values listed below. Walnut stock. The barrel marked "Beals Patent June 28, 1864 Jan. 30, 1866 E. Remington & Sons, Ilion, New York." Approximately 800 were manufactured between 1866 and 1888. A few examples are known to have been factory engraved. Prospective purchasers are advised to secure a qualified appraisal prior to acquisition.

Courtesy Milwaukee Public Museum, Milwaukee, Wisconsin

Exc.	V.G.	Good	Fair	Poor
—	—	950	400	150

U.S. Navy Rolling Block Carbine

Exc.	V.G.	Good	Fair	Poor
—	—	2000	850	350

Model 1867 Navy Cadet Rifle

Paul Goodwin Photo

Exc.	V.G.	Good	Fair	Poor
—	—	2000	850	350

Rolling Block Military Rifles

Exc.	V.G.	Good	Fair	Poor
—	—	750	400	100

No. 1 Rolling Block Sporting Rifle
Standard No. 1 Sporting Rifle

A single shot rolling block rifle produced in a variety of calibers from .40-50 to .50-70 centerfire as well as .44 and .46 rimfire. Standard barrel lengths were either 28" or 30" and of octagonal form.

Courtesy Milwaukee Public Museum, Milwaukee, Wisconsin

Exc.	V.G.	Good	Fair	Poor
—	4500	2000	600	250

Long-Range Creedmoor Rifle

A .44-90, .44-100, or .44-105 caliber rolling block rifle with a 34" half octagonal barrel, long range vernier tang sights and globe front sights. Blued, case hardened with a walnut stock having a checkered pistol grip. This rifle was available with a number of optional features and a qualified appraisal should be secured if those features are in doubt. Produced from 1873 to 1890.

Courtesy Butterfield & Butterfield, San Francisco, California

Exc.	V.G.	Good	Fair	Poor
—	7500	3750	1500	500

Mid-Range Target Rifle

As above, except chambered for .40-70, .44-77, .45-70, or .50-70 caliber with 28" or 30" half octagonal barrels. Produced from 1875 to 1890.

Exc.	V.G.	Good	Fair	Poor
—	5000	2000	750	300

Short-Range Rifle

As above, chambered for cartridges between .38 and .44 caliber with 26" or 30" round or octagonal barrels. Open rear sight with beach front sight. The walnut stock checkered. Produced from 1875 to 1890.

Exc.	V.G.	Good	Fair	Poor
—	4000	1750	600	250

Black Hills Rifle

As above, in .45-60 caliber with a 28" round barrel fitted with open sights and a plain straight grip stock. Produced from 1877 to 1882.

Exc.	V.G.	Good	Fair	Poor
—	4000	2000	850	300

Shotgun

As above, in 16 gauge with either a 30" or 32" Damascus or fluid steel barrels. Produced from 1870 to 1892.

Exc.	V.G.	Good	Fair	Poor
—	1000	500	250	100

Baby Carbine

As above, with a 20" thin round barrel chambered for the .4440 cartridge and fitted with a saddle ring on the left side of the frame. Blued, case hardened with a walnut stock having a carbine buttplate. Manufactured from 1892 to 1902.

Exc.	V.G.	Good	Fair	Poor
—	3000	1250	600	200

Model 1-1/2 Sporting Rifle

A lightweight variation of the above using a 1.25" wide, No. 1 rolling block action. Chambered for rimfire cartridges from .22 to the .38 extra long, as well as centerfire cartridges from .32-20 to the .44-40. Medium weight octagonal barrels from 24" to 28" in length, with open rear and a blade-type front sight. Blued, case hardened with a walnut stock. There were several thousand manufactured between 1888 and 1897.

Paul Goodwin Photo

Exc.	V.G.	Good	Fair	Poor
—	1750	950	400	100

Model 2 Sporting Rifle

As above, using a No. 2 action and chambered for various cartridges from .22 to .38 caliber with 24" or 26" octagonal barrels. Blued, case hardened with a walnut stock. This model was produced with a number of optional features that affect its value. Prospective purchasers are advised to secure a qualified appraisal prior to acquisition. Manufactured from 1873 to 1910.

Paul Goodwin Photo

Exc.	V.G.	Good	Fair	Poor
—	1350	600	250	100

No. 4 Rolling Block Rifle

Built on the lightweight No. 4 action, this rifle was available in .22, .25 Stevens, or .32 caliber, with either a 22.5" or 24" octagonal barrel. Blued, case hardened with a walnut stock. A takedown version was also made and these are worth approximately 10% more than the values listed below. Approximately 50,000 were made between 1890 and 1933.

Exc.	V.G.	Good	Fair	Poor
—	750	400	200	75

Model No. 4 S Military Rifle

At the request of the United States Boy Scouts in 1913, the Remington Company designed a military style rifle having a 28" barrel and full length forend secured by one barrel band. A short upper hand guard was also fitted and a bayonet stud is to be found at the muzzle. In 1915 the designation of this model was changed from "Boy Scout" to "Military Model." Approximately 15,000 were made between 1913 and 1923.

Paul Goodwin Photo

Exc.	V.G.	Good	Fair	Poor
—	2250	950	400	275

No. 5 Rolling Block Rifle

Built on the No. 5 action, this rifle was designed for smokeless cartridges and was made in a variety of barrel lengths, calibers and in a carbine version. Blued, case hardened with a walnut stock.

Exc.	V.G.	Good	Fair	Poor
—	1150	550	250	100

No. 5 Sporting or Target Rifle

Chambered for the .30-30, .303 British, 7mm, .30 U.S., .32-40, .32 U.S., and the .38-55 cartridges. This rifle was offered with 28" or 30" round barrels and features a plain, straight-grip stock with a half-length forend. It has open rear sights and was available with double-set triggers that would add approximately 10% to the value. It was manufactured between 1898 and 1905.

Exc.	V.G.	Good	Fair	Poor
—	5000	2250	850	300

Model 1897

A 7x57mm and .30 U.S. caliber full stock rolling block rifle. The Model 1902 is of identical form except that it was fitted with an automatic ejector. Manufactured from 1897 to 1902.

Paul Goodwin Photo

Exc.	V.G.	Good	Fair	Poor
—	1150	550	250	100

Carbine

As above, fitted with a 20" round barrel and a half-length forend secured by one barrel band.

Exc.	V.G.	Good	Fair	Poor
—	1500	650	250	100

No. 6 Rolling Block Rifle

A lightweight, small rifle designed expressly to be used by young boys. It is chambered for the .22 rimfire cartridge, as well as the .32 Short or Long. It was also produced with a smoothbore barrel to be used with shot cartridges. The round barrel is 20" in length. It has a takedown action with a barrel held on by a knurled knob underneath the frame. It is a lightweight rolling block, with a thin operating knob on the breech. The finish is blued overall. Early models featured a case-colored frame, and these versions would be worth approximately 10% additional. It has a straight-grip walnut stock with a small forearm. Over 250,000 manufactured between 1902 and 1903.

Paul Goodwin Photo

Exc.	V.G.	Good	Fair	Poor
—	550	300	100	75

No. 7 Rolling Block Rifle

Readily identifiable by its accentuated checked pistol grip, this model was available in .22 or .25-10 Stevens caliber with 24", 26", or 28" half octagonal barrels. Fitted with a tang mounted aperture rear sight. Blued, case hardened with a walnut stock. Approximately 1,000 were made between 1903 and 1911.

Exc.	V.G.	Good	Fair	Poor
—	5250	2000	750	300

Remington-Hepburn No. 3 Rifle

A lever activated falling block single shot rifle designed by Lewis Hepburn available in a variety of calibers from .22 Winchester centerfire to .50-90 Sharps with octagonal or round barrels of 26", 28", or 30" length. Blued, case hardened with a walnut stock. This model was available with a variety of optional features that affect the value considerably. Prospective purchasers are advised to secure a qualified appraisal prior to acquisition. Approximately 10,000 were made between 1883 and 1907.

Exc.	V.G.	Good	Fair	Poor
—	4000	1750	800	350

No. 3 Match Rifle

As above, but fitted with a high comb buttstock and a nickel-plated Schuetzen buttplate. Manufactured in various calibers from .25-20 Stevens to .40-65 with 30" half octagonal barrels. This model was made in two versions: "A Quality" with a plain stock, tang mounted rear sight and a Beach front sight, and; "B Quality" with a checkered walnut stock having a cheek rest, checkered forend, vernier rear sight and a combination wind gauge and spirit level front sight. Double set triggers were also available and these would add approximately 10% to the values listed below. Approximately 1,000 were made between 1883 and 1907.

A Quality

Paul Goodwin Photo

Exc.	V.G.	Good	Fair	Poor
—	4250	2000	800	350

B Quality

Paul Goodwin Photo

Exc.	V.G.	Good	Fair	Poor
—	5250	2500	1200	500

No. 3 Long-Range Creedmoor Rifle

As above, in .44 caliber with a 32" or 34" half octagonal barrel, long range vernier rear sight, combination wind gauge and spirit level front sight, with a deluxe checkered walnut stock having a rubber shotgun buttplate. Produced with a number of optional features that affect the value. Prospective purchasers are advised to secure a qualified appraisal prior to acquisition. Manufactured from 1880 to 1907.

Paul Goodwin Photo

Exc.	V.G.	Good	Fair	Poor
—	7500	3500	1250	500

No. 3 Mid-Range Creedmoor Rifle

As above, but chambered for the .40-65 cartridge and fitted with a 28" barrel.

Exc.	V.G.	Good	Fair	Poor
—	5000	2250	950	350

No. 3 Long-Range Military Rifle

This is a rare variation that is chambered for the .44-20 Remington cartridge. It has a round 34" barrel and a full length forearm held on by two barrel bands. The finish is blued and case-colored, and the stock is walnut. There are two basic versions. The plain grade has an uncheckered, straight-grip stock with military-type sights. There is also a fancy grade that features a high-grade, checkered, pistol grip stock with a full-length, checkered forend, vernier tang sight, and wind gauge, spirit lever front sight. There were a few manufactured in the 1880s.

Paul Goodwin Photo

Plain Grade

Exc.	V.G.	Good	Fair	Poor
—	4500	2500	1200	400

Fancy Grade

Exc.	V.G.	Good	Fair	Poor
—	7500	3750	1500	600

No. 3 Schuetzen Match Rifle

As above, with the exception that instead of the side lever, the action is raised or lowered by means of the lever on the triggerguard. Chambered for various popular cartridges and offered with a 30" or 32" part-octagonal, heavy barrel. It features a vernier tang sight with a hooded front sight. It was standard with double-set triggers and a palm rest. The finish is blued and case-colored, with a high-grade checkered walnut stock and forend. It has an ornate, Swiss-type Schuetzen buttplate and is also known as the "Walker-Hepburn Rifle." There were two versions available. One, a standard breechloader with the Remington Walker-marked barrel; and the other, a muzzle-loading variation that was fitted with a removable false muzzle. This version was supplied with a brass bullet starter and other accessories. Prospective purchasers are advised to secure a qualified appraisal prior to acquisition.

Breechloading Version

Exc.	V.G.	Good	Fair	Poor
—	22500	12500	3500	900

Muzzleloading Version

Exc.	V.G.	Good	Fair	Poor
—	37500	17500	5000	1500

No. 3 High-Power Rifle

The Model No. 3 was also made available in a variety of smokeless cartridges; .30-30, .30-40, .32 Special, .32-40 and .38-55. Standard barrel lengths were 26", 28", or 30". Produced from 1900 to 1907.

Exc.	V.G.	Good	Fair	Poor
—	3250	1750	650	250

Remington-Keene Magazine Rifle

A bolt-action rifle chambered for the .40, .43, and .45-70 centerfire cartridges with 22", 24.5", 29.25", or 32.5" barrels. It is readily identifiable by the exposed hammer at the end of the bolt. Blued, case hardened hammer and furniture, with a walnut stock. The receiver marked "E. Remington & Sons, Ilion, N.Y." together with the patent dates 1874, 1876, and 1877. The magazine on this rifle was located beneath the barrel and the receiver is fitted with a cut-off so that the rifle could be used as a single shot. Approximately 5,000 rifles were made between 1880 and 1888 in the following variations:

Sporting Rifle-24.5" Barrel

Paul Goodwin Photo

Remington-Keene Repeating Sporting Rifle Fancy Grade

Paul Goodwin Photo

Exc.	V.G.	Good	Fair	Poor
—	1500	750	350	150

Army Rifle

Barrel length 32.5" with a full-length stock secured by two barrel bands.

Courtesy Milwaukee Public Museum, Milwaukee, Wisconsin

Exc.	V.G.	Good	Fair	Poor
—	4500	2250	950	450

Navy Rifle

As above, with a 29.25" barrel.

Exc.	V.G.	Good	Fair	Poor
—	4500	2250	950	450

Carbine

As above, with a 22" barrel and a half-length forend secured by one barrel band.

Courtesy Milwaukee Public Museum, Milwaukee, Wisconsin

Exc.	V.G.	Good	Fair	Poor
—	3250	1500	750	350

Frontier Model

As above, with a 24" barrel and half-length forend secured by one barrel band. Those purchased by the United States Department of the Interior for arming the Indian Police are marked "U.S.I.D." on the receiver.

Exc.	V.G.	Good	Fair	Poor
—	—	4500	2500	850

Remington-Lee Magazine Rifle

Designed by James Paris Lee, rifles of this type were originally manufactured by the Sharps Rifle Company in 1880. The Remington Company began production of this model in 1881 after the Sharps Company ceased operations. Approximately 100,000 Lee magazine rifles were made between 1880 and 1907. Their variations are as follows:

Courtesy Milwaukee Public Museum, Milwaukee, Wisconsin

Model 1879-Sharps Mfg.

Barrel length 28" with a full-length stock secured by two barrel bands. The barrel marked "Sharps Rifle Co. Bridgeport, Conn." and "Old Reliable" in a rectangular cartouche. Approximately 300 were made prior to 1881.

Exc.	V.G.	Good	Fair	Poor
—	—	4250	2000	600

Model 1879 U.S. Navy Model

Exc.	V.G.	Good	Fair	Poor
—	—	1750	750	250

Model 1879 Sporting Rifle

Barrel length 28" or 30", .45-70 or .45-90 caliber, checkered pistol grip stock with a sporting style forend. Markings on the receiver as above. Approximately 450 made.

Exc.	V.G.	Good	Fair	Poor
—	—	1500	700	250

Model 1879 Military Rifle

Identical to the Navy model, except chambered for the .43 Spanish cartridge. A limited number were also produced in .45-70 caliber. The Spanish versions are worth approximately 25% less than the values listed below. Approximately 1,000 were made. The majority of these rifles were made for export.

Exc.	V.G.	Good	Fair	Poor
—	—	1000	450	150

Model 1882 Army Contract

Exc.	V.G.	Good	Fair	Poor
—	—	1750	750	300

Model 1885 Navy Contract

Exc.	V.G.	Good	Fair	Poor
—	—	1750	750	300

Model 1882 & 1885 Military Rifles

Barrel length 32", full-length stock secured by two barrel bands, chambered for .42 Russian, .43 Spanish, .45 Gardner or .45-70 cartridges. The values for those rifles not in .45-70 caliber would be approximately 25% less than those shown below. Approximately 10,000 Model 1882 rifles were made and 60,000 Model 1885 rifles. The two models can be differentiated by the fact that the cocking piece on the bolt of the Model 1885 is larger. The majority of these rifles were made for foreign contracts and commercial sales.

Exc.	V.G.	Good	Fair	Poor
—	—	950	400	150

Model 1882 & 1885 Sporting Rifle

As above, chambered for .45-70 and .45-90 caliber with 26" or 30" octagonal barrels and walnut sporting stocks. Approximately 200 were made.

Exc.	V.G.	Good	Fair	Poor
—	—	1750	750	200

Model 1882 & 1885 Carbine

As above, with a 24" barrel and a half-length forend secured by one barrel band. Prospective purchasers are advised to secure a qualified appraisal prior to acquisition.

Exc.	V.G.	Good	Fair	Poor
—	—	1750	750	200

Model 1899

Designed for use with smokeless and rimless cartridges, this model is marked on the receiver "Remington Arms Co. Ilion, N.Y. Patented Aug. 26th 1884 Sept. 9th 1884 March 17th 1885 Jan 18th 1887." Produced from 1889 to 1907 in the following variations:

Military Rifle

Exc.	V.G.	Good	Fair	Poor
—	1000	450	200	100

Military Carbine

Exc.	V.G.	Good	Fair	Poor
—	1500	700	300	100

Sporting Rifle

As above, with a 24", 26", or 28" round or octagonal barrel and a half-length sporting stock with a checkered pistol grip. Approximately 7,000 were manufactured.

Exc.	V.G.	Good	Fair	Poor
—	1000	450	200	100

Remington Lebel Bolt-Action Rifle

Exc.	V.G.	Good	Fair	Poor
—	600	300	150	100

Remington Mosin-Nagant Bolt-Action Rifle

Exc.	V.G.	Good	Fair	Poor
—	500	275	100	75

U.S. Model 1917 Magazine Rifle

Exc.	V.G.	Good	Fair	Poor
—	950	400	150	100

Remington-Whitmore Model 1874

A sidelock double-barrel shotgun, combination shotgun rifle or double-barrel rifle with 28" or 30" fluid steel barrels. Also available with Damascus barrels. The barrels released by pushing forward the top lever. Blued, case hardened with a straight or semi-pistol grip walnut stock. The barrels marked "A. E. Whitmore's Patent Aug. 8, 1871, April 16, 1872." The rib between the barrels is marked "E. Remington & Sons, Ilion, N.Y." Several thousand were manufactured between 1874 and 1882.

Shotgun

Exc.	V.G.	Good	Fair	Poor
—	1500	650	250	100

Combination Gun (Rare)

Exc.	V.G.	Good	Fair	Poor
—	3250	1500	450	200

Double Rifle

Prospective purchasers are advised to secure a qualified appraisal prior to acquisition. Very rare.

Exc.	V.G.	Good	Fair	Poor
—	8000	3750	1500	500

Model 1882 Shotgun

A sidelock double-barrel 10 or 12 gauge shotgun with 28" or 30" fluid steel or Damascus barrels. Blued, case hardened with a checkered pistol grip stock and hard rubber buttplate. The barrels are marked "E. Remington & Sons, Ilion, N.Y." and the lock is marked "Remington Arms Co." This model has a conventional top lever that moves to the side. Offered with optional engraving, and such models should be individually appraised. Approximately 7,500 were manufactured between 1882 and 1889.

Exc.	V.G.	Good	Fair	Poor
—	1250	550	250	100

Model 1883 through 1889 Shotgun

A sidelock 10, 12, or 16 gauge double-barrel shotgun with fluid steel or Damascus barrels 28" to 32" in length. The models 1883, 1885, 1887, and 1889 are all somewhat alike, varying only in the form of their hammers and internal mechanisms. Blued, case hardened, checkered pistol grip stock with a grip cap. Available in a variety of styles including highly engraved models that should be individually appraised. Approximately 30,000 were made between 1883 and 1909.

Exc.	V.G.	Good	Fair	Poor
—	1250	550	250	100

Model 1893 (No. 9)

Single barrel hammer gun in 10, 12, 16, 20, 24, and 28 gauge. Barrel lengths from 28" to 34". Case colored frame with hard rubber buttplate.

Courtesy William F. Krause

Exc.	V.G.	Good	Fair	Poor
—	—	350	200	100

Hammerless Shotgun Model 1894

A boxlock 10, 12, or 16 gauge double shotgun with fluid steel or Damascus barrels 26" to 32" in length. Blued, case hardened with a pistol grip stock. Available in a variety of styles and

---

it is advised that highly engraved examples should be individually appraised.

NOTE: Fluid steel barrels add 25% premium.

Exc.	V.G.	Good	Fair	Poor
—	700	350	200	100

Model 1900 Shotgun

As above, in 12 and 16 gauge only. The same cautions apply to highly engraved examples.

Exc.	V.G.	Good	Fair	Poor
—	600	300	200	100

Model 8

A .25, .30, .32, or .35 Remington semiautomatic rifle with a 22" barrel having open sights. The barrel is covered by a full length tube that encloses the recoil spring. Blued with walnut stock. Approximately 60,000 were made between 1906 and 1936 in the following styles.

Standard Grade

Exc.	V.G.	Good	Fair	Poor
400	325	250	175	125

Courtesy Remington Arms

Model SA-Checkered Stock

Exc.	V.G.	Good	Fair	Poor
550	450	350	225	150

Model 8C

Exc.	V.G.	Good	Fair	Poor
600	500	375	300	200

Model 8D Peerless-Light Engraving

Exc.	V.G.	Good	Fair	Poor
1200	850	500	400	300

Model 8E Expert

Exc.	V.G.	Good	Fair	Poor
1500	1200	900	600	450

Model 8F Premier-Heavily Engraved

Exc.	V.G.	Good	Fair	Poor
1800	1475	1000	750	550

Model 81 Woodsmaster

An improved variation of the Model 8, chambered for the same calibers as well as the .300 Savage cartridge. Produced from 1936 to 1950 in the following styles.

Standard Model

Exc.	V.G.	Good	Fair	Poor
400	325	250	175	125

Model 81A-Takedown

Exc.	V.G.	Good	Fair	Poor
450	375	300	225	150

Model 81D Peerless-Engraved

Exc.	V.G.	Good	Fair	Poor
1200	900	600	400	300

Model 81F Premier-Heavily Engraved

Exc.	V.G.	Good	Fair	Poor
1800	1475	900	750	550

Model 12 or 12 A

A .22 caliber slide action rifle with a 22" round or octagonal barrel having open sights. Blued with a walnut stock. Manufactured from 1909 to 1936 in the following styles.

Model 12A

Courtesy Remington Arms

Exc.	V.G.	Good	Fair	Poor
550	375	300	225	150

Model 12B-.22 Short, Gallery Model

Exc.	V.G.	Good	Fair	Poor
550	375	300	225	150

Model 12C-24" Octagon Barrel

Exc.	V.G.	Good	Fair	Poor
500	425	350	250	175

Model 12C N.R.A. Target-Limited Production

Exc.	V.G.	Good	Fair	Poor
750	550	450	250	200

Model 12CS-.22 Remington Special

Exc.	V.G.	Good	Fair	Poor
500	400	325	250	175

Model 12D Peerless-Light Engraving

Exc.	V.G.	Good	Fair	Poor
2250	1750	1200	1000	500

Model 12E Expert

Exc.	V.G.	Good	Fair	Poor
2500	2250	1750	1200	800

Model 12F Premier-Heavily Engraved

Exc.	V.G.	Good	Fair	Poor
3000	2250	1850	1200	800

Model 121 and/or 121A

A .22 caliber slide action rifle with a 24" round barrel. Blued with a walnut stock. Manufactured from 1936 to 1954 in the following styles.

Standard Grade

Exc.	V.G.	Good	Fair	Poor
495	350	225	175	100

Model 121D Peerless-Engraved

Exc.	V.G.	Good	Fair	Poor
2250	2000	1250	1000	750

Model 121F Premier-Heavily Engraved

Exc.	V.G.	Good	Fair	Poor
3250	2500	1750	1200	1000

Model 121S-.22 WRF

Exc.	V.G.	Good	Fair	Poor
850	700	400	350	250

Model 121SB-Smooth Bore

There are four different variations of this smooth bore rifle. Seek expert advice before a sale.

Exc.	V.G.	Good	Fair	Poor
600	450	350	250	200

Model 14 or 14A

A .25, .30, .32 or .35 Remington caliber slide action rifle with a 22" round barrel having open sights. Blued, plain walnut stock. Manufactured from 1912 to 1936.

Model 8F Premier Grade

Paul Goodwin Photo

Remington Model 12F Grade   Paul Goodwin Photo

Exc.	V.G.	Good	Fair	Poor
350	275	225	150	100

Model 14R
As above, with an 18.5" barrel.

Exc.	V.G.	Good	Fair	Poor
500	400	300	250	175

Model 14-1/2
As above, except chambered for the .38-40 or .44-40 cartridge with a 22.5" barrel. A carbine with an 18.5" barrel known as the Model 14-1/2R, would be worth approximately 10% more than the values listed below. Manufactured from 1912 to 1922.

Exc.	V.G.	Good	Fair	Poor
1100	750	500	350	250

Model 141
A .30, .32, or .35 Remington caliber slide action rifle with a 24" barrel having open sights. Blued with a plain walnut stock. Later production versions of this rifle were known as the Model 141A. Manufactured from 1936 to 1950.

Courtesy Remington Arms

Exc.	V.G.	Good	Fair	Poor
500	400	300	250	175

Model 25
A .25-20 or .32-20 caliber slide action rifle with a 24" barrel having open sights. Blued with a walnut stock. Later production examples were known as the Model 25A and a carbine version with an 18" barrel as the Model 25R. Manufactured from 1923 to 1936.

Model 25   Courtesy Remington Arms

Model 25R   Courtesy Remington Arms

Exc.	V.G.	Good	Fair	Poor
550	450	350	250	200

NOTE: For rifles with 18" barrels add 100%.

Model 16
A .22 caliber semiautomatic rifle with a 22" barrel having open sights. Blued with a walnut stock. Later production examples were known as the Model 16A. Manufactured from 1914 to 1928.

Courtesy Remington Arms

Exc.	V.G.	Good	Fair	Poor
400	350	250	125	75

Model 24
Designed by John M. Browning, this semiautomatic rifle is of .22 caliber with a 19" barrel having open sights. Blued with a walnut pistol grip stock. Later production versions were known as the Model 24A. Produced from 1922 to 1935.

Courtesy Wallis & Wallis, Lewes, Sussex, England

Exc.	V.G.	Good	Fair	Poor
400	350	250	150	100

Model 241 Speedmaster
A .22 caliber takedown semiautomatic rifle with a 24" barrel having open sights. Blued with a walnut stock. Later production versions were known as the Model 241A. Approximately 56,000 were made between 1935 and 1949 in the following styles:

Model 241

Courtesy Remington Arms

Exc.	V.G.	Good	Fair	Poor
450	350	250	200	150

Model 241 D Peerless-Engraved
Exc.	V.G.	Good	Fair	Poor
2500	2000	1500	1000	600

Model 241 E Expert

Exc.	V.G.	Good	Fair	Poor
2750	2250	1700	1000	500

Model 241 F Premier-Heavily Engraved

Exc.	V.G.	Good	Fair	Poor
3250	2500	2100	1500	1000

Model 550A

A .22 short, long, or long rifle caliber semiautomatic rifle with a 24" barrel and open sights. Blued with a walnut pistol grip stock. Approximately 220,000 were made between 1941 and 1971.

Exc.	V.G.	Good	Fair	Poor
200	175	150	100	75

Model 550P

As above, with an aperture rear sight.

Exc.	V.G.	Good	Fair	Poor
225	200	175	125	100

Model 55-2G

As above, except fitted with a shell deflector and a screw eye for securing it to a shooting gallery counter.

Exc.	V.G.	Good	Fair	Poor
200	175	150	100	75

Model 30A

A sporting rifle using the U.S. Model 1917 Enfield bolt action chambered for various Remington cartridges as well as the 7x57mm and .30-06 cartridges. Barrel length 22". Checkered walnut stock. A carbine model fitted with a 20" barrel was known as the Model 30R. Manufactured from 1921 to 1940.

Courtesy Remington Arms

Exc.	V.G.	Good	Fair	Poor
450	350	250	175	100

Model 30S

As above, chambered for the .257 Roberts, 7x57, and the .30-06 cartridges and with 24" barrel with a Lyman receiver sight. Select checkered walnut stock. Manufactured from 1930 to 1940.

Exc.	V.G.	Good	Fair	Poor
550	450	325	250	150

Model 41A "Targetmaster"

This is a bolt action rimfire rifle chambered for the .22 caliber short, Long, long rifle. It is fitted with a 27" barrel with an open rear sight and bead front sight. The pistol grip stock is plain. It was produced from 1936 to 1940.

Exc.	V.G.	Good	Fair	Poor
150	125	85	70	50

Model 41AS

Same as above but chambered for the .22 Remington Special or .22 WRF cartridge.

Exc.	V.G.	Good	Fair	Poor
175	150	125	100	75

Model 41P

Same as Model 41A with the addition of a rear peep sight and hooded front sight.

Exc.	V.G.	Good	Fair	Poor
135	115	90	70	50

Model 41SB

Same as Model 41A except for use with .22 shot cartridge. Barrel is smoothbore.

Exc.	V.G.	Good	Fair	Poor
250	200	150	100	75

From 1930 to 1970 the Remington Company produced a variety of single shot and repeating .22 caliber rifles. The values for these are much the same so consequently we list them for reference only.

Model 33	Model 510 X
Model 33 NRA	Model 511 A
Model 34	Model 511 P
Model 34 NRA	Model 511 X
Model 341 A	Model 512 A
Model 341 P	Model 512 P
Model 341 SB	Model 512 X
Model 510	Model 514
Model 510 P	Model 514 P
Model 510 SB	Model 514 BC

Smooth-Bore Models-Add 50%.

Model 510   Courtesy Remington Arms

Model 510 Carbine   Courtesy Remington Arms

Exc.	V.G.	Good	Fair	Poor
125	100	75	50	25

Model 37

A .22 caliber bolt action magazine target rifle with a heavy 28" barrel having target sights and telescope bases. Blued with a walnut target style stock. Manufactured from 1937 to 1940.

Courtesy Remington Arms

Exc.	V.G.	Good	Fair	Poor
600	500	400	300	250

Model 37-1940

As above, with an improved lock, trigger pull and redesigned stock. Manufactured from 1940 to 1954.

Courtesy Remington Arms

Exc.	V.G.	Good	Fair	Poor
650	525	400	300	200

Model 511 Scoremaster

A .22 caliber bolt action magazine sporting rifle with a 22" barrel. Blued with a walnut stock.

Exc.	V.G.	Good	Fair	Poor
250	200	175	125	75

Model 513 TR Matchmaster

A .22 caliber bolt action magazine target rifle with a heavy 27" barrel and Redfield aperture rear sight. Blued with a target style walnut stock. Manufactured from 1940 to 1969.

Exc.	V.G.	Good	Fair	Poor
350	300	200	150	100

Model 513 S

As above, with Marble sights and a checkered walnut sporting style stock. Manufactured from 1941 to 1956.

Exc.	V.G.	Good	Fair	Poor
600	500	400	275	225

Model 521 TL Jr.

A .22 caliber bolt action magazine target rifle with a heavy 25" barrel and Lyman sights. Blued with a target style walnut stock. Manufactured from 1947 to 1969.

Exc.	V.G.	Good	Fair	Poor
250	200	175	125	75

Model 760

A slide-action sporting rifle chambered for various popular centerfire cartridges from the .222 up to the .35 Remington cartridge, with a 22" round barrel having open sights. It features a detachable box magazine. Blued with a checkered, walnut, pistol grip stock. Manufactured between 1952 and 1982. Examples of this rifle chambered for the .222, .223, .244, and the .257 Roberts are worth a premium over other calibers. Prospective purchasers are advised to secure a qualified appraisal prior to acquisition. This model was produced in the following styles.

Standard Model

Exc.	V.G.	Good	Fair	Poor
275	200	175	125	100

Model 760 Carbine-18.5" Barrel

Exc.	V.G.	Good	Fair	Poor
375	300	250	175	150

Model 760D Peerless-Engraved

Exc.	V.G.	Good	Fair	Poor
1000	850	650	550	450

Model 760F Premier-Game Scene Engraved

Exc.	V.G.	Good	Fair	Poor
2500	2000	1500	1200	1000

Model 760F Gold Inlaid

Exc.	V.G.	Good	Fair	Poor
5000	4000	3000	2200	1750

Model 760 Bicentennial-1976 Only

Exc.	V.G.	Good	Fair	Poor
350	300	250	175	100

Model 760 ADL

Exc.	V.G.	Good	Fair	Poor
275	225	175	125	75

Model 760 BDL-Basketweave Checkering

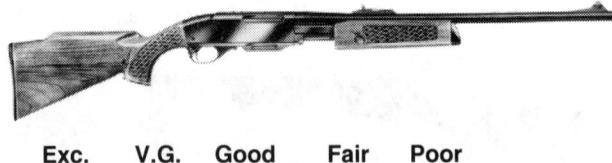

Exc.	V.G.	Good	Fair	Poor
300	250	200	150	100

Model 552A Speedmaster

A .22 caliber semiautomatic rifle with a 23" barrel having open sights. Blued with a pistol grip walnut stock. Manufactured from 1959 to 1988.

Exc.	V.G.	Good	Fair	Poor
150	125	100	75	50

Model 552 BDL

As above, with a more fully figured stock and impressed checkering. Introduced in 1966.

Courtesy Remington Arms

NIB	Exc.	V.G.	Good	Fair	Poor
200	175	150	125	100	75

Model 572 Fieldmaster

A .22 caliber slide-action rifle with a 21" barrel having open sights. Blued with a walnut stock. Manufactured from 1955 to 1988.

Courtesy Remington Arms

Exc.	V.G.	Good	Fair	Poor
150	125	100	75	50

Model 572 BDL

As above, but with a more fully figured walnut stock with impressed checkering. Introduced in 1966.

NIB	Exc.	V.G.	Good	Fair	Poor
210	185	165	145	110	85

Model 572SB

This is the same as the Model 572 but it has a smooth bore barrel and is chambered for the .22 Long Rifle cartridge.

NIB	Exc.	V.G.	Good	Fair	Poor
200	175	125	100	75	60

Model 580

A .22 caliber single shot bolt-action rifle with a 24" barrel having open sights and a Monte Carlo-style stock. Blued. The Model 580BR has a 1" shorter stock and would be worth approximately 10% more than the values listed below. Manufactured from 1968 to 1978.

Courtesy Remington Arms

Exc.	V.G.	Good	Fair	Poor
100	80	60	50	25

Model 580 BR

Same as above but with 1" shorter buttstock.

NIB	Exc.	V.G.	Good	Fair	Poor
130	100	75	60	50	40

Model 580SB

This is the same as the Model 580 except with a smoothbore barrel for .22 Long Rifle cartridges.

NIB	Exc.	V.G.	Good	Fair	Poor
175	125	100	75	60	50

Model 581

A .22 caliber bolt-action magazine rifle, blued with a 24" barrel and walnut stock. Manufactured from 1967 to 1983.

Exc.	V.G.	Good	Fair	Poor
150	125	100	75	50

Model 581 Left Hand

Same as above but built for a left handed shooter.

NIB	Exc.	V.G.	Good	Fair	Poor
175	150	100	75	60	50

Model 582

As above, fitted with a tubular magazine in place of the detachable box magazine. Manufactured from 1967 to 1983.

Courtesy Remington Arms

Exc.	V.G.	Good	Fair	Poor
150	125	100	75	50

Model 581-S

As above, fitted with a 5-round detachable magazine. Introduced in 1986.

Exc.	V.G.	Good	Fair	Poor
185	165	145	110	85

Model 591

A 5mm rimfire Magnum bolt-action rifle with a 24" barrel and Monte Carlo-style stock. Approximately 20,000 were made between 1970 and 1973.

Exc.	V.G.	Good	Fair	Poor
175	150	125	100	75

Model 592

As above, with a tubular magazine. Approximately 7,000 were made.

Exc.	V.G.	Good	Fair	Poor
300	250	200	150	100

Model 740

A .308 or .30-06 semiautomatic rifle with a 22" barrel and detachable box magazine. Blued with a plain walnut stock. Also available with an 18.5" barrel that would be worth approximately 10% more than the values listed below. Manufactured from 1955 to 1960.

Exc.	V.G.	Good	Fair	Poor
250	225	200	150	100

Model 740 ADL

As above, with a checkered walnut stock with a pistol grip.

Exc.	V.G.	Good	Fair	Poor
275	250	225	150	100

Model 740 BDL

As above, with a more finely figured walnut stock.

Exc.	V.G.	Good	Fair	Poor
300	275	250	150	100

Model 742

A 6mm Remington, .243, .280, .30-06, or .308 caliber semiautomatic rifle with a 22" barrel and 4-shot magazine. Also available with an 18" barrel in calibers .308 and .30-06 that are worth approximately 10% more than the values listed below. Blued with a checkered walnut stock. Manufactured from 1960 to 1980.

Exc.	V.G.	Good	Fair	Poor
300	275	250	150	100

Model 742 BDL

As above, with a Monte Carlo-style stock having basketweave checkering.

Standard Grade

Exc.	V.G.	Good	Fair	Poor
325	275	225	175	125

Model 742D Peerless-Engraved

Exc.	V.G.	Good	Fair	Poor
2100	1750	1500	1150	800

Model 742F Premier-Game Scene Engraved

Exc.	V.G.	Good	Fair	Poor
4000	3500	2750	1850	1300

Model 742F Premier-Gold Inlaid

Exc.	V.G.	Good	Fair	Poor
6500	5500	4000	3000	2250

Model 742 Bicentennial-Mfg. 1976 Only

Exc.	V.G.	Good	Fair	Poor
340	300	250	175	125

Model 76 Sportsman

A .30-06 slide action rifle with a 22" barrel and 4-shot magazine. Blued with walnut stock. Manufactured from 1985 to 1987.

Exc.	V.G.	Good	Fair	Poor
250	225	175	125	75

Model 7600

A variation of the above, chambered for a variety of cartridges from 6mm Remington to .35 Whelen with a 22" barrel and a detachable magazine. Also available with an 18.5" barrel. Blued with a checkered walnut stock. In 1996 fine line engraving on the receiver was offered as standard.

Model 7600 with new engraving

Closeup of new engraving on Model 7600

Standard Grade

NIB	Exc.	V.G.	Good	Fair	Poor
450	300	250	200	150	100

Model 7600D Peerless-Engraved

NIB	Exc.	V.G.	Good	Fair	Poor
2250	1800	1400	1200	950	750

Model 7600F Premier-Game Scene Engraved

NIB	Exc.	V.G.	Good	Fair	Poor
4750	4000	3500	2750	1850	1250

Model 7600 Premier-Gold Inlaid

NIB	Exc.	V.G.	Good	Fair	Poor
7000	6250	5000	4000	2750	1850

Model 7600 Synthetic

Same as the standard grade Model 7600 with black synthetic stock. A .30-06 carbine version is also available. Introduced in 1998.

NIB	Exc.	V.G.	Good	Fair	Poor
440	325	250	200	150	100

Model 7600 Special Purpose

The same configuration as the standard Model 7600 but equipped with a special finish on both the wood and metal that is nonreflective. First offered in 1993.

NIB	Exc.	V.G.	Good	Fair	Poor
350	300	250	200	150	100

**Model 7600 Buckmasters ADF
(American Deer Foundation)**

Introduced in 1997 and built only for that year this model is chambered for the .30-06 cartridge and is a limited edition item. Fitted with a 22" barrel and special fine line engraved receiver.

Remington Model 7600 Buckmasters ADF

Remington Model 7600 engraving

NIB	Exc.	V.G.	Good	Fair	Poor
560	450	—	—	—	—

Model 7600 Custom Grade

This Custom Shop model is available in three levels of engraving, gold inlay, wood grade and finish, metal work finish, recoil pad/buttplate, and dimensions. Each gun should be individually appraised prior to a sale.

D Grade

NIB	Exc.	V.G.	Good	Fair	Poor
2600	—	—	—	—	—

F Grade

NIB	Exc.	V.G.	Good	Fair	Poor
5375	—	—	—	—	—

F Grade with Gold Inlay

NIB	Exc.	V.G.	Good	Fair	Poor
8050	—	—	—	—	—

Model Six

A centerfire slide action rifle with a 22" barrel and a 4-shot detachable magazine. Blued with a walnut stock. Manufactured from 1981 to 1987.

Exc.	V.G.	Good	Fair	Poor
400	350	275	200	125

Model 74 Sportsman

A .30-06 caliber semiautomatic rifle with a 22" barrel and a 4-shot detachable magazine. Blued with a walnut stock. Manufactured from 1985 to 1987.

Exc.	V.G.	Good	Fair	Poor
300	250	175	125	75

Model Four

As above, with a select Monte Carlo-style stock. Manufactured from 1982 to 1987.

Exc.	V.G.	Good	Fair	Poor
450	400	350	275	175

Model 7400

This is a semiautomatic rifle with a 22" barrel. It is chambered for the .243, .270, .280, .30-06, .308, and the .35 Whelen. Blued with a checkered walnut stock. Average weight is about 7.5 lbs. Introduced in 1982. In 1996 this model was offered with fine line engraving on the receiver as standard.

Model 7400 with new engraving

Courtesy Remington Arms

Closeup detail on engraving for Model 7400

Courtesy Remington Arms

NIB	Exc.	V.G.	Good	Fair	Poor
500	375	300	250	200	100

Model 7400 Synthetic

Similar to the Model 7400 with black nonreflective synthetic stock. A .30-06 carbine is also offered. Introduced in 1998.

NIB	Exc.	V.G.	Good	Fair	Poor
450	350	250	200	150	100

Model 7400 Carbine

Same as above but with 18.5" barrel and chambered for the .30-06 cartridge.

NIB	Exc.	V.G.	Good	Fair	Poor
500	375	300	250	200	100

Model 7400 Special Purpose

The same configuration as the standard Model 7400 but equipped with a special finish on both the wood and metal that is nonreflective. First offered in 1993.

NIB	Exc.	V.G.	Good	Fair	Poor
400	350	300	250	200	100

Model 7400 Buckmasters ADF (American Deer Foundation)

Introduced in 1997, and built only in that year this model is limited. Chambered for the .30-06 cartridge and fitted with a 22" barrel. Special fine line engraving and polished blue finish. American walnut stock with Monte Carlo and cut checkering. Weight is 7.5 lbs.

Remington 7400 Buckmasters ADF

Remington Model 7400 Buckmasters ADF engraving

NIB	Exc.	V.G.	Good	Fair	Poor
600	500	400	300	—	—

Model 7400 Custom Grade

This Custom Shop model is available in three levels of engraving, gold inlay, wood grade and finish, metal work finish, recoil pad/buttplate, and dimensions. Each gun should be individually appraised prior to a sale.

D Grade

NIB	Exc.	V.G.	Good	Fair	Poor
2600	—	—	—	—	—

F Grade

NIB	Exc.	V.G.	Good	Fair	Poor
5375	—	—	—	—	—

F Grade with Gold Inlay

NIB	Exc.	V.G.	Good	Fair	Poor
8050	—	—	—	—	—

Model 11

A .22 caliber bolt-action magazine rifle with a 20" barrel. Blued with a nylon stock. Manufactured from 1962 to 1964.

Exc.	V.G.	Good	Fair	Poor
150	125	100	75	50

Model 12

As above. Fitted with a tubular magazine. Manufactured from 1962 to 1964.

Exc.	V.G.	Good	Fair	Poor
175	150	125	100	75

Model 10

A bolt-action .22 caliber single shot rifle with a nylon stock. Manufactured from 1962 to 1964.

Courtesy Remington Arms

Exc.	V.G.	Good	Fair	Poor
125	100	75	50	25

Model 66

A .22 caliber semiautomatic rifle with a 20" barrel and tubular magazine in the butt. Black or chrome-plated finish with a black, brown or green checkered nylon stock. Manufactured from 1959 to 1988.

NOTE: Apache Black models are worth 15% more than the values listed below and the Seneca Green model is worth an additional 25%.

Exc.	V.G.	Good	Fair	Poor
150	125	100	75	50

Model 66 Bicentennial Commemorative

As above, but with a 1976 commemorative inscription on the barrel. Manufactured in 1976.

Exc.	V.G.	Good	Fair	Poor
125	100	85	70	55

Model 77

As above, with a 5-round detachable box magazine. Manufactured during 1970 and 1971.

Exc.	V.G.	Good	Fair	Poor
150	125	100	75	50

Model 76

A .22 caliber lever action magazine rifle with a nylon stock. Manufactured from 1962 to 1964.

Courtesy Remington Arms

Exc.	V.G.	Good	Fair	Poor
175	150	125	100	75

Model 522 Viper

Introduced in 1993 the Model 522 Viper is a new Remington .22 rimfire caliber semiautomatic design. The black stock is made from synthetic resin, while the receiver is made from a synthetic as well. It features a 20" barrel and a 10-shot detachable clip. The rifle weighs 4.6 lbs.

NIB	Exc.	V.G.	Good	Fair	Poor
140	120	100	80	60	40

Model 541 S Custom

A .22 caliber bolt-action magazine rifle with a 24" barrel. Blued with a scroll engraved receiver, and checkered walnut stock having a rosewood pistol grip cap and forend tip. Manufactured from 1972 to 1984.

Exc.	V.G.	Good	Fair	Poor
400	325	275	200	125

Model 541T

As above, drilled and tapped for telescopic sights. Introduced in 1986.

NIB	Exc.	V.G.	Good	Fair	Poor
335	275	200	175	125	75

Model 541T Heavy Barrel

This model is the same as the standard 541-T with the exception of a 24" heavy barrel. First introduced in 1993.

NIB	Exc.	V.G.	Good	Fair	Poor
400	350	300	250	200	125

Model 597

Introduced in 1997 this automatic .22 long rifle rimfire rifle features a carbon steel barrel with alloy receiver. All metal has a nonreflective matte black finish. Stock is dark gray synthetic. Barrel length is 20" and weight is approximately 5.5 lbs.

NIB	Exc.	V.G.	Good	Fair	Poor
150	125	—	—	—	—

Model 597 Sporter

Introduced in 1998 this version of the Model 597 has a blued finish with a hardwood stock with beavertail style forearm. Magazine capacity is 10 rounds.

NIB	Exc.	V.G.	Good	Fair	Poor
150	125	—	—	—	—

Model 597 Stainless Sporter

Same as the Model 597SS but fitted with a hardwood stock. Introduced in 2000.

NIB	Exc.	V.G.	Good	Fair	Poor
225	175	—	—	—	—

Model 597 LSS

This version of the Model 597 is similar to the above but with the addition of a laminated stock and stainless steel finish.

NIB	Exc.	V.G.	Good	Fair	Poor
250	200	—	—	—	—

Model 597 SS

This version is also chambered for the .22 LR and has a stainless steel barrel on an alloy receiver. The stock is gray synthetic with beavertail style forearm. Magazine capacity is 10 rounds. Weight is about 5.5 lbs. Introduced in 1998.

NIB	Exc.	V.G.	Good	Fair	Poor
200	160	—	—	—	—

Model 597 HB

Introduced in 2001 this model features a 20" carbon steel heavy barrel chambered for the .22 Long Rifle cartridge. Fitted with a brown laminated stock. No sights. Weight is about 6 lbs.

NIB	Exc.	V.G.	Good	Fair	Poor
265	225	—	—	—	—

Model 597 HB Magnum

Same as model above but chambered for the .22 Winchester Magnum cartridge. Introduced in 2001.

NIB	Exc.	V.G.	Good	Fair	Poor
400	325	—	—	—	—

Model 597 Magnum

This model features a 20" carbon steel barrel, alloy receiver, and black synthetic stock. It is chambered for the .22 Win. Magnum cartridge. Weight is approximately 6 lbs.

NIB	Exc.	V.G.	Good	Fair	Poor
275	225	—	—	—	—

Model 597 Magnum LS

Chambered for the .22 Magnum. The receiver and barrel are blued with a gray laminated hardwood stock with beavertail style forearm. Magazine capacity is 10 rounds. Introduced in 1998.

NIB	Exc.	V.G.	Good	Fair	Poor
350	275	—	—	—	—

Model 597 Custom Target

This model is available on special order from the Custom Shop. It is chambered for the .22 LR cartridge and has a 20" stainless steel heavy target barrel without sights. The stock is a green laminated wood target style with pistol grip. Trigger is custom tuned. Weight is approximately 7.5 lbs. Introduced in 1998.

NIB	Exc.	V.G.	Good	Fair	Poor
600	475	—	—	—	—

Model 597 Custom Target Magnum

Similar to the model above but chambered for the .22 Win. Mag. Weight is approximately 8 lbs. Introduced in 1998. This is special order item only.

NIB	Exc.	V.G.	Good	Fair	Poor
750	600	—	—	—	—

Model 40X-BR

A .22 caliber single-shot bolt action rifle with a heavy 28" barrel fitted with Redfield Olympic sights or telescopic sight bases. Blued with a walnut target style stock having a hard rubber buttplate. Manufactured from 1955 to 1964.

Courtesy Remington Arms

Exc.	V.G.	Good	Fair	Poor
500	400	325	250	150

Model 40X Sporter

As above, with a 24" barrel, 5-shot magazine and a walnut sporting style stock. Less than 700 were made between 1969 and 1980.

Courtesy Remington Arms

Exc.	V.G.	Good	Fair	Poor
2500	1500	1000	750	500

Model 40X Centerfire

As above, chambered for .22, .22 Magnum, .308, or .30-06 centerfire cartridges. Manufactured from 1961 to 1964.

Exc.	V.G.	Good	Fair	Poor
550	450	350	300	200

Model 40XB Stainless

This model is built in the Custom Shop and features stainless steel barrel, receiver, and bolt. The receiver is drilled and tapped and fitted with a 27-1/4" heavy target barrel. The trigger is fully adjustable. There is a choice of walnut stock or synthetic stock. As of 1998 this model will be offered with a special laminated thumbhole stock. Offered in calibers from .222 to .300 Win. Mag. This rifle is built to order. Retail prices range from $1,200 to $1,500 depending on configuration and finish.

Model 40-XB with laminated thumbhole stock

Model 40XB BR

This is a bench rest Custom Shop version of the above model. This rifle has a 22" stainless heavy barrel chambered for the .22 Long Rifle. Adjustable trigger. Built to order. Retail prices begin around $1,350.

Model 40XR KS Sporter

This Custom Shop version is also chambered for the .22 Long Rifle and is fitted with a 24" barrel. Fully adjustable trigger. This model is also built to special order and prices begin around $1,350.

Model XC

This is a Custom Shop position rifle with 24" stainless steel heavy barrel chambered for .223 Rem. and .308 Win. cartridges. Kevlar stock with palm rail. Weight is approximately 11 lbs. Prices begin around $1,550.

Model 720A

A .257 Roberts, .270, or .30-06 bolt-action sporting rifle with a 22" barrel and a 5-shot integral magazine. Blued with a checkered walnut stock. Approximately 2,500 were manufactured in 1941.

Courtesy Remington Arms

Exc.	V.G.	Good	Fair	Poor
1250	1000	800	600	475

Model 721

A .264 Magnum, .270, or .30-06 bolt action rifle with a 24" barrel and a 4-shot magazine. Blued with a plain walnut stock. Manufactured from 1948 to 1962.

Courtesy Remington Arms

Standard Version

Exc.	V.G.	Good	Fair	Poor
300	250	200	150	100

Model 721 ADL

Exc.	V.G.	Good	Fair	Poor
350	300	250	200	125

Model 721 BDL-Select Stock

Exc.	V.G.	Good	Fair	Poor
400	350	300	250	150

Model 721A Magnum-.300 H&H

Exc.	V.G.	Good	Fair	Poor
450	400	350	275	150

Model 722 BDL

As above, with a shorter action chambered for .222 Remington cartridge. Manufactured from 1948 to 1962.

NIB	Exc.	V.G.	Good	Fair	Poor
550	450	300	200	150	100

Model 725 ADL

A centerfire bolt action sporting rifle with a 22" barrel, 4-shot magazine and Monte Carlo-style stock. The .222 caliber version was produced in limited quantities and should be individually appraised. Manufactured from 1958 to 1961.

Courtesy Remington Arms

Exc.	V.G.	Good	Fair	Poor
375	325	275	225	150

Model 725 Kodiak

A .375 Holland & Holland Magnum or .458 Winchester Magnum, bolt-action sporting rifle with a 26" barrel having a muzzle brake and open sights, and 3-shot magazine. Blued with a checkered walnut stock. Manufactured in 1961.

Exc.	V.G.	Good	Fair	Poor
800	700	550	400	300

Model 600

A centerfire bolt action sporting rifle with an 18.5" ventilated rib barrel and a checkered walnut stock. Manufactured from 1964 to 1967.

Courtesy Remington Arms

Exc.	V.G.	Good	Fair	Poor
450	350	275	200	125

Model 600 Mohawk

As above, but with a plain barrel and chambered only for the .222 Remington, .243 Winchester or .308 Winchester cartridges. Manufactured from 1971 to 1979.

Exc.	V.G.	Good	Fair	Poor
300	275	225	175	125

Model 660 Magnum

As above, chambered for the 6.5mm Remington Magnum and .350 Remington Magnum cartridges. Stock of laminated walnut and beechwood. Manufactured from 1965 to 1967.

Exc.	V.G.	Good	Fair	Poor
575	500	425	350	275

Model 660 (improved)

An improved version of the Model 600. Manufactured from 1968 to 1971.

Exc.	V.G.	Good	Fair	Poor
500	425	350	250	200

Model 660 Magnum (improved)

As above, but chambered for either the 6.5mm Remington Magnum or .350 Remington Magnum cartridges and fitted with a laminated stock.

Exc.	V.G.	Good	Fair	Poor
600	500	450	350	275

Model 78 Sportsman

A centerfire bolt action sporting rifle with a 22" barrel and 4-shot magazine. Blued with a walnut stock. Introduced in 1985.

NIB	Exc.	V.G.	Good	Fair	Poor
335	275	225	200	150	100

MODEL 700 SERIES

WHAT'S IT LIKE-THE REMINGTON MODEL 700

What the Volkswagen Beetle was to automobiles, the Remington Model 700 was/is to rifles. Reliable, affordable, accurate and readily available are adjectives often used to describe the rifle. One of the most accurate rifles that I've ever owned is a Model 700 Light Mountain rifle. Chambered for my pet .270 Winchester cartridge, it will consistently put three shots inside .5 MOA. That's wonderful accuracy for a heavy varmint rifle, much less the little mountain rifle. I haven't taken the time to count the different variations of the 700 but they are numerous. Remington seems to simply come out with a new variation of their old standard rather than tinker with a new design for a rifle. They wisely follow the old adage, "if it ain't broke, don't fix it."

The model was introduced in 1962 and has been going strong since. Although we didn't know it at the time, Remington was preparing to introduce the Model 700 at the same time that Winchester executives were taking steps to discontinue the famous Model 70 as we knew it. It's replacement was so bad that Remington probably owes Winchester management a debt of gratitude for their decision. As they say, the rest is history. The 700 is a good rifle, as functional as any and better than most. It has a few shortcomings but all rifles I'm aware of in the 700 price range do as well. The mere fact that it has been going strong for almost four decades now attests to its performance and value. We may be still writing about it in another four decades.

Tom Turpin

NOTE #1: In 1996 Remington added fine line engraving to its Model 700 line. All Model 700 BDL rifles will have this new engraving on them at no extra charge.

NOTE #2: In 1999 Remington introduced a new cartridge; the .300 Remington Ultra Magnum. It will be offered in the following production models: Model 700 BDL, Model 700 BDL SS, Model 700 LSS, Model 700 LSS LH, Model 700 Sendero SF. Custom shop rifles are: Model 700 APR, Model 700 AWR, Model 700 Custom KS Mountain Rifle, Model 700 Custom KS Stainless Mountain Rifle. In 2000 the company added the .338 Ultra Magnum cartridge.

Model 700 ADL

A centerfire bolt action sporting rifle with either a 22" or 24" barrel having open sights and a 4-shot magazine. Blued with a checkered Monte Carlo-style walnut stock. Introduced in 1962. In 1998 this model was available in .223 Rem. and .300 Win. Mag.

NIB	Exc.	V.G.	Good	Fair	Poor
425	325	250	200	150	100

Model 700 ADL Synthetic

This model features a black matte metal finish with 22" barrel or 24" on Magnums. The synthetic stock is black with checkering, recoil pad, and sling swivel studs. Receiver is drilled and tapped for scope. Offered in .243, .270, .30-06 and 7mm Rem. Mag. In 1998 this model was available in .223 Rem. and .300 Win. Mag.

Courtesy Remington Arms

NIB	Exc.	V.G.	Good	Fair	Poor
350	300	250	200	150	100

Model 700 ADL Synthetic Youth

Introduced in 1998 this model has a shortened synthetic stock with a 13" lop. Offered in .243 and .308 calibers.

NIB	Exc.	V.G.	Good	Fair	Poor
400	300	250	200	150	100

Model 700 BDL

Same as above, with a hinged floorplate, hand cut checkering, black forend tip and pistol grip cap. Offered in a wide variety of calibers from the .17 Rem. to the .338 Rem. Ultra Mag. Weights are between 7.25 lbs. to 7.62 lbs. depending on caliber and barrel length.

NIB	Exc.	V.G.	Good	Fair	Poor
465	400	325	275	225	150

Courtesy Remington Arms

Model 700 BDL LH (Left Hand)

This model is also offered in selected calibers for left hand shooters. They are: .270 Win., 7mm Rem. Mag., .30-06, and .300 Rem. Ultra Mag.

NIB	Exc.	V.G.	Good	Fair	Poor
650	500	400	300	—	—

Model 700 BDL (DM)

Same as above but introduced in 1995 with detachable magazine.

NIB	Exc.	V.G.	Good	Fair	Poor
475	425	350	275	225	150

Model 700 BDL LSS

This is a Model 700, introduced in 1996, with a synthetic stock and stainless steel bolt, floor plate, triggerguard, and sling swivels. The action and barrel are stainless steel as well. In 1997 the .260 Rem. cartridge was also available.

Courtesy Remington Arms

NIB	Exc.	V.G.	Good	Fair	Poor
600	475	400	350	300	200

Courtesy Remington Arms

Model 700 BDL SS DM-Magnum Rifle

Introduced in 1996 this Model 700 version is fitted with a factory installed muzzle brake on its Magnum calibers; 7mm Rem. Mag., .300 Win. Mag., .300 Wthby. Mag., and the .338 Win. Mag. and the .338 Rem. Ultra Mag. Weight is approximately 7.5 lbs. In 1997 the 7mm STW cartridge was added to this model.

Courtesy Remington Arms

NIB	Exc.	V.G.	Good	Fair	Poor
675	500	400	300	200	150

Model 700 BDL SS Camo Special Edition

This is a special edition rifle for the Rocky Mountain Elk Foundation. Fitted with a 24" barrel and chambered for the .300 Rem. Ultra Mag cartridge. Camo stock with stainless steel receiver and barrel. Weight is about 7.5 lbs. Introduced in 2001.

NIB	Exc.	V.G.	Good	Fair	Poor
775	625	—	—	—	—

Model 700 EtronX

Introduced in 2000 this rifle features a new technology that electronically discharges the round resulting in nearly instant ignition.

LED located on top of the grip that shows safe or fire and chamber status. There is also a low battery indicator and malfunction indicators as well. The rifle is fitted with a 26" stainless steel fluted barrel. The stock is fiberglass and graphite reinforced with Kevlar. Chambers are .220 Swift, .22-250 Rem., and .243 Win. cartridges. Average weight is about 8.88 lbs.

NIB	Exc.	V.G.	Good	Fair	Poor
1950	1500				

Model 700 EtronX Cutaway

Model 700 Sendero

This Model 700 configuration is chambered for the .25-06, .270, 7mm Rem. Mag., .300 Win. Mag. It is fitted with a synthetic stock and a 26" heavy barrel.

NIB	Exc.	V.G.	Good	Fair	Poor
600	475	400	300	200	150

Model 700 Sendero SF

Introduced in 1996 this model features a stainless steel fluted barrel. It has a synthetic stock with full length bedding. It weighs about 8.5 lbs. Chambered for same calibers as the standard Sendero above except for the .270. In 1997 the 7mm STW cartridge was made available for this model.

Courtesy Remington Arms

NIB	Exc.	V.G.	Good	Fair	Poor
750	600	450	350	250	150

Model 700 Sendero Composite

Introduced in 1999, this model features a composite barrel of graphite fiber with a stainless steel liner. Stock is synthetic. Calibers available are .25-06, 7mm STW, and .300 Win. Mag. Barrel length is 26". Weight is just under 8 lbs.

NIB	Exc.	V.G.	Good	Fair	Poor
1675	1250	—	—	—	—

Model 700 Mountain Rifle

As above, with a tapered 22" lightweight barrel, blued with checkered walnut stock. Introduced in 1986.

NIB	Exc.	V.G.	Good	Fair	Poor
425	325	250	200	150	100

Model 700KS Mountain Rifle

As above, with a lightweight Kevlar stock. Introduced in 1986.

NIB	Exc.	V.G.	Good	Fair	Poor
750	700	600	500	400	300

Model 700 Mountain Rifle (DM)

Same as standard mountain rifle but introduced in 1995 with detachable magazine. In 1998 this model was available in .260 Rem. caliber.

Courtesy Remington Arms

NIB	Exc.	V.G.	Good	Fair	Poor
475	425	350	300	250	175

Model 700 Safari Grade

As the Model 700BDL chambered for 8mm Remington Magnum, .375 Holland & Holland, .416 Remington Magnum or .458 Winchester Magnum cartridges, 24" barrel and 3-shot magazine. Blued with a finely figured walnut checkered stock. The Model KS Safari Grade was fitted with a Kevlar stock and would be worth approximately 20% more than the values listed below. Introduced in 1962.

NIB	Exc.	V.G.	Good	Fair	Poor
875	750	600	500	400	300

Model 700 RS

As above, chambered for the .270 Winchester, .280 Remington, or .30-06 cartridges, 22" barrel and 4-shot magazine. Blued with a DuPont Rynite stock. Manufactured during 1987 and 1988.

Exc.	V.G.	Good	Fair	Poor
500	425	350	250	150

Model 700 FS

As above, with a Kevlar stock.

Exc.	V.G.	Good	Fair	Poor
550	475	400	300	200

Model 700 BDL European

Available for the first time in 1993, this new model features an oil finish stock with Monte Carlo comb and raised cheekpiece. The checkering is fine line. In addition the rifle is standard with hinged floorplate, sling swivel studs, hooded ramp front sight, and adjustable rear sight. Offered in the following calibers: .243, .207, .280, 7mm-08, 7mm Mag. .30-06, and .308.

NIB	Exc.	V.G.	Good	Fair	Poor
400	350	300	250	200	125

Model 700 BDL Stainless Synthetic

Offered in 1993 this model features a stainless steel receiver, barrel, and bolt. Synthetic stock has straight comb, raised cheekpiece, and hinged floor plate. Metal is finished in a black matte nonreflective finish. Available in 14 calibers from .223 to .338 Win. Mag. All barrel lengths regardless of caliber are 24".

NIB	Exc.	V.G.	Good	Fair	Poor
550	450	350	300	200	150

Model 700 BDL Stainless Synthetic (DM)

Same as above but introduced in 1995 with detachable magazine.

Courtesy Remington Arms

NIB	Exc.	V.G.	Good	Fair	Poor
575	475	350	300	200	150

Model 700 Mountain Rifle Stainless Synthetic

This model is the same as the Mountain rifle but with stainless steel receiver, bolt, and barrel. Offered in .25-06 Rem., .270, .280, and .30-06. All calibers are supplied with a 22" barrel. In 1998 this model was available in .260 Rem. caliber.

NIB	Exc.	V.G.	Good	Fair	Poor
450	400	350	300	225	150

Model 700 LSS Mountain Rifle

This model, introduced in 1999, is fitted with a two-tone laminated stock with black forend tip and cheekpiece. Stainless steel barrel and action. Offered in .260 Remington, 7mm-08 Rem., .270 Win., and .30-06. Barrel length is 22". Weight is approximately 6.5 lbs.

NIB	Exc.	V.G.	Good	Fair	Poor
675	550	—	—	—	—

Model 700 Titanium

Introduced in 2001 this model features a titanium receiver drilled and tapped for scope mounts. Fitted with a 22" stainless steel barrel chambered for both long and short calibers. Synthetic stock. Weight is approximately 5.5 lbs.

NIB	Exc.	V.G.	Good	Fair	Poor
1300	1050	—	—	—	—

Model 700 Varmint Special Synthetic

The stock on this model is reinforced with DuPont Kevlar, fiberglass, and graphite. Rifle is offered with a heavy barrel and all metal has a fine matte black finish. The barrel rest on a machined aircraft-grade aluminum bedding stock. The receiver is drilled and tapped for scope mounts. Offered in .22-250, .223,

and .308 calibers. In 1993 the .220 Swift was added to the line. This model was later dropped from the product line. In 2000 it was reintroduced in all calibers above but the .220 Swift.

NIB	Exc.	V.G.	Good	Fair	Poor
500	450	400	350	300	200

Model 700 VS SF (Varmint Synthetic Stainless Fluted)

Introduced in 1994 this model features a stainless steel barrel, receiver and action. It is fitted with a 26" heavy varmint barrel that has a spherical concave crown contour. Six flutes reduce barrel weight and help cooling. A synthetic stock made from fiberglass reinforced with graphite is standard. The stock is dark gray. Offered in .223, .220 Swift, .22-250, and .308 calibers. The .243 Win. cartridge was added to this model in 1997. The rifle weighs about 8-3/8 lbs. In 1998 the barrel was fluted and ported.

Model 700 VS SF-P fluted and ported barrel

NIB	Exc.	V.G.	Good	Fair	Poor
800	650	500	400	300	200

Model 700 Varmint Special Wood

Same as above but furnished with walnut stock and offered in the following calibers: .222, .22-250, .223, 6mm, .243, 7mm-08, and .308.

NIB	Exc	V.G.	Good	Fair	Poor
450	400	350	300	250	150

Model 700 Varmint Laminated Stock (VLS)

Same as above but furnished with special laminated stock. Introduced in 1995. The 7mm-08 Rem. cartridge was added to this model in 1997. In 1998 a beavertail forend was added to this model, as well as the .260 Rem and the 6mm Rem. calibers.

Courtesy Remington Arms

Model 700 VLS with beavertail forearm

NIB	Exc.	V.G.	Good	Fair	Poor
600	475	350	300	250	150

Model 700 VS Composite (Varmint Synthetic Composite)

This model is fitted with a graphite fiber composite barrel and chambered for the .223 Rem., .22-250, or .308 cartridges. Stock is synthetic. Barrel lengths are 26". Weight is 7.9 lbs. Introduced in 1999.

NIB	Exc.	V.G.	Good	Fair	Poor
1675	1250	—	—	—	—

Model 700 LSS LH (Laminated Stock SS Left Hand)

Introduced in 1998 this model features a stainless steel barreled action with satin finish. Stock is similar to the BDL style with Monte Carlo comb and cheekpiece with hinged floor plate. Barrel is 24" with no sights. Offered in .270, .30-06, 7mm Rem. Mag, and .300 Win. Mag.

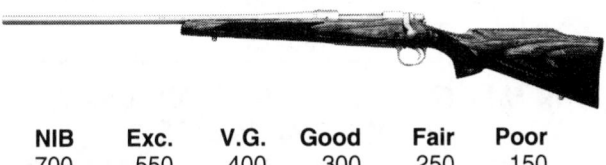

NIB	Exc.	V.G.	Good	Fair	Poor
700	550	400	300	250	150

Model 700 Classic

This limited edition model is furnished with a straight comb, satin finished walnut stock, sling swivel studs, and hinged magazine floorplate. The series began in 1981 and each year Remington has offered the Model 700 Classic in a special chambering. The following is a list of these chamberings by year.

1981-7MM	1990-.25-06 Rem.
1982-.257 Roberts	1991-7mm Wthby. Magnum
1983-.300 H&H Magnum	1992-.220 Swift
1984-.250-3000	1993-.222 Rem.
1985-.350 Rem. Magnum	1994-6.5X55 Swedish
1986-.264 Win. Magnum	1995-.300 Win. Magnum
1987-.338 Win. Magnum	1996-.375 H&H Magnum
1988-.35 Whelen	1997-.280 Rem.
1989-.300 Wthby. Magnum	1998-8mm Rem. Magnum
	1999-.17 Remington
	2000-.223 Win.
	2001-7mm-08

NIB	Exc.	V.G.	Good	Fair	Poor
645	475	350	300	250	150

Model 700 Custom

A special order rifle available in either American, English, or California walnut. Stock can be fitted to customer's own dimensions. Engraving is available as is a large selection of calibers. Model 700 Custom rifles should be priced individually and an appraisal should be obtained.

Model 700 AWR (Alaskan Wilderness Rifle)

This model is built in the Custom Shop and features a blind magazine and stainless steel components on a black matte synthetic stock. Fitted with a 24" barrel, all metal parts are finished in a black satin. Offered in .300 Weatherby Magnum, 7mm Rem. Mag., .300 Win. Mag., .338, and .375 calibers. In 1998 the 7mm STW was added as an additional caliber to this model. Weighs about 6-3/4 lbs. Built to order with a retail price of $1200 in 1995.

Model 700 APR (African Plains Rifle)

This Custom Shop model features a hinged floorplate, a 26" barrel, and blue metal finish. The stock is a laminated Monte Carlo style with cheekpiece and is fitted with black rubber recoil pad. Offered in same calibers as Model 700 AWR. Weighs about 7-3/4 lbs. Retail price in 1995 is $1500 on a special order basis.

Model 700 ABG (African Big Game)

This Custom Shop rifle is fitted with a laminated stock, matte finished receiver and barrel, and 3-round detachable magazine. Chambered for the .375 Rem. Ultra Mag., .375 H&H, .416 Rem. Mag., and .458 Win. Mag. Introduced in 2001. Many extra cost options are offered for Custom Shop firearms. Retail prices in 2001 for this rifle begin at $1727.

Model 700 Safari KS Stainless

A new addition to the Remington line in 1993, the Safari KS Stainless has a special reinforced Kevlar stock in a nonreflective gray finish. Checkering is 18 lines to the inch. Offered in the following calibers: .375 H&H Mag., .416 Rem. Mag., and the .458 Win. Mag.

NIB	Exc.	V.G.	Good	Fair	Poor
500	450	400	350	300	150

Model 700 ML

This model was introduced in 1996. It is an in-line design and the first built on a modern action. It is chambered for the .50 or .54 caliber bullet. It is fitted with a synthetic stock and rubber recoil pad. The barrel length is 24" and the approximate weight is 7.75 lbs. A camo stock option was added to this model in 1997.

Courtesy Remington Arms

Remington Model 700 ML Camo

NIB	Exc.	V.G.	Good	Fair	Poor
350	250	200	150	100	75

Model 700 Classic

Model 700 ML Custom

Introduced in 1997 this new model is similar to the above model but features a satin metal finish and gray laminated thumbhole stock with roll-over cheekpiece.

NIB	Exc.	V.G.	Good	Fair	Poor
775	650	—	—	—	—

Model 700 MLS

Same as above but with stainless steel barrel and action.

Courtesy Remington Arms

Remington Model 700 MLS Camo

NIB	Exc.	V.G.	Good	Fair	Poor
400	300	250	200	150	100

Model 700 MLS Custom

Similar to the above model but with a satin stainless steel finish and a two-toned gray laminated thumbhole stock with roll-over cheekpiece. Introduced in 1997.

NIB	Exc.	V.G.	Good	Fair	Poor
875	725	—	—	—	—

Model 700 ML Youth

This model is similar to the Model ML with a shortened stock with 13" lop with a rubber recoil pad.

NIB	Exc.	V.G.	Good	Fair	Poor
370	300	250	200	150	100

Model 700 Police

Chambered for the .223 cartridge and fitted with a 26" heavy barrel (1-9" twist), black synthetic stock, and parkerized finish.

NIB	Exc.	V.G.	Good	Fair	Poor
630	500	—	—	—	—

Model 700 Police DM

Same as above but chambered for .308 Win. (1-12" twist) or .300 Win. Mag (1-10" twist). Detachable magazine standard.

NIB	Exc.	V.G.	Good	Fair	Poor
670	525	—	—	—	—

NOTE: Add $20 for .300 Win. Mag model.

Model 700 Tactical Weapons System

This set is designed for law enforcement use and features a Model 700 Police chambered for the .308 Win. cartridge, a 24" barrel (1-12" twist), and detachable magazine. Also furnished with a Leupold VARI X III scope with rings and base, and a Harris 1A2 bipod, sling, lens covers, and case.

NIB	Exc.	V.G.	Good	Fair	Poor
N/A	—	—	—	—	—

WHAT'S IT LIKE-THE REMINGTON MODEL 700 POLICE

Remington is a legendary name in firearms manufacturing in the United States. For over 150 years the company has built civilian and military firearms. The Model 700 has been produced by Remington since the late 1960s. During the Vietnam War, the U.S. forces utilized the Model 700 Varmint heavy barrel in .308 caliber as a sniper weapon. During the war the U.S. military upgraded the rifle and changed its name to the M40 sniper rifle. Today, the Army and Marines still use this sniper rifle as a further upgraded system named the M24. The M24 rifles of today are capable of extreme accuracy to over 1,000 yards. The price of the M24 system is over $5,000 per rifle without optics. Remington markets the Model 700PSS as a complete system. It is a bolt action heavy barrel sniper with or without detachable magazine. It comes standard with a synthetic stock rather than the less durable wood. The barrel is 24" and chambered in .223, .308 or .300 Winchester Magnum calibers. By far the most popular caliber is the .308. It is used by many police department SWAT teams in the U.S. One reason is its reasonable price. Police departments get an off-the-shelf world call sniper weapon for a fraction of the cost of the military system. Not as accurate as the military version the Police model is an accurate rifle that will perform well out to 200 yards, which is more than enough for police engagements.

J.R. Moody

Model 700 Police Lightweight Tactical

This model is chambered for the .308 Win. cartridge and fitted with a 20" fluted barrel (1-12" twist). Stock is slim composite Kevlar with dual front swivel studs. Parkerized finish. Detachable magazine. Weight is approximately 7.5 lbs. Introduced in 1998.

NIB	Exc.	V.G.	Good	Fair	Poor
700	550	—	—	—	—

Model 710

Introduced in 2001 this rifle is chambered for the .270 Win. or .30-06 cartridge. Fitted with a 22" barrel and dark gray synthetic stock. Detachable box magazine. Supplied with pre-mounted Bushnell Sharpshooter 3-9x scope. Barrel finish is ordnance gray steel with a matte finish. Weight is about 7.12 lbs.

NIB	Exc.	V.G.	Good	Fair	Poor
359	285	—	—	—	—

Model 788

A centerfire bolt action sporting rifle with either a 22" or 24" barrel and a plain walnut stock. An 18" barrel carbine was also manufactured and is worth approximately 10% more than the values listed below. Manufactured from 1967 to 1984.

Exc.	V.G.	Good	Fair	Poor
325	275	225	150	100

Model Seven

A centerfire bolt action sporting rifle with an 18.5" barrel and 4- or 5-shot magazine. Blued with a checkered walnut stock. Chambered for .223 Rem., .243 Rem., 7mm-08 Rem., .308 Win., and for 1997 the .260 Rem. cartridge. Introduced in 1982.

NIB	Exc.	V.G.	Good	Fair	Poor
450	400	325	275	200	100

Model Seven FS

As above with a Kevlar stock. Introduced in 1987.

NIB	Exc.	V.G.	Good	Fair	Poor
600	525	450	375	275	150

Model Seven SS (Stainless Synthetic)

Introduced in 1994 this model features a stainless steel barrel, receiver, and bolt with a matte finish. It is fitted with a 20" barrel, and a hinged floorplate. The synthetic stock is textured black. Available in .243, 7mm-08, and .308. In 1997 the .260 Rem. cartridge was also offered. Weight approximately 6.25 lbs.

NIB	Exc.	V.G.	Good	Fair	Poor
475	400	350	300	200	150

Model Seven LSS

This model has a stainless steel barrel and action but is fitted with a satin finished laminated stock. Chambered for .22-250, .243, and 7mm-08 Rem. Weight is about 6.5 lbs. Introduced in 2000.

NIB	Exc.	V.G.	Good	Fair	Poor
725	550	—	—	—	—

Model Seven LS

This model offers a laminated stock but with a carbon steel blued barrel. Offered in 5 calibers: .22-250, .243, .260 Rem., 8mm-08 Rem., and .308 Win. Weight is about 6.5 lbs. Introduced in 2000.

NIB	Exc.	V.G.	Good	Fair	Poor
625	450	—	—	—	—

Model Seven MS

First introduced in 1993 and available through the Remington Custom Shop. This rifle features a 20" barrel with Mannlicher stock made from select grain wood and laminated for strength. Available in calibers for .270 Rem. to .308. In 1998 this model was available in .260 Rem. caliber.

NIB	Exc.	V.G.	Good	Fair	Poor
800	700	550	350	250	150

Model Seven Youth

First offered in 1993 this variation is a youth version of the standard Model 7. The buttstock is 1" shorter than standard. Available in 6mm, .243, and 7mm-08. In 1998 this model was available in .260 Rem. caliber.

NIB	Exc.	V.G.	Good	Fair	Poor
350	300	250	200	150	100

Model 1816 Commemorative Flint Lock Rifle

Introduced in 1995. It features a 39", .50 caliber octagonal barrel. Stock is hand finished extra fancy curly maple. Built for one year only. Special order only.

Courtesy Remington Arms

NIB	Exc.	V.G.	Good	Fair	Poor
1800	1200	850	700	500	300

Remington No. 1 Rolling Block Mid-Range

This classic rifle was reintroduced into the Remington in 1997 and features a 30" half octagon, half-round barrel chambered for the .45-70 Gov't cartridge. Designed for use with black powder and lead cast bullets. The receiver is case colored. All barrel, receiver, and metalwork markings match the original rifle. Rear tang-mounted vernier sight and front globe sight with interchangeable inserts. A single set trigger is standard. Steel buttplate. Weight is approximately 9.75 lbs.

NIB	Exc.	V.G.	Good	Fair	Poor
2750	2250	—	—	—	—

Remington Mid-Range Sporter Rolling Block

Introduced in 1998 this model features a 30" round barrel with pistol grip sporter stock. Adjustable rear sight. Chambered for .30-30, .444 Marlin, and .45-70 Gov't. A number of extra costs options are available for this model including barrels, sights, fancy wood, etc. Prices listed below are for standard model.

NIB	Exc.	V.G.	Good	Fair	Poor
1275	1000	—	—	—	—

Model 10A

A 12, 16, or 20 gauge slide action shotgun with barrels ranging from 26" to 32". Takedown, blued with a plain walnut stock. Manufactured from 1907 to 1929.

Courtesy Remington Arms

Exc.	V.G.	Good	Fair	Poor
375	300	250	200	100

Model 11

A 12, 16, or 20 gauge semiautomatic shotgun with barrels ranging in length from 26" to 32". Designed by John M. Browning and produced under license from Fabrique Nationale. Blued with a checkered walnut stock. Approximately 300,000 were made from 1911 to 1948.

Solid Rib or Vent Rib-Add 30%.

Exc.	V.G.	Good	Fair	Poor
300	250	200	150	100

Model 11B Special-Engraved
Exc.	V.G.	Good	Fair	Poor
550	475	375	275	175

Model 11D Tournament
Exc.	V.G.	Good	Fair	Poor
850	750	650	450	300

Model 11E Expert-Engraved
Exc.	V.G.	Good	Fair	Poor
1300	1150	1000	650	450

Model 11F Premier-Heavily Engraved
Exc.	V.G.	Good	Fair	Poor
2250	1900	1600	1150	600

Model 11R-20" Barrel Riot Gun
Exc.	V.G.	Good	Fair	Poor
350	300	250	175	100

Model 17

A 20 gauge slide-action shotgun with barrels ranging in length from 26" to 32". Takedown, blued with a plain walnut stock. Approximately 48,000 were made from 1917 to 1933.

Vent Rib-Add 25%.

Courtesy Remington Arms

Exc.	V.G.	Good	Fair	Poor
350	300	250	175	100

Model 29

As above, chambered for 12 gauge cartridges. Approximately 24,000 manufactured from 1929 to 1933.

Vent Rib-Add 25%.

Exc.	V.G.	Good	Fair	Poor
450	350	300	200	175

NOTE: For guns with 32" barrels add 40%.

Model 31

A 12, 16, or 20 gauge slide-action shotgun with barrels ranging in length from 26" to 32" and a magazine capacity of either 2 or 4 rounds. Takedown, blued with a walnut stock. Approximately 160,000 were made from 1931 to 1949.

Solid Rib or Vent Rib-Add 25%. For early banded barrels add 25%.

Exc.	V.G.	Good	Fair	Poor
400	325	275	200	125

NOTE: For guns with 32" barrel add 50%. For early models with checkered stocks add 40%.

MODEL 870 SERIES

In 1996 Remington offered as standard a new fine line engraving pattern on all Model 870 receivers.

Close-up detail of new engraving on the Model 870

Courtesy Remington Arms

Model 870 Wingmaster

A 12, 16, or 20 gauge slide action shotgun with 26", 28", or 30" barrels and a 5-shot tubular magazine. Blued with a plain walnut stock. Manufactured from 1950 to 1963.

Vent Rib-Add 10%.

Exc.	V.G.	Good	Fair	Poor
250	225	200	150	100

Model 870 Field Wingmaster

As above, with a checkered walnut stock and screw-in choke tubes. Introduced in 1964.

NIB	Exc.	V.G.	Good	Fair	Poor
550	450	300	225	150	100

THE SHOTGUN FOR HOME DEFENSE

For home defense use, my choice of shotgun is relatively easy. I use the ones with which I'm most familiar and that are simple to operate and can be safely stored. This means no cocked internal or visible hammers, no round in the chamber but easily charged, and no safety that must be released. For me, the Remington Model 870 pump shotguns fit the bill. Mine are chambered in 12 gauge, have short, 18-20" barrels and are cylinder bored. Although it can be loaded with seven rounds, I load only five. I use OO buckshot or slugs based on its location and possible use in terms of distance.

With the short barrels, I can more easily store them in safe places, yet I'm able to get them out and charged without becoming entangled in such furnishings of the home as hanging clothing or furniture. The standard open or aperture sights are just fine, with a red or gold bead front sight. I also stay with the standard, full-sized stocks, for the "trick" folding and pistol grip stocks seem to not always work for me. I simply want to be able the chamber a round, shoulder the gun and have some sort of "always there and on" sights to verify my index on a threat; nothing fancy, just something that does the job on demand, regardless of how many "dust bunnies" have accumulated in and on them over time.

Walt Rauch

Model 870 Field Wingmaster Small Bores

Introduced in 1999 this model is now offered in both 28 gauge and .410 bore. Checkered walnut stock. High polish blue finish. Both guns are fitted with 25" barrels. The 28 gauge has Rem chokes while the .410 comes with fixed modified chokes. Weight is approximately 6 lbs. Price below is for the .410 bore.

Wingmaster 28 gauge

Wingmaster .410 bore

NIB	Exc.	V.G.	Good	Fair	Poor
550	450	—	—	—	—

NOTE: Add $50 for 28 gauge gun.

Model 870 Magnum

As above, chambered for 12 or 20 gauge 3" Magnum shells Introduced in 1964. Choke tubes introduced in 1987.

NIB	Exc.	V.G.	Good	Fair	Poor
550	450	300	225	150	100

Model 870 Express

As above, for 3", 12 gauge shells with a 28" ventilated rib and one choke tube. Parkerized with a matte finished stock. Introduced in 1987.

NIB	Exc.	V.G.	Good	Fair	Poor
325	250	200	150	100	75

Model 870 Express Super Magnum

Similar to the Model 870 Express but chambered for the 12 gauge 3.5" shell. Offered in four different configurations. Standard offering is hardwood stock with 28" vent rib barrel. Synthetic stock with 26" vent rib barrel. Turkey camo with 23" vent rib barrel, and a combo with hardwood stock 26" vent rib barrel and #20 fully rifled barrel. Introduced in 1998.

NIB	Exc.	V.G.	Good	Fair	Poor
325	250	—	—	—	—

Model 870TA Trap

As above, with a competition ventilated rib and checkered stock. Produced in 12 gauge only. Discontinued in 1986.

NIB	Exc.	V.G.	Good	Fair	Poor
500	400	300	200	150	100

Model 870TB Trap

As above, with a 28" or 30" full choke, ventilated rib barrel and a trap style walnut stock. Manufactured from 1950 to 1981.

Exc.	V.G.	Good	Fair	Poor
400	325	275	200	125

Model 870TC Trap

As above, with a finely figured walnut stock and screw-in choke tubes.

NIB	Exc.	V.G.	Good	Fair	Poor
575	475	400	350	250	150

Model 870 Classic Trap

Introduced in 2000 this model features special fine line engraving with gold enlays. Stock is select walnut with Monte Carlo comb. Barrel length is 30" with a contoured vent rib. Ventilated recoil pad with white-line spacers. Choke tubes. Weight is about 8 lbs.

NIB	Exc.	V.G.	Good	Fair	Poor
775	575	—	—	—	—

Model 870 Special Field

This Remington pump action shotgun is available in either 12 or 20 gauge and features an English style straight grip stock, 21" vent rib barrel and slim shortened slide handle. In 12 gauge the gun weighs 7 lbs. and in 20 gauge it weighs 6.25 lbs. Comes with a set of Remington choke tubes.

NIB	Exc.	V.G.	Good	Fair	Poor
350	300	250	200	150	100

Model 870 Brushmaster Deer Gun

This 12 gauge slide action shotgun is fitted with a 20" Remington choke plain barrel and Monte Carlo stock. Available for either left-hand or right-hand shooters.

NIB	Exc.	V.G.	Good	Fair	Poor
350	300	250	200	150	100

Model 870 Express Turkey

Furnished in 12 gauge with 21" vent rib barrel with extra-full Remington choke Turkey tube.

NIB	Exc.	V.G.	Good	Fair	Poor
225	200	175	150	125	100

Model 870 Express Camo Turkey

Similar to the Express Turkey but with complete coverage of camo stock. Metal is matte black.

NIB	Exc.	V.G.	Good	Fair	Poor
350	250	200	150	100	75

Model 870 20 Gauge Express Youth Camo Turkey

Similar to the Model 870 Express Camo but in 20 gauge with shortened stock (13" lop).

NIB	Exc.	V.G.	Good	Fair	Poor
350	250	200	150	100	75

Model 870 Express Left Hand

This is a left had version of the Express model fitted with a 28" vent rib barrel and checkered hardwood stock. Black matte finish.

NIB	Exc.	V.G.	Good	Fair	Poor
325	250	200	150	100	75

Model 870 Express Deer Gun

This model is fitted with a 20" fully rifled barrel, iron sights, and Monte Carlo stock. Also offered with a 20" IC rifle sighted barrel. Available in 12 gauge only.

NIB	Exc.	V.G.	Good	Fair	Poor
225	200	175	150	125	100

Model 870 Express Super Magnum Turkey

This 12 gauge gun will handle 2.75", 3", or 3.5" shells. Fitted with a 23" vent rib barrel, black synthetic stock, and matte black metal finish. Weight is about 7.25 lbs. Introduced in 1999.

NIB	Exc.	V.G.	Good	Fair	Poor
350	275	—	—	—	—

Model 870 Express Synthetic Deer

This model is fitted with a 20" fully rifled barrel with adjustable rifle sights. Black synthetic stock with Monte Carlo comb and matte black finish. Weight is about 7 lbs. Introduced in 1999.

NIB	Exc.	V.G.	Good	Fair	Poor
250	200	—	—	—	—

Model 870 Express Combos

Offered in both 12 and 20 gauge with a 26" vent rib modified barrel and a 20" fully rifled deer barrel.

NIB	Exc.	V.G.	Good	Fair	Poor
400	325	250	200	150	100

Model 870 Express HD (Home Defense)

Introduced in 1995 this model features an 18" 12 gauge barrel with cylinder barrel with front bead sight. Weight approximately 7.25 lb.

NIB	Exc.	V.G.	Good	Fair	Poor
225	200	175	150	125	100

Courtesy Remington Arms

Model 870 Rifle Deer Gun

This new 20 gauge model was introduced in 1994 and features a fully rifled 20" barrel. It has a new scope rail design that is more rigid. The finish is blue and the Monte Carlo stock is walnut. Is equipped with recoil pad and checkering.

Close-up of new engraving detail on Model 870 Deer Gun

Courtesy Remington Arms

NIB	Exc.	V.G.	Good	Fair	Poor
450	400	350	300	200	100

Model 870 Express Small Game

Offered in 20 gauge or .410, this model has a nonreflective metal and wood finish. The .410 bore is furnished with a 25" vent rib full choke barrel, while the 20 gauge is available with a 26" or 28" vent rib barrel with Modified Rem. choke tube.

NIB	Exc.	V.G.	Good	Fair	Poor
225	200	175	150	125	100

Model 870 Express Youth Gun

Available in 20 gauge only, this shotgun is built for children. It has a 13" length of pull, a 21" vent rib barrel, and is sold with a Modified Rem. choke tube.

NIB	Exc.	V.G.	Good	Fair	Poor
225	200	175	150	125	100

Model 870 SPS-T Youth Turkey Camo

This shotgun is finished in Mossy Oak Break-Up and chambered for the 12 gauge shell. Fitted with a 20" super full choke. Weight is about 7.125 lbs. Introduced in 2001.

NIB	Exc.	V.G.	Good	Fair	Poor
565	450	—	—	—	—

Model 870 Express Youth Turkey Camo

Similar to the model above but chambered for the 20 gauge shell and finished with Real Tree Camo. Weight is about 6 lbs.

NIB	Exc.	V.G.	Good	Fair	Poor
250	200	—	—	—	—

Model 870 Youth Deer Gun

Chambered for the 20 gauge shell and fitted with a 21" full choked barrel. Real Tree Camo finish. Magazine capacity is 4 rounds. Weight is about 6 lbs.

NIB	Exc.	V.G.	Good	Fair	Poor
250	200	—	—	—	—

Model 870 Security

Offered in 12 gauge only this personal protection shotgun has a 18.5 cylinder choked plain barrel with front bead sight.

NIB	Exc.	V.G.	Good	Fair	Poor
225	200	175	150	125	100

Model 870 SPS-Camo

Offered in 12 gauge only and a choice of 26" or 28" vent rib barrel with Rem. choke tubes. The wood and metal are finished in a brown camo color. Introduced in 2001.

NIB	Exc.	V.G.	Good	Fair	Poor
565	425	—	—	—	—

Model 870 SPS Super Magnum Camo

This model is chambered for 12 gauge shells with chambers that will handle both 3" magnum and 3.5" magnum shells as well as all 2.75" shells. Barrel is 23" vent ribs with Rem. chokes. Finish is Mossy Oak camo. Weight is about 7.25 lbs. Introduced in 1999.

NIB	Exc.	V.G.	Good	Fair	Poor
585	425	—	—	—	—

Model 870 SPS-BG Camo

Available for the first time in 1993 this model features a 12 gauge 20" plain barrel with IC and Turkey Super Full Rem. choke tubes. The wood and metal are finished in a brown camo color.

NIB	Exc.	V.G.	Good	Fair	Poor
325	275	225	175	125	100

Model 870 SPS Super Slug Deer Gun

This model features a 23" fully rifled modified contour barrel which is equipped with a barrel mounted cantilever scope mount. Stock is black synthetic. Weight is approximately 8 lbs. Introduced in 1999.

NIB	Exc.	V.G.	Good	Fair	Poor
525	425	—	—	—	—

Model 870 SPS-T Camo

Same as above with the exception of a 21" vent rib barrel with IC and Turkey Super Full Rem. choke tubes. Both wood and metal are finished in a green camo color.

NIB	Exc.	V.G.	Good	Fair	Poor
325	275	225	175	125	100

Model SPS-T Super Magnum Camo

This 12 gauge model will handle 2.75", 3", and 3.5" shells. Fitted with a 23" barrel with Rem chokes. Finish is Mossy Oak camo. Weight is about 7.25 lbs. Introduced in 1999.

NIB	Exc.	V.G.	Good	Fair	Poor
525	425	—	—	—	—

Model 870 SPS-T Camo NWTF 25th Anniversary

This model is fitted with a 21" barrel with special fiber optic sighting system. NWTF logo on left side of receiver. Introduced in 1998.

NIB	Exc.	V.G.	Good	Fair	Poor
550	450	—	—	—	—

Model 870 Marine Magnum

This 12 gauge shotgun has a nickel finish on the receiver and barrel both inside and outside. Synthetic stock is checkered. The 18" barrel is bored cylinder and is fitted with a 7-round magazine. Sling swivel studs are standard.

NIB	Exc.	V.G.	Good	Fair	Poor
325	275	225	175	125	100

Model 870 SPS

Offered in 12 gauge only with synthetic stock and black matte finish. The barrel is either 26" or 28" vent rib with Rem. choke tubes.

NIB	Exc.	V.G.	Good	Fair	Poor
325	275	225	175	125	100

Model 870 SPS-Deer

Available with a 20" rifle with plain barrel, this 12 gauge shotgun has a black synthetic stock and black matte finish. First introduced in 1993.

NIB	Exc.	V.G.	Good	Fair	Poor
300	250	225	175	125	100

Model 870 SPS-T

This 12 gauge model comes standard with a 21" vent rib barrel, Rem. choke tubes in IC and Turkey Super Full, black synthetic stock, and black matte finish.

NIB	Exc.	V.G.	Good	Fair	Poor
300	250	225	175	125	100

Model 870 Police

This model comes in a wide variety (21) of 12 gauge configurations. Fitted with barrel from 14" (Class III), 18", or 20". Most with parkerized finish, although some variations have blued finish. Wood stock, folding stock, Speedfeed stock, or synthetic stock. Rifle or bead sights, and some configurations with Ghost ring and tritium night sights. Some variations have 7 or 8-round magazine extensions depending on barrel length.

Model 870 Custom Grade

This Custom Shop model is available in three levels of engraving, gold inlay, wood grade and finish, metal work finish, recoil pad/buttplate, and dimensions. Each gun should be individually appraised prior to a sale.

D Grade

NIB	Exc.	V.G.	Good	Fair	Poor
2600	—	—	—	—	—

F Grade

NIB	Exc.	V.G.	Good	Fair	Poor
5375	—	—	—	—	—

F Grade with Gold Inlay

NIB	Exc.	V.G.	Good	Fair	Poor
8050	—	—	—	—	—

Model 48 Sportsman

A 12, 16, or 20 gauge semiautomatic shotgun with 26", 28", or 32" barrels and a 3-shot tubular magazine. Blued with a checkered walnut stock. Approximately 275,000 were made from 1949 to 1959.

Vent Rib-Add 20%.

Exc.	V.G.	Good	Fair	Poor
325	300	250	175	100

Model 11-48

As above, with the addition of 28 gauge and .410 bore. Approximately 425,000 were made from 1949 to 1968.

Exc.	V.G.	Good	Fair	Poor
300	250	200	150	75

Model 58 Sportsman

A 12, 16, or 20 gauge semiautomatic shotgun with 26", 28", or 30" barrels and a 3-shot tubular magazine. The receiver scroll engraved and blued, checkered walnut stock. Approximately 270,000 were made from 1956 to 1963.

Exc.	V.G.	Good	Fair	Poor
300	250	200	150	75

Model 878 Automaster

As above, in 12 gauge only. Approximately 60,000 were made from 1959 to 1962.

Exc.	V.G.	Good	Fair	Poor
275	225	175	125	75

MODEL 1100 SERIES

A 12, 16, 20 or 28 gauge or .410 bore semiautomatic shotgun with barrels ranging in length from 26" to 30" fitted with choke tubes after 1987. The smaller bore versions are worth approximately 20% more than the values listed below. Blued with a checkered walnut stock. Manufactured beginning in 1963.

Exc.	V.G.	Good	Fair	Poor
375	300	250	200	100

Model 1100 Youth Gun

Offered in 20 gauge only with a 21" vent rib 2-3/4" barrel. The stock has a special 13" length of pull. Gun is supplied with a set of Rem. choke tubes.

NIB	Exc.	V.G.	Good	Fair	Poor
425	400	350	300	200	150

Model 1100 Youth Synthetic

Fitted with a 21" vent rib barrel this 20 gauge gun has a 1" shorter length of pull than standard. Matte black finish. Black synthetic stock. Weight is approximately 6.5 lbs. Introduced in 1999.

NIB	Exc.	V.G.	Good	Fair	Poor
500	400	—	—	—	—

Model 1100 Youth Synthetic Camo

Same as model above but with RealTree camo finish and chambered for 20 gauge 3" magnum shells. Weight is about 6.75 lbs. Introduced in 1999.

NIB	Exc.	V.G.	Good	Fair	Poor
550	450	—	—	—	—

Model 1100 Small Game

Available in 20, 28 gauge or .410 bore fitted with 25" vent rib barrels. The 28 gauge and .410 have fixed chokes while the 20 gauge has Rem. choke tubes.

NIB	Exc.	V.G.	Good	Fair	Poor
500	450	400	350	250	150

Model 1100 Tournament Skeet

Offered in 20, 28 gauge, and .410 bore. The 28 gauge and .410 come with 25" Skeet choked vent rib barrels while the 20 gauge is supplied with a 26" Skeet choked vent rib barrel.

Courtesy Remington Arms

NIB	Exc.	V.G.	Good	Fair	Poor
550	475	425	350	250	150

Model 1100 Classic Trap

This model features a 30" low profile vent rib barrel. The stock is semi-fancy walnut with Monte Carlo comb and ventilated recoil pad. Receiver has fine line engraving with gold inlays and the trigger is gold. Weight is about 8.25 lbs.

NIB	Exc.	V.G.	Good	Fair	Poor
875	650	—	—	—	—

Model 1100 Sporting 12

Introduced in 2000 this 12 gauge model features a 28" low profile vent rib barrel. Stock is walnut with cut checkering and Sporting Clays-style recoil pad. Gold trigger and fine line engraving on the receiver. Weight is about 8 lbs.

NIB	Exc.	V.G.	Good	Fair	Poor
850	625	—	—	—	—

Model 1100 Sporting 20

This model has a high grade walnut stock with glass finish and recoil pad. It is fitted with a 28" barrel with target sights. Interchangeable chokes. Introduced in 1998.

NIB	Exc.	V.G.	Good	Fair	Poor
775	625	—	—	—	—

Model 1100 Sporting 28

Introduced in 1996 this version is chambered for the 28 gauge shell. It is fitted with interchangeable chokes and a 25" vent rib barrel. The stock is walnut with Tournament grade checkering and recoil pad.

Courtesy Remington Arms

NIB	Exc.	V.G.	Good	Fair	Poor
550	475	425	350	250	150

Model 1100 LT-20

This 20 gauge model features a choice of 26" or 28" vent rib barrels with Rem choke tubes. It has a blue finish and walnut Monte Carlo stock. Recoil pad and cut checkering are standard. Weight is 6.75 to 7 lbs. depending on barrel length.

NIB	Exc.	V.G.	Good	Fair	Poor
525	450	400	300	200	150

Model 1100 LT-20 Deer Gun

Same as above but fitted with a 21" barrel with adjustable sights and an improved cylinder choke. Satin finish with American walnut stock. Weight is approximately 6.5 lbs.

NIB	Exc.	V.G.	Good	Fair	Poor
525	450	400	300	200	150

Model 1100 LT-20 Synthetic

Same as above but fitted with a synthetic stock with recoil pad.

NIB	Exc.	V.G.	Good	Fair	Poor
425	375	325	275	200	150

Model 1100 LT-20 Magnum

This 20 gauge Model 1100 is chambered for the 3" 20 gauge shell. It is fitted with a 28" vent rib barrel with interchangeable chokes. Checkered walnut stock. Weight is about 7 lbs.

NIB	Exc.	V.G.	Good	Fair	Poor
550	475	400	300	200	150

Model 1100 Synthetic

Introduced in 1995 this model is furnished with a black synthetic stock with black matte metal finish. Available in both 12 and 20 gauge.

Courtesy Remington Arms

NIB	Exc.	V.G.	Good	Fair	Poor
400	350	300	250	200	100

Model 1100 Synthetic Deer Gun

Same as above but fitted with a 21" fully rifled barrel with cantilever rail for scope mounting. Furnished with 2-3/4" chamber.

Stock is black synthetic with checkering and Monte Carlo style cheekpiece. Recoil pad is standard.

NIB	Exc.	V.G.	Good	Fair	Poor
525	450	400	300	200	150

Model 1100 LT-20 Synthetic Camo NWTF 25th Anniversary

This model is fitted with a 21" barrel with special fiber optic sighting system. NWTF logo on left side of receiver. Introduced in 1998.

NIB	Exc.	V.G.	Good	Fair	Poor
650	525	—	—	—	—

Model 1100 Custom Grade

This Custom Shop model is available in three levels of engraving, gold inlay, wood grade and finish, metal work finish, recoil pad/buttplate, and dimensions. Each gun should be individually appraised prior to a sale.

D Grade

NIB	Exc.	V.G.	Good	Fair	Poor
2600	—	—	—	—	—

F Grade

NIB	Exc.	V.G.	Good	Fair	Poor
5375	—	—	—	—	—

F Grade with Gold Inlay

NIB	Exc.	V.G.	Good	Fair	Poor
8050	—	—	—	—	—

MODEL 11-87 SERIES

Model 11-87 Premier

A 3", 12 gauge semiautomatic shotgun with 26" to 32" ventilated rib barrels having screw-in choke tubes. Blued with a checkered walnut stock. Weight is approximately 7.75 lbs. Introduced in 1987. In 1999 this model was offered in a left hand version.

NIB	Exc.	V.G.	Good	Fair	Poor
560	475	425	350	275	175

Model 11-87 Premier Left Hand model

Model 11-87 Premier 20 Gauge

Introduced in 1999 this model is built on a small frame receiver. It will chamber both 2.75" and 3" shells. Available in both 26" and 28" vent rib barrels with twin beads. Barrels are built for Rem. chokes. Stock is walnut with gloss finish. Weight is about 7 lbs.

NIB	Exc.	V.G.	Good	Fair	Poor
700	550	—	—	—	—

Model 11-87 Premier Cantilever Scope Mount Deer Gun

This semiautomatic model has a Monte Carlo stock and the option of a barrel mounted scope (not included). Optional with a fully rifled barrel 21" long with a 1 in 35" twist. Also available in a 21" nonrifled barrel with Rifled and IC Rem. choke tubes. Available in 12 gauge only. Sling swivel studs and camo are standard.

NIB	Exc.	V.G.	Good	Fair	Poor
500	450	400	300	200	150

Model 11-87 Premier Trap

Available in either right or left hand models. Is available with either a straight or Monte Carlo comb, 2.75" chamber, 30" vent rib overbored barrel and special Rem. Trap choke tubes. This model is set up to handle 12 gauge target loads only.

NIB	Exc.	V.G.	Good	Fair	Poor
525	475	425	300	200	150

Model 11-87 Premier SC (Sporting Clays)

This model features a special target stock with a 3.16" length of pull longer than standard and 1/4" higher at the heel. The butt pad is radiused at the heel and rounded at the toe. The receiver top, barrel, and rib have a fine matte finish on the blueing. The vent rib is a medium wide 8mm with stainless steel mid bead and a Bradley style front bead sight. Gun is supplied new with the following Rem. choke tubes: Skeet, Improved Skeet, Imp. Cyl., Model., and Full. Supplied from the factory with a two-barrel custom fitted hard case.

Model 11-87 Sporting Clays with new engraving

Courtesy Remington Arms

Remington Model 11-87 Sporting Clays with nickel plated receiver and ported barrel

NIB	Exc.	V.G.	Good	Fair	Poor
750	600	500	350	200	150

Model 11-87 SC NP (Sporting Clays Nickel Plated)

Same as above but with nickel plated receiver.

NIB	Exc.	V.G.	Good	Fair	Poor
825	650	500	400	300	200

Model 11-87 Upland Special

This model is offered in 12 or 20 gauge with 23" barrel with twin bead sights. Chambered for 3" shells. Stock is walnut with straight grip. Choke tubes standard. Weight is about 7.25 for 12 gauge and 6.5 lbs. for 20 gauge. Introduced in 2000.

NIB	Exc.	V.G.	Good	Fair	Poor
750	550	—	—	—	—

Model 11-87 SPS-BG Camo

This 12 gauge model is fitted with a rifle sighted 21" barrel with a brown camo finish on the stock and metal parts. Introduced in 1993.

NIB	Exc.	V.G.	Good	Fair	Poor
525	475	425	300	200	150

Model 11-87 SPS-T Camo

Same as above but supplied with a 21" vent rib barrel with IC and Turkey Super Full Rem. choke tubes. Camo finish is green. Introduced in 1993.

NIB	Exc.	V.G.	Good	Fair	Poor
550	450	350	250	200	150

Model 11-87 SPS

This 12 gauge model is furnished with a 26" or 28" vent rib barrel with IC, Mod., and Full Rem. choke tubes. The stock is a black synthetic material and the metal is finished in a black matte. In 1997 a camo version of this model was introduced.

Remington Model 11-87 SPS Camo

NIB	Exc.	V.G.	Good	Fair	Poor
450	400	300	250	200	150

Model 11-87 SPS-Deer

The same as above but fitted with a 21" rifle sighted barrel. First introduced in 1993.

NIB	Exc.	V.G.	Good	Fair	Poor
525	475	425	300	200	150

Model 11-87 SPS-T

Same as above but fitted with a 21" vent rib barrel with IC and Turkey Super Full Rem. choke tubes. In 1997 a camo version of this model was introduced.

Remington Model 11-87 SPS-T Camo

NIB	Exc.	V.G.	Good	Fair	Poor
525	475	425	300	200	150

Model 11-87 SPS-T Camo NWTF 25th Anniversary

This model has a 21" barrel with special fiber optic sighting system. NWTF logo on left side of receiver. Introduced in 1998.

NIB	Exc.	V.G.	Good	Fair	Poor
825	650	—	—	—	—

Model 11-87 SP Super Magnum

Introduced in 2000 this model is chambered for the 12 gauge 3.5" magnum shell. Fitted with a 26" or 28" vent rib barrel. Walnut stock with flat finish. Recoil pad. Matte black finish. Weight is about 8.25 lbs.

NIB	Exc.	V.G.	Good	Fair	Poor
850	650	—	—	—	—

Model 11-87 SPS Super Magnum

Same as above but with a black synthetic stock. Introduced in 2000. Weight is about 8.25 lbs.

NIB	Exc.	V.G.	Good	Fair	Poor
850	650	—	—	—	—

Model 11-87 Police

Offered chambered for 12 gauge shells, this model features a synthetic stock, 18" barrel with bead, rifle, or Ghost Ring sights, and 7-shot magazine extension. Restricted to law enforcement.

NIB	Exc.	V.G.	Good	Fair	Poor
N/A	—	—	—	—	—

NOTE: Add $20.00 for rifle sights and $60.00 for Ghost Ring sights.

Model 11-87 Custom Grade

This Custom Shop model is available in three levels of engraving, gold inlay, wood grade and finish, metal work finish, recoil pad/buttplate, and dimensions. Each gun should be individually appraised prior to a sale.

D Grade

NIB	Exc.	V.G.	Good	Fair	Poor
2600	—	—	—	—	—

F Grade

NIB	Exc.	V.G.	Good	Fair	Poor
5375	—	—	—	—	—

F Grade with Gold Inlay

NIB	Exc.	V.G.	Good	Fair	Poor
8050	—	—	—	—	—

Model 11-96 Euro Lightweight

Introduced in 1996 this model is based on the Model 11-87 action. Two vent rib barrel lengths are offered: 26" and 28" supplied with 3 Rem chokes. Fine line engraving on the receiver and checkered Claro walnut stocks are standard. Blued finish. Weight is approximately 7 lbs.

NIB	Exc.	V.G.	Good	Fair	Poor
775	700	—	—	—	—

Model SP-10

A 3.5", 10 gauge semiautomatic shotgun with 26" or 30" ventilated rib barrels having screw-in choke tubes. Matte blued with a checkered walnut stock.

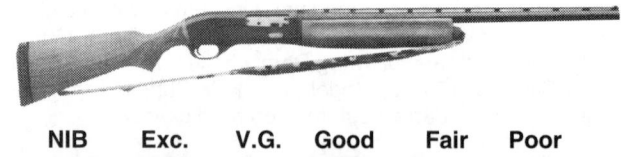

NIB	Exc.	V.G.	Good	Fair	Poor
1275	1000	800	650	550	400

Model SP-10 Magnum Camo

A new model introduced in 1993, this 10 gauge semiautomatic is designed for the turkey or deer hunter. Available with either 26" or 30" vent rib barrel or a 26" vent rib barrel with a 22" deer barrel. An additional barrel option is a 23" vent rib barrel with a camo finish. All barrels are fitted with Remington choke tubes.

NIB	Exc.	V.G.	Good	Fair	Poor
1150	800	700	500	350	200

Model SP-10 Magnum Camo NWTF 25th Anniversary

This model has a special fiber optic sighting system. The "NWTF" logo is on the left side of the receiver. Barrel length is 23". Introduced in 1998.

NIB	Exc.	V.G.	Good	Fair	Poor
1200	950	—	—	—	—

Model SP-10 Synthetic

This model features a black synthetic stock with 26" barrel chambered for 10 gauge shells. Matte black metal finish. Choke tubes standard. Introduced in 2000. Weight is about 10 lbs.

NIB	Exc.	V.G.	Good	Fair	Poor
1175	875	—	—	—	—

Model SP-10 Custom Grade

This Custom Shop model is available in three levels of engraving, gold inlay, wood grade and finish, metal work finish, recoil pad/buttplate, and dimensions. Each gun should be individually appraised prior to a sale.

Model 32

A 12 gauge Over/Under shotgun with 26", 28", or 30" separated barrels and a single selective trigger. Approximately 15,000 were made from 1932 to 1942.

Standard Grade

Solid or vent rib-Add 10%.

Exc.	V.G.	Good	Fair	Poor
2200	1900	1600	1250	1000

Model 32 Skeet

Exc.	V.G.	Good	Fair	Poor
2750	2250	1950	1500	1250

Model 32 TC

Exc.	V.G.	Good	Fair	Poor
2750	2500	2250	1750	1450

Model 32D

Exc.	V.G.	Good	Fair	Poor
3500	3000	2500	2000	1650

Model 32E Expert

Exc.	V.G.	Good	Fair	Poor
4500	3500	3000	2500	2000

Model 32F Premier

Exc.	V.G.	Good	Fair	Poor
7000	5500	4000	3250	2500

Model 3200

A 12 gauge Over/Under shotgun with 26", 28", or 30" separated ventilated rib barrels, single selective trigger, and automatic ejector. Blued with a checkered walnut stock. Manufactured from 1972 to 1984.

Field Grade

Exc.	V.G.	Good	Fair	Poor
800	725	600	450	300

Model 3200 Magnum-3" Chambers

Exc.	V.G.	Good	Fair	Poor
1000	850	750	550	450

Model 3200 Skeet

Exc.	V.G.	Good	Fair	Poor
800	725	600	450	300

Model 3200 4-Gauge Set

Exc.	V.G.	Good	Fair	Poor
4500	3750	3000	2250	1500

Model 3200 Trap

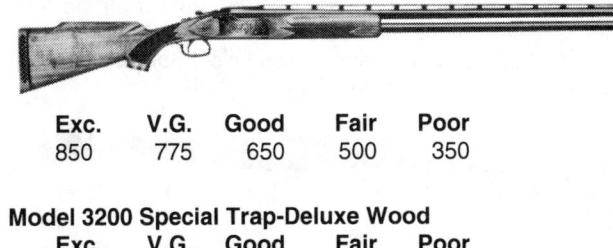

Exc.	V.G.	Good	Fair	Poor
850	775	650	500	350

Model 3200 Special Trap-Deluxe Wood

Exc.	V.G.	Good	Fair	Poor
1150	950	750	550	450

Model 3200 Competition Trap-Engraved

Exc.	V.G.	Good	Fair	Poor
1250	1000	850	650	550

Model 3200 Premier-Heavily Engraved

Exc.	V.G.	Good	Fair	Poor
2250	2000	1750	1500	1000

Model 3200 "One of One Thousand"-1,000 Produced

Exc.	V.G.	Good	Fair	Poor
2500	2000	1500	1100	500

Remington Peerless

Introduced in 1993 this new Remington Over/Under shotgun is offered in 12 gauge only. Available in 26", 28", and 30" vent rib barrel lengths and fitted with Remington choke tubes (IC, M, F). The sideplates are removable and the stock is American walnut.

NIB	Exc.	V.G.	Good	Fair	Poor
1000	900	750	600	400	300

Model 90-T Single Barrel Trap

Offered in 12 gauge only, this single barrel Trap shotgun is fitted with either a 32" or 34" overbored full choke barrel.

NIB	Exc.	V.G.	Good	Fair	Poor
2500	1800	1300	900	600	300

Model 90-T Single Barrel Trap (High Rib)

The same shotgun as described above with the exception of an adjustable high rib for shooters who prefer a more open target picture and higher head position.

NIB	Exc.	V.G.	Good	Fair	Poor
2500	2200	1650	1200	750	400

Model 300 Ideal

This 12 gauge over and under shotgun, was introduced in 2000, and is offered with a choice of 26", 28", or 30" barrels. Single selective trigger and automatic ejectors. Metal finish is blue. Stock is walnut with semi-gloss finish. Solid black recoil pad. Weight is about 7.62 lbs. for 28" barrels.

NIB	Exc.	V.G.	Good	Fair	Poor
1950	1500	—	—	—	—

Model 396 Sporting

Introduced in 1996 this Over and Under shotgun is designed for sporting clays shooting. It is offered in 12 gauge only with 30" barrels. Chokes are interchangeable Rem. choke system. Fancy American stock with satin finish. Scroll engraving on the receiver and blue finish. Weight is about 8 lbs.

Courtesy Remington Arms

NIB	Exc.	V.G.	Good	Fair	Poor
2150	1700	1150	—	—	—

Model 396 Skeet

Same but with a choice of 28" or 30" barrels.

Courtesy Remington Arms

NIB	Exc.	V.G.	Good	Fair	Poor
1975	1500	950	—	—	—

Model 396 Custom Grade

This Custom Shop model is available in three levels of engraving, gold inlay, wood grade and finish, metal work finish, recoil pad/buttplate, and dimensions. Each gun should be individually appraised prior to a sale.

Model XP-100

A .221 Remington Fireball or .223 Remington caliber bolt action single shot pistol with a 14.5" ventilated rib barrel and adjustable sights. Blued with a nylon stock. Introduced in 1963.

NIB	Exc.	V.G.	Good	Fair	Poor
375	325	275	225	175	100

Model XP-100 Silhouette

As above, chambered for either the 7mm Remington or .35 Remington cartridges and fitted with a 15" barrel drilled and tapped for a telescope.

NIB	Exc.	V.G.	Good	Fair	Poor
500	400	300	225	175	100

Model XP-100 Custom

A custom made version of the above with a 15" barrel and either a nylon or walnut stock. Available in .223 Remington, .250 Savage, 6mm Benchrest, 7mm Benchrest, 7mm-08, or .35 Remington calibers. Introduced in 1986.

NIB	Exc.	V.G.	Good	Fair	Poor
900	800	650	550	425	300

Model XP-100 Hunter

This model features a laminated wood stock, 14.5" drilled and tapped barrel, and no sights. It is offered in the following calibers: .223 Rem., 7mm BR Rem., 7mm-08 Rem., and .35 Rem.

NIB	Exc.	V.G.	Good	Fair	Poor
500	400	300	225	175	100

Model XP-100R

Introduced in 1998 this model is chambered for the 9.22-250, .223, .260, and .35 Rem. cartridges. It is fitted with a 14.5" barrel that is drilled and tapped for sights. The receiver is drilled and tapped for scope mounts. Fiberglass stock. Weight is approximately 4.5 lbs.

NIB	Exc.	V.G.	Good	Fair	Poor
650	500	400	—	—	—

REMINGTON CUSTOM SHOP

The Remington Custom Shop builds a number of speciality rifles and shotguns as well as specific custom guns for its customers. Remington will build a wide number of special features from special wood type, finish, and styling options to engraving. These special order features add considerably to the costs of a gun and will affect its price. It is suggested that both the buyer and seller contact the Custom Shop in order to ascertain price and availability of options before a sale. The Custom Shop can be reached at 1-800-243-9700 for current prices and availability.

MODEL 700™ CUSTOM • MODEL 40-XR™ RIMFIRE SPORTER • OPTIONS SELECTION GUIDE

See Remington Custom Gun Shop Order Worksheet for details.

Shown is a Custom Model 40-XR™ Rimfire Sporter featuring satin finished English Walnut stock with classic, straight comb. The pistol grip and fore-end are accentuated with hand-cut, 20 lines per inch, point pattern checkering. The metal work features a deep-luster blued finish.

WOOD TYPE • FINISH • STYLING OPTIONS

Classic, Straight Comb with optional Cheekpiece. Fancy American Walnut with Satin finish.

FORE-END TIPS

Ebony or Rosewood is available for optional fore-end tips.

Classic, Straight Comb with optional Shadowline Cheekpiece. Optional Extra-Fancy English Walnut with hand-rubbed oil finish.

GRIP CAPS

A choice of five is available: (left to right) none (standard), or optional Ebony, Rosewood, Skeleton Steel, and Solid Steel.

Monte Carlo comb with optional Cheekpiece. Optional Extra-Fancy American Walnut with gloss finish.

Monte Carlo comb with optional Shadowline Cheekpiece. Optional Extra Fancy English Walnut with hand-rubbed oil finish.

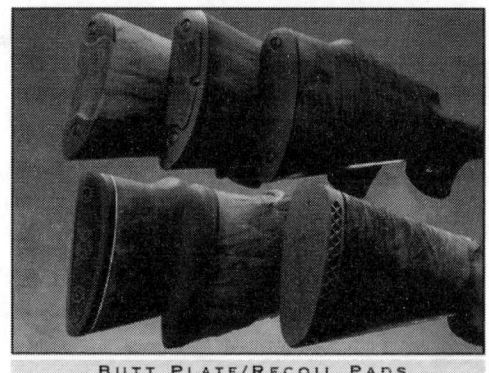

BUTT PLATE/RECOIL PADS

A choice of six is available: (from top left) optional Steel Heel and Toe plates, Skeleton Steel, and Solid Steel butt plate; (bottom row) Standard butt plate, optional "Old English" recoil pad, and Ventilated recoil pad.

REMINGTON 180TH ANNIVERSARY LIMITED EDITION RIFLES AND SHOTGUNS

Remington will manufacture 180 each of the following firearms to commemorate the founding of the company in 1816:

Model 700, Model 7600, Model 7400, Model 870, and the Model 11-87.

These firearms will feature fine line hand engraving with gold embellishments. The rifles will be chambered for the .30-06 cartridge with 22" barrels and the shotguns will be chambered for the 12 gauge shell with 26" vent rib barrels with Rem chokes. All guns will feature blue finishes with high gloss semi-fancy walnut stocks. If sold in a five gun set each will have matching serial numbers. The suggested retail price for the five gun set is $6,925. Individual guns will carry suggested retail prices as follows:

Model 700 180th Anniversary Commemorative-$1,372
Model 7400 180th Anniversary Commemorative-$1,372
Model 7600 180th Anniversary Commemorative-$1,332
Model 870 180th Anniversary Commemorative-$1,305
Model 11-87 180th Anniversary Commemorative-$1,465

Remington Model 11-87 SP deer gun autoloading action with 3" chamber (21" barrel with rifle sights)

Remington Model 11-87 Police 12 gauge autoloading shotgun (21" barrel with 3" chamber and rifle sights)

The Remington Model 11-87 Premier with new engraving. Introduced in 1996

Remington Model 11-87 "Premier" autoloading trap gun with 3 interchangeable "REM" chokes (shown with Monte Carlo stock)

Remington Model 11-87 "Premier" 12 gauge autoloading shotgun with interchangeable "REM" chokes (handles all 2-3/4" & 3" magnum shells)

Remington Model 11-87 SP Magnum autoloading shotgun with interchangeable "REM" chokes (handles all 2-3/4" & 3" magnum shells)

Remington Model 11-87 SP deer gun autoloading shotgun with 3" chamber, cantilever scope mount and interchangeable rifled and improved cylinder "REM" chokes

Remington "XP-100" Custom HB heavy barrel long range single shot pistol; Calibers: .223 Rem., .250 Sav., 6mm BR Rem., 7mm BR Rem. and 7mm-08 Rem. (in right- and left-hand versions)

Remington XP-100R custom pistol bolt action centerfire repeater (with synthetic stock of "Kevlar" ®); Calibers: .223 Rem. (without sights), 7mm-08 Rem. & .35 Rem. (as shown)

Remington Model 7400 Carbine autoloading centerfire rifle with 18-1/2" barrel

Remington Model 7600 Carbine centerfire pump action rifle with 18-1/2" barrel

Remington Model 40-XB "Varmint Special" bolt action centerfire rifle with synthetic stock of "Kevlar"®

Remington Model 40-XBBR bench rest bolt action centerfire rifle

Remington Model 40-XB "Rangemaster" bolt action centerfire target rifle

Remington Model Seven custom "KS" lightweight centerfire rifle, synthetic stock of "Kevlar"® aramid fiber; calibers: .223 Rem., 7mm BR Rem., 7mm-08 Rem., .35 Rem. and .350 Rem. Mag.

Remington Model 700 "AS" bolt action centerfire rifle with synthetic stock

Remington Model 700 mountain rifle, short action version; Calibers: 234 Win., 7mm-08 Rem., & 308 Win.

Remington Model 700 BDL, bolt action centerfire rifle (short action with 24" barrel)

Remington Model 700 BDL Magnum; calibers: 7mm Rem. Mag., .300 Win. Mag., .338 Win. Mag. and .35 Whelen

Remington Model 700 BDL left-hand bolt action centerfire rifle

Remington Model 700 Classic bolt action centerfire rifle, Magnum caliber version

Remington Model 700 BDL "Varmint Special" bolt action centerfire rifle

Remington Model 700 BDL Magnum, left-hand action; calibers: 7mm Rem. Mag. and .338 Win. Mag.

Remington Model 700 BDL left-hand bolt action (short) centerfire rifle; calibers: .22-250 Rem., .243 Win. and .308 Win.

Remington Model 700 Custom bolt action centerfire rifle, Grade IV

Remington Model 700 Custom bolt action centerfire rifle, Grade III

Remington Model 700 Custom Grade II, left-hand short action centerfire rifle, available in Grades I to IV

Remington Model 700 custom bolt action centerfire rifle, Grade II

Remington Model 700 Custom bolt action centerfire rifle, Grade I

Remington Model 700 "Classic" bolt action centerfire rifle, limited edition — .25-06 Rem.

Remington Model 700 Safari Classic with sights: .416 Rem. Mag. and .458 Win. Mag.

Remington Model 700 Safari KS, synthetic stock of "Kevlar"® aramid fiber; Calibers: 8mm Rem. Mag., .375 H&H Mag. 416 Rem. Mag and .458 Win. Mag.

Remington Model 700 ADL "LS" bolt action centerfire rifle with laminated stock; calibers: .243 Win., .270 Win., 30-06 and 7mm Rem. Magnum

Remington Model 90-T super single trap gun, barrel lengths: 30", 32" and 34"

Remington Model 870 "Wingmaster" left-hand field grade pump action shotgun; 12- and 20-gauges (shown with ventilated rib)

Remington Model 870 pump action 20 gauge "lightweight" deer gun

Remington Model 870 SP deer gun, pump action shotgun with 3" chamber, cantilever scope mount and interchangeable rifled and improved cylinder "REM" chokes

Remington Model 870 SP Magnum pump action shotgun, 3" chamber (shown with a 26" barrel)

Remington Model 870 youth gun, 20 gauge lightweight pump action shotgun with interchangeable "REM" chokes. Stock: shortened 1-1/2" Barrel: 21"

Remington Model 870 "Special Field" pump action shotgun with 21" vent rib barrel (20 gauge lightweight version)

Remington Model 870 "Special Field" pump action shotgun with 21" vent rib barrel

Remington Model 870 pump action shotgun, field grade small bore: 28 gauge and .410

Remington Model 870 D tournament grade pump action shotgun

Remington Model 870 F pump action shotgun, premier grade with gold inlay

Remington Model 870 pump action shotgun, 20 gauge "lightweight" with interchangeable "REM" chokes

Remington Model 110 LT-20 "Special Field" 20 gauge autoloading shotgun with 21" vent rib barrel

Remington Model 110 LT-20 autoloader, 20 gauge lightweight shotgun with interchangeable "REM" chokes

Remington Model 110 LT-20 youth gun, 20 gauge lightweight autoloading shotgun with interchangeable "REM" chokes. Stock: shortened 1-1/2". Barrel: 21"

Remington Model 1100 LT-20 Magnum 20 gauge lightweight autoloader with interchangeable "REM" chokes

Remington Model 1100 LT-20 20 gauge lightweight autoloading deer gun

Remington Model 1100 LT-20 tournament skeet 20 gauge autoloading shotgun

Remington Model 1100 tournament skeet autoloading shotgun, small bore version: .410 and 28 gauges

Remington Model 1100 D tournament grade 12 gauge, 5 shot

Remington Model 1100 F autoloading shotgun, premier grade with gold inlay

Remington 541T-HB Heavy Barrel

Model 396 Skeet

Model 870 Wingmaster & Peerless

RENETTE, GASTINNE
Paris, France

SHOTGUNS

Model 105
An Anson & Deeley action 12 or 20 gauge double barrel shotgun available in a variety of barrel lengths, with double triggers and automatic ejectors. Blued, case hardened with a checkered walnut stock.

Exc.	V.G.	Good	Fair	Poor
2000	1600	1250	900	500

Model 98
As above, except more finely finished.

Exc.	V.G.	Good	Fair	Poor
2750	2250	1750	1400	750

Model 202
A 12 or 20 gauge sidelock double barrel shotgun made only on custom order. French case hardened and blued with a checkered walnut stock.

Exc.	V.G.	Good	Fair	Poor
4500	3500	2500	1750	950

Model 353
A custom manufactured double-barrel shotgun with detachable sidelocks. Highly finished.

Exc.	V.G.	Good	Fair	Poor
18000	15000	9500	4250	1500

RIFLES

Type G Rifle
A .30-06, 9.3x74R, or .375 Holland & Holland double barrel rifle with 24" barrels, express sights, double triggers and automatic ejectors. Engraved, blued with a checkered walnut stock.

Exc.	V.G.	Good	Fair	Poor
2750	1850	1500	1150	650

Type R Deluxe
As above, engraved with hunting scenes and with a more finely figured walnut stock.

Exc.	V.G.	Good	Fair	Poor
3500	2750	1750	1450	750

Type PT President
As above, inlaid in gold with extremely well figured walnut stock.

Exc.	V.G.	Good	Fair	Poor
4000	3250	2250	1750	950

Mauser Bolt Action
A custom made bolt action rifle built on a Mauser action. Choice of calibers and stock styles. Base price listed below.

Exc.	V.G.	Good	Fair	Poor
5750	4500	3250	1500	750

Deluxe Mauser Bolt Action
Same as above but with fancy wood and other options.

Exc.	V.G.	Good	Fair	Poor
10000	7000	4500	3250	1250

RENWICK ARMS CO.
SEE—Perry & Goddard

REPUBLIC ARMS, INC.
Chino, California

Republic Patroit
This is a double action only .45 ACP caliber pistol with a 3" barrel and fixed sights. Black polymer frame with checkered grips and stainless steel slide. Magazine capacity is 6 rounds. Weight is about 20 oz. Introduced in 1997.

NIB	Exc.	V.G.	Good	Fair	Poor
325	250	200	—	—	—

RAP 440

This pistol is chambered for the .40 S&W or 9mm cartridges. It is double action/single action operation. Fitted with a 3-3/4" barrel, it has a magazine capacity of 7 rounds. Grips are two-piece black plastic. Weight is approximately 32 oz. Sights are three dot with fixed ramp front and windage adjustable rear. Introduced in 1998. Imported by TSF of Fairfax, VA.

NIB	Exc.	V.G.	Good	Fair	Poor
545	450	—	—	—	—

RETOLAZA HERMANOS
Eibar, Spain

Brompetier

A folding trigger 6.35mm or 7.65mm caliber double action revolver with a 2.5" barrel and a safety mounted on the left side of the frame. Manufactured until 1915.

Exc.	V.G.	Good	Fair	Poor
150	100	85	70	45

Gallus or Titan

A 6.35mm semiautomatic pistol normally marked "Gallus" or "Titan". Blued with plastic grips.

Exc.	V.G.	Good	Fair	Poor
175	125	100	75	50

Liberty, Military, Retolaza, or Paramount

A 6.35mm or 7.65mm semiautomatic pistol with a 3" barrel and 8-shot magazine. The slide marked with any of the trade names listed above.

Exc.	V.G.	Good	Fair	Poor
175	125	100	75	50

Puppy

A folding trigger .22 caliber double action revolver with a 5-shot cylinder. The trade name "Puppy" stamped on the barrel.

Exc.	V.G.	Good	Fair	Poor
150	100	75	50	25

Stosel

A 6.35mm semiautomatic pistol marked on the slide "Automatic Pistol Stosel No. 1 Patent". Blued with plastic grips.

Exc.	V.G.	Good	Fair	Poor
175	125	100	75	50

Titanic

A 6.35mm semiautomatic pistol with a 2.5" barrel, the slide marked "1913 Model Automatic Pistol Titanic Eibar". Blued with plastic grips.

Exc.	V.G.	Good	Fair	Poor
175	125	100	75	50

REUNIES
Liege, Belgium

Dictator

A 6.35mm semiautomatic pistol with a 1.5" barrel, 5-shot magazine and the name "Dictator" together with the company's details stamped on the slide. This pistol features a bolt of tubular form the front end of which is hollow and encloses the barrel breech. Manufactured from 1909 to approximately 1925.

Exc.	V.G.	Good	Fair	Poor
250	150	125	100	75

Texas Ranger or Cowboy Ranger

Patterned after the Colt Model 1873 revolver. This pistol is of .38 Special caliber and has a 5.5" barrel. The barrel marked with the company's details and either the legend "Cowboy Ranger" or "Texas Ranger". Manufactured from 1922 to 1931.

Exc.	V.G.	Good	Fair	Poor
200	125	100	75	50

REUTH, F.
Hartford, Connecticut

Animal Trap Gun

A cast iron .28 to .50 caliber percussion trap gun with either single or double barrels 3.5" or 5" in length. This firearm fires a barbed arrow and is triggered by a cord attached to an animal trap or bait. The barrels marked "F. Reuth's Patent, May 12, 1857." Several hundred were made between 1858 and 1862. The single-barrel model is more common than the single barrel and is worth approximately 20% less.

Exc.	V.G.	Good	Fair	Poor
—	—	1150	500	150

REXIODE ARMAS
Argentina
Importer-VAM Distribution Comp
Wooster, Ohio

RJ 22

This revolver is chambered for the .22 Long Rifle cartridge and fitted with a 3", 4", or 6" barrel. Checkered walnut grips or synthetic grips. Adjustable rear sight. Blued finish. Melting point is 716 degrees F.

NIB	Exc.	V.G.	Good	Fair	Poor
165	125	100	75	50	—

RJ 38

Same as above but chambered for .38 Special cartridge.

NIB	Exc.	V.G.	Good	Fair	Poor
165	125	—	—	—	—

RS 22

A 9-shot revolver chambered for the .22 Long Rifle cartridge. Choice of blued or stainless steel frame. Fixed or adjustable sights. Barrel lengths are 4" or 6". Fitted with rubber grips.

NIB	Exc.	V.G.	Good	Fair	Poor
235	175	—	—	—	—

NOTE: Add $30 for stainless steel.

RS 22M

Same as above but chambered for the .22 Win. mag cartridge.

NIB	Exc.	V.G.	Good	Fair	Poor
235	175	—	—	—	—

NOTE: Add $30 for stainless steel.

RS 357

Same as above but chambered for the .357 magnum cartridge and offered with 3", 4", or 6" barrels.

NIB	Exc.	V.G.	Good	Fair	Poor
235	175	—	—	—	—

NOTE: Add $30 for stainless steel.

Outfitter Single Shot

This is a break down single pistol chambered for the .45 Long Colt .410 . 22 Long Rifle or .22 Win. mag. Blued 10" barrel with synthetic grip. Weight is about 43 oz.

NIB	Exc.	V.G.	Good	Fair	Poor
200	150	—	—	—	—

Outfitter Single Shot Compact

Same as above but with 6" barrel in .22 Win. mag or .45 Long Colt .410 .

NIB	Exc.	V.G.	Good	Fair	Poor
200	150	—	—	—	—

RHEINMETALL
Sommerda, Germany

Dreyse 6.35mm

A 6.35mm semiautomatic pistol with a 2" barrel, manual safety and 6-shot magazine. The slide marked "Dreyse". Blued with plastic grips having the trademark "RFM" cast in them. The patent for this design was issued in 1909 to Louis Scmeisser.

Courtesy James Rankin

Exc.	V.G.	Good	Fair	Poor
400	250	200	150	100

Dreyse 7.65mm

As above, but chambered for the 7.65mm cartridge, with a 3.6" barrel and a 7-shot magazine. The slide marked "Dreyse Rheinmetall Abt. Sommerda." Blued with plastic grips.

Courtesy Orvel Reichert

Exc.	V.G.	Good	Fair	Poor
500	350	250	200	100

Dreyse 9mm

As above, but chambered for the 9mm cartridge with a 5" barrel and an 8-shot magazine. The slide marked "Rheinische Mettellwaaren Und Maschinenfabrik, Sommerda." Blued with plastic grips.

Courtesy James Rankin

Exc.	V.G.	Good	Fair	Poor
1000	800	650	450	300

Rheinmetall 32

A 7.65mm semiautomatic pistol with a 3.65" barrel and an 8-shot magazine. The slide marked "Rheinmetell ABT. Sommerda." Blued with walnut grips. Overall length is 6.5" and weight is about 23.5 oz. Production of this pistol began in 1920.

Courtesy James Rankin

Exc.	V.G.	Good	Fair	Poor
350	225	175	125	90

Rheinmetall 9mm

This is a 9mm version of the Rheinmetall and was built in 1935 to compete with the 9mm Parabellum German military pistols of that time. It was unsuccessful.

Courtesy James Rankin

Exc.	V.G.	Good	Fair	Poor
5000	4500	3800	2500	1000

Dreyse Light Rifle or Carbine

Model 1907 in caliber 7.65 Dreyse. Fitted with a fixed stock and 6-round magazine.

Courtesy James Rankin

Exc.	V.G.	Good	Fair	Poor
4800	4000	3000	2000	1000

RHODE ISLAND ARMS CO.
Hope Valley, Rhode Island

Morrone

A 12 or 20 gauge Over/Under boxlock shotgun with 26" or 28" barrels, single trigger and automatic ejectors. Blued with either a straight or pistol grip walnut checkered stock. 450 were made in 12 gauge and 50 in 20 gauge. Manufactured from 1949 to 1953.

Exc.	V.G.	Good	Fair	Poor
1500	1000	750	600	350

RICHLAND ARMS CO.
Blissfield, Michigan

This company, which ceased operation in 1986, imported a variety of Spanish-made shotguns.

Model 41 Ultra O/U

A 20, 28, or .410 bore double-barrel shotgun with 26" or 28" ventilated rib barrels, single nonselective trigger and automatic ejectors. French Case hardened receiver and checkered walnut stock.

Exc.	V.G.	Good	Fair	Poor
300	250	200	150	100

Model 747 O/U

As above, in 20 gauge only with a single selective trigger.

Exc.	V.G.	Good	Fair	Poor
425	350	300	250	175

Model 757 O/U

A Greener style boxlock 12 gauge double barrel shotgun with 26" or 28" ventilated rib barrels, double triggers and automatic ejectors. Finished as above.

Exc.	V.G.	Good	Fair	Poor
300	250	200	175	125

Model 787 O/U

As above, fitted with screw-in choke tubes.

Exc.	V.G.	Good	Fair	Poor
450	375	325	275	200

Model 808 O/U

A 12 gauge double-barrel shotgun with 26", 28" or 30" ventilated rib barrels, single trigger and automatic ejectors. Blued with checkered walnut stock. Manufactured in Italy from 1963 to 1968.

Exc.	V.G.	Good	Fair	Poor
425	350	300	250	175

Model 80 LS

A 12, 20 or .410 bore single barrel shotgun with 26" or 28" barrels. Blued with checkered walnut stock.

Exc.	V.G.	Good	Fair	Poor
175	125	100	80	60

Model 200

An Anson & Deeley style 12, 16, 20, 28 or .410 bore double barrel shotgun with 22", 26" or 28" barrels, double triggers, and automatic ejectors. Blued with a checkered walnut stock.

Exc.	V.G.	Good	Fair	Poor
350	300	250	200	125

Model 202

As above, with an extra set of interchangeable barrels. Imported from 1963 to 1985.

Exc.	V.G.	Good	Fair	Poor
325	275	225	175	100

Model 711 Magnum

As above, chambered for 3" shells and fitted with 30" or 32" barrels.

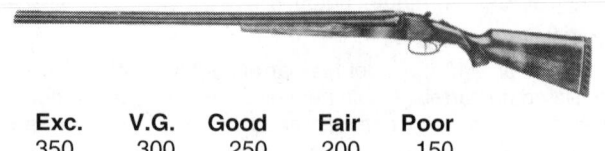

Exc.	V.G.	Good	Fair	Poor
350	300	250	200	150

Model 707 Deluxe

As above, more finely finished and fitted with well figured walnut stocks.

Exc.	V.G.	Good	Fair	Poor
350	300	250	200	150

RICHMOND ARMORY
Richmond, Virginia

Carbine

This weapon was manufactured for use by the Confederate States of America and is extremely collectible. We recommend qualified individual appraisal if a transaction is contemplated. This muzzle-loading carbine is chambered for .58 caliber percussion and has a 25" round barrel and a full-length stock that is held on by two barrel bands. It was manufactured from parts that were captured at the Harper's Ferry Armory in 1861. The locks are marked "Richmond, VA" and dated from 1861 to 1865. There are sling swivels in front of the triggerguard and on the front barrel band; a third swivel is on the underside of the buttstock. The quantity manufactured is not known. They were made between 1861 and 1865.

Courtesy Milwaukee Public Museum, Milwaukee, Wisconsin

Exc.	V.G.	Good	Fair	Poor
—	—	20000	7500	1000

A Richmond Carbine in .62 caliber with 25" barrel was sold at auction for $8,337.50. Condition is fair. Amoskeag Auction Company, August 2001

Musketoon

This weapon is similar to the carbine except that the barrel is 30" in length and the front sight is also the bayonet lug. There is no sling swivel on the buttstock. This weapon was also manufactured between 1861 and 1865.

Exc.	V.G.	Good	Fair	Poor
—	—	17500	7000	1000

Rifled Musket

This model is also similar to the Carbine, with a 40" barrel and a full-length stock held on by three barrel bands. The front sling swivel is on the middle barrel band instead of on the front band. The Rifled Musket was also manufactured between 1861 and 1865.

Courtesy Milwaukee Public Museum, Milwaukee, Wisconsin

Exc.	V.G.	Good	Fair	Poor
—	—	20000	7500	1000

RIEDL RIFLE CO.
Westminster, California

Single-Shot Rifle

This company produced custom order dropping block single-shot rifles in a variety of calibers and barrel lengths. Rifles were normally fitted only with telescopic or target sight bases. Blued with a checkered walnut stock.

Exc.	V.G.	Good	Fair	Poor
500	450	400	300	225

RIFLESMITH INC.
Sheridan, MT
SEE Axtell Rifle Co.

RIGBY, JOHN & CO., LTD.
London, England
SEE—British Double Guns

This company was established in the early 19th century and has produced a variety of shotguns and rifles over the years. Many of the arms produced by this company were custom ordered and prospective purchasers are advised to secure individual appraisals prior to the acquisition of such pieces.

RIFLES

Magazine Rifle

Utilizing a Mauser action, this rifle is available in a number of calibers, barrel lengths and with either a 3- or 5-shot magazine. Blued checkered walnut stock.

Courtesy Faintich Auction Service. Photo Paul Goodwin

NIB	Exc.	V.G.	Good	Fair	Poor
6500	4750	3000	2250	1250	—

Large Bore Magazine Rifle
Utilizing a Bruno square bridge Mauser action, this rifle is chambered for .375 Holland & Holland, .404 Gibbs, .416 Rigby, .458 Winchester Magnum and .505 Gibbs cartridges. Barrel lengths vary from 2" to 24" and a 4-shot magazine is standard.

NIB	Exc.	V.G.	Good	Fair	Poor
7500	5000	3750	2500	1000	—

Single-Shot Rifle
Utilizing a Farquharson dropping block action, this rifle is chambered for a variety of cartridges and has a 24" barrel. The receiver finely engraved and blued. Stock of well figured walnut.

Exc.	V.G.	Good	Fair	Poor
8000	7000	5500	2500	—

Third Quality Boxlock Double Rifle
A double barrel rifle chambered for cartridges from .275 Magnum to .577 Nitro Express with a 24" to 28" barrel fitted with express sights. Double triggers and automatic ejectors. Blued with light engraving and a checkered walnut stock.

Exc.	V.G.	Good	Fair	Poor
12500	10500	8500	4000	—

Second Quality Boxlock Double Rifle
As above, but more finely engraved and with better quality walnut stocks.

Exc.	V.G.	Good	Fair	Poor
16000	14000	10500	50000	—

Best Quality Sidelock Double Rifle
As above, but fitted with full sidelocks, with best bouquet engraving and finely figured walnut stocks.

NIB	Exc.	V.G.	Good	Fair	Poor
35000	30000	25000	20000	10000	—

RIGDON, ANSLEY & CO.
Augusta, Georgia

1851 Colt Navy Type
A .36 caliber percussion revolver with a 7.5" barrel and 6-shot cylinder. Blued with walnut grips. Initial production examples marked "Augusta, GA. C.S.A." and later models "C.S.A." Approximately 1,000 were manufactured in 1864 and 1865.

Courtesy Milwaukee Public Museum, Milwaukee, Wisconsin

Early Production Model

Exc.	V.G.	Good	Fair	Poor
—	—	40000	17500	2000

Standard Production Model

Exc.	V.G.	Good	Fair	Poor
—	—	30000	15000	1500

RIPOMANTI, GUY
St. Etienne, France
Importer - Wes Gilpin
Dallas, Texas
Morton's Ltd.
Lexington, Kentucky

Side-x-Side Shotgun
A high-grade shotgun offered on a strictly made-to-order basis. There is a boxlock model that begins at $8,500 and a sidelock that is priced from $22,500. These prices rise depending on the options and embellishments desired. These guns are rarely seen on the used-gun market; but if a transaction is contemplated, we strongly urge competent individual appraisal. The shotguns are imported by Gilpin's.

Side-x-Side Double Rifles
Extremely high-grade and basically made to order. They are rarely encountered on today's market. They have been imported since 1988. They range in price from $11,000 up. If a transaction is contemplated, we strongly urge competent individual appraisal. These guns are imported by Morton's.

Over/Under Double Rifle
A boxlock action Over/Under chambered for the 9.3x74R cartridge. The barrels are 23.5" in length and have express sights. There are double triggers and automatic ejectors. This model is highly engraved and features a high-grade, hand-checkered walnut stock. It was introduced in 1989 and is imported by Morton's.

NIB	Exc.	V.G.	Good	Fair	Poor
7000	5750	4750	4000	3000	2250

RIVERSIDE ARMS CO.
Chicopee Falls, Massachusetts
Double Barrel Shotguns

Courtesy William Hammond

Brand name used by J. Stevens Arms Co. on many good quality double barrel shotguns. Value depends on model, gauge, and condition. From $100 to $1,600. See also Stevens.

RIZZINI, BATTISTA
Bresica, Italy
Importer - W. L. Moore & Co.
Scottsdale, Arizona

NOTE: There are a number of extra cost options for Rizzini guns that can greatly effect price. Extra barrels and upgraded wood are such options. An expert opinion is suggested prior to a sale.

SHOTGUNS

Aurum Light 16 Gauge

This over/under model is offered in 16 gauge and features a choice of 24.5" to 27.5". Vent rib barrel. Figured oil finish walnut stock with hand checkering and pistol grip. Game scene engraved receiver. Auto ejectors and single selective trigger. Weight is about 6 lbs.

Courtesy William Larkin Moore & Co.

NIB	Exc.	V.G.	Good	Fair	Poor
2250	1650	1250	—	—	—

Artemis

This model features engraved sideplates with game scenes. Offered in 12, 16, 20, 28 gauge as well as .410 bore. Barrel lengths from 24" to 27.5". Auto ejectors and single selective trigger. Figured walnut stock with hand checkering and pistol grip. Weight is about 6 lbs.

Courtesy William Larkin Moore & Co.

NIB	Exc.	V.G.	Good	Fair	Poor
2375	1750	1250	—	—	—

Upland EL

NIB	Exc.	V.G.	Good	Fair	Poor
3600	2700	2000	—	—	—

Artemis Deluxe

Similar to the standard Artemis with the addition of gold inlaid game scenes and fancy walnut stock. Cased.

NIB	Exc.	V.G.	Good	Fair	Poor
4675	3500	2750	—	—	—

S780 Emel

This boxlock model is offered in 12, 16, 20, 28, or .410. Barrel lengths from 24" to 27.5". Hand engraved receiver with game scenes. Auto ejectors and single selective trigger. Fancy walnut stock with hand checkering. Leather case. Weight for 12 gauge is about 6.8 lbs. and the smaller gauges about 6 lbs.

NIB	Exc.	V.G.	Good	Fair	Poor
10300	7750	6000	—	—	—

S790 Emel

This model is similar to the S780 with the exception of the engraving pattern. This model has a thistle-leaf style pattern.

NIB	Exc.	V.G.	Good	Fair	Poor
10250	7750	6000	—	—	—

S792 Emel

This model features sideplates engraved with English scroll and game scenes. Extra select walnut stock. Available in 12, 16, 20, 28, and .410 with barrel lengths from 24" to 27.5".

NIB	Exc.	V.G.	Good	Fair	Poor
9750	7250	5500	—	—	—

S782 Emel

This model is similar to the S792 but with the addition of hand engraved gold inlaid game scenes.

NIB	Exc.	V.G.	Good	Fair	Poor
12250	9200	7200	—	—	—

Artemis EL

This model features sideplates with hand engraved English scroll and game scenes. Extra fancy walnut stock. Cased.

NIB	Exc.	V.G.	Good	Fair	Poor
15600	11500	9000	—	—	—

Premier Sporting

This model is offered in 12 or 20 gauge with choice of barrel lengths from 27.5" to 31.5". Blued boxlock action with auto ejectors and single selective trigger. Select walnut stock with hand checkering and oil finish. Pistol grip stock and beavertail forend. Weight is about 7.5 lbs.

NIB	Exc.	V.G.	Good	Fair	Poor
2750	2100	1600	—	—	—

Sporting EL

NIB	Exc.	V.G.	Good	Fair	Poor
3750	2800	2200	—	—	—

S790 EL Sporting

This model is offered in 12 gauge only and choice of barrel from 27.5" to 31.5". Boxlock action with chrome plate. Auto ejectors and single selective trigger. Pistol grip stock with fancy walnut. Weight is about 7.5 lbs.

NIB	Exc.	V.G.	Good	Fair	Poor
6250	4650	3750	—	—	—

EXPRESS RIFLES

Express 90 L

This over and under rifle is chambered for the 7x65R, 8x57JRS, 9.3x74R, .30-06, .308 Win., and .444 Marlin. Barrel length is 16". Boxlock action with case colored receiver. Auto ejectors and single trigger. Pistol grip walnut stock with Bavarian cheekpiece. Hand checkered and oil finish stock. Weight is about 8 lbs.

NIB	Exc.	V.G.	Good	Fair	Poor
4600	3250	2500	—		

Express 92 EL

Same calibers as above model but with sideplates engraved with English scroll and game scenes. Extra select walnut stock with pistol grip and round cheekpiece.

NIB	Exc.	V.G.	Good	Fair	Poor
9750	7250	5750	—	—	—

RIZZINI, F.ILLI
Brescia, Italy
Importer - W. L. Moore & Co.
Scottsdale, Arizona

Early guns were manufactured with Antonio Zoli. As a result, these were off-the-shelf guns of lower prices. These early guns were imported by Abercombie and Fitch of New York. Some of these guns will be stamped with the A&F address on the barrel. These side-by-side guns have a box lock action.

Lusso Grade

12 gauge

NIB	Exc.	V.G.	Good	Fair	Poor
1200	850	700	600	400	200

20 gauge

NIB	Exc.	V.G.	Good	Fair	Poor
1700	1250	800	600	500	250

28 gauge and .410 bore

NIB	Exc.	V.G.	Good	Fair	Poor
2000	1600	1250	800	600	300

Extra Lusso Grade-Scalloped receiver

12 gauge

NIB	Exc.	V.G.	Good	Fair	Poor
2800	2450	1750	1200	800	400

20 gauge

NIB	Exc.	V.G.	Good	Fair	Poor
3450	3450	2000	1500	1150	600

28 gauge

NIB	Exc.	V.G.	Good	Fair	Poor
3850	3850	2250	1750	1300	700

.410 bore

NIB	Exc.	V.G.	Good	Fair	Poor
4250	4250	2400	1800	1350	750

NOTE: At the present time this Italian gun company builds about 24 shotguns a year. Each gun is highly individualized for the customer. It is therefore advisable to secure a qualified appraisal before purchase. The company only produces two models. These are listed below to give the reader some idea of the value of one of these models. None of these models includes the cost of engraving and multi barrel set and multi gauge sets are extra.

Rizzini models with serial numbers above #1709 have their own patented action and the prices below reflect that action. Guns below have a H&H style action and should deduct approximately 30% from the prices listed below. Sellers and purchasers should note the the R-1 and R-2 models are some of the finest shotguns produced in the world.

Model R-1

Available in 12 to .410 bore with choice of barrels from 25" to 30". Choice of single or double trigger, pistol or straight grip, rib, barrel length and chokes are standard items on this model. This model features a Holland & Holland sidelock action.

12, 16, or 20 gauge

NIB	Exc.	V.G.	Good	Fair	Poor
40000	30000	19000	—	—	—

.28 gauge or .410 bore

NIB	Exc.	V.G.	Good	Fair	Poor
46000	34500	22000	—	—	—

Model R-2

This model has a box lock action and a removable inspection plate on the bottom of the frame. The stock and forearm is fitted with Turkish Circassian walnut. Offered in 12 gauge to .410 bore.

NIB	Exc.	V.G.	Good	Fair	Poor
15000	12000	8500	—	—	—

NOTE: Engraving extras for above models will add $8,700 for English scroll pattern and $22,000 for Fracassi style engraving. Other types of engraving are offered and it is advisable to secure a qualified appraisal of an engraved Rizzini before purchase.

Extra set of barrels in same gauge add 15%.

ROBAR ET CIE
Liege, Belgium

Jieffeco
A 6.35mm or 7.65mm caliber semiautomatic pistol with a 3" barrel. The slide is marked "Pistolet Automatique Jieffeco Depose Brevete SGDG." Blued with plastic grips. Manufactured from 1910 to 1914.

Exc.	V.G.	Good	Fair	Poor
200	150	125	100	75

Melior
As above, with a 2.5" barrel and the slide marked "Melior Brevete SGDG." Manufactured from 1910 to 1914.

Exc.	V.G.	Good	Fair	Poor
200	150	125	100	75

New Model Melior
A .22, 6.35mm, 7.65mm, or 9mm short caliber semiautomatic pistol resembling the Browning Model 1910 with a 2" barrel. The barrel marked "Melior Brevets-Liege, Belgium." Blued, with plastic grips. Manufactured prior to 1958.

Exc.	V.G.	Good	Fair	Poor
200	150	125	100	75

Mercury
As above, in .22 caliber and imported by Tradewinds of Tacoma, Washington. The slide marked "Mercury Made in Belgium." Blue or nickel-plated. Manufactured from 1946 to 1958.

Exc.	V.G.	Good	Fair	Poor
200	150	125	100	75

ROBBINS & LAWRENCE
Windsor, Vermont

Pepperbox
A .28 or .31 caliber percussion 5 barrel pistol with the barrel groups measuring 3.5" or 4.5" in length. Ring trigger, blued iron frame with simple scroll engraving and browned barrels, which are marked "Robbins & Lawrence Co. Windsor, VT. Patent. 1849." The barrel groups for this pistol were made in two types: fluted in both calibers, and ribbed in .31 caliber only. Approximately 7,000 were made between 1851 and 1854.

Exc.	V.G.	Good	Fair	Poor
—	—	1750	600	200

ROBERTSON
Philadelphia, Pennsylvania

Pocket Pistol
A .41 caliber single-shot percussion derringer with barrels ranging in length from 3" to 4.5". The barrel marked "Robertson, Phila."

Exc.	V.G.	Good	Fair	Poor
—	—	1000	500	200

ROBINSON ARMAMENT CO.
Salt Lake City, UT

Super VEPR
This semiautomatic rifle is made in Russia and is chambered for the .308 cartridge. Uses an RPK-type receiver. Chrome lined 21.65" barrel. Walnut thumbhole stock. Black oxide finish. Weight is about 8.5 lbs.

NIB	Exc.	V.G.	Good	Fair	Poor
600	475	—	—	—	—

M-96 Expeditonary Rifle
Chambered for the .223 or 7.62x39mm cartridge. Can use either AK or AR magazines. With quick change barrel. Adjustable gas operating system. Can interchange calibers without tools. Built in the U.S.A.

NIB	Exc.	V.G.	Good	Fair	Poor
1500	1250	—	—	—	—

ROBINSON, ORVIL
SEE—Adirondack Arms Company

ROBINSON, S.C.
Richmond, Virginia

From December of 1862 through March 1 of 1863, S.C. Robinson produced copies of the Sharps carbine. These arms had an overall length of 38-1/2", with .52 caliber barrels 21-1/2" long. The lockplates were marked "S.C. ROBINSON/ARMS MANUFACTORY/RICHMOND VA/1862" along with the serial number. The barrels were marked forward of the rear sight "S.C. ROBINSON/ARMS MANUFACTORY," as well as "RICHMOND VA/1862" to the rear of the sight. Total number made estimated to be slightly over 1900.

In March of 1863, the Robinson factory was taken over by the Confederate States Government. Carbines produced after that date are only stamped with the serial number on their lockplates and "RICHMOND VA" on their barrels. Total number made in excess of 3,400. Prospective purchasers are strongly advised to secure an expert appraisal prior to acquisition.

Robinson Sharps

Exc.	V.G.	Good	Fair	Poor
—	—	8000	4000	1500

Confederate Sharps

Exc.	V.G.	Good	Fair	Poor
—	—	8500	4500	1500

ROCK RIVER ARMS, INC.
Cleveland, IL

NOTE: This company builds Model 1911-style pistols with a number of custom features and offer many options and upgrades. Consult the company or an expert prior to a sale.

PISTOLS

Elite Commando
Built on a National Match frame with 4" National Match slide with double serrations and lowered ejection port (5" barrel op-

tional). Front strap is 30 lpi. Night sights standard. Aluminum trigger and many more customs features. Checkered cocobolo grips. Guaranteed 2.5" groups at 50 yards. Chambered for the .45 ACP cartridge.

NIB	Exc.	V.G.	Good	Fair	Poor
1275	1000	—	—	—	—

Standard Match
Many of the same features as the above model without the night sights. Also chambered for the .45 ACP cartridge.

NIB	Exc.	V.G.	Good	Fair	Poor
1025	750	—	—	—	—

National Match Hardball
Similar features as above models but with adjustable rear Bomar sight with dovetail front sight. Chambered for .45 ACP cartridge.

NIB	Exc.	V.G.	Good	Fair	Poor
1275	1000	—	—	—	—

Bullseye Wadcutter
This model features Rock River slide scope mount. Guaranteed to shoot 1.5" groups at 50 yards. Chambered for .45 ACP.

NIB	Exc.	V.G.	Good	Fair	Poor
1380	1100	—	—	—	—

Basic Limited Match
Similar to the Bullseye Wadcutter but with Bomar adjustable rear sight and dovetail front sights. Chambered for the .45 ACP.

NIB	Exc.	V.G.	Good	Fair	Poor
1395	1100	—	—	—	—

Limited Match
This match pistol comes standard with many custom features. Guaranteed to shoot 1.5" groups at 50 yards. Chambered for the .45 ACP.

NIB	Exc.	V.G.	Good	Fair	Poor
1795	1400	—	—	—	—

Hi-Cap Basic Limited
This model gives the customer the choice of STI, SVI, Para-Ordnance, or Entreprise frames. Many special features. Chambered for the .45 ACP.

NIB	Exc.	V.G.	Good	Fair	Poor
1895	1500	—	—	—	—

NOTE: Add $200 for Para-Ordnance or Entreprise frames.

Ultimate Match Achiever

This is an IPSC-style pistol with scope and three port muzzle compensator with many special features. Chambered for the .38 Super cartridge.

NIB	Exc.	V.G.	Good	Fair	Poor
2250	1750	—	—	—	—

Match Master Steel

This is a Bianchi-style pistol with scope and three port muzzle brake. Chambered fo the .38 Super Cartridge.

NIB	Exc.	V.G.	Good	Fair	Poor
2350	1850	—	—	—	—

RIFLES

CAR A2

These are AR-15-style rifles chambered for the .223 cartridge. Fitted with a 16" barrel with CAR handguards. Two stage trigger. Choice of A2 or non-collapsible butt stock. Choice of black or green furniture. Weight is about 7 lbs.

NIB	Exc.	V.G.	Good	Fair	Poor
925	750	—	—	—	—

NOTE: Add $25 for non-collapsible butt stock.

CAR A2M

Same as above but with mid-length handguard.

NIB	Exc.	V.G.	Good	Fair	Poor
925	750	—	—	—	—

NOTE: Add $25 for non-collapsible butt stock.

CAR A4

Similar to the models above but with flattop receiver and CAR handguard.

NIB	Exc.	V.G.	Good	Fair	Poor
890	725	—	—	—	—

NOTE: Add $25 for non-collapsible butt stock.

CAR A4M

Flattop receiver with mid-length handguard.

NIB	Exc.	V.G.	Good	Fair	Poor
890	725	—	—	—	—

NOTE: Add $25 for non-collapsible butt stock.

Standard A2

The AR-15-style rifle is fitted with a 20" barrel and chambered for the .223 cartridge. Two stage trigger. Fixed stock and full-length hand guard. Weight is about 8.2 lbs.

NIB	Exc.	V.G.	Good	Fair	Poor
925	750	—	—	—	—

Standard A4 Flattop

Same as Standard A2 but with flattop receiver.

NIB	Exc.	V.G.	Good	Fair	Poor
890	725	—	—	—	—

Varmint Rifle

This flattop model is fitted with a 24" stainless steel barrel without sights. Chambered for the .223 cartridge. Fixed stock. Two stage trigger. Weight is about 9.5 lbs.

NIB	Exc.	V.G.	Good	Fair	Poor
950	750	—	—	—	—

NM A2-DCM Legal

Fitted with a 20" stainless steel barrel with National Match sleeve and specially selected upper and lowers to insure tight fit. Special high temp handguards. Two stage trigger. National Match sights. Weight is about 9 lbs.

NIB	Exc.	V.G.	Good	Fair	Poor
1200	950	—	—	—	—

ROGERS & SPENCER
Utica, New York

Army Revolver

A .44 caliber 6-shot percussion revolver with a 7.5" octagonal barrel. The barrel marked "Rogers & Spencer/Utica, N.Y." Blued, case hardened hammer with walnut grips bearing the inspector's mark "RPB". Approximately 5,800 were made between 1863 and 1865.

Courtesy Milwaukee Public Museum, Milwaukee, Wisconsin

Exc.	V.G.	Good	Fair	Poor
—	4000	1750	750	250

ROGUE RIFLE COMPANY
Prospect, Oregon
SEE—Chipmunk Rifles

ROGUE RIVER RIFLEWORKS
Paso Robles, California

Boxlock Double Rifle

These rifles are custom fitted and available in any barrel length or caliber from .22 Hornet to .577 NE. Anson & Deeley boxlocks. Choice of finish, forend, engraving, wood, and various other options. Each rifle should be appraised individually before a sale. Prices below are for basic rifle with no extras.

NIB	Exc.	V.G.	Good	Fair	Poor
12500	—	—	—	—	—

Sidelock Double Rifle

These rifles are custom fitted and available in any barrel length or caliber from .22 Hornet to .577 NE. Holland & Holland pattern sidelocks. Choice of finish, forend, engraving, wood, and various other options. Each rifle should be appraised individually before a sale. Prices below are for basic rifle with no extras.

NIB	Exc.	V.G.	Good	Fair	Poor
18500	—	—	—	—	—

ROHM GMBH
Sonthein/Brenz, Germany

This firm produced a variety of revolvers marked with various trade names that were imported into the United States prior to 1968. Essentially, they are of three types: 1) solid-frame, gate-loading models; 2) solid-frame, swingout-cylinder revolvers; and 3) solid-frame, swingout-cylinder revolvers. They are of low quality and little collector interest.

Courtesy John J. Stimson, Jr.

ROMERWERKE
Suhl, Germany

Romer

.22 caliber semiautomatic pistol with a 2.5" or 6.5" barrel and 7-shot magazine. The barrels are interchangeable and marked "Kal. .22 Long Rifle," the slide marked "Romerwerke Suhl." Blued, with plastic grips. Manufactured between 1924 and 1926.

Exc.	V.G.	Good	Fair	Poor
550	450	400	300	225

RONGE, J. B.
Liege, Belgium

Bulldog
A .32, .380, or .45 caliber double action revolver with a 3" barrel. Unmarked except for the monogram "RF" on the grips. Various trade names have been noted on these revolvers and are believed to have been applied by retailers. Manufactured from 1880 to 1910.

Exc.	V.G.	Good	Fair	Poor
200	150	100	75	50

ROSS RIFLE CO.
Quebec, Canada
Designed in 1896 by Sir Charles Ross, this straight pole rifle was manufactured in a variety of styles. Due to problems with the bolt design, it never proved popular and was discontinued in 1915.

Mark I
Barrel length 28", .303 caliber with a "Harris Controlled Platform Magazine" that can be depressed by an external lever to facilitate loading.

Courtesy Buffalo Bill Historical Center, Cody, Wyoming

Exc.	V.G.	Good	Fair	Poor
500	350	250	150	100

Mark I Carbine
As above, with a 22" barrel.

Exc.	V.G.	Good	Fair	Poor
450	300	250	200	150

Mark 2
As above, with a modified rear sight.

Exc.	V.G.	Good	Fair	Poor
500	350	250	150	100

Mark 3
Introduced in 1910 with improved lockwork and stripper clip guides.

Courtesy Buffalo Bill Historical Center, Cody, Wyoming

Exc.	V.G.	Good	Fair	Poor
500	350	275	175	125

Mark 3B
As above, with a magazine cut-off.

Exc.	V.G.	Good	Fair	Poor
450	300	250	200	150

Sporting Rifle
A .280 Ross or .303 caliber straight pole sporting rifle with a 24" barrel having open sights. Blued with a checkered walnut stock.

Courtesy Buffalo Bill Historical Center, Cody, Wyoming

Courtesy Buffalo Bill Historical Center, Cody, Wyoming

Exc.	V.G.	Good	Fair	Poor
425	300	200	150	125

ROSSI, AMADEO
Leopoldo, Brazil
Importer-BrazTech, L.C., Miami, Florida

SHOTGUNS

Overland Shotgun
An exposed hammer sidelock 12, 20 or .410 bore double barrel shotgun with 26" or 28" barrels and double triggers. Manual extractors. Blued with a walnut stock. Discontinued in 1988.

NIB	Exc.	V.G.	Good	Fair	Poor
250	225	200	150	100	75

Squire Shotgun
A 12, 20 or .410 bore double barrel shotgun with 20", 26", or 28" barrels, double triggers and manual ejectors. Blued with a walnut stock.

NIB	Exc.	V.G.	Good	Fair	Poor
350	300	250	200	150	100

Field Grade Shotgun
This is single shot tip open gun with oil finish hardwood stock, low profile hammer, and pistol grip. No checkering. Offered in 12 and 20 gauge, as well as .410 bore. Barrel length is 28". Weight is about 5.25 lbs. for 12 and 20 gauge and 4 lbs. for the .410 bore.

NIB	Exc.	V.G.	Good	Fair	Poor
100	75	—	—	—	—

Youth Model Shotgun
Same as above but with shorter length of pull and 22" barrel. Offered in 20 gauge and .410 bore only. Weight for 20 gauge is about 5 lbs. and 3.75 lbs. for the .410 bore.

NIB	Exc.	V.G.	Good	Fair	Poor
100	75	—	—	—	—

Match Pair Combo Guns
This model matches a single barrel shotgun with a .22 Long Rifle barrel. Offered in 12/22, 20/22, and .410/22. Adjustable sights on the rifle barrel. Blued finish.

NIB	Exc.	V.G.	Good	Fair	Poor
130	100	—	—	—	—

RIFLES

Model 92

A copy of the Winchester Model 1892, chambered for .357 Magnum, .44 Magnum or .44-40 with either a 16" or 20" barrel. Blued with a walnut stock. The engraved version of this model is worth approximately 20% more than the values listed below. Add $50.00 for a 20" stainless steel version introduced in 1997.

NIB	Exc.	V.G.	Good	Fair	Poor
300	225	175	150	100	75

Model 92 Rifle

Introduced in 1997 this model is fitted with a 24" half octagon barrel and brass blade front sight. Magazine capacity is 13 rounds of .45 Colt. Weight is about 6.8 lbs.

NIB	Exc.	V.G.	Good	Fair	Poor
425	350	—	—	—	—

Model 92 Large Loop

This model has a 16: barrel and is chambered for the .44 Magnum or .45 Colt cartridge. Weight is about 5.5 lbs. Finish is blue. Introduced in 1997.

NIB	Exc.	V.G.	Good	Fair	Poor
325	250	—	—	—	—

Model 62

A copy of the Winchester Model 1890 rifle with either 16.5" or 23" round or octagonal barrels. Blued or stainless steel with a walnut stock.

NIB	Exc.	V.G.	Good	Fair	Poor
200	175	150	125	100	75

Model 59

As above, in .22 Magnum caliber.

NIB	Exc.	V.G.	Good	Fair	Poor
210	175	150	125	100	75

Model 65

Similar to the Model 92, but chambered for either the .44 Special or .44 Magnum cartridge. Barrel length 20". Blued with a walnut stock. Introduced in 1989.

NIB	Exc.	V.G.	Good	Fair	Poor
300	250	200	175	150	125

HANDGUNS

Model 31

A .38 Special caliber double action revolver with a 4" barrel and 5-shot cylinder. Blued or nickel-plated with walnut grips. Imported prior to 1986.

Exc.	V.G.	Good	Fair	Poor
125	100	75	50	40

Model 51

A .22 caliber double action revolver with a 6" barrel, adjustable sights and a 6-shot cylinder. Blued with walnut grips. Imported prior to 1986.

Exc.	V.G.	Good	Fair	Poor
125	100	75	50	40

Model 511 Sportsman

As above, with a 4" barrel and made of stainless steel with walnut grips. Introduced in 1986.

NIB	Exc.	V.G.	Good	Fair	Poor
225	200	150	125	100	75

Model 677

This model was first introduced in 1997 and is chambered for the .357 magnum cartridge. It has a matte blue finish with 2" barrel and black rubber grips. Weight is about 26 oz.

NIB	Exc.	V.G.	Good	Fair	Poor
250	200	—	—	—	—

Model 68

A .38 Special double action revolver with a 2" or 3" barrel and 5-shot cylinder. Blued or nickel-plated with walnut grips.

NIB	Exc.	V.G.	Good	Fair	Poor
185	150	125	100	75	50

Model 68S

This new version was introduced in 1993 and features a shrouded ejector rod and fixed sights. Chambered for the .38 Special cartridge it is offered with either 2" or 3" barrel. Grips or wood or rubber. Finish is blue or nickel. Weighs about 23 oz.

NIB	Exc.	V.G.	Good	Fair	Poor
175	150	125	100	75	60

Model 69

As above, in .32 Smith & Wesson caliber with a 3" barrel and 6-shot cylinder. Imported prior to 1986.

Exc.	V.G.	Good	Fair	Poor
125	100	75	50	40

Model 70

As above, in .22 caliber with a 3" barrel and 6-shot cylinder. Imported prior to 1986.

Exc.	V.G.	Good	Fair	Poor
125	100	75	50	40

Model 84

A stainless steel, .38 Special caliber double action revolver with ribbed 3" or 4" barrel. Blued with walnut grips. Imported in 1985 and 1986.

Exc.	V.G.	Good	Fair	Poor
175	150	125	100	75

Model 851

As above, with either a 3" or 4" ventilated rib barrel and adjustable sights.

NIB	Exc.	V.G.	Good	Fair	Poor
200	175	150	125	100	75

Model 877

Introduced in 1996 this 6-shot revolver is chambered for the .357 magnum cartridge. It is fitted with a 2" heavy barrel. Stainless steel with black rubber grips. Weight is about 26 oz.

NIB	Exc.	V.G.	Good	Fair	Poor
275	200	175	150	100	80

Model 88S

Introduced in 1993 this improved model has the same features of the Model 68 with the addition of a stainless finish. It is chambered for the .38 Special cartridge and is fitted with either a 2" or 3" barrel. Available with either wood or rubber grips. Cylinder holds 5 cartridges. Weighs approximately 22 oz.

NIB	Exc.	V.G.	Good	Fair	Poor
200	175	150	125	100	75

Model 89

As above, in .32 Smith & Wesson caliber with a 3" barrel.

NIB	Exc.	V.G.	Good	Fair	Poor
200	175	150	125	100	75

Model 351

This revolver is chambered for the .38 Special +P cartridge. Fitted with a 2" barrel and rubber grips. 5 round cylinder. Blued finish. Weight is about 24 oz.

NIB	Exc.	V.G.	Good	Fair	Poor
250	200	—	—	—	—

Model 352

Same as above but with stainless steel finish.

NIB	Exc.	V.G.	Good	Fair	Poor
300	225	—	—	—	—

Model 461

This is a 6-round revolver chambered for the .357 Magnum cartridge. Fitted with a 2" barrel. Rubber grips and blued finish. Weight is about 26 oz.

NIB	Exc.	V.G.	Good	Fair	Poor
300	225	—	—	—	—

Model 462

Same as above but with stainless steel finish.

NIB	Exc.	V.G.	Good	Fair	Poor
350	275	—	—	—	—

Model 951

A .38 Special caliber double action revolver with a 3" or 4" ventilated rib barrel and 6-shot cylinder. Blued with walnut grips. Introduced in 1985.

NIB	Exc.	V.G.	Good	Fair	Poor
200	175	150	125	100	75

Model 971

As above, in .357 Magnum caliber with a solid ribbed 4" barrel and enclosed ejector rod. Adjustable sights. Blued with walnut grips. Introduced in 1988.

NIB	Exc.	V.G.	Good	Fair	Poor
225	175	150	125	100	75

Model 971 Comp

Introduced in 1993. Similar to the Model 971 with the addition of a compensator on a 3.25" barrel. Overall length is 9" and weight is 32 oz. Chambered for .357 Magnum cartridge.

NIB	Exc.	V.G.	Good	Fair	Poor
200	175	150	125	100	75

Model 971 Stainless

As above, but constructed of stainless steel with checkered black rubber grips. Introduced in 1989.

NIB	Exc.	V.G.	Good	Fair	Poor
225	200	150	125	100	75

Model 971 VRC (vented rib compensator)

Introduced in 1996 this variation features a choice of a 6", 4", or 2.5" vent rib barrel with integral compensator. Stainless steel with black rubber grips. Weight is from 30 oz. to 39 oz. depending on barrel length.

NIB	Exc.	V.G.	Good	Fair	Poor
300	250	200	175	150	100

Model 988 Cyclops

Introduced in 1997 this model is chambered for the .357 Magnum cartridge and is fitted with four recessed compensator ports on each side of the muzzle. Offered in 8" or 6" barrel lengths this six-shot double action revolver weighs about 44 ozs. for the 6" model and 51 ozs. for the 8" model. Stainless steel finish.

Cyclops with scope mounted

NIB	Exc.	V.G.	Good	Fair	Poor
425	350	—	—	—	—

Model 720

This double action revolver is chambered for the .44 Special and features a 5-round cylinder and 3" barrel. Overall length is 8" and weight is about 27.5 oz. Finish is stainless steel.

NIB	Exc.	V.G.	Good	Fair	Poor
250	200	175	150	125	100

ROTH-SAUER
SEE—J. P. Sauer & Son

ROTH-STEYR
Austria-Hungary
SEE-Steyer

TH. ROTTME
SEE—Austrian Military Firearms

ROTTWIEL
Rotwiel, West Germany
Importer - Dynamit Nobel of America
Northvale, New Jersey

Model 650

A 12 gauge Over/Under shotgun with 28" ventilated rib barrels having screw-in choke tubes, single selective trigger, and automatic ejectors. The receiver engraved and in French case hardened, checkered stock of well figured walnut. Imported prior to 1987.

Exc.	V.G.	Good	Fair	Poor
700	550	400	300	150

Model 72

A 12 gauge Over/Under shotgun with 28" ventilated rib barrels having screw-in choke tubes, single selective trigger and automatic ejectors. Blued with a well figured checkered walnut stock. Imported prior to 1988.

Exc.	V.G.	Good	Fair	Poor
1750	1200	750	500	250

Model 72 American Skeet

As above, with a 26.75" ventilated rib barrel, single selective trigger, and automatic ejectors. The receiver is also engraved. Imported prior to 1988.

Exc.	V.G.	Good	Fair	Poor
1750	1200	750	500	250

Model 72 Adjustable American Trap

As above, with a 34" ventilated rib barrel, adjustable to point of impact. Imported prior to 1987.

Exc.	V.G.	Good	Fair	Poor
1500	1000	600	300	150

Model 72 American Trap

As above, without the barrel being adjustable to the point of impact.

Exc.	V.G.	Good	Fair	Poor
1750	1200	750	500	250

Model 72 International Skeet

As above, with 26.75" ventilated rib barrels having skeet chokes. Imported prior to 1988.

Exc.	V.G.	Good	Fair	Poor
1750	1200	750	500	250

Model 72 International Trap

As above, with 30" high ventilated rib barrels that are im-proved-modified and full choked. Imported prior to 1988.

Exc.	V.G.	Good	Fair	Poor
1750	1200	750	500	250

ROYAL AMERICAN SHOTGUNS
Woodland Hills, California
Importer - Royal Arms International

Model 100

A 12 or 20 gauge Over/Under shotgun with 26", 28", or 30" ventilated rib barrels, double triggers and extractors. Blued with a walnut stock. Imported from 1985 to 1987.

Exc.	V.G.	Good	Fair	Poor
400	300	250	175	150

Model 100AE

As above, with a single trigger and automatic ejectors.

Exc.	V.G.	Good	Fair	Poor
450	325	275	200	175

Model 600

A 12, 20, 28 or. 410 bore double barrel shotgun with 25", 26", 28", or 30" ventilated rib barrels, double triggers and extrac-tors. Blued with a walnut stock. Imported from 1985 to 1987.

Exc.	V.G.	Good	Fair	Poor
450	325	275	200	175

Model 800

A 28 or .410 bore detachable sidelock double barrel shotgun with 24", 26", or 28" barrels, double triggers and automatic ejectors. Blued, French case hardened with an English style walnut stock. Imported from 1985 to 1987.

Exc.	V.G.	Good	Fair	Poor
900	650	600	475	400

RUBY ARMS COMPANY
Guernica, Spain

Ruby

A 6.35mm or 7.35mm caliber semiautomatic pistol with a 3.5" barrel and 6-shot magazine. The slide marked "Ruby". Blued with plastic grips.

Exc.	V.G.	Good	Fair	Poor
200	150	100	75	50

RUGER
SEE—Sturm, Ruger Co.

RUPERTUS, JACOB
Philadelphia, Pennsylvania

Army Revolver

This is an extremely rare revolver chambered for .44 caliber percussion. It has a 7.25" octagon barrel with an integral load-ing lever that pivots to the side instead of downward. The ham-mer is mounted on the side, and there is a pellet priming device located on the backstrap. There is only one nipple on the breach that lines up with the top of the cylinder. The cylin-der is unfluted and holds 6-shots. The finish is blued, with wal-nut grips; and the frame is marked "Patented April 19, 1859". There were less than 12 manufactured in 1859. It would be-hoove one to secure a qualified independent appraisal if a transaction were contemplated.

Exc.	V.G.	Good	Fair	Poor
—	—	10500	5000	1500

Navy Revolver

This model is equally as rare as the Army model. It is cham-bered for .36 caliber percussion. Otherwise it is quite similar in appearance to the Army model. There were approximately 12 manufactured in 1859. Both of these revolvers were manufac-tured for test purposes and were not well-received by the mil-itary, so further production was not accomplished.

Exc.	V.G.	Good	Fair	Poor
—	—	10500	5000	1250

Pocket Model Revolver

This is a smaller version of the Army and Navy model, cham-bered for .25 caliber percussion. It has no loading lever and has a 3-1/8" octagonal barrel. There were approximately 12 manufactured in 1859.

Exc.	V.G.	Good	Fair	Poor
—	—	7000	3250	950

Single-Shot Pocket Pistol

A .22, .32, .38, or .41 rimfire single-shot pistol with half-octag-onal barrels, ranging in length from 3" to 5". The barrel marked "Rupertus Pat'd. Pistol Mfg. Co. Philadelphia". Blued with wal-nut grips. Approximately 3,000 were made from 1870 to 1885. The .41 caliber variety is worth approximately 200% more than the values listed below.

Exc.	V.G.	Good	Fair	Poor
—	—	500	200	75

Double Barrel Pocket Pistol

A .22 caliber double barrel pistol with 3" round barrels and a spur trigger. The hammer fitted with a sliding firing pin. Blued with walnut grips.

Exc.	V.G.	Good	Fair	Poor
—	—	1750	750	200

Spur Trigger Revolver

A .22 caliber spur trigger revolver with a 2.75" round barrel and unfluted cylinder. The top strap marked "Empire Pat. Nov. 21, 71". Blued or nickel-plated with walnut grips. A .41 caliber spur trigger revolver with a 2-7/8" round barrel and a 5-shot fluted cylinder. Blued or nickel-plated with walnut grips. The top strap marked "Empire 41" and the barrel "J. Rupertus Phila. Pa." The .41 caliber variety is worth approximately 25% more than the values listed below. Manufactured during the 1870s and 1880s.

Exc.	V.G.	Good	Fair	Poor
—	—	300	125	75

S

S.A.C.M.
SEE—French State

S.A.E.
Eibar, Spain
Importer - Spain America Enterprises, Inc.
Miami, Florida

Model 210S

A 12, 20 or .410 bore double barrel shotgun with 26" or 28" barrels, double triggers and manual extractors. Blued, French case hardened with a checkered walnut stock. Imported in 1988.

Exc.	V.G.	Good	Fair	Poor
425	375	300	225	150

Model 340X

A Holland & Holland-style sidelock 10 or 20 gauge double barrel shotgun with 26" barrels, double triggers and automatic ejectors. Blued, case hardened with a checkered English style walnut stock. Imported in 1988.

Exc.	V.G.	Good	Fair	Poor
800	650	500	400	200

Model 209E

As above, with the exception that it was also chambered for .410 bore cartridges, and was more finely engraved. Imported in 1988.

Exc.	V.G.	Good	Fair	Poor
1000	800	700	550	250

Model 70

A 12 or 20 gauge Over/Under shotgun with 26" ventilated rib barrels having screw-in choke tubes, single trigger and automatic ejectors. The modestly engraved receiver either blued or French case hardened. Stock of finely figured walnut. Imported in 1988.

Exc.	V.G.	Good	Fair	Poor
450	300	250	200	100

Model 66C

A 12 gauge Over/Under shotgun with 26" or 30" ventilated rib barrels choked for skeet or trap, single trigger and automatic ejectors. The boxlock action lifted with false sideplates, which are engraved and gold inlaid. Blued with a checkered Monte Carlo-style stock and a beavertail forearm. Imported in 1988.

Exc.	V.G.	Good	Fair	Poor
1000	800	700	575	300

S.E.A.M.
Eibar, Spain

This retailer sold a number of pistols produced by the firm of Urizar prior to 1935.

Praga

A 7.65 caliber semiautomatic pistol marked "Praga Cal 7.65" on the slide. Blued with plastic grips impressed with the trademark S.E.A.M.

Exc.	V.G.	Good	Fair	Poor
200	150	125	90	65

S.E.A.M.

A 6.35mm semiautomatic pistol with a 2" barrel. The slide marked "Fabrica de Armas SEAM". Blued with black plastic grips, having the trademark "SEAM" cast into them.

Exc.	V.G.	Good	Fair	Poor
200	150	125	90	65

Silesia

As above, but of 7.65mm caliber with a 3" barrel and having the word "Silesia" stamped on the slide.

Exc.	V.G.	Good	Fair	Poor
200	150	125	90	65

SKB ARMS COMPANY
Tokyo, Japan
Importer - SKB Company U.S.A.
Omaha, Nebraska

SIDE-BY-SIDE GUNS

Model 100

A boxlock 12 or 20 gauge double barrel shotgun with 25" to 30" barrels, single selective trigger and automatic ejectors. Blued with a walnut stock. Imported prior to 1981.

NIB	Exc.	V.G.	Good	Fair	Poor
500	425	375	300	200	100

Model 150

As above, with some engraving, a beavertail forearm and a figured walnut stock. Imported from 1972 to 1974.

NIB	Exc.	V.G.	Good	Fair	Poor
550	450	400	300	200	100

Model 200

As above, with a French case hardened and scalloped receiver.

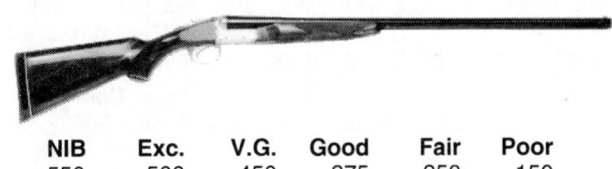

NIB	Exc.	V.G.	Good	Fair	Poor
550	500	450	375	250	150

Model 200E

As above, with an English style stock. Imported prior to 1989.

NIB	Exc.	V.G.	Good	Fair	Poor
800	675	600	475	275	150

Model 280

Same as the Model 200 but fitted with a straight grip stock.

NIB	Exc.	V.G.	Good	Fair	Poor
800	675	600	475	275	150

Model 300

As above, with more engraving and a figured walnut stock.

NIB	Exc.	V.G.	Good	Fair	Poor
750	675	600	475	275	150

Model 385

Similar to the Model 300 but chambered for the 12, 20 or 28 gauge shell. Scroll engraved frame with semi-fancy walnut. Pistol grip or straight grip stock. Limited quantities imported. Weight is approximately 7 lbs. depending on barrel length and gauge.

NIB	Exc.	V.G.	Good	Fair	Poor
2000	1500	1000	700	450	200

Model 385 2 barrel set

Same as above but with a 20 and 28 gauge set of barrels in either 26" or 28".

NIB	Exc.	V.G.	Good	Fair	Poor
2900	2250	1300	—	—	—

Model 385 Sporting Clays

This model is chambered for 12, 20, or 28 gauge and fitted with a 28" barrel. Pistol grip stock. Weight is about 7 lbs. depending on gauge.

NIB	Exc.	V.G.	Good	Fair	Poor
2150	1700	1150	750	500	300

NOTE: For extra set of 20 or 28 gauge barrels add $900.

Model 400E

As above, with engraved false sideplates and an English style stock. Imported prior to 1990.

NIB	Exc.	V.G.	Good	Fair	Poor
975	875	750	600	300	150

Model 480E

As above, with a French case hardened receiver and more finely figured walnut stocks.stocks.

NIB	Exc.	V.G.	Good	Fair	Poor
1200	1000	850	650	350	150

Model 485

This model features an engraved sideplate boxlock action chambered for 12, 20, or 28 gauge with 26" or 28" barrels. Choke tubes. Weight is approximately 7.7 lbs.

NIB	Exc.	V.G.	Good	Fair	Poor
2750	2100	1500	900	650	300

Model 485 2 barrel set

Same as above but with an extra set of barrels in 20/28 gauge combinations with 26" barrels. Choice of pistol grip or straight grip stock.

NIB	Exc.	V.G.	Good	Fair	Poor
3900	3000	1850	—	—	—

OVER AND UNDER GUNS

Model 500

A 12, 20, 28 gauge or .410 bore Over/Under shotgun with 26", 28" or 30" ventilated rib barrels. Blued with a walnut stock. Imported from 1966 to 1979. Blued with a walnut stock. Imported from 1966 to 1979.

NIB	Exc.	V.G.	Good	Fair	Poor
500	450	375	300	150	100

Model 505

A 12 or 20 gauge Over/Under shotgun with screw-in choke tubes, single selective trigger and automatic ejectors. Blued, checkered walnut stock.

NIB	Exc.	V.G.	Good	Fair	Poor
900	750	550	400	350	—

The 505 Series is also produced in sporting clays, trap and skeet configurations, which are valued at approximately 10% additional.

Model 505 3-Gauge Skeet Set

As above, with 3 sets of barrels.

NIB	Exc.	V.G.	Good	Fair	Poor
1850	1650	1400	1100	900	750

Model 585

Similar to the Model 505 but offered in12, 20, and 28 gauge and .410 bore as well. Barrel lengths are 26" or 28". Weight is about 7.25 lbs. for small bores and 8 lbs. for 12 gauge guns.

NIB	Exc.	V.G.	Good	Fair	Poor
1150	900	750	500	400	200

Model 585 Gold Package

Has all of the features of the 585 series with the addition of a gold plated trigger, gold plated game scenes, and schnabel forend. Choice of blued or ssilver receiver.

NIB	Exc.	V.G.	Good	Fair	Poor
1675	1300	850	—	—	—

Model 585 Skeet

Offered in 12, 20, or 28 gauge as well as .410 bore with 28" barrels. Skeet stock and beavertail forearm. Black recoil pad. Weight in 12 gauge about 8 lbs.

NIB	Exc.	V.G.	Good	Fair	Poor
1200	950	750	—	—	—

Model 585-3 barrel Skeet Set

Fitted with 20, 28 gauge and .410 bore barrels. Skeet choked.

NIB	Exc.	V.G.	Good	Fair	Poor
2750	2250	1700	1200	850	400

Model 585-3 barrel Skeet Set Gold Package

Same as above but with engraving and choice of silver or blued receiver.

NIB	Exc.	V.G.	Good	Fair	Poor
3125	2500	1850			

Model 585 Youth/Ladies

This model is similar to the 585 but with a shortened length of pull to 13.5". Weight of 20 gauge model is approximately 6.6 lbs. Weight of 12 gauge is about 7.5 lbs.

NIB	Exc.	V.G.	Good	Fair	Poor
1500	1150	750	500	400	200

Model 585 Youth Gold Package

Same as above but with gold trigger, gold plated game scenes, and schnabel forend. Choice of silver or blued receiver.

NIB	Exc.	V.G.	Good	Fair	Poor
1675	1300	850	—	—	—

Model 585 Upland

Similar to the 585 series except for straight grip stock. Offered in 12, 20, and 28 gauge all with 26" barrels. Weight for 12 gauge is about 7.75 lbs. and for 20 and 28 gauge about 6.75 lbs.

NIB	Exc.	V.G.	Good	Fair	Poor
1500	1150	750	500	400	200

Model 585 Upland Gold Package

This model has the additional gold package features of gold trigger, gold game scenes, and schnabel forend. Choice of silver or blued receiver.

NIB	Exc.	V.G.	Good	Fair	Poor
1675	1300	850	—	—	—

Model 600

As above, with a silver-plated receiver and better quality wood.

NIB	Exc.	V.G.	Good	Fair	Poor
700	625	550	450	325	150

Model 600 Magnum

As above, chambered for 3", 12 gauge cartridges. Imported from 1969 to 1972.

Exc.	V.G.	Good	Fair	Poor
725	650	575	475	350

Model 600 Trap Gun

As above, with 30" or 32" barrels trap choked, with a high comb walnut stock.

NIB	Exc.	V.G.	Good	Fair	Poor
675	600	525	425	300	150

Model 600 Skeet Gun

As above, chambered for 12, 20, 28 or .410 bore cartridges with 26" or 28" barrels that are skeet choked.

NIB	Exc.	V.G.	Good	Fair	Poor
700	625	550	450	325	150

Model 600 Skeet Combo Set

As above, with an extra set of interchangeable barrels. Furnished with a carrying case.

NIB	Exc.	V.G.	Good	Fair	Poor
700	625	550	450	325	150

Model 605

As above, with an engraved and French case hardened receiver.

NIB	Exc.	V.G.	Good	Fair	Poor
900	750	650	550	400	350

The 605 Series is also available in trap or skeet configurations. The values are similar.

Model 605 3-Gauge Skeet Set

As above, with 3 extra sets of barrels.

NIB	Exc.	V.G.	Good	Fair	Poor
2000	1800	1550	1250	1000	850

Model 680E

Similar to the Model 600, with an engraved receiver and English style stock. Imported from 1973 to 1976.

NIB	Exc.	V.G.	Good	Fair	Poor
725	650	575	475	350	200

Model 685

This over and under shotgun is offered in 12, 20, and 28 gauge as well as .410 bore. Barrel lengths are 26" or 28" with choke tubes. The engraved receiver has a silver finish with gold inlays. The walnut stock is semi-fancy.

NIB	Exc.	V.G.	Good	Fair	Poor
1400	1100	850	600	500	250

Model 700 Trap Gun

Similar to the Model 600 Trap, with a wider rib, additional engraving and a figured walnut stock. Imported from 1969 to 1975.

NIB	Exc.	V.G.	Good	Fair	Poor
825	750	675	575	450	250

Model 700 Skeet Gun

As above, with skeet chokes.

NIB	Exc.	V.G.	Good	Fair	Poor
850	775	700	600	475	250

Model 785

Offered in 12, 20, and 28 gauge as well as .410 bore this over and under features 26" or 28" barrels with choke tubes, single trigger, ejectors, and checkered walnut stock. the silver receiver is scroll engraved. Weight is about 8 lbs. for 12 gauge and 7.25 lbs. for small bores.

NIB	Exc.	V.G.	Good	Fair	Poor
2100	1500	900	750	500	300

Model 785-2 barrel set

These two barrel sets are in combination 12/20, 20/28, and 28/.410 bore with 26" and 28" barrels.

NIB	Exc.	V.G.	Good	Fair	Poor
2450	1900	1400	—	—	—

Model 785 Sporting Clays

Chambered for 12, 20, and 28 gauge with barrels lengths from 28" to 32" in 12 gauge and 28" in 20 and 28 gauge. Recoil pad standard.

NIB	Exc.	V.G.	Good	Fair	Poor
2250	1750	1150	—	—	—

NOTE: For Sporting Clays set add $900.

Model 785 Skeet

Offered in 12, 20, 28, and .410 bore with 28" barrels. Recoil pad standard.

NIB	Exc.	V.G.	Good	Fair	Poor
2200	1700	1150	—	—	—

Model 785 3-Gauge Skeet Set

This model furnished with 12, 20, and 28 gauge barrel all 28" in length. Weight is about 7.3 lbs. regardless of gauge.

NIB	Exc.	V.G.	Good	Fair	Poor
4400	3250	2500	—	—	—

Model 785 Trap

Offered in 12 gauge with or without Monte Carlo stock. Barrel length either 30" or 32". Ventilated recoil pad standard.

NIB	Exc.	V.G.	Good	Fair	Poor
2200	1700	1100	—	—	—

Model 785 Trap Combo

Features a 30" or 32" over and under barrels with a single 32" or 34" barrel. Choice of standard stock or Monte Carlo.

NIB	Exc.	V.G.	Good	Fair	Poor
3050	2250	1250	—	—	—

Model 800 Trap Gun

As above, but with trap chokes and more engraving. Imported from 1969 to 1975.

NIB	Exc.	V.G.	Good	Fair	Poor
2000	1000	850	650	550	250

Model 800 Skeet Gun

As above, in 12 or 20 gauge with 26" or 28" skeet choked barrels. Imported from 1969 to 1975.

NIB	Exc.	V.G.	Good	Fair	Poor
2000	1000	850	650	550	250

Model 880 Crown Grade

A false sidelock 12, 20, 28 or .410 bore boxlock double barrel shotgun with a single selective trigger and automatic ejectors. The engraved sideplates and receiver French case hardened, and the figured walnut stock checkered. Imported prior to 1981.

NIB	Exc.	V.G.	Good	Fair	Poor
1700	1500	1250	1100	900	450

Model 885

A false sidelock 12, 20, 28 or .410 bore boxlock shotgun. Similar to the model 800.

NIB	Exc.	V.G.	Good	Fair	Poor
1250	1050	900	700	600	300

Model 5600

This over and under gun is offered in 12 gauge only in either Trap or Skeet configurations.

NIB	Exc.	V.G.	Good	Fair	Poor
600	450	400	350	300	150

Model 5700

Similar to the above but with light scroll engraving on the receiver and figured walnut stock.

NIB	Exc.	V.G.	Good	Fair	Poor
750	575	500	400	300	150

Model 5800

Similar to the Model 5600 but with more engraving coverage on the receiver and fancy walnut stock.

NIB	Exc.	V.G.	Good	Fair	Poor
950	800	700	500	350	175

Model 7300

A 12 or 20 gauge slide action shotgun. Blued with a walnut stock. Imported prior to 1981.

Exc.	V.G.	Good	Fair	Poor
300	250	200	150	100

Model 7900

As above, but skeet choked.

NIB	Exc.	V.G.	Good	Fair	Poor
400	300	250	200	150	100

Model 300

A 12 or 20 gauge semiautomatic shotgun with 26", 28", or 30" barrels. Blued with a walnut stock. Imported from 1968 to 1972.
Ventilated Rib Barrel-Add 20%.

Exc.	V.G.	Good	Fair	Poor
300	250	200	150	100

Model 1300

A redesigned version of the Model 300 with a ventilated rib barrel and screw-in choke tubes. Imported since 1988.

NIB	Exc.	V.G.	Good	Fair	Poor
450	400	350	300	200	150

Model XL 900 MR

A 12 gauge, semiautomatic shotgun with 26" to 30" ventilated rib barrels, and etched alloy receiver and checkered walnut stock. Imported prior to 1981.

Exc.	V.G.	Good	Fair	Poor
325	275	225	175	125

Model 1900
As above, but also chambered for 20 gauge cartridges and available with 22", 26", or 28" ventilated rib barrels having screw-in choke tubes. Blued with a walnut stock.

NIB	Exc.	V.G.	Good	Fair	Poor
500	425	375	300	250	175

Model 3000
Similar to the above, with a modified receiver design. Imported prior to 1990.

Exc.	V.G.	Good	Fair	Poor
475	400	350	250	150

SKS
Former Communist Bloc
NOTE: For history, technical data, descriptions, and prices see the *Standard Catalog of Military Firearms, 1870 to the Present* under country of issue.

SSK INDUSTRIES
Bloomingdale, Ohio

SSK-Contender
A custom made pistol available in 74 different calibers from .178 Bee to .588 JDJ built on a Thompson Center action.

NIB	Exc.	V.G.	Good	Fair	Poor
575	500	475	425	350	275

SSK-XP100
A custom made pistol utilizing a Remington XP100 action. Available in a variety of calibers and sight configurations.

NIB	Exc.	V.G.	Good	Fair	Poor
650	600	550	500	400	300

.50 Caliber XP100
As above, with an integral muzzle brake and reinforced composition stock.

NIB	Exc.	V.G.	Good	Fair	Poor
1750	1500	1250	1000	750	500

S.W.D., INC.
Atlanta, Georgia

Cobray M-11
A 9mm semiautomatic pistol with a 32-round magazine. Parkerized finish.

Exc.	V.G.	Good	Fair	Poor
300	200	175	125	100

M-11 Carbine
As above, with a 16.25" barrel enclosed in a shroud and fitted with a telescoping wire stock.

Exc.	V.G.	Good	Fair	Poor
325	225	200	150	125

Terminator
A 12 or 20 gauge single shot shotgun with an 18" cylinder bored barrel. Parkerized finish.

Exc.	V.G.	Good	Fair	Poor
100	80	70	60	50

SABATTI
SEE—European American Armory

SACKET, D. D.
Westfield, Massachusetts
Under Hammer Pistol
A .34 or .36 single shot percussion pistol with a half octagonal 3" or 4" barrel marked "D. D. Sacket/Westfield/Cast Steel." Manufactured during the 1850s.

Exc.	V.G.	Good	Fair	Poor
—	—	950	475	150

SAFARI ARMS
Phoenix, Arizona
In operation from 1978 to 1987, this company was purchased by Olympic Arms of Olympia, Washington, in 1987 and the models listed below are currently produced by that company under different trade names.

Enforcer
A .45 caliber semiautomatic pistol with a 3.9" barrel and 5-shot magazine. Patterned after the Colt Model 1911. Blued, Armaloy, electroless nickel-plate or parkerized finish with checkered walnut or neoprene grips.

NIB	Exc.	V.G.	Good	Fair	Poor
700	600	500	400	350	150

Match Master
As above, with a 5" barrel.

NIB	Exc.	V.G.	Good	Fair	Poor
700	600	500	400	350	150

Black Widow
As above, with ivory Micarta grips etched with a Black Widow.

NIB	Exc.	V.G.	Good	Fair	Poor
700	600	500	400	350	150

Model 81

As above, without the grip etching and also offered in .38 caliber.

NIB	Exc.	V.G.	Good	Fair	Poor
800	700	600	500	400	200

Model 81L

As above, with a 6" barrel.

NIB	Exc.	V.G.	Good	Fair	Poor
850	750	650	550	450	200

Ultimate Unlimited

A bolt action single shot pistol with a 15" barrel chambered for variety of cartridges. Blued with a laminated stock.

NIB	Exc.	V.G.	Good	Fair	Poor
850	750	650	550	450	200

Survivor I Conversion Unit

A conversion unit lifted to the Model 1911 frame that alters that pistol to a bolt action carbine. Barrel length 16.25", caliber .223, folding stock.

NIB	Exc.	V.G.	Good	Fair	Poor
300	275	250	200	150	100

Counter Sniper Rifle

A .308 caliber bolt action target rifle with a heavy 26" barrel and 20-round detachable magazine. Matte blued with a colored composite stock.

NIB	Exc.	V.G.	Good	Fair	Poor
1200	1050	850	650	450	200

SAKO
Riihimaki, Finland
Importer - Beretta USA
Accokeek, MD

NOTE: Arms produced by this company prior to 1972 are worth approximately 25% more than arms of the same type produced thereafter. Prices for fair and poor condition reflect the worth of the action.

In 2000 Beretta Holding Co. purchased SAKO and distributes the product line through Beretta USA.

Standard Sporter

A bolt action magazine rifle produced in a wide variety of calibers with varying barrel lengths, etc. Blued with checkered walnut stocks.

Exc.	V.G.	Good	Fair	Poor
750	650	450	400	400

Deluxe Model

As above, with an engraved floorplate and checkered Monte Carlo-style stock having a rosewood pistol grip cap and forend tip.

Exc.	V.G.	Good	Fair	Poor
900	750	600	450	400

Finnbear

As above, with a long action available in a variety of large bore calibers fitted with a 20" or 23.5" barrel. Blued with a checkered stock. .458 Winchester Magnum, 20 produced, values doubled.

Exc.	V.G.	Good	Fair	Poor
750	650	550	400	400

Forester

As above, with a shorter action suitable for use with intermediate cartridges.

Exc.	V.G.	Good	Fair	Poor
750	650	550	400	400

Vixen

As above, with a short action.

Exc.	V.G.	Good	Fair	Poor
750	650	550	400	400

FN Action

Manufactured from 1950 to 1957, this model utilized a Fabrique Nationale manufactured receiver and was chambered for .270 Winchester and .30-06 cartridges. Otherwise, as above.

Exc.	V.G.	Good	Fair	Poor
600	500	400	400	400

FN Magnum Action

As above, with a long action for .300 and .375 Holland & Holland.

Exc.	V.G.	Good	Fair	Poor
650	600	500	400	400

Finnwolf

A 4-shot lever action rifle produced in .243 and .308 calibers. Blued, checkered walnut stock. Manufactured from 1962 to 1974.

Exc.	V.G.	Good	Fair	Poor
850	700	550	450	400

Anniversary Model

A 7mm Remington Magnum bolt action rifle with a 24" barrel. Blued, checkered walnut stock. A total of 1,000 were manufactured. As with any commemorative firearm, this model should be NIB to realize its full resale potential.

NIB	Exc.	V.G.	Good	Fair	Poor
2500	850	750	450	400	400

Finnfire

This bolt action rifle is chambered for the .22 long rifle cartridge. It is fitted with a 22" barrel with choice of iron sights or no sights, and a European walnut stock. A 5 shot detachable magazine is standard. Weight is about 5.25 lbs.

Courtesy Stoeger

NIB	Exc.	V.G.	Good	Fair	Poor
750	600	450	400	400	400

Finnfire Heavy Barrel

Same as above but fitted with a heavy barrel.

Courtesy Stoeger

NIB	Exc.	V.G.	Good	Fair	Poor
850	675	500	400	400	400

Finnfire Hunter

Introduced in 2000 this bolt action model is chambered for the .22 Long Rifle cartridge. It is fitted with a 22" barrel and a Sako 75 style select walnut stock. Weight is about 5.75 lbs.

NIB	Exc.	V.G.	Good	Fair	Poor
875	650	—	—	—	—

Finnfire Sporter

This model is chambered for the .22 Long Rifle cartridge and is built on the P94S action. It has a walnut stock with adjustable cheekpiece and buttplate spacer system that allows for length of pull and buttplate angle adjustment. Trigger is adjustable. Introduced in 1999.

NIB	Exc.	V.G.	Good	Fair	Poor
925	750	—	—	—	—

Hunter

This model is offered in three action lengths; short, medium, and long. In the short action the calibers available are .17 Rem., .222, .223 in 21.25" barrel. In medium action the calibers are: .22-250, .243, .308, and 7mm-08 in 21.75" barrel. The long action calibers are: .25-06, .270 Win., .280 Rem., .30-06 22" barrel length. In 24" barrel the long action calibers are: 7mm Rem. Mag., .300 Win. and .300 Wby. Mag., .338 and .375 Win. Mag., and .416 Rem. Mag. In 1996 the .270 Wthby Mag., 7mm Wthby Mag., and the .340 Wthby was added to the long action calibers. Available in left-handed version for all but short action calibers. Adjustable trigger is standard. Checkered European walnut stock. Weight for short action is 6.25 lbs., for medium action 6.5 lbs., and long action calibers 7.75 to 8.25 depending on caliber.

Medium Action

NIB	Exc.	V.G.	Good	Fair	Poor
795	600	500	400	400	400

Short Action

Add 10% for .222 Rem. and .223 Rem. For .17 Rem. add 20% to above prices.

Long Action

NIB	Exc.	V.G.	Good	Fair	Poor
795	600	500	400	400	400

NOTE: For long action calibers in .300 and .338 Win. Mag. add 10%. For .375 H&H Mag. add 20%. For .416 Rem. Mag. add 25%.

Carbine

As above, with an 18.5" barrel. Produced with either a medium or long-length action.

NIB	Exc.	V.G.	Good	Fair	Poor
795	600	500	400	400	400

Long Range Hunting Rifle

Similar to the long action Hunter but fitted with a 26" fluted barrel. chambered for the .25-06, .270 Win., 7mm Rem. Mag., and .300 Win. Mag. Introduced in 1996.

NIB	Exc.	V.G.	Good	Fair	Poor
1250	1000	—	—	—	—

FiberClass

This model features a black plain fiberglass stock. Offered in long action calibers only. The .25-06, .270, .280, and .30-06 are fitted with 22" barrels and weigh 7.25 lbs. The 7mm Rem. Mag., .300 Win. Mag., .338 Win. Mag., and .375 H&H are fitted with 24" barrel and weighs 7.25 lbs. The .416 Rem. Mag. has a 24" barrel and weighs 8 lbs.

NIB	Exc.	V.G.	Good	Fair	Poor
1050	800	600	500	400	400

NOTE: For long action calibers in .300 and .338 Win. Mag. add 10%. For .375 H&H Mag. add 20%. For .416 Rem. Mag. add 25%.

FiberClass Carbine

As above, with a fiberglass stock.

NIB	Exc.	V.G.	Good	Fair	Poor
1050	800	600	500	400	400

Carbine

This model features a Mannlicher-style stock with a two-piece forearm. It has a checkered walnut stock with oil finish. It is offered in both medium and short actions, all with 18.5" barrels. In medium action the .243 and .308 are available and weigh 6 lbs. The long action calibers are: .270, and .30-06 weighing 7.25 lbs.; and the .338 Win. Mag. and .375 H&H weighing 7.75 lbs.

Medium Action

NIB	Exc.	V.G.	Good	Fair	Poor
900	700	500	400	400	400

Long Action

NIB	Exc.	V.G.	Good	Fair	Poor
900	700	500	400	400	400

NOTE: For long action calibers in .338 Win. Mag. add 10%. For .375 H&H Mag. add 20%.

Laminated Model

This model features a laminated checkered hardwood stock made up of 36 layers. Solid recoil pad is standard as are quick detachable sling swivels. Available in both medium and long action calibers. Medium action calibers are: .22-250, .243, .308, and 7mm-08 with 21.75" barrel and weigh 6.5 lbs. Long action calibers are: .25-06, .270, .280, .30-06 with 22" barrel weighing 7.75 lbs. Offered with 24" barrels are: 7mm Rem. Mag., .300 and .338 Win. Mag., and .375 H&H which weighs 7.75 lbs.

Medium Action

NIB	Exc.	V.G.	Good	Fair	Poor
950	750	600	500	400	400

Long Action

NIB	Exc.	V.G.	Good	Fair	Poor
950	750	600	500	400	400

NOTE: For long action calibers in .300 and .338 Win. Mag. add 10%. For.375 H&H Mag. add 20%. For .416 Rem. Mag. add 25%.

Varmint-Heavy Barrel

The checkered walnut stock on this model features an extra wide beavertail forearm with oil finish. Offered in both short and medium action all are fitted with a 23" heavy barrel weighing 8.5 lbs. Short action calibers are .17 Rem., 222, and .223. Medium action calibers are: .22-250, .243, 308, and 7mm-08.

Short Action

NIB	Exc.	V.G.	Good	Fair	Poor
875	700	500	400	400	400

NOTE: Add 10% for .222 and .223 Rem. Add 20% for .17 Rem. to above prices.

Medium Action

NIB	Exc.	V.G.	Good	Fair	Poor
875	700	500	400	400	400

PPC Bench Rest/Varmint

Similar to the Varmint but single shot. Fitted with 23.75" barrel and weighs 8.75 lbs. Available in short action special calibers .22 PPC and 6mm PPC.

NIB	Exc.	V.G.	Good	Fair	Poor
1050	800	600	400	400	400

Classic-Grade

Hand checkered select grade walnut stock with matte lacquer finish are featured on this grade. Offered in medium and long action. Long action rifles are offered in left-hand model. The medium action caliber is .243 Win. with a 21.75" barrel weighing 6 lbs. The long action calibers are: .270, .30-06, and 7mm Rem. Mag. with 24" barrels. Long action calibers weighs about 7.5 lbs.

NIB	Exc.	V.G.	Good	Fair	Poor
750	600	500	400	400	400

Deluxe Grade

This grade features a high grade European walnut stock with hand cut basket weave checkering. The forend tip and grip are fitted with rosewood. English style recoil pad is standard. Long action models are offered in left-hand configuration. As with the Hunter model short, medium, and long action are available in the same calibers, barrel lengths and weights as the Hunter.

Medium Action

NIB	Exc.	V.G.	Good	Fair	Poor
1100	900	650	500	400	400

Short Action

Add 10% for .222 and .223 Rem. Add 20% for .17 Rem. to above prices.

Long Action

NIB	Exc.	V.G.	Good	Fair	Poor
1100	900	650	500	400	400

NOTE: For long action calibers in .300 and .338 Win. Mag. add 10%. For.375 H&H Mag. add 20%. For.416 Rem. Mag. add 25%. For left hand models add $100.

Super Grade/Super Deluxe

Similar to Deluxe Grade but offered with fancy walnut stock with oak-leaf carving. Floor plate and triggerguard are engraved. Pistol grip cap has inlaid silver plate. Offered in same actions and calibers as Hunter and Deluxe Grades.

Medium Action

NIB	Exc.	V.G.	Good	Fair	Poor
2250	1500	900	600	400	400

Short Action

Add 10% for .222 and .223 Rem.

Long Action

NIB	Exc.	V.G.	Good	Fair	Poor
2250	1500	900	600	400	400

NOTE: For long action calibers in .300 and .338 Win. Mag. add 10%. For .375 H&H Mag. add 20%. For .416 Rem. Mag. add 25%.

Safari Grade

As above, chambered for .300 Winchester Magnum, .338 Winchester Magnum, or .375 Holland & Holland cartridges.

NIB	Exc.	V.G.	Good	Fair	Poor
2250	1500	900	800	400	400

MODEL 75 SERIES

This model was introduced in March 1997. It is based on a new design by Sako. Each of the five different action sizes is manufactured for a specific range of calibers. Its action, barrel, and stocks are all redesigned components. It is offered in a variety of configurations and calibers. Sako actions are offered separately in carbon steel, in white, and stainless steel.

Sako 75 action

Model 75 Hunter

This model is available in five different action sizes for calibers from .17 Rem. to .416 Rem. Mag. Weight varies from 6.37 lbs. to 9 lbs. and barrel lengths from 22" to 24.37". Choice of checkered walnut stock or black synthetic stock. All Hunter models are sold without sights as standard but open sights are an option. Magazine is detachable except for .300 Rem. Ultra Mag and the .416 Rem. Mag. Single set trigger is an option.

NIB	Exc.	V.G.	Good	Fair	Poor
1100	800	650	500	400	400

NOTE: Add $30 for long action calibers from .270 to .416.

Model 75 Stainless Synthetic

Same as above but available with synthetic stock and stainless steel barrel and action. Offered in calibers from .22-250 to .375 H&H.

NIB	Exc.	V.G.	Good	Fair	Poor
1200	900	700	600	400	400

NOTE: Add $30 for long action calibers.

Model 75 Deluxe

This model features all of the elements of the Hunter model with the addition of special checkering on select walnut stock with special black finish. All models have a hinged floor plate.

NIB	Exc.	V.G.	Good	Fair	Poor
1600	1250	950	800	500	400

NOTE: Add $100 for long action calibers.

Model 75 Varmint

This model is chambered for the .17 Rem., .222 Rem., .223, and .22-250, all with 24" heavy barrels. In 1999 Sako added the .22PPC and 6PPC calibers. It weighs about 8.4 lbs. Walnut stock.

NIB	Exc.	V.G.	Good	Fair	Poor
1250	950	750	600	450	400

Model 75 Varmint Stainless

Introduced in 1999 this model is similar to the Varmint 75 but with stainless steel barrel. Magazine is detachable but can be loaded through the ejection port. Trigger is adjustable. Offered in all of the calibers as the standard Model 75 Varmint. Weights vary from about 8 lbs. to 8.6 lbs. The stock is laminated.

NIB	Exc.	V.G.	Good	Fair	Poor
1475	1150	—	—	—	—

Model 75 Finnlight

Introduced in 2001 this bolt action rifle features short, medium, and long action calibers with stainless steel barrel lengths from 20.25" to 22.5" depending on caliber. Barrels are fluted. Synthetic stock. Weight is about 6.5 lbs. depending on caliber.

NIB	Exc.	V.G.	Good	Fair	Poor
1225	975	—	—	—	—

Model 75 Super Deluxe

This is a special order rifle. Advise expert opinion before a sale. Price listed below is for the base rifle.

NIB	Exc.	V.G.	Good	Fair	Poor
3400	2400	1850	—	—	—

Model 78

A .22 or .22 Hornet bolt action rifle with a 22" barrel. Blued with a checkered walnut stock. Discontinued in 1986.

Exc.	V.G.	Good	Fair	Poor
500	450	350	250	150

Model 2700 Finnsport

A .270 to .300 Winchester Magnum bolt action rifle with a 22" barrel. Blued, checkered walnut stock. Discontinued in 1985.

Exc.	V.G.	Good	Fair	Poor
600	500	400	400	400

TRG-S

This model features a unique cold forged receiver. The stock is a special reinforced polyurethane Monte Carlo without checkering. The recoil pad has spacer for adjustable length of pull. The trigger is adjustable and the detachable magazine holds 5 rounds. Offered in a variety of calibers from .243 to .375 H&H. Non Magnum calibers are fitted with a 22" barrel and weighs 7.75 lbs. and Magnum calibers are fitted with a 24" barrel and also weighs 7.75 lbs. In 1996 the .270 Wthby Mag., 7mm Wthby Mag., and the .340 Wthby Mag. as well as the 6.5x55S was added.

NIB	Exc.	V.G.	Good	Fair	Poor
800	650	500	450	400	400

TRG-21

The receiver is similar to the TRG-S but the polyurethane stock features a unique design. The trigger is adjustable for length and two-stage pull and also for horizontal or vertical pitch. This model also has several options that would affect the price; muzzle brake, one-piece scope mount, bipod, quick detachable sling swivels, and military nylon sling. The rifle is offered in .308 Win. only. It is fitted with a 25.75" barrel and weighs 10.5 lbs.

NIB	Exc.	V.G.	Good	Fair	Poor
3500	2750	1850	—	—	—

WHAT'S IT LIKE-THE SAKO TRG 21 SNIPER RIFLE

The Sako company of Finland is world renown for its ability to produce very accurate rifles. The Sako TRG 21 is a sniper/precision rifle in every sense of the word. This rifle is a bolt action repeater with a 10-shot magazine in .308 caliber. The barrel is a 26" free floating high precision masterpiece with a muzzle break to further aid in accuracy. The bolt locking system is a 3 lug affair that locks every round with a tight interface in the chamber. This feature gives the rifle the ability to produce surgical precision shots with repeatability. Also the 60 degree turn on the bolt is all that is required to unlock it and rechamber a fresh round. This quick action allows one to fire and reload with incredible smoothness and rapidity. The system is also engineered to fit the operator like a glove. The trigger is adjustable for overtravel and pull with the capacity to eke-out a super smooth, very light trigger. The trigger is also adjustable for angle both right and left to fit the operator. This is a rare but useful feature on any rifle. I have fired many of the world's most accurate sniper rifles and the majority are incredible. When I want to produce a 3 shot, one hole group of no more than 1/4" at 100 yards on demand I take my Sako TRG 21 out on the range or into the field. This the Sako does with consistency without regard to ammunition. This weapon seems to fire most brands with incredible accuracy.

J.R. Moody

TRG-22

This model is similar to the TRG-21 but meets the exact specifications to comply with the Finish military requirements. Introduced in 2000.

NIB	Exc.	V.G.	Good	Fair	Poor
2700	2000	—	—	—	—

TRG-41

Exactly the same as the TRG-21 except chambered for the .338 Lapua Magnum cartridge.

NIB	Exc.	V.G.	Good	Fair	Poor
4350	3500	2500	1500	—	—

TRG-42

This model is similar to the TRG-41 but meets the exact specifications to comply with the Finish military requirements. Introduced in 2000.

NIB	Exc.	V.G.	Good	Fair	Poor
3100	2300	—	—	—	—

SAM, INC.
Reston, Virginia
Special Service Arms Mfg., Inc.

Model 88 Crossfire

A semiautomatic combination 12 gauge .308 caliber shotgun/rifle, with a 7-shot shotgun magazine and 20-shot rifle magazine. Barrel length 20", matte black finished with a composition stock. This weapon can be fired in either mode by means of a selector switch mounted on the receiver.

NIB	Exc.	V.G.	Good	Fair	Poor
1900	1500	—	—	—	—

SAMCO GLOBAL ARMS, INC.
Miami, Florida

This firm imports a variety of military surplus firearms that under current law are marked with the importer's name.

SARASQUETA, FELIX
Eibar, Spain
Importer - SAE, Inc.Miami, Florida

Merke

A 12 gauge Over/Under double barrel shotgun with 22" or 27" ribbed and separated barrels, nonselective trigger and manual extractors. Blued, checkered walnut stock. Imported in 1986 only.

Exc.	V.G.	Good	Fair	Poor
275	225	200	150	100

SARASQUETA, J. J.
Eibar, Spain
Importer - American Arms, Inc.
Overland Park, Kansas

Model 107E

A 12, 16, or 20 gauge boxlock double barrel shotgun with a variety of barrel lengths, double triggers and automatic ejectors. Blued with a checkered walnut stock. Discontinued in 1984.

Exc.	V.G.	Good	Fair	Poor
375	300	275	225	100

Model 119E

As above, with a more finely figured walnut stock.

Exc.	V.G.	Good	Fair	Poor
475	400	375	325	150

Model 130E

As above, but engraved.

Exc.	V.G.	Good	Fair	Poor
800	700	600	450	250

Model 131E

As above, with considerably more engraving.

Exc.	V.G.	Good	Fair	Poor
1100	900	800	650	350

Model 1882 E LUXE

As above, with a single selective trigger and gold inlays. A silver inlaid version is sold for approximately 10% less.

Exc.	V.G.	Good	Fair	Poor
800	700	600	450	250

SARASQUETA, VICTOR
Eibar, Spain

Model 3

A 12, 16, or 20 gauge boxlock or sidelock double barrel shotgun available in a variety of barrel lengths, with double triggers and automatic ejectors. Blued with a checkered straight stock. The sidelock version is worth approximately 20% more than the values listed below. The basic Model 3 was offered in a variety of grades featuring different amounts of engraving and better quality wood. These shotguns are listed under the model designations of 4 to 12E below.

Exc.	V.G.	Good	Fair	Poor
600	500	450	350	300

Model 4

Exc.	V.G.	Good	Fair	Poor
600	550	475	400	300

Model 4E (Auto-ejectors)

Exc.	V.G.	Good	Fair	Poor
675	625	550	450	350

Model 203

Exc.	V.G.	Good	Fair	Poor
650	600	525	425	325

Model 203E

Exc.	V.G.	Good	Fair	Poor
700	650	575	475	375

Model 6E

Exc.	V.G.	Good	Fair	Poor
800	750	625	525	425

Model 7E

Exc.	V.G.	Good	Fair	Poor
850	800	675	575	475

Model 10E

Exc.	V.G.	Good	Fair	Poor
1750	1500	1250	950	750

Model 11E

Exc.	V.G.	Good	Fair	Poor
1850	1600	1350	1150	850

Model 12E

Exc.	V.G.	Good	Fair	Poor
2200	1850	1500	1300	1000

SARDIUS
Israel
Importer - Armscorp of America, Inc.

SD-9
A 9mm double action semiautomatic pistol with a 3" barrel and 6-shot magazine. Matte black finish with composition grips. Imported since 1988.

NIB	Exc.	V.G.	Good	Fair	Poor
350	300	250	200	150	100

SAUER, J. P. & SON
Suhl and Eckernfoerde, German

This is the oldest firearms manufacturing firm in Germany. It was founded in 1751 in Suhl. During this period the company produced high quality handguns and long guns. In 1938 it introduced a new double action semiautomatic pistol, the Sauer 38H. This pistol had the first decocking lever ever used on a mass produced pistol. In 1951 the company relocated to Eckernfoerde where it continued to produced high quality forearms.

NOTE: The Model 90 Supreme and Model 202 are currently imported by Sigarms Inc.

Bolt Action Rifle
A Mauser action sporting rifle chambered for a variety of cartridges with either a 22" or 24" barrel having a raised rib. Double set triggers, express sights, blued with a checkered walnut stock. Manufactured prior to WWII.

Exc.	V.G.	Good	Fair	Poor
700	600	500	400	300

Model 200
A bolt action rifle chambered for a variety of cartridges with short or medium length actions, 24" barrels, set trigger, 4-round magazine. Blued, checkered walnut stock. Discontinued 1987.
Extra barrels-Add $235.

NIB	Exc.	V.G.	Good	Fair	Poor
850	650	550	500	425	350

Model 200 Lightweight

As above, with an alloy receiver. Discontinued in 1987.

Exc.	V.G.	Good	Fair	Poor
600	500	400	325	250

Model 200 Lux

As above, with a finely figured walnut stock, rosewood pistol grip cap and forend tip, gold plated trigger and a machine jewelled bolt. Imported prior to 1988.

Exc.	V.G.	Good	Fair	Poor
700	600	550	475	400

Model 200 Carbon Fiber

The Model 200 fitted with a carbon composition stock. Imported in 1987 and 1988.

Exc.	V.G.	Good	Fair	Poor
800	750	650	500	400

Model 202 Supreme

This is a bolt action rifle with a takedown feature. It is fitted with an adjustable two stage trigger, quick change barrel, black rubber recoil pad, and removable box magazine. The stock is select American claro walnut with high gloss finish and rosewood forend and grip cap. buttstock has a Monte Carlo comb and cheekpiece. It is offered in .243, .270, .308, and .30-06. Barrel length for these calibers is 23.6". Weight for these calibers is about 7.7 lbs. In the Supreme Magnum series it is available in 7mm magnum, .300 Win. Mag., and .375 H&H mag. Barrel for these magnum calibers is 26". Weight for these caliber is 8.4 lbs.

NIB	Exc.	V.G.	Good	Fair	Poor
950	800	750	—	—	—

Model 90

A bolt action rifle produced in a number of calibers in all action lengths with 23" or 26" barrels, with a detachable magazine. Blued with a checkered walnut stock.

Exc.	V.G.	Good	Fair	Poor
800	700	600	450	400

Model 90 Stutzen

As above, with a full-length Mannlicher-style stock. Imported prior to 1990.

Exc.	V.G.	Good	Fair	Poor
825	725	625	475	425

Model 90 Safari

The Model 90 made for use with the .458 Winchester Magnum cartridge and fitted with a 24" barrel. Imported from 1986 to 1988.

Exc.	V.G.	Good	Fair	Poor
1250	1100	950	750	600

The Model 90 Series of bolt action rifles was available in a deluxe version that differed with the grade of workmanship and materials utilized. This deluxe series would be worth approximately 60% additional. There were optional engraved models; these should be individually appraised.

Model 90 Supreme

Similar to the above, with a gold-plated trigger, machine jewelled bolt and finely figured checkered walnut stock. Introduced in 1987.

NIB	Exc.	V.G.	Good	Fair	Poor
1500	1250	1100	950	750	650

SSG-3000

NIB	Exc.	V.G.	Good	Fair	Poor
8800	8000	—	—	—	—

SG 550 Sniper

NIB	Exc.	V.G.	Good	Fair	Poor
14200	12500	10700	—	—	—

NOTE: For other current Sauer rifles see SIG Arms.

SHOTGUN/RIFLE COMBINATIONS

Luftwaffe Survival Drilling

A double barrel 12 gauge by 9.3x74R combination shotgun/rifle with 28" barrels. Blued with a checkered walnut stock and marked with Nazi inspection. Stampings on the stock and barrel breech. Normally, furnished with an aluminum case.

NOTE: Add 50% to prices below for case.

Courtesy Richard. M. Kumor, Sr.

Courtesy Richard M. Kumor, Sr.

Exc.	V.G.	Good	Fair	Poor
7000	6000	4200	2500	—

Model 3000 Drilling

This model was chambered for a variety of gauges and calibers and is built upon a boxlock action having a Greener crossbolt. The action lightly engraved. Blued, checkered walnut stock.

NIB	Exc.	V.G.	Good	Fair	Poor
3400	2900	2500	2000	1500	1250

Model 54 Combo

A combination rifle/shotgun chambered for a variety of gauges and calibers with an action as above. Discontinued in 1986.

Exc.	V.G.	Good	Fair	Poor
2200	2000	1750	1400	1200

SHOTGUNS

Model 60

A 12, 16 or 20 gauge double barrel boxlock shotgun produced in a variety of barrel lengths with double triggers and manual extractors. Blued with checkered walnut stock. Produced prior to WWII.

Exc.	V.G.	Good	Fair	Poor
700	625	550	400	300

Royal Model

A 12 or 20 gauge boxlock double barrel shotgun with 26", 28", or 30" barrels, single selective triggers with automatic ejectors. The frame is scalloped, blued with a checkered walnut stock. Manufactured from 1955 to 1977.

Exc.	V.G.	Good	Fair	Poor
1500	1250	1000	750	500

Grade I Artemis

A 12 gauge sidelock double barrel shotgun with 28" barrels, single selective trigger and automatic ejector. Engraved, blued with checkered walnut stock. Manufactured from 1966 to 1977.

Exc.	V.G.	Good	Fair	Poor
5000	4250	3500	2500	2000

Grade II Artemis

As above, but more finely finished.

Exc.	V.G.	Good	Fair	Poor
6500	5750	4750	3500	3000

Model 66

A 12 gauge sidelock double barrel shotgun having a 26", 28", or 30" barrel, single selective trigger and automatic ejectors. Blued, checkered walnut stock. This model was produced in three different grades that have different degrees of engraving. Produced from 1966 to 1975.

Grade I

Exc.	V.G.	Good	Fair	Poor
2000	1800	1500	1150	800

Grade II

Exc.	V.G.	Good	Fair	Poor
3000	2800	2500	2150	1800

Grade III

Exc.	V.G.	Good	Fair	Poor
3750	3500	2850	2500	2000

PISTOLS
Written and compiled by Jim Cate

Roth-Sauer Model

The very first automatic pistol produced by J.P. Sauer & Sohn but not designed by this firm. It is available only in 7.65 Roth-Sauer caliber. It is a locked breech design, beautifully finished and extremely well made. Later this design was modified and became the Roth-Steyr military pistol which was adopted by Austria in 1907. A difficult to find pistol.

Exc.	V.G.	Good	Fair	Poor
2250	1500	900	500	300

SAUER MODEL 1913

First Series, which incorporates an extra safety button on the left side of the frame near the trigger and the rear sight is simply a milled recess in the cocking knob itself. The serial number range runs from 1 to approximately 4750 and this first series is found only in 7.65mm caliber. All were for commercial sales as far as can be determined. Some were tested by various militaries, no doubt.

A. European variation—all slide legends are in the German language

B. English Export variation—slide legends are marked, J.P. Sauer & Son, Suhl - Prussia, "Sauer's Patent" Pat'd May 20 1912

Both were sold in thick paper cartons or boxes with the color being a reddish purple with gold colored letters, etc. Examples of the very early European variation are found with the English language brochure or manual as well as an extra magazine, cleaning brush and grease container. These were shipped to England or the U.S. prior to Sauer producing the English Export variation.

A. European variation:

Exc.	V.G.	Good	Fair	Poor
1100	900	650	400	250

B. English Export variation:

Exc.	V.G.	Good	Fair	Poor
1450	1150	800	500	300

Original box with accessories and manual: Add $500 if complete and in very good to excellent condition.

Second Series, extra safety button eliminated, rear sight acts as cocking knob retainer.

A. Commercial variation

Normal European/German slide markings are normally found; however it has been called to my attention that there are English Export pistols in this **SECOND SERIES** which have the English markings on the slide which are similar to those found on the **FIRST SERIES** of the Model 1913. This is applicable to both the 7.65mm and 6.35mm model pistols. These are exceptional scarce pistols and should command at least a 50% premium, perhaps more due to their rarity. This commercial variation had factory manuals printed in English, Spanish and German which came with the cardboard boxed pistols. With the original Sauer box accessories and manual: Add $300 if in very good to excellent condition.

Caliber 7.65mm variation

Exc.	V.G.	Good	Fair	Poor
450	375	300	250	100

Caliber 7.65 variation with all words in English (i.e Son, Prussia, etc.)

Exc.	V.G.	Good	Fair	Poor
700	575	450	300	200

Caliber 6.35mm variation

This particular pistol must be divided into three (3) subvariations.

This variation appears to be in a serial number range of its own. The first subvariation appears to run from 1 to 40,000. It is highly doubtful if this quantity was manufactured. The second subvariation incorporates a Zusatzsicherung or Additional Safety which can be seen between the normal safety lever and the top of the left grip. It locked the trigger bar when in use. This second range appears to run from approximately serial number 40,000 to 51,000 which probably was continuous in the number produced. Lastly, the third subvariation examples were manufactured during or after 1926. The triggerguard has a different shape; the slide has a greater area of vertical milled finger grooves; the added Additional safety (Zusatzsicherung) now acts as the hold open device as well. These are found up to approximately 57,000. Then a few examples of the first subvariation are found from 57,000 up to about 62,500. This was, no doubt, usage of remaining parts.

Caliber 6.35mm first subvariation

Exc.	V.G.	Good	Fair	Poor
350	300	250	150	75

Caliber 6.35mm second subvariation

Exc.	V.G.	Good	Fair	Poor
350	300	250	150	75

Caliber 6.35mm third subvariation

Exc.	V.G.	Good	Fair	Poor
450	375	300	200	100

Caliber 6.35mm English export variation (all words in English; i.e. Son, Prussia, etc.). Very Rare, only one example known.

Exc.	V.G.	Good	Fair	Poor
850	700	500	300	200

Please note that any commercial pistol could be special ordered with a factory nickel finish, special grip material (Pearl, wood, etc.) as well as different types of engraving. It would be in your best interest to have these pistols examined by an expert.

B. Police variations

These will be of the standard German Commercial configuration but nearly always having the Zusatzsicherung (additional safety) added to the pistol. This safety is found between the regular safety lever and the top of the left grip. Police used both calibers, 7.65mm and 6.35mm but the 7.65 was predominant. After the early part of the 1930s the 6.35 was not available to police departments. Thus the 6.35mm police marked Sauer is rather scarce in relation to the 7.65mm caliber. A few in 7.65mm are dated 1920 on the left side of the frame and were used by auxiliary policemen in Bavaria. Normal police property markings are on the front or rear gripstraps. Most were originally issued with at least two magazines and a police accepted holster. The mags were usually numbered and the holsters are found with and without pistol numbers.

Caliber 6.35mm police marked but without Zusatzsicherung

Exc.	V.G.	Good	Fair	Poor
400	350	275	200	75

Caliber 6.35mm police marked with Zusatzsicherung

Exc.	V.G.	Good	Fair	Poor
450	375	275	200	75

Caliber 7.65mm police marked without Zusatzsicherung

Exc.	V.G.	Good	Fair	Poor
375	325	275	175	125

Caliber 7.65mm police marked with Zusatzsicherung

Exc.	V.G.	Good	Fair	Poor
400	350	275	175	125

NOTE: Add 10% for one correctly numbered magazine, or 20% if found with both correctly numbered magazines. Add 30% if found with correct holster and magazines.

C.R.F.V. (Reich Finanz Verwaltung)

This Sauer variation is rarely found in any condition. The R.F.V. markings and property number could be 1 to 4 digits. This variation is found in both calibers and were used by the Reich's Customs and Finance department personnel.

Caliber 6.35mm R.F.V. marked pistols

Exc.	V.G.	Good	Fair	Poor
800	650	500	350	250

Caliber 7.65mm R.F.V. marked pistols

Exc.	V.G.	Good	Fair	Poor
750	600	400	300	200

D. Imperial Military variations

These were normal German commercial variations of the time period having either the Imperial Eagle acceptance marking applied on the front of the triggerguard and having the small Imperial Army inspector's acceptance marking (crown over a scriptic letter) on the right side of the frame close to the Nitro proof; or having just the Imperial Army inspector's marking alone. Usually these pistols are found in the 40,000 to 85,000 range. However, the quantity actually Imperial Military accepted is quite low even though thousands were privately purchased by the officer corps. There are examples in 6.35mm which are Imperial Military accepted but these are very scarce.

Caliber 7.65mm Imperial Military accepted pistols

Exc.	V.G.	Good	Fair	Poor
550	450	350	275	150

E. Paramilitary marked Sauer pistols, of the 1925-35 period.

A very few of the Model 1913 pistols will have been marked by paramilitary groups or organizations of this period. Usually this marking is no more than a series of numbers above another series of numbers, such as 23 over 12. These are found usually on the left side of the frame next to the left grip. Most of these numbers are indicative of property numbers assigned to a particular pistols belonging to a particular SA Group, Stahlhelm, or a rightwing organization such as the Red Front (early communist). Any pistol of this type should be examined by an expert to determine if it is an original example.

Exc.	V.G.	Good	Fair	Poor
350	300	275	200	100

F. Norwegian police usage, post World War II

After the war was over many surplus German weapons were put back into use by the government of Norway. The Germans had occupied this country and large numbers of weapons remained when the fighting ended. This included a large number of surplus Sauer pistols being utilized by the police (POLITI) forces. Most of the Sauers that were used by the Politi which have been imported into the U.S. have been the Model 1913; however there were a number of the Model 1930 pistols which reached our country as well. All examples, regardless of the model, have the word POLITI stamped on the slide as well as a rampant lion on a shield under a crown marking. Following this is the property number and this number is also stamped into the left side of the frame. Most saw much usage during the postwar period. All are in 7.65mm caliber.

Exc.	V.G.	Good	Fair	Poor
350	300	200	15	100

1926 EXPORT MODEL

This variation's name comes from actual Sauer factory records found in the Suhl Archive. It is an interim pistol produced during the 1926 to early 1929 period. It is found only in the 7.65mm caliber. This was an advancement of the normal 1913 design which included changes in (1) the safety lever's design that became a slide hold open device as well, (2) shape of the frame was altered in that the triggerguard became more streamlined and the rear of the frame was shortened, and serrations were added to the slide as well as the cocking knob. These are found in the 162,000 to 169,000 range in relatively small clusters. Two to four thousand are presumed to have been manufactured. A scarce Sauer pistol! To date, none have been seen in nickel.

Exc.	V.G.	Good	Fair	Poor
750	625	475	300	150

W.T.M.- Westentaschen Model-Vest Pocket Model

Several variations of vest pocket pistols were manufactured. The first was called a Model 1920 by the Sauer firm. We usually refer to it as the Model 1924. This pistol, as well as all other W.T.M. examples, were designed to carry in "your pocket." They are quite small in size and are found only in the 6.35mm or .25acp caliber. Later on in 1928 an updated version became available and was referred to a Model 1928. These differed in internal parts design, slide configuration and the bottom of the grip was marked, Cal.6.35.28. The last version appeared in 1933 and still utilized the same grips but the trigger and some other small parts differed. All three were available in blue or nickel finish, as well as engraving and fancy grip material. A very few of the Model 1933 had stainless steel (NIROSTA marked) barrels.

Model 1920: Having serrations on the front and rear of the slide

Exc.	V.G.	Good	Fair	Poor
550	450	300	200	75

Model 1928: Having Cal. 6.35.28 on the black bakelite grips

Exc.	V.G.	Good	Fair	Poor
450	400	275	185	75

Model 1933: Having a different type of trigger and found in the 253,000 to early 254,000 serial number range

Exc.	V.G.	Good	Fair	Poor
700	575	400	275	150

NOTE: Add $200 for factory nickel, $250 for factory engraving, $250 for exotic grip material, $500 for factory paper box with cleaning brush, extra magazine and brochure, $750 in original factory imitation leather covered metal presentation case with accessories, $500 for NIROSTA marked stainless barrel.

Model 1930 variations

A. Dutch models: These different types of Dutch pistols will have JOH MUNTS - AMSTERDAM on the left side of the slide. The grips are usually a mottled grey color. Sauer manufactured different pistols for the Dutch police, Navy, Army, Department of Finance, S.M.N. (Steam Ships Netherlands) and possibly other agencies.

1. Dutch Police-First variation manufactured w/o adjustable front sight and w/o lanyard loop.

Exc.	V.G.	Good	Fair	Poor
650	450	350	250	125

2. Amsterdam Police-manufactured w/o adjustable sight but having a lanyard loop.

Exc.	V.G.	Good	Fair	Poor
650	450	350	250	125

3. Navy-made without adjustable sight and having the Anchor & Crown marked on the rear gripstrap.

Exc.	V.G.	Good	Fair	Poor
800	500	375	250	125

4. S.M.N.-found with and w/o adjustable front sights, no lanyard loop, S.M.N. marked horizontally near bottom of rear gripstrap

Exc.	V.G.	Good	Fair	Poor
900	600	375	225	100

5. Department of Finance-found with and w/o adjustable front sight, no lanyard loop, DF over date-1933-on rear grip strap

Exc.	V.G.	Good	Fair	Poor
650	500	385	250	150

NOTE: Accessories: cleaning rod, brush, aluminum oil bottle and manuals, add accordingly.

B. 1930 Commercial Model

These pistols were for sale in Germany and other countries through normal commercial outlets. A very few are factory nickeled, engraved or both; some are with the NIROSTA marked barrels and a very few were made in Duralumin or Dural. The standard caliber was 7.65mm hut a very limited number were made in .22 Long Rifle (.22 lang). Standard grip material is the black bakelite material. Most of the regular pistols were purchased by military officers, some went to paramilitary group, such as the SA.

1. Standard Commercial

Exc.	V.G.	Good	Fair	Poor
600	450	300	200	125

2. Standard Commercial with NIROSTA marked barrel, 7.65mm

Exc.	V.G.	Good	Fair	Poor
700	500	350	275	150

3. Standard Commercial in .22 long rifle (.22 lang)

Exc.	V.G.	Good	Fair	Poor
1000	800	550	375	300

4. Duralumin (rural) Variation, 7.65mm

Exc.	V.G.	Good	Fair	Poor
3500	2750	2000	1200	450

For any variation above: Add: Nickel finish $100; with engraving $500; both nickel and engraving $600; with nickel, engraving, and with a fancy grip material (pearl or ebony, etc.) $750.

BEHORDEN MODEL

The Behorden (Authority) Model is different from the Model 1930 in that it has a trigger safety and a loaded indicator provided.

A. Behorden Commercial

These are normally found with a high polished blued finish. It was available with a nickel finish, engraving, or both, as well as fancy grip material and a NIROSTA marked barrel. The regular caliber is 7.65mm, but a very few are know in .22 L.R.

Exc.	V.G.	Good	Fair	Poor
675	550	409	350	200

NOTE: Add $100 for Nickel finish, $250 for engraving, $350 for both, $500 with nickel, engraving, and a fancy grip material; $250 for NIROSTA marked stainless barrel. Add 100% for .22 caliber.

B. Late Behorden Commercial

These are actually Model 1930 pistols found in the 220,000 to 223,000 serial number range which do not have the trigger safety and/or the indicator pin.

Exc.	V.G.	Good	Fair	Poor
600	450	300	200	125

C. Duralumin Model (Dural)

The frame and slide are made of the Duralumin material. These are rare pistols!

1. Blue anodized variation
Found with and w/o NIROSTA marked barrels. Add: $250 for the stainless barrel.

Exc.	V.G.	Good	Fair	Poor
3850	3250	2500	1500	850

2. Nonanodized variation
Found with and w/o NIROSTA marked barrels. Add: $250 for the stainless barrel.

Exc.	V.G.	Good	Fair	Poor
3850	3250	2500	1500	850

3. Presentation examples of a. and b. above—please consult an expert for pricing

D. Police Models
Examples will be found with police acceptance on the left side of the triggerguard and in a few cases on the front or rear grip straps. Black bakelite grips are standard.

1. Sunburst K police acceptance, with nonadjustable front sight (a round blade)

Exc.	V.G.	Good	Fair	Poor
600	500	350	275	200

2. Sunburst K police acceptance, with adjustable front sight

Exc.	V.G.	Good	Fair	Poor
750	625	450	300	225

3. Diamond in Sunburst police acceptance. All known are with the adjustable front sight

Exc.	V.G.	Good	Fair	Poor
750	625	450	300	225

4. Grip strap marked variation.
(Having abbreviations of a city and the property number of the pistol on the grip strap.) Very few of these are known. Examples are S.Mg. 52, Sch. 78, etc.

Exc.	V.G.	Good	Fair	Poor
500	450	375	250	150

MODEL 36/37
These very few pistols are all prototype Sauer pistols which preceded the Model 38. They are in the 210,000 range. Please consult an expert to determine value! EXTREMELY RARE.

MODEL 38 AND 38-H (H MODEL) VARIATIONS
A. MODEL 38
This pistol started at 260,000. It is Crown N Nitro proofed, has a cocking/decocking lever, and a loaded indicator pin, and is double action. It has a high polish blue; is in 7.65m/m (the standard production pistol); is found without the thumbsafety on the slide; with a pinned mag release. VERY RARE

1. One Line Slide Legend variation (about 250 produced)

Exc.	V.G.	Good	Fair	Poor
2500	1600	1200	600	300

2. Two Line Slide Legend variation, C/N proofs, blued, with pinned magazine release. (about 850 produced) VERY RARE

Exc.	V.G.	Good	Fair	Poor
1850	1400	1000	500	275

3. Two Line Slide Legend variation, C/N proofs, blued, magazine release button retained by a screw. RARE

Exc.	V.G.	Good	Fair	Poor
1000	850	600	400	275

NOTE: Add $250 for factory nickel; $350 for factory chrome; $1000 for engraving; $500 for NIROSTA marked barrel.

4. SA der NSDAP Gruppe Thuringen marked variation blued, C/N proofs, with mag release button held by a screw. VERY RARE

Exc.	V.G.	Good	Fair	Poor
3000	2000	1000	500	275

B. MODEL 38-H or H MODEL

This model has a thumbsafety on the slide, Crown N Nitro proof, high polish blued finish, a cocking/decocking lever, double action, and is found in 7.65m/m caliber as the standard production pistol. This model is found only with the two line slide legend or logo. Type 1, variation 2.

1. Standard Commercial variation as described above:

Exc.	V.G.	Good	Fair	Poor
850	700	475	300	175

NOTE: Add $100 for factory nickel (factory chromed has not been identified); $1000 for factory engraving; $250 for exotic grip material; $500 for NIROSTA marked stainless barrel.

2. SA der NSDAP Gruppe Thuringia variation

Same as 1. above except having SA markings on slide, with blued finish, VERY RARE.

Exc.	V.G.	Good	Fair	Poor
2500	1800	600	350	200

NOTE: Add $700 for SA marked Akah holster in excellent condition.

3. L.M. MODEL

(Leicht Model-lightweight model); frame and slide made of DURAL (Duralumin), in the 264800 range, with thumb safety, and regular black bakelite grips. EXTREMELY RARE.

Exc.	V.G.	Good	Fair	Poor
3850	3250	2500	1500	850

4. Police accepted variation; found with Police Eagle C acceptance on left triggerguard and having Crown N proofs. RARE

Exc.	V.G.	Good	Fair	Poor
850	700	500	300	175

TYPE TWO MODEL 38-H (H MODEL)

There are no Model 38 pistols in the Type Two description, only the H Model with thumbsafety. These begin at serial number 269,100 and have the Eagle N Nitro proofs, with a blued high polish finish and black bakelite grips. The normal caliber is 7.65mm.

A. H Model

1. Standard Commercial

Exc.	V.G.	Good	Fair	Poor
750	550	475	300	200

NOTE: Add $1500 for boxed examples complete with factory manual, clean ring rod, all accessories, extra magazine, etc. $250 for factory nickel, $350 for factory chrome, $1000 for factory engraving.

2. .22 Caliber variation, found in 269,900 range.

Slide and magazines are marked CAL .22 LANG. (Some with steel frame and slides; some with Dural frames and slides). Very Rare.

Exc.	V.G.	Good	Fair	Poor
2500	1800	1000	400	250

3. Jager Model

A special order pistol in .22 Caliber which is similar in appearance to Walther's 1936 Jagerschafts pistol. Very Rare, and watch for fakes.

Exc.	V.G.	Good	Fair	Poor
2500	1850	1200	600	250

4. Police Eagle C and Eagle F acceptance variations.

These are the first Eagle N (post January 1940) police accepted pistols are found in the 270,000 to 276,000 ranges. (Add: 25% for E/F).

Exc.	V.G.	Good	Fair	Poor
650	500	400	325	200

5. German Military variation.

This is the first official military accepted range of 2000 pistols. It is in a TEST range found between 271000 to 273000. Two Eagle 37 military acceptance marks are found on the triggerguard.

Exc.	V.G.	Good	Fair	Poor
1200	900	675	475	300

6. Second Military variation.

These pistols are found with the high polish finish but have only one Eagle 37 acceptance marks. The letter H is found on all small parts.

Exc.	V.G.	Good	Fair	Poor
600	425	350	275	175

7. Police Eagle C acceptance.

This variation includes the remainder of the high polish blued police accepted pistols.

Exc.	V.G.	Good	Fair	Poor
575	425	350	275	175

NOTE: Add $50 for matching magazine, $200 for both matching mags and correct police holster; $300 for both matching mags and correct matching numbered, police accepted & dated holster.

TYPE THREE 38-H MODEL (H MODEL)

This terminology is used because of the change of the exterior finish of the Sauer pistols. Due to the urgency of the war, the order was received to not polish the exterior surfaces of the pistols as had been done previously. There was also a change in the formulation of the grip's material. Later in this range there will be found stamped parts, zinc triggers and magazine bottoms, etc. used to increase the pistol's production. Type Three has a full slide legend.

A. H Model

1. Military accepted with one Eagle 37 Waffenamt mark

Exc.	V.G.	Good	Fair	Poor
500	450	350	275	150

2. Commercial, having only Eagle N Nitro proof marks

Exc.	V.G.	Good	Fair	Poor
450	400	350	25	150

NOTE: See Type Two Commercial info above, prices apply here also.

3. Police accepted with the Police Eagle C acceptance

Exc.	V.G.	Good	Fair	Poor
500	425	350	250	150

NOTE: See Type Two Police info above, prices apply here also.

TYPE FOUR 38-H MODEL (H MODEL)

This is a continuation of the pistol as described in Type Three except the J.P. Sauer & Sohn, Suhl legend is dropped from the slide and only CAL. 7.65 is found on the left side. The word PATENT may or may not appear on the right side. Many are found with a zinc trigger.

A. H Model

1. Military accepted with one Eagle 37 Waffenamt mark

Exc.	V.G.	Good	Fair	Poor
500	450	350	275	150

2. Commercial, having only the Eagle N Nitro proofs

Exc.	V.G.	Good	Fair	Poor
450	400	350	250	150

NOTE: See Type Two Commercial info above, prices apply here also.

3. Police accepted with the Police Eagle C acceptance

Exc.	V.G.	Good	Fair	Poor
500	450	350	275	150

NOTE: See Type Two Price info above, prices apply here also.

4. Eigentum NSDAP SA Gruppe Alpenland slide marked pistols.

These unique pistols are found in the 456000 and 457000 serial number ranges. They have thumb safety levers on the slides.

Exc.	V.G.	Good	Fair	Poor
2800	1800	1000	45	250

5. NSDAP SA Gruppe Alpenland slide marked pistols.
These unique pistols are found in the 465000 serial number range. They have thumbsafety levers on the slide.

Exc.	V.G.	Good	Fair	Poor
2800	1800	1000	450	250

6. H. HIMMLER PRESENTATION PISTOLS
These desirable pistols have a high polish finish with DEM SCHARFSCHUTZEN - H. HIMMLER on the left side of the slide (with no other markings), and J.P. SAUER & SOHN over CAL.7,65 on the right side (opposite of normal). These pistols came in imitation leather cover metal cases with cloth interiors having a cleaning brush, extra magazine and cartridges.

Exc.	V.G.	Good	Fair	Poor
15000	12000	8500	3500	1000

B. MODEL 38
To speed up production even more, the thumbsafety (Hand-sicherung-Hammer safety) was eliminated. The side continues to be marked only with CAL. 7,65. The frame's serial number changes from the right side to the left side at 472000 with overlaps up to 489000.

1. Military accepted with one Eagle 37 Waffenamt mark

Exc.	V.G.	Good	Fair	Poor
450	400	350	25	175

2. Commercial, having only the Eagle N Nitro proofs

Exc.	V.G.	Good	Fair	Poor
450	400	350	250	175

NOTE: See Type Two Commercial info above, prices apply here also.

3. Police accepted with the Police Eagle C acceptance

Exc.	V.G.	Good	Fair	Poor
575	450	400	300	200

4. Police accepted with the Police Eagle F acceptance

Exc.	V.G.	Good	Fair	Poor
475	400	350	250	175

NOTE: (3&4) See Type Two Police info above, prices apply here also.

TYPE FIVE MODEL 38 & H MODEL PISTOLS
There are two different basic variations of the Type Five Sauer pistols. Either may or may not have a thumbsafety lever on the slide. The main criteria is whether the frame is factory numbered as per normal and follows the chronological sequence of those pistols in the preceding model. After the frames were used which were already numbered and finished upon the arrival of the U.S. Army, the last variation came about. Neither variation has any Nitro proof marks.

A. First variation
Factory numbered sequential frames starting on or near serial number 506800. Slides and breech blocks may or may not match.

Exc.	V.G.	Good	Fair	Poor
475	350	275	225	100

B. Second variation
Started with serial number 1; made from mostly rejected parts, generally have notched triggerguards, may or may not be blued, no Nitro proofs, slides may or may not have factory legends, etc. Approximately 300 assembled.

Exc.	V.G.	Good	Fair	Poor
750	500	300	200	100

NOTE: There are some pistols which have postwar Russian Crown N Nitro proofs. The Russians may have assembled a very few pistols after the U.S. Army left this section after the war. Several have been found with newly made barrels in 7.65mm with a C/N proof.

SAVAGE ARMS CORPORATION
Utica, New York
Westfield, Massachusetts

Established in 1894 by Arthur W. Savage, this company has manufactured a wide variety of firearms of which their Model 99 is the best known. By 1915, Savage Arms was manufacturing centerfire and rimfire rifles, pistols, and ammunition. During World War I the company produced the Lewis machine guns. In 1920 Savage purchased J. Stevens Arms Company which was associated with Harry Pope, the famous barrel maker. Later in the decade the company acquired the Page Lewis Company, Davis-Warner, Crescent Firearms, and A.H. Fox. At one time Savage was the largest firearms manufacturing company in the free world. During World War II Savage/Stevens produced military small arms and machine guns. In 1947 the Sporting Arms division moved to Chicopee Falls, MA where it was incorporated into Stevens Arms Company. In 1960 the entire operation was moved to Westfield, MA.

ADVICE FOR THE NEW SAVAGE M-99 COLLECTOR

Comparative values are based on scarcity, originality and condition, as with all collectible guns.

Non-original Savage 99s that have been drilled for scope mounts, sling swivels, or cut down for shotgun recoil pads fall into the fair-to-good category, as described in the grading system outlined near the front of this guide. Sanded/refinished or altered wood, and reblued finish also earn the fair rating no matter whether it was done in a hot-blue tank or with cold-blue on a cleaning patch.

Original wood on a Model 99 is easy to determine. Virtually every 99 up until the 1950s carried the matching serial number of the gun on the forearm wood, buttstock end, and on the but-

tplate underside. This was done so the fitted parts could be re-assembled after final finishing, (fortunately for us collectors, many years later). The few scarce 1899 models with hard rubber buttplates such as the 1899-H featherweight rifle of 1905-1919 had the serial number scratched on the underside instead of being stamped.

Takedown barrel fit and condition should be examined carefully. Be sure the barrel caliber belongs with the apparent Model 99 in hand; the barrel "takes up" <u>tightly</u> against the receiver with no wobbling; the barrel locking groove on the underside and the receiver groove line up; and the forearm snaps into place with authority. Some later takedown barrels were stamped with the last few serial number digits – especially on a 99 set with multiple rifle barrels.

Give attention to the bore. Have a cleaning rod and patches handy, or borrow one to give a dirty bore a closer look. Watch for a ring in the bore indicating a bulged barrel caused by an obstruction or congealed grease in the bore, and sight along the <u>outside</u> of the barrel at a bright light to see if a bulge is evident. If one is there, you can't miss it.

Don't attempt to loosen or tighten up a takedown barrel by grasping the buttplate end of the stock for torque. Most old 1899 takedowns with cracked stocks were probably damaged that way. Hold the receiver instead. All Savage takedown rifles have a metal plug in the forearm barrel channel with a square hole in it. It's there to provide twisting action to unscrew the barrel. Simply remove the forend from the gun, then <u>replace</u> the forend onto the barrel so the hook-lug on the barrel underside fits into the square hole in the forearm. Now, grasping the forearms and barrel together <u>tightly</u>, give it a slow steady twist in the direction of the arrow (to the right). Note, before turning the barrel to remove it or reinstall it, crack open the lever 1/4" or so to withdraw the bolt guide and cartridge extractor from the cuts in the rear of the barrel.

Scope sights are always a question of originality on Savage 99s. Starting in 1937, Savage offered mounted Weaver 29-S 3X scopes on special order; however, these were all mounted on the left side of the receiver with two large screws.

Then in 1939, the Stith Co. brand no-drill scope mount was offered for the Savage 99 to accommodate the Weaver M-330 3/4" and Lyman Alaskan 7/8" diameter scopes for $15 each. The Stith mount was a very clever and durable mount that utilized the barrel rear sight dovetail slot and the two tang sight holes to bridge across the breech area, without the need for altering the gun in any way. The Stith mount is a gun show item since it went out of production in the late 1950s. Typically the Stith is found with the 1" diameter rings for the Weaver 2.5, introduced in January 1946; the Lyman 2.5X Alaskan 7/8" diameter; the Weaver 3/4" diameter 330 and 440; and the Weaver 4X with larger objective lens.

For the collector/shooter, the Stith mount is a very desirable addition to any Savage 99 collection that can be occasionally found at gun shows for $75 to $100 in 85% condition. Be sure it includes the correct 3/8" dovetail fitting and correct screws to mount at the tang.

The first standard Model 99s that were factory drilled and tapped for scope mounts were the 99-R and 99-RS in 1950 at about 560,000 serial number. At that time, the SAVAGE MODEL 99 marking on the top of the receiver ring was rolled over to the left side to avoid the two front scope mounting holes. Even with the scope mount in place, that SAVAGE MODEL 99 marking was clearly visible to confirm that the gun was indeed factory drilled. Finally in 1955, the popular 99-F was introduced with taps for scope mounting, and all other Model 99s followed suit about that time. Incidentally, the 99-F was the first 99 where the model designation was visible on the outside, beside the rear sight right-hand side.

Much more collecting and historical data such as barrel address markings, cartridge details, engraved 99s, and special order 1899s are covered in my book *The Ninety-Nine*. I'm listed as the contributing editor at the front of this guide.

The data on the Savage Model 1899 and 99 are provided by Doug Murray, author/publisher, and are excerpted from his book, *The Ninety-Nine: A History of the Savage Model 99 Rifle*, revised 3rd edition, and is only for the exclusive use in the *Standard Catalog of Firearms*. The pricing is provided by Murray as a reference for this publication.

Model 1895

A .303 Savage caliber lever action rifle with a 26" or 30" barrel and 5-shot rotary magazine. Identifiable by the hole in the breechbolt. The barrel marked "Savage Repeating Arms Co. Utica, N.Y. U.S.A. Pat. Feb. 7, 1893, July 25, 1893. CAL. .303." Blued with a walnut stock. Approximately 8,000 were manufactured between 1895 and 1899.
22" or 30" Barrel-Add 10%.

Exc.	V.G.	Good	Fair	Poor
1800	1400	900	300	200

Model 1899-A-26" Round Barrel Rifle

A .25-35, .30-30, .303 Savage, .32-40 or .38-55, .300 Savage caliber lever action rifle with 26" barrel marked "Savage Arms Company, Utica, N.Y. Pat. Feb. 7, 1893, July 25.'93, Oct.3.'99 .CAL.30." Manufactured between 1899 and 1926/27. Blued with a walnut stock. Serial number range 10000 to 300000. Block cocking indicator on bolt to s/n 90000 then changed to pin indicator on tang.

Exc.	V.G.	Good	Fair	Poor
1200	800	500	250	100

NOTE: Add 50% for .25-35, .32-40, and .38-55 calibers.

Model 1899-A-22" Barrel Short Rifle

Chambered for .303, .30-30, .25-35, .32-40, .38-55. Serial number range from 10000 to 220000. Produced from 1899 to 1922. Same cocking indicator as the 1899-A rifle.

Exc.	V.G.	Good	Fair	Poor
1200	900	600	300	100

NOTE: Add 50% for .25-35, .32-40, and .38-55 calibers.

Model 1899-B 26" Octagon Barrel Rifle

In calibers .303, .30-30, .25-35, .32-40, .38-55. Manufactured between 1899 and 1915. Serial number range 10000 to 175000. Same cocking indicator as 1899-A rifle.

Exc.	V.G.	Good	Fair	Poor
1600	1100	700	350	150

NOTE: Add 50% for .25-35, .32-40, and .38-55 calibers.

Model 1899-C 26" Half Octagon Barrel Rifle

In calibers .303, .30-30, .25-35, .32-40, .38-55. Manufactured between 1899 and 1915. Serial number range 10000 to 175000. Same cocking indicator as 1899-A rifle.

Exc.	V.G.	Good	Fair	Poor
2000	1500	1000	400	150

NOTE: Add 50% for .25-35, .32-40, and .38-55 calibers.

Model 1899-D Military Musket

Chambered for .303 Savage only with 28" barrel. Fitted with full military stocks. Produced from 1899 to 1915. Several hundred produced for Canadian Home Guard during WWI. These will have rack number on buttplate.

Exc.	V.G.	Good	Fair	Poor
3000	2000	1500	700	300

Model 1899-F Saddle Ring Carbine

Fitted with 20" barrel only in calibers .303, .30-30, .25-35, .32-40, .38-55. Built from 1899 to 1919 in serial number range 19000 to 200000. Same cocking indicator as 1899-A rifle. Earliest style with barrel band is rarest variation.

Exc.	V.G.	Good	Fair	Poor
850	600	400	250	100

NOTE: Add 100% for .25-35, .32-40, and .38-55 calibers. Add 200% for barrel band carbine.

Model 1899-CD Deluxe Rifle

In calibers .303, .30-30, .25-35, .32-40, .38-55. Serial number range 50000 to 175000. Built from 1905 to 1917. Same cocking indicator as the 1899-A rifle. The standard Deluxe 1899 rifle with 26" round, octagon, or half octagon barrel with pistol grip stock and checkering. Takedown barrel or short 22" barrel.

Exc.	V.G.	Good	Fair	Poor
3000	2000	1500	600	250

NOTE: Add 30% for .25-35, .32-40, and .38-55 calibers.

A Savage Model 1895 factory engraved rifle sold at auction for $12,650. Chambered for .303 Savage cartridge and fitted with a 26" octagon barrel. Fancy checkered stock with English walnut. Factory records.
Amoskeag Auction Co. Inc., August 2000

Model 1899-H Featherweight Rifle

Chambered for .303, .30-30, .25-35, and .22 HP Savage in 20" barrel. Serial number range 50000 to 220000. Built from 1905 to 1919. The revolutionary .22HP cartridge was introduced in this model in 1912. Most 1899-Hs are found with takedown barrels.

Paul Goodwin Photo

Exc.	V.G.	Good	Fair	Poor
1600	1200	600	300	100

NOTE: Add 50% for .25-35, add 25% for .22HP.

Model 1899 .250-3000 Savage Rifle

This deluxe Model 1899 was developed to introduce the Charles Newton designed .250-3000 Savage cartridge. Fitted with a 22" featherweight takedown barrel, pistol grip, checkered perch belly stock, unique checkered trigger. Built from 1914 to 1921 in the 146500 to 237500 serial number range.

Exc.	V.G.	Good	Fair	Poor
1800	1400	800	350	100

Model 99-B 26"/24" Standard Weight Takedown

Chambered for .303, .30-30, and .300 Savage. Serial number range 200000 to 344000. Produced from 1920 to 1934. In 1926 a new 24" barrel with ramp front sight was introduced.

Exc.	V.G.	Good	Fair	Poor
700	600	400	300	100

Model 99-C 22" Standard Weight Short Rifle

Chambered for .303, .30-30, and .300 Savage. Serial number range 238000 to 290000. built from 1922 to 1926. This model looks like a shortened 26" rifle but with a heavily crowned muzzle.

Exc.	V.G.	Good	Fair	Poor
600	500	400	200	100

Model 99-D 22" Standard Weight Takedown Rifle

Chambered for .303, .30-30, and .300 Savage. Serial number range 238000 to 290000. Built from 1922 to 1926. Same heavily crowned muzzle as 99-C.

Exc.	V.G.	Good	Fair	Poor
700	600	400	200	100

Model 99-E Lightweight Rifle

Chambered for .22HP, .30-30, .303, .250-3000, and .300 Savage. Manufactured between 1922 and 1934. Serial number range 238000 to 344000. In 1926 new ramp front sight introduced.

Exc.	V.G.	Good	Fair	Poor
800	650	500	300	100

NOTE: Add 25% for .22 Hi Power and .250-3000 calibers.

Model 99-F Lightweight Takedown Rifle

As above, but in lightweight takedown barrels in 20", 22", and 24". Chambered for .22HP, .30-30, .303, .250-3000, and .300 Savage.These barrels were tapered lightweight barrels. Manufactured between 1920 and 1940. Serial number range 200000 to 398000. In 1926 new ramp front sight introduced. Early versions look similar to Model 1899-H featherweight. In 1938 checkered stocks offered this option is rare.

Exc.	V.G.	Good	Fair	Poor
1000	700	500	300	100

NOTE: Add 50% for .22HP, and .250-3000. Add 75% for 1938 checkered stocks.

Model 99-G Deluxe Takedown Pistol Grip Rifle

Calibers and barrel lengths as above, with a pistol grip checkered stock. Manufactured between 1922 and 1941. Serial number range 238000 to 407000. No takedown Model 99s made after 1941.

Exc.	V.G.	Good	Fair	Poor
1500	1000	700	300	100

NOTE: Add 50% for .22 Hi Power and 25% for .250-3000

Model 99-H Carbine/Barrel Band Carbine

Fitted with 20" or 22" barrels and chambered for .30-30, .303, .250-3000, and .300 Savage. serial number range 220000 to 400000. Built between 1923 and 1940. Distinctive plain stocks with no flat pads on side of buttstock. Curved carbine style butt-plate. In 1931 barrel band added to forend, then commonly called the "barrel band carbine". In 1935 flat pads added to buttstock sides. Also front ramp sight added.

Exc.	V.G.	Good	Fair	Poor
800	500	300	200	100

NOTE: Add 50% for 1935 barrel band carbine. Add 25% for .250-3000, and .300 Savage.

Combination Cased Set .300 Savage/.410 Barrel

Fitted with 22" or 24" barrels with .410 barrels and .300 Savage in Model 99-F, 99-G, or 99-K configuration. In black fitted case. Serial number range 240000 to 350000. built from 1922 to 1934. Be aware that the barrel address on the .410 barrel matches that on the rifle barrel and that the.410 barrel takes up correctly on the receiver, and that the case fits the .410 barrel and receiver.

Courtesy Amoskeag Auction Company

Exc.	V.G.	Good	Fair	Poor
2500	1800	1200	600	300

Model 99-A 24" Featherweight Rifle

Fitted with a 24" barrel with new 1926 ramp front sight. Chambered for .303, .30-30, or .300 Savage. Serial number range 290000 to 370000. Built from 1926 to 1937. Buttplate is older 1899 crescent style.

Exc.	V.G.	Good	Fair	Poor
600	500	400	250	75

Model 99-K Deluxe Engraved Rifle

The premier Savage Model 99 with an engraved receiver. Fitted with a checkered pistol grip stock of select American walnut, and a takedown frame. Hand honed and hand fitted. Chambered for .22HP, .30-30, .303, .250-3000, and .300 Savage. Fitted with 22" or 24" barrels. Serial number range 285000 to 398000. Manufactured between 1926 and 1940.

Exc.	V.G.	Good	Fair	Poor
2800	1800	1200	600	200

NOTE: Add 30% for .22 caliber Hi Power. Some of these models found with cased set with .410 barrel. Add $700 for V.G. case and barrels.

Model 99-R Heavy Stocked Rifle

This model features a heavy pistol grip checkered stock with rounded forend tip. Fitted with a 22" or 24" barrel and chambered for .250-3000, .303, .300 Savage, .308, .243, and .358 calibers. Serial number range 340000 to 1060000. Manufactured between 1932 and 1960.

Exc.	V.G.	Good	Fair	Poor
750	500	350	200	75

NOTE: Add 50% for .358 and 100% for rare uncataloged .30-30. Approximately 10 made for A.F. Stoeger of N.Y.C. for N.Y. State Police in 1935 in serial number range 348,600. Most of these are found with Redfield No. 102 side peep sight and 1/4" rack number stamped in stock below pistol grip.

Model 99-RS Special Sights

As above, with a Lyman aperture rear tang sight. In 1940 this was changed to a Redfield micrometer tang sight. This was the first model fitted with Savage quick release sling swivels. No .30-30 calibers made in this model. Manufactured between 1932 and 1942.

Exc.	V.G.	Good	Fair	Poor
900	650	500	350	200

NOTE: Add 50% for .358.

Model 99-EG Standard Weight Rifle

Produced with plain uncheckered pistol grip stock until 1940. Available in .22 Hi Power, .250 Savage, .30-30, .303 Savage, .300 Savage, .308, .243, and .358. Serial number range 350000 to 1060000. Manufactured between 1935 and 1960.

Exc.	V.G.	Good	Fair	Poor
700	500	300	200	75

NOTE: For pre-1940 uncheckered stocks add 20%. Add 100% for rifles chambered for .22 Hi Power and .358

Model 99-T Deluxe Featherweight Rifle

This is the classic short barrel deluxe Model 99 with semi-beavertail forend and distinct long checkering pattern. Fitted with 20" or 22" barrels and chambered for .250-3000, .30-30, .303, .22 HP, or .300 Savage. Serial number range 350000 to 400000. Manufactured between 1935 and 1940.

Exc.	V.G.	Good	Fair	Poor
1500	1000	700	350	100

NOTE: Add 100% for .22 Hi Power caliber, 20% for .250-3000.

Model 99-F Featherweight Rifle

The first Savage made with the model designation visible on the outside. Located at the rear on the right side of the barrel. A true featherweight with slender 22" barrel, lightweight stocks with buttend hollowed out. Chambered for .250-3000, .300 Savage, .308, .243, .284, and .358 calibers. Serial number range 755000 to present. Built from 1955 to 1973.

Exc.	V.G.	Good	Fair	Poor
700	550	400	250	75

NOTE: Add 100% for .284 and .358 calibers, add 50% for .243 and .250-3000 Savage.

Model 99-DL Deluxe Monte Carlo Rifle

A deluxe version of the Model 99EG. Available in .243, .250 Savage, .300 Savage, .284, .358, and .308 calibers with a Monte Carlo-style stock. Serial number range 1,000,000 to present. Manufactured between 1960 and 1973.

Exc.	V.G.	Good	Fair	Poor
500	350	250	150	50

NOTE: Add 75% for .358 and .284 calibers.

Model 99-E Economy Rifle

The ugly duckling of the Savage line. The Model 99-E lacked many of the standard features such as left side cartridge counter, tang sight holes, walnut stocks, and capped pistol grip. Fitted with 20", 22", or 24" barrels and chambered for .250-3000, .300 Savage, .243, and .308 calibers. Serial number range 1000000 to present. Built from 1960 to 1984.

Exc.	V.G.	Good	Fair	Poor
300	250	200	150	50

NOTE: The Model 99-E was the last original rotary magazine Model 99 when production discontinued in 1984.

Model 99-C Clip Magazine Rifle

The current production model in .22-250, .243, .284 Winchester, 7mm-08, or .308 caliber with a 22" barrel having open sights. Blued with a walnut stock. This model features a clip magazine and is the first modification in the Model 99 in 66 years. Introduced in 1965. Dropped from production and reintroduced in 1995 in .243 and .308 calibers. Approximate weight is 7.75 lbs.

NIB	Exc.	V.G.	Good	Fair	Poor
550	350	300	250	150	50

NOTE: Add 100% for .22-250, .284, and .7mm-08.

Model 99-DE Citation Grade Rifle

A premier Savage with an engraved receiver with nickel-like finish and impressed checkering on select walnut stocks. Marked 99-M. Offered in .243, .284, and .308 calibers with 22" barrel only. Serial number range 1140000 to present. Manufactured between 1965 and 1970.

Exc.	V.G.	Good	Fair	Poor
1500	1000	600	—	—

NOTE: Add 30% for .284 caliber.

Model 99-PE Presentation Grade Rifle

This model is a presentation grade Model 99 with an engraved receiver as well as a hand-checkered finely figured walnut stock. Mountain lion on right side of receiver and elk on left side. Chambered for .243, .284, and .308 caliber with 22" barrel. Serial number range 1140000 to present. Manufactured between 1965 and 1970.

Exc.	V.G.	Good	Fair	Poor
2000	1500	800	—	—

NOTE: Add 30% for .284 caliber.

A Savage Model PE factory engraved rifle was sold at auction for $6,785. Chambered for the .250-3000 cartridge and fitted with a 22" barrel. This rifle was the only Model 99-PE made in .250-3000 caliber. Condition is 99%. Built in 1981.
Amoskeag Auction Company, March 2001

Model 1895 Anniversary Edition

A .308 caliber reproduction of the Model 1895 with a 24" octagonal barrel, engraved receiver and walnut stock having a schnabel forend. Brass crescent buttplate, brass medallion inlaid in stock. There were 9,999 manufactured in 1970.

NIB	Exc.	V.G.	Good	Fair	Poor
550	300	250	200	—	—

Model 99A-Saddle Gun

A variation of the original Model 99A with a 20" or 22" barrel. Chambered for the .243, .250 Savage, .300 Savage, .308, and .375. Serial number range in new "A" series on left side. Manufactured between 1971 and 1982.

NIB	Exc.	V.G.	Good	Fair	Poor
700	500	300	250	—	—

NOTE: Add 25% for .375 caliber.

Model 99-CD Deluxe Clip Model

The North American classic rifle with distinct stocks of checkered walnut with long grooved forend, deep shaped pistol grip, and Monte Carlo stock with cheekpiece. Fitted with 22" barrel and chambered for .250-3000, .308, or .243. Serial number range in new "A" series on left side. Built from 1975 to 1980.

NIB	Exc.	V.G.	Good	Fair	Poor
750	550	400	300	—	—

Model 99-.358 and 99-.375 Brush Guns

Similar to the Model 99-A straight grip saddle gun, but in .358 and .375 Win. (1980) calibers. Has plain grooved forend, rubber recoil pad. Serial number range in the "A" series on left side. Built from 1977 to 1980.

NIB	Exc.	V.G.	Good	Fair	Poor
700	500	300	250	—	—

NOTE: Add 25% for .358 Win. caliber.

Model 99CE (Centennial Edition)

Introduced in 1995 this limited edition rifle is chambered for the .300 Savage cartridge. Limited to 1,000 rifles with serial numbers from AS0001 to AS1000. Engraved receiver with gold inlays. Select American walnut stock with Monte Carlo comb.

Courtesy Savage Arms

NIB	Exc.	V.G.	Good	Fair	Poor
1600	1300	900	750	500	250

Model 1903

A .22 caliber slide action rifle with a 24" barrel having open sights. Blued with a walnut stock. Manufactured between 1903 and 1922. Late model rifles have updated slide handle and pistol grip stock in same style as Model 1914.

Exc.	V.G.	Good	Fair	Poor
250	200	150	100	75

Model 1903 Gallery Model

Same general specifications as Model 1903 except for a mechanical counter attached to record shots fired.

Exc.	V.G.	Good	Fair	Poor
350	275	200	150	100

Model 1903 Factory Engraved Models

NOTE: These models are seldom seen. Secure a qualified appraisal prior to a sale.

Grade EF

Grade "B" checkering, fancy English walnut stock, Savage 22B front sights, and 21B rear sight.

Exc.	V.G.	Good	Fair	Poor
N/A	—	—	—	—

Expert Grade

Fancy American walnut stock, Grade "A" engraving, Grade "B" checkering, and standard sights.

Exc.	V.G.	Good	Fair	Poor
N/A	—	—	—	—

Grade GH

Plain American walnut stock, Grade "A" checkering, 22B front sight, and 21B rear sight.

Exc.	V.G.	Good	Fair	Poor
N/A	—	—	—	—

Gold Medal Grade

Plain American walnut stock, animal ornamentation on receiver, Grade "A" checkering, and standard sights.

Exc.	V.G.	Good	Fair	Poor
N/A	—	—	—	—

Model 1909

As above, with a 20" barrel. Manufactured between 1909 and 1915.

Exc.	V.G.	Good	Fair	Poor
250	200	150	100	75

Model 1911

Produced from 1911 to 1915 in .22 short only. Bolt action repeater. American walnut stock. Shotgun steel buttplate, bead front sight with adjustable open rear sight. Tubular magazine is loaded through butt stock and has capacity of 20 rounds. Weight is approximately 4 lbs.

Exc.	V.G.	Good	Fair	Poor
275	225	175	125	100

Model 1912

A .22 caliber semiautomatic rifle with a 20" barrel, open sights and in takedown form. Magazine capacity is 7 rounds. Blued with a walnut stock. Manufactured between 1912 and 1916. Weight is about 4.5 lbs.

Exc.	V.G.	Good	Fair	Poor
350	300	200	125	90

Model 6

Similar to the above, with a 24" barrel and tubular magazine. The walnut stock checkered prior to 1938 and plain after 1965.

Exc.	V.G.	Good	Fair	Poor
150	125	100	75	50

Model 7

As above, with a detachable magazine. Manufactured between 1938 and 1954.

Exc.	V.G.	Good	Fair	Poor
150	125	100	75	50

Model 1914

As above, with a 24" octagonal barrel. Manufactured between 1914 and 1926.

Exc.	V.G.	Good	Fair	Poor
275	225	175	125	100

Model 25

A .22 caliber slide action rifle with a 24" octagonal barrel, open sights and tubular magazine. Blued with a plain walnut stock. Manufactured between 1925 and 1929.

Exc.	V.G.	Good	Fair	Poor
350	300	250	200	125

Model 29

Similar to above but with a 22" octagonal barrel later changed to round on post war rifles and a checkered walnut stock, later changed to plain on post war rifles. Manufactured between 1929 and 1967.

Exc.	V.G.	Good	Fair	Poor
300	250	200	150	100

Model 170

A .30-30 or .35 Remington caliber slide action rifle with a 22" barrel and 3-shot tubular magazine. Blued with a walnut stock. Manufactured between 1970 and 1981.

Exc.	V.G.	Good	Fair	Poor
200	175	125	100	75

Model 1904

A .22 caliber single shot bolt action rifle with an 18" barrel and walnut stock. Manufactured between 1904 and 1931. After 1915 this model became known as the Model 04.

Exc.	V.G.	Good	Fair	Poor
150	125	100	75	50

Model 1905

As above, with a 24" barrel. Manufactured between 1905 and 1919.

Exc.	V.G.	Good	Fair	Poor
150	125	100	75	50

Model 1905 Style "B"

Same as the Model 1905 target but with shotgun buttplate.

Exc.	V.G.	Good	Fair	Poor
175	150	100	75	50

Model 1905 Special Target Rifle

This model is the same as the Model 1905 Target Rifle except for hand checkered fancy American walnut stock.

Exc.	V.G.	Good	Fair	Poor
350	250	200	150	100

Model 19 NRA

A .22 caliber bolt action rifle with a 25" barrel, detachable magazine and full length military style stock. Approximately 50,000 were manufactured total between 1919 and 1937.

Exc.	V.G.	Good	Fair	Poor
225	175	150	100	75

Model 19L

As above, with a Lyman receiver sight. Manufactured between 1933 and 1942.

Exc.	V.G.	Good	Fair	Poor
350	300	250	200	150

Model 19M

As above, with a 28" barrel fitted with telescope sight bases. Manufactured between 1933 and 1942.

Exc.	V.G	Good	Fair	Poor
350	300	250	200	150

Model 19H

The Model 19 chambered for .22 Hornet. Manufactured between 1933 and 1942.

Exc.	V.G.	Good	Fair	Poor
500	450	350	300	200

Model 3

A .22 caliber single shot bolt action rifle with a 24" barrel, open sights and walnut stock. Manufactured between 1933 and 1952.

Exc.	V.G.	Good	Fair	Poor
100	80	60	50	35

Model 4

Similar to the above, with a 24" barrel and 5-shot magazine. Produced from 1932 to 1964.

Exc.	V.G.	Good	Fair	Poor
125	100	80	60	50

Model 4M

As above, in .22 Magnum. Produced from 1932 to 1964.

Exc.	V.G.	Good	Fair	Poor
125	100	80	60	50

Model 5

The Model 4 with a tubular magazine. Manufactured between 1933 and 1964.

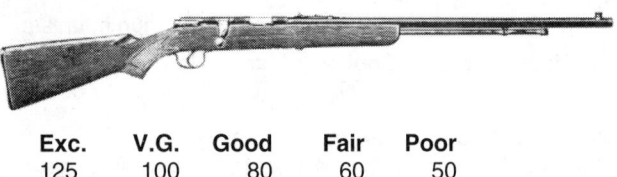

Exc.	V.G.	Good	Fair	Poor
125	100	80	60	50

Model 1920

A .250-3000 or .300 Savage caliber bolt action rifle with a 22" or 24" barrel, open sights and 5-shot magazine. Blued, with a walnut stock having a schnabel forend. Manufactured between 1920 and 1929. An improved version of this rifle was introduced in 1926 that was heavier and had a Lyman #54 peep sight.

Exc.	V.G.	Good	Fair	Poor
350	300	250	175	125

Model 1922

This model is a variation of the Model 19 NRA with a sporting style stock with Schnabel forend. Fitted with a 23" round barrel it was chambered for the .22 caliber cartridge. This model superceded the Model 23 and looks like a Model 23 sporter. Introduced in 1922 and discontinued in 1923. VERY RARE.

Exc.	V.G.	Good	Fair	Poor
750	600	500	—	—

Model 23A

This bolt action .22 l.r. rifle was introduced in 1923 and features a 5-round detachable box magazine and 23" barrel with open sights. The large loading port on the left side of the receiver permitted easy single shot loading. The stock was plain with pistol grip and a schnabel forearm. A varnish wood finish was applied to this model. Production stopped in 1933.

Exc.	V.G.	Good	Fair	Poor
250	200	150	125	100

Model 23AA

This was an improved version of the Model 23A introduced in 1933. It features better speed lock, redesigned stock with oil finish. The receiver was tapped for No. 15 Savage extension peep sight. The rifle weighs approximately 6 lbs. Production ceased in 1942.

Exc.	V.G.	Good	Fair	Poor
290	250	200	150	125

Model 23B

Similar to the Model 23A except chambered for the .25-20 cartridge. Barrel length was 25" and forearm was a full 1.5" wide beavertail. Receiver was tapped for peep sight and magazine capacity was 4 rounds. Production on the Model 23B was from 1923 to 1940.

Exc.	V.G.	Good	Fair	Poor
250	200	150	125	100

Model 23C

The same configuration as the Model 23B with the exception of the caliber; .32-20. Manufactured from 1923 to 1946.

Exc.	V.G.	Good	Fair	Poor
250	200	150	125	100

Model 23D

The same configuration as the Model 23B but chambered for the .22 Hornet cartridge. Manufactured from 1932 to 1948.

Exc.	V.G.	Good	Fair	Poor
325	300	250	200	150

Model 40

Similar to the above but in .250-3000, .300 Savage, .30-30, and .30-06 caliber. Manufactured between 1928 and 1940.

Exc.	V.G.	Good	Fair	Poor
350	300	250	175	125

Model 45 Super

As above, with a Lyman receiver sight and checkered walnut stock. Manufactured between 1928 and 1940.

Exc.	V.G.	Good	Fair	Poor
400	350	300	200	150

Model 35

A .22 caliber bolt action rifle with a 22" barrel, open sights and 5-shot magazine. Blued with a Monte Carlo-style hardwood stock.

Exc.	V.G.	Good	Fair	Poor
100	80	70	50	35

Model 46

As above with a tubular magazine. Manufactured between 1969 and 1973.

Exc.	V.G.	Good	Fair	Poor
100	80	70	50	35

Model 340

A .22 Hornet, .222 Remington, .223, or .30-30 caliber bolt action rifle with a 22" or 24" barrel, open sights and 4- or 5-shot magazine. Blued, with a plain walnut stock. Manufactured between 1950 and 1985.

Exc.	V.G.	Good	Fair	Poor
250	200	175	125	90

Model 342

As above, but in .22 Hornet caliber. Manufactured between 1950 and 1955.

Exc.	V.G.	Good	Fair	Poor
250	200	175	125	90

MODEL 110 SERIES

Model 110 Sporter

A bolt action rifle manufactured in a variety of calibers with a 22" barrel, open sights and 4-shot magazine. Blued with a walnut stock. Manufactured between 1958 and 1963.

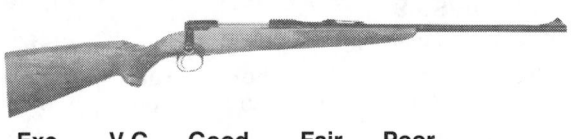

Exc.	V.G.	Good	Fair	Poor
200	150	125	100	75

Model 110-M

Similar to the above, in 7mm Magnum to .338 Winchester Magnum. Manufactured between 1963 and 1969.

Exc.	V.G.	Good	Fair	Poor
275	225	175	150	100

Model 110-D

Similar to the Model 110 in .22-250 to .338 Winchester Magnum caliber with a detachable magazine. Manufactured between 1966 and 1988.

Exc.	V.G.	Good	Fair	Poor
350	300	250	200	150

Model 110-P Premier Grade

As above, with a finely figured walnut stock, rosewood forend tip and pistol grip cap. Manufactured between 1964 and 1970.

Exc.	V.G.	Good	Fair	Poor
450	375	325	250	200

Model 110-PE

As above, with an engraved receiver, magazine floorplate and triggerguard. Manufactured between 1968 and 1970.

Exc.	V.G.	Good	Fair	Poor
850	650	500	400	300

NOTE: Current production Model 110-F are made in the following styles:

Model 110-F-DuPont Rynite Stock and Sights

NIB	Exc.	V.G.	Good	Fair	Poor
450	400	350	300	250	200

Model 110-FX-Without Sights

NIB	Exc.	V.G.	Good	Fair	Poor
400	350	300	250	200	150

Model 110-FP-Composite Stock and 24" heavy barrel

NIB	Exc.	V.G.	Good	Fair	Poor
400	350	300	250	200	150

Model 110-G-Checkered Hardwood Stock and Sights

NIB	Exc.	V.G.	Good	Fair	Poor
375	325	275	225	175	125

Model 110-GX-Without Sights

NIB	Exc.	V.G.	Good	Fair	Poor
350	300	250	200	150	100

Model 110-CY

A compact version of the Model 110 series. Shorter length of pull on walnut stock and 22" barrel. Overall length is 42-1/2". Weight is about 6-1/2 lbs. Chambered in .223, .243, .270, .300 Savage, and .308 calibers.

NIB	Exc.	V.G.	Good	Fair	Poor
350	300	250	200	150	100

Model 110FP-Tactical

Offered in calibers from .223 Rem. to .300 Win. Mag this bolt action rifle has a 24" heavy barrel with recessed muzzle. The synthetic stock is black as are all other surfaces. Available in both right and left hand versions. Weight is approximately 8.5 lbs.

NIB	Exc.	V.G.	Good	Fair	Poor
400	350	300	250	200	150

MODEL 111 SERIES

Model 111 Classic Hunter Series

All models under this series are fitted with a classic American designed straight comb stock with pistol grip. Chambered in 13 different calibers from .223 Rem. to the .338 Win. Mag. Weights vary with caliber and stock type but range from 6-3/8 to 7 lbs. Models are fitted with a detachable or internal magazine. All Hunter series rifles are drilled and tapped for scope mounts.

Model 111 G-Top loading with walnut stock with recoil pad.

NIB	Exc.	V.G.	Good	Fair	Poor
350	300	250	200	150	100

Model 111 GC-Detachable magazine with walnut stock and recoil pad.

Savage Model 111 GC

NIB	Exc.	V.G.	Good	Fair	Poor
400	350	300	250	200	150

Model 111 F-Top loading with graphite stock.

NIB	Exc.	V.G.	Good	Fair	Poor
375	300	250	200	150	100

Model 111 FC-Detachable magazine with graphite stock

NIB	Exc.	V.G.	Good	Fair	Poor
400	350	300	250	200	150

Model 111 FXP3-Top loading with graphite stock and 3x9 scope, rings, and bases, and sling

NIB	Exc.	V.G.	Good	Fair	Poor
475	400	350	300	200	150

Model 111 FCXP3-Same as above but detachable magazine

NIB	Exc.	V.G.	Good	Fair	Poor
475	400	350	300	200	150

Model 111 FAK-blued steel barrel, composite stock, muzzle brake

NIB	Exc.	V.G.	Good	Fair	Poor
400	350	300	250	200	150

MODEL 112 SERIES

Model 112 BT / 112 BT-S (Long Action)

Introduced for the first time in 1994 this model is a competition grade rifle. Chambered for the .223 Rem. and the .308 Win. it features a 26" heavy stainless steel barrel fitted to an alloy steel receiver. In 1995 the .300 Win. Magnum was added to the line referred to as the Model 112 BT-S. The barrel finish is black. The stock is laminated with ambidextrous palm swell and adjustable cheek rest. Weight is about 11 lbs.

Savage Model 112 BT

NIB	Exc.	V.G.	Good	Fair	Poor
1025	850	700	500	300	250

Model 112 Series Varmint Rifles

This series of varmint rifles features 26" barrels. Offered with either composite or laminated wood stocks all Model 112s are top loading and all are drilled and tapped for scope mounting. Available in .223, .22-250, and .220 Swift the BV configuration weighs about 10-1/2 lbs. while the FV configuration weighs about 9 lbs.

Model 112 BVSS (Long Action)

This model has a laminated wood stock with high comb and ambidextrous palm swell. It is fitted with a stainless steel barrel, bolt and triggerguard. In 1996 the .300 Win. Mag., 7mm Rem. Mag., .308 Win., .30-06, and .25-06 was added to this model.

NIB	Exc.	V.G.	Good	Fair	Poor
575	425	350	300	200	150

Model 112 BVSS-S

Same as above but single shot.

NIB	Exc.	V.G.	Good	Fair	Poor
500	400	350	300	200	150

Model 112 FVSS

This version also is fitted with a stainless steel barrel and a composite stock This version was fitted with a stainless steel "fluted" barrel in 1995. Several new calibers were added as well: 300 Win. Mag., 7mm Rem. Mag., .25-06 Rem.

NIB	Exc.	V.G.	Good	Fair	Poor
475	400	350	300	200	150

Model 112 FVSS-S

This is a single shot version of the above model.

NIB	Exc.	V.G.	Good	Fair	Poor
475	400	350	300	200	150

Model 112 FV

This is similar to the model above but with a blued barrel.

NIB	Exc.	V.G.	Good	Fair	Poor
375	300	250	200	150	100

Model 112 BT-Competition Grade

This model was introduced in 1996. It is a competition rifle. It features a 26" blackened stainless steel barrel and custom target style laminated stock with adjustable cheek rest. Chambered for .223 or .308 cartridges. Weight is approximately 11 lbs. The barrel is pillar bedded.

NIB	Exc.	V.G.	Good	Fair	Poor
950	850	700	500	300	250

MODEL 114 SERIES

Model 114 CU

This model has a select grade walnut oil finished stock. The finish is a high polish blue and the bolt has a laser etched Savage logo. A detachable magazine is standard. The receiver is drilled and tapped for a scope mount. Offered in .270, .30-06, 7mm Rem. Mag., and .300 Win. Mag. Weights are about 7-1/8 lbs.

NIB	Exc.	V.G.	Good	Fair	Poor
500	425	325	250	200	150

Model 114 C-Classic

This model, introduced in 2000, features a select grade oil finished walnut stock with cut checkering. No sights. Chambered for .270 and .30-06 with 22" barrel, and .7mm Mag. and .300 Win. Mag with 24" barrel.

NIB	Exc.	V.G.	Good	Fair	Poor
550	425	—	—	—	—

Model 114 CE-Classic European

Introduced in 1996 this rifle is chambered for the .270 Win., .30-06, 7mm Rem. Mag., and .300 Win. Mag. Barrel lengths are 22" or 24" depending on caliber. It has an oil finished stock with skip line checkering and cheekpiece. The forend tip is a schnable type. Rubber recoil pad and pistol grip cap are standard. High luster blue finish. Approximate weight is 7.12 lbs.

NIB	Exc.	V.G.	Good	Fair	Poor
550	475	400	350	300	150

Courtesy Savage Arms

Model 114 U-Ultra

Introduced in 1999 this model features a high gloss walnut stock with custom checkering. Blued finish is high luster with a laser-etched Savage logo on the bolt body. Chambered for the .270 Win., .30-06, 7mm-08 Rem., and .300 Win. Mag cartridges. Barrel length is 22" and 24" depending on caliber. Weight is about 7 lbs.

NIB	Exc.	V.G.	Good	Fair	Poor
500	375	—	—	—	—

MODEL 116 SERIES

This series of rifles feature graphite stocks and stainless steel barreled actions. An adjustable muzzle brake is also included. All rifles in the 116 series are drilled and tapped for scope mounts.

Model 116 FCSAK (Long Action)

Features a detachable box magazine. The 22" barrel is fluted. Offered in .270, .30-06, 7mm Rem. Mag., .300 Win. Mag., and .338 Win. Mag. Weighs about 6-1/2 lbs.

NIB	Exc.	V.G.	Good	Fair	Poor
625	550	450	400	300	200

Model 116 FSAK (Long Action)

Same as model above but with on-off choice for muzzle brake given to shooter.

NIB	Exc.	V.G.	Good	Fair	Poor
575	500	400	300	200	150

Model 116 BSS

Introduced in 2001 this model features a laminated stock. It is chambered for the .270 Win., .30-06, 7mm Rem. Mag., .300 Win. Mag., and the .300 Rem. Ultra Mag. cartridges. Fitted with either a 24" or 26" stainless steel barrel depending on caliber. No sights. Weight is about 7.5 lbs. depending on caliber.

NIB	Exc.	V.G.	Good	Fair	Poor
625	500	—	—	—	—

Model 116 FSS (Long Action)

This is the standard configuration for the 116 series. This model features a top loading action with 22" or 24" barrel depending on caliber. There is no muzzle brake fitted to this model. Weight is approximately 6-3/4 lbs. Offered in 7 calibers from .223 to .338 Win. Mag.

NIB	Exc.	V.G.	Good	Fair	Poor
475	400	300	200	150	100

Model 116 FCS

Same as above but with stainless steel removable box magazine.

NIB	Exc.	V.G.	Good	Fair	Poor
550	475	375	300	200	150

Model 116 FSK-Kodiak (Long Action)

This model features a top loading action with a 22" barrel with muzzle brake. Weight is approximately 7.25 lbs.

NIB	Exc.	V.G.	Good	Fair	Poor
550	475	375	300	200	150

Model 116 SE-Safari Express

Introduced in 1994 this rifle features select grade walnut stock with ebony tip and deluxe checkering. Barrel and action are stainless steel with adjustable muzzle brake. Offered in .300 Win. Mag., .338 Win. Mag., and .458 calibers. In 1995 the .425 Express cartridge was added. In 2000 this model had a stainless steel action and barrel. Weight is approximately 8-1/2 lbs.

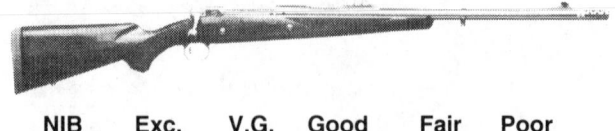

NIB	Exc.	V.G.	Good	Fair	Poor
925	750	600	500	300	200

Model 116 US

Introduced in 1995 this model features a stainless steel action and barrel with a high gloss American walnut stock with ebony tip and custom checkering. Offered in .270 Win., .30-06, 7mm Rem. Mag., and .300 Win. Mag. Barrel is 22" on the two smaller calibers and 24" on the magnum calibers.

NIB	Exc.	V.G.	Good	Fair	Poor
600	500	400	300	250	200

MODEL 12 SERIES

Introduced in 1998 this series features a short action heavy barrel line of rifles designed for long range shooting.

Model 12 BVSS

This model features a 26" fluted stainless steel barrel with recessed crown and a brown laminated stock with beavertail forend. Chambered for .223, .22-250, and .308. Magazine capacity is 4 rounds. Weight is approximately 9.5 lbs. Introduced in 1998.

NIB	Exc.	V.G.	Good	Fair	Poor
575	450	—	—	—	—

Model 12 BVSS-S

Same as above but in a single shot version chambered for .223 and .22-250. Weight is 9 lbs.

NIB	Exc.	V.G.	Good	Fair	Poor
575	450	—	—	—	—

Model 12 FVSS

This model has a 26" stainless steel fluted barrel and a synthetic stock. Offered in .223, .22-250, and .308 calibers. Weight is about 9 lbs. Introduced in 1998. A left version is also offered.

NIB	Exc.	V.G.	Good	Fair	Poor
550	450	—	—	—	—

Model 12 FVSS-S

Same as above but in a single shot configuration chambered for .223 or .22-250. Weight is about 9 lbs.

NIB	Exc.	V.G.	Good	Fair	Poor
550	450	—	—	—	—

Model 12 FV (Short Action)

This model is similar to the other 12 Series rifles but with blued actions and 26" barrels that are nonfluted. Synthetic stock. Chambered for .223 or .22-250. Weight is about 9 lbs. Introduced in 1998. Offered in a left hand model.

NIB	Exc.	V.G.	Good	Fair	Poor
450	350	—	—	—	—

Model 12 VSS-Varminter (Short Action)

Introduced in 2000 this model features a Choate adjustable black synthetic stock. A heavy fluted stainless steel barrel. Box magazine holds 4 rounds. Chambered for .223 or .22-250 cartridges. Weight is approximately 15 lbs.

NIB	Exc.	V.G.	Good	Fair	Poor
850	650	—	—	—	—

MODEL 10 SERIES

Model 10 FP-Tactic (Short Action)

This is a short action model chambered for the .223 or .308 calibers. Fitted with a 24" barrel. Black synthetic stock. Drilled and tapped for scope mount. Weight is approximately 8 lbs. Introduced in 1998.

NIB	Exc.	V.G.	Good	Fair	Poor
475	350	275	200	—	—

Model 10 FLP

Same as above but in left hand.

NIB	Exc.	V.G.	Good	Fair	Poor
450	350	275	200	—	—

Model 10 FM-Sierra

This model features a 20" barrel chambered for .223, .243, or .308 calibers. Black synthetic stock. Magazine capacity is 4 rounds. Weight is approximately 6 lbs. Introduced in 1998.

NIB	Exc.	V.G.	Good	Fair	Poor
450	350	—	—	—	—

Model 10 FCM -Scout Rifle

Chambered for the 7mm-08 Rem. or .308 Win. cartridge this model is fitted with a 20" barrel, removable ghost ring rear sight, one piece scope mount, and other special features. Weight is about 6.2 lbs. Introduced in 1999.

NIB	Exc.	V.G.	Good	Fair	Poor
500	400	—	—	—	—

Model 10 GY-Youth

This model is similar to the Model 1-FM but features a shortened hardwood stock. It is fitted with a 22" barrel and has open sights. It is chambered for .223, .243, or .308 calibers. Weight is about 6.25 lbs. Introduced in 1998.

NIB	Exc.	V.G.	Good	Fair	Poor
375	300	—	—	—	—

MODEL 11 SERIES

Model 11 F

This model features a short action chambered for the .223, .22-250, .243, or .308 calibers. Barrel lengths are 22" with open sights. Black synthetic stock. Weight is approximately 6.75 lbs. Introduced in 1998.

NIB	Exc.	V.G.	Good	Fair	Poor
400	325	—	—	—	—

Model 11FL

Same as above but with left hand action.

NIB	Exc.	V.G.	Good	Fair	Poor
400	325	—	—	—	—

Model 11FNS

Same as Model 11F but without sights.

NIB	Exc.	V.G.	Good	Fair	Poor
400	325	—	—	—	—

Model 11G

Chambered for .223, .243, .22-250, or .308 calibers and fitted with a 22" barrel. Wood stock has fancy checkering pattern, black recoil pad, and a gold medallion. Fitted with open sights. Weight is about 6.75 lbs. Introduced in 1998.

NIB	Exc.	V.G.	Good	Fair	Poor
375	300	—	—	—	—

Model 11GL

Same as above but with left hand action.

NIB	Exc.	V.G.	Good	Fair	Poor
375	300	—	—	—	—

Model 11GNS

Same as above but without sights.

NIB	Exc.	V.G.	Good	Fair	Poor
375	300	—	—	—	—

MODEL 16 SERIES

Model 16FSS

This is a short action with a top-loading design and a magazine capacity of 4 rounds. Chambered for the .223, .243, or .308 calibers. Fitted with a 22" stainless steel barrel. Black synthetic stock. Introduced in 1998.

NIB	Exc.	V.G.	Good	Fair	Poor
525	425	—	—	—	—

Model 16FLSS

Same as above but with left hand action.

NIB	Exc.	V.G.	Good	Fair	Poor
525	425	—	—	—	—

RIMFIRE RIFLES

Model 60

A .22 caliber semiautomatic rifle with a 20" barrel, open sights, and tubular magazine. Blued with a Monte Carlo-style walnut stock. Manufactured between 1969 and 1972.

Exc.	V.G.	Good	Fair	Poor
100	80	70	50	35

Model 64G

Introduced in 1996 this semiautomatic .22 long rifle has a 20.25" barrel and 10-shot detachable magazine. The finish is blue and the stock has a Monte Carlo with checkered pistol grip. Bead front sight with adjustable open rear sight is standard. Weight is about 5.5 lbs.

NIB	Exc.	V.G.	Good	Fair	Poor
125	95	75	60	50	40

Model 64GXP

As above but with unmounted 4x15mm scope.

NIB	Exc.	V.G.	Good	Fair	Poor
150	120	100	80	60	50

Model 64-F

Introduced in 1997 this model features a black synthetic stock with blue finish. Chambered for .22 long rifle and fitted with a 20.25" barrel. Weight is approximately 5.5 lbs.

NIB	Exc.	V.G.	Good	Fair	Poor
140	120				

Model 64FV

Introduced in 1998 this model features a heavy 21" target barrel with no sights. A black synthetic stock is standard. Chambered for the .22LR cartridge. Weight is about 6 lbs.

NIB	Exc.	V.G.	Good	Fair	Poor
150	125	—	—	—	—

Model 64FXP

This is a package model that offers a .22LR gun with 20.25" barrel with detachable 10-round magazine. It comes with a 4x15mm scope as well as open sights. Introduced in 1998. Weight is about 5.25 lbs.

NIB	Exc.	V.G.	Good	Fair	Poor
120	100	—	—	—	—

Model 88

As above, with a hardwood stock. Manufactured between 1969 and 1972.

Exc.	V.G.	Good	Fair	Poor
100	80	70	50	35

Model 90 Carbine

As above, with a 16.5" barrel and carbine style stock having the forend secured to the barrel by a barrel band.

Exc.	V.G.	Good	Fair	Poor
100	80	70	50	35

Model 93G

Introduced in 1996 this model is a bolt action repeating rifle chambered for the .22 WMR cartridge. It is fitted with a 20.75" barrel with 5-shot magazine. It has a walnut stained hardwood stock with cut checkering. Open sights standard. Weight is about 5.75 lbs. In 2001 this model was offered in a left-hand version (Model 93GL).

NIB	Exc.	V.G.	Good	Fair	Poor
140	120	95	75	60	50

Model 93-FS

This .22 WMR model features a stainless steel finish with a 20.75" barrel and black synthetic stock. 5-round magazine.

Front bead sight and sporting rear sight. Introduced in 1997. Weight is about 5.5 lbs.

NIB	Exc.	V.G.	Good	Fair	Poor
175	150	—	—	—	—

Model 93FVSS

This model features a 21" heavy barrel chambered for the .22 WMR cartridge, recessed target muzzle and stainless steel barreled action. Equipped with black synthetic stock. Magazine capacity is 5 rounds. Weight is about 6 lbs. Introduced in 1998.

NIB	Exc.	V.G.	Good	Fair	Poor
200	150	—	—	—	—

Model 93F

Similar to the above model but with blued finish and a synthetic stock with open sights. Weight is approximately 5 lbs. Introduced in 1998.

NIB	Exc.	V.G.	Good	Fair	Poor
140	110	—	—	—	—

Model 30G "Stevens Favorite"

Based on the Stevens Favorite model this lever action single shot .22 caliber rifle is fitted with a 21" half octagonal barrel. Walnut stock with schnabel forend. Blued finish. Weight is about 4.25 lbs. Introduced in 1999.

NIB	Exc.	V.G.	Good	Fair	Poor
190	150	—	—	—	—

MARK I & II SERIES

Introduced in 1996 this series of .22 caliber rifles feature both single shot and repeating models. They are available in both right and left hand models.

Mark I-G

This is a bolt action single shot rifle chambered for the .22 short, long, or long rifle cartridges. It is fitted with a 20.75" barrel and has a cut checkered walnut finished stock. Bead front sight and open adjustable rear sight. Offered in both right and left hand models. Weight is about 5.5 lbs.

NIB	Exc.	V.G.	Good	Fair	Poor
125	100	80	70	60	50

Mark I-GY (Youth Model)

Same as above but fitted with a 19" barrel and shorter buttstock. Weight is about 5 lbs.

NIB	Exc.	V.G.	Good	Fair	Poor
125	100	80	70	60	50

Mark I-SB

This version of the Mark I is a smooth bore model made for .22 caliber shot cartridges. Barrel length is 20.75" and weight is about 5.5 lbs.

NIB	Exc.	V.G.	Good	Fair	Poor
1255	100	80	70	60	50

Mark II-G

This model is a bolt action repeater with 10 shot magazine. It is chambered for the .22 long rifle cartridge. Checkered walnut finished stock. Open sights. Barrel length is 20.75". Offered in both right and left hand versions. Weight is approximately 5.5 lbs.

NIB	Exc.	V.G.	Good	Fair	Poor
125	100	80	70	60	50

Mark II-GY (Youth Model)

Same as above but with 19" barrel and shorter stock.

NIB	Exc.	V.G.	Good	Fair	Poor
125	100	80	70	60	50

Mark II-GXP

Same as the Mark II-G model but includes an unmounted 4x15mm scope.

NIB	Exc.	V.G.	Good	Fair	Poor
130	100	80	70	60	50

Mark II-FSS

This is a stainless steel .22 caliber rifle with 20.75" barrel and 10-round magazine. Receiver is dovetailed for scope mounting. Stock is black synthetic. Weight is about 5 lbs.

NIB	Exc.	V.G.	Good	Fair	Poor
150	125	—	—	—	—

Mark II-LV

This .22 caliber is fitted with a 21" heavy barrel. It has a laminated hardwood stock with cut checkering. Blue finish and 10-round magazine. Weight is approximately 6.5 lbs. Introduced in 1997.

NIB	Exc.	V.G.	Good	Fair	Poor
200	150	—	—	—	—

Mark II-FV

Introduced in 1998 this model features a 21" heavy barrel with blue alloy steel receiver. Stock is black synthetic. Magazine capacity is 5-round detachable magazine. Weight is about 6 lbs.

NIB	Exc.	V.G.	Good	Fair	Poor
175	150	—	—	—	—

Mark II-F

This model has the standard Mark II barreled action with a black synthetic stock. Detachable 10-round magazine is standard. Weight is about 5 lbs. Introduced in 1998.

NIB	Exc.	V.G.	Good	Fair	Poor
120	100	—	—	—	—

Mark II-FXP

Similar to the Mark II-F but with a 4x15mm scope. Weight is approximately 5.25 lbs. First offered in 1998.

NIB	Exc.	V.G.	Good	Fair	Poor
125	100	—	—	—	—

Model 900 Series

First offered in 1996 this series consist of .22 caliber rimfire target rifles in various configurations. All are available in both right or left hand versions.

Model 900B-Biathlon

This rifle features a hardwood stock with 5-round magazine, carrying and shooting rails, butt hook, and hand stop. The barrel length is 21" and comes with a snow cover. Receiver sight are peep variety and the front sight has 7 aperture inserts as standard. Weight is about 8.25 lbs.

NIB	Exc.	V.G.	Good	Fair	Poor
475	400	350	250	200	150

Model 900 TR-Target

This model has a one piece hardwood stock with shooting rail and hand stop. Rear sight is adjustable peep and front sight has 7 aperture inserts. Barrel length is 25". Five-shot magazine is standard. Weight is about 8 lbs.

NIB	Exc.	V.G.	Good	Fair	Poor
400	325	275	225	175	125

Model 900S-Silhouette

This version features a 21" heavy barrel with recessed target style crown. Fitted with a one piece silhouette style stock with high comb and satin walnut finish. Receiver is drilled and tapped for scope mount. Weight is about 8 lbs.

NIB	Exc.	V.G.	Good	Fair	Poor
325	250	225	175	150	100

Model 210F

Introduced in 1996 this bolt action shotgun has a 24" rifled barrel for slugs. It is chambered for the 3" 12 gauge shell. No sights. Magazine holds 2 rounds. Weight is about 7.5 lbs.

NIB	Exc.	V.G.	Good	Fair	Poor
375	300	250	200	150	100

Model 24

An external hammer combination rifle/shotgun with 24" barrels. Blued with a walnut stock. Manufactured from 1950 to 1965 in a variety of styles. The standard chambering was .22 by .410.

Exc.	V.G.	Good	Fair	Poor
150	125	100	75	50

Model 24S-20 Gauge

Exc.	V.G.	Good	Fair	Poor
160	140	125	100	75

Model 24MS-22 Rimfire Magnum

Exc.	V.G.	Good	Fair	Poor
150	125	100	75	50

Model 24DL-Satin Chrome With Checkered Stock

Exc.	V.G.	Good	Fair	Poor
150	125	100	75	50

Model 24 Field-Lightweight Version

Exc.	V.G.	Good	Fair	Poor
175	150	125	100	75

Model 24C-Nickel Finish

Exc.	V.G.	Good	Fair	Poor
200	175	150	125	100

Model 24VS-.357 Magnum/20 Gauge, Nickel Finish

Exc.	V.G.	Good	Fair	Poor
250	200	175	150	125

Model 24F-DuPont Rynite Stock

NIB	Exc.	V.G.	Good	Fair	Poor
350	300	250	200	150	100

Model 2400

A combination 12 gauge by .222 or .308 caliber Over/Under rifle/shotgun with 23.5" barrels and a Monte Carlo-style stock. Made by Valmet and imported between 1975 and 1980.

Exc.	V.G.	Good	Fair	Poor
600	525	450	350	275

SAVAGE SHOTGUNS

Model 420

A 12, 16, or 20 gauge boxlock Over/Under shotgun with 26", 28", or 30" barrels, double triggers and extractors. Manufactured between 1937 and 1943.

Courtesy Nick Niles. Photo Paul Goodwin.

Exc.	V.G.	Good	Fair	Poor
500	400	300	200	150

Model 420 with Single Trigger

Exc.	V.G.	Good	Fair	Poor
500	400	300	200	150

Model 430

As above, with a checkered walnut stock and solid barrel rib. Produced from 1937 to 1943.

Courtesy Nick Niles. Photo Paul Goodwin.

Exc.	V.G.	Good	Fair	Poor
550	450	350	200	150

Model 430 with Single Trigger

Exc.	V.G.	Good	Fair	Poor
600	450	300	200	150

Model 320

This is a side-by-side model.

Exc.	V.G.	Good	Fair	Poor
800	650	500	400	300

Model 412-.410 Bore Adapter

Exc.	V.G.	Good	Fair	Poor
80	60	50	40	30

Model 412F-.410 Bore Adapter

Exc.	V.G.	Good	Fair	Poor
50	45	40	35	25

Model 220

A 12, 16, 20 or .410 bore boxlock single barrel shotgun with 26" to 32" barrels. Blued with a walnut stock. Manufactured between 1938 and 1965.

Exc.	V.G.	Good	Fair	Poor
100	80	70	50	35

Model 210FT

Introduced in 1997 this is a 12 gauge bolt action shotgun with a camouflage finish. Chambered for 3" shells and fitted with a 24" barrel. 2-round magazine. Approximate weight is 7.5 lbs. Drilled and tapped for scope mounting.

NIB	Exc.	V.G.	Good	Fair	Poor
400	325	—	—	—	—

Model 720

A 12 or 16 gauge semiautomatic shotgun with 26" to 32" barrels. Blued with a walnut stock. Manufactured between 1930 and 1949.

Exc.	V.G.	Good	Fair	Poor
300	250	200	150	100

Model 726 Upland Sporter

As above, with a 2-shot magazine. Manufactured between 1931 and 1949.

Exc.	V.G.	Good	Fair	Poor
300	250	200	150	100

Model 740C Skeet

The Model 726 with a 24.5" barrel having a Cutts compensator and skeet-style stock. Manufactured between 1936 and 1949.

Exc.	V.G.	Good	Fair	Poor
300	250	200	150	100

Model 745

The Model 720 in 12 gauge with an alloy receiver and 28" barrel. Manufactured between 1940 and 1949.

Exc.	V.G.	Good	Fair	Poor
275	225	175	125	75

Model 755

A 12 or 16 gauge semiautomatic shotgun with 26" to 30" barrels. Blued with a walnut stock. Also available with Savage Super Choke. Manufactured between 1949 and 1958.

Exc.	V.G.	Good	Fair	Poor
275	225	175	125	75

Model 775

As above, with an alloy receiver. Manufactured between 1950 and 1966.

Exc.	V.G.	Good	Fair	Poor
275	225	175	125	75

Model 750

A 12 gauge semiautomatic shotgun with a 26" or 28" barrel. The Model 750SC fitted with the Savage Super Choke and the Model 750AC with a Poly Choke. Blued with a walnut stock. Manufactured between 1960 and 1967.

Exc.	V.G.	Good	Fair	Poor
275	225	175	125	75

Model FA-1

This is Savage Fox semiautomatic shotgun imported from the Japanese marked KTG from 1981 to 1982. Offered in 12 gauge only with 28" or 30" vent rib barrels. Walnut stock with cut checkering. Magazine capacity is 4 rounds. Weight is about 7.5 lbs.

Exc.	V.G.	Good	Fair	Poor
350	300	250	200	150

Model FP-1

Similar to the above model but with 3" chambers and a 5-round magazine capacity.

Exc.	V.G.	Good	Fair	Poor
350	300	250	200	150

Model 21

This is a slide action shotgun built between 1920 and 1928. Chambered for 12 gauge with 26", 28", 30", or 32" barrel. Walnut pistol grip stock and slide handle. Takedown. Almost identical to the famous Winchester Model 12. Offered in a number of different configurations including standard grade, Trap grade, Tournament grade, and Riot Model. About 13,000 were built.

Exc.	V.G.	Good	Fair	Poor
350	300	250	200	150

Model 28

This slide action shotgun is an improved version of the Model 21. It was manufactured from 1928 to 1934. There are several variations of this gun including the Model 28-A, a standard grade; the Model 28-B, a standard grade with raised matted rib; a Model 28-C, a Riot gun; a Model 28-D, a Trap grade; and in 1931 a Model 28-3, an improved version with checkering and roll marked game scenes on the receiver.

Exc.	V.G.	Good	Fair	Poor
375	325	275	200	150

Model 30

A 12, 16, 20 or .410 bore slide action shotgun with 26" to 30" ventilated rib barrels. Blued with a walnut stock. Manufactured between 1958 and 1978.

Exc.	V.G.	Good	Fair	Poor
225	175	150	100	75

Model 242

A .410 bore boxlock double barrel over and under shotgun with 26" barrels, single trigger, extractors and exposed hammer. Manufactured between 1977 and 1981.

Courtesy Nick Niles. Photo Paul Goodwin

Exc.	V.G.	Good	Fair	Poor
375	300	250	200	150

Model 550

A 12 or 20 gauge boxlock side-by-side double barrel shotgun with 26", 28", or 30" barrels, single triggers and automatic ejectors. Blued with a hardwood stock. Manufactured between 1971 and 1973. Barrels were built by Valmet.

Courtesy Nick Niles. Photo Paul Goodwin

Exc.	V.G.	Good	Fair	Poor
500	400	300	200	150

Model 440

An Italian made 12 or 20 gauge boxlock Over/Under shotgun with 26", 28", or 30" ventilated rib barrels, single selective trigger and extractors. Blued with a walnut stock. Manufactured between 1968 and 1972.

Exc.	V.G.	Good	Fair	Poor
600	500	400	300	200

Model 440A

Courtesy Nick Niles. Photo Paul Goodwin

Exc.	V.G.	Good	Fair	Poor
600	500	400	300	200

Model 440B-T

Exc.	V.G.	Good	Fair	Poor
800	650	500	350	250

Model 444 Deluxe

As above, with a more finely figured stock and automatic ejectors. Imported between 1969 and 1972.

Exc.	V.G.	Good	Fair	Poor
550	475	400	300	225

Model 444

Exc.	V.G.	Good	Fair	Poor
600	500	400	300	200

Model 444B

Exc.	V.G.	Good	Fair	Poor
700	550	400	300	250

Model 440T

A 12 gauge Model 440 with 30" barrels and a trap style stock. Imported between 1969 and 1972.

Exc.	V.G.	Good	Fair	Poor
600	500	400	300	200

Model 330

A Valmet manufactured 12 or 20 gauge Over/Under shotgun with 26", 28", or 30" barrels, single selective trigger and extractors. Blued with a walnut stock. Imported between 1970 and 1978.

Courtesy Nick Niles. Photo Paul Goodwin

Exc.	V.G.	Good	Fair	Poor
800	650	500	350	250

Model 333

As above, with a ventilated rib and automatic ejectors. Imported between 1973 and 1980.

Exc.	V.G.	Good	Fair	Poor
700	550	400	300	200

Model 333T
As above, with a 30" barrel and trap style stock. Imported between 1972 and 1980.

Exc.	V.G.	Good	Fair	Poor
800	650	500	350	250

Model 312 Field O/U

Exc.	V.G.	Good	Fair	Poor
800	600	450	300	200

Model 312 Trap
Exc.	V.G.	Good	Fair	Poor
700	600	550	350	200

Model 312 Sporting Clay
Exc.	V.G.	Good	Fair	Poor
800	600	450	300	200

Model 320 Field
Exc.	V.G.	Good	Fair	Poor
800	600	450	300	200

(SAVAGE) FOX B MODELS
The Fox Model B was introduced about 1939 by Savage for the hunter who wanted better fit and finish than offered by the Stevens brand Model 530. It was made in many variations until 1988.

Fox Model B-Utica, NY
NIB	Exc.	V.G.	Good	Fair	Poor
1000	800	600	450	400	350

Fox Model B-Chicopee Falls, Mass. (later Westfield, Mass.)

Courtesy Nick Niles. Photo Paul Goodwin

NIB	Exc.	V.G.	Good	Fair	Poor
800	750	500	400	350	300

Fox Model B-Single Trigger
NIB	Exc.	V.G.	Good	Fair	Poor
900	800	600	500	400	300

Fox Model BDL
NIB	Exc.	V.G.	Good	Fair	Poor
1000	800	700	600	400	350

Fox Model BDE

Courtesy Nick Niles. Photo Paul Goodwin

NIB	Exc.	V.G.	Good	Fair	Poor
1000	800	700	600	400	350

Fox Model BST
NIB	Exc.	V.G.	Good	Fair	Poor
800	700	600	500	400	300

Fox Model BSE

Courtesy Nick Niles. Photo Paul Goodwin

NIB	Exc.	V.G.	Good	Fair	Poor
1000	750	650	550	450	350

Fox Model BE
NIB	Exc.	V.G.	Good	Fair	Poor
1000	800	600	450	400	350

PISTOLS

Model 1907
A .32 or .380 semiautomatic pistol with a 3.75" or 4.25" barrel depending upon caliber and a 9- or 10-shot magazine. Blued with hard rubber grips. The .380 caliber model is worth approximately 20% more than the values listed below.

Courtesy Orvel Reichert

Exc.	V.G.	Good	Fair	Poor
300	250	200	125	75

Model 1915

Similar to the above, except fitted with a grip safety and having an internal hammer. Manufactured between 1915 and 1917.

Courtesy Orvel Reichert

Exc.	V.G.	Good	Fair	Poor
375	300	250	150	100

Model 1917

As above, with an external hammer and without the grip safety. The form of the grip frame widened. Manufactured between 1917 and 1928.

Exc.	V.G.	Good	Fair	Poor
275	225	175	100	75

Model 6.35mm

A small number of .25 caliber Savage pistols were manufactured between 1915 and 1919. There were several variations. Magazine capacity was 6 to 7 rounds.

Courtesy James Rankin

Exc.	V.G.	Good	Fair	Poor
7000	5000	4000	2500	1000

Model 1905

Manufactured in 1905 in .45ACP this pistol was tested in the US Army trials. A few were sold commercially. It weighs 36 oz., and has an overall length of 9". Magazine capacity is 8 rounds.

Courtesy James Rankin

Exc.	V.G.	Good	Fair	Poor
5500	4500	3500	2000	1000

Model 101

.22 caliber single shot pistol resembling a revolver with a 5.5" barrel. Blued with hardwood grips. Manufactured between 1960 and 1968.

Exc.	V.G.	Good	Fair	Poor
175	150	125	90	75

500 HANDGUN SERIES

Introduced in 1998 this line of short action handguns feature a left hand bolt and a right hand ejection. All are fitted with an internal box magazine, composite stock and 14" barrel.

Model 501F-Sport Striker

This handgun is fitted with a left hand bolt and 10" free floating barrel. Detachable clip holds 10 rounds of .22 Long Rifle cartridges. Drilled and tapped for scope mount. Weight is about 4 lbs. Introduced in 2000.

NIB	Exc.	V.G.	Good	Fair	Poor
200	150	—	—	—	—

Model 502F-Sport Striker
Same as above but chambered for .22 WMR cartridge. Magazine capacity is 5 rounds. Introduced in 2000.

NIB	Exc.	V.G.	Good	Fair	Poor
220	170	—	—	—	—

Model 510F Striker
Blued barrel action and chambered for .22-250, .243, or .308 calibers. Weight is approximately 5 lbs.

NIB	Exc.	V.G.	Good	Fair	Poor
400	325	—	—	—	—

Model 516FSS
Similar to the model above but with stainless steel barreled action.

NIB	Exc.	V.G.	Good	Fair	Poor
450	350	—	—	—	—

Model 516FSAK
Features a stainless steel barreled action with adjustable muzzle brake.

NIB	Exc.	V.G.	Good	Fair	Poor
500	400	—	—	—	—

Model 516BSS
Fitted with a laminated thumbhole stock, left hand bolt for right hand ejection, 14" barrel. This model is chambered for the .223, .243, 7mm-08 Rem., .260 Rem., and .308 Win. calibers. Magazine capacity is 2 rounds. Weight is about 5 lbs. Introduced in 1999.

NIB	Exc.	V.G.	Good	Fair	Poor
550	450	—	—	—	—

Model 516BSAK
Similar to the model above but chambered for the .223 or 22-250 cartridges. The 14" barrel is fitted with an adjustable muzzle brake. Introduced in 1999.

NIB	Exc.	V.G.	Good	Fair	Poor
600	475	—	—	—	—

SAVAGE & NORTH
Middletown, Connecticut

Figure 8 Revolver
A .36 caliber percussion revolver with a 7" octagonal barrel and 6-shot cylinder. The barrel marked "E. Savage, Middletown. CT./H.S. North. Patented June 17, 1856." The four models of this revolver are as follows: (1) With a rounded brass frame, and the mouths of the chamber fitting into the end of the barrel breech; (2) with a rounded iron frame and a modified loading lever that is marked "H.S. North, Patented April 6, 1858"; (3) with a flat-sided brass frame having a round recoil shield; (4) with an iron frame. Approximately 400 of these revolvers were manufactured between 1856 and 1859.

Courtesy Butterfield & Butterfield

First Model

Exc.	V.G.	Good	Fair	Poor
—	—	15000	6500	1500

Second Model

Exc.	V.G.	Good	Fair	Poor
—	—	8500	3500	850

Third Model

Exc.	V.G.	Good	Fair	Poor
—	—	8500	3500	850

Fourth Model

Exc.	V.G.	Good	Fair	Poor
—	—	9500	4000	1000

SAVAGE REVOLVING FIREARMS CO.
Middletown, Connecticut

Navy Revolver
A .36 caliber double action percussion revolver with a 7" octagonal barrel and 6-shot cylinder. The frame marked "Savage R.F.A. Co./H.S. North Patented June 17, 1856/Jan. 18, 1859, May 15, 1860." Approximately 20,000 were manufactured between 1861 and 1865, of which about 12,000 were purchased by the U.S. Government.

Courtesy Milwaukee Public Museum, Milwaukee, Wisconsin

Exc.	V.G.	Good	Fair	Poor
—	—	3750	1500	700

SCATTERGUN TECHNOLOGIES
Formerly-Nashville, Tennessee
Berryville, Arkansas

NOTE: In 1999 Scattergun Technologies was purchased by Wilson Combat and became a division of Wilson Combat. As of that date Wilson Combat Scattergun Technologies firearms will have the Berryville, Arkansas address stamped on the receiver.

TR-870
This model is based on the Remington Model 870 slide action shotgun. It is offered in a wide variety of configurations with different features. The standard model is fitted with an 18" barrel and chambered for the 12 gauge shell. The stock is composite with recoil pad. Tactical forend has flashlight built in. Ghost ring rear sight. Front sight has tritium insert. Six-round shell carrier on left side of receiver. Introduced in 1991. Weight for standard model is approximately 9 lbs. Prices listed below are for the standard model.

NIB	Exc.	V.G.	Good	Fair	Poor
800	650	550	—	—	—

Wilson Combat Current Production Models

Standard Model
Based on the Remington 12 gauge 3" 870 Magnum this model is fitted with an 18" barrel with cylinder bore. Adjustable Ghost ring rear sight with tritium front sight. Seven round extended magazine. Side saddle shell carrier. Synthetic stock. Tactical sling is standard. Parkerized finish. Fitted with a SURE-FIRE tactical light.

NIB	Exc.	V.G.	Good	Fair	Poor
875	650	—	—	—	—

NOTE: Add $100 for Armor-Tuff finish.

Border Patrol Model
Similar to the standard model but without the tactical light. A 14" barrel is offered on this model but all NFA rules apply to the purchase of a short barrel shotgun.

NIB	Exc.	V.G.	Good	Fair	Poor
675	500	—	—	—	—

NOTE: Add $100 for Armor-Tuff finish.

Professional Model
This model features all of the standard model components but it is fitted with a 14" barrel. Magazine capacity is 6 rounds. All NFA rules apply to purchase of short barrel shotgun.

NIB	Exc.	V.G.	Good	Fair	Poor
900	675	—	—	—	—

NOTE: Add $100 for Armor-Tuff finish.

Entry Model
This model has all the features of the standard model butt is fitted with a 12.5" barrel. Magazine capacity is 5 rounds. All NFA rules apply to the purchase of a short barrel shotgun.

NIB	Exc.	V.G.	Good	Fair	Poor
950	700	—	—	—	—

NOTE: Add $100 for Armor-Tuff finish.

K-9 Model
This model is built on a Remington 12 gauge 3" 1187 Magnum semiautomatic. Fitted with Ghost ring rear sights and tritium front sight. Extended magazine holds 7 rounds. Barrel is 18". Synthetic stock with side saddle shell carrier. Parkerized finish.

NIB	Exc.	V.G.	Good	Fair	Poor
1075	800	—	—	—	—

NOTE: Add $100 for Armor-Tuff finish.

SWAT Model
Similar to the K-9 model but fitted with a tactical light and 14" barrel. All NFA rules apply to the purchase of a short barrel shotgun.

NIB	Exc.	V.G.	Good	Fair	Poor
1350	1000	—	—	—	—

NOTE: Add $100 for Armor-Tuff finish.

SCHALK, G. S.
Pottsville, Pennsylvania

Rifle Musket
A .58 caliber percussion rifle with a 40" round barrel and full length stock secured by three barrel bands. The barrel marked "G. Schalk Poftsville 1861." Finished in white with a walnut stock. Approximately 100 were manufactured.

Courtesy Milwaukee Public Museum, Milwaukee, Wisconsin

Exc.	V.G.	Good	Fair	Poor
—	—	6250	3000	750

SCHALL & CO.
New Haven, Connecticut

Manufactured the Fiala repeating pistol for Fiala. Later after Fiala's bankruptcy Schall provided parts, repair service, and produced repeating pistols with the Schall name.

Repeating Pistol
A .22 caliber pistol with 10-shot magazine. Tapered 7.5" barrel with fixed sights and blued finish. Rear sight is much simpler than those of the Fiala. Grips are wood with ribs running lengthwise. Typically marked "SCHALL & CO./NEW HAVEN, CONN USA" but guns exist with no markings.

Courtesy Dr. Jon Miller

Courtesy Dr. Jon Miller

Exc.	V.G.	Good	Fair	Poor
600	400	325	250	175

SCHMIDT, HERBERT
Ostheim, West Germany

Model 11, Liberty 11, and Eig Model E-8
A .22 caliber double action revolver with a 2.5" barrel and 6-shot cylinder. Blued with plastic grips.

Exc.	V.G.	Good	Fair	Poor
100	70	50	40	25

Model 11 Target
As above, with a 5.5" barrel and adjustable sights.

Exc.	V.G.	Good	Fair	Poor
125	90	55	45	30

Frontier Model or Texas Scout
.22 caliber revolver with a 5" barrel and 6-shot cylinder. Blued with plastic grips.

Exc.	V.G.	Good	Fair	Poor
100	70	50	40	25

SCHMIDT, E. & COMPANY
Houston, Texas

Pocket Pistol
A .45 caliber percussion single shot pistol with a 2.5" barrel, German silver mounts and walnut stock. The barrel marked "E. Schmidt & Co. Houston." Manufactured between 1866 and 1870. Prospective purchasers are advised to secure a qualified appraisal prior to acquisition.

Exc.	V.G.	Good	Fair	Poor
—	—	8250	4000	1000

SCHMIDT-RUBIN
Neuhausen, Switzerland

NOTE: For history, technical data, descriptions, and photos see the *Standard Catalog of Military Firearms, 1870 to the Present* under Switzerland.

SCHNEIDER & CO.
Memphis, Tennessee

Pocket Pistol
A .41 caliber single shot percussion pocket pistol with a 3.5" octagonal barrel, iron or German silver mounts and a walnut stock. The lock marked "Schneider & Co./Memphis, Tenn." Manufactured 1859 and 1860.

Exc.	V.G.	Good	Fair	Poor
—	—	4250	1850	650

SCHNEIDER & GLASSICK
Memphis, Tennessee

Pocket Pistols

A .41 caliber percussion pocket pistol with a 2.5" barrel, German silver mounts and walnut stock. The barrel marked "Schneider & Glassick, Memphis, Tenn." Manufactured 1860 to 1862.

Exc.	V.G.	Good	Fair	Poor
—	—	4500	2250	800

SCHOUBOE
See Dansk Rekylriffel Syndikat

SCHULER, AUGUST
Suhl, Germany

Reform

A 6.35mm caliber four barreled pocket pistol with 2.5" barrels. The barrel unit rises as the trigger is pulled. Blued with walnut or hard rubber grips. Manufactured between 1907 and 1914.

Exc.	V.G.	Good	Fair	Poor
850	750	650	450	300

SCHULTZ & LARSEN
Ofterup, Denmark

Model 47 Match Rifle

A .22 caliber single shot bolt action rifle with a 28" barrel, adjustable sights and adjustable trigger. Blued with an ISU style stock.

Exc.	V.G.	Good	Fair	Poor
800	650	550	400	250

Model 61 Match Rifle

As above, but fitted with a palm rest.

Exc.	V.G.	Good	Fair	Poor
1000	850	750	600	300

Model 62 Match Rifle

Similar to the above, but manufactured for centerfire cartridges.

Exc.	V.G.	Good	Fair	Poor
1250	900	750	650	350

Model 54 Free Rifle

Similar to the above, with a 27" barrel and ISU stock.

Exc.	V.G.	Good	Fair	Poor
950	800	700	550	300

Model 68 DL

A .22-250 to .458 Winchester Magnum bolt action rifle with a 24" barrel, adjustable trigger and well figured walnut stock.

Exc.	V.G.	Good	Fair	Poor
850	700	600	450	200

SCHWARZLOSE, ANDREAS
Berlin, Germany

Military Model 96

A 7.63 Mauser caliber semiautomatic pistol with a 6.5" barrel, 7-shot magazine and adjustable rear sight. Blued with walnut grips.

Exc.	V.G.	Good	Fair	Poor
5000	3000	2250	1500	700

Model 08

A 7.65mm semiautomatic pistol with a 4" barrel and 7-shot magazine. The right side of the frame stamped "Schwarlose" over a machine gun. Blued with plastic grips.

Exc.	V.G.	Good	Fair	Poor
500	400	350	300	200

SCOTT, W. C., LTD.
Birmingham, England
SEE—British Double Arms

SEARCY & MOORE
Hogans Creek, Guilford County, North Carolina

Alexander M. Searcy and Dr. J.S. Moore founded this firm in 1862. They were awarded a contract from the State of North Carolina for rifles. Out of the 500 ordered, 105 were delivered in three styles. First 15 had tumblerless locks in .50 caliber; 49 had "improved" or standard locks; and 41 had standard locks in .577 caliber. Rifles of the final style had overall lengths of 48-1/2", and barrel lengths of 33". Locks are marked "SC/1863". Serial numbered internally, as well as on the top of the barrel and top of the breech plug tang.

Prospective purchasers are strongly advised to secure an expert appraisal prior to acquisition.

Exc.	V.G.	Good	Fair	Poor
—	—	9000	5000	3000

SEARS, ROEBUCK & CO. BRAND
Chicago, Illinois

Double Barrel Shotguns

Between 1892 and 1988 the world's largest mail order house carried a huge inventory of sporting doubleguns including any foreign and domestic brands whose makers did not object to Sears' famous price discounts. To increase sales volume, however, Sears also created its own brands which they supported with innovative design, extravagant advertising claims, unbeatable pricing and excellent quality control. These doubles, like many other firearms products handled by Sears, were listed in its very detailed semiannual catalog from about 1892, when the company first offered doubleguns, until about 1988 when social and political pressures made the company stop handling firearms.

Sears marketing people gave birth to and successfully exploited many house and private brands which we no longer associate with Sears at all. In fact, many of these brands clearly rollmarked on guns are now unfamiliar to many collectors. Frequently seen and important in the market segment which many might describe as affordable doubles are some of the most often seen Sears trade names or brands. Listed in chronological order: T. Barker, S.R. & Co., Triumph, Thomas Barker, Sam Holt, Chicago Long Range Wonder, American Bar Lock, Meriden Fire Arms Co., Norwich, A. J. Arbrey Gun Co., New England, Gladiator, Berkshire, Ranger, Eastern Arms Co., J.C. Higgins, Sears, and Ted Williams. These guns were of good quality but sold at bargain prices which gave them tremendous appeal. They were made for Sears to Sears specifications by a number of American firms and a few foreign ones as well, all of which produced excellent shotguns under their own names. among the best known American companies were J. Stevens, Savage Arms, A.H. Fox, N.R. Davis, Crescent Firearms, Ithaca, A. Fyrberg, Colton Mfg. Co., Marlin, Hunter Gun Co., Baker Gun Co., and probably a few others. among the foreign makers were AYA, H. Pieper, Janssen, SKB, Rossi, CBC, and A. Zoli.

Sears customers were not aware of this but they did trust Sears name and brought many millions of these shotguns over nearly a hundred years Sears was in the business. Today these guns are becoming recognized as interesting and valuable collectibles in their own special niche. their values range from $100 to $3,500 or more depending on make, model, decoration, in any, and relative rarity. There will be more information forthcoming in subsequent editions of the Catalog.

SEAVER, E.R.
New York, New York

Pocket Pistol

A .41 caliber percussion pocket pistol with a 2.5" barrel, German silver mounts and a walnut stock.

Exc.	V.G.	Good	Fair	Poor
—	—	1750	900	400

SECURITY INDUSTRIES
Little Ferry, New Jersey

Model PSS

A .38 Special double action revolver with a 2" barrel, fixed sights and 5-shot cylinder. Stainless steel with walnut grips. Manufactured between 1973 and 1978.

Exc.	V.G.	Good	Fair	Poor
200	150	125	100	75

Model PM357

As above, with a 2.5" barrel and in .357 Magnum caliber. Manufactured between 1975 and 1978.

Exc.	V.G.	Good	Fair	Poor
250	200	175	150	100

Model PPM357

As above, with a 2" barrel and a hammer without a finger spur. Manufactured between 1975 and 1978.

Exc.	V.G.	Good	Fair	Poor
250	200	175	150	100

SEDCO INDUSTRIES, INC.
Lake Elsinore, California

Model SP22

A .22 caliber semiautomatic pistol with a 2.5" barrel. Blackened or nickel-plated with plastic grips. Introduced in 1989.

NIB	Exc.	V.G.	Good	Fair	Poor
100	70	60	50	35	25

TH. SEDERE
SEE—Austrian Military Firearms

SEDGELY, R. F., INC.
Philadelphia, Pennsylvania

R.F. Sedgely produced specialized bolt action rifles using the Model 1903 Springfield action. As these arms were for the most part custom order pieces, it is impossible to provide standardized values. It should be noted that his prime engraver was Rudolph J. Kornbrath.

Sedgely also made a .22 caliber hammerless pistol. **SEE-KOLB.**

SEECAMP, L. W. CO., INC.
Milford, Connecticut

LWS .25 ACP Model

A .25 caliber semiautomatic pistol with a 2" barrel, fixed sights and 7-shot magazine. Stainless steel with plastic grips. Approximately 5,000 were manufactured between 1982 and 1985.

NIB	Exc.	V.G.	Good	Fair	Poor
500	400	300	200	150	100

LWS .32 ACP Model

A .32 caliber double action semiautomatic pistol with a 2" barrel and 6-shot magazine. Matte or polished stainless steel with plastic grips.

NIB	Exc.	V.G.	Good	Fair	Poor
750	650	500	400	200	150

Matched Pair

A matched set of the above, with identical serial numbers. A total of 200 sets were made prior to 1968.

Exc.	V.G.	Good	Fair	Poor
900	800	700	500	350

LWS .380 Model

Same as the .32 caliber but chambered for the .380 cartridge. Essential the same weight and dimensions as the .32 caliber pistol. Introduced in 1999.

NIB	Exc.	V.G.	Good	Fair	Poor
750	650	—	—	—	—

NOTE: Seecamp pistols are entirely handmade and as such production is very limited. There may be periods where demand has outstriped supply and prices will rise accordingly.

SEMMERLING
Waco, Texas
SEE—American Derringer Corporation

SHARPS RIFLE
MANUFACTURING COMPANY
Hartford, Connecticut

The first Sharps rifles to be manufactured were made by A.S. Nippes of Mill Creek, Pennsylvania. Later they were made by Robbins & Lawrence of Windsor, Vermont. It was not until 1855 that Sharps established his own factory in Hartford, Connecticut. After his death in 1874, the company was reorganized as the Sharps Rifle Company and remained in Hartford until 1876 when it moved to Bridgeport, Connecticut. It effectively ceased operations in 1880.

NOTE: Sharps rifles and carbines were produced in an almost endless variety. Collectors should note that particular features and calibers can drastically affect the value of any given Sharps. They are, therefore, strongly advised to read: *Frank Sellers, Sharps Firearms* (North Hollywood, California: 1978).

The following descriptions are just a brief guide and are by no means exhaustive.

Model 1849

A breechloading .44 caliber percussion rifle with a 30" barrel having a wooden cleaning rod mounted beneath it. The breech is activated by the triggerguard lever, and there is an automatic disk-type capping device on the right side of the receiver. The finish is blued and case colored. The stock is walnut with a brass patch box, buttplate, and forend cap. It is marked "Sharps Patent 1848." There were approximately 200 manufactured in 1849 and 1850 by the A.S. Nippes Company.

Exc.	V.G.	Good	Fair	Poor
—	—	15000	6500	1500

Model 1850

As above, with a Maynard priming mechanism mounted on the breech. Marked "Sharps Patent 1848" on the breech and the barrel "Manufactured by A.S. Nippes Mill Creek, Pa." The priming device marked "Maynard Patent 1845." There were approximately 200 manufactured in 1850. This model is also known as the 2nd Model Sharps.

Exc.	V.G.	Good	Fair	Poor
—	—	10500	4750	1000

Model 1851 Carbine

A single shot breechloading percussion rifle in .36, .44, or .52 caliber with a 21.75" barrel and Maynard tape priming device. Blued and case hardened with a walnut stock and forearm held on by a single barrel band. The buttplate and barrel band are brass, and the military versions feature a brass patch box. The tang marked "C. Sharps Patent 1848," the barrel "Robbins & Lawrence," and the priming device "Edward Maynard Patentee 1845." Approximately 1,800 carbines and 180 rifles were manufactured by Robbins & Lawrence in Windsor, Vermont, in 1851. Those bearing U.S. inspection marks are worth approximately 75% more than the values listed below.

Courtesy Milwaukee Public Museum, Milwaukee, Wisconsin

Exc.	V.G.	Good	Fair	Poor
—	—	8000	3750	1000

Model 1852

Similar to the above, but with Sharps' Patent Pellet Primer. The barrel marked "Sharps Rifle Manufg. Co. Hartford, Conn." Blued, case hardened, brass furniture and a walnut stock. Manufactured in carbine, rifle, sporting rifle and shotgun form. Approximately 4,600 carbines and 600 rifles were made between 1853 and 1855.

Military Carbine

Courtesy Butterfield & Butterfield

Exc.	V.G.	Good	Fair	Poor
—	—	6000	2750	750

Military Rifle-27" Barrel, Bayonet Lug

Exc.	V.G.	Good	Fair	Poor
—	—	8500	4000	1000

Sporting Rifle

Exc.	V.G.	Good	Fair	Poor
—	—	3750	1500	500

Shotgun

Exc.	V.G.	Good	Fair	Poor
—	—	3000	1250	500

Model 1853

As above, but without the spring retainer for the lever hinge being mounted in the forestock. Approximately 10,500 carbines and 3,000 rifles were made between 1854 and 1858.

Military Carbine

Courtesy Milwaukee Public Museum, Milwaukee, Wisconsin

Exc.	V.G.	Good	Fair	Poor
—	—	6250	2750	750

Military Rifle

Exc.	V.G.	Good	Fair	Poor
—	—	7500	3500	850

Sporting Rifle

Courtesy Butterfield & Butterfield

Exc.	V.G.	Good	Fair	Poor
—	—	2750	1250	450

Shotgun

Courtesy Butterfield & Butterfield

Exc.	V.G.	Good	Fair	Poor
—	—	2500	1000	450

Model 1855

As above, in .52 caliber and fitted with a Maynard tape primer that is marked "Edward Maynard Patentee 1845." Approximately 700 were made between 1855 and 1856.

Exc.	V.G.	Good	Fair	Poor
—	—	10500	4250	1000

Model 1855 U.S. Navy Rifle

As above, with a 28" barrel, full-length stock and bearing U.S. Navy inspection marks. Approximately 260 were made in 1855.

Courtesy Milwaukee Public Museum, Milwaukee, Wisconsin

Exc.	V.G.	Good	Fair	Poor
—	—	9000	4000	1000

Model 1855 British Carbine

The Model 1855 with British inspection marks. Approximately 6,800 were made between 1855 and 1857.

Courtesy Milwaukee Public Museum, Milwaukee, Wisconsin

Exc.	V.G.	Good	Fair	Poor
—	—	6000	3000	850

SHARPS STRAIGHT BREECH MODELS

Similar to the above models, but with the breech opening cut on an almost vertical angle.

Model 1859 Carbine-22" Barrel, Brass Mountings

Courtesy Milwaukee Public Museum, Milwaukee, Wisconsin

Exc.	V.G.	Good	Fair	Poor
—	—	5750	2000	500

Model 1859 Carbine-Iron Mountings

Courtesy Milwaukee Public Museum, Milwaukee, Wisconsin

Exc.	V.G.	Good	Fair	Poor
—	—	3250	1500	500

Model 1863 Carbine

Courtesy Mike Stuckslager

Exc.	V.G.	Good	Fair	Poor
—	—	3250	1500	500

Model 1865 Carbine

Exc.	V.G.	Good	Fair	Poor
—	—	3750	1750	500

Model 1859 Rifle-30" Barrel

Exc.	V.G.	Good	Fair	Poor
—	—	4250	2000	800

Model 1859 Rifle-36" Barrel

Exc.	V.G.	Good	Fair	Poor
—	—	4250	2000	800

Model 1863 Rifle-Without Bayonet Lug

Exc.	V.G.	Good	Fair	Poor
—	—	3750	1500	500

Model 1865 Rifle-Without Bayonet Lug

Exc.	V.G.	Good	Fair	Poor
—	—	3250	1000	500

A Sharps Model 1865 Carbine was sold at auction for $8,625. Chambered for .52 caliber and fitted with a 22" barrel. Only 5,000 of these carbines were built. Not converted. 90% original blue. 95% case colors. Amoskeag Auction Company, August 2001

Sporting Rifle

As above, with octagonal barrels, set triggers and finely figured walnut stocks.

Exc	V.G.	Good	Fair	Poor
—	—	5000	2000	700

Coffee-Mill Model

Some Sharps' carbines were fitted with coffee-mill style grinding devices set into their buttstocks. **CAUTION**. These arms are exceptionally rare and extreme caution should be exercised prior to purchase.

Courtesy Milwaukee Public Museum, Milwaukee, Wisconsin

Exc.	V.G.	Good	Fair	Poor
—	—	32500	12500	—

Metallic Cartridge Conversions

In 1867 approximately 32,000 Model 1859, 1863 and 1865 Sharps were altered to .52-70 rimfire and centerfire caliber.

Courtesy Mike Stuckslager

Exc.	V.G.	Good	Fair	Poor
—	—	3000	1000	500

A Sharps New Model 1863 Metallic Cartridge Conversions sold at auction for $2,750. Fitted with a 22" round barrel and military marked. Condition was good. Amoskeag Auction Company, January 1999

Model 1869

A .40-50 to .50-70 caliber model produced in a military form with 26", 28", or 30" barrels; as a carbine with 21" or 24" barrels and in a sporting version with various barrel lengths and a forend stock fitted with a pewter tip. Approximately 650 were made.

Carbine - .50-70, Saddle Ring on Frame

Exc.	V.G.	Good	Fair	Poor
—	—	3750	1750	500

Military Rifle - .50-70, 30" Barrel With Three Barrel Bands

Exc.	V.G.	Good	Fair	Poor
—	—	5000	2000	800

Sporting Rifle - 26" Barrel, .44-77 and .50-70

Exc.	V.G.	Good	Fair	Poor
—	—	6000	2750	950

WHAT'S IT LIKE-THE SHARPS SINGLE-SHOT RIFLE

Operate the lever on a 1874 Sharps opening up the action and revealing that cavernous chamber and barrel. Retrieve a .45-110 black powder cartridge round from your canvas web belt. Slowly close the lever. Cock the large Sharps hammer. Adjust the elevation on the tang-mounted rear sight. Center the bead front sight in the rear aperture and place it on the target. Slowly squeeze the trigger. Ka-Booooom! Your shoulder is shoved backwards, black powder smoke surrounds you. You may not be Matthew Quigley, but if you can go through all this without having your heart, mind, soul, and spirit deeply stirred you are in deep trouble! The number one use of the Sharps 125 years ago was for the hunting of buffalo. I would guess that most people today, when they pick up a Sharps, still receive a vision of vast herds of buffalo roaming over endless acres of prairie grass. The buffalo are mostly gone, however, thanks to companies such as Shiloh Sharps, C. Sharps Arms, and Pedersoli, replicas of the Sharps rifles are available today, although pricey they may be. Not only are Sharps rifles available, thanks to Black Powder Cartridge Shooting we actually have a sound reason for owning one. There are also a few private herds of buffalo still around and I hope to someday use my Shiloh .45-110 to take an old bull. It is also powerful enough to take care of any other animal I may choose to hunt. If you think the old guns were not that accurate take a good look at what a black powder cartridge shooter can do with one and a good pair of cross sticks shooting at 500 yards. One important thing to remember: if you want the greatest benefit to heart, mind, soul, and spirit when shooting a Sharps rifle please do not commit blasphemy by loading one with anything but black powder.

John Taffin

Model 1870 Springfield Altered

Chambered for .50-70 caliber and fitted with a 35.5" barrel with two barrel bands, walnut stock, case hardened lock and breechlock. Buttplate stamped "US". Also built for Army trials with 22" barrel converted to centerfire.

First Type-most common, straight breech

Courtesy Butterfield & Butterfield

Exc.	V.G.	Good	Fair	Poor
—	—	3250	1500	500

Second Type-Model 1874 action, serial #1 to 300

Exc.	V.G.	Good	Fair	Poor
—	—	5000	2250	750

Carbine-22" barrel converted to centerfire

Exc.	V.G.	Good	Fair	Poor
—	—	7500	4250	900

Model 1874

This model was manufactured in a variety of calibers, barrel lengths, and stock styles. The barrel markings are of three forms: initially, "Sharps Rifle Manufg. Co. Hartford, Conn."; then, "Sharps Rifle Co. Hartford, Conn."; and finally "Sharps Rifle Co. Bridgeport, Conn." As of 1876 "Old Reliable" was stamped on the barrels. This marking is usually found on Bridgeport-marked rifles only. The major styles of this model are as follows:

Military Carbine - .50-70, 21" Barrel (460 made)

Exc.	V.G.	Good	Fair	Poor
—	—	5000	2750	750

Military Rifle

In .45-70 and .50-70 centerfire caliber with a 30" barrel and full-length forend secured by three barrel bands. Approximately 1,800 made.

Courtesy Dennis Callender

Exc.	V.G.	Good	Fair	Poor
—	—	4250	2000	800

Hunter's Rifle

In .40, .44, .45-70, and .50-70 caliber with 26", 28", or 30" round barrels having open sights. Approximately 600 were manufactured.

Exc.	V.G.	Good	Fair	Poor
—	—	6000	2750	800

Business Rifle

In .40-70 and .45-75 Sharps caliber with a 26", 28", or 30" round barrel, adjustable sights and double-set triggers. Approximately 1,600 manufactured.

Courtesy Mike Stuckslager

Exc.	V.G.	Good	Fair	Poor
—	—	5000	2750	750

Sporting Rifle

Offered in a variety of calibers, barrel lengths, barrel weights, barrel styles and stock styles. Approximately 6,000 were manufactured.

Courtesy Milwaukee Public Museum, Milwaukee, Wisconsin

Exc.	V.G.	Good	Fair	Poor
—	—	8000	3500	750

Creedmoor Rifle

With a checkered pistol grip stock, vernier sights, combination wind gauge and spirit level front sight, set trigger and shotgun style butt. Approximately 150 were made.

Exc.	V.G.	Good	Fair	Poor
—	—	17500	6500	1500

Mid-Range Rifle

Similar to the above, with a crescent buttplate. Approximately 180 were made.

Courtesy Butterfield & Butterfield

Exc.	V.G.	Good	Fair	Poor
—	—	10500	5000	1500

Long-Range Rifle

As above with a 34" octagonal barrel. Approximately 425 were manufactured.

Exc.	V.G.	Good	Fair	Poor
—	—	14000	6000	1500

Schuetzen Rifle

Similar to the above, with a checkered pistol grip stock and forend, a large Schuetzen style buttplate, double-set triggers and a vernier tang sight. Approximately 70 were manufactured.

Courtesy Butterfield & Butterfield

Exc.	V.G.	Good	Fair	Poor
—	—	12500	5500	2000

Model 1877

Similar to the Model 1874, and in .45-70 caliber with a 34" or 36" barrel which is marked "Sharps Rifle Co. Bridgeport, Conn. Old Reliable." Approximately 100 were manufactured in 1877 and 1878.

Exc.	V.G.	Good	Fair	Poor
—	25000	10000	5000	2000

Model 1878 Sharps-Borchardt

An internal hammer breechloading rifle manufactured from 1878 to approximately 1880. The frame marked "Borchardt Patent Sharps Rifle Co. Bridgeport Conn. U.S.A."

Carbine

Approximately 385 were made in .45-70 caliber with a 24" barrel. The forend is secured by one barrel band.

Courtesy Milwaukee Public Museum, Milwaukee, Wisconsin

Exc.	V.G.	Good	Fair	Poor
—	—	3750	1500	500

Military Rifle

Approximately 12,000 were made in .45-70 caliber with 32.25" barrels and full stocks secured by two barrel bands.

Courtesy Butterfield & Butterfield

Exc.	V.G.	Good	Fair	Poor
—	2750	1250	600	300

Sporting Rifle

Approximately 1,600 were made in .45-70 caliber with 30" round or octagonal barrels.

Exc.	V.G.	Good	Fair	Poor
—	5000	2000	800	500

Hunter's Rifle

Approximately 60 were made in .40 caliber with 26" barrels and plain walnut stocks.

Exc.	V.G.	Good	Fair	Poor
—	4000	1500	700	500

Business Rifle

Approximately 90 were made with 28" barrels in .40 caliber.

Exc.	V.G.	Good	Fair	Poor
—	4000	1500	700	500

Officer's Rifle

Approximately 50 were made in .45-70 caliber with 32" barrels and checkered walnut stocks.

Exc.	V.G.	Good	Fair	Poor
—	6500	3750	1000	500

Express Rifle

Approximately 30 were made in .45-70 caliber with 26" barrels, set triggers and checkered walnut stocks.

Exc.	V.G.	Good	Fair	Poor
—	9500	5000	1750	750

Short-Range Rifle

Approximately 155 were made in .40 caliber with 26" barrels, vernier rear sights, wind gauge front sight and a checkered walnut stock.

Exc.	V.G.	Good	Fair	Poor
—	7500	3750	1000	600

Mid-Range Rifle

Similar to the above, with a 30" barrel. Approximately 250 were manufactured.

Exc.	V.G.	Good	Fair	Poor
—	6500	3750	1000	600

Long-Range Rifle

Similar to the above, with different sights. Approximately 230 were manufactured.

Exc.	V.G.	Good	Fair	Poor
—	12500	5000	1750	800

C. Sharps & Company and Sharps & Hankins Company Breech-Loading, Single-Shot Pistol

A .31, .34, or .36 caliber breechloading percussion pistol with 5" or 6.5" round barrels. Blued, case hardened with walnut stock.

Courtesy Buffalo Bill Historical Center, Cody, Wyoming

Exc.	V.G.	Good	Fair	Poor
—	—	4000	1750	600

Pistol-Grip Rifle

A .31 or .38 caliber breechloading percussion rifle resembling the above. Manufactured in a variety of barrel lengths. Blued, case hardened with a walnut stock having German silver mounts.

Courtesy Butterfield & Butterfield

Exc.	V.G.	Good	Fair	Poor
—	—	4250	1750	750

Percussion Revolver

A .25 caliber percussion revolver with a 3" octagonal barrel and 6-shot cylinder. Blued with walnut grips. The barrel marked "C. Sharps & Co., Phila. Pa." Approximately 2,000 were manufactured between 1857 and 1858.

Exc.	V.G.	Good	Fair	Poor
—	—	2750	1250	500

4-Shot Pepperbox Pistols

Between 1859 and 1874, these companies manufactured 4 barrel cartridge pocket pistols in a variety of calibers, barrel lengths and finishes. The barrels slide forward for loading. The major models are as follows:

Courtesy Buffalo Bill Historical Center, Cody, Wyoming

Model 1

Manufactured by C. Sharps & Co. and in .22 rimfire caliber.

Exc.	V.G.	Good	Fair	Poor
—	—	600	250	100

Model 2

As above, in .30 rimfire caliber.

Exc.	V.G.	Good	Fair	Poor
—	—	600	250	100

Model 3

Manufactured by Sharps & Hankins and marked "Address Sharps & Hankins Philadelphia Penn." on the frame. Caliber.32 short rimfire.

Exc.	V.G.	Good	Fair	Poor
—	—	750	300	150

Model 4

Similar to the above, in .32 long rimfire and having a rounded birdshead grip.

Courtesy John J. Stimson, Jr.

Exc.	V.G.	Good	Fair	Poor
—	—	750	300	150

Model 1861 Navy Rifle

A .54 Sharps and Hankins caliber breechloading single shot rifle with a 32.75" barrel and full stock secured by three barrel bands. Blued, case hardened with a walnut stock. Approximately 700 were made in 1861 and 1862.

Courtesy Milwaukee Public Museum, Milwaukee, Wisconsin

Exc.	V.G.	Good	Fair	Poor
—	—	3750	1500	700

Model 1862 Navy Carbine

A .54 caliber breechloading carbine with a 24" leather covered barrel. Case hardened with a walnut stock. The frame marked "Sharps & Hankins Philada." Approximately 8,000 were manufactured between 1861 and 1862.

Courtesy Milwaukee Public Museum, Milwaukee, Wisconsin

Exc.	V.G.	Good	Fair	Poor
—	—	3000	1200	500

Short Cavalry Carbine

Similar to the above, with a 19" blued barrel. Approximately 500 were manufactured.

Exc.	V.G.	Good	Fair	Poor
—	—	3750	1500	700

Army Model

Similar to the above, with a 24" barrel that does not have a leather covering. Approximately 500 were purchased by the Army.

Exc.	V.G.	Good	Fair	Poor
—	—	3750	1500	700

SHATTUCK, C. S.
Hatfield, Massachusetts

Double Barrel Shotguns

In addition to single barrel shotguns, Shattuck made about 1,000 hammerless doubles.

Courtesy Nick Niles

Exc.	V.G.	Good	Fair	Poor
1000	500	400	300	200

Boom

A .22 caliber spur trigger revolver with a 2" octagonal barrel and 6-shot cylinder. Nickel-plated with rosewood or walnut grips. The barrel marked "Boom" and "Pat. Nov. 4. 1879". Manufactured during the 1880s.

Exc.	V.G.	Good	Fair	Poor
—	350	150	100	75

Pocket Revolver

A .32 caliber spur trigger revolver with a 3.5" octagonal barrel and 5-shot cylinder. Nickel-plated with hard rubber grips. The barrel marked "C. S. Shattuck Hatfield, Mass. Pat. Nov. 4, 1879." Manufactured during the 1880s.

Exc.	V.G.	Good	Fair	Poor
—	400	200	150	100

SHAW & LEDOYT
Stafford, Connecticut

Under Hammer Pistol

A .31 caliber under hammer percussion pistol with a 2.5" to 3.5" half-octagonal barrel. Blued with a brass mounted walnut grip. The frame marked "Shaw & LeDoyt/Stafford. Conn." Manufactured during the 1850s.

Exc.	V.G.	Good	Fair	Poor
—	—	950	500	150

SHAWK & McLANAHAN
St. Louis, Missouri

Navy Revolver

A .36 caliber percussion revolver with an 8" round barrel and 6-shot cylinder. Blued with a brass frame and walnut grips. Marked "Shawk & McLanahan, St. Louis, Carondelet, Mo." Produced in limited quantities prior to 1860. Prospective purchasers are advised to secure a qualified appraisal prior to acquisition.

Exc.	V.G.	Good	Fair	Poor
—	—	9500	4750	2000

SHERIDEN PRODUCTS, INC.
Racine, Wisconsin

Knockabout

A .22 caliber single shot pistol with a 5" barrel having fixed sights. Blued with plastic grips. Manufactured between 1953 and 1960.

Exc.	V.G.	Good	Fair	Poor
150	100	90	75	50

SHILEN RIFLES, INC.
Ennis, Texas

Model DGA Sporter

A .17 Remington to .258 Winchester caliber bolt action sporting rifle with a 24" barrel furnished without sights. Blued with a walnut stock.

Exc.	V.G.	Good	Fair	Poor
650	550	450	400	350

Model DGA Varminter

As above, in varmint calibers with a 25" barrel.

Exc.	V.G.	Good	Fair	Poor
650	550	450	400	350

Model DGA Silhouette Rifle

As above, in .308 Winchester only.

Exc.	V.G.	Good	Fair	Poor
650	550	450	400	350

Model DGA Bench Rest Rifle

A centerfire single shot bolt action rifle with a 26" barrel and either fiberglass or walnut stock.

Exc.	V.G.	Good	Fair	Poor
750	650	550	500	450

SHILOH RIFLE MFG. CO., INC.
Big Timber, Montana

Established in Farmingdale, New York, in 1976, this company moved to Big Timber, Montana, in 1983 with the name Shiloh Products. It changed its name to Shiloh Rifle Manufacturing Co. in that same year. In 1985 the company began marketing its products factory direct. In 1991 Robert, Phyllis, and Kirk Bryan purchased the company. Those interested in the Sharps reproduction rifles manufactured by this company are advised to contact them in Big Timber.

NOTE: The company will build a rifle to the customers specifications. It is therefore possible that many of these rifles have special order features that are not reflected in the base model price.

Model 1863 Military Rifle

A .54 caliber percussion rifle with a 30" barrel, single or double set triggers and full-length walnut stock secured by three barrel bands.

NIB	Exc.	V.G.	Good	Fair	Poor
850	800	700	600	500	400

Model 1863 Sporting Rifle

As above, with a 30" octagonal barrel, sporting sights and a half-length stock.

NIB	Exc.	V.G.	Good	Fair	Poor
750	700	600	500	400	350

Model 1863 Military Carbine

The Model 1863 with a 22" round barrel and carbine stock secured by one barrel band.

NIB	Exc.	V.G.	Good	Fair	Poor
750	700	600	500	400	350

Model 1862 Confederate Robinson

As above, with a 21.5" barrel, brass buttplate and barrel band.

NIB	Exc.	V.G.	Good	Fair	Poor
800	750	650	550	450	400

Model 1874 Express Rifle

Manufactured in a variety of calibers with a 34" octagonal barrel, double set triggers, vernier rear sight and globe front sight.

NIB	Exc.	V.G.	Good	Fair	Poor
1175	800	700	600	500	400

Montana Roughrider Rifle

As above, with either octagonal or half-octagonal barrels ranging in lengths from 24" to 34".

NIB	Exc.	V.G.	Good	Fair	Poor
1050	700	600	500	400	350

No. 1 Sporter Deluxe Rifle

Similar to the above, with a 30" octagonal barrel.

NIB	Exc.	V.G.	Good	Fair	Poor
1150	750	650	550	450	400

No. 3 Standard Sporter

As above, with a military-style stock.

NIB	Exc.	V.G.	Good	Fair	Poor
1050	700	600	500	400	350

The Business Rifle

As above, with a heavy 28" barrel.

NIB	Exc.	V.G.	Good	Fair	Poor
1050	700	600	500	400	350

The Saddle Rifle

As above, with a 26" barrel and shotgun butt.

NIB	Exc.	V.G.	Good	Fair	Poor
1100	750	650	550	450	400

Model 1874 Military Rifle

The Model 1874 with a 30" round barrel, military sights and full-length stocks secured by three barrel bands.

NIB	Exc.	V.G.	Good	Fair	Poor
850	800	700	600	500	400

Model 1874 Carbine

Similar to the above, with a 24" round barrel.

NIB	Exc.	V.G.	Good	Fair	Poor
750	700	600	500	400	350

The Jaeger

The Model 1874 with a 26" half-octagonal barrel, open sights and pistol grips stock having a shotgun butt.

NIB	Exc.	V.G.	Good	Fair	Poor
800	750	650	550	450	400

Hartford Model

A reproduction of the Sharps Hartford Model.

NIB	Exc.	V.G.	Good	Fair	Poor
1200	900	700	550	450	350

Model 1874 Military Carbine

Similar to the Military Rifle, but with a 22" round barrel.

NIB	Exc.	V.G.	Good	Fair	Poor
750	700	600	500	400	350

SIG
Neuhausen, Switzerland
Importer - Sigarms
Exeter, New Hampshire

P210

A 7.65mm or 9mm semiautomatic pistol with a 4.75" barrel and 8-shot magazine. Blued with plastic grips. In 1996 the 9mm version was the only one imported. Weight is about 32 oz.

NIB	Exc.	V.G.	Good	Fair	Poor
2300	1500	1300	1100	800	500

NOTE: For 1996 a .22 caliber conversion unit serialized to the gun was available. Add $600 for this option.

P 210-1

As above, with an adjustable rear sight, polished finish and walnut grips. Imported prior to 1987.

NIB	Exc.	V.G.	Good	Fair	Poor
2150	1700	1500	1150	800	400

P 210-2

NIB	Exc.	V.G.	Good	Fair	Poor
2000	1750	1350	1000	750	300

P 210-5

As above, with an extended length barrel, adjustable rear sight and walnut grips.

NIB	Exc.	V.G.	Good	Fair	Poor
2250	1850	1650	1000	800	400

P 210-6
As above, with a 4.75" barrel.

NIB	Exc.	V.G.	Good	Fair	Poor
2750	2250	1500	1150	800	400

SIG-HAMMERLI
Lenzburg, Switzerland
Importer-Sigarms
Exeter, New Hampshire

Model P240 Target Pistol
A .32 Smith & Wesson Long Wadcutter or .38 Midrange caliber semiautomatic pistol with a 5.9" barrel, adjustable rear sight, adjustable trigger and 5-shot magazine. Blued, with adjustable walnut grips. Imported prior 1987.

Courtesy John J. Stimson, Jr.

Exc.	V.G.	Good	Fair	Poor
1300	1150	950	750	600

.22 Conversion Unit
A barrel, slide, and magazine used to convert the above to .22 caliber.

Exc.	V.G.	Good	Fair	Poor
500	450	400	300	200

Model 208S
This is a semiautomatic target pistol chambered for the .22 Long Rifle cartridge. The barrel length is 5.9" long with adjustable sights. Sight radius is 8.2". Trigger has adjustable pull weight, travel, slack weight, and creep. Grips are stippled walnut with adjustable palm shelf. Weight is approximately 37 oz. empty.

NIB	Exc.	V.G.	Good	Fair	Poor
1900	1600	—	—	—	—

Model 280
This model is a semiautomatic pistol chambered for the .22 Long Rifle cartridge or the .32 S&W Long Wadcutter. Single action only. Barrel length is 4.6" with a sight radius of 8.7". Adjustable sights. Trigger is adjustable for pull weight, take-up, let-off, and creep. Stippled walnut grip with adjustable palm shelf. Weight is 35 oz. for the .22 caliber and 42 oz. for the .32

caliber. Magazine capacity is six .22 caliber rounds and five .32 caliber rounds.

NIB	Exc.	V.G.	Good	Fair	Poor
1200	1200	—	—	—	—

Model 160/162
This .22 caliber Long Rifle single shot pistol is designed for international free pistol competition. Barrel length is 11.3" with a sight radius of 14.6". Trigger is fully adjustable as are the sights. Stippled walnut grips with adjustable palm shelf and rake angle. The Model 160 has a mechanical trigger while the Model 162 is fitted with an electric trigger.

NIB	Exc.	V.G.	Good	Fair	Poor
2000	1600	—	—	—	—

Trailside PL 22
Introduced in 1999 this semiautomatic pistol is chambered for the .22 Long Rifle cartridge. Barrel length is 4.5" or 6" with fixed sights. Synthetic grips. Two-tone finish. Magazine capacity is 10 rounds. Weight is about 28 oz. with 4.5" barrel and 30 oz. with 6" barrel.

NIB	Exc.	V.G.	Good	Fair	Poor
N/A	—	—	—	—	—

Trailside PL 22 Target
Similar to the PL 22 with the addition of adjustable sights and walnut grips. Introduced in 1999.

NIB	Exc.	V.G.	Good	Fair	Poor
N/A	—	—	—	—	—

SIG-ARMS
Eckernforde, West Germany
Importer - Sigarms
Exeter, New Hampshire

This old-line Swiss firm was established in 1853 and is now a broadly based engineering consortium. Its first successful commercial design was the SP 47/8 introduced in 1948. Sig, a Swiss company, associated itself with the German firm of Sauer in 1970. SIG-Sauer pistols are SIG designs assembled in Germany. At the present time the P239 and P229 Sig pistols are produced in New Hampshire.

PISTOLS
CLASSIC SERIES

NOTE: Maximum magazine capacity for all currently manufactured Sig pistols is 10 rounds regardless of caliber and previous capacity.

NOTE: For pistols with factory installed night sights add $90. Add $45 for pistols with K-Kote finish. Add $35 for nickel slides.

P210

This model was reintroduced into the U.S. in 2001 and is based on the Swiss military version first built in 1949. It is designed primarily as a target pistol and is furnished in four different variations. All variations are chambered for the 9mm cartridge.

NOTE: Older P210 models imported before 1968 without importer stamps and pistols built during the late 1940s and early 1950s may bring a premium to the collector. Be aware that extra barrels, conversion kits, and other special order features will add additional value.

P210-8-9

This variation has adjustable target sights, select wood grips, lateral magazine catch, blued sandblasted finish, and adjustable trigger stop. Heavy frame. Barrel length is 4.8". Weight is about 37 oz.

NIB	Exc.	V.G.	Good	Fair	Poor
4275	3500	—	—	—	—

P210-6-9

This variation has adjustable target sights, wood grips, target grade trigger, and blued sandblasted finish. Barrel length is 4.8". Weight is about 32 oz.

NIB	Exc.	V.G.	Good	Fair	Poor
2075	1650	—	—	—	—

P210-5-9

This variation has extended 5.85" barrel with compensator, ribbed front frame grip, wood grip plates, adjustable target sights, and target trigger. Weight is about 34 oz.

NIB	Exc.	V.G.	Good	Fair	Poor
2325	1850	—	—	—	—

P210-2-9

This variation is similar to the Swiss Army service pistol and has wood grip plates and standard fixed sights. Barrel length is 4.8". Weight is about 32 oz.

NIB	Exc.	V.G.	Good	Fair	Poor
1675	1350	—	—	—	—

P220

This is a high-quality, double action semiautomatic pistol chambered for .38 Super, .45 ACP, and 9mm Parabellum. It has a 4.41" barrel and fixed sights and features the de-cocking lever that was found originally on the Sauer Model 38H. There are two versions of this pistol—one with a bottom magazine release (commonly referred to as the European model) and the other with the release on the side (commonly referred to as the American model) as on the Model 1911 Colt. The frame is a lightweight alloy that is matte-finished and is available in either blue, nickel, or K-Kote finish with black plastic grips. The .45 ACP magazine capacity is 7 rounds and the pistol weighs 25.7 oz.; the .38 Super magazine capacity is 9 rounds and the pistol weighs 26.5 oz.; the 9mm magazine holds 9 rounds and the overall weight is 26.5 oz. This model was manufactured from 1976 and is still in production. The 9mm version in this model is no longer in production. The prices listed below are for guns with a standard blue finish.

NOTE#1: For the K-Kote finish add $40, for nickel slide add $40. Stainless steel add $100.

NOTE#2: At the present the P220 pistol is offered only in .45ACP.

NIB	Exc.	V.G.	Good	Fair	Poor
800	550	400	300	200	150

P220 Sport

Introduced in 1999, this .45ACP pistol is similar to the P220 with the addition of 5.5" barrel with stainless steel compensator. The frame and slide are stainless steel. Magazine capacity is 7 rounds. Weight is about 44 oz.

NIB	Exc.	V.G.	Good	Fair	Poor
1300	1000	700	—	—	—

P225

This is similar to the Model P220 except that it is chambered for 9mm cartridge. It is a more compact pistol, with a 3.86" barrel. It has an 8-shot detachable magazine and adjustable sights. The finish is matte blued. K-Kote, or electrolysis nickel plate with black plastic grips. The overall length is 7.1" with an overall height of 5.2". The pistol weighs 26.1 oz. For K-Kote finish add $70. For nickel slide add $70. No longer in production.

NIB	Exc.	V.G.	Good	Fair	Poor
625	575	500	400	200	150

P226

This model is a full size, high-capacity pistol with a 4.41" barrel chambered for the 9mm or .40S&W cartridge. In 1996 this model was also available chambered for the .357 SIG cartridge. It is available with a 15- or 20-round detachable magazine and high-contrast sights. It is either blued, electrolysis nickel plated, or has a polymer finish known as K-Kote. Overall length is 7.7" and overall height is 5.5". The pistol weighs 26.5 oz. This model was introduced in 1983. Add $50 for K-Kote finish and $50 for nickel slide.

NIB	Exc.	V.G.	Good	Fair	Poor
825	600	550	450	300	200

P226 Sport

Introduced in 2001 this model is similar to the other SIG Sport models and is chambered for the 9mm Luger cartridge. Stainless steel slide and frame with adjustable target sights and competition barrel weight.

NIB	Exc.	V.G.	Good	Fair	Poor
1350	1000	—	—	—	—

JP226 Jubilee Pistol

This variation is a special limited edition of the P226. Each gun carries a special serial number prefixed JP. The grips are hand carved select European walnut. The slide and frame are covered with solid gold wire inlays, while the trigger, hammer, decocking lever, slide catch lever, and magazine catch are all gold plated. Each pistol comes in a custom fitted hard case of full leather. This pistol is no longer imported into the U.S. Fewer than 250 were imported between 1991 and 1992.

NIB	Exc.	V.G.	Good	Fair	Poor
1200	850	600	500	400	200

P228

This model is a compact version of the P226 fitted with a 3.86" barrel and chambered for the 9mm cartridge. Like the P 226 it is available in blue, K-Kote, of nickel finish with black grips. Overall length is 7.1" and overall height is 5.4". Pistol weighs 26.1 oz. For K-Kote finish add $50 and for nickel slide add $50. No longer in production.

NIB	Exc.	V.G.	Good	Fair	Poor
650	600	550	450	350	250

P229

This model is similar to the P228 except that it is chambered for the .40 S&W cartridge and has a blackened stainless steel slide and lightweight aluminum alloy frame. The slide is slightly larger to accommodate the more powerful cartridge. In 1996 the 9mm chamber was also offered in this model. Its overall length is 7.1" and overall height is 5.4". Introduced in 1992. The pistol weighs 27.54 oz. and has a magazine capacity of 12 rounds. In 1994 the company introduced a new caliber for this model; the .357 SIG developed by Federal. Magazine capacity is 12 rounds.

NIB	Exc.	V.G.	Good	Fair	Poor
825	600	550	450	350	250

P229 Nickel

Same as the standard P229 but with full nickel finish over a stainless steel slide and alloy frame. Weight is about 27.5 oz. Introduced in 1998.

NIB	Exc.	V.G.	Good	Fair	Poor
875	650	500	—	—	—

P229 Sport

Chambered for the .357 SIG cartridge this model is fitted with a 4.8" barrel with a muzzle compensator. Adjustable target sights. Both frame and slide are stainless steel. Magazine capacity is 10 rounds. Weight is approximately 41 oz. Introduced in 1998.

NIB	Exc.	V.G.	Good	Fair	Poor
1300	975	—	—	—	—

P239

Introduced in 1996 this pistol is chambered for the 9mm, .40S&W, or .357 SIG cartridge. It is double/single action or double action only. The barrel is 3.6" long and the overall length is 6.6". Weight is 25 oz. It is fitted with a single column magazine with 7 rounds for the .357 SIG and 8 rounds for the 9mm.

NIB	Exc.	V.G.	Good	Fair	Poor
600	450	350	250	200	150

NOTE: All of the above SIG pistols from the P220 to the P239 are available with "SIGLITE" night sights. Add $80 for these optional sights.

P230

This is a semiautomatic, compact, pocket-type pistol chambered for .22 l.r., .32 ACP, .380 ACP, and 9mm Ultra. It has a 3.62" barrel and either a 10-, 8-, or 7-round magazine, depending on the caliber chambered. The pistol weighs between 16.2 oz. and 20.8 oz. The finish is blued or stainless, with black plastic grips; and it was manufactured from 1976. In 1996 a two-tone finish was offered. The .32 ACP and the .380 ACP versions are the only ones currently available. For stainless steel finish add $85 and for stainless steel slide add $35. No longer in production.

NIB	Exc.	V.G.	Good	Fair	Poor
450	375	300	250	200	150

P232

An improved model of the P230. Incorporates numerous changes to improve function and reliability. Basic features, operation, and dimensions remain the same as the P230.

NIB	Exc.	V.G.	Good	Fair	Poor
450	375	300	250	200	150

P232 (1998 Model)

In 1998 this model has as standard features night sights and Hogue grips with an all stainless steel finish. Chambered for .380 ACP, the pistol has a 7-round magazine capacity. Weight is about 21 oz.

NIB	Exc.	V.G.	Good	Fair	Poor
500	375	300	—	—	—

P245 Compact

Introduced in 1999 this model is chambered for the .45ACP cartridge. It is fitted with a 3.9" barrel. Magazine capacity is 6 rounds. Overall length is 7.3". Weight is about 28 oz. Available finishes are blue and K-Kote. SIGLITE night sights are also available.

NIB	Exc.	V.G.	Good	Fair	Poor
775	600	—	—	—	—

SIG PRO SERIES

SP2340

Introduced in 1998 this model is chambered for the .357 SIG or .40 S&W cartridge. It is built on a polymer frame with accessory rails on the dust cover. Barrel length is 3.9". Standard finish is blue. Weight is about 28 oz. Comes with two sets of interchangeable grips and two 10-round magazines. Available in single action/double action or double action only.

SP2340 with laser sights

NIB	Exc.	V.G.	Good	Fair	Poor
600	475	—	—	—	—

SP2009

Similar to the SP2340 but chambered for the 9mm cartridge. Weight is about 25 oz. Magazine capacity is 10 rounds.

NIB	Exc.	V.G.	Good	Fair	Poor
600	475	—	—	—	—

RIMFIRE PISTOLS

Trailside PL 22 Standard

This .22 caliber is offered with either a 4.5" or 6" barrel. Magazine capacity is 10 rounds. Two-tone finish. Fixed sights. Weight is about 28 oz. Introduced in 2000.

NIB	Exc.	V.G.	Good	Fair	Poor
400	300	—	—	—	—

Trailside PL 22 Target

This model features a 4.5" or 6" barrel with adjustable rear sight and laminated grip. Two-tone finish. Weight is about 28 oz. Introduced in 2000.

NIB	Exc.	V.G.	Good	Fair	Poor
475	350	—	—	—	—

Trailside PL 22 Competition

This model features a 6" barrel with adjustable rear sight. The grip is fully adjustable with interchangeable barrel weights. Two-tone finish. Weight is about 36 oz. Introduced in 2000.

NIB	Exc.	V.G.	Good	Fair	Poor
550	400	—	—	—	—

SHOTGUNS

Model SA3 Hunter

Introduced in 1997 this over and under shotgun is chambered for the 20 gauge shell and fitted with 26" or 28" barrels. It has single selective trigger and automatic ejectors. The stock is figured walnut with pistol grip. The receiver is polished steel with engraved game scenes. Weight is approximately 6.8 lbs.

NIB	Exc.	V.G.	Good	Fair	Poor
1325	1050	750	—	—	—

Model SA3 Sporting

This 12 gauge over and under gun was introduced in 1998 and features a 28" or 29.5" barrel with wide 11mm rib and front and mid-target sights. Both barrels and action are blued. Walnut stock with pistol grip and recoil pad. Weight is about 7.3 lbs.

NIB	Exc.	V.G.	Good	Fair	Poor
1675	1250	—	—	—	—

Model SA5 Sporting

Introduced in 1998 this 12 gauge is fitted with a choice of 28" or 29.5" barrels. Single selective trigger and automatic ejectors are standard. Barrels are fitted with a 10mm rib. Receiver is polished steel with engraved clay target on each side. Weight is about 7.6 lbs.

NIB	Exc.	V.G.	Good	Fair	Poor
3175	2500	—	—	—	—

AURORA SERIES

These shotguns were first imported and introduced into the SIG product line in 2000. They are made in Italy by B. Rizzini. All the guns in this series are over and under guns.

AURORA TR FIELD SHOTGUNS

All of the TR field guns are offered in 12, 20, and 28 gauge as well as .410 bore. All have single triggers and ejectors. Barrel lengths are 26" or 28". Weights vary from 7 lbs. for the 12 gauge to 6 lbs. for the .410. Select walnut stock with oil finish. Cut checkering of 20 lpi. Choke tubes on the 12 and 20 gauge model and fixed chokes on the 28 and .410 models.

TR 20U

This model features a box lock action with case hardened frame. No engraving. Straight grip stock.

Aurora TR 20U 28 gauge

NIB	Exc.	V.G.	Good	Fair	Poor
1850	1400	—	—	—	—

TR 20

This model features a box lock action with nickel finish and no engraving. Pistol grip.

Aurora TR 20 .410 bore

NIB	Exc.	V.G.	Good	Fair	Poor
1850	1400	—	—	—	—

TR 30

This model features a case hardened action with side plates. No engraving. Pistol grip.

Aurora TR 30 12 gauge

NIB	Exc.	V.G.	Good	Fair	Poor
2225	1650	—	—	—	—

TR 40 Silver

This model features a silver action with side plates with gold inlaid game scenes. Pistol grip.

Aurora TR 40 Silver

Aurora TR 40 Silver receiver

NIB	Exc.	V.G.	Good	Fair	Poor
2575	1950	—	—	—	—

TR 40 Gold

This features a case hardened action with side plates and gold inlaid game scenes. Pistol grip.

Aurora TR 40 Gold

NIB	Exc.	V.G.	Good	Fair	Poor
2675	2000	—	—	—	—

New Englander

Introduced in 2000 jointly by SIG and L.L. Bean this over/under gun is chambered in 12 and 20 gauge with choice of 26" or 28" barrels. Single selective trigger, auto ejectors, choke tubes all standard. L.L. Bean logo inlaid in gold on receiver. Select turkish walnut stock with oil finish. Prince of Wales style pistol grip and rubber recoil pad.

NIB	Exc.	V.G.	Good	Fair	Poor
1995	1500	—	—	—	—

AURORA TT 25 COMPETITION SHOTGUNS

TT25

This model is offered in both 12 and 20 gauge with a choice of 28" to 32" barrels for the 12 gauge and 28" or 30" barrels for the 20 gauge. Choke tubes. Single selective auto ejectors are standard. Wide competition vent rib. Pistol grip on select walnut stock with 20 lpi checkering. Weight for 12 gauge is about 7.25 lbs. while the 20 gauge weighs about 6.75 lbs.

Aurora TT 25 12 gauge

NIB	Exc.	V.G.	Good	Fair	Poor
1995	1500	—	—	—	—

TT45

Similar to the TT25 but with the addition of a case hardened receiver and side plates with engraving and gold inlay game scenes.

NIB	Exc.	V.G.	Good	Fair	Poor
2795	2200	—	—	—	—

RIFLES

SIG AMT

This is a semiautomatic rifle chambered for .308 cartridge. Fitted with a 19" barrel and wooden buttstock and forearm. Folding bipod standard. Box magazine capacity is 5, 10, or 20 rounds. Weight is about 10 lbs. Built from 1960 to 1974.

NIB	Exc.	V.G.	Good	Fair	Poor
5000	4500	3250	2500	1500	1000

SIG PE57

Similar to the above but chambered for the 7.5x55 Swiss cartridge.

NIB	Exc.	V.G.	Good	Fair	Poor
6000	5000	3500	2700	1700	1300

SIG 550

This semiautomatic rifle is chambered for .223 cartridge and fitted with a 18" barrel.

Courtesy Rock Island Auction Company

NIB	Exc.	V.G.	Good	Fair	Poor
9000	7000	5500	3000	—	—

SIG 551

Same as above but fitted with a 16" barrel.

NIB	Exc.	V.G.	Good	Fair	Poor
9500	7500	6500	4000	—	—

SSG 2000

This is a high-grade, bolt action, sniping-type rifle chambered for .223, 7.5mm Swiss, .300 Weatherby Magnum, and .308 Winchester. It has a 24" barrel and was furnished without sights. It has a 4-round box magazine. The finish is matte blued with a thumbhole-style stippled walnut stock with an adjustable cheekpiece. This model was discontinued in 1986.

NIB	Exc.	V.G.	Good	Fair	Poor
8000	6000	3500	1500	—	—

SSG 3000

Chambered for the .308 Win. cartridge this model is fitted with a 23.4" barrel and ambidextrous McMillian Tactical stock. Magazine capacity is 5 rounds. Overall length is 46.5", and approximate weight is 12 lbs. This model comes in three different packages. They are listed below:

Level I

Base model with no bipod or scope, but with carrying case.

NIB	Exc.	V.G.	Good	Fair	Poor
2550	2000	—	—	—	—

Level II

At this level a Leupold Vari-X III 3.5-10x40mm Deplex scope and Harris bipod with carrying case.

NIB	Exc.	V.G.	Good	Fair	Poor
3500	2750	—	—	—	—

Level III

Rifle is supplied with a Leupold Mark 4 M1-10x40mm Mil-Dot Scope with Harris bipod and carrying case.

NIB	Exc.	V.G.	Good	Fair	Poor
4500	3500	—	—	—	—

WHAT'S IT LIKE-THE SIG SSG 3000

The SIG company of Switzerland is a world renown name in the firearms industry, both in the military and civilian sporting market with many innovative designs under its belt. In the late 1990s, SIG brought to the market the SIG SSG 3000 rifle, a high precision sniper rifle in calibers 7.62x51mm NATO (.308). This model is a dedicated sniper rifle, not a hunting rifle upgraded to higher accuracy standards. The SSG 3000 utilizes a new chassis receiver system or modular construction. This means that unlike other bolt action rifles which incorporate a barrel that is threaded into the receiver, the SIG rifle uses a quick change barrel that enables a sniper to change his own barrel, if need be, rather than sending the rifle back to the depot for replacement. The SIG rifle is a bolt action ten shot repeater with a quick change magazine. The bolt is a 6 lug locking bolt which locks directly into the barrel rather than previous designs that lock into the receiver. The SIG system is a much tighter lock-up. This very tight locking system of the bolt and the barrel equates to a more rigid and accurate rifle. The SIG SSG 3000 comes from the factory with a test target. Most of these test targets that I have seen a 5 shot one hole groups of no more than 3/8" spread. The stock is also ergonomically adjustable for the operator. The trigger is adjustable as well as one would expect from the SIG company: excellence in design and execution.

J.R. Moody

Conversion Kit-.22 LR

In 2001 a .22 caliber conversion was offered for the SSG 3000 rifle. The kit includes a heavy contured barrel, bolt, and 5-round magazine.

NIB	Exc.	V.G.	Good	Fair	Poor
750	—	—	—	—	—

Model SHR 970

Introduced in 1998 this bolt action rifle is chambered for the .25-06 Rem., .270, .280 Rem., .30-06, or .308 cartridges. It has a 22" barrel and the receiver is drilled and tapped for scope mounts. Detachable box magazine. Stock is black synthetic or walnut. Barrels are interchangeable. Weight is about 7.2 lbs.

NIB	Exc.	V.G.	Good	Fair	Poor
500	400	—	—	—	—

NOTE: Add $30 for walnut stock.

Model SHR 970 Magnum

Same as above but chambered for 7mm Rem. Mag or .300 Win. Mag. Barrel length is 24". Weight is about 7.4 lbs.

NIB	Exc.	V.G.	Good	Fair	Poor
500	400	—	—	—	—

NOTE: Add $30 for walnut stock.

Model SHR 970 Tactical

This model was introduced in 2000 and features a McMillan stock, non-reflective metal coating heavy fluted contoured barrel, integral muzzle break. The rifle is chambered for .308 Win. or .300 Win. Mag cartridges. Receiver is drilled and tapped for scope mount and the stock has a fitted rubber recoil pad.

NIB	Exc.	V.G.	Good	Fair	Poor
500	400	—	—	—	—

Model 202 Standard

This bolt action rifle features a choice of synthetic or Turkish walnut stock. Bolt is jeweled. Detachable 3-round box magazine. Offered in standard calibers from .22-250 to .30-06 and magnum calibers from 7mm Rem. Mag. to .375 H&H Mag. Barrel length is 24" for standard calibers and 26" for magnum calibers. Weight is about 7.5 lbs. depending on caliber.

NIB	Exc.	V.G.	Good	Fair	Poor
1250	950	—	—	—	—

Model 202 Lightweight

This model features a black synthetic stock fluted barrel chambered for the .22-250, .243, .25-06, .270, or .30-05 calibers. Barrel length is 24". Magazine capacity is 3 rounds. Alloy receiver and quick change barrel system are standard. Weight is about 6.5 lbs. Introduced in 2001.

NIB	Exc.	V.G.	Good	Fair	Poor
1395	1100	—	—	—	—

Model 202 Varmint

This model is chambered for the .22-250, .243, or .25-06 cartridge. Fitted with a 26" fluted bull barrel. Stock is Turkish walnut with adjustable cheekpiece. Three-round detachable box magazine. Quick change barrel system. Weight is approximately 9.5 lbs.

NIB	Exc.	V.G.	Good	Fair	Poor
1495	1200	—	—	—	—

Model 202 Supreme

This bolt action model is chambered for .243, .25-06, 6.5x55 Swedish, .270 Win., .308 Win., or .30-06. It is fitted with a 24" barrel with choice of synthetic or walnut stock. Magazine capacity is 3 rounds. Weight is approximately 7.7 lbs. No sights.

NIB	Exc.	V.G.	Good	Fair	Poor
1050	775	—	—	—	—

NOTE: Add $50 for walnut stock.

Model 202 Supreme Magnum

As above but chambered for 7mm Rem. Mag., .300 Win. Mag., .300 Wby Mag., or .375 H&H Mag. Magazine capacity is 3 rounds. Choice of synthetic or walnut stock. Weight is about 8.4 lbs.

NIB	Exc.	V.G.	Good	Fair	Poor
1250	850	—	—	—	—

NOTE: Add $50 for walnut stock.

SIMPLEX
Unknown

Simplex

A German design based on the Bergmann-Mars pistol. An 8mm caliber semiautomatic pistol with a 2.6" barrel and a front mounted 5-round magazine. Blued with hard rubber grips having the trade name "Simplex" cast in them. Manufactured from approximately 1901 to around 1906. Early samples may have come from Germany and later pistols are thought to have been produced in Belgium.

Exc.	V.G.	Good	Fair	Poor
1500	950	500	400	200

SIMPSON, R. J.
New York, New York

Pocket Pistol

A .41 caliber single shot percussion pocket pistol with a 2.5" barrel, German silver mounts and walnut stock. Manufactured during the 1850s and 1860s.

Exc.	V.G.	Good	Fair	Poor
—	—	1750	700	300

SIMSON & COMPANY
Suhl, Germany
SEE—Luger

Model 1922

A 6.35mm semiautomatic pistol with a 2" barrel and 6-shot magazine. The slide marked "Selbstlade Pistole Simson DRP" and "Waffenfabrik Simson & Co Suhl." Blued, with black plastic grips.

Exc.	V.G.	Good	Fair	Poor
500	450	400	300	100

Model 1927

Similar to the above, with a slimmer frame stamped with the trademark of three overlapping triangles having the letter "S" enclosed.

Exc.	V.G.	Good	Fair	Poor
500	450	400	300	100

SIRKIS INDUSTRIES, LTD.
Ramat-Gan, Israel
Importer-Armscorp of America
Baltimore, Maryland

SD9

A 9mm double action semiautomatic pistol with a 3" barrel, fixed sights and 7-shot magazine. Blued with plastic grips. Also known as the Sardius.

Exc.	V.G.	Good	Fair	Poor
325	275	225	175	100

Model 35 Match Rifle

A .22 caliber single shot bolt action rifle with a 26" free floating barrel, adjustable rear sight and adjustable trigger. Blued with a walnut stock.

Exc.	V.G.	Good	Fair	Poor
600	550	500	400	200

Model 36 Sniper's Rifle

A 7.62x54mm caliber semiautomatic rifle with a 22" barrel. Matte blued with a composition stock.

Exc.	V.G.	Good	Fair	Poor
675	600	550	450	200

SLOTTER & CO.
Philadelphia, Pennsylvania

Pocket Pistol

A .41 caliber percussion pocket pistol with a 2.5" to 3.5" barrel, German silver mounts and walnut stock. Marked "Slotter & Co. Phila." Manufactured during 1860s.

Exc.	V.G.	Good	Fair	Poor
—	—	1250	600	250

SMITH
AMERICAN ARMS COMPANY
Springfield, Massachusetts

Smith Carbine

A .50 caliber breechloading percussion carbine with a 21.75" round barrel having an octagonal breech. Blued, case hardened with a walnut stock. The barrel marked "Address/Poultney & Trimble/Baltimore, USA" and the frame "Smith's Patent/June 23, 1857" as well as "American Arms Co./Chicopee Falls." Approximately 30,000 were manufactured, most of which were purchased by the United States government. The sales agents were Poultney & Trimble of Baltimore, Maryland.

Exc.	V.G.	Good	Fair	Poor
—	2500	1000	500	200

SMITH, L. C.
Syracuse, New York
Hunter Arms Company
Fulton, New York

One of the finest American-made double barrel shotguns and very collectible in today's market. It was manufactured between 1880 and 1888 in Syracuse, New York; and between 1890 and 1945, in Fulton, New York, by the Hunter Arms Company. In 1945 Marlin Firearms Company acquired Hunter Arms, and the L.C. Smith was made until 1951. In 1968 the L.C. Smith was resurrected for five years, and production ceased totally in 1973. The values given are approximate for standard production models; and we strongly feel that competent, individual appraisals should be secured, especially on the rarer and higher grade models, if a transaction is contemplated.

The values given are for fluid steel, hammerless guns only. Damascus-barreled guns have become collectible if they are in very good or better condition, and values are approximately the same as for the fluid steel models. Damascus guns in less than good condition are worth considerably less.

Early Hammerless Shotguns

The following models were manufactured between 1890 and 1913. They are chambered for 10, 12, 16, and 20 gauge and were produced with various barrel lengths and choke combinations. They feature full sidelock actions. The difference in the models and their values is based on the degree of ornamentation and the quality of materials and workmanship utilized in their construction. The general values furnished are for 10, 12 or 16 gauge guns only.
20 Gauge-Add 50%.
Single-Selective Trigger-Add $250.
Automatic Ejectors-Add 30%.

00 Grade-60,000 Manufactured

Exc.	V.G.	Good	Fair	Poor
1500	1250	1000	650	400

0 Grade-30,000 Manufactured

Exc.	V.G.	Good	Fair	Poor
1600	1350	1050	700	450

No. 1 Grade-10,000 Manufactured

Exc.	V.G.	Good	Fair	Poor
2500	2000	1500	800	550

No. 2 Grade-13,000 Manufactured

Exc.	V.G.	Good	Fair	Poor
3000	2250	1750	900	700

No. 3 Grade-4,000 Manufactured

Exc.	V.G.	Good	Fair	Poor
3500	2750	1800	1000	750

Pigeon Grade-1,200 Manufactured

Exc.	V.G.	Good	Fair	Poor
3500	2750	1800	1000	750

No. 4 Grade-500 Manufactured

Exc.	V.G.	Good	Fair	Poor
10000	7500	5000	3000	2000

A-1 Grade-700 Manufactured, All Damascus, No 20-Gauge

Exc.	V.G.	Good	Fair	Poor
5000	3500	2500	1750	1000

No. 5 Grade-500 Manufactured

Exc.	V.G.	Good	Fair	Poor
8500	7000	5000	2750	2000

Monogram Grade-100 Manufactured

Exc.	V.G.	Good	Fair	Poor
11000	8500	6000	3750	2500

A-2 Grade-200 Manufactured

Exc.	V.G.	Good	Fair	Poor
15000	10000	7500	4500	3750

A-3 Grade-20 Manufactured

This is too rare to generalize a value.

Later Production Hammerless Shotguns

These were manufactured at Fulton, New York, between 1914 and 1951. They are side-by-side double barrel shotguns chambered for 12, 16, and 20 gauge, as well as the .410. They are offered with various barrel lengths and choke combinations. They feature a full sidelock action and are available with double or single triggers, extractors, and automatic ejectors. The finishes are blued and case colored, with checkered walnut stocks that are of either straight, semi-pistolgrip, or pistol-grip configurations. The various models differ as to the degree of ornamentation and the quality of materials and workmanship utilized in their construction. These are highly collectible

American shotguns. Because these guns were manufactured as late as 1951, mint original specimens and even unfired new in the box guns will be offered for sale occasionally. These guns are worth considerably more than excellent condition guns and more than ever an individual, expert authentication and appraisal is recommended if a transaction is anticipated.

The values supplied are for 12 gauge models only.
For 16 gauge add 15% premium.
For 20 gauge add 50% premium.
For .410 bore add 200% premium (field grade), 300% to 400% for higher grades.
Single selective triggers add $250 premium.
For automatic ejectors add 30% premium.

Courtesy Milwaukee Public Museum, Milwaukee, Wisconsin

Field Grade

L.C. Smith 12 gauge and .410 bore Field Grade

Courtesy William Hammond

Exc.	V.G.	Good	Fair	Poor
1250	1000	750	500	350

Ideal Grade

Exc.	V.G.	Good	Fair	Poor
1500	1200	900	600	450

Trap Grade

Exc.	V.G.	Good	Fair	Poor
1800	1450	1100	800	500

Specialty Grade

L.C. Smith Specialty Grade

Courtesy William Hammond

Exc.	V.G.	Good	Fair	Poor
3000	2500	1750	1000	600

Skeet Special Grade

12 gauge Skeet Special

Courtesy William Hammond

Exc.	V.G.	Good	Fair	Poor
3000	2500	1750	1000	600

Premier Skeet Grade

Exc.	V.G.	Good	Fair	Poor
3000	2500	1750	1000	600

Eagle Grade

Exc.	V.G.	Good	Fair	Poor
4500	3600	2600	1500	1050

Crown Grade

With this grade, automatic ejectors became standard equipment. The .410 is extremely rare in this model and nonexistent in higher grades; there were only six manufactured, and they cannot be generally evaluated.

12 and 20 gauge Crown Grades

Courtesy William Hammond

Exc.	V.G.	Good	Fair	Poor
6000	4500	3750	2750	2000

Monogram Grade

This version is offered standard with automatic ejectors and a single selective trigger.

Exc.	V.G.	Good	Fair	Poor
12500	10000	7500	5000	3750

There were two higher grades offered-the Premier Grade and the Deluxe Grade. They are extremely rare, and there have not been enough transactions to generally evaluate them.

HUNTER ARMS BOXLOCKS

These shotguns have been maligned over the years being refered to as "cheap boxlocks not to be confused with the L.C. Smith". These guns, in fact, are inexpensive, high quality boxlocks built with quality equal to the Field Grade L.C. Smith. The receiver, forend iron, triggerguard and triggers are all machined from forgings. Durablity of these guns has proven to be excellent.

16 gauge Fultom and Hunter Special   Courtesy William Hammond

Fulton Model

A utility side-by-side boxlock shotgun chambered for 12, 16, 20 gauge and .410 bore. It was offered with various barrel length and choke combinations. It has double triggers and extractors with a non-selective single trigger option. Values given are for 12 and 16 gauge only.

NOTE: For 20 gauge add 50% premium. For .410 bore add 200% premium. For single trigger add $150.

Exc.	V.G.	Good	Fair	Poor
500	400	300	225	150

Fulton Special

A slightly higher grade version of the Fulton Model featuring modest engraving and pointed checkering.

NOTE: For 20 gauge add 50% premium. For single trigger add $200.

Exc.	V.G.	Good	Fair	Poor
650	550	450	300	200

Hunter Special

Similar to the Fulton Model but features the L.C. Smith rotary locking bolt.

NOTE: For 20 gauge add 50% premium. For .410 bore add 300% premium.

Exc.	V.G.	Good	Fair	Poor
650	550	450	300	200

A factory engraved gold inlaid Deluxe L.C. Smith sold at auction for $43,125. Chambered for 12 gauge with 30" barrels. Matted rib with double ivory beads. Animal and floral gold inlays on receiver and sidelocks. This was the last Deluxe gun made by Hunter Arms. Condition was excellent to mint.
Butterfield & Butterfield, August 2000

Single Barrel Trap Guns

High quality, break-open, single-shot trap guns chambered for 12 gauge only. They feature 32" or 34" vent rib barrels that are full-choked. They have boxlock actions and are standard with automatic ejectors. The finish is blued and case colored, and they have a checkered walnut stock with a recoil pad. The various models differ in the amount of ornamentation and the quality of the materials and workmanship utilized in their construction. There was a total of approximately 2,650 manufactured between 1917 and 1951. Although these firearms are actually rarer and just as high a quality as their side-by-side counterparts, they are simply not as collectible as the side-by-side variations. It would still behoove the astute firearms investor to secure a qualified, individual appraisal if a transaction is contemplated.

Olympic Grade

Exc.	V.G.	Good	Fair	Poor
1500	1250	950	700	600

Specialty Grade

Exc.	V.G.	Good	Fair	Poor
2000	1750	1300	1000	800

Crown Grade

Exc.	V.G.	Good	Fair	Poor
3500	3000	2250	1500	1250

Monogram Grade

Exc.	V.G.	Good	Fair	Poor
6500	5500	3800	2600	1750

Premier Grade

Exc.	V.G.	Good	Fair	Poor
12000	10000	7000	5000	3000

Deluxe Grade

Exc.	V.G.	Good	Fair	Poor
16000	14000	10500	8000	4500

1968 Model

A side-by-side double barrel shotgun chambered for 12 gauge with a 28" vent rib barrel, choked full-and-modified. It features a sidelock action with double triggers and extractors. The finish is blued and case colored, with a checkered walnut stock. This shotgun was manufactured by Marlin between 1968 and 1973.

These are less desirable than earlier models because of manufacturing expedients used. Investment cast receiver rather than machined forgings were used. Cyanide casehardening replaced bone charcoal hardening and aluminum vent ribs were used. A thin brown polymer layer was used to create the fit between the lock plates and buttstock which is a departure from traditional fitting.

Exc.	V.G.	Good	Fair	Poor
700	600	550	450	300

1968 Deluxe Model

Similar to the 1968 model but features a Simmons floating rib and a beavertail-type forearm. It was manufactured by Marlin between 1971 and 1973.

Exc.	V.G.	Good	Fair	Poor
1000	850	750	600	400

SMITH, OTIS
Rockfall, Connecticut

This company manufactured a line of single action, spur-trigger revolvers that are chambered for .22, .32, .38, and .41 rimfire cartridges. The pistols have varying barrel lengths. The cylinder access pin is retained by a button on the left side of the frame. The cylinder usually holds five shots. The finishes are either blued or nickel-plated, with birdshead grips. The quality was considered to be mediocre.

Model 1883 Shell-Ejector

A single action, break-open, self ejecting revolver with a ribbed 3.5" barrel chambered for .32 centerfire. It has a 5-shot fluted cylinder and a spur trigger. It was quite well made. The finish is nickel-plated, with black plastic grips.

Exc.	V.G.	Good	Fair	Poor
—	400	200	100	75

Model 1892

A double action, concealed-hammer revolver chambered for the .38 centerfire cartridge. It has a 4" barrel and, for the first time, a conventional trigger and triggerguard. It is gateloaded and has a solid frame. It is nickel-plated with black plastic grips and also appeared under the Maltby, Henley & Company banner marked "Spencer Safety Hammerless" or "Parker Safety Hammerless." The Otis Smith Company ceased operations in 1898.

Exc.	V.G.	Good	Fair	Poor
—	400	200	100	75

SMITH & WESSON
Springfield, Massachusetts
By Roy G. Jinks
Smith & Wesson Historian

Smith & Wesson was founded by two men who shared the dream of developing a new type of firearm...one capable of being fired repeatedly without the annoyance of having to reload it using loose powder, balls and a primer. Their idea was to direct the firearms makers out of the era of muzzleloading, which had dominated the firearms industry since the invention of hand cannons in the 14th century.

Their dream became a reality when Horace Smith and Daniel B. Wesson formed their first partnership in 1852 to manufacture a lever action pistol incorporating a tubular magazine and firing a fully self-contained cartridge. This new repeating pistol could be fired as rapidly as an individual could operate the lever that loaded the pistol and cocked the hammer, making it ready to be fired. The firing power of this lever action pistol was so impressive that, in 1854 when the gun was reviewed by *Scientific America*, it was nicknamed the Volcanic since to the reviewer the rapid fire sequence appeared to have the force of an erupting volcano.

The original site of the Smith & Wesson Arms Company was in Norwich, Connecticut, and the company operated in those facilities until it ran into financial difficulties in 1854. In the reorganization of the company during that year, a new investor, Oliver Winchester, provided the additional financial support to continue the manufacture of this particular type of pistol. The factory was moved to New Haven, Connecticut, the site of some of Winchester's holdings, and at this time the name was changed to Volcanic Repeating Arms Company and Smith & Wesson sold the majority of their interests. It is interesting to note that this early company continued to develop using the original Smith & Wesson patents and emerged in 1866 as the Winchester Repeating Arms Company.

Horace Smith and D.B. Wesson moved from Connecticut to Springfield, Massachusetts, and in 1856 established their company for the purpose of manufacturing a revolving pistol that would fire a small .22 caliber rimfire cartridge, patented by the partners in 1854. This new rimfire cartridge was the beginning of one of the most famous cartridges developed in the world. It was originally called the "Number One Cartridge" but is today more commonly known as the .22 rimfire. The new revolver was called the Model 1 and it gained immediate popularity because of the advantages offered by the new cartridge. In 1859, finding that demand could no longer be met in the small 25-man shop, Smith & Wesson built a new factory located on Stockbridge Street, close to the United States Armory in the center of Springfield, Massachusetts. The factory continued in a progressive manner, improving on the Model 1, and introducing a larger frame gun more suitable to military and law enforcement use. This revolver was called the Model 2 and used a .32 rimfire cartridge.

The demand for the Smith & Wesson product was greatly accelerated in 1861 with the advent of the Civil War. In fact, by mid-1862, the demand for Smith & Wesson products had grown so great that it exceeded factory capacity and it was necessary to close the order books and only supply products against its heavy backlog. Wartime production helped firmly establish Smith & Wesson as one of the leading firearm manufacturers in the United States. However, in the postwar depression Smith & Wesson, like many other businesses, suffered severe business curtailments and sales dropped to only a few guns per month.

By 1867, the partners realized that a new approach was necessary. They had been experimenting with a new design but had lacked the necessary market. For this reason, in April 1867, they authorized Henry W. Hallott to negotiate contracts and establish a market in Europe, and sales agencies in England, France, and Germany. One of Hallott's first functions was to organize a display of Smith & Wesson arms at a major exposition being held in Paris. The display included the total product line as well as some of their highly engraved works of art to further illustrate the quality craftsmen employed by the firm.

Courtesy Smith & Wesson

The Smith & Wesson arms exhibit was extremely popular and many nations expressed interest in its products. One of the most important persons to view their product line was the Russian Grand Duke Alexis. He was so impressed with Smith & Wesson's revolvers that he purchased several small pistols for himself and his aides. This marketing approach proved highly successful and European orders helped to relieve the effects of the domestic depression. With this new marketplace and the increase in sales, Smith & Wesson introduced their first large caliber 44 revolver called the Model 3.

The Model 3 was a totally new design known as a "top break" revolver that incorporated a fully automatic ejection system allowing rapid unloading and reloading of cartridges.

One of the first customers to receive the Model 3 was the Russian military attache, General Gorloff. He promptly sent this sample to Russia for evaluation, and it was so well received that in May 1871 the Russian government signed a contract for 20,000 Model 3s, paying Smith & Wesson in advance with gold. This contract proved to be one of many signed with the Russian government but, more significantly, it influenced the total market and soon orders poured into the factory far exceeding its ability to supply handguns. The Model 3 became extremely popular throughout the world and on our own western frontier. One of the most interesting notes on the Model 3 appeared in an editorial in the *Army/Navy Journal* shortly after the Custer massacre. This article noted that if Custer and his men had been armed with Schofield's variation of the Smith & Wesson Model 3, rather than the slower loading Colt Single Action revolver, they might have possibly survived the Indian attack.

Smith & Wesson continued to grow and in 1880 expanded their line by introducing the first group of "double action" revolvers, the result of more than four years of extensive research.

In 1899, Smith & Wesson developed one of its most famous revolvers, the .38 Military & Police, which was the predecessor of the Model 10. This revolver was designed to fire another first, the .38 Smith & Wesson Special.

In the summer of 1914 at the request of the British government, Smith & Wesson began development of its first side swing revolvers in .45 caliber. As WWI was engulfing the European continent, England needed a supply of service revolvers. Smith & Wesson responded by producing more than 75,000 revolvers chambered for the .455 Mark 11 British Service cartridge in slightly more than one year, thus helping to provide the British Army with the finest revolver available in the world.

During the 1930s, Smith & Wesson introduced two more famous revolvers, the K-22 Outdoorsman for the competitive shooter and the .357 Magnum for the law enforcement officers who needed a powerful handgun to continue their fight against crime. The .357 Magnum also was significant as it was the beginning of the era of Magnum handguns; an important first in the growth of handgunning in the world.

As it had done in WWI, Smith & Wesson answered the needs of WWII's fighting forces and by 1941 its total plant production was geared to supplying arms for the United States and all her allies. By March 1945 when WWII production was ended, Smith & Wesson had supplied 568,204 .38 military and police revolvers to its close ally Great Britain. These revolvers were produced in the British Service caliber of .38/200.

At the close of WWII, Smith & Wesson continued its progressive leadership under the management of Mr. C.R. Hellstrom, who became president in 1946 and the first person outside the Wesson family to serve in this capacity. In 1949, the company moved to a totally new facility in Springfield, Massachusetts, where it has continued to expand. It introduced the first American-made 9mm double action pistol called the Model 39, followed by the introduction of a gun that has become a legend with sportsmen and gun enthusiasts throughout the world, the Model 29, .44 Magnum, the most powerful handgun.

In 1964 Smith & Wesson entered into a completely new era as the independently owned company was purchased by Bangor Panta Corporation. Bangor Panta, recognizing an even greater potential for this giant of the firearms field, encouraged the president, W.G. Gunn, to further diversify the company. William Gunn succeeded C.R. Hellstrom as president in 1963 following the death of Mr. Hellstrom at the age of 68.

Gunn soon purchased other companies to augment Smith & Wesson's line of handgun and handcuff products to further meet the needs of the law enforcement and sporting markets. By the 1970s Smith & Wesson had increased its products to law enforcement by selling riot control equipment, police Identi-Kit identification equipment, night vision, breath testing equipment and leather products. The sporting dealers were now able to purchase not only Smith & Wesson handguns but ammunition, holsters and long guns, thus allowing them to sell a complete line of Smith & Wesson products.

Even with the expansion of Smith & Wesson's product line in other areas, the management in Springfield continued to concentrate on the development of new handguns. In 1965 the firm introduced the first stainless steel revolver, thus changing again the course of firearms history. The 1970s saw the continued development of stainless models and a new 15-shot 9mm autoloading pistol called the Model 59 to meet the requirement of many law enforcement agencies. Smith & Wesson opened the market of police commemorative handguns, allowing departments to purchase specially designed handguns to commemorate department history. These commemoratives helped further establish Smith & Wessons's position with law enforcement by providing the departments with a memento of their history on a fine quality Smith & Wesson handgun.

The 1970s saw many significant improvements in Smith & Wesson; the further modernization of its manufacturing facilities in Springfield, the development of the stainless steel Model 629, .44 Magnum, the Model 547, 9mm revolver using a special patented extractor system. But most important was the development of the Smith & Wesson L frame line producing the Models 581, 586, 681, and 686, which had a significant impact on both the law enforcement and sporting markets to become the most popular new revolver introduced.

With the new L frame models and the 1980s, Smith & Wesson began to consolidate its widely diversified product line by concentrating on those lines that were most profitable and beneficial to the company. Development was begun on a 9mm autoloading pistol to meet the needs of the United States military and a new .45 autoloading pistol called the Model 645.

In January 1984, Lear Siegler Corporation of Santa Monica, California, purchased Bangor Panta, thus acquiring Smith & Wesson. Lear Siegler, in their evaluation of Smith & Wesson, recognized the fact that Smith & Wesson's total strength laid in the manufacture and sales of handguns, handcuffs, and police Identi-Kits. Under Lear's direction, Smith & Wesson divested itself of all other unrelated lines to concentrate on the product for which they were famous, thus further strengthening their position in the handgun market by concentrating Smith & Wesson's efforts in providing the highest quality, most innovative designs available to handgun users of the world.

In December 1986, Lear Siegler Corporation was purchased by Forstmann Little & Company in an agreed-upon friendly takeover. However, Forstmann Little had no interest in Smith & Wesson. Their primary interest was only in Lear Siegler holdings in the automotive and air space industry. Therefore, they offered Smith & Wesson for sale to help finance the takeover of Lear Siegler. For the first time since 1964, Smith & Wesson was going to be offered for sale on its own merits as one of the finest handgun manufacturers in the United States.

The successful bidder for Smith & Wesson was the F.H. Tomkins p.l.c. of London, England. Tomkins brings to Smith & Wesson a new strong leadership and a renewed dedication to quality and development of the finest handguns in the world.

NOTE: In 2001 Smith & Wesson was purchased by the Saf-T-Hammer Corporation, an American company whose executives are former S&W executives.

SMITH & WESSON ANTIQUE HANDGUNS

Model 1, 1st Issue Revolver

This was the first metallic cartridge arm produced by Smith & Wesson. It is a small revolver that weighs approximately 10 oz. and is chambered for the .22 short rimfire cartridge. The octagonal barrel is 3.25" long. It holds 7 cartridges. The barrel and nonfluted cylinder pivot upward upon release of the under the frame. This model has a square butt with rosewood grips.

The oval brass frame is silver-plated. The barrel and cylinder are blued. The barrel is stamped with the company name and address; the patent dates also appear. The sides of the frame are rounded on the 1st issue. Other characteristics which distinguish the more valuable 1st issue from later issues include a perfectly round side plate and a hinged hammer spur. Smith & Wesson manufactured approximately 11,000 of these revolvers between 1857 and 1860. Since this was the first of its kind, it is not difficult to understand the need for the number of variations within this model designation. Many small improvements were made on the way to the next model. These variations are as follows:

1st Type
Serial range 1 to low 200s, revolving recoil shield, bayonet type catch on frame.

Exc.	V.G.	Good	Fair	Poor
—	15000	10000	8000	—

NOTE: Rarity makes valuation speculative.

2nd Type
Serial range low 200s to 1130, improved recoil plate.

Exc.	V.G.	Good	Fair	Poor
—	9000	5000	2500	—

3rd Type
Serial range 1130 to low 3000s, bayonet catch dropped for spring-loaded side catch.

Typical configuration for 3rd-6th type, Model 1 1st Issue

Courtesy Jim Supica, Old Town Station

Exc.	V.G.	Good	Fair	Poor
—	3500	2500	1500	—

4th Type
Serial range low 3000s to low 4200s, recoil shield made much smaller.

Exc.	V.G.	Good	Fair	Poor
—	3250	2000	1250	—

5th Type
Serial range low 4200s to low 5500s, has 5-groove rifling instead of 3.

Exc.	V.G.	Good	Fair	Poor
—	3250	2000	1250	—

6th Type
Serial range low 5500s to end of production 11670. A cylinder ratchet replaced the revolving recoil shield.

Exc.	V.G.	Good	Fair	Poor
—	3000	1750	1000	—

Model 1 2nd Issue
Similar in appearance to the 1st Issue this 2nd Issue variation has several notable differences that make identification rather simple. The sides of the frame on the 2nd Issue are flat not rounded as on the 1st Issue. The sideplate is irregular in shape—not round like on the 1st Issue. The barrel was 3-3/16" in length. The barrel is stamped "Smith & Wesson" while the

cylinder is marked with the three patent dates: April 3, 1858, July 5 1859, and December 18, 1860. There have been 2nd Issue noted with full silver or nickel-plating. Smith & Wesson manufactured approximately 115,000 of these revolvers between 1860 and 1868. The serial numbers started around 1100 where the 1st Issue left off and continued to 126400. There were approximately 4,400 revolvers marked "2D Quality" on the barrels. These revolvers were slightly defective and were sold at a lesser price. They will bring an approximate 100% premium on today's market.

Courtesy Mike Stuckslager

Exc.	V.G.	Good	Fair	Poor
—	700	400	250	—

Model 1 3rd Issue

This is a redesigned version of its forerunners. Another .22 short rimfire, 7-shot revolver, this model has a fluted cylinder and round barrel with a raised rib. This variation was manufactured totally from wrought iron. The three patent dates are stamped on top of the ribbed barrel as is "Smith & Wesson". It features birdshead type grips of rosewood and is either fully blued nickel-plated, or two-toned with the frame nickel and the barrel and cylinder blued. There are two barrel lengths offered: 3.25" and 2-11/16". The shorter barrel was introduced in 1872. Serial numbering began with #1 and continued to 131163. They were manufactured between 1868 and 1882. The Model 1 3rd Issue was the last of the tip-up style produced by Smith & Wesson.

Courtesy Mike Stuckslager

Shorter Barreled Version-Rare

Exc.	V.G.	Good	Fair	Poor
—	1350	800	400	—

Longer Barreled Version-Standard

Exc.	V.G.	Good	Fair	Poor
—	500	275	200	—

Model 1-1/2 1st Issue (1-1/2 Old Model)

This model was the first of the .32-caliber Rimfire Short revolvers that S&W produced. It is a larger version of the Model 1 but is physically similar in appearance. The Model 1-1/2 was offered with a 3.5" octagonal barrel and has a 5-shot nonfluted cylinder and a square butt with rosewood grips. In 1866 a 4" barrel version was produced for a short time. It is estimated that

about 200 were sold. The finish is blued or nickel-plated. The serial numbering on this model ran from serial number 1 to 26300; and, interestingly to note, S&W had most of the parts for this revolver manufactured on contract by King & Smith of Middletown, Connecticut. Smith & Wesson merely assembled and finished them. They were produced between 1865 and 1868. **NOTE:** Add a 50% premium for the 4" barrel variation.

Courtesy Mike Stuckslager

Exc.	V.G.	Good	Fair	Poor
—	550	350	200	—

Model 1-1/2 2nd Issue (1-1/2 New Model)

The factory referred to this model as the New Model 1-1/2 and it is an improved version of the 1st Issue. It is somewhat similar in appearance with a few notable exceptions. The barrel is 2.5" or 3.5" in length, round with a raised rib. The grip is of the birdshead configuration, and the 5-shot cylinder is fluted and chambered for the .32 rimfire long cartridge. The cylinder stop is located in the top frame instead of the bottom. The finish and grip material are the same as the 1st Issue. There were approximately 100,700 manufactured between 1868 and 1875.

Courtesy Mike Stuckslager

3.5" Barrel-Standard

Exc.	V.G.	Good	Fair	Poor
—	450	275	175	—

Courtesy Mike Stuckslager

2.5" Barrel-Rare

Exc.	V.G.	Good	Fair	Poor
—	1100	600	350	—

Model 1-1/2 Transitional Model

Approximately 650 of these were produced by fitting 1st Issue cylinders and barrels to 2nd Issue frames. They also have 1st Model octagon barrels with 2nd Model birdshead grips. These revolvers fall into the serial number range 27200-28800.

Exc.	V.G.	Good	Fair	Poor
—	3000	1500	800	—

Model 2 Army or Old Model

Similar in appearance to the Model 1 2nd Issue, this revolver was extremely successful from a commercial standpoint. It was released just in time for the commencement of hostilities in the Civil War. Smith & Wesson had, in this revolver, the only weapon able to fire self-contained cartridges and be easily carried as a backup by soldiers going off to war. This resulted in a backlog of more than three years before the company finally stopped taking orders. This model is chambered for .32 rimfire long and has a 6-shot nonfluted cylinder and 4", 5", or 6" barrel lengths. It has a square butt with rosewood grips and is either blued or nickel-plated. There were approximately 77,155 manufactured between 1861 and 1874.

NOTE: A slight premium for early 2 pin model.

Courtesy Chester Krause

Courtesy Mike Stuckslager

5" or 6" Barrel-Standard Barrel

Exc.	V.G.	Good	Fair	Poor
—	1500	950	450	—

4" Barrel-Rare! Use Caution

Exc.	V.G.	Good	Fair	Poor
—	5000	3000	1500	—

A Smith & Wesson Model No. 2 Army was sold at auction for $23,375. It was fitted with an 8" barrel with target sights. Finish was blue and silver plate. Factory extended rosewood grips. Condition is very good with grips 98%. Butterfield & Butterfield, February 2001

.32 Single Action (Model 1-1/2 Centerfire)

This model represented the first .32 S&W centerfire caliber top-break revolver that automatically ejected the spent cartridges upon opening. It is similar in appearance to the Model 1-1/2 2nd Issue. This model has a 5-shot fluted cylinder and a birdshead grip of wood or checkered hard rubber and was offered with barrel lengths of 3", 3.5", 6", 8", and 10". The 8" and 10" barrel are rare and were not offered until 1887. This model pivots downward on opening and features a rebounding hammer that made the weapon much safer to fully load. There were approximately 97,599 manufactured between 1878 and 1892.

Courtesy W.P. Hallstein III and son Chip

Early Model Without Strain Screw-Under #6500

Courtesy Mike Stuckslager

Exc.	V.G.	Good	Fair	Poor
—	500	300	175	—

Later Model With Strain Screw

Courtesy Mike Stuckslager

Exc.	V.G.	Good	Fair	Poor
—	350	250	150	—

8" or 10" Barrel Model-Very Rare, Use Caution

Exc.	V.G.	Good	Fair	Poor
—	3000	2000	800	—

.38 Single Action 1st Model (Baby Russian)

This model is sometimes called the "Baby Russian." It is a top break, automatic-ejecting revolver chambered for the .38 S&W centerfire cartridge. It is offered with either a 3.25" or 4" round barrel with a raised rib, has a 5-shot fluted cylinder, and is finished in blue or nickel plating. A 5" barrel was added as an option a short time later. The butt is rounded, with wood or checkered hard rubber grips inlaid with the S&W medallion. It has a spur trigger. There were approximately 25,548 manufactured in 1876 and 1877 of which 16,046 were nickel and 6,502 were blued.

Courtesy Mike Stuckslager

Exc.	V.G.	Good	Fair	Poor
—	858	375	250	—

.38 Single Action 2nd Model

With the exception of an improved and shortened extractor assembly and the availability of additional barrel lengths of 3.25", 4", 5", 6", 8", and 10" with the 8" and 10" barrel lengths being the most rare, this model is quite similar in appearance to the 1st Model. There were approximately 108,225 manufactured between 1877 and 1891.

Courtesy Mike Stuckslager

8" and 10" Barrel-Very Rare, Use Caution

Exc.	V.G.	Good	Fair	Poor
—	3250	2250	950	—

3.25", 4", 5", and 6" Barrel Lengths-small premium for 5" or 6" lengths

Exc.	V.G.	Good	Fair	Poor
—	375	275	195	—

.38 Single Action 3rd Model

This model differs from the first two models because it is fitted with a triggerguard. It is chambered for the .38 S&W centerfire cartridge, has a 5-shot fluted cylinder, and is a top break design with automatic ejection upon opening. The barrel lengths are 3.25", 4", and 6". The finish is blued or nickel-plated. The butt is rounded, with checkered hard rubber grips featuring S&W medallions. There were approximately 26,850 manufactured between 1891 and 1911.

Courtesy Mike Stuckslager

Exc.	V.G.	Good	Fair	Poor
—	1700	1000	600	—

.38 Single Action Mexican Model

This extremely rare model is quite similar in appearance to the 3rd Model Single Action. The notable differences are the flat hammer sides with no outward flaring of the spur. The spur trigger assembly was not made integrally with the frame but is a separate part added to it. One must exercise extreme caution as S&W offered a kit that would convert the triggerguard assembly of the Third Model to the spur trigger of the Mexican Model. This, coupled with the fact that both models fall within the same serial range, can present a real identification problem. Another feature of the Mexican Model is the absence of a half cock. The exact number of Mexican Models manufactured between 1891 and 1911 is unknown but it is estimated that the number is small.

Exc.	V.G.	Good	Fair	Poor
—	3650	1500	950	—

.32 Double Action 1st Model

This is one of the rarest of all S&W revolvers. There were only 30 manufactured. It also has a straight-sided sideplate that weakened the revolver frame. Perhaps this was the reason that so few were made. This model was the first break-open, double action, automatic-ejecting .32 that S&W produced. It features a 3" round barrel with raised rib, a 5-shot fluted cylinder, and round butt with plain, uncheckered, black hard rubber grips. The finish is blued or nickel-plated. All 30 of these revolvers were manufactured in 1880.

Exc.	V.G.	Good	Fair	Poor
—	12000	7500	4000	—

NOTE: Rarity makes valuation speculative.

.32 Double Action 2nd Model

Courtesy Mike Stuckslager

This revolver is chambered for the .32 S&W cartridge and has a 3" round barrel with a raised rib. The 5-shot cylinder is fluted, and the finish is blued or nickel-plated. It is a top break design with a round butt. The grips are either checkered or floral-embossed hard rubber with the S&W monogram. This model has an oval sideplate, eliminating the weakness of the 1st Model. There were approximately 22,142 manufactured between 1880 and 1882.

Exc.	V.G.	Good	Fair	Poor
—	350	225	175	—

.32 Double Action 3rd Model

This model incorporates internal improvements that are not evident in appearance. The most notable identifiable difference between this model and its predecessors is in the surface of the cylinder. The flutes are longer; there is only one set of stops instead of two; and the free groove is no longer present. There were approximately 21,232 manufactured in 1882 and 1883.

Courtesy Mike Stuckslager

Exc.	V.G.	Good	Fair	Poor
—	350	250	175	—

.32 Double Action 4th Model

This model is quite similar in appearance to the 3rd Model except that the triggerguard is oval in shape instead of the squared back of the previous models. There were also internal improvements. There were approximately 239,600 manufactured between 1883 and 1909.

Courtesy Mike Stuckslager

Exc.	V.G.	Good	Fair	Poor
375	200	175	125	65

NOTE: Add a 50% premium for revolvers built before 1898.

.32 Double Action 5th Model

The only difference between this model and its predecessors is that this model has the front sight machined as an integral part of the barrel rib. On the other models, the sight was pinned in place. There were approximately 44,641 manufactured between 1909 and 1919.

Courtesy Mike Stuckslager

Exc.	V.G.	Good	Fair	Poor
375	275	200	125	100

SAFETY HAMMERLESS

This model was a departure from what was commonly being produced at this time. Some attribute the Safety Hammerless design to D.B. Wesson's hearing that a child had been injured by cocking and firing one of the company's pistols. This story has never been proven. Nevertheless, the concealed hammer and grip safety make this an ideal pocket pistol for those needing concealability in a handgun. This is a small revolver chambered for .32 S&W and .38 S&W cartridges. It has a 5-shot fluted cylinder and is offered with a 2", 3", and 3.5" round barrel with a raised rib. The butt is rounded and has checkered hard rubber grips with the S&W logo. The finish is blue or nickel plated. The revolver is a top break, automatic-ejecting design; and the 1st Model has the latch for opening located in the rear center of the top strap instead of at the sides. The latch is checkered for a positive grip. This model is commonly referred to as the "Lemon Squeezer" because the grip safety must be squeezed as it is fired.

Courtesy Mike Stuckslager

.32 SAFETY HAMMERLESS (AKA .32 NEW DEPARTURE OR .32 LEMON SQUEEZER)

1st Model-push button latch s/n 1- 91417, built 1888-1902

Exc.	V.G.	Good	Fair	Poor
375	225	165	100	50

NOTE: Add a 50% premium for revolvers built before 1898.

.32 Safety Hammerless-2nd Model

T-bar latch, pinned front sight, s/n 91418-169999, built 1902 to 1909.

Courtesy Mike Stuckslager

Exc.	V.G.	Good	Fair	Poor
350	225	165	100	50

.32 Safety Hammerless- 3rd Model

T-bar latch, integral forged front sight, s/n 170000-242981, built 1909 to 1937

Exc.	V.G.	Good	Fair	Poor
400	225	165	100	50

NOTE: For 2" barrel, Bicycle Model-Add 100%.

.38 Double Action 1st Model
This model is similar in appearance to the .32 1st Model, having a straight cut side-plate, but is chambered for the .38 S&W cartridge. The grips are checkered, and there were 4,000 manufactured in 1880.

Exc.	V.G.	Good	Fair	Poor
—	850	500	250	—

.38 Double Action 2nd Model
This is similar in appearance to the .32 2nd Model but is chambered for the .38 S&W cartridge. There were approximately 115,000 manufactured between 1880 and 1884.

Courtesy Mike Stuckslager

Exc.	V.G.	Good	Fair	Poor
—	350	250	200	—

.38 Double Action 3rd Model
Essentially the same in appearance as the .32 Model but chambered for the .38 S&W cartridge, it is also offered with a 3.25", 4", 5", 6", 8", and 10" barrel. There were numerous internal changes in this model similar to the .32 Double Action 3rd Model. There were approximately 203,700 manufactured between 1884 and 1895.

Courtesy Mike Stuckslager

8" and 10" Barrel-Rare, Use Caution
Exc.	V.G.	Good	Fair	Poor
—	2500	1500	800	—

Standard Barrel
Exc.	V.G.	Good	Fair	Poor
—	365	250	200	—

NRA Antique
Exc.	Fine	V.G	Good	Fair
365	300	250	215	185

.38 Double Action 4th Model
This is the .38 S&W version of the 4th Model and is identical in outward appearance to the 3rd Model. The relocation of the sear was the main design change in this model. There were approximately 216,300 manufactured between 1895 and 1909.

Exc.	V.G.	Good	Fair	Poor
385	250	195	150	75

NOTE: Add a 20% premium for revolvers built before 1898.

.38 Double Action 5th Model
This model is the same as the .32 except that it is chambered for the .38 S&W cartridge. There were approximately 15,000 manufactured between 1909 and 1911.

Courtesy Mike Stuckslager

Exc.	V.G.	Good	Fair	Poor
425	285	195	150	75

.38 Double Action Perfected
A unique top-break with both a barrel latch similar to the other top-breaks and a thumbpiece similar to the hand ejectors; also the only top-break where the triggerguard is integral to the frame rather than a separate piece. Produced from 1909 to 1911 in their own serial number range. About 59,400 were built.

Exc.	V.G.	Good	Fair	Poor
550	365	200	165	85

.38 Safety Hammerless 1st Model
Z-bar latch, serial number range 1 to 5250, made 1887 only.
NOTE: Also offered with a 6" barrel. RARE! Add 50%.

Exc.	V.G.	Good	Fair	Poor
—	700	425	250	—

.38 Safety Hammerless 2nd Model
Push button latch protrudes above frame, s/n 5251-42483, built 1887-1890.

Exc.	V.G.	Good	Fair	Poor
—	350	250	175	—

Courtesy Mike Stuckslager

.38 Safety Hammerless 3rd Model
Push button latch flush with frame, s/n 42484-116002, 1890-1898.

Exc.	V.G.	Good	Fair	Poor
—	325	225	165	—

.38 Safety Hammerless Army Test Revolver
There were approximately 100 sold to U.S. government in 1890. They have 3rd Model features but are in the 2nd Model serial number range, 41333-41470. Fitted with 6" barrels and marked "US".

CAUTION: Be very wary of fakes. Seek an expert appraisal prior to a sale.

Exc.	V.G.	Good	Fair	Poor
—	8500	6500	4000	—

NOTE: Rarity makes valuation speculative.

.38 Safety Hammerless 4th Model

This model was produced in .38 S&W only, and the only difference in the 4th Model and the 3rd Model is the adoption of the standard T-bar type of barrel latch as found on most of the top break revolvers. ".38 S&W Cartridge" was also added to the left side of the barrel. There were approximately 104,000 manufactured between 1898 and 1907; serial number range 116003 to 220000.

Courtesy Mike Stuckslager

Exc.	V.G.	Good	Fair	Poor
350	235	175	110	50

.38 Safety Hammerless 5th Model

This is the last of the "Lemon Squeezers," and the only appreciable difference between this model and the 4th Model is that the front sight blade on the 5th Model is an integral part of the barrel and not a separate blade pinned onto the barrel. There were approximately 41,500 manufactured between 1907 and 1940; serial number range 220001 to 261493.
2" Barrel Version-Add 50%.

Courtesy Mike Stuckslager

Exc.	V.G.	Good	Fair	Poor
385	265	175	110	50

Model 3 American 1st Model

This model represented a number of firsts for the Smith & Wesson Company. It was the first of the top break, automatic ejection revolvers. It was also the first Smith & Wesson in a large caliber (it is chambered for the .44 S&W American cartridge as well as the .44 Henry rimfire on rare occasions). It was also known as the 1st Model American. This large revolver is offered with an 8" round barrel with a raised rib as standard. Barrel lengths of 6" and 7" were also available. It has a 6-shot fluted cylinder and a square butt with walnut grips. It is blued or nickel-plated. It is interesting to note that this model appeared three years before Colt's Single Action Army and perhaps, more than any other model, was associated with the historic American West. There were only 8,000 manufactured between 1870 and 1872.

Standard Production Model

Exc.	V.G.	Good	Fair	Poor
—	7000	3500	1500	—

NOTE: Add 25% for "oil hole" variation found on approximately the first 1,500 guns. Add 50% for unusual barrel lengths other than standard 8". Original "Nashville Police" marked guns worth a substantial premium.

Transition Model-Serial Number Range 6466-6744
Shorter cylinder (1.423"), improved barrel catch.

Exc.	V.G.	Good	Fair	Poor
—	6000	3000	1500	—

U.S. Army Order-Serial Number Range 125-2199
One thousand produced with "U.S." stamped on top of barrel; "OWA", on left grip.

Exc.	V.G.	Good	Fair	Poor
—	12000	6000	3000	—

.44 Rimfire Henry Model
Only 200 produced throughout serial range.

Exc.	V.G.	Good	Fair	Poor
—	12000	6000	3000	—

NOTE: Rarity makes valuation speculative.

Model 3 American 2nd Model

An improved version of the 1st Model. The most notable difference is the larger diameter trigger pivot pin and the frame protrusions above the trigger to accommodate it. The front sight blade on this model is made of steel instead of nickel silver. Several internal improvements were also incorporated into this model. This model is commonly known as the American 2nd Model. The 8" barrel length was standard on this model. There were approximately 20,735 manufactured, including 3,014 chambered for .44 rimfire Henry, between 1872 and 1874.

NOTE: There have been 5.5", 6", 6.5", and 7" barrels noted; but they are extremely scarce and would bring a 40% premium over the standard 8" model. Use caution when purchasing these short barrel revolvers.

Courtesy Buffalo Bill Historical Center, Cody, Wyoming

.44 Rimfire Henry
Exc.	V.G.	Good	Fair	Poor
—	6500	3250	1500	—

Standard 8" Model-.44 American centerfire
Exc.	V.G.	Good	Fair	Poor
—	5000	3000	1250	—

A Second Model American was sold at auction for $12,100. It was fitted with a 7" barrel. Blued finish. Chambered for .44 S&W caliber. Condition was antique excellent.
Faintich Auction Service, October 1999

Paul Goodwin Photo

WHAT'S IT LIKE-SMITH & WESSON MODEL #3 RUSSIAN

Shortly after purchasing my first Colt Single Action as a teenager I discovered I had a neighbor who also loved single actions. He had a First Generation Colt that had been converted to a 7 1/2" .44 Special with a 1860 Army grip frame, an 1860 Army that now wore the Colt Single Action Army grip frame, and the most fascinating sixgun of all, a .44 Russian Smith & Wesson. It was 1957 and this teenager up to that time had always believed Smith & Wesson only made double action sixguns. As I was allowed to handle and shoot the .44 Russian I realized it did not have the marvelous balance of the Colt Single Action but even as untrained as I was, I could recognize that this was truly a marvelous piece of engineering. In 1869 Smith & Wesson brought forth the first successful cartridge-firing, big-bore revolver with the S&W .44 American and presented one of their revolvers to the Russian military attaché, General Gorloff. This was a very smart move on the part of Smith and Wesson for two reasons: 1) Russia placed a large order for Smith & Wesson revolvers with over 60,000 Russians going to Russia, and 2) more importantly for the shooters, the Russians modernized the .44 American rim-fire to a center-fire cartridge with the inside lubricated bullet instead of the heel-type bullet used in the American. We still use this same style bullet today. My neighbor's Smith & Wesson was a Model #3 Russian. Over the past 45 years I've let several of these slip by me but that has all been corrected and I now have one of the Model #3 Russians from Navy Arms and unlike many replicas it is offered only in the original chambering of .44 Russian. Shooting one is definitely a great connection to the past.

John Taffin

Model 3 Russian 1st Model

This model is quite similar in appearance to the American 1st and 2nd Model revolvers. S&W made several internal changes to this model to satisfy the Russian government. The markings on this revolver are distinct; and the caliber for which it is chambered, .44 S&W Russian, is different. There were approximately 20,000 Russian-Contract revolvers. The serial number range is 1-20000. They are marked in Russian Cyrillic letters. The Russian double-headed eagle is stamped on the rear portion of the barrel with inspector's marks underneath it. All of the contract guns have 8" barrels and lanyard swivels on the butt. These are rarely encountered, as most were shipped to Russia. The commercial run of this model numbered approximately 4,655. The barrels are stamped in English and include the words "Russian Model." Some are found with 6" and 7" barrels, as well as the standard 8". There were also 500 revolvers that were rejected from the Russian contract series and sold on the commercial market. Some of these are marked in English; some, Cyrillic. Some have the Cyrillic markings ground off and the English restamped. This model was manufactured from 1871 to 1874.

Russian Contract Model-Cyrillic barrel address

Exc.	V.G.	Good	Fair	Poor
—	7000	3500	2000	—

Commercial Model

Exc.	V.G.	Good	Fair	Poor
—	5000	2750	1250	—

Rejected Russian Contract Model

Exc.	V.G.	Good	Fair	Poor
—	5000	2750	1250	—

Model 3 Russian 2nd Model

This revolver was known as the "Old Model Russian." This is a complicated model to understand as there are many variations within the model designation. The serial numbering is quite complex as well, and values vary greatly due to relatively minor model differences. Before purchasing this model, it would be advisable to secure competent appraisal as well as to read reference materials solely devoted to this firearm. This model is chambered for the .44 S&W Russian, as well as the .44 rimfire Henry cartridge. It has a 7" barrel and a round butt featuring a projection on the frame that fits into the thumb web. The grips are walnut, and the finish is blue or nickel-plated. The triggerguard has a reverse curved spur on the bottom. There were approximately 85,200 manufactured between 1873 and 1878.

Courtesy Jim Supica, Old Town Station

Commercial Model

6,200 made, .44 S&W Russian, English markings.

Exc.	V.G.	Good	Fair	Poor
—	3250	1500	850	—

.44 Rimfire Henry Model

500 made.

Exc.	V.G.	Good	Fair	Poor
—	4750	2250	1000	—

Russian Contract Model

70,000 made; rare, as most were shipped to Russia. Cyrillic markings; lanyard swivel on butt.

Exc.	V.G.	Good	Fair	Poor
—	3500	1750	950	—

1st Model Turkish Contract

.44 rimfire Henry, special rimfire frames, serial-numbered in own serial number range 1-1000.

Exc.	V.G.	Good	Fair	Poor
—	6000	3750	1750	—

2nd Model Turkish Contract

Made from altered centerfire frames from the regular commercial serial number range. 1,000 made. Use caution with this model.

Exc.	V.G.	Good	Fair	Poor
—	4500	2250	1000	—

Japanese Govt. Contract

Five thousand made between the 1-9000 serial number range. The Japanese naval insignia, an anchor over two wavy lines, found on the butt. The barrel is Japanese proofed, and the words "Jan.19, 75 REISSUE July 25, 1871" are stamped on the barrel, as well.

Exc.	V.G.	Good	Fair	Poor
—	3500	1700	950	—

Model 3 Russian 3rd Model

This revolver is also known as the "New Model Russian." The factory referred to this model as the Model of 1874 or the Cavalry Model. It is chambered for the .44 S&W Russian and the .44 Henry rimfire cartridge. The barrel is 6.5", and the round butt is the same humped-back affair as the 2nd Model. The grips are walnut; and the finish, blue or nickel-plated. The most notable differences in appearance between this model and the 2nd Model are the shorter extractor housing under the barrel and the integral front sight blade instead of the pinned-on one found on the previous models. This is another model that bears careful research before attempting to evaluate. Minor variances can greatly affect values. Secure detailed reference materials and qualified appraisal. There were approximately 60,638 manufactured between 1874 and 1878.

> A prototype Model 3 Russian with 7" barrel was sold at auction for $14,950. This revolver has a redesigned round butt profile. Factory letter. Condition was very good nickel plate.
> Amoskeag Auction Co. Inc., March 2000

Commercial Model

.44 S&W Russian, marked "Russian Model" in English, 13,500 made.

Exc.	V.G.	Good	Fair	Poor
—	9000	5000	2500	—

.44 Rimfire Henry Model

Exc.	V.G	Good	Fair	Poor
—	4500	2700	900	—

Turkish Model

Five thousand made of altered centerfire frames, made to fire .44 rimfire Henry. "W" inspector's mark on butt. Fakes have been noted; be aware.

Exc.	V.G	Good	Fair	Poor
—	4500	2700	900	—

Japanese Contract Model

One thousand made; has the Japanese naval insignia, an anchor over two wavy lines, stamped on the butt.

Exc.	V.G	Good	Fair	Poor
—	3100	1950	850	—

Russian Contract Model

Barrel markings are in Russian Cyrillic. Approximately 41,100 were produced.

Exc.	V.G	Good	Fair	Poor
—	3100	1950	850	—

Model 3 Russian 3rd Model (Loewe & Tula Copies)

The German firm of Ludwig Loewe produced a copy of this model that is nearly identical to the S&W. This German revolver was made under Russian contract, as well as for commercial sales. The contract model has different Cyrillic markings than the S&W and the letters "HK" as inspector's marks. The commercial model has the markings in English. The Russian arsenal at Tula also produced a copy of this revolver with a different Cyrillic dated stamping on the barrel.

Courtesy Mike Stuckslager

Courtesy Mike Stuckslager

Loewe

Exc.	V.G	Good	Fair	Poor
—	2900	1750	700	—

Tula

Exc.	V.G	Good	Fair	Poor
—	3350	2000	800	—

MODEL 3 SCHOFIELD

Model 3 Schofield 1st Model

"US" Contract-3,000 Issued

Exc.	V.G.	Good	Fair	Poor
—	8000	4250	2250	—

Civilian Model, No "US" markings-35 Made-Very Rare,
NOTE: Use Caution. UNABLE TO PRICE. At least double the military model values. Expert appraisal needed.

Model 3 Schofield 2nd Model

"US" Contract-4,000 Issued

Exc.	V.G.	Good	Fair	Poor
—	7500	4000	2250	—

Civilian Model-646 Made

Exc.	V.G.	Good	Fair	Poor
—	7000	4000	2000	—

Model 3 Schofield-Surplus Models

After the government dropped the Schofield as an issue cavalry sidearm, the remaining U.S. inventory of these revolvers was sold off as military surplus. Many were sold to National Guard units; and the remainder were sold either to Bannerman's or to Schuyler, Hartley & Graham, two large gun dealers who then resold the guns to supply the growing need for guns on the Western frontier. Schuyler, Hartley & Graham sold a number of guns to the Wells Fargo Express Co. These weapons were nickel-plated and had the barrels shortened to 5", as were many others sold during this period. Beware of fakes when contemplating purchase of the Wells Fargo revolvers.

Wells Fargo & Co. Model

Exc.	V.G.	Good	Fair	Poor
—	8000	4000	2000	—

Surplus Cut Barrel-Not Wells Fargo

Exc.	V.G.	Good	Fair	Poor
—	3500	2000	1200	—

New Model No. 3 Single Action

Always interested in perfecting the Model 3 revolver D.B. Wesson redesigned and improved the old Model 3 in the hopes of attracting more sales. The Russian contracts were almost filled so the company decided to devote the effort necessary to improve on this design. In 1877 this project was undertaken. The extractor housing was shortened; the cylinder retention system was improved; and the shape of the grip was changed to a more streamlined and attractive configuration. This New Model has a 3.5", 4", 5", 6", 6.5", 7", 7.5", or 8" barrel length with a 6-shot fluted cylinder. The 6.5" barrel and .44 S&W Russian chambering is the most often encountered variation of this model, but the factory considered the 3-1/2" and 8" barrels as standard and these were kept in stock as well. The New Model No. 3 was also chambered for .32 S&W, .32-44 S&W, .320 S&W Rev. Rifle, .38 S&W, .38-40, .38-44 S&W, .41 S&W, .44 Henry rimfire, .44 S&W American, .44-40, .45 S&W Schofield, .450 Rev., .45 Webley, .455 MkI and .455 MkII. They are either blued or nickel-plated and have checkered hard rubber grips with the S&W logo molded into them, or walnut grips. There are many sub-variations within this model designation, and the potential collector should secure detailed reference material that deals with this model. There were approximately 35,796 of these revolvers manufactured between 1878 and 1912. Nearly 40 percent were exported to fill contracts with Japan, Australia, Argentina, England, Spain, and Cuba. There were some sent to Asia, as well. The proofmarks of these countries will establish their provenance but will not add appreciably to standard values.

Standard Model-6.5" barrel, .44 S&W Russian

Courtesy Mike Stuckslager

Exc.	V.G.	Good	Fair	Poor
—	3700	2000	1000	—

Japanese Naval Contract

This was the largest foreign purchaser of this model. There were over 1,500 produced with the anchor insignia stamped on the frame.

Courtesy Mike Stuckslager

Exc.	V.G.	Good	Fair	Poor
—	3700	2000	1000	—

Japanese Artillery Contract

This variation is numbered in the 25,000 serial range. They are blued, with a 7" barrel and a lanyard swivel on the butt. Japanese characters are stamped on the extractor housing.

Exc.	V.G.	Good	Fair	Poor
—	5000	2500	1250	—

Maryland Militia Model

This variation is nickel-plated, has a 6.5" barrel, and is chambered for the .44 S&W Russian cartridge. The butt is stamped "U.S.," and the inspector's marks "HN" and "DAL" under the date 1878 appear on the revolver. There were 280 manufactured between serial-numbers 7126 and 7405.

Exc.	V.G.	Good	Fair	Poor
—	10000	6000	3000	—

NOTE: Rarity makes valuation speculative.

Australian Contract

This variation is nickel-plated, is chambered for the .44 S&W Russian cartridge, and is marked with the Australian Colonial Police Broad Arrow on the buff. There were 250 manufactured with 7" barrels and detachable shoulder stocks. The stock has the Broad Arrow stamped on the lower tang. There were also 30 manufactured with 6.5" barrels without the stocks. They all are numbered in the 12,000-13,000 serial range.

Courtesy Mike Stuckslager

Courtesy Mike Stuckslager

Courtesy Mike Stuckslager

Courtesy Mike Stuckslager

A Smith & Wesson New Model No. 3 Australian with match numbered holster and shoulder stock sold at auction for $12,650. Nickel finish was good.
Faintich Auction Service, October 1999

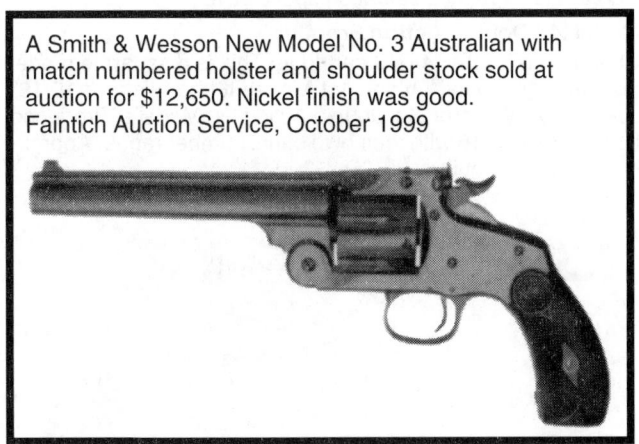

Paul Goodwin Photo

Revolver with stock and holsters

Exc.	V.G.	Good	Fair	Poor
—	8000	4750	2750	—

NOTE: Deduct 40% for no stock.

Argentine Model

This was essentially not a factory contract but a sale through Schuyler, Hartley and Graham. They are stamped "Ejercito/Argentino" in front of the triggerguard. The order amounted to some 2,000 revolvers between the serial numbers 50 and 3400.

Exc.	V.G.	Good	Fair	Poor
—	7000	3500	1750	—

Turkish Model

This is essentially the New Model No. 3 chambered for the .44 rimfire Henry cartridge. It is stamped with the letters "P," "U" and "AFC" on various parts of the revolver. The barrels are all 6.5"; the finish, blued with walnut grips. Lanyard swivels are found on the butt. There were 5,461 manufactured and serial numbered in their own range, starting at 1 through 5,461 between 1879 and 1883.

Courtesy Mike Stuckslager

Exc.	V.G.	Good	Fair	Poor
—	7000	3500	1750	—

New Model No. 3 Target Single Action

This revolver is similar in appearance to the standard New Model No. 3, but was the company's first production target model. It has a 6.5" round barrel with a raised rib and 6-shot fluted cylinder and is finished in blue or nickel-plated. The grips are either walnut or checkered hard rubber with the S&W logo molded into them. This model is chambered in either .32 S&W or .38 S&W. The company referred to these models as either the .32-44 Target or the .38-44 Target depending on the caliber. The designation of .44 referred to the frame size, i.e. a .32 caliber built on a .44 caliber frame. This model was offered with a detachable shoulder stock as an option. These stocks are extremely scarce on today's market. There were approximately 4,333 manufactured between 1887 and 1910.
Shoulder Stock-Add 50%.

Courtesy Mike Stuckslager

Exc.	V.G.	Good	Fair	Poor
—	3100	1350	850	—

New Model No. 3 Frontier Single Action

This is another model similar in appearance to the standard New Model No. 3. It has a 4", 5", or 6.5" barrel and is chambered for the .44-40 Winchester Centerfire cartridge. Because the original New Model No. 3 cylinder was 1-7/16" in length this would not accommodate the longer .44-40 cartridge. The cylinder on the No. 3 Frontier was changed to 1-9/16" in length. Later the company converted 786 revolvers to .44 S&W Russian and sold them to Japan. This model is either blued or nickel-plated and has checkered grips of walnut or hard rubber. They are serial numbered in their own range from 1 through 2072 and were manufactured from 1885 until 1908. This model was designed to compete with the Colt Single Action Army but was not successful.

Courtesy Mike Stuckslager

.44-40-Commercial Model

Exc.	V.G.	Good	Fair	Poor
—	5000	2500	1250	—

Japanese Purchase Converted to .44 S&W Russian

Exc.	V.G.	Good	Fair	Poor
—	4000	2000	1000	—

New Model No. 3-.38 Winchester

This variation was the last of the New Model No. 3s to be introduced. It was offered in .38-40 Winchester as a separate model from 1900 until 1907. The finish is blue or nickel-plate, and the grips are checkered hard rubber or walnut. Barrel lengths of 4" or 6.5" were offered. This model was not at all popular, as only 74 were manufactured in their own serial range 1 through 74. Today's collectors are extremely interested in this extremely rare model.

Courtesy Mike Stuckslager

Exc.	V.G.	Good	Fair	Poor
—	14000	8000	4000	—

NOTE: Rarity makes valuation speculative. A New Model #3 .38 Winchester in Good condition was offered in Old Town Station Dispatch for $6,850 in 1999.

.44 Double Action 1st Model

This model is a top break revolver that automatically ejects the spent cartridge cases upon opening. The barrel latch is located at the top and rear of the cylinder; the pivot, in front and at the bottom. This model was also known as "The D.A. Frontier" or "The New Model Navy." The revolver is chambered for the .44 S&W Russian and was built on a modified Model 3 frame. It is also found on rare occasions chambered for the .38-40 and the .44-40 Winchester. The barrel lengths are 4", 5", 6", and 6.5", round with a raised rib. A 3-1/2" barrel was produced on this model by special request. Collectors should be aware that the barrel for this model and the New Model No. 3 were

interchangeable and the factory did in fact use barrels from either model. The serial number on the rear of the barrel should match the number on the butt, cylinder and barrel latch. The cylinder holds 6 shots and is fluted. It has double sets of stop notches and long free grooves between the stops. It is serial numbered in its own range, beginning at 1. There were approximately 54,000 manufactured between 1881 and 1913.

Courtesy Butterfield & Butterfield, San Francisco, California

Standard .44 S&W Russian

Exc.	V.G.	Good	Fair	Poor
—	1300	700	400	—

Model .44 Double Action Wesson Favorite

The Favorite is basically a lightened version of the 1st Model D.A. .44. The barrel is thinner and is offered in 5" length only. There are lightening cuts in the frame between the triggerguard and the cylinder; the cylinder diameter was smaller, and there is a groove milled along the barrel rib. The Favorite is chambered for the .44 S&W Russian cartridge and has a 6-shot fluted cylinder with the same double-cylinder stop notches and free grooves as the 1st Model Double Action .44. The company name and address, as well as the patent dates, are stamped into the edge of the cylinder instead of on the barrel rib. It is serial-numbered in the same range, between #9000 and 10100. The revolver was most often nickel-plated but was also offered blued. The grips are walnut or checkered hard rubber with the S&W logo molded in. There were approximately 1,000 manufactured in 1882 and 1883. Use caution when purchasing a blued model.
Blued finish-Add 25%.

Exc.	V.G.	Good	Fair	Poor
—	9000	5000	2500	—

NOTE: Rarity makes valuation speculative.

Model .44 Double Action Frontier

Chambered for the .44-40 cartridge. This is a separate model from the .44 Double Action 1st Model. It has a longer 19/16" cylinder like the later .44 Double Action 1st Model's. Produced from 1886 to 1916 with their own serial number range. Approximately 15,340 built.

Courtesy Mike Stuckslager

Exc.	V.G.	Good	Fair	Poor
—	1600	850	450	—

A pair of S&W revolvers were sold at auction for $15,525. They were a .44 Double Action first model and a .38 Double Action. Both belonged to General Leonard Wood. The .44 was delivered in 1905 and the .38 delivered in 1901. Condition was fair for the .44 and good for the .38. Amoskeag Auction Co. Inc., March 2000

Model .38 Winchester Double Action

Similar to the .44 Double Action 1st Model except for the chamber. Fitted with long cylinder. Approximately 276 produced in their own serial number range from 1900 to 1910.

Exc.	V.G.	Good	Fair	Poor
—	5500	3000	1250	—

1st Model Single Shot

This unusual pistol combines the frame of the .38 Single Action 3rd Model with a single shot barrel. This model is a top break and functions exactly as the revolver models do. The barrel length is 6", 8", or 10"; and the pistol is chambered for .22 Long Rifle, .32 S&W, and .38 S&W. The finish is blue or nickel plated, with a square butt. The grips are checkered hard rubber extension types for a proper target hold. This pistol is considered quite rare on today's market, as only 1,251 were manufactured between 1893 and 1905.

.22 L. R.

Exc.	V.G.	Good	Fair	Poor
—	750	500	325	—

.32 S&W

Exc.	V.G.	Good	Fair	Poor
—	950	550	400	—

.38 S&W

Exc.	V.G.	Good	Fair	Poor
—	1100	700	425	—

2nd Model Single Shot

The 2nd Model Single Shot has a frame with the recoil shield removed, is chambered for the .22 l.r. only, and is offered with the 10" barrel. The finish is blue or nickel plated, and the grips are checkered hard rubber extension types. There were approximately 4,617 manufactured between 1905 and 1909.

Courtesy Mike Stuckslager

Exc.	V.G.	Good	Fair	Poor
700	575	450	250	175

3rd Model Single Shot

The basic difference between this model and the 2nd Model is that this pistol could be fired double action as well as single action, and the frame came from the double action perfected model. There were 6,949 manufactured between 1909 and 1923.

Courtesy Mike Stuckslager

Exc.	V.G.	Good	Fair	Poor
700	575	450	250	175

Straight Line Single Shot

This is a unique pistol that very much resembles a semiautomatic. The barrel is 10" in length and pivots to the left for loading. It is chambered for .22 Long Rifle cartridge and is finished in blue, with walnut grips inlaid with the S&W medallions. The hammer is straight-line in function and does not pivot. There were 1,870 manufactured between 1925 and 1936.

Courtesy Butterfield & Butterfield, San Francisco, California

Exc.	V.G.	Good	Fair	Poor
2250	1600	1000	500	300

.32 Hand Ejector Model of 1896 or .32 Hand Ejector 1st Model

This model was the first time S&W made a revolver with a swing-out cylinder. Interestingly, there is no cylinder latch; but the action opens by pulling forward on the exposed portion of the cylinder pin. This frees the spring tension and allows the cylinder to swing free. Another novel feature of this model is the cylinder stop location, which is located in the top of the frame over the cylinder. This model is chambered for the .32 S&W Long cartridge, has a 6-shot fluted cylinder, and is offered with 3.25", 4.25", and 6" long barrels. It is available with either a round or square butt, has checkered hard rubber grips, and is blued or nickel-plated. Factory installed target sights were available by special order. The company name, address, and patent dates are stamped on the cylinder instead of on the barrel. There were approximately 19,712 manufactured between 1896 and 1903.

Courtesy Mike Stuckslager

Exc.	V.G.	Good	Fair	Poor
—	700	500	300	—

Hand Ejector Model of 1903

This model is quite different from its predecessor. The cylinder locks front and back; the cylinder stop is located in the bottom of the frame, and the familiar sliding cylinder latch is found on the left side of the frame. The barrel lengths are 3.25", 4.25", and 6". The 6-shot cylinder is fluted, and the revolver is chambered for .32 S&W Long. It is offered either blued or nickel-plated, and the round butt grips are checkered hard rubber. There were approximately 19,425 manufactured in 1903 and 1904; serial number range 1 to 19425.

Courtesy Mike Stuckslager

Exc.	V.G.	Good	Fair	Poor
300	250	200	150	100

.32 Hand Ejector Model of 1903 1st Change

This model differs from the model of 1903 internally, and the serial number range 19426 to 51126 is really the only way to differentiate the two. There were approximately 31,700 manufactured between 1904 and 1906.

Exc.	V.G.	Good	Fair	Poor
300	200	150	125	90

.32 Hand Ejector Model of 1903 2nd Change

Produced from 1906 to 1909 in serial number range 51127 to 95500. A total of 44,373 manufactured.

.32 Hand Ejector Model of 1903 3rd Change

Produced from 1909 to 1910 in serial number range 95501 to 96125. A total of 624 manufactured.

.32 Hand Ejector Model of 1903 4th Change

Produced in 1910 in serial number range 96126 to 102500. A total of 6,374 manufactured.

.32 Hand Ejector Model of 1903 5th Change

Produced from 1910 to 1917 in serial number range 102500 to 263000. A total of 160,500 manufactured.

.32 Hand Ejector Third Model

Produced from 1911 to 1942 in serial number range 263001 to 536684. A total of 273,683 were manufactured.

Exc.	V.G.	Good	Fair	Poor
300	200	150	125	90

.22 Ladysmith 1st Model

This model was designed primarily as a defensive weapon for women. Its small size and caliber made it ideal for that purpose. The 1st Model Ladysmith is chambered for .22 Long cartridge and has a 7-shot fluted cylinder and 3" and 3.5" barrel lengths. This little revolver weighed 9-5/8 ounces. It is either blued or nickel-plated and has a round butt with checkered hard rubber grips. The 1st Model has a checkered cylinder-latch button on the left side of the frame. There were approximately 4,575 manufactured between 1902 and 1906.

Exc.	V.G.	Good	Fair	Poor
1750	1200	850	650	450

.22 Ladysmith 2nd Model

This is essentially quite similar in appearance to the 1st Model, the difference being in the pull-forward cylinder latch located under the barrel, replacing the button on the left side of the frame. The new method allowed lockup front and back for greater action strength. The 2.25" barrel length was dropped; caliber and finishes are the same. There were approximately 9,374 manufactured between 1906 and 1910; serial number range 4576 to 13950.

Courtesy Mike Stuckslager

Exc.	V.G.	Good	Fair	Poor
1550	900	800	600	400

.22 Ladysmith 3rd Model

This model is quite different in appearance to the 2nd Model, as it features a square butt and smooth walnut grips with inlaid S&W medallions. The barrel lengths remained the same, with the addition of a 2.25" and 6" variation. The under barrel cylinder lockup was not changed, nor were the caliber and finishes. There were approximately 12,200 manufactured between 1910 and 1921; serial number range 13951 to 26154.
NOTE: Add a 50% premium for 2.25" and 6" barrel lengths.

Courtesy W.P. Hallstein III and son Chip

Exc.	V.G.	Good	Fair	Poor
1350	1000	800	600	400

.38 Hand Ejector Military & Police 1st Model or Model of 1899

This was an early swing-out cylinder revolver, and it has no front lockup for the action. The release is on the left side of the frame. This model is chambered for .38 S&W Special cartridge and the .32 Winchester centerfire cartridge (.32-20), has a 6-shot fluted cylinder, and was offered with a 4", 5", 6", 6.5", or 8" barrel in .38 caliber and 4", 5", and 6-1/2" in .32-20 caliber. The finish is blued or nickel-plated; the grips, checkered walnut or hard rubber. There were approximately 20,975 manufactured between 1899 and 1902 in .38 caliber; serial number range 1 to 20,975. In the .32-20 caliber 5,311 were sold between 1899 and 1902; serial number range 1 to 5311.

Courtesy Mike Stuckslager

Commercial Model

Exc.	V.G.	Good	Fair	Poor
750	650	600	450	350

U.S. Navy Model

One thousand produced in 1900, .38 S&W, 6" barrel, blued with checkered walnut grips, "U.S.N." stamped on butt, serial number range 5000 to 6000.

Exc.	V.G.	Good	Fair	Poor
1300	1000	700	500	300

U.S. Army Model

One thousand produced in 1901, same as Navy Model except that it is marked "U.S.Army/Model 1899" on butt, "K.S.M." and "J.T.T." on grips, serial number range 13001 to 14000.

Exc.	V.G.	Good	Fair	Poor
1300	1000	700	500	300

.38 Hand Ejector M&P 2nd Model or Model of 1902

The 2nd Model is similar in appearance to the 1st Model. The major difference is the addition of the front lockup under the barrel, and the ejector rod was increased in diameter. Barrel lengths for the .38 S&W were 4", 5", 6", or 6-1/2" while the .32-20 was available in 4", 5", or 6-1/2" barrel lengths. Both calibers were offered in round butt only configuration. There were approximately 12,827 manufactured in .38 S&W in 1902 and 1903; serial number range 20,976 to 33,803. In the .32-20 caliber 4,499 were produced; serial number range 5312 to 9811.

Exc.	V.G.	Good	Fair	Poor
500	350	300	250	100

.38 Hand Ejector M&P 2nd Model, 1st Change

Built between 1903 and 1905 this variation represents the change to the square butt, which made for better shooting control and standardized frame shape. Both the .38 S&W and the .32-20 were available in 4", 5", or 6-1/2" barrel lengths. The company manufactured 28,645 .38 calibers; serial number range 33,804 to 62,449 and produced 8,313 .32-20s; serial number 9812 to 18125.

Exc.	V.G.	Good	Fair	Poor
500	350	300	250	100

.38 Hand Ejector Model of 1905

This model was a continuation of the .38 M&P Hand Ejector series. Built from 1905 to 1906 it was available in 4", 5", 6", and 6-1/2" barrels for both the .38 and .32-20 calibers. Finished in either blue or nickel with round or square butt the .38 caliber model serial number range was from 62450 to 73250 or about 10,800 produced. The .32-20 caliber serial number range spans 18126 to 22426 or 4,300 produced.

Exc.	V.G.	Good	Fair	Poor
600	425	300	250	150

.38 Hand Ejector Model of 1905, 1st Change

Produced from 1906 to 1908 this model is similar to the original model of 1905 with regard to barrel lengths, finish and butt styles. The 1st change in .38 caliber was produced in serial number range 73251 to 120000 with 46,749 sold. In .32-20 caliber the serial-number range was 22427 to 33500 with 11,073 sold.

.38 Hand Ejector Model of 1905, 2nd Change

Produced from 1908 to 1909 only internal changes were made to this model. The best approach to differentiate this model is by serial number. The .38 caliber serial number range was from 120001 to 146899 with 26,898 produced. In the .32-20 caliber the serial number range is between 33501 and 45200 with 11,699 produced.

.38 Hand Ejector Model of 1905, 3rd Change

Produced from 1909 to 1915 the 3rd Change variation was available in only 4" or 6" barrel lengths for both the .38 and .32-20 models. The .38 caliber serial number range was between 146900 to 241703 with 94,803 sold.

Courtesy Mike Stuckslager

.38 Hand Ejector Model of 1905, 4th Change

Courtesy Mike Stuckslager

This last variation was also the longest production run. Produced from 1915 to 1942 the .38 caliber model was available in 2", 4", 5", or 6", barrel lengths while the .32-20 caliber was offered in 4", 5", or 6" barrel lengths. The .38 caliber serial number range was from 241704 to 1000000. The .32-20 caliber model was produced from 1915 to 1940 in serial number range from 65701 to 144684.

.22-32 Hand Ejector

Courtesy Mike Stuckslager

This is a very interesting model from the collector's point of view. Phillip B. Bekeart, a San Francisco firearms dealer requested that S&W manufacture a .22 caliber target-grade revolver on the heavier .32 frame. He believed in his idea so passionately that he immediately ordered 1,000 of the guns for himself. This initial order is found within the serial number range 1 to 3000 and are known to collectors as the authentic Bekearts. The remainder of the extensive production run are simply .22-.32 Hand Ejectors. This model is chambered for .22 Long Rifle cartridge and has a 6-shot fluted cylinder with 6" barrel. The finish is blue, with square butt and checkered extension-type walnut grips. There were only 292 revolvers of his initial order delivered to Mr. Bekeart, but the first 1,000 pistols are considered to be True Bekearts. The production number of each respective pistol is stamped into the base of the extended wooden grips. S&W went on to manufacture several hundred thousand of these revolvers between 1911 and 1953.

"The True Bekeart"

Serial number range 138226 to 139275 in the .32 Hand Ejector series, production number stamped on butt. Professional appraisal should be secured.

Exc.	V.G.	Good	Fair	Poor
750	500	400	300	250

Standard Model

Exc.	V.G.	Good	Fair	Poor
500	300	250	200	125

.44 Hand Ejector 1st Model

Courtesy Mike Stuckslager

This model is also known by collectors as the ".44 Triple Lock" or "The New Century." The Triple Lock nickname came from a separate locking device located on the extractor rod shroud that is used in addition to the usual two locks. This model is chambered for the .44 S&W Special cartridge or the .44 S&W Russian. On a limited basis it is also chambered in .44-40, .45 Colt, and .38-40. The fluted cylinder holds 6 shots, and the barrel was offered in standard lengths of 5" or 6.5". A limited quantity of 4" barrel was produced. The finish is blued or nickel-plated; and the grips are checkered walnut, with the gold S&W medallion on later models. There were approximately 15,375 manufactured between 1908 and 1915.

Courtesy Mike Stuckslager

.44 S & W Special and .44 S&W Russian

Exc.	V.G.	Good	Fair	Poor
900	700	500	350	200

Other Calibers (Rare)

Exc.	V.G.	Good	Fair	Poor
1100	800	600	450	300

.44 Hand Ejector 2nd Model

This model is quite similar in appearance to the 1st Model. The major difference is the elimination of the third or triple lock device and the heavy ejector rod shroud. Other changes are internal and not readily apparent. This model is also standard in .44 S&W Special chambering but was offered rarely in .38-40, .44-40, and .45 Colt. Specimens have been noted with adjustable sights in 6-1/2" barrel lengths. Standard barrel lengths were 4", 5", and 6-1/2". There were approximately 17,510 manufactured between 1915 and 1937 in serial number range 15376 to 60000.

Courtesy Mike Stuckslager

.44 S & W Special

Exc.	V.G.	Good	Fair	Poor
650	600	500	350	200

.38-40, .44-40 or .45 Colt

Exc.	V.G.	Good	Fair	Poor
750	650	550	400	250

.44 Hand Ejector 3rd Model or Model of 1926

This model is similar in appearance to the 2nd Model but brought back the heavy ejector rod shroud of the 1st Model without the triple lock device. Barrel lengths were 4", 5", and 6-1/2". The .44 Hand Ejector Model was manufactured between 1926 and 1949.

Courtesy Mike Stuckslager

.44 S & W Special

Exc.	V.G.	Good	Fair	Poor
650	450	350	275	150

.44-40 or .45 Colt

Exc.	V.G.	Good	Fair	Poor
800	550	400	300	150

.44 Hand Ejector 4th Model (Target Model)

The 4th Model featured a ribbed barrel, micrometer adjustable sight, and short throw hammer. Never a popular seller this model had only 5,050 pistol produced between 1950 and 1966.

Exc.	V.G.	Good	Fair	Poor
600	400	325	250	200

.45 Hand Ejector U.S. Service Model of 1917

WWI was on the horizon, and it seemed certain that the United States would become involved. The S&W people began to work with the Springfield Armory to develop a hand-ejector model that would fire the .45-caliber Government cartridge. This was accomplished in 1916 by the use of half-moon clips. The new revolver is quite similar to the .44 Hand Ejector in appearance. It has a 5.5" barrel, blued finish with smooth walnut grips, and a lanyard ring on the butt. The designation "U.S. Army Model 1917" is stamped on the butt. After the war broke out, the government was not satisfied with S&W's production and actually took control of the company for the duration of the war. This was the first time that the company was not controlled by a Wesson. The factory records indicate that there were 163,476 Model 1917s manufactured between 1917 and 1919, the WWI years. After the war, the sale of these revolvers continued on a commercial and contract basis until 1949, when this model was finally dropped from the S&W product line.

Military Model

Exc.	V.G.	Good	Fair	Poor
500	350	300	200	150

Brazilian Contract

25,000 produced for the Brazilian government in 1938. The Brazilian crest is stamped on the sideplate.

Exc.	V.G.	Good	Fair	Poor
300	250	200	150	100

Commercial Model

High gloss blue and checkered walnut grips.

Courtesy Mike Stuckslager

Exc.	V.G.	Good	Fair	Poor
600	450	350	275	200

.455 Mark II Hand Ejector 1st Model

This model was designed the same as the .44 Hand Ejector 1st Model with no caliber stamping on the barrel. It has a barrel length of 6.4". Of the 5,000 revolvers produced and sold only

100 were commercial guns, the rest were military. Produced between 1914 and 1915. The commercial model is worth a premium.

Exc.	V.G.	Good	Fair	Poor
700	575	400	300	200

.455 Mark II Hand Ejector 2nd Model

Similar to the first model without an extractor shroud. Barrel length was also 6.5". Serial number range was 5000 to 74755. Manufactured from 1915 to 1917.

Exc.	V.G.	Good	Fair	Poor
450	300	250	225	175

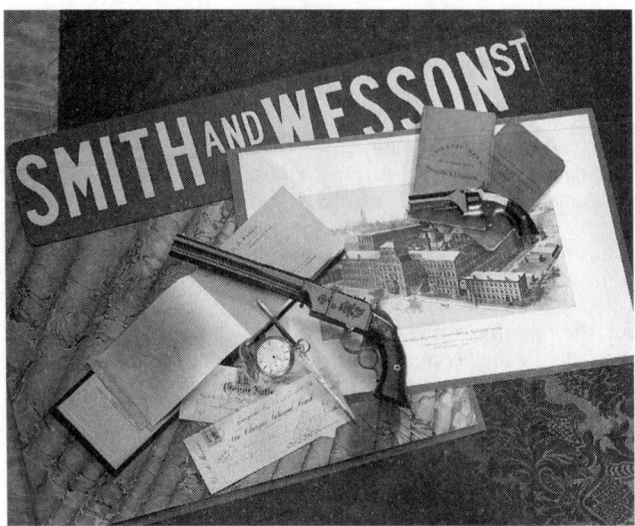

Courtesy Smith & Wesson

S&W .35 Automatic Pistol

Production of the .35 Automatic was S&W's first attempt at an auto-loading pistol. As was always the case, the company strived for maximum safety and dependability. This model has a 3.5" barrel and a 7-shot detachable magazine and is chambered in .35 S&W Automatic, a one-time-only cartridge that eventually proved to be the major downfall of this pistol from a commercial standpoint. There were two separate safety devices—a revolving cam on the backstrap and a grip safety on the front strap that had to be fully depressed simultaneously while squeezing the trigger. The finish is blue or nickel-plated; and the grips are walnut, with the S&W inlaid medallions. The magazine release slides from side to side and is checkered, expensive to manufacture, and destined to be modified. There were approximately 8,350 manufactured.

Exc.	V.G.	Good	Fair	Poor
500	350	250	200	150

S&W .32 Automatic Pistol

In 1921 it became apparent to the powers that controlled S&W that the .35-caliber automatic was never going to be a commercial success. Harold Wesson, the new president, began to redesign the pistol to accept the .32 ACP, a commercially accepted cartridge, and to streamline the appearance to be more competitive with the other pistols on the market, notably Colt's. This new pistol used as many parts from the older model as possible for economy's sake. The pivoting barrel was discontinued, as was the cam-type safety in the rear grip strap. A magazine disconnector and a reduced-strength recoil spring to ease cocking were employed. The barrel length was kept at 3.5", and the 7-shot magazine was retained. The finish is blued only, and the grips are smooth walnut. There were only 957 of these manufactured between 1924 and 1936. They are eagerly sought by collectors.

A S & W .32 Automatic pistol sold at auction for $3,105. Smooth walnut grips with S&W medallions. Shipped in 1924 to Remington Arms. Condition was excellent. Amoskeag Auction Co. Inc., March 2000

Courtesy James Rankin

Exc.	V.G.	Good	Fair	Poor
2000	1500	1000	700	500

SMITH & WESSON MODERN HANDGUNS

With the development of the Hand Ejector Models and the swingout cylinders, Smith & Wesson opened the door to a number of new advancements in the revolver field. This new system allowed for a solid frame, making the weapon much stronger than the old top break design. The company also developed different basic frame sizes and gave them letter designations. The I frame, which later developed into the slightly larger J frame, was used for the .22-.32 and the small, concealable .38 revolvers. The medium K frame was used for .38 duty- and target-type weapons. The N frame was the heavy-duty frame used for the larger .357 and .44 and .45 caliber revolvers. The hand ejector went through many evolutionary changes over the years. We strongly recommend that the collector secure a detailed volume that deals exclusively with Smith & Wesson (see the bibliography), and learn all that is available on this fascinating firearm. Models are catalogued the by their numerical designations, brief description are given, and current values offered. It is important to note that the S&W revolver that we see marketed by the company today has undergone many changes in reaching its present configuration. The early models featured five screws in their construction, not counting the grip screw. There were four screws fastening the sideplate and another through the front of the triggerguard that retained the cylinder stop plunger. The first change involved the elimination of the top sideplate screw, and the five-screw Smith & Wesson became the four-screw. Later the frame was changed to eliminate the cylinder stop plunger screw, and the three-screw was created. Some models were offered with a flat cylinder latch that was serrated instead of the familiar checkering. Recently in 1978, the method of attaching the barrel to the frame was changed; and the familiar pin was eliminated. At the same time, the recessed cylinder commonly found on magnum models was also eliminated. All of these factors have a definite effect on the value and collectibility of a particular S&W handgun.

IMPORTANT PRICING INFORMATION

Values reflected below will be affected by the following factors:

Five Screw Models-Add 40 to 50%.

Four Screw Models-Add 30%. Models with flat latches-Add 20%.

Models not pinned or recessed deduct 10%.

NOTE: The pre-model number designations are listed in parentheses after the model number.

Courtesy Smith & Wesson

Model 10 (.38 Military & Police)

This model has been in production in one configuration or another since 1899. It was always the mainstay of the S&W line and was originally known as the .38 Military and Police Model. The Model 10 is built on the K, or medium frame, and was always meant as a duty gun. It was offered with a 2", 3", 4", 5", or 6" barrel. Currently only the 4" and 6" are available. A round or square butt is offered. It is chambered for the .38 Special and is offered in blue or nickel-plate, with checkered walnut grips. The Model designation is stamped on the yoke on all S&W revolvers. This model, with many other modern S&W pistols, underwent several engineering changes. These changes may affect the value of the pistol and an expert should be consulted. The dates of these changes are as follows:

10-None-1957	10-4-1962
10-1-1959	10-5-1962
10-2-1961	10-6-1962
10-3-1961	

NIB	Exc.	V.G.	Good	Fair	Poor
325	250	200	150	125	90

Victory Model

Manufactured during WWII, this is a Model 10 with a sandblasted and parkerized finish, a lanyard swivel, and smooth walnut grips. The serial number has a V prefix. This model was available in only 2" and 4" barrel lengths. The Victory Model was discontinued on April 27, 1945, with serial number VS811,119.

Victory Model marked "N.Y.M.I."

Courtesy Richard M. Kumor, Sr.

Exc.	V.G.	Good	Fair	Poor
275	200	150	100	75

NOTE: Top strap marked Navy will bring a 75% premium. Navy variation with both top strap and side plate marked will bring a 100% premium. Navy variation marked "N.Y.M.I." will bring a 125% premium. Revolvers marked "U.S.G.C." or "U.S.M.C." will bring a premium of unknown amount. Exercise caution.

Model 11 (.38/200 British)

First produced in 1947 S&W received many contracts for this service pistol. Nicknamed the .38/200 British Service Revolver, the company sold many of these models throughout the 1950s and 1960s. There are several rare variations of this model that will greatly affect its value. Consult an expert if special markings and barrel lengths are encountered.

Exc.	V.G.	Good	Fair	Poor
250	200	150	100	75

Model 12 (.38 Military & Police Airweight)

The Model 12 was introduced in 1952, starting serial number C223,999, and is merely a Model 10 with a lightweight alloy frame and cylinder. In 1954 the alloy cylinder was replaced with one of steel that added an additional 4 ounces in weight. Discontinued in 1986.
Aluminum Cylinder Model-Add 40%.

Exc.	V.G.	Good	Fair	Poor
275	200	150	125	100

USAF M-13 (Aircrewman)

In 1953 the Air Force purchased a large quantity of Model 12s with alloy frames and cylinders. They were intended for use by flight crews as survival weapons in emergencies. This model was not officially designated "13" by S&W, but the Air Force stamped "M13" on the top strap. This model was rejected by the Air Force in 1954 because of trouble with the alloy cylinder.

Exc.	V.G.	Good	Fair	Poor
800	750	600	450	250

Model 13 (.357 Military & Police)

This is simply the Model 10 M&P chambered for the .357 Magnum and fitted with a heavy barrel. It was introduced in 1974.

Exc.	V.G.	Good	Fair	Poor
275	250	200	175	125

Model 14 (K-38 Masterpiece)

Courtesy Mike Stuckslager

This model is also known as the "K-38." In 1957 "Model 14" was stamped on the yoke. This model is offered in a 6" barrel with adjustable sights. In 1961 a single action version with faster lock time was offered. This would be worth a small premium. This model was discontinued in 1981.
Single Action Model-Add 20%.

Exc.	V.G.	Good	Fair	Poor
275	250	200	175	125

Model 15 (K-38 Combat Masterpiece)

Also known as the "Combat Masterpiece" this model was produced at the request of law enforcement officers who wanted the "K-38" fitted with a 4" barrel. The model went into production in 1950 and was discontinued in 1987.

Exc.	V.G.	Good	Fair	Poor
300	250	200	175	125

Model 16 (K-32 Masterpiece)

Also known as the "K-32" until 1957, this model is identical in appearance to the Model 14 except that it is chambered for .32 S&W. The Model 16 did not enjoy the commercial popularity of the Model 14 and was dropped from the line in 1973. Only 3,630 K-32s/Model 16s were sold between 1947 and 1973. Reintroduced in 1990 in .32 Magnum and discontinued in 1993.

Courtesy Mike Stuckslager

Post-War

Exc.	V.G.	Good	Fair	Poor
1000	700	450	300	250

Pre-War

Exc.	V.G.	Good	Fair	Poor
2000	1400	900	600	500

Model 16 (.32 Magnum)

Reintroduced in 1990 in .32 Magnum and discontinued in 1993.

NIB	Exc.	V.G.	Good	Fair	Poor
350	300	250	200	150	100

K-32 Combat Masterpiece

S&W produced a limited number of 4" barreled K-32 revolvers. They were never given a number designation, as they were discontinued before 1957 when the numbering system began.

Exc.	V.G.	Good	Fair	Poor
1100	800	500	350	300

Model 17 (K-22)

This is the numerical designation that S&W placed on the "K-22" in 1957. This target model .22 rimfire revolver has always been popular since its introduction in 1946. It is offered in 4", 6", and 8-3/8" barrel lengths, with all target options. The 8-3/8" barrel was dropped from the product line in 1993. The finish is blued, and it has checkered walnut grips.

Courtesy Mike Stuckslager

NIB	Exc.	V.G.	Good	Fair	Poor
300	275	225	175	125	100

Model 17 Plus

Introduced in 1996 this new version of the old Model 17 has a 10-round cylinder for its .22 long rifle cartridges. It features a 6" full lug barrel with Patridge front sight and adjustable rear sight. The hammer is semi-target style and the trigger is a smooth combat style. Finish is matte black and the grips are Houge black rubber. Drills and tapped for scope mounts. Weight is about 42 oz.

NIB	Exc.	V.G.	Good	Fair	Poor
350	300	250	200	150	100

Model 617 Plus

Identical to the Model 17 but furnished with stainless steel frame and cylinder.

NIB	Exc.	V.G.	Good	Fair	Poor
375	300	250	200	150	100

Model 648

Identical to the Model 617 but chambered for the .22 Magnum rimfire cartridge.

NIB	Exc.	V.G.	Good	Fair	Poor
325	300	275	225	175	100

A Prewar K-22 Combat Masterpiece was sold at auction for $1,320. Fitted with a 6" barrel. Built in 1940. Condition was mint with original box.
Amoskeag Auction Company, May 1999

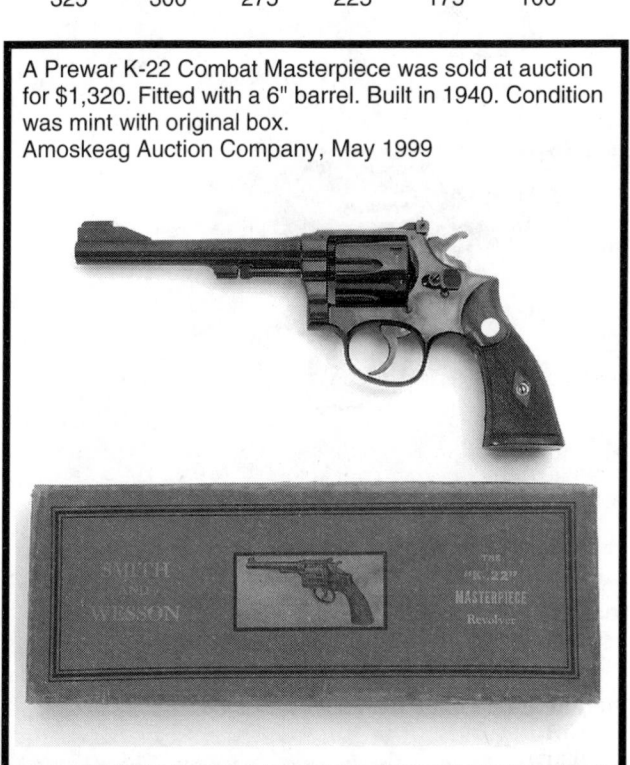

Model 18 (K-22 Combat Masterpiece)

This is the model designation for the 4"-barreled "Combat Masterpiece" chambered for the .22 rimfire.

Exc.	V.G.	Good	Fair	Poor
300	275	250	200	125

> **Note On "K Frame" Target Models:**
> 1. The factory eliminated the upper corner screw from the side plate in 1955. The 5-screw became a 4-screw. This change occurred around serial number K260,000.
> 2. Model number designations were stamped on the yoke in 1957.

Model 19 (.357 Combat Magnum)

Introduced in 1954 at the urging of Bill Jordan, a competition shooter with the U.S. Border Patrol, who went on to become a respected gun writer, this model is one of Smith and Wesson's most popular pistols. It was built on the "K-Frame" and was the first medium frame revolver chambered for the powerful .357 Magnum cartridge. Since its inception the Model 19 has been one of S&W's most popular revolvers. It was the first revolver to be introduced as a three-screw model. Originally it was offered with a 4" heavy barrel with extractor shroud; the 6" became available in 1963. The finish is blued or nickel plated, and the grips are checkered walnut. The Goncalo Alves target stocks first appeared in 1959. In 1968 a 2.5" round butt version was introduced. The Model 19 has been the basis for two commemoratives—the Texas Ranger/with Bowie Knife and the Oregon State Police/with Belt Buckle. This model is no longer in production.

NIB	Exc.	V.G.	Good	Fair	Poor
275	250	225	200	150	100

Texas Ranger Cased with Knife
NIB
700

Oregon State Police Cased with Buckle
NIB
900

THE S&W K-FRAME REVOLVER

The S&W mid-sized K-frame revolver has been around since 1899, so something must be right about it. Just looking at the K-frame, one could easily think this handgun is all "elbows and knees," for the grip frame appears to be ill-suited for grasping and the protruding cylinder and ejector rod look to be parts that will surely be ill-manipulated under stress. The Model 10 K-frame certainly hasn't been the recipient of modern ergonomic design. No free-flowing lines to be sure. But perceptions are often deceiving and the K-frame is no exception. I've owned and used the S&W K-frame revolvers for over 35 years and have found that some are only better than others; none are poor or "worse." In 1964, I settled on the S&W Model 19, the Combat Magnum as it was then called, chambered for the .357 Magnum cartridge, with 4" barrel and the original S&W checkered-wood target grips.

I don't know if I accommodated to the gun or, in fact, the gun is designed correctly. I do know that when I pick up this gun, as I have thousands of times in anticipation of using it for my law enforcement work, I'm as comfortable with it as I am with the steering wheel of my car. Admittedly, I modified the target grips with saw, file and sandpaper to create an almost seamless fit between hand and wood. When firing the Model 19, I feel that I'm in total control of the gun and the fired bullet. Pressing back on the now-slightly-rounded trigger, the smooth-working mechanical double action moves the cylinder around, without hesitation, bringing a cartridge in line to be struck by the dropping hammer and firing pin. When the gun fires and lifts in recoil, I simply "know" I have total control of the gun and the direction of the launched round as I see the red ramp front sight rise in the white outline square of the rear notch. This frozen moment is one I continue to enjoy each and every time. In the aftermath of firing, the slightly stinging recoil serves as an ongoing reminder of the lethality I hold in my hand.

Walt Rauch

Model 20 (.38/.44 Heavy Duty)

Known as the "38/44 Heavy Duty" before the change to numerical designations this model was brought out in 1930 in response to requests from law enforcement personnel for a more powerful sidearm. This model, along with the .38-44 S&W Special cartridge, was an attempt to solve the problem. The revolver was manufactured with a standard 5" long barrel but has been noted rarely as short as 3-1/2" and as long as 8-3/8". It was built on the large N-frame and is blued or nickel-plated, with checkered walnut grips. Eventually the popularity of the .357 Magnum made the Model 20 superfluous, and it was discontinued in 1966. Postwar production for this model was about 20,000 revolvers.
Prewar .44 Special-Add 50%.

Courtesy Mike Stuckslager

Exc.	V.G.	Good	Fair	Poor
475	350	250	200	150

Model 21 (1950 Military)

This model was known as the "1950 Military" and the "4th Model .44 Hand Ejector" before the Model 21 designation was applied in 1957. The Model 21 was chambered for the .44 Special cartridge and equipped with fixed sights. The Model 21 was built on the N frame and is quite rare, as only 1,200 were manufactured in 16 years of production. It was discontinued in 1966.

Exc.	V.G.	Good	Fair	Poor
1500	1200	950	650	500

Model 696

Introduced in 1997 this model features a 3" underlug barrel. chambered for the .44 Special and fitted on an L-frame, capacity is 5 rounds. Grips are Hogue black rubber. Finish is stainless steel. Weight is approximately 48 oz.

NIB	Exc	V.G.	Good	Fair	Poor
450	400	350	—	—	—

Model 22 (1950 .45 Military)

This model was known as the "1950 .45 Military" before 1957. It was actually introduced in 1951 and is similar in appearance to the Model 21 except that it is chambered for the .45 Auto Rim or .45 ACP cartridge. Half-moon clips are used with the latter. There were 3,976 manufactured between 1951 and 1966. Beginning serial number for this model was S85,000.

Exc.	V.G.	Good	Fair	Poor
750	650	550	300	200

Model 23 (.38/.44 Outdoorsman)

Courtesy Mike Stuckslager

The .38-44 Outdoorsman was the model name of this N-frame revolver before the 1957 designation change. This is simply the Model 20 with adjustable sights. It was introduced in 1931 as a heavy-duty sporting handgun with hunters in mind. S&W produced 4,761 of these prewar revolvers. It features a 6.5" barrel and blued finish and was the first S&W to have the new checkered walnut "Magna" grips. After 1949 this revolver was thoroughly modernized and had the later ribbed barrel. There were a total of 8,365 manufactured before the model was discontinued in 1966. 6,039 were of the modernized configuration.

Exc.	V.G.	Good	Fair	Poor
600	450	350	225	125

Model 24 (.44 Target Model of 1950)

This model was introduced as the .44 Target Model of 1950. It is simply the N-frame Model 21 with adjustable target sights. This revolver was quite popular with the long-range handgunning devotees and their leader, Elmer Keith. The introduction of the .44 Magnum in 1956 began the death knell of the Model 24, and it was finally discontinued in 1966. S&W produced a total of 5,050 Model 24s. It was reintroduced in 1983 and 1984—and then was dropped again.

Exc.	V.G.	Good	Fair	Poor
450	400	300	250	200

Model 25 (.45 Target Model of 1950)

Prior to the model designation change in 1957 this model was also known as the .45 Target Model of 1955, this was an improved version of the 1950 Target .45. The Model 25 features a heavier barrel 4", 6.5", or 8" in length with blued or nickel-plated finish. All target options were offered. The Model 25 is chambered for the .45 ACP or .45 Auto-rim cartridges. This model is still available chambered for .45 Colt as the Model 25-5.

Exc.	V.G.	Good	Fair	Poor
400	350	300	250	200

Model 25-3 125th Anniversary with Case

NIB
450

Model 25-2

This is the discontinued modern version of the Model 25 chambered in .45 ACP. The 6.5" barrel is shortened to 6" and is available in a presentation case.

Exc.	V.G.	Good	Fair	Poor
400	350	300	250	200

Model 625-2

This is the stainless steel version of the Model 25-2. It is fitted with a 5" barrel and has Pachmayr SK/GR gripper stocks as standard. Designed for pin shooting.

NIB	Exc.	V.G.	Good	Fair	Poor
425	350	300	250	200	150

Model 625 Mountain Gun

Offered for the first time in 1996 this model is chambered for the .45 Colt cartridge. It is fitted with a 4" tapered barrel with ramp front sight and adjustable rear sight. The frame is drilled and tapped for a scope mount. In 2000 this model was offered in .45 ACP caliber.

NOTE: The Model 625 Mountain Gun is a limited production revolver limited to between 2,500 and 3,000 guns. When those units are sold the model is no longer in production until re-issued by S&W.

NIB	Exc.	V.G.	Good	Fair	Poor
650	500	400	350	—	—

Model 610

Introduced in 1998 this revolver is chambered for the 10mm cartridge. It is fitted with a 6.5" full lug barrel and an unfluted cylinder. Hogue grips are standard. Adjustable rear sight. Interchangeable front sight. Weight is approximately 52 oz.

NIB	Exc.	V.G.	Good	Fair	Poor
650	525	—	—	—	—

Model 26 (1950 .45 Target)

This is the numerical designation of the 1950 .45 Target Model. This large N-frame revolver is basically the same as the Model 25 but has a lighter, thinner barrel. This caused its unpopularity among competitive shooters who wanted a heavier revolver. This brought about the Model 25 and the demise of the Model 26 in 1961 after only 2,768 were manufactured. The Model 26 also has two additional variations and are marked 26-1 and 26-2.

Exc.	V.G.	Good	Fair	Poor
750	650	500	400	250

Factory Registered .357 Magnum

In the early 1930s, a gun writer named Phillip B. Sharpe became interested in the development of high performance loads to be used in the then popular .38-44 S&W revolvers. He repeatedly urged the company to produce a revolver especially made to handle these high pressure loads. In 1934 S&W asked Winchester to produce a new cartridge that would create the ballistics that Sharpe was seeking. This new cartridge was made longer than the standard .38 Special case so that it could not inadvertently be fired in an older gun. The company never felt that this would be a commercially popular venture and from the onset visualized the ".357 Magnum" as a strictly deluxe hand-built item. They were to be individually numbered, in addition to the serial number, and registered to the new owner. The new Magnum was to be the most expensive revolver in the line. The gun went on the market in 1935, and the first one was presented to FBI Director J. Edgar Hoover. The gun was to become a tremendous success. S&W could only produce 120 per month, and this did not come close to filling orders. In 1938 the practice of numbering and registering each revolver was discontinued after 5,500 were produced. The ".357 Magnum," as it was designated, continued as one of the company's most popular items.

The Factory Registered Model was built on the N-frame. It could be custom ordered with any barrel length from 3.5" up to 8-3/8". The finish is blue, and the grips are checkered walnut. This model was virtually hand-built and test targeted. A certificate of registration was furnished with each revolver. The registration number was stamped on the yoke of the revolver with the prefix "Reg." This practice ceased in 1938 after 5,500 were produced.

Courtesy Mike Stuckslager

Exc.	V.G.	Good	Fair	Poor
1800	1200	800	550	400

Prewar .357 Magnum

This is the same as the Factory Registered Model without the certificate and the individual numbering. Approximately 1,150 were manufactured between 1938 and 1941. Production ceased for WWII weapons production.

Exc.	V.G.	Good	Fair	Poor
750	550	450	300	250

Model 27 (.357 Magnum)

In 1948 after the end of WWII, production of this revolver commenced. The new rebound slide operated hammer block and short throw hammer were utilized, and the barrel lengths offered were 3.5", 5", 6", 6-1/2", and 8-3/8". In 1957 the model designation was changed to Model 27; and in 1975 the target trigger, hammer and Goncalo Alves target grips were made standard. This revolver is still available from S&W and has been in production longer than any other N-frame pistol. Some additional variations may be of interest to the collector. Around serial number SI 71,584 the 3 screw side plate model was first produced. In 1960 the model designation -1 was added to the model to indicate the change to a left-hand thread to the extractor rod. In 1962 the cylinder stop was changed, which disposed of the need for a plunger spring hole in front of the triggerguard. This change was indicated by a -2 behind the model number.

NIB	Exc.	V.G.	Good	Fair	Poor
350	325	300	250	200	150

Model 627

This is special edition stainless steel version of the Model 27 and is offered with a 5-1/2" barrel. Manufactured in 1989 only. Approximately 4,500 produced.

NIB	Exc.	V.G.	Good	Fair	Poor
500	400	350	300	200	150

Model 28 (Highway Patrolman)

The Model 27 revolver was extremely popular among law enforcement officers, and many police agencies were interested in purchasing such a weapon-except for the cost. In 1954 S&W produced a new model called, at the time, the "Highway Patrolman." This model had all the desirable performance features of the deluxe Model 27 but lacked the cosmetic features that drove up the price. The finish is a matte blue; the rib is sandblasted instead of checkered or serrated, and the grips are the standard checkered walnut. Barrel lengths are 4" and 6.5". On late models the 6.5" barrel was reduced to 6", as on all S&Ws. The model designation was changed to Model 28 in 1957. S&W discontinued the Model 28 in 1986.

Exc.	V.G.	Good	Fair	Poor
275	250	225	175	100

Model 29 (.44 Magnum)

In the early 1950s, handgun writers, under the leadership of Elmer Keith, were in the habit of loading the .44 Special cartridge to high performance levels and firing them in the existing .44 Hand Ejectors. They urged S&W to produce a revolver strong enough to consistently fire these heavy loads. In 1954 Remington, at the request of S&W produced the .44 Magnum cartridge. As was the case with the .357 Magnum, the cases were longer so that they would not fit in the chambers of the older guns. The first .44 Magnum became available for sale in early 1956. The first 500 were made with the 6.5" barrel; the 4" became available later that year. In 1957 the model designation was changed to 29, and the 8-3/8" barrel was introduced. The Model 29 is available in blue or nickel-plate. It came standard with all target options and was offered in a fitted wood case. The Model 29 is considered by many knowledgeable people to be the finest revolver S&W has ever produced. The older Model 29 revolvers are in a different collector category than most modern S&W revolvers. The early four-screw models can be worth a 50% premium in excellent condition. These early models were produced from 1956 to 1958 and approximately 6,500 were sold. One must regard these revolvers on a separate basis and have them individually appraised for proper valuation. In 1993 the 4" barrel was dropped from production. This model is no longer in production.

NIB	Exc.	V.G.	Good	Fair	Poor
500	400	300	250	200	150

WHAT'S IT LIKE-SMITH & WESSON MODEL 29 .44 MAGNUM

It was certainly the most awe-inspiring sixguns I had ever seen! I had heard reports about this gun now here it was at the local gunshop. It was not for sale as the savvy proprietor knew he could make a lot of money renting it. After all how many people up to this time could boast that they had actually fired a .44 Magnum! The three of us, all teenagers and accustomed to shooting .22's, .357 Magnums, even the .45 ACP and .45 Colt, all paid our money, all shot the new .44, and also in unison, we all lied and said: "It didn't kick bad at all!" In reality it kicked like the proverbial mule! Fortunately over the ensuing years we have learned to handle its recoil and even heavier-kickin' sixguns. In the late 1920s, Elmer Keith started promoting the heavy loads in his .44 Specials that led directly to Smith & Wesson and Remington getting together and offering the .44 Magnum. Keith received the call in December of 1955 that his dream was a reality. He had asked for a 250 gr. bullet at a full 1200 fps; he got a 240 gr. bullet at 1400 fps plus and new era of big game hunting with a handgun was about to begin. Twenty years earlier, Col. Doug Wesson had used then new .357 Magnum to take several head of big game but now we had a sixgun that was truly capable of taking any North American big game animals. First known as simply "The .44 Magnum", it became that Model 29 when Smith and Wesson went to a numbering system in 1957. In my mind the Model 29 is a magnificently beautiful revolver. Originally available in both blue and nickle finishes, with barrel lengths of 4", 6 1/2", and 8 3/8" (if you have an original 5" you have struck gold!), the Model 29 is and always will be the King of .44 Magnum sixguns.

Long Live the King.

John Taffin

Early 5" Barrel Model 29

This is the rarest of the Model 29s. A total of 500 were manufactured in 1958. Collectors are cautioned to exercise care before purchasing one of these rare Model 29 variations.

NIB	Exc.	V.G.	Good	Fair	Poor
2000	1500	1200	800	500	300

Notes on N Frame Revolvers:
1. N-frame models were changed from 5-screw to 4-screw between 1956 and 1958. Serial number SI75,000.
2. Triggerguard screw was eliminated in 1961.
3. The pinned barrel and recessed cylinder were discontinued in 1978.

Model 629

This revolver is simply a stainless steel version of the Model 29 chambered for the .44 Magnum.

NIB	Exc.	V.G.	Good	Fair	Poor
475	400	300	250	225	200

Model 629 Backpacker

This 1994 variation of the Model 629 is built on the N-frame with round butt. Cylinders are fluted and chamfered. Barrel length is 3" with adjustable rear sight. The finish is stainless steel and Hogue rubber grips are standard. Weight is approximately 40 oz.

NIB	Exc.	V.G.	Good	Fair	Poor
700	600	500	400	300	200

Model 629 Mountain Gun

This limited edition 6-shot revolver, introduced in 1993, features a 4" barrel chambered for the .44 Magnum. Built on the large N-frame this pistol is made from stainless steel and is drilled and tapped for scope mounts. It is equipped with a Hogue round butt rubber monogrip. Standard sights are a pinned black ramp front sight and an adjustable black rear blade. Weight is approximately 40 oz. Model was re-introduced in 1999.

NIB	Exc.	V.G.	Good	Fair	Poor
500	450	400	350	300	150

Model 629 Classic

This model has additional features that the standard Model 629 does not have such as: Chamfered cylinder, full lug barrel, interchangeable front sights, Hogue combat grips, and a drilled and tapped frame to accept scope mounts.

NIB	Exc.	V.G.	Good	Fair	Poor
400	375	325	250	225	200

Model 629 Classic DX

Has all of the features of the Model 629 Classic, introduced in 1991, plus two sets of grips and five interchangeable front sights. Available in 6.5" or 8-3/8" barrel. A 5" barrel option was offered in 1992 but dropped in 1993.

NIB	Exc.	V.G.	Good	Fair	Poor
650	500	450	350	300	150

Model 629 Classic Powerport

Introduced in 1996 this model offers a integral compensator with a 6.5" full lug barrel. The Patridge front sight is pinned and the rear sight is fully adjustable. The frame is drilled and tapped for scope mounts. Synthetic Houge combat-style grips are standard. Weight is approximately 52 oz.

NIB	Exc.	V.G.	Good	Fair	Poor
600	550	—	—	—	—

Model 30 (The .32 Hand Ejector)

This model was built on the small I frame and based on the .32 Hand Ejector Model of 1903. This older model was dropped from production in 1942. It was re-introduced in 1949 in a more modern version but still referred to as the .32 Hand Ejector. In 1957 the model designation was changed to Model 30. In 1960 this frame size was dropped, and the J-frame, which had been in use since 1950, became standard for the Model 30. S&W stamped -1 behind the model number to designate this important change in frame size. The Model 30 is chambered for the .32 S&W long cartridge. It has a 6-shot cylinder and 2", 3", 4", and 6" barrel lengths. It has fixed sights and is either blued or nickel-plated. The butt is round, with checkered walnut grips. It was discontinued in 1976.

Courtesy W.P. Hallstein III and son Chip

Exc.	V.G.	Good	Fair	Poor
350	250	200	150	100

Model 31 (.32 Regulation Police)

This model is the same as the Model 30 with a square butt. It was known as the .32 Regulation Police before 1957. It is now discontinued.

Exc.	V.G.	Good	Fair	Poor
275	250	200	150	100

Model 31 (.32 Regulation Police Target)

The Target model of the Regulation Police is rare. Only 196 of these special variations were produced in 1957. All specifications are the same as the Model 31 except for the addition of adjustable sights.

Exc.	V.G.	Good	Fair	Poor
500	400	250	200	150

Model 32 (.38/.32 Terrier)

This model, known as the Terrier prior to 1957, was introduced in 1936. It is essentially a .38 Regulation Police chambered for .38 S&W and having a 2" barrel and round butt. Like the Model 30 and 31 this revolver was originally built on the I-frame, which was changed to the J-frame in 1960. The -1 behind the model number signifies this change. It is offered in blue or nickel-plate and has a 5-shot cylinder, fixed sights, and checkered walnut grips. This model was discontinued in 1974.

Exc.	V. G.	Good	Fair	Poor
300	200	150	100	75

NOTE: A limited production version with alloy frame and steel cylinder was produced as the Model 032. Add 30% for this model.

Model 33 (.38 Regulation Police)

This model is simply the .38 Regulation Police with a square butt and 4" barrel chambered for the .38 S&W. The factory referred to this model as the .38-.32 revolver. It, too, was built on the small I-frame and later changed to the J-frame in 1960. The Model 33 was discontinued in 1974.

Courtesy Mike Stuckslager

Exc.	V.G.	Good	Fair	Poor
350	250	200	150	100

Model 34 (.22/.32 Kit Gun)

Courtesy Mike Stuckslager

Introduced in 1936 as the .22-32 Kit Gun, it has a 2" or 4" barrel, either round or square butt, and adjustable sights. This model underwent several modifications before it reached its present form. S&W modernized this revolver in 1953 with the addition of a coil mainspring and micro-click sights. The Model 34 is built on this improved version. The revolver is a .32 Hand Ejector chambered for the .22 rimfire. It is built on the I-frame until 1960 when the changeover to the improved J-frame occurred. The -1 behind the model number indicates this varia-

tion. The Model 34 is offered blued or nickel-plate and is currently in production.

NIB	Exc.	V.G.	Good	Fair	Poor
375	300	250	225	175	100

Model 35 (.22/.32 Target)

This is a square-butt, 6"-barreled version of the .22/32 Hand Ejector. It was known prior to 1957 as the .22/32 Target. It underwent the same changes as the Model 34 but was discontinued in 1973.

Courtesy Mike Stuckslager

Exc.	V.G.	Good	Fair	Poor
350	300	250	200	100

AIRLITE SERIES
(titanium cylinder-aluminum alloy frame)

Model 317 AirLite

This 8-round revolver was introduced in 1997 and is chambered for the .22 Long Rifle cartridge. It is fitted with a 2" barrel, serrated ramp front sight, fixed rear sight, and Dymondwood boot grips. It is produced from carbon and stainless steel and also aluminum alloy on a J-frame. Its weight is about 9.9 oz.

NIB	Exc.	V.G.	Good	Fair	Poor
425	375	325	—	—	—

Model 317 AirLite Kit Gun

This version of the Model 317 was introduced in 1998 and is fitted with a 3" barrel with adjustable rear sight. Choice of Dymondwood grips or Uncle Mike's Combat grips. Weight is about 12 oz. In 2001 this model was offered with Hi-Viz green dot front sight.

NIB	Exc.	V.G.	Good	Fair	Poor
500	400	325	—	—	—

Model 317 AirLite Ladysmith

This model features a 2" barrel and Dymondwood grips. Display case is standard. Weight is about 10 oz.

NIB	Exc.	V.G.	Good	Fair	Poor
500	400	325	—	—	—

Model 331 AirLite

This model is chambered for the .32 H&R Magnum cartridge on a J-frame. Barrel length is 1-7/8". Exposed hammer offers single or double action. The frame is aluminum, as is the barrel shroud and yoke. The cylinder is titanium. The barrel has a stainless steel liner. Matte finish. Because the revolver is made from aluminum and titanium it has a two tone appearance because of the two different materials. Choice of wood or rubber boot grips. Capacity is 6 rounds. Weight is about 12 oz. with rubber grip and 11.2 oz. with wood grip. Introduced in 1999.

NIB	Exc.	V.G.	Good	Fair	Poor
550	450	—	—	—	—

Model 332 AirLite

This model is similar to the Model 331 above but with a concealed hammer, double action configuration. Weight is 12 oz. with rubber grips and 11.3 oz. with wood grips.

NIB	Exc.	V.G.	Good	Fair	Poor
550	450	—	—	—	—

Model 337 AirLite

This model has an aluminum frame, exposed hammer, titanium cylinder. Front sight is black and pinned. Smooth trigger.

Cylinder capacity is five rounds. Chambered for .38 Special +P ammo. Barrel length is 1-7/8". Wood or rubber grips. Weight with wood groups is about 11.2 oz., with rubber grips about 12 oz. Introduced in 1999.

NIB	Exc.	V.G.	Good	Fair	Poor
575	450	—	—	—	—

Model 337 Kit Gun

Similar to the Model 337 but fitted with a 3" barrel. Adjustable rear sight. Weight is about 13.5 oz. In 2001 this model was offered with Hi-Viz green dot front sighht.

NIB	Exc.	V.G.	Good	Fair	Poor
650	475	—	—	—	—

Model 337 PD

Similar to the Model 337 but with a matte black finish over the aluminum frame and Hogue Batam grips. Weight is 10.7 oz. Introduced in 2000.

NIB	Exc.	V.G.	Good	Fair	Poor
600	450	—	—	—	—

Model 340

Introduced in 2001 this hammerless model features a Scandium alloy frame and is fitted with a 1.875" barrel. Chambered for the .357 magnum cartridge with a 5-round cylinder. Matte stainless grey finish. Pinned black front sight. Hogue Batam grips standard. Weight is about 12 oz.

NIB	Exc.	V.G.	Good	Fair	Poor
750	600	—	—	—	—

Model 340 PD

Same as the Model 340 but with a black grey finish. Also introduced in 2001.

NIB	Exc.	V.G.	Good	Fair	Poor
775	625	—	—	—	—

Model 342 AirLite

This is similar to the above model but with double action only concealed hammer. Weight is 11.3 oz. with wood grips and 12 oz. with rubber grips. Introduced in 1999.

NIB	Exc.	V.G.	Good	Fair	Poor
575	450	—	—	—	—

Model 342 PD

Similar to the Model 337 but with matte black finish over the aluminum frame and Hogue Batam grips. Weight is about 10.8 oz. Introduced in 2000.

NIB	Exc.	V.G.	Good	Fair	Poor
600	450	—	—	—	—

Model 360

This J frame model features a Scandium alloy frame with exposed hammer and 5-shot cylinder. Fixed sights on a 1.875" barrel. Matte stainless grey finish. Weight is about 12 oz. Introduced in 2001.

NIB	Exc.	V.G.	Good	Fair	Poor
750	600	—	—	—	—

Model 360 Kit Gun

This version of the M360 is fitted with a 3.125" barrel with Hi-Viz green dot front sight and adjustable rear sight. Weight is about 14.5 oz. Introduced in 2001.

NIB	Exc.	V.G.	Good	Fair	Poor
875	700	—	—	—	—

Model 386

Introduced in 2001 this L frame model features a 6-shot cylinder chambered for the .357 magnum cartridge. Fitted with a 3.125" barrel with Hi-Viz green dot front sight and adjustable rear sight. Scandium alloy frame with matte stainless grey finish. Weight is about 18.5 oz. Hogue Batam grips.

NIB	Exc.	V.G.	Good	Fair	Poor
825	650	—	—	—	—

Model 386 PD

Same as above but with black grey finish and 2.5" barrel with red ramp front sight and adjustable rear sight. Weight is about 17.5 oz.

NIB	Exc.	V.G.	Good	Fair	Poor
795	625	—	—	—	—

Model 396 Mountain Lite

This L-frame revolver is chambered for the .44 Special cartridge. It is fitted with a five round titanium cylinder and aluminum alloy frame. Barrel length is 3" and has a green Hi-Viz front sight and an adjustable rear sight. Introduced in 2000. Weight is approximately 19 oz.

NIB	Exc.	V.G.	Good	Fair	Poor
775	625	—	—	—	—

Model 242

This medium frame revolver is chambered for the .38 Special +P cartridge. Semi-concealed hammer and 2.5" barrel. Pinned black ramp front sight. Black rubber boot grips. Seven-round cylinder. Matte alloy and titanium finish. Weight is about 19 oz. Introduced in 1999. This model is no longer in production.

NIB	Exc.	V.G.	Good	Fair	Poor
550	450	—	—	—	—

Model 296

Also a medium frame revolver chambered for the .44 Special cartridge. Fitted with a 2.5" barrel. Concealed hammer. Cylinder capacity is 5 rounds. Weight is about 19 oz. Introduced in 1999.

NIB	Exc.	V.G.	Good	Fair	Poor
550	450	—	—	—	—

Model 610

This N frame model is chambered for the 10mm cartridge and fitted with a 4" barrel with interchangeable ramp sight. Adjustable rear sight. Six-round non-fluted cylinder. Hogue rubber combat grips. Stainless steel finish. Weight is about 50 oz. Introduced in 2001.

NIB	Exc.	V.G.	Good	Fair	Poor
775	625	—	—	—	—

THE S&W FIVE-SHOOTERS
(Genre - Chiefs Special)

If there is a go-everywhere handgun, it is the genre known as the "Chiefs Special," which was originally a five-shot, steel-frame, exposed-hammer revolver built on a small frame bearing the factory connotation "J." I use the "Centennial" or hammerless version made from either all steel or steel and aluminum and they are my "go-everywhere" guns of choice. As the gun has continued in popularity, it has been made without an exposed hammer, with a shrouded hammer, with a 2" and a 3" barrel and with various sights and barrel configurations as well as in a number of calibers, including .32 Magnum, .38 Special, 9x19mm and .357 Magnum. There are also .22 LR and .22 Magnum rimfire versions with adjustable sights. All the styles and calibers are made in blued steel, stainless steel or with a combination of steel and alloy materials to make the guns even lighter to carry.

The J-frame revolver is like the observation made by Goldilocks in "Goldilocks and the Three Bears," "It's just right!" From a functional design perspective, the grip is too small; the barrel, normally a nominal 2", is too short; the vestal sights are too small; and it only holds five rounds. When shooting the larger and more powerful cartridges, there's an upper limit of just plain physical discomfort reached when the ammunition is loaded too much above standard velocities. The little guys can safely handle +P and Magnum rounds, but not the person firing them. To use a J-frame revolver effectively, a regime of regular practice should be established, say 20 rounds every other month, shot at man-sized targets up close. Even though I carry the Centennials with the thought that I will probably never need them, I do want to be able to solve the problem should it present itself.

Walt Rauch

NIB	Exc.	V.G.	Good	Fair	Poor
300	250	200	175	125	100

Model 36LS (.38 Ladysmith)

This model is similar to the Model 36 with the exception that it is only offered with a 2" barrel, comes with rosewood grips and a soft carrying case. Weighs 20 oz.

NIB	Exc.	V.G.	Good	Fair	Poor
325	250	200	175	125	100

Model 36 (Chief's Special Target)

Since 1955 a limited number of Chief's Specials with adjustable sights have been manufactured. They have been offered with 2" or 3" barrels, round or square butts, and either blue or nickel-plated. Between 1957 and 1965, these target models were stamped Model 36 on the yoke. The revolvers manufactured between 1965 and the model discontinuance in 1975 were marked Model 50. This is a very collectible revolver. A total of 2,313 of these special target models were sold in various model designations. Some are more rare than others.

Model 36 (.38 Chief's Special)

This model, known as the Chief's Special, was introduced in 1950. It was built on the J-frame and is chambered for the .38 Special cartridge. It holds 5 shots, has a 2" or 3" barrel, and was initially offered in a round butt. In 1952 a square butt version was released. It is finished in blue or nickel-plate and has checkered walnut grips. A 3" heavy barrel was first produced in 1967 and became standard in 1975. The 2" barrel was dropped from production in 1993.

Courtesy W.P. Hallstein III and son Chip

Exc.	V.G.	Good	Fair	Poor
450	375	325	275	200

Model 37

Introduced in 1952 as the Chief's Special Airweight, this revolver initially had an alloy frame and cylinder. In 1954, following many complaints regarding damaged revolvers, the cylinders were made of steel. Barrel lengths, finishes, and grip options on the Airweight are the same as on the standard Chief Special. In 1957 the Model 37 designation was adopted. These early alloy frame and cylinder revolvers were designed to shoot only standard velocity .38 Special cartridges. The use of high velocity ammunition was not recommended by the factory.

NIB	Exc.	V.G.	Good	Fair	Poor
350	300	275	225	175	125

NOTE: All 1998 production models are now rated for +P ammunition.

Model 637

Same as the model above but with aluminum frame and stainless steel finish.

NIB	Exc.	V.G.	Good	Fair	Poor
400	325	275	225	175	125

NOTE: All 1998 production models are now rated for +P ammunition.

Model 38 (Airweight Bodyguard)

This model was introduced in 1955 as the Airweight Bodyguard. This was a departure from S&W's usual procedure in that the alloy-framed version came first. The Model 38 is chambered for .38 Special and is available with a 2" barrel standard. Although a 3" barrel was offered, it is rarely encountered. The frame of the Bodyguard is extended to conceal and shroud the hammer but at the same time allow the hammer to be cocked by the thumb. This makes this model an ideal pocket revolver, as it can be drawn without catching on clothing. It is available either blue or nickel-plated, with checkered walnut grips.

NIB	Exc.	V.G.	Good	Fair	Poor
325	250	225	175	125	100

NOTE: All 1998 production models are now rated for +P ammunition.

Model 638

Same as the model above but with aluminum frame and stainless steel finish.

NIB	Exc.	V.G.	Good	Fair	Poor
450	350	300	225	175	125

NOTE: All 1998 production models are now rated for +P ammunition.

Model 49 (Bodyguard)

This model was introduced in 1959 and is identical in configuration to the Model 38 except that the frame is made of steel.

NIB	Exc.	V.G.	Good	Fair	Poor
350	250	225	200	150	100

Model 649 (Bodyguard Stainless)

This stainless steel version of the Model 49 was introduced in 1985. It is also available in .357 Magnum. As of 1998 this model was also offered in a .38 Special only version.

NIB	Exc.	V.G.	Good	Fair	Poor
350	300	225	200	175	125

Model 40 (aka Model 42) Centennial

This model was introduced in 1952 as Smith & Wesson's 100th anniversary and appropriately called the "Centennial Model". It is of the Safety Hammerless design. This model was built on the J-frame and features a fully concealed hammer and a grip safety. The Model 40 is chambered for the .38 Special cartridge. It is offered with a 2" barrel in either blue or nickel plate. The grips are checkered walnut. The Centennial was discontinued in 1974.

Courtesy Mike Stuckslager

Exc.	V.G.	Good	Fair	Poor
475	350	300	250	200

Model 640 Centennial

A stainless steel version of the Model 40 furnished with a 2- or 3" barrel. Both the frame and cylinder are stainless steel. The 3" barrel was no longer offered as of 1993. As of 1998 this model was also offered in a .38 Special only version.

NIB	Exc.	V.G.	Good	Fair	Poor
375	300	250	200	150	100

Model 640 Centennial .357 Magnum

Introduced in 1995 this version of the Model 640 is chambered for the .357 cartridge and fitted with a 2-1/8" barrel. The gun is stainless steel with a fixed notch rear sight and pinned black ramp front sight. It is 6-3/4" in length and weighs 25 oz.

NIB	Exc.	V.G.	Good	Fair	Poor
375	300	250	200	150	100

Model 642 Centennial Airweight

Identical to the Model 640 with the exception of a stainless steel cylinder and aluminum alloy frame. Furnished with a 2" barrel. Discontinued in 1992. Replaced by the Model 442 which was introduced in 1993. This model was reintroduced in 1996.

NIB	Exc.	V.G.	Good	Fair	Poor
400	300	250	200	150	100

NOTE: All 1998 production models are now rated for +P ammunition.

Model 642LS

Same as above but fitted with smooth combat wood grips and a softside carry case.

NIB	Exc.	V.G.	Good	Fair	Poor
350	275	225	175	125	100

NOTE: All 1998 production models are now rated for +P ammunition.

Model 940

Styled like the other Centennial models, this model is chambered for the 9mm Parabellum cartridge. It has a stainless steel cylinder and frame and is furnished with a 2" or 3" barrel. The 3" barrel version was dropped from production in 1993.

NIB	Exc.	V.G.	Good	Fair	Poor
375	300	225	175	125	100

Model 631

This revolver is chambered for the .32 Magnum cartridge and is fitted with a 2" (fixed sights) or 4" (adjustable sights) barrel. Stainless steel finish. Weight with 23" barrel is 22 oz. Produced in 1990.

NIB	Exc.	V.G.	Good	Fair	Poor
450	350	275	200	150	100

Model 631 Lady Smith
Similar to the above model but with rosewood grips and laser etched. Fitted with 2" barrel.

NIB	Exc.	V.G.	Good	Fair	Poor
450	350	275	200	150	100

Model 632 Centennial
This model is similar to the other Centennial models but is chambered for the .32 H&R Magnum cartridge. It comes standard with a 2" barrel, stainless steel cylinder and aluminum alloy frame. Dropped from the product line in 1993.

NIB	Exc.	V.G.	Good	Fair	Poor
325	275	225	175	125	100

Model 42 - Airweight Centennial
This model is identical in configuration to the Model 40 except that it was furnished with an aluminum alloy frame. It was also discontinued in 1974.

Editors Note: The first 37 Model 42s were manufactured with aluminum alloy cylinders. They weigh 11-1/4 ounces compared to 13 ounces for the standard model. The balance of Model 42 production was with steel cylinders. Add 300% for this extremely rare variation.

NIB	Exc.	V.G.	Good	Fair	Poor
450	400	325	200	150	100

Model 042 Centennial Airweight
This model was produced in 1992 but is not catalogued. It is chambered for .38 Special and fitted with a 2" barrel. The frame is alloy. Marked "MOD 042". No grip safety. Blued finish. Weight is about 16 oz.

NIB	Exc.	V.G.	Good	Fair	Poor
450	350	300	200	150	100

Model 442 Centennial Lightweight

This 5-shot revolver is chambered for the .38 Special and is equipped with a 2" barrel, aluminum alloy frame, and carbon steel cylinder. It has a fully concealed hammer and weighs 15.8 oz. The front ramp sight is serrated and the rear sight is a fixed square notch. Rubber combat grips from Michael's of Oregon are standard. Finish is either blue or satin nickel. Introduced in 1993.

NIB	Exc.	V.G.	Good	Fair	Poor
350	300	250	200	150	100

NOTE: All 1998 production models are now rated for +P ammunition.

Model 43 (.22/.32 Kit Gun Airweight)
This model was built on the J-frame, is chambered for .22 rimfire, has a 3.5" barrel, and is offered in a round or square butt, with checkered walnut grips. It has adjustable sights and is either blued or nickel-plated. The frame is made of aluminum alloy. Except for this, it is identical to the Model 34 or .22/.32 Kit Gun. This model has a rare 2" barrel configuration as well as a .22 MRF model. The Model 43 was introduced in 1954 and was discontinued in 1974.

Courtesy Mike Stuckslager

NIB	Exc.	V.G.	Good	Fair	Poor
375	300	250	200	150	100

Model 51 (.22/.32 Kit Gun Magnum)
This model is simply the Model 34 chambered for the .22 Winchester Magnum rimfire. It was first introduced in 1960 beginning with serial number 52637. Available in both round and square butt with the round butt variation having a total production of only 600. The Model 51 was discontinued in 1974.

NIB	Exc.	V.G.	Good	Fair	Poor
450	325	275	250	200	125

Model 651
This stainless steel version of the Model 51 .22 Magnum Kit Gun was manufactured between 1983 and 1987.

Exc.	V.G.	Good	Fair	Poor
350	300	250	200	125

Model 73

Produced in about 1973 this revolver was built on a special "C" size frame. Cylinder holds 6 rounds and is chambered for the .38 Special cartridge. Fitted with a 2" barrel. A total of 5,000 were built. All but 20 were destroyed. An extremely rare S&W revolver. Marked, "MOD 73" on yoke.

Courtesy Jim Supica, Old Town Station

NIB	Exc.	V.G.	Good	Fair	Poor
—	8500	—	—	—	—

Notes on J-frame Revolvers:

1. In 1953 the cylinder stop plunger screw was eliminated.
2. In 1955 the top corner sideplate screw was eliminated.
3. In 1957 the numerical model designation was stamped on the yoke.
4. In 1966 the flat latch was changed to the present contoured cylinder release.

Model 45 (Post Office)

This model is a special purpose K-frame Military & Police Model chambered for the .22 rimfire. It was designed as a training revolver for police departments and the U.S. Postal Service. This model was manufactured in limited quantities between 1948 and 1957. In 1963 production abruptly began and ended again. There were 500 of these revolvers released on a commercial basis, but they are rarely encountered.

NIB	Exc.	V.G.	Good	Fair	Poor
750	600	550	350	200	100

Model 48 (K-22 Masterpiece Magnum)

Introduced in 1959 and is identical to the Model 17 or K-22 except that it is chambered for the .22 WRM cartridge. Offered in 4", 6", and 8-3/8" barrel lengths, it has a blued finish. Discontinued in 1986.

NIB	Exc.	V.G.	Good	Fair	Poor
400	350	275	225	150	100

Model 53 (Magnum Jet)

Introduced in 1961 and chambered for the .22 Jet, a Remington cartridge. The barrel lengths were 4, 6, and 8-3/8" and the finish is blued. Sights were adjustable and the revolver was furnished with cylinder inserts that would allow .22 rimfire cartridges to be fired. The frame had two firing pins. Approximately 15,000 were produced before it was discontinued in 1974. Price includes guns with individual chambered inserts.

NIB	Exc.	V.G.	Good	Fair	Poor
800	650	450	350	250	200

NOTE: Add $150 for auxiliary .22 LR cylinder.

A Model 53-2 factory engraved S&W sold at auction for $2,300. "A" coverage with factory letter. Original box. Condition was excellent to mint.
Amoskeag Auction Company, March 2000

Model 56 (KXT-38 USAF)

Introduced in 1962 this is a 2" heavy barrel built on the K-frame. It is chambered for the .38 Special. There were approximately 15,000 of these revolvers built when it was discontinued in 1964. It was marked "US" on the backstrap. A total of 15,205 produced but most destroyed.

NIB	Exc.	V.G.	Good	Fair	Poor
2500	1750	1250	750	500	250

Model 57

This revolver was introduced in 1964 and is chambered for the .41 Magnum cartridge. It is built on the N-frame. Offered in 4", 6", and 8-3/8" barrel lengths, it has a blued frame and adjustable sights. Model designations are: 57-1 1982; 57-2 1988; 57-3 1990; 57-4 1993.

NIB	Exc.	V.G.	Good	Fair	Poor
450	350	275	225	200	150

Model 657

This is a stainless steel version of the Model 57 and was introduced in 1980. Still in production. In 2001 this model was reintroduced again with a 7.5" barrel with pinned front sight and adjustable rear sight. Hogue rubber combat grips. Weight is about 52 oz.

NIB	Exc.	V.G.	Good	Fair	Poor
670	525	425	—	—	—

Model 58

This model is chambered for the .41 Magnum and is fitted with fixed sights. Offered in blued or nickel finish and with 4" barrel. Checkered walnut grips are standard. Introduced in 1964.

NIB	Exc.	V.G.	Good	Fair	Poor
400	325	250	200	150	100

Model 547

Introduced in 1980 and chambered for the 9mm cartridge and offered with either 3" or 4" barrel. Finish is blued. Discontinued.

NIB	Exc.	V.G.	Good	Fair	Poor
375	300	250	200	150	100

Model 60

Introduced in 1965 this model is similar to the Model 36 but in stainless steel. Offered in 2" barrel with fixed sights, walnut grips, and smooth trigger. Some 2" Model 60s were produced with adjustable sights-Add 50%. The 3" barrel version comes with a full underlug, adjustable sights, serrated trigger, and rubber grips. The 2" version weighs about 20 oz. while the 3" version weighs approximately 25 oz. In 1996 this model was offered chambered for the .357 Magnum cartridge. This new version is fitted with a 2-1/8" barrel. The 2-1/8" barrel weighs about 23 oz. As of 1998 this model was also offered in a .38 Special only version.

2" Barrel

NIB	Exc.	V.G.	Good	Fair	Poor
350	275	200	175	125	100

3" Barrel

NIB	Exc.	V.G.	Good	Fair	Poor
350	275	200	175	125	100

Model 60LS (LadySmith)

Chambered for the .38 Special with 2" barrel and stainless steel frame and cylinder. This slightly smaller version of the Model 60 is made for small hands. A new version offered in 1996 is chambered for the .357 Magnum cartridge.

NIB	Exc.	V.G.	Good	Fair	Poor
300	275	250	200	150	100

Model 63

This model, introduced in 1977, is simply the Model 34 made of stainless steel.

NIB	Exc.	V.G.	Good	Fair	Poor
350	275	250	225	200	150

Model 64 (Military & Police Stainless)

This model is the stainless steel version of the Model 10 M&P. It was introduced in 1970. The Model 64-1 variation was introduced in 1972 and is the heavy barrel version.

NIB	Exc.	V.G.	Good	Fair	Poor
350	300	275	225	175	125

Model 65 (.357 Military & Police Heavy Barrel Stainless)

This is the stainless steel version of the Model 13 M&P .357 Magnum. It was introduced in 1974.

NIB	Exc.	V.G.	Good	Fair	Poor
350	300	275	225	175	125

Model 66 (.357 Combat Magnum Stainless)

Released in 1970, this is the stainless steel version of the Model 19 or Combat Magnum. It is chambered for the .357 Magnum, has adjustable sights, a square butt with checkered walnut grips, and was initially offered with a 4" barrel. In 1974 a 2.5" barrel, round butt version was made available. It was available in a 6" barrel, as well as all target options until discontinued in 1993.

NIB	Exc.	V.G.	Good	Fair	Poor
350	300	250	200	150	125

Model 67 (.38 Combat Masterpiece Stainless)

Introduced in 1972 this is a stainless steel version of the Model 15 with a 4" barrel. It is chambered for the .38 Special cartridge. Model designation changes are as follows: {None} 1972 to 1977; {-1} 1977 to 1988; {-2} 1988 to 1993; {-3} 1993 to present.

NIB	Exc.	V.G.	Good	Fair	Poor
350	300	250	200	150	100

Model 650

Introduced in 1983 this stainless steel model is built on a J-frame with a 3" heavy barrel chambered for the .22 WRM. It has a round butt and fixed sights. Discontinued in 1988.

NIB	Exc.	V.G.	Good	Fair	Poor
425	350	250	175	125	100

Model 651

This J-frame model was introduced in 1983 and chambered for the .22 WRM and fitted with a 4" barrel. Stainless steel finish and adjustable sights. Designation changes are: {None} 1983 to 1988; {-1} 1988 to 1990; {-2} 1988 to 1990.

NIB	Exc.	V.G.	Good	Fair	Poor
400	350	250	175	125	100

Model 520

Introduced in 1980 and built on the N-frame. Chambered for the .357 Mag. cartridge with a 4" barrel. It has fixed sights, blued finish and checkered walnut grips.

NIB	Exc.	V.G.	Good	Fair	Poor
350	300	250	225	150	100

Model 581

Introduced in 1980. Built on the L-frame with a full barrel underlug. Chambered for the .357 Mag. cartridge with a 4" barrel and blued or nickel finish. Rear sight is fixed. Sometimes referred to as the Distinguished Service Magnum. Designation changes are: {None} 1980 to 1986; {-1} 1986 to 1987; {-2} 1987 to 1988; {-3} 1988 to present.

NIB	Exc.	V.G.	Good	Fair	Poor
350	300	275	225	150	100

Model 681

This model is identical as the Model 581 but with a stainless steel frame and barrel. Introduced in 1981 and discontinued in 1992.

NIB	Exc.	V.G.	Good	Fair	Poor
350	300	250	200	150	100

Model 586

Introduced in 1980 this L-frame revolver is furnished with target sights, target stocks, and target trigger. Barrels in 4", 6", or 8" lengths. Choice of blued or nickel finish. Designation changes are: {None} 1980 to 1986; {-1} 1986 to 1987; {-2} 1987 to 1988; {-3} 1988 to 1993; {-4} 1993 to present; {-5} 1993 to present (export to Brazil in .38 caliber). This model is no longer in production.

NIB	Exc.	V.G.	Good	Fair	Poor
375	300	250	200	150	100

Model 686

Introduced in 1980 this is a stainless steel version of the Model 586. There is no {-5} designation for this model.

NIB	Exc.	V.G.	Good	Fair	Poor
375	300	250	200	150	100

Model 686 Powerport

Introduced in 1995 this version of the Model 686 features a 6" full lug barrel with integral compensator. The frame is drilled and tapped for scope mounts. Hogue grips are furnished as standard.

NIB	Exc.	V.G.	Good	Fair	Poor
600	550	450	400	300	200

Model 686 Magnum Plus

Offered for the first time in 1996 this model features a 7 shot cylinder. It is available with 2.5", 4", or 6" barrel lengths. It is fitted with a red ramp front sight and a fully adjustable rear sight. The frame is drilled and tapped for scope mounts. Hogue synthetic grips are standard. The stainless steel is satin finished. Weight is between 35 oz. and 45 oz. depending on barrel length.

NIB	Exc.	V.G.	Good	Fair	Poor
450	400	—	—	—	—

Model 686 Plus Mountain Gun

This model is fitted with a 4" tapered barrel and chambered for the .357 magnum cartridge. It has adjustable rear sights. Hogue rubber grips are standard. Stainless steel finish. Weight is about 44 oz.

NIB	Exc.	V.G.	Good	Fair	Poor
550	450	—	—	—	—

WHAT'S IT LIKE-THE SCHOFIELD MODEL

About the same time that I began shooting six-guns seriously, Val Forgett of Navy Arms started importing replica percussion revolvers. I early on shot both an 1860 Army and an 1858 Remington from Navy Arms. Over the last 40 years, thousands of replica Colt and Remington revolvers, both cartridge firing and cap and ball style have been imported. The quality has run the full gamut from poor to excellent and the latter attribute can be directly assessed to Forgett's efforts. Although we have seen so many Colt and Remington replicas, it would not be until the mid-1990s when a Smith & Wesson single action would be offered again thanks to Val Forgett. The Smith & Wesson Schofield was an improvement on the Smith & Wesson American that placed the opening latch on the frame instead of the barrel frame allowing it to be opened with one hand. All Smith and Wesson single actions were of the break-top variety with the latch in front of the hammer and the hinge at the bottom of the frame in front of the cylinder. Even today this system makes for very fast unloading and reloading of single action revolvers. The Schofield Model from Navy Arms is offered in both blue and nickel, 7" or 5" barrel lengths and in .45 Colt or .44-40. Except for the longer length of the cylinder to accept these cartridges, they are faithful replicas. Now, thanks to the Performance Center at Smith & Wesson one can have an S&W Model 3 Schofield chambered in the original .45 S&W. In either case, these big bore sixguns are a real piece of history and give the shooter a different experience and feel than the traditional replicas that are patterned after Colt and Remington single actions.

John Taffin

Model 3 Schofield

A reintroduction of the famous Schofield revolver. This is a single action top break model chambered for the .45 S&W cartridge. Barrel length is 7". Frame and barrel are blue while hammer and trigger are case hardened. Sights are a fixed rear notch and half moon post front. Walnut grips. Weight is 40 oz. Reintroduced in 2000.

NIB	Exc.	V.G.	Good	Fair	Good
1350	1100	—	—	—	—

SEMIAUTOMATIC PISTOLS

Courtesy Smith & Wesson

NOTE: For pistols with Smith and Wesson factory installed night sights add $100 to NIB and Exc. prices. For S&W factory engraving add $1,000 for Class C (1/3 coverage), $1,250 for Class B (2/3 coverage), $1,500 for Class A (full coverage).

Model 39

This was the first double action semiautomatic pistol produced in the United States. It was introduced in 1957. It had an alloy frame and was chambered for the 9mm Parabellum cartridge. The barrel was 4" and the finish was either blued or nickel with checkered walnut grips. The rear sight was adjustable. Magazine capacity is 8 rounds. Discontinued in 1982.

NIB	Exc.	V.G.	Good	Fair	Poor
400	350	250	200	150	100

Model 39 Steel Frame

A total of 927 steel frame Model 39s were produced. A rare pistol, use caution.

NIB	Exc.	V.G.	Good	Fair	Poor
1250	1000	700	550	400	250

Model 59

Introduced in 1971 this pistol is similar to the Model 39 but with a wide grip to hold a double column magazine of 14 rounds. Furnished with black checkered plastic grips. Discontinued in 1982.

NIB	Exc.	V.G.	Good	Fair	Poor
400	300	250	200	150	100

Model 439

Introduced in 1979 this is an improved version of the Model 39. Furnished with adjustable rear sight. Discontinued in 1988.

NIB	Exc.	V.G.	Good	Fair	Poor
450	400	350	325	250	100

Model 639

This is a stainless steel version of the Model 439. Introduced in 1984 and discontinued in 1988.

NIB	Exc.	V.G.	Good	Fair	Poor
400	325	300	250	200	100

Model 459

This improved-sight version of the 15-shot Model 59 9mm pistol was introduced in 1979 and discontinued in 1987.

NIB	Exc.	V.G.	Good	Fair	Poor
475	400	350	300	250	200

Model 659

This stainless steel version of the Model 459 9mm pistol features an ambidextrous safety and all other options of the Model 459. Introduced in 1982 and discontinued in 1988.

NIB	Exc.	V.G.	Good	Fair	Poor
475	425	350	300	250	150

Model 539

This is yet another version of the Model 439 9mm pistol. It incorporates all the features of the Model 439 with a steel frame instead of aluminum alloy. This model was introduced in 1980 and discontinued in 1983.

NIB	Exc.	V.G.	Good	Fair	Poor
450	400	350	300	250	200

Model 559

This variation of the Model 459 9mm pistol has a steel frame instead of aluminum alloy. It is identical in all other respects.

NIB	Exc.	V.G.	Good	Fair	Poor
450	400	350	300	250	200

Model 469

The Model 469 was brought out in answer to the need for a more concealable high-capacity pistol. It is essentially a "Mini" version of the Model 459. It is chambered for the 9mm Parabellum and has a 12-round detachable magazine with a finger-grip extension and a shortened frame. The barrel is 3.5" long; the hammer is bobbed and does not protrude; the safety is ambidextrous. The finish is matte blue, with black plastic grips. The Model 469 was introduced in 1983 and discontinued in 1988.

NIB	Exc.	V.G.	Good	Fair	Poor
450	375	325	275	200	150

Model 669

This is a stainless steel version of the Model 469 9mm pistol. All of the features of the 469 are incorporated. The Model 669 was manufactured from 1986 to 1988.

NIB	Exc.	V.G.	Good	Fair	Poor
475	425	350	300	250	200

Model 645

The Model 645 is a large-framed, stainless steel double action pistol chambered for the .45 ACP cartridge. It has a 5" barrel, adjustable sights, and a detachable 8-shot magazine. It is offered with fixed or adjustable sights and an ambidextrous safety. The grips are molded black nylon. S&W manufactured this pistol between 1985 and 1988.

NIB	Exc.	V.G.	Good	Fair	Poor
500	425	375	325	250	150

Model 745 - IPSC

This model is similar in outward appearance to the Model 645 but is quite a different pistol. The Model 745 is a single action semiautomatic chambered for the .45 ACP cartridge. The frame is made of stainless steel, and the slide of blued carbon steel. The barrel is 5", and the detachable magazine holds 8 rounds. The sights are fully adjustable target types. The grips are checkered walnut. Introduced in 1986 and discontinued in 1990.

NIB	Exc.	V.G.	Good	Fair	Poor
700	600	500	400	350	250

Model 41

The Model 41 was introduced to the shooting public in 1957. It is a high quality .22 rimfire target pistol. It has an steel frame, steel slide, and either a 5.0", 5.5" or 7.375" barrel. It has a detachable 10-shot magazine, adjustable target sights, and checkered walnut target grips with thumb rest. The finish is blued. Weight with 5.5", barrel is about 41 oz. and for 7.375" barrel about 44 oz. Prices below are for 5" lightweight barrel.

Other Barrel Options:
5.5" With Extended Sight-Add $100.
5.5" Heavy With Extended Sight-Add $100.
7.375" With Muzzle Brake-Add $75.

Model 41 barrel types

Courtesy John J. Stimson, Jr.

NOTE: For full set of steel and aluminum barrel weights add up to $500 depending on condition. For .22 short conversion kit add $750 depending on condition. For military marked pistols add 400%.

NIB	Exc.	V.G.	Good	Fair	Poor
850	600	400	300	225	150

Model 41 (New Model)

This model was restyled in 1994 featuring recontoured hardwood stocks, a Millet adjustable rear sight, and a drilled and tapped barrel for scope mounting.

NIB	Exc.	V.G.	Good	Fair	Poor
650	575	500	400	300	150

Model 41-1

This model was introduced in 1960 and is chambered for the .22 Short rimfire only. It was developed for the International Rapid Fire competition. In appearance it is quite similar to the Model 41 except that the slide is made of aluminum alloy, as well as the frame, in order to lighten it to function with the .22 short cartridge. This model was not a commercial success like the Model 41, so it was discontinued after fewer than 1,000 were manufactured.

Model 41-1 .22 Short with optional weights

Courtesy John J. Stimson, Jr.

NIB	Exc.	V.G.	Good	Fair	Poor
1200	900	725	500	375	225

Model 46

This was a lower-cost version of the Model 41. It was developed for the Air Force in 1959. Its appearance was essentially the same as the Model 41 with a 7" barrel. Later a 5" barrel was introduced, and finally in 1964 a heavy 5.5" barrel was produced. This economy target pistol never had the popularity that the more expensive Model 41 had, and it was discontinued in 1968 after approximately 4,000 pistols were manufactured.

Courtesy Mike Stuckslager

NIB	Exc.	V.G.	Good	Fair	Poor
700	600	450	350	250	200

Model 61 Escort

In 1970 the Model 61 was introduced as the only true pocket automatic that S&W produced. It was chambered for the .22 l.r. cartridge with a 2-1/2" barrel and 5-round magazine. It was offered in either blued or nickel finish with black checkered plastic grips. It was dropped from the product line in 1974.

NIB	Exc.	V.G.	Good	Fair	Poor
250	175	150	125	100	75

Model 52A

Introduced in 1961 in the .38 AMU caliber for the Army marksmanship training. Army rejected the pistol and the 87 units built were released to the public. The letter "A" is stamped behind the model designation. A rare find; only 87 were produced. Use caution.

NIB	Exc.	V.G.	Good	Fair	Poor
3000	2500	2000	1500	750	500

Model 52 (.38 Master)

Introduced in 1961 as a target pistol chambered for the .38 Special mid-range wad cutter cartridge. It is similar in appearance to the Model 39 but is single action only by virtue of a set screw. Fitted with a 5" barrel and a 5-round magazine. It has a blued finish with checkered walnut grips. About 3,500 of these pistols were produced in this configuration until discontinued in 1963.

NIB	Exc.	V.G.	Good	Fair	Poor
900	750	550	450	300	200

Model 52-1

In 1963 this variation featured a true single action design and were produced until 1971.

NIB	Exc.	V.G.	Good	Fair	Poor
750	650	450	350	300	200

Model 52-2

Introduced in 1971 with a coil spring style extractor. Model was discontinued in 1993.

NIB	Exc.	V.G.	Good	Fair	Poor
700	600	475	400	300	200

Model 2214 (The Sportsman)

This semiautomatic pistol is chambered for the .22 Long Rifle and designed for casual use. It is fitted with a 3" barrel and has a magazine capacity of 8 rounds. The slide is blued carbon steel and the frame is alloy. Introduced in 1990.

NIB	Exc.	V.G.	Good	Fair	Poor
200	175	150	125	100	50

Model 2206

This .22 Long Rifle pistol is offered with either a 4-1/2" or 6" barrel. Magazine capacity is 12 rounds. Adjustable rear sight. Stainless steel frame and slide.

NIB	Exc.	V.G.	Good	Fair	Poor
250	200	175	125	100	50

Model 2206 TGT (Target)

Introduced in 1995 this version of the Model 2206 features a selected 6" barrel, bead blasted sighting plane and polished flat side surfaces. A Patridge front sight and Millet adjustable rear sight are standard. In addition the model has a serrated trigger with adjustable trigger stop and a 10-round magazine.

NIB	Exc.	V.G.	Good	Fair	Poor
350	300	250	200	150	100

Model 422 Field

Introduced in 1987 this .22 Long Rifle pistol has a 4-1/2" barrel or 6" barrel with an alloy frame and steel slide. The magazine capacity is 10 rounds. This model has fixed sights and black plastic grips. Finish is matte blue.

NIB	Exc.	V.G.	Good	Fair	Poor
200	175	150	125	100	50

Model 422 Target

Same as the Field model but fitted with adjustable sights and checkered walnut grips.

NIB	Exc.	V.G.	Good	Fair	Poor
250	200	175	150	100	50

Model 622 Field

This is a stainless steel version of the Model 422 Field.

NIB	Exc.	V.G.	Good	Fair	Poor
225	200	175	150	125	75

Model 622 Target

This is the stainless steel version of the Model 422 Target.

NIB	Exc.	V.G.	Good	Fair	Poor
275	225	200	175	125	75

Model 622VR

Redesigned in 1996 this .22 caliber model features a 6" ventilated rib barrel. It is fitted with a matte black trigger and a new triggerguard. The front sight is a serrated ramp style with an adjustable rear sight. Weight is approximately 23 oz. Grips are black polymer.

NIB	Exc.	V.G.	Good	Fair	Poor
300	250	200	150	100	75

Model 22A Sport

Introduced in 1997 this model features a choice of 4", 5.5", or 7" barrel. It is chambered for the .22 Long Rifle cartridge. Magazine capacity is 10 rounds. Rear sight is adjustable. Grips are either two-piece polymer or two-piece Soft Touch. Frame and slide are aluminum alloy and stainless steel. Finish is blue. Weight is approximately 28 oz. for 4" model and 32 oz. for 5.5" model. Weight of 7" model is about 33 oz. Prices quoted below are for 4" model. In 2001 this model was furnished with a Hi-Viz green dot front sight.

NIB	Exc.	V.G.	Good	Fair	Poor
200	150	100	75	—	—

Model 22S Sport

This model, also introduced in 1997, is similar to the above model but with 5.5" and 7" barrel on stainless steel frames. Weight is about 41 oz. and 42 oz. respectively. In 2001 this model was fiurnished with a Hi-Viz green dot front sight.

NIB	Exc.	V.G.	Good	Fair	Poor
275	225	200	150	—	—

Model 22A Target

This .22 caliber target pistol has a 10-round magazine, adjustable rear sight, and target grips with thumb rest. The barrel is 5.5" bull barrel. Finish is blue. Weight is about 39 oz. Introduced in 1997.

NIB	Exc.	V.G.	Good	Fair	Poor
275	225	—	—	—	—

Model 22S Target

Same as above but with stainless steel frame and slide. Weight is approximately 48 oz.

NIB	Exc.	V.G.	Good	Fair	Poor
350	300	—	—	—	—

Model 3904

In 1989 S&W redesigned the entire line of 9mm semiautomatic handguns. The 3904 is chambered for the 9mm Parabellum and has an 8-shot detachable magazine and 4" barrel with a fixed bushing. The frame is alloy, and the triggerguard is squared for two-hand hold. The magazine well is beveled, and the grips are one-piece wrap-around made of delrin. The three dot sighting system is employed. This model has been discontinued.

NIB	Exc.	V.G.	Good	Fair	Poor
450	400	325	300	275	225

Model 3906

This is the stainless steel version of the Model 3904. The features are the same. It was introduced in 1989. This model has been discontinued.

NIB	Exc.	V.G.	Good	Fair	Poor
450	400	325	300	275	225

Model 3914

Offered as a slightly smaller alternative to the Model 3904, this 9mm pistol has a 3-1/2" barrel, 8-round magazine, and blued carbon steel slide and alloy frame.

NIB	Exc.	V.G.	Good	Fair	Poor
525	450	400	350	300	250

Model 3913

This version is similar to the Model 3914 but features a stainless steel slide and alloy frame.

NIB	Exc.	V.G.	Good	Fair	Poor
525	450	400	350	300	250

Model 3914LS

This is a redesigned Model 3914 that has a more modern appearance. The LS refers to LadySmith and is chambered for the 9mm cartridge. All other features are the same as the Model 3914 including the blued carbon slide and alloy frame.

NIB	Exc.	V.G.	Good	Fair	Poor
525	450	400	350	300	200

Model 3913LS

This model is identical to the Model 3914LS with the exception of the stainless steel slide.

NIB	Exc.	V.G.	Good	Fair	Poor
525	450	400	350	300	200

Model 3954

Similar to the Model 3914 but offered in double action only. Discontinued in 1993.

NIB	Exc.	V.G.	Good	Fair	Poor
525	450	400	350	300	200

Model 915

Introduced in 1993 this model is chambered for the 9mm cartridge and features a 4" barrel, matte blue finish, fixed rear sight, and wrap-around rubber grips. Overall length is 7.5" and weight is about 28 oz.

NIB	Exc.	V.G.	Good	Fair	Poor
400	350	250	200	150	100

Model 5904

This is a full high capacity, 15-shot version of the Model 3904. It was introduced in 1989 and features a slide mounted decocking lever and 4" barrel. This version has a blued carbon steel slide and alloy frame. This model is no longer in production.

NIB	Exc.	V.G.	Good	Fair	Poor
525	450	375	325	275	200

Model 5906

This is a stainless steel version of the Model 5904. Both the slide and frame are stainless steel.

NIB	Exc.	V.G.	Good	Fair	Poor
525	450	375	275	200	

Model 5906 Special Edition

A double action semiautomatic pistol chambered for the 9mm with a 15-round magazine. The frame and slide have a special machine finish while the grips are one-piece wrap-around Xenoy. The front sight is a white dot post and the rear sight is a Novak L-Mount Carry with two white dots. This model has a manual safety/decocking lever and firing pin safety. Introduced in 1993.

NIB	Exc.	V.G.	Good	Fair	Poor
525	450	350	300	250	150

Model 5903

The same caliber and features as the Model 5904 and Model 5906, but furnished with a stainless steel slide and alloy frame.

NIB	Exc.	V.G.	Good	Fair	Poor
525	450	400	350	300	250

Model 5926

S&W offers a 9mm pistol similar to the 5906 but with a frame mounted decocking lever. Both the slide and frame are stainless steel. Discontinued in 1993.

NIB	Exc.	V.G.	Good	Fair	Poor
525	450	375	300	250	150

Model 5946

This 9mm pistol offers the same features as the Model 5926, but in a double action only mode. The hammer configuration on this model is semi-bobbed instead of serrated.

NIB	Exc.	V.G.	Good	Fair	Poor
525	450	400	350	300	250

Model 5967

This is a 9mm model with a M5906 frame and a 3914 slide. It has a stainless steel frame and blued slide. Novak Lo-Mount fixed sights. Introduced in 1990 and sold through Lew Horton.

NIB	Exc.	V.G.	Good	Fair	Poor
600	475	400	350	300	250

Model 6904

This is the concealable, shortened version of the Model 5904. It has a 12-shot magazine, fixed sights, bobbed hammer, and a 3.5" barrel.

NIB	Exc.	V.G.	Good	Fair	Poor
525	450	400	350	300	250

Model 6906

This version has a stainless steel slide and alloy frame but otherwise is similar to the Model 6904.

NIB	Exc.	V.G.	Good	Fair	Poor
525	450	400	350	300	200

Model 6946

This is a double action version of the Model 6906.

NIB	Exc.	V.G.	Good	Fair	Poor
525	450	400	350	300	200

Model 4003

This pistol is chambered for the .40 S&W cartridge and is fitted with a 4" barrel, 11-round magazine, serrated hammer with a stainless steel slide and alloy frame.

NIB	Exc.	V.G.	Good	Fair	Poor
575	500	400	350	300	200

Model 4004

Identical to the Model 4003 except for a blue carbon steel slide and alloy frame. Discontinued in 1993.

NIB	Exc.	V.G.	Good	Fair	Poor
575	500	400	350	300	200

Model 4006

This model is identical to the Model 4003 except that both the slide and frame are made from stainless steel. This adds 8 oz. to the weight of the pistol.

NIB	Exc.	V.G.	Good	Fair	Poor
575	500	400	350	300	200

Model 4026

Similar to the Model 4006 this version has a frame-mounted decocking lever.

NIB	Exc.	V.G.	Good	Fair	Poor
575	500	400	350	300	200

Model 4046

Similar to the Model 4006 but with a double action only configuration.

NIB	Exc.	V.G.	Good	Fair	Poor
575	500	400	350	300	250

Model 4013

A compact version of the 4000 series, this .40 caliber model features a 3-1/2" barrel, 8-round magazine, and stainless steel slide and alloy frame.

NIB	Exc.	V.G.	Good	Fair	Poor
575	500	400	350	300	200

Model 4013 TSW

Similar to the Model 4013 but traditional double action only with some improvements. Magazine capacity is 9 rounds of .40 S&W cartridges. Finish is satin stainless. Weight is approximately 26 oz. Introduced in 1997.

NIB	Exc.	V.G.	Good	Fair	Poor
700	625	—	—	—	—

Model 4014

Identical to the Model 4013 except for a blued carbon steel slide and alloy frame.

NIB	Exc.	V.G.	Good	Fair	Poor
575	500	400	350	300	200

Model 4053

Identical to the Model 4013, stainless steel slide and alloy frame, except offered in a double action only configuration.

NIB	Exc.	V.G.	Good	Fair	Poor
575	500	400	350	300	200

Model 4054

This model is the same as the Model 4053 except for a blued carbon steel slide and alloy frame. Dropped from S&W product line in 1992.

NIB	Exc.	V.G.	Good	Fair	Poor
575	500	400	300	250	200

Model 4056 TSW

This is a double action only pistol chambered for the .40 S&W cartridge. Fitted with a 3.5" barrel with white dot sights. Curved backstrap. Stainless steel and alloy frame. Stainless steel finish. Magazine capacity is 9 rounds. Introduced in 1997. Weight is approximately 36 oz.

NIB	Exc.	V.G.	Good	Fair	Poor
725	625	—	—	—	—

Model 411

This model was introduced in 1993 as a no frills model and features an alloy frame, 4" barrel, matte blue finish, fixed sights, and wrap-around rubber grips. Chambered for .40 S&W cartridge with 11-round magazine capacity. Overall length is 7.5" and weight is approximately 29 oz.

NIB	Exc.	V.G.	Good	Fair	Poor
400	350	300	250	200	150

Model 1006

This is a full size 10mm pistol with a 5" barrel, 9-round magazine, and choice of fixed or adjustable sights. Both the slide and frame are stainless steel.

NIB	Exc.	V.G.	Good	Fair	Poor
475	450	400	350	300	200

Model 1066

This is a slightly smaller version of the Model 1006 and is furnished with a 4-1/4" barrel. Discontinued in 1993.

NIB	Exc.	V.G.	Good	Fair	Poor
475	450	400	350	300	200

Model 1076

Identical to the Model 1066 with the exception of the frame mounted decocking lever.

NIB	Exc.	V.G.	Good	Fair	Poor
475	450	400	350	300	200

Model 1086

Similar to the Model 1066 but offered in double action only. This model was discontinued in 1993.

NIB	Exc.	V.G.	Good	Fair	Poor
475	425	375	300	250	200

Model 1026

Similar to the Model 1006 with a 5" barrel this model has a frame mounted decocking lever.

NIB	Exc.	V.G.	Good	Fair	Poor
475	450	400	350	300	200

Model 4506

This is the newly designed double action .45 ACP pistol. It is all stainless steel and has a 5" barrel, 8-shot detachable magazine, and wrap-around black delrin grips. This model is no longer in production.

NIB	Exc.	V.G.	Good	Fair	Poor
550	475	400	350	300	250

Model 4505

This version is identical to the Model 4506 with the exception of a blued slide and frame.

NIB	Exc.	V.G.	Good	Fair	Poor
550	475	400	350	300	250

Model 4516

Offered in a .45 caliber this 4500 series is a compact version of the full size .45 caliber S&W autos. Furnished with a 3-3/4" barrel and a 7-round magazine this model has a stainless slide and frame. Discontinued in 1991. This model was reintroduced in 1994.

NIB	Exc.	V.G.	Good	Fair	Poor
550	475	425	375	300	250

Model 4536

A compact version and similar to the Model 4616 this pistol is offered with a decock lever on the frame.

NIB	Exc.	V.G.	Good	Fair	Poor
550	475	400	350	300	250

Model 4546

A full size version of the Model 4506 but offered in double action only.

NIB	Exc.	V.G.	Good	Fair	Good
550	475	400	350	300	250

TSW SERIES (Tactical Smith & Wesson)

This series is an upgrade of the older Smith & Wesson pistol series many of which have been discontinued. These pistols come with either a traditional double action trigger or a double action only trigger. All TSW pistol have an equipment rail for mounting lights or lasers. All are marked "TACTICAL S&W" on the slide.

3913/3953 TSW

Chambered for 9mm cartridge and fitted with a 3.5" barrel. White dot front sight and Novak Lo-Mount rear sight. Aluminum alloy frame. Magazine capacity is 7 rounds. Weight is about 25 oz. Stainless steel finish. The 3913 is traditional double action while the 3953 is double action only.

NIB	Exc.	V.G.	Good	Fair	Good
700	525	400	—	—	—

4013/4053 TSW

This pistol is chambered for the .40S&W cartridge and fitted with a 3.5" barrel. White dot front sight and Novak Lo-Mount rear sight. Aluminum alloy frame and stainless steel slide. Magazine capacity is 9 rounds. Weight is about 27 oz. The 4013 is traditional double action while the 4053 is double action only.

NIB	Exc.	V.G.	Good	Fair	Good
800	600	450	—	—	—

4513/4553 TSW

This model is chambered for the .45 ACP cartridge and fitted with a 3.75" barrel. White dot front sight and Novak Lo-Mount rear sight. Aluminum alloy frame with stainless steel slide. Magazine capacity is 7 rounds. Weight is about 29 oz. The 4513 is traditional double action while the 4553 is double action only.

NIB	Exc.	V.G.	Good	Fair	Good
850	625	475	—	—	—

NOTE: The double action only model 4553 is $50 less.

5903/5906/5943/5946 TSW

These pistols are chambered for the 9mm cartridge and fitted with a 4" barrel. Fixed sights standard (5903, 5906, 5943, 5946) adjustable sights (5906) optional as well as night sights (5906). Offered in traditional double action (5903, 5906) as well as double action only (5943, 5946). Magazine capacity is 10 rounds and weight is about 38 oz. Stainless steel finish.

NIB	Exc.	V.G.	Good	Fair	Good
750	550	400	—	—	—

NOTE: Add $100 for night sights, add $50 for adjustable sights.

4003/4006/4043/4046 TSW

This model comes in the same configurations as the 5903 group except these pistols are chambered for the .40S&W cartridge. Magazine capacity is 10 rounds. Weight is about 28 oz.

NIB	Exc.	V.G.	Good	Fair	Good
800	600	450	—	—	—

NOTE: Add $100 for night sights, add $50 for adjustable sights.

4563/4566/4583/4586 TSW

Similar to the above model but chambered for the .45 ACP cartridge and fitted with a 4.25" barrel. Same configurations as above. Weight is about 31 oz.

NIB	Exc.	V.G.	Good	Fair	Good
800	600	450	—	—	—

NOTE: Add $100 for night sights, add $50 for adjustable sights.

CHIEF'S SPECIAL SERIES

CS9

Chambered for 9mm cartridge and fitted with a 3" barrel this model has a stainless steel slide and aluminum alloy frame. Also available in blued finish. Hogue wrap around grips is standard. Fixed sights. Magazine capacity is 7 rounds. Weight is approximately 21 oz.

NIB	Exc.	V.G.	Good	Fair	Poor
—	—	—	—	—	—

CS45

Similar to the model above but chambered for the .45 ACP cartridge. Barrel length is 3.25". Magazine capacity is 6 rounds. Weight is about 24 oz.

NIB	Exc.	V.G.	Good	Fair	Poor
—	—	—	—	—	—

CS40

This Chief's Special model is chambered for the .40S&W cartridge. Barrel length is 3.25". Magazine capacity is 7 rounds. Weight is about 24 oz.

NIB	Exc.	V.G.	Good	Fair	Poor
—	—	—	—	—	—

CS40 Two-Tone

Same as above but with alloy frame and black slide. Limited edition. Introduced in 2000.

NIB	Exc.	V.G.	Good	Fair	Good
650	475	375	—	—	—

SIGMA SERIES

This new pistol was introduced in 1994 and features a departure from the traditional S&W pistol. The pistol features a stainless steel barrel, carbon steel slide, and polymer frame. Offered in .40 S&W and 9mm calibers with 15-round and 17-round capacities. Magazines built after 9/13/94 will be limited to 10 rounds for all calibers per Federal law.

NIB	Exc.	V.G.	Good	Fair	Poor
450	400	350	300	250	200

Sigma Series Compact

Same as above but with barrel and slide 1/2" shorter than full size Sigma. Offered in both .40 S&W and 9mm.

NIB	Exc.	V.G.	Good	Fair	Poor
450	400	350	300	250	200

Sigma Series SW9M

Introduced in 1996 this pistol is chambered for the 9mm cartridge. It is fitted with a 3.25" barrel and has a magazine capacity of 7 rounds. The frame is polymer and the slide carbon steel. Height is 4.5" and overall length is 6.25". Weight is 18 oz.

NIB	Exc.	V.G.	Good	Fair	Poor
450	400	—	—	—	—

Sigma SW 9V

Chambered for the 9mm cartridge this model is fitted with a 4" barrel and 10-round magazine. It has a traditional double action. White dot sights are standard. Grips are integral to the frame. Stainless steel slide. Satin stainless finish with choice of gray or black frame. Weight is about 25 oz. Introduced in 1997.

NIB	Exc.	V.G.	Good	Fair	Poor
425	325	—	—	—	—

Sigma SW9P
Same as the Model SW9V with the addition of a ported barrel. Introduced in 2001.

NIB	Exc.	V.G.	Good	Fair	Poor
425	325	—	—	—	—

Sigma SW40P
Same as the Model SW40V but with the addition of a ported barrel. Introduced in 2001.

NIB	Exc.	V.G.	Good	Fair	Poor
495	400	—	—	—	—

Sigma SW9G
Same as the standard SW9 but with a black Melonite stainless steel slide and NATO green polymer frame. Introduced in 2001.

NIB	Exc.	V.G.	Good	Fair	Poor
495	400	—	—	—	—

Sigma SW40G
Same as the standard SW40 pistol but with a black Melonite stainless steel slide and NATO green polymer frame. Introduced in 2001.

NIB	Exc.	V.G.	Good	Fair	Poor
425	325	—	—	—	—

Sigma SW40V
Same as above but chambered for .40 S&W cartridge. Weight is 25 oz. Introduced in 1997.

NIB	Exc.	V.G.	Good	Fair	Poor
425	325	—	—	—	—

Sigma SW 380
Introduced in 1995 this model is chambered for the .380 ACP cartridge. Barrel length is 3" with overall length 5.8". Empty weight is 14 oz. with a magazine capacity of 6 rounds.

NIB	Exc.	V.G.	Good	Fair	Poor
300	250	200	150	100	75

ENHANCED SIGMA SERIES

Introduced in 1999 this series features a shorter trigger pull, slide stop guard, redesigned extractor and ejector. The ejection port is also lower. These pistols are also fitted with an accessory grove. Checkering pattern is more aggressive.

Model SW9E

Chambered for the 9mm cartridge this model has a 4" barrel with Tritium sights. Stainless steel slide with black Melonite finish. Magazine capacity is 10 rounds. Weight is about 25 oz.

NIB	Exc.	V.G.	Good	Fair	Poor
—	—	—	—	—	—

Model SW40E

Similar to the above model but chambered for the .40 S&W cartridge. Weight is about 24 oz.

NIB	Exc.	V.G.	Good	Fair	Poor
—	—	—	—	—	—

Model SW9VE

This model is chambered for the 9mm cartridge and fitted with a 4" barrel. Fixed sights and stainless steel slide. Weight is about 25 oz.

NIB	Exc.	V.G.	Good	Fair	Poor
—	—	—	—	—	—

Model SW40VE

Similar to the model above but chambered for the .40 S&W cartridge.Weight is about 24 oz.

NIB	Exc.	V.G.	Good	Fair	Poor
—	—	—	—	—	—

Model SW99

This model features a polymer frame designed and manufactured in Germany by Walther. The slide and barrel are manufactured by S&W in the U.S. chambered for either the 9mm or .40 S&W cartridge this model is fitted with a 4" barrel on the 9mm model and a 4.125" barrel on the .40 S&W model. Adjustable rear sights. Decocking slide mounted lever. Barrel and slide are stainless steel with black Melonite finish. Trigger is traditional double action. Magazine capacity is 10 rounds. Weight is about 25 oz. Introduced in 1999.

NIB	Exc.	V.G.	Good	Fair	Poor
735	—	—	—	—	—

Model 410

This model was first introduced in 1996. It features an alloy frame with carbon steel slide. It is chambered for the .40 S&W cartridge. Barrel length is 4". The magazine capacity is 10 rounds and the overall length is 7.5". Weight is approximately 29 oz.

NIB	Exc.	V.G.	Good	Fair	Poor
450	400	—	—	—	—

Model 410 Two-Tone
Same as the Model 410 but with alloy finish frame and black slide. Limited edition.

NIB	Exc.	V.G.	Good	Fair	Good
550	400	325	—	—	—

Model 457
Introduced in 1996 this .45 ACP model features a 3.75" barrel with rounded triggerguard and double action. It is fitted with a single side decocker. Magazine capacity is 7 rounds. Overall length is 7.25" and weight is about 29 oz. The frame is alloy and the slide a carbon steel. Finish is matte black.

NIB	Exc.	V.G.	Good	Fair	Poor
450	400	—	—	—	—

Model 908

Introduced in 1996 this is an economy compact pistol. It is chambered for the 9mm cartridge and is fitted with a 3.5" barrel. The action is traditional double action. Fixed rear sight. Magazine capacity is 8 rounds. Overall length is 6-7/8" and weight is about 26 oz.

NIB	Exc.	V.G.	Good	Fair	Poor
400	350	—	—	—	—

Model 909
Introduced in 1995 this pistol is chambered for the 9mm cartridge. It has a blue carbon steel slide, aluminum alloy frame, and is double action. It has a single column magazine and curved backstrap.

NIB	Exc.	V.G.	Good	Fair	Poor
400	350	300	200	150	100

Model 910
Also introduced in 1995. Same as above model but with double column magazine and straight backstrap.

NIB	Exc.	V.G.	Good	Fair	Poor
400	350	300	200	150	100

NOTE: All detachable magazines manufactured after 9/13/94 will be limited to 10 rounds of ammunition per Federal law regardless of caliber and original capacity of the pistol.

SMITH & WESSON COMMEMORATIVES
Smith & Wesson has over the years built many special edition handguns. These guns have been to commemorate some important national or regional event or group. The company has also built a large number of special edition handguns for certain distributors such as Lew Horton which is listed below. There are well over 200 special production guns not reflected in this pricing guide. Not even Smith & Wesson has all of the information on these guns and with many the number is so small that a market price would not be possible to establish. Listed below are a number of Smith & Wesson Commemoratives that we do have information on. Due to the difficulty in determining value only the original retail price is listed. Remember to receive full value for these guns they must be NIB, unfired with unturned cylinders.

Model 14 Texas Ranger Comm.

Introduced in 1973. Supplied with 4" barrel and cased. Edition limited to 10,000. 8,000 of these had knives. Serial numbers TR 1 to TR 10000.

Original Retail Price: $250.00

Model 25-3 S&W 125th Anniversary Comm.

Introduced in 1977. Limited edition of 10,000. Serial numbers SW0000 to SW10000. Deluxe models marked 25-4.

Original Retail Price: $350.00

Model 26-4 Georgia State Police Comm.

Introduced in 1988/1989 and supplied with a 5" barrel. Total production of 802 guns. Known Serial numbers BBY00354 to BBY0434.

Original Retail Price: $405.00

Model 27 .357 50th Anniversary Comm.

Introduced in 1985 and supplied with a 5" barrel and cased. Limited edition to 2,500 guns. Serial numbers REG0001 to REG2500.

Original Retail Price: N/A

Model 29-3 Elmer Keith Comm.

Introduced in 1986 and supplied with a 4" barrel. Gun etched in gold. Limited edition of 2,500 guns. Serial numbers EMK0000 to EMK0100 for Deluxe models and EMK 010 to EMK2500 for standard model.

Original Retail Price: $850.00

Model 544 Texas Wagon Train 150 Anniversary Comm.

Introduced in 1986 and limited to 7801 guns. Serial numbers TWT0000 to TWT7800.

Original Issue Price: N/A

Model 586 Mass. State Police Comm.

Introduced in 1986 and fitted with a 6" barrel. Limited to 631 guns. Serial numbers with ABT-AUC prefix.

Original Issue Price: N/A

Model 629-1 Alaska 1988 Iditarod Comm.

Introduced in 1987 and limited to 545 guns. Serial numbers from AKI0001 to AKI0545.

Original Retail Price: N/A

Model 745 IPSC Comm.

Introduced in 1986 and limited to 5362 guns. Serial numbers DVC0000 to DVC5362.

Original Retail Price: N/A

Model 4516-1 U.S. Marshall Comm.

Introduced in 1990 and limited to 500 guns. Serial numbers USM0000 to USM0499.

Original Retail Price: $599.95

Courtesy Smith & Wesson

SMITH & WESSON
PERFORMANCE CENTER HANDGUNS

The role of Smith & Wesson's Performance Center has changed since it was established in 1990. What was once a specialized tune-up and competition one-off production department has now become a separate facility in providing specialized and limited handguns to the public often with distributors participation. This change came about around 1991, when the Performance Center initiated its own limited edition designs. These editions are generally limited to between 300 and 600 pistols for each model. The Performance Center, in fact, has its own distinct product line. Performance Center pistols are made in its own shop using its own designers. One of these distributors that has played a major role in offering these special guns to the public is the Lew Horton Distribution Company. The Center still continues to offer action jobs and accurate work but no longer executes one-of-a-kind customizing. The Performance Center has built about eight to twelve different models in the last two years. Plans call for more of these unique handguns to be built in the future. Pistols that are available from a certain distributor or the Performance Center will be noted in the description of each pistol.

Limited Edition Pistols and Revolvers of 1990

One of the first limited special series of Performance Center handguns was this offering, which consisted of custom engraved S&W handguns limited to 15 units on any current (1990) production pistol or revolver. This Limited Edition featured: 24 karat gold and sterling inlays, special bright mirror finish, decorated in light scroll pattern, specially assigned serial number beginning with the prefix "PEC", tuned action, solid walnut presentation case inlaid with blue or burgundy leather insert, embossed with gold with performance center logo. Interior of case is custom fitted with a matching colored velvet. Each handgun is hand numbered and has a signed certificate of authenticity. Because of the unique nature of the Limited Edition offering it is strongly recommended to secure a professional appraisal.

.40 S&W Tactical

A limited edition semiautomatic handgun offered exclusively by Lew Horton through the Performance Center. This special pistol is fitted with a 5" match-grade barrel, hand fit spherical barrel bushing, custom tuned action, special trigger job, oversized frame and slide rails, wrap-around straight backstrap grip. Replaceable front and Novak rear sights. Special serial numbers. Offered in 1992 and limited to 200 units.

Suggested Retail Introductory Price: $1500

Horton/Performance pistol. A production of 250 units. Offered in 1992.

.40 S&W Compensated
Similar to the .40 S&W Tactical but furnished with a 4.625" barrel and single chamber compensator. This is also a Lew

Suggested Retail Introductory Price: $1700

.40 S&W Performance Action Pistol

Offered in limited quantities in 1990, this Performance Center .40 S&W semiaction pistol was used by the Smith & Wesson shooting team. The frame and barrel are stainless steel with blued carbon steel slide, two port compensator, two fitted and numbered 13-round magazines, 5.25" match grade barrel extended frame beavertail, square combat triggerguard, oversize magazine release button, spherical barrel bushing, wraparound straight backstrap grip, extended magazine funnel, and BoMar adjustable rear sight. The action is tuned for accuracy and precision.

Suggested Retail Introductory Price: N/A

Model 681 Quadport

A Lew Horton revolver limited to 300 guns with special serial numbers. This 7-shot revolver has a 3" barrel underlug quadport barrel. The action is tuned cylinders are chambered and the trigger has an overtravel stop. Sights are fixed combat type.

Suggested Retail Introductory Price: $675

Model 686 Competitor

Introduced by Lew Horton and the Performance Center for 1993 this limited edition revolver features a match grade barrel and unique under barrel weight system. The action has been custom tuned and the receiver is drilled and tapped for scope mounts. Charge holes are chambered, ejector rod housing is enclosed, and the grip is an extended competition type. Special serial numbers.

Suggested Retail Introductory Price: $1100

Model 686 Hunter

Similar to the Model 686 Competitor. This is also a limited edition Lew Horton revolver chambered for the .357 Magnum and features the under barrel weight system, internal scope mount, and custom tuned action. Special serial numbers.

Suggest Retail Introductory Price: $1154

Model 686 Carry Comp 4"

Offered in limited quantities by Lew Horton and the Performance Center in 1992 this new design features the unique single chamber integral barrel compensator. Front is windage adjustable and the action is custom tuned. Chambered for the .357 Magnum cartridge. Special serial numbers.

Suggested Retail Introductory price: $1000

Model 686 Carry Comp 3"

The 1993 Lew Horton limited edition version of the Model 686 Carry Comp 4" model with a 3" barrel. The same features apply to both models.

Suggested Retail Introductory Price: $1000

Model 686 Plus

This Lew Horton model features a 7-round cylinder with chamfered charge holes for use with full moon clips for both .38 Special and .357 Magnum cartridges. Fitted with a tapered 6" barrel with counter sunk muzzle. Gold bead front sight and adjustable rear sight. Altamont wood grips are standard. Stainless steel finish. Weight is approximately 44 oz.

Suggested Retail Price: $930

Model 629 Hunter

Introduced in 1992 by Lew Horton and the Performance Center this limited edition revolver features a new design that utilizes a 6" under barrel weight system, special integral barrel compensator. The action has been custom tuned and the receiver has an integral scope mount. Chambered for the .44 Magnum. Special finger groove grips are standard. Special serial numbers.

Suggested Retail Introductory Price: $1234

Model 629 Hunter II

Another Lew Horton/Performance Center limited edition revolver that features 2x Nikon scope with steel see-through rings. The barrel is Mag-Na-Ported and incorporates the Performance Center's under barrel weight arrangement. The action is custom tuned and the revolver is supplied with a ballistic nylon range carry bag. Special serial numbers.

Suggested Retail Introductory Price: $1234

Model 629 Comped Hunter

Offered through RSR this model features a 6" barrel with 4-port detachable compensator. The cylinder is unfluted. Sights are adjustable, fitted with Altamount wood grips. Tuned action. Stainless steel. Weight is approximately 59 oz.

Suggested Retail Price: $1100

Model 629 12" Hunter

Introduced in 2000 this Lou Horton revolver is fitted with a 12" barrel with Patridge front sight and Wilson silhouette adjustable rear sight. Hogue Combat grips. Finish is glassbead stainless steel. Comes with a Waller 21" gun rug. Weight is about 65 oz.

Suggested Retail Price: $

Model 629 Magnum Hunter Trail Boss

Exclusive to RSR this limited edition model is chambered for the .44 magnum cartridge and is fitted with a 3" barrel. Stainless steel finish.

Suggested Retail Introductory Price: $733

Model 629 Compensated Hunter

Chambered for the .44 magnum cartridge and fitted with a 7.5" barrel with compensator. Barrel also has removable stainless steel scope mount. Open sights fitted with adjustable orange ramp front and adjustable rear sight. Rosewood grips. Six-round cylinder. Weight is 52 oz. Talo exclusive. Introduced in 2001.

Suggested Retail Introductory Price: $900

Model 629 Stealth Hunter

Fitted with a 7.5" ported barrel and chambered for the .44 magnum cartridge. Six-round cylinder. The finish is black-T and NATO green. Red ramp Millett front sight and adjustable rear sight. Hogue rubber combat grips standard. Furnished with lockable aluminum case. Weight is about 56 oz. Introduced in 2001. Camfour Distributor exclusive.

Suggested Retail Introductory Price: $

Model 629 Carry Comp

Introduced in 1992 by Lew Horton and the Performance Center this limited edition revolver is chambered for the .44 Magnum cartridge. It features an integral ported 3" barrel, fluted cylinder, radiused charge holes, dovetail front and fixed groove rear sight. Fitted with a rubber combat grip. The action is custom by the Performance Center. Special serial numbers.

Suggested Retail Introductory Price: $1000

Model 629 Carry Comp II

A limited edition 1993 offering by Lew Horton and the Performance Center similar to the 1992 Model 629 Carry Comp with the exception that this 1993 model has a special unfluted cylinder and fully adjustable rear sight. Special serial numbers.

Suggested Retail Introductory Price: $1000

Model 610

Introduced in 1998 by Lew Horton this model features a 3" full lug barrel chambered for the 10mm cartridge. Nonfluted cylinder, red ramp front sight and white outline rear sight. Rosewood grips. Limited to 300 revolvers.

Suggested Retail Introductory Price: $740

Model 640 Carry Comp

Introduced in 1991 by Lew Horton and the Performance Center this revolver is chambered for the .38 S&W Special, but with a strengthened action to handle + P + loads. Fitted with a heavy 2.625" barrel with unique integral barrel compensator. The front sight is replaceable and adjustable for windage. The rear sight is a fixed groove. Custom trigger job and custom tuned action are also part of the package. Special serial numbers.

Suggested Retail Introductory Price: $750

Model 640 .357 Quadport

Introduced in 1996. Similar to the model above but chambered for the .357 magnum cartridge and quadported. Limited to 190 revolvers. Special serial numbers.

Suggested Retail Introductory Price: $675

Model 460 Airweight

Chambered for the .38 Special cartridge, this model is fitted with a 2" Mag-Na-Ported barrel and a five shot cylinder. Fixed sights. Eagle Secret Service grips. Weight is about 16 oz. Limited to 450 revolvers. Introduced in 1994.

Suggested Retail Price: $580

Model 625 Light Hunter

This is a large frame revolver chambered for the .45 Colt. It is fitted with a 6" Mag-Na-Ported barrel with integral Weaver style base. It has a stainless steel finish and black Hogue rubber grips. Drift adjustable Millet front and fully adjustable rear sight. Offered in limited quantities. Introduced in 1997 by RSR.

Suggested Retail Introductory Price: $580

Model 625

Introduced in 1998 this model is chambered for the .45 ACP or .45 Colt cartridge. Fitted with a 3" full lug barrel, fluted cylinder, and rosewood grips. Limited to 150 revolvers in each chambering.

Suggested Retail Introductory Price: $755

Model 625 V-Comp

Chambered for the .44 Magnum cartridge this model is fitted with a 4" barrel and removable three port compensator. Front sight is a red ramp with black adjustable rear sight. Hogue wood combat grips. Furnished with aluminum case. Weight is about 43 oz. Finish is stainless steel. Distributed by RSR. Introduced in 1999.

Suggested Retail Price: $1000

Model 625-5.25"

Introduced in 2001 this model features a special Jerry Miculek Hogue laminated combat grip. Chambered for the .45 ACP cartridge and fitted with a 5.25" barrel. Stainless steel finish. Interchangeable gold bead front sight amd adjustable rear sight. Weight is about 42 oz. Camfour exclusive.

Suggested Retail Introductory Price: $

Model 627-8 Shot

Chambered for the .357 Magnum cartridge this revolver has an 8-round capacity. Drilled and tapped with adjustable sights on a 5" tapered and contoured barrel. Tuned action. Hogue wood grips. Satin stainless steel finish. Weight is approximately 44 oz. A Lew Horton exclusive. Introduced in 1997.

Suggested Retail Introductory Price: $1000

Model 627 Defensive-8 Shot

Chambered for the .357 Magnum this model is fitted with an eight-round unfluted cylinder recessed for full moon clips. Barrel length is 2-5/8". Adjustable rear sight and drift adjustable front sight. Wooden eagle boot grips. Weight is about 38 oz. Introduced in 1999. Furnished with aluminum case.

Suggested Retail Price: $1025

Model 651

This is a limited edition revolver by RSR chambered for the .22 WMR cartridge. Fitted with a 2" barrel and boot grips. Stainless steel finish.

Suggested Retail Price: $492

"Shorty-Forty" .40 S&W

Introduced in 1992 and available exclusively from Lew Horton, this limited edition Performance Center pistol features a light alloy frame, oversize slide rails, and spherical barrel bushing. A match grade barrel is joined to a custom tuned action. Special serial numbers.

Suggested Retail Introductory Price: $950

"Shorty Forty" Mark III

Offered in 1995 this Lew Horton exclusive features low-mount adjustable sights, hand-fitted titanium barrel bushing, checkered front strap. The action as been hand honed and the pistol is sold with two magazines; one 11 rounds and the other 9 rounds.

Suggested Retail Price: $1000

Shorty .45

Introduced by Lew Horton in 1996 this .45 ACP pistol has a hand-fitted titanium barrel bushing, oversize frame and slide rails, match grade barrel, checkered front strap, hand honed double action, and special serial numbers.

Suggested Retail Price: $1095

Shorty Nine

This Lew Horton exclusive is limited to 100 units. It features a hand-fitted titanium barrel bushing, oversize slide rails, action job, low mount adjustable sights, checkered front strap, match grade barrel, and two tone finish. Furnished with two 12-round magazines.

Suggested Retail Price: $1000

9 Recon

This is an RSR exclusive and introduced in 1999. Chambered for the 9mm cartridge this model is fitted with a 3.5" barrel. Rear sight is Novak Lo-Mount. Hogue wrap around rubber grips. The slide is black carbon steel with an alloy frame. Magazine capacity is 12 rounds. Weight is about 27 oz.

Suggested Retail Price: $1178

45 Recon

Another RSR pistol chambered for the .45 ACP cartridge. The 4.25" barrel is ported with Novak Lo-Mount sights. Hogue wrap around rubber grips. Stainless steel slide and barrel with aluminum frame. Weight is about 28 oz. Magazine capacity is 7 rounds. Furnished with aluminum case.

Suggested Retail Price: $1221

Suggested Retail Introductory Price: $1350

Performance Center .45 Limited
This Lew Horton model is a full size single action pistol. Hand-fitted titanium barrel bushing, fitted slide lock, match grade barrel, adjustable sights, oversize magazine well, tuned action, and checkered front strap.

Suggested Retail Price: $1400

Shorty .356 TSW
This new cartridge is also available in another Lew Horton/Performance Center limited edition pistol with a 4" barrel. It features a steel frame and hand-fitted slide, with spherical barrel bushing. The double action is custom tuned by the Performance Center. Magazine holds 12 rounds. Similar in appearance to the "Shorty-Forty". Offered in 1993. Special serial numbers.

Model 5906 Performance Center
Introduced in 1998 this 9mm pistol features front slide serrations, ambidextrous decocker, titanium coated barrel bushing, match grade barrel, and Noval Lo-Mount sights. Sold with one 15-round magazine and one 10-round magazine. Stainless steel finish.

Suggested Retail Introductory Price: $1000

Suggested Retail Introductory Price: $1200

Model 45 Recon
Chambered for the .45 ACP cartridge, this model is an enhanced version of the "Shorty 45." It has a ported 3.75" match grade barrel with titanium barrel bushing. Novak Lo-Mount sights. Fitted with Hogue grips. Magazine capacity is 7 rounds. Matte black finish. Weight is approximately 28 oz.

Suggested Retail Price: $1200

Model .356 TSW "Limited" Series
This is a Lew Horton gun. This model is chambered for the new .356 TSW caliber (TSW stands for Team Smith & Wesson). This is a new caliber, actually a 9mm x 21.5mm cartridge, with ballistics of around 1,235 fps. with a 147 grain bullet. Designed as a low end .357 competition pistol. Built for the competitive shooter (IPSC) it features a 15-round magazine and distinctive profile and markings. The single action trigger is adjustable for reach while the slide, frame, and barrel are custom fitted. The gun comes with a spherical barrel bushing and adjustable BoMar sights. The frame grip is checked 20 line to the inch, the magazine well is extended as is the magazine release. The magazine is fitted with a pad.

Model 845 of 1998
This .45 ACP caliber model has a 5" match grade barrel with hand lapped rails on frame and slide. Patridge front sight and adjustable Bomar rear sight. Single action trigger is tuned and the slide has front serrations. Magazine capacity is 8 rounds. Stainless steel finish. Limited to 150 pistols.

Suggested Retail Price: $1500

Model .45 CQB Combat

Introduced in 1998 this Lew Horton model features a 4" match grade barrel. Novak Lo-Mount sights. Double action trigger with ambidextrous de-cocker. Available in both a matte black and stainless steel finish. Matte black model has alloy frame and weighs about 30 oz. Stainless steel version has stainless frame and weighs about 38 oz.

Suggested Retail Price: $1200

Model 945

This is a single action only pistol chambered for the .45 ACP cartridge. Fitted with a 5" match grade barrel and Bomar adjustable rear sight. Grips are checkered black/silver wood laminate with matte stainless slide and frame. Magazine capacity is 8 rounds. Empty weight is approximately 44 oz. Introduced in 1998.

Suggested Retail Price: $1600

Model 945 Black Model

This Performance Center Model features a 3.25" barrel with black stainless steel slide. Frame is aluminum. Novak Lo-Mount sights. Hogue checkered wood laminate grips. Furnished with two 6-round magazines and a locking aluminum gun case. Weight is about 24 oz. Exclusive with RSR.

Suggested Retail Introductory Price: $

Model 945-40

This PC model is fitted with a 3.75" barrel chambered for the .40 S&W cartridge. Novak Lo-Mount sights and Hogue checkered wood laminate grips are standard. Furnished with two 7-round magazines and a locking aluminum case. Clear glass-bead finish. Exclusive with Sports South.

Suggested Retail Introductory Price: $

Model 945 Micro

Similar to the Model 945 Black Model but with stainless steel finish. Exclusive with Camfour Distributor.

Suggested Retail Introductory Price: $

Model 66 .357 Magnum F-Comp

A Performance Center revolver designed as a carry gun. Furnished with a 3" ported barrel and full underlug. The thumbpiece has been cut down to accommodate all speed loaders, the charge holes are countersunk, and the pistol comes standard with a stainless steel finish. The K-frame action has been custom tuned and the rear sight is a fully adjustable black blade while the front sight features a Tritium dot night sight. Furnished with a round butt combat style rubber grip. This revolver has a stainless steel finish. This is a Lew Horton special limited edition, 300 units, revolver.

Suggested Retail Introductory Price: $800

Model 66

An RSR exclusive this model is chambered for the .357 magnum cartridge and fitted with a 3" barrel. Red ramp front sight. Stainless steel finish. Limited edition.

Suggested Retail Price: $490

Model 681 Quad Port

Chambered for the .357 magnum cartridge and fitted with a 3" barrel with Quad porting. Fixed rear sight. Seven-round cylinder with moon clips. Two sets of grips are standard: Hogue Bantam and checkered wood laminate. Stainless steel finish. Weight is about 35 oz. Camfor exclusive. A 4" barrel version is also available.

Suggested Retail Introductory Price: $

Model 25

This PC model is a reintroduction of the original Model 25. Chambered for the .45 Colt cartridge and fitted with a tapered 6" barrel with pinned gold bead patridge front sight. Four screw frame. Furnished with locking aluminum case. Weight is about 42 oz. Sports South exclusive.

Suggested Retail Introductory Price: $

Model 19 .357 Magnum K-Comp

This is the same gun as the F-Comp but furnished with a black matte finish and is sold through stocking dealers on a unlimited basis.

Suggested Retail Introductory Price: $800

Model 657 Classic

Offered in limited quantities of 350 units this Lew Horton/Performance Center revolver features an unfluted cylinder and 6.5" barrel on a drilled and tapped N-frame. Chambered for the .41 Magnum cartridge this handgun is fitted with adjustable rear sight. Special serial numbers.

Suggested Retail Introductory Price: $550

Model 657

This Lew Horton/Performance Center revolver is fitted with a 3" full lug barrel chambered for the .41 Magnum cartridge. Fluted cylinder with red ramp front sight and white outline rear. Rosewood grips. Limited to 150 revolvers in 1998.

Suggested Retail Introductory Price: $720

Model 657 Defensive

Introduced in 1999 by Lou Horton, this .41 Magnum revolver is fitted with a 2-5/8" barrel with drift adjustable Millet front sight and fully adjustable rear sight. Stainless steel finish with 6-shot nonfluted cylinder. Hogue combat grips. Weight is about 40 oz. Furnished with aluminum case.

Suggested Retail Price: $1025

Model 657 Hunter

Introduced in 1995 this is an RSR Wholesale Guns exclusive. Fitted with an integral weaver base, Mag-Na-Ported 6" barrel with Millet red ramp front sight and adjustable rear sight this model has a stainless steel finish special serial numbers, chamfered charge holes, and adjustable trigger stop. Limited to 500 guns.

Suggested Retail Introductory Price: $1000

Model 60 Carry Comp

Introduced in the summer of 1993 this J-frame revolver is fitted with a 3" full underlug barrel with integral compensator. The charge holes are radiused for quick loading and the action is tuned by the Performance Center. The pistol is rated for + P ammunition. The grips are fancy wood contoured for speed loaders. This Lew Horton revolver is limited to 300 guns and has special serial numbers.

Suggested Retail Introductory Price: $795

Paxton Quigley Model 640

This is a Performance Center offering restricted to 300 revolvers. Built around the Model 640 this limited edition handgun has a 2" compensated barrel, windage adjustable front sight, specially tuned action, and a tapestry soft gun case. Each gun has a distinct serial number range.

Suggested Retail Price: $720

Model 640 Centennial Powerport

Introduced in 1996 this model is a Lew Horton exclusive. It is fitted with a 2-1/8" barrel with integral compensator. The front sight is a black blade with Tritium insert and the rear is a fixed notch. The cylinder holds five .357 or .38 rounds. Stainless steel with Pachmayr decelerator compact grips. Overall length is 6.75" and weight is about 25 oz. Limited to 300 units.

Suggested Retail Price: $675

Model 940 Centennial .356

Offered exclusively from Lew Horton this J-frame revolver is chambered for the new .356 cartridge and has a 2" compensated barrel. It will also fire the 9mm cartridge. This gun features a tuned action, radius hammer and trigger and special serial numbers.

Suggested Retail Price: $760

Model 13 .357

This is a Lew Horton exclusive that features a 3" barrel with 4 Mag-Na-Ports, a bobbed hammer for double action only, chambered charge holes, beveled cylinder, contoured grip and thumb latch for speed loader clearance, overtravel trigger stop, and FBI grips. Limited to 300 guns.

Suggested Retail Price: $730

Model 845 Single Action

Offered by Lew Horton this pistol is chambered for the .45 ACP and is designed for the competitive shooter. Adjustable reach trigger precision fitted slide, frame and barrel are some of the special features. The barrel bushing is spherical and the front sight is dovetailed. The magazine well is extended as is the magazine release and safety. Both front and rear sight are adjustable.

Suggested Retail Price: $1470

SMITH & WESSON LONG ARMS

.320 Revolving Rifle Model

This model is rare and unique—a prize to a S&W collector. The Revolving Rifle is chambered for the .320 S&W Revolving Rifle cartridge, has a 6-shot fluted cylinder and is offered with a 16", 18", and 20" barrel. Only 76 of the rifles are nickel-plated, and the remainder of the production is blued. The butt is rounded, with red hard rubber checkered grips and a forearm of the same material. There is a detachable shoulder stock with a black hard rubber buttplate featuring the S&W logo. The rifle was furnished in a leather carrying case with accessories. As fine a firearm as this was, it was a commercial failure for S&W; and they finally came to the realization that the public did not want a revolving rifle. They manufactured only 977 of them between 1879 and 1887.

NOTE: Values are for complete unit. Deduct 40% without stock. Add 10% for 16" or 20" barrels.

Exc.	V.G.	Good	Fair	Poor
8000	5500	3500	2000	1500

Model A Rifle

A bolt action with 23.75" barrel, chambered for .22-250, .243, .270, .308, .30-06, 7mm Magnum, and .300 Winchester Magnum. It has a folding rear sight and a checkered Monte Carlo stock with contrasting rosewood forend tip and pistol grip cap. It was manufactured for S&W by Husqvarna of Sweden.

NIB	Exc.	V.G.	Good	Fair	Poor
400	325	275	200	150	100

Model B

As above, with a schnabel forend and 20.75" barrel.

NIB	Exc.	V.G.	Good	Fair	Poor
400	325	275	200	150	100

A Smith & Wesson Model 320 Revolving Rifle sold at auction for $18,700. Fitted with an 18" barrel and detachable shoulder stock. Comes with leather carrying case. Stock is Circassian walnut. Condition was very good to excellent.
Faintich Auction Service, October 1999

Paul Goodwin Photo

Model C
As above, with a cheekpiece.

NIB	Exc.	V.G.	Good	Fair	Poor
425	350	300	225	175	125

Model D
As above, with a Mannlicher-style stock.

NIB	Exc.	V.G.	Good	Fair	Poor
550	500	400	350	250	150

SNAKE CHARMER
Little Field, Texas
Sporting Arms Manufacturing, Inc.

Snake Charmer
A .410 bore single shot shotgun with an 18.5" barrel. Stainless steel with a composition stock.

NIB	Exc.	V.G.	Good	Fair	Poor
175	125	100	75	50	25

SNEIDER, CHARLES E.
Baltimore, Maryland

2-Cylinder Revolver
A .22 caliber spur trigger revolver with a 2.75" octagonal barrel and twin 7-shot cylinders that can be pivoted. The barrel marked "E. Sneider Pat. March 1862". Produced in limited quantities during the 1860s. Prospective purchasers are advised to secure a qualified appraisal prior to acquisition.

Courtesy Butterfield & Butterfield

Exc.	V.G.	Good	Fair	Poor
—	—	10000	5000	1250

SODIA, FRANZ
Ferlach, Austria

A wide variety of double barrel shotguns, drillings, and combination shotgun/rifles are made by this maker. As these arms are essentially custom order pieces, it is advised that perspective purchasers secure individual appraisals.

SOKOLOVSKY CORP. SPORT ARMS
Sunnyvale, California

.45 Automaster

A .45 caliber stainless steel semiautomatic pistol with a 6" barrel fitted with Millet adjustable sights and 6-shot magazine. Approximately 50 of these pistols have been made since 1984.

NIB	Exc.	V.G.	Good	Fair	Poor
3250	2750	2250	1750	1250	800

SPALDING & FISHER
Worcester, Massachusetts

Double Barreled Pistol

A .36 caliber percussion double-barrel pocket pistol with 5.5" barrels, blued iron frame and walnut grips. The top of the barrels marked "Spalding & Fisher". Produced during the 1850s.

Exc.	V.G.	Good	Fair	Poor
—	—	850	350	100

SPANG & WALLACE
Philadelphia, Pennsylvania

Pocket Pistol

A .36 caliber percussion pocket pistol with a 2.5" to 6" barrel, German silver furniture and checkered walnut stock. The barrel marked "Spang & Wallace/Phila." Manufactured during late 1840s and early 1850s.

Exc.	V.G.	Good	Fair	Poor
—	—	1250	650	200

SPENCER
Boston, Massachusetts

Spencer Carbine

This was one of the most popular firearms used by Union forces during the Civil War. It is chambered for a metallic rimfire cartridge known as the "No. 56." It is actually a .52 caliber and was made with a copper case. The barrel is 22" in length. The finish is blued, with a carbine-length walnut stock held on by one barrel band. There is a sling swivel at the butt. There were approximately 50,000 manufactured between 1863 and 1865.

Courtesy Butterfield & Butterfield, San Francisco, California

Exc.	V.G.	Good	Fair	Poor
—	—	4000	1750	500

Military Rifle-Navy Model

This model is similar to the carbine, with a 30" round barrel and a full-length walnut stock held on by three barrel bands. It features an iron forend tip and sling swivels. The Civil War production consisted of two models. A Navy model was manufactured between 1862 and 1864 (there were approximately 1,000 of these so marked).

Exc.	V.G.	Good	Fair	Poor
—	—	4500	1850	600

Military Rifle-Army Model

There were approximately 11,450 produced for the Army during the Civil War. They are similar to the Navy model except that the front sight doubles as a bayonet lug. They were manufactured in 1863 and 1864.

Courtesy Milwaukee Public Museum, Milwaukee, Wisconsin

Exc.	V.G.	Good	Fair	Poor
—	—	3500	1500	600

A Spencer Model 1860 Military Rifle sold at auction for $19,550. Chambered for .50 caliber and fitted with a 30" round barrel. Martially marked. Civil War provenance. Condition is very fine.
Rock Island Auction Company, September 2001

Springfield Armory Postwar Alteration

After the conclusion of the Civil War, approximately 11,000 carbines were refurbished and rechambered for .50 caliber rimfire. The barrels were sleeved, and a device known as the "Stabler cut-off" was added to convert the arm to single shot function. Often they were refinished and restocked. The inspector's marks "ESA" will be found in an oval cartouche on the left side of the stock. These alterations took place in 1867 and 1868.

Exc.	V.G.	Good	Fair	Poor
—	—	3500	1500	500

Model 1865 Contract

This model was manufactured by the Burnside Rifle Company in 1865. They are similar to the Civil War-type carbine and are marked "By Burnside Rifle Co./Model 1865". There were approximately 34,000 manufactured. Old records show that 30,500 were purchased by the United States government, and 19,000 of these had the Stabler cut-off device.

Courtesy Wallis & Wallis, Lewes, Sussex, England

Exc.	V.G.	Good	Fair	Poor
—	—	2500	1150	400

A Spencer Model 1865 SRC was sold at auction for $9,775. "A" markings correct. Condition was very good to excellent.
Rock Island Auction Company, April 1999

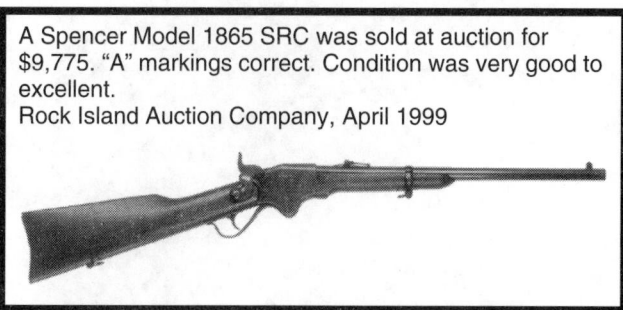

NOTE: There were a number of other variations in the Spencer line. It would behoove anyone interested in collecting this fine Civil War firearm to educate oneself on these variances and to secure individual appraisal if transactions are contemplated. This is a complex model with many subtle variations.

SPENCER ARMS CO.
Windsor, Connecticut

From 1882 to 1889 they manufactured the first successful slide action repeating shotgun. Designed by Christopher M. Spencer who also designed the Civil War era Spencer military carbines. The shotgun came in both solid and takedown models in both 12 and 10 gauge. In 1890 Francis Bannerman & Sons of New York bought the patents and machinery and moved the operation to Brooklyn, New York. They produced what is known as the Spencer Bannerman models from 1890 to 1907. The takedown model is worth 20% premium and 10 gauge models are worth a 10% premium. The later Bannerman models are worth 20% less than the Spencer models.

Exc.	V.G.	Good	Fair	Poor
—	950	400	200	125

SPENCER REVOLVER
Maltby, Henley & Company
New York, New York

Safety Hammerless Revolver

A .32 caliber hammerless double action revolver with a 3" barrel. The frame and barrel made of brass, the cylinder of steel and the grips are of walnut. The barrel is marked "Spencer Safety Hammerless Pat. Jan. 24, 1888 & Oct. 29, 1889". Manufactured by the Norwich Pistol Company circa 1890.

Exc.	V.G.	Good	Fair	Poor
—	375	200	150	100

SPHINX
Sphinx Engineering SA
Porrentru, Switzerland
Imported by
Sile Distributors Inc.

This Swiss-based company was founded in 1876 and produced the first automatic turning machine. The company made small drills, tungsten carbine tools, and tool coatings. After WWII Sphinx developed more exotic machines and drills. In 1990 Sphinx Engineering SA was established for the development and production of pistols. In 1991 the AT .380 was introduced to the market. The following year the AT 2000 was placed on the market. Sphinx purchased the rights to its current line of pistols from ITM AG, a Swiss firm that experienced financial problems with the development of its pistol line, in 1989. The AT series is essentially a copy of the famous Czech CZ 75 semiautomatic pistol.

AT-380

This semiautomatic pistol is a small .380 caliber in double action only. The magazine capacity is 11 rounds. It is offered in stainless steel, blued, or two-tone finish. The barrel is 3.27" and overall length is 6.03". Sights are fixed and grips are black checkered plastic. Weight is 25 oz.

NIB	Exc.	V.G.	Good	Fair	Poor
450	400	350	300	200	100

AT-2000

This is a series number applied to several different variations of the same basic design. Based on the CZ 75 pistol the AT-2000 is a semiautomatic pistol offered in 9mm and .40 S&W. Barrel lengths are different depending on variation, but the AT-2000 can be converted from double action to double only in just a matter of minutes.

AT-2000S/SDA

This model is chambered for the 9mm or .40 S&W cartridge. The barrel length is 4.53" and overall length is 8.12". Magazine capacity is 15 rounds for 9mm and 13 rounds for .40 S&W. Available in double action (S) or double action only (SDA). Offered with two-tone or all blued finish. Weighs 35 oz.

NIB	Exc.	V.G.	Good	Fair	Poor
675	600	500	400	300	200

AT-2000P/PDA

This is a slightly smaller of the AT-2000S. Magazine capacity is 13 rounds for 9mm and 11 rounds for .40 S&W. The features are the same except that the barrel length is 3.66", overall length 7.25", and weight is 31 oz.

NIB	Exc.	V.G.	Good	Fair	Poor
650	600	500	400	300	200

AT-2000PS

This version, sometimes referred to as the Police Special, features the shorter barrel of the AT-2000P model on the larger AT-2000S frame. Barrel length is 3.66" and magazine capacity is 15 rounds for 9mm and 13 rounds for the .40 S&W.

NIB	Exc.	V.G.	Good	Fair	Poor
650	600	500	400	300	200

AT-2000H/HDA

This is the smallest version of the AT-2000 series. Magazine capacity is 10 rounds for 9mm and 8 rounds for .40 S&W. The barrel length is 3.34" and overall length is 6.78". Weight is 26 oz.

AT-2000C

This is the competitor model. It features a competition slide, dual port compensator, match barrel, and Sphinx scope mount. Offered in double action/single action. Available in 9mm, 9x21, and .40 S&W.

NIB	Exc.	V.G.	Good	Fair	Poor
1600	1200	800	600	400	200

AT-2000CS

Same as above model but fitted with BoMar adjustable sights.

NIB	Exc.	V.G.	Good	Fair	Poor
1400	1000	600	400	300	200

AT-2000GM

The Grand Master model. Features are similar to the AT-2000C but offered in single action only.

NIB	Exc.	V.G.	Good	Fair	Poor
2100	1750	1250	600	300	200

AT-2000GMS

Same as above but fitted with BoMar adjustable sights.

NIB	Exc.	V.G.	Good	Fair	Poor
2000	1650	1200	600	300	200

SPIES, A. W.
New York, New York

Pocket Pistol

A .41 caliber percussion pocket pistol with a 2.5" barrel, German silver furniture and a checkered walnut stock. Produced during the 1850s.

Exc.	V.G.	Good	Fair	Poor
—	—	1750	900	300

SPILLER & BURR
Atlanta, Georgia

Navy Revolver

A .36 caliber percussion revolver with a 6" or 6.5" octagonal barrel and 6-shot cylinder. The barrel and cylinder blued, the frame of brass with walnut grips. Some pistols are marked "Spiller & Burr" while others are simply marked "C.S." Approximately 1,450 were made between 1862 and 1865. Prospective purchasers are advised to secure a qualified appraisal prior to acquisition.

Courtesy Milwaukee Public Museum, Milwaukee, Wisconsin

Exc.	V.G.	Good	Fair	Poor
—	—	30000	15000	—

SPIRLET, A.
Liege, Belgium

Spirlet was erroneously credited with inventing the top-hinged tip-up revolver. This weapon was around well before Spirlet's time. Actually, the patent that he held covers lockwork and an ejection system that was used on tip-up revolvers. Although he manufactured some of these tip-up revolvers himself, there were never enough of them to establish him as little more than a small custom gunmaker. Revolvers that he manufactured bear his name and address on the breech end of the barrel. Many other makers utilized his developments.

SPITFIRE
JSL (Hereford) Ltd.
Hereford, England
Importer - Specialty Shooters
Ft. Lauderdale, Florida

This semiautomatic pistol is a design based on the CZ 75. This is a hand-built pistol designed by John Slough and built from a solid block of steel. The stainless steel frame and slide are cut with spark erosion and diamond grinding. Barrels are built and bored in the same factory. This is primarily a competition pistol.

Spitfire Standard Model (G1)

Chambered for the 9x21, 9mm Parabellum, or .40 S&W cartridges this pistol uses the locked breech concept. The trigger system is single and double action and it is fitted with an ambidextrous safety. The barrel is 3.7" and the overall length is 7.1". Magazine capacity of the 9mm is 15 rounds. Sights are fixed. Empty weight is 35 oz. Finish is stainless steel. Comes supplied with presentation box, 2 magazines, and allen key.

NIB	Exc.	V.G.	Good	Fair	Poor
1300	900	700	500	300	200

Spitfire Sterling Model (G2)

This model is chambered for the 9x21, 9mm Parabellum, or .40 S&W cartridges. Its features are the same as the Standard Model with the exception that it has adjustable sights.

NIB	Exc.	V.G.	Good	Fair	Poor
1400	1000	800	600	300	200

NIB	Exc.	V.G.	Good	Fair	Poor
1800	1400	1000	800	400	200

Spitfire Master Model

This is similar to the Standard Model but without sights. It is fitted with a stainless steel bridge mount to take an Aimpoint sight. Also has a dual port compensator. Supplied with presentation box and 2 magazines.

NIB	Exc.	V.G.	Good	Fair	Poor
2100	1750	1250	800	400	200

Spitfire Squadron Model

This model has a Standard Model frame, adjustable rear sight slide, adjustable rear sight slide with compensator, Master Model slide and barrel with stainless steel bridge mount and Aimpoint sight, 4 magazines, screwdriver, allen key, oil bottle, spare springs, cleaning kit, and fitted leather case.

NIB	Exc.	V.G.	Good	Fair	Poor
6000	4800	2100	900	450	200

Spitfire Super Sterling (G7)

Also chambered for the 9x21, 9mm Parabellum, and .40 S&W this model features a single port compensator, 4.3" barrel, and overall length of 8.25". Weight is approximately 36 oz.

NIB	Exc.	V.G.	Good	Fair	Poor
1600	1200	900	700	350	200

Spitfire Battle of Britain Commemorative

This is a limited edition of 1,056 Spitfires in 9mm Parabellum. Each one represents one of the Spitfire aircraft. The stainless steel slide has the inscription "Battle of Britain-50th Anniversary", the grips are checkered walnut, log book of history of that particular aircraft, and a wooden presentation box with engraved plaque.

Retail Price: $1900

Spitfire Competition Model (G3)

Chambered for 9x21, 9mm Parabellum, or .40 S&W cartridge this model features a tapered slide rib, adjustable rear sight, dual pod compensator, match hammer, adjustable trigger stop with presentation box. Barrel is 5.27" with compensator and weight is 40 oz.

Westlake Britarms

This is a .22 Long Rifle Match pistol. Barrel length is 5.77", sight base is 8.42", magazine capacity is 5 rounds. Weight is approximately 47 oz. Trigger is adjustable for length, front and rear trigger stops, adjustable palm rest on contoured wood grips, take-down barrel design with removable weight. Limited importation.

NIB	Exc.	V.G.	Good	Fair	Poor
1850	1400	1000	800	400	200

SPRINGFIELD ARMORY (MODERN)
SEE—Springfield Inc.

SPRINGFIELD INC.
Geneseo, Illinois

RIFLES

MI Garand Rifle

A .270 (discontinued), .308 or .30-06 caliber semiautomatic rifle with a 24" barrel and 8-shot magazine. Patterned directly after the U.S. M1 Rifle.

Courtesy Milwaukee Public Museum, Milwaukee, Wisconsin

Exc.	V.G.	Good	Fair	Poor
775	650	550	400	300

NOTE: As of January 1993 Springfield Inc. purchased the inventory, name, patents, trademarks, and logo of the Springfield Armory Inc. and intends to carry on the tradition of quality products and service in the future. Products, services, and distribution patterns remain unchanged. The Springfield Custom Shop, producing "Raceguns", will continue as before.

M1A Basic Rifle

Chambered for .308 Win. and fitted with a painted black fiberglass stock. Barrel length is 22" without flash suppressor. Front sights are military square post and rear military aperture (battle sights). Magazine capacity is 5, 10, or 20 box. Rifle weighs 9 lbs.

NIB	Exc.	V.G.	Good	Fair	Poor
1250	1000	850	650	400	250

M1A Standard Rifle

This model is chambered for the .308 Win., .243, or 7mmx08 cartridges. Also fitted with a 22" barrel but with adjustable rear sight. Fitted with a walnut stock with fiberglass hand guard, it comes equipped with a 20-round box magazine. Weighs 9 lbs.

NIB	Exc.	V.G.	Good	Fair	Poor
1375	1100	850	650	400	250

M1A-A1 Bush Rifle

Chambered for .308, .243, or 7mmx08 cartridge with choice of walnut stock, black fiberglass, or folding stock (no longer produced). Fitted with 18.25" barrel. Rifle weighs 8.75 lbs.

NIB	Exc.	V.G.	Good	Fair	Poor
1400	1100	850	650	400	250

NOTE: Add $250 for folding stock.

M1A Scout Squad Rifle

This .308 model is fitted with an 18" barrel and a choice of fiberglass or walnut stock. Military sights. Supplied with 10-round magazine. Weight with fiberglass stock is about 9 lbs., with walnut stock about 9.3 pounds.

NIB	Exc.	V.G.	Good	Fair	Poor
1500	1100	750	550	—	—

M1A National Match

Chambered for .308 as standard with choice of .243 or 7mmx08 cartridge. Fitted with a medium weight National Match 22" glass bedded barrel and walnut stock. Special rear sight adjustable to half minute of angle clicks. Weighs 10.06 lbs.

NIB	Exc.	V.G.	Good	Fair	Poor
1900	1400	1000	700	500	250

M1A Super Match

This is Springfield's best match grade rifle. Chambered for .308 as standard and also .243 or 7mmx08 cartridge. Fitted with special oversize heavy walnut stock, heavy Douglas match glass bedded barrel, and special rear lugged receiver. Special rear adjustable sight. Weighs 10.125 lbs.

NIB	Exc.	V.G.	Good	Fair	Poor
2200	1700	1250	850	600	300

M1A Model 25 Carlos Hathcock

Introduced in 2001 this model features a match trigger, stainless steel heavy match barrel, McMillan synthetic stock with adjustable cheek pad, Harris Bi-pod, and other special features. Chambered for the .308 cartridge. Weight is about 12.75 lbs. A special logo bears his signature.

NIB	Exc.	V.G.	Good	Fair	Poor
—	—	—	—	—	—

M21 Law Enforcement/Tactical Rifle

Similar to the Super Match with the addition of a special stock with rubber recoil pad and height adjustable cheekpiece. Available as a special order only. Weighs 11.875 lbs.

NIB	Exc.	V.G.	Good	Fair	Poor
2400	1750	1350	900	650	350

SAR-4800

This is a semiautomatic gas operated rifle, similar in appearance to the FN-FAL/LAR rifle, chambered for the .308 Win. cartridge. It is fitted with a 21" barrel and has a fully adjustable rear sight. Weight is approximately 9.5 lbs. No longer imported.

NIB	Exc.	V.G.	Good	Fair	Poor
1200	1000	800	600	400	250

SAR-8

This semiautomatic rifle is similar in appearance to the HK-91. It is chambered for the .308 Win. and is of the recoil operated delayed roller-lock design. Barrel length is 18" and the rear sight is fully adjustable. Weight is about 8.7 lbs. No longer imported.

NIB	Exc.	V.G.	Good	Fair	Poor
1200	1000	800	600	400	250

SAR-8 Tactical

Similar to the above model but fitted with a heavy barrel. Introduced in 1996. No longer imported.

NIB	Exc.	V.G.	Good	Fair	Poor
1600	1300	950	750	500	300

IDF Mauser Rifle Model 66SP

This is a bolt action rifle chambered for the .308 Win. cartridge. Adjustable trigger for pull and travel. Barrel length is 27". Specially designed stock has broad forend and a thumb hole pistol grip. Cheekpiece is adjustable as is the recoil pad. Supplied with case. This rifle is military issue. Less than 100 imported into the U.S.

NIB	Exc.	V.G.	Good	Fair	Poor
2200	1750	—	—	—	—

M6 Scout

A .22, .22 Magnum, or .22 Hornet and .410 bore Over/Under combination shotgun rifle with an 18" barrel. Black anodized finish with a synthetic stock.

NIB	Exc.	V.G.	Good	Fair	Poor
175	125	90	70	50	40

M6 Scout-Stainless Steel

Same as above but in stainless steel. First introduced in 1996.

NIB	Exc.	V.G.	Good	Fair	Poor
200	150	120	90	75	50

PISTOLS

Model 1911-A1

A 9mm, .38 Super or .45 caliber copy of the Colt Model 1911-A1 semiautomatic pistol. Blued or parkerized. Introduced in 1985.

NIB	Exc.	V.G.	Good	Fair	Poor
425	375	350	300	250	200

Combat Commander

A copy of the Colt Model 1911-A1 Combat Commander chambered for .45 ACP only. Introduced in 1988.

NIB	Exc.	V.G.	Good	Fair	Poor
475	425	400	350	300	250

Model Trophy Match

This model has special features such as fully adjustable target sights, match grade 5" barrel, and special wide trigger. Weight is approximately 36 oz. Available in blue, stainless steel, or bi-tone finish. In 1997 this model was offered chambered for the 9mm cartridge. Values would be the same for both .45 ACP and the 9mm models.

NIB	Exc.	V.G.	Good	Fair	Poor
850	750	650	500	400	300

NOTE: For stainless steel add $40.

Model 1911-A2 S.A.S.S.

This is a single shot pistol built on the Model 1911 frame. Available in two barrel lengths; 10.75" and 14.9". Offered in .22 Long Rifle, .223, 7mm-08, 7mmBR, .357 Magnum, .308, and .44 Magnum calibers. This conversion kit is available for those wishing to use it on their own Model 1911 pistol frames.

NIB	Exc.	V.G.	Good	Fair	Poor
225	200	175	150	100	50

Model 1911-A1 Stainless

Similar to the standard Model 1911 but chambered for the .45 ACP cartridge and offered in stainless steel. Equipped with three dot sights, beveled magazine well, and checkered walnut grips. Weighs about 39.2 oz.

NIB	Exc.	V.G.	Good	Fair	Poor
500	425	400	350	300	200

NOTE: For Bomar sights add $50.

Model 1911-A1 Factory Comp.

Chambered for the .45 ACP or the .38 Super this pistol is fitted with a three chamber compensator. The rear sight is adjustable, an extended thumb safety and Videcki speed trigger are standard features. Also checkered walnut grips, beveled magazine well and Commander hammer are standard. Weighs 40 oz.

NIB	Exc.	V.G.	Good	Fair	Poor
850	700	500	300	200	100

NOTE: Factory Comp pistols chambered for .38 Super may bring a small premium.

Model 1911-A1 Factory Comp. High Capacity

Same as above but with 13-round magazine. New pistols sold in 1996 will be supplied with 10-round magazines except to law enforcement.

NIB	Exc.	V.G.	Good	Fair	Poor
975	850	700	600	400	200

Model 1911-A1 Defender

Chambered for the .45 ACP cartridge this pistol is fitted with a tapered cone dual port compensator. It also is fitted with reversed recoil plug, full length recoil spring guide, fully adjustable rear sight, serrated front strap, rubberized grips, and Commander style hammer. Eight-round magazine capacity. The finish is bi-tone. Weighs 40.16 oz.

NIB	Exc.	V.G.	Good	Fair	Poor
850	700	500	300	200	100

Model 1911-A1 Compact

Available in blue or bi-tone this .45 ACP is fitted with a 4.5" barrel and compact compensator. It is equipped with Commander style hammer and three dot sights. Walnut grips are standard. Comes with 7-round magazine. Weighs 37.2 oz.

NIB	Exc.	V.G.	Good	Fair	Poor
500	400	300	250	200	100

NOTE: For stainless steel add $40.

Lightweight Compact Comp

Fitted with a 4-1/2" barrel and single port compensator. Magazine hold 8 rounds of .45 ACP. Frame is alloy and weight is 30 oz.

NIB	Exc.	V.G.	Good	Fair	Poor
500	400	300	250	200	100

Model 1911-A1 Compact Mil-Spec

This model is the same as the standard blued steel Compact model but with a parkerized finish.

NIB	Exc.	V.G.	Good	Fair	Poor
450	375	250	200	150	100

Model 1911-A1 Long Slide

This model features a 6" barrel, 3-dot fixed sights, checkered wooden grips, and an 8-round magazine capacity. Finish is stainless steel. Weight is about 38 oz. Introduced in 1997.

NIB	Exc.	V.G.	Good	Fair	Poor
625	550	500	—	—	—

Model 1911-A1 Champion

This .45 ACP pistol has a shortened slide, barrel, and reduced size frame. The Champion is fitted with 4" barrel, 8-round magazine, Commander hammer, checkered walnut grips, and special 3-dot sights. Weighs 33.4 oz.

NIB	Exc.	V.G.	Good	Fair	Poor
500	400	350	250	150	100

Model 1911-A1 Champion Mil-Spec

Same as above but with a parkerized finish.

NIB	Exc.	V.G.	Good	Fair	Poor
450	375	300	200	150	100

Model 1911-A1 Stainless Champion

Same as above but offered in stainless steel. Weighs about 33.4 oz.

NIB	Exc.	V.G.	Good	Fair	Poor
525	425	375	275	200	150

Champion Compact

Includes same features as Champion but with a shortened grip frame length and a 7-round magazine. Weighs 32 oz.

NIB	Exc.	V.G.	Good	Fair	Poor
450	350	250	200	150	100

Ultra Compact 1911-A1

This model features a 3-1/2" barrel with a 7-1/8" overall length. It has a stainless steel frame, beveled mag well, speed trigger, match grade barrel, and walnut grips. Weighs 31 oz.

NIB	Exc.	V.G.	Good	Fair	Poor
600	475	350	250	200	150

Ultra Compact Lightweight MD-1

Same as above but in .380 caliber with alloy frame. Weighs 24 oz.

NIB	Exc.	V.G.	Good	Fair	Poor
375	325	275	200	150	100

Ultra Compact 1911-A1 Mil-Spec

Same as the Ultra Compact Model but with a parkerized finish.

NIB	Exc.	V.G.	Good	Fair	Poor
600	475	350	350	200	150

V10 Ultra Compact 1911 A-1

Same as the Ultra Compact 1911 A-1 but fitted with a compensator built into the barrel and slide.

NIB	Exc.	V.G.	Good	Fair	Poor
600	525	400	300	200	150

V10 Ultra Compact 1911-A1 Mil-Spec

Same as above but with parkerized finish.

NIB	Exc.	V.G.	Good	Fair	Poor
525	425	350	300	200	150

Model 1911-A1 High Capacity

This model is chambered in .45 ACP (10-round magazine) or 9mm caliber (16-round magazine). Standard features include Commander hammer, walnut grips, and beveled magazine well. Blued finish. Weighs 42 oz. In 1997 this model was offered in stainless steel and parkerized finish.

NIB	Exc.	V.G.	Good	Fair	Poor
650	525	400	300	200	100

NOTE: For stainless steel add $40, for parkerized finish deduct $25.

Compact High Capacity

Same as above but with an 11-round magazine. New pistols sold in 1996 will have 10-round magazine except to law enforcement.

NIB	Exc.	V.G.	Good	Fair	Poor
650	525	400	300	200	150

Ultra Compact High Capacity

This .45ACP model is offered in three different 3.5" barrel variations; stainless steel, parkerized, and ported. Standard magazine capacity is 10 rounds, 12 for law enforcement. Weight is about 31 oz.

NIB	Exc.	V.G.	Good	Fair	Poor
550	450	350	300	—	—

NOTE: Add $60 for stainless steel and $100 for ported models.

The Springfield P9 Pistol

This is a double action 9mm, .45 ACP, or .40 S&W pistol based on the Czech CZ 75 design. It incorporates several design features including: stainless steel trigger, sear safety mechanism, extended sear safety lever, redesigned back strap, lengthened beavertail grip area, and a new high strength slide stop. This model discontinued in 1993.

NIB	Exc.	V.G.	Good	Fair	Poor
450	375	300	250	200	100

Model P9 Standard

This is the standard pistol fitted with a 4.7" barrel, low profile target sights, and a ribbed slide. The 9mm has a 16-round magazine, the .45 ACP has a 10-round magazine, and the .40 S&W holds 12 rounds. Offered in either blue or stainless finish. Weighs about 35 oz.

NIB	Exc.	V.G.	Good	Fair	Poor
425	350	300	250	200	100

Model P9 Factory Comp.

This is a competition pistol fitted with triple port compensator, extended magazine release, adjustable rear sight, slim competition wood grips, and bi-tone finish. Weighs 34 oz. Dropped from the Springfield product line in 1993.

NIB	Exc.	V.G.	Good	Fair	Poor
500	450	400	300	200	100

Model P9 Ultra (IPSC Approved)

This competition pistol features a longer slide and barrel, 5". Special target sights, rubberized competition grips. Pistol is engraved with IPSC logo. Available in bi-tone finish only. Weighs 34.5 oz. Dropped from production in 1993.

NIB	Exc.	V.G.	Good	Fair	Poor
450	400	350	300	200	100

Omega

A .38 Super, 10mm Norma, or .45 caliber semiautomatic pistol with a 5" or 6" polygon rifled barrel, ported or unported, adjustable sights and Pachmayr grips. Patterned somewhat after the Colt Model 1911. Introduced in 1987.
Caliber Conversion Units-Add $675.

NIB	Exc.	V.G.	Good	Fair	Poor
550	450	350	250	200	125

Super Tuned Champion

Introduced in 1997 this model features a 4" barrel chambered for the .45 ACP cartridge, Novak fixed low-mount sights. Tuned and polished extractor and ejector. Polished feed ramp and barrel throat. Magazine capacity is 7 rounds. Choice of blued or parkerized finish. Weight is approximately 36 oz.

NIB	Exc.	V.G.	Good	Fair	Poor
875	800	—	—	—	—

Super Tuned V10
Similar to the model above but with 3.5" barrel. Finish is bi-tone or stainless steel. Weight is about 33 oz. Introduced in 1997. Add $100 for stainless steel.

NIB	Exc.	V.G.	Good	Fair	Poor
950	825	—	—	—	—

Super Tuned Standard
This model features a 5" barrel with stainless steel finish. Weight is about 39 oz. Has all other super tune features. Introduced in 1997.

NIB	Exc.	V.G.	Good	Fair	Poor
900	775	—	—	—	—

Tactical Response Pistol (TRP)
This .45ACP pistol is fitted with a 5" barrel and choice of stainless steel or black Armory Kote finish. Fully checkered front strap and mainspring housing. Novak Lo-Mount sights. Magazine capacity 8 rounds. Weight is about 37 oz.

NIB	Exc.	V.G.	Good	Fair	Poor
1150	900	750	600	—	—

TRP Champion
Same as above but with a 3.9" barrel and black Armory Kote finish. Weight is about 33 oz.

NIB	Exc.	V.G.	Good	Fair	Poor
1175	950	800	600	—	—

TRP-Pro
This model is fitted with a 5" barrel and many special features including Novak Lo-Mount tritium sights. Magazine capacity is 7 rounds. Meets specifications for FBI Swat team. Weight is 36 oz.

NIB	Exc.	V.G.	Good	Fair	Poor
2350	1750	—	—	—	—

SPRINGFIELD CUSTOM SHOP
This specialty shop was formed to build custom pistols to the customer's own specifications. When these one-of-a-kind pistols are encountered it is advisable for the shooter or collector to get an independent appraisal. The Springfield Custom also offers standard custom and Racegun packages that are readily available and in stock. These pistols are commercially available and priced below.

Custom Carry
Chambered for the following cartridges: .45 ACP, 9mm Parabellum, .38 Super, 10mm, .40 S&W, 9mm x 21. Pistol is fitted with fixed 3-dot sights, speed trigger, Match barrel and bushing, extended thumb safety, beveled magazine well, Commander hammer, polished feed ramp and throated barrel, tuned extractor, lowered and flared ejection port, fitted slide to frame, full length spring guide rod, and walnut grips. Supplied with 2 march magazines and plastic carrying case.

NIB	Exc.	V.G.	Good	Fair	Poor
1300	1000	—	—	—	—

Bureau Model 1911-A1
Introduced in 1998 this model features a 5" match barrel, a speed trigger, lowered and flared ejection port, beavertail grip safety, Lo-Mount Novak night sights, front strap checkering, Black T finish and special serial numbers with FBI prefix. Bureau Model markings on slide.

NIB	Exc.	V.G.	Good	Fair	Poor
1895	1500	—	—	—	—

Basic Competition Model
Chambered for the .45 ACP this model features a variety of special options for the competition shooter. Special BoMar sights, match trigger, custom slide to frame fit, polished feedramp and throated barrel are just some of the features of this pistol.

NIB	Exc.	V.G.	Good	Fair	Poor
1300	1000	—	—	—	—

N.R.A. PPC

Designed to comply with NRA rules for PPC competition this pistol is chambered for the .45 ACP cartridge with a match grade barrel and chamber. It has a polished feedramp, throated barrel, recoil buffer system, walnut grips, and fully adjustable sights. It is sold with a custom carrying case.

NIB	Exc.	V.G.	Good	Fair	Poor
1400	1150	850	—	—	—

Bullseye Wadcutter

Chambered for .45 ACP, .38 Super, 10mm, and .40 S&W. Slide is fitted with BoMar rib. Standard features include full length recoil spring guide rod, speed trigger, Commander hammer, lowered and flared ejection port, tuned extractor, fitted slide to frame, beveled magazine well, checkered front strap, checkered main spring housing, removable grip cope mount, match barrel and bushing, polished feed ramp and throated barrel, walnut grips, and two magazines with slam pads.

NIB	Exc.	V.G.	Good	Fair	Poor
1500	1200	900	—	—	—

Trophy Master Expert Limited Class

Chambered for .45 ACP Adjustable BoMar rear sight, match barrel, polished ramp and throated barrel, extended ambidextrous thumb safety, beveled and polished magazine well, full length recoil spring guide, match trigger, Commander hammer, lowered and flared ejection port, tuned extractor, fitted slide to frame, extended slide release, flat mainspring housing, Pachmayr wrap-around grips, 2 magazines with slam pads and plastic carrying case.

NIB	Exc.	V.G.	Good	Fair	Poor
1800	1500	1000	750	500	300

Expert Pistol

Similar to the above model but progressive triple port compensator.

NIB	Exc.	V.G.	Good	Fair	Poor
1700	1350	950	—	—	—

Springfield Formula "Squirtgun"

Chambered for .45 ACP, .38 Super, 9mmx19, 9mmx21, and 9mmx23. Fitted with a high capacity 20-round frame, customer specifications sights, hard chrome frame and slide, triple chambered tapered cone compensator, full recoil spring guide and reverse plug, shock butt, lowered and flared ejection port, fitted trigger, Commander hammer, polished feed ramp and throated barrel, flat checkered mainspring housing, extended ambidextrous thumb safety, tuned extractor, checkered front strap, bottom of triggerguard checkered, rear of slide serrated, cocking sensations on front of slide, built in beveled magazine well, and checkered wood grips.

NIB	Exc.	V.G.	Good	Fair	Poor
2900	2250	1250	950	400	200

Trophy Master Distinguished Pistol

This model is chambered for the following cartridges: .45 ACP, .38 Super, 10mm, .40 S&W, 9mmx21. Special BoMar adjustable rear sight with hidden rear leaf, triple port compensator on match barrel, full length recoil spring guide rod and recoil spring retainer, shock butt, lowered and flared ejection port, fitted speed trigger, Commander hammer, polished feed ramp and throated barrel, flat checkered magazine well and mainspring housing matched to beveled magazine well, extended ambidextrous thumb safety, tuned extractor, checkered front strap, flattened and checkered triggerguard, serrated slide top and compensator, cocking sensations on front of slide, checkered walnut grips, 2 magazines with slam pads, and carrying case.

NIB	Exc.	V.G.	Good	Fair	Poor
2450	1900	1350	—	—	—

Distinguished Limited Class

Similar to the above model but built to comply with USPSA "Limited Class" competition rules. This model has no compensator.

NIB	Exc.	V.G.	Good	Fair	Poor
2350	1850	1300	—	—	—

CMC Formula "Squirtgun"

Chambered for .45 ACP, .38 Super, 9mmx19, 9mmx21, 9mmx23. This pistol has a 20-round magazine and a modular frame. All other features the same as the Trophy Master.

NIB	Exc.	V.G.	Good	Fair	Poor
2750	2000	1200	800	400	200

National Match Model

As above, with a National Match barrel and bushing, adjustable sights and checkered walnut grips. Introduced in 1988.

NIB	Exc.	V.G.	Good	Fair	Poor
1300	1000	750	—	—	—

Competition Grade

As above, hand-tuned, Match Grade trigger, low-profile combat sights, an ambidextrous safety, and a Commander-type hammer. Furnished with Pachmayr grips. Introduced in 1988.

NIB	Exc.	V.G.	Good	Fair	Poor
1300	1000	750	—	—	—

A Model Master Grade Competition Pistol

Similar to the Custom Carry Gun, with a National Match barrel and bushing. Introduced in 1988.

NIB	Exc.	V.G.	Good	Fair	Poor
1700	1500	1250	850	400	250

Model B-1 Master Grade Competition Pistol
Specially designed for USPSA/IPSC competition. Introduced in 1988.

NIB	Exc.	V.G.	Good	Fair	Poor
2000	1750	1250	850	400	250

High Capacity Full-House Race Gun
Built with all available race gun options. Offered in .45 ACP, 9x25 Dillon, .38 Super, and custom calibers on request.

NIB	Exc.	V.G.	Good	Fair	Poor
2600	2050	1500	—	—	—

Night Light Standard
Introduced in 1996 as a limited edition from Springfield distributor Lew Horton this full size Model 1911A1 pistol is chambered for the .45 ACP. It has a lightweight frame and slide with millett night sights with Houge rubber wrap around grips. Fitted with extended beavertail safety. Weight 29 oz.

NIB	Exc.	V.G.	Good	Fair	Poor
620	500	400	300	—	—

Night Light Compact
This model was also introduced by Lew Horton in 1996 and is similar to the above model but fitted with a 4.25" barrel and lightweight frame and slide. Weight is 27 oz.

NIB	Exc.	V.G.	Good	Fair	Poor
620	500	400	300	—	—

Night Compact
Same as above but with a steel frame and slide.

NIB	Exc.	V.G.	Good	Fair	Poor
595	475	375	—	—	—

Omega
A .38 Super, 10mm Norma, or .45 caliber semiautomatic pistol with a 5" or 6" polygon rifled barrel, ported or unported, adjustable sights and Pachmayr grips. Patterned somewhat after the Colt Model 1911. Introduced in 1987.
Caliber Conversion Units-Add $675.

NIB	Exc.	V.G.	Good	Fair	Poor
550	450	350	250	200	125

SPRINGFIELD ARMORY
Springfield, Massachusetts
This was America's first federal armory. It began producing military weapons in 1795. The armory has supplied military weapons to the United States throughout its history.

Model 1841 Cadet Musket
This is a single shot, muzzle-loading rifle chambered for .57 caliber percussion. It has a 40" round barrel with a full-length stock held on by three barrel bands. This rifle features no rear sight. It is browned and case-colored, with iron mountings. There is a steel ramrod mounted under the barrel. The lockplate is marked "Springfield" with the date of manufacture and "US" over an eagle motif. There were approximately 450 produced between 1844 and 1845.

Exc.	V.G.	Good	Fair	Poor
5000	4000	3000	2500	1850

Model 1842 Musket
This is a single shot muzzleloader chambered for .69 caliber percussion. It has a 42" round barrel and a full-length stock held on by three barrel bands. The finish is white with iron mountings and a steel ramrod mounted beneath the barrel. There were a total of approximately 275,000 manufactured between 1844 and 1855 by both the Springfield Armory and the Harper's Ferry Armory. They are so marked.

Courtesy Milwaukee Public Museum, Milwaukee, Wisconsin

Exc.	V.G.	Good	Fair	Poor
1250	1000	750	450	350

Model 1847 Musketoon
This is a single shot muzzleloader chambered for .69 caliber percussion. It has a 26" round smooth bore barrel. The finish is white, with a full-length walnut stock held on by two barrel bands. The lock is marked "Springfield". There were approximately 3,350 manufactured between 1848 and 1859.

Paul Goodwin Photo

Exc.	V.G.	Good	Fair	Poor
1750	1500	1000	850	600

Model 1851 Percussion Cadet Musket
This single shot muzzleloader in .57 caliber with 40" round barrel is almost identical with the Model 1841 Cadet Musket, the main difference and distinguishing feature is the use of the slightly smaller Model 1847 Musketoon lock. Markings are identical as shown for the Model 1841 Cadet Musket. These weapons were made at the Springfield Armory from 1851 to 1853, with total production of 4,000 guns.

Exc.	V.G.	Good	Fair	Poor
2800	1900	1400	1000	500

Model 1855 Musket

Courtesy Milwaukee Public Museum, Milwaukee, Wisconsin

This is a single shot muzzleloader chambered for .58 caliber percussion. It has a 40" round barrel with a full-length stock held on by three barrel bands. It has iron mountings and a ramrod mounted under the barrel. The front sight acts as a bayonet lug. The finish is white with a walnut stock. The lock is marked "U.S. Springfield". There was also a Harper's Ferry manufactured version that is so marked. There were approximately 59,000 manufactured between 1857 and 1861.

Exc.	V.G.	Good	Fair	Poor
1500	1250	1000	750	550

Model 1855 Rifled Carbine

This is a single shot muzzleloader chambered for .54 caliber percussion. It has a 22" round barrel with a 3/4-length stock held on by one barrel band. The finish is white with iron mountings and a ramrod mounted under the barrel. The lock is marked "Springfield" and dated. There were approximately 1,000 manufactured between 1855 and 1856.

Exc.	V.G.	Good	Fair	Poor
3500	3000	2500	1750	1250

Model 1861 Percussion Rifle-Musket

The Model 1861 was the standard musket in use during the Civil War. This .58 caliber single shot muzzleloader has a 40" barrel with three barrel bands and all iron mountings; all metal parts are finished bright (some rear sights are blued) and the stock is walnut. On the lock there is an eagle motif forward of the hammer, US/SPRINGFIELD, beneath the nipple bolster, and the date at the rear section of the lock. About 256,129 of these muskets were made at the Springfield Armory, while almost 750,000 more were made under contract.

Paul Goodwin Photo

Exc.	V.G.	Good	Fair	Poor
2400	1800	1200	900	400

Model 1863 Rifled Musket

This is a single shot muzzleloader chambered for .58 caliber percussion. It has a 40" round barrel and a full-length stock held on by three barrel bands. The finish is white with iron mountings, and the lock is marked "U.S. Springfield" and dated 1863. There were approximately 275,000 manufactured in 1863.

Courtesy Bob Ball

Exc.	V.G.	Good	Fair	Poor
1250	1000	750	600	400

Model 1863 Rifle Musket, Type II, aka Model 1864

This was the last U.S. martial regulation arm of muzzleloading design, and it was widely used during the latter part of the Civil War. Produced at the Springfield Armory between 1864 and 1865, with total production of 25,540 pieces. This weapon is identical to the Type I with the exception of the dating of the lock, which is either 1864 or 1865, a single leaf rear sight, and solid barrel bands secured by flat springs mounted in the stock. The ramrod was either the tulip head type, or the new knurled and slotted design.

Model 1863 Type II lock

Paul Goodwin Photo

Exc.	V.G.	Good	Fair	Poor
2000	1300	1050	700	400

NOTE: For additional Springfield Armory firearms history, technical data, descriptions, photos, and prices see the *Standard Catalog of Military Firearms, 1870 to the Present* under United States, Rifles.

SPRINGFIELD ARMS COMPANY
Springfield, Massachusetts

Dragoon

A .40 caliber percussion revolver with either a 6" or 7.5" round barrel, some fitted with loading levers, others without. The top strap marked "Springfield Arms Company". Blued with walnut grips. Approximately 110 revolvers were manufactured in 1851.

Exc.	V.G.	Good	Fair	Poor
—	—	7500	3500	950

Navy Model

A .36 caliber percussion revolver with a 6" round barrel, centrally mounted hammer, and 6-shot etched cylinder. The top strap marked "Springfield Arms Company". Blued, case hardened with walnut grips. This model was manufactured in two variations, one with a single trigger and the other with a double trigger, the forward one of which locks the cylinder. Both variations had loading levers. Approximately 250 of these pistols were made in 1851.

Exc.	V.G.	Good	Fair	Poor
—	—	3500	1250	400

Belt Model

A .31 caliber percussion revolver with 4", 5", or 6" round barrels, centrally mounted hammer, and an etched 6-shot cylinder. Made with or without a loading lever. Early production versions of this revolver are marked "Jaquith's P___nt 1838" on the frame and later production were mar___ ___ringfield Arms" on the top strap. Approximately 150 ___ ___e.

Exc.	V.G.	Good	Fair	Poor
—	—			

Warner Model

As above, but ___ ___ ___ ___ approx-
imat___ ___

Courtesy Milwaukee Public Museum, Milwaukee, Wisconsin

A .28 caliber percussion revolver with 2.5" round barrel, centrally mounted hammer, no loading lever and etched 6-shot cylinder. Marked "Warner's Patent Jan. 1851" and "Springfield Arms Company". Blued, case hardened with walnut grips. Early production examples of this revolver do not have a groove on the cylinder and have a rounded frame. Approximately 525 were made in 1851.

Exc.	V.G.	Good	Fair	Poor
—	—	700	300	150

Ring Trigger Model

As above, but fitted with a ring trigger that revolved the cylinder. Approximately 150 were made in 1851.

Courtesy Milwaukee Public Museum, Milwaukee, Wisconsin

Exc.	V.G.	Good	Fair	Poor
—	—	900	450	200

Double Trigger Model

As above, with two triggers set within a conventional trigger-guard. The forward trigger revolves the cylinder. Approximately 350 were made in 1851.

Courtesy Milwaukee Public Museum, Milwaukee, Wisconsin

Exc.	V.G.	Good	Fair	Poor
—	—	900	450	200

Late Model Revolver

As above, except that the cylinder is automatically turned when the hammer is cocked. The top strap marked "Warner's Patent/James Warner, Springfield, Mass." Approximately 500 were made in 1851.

Exc.	V.G.	Good	Fair	Poor
—	—	700	300	100

Double Barrel Shotguns

The Springfield Arms Co. was bought by Stevens who used the Springfield brand name on many good quality single and double barrel shotguns. Values range from $100 to $1,600 depending on model, gauge, and condition. See also Stevens.

SQUIBBMAN
SEE—Squires, Bingham Mfg. Co., Inc.
Rizal, Philippine Islands

SQUIRES BINGHAM MFG. CO., INC.
Rizal, Philippine Islands

Firearms produced by this company are marketed under the trademark Squibbman.

Model 100D

A .38 Special caliber double action swingout cylinder revolver with a 3", 4", or 6" ventilated rib barrel, adjustable sights, matte black finish and walnut grips.

Exc.	V.G.	Good	Fair	Poor
150	100	80	60	40

Model 100DC

As above, without the ventilated rib.

Exc.	V.G.	Good	Fair	Poor
150	100	80	60	40

Model 100

As above, with a tapered barrel and uncheckered walnut grips.

Exc.	V.G.	Good	Fair	Poor
150	100	80	60	40

Thunder Chief

As above, but in .22 or .22 Magnum caliber with a heavier ventilated rib barrel, shrouded ejector, and ebony grips.

Exc.	V.G.	Good	Fair	Poor
150	125	100	80	60

STAFFORD, T. J.
New Haven, Connecticut

Pocket Pistol

A .22 caliber single shot spur trigger pistol with a 3.5" octagonal barrel marked "T.J. Stafford New Haven Ct.," silver-plated brass frame and walnut or rosewood grips.

Courtesy W.P. Hallstein III and son Chip

Exc.	V.G.	Good	Fair	Poor
—	—	600	250	100

Large Frame Model

As above, but in .38 rimfire caliber with a 6" barrel.

Exc.	V.G.	Good	Fair	Poor
—	—	850	400	200

STALCAP, ALEXANDER T.F.M.
Nashville, Tennessee

First in business during the 1850s, Stalcap received a contract in 1862, to modify sporting arms for military use. Overall length 50-7/8" to 51-3/4"; octagonal barrels 35-1/4" - 36" turned round at muzzle for socket bayonets; .54 caliber. Rifles assembled with sporting locks, new stocks and brass furniture. At least 102 rifles were delivered in 1862. These arms are unmarked.

Prospective purchasers are strongly advised to secure an expert appraisal prior to acquisition.

Exc.	V.G.	Good	Fair	Poor
—	—	3750	2000	1000

STANDARD ARMS CO.
Wilmington, Delaware

Model G

Chambered for .25-35, .30-30, .25 Remington, .30 Remington, and .35 Remington, with a 22" barrel, and open sights. Integral box magazine and closable gas port that allowed the rifle to be used as a slide action. Blued with a walnut stock. Produced in limited quantities, circa 1910.

Exc.	V.G.	Good	Fair	Poor
—	750	350	250	150

STAR, BONIFACIO ECHEVERRIA
Eibar, Spain
SEE—Echeverria

STARR, EBAN T.
New York, New York

Single Shot Derringer

Courtesy Milwaukee Public Museum, Milwaukee, Wisconsin

A .41 caliber single shot pistol with a pivoted 2.75" round barrel. The hammer mounted on the right side of the frame and the trigger formed in the shape of a button located at the front of the frame. The frame marked "Starr's Pat's May 10, 1864". The brass frame silver-plated, the barrel blued or silver-plated with checkered walnut grips. Manufactured from 1864 to 1869.

Exc.	V.G.	Good	Fair	Poor
—	—	1500	750	200

Four Barreled Pepperbox

A .32 caliber 4 barreled pocket pistol with 2.75" to 3.25" barrels. The frame marked "Starr's Pat's May 10, 1864". Brass frames, silver-plated. The barrel is blued with plain walnut grips. This pistol was produced in six variations as follows:

Courtesy Milwaukee Public Museum, Milwaukee, Wisconsin

First Model

Fluted breech and a barrel release mounted on the right side of the frame.

Exc.	V.G.	Good	Fair	Poor
—	—	1750	700	200

Second Model

Flat breech.

Exc.	V.G.	Good	Fair	Poor
—	—	1300	550	200

Third Model

Rounded breech with a visible firing-pin retaining spring.

Exc.	V.G.	Good	Fair	Poor
—	—	1100	450	150

Fourth Model
Rounded breech without visible springs.

Exc.	V.G.	Good	Fair	Poor
—	—	1100	450	150

Fifth Model
A larger, more angular grip.

Exc.	V.G.	Good	Fair	Poor
—	—	850	400	150

Sixth Model
The frame length of this variation is of increased size.

Exc.	V.G.	Good	Fair	Poor
—	—	1350	650	200

STARR ARMS COMPANY
New York, New York

1858 Navy Revolver
A .36 caliber double action percussion revolver with a 6" barrel and 6-shot cylinder. Blued, case hardened with walnut grips. The frame marked "Starr Arms Co. New York." Approximately 3,000 were made between 1858 and 1860.

Courtesy Milwaukee Public Museum, Milwaukee, Wisconsin

Standard Model

Exc.	V.G.	Good	Fair	Poor
—	—	2750	1100	300

Martially Marked (JT)

Exc.	V.G.	Good	Fair	Poor
—	—	3750	1600	500

A cased pair of Starr double action revolvers was sold at auction for $22,000. Silver-plated and engraved with accessories. Condition is about 70% original silver. Case is in fine condition.
Little John's Auction Service, Inc., May 2001

1858 Army Revolver
A .44 caliber double action percussion revolver with a 6" barrel and 6-shot cylinder. Blued, case hardened with walnut grips. The frame marked "Starr Arms Co. New York". Approximately 23,000 were manufactured.

Exc.	V.G.	Good	Fair	Poor
—	—	2250	1100	300

1863 Army Revolver
Similar to the above, but single action and with an 8" round barrel. Approximately 32,000 were manufactured between 1863 and 1865.

Courtesy Milwaukee Public Museum, Milwaukee, Wisconsin

Exc.	V.G.	Good	Fair	Poor
—	—	2750	1250	350

Percussion Carbine
A .54 caliber breechloading percussion carbine with a 21" round barrel secured by one barrel band. Blued, case hardened with a walnut stock. The lock marked "Starr Arms Co./Yonkers, N.Y."

Courtesy Milwaukee Public Museum, Milwaukee, Wisconsin

Exc.	V.G.	Good	Fair	Poor
—	—	2750	1250	400

Cartridge Carbine
Similar to the above, but in .52 rimfire caliber. Approximately 5,000 were manufactured.

Courtesy Milwaukee Public Museum, Milwaukee, Wisconsin

Exc.	V.G.	Good	Fair	Poor
—	—	2500	1000	350

STEEL CITY ARMS, INC.
Pittsburgh, Pennsylvania

Double Deuce

A .22 caliber stainless steel double action semiautomatic pistol with a 2.5" barrel, 7-shot magazine and plain rosewood grips. Introduced in 1984.

Exc.	V.G.	Good	Fair	Poor
300	250	200	150	100

STENDA WAFFENFABRIK
Suhl, Germany

Pocket Pistol

A 7.65mm semiautomatic pistol similar to the "Beholla," the "Leonhardt," and the "Menta." Stenda took over the production of the Beholla pistol design at the close of WWI. The only major difference in the Stenda design was the elimination of the Beholla's worst feature, the pin that went through the slide and retained the barrel. It was replaced by a sliding catch that anchored it in place and unlocked the slide so that the barrel could be removed without the need of a vise and drift pin. The Stenda pistol can be identified by the fact that there are no holes through the slide and there is a catch on the frame above the trigger. The finish blued, with plastic grips; and the slide is marked "Waffenfabrik Stendawerke Suhl." Approximately 25,000 manufactured before production ceased in 1926.

Exc.	V.G.	Good	Fair	Poor
400	250	200	150	100

STERLING ARMAMENT LTD.
London, England
Importer-Cassi, Inc.
Colorado Springs, Colorado

Parapistol MK 7 C4

A 9mm semiautomatic pistol with a 4" barrel, and detachable magazines of 10-68-round capacity. Black wrinkled paint finish with plastic grips.

NIB	Exc.	V.G.	Good	Fair	Poor
600	475	400	300	200	100

Parapistol MK 7 C8

As above, with a 7.8" barrel.

NIB	Exc.	V.G.	Good	Fair	Poor
625	500	400	300	200	100

Sterling MK 6

A semiautomatic copy of the Sterling submachine gun with a 16.1" barrel, folding metal stock and side mounted magazine. Finished as above.

NIB	Exc.	V.G.	Good	Fair	Poor
1500	950	750	500	300	200

Sterling AR 180

A copy of the Armalite Model AR18, 5.56mm rifle. Finished with either black wrinkled paint or, more rarely, blued.

NIB	Exc.	V.G.	Good	Fair	Poor
1100	750	600	500	350	200

STERLING ARMS CORPORATION
Gasport, New York

Model 283 Target 300

This pistol is similar in appearance to Hi-Standard semiautomatic pistols. Chambered for the .22 Long Rifle cartridge it was offered with 4", 4-1/2", or 8" barrels. Rear sight is adjustable and magazine holds 10 rounds. Grips are black plastic. Weight is approximately 36 oz.

NIB	Exc.	V.G.	Good	Fair	Poor
200	150	125	100	75	60

Model 284 Target 300L

Similar to the above model except for 4-1/2" or 6" tapered barrel with barrel band.

Courtesy John J. Stimson, Jr.

NIB	Exc.	V.G.	Good	Fair	Poor
225	175	125	100	75	60

Model 285 Husky

Similar to the Model 283 with the exception of fixed sights. Offered with 4-1/2" barrel only.

NIB	Exc.	V.G.	Good	Fair	Poor
200	150	125	100	75	60

Model 286 Trapper

Similar to the Model 284 except for fixed sights.

NIB	Exc.	V.G.	Good	Fair	Poor
200	150	125	100	75	60

Model 287 PPL .380

This is a pocketsize semiautomatic pistol chambered for the .380 ACP cartridge. Fitted with a 1" barrel it has a 5-1/4" length overall. Magazine holds 6 rounds. Weight is approximately 22 oz.

NIB	Exc.	V.G.	Good	Fair	Poor
125	75	60	50	40	30

Model PPL .22

This is a small pocket pistol similar to the Model 287 but chambered for the .22 l.r. cartridge. Barrel is 1" long. Pistol weighs about 24 oz.

NIB	Exc.	V.G.	Good	Fair	Poor
175	125	100	75	60	50

Model 300

Similar to the Model 287 but chambered for the .25 ACP cartridge. It has a 2-1/4" barrel with a 6-round magazine. Length is 5" overall and the weight is about 14 oz.

NIB	Exc.	V.G.	Good	Fair	Poor
150	125	100	75	50	40

Model 300S

This is the stainless steel version of the Model 300.

NIB	Exc.	V.G.	Good	Fair	Poor
165	135	115	75	50	40

Model 302

Identical to the Model 300 except that it is chambered for the .22 Long Rifle cartridge.

NIB	Exc.	V.G.	Good	Fair	Poor
150	125	100	75	50	40

Model 302S

Same as above but in stainless steel.

NIB	Exc.	V.G.	Good	Fair	Poor
165	135	115	75	60	50

Model 400

This is a double action semiautomatic pistol chambered for the .380 ACP cartridge with a 3-1/2" barrel. Magazine holds 7 rounds. Pistol is 6-1/2" overall and the weight is approximately 24 oz.

NIB	Exc.	V.G.	Good	Fair	Poor
200	175	150	125	100	75

Model 400S

This is the stainless steel version of the Model 400.

NIB	Exc.	V.G.	Good	Fair	Poor
225	200	175	125	100	75

Model 402

Similar to the Model 400 except chambered for the .22 Long Rifle cartridge.

NIB	Exc.	V.G.	Good	Fair	Poor
150	125	100	75	60	40

Model 450

This is a double action semiautomatic pistol chambered for the .45 ACP cartridge. Magazine holds 8 rounds. The barrel is 4" in length. Fitted with an adjustable rear sight. Blued finish and walnut grips are standard. Weight is about 36 oz.

NIB	Exc.	V.G.	Good	Fair	Poor
375	325	250	200	150	100

Model X-Caliber

A single shot .22 Long Rifle, .22 WMR, .357 Magnum, or .44 Magnum pistol with interchangeable barrels from 8" and 10". Adjustable rear sight. Finger groove grips.

NIB	Exc.	V.G.	Good	Fair	Poor
200	175	150	125	100	75

STEVENS, J. ARMS CO.
Chicopee Falls, Massachusetts

In 1864 this firm began doing business as J. Stevens & Company. In 1888 it was incorporated as the J. Stevens Arms & Tool Company. It operated as such until 1920, when it was taken over by the Savage Arms Company. It has operated as an independent division in this organization since. This company produced a great many firearms—most that were of an affordable nature. They are widely collected, and one interested in them should take advantage of the literature available on the subject.

Vest Pocket Pistol

This is a single shot pocket pistol chambered for the .22 and the .30 rimfire cartridges. The .22 caliber version is rarely encountered and would be worth approximately 25% more than the values illustrated. It has a 2.75" part-octagonal barrel that pivots upward for loading. It has an external hammer and a spur-type trigger. The frame is nickel-plated or blued, with a blued barrel. The odd shaped flared grips are made of rosewood. The first models were marked "Vest Pocket Pistol" only. Later models have the barrels marked "J. Stevens & Co. Chicopee Falls, Mass." There were approximately 1,000 manufactured between 1864 and 1876.

Courtesy Milwaukee Public Museum, Milwaukee, Wisconsin

Exc.	V.G.	Good	Fair	Poor
3300	2200	1650	1000	850

Pocket Pistol

Courtesy Milwaukee Public Museum, Milwaukee, Wisconsin

This is a more conventional-appearing, single shot pocket pistol chambered for either the .22 or the .30 rimfire cartridges. It has a 3.5" part-octagonal barrel that pivots upward for loading. It features a plated brass frame with either a blued or nickel-plated barrel and rosewood, two-piece grips. The barrel is marked "J. Stevens & Co. Chicopee Falls, Mass." There were approximately 15,000 manufactured between 1864 and 1886.

Exc.	V.G.	Good	Fair	Poor
450	325	225	125	100

Gem Pocket Pistol

This is a single shot, derringer-type pocket pistol chambered for either the .22 or .30 rimfire cartridges. It has a 3" part-octagonal barrel that pivots to the side for loading. It has a nickel-plated brass frame with either a blued or plated barrel. It has bird's-head grips made of walnut or rosewood. The barrel is marked "Gem". The Stevens name or address does not appear on this firearm. There were approximately 4,000 manufactured between 1872 and 1890.

Exc.	V.G.	Good	Fair	Poor
1000	800	550	425	300

.41 Caliber Derringer

This is a single shot pocket pistol chambered for the .22 or .31 caliber rimfire cartridge. It has a 4" part-octagonal barrel that pivots upward for loading. It has a spur trigger and an external hammer. The frame is plated brass with a blued barrel. It has walnut bird's-head grips. This firearm is completely unmarked except for a serial number. There were approximately 100 manufactured in 1875.

.22 Caliber

Exc.	V.G.	Good	Fair	Poor
4500	4000	3000	2100	1200

.41 Caliber

Exc.	V.G.	Good	Fair	Poor
4200	3500	2700	1900	1200

Single Shot Pistol

This is a single shot pistol chambered for the .22 or .30 rimfire cartridges. It has a 3.5" part-octagonal barrel that pivots upward for loading. It is quite similar in appearance to the original pocket pistol. It has a plated brass frame and either a blued or nickel-plated barrel with walnut, square-butt grips. The barrel is marked "J. Stevens A&T Co." There were approximately 10,000 manufactured between 1886 and 1896.

Exc.	V.G.	Good	Fair	Poor
450	300	225	175	125

No. 41 Pistol

This is a single shot pocket pistol chambered for the .22 and .30 Short cartridges. It has a 3.5" part-octagonal barrel that pivots upward for loading. It features an external hammer and a spur-type trigger. It has an iron frame with the firing pin mounted in the recoil shield. It is either blued or nickel-plated, with square-butt walnut grips. There were approximately 90,000 manufactured between 1896 and 1916.

Exc.	V.G.	Good	Fair	Poor
400	350	275	225	125

Stevens Tip Up Rifles

This series of rifles was produced by Stevens beginning in the 1870s through 1895. There are a number of variations, but they are all quite similar in appearance. They feature a distinctive sloped frame made of iron and nickel-plated. Most frames are similar in size, but there is a slightly lighter frame used on the "Ladies Model" rifles. These Tip Up rifles are chambered for various calibers from the .22 rimfire to the .44 centerfire cartridges. They are offered with barrel lengths of 24", 26", 28", or 30". The actions are nickel-plated, as well as the triggerguards and the buttplates. The barrels are blued, and the two-piece stocks are of walnut. They are offered with various buttplates and sights. A shotgun version is also offered. There are a number of variations that differ only slightly, and the model numbers are not marked on the rifles. We suggest securing a qualified appraisal if in doubt. The major variations and their values are as follows:

Courtesy Milwaukee Public Museum, Milwaukee, Wisconsin

Ladies Model-.22 or.25 Rimfire Only, 24" or 26" Barrel.

Exc.	V.G.	Good	Fair	Poor
3000	2500	1800	1200	600

Tip Up Rifle-Without Forend

Exc.	V.G.	Good	Fair	Poor
600	500	350	225	175

Tip Up Rifle-With Forend, Swiss-Type Buttplate

Exc.	V.G.	Good	Fair	Poor
950	750	450	325	200

Tip Up Shotgun-All Gauges, 30" or 32" Barrel

Exc.	V.G.	Good	Fair	Poor
350	300	200	150	100

Ideal Single Shot Rifle

This excellent rifle was manufactured by Stevens between 1896 and 1933. It is a single-shot, falling-block type action that is activated by a triggerguard-action lever. It was produced in many popular calibers from .22 rimfire up to .30-40. It was also manufactured in a number of special Stevens calibers. It was offered with various length barrels in many different grades, from plain Spartan starter rifles up to some extremely high-grade Schuetzen-type target rifles with all available options. In 1901 Harry Pope of Hartford, Connecticut, went to work for Stevens and brought his highly respected barrel to the Stevens Company. He remained an employee for only two years, and the firearms produced during this period have the name "Stevens-Pope" stamped on the top of the barrel in addition to the other factory markings. Rifles marked in this manner and authenticated would be worth an approximate 50% premium if they are in very good to excellent condition. Due to numerous variations and options offered, we strongly recommend securing a qualified appraisal, especially on the higher-grade Ideal series rifles, if a transaction is contemplated.

No. 44

This version is chambered for various calibers and is offered with a 24" or 26" barrel. It has an open rear sight with a Rocky Mountain-type front sight. The finish is blued and case colored, with a walnut stock. There were approximately 100,000 manufactured between 1896 and 1933.

Exc.	V.G.	Good	Fair	Poor
1000	800	550	350	195

No. 44-1/2

This rifle is similar in appearance to the No. 44 but features an improved action. It has barrel lengths up to 34" and will be found with the Stevens-Pope barrel. It was manufactured between 1903 and 1916.

Courtesy J. B. Barnes

Exc.	V.G.	Good	Fair	Poor
1600	1400	1100	850	700

No. 044-1/2

This version is also known as the English Model rifle and is similar to the No. 44-1/2 except that it has a shotgun butt and a tapered barrel. There were a number of options offered that would affect the value. It was manufactured between 1903 and 1916.

Courtesy Mike Stuckslager

Exc.	V.G.	Good	Fair	Poor
1600	1400	1100	850	700

No. 45

This version is also known as the Range Rifle, It is chambered for various calibers from the .22 rimfire to .44-40. Its identifying features are the Beach sights with an additional vernier tang sight and a Swiss-type buttstock. It is offered with a 26" or 28" part-octagonal barrel. It was manufactured between 1896 and 1916. Values for a standard version are as follows:

Exc.	V.G.	Good	Fair	Poor
1700	1500	1150	925	725

NOTE: Deduct 25% for .44 action.

No. 46

Same as the No. 45 but with a fancy wood stock. Manufactured from 1896 to 1902. Built in No. 44 action only.

Exc.	V.G.	Good	Fair	Poor
2200	1900	1550	1325	1000

No. 47

This version is similar to the No. 45, with a pistol grip buttstock.

Exc.	V.G.	Good	Fair	Poor
3000	2700	2200	1600	1000

NOTE: Deduct 25% for .44 action.

No. 48

Same as the No. 47 but with a fancy wood checkered stock. Manufactured from 1896 to 1902. Built in a No. 44 action only. This is a very rare model.

Exc.	V.G.	Good	Fair	Poor
4250	3750	2750	1950	1250

No. 49

This model is also known as the "Walnut Hill Rifle." It is a high grade target rifle chambered for many calibers between the .22 rimfire and the .44-40. It is offered with a 28" or 30" part-octagonal barrel that is medium- or heavy-weight. It was furnished with a globe front sight and a vernier tang sight. It is blued with a case-colored frame and has a high-grade, checkered, varnished walnut stock that has a high comb and features a pistol grip, cheekpiece, Swiss-type buttplate, and a loop-type triggerguard lever that resembles that of a lever-action rifle. The receiver is engraved, and there were a number of options available that would increase the value when present. We recommend an appraisal when in doubt. This rifle was manufactured between 1896 and 1916.

Courtesy J.B. Barnes

Exc.	V.G.	Good	Fair	Poor
6000	5500	3300	2100	1600

Model 50

This version is identical to the Model 49 but was offered with a higher-grade walnut stock. This is a very rare model.

Courtesy J.B. Barnes

Exc.	V.G.	Good	Fair	Poor
7000	6500	3900	2500	1800

Model 51

This version is known as the "Schuetzen Rifle" and is quite similar to the No. 49 except that it features double-set triggers, a higher-grade walnut stock, a wooden insert in the trigger-guard action lever, and a heavy, Schuetzen-type buttplate. There were many options available on this model, and we recommend securing an appraisal when in doubt. It was manufactured between 1896 and 1916.

Courtesy J.B. Barnes

Exc.	V.G.	Good	Fair	Poor
10000	8000	5300	3200	2100

No. 52

This version is also known as the "Schuetzen Junior." It is similar to the No. 51 except that it features more engraving and a higher-grade walnut stock. It was manufactured between 1897 and 1916.

Courtesy J.B. Barnes

Courtesy J.B. Barnes

Exc.	V.G.	Good	Fair	Poor
9500	7400	4700	2700	1600

No. 53

This model is the same as the No. 51 except for the addition of a fancy wood stock and palm rest. Produced from 1896 to 1902 and offered only with a No. 44 action. This is a rare rifle.

Exc.	V.G.	Good	Fair	Poor
11500	8750	6000	3750	2500

No. 54

This is similar to the No. 52 except that it has double-set triggers and a palm rest, as well as a heavy, Swiss-style buttplate. It is offered with a 30" or 32" part-octagonal heavy barrel. This was Stevens' top-of-the-line rifle. It was offered with many options, and an appraisal should be secured if in doubt. It was manufactured between 1897 and 1916.

Courtesy J.B. Barnes

Exc.	V.G.	Good	Fair	Poor
14000	12000	8500	6000	5000

NOTE: The above prices are based on a #44-1/2 action. A #44 action will bring 20% less than the prices listed above.

No. 55

This version is one of the Stevens' Ideal Ladies Models. It is chambered for the smaller rimfire calibers between .22 Short and .32 Long rimfire. It features a 24" or 26" part-octagonal barrel with a vernier tang sight. The finish is blued and case-colored, with a checkered pistol grip walnut stock that features a Swiss-type buttplate. This is a lighter weight rifle that was manufactured between 1897 and 1916.

Exc.	V.G.	Good	Fair	Poor
3600	3100	1700	950	700

No. 56

This Ladies' Model rifle is similar to the No. 55 except that it is chambered for centerfire cartridges and has a higher-grade walnut stock. It was made on the improved No. 44-1/2 action. It was manufactured between 1906 and 1916.

Courtesy J.B. Barnes

Exc.	V.G.	Good	Fair	Poor
4000	3300	2150	1400	800

No. 404

This version is chambered for the .22 rimfire cartridge only. It features a 28" round barrel with a globe front sight and a Lyman No. 42 receiver sight. The finish is blued and case-colored. It has a walnut straight-grip stock with a semi-beavertail forend. It features a shotgun-type buttplate. It was manufactured between 1910 and 1916.

Exc.	V.G.	Good	Fair	Poor
1200	1000	800	700	600

No. 414

This version is also known as the Armory Model and is chambered for the .22 l.r. cartridge only. It was built on a No. 44 action and features a 26" round barrel. It has a Rocky Mountain front sight with a Lyman receiver sight at the rear. The finish is blued and case-colored, with a straight-grip walnut stock and forend held on by a single barrel band. It was manufactured between 1912 and 1932.

Courtesy Mike Stuckslager

Exc.	V.G.	Good	Fair	Poor
700	500	400	250	250

No. 417 Walnut Hill Model

This is a heavy single shot, lever action target rifle chambered for the .22 Long Rifle, .22 Short, or .22 Hornet cartridges. Weight is approximately 10.5 lbs. Produced from 1932 to 1940.

Exc.	V.G.	Good	Fair	Poor
1500	1200	800	600	400

No. 417 1/2 Walnut Hill Model

This model is a sporting version of the Model 417. Weight is about 8.5 lbs. Manufactured from 1932 to 1940.

Exc.	V.G.	Good	Fair	Poor
1600	1300	900	700	450

No. 418 Walnut Hill Jr.

This is a light single shot lever action target rifle chambered for .22 Long Rifle or .22 Short. Weight is about 6.5 lbs. Manufactured from 1932 to 1940.

Exc.	V.G.	Good	Fair	Poor
750	600	400	300	175

No. 418 1/2 Walnut Hill Jr.

Similar to the Model 418 but chambered for .25 rimfire or .22 WRF cartridges. It is also fitted with sporting sights. Manufactured from 1932 to 1940.

Exc.	V.G.	Good	Fair	Poor
750	600	400	300	175

BOY'S RIFLES

The Stevens Company produced an extensive line of smaller, single shot rifles chambered for small calibers and intended primarily for use by young shooters. These firearms have become quite collectible and are considered a field of specialty by many modern collectors.

NOTE: There are many variations that were available with a number of options that would affect their value. We supply information and values for the major variations but would recommend securing a qualified appraisal if in doubt.

"FAVORITE" RIFLES

This series of rifles is chambered for the .22, .25, and .32 rimfire. It has a 22" part-octagonal barrel and is blued, with a case-colored frame. It has a takedown-type action with an interchangeable barrel feature. It was available with optional sights, as well as buttplates. There were approximately 1,000,000 manufactured between 1893 and 1939. The variations are as follows:

Courtesy Mike Stuckslager

Courtesy Buffalo Bill Historical Center, Cody, Wyoming

1st Model Favorite

This version is chambered for the .22 or .25 rimfire cartridge. It has a removable sideplate on the right side of the receiver not found on any other variation. There were approximately 1,000 manufactured between 1893 and 1894.

Exc.	V.G.	Good	Fair	Poor
1200	800	650	500	350

No. 17

This is the standard, plain version with open sights.

Exc.	V.G.	Good	Fair	Poor
450	300	250	175	125

No. 20

This version is chambered for the .22 or .32 rimfire shot cartridges and has a smoothbore barrel and no rear sight.

Exc.	V.G.	Good	Fair	Poor
500	350	250	175	125

No. 21

This version is known as the Bicycle rifle and features a 20" barrel with open sights standard. It was furnished with a canvas carrying case that would be worth approximately a 10% premium. It was manufactured between 1898 and 1903.

Exc.	V.G.	Good	Fair	Poor
550	375	250	150	100

No. 21 Ladies Model

This version bears the same model number as the Bicycle rifle but has a 24" barrel and a high grade, checkered walnut stock with a Swiss buttplate. It features a vernier tang sight. It was manufactured between 1910 and 1916.

Exc.	V.G.	Good	Fair	Poor
3700	3100	1700	950	550

No. 16

This version is known as the "Crack Shot." It is chambered for .22 or .32 rimfire cartridges with a 20" round barrel. It has a rolling-block-type action with a thumb lever on the side. It is a utility-type rifle with open sights, a blued and case-colored finish, and a plain two-piece walnut stock with a rubber buttplate. The barrel is marked "Crack Shot" along with the standard Stevens' barrel address markings. It was manufactured between 1900 and 1913.

Exc.	V.G.	Good	Fair	Poor
350	250	125	100	75

No. 16-1/2

This version is similar to the No. 16 except that it is chambered for the .32 rimfire shot cartridge with a smoothbore barrel. It was manufactured between 1900 and 1913.

Exc.	V.G.	Good	Fair	Poor
400	300	175	125	100

No. 23-Sure Shot

This version is chambered for the .22 rimfire cartridge. It has a 20" round barrel that pivots to the right for loading. There is a barrel release on the frame. This version is blued and case-colored, with a plain walnut buttstock and no forend. It was manufactured between 1894 and 1897.

Exc.	V.G.	Good	Fair	Poor
1800	1400	950	700	400

No. 15

This version is also known as the "Maynard Junior." It is chambered for the .22 rimfire cartridge and has an 18" part-octagonal barrel. The action is similar to the Civil War Maynard rifle with a triggerguard-activating lever. The finish is all blued, with a bored-type buttstock and no forearm. The barrel is marked "Stevens Maynard, J. R." in addition to the standard Stevens' barrel address. It was manufactured between 1902 and 1912.

Courtesy Mike Stuckslager

Exc.	V.G.	Good	Fair	Poor
450	350	200	150	100

No. 15-1/2

This is a smoothbore version of the No. 15.

Exc.	V.G.	Good	Fair	Poor
500	400	250	175	125

No. 14

This version is also known as the "Little Scout." It is a utility, takedown rifle that is blued, with a one-piece bored-type stock. It features a rolling-block-type action and was manufactured between 1906 and 1910.

Exc.	V.G.	Good	Fair	Poor
450	350	200	150	100

No. 14-1/2

This version is similar to the No. 14 except that it has a two-piece stock. It is also marked "Little Scout." It was manufactured between 1911 and 1941.

Exc.	V.G.	Good	Fair	Poor
400	300	225	125	100

No. 65

This version is known as the "Little Krag." It is a single shot bolt-action rifle chambered for the .22 rimfire cartridge. It has a one-piece stock and a 20" round barrel that was marked "Little Krag." This version is quite scarce. It was manufactured between 1903 and 1910.

Exc.	V.G.	Good	Fair	Poor
550	450	300	200	100

No. 12

This version is also known as the "Marksman." It is chambered for the .22, .25, and the .32 rimfire cartridges. It has a 22" barrel that pivots upward for loading. It is activated by an S-shaped triggerguard lever. It was manufactured between 1911 and 1930.

Courtesy Mike Stuckslager

Exc.	V.G.	Good	Fair	Poor
400	350	250	200	150

No. 26

This version is also known as the "Crack Shot." It has a rolling block-type action and is chambered for .22 or the .32 rimfire cartridges. It is offered with an 18" or 20" round barrel. It is blued and has a two-piece stock. It was manufactured between 1912 and 1939.

Courtesy Mike Stuckslager

Exc.	V.G.	Good	Fair	Poor
400	350	225	175	100

No. 26-1/2

This is the smoothbore version of the No. 26.

Exc.	V.G.	Good	Fair	Poor
425	375	250	175	100

No. 11-Junior

This is a single shot, rolling block rifle chambered for the .22 rimfire cartridge. It has a 20" barrel, is blued, and has a bore-type stock without a buttplate. This was the last model offered in the Boy's Rifle series. It was manufactured between 1924 and 1931.

Exc.	V.G.	Good	Fair	Poor
350	300	175	100	75

Model 71

This was a reintroduced version of the "Stevens Favorite." It is chambered for the .22 l.r. cartridge and has a 22" octagonal barrel. The finish is blued and case-colored, with a plain walnut stock that has an inlaid medallion and a crescent buttplate. There were 10,000 manufactured in 1971.

Exc.	V.G.	Good	Fair	Poor
350	275	175	100	75

Model 72

This is a reintroduced version of the "Crack Shot" that features a single-shot, falling block action. It is chambered for the .22 rimfire cartridge and has a 22" octagon barrel with open sights. It is blued and case-colored, with a straight walnut stock. It was introduced in 1972.

Exc.	V.G.	Good	Fair	Poor
175	150	125	100	75

Model 70

This is a slide-action rifle chambered for the .22 rimfire cartridge. It is also known as the "Visible Loading Rifle." It features a 20" round barrel with a 3/4-length, tubular magazine. The finish is blued and case-colored, and it has a walnut stock. It features open sights but was available with other options. It was offered as the No. 70-1/2, 71, 71-112, 72, and 72-1/2. These different model numbers denote various sight combinations. Otherwise, they are identical. They were manufactured between 1907 and 1932.

Exc.	V.G.	Good	Fair	Poor
400	350	225	100	75

No. 80

This is a slide-action repeating rifle chambered for the .22 rimfire cartridge. It has a 24" round barrel with a tubular magazine. It features open sights and is blued, with a walnut stock. It was manufactured between 1906 and 1910.

Exc.	V.G.	Good	Fair	Poor
450	350	225	175	100

High Power Rifle

This is a series of lever-action hunting rifles chambered for the .25, .30-30, .32, and the .35 centerfire cartridges. It features a 22" round barrel with a tubular magazine. The finish is blued, with a walnut stock. It is available in four variations: the No. 425, No. 430, No. 435, and the No. 440. These designations denote increased ornamentation and high quality materials and workmanship used in construction. There were approximately 26,000 manufactured between 1910 and 1917.

No. 425

Exc.	V.G.	Good	Fair	Poor
800	700	500	300	200

No. 430

Exc.	V.G.	Good	Fair	Poor
950	750	650	400	300

No. 435

Exc.	V.G.	Good	Fair	Poor
1600	1300	1000	600	400

No. 440

Exc.	V.G.	Good	Fair	Poor
3100	2800	2400	1600	850

Beginning in 1869 the Stevens Company produced a series of single shot, break-open target and sporting pistols that pivot upward for loading. They are chambered for the .22 and the .25 rimfire cartridges, as well as various centerfire cartridges from the .32 short Colt to the .44 Russian. These pistols were made with various barrel lengths and have either a spur trigger or conventional trigger with a guard. They are all single-actions with exposed hammers. The finishes are nickel-plated frames with blued barrels and walnut grips. These variations and their values are as follows:

Six-inch Pocket Rifle

This version is chambered for the .22 rimfire cartridge and has a 6" part-octagonal barrel with open sights. The barrel is marked "J. Stevens & Co. Chicopee Falls, Mass." There were approximately 1,000 manufactured between 1869 and 1886.

Exc.	V.G.	Good	Fair	Poor
500	400	350	200	100

No. 36

This version is known as the Stevens-Lord pistol. It is chambered for various rimfire and centerfire calibers up to .44 Russian. It is offered with a 10" or 12" part-octagonal barrel and features a firing pin in the frame with a bushing. It has a conventional trigger with a spurred triggerguard. It features the standard Stevens' barrel address. It was named after Frank Lord, a target shooter well-known at this time. There were approximately 3,500 manufactured from 1880 to 1911.

Courtesy J.B. Barnes

Exc.	V.G.	Good	Fair	Poor
1500	1200	900	600	350

First Issue Stevens-Conlin

This version is chambered for the .22 or .32 rimfire cartridges. It has a 10" or 12" part-octagonal barrel. It features a plated brass frame with a blued barrel and checkered walnut grips with a weighted buttcap. This version has a spur trigger either with or without a triggerguard. It was named after James Conlin, the owner of a shooting gallery located in New York City. There were approximately 500 manufactured between 1880 and 1884.

Courtesy J.B. Barnes

Exc.	V.G.	Good	Fair	Poor
2500	2100	1600	900	500

Second Issue Stevens-Conlin No. 38

This version is similar to the First Issue, with a conventional trigger and spurred triggerguard, as well as a fully adjustable rear sight. There were approximately 6,000 manufactured between 1884 and 1903.

Exc.	V.G.	Good	Fair	Poor
1400	1200	1000	700	400

No. 37

This version is also known as the Stevens-Gould and was named after a nineteenth century firearms writer. It resembles the No. 38 without the spur on the triggerguard. There were approximately 1,000 manufactured between 1889 and 1903.

Courtesy J.B. Barnes

Exc.	V.G.	Good	Fair	Poor
1800	1600	1200	800	400

No. 35

This version is chambered for the .22 rimfire, the .22 Stevens-Pope, and the .25 Stevens cartridges. It is offered with a 6", 8", 10", or 12.25" part-octagonal barrel. The firing pin has no bushing. It features an iron frame that is either blued or plated with a blued barrel. It has plain walnut grips with a weighted buttcap. It featured open sights. There were approximately 43,000 manufactured between 1923 and 1942.

Exc.	V.G.	Good	Fair	Poor
450	325	275	175	100

NOTE: Longer barrels worth a premium.

A Stevens Lord pistol was sold at auction for $123,500. It was engraved and was the personal property of Buffalo Bill Cody. Fitted with 10" barrel. Chambered for .32 caliber. Grips are mother-of-pearl. Condition was very good. Butterfield & Butterfield, May 1998

No. 35 Target
This version is similar to the No. 35 but has a better quality triggerguard and sights. There were approximately 35,000 manufactured between 1907 and 1916.

Exc.	V.G.	Good	Fair	Poor
500	400	325	200	100

Stevens No. 35 Off-Hand Shot Gun NFA, CURIO OR RELIC

Stevens No. 35 Auto-Shot
The Stevens No. 35 is a .410 bore pistol manufactured by the J. Stevens Arms Co., Chicopee Falls, Massachusetts. It was available with an 8" or 12.25" smooth bore barrel, for 2.5" shells only, in two variations: the **Off-Hand Shot Gun** (1923 to 1929) and the **Auto-Shot** (1929 to 1934). Total production is unknown because the .410 and .22 rimfire variations of the No. 35 share the same serial number range. Researcher Ken Cope estimates total Auto-Shot production was approximately 2,000, and Off-Hand production at 20,000 to 25,000. Production was halted after the government ruled the .410 Stevens to be a "firearm" in the "any other weapon" category under the NFA in 1934, when its retail price was about $12. The Stevens does not possess the same collector appeal as other .410 smooth bore pistols, because (1) its relatively lightweight makes it an uncomfortable shooter, and (2) the gun is not well made.

Off-Hand Shot Gun: Serial range from 1 to 43357

Courtesy John J. Stimson, Jr.

Exc.	V.G.	Good	Fair	Poor
400	250	200	100	75

Auto-Shot
Exc.	V.G.	Good	Fair	Poor
450	300	200	125	100

NOTE: 8" barrel commands a 25 to 50 percent premium.

No. 43
This version is also called the Diamond and was produced in two distinct variations called the First Issue and the Second Issue. The First Issue has a brass frame; and the Second Issue, an iron frame and no firing pin bushing. Otherwise they are quite similar and would be valued the same. They are chambered for the .22 rimfire cartridge and are offered with either a 6" or 10" part-octagonal barrel. The frames are either nickel-plated or blued with blued barrels and square-butt walnut grips. There were approximately 95,000 manufactured between 1886 and 1916.

Paul Goodwin Photo

Exc.	V.G.	Good	Fair	Poor
400	300	250	150	75

NOTE: Add a 25% premium for 10" barrels.

No. 10 Target Pistol
This version was a departure from its predecessors. It very much resembles a semiautomatic pistol but is, in reality, a single-shot. It is chambered for the .22 rimfire cartridge and has an 8" round barrel that pivots upward for loading. It has a steel frame and is blued, with checkered rubber grips. Instead of the usual exposed hammer, this version has a knurled cocking piece that extends through the rear of the frame. There were approximately 7,000 manufactured between 1919 and 1933.

Courtesy John J. Stimson, Jr.

Exc.	V.G.	Good	Fair	Poor
400	300	200	150	100

POCKET RIFLES
This series of pistols is similar to the target and sporting pistols except that these were produced with detachable shoulder stocks that bear the same serial number as the pistol with which they were sold. They are sometimes referred to as Bicycle rifles. The collector interest in these weapons is quite high; but it would behoove one to be familiar with the provisions of the Gun Control Act of 1968 when dealing in or collecting this variation—as when the stock is attached, they can fall into the category of a short-barreled rifle. Some are considered to be curios and relics, and others have been totally declassified; but some models may still be restricted. We strongly recommend securing a qualified, individual appraisal on these highly collectible firearms if a transaction is contemplated.

NOTE: The values we supply include the matching shoulder stock. If the stock number does not match the pistol, the values would be approximately 25% less; and with no stock at all, 50% should be deducted.

Old Model Pocket Rifle
This version is chambered for the .22 rimfire cartridge and has an 8" or 10" part-octagonal barrel. It has a spur trigger and an external hammer on which the firing pin is mounted. The extractor is spring-loaded. It has a plated brass frame, blued barrel, and either walnut or rosewood grips. The shoulder stock is either nickel-plated or black. The barrel is marked "J. Stevens & Co. Chicopee Falls, Mass." There were approximately 4,000 manufactured between 1869 and 1886.

Exc.	V.G.	Good	Fair	Poor
900	700	550	325	200

Reliable Pocket Rifle
This version is chambered for the .22 rimfire cartridge and in appearance is quite similar to the Old Model. The basic difference is that the extractor operates as a part of the pivoting barrel mechanism instead of being spring-loaded. The barrel is marked "J. Stevens A&T Co." There were approximately 4,000 manufactured between 1886 and 1896.

Exc.	V.G.	Good	Fair	Poor
800	625	500	400	300

No. 42 Reliable Pocket Rifle
This version is similar to the first issue Reliable except that it has an iron frame with the firing pin mounted in it without a

bushing. The shoulder stock is shaped differently. There were approximately 8,000 manufactured between 1896 and 1916.

Exc.	V.G.	Good	Fair	Poor
700	575	475	350	250

First Issue New Model Pocket Rifle

This version is the first of the medium-frame models with a frame width of 1". All of its predecessors have a 5/8" wide frame. This model is chambered for the .22 and .32 rimfire cartridges and is offered with barrel lengths of 10", 12", 15", or 18" that are part-octagonal in configuration. The external hammer has the firing pin mounted on it. It has a plated brass frame, blued barrel, and either walnut or rosewood grips. The shoulder stock is nickel-plated and fitted differently than the small-frame models in that there is a dovetail in the butt and the top leg is secured by a knurled screw. The barrel is marked "J. Stevens & Co. Chicopee Falls, Mass." There were approximately 8,000 manufactured between 1872 and 1875.

Courtesy Mike Stuckslager

Exc.	V.G.	Good	Fair	Poor
800	700	550	400	300

Second Issue New Model Pocket Rifle

This version is similar to the First Issue except that the firing pin is mounted in the frame with a bushing. There were approximately 15,000 manufactured between 1875 and 1896.

Paul Goodwin Photo

Exc.	V.G.	Good	Fair	Poor
700	600	500	400	300

Vernier Model

This version is similar to the Second Issue except that it features a vernier tang sight located on the back strap. There were approximately 1,500 manufactured between 1884 and 1896.

Exc.	V.G.	Good	Fair	Poor
850	650	550	450	200

No. 40

This version is similar to its medium-frame predecessors except that it has a longer grip frame and a conventional trigger with triggerguard. There were approximately 15,000 manufactured between 1896 and 1916.

Exc.	V.G.	Good	Fair	Poor
700	600	500	300	200

No. 40-1/2

This version is similar to the No. 40, with a vernier tang sight mounted on the back strap. There were approximately 2,500 manufactured between 1896 and 1915.

Exc.	V.G.	Good	Fair	Poor
800	700	600	500	350

No. 34 (Hunter's Pet)

This is the first of the heavy-frame pocket rifles that featured a 1.25" wide frame. This version is also known as the "Hunter's Pet". It is chambered for many popular cartridges from the .22 rimfire to the .44-40 centerfire. It is offered with a part-octagonal 18", 20", 22", or 24" barrel. It has a nickel-plated iron frame and blued barrel. The detachable stock is nickel-plated, and the grips are walnut. There were few produced with a brass frame; and if located, these would be worth twice the value indicated. The firing pin is mounted in the frame with the bushing, and it features a spur trigger. There were approximately 4,000 manufactured between 1872 and 1900.

Exc.	V.G.	Good	Fair	Poor
950	800	500	350	250

A factory engraved Stevens No. 34 Hunter's Pet was sold at auction for $6,900. Fitted with an 18" barrel and telescope sight. Checkered walnut grips with gold plated frame. Condition was excellent as refinished. Butterfield & Butterfield, November 1999

No. 34-1/2

This version is similar to the No. 34 except that it features a vernier tang sight mounted on the back strap. There were approximately 1,200 manufactured between 1884 and 1900.

Exc.	V.G.	Good	Fair	Poor
1100	950	675	500	350

STEVENS BOLT ACTION UTILITY RIFLES

The Stevens Company produced a number of inexpensive, utilitarian, bolt-action rifles. These were both single-shot and repeaters. They have been popular over the years as starter rifles for young shooters. Their values are quite similar, and we list them for reference purposes only.

Model 053—Single Shot
Model 056—5-Shot Magazine
Model 066—Tube Magazine
Model 083—Single Shot
Model 084—5-Shot Magazine
Model 086—Tube Magazine
Model 15—Single Shot
Model 15Y—Single Shot
Model 419—Single Shot
Model 48—Single Shot
Model 49—Single Shot
Model 50—Single Shot
Model 51—Single Shot
Model 52—Single Shot
Model 53—Single Shot
Model 56—5-Shot Magazine
Model 66—Tube Magazine

Exc.	V.G.	Good	Fair	Poor
—	200	100	70	50

Model 416

This is a target rifle chambered for the .22 l.r. cartridge. It has a 24" heavy barrel with aperture sights. It features a 5-round detachable magazine and is blued, with a target-type walnut stock.

Exc.	V.G.	Good	Fair	Poor
450	350	200	150	100

Model 322

This is a bolt-action sporting rifle chambered for the .22 Hornet cartridge. It has a 20" barrel with open sights and a detachable box magazine. The finish is blued, with a plain walnut stock.

Exc.	V.G.	Good	Fair	Poor
175	125	100	75	50

Model 322-S

This version features an aperture rear sight.

Exc.	V.G.	Good	Fair	Poor
225	125	100	75	50

Model 89

This is a single shot, Martini-type, falling-block rifle chambered for the .22 l.r. cartridge. It has an 18.5" barrel and a trigger-guard loop-lever activator. The finish is blued, with a straight walnut stock. It was introduced in 1976 and is no longer manufactured.

Exc.	V.G.	Good	Fair	Poor
125	80	70	60	40

Model 87M

Designed to look like the M1 Garand this rifle was chambered for the .22 rimfire cartridge.

Courtesy Richard M. Kumor, Sr.

Exc.	V.G.	Good	Fair	Poor
600	500	375	—	—

Model 987

This is a blowback-operated semiautomatic rifle chambered for the .22 l.r. cartridge. It has a 20" barrel with a 15-round tubular magazine. The finish is blued, with a hardwood stock.

Exc.	V.G.	Good	Fair	Poor
150	100	90	80	60

STEVENS SINGLE SHOT SHOTGUNS

This company manufactured a number of single barrel, break-open, single-shot shotguns. They were produced chambered for various gauges with various-length barrels and chokes. They are quite similar in appearance and were designed as inexpensive, utility-grade weapons. There is little or no collector interest in them at this time, and their values are similar. We list them for reference purposes only.

Model 100	Model 125	Model 94
Model 102	Model 140	Model 944
Model 104	Model 160	Model 94A
Model 105	Model 165	Model 94C
Model 106	Model 170	Model 95
Model 107	Model 180	Model 958
Model 108	Model 89	Model 97
Model 110	Model 90	Model 970
Model 120	Model 93	

Model 107

Model 94C

Exc.	V.G.	Good	Fair	Poor
150	100	75	50	25

Model 182

This is a single shot, break-open shotgun chambered for 12 gauge. It is offered with a 30" or 32" trap choked barrels and features a hammerless action with an automatic ejector and a lightly engraved receiver. The finish is blued, with a checkered trap-grade stock.

Exc.	V.G.	Good	Fair	Poor
175	125	100	75	50

Model 185

This version features a half-octagonal barrel with an automatic ejector and a checkered walnut stock.
Damascus Barrel-Deduct 25%.

Exc.	V.G.	Good	Fair	Poor
175	125	100	75	50

Model 190

This is a 12-gauge hammerless gun with an automatic ejector. It is lightly engraved with a half-octagonal barrel.
Damascus Barrel-Deduct 25%.

Exc.	V.G.	Good	Fair	Poor
175	125	100	75	50

Model 195

This is another deluxe version that features engraving, a half-octagonal barrel, and a high-grade, checkered walnut stock.
Damascus Barrel-Deduct 25%.

Exc.	V.G.	Good	Fair	Poor
350	250	200	150	100

Model 240

This over and under model features a boxlock frame with exposed hammers.

Exc.	V.G.	Good	Fair	Poor
400	300	250	200	150

STEVENS DOUBLE BARREL SHOTGUNS

The firm of J. Stevens and its successors produced a number of utility-grade, side-x-side double-barrel shotguns between 1877 and 1988. They are chambered for 10, 12, 16, or 20 gauge as well as the .410 bore. Stevens shotguns in 10 gauge and .410 bore will normally bring a premium as do guns with single triggers and ejectors. They have various length barrels and choke combinations. They feature double triggers and extractors except where noted. A complete list of Stevens brand models including the three in-house brands: Riverside, Springfield, and Super Value follow:

STEVENS BRAND

Model 1877-Hammer Boxlock

NIB	Exc.	V.G.	Good	Fair	Poor
1000	500	400	300	250	200

Model 250-Hammer Sidelock

NIB	Exc.	V.G.	Good	Fair	Poor
1000	500	400	300	250	200

Model 225-Hammer Boxlock

Courtesy Nick Niles. Photo Paul Goodwin

NIB	Exc.	V.G.	Good	Fair	Poor
1000	500	400	300	250	200

Model 260-Hammer Sidelock

NIB	Exc.	V.G.	Good	Fair	Poor
1000	500	400	300	250	200

Model 270-Hammer Sidelock

NIB	Exc.	V.G.	Good	Fair	Poor
1000	500	400	300	250	200

Model 280-Hammer Sidelock

NIB	Exc.	V.G.	Good	Fair	Poor
1000	500	400	300	250	200

Model 325-Hammerless Boxlock

NIB	Exc.	V.G.	Good	Fair	Poor
800	400	350	300	250	200

Model 350-Hammerless Boxlock

NIB	Exc.	V.G.	Good	Fair	Poor
800	400	350	300	250	200

Model 360-Hammerless Boxlock

NIB	Exc.	V.G.	Good	Fair	Poor
800	400	350	300	250	200

Model 370-Hammerless Boxlock

NIB	Exc.	V.G.	Good	Fair	Poor
800	400	350	300	250	200

Model 380-Hammerless Boxlock

NIB	Exc.	V.G.	Good	Fair	Poor
1000	500	400	350	250	200

Model 235-Hammer Boxlock

NIB	Exc.	V.G.	Good	Fair	Poor
800	400	350	300	250	200

Model 335 (Early)-Hammerless Boxlock

Courtesy Nick Niles. Photo Paul Goodwin

NIB	Exc.	V.G.	Good	Fair	Poor
800	400	350	300	250	200

Model 255-Hammer Sidelock

NIB	Exc.	V.G.	Good	Fair	Poor
800	400	350	300	250	200

Model 265-Hammer Sidelock

Courtesy Nick Niles. Photo Paul Goodwin

NIB	Exc.	V.G.	Good	Fair	Poor
800	400	350	300	250	200

Model 355-Hammerless Boxlock

NIB	Exc.	V.G.	Good	Fair	Poor
1400	700	500	400	300	250

Model 365-Hammerless Boxlock

Courtesy Nick Niles. Photo Paul Goodwin

NIB	Exc.	V.G.	Good	Fair	Poor
1600	800	550	450	350	300

Model 375 (London Proofs)-Hammerless Boxlock

NIB	Exc.	V.G.	Good	Fair	Poor
2400	1200	800	600	400	350

Model 375 (U.S.)-Hammerless Boxlock

NIB	Exc.	V.G.	Good	Fair	Poor
1800	900	600	500	350	300

Model 385 (London Proofs)-Hammerless Boxlock

NIB	Exc.	V.G.	Good	Fair	Poor
2800	1400	900	600	400	350

Model 385 (U.S.)-Hammerless Boxlock

NIB	Exc.	V.G.	Good	Fair	Poor
2000	1000	750	500	400	250

Model 345-Hammerless Boxlock

Courtesy Nick Niles, Photo Paul Goodwin

NIB	Exc.	V.G.	Good	Fair	Poor
1000	500	400	300	250	200

Model 335 (Late)-Hammerless Boxlock

NIB	Exc.	V.G.	Good	Fair	Poor
800	400	350	300	250	200

Model 330-Hammerless Boxlock

NIB	Exc.	V.G.	Good	Fair	Poor
800	400	350	300	250	200

Stevens Model 330 early fork type cocking lever (early)

Stevens Model 330 late spade type cocking lever (late)

Model 331-Single Trigger Hammerless Boxlock

NIB	Exc.	V.G.	Good	Fair	Poor
900	450	350	300	250	200

Model 530-Hammerless Boxlock

NIB	Exc.	V.G.	Good	Fair	Poor
800	400	350	300	250	200

Model 515-Hammerless Boxlock

NIB	Exc.	V.G.	Good	Fair	Poor
1100	550	450	400	350	300

Model 515-Single Trigger Hammerless Boxlock

NIB	Exc.	V.G.	Good	Fair	Poor
1200	600	500	400	300	250

Model 500-Skeet Hammerless Boxlock

Courtesy Nick Niles. Photo Paul Goodwin

NIB	Exc.	V.G.	Good	Fair	Poor
2000	1000	800	700	600	400

Model 530M-Tenite Hammerless Boxlock

NIB	Exc.	V.G.	Good	Fair	Poor
800	400	350	300	250	200

Model 530M-Tenite Single Trigger Hammerless Boxlock

NIB	Exc.	V.G.	Good	Fair	Poor
1200	600	500	400	350	300

Model 530A-Hammerless Boxlock

Courtesy Nick Niles. Photo Paul Goodwin

NIB	Exc.	V.G.	Good	Fair	Poor
800	400	350	300	250	200

Model 530A-Single Trigger Hammerless Boxlock

NIB	Exc.	V.G.	Good	Fair	Poor
900	450	400	350	300	250

Stevens Model 311   Courtesy Nick Niles

Model 311-Tenite Hammerless Boxlock

NIB	Exc.	V.G.	Good	Fair	Poor
800	400	350	300	250	200

Model 311-Tenite Single Trigger Hammerless Boxlock

NIB	Exc.	V.G.	Good	Fair	Poor
1000	500	450	400	350	300

Model 311A-Hammerless Boxlock

NIB	Exc.	V.G.	Good	Fair	Poor
800	400	350	300	250	200

Model 311C-Hammerless Boxlock

Courtesy Nick Niles. Photo Paul Goodwin

NIB	Exc.	V.G.	Good	Fair	Poor
700	350	300	250	200	150

Model 311D-Hammerless Boxlock

Courtesy Nick Niles. Photo Paul Goodwin

NIB	Exc.	V.G.	Good	Fair	Poor
800	400	350	300	250	200

Model 311E-Hammerless Boxlock

NIB	Exc.	V.G.	Good	Fair	Poor
1000	500	400	350	300	250

Model 311 F-Hammerless Boxlock

NIB	Exc.	V.G.	Good	Fair	Poor
800	400	350	300	250	200

Model 311H-Hammerless Boxlock

NIB	Exc.	V.G.	Good	Fair	Poor
800	400	350	300	250	200

Model 311H-Vent Rib Hammerless Boxlock

Courtesy Nick Niles. Photo Paul Goodwin

NIB	Exc.	V.G.	Good	Fair	Poor
900	450	400	350	300	250

Model 311J/R-Hammerless Boxlock

Courtesy Nick Niles. Photo Paul Goodwin

NIB	Exc.	V.G.	Good	Fair	Poor
700	350	300	250	200	150

Model 311J/R-Solid Rib Hammerless Boxlock

NIB	Exc.	V.G.	Good	Fair	Poor
700	350	300	250	200	150

Model 311H-Waterfowler Hammerless Boxlock

NIB	Exc.	V.G.	Good	Fair	Poor
1200	600	500	400	300	200

Model 240-.410 Over/Under Hammer Tenite

NIB	Exc.	V.G.	Good	Fair	Poor
600	500	400	300	250	200

RIVERSIDE BRAND

Model 215 Hammer Boxlock

Courtesy Nick Niles. Photo Paul Goodwin

NIB	Exc.	V.G.	Good	Fair	Poor
1300	650	450	350	250	200

Model 315 (Early)-Hammerless Boxlock

NIB	Exc.	V.G.	Good	Fair	Poor
1000	500	400	350	250	200

Model 315 (Late)-Hammerless Boxlock

NIB	Exc.	V.G.	Good	Fair	Poor
1000	500	400	350	250	200

SUPER VALUE BRAND

Model 511-Hammerless Boxlock

NIB	Exc.	V.G.	Good	Fair	Poor
900	450	350	300	200	150

Model 511-Sunken Rib Hammerless Boxlock

NIB	Exc.	V.G.	Good	Fair	Poor
800	400	350	300	200	150

SPRINGFIELD BRAND

Model 215-Hammer Boxlock

NIB	Exc.	V.G.	Good	Fair	Poor
1000	500	400	350	250	150

Model 311-Hammerless Boxlock

Courtesy Nick Niles. Photo Paul Goodwin

NIB	Exc.	V.G.	Good	Fair	Poor
800	400	350	300	250	150

Model 315-Hammerless Boxlock

Courtesy Nick Niles. Photo Paul Goodwin

NIB	Exc.	V.G.	Good	Fair	Poor
1000	500	400	350	250	200

Model 3150-Hammerless Boxlock

NIB	Exc.	V.G.	Good	Fair	Poor
1200	600	500	350	250	200

Model 3151-Hammerless Boxlock

NIB	Exc.	V.G.	Good	Fair	Poor
1500	750	600	400	300	200

Model 3151-Single Trigger Hammerless Boxlock

NIB	Exc.	V.G.	Good	Fair	Poor
1600	800	700	500	400	300

Model 311-Single Trigger Hammerless Boxlock

NIB	Exc.	V.G.	Good	Fair	Poor
1400	700	600	500	400	200

Model 5151-Hammerless Boxlock

Courtesy Nick Niles. Photo Paul Goodwin

NIB	Exc.	V.G.	Good	Fair	Poor
1000	500	400	350	250	200

Model 5151-Single Trigger Hammerless Boxlock

NIB	Exc.	V.G.	Good	Fair	Poor
1200	600	450	350	250	200

Model 311-New Style Hammerless Boxlock

Courtesy Nick Niles. Photo Paul Goodwin

NIB	Exc.	V.G.	Good	Fair	Poor
800	350	300	250	150	100

Model 311-New Style Tenite Hammerless Boxlock

NIB	Exc.	V.G.	Good	Fair	Poor
800	400	350	300	250	150

Model 511-Sunken Rib Hammerless Boxlock

NIB	Exc.	V.G.	Good	Fair	Poor
800	400	300	250	200	150

Model 511-Hammerless Boxlock

NIB	Exc.	V.G.	Good	Fair	Poor
900	450	300	250	200	150

Model 511A-Hammerless Boxlock

NIB	Exc.	V.G.	Good	Fair	Poor
900	450	300	250	200	150

STEVENS DATE CODE

Collectors will find a date code stamped on every double-barrel shotgun in the Stevens brands produced between March 1949 and December 1968. Usually, it is behind the hinge pin or ahead of the triggerguard on the bottom of the frame. It will appear as a small circle containing a number and letter. The letters correspond to the years shown in the following table. Significance of the numbers is not known.

DATE CODES			
A-1949	B-1950	C-1951	D-1952
E-1953	F-1954	G-1955	H-1956
I-1957	J-1958	K-1959	L-1960
M-1961	N-1962	P-1963	R-1964
S-1965	T-1966	U-1967	V-1968
W-1969	X-1970		

STEVENS BOLT ACTION SHOTGUNS

The Stevens Company produced a number of bolt-action shotguns that are either single shot or repeaters. They are chambered for the 20 gauge or .410 and are blued, with walnut stocks. The values for these utility-grade shotguns are similar.

Model 237—Single Shot   Model 39—Tube Magazine
Model 258—Clip Fed   Model 58—Clip Fed
Model 37—Single Shot   Model 59—Tube Magazine
Model 38—Clip Fed

Model 58

Exc.	V.G.	Good	Fair	Poor
125	100	75	50	35

STEVENS SLIDE ACTION UTILITY GRADE SHOTGUNS

The J. Stevens Arms Company also produced a series of utility-grade slide-action shotguns. They are chambered for various gauges with various barrel lengths and chokes. The finishes are blued, with walnut stocks. The values are similar, and we list them for reference purposes as follows:

Model 520	Model 67	Model 77-AC
Model 522	Model 67-VR	Model 77-M
Model 620	Model 77	Model 820
Model 621	Model 77-SC	

Model 67

Exc.	V.G.	Good	Fair	Poor
200	150	125	100	75

Model 620 U.S. Marked Trench Gun

Courtesy Richard M. Kumor Sr.

Exc.	V.G.	Good	Fair	Poor
1200	975	600	—	—

NOTE: Add $150 for bayonet.

Model 124

This is a recoil-operated semiautomatic shotgun chambered for 12 gauge. It has a 28" barrel with various chokes, is blued, and has a brown plastic stock.

Exc.	V.G.	Good	Fair	Poor
150	100	75	65	50

Model 67

This is a slide-action shotgun chambered for 12 and 20 gauge, as well as .410. It has 3" chambers. It is offered with various length barrels and choke tubes with a 5-shot tube magazine. It features a steel receiver and is blued, with a walnut stock. It was discontinued in 1989.

Exc.	V.G.	Good	Fair	Poor
250	175	150	100	75

Model 675

This is a slide-action shotgun chambered for 12 gauge with a 24" vent rib barrel with iron sights. The finish is blued, with a hardwood stock and recoil pad. It was manufactured in 1987 and 1988.

Exc.	V.G.	Good	Fair	Poor
300	250	200	150	100

Model 69-RXL

This is a matte-finished riot version of the Model 67 series slide-action shotgun. It has an 18.25" cylinder-bore barrel and is furnished with a recoil pad. It was discontinued in 1989.

Exc.	V.G.	Good	Fair	Poor
250	175	150	100	75

STEYR
Steyr, Austria

STEYR & MANNLICHER PISTOLS
Text and prices furnished by Joseph Schroeder.

Not all Mannlicher pistols were made by Steyr, and many of the pistols made by Steyr were not designed by Mannlicher. However, since by far the greatest number of Mannlicher's pistols were made by Steyr we believe it will be appropriate to include all of Ferdinand Ritter von Mannlicher's pistols along with other Steyr designs under this heading.

Schoenberger

Considered by many to be the first "commercial" semiautomatic pistol even though apparently at the most only about two dozen were made in 1892. The Steyr-made 8mm Schoenberger was based on patents granted to Laumann in 1890-91 and had a magazine in front of the triggerguard.

Too rare to price.

Mannlicher Model 1894

Mannlicher's first "successful" self-loading pistol, the Model 1894 had a blow-forward action and double action lockwork. Earliest examples were made in Austria, probably by Steyr, in 7.6mm but the greatest number were made by SIG in 1896-97 for Swiss army tests. These 100 pistols had a shorter barrel and smaller frame and were in 6.5mm. Prices are for Swiss examples; add 20% for 7.6mm pistols.

Courtesy Rock Island Auction Company

Exc.	V.G.	Good	Fair	Poor
12000	9000	6000	5000	3000

Mannlicher Model 1896/03

This is one of the most confusing of Mannlicher's pistols. Earliest examples, which have a fixed magazine and ribbed barrel, may have been made by Steyr and are very rare. Later versions, with a removable box magazine, have been called "Model 1896/03" and "Model 1901", and were made as both a pistol and pistol-carbine, possibly in Switzerland. Chambered for the 7.65mm Mannlicher cartridge, which is really a 7.65mm Borchardt. Prices shown are for the standard later model pistol or pistol-carbine (12" barrel, tangent sight); double prices for early pistol or late model pistol with detachable holster stock.

Courtesy Joseph Schroeder

Exc.	V.G.	Good	Fair	Poor
6500	4500	3000	2000	1500

Mannlicher Model 1899

Earliest version of Mannlicher's final semiautomatic pistol design, only about 250 were made by Dreyse in Soemmerda, Germany. Chambered for a tapered case 7.63mm Mannlicher cartridge. Distinguished by the large safety lever on the left side, takedown screw under the barrel, and the Dreyse markings.

Courtesy Joseph Schroeder

Exc.	V.G.	Good	Fair	Poor
7500	5000	4000	3000	1500

Mannlicher Model 1901

Marked "WAFFENFABRIK Steyr" on the left side and "SYSTEM MANNLICHER" on the right, the Model 1901 is distinguished by its checkered grips, rear sight located on the rear of the barrel, 8-round fixed magazine, and serial numbers to a little over 1000.

Courtesy Joseph Schroeder

Exc.	V.G.	Good	Fair	Poor
2500	1800	1400	900	700

Mannlicher Model 1905

Improved version of the Model 1901, with longer grip holding 10 rounds, grooved wooden grips, rear sight on rear of breech-block, and "MODEL 1905" added to right side. Later production moved all markings to the left side so Argentine crest could be placed on right side. Prices shown are for an original commercial Model 1905, NOT a reblued Argentine contract with the crest ground off.

Courtesy Joseph Schroeder

Exc.	V.G.	Good	Fair	Poor
1850	1250	900	600	400

Argentine Contract (Original crest on right side)

Exc.	V.G.	Good	Fair	Poor
2000	1500	1000	750	500

Roth Steyr Model 1907

Based on the patents granted to Karel Krnka and Georg Roth, the 8mm Model 1907 had a rotating barrel locking system and was the first self-loading pistol adopted by the Austro-Hungarian Army. Add 20% for early Steyr examples without a large pin visible on right side of frame, or for those made in Budapest instead of Steyr.

Courtesy Joseph Schroeder

Exc.	V.G.	Good	Fair	Poor
750	600	500	350	250

Steyr Model 1908 Pocket Pistol

Based on the Belgian patents of Nicholas Pieper, these .25 and .32 caliber pocket pistols featured tipping barrels were built by Steyr under license from Pieper in Liege. Production was suspended during WWI but may have resumed after the war ended. Prices are for either caliber.

Exc.	V.G.	Good	Fair	Poor
300	200	125	100	75

Steyr Hahn Model 1911

Commercially marked

Exc.	V.G.	Good	Fair	Poor
1350	1000	750	500	350

Austrian Military

Exc.	V.G.	Good	Fair	Poor
375	300	200	150	100

Chelean or Rumanian Military

Exc.	V.G.	Good	Fair	Poor
450	375	300	250	200

German WWII Issue (P.08 marked)

Exc.	V.G.	Good	Fair	Poor
500	450	325	250	200

Steyr Model SP

Steyr's first post WWII pistol, the Model SP was a beautifully made .32ACP which, being double action only and more expensive than most of its contemporaries, was not competitive and was discontinued in the early '60s after fewer than 1,000 were made. Slide marked "STEYR-DAIMLER-PUCH A.G. MOD.SP KAL. 7.65mm."

Courtesy Joseph Schroeder

Exc.	V.G.	Good	Fair	Poor
850	750	500	350	200

Steyr Model GB

The GB was introduced in the mid '70s as a 9mm Parabellum military pistol, large in size but with an 18-round magazine capacity. Other features included polygon rifling and a gas trap around the barrel to delay breech opening. Initially produced as the Rogak P-18 by L.E.S. of Morton Grove, Illinois but discontinued due in part to quality control problems after just over 2,000 were made. Later production by Steyr as the GB was to much higher standards, but the GB never achieved much popularity and was discontinued in 1988.

Rogak P-18

Exc.	V.G.	Good	Fair	Poor
375	325	225	175	125

Steyr GB

Exc.	V.G.	Good	Fair	Poor
550	450	325	250	200

RIFLES

Steyr Mannlicher Model 1950

A .257 Roberts, .270 Winchester, or .30-06 caliber bolt-action sporting rifle with a 24" barrel and 5-shot rotary magazine. Blued with a checkered walnut stock having an ebony pistol grip cap and forend tip. Manufactured from 1950 to 1952.

Exc.	V.G.	Good	Fair	Poor
1250	1000	800	650	500

Model 1950 Carbine

As above, with a 20" barrel and Mannlicher-style stock. Fitted with a steel forend cap. Manufactured in 1950 to 1952.

Exc.	V.G.	Good	Fair	Poor
1300	1050	900	700	350

Model 1952

Similar to the above, with a swept back bolt handle. Manufactured from 1952 to 1956.

Exc.	V.G.	Good	Fair	Poor
1500	1200	1000	750	600

Model 1952 Carbine

As above, with a 20" barrel and Mannlicher-style stock.

Exc.	V.G.	Good	Fair	Poor
1500	1200	1000	750	600

Model 1956 Rifle

Similar to the above, in .243 and .30-06 caliber with a 22" barrel and high comb stock. Manufactured from 1956 to 1960.

Exc.	V.G.	Good	Fair	Poor
1250	1100	950	800	650

Model 1956 Carbine

As above, with a 20" barrel and Mannlicher-style stock. Manufactured from 1956 to 1960.

Exc.	V.G.	Good	Fair	Poor
1450	1100	900	700	600

Model 1961 MCA Rifle

As above, with a Monte Carlo-style stock.

Exc.	V.G.	Good	Fair	Poor
1350	1200	1000	850	700

Model 1961 MCA Carbine

As above, with a Mannlicher-style Monte Carlo stock.

Exc.	V.G.	Good	Fair	Poor
1450	1250	1100	700	600

THE FOLLOWING STEYR/MANNLICHER GUNS ARE CURRENTLY IMPORTED BY GSI INC. TRUSSVILLE, ALABAMA

NOTE: Steyr Mannlicher has been for sale for the past year. The present owner of Steyr has sold the land that the factory is located on and that factory and its future owner will have to move locations. Currently GSI Inc. is no longer receiving shipments of Steyr Mannlicher rifles or handguns, nor does GSI, Inc. anticipate futher deliveries. Future sales of Steyr Mannlicher firearms are up to the new owners. When the situation is clarified we will inform our readers.

SPORTER SERIES

This series includes rifles that are lightweight and have a reduced overall length. All Sporter models have an interchangeable 5-round rotary magazine. The stock is oil-finished walnut in either the Mannlicher full stock design or the half stock version. In both stock configurations an oval European cheekpiece is standard. These rifles are offered in four different action lengths: **SL** (super light), **L** (light), **M** (medium), or **S** (magnum). They are also available with either single trigger or double set triggers.

Model M72 L/M

A .243, .270, 7x57mm, 7x64mm, .308 or .30-06 caliber bolt-action rifle with a 23" fluted barrel, and single or double set triggers. Blued, checkered walnut stock. Manufactured from 1972 to 1980.

Exc.	V.G.	Good	Fair	Poor
1100	850	650	500	400

Model SL

This model features the super light action and is offered with 20" barrel in full stock version or 23-1/6" barrel in half stock version. A rubber buttpad is standard. This model does not have a forend tip on its half stock variation. Offered in the following calibers: .222 Rem., .222 Rem. Mag., .223, and 5.6x50 Mag. Weighs approximately 6.2 lbs. with full stock and 6.3 lbs. with half stock.

NIB	Exc.	V.G.	Good	Fair	Poor
1850	1650	1000	750	500	300

Model SL Carbine

As above, with a 20" fluted barrel and Mannlicher-style stock.

NIB	Exc.	V.G.	Good	Fair	Poor
1950	1750	1050	800	550	350

Varmint Model

This model features a heavy 26" barrel chambered for the .222 Rem., .223, 5.6x57, .243 Win., .308 Win., and .22-250. The forend of the stock is ventilated. The grip is enlarged and textured. Choice of single or double set triggers. Recoil pad is standard. Weighs about 8 lbs.

NIB	Exc.	V.G.	Good	Fair	Poor
1950	1750	1050	800	550	350

Model L

This rifle has the light action and is offered in the same stock configuration and barrel lengths as the Model SL. The calibers are: 5.6x57, .243 Win., .308, .22-250, and 6mm Rem. Weighs about 6.3 lbs. with full stock and 6.4 lbs. with half stock.

NIB	Exc.	V.G.	Good	Fair	Poor
1850	1650	1000	750	500	300

Luxus Series

This luxury model offers a choice of full or half stock variations in select walnut with fine line checkering. The pistol grip is steeply angled. The Luxus rifles are fitted with a swept back European cheekpiece. A single set trigger is standard. The box magazine holds 3 rounds. Optional engraving and stock carving may be encountered on these modes that will dramatically affect price. The Luxus rifles are available with light, medium, or magnum length actions.

Luxus Model L

Same dimensions and barrel lengths as the Sporter version. The calibers are: 5.6x57, .243 Win., .308, .22-250, and 6mm Rem.

NIB	Exc.	V.G.	Good	Fair	Poor
2400	2000	1100	800	600	350

Luxus Model M

Same dimensions and barrel lengths as the Sporter Model M. Available in the following calibers: 6.5x57, .270 Win., 7x64, .30-06, 9.3x626.5x55, 7.5 Swiss, 7x57, and 8x57JS.

NIB	Exc.	V.G.	Good	Fair	Poor
2400	2000	1100	800	600	350

Luxus Model S

Same as the Sporter Model S. Offered in the following calibers: 6.5x68, 7mm Rem. Mag., .300 Win. Mag., and 8x685.

NIB	Exc.	V.G.	Good	Fair	Poor
2400	2000	1100	800	600	350

Model M

This model features the medium action and has the same barrel and stock configurations as the other two models listed above with the exception that it has no buttpad and it does have a forend tip on its half stock variation. Available in the following calibers: 6.5x57, .270 Win., 7x64, .30-06, 9.3x62, 6.5x55, 7.5 Swiss, 7x57, and 8x57JS. Weighs approximately 6.8 lbs. with full stock and 7 lbs. with half stock.

NIB	Exc.	V.G.	Good	Fair	Poor
2500	2100	1200	900	600	300

Professional Model M

This model is fitted with a medium weight action and features a black synthetic checkered stock. Comes fitted with a ventilated rubber recoil pad. Offered with 20" or 23.6" barrel it is available with single or double set trigger. Available in the following calibers: 6.5x57, .270 Win., 7x64, .30-06, 9.3x626, .5x55, 7.5 Swiss, 7x57, and 8x57 JS. Weighs approximately 7.25 lbs.

NIB	Exc.	V.G.	Good	Fair	Poor
1500	1200	950	700	600	300

Model M III Professional

Introduced in 1995 this is an economy version of the Model M Professional. It is fitted with a 23.5" barrel, black synthetic stock, and choice of single or double set triggers. Offered in .25-06, .270 Win., .30-06, and 7x64 calibers. Weight is approximately 7 lb. 5 oz.

NIB	Exc.	V.G.	Good	Fair	Poor
1000	800	600	400	300	200

NOTE: With checkered walnut stock add $100.

Model S

This rifle is offered with half stock only and is fitted with a 26" barrel. The action is magnum length and is offered in the following calibers: 6.5x68, 7mm Rem. Mag., .300 Win. Mag., and 8x685. Rifle weighs about 8.4 lbs.

NIB	Exc.	V.G.	Good	Fair	Poor
1950	1750	1150	900	700	300

Model S/T

Similar to the model above but in a heavy barreled version. Offered in the following calibers: 9.3x64, .375 H&H, and .458 Win. Mag. An optional buttstock magazine is available. Weighs about 9 lbs.

NIB	Exc.	V.G.	Good	Fair	Poor
2100	1900	1400	1100	800	500

Tropical Rifle

As above, with a 26" heavy barrel chambered for .375 Holland & Holland and .458 Winchester Magnum. Not imported after 1985.

Exc.	V.G.	Good	Fair	Poor
2000	1750	1100	650	450

Steyr SBS (Safe Bolt System)

This series was introduced in 1997 and features a newly designed bolt. It is offered in two distinct models the SBS Forester and the SBS ProHunter.

SBS ProHunter

This model has a 23.6" barrel with 4-round magazine and single adjustable trigger. Offered in .243 Win., .25-06, .270 Win.,

7mm/08, .308 Win., .30-06, 7mm Rem. Mag., .300 Win. Mag., and several European calibers. Weight is approximately 7.5 lbs. This model is furnished with a black synthetic stock with recoil pad and buttspacers. Introduced in 1999.

NIB	Exc.	V.G.	Good	Fair	Poor
700	550	450	—	—	—

NOTE: Add $150-$300 for custom metric calibers. Add approximately $30 for 7mm mag and .300 Win. Mag calibers.

SBS ProHunter Stainless Steel

Same as the ProHunter model but with stainless steel action and barrel. Introduced in 2000.

NIB	Exc.	V.G.	Good	Fair	Poor
800	600	—	—	—	—

NOTE: Add $150-$300 for custom metric calibers. Add approximately $30 for 7mm mag and .300 Win. Mag calibers.

SBS ProHunter Camo

Same as standard ProHunter but with camo synthetic stock.

NIB	Exc.	V.G.	Good	Fair	Poor
775	550	450	—	—	—

NOTE: Add $150-$300 for custom metric calibers. Add approximately $30 for 7mm mag and .300 Win. Mag calibers.

SBS ProHunter Camo Stainless Steel

Same as above but with stainless steel action and barrel.

NIB	Exc.	V.G.	Good	Fair	Poor
850	625	500	—	—	—

NOTE: Add $150-$300 for custom metric calibers. Add approximately $30 for 7mm mag and .300 Win. Mag calibers.

SBS ProHunter Mountain Rifle

Chambered for .243, .25-06, .270, and 7mm-08 calibers this model is fitted with a 20" barrel with no sights. Receiver engraved "Mountain Rifle". Synthetic stock with recoil pad standard. Weight is 7.25 lbs. Introduced in 1999.

NIB	Exc.	V.G.	Good	Fair	Poor
725	550	400	—	—	—

SBS ProHunter Mountain Stainless Steel

Same as the ProHunter Mountain but with stainless steel action and barrel. Introduced in 2000.

NIB	Exc.	V.G.	Good	Fair	Poor
825	600	—	—	—	—

SBS ProHunter Mountain Camo

Same as the ProHunter but with camo synthetic stock. Introduced in 2000.

NIB	Exc.	V.G.	Good	Fair	Poor
800	600	—	—	—	—

SBS ProHunter Mountain Camo Stainless Steel

Same as above but with stainless steel action and barrel. Introduced in 2000.

NIB	Exc.	V.G.	Good	Fair	Poor
875	650	—	—	—	—

SBS ProHunter (Youth/Ladies)

This model is fitted with a walnut stock with buttspacers to create a shorter length of pull and extra thick recoil pad. Chambered for .243, 7mm-08, and .308. Weight is about 7.25 lbs. Introduced in 1999.

NIB	Exc.	V.G.	Good	Fair	Poor
800	650	550	—	—	—

SBS ProHunter Compact

Same as above but with black synthetic stock. Also offered with stainless steel action and barrel.

NIB	Exc.	V.G.	Good	Fair	Poor
800	650	550	—	—	—

NOTE: Add $80 for stainless steel model.

SBS ProHunter 376 Steyr

This model is chambered for the .376 Steyr cartridge. Fitted with a 20" barrel with iron sights. Synthetic stock with special thick pad. Weight is about 8 lbs. Introduced in 1999.

NIB	Exc.	V.G.	Good	Fair	Poor
800	650	550	—	—	—

SBS Forester

Same as above model but furnished with a walnut stock with recoil pad.

NIB	Exc.	V.G.	Good	Fair	Poor
720	575	475	—	—	—

NOTE: Add $150-$300 for custom metric calibers. Add $30 for 7mm Rem. Mag and .300 Win. Mag.

SBS Forester Mountain Rifle

Walnut stock with 20" barrel and no sights. Chambered for a variety of calibers including .243, .25-06, .270, 7mm-08, .308, .30-06 and 6.5x55. Receiver engraved "Mountain Rifle". Introduced in 1999.

NIB	Exc.	V.G.	Good	Fair	Poor
750	600	500	—	—	—

SBS Classic American

This model features a 23.6" barrel with a single adjustable trigger and stain finish walnut stock with recoil pad. Offered in calibers from .243 to .300 Win. Mag. Weight is about 7.2 lbs. Introduced in 2000.

NIB	Exc.	V.G.	Good	Fair	Poor
1500	1100	—	—	—	—

NOTE: Add $150-$300 for custom metric calibers. Add approximately $30 for 7mm Mag and .300 Win. Mag calibers.

SBS Classic Mannlicher

Offered in the same calibers as above except for 7mm Rem. Mag and .300 Win. Mag. and fitted with a 25.6" barrel. The walnut stock is the full Mannlicher style with recoil pad. Fitted with open sights. Weight is about 7.2 lbs. Introduced in 2000.

NIB	Exc.	V.G.	Good	Fair	Poor
1700	1250	—	—	—	—

Mannlicher SBS European-Half Stock

Fitted with a 23.6" barrel with iron sights and chambered for a wide variety of American and European calibers from .243 to 9.3x62. European style figured walnut stock. Adjustable trigger. Recoil pad. Weight is about 7.5 lbs.

NIB	Exc.	V.G.	Good	Fair	Poor
2795	2200	1750	—	—	—

Mannlicher SBS European-Half Stock Carbine

Same as model above but with 20" barrel.

NIB	Exc.	V.G.	Good	Fair	Poor
2895	2300	1850	—	—	—

Mannlicher SBS European-Full Stock

Same as above but with full European stock covering a 20" barrel.

NIB	Exc.	V.G.	Good	Fair	Poor
3000	2400	1950	—	—	—

Mannlicher SBS Magnum European-Half Stock

This model is chambered for the 7mm Rem. Mag., .300 Win. Mag., and the 6.5x68 and 8x68S calibers. Fitted with a 25.6" barrel with iron sights. Walnut stock. Weight is about 7.75 lbs.

NIB	Exc.	V.G.	Good	Fair	Poor
3000	2400	1950	—	—	—

Steyr Scout-Jeff Cooper Package

Developed by Col. Jeff Cooper this model is chambered for the .308 Win. cartridge. It is fitted with a 19" fluted barrel. Stock is grey synthetic with removable buttspacers and folding bipod. Magazine capacity is 5 rounds with optional 10 round magazines available. Weight is approximately 7 lbs. with scope. Weight is 6.3 lbs with no scope. Adjustable single trigger. Factory installed Leupold M8 2.5x28mm scope. Introduced in 1998.

NIB	Exc.	V.G.	Good	Fair	Poor
2600	2000	1600	—	—	—

Steyr Scout Package

Similar to the Jeff Cooper Package but without the Jeff Cooper logo. Stock is black synthetic. Also offered in .223 Rem., .243 Win., 7mm/08 as well as .308 and .375 Steyr calibers.

NIB	Exc.	V.G.	Good	Fair	Poor
2600	2000	1600	—	—	—

Steyr Scout

Same as above but rifle only.

NIB	Exc.	V.G.	Good	Fair	Poor
1895	1500	1200	—	—	—

Steyr Scout Tactical

This model has a 19.25" fluted barrel and is chambered for the .223 or .308 Win. cartridge. Integral bipod. Emergency Ghost Ring sights.

NIB	Exc.	V.G.	Good	Fair	Poor
2050	1500	1000	—	—	—

NOTE: Add $100 for stainless steel model.

PRECISION/TACTICAL RIFLES

Model SSG-PI

This model features a black synthetic stock originally designed as a military sniper rifle. Fitted with a cocking indicator, single or double set trigger, 5-round rotary magazine, or 10-round magazine. Receiver is milled to NATO specifications for Steyr ring mounts. Barrel length is 26". Rifle weighs about 9 lbs. Offered in .308 Win.

NOTE: This model was originally called the SSG 69.

NIB	Exc.	V.G.	Good	Fair	Poor
1700	1300	1000	—	—	—

WHAT'S IT LIKE-THE STEYR SSG 69/P11

The 7.62x51mm SSG69 is a special purpose precision rifle manufactured by the famous Steyr factory in Austria. SSG stands for Scharf Schuetzen Gewehr, or Sharpshooter's rifle. The SSG was adopted by the Austrian military in 1969. The Austrian military shooting team established world records with the rifle in 1970 and 1975. The accuracy of this system is the result of many factors. the barrel is cold hammer forged. the solid barrel receiver interface is provided by special 57mm sleeve used to increase the rigidity and the bearing surface of the receiver surrounding the barrel. This bolt action system locks tightly by utilizing 6 rear locking lugs. A 60 degree rotation is required to unlock the bolt. The two stage trigger is adjustable. As an option, Steyr offers an adjustable double set trigger. The stock is unique in that it was one of the first to incorporate plastic composites into a sniper rifle system. Plastic is inert, more so than wood, thus more durable to climate changes. It is also more rugged. The SSG incorporates a detachable magazine in 5 or ten rounds. these magazines are rotary design that smoothly guides the cartridge into the chambered without contacting the bullet. the SSG is a remarkable system at an affordable price, one reason why so many countries have adopted it in their military and police units.

J.R. Moody

SSG-PII Police Rifle

This version of the SSG has a heavier 26" barrel and a larger knob style bolt handle. Weighs about 10 lbs. 11 oz.

NIB	Exc.	V.G.	Good	Fair	Poor
1700	1300	1000	—	—	—

SSK-PIIK Police Kurz

Similar to the above model but with a 20" heavy barrel. Weight is about 10 lbs.

NIB	Exc.	V.G.	Good	Fair	Poor
1700	1300	1000	—	—	—

SSG-PII&PIIK McMillian

Fitted with a McMillian A-3 stock with adjustable cheekpiece and removable buttspacers. Special forearm rail.

NIB	Exc.	V.G.	Good	Fair	Poor
2300	1750	1350	—	—	—

SSG-PIV

Again similar to the above PIIK but with a 16.75" heavy barrel with a removable flash hider. Barrel is threaded. Weight is about 9 lbs. 11 oz.

NIB	Exc.	V.G.	Good	Fair	Poor
2500	2000	1500	1000	750	400

Match

NIB	Exc.	V.G.	Good	Fair	Poor
3000	2500	2000	1500	800	400

Match UIT

Designed as an international target rifle this model features special shaped pistol grip, an adjustable trigger for length of pull and pressure. Enlarged bolt handle and nonglare barrel. Chambered for .308 Win. cartridge.

NIB	Exc.	V.G.	Good	Fair	Poor
3900	3500	3000	2000	1500	1000

JAGD Match

Introduced in 1995 this model features a choice of 23.5" or 20" barrel with sights. The stock is laminated. A full stock version is offered on 20" barrel models and a half stock is offered on the 23.5" barrel models. Available in a variety of configurations with calibers from .222 Rem. to .458 Win. Mag.

NIB	Exc.	V.G.	Good	Fair	Poor
1750	1250	900	500	350	200

SBS TACTICAL SERIES

SBS Tactical

Fitted with a black synthetic stock and 20" barrel with no sights. This model is chambered for the .308 cartridge. Removable buttspacers. Black bolt body. Receiver engraved "SBS Tactical". Introduced in 1999. Weight is about 7.25 lbs.

NIB	Exc.	V.G.	Good	Fair	Poor
950	750	600	—	—	—

NOTE: Add $100 for stainless steel model (introduced 2000).

SBS Tactical Heavy Barrel

This model also has a black synthetic stock but is fitted with a 26" heavy barrel and no sights. Black bolt body. Receiver engraved "SBS Tactical HB". Weight is about 8 lbs. Introduced in 1999. Also offered with 20" barrel called "HBC". Both barrel lengths chambered for .308 cartridge.

NIB	Exc.	V.G.	Good	Fair	Poor
950	750	600	—	—	—

SBS Tactical Heavy Barrel Carbine

This model features a 20" heavy barrel, no sights, matte blue finish. Chambered for .308 caliber. Introduced in 2000.

NIB	Exc.	V.G.	Good	Fair	Poor
1000	700	—	—	—	—

SBS Tactical McMillian

This model is fitted with a 26" barrel chambered for the .308 cartridge and has a McMillian A-3 stock. Oversize bolt handle. Weight is about 9.8 lbs. Introduced in 1999.

NIB	Exc.	V.G.	Good	Fair	Poor
1600	1250	950	—	—	—

SBS CISM Rifle

This model is chambered for the .308 cartridge and fitted with a 19.7" heavy barrel. The stock is laminated wood with black lacquer finish. The stock has a forearm rail with handstop, adjustable buttplate, and cheekpiece. The trigger is adjustable. Weight is approximately 10.25 lbs. Introduced in 1999.

NIB	Exc.	V.G.	Good	Fair	Poor
3295	2500	—	—	—	—

SBS Tactical Elite Heavy Barrel

This model, introduced in 2000, features a 26" heavy barrel, no sights, matte blue finish, Zytel stock with adjustable cheekpiece and adjustable butt plate. Full length Picatinney mounting rail. Magazine capacity is 5 or 10 rounds. Chambered for .308 cartridge.

NIB	Exc.	V.G.	Good	Fair	Poor
2400	1750	—	—	—	—

NOTE: Add $100 for stainless steel model. Add $1,000 for ZF optics.

SBS Tactical Elite Heavy Barrel Carbine

Same as the Tactical Elite Heavy Barrel model but fitted with a 20" heavy barrel. Introduced in 2000.

NIB	Exc.	V.G.	Good	Fair	Poor
2400	1750	—	—	—	—

Steyr AUG

A 5.56mm semiautomatic, Bullpup semiautomatic rifle with a 20" barrel incorporating a Swarovski 1.5x telescopic sight. Green carbon composite stock. Weight is about 8.5 lbs. Recommend independent, local appraisals.

NIB	Exc.	V.G.	Good	Fair	Poor
3700	3500	3100	2500	1600	1300

Steyr AUG-Police Model

Same as above but with black stock and 16" barrel.

NIB	Exc.	V.G.	Good	Fair	Poor
4000	3700	3400	2800	1900	1500

Steyr AUG Special Receiver

Receiver only. Special flattop with Stanag mounting.

NIB	Exc.	V.G.	Good	Fair	Poor
2500	2000	1800	1200	800	600

Steyr Zepher

This model is a .22 caliber rimfire bolt action carbine. It has a 5-round detachable magazine, dovetailed receiver for scope rings. It is fitted with a full stock. Made from 1953 to 1968.

Exc.	V.G.	Good	Fair	Poor
1200	1000	900	700	350

PISTOLS

Model SPP

Introduced in 1993 this is a 9mm semiautomatic pistol. It is made from synthetic materials and operates on a delayed blowback, rotating barrel system. The magazine capacity is either 15 or 30 rounds. The barrel is 5.9" in length overall length is 12.75" and weight is about 42 oz. Due to its appearance and design this pistol was banned for importation into the United States shortly after its introduction. Because of this circumstance the price of this pistol may fluctuate widely.

NIB	Exc.	V.G.	Good	Fair	Poor
900	750	600	500	400	300

NIB	Exc.	V.G.	Good	Fair	Poor
600	450	—	—	—	—

Model S

This model is similar to the Model M but is fitted with a 3.58" barrel. Chambered for the .40 S&W, 9mm, or .357 Sig cartridges. Magazine capacity is 10 rounds Weight is approximately 22 oz. Introduced in 2000.

Model M

Chambered for the .40 S&W, pmm, or .357 Sig cartridge this semiautomatic pistol has a polymer frame and 3 user selectable safety systems. Loaded chambered indicator. Triangle/Trapezoid sights. Limited access lock with key. Weight is about 28 oz. Magazine capacity is 10 rounds. Introduced in 1999.

NIB	Exc.	V.G.	Good	Fair	Poor
600	450	—	—	—	—

STEYR HAHN
SEE—Steyr

STEYR MANNLICHER
SEE—Steyr

STOCK, FRANZ
Berlin, Germany

Stock

A .22, 6.35mm or 7.65mm semiautomatic pistol with an open topped slide. The frame marked "Franz Stock Berlin". Blued with black composition grips impressed with the name "Stock" at the top. Manufactured from 1918 to the early 1930s.

Exc.	V.G.	Good	Fair	Poor
450	300	250	150	100

STOCKING & CO.
Worcester, Massachusetts

Pepperbox

Courtesy Wallis & Wallis, Lewes, Sussex, England

A .28 or .316 barreled percussion pepperbox revolver with barrel lengths from 4" to 6" in length. The hammer is fitted with a long cocking piece at the rear and the triggerguard may or may not be made with a spur at the rear. Blued with walnut grips. The barrel group marked "Stocking & Co., Worcester." Manufactured between 1846 and 1854.

Exc.	V.G.	Good	Fair	Poor
—	—	1250	550	200

Single Shot Pistol

A .36 caliber single shot percussion pistol of the same pattern as the pepperbox with a 4" half octagonal barrel. Marked as above. Manufactured from 1849 to 1852.

Exc.	V.G.	Good	Fair	Poor
—	—	650	250	100

STOEGER, A. F.
South Hackensack, New Jersey

American Eagle Luger

This is identical to the German design. It is chambered for the 9mm with a 7-round magazine and fitted with a 4" barrel. Checkered walnut grips. Stainless steel. Weight is about 32 oz.

NIB	Exc.	V.G.	Good	Fair	Poor
650	450	400	250	200	100

American Eagle Navy Model

Same as above but with a 6" barrel.

NIB	Exc.	V.G.	Good	Fair	Poor
650	450	400	250	200	100

.22 Luger

A .22 caliber simplified copy of the German Model P.08 semi-automatic pistol with a 4.5" or 5.5" barrel and an aluminum frame. The word "Luger" is roll engraved on the right side of the frame. Blued with checkered brown plastic grips.

Exc.	V.G.	Good	Fair	Poor
300	250	200	150	100

Target Luger

As above, with adjustable target sights.

Exc.	V.G.	Good	Fair	Poor
325	275	225	175	125

Luger Carbine

As above, with an 11" barrel, walnut forend and checkered walnut grips. Furnished with a red velvet lined black leatherette case. Manufactured during the 1970s.

Exc.	V.G.	Good	Fair	Poor
550	400	350	250	175

SHOTGUNS

Model 2000

This is a semiautomatic shotgun chambered for the 12 gauge shell. Fitted with 26", 28", or 30" vent rib barrel. Single trigger with screw-in chokes. Weight is about 7 lbs. Introduced in 2001.

NIB	Exc.	V.G.	Good	Fair	Poor
490	400	—	—	—	—

Model 2000 Deluxe

Same as above but with high grade walnut stock and etched receiver with gold trigger.

NIB	Exc.	V.G.	Good	Fair	Poor
620	500	—	—	—	—

Coach Gun

This is a side-by-side gun chambered for the 12 or 20 gauge shell as well as the .410 shell. Fitted with 20" barrels with double triggers. Improved cylinder and modified fixed chokes. Weight is about 7 lbs.

NIB	Exc.	V.G.	Good	Fair	Poor
300	250	—	—	—	—

NOTE: Add $50 for nickel finish.

Uplander

This side-by-side shotgun is chambered for the 12, 16, 20, 28 ,and .410 bores. with choice of 26" or 28" barrels. Fixed chokes. Double triggers. Weight is about 7.25 lbs.

NIB	Exc.	V.G.	Good	Fair	Poor
325	275	—	—	—	—

Uplander Supreme

Same as above but with select wood and screw-in chokes.

NIB	Exc.	V.G.	Good	Fair	Poor
425	350	—	—	—	—

Uplander English

This variation is fitted with a straight grip stock and chambered for the 20 gauge or .410 bore. Fitted with 24" barrels. Weight is about 7 lbs. Also available with a short stock.

NIB	Exc.	V.G.	Good	Fair	Poor
340	275	—	—	—	—

Condor

This is an over and under shotgun chambered for the 12 or 20 gauge shell. Fitted with 26" or 28" barrels. Fixed chokes. Single trigger. Blued finish. Weight is about 7.7 lbs.

NIB	Exc.	V.G.	Good	Fair	Poor
390	300	—	—	—	—

Condor Supreme Deluxe

Similar to the above model but with cut checkering and high polish blue. Offered in 12 and 20 gauge with 26" or 28" barrels as well as 24" barrels for the 20 gauge. Automatic ejectors.

NIB	Exc.	V.G.	Good	Fair	Poor
490	400	—	—	—	—

STI INTERNATIONAL
Georgetown, Texas

LS9 & LS40

Single stack pistol chambered for the 9mm or .40 S&W cartridge. Fitted with a 3.4" barrel and short grip. Heine Low Mount sights. Rosewood grips. Matte blue finish. Magazine capacity is 7 rounds for 9mm and 6 rounds for .40 S&W. Weight is about 28 oz.

NIB	Exc.	V.G.	Good	Fair	Poor
745	600	—	—	—	—

BLS9 & BLS40

Same as above but with full length grip. Magazine capacity is 9 rounds for 9mm and 8 rounds for .40 S&W.

NIB	Exc.	V.G.	Good	Fair	Poor
840	675	—	—	—	—

Ranger

Chambered for the .45 ACP cartridge and fitted with a 3.9" barrel with short grip. Fixed sti sights. Blued frame with stainless steel slide. Weight is about 29 oz.

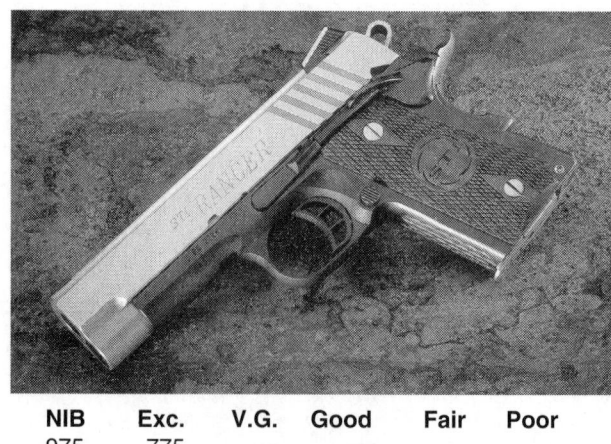

NIB	Exc.	V.G.	Good	Fair	Poor
975	775	—	—	—	—

Trojan

Chambered for the .45 ACP, .40 Super, .40 S&W, and 9mm cartridge. Fitted with a 5" barrel. Rosewood grips. Matte blue finish. Eight-round magazine capacity. Weight is about 36 oz.

NIB	Exc.	V.G.	Good	Fair	Poor
970	775	—	—	—	—

NOTE: For .40 Super with .45 ACP conversion add $275. For Trojan with 6" slide add $250.

Xcaliber Single Stack

Chambered for the .450 SMC cartridge and fitted with a 6" slide. Adjustable rear sight. Weight is about 38 oz. Blue finish. Single stack magazine.

NIB	Exc.	V.G.	Good	Fair	Poor
1465	1175	—	—	—	—

VIP

Chambered for the .45 ACP cartridge and fitted with a 3.9" ramped bull barrel. Stainless steel flat top slide. Fixed rear sight. Ten-round magazine capacity. Weight is about 25 oz.

NIB	Exc.	V.G.	Good	Fair	Poor
1700	1350	—	—	—	—

Edge
Chambered for the 9mm, 10mm, .40 S&W, and .45 ACP cartridge with 5" ramped bull barrel. Dual stack magazine. Bomar style sights. Blue finish. Weight is about 39 oz.

NIB	Exc.	V.G.	Good	Fair	Poor
1775	1400	—	—	—	—

Executive
Chambered for the .40 S&W cartridge. Fitted with a 5" ramped bull barrel. Adjustable rear sight. Gray synthetic grip and hard chrome slide. Weight is about 39 oz. Double stack magazine.

NIB	Exc.	V.G.	Good	Fair	Poor
2260	1800	—	—	—	—

Eagle
Chambered for customer's choice of caliber and fitted with 5" ramped bull barrel. Fixed sights. Blued frame and stainless steel slide. Weight is about 30 oz.

NIB	Exc.	V.G.	Good	Fair	Poor
1795	1400	—	—	—	—

Xcaliber Double Stack
Same as the Xcaliber Single Stack except that this model has a double stack magazine.

NIB	Exc.	V.G.	Good	Fair	Poor
2125	1700	—	—	—	—

Competitor
Chambered for the .38 Super cartridge and fitted with a 5.5" ramped bull barrel with compensator. Fitted with a C-More scope. Stainless steel slide. Weight is about 44 oz with scope and mount.

NIB	Exc.	V.G.	Good	Fair	Poor
2500	1900	—	—	—	—

Grandmaster
Custom built to customer's specifications.

NIB	Exc.	V.G.	Good	Fair	Poor
N/A	—	—	—	—	—

Hawk 4.3
This pistol is modeled on the 1911 design and is equipped with a 4.3" barrel with steel slide. The frame of the pistol is made from polymer and features and increased magazine capacity while retaining the 1911 grip thickness. Chambered for .38 Super, .45 ACP, .40 S&W, 10mm, and 9x25 calibers. Built primarily for competition shooting.

NIB	Exc.	V.G.	Good	Fair	Poor
1775	1400	900	—	—	—

Night Hawk 4.3
Chambered for .45 ACP only with 4.3" bull barrel and a host of special features such a narrow tactical safety, front and rear slide serrations, and extended dust cover. Tritium sights optional. Blued finish. Weight is 33 oz.

NIB	Exc.	V.G.	Good	Fair	Poor
1925	1500	—	—	—	—

Falcon 3.9

Similar to the above model but fitted with a 3.9" barrel. Weight is approximately 30 oz. with steel frame and 25 oz. with Aluminum frame.

NIB	Exc.	V.G.	Good	Fair	Poor
1925	1500	—	—	—	—

Sparrow 5.0

Chambered for the .22 Long Rifle cartridge only and fitted with a 5" bull barrel with fixed sights. Weight is approximately 30 oz.

NIB	Exc.	V.G.	Good	Fair	Poor
990	800	600	—	—	—

Edge 5.1

Chambered for .40 S&W only with 5" bull barrel and many special features. BoMar front and rear sights. Weight is 39 oz.

NIB	Exc.	V.G.	Good	Fair	Poor
2025	1600	1250	—	—	—

Eagle 5.1

Similar to the Model 2011 Hawk but furnished with a 5" barrel. Comes standard with BoMar adjustable sights.

NIB	Exc.	V.G.	Good	Fair	Poor
1775	1400	900	—	—	—

Eagle 5.5

Similar to above model but furnished with a 5-1/2" barrel with compensator.

NIB	Exc.	V.G.	Good	Fair	Poor
2475	1900	1250	—	—	—

Eagle 6.0

Chambered for 9mm, .38 Super, .40S&W, or .45 ACP cartridges. Fitted with a 6" bull barrel. Many special features. BoMar front and rear sights. Blued finish. Weight is about 42 oz.

NIB	Exc.	V.G.	Good	Fair	Poor
1925	1500	—	—	—	—

Hunter 6.0

Chambered for the 10mm cartridge only and fitted with a 6" bull barrel. Heavy extended frame. Many special features. Leupold 2x scope. Blued finish. Weight with scope 51 oz.

NIB	Exc.	V.G.	Good	Fair	Poor
2350	1850	—	—	—	—

STREET SWEEPER
Atlanta, Georgia

Street Sweeper

A 12 gauge semiautomatic double action shotgun with an 18" barrel and 12-shot rotary, drum magazine. Matte black finish. Introduced in 1989.

NOTE: This firearm is now on the restricted list as a Class III weapon and is subject to NFA rules. This model requires registration with the BATF to avoid federal penalties. Make sure that the shotgun is transferable prior to sale.

NIB	Exc.	V.G.	Good	Fair	Poor
750	600	500	400	300	—

STURDIVANT, LEWIS G.
Talladega, Alabama

Received contract from the state of Alabama for 2,000 "Mississippi" or "Enfield" rifles. Two hundred and eighty were received on this contract. These arms resemble U.S. Model 1841 Rifles without patchboxes. Overall length 48-1/2"; barrel length 33"; .577 caliber. Unmarked.

Prospective purchasers are strongly advised to secure an expert appraisal prior to acquisition.

STURM, RUGER & CO.
Southport, Connecticut

In 1946 William B. Ruger applied for his first patent on a blowback operated, semiautomatic, .22 caliber pistol. In 1949 Bill Ruger and Alexander Sturm released this pistol for sale, and the Ruger dynasty began. This pistol was as perfect for the American marketplace as could be. It was accurate, reliable, and inexpensive and insured the new company's success. In 1951 Alexander Sturm passed away, but Mr. Ruger continued forward. At this time the fledgling television industry was popularizing the early American West, and Colt had not reintroduced the Single Action Army after WWII. Ruger decided that a Western-style six shooter would be a successful venture, and the Single Six was born. This was not a Colt copy but a new design based on the Western look. Again Ruger scored in the marketplace, and this has been pretty much the rule ever since. With few exceptions this company has shown itself to be accurate in gauging what the gun-buying public wants. They have expanded their line to include double action revolvers, single shots, semiauto and bolt action rifles, percussion revolvers, and even a semiautomatic wonder nine. They have stayed ahead of the legal profession as much as possible by introducing safety devices and comprehensive instruction manuals and generally insured their future success. For such a relatively new company, collector interest in certain models is quite keen. There are a number of factors that govern Ruger collector values. All models made in 1976 were designated "200th Year of Liberty" models and if in NIB condition will bring up to a 25% premium if a market is found. The newer models that have a safety warning stamped on the barrel are generally purchased only by shooters and have no collector appeal whatsoever. The astute individual must be aware of these nuances when dealing in Rugers. There are some excellent works written on the Ruger (not as many as there are on the Colt or the Smith & Wesson), and the new collector can educate himself if he so desires. We list this company's models in chronological order.

SEMIAUTOMATIC RIMFIRE PISTOLS

Standard Model "Red Eagle Grips"

This is a blowback semiautomatic with a fixed, exposed, 4.75" barrel. The receiver is tubular, with a round bolt. There is a 9-shot detachable magazine, and the sights are fixed. The finish is blued, and the black hard rubber grips on this first model feature a red Ruger eagle or hawk medallion on the left side. There were approximately 25,600 manufactured before Alexander Sturm's death in 1951, but this model may be seen as high as the 35000 serial number range. Because variations of this model exist an expert opinion should be sought before a final price is established.

Exc.	V.G.	Good	Fair	Poor
525	400	300	250	150

NOTE: Factory verfied plated pistols will bring between $2,500 and $5,000 depending on condition. For pistols in factory original wood "cod box" shipping carton add $750 to $1500. For pistols in original hinged cardboard box add 35%.

Standard Model

This model is identical to the Red Eagle except that after Sturm's death the grip medallions were changed from red to black and have remained so ever since. This pistol was produced from 1952-1982 in 4-3/4" and 6" barrels. There are a great many variations of this pistol, but a book dealing with this pistol alone should be consulted as the differences in variations are subtle and valuation of these variations is definitely a matter for individual appraisal.

Exc.	V.G.	Good	Fair	Poor
185	135	125	100	85

Standard Model-Marked "Hecho en Mexico"

These pistols were assembled and sold in Mexico. Approximately 200 were built with 4-3/4" barrels and about 50 were produced with 6" barrels. Only a few of these pistols have been accounted for and for this reason an expert should be consulted.

Exc.	V.G.	Good	Fair	Poor
1500	1200	850	600	400

Mark I Target Model

The success of the Ruger Standard Model led quite naturally to a demand for a more accurate target model. In 1951 a pistol that utilized the same frame and receiver with a 6-7/8", target-type barrel and adjustable sights was introduced. Early target models number 15000 to 16999 and 25000 to 25300 have Red Eagle grips. In 1952 a 5-1/4" tapered barrel model was introduced, but was soon discontinued. In 1963 the popular 5-1/2" bull barrel model was introduced. These models enjoyed well deserved success and were manufactured from 1951-1982.
NOTE: For original hinged box add 35%. With Factory Supplied Muzzle Brake-Add $75-100.

Red Eagle 6-7/8" Barrel.

Exc.	V.G.	Good	Fair	Poor
525	400	250	200	150

Black or Silver Eagle 6-7/8" Barrel

Exc.	V.G.	Good	Fair	Poor
250	195	175	150	125

NOTE: For other Mark I Target models under serial number 72500 in original hinged box-Add 75%.

The 5-1/4" Tapered Barrel Model

Exc.	V.G.	Good	Fair	Poor
500	400	250	175	125

NOTE: Add 50% if in original 5-1/4" marked hinged box.

The 5-1/2" Bull Barrel Model.

Exc.	V.G.	Good	Fair	Poor
225	195	150	125	95

Mark I Target Model-Rollmarked With U.S. On Top Of Frame.

These pistols will have either 1/16" or 1/8" high serial numbers.

Exc.	V.G.	Good	Fair	Poor
500	400	300	200	150

NOTE: Add 25% to price if pistol has 1/8" high serial numbers.

Stainless Steel-1 of 5,000

This model is a special commemorative version of the first standard with the "Red Eagle" grips. It is made of stainless steel and is rollmarked with Bill Ruger's signature on it. The pistol is encased in a wood "salt cod" case.

NIB	Exc.	V.G.	Good	Fair	Poor
395	350	300	225	175	125

MARK II .22 CALIBER PISTOL SPECIFICATIONS:

Supplied in .22 l.r. with various barrel weights and lengths. Magazine capacity is 10 rounds. Trigger is grooved with curved finger surface. High speed hammer provides fast lock time. Grips are sharply checkered and made of black gloss delrin material. Stainless steel models have a brushed satin finish. Today, each model except the MK-10 and KMK-10, come from the factory with a lockable plastic case and Ruger lock.

Mark II Standard Model

This is a generally improved version of the first Ruger pistol. There is a hold-open device, and the magazine holds 10 rounds. This model was introduced in 1982.

Standard Mark II Model MK-4
Blued finish with 4.75" barrel. Checkered composition grips. Weight about 35 oz.

NIB	Exc.	V.G.	Good	Fair	Poor
225	175	150	125	100	75

Standard Mark II Model MK4-50
Introduced in 1999 to commemorate the 50th anniversary of the first Ruger rimfire pistol. Fitted with a 4.75" barrel with fixed sights. Chambered for the .22 Long Rifle cartridge. The pistols grips have a red Ruger medallion and Ruger crest on the barrel. Furnished in a red case. Weight is about 35 oz. Production limited to one year.

NIB	Exc.	V.G.	Good	Fair	Poor
285	225	—	—	—	—

Standard Mark II Model MK-6
Same as above but with 6" barrel. Weight 37 oz.

NIB	Exc.	V.G.	Good	Fair	Poor
225	175	150	125	100	75

Standard Mark II Model KMK-4
This model is the same as the Mark II Standard except that it is made of stainless steel.

NIB	Exc.	V.G.	Good	Fair	Poor
330	260	200	150	125	100

Standard Mark II Model KMK-6
Same as above but with 6" barrel. Weight is about 37 oz.

NIB	Exc.	V.G.	Good	Fair	Poor
330	260	200	150	125	100

NOTE: In 1997, Ruger produced 650 of the Model MK-6 with special features for the "Friends of the NRA" auction of the same year. These guns have high polish blueing, faux ivory grips panels, a gold inlaid National Rifle Association inscription and a gold inlaid number of "1 of 650" to "650 of 650". The NIB price for these pistols is $550.00.

Mark II Target Model
This model incorporates the same improvements as the Mark II Standard but is offered with 5.5" bull, 6-7/8" tapered and 10" heavy barrel. A 5-1/4" tapered barrel was added in 1990 but discontinued in 1994. Blued finish. This model has adjustable target sights and was introduced in 1982.

NIB	Exc.	V.G.	Good	Fair	Poor
311	250	200	150	125	100

NOTE: In 1989, approximately 2,000 5-1/2" bull barrel Mark II pistols with blue barreled receivers and stainless steel grip frames were produced by Ruger on order from a Ruger distributor. They exist in the 215-25xxx to 215-43xxx serial number range. The NIB price for these pistols is $375.

Stainless Steel Mark II Target Model
This model is the same as the blued version but is made of stainless steel.

		V.G.	Good	Fair	Poor
		250	225	175	125

NOTE: Some with U.S. markings. These are found in the serial number range of 210-00001 to 210-18600. Only a small number in civilian hands. The NIB price for these pistols is $1,000.00.

Mark II Competition Model KMK-678GC

The Competition model features a stainless steel frame with checkered laminated hardwood thumb rest grips, heavy 6-7/8" bull barrel factory drilled and tapped for scope mount, Partridge type front sight undercut to prevent glare and an adjustable rear sight. Pistol weighs 45 oz.

NIB	Exc.	V.G.	Good	Fair	Poor
427	350	275	200	125	100

NOTE: In 1997 Ruger produced 204 of these pistols in blue instead of stainless steel for one of their distributors. They are very scarce. The NIB for these pistols is $350.00.
In 1995 Ruger produced a similar blued pistol (1000 total, 500 each with or without scope rings) with 5-1/2" slab side barrels. These are not marked "Competition Target Model" like the previously described variation. The NIB price for these pistols is $350.00 and with rings $375.00.

Ruger 22/45 Model

This .22 Long Rifle caliber pistol has the same grip angle and magazine latch as the Model 1911 .45 ACP. The semiautomatic action is stainless steel and the grip frame is made from Zytel, a fiberglass reinforced lightweight composite material. Front sight is Patridge-type. This model is available in several different configurations. A 4" tapered barrel and standard model sights, a 5.25" tapered barrel with target sights, or a 5.5" bull barrel with target sights. The 5.25" barrel was discontinued in 1994.

KP-4

This model features a 4.75" standard weight barrel with fixed sights. Pistol weighs 28 oz.

NIB	Exc.	V.G.	Good	Fair	Poor
250	175	150	125	100	75

NIB	Exc.	V.G.	Good	Fair	Poor

Mark II Bull Barrel Model MK-10

Introduced in 1996 this bull barrel variation has a blued finish with a 4" barrel. Grips are checkered Composition. Weight is about 39 oz.

	Exc.	V.G.	Good	Fair	Poor
250	195	175	150	125	100

Government Model

This model is similar to the blue Mark II Target, with a 6-7/8" bull barrel. It is the civilian version of a training pistol that the military is purchasing from Ruger. The only difference is that this model does not have the U.S. markings.

NIB	Exc.	V.G.	Good	Fair	Poor
357	285	225	200	150	100

Stainless Steel Government Model

Stainless steel version of the Government Model.

KP-514

Furnished with a target tapered barrel 5.25" in length. Comes with adjustable sights. Pistol weighs 38 oz. Model now discontinued.

NIB	Exc.	V.G.	Good	Fair	Poor
300	200	175	150	100	75

KP-512

This model is equipped with a 5.5" bull barrel with adjustable sights. Weighs 42 oz.

NIB	Exc.	V.G.	Good	Fair	Poor
300	200	175	150	100	75

NOTE: In 1995 Ruger produced 500 22/45s with stainless steel 6-7/8" Government type barreled receivers for one of their distributors. They appear around the 220-59xxx serial number range. The NIB price for these pistols is $350.00.

Also in 1997 another Ruger distributor succeeded in contracting Ruger to make a similar 22/45 only in blue and with 6-7/8" slab side bull barrels. Approximatley 1,000 were produced with serial numbers extending to the 220-87xxx serial number range. The NIB price is $300.00.

P-4

A limited number, about 1,000, of this variation was produced in 1995 with a 4" bull barrel on a P frame. It was introduced into the product line as a production pistol in 1997. Weight is approximately 31 oz.

NIB	Exc.	V.G.	Good	Fair	Poor
325	250	200	150	100	75

P-512

This variation of the stainless steel version has a blued receiver with P-style frame.

NIB	Exc.	V.G.	Good	Fair	Poor
210	175	125	100	75	60

SINGLE ACTION REVOLVERS

Single Six Revolver

This is a .22 rimfire, 6-shot, single action revolver. It was first offered with a 5-1/2" barrel length and a fixed sight. In 1959 additional barrel lengths were offered for this model in 4-5/8", 6-1/2", and 9-1/2". It is based in appearance on the Colt Single Action Army, but internally it is a new design that features coil springs instead of the old-style, flat leaf springs. It also features a floating firing pin and is generally a stronger action than what was previously available. The early model had a flat loading gate and was made this way from 1953-1957, when the contoured gate became standard. Early models had checkered hard rubber grips changed to smooth varnished walnut by 1962. Black eagle grip medallions were used from the beginning of production to 1971 when a silver eagle grip medallion replaced it. No "Red Eagle" single-sixes were ever produced. This model was manufactured from 1953-1972.

Flat Gate Model-60,000 produced

Courtesy John C. Dougan

Courtesy *Know Your Ruger Single Action Revolvers 1953-63*.
Blacksmith Corp.

Exc.	V.G.	Good	Fair	Poor
350	300	225	165	150

NOTE: Be aware that revolvers serial numbered under 1000 will bring a premium of 25% to 125% depending on condition, low serial number, and color of cylinder frame—bright reddish purple the most desirable.

Contoured Gate Model-Introduced 1957

Exc.	V.G.	Good	Fair	Poor
275	225	175	150	125

NOTE: Be aware that 4-5/8" and 9-1/2" barrel lengths will bring a premium. There were 258 5-1/2" barrel factory engraved pistols in this model. Add $2,500 to $3,500 depending on variety and condition.

Single Six Convertible

This model is similar to the Single Six but is furnished with an extra .22 rimfire Magnum cylinder.

Exc.	V.G.	Good	Fair	Poor
300	250	200	150	125

NOTE: Barrel lengths in 4-5/8" and 9-1/2" will bring a premium.

Single Six .22 Magnum Model

This model is similar to the Single Six except that it is chambered for the .22 rimfire Magnum and the frame was so marked. It was offered in the 6.5" barrel length only and was manufactured for three years. An extra long rifle cylinder was added later in production. The serial numbers are in the 300000-340000 range.

Exc.	V.G.	Good	Fair	Poor
350	300	250	200	175

Lightweight Single Six

Courtesy *Know Your Ruger Single Action Revolvers 1953-63.*
Blacksmith Corp.

This model is similar to the Single Six, with an aluminum alloy frame and 4-5/8" barrel. This variation was produced between 1956 and 1958 and was in the 200000-212000 serial number range. Approximately the first 6,500 were produced with alloy cylinders with steel chamber inserts.

Courtesy *Know Your Ruger Single Action Revolvers 1953-63.*
Blacksmith Corp.

Silver Anodized Frame with Aluminum Cylinder Model with Martin Hardcoat Finish

Exc.	V.G.	Good	Fair	Poor
500	400	300	225	195

Black Anodized Aluminum Frame and Cylinder Model

Exc.	V.G.	Good	Fair	Poor
550	450	350	300	250

Black Anodized Frame with Blue Steel Cylinder Model

Exc.	V.G.	Good	Fair	Poor
400	350	250	225	195

Silver Anodized with Blue Steel Cylinder Model

Only a few hundred pistols in this variation were produced by the factory with an "S" suffix.

Exc.	V.G.	Good	Fair	Poor
900	800	600	400	200

NOTE: Stamped after the serial number or on the bottom of the frame. Varieties of "S" marked lightweights exist. Individual evaluation and appraisal is recommended. These are factory seconds and are verifiable.
NOTE: For original Lightweight Single-Six boxes add 25% to 40%.

Super Single Six

Introduced in 1964, this is the Single Six with adjustable sights. Prices given below are for pistols with 5-1/2" and 6-1/2" barrels.

Courtesy *Know Your Ruger Single Actions: The Second Decade.*
Blacksmith Corp.

Exc.	V.G.	Good	Fair	Poor
275	225	150	125	100

Super Single Six with 4-5/8" Barrel (200 built)

Exc.	V.G.	Good	Poor
1000	900	750	400

Super Single Six-Nickel-Plated Model (Approximately 100 built)

Exc.	V.G.	Good	Poor
2250	1600	1200	—

NOTE: The above models are factory verifiable.

Bearcat

This is a scaled-down version of the single action. It is chambered for .22 rimfire and has a 4" barrel and an unfluted, roll engraved cylinder. The frame is alloy, and it has a brass colored anodized alloy triggerguard. The finish is blue, and the grips are plastic impregnated wood until 1963, thereafter walnut with eagle medallions were used. This model was manufactured from 1958-1970.

Courtesy *Know Your Ruger Single Actions: The Second Decade.*
Blacksmith Corp.

Serial Number under 30000

Exc.	V.G.	Good	Fair	Poor
350	275	225	150	125

Alphabet Model

Exc.	V.G.	Good	Fair	Poor
400	350	295	275	225

Black Anodized Triggerguard Model (109 built)

Exc.	V.G.	Good	Fair	Poor
800	600	500	400	—

Serial Number over 30000 or with 90-prefix

Exc.	V.G.	Good	Fair	Poor
350	300	265	225	175

Super Bearcat

This model is similar to the Bearcat, with a steel frame and, on later models, a blued steel triggerguard and grip frame. The early examples still used brass. This model was manufactured from 1971 to 1974.

Courtesy W.P. Hallstein III and son Chip

Exc.	V.G.	Good	Fair	Poor
350	300	250	225	175

Blackhawk Flattop-.357 Magnum

The success of the Single Six led to the production of a larger version chambered for the .357 Magnum cartridge. This model is a single action, with a 6-shot fluted cylinder and a flat top strap with adjustable "Micro sight." The barrel length is 4-5/8", 6.5", and 10". The finish is blue with checkered hard rubber grips on the early examples and smooth walnut on later ones. There were approximately 42,600 manufactured between 1955 and 1962.

Courtesy *Know Your Ruger Single Action Revolvers 1953-63.* Blacksmith Corp.

Courtesy *Know Your Ruger Single Action Revolvers 1953-63.* Blacksmith Corp.

4-5/8" barrel

Exc.	V.G.	Good	Fair	Poor
500	450	275	250	225

6-1/2" barrel

Exc.	V.G.	Good	Fair	Poor
700	550	450	375	350

10" barrel

Exc.	V.G.	Good	Fair	Poor
1200	950	850	750	650

NOTE: Add $150 for NIB.

A Ruger Blackhawk Flattop revolver. sold at auction for $1,610. Two digit serial number. Condition was mint. Amoskeag Auction Company, May 2000

Blackhawk Flattop .44 Magnum

Courtesy *Know Your Ruger Single Action Revolvers 1953-63*.
Blacksmith Corp.

In 1956 the .44 Magnum was introduced, and Ruger jumped on the bandwagon. This is similar in appearance to the .357 but has a slightly heavier frame and a larger cylinder. It was available in a 6.5", 7.5", and 10" barrel. It was manufactured from 1956-1963. There were approximately 28,000 manufactured.

Courtesy *Know Your Ruger Single Action Revolvers 1953-63*.
Blacksmith Corp.

6-1/2" barrel

NIB	Exc.	V.G.	Good	Fair	Poor
850	650	550	450	350	250

7-1/2" barrel

NIB	Exc.	V.G.	Good	Fair	Poor
1000	850	700	600	450	300

10" barrel

NIB	Exc.	V.G.	Good	Fair	Poor
1500	1200	900	800	700	400

Blackhawk

This model is similar to the "Flattop," but the rear sight is protected by two raised protrusions—one on each side. It was available chambered for the .30 Carbine, .357 Magnum, .41 Magnum, or the .45 Colt cartridge. Barrel lengths are 4-5/8" or 6.5" in .357 Magnum and .41 Magnum. .45 Colt version has 4-5/8" and 7.5" barrel lengths. The .30 Carbine is furnished with a 7.5" barrel only. The finish is blue, and the grips are walnut with Ruger medallions. This model was produced from 1962 to 1972.

Courtesy *Know Your Ruger Single Action Revolvers 1953-63*.
Blacksmith Corp.

Exc.	V.G.	Good	Fair	Poor
400	300	200	150	125

NOTE: Original verified factory brass grip frame will add at least $200 to above prices. It was available chambered for the .357 Magnum or .41 Magnum (4-5/8" or 6-1/2" barrel), or .45 Long Colt (4-5/8" or 7-1/2" barrel).

NOTE: The .41 Magnum with factory installed brass frame will bring $800 to $1500 depending on condition.

Blackhawk Convertible

This model is the same as the Blackhawk with an extra cylinder to change or convert calibers. The .357 Magnum has a 9mm cylinder, and the .45 Colt has a .45 ACP cylinder.

.357/9mm

Exc.	V.G.	Good	Fair	Poor
450	400	300	200	—

.45 L.C./.45 ACP

Exc.	V.G.	Good	Fair	Poor
500	400	300	200	—

The 4-5/8" barrel will bring a slight premium.

NOTE: Nonprefix serial numbered .357/9mm Blackhawks will bring a premium.

Super Blackhawk

The formidable recoil of the .44 Magnum cartridge was difficult to handle in a revolver with a small grip such as found on the Blackhawk, so it was decided to produce a larger-framed revolver with increased size in the grip. The rear of the trigger-guard was squared off, and the cylinder was left unfluted to increase mass. This model was offered with a 7.5" barrel; 600 6.5" barrel Super Blackhawks were produced by factory error. This model is blued and has smooth walnut grips with medallions. The first of these revolvers were offered in a fitted wood case and are rare today. The Super Blackhawk was made from 1959-1972.

Exc.	V.G.	Good	Fair	Poor
450	350	250	200	150

Early Model in Wood Presentation Case

Exc.	V.G.	Good	Fair	Poor
850	650	475	400	300

In Fitted White Cardboard Case

Exc.	V.G.	Good	Fair	Poor
1200	1000	950	875	675

With Long Grip Frame in Wood Case (300 guns built)

Exc.	V.G.	Good	Fair	Poor
1250	1150	1050	800	675

Factory Verified 6-1/2" barrel-about 600 guns built in the 23000 to 25000 serial number range.

Exc.	V.G.	Good	Fair	Poor
750	650	550	450	375

NOTE: For pistols with brass grip frames add $150 to above prices.

NOTE: For pistols with verified factory installed brass grip frame add $200. Each example should be appraised.

WHAT'S IT LIKE-THE RUGER SUPER BLACKHAWK

When Ruger caught wind of Smith & Wesson bringing forth the .44 Magnum, they rushed to do the same. Three of their .357 Blackhawks were re-chambered and rebarreled to .44 Magnum, and when one blew with proof loads they went to the larger frame that became the .44 Magnum Blackhawk or Flat-Top. This Model had the same grip frame as the Colt Single Action Army which was designed to comfortably shoot 250 gr. bullets at around 800-900 fps. I purchased one of the first .44 Magnum Rugers to arrive and found it kicked even worse than the Smith & Wesson .44 Magnum. Of course, realize that in those early days none of us had ever experienced recoil anywhere near what the .44 Magnum produced. Apparently most shooters felt the same way and in 1959 Ruger made some significant changes in their .44 Magnum Blackhawk. The grip frame was made larger with a square backed trigger guard, the barrel length was increased from 6 1/2" to 7 1/2", and to add weight, the grip frame was now steel instead of an aluminum alloy, and the cylinder was unfluted. For more than 40 years now the Super Blackhawk has been the true workhorse of the hunting fields and probably the greatest bargain offered to big bore shooters. In 1973 it became the New Model Super Blackhawk with a transfer bar safety that allowed it to be safely carried fully loaded with six rounds. Today the Super Blackhawk is offered in both blue and stainless, and in barrel lengths of 4 5/8", 5 1/2", 7 1/2", and 10 1/2". I particularly prefer the longest length for its easiest shooting qualities using it with great success on both the silhouette range and in the game fields.

John Taffin

Hawkeye Single Shot

Courtesy John C. Dougan

The shooting public wanted a small-caliber, high-velocity handgun. The Smith & Wesson Model 53, chambered for the .22 Jet, appeared in 1961; and the cartridge created extraction problems for a revolver. Ruger solved the problem with the introduction of the Hawkeye-a single shot that looked like a six shooter. In place of the cylinder was a breech block that cammed to the side for loading. This pistol was excellent from an engineering and performance standpoint but was not a commercial success. The Hawkeye is chambered for the .256 Magnum, a bottleneck cartridge, and has an 8.5" barrel and

adjustable sights. The finish is blued with walnut, medallion grips. The barrel is tapped at the factory for a 1" scope base. This pistol is quite rare as only 3,300 were produced in 1963 and 1964.

NIB	Exc.	V.G.	Good	Fair	Poor
1500	1200	1000	850	600	500

Editor's Comment: All of the above single action Ruger pistols fitted with factory optional grips will bring a premium regardless of model. This premium applies to pistols manufactured from 1954 to 1962 only. For the following optional grips the premium is: Ivory $650, Stag $300.

NEW MODEL SERIES

The Ruger firm has always demonstrated keen perception and in 1973 completely modified their single action lockwork to accommodate a hammer block or transfer bar. This hammer block or transfer bar prevented accidental discharge should a revolver be dropped. In doing so, the company circumvented a great deal of potential legal problems and made collectibles out of the previous models. There are many individuals who simply do not care for the "New Models," as they are called, and will not purchase them; but judging from the continued success and growth of the Ruger company, those individuals must be the exception, not the rule.

Super Single Six Convertible (New Model)

This model is similar in appearance to the old model but has the new hammer block safety system. The frame has two pins instead of three screws, and opening the loading gate frees the cylinder stop for loading. Barrel lengths are 4-5/8", 5.5", 6.5", and 9.5". The sights are adjustable; the finish is blued. The grips are walnut with a medallion, and an interchangeable .22 Magnum cylinder is supplied. This model was introduced in 1973 and is currently in production.

NIB	Exc.	V.G.	Good	Fair	Poor
313	245	190	125	100	80

Stainless Steel Single Six Convertible

The same as the standard blued model but made from stainless steel. Offered with a 4-5/8", 6-1/2", and 9-1/2" barrel.

NIB	Exc.	V.G.	Good	Fair	Poor
310	250	200	175	125	100

NOTE: Pistols with 4-5/8" or 9-1/2" barrel will bring an additional 40% premium. Pistols with 4-5/8" barrels with "made in the 200th year of American Liberty" rollmark on the barrel will bring at least 100% premium to the NIB prices.

New Model Single-Six (.22 Long Rifle only) "Star" Model

This model was produced in blue and stainless for one year only in 4-5/8", 5-1/2", 6-1/2", and 9-1/2" barrel lengths. Very low production on this model.

Blue Variation

5.5" or 6.5" barrel

NIB	Exc.	V.G.	Good	Fair	Poor
450	400	350	300	275	—

9.5" barrel-Rare

NIB	Exc.	V.G.	Good	Fair	Poor
550	500	450	400	350	—

4.62" barrel-Very Rare

NIB	Exc.	V.G.	Good	Fair	Poor
800	750	450	400	350	—

Stainless Variation

5.5" or 6.5" barrel

NIB	Exc.	V.G.	Good	Fair	Poor
375	325	275	—	—	—

9.5" barrel

NIB	Exc.	V.G.	Good	Fair	Poor
500	450	400	—	—	—

4.62" barrel-Rare

NIB	Exc.	V.G.	Good	Fair	Poor
600	550	500	—	—	—

Fixed Sight New Model Single Six

First made as drift adjustable rear sight (500 each in 4-5/8", 5-1/2", and 6-1/2" blue) and now a catalogued item as a pinched frame style fixed rear sight. Barrel lengths are offered in 5-1/2" and 6-1/2" lengths. Finish is blued or glossy stainless steel. Rear sight is fixed. Weights are between 32 and 38 oz. depending on barrel length and cylinder.

Blued Finish

NIB	Exc.	V.G.	Good	Fair	Poor
275	225	200	150	125	100

Stainless Steel

NIB	Exc.	V.G.	Good	Fair	Poor
335	300	250	200	150	125

Colorado Centennial Single Six

This model had a stainless steel grip frame, and the balance is blued. It has walnut grips with medallion insert. The barrel is 6-1/2", and the revolver is furnished with a walnut case with a centennial medal insert. There were 15,000 manufactured in 1975.

NIB	Exc.	V.G.	Good	Fair	Poor
300	250	200	—	—	—

NOTE: Add 50% for model with Liberty marked barrel.

Model "SSM" Single Six

This is the Single Six chambered for the .32 H&R Magnum cartridge. The first 800 pistols were marked with "SSM" on the cylinder frame and will bring a slight premium. Sold from 1984 to 1997. Adjustable sights.

NIB	Exc.	V.G.	Good	Fair	Poor
350	300	200	150	125	100

New Model Single Six-Fixed Sight

Introduced in 2000 this revolver is chambered for the .32 H&R Magnum cartridge and fitted with a 4.625" barrel. Offered in blue or stainless steel. Short (1/4" shorter) simulated ivory grips. Vaquero-style frame with fixed sights.

NIB	Exc.	V.G.	Good	Fair	Poor
525	400	—	—	—	—

Buckeye Special

This model was built in 1989 and 1990. It is chambered for the .38-40 or 10mm and .32-20 or .32 H&R cartridges.

NIB	Exc.	V.G.	Good	Fair	Poor
450	350	295	250	125	—

New Model Blackhawk

This model is similar in appearance to the old model Blackhawk, offered in the same calibers and barrel lengths. It has the transfer bar safety device. It was introduced in 1973 and is currently in production.

NIB	Exc.	V.G.	Good	Fair	Poor
325	250	200	175	150	125

Stainless Steel Blackhawk (New Model)

This is simply the New Model Blackhawk made from stainless steel. To date it has been offered in .357, .44, and .45 L.C. calibers.

NIB	Exc.	V.G.	Good	Fair	Poor
375	325	275	225	175	150

Blackhawk Convertible (New Model)

This model is the same as the Blackhawk with interchangeable conversion cylinders—.357 Magnum/9mm and .45 Colt/.45 ACP. Prices below are given for blued model.

NIB	Exc.	V.G.	Good	Fair	Poor
300	250	200	175	150	125

.45 ACP & .45 Long Colt convertable (1998)

NIB	Exc.	V.G.	Good	Fair	Poor
375	300	—	—	—	—

Stainless Model (300 guns built) .357/9mm.

NIB	Exc.	V.G.	Good	Fair	Poor
—	700	600	500	375	250

Model SRM Blackhawk

This is the New Model Blackhawk with a 7.5" or 10.5" barrel. It was chambered for the .357 Maximum and was intended for silhouette shooting. This model experienced problems with gas erosion in the forcing cone and under the top strap and was removed from production in 1984 after approximately 9200 were manufactured.

Exc.	V.G.	Good	Fair	Poor
600	500	400	275	250

Super Blackhawk (New Model)

This model is similar in appearance to the old model but has the transfer bar safety device. It was manufactured from 1973 to the present and commenced at serial number 81-00001.

NIB	Exc.	V.G.	Good	Fair	Poor
425	350	275	225	175	125

Super Blackhawk Stainless Steel

This model is the same as the blued version but is made of stainless steel. In 1998 this model was offered in 4-5/8" or 7-1/2" barrels with hunter grip frame and laminated grip panels. Add $50 to prices below for this feature.

NIB	Exc.	V.G.	Good	Fair	Poor
450	395	300	250	200	150

Bisley Model

This model has the modified features found on the famous old Colt Bisley Target model—the flat top frame, fixed or adjustable sights, and the longer grip frame that has become the Bisley trademark. The Bisley is available chambered for .22 l.r., .32 H&R Magnum, .357 Magnum, .41 Magnum, .44 Magnum, and .45 Long Colt. The barrel lengths are 6.5" and 7.5"; cylinders are either fluted or unfluted and roll engraved. The finish is a satin blue, and the grips are smooth Goncalo Alves with medallions. The Bisley was introduced in 1986.

.22 Long Rifle and .32 H&R Magnum

NIB	Exc.	V.G.	Good	Fair	Poor
380	305	225	200	150	125

NOTE: Add $100 for .32 Magnum Bisley.

.357 Magnum, .41 Magnum, .44 Magnum, and .45 Long Colt

NIB	Exc.	V.G.	Good	Fair	Poor
450	365	275	250	200	175

NOTE: Approximately 750 stainless grip frame .22 caliber Bisleys were made. These will demand a premium.

Shootists Bisley

Produced in 1994 for the Shootist organization in memory of Tom Ruger. Chambered for the .22 cartridge these revolvers were limited to 52 total produced. They were stainless steel and were fitted with 4-5/8" barrels. The barrels were marked, "IN MEMORY OF OUR FRIEND TOM RUGER THE SHOOTIST 1994". Some of these revolvers, but not all, have the name of the owner engraved on the backstrap.

Photo courtesy of Jim Taylor

NIB	Exc.	V.G.	Good	Fair	Poor
1200	—	—	—	—	—

Old Army Percussion Revolver

This model is a .45 caliber percussion revolver with a 7-1/2" barrel. It has a 6-shot cylinder, with a blued finish and walnut grips. For 1994 this model is offered with fixed sights. Weight is about 46 oz.

NIB	Exc.	V.G.	Good	Fair	Poor
413	325	250	100	100	100

NOTE: For pistols with original factory installed brass grip frame add $150 to above prices.

Old Army Stainless Steel

This model is the same as the blued version except that it is made of stainless steel.

NIB	Exc.	V.G.	Good	Fair	Poor
465	350	275	100	100	100

A HISTORY OF THE RUGER OLD ARMY BLACKPOWDER REVOLVER

By J.C. Munnell

In 1972, Sturm, Ruger & Co. once again confounded "modern" thinking, and introduced another "retro" gun—the Old Army percussion revolver. In doing so, Bill Ruger was not attempting to produce a replica of any old-time gun. Instead, he introduced a thoroughly modern black powder revolver.

The Old Army is built on a much-modified Super Blackhawk cylinder frame. It initially had a fully-adjustable rear sight, and a ramp front sight for serious accuracy. It was and is a six-shooter, and always has had a 7-1/2" barrel. The cylinder is circumferentially roll marked with the cautionary words "For Black Powder Only."

Series numbers run from 140-00001-up, although the first 100 numbered guns were not made until over a year later and possess later features. The first 700 or so guns made had a flat-topped front sight.

Initial production was of blued chrome-moly steel, and the early guns all had the standard alloy XR-3 RED grip frame. In 1973, a brass dragoon-style grip frame was added as an option. Although never frequently encountered, these brass frames were available through March of 1975.

In 1975, the Old Army was offered in stainless steel. Initially (for about the first 7,800 guns), no prefix was assigned to the serial numbers of the stainless guns. Later guns were produced in the 145- serial range. (In Nov. of 1980, and after about 46,000 blued guns had been made, all Old Armies with adjustable sights were numbered in the 145- prefix range).

All guns shipped in 1976 bore the barrel inscription "Made in the 200'th Year of American Liberty." Only about 2,300 blued Old Armies were so-marked, while approximately 4,600 non-prefix stainless and only about 1,300 prefix stainless guns were made.

Guns made from 1978 on had the "warning" barrel inscription. This continues today. This is a good place to remark that all Old Army revolvers utilize the "Old Model" lock work, although all parts were not interchangeable with those of Blackhawk models.

By serial number 145-73000, the triggers on the stainless guns were smooth like those on blued buns, instead of serrated.

In 1994, fixed-sight guns were introduced, both in blue and stainless, as companion pieces to the highly successful Ruger Vaquero. Unlike the Vaquero, however, blued Old Armies do not have case-colored frames. These fixed-sight guns were assigned in the 148- prefix.

At the end of 1998, a high-polish stainless finish was added, both to fixed- and adjustable-sighted guns. Many of the high-polish guns also wore faux ivory grips. The current Ruger catalogue lists only high polish for the stainless Old Army.

PACKAGING

Initial shipments of Old Army revolvers were made in 2-piece red and black boxes with the designation .45 caliber. Later, the caliber designation was changed to .44 caliber, although the bore size was **not** changed, and remains .451-.452". Boxes were changed generally to a one-piece orangish box with white and black lettering. Occasionally, an Old Army will be found packaged in a 2-piece yellow and black Old Model Blackhawk box with an added-on end sticker. These were left over boxes after the introduction of the New Model single actions in 1973.

Still later, a yellow and black 1-piece "universal" box was introduced for the entire Ruger handgun line. Current packaging is a lockable plastic box, either with or without a shipping oversleeve.

SPECIAL ISSUES

Since blackpowder guns can be sold to and shipped to non-federally licensed dealers, the Old Army has been popular for commemoratives and special issue. The first such was a spe-cial run of 100 consecutively-numbered blued guns for the national Muzzle Loading Rifle Association in 1974. These guns had the NMLRA emblem in the left grip.

The second special issues was 100 consecutively-numbered stainless guns made for The Ruger Association in 1975. These guns were non-prefix serial number guns, but had a star before the number. **One** of these guns was shipped in 1976 with the "Liberty" barrel inscription!

In 1977, a second R.C.A. issue was made out of the last 200 guns produced in 1976 with the "Liberty" barrel inscription. These guns had the 145- prefix and also had an eagle stamped before the serial number. Both R.C.A. series also had identifying marks, logos or inscriptions on the guns.

Within the past couple of years, another run of stainless Old Armies was made, ostensibly for the R.C.A., although many were sold through The Sportsman's Guide.

ODDITIES

Every collectible gun model with have its "strange" or mis-marked examples, and the Ruger Old Army revolver is no exception. Usually such guns are simply mistakes which, since they have no mechanical or glaring cosmetic defects, find their way into normal commerce. However, there is one example of an Old Army Oddity which occurred fairly frequently throughout 1975. Interspersed throughout the 1975 production of the stainless models are guns on which the cylinder inscription is backwards; in order to read it, the guns must be pointing toward you!! It is my belief that these were intended for the R.C.A. first series guns (or they were the reason the factory agreed to sell the R.C.A. guns in the first place?), because most of the 100 R.C.A. guns had the backwards inscription. However, several such cylinders were installed in general production guns. Incidentally, **one** such blued gun is known.

Other interesting guns are factory "seconds", "show guns", or demonstrators. These guns may be marked in several ways: some have a letter "S" either following the serial number or on the bottom of the cylinder frame, in front of the triggerguard; others have a "U" or an "*" either preceding or following the serial number.

From time to time two frames will be made with the same serial number. When this happens, a letter "D" will be added to the serial number, either preceding or after the number.

Such guns, together with vagaries of grip material or packaging make for interesting—and scarce—sub-variations.

Over the next 28 years of existence, the Ruger Old Army has never been what bean counters would get excited about; sales have been modest but steady. This means that come variations have been produced in extremely small numbers, making the acquisition of one more difficult and more rewarding. Since there are not a lot of Old Army collectors, this may be a real "sleeper" field.

PRICES
Blue: $325, 300, 250, etc.
Stainless: $350, 325, 275, etc.
Add $100 for flat-topped front sight
Add $150 for brass grip frame
Add $200 for backward cylinder inscription stainless gun
Add $100-150 for "Liberty" barrel inscription
Add $50 for high-polish
Add $50 for "ivory" or rosewood grips (not Golcalo Alves grips)
Add $50 for old-style tow-piece red and black boxes.

Add $20 for other style boxes and plastic cases.

Add $50-100 for "D", "S", "U" or "*"-prefix or suffix serial number
NMLRA: $800-750
RCA 1st Series: $750, 700

Ruger Vaquero

This single action pistol was introduced in 1993 and was voted handgun of the year by the shooting industry. It is a fixed sight version of the New Model Blackhawk. It is available in stainless steel or blued with case-colored frame. Offered in three different barrel lengths: 4.62", 5.5", and 7.5". Chambered for the .45 Long Colt. In 1994 the .44-40 and .44 Magnum calibers were added to the Vaquero line. Capacity is 6 rounds. Weighs between 39 and 41 oz. depending on barrel length.

NOTE: Vaqueros with 4-5/8" barrel chambered for .44 Magnum in both blue and stainless are uncatalogued, add 25%.

NIB	Exc.	V.G.	Good	Fair	Poor
435	350	250	200	150	100

Ruger Vaquero Birdshead

Introduced in 2001 this model features a birdshead grip. Chambered for the .45 Long Colt cartridge and fitted with a 5.5" barrel. Offered in stainless steel and blued finish. Weight is about 40 oz.

NIB	Exc.	V.G.	Good	Fair	Poor
545	425	—	—	—	—

Ruger Bisley Vaquero

Introduced in 1997 this model features a 5.5" barrel chambered for .44 Magnum or .45 Long Colt. Grips are smooth rosewood. Finish is blued with case colored frame. Blade front sight and notch rear. Weight is about 40 oz.

NIB	Exc.	V.G.	Good	Fair	Poor
425	350	—	—	—	—

New Ruger Bearcat

The return of an old favorite was made in 1993. This new version is furnished with a .22 Long Rifle cylinder and a .22 WMR cylinder. Barrel length is 4" with fixed sights. Grips are walnut. Offered in both blued finish or stainless steel.

NIB	Exc.	V.G.	Good	Fair	Poor
320	275	225	—	—	—

NOTE: There was a factory recall on the magnum cylinders. Bearcats with both cylinders are very rare and will bring an additional $700-800 premium.

DOUBLE ACTION REVOLVERS

Security Six

This revolver, also known as the Model 117, is chambered for the .357 Magnum cartridge and has a 2.75", 4", or 6" barrel. It features adjustable sights and a square-butt, with checkered walnut grips. It was manufactured between 1970 and 1985. Early guns with fixed sights and square butt were also marked "Security-Six". The model was later termed "Service-Six" and was so marked. The prices listed below are only for the adjustable sight and square butt "Security-Six" models. Round butt Security-Sixes with adjustable are worth a premium.

Exc.	V.G.	Good	Fair	Poor
250	225	200	150	100

NOTE: Fixed sight guns marked Security-Six and round butt Security-Sixes with adjustable sights are worth a premium.

Stainless Steel Model 717

This model is the Security-Six made from stainless steel.

Exc.	V.G.	Good	Fair	Poor
295	250	225	175	125

Speed Six

This model is known as the Model 207, chambered for .357 Magnum; Model 208, chambered for .38 Special; and Model 209, chambered for 9mm. It has a 2.75" or 4" barrel, fixed sights, and a round butt with checkered walnut grips and was blued. There are some with factory bobbed hammers. This model was introduced in 1973.

Exc.	V.G.	Good	Fair	Poor
250	225	200	150	100

Models 737, 738, 739

These are the designations for the stainless steel versions of the Speed-Six. They are the same revolver except for the material used in the manufacture.

Exc.	V.G.	Good	Fair	Poor
275	250	225	175	125

Police Service-Six

This model is also known as the Model 107, chambered for .357 Magnum; the Model 108, chambered for the .38 Special; and the 109, chambered for the 9mm. The barrel is 2.75" or 4". A few 6" barrel Service-Sixes were also produced and these are worth a premium. It has fixed sights and a square butt, with checkered walnut grips. The finish is blued. The 9mm was discontinued in 1984; the other two calibers, in 1988.

Exc.	V.G.	Good	Fair	Poor
250	225	200	150	100

Model 707 and 708

This is the designation for the stainless versions of the Police Service-Six. It was not produced in 9mm, and only the 4" barrel was offered. This model was discontinued in 1988.

Exc.	V.G.	Good	Fair	Poor
270	250	225	175	125

GP-100

This model is chambered for the .357 Magnum/.38 Special. It is available with fixed or adjustable sights in barrel lengths of 3", 4", or 6" barrel and has a frame designed for constant use of heavy magnum loads. The rear sight has a white outline, and the front sight features interchangeable colored inserts. The finish is blued, and the grips are a new design made of rubber with smooth Goncalo Alves inserts. This model was introduced in 1986.

NIB	Exc.	V.G.	Good	Fair	Poor
423	355	275	225	175	125

GP-100 Stainless

This model is the same as the GP-100 except that the material used is stainless steel.

NIB	Exc.	V.G.	Good	Fair	Poor
457	375	300	250	200	150

SP-101

This model is similar in appearance to the GP-100 but has a smaller frame and is chambered for the .22 l.r. (6-shot), 38 Special (5-shot), .357 Magnum (5-shot), and 9mm (5-shot). The grips are all black synthetic, and the sights are adjustable for windage. Barrel lengths are 2" or 3", and construction is of stainless steel. This model was introduced in 1989. 6" barrel is available for .22 caliber.

NIB	Exc.	V.G.	Good	Fair	Poor
445	360	300	250	200	150

SP-101 Spurless-Hammer

This model was introduced in 1993 and features an SP-101 without an exposed hammer spur. Available in two calibers: .38 Special and .357 Magnum with 2-1/4" barrel. This double action revolver has fixed sights, holds 5 rounds and weighs about 26 oz.

NIB	Exc.	V.G.	Good	Fair	Poor
325	250	200	150	100	80

Redhawk

This model is a large-frame, double action revolver which was chambered for the .41 Magnum until 1992, and currently for the .44 Magnum cartridges. The barrel lengths are 5-1/2" and 7-1/2". The finish is blued, and the grips are smooth walnut. The Redhawk was introduced in 1986.

NIB	Exc.	V.G.	Good	Fair	Poor
410	325	275	225	175	125

Redhawk Stainless Steel

The same as the blued version except constructed of stainless steel. It was chambered for .357 Magnum until 1985, the .41 Magnum until 1992, and currently for the .44 Magnum. In 1998 this model was offered chambered for .45 Long Colt cartridge in barrel lengths of 5.5" and 7.5".

NIB	Exc.	V.G.	Good	Fair	Poor
450	350	300	250	200	150

WHAT'S IT LIKE:-THE RUGER .480 SUPER REDHAWK

The rumors had been circulating for quite a while that Ruger would be chambering one of their sixguns for the .454 Casull. We all expected Ruger to choose the Bisley Model as the platform and fit it with a five-shot cylinder. Ruger chose a different path. Instead of a single action, they used a double action; instead of a five-shot cylinder, they went with a six-shot cylinder. So much for prognosticators! Ruger's choice was the super strong Super Redhawk made even more durable by the use of a higher grade of steel. That was two years ago and the .454 Casull has proven to be very popular in the Ruger Super Redhawk. Since that time, Bill Ruger had retired, and to honor him we have the first cartridge to bear the Ruger name with the .480 Ruger chambered in the same Super Redhawk. Although it is called a ".480", this new cartridge actually uses the same diameter bullets as the .475 Linebaugh and is in fact simply a shortened .475 Linebaugh going from 1.4" to an official 1.283". The Linebaugh uses 420 gr. bullets at 1350 fps while the new .480 Ruger is loaded by Hornady with a 325 gr. XTP-JHP bullet at the same speed. Call the .480 a heavy loaded .44 Special to the .475 Linebaugh's .44 Magnum. In its current loading, the .480 Ruger should be an excellent deer, black bear, and wild pig cartridge that most shooters will find not all that difficult to handle in the .480 Ruger Super Redhawk especially with the added weight of a scope which just naturally goes with this large sixgun which comes scope ready with Ruger rings. Several of us baptized the .480 Ruger Super Redhawk and Hornady's factory ammunition with excellent success on wild pigs on a hunt sponsored by Hornady. I welcome the new cartridge and predict large sales for the .480 Super Redhawk from Ruger.

John Taffin

Super Redhawk

This is a more massive version of the Redhawk. It weighs 53 oz. and is offered with a 7.5" or 9.5" barrel. It is made of stainless steel, and the barrel rib is milled to accept the Ruger scope-ring system. The grips are the combination rubber and Goncalo Alves-type found on the GP-100. This revolver was introduced in 1987. In 1999 this model was offered chambered for the .454 Casull cartridge with 7.5" or 9.5" barrel. In 2001 this model was offered in .480 Ruger caliber in 7.5" or 9.5" barrel.

NIB	Exc.	V.G.	Good	Fair	Poor
500	450	400	350	300	225

NOTE: Add $200 for .454 Casull or .480 Ruger caliber. Revolvers chambered for the .454 Casull also accept .45 Long Colt cartridges.

SEMIAUTOMATIC HANDGUNS

P-85 or P-89

This model represents Ruger's entry into the wonder nine market. The P-85 is a double action, high-capacity (15-shot detachable magazine) semiautomatic, with an alloy frame and steel slide. It has a 4.5" barrel, ambidextrous safety, and three dot sighting system. It has a matte black finish and black synthetic grips. The latest option for this model is a decocking device to replace the standard safety. There is also an optional molded locking case and extra magazine with loading tool available. It is more reasonably priced than many of its competitors. This pistol was introduced in 1987 and was sold at large premium for some time due to limited supply and great demand. As of this writing, Ruger is producing this pistol in a new plant in Prescott, Arizona; and the premium situation no longer exists. This model is also produced in a 9x21 cartridge for nonNato countries. In 1991 the internal mechanism was changed slightly with the result that a name change occurred "P85 Mark II".

NIB	Exc.	V.G.	Good	Fair	Poor
335	300	275	250	200	150

P-85 Stainless Steel

This model is the same as the matte black version except that the receiver assembly is made of stainless steel.

NIB	Exc.	V.G.	Good	Fair	Poor
375	335	300	200	200	150

KP-89X

Introduced in 1993 this pistol features a stainless steel convertible safety model which comes with both 9mm and .30 Luger barrels. The barrels are interchangeable without the use of tools. Magazine capacity is 15 rounds. Less than 6,000 produced.

NIB	Exc.	V.G.	Good	Fair	Poor
420	380	345	245	200	150

P-89

Introduced in 1991 this semiautomatic pistol is chambered for the 9mm cartridge. It has a blued finish and a 15-round magazine. The safety is a manual ambidextrous lever type. The barrel is 4.5" and the empty weight is approximately 36 oz.

NIB	Exc.	V.G.	Good	Fair	Poor
335	250	200	150	100	80

KP-89

This model is the same configuration as the P-89 but furnished with a stainless steel finish. Introduced in 1991.

NIB	Exc.	V.G.	Good	Fair	Poor
375	300	250	200	150	100

P-89DC

This model features a blued finish and is chambered for the 9mm Parabellum cartridge but is fitted with a decock-only lever (no manual safety). After decocking the gun can be fired by a double action pull of the trigger.

NIB	Exc.	V.G.	Good	Fair	Poor
375	300	250	200	150	100

KP-89DC

This is the stainless steel version of the P-89DC with decock only.

NIB	Exc.	V.G.	Good	Fair	Poor
375	300	250	200	150	100

KP-89DAO

Chambered for the 9mm cartridge this model is the stainless steel double action only version of the above model.

NIB	Exc.	V.G.	Good	Fair	Poor
375	300	250	200	150	100

KP-90

Chambered for the .45 ACP cartridge, this model is in stainless steel and holds 7 rounds in the magazine. It is fitted with a manual safety. Introduced in 1991.

NIB	Exc.	V.G.	Good	Fair	Poor
475	375	275	200	150	100

P-90

Same as above model but with blued finish. Introduced in 1998.

NIB	Exc.	V.G.	Good	Fair	Poor
450	350	—	—	—	—

KP-90DC

This stainless steel version of the KP-90 has a decock-only system. Chambered for the .45 ACP cartridge.

NIB	Exc.	V.G.	Good	Fair	Poor
460	350	275	200	150	100

KP-91DC

This model features a stainless steel finish and is chambered for the .40 S&W cartridge. Magazine capacity is 11 rounds. It has a decock-only system. Introduced in 1992. Discontinued.

NIB	Exc.	V.G.	Good	Fair	Poor
375	325	275	200	150	100

KP-91 DAO

Chambered for the .40 S&W with stainless steel finish it features a double action only system. Discontinued.

NIB	Exc.	V.G.	Good	Fair	Poor
375	325	275	200	150	100

P93D

This is a blued version with ambidextrous de-cocker and 3.9" barrel. Introduced in 1998.

NIB	Exc.	V.G.	Good	Fair	Poor
400	325	—	—	—	—

KP-93DC

Introduced in 1993 this pistol is a new addition to the P series as a compact model. Stainless steel and chambered for the 9mm cartridge it has a magazine capacity of 15 rounds. Available in decock-only configuration. Barrel length is 3.9" and the weight is about 24 oz. empty.

NIB	Exc.	V.G.	Good	Fair	Poor
500	400	300	250	150	100

KP-93DAO

The double action only version of the KP-93 compact series.

NIB	Exc.	V.G.	Good	Fair	Poor
490	400	300	250	150	100

KP-94

Introduced in 1994 this model is smaller than the full size P series pistols and the compact P93 pistols. Offered in 9mm or .40 S&W calibers this pistol has an aluminum alloy frame and stainless steel slide. Barrel length is 4-1/4" and magazine capacity for the 9mm is 15-rounds and for the .40 11 rounds. Weight is approximately 33 oz. It is offered in double action only as well as traditional double action. A decock only model is available also.

NIB	Exc.	V.G.	Good	Fair	Poor
415	350	300	250	200	150

KP-94DC

This is similar to the model above but in decock only.

NIB	Exc.	V.G.	Good	Fair	Poor
415	350	300	250	200	150

P-94

This is a blued version of the KP-94. Introduced in 1998.

NIB	Exc.	V.G.	Good	Fair	Poor
400	325	—	—	—	—

KP-94DAO

Same as the KP-94 model but in double action only.

NIB	Exc.	V.G.	Good	Fair	Poor
400	350	300	250	200	150

KP-944

Chambered for the .40 S&W cartridge this model has a stainless steel tapered slide, an 11-round magazine, and a manual safety. Models made after September, 1994 have a 10-round magazine.

NIB	Exc.	V.G.	Good	Fair	Poor
415	350	300	250	200	150

KP-944DC

Same as a model above but fitted with a decock only system.

NIB	Exc.	V.G.	Good	Fair	Poor
415	350	300	250	200	150

KP-944DAO

Same as model above but with a double action only model of fire.

NIB	Exc.	V.G.	Good	Fair	Poor
415	350	300	250	200	150

P-95

Introduced in 1996 this 9mm pistol features a 3.9" barrel, polymer frame and stainless steel slide. Decocker only. Fixed 3-dot sights are standard. Overall length is 7.3". Empty weight is about 29 oz. In 2001 this model was offered with a manual safety and blued finish.

NIB	Exc.	V.G.	Good	Fair	Poor
450	350	300	225	150	100

P-95DAO

Same as above but in double action only.

NIB	Exc.	V.G.	Good	Fair	Poor
450	350	300	225	150	100

KP-95DC

This model is the same as the matte black version of the P-95, only this is in stainless steel. It has a decock only safety.

NIB	Exc.	V.G.	Good	Fair	Poor
450	350	300	225	150	100

KP-95DAO

Same as the model above but in double action only. In 2001 this model was offered with a manual safety and blued finish.

NIB	Exc.	V.G.	Good	Fair	Poor
450	350	300	225	150	100

KP97D

Introduced in 1999 this decock only model is chambered for the .45 ACP cartridge. It has a stainless steel slide. magazine capacity is 7 rounds. Fixed sights. Weight is about 27 oz.

NIB	Exc.	V.G.	Good	Fair	Poor
450	350	—	—	—	—

KP97DAO

Same specifications as the model above but in double action only. Introduced in 1999.

NIB	Exc.	V.G.	Good	Fair	Poor
450	350	—	—	—	—

SEMIAUTOMATIC RIFLES

10/22 Standard Carbine With Walnut Stock

This model has an 18.5" barrel and is chambered for the .22 l.r. It has a 10-shot, detachable rotary magazine and a folding rear sight. The stock is smooth walnut, with a barrel band and carbine-style buttplate. This rifle enjoys a fine reputation for accuracy and dependability and is considered an excellent value. It was introduced in 1964.
Birch Stock-Deduct $20.

NIB	Exc.	V.G.	Good	Fair	Poor
250	175	125	100	75	50

10/22 Standard Carbine Stainless Steel

Same as above but with stainless steel barrel and receiver.

NIB	Exc.	V.G.	Good	Fair	Poor
225	185	150	125	100	75

10/22 Magnum

Introduced in 1999 this model is chambered for the .22 Magnum cartridge. Barrel length is 18.5". Folding rear sight and gold bead front sight. Hardwood stock. Weight is about 5.5 lbs.

NIB	Exc.	V.G.	Good	Fair	Poor
425	325	300	—	—	—

10/22 Sporter

This model is similar to the Standard Carbine except that it has a Monte Carlo stock, finger-groove forend, and no barrel band. It was manufactured between 1966 and 1971.

Exc.	V.G.	Good	Fair	Poor
400	300	200	175	125

NOTE: Factory hand checkering-Add 300%.

10/22 Deluxe Sporter

The same as the Sporter with a checkered stock and better buttplate. Introduced in 1971.

NIB	Exc.	V.G.	Good	Fair	Poor
250	200	150	125	100	75

10/22 International Carbine

This model is similar to the Standard Carbine, with a full-length, Mannlicher-style stock. It was manufactured between 1966 and 1971 and is fairly rare on today's market.

Exc.	V.G.	Good	Fair	Poor
550	425	350	300	250

NOTE: Factory hand checkering-Add 50%.

10/22 International Carbine (New Model)

This 1994 model is a reintroduction of the older version. It is offered in either a blued or stainless steel finish. Barrel length is 18-1/2". Magazine capacity is 10 rounds. The hardwood stock had no checkering when this model was first introduced. Shortly after introduced the factory began checkering these stocks. Weight is about 5.2 lbs.

NIB	Exc.	V.G.	Good	Fair	Poor
225	200	150	125	100	75

Model 10/22T

Introduced in 1996 this model is a target version of the 10/22 line. It has a laminated American hardwood stock with blued heavy barrel with hammer-forged spiral finish. Rifle comes standard without sights. Barrel length is 20". Weight is approximately 7.25 lbs.

NIB	Exc.	V.G.	Good	Fair	Poor
450	350	275	200	150	100

Model 10/22TNZ

This target model features a 20" stainless steel barrel and receiver with laminated thumbhole stock. No sights. Weight is about 7 lbs. Introduced in 2001.

NIB	Exc.	V.G.	Good	Fair	Poor
650	475	—	—	—	—

Model 10/22 Canadian Centennial

In 1966 and 1967 approximately 4,500 10/22 Sporters were built for the Canadian Centennial. The first 2,000 were sold with a Remington Model 742 in .308 caliber with matching serial numbers. The Ruger Sporter may be checkered or uncheckered. The two-gun set was either boxed separately or together.

NIB For Two Gun Set
700

NIB For 10/22 Only
450

10/22 Laminated Stock Carbine

Produced in varying quantities since 1986 these models are becoming quite collectible. The stocks range in color from dark green to gray and various shades of brown. Because there are so many different variations each should be individually appraised. Prices listed are for blued carbine models.

NIB	Exc.	V.G.	Good	Fair	Poor
250	200	175	150	125	100

NOTE: In stainless steel add approximately $40 to NIB price.

10/22 Laminated Stock Sporter Model

This model has a tree bark laminated stock.

NIB	Exc.	V.G.	Good	Fair	Poor
325	275	225	175	150	100

10/22 Laminated Stock International

This stainless steel model was an exclusive WalMart product. A few of these models in blue were also produced.

Blue
NIB	Exc.	V.G.	Good	Fair	Poor
400	325	250	200	150	100

Stainless Steel
NIB	Exc.	V.G.	Good	Fair	Poor
350	275	225	175	125	100

10/22 All Weather

This model is fitted with a stainless steel barrel and action and synthetic stock. Introduced in 1997. In 2001 this model was offered with blued finish

NIB	Exc.	V.G.	Good	Fair	Poor
250	200	150	125	100	70

Model 44 Carbine

This model is a short, 18.5" barreled, gas-operated carbine chambered for the .44 Magnum cartridge. It has a 4-shot, non-detachable magazine, a folding rear sight, and a plain walnut stock. This is a handy deer hunting carbine manufactured between 1961 and 1985.

NIB	Exc.	V.G.	Good	Fair	Poor
—	450	350	300	200	150

Deerstalker Model

The same as the Model 44 Carbine with "Deerstalker" stamped on it. This model was manufactured in 1961 and 1962 only.

Exc.	V.G.	Good	Fair	Poor
650	550	400	300	200

Model 44RS

This is the Model 44 with sling swivels and an aperture sight.

Exc.	V.G.	Good	Fair	Poor
525	400	300	200	150

NOTE: "Liberty" marked 44RS carbines are extremely rare and will bring a premium. An individual appraisal is recommended.

Model 44 Sporter

This version has a Monte Carlo stock, finger groove forend, and no barrel band. It was manufactured until 1971.

Exc.	V.G.	Good	Fair	Poor
600	500	350	250	200

NOTE: Factory hand checkered models will bring at least a 75% premium.

Model 44 International Carbine

This version features a full-length, Mannlicher-style stock. It was discontinued in 1971 and is quite collectible.

Exc.	V.G.	Good	Fair	Poor
800	550	425	350	275

NOTE: Factory hand checkered models will bring at least a 50% premium.

Model 44 25th Anniversary Model

This version is lightly engraved, has a medallion in the stock and was only made in 1985, the last year of production.

NIB	Exc.	V.G.	Good	Fair	Poor
550	400	350	300	250	200

Model 99/44 Deerfield Carbine

A new and improved version, introduced in 2000, of the original Model 44 Carbine. Fitted with a 18.5" barrel this gas operated rifle has a hardwood stock and 4-round magazine capacity. Adjustable rear sight. Blued finish. Weight is about 6.2 lbs. This rifle will not cycle .44 Special ammo.

NIB	Exc.	V.G.	Good	Fair	Poor
650	475	—	—	—	—

Mini-14

This is a paramilitary style carbine chambered for the .223 Remington and on a limited basis for the .222 cartridge. It has an 18.5" barrel and is gas-operated. The detachable magazines originally offered held 5, 10, or 20 rounds. The high-capacity magazines are now discontinued, and prices of them are what the market will bear. The Mini-14 has a military-style stock and aperture sight. It was introduced in 1975.

NIB	Exc.	V.G.	Good	Fair	Poor
435	375	325	275	225	150

NOTE: 10 and 20-round magazines are still offered but to law enforcement only.

Mini-14 Stainless Steel
The same as the Mini-14 except constructed of stainless steel.

NIB	Exc.	V.G.	Good	Fair	Poor
465	400	350	300	250	175

Mini-14 All-Weather Rifle
Introduced in 1999 this model has all the features of the stainless steel Mini-14 Rifle with the addition of a black Polymer stock. Weight is about 6.5 lbs.

NIB	Exc.	V.G.	Good	Fair	Poor
500	400	350	300	250	175

Mini-14 Ranch Rifle
This model is similar to the standard Mini-14, with a folding rear sight and the receiver milled to accept the Ruger scope-ring system. The rings are supplied with the rifle.

NOTE: Models chambered in .222 caliber will bring a premium.

NIB	Exc.	V.G.	Good	Fair	Poor
465	400	350	300	250	175

Stainless Steel Mini-14 Ranch Rifle
This model is the same as the blued version except that it is made of stainless steel.

NIB	Exc.	V.G.	Good	Fair	Poor
625	500	400	350	300	225

Mini-14 All-Weather Ranch Rifle
Introduced in 1999 this model has all the features of the stainless steel Ranch Rifle with the addition of a black Polymer stock. Weight is about 6.5 lbs.

NIB	Exc.	V.G.	Good	Fair	Poor
625	500	—	—	—	—

GB Model
This model has a factory-installed folding stock, flash suppressor, and bayonet lug. It was designed and sold by Ruger to law enforcement agencies. A number have come on the civilian market through surplus sales and police trade-ins. With the assault rifle hysteria, prices of this model have fluctuated wildly in some areas. Now that Ruger has discontinued the folding stock and the high capacity magazines, this could become even less predictable. It would behoove anyone contemplating purchase of this model to check their local ordinances and the current market in their area. Note that this is a semiautomatic and totally different than the full-auto version of this weapon available only through Class 3 dealers.

Mini-30
This model was brought out by Ruger in 1987 in answer to the influx of weapons imported from China that were chambered for this cartridge—the 7.62mm x 39 Russian. This cartridge is touted as a fine hunting cartridge for deer-sized game; and by adding this chambering, the handy Mini-14 becomes a legitimate hunting gun—and a new market opened. This model is similar in appearance to the standard Mini-14 and is supplied with Ruger scope rings.

NIB	Exc.	V.G.	Good	Fair	Poor
450	395	300	250	200	150

Mini-30 Stainless with Synthetic stock

NIB	Exc.	V.G.	Good	Fair	Poor
700	550	450	300	200	150

Ruger Carbine
This is a semiautomatic carbine chambered for the 9mm (PC9) or .40 S&W (PC4) cartridges. It is fitted with a 16.25" barrel and black synthetic stock. Post front sight with adjustable rear sight. A receiver is also offered. Detachable magazine has 10 round capacity. Weight is approximately 6.4 lbs. Introduced in 1998.

NIB	Exc.	V.G.	Good	Fair	Poor
550	450	—	—	—	—

NOTE: Add $30 for receiver sight.

SINGLE SHOT RIFLES
All Ruger single shot rifles feature a sliding shotgun-type safety, that engage both the sear and the hammer, all metal parts are polished and blued, each receiver and stock is hand fitted, and the stock is American walnut with a satin finish. The pistol grip and forearm are hand checkered with 20 lines to the inch. Those No. 1 rifles offered with open sights are fitted with an adjustable folding leaf rear sight set into a quarter rib on the barrel and a dovetail-type gold bead front sight. All quarter ribs are machined to accommodate Ruger steel scope rings.

NOTE: There are many rare nonprefixed No. 1 rifles. Unique examples should be individually appraised. "Writers Club" 1 of 21 rifles that are engraved will bring $3000 to $5000 depending on the amount of engraving and gold inlay, caliber, and the person that it was presented to.

Ruger No. 1 Light Sporter (1-A)

This model features open sights, barrel band on lightweight barrel, and Alexander Henry style forearm. Offered with a 22" barrel in four calibers. Rifle weighs 7.25 lbs.

NIB	Exc.	V.G.	Good	Fair	Poor
600	495	400	300	250	200

Ruger No. 1 Standard (1-B)

This model is furnished with no sights, medium barrel, semi-beavertail forearm, and quarter rib with 1" Ruger scope rings. Weighs 8 lbs.

NIB	Exc.	V.G.	Good	Fair	Poor
600	495	400	300	250	200

Ruger No. 1 Standard Stainless (1-B-BBZ)

Introduced in 2000 this model features a laminated wood stock. It is chambered for the .243 Win., .25-06, 7mm Mag., 7mm STW, .30-06, .300 Win. Mag. Fitted with a 26" barrel. Weight is approximately 8 lbs.

NIB	Exc.	V.G.	Good	Fair	Poor
800	600	—	—	—	—

Ruger No. 1 Tropical (1-H)

Fitted with open sights this model has a barrel band on a heavy barrel with Alexander Henry style forearm. Rifle weighs 9 lbs. In 2001 this model was also offered with stainless steel finish and black lamanited stock in .375 H&H.

NIB	Exc.	V.G.	Good	Fair	Poor
800	650	450	300	250	200

NOTE: A few 24" heavy barrel 1-H rifles were chambered for the .45-70 Government cartridge up to 1976. These bring a substantial premium and should be appraised individually. The recently catalogued .404 Jeffery has been discontinued. Only a few of these rifles were produced.

Ruger No. 1 International (1-RSI)

This No. 1 rifle features a lightweight barrel with full length forearm, open sights. Rifle weighs 7.25 lbs.

NIB	Exc.	V.G.	Good	Fair	Poor
700	550	400	300	200	150

Ruger No. 1 Medium Sporter (1-S)

The Medium Sporter is equipped with open sights, a barrel band on a medium weight barrel, and Alexander Henry style forearm. Rifle weighs 8 lbs. In 2001 this model was also offered in stainless steel and black laminated stock in .45-70 caliber.

NIB	Exc.	V.G.	Good	Fair	Poor
800	650	450	300	250	200

Ruger No. 1 Special Varminter (1-V)

This model is furnished with no sights, a heavy barrel, target scope blocks with 1" Ruger scope rings, and semi-beavertail forearm. Rifle weighs about 9 lbs.

NIB	Exc.	V.G.	Good	Fair	Poor
600	495	400	300	250	200

Ruger No. 1 Stainless Varminter (1-V-BBZ)

Introduced in 2000 this model features a laminated wood stock and stainless steel finish. Chambered for .22-250 and fitted with a 24" barrel. Weight is approximately 9 lbs.

NIB	Exc.	V.G.	Good	Fair	Poor
800	600	—	—	—	—

RUGER NO. 1 SINGLE-SHOT RIFLES

Caliber, catalog number, and availability by barrel length.

Caliber	1-A	I-B	1-H	1-RSI	1-S	1-V
.218 Bee	—	26"	—	—	26"	—
.22 Hornet	—	26"	—	—	—	—
.223	—	26"	—	—	—	24"
.22 PPC	—	—	—	—	—	24"
.22-250	—	26"	—	—	—	24"
.220 Swift	—	26"	—	—	—	26"
6mm Rem.	—	26"	—	—	—	24"
6mm PPC	—	—	—	—	—	24"
.243 Win.	22"	26"	—	20"	—	—
.257 Roberts	—	26"	—	—	—	—
.25-06	—	26"	—	—	—	24"
.27O Win.	22"	26"	—	20"	—	—
.270 Wby. Mag.	—	26"	—	—	—	—
7x57mm	22"	—	—	20"	—	—
.280	—	26"	—	—	—	—
7mm Rem. Mag.	—	26"	—	—	26"	—
.30-06	22"	26"	—	20"	—	—
.300 Win. Mag.	—	26"	—	—	26"	—
.300 Wby. Mag.	—	26"	—	—	—	—
.338 Win. Mag.	—	26"	—	—	26"	—
.375 H&H Mag.	—	—	24"	—	—	—
.404 Jeffery	—	—	24"	—	—	—
.416 Rigby	—	—	24"	—	—	—
.416 Rem. Mag.	—	—	—	—	22"	—
.45-70	—	—	—	—	22"	—
.458 Win. Mag.	—	—	24"	—	—	—

Number 3 Carbine

This model is a less elaborate, inexpensive version of the Number 1. The action is the same except that the lever is less ornate in appearance and lacks the locking bar. The uncheckered stock is of a military carbine style with a barrel band. It is similar in appearance to the Model 44 and the 10/22. This serviceable rifle was chambered for the .45-70 when it was released in 1972. Later chamberings added the .22 Hornet, .30-40 Krag, .223, .44 Magnum, and the .375 Winchester. The barrel is 22" long, and there is a folding rear sight. This model was discontinued in 1987.

Exc.	V.G.	Good	Fair	Poor
500	400	300	200	125

BOLT ACTION RIFLES

Ruger introduced the Model 77R in 1968. It filled the need for a good quality, reasonably priced, bolt action hunting rifle. It has been a commercial success. There are certain variations of this rifle that collectors actively seek. One should avail oneself of the specialized literature on this model and secure individual appraisals on the rare variations as the differences are slight and beyond the scope of this book.

Model 77-R/RS

This model was introduced in 1968. It is offered with a 22", 24", or 26" barrel. The Model 77 is chambered for most calibers from .22-250 through .458 Win. Mag. The action is of a modified Mauser-type, finished in blue with a checkered walnut stock and red rubber buttplate. The rifle is available milled for Ruger scope rings or in the round-top style that allows the mounting of any popular scope ring system. This model is designated 77R when supplied with rings only; and 77RS, when supplied with rings and sights. This model was replaced by the Model 77 MK II.

NIB	Exc.	V.G.	Good	Fair	Poor
450	400	350	300	250	200

Model 77-RS

NIB	Exc.	V.G.	Good	Fair	Poor
500	450	400	300	250	200

Model 77 Flat Bolt

This is an example of the slight variations that make this model collectible. This is essentially the same rifle with the knob on the bolt handle flattened. They were only produced in the configuration until 1972. Watch for fakes, and read specialized material. Calibers such as the 6.5 Rem. Mag., .284, and .350 Rem. Mag. will bring a premium especially in the RS model.

Exc.	V.G.	Good	Fair	Poor
550	450	400	350	275

NOTE: Nonprefixed rifles exists in calibers and configurations other than those advertised by Ruger. These should be individually appraised.

Model 77 RL & RLS

This variation is similar to the standard model except that it features an ultralight 20" barrel and black forearm tip. This model was also available in an 18.5" carbine version with sights designated the RLS. This model was also in an 18.5" Carbine version with sights designated the RLS. They were chambered for the .22-250, .243, .257, .270, .250-3000, .308, and .30-06. Weight is only 6 lbs.

NIB	Exc.	V.G.	Good	Fair	Poor
450	400	375	325	275	225

Model 77 RSI

This version of the Model 77 has a full-length, Mannlicher-style stock and was chambered for the .22-250, .250-3000, .243, .270, 7mm/08, .308 and the .30-06.

NIB	Exc.	V.G.	Good	Fair	Poor
500	400	350	300	275	200

Model 77V Varmint

This variation is similar to the standard Model 77 except that it has a 24" heavy barrel that is drilled and tapped for target scope bases and has a wider beavertail forearm. It is chambered for the .22-250, .243, 6mm, .25-06, .280, and .308. This model was also chambered for the .220 Swift in a 26" heavyweight barrel.

NIB	Exc.	V.G.	Good	Fair	Poor
430	395	350	300	250	200

Model 77 RS African

This is a heavier barreled version, with a steel triggerguard and floorplate. Earlier versions were stocked with fine quality Circassian walnut. This rifle is chambered for the .458 Winchester Magnum.

NIB	Exc.	V.G.	Good	Fair	Poor
550	475	400	350	300	250

NOTE: Add $100 for early models with Circassian walnut stocks. Fewer than 50 rifles chambered for the .416 Taylor cartridge were produced up to 1976. Selling prices range from $3000 to $5000 and should be individually appraised.

Model 77/22

This is a high quality, .22 rimfire rifle designed for the serious shooter. This model has a 20" barrel and a 10-shot, detachable rotary magazine. It is made of steel and stocked with checkered walnut. It is available with sights, scope rings, or both as an extra cost ($20) option. This model was introduced in 1984. Early guns without the 77/22 rollmark on the receiver will bring a premium.

NIB	Exc.	V.G.	Good	Fair	Poor
365	325	275	225	175	125

Model 77/22 Synthetic Stock

This version is quite similar to the standard 77/22, with a black matte finished synthetic stock.

NIB	Exc.	V.G.	Good	Fair	Poor
300	275	225	200	150	100

Model 77/22 Stainless Steel/Synthetic Stock

This model is the same as the blued version except that it is made of stainless steel.

NIB	Exc.	V.G.	Good	Fair	Poor
350	300	250	200	150	100

Model 77/22 Varmint

Introduced in 1993 this model features a stainless steel finish, laminated wood stock, heavy 20" varmint barrel with no sights. Scope rings are included as standard. Chambered for the .22 Long Rifle or Win. Mag. Rimfire.

NIB	Exc.	V.G.	Good	Fair	Poor
395	325	250	200	150	100

Model 77/22M

This model is simply the 77/22 chambered for the .22 Magnum cartridge. The finish is blue, and the magazine capacity is 9 rounds.

NIB	Exc.	V.G.	Good	Fair	Poor
370	300	250	225	175	125

Model 77/22 Stainless Steel

This is the same as the blued 77/22M constructed of stainless steel.

NIB	Exc.	V.G.	Good	Fair	Poor
395	325	250	200	150	100

Model 77/22-.22 Hornet

Introduced in 1994 this version of the 77/22 series is chambered for the .22 Hornet cartridge. this model is furnished with or without sights. The barrel is 20" and it has a 6-round detachable rotary magazine. The stock is checkered walnut with sling swivels. Weight is approximately 6 lbs.

NIB	Exc.	V.G.	Good	Fair	Poor
395	325	275	225	200	150

NOTE: This model is offered with (77/22RSH) or without (77/22RH) sights.

Model K77/22VHZ

Introduced in 1995 this .22 Hornet variation features a stainless steel heavy-weight barrel and laminated American hardwood stock. Offered without sights.

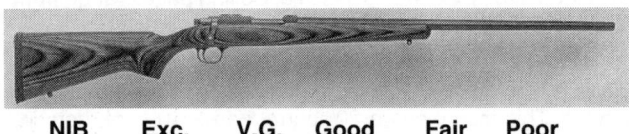

NIB	Exc.	V.G.	Good	Fair	Poor
425	360	300	250	200	150

RUGER MODEL 77: MARK I VS. MARK II

This Ruger bolt action was produced in the Mark I version until November 1991 when it was dropped from the product line. In December 1991 Ruger began producing a new bolt action Model 77 design referred to as the Mark II. There are several noticeable and important differences between the two versions. The Model 77 Mark I features a sliding tang safety while the Mark II has a new three-position wing safety. The Mark I designed Model 77 holds 5 rounds while the newer Mark II holds 4 rounds. The Mark I incorporates and chrome moly bolt and the Mark II has a stainless steel bolt. The Mark I has a spring loaded ejector while the Mark II has a fixed pin design. The Mark I has an adjustable trigger as opposed to the newer Mark II's nonadjustable trigger. The Mark I bolt face does not incorporate a central feed system while the Mark II does have a central feed. The Mark II design also features a slimmer action that the older Mark I design.

Model 77R MKII

Introduced in 1992 this model is the basic Model 77 rifle. Features blued metal parts and no sights. Available in 15 different calibers from .223 to .338 Win. Mag. in barrel lengths from 22" to 24" depending on caliber. Comes from factory with scope bases and rings. Rifle weighs approximately 7 lbs.

NIB	Exc.	V.G.	Good	Fair	Poor
390	350	300	250	200	150

Model 77RP MKII

This model was also introduced in 1992 and differs from the Model 77R with the addition of stainless steel barrel and receiver and synthetic stock. Available in 10 calibers. In 1998 the .25-06 caliber was added to this model.

NIB	Exc.	V.G.	Good	Fair	Poor
390	350	300	250	200	150

Model 77RS MKII

This is a blued version of the basic rifle with the addition of open sights. Available in 9 calibers from .243 Win. to .458 Win. Mag.

NIB	Exc.	V.G.	Good	Fair	Poor
450	400	350	300	250	175

Model 77RSP MKII

The stainless version of the basic rifle with the addition of a synthetic stock and open sights. Available in 6 calibers: .243, .270, 7MM Rem. Mag., .30-06, .330 Win. Mag., .338 Win. Mag. Introduced in 1993.

NIB	Exc.	V.G.	Good	Fair	Poor
425	400	350	300	250	175

Model 77RSI MKII

Also introduced in 1993 this model features a blued barrel and full length walnut stock. Offered in 4 calibers all with 18" barrel. The calibers are: .243, .270, .30-06, and .308.

NIB	Exc.	V.G.	Good	Fair	Poor
450	400	350	300	250	175

Model 77RL MKII

This model features a short action in six calibers from .223 to .308, all with 20" barrel. Rifle weighs about 6 lbs. Introduced in 1992.

NIB	Exc.	V.G.	Good	Fair	Poor
420	350	300	250	200	150

Model 77LR MKII

This model is a left-handed rifle furnished in long action calibers: .270, 7mm Rem. Mag., .30-06, .300 Win. Mag. Introduced in 1992.

NIB	Exc.	V.G.	Good	Fair	Poor
400	350	300	250	200	150

Model 77RLP MKII

Introduced in 1999 this model is similar to the RL model above but with a all-weather synthetic stock. Weight is about 6.5 lbs.

NIB	Exc.	V.G.	Good	Fair	Poor
600	475	—	—	—	—

Model 77VT MKII

This rifle was introduced in 1993 and is a target rifle. Furnished with no sights, heavy laminated wood stock with beavertail forend, and adjustable trigger. Barrel, bolt, and action are stainless steel. Weighs approximately 9.75 lbs. Furnished in eight calibers from .223 to .308.

NIB	Exc.	V.G.	Good	Fair	Poor
430	400	350	300	250	175

Model 77RBZ MKII

This model features a stainless steel barrel and action fitted with laminated hardwood stock. No sights. Weight is approximately 7.25 lbs. Offered in a wide variety of calibers from .223 to .338 Win. Mag. Introduced in 1997.

NIB	Exc.	V.G.	Good	Fair	Poor
600	500	—	—	—	—

Model 77 RSBZ on top and Model RBZ at bottom

Model 77RSBZ MKII

Same as above but fitted with open sights. Also introduced in 1997.

NIB	Exc.	V.G.	Good	Fair	Poor
650	550	—	—	—	—

Model 77CR MKII Compact Rifle

Introduced in 2001 this rifle features a 16.5" barrel with 4-round magazine. Chambered for the .223 Rem., .243 Win., .260 Rem., and .308 Win. cartridges. Blued model is fitted with walnut stock and stainless steel model is fitted with black laminted stock. Weight is about 5.75 lbs.

Ruger M-77 Mark II .223 Remington. Ruger's new M-77 Mark II bolt action is the slender, ideal hunter

NIB	Exc.	V.G.	Good	Fair	Poor
650	475	—	—	—	—

NOTE: Add $50 for stainless steel model (M77CRBBZ).

Model 77 Express MKII

Introduced in 1992 the Ruger Express Mark II rifle features a select Circassian walnut straight comb checkered stock. The checkering is 22 lines to the inch and the butt stock is fitted with a rubber recoil pad. The pistol grip is fitted with a metal grip cap. The barrel length is 22" and features a blade front sight, V-notch rear express sights, and the receiver is machined for scope mounts, which are included. Available in the following calibers: .270, .30-06, 7mm Rem. Mag., .300 Win. Mag., .338 Win. Mag. Rifle weighs about 7.5 lbs.

NIB	Exc.	V.G.	Good	Fair	Poor
1200	850	650	550	400	200

Model 77 Magnum MKII

Similar in all respects to the Model 77 Express MKII except offered in the following calibers: .375 H&H and .416 Rigby. The .375 and weighs about 9.25 lbs. while the .416 weighs about 10.25 lbs.

NIB	Exc.	V.G.	Good	Fair	Poor
1250	850	650	550	400	200

Model 77/44RS

This bolt action is chambered for the .44 Magnum cartridge. It features an 18.5" barrel with open sights. The stock is American walnut with rubber butt pad and checkering on forearm and pistol grip. Detachable rotary magazine has 4-round capacity. Weight is approximately 6 lbs. Introduced in mid-1997.

NIB	Exc.	V.G.	Good	Fair	Poor
575	450	—	—	—	—

Model 77/44RSP

Introduced in 1999 this model has a matte stainless steel barrel and action and a black synthetic stock. chambered for .44 Magnum cartridge. Weight is about 6 lbs.

NIB	Exc.	V.G.	Good	Fair	Poor
575	450	—	—	—	—

Model 77/50RS

This model is an in-line percussion rifle chambered for .50 caliber. It is fitted with a 22" barrel with open sights. Stock is birch with rubber butt plate and no checkering. Blued finish. Weight is approximately 6.5 lbs. Introduced in mid-1997.

NIB	Exc.	V.G.	Good	Fair	Poor
395	325	—	—	—	—

Model 77/50RSO

Similar to the model above but with a straight grip checkered walnut stock with curved buttplate. Introduced in 1998.

NIB	Exc.	V.G.	Good	Fair	Poor
550	450	—	—	—	—

Model 77/50RSBBZ

This model was introduced in 1998 and features all of the specifications of the Model 77/50RS with the addition of a black/grey laminated stock and a stainless steel finish.

NIB	Exc.	V.G.	Good	Fair	Poor
595	475	—	—	—	—

Model 77/50RSP

This model is fitted with a stainless steel barrel and action and fitted with a black synthetic stock with pistol grip. Weight is about 6.5 lbs. Introduced in 1999.

NIB	Exc.	V.G.	Good	Fair	Poor
575	450	—	—	—	—

LEVER ACTION RIFLES

Model 96/22

Introduced into the Ruger line in 1996 this lever action rifle is chambered for the .22 long rifle. The stock is American hardwood and the barrel length is 18.5". Magazine capacity is 10 rounds. Open sights are standard. Weight is approximately 5.25 lbs.

NIB	Exc.	V.G.	Good	Fair	Poor
265	225	200	175	150	100

Model 96/22M

Same as above but chambered for the .22 WMR cartridge. Magazine capacity is 9 rounds.

NIB	Exc.	V.G.	Good	Fair	Poor
290	275	225	175	150	100

Model 96/44

Same as the .22 caliber except chambered for the .44 Magnum cartridge. Magazine capacity is 4 rounds and the weight is about 5-7/8 lbs.

NIB	Exc.	V.G.	Good	Fair	Poor
325	300	250	200	150	100

SHOTGUNS

Red Label Over/Under Early Production

Ruger introduced the Red Label in 20 gauge in 1977; the 12 gauge followed five years later. This high quality shotgun is offered with 3" chambers in 26" or 28" barrel lengths. Various chokes are available. They are boxlocks with automatic ejectors. The stock is of checkered walnut. The finish is blue on the earlier guns.

NIB	Exc.	V.G.	Good	Fair	Poor
700	650	550	400	300	250

Super Blackhawk in scarce mahogany case, serial numbers 1-8500
Courtesy *Know Your Ruger Single Action Revolvers 1953-63*.
Blacksmith Corp.

Super Blackhawk in rare white cardboard case, serial numbers 3500-10500

Courtesy *Know Your Ruger Single Action Revolvers 1953-63*.
Blacksmith Corp.

Red Label Over/Under Current Production

The new 12 and 20 gauge Red Label shotgun has a stainless steel receiver and blued barrels. They are offered with screw-in choke tubes. Otherwise they are similar to the earlier models. In 1994 Ruger added the 28 gauge with 26" or 28" barrels to the Red Label line.

NIB	Exc.	V.G.	Good	Fair	Poor
1000	800	650	500	400	300

Red Label Over/Under Sporting Clays

Courtesy compliments of Bill Ruger, John C. Dougan

Offered in 20 gauge this model was introduced in 1994 with 3" chambers and 30" barrels. Walnut stock has checkering pistol grip. Weight is about 7 lbs.

NIB	Exc.	V.G.	Good	Fair	Poor
1050	950	750	500	—	—

NOTE: Factory engraved Red Label shotguns are catalogued, as of 1996, as available with three different engraving coverages. A total of 375 were produced. Prices for these engraved guns are as follows:
Grade 1 EXC.-$2200
Grade 2 (1/3 coverage)-EXC.-$2400
Grade 3 (2/3 coverage)-EXC.-$2750

Red Label All-Weather Over/Under

Offered in 12 gauge only with 26", 28", or 30" barrels this model is fitted with a black synthetic stock with pistol grip. Weight is about 7.5 lbs. Introduced in 1999.

NIB	Exc.	V.G.	Good	Fair	Poor
1400	1100	—	—	—	—

Engraved Red Label All-Weather Over/Under

Introduced in 2000 this model features a scroll engraved receiver with gold inlaid duck. Offered in 12 gauge only with 26", 28", or 30" barrel.

NIB	Exc.	V.G.	Good	Fair	Poor
1600	1250	—	—	—	—

Engraved Red Label Over/Under

This model features a scroll engraved receiver with a gold inlaid game bird appropiate to gauge. The 12 gauge: pheasant; 20 gauge: grouse; and 28 gauge: woodcock. Walnut stock. Other specifications same as standard Red Label shotguns. Introduced in 2000.

NIB	Exc.	V.G.	Good	Fair	Poor
1600	1250	—	—	—	—

Ruger Woodside Over/Under

Introduced in 1995 this new model features a Circassian walnut stock with either pistol grip or straight grip. Available in 12 or 20 gauge with barrel lengths of 26", 28", or 30". Screw-in chokes are standard.

NIB	Exc.	V.G.	Good	Fair	Poor
1675	1150	850	600	—	—

NOTE: The Woodside shotgun is also available in three different engraving patterns.

Ruger Trap Model

Introduced in 2000 this model is a 12 gauge single barrel trap gun with a 34" barrel choked full and modified. It is fitted with a mechanical trigger and auto ejector. The stock is select walnut with adjustable cheekpiece and butt plate. Receiver is engraved. Weight is approximately 9 lbs.

NIB	Exc.	V.G.	Good	Fair	Poor
2850	2100	—	—	—	—

Ruger New Model Single-Six Revolver

SUNDANCE INDUSTRIES, INC.
North Hollywood, California

Model D-22M
A .22 or .22 Magnum caliber double barrel Over/Under pocket pistol with 2.5" barrels and an aluminum alloy frame. Blackened finish or chrome-plated with either simulated pearl or black grips. Introduced in 1989.

Exc.	V. G.	Good	Fair	Poor
225	175	125	100	75

Model BOA
Introduced in 1991 this semiautomatic pistol is chambered for the .25 ACP cartridge. Fitted with a 2.5" barrel with fixed sights. Grip safety. Choice of black or chrome finish. Magazine capacity is 7 rounds. Weight is about 16 oz.

NIB	Exc.	V.G.	Good	Fair	Poor
95	80	70	50	—	—

Model A-25
Similar to the BOA but without grip safety.

NIB	Exc.	V.G.	Good	Fair	Poor
80	65	50	40	—	—

Model Laser 25
Similar to the Model BOA with grip safety but equipped with a laser sight. Laser activated by squeezing grip safety. Weight with laser 18 oz. Introduced in 1995.

NIB	Exc.	V.G.	Good	Fair	Poor
220	175	125	—	—	—

Sundance Point Blank
This is an over and under derringer chambered for the .22 Long Rifle cartridge. It is fitted with a 3" barrel and double action trigger. Enclosed hammer. Matte black finish. Weight is about 8 oz. Introduced in 1994.

NIB	Exc.	V.G.	Good	Fair	Poor
95	80	70	50	—	—

SUTHERLAND, S.
Richmond, Virginia

Pocket Pistol
A .41 caliber percussion single shot pistol with round barrels of 2.5" to 4" in length, German silver mounts and a walnut stock. The lock normally marked "S. Sutherland" or "S. Sutherland/Richmond". Manufactured during the 1850s.

Exc.	V.G.	Good	Fair	Poor
—	—	1750	800	300

SYMS, J. G.
New York, New York

Pocket Pistol
A .41 caliber single shot percussion pistol with 1.5" to 3.5" barrels, German silver mounts and a walnut stock. The lock normally marked "Syms/New York". Manufactured during the 1850s.

Exc.	V.G.	Good	Fair	Poor
—	—	1750	800	300

TACONIC FIREARMS LTD.
Cambridge, New York

M98 Ultimate Hunter

This bolt action rifle is based on the M98 Mauser action. It is available in calibers from .22-250 to .358 Win. Stainless steel barrel length is 22". Titanium grip cap. Stock is XXX English walnut with cheekpiece and oil finish. Ebony forend tip. Scope bases are integral to the receiver. The price listed below is for the standard rifle. There are an extensive list of options which will greatly affect price. For example an optional quarter rib will add $1000 to the base price of the gun. Seek expert assistance prior to a sale.

NIB	Exc.	V.G.	Good	Fair	Poor
6000	4750	—	—	—	—

TALLASSEE
Tallassee, Alabama

Carbine

A .58 caliber single shot percussion carbine with a 25" round barrel and full-length stock secured by two barrel bands. Fitted with sling swivels. Barrel and lock finished in the bright, brass furniture and walnut stock. The lock marked "C.S./Tallassee/Ala." Approximately 500 of these carbines were manufactured in 1864. Perspective purchasers are advised to secure a qualified appraisal prior to acquisition.

Courtesy Milwaukee Public Museum, Milwaukee, Wisconsin

Exc.	V.G.	Good	Fair	Poor
—	—	7500	3000	800

TANFOGLIO
Valtrompia, Italy

The products of this company, which was established in the late 1940s, have been imported into the United States by various companies including Eig Corporation, F.I.E. of Hialeah, Florida, and Excam.

Sata

A .22 or 6.35mm caliber semiautomatic pistol with a 3" barrel. The slide marked "Pistola SATA Made in Italy" and the grips "SATA". Blued with black plastic grips.

Exc.	V.G.	Good	Fair	Poor
175	150	125	90	75

Titan

A 6.35mm caliber semiautomatic pistol with a 2.5" barrel and external hammer. The slide marked "Titan 6.35" and on U.S. imported examples, "EIG". Blued with plastic grips.

Exc.	V.G.	Good	Fair	Poor
100	75	50	40	30

TA 90 or TZ-75

A 9mm caliber semiautomatic pistol with a 4.75" barrel and 15-shot magazine. Blued or chrome-plated with walnut or rubber grips. Those imported by Excam were known as the Model TA 90, while those imported by F.I.E. are known as the Model TZ-75.

NIB	Exc.	V.G.	Good	Fair	Poor
450	400	350	300	250	200

TA 90B

As above, with a 3.5" barrel, 12-shot magazine and Neoprene grips. Introduced in 1986.

NIB	Exc.	V.G.	Good	Fair	Poor
500	450	400	350	300	250

TA 90 SS

As above, with a ported 5" barrel, adjustable sights and two-tone finish. Introduced in 1989.

NIB	Exc.	V.G.	Good	Fair	Poor
650	600	500	450	400	300

TA 41

As above, in .41 Action Express caliber. Introduced in 1989.

NIB	Exc.	V.G.	Good	Fair	Poor
500	450	400	350	300	250

TA 41 SS

As above, with a ported 5" barrel, adjustable sights and two-tone finish. Introduced in 1989.

NIB	Exc.	V.G.	Good	Fair	Poor
650	600	500	450	400	300

TA 76

A .22 caliber single action revolver with a 4.75" barrel and 6-shot cylinder. Blued or chrome-plated with a brass back strap and triggerguard. Walnut grips.

NIB	Exc.	V.G.	Good	Fair	Poor
100	90	80	65	50	25

TA 76M Combo

As above, with a 6" or 9" barrel and an interchangeable .22 Magnum caliber cylinder.

NIB	Exc.	V.G.	Good	Fair	Poor
110	100	90	75	60	35

TA 38SB

A .38 Special caliber Over/Under double barrel pocket pistol with 3" barrels and a hammer block safety. Blued with checkered nylon grips. Discontinued in 1985.

Exc.	V.G.	Good	Fair	Poor
100	90	80	60	40

TANNER, ANDRE
Switzerland

Model 300 Free Rifle

A 7.5mm Swiss or .308 caliber single shot rifle with varying length barrels having adjustable target sights, adjustable trigger, and a walnut stock fitted with a palm rest and adjustable cheekpiece. Blued.

NIB	Exc.	V.G.	Good	Fair	Poor
4750	3750	3000	2500	1500	750

Model 300S

As above, with a 10-shot magazine and not fitted with a palm rest. Discontinued in 1988.

NIB	Exc.	V.G.	Good	Fair	Poor
4500	3500	2750	2250	1250	750

Model 50F

As above, in .22 caliber with a thumb hole stock. Discontinued in 1988.

NIB	Exc.	V.G.	Good	Fair	Poor
3750	3000	2500	1750	900	500

TARPLEY J. & F.
AND E. T. GARRETT & CO.
Greensboro, North Carolina

Carbine

A .52 caliber breechloading single shot percussion carbine with a 22" round barrel and a plain walnut buttstock. Blued with a case hardened frame. The tang marked "J H Tarpley's./Pat Feb 14./1863". Over 400 of these carbines were manufactured. It is advised that prospective purchasers should seek a qualified appraisal prior to acquisition.

Exc.	V.G.	Good	Fair	Poor
—	—	65000	30000	—

TAURUS INTERNATIONAL MFG. CO.
Porto Alegre, Brazil
Importer-Taurus International
Miami, Florida

PISTOLS

PT-92AF

A 9mm caliber double action semiautomatic pistol with a 4.92" barrel, exposed hammer, and 15-shot magazine. Blued or nickel-plated with plain walnut grips.

NIB	Exc.	V.G.	Good	Fair	Poor
400	350	300	250	200	150

PT-92C

This 9mm model is a large capacity semiautomatic pistol with a 4.25" barrel. Drift adjustable 3-dot combat rear sight. Magazine holds 13 rounds in a double column. Choice of blued, stain nickel, or stainless steel finish. Brazilian hardwood grips are standard. Weighs 31 oz.

NIB	Exc.	V.G.	Good	Fair	Poor
375	325	275	220	160	100

PT-92

A slightly larger and heavier version of the PT-92C. This model has a 5" barrel with drift adjustable 3-dot combat rear sight. Magazine capacity is 15 rounds. This model is 1" longer overall than the above model and weighs 34 oz. Also available in blued, nickel, and stainless steel.

NIB	Exc.	V.G.	Good	Fair	Poor
500	400	300	225	150	100

NOTE: Add $20 for stainless steel and $50 for blue with gold finish, $60 for stainless steel with gold accents. A blued or stainless steel .22 Long Rifle conversion kit will add $250.

PT-99

Similar in appearance and specifications to the PT-92, this version has the additional feature of fully adjustable 3-dot rear sight.

NIB	Exc.	V.G.	Good	Fair	Poor
525	425	325	250	150	100

NOTE: Add $20 for stainless steel finish.

PT-100

This model is similar to the other full size Taurus semiautomatics except that it is chambered for the .40 S&W cartridge. Supplied with a 5" barrel, with drift adjustable rear sight, it has a magazine capacity of 11 rounds. Also available in blued, nickel, or stainless steel. Weighs 34 oz.

NIB	Exc.	V.G.	Good	Fair	Poor
500	400	300	200	150	100

NOTE: For Special Edition with blued steel with gold fixtures and rosewood grips add $50. For blued steel with gold fixtures and pearl grips add $110.

PT-101

Same as the model above but furnished with fully adjustable rear 3-dot combat sight.

NIB	Exc.	V.G.	Good	Fair	Poor
500	350	300	250	150	100

PT-111

This is a double action only pistol chambered for the 9mm cartridge. Fitted with a 3.3" barrel and polymer frame. Magazine capacity is 10 rounds. Weight is about 16 oz. Choice of blue or stainless steel. Introduced in 1997. Add $20.00 for stainless steel.

NIB	Exc.	V.G.	Good	Fair	Poor
350	250	200	175	150	100.

NOTE: Add $20 for stainless steel finish.

PT-908

A semiautomatic double action pistol chambered for the 9mm Parabellum cartridge. It is fitted with a 3.8" barrel, with drift adjustable rear 3-dot combat sight. Magazine capacity is 8 rounds in a single column. Available in blued, satin nickel, or stainless steel. Stocks are black rubber. Pistol weighs 30 oz. Introduced in 1993.

NIB	Exc.	V.G.	Good	Fair	Poor
375	325	275	225	150	100

Deluxe Shooter's Pak

Offered by Taurus as a special package it consists of the pistol, with extra magazine, in a fitted custom hard case. Available for the following models: PT-92, PT-99, PT-100, and PT-101.

NOTE: Add approximately 10% to the above prices of these models for this special feature.

PT-911

This model was introduced in 1997 and is chambered for the 9mm cartridge. It is fitted with a 4" barrel and has a magazine capacity of 10 rounds. Choice of blue or stainless steel. Weight is about 28 oz. Black rubber grips are standard.

NIB	Exc.	V.G.	Good	Fair	Poor
450	350	275	225	175	125

NOTE: Add $20 for stainless steel.

PT-138

Introduced in 1998 this polymer frame pistol is chambered for the .380 cartridge. It is fitted with a 4" barrel in either blue or stainless steel. Weight is about 16 oz. Magazine capacity is 10 rounds.

Blue

NIB	Exc.	V.G.	Good	Fair	Poor
350	250	200	175	—	—

Stainless Steel

NIB	Exc.	V.G.	Good	Fair	Poor
375	275	225	175	—	—

PT-140 Millennium

Chambered for the .40 S&W cartridge and fitted with a 3.25" barrel, this model features a polymer frame and either a blue or stainless steel slide. Fixed sights. Magazine capacity is 10 rounds. Weight is about 19 oz.

Blue Finish

NIB	Exc.	V.G.	Good	Fair	Poor
450	350	275	200	150	100

Stainless Steel

NIB	Exc.	V.G.	Good	Fair	Poor
525	425	325	250	175	100

NOTE: For night sights add $75.

PT-145 Millennium

Similar to the PT-140 but chambered for the .45 ACP cartridge. Barrel length is 3.27". Weight is about 23 oz.

Blue Finish

NIB	Exc.	V.G.	Good	Fair	Poor
490	400	325	225	150	100

Stainless Steel

NIB	Exc.	V.G.	Good	Fair	Poor
550	450	350	250	175	100

NOTE: For night sights add $75.

PT-58

This model was introduced in 1988. Chambered for the .380 ACP cartridge it is fitted with a 4" barrel with drift adjustable rear sight. It is a conventional double action design. Available in blued, satin nickel, or stainless steel. It is fitted with Brazilian hardwood grips. Pistol weighs 30 oz.

NIB	Exc.	V.G.	Good	Fair	Poor
350	300	250	200	150	100

PT400/400SS

Chambered for the .400 CorBon cartridge and fitted with a 4.25" ported barrel with fixed sights. Magazine capacity is 8 rounds. Offered in blue or stainless steel. Rubber grips. Weight is about 30 oz.

Blue Finish

NIB	Exc.	V.G.	Good	Fair	Poor
500	400	300	200	150	100

Stainless Steel

NIB	Exc.	V.G.	Good	Fair	Poor
525	425	325	225	150	100

PT-45

Introduced in 1994 this semiautomatic double action pistol is chambered for the .45 ACP cartridge. The barrel is 3-3/4" in length and the magazine capacity is 8 rounds. Offered in blued or stainless steel with grips of Brazilian hardwood. Fixed sights are standard. Overall length is 7.1" and weight is approximately 30 oz.

Blue Finish

NIB	Exc.	V.G.	Good	Fair	Poor
400	350	275	200	150	100

Stainless Steel

NIB	Exc.	V.G.	Good	Fair	Poor
475	400	325	250	200	150

PT-945C

Introduced in 1995 this .45 ACP double action pistol features a 4" barrel with an 8-round magazine. The grips are black rubber. The sights are drift adjustable 3-dot combat style. Approximate weight is 30 oz. Offered in blue or stainless steel with or without ported barrel. Add $40 for ported barrel.

Blue

NIB	Exc.	V.G.	Good	Fair	Poor
475	350	250	200	150	100

NOTE: Add $45 for blued finish with gold accents and ported barrel. Add $35 for ported barrel and blue finish.

Stainless Steel

NIB	Exc.	V.G.	Good	Fair	Poor
500	400	300	250	150	100

NOTE: Add $40 for ported barrel with stainless steel finish or Stainless steel finish with gold accents.

PT-945S

Same as the model above but chambered for the .45 Super cartridge. Introduced in 1998.

Blue

NIB	Exc.	V.G.	Good	Fair	Poor
450	350	250	200	150	100

Stainless Steel

NIB	Exc.	V.G.	Good	Fair	Poor
475	375	275	225	150	100

PT-940

Similar to the PT-945 except chambered for the .40 S&W cartridge. Fitted with a 4" barrel. Magazine capacity is 10 rounds. Choice of blue or stainless steel. Black rubber grips. Weight is approximately 28 oz. Introduced in 1997. Add $20 for stainless steel.

NIB	Exc.	V.G.	Good	Fair	Poor
450	350	—	—	—	—

PT-938

This model is chambered for the .380 ACP cartridge and fitted with a 3" barrel. Black rubber grips and choice of blue or stainless steel. Weight is about 27 oz. Introduced in 1997.

NIB	Exc.	V.G.	Good	Fair	Poor
425	325	—	—	—	—

PT-22

This is a semiautomatic double action only pistol that features a 2.75" barrel with fixed sights and a manual safety. It is chambered for the .22 Long Rifle cartridge and has a magazine capacity of 8 rounds. The stocks are Brazilian hardwood and the finish is available in either blue, blue with gold trim, nickel, or two-tone . Pistol weighs 12.3 oz.

NIB	Exc.	V.G.	Good	Fair	Poor
200	150	100	75	60	50

NOTE: For Special Edition with blued steel with gold fixtures and rosewood grips add $50. For blued steel with gold fixtures and pearl grips add $110.

PT-25

Similar in appearance to the PT-22, this model is chambered for the .25 ACP cartridge and has a magazine capacity of 9 rounds. This model is also fitted with a 2.75" barrel. Offered in either blue, blue with gold trim, two-tone finish, or nickel.

NIB	Exc.	V.G.	Good	Fair	Poor
200	150	100	75	60	50

NOTE: For Special Edition with blued steel with gold fixtures and rosewood grips add $50. For Blued steel with gold fixtures and pearl grips add $110.

REVOLVERS

Model 22H

This revolver is chambered for the .22 Hornet cartridge and fitted with a 10" vent rib barrel. Sights are fully adjustable. Cylinder holds 8 rounds. Finish is matte stainless steel. Rubber grips. Weight is about 50 oz. Stamped "RAGING HORNET" on the barrel.

NIB	Exc.	V.G.	Good	Fair	Poor
900	725	550	—	—	—

Model 73

A .32 Smith & Wesson Long double action swing-out cylinder revolver, with a 3" barrel and 6-shot cylinder. Blued or nickel plated with walnut grips.

NIB	Exc.	V.G.	Good	Fair	Poor
200	175	150	125	100	75

Model 80

A full size 6-round .38 Special with 3" or 4" heavy tapered barrel. Supplied with fixed sights and offered with blued or stainless steel (offered new in 1993) finish. Brazilian hardwood grips are standard. Weighs 30 oz.

NIB	Exc.	V.G.	Good	Fair	Poor
190	175	135	110	85	70

NOTE: Add $40 for stainless steel.

Model 82

Nearly identical with the Model 80, the Model 82 has a 3" or 4" heavy, solid rib barrel in place of the heavy tapered barrel. Pistol weighs 34 oz.

NIB	Exc.	V.G.	Good	Fair	Poor
190	175	135	110	85	70

NOTE: Add $40 for stainless steel.

Model 82B4

Chambered for the .38 special +P cartridge and fitted with a 4" heavy solid rib barrel. Cylinder holds 6 rounds. Rubber grips. Fixed sights. Blue finish. Weight is about 37 oz.

NIB	Exc.	V.G.	Good	Fair	Poor
295	250	200	—	—	—

Model 82SS4

Same as above but with stainless steel finish. Weight is about 37 oz.

NIB	Exc.	V.G.	Good	Fair	Poor
340	275	225	—	—	—

Model 827B4

Chambered for the .398 Special +P cartridge and fitted with a 4" heavy barrel with solid rib. Cylinder is 7 shots. Rubber grips. Blued finish. Weight is about 37 oz. Fixed sights.

NIB	Exc.	V.G.	Good	Fair	Poor
300	250	200	—	—	—

Model 827SS4

Same as above but with stainless steel finish. Weight is about 35 oz.

NIB	Exc.	V.G.	Good	Fair	Poor
350	300	250	—	—	—

Model 83

Similar to the Model 82 except for a fully adjustable rear sight and Patridge type front sight. Offered with 4" barrel only with

blued or stainless steel (new for 1993) finish. Pistol weighs 34 oz.

NIB	Exc.	V.G.	Good	Fair	Poor
200	175	150	125	100	75

Model 85

A double action revolver chambered for the .38 Special. This model is available in either a 2" or 3" heavy, solid rib barrel fitted with ejector shroud. Sights are fixed. Blued finish and stainless steel (new for 1993) are offered with Brazilian hardwood grips. Pistol weighs 21 oz. with 2" barrel.

NIB	Exc.	V.G.	Good	Fair	Poor
200	175	150	125	100	75

NOTE: Beginning in 1996 this model will be furnished with Uncle Mike's Boot Grips.

NOTE: For Special Edition with blued steel with gold fixtures and rosewood grips add $50. For blued steel with gold fixtures and pearl grips add $110.

Model 85 Stainless
As above, in stainless steel.

NIB	Exc.	V.G.	Good	Fair	Poor
220	190	175	150	125	100

NOTE: Beginning in 1996 this model will be furnished with Uncle Mike's Boot Grips.

Model 85CH
Same as above but offered in 2" or 3" barrel with shrouded hammer. Double action only.

NOTE: Add $50 for stainless steel and $25 for ported barrel on 2" models.

NIB	Exc.	V.G.	Good	Fair	Poor
250	200	150	125	100	75

Model 85 UL
This double action revolver is built on a small aluminum frame and is chambered for the .38 Special cartridge. It is fitted with a 2" barrel. Choice of blue or stainless steel finish. Weight is approximately 17 oz. Introduced in 1997. Add $30.00 for stainless steel.

NIB	Exc.	V.G.	Good	Fair	Poor
300	250	—	—	—	—

NOTE: For Special Edition with blued steel with gold fixtures and rosewood grips add $50. For blued steel with gold fixtures and pearl grips add $110.

Model 86
Similar to the Model 83 with the exception of a 6" barrel, target hammer, adjustable trigger, and blue only finish. Weighs 34 oz.

NIB	Exc.	V.G.	Good	Fair	Poor
250	225	200	150	125	100

Model 94
This double action revolver is chambered for the .22 Long Rifle cartridge. The swing out holds 9 rounds and it is available with either a heavy, solid rib, 3" or 4" barrel. In 1996 a 5" barrel option was added to this model in both blue and stainless steel. Ramp front sight with fully adjustable rear sight. Offered in blued or stainless steel with Brazilian hardwood grips. Pistol weighs 25 oz. with 4" barrel.

Blue

NIB	Exc.	V.G.	Good	Fair	Poor
225	175	150	125	100	75

Stainless Steel

NIB	Exc.	V.G.	Good	Fair	Poor
275	225	175	150	100	75

Model 94 UL
Introduced in 1997 this model is built on a small aluminum frame with 2" barrel and chambered for the .22 Long Rifle cartridge. choice of blue or stainless steel. Weight is approximately 14 oz.

NIB	Exc.	V.G.	Good	Fair	Poor
325	250	200	—	—	—

Model 941

Similar in appearance to the Model 94 this version is chambered for the .22 WMR. Available with a choice of 3" or 4" heavy, solid rib barrel. In 1996 a 5" barrel option was added to this model. This model holds 8 rounds. Ramp front sight with fully adjustable rear sight. Available in blued or stainless steel with Brazilian hardwood grips. Pistol weighs 27.5 oz.

Blue

NIB	Exc.	V.G.	Good	Fair	Poor
250	200	175	125	100	75

Stainless Steel

NIB	Exc.	V.G.	Good	Fair	Poor
300	250	200	150	100	75

Model 941 UL

Same as the standard Model 941 but with an aluminum frame and 2" barrel. Weight is about 18 oz. Introduced in 1997.

NIB	Exc.	V.G.	Good	Fair	Poor
350	275	225	—	—	—

Model 96

A full size .22 caliber Long Rifle revolver with 6" heavy, solid rib barrel. Fully adjustable rear sight with target hammer and adjustable target trigger. Cylinder holds 6 rounds. Available in blued only with Brazilian hardwood grips. Pistol weighs 34 oz.

NIB	Exc.	V.G.	Good	Fair	Poor
250	225	175	125	100	75

Model 741

This double action revolver is chambered for the .32 H&R Mag. cartridge. It features a 3" or 4" heavy, solid rib barrel with fully adjustable rear sight. Swing out cylinder holds 6 rounds. Available in either blued or stainless steel (stainless steel model introduced in 1993) with Brazilian hardwood grips. Pistol weighs 30 oz.

NIB	Exc.	V.G.	Good	Fair	Poor
200	175	150	125	100	75

NOTE: Add $40 for stainless steel.

Model 761

Similar to the Model 741 this version has a 6" barrel, target hammer, adjustable target trigger, and is available in blued only. Weighs 34 oz.

NIB	Exc.	V.G.	Good	Fair	Poor
250	225	175	150	125	100

Model 65

This double action revolver is chambered for the .357 Magnum cartridge. It is offered with 2.5" or 4" heavy, solid rib barrel with ejector shroud. Fitted with fixed sights and Brazilian hardwood grips it is available in blued or stainless steel. The 2.5" barrel is a new addition to the Model 65 for 1993. Pistol weighs 34 oz. with 4" barrel.

NIB	Exc.	V.G.	Good	Fair	Poor
300	250	200	150	125	100

NOTE: Add $40 for stainless steel.

Model 605

Introduced in 1995 this revolver is chambered for the .357 Magnum cartridge. It is fitted with a 2-1/4" or 3" heavy barrel and is offered in blue or stainless steel. Weighs 25 oz.

Stainless Steel

NIB	Exc.	V.G.	Good	Fair	Poor
340	275	225	175	125	100

Blue

NIB	Exc.	V.G.	Good	Fair	Poor
300	250	200	150	125	100

Model 605 Custom (B2C)

Same as above but offered with a 2-1/4" compensated barrel.

Stainless Steel

NIB	Exc.	V.G.	Good	Fair	Poor
340	275	225	175	125	100

Blue

NIB	Exc.	V.G.	Good	Fair	Poor
300	250	200	150	125	100

Model 605CHB2/SS2

Chambered for the .357 Magnum cartridge and fitted with a 2.25" solid rib barrel and 5-shot cylinder this model has a concealed hammer. Weight is about 24 oz.

Stainless Steel

NIB	Exc.	V.G.	Good	Fair	Poor
340	275	225	175	125	100

Blue

NIB	Exc.	V.G.	Good	Fair	Poor
300	250	200	150	125	100

Model 605CHB2C/SS2C

Same as above but with concealed hammer and ported barrels.

Stainless Steel

NIB	Exc.	V.G.	Good	Fair	Poor
360	275	225	175	125	100

Blue

NIB	Exc.	V.G.	Good	Fair	Poor
320	250	200	150	125	100

Model 66

Similar to the Model 65 but offered with a choice of 2.5", 4", or 6" barrel with fully adjustable rear sight. Offered with either blued or stainless steel. Weighs 35 oz. with 4" barrel. The 2.5" barrel was introduced in 1993.

NIB	Exc.	V.G.	Good	Fair	Poor
225	200	175	150	125	100

Model 66CP

This model is similar to the Model 66 but features a compensated heavy, solid rib 4" or 6" ejector shroud barrel. Introduced in 1993. Pistol weighs 35 oz.

NIB	Exc.	V.G.	Good	Fair	Poor
250	225	200	150	125	100

Model 66B4/SS4

Chambered for the .357 magnum cartridge with 4" solid rib barrel and 7-shot cylinder. Adjustable sights. Rubber grips. Weight is about 38 oz.

Stainless Steel

NIB	Exc.	V.G.	Good	Fair	Poor
400	325	275	225	150	100

Blue

NIB	Exc.	V.G.	Good	Fair	Poor
350	275	225	150	125	100

Model 669

This model is chambered for the .357 Magnum cartridge and features a 4" or 6" heavy, solid rib barrel with full shroud. It has fully adjustable rear sight and is available with blued or stainless steel finish. Brazilian hardwood grips are standard. Pistol weighs 37 oz. with 4" barrel.

NIB	Exc.	V.G.	Good	Fair	Poor
250	225	200	150	125	100

NOTE: Add $60 for stainless steel.

Model 669CP

This variation of the Model 699 was introduced in 1993 and features a 4" or 6" compensated barrel. Fully adjustable rear sights are standard and it is offered with either blue or stainless steel finish. Weighs 37 oz. In 1998 this model was fitted with a 7-round cylinder.

NIB	Exc.	V.G.	Good	Fair	Poor
250	225	200	150	125	100

NOTE: Add $60 for stainless steel.

Model 627

This model is chambered for the .357 Magnum cartridge and has a 7-round cylinder. The 4" barrel is ported with a heavy underlug. Adjustable rear sight. Matte stainless steel finish. Introduced in 2000.

NIB	Exc.	V.G.	Good	Fair	Poor
425	325	—	—	—	—

Model 689

This model is chambered for the .357 Magnum cartridge and features a heavy, vent rib barrel in either 4" or 6" lengths. Fully adjustable rear sight is standard. Offered in blued or stainless steel. Pistol weighs 37 oz. In 1998 this model was fitted with a 7-round cylinder.

NIB	Exc.	V.G.	Good	Fair	Poor
250	225	200	150	125	100

Model 606

Introduced in 1997 this 6-round model is chambered for the .357 magnum cartridge. Fitted with a 2" solid rib barrel with ramp front sight and notched rear sight. Available in double action, single or double action only. Offered in blue or stainless steel. Rubber grips are standard. Weight is approximately 29 oz. A number of variations are offered on this model. For stainless steel models add $50.00.

NIB	Exc.	V.G.	Good	Fair	Poor
300	250	—	—	—	—

Model 607

Introduced in 1995 this .357 Magnum model features a choice of 4" or 6-1/2" integral compensated barrel in either blue or stainless steel. The 6-1/2" barrel is fitted with a vent rib.

Stainless Steel

NIB	Exc.	V.G.	Good	Fair	Poor
400	350	300	200	150	100

Blue

NIB	Exc.	V.G.	Good	Fair	Poor
325	275	225	200	150	100

Model 608

Introduced in 1996 this revolver is chambered for the .357 Magnum cartridge. The cylinder is bored for 8 rounds. Offered in 4" and 6.5" barrel lengths with integral compensator. The front sight is serrated ramp with red insert and the rear is adjustable. Offered in both blued and stainless steel versions. Weight is approximately 51.5 oz. with 6.5" barrel.

Stainless Steel

NIB	Exc.	V.G.	Good	Fair	Poor
450	350	300	200	150	100

Blue

NIB	Exc.	V.G.	Good	Fair	Poor
425	325	250	200	150	100

Model 617

Chambered for the .357 Magnum cartridge with 7-round cylinder. It is fitted with a 2" barrel. Choice of blue or stainless steel finish. Some variations offered a ported barrel. Introduced in 1998.

Stainless Steel

NIB	Exc.	V.G.	Good	Fair	Poor
400	325	275	225	—	—

Blue

NIB	Exc.	V.G.	Good	Fair	Poor
450	350	275	—	—	—

NIB	Exc.	V.G.	Good	Fair	Poor
350	275	225	175	—	—

NOTE: Add $20 for ported barrels.

Model 617 with ported barrel

Model 617 CHB2/SS2

Chambered for the .357 Magnum cartridge this model features a concealed hammer, 2" solid rib barrel, and fixed sights.

Stainless Steel

NIB	Exc.	V.G.	Good	Fair	Poor
400	325	275	225	—	—

Blue

NIB	Exc.	V.G.	Good	Fair	Poor
350	275	225	175	—	—

Model 415

Chambered for .41 Magnum cartridge and fitted with a 2.5" ported barrel. Fixed sights. Rubber grips. Matte stainless steel finish. Weight is about 30 oz.

Model 431

Chambered for the .44 Special cartridge this double action revolver is furnished with a 3" or 4" heavy, solid rib barrel with ejector shroud. Cylinder capacity is 5 rounds. Fixed sights are standard. Choice of blued or stainless steel finish. Pistol weighs 35 oz.

NIB	Exc.	V.G.	Good	Fair	Poor
225	200	175	150	125	100

NOTE: Add $60 for stainless steel.

Model 817 (Ultra-Lite)

Chambered for the .357 Magnum cartridge and fitted with a 7 shot cylinder and 2" solid rib barrel this model features an alloy frame. Stainless steel or blued finish. Some models are ported. Weight is about 21 oz.

Stainless Steel

NIB	Exc.	V.G.	Good	Fair	Poor
390	325	275	225	175	100

Blue

NIB	Exc.	V.G.	Good	Fair	Poor
350	275	225	175	125	100

NOTE: Add $20 for ported barrels.

Model 441

Similar to the Model 431 but furnished with an additional choice of a 6" barrel as well as a 3" or 4". Comes standard with fully adjustable rear sight. Cylinder capacity is 5 rounds. Blued or stainless steel finish. Pistol weighs 40.25 oz. with 6" barrel.

NIB	Exc.	V.G.	Good	Fair	Poor
250	225	200	175	125	100

NOTE: Add $60 for stainless steel.

Model 425 Tracker

Chambered for the .41 Magnum cartridge this model features a 4" heavy underlug ported barrel. Adjustable rear sight. Cylinder is chambered for 5 rounds. Matte stainless steel finish. Introduced in 2000.

NIB	Exc.	V.G.	Good	Fair	Poor
425	325	—	—	—	—

Model 445

This small frame revolver is chambered for the .44 Special cartridge. It is fitted with a 2" barrel with ramp front sight and notched rear sight. Cylinder holds 5 rounds. Black rubber grips. Offered in blue or stainless steel. Weight is about 28 oz. Add $50.00 for stainless steel. Factory barrel porting, add $20, is optional. Introduced in 1997.

NIB	Exc.	V.G.	Good	Fair	Poor
325	250	200	175	—	—

Model 450

Chambered for the .45 Long Colt cartridge this model features a 2" heavy solid rib barrel with 5 shot cylinder and fixed sights. Ported barrel. Rubber grips. Stainless steel finish. Weight is about 28 oz.

Stainless Steel

NIB	Exc.	V.G.	Good	Fair	Poor
450	350	275	225	175	125

NOTE: Add $30 for Ultra Lite model

WHAT'S IT LIKE-THE TAURUS .454 RAGING BULL

The Brazilian firm of Taurus has long been offering less expensive options to American shooters but there was always something missing in my mind's eye. Even when the .44 Magnum model was introduced, there was still something that was not quite right. The sixguns from south of the border looked too, well, foreign. All that changed with the introduction of the Raging Bull. This is one good-looking sixgun especially with the 6 1/2" stainless steel model. The combination of heavy under lugged barrel and the stainless steel finish makes it look even more massive than it is, and this is one very sturdily built revolver. Whoever is responsible for the design should be given a medal for artistic achievement. Of course, none of this makes any difference unless the gun also shoots well. And this gun does shoot well. In addition to being capable of excellent accuracy it is also about as comfortable as one can expect in a portable sixgun with the power of the .454 Casull. Four things contribute to making the Raging Bull controllable. We have mentioned the heavy under lugged barrel to which we can add porting and soft rubber finger groove grips. Finally, there is the weight of this big sixgun which when fully loaded comes in at slightly under four pounds with the 6 1/2" barrel and slightly over with the 8 3/8" barrel. It is a revolver designed for shooting. To add to the strength of this five-shot sixgun, the cylinder is latched both at the rear and at the front requiring two hands pushing on both latches to release the cylinder for loading and unloading. And for those who are concerned about such things, the Raging Bull has a built-in locking feature on the back of the hammer.

John Taffin

Model 454

This model is chambered for the .454 Casull. It is built on a large frame with a 5-round capacity. Barrel lengths are 5", 6.5" or 8.375" and are fitted with a ventilated rib and integral compensator. Sights are adjustable. Finish is blue or stainless steel. Black rubber or walnut grips. Weight is 53 oz. with 6.5" barrel. Add $60.00 for stainless steel model. Introduced in 1997.

Taurus Model 44

Blue Finish

NIB	Exc.	V.G.	Good	Fair	Poor
750	600	475	375	—	—

Stainless Steel

NIB	Exc.	V.G.	Good	Fair	Poor
820	650	500	400	—	—

Black Stainless Steel

NIB	Exc.	V.G.	Good	Fair	Poor
845	675	525	425	—	—

Model 44/444

Introduced in 1994 this heavy frame revolver is chambered for the .44 Magnum cartridge. Offered with choice of three barrel lengths: 4" with solid rib barrel, 6-1/2" with vent rib, and 8-3/8" with vent rib. All Model 44s have a built in compensator. The front sight is a serrated ramp with adjustable rear sight. Offered in either blued or stainless finish. Weight of 6-1/2" barrel gun is 53 oz.

Blue Finish

NIB	Exc.	V.G.	Good	Fair	Poor
545	425	300	200	150	100

Stainless Steel

NIB	Exc.	V.G.	Good	Fair	Poor
600	475	375	250	200	125

Model 45

Chambered for the .45 Long Colt and fitted with a choice of 6.5" or 8-3/8" heavy vent rib barrels. Cylinder holds 6 rounds. Rubber grips, ported barrels, and adjustable sights are standard. Weight with 6.5" barrel is about 53 oz.

Blue Finish

NIB	Exc.	V.G.	Good	Fair	Poor
545	425	300	200	150	100

Stainless Steel

NIB	Exc.	V.G.	Good	Fair	Poor
600	475	375	250	200	125

TITANIUM SERIES REVOLVERS

Introduced in 1999 this series of revolvers feature titanium barrels with stainless steel bore liners, titanium frames and cylinders. Hammers, triggers, latches, ejector rod and other small parts are made from case hardened chrome moly steel. All Taurus Titanium revolvers have factory porting and are rated for +P ammunition. Rubber grips are standard. Three different finishes are offered: Bright Spectrum blue, Matte Spectrum blue, and Matte Spectrum gold.

Model 85Ti

Chambered for .38 Special and fitted with a 2" barrel with 5-shot cylinder. Fixed sights.

NIB	Exc.	V.G.	Good	Fair	Poor
525	425	—	—	—	—

Model 731Ti

Chambered for the .32 H&R Magnum and fitted with a 2" barrel with 6-shot cylinder. Fixed sights.

NIB	Exc.	V.G.	Good	Fair	Poor
525	425	—	—	—	—

Model 617Ti

Chambered for .357 Magnum and fitted with a 2" barrel and 7-shot cylinder. Fixed sights. Weight is about 20 oz.

NIB	Exc.	V.G.	Good	Fair	Poor
600	475	—	—	—	—

Model 627Ti

This model features a 7-round cylinder chambered for the .357 Magnum cartridge. Fitted with a ported 4" barrel with adjustable sights. Gray finish. Weight is about 28 oz. depending on barrel length.

NIB	Exc.	V.G.	Good	Fair	Poor
675	500	—	—	—	—

Model 415Ti

Chambered for the .41 Magnum and fitted with a 2.5" barrel with 5-shot cylinder. Fixed sights. Weight is about 21 oz.

NIB	Exc.	V.G.	Good	Fair	Poor
600	475	—	—	—	—

Model 425Ti

This model is chambered for the .41 Magnum cartridge and has a 5-round cylinder. The barrel is ported and 4" with adjustable rear sight. Gray finish. Introduced in 2000.

NIB	Exc.	V.G.	Good	Fair	Poor
675	500	—	—	—	—

Model 450Ti

Chambered for the .45 Long Colt and fitted with a 2" barrel with 5-shot cylinder. Fixed sights. Weight is about 19 oz.

NIB	Exc.	V.G.	Good	Fair	Poor
600	475	—	—	—	—

Model 445Ti

Chambered for the .44 Special and fitted with a 2" barrel with 5 shot cylinder. Fixed sights. Weight is about 20 oz.

NIB	Exc.	V.G.	Good	Fair	Poor
600	475	—	—	—	—

Model UL/Ti

Chambered for the .38 Special this model has a Titanium cylinder and alloy frame. Fitted with a 2" unported barrel. Cylinder is 5 shot. Fixed sights.

NIB	Exc.	V.G.	Good	Fair	Poor
500	400	—	—	—	—

RIFLES

Model 62

Introduced in 2000 this is a replica of the Winchester Model 62 .22 caliber rifle. Fitted with a 23" barrel and adjustable rear sight. Magazine capacity is 13 rounds. Weight is about 5 lbs. Hardwood stock.

NIB	Exc.	V.G.	Good	Fair	Poor
275	200	—	—	—	—

NOTE: Add $15 for stainless steel.

Model 62 Carbine

Same as above but with a 16.5" barrel. Magazine capacity is 12 rounds. Weight is about 4.5 lbs. Introduced in 2000.

NIB	Exc.	V.G.	Good	Fair	Poor
275	200	—	—	—	—

NOTE: Add $15 for stainless steel.

Model 72

Same as the Model 62 but chambered for the .22 magnum cartridge.

NIB	Exc.	V.G.	Good	Fair	Poor
295	225	—	—	—	—

NOTE: Add $15 for stainless steel.

Model 72 Carbine

Same as the Model 62 Carbine but chambered for the .22 magnum cartridge.

NIB	Exc.	V.G.	Good	Fair	Poor
295	225	—	—	—	—

NOTE: Add $15 for stainless steel.

TAYLOR'S & CO., INC.
Winchester, Virginia

PISTOLS

Napoleon Le Page Pistol (Model 551)

A percussion French style duelling pistol. Chambered for .45 caliber and fitted with a 10" octagon barrel. Walnut stock silver plated butt cap and triggerguard. Double set triggers. Made by Uberti.

NIB	Exc.	V.G.	Good	Fair	Poor
350	275	—	—	—	—

Kentucky Pistol (Model 550)

Chambered for the .45 caliber ball and fitted with a 10" barrel. Bird's head grip with brass ramrod thimbles and case hardened sidelock. Made by Uberti.

NIB	Exc.	V.G.	Good	Fair	Poor
185	150	—	—	—	—

Colt Model 1847 Walker (Model 500A)

Fitted with a 9" round barrel and chambered for .44 caliber. This model has a 6-round engraved cylinder. Steel frame and backstrap and brass triggerguard. One piece walnut grips. Made by Uberti.

NIB	Exc.	V.G.	Good	Fair	Poor
370	300	—	—	—	—

Colt Dragoon (Models 485A, 490A, 495A)

Offered in 1st, 2nd, and 3rd models each is fitted with a 7.5" barrel and chambered for .44 caliber. Steel frame and brass backstrap and triggerguard. The 2nd and 3rd models have a square cylinder stop. The loading lever is inverted on the 3rd model. All have one piece walnut grip. Made by Uberti.

NIB	Exc.	V.G.	Good	Fair	Poor
295	250	—	—	—	—

NOTE: Add $15 for 3rd model.

Colt Model 1848 Baby Dragoon (Models 470, 471, 472)

Chambered for the .31 caliber and fitted with a 5-round cylinder. Barrel length is 4". Choice of blued or white steel frame. Brass backstrap and triggerguard. One piece walnut grip. Made by Uberti.

NIB	Exc.	V.G.	Good	Fair	Poor
250	200	—	—	—	—

Colt Model 1851 Navy

Offered with either brass or steel frame with brass backstrap and triggerguard. Chambered for .36 caliber and fitted with a 7.5" barrel. Cylinder holds 6 rounds. One piece walnut grip. Brass frame model made by Armi San Marco. Steel frame model made by F. LLI. Pietta.

Brass frame (Model 210)

NIB	Exc.	V.G.	Good	Fair	Poor
135	100	—	—	—	—

Steel frame (Model 245)

NIB	Exc.	V.G.	Good	Fair	Poor
165	125	—	—	—	—

Remington Model 1858

This is a .44 caliber either a brass frame or steel frame and brass triggerguard model with 8" octagon barrel. Cylinder holds 6 rounds. Two piece walnut grips. Brass frame made by F. LLI. Pietta. Steel frame made by Armi San Marco.

Brass frame (Model 410)

NIB	Exc.	V.G.	Good	Fair	Poor
150	120	—	—	—	—

Steel frame (Model 430)

NIB	Exc.	V.G.	Good	Fair	Poor
185	140	—	—	—	—

Starr Model 1858 (Model 510, 511)

This model is offered in either double action or single action. ly is chambered for the .44 caliber and fitted with a 6" round barrel. Made by F. LLI. Pietta.

NIB	Exc.	V.G.	Good	Fair	Poor
370	300	—	—	—	—

Colt Model 1860 Army

This model features an 8" round barrel except for the Sheriff's model which is 5.5". Choice of brass or steel frame with brass backstrap and triggerguard. Chambered for .44 caliber. One piece walnut grip. Brass frame model made by Armi San Marco and steel frame by Uberti.

Brass frame (Model 300)

NIB	Exc.	V.G.	Good	Fair	Poor
160	250	—	—	—	—

Steel frame (Model 310, 312, 315)

NIB	Exc.	V.G.	Good	Fair	Poor
250	200	—	—	—	—

NOTE: A half-fluted cylinder model is also offered.

Colt Model 1861 Navy (Model 210)

This model is chambered for the .36 caliber and fitted with a 7.5" round barrel. Cylinder is 6 rounds. Brass frame and backstrap and triggerguard. One piece walnut grip. Made by Uberti.

NIB	Exc.	V.G.	Good	Fair	Poor
250	200	—	—	—	—

Colt Model 1862 Police (Model 315B)

Fitted with a 6.5" round barrel and chambered for .36 caliber. Case hardened frame with brass backstrap and triggerguard. Made by Uberti.

NIB	Exc.	V.G.	Good	Fair	Poor
265	200	—	—	—	—

Colt Model 1862 Pocket (Model 315C)

Similar to the above model but fitted with a 6.5" octagonal barrel. Made by Uberti.

NIB	Exc.	V.G.	Good	Fair	Poor
235	185	—	—	—	—

Remington Model 1863 Pocket (Model 435)

This revolver is chambered for the .31 caliber ball and fitted with a 3.5" barrel. Cylinder is 5 rounds. Frame, backstrap and triggerguard are brass. Walnut grip. Made by Armi San Marco.

NIB	Exc.	V.G.	Good	Fair	Poor
150	100	—	—	—	—

Colt Model 1873 Cattleman (Models 700, 701, 702)

This famous replica is made in several different configurations. Offered in barrel lengths of 4.75", 5.5", and 7.5". Calibers are: .45 Colt, .44-40, .44 Special, .38-40, .357 Magnum, and .45ACP. Frame is case hardened with steel backstrap. One piece walnut grip. Made by Uberti.

NIB	Exc.	V.G.	Good	Fair	Poor
400	325	—	—	—	—

NOTE: Add $80 for dual cylinder and $80 for nickel finish.

Colt Model 1873 Birdshead (Models 703A, 703B, 703C)

Same as above but offered with birdshead grip.

NIB	Exc.	V.G.	Good	Fair	Poor
400	325	—	—	—	—

RIFLES

Kentucky Rifle

Offered in either flintlock or percussion this rifle is .40 caliber and fitted with a 3.5" barrel. One piece stock with brass fixtures.

Flintlock (Model 183)

NIB	Exc.	V.G.	Good	Fair	Poor
335	250	—	—	—	—

Percussion (Model 182)

NIB	Exc.	V.G.	Good	Fair	Poor
300	240	—	—	—	—

Model 1842 U.S. Percussion Musket (Model 125)

This model is offered as a smoothbore or rifled musket with 42" .69 caliber barrel. Finish is in the white. One piece walnut stock.

Smoothbore

NIB	Exc.	V.G.	Good	Fair	Poor
540	425	—	—	—	—

Rifled Smoothbore with rear sight (Model 126)

NIB	Exc.	V.G.	Good	Fair	Poor
585	450	—	—	—	—

Model 1855 U.S. Percussion Musket (Model 116)

This model has a .58 caliber 40" barrel with rear sight. One piece walnut stock. White satin finish.

NIB	Exc.	V.G.	Good	Fair	Poor
550	425	—	—	—	—

Model 1853 3-Band Enfield Musket (Model 120)

This rifled musket has a 39" .58 caliber barrel. Blued finish. One piece walnut stock. Brass buttplate, nosecap, and trigger-guard.

NIB	Exc.	V.G.	Good	Fair	Poor
425	325	—	—	—	—

Model 1858 2-Band Enfield Musket (Model 121)

Similar to the above model but fitted with a .58 caliber 33" barrel.

NIB	Exc.	V.G.	Good	Fair	Poor
400	325	—	—	—	—

Model 1861 Springfield Musket (Model 110)

This model has a 40" .58 caliber barrel with one piece walnut stock. White satin finish.

NIB	Exc.	V.G.	Good	Fair	Poor
475	375	—	—	—	—

Model 1862 C.S. Richmond Musket (Model 115)

This rifle is fitted with a 40" .58 caliber barrel with 3 barrel bands. Brass buttplate and nosecap. White satin finish. One piece walnut stock.

NIB	Exc.	V.G.	Good	Fair	Poor
490	400	—	—	—	—

Model 1863 Remington Zouave (Model 140)

Fitted with a 33" barrel chambered for the .58 caliber ball. One piece walnut stock with blued finish, brass butt plate, nosecap, triggerguard, patchbox, and barrel bands.

NIB	Exc.	V.G.	Good	Fair	Poor
375	300	—	—	—	—

Henry Rifle

This lever action rifle is chambered for the .44-40 or .45 Colt cartridge. Fitted with a 24.25" octagon barrel. Walnut stock. Open sights.

Brass frame (Model 198)

NIB	Exc.	V.G.	Good	Fair	Poor
940	750	—	—	—	—

Iron frame (Model 199)

NIB	Exc.	V.G.	Good	Fair	Poor
990	800	—	—	—	—

Winchester Model 1866 (Model 201)

This model is chambered for the .44-40 or .45 Colt cartridge. Fitted with a 24.25" octagon barrel. Brass frame. Open sights. Made by Uberti.

NIB	Exc.	V.G.	Good	Fair	Poor
830	650	—	—	—	—

Winchester Model 1866 Yellowboy Carbine (Model 202)

Same as above but with 19" round barrel and the additional .38 Special caliber. Made by Uberti.

NIB	Exc.	V.G.	Good	Fair	Poor
750	600	—	—	—	—

Winchester Model 1873 (Model 200)

This lever action model is chambered for the .44-40 or .45 Colt cartridge and fitted with a 24.25" octagon barrel. Made by Uberti.

NIB	Exc.	V.G.	Good	Fair	Poor
750	600	—	—	—	—

Winchester Model 1873 Carbine (Model 200B)

Chambered for the .45 Long Colt cartridge and fitted with a 19" barrel. Magazine capacity is 10 rounds. Walnut stock and case colored frame.

NIB	Exc.	V.G.	Good	Fair	Poor
825	650	—	—	—	—

Winchester Model 1873 Sporting Rifle (Model 200C)

Chambered for the .45 Long Colt cartridge and fitted with a 30" octagon barrel. Checkered walnut stock with pistol grip. Case colored frame and blued barrel.

NIB	Exc.	V.G.	Good	Fair	Poor
925	750	—	—	—	—

Winchester Model 1885 Highwall (Model 203)

Offered with 30" or 32" barrels chambered for the .45-70 cartridge. Walnut stock.

NIB	Exc.	V.G.	Good	Fair	Poor
800	650	—	—	—	—

Winchester Model 1885 Low Wall Sporting Rifle (Model 204)

This single shot rifle is chambered for the .22 Long Rifle, .32-20, or .38-40 cartridge. Checkered walnut stock.

NIB	Exc.	V.G.	Good	Fair	Poor
800	650	—	—	—	—

Sharps Model 1859 Infantry (Model 151)

This rifle is fitted with a 30" round barrel and is chambered for the .54 caliber cartridge. One piece walnut with 3 barrel bands. Adjustable rear sight.

NIB	Exc.	V.G.	Good	Fair	Poor
950	750	—	—	—	—

Sharps Model 1859 Berdan Military (Model 152)

This .54 caliber rifle is fitted with a 30" round barrel. One piece walnut stock with 3 barrel bands. Adjustable rear sight. This model is fitted with double set triggers.

NIB	Exc.	V.G.	Good	Fair	Poor
1000	800	—	—	—	—

Sharps Model 1859 Cavalry (Model 153)

This model has a 22" round barrel with adjustable rear sight. Chambered for .54 caliber. Walnut stock is fitted with patch box.

NIB	Exc.	V.G.	Good	Fair	Poor
825	650	—	—	—	—

Sharps Model 1863 Cavalry (Model 154)

Similar to the Model 1859 Cavalry but without the patch box.

NIB	Exc.	V.G.	Good	Fair	Poor
800	650	—	—	—	—

Sharps Model 1863 Sporting Rifle (Model 131)

This .54 caliber model is offered with either 30" or 32" octagon barrel with single or double set triggers. Walnut stock.

NIB	Exc.	V.G.	Good	Fair	Poor
875	700	—	—	—	—

NOTE: Add $20 for double set trigger.

Sharps Model 1874 Sporting Rifle (Model 138)

This model is offered with a variety of features. Available in .45-70 with choice of 30" or 32" octagon barrel with a choice of single trigger or double set triggers. It is also available with Hartford-style pewter forend tip. In this configuration it is available in .45-70, .40-65, .45-90, or .45-120 calibers. Checkered stock with patch is optional.

NIB	Exc.	V.G.	Good	Fair	Poor
895	700	—	—	—	—

NOTE: Add $125 for Hartford style forend tip. Add $250 for checkered stock with patch box.

Sharps Model 1874 Deluxe Sporting Rifle (Model 155)

This .45-70 caliber model features a hand checkered walnut stock with oil finish. Receiver is in the white with standard scroll engraving

NIB	Exc.	V.G.	Good	Fair	Poor
1800	1350	—	—	—	—

NOTE: For Deluxe Model 1874 with gold inlay add $800.

Sharps Model 1874 Infantry Rifle (Model 157)

This .45-70 caliber model features a 30" round barrel with 3 barrel bands. One piece walnut stock. Adjustable rear sight. Single trigger. Patch box in stock.

NIB	Exc.	V.G.	Good	Fair	Poor
1000	800	—	—	—	—

Sharps Model 1874 Berdan Rifle (Model 158)

Similar to the above model but with a double set trigger.

NIB	Exc.	V.G.	Good	Fair	Poor
1050	825	—	—	—	—

Sharps Model 1874 Cavalry (Model 159)

This .45-70 caliber model is fitted with a 22" round barrel. Adjustable rear sight.

NIB	Exc.	V.G.	Good	Fair	Poor
875	700	—	—	—	—

Spencer Model 1865 Carbine (Model 160)

This lever action model is chambered in a choice of calibers: .56-50, .44 Russian, or .45 Schofield. Fitted with a 20" round barrel. Walnut stock. Case hardened receiver and blued barrel. Made by Armi Sport.

NIB	Exc.	V.G.	Good	Fair	Poor
N/A	—	—	—	—	—

TAYLOR, L.B.
Chicopee, Massachusetts

Pocket Pistol

A .32 caliber spur trigger single shot pocket pistol with a 3.5" octagonal barrel marked "L. B. Taylor & Co. Chicopee Mass."

Silver-plated brass frame, blued barrel and walnut grips. Manufactured during the late 1860s and early 1870s.

Exc.	V.G.	Good	Fair	Poor
—	—	800	350	100

TERRIER ONE
Importer-Southern Gun Distributors
Miami, Florida

Terrier One

A .32 caliber double action swing-out cylinder revolver with a 2.25" barrel and 5-shot cylinder. Nickel-plated with checkered walnut grips. Manufactured from 1984 to 1987.

Exc.	V.G.	Good	Fair	Poor
100	75	50	30	25

TERRY, J. C.
New York City

Pocket Pistol

A .22 caliber spur trigger single shot pocket pistol with a 3.75" round barrel. The back strap marked "J.C. Terry/Patent Pending." Silver-plated brass frame, blued barrel and rosewood or walnut grips. Manufactured in the late 1860s.

Exc.	V.G.	Good	Fair	Poor
—	—	950	475	100

A J.C. Terry repeating pocket pistol sold at auction for $2,530. This example is quite unique and may be the only repeating Terry made. Condition is very good. Chambered for the .22 short cartridge and fitted with a 3.75" barrel.
Amoskeag Auction Company, May 2001

TEXAS CONTRACT RIFLES

Three contractors produced rifles for the State of Texas during 1862 and 1863. One of these patterns has a sporting back-action lock, Enfield barrel bands, an overall length of 47-3/8", heavy 32" long barrel of .58 caliber. Total deliveries by all contractors amounted to 1,464 rifles. Quality of these arms was decidedly inferior and often complained about.

Prospective purchasers are strongly advised to secure an expert appraisal prior to acquisition.

TEXAS GUNFIGHTERS
Ponte Zanano, Italy
Importer-Texas Gunfighters
Irving, Texas

Shootist Single Action

A .45 Long Colt caliber single action revolver with a 4.75" barrel. Nickel-plated with one-piece walnut grips. This model is made by Aldo Uberti. Introduced in 1988.

NIB	Exc.	V.G.	Good	Fair	Poor
600	550	500	400	350	200

1 of 100 Edition

As above, with one-piece mother-of-pearl grips fitted in a case with an additional set of walnut grips. 100 were made in 1988.

NIB	Exc.	V.G.	Good	Fair	Poor
1250	1000	850	700	600	300

TEXAS LONGHORN ARMS, INC.
Richmond, Texas

NOTE: As of 1998 this company had suspended operations.

Jezebel

A .22 or .22 Magnum single shot pistol with a 6" barrel. Stainless steel with a walnut stock and forend. Introduced in 1987.

NIB	Exc.	V.G.	Good	Fair	Poor
225	175	150	125	100	75

Texas Border Special

A .44 Special or .45 Colt caliber single action revolver with a 3.5" barrel having Pope style rifling. Blued, case hardened with one-piece walnut grips.

NIB	Exc.	V.G.	Good	Fair	Poor
1500	1250	1000	800	600	300

South Texas Army

As above, but with a 4.75" barrel also chambered for the .357 Magnum cartridge and fitted with conventional one-piece walnut grips.

NIB	Exc.	V.G.	Good	Fair	Poor
1500	1250	1000	800	600	300

West Texas Target

As above, with a 7.5" barrel, flat top frame and in .32-20 caliber in addition to the calibers noted above.

NIB	Exc.	V.G.	Good	Fair	Poor
1500	1250	1000	800	600	300

Grover's Improved Number Five

Similar to the above, in .44 Magnum with a 5.5" barrel. Serial Numbered K1 to K1200. Introduced in 1988.

NIB	Exc.	V.G.	Good	Fair	Poor
1000	800	700	600	500	250

Mason Commemorative

As above, in .45 Colt with a 4.75" barrel and having the Mason's insignia. Gold inlaid. Introduced in 1987.

NIB	Exc.	V.G.	Good	Fair	Poor
1500	1250	1000	800	600	300

Texas Sesquicentennial Commemorative

As above, engraved in the style of Louis D. Nimschke with one-piece ivory grips and a fitted case.

NIB	Exc.	V.G.	Good	Fair	Poor
2500	2000	1500	900	750	400

THAMES ARMS CO.
Norwich, Connecticut

A .22, .32, or .38 caliber double action top break revolver with varying length barrels normally marked "Automatic Revolver", which refers to the cartridge ejector. Nickel-plated with walnut grips.

Exc.	V.G.	Good	Fair	Poor
500	125	100	75	50

THIEME & EDELER
Eibar, Spain

Pocket Pistol

A 7.65mm caliber semiautomatic pistol with a 3" barrel marked "T E". Blued with black plastic grips. Manufactured prior to 1936.

Exc.	V.G.	Good	Fair	Poor
250	150	100	75	50

THOMPSON
SEE—Auto Ordnance

THOMPSON/CENTER ARMS
Rochester, New Hampshire

Contender

Introduced in 1967 this model is the basis for all past and present variations. The standard version is offered with a 10" octagon barrel and is available in 10" Bull barrel, 10" vent rib barrel, 14" Super models, 14" Super with vent rib, 16" Super models, and 16" Super models with vent rib. A stainless steel finish is available on all models except the 10" octagon barrel. The action on these handguns is a single shot, break open design. Unless otherwise stated the barrels are blued. The Competitor grip is walnut with rubber insert mounted on back of grip. A finger groove grip is also available made from walnut with finger notching and thumb rest. Forend is American black walnut in various length and designs depending on barrel size. Stainless steel models have rubber grips with finger grooves. Standard sights are standard Patridge rear with ramp front. An adjustable rear sight is offered as an option. Barrels with vent ribs are furnished with fixed rear sight and bead front sight. Due to the numerous variations of the Contender several breakdowns will be listed to help the reader find the closest possible handgun he may be looking for.

NOTE: Early frames with no engraving, called flatsides, and those with eagle engraving bring between $2,000 and $2,500 on the collector market.

10" Octagon Barrel Model

This was the first Contender design and is offered in .22 Long Rifle only. It is supplied with adjustable rear sight and mounting holes for scope. Grips are Competitor or rubber. Weighs about 44 oz.

NIB	Exc.	V.G.	Good	Fair	Poor
360	300	250	200	150	100

10" Bull Barrel Model

Comes standard with adjustable rear sight, mounting holes for scope mounts, and Competitor grips for blued models and rubber grips on stainless models. Available in blued or stainless steel. Offered in the following calibers as complete pistols: .22 l.r., .22 l.r. Match, .22 Win. Mag. (blued only), .22 Hornet, .223, 7mm T.C.U. (blued only), .30-30, .32-20 (blued only), .357 Mag., .357 Rem. max (blued only), .44 Mag., .45 Colt, .410 bore. In 1994 Thompson/Center introduced the .300 whisper cartridge to its Contender product line. Weighs approximately 50 oz.

NIB	Exc.	V.G.	Good	Fair	Poor
350	300	250	200	150	100

10" Vent Rib Model

This features a raised vent rib and is chambered for the .45 Long Colt/.410 bore. The rear sight is fixed and the front sight is a bead. A detachable choke screws into the muzzle for use with the .410 shell. Furnished with Competitor grips or rubber grips.

NIB	Exc.	V.G.	Good	Fair	Poor
370	320	270	220	150	100

Super 14" Model

This model features a 14" bull barrel. Furnished with adjustable rear sight and ramp front sight. Drilled and tapped for scope mounts. Competitor or rubber grips are offered. Available in blued or stainless steel finish. Furnished in the following calibers in a complete pistol only: .22 Long Rifle, .22 l.r. Match, .17 Rem. (blued only), .22 Hornet, .222 Rem. (blued only), .223 Rem., 7mm T.C.U. (blued only), 7-30 Waters, .30-30, .357 Rem. Max (blued only), .35 Rem., .375 Win. (blued only), .44 Mag. (blued only). weighs approximately 56 oz.

NIB	Exc.	V.G.	Good	Fair	Poor
360	300	250	200	150	100

Super 14" Vent Rib Model

Similar to the 10" vent rib model chambered for the .45 Long Colt/.410 bore but furnished with a 14" vent rib barrel.

NIB	Exc.	V.G.	Good	Fair	Poor
385	325	275	215	150	100

Super 16" Model

Fitted with a 16.25" tapered barrel, two position adjustable rear sight. Drilled and tapped for scope mount. Furnished with Competitor grips or rubber grips and choice of blued or stainless steel finish. Available in the following calibers as complete pistols only: .22 l.r., .22 Hornet, .223 Rem., 7-30 Waters, .30-30, .35 Rem., .45-70 Government. Weighs approximately 56 oz.

NIB	Exc.	V.G.	Good	Fair	Poor
370	320	275	215	150	100

Super 16" Vent Rib Model

Chambered for .45 Long Colt/.410 bore this model was offered for the first time in 1993. All other features are the same as the other Contender .45/.410 bore pistols.

NIB	Exc.	V.G.	Good	Fair	Poor
390	350	300	250	175	125

Contender Hunter Model

This model is designed for handgun hunting and is offered in two barrel lengths: 12" and 14". The barrels are fitted with a compensator and a 2.5 power scope. There are no iron sights fitted. A nylon carrying sling and soft leather carrying case are standard. Offered in the following calibers: 7-30 Waters, .30-30 Win., .35 Rem., .45-70 Government, .44 Mag., .223 Rem., and .375 Win. Fitted with Competitor grips and offered in blued or stainless steel finish. Weighs approximately 64 oz.

NIB	Exc.	V.G.	Good	Fair	Poor
575	500	400	300	200	100

> **NOTE:** Barrel interchangeability is acceptable for blued barrels and frames with stainless steel barrels and frames. DO NOT interchange Alloy II barrels and frames with either blued or stainless steel components.

Encore Pistol

Introduced in 1996 this single shot pistol will feature barrels chambered for the .30-06, .308 Win., 7mm-08 Rem., .223 Rem., .22-250 Rem., .44 Magnum, and 7mmBR. Offered with 10.625", 15", or 24" barrels this new handgun is designed for use with higher pressure cartridges. Barrels will not interchange with the Contender. Weight with 10.625" barrel is 56 oz., with 15" barrel about 4 lbs. and with 24" barrel about 6.75 lbs.

NIB	Exc.	V.G.	Good	Fair	Poor
500	450	—	—	—	—

NOTE: Add $60 for stainless steel frame and barrels.

Encore Rifle

Similar to the Encore pistol but with longer barrels and walnut stock and forearm. A wide variety of calibers are offered from .22-250 to .300 Win. Mag. in barrels lengths from 24" to 26". Heavy barrels are offered in 7mm Rem Mag., .300 Win. Mag., and .22-250. These are offered with no sights. Weight is about 6 lbs. 12 oz. for 7mm-08 with 24" barrel. Introduced in 1997. In 1998 the .260 Rem., .280 Rem., and .45-70 Gov't cartridges were added. In 1999 stainless steel frame and barrels were offered as well as blued.

NIB	Exc.	V.G.	Good	Fair	Poor
550	450	—	—	—	—

NOTE: Add about $60 for stainless steel frame and barrels.

Encore Shotgun

Introduced in 1998 this model is fitted with a 26" 20 gauge vent rib barrel with walnut stock and forend. Choke tubes are standard.

NIB	Exc.	V.G.	Good	Fair	Poor
625	475	—	—	—	—

Encore Rifled Shotgun

Introduced in 2000 this model features a 26" rifled shotgun barrel chambered for the 20 gauge shell. Adjustable rear sight. Walnut stock and blued finish.

NIB	Exc.	V.G.	Good	Fair	Poor
600	450	—	—	—	—

Encore 209x50 Mag Rifle

This muzzleloading rifle is chambered for .50 caliber and fitted with a 26" barrel. Designed to handle magnum loads of up to 150 grains of FFG black powder. Blued or stainless steel finish. Introduced in 1998.

NIB	Exc.	V.G.	Good	Fair	Poor
550	450	400	—	—	—

NOTE: Add $75 for stainless steel.

Encore 209x50 Pistol

This model features a 15" barrel chambered for .50 caliber. Walnut stock and blued finish. Approximate weight is 16 oz. Introduced in 2000.

NIB	Exc.	V.G.	Good	Fair	Poor
550	425	—	—	—	—

Contender Carbine Model

This model is built from the same design as the Contender Model. It features completely interchangeable barrels chambered for 12 different cartridges from .22 l.r. to .35 Rem. A .410 bore shotgun barrel is also offered. The standard model has a 21" barrel stocked with walnut. For stainless steel models a composite stock in fitted walnut is also available. All are drilled and tapped for scope mounts. Available in blued or stainless steel.

Standard 21" Carbine Model

This model is fitted with a 21" plain barrel and walnut stocks. Offered in the following calibers as a complete gun only: .22 l.r., .22 l.r. Match (blued only), .17 Rem. (blued only), .22 Hornet, .223 Rem., 7-30 Waters, .30-30, .35 Rem. (blued only), .375 Win. (blued only). Weighs 5 lbs. 3 oz.

NIB	Exc.	V.G.	Good	Fair	Poor
400	350	300	250	200	100

21" Carbine .410 Bore

Same as above but fitted with a vent rib barrel and screw in choke.

NIB	Exc.	V.G.	Good	Fair	Poor
410	360	300	250	200	100

16" Youth Model Carbine

A special walnut buttstock with 12" length of pull and 16.25" barrel. Short buttstock can be replaced with standard buttstock. Blued or stainless steel finish. Complete guns are offered in the same calibers as the 21" Carbine with the exception of the .375 Win. and the addition of the .45 Long Colt/.410 bore with vent rib barrel.

NIB	Exc.	V.G.	Good	Fair	Poor
350	300	250	200	150	100

TCR Hunter Model

This single shot top lever rifle is chambered for cartridges from .22 Long Rifle to .308 Win. Fitted with a 23" barrel. The finish is blue with walnut stock. Discontinued as a regular production rifle in 1993 but available from the TC custom shop as a special order.

NIB	Exc.	V.G.	Good	Fair	Poor
425	375	300	250	200	100

T/C 22 LR Classic

Introduced in 2000 this model is a semiautomatic rifle chambered for the .22 Long Rifle cartridge. It is fitted with a 22" match grade barrel. Walnut stock with Monte Carlo comb. Adjustable rear sight. Magazine capacity is 8 rounds. Weight is about 5.5 lbs.

NIB	Exc.	V.G.	Good	Fair	Poor
325	250	—	—	—	—

BLACK POWDER FIREARMS

System 1

Introduced in 1997 this concept features a complete muzzle-loading system with interchangeable barrels. Offered with .32, .50, .54, .58 caliber and 12 gauge shotgun barrels with walnut stock and blued finish. Or stainless steel with synthetic stock. Barrel lengths are 26". Approximate weight is 7.5 lbs. Sights are adjustable. Add $30.00 for synthetic stock and stainless steel.

NIB	Exc.	V.G.	Good	Fair	Poor
350	300	—	—	—	—

Thunder Hawk

Introduced in 1993, this rifle features a .50 caliber cap lock in-line ignition with 21" round barrel. Rear sight is adjustable with ramp front sight. The stock is a plain American black walnut with rubber recoil pad. Trigger is adjustable. In 1994 this model was available in stainless steel. Weighs 6.75 lbs.

NIB	Exc.	V.G.	Good	Fair	Poor
225	200	175	150	100	75

Thunder Hawk Shadow

Introduced in 1996, this model features an in-line ignition in .50 or .54 caliber with a 24" round barrel. It comes standard with a black checkered composite stock. Weight is approximately 7 lbs. In 1997 this model was offered with camouflage stock and blued finish.

NIB	Exc.	V.G.	Good	Fair	Poor
300	250	200	150	100	75

Grey Hawk

This stainless steel composite stock rifle is a .50 caliber cap lock with 24" round barrel. It utilizes a hooked breech system. The lock is a heavy-duty coil spring with floral engraving pattern. Adjustable rear sight and bead front sight are standard. Weighs about 7 lbs.

NIB	Exc.	V.G.	Good	Fair	Poor
225	200	175	150	100	75

Hawken Cap Lock Rifle

Available in .45, .50, and .54 caliber this rifle has a 28" octagonal barrel and hooked breech system. Triggers are fully adjustable and can function as double set or single stage. Adjustable sights with bead front sight are standard. Trim is solid brass and stock is select American walnut with cheekpiece. Weighs about 8.5 lbs.

NIB	Exc.	V.G.	Good	Fair	Poor
300	250	200	150	100	75

Hawken Flint Lock Rifle

Offered in .50 caliber with 28" octagonal barrel. All other features are the same as above.

NIB	Exc.	V.G.	Good	Fair	Poor
310	260	200	150	100	75

Hawken Custom/Elite

Introduced in 1994 this model features a .50 caliber traditional cap lock rifle with double set triggers, Crescent butt, and select American walnut stock with no patch box. The finish is a high luster blue.

NIB	Exc.	V.G.	Good	Fair	Poor
400	350	275	175	100	75

Renegade Cap Lock Rifle

Offered in .50 or .54 caliber with 26" octagonal barrel. Adjustable triggers that can function as double set or single stage. Adjustable sights with blued trim. Walnut stock. Offered in either right hand or left hand models. Weighs about 8 lbs.

NIB	Exc.	V.G.	Good	Fair	Poor
275	225	200	150	100	75

Renegade Flint Lock

Available in .50 caliber only and right hand only. Other features are the same as Cap Lock Model.

NIB	Exc.	V.G.	Good	Fair	Poor
275	250	200	150	100	75

Big Boar Rifle

This hooked breech model features the .58 caliber with 26" octagonal barrel. Single trigger and adjustable sights are standard. Trim is blued steel. American walnut stock with rubber pad. Weighs about 7.75 lbs.

NIB	Exc.	V.G.	Good	Fair	Poor
275	250	200	150	100	75

High Plains Sporter

This is a .50 caliber cap lock with a 24" round barrel. The lock is case-colored. Choice of adjustable open sights or tang sight. Trim is blued. The stock is walnut with rubber recoil pad, pistol grip, and sling swivel studs. Weighs about 7 lbs.

NIB	Exc.	V.G.	Good	Fair	Poor
275	250	200	150	100	75

Tree Hawk

Available in either .50 caliber cap lock or 12 gauge cap lock. The .50 caliber carbine has a 21" barrel and is offered in camo colors. The 12 gauge shotgun is fitted with a 27" barrel and also comes in camo colors. Weight is about 6.75 lbs.

Rifle

NIB	Exc.	V.G.	Good	Fair	Poor
275	250	200	150	100	75

Shotgun

NIB	Exc.	V.G.	Good	Fair	Poor
275	250	200	150	100	75

White Mountain Carbine

Available in either .45, .50, or .54 caliber cap lock or .50 flint lock. Fitted with a 20-1/2" octagon barrel. The lock is case-colored and trim is blued. Stock is walnut with rubber recoil pad. Weighs about 6.5 lbs.

NIB	Exc.	V.G.	Good	Fair	Poor
250	225	200	150	100	75

Black Mountain Magnum

Introduced in 1999 this model features a 26" round barrel with choice of walnut or composite stock. Chambered for .50 or .54 caliber or 12 gauge with 27" round barrel. All models are cap lock. Blued finish.

NIB	Exc.	V.G.	Good	Fair	Poor
350	275	—	—	—	—

Pennsylvania Hunter

Offered in .50 caliber cap or flint lock and fitted with either a 31-1/2" octagon/round barrel or a 21-1/2" octagon/round barrel. Fully adjustable sights, walnut stock, and blued trim are standard. Rifle weighs about 7.5 lbs. while the carbine weighs about 6.5 lbs.

Rifle

NIB	Exc.	V.G.	Good	Fair	Poor
400	325	250	200	150	100

Carbine

NIB	Exc.	V.G.	Good	Fair	Poor
400	325	250	200	150	100

Pennsylvania Match Rifle

Similar to the Pennsylvania Hunter Rifle except equipped with a tang peep sight and a globe front sight.

NIB	Exc.	V.G.	Good	Fair	Poor
350	275	200	150	100	75

New Englander Rifle

Offered in either .50 or .54 caliber cap lock with walnut stock and 26" round barrel. Adjustable sights. Weighs about 7 lbs. 15 oz. A 12" barrel is optional.

NIB	Exc.	V.G.	Good	Fair	Poor
200	175	150	125	90	75

NOTE: Add $150 for interchangeable shotgun barrel.

New Englander Shotgun

Same as above, but fitted with a 27" 12 gauge barrel with screw in full choke. Weighs about 6 lbs. 8 oz.

NIB	Exc.	V.G.	Good	Fair	Poor
230	200	175	150	100	75

New Englander Composite

Offered with composite stock. The .50 or .54 caliber rifle has a 24" barrel and the 12 gauge shotgun has a 27" barrel.

Rifle

NIB	Exc.	V.G.	Good	Fair	Poor
200	175	150	125	100	75

Shotgun

NIB	Exc.	V.G.	Good	Fair	Poor
225	200	175	150	100	75

Scout Carbine

This is a muzzleloading carbine of .50 or .54 caliber with an in-line ignition system. Offered with either walnut stock or composite stock (first offered in 1993) it is fitted with a 21" round barrel. Adjustable rear sight and fixed blade front sight. Brass barrel band and triggerguard on walnut stock and blued barrel band and triggerguard on composite stock model. Weighs about 7 lbs. 4 oz.

Walnut stock

NIB	Exc.	V.G.	Good	Fair	Poor
325	275	200	150	100	75

Composite stock

NIB	Exc.	V.G.	Good	Fair	Poor
250	225	175	150	100	75

Scout Rifle

Similar to the Scout Carbine but fitted with a 24" stepped half-round, half-octagonal barrel. Weight is approximately 8 lbs.

Walnut Stock

NIB	Exc.	V.G.	Good	Fair	Poor
350	300	225	175	125	100

Composite Stock

NIB	Exc.	V.G.	Good	Fair	Poor
275	250	200	150	100	75

Scout Pistol

The same design as the Scout carbine this single action pistol is available in .45, .50, or .54 caliber. Fitted with a 12" barrel, adjustable rear sight, and blued finish with brass triggerguard. Black walnut grips. Weighs 4 lbs. 6 oz.

NIB	Exc.	V.G.	Good	Fair	Poor
250	225	200	175	100	75

Fire Hawk Deluxe

Introduced in 1996 this is an in-line muzzleloader. Offered in either .50 or .54 caliber with blued or stainless steel. Semi-fancy checkered walnut stock has a cheekpiece. The round barrel is 24" long. Adjustable rear leaf sight with ramp style front bead. Weight is about 7 lbs.

NIB	Exc.	V.G.	Good	Fair	Poor
400	325	250	200	—	—

Fire Hawk

Similar to the Deluxe Fire Hawk but with standard American walnut stock or composition stock.

NIB	Exc.	V.G.	Good	Fair	Poor
300	250	200	150	—	—

Fire Hawk Thumbhole Stock

NIB	Exc.	V.G.	Good	Fair	Poor
325	275	225	175	—	—

Fire Hawk Camo Stock

NIB	Exc.	V.G.	Good	Fair	Poor
325	275	225	175	—	—

Fire Hawk Bantam

NIB	Exc.	V.G.	Good	Fair	Poor
275	225	175	125	—	—

Fire Hawk .32 & .58 caliber models

NIB	Exc.	V.G.	Good	Fair	Poor
300	250	200	150	—	—

Fire Storm

Offered as a percussion or flintlock and fitted with a 26" barrel chambered for .50 caliber. Black composite stock. Adjustable fiber optics rear sight. Weight is about 7 lbs. Introduced in 2000.

NIB	Exc.	V.G.	Good	Fair	Poor
375	300	—	—	—	—

Black Diamond

This is an in-line muzzleloading rifle with removable breech plug. Fitted with a 22.5" .50 caliber barrel. Stock is Rynite. Choice of blue or stainless steel. Add $50 for stainless steel. Introduced in 1998.

NIB	Exc.	V.G.	Good	Fair	Poor
325	250	200	—	—	—

Thompson/Center Hawken Flint Lock

Thompson/Center Renegade Flint Lock

Thompson/Center White Mountain Carbine .50 caliber Cap Lock

Thompson/Center Renegade Cap Lock Rifle

Thompson/Center Renegade Cap Lock (left hand)

Thompson/Center Renegade Hunter Model

THUNDER FIVE
MIL Inc.
Piney Flats, Tennessee

Five shot, double action, 2" rifled barrel, matte finish, ambidextrous hammer block safety, Pachmayr grips, chambered in .45 Long Colt/.410 shotgun and .47-70 Government.

NIB	Exc.	V.G.	Good	Fair	Poor
500	400	350	300	200	100

TIKKA
Tikkakoski, Finland
Importer-Beretta USA

RIFLES

Whitetail Hunter

This rifle features a hand checkered walnut stock with matte lacquer finish. These rifles are furnished without sights, but receiver is grooved. Magazine is detachable box type. Three action lengths are offered: short, medium, and long. In short action calibers the choices are: .17 Rem., .223, .22-250, .243, and .308 with 22.4" barrels and weigh 7 lbs. The medium action calibers are: .270 and .30-06 with 22.4" barrels and weigh 7.3 lbs. In long are the 7mm Rem. Mag., .300 and .338 Win. Mag. with 24.4" barrel and weigh 7.5 lbs.

NIB	Exc.	V.G.	Good	Fair	Poor
725	600	500	400	200	150

Hunter Deluxe

Similar to standard model above but furnished with cheekpiece, select walnut stock, rosewood pistol grip cap and forend tip. Metal surfaces are a highly polished blue. Same calibers as offered above.

NIB	Exc.	V.G.	Good	Fair	Poor
875	700	600	400	200	150

Whitetail/Battue Rifle

This rifle was originally designed for the French market. The barrel is 20.5" long and is fitted with a raised quarter rib. The walnut is checkered with rubber recoil pad standard. A black fiberglass stock is offered as an option. In the medium action the only caliber is .308. In a long action the calibers are: .270, .30-06, 7mm Rem. Mag., .300 and .338 Win. Mag. All models weigh about 7 lbs. In 2000 this model was offered in a left hand model.

NIB	Exc.	V.G.	Good	Fair	Poor
600	475	375	—	—	—

NOTE: Add $50 for stainless steel finish. Add $20 for magnum calibers. Add $60 for left hand model.

Varmint/Continental Rifle

This model features a 23.5" heavy barrel without sights. The checkered walnut stock has a wide forend. Offered in .17 Rem., .223, .22-250, .243, and .308. Weighs approximately 8.5 lbs.

NIB	Exc.	V.G.	Good	Fair	Poor
700	550	—	—	—	—

Long Range Hunting

Same as above but in .25-06, .270, .7mm Mag., and .300 Win. Mag. Fitted with 26" heavy barrel.

NIB	Exc.	V.G.	Good	Fair	Poor
700	550	—	—	—	—

Sporter

Introduced in 1998 this model features a select walnut stock, adjustable cheekpiece, adjustable buttplate, adjustable trigger. Comes without open sights. Detachable 5-round magazine. Chambered for .223, .22-250, and .308 calibers.

NIB	Exc.	V.G.	Good	Fair	Poor
950	725	—	—	—	—

SHOTGUNS/DOUBLE RIFLES (FORMERLY VALMET)

Tikka, Valmet and Sako have been merged into one company, SAKO Ltd. These firearms are now manufactured under the brand name Tikka and are manufactured in Italy. Parts are interchangeable between the Valmet guns, made in Finland and the Tikka guns, made in Italy.

412S Shotgun

This Over/Under shotgun is available in 12 gauge only with 26" or 28" barrels. The stock is checkered European walnut. Weighs about 7.25 lbs.

NIB	Exc.	V.G.	Good	Fair	Poor
950	800	650	500	300	200

412S Shotgun/Rifle

Same as above but with 12 gauge barrel and choice of .222 or .308 barrel. Barrel length is 24" and weighs 8 lbs.

NIB	Exc.	V.G.	Good	Fair	Poor
1000	850	700	500	300	200

412S Double Rifle

Same as above but fitted with a 24" Over/Under rifle barrel in 9.3x74R. Weighs about 8.5 lbs.

NIB	Exc.	V.G.	Good	Fair	Poor
1150	950	750	500	300	200

412S Sporting Clays

Introduced in 1993 this model is offered in 12 gauge with 28" barrels with choke tubes.

NIB	Exc.	V.G.	Good	Fair	Poor
1000	850	700	500	300	200

512S Field Grade

Introduced in 2000 this over and under gun is chambered for the 12 gauge 3" shell and fitted with either a 26" or 28" choke tube barrels.

NIB	Exc.	V.G.	Good	Fair	Poor
1125	850	—	—	—	—

NOTE: For shotgun/rifle barrel sets add $650 per set.

512S Sporting Clays

This 12 gauge 3" model is fitted with a 30" barrel with choke tubes.

NIB	Exc.	V.G.	Good	Fair	Poor
1175	900	—	—	—	—

TIMBER WOLF
SEE—Action Arms

TIPPING & LAWDEN
Birmingham, England

Thomas Revolver

A .320, .380, or .450 double action revolver with a 4.5" barrel and 5-shot cylinder, utilizing a cartridge extraction system designed by J. Thomas of Birmingham in which the barrel and cylinder may be moved forward. Manufactured from 1870 to 1877.

Exc.	V.G.	Good	Fair	Poor
—	—	600	300	175

TIPPMAN ARMS
Fort Wayne, Indiana

Model 1917

A .22 caliber semiautomatic one-half scale reproduction of the Browning Model 1917 water cooled machine gun. Barrel length 10". A tripod was sold with this model. Manufactured in 1986 and 1987.

NIB	Exc.	V.G.	Good	Fair	Poor
5750	5250	—	—	—	—

Model 1919 A-4

A .22 caliber semiautomatic one-half scale reproduction of the Browning Model 1919 A-4 machine gun. Barrel length 11" and furnished with a tripod. Manufactured in 1986 and 1987.

NIB	Exc.	V.G.	Good	Fair	Poor
3000	2750	—	—	—	—

Model .50 HB

A .22 Magnum caliber semiautomatic one-half scale reproduction of the Browning .50 caliber machine gun. Barrel length 18.25", furnished with a tripod. Manufactured in 1986 and 1987.

NIB	Exc.	V.G.	Good	Fair	Poor
6000	5500	—	—	—	—

TOBIN ARMS MANUFACTURING CO.
Norwich, Connecticut and Windsor, Ontario, Canada

The Tobin Arms Manufacturing Co. operated from about 1905 to 1925 making an exposed hammer double and two hammerless models in four grades. The "Simplex" was cleverly designed (based on a patent by C.M. Wollam) side plated double barrel internal hammer shotgun which resembled the Hopkins and Allen guns of that time. Some may have been private branded. Most of the Tobin doubles were made in Norwich, CT and are so marked. After 1909 operations were transferred to Windsor, Ont, Canada and some guns will be found with that address. Tobin guns are not often seen by collectors and are highly prized because of their relative rarity and because they were considered good guns by top dealers such as C.J. Godfrey Co. of New York City and Iver Johnson Sporting Goods of Boston. Values depend on condition and range from $200 in poor condition to $1000 and up for engraved versions in good to very good condition.

TODD, GEORGE H.
Montgomery, Alabama

Rifled Musket

A .58 caliber single shot percussion rifle with a 40" barrel and full length stock secured by three barrel bands. Barrel and lock finished in the bright, brass furniture and walnut stock. The lock marked "George H. Todd/ Montgomery, Ala." Very Rare. Prospective purchasers are advised to secure a qualified appraisal prior to acquisition.

Exc.	V.G.	Good	Fair	Poor
—	—	20000	8500	—

TOKAREV
Soviet State Arsenals

NOTE: For history, technical data, descriptions, photos, and prices see the *Standard Catalog of Military Firearms, 1870 to the Present* under Russia.

TOMISKA, ALOIS
Pilsen, Czechoslovakia

Little Tom

A 6.35mm or 7.65mm caliber semiautomatic pistol with a 2.5" barrel. The slide marked "Alois Tomiska Plzen Patent Little Tom" and the grips inlaid with a medallion bearing the monogram "AT". Blued with checkered walnut grips. Manufactured from 1908 to 1918. Subsequently produced by the Wiener Waffenfabrik.

Exc.	V.G.	Good	Fair	Poor
550	425	350	250	125

TORKALSON MFG CO
Harfield, Warren, and Worcester, Massachusetts
Double Barrel Shotguns

Reinhard T. Torkalson's company made double barrel, box-lock, side-by-side, hammerless shotguns in four models at several locations between 1885 and 1910. He worked with Iver Johnson at Fitchburg, MA and also built guns carrying the Lovell (Boston) name. His "New Worcester" marked guns are quite common. they were sold by Sears and other large and well known houses.

Exc.	V.G.	Good	Fair	Poor
450	300	200	150	100

TRADEWINDS
Tacoma, Washington

Model H-170

A 12 gauge semiautomatic shotgun with a 26" or 28" ventilated rib barrel and 5-shot tubular magazine. Blued, anodized alloy receiver and walnut stock.

Exc.	V.G.	Good	Fair	Poor
300	250	225	150	100

Model 260-A

A .22 caliber semiautomatic rifle with a 22.5" barrel, open sights and 5-shot magazine. Blued with a walnut stock.

Exc.	V.G.	Good	Fair	Poor
200	175	125	100	75

Model 311-A

A .22 caliber bolt action rifle with a 22.5" barrel, open sights and a 5-shot magazine. Blued with a walnut stock.

Exc.	V.G.	Good	Fair	Poor
175	150	100	75	50

Model 5000 "Husky"

A centerfire bolt action rifle with a 24" barrel, adjustable sights and 4-shot magazine. Blued with a walnut stock.

Exc.	V.G.	Good	Fair	Poor
350	300	275	200	100

TRADITIONS
Old Saybrook, CT

OVER AND UNDER SHOTGUNS

NOTE: These shotguns are built by the Italian firm of Fausti Stefano.

Hunter

Introduced in 2001 this model features a choice of 12 or 20 gauge chambers with 26" or 28" vent rib barrels with fixed chokes. Single selective trigger. Extractors. Checkered walnut stock. Blued frame and barrels. Black rubber recoil pad. Weight is about 7.25 lbs. for 12 gauge and 6.75 lbs. for 20 gauge.

NIB	Exc.	V.G.	Good	Fair	Poor
650	500	—	—	—	—

Field I

This model is offered in 12, 20 and 28 gauge as well as .410 bore. Barrel lengths are 26". Fixed chokes. Single selective trigger and extractors. Coin finish engraved receiver. Checkered walnut stock. Black rubber recoil pad. Weight is similar to the Hunter model with the .410 bore weighing about 6.5 lbs.

NIB	Exc.	V.G.	Good	Fair	Poor
575	450	—	—	—	—

Field II

Similar to the Field I but with the additional choice of a 16 gauge with 28" barrels. This model also features screw-in chokes and automatic ejectors.

NIB	Exc.	V.G.	Good	Fair	Poor
750	600	—	—	—	—

Field III Gold

Similar to the other Field series of guns but offered in 12 gauge only with 26" or 28" barrels. Select oil finish walnut stock. Engraved receiver with gold pheasants and woodcock.

NIB	Exc.	V.G.	Good	Fair	Poor
975	775	—	—	—	—

Upland III

Introduced in 2001 this model features a 12 gauge gun with 26" vent rib barrels. High grade checkered walnut stock with hand engraved receiver with gold. Schnabel forend. Single selective trigger and auto ejectors standard. Screw-in chokes. Black rubber recoil pad. Weight is about 7.25 lbs.

NIB	Exc.	V.G.	Good	Fair	Poor
1000	800	—	—	—	—

Sporting Clay II

This 12 gauge gas operated model has either 28" or 30" vent rib ported barrels. Screw-in extended choke tubes. Checkered walnut stock with blued receiver and barrels. Weight is about 8 lbs.

NIB	Exc.	V.G.	Good	Fair	Poor
900	725	—	—	—	—

Upland II

Offered in both 12 and 20 gauge with 26" barrels in 12 gauge and 24" or 26" barrels in 20 gauge. Straight grip walnut stock. Engraved blued receiver. Schnabel forend. Choke tubes. Single selective trigger and auto ejectors. Weight for 12 gauge gun is about 7.25 lbs. and for 20 gauge about 6.25 lbs.

NIB	Exc.	V.G.	Good	Fair	Poor
800	650	—	—	—	—

Waterfowl II

Introduced in 2001 this 12 gauge model is fitted with 28" vent rib barrels and 3.5" chambers. Finish on stock and barrels is Advantage Wetlands camo. Blued engraved receiver. Recoil pad. Single selective trigger with auto ejectors. Weight is about 7.25 lbs.

NIB	Exc.	V.G.	Good	Fair	Poor
850	700	—	—	—	—

Turkey II

Offered in 12 gauge with choice of 24" or 26" vent rib barrels with Mossy break-up finish camo with blued receiver. X-full choke. Single selective trigger and auto ejectors. Weight is about 7 lbs.

NIB	Exc.	V.G.	Good	Fair	Poor
850	700	—	—	—	—

Mag Hunter II

This is a 12 gauge gun with 28" barrels with 3.5" chambers. Engraved blued receiver. Walnut stock. Rubber recoil pad. Single selective trigger with auto ejectors. Screw-in chokes. Weight is about 7 lbs.

NIB	Exc.	V.G.	Good	Fair	Poor
750	600	—	—	—	—

SIDE-BY-SIDE SHOTGUNS

NOTE: These side-by-side guns are imported from the Italian firm of Fausti Stanfano.

Elite I DT

This model is offered in 12, 20, and 28 gauge as well as .410 bore. All gauges are fitted wtih 26" barrels with fixed chokes. Double triggers and extractors. Walnut stock. Weight about 6 lbs.

NIB	Exc.	V.G.	Good	Fair	Poor
750	600	—	—	—	—

NOTE: Add $60 for 28 and .410 models.

Elite I ST

Same as above but with single selective trigger.

NIB	Exc.	V.G.	Good	Fair	Poor
890	700	—	—	—	—

Elite Hunter

Introduced in 2001 this model features either a 12 or 20 gauge gun with 26" barrels with screw-in chokes. Walnut stock with beavertail forend. Single non-selective trigger. Weight is about 6.5 lbs.

NIB	Exc.	V.G.	Good	Fair	Poor
950	750	—	—	—	—

Elite Field III ST

Introduced in 2001 this model is offered in either 28 or .410 bore with 26" barrels. High grade walnut stock with straight grip. Fixed chokes. Engraved receiver with gold. Weight is about 6.25 lbs.

NIB	Exc.	V.G.	Good	Fair	Poor
2000	1500	—	—	—	—

SEMIAUTOMATIC SHOTGUNS

ALS Field

Introduced in 2001 this model is offered in both 12 and 20 gauge with 24", 26", or 28" vent rib barrel. Walnut stock with black pad. Blued receiver and barrels. Screw-in chokes. Weight is about 6.25 lbs.

NIB	Exc.	V.G.	Good	Fair	Poor
450	350	—	—	—	—

ALS Hunter

Same as above but with synthetic stock with 26" or 28" barrels.

NIB	Exc.	V.G.	Good	Fair	Poor
425	325	—	—	—	—

ALS Waterfowl

This 12 gauge model has Advantage Wetlands camo and is fitted with a 28" barrel with screw-in chokes. Weight is about 6.5 lbs.

NIB	Exc.	V.G.	Good	Fair	Poor
500	400	—	—	—	—

ALS Turkey

Same as above but with 21" barrel and Mossy Oak Break-up camo. Weight is about 6 lbs.

NIB	Exc.	V.G.	Good	Fair	Poor
500	400	—	—	—	—

TRANTER, WILLIAM
Birmingham, England

William Tranter produced a variety of revolvers on his own and a number of other makers produced revolvers based upon his designs. Consequently, "Tranter's Patent" is to be found on revolvers made by such firms as Deane, Adams and Deane, etc.

Courtesy Wallis & Wallis, Lewes, Sussex, England

Model 1872

A .38 caliber double action revolver with a 6" octagonal barrel and 6-shot cylinder. Blued with walnut grips.

Exc.	V.G.	Good	Fair	Poor
—	1000	500	300	200

Model 1878

A .450 caliber double action revolver with a 6" octagonal barrel. Blued with a walnut grip. Manufactured from 1878 to 1887.

Exc.	V.G.	Good	Fair	Poor
—	1200	500	275	175

TRIPPLET & SCOTT
MERIDAN MANUFACTURING COMPANY
Meridan, Connecticut

Repeating Carbine

A .50 caliber carbine with either a 22" or 30" round barrel and a 7-shot magazine located in the butt. This model is loaded by turning the barrel until it comes in line with the magazine. Blued, case hardened with a walnut stock. Approximately 5,000 were made in 1864 and 1865.

Courtesy Milwaukee Public Museum, Milwaukee, Wisconsin

Exc.	V.G.	Good	Fair	Poor
—	2500	1150	500	200

TRISTAR SPORTING ARMS
N. Kansas City, Missouri

Tristar 300 series over and under guns are imported from Turkey. Tristar Nova series are imported from Italy.

NOTE: In 2000 Tristar bought American Arms. American Arms no longer exists but some of its models will appear under the Tristar name. For American Arms firearms built prior to the sale see that section.

SILVER SERIES

Silver Sporting

Offered in 12 gauge with 28" or 30" barrels with single selective trigger, auto ejectors, choke tubes, ported barrels with target rib, checkered walnut stock with pistol grip and recoil pad.

NIB	Exc.	V.G.	Good	Fair	Poor
750	600	—	—	—	—

Specialty Magnums

This is a 12 gauge magnum chambered for the 3.5" shell and fitted with a 28" barrel. Choke tubes. Checkered black walnut stock with pistol grip.

NIB	Exc.	V.G.	Good	Fair	Poor
600	475	—	—	—	—

Silver Hunter

Offered in both 12 and 20 gauge with 26" or 28" vent rib barrels with single selective trigger, choke tubes, engraved receiver with silver finish. Checkered walnut stock with pistol grip.

NIB	Exc.	V.G.	Good	Fair	Poor
500	400	—	—	—	—

Silver II

As above but also in 16 and 28 gauge as well as .410 bore. Fixed chokes for 16, 28, and .410 models.

NIB	Exc.	V.G.	Good	Fair	Poor
550	450	—	—	—	—

300 SERIES

NOTE: This series of over and under shotguns is no longer imported by Tristar.

Model 333

This over and under gun is available in 12 or 20 gauge with 26", 28", or 30" barrels in 12 gauge. Hand engraved frame. Fitted with 3" chambers and choke tubes. Single selective triggers and auto ejectors. Fancy Turkish walnut stock. Weighs around 7.75 lbs for 12 gauge and 7.5 lbs for 20 gauge.

NIB	Exc.	V.G.	Good	Fair	Poor
800	650	600	—	—	—

Model 333 SC

Similar to above model but with addition of 11mm sporting rib, recoil pad, forcing cones, and ported barrels. Extended choke tubes.

NIB	Exc.	V.G.	Good	Fair	Poor
900	700	650	—	—	—

Model 333L

This shotgun has the same features as the Model 333 but with a special stock designed for women. Length of pull is shorter with special Monte Carlo comb.

NIB	Exc.	V.G.	Good	Fair	Poor
800	650	600	—	—	—

Model 333SCL

Same features as Model 333SC but with special stock.

NIB	Exc.	V.G.	Good	Fair	Poor
900	700	650	—	—	—

Model 330

This over and under model has a standard Turkish walnut stock with etched engraved frame. Offered in 12 and 20 gauge. Single trigger with extractors and fixed chokes.

NIB	Exc.	V.G.	Good	Fair	Poor
575	475	400	—	—	—

Model 330 D

This model is the same as the above but with the addition of selective auto ejectors.

NIB	Exc.	V.G.	Good	Fair	Poor
700	575	500	—	—	—

Model 300

This model features an underlug action lock with double triggers and extractors. Frame is etched. Offered in 12 gauge only with 26" or 28" barrels with fixed chokes.

NIB	Exc.	V.G.	Good	Fair	Poor
425	350	300	—	—	—

Model 311

This is a side-by-side gun in 12 or 20 gauge with 26" or 28" barrels with choke tubes. Standard Turkish walnut. Blued frame.

NIB	Exc.	V.G.	Good	Fair	Poor
600	500	450	—	—	—

Model 311R

Same as above but with 20" barrel choked cylinder and cylinder.

NIB	Exc.	V.G.	Good	Fair	Poor
425	350	300	—	—	—

EMILIO RIZZINI (Old Nova Series)

TR-L (Nova L)

Offered in 12 or 20 gauge with choice of 28" or 30" vent rib barrels. Choke tubes standard. Standard grade walnut with pistol grip. Action is silver finish boxlock with auto ejectors and single selective trigger. Weight is approximately 7.5 lbs. Stock dimensions are made for a smaller shooter. Introduced in 1998.

NIB	Exc.	V.G.	Good	Fair	Poor
1000	750	—	—	—	—

TR-SC (Nova SC)

Similar to the Nova L but offered in 12 gauge only with standard stock dimensions and semi-fancy walnut stock with pistol grip. Black sporting clays style recoil pad. Weight is between 7.5 and 8 lbs. depending on barrel length. Introduced in 1998.

NIB	Exc.	V.G.	Good	Fair	Poor
1000	750	—	—	—	—

TR-1 (Nova I)

Offered in 12 and 20 gauge with in 26" or 28" barrels with fixed chokes. Walnut stock with hand checkering and pistol grip. Beavertail forend. Boxlock action is blue with single selective trigger and extractors. Weight is about 7.5 lbs. Introduced in 1998.

NIB	Exc.	V.G.	Good	Fair	Poor
585	475	—	—	—	—

TR-II (Nova II)

Same as above but fitted with automatic ejectors.

NIB	Exc.	V.G.	Good	Fair	Poor
875	700	—	—	—	—

TR-Mag (Nova Mag)

Similar to the Nova I but chambered for 10 and 12 gauge 3.5" shell. Choice of 24" or 28" vent rib barrels with choke tubes. Nonreflective non glare blue finish. Introduced in 1998.

NIB	Exc.	V.G.	Good	Fair	Poor
750	600	—	—	—	—

NOTE: Add $175 for 12 gauge with ejectors and $350 for 10 gauge guns.

TTR-Royal

This model is offered in 12, 20 or 28 gauge with 28" ported choke tube barrels, straight grip semi-fancy walnut stock, and auto ejectors. Silver receiver with gold engraving.

NIB	Exc.	V.G.	Good	Fair	Poor
1300	1000	—	—	—	—

TR-Class SL

Top-of-the-line model with sculptured frame and engraved side plates. offered in 12 gauge only.

NIB	Exc.	V.G.	Good	Fair	Poor
1775	1350	—	—	—	—

411 SERIES

Model 411

This side-by-side double is imported from Italy and introduced in 1998. Chambered for 12, 20, and .410 bore with choice of 26" or 28" barrels with choke tubes or fixed chokes. Boxlock action with engraving and case coloring. Double triggers and extractors. Standard walnut stock with pistol grip and splinter forearm. Weight is between 6 and 6.5 lbs.

NIB	Exc.	V.G.	Good	Fair	Poor
750	600	—	—	—	—

Model 411R

Offered in 12 or 20 gauge with 20" barrel with fixed cylinder chokes. Extractors. Weight is about 6.5 lbs for 12 gauge and 6 lbs for 20 gauge.

NIB	Exc.	V.G.	Good	Fair	Poor
750	600	—	—	—	—

Model 411D

This model is similar to the Model 411 but with engraved case, colored finish on the receiver, auto ejectors, single trigger, and straight grip stock. Weight for 28 gauge is about 6.25 lbs. and for the 12 gauge about 7 lbs.

NIB	Exc.	V.G.	Good	Fair	Poor
1100	850	—	—	—	—

Model 411F

Same as the Model 411D but with silver engraved receiver.

NIB	Exc.	V.G.	Good	Fair	Poor
1600	1200	—	—	—	—

PHANTOM SERIES

Phantom Field

This is a gas operated semiautomatic shotgun that is chambered for the 12 gauge 2.75" or 3" shell. Fitted with 24", 26", or 28" barrel. Checkered walnut stock with pistol grip. Screw-in chokes. Five-round magazine.

NIB	Exc.	V.G.	Good	Fair	Poor
425	325	—	—	—	—

NOTE: For magnum models add $75.

Phantom Synthetic

Same as above but with synthetic stock.

NIB	Exc.	V.G.	Good	Fair	Poor
375	300	—	—	—	—

NOTE: For magnum models add $75.

Phantom HP

Same features as the phantom field except with synthetic stock, 19" barrel, and swivel studs.

NIB	Exc.	V.G.	Good	Fair	Poor
375	300	—	—	—	—

Pee Wee

This is a single shot bolt action rifle chambered for .22 Long Rifle cartridges. Stock is walnut and it is about 1/2 the size of an adult rifle. Weight is about 2.75 lbs. Open sights. Finish is blue.

NIB	Exc.	V.G.	Good	Fair	Poor
200	150	100	—	—	—

Model 1887

This is a reproduction of the Winchester Model 1887 lever action shotgun. Offered in 12 gauge only with 22" cylinder choked barrel. Walnut stock. Five-round magazine. Weight is about 8.75 lbs. Made in Australia by ADI, Limited, Lithgow.

NIB	Exc.	V.G.	Good	Fair	Poor
1195	900	750	—	—	—

TROCAOLA
Eibar, Spain

This maker produced a variety of .32, .38, and .44 caliber top break revolvers between approximately 1900 and 1936. These pistols can be identified by the monogram "TAC" stamped on the left side of the frame. The value of all these revolvers is as follows:

Exc.	V.G.	Good	Fair	Poor
200	125	100	75	50

TRYON, EDWARD K. & COMPANY
Philadelphia, Pennsylvania

Pocket Pistol

A .41 caliber single shot percussion pocket pistol with a 2" or 4" barrel, German silver mounts and a walnut stock. The lock marked "Tryon/Philada." Manufactured during the 1860s and 1870s.

Exc.	V.G.	Good	Fair	Poor
—	—	1650	750	200

TUCKER SHERARD & COMPANY
Lancaster, Texas

Dragoon

A .44 caliber percussion revolver with a 7.75" round barrel fitted with a loading lever and a 6-shot cylinder. The barrel marked "Clark, Sherard & Co., Lancaster, Texas," and the cylinder etched in two panels with crossed cannons and the legend "Texas Arms." Approximately 400 revolvers of this type were made between 1862 and 1867. Prospective purchasers are advised to secure a qualified appraisal prior to acquisition.

Exc.	V.G.	Good	Fair	Poor
—	—	50000	20000	—

TUFTS & COLLEY
New York, New York

Pocket Pistol

A .44 caliber single shot percussion pocket pistol with a 3.5" barrel, German silver mounts and walnut stock. The lock marked "Tufts & Colley" and the barrel "Deringer/Pattn". Manufactured during the 1860s.

Exc.	V.G.	Good	Fair	Poor
—	—	1500	750	200

TURBIAUX, JACQUES
Paris, France
SEE—Ames

TURNER, THOMAS
Redding, England

Pepperbox

A .476 double action percussion pepperbox having 6 barrels. Blued, case hardened with walnut grips. The left side of the frame is engraved in an oval "Thomas Turner, Redding."

Courtesy Butterfield & Butterfield, San Francisco, California

Exc.	V.G.	Good	Fair	Poor
—	4000	1500	900	400

TYLER ORDNANCE WORKS
Tyler, Texas

This company produced 56 Austrian rifles, 508 Enfield rifles, 423 Hill rifles and 1,009 Texas rifles during the Civil War.

NOTE: Extreme caution is urged prior to purchasing any of these arms and a qualified appraisal should be sought. These rifles are very rare.

Tyler Texas Rifle

A .57 caliber single shot rifle with a 27" barrel and a full stock secured by two barrel bands. The lock marked "Texas Rifle/Tyler/Cal. .57".

Exc.	V.G.	Good	Fair	Poor
—	—	37500	15000	—

Hill Rifle

A .54 caliber single shot percussion rifle with a 27" barrel, full stock secured by two brass barrel bands and an iron triggerguard and buttplate. The lock marked "Hill Rifle/Tyler/Tex/ Cal. .54".

Exc.	V.G.	Good	Fair	Poor
—	—	37500	15000	—

USAS 12
DAEWOO PRECISION IND., LTD.
South Korea
Importer-Gilbert Equipment Company
Mobile, Alabama

USAS 12
A 12 gauge semiautomatic shotgun with a 18.25" cylinder bored barrel, and either a 10-shot box magazine or 20-shot drum magazine. Parkerized, with a composition stock. This model is no longer imported.

NOTE: A local appraisal of this model is strongly recommended.

WARNING: As of May 1, 2001 this firearm must be registered with the ATF and a transfer tax of $200 paid. This firearm is classified as a destructive device. Unreistered guns ewill be considered contraband after this date and persons in possission will be in violation of federal law.

U.S. ARMS CO.
Riverhead, New York
SEE—United Sporting Arms, Inc.

U.S. ORDNANCE
Reno, Nevada
The following models are machined to military specifications and are semi-automatic only.

M-60
This is a 7.62mm belt-fed semi-automatic weapon modeled after the famous machine gun used in Vietnam. Fitted with a 22" barrel, the weight of the gun is about 24 lbs.

NIB	Exc.	V.G.	Good	Fair	Poor
5995	—	—	—	—	—

M-60E3
A shorter more lightweight version of the standard M-60 fitted with a 17" barrel. Weight reduced to about 18 lbs.

NIB	Exc.	V.G.	Good	Fair	Poor
6495	—	—	—	—	—

Browning Model 1919
This belt-fed model is chambered for the 7.62mm/.30-06 cartridges. Fitted with a 23" barrel. Weight is about 30 lbs. Prices listed are for gun only.

Model 1919 A6

Model 1919 with A4 tripod

NIB	Exc.	V.G.	Good	Fair	Poor
1995	—	—	—	—	—

NOTE: For A6 stock, bipod, and carry handle add $125. For A4 tripod add $450.

Vickers
This model is chambered for the .303 cartridge and is belt-fed. Weight is about 40 lbs. Prices listed are for gun only.

NIB	Exc.	V.G.	Good	Fair	Poor
4495	—	—	—	—	—

NOTE: For tripod add $500.

U.S. REPEATING ARMS CO.
SEE—Winchester

UNITED STATES REVOLVER ASSOCIATION
SEE—Harrington & Richardson Arms Co.

UBERTI, ALDO
Ponte Zanano, Italy
Importers - Cimarron Firearms, E.M.F., Inc., Uberti USA, American Arms, Navy Arms, Taylors, Traditions

This company manufactures high-grade reproductions of famous Western-style American firearms. Their products have been imported over the years by a number of different companies. They produce both black powder guns and the cartridge firearms that are included in this section. This Italian manufacturer builds high quality firearms of the American West. Featured are Colt, Winchester, and Remington. Each importer stamps its name on the firearm in addition to the Uberti address.

There may be small variations in stampings on the barrel address if requested by the importer. Perhaps the most noticeable difference between importers is the exclusive use of original stampings and patent dates on Colt single actions and Winchester rifles by Cimarron Arms. This firm also has a case hardened hammer on its Colt single action as well as a high polish charcoal blue.

NOTE: In 2000 Beretta Holding company purchased Uberti.

UBERTI U.S.A.
Lakeville, CT

The prices listed represent the Uberti line as imported into the United States. Uberti offeres a number of options that will affect price. Many of these options are special finishes and grips. It is strongly suggested that before a sale that expert opinion is sought.

Patterson Revolver

This is an exact copy of the famous and rare Colt pistol. Offered in .36 caliber with engraved 5-shot cylinder, the barrel is 7.5" long and octagonal forward of the lug. The frame is case hardened steel as is the backstrap. Grips are one-piece walnut. Overall length is 11.5" and weight is about 2.5 lbs.

NIB	Exc.	V.G.	Good	Fair	Poor
375	300	200	125	100	75

Walker Colt Revolver

This is a faithful reproduction of the famous and highly sought after Colts. Caliber is .44 and the round barrel is 9" in length. The frame is case hardened steel and the triggerguard is brass. The 6-shot cylinder is engraved with fighting dragoons scene. Grip is one piece walnut. Overall length is 15.75" and weight is a hefty 70 oz.

NIB	Exc.	V.G.	Good	Fair	Poor
350	300	200	125	100	75

Colt Whitneyville Dragoon

This was the transition Walker. A reduced version of the Model 1847 Walker. Fitted with a 7.5" barrel and chambered for the .44 caliber.

NIB	Exc.	V.G.	Good	Fair	Poor
330	275	200	125	100	75

Colt 1st Model Dragoon Revolver

This was a shorter version of the Walker and evolved directly from that original design. This model is a 6-shot .44 caliber with a 7.5" barrel. The frame is color case hardened steel while the backstrap and triggerguard are brass. Grips are one-piece walnut. Overall length is 13.5" and weight is about 63 oz.

NIB	Exc.	V.G.	Good	Fair	Poor
300	200	175	125	100	75

Colt 2nd Model Dragoon Revolver

This differs from the 1st model in that the cylinder bolt slot is square instead of oval.

NIB	Exc.	V.G.	Good	Fair	Poor
300	200	175	125	100	75

Colt 3rd Model Dragoon Revolver

This model varies from the 2nd model as follows:
a: Loading lever taper is inverted.
b: Loading lever latch hook is different shape.
c: Loading lever latch.
d: Backstrap is steel and triggerguard is brass oval.
e: Frame is cut for a shoulder stock.

NIB	Exc.	V.G.	Good	Fair	Poor
300	225	175	125	100	75

Colt Model 1849 Wells Fargo

This model has no loading lever. Chambered for .31 caliber cartridge. The barrel is octagonal. The frame is case colored and hardened steel while the backstrap and triggerguard are brass. Cylinder is engraved and holds 5 rounds. Grip is one piece walnut. Overall length is 9.5" and weight is 34 oz.

NIB	Exc.	V.G.	Good	Fair	Poor
275	200	150	125	100	75

Colt Model 1849 Pocket Revolver

Same as the Wells Fargo with the addition of a loading lever.

NIB	Exc.	V.G.	Good	Fair	Poor
265	200	150	125	100	75

Colt Model 1848 Baby Dragoon

Similar is appearance to the Model 1849 but with a 4" tapered octagonal barrel and a square back triggerguard. No loading lever. Weight is about 23 oz.

NIB	Exc.	V.G.	Good	Fair	Poor
275	200	150	125	100	75

The Model 1851 Navy Colt

Chambered for .36 caliber with an engraved 6-shot cylinder. The tapered octagonal barrel is 7.5". The frame is case colored steel and the backstrap and oval triggerguard are brass. Grips are one-piece walnut. Overall length is 13" and weight is about 44 oz.

NIB	Exc.	V.G.	Good	Fair	Poor
250	175	150	125	100	75

Model 1861 Navy Colt

Sometime referred to as the "New Navy" this model is similar in appearance to the Model 1851. Offered in two variations. The military version has a steel backstrap and triggerguard and is cut for a shoulder stock. The civilian version has a brass backstrap and triggerguard and is not cut for a shoulder stock.

Military Model

NIB	Exc.	V.G.	Good	Fair	Poor
250	200	150	125	100	75

Civilian Model

NIB	Exc.	V.G.	Good	Fair	Poor
250	200	150	125	100	75

Colt Model 1860 Army

Chambered for the .44 caliber ball and fitted with a round tapered 8" barrel this revolver has a 6-shot engraved cylinder. Grips are one-piece walnut. Overall length is 13.75" and weight is approximately 42 oz.

Military version has steel backstrap and brass triggerguard and is cut for a shoulder stock.

NIB	Exc.	V.G.	Good	Fair	Poor
250	200	150	125	100	75

Civilian version has brass backstrap and triggerguard and is not cut for a shoulder stock.

NIB	Exc.	V.G.	Good	Fair	Poor
250	200	150	125	100	75

Fluted Cylinder Version-Military

NIB	Exc.	V.G.	Good	Fair	Poor
260	200	160	125	100	75

Fluted Cylinder Version-Civilian

NIB	Exc.	V.G.	Good	Fair	Poor
250	200	150	125	100	75

Colt Model 1862 Police Revolvers

Chambered for .36 caliber and fitted with a round tapered barrel in 4.5", 5.5", or 6.5" barrel. The 5-shot cylinder is fluted, the frame color case hardened, and the backstrap and triggerguard are brass. Grips are one-piece walnut. Weight is about 25 oz.

NIB	Exc.	V.G.	Good	Fair	Poor
275	200	175	150	125	100

Colt Model 1862 Pocket Navy Revolver

Similar to the Model 1862 Police model but fitted with a 5-shot engraved nonfluted cylinder. Barrel lengths are 4.5", 5.5", and 6.5". Weight is about 27 oz.

NIB	Exc.	V.G.	Good	Fair	Poor
225	200	175	150	125	100

Colt Model 1868 Army Thuer Conversion

NIB	Exc.	V.G.	Good	Fair	Poor
400	325	225	175	150	100

Remington Model 1858 New Army .44 Caliber

Chambered for .44 caliber and fitted with a tapered octagonal 8" barrel. Cylinder holds 6 shots and the frame is blued steel. triggerguard is brass. Grips are two-piece walnut. Overall length is 13.75" and weight is about 42 oz.

NIB	Exc.	V.G.	Good	Fair	Poor
250	200	150	125	100	75

Remington Model 1858 New Army .36 Caliber

Similar to above model but fitted with a 7-3/8" tapered octagonal barrel. Weight is approximately 40 oz.

NIB	Exc.	V.G.	Good	Fair	Poor
250	200	150	125	100	75

Remington Model 1858 New Army .44 Caliber Target

This version is fitted with a fully adjustable rear sight and ramp front sight.

NIB	Exc.	V.G.	Good	Fair	Poor
275	225	175	150	100	75

Remington Model 1858 New Army .44 Caliber Stainless Steel

All parts are stainless steel.

NIB	Exc.	V.G.	Good	Fair	Poor
350	275	225	150	100	75

Remington Model 1858 New Army .44 Cal. SS Target

Same as Target Model but all parts are stainless steel.

NIB	Exc.	V.G.	Good	Fair	Poor
375	300	225	175	100	75

Remington Model 1858 Target Revolving Carbine
Chambered for .44 caliber and fitted with an 18" octagon barrel. The frame is blued steel and the triggerguard is brass. Stock is select walnut. Overall length is 35" and weight is about 4.4 lbs.

NIB	Exc.	V.G.	Good	Fair	Poor
400	300	200	150	100	75

1875 Remington "Outlaw"
This is a replica of the original Remington cartridge pistol chambered for .357 Magnum, .44-40, .45 ACP, .45 ACP/.45 L.C. conversion, and .45 Colt. The frame is case colored steel and the triggerguard is brass. It is offered with a 7.5" round barrel and is either blued or nickel-plated, with two-piece walnut grips. Overall length is 13.75" and weight is about 44 oz.

NIB	Exc.	V.G.	Good	Fair	Poor
475	350	275	225	175	125

Remington Model 1890 Police
This is a 5.5"-barreled replica of the original Remington Pistol. It is chambered for .357 Magnum, .44-40, .45 ACP, .45 ACP/.45 L.C. conversion, and .45 Colt. The frame is case colored steel and the triggerguard is brass. It was available in either blued or nickel-plate. Grips are two-piece walnut and are fitted with a grip ring. Overall length is 11.75" and weight is about 41 oz.

NIB	Exc.	V.G.	Good	Fair	Poor
475	350	300	275	225	175

Model 1871 Rolling Block Pistol

This is a single-shot target pistol chambered for .22 l.r., .22 Magnum, .22 Hornet, .222 Rem., 223 Rem., .45 Long Colt, or .357 Magnum. It has a 9.5" half-octagonal, half-round barrel and is blued, with a case colored receiver and walnut grip and forearm. The triggerguard is brass. Overall length is 14" and weight is about 44 oz.

NIB	Exc.	V.G.	Good	Fair	Poor
400	300	225	200	150	100

Model 1871 Rolling Block Carbine
This model is similar to the pistol, with a 22.5" half-octagonal, half-round barrel and a full-length walnut stock. triggerguard and buttplate are brass. Overall length is 35.5" and weight is approximately 4.8 lbs.

NIB	Exc.	V.G.	Good	Fair	Poor
475	350	275	225	175	125

Henry Rifle
This is a brass-framed reproduction of the famous Winchester/Henry Rifle. It is chambered for the .44-40 cartridge, and this is basically the only departure from being a true and faithful copy. The octagonal barrel is 24.25" on the rifle model and 22.25" on the carbine model. There are also two Trapper models offered; an 18.5" barrel and a 16.5" version. This is high quality rifle and amazingly close to the original in configuration. There are three grades of engraving also available. Weights are as follows: rifle 9.2 lbs., carbine 9 lbs., 18.5" trapper 7.9 lbs., 16.5" trapper 7.4 lbs. Finish can be steel, standard blued or charcoal blue.
Grade A-Add $350.
Grade B-Add $450.
Grade C-Add $600.

NIB	Exc.	V.G.	Good	Fair	Poor
900	700	550	450	350	200

Winchester Model 1866
This is a faithful replica of the Winchester 1866. It is chambered for .22 l.r., .22 Magnum, .38 Special, and .44-40, and .45 Long Colt. The rifle version has a brass frame and a 24.25" tapered octagon barrel. The frame finish is brass, with a walnut stock. Weight is about 8 lbs.

NIB	Exc.	V.G.	Good	Fair	Poor
800	650	550	450	350	200

1866 Yellowboy Carbine

This model is similar to the standard rifle, but is offered with a 19" round tapered barrel.

NIB	Exc.	V.G.	Good	Fair	Poor
700	600	500	450	350	200

Winchester Model 1873 Carbine

This is a reproduction of the Winchester 1873 chambered for .357 Magnum, .45 Long Colt, and .44-40. It has a case colored steel receiver and a 19" round tapered barrel. The lever is also case colored. The stock and forearm are walnut. Overall length is 38.25" and weight is about 7.4 lbs.

NIB	Exc.	V.G.	Good	Fair	Poor
900	700	500	450	350	200

Winchester Model 1873 Rifle

This model is similar to the Carbine, with a 24.25" octagonal barrel. Overall length is 43.25" and weight is approximately 8.2 lbs.

NOTE: Extra barrel lengths from 30" to 20" in .45 L.C. and .44-40 are also offered at extra cost.

NIB	Exc.	V.G.	Good	Fair	Poor
950	750	600	450	350	200

Winchester 1873 Half-Octagon Rifle

Same as above but with 24.25" half octagon barrel. Stock has a checkered pistol grip.

NIB	Exc.	V.G.	Good	Fair	Poor
1000	800	600	450	350	200

Winchester 1873 Musket

Chambered for the .44-40 or .45 Long Colt cartridge and fitted with a 30" barrel with full stock and three barrel bands. Magazine capacity is 14 rounds. Weight is about 9 lbs.

NIB	Exc.	V.G.	Good	Fair	Poor
1000	800	600	450	350	200

Model 1885 High Wall Single Shot Carbine

Chambered for .38-55, .30-30, .44-40, .45 Colt, .40-65, or .45-70 with 28" barrel. Walnut stock.

NIB	Exc.	V.G.	Good	Fair	Poor
825	600	450	350	250	—

Model 1885 High Wall Single Shot Rifle

Same as above but with 30" barrel.

NIB	Exc.	V.G.	Good	Fair	Poor
900	675	500	400	300	—

Model 1885 High Wall Single Shot Rifle Pistol Grip

Fittted with a 30" or 32" barrel and checkered pistol stock. Same calibers as above.

NIB	Exc.	V.G.	Good	Fair	Poor
1000	800	600	450	350	—

Hawken Santa Fe

Based on the famous original rifle this reproduction is bored for .54 caliber and fitted with a 32" octagon barrel. A double set trigger and case hardened lock plate are standard. The stock ferrule and wedge plates are German silver. The stock is walnut with cheekpiece. Overall length is 50" and weight is about 9.5 lbs. Also available in kit form.

NIB	Exc.	V.G.	Good	Fair	Poor
350	300	250	200	150	100

Cattleman

This is a single action revolver patterned closely after the Colt Single Action Army. It is chambered in various popular calibers; .357 Magnum, .44-40, .44 Special, .45 ACP, .45 L.C./.45 ACP convertible, and .45 Colt. It is offered with barrel lengths of 4.75", 5.5", and 7.5". It is offered with either a modern or black powder-type frame and brass or steel backstraps. The finish is blued, with walnut grips. A Sheriff's Model with a 3" barrel and no ejector rod chambered for .44-40 and .45 Colt is also available and is valued the same. Weight is approximately 38 oz. for 5.5" barrel gun.

NIB	Exc.	V.G.	Good	Fair	Poor
325	275	250	200	150	100

Cattleman Flattop Target Model
This model is similar to the standard Cattleman, with an adjustable rear sight.

NIB	Exc.	V.G.	Good	Fair	Poor
435	350	275	225	175	125

Bisley
Chambered for the .32-20, .38 Special, .357 mag, .38-40, .44-40, and .44 Special and fitted with either 4.75", 5.5", or 7.5" barrel. Case hardned frame with two piece walnut grips.

NIB	Exc.	V.G.	Good	Fair	Poor
435	350	275	225	175	125

Bisley Flattop
As above but with adjustable rear sight.

NIB	Exc.	V.G.	Good	Fair	Poor
435	350	275	225	175	125

New Thunderer Model
Designed and imported exclusively by Cimarron Arms for single action shooting competition. Fitted with birdshead grip with hard rubber this model is chambered for the .357 Magnum, .44 Special, .44 WCF, and .45 Colt. Offered in barrel lengths of 3.5" and 4.75". Finish in nickel or blued with case colored frame.

4 3/4" WITH EJECTOR

3 1/2" WITH EJECTOR

NIB	Exc.	V.G.	Good	Fair	Poor
450	350	300	250	200	100

Buckhorn Buntline
This version is chambered for the .44 Magnum. It has an 18" round barrel, and it is cut for attaching a shoulder stock. Steel backstrap and triggerguard. Overall length is 23" and weight is about 57 oz.

Detachable Shoulder Stock-Add 25%.

NIB	Exc.	V.G.	Good	Fair	Poor
400	325	300	250	200	100

Buckhorn Target

Same as above but fitted with an adjustable rear sight and ramp front sight. Has a flat upper frame.

NIB	Exc.	V.G.	Good	Fair	Poor
450	350	300	250	200	100

Phantom

Similar to the Buckhorn, but chambered for the .44 Magnum and the .357 Magnum. The barrel is a round 10.5" and the frame is blued with blued steel backstrap. One-piece walnut grips with anatomic profile. Adjustable sight. Weight is approximately 53 oz.

NIB	Exc.	V.G.	Good	Fair	Poor
350	325	300	250	200	100

Buntline Carbine

This version has the 18" barrel but is fitted with a permanently mounted shoulder stock with a brass buttplate and sling swivel. Chambered for .44-40, .45 Long Colt, .357 Magnum, and .44 Magnum. Offered with fixed or adjustable sights.

NIB	Exc.	V.G.	Good	Fair	Poor
450	400	350	300	250	200

Tornado

This r shot revolver is chambered for the .454 Casull and fitted with a 4.75", 5.5" or 7.5" with ported barrel. Sandblasted nickel finish. Weight is about 47 oz.

NIB	Exc.	V.G.	Good	Fair	Poor
750	600	500	—	—	—

1873 Stallion

This is a scaled-down version, chambered for .22 l.r./.22 Magnum. It is blued with a case colored frame and features one-piece walnut grips.

NIB	Exc.	V.G.	Good	Fair	Poor
325	275	250	200	150	100

Schofield Revolver

Patterned after the original S&W revolver this model is chambered for the .44-40 or .45 Colt cartridge. It is fitted with a 7", 5", or 3.5" barrel . Weight with 7.5" barrel is approximately 40 oz.

NIB	Exc.	V.G.	Good	Fair	Poor
750	550	400	300	—	—

Model 1874 Russian

Chambered for the .44 Russian cartridge and fitted with a 6" or 7" barrel.

NIB	Exc.	V.G.	Good	Fair	Poor
800	650	450	350	—	—

Inspector Model

This is a double action revolver built on the same general lines as the Colt Detective model. Cylinder holds 6 cartridges and is chambered for the .38 Special. Offered in the following barrel lengths with fixed sights: 2", 2.125", 2.5", 3", 4", 6" and also offered in 4" and 6" barrel lengths with adjustable sights. Grips are walnut and finish is blued or chrome. With the 3" barrel the weight is about 24 oz.

NIB	Exc.	V.G.	Good	Fair	Poor
250	200	150	125	100	75

UHLINGER, WILLIAM P.
Philadelphia, Pennsylvania

Pocket Revolver

A .32 caliber spur trigger revolver with a 2.75" or 3" octagonal barrel and an unfluted 6-shot cylinder. Blued with rosewood or walnut grips. Manufactured during the late 1860s and early 1870s.

NOTE: Uhlinger-manufactured pistols will often be found with retailer's names on them, such as: D.D. Cone, Washington, D.C.; J.P. Lower; and W.L. Grant.

Long Cylinder (1-3/16")

Exc.	V.G.	Good	Fair	Poor
—	—	500	250	100

Short Cylinder (1")

Exc.	V.G.	Good	Fair	Poor
—	—	375	175	75

.32 Rimfire Model (5", 6", or 7" Barrel)

Exc.	V.G.	Good	Fair	Poor
—	—	600	250	100

ULTIMATE
SEE—Camex-Blaser

ULTRA LIGHT ARMS, INC.
Granville, West Virginia

This maker manufactures a variety of bolt action rifles fitted with Douglas barrels of varying lengths, custom triggers, and reinforced graphite stocks. The values for standard production models are as follows:

Model 20 (Short Action)

Weight is 4.5 lbs with 22" barrel. Composte stock with choice of colors or camo finish. Adjustable trigger. No sights. Offered in left or right hand.

NIB	Exc.	V.G.	Good	Fair	Poor
2500	1850	1500	1250	900	700

Model 20 RF-Rimfire

Weight is about 4.5 lbs. with 22" barrel. Stock is synthetic with choice of colores or camo finish. No sights. Adjustable trigger. Available as a single shot or repeater.

NIB	Exc.	V.G.	Good	Fair	Poor
800	650	600	500	400	300

Model 24 (Long Action)

Weight is approximately 5.25 lbs. with 22" barrel.

NIB	Exc.	V.G.	Good	Fair	Poor
2600	1850	1500	1250	900	700

Model 28 Magnum

Weight is about 5.75 lbs. with 24" barrel.

NIB	Exc.	V.G.	Good	Fair	Poor
2500	2250	1750	1500	1000	750

Model 40 Magnum

Weight is about 7.5 lbs with 26" barrel.

NIB	Exc.	V.G.	Good	Fair	Poor
2900	2250	1750	1500	1000	700

Model 20 Hunter's Pistol

A bolt action repeating pistol designed with the serious hunter in mind. It is offered in various popular calibers with a 14", high quality, Douglas heavy barrel. It has a 5-shot magazine and is matte blued, with a reinforced graphite Kevlar stock. It was introduced in 1987.

NIB	Exc.	V.G.	Good	Fair	Poor
1250	1000	850	750	600	500

Model 90

This is a muzzle loading rifle built with either a 45 or 50 caliber barrel. Graphit stock. Williams sights. Barrel length is 28". Adjustable trigger. Weight is about 6 lbs.

NIB	Exc.	V.G.	Good	Fair	Poor
950	750	600	—	—	—

UNCETA
SEE—Astra-Unceta SA

UNION FIRE ARMS COMPANY
Toledo, Ohio

This company was incorporated in 1902 and used the names of Union Fire Arms, Union Arms Company, Illinois Arms Company (made for Sears) and Bee Be Arms Company. In 1917 the company was either bought up or absorbed by Ithaca Gun Company.

Double Barrel Shotguns

Union's predecessor, Colton Manufacturing Co. (1894-1902) made a double for Sears. It was cleverly designed with coil mainspring striker locks set into sideplates. the Union double in 12 and 16 gauge with steel or Damascus barrels derived from it, but was a traditional hammerless sidelock side-by-side well made gun (1902-1913) and also sold by Sears. Values depend on grade and condition.

Union also offered, about 1905, an unusual boxlock hammer gun, the Model 25 in 12 gauge only. It employs external hammers but they are mounted within the frame and the spurs protrude in front of the topsnap opener. These guns are hard to find and values range from $300 to $1,200 depending on condition. They are produced with steel, twist, or Damascus barrels but only in a plain grade.

Courtesy Nick Niles

Exc.	V.G.	Good	Fair	Poor
1000	500	400	300	200

Model 24

Slide action, Model 25 Peerless that was a fancy version of the Model 24 and the Model 25A, which was a trap model, were manufactured from 1902 to 1913 in 12 or 16 gauge with 24", 26", 28", or 32" steel or Damascus barrels. This gun had a unique double trigger. The front trigger cocked and decocked an internal firing pin and the back trigger fired the gun. The gun is marked on the left side of the frame and the pump release is on the right side. This model had one serious drawback, in that the slide that extracted a spent shell extended back over the comb of the stock. This often hit the shooter's thumb knuckle and caused injury. In 1907 Union redesigned their slide by reducing its length and shielding it behind a steel plate that covered the rear half of the opening. These are the Model 24, 25, and 25A improved versions. Approximately 17,000 of all models combined were made.

Exc.	V.G.	Good	Fair	Poor
—	600	300	200	100

Model 50

Manufactured 1911 to 1913. This was basically a redesign of the Model 24. The main distinguishing feature of the Model 50 was that the frame sloped down to meet the comb of the stock and the double trigger system was replaced by a single trigger. It came in 12 or 16 gauge with a 26", 28", 30", or 32" Krupp steel barrel. Fewer than 3,000 were made.

Exc.	V.G.	Good	Fair	Poor
—	700	400	300	200

Model 23

Hammerless double, manufactured between 1902 and 1913 with or without automatic ejectors. With some engraving, it came in both single and double trigger models; this was their top grade gun. Came in 12 and 16 gauge with 28", 30", or 32" steel, twist, or Damascus barrels.

Exc.	V.G.	Good	Fair	Poor
—	300	150	125	100

Model 22

This was essentially a no frills Model 23. It had the same barrel length and steel options, but it had a plain walnut stock and no engraving. There were fewer than 10,000 Model 22 and 23s made.

Courtesy Nick Niles, Photo Paul Goodwin

Exc.	V.G.	Good	Fair	Poor
—	200	100	75	50

Diamond Grade

Single shot, manufactured between 1905 and 1910. It had a unique octagonal breech in 12 gauge only with 30" steel, laminated, or Damascus barrel. This was their premium grade single shot. Few of these were made.

Exc.	V.G.	Good	Fair	Poor
—	350	200	100	50

Model 18

Single shot, manufactured 1906 to 1913 came in 12 or 16 gauge. 30", 32", 34", or 36" steel barrel. A plain single shot. Very few made.

Exc.	V.G.	Good	Fair	Poor
—	150	75	50	25

Reifengraber

A .32 or .38 S&W caliber gas operated semiautomatic pistol, with a 3" barrel. Blued with walnut grips, approximately 100 of these pistols were manufactured.

Exc.	V.G.	Good	Fair	Poor
—	2250	1100	500	350

Automatic Revolver

.32 S&W caliber, copy of the Webley Fosbery semiautomatic revolver with a 3" barrel. Blued with either walnut or plastic grips. The cylinder has zigzag grooves.

Exc.	V.G.	Good	Fair	Poor
—	2000	1000	400	250

UNION
Unknown

Pocket Pistol

.22 caliber spur trigger single shot pistol with a 2.75" barrel marked "Union". Nickel-plated with walnut grips.

Exc.	V.G.	Good	Fair	Poor
—	—	400	100	75

UNIQUE
Hendaye, France
SEE—Pryrenees

UNITED SPORTING ARMS, INC.
Tucson, Arizona

THE HISTORY OF SEVILLE AND EL DORADO REVOLVERS

by J.C. Munnell

The history of United Sporting Arms, its related companies, and the Seville and El Dorado line of single action revolvers is a long and torturous one. It actually begins in 1973 or 1974, with the formation of United States Arms in Riverhead, New York, by three individuals. Before any but a few prototype guns were made, the partners split up, with one remaining as United States Arms, and the other two forming United Sporting Arms in nearby Hauppauge, New York.

United States Arms produced the Abilene revolver, intended to compete head-on price-wise with the Ruger Blackhawk, while United Sporting Arms, intending to make a superior (and higher-priced) product, initially produced the Seville in chrome moly steel, and slightly later, the El Dorado revolver out of stainless steel.

The Abilene was manufactured in Riverhead until 1979 or 1980 in calibers .357 and .44 magnum, and possibly the .45 Colt, all in blued steel. The assets of this company were eventually sold to A.I.G., Inc., which was a division of Mossberg. A.I.G. assembled guns from existing parts until 1983, at which time the Abilene production ended. These guns bore a North Haven, CT address, and utilized a distinctive hammer-nose safety device instead of the former transfer bar system. Calibers were the same, and all guns were made from carbon steel. Some guns had a Magnaloy finish, thereby giving rise to the misconception that some Abilenes were made from stainless steel, none were.

Meanwhile, the two remaining original partners began production of the United Sporting Arms Seville revolver in 1977. By late in that year, this company had accomplished several firearms "firsts" with production of the stainless steel El Dorado revolver. This was the first use of 17-4 pH stainless for a revolver frame, far pre-dating Freedom Arms, and was made at a time when Sturm Ruger engineering department was sending lengthy letters explaining why stainless steel was totally unsuitable for guns chambered for the .44 magnum cartridge. It would be years until the rest of the firearms industry caught up to this fledgling company

In 1979, one of the remaining partners established a second production facility in Tombstone, Arizona, under the name of United Sporting Arms of Arizona, Inc. Guns made in this plant still utilized frames made in New York, and therefore bore the Hauppauge, New York frame inscription. However, Tombstone built guns will contain the letter "T" as a suffix to the serial number. In Tombstone, the Silver Seville was born, having a highly-polished stainless grip frame on an otherwise blued gun. This is a striking combination, and has become quite popular on custom guns as well as some limited production runs from other makers. (Neither the guns themselves, nor the official company records reflect this designation, only the boxes for the guns do.) Here, to the .41 magnum and .45 Colt calibers were added to the Seville line. No stainless steel guns were made in Tombstone, Arizona.

Later in 1979, the Arizona facility was re-located to the town of Bisbee, Arizona. Less than 200 guns were made with the Bisbee address. These were all made from blued steel, and were all in .45 Colt or.44 Magnum, except as noted. Oddly enough, in the short time the company was at this location, three very distinct models were produced.

First was the Tombstone Commemorative. Although 200 were commissioned by the city of Tombstone, only about 60 were ever completed. These guns had blued frames, and stainless steel cylinders, barrels and grip frames. Some engraving was present on the cylinder and barrel, and the legend "Tombstone, Arizona 100 years of history 1879-1979" appears in three lines on the barrel. The guns came in a wooden case, and serial numbers began with TC-1. All were in .44-40 WCF caliber.

The second Bisbee gun was the Helldorado. Originally designed for the Old Tucson stunt man group "The Fall Guys", the gun had a flat-top frame with no sights, and was intended for blanks only. Only 4 were made. The final Bisbee introduction, and the only one to survive the next location change, was the Quik Kit. This was an ingenious multi-caliber system of interchangeable barrels and cylinders; invented by Ray Herriott of Centaur Systems. Only about thirty such guns were produced in Bisbee, some in blue and some in stainless. All bore the Centaur logo on the frame and all had the serial number prefix of "QK".

In late 1979, the company moved once again, this time to Tucson, Arizona. By now, the split from the New York concern was completed legally as well as physically, new guns were in blue and stainless, but all were called Sevilles. (The New York operation retained exclusive rights to the El Dorado name.) Also at this time, the frame marking on the guns simply read "Sporting Arms, Inc."

Between late 1979 and the end of 1981, several new variations of the Seville revolver were introduced. Shortly after Ruger announced the Blackhawk SRM in .357 Maximum caliber, United Sporting Arms offered a lengthened frame stainless steel gun in this caliber. This gun did not suffer from the various maladies which eventually doomed the Ruger version, and was winning silhouette matches long after the demise of the Blackhawk SRM. This model also spawned the awesome .375 USA Seville--the same caliber later re-named the .375 Super Magnum by Dan Wesson. Although only two prototypes of this caliber were made before the next company change, several hundred guns were made in .357 Maximum.

Also during this period the Sheriffs' Model with 3-1/2" barrel was introduced. Most of these guns were produced in chrome moly steel, and most were shipped with a distinctive round-butt "birdshead" grip frame. This proved very popular, and these guns became a mainstay of the company's line right until the end. Most of these Sheriffs' Models had fully adjustable sights, but at least three were made with Colt-like fixed sights, all of which, oddly, were convertibles in.45 Colt and.45 ACP.

Guns were produced in calibers 9mm Winchester Magnum, and .45 Winchester Magnum, primarily for export to Europe. A few guns were made in .44-40 and .44 Special. Also introduced was the Hunter Finish, a bead-blasted stainless steel, and the Rawhide finish, with the same treatment to a blued gun. A very few blued guns were made with a brass grip frame, as well as the "Silver Seville" configuration.

In early February of 1982, the company again changed ownership. The company name, and the frame marking on the guns, returned to United Sporting Arms, Inc. About half of the production was devoted to the so-called long-frame guns-.357 Maximum and .375 USA-and about half of these were silhou-

ette guns with 10-1/2" barrels. The .454 magnum (.454 Casull) was added to the line. However, only 30 of these guns were ever made. (Note: perhaps as many as 50 guns in this chambering were made and marked "Sporting Arms, Inc." These guns were NOT made in any United Sporting Arms factory, and are very definitely of sub-standard quality.) These guns were made on a special frame, different from all other caliber guns.

Prototype guns were made-usually two in each caliber. Produced were .41 Super Magnum and .44 Super Magnum (long before Dan Wesson made guns available in .445 and .414 Super Magnums), as well as .375 Special, and, oddly enough, .218 Mashburn Bee. None of these went into regular; production.

Normal production guns were, as to be expected, with blued, stainless steel, "silver" and brass grip-frame guns were all produced. Quite a few birdshead-grip guns were made, not only in the Sheriffs Model configuration. Guns in heavy-recoiling calibers are particularly comfortable to shoot two-handed with this grip configuration. The author has a .454 Magnum Seville with a 6-1/2" barrel and the birdshead grip frame, and it is by far the most comfortable gun I've ever shot, even with 325 grain bullets at over 1700 f.p.s.!

In November of 1985, the company was again sold, and this time it was moved to Post Fails, Idaho. Problems developed almost immediately, and even though it would be three years until the assets were sold (to the previous owners from Tucson), very few guns were ever made; less than 200. The only new product introduced in Idaho was the .32 H&R magnum chambering.

Caution: Several hundred frames "disappeared" from the Idaho plant right before the bankruptcy sale, and several bootleg guns have turned up. These guns are of distinctly dubious quality, as are many of the Idaho-marked guns. Supposedly, the BATF is aware of the situation, and arrests may yet happen.

When the assets of the Idaho plant were sold to the former owners they had no desire to resume the firearm manufacturing business, so they shipped the remaining parts, tooling and moulds to Chimney Rock, North Carolina. In a moment you'll see why.

While all this changing of location and ownership was going on, the remaining original partner in Hauppauge, New York had reorganized as El Dorado Arms, Inc., and had been in continuous production of the El Dorado revolver (although on a very limited basis) since 1979. Until the mid-1980's, all El Dorados were made from 17-4 pH stainless steel, and nearly all were chambered for the .44 magnum cartridge.

In 1985, El Dorado Arms relocated to Chimney Rock, N.C., where production continued, and the model line was expanded to include the Laredo in blued steel, and the fixed-sight Rebel in both blued and stainless steel. Also introduced at this time (although at least two prototype guns so chambered had been made in New York) was the .22 long rifle chambering, complete with match chambers, specifically for the silhouette market. Eventually .22 rimfire magnum guns were added.

The only thing lacking from the North Carolina lineup was a long frame revolver for the Super Magnum calibers. When the remaining Idaho assets were received in North Carolina, not only were there parts for the long-frame gun, but also the molds to produce more parts for these guns. In fact quite a few El Dorado .357 and .375 Super Magnum chambered guns found there way into the silhouette winners circle, alongside their smaller brothers.

Ironically, it had taken nine years, but all the components of United Sporting Arms had came full circle, and were re-united under one roof. And this was under the ownership of one of the founders of the original United States Arms!

Production of El Dorado revolvers always was very limited, and it finally ceased for good in 1997 or 1998.

Altogether, only about 6,000 or 7,000 guns were produced by all of the United Sporting Arms/El Dorado Arms companies. (Total production of the Abilene revolver by either United States Arms or A.I.G. is not available). However, even forgetting the eight different frame inscriptions, barrel lengths between 3-1/2" and 10-1/2" were made; there were all-blue, all stainless, blue and stainless, and blue and brass guns, standard finish, "hunter" and "rawhide" finishes as well as high-polish stainless; standard and birdshead grip-frame guns; Quik-Kits, convertibles and Tombstone Commemoratives; long-frame, short-frame and .454-frame guns. There were also at least 21 different chamberings. Thus, the variations are practically endless.

Quality, except for the very few noted instances, was always very high. An informal United Sporting Arms slogan was that a Seville was what a Super Blackhawk could be if Ruger had a custom shop. Given the truth of this statement, it must be admitted that an El Dorado Arms gun as what a custom Seville could have been.

Advertised prices for Sevilles and El Dorados run the full gamut from bargain "orphaned" gun prices to those reflecting the semi-custom nature of these guns For the most part, what price stability does exist is on the higher end. and this is as it should be.

For most of the production of United Sporting Arms guns, and some of the El Dorado Arms guns, copies of original factory records are available. For a letter of verification for any particular gun (refunded if no records are available, send $20 to J.C. Munnell, 633 Long Run Rd, McKeesport, PA 15132. Phone information is not available.

Three different barrel lengths of the long frame Seville. From top to bottom; 10-1/2", 7-1/2", and 6-1/2". All of these revolvers were made by United Sporting Arms, Inc. of Tucson, Arizona.

Two examples of Quik-Kit revolvers. At the top is a Ruger reworked by United Sporting Arms, Inc. of Tucson and at the bottom is a standard production revolver from the same company.

Four birdshead grip revolvers, all made by United Sporting Arms, Inc. of Tucson. Note that the bottom two examples are a Sheriff's model and a very rare convertible.

These two United Sporting Arms, Inc. of Bisbee, Arizona revolvers are the sightless Heldorados

Blued Guns

NIB	Exc.	V.G.	Good	Fair	Poor
N/A	500	450	350	N/A	N/A

Blue Silhouette (10.5" barrels)

NIB	Exc.	V.G.	Good	Fair	Poor
N/A	600	550	500	N/A	N/A

NOTE: Add $100 for stainless, $250 for stainless long-frame models (calibers .357 Maximum/Super Mag. and .357 USA/Super Mag)

Silver Sevilles

NIB	Exc.	V.G.	Good	Fair	Poor
N/A	550	475	400	N/A	N/A

Stainless Steel Guns

NIB	Exc.	V.G.	Good	Fair	Poor
N/A	600	525	450	N/A	N/A

Tombstone Commemorative

NIB	Exc.	V.G.	Good	Fair	Poor
1000	750	N/A	N/A	N/A	N/A

Quik-Kit Stainless Steel

NIB	Exc.	V.G.	Good	Fair	Poor
1500	1250	N/A	N/A	N/A	N/A

Quik-Kit Blued

NIB	Exc.	V.G.	Good	Fair	Poor
1200	1000	N/A	N/A	N/A	N/A

NOTE: For Quik-Kit guns with extra barrel and cylinder add $200 for each barrel and cylinder.

Deduct 10% if United Sporting Arms, Hauppauge, N.Y.

Deduct 20% if United Sporting Arms, Post Falls, ID.

Add 20% if El Dorado Arms (either N.Y. or N.C.)
Add 10% for 1-1/2" barrel Sheriff's Model
Add 20% for 10-1/2" barrel
Add 20% for birdshead grip frame
Add 20% if brass grip frame

UNITED STATES ARMS
Otis A. Smith Company
Rockfall, Connecticut

Single Action Revolver

A .44 rimfire and centerfire single action revolver with a 7" barrel and integral ejector. The hammer nose is fitted with two firing pins so that rimfire or centerfire cartridges can be used interchangeably. The barrel marked "United States Arms Company - New York", the top strap "No. 44". Blued with either hard rubber or rosewood grips. Manufactured in limited quantities. Circa 1870 to 1875.

Exc.	V.G.	Good	Fair	Poor
—	—	2750	1250	500

UNITED STATES HISTORICAL SOCIETY
Richmond, Virginia

The following arms are manufactured by the Williamsburg Firearms Manufactory and the Virginia Firearms Manufactory. This company ceased business under this name in 1994 and resumed business under the name of America Remembers in Mechanicsville, VA. No current prices are given for these models due to the lack of an active secondary market. Issue prices only are given.

George Washington

A reproduction of a flintlock pistol originally owned by George Washington. A total of 975 were made and were issued at a price of $3,000.

Thomas Jefferson

A reproduction of a flintlock pistol originally owned by Thomas Jefferson. A total of 1,000 were made and were issued at a price of $1,900.

Hamilton-Burr Dueling Pistols

Reproductions of the flintlock pistols used in the Hamilton-Burr duel. A total of 1,200 sets were made and sold at an issue price of $2,995.

Stonewall Jackson Pistol

A reproduction of a Colt Model 1851 Navy cased with accessories. Total of 2,500 were made in 1988. Issue Price was $2,100.

Texas Paterson Edition

A reproduction of a Colt Paterson revolver cased with accessories. Total of 1,000 were made in 1988. Issue price was $2,500.

Buffalo Bill Centennial

A reproduction of a Colt Model 1860 Army revolver with acid-etched scenes inlaid in gold, cased with accessories. Total of 2,500 were made in 1983 and issued at a price of $1,950.

U.S. Cavalry Model

A reproduction of a Colt Model 1860 Army revolver with a gold-plated cylinder and stag grips, cased with a brass belt buckle. Total of 975 were made beginning in 1988. Issue price was $1,450

Sam Houston Model

Reproduction of a Colt Model 1847 Army revolver with etched and gilt additions. Total of 2,500 were made. Issue price was $2,300.

Robert E. Lee Model

Reproduction of the Colt Model 1851 Navy revolver with gilt additions and cased with accessories. A total of 2,500 were made. Issue price was $2,100.

H. Deringer Set

Cased pair of reproduction .41 caliber Henry Deringer percussion pocket pistols available in three grades as follows:

Silver Mounted: 1,000
Issue Price $1,900

14 Kt. Gold Mounted: 100
Issue Price $2,700

18 Kt. Mounted with Gemstone: 5
Issue Price-$25,000

UNITED STATES PATENT FIREARMS MANUFACTURING COMPANY
Hartford, Connecticut

This company began business in 1995. The company imports its parts from Uberti in Italy and fits, finishes, and assembles the gun in Hartford. Produces only reproductions of Colt revolvers.

Single Action Army Revolver

Offered in a wide variety of calibers including .22 rimfire, .38 S&W, .357 magnum, .38-40, .44 Russian, .44-40, .45 Colt, and .45 ACP. Barrel lengths are 3", 4", 4.75", 5.5", and 7.5". Guns with 3" and 4" barrels are available in .44-40 or .45 Colt only. The standard gun is supplied with the original "P" frame. A modern cross pin frame is available for an additional $10. Prices listed are for standard grips and finish.

NIB	Exc.	V.G.	Good	Fair	Poor
650	450	375	—	—	—

Flattop Target Model

This model is offered with the same calibers as the Single Action Army above. Barrel lengths are 4.75", 5.5", and 7.5". Grips are two piece hard rubber. Prices listed are given for standard finish. Introduced in 1997.

NIB	Exc.	V.G.	Good	Fair	Poor
750	550	450	—	—	—

Model 1873 Cut Away

Chambered for the .45 Colt cartridge **but not to be fired**. Fitted with a 7.5" barrel and brushed steel finish. Parts cut away for display.

NIB	Exc.	V.G.	Good	Fair	Poor
N/A	—	—	—	—	—

Henry Nettleton Revolver

This is an exact reproduction of the U.S. Government inspector model produced in the Springfield Armory. Offered in 7.5" and 5.5" models. Introduced in 1997.

NIB	Exc.	V.G.	Good	Fair	Poor
1100	800	600	—	—	—

Buntline Special

Fitted with a 16" barrel and chambered for the .45 Colt cartridge. Supplied with nickel stock. Limited edition. Cased.

NIB	Exc.	V.G.	Good	Fair	Poor
2175	1600	—	—	—	—

China Camp Cowboy Action Gun

Chambered for .45 Colt cartridge but other calibers also available from .32WCF to .44WCF. Barrel lengths are 4.75", 5.5", and 7.5". Special action job. Two piece hard rubber grips standard. Finish is silver steel.

NIB	Exc.	V.G.	Good	Fair	Poor
975	800	600	—	—	—

Omni-Potent Bird Head Model

Offered with birdshead grips and available with 3.5", 4", or 4.75" barrel lengths. Also offered in a snubnose version with 2" or 3" barrel with no ejector.

NIB	Exc.	V.G.	Good	Fair	Poor
1100	800	600	—	—	—

Bisley Model

Based on the famous Bisley model this reproduction features barrel lengths of 4.75", 5.5", 7.5", and 10". the .45 Colt caliber is standard but .32WCF, .38S&W, .44S&W, .41 Colt, .38WCF, .44WCF are optional. Add $60.00 for 10" models. Introduced in 1997.

NIB	Exc.	V.G.	Good	Fair	Poor
975	750	550	—	—	—

NOTE: This company offers a wide variety of special order options on its revolvers from special bluing to grips to engraving. These special order options will affect price to a significant degree. Seek qualified assistance prior to a sale.

UNITED STATES SMALL ARMS CO.
Chicago, Illinois
Huntsman Model Knife Pistol
Made from approximately 1918-1930.

UNIVERSAL FIREARMS
Sacksonville, Arkansas

Model 7312
A 12 gauge Over/Under shotgun with separated 30" ventilated rib barrels, single selective trigger and automatic ejectors. The case hardened receiver engraved. Blued with a walnut stock. Discontinued in 1982.

Exc.	V.G.	Good	Fair	Poor
1700	1500	1250	900	450

Model 7412
As above, with extractors. Discontinued in 1982.

Exc.	V.G.	Good	Fair	Poor
1500	1250	1000	750	400

Model 7712
As above, with 26" or 28" barrels, nonselective single trigger and extractors. Discontinued in 1982.

Exc.	V.G.	Good	Fair	Poor
450	400	350	250	100

Model 7812
As above, with more detailed engraving and automatic ejectors. Discontinued in 1982.

Exc.	V.G.	Good	Fair	Poor
600	550	450	350	150

Model 7912
As above, with a gold wash frame and single selective trigger. Discontinued in 1982.

Exc.	V.G.	Good	Fair	Poor
1200	1000	750	600	300

Model 7112
A 12 gauge double barrel boxlock shotgun with 26" or 28" barrels, double triggers and extractors. Blued, case hardened with a walnut stock. Discontinued in 1982.

Exc.	V.G.	Good	Fair	Poor
350	300	250	200	100

Double Wing

A 10, 12, 20 or .410 bore boxlock double barrel shotgun with 26", 28", or 30" barrels, double triggers and extractors. Blued with a walnut stock. Discontinued in 1982.

Exc.	V.G.	Good	Fair	Poor
350	300	250	200	100

Model 7212

A 12 gauge single barrel trap shotgun with a 30" ventilated rib ported barrel, and automatic ejector. Engraved, case hardened receiver and walnut stock. Discontinued in 1982.

Exc.	V.G.	Good	Fair	Poor
1000	850	650	450	300

Model 1000 Military Carbine

A copy of the U.S. M1 Carbine with an 18" barrel. Blued with a birch wood stock.

Exc.	V.G.	Good	Fair	Poor
350	250	200	100	75

Model 1003

As above, with a 16", 18", or 20" barrel.

Exc.	V.G.	Good	Fair	Poor
250	200	150	100	75

Model 1010

As above, but nickel-plated.

Exc.	V.G.	Good	Fair	Poor
275	225	175	125	100

Model 1015

As above, but gold-plated.

Exc.	V.G.	Good	Fair	Poor
300	250	200	150	125

Model 1005 Deluxe

As above, with a polished blue finish and Monte Carlo-style stock.

Exc.	V.G.	Good	Fair	Poor
275	225	150	100	75

Model 1006 Stainless

As the Model 1000, but in stainless steel.

Exc.	V.G.	Good	Fair	Poor
400	300	225	125	100

Model 1020 Teflon

As above, with a black or gray Dupont Teflon-S finish.

Exc.	V.G.	Good	Fair	Poor
300	225	175	125	100

Model 1256 Ferret

The Model 1000 in .256 Winchester Magnum caliber.

Exc.	V.G.	Good	Fair	Poor
275	200	175	125	100

Model 3000 Enforcer

A pistol version of the Model 1000 with an 11.25" barrel and 15- or 30-shot magazines.

Nickel Finish-Add 20%
Gold-Plated-Add 40%

Stainless Steel-Add 30%
Teflon-S-Add 20%

Blued

Exc.	V.G.	Good	Fair	Poor
300	225	200	150	100

Model 5000 Paratrooper

The Model 1000, with a 16" or 18" barrel and folding stock. This model, in stainless steel, is known as the Model 5006.

Exc.	V.G.	Good	Fair	Poor
350	250	200	125	100

1981 Commemorative Carbine

A limited production version of the Model 1000 cased with accessories. Produced in 1981.

NIB	Exc.	V.G.	Good	Fair	Poor
500	350	250	200	100	75

Model 2200 Leatherneck

A .22 caliber version of the U.S. M1 Carbine with an 18" barrel and blowback action. Blued with a birch wood stock.

Exc.	V.G.	Good	Fair	Poor
200	175	150	100	75

U.S. M1 CARBINE
Various Manufacturers

NOTE: For history, techinical data, descriptions, photos, and prices see the *Standard Catalog of Military Firearms, 1870 to the Present* under United States, Rifles.

URIZAR, TOMAS
Eibar, Spain

Celta, J. Cesar, Premier, Puma, and Union

A 6.35mm semiautomatic pistol with a 3" barrel. The slide marked with the trade names listed above. Blued with black plastic grips, cast with a wild man carrying a club.

Exc.	V.G.	Good	Fair	Poor
200	150	125	90	75

Dek-Du

A 5.5mm folding trigger double action revolver with a 12-shot cylinder. Later versions were made in 6.35mm. Manufactured from 1905 to 1912.

Exc.	V.G.	Good	Fair	Poor
175	125	100	75	50

Express

A 6.35mm semiautomatic pistol with a 2" barrel. The slide marked "The Best Automatic Pistol Express". Blued with walnut grips. A 7.65mm variety exists with a 4" barrel.

Exc.	V.G.	Good	Fair	Poor
175	125	100	75	50

Imperial

A 6.35mm caliber semiautomatic pistol with a 2.5" barrel. This model was actually made by Aldazabal. Manufactured circa 1914.

Exc.	V.G.	Good	Fair	Poor
175	125	100	75	50

Le Secours or Phoenix

A 7.65mm semiautomatic pistol marked with either of the trade names listed above.

Exc.	V.G.	Good	Fair	Poor
175	125	100	75	50

Princeps

A 6.35mm or 7.65mm semiautomatic pistol marked on the slide "Made in Spain Princeps Patent."

Exc.	V.G.	Good	Fair	Poor
175	125	100	75	50

Venus

A 7.65mm semiautomatic pistol with the grips having the trade name "Venus" cast in them.

Exc.	V.G.	Good	Fair	Poor
175	125	100	75	50

UZI ISRAELI MILITARY INDUSTRIES
Importer-None
SEE-also Vector Arms, Inc.

Uzi Carbine Model A

Chambered for 9mm cartridge and fitted with a 16" barrel with 25-round magazine. Gray parkerized finish. Built from 1980 to 1983.

NIB	Exc.	V.G.	Good	Fair	Poor
1850	1600	1200	1000	600	450

Uzi Carbine Model B

A 9mm, .41 Action Express or .45 caliber semiautomatic carbine with a 16.1" barrel and 20-, 25-, or 32-shot box magazines. A 50-shot drum magazine is available in 9mm caliber. Black parkerized finish, plastic grips and a folding stock. It is strongly suggest that a buyer or seller seek a qualified local appraisal. First produced in 1983. This model is no longer imported as of 1989.

NIB	Exc.	V.G.	Good	Fair	Poor
1650	1450	1000	800	500	400

Uzi Mini-Carbine

As above, in 9mm or .45 caliber with a 19.75" barrel. This model is no longer imported.

NIB	Exc.	V.G.	Good	Fair	Poor
2000	1500	1150	800	600	400

Uzi Pistol

As above in 9mm or .45 ACP, with a 4.5" barrel, pistol grip, no rear stock and a 20-shot magazine. This model is no longer imported.

NIB	Exc.	V.G.	Good	Fair	Poor
850	700	550	450	350	250

UZI EAGLE PISTOLS

NOTE: As of 1999 these pistols were no longer imported into the U.S.

Full Size Model

Introduced in 1997 this is a double action pistol chambered for the 9mm and .40 S&W cartridge. Barrel length is 4.4". Overall length is 8.1". Tritium night sights are standard.

NIB	Exc.	V.G.	Good	Fair	Poor
475	375	—	—	—	—

Short Slide Model

Introduced in 1997 this is a double action pistol chambered for the 9mm, .40 S&W and .45 ACP cartridge. Barrel length is 3.7". Overall length is 7.5". Tritium night sights are standard.

NIB	Exc.	V.G.	Good	Fair	Poor
500	400	—	—	—	—

Compact Model

Introduced in 1997 this is a double action pistol chambered for the 9mm, .40 S&W and .45 ACP cartridge. Barrel length is 3.5". Overall length is 7.2". Tritium night sights are standard. Magazine capacity is 8 rounds for the .45 ACP and 10 rounds for the other calibers. Double action only is an option for this model.

NIB	Exc.	V.G.	Good	Fair	Poor
500	400	—	—	—	—

Polymer Compact Model

Introduced in 1997 this is a double action pistol chambered for the 9mm and .40 S&W cartridge. Barrel length is 3.5". Overall length is 7.2". Tritium night sights are standard.

NIB	Exc.	V.G.	Good	Fair	Poor
475	375	—	—	—	—

VALKYRIE ARMS, LTD.
Olympia, Washington

Browning 1919 A4 .30 Caliber

This is a semiautomatic version of the famous Browning machine gun. It is chambered for the .30-06 or the .308 cartridge. It come equipped with a tripod, pintle, T&E, belly linker and 200 links. An A6 configuration is available. Available in late 1996.

NIB	Exc.	V.G.	Good	Fair	Poor
2850	2000	1500	—	—	—

U.S. M3-A1

A re-creation of the famous "grease gun" but in semi-auto. Barrel length is 16.5". Supplied with three 30-round magazines.

NIB	Exc.	V.G.	Good	Fair	Poor
695	550	—	—	—	—

NOTE: For dummy suppressor add $50. For real suppressor add $300 plus transfer tax of $200. All NFA rules and state laws must be followed for suppressors.

DeLisle Carbine

A copy of the famous World War II commando carbine used by British forces. Chambered for .45ACP. Integral suppressor. All NFA rules must be followed. Only 167 carbines will be produced.

NIB	Exc.	V.G.	Good	Fair	Poor
1595	1250	—	—	—	—

NOTE: For dummy suppressor deduct $300.

VALMET, INC.
Jyvaskyla, Finland
Importer-Stoeger, Inc.
South Hackensack, New Jersey

M-62S

A semiautomatic copy of the Finnish M-62 service rifle in 7.62x39 caliber that is patterned after the Russian AK47. Fitted with a walnut or tubular steel stock. Manufactured after 1962.

NIB	Exc.	V.G.	Good	Fair	Poor
2000	1600	1200	900	750	300

M-71S

As above, in 5.56mm caliber and available with a composition stock.

NIB	Exc.	V.G.	Good	Fair	Poor
2000	1600	1200	900	750	300

Model 76

As above, in 5.56mm, 7.62x39mm, or 7.62x51mm with either a 16.75" or 20.5" barrel.

NIB	Exc.	V.G.	Good	Fair	Poor
1500	1250	950	750	550	200

Model 78

As above, in 7.62x51mm, 7.62x39, or .223 with a 24.5" barrel, wood stock, and integral bipod.

NIB	Exc.	V.G.	Good	Fair	Poor
1750	1350	1000	850	600	300

Lion

A 12 gauge Over/Under shotgun with 26", 28", or 30" barrels, single selective trigger and extractors. Blued with a walnut stock. Manufactured from 1947 to 1968.

Exc.	V.G.	Good	Fair	Poor
450	375	300	250	100

VALTION (LAHTI)
SEE—Lahti

VALTRO
Italy
Importer-Valtro U.S.A.

1998 A1

A Model 1911 clone chambered for .45 ACP and fitted with a match grade 5" barrel. Many special features include a checkered front strap, beavertail grip safety, deluxe wood grips, serrated slide front and back, beveled magazine well. Weight is approximately 40 oz. Introduced in 1998.

NIB	Exc.	V.G.	Good	Fair	Poor
900	700	—	—	—	—

Tactical 98 Shotgun

Chambered for 12 gauge and fitted with a 18.5" or 20" ported barrel. Choice of pistol grip or standard stock. Extended magazine with 5 or 7 rounds. Ghost ring sights.

NIB	Exc.	V.G.	Good	Fair	Poor
850	675	—	—	—	—

VARNER SPORTING ARMS, INC.
Marietta, Georgia

The rifles listed below are all patterned after the Stevens Favorite model.

Hunter

.22 caliber single shot rifle with a 21.5" half-octagonal, takedown barrel fitted with an aperture rear sight. Blued with well figured walnut stocks. Introduced in 1988.

NIB	Exc.	V.G.	Good	Fair	Poor
375	300	250	200	150	100

Hunter Deluxe

As above, with a case hardened receiver and a more finely figured stock.

NIB	Exc.	V.G.	Good	Fair	Poor
500	400	350	250	175	125

Presentation Grade

As above, with a target hammer and trigger, and a hand checkered stock.

NIB	Exc.	V.G.	Good	Fair	Poor
575	475	425	350	250	200

Engraved Presentation Grade No. 1 Grade

NIB	Exc.	V.G.	Good	Fair	Poor
650	550	500	450	350	200

No. 2 Grade

NIB	Exc.	V.G.	Good	Fair	Poor
775	650	600	500	400	200

No. 3 Grade

NIB	Exc.	V.G.	Good	Fair	Poor
1100	850	700	550	350	200

NOTE: This company made several over and under shotguns and rifle/shotgun combination guns for the Savage Company. These are no longer being imported into this country.

VECTOR ARMS, INC
North Salt Lake, UT

UZI

This is a semiautomatic, pre-ban Uzi carbine with 18" barrel chambered for the 9mm cartridge. Receiver built by Group Industries of Louisville, KY prior to May, 1986. Receiver fixed parts manufacturing and receiver assembly by Vector Arms. Only 97 of these semiautomatic receivers were manufactured.

NIB	Exc.	V.G.	Good	Fair	Poor
1600	1300	—	—	—	—

NOTE: For .45 ACP or .22 caliber conversion kit add $200.

VEKTOR
South Africa
Importer-Vektor U.S.A.
Norfolk, VA

NOTE: As of 2001 the importer, Vecktor, USA, is no longer in business.

Model Z88

This is a semiautomatic pistol chambered for the 9mm cartridge. It has a 5" barrel and fixed sights. Weight is about 35 oz. Blue finish. Magazine capacity is 15 rounds or 10 in U.S.

NIB	Exc.	V.G.	Good	Fair	Poor
600	475	—	—	—	—

Model SP1 Service Pistol

This model is chambered for the 9mm cartridge and is fitted with a 4-5/8" barrel. Fixed sights. Weight is 35 oz. Blue finish. Magazine capacity is 15 rounds or 10 in U.S.

NIB	Exc.	V.G.	Good	Fair	Poor
600	475	—	—	—	—

NOTE: Add $30 for anodized or nickel finish.

Model SP1 Sport

Similar to the SP1 this model features a 5" barrel with 3 chamber compensator. Blue finish. Weight is about 38 oz.

NIB	Exc.	V.G.	Good	Fair	Poor
725	575	—	—	—	—

Model SP1 Tuned Sport

This model also has a 3 chamber compensator on a 5" barrel but it has an adjustable straight trigger and LPA 3 dot sighting system. Nickel finish. Weight is about 38 oz.

NIB	Exc.	V.G.	Good	Fair	Poor
1200	950	—	—	—	—

Model SP1 Target

This 9mm model is fitted with a 6" barrel with adjustable straight trigger. LPA 3 dot sighting system. Weight is about 40.5 oz. Two tone finish.

NIB	Exc.	V.G.	Good	Fair	Poor
1225	975	—	—	—	—

Model SP1 Compact (General's Model)

A compact version of the 9mm pistol fitted with a 4" barrel. Fixed sights. Blue finish. Magazine capacity is 15 rounds or 10 for U.S. Weight is about 31.5 oz.

NIB	Exc.	V.G.	Good	Fair	Poor
650	525	—	—	—	—

Model SP2

A full size service pistol chambered for the .40 S&W cartridge. fitted with a 4-5/8" barrel. Fixed sights. Magazine capacity is 11 rounds or 10 for U.S. Blued finish. Weight is about 35 oz.

NIB	Exc.	V.G.	Good	Fair	Poor
600	475	—	—	—	—

Model SP2 Compact (General's Model)

A compact .40 S&W pistol with 4" barrel. Magazine capacity is 11 rounds or 10 for U.S. Weight is about 31.5 oz. Blue finish. Fixed sights.

NIB	Exc.	V.G.	Good	Fair	Poor
650	525	—	—	—	—

Model SP2 Competition

This model is chambered for the .40S&W cartridge and fitted with a 5.88" barrel. It features enlarged safety levers and magazine catch. The frame has been thickened for scope mount. Beavertail grip and straight trigger. Weight is about 42 oz.

NIB	Exc.	V.G.	Good	Fair	Poor
1000	750	—	—	—	—

Model SP1 Ultra Sport

This model is designed for IPSC open class competition. Barrel length is 6" with 3 chamber compensator. Chambered for 9mm cartridge. Optical scope mount with Weaver rails. Magazine capacity is 19 rounds or 10 for U.S. Weight is about 41.5 oz. Priced with Lynx scope.

NIB	Exc.	V.G.	Good	Fair	Poor
2150	1700	—	—	—	—

Model SP2 Ultra Sport

Same as model above but chambered for .40 S&W cartridge. Magazine capacity is 14 rounds or 10 for U.S.

NIB	Exc.	V.G.	Good	Fair	Poor
2150	1700	—	—	—	—

Model SP2 Conversion Kit

Made for the SP2 this is a 9mm conversion kit that consists of a 9mm barrel, recoil spring, and 9mm magazine.

NIB	Exc.	V.G.	Good	Fair	Poor
190	150	—	—	—	—

Model CP-1 Compact

Chambered for the 9mm cartridge and fitted with a 4" barrel this model has a polymer frame. Fixed sights. Weight is about 25 oz. Magazine capacity is 13 rounds standard, 12 rounds compact or 10 rounds for U.S. Offered with black or nickel slide.

NIB	Exc.	V.G.	Good	Fair	Poor
475	375	—	—	—	—

NOTE: Add $20 for nickel slide.

RIFLES

Vektor H5 Pump Action Rifle

This pump action rifle is chambered for the .233 cartridge. It is fitted with a thumbhole stock and a 22" barrel. Magazine capacity is 5 rounds.

NIB	Exc.	V.G.	Good	Fair	Poor
850	625	—	—	—	—

Vektor 98

Built on a Mauser action this rifle is chambered for a variety of calibers from .243 to .375H&H. Fitted with a one piece walnut stock with hand checkering. Magazine capacity is 5 rounds. Open sights on Magnum calibers only.

NIB	Exc.	V.G.	Good	Fair	Poor
1150	850	—	—	—	—

Vektor Lyttelton

This rifle features numerous special features and is fitted with a classic walnut stock with wrap-around checkering. Fixed sights. Calibers offered are from .243 to .375H&H.

NIB	Exc.	V.G.	Good	Fair	Poor
1595	1100	—	—	—	—

VENUS WAFFENWERKE
Zella Mehlis, Germany

Venus

A 6.35mm, 7.65mm, or 9mm semiautomatic pistol with a 3.5" barrel. Slide is marked "Original Venus Patent" and the grips bear the monogram "OW". Designed by Oskar Will. Blued, plastic grips. Manufactured from 1912 to 1914.

Exc.	V.G.	Good	Fair	Poor
700	550	400	250	100

VERNEY-CARRON
St. Etienne, France
Importer-Ventura
Seal Beach, California

Concours

A 12 gauge Over/Under boxlock shotgun with 26" or 28" ventilated rib barrels, single selective triggers, automatic ejectors and profuse engraving. Blued, French case hardened with checkered walnut stock. First imported in 1978.

Exc.	V.G.	Good	Fair	Poor
1250	800	700	600	300

Skeet Model

As above, with a 28" skeet choked barrel and a pistol grip stock.

Exc.	V.G.	Good	Fair	Poor
1400	950	700	600	300

VERONA
Italy
Importer-B.C. Outdoors
Boulder City, Nevada

HUNTING SHOTGUNS

LX501

This over and under shotgun is chambered for the 12, 20, 28, and .410 bore. Single selective trigger. Ejectors. Blued steel receiver. Walnut stock with machine checkering. It is offered with 28" vent rib barrels. Screw-in chokes for 12 and 20 gauges models. Fixed chokes for 28 and .410 bore. Chambers are 3" for all gauges except 28 gauge. Weight is between 6.25 lbs. and 6.75 lbs. depending on gauge.

NIB	Exc.	V.G.	Good	Fair	Poor
800	600	—	—	—	—

NOTE: For 28 gauge and .410 bore add $30.

LX692G

This model is also offered in 12, 20, 28, and .410 bore with 28" vent rib barrels. Receiver is fitted with sideplates with gold inlaid hunting scenes on three sides. Matte finish walnut stock with Schnabel forearm, hand cut checkering. Weight is between 7.25 lbs. and 7.75 lbs. depending on gauge.

NIB	Exc.	V.G.	Good	Fair	Poor
1390	1050	—	—	—	—

NOTE: For 28 gauge add $40 for .410 bore add $25.

LX692G-20/28

This model has the features ads above but features a 20 gauge gun with extra set of 28 gauge barrels. Choke tubes standard. Weight is about 7.5 lbs. with 20 gauge barrels.

NIB	Exc.	V.G.	Good	Fair	Poor
2000	1500	—	—	—	—

LX702G

This model is offered in both 12 and 20 gauge with 28" barrel chambered for 3" shells. This model features a case colored receiver with side plates. The reciever is engraved on three side with gold inlaid upland bird hunting scenes. Full figured Turkish walnut with hand checkering and oil finish. Single selective trigger, black recoil pad, ejectors and Schnabel forearm. Weight for 12 gauge is about 7 lbs. For the 20 gauge about 6 lbs.

NIB	Exc.	V.G.	Good	Fair	Poor
1550	1150	—	—	—	—

SPORTING SHOTGUNS

LX680

Chambered for 12 or 20 gauge shells with 2.75" chambers. Single selective trigger, ejectors, lightly engraved steel receiver. Walnut stock with beavertail firearm and hand cut checkering. Ventilated recoil pad standard. Fitted with 28" barrels with ventilated rib between barrels. Choke tubes. Weight is about 6.5 lbs. depending on gauge.

NIB	Exc.	V.G.	Good	Fair	Poor
1075	800	—	—	—	—

LX692GS

Similar to the above model but fitted with sideplates with gold inlaid hunting scenes.

NIB	Exc.	V.G.	Good	Fair	Poor
1425	1075	—	—	—	—

COMPETITION SHOTGUNS

LX680C S&T

This over and under model features a choice of 28" or 30" 11mm vent rib barrels on a 12 gauge frame. Single selective trigger, ejectors. Matte finish Turkish walnut stock with hand cut checkering, beavertail forearm, wider comb. Lightly engraved steel receiver. Ventilated rib between barrels. Choke tubes. Weight is approximately 7.75 lbs. depending on barrel length. The 28" barrel model is designated as Skeet/Sporting and the 30" model is designated Trap.

NIB	Exc.	V.G.	Good	Fair	Poor
1175	875	—	—	—	—

LX692GC S&T

Same as above but with sideplates with gold inlaid game scenes.

NIB	Exc.	V.G.	Good	Fair	Poor
1550	1150	—	—	—	—

LX702GC S&T

This model features a case colored receiver and side plates with gold inlaid birds. Offered in 12 gauge only with choice of 28" or 30" barrels. Weight is about 7.5 lbs.

NIB	Exc.	V.G.	Good	Fair	Poor
1625	1225	—	—	—	—

VETTERLI
Switzerland
Various Manufacturers

NOTE: for techinical data, history, description, photos and prices see the *Standard Catalog of Military Firearms, 1870 to the Present* under Switzerland, Rifles.

VICKERS, LTD.
Crayford/Kent, England

Jubilee

A .22 caliber single shot Martini-action single shot rifle with a 28" barrel, adjustable sights and pistol grip walnut stock. Blued. Manufactured prior to WWII.

Exc.	V.G.	Good	Fair	Poor
500	400	350	275	200

Empire

As above, with a 27" or 30" barrel and a straight stock.

Exc.	V.G.	Good	Fair	Poor
500	350	300	225	150

VICTOR EJECTOR
SEE—Crescent Fire Arms Co.

VICTORY ARMS COT., LTD.
North Hampton, England

Model MC5

A 9mm, .38 Super, .41 Action Express, 10mm, or .45 caliber semiautomatic pistol with a 4.25", 5.75", or 7.5" barrel, 10-, 12-, or 17-shot magazine, decocking lever and Millett sights. Interchangeable barrels were available. Introduced in 1989.

NIB	Exc.	V.G.	Good	Fair	Poor
500	400	300	250	200	150

VIRGINIAN
SEE Interarms

VOERE
Kufstein, Austria

In 1987 this company was purchased by Mauser-Werke. Voere actions are used in rifles made and sold by KDF, Inc., of Seguin, Texas. Values for older-production rifles are as follows:

Model 1007

Bolt action rifle chambered for .22 LR cartridge and fitted with an 18" barrel. Open sights. Beech stock. Introduced in 1984. Discontinued in 1991.

NIB	Exc.	V.G.	Good	Fair	Poor
225	175	150	125	100	75

Model 1013

This bolt action rifle is chambered for the .22 WMR cartridge and fitted with an 18" barrel. Magazine capacity is 8 rounds. Open sight with adjustable rear. Military-style stock that is oil finished. Double set triggers.

NIB	Exc.	V.G.	Good	Fair	Poor
275	225	200	150	125	100

Model 2107

This .22 LR bolt action rifle has a 19.5" barrel with Monte Carlo stock. 8-round magazine. Weight is about 6 lbs.

NIB	Exc.	V.G.	Good	Fair	Poor
325	250	225	200	150	125

Model 2107 Deluxe

Bolt action rifle chambered for .22 LR cartridge has checkered stock with raised cheekpiece. Discontinued in 1988.

NIB	Exc.	V.G.	Good	Fair	Poor
350	275	225	200	150	125

Model 2114S

This is a semiautomatic rifle chambered for .22 LR cartridge and fitted with a 18" barrel. Magazine capacity is 15 rounds. Open sight. Stock is beechwood. Single-stage trigger. No longer in production.

NIB	Exc.	V.G.	Good	Fair	Poor
275	225	200	150	125	100

Model 2115

Similar to the model above but with checkered stock. Weight is about 5.75 lbs. Discontinued in 1995.

NIB	Exc.	V.G.	Good	Fair	Poor
300	250	225	175	150	100

Model 2150

This is a bolt action centerfire rifle chambered for calibers from .22-250 to .338 Win. Mag. Fitted with 22" barrels (24" on magnums). Open sights with adjustable rear sight. Checkered walnut stock with oil finish. Built on M98 Mauser action. Weight is about 8 lbs. depending on caliber. Discontinued in 1995.

NIB	Exc.	V.G.	Good	Fair	Poor
800	650	550	450	300	200

Model 2155

Similar to the Model 2150 but with no sights and double set triggers. Discontinued in 1995.

NIB	Exc.	V.G.	Good	Fair	Poor
800	650	550	450	300	200

Model 2165

Similar to the above model but with open sights, walnut stock with Bavarian cheekpiece and schnabel forearm. Rosewood grip cap. Discontinued.

NIB	Exc.	V.G.	Good	Fair	Poor
850	675	550	450	300	200

Model 2185

This is a semiautomatic centerfire rifle chambered for 7x64, .308, and .30-06 cartridges. Fitted with a 20" barrel and open sights with adjustable rear sight. Checkered walnut stock. Available with full stock as well. Add $100 for Mannlicher stock.

NIB	Exc.	V.G.	Good	Fair	Poor
1700	1300	850	700	500	300

Model 2185 Match

Same as the Model 2185 except for a 5-round magazine, hooded front sight, laminated stock with adjustable cheekpiece. Discontinued in 1994.

NIB	Exc.	V.G.	Good	Fair	Poor
3000	2400	1750	1150	650	400

Model Titan

This is a centerfire bolt action rifle chambered in calibers from .243 to .375 H&H. Fitted with 24" or 26" barrels depending on caliber. No sights. Checkered Monte Carlo walnut stock with oil finish. Discontinued in 1988.

NIB	Exc.	V.G.	Good	Fair	Poor
800	650	550	450	300	200

Model Titan Menor

Bolt action rifle chambered for .222 Rem, .223 Rem. Fitted with a 23.5" barrel and 3-round magazine. No sights. Checkered Monte Carlo walnut stock with rosewood grip cap. Introduced in 1986 and dropped in 1988.

NIB	Exc.	V.G.	Good	Fair	Poor
600	475	375	250	200	150

Model VEC-91 Lightning

Bolt action rifle that fires caseless 6mm ammo. Adjustable rear sight on a 20" barrel. Checkered walnut stock with cheekpiece. Electronic trigger. Introduced in 1991.

NIB	Exc.	V.G.	Good	Fair	Poor
1700	1300	850	700	500	300

Model VEC-91BR
Same as model above but in single shot with heavy 20" barrel. Synthetic target stock. Introduced in 1995.

NIB	Exc.	V.G.	Good	Fair	Poor
1700	1300	850	700	500	300

Model VEC-91HB
Same as the VEC-91 except single shot with heavy 22" barrel. Choice of synthetic stock or laminated wood stock. Introduced in 1995.

NIB	Exc.	V.G.	Good	Fair	Poor
1400	1100	750	600	450	200

Model VEC-91SS
This version has no sights and a synthetic stock. Introduced in 1995.

NIB	Exc.	V.G.	Good	Fair	Poor
1200	900	650	550	400	200

VOLCANIC ARMS COMPANY
New Haven, Connecticut
SEE—Winchester Repeating Arms Co.

VOLUNTEER ENTERPRISES
Knoxville, Tennessee
SEE—Commando Arms

VOLKSPISTOLE
Various Makers
Germany

Volkspistole
Quite mysterious, a few have ever been noted. It was designed as a cheaply manufactured, last-ditch weapon that was supposed to be used to flood the German countryside and cause casualties among the invaders at the close of WWII. It is chambered for the 9mm Parabellum cartridge and features a gas-operated, delayed blowback action. It has a 5.1" barrel with an 8-round, detachable box magazine. The construction is of steel stampings. It has no safety devices and no markings whatsoever. Examples noted are in the white, and there are no sights affixed to them. It appears that this weapon never actually went into production, and it would be impossible to estimate a value. Anyone encountering such a weapon would be wise to secure a qualified appraisal.

VOUZLAUD
Paris, France
Importer-Waverly Arms Co.
Suffolk, Virginia

Model 315 E
A 12, 16, or 20 gauge boxlock shotgun with 20" barrels, double triggers, and straight gripped stock. Blued, case hardened. Imported prior to 1988.

Exc.	V.G.	Good	Fair	Poor
7500	6000	4000	2000	900

Model 315 EL
As above, with more engraving and also available in .28 or .410 bore, which are worth approximately $1,000 more than the values listed below.

Exc.	V.G.	Good	Fair	Poor
10000	8000	5000	2500	1100

Model 315 EGL
As above, with a French case hardened receiver. Discontinued in 1987.

Exc.	V.G.	Good	Fair	Poor
15000	12000	8500	4000	1500

Model 315 EGL-S
As above, with engraved hunting scenes. Discontinued in 1987.

Exc.	V.G.	Good	Fair	Poor
5500	4500	3500	2000	1000

WALCH, JOHN
New York, New York

Navy Revolver

A .36 caliber superimposed load percussion revolver with a 6" octagonal barrel and a 6-shot cylinder fitted with 12 nipples, 2 hammers, and 2 triggers. The barrel marked "Walch Firearms Co. NY." and "Patented Feb. 8, 1859". Blued with walnut grips.

Exc.	V.G.	Good	Fair	Poor
—	—	8250	3250	950

Pocket Revolver

A spur trigger .31 caliber 10-shot percussion revolver with either a brass or iron frame and walnut grips. The iron frame version is worth approximately 50% more than the brass variety.

Exc.	V.G.	Good	Fair	Poor
—	—	2500	1000	300

WALDMAN
Germany

Waldman

A 7.65mm semiautomatic pistol with a 3.5" barrel and 8-shot magazine. The slide marked "1913 Model Automatic Pistol" and some examples are marked "American Automatic Pistol". Blued with checkered walnut grips inlaid with a brass insert marked "Waldman".

Exc.	V.G.	Good	Fair	Poor
300	225	200	150	100

WALLIS & BIRCH
Philadelphia, Pennsylvania

Pocket Pistol

A .41 caliber single shot percussion pocket pistol with a 2.5" or 3" barrel, German silver furniture and walnut stock. The barrels marked "Wallis & Birch Phila." Produced during the 1850s.

Exc.	V.G.	Good	Fair	Poor
—	—	1750	800	250

WALTHER, CARL
Zella Mehilis and Ulm/Donau, Germany

In 1886 Carl Walther set up a workshop to make sporting arms. Until 1900 his operation remained small. In 1907 he designed the 6.35mm blowback pistol. This design was offered for sale in 1908. In less than a year after the introduction of the first pistol the second model was introduced. Called the Model 2, this pistol was more advanced than the first design and became a popular handgun in Germany prior to WWI. Two years later the Model 3 was introduced and successive models were designed and produced through 1921 when the Model 9 was announced. In 1929 Walther built the now famous Model PP, Polizei Pistole, which became synonymous with quality and advanced design. The Walther legend was born and has been maintained up to this date as a fine high quality German built pistol. After WWII the Walther company relocated in Ulm/Donau, Germany.

Editors Comment: There are a large number of Walther variations, especially during the WWII era and it requires years of experience to learn the subtleties of these variations. When dealing with expensive Walther pistols it is suggested that an expert appraisal be obtained before buying or selling these highly collectable handguns.

Model 1

A 6.35mm semiautomatic pistol barrel lengths of 2-6". Blued with checkered hard rubber grips with the Walther logo on each grip. Introduced in 1908.

Courtesy James Rankin

Courtesy James Rankin

Exc.	V.G.	Good	Fair	Poor
800	450	350	200	200

Model 2

A 6.35mm semiautomatic pistol having a knurled bushing at the muzzle that retains the mainspring. There are two variations. One with a fixed rear sight, and one with a pop up rear sight. Blued with checkered hard rubber grips with the Walther logo on each grip. Introduced in 1909.

Courtesy James Rankin

Courtesy James Rankin

Fixed Sights

Exc.	V.G.	Good	Fair	Poor
650	500	300	200	150

Pop Up Sights

Exc.	V.G.	Good	Fair	Poor
1500	800	600	400	300

Model 3

A 7.65mm semiautomatic pistol having a smooth barrel bushing. Blued with checkered hard rubber grips with the Walther logo on each. Introduced in 1910.

Courtesy James Rankin

Courtesy James Rankin

Exc.	V.G.	Good	Fair	Poor
1500	1000	600	350	200

Model 4

A 7.65mm semiautomatic pistol larger than the preceding models. There were many variations of this model produced. Blued with checkered hard rubber grips with the Walther logo on each grip. Introduced 1910.

Courtesy James Rankin

Courtesy James Rankin

Exc.	V.G.	Good	Fair	Poor
450	375	300	200	150

Model 5

A 6.35mm semiautomatic pistol which is almost identical to the Model 2. Fixed sights. Blued with checkered hard rubber grips with the Walther logo on each grip.

Courtesy James Rankin

Courtesy James Rankin

Exc.	V.G.	Good	Fair	Poor
500	400	300	200	150

Model 6

A 9mm semiautomatic pistol. The largest of the Walther numbered pistols. Approximately 1,500 manufactured. Blued with checkered hard rubber grips with the Walther logo on each grip. Sometimes seen with plain checkered wood grips. Introduced 1915.

Courtesy James Rankin

Courtesy James Rankin

Exc.	V.G.	Good	Fair	Poor
7000	5000	3000	1500	700

Model 7

A 6.35mm semiautomatic pistol in the same style as the Model 4. Blued with checkered hard rubber grips with the Walther logo on each side. Introduced in 1917.

Courtesy James Rankin

Courtesy James Rankin

Exc.	V.G.	Good	Fair	Poor
550	400	300	200	150

Model 8

A 6.35mm semiautomatic pistol. Finishes in blue, silver, and gold. Three types of engraving coverage; slide only, slide and frame and complete coverage overall. The grips are checkered hard rubber with the WC logo on one grip, and 6.35mm on the opposite side. Ivory grips are seen with many of the engraved models. Introduced in 1920 and produced until 1944.

Courtesy James Rankin

Courtesy James Rankin

Courtesy James Rankin

Courtesy James Rankin

Blue, Silver, and Gold Finish

Exc.	V.G.	Good	Fair	Poor
575	375	300	200	150

Engraved Slide

Exc.	V.G.	Good	Fair	Poor
1000	700	500	300	200

Engraved Slide and Frame

Exc.	V.G.	Good	Fair	Poor
2000	1400	850	450	300

Engraved, Complete Coverage

Exc.	V.G.	Good	Fair	Poor
2500	1750	900	500	300

Model 9

A 6.35mm semiautomatic pistol. Smaller than the Model 8, but built as the Model 1 with exposed barrel. Same finishes and engraving as the Model 8. Introduced 1921 and produced until 1944.

All values the same as the Model 8.

Sport Model 1926   Walther Hammerless Target 22
Walther Standard Sport   Walther 1932 Olympia

Sport Model Target, Special Stoeger Model

All of these 22 l.r. caliber semiautomatic pistols are the same target pistol introduced by Walther in 1926. A well-made pistol with a barrel length of between 6"-16". It has one-piece checkered wrap-around wood grips. There was also a .22 Short version of the Olympia model produced for rapid fire Olympic shooting. There was also a torpedo shape target weight available for shooters.

Courtesy Orvel Reichert

Courtesy James Rankin

Exc.	V.G.	Good	Fair	Poor
850	650	450	350	250

Add $200 for target weight. Add $500 for case.

Walther 1936 Olympia

This semiautomatic target pistol in .22 caliber resembled the earlier 1932 Olympia, but with many improvements. There were four standard models produced with many variations of each one. These variations included many barrel lengths, and both round and octagon barrels. There were duraluminum slides, frames and triggers. Various weight configurations to as many as four separate weights to one gun. One-piece wrap-around checkered wood grips in different configurations for the individual shooter. Produced until 1944. The four models were:

Funfklamph Pentathlon
Jagerschafts-Hunter
Sport or Standard Model
Schnellfeur-Rapid Fire

Courtesy James Rankin

Olympia without weights   Courtesy John J. Stimson, Jr.

Exc.	V.G.	Good	Fair	Poor
1200	800	600	475	250

Add $250 for weights.

Model MP

A 9mm semiautomatic pistol which was the forerunner of the Model AP and P.38 series. Found in variations that resemble a large Model PP or the P.38. Blued finish with one-piece wrap-around checkered wood grips.

Courtesy James Rankin

Exc.	V.G.	Good	Fair	Poor
35000	30000	25000	20000	15000

Model AP

A 9mm semiautomatic pistol which was the forerunner of the Model P.38. A hammerless pistol in various barrel lengths. Sometimes with duraluminum frames, and some with stocks. Blued finish with one-piece wrap-around checkered wood grips.

Exc.	V.G.	Good	Fair	Poor
28000	25000	20000	15000	10000

NOTE: With stock add $4000.

Model PP

Courtesy James Rankin

A semiautomatic pistol in .22, .25, .32 and .380 caliber. Introduced in 1928. It was the first successful commercial double action pistol. It was manufactured in finishes of blue, silver, and gold, and with three different types of engraving. Grips were generally two-piece black or white plastic with the Walther banner on each grip. Grips in wood or ivory are seen, but usually on engraved guns. There are many variations of the Model PP and numerous NSDAP markings seen on the pre-1946 models that were produced during the Nazi regime. All reflect various prices.

Model PP .22 Caliber

Exc.	V.G.	Good	Fair	Poor
800	600	350	250	150

Model PP .25 Caliber

Exc.	V.G.	Good	Fair	Poor
5800	4000	2500	1500	600

Model PP .32 Caliber High Polished Finish

Exc.	V.G.	Good	Fair	Poor
450	325	275	225	175

Model PP .32 Caliber Milled Finish

Exc.	V.G.	Good	Fair	Poor
425	325	250	200	125

Model PP .380 Caliber

Exc.	V.G.	Good	Fair	Poor
950	750	550	475	350

Model PP .32 Caliber with Duraluminum Frame

Exc.	V.G.	Good	Fair	Poor
800	675	550	400	200

Model PP .32 Caliber with Bottom Magazine Release

Exc.	V.G.	Good	Fair	Poor
950	750	600	400	200

Model PP .32 Caliber with Verchromt Finish

Exc.	V.G.	Good	Fair	Poor
2000	1450	1000	700	400

Model PP .32 Caliber in Blue, Silver or Gold Finish and Full Coverage Engraving

Blue

Exc.	V.G.	Good	Fair	Poor
5000	3000	2500	1200	700

Silver

Exc.	V.G.	Good	Fair	Poor
5000	3000	2500	1200	700

Gold

Exc.	V.G.	Good	Fair	Poor
5000	3000	2500	1200	700

NOTE: Add $250 for ivory grips with any of the three above.
Add $700 for leather presentation cases.
Add $500 for .22 caliber.
Add $1000 for .380 caliber.

Model PP .32 Caliber, Allemagne Marked

Exc.	V.G.	Good	Fair	Poor
850	700	550	325	250

Model PP .32 Caliber, A. F. Stoeger Contract

Exc.	V.G.	Good	Fair	Poor
2000	1450	1050	700	400

Model PP .32 Caliber with Waffenampt Proofs. High Polished Finish

Exc.	V.G.	Good	Fair	Poor
900	650	375	275	150

Model PP .32 Caliber with Waffenampt Proofs. Milled Finish

Exc.	V.G.	Good	Fair	Poor
450	375	325	250	150

Model PP .32 Caliber. Police Eagle/C Proofed. High Polished Finish

Exc.	V.G.	Good	Fair	Poor
800	475	375	250	150

Model PP .32 Caliber. Police Eagle/C and Police Eagle/F Proofed. Milled Finish

Exc.	V.G.	Good	Fair	Poor
600	400	375	275	150

Model PP .32 Caliber. NSKK Marked On The Slide

Exc.	V.G.	Good	Fair	Poor
2200	1500	850	550	300

NOTE: Add $700 with proper NSKK DRGM AKAH holster.

Model PP .32 Caliber. NSDAP Gruppe Markings

Exc.	V.G.	Good	Fair	Poor
2000	1500	1000	500	300

NOTE: Add $600 with proper SA DRGM AKAH holster.

Model PP .32 Caliber. PDM Marked with Bottom Magazine Release

Exc.	V.G.	Good	Fair	Poor
850	700	550	475	300

Model PP .32 Caliber. RJ Marked

Exc.	V.G.	Good	Fair	Poor
750	600	475	400	150

Model PP .32 Caliber. RFV Marked. High Polished or Milled Finish

Exc.	V.G.	Good	Fair	Poor
700	600	475	400	150

Model PP .32 Caliber. RBD Munster Marked

Exc.	V.G.	Good	Fair	Poor
2200	1750	1200	650	400

Model PP .32 Caliber. RpLt Marked

Exc.	V.G.	Good	Fair	Poor
950	750	475	375	200

Model PP .32 Caliber. Statens Vattenfallsverk Marked

Exc.	V.G.	Good	Fair	Poor
850	700	550	375	200

Model PP .32 Caliber. AC Marked

Exc.	V.G.	Good	Fair	Poor
450	375	300	250	150

Model PP .32 Caliber. Duraluminum Frame

Exc.	V.G.	Good	Fair	Poor
750	600	500	400	150

Model PP .380 Caliber. Bottom Magazine Release and Waffenampt Proofs

Exc.	V.G.	Good	Fair	Poor
1550	1100	700	500	300

Model PPK

A semiautomatic pistol in .22, .25, .32 and .380 caliber. Introduced six months after the Model PP in 1929. A more compact version of the Model PP with one less round in the magazine and one-piece wrap-around checkered plastic grips in brown, black, and white with the Walther banner on each side of the grips. The Model PPK will be found with the same types of finishes as the Model PP as well as the same styles of engraving. Grips in wood or ivory are seen with some of the engraved models. As with the Model PP there are many variations of the Model PPK and numerous NSDAP markings seen on the pre-1946 models that were produced during the Nazi regime. All reflect various prices.

Courtesy Orvel Reichert

Courtesy James Rankin

Model PPK .22 Caliber

Exc.	V.G.	Good	Fair	Poor
1200	700	475	325	175

Model PPK .25 Caliber

Exc.	V.G.	Good	Fair	Poor
6000	4000	1850	1000	500

Model PPK .32 Caliber. High Polished Finish

Exc.	V.G.	Good	Fair	Poor
550	450	325	250	150

Model PPK .32 Caliber. Milled Finish

Exc.	V.G.	Good	Fair	Poor
500	400	325	250	150

Model PPK .380 Caliber

Courtesy Orvel Reichert

Exc.	V.G.	Good	Fair	Poor
2200	1750	1300	750	375

Model PPK .32 Caliber with Duraluminum Frame

Exc.	V.G.	Good	Fair	Poor
950	800	600	400	200

Model PPK .32 Caliber with Verchromt Finish

Exc.	V.G.	Good	Fair	Poor
2500	1800	1200	700	350

Model PPK .32 Caliber in Blue, Silver or Gold Finish and Full Coverage Engraving

Blue

Exc.	V.G.	Good	Fair	Poor
5000	3500	2500	1200	700

Silver

Exc.	V.G.	Good	Fair	Poor
5000	3500	2750	1200	700

Gold

Exc.	V.G.	Good	Fair	Poor
5000	3500	3000	1200	700

Add $750 for ivory grips with any of the three above.
Add $700 for leather presentation cases.
Add $500 for .22 caliber.
Add $1000 for .380 caliber.

Model PPK .32 Caliber Marked Mod. PP on Slide

Exc.	V.G.	Good	Fair	Poor
5000	4000	2500	1500	1000

Model PPK .32 Caliber with Panagraphed Slide

Exc.	V.G.	Good	Fair	Poor
750	550	450	300	200

Model PPK .32 Caliber. Czechoslovakian Contract

Exc.	V.G.	Good	Fair	Poor
1850	1500	1000	550	300

Model PPK .32 Caliber. Allemagne Marked

Exc.	V.G.	Good	Fair	Poor
800	700	600	400	250

Model PPK .32 Caliber with Waffenampt Proofs and a High Polished Finish

Exc.	V.G.	Good	Fair	Poor
1200	800	550	400	250

Model PPK .32 Caliber with Waffenampt Proofs and a Milled Finish

Exc.	V.G.	Good	Fair	Poor
900	700	375	300	175

Model PPK .32 Caliber. Police Eagle/C Proofed. High Polished Finish

Exc.	V.G.	Good	Fair	Poor
725	600	450	300	175

Model PPK .32 Caliber. Police Eagle/C Proofed. Milled Finish

Exc.	V.G.	Good	Fair	Poor
650	500	375	275	175

Model PPK .32 Caliber. Police Eagle/F Proofed. Duraluminum Frame. Milled Finish

Exc.	V.G.	Good	Fair	Poor
900	700	550	350	225

Model PPK .22 Caliber. Late War, Black Grips

Exc.	V.G.	Good	Fair	Poor
1200	750	600	450	300

Model PPK .32 Caliber. Party Leader Grips. Brown

Exc.	V.G.	Good	Fair	Poor
3000	2550	2350	2250	2000

Model PPK .32 Caliber. Party Leader Grips. Black

Exc.	V.G.	Good	Fair	Poor
3250	3000	2750	2550	2500

NOTE: If grips are badly cracked or damaged on the two Party Leaders above, reduce $2000 each valuation.
Add $500 with proper Party Leader DRGM AKAH holster.

Model PPK .32 Caliber. RZM Marked

Exc.	V.G.	Good	Fair	Poor
1200	900	500	400	300

Model PPK .32 Caliber. PDM Marked with Duraluminum Frame and Bottom Magazine Release

Exc.	V.G.	Good	Fair	Poor
2500	1800	1150	750	450

Model PPK .32 Caliber. RFV Marked

Exc.	V.G.	Good	Fair	Poor
2000	1750	1150	650	400

Model PPK .32 Caliber. DRP Marked

Exc.	V.G.	Good	Fair	Poor
800	650	550	450	275

Model PPK .32 Caliber. Statens Vattenfallsverk

Exc.	V.G.	Good	Fair	Poor
1400	1200	700	450	300

WALTHER POST WORLD WAR II

Models PP and PPK

Manufactured by the firm of Manufacture de Machines du Haut Rhin at Mulhouse, France under license by Walther.

Model PP Some with Duraluminum Frames. Model PP .22 Caliber

Exc.	V.G.	Good	Fair	Poor
750	600	400	275	175

Model PP 32 Caliber

Exc.	V.G.	Good	Fair	Poor
500	375	350	275	175

Model PP 380 Caliber

Exc.	V.G.	Good	Fair	Poor
750	600	400	275	175

Model PP. All Three Calibers Finished In Blue, Silver and

Gold With Full Coverage Engraving
Blue
Exc.	V.G.	Good	Fair	Poor
1700	1300	900	600	300

Silver
Exc.	V.G.	Good	Fair	Poor
1700	1300	900	600	300

Gold
Exc.	V.G.	Good	Fair	Poor
1700	1300	900	600	300

Model PP Mark II
These Walthers were manufactured under license by Walther and produced by the Manurhin Company. They were sold exclusively by Interarms, Alexandria, Virginia. The Mark IIs were the same pistols as those above and have the same types of finish and engraving as well as the same value.

Model PP Manurhin
Manurhin Company manufactured with Manurhin logo and inscription. Usually "licensed by Walther" somewhere on the pistol. The same pistols as those above, bearing the same types of finish and engraving, and having the same values.

Model PP Sport, Manurhin
.22 caliber. This is the same gun as the Model PP with different barrel lengths running from 5-3/4" to 7-3/4". It is basically a target .22 with adjustable rear sights for elevation and windage. The front sight is also adjustable. There is a barrel bushing at the muzzle that attaches the front sight to the barrel. The grips are contoured checkered plastic and are either squared at the bottom of the grips or are in the shape of an inverted bird's head.

Exc.	V.G.	Good	Fair	Poor
900	600	450	375	275

Mode PP Sport C, Manurhin
.22 caliber. This is the same gun as the Model PP Sport but in single action with a spur hammer. It has front and rear adjustable sights and squared target grips in checkered black, brown and plastic. Blued and silver finish.

Exc.	V.G.	Good	Fair	Poor
900	600	450	375	275

Model PP Sport, Walther
A .22 caliber Sport was manufactured by Manurhin, but sold by the Walther with the Walther logo and inscription. This is the same gun as the Model PP Sport, Manurhin. Only sold for a period of two years.

Walther PP Sport   Courtesy John J. Stimson, Jr.

Exc.	V.G.	Good	Fair	Poor
900	600	450	375	275

Model PP Fiftieth Anniversary Commemorative Model
In .22 or .380 caliber. Blued with gold inlays and hand carved grips with oak leaves and acorns. Walther banner carved into each side of the grips. Wood presentation case.

Exc.	V.G.	Good	Fair	Poor
1500	1000	750	500	300

Model PPK. Some With Duraluminum Frames
Model PPK. .22 Caliber
Exc.	V.G.	Good	Fair	Poor
750	600	400	275	175

Model PPK. .32 Caliber
Exc.	V.G.	Good	Fair	Poor
550	400	350	275	175

Model PPK. .380 Caliber
Exc.	V.G.	Good	Fair	Poor
750	600	400	275	175

Model PPK. All Three Calibers Finished In Blue, Silver and Gold With Full Coverage Engraving
Blue
Exc.	V.G.	Good	Fair	Poor
1750	1300	750	450	300

Silver
Exc.	V.G.	Good	Fair	Poor
1750	1300	750	450	300

Gold
Exc.	V.G.	Good	Fair	Poor
1850	1400	750	450	300

Model PPK Mark II
These Walthers were manufactured under license by Walther and produced by the Manurhin Company. They were sold exclusively by Interarms, Alexandria, Virginia. The Mark IIs were the same pistols as those above and have the same types of finish and engraving as well as the same value.

Model PPK Manurhin
Manurhin Company manufactured with Manurhin logo and inscription. Usually "Licensed by Walther" somewhere on the pistol. The same pistols as above, bearing the same types of finish and engraving, and having the same value.

Courtesy James Rankin

Model PPK Fiftieth Anniversary Commemorative Model
In .22 or .380 caliber. Blued with gold inlays and hand carved grips with oak leaves and acorns. Walther banner carved into each side of the grips. Wood presentation case.

Exc.	V.G.	Good	Fair	Poor
2100	1800	1250	1000	500

Model PPK/S

This Walther was manufactured in .22, .32 and .380 caliber for sale in the United States market after the introduction of the United States Gun Control Act of 1968. It is basically a Model PP with a cut-off muzzle and slide. It has two-piece black checkered plastic grips as seen on the Model PP. It was finished in blue, nickel, dull gold and verchromt.

Exc.	V.G.	Good	Fair	Poor
550	475	375	300	200

Model PPK American

In 1986 the Model PPK was licensed by the Walther Company to be manufactured in the United States. The finish is stainless steel. Caliber is .380.

Exc.	V.G.	Good	Fair	Poor
500	375	300	200	150

Model PPK/S American

Manufactured in the United States. The same as the German Model PPK/S. This pistol is finished in blue and stainless steel. Caliber is 380.

Exc.	V.G.	Good	Fair	Poor
500	375	300	200	150

Model TP

A Walther manufactured semiautomatic pistol in .22 and .25 calibers patterned after the earlier Model 9. Finish is blue and silver black plastic checkered grips with Walther banner medallions in each grip.

Exc.	V.G.	Good	Fair	Poor
750	600	500	375	250

Model TPH

A Walther manufactured semiautomatic pistol in .22 and .25 calibers. This is a double action pistol with a duraluminum frame. Finished in blue or silver. Two-piece black checkered plastic grips. Full coverage engraving available.

Exc.	V.G.	Good	Fair	Poor
650	500	450	350	250

Add $300 for the engraved model.

Model TPH American

This semiautomatic is produced in both .22 and .25 calibers. It is licensed by Walther and manufactured in the United States. It is produced in stainless steel and has two-piece black plastic checkered grips. It is a double action pistol.

Exc.	V.G.	Good	Fair	Poor
400	300	200	150	100

Model PP Super

This is a .380 and 9x18 caliber, double action semiautomatic manufactured by Walther. It is similar in design to the Model PP, but with a P.38 type of mechanism. Finish is blue and the grips are wrap-around black checkered plastic or a type of molded wood colored plastic.

Courtesy Orvel Reichert

Exc.	V.G.	Good	Fair	Poor
550	450	350	250	150

P-38 GERMAN MILITARY SERVICE PISTOLS-*SEE P-38 SECTION*

Model P-38

Following WWII, the P-38 was reintroduced in variety of calibers with a 5" barrel and alloy or steel frame.

.22 Caliber

NIB	Exc.	V.G.	Good	Fair	Poor
1000	800	650	500	350	200

Other Calibers

NIB	Exc.	V.G.	Good	Fair	Poor
750	600	500	400	300	200

Steel-Framed (Introduced 1987)

NIB	Exc.	V.G.	Good	Fair	Poor
1400	1250	1000	750	500	400

Factory-engraved versions of the P-38 pistol were blued, chrome, or silver or gold-plated. We suggest that a qualified appraisal be secured when contemplating purchase.

Model P-38K

As above, with a 2.8" barrel and front sight is mounted on the slide. Imported between 1974 and 1980.

Exc.	V.G.	Good	Fair	Poor
800	600	450	400	300

Model P-38 IV

A redesigned version of the above, with a 4.5" barrel and 8-shot magazine. Fitted with a decocking lever and adjustable sights. Imported prior to 1983.

Exc.	V.G.	Good	Fair	Poor
700	600	450	400	300

CURRENTLY IMPORTED WALTHER PISTOLS-WALTHER USA

In 1999 Carl Walther Gmbh of Germany and Smith & Wesson entered into a joint agreement to import and distribute Walther branded firearms and accessories into the U.S. beginning August 1, 1999.

Model PP Limited Edition

This model was introduced in 2000 and is a limited edition of 100 pistols chambered in .380ACP and 50 pistols chambered in .32ACP. The finish is a high polish blue with the slide marked "LAST EDITION 1929-1999". Supplied with a special case with certificate and video of history of Walther.

NIB	Exc.	V.G.	Good	Fair	Poor
1100	—	—	—	—	—

Model PPK/E-Walther USA

Introduced in 2000 this pistol is chambered for the .380 or .32ACP cartridges and later in that year the .22 Long Rifle. It has a double action trigger. Produced in Hungary by Walther. Barrel length is 3.4". Magazine capacity is 7 rounds for the .380 and 8 rounds for the .32ACP and .22 Long Rifle. Blued finish and plastic grips.

NIB	Exc.	V.G.	Good	Fair	Poor
275	225	—	—	—	—

Model PPK

Chambered for the .380 ACP or .32 ACP cartridge and fitted with a 3.35" barrel. Offered in blue or stainless steel. Black plastic grips. Fixed red dot sights. Magazine is 6 for the .380 ACP and 7 for the .32 ACP. Weight is about 21 oz.

NIB	Exc.	V.G.	Good	Fair	Poor
525	425	—	—	—	—

Model PPK/S

Same as the PPK but with .25" longer grip. Magazine capacity is 7 rounds for the .380 ACP and 8 rounds for the .32 ACP. Weight is about 23 oz. Offered in blue, stainless steel and two-tone finish.

NIB	Exc.	V.G.	Good	Fair	Poor
525	425	—	—	—	—

Model P 5

A 9mm semiautomatic pistol with a double action firing mechanism. One of the first Walthers to have a decocker lever. Finish is a combination of black matte and high polish. It has black plastic checkered grips.

NIB	Exc.	V.G.	Good	Fair	Poor
875	650	500	400	300	—

Model P 5, Compact

A shorter version of the standard Model P 5.

NIB	Exc.	V.G.	Good	Fair	Poor
850	700	600	375	250	—

Model P 5 One Hundred Year Commemorative

Blued with gold inlays and hand carved grips with oak leaves and acorns. Walther banner carved into each side of the grips.

Wood presentation case

NIB	Exc.	V.G.	Good	Fair	Poor
2000	1500	—	—	—	—

Model P 88

A 9mm semiautomatic in double action with ambidextrous decocking lever. Fifteen shot magazine and two-piece black checkered plastic grips. Combination of high polish and black matte finish.

NIB	Exc.	V.G.	Good	Fair	Poor
875	700	600	500	300	—

Model P 88 Compact

A shorter version of the standard Model P88.

NIB	Exc.	V.G.	Good	Fair	Poor
850	700	600	500	300	—

Model P 99

Introduced in 1997 this is a single and double action design with a 4" barrel and polymer frame. Chambered for 9mm or .40S&W cartridge it has a magazine capacity of 10 rounds (16 rounds in 9mm and 12 rounds in .40S&W for law enforcement). Front is interchangeable and rear is windage adjustable. Total length of pistol is 7" and weight is approximately 25 oz. Finish is blue tenifer.

NIB	Exc.	V.G.	Good	Fair	Poor
700	550	450	—	—	—

Model P 990

A double action only version of the P 99.

NIB	Exc.	V.G.	Good	Fair	Poor
700	550	450	—	—	—

Model P 99 QPQ

Similar to the P 99 but with silver tenifer finish.

NIB	Exc.	V.G.	Good	Fair	Poor
700	550	450	—	—	—

Model P 990 QPQ

A double action only version of the P 99 QPQ.

NIB	Exc.	V.G.	Good	Fair	Poor
700	550	450	—	—	—

Model P 99 QA

Similar to the P99 pistol but with a constant short trigger pull. Trigger pull is approximately 6.5 lbs. Offered in both 9mm and .40S&W calibers. Introduced in 2000.

NIB	Exc.	V.G.	Good	Fair	Poor
700	550	450	—	—	—

Model P 99 Military

Similar to the P99 but with military finish.

NIB	Exc.	V.G.	Good	Fair	Poor
700	550	450	—	—	—

Model P 99 La Chasse DU

This model features laser engraving on the blue tenifer slide.

NIB	Exc.	V.G.	Good	Fair	Poor
750	600	—	—	—	—

Model P 99 La Chasse

This model features hand engraving on a gray tenifer slide.

NIB	Exc.	V.G.	Good	Fair	Poor
1675	1250	—	—	—	—

Model P 99 Commemorative

This is a limited edition P99 that features a high polish blue slide with a special serial number and the marking" COMMEMORATIVE FOR THE YEAR 2000". Offered in both 9mm and .40S&W calibers. Each handgun comes with a special certificate and video of the history of Walther.

NIB	Exc.	V.G.	Good	Fair	Poor
720	—	—	—	—	—

Model FP

A .22 Long Rifle caliber, single-shot target pistol that fires electrically. It has micro adjustable electric firing system along with micrometer sights and contoured wooden grips that are adjustable. The barrel is 11.7" and the finish is blued.

Exc.	V.G.	Good	Fair	Poor
2000	1600	1000	500	400

Model GSP

A semiautomatic target pistol in .22 l.r. and .38 calibers. This target pistol has a 4-1/2" barrel, 5-shot magazine and contoured wood target grips. Blued finish and sold with attache case and accessories.

Courtesy John J. Stimson, Jr.

Exc.	V.G.	Good	Fair	Poor
1600	1200	750	650	300

Model GSP-C

Almost the same pistol as the Model GSP, but in .32 caliber S&W wadcutter.

Exc.	V.G.	Good	Fair	Poor
1500	1100	750	650	300

Model OSP

A .22 Short semiautomatic target pistol that is similar to the Model GSP. This pistol is made for rapid fire target shooting. Blued finish with contoured wood grips.

Exc.	V.G.	Good	Fair	Poor
1800	1200	750	650	300

Free Pistol

A .22 caliber single shot target pistol with an 11.7" barrel, micrometer sights, adjustable grips and an electronic trigger. Blued.

NIB	Exc.	V.G.	Good	Fair	Poor
1900	1600	1200	900	700	550

Model R99

This 6 shot revolver is chambered for the .357 Magnum cartridge. Barrel length is 3". Weight is about 28 oz. Offered in blue or stainless steel. Introduced in 1999.

NIB	Exc.	V.G.	Good	Fair	Poor
N/A	—	—	—	—	—

Model B

A .30-06 caliber bolt action rifle with a 22" barrel, 4-shot magazine and single or double set triggers. Double set triggers are worth approximately 20% more than the values listed below. Blued with a walnut stock.

Exc.	V.G.	Good	Fair	Poor
575	500	350	250	175

Olympic Single Shot

A .22 caliber bolt action rifle with a 26" barrel, adjustable target sights and a walnut stock fitted with a palm rest and adjustable buttplate. Blued.

Exc.	V.G.	Good	Fair	Poor
950	850	700	500	400

Model V

A .22 caliber single-shot bolt action rifle with a 26" barrel and adjustable sights. Blued with a plain walnut stock. Manufactured before WWII.

Exc.	V.G.	Good	Fair	Poor
450	400	300	200	150

Model V Champion

As above, with a checkered walnut stock.

Exc.	V.G.	Good	Fair	Poor
500	400	350	250	200

Model KKM International Match

A .22 caliber single shot bolt action rifle with a 28" barrel and adjustable sights. Blued with a walnut stock fitted for a palm rest and with an adjustable buttplate. Manufactured after WWII.

Exc.	V.G.	Good	Fair	Poor
1400	1100	850	450	350

Model KKM-S

As above, with an adjustable cheekpiece.

Exc.	V.G.	Good	Fair	Poor
1400	1100	850	500	400

Model KKW

As above, with a military-style stock.

Exc.	V.G.	Good	Fair	Poor
900	700	500	350	300

Model KKJ Sporter

A .22 caliber bolt action rifle with a 22.5" barrel and 5-shot magazine. Blued with a checkered walnut stock. This model was available with double set triggers and their presence would add approximately 20% to the values listed below. Manufactured after WWII.

Exc.	V.G.	Good	Fair	Poor
700	600	450	350	300

Model KKJ-MA

As above, in .22 rimfire Magnum.

Exc.	V.G.	Good	Fair	Poor
650	550	450	350	300

Model KKJ-HO

As above, in .22 Hornet.

Exc.	V.G.	Good	Fair	Poor
750	700	600	450	350

Model SSV Varmint

A .22 caliber bolt action single shot rifle with a 25.5" barrel not fitted with sights and Monte Carlo-style stock. Blued. Manufactured after WWII.

Exc.	V.G.	Good	Fair	Poor
700	600	475	375	300

Model UIT BV Universal

As above, with adjustable target sights and a walnut stock fitted with a palm rest and adjustable buttplate.

NIB	Exc.	V.G.	Good	Fair	Poor
1750	1500	1250	900	650	500

Model UIT Match

As above, with a stippled pistol grip and forend. Also available with an electronic trigger that would add approximately $50 to the values listed below.

NIB	Exc.	V.G.	Good	Fair	Poor
1350	1100	800	600	450	400

GX 1

As above, with an adjustable Free Rifle stock.

NIB	Exc.	V.G.	Good	Fair	Poor
2250	2000	1750	1250	850	700

Prone Model 400
As above, with a prone position stock.

NIB	Exc.	V.G.	Good	Fair	Poor
750	700	600	450	350	300

Model KK/MS Silhouette
A .22 caliber bolt action rifle with a 25.5" front-weighted barrel furnished without sights and a thumb hole stock having an adjustable buttplate. Introduced in 1984.

NIB	Exc.	V.G.	Good	Fair	Poor
1300	1100	850	700	550	400

Running Boar Model 500
As above, with a 23.5" barrel.

NIB	Exc.	V.G.	Good	Fair	Poor
1550	1350	950	750	600	450

Model WA-2000
A .300 Winchester Magnum or .308 caliber bolt action sporting rifle produced on custom order. Prospective purchasers are advised to secure an appraisal prior to acquisition. Imported prior to 1989.

Exc.	V.G.	Good	Fair	Poor
6500	4750	3500	3000	2000

Model SF
A 12 or 16 gauge boxlock double barrel shotgun fitted with double triggers and extractors. Blued with a checkered walnut stock fitted with sling swivels.

Exc.	V.G.	Good	Fair	Poor
900	600	500	250	100

Model SFD
As above, with the stock having a cheekpiece.

Exc.	V.G.	Good	Fair	Poor
1000	750	650	425	250

WALTHER MANURHIN
Mulhouse, France
The Manurhin-manufactured Walther pistols are listed in the Walther section of this text under their respective model headings.

WANZEL
SEE—Austrian Military Firearms

WARNANT, L. AND J.
Ognee, Belgium

Revolver
Modeled after pistols manufactured by Smith & Wesson, the Warnants produced a variety of revolvers in .32, .38, or .45 caliber, between 1870 and 1890.

Exc.	V.G.	Good	Fair	Poor
—	175	75	60	50

Semiautomatic Pistol
A 6.35mm semiautomatic pistol with a 2.5" barrel and 5-shot magazine. The slide marked "L&J Warnant Bte 6.35mm". Blued with black plastic grips bearing the monogram "L&JW." Manufactured after 1908.

Exc.	V.G.	Good	Fair	Poor
300	200	150	100	75

1912 Model
A 7.65mm caliber semiautomatic pistol with a 3" barrel and 7-shot magazine. The slide marked "L&J Warnant Brevetes Pist Auto 7.65mm". Manufactured prior to 1915.

Exc.	V.G.	Good	Fair	Poor
300	200	150	100	75

WARNER ARMS CORPORATION
Brooklyn, New York and Norwich, Connecticut
Established in 1912, this firm marketed revolvers, rifles, semiautomatic pistols and shotguns made for them by other companies (including N.R. Davis & Sons, Ithaca Gun Company and so forth). In 1917, the company was purchased by N.R. Davis & Company. *See also Davis-Warner.*

The arms marketed by Warner Prior to 1917 are as follows:

SHOTGUNS

Single Trigger Hammerless Utica Special Double Barrel
In 12 gauge with 28", 30", or 32" barrels.

Double Trigger Hammerless Double Barrel
In 12 or 16 gauge with 28", 30", or 32" barrels.

Grade X, SF, XT, SFT, XD and XDF Hammer Guns
In 12, 16 or 20 gauge with 28", 30", or 32" barrels.

Field Grade Hammer Gun
In 12 or 16 gauge with 28" or 30" barrels.

Box Lock Hammerless
In 12 or 16 gauge with 28", 30", or 32" barrels.

RIFLES

Number 522
A .22 caliber single-shot rifle with an 18" barrel.

Number 532
A .32 caliber single-shot rifle with an 18" barrel.

REVOLVERS

Double Action
.32 and .38 caliber with 4" or 5" barrels.

Double Action Hammerless
.32 and .38 caliber with 4" or 5" barrels.

SEMIAUTOMATIC PISTOLS

"Faultless": Warner-Schwarzlose Model C, .32 ACP.

Exc.	V.G.	Good	Fair	Poor
—	500	300	200	100

WARNER, CHAS.
Windsor Locks, Connecticut

Pocket Revolver
A .31 caliber percussion revolver with a 3" round barrel and 6-shot unfluted cylinder. The cylinder marked "Charles Warner. Windsor Locks, Conn." Blued with walnut grips. Approximately 600 were made between 1857 and 1860.

Exc.	V.G.	Good	Fair	Poor
—	—	850	350	100

WARNER, JAMES
Springfield, Massachusetts

Revolving Carbines
A variety of revolving carbines were made by this maker, nearly all of which are of .40 caliber, with octagonal barrels measuring 20" to 24" in length. The most commonly encountered variations are as follows:

Manually Revolved Grooved Cylinder

This model is fitted with two triggers one of which is a release so that the cylinder can be manually turned. Not fitted with a loading lever. The top strap marked "James Warner/Springfield, Mass." Approximately 75 were made in 1849.

Courtesy Milwaukee Public Museum, Milwaukee, Wisconsin

Exc.	V.G.	Good	Fair	Poor
—	—	4250	2000	500

Retractable Cylinder Model

This version has a cylinder that fits over the breech, and it must be retracted before it can be manually rotated. The cylinder release is a button located in front of the trigger. It is marked "James Warner/Springfield Mass" and with an eagle over the letters "U.S." The cylinder is etched, and there is no loading lever. It also has a walnut stock with patch box and no forearm. There were approximately 25 manufactured in 1849.

Exc.	V.G.	Good	Fair	Poor
—	—	5750	2500	800

Automatic Revolving Cylinder

The cylinder is automatically turned when the hammer is cocked. This model is fitted with a loading lever and is marked "Warner's Patent/Jan. 1851" and "Springfield Arms Co." Approximately 200 were made during the 1850s.

Courtesy Milwaukee Public Museum, Milwaukee, Wisconsin

Exc.	V.G.	Good	Fair	Poor
—	—	4000	1750	500

Belt Revolver

A .31 caliber double action percussion revolver with a 4" or 5" round barrel and 6-shot etched cylinder. Blued with walnut grips. No markings appear on this model except for the serial number. Manufactured in 1851.

Courtesy Milwaukee Public Museum, Milwaukee, Wisconsin

Exc.	V.G.	Good	Fair	Poor
—	—	1500	600	100

Pocket Revolver

A .28 caliber percussion revolver with a 3" octagonal barrel marked "James Warner, Springfield, Mass., USA" and a 6-shot cylinder. Blued with walnut grips. Approximately 500 were made.

Exc.	V.G.	Good	Fair	Poor
—	—	500	200	100

Second Model

As above, with either a 3" or 4" barrel and marked "Warner's Patent 1857."

Courtesy Wallis & Wallis, Lewes, Sussex, England

Exc.	V.G.	Good	Fair	Poor
—	—	650	300	100

Third Model

As above, but in .31 caliber.

Exc.	V.G.	Good	Fair	Poor
—	—	500	250	100

Single Shot Derringer

A .41 caliber rimfire single shot pocket pistol with a 2.75" round barrel, brass frame and walnut grips. As this model is unmarked, it can only be identified by the large breechblock which lifts upward and to the left for loading.

Exc.	V.G.	Good	Fair	Poor
—	—	17500	6500	1000

Pocket Revolver

A .30 caliber rimfire revolver with a 3" barrel marked "Warner's Patent 1857" and 5-shot cylinder. Blued or nickel-plated with walnut grips. Approximately 1,000 were made during the late 1860s.

Exc.	V.G.	Good	Fair	Poor
—	—	350	150	75

WATSON BROTHERS
London, England
SEE—British Double Guns

WEATHERBY
Atascadero, California

This corporation was founded in 1945 by Roy Weatherby. He pioneered the high-velocity hunting rifle. His rifles were designed to fire cartridges that he also produced. They are examples of fine craftsmanship and have been used to take some of the top trophy animals from all around the world. Formerly these rifles were manufactured in West Germany. They are currently produced in Japan. Although the Japanese rifles are, in the opinion of the editors, every bit as fine a firearm as the German versions, collectors have dictated an approximate 15% premium assessed to the German-manufactured versions. The values given are for the current-production Japanese weapons. Simply add the premium for a German-manufactured rifle. There are other premiums that collectors are paying in 1994 and these are as follows:

NOTE: For German calibers .224 through .300 add 25% for 24" barrels and 35% for 26" barrels.

Mark V

This is a deluxe, bolt action repeating rifle chambered for various popular standard calibers, as well as the full line of Weatherby cartridges from .240 Weatherby Magnum to .300 Weatherby Magnum. It is furnished with either a 24" or 26" barrel without sights. It has either a 3- or 5-round magazine, depending on the caliber. It has a deluxe, high-polish blued finish with a select, skip-line checkered walnut stock with a rosewood forearm tip and pistol grip cap. This rifle is available with a left-hand action.

NIB	Exc.	V.G.	Good	Fair	Poor
1000	850	700	600	500	400

Mark V Sporter

Introduced in 1993 this model is identical to the Mark V Deluxe without the custom features. The metal is a low luster finish, the stock is claro walnut with high gloss finish. A Monte Carlo comb with raised cheekpiece and black 1" recoil pad are standard features on this model. Available in Weatherby calibers from .257 through .340 plus .270 Win., .30-06, 7mm Rem. Mag., .300 Win Mag., .338 Win. Mag. Weighs 8 to 8.5 lbs. depending on caliber.

NIB	Exc.	V.G.	Good	Fair	Poor
660	600	500	400	350	300

Mark V .340 Weatherby Magnum

This version is chambered for a larger magnum cartridge and is offered with the 26" barrel only.
For German guns in this caliber-Add 70%.

NIB	Exc.	V.G.	Good	Fair	Poor
1050	900	750	650	550	400

Mark V .375 Weatherby Magnum

This version was manufactured in Germany only and is chambered for the currently obsolete .375 Weatherby Magnum cartridge. This version has become very collectible.

NIB	Exc.	V.G.	Good	Fair	Poor
5000	3500	3000	2500	2000	1500

Mark V .378 Weatherby Magnum

This version is chambered for the .378 Weatherby Magnum cartridge and is considered to be one of the most powerful rifles currently available in the world. It is furnished with a 26" barrel only.
For German guns in this caliber-Add 50%.

NIB	Exc.	V.G.	Good	Fair	Poor
1100	900	700	500	450	400

Mark V .416 Weatherby Magnum

This is an extremely powerful rifle suitable for hunting the biggest game. It is the first new caliber to be released by Weatherby since 1965. It was introduced in 1989.

NIB	Exc.	V.G.	Good	Fair	Poor
1100	900	700	—	—	—

Mark V .460 Weatherby Magnum

This is the most powerful commercial rifle available in the world. It is considered to be overkill for any game except the largest and most dangerous creatures that roam the African continent. It is available with a 24" or 26" heavy barrel with an integral, recoil-reducing muzzle brake. It has a custom reinforced stock.
For German guns in this caliber-Add 100%.

NIB	Exc.	V.G.	Good	Fair	Poor
1350	1200	1000	800	—	—

Mark V Dangerous Game Rifle

This model was introduced in 2001 and features a synthetic stock with Monte Carlo and 24" or 26" barrel with barrel band and hooded front sight depending on caliber. Chambered for the .378 Weatherby Mag., .416 Weatherby Mag., and the .460 Weatherby Mag. Adjustable trigger. Weight is between 8.74 and 9.5 lbs. depending on caliber.

NIB	Exc.	V.G.	Good	Fair	Poor
2600	2000	—	—	—	—

Mark V Fluted Stainless

Introduced late in 1996 this model features a fluted stainless steel barrel chambered for the .257 Weatherby Magnum to the .300 Weatherby Magnum calibers as well as the 7mm Rem. Mag. and the .300 Win. Mag. The stock is synthetic with raised comb and checkered stock. Weight varies depending on caliber.

NIB	Exc.	V.G.	Good	Fair	Poor
1100	850	700	500	—	—

Mark V Fluted Synthetic

This model is similar to the above model with a blued carbon steel action and barrel with synthetic stock. Introduced late in 1996.

NIB	Exc.	V.G.	Good	Fair	Poor
900	725	600	—	—	—

Mark V SLS

This model features a stainless steel barreled action with laminated wood stock fitted with a 1" black recoil pad. Rifle is chambered for .257 through .340 Weatherby Magnum calibers as well as .7mm Rem. Mag., .300 and .338 Win. Mag., and the .375 H&H Mag. Weight is about 8.25 lbs. depending on caliber. Introduced in late 1996.

NIB	Exc.	V.G.	Good	Fair	Poor
1200	950	750	—	—	—

Mark V Varmint

This version is chambered for the .22-250 and the .224 Weatherby cartridge. It is offered with a 24" or 26" heavy barrel.

NIB	Exc.	V.G.	Good	Fair	Poor
975	800	750	550	450	400

NOTE: For German built add 50%.

Mark V Euromark

This model features a hand-checkered, oil-finished, claro walnut stock with an ebony forend tip and pistol grip cap. It has a satin blued finish. It was introduced in 1986.

NIB	Exc.	V.G.	Good	Fair	Poor
1050	900	750	650	—	—

Mark V Lazermark

This version had a laser-carved pattern on the stock and forearm in place of the usual checkering. It was introduced in 1985.

NIB	Exc.	V.G.	Good	Fair	Poor
1100	1000	800	700	—	—

Mark V Fibermark

This version has a matte blue finish and is furnished with a synthetic black, wrinkle-finished stock. Chambered for calibers from .22-250 to .375 H&H with barrel lengths from 24" to 26" depending on caliber.

NIB	Exc.	V.G.	Good	Fair	Poor
900	700	—	—	—	—

NOTE: Add $200 for stainless steel models.

Mark V Ultramark

This is a custom-finished version with a glass-bedded action and a special, high-polish blue. The action is hand-honed, and the walnut stock features basket weave checkering. It was introduced in 1989.

NIB	Exc.	V.G.	Good	Fair	Poor
1250	1150	900	750	—	—

Mark V Accumark

Introduced in 1995 this rifle features a Mark V Magnum action. The trigger is preset at the factory for 3.5 lbs. of pull. It is fully adjustable for sear engagement at let-off weight. The action metal is black oxide coated with a bead blast matte finish. The stainless steel barrel is 26" in length with a low luster brushed finish. Weight is approximately 8 lbs. and is offered in caliber from .257 to .340 Weatherby Magnum, 7mm Rem. Magnum, and .300 Win. Magnum. In August the company announced that this model would also be offered in the .30-.378 Weatherby caliber. In 1997 this model was offered chambered for the 7mm STW cartridge. Available in right hand only.

Mark V Accumark

Mark V Accumark for .30-.378 Weatherby Magnum

NIB	Exc.	V.G.	Good	Fair	Poor
1250	1000	850	—	—	—

Mark V Accumark Left Hand

This is a left hand version of the Accumark. Introduced in 1999.

NIB	Exc.	V.G.	Good	Fair	Poor
1400	1100	950	800	—	—

35th Anniversary Commemorative Mark V

This specially embellished rifle commemorated the 35th anniversary of the company. There were 1,000 produced in 1980. As with all commemoratives, it must be NIB with all furnished materials to be worth top dollar.

NIB	Exc.	V.G.	Good	Fair	Poor
1500	1150	900	750	—	—

1984 Olympic Commemorative Mark V

This is a specially embellished Mark V rifle that has gold-plated accents and an exhibition-grade walnut stock with a star inlay. There were 1,000 manufactured in 1984. This is a commemorative rifle and must be NIB to bring premium value.

NIB	Exc.	V.G.	Good	Fair	Poor
1500	900	750	600	—	—

Safari Grade Mark V

This is a custom-order version that is available chambered from the .300 Weatherby Magnum through the .460 Weatherby Magnum. It is available with a number of custom options and can be ordered with an 8- to 10-month delivery delay.

NIB	Exc.	V.G.	Good	Fair	Poor
3000	2750	2000	1200	—	—

Crown Grade Mark V

This is Weatherby's best-grade rifle and is available on a custom-order basis only. It features an engraved receiver and barrel with an exhibition-grade, hand-checkered walnut stock. It is also furnished with an engraved scope mount.

NIB	Exc.	V.G.	Good	Fair	Poor
4500	3500	2750	1500	—	—

Mark V Super Varmint Master (SVM)

Introduced in 2000 this model features a 26" stainless steel barrel. The stock is laminated with Monte Carlo comb. Fully adjustable trigger. Chambered for .220 Swift, .223 Rem., .22-250, .243 Win., 7mm-08, and .308 Win. Also offered in a single shot configuration. Weight is about 8.5 lbs.

NIB	Exc.	V.G.	Good	Fair	Poor
1375	1000	—	—	—	—

MARK V LIGHTWEIGHT RIFLES

Mark V Synthetic Lightweight

Chambered in calibers from .22-250 to .308 Win. fitted with a 24" barrel. Synthetic stock with Monte Carlo comb. Magazine capacity is 5 rounds. Weight is approximately 6.5 lbs. A carbine version is offered with 20" barrel in .243, 7mm-08, and .308. Weight is about 6 lbs.

NIB	Exc.	V.G.	Good	Fair	Poor
700	550	—	—	—	—

Mark V Stainless Lightweight

Similar to the model above but with stainless steel barrel and action. Weight is about 6.5 lbs. Carbine version also available.

NIB	Exc.	V.G.	Good	Fair	Poor
900	725	600	500	—	—

Mark V Sporter Lightweight

Chambered for calibers ranging from .22-250 to .308 Win. and fitted with a 24" barrel. Stock is claro walnut with Monte Carlo comb. Weight is approximately 6.75 lbs.

NIB	Exc.	V.G.	Good	Fair	Poor
850	675	500	—	—	—

Mark V Accumark Lightweight

Chambered for calibers from .22-250 to .300 Wby. and fitted with a 24" barrel. Magazine capacity is 5 rounds. Special laminated synthetic stock. Weight is approximately 7 lbs. Introduced in 1998.

NIB	Exc.	V.G.	Good	Fair	Poor
1100	850	750	600	—	—

Mark V Ultra Lightweight

Similar to the above model but with lightened components. Calibers begin with .243 and go to .300 Wby. Fitted with a 24" or 26" barrel depending on caliber. Weight is about 5.75 lbs. Introduced in 1998. In 2000 this model was offered in a left hand version. In 2001 this model was available chambered for the .338-06 A-Square cartridge.

NIB	Exc.	V.G.	Good	Fair	Poor
1250	850	700	—	—	—

Mark V Deluxe Lightweight

This model, in its lightweight configuration, is offered In calibers from .22-25- to .30-06. These calibers are fitted to a 24" barrel. Fitted with hand select walnut Monte Carlo stock with rosewood forend tip and pistol grip cap. Fine line checkering. Weight is about 6.75 lbs. Introduced in 1999.

NIB	Exc.	V.G.	Good	Fair	Poor
1450	1100	950	800	—	—

Mark V SPM (Super Predator Master)

Introduced in 2001 this rifle features a 24" blackened stainless steel fluted barrel. Chambered for the .223 Rem., .22-250 Rem., .243 Win., 7mm-08 Rem., and the .308 Win. cartridges.

Fully adjustable trigger. Synthetic stock. Weight is about 6.5 lbs. Right hand only.

NIB	Exc.	V.G.	Good	Fair	Poor
1450	1150	—	—	—	—

WARNING: WEATHERBY VANGUARD

DO NOT use this model until the company performs a safety upgrade to the bolt. The rifle can accidentally discharge without the bolt being fully engaged. The affected rifles bear serial numbers from one of the following series on the receiver: 00001 through 03810; V00001 through V80966; VX00001 through VX44065; VS00001 through VS23699; VL00001 through VL46984; W00001 through W0099; NV0001 through NV0099.

Vanguard VGX

This was Weatherby's Japanese-manufactured economy rifle. It is chambered for various popular standard American cartridges from .22-50 to the .300 Winchester Magnum cartridge. It is a bolt action repeater with a 24" barrel furnished without sights. It has either a 3-shot or 5-shot magazine; and the finish is polished blue, with a select, checkered walnut stock with a rosewood forend tip and pistol grip cap. This model was discontinued in 1988.

Exc.	V.G.	Good	Fair	Poor
500	400	350	300	250

Vanguard VGS

This satin-finish version was also discontinued in 1988.

Exc.	V.G.	Good	Fair	Poor
450	350	300	250	200

Vanguard VGL

This is a lightweight carbine version that has a 20" barrel. It was discontinued in 1988.

Exc.	V.G.	Good	Fair	Poor
450	350	300	250	200

Fiberguard

This version has a matte-blued finish with a green fiberglass stock. It was discontinued in 1988.

Exc.	V.G.	Good	Fair	Poor
500	400	350	300	250

Vanguard Classic I

This version is chambered for various popular standard calibers and has a 24" barrel and either a 3- or 5-shot magazine. It has a satin blue finish and a select checkered, oil-finished walnut stock. It was introduced in 1989.

NIB	Exc.	V.G.	Good	Fair	Poor
475	400	375	300	250	200

Vanguard Classic II

This is a more deluxe version with a higher-grade walnut stock.

NIB	Exc.	V.G.	Good	Fair	Poor
600	550	475	400	300	250

Vanguard VGX Deluxe

This version has a high-gloss, Monte Carlo-type stock and a high-polished blued finish. It was introduced in 1989.

NIB	Exc.	V.G.	Good	Fair	Poor
600	550	475	400	300	250

Vanguard Weatherguard

This version has a wrinkle-finished, black synthetic stock. It was introduced in 1989.

NIB	Exc.	V.G.	Good	Fair	Poor
400	300	250	—	—	—

Weathermark

Introduced in 1993 this model features a checkered composite stock with matte blue metal finish. Available in Weatherby calibers from .257 through .340 and .270 Win., 7mm Rem. Mag., .30-06, .300 and .338 Win. Mag. Weighs 7.5 lbs.

NIB	Exc.	V.G.	Good	Fair	Poor
550	450	—	—	—	—

Weathermark Alaskan

Similar to the Weathermark with checkered composite stock the barreled action is electroless nickel with nonglare finish. Muzzle brake is optional. Available in same calibers as Weathermark. Weighs 7.7 lbs.

NIB	Exc.	V.G.	Good	Fair	Poor
725	600	500	—	—	—

Mark XXII

This is a semiautomatic rifle chambered for the .22 l.r. cartridge. There are two versions—one with a detachable magazine and the other with a tubular magazine. It has a 24" barrel with adjustable sights and a select checkered walnut stock with a rosewood forearm tip and pistol grip cap. This model was originally produced in Italy and was manufactured in Japan. It is now discontinued.

Mark XXII

Mark XXII Tube Model

NIB	Exc.	V.G.	Good	Fair	Poor
550	350	300	250	200	150

For Italian guns-Add 35%.

CUSTOM RIFLES

NOTE: Weatherby custom rifles are offered with many different options that will affect price. Consult an expert prior to a sale.

Weatherby Custom Grade engraving patterns

Classic Custom

This model features an oil finished French walnut stock with 20 lpi checkering, ebony forend tip, metal grip cap, and skeltonized steel buttplate. All metal work is matte blue. Calibers are all Weatherby from .257 Wby Mag to .340 Wby Mag.

NIB	Exc.	V.G.	Good	Fair	Poor
5075	3800	—	—	—	—

Safari Grade Custom

This model features an oil finish French walnut stock with Monte Carlo comb with fleur-de-lis checkering. Ebony forend tip and pistol grip cap. Damascened bolt and follower with checkered bolt handle. Quarter rib. Engraved floorplate "Safari Custom". Calibers from .257 Wby Mag to .460 Wby Mag.

NIB	Exc.	V.G.	Good	Fair	Poor
5175	3900	—	—	—	—

Crown Custom

This model features a hand carved walnut stock with buttstock inlay, damascened bolt and follower with checkered bolt handle. Engraved barrel, receiver and triggerguard. Floorplate engraved with gold inlays.

NIB	Exc.	V.G.	Good	Fair	Poor
6575	4900	—	—	—	—

Outfitter Custom

This model features a Bell & Carlson synthetic stock with custom camo and Pachmayr pad. Lightweight stainless steel fluted barrel. Titanium nitride finish on all metalwork.

NIB	Exc.	V.G.	Good	Fair	Poor
2150	1600	—	—	—	—

Outfitter Krieger Custom

This model features a Bell & Carlson synthetic stock with custom camo and Pachmayr pad. Custom Krieger stainless steel fluted barrel. Titanium nitride finish on all metalwork.

NIB	Exc.	V.G.	Good	Fair	Poor
3500	2500	—	—	—	—

HANDGUNS

Mark V Center Fire Pistol (CFP)

Introduced in 1998 this bolt action centerfire pistol is chambered for .22-250, .243, .7mm-08, and .308 calibers. Fitted with a 15" fluted barrel. Laminated stock. Magazine capacity is 3 rounds. Weight is approximately 5.25 lbs.

NIB	Exc.	V.G.	Good	Fair	Poor
1050	800	725	—	—	—

Mark V Accumark CFP

This model is similar to the Accumark rifle and features a synthetic stock of Kevlar and fiberglass. The stock has a matte black gel coat finish. Offered in .223 Rem., .22-250, .243 Win., 7mm-08, and .308 Win. calibers. Fluted barrel length is 15". Weight is about 5 lbs. Introduced in 2000.

NIB	Exc.	V.G.	Good	Fair	Poor
1050	800	—	—	—	—

SHOTGUNS

Centurion

This is a gas-operated semiautomatic shotgun chambered for 12 gauge. It is offered with various barrel lengths and chokes. It has a checkered walnut stock. It was manufactured between 1972 and 1981.

Exc.	V.G.	Good	Fair	Poor
350	300	250	200	150

Centurion Deluxe

This version is slightly engraved and features a vent ribbed barrel and higher-grade wood.

Exc.	V.G.	Good	Fair	Poor
375	325	275	225	175

Model 82

This is a gas-operated semiautomatic shotgun chambered for 12 gauge with 2.75" or 3" chambers. It has various barrel lengths with vent ribs and screw-in choke tubes. It features an alloy receiver and a deluxe, checkered walnut stock. It is also available as the Buckmaster with a 22" open-choked barrel. This model was introduced in 1983.

NIB	Exc.	V.G.	Good	Fair	Poor
500	450	400	350	300	250

Model SAS Field

Introduced in 1999 this gas operated semiautomatic model features a high grade claro walnut stock with black pistol grip cap. Fine line checkering. Chambered for 12 or 20 gauge and fitted with 26", 28", or 30" vent rib barrels in 12 gauge and 26" or 28" vent rib barrels in 20 gauge. The 12 gauge models weigh around 7.5 lbs. depending on barrel length and the 20 gauge weigh around 7 lbs. depending on barrel length. Fitted with Briley choke tubes.

NIB	Exc.	V.G.	Good	Fair	Poor
875	650	500	—	—	—

Model SAS Synthetic

This model features a black synthetic stock chambered for 12 or 20 gauge barrels as above. Introduced in 2000.

NIB	Exc.	V.G.	Good	Fair	Poor
925	675	—	—	—	—

Model SAS Camo

This model is offered with either shadowgrass or superflauge camo stocks. Available in 12 gauge only with 3" chambers. Shadowgrass model offered with 26" or 28" barrels the Superflauge model with 24" or 26" barrels. Weight is about 7.5 lbs.

Shadow Grass

NIB	Exc.	V.G.	Good	Fair	Poor
1050	800	—	—	—	—

Superflauge

NIB	Exc.	V.G.	Good	Fair	Poor
1050	800	—	—	—	—

Patrician

This is a slide action shotgun chambered for 12 gauge. It is offered with various barrel lengths and choke combinations. It has a vent rib barrel, a blued finish, and a checkered walnut stock. It was manufactured between 1972 and 1981.

Exc.	V.G.	Good	Fair	Poor
300	250	225	175	125

Patrician Deluxe

This is a slightly engraved version with fancier-grade walnut.

NIB	Exc.	V.G.	Good	Fair	Poor
500	350	300	250	200	150

Model 92

This is a slide action shotgun chambered for 12 gauge with 2.75" or 3" chambers. It is offered with 26", 28", or 30" ventilated rib barrels with screw-in choke tubes. It features a short, twin rail slide action and an engraved alloy receiver. The finish is blued, with a deluxe checkered walnut stock. A Buckmaster model with a 22" open-choke barrel and rifle sights is also available.

NIB	Exc.	V.G.	Good	Fair	Poor
350	300	250	200	175	125

Regency Field Grade

This is an Over/Under double barrel shotgun chambered for 12 or 20 gauge. It has various length vent ribbed barrels and a boxlock action with engraved false sideplates. It features a single selective trigger and automatic ejectors. The finish is blued, with a checkered walnut stock. This model was imported from Italy between 1972 and 1980. It is also offered as a trap-grade with the same value.

Exc.	V.G.	Good	Fair	Poor
1000	800	650	—	—

Olympian

This model is similar to the Regency, with less engraving. It was not imported after 1980. A skeet and a trap model, as well as a field-grade model, were available. The values were similar.

Exc.	V.G.	Good	Fair	Poor
800	700	600	—	—

Orion Upland

This 12 or 20 gauge model features a claro walnut stock with rounded pistol grip and slim forearm. Plain blued receiver. Choice of 26" or 28" vent rib barrel with 3" chambers. Multi choke system. Introduced in 1999.

NIB	Exc.	V.G.	Good	Fair	Poor
1050	800	700	550	—	—

Orion Grade I

This is an Over/Under double barrel shotgun chambered for 12 or 20 gauge with 3" chambers. It is offered with 26" or 28" vent rib barrels with screw-in chokes. It has a single selective trigger and automatic ejectors. The boxlock action features no engraving. The finish is blued, with a checkered walnut stock. It was introduced in 1989.

NIB	Exc.	V.G.	Good	Fair	Poor
850	750	700	600	500	400

Orion Grade II Skeet

This model is supplied with a claro walnut checkered stock with full pistol grip with rosewood grip cap. The receiver is a matte blue with scroll engraving. The barrel has a matte vent rib with side vents and mid-point head with white bead front sight. Special ventilated recoil pad. Offered in 12 gauge and 20 gauge with 26" barrels. Fixed skeet chokes are standard. The 12 gauge weighs 7.5 lbs. while the 20 gauge weighs 7.25 lbs.

NIB	Exc.	V.G.	Good	Fair	Poor
950	800	700	600	500	400

Orion Grade II Sporting Clays

Similar to the Classic model but with a full pistol grip with rosewood grip cap. The receiver is silver gray with scroll engraving. The claro walnut stock is checkered with a high gloss finish. Offered in 12 gauge with 28" to 30" vent rib barrels. Supplied with 5 screw in choke tubes.

NIB	Exc.	V.G.	Good	Fair	Poor
1000	850	750	600	450	400

Orion Grade II Double Trap

This model features an integral multi-choke tube. The Monte Carlo stock has a rosewood pistol grip cap with diamond shaped inlay. The receiver is blue with scroll engraving. Available with 30" or 32" vent rib barrels. Weighs 8 lbs.

NIB	Exc.	V.G.	Good	Fair	Poor
950	800	700	550	—	—

Orion Grade II Single Trap

Similar to the Double Trap but furnished with a single 32" barrel. Weighs 8 lbs.

NIB	Exc.	V.G.	Good	Fair	Poor
950	800	700	550	450	400

Orion Grade II

This version is lightly engraved and has a high-gloss finish. Otherwise, it is similar to the Grade I.

NIB	Exc.	V.G.	Good	Fair	Poor
1000	900	800	650	550	400

Orion Grade II Classic Field

Introduced in 1993 this model features a rounded pistol grip and slim forearm design. The walnut stock is oil finished. The receiver is blued with game scene engraving. A solid recoil pad is standard. Available in 12 gauge, 20 gauge, and 28 gauge with vent rib barrel lengths from 26" to 30" depending on gauge. Screw in choke tubes standard. Weighs 6.5 lbs. to 8 lbs. depending on gauge.

NIB	Exc.	V.G.	Good	Fair	Poor
900	800	700	550	450	400

Orion Grade II Classic Sporting Clays

Introduced in 1993 this model has a rounded pistol grip with slender forearm with an oil finished stock. The receiver is blued with scroll engraving. A stepped competition matte vent rib with additional side vents is supplied. The recoil pad has a special radius heel. Offered in 12 gauge with 28" barrel. Furnished with 5 screw in choke tubes. Weighs 7.5 lbs.

NIB	Exc.	V.G.	Good	Fair	Poor
1000	850	750	600	450	400

Orion Super Sporting Clays (SSC)

Introduced in 1999 this 12 gauge model features a walnut stock with sporter style pistol grip and cast off. Barrel lengths are 28", 30" or 32" with 3" chambers and 12mm grooved rib. Barrels are also ported and backbored. Comes with 5 choke tubes. Weight is approximately 8 lbs.

NIB	Exc.	V.G.	Good	Fair	Poor
1750	1400	1150	925	750	—

Orion Grade III

This version has a game scene-engraved, coin-finished receiver and higher-grade walnut. It was introduced in 1989.

NIB	Exc.	V.G.	Good	Fair	Poor
1100	1000	900	750	650	—

Orion Grade III Classic Field

New for 1993 this model features a rounded pistol grip and slim forearm with oil finish claro walnut with fine line checkering. The receiver is silver gray with scroll engraving and gold game bird overlays. Available in 12 gauge with 28" vent rib barrels and 20 gauge with 26" vent rib barrels. Screw in choke tubes standard.

NIB	Exc.	V.G.	Good	Fair	Poor
1100	950	850	650	500	400

Weatherby Orion O/U Shotgun, IMC - Integral "Multi-choke"™ flush-fitting interchangeable choke tubes

Weatherby Athena O/U Shotgun, IMC - Integral "Multi-choke" ™ flush fitting interchangeable choke tubes

Orion Grade III Classic English Field

This model features an English style straight grip stock with a choice of 12 gauge with 28" barrel or 20 gauge with 26" or 28" barrels. The receiver is engraved and the oil finished is hand checkered. Weight of 12 gauge gun is about 7 lbs. and 20 gauge gun is about 6.5 lbs. Introduced in 1996.

NIB	Exc.	V.G.	Good	Fair	Poor
1250	1000	800	—	—	—

Athena Grade III Classic Field

Offered in 12 or 20 gauge this model features a hand select claro walnut stock with oil finish. The pistol grip is rounded. The silver-gray sideplates feature a rose and scroll engraving pattern with gold overlaid hunting scenes. Available with 26" or 28" vent rib barrels with multi-choke system. Weight is around 7.5 lbs. for 12 gauge and 7 lbs. for 20 gauge. Introduced in 1999. In 2001 a 28 gauge version was offered with 26" or 28" barrels.

NIB	Exc.	V.G.	Good	Fair	Poor
2000	1500	1250	—	—	—

Athena Grade IV

This is an Over/Under double barrel shotgun chambered for 12, 20, and 28 gauge, as well as .410. It has 3" chambers. It is offered with various barrel lengths with vent ribs and screw-in choke tubes. It has a boxlock action with Greener crossbolt, single selective trigger, and automatic ejectors. It has en-

graved false sideplates and a satin nickel-plated action. The barrels are blued, with a select checkered walnut stock. This model was introduced in 1989.

NIB	Exc.	V.G.	Good	Fair	Poor
2000	1750	1500	1200	950	750

Competition Model Athena

This is either a trap or skeet version with stock dimensions designed for either skeet or trap and competition-type ribs.

NIB	Exc.	V.G.	Good	Fair	Poor
1650	1400	1150	1000	750	600

Athena Grade V Classic Field

Introduced in 1993 this model features a rounded pistol grip with slender forearm. The high grade claro walnut stock is oil finished with fine line checkering. The receiver has a side plate that is silver gray with rose and scroll engraving. The vent rib barrels also have side vents. A solid recoil is supplied. Offered in 12 gauge with 26", 28", or 30" barrels and 20 gauge with 26" and 28" barrels. Choke tubes are standard. Weatherby Athena Master skeet tube set, 12 gauge 28" skeet shotgun, plus two each 20, 28 and .410 gauge fitted, full length Briley tubes with integral extractors. Packed in custom fitted aluminum case (not shown).

NIB	Exc.	V.G.	Good	Fair	Poor
1950	1750	1100	700	600	—

NOTE: Add 50% for Master Skeet Set.

WEAVER ARMS
Escondido, California

Nighthawk Assault Pistol
A 9mm semiautomatic pistol with a 10" or 12" barrel, alloy receiver and ambidextrous safety. Blackened with plastic grips. Introduced in 1987.

NIB	Exc.	V.G.	Good	Fair	Poor
550	450	400	350	300	150

Nighthawk Carbine
As above, with a 16.1" barrel, retractable shoulder stock, 25-, 32-, 40-, or 50-shot magazine. Introduced in 1984.

NIB	Exc.	V.G.	Good	Fair	Poor
600	500	450	350	300	150

WEBLEY & SCOTT, LTD.
Birmingham, England
SEE ALSO—British Double Guns
Established in 1860, this firm has produced a wide variety of firearms over the years and has been known as Webley & Scott, Ltd. since 1906.

Model 1872 Royal Irish Constabulary
A .450 double action revolver with a 3.25" barrel, 5-shot cylinder and rotating ejector. This model was also offered with 2.5" and 3.5" barrels. Blued with checkered walnut grips.

Exc.	V.G.	Good	Fair	Poor
650	400	250	200	150

Model 1880 Metropolitan Police
As above, with a 2.5" barrel and 6-shot cylinder.

Exc.	V.G.	Good	Fair	Poor
400	325	250	200	150

Model 1878 Webley-Pryse
Chambered for the .455 and .476 Eley cartridge.

Exc.	V.G.	Good	Fair	Poor
1100	900	750	550	300

NOTE: Add 200% premium for revolvers chambered for .577. Deduct 50% for revolvers chambered for cartridges below .442.

New Model 1883 R.I.C.
Similar to the Model 1880, but in .455 caliber with a 4.5" barrel. Also made with a 2.5" barrel.

Exc.	V.G.	Good	Fair	Poor
550	400	300	200	100

Model 1884 R.I.C. Naval
As above, with a brass frame and oxidized finish. Barrel length 2.75" and of octagonal form.

Exc.	V.G.	Good	Fair	Poor
1000	800	700	600	500

British Bulldog
Similar to the new Model 1883 R.I.C. blued, checkered walnut grips. Those engraved on the back strap "W.R.A. Co." were sold through the Winchester Repeating Arms Company's New York sales agency and are worth a considerable premium over the values listed below. Manufactured from 1878 to 1914.

Exc.	V.G.	Good	Fair	Poor
350	300	250	200	150

NOTE: Add a premium for U.S. dealer markings, see above.

Model 1878 Army Express Revolver
A .455 caliber double action revolver with a 6" barrel and integral ejector. Blued with one-piece walnut grips.

Exc.	V.G.	Good	Fair	Poor
1300	1000	750	500	350

NOTE: Add 100% premium for single action version.

Webley Kaufmann Model 1880
A top break, hinged-frame double action revolver chambered for the .450 centerfire cartridge, with a 5.75" barrel and a curved bird's-head butt. Blued, with walnut grips.

Exc.	V.G.	Good	Fair	Poor
1200	1000	800	—	—

Webley-Green Model
A double action, top break revolver chambered for the .455 cartridge, with a 6" ribbed barrel and a 6-shot cylinder. The cylinder flutes on this model are angular and not rounded in shape. Blued, with checkered walnut, squared butt grips with a lanyard ring on the butt. Introduced in 1882 and manufactured until 1896.

Exc.	V.G.	Good	Fair	Poor
1000	800	600	—	—

Mark I
A .442, .455, or .476 double action top break revolver with a 4" barrel and 6-shot cylinder. Blued with checkered walnut grips. Manufactured from 1887 to 1894.

Courtesy Faintich Auction Services, Inc. Photo Paul Goodwin

Exc.	V.G.	Good	Fair	Poor
600	500	350	250	150

Mark II

As above, with a larger hammer spur and improved barrel catch. Manufactured from 1894 to 1897.

Exc.	V.G.	Good	Fair	Poor
550	450	300	200	100

Mark III

As above, with internal improvements. Introduced in 1897.

Exc.	V.G.	Good	Fair	Poor
400	325	225	150	75

Mark IV

As above, with a .455 caliber 3", 4", 5", or 6" barrel. This model was also available in .22 caliber with 6" barrel, .32 caliber with 3" barrel, and .38 caliber with 3", 4", or 5" barrel.

Courtesy Faintich Auction Services, Inc. Photo Paul Goodwin

Exc.	V.G.	Good	Fair	Poor
400	325	225	150	75

Mark V

As above, with a 4" or 6" barrel. Manufactured from 1913 to 1915.

Courtesy Faintich Auction Services, Inc. Photo Paul Goodwin

Exc.	V.G.	Good	Fair	Poor
500	400	250	200	150

Mark VI

As above, with a 4" or 6" barrel and modified grip.

Courtesy Faintich Auction Services, Inc. Photo Paul Goodwin

Exc.	V.G.	Good	Fair	Poor
375	325	250	175	100

Mark VI .22 Rimfire

A standard-size Mark V chambered for the .22 rimfire cartridge used as a training pistol. Manufactured in 1918 and quite scarce.

Courtesy Faintich Auction Services, Inc. Photo Paul Goodwin

Exc.	V.G.	Good	Fair	Poor
750	600	500	350	200

WEBLEY SEMIAUTOMATIC PISTOLS

Text and prices by Joseph Schroeder

Webley's first attempt to enter the new self-loading pistol field occurred in the 1890s, when they actually made a few proto-type Gabbet-Fairfax "Mars" pistols (see under Gabbet-Fairfax) before deciding that the design was hopelessly complicated and impractical. They then enjoyed some success with the Webley-Fosbery automatic Revolver, a natural for England's premier revolver maker, while experimenting with semiautomatic pistol designs in the 1903-1905 period. Their first commercial pistol, the .32 caliber 1905, was quickly followed by a variety of related designs in various calibers. An interesting sidebar on Webley commercial self-loading pistols is that they were all numbered in the same series, so serial numbers bear no relation to the quantity of a given model actually produced but do indicate when they were made.

Webley-Fosbery Automatic Revolver

Recoil forces the top half of this unusual pistol back to cock the hammer, while a stud in the frame cams the cylinder around to bring a fresh chamber into position. Early examples under serial number 75 or so appear to be hand-made as no two seem to be identical; these bring a 100% premium over late model pistols. Other low number guns, under serial number 300 or so, also differ in appearance from the later production and bring a 25% premium. Early production was all in .455 Webley with a 6-round cylinder; a .38 ACP version with an 8-round cylinder was introduced about 1903 but is much scarcer than the .455.

Courtesy Joseph Schroeder

.455 Caliber

Exc.	V.G.	Good	Fair	Poor
4500	3750	2750	1750	1250

.38 Caliber

Exc.	V.G.	Good	Fair	Poor
6500	5000	4000	2500	1500

Model 1904

Made experimentally in both .38 ACP and .455 calibers, the highest serial numbered 1904 known is in the 30s and very few seem to have survived. A later Webley experimental, the Model 1906, made in .45 for the U.S. Army trial but apparently never submitted. Either model is too rare to price.

Model 1904

Courtesy Joseph Schroeder

Model 1906

Courtesy Joseph Schroeder

Model 1905

Webley's first commercial semiautomatic pistol was this compact .32 caliber. The earliest Model 1905s have a diagonal flat machined on the slide and a hammer-mounted safety; these bring about a 50% premium. The Model 1905 was replaced by the Model 1908 after about perhaps 20,000 were made.

Courtesy Joseph Schroeder

Exc.	V.G.	Good	Fair	Poor
750	600	400	250	150

Model 1907

The 1907 is a very popular .25 caliber with an outside hammer and was one of Webley's most popular pistols; it remained in production until WWII and over 50,000 were made.

Courtesy Joseph Schroeder

Exc.	V.G.	Good	Fair	Poor
300	225	150	125	100

Model 1908

The Model 1908 is a slight redesign of the Model 1905. Webley's most popular self-loading pistol, it remained in production until WWII. Examples bearing a crown and the letters "MP" were made for the Metropolitan Police and bring a slight premium.

Exc.	V.G.	Good	Fair	Poor
350	275	200	150	125

Model 1909

The Model 1909 is a modified and enlarged version of the Model 1908, chambered for the 9mm Browning Long cartridge. It was never popular, and manufacture ended in 1914 with just under 1,700 made. Its most unusual feature was the slide release on top of the slide.

Courtesy Joseph Schroeder

Exc.	V.G.	Good	Fair	Poor
1000	750	500	300	200

Model 1910 .380

The Model 1910 .380 was simply a Model 1908 modified to accept the .380 cartridge. Never very popular, under 2,000 were sold.

Courtesy Joseph Schroeder

Exc.	V.G.	Good	Fair	Poor
750	500	300	200	150

Model 1910 .38 ACP

This was Webley's first locked breech pistol, based closely on the experimental Model 1906 design and chambered for the .38 ACP cartridge. There are two models, both with internal hammers but one with a grip safety and the later without. Total production for both was under 1,000, so both are rare.

Courtesy Joseph Schroeder

Exc.	V.G.	Good	Fair	Poor
1500	1200	900	500	350

Model 1911

The Model 1911 is a single shot .22 caliber training version of the Model 1908, and developed specifically for the Metropolitan Police. It features a "blow open" action which ejects the fired cartridge but remains open for reloading, and the bottom of the frame is slotted for attaching a shoulder stock. Stocks are quite rare, and will probably add more than 100% to the value of the pistol.

Courtesy Joseph Schroeder

Exc.	V.G.	Good	Fair	Poor
750	600	450	300	200

Model 1912

A perceived need for a hammerless version of the Model 1907 .25 caliber led to the introduction of the Model 1912. It actually does have an internal hammer, but the recoil spring is two coils in the slide instead of the large V-spring under the right grip frame found in all other Webley semiautomatic pistols. Not as popular as the Model 1907, production totaled almost 15,000 vs over 50,000 for the hammer model.

Exc.	V.G.	Good	Fair	Poor
400	300	250	175	125

Model 1913

The Model 1913 was the result of years of development in conjuction with the British government and was finally adopted in 1913 as the Model 1913 MK1N for Royal Navy issue. It has the same breech-locking system as the Model 1910, but has an external hammer and is chambered for the .455 Webley Self-Loading cartridge. About 1,000 Model 1913s were sold commercially and serial numbered along with the smaller caliber pistols. In 1915 a variation of the Model 1913 with butt slotted for a shoulder stock, an adjustable rear sight, and a hammer safety adopted for use by the Royal Horse Artillery. Shoulder stocks are very rare, and will double values shown for the RHA model. All militaries were numbered in their own series; about 10,000 made in both variations.

Courtesy Joseph Schroeder

Model 1913

Exc.	V.G.	Good	Fair	Poor
1500	1200	800	500	300

Model 1913 (RHA model)

Courtesy Joseph Schroeder

Exc.	V.G.	Good	Fair	Poor
2500	2000	1500	850	600

Model 1922

The Model 1922 was a redesign of the Model 1909 in hopes of military adoption. The grip safety was replaced by a manual safety mounted on the slide, the grip angle was changed, and a lanyard ring added to the butt. Unfortunately for Webley its only official use was by the Union Defence Force of South Africa (1,000 pistols). South African guns are marked with a large "U" with an arrow in it and bring a 20% premium.

Exc.	V.G.	Good	Fair	Poor
1200	800	600	350	200

WEIHRAUCH, HANS HERMANN
Melrichstadt, West Germany

Model HW 60M

A .22 caliber single shot bolt action rifle with a 26.75" barrel and adjustable sights. Blued with a walnut stock.

NIB	Exc.	V.G.	Good	Fair	Poor
800	650	550	400	350	250

Model HW 66

A .22 Hornet or .222 Remington bolt action rifle with a stainless steel 26" barrel and single or double set triggers. Blued with a walnut stock.

NIB	Exc.	V.G.	Good	Fair	Poor
700	550	500	350	300	200

Model HW-3

A double action, solid-frame, swing-out cylinder revolver chambered for .22 l.r. or .32 Smith & Wesson long cartridges with a barrel length of 2.75", and a cylinder holding either seven or eight cartridges. Blued, with walnut grips. In America this revolver was known as the Dickson Bulldog. In Europe it was known as the Gecado.

Exc.	V.G.	Good	Fair	Poor
100	75	50	35	25

Model HW-5

As above, with a 4" barrel. Sold in the United States under the trade name "Omega."

Exc.	V.G.	Good	Fair	Poor
100	75	50	35	25

Model HW-7

As above, in .22 caliber with a 6" barrel and 8-shot cylinder. Sold in the United States as the "Herter's Guide Model". Also available with target sights and thumb rest grips as the Model HW-7S.

Exc.	V.G.	Good	Fair	Poor
100	75	50	35	25

Model HW-9

Similar to the HW-7, with a 6-shot cylinder and 6" ventilated rib barrel fitted with target sights and target grips.

Exc.	V.G.	Good	Fair	Poor
100	75	50	35	25

These pistols all carry the Arminius trademark, a bearded head wearing a winged helmet. The model number will be found on the cylinder crane; the caliber, on the barrel; and the words "Made in Germany" on the frame.

WEISBURGER, A.
Memphis, Tennessee

Pocket Pistol

A .41 caliber percussion single shot pocket pistol with 2.5" barrel, German silver furniture and a walnut stock. Manufactured during the 1850s.

Exc.	V.G.	Good	Fair	Poor
—	—	4750	3250	—

WESSON, DAN FIREARMS/NYI CORP.
Norwich, New York

In 1996 the assets of the Wesson Firearms Co. were purchased by the New York International Corp. All interchangeable barrel models were produced. There are no plans at this time to build fixed barrel models. At the present time parts and service for original Dan Wesson revolvers are available from the new company. Full production of new models occurred in 1997. These firearms will be laser marked on the barrel or frame with: "NYI" in an oval and below "DAN WESSON FIREARMS" on the next line "NORWICH, NEW YORK USA".

NEW GENERATION SMALL FRAME SERIES

NOTE: The "7" prefix denotes stainless steel frame and barrel.

Model 22/722

This is a 6 shot revolver chambered for .22 caliber cartridge. Interchangeable barrel lengths are 2.5", 4", 5.6", 8", and 10". Adjustable rear sight and interchangeable front sight. Hogue finger groove rubber grips. Weight is 36 oz. for 2.5" barrel and 58 oz. for 10" barrel.

NIB	Exc.	V.G.	Good	Fair	Poor
485	375	—	—	—	—

NOTE: Add between 4% and 9% depending on barrel length and for stainless steel.

Model 22M/722M

Same as above but chambered for .22 Win. Mag. cartridge.

NIB	Exc.	V.G.	Good	Fair	Poor
520	400	—	—	—	—

NOTE: Add between 4% and 9% depending on barrel length and for stainless steel.

Model 32/732

Same as above. Chambered for .32 H&R cartridge.

NIB	Exc.	V.G.	Good	Fair	Poor
550	425	—	—	—	—

NOTE: Add between 4% and 9% depending on barrel length and for stainless steel.

Model 3220/73220

Same as above but chambered for the .32-20 cartridge.

NIB	Exc.	V.G.	Good	Fair	Poor
550	425	—	—	—	—

NOTE: Add between 4% and 9% depending on barrel length and for stainless steel.

Model 15/715

Same as above but chambered for the .38 Special and .357 Magnum cartridges.

NIB	Exc.	V.G.	Good	Fair	Poor
485	375	—	—	—	—

NOTE: Add between 4% and 9% depending on barrel length and for stainless steel.

WHAT'S IT LIKE-THE DAN WESSON

Dan Wesson, grandson of the original Daniel Baird Wesson of Smith & Wesson, was a true firearms innovator. The revolver, which would bear his name, had several remarkable features. Instead of a grip frame there was a grip stud allowing greater latitude in size and shape of grips. The cylinder locked at the front instead of at the end of the ejector rod, and front sight blades were made interchangeable offering several shapes and sizes, as well as different colored inserts. The most radical element of the Dan Wesson revolver is the fact that instead of a firmly fitted barrel, this new design featured a smaller diameter barrel and an over fitting shroud, both of which were easily removable by using the special tool supplied by Dan Wesson to unlock the barrel nut at the muzzle end of the barrel. This latter innovation allowed one cylinder and frame to be fitted with many barrel lengths and, in fact, Pistol Pacs were offered with three different easily changeable barrel lengths. As an extra added bonus the easy interchangeability of barrels and the solid locking barrel nut resulted in excellent accuracy and the Dan Wesson revolvers early on gained great popularity with silhouette shooters. Today, Wesson Firearms is under new ownership and management using all new machinery and turning out the best Dan Wesson revolvers ever offered. In addition to the traditional calibers such as .357 Magnum and .44 Magnum, and the Super-Mags, .357 and .445, the .414 SuperMag is now reality and such new cartridges as the .460 Rowland and the .360 Dan Wesson are being offered. Unlike previous offerings, the new Dan Wessons feature smooth chambers and the front of the cylinder and the back of the barrel are square and parallel allowing for tight and precise barrel/cylinder gaps. Excellent sixguns.

John Taffin

NEW GENERATION LARGE FRAME SERIES

NOTE: The "7" prefix denotes stainless steel frame and barrel.

Model 41/741

This is a large frame revolver with 6 shot cylinder. Interchangeable barrels in 4", 6", 8", and 10". Adjustable rear sight with interchangeable front sight. Hogue finger grip rubber grips standard. Weight is from 49 oz. for 4" barrel to 69 oz. for 10" barrels.

NIB	Exc.	V.G.	Good	Fair	Poor
575	450	—	—	—	—

NOTE: Add between 4% and 9% depending on barrel length and for stainless steel.

Model 44/744

Same as above but chambered for .44 Magnum cartridge.

NIB	Exc.	V.G.	Good	Fair	Poor
575	450	—	—	—	—

NOTE: Add between 4% and 9% depending on barrel length and for stainless steel.

Model 45/745

Same as above but chambered for .45 Colt cartridge.

NIB	Exc.	V.G.	Good	Fair	Poor
600	475	—	—	—	—

NOTE: Add between 4% and 9% depending on barrel length and for stainless steel.

Model 360/7360

Same as above but chambered for .357 Magnum cartridge.

NIB	Exc.	V.G.	Good	Fair	Poor
640	500	—	—	—	—

NOTE: Add between 4% and 9% depending on barrel length and for stainless steel.

Model 460/7460

Same as above but chambered for the .45ACP, .45 Auto Rim, .45 Super, .45 Win. Mag, or .460 Rowland.

NIB	Exc.	V.G.	Good	Fair	Poor
650	525	—	—	—	—

NOTE: Add between 4% and 9% depending on barrel length and for stainless steel.

NEW GENERATION SUPERMAG FRAME SERIES

NOTE: The "7" prefix denotes stainless steel frame and barrel.

Model 40/740

This is a 6 shot revolver chambered for .the .357 Magnum, .357 Super Magnum/Maximum cartridges with interchangeable barrels in 4", 6", 8", or 10" lengths. Adjustable rear sight and interchangeable front sights. Hogue finger groove rubber grips standard. Weight range from 51 oz. for 4" barrel to 76 oz. for 10" barrel.

NIB	Exc.	V.G.	Good	Fair	Poor
795	650	—	—	—	—

NOTE: Add between 4% and 9% depending on barrel length and for stainless steel.

Model 414/7414

Same as above but chambered for .414 Super Magnum cartridge.

NIB	Exc.	V.G.	Good	Fair	Poor
795	650	—	—	—	—

NOTE: Add between 4% and 9% depending on barrel length and for stainless steel.

Model 445/7445

Same as above but chambered for .445 Super Mag. cartridge.

NIB	Exc.	V.G.	Good	Fair	Poor
795	650	—	—	—	—

NOTE: Add between 4% and 9% depending on barrel length and for stainless steel.

NEW GENERATION COMPENSATED SERIES

NOTE: The "7" prefix denotes stainless steel frame and barrel.

Model 15/715

This is a 6 shot revolver that is chambered for the .357 Magnum cartridge and offered with interchangeable barrels in 4", 6", or 10" lengths. Barrels have an integral compensator. Adjustable rear sight and interchangeable front sight. Hogue finger groove rubber grips.

NIB	Exc.	V.G.	Good	Fair	Poor
575	450	—	—	—	—

NOTE: Add between 4% and 9% depending on barrel length and for stainless steel.

Model 41/741

Same as above but chambered for .41 Magnum cartridge.

NIB	Exc.	V.G.	Good	Fair	Poor
675	550	—	—	—	—

NOTE: Add between 4% and 9% depending on barrel length and for stainless steel.

Model 44/744

Same as above but chambered for .44 Magnum cartridge.

NIB	Exc.	V.G.	Good	Fair	Poor
675	550	—	—	—	—

NOTE: Add between 4% and 9% depending on barrel length and for stainless steel.

Model 45/745

Same as above but chambered for .45 Colt cartridge.

NIB	Exc.	V.G.	Good	Fair	Poor
675	550	—	—	—	—

NOTE: Add between 4% and 9% depending on barrel length and for stainless steel.

Model 360/7360

Same as above but chambered for .357 Magnum on large frame.

NIB	Exc.	V.G.	Good	Fair	Poor
765	600	—	—	—	—

NOTE: Add between 4% and 9% depending on barrel length and for stainless steel.

Model 460/7460

Same as above but chambered for the .45ACP, .45Auto Rim, .45 Super, .45 Win. Mag., or the .460 Rowland cartridges.

NIB	Exc.	V.G.	Good	Fair	Poor
825	650	—	—	—	—

NOTE: Add between 4% and 9% depending on barrel length and for stainless steel.

STANDARD SILHOUETTE SERIES
NOTE: All Standard Silhouette series revolvers are stainless steel.

Model 722 VH10
This is a 6-shot revolver chambered for the .22 caliber cartridge. Interchangeable barrel system. Choice of fluted or non-fluted cylinders. Patridge front sight and adjustable rear sight. Hogue finger groove rubber grips standard. Lightweight slotted 8" shroud.

NIB	Exc.	V.G.	Good	Fair	Poor
800	650	—	—	—	—

Model 7360 V8S
Same as above but chambered for the .357 Magnum cartridge.

NIB	Exc.	V.G.	Good	Fair	Poor
820	670	—	—	—	—

Model 741 V8S
Same as above but chambered for the .41 Magnum cartridge with 8" slotted shroud.

NIB	Exc.	V.G.	Good	Fair	Poor
800	650	—	—	—	—

Model 741 V10S
Same as above but with 10" slotted shroud.

NIB	Exc.	V.G.	Good	Fair	Poor
925	750	—	—	—	—

Model 744 V8S
Chambered for .44 Magnum cartridge and fitted with an 8" slotted shroud.

NIB	Exc.	V.G.	Good	Fair	Poor
825	675	—	—	—	—

Model 744 V10S
Same as above but fitted with a 10" slotted shroud.

NIB	Exc.	V.G.	Good	Fair	Poor
925	750	—	—	—	—

Model 740V8S
Chambered for the .357 Super Mag. and fitted with an 8" slotted shroud.

NIB	Exc.	V.G.	Good	Fair	Poor
950	800	—	—	—	—

Model 7414 V8S
Chambered for the .414 Super Mag and fitted with an 8" slotted shroud.

NIB	Exc.	V.G.	Good	Fair	Poor
950	800	—	—	—	—

Model 7445 V8S
Chambered for the .445 Super Mag. and fitted with a 8" slotted shroud.

NIB	Exc.	V.G.	Good	Fair	Poor
950	800	—	—	—	—

SUPER RAM SILHOUETTE SERIES
NOTE: All Super Ram Silhouette series revolvers are stainless steel.

Model 722 VH10 SRS1
This model is chambered for the .22 caliber cartridge and is fitted with a 10" slotted shroud barrel. Interchangeable barrel system. Adjustable Bomar rear sight. Bomar SRS-1 hood front sight. Fluted or non-fluted cylinders. Hogue finger groove rubber grips.

NIB	Exc.	V.G.	Good	Fair	Poor
950	800	—	—	—	—

Model 7360 V8S SRS1
Same as above but chambered for .357 Magnum cartridge. Fitted with an 8" slotted shroud.

NIB	Exc.	V.G.	Good	Fair	Poor
1100	875	—	—	—	—

Model 741 V8S SRS1
Same as above but chambered for.41 Magnum cartridge and fitted with an 8" slotted shroud.

NIB	Exc.	V.G.	Good	Fair	Poor
1100	875	—	—	—	—

Model 741 V10S SRS1
Same as above but fitted with a 10" slotted shroud.

NIB	Exc.	V.G.	Good	Fair	Poor
1125	900	—	—	—	—

Model 744 V8S SRS1
Same as above but chambered for the .44 Magnum cartridge and fitted with an 8" slotted shroud.

NIB	Exc.	V.G.	Good	Fair	Poor
1100	875	—	—	—	—

Model 744 V10S SRS1
Same as above but fitted with a 10" slotted shroud.

NIB	Exc.	V.G.	Good	Fair	Poor
1125	900	—	—	—	—

Model 740 V8S SRS1
Same as above but chambered for .357 Super Mag. and fitted with an 8" slotted shroud.

NIB	Exc.	V.G.	Good	Fair	Poor
1200	950	—	—	—	—

Model 7414 V8S SRS1
Same as above but chambered for .414 Super Mag. and fitted with an 8" slotted shroud.

NIB	Exc.	V.G.	Good	Fair	Poor
1200	950	—	—	—	—

Model 7445 V8S SS1
Same as above but chambered for .445 Super Mag. and fitted with an 8" slotted shroud.

NIB	Exc.	V.G.	Good	Fair	Poor
1200	950	—	—	—	—

PISTOL PACK SERIES

This series consist of a Dan Wesson revolver of the customer's choice with adjustable rear sight and four barrel assemblies in the small frame calibers (2.5", 4", 6", and 8"); the large frame and supermag frame have three barrel assemblies (4", 6", and 8"). Also included is a cleaning kit, wrench kit, extra exotic wood grips, instruction manual and fitted hard case. Choice of blue or stainless steel finish ("7" prefix).

Model 22/722
Chambered for .22 Long Rifle.

NIB	Exc.	V.G.	Good	Fair	Poor
1200	950	—	—	—	—

Model 32/732
Chambered for .32 H&R Magnum.

NIB	Exc.	V.G.	Good	Fair	Poor
1200	950	—	—	—	—

Model 3220/73220
Chambered for the .32-20.

NIB	Exc.	V.G.	Good	Fair	Poor
1200	950	—	—	—	—

Model 15/715
Cumbered for the .357 Magnum.

NIB	Exc.	V.G.	Good	Fair	Poor
1200	950	—	—	—	—

Model 41/741
Chambered for the .41 Magnum.

NIB	Exc.	V.G.	Good	Fair	Poor
1450	1150	—	—	—	—

Model 44/744
Chambered for the .44 Magnum.

NIB	Exc.	V.G.	Good	Fair	Poor
1450	1150	—	—	—	—

Model 45/745
Chambered for the .45 Colt.

NIB	Exc.	V.G.	Good	Fair	Poor
1450	1150	—	—	—	—

Model 460/7460
Chambered for the .45ACP, .45 Auto Rim, .45 Super, .45 Win. Mag, .460 Rowland.

NIB	Exc.	V.G.	Good	Fair	Poor
1450	1150	—	—	—	—

Model 40/740
Chambered for the .357 Maximum.

NIB	Exc.	V.G.	Good	Fair	Poor
1650	1300	—	—	—	—

Model 414/7414
Chambered for the .414 Super Mag.

NIB	Exc.	V.G.	Good	Fair	Poor
1650	1300	—	—	—	—

Model 445/7445
Chambered for the .445 Super Mag.

NIB	Exc.	V.G.	Good	Fair	Poor
1650	1300	—	—	—	—

HUNTER PACK SERIES

The Hunter Pack comes with a Dan Wesson of the customer's choice with adjustable rear sight and two 8" barrel assemblies, one with open sights and one drilled and tapped with Burris or Weaver mount installed. Extra set of exotic wood grips, wrench kit, cleaning kit, and manual. Offered in blue or stainless steel ("7" prefix).

Model 22/722
Chambered for .22 Long Rifle.

NIB	Exc.	V.G.	Good	Fair	Poor
1200	950	—	—	—	—

Model 32/732
Chambered for .32 H&R Magnum.

NIB	Exc.	V.G.	Good	Fair	Poor
1200	950	—	—	—	—

Model 3220/73220
Chambered for the .32-20.

NIB	Exc.	V.G.	Good	Fair	Poor
1200	950	—	—	—	—

Model 15/715
Chambered for .357 Mag.

NIB	Exc.	V.G.	Good	Fair	Poor
1200	950	—	—	—	—

Model 41/741
Chambered for the .41 Mag.

NIB	Exc.	V.G.	Good	Fair	Poor
1450	1150	—	—	—	—

Model 44/744
Chambered for the .44 Mag.

NIB	Exc.	V.G.	Good	Fair	Poor
1450	1150	—	—	—	—

Model 45/745
Chambered for the .45 Colt.

NIB	Exc.	V.G.	Good	Fair	Poor
1450	1150	—	—	—	—

Model 460/7460
Chambered for the .45ACP, .45 Auto Rim, .45 Super, .45 Win. Mag., .460 Rowland.

NIB	Exc.	V.G.	Good	Fair	Poor
1450	1150	—	—	—	—

Model 40/740
Chambered for the .357 Maximum.

NIB	Exc.	V.G.	Good	Fair	Poor
1650	1300	—	—	—	—

Model 414/7414
Chambered for the .414 Super Mag.

NIB	Exc.	V.G.	Good	Fair	Poor
1650	1300	—	—	—	—

Model 445/7445
Chambered for the .445 Super Mag.

NIB	Exc.	V.G.	Good	Fair	Poor
1650	1300	—	—	—	—

PISTOLS

Pointman Major
This is a semiauto pistol chambered for the .45 ACP cartridge. Many special features including interchangeable front sight, Jarvis match barrel, adjustable rear sight, beveled magazine well, and others. Stainless steel slide and frame. Rosewood checkered grips. Slide serrations both front and rear. A high sighting rib with interchangeable sights. Introduced in 2000.

NIB	Exc.	V.G.	Good	Fair	Poor
775	625	—	—	—	—

Pointman Minor
Same as above except blued slide and frame and no match barrel.

NIB	Exc.	V.G.	Good	Fair	Poor
600	450	—	—	—	—

Pointman Seven
Has many of the same features as the Pointman Major with blued slide and frame and no sighting rib.

NIB	Exc.	V.G.	Good	Fair	Poor
1000	750	—	—	—	—

Pointman Seven Stainless
Same as above with stainless steel frame and slide.

NIB	Exc.	V.G.	Good	Fair	Poor
1100	800	—	—	—	—

Pointman Guardian
This model is fitted with a 4.25" barrel and match trigger group. Adjustable rear sight plus many other specail features. Blued frame and slide with sighting rib.

NIB	Exc.	V.G.	Good	Fair	Poor
775	575	—	—	—	—

Pointman Guardian Duce
Same as above but with blued steel slide and stainless steel frame

NIB	Exc.	V.G.	Good	Fair	Poor
825	600	—	—	—	—

WESSON FIREARMS CO., INC.
Palmer, Massachusetts
The company was founded in 1968 by Daniel B. Wesson, the great-grandson of D.B. Wesson, co-founder of Smith & Wesson. This line of handguns is unique for its barrel/shroud interchangeability. Dan Wesson revolvers have established themselves as champion metallic silhouette competition guns.

The company offers a comprehensive line of handguns for almost every use. The company will also custom build a handgun to customer specifications. Dan Wesson Arms was restructured on January 4, 1991, and identified as Wesson Firearms Company, Inc. Wesson handguns made after this date will be stamped with this new corporate name. In 1995 the company declared bankruptcy.

Model II

A .357 Magnum caliber double action swing-out cylinder revolver with interchangeable 2.5", 4", or 6" barrels and a 6-shot cylinder. Blued with walnut grips. Manufactured in 1970 and 1971.
Extra Barrels-Add 25% per barrel.

NIB	Exc.	V.G.	Good	Fair	Poor
200	175	150	125	100	75

Model 12

As above, with adjustable target sights.

NIB	Exc.	V.G.	Good	Fair	Poor
250	225	200	175	125	100

Model 14

As above, with a recessed barrel locking nut and furnished with a spanner wrench. Manufactured from 1971 to 1975.

NIB	Exc.	V.G.	Good	Fair	Poor
250	200	175	150	100	75

Model 15

As above, with adjustable target sights.

NIB	Exc.	V.G.	Good	Fair	Poor
275	225	200	175	125	100

Model 8

As above, in .38 Special caliber.

NIB	Exc.	V.G.	Good	Fair	Poor
225	175	150	125	100	75

Model 9

As the Model 15, with adjustable sights and in .38 Special caliber. Manufactured from 1971 to 1975.

NIB	Exc.	V.G.	Good	Fair	Poor
250	225	200	175	125	100

.22 CALIBER REVOLVERS

Model 22

This is a double action target revolver chambered for the .22 Long Rifle cartridge. It is available in 2", 4", 6", and 8" barrel length with a choice of standard rib shroud, ventilated rib shroud, or ventilated heavy rib shroud. All variations feature an adjustable rear sight, red ramp interchangeable front sight and target grips. Offered in bright blue or stainless steel finish. For

revolvers with standard barrel assembly weights are: 2"-36 oz., 4"-40 oz., 6"-44 oz., and 8"-49 oz.

Model 722

Same as above but with stainless steel finish.

Model 22M

Same as above but chambered for .22 Magnum with blued finish.

Model 722M

Same as above but chambered for .22 Magnum with stainless steel finish.

Standard Rib Shroud

NIB	Exc.	V.G.	Good	Fair	Poor
280	250	200	150	100	75

Ventilated Rib Shroud

NIB	Exc.	V.G.	Good	Fair	Poor
300	275	225	150	100	75

Ventilated Heavy Rib Shroud

NIB	Exc.	V.G.	Good	Fair	Poor
330	280	240	200	125	100

NOTE: Add 10% to above prices for stainless steel finish.

P22 Pistol Pac

This model is also a target revolver similar to the Model 22 and its variations. Chambered for the .22 l.r. or .22 Magnum it is also offered with three types of barrel shrouds: standard, ventilated, or ventilated heavy. It is available in blued or stainless steel finish. The principal feature of the Pistol Pac is the 3 barrel assemblies in 2.5", 4", 6", and 8" with extra grips, four additional front sights, and a fitted carrying case.

Standard Rib Shroud

NIB	Exc.	V.G.	Good	Fair	Poor
500	450	400	350	300	150

Ventilated Rib Shroud

NIB	Exc.	V.G.	Good	Fair	Poor
600	550	500	450	350	150

Ventilated Heavy Rib Shroud

NIB	Exc.	V.G.	Good	Fair	Poor
650	600	550	475	350	150

NOTE: Add 10% to above prices for stainless steel finish.

HP22 Hunter Pac

This model is chambered for the .22 Magnum cartridge. The set includes a ventilated heavy 8" shroud, a ventilated 8" shroud only with Burris scope mounts and Burris scope in either 1.5x4X variable or fixed 2X, a barrel changing tool, and fitted carrying case. Finish is blued or stainless steel.

NOTE: Hunter Pacs are a special order item and should be evaluated at the time of sale.

.32 CALIBER REVOLVERS

Model 32

This model is a target revolver chambered for the .32 H&R Magnum cartridge. It is offered in 2", 4", 6", or 8" barrel lengths with choice of rib shrouds. All variations are fitted with adjustable rear sight, red ramp interchangeable front sight, and target grips. Available in blued or stainless steel finish. Weights depend on barrel length and shroud type but are between 35 oz. and 53 oz.

Model 732
Same as above but with stainless steel finish.

Model 322
Same as above but chambered for .32-20 cartridge with blued finish.

Model 7322
Same as above but chambered for .32-20 cartridge with stainless steel finish.

Standard Rib Shroud

NIB	Exc.	V.G.	Good	Fair	Poor
275	225	200	150	100	75

Ventilated Rib Shroud

NIB	Exc.	V.G.	Good	Fair	Poor
300	250	225	150	100	75

Ventilated Heavy Rib Shroud

NIB	Exc.	V.G.	Good	Fair	Poor
325	275	250	150	100	75

NOTE: Add 10% to above prices for stainless steel finish.

P32 Pistol Pac

This set offers the same calibers, barrel shrouds, and finishes as the above models but in a set consisting of 2", 4", 6", and 8" barrels with extra grips, four additional sights, and fitted case.

Standard Rib Shroud

NIB	Exc.	V.G.	Good	Fair	Poor
500	450	400	300	150	100

Ventilated Rib Shroud

NIB	Exc.	V.G.	Good	Fair	Poor
575	500	450	325	150	100

Ventilated Heavy Rib Shroud

NIB	Exc.	V.G.	Good	Fair	Poor
650	600	500	400	200	125

NOTE: Add 10% to above prices for stainless steel finish.

HP32 Hunter Pac

This model is chambered for the .32 H&R Magnum or .32-20 cartridge. The set includes a ventilated heavy 8" shroud, a ventilated 8" shroud only with Burris scope mounts and Burris scope in either 1.5x4X variable or fixed 2X, a barrel changing tool, and fitted carrying case. Finish is blued or stainless steel.

NOTE: Hunter Pacs are a special order item and should be evaluated at the time of sale.

.357 MAGNUM AND .38 CALIBER REVOLVERS

Model 14

This is a double action service revolver chambered for the .357 Magnum cartridge. Available with 2", 4", or 6" barrel with service shroud. It has fixed sights, service grip, and is offered in blued or stainless steel finish.

Model 714
Same as above but with stainless steel finish.

Model 8

Same as above but chambered for .38 Special cartridge with blued finish.

Model 708

Same as above but chambered for .38 Special with stainless steel finish.

NIB	Exc.	V.G.	Good	Fair	Poor
225	175	150	125	100	75

NOTE: Add 10% to above prices for stainless steel finish.

P14/8 Pistol Pac

This set consists of a 2", 4", and 6" barrel with service shroud and fixed sights. It has an extra grip and fitted carrying case. The P14 is chambered for the .357 Mag. and the P8 is chambered for the .38 Special.

NIB	Exc.	V.G.	Good	Fair	Poor
375	300	250	200	150	100

NOTE: Add 10% to above prices for stainless steel finish.

Model 15

This model is designed as a double action target revolver chambered for the .357 Magnum cartridge. It is available with 2", 4", 6", 8", and 10" barrels lengths with standard rib shroud. It features adjustable rear sight, red ramp interchangeable front sight, and target grips. Offered with blued finish. Weights according to barrel length are: 2"-32 oz., 4"-36 oz., 6"-40 oz., 8"-44 oz., 10"-50 oz.

Model 715

Same as above but with stainless steel finish.

Model 9

Same as above but chambered for .38 Special cartridge with blued finish.

Model 709

Same as above but with stainless steel finish.

Standard Rib Shroud

NIB	Exc.	V.G.	Good	Fair	Poor
275	225	200	150	100	75

Ventilated Rib Shroud

NIB	Exc.	V.G.	Good	Fair	Poor
300	250	225	150	100	75

Ventilated Heavy Rib Shroud

NIB	Exc.	V.G.	Good	Fair	Poor
325	275	250	150	100	75

NOTE: Add 10% to above prices for stainless steel finish.

P15/9 Pistol Pac

This model is a set with 2", 4", 6", and 8" barrels with standard rib shroud. Chambered for the .357 or .38 Special with standard rib shroud, four additional sights, and extra grip, and carrying case. The P15 is chambered for the .357 Mag. while the P9 is chambered for the .38 Special.

Standard Rib Shroud

NIB	Exc.	V.G.	Good	Fair	Poor
500	450	400	350	150	100

Ventilated Rib Shroud

NIB	Exc.	V.G.	Good	Fair	Poor
575	500	450	350	150	100

Ventilated Heavy Rib Shroud

NIB	Exc.	V.G.	Good	Fair	Poor
650	575	500	400	200	100

NOTE: Add 10% to above prices for stainless steel finish.

HP 15 Hunter Pac

This model is chambered for the .357 Magnum cartridge. The set includes a ventilated heavy 8" shroud, a ventilated 8" shroud only with Burris scope mounts and Burris scope in either 1.5x4X variable or fixed 2X, a barrel changing tool, and fitted carrying case. Finish is blued or stainless steel.

NOTE: Hunter Pacs are a special order item and should be evaluated at the time of sale.

Model 40/Supermag

This model is a target revolver chambered for the .357 Maximum cartridge. It has an adjustable rear sight, red ramp interchangeable front sight, ventilated rib shroud, and target grip. Barrel lengths are 4", 6", 8", or 10". A ventilated slotted shroud is available in 8" only. For 1993 a compensated barrel assembly, "CBA", as been added to the product line as a complete gun. Finish is blued. Weighs approximately 64 oz. with ventilated rib shroud barrel.

Model 740

Same as above but with stainless steel finish.

Ventilated Rib Shroud

NIB	Exc.	V.G.	Good	Fair	Poor
400	350	300	250	200	100

Ventilated Slotted Shroud-8" barrel only

NIB	Exc.	V.G.	Good	Fair	Poor
450	400	350	300	200	100

Ventilated Heavy Rib Shroud

NIB	Exc.	V.G.	Good	Fair	Poor
475	425	375	300	200	100

NOTE: Add 10% to above prices for stainless steel finish.

NOTE: For .357 Supermag with compensated barrel assembly add $30.

HP40 Hunter Pac

This model is chambered for the .357 Supermag cartridge. The set includes a ventilated heavy 8" shroud, a ventilated 8" shroud only with Burris scope mounts and Burris scope in either 1.5x4X variable or fixed 2X, a barrel changing tool, and fitted carrying case. Finish is blued or stainless steel.

NOTE: Hunter Pacs are a special order item and should be evaluated at the time of sale.

Model 375

This model, also known as the .375 Supermag, is chambered for the .357 Maximum cartridge, based on the .375 Winchester cartridge. Offered in 6", 8", 10" barrels in ventilated, ventilated heavy, or ventilated slotted rib barrels. Sights are interchangeable and adjustable. Available in bright blue finish only. Weighs approximately 64 oz. with ventilated rib shroud barrel.

Ventilated Rib Shroud

NIB	Exc.	V.G.	Good	Fair	Poor
400	350	300	250	200	100

Ventilated Heavy Rib Shroud

NIB	Exc.	V.G.	Good	Fair	Poor
450	400	350	300	200	100

Ventilated Slotted Shroud-8" barrel only

NIB	Exc.	V.G.	Good	Fair	Poor
475	425	375	300	200	100

HP375 Hunter Pac

This model is chambered for the .375 Supermag cartridge. The set includes a ventilated heavy 8" shroud, a ventilated 8" shroud only with Burris scope mounts and Burris scope in either 1.5x4X variable or fixed 2X, a barrel changing tool, and fitted carrying case. Finish is blued or stainless steel.

NOTE: Hunter Pacs are a special order item and should be evaluated at the time of sale.

.41, .44 MAGNUM, AND 45 LONG COLT REVOLVERS

Model 44

This model is a target double action revolver chambered for the .44 Magnum. It has 4", 6", 8", or 10" barrels with ventilated rib shrouds. Other features include: adjustable rear sight, red ramp interchangeable front sight, and target grips. Finish is bright blue. Weights with 4" barrel-40 oz., 6"-56 oz., 8"-64 oz., and 10"-69 oz.

Model 744

Same as above but with stainless steel finish.

Model 41

Same as above but chambered for .41 Magnum with blued finish.

Model 741

Same as above but with stainless steel finish.

Model 45

Same as above but chambered for .45 Long Colt with bright blue finish.

Model 745

Same as above but with stainless steel finish. Ventilated rib shroud.

NIB	Exc.	V.G.	Good	Fair	Poor
350	300	250	200	100	75

Ventilated Heavy Rib Shroud

NIB	Exc.	V.G.	Good	Fair	Poor
375	325	275	200	100	75

NOTE: Add 10% to above prices for stainless steel finish.

P44/P41/P45 Pistol Pac

This set features a 6" and 8" barrel assembly with ventilated rib shroud, an extra grip, two additional front sights, and a fitted carrying case. Chambered for .41 Magnum, .44 Magnum, or .45 Long Colt.

Ventilated Rib Shroud

NIB	Exc.	V.G.	Good	Fair	Poor
525	475	400	300	200	100

Ventilated Heavy Rib Shroud

NIB	Exc.	V.G.	Good	Fair	Poor
575	525	425	300	200	100

NOTE: Add 10% to above prices for stainless steel finish.

HP41/44 Hunter Pac

This model is chambered for either the .41 or .44 Magnum cartridge. The set includes a ventilated heavy 8" shroud, a ventilated 8" shroud only with Burris scope mounts and Burris scope in either 1.5x4X variable or fixed 2X, a barrel changing tool, and fitted carrying case. Finish is blued or stainless steel.

NOTE: Hunter Pacs are a special order item and should be evaluated at the time of sale.

Model 445

This double action target revolver is chambered for the .445 Supermag cartridge. Barrel lengths offered are 8" with ventilated slotted rib shroud, 8" ventilated heavy slotted rib shroud, or 10" ventilated slotted rib shroud. Barrel lengths are also available in 4", 6", 8", and 10" with choice of ventilated rib or ventilated heavy rib shrouds. Introduced in 1993 is a compensated barrel assembly available as a complete gun. This is designated the "CBA". Fitted with adjustable rear sights, red ramp interchangeable front sight, and target grips. Finish is bright blue. Typical weight with 8" ventilated rib shroud barrel is about 62 oz.

Model 7445

Same as above but with stainless steel finish.

Ventilated Rib Shroud

NIB	Exc.	V.G.	Good	Fair	Poor
400	350	300	250	200	100

Ventilated Heavy Rib Shroud

NIB	Exc.	V.G.	Good	Fair	Poor
430	380	330	250	200	100

NOTE: Add 10% to above prices for stainless steel finish.

NOTE: For .44 Magnum and .445 Supermag with compensated barrel assembly add $30.

Model 7445 Alaskan Guide Special

This limited edition model (only 500 will be produced) is chambered for the .445 Supermag cartridge. It features a 4" ventilated heavy compensated shroud barrel assembly, synthetic grips, and a matte black titanium nitride finish. Overall barrel length is 5.5" and the revolver weighs 56 oz.

NIB	Exc.	V.G.	Good	Fair	Poor
900	700	600	350	200	100

HP455 Hunter Pac

This model is chambered for the .445 Supermag cartridge. The set includes a ventilated heavy 8" shroud, a ventilated 8" shroud only with Burris scope mounts and Burris scope in either 1.5x4X variable or fixed 2X, a barrel changing tool, and fitted carrying case. Finish is blued or stainless steel.

NOTE: Hunter Pacs are a special order item and should be evaluated at the time of sale.

FIXED BARREL HANDGUNS

Model 38P

This model is a 5-shot double action revolver designed for the .38 Special cartridge. Barrel is 2.5" with fixed sights. Choice of wood or rubber grips. Finish is blued. Weighs 24.6 oz.

Model 738P

Same as above but with stainless steel finish.

NIB	Exc.	V.G.	Good	Fair	Poor
200	175	150	125	100	75

NOTE: Add 10% to above prices for stainless steel finish.

Model 14/714 Fixed Barrel Service

Same features as the .357 Magnum Model 14 without the interchangeable barrels. Barrel length are either 2.5" or 4" with fixed sights. Offered in either blued or stainless steel. Weighs 30 oz. with 2.5" barrel and 34 oz. with 4" barrel.

NIB	Exc.	V.G.	Good	Fair	Poor
200	175	150	125	100	75

NOTE: Add 10% to above prices for stainless steel finish.

Model 15/715 Fixed Barrel Target

Same as the .357 Magnum Model 15 with target sights and grips. Fixed barrel lengths are either 3" or 5". Available in blued or stainless steel. Weighs 37 oz. with 3" barrel and 42 oz. with 5" barrel.

NIB	Exc.	V.G.	Good	Fair	Poor
220	195	160	125	100	75

NOTE: Add 10% to above prices for stainless steel finish.

Model 45/745 Pin Gun

This model uses a .44 Magnum frame with 5" barrel with two-stage compensator. Choice of ventilated or ventilated heavy rib shroud configuration. Chambered for .45 ACP with or without half moon clips. Finish is blued or stainless steel. Weighs 54 oz.

Ventilated Rib Shroud

NIB	Exc.	V.G.	Good	Fair	Poor
550	500	450	400	200	100

Ventilated Heavy Rib Shroud

NIB	Exc.	V.G.	Good	Fair	Poor
600	550	500	400	200	100

NOTE: Add 10% to above prices for stainless steel finish.

Wesson Firearms Silhouette .22

This model is a 6-shot .22 l.r. single action only revolver with a 10" barrel. Fitted with compact style grips, narrow notch rear sight with choice of ventilated or ventilated heavy rib shroud. Finish is blued or stainless steel. Weighs 55 oz. with ventilated rib shroud and 62 oz. with ventilated heavy rib shroud.

Ventilated Rib Shroud

NIB	Exc.	V.G.	Good	Fair	Poor
375	325	275	225	150	100

Ventilated Heavy Rib Shroud

NIB	Exc.	V.G.	Good	Fair	Poor
390	350	290	225	150	100

NOTE: Add 10% to above prices for stainless steel finish.

WESSON, EDWIN
Hartford, Connecticut

Dragoon

A .45 caliber percussion revolver with a 7" round barrel and 6-shot unfluted cylinder. The barrel blued, the frame case hardened and the walnut grips fitted with a brass buttcap. Manufactured in 1848 and 1849.

Exc.	V.G.	Good	Fair	Poor
—	—	9000	5000	—

WESSON, FRANK
Worcester, Massachusetts
Springfield, Massachusetts

Manual Extractor Model

A .22 caliber spur trigger single shot pistol with a 4" octagonal barrel and thin brass frame. The barrel release is located in the front of the trigger. No markings. Approximately 200 were made in 1856 and 1857.

Exc.	V.G.	Good	Fair	Poor
—	—	700	300	100

First Model Small Frame

As above, with a 3", 3.5", or 6" half-octagonal barrel. Blued with rosewood or walnut grips. The barrel marked "Frank Wesson Worcester Mass/Pat'd Oct. 25, 1859 & Nov. 11, 1862". Serial numbered from 1 to 2500.

Exc.	V.G.	Good	Fair	Poor
—	—	450	200	75

Second Type

As above, with a flat sighted frame and a circular sideplate.

Exc.	V.G.	Good	Fair	Poor
—	—	400	175	75

First Model Medium Frame

As above, in .30 or .32 rimfire with a 4" half-octagonal barrel and an iron frame. Approximately 1,000 were made between 1859 and 1862.

Exc.	V.G.	Good	Fair	Poor
—	—	450	200	75

Medium Frame Second Model

As above, with a longer spur trigger and a slightly wider frame at the barrel hinge. Manufactured from 1862 to 1870.

Exc.	V.G.	Good	Fair	Poor
—	—	450	200	75

Small Frame Pocket Rifle

A .22 caliber spur trigger single-shot pistol with a 6" half octagonal barrel and narrow brass frame. This model is adopted for use with a detachable skeleton shoulder stock. The barrel marked "Frank Wesson Worcester, Mass." Manufactured from 1865 to 1875 with approximately 5,000 made.

Matching Shoulder Stock-Add 100%.

Pistol Only

Exc.	V.G.	Good	Fair	Poor
—	—	700	300	100

Medium Frame Pocket Rifle

As above, in .22, .30, or .32 rimfire with a 10" or 12" half octagonal barrel. Approximately 1,000 were made from 1862 to 1870.

Matching Shoulder Stock-Add 100%.

Pistol Only

Exc.	V.G.	Good	Fair	Poor
—	—	425	200	75

Model 1870 Small Frame Pocket Rifle

As above, in .22 caliber with a 10", 12", 15", or 18" or 20" half octagonal barrel that rotates to the side for loading. This model was made with either a brass or iron frame. It has a half cocked notch on the hammer.

Matching Shoulder Stock-Add 100%.

Pistol Only

Exc.	V.G.	Good	Fair	Poor
—	—	450	200	75

1870 Medium Frame Pocket Rifle First Type

As above, but with a slightly larger frame chambered for .32 rimfire. Approximately 5,000 were made from 1870 to 1893.

Matching Shoulder Stock-Add 100%.

Pistol Only

Exc.	V.G.	Good	Fair	Poor
—	—	400	175	75

1870 Medium Frame Pocket Rifle Second Type

As above, with an iron frame and a push-button half cocked safety.

Match Shoulder Stock-Add 100%.

Pistol Only

Exc.	V.G.	Good	Fair	Poor
—	—	400	175	75

1870 Medium Frame Pocket Rifle Third Type

As above, with 3 screws on the left side of the frame.

Matching Shoulder Stock-Add 100%.

Pistol Only

Exc.	V.G.	Good	Fair	Poor
—	—	400	175	75

1870 Large Frame Pocket Rifle First Type

As above, in .32, .38, .42, or .44 rimfire with an octagonal barrel from 15" to 24" in length. The barrel marked "Frank Wesson

Worcester, Mass Patented May 31, 1870". Less than 250 of these rifles were made between 1870 and 1880.

Matching Shoulder Stock-Add 100%.

Pistol Only

Exc.	V.G.	Good	Fair	Poor
—	—	950	400	150

1870 Large Frame Pocket Rifle Second Type

As above, with a sliding extractor.

Matching Shoulder Stock-Add 100%.

Pistol Only

Exc.	V.G.	Good	Fair	Poor
—	—	950	400	150

Small Frame Superposed Pistol

A .22 caliber spur trigger Over/Under pocket pistol with 2" or 2.5" octagonal barrels that revolve. Approximately 3,500 were made between 1868 and 1880. On occasion this pistol is found with a sliding knife blade mounted on the side of the barrels. The presence of this feature would add approximately 25% to the values listed below.

Exc.	V.G.	Good	Fair	Poor
—	—	1750	850	250

Medium Frame Superposed Pistol

As above, in .32 rimfire with 2.5" or 3.5" barrels. As with the smaller version, this pistol is occasionally found with a sliding knife blade mounted on the barrels that would add 25% to the values listed below. Manufactured from 1868 to 1880.

First Type Marked "Patent Applied For"

Exc.	V.G.	Good	Fair	Poor
—	—	950	400	100

Second Type Marked "Patent December 15, 1868"

Exc.	V.G.	Good	Fair	Poor
—	—	950	400	100

Third Type Full-Length Fluted Barrels

Courtesy W.P. Hallstein III and son Chip

Courtesy W.P. Hallstein III and son Chip

Exc.	V.G.	Good	Fair	Poor
—	—	1000	450	150

Large Frame Superposed Pistol

Courtesy W.P. Hallstein III and son Chip

Courtesy W.P. Hallstein III and son Chip

As above, in .41 rimfire with a 3" octagonal barrel fitted with a sliding knife blade. Approximately 2,000 were made from 1868 to 1880.

Exc.	V.G.	Good	Fair	Poor
—	—	2500	1000	300

No. 1 Long Range Rifle

A .44-100 or .45-100 caliber single-shot dropping block rifle with a 34" octagonal barrel. Blued with a checkered walnut stock. The barrel marked "F. Wesson Mfr. Worcester, Mass. Long Range Rifle Creedmoor". Manufactured in 1876.

Exc.	V.G.	Good	Fair	Poor
—	10000	4000	1750	500

No. 2 Mid-Range or Hunting Rifle

Similar to the above, with the firing pin located in a bolster on the right side of the receiver. The triggerguard has a rear finger loop. Standard barrel length 28", 32", and 34" and marked "F. Wesson Maker Worcester, Mass." The 32" and 34" barrels are occasionally marked "Long Range Rifle Creedmoor". Approximately 100 were made.

Courtesy Buffalo Bill Historical Center, Cody, Wyoming

Exc.	V.G.	Good	Fair	Poor
—	6750	3250	1500	500

No. 2 Sporting Rifle

A .38-100, .40-100, or .45-100 caliber single shot dropping barrel action rifle with barrels ranging from 28" to 34" in length. Approximately 25 were made.

Courtesy Buffalo Bill Historical Center, Cody, Wyoming

Exc.	V.G.	Good	Fair	Poor
—	7500	3000	1250	500

WESSON & LEAVITT
MASSACHUSETTS ARMS COMPANY
Chicopee Falls, Massachusetts

Revolving Rifle

A .40 caliber percussion revolving rifle with a 16" to 24" round barrel and 6-shot cylinder. Blued with a walnut stock. Approximately 25 were made in 1849.

Exc.	V.G.	Good	Fair	Poor
—	—	7500	3500	950

Dragoon

A .40 caliber percussion revolver with a 6.25" or 7" round barrel and 6-shot cylinder. These pistols are marked "Mass. Arms Co./Chicopee Falls". Approximately 30 were made with the 6.25" barrel and 750 with the 7" barrel. Manufactured in 1850 and 1851.

Courtesy Milwaukee Public Museum, Milwaukee, Wisconsin

Exc.	V.G.	Good	Fair	Poor
—	—	4750	2000	500

WESTERN ARMS
SEE—Bacon

WESTERN ARMS CORPORATION
SEE—Ithaca

WESTERN FIELD
Montgomery Ward

"Western Field" is the trade name used by Montgomery Ward & Company on arms that they retail. See Firearms Trade Names List at the end of this book.

WESTLEY RICHARDS & CO., LTD.
Birmingham, England
SEE—British Double Guns

A wide variety of firearms have been produced by this company since its founding. Presently, it produces boxlock and sidelock double barrel shotguns of both side-by-side and Over/Under form, bolt action rifles and double barrel rifles. Prospective purchasers are advised to secure individual appraisals prior to acquisition.

Westley Richards Deluxe Sidelock

Westley Richards Magazine Rifle

ROBERT WHEELER
SEE—English Military Firearms

WHITE, ROLLIN
Lowell, Massachusetts

Pocket Pistol

A .32 or .38 rimfire spur trigger single shot pistol with a 3" or 5" octagonal barrel. Brass or iron frames with walnut grips. The .38 caliber version with the 5" barrel was not produced in large quantities and therefore is worth approximately 25% more than the values listed below. The barrels are marked "Rollin White Arms Co., Lowell, Mass."

Exc.	V.G.	Good	Fair	Poor
—	—	750	350	150

Pocket Revolver

A .22 caliber spur trigger revolver with a 3.25" octagonal barrel and 7-shot cylinder. The brass frame silver-plated, barrel blued and grips of walnut. This revolver was marked in a variety of ways including "Rollin White Arms Co., Lowell, Mass.", "Lowell Arms Co., Lowell, Mass.", or "Made for Smith & Wesson by Rollin White Arms Co., Lowell, Mass." Approximately 10,000 were made during the late 1860s.

Exc.	V.G.	Good	Fair	Poor
—	—	600	250	75

WHITNEY ARMS COMPANY
(INCLUDING)
ELI WHITNEY, SR. / P. & E.W. BLAKE /
ELI WHITNEY, JR.

As the United States' first major commercial arms maker, Eli Whitney's New Haven plant, which began production in 1798 and continued under family control for the next ninety years, was one of the more important American arms manufactories of the nineteenth century. Its products, accordingly, are eminently collectible. Moreover, during its ninety years of operation, the Whitney clan produced a number of unusual arms, some exact copies of regulation U.S. martial longarms, others variations and derivatives of U.S. and foreign longarms, a variety of percussion revolvers, and finally a variety of single shot and repeating breechloading rifles in an attempt to capture a portion of the burgeoning market in these cartridge arms during the post Civil War period. Contrary to the prevailing myth, Eli Whitney, Sr., who also invented the cotton gin, did NOT perfect a system of interchangeability of parts in the arms industry. His contributions in this line were more as a propagandist for the concept that was brought to fruition by others, notably Simeon North and John Hall.

Eli Whitney, Sr. Armory Muskets, 1798-1824. 1798 U.S. Contract Muskets, Types I-IV

On 14 January 1798 Eli Whitney, Sr., having convinced the U.S. War Department that he could mass produce inter-changeable parts muskets, was awarded a contract for 10,000 muskets following the "Charlesville" (French M1766) pattern then also being copied at the newly opened Springfield Armory and most of the U.S. musket contractors. Whitney's 1798 con-tract muskets measure between 58-7/8" and 57-3/4" in overall length, with the longer arms delivered earlier. The .69 caliber smoothbore barrels measure approximately 44", though most are shy of that length by anywhere from 1/16" to a maximum of 1-1/4". Lockplates are flat with a beveled edge and are marked "U.STATES" in a curve on the pointed tail and with a perched eagle with down folded wings over "NEW HAVEN" forward of the cock. Four differences in the material and man-ner of attachment of the pan distinguish the subtypes. The first deliver of 500 muskets in September of 1801 had an integral, faceted iron pan (Type I); the second delivery of 500 muskets in June of 1802 also had faceted iron pans, but were detach-able (Type II). The 1,000 muskets delivered in September of 1802 and March of 1803 had faceted, detachable pans, but these were made of brass instead of iron (Type III). The final 8,000 muskets, delivered between 1803 and 1809, had de-tachable brass pans with a rounded bottom that Whitney cop-ied from the French M1777 musket (Type IV) and a rounded cock, also copied from the French M1777 musket. Generally speaking, due to the limited production of Types I - III, they should command a higher price; prices are given for the more common Type IV 1798 contract musket. It should be noted however, that about 1804 Whitney delivered 112 Type IV mus-kets to Connecticut's "1st Company of Governor's Foot Guards". Although similar to the Type IV musket, these 112 arms are distinguished by the absence of the "U.STATES" on the tail of the lock and the addition of the name "CONNECTI-CUT" to the left side plate. Such an arm should demand a con-siderable premium over the usual Type IV musket.

Exc.	V.G.	Good	Fair	Poor
—	—	4250	2000	500

Whitney Connecticut, New York, and U.S. 1812 Contract Muskets

In 1808 Whitney received a contract from the state of New York for 2,000 muskets. In 1810, he received a second con-tract from the same source for an additional 2,000 muskets, all of which were eventually delivered by mid-1813. In the interim, in 1809, the state of Connecticut contracted with Whitney to deliver 700 muskets per year over the next three years. With the outbreak of the War of 1812, in July of 1812, a contract was let to Eli Whitney for 15,000 muskets (later extended by another 3,000 muskets), conforming to the pattern he had made for the state of New York, but with 42" long barrels. All of these contract muskets shared most of the same features. Overall length was 58". The .69 caliber smoothbore barrel was nominally 42", though the two state contracts did not rigidly en-force that dimension. The lockplate of these muskets bore the inscription "NEW HAVEN" within a curving scroll forward of the cock. Like the Type III 1798 U.S. contract muskets, the lock-plates incorporated a detachable round bottomed brass pan and a round faced cock. The stock was distinguished by hav-ing a low, virtually nonexistent comb similar to that of the 1816 musket pattern. The New York state contract muskets are dis-tinguished by having the state ownership mark "SNY" on the axis of the barrel near the breech. (It should be noted that the first 1,000 muskets delivered under the U.S. 1812 contract were also delivered to New York, but these have the mark across the breech at right angles to the axis of the barrel.) The Connecticut contract muskets are distinguishable by having the state ownership mark "S.C." (for "state of Connecticut" on the barrel and the top of the comb of the stock. On Connecticut muskets in better condition, the Connecticut coat-of-arms (a shield with three clusters of grape vines) should also be visible struck into the wood on the left side of the musket opposite the lock. Verifiable Connecticut and New York contract muskets should bring a premium over the U.S. contract muskets.

Exc.	V.G.	Good	Fair	Poor
—	—	3250	1500	500

Whitney Armory Muskets, 1825-1842

Eli Whitney died in 1825. Although he had a son destined to take over the family business, Eli Whitney, Jr. was only 5 years old when his father passed away and could not assume legal possession until he turned 21 in 1842. In the interim, the company was administered by the senior Whitney's trustees, Henry Edwards and James Goodrich, while the plant itself was run by Whitney's nephews, Philo and Eli Whitney Blake. During their control of the factory, three contracts were fulfilled for the U.S. government, one awarded in August of 1822 for 15,000 muskets (delivered between 1826 and 1830), a second awarded in March of 1830 for 8,750 muskets (delivered between 1831 and 1836) and a final contract in January of 1840 for 3,000 muskets (delivered between 1840 and 1842). An additional 6,750 were delivered under annual allotments granted by the War Department between 1835 and 1839 over and above the contracts for distribution to the states under the 1808 Militia Act. Although the 1840 contract had originally called for U.S. M1840 muskets, in April of that year, the contract was altered so that Whitney's plant could continue to deliver what it had delivered consistently from 1824, the U.S. M1816/1822 flintlock musket.

Whitney (and P. & E.W. Blake) U.S. M1816/1822 Contract Muskets

The U.S. M1816/1822 muskets manufactured at Whitney's Armory were identical to those produced at the U.S. Armories at Springfield and Harpers Ferry. The overall length was 57-3/4". The 42" long, .69 caliber smoothbore barrels were finished with a browning solution until 1831; after that date the metal was left in the polished "bright." The stock and the lock reflect Whitney's earlier attempts impart his design elements into the U.S. patterns. The stock had the low comb of his M1812 musket and the lock incorporated the rounded cock and round bottomed brass pan that he had championed from the French M1777 musket. The lock markings varied during the period that the arm was produced, though all were marked on the pointed tail with the vertical stamp: "NEW HAVEN" arced around the date (1825-1830), or in three vertical lines: "NEW / HAVEN / (date: 1831-1842)". Those made between 1825 and 1830 under the direct supervision of Whitney's nephews bore the two line mark "U.S. / P. & E.W. BLAKE" forward of the cock; those made from 1830 to 1837 bear the "U.S" over "E. WHITNEY" with a crossed arrow and olive branch between; after 1837 the crossed arrow and olive branch motif was eliminated in favor of the simple two lines. In addition to the Whitney Armory's federal contracts, Whitney executed at least one contract with the state of South Carolina in the mid-1830s for an estimated 800 to 2,000 muskets. Basically identical in configuration to the federal contract muskets, the South Carolina muskets were distinguished by the substitution of "S.C." for "U.S." over the "E. WHITNEY" stamp of the lockplate. They also bear the state ownership mark "So. CAROLINA" on the top of the barrel. Due to their relative rarity and Confederate usage (especially if altered to percussion by means of a brazed bolster), the South Carolina contract arms should bring a considerable premium.

Exc.	V.G.	Good	Fair	Poor
—	—	3250	1500	500

Whitney Armory U.S. M1816/M1822 Muskets, Altered to Percussion

From 1850 through 1856, many of the contract muskets in store at the U.S. arsenals were altered from flintlock to percussion by means of the "Belgian" or "cone-in barrel" method. The system of alteration involved the removal of the flintlock battery from the lock, filing in the screw holes from those parts, substituting a percussion hammer for the cock, plugging the vent, removing the breech plug so as to "upset" the upper, right hand side top of the barrel, drilling and threading the "upset" section for a cone, reinserting the breech plug, and screwing in a new percussion cone. The percussioned musket was effective but the barrel was considerably weakened by the process, and while some were rifled during the American Civil War, most saw service in that conflict as smoothbores. As a general rule, the muskets so altered generally command about one-third the price of the arm in original flintlock. Exceptions are those with state ownership marks (eg. "OHIO" in the stock), with regimental marks, or with the so-called "Sea Fencible" buttplate.

Whitney Armory U.S. M1816/M1822 Muskets, Flintlock or Altered to Percussion and Adapted with "Sea Fencible" Heavy Butt Plates

A number of the Whitney U.S. M1816/1822 muskets were delivered to the Commonwealth of Massachusetts under the terms of the 1808 Militia Act. Many of these were subsequently altered to percussion at the Watertown Arsenal near Boston for the state after 1850. At some time in their career both some of the flintlock arms and those that had been altered to percussion were adapted to a heavy brass buttplate with a peculiar knob at its heel. In the process the buttstock was usually narrowed to conform to the width of the new buttplate. Because many of the muskets encountered with this buttplate bore the inspection mark of Samuel Fuller ("SF/V" within a lozenge), these arms were initially considered to have been made for the Massachusetts "Sea Fencible" organizations formed during and after the War of 1812. That appellation, however, has been dismissed, although the exact purpose of the new buttplate and the date of its application are not known. These butt-plates are usually (but not necessarily) found on Whitney contract muskets and invariably are marked with the Massachusetts state ownership mark "MS" on the barrel as well as rack numbers on the tang of the buttplate itself. Despite the unknown purpose of these arms, they command a considerable premium over standard flintlock or altered to percussion Whitney muskets.

Exc.	V.G.	Good	Fair	Poor
—	—	1900	950	250

Eli Whitney Jr. Armory Rifles and Rifle-Muskets, 1842-1865

Upon reaching the age of 21 in 1842, Eli Whitney, Jr. assumed command of his late father's gun making empire. Although he realized that the armory required updating to meet the improved tolerances adopted by the U.S. War Department, he also realized that a profit might be made in turning out arms of lesser standards for independent sale to the militia or the states. As a result, the younger Whitney's product line included not only several of the regulation U.S. longarms, but also a number of "good and serviceable" militia arms, including:

Whitney U.S. M1841 Contract Rifle (unaltered)

Between 1842 and 1855 Eli Whitney, Jr. received five contracts from the U.S. War Department to manufacture the newly adopted U.S. M1841 percussion rifle: 7,500 on October of 1842 (delivered between 1844 and 1847), 7,500 in March of 1848, subsequently extended to 10,000 in January of 1849 (delivered between 1849 and 1853) 5,000 (previously contracted for by Edward K. Tryon) in October of 1848 (delivered contiguous with the 1848 contract for 10,000), 5,000 in 1853 (delivered between 1853 and 1855), and 100 in 1855 (delivered that year). All except the final 1,100 delivered in 1855 conformed to the model made at Harpers Ferry, and of those 1,100, the only difference of 500 of them was the ramrod. This rifle was 49" in length, overall, having a 33" long browned barrel with .54 caliber rifled (7 groove) bore. The barrel bears the stamp of inspection at the breech, usually "U S /(inspectors' initials) / P", while the left flat (after mid-1848 for Whitney rifles) should also bear the stamping "STEEL" to indicate that the barrel had been rolled from "cast steel". Furniture is brass, the buttplate bearing the stamped letters, "U S". The lockplate is flat with a beveled edge and bears the horizontal two line inscription "E. WHITNEY" / "U S" forward of the hammer and the vertical, two line inscription "N. HAVEN" / (date) on the tail. (The date also appears on the breech plug tang). As originally made, the M1841 rifle was not adapted for a bayonet, though several modifications were made to the rifle between 1855 and 1862 to effect that adaptation.

Exc.	V.G.	Good	Fair	Poor
—	—	4250	1750	500

Whitney U.S. M1841/1855 Contract Rifle, Adapted to Saber Bayonet & Long Range Sights

Before the final 600 rifles (of the 2,600 made in 1855) left the factory, the U.S. War Department contracted with Whitney to bring them up to the standards of the modified U.S. M1841 rifle then being produced or adapted at the Harpers Ferry Armory. The adaptation was two fold. First, a long range rear "ladder" style rear sight, having a 2-1/4" base was soldered to the top of the barrel; then a 1/2" long bayonet lug with 1" guide was

brazed to the right side of the barrel, 2-1/2" from the muzzle. To permit disassembly, the old front band was removed and replaced with a shortened version. A new ramrod (also applied to 500 rifles without this adaptation), having an integral iron head cupped for the newly adopted "Minie ball" replaced the flat brass headed ramrod to complete the process; the rifle remained in .54 caliber with 7 grooves. Neither was the front sight modified. Bayonets were furnished by the Ames Manufacturing Company on a separate contract. Rifles so adapted at the Whitney Armory are among the rarer variants of the U.S. M1841 line and prices reflect that rarity.

Exc.	V.G.	Good	Fair	Poor
—	—	4750	1750	650

Whitney U.S. M1841 Contract Rifles, Adapted to Saber Bayonets and Long Range rear sights (Colt 1862 Adaptation)

A large number of unaltered U.S. M1841 rifles remained on hand in U.S. Arsenals when the Civil War broke out, primarily those of Whitney's and Robbins & Lawrence's manufacture. To upgrade these rifles, revolver maker, Samuel Colt arranged to purchase 10,500 and adapt them to bayonets and long range sights. The sight that he affixed consisted of the two leaf rear sight he had been using on his revolving rifles, with one leaf flopping forward and one flopping backward from the 100 yard block. The saber bayonet lug he attached consisted of a blued clamping ring with integral 1/2" long lug attached that could fastened to the barrel so that the lug projected from the right side. These lugs were numbered both to the bayonet and the rifle's barrel, the number appearing on the lower surface of the barrel just behind the location of the clamping ring. Colt also bored the rifles up to .58 caliber, leaving some with 7 grooves but rerifling others with 3 wide grooves. An estimated half of the 10,200 rifles so modified by Colt were of Whitney's earlier production. Due to the Colt association, rifles so modified usually command slightly higher prices than other Civil War adaptations for saber or socket bayonets.

Exc.	V.G.	Good	Fair	Poor
—	—	4750	1750	650

Whitney South Carolina Contract M1841 Rifle

To meet the perceived needs of South Carolina during the anti-slavery debates following the Mexican War Annexation, Whitney produced a variant of the U.S. M1841 rifle for that state, delivering only 274 in 1849. The marking of this rifle differed only in having the letters "S C" on the plate beneath the "E. WHITNEY" stamp. Because South Carolina had previously contracted for 1,000 variant M1841 rifles from William Glaze & Co. in 1853 which accepted a socket bayonet, Whitney provided the 274 1849 dated rifles with that provision also, although the lug was located under the barrel instead of atop it. Because the socket bayonet dominated the forward 3" of the barrel, the front sight was relocated to the top of the upper strap of the front band. Rifles from this contract are exceedingly rare.

Exc.	V.G.	Good	Fair	Poor
—	—	6250	3000	950

Whitney "Good & Serviceable" M1841 Derivatives

From parts or entire rifles rejected for his federal contracts for U.S. M1841 rifles, between 1848 and 1860, Eli Whitney, Jr. assembled a number of rifles similar in overall characteristics to the federal contract rifles but differing both in quality and in a number of minor details. At least four variants were produced between 1855 and 1862 and sold to various states or independent militia companies. Distinguishing characteristics of these four are:

Type I. M1841 rifle adapted to saber bayonet but not to long range sights.

A 1/2" long saber bayonet lug (either with or without the 1" guide) brazed to the right side of the barrel; long front band replaced with short double strapped band left over from 1855 contract. Some of this type (without 1" guide) are known with "OHIO" state ownership marks and are thought to be from among the 420 purchased by the state in 1861 from Schuyler, Hartley & Graham. Examples are known with the lockplate dated 1855 and without any date or "US" stamp below "E. WHITNEY".

Type II. M1841 rifle adapted to saber bayonet and Sharps long range sight.

These rifles also bear the 1/2" brazed saber bayonet lug (with the 1" guide) and the short front band, but they also have a Sharps M1853 "ladder" rear sight added in lieu of the standard notched iron block. Moreover, rifles in this configuration lack the brass patchbox lid and its underlying cavity for implements and greased patches.

Type III. M1841 rifle adapted to socket bayonet and Sharps long range sight.

These late production (1859-1860) derivatives of the M1841 rifle are adapted to the Sharps long range sight used on the Type II. rifles but have a patch box. Unlike standard production, however, it is covered with an iron lid and hingle. The triggerguard strap is also iron. Lock plates delete both the date from the tail and the "US" under "E. WHITNEY." An iron stud is added below the barrel near the muzzle for a socket bayonet, necessitating the relocation of the brass blade front sight to the upper strap of the forward band. Probably less than 100 of this configuration were made, making it the most desirable of the derivative M1841 rifles.

Type IV. M1841 rifle unadapted using modified parts.

Rifles of this configuration use the same markings as the type III rifles but delete entirely the patch box and its lid (like the type II rifles). The triggerguard strap is iron and the lock screws seem to be the same as Whitney used for his Whitney short Enfield derivative rifles. It is suspected that these rifles were purchased from New York dealers and sold to Georgia during the secession crisis of 1860-1861, thereby enhancing their collector's value, though in general Whitney M1841 derivative rifles are equal in pricing:

Exc.	V.G.	Good	Fair	Poor
—	—	3250	1250	500

Whitney M1842 Rifled Musket Derivative

Using rejected U.S. M1842 barrels sold at auction by the Springfield Armory, Whitney assembled approximately 2,000 .69 caliber rifled muskets that he exchanged with the state of New Hampshire in 1858 for a number of old flintlock muskets owned by that state. These rifled muskets exhibit a number of anomalies from the U.S. M1842 musket, although overall length (57-3/4") and the barrel length (42") remain the same as that musket, the bores are rifles with 7 narrow grooves, and in addition to the dates and inspection marks placed at Springfield usually bear the state ownership mark "NEW HAMPSHIRE" on the top of the barrel. In finishing these rifled muskets, Whitney utilized a number of parts from other gun makers, including Sharps M1853 "ladder" style carbine rear sights, bands from the Robbins & Lawrence P1853 Enfield rifle-musket contract, and internal lock parts remaining from his M1841 rifles. Parts that are unique to these arms include the iron nosecap and the flat lockplate. The lockplates are unmarked, but the barrels usually show a letter/number code common to Whitney's production during this period. Despite a production of approximately 2,000 muskets, the survival rate for this type of arm is quite low.

Exc.	V.G.	Good	Fair	Poor
—	—	3250	1250	400

Whitney P1853 "Long Enfield" Rifle-Musket Derivative

Having secured a number of bands and other furniture from the Robbins & Lawrence contract for P1853 Enfield rifle-muskets, about 1859 Whitney developed a derivative of that arm that combined those bands with a 40" barrel .58 caliber, rifled with 7 grooves that basically resembled the configuration of the U.S. M1855 rifle-musket, a copy of which Whitney was also making. The 56" long rifle-musket that resulted was sold to state militia companies and two states, Maryland purchasing 2,000 and Georgia contracting for 1,700 (of which 1,225 were delivered). Although several of the components of the furniture were from the Robbins & Lawrence contract, the nosecap was pewter (Enfield style), and the iron buttplate and brass triggerguard bow/iron strap were of a style peculiar to Whitney' Enfield series. The rear sight resembled the ladder pattern of the U.S. M1855 rifle musket. The unique flat, unbeveled lockplate simply bears the one line stamp, "E. WHITNEY" forward of the hammer.

Exc.	V.G.	Good	Fair	Poor
—	—	3250	1250	600

Whitney P1853 "Short Enfield" Rifle Derivative

At the same time that Whitney developed his "Long Enfield" Derivative Rifle-Musket, he also prepared a short version of it similar to the British P1856 sergeant's rifle. Having an overall length of 49", the rifle version had a 33" long barrel in .58 caliber and rifled with 7 grooves like the rifle-musket. The furniture was basically the same as the rifle-musket as well, with a pewter nosecap, iron buttplate, and combination brass bow and iron strap triggerguard (although some variants are known with all brass P1853 triggerguards). The two iron bands were from the Robbins & Lawrence contract salvage, as were the brass lock screw washers. The flat, unbeveled lockplate is the same style as used in the Long Enfield derivative rifle-muskets and is similarly marked "E. WHITNEY" forward of the hammer. In the manufacture of the rifle, four variants evolved, as follows:

Type I. Butt stock incorporated an oval iron patch box; front and rear sights were of standard U.S. M1841 configuration and no provision was made for a saber bayonet.

Type II. Butt stock continued to incorporate an oval iron patch box; rear sight was now the long range "ladder" type on a 2-5/16" base as used on the long Enfield rifle-musket derivative. Front sight was an iron block with integral blade. A 1/2" long saber bayonet lug was added to the right side of the barrel.

Type III. The oval iron patchbox was deleted from the buttstock. Front and rear sights remain as in Type II, as does bayonet lug.

Type IV. Identical to type III but with a new single leaf rear sight on a 1-1/4" long base.

Total production of these rifles is estimated to have been between 800 and 1,000, with approximately half of the number going to southern states. Prices should not vary between the four types; however, confirmed Confederate usage will increase the value significantly.

Exc.	V.G.	Good	Fair	Poor
—	—	3500	1250	600

Whitney M1855 Rifle Derivative

At the same time that Whitney advertised his Enfield derivative series of rifle-muskets and rifles, he also indicated the availability of a short rifle with saber bayonet. This rifle combined rejected barrels made at Harpers Ferry in 1858 for the U.S. M1855 rifles with rejected, unmilled Maynard tape primer lockplates that had been shaved of their top "hump", marked forward of the hammer with the single line stamp, "E. WHITNEY." The buttplate and the triggerguard also conform to that of the U.S. M1855 rifle, but the bands are brass, remaining from Whitney's M1841/1855 rifle contract. Early in production these rifles used round brass lock screw washers following the M1855 pattern; later production used the winged brass lock screw washers that Whitney inherited from the Robbins & Lawrence P1853 rifle-musket contract and that he used on his Enfield series derivatives. At least two patterns of saber bayonet were used on this rifle.

Exc.	V.G.	Good	Fair	Poor
—	—	3500	1250	500

Whitney M1855 Rifle-Musket Derivative

In 1861, Whitney accepted a U.S. contract to produce 40,000 U.S. "M1855" rifle-muskets. What Whitney had in mind under this contract and what the War Department demanded were two different arms. Whitney's product was similar to the U.S. M1855 rifle-musket but differed in a number of respects. The 40" barrel was .58 caliber but was rifled with 7 rather than 3 grooves and was adapted to the English P1853 socket bayonet he had been using on his Enfield derivative rifle-muskets. The initial rear sight, while similar to the U.S. M1855 type, was slightly shorter, having a 2-5/16" base. (On later production, Whitney substituted a shorter, 1-1/4" long base with a single, pierced leaf sight.) The nosecap, moreover was made of pewter, and followed the Enfield pattern rather than being malleable iron of the U.S. M1855 pattern. On later production, Whitney also substituted brass winged lock screw washers from his Enfield derivative series. The lockplates for these arms were drawn from complete Maynard locks made at the federal armories in 1858 and 1859 but later rejected for flaws. Upon these plates Whitney stamped "E. WHITNEY / N. HAVEN", as on his early Connecticut contract M1861 derivative rifle-muskets. Except for the letter/number code, the barrels are unmarked. Examples are known whose stocks bear indications of issue to the 8th Connecticut Infantry during the Civil War, suggesting Whitney may have sold the few made to Connecticut under his first state contract. Arms with these regimental marks should command a premium over unmarked arms.

Exc.	V.G.	Good	Fair	Poor
—	—	3500	1250	500

Whitney M1861 Connecticut Contract Rifle-Musket Derivative

In 1861 and 1862, Eli Whitney, Jr. entered into two contracts with his home state of Connecticut for respectively 6,000 and 8,000 rifle-muskets generally conforming to the U.S. M1861 rifle musket. A number of exceptions to U.S. model, however, were permitted. On the first contract, the 40" barrels were in .58 caliber but were made with 7 groove rifling instead of 3 groove; on the second contract the arms were made with 3 groove rifling. Nosecaps for both contracts were of the U.S. M1855/1861 pattern but were cast in pewter instead of malleable iron. An exception was also permitted in the rear sights, which initially were the same 1-1/4" long base with pierced single leaf that Whitney had used on his Type IV short Enfield derivative rifles, though later the base was changed to conform to the pattern adopted for the U.S. M1861 rifle-musket but still retaining the single leaf. Lockplates were M1861 style, marked forward of the hammer "E. WHITNEY / N. HAVEN" on early production and with an eagle surmounting a panoply of flags and trophies over "WHITNEYVILLE" on later production. The barrels bore the typical Whitney letter/number code and were adapted to the Enfield pattern socket bayonets rather than the U.S. M1855 socket bayonets. Later production occasionally bears the inspection letters "G.W.Q."

Exc.	V.G.	Good	Fair	Poor
—	—	2500	950	400

Whitney "High Humpback" Lockplate M1861 Rifle-Musket Derivative

With the completion of his Connecticut contracts, Whitney combined the excess parts from its production with some of the unmilled and unshaved lockplates that he still had on hand from his M1855 Rifle Derivatives. The 56" long rifle-muskets that resulted have 40" barrels in .58 caliber with 3 groove rifling and a rear sight that conforms to the U.S. M1861 pattern that Whitney began making in 1863. The flat,

beveled unmilled lockplates bear the two line stamp "E. WHITNEY / N. HAVEN" that Whitney had used on his M1855 rifle-musket derivative and on the early M1861 Connecticut contract rifle-muskets, but showing considerable wear, to the extent that the second line is often incomplete or missing entirely. Photograph evidence indicates that the 21st Connecticut Infantry received some of these rifle-muskets. They are often mistaken as a southern purchase, which artificially raises the asking prices.

Exc.	V.G.	Good	Fair	Poor
—	—	3250	1250	500

Whitney "Manton" M1861 Rifle-Musket Derivative

In order to dispose of some of his inferior arms from the second Connecticut state contract, Whitney assembled at least 1,300 bearing a fictitious Old English lock stamp "Manton" forward of the hammer and the date "1862" on its tail. In most respects this arm resembled the U.S. M1861 rifle musket, complete with 3 groove rifling in its .58 caliber, 40" barrel with typical Whitney letter/number code near the muzzle (and often also marked "G.W.Q. on its left flat). Nosecaps, in typical Whitney style, were case from pewter instead of being formed from malleable iron. The rear sight closely follows the M1861 pattern but lacks the step on its side walls since it utilized a simple pierced leaf instead of the compound double leaf of the M1861 rifle-musket. These arms were disposed of in the New York City market after the 1863 Draft Riot and issued to the New York National Guard.

Exc.	V.G.	Good	Fair	Poor
—	—	4250	2000	600

Whitney "Direct Vent" M1861 Rifle-Musket Derivatives

In his continued efforts to dispose of surplus and rejected parts from his Connecticut and federal contracts, Whitney devised in 1863 a rifle-musket generally conforming to the M1861 rifle-musket except in two notable features. The bolster, instead of projecting considerably away from the barrel and having a clean-out screw was relatively short and flat faced. The process of making this bolster eliminated one production sequence, since it was not possible to drill the hole for the cone directly to the barrel. To accommodate the new cone position, the lockplates were made flat, without the bevel, and inletted flush with the stock. Lockplates bear the eagle surmounting the panoply of flags and trophies over "WHITNEYVILLE" stamp forward of the hammer, and are known with "1863" on the tail or without any date. The rear sight is the same as used on the "Manton" rifle-musket derivative. Arms with barrels than 40", 39", and 30" exist, all in .58 caliber with 3 groove rifling; however, the shortest of these may be postwar modifications for cadet use. Quantities made are not known, but surviving examples suggest limited production, probably to use faulty parts from the 1863 federal contract.

Exc.	V.G.	Good	Fair	Poor
—	—	3250	1250	400

Whitney U.S. M1861 Contract Rifle-Musket

In October of 1863, Whitney secured a contract with the U.S. War Department to produce 15,000 U.S. M1861 rifle-muskets. The arms manufactured under this contract conform in all respects to the Springfield Model adopted in 1861. The 40" barrel is in .58 caliber and rifled with 3 grooves; its rear sight conforms to the two leaf model with stepped side walls. Nose-cap is M1861 style and made of malleable iron. Socket bayonets furnished with them conform to the U.S. M1855/M1861 pattern. Marks include "US" on buttplate and standard inspection marks on barrel and stock. Lockplate marked with eagle surmounting letters "US" forward of the hammer and "WHIT-NEYVILLE" on the forward projection of the plate; date, "1863" or "1864" stamped on tail of the plate.

Exc.	V.G.	Good	Fair	Poor
—	—	3250	1250	400

Whitney U.S. Navy Contract Rifle

In July of 1861, Whitney entered a contact with the U.S. Navy to produce 10,000 rifles of the "Plymouth Pattern". So called after the U.S. Navy warship whereupon the first Harpers Ferry trial rifles had been developed, the new Navy rifle borrowed many of its characteristics from the French M1846 "carbine a tige." Overall length was 50" with a 34" long barrel bearing a saber bayonet lug with guide extending nearly to the muzzle on its right side. The bore was .69 caliber, rifled with three broad lands and grooves. The rear sight copied the French M1846 and M1859 styles, i.e. it has an elevating ladder but no sidewalls. On early production the sights are serially numbered to the rifle's serial number (appearing on the breech plug tang). Barrels bear the standard U.S. inspection marks on the left quarter flat and the production date ("1863" or "1864") on the top of the barrel near the breech. Two lock markings have been encountered. The earlier production uses flat beveled plate marked with the date "1863" on its tail and an eagle surmounting a panoply of flags and trophies over the name "WHITNEYVILLE." In later (after serial no. 3,000) the lock's tail is marked "1864" and the stamping forward of the hammer matches that on the U.S. M1861 Whitney contract rifle-muskets, i.e. a small eagle over "U S" and "WHITNEYVILLE" in the forward projection of the plate. Inspector's initials (F.C.W.) appear on the barrel and in a cartouche on the stock.

Exc.	V.G.	Good	Fair	Poor
—	—	4250	1750	600

The Whitney Arms Company, 1865-1888

With the close of the American Civil War, Eli Whitney, Jr. again turned his eyes to the manufacture of inexpensive arms from parts remaining on hand from his Civil War contracts. Extra barrels were turned into inexpensive muzzleloading shotguns, and a few breechloading designs were toyed with. Following Remington's example, Whitney soon realized that a substantial profit could be made in the production of single shot martial arms for foreign governments. The result was a series of breechloading arms that copied many salient features of the Remington line, including a direct copy after the expiration of the Remington patent for the "rolling block" mechanism. Not until the late 1870's did Whitney acquire the rights to several patents that led to the production of a lever action repeating rifle. During the postwar period, revolver production, which had begun with evasions of Colt's patents in the decade prior to the Civil War, mushroomed with the production of small, spur trigger rimfire cartridge revolvers. Despite the variety of arms produced, by 1883 Whitney was considering the sale of his company. Business reverses over the next five years necessitated the sale of the firm to Winchester in 1888. Primarily interested securing in the patent rights for Whitney's lever action series of rifles, Winchester closed the plant and moved its machinery to New Haven. After ninety years of production the Whitneyville Armory ceased to exist.

Single Barreled Percussion Shotgun

This firearm was manufactured by Whitney out of surplus .58 caliber rifle barrels that were opened up and converted to smoothbore .60 caliber shotgun barrels. They are offered in lengths of 28" to 36" and are marked "Whitney Arms Co., Whitneyville, Conn. Homogeneous Wrought Steel". The finish is blued, with varnished walnut stocks that are crudely checkered. There were approximately 2,000 manufactured between 1866 and 1869. These guns are rarely encountered on today's market.

Exc.	V.G.	Good	Fair	Poor
—	—	950	400	150

Double Barreled Percussion Shotgun

The specifications for this version are similar to that of the single barrel except that there are two side-by-side barrels with double locks and hammers and double triggers. They are slightly more common than the single barreled version.

Exc.	V.G.	Good	Fair	Poor
—	—	950	400	150

Swing-Breech Carbine

This is a single shot breechloading carbine chambered for the .46-caliber rimfire cartridge. It has a 22" round barrel with a button-released breechblock that swings to the side for loading. The finish is blued, with a walnut stock. There were fewer than 50 manufactured in 1866.

Exc.	V.G.	Good	Fair	Poor
—	—	3250	1750	600

Whitney-Cochran Carbine

This is a single shot breechloading carbine chambered for the .44 rimfire cartridge. It has a 28" round barrel with a lever activated breechblock that raises upward for loading. It was manufactured under license from J.W. Cochran. The finish is blued, with a walnut stock. There is a saddle ring on the left side of the frame. It is marked "Whitney Arms Co. - Whitneyville, Conn." This gun was produced for the 1867 Government Carbine Trials. There were fewer than 50 manufactured in 1866 and 1867.

Courtesy Milwaukee Public Museum, Milwaukee, Wisconsin

Exc.	V.G.	Good	Fair	Poor
—	—	4250	1750	600

Excelsior

This is a single-shot rifle chambered for the .38, .44, or .50 rimfire cartridges. It is found with various-length octagonal or round barrels. The finish is blued, with a walnut stock and forearm held on by one barrel band. The breechblock pivots downward for loading. There is a center-mounted hammer. It is marked "Whitney Arms Co. Whitneyville Conn." The shorter barreled carbine versions have a saddle ring on the frame. There were approximately 200 manufactured between 1866 and 1870.

Exc.	V.G.	Good	Fair	Poor
—	—	2500	950	300

Whitney-Howard Lever Action

This is a single-shot breechloader that is chambered for the .44 rimfire cartridge. It has also been noted as a shotgun chambered for 20 gauge smoothbore with barrels from 30" to 40" in length. The rifle version has barrel lengths from 22" to 28". The breechblock is opened by means of a combination lever and triggerguard. There is also a carbine version with barrel lengths of 18.5" or 19". There were approximately 2,000 manufactured totally between 1866 and 1870. Values are as follows:

Shotgun

Courtesy Buffalo Bill Historical Center, Cody, Wyoming

Exc.	V.G.	Good	Fair	Poor
—	—	600	250	100

Rifle

Courtesy Milwaukee Public Museum, Milwaukee, Wisconsin

Exc.	V.G.	Good	Fair	Poor
—	—	750	350	150

Carbine

Courtesy Milwaukee Public Museum, Milwaukee, Wisconsin

Exc.	V.G.	Good	Fair	Poor
—	—	950	400	200

Whitney Phoenix

There is little known about the origin of this model. It is built on a patent issued to Whitney in 1874. There are a number of variations that are all marked "Phoenix, Patent May 24, 74." The

Whitney name is not marked on any of the versions. They are all single-shot breechloaders with a breechblock that lifts to the right side and upward for loading. The barrels are all blued, with either case colored or blued receivers and walnut stocks. There were approximately 25,000 total manufactured between 1867 and 1881. The models and values are as follows:

Courtesy Milwaukee Public Museum, Milwaukee, Wisconsin

Courtesy Milwaukee Public Museum, Milwaukee, Wisconsin

Gallery Rifle

This version is chambered for the .22 rimfire caliber and has a 24" half-octagonal barrel. Its production was quite limited.

Exc.	V.G.	Good	Fair	Poor
—	—	1250	500	200

Shotgun

This is a smoothbore version chambered for 10, 12, 14, 16, or 22 gauge. It has smoothbore barrels between 26" and 32" in length. There were approximately 5,000 manufactured.

Exc.	V.G.	Good	Fair	Poor
—	—	500	200	100

Military Rifle

This version is chambered for the .433, .45, or .50 caliber centerfire cartridges. It has a 35" round barrel with a full-length, two-piece walnut stock held on by three barrel bands. There were approximately 15,000 manufactured. Many were sent to Central or South America.

Exc.	V.G.	Good	Fair	Poor
—	—	2500	1000	400

Schuetzen Rifle

This is a target-shooting version chambered for the .38, .40, or .44 centerfire cartridges. It has either a 30" or 32" octagonal barrel with a Schuetzen-type walnut stock and forearm that features hand checkering. It has a nickel-plated, Swiss-style buttplate and adjustable sights with a spirit level. This model has been noted with double-set triggers. There were few manufactured.

Exc.	V.G.	Good	Fair	Poor
—	—	2750	1200	450

Civilian Carbine

This version is chambered for the .44 caliber centerfire and has a 24" round barrel. The finish is blued, with a case colored frame and a walnut stock and forearm held on by one barrel band. It has military-type sights, buttplate, and a saddle ring mounted on the frame. There were approximately 500 manufactured.

Courtesy Milwaukee Public Museum, Milwaukee, Wisconsin

Exc.	V.G.	Good	Fair	Poor
—	—	2500	850	400

Military Carbine

This version is chambered for the .433, .45, or .50 centerfire cartridges. It has a 20.5" round barrel and was manufactured for Central and South America. It is very rarely encountered on today's market.

Courtesy Milwaukee Public Museum, Milwaukee, Wisconsin

Courtesy Milwaukee Public Museum, Milwaukee, Wisconsin

Exc.	V.G.	Good	Fair	Poor
—	—	2500	850	400

Whitney-Laidley Model I Rolling Block

Whitney acquired manufacturing rights for this model from the inventors T. Laidley and C.A. Emery, who had received the patent in 1866. Whitney immediately started to modify the action to become competitive with the Remington Rolling Block. There were approximately 50,000 manufactured total between 1871 and 1881. There are a number of variations of this model as follows:

Military Carbine

There were approximately 5,000 manufactured chambered for the .433, .45, or .50 centerfire cartridges. It has a 20.5" round barrel with military-type sights and a saddle ring on the receiver. The finish is blued, with a case colored frame and a walnut stock. Most of them were shipped to Central or South America.

Exc.	V.G.	Good	Fair	Poor
—	—	1750	700	250

Civilian Carbine

This version is chambered for .44 rimfire or centerfire and .46 rimfire. It has either an 18.5" or 19.5" barrel. It is blued, with a case colored frame. The stock is walnut. A nickel-plated version is also available. There were approximately 1,000 of this version manufactured.

Exc.	V.G.	Good	Fair	Poor
—	—	1500	600	200

Military Rifle

This version is chambered the same as the Military Carbine but has either a 32.5" or 35" round barrel with a full-length two-piece stock held on by three barrel bands. The finish is blued, with a case colored receiver and a walnut stock. There were approximately 30,000 manufactured. Most were shipped to Central or South America.

Courtesy Milwaukee Public Museum, Milwaukee, Wisconsin

Exc.	V.G.	Good	Fair	Poor
—	—	1600	700	250

Gallery Rifle

This is a .22 caliber sporting-rifle version with a 24" octagonal barrel. The finish is similar to the Military Rifle. There were approximately 500 manufactured.

Exc.	V.G.	Good	Fair	Poor
—	—	1150	475	200

Sporting Rifle

This version is chambered for .38, .40, .44, .45, or .50 centerfire, as well as .32, .38, or .44 rimfire. It features barrel lengths from 24" to 30" in either round or octagonal configurations. The finish is similar to the Military Rifle, and there were approximately 5,000 manufactured.

Exc.	V.G.	Good	Fair	Poor
—	—	1750	750	300

Creedmoor No. 1 Rifle

This version is chambered for the .44 caliber cartridge and has a 32" or 34" barrel that is either round or octagonal in configuration. It has a blued finish with case colored frame and a hand checkered, select walnut stock and forearm. It features vernier adjustable sights with a spirit level. It is marked "Whitney Creedmoor". There were fewer than 100 manufactured.

Exc.	V.G.	Good	Fair	Poor
—	—	5250	2750	850

Creedmoor No. 2 Rifle

This version is similar to the No. 1 Rifle except that it is chambered for the .40 caliber cartridge with either a 30" or 32" barrel.

Exc.	V.G.	Good	Fair	Poor
—	—	4250	1750	500

Whitney-Remington Model 2 Rolling Block

When Remington's patent for the Rolling Block action expired, Whitney was quick to reproduce the action, labeling it his "New Improved System." It is essentially quite similar to Remington's Rolling Block and is easily recognized when compared with the Model 1 because it has only two parts — the hammer and the breechblock. The frame is also rounded. The tang on this model is marked "Whitney Arms Company, New Haven Ct USA". There were approximately 50,000 total manufactured between 1881 and 1888. There are a number of variations as follows:

Shotgun

This is a smoothbore version chambered for 12, 14, 16, or 20 gauge. It is offered with barrel lengths between 26" and 30". Twenty inch barrels have also been noted.

Exc.	V.G.	Good	Fair	Poor
—	—	550	200	100

Military Carbine

This version is chambered for the .433 and .45 centerfire cartridges. It has a 20.5" barrel and is blued, with a case colored receiver and walnut stock. There were approximately 5,000 manufactured. Most were sent to South or Central America.

Exc.	V.G.	Good	Fair	Poor
—	—	1250	550	250

Civilian Carbine

This version is chambered for the .44 rimfire or centerfire cartridge with an 18.5" round barrel. The finish is similar to the Military Carbine. There were approximately 2,000 manufactured.

Exc.	V.G.	Good	Fair	Poor
—	—	1250	550	250

Military Rifle

This version is chambered for the .433, .45, or .50 centerfire cartridge. It has a 32.5" or 35" barrel. It is finished similarly to the Military Carbine. There were approximately 39,000 manufactured.

Courtesy Buffalo Bill Historical Center, Cody, Wyoming

Exc.	V.G.	Good	Fair	Poor
—	—	1500	650	250

No. 1 Sporting Rifle

This version is chambered for various popular sporting cartridges and is offered with barrel lengths from 26" to 30", either round or octagonal in configuration. The finish is blued, with a case colored receiver and a varnished walnut stock. There were many options available that could radically affect the value, and a qualified appraisal would be advisable. There were approximately 3,000 manufactured.

Exc.	V.G.	Good	Fair	Poor
—	—	1750	750	300

No. 2 Sporting Rifle

This is a smaller version of the No. 1 Rifle, chambered for the .22 rimfire, .32, .38, and .44-40 centerfire cartridges. Again, a qualified appraisal would be helpful, as many options can affect the value.

Exc.	V.G.	Good	Fair	Poor
—	—	1250	550	200

Whitney-Burgess-Morse Rifle

This is a lever action repeating rifle chambered for the .45-70 Government cartridge. There are three variations. All have a magazine tube mounted beneath the barrel with blued finishes and walnut stocks. The barrels are marked "G. W. Morse Patented Oct. 28th 1856". The tang is marked "A. Burgess Patented Jan. 7th, 1873, Patented Oct 19th 1873". There were approximately 3,000 total manufactured between 1878 and 1882. The variations areas follows:

Sporting Rife

This version has a 28" octagonal or round barrel. The magazine tube holds 9 rounds. There are a number of options available that can increase the value drastically; and we recommend competent, individual appraisal. Value given is for a standard model.

Exc.	V.G.	Good	Fair	Poor
—	—	3250	1250	400

Military Rifle

This version has a 33" round barrel with a full-length forearm held on by two barrel bands. It features military sights and has an 11-round tubular magazine. It has a bayonet lug and sling swivels. This variation is also found chambered for the .43 Spanish and .42 Russian cartridges. There were approximately 1,000 manufactured.

Exc.	V.G.	Good	Fair	Poor
—	—	4250	2000	700

Carbine

This version has a 22" round barrel with a full-length forearm held on by one barrel band. It has a 7-round tubular magazine and a saddle ring attached to the frame. There were approximately 500 manufactured.

Exc.	V.G.	Good	Fair	Poor
—	—	4750	2250	750

Whitney-Kennedy Rifle

This is a lever action repeating rifle that was manufactured in two sizes. It has a magazine tube mounted under the barrel and a blued finish with a case colored lever. The stock is walnut. The barrel is marked "Whitney Arms Co New Haven, Conn. U.S.A." Occasionally, the word "Kennedy" is marked after the Whitney name. There are two major variations. One features a standard-type action lever; and the other, the same "S"-shaped lever that is found on the Burgess model. This version would be worth approximately 10% additional. As with many of the rifles of this era, there were many options available that will affect the values. We strongly recommend securing a qualified appraisal for all but the standard models if a transaction is contemplated. There were approximately 15,000 manufactured between 1879 and 1886. The variations of the Whitney-Kennedy and their values are as follows:

Courtesy Buffalo Bill Historical Center, Cody, Wyoming

Small Frame Sporting Rifle

This version is chambered for the .32-20, .38-40, and the .40-40 cartridges. It has a 24" barrel that is either round or octagonal in configuration. Examples will be noted with either a full-length or half-length tubular magazine.

Exc.	V.G.	Good	Fair	Poor
—	—	2250	900	350

Large Frame Sporting Rifle

This version is chambered for the .40-60, .45-60, .45-75, and the .50-90 cartridges. The .50-caliber version is uncommon and will bring a 20% premium. The barrel lengths offered are 26" or 28".

Exc.	V.G.	Good	Fair	Poor
—	—	2500	1150	450

Military Rifle

This is a large-frame model, chambered for the .40-.60, .44-.40, and the .45-60 cartridges. It has a 32.25" round barrel and either an 11- or 16-round tubular magazine. It has a full-length walnut forend held on by two barrel bands and features a bayonet lug and sling swivels. There were approximately 1,000 manufactured. Most were shipped to Central or South America.

Exc.	V.G.	Good	Fair	Poor
—	—	3750	1750	550

Military Carbine

This is built on either the small-frame or large-frame action and is chambered for the .38-40, .44-40, .40-60, or .45-60 cartridges. It has either a 20" or 22" round barrel and a 9- or 12-round tubular magazine, depending on the caliber. It has a short forend held on by a single barrel band. There were approximately 1,000 manufactured. Most were sent to Central or South America.

Courtesy Buffalo Bill Historical Center, Cody, Wyoming

Exc.	V.G.	Good	Fair	Poor
—	—	3750	1750	550

Hooded Cylinder Pocket Revolver

This is an unusual revolver that is chambered for .28 caliber percussion. It has a manually rotated, 6-shot hooded cylinder that has etched decorations. The octagonal barrel is offered in lengths of 3" to 6". There is a button at the back of the frame that unlocks the cylinder so that it can be rotated. The finish is blued, with a brass frame and two-piece rounded walnut grips.

It is marked "E. Whitney N. Haven Ct." There were approximately 200 manufactured between 1850 and 1853.

Exc.	V.G.	Good	Fair	Poor
—	—	3250	1500	600

Two Trigger Pocket Revolver

This is a conventional-appearing pocket revolver with a manually rotated cylinder. There is a second trigger located in front of the conventional triggerguard that releases the cylinder so that it can be turned. It is chambered for .32 caliber percussion and has an octagonal barrel from 3" to 6" in length. It has a 5-shot unfluted cylinder that is etched and a brass frame. The remainder is blued, with squared walnut two-piece grips. An iron-frame version is also available, but only 50 were produced. It would bring approximately 60% additional. There were approximately 650 total manufactured between 1852 and 1854.

Courtesy Milwaukee Public Museum, Milwaukee, Wisconsin

Exc.	V.G.	Good	Fair	Poor
—	—	1750	750	250

Whitney-Beals Patent Revolver

This was an unusual, ring-trigger pocket pistol that was made in three basic variations.

Courtesy Milwaukee Public Museum, Milwaukee, Wisconsin

First Model

This version is chambered for .31-caliber percussion and has barrels of octagonal configuration from 2" to 6" in length. It has a brass frame and a 6-shot cylinder. It is marked "F. Beals/New Haven, Ct." There were only 50 manufactured.

Exc.	V.G.	Good	Fair	Poor
—	—	3500	1500	450

.31 Caliber Model

This version has an iron frame and a 7-shot cylinder. The octagonal barrels are from 2" to 6" in length. It is marked "Address E. Whitney/Whitneyville, Ct." There were approximately 2,300 manufactured.

Exc.	V.G.	Good	Fair	Poor
—	—	1250	550	200

.28 Caliber Model

Except for the caliber, this model is similar to the .31 Caliber Model. There were approximately 850 manufactured.

Exc.	V.G.	Good	Fair	Poor
—	—	1500	600	250

Whitney 1851 Navy

This is a faithful copy of the 1851 Colt Revolver. It is virtually identical. There is a possibility that surplus Colt parts were utilized in the construction of this revolver. There were approximately 400 manufactured in 1857 and 1858.

Exc.	V.G.	Good	Fair	Poor
—	—	4250	1750	650

Whitney Navy Revolver

This is a single action revolver chambered for .36 caliber percussion. It has a standard octagonal barrel length of 7.5". It has an iron frame and a 6-shot unfluted cylinder that is roll engraved. The finish is blued, with a case colored loading lever and two-piece walnut grips. The barrel is marked either "E. Whitney/N. Haven" or "Eagle Co." There are a number of minor variations on this revolver, and we strongly urge competent appraisal if contemplating a transaction. There were 33,000 total manufactured between 1858 and 1862.

Courtesy Wallis & Wallis, Lewes, Sussex, England

FIRST MODEL

Nearly the entire production of the First Model is marked "Eagle Co." The reason for this marking is unknown. There are four distinct variations of this model. They are as follows:

First Variation

This model has no integral loading-lever assembly and has a thin top strap. There were only 100 manufactured.

Exc.	V.G.	Good	Fair	Poor
—	—	3250	1250	550

Second Variation

This version is similar to the First Variation, with an integral loading lever. There were approximately 200 manufactured.

Exc.	V.G.	Good	Fair	Poor
—	—	2750	900	400

Third Variation

This is similar to the Second, with a three-screw frame instead of four screws. The loading lever is also modified. There were approximately 500 manufactured.

Exc.	V.G.	Good	Fair	Poor
—	—	2000	700	300

Fourth Variation

This version has a rounded frame and a safety notch between the nipples on the rear of the cylinder. There have been examples noted marked "E. Whitney/N. Haven." There were approximately 700 manufactured.

Exc.	V.G.	Good	Fair	Poor
—	—	2250	650	300

SECOND MODEL

First Variation

This version features a more robust frame with a brass triggerguard. The barrel is marked "E. Whitney/N. Haven." The cylinder pin is secured by a wing nut, and there is an integral loading lever. There were approximately 1,200 manufactured.

Exc.	V.G.	Good	Fair	Poor
—	—	1750	800	300

Second Variation

This version has six improved safety notches on the rear of the cylinder. There were approximately 10,000 manufactured.

Exc.	V.G.	Good	Fair	Poor
—	—	1500	600	250

Third Variation

This version has an improved, Colt-type loading-lever latch. There were approximately 2,000 manufactured.

Exc.	V.G.	Good	Fair	Poor
—	—	1500	600	250

Fourth Variation

This is similar to the Third except the cylinder is marked "Whitneyville". There were approximately 10,000 manufactured.

Exc.	V.G.	Good	Fair	Poor
—	—	1500	600	250

Fifth Variation

This version has a larger triggerguard. There were approximately 4,000 manufactured.

Exc.	V.G.	Good	Fair	Poor
—	—	1500	600	250

Sixth Variation

This version has the larger triggerguard and five-groove rifling instead of the usual seven-groove. There were approximately 2,500 manufactured.

Exc.	V.G.	Good	Fair	Poor
—	—	1500	600	250

Whitney Pocket Revolver

This is a single action revolver chambered for .31 caliber percussion. It has octagonal barrels between 3" and 6" in length. It has a 5-shot unfluted cylinder that is roll engraved and marked "Whitneyville". The frame is iron with a blued finish and a case colored integral loading lever. The grips are two-piece walnut. The development of this model, as far as models and variations go, is identical to that which we described in the Navy Model designation. The values are different, and we list them for reference. Again, we recommend securing qualified appraisal if a transaction is contemplated. There were approximately 32,500 manufactured from 1858 to 1862.

Courtesy Buffalo Bill Historical Center, Cody, Wyoming

First Model

First Variation

Exc.	V.G.	Good	Fair	Poor
—	—	1750	750	250

Second Variation

Exc.	V.G.	Good	Fair	Poor
—	—	1250	500	200

Third Variation

Exc.	V.G.	Good	Fair	Poor
—	—	1000	400	150

Fourth Variation

Exc.	V.G.	Good	Fair	Poor
—	—	1000	400	150

Fifth Variation

Exc.	V.G.	Good	Fair	Poor
—	—	1000	400	150

Second Model

First Variation

Exc.	V.G.	Good	Fair	Poor
—	—	750	300	100

Second Variation

Exc.	V.G.	Good	Fair	Poor
—	—	750	300	100

Third Variation

Exc.	V.G.	Good	Fair	Poor
—	—	750	300	100

Fourth Variation

Exc.	V.G.	Good	Fair	Poor
—	—	900	375	125

New Model Pocket Revolver

This is a single action, spur-triggered pocket revolver chambered for .28-caliber percussion. It has a 3.5" octagonal barrel and a 6-shot roll engraved cylinder. It features an iron frame with a blued finish and two-piece walnut grips. The barrel is marked "E. Whitney/N. Haven". There were approximately 2,000 manufactured between 1860 and 1867.

Courtesy Milwaukee Public Museum, Milwaukee, Wisconsin

Exc.	V.G.	Good	Fair	Poor
—	—	1000	450	200

Rimfire Pocket Revolver

This is a spur-trigger, single action, solid-frame pocket revolver that was produced in three frame sizes, depending on the caliber. It is chambered for the .22, .32, and .38 rimfire cartridges. The frame is brass, and it is found in a variety of finishes- nickel-plated or blued, or a combination thereof. The bird's-head grips are rosewood or hard rubber; ivory or pearl grips are sometimes encountered and will bring a slight premium in value. The barrels are octagonal and from 1.5" to 5" in length. The barrels are marked "Whitneyville Armory Ct. USA". They have also been noted with the trade names "Monitor," "Defender," or "Eagle." They were commonly referred to as the Model No. 1, No. 1.5, Model 2, or Model 2.5. The values for all are quite similar. There were approximately 30,000 manufactured of all types between 1871 and 1879.

Courtesy Milwaukee Public Museum, Milwaukee, Wisconsin

Courtesy Milwaukee Public Museum, Milwaukee, Wisconsin

Exc.	V.G.	Good	Fair	Poor
—	—	350	100	50

WHITNEY FIREARMS COMPANY
Hartford, Connecticut

Wolverine
A .22 caliber semiautomatic pistol with a 4.75" barrel. Blued or nickel-plated with plastic grips and an aluminum alloy frame. This pistol is readily distinguishable by its streamlined form. Approximately 13,000 examples were made with the blued finish and 900 with a nickel-plated finish. The slide marked "Wolverine Whitney Firearms Inc., New Haven, Conn USA". Some examples are also marked "Lightning". Manufactured from 1955 to 1962.

Blue Finish

Exc.	V.G.	Good	Fair	Poor
500	400	350	250	200

Nickel-Plated

Exc.	V.G.	Good	Fair	Poor
600	500	450	300	250

WHITWORTH
SEE—Interarms

WICHITA ARMS, INC.
Wichita, Kansas

Classic Rifle
A single shot bolt action rifle produced in a variety of calibers with a 21" octagonal barrel. Offered with Canjar adjustable triggers. Blued with a checkered walnut stock.

NIB	Exc.	V.G.	Good	Fair	Poor
3000	2500	2250	1850	1250	1000

Varmint Rifle
As above, with a round barrel.

NIB	Exc.	V.G.	Good	Fair	Poor
2000	1750	1500	1250	1000	800

Silhouette Rifle
As above, with a 24" heavy barrel, gray composition stock and 2-oz. Canjar trigger.

NIB	Exc.	V.G.	Good	Fair	Poor
2200	1900	1700	1000	850	650

Wichita International Pistol
A single shot pivoted barrel target pistol produced in a variety of calibers from .22 to .357 Magnum with a 10.5" or 14" barrel fitted with either adjustable sights or telescopic sight mounts. Stainless steel with walnut forestock and grips.

NIB	Exc.	V.G.	Good	Fair	Poor
500	450	400	350	300	200

Wichita Classic Pistol

A bolt action single shot pistol chambered for a variety of calibers up to .308, with a left hand action and 11.25" barrel. Blued with a walnut stock.

NIB	Exc.	V.G.	Good	Fair	Poor
3000	2500	2250	1850	1250	1000

Wichita Classic Engraved As Above, But Embellished

NIB	Exc.	V.G.	Good	Fair	Poor
5000	4250	3500	2500	2000	1500

Wichita Silhouette Pistol

As above, in 7mm HMSA or .308 with a 15" barrel. The walnut stock is made so that the pistol grip is located beneath the forward end of the bolt.

NIB	Exc.	V.G.	Good	Fair	Poor
1100	950	750	600	500	400

Wichita MK40

As above, with a 13" barrel having multi-range sights and either a composition or walnut stock. Standard finish is blued, however, this model was also made in stainless steel.

NIB	Exc.	V.G.	Good	Fair	Poor
1100	950	750	600	500	400

WICKLIFFE RIFLES
Triple S Development
Wickliffe, Ohio

Model 76

A single-shot falling-block rifle produced in a variety of calibers from .22 Hornet to .45-70 with a 22" lightweight or 26" heavyweight barrel. Blued with a walnut stock. Introduced in 1976.

Exc.	V.G.	Good	Fair	Poor
550	350	300	250	175

Model 76 Deluxe

As above, with a nickel-silver pistol grip cap, machine jeweled breechblock and more finely figured walnut stock. Introduced in 1976.

Exc.	V.G.	Good	Fair	Poor
600	400	350	300	200

Traditionalist

The Model 76 in .30-06 or .45-70 caliber with a 24" barrel having open sights and a checkered walnut buttstock. Introduced in 1979.

Exc.	V.G.	Good	Fair	Poor
550	350	300	250	175

Stinger

Similar to the Model 76, but chambered for .22 Hornet or .223 Remington with a 22" barrel fitted with a Burris 6X power telescope. Blued with a checkered Monte Carlo-style stock. Introduced in 1979.

Exc.	V.G.	Good	Fair	Poor
550	350	300	250	175

Stinger Deluxe

As above, with a superior grade of finish and more finely figured walnut stock.

Exc.	V.G.	Good	Fair	Poor
600	400	350	300	200

WIENER WAFFENFABRIK
Vienna, Austria

Little Tom

A 6.35mm or 7.65mm double action semiautomatic pistol with a 2.5" barrel. The slide marked "Wiener Waffenfabrik Patent Little Tom", and the caliber. Blued with either walnut or plastic grips inlaid with a medallion bearing the company's trademark. Approximately 10,000 were made from 1919 to 1925.

Courtesy Faintich Auction Service, Photo Paul Goodwin

Exc.	V.G.	Good	Fair	Poor
500	450	400	250	175

WILDEY FIREARMS CO., INC.
Cheshire, Connecticut
New Burg, New York
Brookfield, Connecticut

Wildey Auto Pistol

A gas-operated, rotary-bolt, double action semiautomatic pistol chambered for the .357 Peterbuilt, the .45 Winchester Magnum, or the .475 Wildey Magnum cartridges. with 5", 6", 7", 8", or 10" ventilated rib barrels. The gas-operated action is adjustable and features a single shot cutoff. The rotary bolt has three heavy locking lugs. Constructed of stainless steel with adjustable sights and wood grips. The values of this rarely encountered pistol are based on not only the condition, but the caliber—as well the serial number range, with earlier-numbered guns being worth a good deal more than the later or current production models.

Cheshire CT Address
Produced in .45 Winchester Magnum only and is serial numbered from No. 1 through 2489.

Serial No. 1 through 200

NIB	Exc.	V.G.	Good	Fair	Poor
2000	1500	1200	—	—	—

Serial numbers above 200 would be worth approximately $200 less respectively in each category of condition.

Survivor Model
This pistol is presently manufactured in Brookfield, Connecticut.

NIB	Exc.	V.G.	Good	Fair	Poor
1100	875	750	550	450	300

Presentation Model
As above, but engraved and fitted with hand checkered walnut grips.

NIB	Exc.	V.G.	Good	Fair	Poor
2500	2000	1500	—	—	—

WILKES, JOHN
London, England
SEE—British Double Guns

WILKINSON ARMS CO.
Covina, California

Diane
A .25 caliber semiautomatic pistol with a 2.25" barrel and 6-shot magazine. Blued with plastic grips.

Exc.	V.G.	Good	Fair	Poor
175	125	100	75	50

Terry Carbine
A 9mm caliber semiautomatic carbine with a 16.25" barrel, adjustable sights, and 30-shot magazine. Matte blued with either a black composition or maple stock.

Exc.	V.G.	Good	Fair	Poor
400	300	250	175	125

WILLIAMSON
MOORE FIREARMS COMPANY
New York, New York

Derringer
A .41 caliber single shot pocket pistol with a 2.5" sliding barrel. Blued, with a silver-plated furniture and a checkered walnut grip. Barrel marked "Williamson's Pat. Oct. 2, 1866 New York". This pistol was fitted with an auxiliary percussion cap chamber adaptor. Manufactured from 1866 to approximately 1870.

Exc.	V.G.	Good	Fair	Poor
—	—	950	400	100

WILSON & CO.
SEE—English Military Firearms

WILSON, J. P.
Ilion, New York

Percussion Alarm Gun
This unusual little device is chambered for .22 caliber percussion. It consists of approximately a 1" rectangular brass block with a chamber bored into it that accepts a black-powder charge. There is no provision for a projectile. There is a spring retained arm on top, that works as a hammer. As the device is activated by a door or a window, the hammer snaps closed, striking a percussion cap that causes the charge to fire, thereby creating an alarm notifying that the perimeter has been breached. It is marked "J. P. Wilson/Patented Feb. 8, 1859/Ilion, NY".

Exc.	V.G.	Good	Fair	Poor
—	—	700	250	100

WILSON COMBAT
Berryville, Arkansas

Wilson's began making custom 1911 style pistols using Colt slides and frames in 1977. This company produces a wide range of quality components for the 1911 pistol such as slides, triggers, safeties, barrels, etc. The models listed below are for complete factory built and assembled guns. These factory built pistols are sold with a lifetime warranty even to subsequent buyers. The pistols listed below are divided into two categories. Semi-custom pistols are off-the-shelf guns available through participating dealers. Custom pistols are special order guns.

POLYMER FRAME PISTOLS

Tactical Carry (KZ-45)

Chambered for .45 ACP cartridge and fitted with a 5" stainless steel match barrel this model has numerous special features such as night sights and front and rear slide serrations. Frame is stainless steel and reinforced polymer. Magazine capacity is 10 rounds. Finish is black polymer. Weight is approximately 31 oz. Introduced in 1999.

NIB	Exc.	V.G.	Good	Fair	Poor
995	800	—	—	—	—

SEMI-CUSTOM PISTOLS

These pistols were first built in 1996 using Springfield Armory pistols as the base gun. The Protector Compact was built on the Springfield Compact pistol. In 1997 all Service Grade pistols are built on the new Wilson Combat slide and frame with the exception of the Protector compact which is built on a Colt commander slide and a Colt Officer Model frame. The semi-custom pistols are all marked with 1996A2 on the left-hand side of the slide. Service Grade pistols bear the name Protector, Protector Compact, or Classic on the rights side of the frame's dust cover.

Wilson Model 1996A2

This pistol, introduced in 1996, is offered in a number of different configurations. These configurations affect price. The base pistol is chambered for the .45 ACP cartridge, has snag free sights and blue finish. Barrel length is 5", magazine capacity is 8 rounds and weight is approximately 38 oz. There are numerous special features on the standard pistol.

NIB	Exc.	V.G.	Good	Fair	Poor
1350	1050	—	—	—	—

NOTE: Add $70 for tritium night sights, $125 for Wilson adjustable sights, $275 for nights sights, ambi safety, hard chrome frame, $325 for Wilson adjustable sights, ambi safety, hard chrome frame.

Service Grade Protector

This model is fitted to a 5" slide with match barrel adjustable sights, and numerous other special features. Weight is about 38 oz. Black polymer finish on slide and frame. Introduced in 1996.

NIB	Exc.	V.G.	Good	Fair	Poor
1695	1350	—	—	—	—

NOTE: Add $100 for stainless steel.

Service Grade Protector Compact

Same as above but fitted with a 4.25" match grade barrel. Weight is about 34 oz. Introduced in 1996.

NIB	Exc.	V.G.	Good	Fair	Poor
1695	1350	—	—	—	—

Service Grade Sentinel Ultra Compact

This .45 ACP pistol is fitted with a 3.6" heavy tapered cone handfitted barrel, night sights, high ride beavertail and numerous special features. Magazine capacity is 6 rounds. Weight is about 29 oz. Finish is a black polymer.

NIB	Exc.	V.G.	Good	Fair	Poor
1995	1550	—	—	—	—

Service Grade Tactical

This .45 ACP pistol is fitted with a 5" tapered cone handfitted barrel. Cocking serrations on front and rear of slide. High ride beavertail safety and other special features. Night sights are standard. Coco Bolo grips. Weight is about 38 oz. finish is black polymer. Magazine capacity is 8 rounds. Introduced in 1999.

NIB	Exc.	V.G.	Good	Fair	Poor
1725	1350	—	—	—	—

Service Grade Target

Chambered for the .45 ACP cartridge this model features a 5" stainless steel match handfitted barrel with full length guide rod. Front and rear cocking serrations. Magazine well is beveled and grips are Coco Bolo. Numerous other special features. Weight is about 38 oz. Finish is black polymer. Magazine capacity is 8 rounds.

NIB	Exc.	V.G.	Good	Fair	Poor
1725	1350	—	—	—	—

Service Grade Classic

This model has a 5" barrel, adjustable sights, hard chrome finish on frame, and other special features. Weight is about 38 oz. Introduced in 1996.

NIB	Exc.	V.G.	Good	Fair	Poor
1795	1400	—	—	—	—

NOTE: Add $100 for stainless steel.

.22 Classic Rimfire Pistol

Chambered for the .22 caliber rimfire cartridge and fitted with a 5" barrel. Hard chrome frame and black anodized slide. Weight is less than standard .45 caliber pistol. Introduced in 1996.

NIB	Exc.	V.G.	Good	Fair	Poor
1145	875	—	—	—	—

Custom Carry Revolver

Built on a Smith & Wesson .357 Magnum Model 66 this model features a 2.5" barrel with adjustable night sights. Cylinder is chambered and grip is black nylon with smooth finish. Stainless steel finish. Weight is about 30 oz.

NIB	Exc.	V.G.	Good	Fair	Poor
1075	850	—	—	—	—

CUSTOM BUILT PISTOLS

Wilson Custom pistols bear the Wilson Combat or Wilson Custom label on the right side of the frame on the dust cover. Full custom guns are typically built on a Colt, Springfield Armory, Norinco, STI, Strayer Voight or Wilson Combat gun.

Combat Classic Super Grade

Fitted with a 5" match grade handfit stainless steel barrel. Adjustable sights, high ride beavertail safety, contoured magazine well and polymer slide with hard chrome frame. Weight is approximately 45 oz.

NIB	Exc.	V.G.	Good	Fair	Poor
3495	2750	—	—	—	—

Stealth Defense System

Built with a 4.25" slide with match grade stainless steel barrel. This model features night sights checkered front strap and mainspring spring housing with numerous special features. Black polymer finish. Weight is approximately 34 oz.

NIB	Exc.	V.G.	Good	Fair	Poor
2895	2250	1500	—	—	—

Defensive Combat Pistol

This .45 ACP pistol is built with a 5" match grade stainless steel barrel, night sights, and numerous special features. Finish is black polymer. Weight 38 oz.

NIB	Exc.	V.G.	Good	Fair	Poor
2395	1850	1250	—	—	—

Classic Master Grade

This .45 ACP pistol is fitted with a 5" stainless steel handfitted match grade barrel. Numerous special features such as ultralight hammer, ambidextrous safety, etc. Finish is stainless steel frame and black polymer slide. Weight is about 38 oz. and magazine capacity is 8 rounds.

NIB	Exc.	V.G.	Good	Fair	Poor
2895	2250	—	—	—	—

Tactical Elite

This is similar to other Wilson pistol but with the exception of the special tactical heavy tapered cone hand.

NIB	Exc.	V.G.	Good	Fair	Poor
2950	2250	1500	—	—	—

Defensive Combat Pistol Deluxe

This model has a 5" match grade stainless steel barrel and numerous special features. fItted with adjustable sights. Weight is about 38 oz. Finish is black polymer.

NIB	Exc.	V.G.	Good	Fair	Poor
2595	2000	1350	—	—	—

Competition Pistols

Wilson Combat offers a custom built pistol to the customer's specifications. An expert appraisal is recommended prior to sale.

TACTICAL RIFLES

UT-15 Urban Tactical

This semiauto rifle is fitted with a 16.25" fluted barrel with tactical muzzle brake. Flat top receiver. Aluminum handguard. Chambered for the .223 cartridge. Parkerized finish. Accepts all M-16/AR-15 magazines. Weight is about 6.5 lbs.

NIB	Exc.	V.G.	Good	Fair	Poor
1600	1200	—	—	—	—

NOTE: Add $100 for Armor-Tuff finish.

TPR-15 Tactical Precision Rifle

This model is fitted with a match grade 18" fluted barrel. Free floating aluminum handguard. Chambered for .223 cartridge. Weight is about 6.5 lbs. Parkerized finish.

NIB	Exc.	V.G.	Good	Fair	Poor
1600	1200	—	—	—	—

Note: Add $100 for Armor-Tuff finish.

M-4T Tactical Carbine

This model features a 16.25" M-4 style heavy barrel with muzzle brake. Flat top receiver. Chambered for .223 cartridge. Parkerized finish. Weight is about 6.5 lbs.

NIB	Exc.	V.G.	Good	Fair	Poor
1575	1150	—	—	—	—

NOTE: Add $100 for Armor-Tuff finish.

WINCHESTER
R I F L E S   A N D   S H O T G U N S

WINCHESTER REPEATING ARMS COMPANY
New Haven, Connecticut

Winchester is a name that is identified with the Old West and the frontier days of America. Winchester rifles and shotguns are prized for their historical significance as well as their collectiblity. The Winchester Repeating Arms Company was formally established by Oliver F. Winchester on February 20, 1866, and the first model to bear the name of the company was the Model 1866 lever action rifle chambered for the .44 caliber rimfire cartridge. As with any enterprise it is helpful to study the background and beginnings of the Winchester company so as to better understand the chronological sequence of various rifles and pistols that preceded the Winchester Model 1866.

The story begins with Walter Hunt of New York City who, in 1848, developed the Rocket Ball and Volition Repeater, a unique lever action, breechloading, under barrel magazine tube repeater. This rifle was the origin for future concepts. Hunt's business partner, George Arrowsmith, had as his machinist a man named Lewis Jennings, who improved and simplified Walter Hunt's original concept. Jennings' improvements were granted a U.S. patent in 1849. This 25-shot repeating rifle was promoted by Arrowsmith who found a willing investor in Courtland Palmer, a Connecticut merchant. Palmer bought both the Hunt and Jennings patents and had 5,000 Jennings rifles built by Robbins and Lawrence in Vermont in 1850. The foreman at Robbins and Lawrence was Benjamin Tyler Henry, a man who would play an important role in future repeating rifle developments. By 1851 two additional individuals would enter the Hunt-Jennings story: Daniel Wesson and Horace Smith. These two men improved on Lewis Jennings' design, and Smith was granted a patent in 1851, which he assigned to Palmer. Despite the initial achievements with the Jennings rifle, the action proved too complex and the cartridges too light for successful marketability.

In 1854 Horace Smith and Daniel Wesson were granted a U.S. patent for a repeating firearm similar to earlier Horace Smith design. Courtland Palmer funded the experimental work on the new pistol, which featured a 4" barrel and a full-length under barrel magazine. Palmer, Smith, and Wesson formed a partnership incorporating the Hunt, Jennings, Smith, and new Smith & Wesson patents. The pistols were made in Norwich, Connecticut, under the name of Smith & Wesson. B. Tyler Henry was an employee of the new firm. Only about 1,000 of these pistol were produce before the company name was changed to Volcanic Repeating Arms Company, an incorporated firm, in 1855. The new company was formed by Palmer, Smith, and Wesson with the additional financial assistance of Oliver F. Winchester. Winchester was at the time a successful manufacturer of men's clothing in New Haven, Connecticut. The new company bought out Palmer and Smith, while Daniel Wesson stayed on as shop foreman to work on his metallic rimfire cartridge. Volcanic pistols and rifles were first built at the original Smith & Wesson factory in Norwich until 1856 when a new plant was located at New Haven. In 1857 the majority of stock in the Volcanic Repeating Arms Company was owned by Oliver Winchester

The New Haven Arms Company was structured in April 1857 to assume the business of Volcanic Repeating Arms Company. This new company continued the production of Volcanic pistols and rifles, but these were now marked as "NEW HAVEN CONN. PATENT FEB. 14, 1854". These Volcanics received favorable reports as to their rapidity of fire and ease of operation, but they suffered from low velocity, energy, and small calibers. These difficulties affected sales, which remained slow. Perhaps this would be the end of the story had it not been for B. Henry Tyler, who was the shop foreman at New Haven Arms Company after the departure of Daniel Wesson. Tyler had been involved with the predecessors for the past 10 years and he received a patent in 1860 for the improvement in magazine firearms. The success of Henry's new design was twofold: First, the development of a new, more powerful .44 caliber metallic rimfire cartridge was sufficiently potent enough to compete with the single shot rifles of the day, and second, the advancement in the firing pin design, the addition of an extractor, and improvements in the bolt and feeding mechanisms all helped to make the Henry rifle a success. The first production Henry rifles were delivered in 1862. In 1866 the New Haven Arms Company name was changed to Winchester Repeating Arms Company.

The subsequent models offered by Winchester are highly prized by collectors. Winchester Repeating Arms Company went on to establish itself as one of the world's leading firearms manufacturers. Winchester provided repeating rifles that played an important role in this nation's history and will forever have a place as the company that built the guns that "Won the West." By the beginning of World War I, 1914, Winchester was the leading domestic firearms producer in the United States and also exported guns around the world. After World War I ended and beginning in the early 1920s, the company began to lose its dominant position in the firearms industry. The decade of the '20s marked a difficult financial period for Winchester with the company finally being forced into receivership by the end of the decade. In 1931, Winchester was purchased by the Western Cartridge Company owned by the Olin family. Because of the changing times, the company's focus was now on sporting arms and the drive for new models and manufacturing techniques came from the vision and foresight of John M. Olin.

From 1931 until 1963, Winchester Repeating Arms regained its reputation for quality firearms, and the rifles and shotguns produced during this period in the company's history are as collectible as those guns that preceded it. In 1964, the company could no longer afford to mass produce firearms that in reality were hand fitted and hand machined. Production changes were implemented that reflected the mass production psychology that was becoming so commonplace in American industry. With the exception of the Model 21 and a few other select models of Winchester rifles and shotguns, many Winchester guns produced after 1963 are not viewed by collectors necessarily as collectibles. Nevertheless, they were excellent guns for the hunting fields and duck blinds. In 1981 Winchester Repeating Arms Company sold its firearms division to U.S. Repeating Arms Company. This new company continues to the present day to build rifles and shotguns under license from Winchester. U.S. Repeating Arms Company has itself been the object of several buyouts. Nevertheless, the Winchester legend lives on; collected and respected by many.

A brief guide to the Winchester Repeating Arms Company corporate and divisional name changes will be of help to the collector to establish the proper company name on various firearms and advertising materials.

The prices given here are for the most part standard guns without optional features that were so often furnished by the factory. These optional or extra cost features are too numerous to list and can affect the price of a shotgun or rifle to an enormous degree. In some cases these options are one of a kind. Collectors and those interested in Winchester firearms have the benefit of some of the original factory records. These records are now stored in the Cody Firearms Museum, Buffalo Bill Historical Center, P.O. Box 1000, Cody, Wyoming (307)587-4771. For a $25 fee the museum will provide factory letters containing the original specifications of certain Winchester models using the original factory records.

CAUTION: Buyers should confirm by Cody letter any special order feature on any Winchester within the Cody record range before paying a premium for a scarce feature.

Hunt Repeating Rifle

Walter Hunt described his repeating rifle as the Volition Repeater. Hunt was granted U.S. patent number 6663 in August 1849 for his repeating rifle that was to pave the way for future generations of Winchester repeating rifles. Hunt's rifle design was unique and innovative as was his patent number 5701 for a conical lead bullet that was to be fired in his rifle. This ingenious bullet had a hole in its base filled with powder and closed by a disc with an opening in the middle to expel the ignition from an independent priming source that used priming pellets made of fulminate of mercury. The rifle actually worked but only the patent model was built; it is now in the Cody Firearms Museum.

WINCHESTER CORPORATE AND DIVISIONAL NAME CHANGES 1931-1991

WINCHESTER REPEATING ARMS COMPANY
Dec. 22, 1931 - Dec. 31, 1938

WINCHESTER REPEATING ARMS COMPANY
A Division of Western Cartridge Company
Dec. 31, 1938 - Dec. 30, 1944

WINCHESTER REPEATING ARMS COMPANY
A Division of Olin Industries, Inc.
Dec. 30, 1944 - January 1952

WINCHESTER-WESTERN DIVISION
Olin Industries, Inc.
January 1952 - Aug. 31, 1954

WINCHESTER-WESTERN DIVISION
Olin Mathieson Chemical Corporation
Aug. 31, 1954 - Sept. 1, 1969

WINCHESTER-WESTERN DIVISION
OLIN CORPORATION
Sept. 1, 1969 - July 21, 1981

U.S REPEATING ARMS COMPANY
July 21, 1981 - Present

Jennings

Second in the evolutionary line of Winchester rifles is the Jennings. Made by Robbins & Lawrence of Windsor, Vermont, this rifle incorporated the original concept of the Hunt design with the additional improvements utilized by Lewis Jennings. The Jennings rifle is important not only as a link in the chain of repeating rifle development but also because it introduced Benjamin Henry Tyler to the concept of the tubular magazine lever action repeating rifle. The Jennings rifle was built in three separate and distinct models. While total production of the three types was contracted for 5,000 guns, it is probable that only about 1,000 were actually produced.

MODEL	SERIAL NUMBER
1866	124995 to 170101
1873	1 to 720496 (N/A 497-610 and 199551-199598)
1876	1 to 63871
Hotchkiss	1 to 84555
1885*	1 to 109999 (N/A 74459-75556)
1886	1 to 156599 (N/A 146000-150799)
1887 & 1901	1 to 72999
1890	1 to 329999 (N/A 20000-29999)
1906	1 to 79999
1892	1 to 379999
1893	1 to 34050
1897	1 to 377999
1894	1 to 353999
1895	1 to 59999
Lee	1 to 19999
1903	1 to 39999
1905	1 to 29078
1906	1 to 79999
1907	1 to 9999
21	1 to 35000

* Single-Shot

> A Smith-Jennings repeating rifle was sold at auction for $23,100. Serial number 1. Condition is very good overall with brown patina. Wood is very good as well.
> Little John's Auction, Inc., May 2001

First Model

The First Model Jennings was built in a .54 caliber, breech-loading, single shot configuration with a ring trigger, oval triggerguard, and 26" barrel. A ramrod was fixed to the underside of the barrel as well. This variation was made from 1850 to 1851.

Courtesy Milwaukee Public Museum, Milwaukee, Wisconsin

Exc.	V.G.	Good	Fair	Poor
—	—	6250	3250	1000

Second Model

The Second Model Jennings was produced adopting the improvements made by Horace Smith. This Second Model is a breech-loading repeating rifle with an under barrel magazine tube and a 26" barrel. The frame is sculptured, unlike the First Model. The ring trigger is still present, but the triggerguard was removed as part of the design change. The caliber remained a .54, and the rifle was fitted with a 25" barrel. The Second Model was produced in 1851 and 1852.

Courtesy Milwaukee Public Museum. Milwaukee, Wisconsin

Exc.	V.G.	Good	Fair	Poor
—	—	7000	4000	1500

Third Model

The Third Model represents an attempt by investors to use the remaining parts and close out production. The .54 caliber Third Model was a muzzleloading rifle with a ramrod mounted under the barrel and a 26-1/2" barrel. The frame was the same as that used on the First Model, but the trigger was more of the conventional type. The triggerguard had a bow in the middle giving this model a distinctive appearance. This variation was produced in 1852 and marks the end of the early conceptual period in repeating rifle development.

Exc.	V.G.	Good	Fair	Poor
—	—	8500	5000	2500

Smith & Wesson Volcanic Firearms

An interesting connection in the evolution of the lever action repeating firearm is found in the production of a small group of pistols and rifles built in Norwich, Connecticut, by Horace Smith and Daniel Wesson under the firm name of Smith & Wesson. The company built two types of Volcanic pistols. One was a large frame model with an 8" barrel and chambered in .41 caliber. About 500 of these large frames were produced. The other pistol was a small frame version with a 4" barrel

chambered in .31 caliber. Slightly more of these small frame pistols were built, about 700, than the large frame version. In both variations the barrel, magazine, and frame were blued. Smith & Wesson also produced a lever action repeating rifle. These rifles are exceedingly rare with less than 10 having been built. They were chambered for the .528 caliber and were fitted with 23" barrels. Because of the small number of rifles built, no value is offered.

Courtesy Buffalo Bill Historical Center, Cody, Wyoming

Courtesy Buffalo Bill Historical Center, Cody, Wyoming

8" Pistol

Exc.	V.G.	Good	Fair	Poor
—	—	12500	5500	1000

Courtesy Buffalo Bill Historical Center, Cody, Wyoming

4" Pistol

Exc.	V.G.	Good	Fair	Poor
—	—	10000	4000	1000

Volcanic Firearms (Volcanic Repeating Arms Company)

With the incorporation of the Volcanic Repeating Arms Company, a new and important individual was introduced who would have an impact on the American arms industry for the next 100 years: Oliver F. Winchester. This new company introduced the Volcanic pistol using the improvements made by Horace Smith and Daniel Wesson. Volcanic firearms are marked on the barrel, "THE VOLCANIC REPEATING ARMS CO. PATENT NEW HAVEN, CONN. FEB. 14, 1854". The Volcanic was offered as a .38 caliber breechloading tubular magazine repeater with blued barrel and bronze frame. These pistols were available in three barrel lengths.

6" Barrel

Exc.	V.G.	Good	Fair	Poor
—	—	6500	3500	1500

8" Barrel

Exc.	V.G.	Good	Fair	Poor
—	—	6500	3500	1500

16" Barrel

Exc.	V.G.	Good	Fair	Poor
—	—	12500	5500	2500

Courtesy Milwaukee Public Museum, Milwaukee, Wisconsin

Courtesy Buffalo Bill Historical Center, Cody, Wyoming

NOTE: A few Volcanic pistols were produced with detachable shoulder stocks. These are considered quite rare. For original guns with this option, the above prices should be increased by 25%.

Two large frame Volcanic pistols were sold at auction. One with 8" barrel sold for $9,900 and the other with 6" barrel sold for $8,800. The 8" barrel gun had 75% blue and the 6" barrel pistol had 55% blue. Grips are very good on both pistols.
Little John's Auction, Inc., May 2001

Volcanic Firearms (New Haven Arms Company)

In 1857 the New Haven Arms Company was formed to continue the production of the former Volcanic Repeating Arms Company. Volcanic firearms continued to be built but were now marked on the barrel, "NEW HAVEN, CONN. PATENT FEB. 14, 1854". The Volcanic pistols produced by the New Haven Arms Company were built in .30 caliber and used the same basic frame as the original Volcanic. These pistols were produced in 3-1/2" and 6" barrel lengths.

3-1/2" Barrel

Exc.	V.G.	Good	Fair	Poor
—	—	5000	2500	1500

6" Barrel

Exc.	V.G.	Good	Fair	Poor
—	—	5500	3000	1750

Lever Action Carbine

New Haven Arms introduced, for the first time, a Volcanic rifle that featured a full length slotted magazine tube with a spring activated thumb piece follower that moved along the entire length of the magazine tube. These rifles were chambered for .38 caliber cartridge and were offered in three barrel lengths: 16", 20", and 24".

Courtesy Buffalo Bill Historical Center, Cody, Wyoming

16" Barrel

Exc.	V.G.	Good	Fair	Poor
—	—	12500	6000	2000

20" Band

Exc.	V.G.	Good	Fair	Poor
—	—	16000	8000	3000

24" Band

Exc.	V.G.	Good	Fair	Poor
—	—	20000	10000	3000

Henry Rifle

With the development of B. Tyler Henry's improvements in the metallic rimfire cartridge and his additional improvements in the Volcanic frame, the direct predecessor to the Winchester lever action repeater was born. The new cartridge was the .44 caliber rimfire, and the Henry rifle featured a 24" octagon barrel with a tubular magazine holding 15 shells. The rifle had no forearm, but was furnished with a walnut buttstock with two styles of buttplates: an early rounded heel crescent shape seen on guns produced from 1860 to 1862 and the later sharper heel crescent butt found on guns built from 1863 to 1866. The early models, produced from 1860 to 1861, were fitted with an iron frame, and the later models, built from 1861 to 1866, were fitted with brass frames. About 14,000 Henry rifles were made during the entire production period; only about 300 were iron frame rifles.

Courtesy Butterfield & Butterfield, San Francisco, California

Iron Frame Rifle

Courtesy Butterfield & Butterfield, San Francisco, California

Exc.	V.G.	Good	Fair	Poor
—	—	75000	25000	—

WHAT'S IT LIKE-THE 1860 HENRY

Someone recently posed the question, "If money was no object, and you could have any rifle you wanted, what would you choose?" Without hesitation I said an original 1860 Henry and a boxcar load full of ammunition. It is a rare individual today who has ever fired an 1860 Henry in its original persuasion not due to lack of rifles but the great dearth of .44 Rimfire ammunition. It was my rare privilege this past year to be called in to examine an original .44 Henry by a fellow who was dying of cancer and wanted to get the best possible price for his wife. It was quite an emotional experience not only because of the situation, but I was actually able to hold and work the action on a real 1860 Henry. This particular gun had spent 40 years setting in a barn being used as the pest gun on the farm! In spite of this, much of the bluing was still intact; the stock did have a few minor dings but was still solid; and the barrel was in excellent shape. That gun eventually sold for $15,000! B. Tyler Henry was an absolute genius. Consider this, when the seventeen-shot, lever action 1860 Henry arrived on the scene, military units were still armed with single shot muzzle loading rifles. Suddenly firepower made a tremendous leap forward. By today's standards the .44 Rimfire is a very low power cartridge, however, for battle the ability to fire seventeen shots in rapid succession was far more important than single-shot power. We may not be able to shoot an original Henry but thanks to the world of replica firearms we can come close. The 1860 Henry made in Italy is a faithful reproduction of the originals allowing us to hold a piece of history in our hand and by being chambered in .44-40, the ammunition availability problem is solved.

John Taffin

An iron frame Henry sold at auction for $82,500. Part of the Winchester collection at the Cody Firearms Museum. About 40% original blue. Wood has most of its original varnish. An excellent example of an iron frame Henry.
Little John's Auction Service, Inc., May 2001

An early Henry without locking latch was sold at auction for $96,000. It was part of the Colt Museum collection. Condition was very good to excellent.
Butterfield & Butterfield, November 1999

A Henry rifle sold at auction for $28,750. It was fitted with a rare Globe front sight. Condition was good.
Butterfield & Butterfield, June 2000

An engraved presentation Henry, serial number 7, was sold at auction for $80,500. Receiver was gold finish with scroll engraving. Rosewood stock. Condition was very good.
Rock Island Auction Company, December 1999

Brass Frame Rifle

Exc.	V.G.	Good	Fair	Poor
—	—	25000	8000	—

Martially Inspected Henry Rifles

Beginning in 1863 the Federal Government ordered 1730 Henry Rifles for use in the Civil War. Most of these government inspected rifles fall into serial number range 3000 to 4000 while the balance are close to this serial number range. They are marked "C.G.C." for Charles G. Chapman, the government inspector. These Henry rifles were used under actual combat conditions and for that reason it is doubtful that there are any rifles that would fall into the excellent condition category. Therefore no price is given.

NOTE: There are many counterfeit examples of these rifles. It is strongly advised that an expert in this field be consulted prior to a sale.

Exc.	V.G.	Good	Fair	Poor
—	—	50000	15000	7000

Winchester's Improvement Carbine

Overall length 43-1/2"; barrel length 24"; caliber .44 r.f. Walnut stock with a brass buttplate; the receiver and magazine cover/forend of brass; the barrel and magazine tube blued. The magazine loading port is exposed by sliding the forend forward. This design was protected by O.F. Winchester's British Patent Number 3285 issued December 19, 1865. Unmarked except for internally located serial numbers. Approximately 700 manufactured in December of 1865 and early 1866, the majority of which were sold to Maximilian of Mexico. Prospective purchasers are strongly advised to secure an expert appraisal prior to acquisition.

Exc.	V.G.	Good	Fair	Poor
—	—	17500	10000	7500

A Winchester Model 1866 rifle, engraved by Conrad Ulrich, was sold at auction for $74,000. Condition was very good.
Butterfield & Butterfield, November 1999

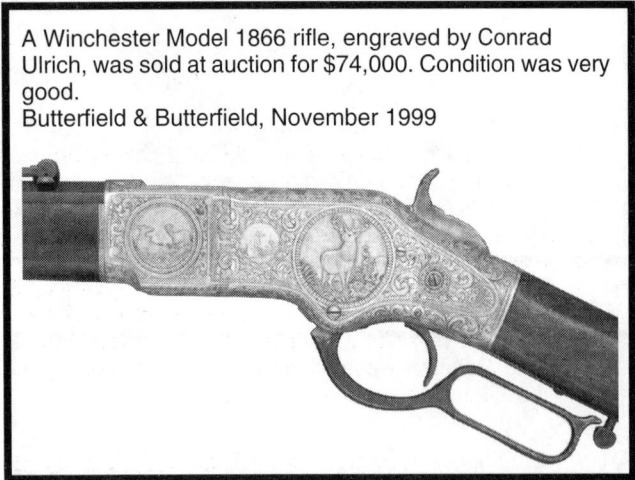

Model 1866

In 1866 the New Haven Arms Company changed its name to the Winchester Repeating Arms Company. The first firearm to be built under the Winchester name was the Model 1866. This first Winchester was a much improved version of the Henry. A new magazine tube developed by Nelson King, Winchester's plant superintendent, was a vast improvement over the slotted magazine tube used on the Henry and its predecessor. The old tube allowed dirt to enter through the slots and was weakened because of it. King's patent, assigned to Winchester, featured a solid tube that was much stronger and reliable. His patent also dealt with an improved loading system for the rifle. The rifle now featured a loading port on the right side of the receiver with a spring loaded cover. The frame continued to be made from brass. The Model 1866 was chambered for the .44 caliber Flat Rimfire or the .44 caliber Pointed Rimfire. Both cartridges could be used interchangeably.

The barrel on the Model 1866 was marked with two different markings. The first, which is seen on early guns up to serial number 23000, reads "HENRY'S PATENT-OCT. 16, 1860 KING'S PATENT-MARCH 29, 1866". The second marking reads, "WINCHESTER'S-REPEATING-ARMS.NEW HAVEN, CT. KING'S-IMPROVEMENT-PATENTED MARCH 29, 1866 OCTOBER 16, 1860". There are three basic variations of the Model 1866:

Courtesy Milwaukee Public Museum, Milwaukee, Wisconsin

1. Sporting Rifle round or octagon barrel. Approximately 28,000 were produced.

2. Carbine round barrel. Approximately 127,000 were produced.

3. Musket round barrel. Approximately 14,000 were produced.

The rifle and musket held 17 cartridges, and the carbine had a capacity of 13 cartridges. Unlike the Henry, Model 1866s were fitted with a walnut forearm. The Model 1866 was discontinued in 1898 with approximately 170,000 guns produced. The Model 1866 was sold in various special order configurations, such as barrels longer or shorter than standard, including engraved guns. The prices listed below represent only standard Model 1866s. For guns with special order features, an independent appraisal from an expert is highly recommended.

Courtesy Butterfield & Butterfield, San Francisco, California

First Model

This first style has both the Henry and King patent dates stamped on the barrel, a flat loading port cover, and a two-screw upper tang. Perhaps the most distinctive feature of the First Model is the rapid drop at the top rear of the receiver near the hammer. This is often referred to as the "Henry Drop," a reference to the same receiver drop found on the Henry rifle. First Models will be seen up through the 15000 serial number range.

Courtesy Butterfield & Butterfield, San Francisco, California

Rifle

Exc.	V.G.	Good	Fair	Poor
—	20000	12000	5000	2000

Carbine

Exc.	V.G.	Good	Fair	Poor
—	15000	10000	500	2000

A Winchester Model 1866 rifle was sold at auction for $46,750. An early flatside rifle with saddle ring. Stamped with Japanese inspection marks. Condition is about 90% barrel blue. Excellent stock. Excellent frame.
Little John's Auction Service, Inc., May 2001

Second Model

The second style differs from the first most noticeably in its single screw upper tang and a flare at the front of the receiver to meet the forearm. The Second Model also has a more gradual drop at the rear of the receiver than the First Model. The Second Style Model 1866 appears through serial number 25000.

Courtesy Butterfield & Butterfield, San Francisco, California

Rifle

Exc.	V.G.	Good	Fair	Poor
—	15000	7500	4000	3000

Courtesy Butterfield & Butterfield, San Francisco, California

Carbine

Exc.	V.G.	Good	Fair	Poor
—	12000	7500	5000	2000

This Winchester Model 1866 was found at the Battle of the Little Big Horn site. It is marked with an Indian symbol on the reciever. Condition was good. All original. Auction price was $684,500.
James D. Julia, Inc., April 2000

Third Model

The third style's most noticeable characteristic is the more moderately curved receiver shape at the rear of the frame. The serial number is now stamped in block numerals behind the trigger thus allowing the numbers to be seen for the first time without removing the stock. The barrel marking is stamped with the Winchester address. The Third Model is found between serial numbers 25000 and 149000. For the first time a musket version was produced in this serial number range.

Rifle

Courtesy Butterfield & Butterfield, San Francisco, California

Exc.	V.G.	Good	Fair	Poor
—	12000	7000	4000	2000

Carbine

Exc.	V.G.	Good	Fair	Poor
—	10000	7500	3500	2000

Musket

Courtesy Butterfield & Butterfield, San Francisco, California

Exc.	V.G.	Good	Fair	Poor
—	8000	5000	2000	1000

Fourth Model

The fourth style has an even less pronounced drop at the top rear of the frame, and the serial number is stamped in script on the lower tang under the lever. The Fourth Model is seen between serial number 149000 and 170100 with the late guns having an iron buttplate instead of brass.

Iron

Exc.	V.G.	Good	Fair	Poor
—	12000	7500	3500	2000

Carbine

Exc.	V.G.	Good	Fair	Poor
—	10000	5000	2000	1000

Musket

Exc.	V.G.	Good	Fair	Poor
—	9500	5000	1800	1000

Model 1866 Iron Frame Rifle Musket

Overall length 54-1/2"; barrel length 33-1/4"; caliber .45 c.f. Walnut stock with case hardened furniture, barrel burnished bright, the receiver case hardened. The finger lever catch mounted within a large bolster at the rear of the lever. Unmarked except for serial numbers that appear externally on the receiver and often the buttplate tang. Approximately 25 made during the early autumn of 1866. Prospective purchasers are strongly advised to secure an expert appraisal prior to acquisition. Due to the recent identification of this model pricing schedules have yet to be established.

Model 1866 Iron Frame Swiss Sharpshooters Rifle

As above, but in .41 Swiss caliber and fitted with a Scheutzen style stock supplied by the firm of Weber Ruesch in Zurich. Marked Weber Ruesch, Zurich on the barrel and serial numbered externally. Approximately 400 to 450 manufactured in

1866 and 1867. Prospective purchasers are strongly advised to secure an expert appraisal prior to acquisition. Due to the recent identification of this model pricing schedules have yet to be established.

Model 1867 Iron Frame Carbine

Overall length 39-1/4"; barrel length 20"; caliber .44 r.f. Walnut stock with case hardened furniture; the barrel and magazine tube blued; the receiver case hardened. The finger lever catch mounted within the rear curl of the lever. Unmarked except for serial numbers that appear externally on the receiver and often the buttplate tang. Approximately 20 manufactured. Prospective purchasers are strongly advised to secure an expert appraisal prior to acquisition. Due to the recent identification of this model pricing schedules have yet to be established.

Model 1868 Iron Frame Rifle Musket

Overall length 49-1/2" (.455 cal.), 50-1/2" or 53" (.45 and .47 cal.); barrel length 29-1/2" (.455 cal.) and 30-1/4" or 33" (.45 and .47 cal.); calibers .45 c.f., .455 c.f., and .47 c.f. Walnut stock with case hardened or burnished bright (.45 and .47 cal.) furniture; the barrel burnished bright; the receiver case hardened or burnished bright (.45 and .47 cal.). The finger lever catch mounted on the lower receiver tang. The rear of the finger lever machined with a long flat extension on its upper surface. Unmarked except for serial number. Approximately 30 examples made in .45 and .455 caliber and 250 in .47 caliber. Prospective purchasers are strongly advised to secure an expert appraisal prior to acquisition. Due to the recent identification of this model pricing schedules have yet to be established.

Model 1868 Iron Frame Carbine

Overall length 40"; barrel length 20"; caliber .44 c.f. Walnut stock with case hardened furniture; barrel and magazine tube blued; the receiver case hardened. The finger lever catch as above. Unmarked except for serial numbers (receiver and buttplate tang). Approximately 25 manufactured. Prospective purchasers are strongly advised to secure an expert appraisal prior to acquisition. Due to the recent identification of this model pricing schedules have yet to be established.

Model 1873

This Winchester rifle was one of the most popular lever actions the company ever produced. This is the "gun that won the West" and with good reason. It was chambered for the more powerful centerfire cartridge, the .44-40. Compared to the .44 Henry, this cartridge was twice as good. With the introduction of the single action Colt pistol in 1878, chambered for the same cartridge, the individual had the convenience of a pistol for protection and the accuracy of the Winchester for food and protection. The .44-40 was the standard cartridge for the Model 1873. Three additional cartridges were offered but were not as popular as the .44. The .38-40 was first offered in 1879 and the .32-20 was introduced in 1882. In 1884 the Model 1873 was offered in .22 caliber rimfire, with a few special order guns built in .22 extra long rimfire. Approximately 19,552 .22 caliber Model 1873s were produced.

Early Model 1873s were fitted with an iron receiver until 1884, when a steel receiver was introduced. The Model 1873 was offered in three styles:

1. Sporting Rifle, 24" round, octagon, or half-octagon barrel. Equipped standard with a crescent iron buttplate, straight grip stock and capped forearm.

2. Carbine, 20" round barrel. Furnished standard with a rounded iron buttplate, straight grip stock, and carbine style forend fastened to the barrel with a single barrel band.

3. Musket, 30" round barrel. Standard musket is furnished with a nearly full-length forearm fastened to the barrel with three barrel bands. The buttstock has a rounded buttplate.

The upper tang was marked with the model designation and the serial number was stamped on the lower tang. Caliber stampings on the Model 1873 are found on the bottom of the frame and on the breech end of the barrel. Winchester discontinued the Model 1873 in 1919 after producing about 720,000 guns.

The Winchester Model 1873 was offered with a large number of extra cost options that greatly affect the value of the gun. For example, Winchester built two sets of special Model 1873s; the 1-of-100 and the 1-of-1000. Winchester sold only 8 1-of-100 Model 1873s, and 136 of the 1-of-1000 guns that were built. In 1991 a few of these special guns were sold at auction and brought prices exceeding $75,000. The prices listed here are for standard guns only. For Model 1873 with special features, it is best to secure an expert appraisal. Model 1873s with case colored receivers will bring a premium.

Courtesy Butterfield & Butterfield, San Francisco, California

First Model

The primary difference between the various styles of the Model 1873 is found in the appearance and construction of the dust cover. The First Model has a dust cover held in place with grooved guides on either side. A checkered oval finger grip is found on top of the dust cover. The latch that holds the lever firmly in place is anchored into the lower tang with visible threads. On later First Models, these threads are not visible. First Models appear from serial number 1 to about 31000.

Courtesy Milwaukee Public Museum, Milwaukee, Wisconsin

Rifle

Exc.	V.G.	Good	Fair	Poor
—	7500	4000	2000	750

Carbine

Exc.	V.G.	Good	Fair	Poor
—	10000	5000	3000	1000

Musket

Exc.	V.G.	Good	Fair	Poor
—	3500	1500	1000	500

Second Model

The dust cover on the Second Model operates on one central guide secured to the receiver with two screws. The checkered oval finger grip is still used, but on later Second Models this is changed to a serrated finger grip on the rear of the dust cover. Second Models are found in the 31000 to 90000 serial number range.

Courtesy Butterfield & Butterfield, San Francisco, California

Rifle

Exc.	V.G.	Good	Fair	Poor
9500	6000	2500	1000	500

Carbine

Exc.	V.G.	Good	Fair	Poor
12000	7500	4000	1500	800

Musket

Exc.	V.G.	Good	Fair	Poor
3500	1500	1000	750	500

Third Model

The central guide rail is still present on the Third Model, but it is now integrally machined as part of the receiver. The serrated rear edges of the dust cover are still present on the Third Model.

Courtesy Butterfield & Butterfield, San Francisco, California

Courtesy Butterfield & Butterfield, San Francisco, California

Rifle

Exc.	V.G.	Good	Fair	Poor
9500	5000	2000	800	400

Carbine

Exc.	V.G.	Good	Fair	Poor
12000	6500	3500	1200	800

Musket

Exc.	V.G.	Good	Fair	Poor
3500	1500	1000	750	300

Model 1873 .22 Rimfire Rifle

Winchester's first .22 caliber rifle and the first .22 caliber repeating rifle made in America was introduced in 1884 and discontinued in 1904. Its drawback was the small caliber. The general preference during this period of time was for the larger caliber rifles. Winchester sold a little more than 19,000 .22 caliber Model 1873s.

Exc.	V.G.	Good	Fair	Poor
10000	5500	2500	1500	750

Model 1876

Winchester's Model 1876, sometimes referred to as the Centennial Model, was the company's response to the public's demand for a repeater rifle capable of handling larger and more potent calibers. Many single shot rifles were available at this time to shoot more powerful cartridges, and Winchester redesigned the earlier Model 1873 to answer this need. The principal changes made to the Model 1873 were a larger and stronger receiver to handle more powerful cartridges. Both the carbine and the musket had their forearms extended to cover the full length of the magazine tube. The carbine barrel was increased in length from 20" to 22", and the musket barrel length was increased from 30 to 32". The Model 1876 was the first Winchester to be offered with a pistol grip stock on its special Sporting Rifle. The Model 1876 was available in the following calibers: .45-77 W.C.F., .50-95 Express, .45-60 W.C.F., .40-60 W.C.F. The Model 1876 was offered in four different styles:

1. Sporting Rifle, 28" round, octagon, or half-octagon barrel. This rifle was fitted with a straight grip stock with crescent iron buttplate. A special sporting rifle was offered with a pistol grip stock.

2. Express Rifle, 26" round, octagon, or half-octagon barrel. The same sporting rifle stock was used.

3. Carbine, 22" round barrel with full length forearm secured by one barrel band and straight grip stock.

4. Musket, 32" round barrel with full-length forearm secured by one barrel band and straight grip stock. Stamped on the barrel is the Winchester address with King's patent date. The caliber marking is stamped on the bottom of the receiver near the magazine tube and the breech end of the barrel. Winchester also furnished the Model 1876 in 1-of-100 and 1-of-1000 special guns. Only 8 1-of-100 Model 1876s were built and 54 1-of-1000 76s were built. As with their Model 1873 counterparts, these rare guns often sell in the $75,000 range or more. Approximately 64,000 Model 1876s were built by Winchester between 1876 and 1897. As with other Winchesters, the prices given below are for standard guns.

First Model

As with the Model 1873, the primary difference in model types lies in the dust cover. The First Model has no dust cover and is seen between serial number 1 and 3000.

Courtesy Butterfield & Butterfield, San Francisco, California

Rifle

Exc.	V.G.	Good	Fair	Poor
—	6500	3000	1500	1000

Courtesy Butterfield & Butterfield, San Francisco, California

Carbine

Exc.	V.G.	Good	Fair	Poor
—	5000	3000	1500	1000

Musket

Exc.	V.G.	Good	Fair	Poor
—	7000	4000	2000	1000

Second Model

The Second Model has a dust cover with guide rail attached to the receiver with two screws. On the early Second Model an oval finger guide is stamped on top of the dust cover while later models have a serrated finger guide along the rear edge of the dust cover. Second Models range from serial numbers 3000 to 30000.

Rifle

Exc.	V.G.	Good	Fair	Poor
—	3500	2500	1000	500

Carbine

Exc.	V.G.	Good	Fair	Poor
—	4500	2500	1500	700

Northwest Mounted Police Carbine

The folding rear sight is graduated in meters instead of yards.

Exc.	V.G.	Good	Fair	Poor
8000	4000	2000	1000	700

NOTE: A Model 1876 NWP in excellent condition is very rare. Proceed with caution.

Musket

Exc.	V.G.	Good	Fair	Poor
8000	4000	2000	1000	700

Third Model

The dust cover guide rail on Third Model 76s is integrally machined as part of the receiver with a serrated rear edge on the dust cover. Third Model will be seen from serial numbers 30000 to 64000.

Rifle

Exc.	V.G.	Good	Fair	Poor
6000	3500	2000	800	500

Carbine

Exc.	V.G.	Good	Fair	Poor
7000	4000	2500	1500	700

Northwest Mounted Police Carbine

The folding rear sight is graduated in meters instead of yards.

Exc.	V.G.	Good	Fair	Poor
7500	3500	1750	900	650

NOTE: A Model 1876 NWP in excellent condition is very rare. Proceed with caution.

Musket

Exc.	V.G.	Good	Fair	Poor
7500	3500	1750	900	650

A Model 1876 rifle was sold at auction for $7,360. Chambered for .45-75 and fitted with a 28" round barrel with full magazine. Condition was excellent.
Amoskeag Auction Co. Inc., May 2000

A First Model 1876 1 of 1000 was sold at auction for $96,000. Chambered for .45 caliber and fitted with a 28" octagon barrel. Scroll engraved and inlaid silver bands at muzzle and breech. Condition was very good. Shipped 1877.
Butterfield & Butterfield, February 1999

Winchester Hotchkiss Bolt Action Rifle

This model is also known as the Hotchkiss Magazine Gun or the Model 1883. This rifle was designed by Benjamin Hotchkiss in 1876, and Winchester acquired the manufacturing rights to the rifle in 1877. In 1879 the first guns were delivered for sale. The Hotchkiss rifle was a bolt action firearm designed for military and sporting use. It was the first bolt action rifle made by Winchester. The rifle was furnished in .45-70 Government, and although the 1884 Winchester catalog lists a .40-65 Hotchkiss as being available, no evidence exists that such a chamber was ever actually furnished. The Model 1883 was available in three different styles:

1. Sporting Rifle, 26" round, octagon, or half-octagon barrel fitted with a rifle-type stock that included a modified pistol grip or straight grip stock.

2. Carbine, 24" round or 22-1/2" round barrel with military style straight grip stock.

3. Musket, 32" or 28" round barrel with almost full length military-style straight grip stock. Winchester produced the Model 1883 until 1899, having built about 85,000 guns.

First Model

This model has the safety and a turn button magazine cut-off located above the triggerguard on the right side. The Sporting Rifle is furnished with a 26" round or octagon barrel while the carbine has a 24" round barrel with a saddle ring on the left side of the stock. The musket has a 32" round barrel with two barrel bands, a steel forearm tip, and bayonet attachment under the barrel. The serial number range for the First Model is between 1 and about 6419.

Sporting Rifle

Courtesy Butterfield & Butterfield, San Francisco, California

Exc.	V.G.	Good	Fair	Poor
5500	2500	1500	900	500

Courtesy George Hoyem

Carbine

Exc.	V.G.	Good	Fair	Poor
5500	2500	1500	900	500

Musket

Exc.	V.G.	Good	Fair	Poor
5500	2500	1500	900	500

Second Model

On this model the safety is located on the top left side of the receiver, and the magazine cutoff is located on the top right side of the receiver to the rear of the bolt handle. The sporting rifle remains unchanged from the First Model with the above exceptions. The carbine has a 22-1/2" round barrel with a nickeled forearm cap. The musket now has a 28" barrel. Serial number range for the Second Model runs from 6420 to 22521.

Sporting Rifle

Courtesy Milwaukee Public Museum, Milwaukee, Wisconsin

Exc.	V.G.	Good	Fair	Poor
4500	2500	1000	750	500

Courtesy George Hoyem

Carbine

Exc.	V.G.	Good	Fair	Poor
4500	2250	1000	750	500

Musket

Exc.	V.G.	Good	Fair	Poor
4500	2250	1000	750	500

Third Model

The Third Model is easily identified by the two-piece stock separated by the receiver. The specifications for the sporting rifle remain the same as before, while the carbine is now fitted with a 20" barrel with saddle ring and bar on the left side of the frame. The musket remains unchanged from the Second Model with the exception of the two-piece stock. Serial numbers of the Third Model range from 22552 to 84555.

Sporting Rifle

Exc.	V.G.	Good	Fair	Poor
4250	2500	1000	750	500

Carbine

Exc.	V.G.	Good	Fair	Poor
4250	2500	1000	700	400

Courtesy Butterfield & Butterfield, San Francisco, California

Musket

Exc.	V.G.	Good	Fair	Poor
4250	2500	750	500	300

Model 1885 (Single Shot)

The Model 1885 marks an important development between Winchester and John M. Browning. The Single Shot rifle was the first of many Browning patents that Winchester would purchase and provided the company with the opportunity to diversify its firearms line. The Model 1885 was the first single shot rifle built by Winchester. The company offered more calibers in this model than any other. A total of 45 centerfire calibers were offered from the .22 extra long to the 50-110 Express, as well as 14 rimfire caliber from .22 B.B. cap to the .44 Flat Henry. Numerous barrel lengths, shapes, and weights were available as were stock configurations, sights, and finishes. These rifles were also available in solid frame and takedown styles. One could almost argue that each of the 139,725 Model 1885s built are unique. Many collectors of the Winchester Single Shot specialize in nothing else. For this reason it is difficult to provide pricing that will cover most of the Model 1885s that the collector will encounter. However the prices given here are for standard guns in standard configurations.

The Model 1885 was offered in two basic frame types:

A. The High Wall was the first frame type produced and is so called because the frame covers the breech and hammer except for the hammer spur.

B. The breech and hammer are visible on the Low Wall frame with its low sides. This frame type was first introduced around the 5000 serial number range.

Both the High Wall and the Low Wall were available in two type frame profiles; the Thickside and the Thinside. The Thickside frame has flat sides that do not widen out to meet the stock. The Thickside is more common on the low wall rifle and rare on the High Walls.

The Thinside frame has shallow milled sides that widen out to meet the stock. Thinside frames are common on High Wall guns and rare on Low Wall rifles.

1. The standard High Wall rifle was available with octagon or round barrel with length determined by caliber. The butt stock and forearm were plain walnut with crescent buttplate and blued frame.

2. The standard Low Wall featured a round or octagon barrel with length determined by caliber and a plain walnut stock and forearm with crescent buttplate.

3. The High Wall musket most often had a 26" round barrel chambered for the .22 caliber cartridge. Larger calibers were available as were different barrel lengths. The High Wall Musket featured an almost full length forearm fastened to the barrel with a single barrel band and rounded buttplate.

4. The Low Wall musket is most often referred to as the Winder Musket named after the distinguished marksman, Colonel C.B. Winder. This model features a Lyman receiver sight and was made in .22 caliber.

5. The High Wall Schuetzen rifle was designed for serious target shooting and was available with numerous extras including a 30" octagon barrel medium weight without rear sight seat; fancy walnut checkered pistol grip Schuetzen-style cheekpiece; Schuetzen-style buttplate; checkered forearm; double set triggers; spur finger lever, and adjustable palm rest.

6. The Low Wall carbine was available in 15", 16", 18", and 20" round barrels. The carbine featured a saddle ring on the left side of the frame and a rounded buttplate.

7. The Model 1885 was also available in a High Wall shotgun in 20 gauge with 26" round barrel and straight grip stock with shotgun style rubber buttplate. The Model 1885 was manufactured between 1885 and 1920 with a total production of about 140000 guns.

NOTE: Add a 10% premium for rifles built before 1898.

Courtesy Butterfield & Butterfield, San Francisco, California

Standard High Wall Rifle

Courtesy Butterfield & Butterfield, San Francisco, California

Exc.	V.G.	Good	Fair	Poor
3750	3000	2250	1300	850

Standard Low Wall Rifle

Courtesy Butterfield & Butterfield, San Francisco, California

Exc.	V.G.	Good	Fair	Poor
3500	2500	1750	1100	750

High Wall Musket

Exc.	V.G.	Good	Fair	Poor
2750	2000	1200	900	700

Courtesy Buffalo Bill Historical Center, Cody, Wyoming

Low Wall Musket (Winder Musket)

Exc.	V.G.	Good	Fair	Poor
2250	1500	700	400	250

High Wall Schuetzen Rifle

Exc.	V.G.	Good	Fair	Poor
10500	6000	4000	2000	1200

Low Wall Carbine

Courtesy Buffalo Bill Historical Center, Cody, Wyoming

Exc.	V.G.	Good	Fair	Poor
17500	10000	7000	3000	1500

High Wall Shotgun

Exc.	V.G.	Good	Fair	Poor
3500	2500	1750	1250	850

NOTE: Model 1885s with case colored frames bring a premium of 25% over guns with blued frames.
NOTE: Model 1885s in calibers .50-110 and .50-100 will bring a premium depending on style and configuration.

Model 1886

Based on a John Browning patent, the Model 1886 was one of the finest and strongest lever actions ever utilized in a Winchester rifle. Winchester introduced the Model 1886 in order to take advantage of the more powerful centerfire cartridges of the time.

Model 1886 rifles and carbines were furnished with walnut stocks, case hardened frames, and blued barrels and magazine tubes. In 1901 Winchester discontinued the use of case hardened frames on all its rifles and used blued frames instead. For this reason, case hardened Model 1886 rifles will bring a premium. Winchester provided a large selection of extra cost options on the Model 1886, and for rifles with these options, a separate valuation should be made by a reliable source. The Model 1886 was produced from 1886 to 1935 with about 160,000 in production.

The rifle was available in 10 different chambers:

45-70 U.S. Gov't	50-110 Express
45-90 W.C.F.	40-70 W.C.F.
40-82 W.C.F.	38-70 W.C.F.
40-65 W.C.F.	50-100-450
38-56 W.C.F.	33 W.C.F.

The most popular caliber was the 45-70 Government. Prices of the Model 1886 are influenced by caliber, with the larger calibers bringing a premium. The 1886 was available in several different configurations.

1. Sporting Rifle, 26", round, octagon, or half-octagon barrel, full or half magazine and straight grip stock with plain forearm.

2. Fancy Sporting Rifle, 26", round or octagon barrel, full or half magazine and fancy checkered walnut pistol grip stock with checkered forearm.

3. Takedown Rifle, 24" round barrel, full or half magazine with straight grip stock fitted with shotgun rubber buttplate and plain forearm.

4. Extra Lightweight Takedown Rifle, 22" round barrel, full or half magazine with straight grip stock fitted with shotgun rubber buttplate and plain forearm.

5. Extra Lightweight Rifle, 22" round barrel, full or half magazine with straight grip stock fitted with a shotgun rubber butt-plate and plain forearm.

6. Carbine, 22" round barrel, full or half magazine, with straight grip stock and plain forearm.

7. Musket, 30" round barrel, musket style forearm with one barrel band. Military style sights. About 350 Model 1886 Muskets were produced.

NOTE: Add a 10% premium for rifles built before 1898.

Courtesy Milwaukee Public Museum, Milwaukee, Wisconsin

Sporting Rifle

Courtesy Butterfield & Butterfield, San Francisco, California

Exc.	V.G.	Good	Fair	Poor
10000	6000	3500	1500	650

Fancy Sporting Rifle

Exc.	V.G.	Good	Fair	Poor
15000	9500	5000	3500	2000

Takedown Rifle-Standard

Exc.	V.G.	Good	Fair	Poor
10000	7000	3500	1750	700

Extra Lightweight Takedown Rifle-.33 caliber

A Winchester Model 1886 takedown rifle in .33WCF caliber was sold at auction for $101,500. It was engraved by John Unrich with scroll and gold and platinum inlays. Stock was done with Grade A checkering. Condition was excellent.
Butterfield & Butterfield, November 1999

Exc.	V.G.	Good	Fair	Poor
3750	2500	1250	600	400

Extra Lightweight Takedown Rifle

Exc.	V.G.	Good	Fair	Poor
6500	4500	1500	1000	500

Extra Lightweight Rifle-.33 caliber

Exc.	V.G.	Good	Fair	Poor
3750	2500	1100	550	400

Extra Lightweight Rifle

Courtesy Butterfield & Butterfield, San Francisco, California

Exc.	V.G.	Good	Fair	Poor
6500	4500	1750	850	500

Carbine

Exc.	V.G.	Good	Fair	Poor
15000	10000	5000	2000	1000

Musket

Exc.	V.G.	Good	Fair	Poor
—	15000	7500	3000	1500

NOTE: For .50 Express add a premium of 20%. Case colored Model 1886s will bring a premium of 20% .

A factory cut-away of a Winchester Model 1886 was sold at auction for $12,075. No serial number. Chambered for the .45-70 cartridge and fitted with a 26" octagon barrel with full magazine. Condition is very good nickel finish. Amoskeag Auction Co. Inc., May 2000

Model 71

When Winchester dropped the Model 1886 from its line in 1935 the company replaced its large bore lever action rifle with the Model 71 chambered for the .348 caliber. The Model 71 is similar in appearance to the Model 1886 with some internal parts strengthened to handle the powerful .348 cartridge. The rifle was available in three basic configurations:

1. Standard Rifle, 24" round barrel, 3/4 magazine, plain walnut pistol grip stock and semi-beavertail forearm.

2. Standard Rifle (Carbine), 20" round barrel, 3/4 magazine, plain walnut pistol grip stock and semi-beavertail forearm.

3. Deluxe Rifle, 24" round barrel, 3/4 magazine, checkered walnut pistol grip stock and checkered semi-beavertail forearm. The frames and barrels were blued on all models of this rifle.

4. Deluxe Rifle (Carbine), 20" round barrel, 3/4 magazine, checkered walnut pistol grip stock and checkered semi-beavertail forearm. The frames and barrels were blued on all models of this rifle.

The Model 71 was produced from 1935 to 1957 with about 47,000 built.

Standard Rifle-24" Barrel

Exc.	V.G.	Good	Fair	Poor
1000	800	600	400	300

Standard Rifle (Carbine)-20" Barrel

Courtesy Butterfield & Butterfield, San Francisco, California

Exc.	V.G.	Good	Fair	Poor
3250	2000	1600	1200	650

Deluxe Rifle-24" Barrel

Exc.	V.G.	Good	Fair	Poor
1600	950	700	525	425

Deluxe Rifle (Carbine)-20" Barrel

Exc.	V.G.	Good	Fair	Poor
3750	3000	2000	1250	700

NOTE: For prewar Model 71s add a premium of 20%. The prewar Model 71 has a longer tang than its post-war predecessor. for a bolt peep sight add 10%.

WHAT'S IT LIKE-THE WINCHESTER MODEL 1892

It is a scene that few Western movie fans will ever forget. The "One-eyed Fat Man" shouts: "Fill your hand you sunnavabitch!", puts the reins between his teeth, and with his Colt in his left hand and Winchester Model ' 92 it is right, Rooster Cogburn charges the Ned Pepper gang single-handedly. There's no doubt that the Colt Single Action Army was the #1 firearms star in Western movies, however, the lever action Model 1892 played a close second. Remember, John Wayne as Ringo, twirling his short barreled carbine as he stops the stagecoach to Lordsburg? Or Lucas McCain as he fires his Winchester Model '92 with near machine gun rapidity? Or even Josh Randall with his cut down Mare's Leg? Of course all of these were simply Hollywood props. In reality the Model 1892 Winchester did not need large loop lovers, trigger actuated by a screw in the lever, cut down stocks and short barrels, or anything else to improve it. It is simply a magnificent little lever action rifle and probably the handiest ever offered. Original 1892s were mostly chambered in .32-20, .38-40, and .44-40. Designed by John Browning who simply scaled down the huge 1886 Winchester that was offered in such calibers as .45-70, .45-90, and .50-90, the 1892 became the ultimate, easy-handling, fast-operating saddle gun. I know of no other rifle, no matter what it's operating mechanism, that is as easily handled as a Model 1892. I am fortunate to have both a .32-20 and .38-40 which are just about the most enjoyable rifles I own. Not only can originals still be found at reasonable prices, replicas abound in the original .44-40 as well as .45 Colt, which was never chambered in any of the original lever action rifles, plus the modern .357 and .44 Magnums. The '92 is a great tribute to a great gun designer.

John Taffin

Model 1892

The Model 1892 was an updated successor to the Model 1873 using a scaled down version of the Model 1886 action. The rifle was chambered for the popular smaller cartridges of the day, namely the .25-20, .32-20, .38-40, .44-40, and the rare .218 Bee. The rifle was available in several different configurations:

1. Sporting Rifle, solid frame or takedown (worth an extra premium of about 20%), 24" round, octagon, or half-octagon barrel with 1/2, 2/3, or full magazines. Plain straight grip walnut stock with capped forearm.

2. Fancy Sporting Rifle, solid frame or takedown (worth 20% premium), 24" round, octagon, or half-octagon barrel with 1/2, 2/3, or full magazine. Checkered walnut pistol grip stock with checkered capped forearm.

3. Carbine, 20" round barrel, full or half magazine, plain walnut straight grip stock with one barrel band forearm. Carbines were offered only with solid frames.

4. Trapper's Carbine, 18", 16", 15", or 14" round barrel with the same dimensions of standard carbine. Federal law prohibits the possession of rifles with barrel lengths shorter than 16". The Model 1892 Trapper's Carbine can be exempted from this law as a curio and relic with a federal permit providing the trapper is an original trapper and left the factory with the short trapper barrel.

5. Musket, 30" round barrel with full magazine. Almost full length forearm held by two barrel bands. Buttstock is plain walnut with straight grip.

The Model 1892 was built between 1892 and 1932 with slightly more than 1 million sold. The Model 1892 carbine continued to be offered for sale until 1941.

NOTE: Antique Winchester Model 1892s (pre-1898 manufacture) will bring a premium of 10%.

Courtesy Butterfield & Butterfield, San Francisco, California

Sporting Rifle

Exc.	V.G.	Good	Fair	Poor
3500	2500	700	450	200

Courtesy Butterfield & Butterfield, San Francisco, California

Fancy Sporting Rifle

Exc.	V.G.	Good	Fair	Poor
8500	5500	2500	1500	500

Courtesy Butterfield & Butterfield, San Francisco, California

Carbine

Courtesy Butterfield & Butterfield, San Francisco, California

Exc.	V.G.	Good	Fair	Poor
4000	3000	1250	700	300

Trapper's Carbine

Exc.	V.G.	Good	Fair	Poor
7500	4800	2000	850	400

NOTE: Add 20% for 15" barrel. Add 50% for carbines chambered for 25-20 cartridge.

Musket

Exc.	V.G.	Good	Fair	Poor
—	7500	2500	1000	500

A deluxe Winchester Model 1892 saddle ring carbine was sold at auction for $11,500. Chambered for .44-40 and fitted with a 20" barrel. Checkered pistol grip. Nickel plated barrel bands and buttplate. Fancy walnut stock. Factory letter. Condition was very good.
Rock Island Auction Company, August 1999

Model 53

This model was in fact a slightly more modern version of the Model 1892 offered in the following calibers: .25-20, .32-20, and the .44-40. It was available in only one style: the Sporting Rifle, 22" round barrel, half magazine, straight or pistol grip plain walnut stock with shotgun butt. It was available in solid frame or takedown with blued frame and barrel. The Model 53 was produced from 1924 to 1932 with about 25,000 built.

Sporting Rifle

Exc.	V.G.	Good	Fair	Poor
3500	2500	1000	500	300

NOTE: Add 10% for takedown model. Add 40% for rifles chambered for .44-40 cartridge. A few of these rifles were fitted with stainless steel barrel in the early 1930s. If the black paint on these barrels is in good condition they will bring a substantial premium

Model 65

This model was a continuation of the Model 53 and was offered in three calibers: .25-20, .32-20, and .218 Bee. It had several improvements over the Model 53, namely the magazine capacity was increased to 7 cartridges, forged ramp for front sight, and a lighter trigger pull. The Model 65 was available only in solid blued frame with blued barrel and pistol grip with plain walnut stock. Only about 5,700 of these rifles were built between 1933 and 1947.

Model 65 in .218 Bee, Courtesy Rock Island Auction Company

Standard Rifle

Exc.	V.G.	Good	Fair	Poor
3500	2500	1000	550	250

NOTE: Add 10% for bolt peep sight. Model 65s in .218 Bee left the factory with bolt peep sights as original equipment.

Model 1894

Based on a John M. Browning patent, the Model 1894 was the most successful centerfire rifle Winchester ever produced. This model is still in production, and the values given here reflect those rifles produced before 1964, or around serial number 2550000. The Model 1894 was the first Winchester developed especially for smokeless powder and was chambered for the following cartridges: .32-40, .38-55, .25-35 Winchester, .30-30 Winchester, and the .32 Winchester Special. The rifle was available in several different configurations:

1. Sporting Rifle, 26" round, octagon, or half-octagon barrel, in solid frame or takedown. Full, 2/3 or 1/2 magazines were available. Plain walnut straight or pistol grip stock with crescent buttplate and plain capped forearm.

A Model 94 takedown deluxe short rifle was sold at auction for $49,500. Chambered for .25-35 caliber and fitted with an 18-1/2" octagon barrel. Engraved in style No. 4 with D carved wood. Steel shotgun butt engraved and inlaid with gold line work. Special Lyman sights. Fancy walnut stock. Condition was excellent.
Faintich Auction Service, April 1999

Photo by Paul Goodwin

2. Fancy Sporting Rifle, 26" round, octagon, or half-octagon barrel, in solid frame or takedown. Full, 2/3, or 1/2 magazines were available. Fancy walnut checkered straight or pistol grip stock with crescent buttplate and checkered fancy capped forearm.

3. Extra lightweight Rifle, 22" or 26" round barrel with half magazine. Plain walnut straight grip stock with shotgun buttplate and plain capped forearm.

4. Carbine, 20" round barrel, plain walnut straight grip stock with carbine style buttplate. Forearm was plain walnut uncapped with one barrel band. Carbines were available with solid frame only. Carbines made prior to 1925 were fitted with a saddle ring on the left side of receiver and worth a premium over carbines without saddle ring.

5. Trapper's Carbine, 18", 16", 15", or 14". Buttstock, forearm, and saddle ring specifications same as standard carbine. All Model 1894s were furnished with blued frames and barrels, although case hardened frames were available as an extra cost option. Case colored Model 1894s are rare and worth a considerable premium, perhaps as much as 1000 percent. Guns with extra cost options should be evaluated by an expert to determine proper value. Between 1894 and 1963, approximately 2,550,000 Model 1894s were sold.

NOTE: Antique Winchester Model 1894s (pre-1898 manufacture) will bring a premium of 10%. First year production guns documented by the Cody Museum will command a 50% premium.

Courtesy Butterfield & Butterfield, San Francisco, California

First Model Sporting Rifle
Very early model that incorporates a screw entering the receiver over the loading port from the outside. Rare.

Exc.	V.G.	Good	Fair	Poor
4500	3000	1000	750	400

Sporting Rifle

Exc.	V.G.	Good	Fair	Poor
3000	2000	750	500	200

NOTE: Takedown versions are worth approximately 20% more.

Courtesy Butterfield & Butterfield, San Francisco, California

Fancy Sporting Rifle

Exc.	V.G.	Good	Fair	Poor
9000	5500	2000	1000	500

NOTE: Takedown versions are worth approximately 20% more. Fancy Sporting Rifles were also engraved at the customer's request. Check factory where possible and proceed with caution. Factory engraved Model 1894s are extremely valuable.

Extra Lightweight Rifle

Exc.	V.G.	Good	Fair	Poor
4250	3000	1100	600	300

Courtesy Butterfield & Butterfield, San Francisco, California

Carbine

Exc.	V.G.	Good	Fair	Poor
3000	2000	600	400	200

NOTE: Above values are for guns with saddle rings. For carbines without saddle rings deduct 35%. Add 25% for carbines chambered for .25-20 cartridge.

Courtesy Butterfield & Butterfield, San Francisco, California

Trappers Carbine

Exc.	V.G.	Good	Fair	Poor
6500	4250	1500	750	400

NOTE: Add 30% for carbines chambered for 25-35 or 38-55 calibers.

A gold inlaid Pan-American Exposition Winchester Model 1894 sold at auction for $20,700. Built in 1895 and used for factury display. Caliber 30-30 with 26" round barrel with full magazine. Fancy checkered stock with pistol grip. Condition was very good to excellent factory refinish. Rock Island Auction Company, August 1999

Model 55

This model was a continuation of the Model 1894 except in a simplified version. Available in the same calibers as the Model 1894, this rifle could be ordered only with a 24" round barrel, plain walnut straight grip stock with plain forend and shotgun butt. Frame and barrel were blued with solid or takedown features. This model was produced between 1924 and 1932 with about 21,000 sold. Serial numbers for the Model 55 were numbered separately until about serial number 4500; then the guns were numbered in the Model 1894 sequence.

Standard Rifle

Exc.	V.G.	Good	Fair	Poor
1500	1000	650	450	200

NOTE: .25-35 caliber will bring about a 60% premium. Add 10% for models with solid frame.

Model 64

An improved version of the Model 55, this gun featured a larger magazine, pistol grip stock, and forged front sight ramp. The trigger pull was also improved. Frame and barrel were blued. chambered for the .25-35 Win., 30-30 Win., .32 Win. Special, and the .219 zipper added in 1938 and discontinued in the Model 64 in 1941). Serial number of the Model 64 was concurrent with the Model 1894. Built between 1933 and 1957, approximately 67,000 were sold. This model was reintroduced in 1972 and discontinued in 1973. The values listed below are for the early version only.

Courtesy Butterfield & Butterfield, San Francisco, California

Standard Rifle
Exc.	V.G.	Good	Fair	Poor
1200	900	500	300	200

Carbine-20" Barrel
Exc.	V.G.	Good	Fair	Poor
1550	1000	650	500	250

NOTE: For Deluxe model add 50% to above prices. For Carbine model add 50% to above prices. For rifles chambered for the .219 Zipper and .25-35 cartridges add 50%. Add 10% for bolt peep sight. Model 64s in .219 Zipper left the factory with bolt peep sights as original equipment.

Model 1895

The Model 1895 was the first nondetachable box magazine rifle offered by Winchester. Built on a John M. Browning patent,

this rifle was introduced by Winchester to meet the demand for a rifle that could handle the new high power, smokeless hunting cartridges of the period. The Model 1895 was available in the following calibers: .30-40 Krag, .38-72 Winchester, .40-72 Winchester, .303 British, .35 Winchester, .405 Government, 7.62 Russian, .30-03, and .30-06. The rifle gained fame as a favorite hunting rifle of Theodore Roosevelt. Because of its box magazine, the Model 1895 has a distinctive look like no other Winchester lever action rifle. The rifle was available in several different configurations:

1. Sporting Rifle, 28" or 24" (depending on caliber) round barrel, plain walnut straight grip stock with plain forend. The first 5,000 rifles were manufactured with flat sided receivers, and the balance of production were built with the receiver sides contoured. After serial-number 60000 a takedown version was available.

2. Fancy Sporting Rifle, 28" round barrel, fancy walnut checkered straight grip stock and fancy walnut checkered forearm. Rifles with serial numbers below 5000 had flat sided frames.

3. Carbine, 22" round barrel, plain walnut straight grip stock with military style hand guard forend. Some carbines are furnished with saddle rings on left side of receiver.

4. Musket:

A. Standard Musket, 28" round, plain walnut straight grip stock with musket style forend with two barrel bands.

B. U.S. Army N.R.A. Musket, 30" round barrel, Model 1901 Krag-Jorgensen rear sight. Stock similar to the standard musket. This musket could be used for "Any Military Arm" matches under the rules of the National Rifle Association.

C. N.R.A. Musket, Models 1903 and 1906, 24" round barrel with special buttplate. Also eligible for all matches under "Any Military Arm" sponsored by the N.R.A. This musket was fitted with the same stock as listed above.

D. U.S. Army Musket, 28" round barrel chambered for the .30-40 Krag. Came equipped with or without knife bayonet. These muskets were furnished to the U.S. Army for use during the Spanish-American War and are "US" marked on the receiver.

E. Russian Musket, similar to standard musket but fitted with clip guides in the top of the receiver and with bayonet. Approximately 294,000 Model 1895 Muskets were sold to the Imperial Russian Government between 1915 and 1916. The first 15,000 Russian Muskets had 8" knife bayonets, and the rest were fitted with 16" bayonets.

The Model 1895 was produced from 1895 to 1931 with about 426,000 sold.

NOTE: Add a 10% premium for rifles built before 1898.

Courtesy Butterfield & Butterfield, San Francisco, California

Sporting Rifle

Courtesy Butterfield & Butterfield, San Francisco, California

Exc.	V.G.	Good	Fair	Poor
5000	3000	1200	700	300

NOTE: Flat side rifles will bring a premium of 100%. Takedown rifles will add an additional 15%.

Fancy Sporting Rifles

Exc.	V.G.	Good	Fair	Poor
6500	4500	1500	1100	500

NOTE: Flat side rifles will bring a premium of 100%. Takedown rifles will add an additional 15%.

Courtesy Butterfield & Butterfield, San Francisco, California

Carbine

Exc.	V.G.	Good	Fair	Poor
3000	1750	1050	600	300

A Winchester Model 1895 carbine with saddle ring sold at auction for $6,900. Condition was near mint.
Rock Island Auction Company, August 1999

Standard Musket

Exc.	V.G.	Good	Fair	Poor
3000	1750	1050	600	300

U.S. Army N.R.A. Musket

Exc.	V.G.	Good	Fair	Poor
4500	2000	1200	800	400

N.R.A. Musket, Model 1903 and 1906

Exc.	V.G.	Good	Fair	Poor
5500	2500	1200	800	400

U.S. Army Musket

Exc.	V.G.	Good	Fair	Poor
—	3000	1500	850	450

Russian Musket

Exc.	V.G.	Good	Fair	Poor
4000	2500	1000	500	250

A factory crate of 10 Winchester Model 1895 saddle ring carbines was sold at auction for $48,875. Crate was original Winchester. All chambered in .30 Army. Condition was mint and unfired. Factory hang tags.
Butterfield & Butterfield, November 1999

A Winchester Match Grade double barrel shotgun sold at auction for $3,795. This gun was a 20 gauge with damascus barrels. Engraved receiver. This may be the only 20 guage Match grade imported into U.S. Condition was good with refinished stock.
Rock Island Auction Company, August 1999

Breechloading Double Barrel Shotgun

Winchester imported an English made shotgun sold under the Winchester name between 1879 and 1884. The gun was available in 10 and 12 gauge with 30" or 32" Damascus barrels. It was sold in five separate grades referred to as "classes." The lowest grade was the "D" and the best grade was called the "Match Grade." These were marked on the sidelocks. The center rib was stamped "Winchester Repeating Arms Co., New Haven, Connecticut, U.S.A." About 10,000 of these guns were imported by Winchester.

Class A,B,C, and D

Exc.	V.G.	Good	Fair	Poor
2500	2250	1250	850	500

Match Gun

Exc.	V.G.	Good	Fair	Poor
2500	2250	1250	850	500

Model 1887 Shotgun

Winchester enjoyed a great deal of success with its imported English shotgun, and the company decided to manufacture a shotgun of its own. In 1885 it purchased the patent for a lever action shotgun designed by John M. Browning. By 1887 Winchester had delivered the first model 1887 in 12 gauge and shortly after offered the gun in 10 gauge. Both gauges were offered with 30" or 32" full choked barrels, with the 30" standard on the 12 gauge and 32" standard on the 10 gauge. A Riot Gun was offered in 1898 both in 10, and 12 gauge with 20" barrels choked cylinder. Both variations of the Model 1887 were offered with plain walnut pistol grip stocks with plain forend. The frame was case hardened and the barrel blued. Between 1887 and 1901 Winchester sold approximately 65,000 Model 1887 shotguns.

Courtesy Milwaukee Public Museum, Milwaukee, Wisconsin

Courtesy Butterfield & Butterfield, San Francisco, California

Standard Shotgun

Exc.	V.G.	Good	Fair	Poor
1700	1200	850	500	300

Riot Shotgun

Exc.	V.G.	Good	Fair	Poor
2000	1500	950	600	400

Model 1901 Shotgun

This model is a redesign of the Model 1887 shotgun and was offered in 10 gauge only with a 32" barrel choked full, modified, or cylinder. The barrel was reinforced to withstand the new smokeless powder loads and the frame was blued instead of case hardened. The stock was of plain walnut with a modified pistol and plain forearm. The Model 1901 was built between 1901 and 1920 with about 65,000 guns sold.

Standard Shotgun

Exc.	V.G.	Good	Fair	Poor
1200	800	600	400	250

Model 1893

This was the first slide action repeating shotgun built by Winchester. It featured an exposed hammer and side ejection. Based on a John M. Browning patent this model was not altogether satisfactory. The action proved to be too weak to handle smokeless loads even though the gun was designed for black powder. The gun was offered in 12 gauge with 30" or 32" barrels choked full. Other chokes were available on special order and will command a premium. The stock was plain walnut with a modified pistol grip, grooved slide handle, and hard rubber buttplate. The receiver and barrel were blued. Winchester produced the Model 1893 between 1893 and 1897, selling about 31000 guns.

Courtesy Butterfield & Butterfield, San Francisco, California

Standard Shotgun

Exc.	V.G.	Good	Fair	Poor
850	700	600	325	250

Model 1897

The Model 1897 replaced the Model 1893, and while similar to the Model 1893, the new model had several improvements such as a stronger frame, chamber made longer to handle 2-3/4" shells, frame top was covered to force complete side ejection, the stock was made longer and with less drop. The Model 1897 was available in 12 or 16 gauge with the 12 gauge offered either in solid or takedown styles and the 16 gauge available in takedown only. The Model 1897 was available with barrel lengths of 20", 26", 28", 30", and 32" and in practically all choke options from full to cylinder. The shotgun could be ordered in several different configurations:

1. Standard Gun, 12 or 16 gauge, 30" barrel in 12 gauge and 28" barrel in 16 gauge, with plain walnut modified pistol grip stock and grooved slide handle. Steel buttplate standard.

2. Trap Gun 12 or 16 gauge, 30" barrel in 12 gauge and 28" barrel in 16 gauge, fancy walnut stock with oil finish checkered pistol grip or straight grip stock with checkered slide handle. Marked "TRAP" on bottom of frame.

3. Pigeon Gun, 12 or 16 gauge, 28" barrel on both 12 and 16 gauge, straight or pistol grip stock same as Trap gun, receiver hand engraved.

4. Tournament Gun, 12 gauge only with 30" barrel, select walnut checkered straight grip stock and checkered slide handle, top of receiver is matted to reduce glare.

5. Brush Gun, 12 or 16 gauge, 26" barrel, cylinder choke, has a slightly shorter magazine tube than standard gun, plain walnut modified pistol grip stock with grooved slide handle.

6. Brush Gun, Takedown, same as above with takedown feature and standard length magazine tube.

7. Riot Gun, 12 gauge, 20" barrel bored to shoot buckshot, plain walnut modified pistol grip stock with grooved slide handle. Solid frame or takedown.

8. Trench Gun, same as Riot Gun but fitted with barrel hand guard and bayonet.

The Winchester Model 1897 was a great seller for Winchester. During its 60-year production span 1,025,000 guns were sold.

Standard Gun

Exc.	V.G.	Good	Fair	Poor
750	650	450	300	200

Trap Gun

Exc.	V.G.	Good	Fair	Poor
1050	900	600	500	400

Pigeon Gun

Exc.	V.G.	Good	Fair	Poor
2700	2200	1600	1250	1000

Tournament Gun

Exc.	V.G.	Good	Fair	Poor
1100	900	700	500	400

Brush Gun

Exc.	V.G	Good	Fair	Poor
950	750	600	500	400

Courtesy Butterfield & Butterfield, San Francisco, California

Riot Gun

Exc.	V.G.	Good	Fair	Poor
700	600	500	350	200

Trench Gun

Courtesy Butterfield & Butterfield, San Francisco, California

Exc.	V.G.	Good	Fair	Poor
2000	1500	1000	500	300

NOTE: Add 25% for 16 gauge guns in excellent, very good, and good condition.

WHAT'S IT LIKE-THE WINCHESTER MODEL 1897

We have good news and we have bad news. The good news is that thanks to the great interest in the sport of Cowboy Action Shooting, which requires a double barreled or pump shotgun that was available before 1899, the Model 1897 has been resurrected to a new life with a whole new generation of shooters. The bad news is because of this prices on shootable Model '97's have sky rocketed. Five years ago I paid $125 for a take-down Model '97 12 gauge with 90 percent plus finish and in excellent shooting condition. A glance at the shelves of the local gun shops today reveal that a similar condition Model '97 is more in the neighborhood of $500! There has always been something very businesslike about pump shotguns. It is a rare bad guy who would not be stopped in his tracks when he hears a round being racked into the chamber of Model 97. All of today's modern pump shotguns are of the "hammerless" style, that is the hammer is concealed within the shotgun's frame. Not so with the Model '97. Its businesslike appearance is added to with the presence of an external hammer. Model '97's are extremely popular with Cowboy Action Shooters for the simple reason that they are very fast to operate. A shooter with quick hands and nimble fingers can drop shotgun shells into the Model '97 coming over the top and into the ejection port and operate the '97 as a single shot very rapidly. Certainly one who knows what he or she is about can trigger six aimed shots faster from a Model '97 than from a double barreled shotgun. The Model '97 saw a lot of use in the trenches of World War I, is a mainstay in Cowboy Action Shooting, and still makes a mighty fine home defense gun. Not bad for shotgun designed over 100 years ago.

John Taffin

Winchester-Lee Straight Pull Rifle

U.S. Navy Musket

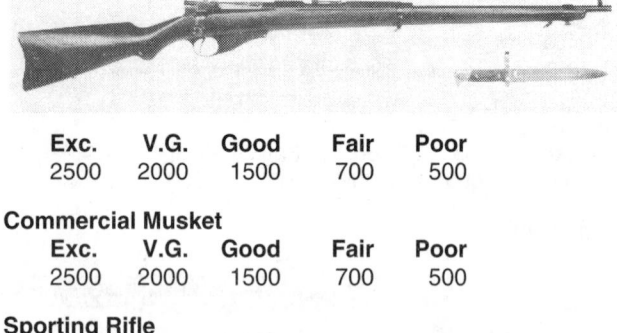

Exc.	V.G.	Good	Fair	Poor
2500	2000	1500	700	500

Commercial Musket

Exc.	V.G.	Good	Fair	Poor
2500	2000	1500	700	500

Sporting Rifle

Exc.	V.G.	Good	Fair	Poor
2500	2000	1500	700	500

Model 1890

The Model 1890 was the first slide action rifle ever produced by Winchester. Designed by John and Matthew Browning, this rifle was chambered for the .22 Short, Long, and Winchester Rimfire cartridges (the WRF cartridge was developed by Winchester specifically for the Model 1890) not on an interchangeable basis. In 1919 the .22 l.r. cartridge was offered as well.

The rifle was a slide action top ejecting rifle with an 18" under barrel magazine tube. All Model 1890s were furnished standard with plain walnut straight stocks with crescent buttplate and 12 groove slide handle. This rifle was one of the company's best selling small caliber firearms and was in worldwide use. The Model 1890 came in three separate and distinct variations that greatly affect its value:

1. First Model, solid frame, 24" octagon barrel, case hardened frame, and fixed rear sight. Approximately 15,552 of these First Model guns were produced, and their distinctive feature is concealed locking lugs and solid frame. Serial numbered on the lower tang only. Built from 1890 to 1892.

2. Second Model, takedown, 24" octagon barrel, case hardened frame, and adjustable rear sight. Serial numbered from 15,553 to 112,970 (on lower tang only) these Second Model guns feature the same concealed locking lugs but with the added takedown feature. A Deluxe version was offered with fancy walnut checkered straight or pistol grip stock and grooved slide handle.

2A. Second Model (Blued Frame Variation), same as above but with blued frame. Serial numbered from 112,971 to 325,250 (on lower tang until 232,328, then also on bottom front end of receiver) these blued frame Second Models are much more numerous than the case hardened variety. A Deluxe version was offered with fancy walnut checkered straight or pistol grip stock and grooved slide handle.

3. Third Model, takedown, 24" octagon barrel, blued frame, adjustable rear sight. Serial numbered from 325,251 to as high as 853,000 (numbered on both the lower tang and bottom front of receiver) the distinctive feature of the Third Model is the locking cut made on the front top of the receiver to allow the breech bolt to lock externally. A Deluxe version was offered with fancy walnut checkered stock, straight or pistol grip with grooved slide handle. Winchester offered many extra cost options for this rifle that will greatly affect the value. Secure an expert appraisal before proceeding. The Model 1890 was produced from 1890 to 1932 with approximately 775,000 guns sold.

First Model-Standard Grade

Exc.	V. G.	Good	Fair	Poor
9000	5000	2500	1250	750

Second Model-Case Hardened Frame
Standard

Exc.	V. G.	Good	Fair	Poor
5500	3500	2000	1000	500

Deluxe

Exc.	V. G.	Good	Fair	Poor
10000	7000	3500	2000	1000

Courtesy Butterfield & Butterfield, San Francisco, California

Courtesy Butterfield & Butterfield, San Francisco, California

Second Model-Blued Frame

Standard

Exc.	V.G.	Good	Fair	Poor
4000	2250	1500	750	500

Deluxe

Exc.	V.G.	Good	Fair	Poor
7500	5500	3000	1500	1000

Courtesy Butterfield & Butterfield, San Francisco, California

Third Model

Standard

Exc.	V.G.	Good	Fair	Poor
2750	1750	1200	750	500

Deluxe

Exc.	V.G.	Good	Fair	Poor
6000	4000	2000	1000	750

NOTE: For Third Models chambered for .22 Long Rifle add 25% premium.

WHAT'S IT LIKE-THE WINCHESTER MODEL 1890

Another in a long line of John M. Browning designs: the Winchester Model 1890. This slide action .22 caliber rifle was a sharp departure for Winchester. It's first slide action rifle proved to be a resounding success. The rifle was offered in .22 short, .22 Long, and .22 WRF (expressly developed by Winchester for the Model 90) but not interchangeably. In 1919 the .22 Long Rifle was added to the list of available calibers. These rifles are divided into three separate categories by collectors; 1st Model, 2nd Model, and 3rd Model. Earlier models with beautifully case colored receivers are worth more than later blued receiver models because of scarcity and desirability. The vast majority of Model 90s are plain guns with American black walnut stocks of straight but handsome grain. Barrel were 24" blued octagon with a positive lock-up on the receiver. The slide action was smooth and fast with positive ejection of spent shells. It is a good shooting rifle yet solid and reliable. A few of these rifles were built with special features. These are few and far between but when encountered demand quite a premium. Checkered stocks with pistols grip, engraved receivers, fancy wood, shorter or longer barrels than standard, and special order sights are just some of the extras found on Model 90s. The Model 90 soon became a symbol of the American spirit that so invokes images of the past that Americans began to view it as the all-American .22 caliber rifle. So successful was this design that Winchester sold approximately 850,000 rifles, and its success led to the production of the Model 1906, the Model 62, and the Model 61, all of which were slide action rifles.

Ned Schwing

Model 1906

In 1906 Winchester decided to offer a lower cost version of the Model 1890. The Model 1906 used the same receiver but was fitted with a 20" round barrel and plain gumwood straight grip stock. When the Model 1906 was first introduced, it sold for two-thirds of the price of the Model 1890. For the first two years the gun was chambered for the .22 Short cartridge only. In 1908 the rifle was modified to shoot .22 Short, Long, and Long Rifle cartridges interchangeably. This modification insured the Model 1906's success, and between 1906 and 1932 about 800,000 were sold. All Model 1906s were of the takedown variety. The Model 1906 is available in three important variations:

1. 22 Short Only, 20" round barrel, straight grip gumwood stock and smooth slide handle. These were built from serial number 1 to around 113000.

2. Standard Model 1906, 20" round barrel, straight grip gumwood stock with 12 groove slide handle. Serial numbered from 113000 to 852000.

3. Model 1906 Expert, 20" round barrel, pistol grip gumwood stock with fluted smooth slide handle. Expert was available from 1918 to 1924 and was offered in three different finishes regular blued finish, half nickel (receiver, guard, and bolt), and full nickel (receiver, guard, bolt, and barrel nickeled).

Courtesy Butterfield & Butterfield, San Francisco, California

Model 1906 .22 Short Only

Courtesy Butterfield & Butterfield, San Francisco, California

Exc.	V.G.	Good	Fair	Poor
3250	1750	750	500	200

Standard Model 1906

NIB	Exc.	V.G.	Good	Fair	Poor
3500	2000	1000	650	400	200

Model 1906 Expert

Courtesy Butterfield & Butterfield, San Francisco, California

Exc.	V.G.	Good	Fair	Poor
3250	1700	850	500	300

NOTE: Prices are for all blued Experts. Add 25% for half nickel and 100% for full nickel.

Model 62 and 62A

When the Model 1890 and Model 1906 were dropped from the Winchester product line in 1932, the company introduced the Model 62 to take their place. An updated version of the earlier slide action .22 rifles, the Model 62 was fitted with a 23" round barrel and was capable of shooting .22 Short, Long, and Long Rifle cartridges interchangeably. Winchester offered a Gallery version of the Model 62 that was chambered for .22 Short only. Some of these Gallery guns have "Winchester" stamped on the left side of the receiver. Winchester Model 62 Gallery rifles have a triangular loading port on the loading tube that the standard models did not have. A change in the breech bolt mechanism brought about a change in the name designation from Model 62 to Model 62A. This occurred around serial number 98000. The letter "A" now appears behind the serial number. This model stayed in production until 1958, and collectors will concede a premium for guns built prior to WWII with small slide handles. The stock was of plain walnut with straight grip and grooved slide handle. Both the receiver and barrel were blued. All Model 62 and 62As were takedown. Approximately 409,000 guns were sold.

Courtesy Butterfield & Butterfield, San Francisco, California

Prewar Model 62

NIB	Exc.	V.G.	Good	Fair	Poor
2000	1500	700	400	250	150

NOTE: Barrels marked with Model 62 are worth more than barrels marked with Model 62A by approximately 15%. Gallery models will bring a premium of 400%.

Postwar Model 62

NIB	Exc.	V.G.	Good	Fair	Poor
1300	750	450	325	225	125

Model 62 Gallery-.22 Short Only w/triangular loading port & "WINCHESTER" stamped on side of receiver.

NIB	Exc.	V.G.	Good	Fair	Poor
4000	1750	1000	650	400	200

NOTE: A Model 62 with "WINCHESTER" stamped on the side of the receiver is more desirable than one without the stamping. Deduct 10% for Gallery rifles without this stamping.

Model 61

Winchester developed the Model 61 in an attempt to keep pace with its competitors' hammerless .22 rifles. The Model 61 featured a 24" round or octagonal barrel and could be ordered by the customer in a variety of configurations. Collector interest in this rifle is high because of the fairly large number of variations. The Model 61 is often considered a companion to the Winchester Model 12 and Model 42 shotguns. The following is a list of chamber and barrel variations found in this model:

1. 24" round barrel, .22 Short, Long, Long Rifle.
2. 24" octagonal barrel, .22 Short only-add 300%.
3. 24" octagonal barrel, .22 Long Rifle only-add 200%.
4. 24" octagonal barrel, .22 W.R.F. only-add 200%.
5. 24" round barrel, .22 Long Rifle Shot only add 300%.
5A. 24" round barrel, Shot only Routledge bore add 500%.
6. 24" round barrel, .22 W.R.F. only-add 200%.
7. 24" round barrel, .22 Long Rifle only-add 200%.
8. 24" round barrel, .22 Winchester Magnum-add 300%.
9. 24" round barrel, .22 Short only-add 500%.

The Model 61 was fitted with a plain walnut pistol grip stock with grooved slide handle. All Model 61s were of the take down variety. Prewar models will have a short slide handle. Manufactured between 1932 and 1963, approximately 342,000 guns were sold.

Courtesy Butterfield & Butterfield, San Francisco, California

Prewar Model 61

NIB	Exc.	V.G.	Good	Fair	Poor
2500	1500	800	600	325	200

NOTE: Single caliber models will command a premium of 50% depending on caliber. Octagon barrel models will command a premium of 75%. .22 Long Rifle Shot only models will bring a premium of 250%.

Postwar Model 61

NIB	Exc.	V.G.	Good	Fair	Poor
1500	700	500	450	250	150

Model 61 Magnum

NIB	Exc.	V.G.	Good	Fair	Poor
1600	950	775	600	400	250

NOTE: This variation (Model 61 Magnum) was produced from 1960 to 1963.

WHAT'S IT LIKE-THE WINCHESTER MODEL 61

Introduced in 1932 the Winchester Model 61 bears a remarkable resemblance to the Model 12 and Model 42. A hammerless .22 caliber rifle that is finely balanced and built by hand using only the best materials. This is quite a tribute to a .22 caliber rifle, but after all it is a Winchester. Its pump action is smooth and fast, and its adult size butt stock makes for a easy to handle rifle. With butt stock and forearm of straight grain American walnut the Model 61 is a handsome rifle, and it shoots well too. The takedown feature makes the gun easy to transport and store. I think what makes this model so appealing to collectors besides its good looks and handling qualities are the numerous configurations the rifle was offered to the customer. The Model 61 was available with round or octagon barrel in short, long, and long rifle calibers interchangeably or dedicated calibers such as Long Rifle only; Short only, W.R.F. only, Winchester Magnum Rim Fire only, and perhaps the most appealing of all Long Rifle Shot only. During the 1930s and 1940s miniature hand traps and targets were a popular pastime for Model 61 shot only rifles. Model 61s were also used in shooting gallery's around the world in .22 short only configurations. Some of these were stamped "WINCHESTER" in red letters on the side of the receiver. These gallery rifles bring a big premium as do the shot only guns. I have owned a Model 61 for about 48 years. It has never let me down and it functions as well today as it did in 1953. What else can I say.

Ned Schwing

Model 1903

The first semiautomatic rifle produced by Winchester was designed by T.C. Johnson. This rifle was offered in a takedown version only and was available in a 20" round barrel chambered for the .22 Winchester Automatic Rimfire. This ammunition is no longer produced and when found is very expensive. The tubular magazine is located in the butt stock and holds 10 cartridges. The rifle was available in two different configurations:

1. Standard Rifle, 20" round barrel, plain walnut straight grip stock with plain forend. Steel crescent butt was standard.

2. Deluxe Rifle, 20" round barrel, fancy checkered walnut pistol grip stock with checkered forearm. Manufactured from 1903 to 1932, about 126,000 were sold.

Standard Rifle

Courtesy Butterfield & Butterfield, San Francisco, California

Exc.	V.G.	Good	Fair	Poor
850	550	325	200	100

Deluxe Rifle

Exc.	V.G.	Good	Fair	Poor
2250	1000	700	500	250

NOTE: The first 5,000 guns were built without safeties, and the first 15,000 guns were furnished with bronze firing pins instead of steel. These early Model 1903s will bring a premium of 30%.

Model 63

The Model 63 took the place of the Model 1903 in 1933 in an attempt by Winchester to solve the problem of having to use a special .22 caliber cartridge in the gun to operate the blowback system. It is a very high quality semiautomatic rifle. Many collectors and shooters considered it the best rimfire semiautomatic rifle ever produced. The Model 63 was chambered for the .22 Long Rifle cartridge and was available in a 20" barrel for the first four years or until about serial number 9800. Thereafter, the model was offered with a 23" round barrel for the remainder of the production period. The gun was fitted with a plain walnut pistol grip stock and forearm. The tubular magazine was located in the butt stock that came with a steel buttplate. The last 10,000 Model 63s were sold with a grooved receiver top to make the addition of a scope easier. Manufactured between 1933 and 1958, about 175,000 guns were sold.

Courtesy Butterfield & Butterfield, San Francisco, California

20" Barrel Model 63

Courtesy Butterfield & Butterfield, San Francisco, California

NIB	Exc.	V.G.	Good	Fair	Poor
2750	1400	800	500	400	250

23" Barrel Model 63

NIB	Exc.	V.G.	Good	Fair	Poor
1750	1000	700	600	400	200

NOTE: Grooved top receivers command a premium of 20%.

Model 1905

The Model 1905 was a larger version of the Model 1903, developed by T.C. Johnson to handle the more powerful centerfire cartridges. It was chambered for the .32 Winchester Self-Loading and .35 Self-Loading cartridges, loading by means of a detachable box magazine. Available in takedown only, this model was offered in two different styles:

1. Sporting Rifle, 22" round barrel, plain walnut straight grip (changed to pistol grip in 1908) stock with plain forend.

2. Fancy Sporting Rifle, 22" round barrel, fancy walnut checkered pistol grip stock with checkered forend. This model was the first Winchester semiautomatic rifle to fire centerfire cartridges. Produced from 1905 to 1920 with about 30,000 rifles sold.

Sporting Rifle

Exc.	V.G.	Good	Fair	Poor
500	350	250	175	125

Fancy Sporting Rifle

Exc.	V.G.	Good	Fair	Poor
600	400	300	200	150

Model 1907

The Model 1907 was an improved version of the Model 1905 and chambered for the new .351 Winchester Self-Loading cartridge. Outward appearance was the same as Model 1905 except for 20" round barrel. This rifle was available in three different styles:

1. Sporting Rifle, 20" round barrel, plain walnut pistol grip stock with plain forend. Discontinued in 1937.

2. Fancy Sporting Rifle, 20" round barrel, fancy walnut checkered pistol grip stock and checkered forend.

3. Police Rifle, 20" round barrel, plain walnut pistol grip stock and beavertail forend. This version was fitted with a leather sling and with or without knife bayonet. First introduced in 1937. Winchester discontinued this model in 1957 after having sold about 59,000 guns.

Sporting Rifle

Exc.	V.G.	Good	Fair	Poor
400	300	250	175	125

Fancy Sporting Rifle

Exc.	V.G.	Good	Fair	Poor
550	400	300	200	150

Police Rifle

Exc.	V.G.	Good	Fair	Poor
450	350	275	200	150

Model 1910

This model was similar to the Model 1907 but the action was made stronger to handle the new Winchester .401 Self-Loading cartridge. The specifications for this model are the same as the Model 1907. Built between 1907 and 1936, only about 21,000 of these guns were sold.

Courtesy Butterfield & Butterfield, San Francisco, California

Sporting Rifle

Exc.	V.G.	Good	Fair	Poor
400	300	250	175	125

Fancy Sporting Rifle

Exc.	V.G.	Good	Fair	Poor
550	400	300	200	150

Model 55 (Rimfire Rifle)

Not to be confused with the lever action model, this .22 caliber rifle was a semiautomatic single shot with a 22" round barrel. Fitted with a plain walnut pistol grip one-piece stock and forend. The safety goes on when each cartridge is inserted into the chamber. This model was not serial numbered and was produced from 1957 to 1961 with about 45,000 guns sold.

Standard Rifle

Exc.	V.G.	Good	Fair	Poor
250	200	125	100	60

Model 74

This was a semiautomatic chambered for either the .22 Short or the .22 Long Rifle. The rifle has a tubular magazine in the buttstock and a 24" round barrel. The bolt on this rifle was designed to be easily removed for cleaning or repair. The stock was plain walnut pistol grip with semi-beavertail forend. A Gallery Special was offered that was chambered for the .22 Short and fitted with a steel shell deflector. This gallery model was also available with chrome trimmings at extra cost.

Courtesy C.H. Wolfersberger

Sporting Rifle

Exc.	V.G.	Good	Fair	Poor
400	300	225	150	100

Gallery Special-.22 Short Only

Exc	V.G.	Good	Fair	Poor
600	450	325	225	150

NOTE: For Gallery models with chrome trimmings, add a premium of 50%.

Model 77

This rifle was built on the blow-back design for semiautomatic rifles and is chambered for the .22 Long Rifle. It features a 22" round barrel and either a detachable box magazine or under barrel tubular magazine. The rifle has a triggerguard made of nylon. It has a plain walnut pistol grip stock with semi-beavertail forend and composition buttplate. Built between 1955 and 1963, Winchester sold about 217,000 of these rifles.

Standard Rifle

Exc.	V.G.	Good	Fair	Poor
300	200	150	100	50

NOTE: Models with tubular magazines will bring a premium of 10% to 20%.

Model 100

This rifle is gas operated, semiautomatic and chambered for the .243, .308, and .284 caliber center cartridges. It was available in a rifle version with a 22" round barrel and a carbine version with a 19" barrel. Both were furnished with a detachable box magazine. The stock was a one-piece design with pistol grip and was offered in either hand cut checkering or pressed basket weave checkering. Rifles were introduced in 1961 and the carbine in 1967. The Model 100 was last produced in 1973 with about 263,000 guns sold.

WARNING: The Model 100 has been recalled. Do not purchase this model without first determining if the problem has been repaired.

Model 100 Rifle

Exc.	V.G.	Good	Fair	Poor
475	400	300	250	200

NOTE: Pre-1964 models 15% premium. Prices given are for .308 caliber; for .243 add 15%, for .284 add 20%.

Model 100 Carbine

Exc.	V.G.	Good	Fair	Poor
575	475	375	325	225

NOTE: Add 25% premium for .243, and 100% for .284.

Model 88

The Model 88 was a modern short stroke lever action chambered for the .243, .308, 284, and .358 calibers. It was available in a rifle version with 22" round barrel and a carbine version with 19" round barrel. The carbine model was not chambered for the .358 cartridge. Both were furnished with a detachable box magazine. The stock was a one-piece design with pistol grip and was offered with hand cut checkering or pressed basket weave checkering after 1964. The rifle was introduced in 1955 and the carbine was first offered in 1968. Both versions were discontinued in 1973 with about 283,000 sold.

Model 88 Rifle

Exc.	V.G.	Good	Fair	Poor
500	400	300	250	150

NOTE: Pre-1964 models add 25% premium. Prices above are for .308 caliber; for .243 add 15%, .284 add 75%, and for 358 add 100%.

Model 88 Carbine

Exc.	V.G.	Good	Fair	Poor
950	800	650	400	300

NOTE: Add 25% for .243, add 100% for .284 calibers.

Model 1900

This single shot bolt action .22 caliber rifle was based on a John M. Browning design. The rifle was furnished with an 18" round barrel and chambered for the .22 Short and Long interchangeably. The stock was a one-piece plain gumwood straight grip without a buttplate. The rifle was not serial numbered. It was produced from 1899 to 1902 with about 105,000 sold.

Exc.	V.G.	Good	Fair	Poor
2500	1250	450	300	200

Model 1902

Also a single shot, this model was of the same general design as the Model 1900 with several improvements: a special shaped metal triggerguard was added, a shorter trigger pull, a steel buttplate, a rear peep sight, and the barrel was made heavier at the muzzle. The rifle was chambered for the .22 Short and Long cartridges until 1914 when the .22 Extra Long was added. In 1927 the .22 Extra Long was dropped in favor of the more popular .22 Long Rifle. All of these cartridges were interchangeable. The stock was a one-piece plain gumwood with straight grip (the metal triggerguard added a pistol grip feel) and steel buttplate, which was changed to composition in 1907. This model was not serial numbered. About 640,000 Model 1902s were sold between 1902 and 1931 when it was discontinued.

Exc.	V.G.	Good	Fair	Poor
1000	750	400	225	125

Model 99 or Thumb Trigger

This rifle was a modification of the Model 1902 without a traditional trigger. The rifle was fired by depressing the trigger with the thumb, which was part of the sear and extractor located behind the bolt. The rifle was chambered for the .22 Short and Long until 1914 when it was also chambered for the .22 Extra Long. All cartridges could be shot interchangeably. The stock was the same as the Model 1902, Gumwood stained walnut, without the trigger or triggerguard. This model was not serial numbered. Built between 1904 and 1923. Winchester sold about 76,000 rifles.

Exc.	V.G.	Good	Fair	Poor
3000	1250	600	300	200

Model 1904

This model was a slightly more expensive version of the Model 1902. It featured a 21" round barrel, a one-piece plain gumwood straight grip stock (the metal triggerguard gave the rifle a pistol grip feel) with a small lip on the forend. Rifle was chambered for the .22 Short and Long until 1914 when the .22 Extra Long was added. The .22 Long Rifle cartridge was added in place of the Extra Long in 1927. This model was not serial numbered. Produced between 1904 and 1931, about 303,000 rifles were sold.

Exc.	V.G.	Good	Fair	Poor
850	600	350	200	100

Model D Military Rifle

Overall length 46-3/8"; barrel length 26"; caliber 7.62mm. Walnut stock with blued barrel, receiver, magazine housing and furniture. Receiver ring over barrel breech stamped with serial number and Winchester proofmark. A total of 500 Model D Rifles were shipped to Russia for trial in March of 1917.

Prospective purchasers are strongly advised to secure an expert appraisal prior to acquisition. Due to the recent identification of this model pricing schedules have yet to be established.

Imperial Bolt Action Magazine Rifle (Model 51)

Designed by T.C. Johnson, approximately 25 of these rifles were made during 1919 and 1920 in two different styles and three calibers. The takedown variation has an overall length of 42-1/4", barrel length 22" and was made in .27, .30-06 and .35 Newton calibers. The solid frame version is identical in form, dimensions and calibers. Sight configurations and markings vary.

Winchester Imperial Takedown

Winchester Imperial Solid Frame

Model 43

Introduced in 1949, this rifle was chambered for the .218 Bee, .22 Hornet, .25-20 Winchester, and the .32-20 Winchester. The rifle was a bolt action with detachable box magazine, fitted with a 24" round barrel and front sight ramp forged integrally with barrel. **This model was not drilled and tapped for scope blocks except for a few late rifles.** This model was available in two styles:

1. Standard Rifle, 24" round barrel, plain walnut pistol grip stock and forend. One inch sling swivels are standard.

2. Special Rifle, 24" round barrel, select walnut checkered pistol grip stock and checkered forend. Furnished with either open sporting rear sight or Lyman 57A micrometer receiver sight.

The Model 43 was produced from 1949 to 1957 with about 63,000 sold.

Standard Rifle

Exc.	V.G.	Good	Fair	Poor
650	550	400	300	200

Special Rifle or Deluxe

Exc.	V.G.	Good	Fair	Poor
750	650	550	250	175

NOTE: For rifles chambered for .25-20 and .32-20 add a 50% premium. For rifles with non-factory drilled and tapped scope holes deduct 40%.

Model 47

This model was a single shot bolt action rifle chambered for the .22 Short, Long, and Long Rifle interchangeably. The rifle was furnished with a 25" round barrel, plain walnut pistol grip stock and forend. The bolt, bolt handle, and trigger are chrome plated. This model has a special bolt with a post on the underside. This moves into the safety position when the bolt is closed. This model was not serial numbered. Produced between 1948 and 1954, Winchester sold about 43,000 guns.

Courtesy Buffalo Bill Historical Center, Cody, Wyoming

Model 47 Target Rifle

Fitted with a 28" round standard weight or heavyweight barrel, plain walnut modified pistol grip stock with correct bolt.

Exc.	V.G.	Good	Fair	Poor
400	350	250	200	150

NOTE: Add 10% premium for Model 47 with factory peep sight.

Model 52

One of the finest small caliber bolt action rifles ever built, the Model 52 was Winchester's answer to the increased demand for a military style target rifle following WWI. The Model 52 was a well-made quality-built bolt action rifle. The rifle was chambered for the .22 Long Rifle cartridge. Designed by T.C. Johnson, this rifle was built in several different configurations over its production life:

1. Model 52 with finger groove in forend and one barrel band. Produced from 1920 to 1929.

2. Model 52 Target Rifle, same as above but without finger groove in forend and has first speed lock. Made from 1929 to 1932.

3. Model 52A Target Rifle, same as above with addition of reinforced receiver and locking lug. Made from 1932 to 1935.

4. Model 52B Target Rifle, same as above with addition of adjustable sling swivel and single shot adaptor. Made from 1935 to 1947.

5. Model 52C Target Rifle, same as above with addition of an easily adjustable vibration-free trigger mechanism. Made from 1947 to 1961.

6. Model 52D Target Rifle, this is a single shot rifle with free-floating barrel and new design stock with adjustable hand-stop channel.

7. Model 52 Bull Gun, same as target rifle but fitted with extra heavyweight barrel. Made from 1939 to 1960. The Bull Barrel measures 1.125" at the receiver juncture while the heavyweight measures 1". Both barrels measure .875" at the muzzle.

8. Model 52 International Match, a free style stock with thumb hole and adjustable buttstock and forend introduced in 1969 and an International Prone model with no thumb hole or adjustable buttplate and forend was introduced in 1975. Both discontinued in 1980.

9. Model 52 Sporter, 24" round barrel, select walnut checkered pistol grip stock with cheekpiece and forend with black plastic tip. Pistol grip was furnished with hard rubber grip cap. The Model 52 Sporter was introduced in 1934 and discontinued in 1958. It went through the same improvements as the Target Rifle, thus the designation Model 52A Sporter etc.

Model 52 Target

Exc.	V.G.	Good	Fair	Poor
550	450	350	300	225

Model 52 Target-Speed Lock

Exc.	V.G.	Good	Fair	Poor
550	450	350	300	250

Model 52A Target Heavy Barrel-Rare

Exc.	V.G.	Good	Fair	Poor
700	600	500	400	300

Model 52B Target Heavy & Standard Barrel

Exc.	V.G.	Good	Fair	Poor
650	550	450	350	250

Model 52B Target Bull Barrel

Exc.	V.G.	Good	Fair	Poor
900	800	700	500	400

Model 52C Target

Exc.	V.G.	Good	Fair	Poor
750	650	550	400	300

Model 52D Target

Exc.	V.G.	Good	Fair	Poor
850	750	600	500	300

Model 52B Bull Gun

Exc.	V.G.	Good	Fair	Poor
850	750	600	500	300

Model 52C Bull Gun

Exc.	V.G.	Good	Fair	Poor
900	800	650	550	300

Model 52 International Match

Approximately 300 manufactured.

Free Style

Exc.	V.G.	Good	Fair	Poor
2750	1500	950	600	400

Prone

Exc.	V.G.	Good	Fair	Poor
850	750	600	500	300

Model 52 Sporter-C Model

Exc.	V.G.	Good	Fair	Poor
3600	3000	2000	1600	900

NOTE: Add 50% to above prices for "A" or pre-"A" series sporters. These are very rare early models in the sporter series.

Editor's Comment: According to Winchester factory records, Model 52 barrels were, "originally drilled and tapped for Winchester telescope bases designed for use with the Winchester 3A, 5A, and Lyman telescopes. These bases had a 6.2" center to center spacing ... a change in the bases and the spacing to be used was authorized on January 11, 1933. These new bases had a specially shaped Fecker type notch added on the right hand side of both bases. They are known as Winchester Combination Telescope Sight Bases and are satisfactory for use with Winchester, Lyman, Fecker, and Unertl telescopes. Bases are spaced 7.2" center to center ... All Model 52 targets were factory drilled for scope mounting but only the "C" series Sporters were factory drilled for scopes.

Model 54

The Model 54 was to centerfire cartridges what the Model 52 was to rimfire cartridges. The Model 54 was also a quality made bolt action rifle with a nondetachable box magazine and was chambered for a variety of calibers: .270, .30-06, .30-30, 7mm, 7.65, 9.mm, .250-3000, .22 Hornet, .220 Swift, and .257 Roberts. This was Winchester's first bolt action rifle built for heavy, high velocity ammunition. The rifle was available in several different styles:

1. Standard Rifle, 24" or 20" round barrel (except .220 Swift which was 26"), plain walnut checkered pistol grip stock and forend.

2. Carbine, 20" round barrel, plain walnut pistol grip stock with finger groove on each side of forend.

3. Sniper's Rifle, 26" round heavyweight barrel, plain walnut pistol grip stock and forend.

4. N.R.A. Rifle, 24" round barrel, select walnut checkered pistol grip stock and forend.

5. Super Grade Rifle, 24" round barrel, select walnut checkered pistol grip stock with cheekpiece and checkered forend with black plastic tip. Pistol grip was capped with hard rubber cap. Super Grade was equipped with 1" detachable sling swivels.

6. Target Rifle, 24" round heavyweight barrel, plain walnut checkered pistol grip stock and forend.

7. National Match Rifle, 24" round barrel, plain walnut special target stock and forend.

The Model 54 was introduced in 1925 and was discontinued in 1936 with about 50,000 guns sold.

Standard Rifle

Exc.	V.G.	Good	Fair	Poor
650	550	400	300	225

Carbine

Exc.	V.G.	Good	Fair	Poor
700	600	450	350	275

Sniper's Rifle

Exc.	V.G.	Good	Fair	Poor
900	750	600	500	350

N.R.A. Rifle

Exc.	V.G.	Good	Fair	Poor
900	750	600	500	350

Super Grade Rifle

Exc.	V.G.	Good	Fair	Poor
900	750	600	450	375

Target Rifle

Exc.	V.G.	Good	Fair	Poor
900	750	600	450	375

National Match Rifle

Exc.	V.G.	Good	Fair	Poor
900	750	600	450	375

NOTE: The rare calibers are the 7mm, 7.65 and the .9mm, which bring considerable premiums (in some cases as much as 250%) over standard calibers. Popular calibers such as .22 Hornet, .220 Swift, 30-30, and .257 Roberts will also bring a premium. Proceed with caution on Model 54s with rare caliber markings.

Model 56

This model was designed to be a medium priced bolt action rimfire rifle. It featured a detachable box magazine and was chambered for the .22 Short or .22 Long Rifle cartridges. The rifle was offered in two styles;

1. Sporting Rifle, 22" round barrel, plain walnut pistol grip stock and forend.

2. Fancy Sporting Rifle, 22" round barrel, fancy walnut checkered pistol grip stock and forend.

Both styles had a forend with a distinctive lip on the forend tip. The rifle was introduced in 1926 and was discontinued in 1929 with about 8,500 rifles sold.

Sporting Rifle

Exc.	V.G.	Good	Fair	Poor
1500	1000	750	525	400

Fancy Sporting Rifle (Very Rare, Use Caution)

Exc.	V.G.	Good	Fair	Poor
3000	2000	1500	900	750

NOTE: Add a 50% premium for rifles chambered for .22 Short only.

Model 57

The Model 57 was close in appearance to the Model 56 with the addition of a heavier stock, target sights, and swivel bows attached to the stock. The rifle was chambered for the .22 Short or .22 l.r. and featured a 22" round barrel with detachable box magazine. The stock was plain walnut with pistol grip and plain forend. The rifle was introduced in 1927 and dropped from the Winchester line in 1936 having sold only about 19,000 guns.

Model 57

Exc.	V.G.	Good	Fair	Poor
750	600	450	325	250

NOTE: Add 20% premium for web sling.

Model 58

This model was an attempt by the company to market a low priced .22 caliber rimfire rifle in place of its Models 1902 and 1904. This was a single shot bolt action, cocked by pulling the firing pin head to the rear. It had an 18" round barrel and was chambered for the .22 Short, Long, and Long Rifle interchangeably. The stock was a one-piece plain wood with straight grip. This model was not serial-numbered. The Model 58 was introduced in 1928 and discontinued in 1931. About 39,000 were sold.

Exc.	V.G.	Good	Fair	Poor
2000	1000	425	250	125

Model 59

The Model 59 was essentially a Model 58 with the addition of a pistol grip stock and a 23" round barrel. Introduced in 1930, it was dropped from the product line in the same year with a total sales of about 9,000 guns.

Courtesy Olin Corporation

Exc.	V.G.	Good	Fair	Poor
2000	1000	400	200	125

Model 60 and 60A

This rifle used the same action as that of the Model 59. When the rifle was first introduced in 1931, it was furnished with a 23" round barrel which was changed to 27" in 1933. Several other mechanical improvements were included with this model; perhaps the most noticeable were the chrome-plated bolt, bolt handle, and trigger. The stock was plain wood with pistol grip. In 1933 the Model 60A was added, which was the same rifle but in a target configuration. The front sight was a square top military blade with a Lyman 55W receiver sight. The Model 60 was discontinued in 1934 with about 166,000 rifles sold. The Model 60A was dropped in 1939 with only about 6,100 rifles sold.

Courtesy Buffalo Bill Historical Center, Cody, Wyoming

Model 60

Exc.	V.G.	Good	Fair	Poor
400	250	200	150	100

Model 60A

Exc.	V.G.	Good	Fair	Poor
400	300	250	150	100

Model 67

Winchester again upgraded and improved the Model 60 with an expansion of the styles offered to the shooting public. The standard chamber for the rifle was .22 Short, Long, and Long Rifle interchangeably with the W.R.F. only added in 1935:

1. Sporting Rifle, 27" round barrel, stock similar to the Model 60.

2. Smoothbore Rifle, 27" barrel, chambered for the .22 Long Shot or .22 Long Rifle Shot.

3. Junior Rifle, 20" round barrel and shorter stock.

4. Rifle with miniature target boring, 24" round barrel, chambered for .22 l.r. Shot.

Model 67s were not serial numbered for domestic sales but were numbered for foreign sales. Introduced in 1934 the gun was dropped from the line in 1963 having sold about 384,000. Many of these models were fitted at the factory with telescopes, and the bases were mounted on the rifle and the scope was packed separately.

Courtesy C.H. Wolfersberger

Courtesy Buffalo Bill Historical Center, Cody, Wyoming

Sporting Rifle

Exc.	V.G.	Good	Fair	Poor
200	150	125	100	75

Smoothbore Rifle

Courtesy Buffalo Bill Historical Center, Cody, Wyoming

Exc.	V.G.	Good	Fair	Poor
800	600	400	250	200

Junior Rifle

Exc.	V.G.	Good	Fair	Poor
250	200	175	150	125

Miniature Target Rifle

This model is marked "FOR SHOT ONLY" and has beads instead of standard iron rifle sights.

Exc.	V.G.	Good	Fair	Poor
1200	900	700	400	300

Model 677

This model looked the same as the Model 67 but was manufactured without iron sights and therefore will have no sight cuts in the barrel. The rifle was furnished with either 2-3/4 power scopes or 5 power scopes. This model was not serial numbered. Introduced in 1937 and discontinued in 1939.

Exc.	V.G.	Good	Fair	Poor
2250	1350	900	600	300

NOTE: Add a 50% premium for rifles chambered for .22WRF.

Model 68

Another takeoff on the Model 67, this model differed only in the sight equipment offered. Winchester fitted this rifle with its own 5 power telescopes. First sold in 1934 the Model 68 was dropped in 1946 with sales of about 101,000.

Courtesy C.H. Wolfersberger

With Scope

Exc.	V.G.	Good	Fair	Poor
750	500	300	200	150

Without Scope

Exc.	V.G.	Good	Fair	Poor
300	225	150	100	75

NOTE: Rifles with factory scopes and no sights add 50%. For rifles with factory scopes and no sights chambered for .22 WRF add 200%.

Model 69 and 69A

This model was designed by Winchester to answer the demand for a medium priced hunting and target .22 rimfire bolt action rifle. The rifle had a detachable box magazine, and many were offered with factory-installed telescopes in 2-3/4 and 5 power. The stock was plain walnut with pistol grip and plain forend. This model was not serial numbered. The 69A version was introduced in 1937 and featured an improved cocking mechanism. Introduced in 1935 as the Model 69, this gun was dropped in 1963 with sales of about 355,000 guns.

Exc.	V.G.	Good	Fair	Poor
450	375	300	200	100

NOTE: Add 25% for Target Model. Add 20% for grooved receiver.

Model 697

The Model 697 was similar in appearance to the Model 69 except A was equipped exclusively for a telescope. Winchester offered either a 2-3/4 or 5 power scope with the bases attached at the factory and the scope packed separately. Built between 1937 and 1941 with small sales, this model was not serial numbered.

Exc.	V.G.	Good	Fair	Poor
2000	1200	800	600	400

NOTE: For factory scopes with no sights add 50%.

Model 70

Considered by many as the finest bolt action rifle ever built in the United States, the pre-1964 Model 70 is highly sought after by shooters and collectors alike. Its smooth, strong action has no peer. It is often referred to as "The Riflemen's Rifle." The Model 70 is an updated and improved version of the Model 54 and features a hinged floorplate, new speed locks, new safety design that does not interfere with telescope, manually releasable bolt stop, more attractive buttstock and forend, and forged steel triggerguard. Like many Winchesters, the Model 70 was available with several extra cost options that should be evaluated by an expert. The values listed below are given for pre-1964 Model 70s with serial numbers from 1 to 581471. This rifle was available in several different styles:

1. Standard Grade, 24" round barrel (except 26" round barrel for .220 Swift and .300 H&H Magnum—25-inch round barrel for .375 H&H Magnum after 1937), plain walnut checkered pistol stock and forend. Built from 1936 to 1963.

2. Standard Grade Carbine, 20" round barrel, chambered for .22 Hornet, .250-3000, .257 Roberts, .270, 7mm, and 30-06, same stock as Standard Grade. Built from 1936 to 1946.

3. Super Grade Rifle, same barrel and calibers as Standard Grade, select walnut checkered and capped pistol grip stock with cheekpiece and checkered forend with plastic tip. Built from 1936 to 1960.

4. Featherweight, 22" round barrel chambered for .243, .264, .270, .308, .30-06, and .358. Fitted with aluminum triggerguard, aluminum buttplate, and aluminum floor plate. Later versions with plastic buttplate. Built from 1952 to 1963.

5. Featherweight Super Grade, same as above except not chambered for the .358 cartridge, but fitted with Super Grade stock. Built from 1952 to 1963.

6   National Match, same as Standard Grade but fitted with target type stock and telescope bases. Chambered for .30-06 only. Discontinued in 1960.

7. Target, 24" round medium-weight barrel with same stock as National Match in .243 and 30-06 calibers. Discontinued in 1963.

8. Varmint, 26" round heavy barrel, with heavier stock, chambered for .243 and the rare .220 Swift. Built from 1956 to 1963.

9. Westerner, 26" round barrel with Standard Grade stock, chambered for .264 Winchester Magnum. Built from 1960 to 1963. Fitted with a solid rubber pad for early production guns and a vented pad for later guns.

10. Alaskan, 25" round barrel, with Standard Grade stock, chambered for .338 Winchester Magnum and .375 H&H Magnum. Built from 1960 to 1963. Fitted with a solid rubber pad for early production guns and a vented pad for later guns.

11. Bull Gun, 28" round barrel, same stock as National Match, chambered for .30-06 and .300 H&H Magnum. Built from 1936 to 1963.

The standard calibers offered for the Model 70 are as follows in order of rarity: .300 Savage, .35 Rem., .458 Win Magnum, 7mm, .358 Win., .250-3000 Savage, .300 Win Magnum, .338 Win. Magnum, .375 H&H Magnum, .257 Roberts, .220 Swift, .22 Hornet, .264 Win. Magnum, .300 H&H Magnum, .308 Win., .243 Win., .270 W.C.F., .30-06.

NOTE: Prices for the Model 70 are, in many cases, based on the caliber of the rifle; the more rare the caliber, the more premium the gun will command. Many pre-1964 Model 70s are still available in new condition in the original box with all papers. Add 100% if the box is serial numbered to the gun. **Use caution** prior to purchase of NIB guns due to fake boxes and papers.

PRICING NOTE: The asterisk (*) signifies the value of the rifle with respect to a usable action. Model 70 receivers bring $500 regardless of the condition of the barrel and stock. If the receiver is unusable then the rifle is worth the value of its usable parts, i.e. less than $500.

For Model 70s with "X" or "D" prefex add a premium of 10%. These letters indicate that there were two rifles mistakenly stamped with the same serial number.

Standard Rifle

.30-06 Springfield (1937-1963)

Prewar

Exc.	V.G.	Good	Fair	Poor
1100	800	500*	365*	300*

Postwar

Exc.	V.G.	Good	Fair	Poor
700	550	500*	365*	300*

Relative Caliber Rarity*
Model 70
1936 - 1963

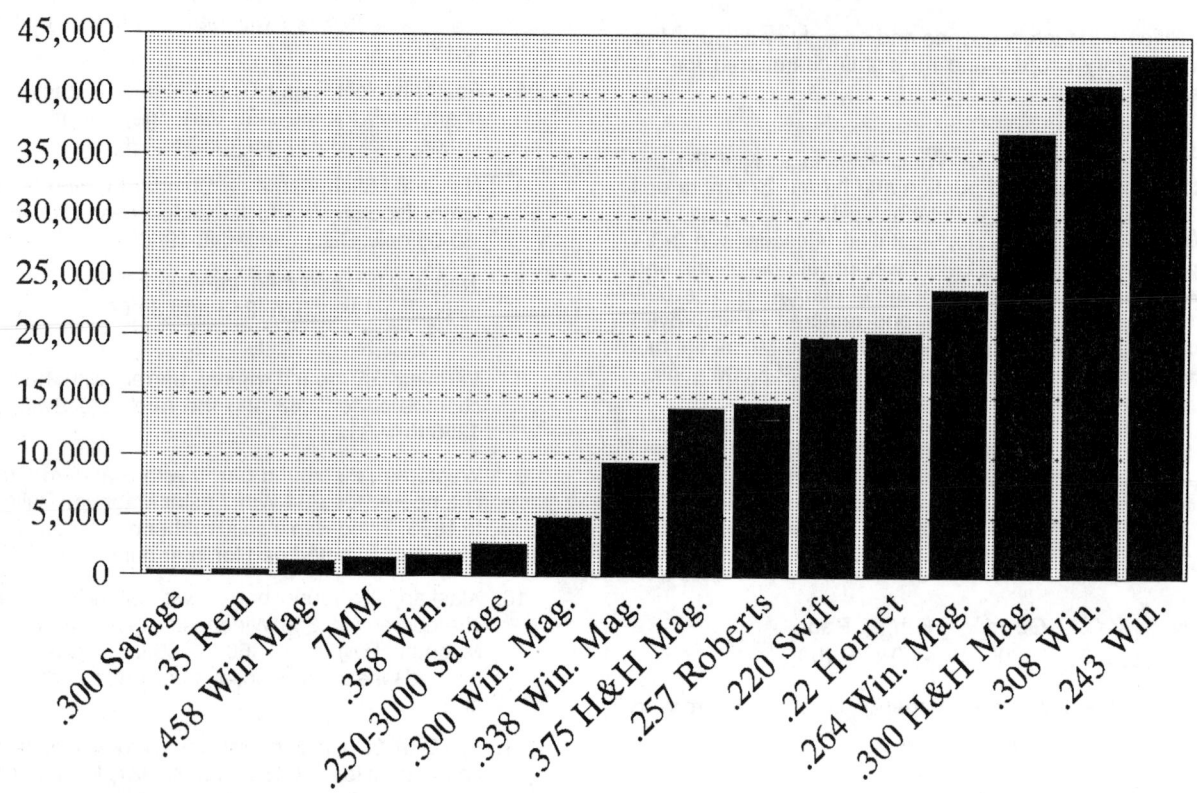

* Excluding the .270 W.C.F.(approx. 100,000) and 30-06 (approx. 200,000) which were the most common.

.270 Win. (1937-1963)
Prewar

Exc.	V.G.	Good	Fair	Poor
1250	900	500*	365*	300*

Postwar

Exc.	V.G.	Good	Fair	Poor
850	700	500*	365*	300*

.243. Win. (1955-1963)

Exc.	V.G.	Good	Fair	Poor
1100	900	700	420*	315*

.300 H&H Magnum (1937-1963)
Pre-War

Exc.	V.G.	Good	Fair	Poor
1500	1200	850	600	370*

Postwar

Exc.	V.G.	Good	Fair	Poor
1200	950	700	600	370*

.264 Win. Magnum (1959-1963)

Exc.	V.G.	Good	Fair	Poor
1150	950	750	600	370*

.22 Hornet (1937-1958)
Prewar

Exc.	V.G.	Good	Fair	Poor
1950	1500	1250	700	400*

Postwar

Exc.	V.G.	Good	Fair	Poor
1500	1200	900	600	400*

.220 Swift (1937-1963)
Prewar

Exc.	V.G.	Good	Fair	Poor
1250	1050	800	650	400*

Postwar

Exc.	V.G.	Good	Fair	Poor
1000	850	700	500	370*

.257 Roberts (1937-1959)
Prewar

Exc.	V.G.	Good	Fair	Poor
1900	1650	1150	750	400*

Postwar

Exc.	V.G.	Good	Fair	Poor
1250	1050	850	650	370*

.375 H&H Magnum (1937-1963)
Prewar

Exc.	V.G.	Good	Fair	Poor
2200	1750	1300	900	500*

Postwar

Exc.	V.G.	Good	Fair	Poor
1750	1400	950	650	500*

.338 Win. Magnum (1959-1963)

Exc.	V.G.	Good	Fair	Poor
1550	1250	850	650	500*

.300 Win. Magnum (1962-1963)

Exc.	V.G.	Good	Fair	Poor
1500	1250	800	600	500*

.250-3000 Savage (1937-1949)

Exc.	V.G.	Good	Fair	Poor
2250	1750	950	750	500*

7mm (1937-1949)

Exc.	V.G.	Good	Fair	Poor
3100	2500	1750	1100	700

.35 Rem. (1944-1947)

Exc.	V.G.	Good	Fair	Poor
4250	3250	2250	1260	950

.300 Savage (1944-1950s?)

Exc.	V.G.	Good	Fair	Poor
4250	3250	2250	1260	950

.458 African (Built in Supergrade only, 1956-1963)

Exc.	V.G.	Good	Fair	Poor
4500	3750	3000	2000	1200

Featherweight

Exc.	V.G.	Good	Fair	Poor
1000	850	700	550	450

NOTE: Add 100% for .358 Win. For .264 and .270 calibers add 25%.

Featherweight Super Grade

Exc.	V.G.	Good	Fair	Poor
3500	3000	2200	1250	1000

Standard Grade Carbine

Exc.	V.G.	Good	Fair	Poor
2250	1750	1150	850	650

NOTE: For Supergrade rifles add 100%.

National Match

Exc.	V.G.	Good	Fair	Poor
1800	1500	1200	800	600

Target

Exc.	V.G.	Good	Fair	Poor
1400	1200	825	650	550

Varmint

Exc.	V.G.	Good	Fair	Poor
1000	850	600	500	375*

NOTE: Add 40% premium for .220 Swift.

Bull Gun

Exc.	V.G.	Good	Fair	Poor
2100	1450	950	700	600

WHAT'S IT LIKE-THE PRE-64 MODEL 70

Which rifle looks like a rifle is supposed to look, functions like a rifle is supposed to function and smells like a rifle is supposed to smell? The pre-64 Winchester Model 70, of course. Only the old Mauser Model 98 will rival it in those three categories. I was introduced to the Winchester Model 70 in the 1950's by the legendary outdoor scribe, Jack O'Connor. My infatuation with the rifle still exists, even a half-century later. Over the years, it was produced in many different variations and in about every caliber known to man. My favorite though is the .270 Winchester, also an O'Connor favorite. Mated together, this rifle and cartridge combo is probably the closest to ideal for most North American game as one will ever find. The action, as it comes from the box, is glass smooth. The trigger, as simple and uncomplicated as they come, is still one of the very best. The stock, crafted from American black walnut, is generally pretty devoid of figure but fits the shooter like a rifle stock should. Finally, the factory barrel is generally as accurate as a custom one costing many times more. Someone in our past (Col. Whelen???) labeled the Model 70 as the "Rifleman's Rifle." It truly is. Whether after varmints, whitetail deer or the world's largest and most dangerous game, the pre-64 Model 70 is always up to the task. Without my Model 70 in .338 Winchester, I might not be penning these lines. A mad Alaska brown bear confused me with a Big Mac. The .338 and I won the battle - barely! Clean it and keep it lubricated and it will last several lifetimes. It is a great rifle and always will be.

Tom Turpin

Model 72

This model is a bolt action rifle with tubular magazine. It is chambered for the .22 Short, Long, and Long Rifle cartridges interchangeably. Early rifles were available with 2-3/4 or 5 power telescopes, but the majority were furnished with either open sights or peep sights. This rifle was available in two different configurations:

1. Sporting Rifle, 25" round barrel, chambered for the .22 Short, Long, and l.r. cartridges, one piece plain walnut pistol grip stock and forend.

2. Gallery Special, 25" round barrel, chambered for .22 Short only, stock same as Sporting Rifle.

This model was not serial numbered. It was built between 1938 and 1959 with about 161,000 rifles sold.

Courtesy C.H. Wolfersberger

Exc.	V.G.	Good	Fair	Poor
425	350	300	225	125

NOTE: Gallery Special will command a premium of 100%. For rifles with factory scopes and no sights add 200% depending on condition. Add 25% premium for peep sights. Add 20% for Model 72A with grooved receiver.

Model 75

Styles:

1. Sporting Rifle, 24" round barrel, chambered for .22 Long Rifle, select walnut checkered pistol grip stock and forend. This rifle was furnished with either open rear sights or a Lyman 57 E receiver sight.

Target Rifle, 28" round barrel, chambered for .22 Long Rifle, plain walnut pistol grip stock and forend. The Target Rifle was furnished with either a Winchester 8 power telescope or a variety of target sights.

This model was discontinued in 1958 with about 89,000 sold.

Model 75 Sporter

NIB	Exc.	V.G.	Good	Fair	Poor
1400	900	700	500	350	200

Model 75 Target

Exc.	V.G.	Good	Fair	Poor
700	600	500	350	200

Model 12

This model was designed by T.C. Johnson and was the first slide action hammerless shotgun built by Winchester. The Model 12 has enjoyed great success in its 51-year history, and over 1,900,000 were sold. This was a high quality, well-made shotgun that is still in use in the hunting and shooting fields across the country. All Model 12s were of the takedown variety. The Model 12 was dropped from regular product line in 1963, but a special model was produced in the Custom Shop until 1979. In 1972 Winchester resurrected the Model 12 in its regular production line in 12 gauge only and ventilated rib. This reintroduced Model 12 was dropped in 1980. The prices listed below are for guns made prior to 1964 or for guns with serial numbers below 1968307. This shotgun was offered in several different styles:

1. Standard Grade, 12, 16, 20, and 28 gauge, with plain, solid rib, or vent rib round barrels of standard lengths (26", 28", 30", 32"), plain walnut pistol grip stock with grooved slide handle. Built from 1912 to 1963.

2. Featherweight, same as above with lightweight alloy triggerguard. Built between 1959 and 1962.

3. Riot Gun, in 12 gauge only with 20" round choked cylinder, stock same as Standard Grade. Built between 1918 and 1963.

4. Trench Gun, chambered for 12 gauge only with 20" round barrel with ventilated hand guard over barrel, fitted with bayonet lug. All metal surfaces are "Parkerized," and these shotguns should be U.S. marked as a military firearm. Introduced in 1918 and built for U.S. Armed Forces on special order.

5. Skeet Grade, chambered for 12, 16, 20, and 28 gauge with 26" round barrel with solid or ventilated rib, select walnut checkered pistol stock and special checkered extension slide handle (longer than standard). Built from 1933 to 1963.

6. Trap Grade, chambered for 12 gauge only with 30" round barrel with solid rib or ventilated rib, select walnut pistol or straight grip stock, checkered extension slide handle. Built from 1914 to 1963.

7. Heavy Duck Gun, chambered in 12 gauge only with 30" or 32" round barrel with plain, solid, or ventilated rib, plain walnut pistol grip stock fitted with Winchester solid red rubber recoil pad, plain grooved slide handle. Built from 1935 to 1963.

8. Pigeon Grade, chambered for 12, 16, 20, and 28 gauges with standard barrel lengths and choice of ribs. This was a special order shotgun and will be seen in many different variations, most of these guns were factory engraved. Built 1914 to 1963.

The Model 12 shotgun will be seen in many different combinations of gauges, barrel lengths, ribs, and stocks, all of which determine value. The more rare a particular combination, the higher the price. The buyer is urged to be extremely cautious before purchasing the more rare combinations, such as a 28 gauge. The best advice is to seek assistance from an expert and get as many opinions as possible. The prices listed below are for guns in standard configurations.

Courtesy Butterfield & Butterfield, San Francisco, California

Standard Grade-12 gauge

Exc.	V.G.	Good	Fair	Poor
675	400	300	300	200

Featherweight

Exc.	V.G.	Good	Fair	Poor
575	400	325	275	200

Riot Gun

Exc.	V.G.	Good	Fair	Poor
825	650	550	400	250

Trench Gun

Exc.	V.G.	Good	Fair	Poor
1800	1200	950	550	400

Skeet Grade

Exc.	V.G.	Good	Fair	Poor
1300	850	700	400	350

Trap Grade

Exc.	V.G.	Good	Fair	Poor
900	700	600	450	400

Heavy Duck Gun

Exc.	V.G.	Good	Fair	Poor
700	600	450	325	300

NOTE: For Heavy Duck Guns with solid ribs add 25% premium.

Pigeon Grade

Exc.	V.G.	Good	Fair	Poor
2000	1400	1200	650	500

NOTE: For 16 Gauge deduct 20%. For 20 gauge add 20%. For 28 gauge add 600%. For guns with solid rib add 20%. For guns with Winchester Special Ventilated Rib add 30%. For guns with Milled Rib add 40%. Add 20% for 32" barrels on any Model 12 model. Add 30% premium for original box and papers.

Winchester engraving patterns for the Model 12 shotgun. Winchester also used these patterns on the Model 42, but with different birds.

Model 25

This model is similar in appearance to the Model 12 but does not have the takedown feature. All guns were solid frame. The Model 25 was furnished in 12 gauge with 26" or 28" plain round barrel, plain walnut pistol grip stock with grooved slide handle. This was an attempt by Winchester to introduce a less expensive version of the Model 12. Introduced in 1949 it was dropped from the product line in 1954 having sold about 88,000 guns.

Exc.	V.G.	Good	Fair	Poor
350	250	200	150	100

Model 20

In order to utilize the expanded production facilities left over from WWI, Winchester introduced a series of three different models of single shot shotguns; the Model 20 was the first of the three. This model has a visible hammer and a top lever frame. It was the first Winchester to have this type of breakdown action. It was chambered for the .410, 2-1/2" shell. The barrel is 26" round choked full, plain walnut pistol grip stock with hard rubber buttplate. The forend has a small lip on the front end. The Model 20 was dropped from the product line in 1924 having sold about 24,000 guns.

Courtesy C.H. Wolfersberger

Exc.	V.G.	Good	Fair	Poor
700	500	350	200	150

Model 36

The Model 36 was the second of the single shot shotguns to be introduced in 1920. This model features a bolt action that is cocked by pulling the firing pin head to the rear. It is fitted with an 18" round barrel, chambered for the 9mm Long Shot, 9mm Short Shot, and 9mm Ball interchangeably, plain gumwood straight grip stock with special metal pistol grip triggerguard. Winchester referred to this model as the "Garden Gun" for use against birds and pests around the house and barn. This model was not serial numbered. It was dropped from the product line in 1927 having sold about 20,000 guns.

Exc.	V.G.	Good	Fair	Poor
750	475	375	300	225

Model 41

This was the third of the low-priced single shot shotguns to be announced in 1920. Like the Model 36, the Model 41 was a bolt action arrangement but of much stronger construction and design. It features a 24" round barrel, chambered for the .410 2-1/2" shell, plain walnut pistol grip stock and forend. Straight grip stock was furnished at no extra charge. This model was not serial numbered. It was discontinued in 1934 having sold about 22,000 guns.

Courtesy C.H. Wolfersberger

Exc.	V.G.	Good	Fair	Poor
600	500	350	300	200

Model 21

The Model 21 was Winchester's finest effort with regard to quality, reliability, and strength. Developed in the late 1920s the introduction of this fine side-x-side shotgun was delayed by the company's financial troubles. When Winchester was purchased by the Olin family, the Model 21 was assured the attention it richly deserved due to John M. Olin's love for the gun. Despite the Model 21 being offered as a production gun it was, in fact, a hand-built custom made shotgun. Almost each Model 21 built has a personality of its own because each shotgun is slightly different with regard to chokes, barrel lengths, stock dimensions, and embellishments. The gun was introduced in 1931. From 1931 to 1959 the Model 21 was considered a production line gun and about 30,000 were sold. In 1960, when the Custom Shop was opened, the Model 21 was built there using the same procedures. Sales during the Custom Shop era were about 1,000 guns. Winchester changed the name of some of the Model 21 styles but the production methods stayed the same. In 1981 Winchester sold its firearms division to U.S. Repeating Arms Company including the right to build the Model 21. Again the production procedures stayed the same as did many of the former employees. U.S. Repeating Arms expanded and changed some of the style designations for the Model 21. Production was discontinued in about 1991. No sales figures are available for this time period. Collectors and shooters will be given the price breakdown for all three eras of production separately.

Model 21-1931 to 1959

The Model 21 was available in several different styles and configurations:

1. Standard Grade, chambered in 12, 16, and 20 gauge with barrel length from 26", 28", 30", and 32" with matted rib or ventilated rib, select walnut checkered pistol or straight grip stock with checkered beavertail forend. Built from 1931 to 1959.

2. Tournament Grade, same as above with special dimension stock. Marked "TOURNAMENT" on bottom of trigger plate. Built from 1933 to 1934.

3. Trap Grade, same as above with slightly better grade wood and stock made to customers' dimensions. Marked "TRAP" on trigger plate. Built from 1940 to 1959.

4. Skeet Grade, same as above with the addition of the 28 gauge, stock furnished with checkered butt. Marked "SKEET" on trigger plate. Built from 1936 to 1959.

5. Duck Gun, chambered for 12 gauge 3" magnum shells, 30" or 32" barrels, Standard Grade stock except for shorter length of pull. Marked "DUCK" on trigger plate. Built from 1940 to 1952.

6. Magnum Gun, chambered for 3" 12 or 20 gauge, same stock as Duck Gun. Not marked on trigger plate. Built from 1953 to 1959.

7. Custom Built/Deluxe Grade, chambered for 12, 16, 20, 28, and .410, barrel lengths from 26" to 32", stock built to customer's specifications using fancy walnut. Marked "CUSTOM BUILT" on top of rib or "DELUXE" on trigger plate. These grades are frequently but not always engraved. Built from 1933 to 1959.

NOTE: Some early Model 21s were furnished with double triggers, extractors, and splinter forends. This combination reduces the price of the gun regardless of grade. Deduct about 25%.

Standard Grade

	Exc	V.G.	Good	Fair	Poor
12 gauge	4400	3800	3200	3000	2600
16 gauge	5500	5000	4500	4300	3700
20 gauge	6000	5500	5000	4600	4000

Tournament Grade

	Exc.	V.G.	Good	Fair	Poor
12 gauge	4600	4000	3500	3200	2800
16 gauge	6000	5500	5000	4500	4000
20 gauge	6400	5900	5400	5000	4200

Trap Grade

	Exc.	V.G.	Good	Fair	Poor
12 gauge	4800	4200	3700	3300	3000
16 gauge	6300	5700	5200	4500	4000
20 gauge	6600	6100	5600	5200	4500

Skeet Grade

	Exc.	V.G.	Good	Fair	Poor
12 gauge	4500	3900	3300	3100	2700
16 gauge	5600	5100	4700	4400	3800
20 gauge	6200	5700	5200	4800	4200

Duck/Magnum Gun

Exc	V.G.	Good	Fair	Poor
4800	4300	3700	3200	2800

NOTE: Add 30% for 20 gauge Magnum.

NOTE: Factory ventilated ribs command a premium of about $1,800 on 12 gauge guns and $2,500 on 20 and 16 gauge guns. Models 21s with factory furnished extra barrels will bring an additional premium of about $2,500.

NOTE: Refinished and restored Model 21s are in a somewhat unique category of American made collectible shotguns. A gun that has been professionally refinished by a master craftsman will approximate 90% of the value of factory original guns.

Custom Built/Deluxe Grade

The prices paid for guns of this grade are determined by gauge, barrel and choke combinations, rib type, stock specifications, and engraving.

	Exc.	V.G.	Good	Fair	Poor
12 gauge	6500	6000	5000	4000	3500
16 gauge	7500	7000	6000	5000	4000
20 gauge	800	7500	6500	5500	4500

It is best to secure a factory letter from the Cody Firearms Museum. With respect to such letter it is important to note that these records are incomplete and may be inaccurate in a few cases. Records for Model 21s built during the 1930s may be missing. Special order guns may have incomplete records. In such cases a written appraisal from an authoritative collector or dealer may be helpful.

Custom Built .410 Bore

Exc.	V.G.	Good	Fair	Poor
45000	35000	30000	26000	22000

NOTE: Less than 50 .410 Model 21s were built between 1931 and 1959 in all grades. The number of 28 gauge Model 21s built is unknown but the number is probably no greater than the .410 bore.

A Winchester Model 21 Grand American was sold at auction for $40,250. It was engraved by Nick Kusmit and fitted with 3 barrels: two 20 gauge and one .410 bore. All barrels are 28" with vent ribs. Cased. Condition is near mint.
Rock Island Auction Company, October 2000

Custom Shop Model 21s - 1960 to 1981

When Winchester moved the production of the Model 21 into the Custom Shop the number of styles was greatly reduced. There were now three distinct styles:

1. Custom Grade, chambered in 12, 16, 20, 28 gauge, and .410 bore in barrel lengths from 26" to 32". Matted rib, fancy walnut checkered pistol or straight grip stock with checkered forend. Guns with pistol grips furnished with steel grip cap. A small amount of scroll engraving was provided on the frame of this grade.

2. Pigeon Grade, same chambers and barrel lengths as above with the addition of choice of matted or ventilated-rib, leather covered recoil pad, style "A" carving on stock and forend, and gold engraved pistol grip cap. The frame was engraved with the 21-6 engraving pattern.

3. Grand American Grade, same chambers and barrel lengths as Pigeon Grade with the addition of "B" carving on the stock and forend, 21-6 engraving with gold inlays, extra set of interchangeable barrels with extra forend. All of this was enclosed in a leather trunk case.

Custom Grade - 12 Gauge

Exc.	V.G.	Good	Fair	Poor
8500	7000	6200	5500	4800

NOTE: Add $4000 for 16 gauge. Add $3000 for 20 gauge.

Pigeon Grade - 12 Gauge

Exc.	V.G.	Good	Fair	Poor
15000	12000	10000	8000	6500

NOTE: Add $5000 for 16 gauge. Add $4000 for 20 gauge.

Grand American - 12 Gauge

Exc.	V.G.	Good	Fair	Poor
22000	18000	15000	13000	11500

NOTE: Add $15,000 for 16 gauge (extremely rare). Add $4,000 for 20 gauge.

Editor's Comment: There were eight 28 gauge Model 21s built during this period and five .410 bores built. These guns obviously command a large premium. Factory letters are available on these guns.

ENGRAVED MODEL 21s

Winchester catalogued a number of special order engraving patterns which ranged from a small amount of scroll (#1) to full coverage game scene and scroll (#6). In addition, there were a few guns engraved on special order to the customer's request. Engraved guns are extremely rare, and the value added will vary with the rarity of the gauge and the date of manufacture. The following table represents the value added for various standard engraving patterns on 12 gauge guns for the "Custom Shop" (1960-1982) and "Pre-Custom Shop"

(1932-1959) periods. However, it is advisable to seek the opinion of an authorative collector or dealer prior to a sale.

Engraving Pattern	Pre-Custom Shop	Custom Shop
#1	30%	20%
#2	40%	30%
#3	60%	45%
#4	70%	50%
#5	90%	70%
#6	100%	80%

WHAT'S IT LIKE-THE WINCHESTER MODEL 21

This shotgun is built like a tank. It has a long blued receiver that can withstand pressures far in excess of what may be encounter by the shooter. This is a real plus for the American shooter who likes high brass loads. The barrels are locked together in such a way as to reduce looseness even after thousands of rounds. Winchester fit its classic American black walnut to the butt stock and forend so that its appearance is decidedly American. Offered in 12, 16, 20 , 28 gauge as well as .410 bore the Winchester Model 21 is probable the most rugged and dependable American double barrel shotgun ever built. All of this is at a cost though; it's heavy. A 12 gauge Model 21 weighs in at about 7.5 lbs., while a 20 gauge gun can approach 7 lbs. Even the .410 bore, rare that it is, is about 7 lbs. The 28 gauge guns are 7.5 pound barrel heavy guns that are really not suitable for field shooting. But this weight is a plus when shooting magnum loads as it helps to tame recoil. Its long receiver, while not its most attractive feature, allows the action to be opened in a minimum of space; an excellent feature in the field especially the duck or goose blind. Despite these criticisms the Model 21 is a quality shotgun that remained in production for 60 years; from 1930 through about 1990. The Model 21 is fitted with beautiful walnut stocks, finely checkered, hand fitted and finished. Engraved examples of this gun are scarce and most are executed in American scroll with the higher grades done in game scenes. For over 50 years the Model 21 was the flagship of the Winchester line and with only a total production of about 33,000 guns it is truly a collectable firearm built for several lifetimes of hard use.

Ned Schwing

Custom Shop Model 21s 1982 to Present

When U.S. Repeating Arms Company took over the production of the Model 21 the Pigeon Grade was dropped from the line. The Grand American Grade was retained with all the features of its predecessor but with the addition of a small bore set featuring a 28 gauge and .410 bore set of barrels. Two new grades were introduced in 1983; the Standard Custom Grade and the Special Custom Built. In addition to these grades the factory would undertake to build for its customers whatever was desired. Due to the unique nature of these guns it is advised that an expert appraisal be sought to establish a value. While the changeover from Winchester to U.S. Repeating Arms was a transfer of business assets and the craftsmen and personnel remained the same, collectors are reluctant to assign the same values to U.S. Repeating Arms Model 21s as those produced by Winchester. No official production figures are available for U.S.R.A. Model 21s but the number is most likely small; perhaps around 200 guns.

Standard Custom Built

NIB	Exc.	V.G	Good	Fair	Poor
7500	6000	5000	4500	4000	3500

Grand American

NIB	Exc.	V.G	Good	Fair	Poor
16000	10000	8500	7500	5500	4500

Grand American - Small Gauge Set - 28 or .410 bore

NIB	Exc.	V.G	Good	Fair	Poor
47000	35000	30000	23000	20000	17000

Model 24

The Model 24 was Winchester's attempt to develop a medium-priced double barrel shotgun. Like the Model 21, it was a top lever breakdown model that was available in 12, 16, and 20 gauge in various barrel lengths from 26" to 30". Offered in a Standard model only with double triggers, raised matted rib, plain walnut pistol or straight grip stock with semi-beavertail forend, the Model 24 was introduced in 1939 and was discontinued in 1957 with about 116,000 guns sold.

Top: Model 24 Standard; bottom: Model 24 Improved

Exc.	V.G.	Good	Fair	Poor
650	500	400	250	200

NOTE: Add 10% for 16 gauge. Add 25% for 20 gauge.

Model 37

This model was developed to keep pace with Winchester's competitors in the low-price single barrel exposed hammer shotgun market. The shotgun was available in 12, 16, 20, 28 gauge, and .410 bore with barrel lengths from 26" to 30". The stock was plain walnut with pistol grip and semi-beavertail forend. This model was not serial numbered. Introduced in 1936 it stayed in the company line until 1963 having sold slightly over 1,000,000 guns.

Courtesy C.H. Wolfersberger

	Exc.	V.G.	Good	Fair	Poor
12 gauge	350	300	250	150	50
16 gauge	250	200	150	100	60
20 gauge	300	275	225	135	90
28 gauge	1750	1200	900	600	450

Youth Model-26" modified barrel, Win. factory pad.

	Exc.	V.G.	Good	Fair	Poor
28 gauge	1500	1000	800	600	450
.410 bore	350	300	275	200	100

NOTE: For 12 and 16 gauge guns add a 50% premium for 32" barrels. Use caution for 28 gauge guns. Many fakes are seen for sale.

THE lines of a double gun are particularly suited to tasteful ornamentation through genuine hand engraving. The six styles shown here and on the following pages have been executed by WINCHESTER custom engravers and designed exclusively for the Model 21. Other designs to meet a desire for something more elaborate can be submitted to our Custom Gun Department. For personalized engraving we will work from sketches or ideas offered by the purchaser.

Engravings for Model 21 Shotguns

Engraving patterns used by Winchester for the Model 21 between 1932 and 1959

Engravings for Model 21 Shotguns

WINCHESTER custom engravers have specialized for many years in executing high fidelity game scenes; game animals and birds; hunting dogs; beautiful floral designs and artistic pattern or scroll work; as well as monogrammed shields or nameplates in the stock. Techniques range from very fine flat designs to heavy relief work and all types of inlay work in gold, silver or platinum.

Engraving patterns used by Winchester for the Model 21 between 1932 and 1959

Model 42

This was the first slide action shotgun ever developed exclusively for the .410 bore. Invented by William Roemer, the Model 42 was in effect, at least in outward appearance, a miniature Model 12. This shotgun was a quality built, fast handling, racy looking shotgun that many refer to as "Everybody's Sweetheart." The Model 42 was offered in several different configurations throughout its production. These configurations will greatly influence value:

1. Standard Grade, 26" or 28" plain or solid rib barrel, plain walnut pistol grip stock with grooved slide handle, fitted with composition buttplate. Built from 1933 to 1963.

2. Skeet Grade, 26" or 28" plain, solid rib, or ventilated-rib barrel, select walnut checkered pistol or straight grip stock with checkered extension slide handle. The Skeet Grade was offered in chokes other than skeet. Skeet Grade Model 42s are seen in full, modified cylinder, improved cylinder, and skeet chokes. Built from 1933 to 1963.

3. Trap Grade, 26" or 28" plain or solid rib barrel, fancy walnut special checkered pistol or straight grip stock with special checkered extension slide handle. The Trap Grade checkering pattern has one closed diamond on each side of the pistol grip or, in the case of the straight grip, the diamond is located on the underside of the grip. The extension slide handle has two diamonds on each side. Stamped "TRAP" on the bottom of the receiver. Built from 1934 to 1939.

4. Deluxe Grade, same as above, available with ventilated rib in 1954. Some early models stamped "DELUXE" on bottom of receiver. Built from 1940 to 1963.

5. Pigeon Grade, same as above Deluxe Grade but engraved with a pigeon on the lower magazine tube. Very few of this grade were built by Winchester, and the majority were done in the late 1940s.

Engraved Model 42s will occasionally be seen. Collectors are urged to seek expert advice on these rare and expensive guns. The Model 42 was produced from 1933 to 1963. About 160,000 were sold.

Standard Grade

NIB	Exc.	V.G.	Good	Fair	Poor
1750	1000	850	600	350	250

NOTE: For Standard Grade guns with solid ribs add 50%. For pre-war guns add 30%.

Skeet Grade-Solid Rib

NIB	Exc.	V.G.	Good	Fair	Poor
3500	2750	2250	1500	750	400

NOTE: Add 25% guns chambered for 2-1/2" shells. For pre-war guns add 30%. For Skeet Grade guns with no rib deduct 20%.

Skeet Grade-Ventilated Rib

NIB	Exc.	V.G.	Good	Fair	Poor
5000	4000	3000	1250	850	600

NOTE: Add 25% of guns chambered for 2-1/2" shells.

Editor's Comment: Contrary to traditional views, Winchester did install factory ventilated ribs on its Model 42. Former employees and factory drawings substantiate this fact. However, the subject of what is a factory rib and what is not has been covered in great detail in an excellent book on the Model 42. Seek expert advice before selling or purchasing any Model 42 with a ventilated rib.

Trap Grade

Exc.	V.G.	Good	Fair	Poor
8500	5500	3500	1750	700

Deluxe Grade-Solid Rib

Exc.	V.G.	Good	Fair	Poor
5500	3000	1500	750	400

Deluxe Grade-Ventilated Rib

Exc.	V.G.	Good	Fair	Poor
7500	4500	2250	900	500

NOTE: For Pigeon Grade Model 42s add 50%.

WHAT'S IT LIKE-THE WINCHESTER MODEL 42

Designed by William Roemer in 1933 the Winchester Model 42 slide action shotgun appears at first glance to be a miniature Model 12. It is, sort of. The Model 42 was really a stand alone design that merely resembled its big brother, the Model 12. For pump gun enthusiasts the Model 42 is a real sweetheart. Light and fast this little .410 weighs around 6 pounds. Offered with 26 inch or 28 inch barrel with chokes ranging from full to cylinder the Model 42 was able to handle a variety of shooting task if used with discretion. Developed at a time when the .410 bore was somewhat of a novelty. The Model 42 was the first American shotgun chambered for the new 3 inch shell as well as being able to handle the older 2 1/2 inch shell. The gun was designed for small game shooting as well as sub-bore skeet shooting, a very fashionable sport at the time. Winchester stocked its little .410 with nice straight grain American black walnut and used, during the pre-war years, a shellac finish that gave a rich look to the butt stock and forearm. Offered with both pistol grip and straight grip with or without checkering the Model 42 became a popular sub-bore gun during the 1930s. A few were factory engraved and those examples will bring a big premium to the collector. In addition to all of the attractive qualities of the Model 42 nothing compares to its wonderful handling qualities. Just to pick it up and swing through an imaginary bird, the Model 42 becomes a joy to hold. But perhaps there is another reason for this appreciation. The Model 42 symbolizes an important part of this country's industrial history when hand machining and hand fitting were commonplace. This shotgun is a symbol of American excellence of a bygone era.

Ned Schwing

Model 1911

This was Winchester's first self-loading shotgun and was developed by T.C. Johnson in order to keep pace with the Remington Auto-Loading Shotgun Model 11, which was developed by John M. Browning with help from T.C. Johnson. Because of the delays involved in developing a brand new design, the Model 1911 was introduced on October 7, 1911. The shotgun was a recoil operated mechanism, had a tubular magazine and had the takedown feature. The shotgun was available in two styles:

1. Plain Model 1911, 26" or 28" barrel, 12 gauge, choked full, modified, or cylinder, plain birch laminated pistol grip stock and forend with hard rubber buttplate.

2. Fancy Model 1911, same as above with fancy birch laminated stock.

Because of the hurry in getting the model ready for production, the shotgun demonstrated design weakness and never proved satisfactory. It was discontinued in 1925 with about 83,000 guns sold.

Model 1911-Plain

Exc.	V.G.	Good	Fair	Poor
550	375	300	250	200

Model 1911-Fancy

Exc.	V.G.	Good	Fair	Poor
800	500	400	300	250

Model 40

This model represents Winchester's second attempt to build a self-loading long recoil-operated repeating shotgun. This shotgun was a hammerless tubular magazine gun without the hump at the rear of the receiver. Available in 12 gauge only with barrel lengths from 28" to 30". The Standard Grade had plain walnut pistol grip stock and forend. The Skeet Grade was fitted with select walnut checkered pistol grip stock and checkered forend. The Model 40 suffered from the same design problems as the Model 11, and sales were small. Introduced in 1940 and discontinued in 1941, Winchester sold about 12,000 guns.

Standard Grade

Exc.	V.G.	Good	Fair	Poor
600	500	400	275	200

Skeet Grade

Exc.	V.G.	Good	Fair	Poor
800	600	500	300	250

Model 50

The Model 50 was the company's third attempt to produce a satisfactory self-loading repeating shotgun. Winchester went to the short recoil system, utilizing a floating chamber design. This model was available in several different styles:

1. Standard Grade, 12 or 20 gauge with plain or ventilated rib in lengths from 26" to 30", plain walnut checkered pistol grip stock and forend.

2. Skeet Grade, 12 or 20 gauge with 26" ventilated rib barrel. Walnut checkered pistol grip stock and forend.

3. Trap Grade, 12 gauge with 30" ventilated rib barrel, walnut checkered Monte Carlo stock and forend.

4. Pigeon Grade, 12 or 20 gauge with barrel lengths to customers' specifications. Fancy walnut checkered stock and forend. Made on special orders only.

5. Featherweight, a lighter version of all the above except Trap Grade.

This model begins with serial number 1000. This model was successful and was built between 1954 and 1961. Winchester sold about 200,000 guns.

Standard Grade

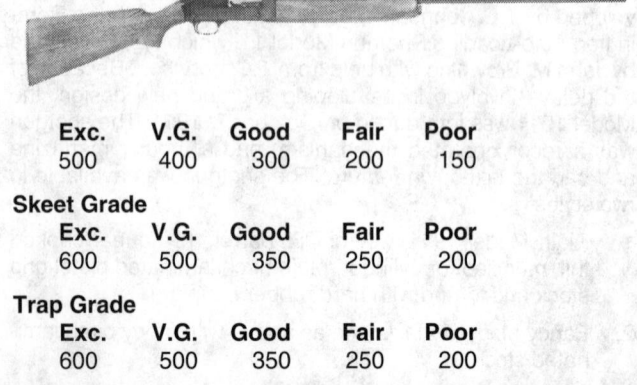

Exc.	V.G.	Good	Fair	Poor
500	400	300	200	150

Skeet Grade

Exc.	V.G.	Good	Fair	Poor
600	500	350	250	200

Trap Grade

Exc.	V.G.	Good	Fair	Poor
600	500	350	250	200

Pigeon Grade

Exc.	V.G.	Good	Fair	Poor
1250	900	750	450	250

Featherweight

Exc.	V.G.	Good	Fair	Poor
500	400	325	225	150

NOTE: Add 10% for 20 gauge.

Model 59

The fourth and final pre-1964 Winchester self-loading shotgun featured a steel and fiberglass barrel with aluminum alloy receiver. The gun was available in 12 gauge only with barrel lengths from 26" to 30" with a variety of chokes. In 1961 Winchester introduced the "Versalite" choke tube, which gave the shooter a choice of full, modified, or improved cylinder chokes in the same barrel. This model was available in two different styles:

1. Standard Grade, plain walnut checkered pistol grip stock and forend.

2. Pigeon Grade, select walnut checkered pistol grip and forend.

Winchester sold about 82,000 of these guns between 1960 and 1965.

Courtesy Butterfield & Butterfield, San Francisco, California

Standard Grade

Exc.	V.G.	Good	Fair	Poor
600	500	375	225	150

Pigeon Grade

Exc.	V.G.	Good	Fair	Poor
1500	1100	850	600	300

NOTE: Add 4

Exc.	V.G.	Good	Fair	Poor
650	550	450	350	250

0% premium for barrels with 3 Versalite chokes and wrench. Add 20% premium for original box and papers.

This shotgun was also made in 10 gauge (very rare), 20 gauge, and 14 gauge. If any of these very low production or prototype guns are encountered use extreme caution and seek an expert appraisal.

POST-1963 RIFLES AND SHOTGUNS

RIFLES

Model 121

This is a single shot, bolt action rifle chambered for the .22 rimfire cartridge. It has a 20.75" barrel with open sights. The finish is blued, with a plain walnut stock. It was manufactured between 1967 and 1973. A youth model with a shorter stock was designated the 121Y and is valued the same.

Courtesy Buffalo Bill Historical Center, Cody, Wyoming

Exc.	V.G.	Good	Fair	Poor
125	100	80	60	40

Model 131

This is a bolt action repeater chambered for the .22 rimfire cartridge. It has a 20.75" barrel with open sights and a 7-round, detachable magazine. The finish is blued, with a plain walnut stock. It was manufactured between 1967 and 1973. A tubular magazine version was designated the Model 141 and is valued the same.

Exc.	V.G.	Good	Fair	Poor
140	110	90	75	50

Model 310

This is a single shot, bolt action rifle chambered for the .22 rimfire cartridge. It features a 22" barrel with open sights. The finish is blued, with a checkered walnut stock. It was manufactured between 1972 and 1975.

Courtesy Buffalo Bill Historical Center, Cody, Wyoming

Exc.	V.G.	Good	Fair	Poor
200	150	125	100	75

Model 320

This is a bolt action repeating rifle that is similar in configuration to the Model 310 single shot. It has a 5-round, detachable box magazine. It was manufactured between 1972 and 1974.

Exc.	V.G.	Good	Fair	Poor
350	300	250	175	125

Model 250

This is a lever action repeating rifle with a hammerless action. It is chambered for the .22 rimfire cartridge and has a 20.5" barrel with open sights and a tubular magazine. The finish is blued, with a checkered pistol grip stock. It was manufactured between 1963 and 1973.

Exc.	V.G.	Good	Fair	Poor
125	100	80	60	40

Model 250 Deluxe

This version is similar to the Model 250 and is furnished with select walnut and sling swivels. It was manufactured between 1965 and 1971.

Exc.	V.G.	Good	Fair	Poor
165	135	100	75	50

Model 255

This version is simply the Model 250 chambered for the .22 WMR cartridge. It was manufactured between 1964 and 1970.

Exc.	V.G.	Good	Fair	Poor
160	130	100	70	50

Model 255 Deluxe

This version was offered with select walnut and sling swivels. It was manufactured between 1965 and 1973.

Exc.	V.G.	Good	Fair	Poor
195	165	125	100	75

Model 270

This is a slide action rifle chambered for the .22 rimfire cartridge. It has a 20.5" barrel and a tubular magazine. The finish is blued, with a checkered walnut stock. It was manufactured between 1963 and 1973.

Exc.	V.G.	Good	Fair	Poor
135	115	85	50	35

Model 490

This is a blowback-operated, semiautomatic rifle chambered for the .22 l.r. cartridge. It has a 22" barrel with open sights and a 5-round, detachable magazine. The finish is blued, with a checkered stock. It was manufactured between 1975 and 1980.

Exc.	V.G.	Good	Fair	Poor
275	225	165	100	75

Model 63

Introduced in 1997 this is a recreation of the famous Model 63 .22 caliber auto. Fitted with a 23" barrel and 10-round tubular magazine. the receiver top is grooved for scope mounting.

Grade I

NIB	Exc.	V.G.	Good	Fair	Poor
675	525	—	—	—	—

High Grade-engraved receiver with gold accents and select walnut stock.

NIB	Exc.	V.G.	Good	Fair	Poor
1075	850	—	—	—	—

Model 94

This is the post-'64 lever action carbine chambered for the .30-30, .7-30 Waters, and the .44 Magnum cartridges. It is offered with a 20" or 24" barrel and has a 6- or 7-round, tubular magazine depending on barrel length. The round barrel is offered with open sights. The forearm is held on by a single barrel band. The finish is blued, with a straight grip walnut stock. In 1982 it was modified to angle ejection to simplify scope mounting. It was introduced as a continuation of the Model 94 line in 1964.

NIB	Exc.	V.G.	Good	Fair	Poor
275	225	175	125	100	75

Model 94 Ranger-Base Model

NIB	Exc.	V.G.	Good	Fair	Poor
240	200	175	150	100	75

Model 94 Ranger Compact

Introduced in 1998 this model features a 16" barrel with 12.5" lop. Chambered for .30-30 or .357 Magnum. Furnished with black recoil pad. Post-style front sight with adjustable rear sight. Hardwood stock. Weight is approximately 5.87 lbs

NIB	Exc.	V.G.	Good	Fair	Poor
325	250	225	200	—	—

Model 94 Black Shadow

This model features a black synthetic stock with nonglare finish and black recoil pad. Offered in .30-30, .44 Magnum, or .444 Marlin. Fitted with a 20" barrel. Weight is about 6.5 lbs. Introduced in 1998.

NIB	Exc.	V.G.	Good	Fair	Poor
350	275	250	225	—	—

Model 94 Deluxe-Checkered Stock

NIB	Exc.	V.G.	Good	Fair	Poor
300	250	200	150	125	100

Model 94 Win-Tuff-Laminated Stock

NIB	Exc.	V.G.	Good	Fair	Poor
325	275	225	165	125	100

Model 94 XTR-Select, Checkered Walnut Stock-Discontinued 1988

Exc.	V.G.	Good	Fair	Poor
300	250	165	100	85

Model 94 XTR Deluxe-Fancy Checkering

Exc.	V.G.	Good	Fair	Poor
385	325	225	150	110

Model 94 Trapper-16" Barrel

NIB	Exc.	V.G.	Good	Fair	Poor
325	250	200	135	100	75

Model 94 Antique Carbine-Gold-plated Saddle Ring

Exc.	V.G.	Good	Fair	Poor
275	225	190	125	90

Model 94 Wrangler-.32 Win. Special

Exc.	V.G.	Good	Fair	Poor
350	300	190	125	100

Model 94 Wrangler II-Loop Lever

NIB	Exc.	V.G.	Good	Fair	Poor
375	300	250	200	150	100

Model 94 Legacy

This Model 94 is fitted with a 20" barrel and chambered for the .30-30 Win. but it is fitted with a half pistol grip stock. Both walnut butt stock and forearm are cut checkered. Weight is 6.5 lbs.

NIB	Exc.	V.G.	Good	Fair	Poor
390	330	275	225	150	100

Model 94 XTR Big Bore

This version is chambered for the .307, .356, or the .375 Win. cartridges. It features the angle-ejection and is blued with a walnut, Monte Carlo-type stock and recoil pad. The round barrel is 20" in length. It has a 6-round, tubular magazine. It was introduced in 1978.

NIB	Exc.	V.G.	Good	Fair	Poor
330	275	225	165	125	100

Model 94 Centennial Limited Editions

Introduced in 1994 these models celebrate the 100-year anniversary of the Winchester Model 1894. Offered in three grades these models are of limited production. The Grade I is limited to 12,000 rifles while the High Grade is limited to 3,000 rifles. Only 94 of the Custom Limited model will be produced. Each Limited model has different grades of select walnut and engraving coverage. All are chambered for the .30-30 Winchester cartridge.

Grade I

NIB	Exc.	V.G.	Good	Fair	Poor
750	700	600	450	300	200

High Grade

NIB	Exc.	V.G.	Good	Fair	Poor
1200	950	700	500	300	200

Custom High Grade

NIB	Exc.	V.G.	Good	Fair	Poor
4500	3900	2500	1000	750	450

Model 94 Trails End

This model is chambered for the .357 Mag., .44 Mag., and .45 Colt. Offered with standard size loop lever or Wrangler-style loop. Introduced in 1997.

NIB	Exc.	V.G.	Good	Fair	Poor
400	325	250	—	—	—

Model 94 Timber Carbine

Introduced in 1999 this model is chambered for the .444 Marlin cartridge. Barrel is 17.75" long and ported. Hooded front sight. Magazine capacity is 5 rounds. Weight is about 6 lbs. Finish is blue. Walnut stock.

NIB	Exc.	V.G.	Good	Fair	Poor
520	400	—	—	—	—

Model 94 Pack Rifle

This lever action model features an 18" barrel chambered for the 30-30 or .44 Magnum. It has a walnut stock with pistol grip and no checkering. Magazine is 3/4 style and has a 4-round capacity for ther 30-30 and 5 rounds for the .44 Mag. Open sights. Weight is about 6.25 lbs. Introduced in 2000.

NIB	Exc.	V.G.	Good	Fair	Poor
475	350	—	—	—	—

Model 9410

Introduced in 2001 this model features a .410 shotgun in a lever action configuration. Barrel length is 24" and is smooth bore with cylinder choke. Chambered is 2.5". Magazine capacity is 9 rounds. Truglo front sight. Weight is about 6.75 lbs.

NIB	Exc.	V.G.	Good	Fair	Poor
525	400	—	—	—	—

Model 9422

Introduced in 1972 this model is chambered for the .22 rimfire and .22 Magnum rimfire cartridges. It was fitted with a 20.5" barrel, front ramp sight with hood, and adjustable semi-buckhorn rear sight. Tubular magazine holds 21 Shorts, 17 Longs, and 15 Long Rifle cartridges. The Magnum version holds 11 cartridges. Weight is about 6.25 lbs. Two-piece American walnut stock with no checkering. Between 1972 and 1992 approximately 750,000 Model 9422s were produced.

NIB	Exc.	V.G.	Good	Fair	Poor
300	250	225	190	165	100

Model 9422 XTR

This is a deluxe lever action rifle chambered for the .22 rimfire cartridge. It is a takedown rifle with a 20.5", round barrel and a tubular magazine. The finish is blued with a checkered, high-gloss, straight grip walnut stock. It was introduced in 1978. A .22 Magnum version is also available and would be worth approximately $10 additional.

NIB	Exc.	V.G.	Good	Fair	Poor
350	300	250	200	125	100

Model 9422 XTR Classic

This version is similar to the standard Model 9422 XTR except that it features a 22.5" barrel and a satin-finished, plain, pistol grip walnut stock. It was manufactured between 1985 and 1987.

NIB	Exc.	V.G.	Good	Fair	Poor
650	550	350	250	200	125

Model 9422 WinTuff

This model features an uncheckered laminated wood stock that is brown in color. Chambered for both the .22 Rimfire and the .22 Winchester Magnum Rimfire. Weighs 6.25 lbs. Other features are the same as the standard Model 9422.

NIB	Exc.	V.G.	Good	Fair	Poor
325	275	225	165	100	75

Model 9422 WinCam

This model is chambered only for the .22 Winchester Magnum Rimfire. The laminated stock is a green color. Weighs 6.25 lbs.

NIB	Exc.	V.G.	Good	Fair	Poor
350	280	225	165	100	75

Model 9422 Trapper

Introduced in 1996 this model features a 16.5" barrel. It has an overall length of 33". Weight is 5.5 lbs.

NIB	Exc.	V.G.	Good	Fair	Poor
350	300	250	200	150	100

Model 9422 High Grade

This variation of the Model 9422 series features a specially engraved receiver and fancy wood stock. Barrel length is 20.5". Weight is about 6 lbs.

NIB	Exc.	V.G.	Good	Fair	Poor
450	400	300	250	175	125

Model 9422 25th Anniversary Rifle

Introduced in 1997 this model features 20.5" barrel. Limited quantities.

Grade I-engraved receiver

NIB	Exc.	V.G.	Good	Fair	Poor
600	475	—	—	—	—

High Grade-engraved receiver with silver border

NIB	Exc.	V.G.	Good	Fair	Poor
1350	1100	—	—	—	—

Model 9422 Legacy

This model has a semi-pistol grip stock of checkered walnut. Will shoot .22 caliber LR, L, or S cartridges. Fitted with a 16" barrel. Weight is about 6 lbs. Introduced in 1998.

NIB	Exc.	V.G.	Good	Fair	Poor
400	325	—	—	—	—

Model 9422 Large Loop & Walnut

Introduced in 1998 this model features a walnut stock with large loop lever. Large loop offered on .22 LR, L, or S model. Standard lever on .22 WMR version. Fitted with 16" barrel. Weight is about 6 lbs.

NIB	Exc.	V.G.	Good	Fair	Poor
400	300	—	—	—	—

Model 9422 High Grade Series II

This model features a high grade walnut stock with cut checkering. Receiver engraved with dogs and squirrels. Fitted with 16" barrel. Weight is about 6 lbs. Introduced in 1998.

NIB	Exc.	V.G.	Good	Fair	Poor
500	400	—	—	—	—

Model 64

This is a post-1964 version of the lever action Model 64. It is chambered for the .30-30 cartridge and has a 24" round barrel with open sights and a 5-round, 2/3-length tubular magazine. The finish is blued with a plain walnut pistol grip stock. It was manufactured between 1972 and 1974.

Exc.	V.G.	Good	Fair	Poor
300	250	190	125	100

Model 1885 Low Wall

Introduced in fall of 1999 this single shot model is chambered for the .22 Long Rifle cartridge. It is fitted with a 24.5" half octagon barrel with leaf rear sight. Drilled and tapped for a tang sight. Crescent steel buttplate. Walnut stock. Weight is about 8 lbs. Limited to 2,400 rifles.

Grade I

NIB	Exc.	V.G.	Good	Fair	Poor
750	600	—	—	—	—

High Grade

Right and left side detail of High Grade 1885 Low Wall

NIB	Exc.	V.G.	Good	Fair	Poor
1225	925	—	—	—	—

Model 1892

Introduced in mid-1997 this model is chambered for the .45 Colt cartridge. It features a straight grip, full magazine, and crescent butt plate.

Grade I-2,500 rifles with engraved receiver

NIB	Exc.	V.G.	Good	Fair	Poor
725	575	—	—	—	—

High Grade-1,000 rifle with gold accents.

NIB	Exc.	V.G.	Good	Fair	Poor
1275	1050	—	—	—	—

Model 1892 Short Rifle

This model is fitted with a 20" barrel and chambered for the .45 Colt, .357 Magnum, .44 Magnum, and .44-40 cartridges. Walnut stock and blued barrel and receiver. Weight is about 6.25 lbs. Introduced in 1999.

NIB	Exc.	V.G.	Good	Fair	Poor
740	575	—	—	—	—

Model 1886

Introduced to the Winchester line in 1997 this was a noncatalogued item. This model features a 26" octagon barrel, semi pistol grip, and cresent butt plate.

Grade I-2,500 rifles blued receiver

NIB	Exc.	V.G.	Good	Fair	Poor
1000	800	—	—	—	—

High Grade-1,000 rifles with gold accents on receiver.

NIB	Exc.	V.G.	Good	Fair	Poor
1575	1300	—	—	—	—

Model 1886 Take Down Classic

Introduced in 1999 this model is chambered for the .45-70 cartridge and features a 26" barrel with take down feature. Walnut stock with pistol grip and crescent butt. Magazine capacity is 8 rounds. Weight is about 9.25 lbs.

NIB	Exc.	V.G.	Good	Fair	Poor
1140	900	—	—	—	—

Model 1886 Extra Light

This model is similar to the Model 1886 Classic but fitted with a 22" round tapered barrel and half magazine. Chambered for the .45-70 cartridge. Shotgun butt. Weight is about 7.25 lbs. Limited edition. Introduced in 2000.

Grade I (3,500)

NIB	Exc.	V.G.	Good	Fair	Poor
1150	850	—	—	—	—

High Grade (1,000)

NIB	Exc.	V.G.	Good	Fair	Poor
1450	1050	—	—	—	—

Model 1895 Limited Edition

Introduced in 1995 this reproduction of the famous Model 1895 is offered in .30-06 caliber with 24" barrel. Magazine capacity is 4 rounds. Weight is approximately 8 lbs. Available in two grades each limited to 4,000 rifles.

Grade I

NIB	Exc.	V.G.	Good	Fair	Poor
800	700	—	—	—	—

High Grade

NIB	Exc.	V.G.	Good	Fair	Poor
1300	1000	—	—	—	—

Model 1895 Limited Edition for the year 2000

Same as above but chambered for the .404 Win. cartridge. Introduced in 2000.

Grade I

NIB	Exc.	V.G.	Good	Fair	Poor
1150	800	—	—	—	—

High Grade

NIB	Exc.	V.G.	Good	Fair	Poor
1550	1150	—	—	—	—

Model 52B Sporting Rifle

A 1993 limited edition rifle (6,000 guns) that is a faithful reproduction of the famous Winchester Model 52 Sporter. Equipped with a 24" barrel, adjustable trigger, and "B" style cheekpiece. This model was reissued in 1997 and limited to 3,000 rifles.

NIB	Exc.	V.G.	Good	Fair	Poor
575	500	450	325	225	100

POST-'64 MODEL 70S

These post Model 70 rifles were fitted with redesigned actions and bolt with free floating barrels, and new style stock with impressed checkering.

Model 70-Standard Grade

This is a bolt action sporting rifle chambered for various popular calibers such as the .22-250, .222 Rem., .243 Win., .270 Win., .30-06, and .308 Win. It features a 22" barrel with open sights and a 5-round, integral box magazine. The finish is blued with a Monte Carlo-type stock furnished with sling swivels. It was manufactured between 1964 and 1971.

Exc.	V.G.	Good	Fair	Poor
350	250	200	150	100

Model 70 Varmint

Chambered for the .22-25, .222 Rem., and .243 Win. cartridges this rifle is fitted with a 24" heavyweight barrel with no sights. Magazine capacity is 5 rounds. Weight is about 9.75 lbs. Built from 1964 to 1971.

Exc.	V.G.	Good	Fair	Poor
400	250	200	150	100

Model 70 Westerner

This model is chambered for the .264 Win. Magnum and .3-- Win. Magnum cartridges. Open sights, 24" barrel. Ventilated recoil pad. Weight is about 7.25 lbs. Built from 1964 to 1971.

Exc.	V.G.	Good	Fair	Poor
400	250	200	150	100

Model 70 African

Chambered for the .458 Win. Magnum cartridge this rifle is fitted with a 22" barrel with open sights. Magazine capacity is 3 rounds. Weight is about 8.5 lbs. Built from 1964 to 1971.

Exc.	V.G.	Good	Fair	Poor
600	450	350	250	150

Model 70 Magnum

Chambered for the 7mm Rem. Mag., .300 Win. Mag., and .375 H&H cartridges. Barrel length is 24". Weight is about 7.75 lbs. Built from 1964 to 1971.

Exc.	V.G.	Good	Fair	Poor
450	350	250	200	150

Model 70 Deluxe

Built from 1964 to 1971 this rifle features a Monte Carlo stock with hand checkering and ebony forend tip. Offered in .243, .270, 30-06, .300 Win. Mag. fitted with 22" barrel except magnums with 24" barrel. Weight is about 7.5 lbs.

Exc.	V.G.	Good	Fair	Poor
400	300	200	150	100

Model 70 Mannlicher

This is a full-length, Mannlicher-type stocked version of the Model 70 bolt action rifle that is chambered for the .243, .270, .308, and the .30-06 cartridges. It was introduced in 1969. It features a 19" barrel with open sights. The finish is blued. It was discontinued in 1972. Only 2401 were produced. Excellent quality.

Exc.	V.G.	Good	Fair	Poor
750	600	500	400	300

Model 70 Target Rifle

This version is chambered for the .308 or the .30-06 cartridges. It was offered with a 24" heavy barrel without sights. It is furnished with bases for a target scope. The finish is blued with a heavy walnut target stock with a palm rest. Weight is approximately 10.25 lbs.

Exc.	V.G.	Good	Fair	Poor
650	550	450	350	250

Model 70 International Match Army

This version is chambered for the .308 cartridge and has a 24" heavy barrel furnished without sights. It has an adjustable trigger and is blued, with a target-type heavy stock that had an accessory rail and an adjustable butt.

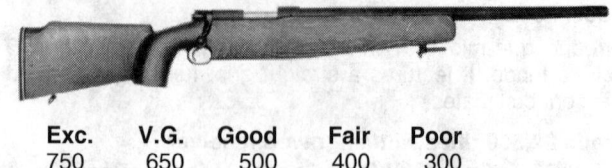

Exc.	V.G.	Good	Fair	Poor
750	650	500	400	300

Model 70A

This is a utility version of the bolt action post-1964 Model 70. It was furnished without a hinged floorplate. The finish is blued, with a walnut stock. It was manufactured between 1972 and 1978.

Exc.	V.G.	Good	Fair	Poor
300	275	225	175	100

Model 70 XTR Featherweight

This gun was built after the takeover by the U.S.R.A. Company. It is a bolt action sporting rifle chambered for various calibers from .22-250 up to the .30-06 cartridges. It has a 22" barrel that is furnished without sights and features either a short- or medium-length action. It has a 5-round, integral magazine. The finish is blued, with a checkered walnut stock. It was introduced in 1981.

NIB	Exc.	V.G.	Good	Fair	Poor
450	400	325	300	250	200

Model 70 Fiftieth Anniversary Model

This is a commemorative version of the post-1964 Model 70 bolt action rifle. It is chambered for the .300 Win. Mag. and is offered with a 24" barrel. It is engraved and high-gloss blued with a deluxe, checkered walnut stock. There were 500 manufactured in 1987. In order to realize collector potential, it must be NIB with all supplied materials.

NIB	Exc.	V.G.	Good	Fair	Poor
1000	—	—	—	—	—

Model 70 XTR Super Express

This is a heavy-duty version of the Post-'64 Model 70 chambered for the .375 H&H and the .458 Win. Mag. cartridges. It is offered with a 22" or 24" heavy barrel and a 3-round, integral box magazine. This version has extra recoil lugs mounted in the stock and is blued with a select, straight-grain walnut stock and a recoil pad standard.

NIB	Exc.	V.G.	Good	Fair	Poor
650	500	400	300	200	100

Model 70 XTR Varmint

This version is chambered for the .22-250, .223, and the .243 cartridges. It has a 24" heavy barrel and is furnished without sights. It has a 5-round magazine and is blued with a heavy walnut stock. It was introduced in 1972.

NIB	Exc.	V.G.	Good	Fair	Poor
400	350	300	250	200	100

Model 70 Winlight

This version is offered in various calibers between .270 and the .338 Win. Mag. It features a matte-blue finish and a fiber-glass stock. It is offered with a 22" or a 24" barrel and a 3- or 4-round magazine. It was introduced in 1986.

NIB	Exc.	V.G.	Good	Fair	Poor
400	350	300	250	200	100

Ranger

This is a utility-grade, bolt action rifle chambered for the .270 Win., .30-06, and the 7mm Rem. Mag. cartridges. It is offered with a 22" or a 24" barrel with open sights and has a 3- or 4-round box magazine. The finish is blued with a plain hardwood stock.

NIB	Exc.	V.G.	Good	Fair	Poor
350	300	275	225	150	100

Model 70 Featherweight Classic

A U.S.R.A. model with 22" barrel, walnut stock, and claw controlled round feeding. The bolt is jeweled and the bolt handle knurled. Comb is straight. Available in .270, .280, and .30-06 calibers. In 1997 this model was offered in the 6.5x55mm Swedish caliber. Rifle weighs about 7.25 lbs. In 2001 this model was offered chambered for the .300 Winchester Short Magnum (WSM) cartridge.

NIB	Exc.	V.G.	Good	Fair	Poor
700	550	400	300	200	100

Model 70 Featherweight Classic All-Terrain

Introduced in 1996 this model features a weather-resistant stainless steel barrel and action with fiberglass/graphite black synthetic stock. Offered in .270 Win., .30-06, 7mm Rem. Mag., .330 Win. Mag. Weight is about 7.25 lbs. Also offered with the BOSS system.

NIB	Exc.	V.G.	Good	Fair	Poor
600	550	450	300	200	150

NOTE: Add $100 for BOSS.

Model 70 Classic Laredo

First offered in 1996 this model features a heavy 26" barrel with pre-64 action on a gray synthetic stock. Chambered for the 7mm Rem. Mag and the .300 Win. Mag. The forearm is a beavertail. Finish is matte blue. In 1997 this model was offered chambered for the 7mm STW cartridge. In 1998 this model was offered with fluted barrel.

NIB	Exc.	V.G.	Good	Fair	Poor
750	650	550	500	400	300

NOTE: Add $100 for BOSS. Add $125 for fluted barrel.

Model 70 Classic Compact

Introduced in 1998 this model is a scaled down version of the Featherweight. It has a lop of 12.5" and a 20" barrel. Chambered for .243, .308, and 7mm-08 calibers. Checkered walnut stock. Weight is about 6.5 lbs.

NIB	Exc.	V.G.	Good	Fair	Poor
525	425	—			

Model 70 Classic Sporter LT

Introduced in 1999 this model is chambered for a wide variety of calibers from .25-06 to .338 Win. Mag. Fitted with a 24" or 26" barrel depending on caliber and no sights. Walnut stock with butt pad. Blued finish. Also offered in left hand models from .270 to .338 Win. Mag. Weight is about 8 lbs.

NIB	Exc.	V.G.	Good	Fair	Poor
630	500	—	—	—	—

NOTE: Add $30 for left hand models.

Model 70 Classic Safari Express

This model is chambered for the .375 H&H Mag, .416 Rem. Mag, and .458 Win. Mag. fitted with a 24" barrel magazine capacity is 4 rounds. Walnut stock. with open sights. Left hand model offered in .375 H&H. Weight is about 8.5 lbs. Introduced in 1999.

NIB	Exc.	V.G.	Good	Fair	Poor
925	750	—	—	—	—

NOTE: Add $30 for .375 H&H left hand model.

Model 70 Super Grade

Another U.S.R.A. rifle that features a select walnut stock, claw controlled round feed, a single reinforced cross bolt, 24" barrel shipped with bases and rings. The butt stock has a straight comb with classic cheekpiece and deep cut checkering. Available in .270, .30-06, 7mm Rem. Mag., .300 Win. Mag., .338 Win. Mag. Rifle weighs approximately 7.75 lbs. Currently in production.

NIB	Exc.	V.G.	Good	Fair	Poor
800	650	550	450	300	150

Model 70 Super Express

A U.S.R.A. version of the post-1964 XTR Super Express. Specifications are the same as the earlier model. Rifle weighs 8.5 lbs. Introduced in 1993.

NIB	Exc.	V.G.	Good	Fair	Poor
650	500	400	300	200	100

Model 70 Heavy Varmint

Introduced by U.S.R.A. in 1993 this rifle features a fiberglass/graphite stock with heavy 26" stainless steel barrel. Offered in .223, .22-250, .243, and .308. In 1997 this model was offered chambered for the .222 Rem. cartridge. Rifle weighs about 10.75 lbs.

NIB	Exc.	V.G.	Good	Fair	Poor
550	475	400	300	200	100

Model 70 Heavy Varmint-Fluted Barrel

Introduced in 1997 this model is similar to the above Varmint with the addition of a fluted barrel. Calibers are also the same as the above model.

NIB	Exc.	V.G.	Good	Fair	Poor
550	475	400	—	—	—

Model 70 Stainless

All metal parts are stainless steel, including the barrel, with synthetic stock. Available with 24" barrel and chambered for .270, .30-06, 7mm Rem. Mag., .300 Win. Mag., and .338 Win. Mag. Weighs about 7.5 lbs. Currently in production. In 2001 this model was offered chambered for the .300 Winchester Short Magnum (WSM) cartridge.

NIB	Exc.	V.G.	Good	Fair	Poor
550	425	375	300	200	100

Model 70 Classic Laminated Stainless

Introduced in 1998 this model features a laminated stock and stainless steel barrel and action. Offered in .270, .30-06, 7mm Rem. Mag., .300 Win. Mag., and .338 Win. Mag. Pre-64 action. Bolt is jeweled and bolt handle is knurled. Barrel lengths are 24" and 26" depending on caliber. Weight is about 8 lbs. In 2001 this model was offered chambered for the .300 Winchester Short Magnum (WSM) cartridge.

NIB	Exc.	V.G.	Good	Fair	Poor
750	600	—	—	—	—

Classic Camo Stainless

This model features a Sporter-style stock with 24" or 26" barrel and Mossy Oak Treestand camo on the stock. Chambered for .270 Win., .30-06, 7mm Rem. Mag., and .300 Win Mag. Magazine capacity is 5 rounds. Weight is about 7.5 lbs. Introduced in 1998.

NIB	Exc.	V.G.	Good	Fair	Poor
725	550	—	—	—	—

Model 70 SM

This rifle features a synthetic stock with black matte finish. Barrel length is 24". Available in 10 calibers from .223 Rem. to .375 H&H Mag. Depending on caliber rifle weighs between 7 and 8 lbs. Currently in production.

NIB	Exc.	V.G.	Good	Fair	Poor
475	400	300	200	150	100

Model 70 DBM-S

Similar to the Model 70 SM but fitted with a detachable box magazine. The metal parts are blued and the stock is synthetic. Offered in 8 calibers from .223 Rem. to .338 Win. Mag. Furnished with scope bases and rings are open sights. Rifle weighs about 7.25 lbs. depending on caliber. Introduced in 1993.

NIB	Exc.	V.G.	Good	Fair	Poor
500	425	325	225	150	100

Model 70 Varmint

Similar to the Model 70 Heavy Varmint but furnished with a traditional walnut stock and 26" medium heavy barrel. Offered in .223 Rem., .22-250, .243, and .308. Weighs 9 lbs.

NIB	Exc.	V.G.	Good	Fair	Poor
465	400	300	200	150	100

Model 70 DBM

DBM stands for detachable box magazine. Fitted with a straight comb walnut stock. Jeweled bolt with blued receiver. Shipped with scope bases and rings or open sights. Rifle offered in 8 calibers from .223 Rem. to .300 Win. Mag. Rifle weighs about 7.35 lbs. depending on caliber. Introduced in 1993.

NIB	Exc.	V.G.	Good	Fair	Poor
480	425	325	225	150	100

Model 70 Sporter

U.S.R.A.'s basic Model 70 offering. Straight comb walnut stock with checkering, jeweled bolt and blued receiver and barrel are standard. Available in 12 calibers from .223 Rem. to .338 Win. Mag. including .270 Weatherby Mag. and .300 Weatherby Mag. Barrel length is 24" and is available with either scope bases and rings or open sights. Rifle weighs about 7.5 lbs.

NIB	Exc.	V.G.	Good	Fair	Poor
450	400	300	200	150	100

Model 70 WinTuff

Similar to the Sporter except fitted with a laminated hardwood straight comb stock with cheekpiece. Offered in 24" barrel lengths with a choice of 6 calibers from .270 Win. to .338 Win. Mag. Furnished with scope bases and rings. Rifle weighs about 7.65 lbs. depending on caliber.

NIB	Exc.	V.G.	Good	Fair	Poor
450	400	300	200	150	100

Model 70 Lightweight

Similar to the Model 70 Winlight. Offered with straight comb checkered walnut stock with knurled bolt and blued receiver and barrel. The barrel is 22" without sights. Offered in 5 calibers: .223, .243, .270, .308, and .30-06. Rifle weighs about 7 lbs. depending on caliber.

NIB	Exc.	V.G.	Good	Fair	Poor
400	350	300	200	150	100

Model 70 Black Shadow

Chambered for the .270, .30-06, 7mm Rem. Mag., and .300 Win. Mag. and fitted with a 22" or 24" barrel depending on caliber. Finish is matte black with composite stock. Push feed action. Weight is 7.25 lbs. Introduced in 1998.

NIB	Exc.	V.G.	Good	Fair	Poor
425	350	—	—	—	—

Model 70 Stealth

This is a varmint model with 26" heavy barrel chambered for .223 Rem., .22-250, or .308 Win. It has a push feed bolt action. Black synthetic stock. Matte black finish. Weight is approximately 10.85 lbs.

NIB	Exc.	V.G.	Good	Fair	Poor
725	550	450	—	—	—

Model 70 Coyote

This model, introduced in 2000, has a push feed bolt action and is chambered for the .223 Rem, .22-250, and .243 Win. calibers. Fitted with a medium heavy 24" stainless steel barrel with laminated stock and large forend. Weight is about 9 lbs.

NIB	Exc.	V.G.	Good	Fair	Poor
675	500	—	—	—	—

Model 70 Ladies/Youth Ranger

A scaled down version of the Ranger. Length of pull is 1" shorter than standard. Rifle weighs 6.5 lbs. Chambered in .243 and .308. In 1997 this model was offered chambered for the .223 Rem. and the 7mm-08 Rem. cartridges.

NIB	Exc.	V.G.	Good	Fair	Poor
375	350	300	200	150	100

NOTE: In 1994 U.S. Repeating Arms reintroduced the pre-1963 Model 70 action on many of its Model 70 rifles. At the present time this new action does not affect values but may do so in the future depending on shooter reaction.

WINCHESTER CUSTOM GUN SHOP

NOTE: There a number of special order options offered by the Custom shop that will greatly effect prrice such as special order engraving, stock carving, wood, sights, etc. It is strongly suggested that an independent appraisial be secured prior to a sale.

Model 70 Featherweight Ultra Grade

Limited to 1,000 rifles this model is profusely engraved with game scene and gold line inlaid. Serial number inlaid in gold. Offered in .270 caliber with very fine figured walnut stock with fine line checkering. Mahogany fitted case. Strongly suggest a qualified appraisal before sale.

NIB	Exc.	V.G.	Good	Fair	Poor
5000	—	—	—	—	—

Model 70 Custom Sharpshooter

A U.S.R.A. Custom Shop gun. This model is fitted with a stainless steel Schneider barrel with hand-honed action and hand fitted. The stock is a custom McMillan A-2 glass bedded stock. Offered in .223 Rem., .22-250 Rem., .308 Win. and .300 Win. Mag. Comes from the factory with a hard case. Currently in production.

NIB	Exc.	V.G.	Good	Fair	Poor
1300	950	750	500	300	150

Model 70 Custom Classic Sharpshooter II

Same as above but introduced in 1996 with an H-S heavy target stock, a pre-64 action stainless steel H-S barrel. Weight is about 11 lbs. Offered in .22-250, .308, .30-06, and .300 Win. Mag.

NIB	Exc.	V.G.	Good	Fair	Poor
1800	1400	—	—	—	—

Model 70 Custom Sporting Sharpshooter

Essentially a take off on the Custom Sharpshooter but configured for hunting. Fitted with a McMillan sporter style gray stock and Schneider stainless steel barrel. Offered in .270 Win., .300 Win., and 7mm STW. Introduced in 1993.

NIB	Exc.	V.G.	Good	Fair	Poor
1250	900	750	500	300	150

Model 70 Custom Classic Sporting Sharpshooter II

Introduced in 1996 this is an updated version of the model above. It features a pre-1964 action with H-S special fiber-glass stock and stainless steel barrel. Available in .7mm S.T.W., .300 Win. Mag. Weight is about 8.5 lbs.

NIB	Exc.	V.G.	Good	Fair	Poor
1700	1400	—	—	—	—

Model 70 Custom Grade

This custom built Model 70 is hand finished, polished, and fitted in the Custom Shop. Internal parts are hand honed while the barrel is lead lapped. The customer can order individual items to his or her own taste, including engraving, special stock dimensions and carvings, etc. Each Custom Grade Model 70 should be priced on an individual basis.

Model 70 Custom Express

Also built in the Custom Shop this model features figured walnut, hand-honed internal parts, bolt and follower are engine turned. A special 3-leaf rear sight is furnished also. Offered in .375 H&H Mag., .375 JRS, .416 Rem. Mag., .458 Win. Mag., and .470 Capstick.

NIB	Exc.	V.G.	Good	Fair	Poor
1850	1550	1000	600	400	200

Model 70 Custom African Express

Introduced in 1999 this model is chambered for the .340 Wby., .358 STA, .375 H&H, .416 Rem. Mag., and the .458 Win. Mag. Fitted with a 24" barrel and a magazine capacity of 4 rounds. Express sights. Weight is about 9.75 lbs. Ebony pistol grip cap, and select walnut stock.

NIB	Exc.	V.G.	Good	Fair	Poor
3850	3000	—	—	—	—

Model 70 Custom Safari Express

This model has a figured walnut stock with the bolt and follower engine turned. Express sights. Chambered in .340 Wby., .358 STA, .375 H&H, .416 Rem. Mag., and .458 Win. Mag. Barrel length is 24". Weight is about 9.5 lbs. Introduced in 1999.

NIB	Exc.	V.G.	Good	Fair	Poor
2395	1750	—	—	—	—

Model 70 Custom "Ultra Light" Mannlicher

This model features a full length stock of figured walnut with smooth tapered barrel and blued action. Chambered for .260 Rem., .308 Win., and 7mm-08. Fitted with a 19" barrel with optional open sights. Weight is about 6.75 lbs. Introduced in 1999.

NIB	Exc.	V.G.	Good	Fair	Poor
2475	1850	—	—	—	—

Model 70 Ultimate Classic

This model features a number of special options as standard. Included is a pre-1964 action, choice of round, round fluted, 1/2 octagon 1/2 round barrel, full tapered octagon barrel, blued or stainless steel barrel actions, fancy American walnut stock, special Custom Shop serial numbers and proof stamp, inletted swivel bases, red recoil pad, fine cut checkering, and a hard case. Offered in a wide variety of calibers from .25-06 to .338 Win. Mag. Weight is about 7.5 to 7.75 lbs. depending on caliber. Also available in stainless steel.

NIB	Exc.	V.G.	Good	Fair	Poor
2450	1950	1500	—		

NOTE: In 1997 this model was introduced in a left hand version.

Model 70 Custom Take Down

Introduced in 1998 this composite stock rifle has a special take down feature. Chambered for .375 H&H, .416 Rem. Mag., .300 Win Mag., 7mm STW. Magazine capacity is 3 rounds. Barrel length is 26". Weight is between 8.5 and 9 lbs. Offered in fluted barrel in .300 Win. Mag. and 7mm STW.

NIB	Exc.	V.G.	Good	Fair	Poor
3300	2500	—			

Model 70 Custom Short Action

This custom shop model is fitted with a 22" match grade barrel Controlled feed. Chambered for short action calibers from .243 to .358. Semi-fancy walnut stock. Hand cut checkering. Supplied with hard case. Weight is about 7.5 lbs. Introduced in 2000.

NIB	Exc.	V.G.	Good	Fair	Poor
2700	1950	—	—	—	—

Model 70 Custom Extreme Weather

This custom shop model is fitted with a round or fluted 24" match grade barrel. Both barrel and action are stainless steel. McMillian fiberglass stock with cheek piece. Chambered in calibers from .25-06 to .338 Win. Mag. Weight is about 7.5 lbs. Introduced in 2000.

NIB	Exc.	V.G.	Good	Fair	Poor
1950	1500	—	—	—	—

Model 94 Custom Limited Edition

This is essentially a special order Model 94 with choice of engraving and stock carving. Chambered for the .44-40 and fitted with a 24" octagonal barrel. Fancy walnut stock. Limited to 75 rifles. Weight is about 7.75 lbs. Suggest an appraisal prior to a sale.

NIB	Exc.	V.G.	Good	Fair	Poor
2250	1750	—	—	—	—

POST-1964 SHOTGUNS

MODEL 12 "Y" SERIES

Model 12 Field Grade

This is a later version of the slide action Model 12, chambered for 12 gauge only. It was offered with a 26", 28", or 30" vent rib barrel with various chokes. The finish is blued with a jeweled bolt and a hand-checkered, select walnut stock. This version is easily recognizable as it has the letter Y serial number prefix. It was manufactured between 1972 and 1976.

Exc.	V.G.	Good	Fair	Poor
650	550	400	350	275

Model 12 Super Pigeon Grade

This is a deluxe version that features extensive engraving and fancy checkering. It was offered with a turned action and select, fancy-grade walnut. It was a limited-production item produced between 1964 and 1972. It was briefly reintroduced in 1984 and discontinued again in 1985.

Exc.	V.G.	Good	Fair	Poor
3000	2500	1850	1400	950

Model 12 Skeet

This version is similar to the Field Grade but is offered with a 26", vent rib, skeet-bored barrel. The finish is blued, with a skeet-type stock and recoil pad. It was manufactured between 1972 and 1975.

Exc.	V.G.	Good	Fair	Poor
700	650	550	350	300

Model 12 Trap Grade

This version features a 30" vent rib barrel with a full choke. It is blued with a trap-type, standard, or Monte Carlo stock with a recoil pad. It was manufactured between 1972 and 1980.

Exc.	V.G.	Good	Fair	Poor
650	600	500	300	200

Model 12 (Limited Edition)

Available in 20 gauge only. Furnished with a 26" vent rib barrel choked improved cylinder. The walnut stock is checkered with pistol grip. Introduced in 1993 and available in three different grades.

Grade 1 (4,000 guns)

NIB	Exc.	V.G.	Good	Fair	Poor
700	600	450	350	200	100

Grade IV (1,000 guns) Gold Highlights

NIB	Exc.	V.G.	Good	Fair	Poor
1150	900	650	400	200	100

Ducks Unlimited Model

Available through Ducks Unlimited chapters. An independent appraisal is suggested.

Model 42 (Limited Edition)

A reproduction of the famous Winchester Model 42 .410 bore slide action shotgun. Furnished with a 26" ventilated rib barrel choked full. The receiver is engraved with gold border. Introduced in 1993 and limited to 850 guns.

NIB	Exc.	V.G.	Good	Fair	Poor
1250	900	600	400	300	150

Model 1200

This is a slide action shotgun chambered for 12, 16, or 20 gauge. It was offered with a 26", 28", or 30", vent rib barrel with various chokes. It has an alloy receiver and is blued, with a checkered walnut stock and recoil pad. It was manufactured between 1964 and 1981. This model was offered with the plastic Hydrocoil stock, and this would add approximately 35% to the values given.

Exc.	V.G.	Good	Fair	Poor
225	175	150	100	75

MODEL 1300 SERIES

Model 1300 XTR

This is the current slide action shotgun offered by Winchester. It is chambered for 12 and 20 gauge with 3" chambers. It is a takedown gun that is offered with various-length vent rib barrels with screw-in choke tubes. It has an alloy frame and is blued with a walnut stock. It was introduced in 1978.

Exc.	V.G.	Good	Fair	Poor
300	250	200	150	100

Model 1300 Waterfowl

This version is chambered for 12 gauge, 3" only. It has a 30" vent rib barrel with screw-in choke tubes. It is matte-blued, with a satin-finished walnut stock and a recoil pad. It was introduced in 1984. A laminated WinTuff stock was made available in 1988 and would add $10 to the value.

NIB	Exc.	V.G.	Good	Fair	Poor
350	300	250	200	150	100

Model 1300 WinCam Turkey Gun

This version is similar to the Model 1300 Turkey Gun, with a green, laminated hardwood stock. It was introduced in 1987. A WinTuff version is also available and would add $20 to the values given.

NIB	Exc.	V.G.	Good	Fair	Poor
375	325	250	200	150	125

Model 1300 Stainless Security

This version is chambered for 12 or 20 gauge and is constructed of stainless steel. It has an 18" cylinder-bore barrel and a 7- or 8-shot tubular magazine. It is available with a pistol grip stock, which would add approximately 50% to the values given.

NIB	Exc.	V.G.	Good	Fair	Poor
275	250	225	165	125	100

Model 1300 Turkey

This slide action model features a 22" vent rib barrel chambered for 3" 12 gauge shells. Supplied with choke tubes. Gun weighs 7.25 lbs.

NIB	Exc.	V.G.	Good	Fair	Poor
350	300	250	200	150	100

Model 1300 Realtree Turkey

Introduced in 1994 this model features a synthetic stock camouflaged with Realtree. The receiver and 22" barrel are matte finish.

NIB	Exc.	V.G.	Good	Fair	Poor
375	275	225	200	150	100

Model 1300 Mossy Oak Break-Up Turkey

Same as above but with Mossy Oak Break-Up camo stock and gun. Introduced in 2000.

NIB	Exc.	V.G.	Good	Fair	Poor
450	325	—	—	—	—

Model 1300 Black Shadow Turkey

This model was also introduced in 1994 and features a black composite stock with a nonglare finish on the barrel, receiver, bolt, and magazine. Barrel has vent rib and is 22" in length.

NIB	Exc.	V.G.	Good	Fair	Poor
275	225	190	165	125	100

Model 1300 National Wild Turkey Federation Series III

Engraved receiver, camo stock, open sights on a 22" plain barrel, and all metal and wood parts are nonglare. Comes with a quick detachable sling. Offered in 12 gauge only. Gun weighs 7.25 lbs.

NIB	Exc.	V.G.	Good	Fair	Poor
370	320	250	200	150	100

Model 1300 National Wild Turkey Federation Series IV

Introduced in 1993 this model is similar to the Series II with the addition of a 22" vent rib barrel. Stock is black laminated. Comes with quick detachable sling. Gun weight 7 lbs.

NIB	Exc.	V.G.	Good	Fair	Poor
370	320	250	200	150	100

Model 1300 Whitetails Unlimited Slug Hunter

This slide action model features a full length rifle barrel chambered for 3" 12 gauge shells. Barrel is choked cylinder. Fitted with a checkered walnut stock with engraved receiver. Receiver is drilled and tapped for bases and rings, which are included. Comes equipped with camo sling. Weighs 7.25 lbs.

NIB	Exc.	V.G.	Good	Fair	Poor
350	300	250	200	150	100

Model 1300 Slug Hunter

Similar to the Whitetails Unlimited model, but without the engraved receiver.

NIB	Exc.	V.G.	Good	Fair	Poor
350	300	250	200	150	100

Model 1300 Black Shadow Deer

Introduced in 1994 this 12 gauge Model 1300 features a black composite stock with nonglare finish on the bolt, barrel, receiver, and magazine. Barrel is 22" with ramp front sight and adjustable rear sight. In 2000 this model was offered with a rifle's barrel.

NIB	Exc.	V.G.	Good	Fair	Poor
325	250	175	150	125	100

NOTE: Add $25 for rifled barrel.

Model 1300 Black Shadow Field

Same as above but fitted with a 26" or 28" vent rib barrel chambered for 3" Mag. shells. Weight is about 7 lbs.

NIB	Exc.	V.G.	Good	Fair	Poor
275	225	200	150	100	80

Model 1300 Slug Hunter Sabot (Smoothbore)

Similar to the Slug Hunter but furnished with a smoothbore barrel with a special extended screw-in choke tube that is rifled.

NIB	Exc.	V.G.	Good	Fair	Poor
275	250	200	175	150	100

Model 1300 Upland Special

This 12 gauge slide action shotgun is fitted with a 24" vent rib barrel and straight grip walnut stock. Weight is about 7 lbs. Introduced in 1999. In 2000 this model was offered in 20 gauge with 24" vent rib barrel.

NIB	Exc.	V.G.	Good	Fair	Poor
375	275	200	—	—	—

Model 1300 Ranger

This slide action shotgun is a lower cost version of the Model 1300. Furnished with a hardwood stock and available in 12 or 20 gauge with 26" or 28" vent rib barrel. Win. chokes are included.

NIB	Exc.	V.G.	Good	Fair	Poor
260	225	190	165	125	100

Model 1300 Ranger Ladies/Youth-Compact

Available in 20 gauge only this model has a 1" shorter than standard length of pull and a 22" vent rib barrel. Choke tubes are included. Gun weighs 6.75 lbs.

NIB	Exc.	V.G.	Good	Fair	Poor
275	225	190	165	125	100

Model 1300 Ranger Deer Slug

Comes in two principal configurations: a 12 gauge 22" smooth barrel with cylinder choke; and a 12 gauge 22" rifled barrel. Both are chambered for 3" shells and weigh 6.75 lbs.

NIB	Exc.	V.G.	Good	Fair	Poor
250	200	175	150	125	100

Model 1300 Ranger Deer Combo

The Model 1300 Ranger Deer Combos are available in three different configurations. One: 12 gauge 22" smooth barrel and 28" vent rib barrel with WinChokes. Two: 12 gauge 22" rifled barrel with 28" vent rib barrel with WinChokes. Three: 20 gauge 22" smooth barrel with 28" vent rib barrel with Win-Chokes.

12 Gauge Combo

NIB	Exc.	V.G.	Good	Fair	Poor
325	275	225	190	165	100

20 Gauge Combo

NIB	Exc.	V.G.	Good	Fair	Poor
325	275	225	190	165	100

Model 1300 Defender Combo

This personal defense slide action shotgun features an 18" cylinder choked barrel and a 28" vent rib barrel with modified WinChoke and an accessory pistol grip. A hardwood stock comes fitted to the gun.

NIB	Exc.	V.G.	Good	Fair	Poor
300	250	200	175	150	100

Model 1300 Defender 5-Shot

Same as above but furnished with a hardwood stock only and 18" barrel.

NIB	Exc.	V.G.	Good	Fair	Poor
250	200	175	150	125	100

Model 1300 Camp Defender

Introduced in 1999 this 12 gauge model features a 22" barrel and walnut stock. Magazine capacity is 5 rounds. Barrel fitted with rifle sights. Weight is about 7 lbs. Comes with cylinder choke tube.

NIB	Exc.	V.G.	Good	Fair	Poor
350	275	—	—	—	—

Model 1300 Defender 8-Shot

Same as above but furnished with an 18" barrel with extended magazine tube.

NIB	Exc.	V.G.	Good	Fair	Poor
250	200	175	150	125	100

Model 1300 Defender Synthetic Stock

Same as above but fitted with a black synthetic full stock. Available in either 12 or 20 gauge.

NIB	Exc.	V.G.	Good	Fair	Poor
250	200	175	150	125	100

Model 1300 Defender Pistol Grip

Same as above but fitted with a black synthetic pistol grip and extended magazine tube.

NIB	Exc.	V.G.	Good	Fair	Poor
250	200	175	150	125	100

Model 1300 Lady Defender

Chambered for the 20 gauge shell this model features a 18" barrel with 8-round capacity. Pistol grip stock. Introduced in 1997.

NIB	Exc.	V.G.	Good	Fair	Poor
275	225	—	—	—	—

Model 1300 Stainless Marine

This 12 gauge slide action shotgun comes with a black synthetic full stock with all metal parts chrome plated. Barrel is 18" and magazine tube holds 7 rounds. Gun weighs 6.75 lbs.

NIB	Exc.	V.G.	Good	Fair	Poor
400	325	275	225	165	100

Model 1300 Stainless Marine with Pistol Grip

Same as above with black synthetic pistol grip in place of full butt stock. Gun weighs 5.75 lbs.

NIB	Exc.	V.G.	Good	Fair	Poor
350	300	250	200	150	100

Model 1500 XTR

This is a gas-operated, semiautomatic shotgun chambered for 12 or 20 gauge, with a 28" vent rib barrel with screw-in chokes. The finish is blued, with a walnut stock. It was manufactured between 1978 and 1982.

Exc.	V.G.	Good	Fair	Poor
300	250	225	175	125

Super X Model I

This is a self-compensating, gas-operated, semiautomatic shotgun chambered for 12 gauge. It was offered with a 26", 28", or 30" vent rib barrel with various chokes. It features all-steel construction and is blued, with a checkered walnut stock. It was manufactured between 1974 and 1981.

Exc.	V.G.	Good	Fair	Poor
500	375	300	250	150

Super X Model 1 Custom Competition

This is a custom-order trap or skeet gun that features the self compensating, gas-operated action. It is available in 12 gauge only from the Custom Shop. It is offered with a heavy degree of engraving on the receiver and a fancy, checkered walnut stock. Gold inlays are available and would add approximately 50% to the values given. This model was introduced in 1987.

NIB	Exc.	V.G.	Good	Fair	Poor
1450	1100	925	775	650	500

Super X2 Magnum

Introduced in 1999 this model is a gas operated design chambered for 3.5" 12 gauge shells. Fitted with a black synthetic stock and choice of 24", 26", or 28" vent rib barrels. Invector chokes. Magazine capacity is 5 rounds. Weight is about 7.5 lbs depending on barrel length. Matte black finish.

NIB	Exc.	V.G.	Good	Fair	Poor
850	675	—	—	—	—

Super X2 Turkey

Similar to the X2 Magnum but with 24" vent rib barrel with tru-glo sights. Extra full choke. Weight is about 7.25 lbs. Black synthetic stock. Introduced in 1999.

NIB	Exc.	V.G.	Good	Fair	Poor
860	675	—	—	—	—

Super X2 Turkey Mossy Oak Break-Up

Same as above but with Mossy Oak Break-Up camo on stock and gun. Introduced in 2000.

NIB	Exc.	V.G.	Good	Fair	Poor
1025	750	—	—	—	—

Super X2 Camo Waterfowl

Chambered for 12 gauge 3.5" shells and fitted with a 28" vent rib barrel this model features a Mossy Oak camo finish. Introduced in 1999.

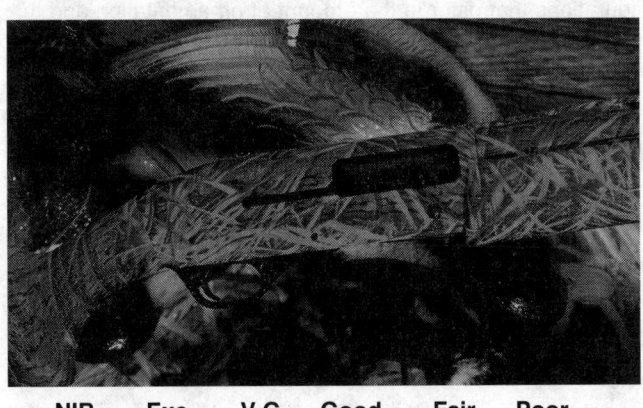

NIB	Exc.	V.G.	Good	Fair	Poor
930	725	—	—	—	—

Super X2 Magnum Field

This model is chambered for the 12 gauge 3" shell and is offered with either a walnut stock or black synthetic stock. Choice of 26" or 28" vent rib barrel with invector chokes. Weight is about 7.25 lbs. Introduced in 1999.

NIB	Exc.	V.G.	Good	Fair	Poor
800	625	—	—	—	—

Super X2 Sporting Clays

Introduced in 2001 this model features a 12 gauge gun with choice of 28" or 30" barrels with high post rib. Barrels are back bore with Invector chokes. Adjust6able comb. Weight is about 8 lbs.

NIB	Exc.	V.G.	Good	Fair	Poor
1200	950	—	—	—	

Model 1400

This is a gas-operated, semiautomatic shotgun chambered for 12, 16, or 20 gauge. It was offered with a 26", 28", or 30" vent rib barrel with various chokes. The finish is blued, with a checkered walnut stock. It was manufactured between 1964 and 1981. The Hydrocoil plastic stock was available on this model and would add approximately 35% to the values given.

Exc.	V.G.	Good	Fair	Poor
250	225	200	150	100

New Model 1400

This is a gas-operated, semiautomatic shotgun chambered for 12 or 20 gauge. It is offered with a 22" or 28" vent rib barrel with screw-in chokes. The finish is blued, with a checkered walnut stock. It was introduced in 1989.

NIB	Exc.	V.G.	Good	Fair	Poor
400	350	300	250	200	125

Model 1400 Ranger

This is a utility-grade, gas-operated, semiautomatic shotgun chambered for 12 or 20 gauge. It is offered with a 28" vent rib barrel with screw-in chokes, as well as a 24" slug barrel with rifle sights. The finish is blued, with a checkered stock. A combination two barrel set that includes the deer barrel would be worth approximately 20% additional. This model was introduced in 1983 and is currently produced.

NIB	Exc.	V.G.	Good	Fair	Poor
340	300	250	200	150	100

Model 1400 Quail Unlimited

This 12 gauge semiautomatic shotgun model was introduced in 1993. It features compact engraved receiver with 26" vent rib barrel supplied with WinChoke tubes. Stock is checkered walnut. Gun weighs 7.25 lbs.

NIB	Exc.	V.G.	Good	Fair	Poor
340	300	250	200	150	100

Model 1400 Ranger Deer Combo

This model features a 12 gauge 22" smooth barrel and a 28" vent rib barrel with three WinChokes.

NIB	Exc.	V.G.	Good	Fair	Poor
340	300	250	200	150	100

Model 37A

Introduced in 1973. It is single shot shotgun with exposed hammer. Offerd in 12, 16, 20, and 28 guage as well as .410 bore. All guns chokes full except youth model cjoked modified. Walnut finish on wardwood stock. Pistol grip cap with white spacer. Weight is about 6 lbs. About 395,000 were produced until 1980.

Exc.	V.G.	Good	Fair	Poor
275	225	200	150	100

Model 22

Introduced in 1975 this side by side shotgun was manufactured by Laurona in Spain to Winchester's specifications for the European market. It had an oil finished stock with checked pistol grip semi-beavertail forearm and hand engraved receiver. The finish was black chrome. The gun was fitted with double triggers, matted rib and offered in 12 gauge only with 28 inch barrels. It weighted 6-3/4 lbs.

NIB	Exc.	V.G.	Good	Fair	Poor
1250	950	700	550	400	200

Model 91

This over and under shotgun was built for Winchester by Laurona for its European markets. Offered in 12 gauge only with 28" barrels the barrels were fitted with a ventilated rib. The gun was offered with single or double triggers with hand checkered walnut stock with oil finish and hand engraved receiver. The finish was black chrome. Gun weighs 7-1/2 lbs.

NIB	Exc.	V.G.	Good	Fair	Poor
1000	800	600	500	400	200

Supreme Field

Introduced in 2000 this over and under gun is chambered for the 12 gauge 3" shell and fitted with 28" vent rib barrels with Invector chokes. Walnut stock with pistol grip and blued engraved receiver. Weight is about 7.5 lbs.

NIB	Exc.	V.G.	Good	Fair	Poor
1325	1000	—	—	—	—

Supreme Sporting

Similar to the above model but fitted with a choice of 28" or 30" barrels chambered for 12 gauge 2.75" shells. Barrels are ported. Adjustable trigger. Polished silver receiver with blued barrels. Weight is about 7.5 lbs. Introduced in 2000.

NIB	Exc.	V.G.	Good	Fair	Poor
1475	1100	—	—	—	—

MODEL 23 SERIES

Model 23 XTR

This is a side-by-side, double barrel shotgun chambered for 12 or 20 gauge. It is offered with 25.5", 26", 28", or 30" vent rib barrels with 3" chambers and various choke combinations. It is a boxlock gun that features a single trigger and automatic ejectors. It is scroll-engraved with a coin-finished receiver, blued barrels, and a checkered, select walnut stock. It was introduced in 1978. This model is available in a number of configurations that differ in the amount of ornamentation and the quality of materials and workmanship utilized in their construction. These models and their values are as follows:

Grade I-Discontinued

Exc.	V.G.	Good	Fair	Poor
1325	1100	900	725	450

Pigeon Grade-With WinChokes

Exc.	V.G.	Good	Fair	Poor
1450	1200	1075	900	550

Pigeon Grade Lightweight-Straight Stock

Exc.	V.G.	Good	Fair	Poor
1850	1450	1250	950	650

Golden Quail

This series was available in 28 gauge and .410, as well as 12 or 20 gauge. It features 25.5" barrels that are choked improved cylinder/modified. It features a straight grip, English-style stock with a recoil pad. The .410 version would be worth approximately 10% more than the values given. This series was discontinued in 1987.

Exc.	V.G.	Good	Fair	Poor
2150	1800	1500	1100	850

Model 23 Light Duck

This version is chambered for 20 gauge and was offered with a 28" full and full-choked barrel. There were 500 manufactured in 1985.

Exc.	V.G.	Good	Fair	Poor
1500	1250	1100	850	750

Model 23 Heavy Duck

This version is chambered for 12 gauge with 30" full and full-choked barrels. There were 500 manufactured in 1984.

Exc.	V.G.	Good	Fair	Poor
1500	1250	1100	850	750

Model 21

This is a high-quality, side-by-side, double barrel shotgun that features a boxlock action and is chambered for 12, 16, 20, and 28 gauges, as well as .410. It is featured with various barrel lengths and choke combinations. Since 1960 the Model 21 has been available on a custom-order basis only. It is available in five basic configurations that differ in the options offered, the amount of ornamentation, and the quality of materials and workmanship utilized in their construction. See previous Model 21 entry.

MODEL 101 SERIES

Model 101 Field Grade

This is an Over/Under, double barrel shotgun chambered for 12, 20, and 28 gauge, as well as .410. It was offered with 26", 28", or 30" vent rib barrels with various choke combinations. As of 1983 screw-in chokes have been standard, and models so furnished would be worth approximately $50 additional. This is a boxlock gun with a single selective trigger and automatic ejectors. The receiver is engraved; the finish, blued with a checkered walnut stock. It was manufactured between 1963 and 1987.
28 Gauge-Add 40%.
.410-Add 50%.

Exc.	V.G.	Good	Fair	Poor
825	700	550	425	300

Waterfowl Model

This version of the Model 101 is chambered for 12 gauge with 3" chambers. It has 30" or 32" vent rib barrels and a matte finish.

Exc.	V.G.	Good	Fair	Poor
1250	1000	850	650	500

Model 101 Magnum

This version is similar to the Field Grade, chambered for 12 or 20 gauge with 3" Magnum chambers. It was offered with 30" barrels with various chokes. The stock is furnished with a recoil pad. It was manufactured between 1966 and 1981.

Exc.	V.G.	Good	Fair	Poor
850	750	575	450	325

Model 101 Skeet Grade

This version was offered with 26" skeet-bored barrels with a competition rib and a skeet-type walnut stock. It was manufactured between 1966 and 1984.

Exc.	V.G.	Good	Fair	Poor
1050	925	825	550	400

Model 101 Three-Gauge Skeet Set

This combination set was offered with three barrels, chambered for 20 and 28 gauge, as well as .410. It was furnished with a fitted case and manufactured between 1974 and 1984.

Exc.	V.G.	Good	Fair	Poor
2150	1600	1100	800	650

Model 101 Trap Grade

This version is chambered for 12 gauge only and was offered with 30" or 32" competition ribbed barrels, choked for trap shooting. It is furnished with a competition-type stock. It was manufactured between 1966 and 1984.

Exc.	V.G.	Good	Fair	Poor
1400	1100	925	700	500

Model 101 Pigeon Grade

This is a more deluxe engraved version of the Model 101, chambered for 12, 20, or 28 gauge, as well as .410. It features a coin-finished receiver with a fancy checkered walnut stock. It was introduced in 1974.

Exc.	V.G.	Good	Fair	Poor
2000	1600	1300	975	750

Super Pigeon Grade

This is a deluxe version of the Model 101, chambered for 12 gauge. It is heavily engraved with several gold inlays. The receiver is blued, and it features a high-grade walnut stock with fleur-de-lis checkering. It was imported between 1985 and 1987.

Exc.	V.G.	Good	Fair	Poor
4500	3750	2950	2200	1650

Model 101 Diamond Grade

This is a competition model, chambered for all four gauges. It was offered in either a trap or skeet configuration with screw-in chokes, an engraved matte-finished receiver, and a select checkered walnut stock. The skeet model features recoil-reducing muzzle vents.

Exc.	V.G.	Good	Fair	Poor
1900	1550	1200	850	650

Model 501 Grand European

This is an Over/Under, double barrel shotgun chambered for 12 or 20 gauge. It was available in trap or skeet configurations and was offered with a 27", 30", or 32" vent rib barrel. It is heavily engraved and matte-finished, with a select checkered walnut stock. It was manufactured between 1981 and 1986.

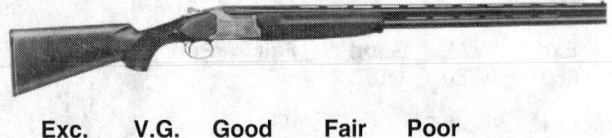

Exc.	V.G.	Good	Fair	Poor
1650	1300	1000	750	550

Model 501 Presentation Grade

This is a deluxe version chambered in 12 gauge only. It is ornately engraved and gold-inlaid. The stock is made out of presentation-grade walnut. It was furnished with a fitted case. It was manufactured between 1984 and 1987.

Exc.	V.G.	Good	Fair	Poor
3400	2750	2200	1600	1250

Combination Gun

This is an Over/Under rifle/shotgun combination chambered for 12 gauge over .222, .223, .30-06, and the 9.3x74R cartridges. It features 25" barrels. The shotgun tube has a screw-in choke. It is engraved in the fashion of the Model 501 Grand European and features a select checkered walnut stock. It was manufactured between 1983 and 1985.

Exc.	V.G.	Good	Fair	Poor
2500	2200	1950	1450	1000

Express Rifle

This is an Over/Under, double barreled rifle chambered for the .257 Roberts, .270, 7.7x65R, .30-06, and the 9.3x74R cartridges. It features 23.5" barrels with a solid rib and express sights. It is engraved with game scenes and has a satin-finished receiver. The stock is checkered select walnut. It was manufactured in 1984 and 1985.

Exc.	V.G.	Good	Fair	Poor
2000	1650	1350	1100	750

Model 96 Xpert

This is a utility-grade, Over/Under, double barrel shotgun that is mechanically similar to the Model 101. It is chambered for 12 or 20 gauge and was offered with various barrel lengths and choke combinations. It has a boxlock action with single selective trigger and automatic ejectors. The plain receiver is blued, with a checkered walnut stock. It was manufactured between 1976 and 1982. A competition-grade model for trap or skeet was also available and would be worth approximately the same amount.

Exc.	V.G.	Good	Fair	Poor
650	550	450	350	275

Model 1001 Field

A new addition to the U.S.R.A. product line for 1993. This Over/Under shotgun is available in 12 gauge only, with a 28" ventilated rib barrel furnished with WinPlus choke tubes. A walnut checkered pistol stock is standard. The finish is blued with scroll engraving on the receiver. The receiver top has a matte finish. The gun weighs 7 lbs.

NIB	Exc.	V.G.	Good	Fair	Poor
875	750	650	500	300	150

Model 1001 Sporting Clays I & II

This model features different stock dimensions, a fuller pistol grip, a radiused recoil pad, and a wider vent rib fitted on a 28" barrel (Sporting Clays I model, the Sporting Clays II features a 30" barrel). Comes complete with choke tubes. The frame has a silver nitrate finish and special engraving featuring a flying clay target. Introduced in 1993. Gun weighs 7.75 lbs.

NIB	Exc.	V.G.	Good	Fair	Poor
1000	800	700	550	300	150

WINCHESTER COMMEMORATIVE RIFLES

Since the early 1960s, Winchester has produced a number of special Model 1894 rifles and carbines that commemorated certain historic events, places, or individuals. In some cases they are slightly embellished and in others are quite ornate. The general liquidity of these commemoratives has not been as good as would be expected. In some cases they were produced in excessive amounts and could not, in all honesty, be considered limited-production items. In any case, in our opinion one should purchase weapons of this nature for their enjoyment factor as the investment potential is not sufficient reason for their purchase. As with all commemoratives, in order to realize the collector potential they must be NIB with all supplied materials including, in the case of Winchester, the colorful outer sleeve that encased the factory carton. If a Winchester commemorative rifle has been cocked leaving a line on the hammer or the lever, many collectors will show little or no interest in its acquisition. If they have been fired, they will realize little premium over a standard, Post-'64 Model 94. A number of commemoratives have been ordered by outside concerns and are technically not factory issues. Most have less collectibility than the factory-issued models. There are a number of concerns that specialize in marketing the total range of Winchester commmemorative rifles. We list the factory-issue commemoratives with their current value, their issue price, and the number manufactured.

1964 Wyoming Diamond Jubilee-Carbine

NIB	Issue	Amt. Mfg.
1295	100	1,500

1966 Centennial-Rifle

NIB	Issue	Amt. Mfg.
450	125	102,309

1966 Centennial-Carbine

NIB	Issue	Amt. Mfg.
425	125	102,309

1966 Nebraska Centennial-Rifle

NIB	Issue	Amt. Mfg.
1195	100	2,500

1967 Canadian Centennial-Rifle

NIB	Issue	Amt. Mfg.
450	125	

1967 Canadian Centennial-Carbine

NIB	Issue	Amt. Mfg.
425	125	90,301

1967 Alaskan Purchase Centennial-Carbine

NIB	Issue	Amt. Mfg.
1495	125	1,500

1968 Illinois Sesquicentennial-Carbine

NIB	Issue	Amt. Mfg.
395	110	37,648

1968 Buffalo Bill-Carbine

NIB	Issue	Amt. Mfg.
425	130	112,923

1968 Buffalo Bill-Rifle

NIB	Issue	Amt. Mfg.
450	130	

1968 Buffalo Bill "1 or 300"-Rifle

NIB	Issue	Amt. Mfg.
2650	1000	300

1969 Theodore Roosevelt-Rifle

NIB	Issue	Amt. Mfg.
450	135	—

1969 Theodore Roosevelt-Carbine

NIB	Issue	Amt. Mfg.
425	135	52,386

1969 Golden Spike Carbine

NIB	Issue	Amt. Mfg.
450	120	69,996

1970 Cowboy Commemorative Carbine

NIB	Issue	Amt. Mfg.
450	125	27,549

1970 Cowboy Carbine "1 of 300"

NIB	Issue	Amt. Mfg.
2650	1000	300

1970 Northwest Territories (Canadian)

NIB	Issue	Amt. Mfg.
850	150	2,500

1970 Northwest Territories Deluxe (Canadian)

NIB	Issue	Amt. Mfg.
1100	250	500

1970 Lone Star-Rifle

NIB	Issue	Amt. Mfg.
450	140	—

1970 Lone Star-Carbine

NIB	Issue	Amt. Mfg.
425	140	38,385

1971 NRA Centennial-Rifle

NIB	Issue	Amt. Mfg.
425	150	21,000

1971 NRA Centennial-Musket

NIB	Issue	Amt. Mfg.
425	150	23,400

1971 Yellow Boy (European)

NIB	Issue	Amt. Mfg.
1150	250	500

1971 Royal Canadian Mounted Police (Canadian)

NIB	Issue	Amt. Mfg.
795	190	9,500

1971 Mounted Police (Canadian)

NIB	Issue	Amt. Mfg.
795	190	5,100

1971 Mounted Police, Presentation

NIB	Issue	Amt. Mfg.
9995	—	10

1974 Texas Ranger-Carbine

NIB	Issue	Amt. Mfg.
695	135	4,850

1974 Texas Ranger Presentation Model

NIB	Issue	Amt. Mfg.
2650	1000	150

1974 Apache (Canadian)

NIB	Issue	Amt. Mfg.
795	150	8,600

1974 Commanche (Canadian)

NIB	Issue	Amt. Mfg.
795	230	11,500

1974 Klondike Gold Rush (Canadian)

NIB	Issue	Amt. Mfg.
795	240	10,500

1975 Klondike Gold Rush-Dawson City Issue (Canadian)

NIB	Issue	Amt. Mfg.
8500	—	25

1976 Sioux (Canadian)

NIB	Issue	Amt. Mfg.
795	280	10,000

1976 Little Bighorn (Canadian)

NIB	Issue	Amt. Mfg.
795	300	11,000

1976 U.S. Bicentennial Carbine

NIB	Issue	Amt. Mfg.
595	325	19,999

1977 Wells Fargo

NIB	Issue	Amt. Mfg.
495	350	19,999

1977 Legendary Lawman

NIB	Issue	Amt. Mfg.
495	375	19,999

1977 Limited Edition I

NIB	Issue	Amt. Mfg.
1395	1500	1,500

1977 Cheyenne-.22 Cal. (Canadian)

NIB	Issue	Amt. Mfg.
695	320	5,000

1977 Cheyenne-.44-40 Cal. (Canadian)

NIB	Issue	Amt. Mfg.
795	300	11,225

1977 Cherokee-.22 Cal. (Canadian)

NIB	Issue	Amt. Mfg.
695	385	3,950

1977 Cherokee-.30-30 Cal. (Canadian)

NIB	Issue	Amt. Mfg.
795	385	9,000

1978 "One of One Thousand" (European)

NIB	Issue	Amt. Mfg.
7500	5000	250

1978 Antler Game Carbine

NIB	Issue	Amt. Mfg.
550	375	19,999

1979 Limited Edition II

NIB	Issue	Amt. Mfg.
1395	1500	1,500

1979 Legendary Frontiersman Rifle

NIB	Issue	Amt. Mfg.
550	425	19,999

1979 Matched Set of 1,000

NIB	Issue	Amt. Mfg.
2250	3000	1,000

1979 Bat Masterson (Canadian)

NIB	Issue	Amt. Mfg.
795	650	8,000

1980 Alberta Diamond Jubilee (Canadian)

NIB	Issue	Amt. Mfg.
795	650	2,700

1980 Alberta Diamond Jubilee Deluxe (Canadian)

NIB	Issue	Amt. Mfg.
1495	1900	300

1980 Saskatchewan Diamond Jubilee (Canadian)

NIB	Issue	Amt. Mfg.
795	695	2,700

1980 Saskatchewan Diamond Jubilee Deluxe (Canadian)

NIB	Issue	Amt. Mfg.
1495	1995	300

1980 Oliver Winchester

NIB	Issue	Amt. Mfg.
695	375	19,999

1981 U.S. Border Patrol

NIB	Issue	Amt. Mfg.
595	1195	1,000

1981 U.S. Border Patrol-Member's Model

NIB	Issue	Amt. Mfg.
595	695	800

1981 Calgary Stampede (Canadian)

NIB	Issue	Amt. Mfg.
1250	2200	1,000

1981 Canadian Pacific Centennial (Canadian)

NIB	Issue	Amt. Mfg.
550	800	2,000

1981 Canadian Pacific Centennial Presentation (Canadian)

NIB	Issue	Amt. Mfg.
1100	2200	300

1981 Canadian Pacific Employee's Model (Canadian)

NIB	Issue	Amt. Mfg.
550	800	2,000

1981 John Wayne (Canadian)

NIB	Issue	Amt. Mfg.
1195	995	1,000

1981 John Wayne

NIB	Issue	Amt. Mfg.
995	600	49,000

1981 Duke

NIB	Issue	Amt. Mfg.
2950	2250	1,000

1981 John Wayne "1 of 300" Set

NIB	Issue	Amt. Mfg.
6500	10000	300

1982 Great Western Artist I

NIB	Issue	Amt. Mfg.
1195	2200	999

1982 Great Western Artist II

NIB	Issue	Amt. Mfg.
1195	2200	999

1982 Annie Oakley

NIB	Issue	Amt. Mfg.
695	699	6,000

1983 Chief Crazy Horse

NIB	Issue	Amt. Mfg.
595	600	19,999

1983 American Bald Eagle

NIB	Issue	Amt. Mfg.
595	895	2,800

1983 American Bald Eagle-Deluxe

NIB	Issue	Amt. Mfg.
3000	2995	200

1983 Oklahoma Diamond Jubilee

NIB	Issue	Amt. Mfg.
1395	2250	1,001

1984 Winchester-Colt Commemorative Set

NIB	Issue	Amt. Mfg.
2250	3995	2,300

1985 Boy Scout 75th Anniversary-.22 Cal.

NIB	Issue	Amt. Mfg.
595	615	15,000

1985 Boy Scout 75th Anniversary-Eagle Scout

NIB	Issue	Amt. Mfg.
3000	2140	1,000

Texas Sesquicentennial Model-Rifle-.38-55 Cal.

NIB	Issue	Amt. Mfg.
2400	2995	1,500

Texas Sesquicentennial Model-Carbine-.38-55 Cal.

NIB	Issue	Amt. Mfg.
695	695	15,000

Texas Sesquicentennial Model Set with Bowie Knife

NIB	Issue	Amt. Mfg.
6250	7995	150

1986 Model 94 Ducks Unlimited

NIB	Issue	Amt. Mfg.
650	—	2,800

1986 Statue of Liberty

NIB	Issue	Amt. Mfg.
7000	6500	100

1986 120th Anniversary Model-Carbine-.44-40 Cal.

NIB	Issue	Amt. Mfg.
895	995	1,000

1986 European 1 of 1,000 Second Series (European)

NIB	Issue	Amt. Mfg.
7000	6000	150

1987 U.S. Constitution 200th Anniversary-44-40

NIB	Issue	Amt. Mfg.
13500	12000	17

1990 Wyoming Centennial-30-30

NIB	Issue	Amt. Mfg.
1095	895	500

1991 Winchester 125th Anniversary

NIB	Issue	Amt. Mfg.
5500	4995	61

1992 Arapaho-30-30

NIB	Issue	Amt. Mfg.
1095	895	500

1992 Ontario Conservation-30-30

NIB	Issue	Amt. Mfg.
1195	1195	400

1992 Kentucky Bicentennial-30-30

NIB	Issue	Amt. Mfg.
1095	995	500

1993 Nez Perce-30-30

NIB	Issue	Amt. Mfg.
1095	995	600

1995 Florida Sesquicentennial Carbine

NIB	Issue	Amt. Mfg.
1195	1195	360

1996 Wild Bill Hickok Carbine

NIB	Issue	Amt. Mfg.
1195	1195	350

Winchester 120th Commemorative Anniversary carbine

Winchester Model 9422 Boy Scouts of America Commemorative

John Wayne Commemorative Gun

Winchester Chief Crazy Horse Commemorative

Winchester Wells Fargo & Co. Commemorative carbine

Winchester Model 9422 Annie Oakley Commemorative

Close-up of Model 9422 Annie Oakley Commemorative engraving

Winchester Texas Ranger Commemorative

Receiver of the Winchester Legendary Lawmen Model 94 carbine. The antique silver finish is decoratively engraved on both sides.

Winchester Serial Numbers

Records at the factory indicate the following serial numbers were assigned to guns at the end of the calendar year.

MODEL 100

Year	Serial	Year	Serial
1961 —	1 to 32189	1968 —	210053
62 —	60760	69 —	A210999
63 —	78863	70 —	229995
64 —	92016	71 —	242999
65 —	135388	72 —	A258001
66 —	145239	73 —	A262833
67 —	209498		

Records at the factory indicate the following serial numbers were assigned to guns at the end of the calendar year.

MODEL 88

Year	Serial	Year	Serial
1955 —	1 to 18378	1965 —	162699
56 —	36756	66 —	192595
57 —	55134	67 —	212416
58 —	73512	68 —	230199
59 —	91890	69 —	H239899
60 —	110268	70 —	H258229
61 —	128651	71 —	H266784
62 —	139838	72 —	H279014
63 —	148858	73 —	H283718
64 —	160307		

Records at the factory indicate the following serial numbers were assigned to guns at the end of the calendar year.

MODEL 74

Year	Serial	Year	Serial
1939 —	1 to 30890	1948 —	223788
40 —	67085	49 —	249900
41 —	114355	50 —	276012
42 —	128293	51 —	302124
43 —	None	52 —	328236
44 —	128295	53 —	354348
45 —	128878	54 —	380460
46 —	145168	55 —	406574
47 —	173524		

Records at the factory indicate the following serial numbers were assigned to guns at the end of the calendar year.

MODEL 71

Year	Serial	Year	Serial
1935 —	1 to 4	1947 —	25758
36 —	7821	48 —	27900
37 —	12988	49 —	29675
38 —	14690	50 —	31450
39 —	16155	51 —	33225
40 —	18267	52 —	35000
41 —	20810	53 —	37500
42 —	21959	54 —	40770
43 —	22048	55 —	43306
44 —	22051	56 —	45843
45 —	22224	57 —	47254
46 —	23534		

Records at the factory indicate the following serial numbers were assigned to guns at the end of the calendar year.

MODEL 70

Year	Serial	Year	Serial
1935 —	1 to 19	1950 —	173150
36 —	2238	51 —	206625
37 —	11573	52 —	238820
38 —	17844	53 —	282735
39 —	23991	54 —	323530
40 —	31675	55 —	361025
41 —	41753	56 —	393595
42 —	49206	57 —	425283
43 —	49983	58 —	440792
44 —	49997	59 —	465040
45 —	5 0921	60 —	504257
46 —	58382	61 —	545446
47 —	75675	62 —	565592
48 —	101680	63 —	581471
49 —	131580		

All post-64 Model 70s began with the serial number 700000

Year	Serial	Year	Serial
1964 —	740599	1973 —	G1128731
65 —	809177	74 —	G1175000
66 —	833795	75 —	G1218700
67 —	869000	76 —	G1266000
68 —	925908	77 —	G1350000
69 —	G941900	78 —	G1410000
70 —	G957995	79 —	G1447000
71 —	G1018991	80 —	G1490709
72 —	G1099257	81 —	G1537134

Records at the factory indicate the following serial numbers were assigned to guns at the end of the calendar year.

MODEL 63

Year	Serial	Year	Serial
1933 —	1 to 2667	1946 —	61607
34 —	5361	47 —	71714
35 —	9830	48 —	80519
36 —	16781	49 —	88889
37 —	25435	50 —	97259
38 —	30934	51 —	105629
39 —	36055	52 —	114000
40 —	41456	53 —	120500
41 —	47708	54 —	127000
42 —	51258	55 —	138000
43 —	51631	56 —	150000
44 —	51656	57 —	162345
45 —	53853	58 —	174692

Factory records indicate the following serial numbers were assigned to guns at the end of the calendar year.

MODEL 62

Year	Serial	Year	Serial
1932 —	1 to 7643	1946 —	183756
33 —	10695	47 —	219085
34 —	14090	48 —	252298
35 —	23924	49 —	262473
36 —	42759	50 —	272648
37 —	66059	51 —	282823
38 —	80205	52 —	293000
39 —	96534	53 —	310500
40 —	116393	54 —	328000
41 —	137379	55 —	342776
42 —	155152	56 —	357551
43 —	155422	57 —	383513
44 —	155425	58 —	409475
45 —	156073		

Records at the factory indicate the following serial numbers were assigned to guns at the end of the calendar year.

MODEL 61

Year	Serial	Year	Serial
1932 —	1 to 3532	1948 —	115281
33 —	6008	49 —	125461
34 —	8554	50 —	135641
35 —	12379	51 —	145821
36 —	20615	52 —	156000
37 —	30334	53 —	171000
38 —	36326	54 —	186000
39 —	42610	55 —	200962
40 —	49270	56 —	215923
41 —	57493	57 —	229457
42 —	59871	58 —	242992
43 —	59872	59 —	262793

44 —	59879	60 —	282594
45 —	60512	61 —	302395
46 —	71629	62 —	322196
47 —	92297	63 —	342001

This model was discontinued in 1963. For some unknown reason there are no actual records available from 1949 through 1963. The serial number figures for these years are arrived at by taking the total production figure of 342,001, subtracting the last known number of 115281, and dividing the difference equally by the number of remaining years available, (15).

Records at the factory indicate the following serial numbers were assigned to guns at the end of the calendar year.

MODEL 55 CENTERFIRE

1924 —	1 to 836	1929 —	12258
25 —	2783	30 —	17393
26 —	4957	31 —	18198
27 —	8021	32 —	19204
28 —	10467	33 —	Clean-up 20580

Records at the factory indicate the following serial numbers were assigned to guns at the end of the calendar year.

MODEL 54

1925 —	1 to 3140	1931 —	36731
26 —	8051	32 —	38543
27 —	14176	33 —	40722
28 —	19587	34 —	43466
29 —	29104	35 —	47125
30 —	32499	36 —	50145

Records at the factory indicate the following serial numbers were assigned to guns at the end of the calendar year.

MODEL 53

In the case of the Model 53 the following list pertains to the number of guns produced each year rather than a serial number list.

The Model 53 was serially numbered concurrently with the Model 92.

MODEL 53s PRODUCED

1924 —	1488	1929 —	1733
25 —	2861	30 —	920
26 —	2531	31 —	621
27 —	2297	32 —	206
28 —	1958		

This model was discontinued in 1932, however, a clean-up of production continued for nine more years with an additional 486 guns.

TOTAL PRODUCTION APPROXIMATELY - 15,100

Records at the factory indicate the following serial numbers were assigned to guns at the end of the calendar year.

1920 —	None indicated	1950 —	70766
21 —	397	51 —	73385
22 —	745	52 —	76000
23 —	1394	53 —	79500
24 —	2361	54 —	80693
25 —	3513	55 —	81831
26 —	6383	56 —	96869
27 —	9436	57 —	97869
28 —	12082	58 —	98599
29 —	14594	59 —	98899
30 —	17253	60 —	102200
31 —	21954	61 —	106986
32 —	24951	62 —	108718
33 —	26725	63 —	113583
34 —	29030	64 —	118447

35 —	32448	65 —	120992
36 —	36632	66 —	123537
37 —	40419	67 —	123727
38 —	43632	68 —	123917
39 —	45460	69 —	E124107
40 —	47519	70 —	E124297
41 —	50317	71 —	E124489
42 —	52129	72 —	E124574
43 —	52553	73 —	E124659
44 —	52560	74 —	E124744
45 —	52718	75 —	E124828
46 —	56080	76 —	E125019
47 —	60158	77 —	E125211
48 —	64265	78 —	E125315
49 —	68149		

This model was discontinued in 1978. A small clean-up of production was completed in 1979 with a total of 125,419.

Records at the factory indicate the following serial numbers were assigned to guns at the end of the calendar year.

MODEL 50

1954 —	1 to 24550	1958 —	122750
55 —	49100	59 —	147300
56 —	73650	60 —	171850
57 —	98200	61 —	196400

Records at the factory indicate the following serial numbers were assigned to guns at the end of the calendar year.

MODEL 42

1933 —	1 to 9398	1949 —	81107
34 —	13963	50 —	87071
35 —	17728	51 —	93038
36 —	24849	52 —	99000
37 —	30900	53 —	108201
38 —	34659	54 —	117200
39 —	38967	55 —	121883
40 —	43348	56 —	126566
41 —	48203	57 —	131249
42 —	50818	58 —	135932
43 —	50822	59 —	140615
44 —	50828	60 —	145298
45 —	51168	61 —	149981
46 —	54256	62 —	154664
47 —	64853	63 —	159353
48 —	75142		

Records at the factory indicate the following serial numbers were assigned to guns at the end of the calendar year.

MODEL 24

1939 —	1 to 8118	1944 —	33683
40 —	21382	45 —	34965
41 —	27045	46 —	45250
42 —	33670	47 —	58940
43 —	None recorded	48 —	64417

There were no records kept on this model from 1949 until its discontinuance in 1958. The total production was approximately 116,280.

Records at the factory indicate the following serial numbers were assigned to guns at the end of the calendar year.

MODEL 12

1912 —	5308	1938 —	779455
13 —	32418	39 —	814121
14 —	79765	40 —	856499
15 —	109515	41 —	907431
16 —	136412	42 —	958303
17 —	159391	43 —	975640
18 —	183461	44 —	975727
19 —	219457	45 —	990004

20 —	247458	46 —	1029152
21 —	267253	47 —	1102371
22 —	304314	48 —	1176055
23 —	346319	49 —	1214041
24 —	385196	50 —	1252028
25 —	423056	51 —	1290015
26 —	464564	52 —	1328002
27 —	510693	53 —	1399996
28 —	557850	54 —	1471990
29 —	600834	55 —	1541929
30 —	626996	56 —	1611868
31 —	651255	57 —	1651435
32 —	660110	58 —	1690999
33 —	664544	59 —	1795500
34 —	673994	60 —	1800000
35 —	686978	61 —	1930029
36 —	720316	62 —	1956990
37 —	754250	63 —	1962001

A clean-up of production took place from 1964 through 1966 with the ending serial number 70875

New Style M/12

1972 —	Y2000100-Y2006396
73 —	Y2015662
74 —	Y2022061
75 —	Y2024478
76 —	Y2025482
77 —	Y2025874
78 —	Y2026156
79 —	Y2026399

Records at the factory indicate the following serial numbers were assigned to guns at the end of the calendar year.

MODEL 1911 S.L.

1911 —	1 to 3819	1919 —	57337
12 —	27659	20 —	60719
13 —	36677	21 —	64109
14 —	40105	22 —	69132
15 —	43284	23 —	73186
16 —	45391	24 —	76199
17 —	49893	25 —	78611
18 —	52895		

The model 1911 was discontinued in 1925. However, guns were produced for three years after that date to clean up production and excess parts. When this practice ceased there were approximately 82,774 guns produced.

Records at the factory indicate the following serial numbers were assigned to guns at the end of the calendar year.

MODEL 1910

1910 —	1 to 4766	1924 —	17030
11 —	7695	25 —	17281
12 —	9712	26 —	17696
13 —	11487	27 —	18182
14 —	12311	28 —	18469
15 —	13233	29 —	18893
16 —	13788	30 —	19065
17 —	14255	31 —	19172
18 —	14625	32 —	19232
19 —	15665	33 —	19281
20 —	Not Available	34 —	19338
21 —	15845	35 —	19388
22 —	16347	36 —	19445
23 —	16637		

A clean-up of production continued into 1937 when the total of the guns were completed at approximately 20786.

Records at the factory indicate the following serial numbers were assigned to guns at the end of the calendar year.

MODEL 1907

1907 —	1 to 8657	1933 —	44806
08 —	14486	34 —	44990
09 —	19707	35 —	45203
10 —	23230	36 —	45482
11 —	25523	37 —	45920
12 —	27724	38 —	46419
13 —	29607	39 —	46758
14 —	30872	40 —	47296
15 —	32272	41 —	47957
16 —	36215	42 —	48275
17 —	38235	43 —	None
18 —	39172	44 —	None
19 —	40448	45 —	48281
20 —	Not Available	46 —	48395
21 —	40784	47 —	48996
22 —	41289	48 —	49684
23 —	41658	**49 —	50662
24 —	42029	**50 —	51640
25 —	42360	**51 —	52618
26 —	42688	**52 —	53596
27 —	43226	**53 —	54574
28 —	43685	**54 —	55552
29 —	44046	**55 —	56530
30 —	44357	**56 —	57508
31 —	44572	**57 —	58486
32 —	44683		

Actual records on serial numbers stops in 1948. The serial numbers ending each year from 1948 to 1957 were derived at by taking the last serial number recorded (58486) and the last number from 1948, (49684) and dividing the years of production, (9), which relates to 978 guns each year for the nine year period.

Records at the factory indicate the following serial numbers were assigned to guns at the end of the calendar year.

MODEL 1906

1906 —	1 to 52278	1920 —	None
07 —	89147	21 —	598691
08 —	114138	22 —	608011
09 —	165068	23 —	622601
10 —	221189	24 —	636163
11 —	273355	25 —	649952
12 —	327955	26 —	665484
13 —	381922	27 —	679692
14 —	422734	28 —	695915
15 —	453880	29 —	711202
16 —	483805	30 —	720116
17 —	517743	31 —	725978
18 —	535540	32 —	727353
19 —	593917		

A clean-up of production took place for the next few years with a record of production reaching approximately 729,305.

Records at the factory indicate the following serial numbers were assigned to guns at the end of the calendar year.

MODEL 1905

1905 —	1 to 5659	1913 —	25559
06 —	15288	14 —	26110
07 —	19194	15 —	26561
08 —	20385	16 —	26910
09 —	21280	17 —	27297
10 —	22423	18 —	27585
11 —	23503	19 —	28287
12 —	24602	20 —	29113

Records at the factory indicate the following serial numbers were assigned to guns at the end of the calendar year.

MODEL 1903

Year	Serial	Year	Serial
1903 —	Not Available	1918 —	92617
04 —	6944	19 —	96565
05 —	14865	20 —	Not Available
06 —	23097	21 —	97650
07 —	31852	22 —	99011
08 —	39105	23 —	100452
09 —	46496	24 —	101688
10 —	54298	25 —	103075
11 —	61679	26 —	104230
12 —	69586	27 —	105537
13 —	76732	28 —	107157
14 —	81776	29 —	109414
15 —	84563	30 —	111276
16 —	87148	31 —	112533
17 —	89501	32 —	112992

This model was discontinued in 1932, however, a clean up of parts was used for further production of approximately 2,000 guns. Total production was stopped at serial number 114962 in 1936.

Records at the factory indicate the following serial numbers were assigned to guns at the end of the calendar year.

MODEL 1901 SHOTGUN

Year	Serial	Year	Serial
1904 —	64856 to 64860	1913 —	72764
05 —	66483	14 —	73202
06 —	67486	15 —	73509
07 —	68424	16 —	73770
08 —	69197	17 —	74027
09 —	70009	18 —	74311
10 —	70753	19 —	74872
11 —	71441	20 —	77000
12 —	72167		

Records at the factory indicate the following serial numbers were assigned to guns at the end of the calendar year.

MODEL 1897

Year	Serial	Year	Serial
1897 —	to 32335	1928 —	796806
98 —	64668	29 —	807321
99 —	96999	30 —	812729
1900 —	129332	31 —	830721
01 —	161665	32 —	833926
02 —	193998	33 —	835637
03 —	226331	34 —	837364
04 —	258664	35 —	839728
05 —	296037	36 —	848684
06 —	334059	37 —	856729
07 —	377999	38 —	860725
08 —	413618	39 —	866938
09 —	446888	40 —	875945
10 —	481062	41 —	891190
11 —	512632	42 —	910072
12 —	544313	43 —	912265
13 —	575213	44 —	912327
14 —	592732	45 —	916472
15 —	607673	46 —	926409
16 —	624537	47 —	936682
17 —	646124	48 —	944085
18 —	668383	49 —	953042
19 —	691943	50 —	961999
20 —	696183	51 —	970956
21 —	700428	52 —	979913
22 —	715902	53 —	988860
23 —	732060	54 —	997827
24 —	744942	55 —	1006784
25 —	757629	56 —	1015741
26 —	770527	57 —	1024700
27 —	783574		

Records on this model are incomplete. The above serial numbers are estimated from 1897 through 1903 and again from 1949 through 1957. The actual records are in existence from 1904 through 1949.

Records at the factory indicate the following serial numbers were assigned to guns at the end of the calendar year.

MODEL 1895

Year	Serial	Year	Serial
1895 —	1 to 287	1914 —	72082
96 —	5715	15 —	174233
97 —	7814	16 —	377411
98 —	19871	17 —	389106
99 —	26434	18 —	392731
1900 —	29817	19 —	397250
01 —	31584	20 —	400463
02 —	35601	21 —	404075
03 —	42514	22 —	407200
04 —	47805	23 —	410289
05 —	54783	24 —	413276
06 —	55011	25 —	417402
07 —	57351	26 —	419533
08 —	60002	27 —	421584
09 —	60951	28 —	422676
10 —	63771	29 —	423680
11 —	65017	30 —	424181
12 —	67331	31 —	425132
13 —	70823	32 —	425825

Records at the factory indicate the following serial numbers were assigned to guns at the end of the calendar year.

MODEL 94

Year	Serial	Year	Serial
1894 —	1 to 14579	1939 —	1101051
95 —	44359	40 —	1142423
96 —	76464	41 —	1191307
97 —	111453	42 —	1221289
98 —	147684	43 —	No Record Avail.
99 —	183371	44 —	No Record Avail.
1900 —	204427	45 —	No Record Avail.
01 —	233975	46 —	No Record Avail.
02 —	273854	47 —	No Record Avail.
03 —	291506	48 —	1500000
04 —	311363	49 —	1626100
05 —	337557	50 —	1724295
06 —	378878	51 —	1819800
07 —	430985	52 —	1910000
08 —	474241	53 —	2000000
09 —	505831	54 —	2071100
10 —	553062	55 —	2145296
11 —	599263	56 —	2225000
12 —	646114	57 —	2290296
13 —	703701	58 —	2365887
14 —	756066	59 —	2410555
15 —	784052	60 —	2469821
16 —	807741	61 —	2500000
17 —	821972	62 —	2551921
18 —	838175	63 —	2586000
19 —	870762	*1964 —	2700000
20 —	880627	64 —	2797428
21 —	908318	65 —	2894428
22 —	919583	66 —	2991927
23 —	938539	67 —	3088458
24 —	953198	68 —	3185691
25 —	978523	69 —	3284570
26 —	997603	70 —	3381299
27 —	1027571	71 —	3557385
28 —	1054465	72 —	3806499
29 —	1077097	73 —	3929364
30 —	1081755	74 —	4111426
31 —	1084156	75 —	4277926
32 —	1087836	76 —	4463553
33 —	1089270	77 —	4565925

34 —	1091190	78 —	4662210
35 —	1099605	79 —	4826596
36 —	1100065	80 —	4892951
37 —	1100679	81 —	5024957
38 —	1100915	62 —	5103248

*The post-64 Model 94 began with serial number 2700000.

Serial number 1000000 was presented to President Calvin Coolidge in 1927.

Serial number 1500000 was presented to President Harry S. Truman in 1948.

Serial number 2000000 was presented to President Dwight D. Eisenhower in 1953.

Serial numbers 2500000 and 3000000 were presented to the Winchester Gun Museum, now located in Cody, Wyoming.

Serial number 3500000 was not constructed until 1979 and was sold at auction in Las Vegas, Nevada. Serial number 4000000—whereabouts unknown at this time.

Serial number 4500000—shipped to Italy by Olin in 1978. Whereabouts unknown.

Serial number 5000000—in New Haven, not constructed as of March 1983.

Records at the factory indicate the following serial numbers were assigned to guns at the end of the calendar year.

MODEL 1892

1892 —	1 to 23701	1913 —	742675
93 —	35987	14 —	771444
94 —	73508	15 —	804622
95 —	106721	16 —	830031
96 —	144935	17 —	853819
97 —	159312	18 —	870942
98 —	165431	19 —	903649
99 —	171820	20 —	906754
1900 —	183411	21 —	910476
01 —	191787	22 —	917300
02 —	208871	23 —	926329
03 —	253935	24 —	938641
04 —	278546	25 —	954997
05 —	315425	26 —	973896
06 —	376496	27 —	990883
07 —	437919	28 —	996517
08 —	476540	29 —	999238
09 —	522162	30 —	999730
10 —	586996	31 —	1000727
11 —	643483	32 —	1001324
12 —	694752		

Records on the Model 1890 are somewhat incomplete. Our records indicate the following serial numbers were assigned to guns at the end of the calendar year beginning with 1908. Actual records on the firearms that were manufactured between 1890 and 1907 will be available from the "Winchester Museum," located at The "Buffalo Bill Historical Center", P.O. Box 1020, Cody, WY 82414

MODEL 1890

1908 —	330000 to 363850	1920 —	None
09 —	393427	21 —	634783
10 —	423567	22 —	643304
11 —	451264	23 —	654837
12 —	478595	24 —	664613
13 —	506936	25 —	675774
14 —	531019	26 —	687049
15 —	551290	27 —	698987
16 —	570497	28 —	711354
17 —	589204	29 —	722125
18 —	603438	30 —	729015
19 —	630801	31 —	733178
		32 —	734454

The Model 1890 was discontinued in 1932, however, a clean-up of the production run lasted another 8+ years and included another 14,000 to 15,000 guns. Our figures indicate approximately 749,000 guns were made.

Records at the factory indicate the following serial numbers were assigned to guns at the end of the calendar year.

MODEL 1887

1887 —	1 to 7431	1993 —	54367
88 —	22408	94 —	56849
89 —	25673	95 —	58289
90 —	29105	96 —	60175
91 —	38541	97 —	63952
92 —	49763	98 —	64855

According to these records no guns were produced during the last few years of this model and it was therefore discontinued in 1901.

Records at the factory indicate the following serial numbers were assigned to guns at the end of the calendar year.

MODEL 1886

1886 —	1 to 3211	1905 —	138838
87 —	14728	06 —	142249
88 —	28577	07 —	145119
89 —	38401	08 —	147322
90 —	49723	09 —	148237
91 —	63601	10 —	150129
92 —	73816	11 —	151622
93 —	83261	12 —	152943
94 —	94543	13 —	152947
95 —	103708	14 —	153859
96 —	109670	15 —	154452
97 —	113997	16 —	154979
98 —	119192	17 —	155387
99 —	120571	18 —	156219
1900 —	122834	19 —	156930
01 —	125630	20 —	158716
02 —	128942	21 —	159108
03 —	132213	22 —	159337
04 —	135524		

No further serial numbers were recorded until the discontinuance of the model, which was in 1935 at 159994.

Records at the factory indicate the following serial numbers were assigned to guns at the end of the calendar year.

MODEL 1885
SINGLE SHOT

1885 —	1 to 375	1900 —	88501
86 —	6841	01 —	90424
87 —	18328	02 —	92031
88 —	30571	03 —	92359
89 —	45019	04 —	92785
90 —	None	05 —	93611
91 —	53700	06 —	94208
92 —	60371	07 —	95743
93 —	69534	08 —	96819
94 —	None	09 —	98097
95 —	73771	10 —	98506
96 —	78253	11 —	99012
97 —	78815	12 —	None
98 —	84700	13 —	100352
99 —	85086		

No further serial numbers were recorded until the end of 1923. The last number recorded was 139700.

Records at the factory indicate the following serial numbers were assigned to guns at the end of the calendar year.

MODEL 1876

1876 —	1 to 1429	1988 —	63539
77 —	3579	89 —	None
78 —	7967	90 —	None
79 —	8971	91 —	None
80 —	14700	92 —	63561
81 —	21759	93 —	63670
82 —	32407	94 —	63678
83 —	42410	95 —	None
84 —	54666	96 —	63702
85 —	58714	97 —	63869
86 —	60397	98 —	63871
87 —	62420		

Records at the factory indicate the following serial numbers were assigned to guns at the end of the calendar year.

MODEL 1873

1873 —	1 to 126	1897 —	513421
74 —	2726	98 —	525922
75 —	11325	99 —	541328
76 —	23151	1900 —	554128
77 —	23628	01 —	557236
78 —	27501	02 —	564557
79 —	41525	03 —	573957
80 —	63537	04 —	588953
81 —	81620	05 —	602557
82 —	109507	06 —	613780
83 —	145503	07 —	None
84 —	175126	08 —	None
85 —	196221	09 —	630385
86 —	222937	10 —	656101
87 —	225922	11 —	669324

88 —	284529	12 —	678527
89 —	323956	13 —	684419
90 —	363220	14 —	686510
91 —	405026	15 —	688431
92 —	441625	16 —	694020
93 —	466641	17 —	698617
94 —	481826	18 —	700734
95 —	499308	19 —	702042
96 —	507545		

No last number available: 1920, 21, 22, 23—720609.

Records at the factory indicate the following serial numbers were assigned to guns at the end of the calendar year.

MODEL 1866

1866 —	12476 to 14813	1883 —	162376
67 —	15578	84 —	163649
68 —	19768	85 —	163664
69 —	29516	86 —	165071
70 —	52527	87 —	165912
71 —	88184	88 —	167155
72 —	109784	89 —	167401
73 —	118401	90 —	167702
74 —	125038	91 —	169003
75 —	125965	92 —	None
76 —	131907	93 —	169007
77 —	148207	94 —	169011
78 —	150493	95 —	None
79 —	152201	96 —	None
80 —	154379	97 —	169015
81 —	156107	98 —	170100
82 —	159513	99 —	Discontinued

Winchester Ranger lever action rifle

Winchester Model 9422 walnut

Winchester Model 70 lightweight Win-Tuff, laminated stock

WINDSOR
Windsor, Vermont
Robbins & Lawrence
Hartford, Connecticut

Windsor Rifle-Musket

A .577 caliber single shot percussion rifle with a 39" round barrel secured by three barrel bands. The lock marked "Windsor". Rifles of this pattern were contracted for by the British Government. The lock and barrel finished in the white, brass furniture, and a walnut stock. Approximately 16,000 were made from 1855 to 1858.

Exc.	V.G.	Good	Fair	Poor
—	—	3000	950	300

WINSLOW ARMS CO.
Camden, South Carolina

Bolt Action Rifle

A high-grade, semi-custom sporting rifle built upon a number of actions and offered in all popular calibers from .17 Remington to the .458 Winchester Magnum with a 24" barrel and a 3-shot magazine. The larger Magnum models have a 26" barrel and a 2-shot magazine. Two basic stocks are offered—the Conventional Bushmaster, which features a standard pistol grip and a beavertail forearm; and also the Plainsmaster, which has a full curled, hooked pistol grip and a wide, flat beavertail forearm. Both have Monte Carlo-style stocks with recoil pads and sling swivels. Offered in a choice of popular woods with rosewood forend tips and pistol gripcaps. Eight different grades of this rifle are available and the following lists the values applicable for each.

Commander Grade

Figured walnut stock. Rosewood forearm tip and grip cap. White line recoil pad. FN Supreme action.

Exc.	V.G.	Good	Fair	Poor
550	450	400	350	300

Regal Grade

All features of Commander Grade plus ivory and ebony inlay on stock, French style checkering, jeweled bolt.

Exc.	V.G.	Good	Fair	Poor
650	550	450	375	200

Regent Grade

As above with addition of hand carved checkering.

Exc.	V.G.	Good	Fair	Poor
800	700	500	450	200

Regimental Grade

As above but with addition of basket weave carving, 2 ivory stock inlays and large ivory and ebony inlay on both side of butt stock with animal silhouette.

Exc.	V.G.	Good	Fair	Poor
950	850	650	550	250

Crown Grade

As above but with more elaborate ivory inlays on stock.

Exc.	V.G.	Good	Fair	Poor
1500	1250	1000	750	350

Royal Grade

As above but with addition even more elaborate stock carving and ivory and ebony inlay.

Exc.	V.G.	Good	Fair	Poor
1750	1400	1150	850	400

Imperial Grade

As above but with addition of engraved barrel from receiver to 11" forward. Engraved receiver ring, bolt handel and trigger guard. Engraved scope mounts and rings.

Exc.	V.G.	Good	Fair	Poor
4000	3000	2500	2000	1000

Emperor Grade

As above but with addition of gold raised relief animals engraved receiver and forward part of barrel with muzzle tip engraved engraved as well. Highest Winslow grade.

Exc.	V.G.	Good	Fair	Poor
6250	5000	4000	3000	1500

WISEMAN, BILL & CO.
Bryan, Texas

A custom order bolt action rifle utilizing a Sako action, McMillan stainless steel barrel and laminated stock. The action components Teflon coated. It is made in four styles: the Hunter, Hunter Deluxe, Maverick, and the Varminter.

Exc.	V.G.	Good	Fair	Poor
1500	1250	950	—	—

Silhouette Pistol

A custom made single shot pistol produced in a variety of calibers with a 14" fluted stainless steel barrel and laminated pistol grip stock. Furnished without sights. Introduced in 1989.

Exc.	V.G.	Good	Fair	Poor
1300	1000	800	—	—

WITNESS
SEE—European American Armory

WOLF SPORTING PISTOLS
Importer-Handgunner Gunshop
Topton, PA

Wolf SV Target

Chambered for 9x19, 9x21, 9x23, .38 Super, .40 S&W, or .45 ACP. Barrel is 4.5" long. Weight is 44 oz. Many special features. Built in Austria. Price listed below is for basic pistol. A number of special order items are offered. Check with importer before a sale. First imported in 1998.

NIB	Exc.	V.G.	Good	Fair	Poor
2000	1600	—	—	—	—

Wolf SV Match

Chambered for 9x19, 9x21, 9x23, .38 Super, .40 S&W, or .45 ACP. Barrel is 5.5" long. Weight is 44 oz. Many special features. Built in Austria. Price listed below is for basic pistol. A number of special order items are offered. Check with importer before a sale. First imported in 1998.

NIB	Exc.	V.G.	Good	Fair	Poor
2000	1600	—	—	—	—

WOODWARD, JAMES & SONS
London, England
SEE—British Double Guns

Prior to WWII, this company produced a variety of boxlock and sidelock shotguns that are regarded as some of the best made. Prospective purchasers should secure a qualified appraisal prior to acquisition.

WURFFLEIN, ANDREW & WILLIAM
Philadelphia, Pennsylvania

Pocket Pistol

A .41 caliber percussion single shot pocket pistol with either a 2.5" or 3" barrel, German silver furniture and checkered walnut stock. The lock marked "A. Wurfflein / Phila." Manufactured during the 1850s and 1860s.

Exc.	V.G.	Good	Fair	Poor
—	—	950	500	200

Single-Shot Target Pistol

A .22 caliber single-shot pistol with half-octagonal barrels measuring from 8" to 16" in length. The barrel pivots downward for loading and is marked "W. Wurfflein Philad'a Pa. U.S.A. Patented June 24th, 1884". Blued with walnut grips. This model is also available with a detachable shoulder stock, which if present would add approximately 35% to the values listed below. Manufactured from 1884 to 1890.

Exc.	V.G.	Good	Fair	Poor
—	—	800	400	200

Single-Shot Rifle

A single-shot rifle produced in a variety of calibers with octagonal barrels of 24" to 28" length. This rifle was available with a wide variety of optional features and a qualified appraisal should be sought if any features are in doubt.

Exc.	V.G.	Good	Fair	Poor
—	—	750	350	150

Mid-range Model

As above, with a 28" or 30" half-octagonal barrel.

Exc.	V.G.	Good	Fair	Poor
—	—	2500	950	400

Model No. 25

The highest grade rifle manufactured by Wurfflein.

Exc.	V.G.	Good	Fair	Poor
—	—	3000	1250	600

XL
HOPKINS & ALLEN
Norwich, Connecticut

Derringer

A .41 caliber spur trigger single-shot pistol with a 2.75" octagonal barrel and either iron or brass frame. Blued, nickel-plated with rosewood grips. The barrel marked "XL Derringer". Manufactured during the 1870s.

Exc.	V.G.	Good	Fair	Poor
—	—	950	400	150

Vest Pocket Derringer

As above, in .22 caliber with a 2.25" round barrel and normally full nickel-plated. The barrel marked "XL Vest Pocket". Manufactured from 1870s to 1890s.

Exc.	V.G.	Good	Fair	Poor
—	—	500	275	75

XPERT
HOPKINS & ALLEN
Norwich, Connecticut

Xpert Derringer

A .22 or .30 caliber spur trigger single-shot pistol with round barrels, 2.25" to 6" in length and a nickel-plated finish with rosewood grips. The breechblock pivots to the left side for loading. The barrel marked "Xpert-Pat. Sep. 23. 1878". Manufactured during the 1870s.

Exc.	V.G.	Good	Fair	Poor
—	—	650	250	75

Z

Z-B RIFLE CO.
Brno, Czechoslovakia

Model ZKW-465 Varmint Rifle

A Mauser bolt action rifle chambered for the .22 Hornet cartridge. It has a 23" barrel with a three-leaf, folding rear sight. It is offered standard with double-set triggers. The finish is blued, with a select walnut checkered stock.

Exc.	V.G.	Good	Fair	Poor
1300	1100	950	800	500

ZM WEAPONS
Bernardton, MA

LR-300 sport rifle

This is a highly modified AR-15 chambered for the .223 cartridge. It is fitted with a 16.25" barrel and a true folding stock. A ghost ring rear sight and an adjustable post front sight with tritium insert is standard. Weight is approximately 7.2 pounds. Introduced in 1997.

NIB	Exc.	V.G.	Good	Fair	Poor
1995	1600	1200	—	—	—

ZANOTTI, FABIO
Brescia, Italy
Importer - New England Arms Co.
Kittery Point, Maine

Model 625

A 12 to .410 bore boxlock double barrel shotgun with automatic ejectors and single selective trigger. Blued with checkered walnut stock.

NIB	Exc.	V.G.	Good	Fair	Poor
4500	3500	2500	2000	1500	750

Model 626

As above, engraved with either scroll work or hunting scenes.

NIB	Exc.	V.G.	Good	Fair	Poor
5000	4500	3000	2500	1500	750

Giacinto

An external hammer boxlock shotgun produced in a variety of gauges with double triggers.

NIB	Exc.	V.G.	Good	Fair	Poor
4750	3500	2750	2000	1200	750

Maxim

Similar to the Model 625, but fitted with detachable sidelocks.

NIB	Exc.	V.G.	Good	Fair	Poor
7500	6500	5000	3500	2250	1200

Edward

As above, but more intricately engraved.

NIB	Exc.	V.G.	Good	Fair	Poor
10000	8000	6500	4500	3000	1500

Cassiano I

As above, with exhibition grade engraving.

NIB	Exc.	V.G.	Good	Fair	Poor
11000	9000	7000	6000	4000	2000

Cassiano II

As above, with gold inlays.

NIB	Exc.	V.G.	Good	Fair	Poor
12500	10000	8500	7000	5000	2500

Cassiano Executive

A strictly custom made shotgun produced to the client's specifications. Prospective purchasers should secure a qualified appraisal prior to acquisition. Prices listed below are for base model only.

NIB	Exc.	V.G.	Good	Fair	Poor
15000	12500	—	—	—	—

ZEHNER, E. WAFFENFABRIK
Suhl, Germany

Zehna

A 6.35mm semiautomatic pistol with a 2.5" barrel and 5-shot magazine. The slide marked "Zehna DRPA," and the caliber on later production models. Blued with a black plastic grips bearing the monogram "EZ". Approximately 20,000 were made from 1921 to 1927.

Exc.	V.G.	Good	Fair	Poor
400	300	250	175	100

ZEILINGER
SEE—Austrian Military Firearms

ZEPHYR
Eibar, Spain
Importer - Stoegers

Woodlander II

A 12 or 20 gauge boxlock shotgun with varying length barrels, double triggers and extractors. Blued with a walnut stock.

NIB	Exc.	V.G.	Good	Fair	Poor
500	450	400	300	200	100

Uplander

A 12, 16, 20, 28 or .410 bore sidelock double barrel shotgun with varying length barrels, double triggers, and automatic ejectors. Blued with a walnut stock.

NIB	Exc.	V.G.	Good	Fair	Poor
800	700	500	400	300	150

Upland King

As above, in 12 or 16 gauge with ventilated rib barrels.

NIB	Exc.	V.G.	Good	Fair	Poor
1000	800	700	600	400	250

Vandalia

A 12 gauge single barrel trap gun with a 32" full choked barrel. Blued with a walnut stock.

NIB	Exc.	V.G.	Good	Fair	Poor
700	600	550	450	300	150

Sterlingworth II

Identical to the Woodlander, but with sidelocks.

NIB	Exc.	V.G.	Good	Fair	Poor
850	700	550	450	300	150

Victor Special

A 12 gauge boxlock double barrel shotgun with 25", 28", or 30" barrels, double triggers and extractors. Blued with a walnut stock.

NIB	Exc.	V.G.	Good	Fair	Poor
450	400	300	250	175	100

Thunderbird

A 10 gauge Magnum boxlock double barrel shotgun with 32" full choked barrels, double triggers, and automatic ejectors. Blued with a walnut stock.

NIB	Exc.	V.G.	Good	Fair	Poor
900	700	600	500	400	200

Honker

A 10 gauge Magnum single barrel shotgun with a 36" full choked and ventilated rib barrel. Blued with a walnut stock.

NIB	Exc.	V.G.	Good	Fair	Poor
500	450	400	300	200	100

ZOLI USA, ANGELO
Brescia, Italy

Slide Action Shotgun

A 12 gauge Magnum slide action shotgun produced with a variety of barrel lengths with detachable choke tubes. Blued with a walnut stock.

NIB	Exc.	V.G.	Good	Fair	Poor
350	300	250	200	150	100

Diano I

A 12, 20 or .410 bore single-shot folding barrel shotgun. Produced in a variety of barrel lengths. Blued with a walnut stock.

NIB	Exc.	V.G.	Good	Fair	Poor
125	100	90	80	60	40

Diano II

As above, but with a bottom lever instead of a top release lever.

NIB	Exc.	V.G.	Good	Fair	Poor
125	100	90	80	60	40

Apache

A 12 gauge Magnum lever action shotgun with a 20" barrel fitted with detachable choke tubes. Blued with a walnut stock.

NIB	Exc.	V.G.	Good	Fair	Poor
450	400	350	300	250	150

Quail Special

A .410 Magnum bore double barrel shotgun with 28" barrels and a single trigger. Blued with a walnut stock.

NIB	Exc.	V.G.	Good	Fair	Poor
225	175	150	125	100	75

Falcon II

As above with 26" or 28" barrels and double triggers.

NIB	Exc.	V.G.	Good	Fair	Poor
225	175	150	125	100	75

Pheasant

A 12 gauge Magnum double barrel shotgun with 28" barrels, single trigger, and automatic ejectors. Blued with a walnut stock.

NIB	Exc.	V.G.	Good	Fair	Poor
400	350	300	250	200	150

Classic

As above, with 26" to 30" barrels fitted with detachable choke tubes, single selective trigger, and automatic ejectors. Blued with a walnut stock.

NIB	Exc.	V.G.	Good	Fair	Poor
850	700	600	500	300	200

Snipe

A .410 bore Over/Under shotgun with 26" or 28" barrels and a single trigger.

NIB	Exc.	V.G.	Good	Fair	Poor
275	225	200	175	150	100

Dove

Similar to the above.

NIB	Exc.	V.G.	Good	Fair	Poor
275	225	200	175	150	100

Texas

A 12, 20 or .410 bore Over/Under shotgun with 26" or 28" barrels, double triggers, and a bottom barrel release lever.

NIB	Exc.	V.G.	Good	Fair	Poor
300	250	200	150	100	75

Field Special

A 12 or 20 gauge Magnum double barrel shotgun produced in a variety of barrel lengths with a single trigger and extractors. Blued with a walnut stock.

NIB	Exc.	V.G.	Good	Fair	Poor
500	400	300	250	200	100

Pigeon Model

As above, but more finely finished.

NIB	Exc.	V.G.	Good	Fair	Poor
500	400	300	250	200	100

Standard Model

Similar to the above but in 12 and 20 gauge only.

NIB	Exc.	V.G.	Good	Fair	Poor
450	400	300	250	200	100

Special Model

As above, with detachable choke tubes and a single selective trigger.

NIB	Exc.	V.G.	Good	Fair	Poor
500	400	300	250	200	100

Deluxe Model

As above, but engraved and with better quality walnut.

NIB	Exc.	V.G.	Good	Fair	Poor
700	600	500	400	300	150

Presentation Model

As above, with false sidelocks and finely figured walnut stock.

NIB	Exc.	V.G.	Good	Fair	Poor
800	700	600	450	350	200

St. George's Target

A 12 gauge Over/Under shotgun trap or skeet bore with various length barrels, single selective trigger, and automatic ejectors. Blued with a walnut stock.

NIB	Exc.	V.G.	Good	Fair	Poor
1000	850	700	600	550	250

St. George Competition

A 12 gauge single barrel gun with an extra set of over and under barrels.

NIB	Exc.	V.G.	Good	Fair	Poor
1750	1600	1200	950	500	300

Express Rifle

A .30-06, 7x65Rmm or 9.3x74Rmm Over/Under double barrel rifle with single triggers and automatic ejectors. Blued with a walnut stock.

NIB	Exc.	V.G.	Good	Fair	Poor
4000	3500	2500	1750	1200	600

Express EM

As above, but more finely finished.

NIB	Exc.	V.G.	Good	Fair	Poor
5000	4000	3000	1500	1000	750

Savana E

As above, with double triggers.

NIB	Exc.	V.G.	Good	Fair	Poor
6000	5250	4500	3500	2750	1500

Savana Deluxe

As above, but engraved with hunting scenes.

NIB	Exc.	V.G.	Good	Fair	Poor
8000	7000	6000	4750	3500	2000

AZ 1900C

A .243, .270, 6.5x55mm, .308, or .30-06 bolt action rifle with a 24" barrel having open sights. Blued with a walnut stock.

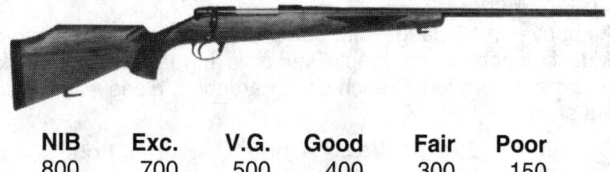

NIB	Exc.	V.G.	Good	Fair	Poor
800	700	500	400	300	150

AZ 1900M

Same as above but fitted with a Bell & Carlson composite stock.

NIB	Exc.	V.G.	Good	Fair	Poor
700	600	450	350	275	200

AZ 1900 Deluxe

As above, but more finely finished.

NIB	Exc.	V.G.	Good	Fair	Poor
950	800	650	500	400	200

AZ 1900 Super Deluxe

As above, but engraved with a finely figured walnut stock.

NIB	Exc.	V.G.	Good	Fair	Poor
1350	1000	800	600	450	250

Patricia Model

As above, in .410 Magnum bore with 28" ventilated rib barrels, various chokes, single selective trigger, and automatic ejectors. Engraved, blued with finely figured walnut stock.

NIB	Exc.	V.G.	Good	Fair	Poor
1300	1100	950	750	650	400

Condor

A .30-06 or .308 and 12 gauge Over/Under combination shotgun rifle with double triggers, extractors and sling swivels. Blued with a walnut stock.

NIB	Exc.	V.G.	Good	Fair	Poor
1250	1050	850	700	500	300

Airone

As above, with false sidelocks.

NIB	Exc.	V.G.	Good	Fair	Poor
1500	1250	1000	800	600	300

Leopard Express

A .30-06, .308, 7x65Rmm, or .375 Holland & Holland Over/Under double barrel rifle with 24" barrels having express sights, double triggers and extractors. Blued with a walnut stock.

NIB	Exc.	V.G.	Good	Fair	Poor
1500	1250	1000	800	600	300

ZOLI, ANTONIO
Brescia, Italy

Silver Hawk

A 12 or 20 gauge boxlock double barrel shotgun produced in a variety of barrel lengths and chokes with a double trigger. Engraved, blued with walnut stock.

NIB	Exc.	V.G.	Good	Fair	Poor
450	400	350	300	250	100

Ariete M2

A 12 gauge boxlock double barrel shotgun with 26" or 28" barrels, non-selective single trigger and automatic ejectors. Engraved, blued with a walnut stock.

NIB	Exc.	V.G.	Good	Fair	Poor
600	500	450	400	350	200

Empire

As above, in 12 or 20 gauge with 27" or 28" barrels. Engraved, French case hardened, blued with a walnut stock.

NIB	Exc.	V.G.	Good	Fair	Poor
1650	1450	1200	950	750	400

Volcano Record

A 12 gauge sidelock double barrel shotgun with 28" barrels available in a variety of chokes, single selective trigger and automatic ejectors. Engraved, French case hardened, blued with a walnut stock.

NIB	Exc.	V.G.	Good	Fair	Poor
5500	5000	4000	3000	2000	1000

Volcano Record ELM

This model is strictly a custom-ordered shotgun produced to the purchaser's specifications. A qualified appraisal is suggested prior to acquisition.

NIB	Exc.	V.G.	Good	Fair	Poor
14000	11500	8500	6500	3500	1500

Silver Snipe

A 12 or 20 gauge Over/Under shotgun produced with varying lengths, ventilated rib barrels, single trigger and extractors. Engraved, blued with a walnut stock.

NIB	Exc.	V.G.	Good	Fair	Poor
500	450	400	325	275	150

Golden Snipe

As above, but more finely finished and fitted with automatic ejectors.

NIB	Exc.	V.G.	Good	Fair	Poor
600	500	450	350	300	150

Delfino

As above, in 12 or 20 gauge Magnum with 26" or 28" ventilated rib barrels, non-selective single trigger and automatic ejectors. Engraved, blued with walnut stock.

NIB	Exc.	V.G.	Good	Fair	Poor
525	425	325	275	250	150

Ritmo Hunting Gun

As above, in 12 gauge Magnum with 26" or 28" separated ventilated rib barrels, single selective trigger and automatic ejectors. Engraved, blued with a walnut stock.

NIB	Exc.	V.G.	Good	Fair	Poor
600	500	450	400	350	200

Condor Model

As above, in 12 gauge with 28" skeet bored barrels having a wide competition rib, single selective trigger and automatic ejectors. Engraved, French case hardened, blued with a walnut stock.

NIB	Exc.	V.G.	Good	Fair	Poor
850	800	650	500	400	200

Angel Model

As above, in a field grade version.

NIB	Exc.	V.G.	Good	Fair	Poor
900	800	600	500	400	200

Ritmo Pigeon Grade IV

As above, with 28" separated ventilated rib barrels, single selective trigger, automatic ejectors and extensively engraved. French case hardened, blued with a finely figured walnut stock.

NIB	Exc.	V.G.	Good	Fair	Poor
1800	1600	1200	800	600	300

Model 208 Target

As above, with 28" or 30" trap or skeet bored barrels fitted with a wide ventilated rib.

NIB	Exc.	V.G.	Good	Fair	Poor
1000	850	700	600	500	250

Model 308 Target

As above, but more finely finished.

NIB	Exc.	V.G.	Good	Fair	Poor
1400	1100	850	700	500	250

Combinato

A .222 or .243 and 12 or 20 gauge Over/Under combination rifle/shotgun with an engraved boxlock action, double triggers, and a folding rear sight. French case hardened, blued with a walnut stock.

NIB	Exc.	V.G.	Good	Fair	Poor
1700	1250	950	850	600	300

Safari Deluxe

As above, but with false sidelocks that are engraved with scrolls or hunting scenes.

NIB	Exc.	V.G.	Good	Fair	Poor
5000	4000	2850	1500	1200	650

ZULAICA, M.
Eibar, Spain

Zulaica

A solid-frame .22 caliber revolver having a 6-shot cylinder that has zigzag grooves on its exterior surface. It is fired by an external hammer and the frame is hollow with a rod inside of it that connects to the breechblock. There is a serrated cocking piece connected to this rod that is found at the top rear of the frame. When fired, the cartridge case blows from the cylinder and activates the breechblock similar to a semiautomatic pistol.

Exc.	V.G.	Good	Fair	Poor
750	600	500	350	250

ROYAL

The name Royal was applied to a number of pistols produced by this company, as noted below.

Royal

A 6.35mm or 7.65mm semiautomatic pistol that is normally marked on the slide "Automatic Pistol 6.35 Royal" or "Automatic Pistol 7.65 Royal".

Exc.	V.G.	Good	Fair	Poor
175	125	100	75	50

Royal

As above, in 7.65mm caliber with a 5.5" barrel and 12-shot magazine.

Exc.	V.G.	Good	Fair	Poor
200	150	125	100	75

Royal

A rather poor copy of the Mauser Model C/96 semiautomatic pistol with fixed lockwork.

Exc.	V.G.	Good	Fair	Poor
600	500	400	300	150

Vincitor

A 6.35mm or 7.65mm caliber semiautomatic pistol patterned after the Model 1906 Browning. The slide marked "SA Royal Vincitor". Blued with plastic grips.

Exc.	V.G.	Good	Fair	Poor
175	150	125	100	75

FIREARMS TRADE NAMES

A.A. Co.: Inexpensive pocket revolvers of unknown manufacture.

Acme:
a) Trade name used by the W.H. Davenport Firearms Company on shotguns.
b) Trade name used by the Hopkins and Allen Company on revolvers produced for the Merwin, Hulbert and Company and the Herman Boker Company of New York.
c) Trade name used by the Maltby, Henley and Company of New York on inexpensive pocket revolvers.

Acme Arms Company: Trade name used by the J. Stevens Arms and Tool Company on pistols and shotguns produced for the Cornwall Hardware Company of New York.

N.R. Adams: Trade name used by the N.R. Davis and Company on shotguns.

Aetna: Trade name used by the firm of Harrington and Richardson on inexpensive pocket revolvers.

Alamo Ranger: The name found on inexpensive Spanish revolvers.

Alaska: Trade name used by the Hood Firearms Company on inexpensive pocket revolvers.

Alert: Trade name used by the Hood Firearms Company on inexpensive pocket revolvers.

Alexander Gun Company: Trade name believed to have been used by E.K. Tryon of Philadelphia on imported shotguns.

Alexis: Trade name used by the Hood Firearms Company on inexpensive pocket revolvers.

Allen 22: Trade name used by the Hopkins and Allen Company on inexpensive pocket revolvers.

America: Trade name used by the Crescent Firearms Company on inexpensive pocket revolvers.

American: Trade name used by the Ely and Wray on inexpensive pocket revolvers.

American Barlock Wonder: Trade name used by the H. & D. Folsom Arms Company on Shotguns made for the Sears, Roebuck Company of Chicago.

American Boy: Trade name used on firearms retailed by the Townley Metal and Hardware Company of Kansas City, Missouri.

American Bulldog: Trade name used by the Iver Johnson Arms and Cycle Works on inexpensive pocket revolvers.

American Bulldog Revolver: Trade name used by Harrington and Richardson Arms Company on an inexpensive pocket revolver.

American Eagle: Trade name used by the Hopkins and Allen Company on inexpensive pocket revolvers.

American Gun Company: Trade name used by H. & D. Folsom Arms Company on pistols and shotguns that firm retailed.

American Gun Barrel Company: Trade name used by R. Avis of West Haven, Connecticut, between 1916 and 1920.

American Nitro: Trade name used by H. & D. Folsom Arms Co. on shotguns.

Americus: Trade name used by the Hopkins and Allen Company on inexpensive pocket revolvers.

Angel: Trade name found on inexpensive pocket revolvers of unknown manufacture.

The Arab: Trade name used by the Harrington and Richardson Arms Company on shotguns.

Aristocrat:
a) Trade name used by the Hopkins and Allen Company on inexpensive pocket revolvers.
b) Trade name used by the Supplee-Biddle Hardware Company of Philadelphia on firearms they retailed.

Armory Gun Company: Trade name used by H. & D. Folsom Arms Co. on shotguns.

Aubrey Shotgun: Trade name found on shotguns made for the Sears, Roebuck and Company of Chicago by Albert Aubrey of Meriden, Connecticut.

Audax: Trade name used by the Manufacture d'Armes Pyrenees on semiautomatic pistols.

Aurora: Trade name found on inexpensive Spanish semiautomatic pistols.

Autogarde: Trade name used by the Societe Francaise des Munitions on semiautomatic pistols.

Automatic:
a) Trade name used by the Forehand and Wadsworth Company on inexpensive pocket revolvers.
b) Trade name used by the Harrington and Richardson Arms Company on inexpensive pocket revolvers.
c) Trade name used by the Iver Johnson Arms and Cycle Works on inexpensive pocket revolvers.

Auto Stand: Trade name used by the Manufacture Francaise d'Armes et Cycles, St. Etiene on semiautomatic pistols.

Avenger: Trade name found on inexpensive pocket revolvers of unknown manufacture.

Baby Hammerless: Trade mark used successively by Henry Kolb and R.F. Sedgley on pocket revolvers they manufactured.

Baby Russian: Trade name used by the American Arms Company on revolvers they manufactured.

Baker Gun Company: Trade name used by the H. & D. Folsom Arms Company on shotguns they retailed.

Baker Gun and Forging Company: Trade name used by the H. & D. Folsom Arms Company on shotguns they retailed.

Bang: Trade name found on inexpensive pocket revolvers of unknown manufacture.

Bang Up: Trade name used on inexpensive pocket revolvers retailed by the Graham and Haines Company of New York.

T. Barker: Trade name used by the H. & D. Folsom Arms Company of New York on shotguns they retailed.

Bartlett Field: Trade name used on shotguns retailed by Hibbard, Spencer, Bartlett and Company of Chicago.

Batavia: Trade name used on shotguns produced by the Baker Gun Company.

Batavia Leader: Trade name used on shotguns produced by the Baker Gun Company.

Bay State: Trade name used by the Harrington and Richardson Arms Company on both inexpensive pocket revolvers and shotguns.

Belknap: Trade name used by the Belknap Hardware Company of Louisville, Kentucky, on shotguns made by the Crescent Fire Arms Company, which they retailed.

Bellmore Gun Company: Trade name used by the H. & D. Folsom Arms Company on shotguns made for them by the Crescent Fire Arms Company.

Berkshire: Trade name used by the H. & D. Folsom Arms Company on shotguns made for the Shapleigh Hardware Company of St. Louis, Missouri.

Bicycle: Trade name used on firearms made by the Harrington and Richardson Arms Company.

Big All Right: Trade name used on shotguns manufactured by the Wright Arms Company.

Big Bonanza: Trade name found on inexpensive pocket revolvers of unknown manufacture.

Bismarck: Trade name found on inexpensive pocket revolvers of unknown manufacture.

Black Beauty: Trade name used by the Sears, Roebuck and Company on imported shotguns they retailed.

Black Diamond: Trade name found on Belgian made shotguns retailed by an unknown American wholesale house.

Black Diana: Trade name used by the Baker Gun Company on shotguns.

Blackfield: Trade name used by the Hibbard, Spencer, Bartlett and Company of Chicago on shotguns they retailed.

Blackhawk: Trade name found on inexpensive pocket revolvers of unknown manufacture.

Black Prince: Trade name used by the Hopkins and Allen Company on inexpensive pocket revolvers.

Bliss: Trade name believed to have been used by the Norwich Arms Company.

Blood Hound: Trade name found on inexpensive pocket revolvers of unknown manufacture.

Bluefield: Trade name used by the W.H. Davenport Firearms Company on shotguns.

Bluegrass: Trade name used by the Belknap Hardware Company of Louisville, Kentucky, on shotguns they retailed.

Bluegrass Arms Company: Trade name of shotguns made by H. & D. Folsom Arms Co. for Belknap Hardware of Louisville, Kentucky.

Blue Jacket: Trade name used by the Hopkins and Allen Company on inexpensive pocket revolvers they made for the Merwin, Hulbert and Company of New York.

Blue Leader: Trade name found on inexpensive pocket revolvers of unknown manufacture.

Blue Whistler: Trade name used by the Hopkins and Allen Company on inexpensive pocket revolvers they made for the Merwin, Hulbert and Company of New York.

Bogardus Club Gun: Trade name found on Belgian made shotguns retailed by an unknown American wholesaler (possibly B. Kittredge and Company of Cincinnati, Ohio).

Boltun: Trade name used by F. Arizmendi on semiautomatic pistols.

Bonanza: Trade name used by the Bacon Arms Company on inexpensive pocket revolvers.

Boom: Trade name used by the Shattuck Arms Company on inexpensive pocket revolvers.

Daniel Boone Gun Company: Trade name used by the Belknap Hardware Company of Louisville, Kentucky, on firearms they retailed.

Boone Gun Company: Trade name used by the Belknap Hardware Company of Louisville, Kentucky, on firearms they retailed.

Boss:
a) Trade name used by E.H. and A.A. Buckland of Springfield, Massachusetts, on single-shot derringers designed by Holt & Marshall.
b) Trade name used on inexpensive pocket revolvers of unknown American manufacture.

Boys Choice: Trade name used by the Hood Firearms Company on inexpensive pocket revolvers.

Bride Black Prince: Trade name used by H. & D. Folsom Arms Co. on shotguns.

Bridge Gun Company: Registered trade name of the Shapleigh Hardware Company, St. Louis, Missouri.

Bridgeport Arms Company: Trade name used by H. & D. Folsom Arms Co. on shotguns.

Bright Arms Company: Trade name used by H. & D. Folsom Arms Company

British Bulldog: Trade name found on inexpensive pocket revolvers of unknown American and English manufacture.

Brownie:
a) Trade name used by the W.H. Davenport Firearms Company on shotguns.
b) Trade name used by the O.F. Mossberg Firearms Company on a four-shot pocket pistol.

Brutus: Trade name used by the Hood Firearms Company on inexpensive pocket revolvers.

Buckeye: Trade name used by the Hopkins and Allen Company on inexpensive pocket revolvers.

Buffalo: Trade name used by Gabilongo y Urresti on semiautomatic pistols.
Buffalo: Trade name found on bolt action rifles made in France.
Buffalo: Trade name used by the Western Arms Company on an inexpensive pocket revolver.
Buffalo Bill: Trade name used by the Iver Johnson Arms and Cycle Works on an inexpensive pocket revolver.
Buffalo Stand: Trade name used by the Manufacture Francaise d'Armes et Cycles on target pistols.
Bull Dog: Trade name used by the Forehand and Wadsworth Company on inexpensive pocket revolvers.
Bull Dozer:
a) Trade name used by the Norwich Pistol Company on inexpensive pocket revolvers.
b) Trade name used by the Forehand and Wadsworth Company on inexpensive pocket revolvers.
c) Trade name on Hammond Patent pistols made by the Connecticut Arms and Manufacturing Company.
Bull Frog: Trade name used by the Hopkins and Allen Company on rifles.
Bulls Eye: Trade name used by the Norwich Falls Pistol Company (O.A. Smith) on inexpensive pocket revolvers.
Burdick: Trade name used by the H. & D. Folsom Arms Company on shotguns made for the Sears, Roebuck and Company of Chicago.
General Butler: Trade name found on inexpensive pocket revolvers of unknown manufacture.
Cadet: Trade name used by the Crescent Firearms Company on rifles.
Canadian Belle: Trade name used by H. & D. Folsom Arms Co. on shotguns.
Cannon Breech: Trade name used by the Hopkins and Allen Company on shotguns.
Captain: Trade name used by Manufacture d'Armes de Pyrenees on semiautomatic pistols.
Captain Jack: Trade name used by Hopkins & Allen on inexpensive pocket revolvers.
Carolina Arms Company: Trade name used by the H. & D. Folsom Arms Company on shotguns produced for the Smith, Wadsworth Hardware Company of Charlotte, North Carolina.
Caroline Arms: Trade name used by the H. & D. Folsom Arms Co.
Caruso: Trade name used by the Crescent Firearms Company on shotguns made for the Hibbard, Spencer, Bartlett and Company of Chicago.
Centennial 1876:
a) Trade name used by the Deringer Pistol Company on inexpensive pocket revolvers.
b) Trade name used by the Hood Firearms Company on inexpensive pocket revolvers.
Central Arms Company: Trade name used by the W. H. Davenport Firearms Company on shotguns made for the Shapleigh Hardware Company of St. Louis, Missouri.
Century Arms Company: Trade name used by the W. H. Davenport Firearms Company on shotguns made for the Shapleigh Hardware Company of St. Louis, Missouri.
Challenge:
a) Trade name found on inexpensive pocket revolvers of unknown manufacture.
b) Trade name used by the Sears, Roebuck and Company of Chicago on shotguns made by Albert Aubrey of Meriden, Connecticut.
Challenge Ejector: Trade name used by the Sears, Roebuck and Company of Chicago on shotguns made by Albert Aubrey of Meriden, Connecticut.
Champion:
a) Trade name used by H.C. Squires on shotguns.
b) Trade name used by J.P. Lovell on shotguns.
c) Trade name used by the Iver Johnson Arms and Cycle Works on shotguns and inexpensive pocket revolvers.
d) Trade name used by the Norwich Arms Company on inexpensive pocket revolvers.

Chantecler: Trade name used by Manufacture d'Armes de Pyrenees on semiautomatic pistols.
Chatham Arms Company: Trade name used by H. & D. Folsom Arms Company used on shotguns.
Cherokee Arms Company: Trade name used by the H. & D. Folsom Arms Company on shotguns made for C.M. McLung and Company of Knoxville, Tennessee.
Chesapeake Gun Company: Trade name used by the H. & D. Folsom Arms Company of New York.
Chicago: Trade name found on shotguns retailed by the Hibbard, Spencer, Bartlett and Company of Chicago.
Chicago Ledger: Trade name used by the Chicago Firearms Company on inexpensive pocket revolvers.
Chicago Long Range Wonder: Trade name used by the H. & D. Folsom Arms Company on shotguns made for the Sears, Roebuck and Company of Chicago.
Chichester: Trade name used by Hopkins & Allen on inexpensive pocket revolvers.
Chicopee Arms Company: Trade name used by the H. & D. Folsom Arms Company of New York.
Chieftan: Trade name found on inexpensive pocket revolvers of unknown manufacture.
Christian Protector: Trade name found on inexpensive pocket revolvers of unknown manufacture.
Climax XL: Trade name used by Herman Boker and Company of New York on revolvers, rifles and shotguns.
Club Gun: Trade name used by B. Kittredge and Company of Cincinnati, Ohio, on shotguns they retailed.
Cock Robin: Trade name used by the Hood Firearms Company on inexpensive pocket revolvers.
Colonial: Trade name used by Manufacture d'Armes de Pyrenees on semiautomatic pistols.
Colonial: Trade name used by H. & D. Folsom Company on shotguns.
Columbian Automatic: Trade name used by Foehl & Weeks on inexpensive pocket revolvers.
Colton Arms Company: Trade name used by the Shapleigh Hardware Company of St. Louis, Missouri, on imported shotguns they retailed.
Colton Firearms Company: Trade name used by the Sears, Roebuck and Company of Chicago on shotguns they retailed.
Columbia:
a) Trade name found on inexpensive pocket revolvers of unknown manufacture.
b) Trade name used by H.C. Squires on shotguns.
Columbia Arms Company: Registered trade name of Henry Keidel, Baltimore, Maryland.
Columbian: Trade name found on inexpensive pocket revolvers of unknown manufacture.
Columbian Firearms Company:
a) Trade name used by the Maltby, Henly and Company on inexpensive pocket revolvers.
b) Trade name used by the Crescent Firearms Company on shotguns.
Combat: Trade name used by Randall Firearms Co. for its service model with a flat rib top and fixed sights.
Comet: Trade name used by the Prescott Pistol Company on inexpensive pocket revolvers.
Commander: Trade name used by the Norwich Arms Company on inexpensive pocket revolvers.
Commercial: Trade name used by the Norwich Falls Pistol Company (O.A. Smith) on inexpensive pocket revolvers.
Compeer: Trade name used by the H. & D. Folsom Arms Company on firearms made for the Van Camp Hardware and Iron Company of Indianapolis, Indiana.
Competition: Trade name used by John Meunier of Milwaukee, Wisconsin, on rifles.

Conestoga Rifle Works: Trade name of Henry Leman, Philadelphia, Pennsylvania.
Connecticut Arms Company: Trade name used by H. & D. Folsom Arms Company on shotguns.
Constable: Trade name used by Astra on semiautomatic pistols.
Constabulary: Trade name used by L. Ancion-Marx of Liege on revolvers.
Continental: Trade name used by the Great Western Gun Works of Pittsburgh, Pennsylvania, on firearms they retailed.
Continental Arms Company: Trade name used by the Marshall Wells Company of Duluth, Minnesota, on firearms they retailed.
Cotton King: Trade name found on inexpensive pocket revolvers of unknown manufacture.
Cowboy: Trade name used by the Hibbard, Spencer, Bartlett and Company of Chicago on imported, inexpensive pocket revolvers they retailed.
Cowboy Ranger: Trade name used by the Rohde Spencer Company of Chicago on inexpensive pocket revolvers.
Crack Shot: Trade name used by the J. Stevens Arms and Tool Company on rifles.
Cracker Jack: Trade name used by the J. Stevens Arms and Tool Company on pistols.
Creedmoore:
a) Trade name used by the Hopkins and Allen Company on inexpensive pocket revolvers.
b) Trade name used by the Chicago Firearms Company on inexpensive pocket revolvers.
c) Trade name used by William Wurflein on rifles.
Creedmoore Armory: Trade name used by A.D. McAusland of Omaha, Nebraska on rifles.
Creedmoore Arms Company: Trade name found on imported shotguns retailed by an unknown American wholesaler.
Crescent: Trade name used by the Crescent Arms Company on inexpensive pocket revolvers.
Crescent International 1XL: Trade name used by Herman Boker and Company of New York on shotguns.
Creve Coeur: Trade name used by the Isaac Walker Hardware Company of Peoria, Illinois, on imported shotguns they retailed.
Crown: Trade name used by the Harrington and Richardson Arms Company on inexpensive pocket revolvers.
Crown Jewel: Trade name used by the Norwich Arms Company on inexpensive pocket revolvers.
Cruso: Trade name used by the H. & D. Folsom Arms Company on shotguns made for Hibbard, Spencer, Bartlett and Company of Chicago.
Cumberland Arms Company: Trade name used by the H. & D. Folsom Arms Company on shotguns made for the Gray and Dudley Hardware Company of Nashville, Tennessee.
Czar:
a) Trade name used by the Hopkins and Allen Company on inexpensive pocket revolvers.
b) Trade name used by the Hood Firearms Company on inexpensive pocket revolvers.
Daisy:
a) Trade name used by the Bacon Arms Company on inexpensive pocket revolvers.
b) Registered proprietary trade name engraved on firearms made by the Winchester Repeating Arms Company for the F. Lassetter and Company, Limited of Sydney, Australia.
Daniel Boone Gun Company: Trade name used by H. & D. Folsom Arms Company on shotguns made for Belknap Hardware Company of Louisville, Kentucky.
Daredevel: Trade name used by Lou J. Eppinger of Detroit, Michigan, on pistols.
Dash: Trade name found on inexpensive pocket revolvers of unknown manufacture.
Davis Guns: Trade names used successively by N.R. Davis, Davis Warner, and the Crescent-Davis Arms Company on various firearms.

Dead Shot:
a) Trade name found on inexpensive pocket revolvers of unknown manufacture.
b) Trade name used by the Meriden Firearms Company on rifles.

Deer Slayer: Trade name used by J. Henry and Son of Boulton, Pennsylvania on rifles.

Defender:
a) Trade name used by the Iver Johnson Arms and Cycle Works on inexpensive pocket revolvers.
b) Trade name used by the U.S. Small Arms Company on knife pistols.

Defiance: Trade name used by the Norwich Arms Company on inexpensive pocket revolvers.

Delphian Arms Company:
a) Trade name used by the Supplee-Biddle Hardware Company of Philadelphia, Pennsylvania, on shotguns they retailed that were supplied by the H. & D. Folsom Company of New York.
b) Trade name used by the H. & D. Folsom Arms Company of New York on shotguns.

Delphian Manufacturing Company: Trade name used by the H. & D. Folsom Arms Company of New York on shotguns.

Demon: Trade name used by Manufacture d'Armes de Pyrenees on semiautomatic pistols.

Demon Marine: As above.

Dexter: Trade name found on inexpensive pocket revolvers of unknown manufacture.

Diamond Arms Company: Trade name used by the Shapleigh Hardware Company of St. Louis, Missouri, on imported shotguns they retailed.

Dictator: Trade name used by the Hopkins and Allen Company on inexpensive pocket revolvers.

Dominion Pistol: Trade name found on inexpensive pocket revolvers of unknown manufacture.

Double Header: Trade name used by E.S. Renwick on Perry and Goddard Patent derringers.

Douglas Arms Company: Trade name used by the Hopkins and Allen Company on shotguns.

Dreadnought: Trade name used by the Hopkins and Allen Company on shotguns and inexpensive pocket revolvers.

Duchess: Trade name used by the Hopkins and Allen Company on inexpensive pocket revolvers.

Duke: Trade name found on inexpensive pocket revolvers which may have been made by the Hopkins and Allen Company.

Dunlop Special: Trade name used by the Davis Warner Arms Company on shotguns made for the Dunlop Hardware Company of Macon, Georgia.

Duplex: Trade name used by the Osgood Gun Works of Norwich, Connecticut.

E.B.A.C.: Trade name used by Manufacture d'Armes de Pyrenees on semiautomatic pistols.

Eagle: Trade name used by the Iver Johnson Arms and Cycle Works on inexpensive pocket revolvers.

Eagle Arms Company: Trade name used by the Iver Johnson Arms and Cycle Works on inexpensive pocket revolvers.

Earlhood: Trade name used by E.L. Dickinson on inexpensive pocket revolvers.

Earnest Companion: Trade name found on inexpensive pocket revolvers of unknown manufacture.

Earthquake: Trade name used by E.L. Dickinson on inexpensive pocket revolvers.

Eastern Arms Company: Trade name used by the Sears, Roebuck and Company of Chicago on both shotguns and inexpensive revolvers made by the Iver Johnson Arms and Cycle Works.

Eclipse:
a) Trade name found on single-shot derringers of unknown manufacture.
b) Trade name used by E.C. Meacham on imported shotguns.

Electric: Trade name found on inexpensive pocket revolvers of unknown manufacture.

Electric City Single Hammer: Trade name found on single-shot shotguns retailed by the Wyeth Hardware and Manufacturing Company of St. Joseph, Missouri.

Elector: Trade name found on inexpensive pocket revolvers of unknown manufacture.

Elgin Arms Company: Trade name used by the H. & D. Folsom Arms Company on shotguns made for the Strauss and Schram Company of Chicago.

Elita: Trade name used by the W.H. Davenport Fire Arms Company on shotguns.

Empire:
a) Trade name used by the Rupertus Patented Pistol Manufacturing Company on inexpensive pocket revolvers.
b) Trade name used by the Crescent Firearms Company on shotguns.

Empire Arms Company: Trade name used by the H. & D. Folsom Arms Company on firearms made for the Sears, Roebuck and Company of Chicago.

Enders Royal Shotgun: Trade name used by the Crescent Davis Firearms Company on shotguns made for the Simmons Hardware Company of St. Louis, Missouri.

Enders Special Service: Trade name used by the Crescent Davis Firearms Company on shotguns made for the Simmons Hardware Company of St. Louis, Missouri.

Enterprise: Trade name used by the Enterprise Gun Works on inexpensive pocket revolvers.

Essex Gun Works: Trade name used by the Crescent - Davis Firearms Company on shotguns made for the Belknap Hardware Company of Louisville, Kentucky.

Eureka: Trade name used by the Iver Johnson Arms and Cycle Works on inexpensive pocket revolvers.

Excel: Trade name used by both the H. & D. Folsom Arms Company and the Iver Johnson Arms and Cycle Works on shotguns made for the Montgomery Ward and Company of Chicago.

Excelsior:
a) Trade name found on inexpensive pocket revolvers of unknown manufacture.
b) Trade name used by the Iver Johnson Arms and Cycle Works on shotguns.

Expert:
a) Trade name found on single-shot derringers of unknown manufacture.
b) Trade name used by the W.J. Davenport Firearms Company on shotguns made for the Witte Hardware Company of St. Louis, Missouri.

Express: Trade name used by the Bacon Arms Company on inexpensive pocket revolvers.

Express: Trade name used by Tomas de Urizar on a variety of semiautomatic pistols.

Farwell Arms Company: Trade name used by the Farwell, Ozmun, Kirk and Company of St. Paul, Minnesota, on shotguns.

Fashion: Trade name found on inexpensive pocket revolvers of unknown manufacture.

Faultless: Trade name used by the H. & D. Folsom Arms Company on shotguns made for the John M. Smythe Merchandise Company of Chicago.

Faultless Goose Gun: Trade name used by the H. & D. Folsom Arms Company on shotguns made for the John M. Smythe Merchandise Company of Chicago.

Favorite:
a) Trade name used by the J. Stevens Arms and Tool Company on rifles.
b) Trade name used by the Iver Johnson Arms and Cycle Works on inexpensive pocket revolvers.

Favorite Navy: Trade name used by the Iver Johnson Arms and Cycle Works on inexpensive pocket revolvers.

Featherlight: Trade name used by the Sears, Roebuck and Company of Chicago on firearms they retailed.

Federal Arms Company: Trade name used by Meriden Firearms Company.

Folks Gun Works: Trade name of William and Samuel Folk of Bryan, Ohio on rifles and shotguns.

Freemont Arms Company: Trade name found on shotguns distributed by an unknown retailer.

Frontier: Trade name used by the Norwich Falls Pistol Company (O.A. Smith) on inexpensive pocket revolvers made for the firm of Maltby, Curtis and Company of New York.

Fulton: Trade name used by the Hunter Arms Company on shotguns.

Fulton Arms Company: Trade name used by the W.H. Davenport Firearms Company on shotguns.

Furor: Trade name used by Manufacture d'Armes de Pyrenees on semiautomatic pistols.

Gallia: Trade name used by Manufacture d'Armes de Pyrenees on semiautomatic pistols.

Game Getter: Registered trade mark of the Marble Arms and Manufacturing Company on combination rifle-shotguns.

Gaulois: Trade name used by Manufacture d'Armes et Cycles on squeezer type pistols (see also Mitrailleuse).

Gem:
a) Trade name used by the J. Stevens Arms and Tool Company on single-shot pocket pistols.
b) Trade name used by the Bacon Arms Company on inexpensive pocket revolvers.

General: Trade name used by the Rupertus Patented Pistol Manufacturing Company on inexpensive pocket revolvers.

Gerrish: Trade name of G.W. Gerrish of Twin Falls, Idaho, used on shotguns.

Gibralter: Trade name of Albert Aubrey on shotguns made for the Sears, Roebuck and Company of Chicago.

Gladiator: Trade name of Albert Aubrey on shotguns made for the Sears, Roebuck and Company of Chicago.

Gold Field: Trade name found on inexpensive pocket revolvers of unknown manufacture.

Gold Hibbard: Trade name used by Hibbard, Spencer, Bartlett and Company of Chicago on firearms they retailed.

Gold Medal Wonder: Trade name used by H. & D. Folsom Arms Co. on shotguns.

Governor: Trade name used by the Bacon Arms Company on inexpensive pocket revolvers.

Guardian: Trade name used by the Bacon Arms Company on inexpensive pocket revolvers.

Gut Buster: Trade name found on inexpensive pocket revolvers of unknown manufacture.

Gypsy: Trade name found on inexpensive pocket revolvers of unknown manufacture.

Half Breed: Trade name found on inexpensive pocket revolvers of unknown manufacture.

Hamilton Arms: Registered trade name of the Wiebusch and Hilger Company, New York.

Hammerless Auto Ejecting Revolver: Trade name of the Meriden Firearms Company used on revolvers made for the Sears, Roebuck and Company of New York.

Hanover Arms Co.: If no foreign proofmarks then trade name used by H. & D. Folsom Arms Company.

Hardpan: Trade name found on inexpensive American pocket revolver.

Hard Pan: Trade name used by Hood Arms Company on inexpensive pocket revolvers.

S.H. Harrington: If no foreign proofmarks then trade name used by H. & D. Folsom Arms Company.

Frank Harrison Arms Company: Trade name used by the Sickles and Preston Company of Davenport, Iowa, on firearms they retailed.

Hart Arms Company: Trade name used by a Cleveland, Ohio, wholesaler (possibly the George Worthington Company).

Hartford Arms Company: Trade name used by the H. & D. Folsom Arms on shotguns made for the Simmons Hardware Company of St. Louis, Missouri.

Harvard: Trade name used by the H. & D. Folsom Arms Company on shotguns made for the George Worthington Company of Cleveland, Ohio.

Hercules: Trade name used by the Iver Johnson Arms and Cycle Works on shotguns made for the Montgomery Ward and Company of Chicago.

Hermitage Arms Company: Trade name used by the H. & D. Folsom Arms Company on shotguns made for the Gray and Dudley Hardware Company of Nashville, Tennessee.

Hero:
a) Trade name used by the American Standard Tool Company on percussion pistols.
b) Trade name used by the Manhattan Firearms Manufacturing Company on percussion pistols.

Hexagon: Trade name used by the Sears, Roebuck and Company of Chicago on shotguns they retailed.

Hinsdale: Trade name used by the Hopkins and Allen Company on inexpensive pocket revolvers.

S. Holt Arms Company: Trade name used by the Sears, Roebuck and Company of Chicago on shotguns they retailed.

Hornet: Trade name used by the Prescott Pistol Company on inexpensive pocket revolvers.

Howard Arms Company: Trade name used by the H. & D. Folsom Arms Company on shotguns they distributed.

Hudson: Trade name used by the Hibbard, Spencer, Bartlett and Company of Chicago on shotguns they retailed.

Hunter: Trade name used by the H. & D. Folsom Arms Company on shotguns made for the Belknap Hardware Company of Louisville, Kentucky.

The Hunter: Trade name used by the Hunter Arms Company on shotguns.

Hurricane: Trade name found on inexpensive pocket revolvers of unknown manufacture.

Illinois Arms Company: Trade name used by the Rohde, Spencer Company of Chicago on firearms they retailed.

Imperial: Trade name used by the Lee Arms Company on inexpensive pocket revolvers.

Imperial Arms Company: Trade name used by the Hopkins and Allen Company on inexpensive pocket revolvers.

Infallible: Trade name used by the Lancaster Arms Company of Lancaster, Pennsylvania on shotguns they retailed.

Infallible Automatic Pistol: Trade name used by the Kirtland Brothers Company of New York on inexpensive pistols they retailed.

International:
a) Trade name found on inexpensive pocket revolvers of unknown manufacture.
b) Trade name used by E.C. Meacham on shotguns.

Interstate Arms Company: Trade name used by the H. & D. Folsom Arms Company on shotguns made for the Townley Metal and Hardware Company of Kansas City, Missouri.

I.O.A.: Trade name used by the Brown, Camp Hardware Company of Des Moines, Iowa on firearms they retailed.

Invincible: Trade name used by the Iver Johnson Arms and Cycle Works on both shotguns and inexpensive pocket revolvers.

I.X.L.:
a) Trade name used by B.J. Hart on percussion revolvers.
b) Trade name used by the W.H. Davenport Firearms Company on shotguns made for the Witte Hardware Company of St. Louis, Missouri.

Ixor: Trade name used by Manufacture d'Armes de Pyrenees on semiautomatic pistols.

J.S.T. & Company: Trade name used by the Iver Johnson Arms and Cycle Works on inexpensive pocket revolvers.

Jackson Arms Company: Trade name used by the H. & D. Folsom Arms Company on shotguns made for C.M. McLung and Company of Knoxville, Tennessee.

Jewel: Trade name used by the Hood Fire Arms Company on inexpensive pocket revolvers.

Joker: Trade name used by the Marlin Firearms Company on inexpensive pocket revolvers.

Joseph Arms Company (Norwich, Connecticut): Trade name used by H. & D. Folsom Arms Company.

Judge: Trade name found on inexpensive pocket revolvers of unknown manufacture.

Jupitor: Trade name used by Fabrique d'Armes de Grand Precision, Eibar, Spain, on semiautomatic pistols.

K.K.: Trade name used by the Hopkins and Allen Company on shotguns made for the Shapleigh Hardware Company of St. Louis, Missouri.

Keno: Trade name found on inexpensive pocket revolvers of unknown manufacture.

Kentucky: Trade name used by the Iver Johnson Arms and Cycle Works on inexpensive pocket revolvers.

Keystone Arms Company: Trade name used by the W.H. Davenport Firearms Company on shotguns made for the E.K. Tryon Company of Philadelphia, Pennsylvania.

Kill Buck: Trade name of the Enterprise Gun Works (James Bown), Pittsburgh, Pennsylvania.

Killdeer: Trade name used by the Sears, Roebuck and Company of Chicago on firearms bearing their trade name Western Arms Company.

King Nitro: Trade name used by the W.H. Davenport Firearms Company on shotguns made for the Shapleigh Hardware Company of St. Louis, Missouri.

King Pin: Trade name found on inexpensive single-shot and revolving pocket pistols.

Kingsland Gun Company: Trade name used by the H. & D. Folsom Arms Company on shotguns made for the Geller, Ward and Hasner Company of St. Louis, Missouri.

Kirk Gun Company: Trade name used by Farwell, Ozmun, and Kirk Company of St. Paul, Minnesota.

Knickerbocker: Trade name used by the Crescent-Davis Firearms Company on shotguns.

Knickerbocker Club Gun: Trade name used by Charles Godfrey of New York on imported shotguns he retailed.

Knockabout: Trade name used by the Montgomery Ward and Company of Chicago on shotguns they retailed.

Knox-All: Trade name used by the Iver Johnson Arms and Cycle Works on firearms they made for the H. & D. Folsom Arms Company of New York.

L'Agent: Trade name used by Manufacture Francaises d'Armes et Cycles on revolvers.

Lakeside: Trade name used by the H. & D. Folsom Arms Company on firearms they made for the Montgomery Ward and Company of Chicago.

Leader:
a) Trade name used by the Shattuck Arms Company on inexpensive pocket revolvers.
b) Trade name used by the Harrington and Richardson Arms Company on inexpensive pocket revolvers.

Leader Gun Company: Trade name used by the H. & D. Folsom Arms Company on shotguns they made for the Charles Williams Stores, Inc. of New York.

Le Colonial: Trade name used by Manufacture Francaises d'Armes et Cycles on revolvers.

Le Colonial: As above.

Lee's Hummer: Trade name used by the H. & D. Folsom Arms Company on firearms they made for the Lee Hardware Company of Salina, Kansas.

Lee's Special: Trade name used by the H. & D. Folsom Arms Company on firearms they made for the Lee Hardware Company of Salina, Kansas.

Le Francais: Trade name used by Manufacture Francaises d'Armes et Cycles on semiautomatic pistols.

Le Francais: As above on semiautomatic pistols.

Gen Curtis E. LeMay: Trade name used for Randall Firearms Co. for its small compact pistol made from the General's own gun.

Le Petit Forminable: Trade name used by Manufacture Francaises d'Armes et Cycles on revolvers.

Le Petit Forminable: As above on revolvers.

Le Protecteur: Trade name used by J.E. Turbiaux of Paris on squeezer pistols of the type later made by the Ames Sword Company.

Le Terrible: Trade name used by Manufacture Francaises d'Armes et Cycles on revolvers.

Liberty: Trade name used by the Norwich Falls Pistol Company (O.A. Smith) on inexpensive pocket revolvers.

Liege Gun Company: Trade name used by the Hibbard, Spencer, Bartlett and Company of Chicago on imported shotguns they retailed.

Lion: Trade name used by the Iver Johnson Arms and Cycle Works on inexpensive pocket revolvers.

Lion: Trade name used by the Iver Johnson Arms and Cycle Works on inexpensive pocket revolvers.

Little Giant: Trade name used by the Bacon Arms Company on inexpensive pocket revolvers.

Little John: Trade name used by the Hood Firearms Company on inexpensive pocket revolvers.

Little Joker: Trade name found on inexpensive pocket revolvers of unknown manufacture.

Little Pal: Registered trade name for knife pistols made by L.E. Pulhemus.

Little Pet: Trade name used by the Sears, Roebuck and Company of Chicago on inexpensive pocket revolvers they retailed.

London Revolver: Trade name found on inexpensive pocket revolvers of unknown manufacture.

Lone Star: Trade name found on inexpensive pocket revolvers of unknown manufacture.

Long Range Winner: Trade name used by the Sears, Roebuck and Company of Chicago on shotguns they retailed.

Long Range Wonder: Trade name used by the Sears, Roebuck and Company of Chicago on shotguns they retailed.

Long Tom: Trade name used by the Sears, Roebuck and Company of Chicago on shotguns they retailed.

Looking Glass: Trade name used on semiautomatic pistols of unknown Spanish manufacture.

Marquis of horne: Trade name used by Hood Arms Company on inexpensive pocket revolvers.

Mars: Trade name used by Manufacture d'Armes de Pyrenees on semiautomatic pistols.

Marshwood: Trade name used by the H. & D. Folsom Arms Company on shotguns they made for the Charles Williams Stores Inc. of New York.

Marvel: Trade name used by the J. Stevens Arms and Tool Company on various firearms.

Massachusetts Arms Company: Trade name used by both the J. Stevens Arms and Tool Company and the H. & D. Folsom Arms Company on firearms made for the Blish, Mizet and Silliman Hardware Company of Atchinson, Kansas.

Maximum: Trade name found on inexpensive pocket revolvers of unknown manufacture.

Metropolitan: Trade name used by the H. & D. Folsom Arms Company on firearms they made for the Siegal-Cooper Company of New York.

Metropolitan Police:
a) Trade name used by the Maltby, Curtiss and Company on inexpensive pocket revolvers.
b) Trade name used by the Rohde-Spencer Company of Chicago on inexpensive pocket revolvers.

Midget Hammerless: Trade name used by the Rohde-Spencer Company of Chicago on inexpensive pocket revolvers.

Mikros: Trade name used by Manufacture d'Armes de Pyrenees on semiautomatic pistols.

Minnesota Arms Company: Trade name used by the H. & D. Folsom Arms Company on shotguns they made for the Farwell, Ozmun, Kirk and Company of St. Paul, Minnesota.

Missaubi Arms Company: Trade name used by the Hunter Arms Company, possibly for the Farwell, Ozmun, Kirk and Company of St. Paul, Minnesota.

Mississippi Arms Company: Trade name used by the H. & D. Folsom Arms Company on firearms made for the Shapleigh Hardware Company of St. Louis, Missouri.

Mississippi Valley Arms Company: Trade name used by the H. & D. Folsom Arms Company on firearms made for the Shapleigh Hardware Company of St. Louis, Missouri.

Mitrailleuse: Alternate trade name of the Gaulois squeezer pistol.

Mohawk: Trade name used by the H. & D. Folsom Arms Company on firearms made for the Blish, Mizet and Silliman Hardware Company of Atchison, Kansas.

Mohegan: Trade name used by the Hood Firearms Company on inexpensive pocket revolvers.

Monarch:
a) Trade name used by the Hopkins and Allen Company on inexpensive pocket revolvers.
b) Trade name used by the Osgood Gun Works on Duplex revolvers.

Monitor:
a) Trade name used by the Whitneyville Armory on inexpensive pocket revolvers.
b) Trade name used by the H. & D. Folsom Arms Company on firearms made for the Paxton and Gallagher Company of Omaha, Nebraska.

Montgomery Arms Company: Trade name used by the H. & D. Folsom Arms Company on a variety of firearms.

Mountain Eagle: Trade name used by the Hopkins and Allen Company on inexpensive pocket revolvers.

Mount Vernon Arms Company: Trade name used by the H. & D. Folsom Arms Company on firearms made for the Carlin, Hullfish Company of Alexandria, Virginia.

My Companion: Trade name found on inexpensive pocket revolvers of unknown manufacture.

My Friend: Trade name used by James Reid of New York.

Napoleon: Trade name used by the Thomas J. Ryan Pistol Manufacturing Company of Norwich, Connecticut, on inexpensive pocket revolvers.

National Arms Company: Trade name used by the H. & D. Folsom Arms Company on firearms made both for the May Hardware Company of Washington, D.C., and the Moskowitz and Herbach Company of Philadelphia, Pennsylvania.

Nevermiss: Trade name used by the Marlin Firearms Company on single-shot pocket pistols.

New Aubrey: Trade name used by Albert Aubrey of Meriden, Connecticut, on both revolvers and shotguns made for the Sears, Roebuck and Company of Chicago.

New Britain Arms Company: Trade name used by H. & D. Folsom Arms Company.

New Defender: Trade name used by Harrington & Richardson on revolvers.

New Elgin Arms Company: Trade name used by H. & D. Folsom Arms Company.

New Empire: Trade name used by H. & D. Folsom Arms Company.

New England Arms Company: Trade name believed to have been used by Charles Godfrey on shotguns made for the Rohde-Spencer Company of Chicago.

New Era Gun Works: Trade name used by the Baker Gun Company on firearms made for an unknown retailer.

New Haven Arms Company: Trade name found on Belgian shotguns imported by either E.K. Tryon of Philadelphia or the Great Western Gun Works of Pittsburgh, Pennsylvania.

New Liberty: Trade name used by the Sears, Roebuck and Company of Chicago on inexpensive pocket revolvers they retailed.

Newport:
a) Trade name found on inexpensive pocket revolvers of unknown manufacture.
b) Trade name used by the H. & D. Folsom Arms Company on shotguns made for Hibbard, Spencer, Bartlett and Company of Chicago.

New Rival: Trade name used by the H. & D. Folsom Arms Company on firearms made for the Van Camp Hardware and Iron Company of Indianapolis, Indiana.

New Worcester: Trade name used by the Torkalson Manufacturing Company of Worcester, Massachusetts.

New York Arms Company: Trade name used by the H. & D. Folsom Arms Company on firearms made for the Garnet Carter Company of Chattanooga, Tennessee.

New York Gun Company: Trade name used by the H. & D. Folsom Arms Company on firearms made for the Garnet Carter Company of Chattanooga, Tennessee.

New York Club: Trade name used by the H. & D. Folsom Arms Company on rifles.

New York Machine Made: Trade name used by the H. & D. Folsom Arms Company.

New York Pistol Company: Trade name used by the Norwich Falls Pistol Company (O.A. Smith) on inexpensive pocket revolvers.

Nightingale: Trade name found on inexpensive pocket revolvers of unknown manufacture.

Nitro Bird: Trade name used by the Richards and Conover Hardware Company of Kansas City, Missouri.

Nitro Hunter: Trade name used by the H. & D. Folsom Arms Company on shotguns made for the Belknap Hardware Company of Louisville, Kentucky.

Nitro King: Trade name used by the Sears, Roebuck and Company of Chicago on shotguns of unknown manufacture.

Nitro Special: Trade name used by the J. Stevens Arms and Tool Company on shotguns.

Northfield Knife Company: Trade name used by the Rome Revolver and Novelty Works of Rome, New York, on inexpensive pocket revolvers.

Norwich Arms Company:
a) Trade name used by the Hood Firearms Company on inexpensive pocket revolvers.
b) Trade name found on shotguns retailed by the Marshall, Wells Company of Duluth, Minnesota, and Winnipeg, Manitoba, Canada.

Norwich Falls Pistol Company: Trade name used by the O.A. Smith Company on inexpensive pocket revolvers made for Maltby, Curtis and Company of New York.

Norwich Lock Manufacturing Company: Trade name used by F.W. Hood Firearms Company on inexpensive pocket revolvers.

Not-Nac Manufacturing Company: Trade name used by the H. & D. Folsom Arms Company on firearms made for the Canton Hardware Company of Canton, Ohio.

Novelty: Trade name used by D.F. Mossberg & Sons on Shattuck Unique pistols.

OK:
a) Trade name used by the Marlin Firearms Company on single-shot pocket pistols.
b) Trade name used by Cowles and Son of Chicopee Falls, Massachusetts, on single-shot pocket pistols.
c) Trade name found on inexpensive pocket revolvers of unknown manufacture.

Old Hickory:
a) Trade name found on inexpensive pocket revolvers of unknown manufacture.
b) Trade name used by the Hibbard, Spencer, Bartlett and Company of Chicago on shotguns they retailed.

Old Reliable: Trade name used by the Sharps Rifle Company.

Olympic:
a) Trade name used by the J. Stevens Arms and Tool Company on rifles and pistols.
b) Trade name used by the Morley and

Murphy Hardware Company of Green Bay, Wisconsin, on firearms they retailed (possibly made by the J. Stevens Arms and Tool Company).

Osprey: Trade name used by Lou J. Eppinger of Detroit, Michigan, on firearms he made.

Our Jake: Trade name used by E.L. and J. Dickinson of Springfield, Massachusetts, on inexpensive pocket revolvers.

Oxford Arms Company: Trade name used by the H. & D. Folsom Arms Company on firearms made for the Belknap Hardware Company of Louisville, Kentucky.

Pagoma: Trade name used by the H. & D. Folsom Arms Company on firearms made for the Paxton and Gallagher Company of Omaha, Nebraska.

Peoria Chief: Trade name found on inexpensive pocket revolvers.

Perfect: Trade name used by the Foehl and Weeks Firearms Manufacturing Company of Philadelphia, Pennsylvania, on inexpensive pocket revolvers.

Perfect: Trade name used by Manufacture d'Armes de Pyrenees on semiautomatic pistols.

Perfection:
a) Trade name used by the H. & D. Folsom Arms Company on firearms made for the H.G. Lipscomb and Company of Nashville, Tennessee.
b) Trade name used by the John M. Smythe Merchandise Company of Chicago on firearms they retailed.

Pet: Trade name found on inexpensive pocket revolvers of unknown manufacture.

Petrel: Trade name found on inexpensive pocket revolvers of unknown manufacture.

Phenix: Trade name used by J. Reid of New York on revolvers.

Phoenix:
a) Trade name used by J. Reid of New York on revolvers.
b) Trade name used by the Whitneyville Armory on percussion revolvers.

Piedmont: Trade name used by the H. & D. Folsom Arms Company on firearms made for the Piedmont Hardware Company of Danville, Pennsylvania.

Pinafore: Trade name used by the Norwich Falls Pistol Company (O.A. Smith) on inexpensive pocket revolvers.

Pioneer: Trade name found on inexpensive pocket revolvers of unknown manufacture.

Pioneer Arms Company: Trade name used by the H. & D. Folsom Arms Company on firearms made for the Kruse and Baklmann Hardware Company of Cincinnati, Ohio.

Pittsfield: Trade name used by the Hibbard, Spencer, Bartlett and Company of Chicago on firearms probably made by the H. & D. Folsom Arms Company.

Plug Ugly: Trade name found on inexpensive pocket revolvers of unknown manufacture.

Plymouth: Trade name used by Spear and Company of Pittsburgh, Pennsylvania, on firearms they retailed.

Pocahontas: Trade name found on inexpensive pocket revolvers of unknown manufacture.

Pointer: Trade name found on single-shot pocket pistols of unknown manufacture.

Prairie Fire: Trade name found on inexpensive pocket revolvers of unknown manufacture.

Prairie King:
a) Trade name used by the Bacon Arms Company on inexpensive pocket revolvers.
b) Trade name used by the H. & D. Folsom Arms Company on inexpensive pocket revolvers.

Premier:
a) Trade name used by the Thomas E. Ryan Company on inexpensive pocket revolvers.
b) Trade name used by the Harrington and Richardson Arms Company on revolvers.
c) Trade name used by the Montgomery Ward and Company of Chicago on firearms they retailed.
d) Registered trade name of Edward K. Tryon and Company of Philadelphia, Pennsylvania.

Premium: Trade name used by the Iver Johnson Arms and Cycle Works on inexpensive pocket revolvers.

John W. Price: Trade name used by the Belknap Hardware Company of Louisville, Kentucky, on firearms they retailed.

Princess: Trade name found on inexpensive pocket revolvers of unknown American manufacture.

Progress: Trade name used by Charles J. Godfrey of New York on shotguns.

Protection: Trade name used by the Whitneyville Armory on revolvers.

Protector:
a) Trade name found on inexpensive pocket revolvers of unknown manufacture.
b) Trade name used by the Chicago Firearms Company on inexpensive pocket revolvers.

Protector Arms Company: Trade name used by the Rupertus Patented Pistol Manufacturing Company on inexpensive pocket revolvers.

Providence: Trade name found on inexpensive pocket revolvers of unknown manufacture.

Puppy: Trade name found on inexpensive pocket revolvers made by several European makers.

Quail: Trade name used by the Crescent-Davis Arms Company on shotguns.

Queen:
a) Trade name used by the Hood Firearms Company on inexpensive pocket revolvers.
b) Trade name used by the Hyde and Shattuck Company on inexpensive single-shot pocket pistols.

Queen City: Trade name used by the H. & D. Folsom Arms Company on firearms made for the Elmira Arms Company of Elmira, New York.

Raider: Randall Firearms Co. Commander size pistol named after Gen Randall's flight squadron; "Randall's Raiders".

Ranger:
a) Trade name found on inexpensive pocket revolvers of unknown manufacture.
b) Trade name used by the Eastern Arms Company on various firearms made for the Sears, Roebuck and Company of Chicago.
c) Trade name of the Sears, Roebuck and Company of Chicago on a wide variety of firearms marketed by that firm.

Rapid-Maxim: Trade name used by Manufacture d'Armes de Pyrenees on semiautomatic pistols.

Reassurance: Trade name found on inexpensive pocket revolvers of unknown manufacture.

Red Chieftan: Trade name used by the Supplee Biddle Hardware Company of Philadelphia, Pennsylvania, on inexpensive pocket pistols they retailed.

Red Cloud: Trade name used by the Ryan Pistol Manufacturing Company on inexpensive pocket revolvers.

Red Hot: Trade name found on inexpensive pocket revolvers of unknown manufacture.

Red Jacket.
a) Trade name used by the Lee Arms Company on inexpensive pocket revolvers.
b) Trade name used by the Hopkins and Allen Company on inexpensive pocket revolvers.

Reliable: Trade name found on inexpensive pocket revolvers of unknown manufacture.

Reliance: Trade name used by John Meunier of Milwaukee, Wisconsin, on rifles.

Rev-O-Noc: Trade name used by the H. & D. Folsom Arms Company on firearms made for the Hibbard, Spencer, Bartlett and Company of Chicago.

Rich-Con: Trade name used by the H. & D. Folsom Arms Company for shotguns made for Richardson & Conover Hardware Company.

Richmond Arms Company: Trade name used by the H. & D. Folsom Arms Company on firearms made for an unknown retailer.

Charles Richter Company: Trade name used by the H. & D. Folsom Arms Company on firearms made for the New York Sporting Goods Company of New York.

Rickard Arms Company: Trade name used by the H. & D. Folsom Arms Company on firearms made for the J.A. Rickard Company of Schenectady, New York.

Rip Rap: Trade name used by the Bacon Arms Company on inexpensive pocket revolvers.

Rival: Trade name used by the H. & D. Folsom Arms Company on firearms made for the Van Camp Hardware and Iron Company of Indianapolis, Indiana.

Riverside Arms Company: Trade name used by the J. Stevens Arms and Tool Company on various types of firearms.

Robin Hood: Trade name used by the Hood Firearms Company on inexpensive pocket revolvers.

Rocky Hill: Trade name found on inexpensive cast iron percussion pocket pistols made in Rocky Hill, Connecticut.

Rodgers Arms Company: Trade name used by the Hood Firearms Company on firearms made for an unknown retailer.

Royal Gun Company: Trade name used by the Three Barrel Gun Company.

Royal Service: Trade name used by the Shapleigh Hardware Company of St. Louis, Missouri, on firearms they retailed.

Rummel Arms Company: Trade name used by the H. & D. Folsom Arms Company on firearms made for the A.J. Rummel Arms Company of Toledo, Ohio.

Russel Arms Company: Registered trade name of the Wiebusch and Hilger Company of New York.

Russian Model: Trade name used by the Forehand and Wadsworth Company on inexpensive pocket revolvers.

S.A.: Trade mark of the Societe d'Armes Francaises.

Safe Guard: Trade name found on inexpensive pocket revolvers of unknown manufacture.

Safety Police: Trade name used by the Hopkins and Allen Company on inexpensive pocket revolvers.

St. Louis Arms Company: Trade name used by the H. & D. Folsom Arms Company on firearms made for the Shapleigh Hardware Company of St. Louis, Missouri.

Scott: Trade name used by the Hopkins and Allen Company on inexpensive pocket revolvers.

Secret Service Special: Trade name used by the Rohde-Spencer Company of Chicago on inexpensive pocket revolvers.

Selecta: Trade name used by Manufacture d'Armes de Pyrenees on semiautomatic pistols.

Senator: Trade name found on inexpensive pocket revolvers of unknown manufacture.

Sentinal: Trade name found on inexpensive pocket revolvers of unknown manufacture.

Service Model C: The predecessor to the "Raider" pistol.

The Sheffield: Trade name used by the A. Baldwin and Company, Limited of New Orleans, Louisiana, on shotguns they retailed.

Sickels-Arms Company: Trade name used by the Sickels and Preston Company of Davenport, Iowa, on firearms they retailed.

Simson: Trade name used by the Iver Johnson Arms and Cycle Works on firearms made for the Iver Johnson Sporting Goods Company of Boston, Massachusetts.

Sitting Bull: Trade name found on inexpensive pocket revolvers of unknown manufacture.

Skue's Special: Trade name used by Ira M. Skue of Hanover, Pennsylvania, on shotguns.

Smoker: Trade name used by the Iver Johnson Arms and Cycle Works on inexpensive pocket revolvers.

John M. Smythe & Company: Trade name used by H. & D. Folsom Arms Company for shotguns made for John M. Smythe Hardware Company of Chicago.

Southern Arms Company: Trade name used by the H. & D. Folsom Arms Company on firearms made for an unknown retailer.

Southerner:
a) Trade name used by the Brown Manufacturing Company and the Merrimac Arms Manufacturing Company on single-shot pocket pistols.
b) Registered trade name of Asa Farr of New York on pistols.

Southron: Trade name found on inexpensive pocket pistols of unknown manufacture.

Special Service: Trade name used by the Shapleigh Hardware Company of St. Louis, Missouri, on inexpensive pocket revolvers.

Spencer Gun Company: Trade name used by the H. & D. Folsom Arms Company.

Splendor: Trade name found on inexpensive pocket revolvers of unknown manufacture.

The Sportsman: Trade name used by the H. & D. Folsom Arms Company on firearms made for the W. Bingham Company of Cleveland, Ohio.

Springfield Arms Company: Trade name used by the J. Stevens Arms and Tool Company.

Spy: Trade name found on inexpensive pocket revolvers of unknown manufacture.

Square Deal: Trade name used by the H. & D. Folsom Arms Company on firearms made for the Stratton, Warren Hardware Company of Memphis, Tennessee.

Standard: Trade name used by the Marlin Firearms Company on revolvers.

Stanley Arms: Registered trade name of the Wiebusch and Hilger Company of New York on firearms they retailed.

Stanley Double Gun: Trade name used by the H. & D. Folsom Arms Company on shotguns they retailed.

Star:
a) Trade name found on inexpensive single-shot pocket pistols of unknown manufacture.
b) Trade name used by the Prescott Pistol Company on inexpensive pocket revolvers.
c) Trade name used by Johnson & Bye on single-shot cartridge derringers.

State Arms Company: Trade name used by the H. & D. Folsom Arms Company on firearms made for the J.H. Lau and Company of New York.

Sterling:
a) Trade name used by E.L. and J. Dickinson of Springfield, Massachusetts, on single-shot pistols.
b) Trade name used by the H. & D. Folsom Arms Company on shotguns they retailed.

Stinger: Registered proprietary trade name engraved on firearms made by the Winchester Repeating Arms Company for the Perry Brothers Limited of Brisbane, Australia.

Stonewall:
a) Trade name used by the Marlin Firearms Company on single-shot derringers.
b) Trade name used by T.F. Guion of Lycoming, Pennsylvania, on single-shot percussion pistols he retailed.

Striker: Trade name found on inexpensive pocket revolvers of unknown manufacture.

Sullivan Arms Company: Trade name used by the H. & D. Folsom Arms Company on firearms made for the Sullivan Hardware Company of Anderson, South Carolina.

Superior: Trade name of the Paxton and Gallagher Company of Omaha, Nebraska, on revolvers and shotguns.

Super Range: Trade name of the Sears, Roebuck and Company of Chicago on shotguns.

Sure Fire: Trade name found on inexpensive pocket revolvers of unknown manufacture.

Swamp Angel: Trade name used by the Forehand and Wadsworth Company on inexpensive pocket revolvers.

Swift: Trade name used by the Iver Johnson Arms and Cycle Works on firearms made for the John P. Lovell & Sons, Boston, Massachusetts.

Syco: Trade name used by the Wyeth Hardware Company of St. Joseph, Missouri, on firearms they retailed.

Sympathique: Trade name used by Manufacture d'Armes de Pyrenees on semiautomatic pistols.

Ten Star: Trade name used by the H. & D. Folsom Arms Company on firearms made for the Geller, Ward and Hasner Company of St. Louis, Missouri.

Terrier: Trade name used by the Rupertus Patented Pistol Manufacturing Company on inexpensive pocket revolvers.

Terror: Trade name used by the Forehand and Wadsworth Company on inexpensive pocket revolvers.

Texas Ranger: Trade name used by the Montgomery Ward and Company of Chicago on inexpensive pocket revolvers they retailed.

Thames Arms Company: Trade name used by the Harrington and Richardson Arms Company on firearms they made for an unknown wholesaler.

Tiger:
a) Trade name used by the Iver Johnson Arms and Cycle Works on inexpensive pocket revolvers.
b) Trade name used by the J.H. Hall and Company of Nashville, Tennessee, on shotguns they retailed.

Tobin Simplex: Trade name used on shotguns of unknown manufacture that were retailed by the G.B. Crandall Company, Limited of Woodstock, Ontario, Canada.

Toledo Firearms Company:
a) Trade name used by the Hopkins and Allen Company on inexpensive pocket revolvers.
b) Trade name used by E.L. and J. Dickinson on inexpensive pocket revolvers.

Toronto Belle: Trade name found on inexpensive pocket revolvers of unknown manufacture.

Touriste: Trade name used by Manufacture d'Armes de Pyrenees on semiautomatic pistols.

Tower's Police Safety: Trade name used by Hopkins & Allen on inexpensive pocket revolvers.

Townley's Pal and Townley's American Boy: Trade name used by H. & D. Folsom Arms Company for shotguns made for Townley Metal and Hardware Company of Kansas City, Missouri.

Tramps Terror: Trade name used by the Forehand and Wadsworth Company on inexpensive pocket revolvers.

Traps Best: Trade name believed to have been used by the H. & D. Folsom Arms Company on firearms made for the Watkins, Cottrell Company of Richmond, Virginia.

Triumph: Trade name used by the H. & D. Folsom Arms Company on shotguns.

Trojan: Trade name found on inexpensive pocket revolvers of unknown manufacture.

True Blue: Trade name found on inexpensive pocket revolvers of unknown manufacture.

Tryon Special: Trade name used by the Edward K. Tryon Company of Philadelphia, Pennsylvania, on shotguns they retailed.

Tycoon: Trade name used by the Iver Johnson Arms and Cycle Works on inexpensive pocket revolvers.

Uncle Sam: Trade name used by Johnson & Bye on percussion pocket pistols.

Union:
a) Trade name found on inexpensive single-shot pocket pistols of unknown manufacture.
b) Trade name used by the Hood Firearms Company on inexpensive pocket revolvers.
c) Trade name used by the Prescott Pistol Company on inexpensive pocket revolvers.

Union Arms Company: Trade name used by the H. & D. Folsom Arms Company on firearms made for the Bostwick, Braun Company of Toledo, Ohio.

Union Jack: Trade name found on inexpensive pocket revolvers of unknown manufacture.

Union N.Y.: Trade name used by the Whitneyville Armory on inexpensive pocket revolvers.

Unique: Trade name used by the C.S. Shattuck Arms Company on revolvers and four barrel pocket pistols.

United States Arms Company: Trade name used by Norwich Falls Pistol Company (O.A. Smith) on inexpensive pocket revolvers.

U.S. Arms Company: Trade name used successively by the Alexander Waller and Company (1877), the Barton and Company (1878) and the H. & D. Folsom Arms Company (1879 forward) on a variety of firearms.

U.S. Revolver: Trade name used by the Iver Johnson Arms and Cycle Works on inexpensive pocket revolvers.

U.S. Single Gun: Trade name used by the Iver Johnson Arms and Cycle Works on single barrel shotguns.

Universal: Trade name used by the Hopkins and Allen Company on inexpensive pocket revolvers.

Utica Firearms Company: Trade name used by the Simmons Hardware Company of St. Louis, Missouri, on firearms they retailed.

Valient: Trade name used by the Spear and Company of Pittsburgh, Pennsylvania, on firearms they retailed.

Veiled Prophet: Trade name used by the T.E. Ryan Pistol Manufacturing Company on inexpensive pocket revolvers.

Venus: Trade name used by the American Novelty Company of Chicago on inexpensive pocket revolvers.

Veteran: Trade name found on inexpensive pocket revolvers of unknown manufacture.

Veto: Trade name found on inexpensive pocket revolvers of unknown manufacture.

Victor:
a) Trade name used by the Marlin Firearms Company on single-shot pocket pistols.
b) Trade name used by the Harrington and Richardson Arms Company on inexpensive pocket revolvers.
c) Trade name used by the H. & D. Folsom Arms Company on inexpensive pocket pistols and revolvers.

Victor Arms Company: Trade name used by the H. & D. Folsom Arms Company on firearms made for the Hibbard, Spencer, Bartlett and Company of Chicago.

Victor Special: Trade name used by the H. & D. Folsom Arms Company on firearms made for the Hibbard, Spencer, Bartlett and Company of Chicago.

Victoria: Trade name used by the Hood Firearms Company on inexpensive pocket revolvers.

Vindix: Trade name used by Manufacture d'Armes de Pyrenees on semiautomatic pistols.

Viper: Trade name used on inexpensive pocket revolvers of unknown American manufacture.

Virginia Arms Company: Trade name used by the H. & D. Folsom Arms Company and later the Davis-Warner Arms Company on firearms made for the Virginia-Carolina Company of Richmond, Virginia.

Volunteer: Trade name used by the H. & D. Folsom Arms Company on inexpensive pocket revolvers made for the Belknap Hardware Company of Louisville, Kentucky.

Vulcan: Trade name used by the H. & D. Folsom Arms Company on firearms made for the Edward K. Tryon Company of Philadelphia, Pennsylvania.

Walnut Hill: Trade name used by the J. Stevens Arms and Tool Company on rifles.

Warner Arms Corporation: Trade name used by the H. & D. Folsom Arms Company on firearms made for the Kirtland Brothers, Inc. of New York.

Wasp: Trade name found on inexpensive pocket revolvers of unknown manufacture.

Wautauga: Trade name used by the Whitaker, Holtsinger Hardware Company of Morristown, Tennessee on firearms they retailed.

Western: Trade name used by the H. & D. Folsom Arms Company on firearms made for the Paxton and Gallagher Company of Omaha, Nebraska.

Western Arms Company:
a) Trade name used by the Bacon Arms on various types of firearms.
b) Trade name used by W.W. Marston on revolvers.
c) Trade name used by Henry Kolb and later R.F. Sedgly of Philadelphia, Pennsylvania, on Baby Hammerless revolvers.
d) Trade name used by the Ithaca Gun Company on shotguns believed to have been made for the Montgomery Ward and Company of Chicago.

Western Field: Trade name used by Montgomery Ward and Company of Chicago on shotguns of various makes that they retailed.

Western Field: Trade name used by Manufacture d'Armes de Pyrenees on revolvers.

J.J. Weston: Trade name used by the H. & D. Folsom Arms Company on shotguns.

Whippet: Trade name used by the H. & D. Folsom Arms Company on firearms made for the Hibbard, Spencer, Bartlett and Company of Chicago.

Whistler: Trade name used by the Hood Firearms Company on inexpensive pocket revolvers.

White Powder Wonder: Trade name used by Albert Aubrey of Meriden, Connecticut on shotguns made for the Sears, Roebuck and Company of Chicago.

Wildwood: Trade name used by the H. & D. Folsom Arms Company for shotguns made for Sears, Roebuck & Company.

Wilkinson Arms Company: Trade name used by the H. & D. Folsom Arms Company on firearms made for the Richmond Hardware Company of Richmond, Virginia.

Wiltshire Arms Company: Trade name used by the H. & D. Folsom Arms Company on firearms made for the Stauffer, Eshleman and Company of New Orleans, Louisiana.

Winfield Arms Company: Trade name used by the H. & D. Folsom Arms Company on various types of firearms.

Winner: Trade name found on inexpensive pocket revolvers of unknown manufacture.

Winoca Arms Company: Trade name used by the H. & D. Folsom Arms Company on firearms made for the N. Jacobi Hardware Company of Wilmington, North Carolina.

Witte's Expert: Trade name used by the Witte Hardware Company of St. Louis, Missouri, on shotguns they retailed.

Witte's IXL: Trade name used by the Witte Hardware Company of St. Louis, Missouri, on shotguns they retailed.

Wolverine Arms Company: Trade name used by the H. & D. Folsom Arms Company on firearms made for the Fletcher Hardware Company of Wilmington, North Carolina.

Woodmaster: Trade name found on Belgian shotguns imported by an unknown wholesaler.

Worlds Fair: Trade name used by the Hopkins and Allen Company on shotguns.

Worthington Arms Company: Trade name used by the H. & D. Folsom Arms Company on various types of firearms.

Wyco: Trade name used by the Wyeth Hardware and Manufacturing Company of St. Joseph, Missouri, on firearms they retailed.

XL:
a) Trade name used by the Hopkins and Allen Company on inexpensive pocket revolvers.
b) Trade name used by the Marlin Firearms Company on single-shot pocket pistols.

XPERT:
a) Trade name used by the Hopkins and Allen Company on inexpensive pocket revolvers.
b) Trade name used by the Iver Johnson Arms and Cycle Works on inexpensive single-shot pocket pistols.

XXX Standard: Trade name used by the Marlin Firearms Company on revolvers.

You Bet: Trade name used on inexpensive pocket revolvers of unknown American manufacture.

Young America: Trade name used by J.P. Lindsay of New York on superimposed - load percussion pistols.

Young American: Trade name used by the Harrington and Richardson Arms Company on revolvers.

FIREARMS MANUFACTURERS AND IMPORTERS

AcuSport Corporation
One Hunter Place
Bellecontaine, OH 43311
937-593-7010
FAX: 937-592-5625

Accu-Tek
4510 Carter CT.
Chino, CA 91710
909-627-2404
FAX: 909-627-7817

AMAC, Inc.
2202 Redmond Road
Jacksonville, AR 72076

American Arms, Inc.
715 E. Armour Road
N. Kansas City, MO 64116
816-474-3161
FAX: 816-474-1225

American Derringer Corp.
127 N. Lacy Drive
Waco, TX 76705
817-799-9111
FAX: 817-799-7935

American Frontier Firearms
40725 Brook Trails Way
Aguanga, CA 92536
909-763-0014
FAX: 909-763-0014

AMT
6226 Santos Diaz St.
Irwindale, CA 91702
818-334-6629
FAX: 818-969-5247

ArmaLite, Inc.
P.O. Box 299
Geneseo, IL 61254
309-944-6939
FAX: 309-944-6949

Armes De Chasse
Suite 8A, House Road
Hertford, NC 27944

Arminex Ltd.
7127 E. Sahuaro Drive #107A
Scottsdale, AZ 85254

Armscorp of America
4424 John Avenue
Baltimore, MA 21227
410-247-6200
FAX: 410-247-6205

Armsport, Inc.
3590 NW 49th St.
Miami, FL 33142
305-635-7850
FAX: 305-633-2877

Arnold Arms Co., Inc.
P.O. Box 1011
Arlington, WA 98223
360-435-1011
FAX: 360-435-7304

A-Square Co. Inc.
One Industrial Park
Bedford, KY 40006
502-255-7456
FAX: 502-255-7657

Austin & Halleck
1099 Welt
Weston, MO 64098
816-386-2176
FAX: 816-386-2177

Autauga Arms
Pratt Plaza Mall No. 13
Pratville, AL 36067
800-262-9563
FAX: 334-361-2961

Auto-Ordnance Corp.
Williams Lane
West Hurley, NY 12491
914-679-4190

Axtell Rifle Company
Riflesmith, Inc.
353 Mill Creek Road
Sheridan, MT 59749
406-842-5814

Aya-Agiurre Y Aranzabal, S.A.L.
P.O. Box 45
Eibar (Guipuzcoa), Spain

Baer Custom, Les
29601 34th Avenue
Hillsdale, IL 61257
309-658-2716
FAX: 309-658-2610

Bailons Gunmakers, Ltd.
94-95 Bath Street
Birmingham, England B4 6HG

Ballard Rifle and Cartridge Co.
113 W. Yellowstone Ave.
Cody, WY 82414
307-587-4914
FAX: 307-527-6097

Barrett Firearms Mfg.
8211 Manchester Highway
P.O.Box 1077
Murfreesboro, TN 37130
615-896-2938
FAX: 615-896-7313

Benelli U.S.A.
17603 Indian Head Highway
Accokeek, MD 20607
301-283-6981
FAX: 301-283-6988

Beretta U.S.A. Corp.
17601 Beretta Drive
Accokeek, MD 20607
301-283-2191
FAX: 301-283-0435

Bernardelli Vincenzo, S.P.A.
P.O. Box 74
Gardone, V.T., Brescia, Italy 25063

Bond Arms
P.O. Box 1296
Grandbury, TX 76048
817-573-5733
FAX: 817-573-5636

Boswell, Charles, Gunmakers
212 East Morehead Street
Charlotte, NC 28202

Briley Mfg. Company
1230 Lumpkin
Houston, TX 77043
800-331-5718

British Game Gun
P.O. Box 5795
Kent, WA 98064-5795

Brolin Arms
2755 Thompson Creek Road
Pomona, CA 91767
909-392-0401
FAX: 909-392-7824

Brown, E.A. Manufacturing Co.
P.O. Box 9219
Akron, OH 44305
800-834-GUNS

Browning
One Browning Place
Morgan, UT 84050
801-876-2711
FAX: 801-876-3331

Browning-Parts & Service
3005 Arnold Tenbrook Rd.
Arnold, MO 63010
314-287-6800
FAX: 314-287-9751

Calico
405 East 19th Street
Bakersfield, CA 93305
805-835-9605
FAX: 805-835-9605

Caspian Arms, Ltd.
14 North Main Street
Hardwick, VT 05843
802-4726454
FAX: 802-472-6709

Casull Arms Company, Inc.
P.O. Box 4155
Jackson, WY 83001
307-733-1530
FAX: 307-886-0300

Century International Arms
P.O. Box 714
St. Albans, VT 05478
802-527-1252
FAX: 802-527-0470

Champlin Firearms
P.O. Box 3191/Woodring Airport
Enid, OK 73702
580-237-7388
FAX: 580-242-6922

Charter 2000
273 Canal Street
Shelton, CT 06484
203-922-1652
FAX: 203-922-1469

Churchill, E. J., Ltd.
Ockley Road, Dorking
Surrey, England RH5 4PU

Cimarron Arms
P.O. Box 906
Fredericksburg, TX 78624
830-997-9090
FAX: 830-997-0802

Colt Firearms
P.O. Box 1868
Hartford, CT 06144
800-962-COLT
FAX: 860-244-1449

Colt Blackpowder Arms Co.
110 8th Street
Brooklyn, NY 11215
212-925-2159
FAX: 212-966-4986

Competitor Corp.
30 Tricnit Road, Unit 16
New Ipswich, NH 03071
603-878-3891
FAX: 603-878-3950

Connecticut Shotgun Manufacturing Co.
A. H. Fox Shotguns
35 Woodland Street
Box 1692
New Britain, CT 06051
860-225-6581
FAX: 860-832-8708

Connecticut Valley Arms, Inc.
5988 Peachtree Corners East
Norcross, GA 30071
800-251-9412
FAX: 404-242-8546

Coonan Arms
1745 HWY. 36E
Maplewood, MN 55109
612-777-3156
FAX: 612-777-3683

Cooper Arms
P.O. Box 114
Stevensville, MT 59870
406-777-5534
FAX: 406-777-5228

CZ-U.S.A.
P.O. Box 171073
Kansas City, KS 66117-0073
913-321-1811
FAX: 913-321-4901

Dakota Arms, Inc.
HC55, Box 326
Sturgis, SD 57785
605-347-4686
FAX: 605-347-4456

Dixie Gun Works
P.O. Box 130
Union City, TN 38261
901-885-0561
FAX: 901-885-0440

Doug Turnbull Restoration, Inc.
6680 Route 5 & 20
Bloomfield, NY 14469
716-657-6338
FAX: 716-657-6338

Downsizer Corp.
P.O. Box 710316
Santee, CA 92072
619-448-5510
FAX: 619-448-5780

DSA, Inc
P.O. Box 387
Round Lake, IL 60073

DuBiel Arms Co.
1800 West Washington Avenue #205
Sherman, TX 75090-5359

Dumoulin Ernst-U.S.A.
10 Rue Boclinville
Herstal, Belgium B-4041

Eagle Imports
1750 Brielle Ave., Unit B1
Wanamassa, NJ 07712
908-493-0333
FAX: 908-493-0301

Ed Brown Products
43825 Muldrow Trail
Perry, MO 63462
573-565-3261
FAX: 573-565-2791

Ellett Bros.
P.O. Box 128
Chapin, SC 29036
803-345-3751
FAX: 803-345-1820

EMF Co., Inc.
1900 E. Warner Avenue
1-D
Santa Ana, CA 92705
714-260-6611
FAX: 714-756-0133

Entreprise Arms Inc.
15861 Business Center Dr.
Irwindale, CA 91706

Euro-Imports
614 Millar Ave.
El Cajon, CA 92929
619-442-7005
FAX: 619-442-7005

European American
Armory
P.O. Box 122
Sharpes, FL 32959
407-639-4842
FAX: 407-639-7006

F.M.J.
P.O. Box 759
Copperhill, TN 37317

F.N. Manufacturing, Inc.
P.O. Box 104
Columbia, SC 29202

Falcon Firearms Mfg.
Corporation
P.O. Box 3748
Granada Hills, CA 91344

Feather Industries
37600 Liberty Dr.
Trinidad, CO 81082

Federal Ordnance, Inc.
1443 Potrero Avenue
S. El Monte, CA 91733

Fieldsport
3313 W. South Airport
Road
Traverse City, MI 49684

Fiocchi Of American
Route 2, Box 90-8
Ozark, MO 65721
417-725-4118
FAX: 417-725-1039

Fletcher Bidwell
305 E. Terhune Street
Viroqua, WI 54665
866-637-1860
FAX: 608-637-6922

Francotte, Aug.
Rue du 3 Juin, 109
Liege, Belgium B-4040

Freedom Arms
P.O. Box 1776
Freedom, WY 83120
307-883-2468
FAX: 307-883-2005

Furr Arms
91 North 970 West
Orem, UT 84057
801-226-3877
FAX: 801-226-3877

Galaxy Imports
P.O. Box 3361
Victoria, TX 77903
512-573-4867
FAX: 512-576-9622

Gamba, Renato
Via Michelangelo, 64
Gardone, Italy 1-25063

Gamba, U.S.A.
P.O. Box 60452
Colorado Springs, CO
80960
719-578-1145
FAX: 719-444-0731

Gary Reeder Custom Guns
2710 N. Steves Blvd. Suite
22
Flagstaff, AZ 86004
520-526-3313
FAX: 520-526-1287

Glock, Inc.
6000 Highlands Parkway
Smyrna, GA 30082
770-432-1202
FAX: 770-433-8719

Goncz Company
11526 Burbank #18
N. Hollywood, CA 91601

Griffin & Howe
36 West 44th Street #1011
New York, NY 10036
212-921-0980

Griffin & Howe, Inc.
33 Claremont Road
Bernardsville, NJ 07924
908-766-2287
FAX: 908-766-1068

GSI, Inc.
108 Morrow Ave.
Trussville, AL 35173
205-655-8299
FAX: 205-655-7078

H-S Precision, Inc.
1301 Turbine Drive
Rapid City, SD 57703
605-341-3006
FAX: 605-342-8964

Hatfield International
224 North 4th
St. Joseph, MO 64501

Harrington & Richardson
60 Industrial Rowe
Gardner, MA 01440
508-632-9393
FAX: 508-632-2300

Hanus Birdguns
P.O. Box 533
Newport, OR 97365
541-265-7433
FAX: 541-265-7400

Harris Gunworks
12001 N. Cave Creek Rd.
Phoenix, AZ 85020
602-997-5370
FAX: 602-997-5335

Heavy Express Inc.
P.O. Box 60698
Colorado Springs, CO
80960

Heckler & Koch, Inc.
21480 Pacific Boulevard
Sterling, VA 20166
703-450-1900
FAX: 703-450-8160

Henry Repeating Arms Co
110 8th Street
Brooklyn, New York 11215
718-499-5600

Heritage Manufacturing,
Inc.
4600 NW 135th St.
Opa Locla, FL 33054
305-685-5966
FAX: 305-687-6721

Hesse Arms
1126 70th Street East
Inver Grove Heights, MN
55077

High Standard
Manufacturing Co.
4601 South Pinemont
#148B
Houston, TX 77041
713-462-4200
FAX: 713-462-6437

Hi-Power Firearms
MKS Supply
5990 Philadaphia Dr.
Dayton, OH 45415
513-275-4991
FAX: 513-522-8330

Holmes Firearms
Route 6, Box 242
Fayetteville, AR 72703

Horton, Lew, Distributing
Co., Inc.
15 Walkup Drive
Westboro, MA 01581
508-366-7400
FAX: 508-366-5332

Hyper Single, Inc.
520 East Beaver
Jenks, OK 74037
918-299-2391

IAR
33171 Camino Capistrano,
San Juan Capistrano,
CA 92675
714-443-3642
FAX: 714-443-3647

Illinois Arms
2300 Central Avenue,
Suite K
Boulder, CO 80301

Import Sports, Inc.
1750 Brielle Ave
Unit B-1
Wanamassa, NJ 07712
908-493-0302
FAX: 908-493-0301

Intertex
1100 Culp Road
Pineville, NC 28134

Intratec
12405 SW 130th Street
Miami, FL 33186
305-232-1821
FAX: 305-253-7207

Ithaca Classic Doubles
No. 5 Railroad Street
Victor, NY 14564

Ithaca Gun/Ithaca Acq.
Corp.
891 Route 34B
King Ferry, NY 13081
315-364-7171
FAX: 315-364-5134

Jennings Firearms
3680 Research Way
Carson City, NV 89706

J.O. Arms Inc.
5709 Hartsdale
Houston, TX 77036

K.B.I. Inc.
P.O. Box 5440
Harrisburg, PA 17110
717-540-8518
FAX: 717-540-8567

KDF
2485 Highway 46 North
Seguin, TX 78155

Kahr Arms
P.O. Box 220
Blauvelt, NY 10913
914-353-5996
FAX: 914-353-7833

Kel-Tec CNC, Inc.
1485 Cox Rd.
P.O. Box 3427
Cocoa, FL 32924
407-631-0068
FAX: 407-631-1169

Kimber
Sales & Marketing Office
2590 Highway 35
Kalispell, MT 59901
Corporate Offices
1 Lawton Street
Yonkers, NY 10705
800-880-2418
FAX: 914-964-9340

Knight Rifles
P.O. Box 130
234 Airport road
Centerville, IA 52544
515-856-2626
FAX: 515-856-2628

Knight's Manufacturing
Co.
7750 Ninth St., SW
Vero Beach, FL 32968
561-562-5697
FAX: 561-569-2955

Kongsberg America
P.O. Box 252
Fairfield, CT 06430

Krieghoff International
P.O. Box 549
Ottsville, PA 18942
610-847-5173
FAX: 610-847-8691

L.A.R. Manufacturing
4133 West Farm Road
West Jordan, UT 84088
801-280-3505
FAX: 801-280-1972

Lakelander U.S.A.
P.O. Box 4208
Gulfport, MS 39502

Laurona
P.O. Box 260
20600 Eibar (Guipuzcoa),
Spain

Lazzeroni Arms Co.
1415 South Cherry Av.
Tucson, AZ 85726
888-492-7247
FAX: 520-624-4250

Baer, Les, Custom Inc.
29601 34th Av North
Hillsdale, IL 61257
309-658-2716
FAX: 309-658-2610

Ljutic Industries
732 North 16th Avenue
P.O. Box 2117, Suite 22
Yakima, WA 98907
509-248-0476
FAX: 509-576-8233

Lone Star Rifle Company
11231 Rose Road
Conroe, TX 77303
409-856-3363

Lyman
475 Smith Street
Middletown, CT 06457
860-632-2020
FAX: 860-632-1699

Magnum Research, Inc.
7110 University Avenue
N.E.
Minneapolis, MN 55432
800-772-6168
FAX: 612-574-0109

Marlin Firearms
100 Kenna Drive
North Haven, CT 06473
203-239-5621
FAX: 203-234-7991

Maverick Arms Inc.
P.O. Box 586
Industrial Boulevard
Eagle Pass, TX 78853

McMillan, G., & Co.
21421 North 7th Avenue
Phoenix, AZ 85027
602-582-9635
FAX: 602-581-3825

Military Armament Corp.
P.O. Box 120, Mt. Zion Rd.
Lingeville, TX 76461
817-965-3253

Miltex, Inc
700 South Lee Street
Alexandria, VA 22314
888-642-9123
FAX: 301-645-1430

M.O.A. Corp.
2451 Old Camden Pike
Eaton, OH 45320
513-456-3669

Moore, William Larkin, &
Co.
31360 Via Colinas #109
Westlake Village, CA
91301

Mossberg, O. F., & Sons, Inc.
Seven Grasso Avenue
North Haven, CT 06473
203-230-5300
FAX: 203-230-5420

Navy Arms Co.
689 Bergen Blvd.
Ridgefield, NJ 07657
201-945-2500
FAX: 201-945-6859

New England Arms Co.
Lawrence Lane
Kittery Point, ME 03905
207-439-0593
FAX: 207-439-6726

New England Custom Gun Service
438 Willow Brook Road
Plainfield, NH 03781
306-469-3450

New England Firearms
60 Industrial Rowe
Gardner, MA 01440
508-632-9393
FAX: 508-632-2300

North American Arms
2150 South 950 East
Provo, UT 84606
801-374-9990
FAX: 801-374-9998

Nowlin Manufacturing Co.
Rt. 1, Box 308
Claremore, OK 74017
918-342-0689
FAX: 918-342-0624

Ohio Ordnance Works
P.O. Box 687
Chardon, Ohio

Olympic Arms, Inc.
624 Old Pacific Highway Southeast
Olympia, WA 98513
360-491-3447
FAX: 360-491-3447

Para-Ordnance
980 Tapscott Rd.
Scarborough, Ontario
M1X 1E7
416-297-7855
FAX: 416-297-1289

Parker Reproductions
124 River Road
Middlesex, NJ 08846
908-469-0100
FAX: 908-469-9692

Pedersoli Davide & Co.
Via Artigiani N. 57
Gardone Valtrompia, Brescia
Italy 25063

Perazzi U.S.A. Inc.
1207 South Shamrock Avenue
Monrovia, CA 91016
626-303-0068
FAX: 626-303-2081

Prairie Gun Works
1-761 Marion Street
Winnipeg, Manitoba
Canada R2J OK6

Precision Imports
5040 Space Center Dr.
San Antonio, TX 78218

Professional Ordnance Inc.
1215 E. Airport Dr.
Ontario, CA 91761
909-923-5559
FAX: 909-923-0899

Phillips & Rodgers, Inc.
100 Hilbig, Suite C
Conroe, TX 77301
800-682-2247
FAX: 409-756-0976

Phoenix Arms
1420 South Archibald Ave.
Ontario, CA 91761
909-947-4843
FAX: 909-947-6798

P.S.M.G. Gun Co.
10 Park Avenue
Arlington, MA 02174
617-646-8845
FAX: 617-646-2133

Raptor Arms Co.
115 S. Union St., Suite 308
Alexandria, VA 22314
203-924-7618
FAX: 203-924-7624

Raven Arms
1300 Bixby Drive
City of Industry, CA 91745

Remington Arms Co., Inc.
P.O. Box 700
870 Remington Drive
Madison, NC 27025-0700
800-243-9700
FAX: 910-548-8700

Republic Arms, Inc.
15167 Sierra Bonita Lane
Chino, CA 91710
909-597-3873
FAX: 909-597-2612

Rock River Arms Inc.
101 Noble Street
Cleveland, IL 61241
309-792-5780
FAX: 309-792-5781

Rogue Rifle Co.
P.O. Box 20
Prospect, OR 97536
541-560-4040
FAX: 541-560-4041

Rogue River Rifleworks
1317 Spring Street
Paso Robles, CA 93446
805-227-4706
FAX: 805-227-4723

Rowe, John F.
2501 Rockwood Road
Enid, OK 73702

Savage Arms
Springdale Road
Westfield, MA 01085
413-568-7001
FAX: 413-562-7764

Scattergun Technologies, Inc.
620 8th Street S.
Nashville, TN 37203
615-254-1441
FAX: 615-254-1449

Seecamp, L.W.C.
301 Brewster Rd.
Milford, CT 06460
203-877-3429

SGS Importers International
1750 Brielle Ave.
Unit B-1
Wanamassa, NJ

Shiloh Rifle Mfg. Co., Inc.
P.O. Box 279
Ind. Park
Big Timber, MT 59011
406-932-4454
FAX: 406-932-5627

SigArms, Inc.
Corporate Park
Exeter, NH 03833
603-772-2302
FAX: 603-772-9082

Sile Distributors
7 Centre Market Place
New York, NY 10013
212-925-4111
FAX: 212-925-3149

S.K.B.
4325 South 120th St.
P.O. Box 37669
Omaha, NE 68137
800-752-2767
FAX: 402-330-8029

Smith & Wesson
2100 Roosevelt Road
Springfield, MA 01102
413-781-8300
FAX: 413-731-8980

Sokolovsky Inc.
P.O. Box 70113
Sunnyvale, CA 94086

Sphinx U.S.A., Inc.
998 North Colony Rd.
Meridan, CT 06450

Specialty Shooters
3325 Griffin Road
Suite 9M/M
Fort Lauderdale, FL 33312

Springfield Armory, Inc.
420 West Main Street
Geneseo, IL 61254
309-944-5631
FAX: 309-944-3676

SSK Industries
721 Woodvue Lane
Wintersville, OH 43952
740-264-0176
FAX: 740-264-2257

S.T.I. International, Inc.
114 Halmar Cove
Georgetown, TX 78628
800-959-8201
FAX: 512-819-0465

Stoeger Industries
5 Mansard Court
Wayne, NJ 07470
201-872-9500
FAX: 201-872-2230

Sturm Ruger & Co., Inc
10 Lacey Place
Southport, CT 06490
520-541-8820
FAX: 520-541-8850

Taconic Firearms Ltd.
P.O. Box 553
Cambridge, NY 12816
518-677-2704
FAX: 518-677-5974

Taurus International
16175 NW 49th Av.
Miami, FL 33014
305-624-1115
FAX: 305-623-7506

Techno-Arms Ltd./VFI
11 Perry Dr., Unit G
Foxboro, MA 02035

Thompson/Center Arms Co.
Farmington Road
P.O. Box 5002
Rochester, NH 03867
603-332-2394
FAX: 603-332-5133

Traditions Performance Firearms
1375 Boston Post Road
Old Saybrook, CT 06475
860-388-4657
FAX: 860-388-4657

Uberti U.S.A., Inc.
P.O. Box 469
Lakeville, CT 06039
860-435-8068
FAX: 860-435-8146

Ultra Light Arms, Inc.
P.O. Box 1270
Granville, WV 26534
304-599-5687
FAX: 304-599-5687

U.S. Repeating Arms/Winchester
275 Winchester Ave.
Morgan, UT 84050
801-876-3440
FAX: 801-876-3737

United States Patent Firearms Manufacturing Co.
25-55 Van Dyke Av.
Hartford, CT 06106
800-877-2832
FAX: 800-644-7265

Valtro U.S.A.
1281 Anderson Drive
San Rafael, CA 94901
415-256-2575
FAX: 415-256-2576

Varner Sporting Arms Inc.
1004-F Cobb Parkway North
Marietta, GA 30062

Vector Arms, Inc.
270 W. 500 N.
North Salt Lake, UT 84054
801-295-1917
FAX: 801-295-9316

Weatherby, Inc.
3100 El Comino Real
Atascadero, CA 93422
805-466-1767
FAX: 805-466-2527

Westley Richards & Co. Ltd.
40 Grange Road,
Bournbrook
Birmingham, England B29 5A

Wichita Arms
444 Ellis
Wichita, KS 67211
316-265-0061
FAX: 316-265-0760

Wildey, Inc.
P.O. Box 475
Brookfield, CT 06804
203-355-9000
FAX: 203-354-7759

Wilkinson Arms
26884 Pearl Road
Parma, ID 83660

Wilson Gun Shop
Box 578
Berryville, AR 72616
870-545-3618
FAX: 870-545-3310

Winslow Arms
P.O. Box 783
Camden, SC 29020

Wolf Sporting Pistols
Handgunner Custom Shop
17 W. Weis Street
Topton, PA 19562

ZM Weapons
203 South Street
Bernardston, MA 01337
413-648-9501
FAX: 413-648-0219

Zoli, Antonio
Via Zanardelli, 39
I-25063 Gardone V.T. (BS)
Italy

GUN COLLECTORS ASSOCIATIONS

Alabama Gun Collectors
P.O. Box 70965
Tuscalossa, AL 35407

Alaska Gun Collectors
Association
5240 Litte Tree
Anchorage, Alaska 99507

American Society of Arms
Collectors
P.O. Box 2567
Waxahachie, TX 75165

Arizona Arms Association
4837 Bryce Ave.
Glendale, AZ 85301

Ark-La-Tex Gun Collectors
Association
919 Hamilton Road
Bossier City, LA 71111

Bay Colony Weapons
Collectors, Inc.
Box 111
Hingham, MA 02043

Boardman Valley Collectors
Guild
County Road 600
Manton, MI 49663

Browning Collectors
Association
2749 Keith Dr.
Villa Ridge, MO 63089

California Arms and Collectors
Assoc.
8290 Carburton St.
Lonf Beach, Ca 90808

Colorado Gun Collectors
2553 South Quitman Street
Denver, CO 80219

Colt Collectors Association
25000 Highland Way
Los Gatos, CA 95030

Derringer Collectors
Association
500 E. Old 66
Shamrock, TX 79079

Florida Gun Collectors
Association
P.O. Box 43
Branford, FL 32008

Freedom Arms Collectors
Association
P.O. Box 160302
Miami, FL 33116

High Standard Collectors
Association
540 W 92nd Street
Indianapolis, In 46260

Houston Gun Collectors
Association
P.O. Box 741429
Houston, TX 77274

Indianhead Firearms
Association
Route 9, Box 186
Chippewa Falls, WI 54729

Indian Territory Gun Collectors
Association
Box 4491
Tulsa, OK 74159

International Society of Mauser
Arms Collectors
P.O. Box 277
Alpharetta, GA 30239

Iroquois Arms Collectors
Association
P.O.Box 142
Ransomville, NY 14131

Jefferson State Arms Collectors
521 South Grape
Medford, OR 97501

Jersey Shore Antique Arms
Collectors
P.O. Box 100
Bayville, NJ 08721

Kentuckiana Arms Collectors
Association
P.O. Box 1776
Louisville, KY 40201

Kentucky Gun Collectors
Association
P.O. Box 64
Owensboro, KY 42376

Lehigh Valley Military
Collectors Association
P.O. Box 72
Whitehall, PA 18052

Long Island Antique Gun
Collectors Association
35 Beach Street
Farmingdale, L.I., NY 11735

Marlin Firearms Collectors
Association
44 Main Street
Champaign, IL 61820

Maryland Arms Collectors
Association
P.O. Box 20388
Baltimore, MD 21284-0388

Memphis Antique Weapons
Association
4672 Barfield Road
Memphis, TN 38117

Minnesota Weapons Collectors
Association
P.O. Box 662
Hopkins, MN 55343

Missouri Valley Arms Collectors
Association
P.O. Box 33033
Kansas City, MO 64114

Montana Arms Collectors
Association
308 Riverview Drive
East Great Falls, MT 59404

National Automatic Pistol
Collectors Association
Box 15738-TOGS
St. Louis, MO 63163

National Rifle Association
11250 Waples Mill Rd.
Fairfax, VA 22030

New Hampshire Arms
Collectors, Inc.
P.O. Box 5
Cambridge, MA 02139

Northeastern Arms Collectors
Association, Inc.
P.O. Box 185
Amityville, NY 11701

Ohio Gun Collectors
Association
P.O. Box 9007
Maumee, OH 43537

Oregon Arms Collectors
P.O. Box 13000-A
Portland, OR 97213

Pelican Arms Collectors
Association
P.O. Box 747
Clinton, LA 70722

Pennsylvania Antique Gun
Collectors Association
28 Fulmer Avenue
Havertown, PA 19083

Pikes Peak Gun Collectors
Guild
406 E. Uintah
Colorado Springs, CO 80903

Potomac Arms Collectors
Association
P.O. Box 1812
Wheaton, MD 20915

Randall Collectors Club
228 Columbine Dr.
Casper WY 82609-3948

Remington Society of America
8267 Lone Feather
Las Vegas, NV 89123

Ruger Collectors Association,
Inc.
P.O. Box 240
Greens Farms, CT 06436

Sako Collectors Association,
Inc.
202 N. Locust
Whitewater, KS 67154

Santa Barbara Antique Arms
Collectors Association
P.O. Box 6291
Santa Barbara, CA 93160-6291

San Bernardino Valley Arms
Collectors
1970 Mesa Street
San Bernardino, CA 92405

Santa Fe Gun Collectors
Association
1085 Nugget
Los Alamos, NM 87544

San Fernando Valley Arms
Collectors Association
P.O. Box 65
North Hollywood, CA 91603

Shasta Arms Collectors
Association
P.O. Box 3292
Redding, CA 96049

Smith & Wesson Collectors
Association
2711 Miami St.
St. Louis, MO 63118

Tampa Bay Arms Collectors
Association
2461 67th Avenue South
St. Petersburg, FL 33712

Texas Gun Collectors
Association
P.O. Box 12067
El Paso, TX 79913

Washington Arms Collectors,
Inc.
P.O. Box 7335
Tacoma, WA 98407

Weapons Collectors Society of
Montana
3100 Bancroft
Missoula, MT 59801

Weatherby Collectors
Association, Inc.
21569 448th Avenue
Oldham, SD 57051

Willamette Valley Arms
Collectors Association,
Inc.
P.O. Box 5191
Eugene, OR 97405

Winchester Arms Collectors
Association
P.O. Box 6754
Great Falls, MT 59406.

Ye Connecticut Gun Guild
U.S. Route 7
Kent Road
Cornwall Bridge, CT 06754

Zumbro Valley Arms Collectors,
Inc.
Box 6621
Rochester, MN 55901

BIBLIOGRAPHY

Bady, Donald *Colt Automatic Pistols.* Alhambra, California: Borden Publishing Company, 1973.

Baer, Larry L. *The Parker Gun.* Los Angeles, California: Beinfeld Publications, 1980.

Bailey, D. and Nie, D. *English Gunmakers.* London: Arms and Armour Press, 1978.

Ball, W.D., *Remington Firearms: The Golden Age of Collecting,* Iola, WI: Krause Publications, 1995.

Ball, W.D., *Mauser Military Rifles of the World.* Iola, WI: Krause Publications, 1996.

Belford, James & Dunlap, Jack *The Mauser Self-Loading Pistol.* Alhambra, California: Borden Publishing, 1969.

Bishop, Chris and Drury, Ian *Combat Guns.* Secaucus, New Jersey: Chartwell Books, 1987.

Blackmore, H. *Gunmakers of London.* York, Pennsylvania: Geo. Shumway, 1986.

Blackmore, H. *Guns and Rifles of the World.* New York, New York: Viking Press, 1965.

Blair, C. *Pistols of the World.* London: B.T. Batsford, Ltd., 1968.

Bogdanovic & Valencak *The Great Century of Guns.* New York, New York: Gallery Books, 1986.

Bowen, T.G. *James Reid and his Catskill Knuckledusters.* Lincoln, Rhode Island: Andrew Mowbray, Inc., 1989.

Breathed, J. and Schroeder, J. *System Mauser.* Glenview, Illinois: Handgun Press, 1967.

Brophy, Lt. Col. William S., USAR, Ret. *The Krag Rifle.* Los Angeles, California: Beinfeld Publications, 1980.

Brophy, Lt. Col. William S., USAR, Ret. *L.C. Smith Shotguns.* Los Angeles, California: Beinfeld Publications, 1977.

Brophy, W. *Marlin Firearms.* Harrisburg, Pennsylvania: Stackpole Books, 1989.

Browning, J. and Gentry, C. *John M. Browning; American Gunmaker.* Ogden, Utah: Browning, 1989.

Butler, David F. *The American Shotgun.* New York, New York: Winchester Press, 1973.

Buxton, Warren *The P 38 Pistol.* Dallas, Texas: Taylor Publishing Company, 1978.

Carr, J. *Savage Automatic Pistols.*

Chant, Christopher *The New Encyclopedia of Handguns.* New York, New York: Gallery Books.

Conley, F.F. *The American Single Barrel Trap Gun.* Carmel Valley, California: F.F. Conley, 1989.

Cope, K.L. *Stevens Pistols and Pocket Rifles.* Ottawa, Ontario: Museum Restoration Service.

Cormack, A.J.R. *Small Arms, a Concise History of Their Development.* Profile Publications, Ltd.

Cormack, A.J.R. *Small Arms in Profile, Volume I.* Garden City, New York: Doubleday & Company, Inc.,1973.

deHass, Frank *Bolt Action Rifles.* Northfield, Illinois: Digest Books, Inc., 1971.

deHass, Frank *Single-shot Rifles and Actions.* Northfield, Illinois: Digest Books, Inc., 1969.

Eastman, Matt, *Browning Sporting Arms of Distinction*; 1903-1992. Fitzgerald, Georgia, 1994.

Eberhart, L. D. & Wilson, R. L. *The Deringer in America: Volume Two - The Cartridge Era.* Lincoln, RI: Andrew Mowbray Inc., 1993.

Dance, T. *High Standard: A Collector's Guide to the Hamden & Hartford Target Pistols.* Lincoln, RI: Andrew Mowbray Inc., 1991

Dunlap, J. *Pepperbox Firearms.* Palo Alto, California: Pacific Books, 1964.

Ezell, Edward C. *Small Arms Today.* Harrisburg, Pennsylvania: Stackpole Books.

Frasca & Hill *The 45-70 Springfield.* Northridge, California: Springfield Publishing Company, 1980.

Fuller, C. *The Whitney Firearms.* Huntington, West Virginia: Standard Pub., Inc., 1946.

Gaier & Francotte, *FN 100 Years; The Story of a Great Liege Company, 1889-1989.* Brussels, Belgium, 1989.

Gander, Terry, editor, *Janes Infantry Weapons*, 23rd edition, Surry, England, 1997.

Goddard, W. H. D. *The Government Models.* The Development of the Colt Model of 1911. Lincoln, RI: Andrew Mowbray Inc., 1988.

Graham, R., Kopec, J., Moore, C. *A Study of the Colt Single Action Army Revolver.* Dallas, Texas: Taylor Publishing Co., 1978.

Greener, W. *The Gun and Its Development.* Secaucus, New Jersey: Chartwell Books, 1988.

Gun Digest 1967 through 1989 Editions. Northfield, Illinois: DBI Books.

Guns of the World Los Angeles, California: Petersen Publishing Company, 1972.

Hayward, J.F. *Art of the Gunmaker, Vol.* 1. London: Barrie & Rockliff, 1962; Vol. 2. London: Barrie & Rockliff, 1963.

Henshaw, Thomas, et. al., *The History of Winchester Firearms 1866-1992, 6th Ed.* Winchester Press, 1993.

Hiddleson, C. *Encyclopedia of Ruger Semi-Automatic Pistols: 1949-1992.* Iola, WI: Krause Publications, 1993.

Hinman, Bob *The Golden Age of Shotgunning,* New York, N.Y., Winchester Press, 1975.

Hoff, A. *Airguns and Other Pneumatic Arms.* London: Barrie & Jenkins, 1972.

Hoffschmidt, E.J. *Know Your. 45 Auto Pistols Models 1911 & Al.* Southport, Connecticut: Blacksmith Corporation, 1974.

Hoffschmidt, E.J. *Know Your Walther PP & PPK Pistols.* Southport, Connecticut: Blacksmith Corporation, 1975.

Hogg, Ian V. *German Pistols and Revolvers 1871-1945.* Harrisburg, Pennsylvania: Stackpole Books, 1971.

Hogg, Ian V. and Weeks, John *Military Small Arms of the 20th Century.* Fifth Edition. Northfield, Illinois: DBI Books, 1985.

Hogg, Ian V. and Weeks, John *Pistols of the World. Revised Edition.* Northfield, Illinois: DBI Books, 1982.

Honeycutt, Fred L., Jr. *Military Pistols of Japan.* Lake Park, Florida: Julin Books, 1982.

Houze, H. *The Winchester Model 52: Perfection in Design,* Iola, WI: Krause Publications, 1997.

Houze, H. *To The Dreams Of Youth: Winchester .22 Caliber Single-shot Rifle.* Iola, WI: Krause Publications, 1993.

Houze, H. *Winchester Repeating Arms Company Its History and Development 1865 to 1981.* Iola, WI: Krause Publications, 1994.

Houze, H. *Colt Rifles & Muskets: 1847-1870.* Iola, WI: Krause Publications, 1996.

Jamieson, G. Scott *Bullard Arms.* Erin, Ontario: Boston Mills Press, 1988.

Jinks, R.G. *History of Smith A. Wesson.* Beinfeld Pub., Inc., 1977.

Karr, C.L. and C.R. *Remington Handguns.* Harrisburg, Pennsylvania: Stackpole Co., 1956.

Kenyon, C. *Lugers at Random.* Glenview, Illinois: Handgun Press, 1990.

Kindig, J., Jr. *Thoughts on the Kentucky Rifle in its Golden Age.* New York, New York: Bonanza Books, 1964.

Laidacker, John S. *Collected Notes Concerning Developmental Cartridge Handguns In .22 Calibre As Produced in the United States and Abroad From 1855 to 1875.* Bloomsburg, PA: J.S. Laidacker, 1994.

Larson, Eric *Variations of the Smooth Bore H&R Handy-Gun.* Takoma Park, Maryland: 1993.

Leithe, Frederick E. *Japanese Handguns.* Alhambra, California: Borden Publishing Company, 1968.

Lenk, T. *The Flintlock, Its Origins and Development.* New York, New York: Bramhall House, 1965.

Lewis, Jack, editor, *Gun Digest Book of Assault Weapons*, 4th edition, Krause Publications, Iola, WI, 1996.

Lippard, K. *Fabbri Shotguns*, Colorado Springs, Colorado, VM Publications, 1998.

Lippard, K, *Perazzi Shotguns*, Colorado Springs, Colorado, VM Publications, 1996.

Lugs, J. *Firearms Past and Present.* London: Grenville, 1975.

Madis, George *The Winchester Model 12.* Brownsboro, Texas: Art & Reference House, 1982.

Madis, George *The Winchester Book.* Brownsboro, Texas: Art & Reference House, 1977.

Marcot, R. *Spencer Repeating Firearms.* Irvine, California: Northwood Heritage Press, 1990.

Markham, George *Japanese Infantry Weapons of World War Two.* New York, New York: Hippocrene Books, Inc., 1976.

McDowell, R. *Evolution of the Winchester.* Tacoma, Washington: Armory Pub., 1985.

McDowell, R. *A Study of Colt Conversions and Other Percussion Revolvers*, Iola, WI; Krause Publications, 1997.

McIntosh, Michael *A.H. Fox; The Finest Gun in the World.* Countrysport Press, 1992.

Moller, G. D. *American Military Shoulder Arms, Volume 1, Colonial and Revolutionary War Arms.* Niwot, CO: University Press of Colorado, 1993.

Murphy, J. M.D. *Confederate Carbines & Musketoons.* J. Murphy, M.D., n.p.: 1986.

Murray, Douglas P. *The 99: A History of the Savage Model 99 Rifle.* Murray, 1976.

Myatt, Major Frederick, M.D. *Pistols and Revolvers.* New York, New York: Crescent Books, 1980.

Nutter, W.E. *Manhattan Firearms.* Harrisburg, Pennsylvania: Stackpole Co., 1958.

Olson, Ludwig *Mauser Bolt Rifles.* Third Edition. Montezuma, Iowa: Brownell & Sons, 1976.

Parsons, J. E. *Henry Deringer's Pocket Pistol.* New York, New York: Wm. Morrow & Co., 1952.

Pender, Roy G. *III Mauser Pocket Pistols 1910-1946.* Houston, Texas: Collectors Press, 1971.

Peterson, H.L. *Arms and Armor in Colonial America.* New York, New York: Brandhall House, 1956.

Petty, Charles E. *High Standard Automatic Pistols 1932-1950.* Highland Park, NJ: The Gun Room Press, 1989.

Rankin, J. *Walther Models PP and PPK.* Coral Gables, Florida: Rankin, 1989.

Rankin, J. *Walther Volume III,* 1908-1980. Coral Gables, Florida: Rankin, 1981.

Reese, Michael *11 Luger Tips.* Union City, Tennessee: Pioneer Press, 1976.

Reilly, R. *United States Martial Flintlocks.* Lincoln, Rhode Island: Andrew Mowbray, Inc., 1986.

Reilly, R. *United States Military Small Arms 1816-1865.* Baton Rouge, Louisiana: Eagle Press, Inc., 1970.

Renneberg, R.C. *The Winchester Model 94: The First 100 Years.* Iola, WI: Krause Publications, 1992.

Riling, R. *The Powder Flask Book.* New York, New York: Bonanza Books, 1953.

Rosenberger, R.F.& Kaufmann, C. *The Long Rifles of Western Pennsylvania-Allegheny and Westmoreland Counties.* Pittsburgh, PA: University of Pittsburgh Press, 1993.

Rule, R. *The Rifleman's Rifle: Winchester's Model 70, 1936-1963.* Northridge, California: Alliance Books, 1982.

Ruth, L. *War Baby! Comes Home-The U.S. Caliber .30 Caliber Carbine Volume II.* Toronto, Ontario: Collector Grade Publications, Inc., 1993.

Ruth, L. *War Baby! The U.S. Caliber .30 Carbine.* Toronto, Ontario: Collector Grade Publications, Inc., 1992.

Schroeder, Joseph J. *Gun Collector's Digest, Volume II* Northfield, Illinois: Digest Books, Inc., 1977.

Schwing, N. *Winchester's Finest, The Model 21.* Iola, WI: Krause Pub., 1990.

Schwing, N. *The Winchester Model 42.* Iola, WI: Krause Pub., 1990.

Schwing, N. *Winchester Slide Action Rifles, Vol. Model 1890 and Model 1906.* Iola, WI: Krause Publications, 1992.

Schwing, N. *Winchester Slide Action Rifles, Vol. Model 61 and Model 62.* Iola, WI: Krause Publications, 1993.

Schwing, N. *The Browning Superposed: John Browning's Last Legacy.* Iola, WI: Krause Publications, 1996.

Sellers, F. *Sharps Firearms.* North Hollywood, California: Beinfeld Pub., Inc., 1978.

Sellers, F. *American Gunsmiths.* Highland Park, New Jersey: Gun Room Press, 1983.

Sellers, F. and Smith, S. *American Percussion Revolvers.* Ottawa, Ontario: Museum Restoration Service, 1971.

Serven, James E. *200 Years of American Firearms.* Chicago, Illinois: Follett Publishing Company, 1975.

Serven, J. *Collecting of Guns.*

Sharpe, P. *The Rifle in America.* Funk and Wagnalls Co., 1953.

Sheldon, Douglas G. *A Collector's Guide to Colt's. 38 Automatic Pistols.* Sheldon, 1987.

Smith, W. *The Book of Pistols and Revolvers.* Harrisburg, Pennsylvania: Stackpole Co., 1962.

Stadt, R.W. *Winchester Shotguns and Shotshells.* Tacoma, Washington: Armory Publications, 1984.

Stevens, R. *The Browning High Power Automatic Pistol.* Toronto, Canada: Collector Grade Publications, 1990.

Stoeger's Catalog & Handbook. 1939 Issue. Hackensack, New Jersey: Stoeger Arms Corporation.

Supica J. & Nahas R., *Standard Catalog of Smith & Wesson.* Iola, WI: Krause Publications, 1996.

Sutherland, R.Q. & Wilson, R. L. *The Book of Colt Firearms.* Kansas City, Missouri: R.Q. Sutherland,1971.

Tivey, T. *The Colt Rifle, 1884-1902.* N.S.W. Australia: Couston & Hall, 1984.

Vorisek, Joleph T *Shotgun Markings:* 1865 to 1940, Canton, CT: Armsco Press 1990.

Wahl, Paul *Wahl's Big Gun Catalog II.* Cut And Shoot, Texas: Paul Wahl Corporation, 1988.

Walter, John *The German Rifle.* Ontario, Canada: Fortress Publishing, Inc., 1979.

Whitaker, Dean H. *The Winchester Model 70 1937-1964.* Dallas, Texas: Taylor Publishing Company, 1978.

Wilkerson, Don *The Post War Colt Single Action Army Revolver.* Dallas, Texas: Taylor Publishing Company, 1978.

Wilson, R.L. *Colt An American Legend.* New York, New York: Abbeville Press, 1985.

Wilson, R.L. *Colt Engraving.* Beinfeld Publishing, Inc., n.p., 1982.

Wilson, R.L. *Winchester Engraving.* Palm Springs, California: Beinfeld Books, 1989.

Wilson, R.L. *The Colt Heritage.* New York, New York: Simon & Schuster, 1979.

Wilson, R.L. *Winchester An American Legend.* New York, New York: 1991.

Winant, L. *Early Percussion Firearms.* New York, New York: Wm. Morrow & Co., 1959.

Winant, L. *Firearms Curiosa.* New York, New York: Greenburg Pub., 1955.

Workman, W.E. *The Ruger 10/22,* Iola, WI: Krause Publications, 1994.

Zhuk, A.B. *The Illustrated Encyclopedia of Handguns.* London, England, Greenhill Books, 1995.

MANUFACTURER & MODEL INDEX